The IDG Books Bible Advantage

The *Access for Windows 95 Bible,* 3rd Edition is part of the Bible series brought to you by IDG Books Worldwide. We designed Bibles to meet your growing need for quick access to the most complete and accurate computer information available.

Bibles work the way you do: They focus on accomplishing specific tasks — not learning random functions. These books are not long-winded manuals or dry reference tomes. In Bibles, expert authors tell you exactly what you can do with your software and how to do it. Easy to follow, step-by-step sections; comprehensive coverage; and convenient access in language and design — it's all here.

The authors of Bibles are uniquely qualified to give you expert advice as well as insightful tips and techniques not found anywhere else. Our authors maintain close contact with end users through feedback from articles, training sessions, e-mail exchanges, user group participation, and consulting work. Because our authors know the realities of daily computer use and are directly tied to the reader, our Bibles have a strategic advantage.

Bible authors have the experience to approach a topic in the most efficient manner, and we know that you, the reader, will benefit from a "one-on-one" relationship with the author. Our research shows that readers make computer book purchases because they want expert advice on a product. Readers want to benefit from the author's experience, so the author's voice is always present in a Bible series book.

In addition, the author is free to include or recommend useful software in a Bible. The software that accompanies a Bible is not intended to be casual filler but is linked to the content, theme, or procedures of the book. We know that you will benefit from the included software.

You will find what you need in this book whether you read it from cover to cover, section by section, or simply one topic at a time. As a computer user, you deserve a comprehensive resource of answers. We at IDG Books Worldwide are proud to deliver that resource with the *Access for Windows 95 Bible,* 3rd Edition.

Brenda McLaughlin
Vice President and Group Publisher
Internet: YouTellUs@IDGBooks.com

ACCESS FOR WINDOWS® 95 BIBLE

3RD EDITION

ACCESS
FOR WINDOWS® 95
BIBLE™
3RD EDITION

by Cary N. Prague & Michael R. Irwin

IDG Books Worldwide, Inc.
An International Data Group Company

Foster City, CA ◆ Chicago, IL ◆ Indianapolis, IN ◆ Braintree, MA ◆ Dallas, TX

Access for Windows® 95 Bible, 3rd Edition

Published by
IDG Books Worldwide, Inc.
An International Data Group Company
919 E. Hillsdale Blvd. Suite 400
Foster City, CA 94404

Library of Congress Catalog Card No.: 95-80474

ISBN:1-56884-493-X

Printed in the United States of America

10 9 8 7 6 5 4 3 2 1

3B/ST/RQ/ZV

Distributed in the United States by IDG Books Worldwide, Inc.

Distributed by Macmillan Canada for Canada; by Computer and Technical Books for the Caribbean Basin; by Contemporanea de Ediciones for Venezuela; by Distribuidora Cuspide for Argentina; by CITEC for Brazil; by Ediciones ZETA S.C.R. Ltda. for Peru; by Editorial Limusa SA for Mexico; by Transworld Publishers Limited in the United Kingdom and Europe; by Al-Maiman Publishers & Distributors for Saudi Arabia; by Simron Pty. Ltd. for South Africa; by IDG Communications (HK) Ltd. for Hong Kong; by Toppan Company Ltd. for Japan; by Addison Wesley Publishing Company for Korea; by Longman Singapore Publishers Ltd. for Singapore, Malaysia, Thailand, and Indonesia; by Unalis Corporation for Taiwan; by WS Computer Publishing Company, Inc. for the Philippines; by WoodsLane Pty. Ltd. for Australia; by WoodsLane Enterprises Ltd. for New Zealand.

For general information on IDG Books Worldwide's books in the U.S., please call our Consumer Customer Service department at 800-762-2974. For reseller information, including discounts and premium sales, please call our Reseller Customer Service department at 800-434-3422.

For information on where to purchase IDG Books Worldwide's books outside the U.S., contact IDG Books Worldwide at 415-655-3021 or fax 415-655-3295.

For information on translations, contact Marc Jeffrey Mikulich, Director, Foreign & Subsidiary Rights, at IDG Books Worldwide, 415-655-3018 or fax 415-655-3295.

For sales inquiries and special prices for bulk quantities, write to the address above or call IDG Books Worldwide at 415-655-3200.

For information on using IDG Books Worldwide's books in the classroom, or ordering examination copies, contact Jim Kelly at 800-434-2086.

About the Authors

Cary Prague

Cary Prague is one of the top authors in the database industry today. He is a winner of the Computer Press Association's Best Software Specific Book of the Year. He has written over 35 best selling books on personal computer database products including Microsoft Access, Borland dBASE and Paradox, and Microrim R:Base. He is a Contributing Editor to *Access Advisor* Magazine and certified in Microsoft Access, having passed the Microsoft certification exams. Recently, one of his software products, Check Writer for Microsoft Access, won the Microsoft Network contest for best software program.

Cary's books include four different *Access Bible*s and he is currently working on *Access 95 SECRETS,* to be published in late 1995 by IDG books. He is also the author of *Everyman's Database Primer for dBASE IV*, and the incredibly successful *Programming with dBASE* series that sold over one million copies and won the book of the year award. He has been writing since 1985.

Cary is the founder of Cary Prague Books and Software, the world's largest Access add-on software company. His current catalog contains many products for Access 95 and Access 2.0, including Yes! I Can Run My Business With Access, a full featured customizable business accounting product, the User Interface Construction Kit, Madonis Menu Machine, Coach Cards Developers Toolkit, Buton Designer Pro, Access Business Forms Library, Access Mail Merge Report Wizard, The Envelope Wizard, The Picture Builder Add-On Picture Pack, and books and videos for all versions of Microsoft Access.

He is a frequent speaker at national computer conferences and is a 1995 speaker at Access Advisor/Microsoft's Database Conference, Microsoft Developer Days, Microsoft Tech-Ed East, and Digital Consulting's Database World Conference. He formerly lectured on Borland's Database Conference and World Tour.

Mr. Prague has a master's degree in Computer Science from Rensselaer Polytechnic University. He also earned Bachelor of Accounting and MBA degrees from the University of Connecticut. He is a Certified Data Processor.

Michael R. Irwin

Michael Irwin is considered one of the leading authorities on automated database management systems. He is a noted worldwide lecturer, award-winning (both national and International), best-selling author, and developer of client/server and PC-based database management systems.

Mr. Irwin has extensive database knowledge, gained by working with the Metropolitan Police Department in Washington, D.C. as a developer and analyst for the Information Systems Division. He retired in June 1992. Now he runs his own consulting firm, specializing in Database Integration and emphasizing client/server solutions. His range of expertise includes database processing in and between mainframe, mini-, and PC-based database systems. His extensive PC-based database knowledge and expertise has made him one of the leading authorities on PC-based database systems today.

He has authored numerous database books over the last three years, with several of them consistently on the best sellers lists. His most recent works include *The OOPs primer* (Borland Press) and *dBASE 5.5 for Windows Programming* (Prentice Hall).

Welcome to the world of IDG Books Worldwide.

IDG Books Worldwide, Inc., is a subsidiary of International Data Group, the world's largest publisher of computer-related information and the leading global provider of information services on information technology. IDG was founded more than 25 years ago and now employs more than 7,500 people worldwide. IDG publishes more than 235 computer publications in 67 countries (see listing below). More than 70 million people read one or more IDG publications each month.

Launched in 1990, IDG Books Worldwide is today the #1 publisher of best-selling computer books in the United States. We are proud to have received 8 awards from the Computer Press Association in recognition of editorial excellence, and our best-selling *...For Dummies*® series has more than 19 million copies in print with translations in 28 languages. IDG Books Worldwide, through a recent joint venture with IDG's Hi-Tech Beijing, became the first U.S. publisher to publish a computer book in the People's Republic of China. In record time, IDG Books Worldwide has become the first choice for millions of readers around the world who want to learn how to better manage their businesses.

Our mission is simple: Every one of our books is designed to bring extra value and skill-building instructions to the reader. Our books are written by experts who understand and care about our readers. The knowledge base of our editorial staff comes from years of experience in publishing, education, and journalism — experience which we use to produce books for the '90s. In short, we care about books, so we attract the best people. We devote special attention to details such as audience, interior design, use of icons, and illustrations. And because we use an efficient process of authoring, editing, and desktop publishing our books electronically, we can spend more time ensuring superior content and spend less time on the technicalities of making books.

You can count on our commitment to deliver high-quality books at competitive prices on topics consumers want to read about. At IDG Books Worldwide, we value quality, and we have been delivering quality for more than 25 years. You'll find no better book on a subject than an IDG book.

John Kilcullen
President and CEO
IDG Books Worldwide, Inc.

IDG Books Worldwide, Inc., is a subsidiary of International Data Group, the world's largest publisher of computer-related information and the leading global provider of information services on information technology. International Data Group publishes over 235 computer publications in 67 countries. More than seventy million people read one or more International Data Group publications each month. The officers are Patrick J. McGovern, Founder and Board Chairman; Kelly Conlin, President; Jim Casella, Chief Operating Officer. International Data Group's publications include: **ARGENTINA'S** Computerworld Argentina, Infoworld Argentina; **AUSTRALIA'S** Computerworld Australia, Computer Living, Australian PC World, Australian Macworld, Network World, Mobile Business Australia, Publish!, Reseller, IDG Sources; **AUSTRIA'S** Computerwelt Oesterreich, PC Test; **BELGIUM'S** Data News (CW); **BOLIVIA'S** Computerworld; **BRAZIL'S** Computerworld, Connections, Game Power, Mundo Unix, PC World, Publish, Super Game; **BULGARIA'S** Computerworld Bulgaria, PC & Mac World Bulgaria, Network World Bulgaria; **CANADA'S** CIO Canada, Computerworld Canada, InfoCanada, Network World Canada, Reseller; **CHILE'S** Computerworld Chile, Informatica; **COLOMBIA'S** Computerworld Colombia, PC World; **COSTA RICA'S** PC World; **CZECH REPUBLIC'S** Computerworld, Elektronika, PC World; **DENMARK'S** Communications World, Computerworld Denmark, Computerworld Focus, Macintosh Produktkatalog, Macworld Danmark, PC World Danmark, PC Produktguide, Tech World, Windows World; **ECUADOR'S** PC World Ecuador; **EGYPT'S** Computerworld (CW) Middle East, PC World Middle East; **FINLAND'S** MikroPC, Tietoviikko, Tietoverkko; **FRANCE'S** Distributique, GOLDEN MAC, InfoPC, Le Guide du Monde Informatique, Le Monde Informatique, Telecoms & Reseaux; **GERMANY'S** Computerwoche, Computerwoche Focus, Computerwoche Extra, Electronic Entertainment, Gamepro, Information Management, Macwelt, Netzwelt, PC Welt, Publish, Publish; **GREECE'S** Publish & Macworld; **HONG KONG'S** Computerworld Hong Kong, PC World Hong Kong; **HUNGARY'S** Computerworld SZT, PC World; **INDIA'S** Computers & Communications; **INDONESIA'S** Info Komputer; **IRELAND'S** ComputerScope; **ISRAEL'S** Beyond Windows, Computerworld Israel, Multimedia, PC World Israel; **ITALY'S** Computerworld Italia, Lotus Magazine, Macworld Italia, Networking Italia, PC Shopping Italy, PC World Italia; **JAPAN'S** Computerworld Today, Information Systems World, Macworld Japan, Nikkei Personal Computing, SunWorld Japan, Windows World; **KENYA'S** East African Computer News; **KOREA'S** Computerworld Korea, Macworld Korea, PC World Korea; **LATIN AMERICA'S** GamePro; **MALAYSIA'S** Computerworld Malaysia, PC World Malaysia; **MEXICO'S** Compu Edicion, Compu Manufactura, Computacion/Punto de Venta, Computerworld Mexico, MacWorld, Mundo Unix, PC World, Windows; **THE NETHERLANDS'** Computer! Totaal, Computable (CW), LAN Magazine, Lotus Magazine, MacWorld; **NEW ZEALAND'S** Computer Buyer, Computerworld New Zealand, Network World, New Zealand PC World; **NIGERIA'S** PC World Africa; **NORWAY'S** Computerworld Norge, Lotusworld Norge, Macworld Norge, Maxi Data, Networld, PC World Ekspress, PC World Nettverk, PC World Norge, PC World's Produktguide, Publish& Multimedia World, Student Data, Unix World, Windowsworld; **PAKISTAN'S** PC World Pakistan; **PANAMA'S** PC World Panama; **PERU'S** Computerworld Peru, PC World; **PEOPLE'S REPUBLIC OF CHINA'S** China Computerworld, China Infoworld, China PC Info Magazine, Computer Fan, PC World China, Electronics International, Electronics Today/Multimedia World, Electronic Product World, China Network World, Software World Magazine, Telecom Product World; **PHILIPPINES'** Computerworld Philippines, PC Digest (PCW); **POLAND'S** Computerworld Poland, Computerworld Special Report, Networld, PC World/Komputer, Sunworld; **PORTUGAL'S** Cerebro/PC World, Correio Informatico/Computerworld, MacIn; **ROMANIA'S** Computerworld, PC World, Telecom Romania; **RUSSIA'S** Computerworld-Moscow, Mir - PK (PCW), Sety (Networks); **SINGAPORE'S** Computerworld Southeast Asia, PC World Singapore; **SLOVENIA'S** Monitor Magazine; **SOUTH AFRICA'S** Computer Mail (CIO), Computing S.A., Network World S.A., Software World; **SPAIN'S** Advanced Systems, Amiga World, Computerworld Espana, Communicaciones World, Macworld Espana, NeXTWORLD, Super Juegos Magazine (GamePro), PC World Espana, Publish; **SWEDEN'S** Attack, ComputerSweden, Corporate Computing, Macworld, Mikrodatorn, Natverk & Kommunikation, PC World, CAP & Design, Datalngenjoren, Maxi Data,Windows World; **SWITZERLAND'S** Computerworld Schweiz, Macworld Schweiz, PC Tip; **TAIWAN'S** Computerworld Taiwan, PC World Taiwan; **THAILAND'S** Thai Computerworld; **TURKEY'S** Computerworld Monitor, Macworld Turkiye, PC World Turkiye; **UKRAINE'S** Computerworld, Computers+Software Magazine; **UNITED KINGDOM'S** Computing/Computerworld, Connexion/Network World, Lotus Magazine, Macworld, Open Computing/Sunworld; **UNITED STATES'** Advanced Systems, AmigaWorld, Cable in the Classroom, CD Review, CIO, Computerworld, Computerworld Client/Server Journal, Digital Video, DOS World, Electronic Entertainment Magazine (E2), Federal Computer Week, Game Hits, GamePro, IDG Books Worldwide, Infoworld, Laser Event, Macworld, Maximize, Multimedia World, Network World, PC Letter, PC World, Publish, SWATPro, Video Event; **URUGUAY'S** PC World Uruguay; **VENEZUELA'S** Computerworld Venezuela, PC World; **VIETNAM'S** PC World Vietnam.
08/30/95

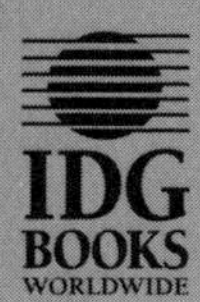

Credits

Publisher
Karen A. Bluestein

Acquisitions Manager
Gregory Croy

Acquisitions Editor
Ellen L. Camm

Brand Manager
Melisa M. Duffy

Editorial Directors
Mary Bednarek
Andy Cummings

Editorial Executive Assistant
Jodi Lynn Semling

Editorial Assistant
Nate Holdread

Production Director
Beth Jenkins

Supervisor of Project Coordinator
Cindy L. Phipps

Supervisor of Page Layout
Kathie S. Schnorr

Pre-Press Coordinator
Steve Peake

Pre-Press Coordinator
Tony Augusburger

Media/Archive Coordinator
Paul Belcastro

Project Editor
Erik Dafforn

Associate Project Editor
Pat O'Brien

Editors
Barry Childs-Helton
Kathy Simpson

Technical Reviewer
Diana Smith

Project Coordinator
Valery Bourke

Production Staff
Gina Scott
Carla C. Radzinkins
Patricia R. Reynolds
Melissa D. Buddendeck
Gwenette Gaddis
Dwight Ramsey
Robert Springer
Theresa Sánchez-Baker
Leslie Poppelwell
Cameron Booker
Dominique deFelice
Jill Lyttle
Todd Klemme
Drew R. Moore

Proofreader
Phil Worthington

Indexer
Liz Cunningham

Book Design
Drew R. Moore

Cover Design
Three 8 Creative Group

Acknowledgments

When we first saw Access in July of 1992, we were instantly sold on this new generation of database management and access tool. We've both spent the last three years using Access daily. In fact, after three short years, there are estimated to be nearly 8 million Access users worldwide.

Now we have rewritten this book again for all the incredible new features in Access for Windows 95. We've covered every new feature and added a programming section. Nearly 250,000 copies of our *Access Bible*s have been sold for Access 1.0, 1.1, and 2.0 and we thank all of our loyal readers.

We've also written countless systems, designed and brought to market many add-on products for Access, and created the largest Access add-on software and book distribution company in the world. We've served nearly 10,000 customers, our staff has answered thousands of technical support questions, and we've received critical acclaim from readers and reviewers alike. Our first acknowledgment is to all the users of Access who have profited and benefitted beyond everyone's wildest dreams.

There are many people who assisted us in writing this book. We'd like to recognize each of them.

To Jennifer Scales for running Cary's business while he disappeared for two months. It's Bonus Time!

To Phuc Phan, student at the University of Connecticut. Phuc helped take many of the screen dumps you see in this book. Without Phuc, this book would not have been on time.

To Jennifer Reardon, one of my top developers, for stepping in and stepping up at the last minute to write Chapters 33 and 34.

To Bill Amo, for always being there when I ask *How do you get this to work?*

To Senor Raul Perez of SNETCO for allowing me to take 6 months to do a two month project so I could write this book and for always buying coffee.

To Lowell Putnam, of VCI Communications for forcing me to learn more about Access than I ever wanted to know.

To Ken Getz, who can answer any question - Including those nobody can answer.

To John S. Dranchak for designing the reports in Chapters 21 and 23, and creating the logo for Mountain Animal Hospital.

To Diana Smith, who wrote the original introductory chapters (2, 3, and 5) and also was the technical editor for this book. To her we offer a special thank you.

Thanks to Mary Lynn Maurice for her assistance in writing Chapters 4 and 6, so long ago.

To our agents, Matt Wagner and Bill Gladstone at Waterside Productions.

To the folks at IDG Books:

To John Kilcullen, President and CEO of IDG books, who still has time to talk to me on the phone and make things happen. Thanks John. Without you, there would be no book. Day and date, John!

To Karen Bluestein, Mary Bednarek, Greg Croy, and all the editors — Pat O'Brien, Barry Childs-Helton, and Kathy Simpson. Thanks for the incredible job you did managing the project and editing our book.

A special thanks to Erik Dafforn, my project editor and one of the best in the business. Enjoy the popcorn of the month club.

(The publisher would like to give special thanks to Patrick J. McGovern, without whom this book would not have been possible.)

Dedication

To Julia Kramer, my niece, in honor of her Bat Mitzvah

CNP

Dra. Arni Lim, MD and the entire Lim Family. Without their support I would be lost in the Philippines.

MRI

Contents at a Glance

Table of Contents

Chapter 26: Creating Action Queries 713

Chapter 27: Advanced Query Topics 739

Part V: Applications in Access 825

Chapter 30: An Introduction to Macros and Events 827

Foreword

Microsoft® Access for Windows 95 represents a milestone in the computer industry and for the millions of personal computer users, software developers, and corporations who rely on Microsoft Access every day to increase their productivity and their access to information. Now, our first release of Microsoft Access for Windows 95 is available for developing Windows 95 applications and accessing data in the Windows 95 and Windows NT 32-bit environments.

Particularly significant is that Microsoft Access for Windows 95 combines so much that is familiar with so much that is new — Microsoft Access 2.0 applications can be easily converted to Microsoft Access for Windows 95, and module code is converted from Access Basic to the new Visual Basic Application Edition common to Microsoft Access, Microsoft Visual Basic, and Microsoft Office applications.

To help both the new user and the user moving from Microsoft Access 2.0 or Microsoft Access 1.1, database gurus Cary Prague and Michael Irwin have charted a path that shows how to take advantage of the capabilities of Microsoft Access for Windows 95.

Working in a tutorial setting, Cary and Michael first introduce database concepts in a few simple and easy-to-understand chapters. They help you understand necessary terminology and they show you how to install and use the most basic features of Microsoft Access.

Building on the beginning of the book, they take you through simple tables, queries, forms, and reports. Working with a concrete set of examples and a real world application, the reader is led from topic to topic through a full range of the new features of Microsoft Access for Windows 95, including the Database Wizard (which creates instant applications), Table Analyzer, Database Splitter Wizard, Performance Analyzer, creating custom toolbars and shortcut menus, and using the new OLE custom controls.

The majority of the book focuses on tasks of increasing complexity, including using linked tables, advanced queries, importing external data, multipage forms, using multitable reports, macros, and the new VBA language.

Whether you are a long-time user of Microsoft Access or a first-time user of Microsoft Access for Windows 95, the Microsoft Access for Windows 95 Bible shows you everything you need to get started and be productive with Microsoft Access.

Scott Horn
Microsoft Access Product Manager

Introduction

Welcome to the *Access for Windows 95 Bible* — your personal guide to a powerful, easy-to-use database management system.

This book examines Microsoft Access for Windows 95. We think that Microsoft Access is an excellent database manager and the best Windows database on the market today. Our goal with this book is to share what we know about Access and, in the process, to help make your work and your life easier.

This book contains everything you need in order to learn Microsoft Access to a fairly advanced level. You'll find that the book starts off with the basics and builds, chapter by chapter, on topics previously covered. In places where it is essential that you understand previously covered topics, we present the concepts again and review how to perform specific tasks before moving on. Although each chapter is an integral part of the book as a whole, each chapter can also stand on its own. You can read the book in any order you want, skipping from chapter to chapter and from topic to topic. (Note that this book's index is particularly thorough; you can refer to the index to find the location of a particular topic you're interested in.)

The examples in this book have been well thought out to simulate the types of tables, queries, forms, and reports most people need to create when performing common business activities. There are many notes, tips, and techniques (and even a few secrets) to help you better understand the product.

Although designed to supplement the Microsoft Access documentation, this book can easily substitute for the manuals included with Access. We even created appendixes to be used as reference manuals for common Access specifications. This book follows a much more structured approach than the Microsoft Access manuals — going into more depth on almost every topic and showing many different types of examples.

Is This Book for You?

We wrote this book for beginning, intermediate, and advanced users of Microsoft Access. With any new product, most users start at the beginning. If, however, you've already read through the Microsoft Access manuals and worked with the North Winds sample files, you may want to start with the later parts of this book. Note, however, that starting at the beginning of a book is usually a good idea so you don't miss out on the secrets and tips in the early chapters.

We think this book covers Microsoft Access in detail better than any other book currently on the market. We hope you will find this book helpful while working with Access, and that you enjoy the innovative style of an IDG book.

Yes — If you have no database experience

If you're new to the world of database management, this book has everything you need to get started with Microsoft Access. It then offers advanced topics for reference and learning.

Yes — If you've used other database managers like dBASE or Paradox

If you're abandoning another database (such as dBASE, Paradox, Approach, R:Base, or Alpha Four) or even upgrading from Access 2.0 to Access for Windows 95, this book is for you. You'll have a head start because you're already familiar with database managers and how to use them. With Microsoft Access, you will be able to do all the tasks you've always performed with character-based databases — *without* programming or getting lost. This book will take you through each subject step by step.

Yes — If you want to learn the basics of Visual Basic Applications Edition (VBA) programming

VBA has replaced the Access Basic language. We know that an entire book is needed to properly cover VBA, but we took the time to put together two introductory chapters that build on what you learn in the macros chapters of this book. The VBA programming chapters use the same examples you will be familiar with by the end of the book.

Conventions Used in This Book

The following conventions are used in this book:

- When you are instructed to press a *key combination* (press and hold down one key while pressing another key), the key combination is separated by a plus sign. Ctrl+Esc, for example, indicates that you must hold down the Ctrl key and press the Esc key; then release both keys.
- *Point the mouse* refers to moving the mouse so that the mouse pointer is on a specific item. *Click* refers to pressing the left mouse button once and releasing it. *Double-click* refers to pressing the left mouse button twice in rapid succession and then releasing it. *Right-click* refers to pressing the right mouse button once and releasing it. *Drag* refers to pressing and holding down the left mouse button while moving the mouse.
- When you are instructed to *select* a menu, you can use the keyboard or the mouse. To use the keyboard, press and hold down the Alt key (to activate the menu bar) and then press the underlined letter of the menu name; press Alt+E to select the Edit menu, for example. Or you can use the mouse to click on the word Edit on-screen. Then, from the menu that drops down, you can press the underlined letter of the command you want (or click on the command name) to select it.
- When you are instructed to select a command from a menu, you will often see the menu and command separated by an arrow symbol. Edit⇨Paste, for example, indicates that you need to select the Edit menu and then choose the Paste command from the menu.
- *Italic* type is used for new terms and for emphasis.
- **Bold** type is used for material you need to type directly into the computer.
- `A special typeface is used for information you see on-screen`— error messages, expressions, and formulas, for example.

Icons and Alerts

You'll notice special graphic symbols, or *icons,* used in the margins throughout this book. These icons are intended to alert you to points that are particularly important or noteworthy. The following icons are used in this book:

Note

This icon highlights a special point of interest about the topic under discussion.

Tip

This icon points to a useful hint that may save you time or trouble.

Warning

This icon alerts you that the operation being described can cause problems if you're not careful.

New!

This icon alerts you to a new feature found in Access for Windows 95.

Cross Ref

This icon points to a more complete discussion in another chapter of the book.

Disk

This icon highlights information for readers who are following the examples and using the sample files included on the disk accompanying this book.

Sidebars

In addition to noticing the icons used throughout this book, you will also notice material placed in grey boxes. This material offers background information, an expanded discussion, or a deeper insight about the topic under discussion. Some *sidebars* offer nuts-and-bolts technical explanations, and others provide useful anecdotal material.

How This Book Is Organized

This book contains 34 chapters, which are divided into five main parts. In addition, the book contains two appendixes.

Part I: First Things First

Part I consists of the first six chapters of the book. In Chapter 1, you receive background information on Microsoft Access and an overview of its features. Chapter 2 covers installation — what you need in terms of hardware and software, as well as how to get Access running properly. In Chapter 3, you learn how to start and stop Access, plus several techniques for moving between Access and other applications. Chapter 4 provides a review of database concepts for new users of a database product. Chapter 5 is a hands-on test drive of Access, provided to give you a quick look at some of its features. And Chapter 6 is a case study of the up-front design that is necessary for properly implementing a database system; otherwise, you must go through many false starts and redesigns when creating an application. You will design on paper the tables, forms, queries, reports, and menus necessary for creating the application.

Part II: Basic Database Usage

The next six chapters make up Part II. You learn how to create a database table in Chapter 7, and you also examine how to change a database table, including moving and renaming fields without losing data. In Chapter 8, you learn how to enter, display, change, and delete data. Chapter 9 teaches the basics of creating data-entry forms, using Wizards to simplify the creation process; using data-entry forms is also discussed. In Chapter 10, you examine the concept of queries, then you create several queries to examine how data can be rearranged and displayed. Chapter 11 covers the basics of report creation and printing. In Chapter 12, you create the many tables used in the case study, and then learn how to relate multiple tables.

Part III: Using Access in Your Work

Part III contains eleven chapters that go into more depth on creating and using forms, queries, and reports. In Chapter 13, you take a look at how to create the expressions and built-in functions that are so important in forms and reports. In Chapter 14, you learn how to create relations and joins in queries. Chapter 15 discusses basic selection queries, using many examples and pictures. In Chapter 16, you examine the concepts of controls and properties, and then learn how to manipulate controls in a form. Chapter 17 examines in detail how to create and use data-entry forms. Chapter 18 covers how to use visual effects to create great-looking forms and reports that catch the eye and increase productivity. In Chapter 19, you learn how to add complex data validation to tables and data-entry forms. Chapter 20 explains the use of pictures, graphs, sound, video, and other OLE objects. Chapters 21–23 cover reports — from simple controls to complex calculations, summaries, printing, and desktop publishing.

Part IV: Advanced Database Features

This part contains six chapters that present advanced topics on each of the basic tasks of Access. Chapter 24 examines how to import, export, and attach external files, along with copying Access objects to other Access databases. Chapter 25 discusses advanced select query topics, including total, cross-tabulation, top value, and union queries. Chapter 26 covers action queries, which change data rather than simply displaying records. Chapter 27 is a compendium of advanced query topics that will leave you amazed at the power of Access. Creating forms and subforms from multiple tables is the subject of Chapter 28; this chapter examines how to create the one-to-many relationship found in many database systems. Part IV ends with Chapter 29, which offers a look at additional types of reports not previously covered, including mail-merge reports and mailing labels.

Part V: Applications in Access

This part looks at Access as an application environment. Chapter 30 covers the concept of event-driven software and how Access uses macros to automate manual processes. This chapter also examines what a macro is, how macros are created, and how to debug them. Chapter 31 explains data manipulation, including posting totals and filling in data-entry fields. In Chapter 32, you learn how to create button menus known as switchboards, as well as traditional pull-down menus, custom toolbars, and dialog boxes. Chapter 33 is an introduction to modules using VBA, which teaches you how to create a basic module and debug a program. Chapter 34 builds on the discussion of modules, teaching you logical constructs, error processing, DAO, and recordset processing.

The appendixes and reference material

Two appendixes are included in this book. Appendix A presents a series of tables listing Access specifications, including maximum and minimum sizes of many of the controls in Access. Appendix B displays a database diagram of the many database tables used in this book so you can create your own system.

First Things First

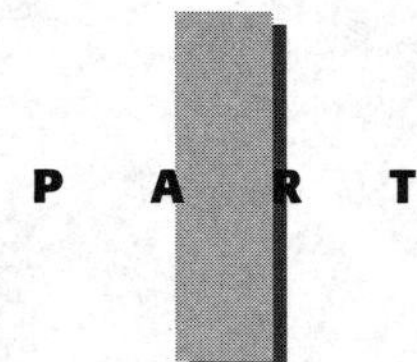

P A R T

✦ ✦ ✦ ✦

In This Part

✦ ✦ ✦ ✦

CHAPTER 1

What Is Access?

◆ ◆ ◆ ◆

In This Chapter

Examining what Access is

Looking at some of the capabilities of Access

Understanding how to work with Access if you're already a database user

Understanding how to work with Access if you're already a spreadsheet user

◆ ◆ ◆ ◆

Before you begin to use a software product, it is important to understand its capabilities and the types of tasks it is designed to perform. Access is a multifaceted product whose use is bounded only by your imagination.

Access Is . . .

Essentially, Access is a *database management system* (DBMS). Like other products in this category, Access stores and retrieves data, presents information, and automates repetitive tasks (such as maintaining accounts payable, inventory control, and scheduling). By using Access, you can develop easy-to-use input forms like the one shown in Figure 1-1. You can process your data and run powerful reports.

Access is also a powerful Windows application; for the first time, the productivity of database management meets the usability of Microsoft Windows. Because both Windows and Access are from Microsoft, the two products work very well together. Access runs on the Windows platform, so all the advantages of Windows are available in Access. You can cut, copy, and paste data from any Windows application to and from Access. You can create a form design in Access and paste it into the report designer. Using OLE (Object Linking and Embedding) objects in Windows 95 and Microsoft Office 95 products (Excel, Word, PowerPoint) you can extend Access into being a true database operating environment through integration with these products.

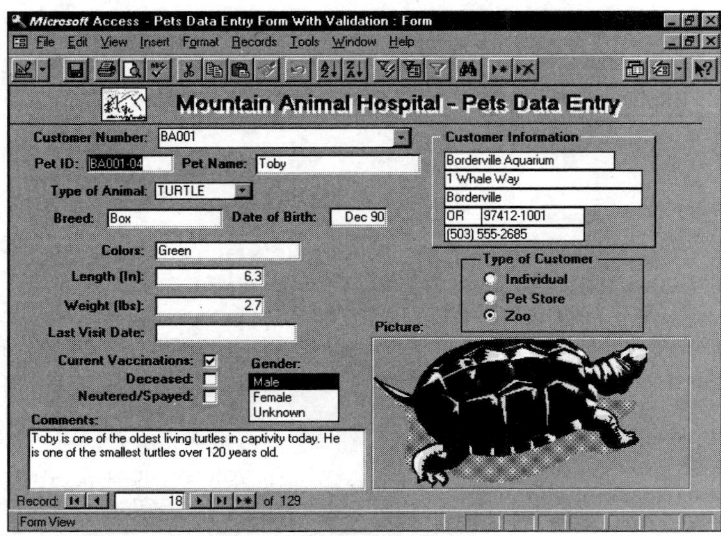

Figure 1-1: A typical Access data entry form.

Even so, Access is more than just a database manager. As a *relational* database manager, it gives you access to all types of data, and gives you the use of more than one database table at a time. It can reduce the complexity of your data and make it easier to get your job done. You can link an Access table with mainframe or server data, or use a table created in Paradox or dBASE. You can take the results of the link and combine the data with an Excel worksheet quickly and easily. If you use Microsoft Office, you will find complete interoperability between Access and Word, Excel, and PowerPoint.

Figure 1-2 shows Microsoft's original marketing concept for Access. This simple figure conveys the message that Access is usable at all levels. Beginning at the lowest level of the hierarchy and moving upward, you see *tools* listed first; these give the end user the capability of creating forms and reports easily. You can perform simple processing by using *expressions* to validate data or display a number with a currency symbol. *Macros* allow for automation without programming, whereas VBA (Visual Basic for Applications) Code lets the user program complex processes. Finally, by using C language like functions or Windows API calls, a programmer can write interfaces to other programs and data sources.

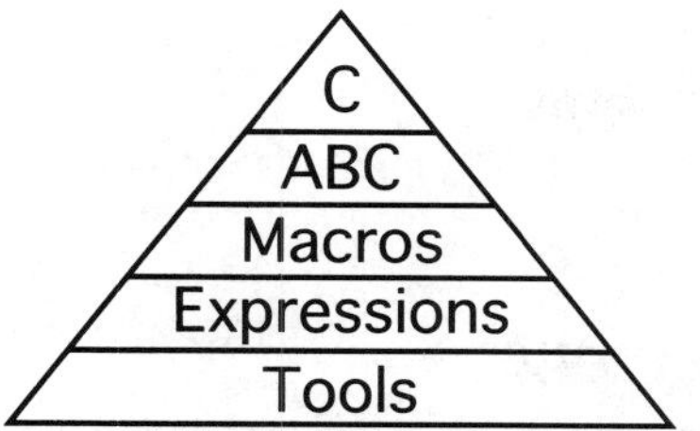

Figure 1-2: The Access usability hierarchy.

Access is a set of tools for end-user database management. Access has a table creator, a form designer, a query manager, and a report writer. Access is also an environment for developing applications. By using macros to automate tasks, you can create user-oriented applications as powerful as those created with programming languages — complete with the buttons, menus, and dialog boxes you see in Figure 1-3. By programming in Visual Basic for Applications (known as VBA), you can actually create programs as powerful as Access itself. In fact, many of the tools in Access (such as the Wizards and Builders) are written in VBA.

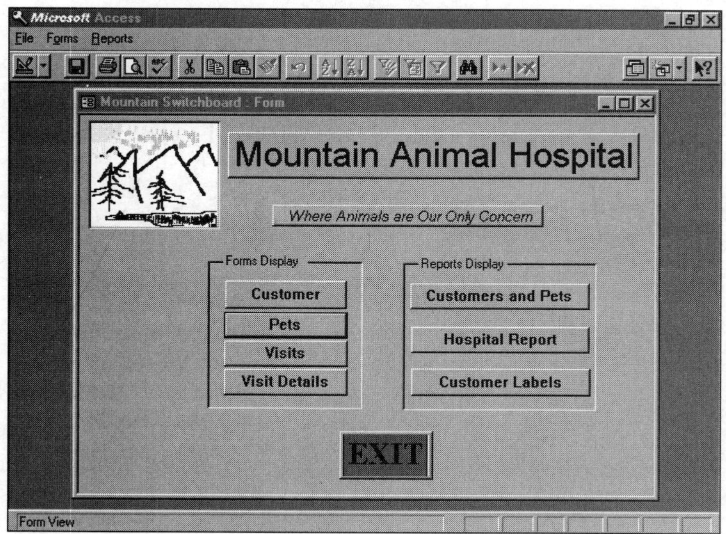

Figure 1-3: A macro switchboard and custom menu.

The power and usability of Access make it the best database management software, by far, on the market today. Simply telling you about what Access can do, however, doesn't begin to cover the material in this book. In the first 450 pages, you learn how to use Access from an end user's point of view. In the next 450 pages, you will learn Access from the power user's view. Finally, the last 100 pages will teach you the basics of VBA; you will examine many topics in a depth that your reference manuals can only begin to touch.

What Access Offers

The following paragraphs briefly describe some key features in Access, and will help prepare you for some of the subjects covered in this book.

True relational database management

Access provides true *relational database management.* Access includes definitions for primary and foreign keys, and has full referential integrity built in at the level of the database engine itself (which prevents inconsistent updates or deletions). In addition, tables in Access have data-validation rules to prevent inaccurate data regardless of how data is entered, and every field in a table has format and default definitions for more productive data entry. Access supports all the necessary field types, including Text, Number, Currency, Date/Time, Memo, Yes/No, and OLE objects. When values are missing in special processing, Access provides full support for null values.

The relational processing in Access fills many needs with its flexible architecture. It can be used as a stand-alone database management system, in a file-server configuration, or as a front-end client to products such as an SQL server. In addition, Access features ODBC (Open Database Connectivity); you'll be able to connect to many more external formats, such as Oracle, RDB, Sybase, or even mainframe IBM DB/2.

The program provides complete support for transaction processing, ensuring the integrity of transactions. In addition, user-level security provides control over assigning user and group permissions to view and modify database objects.

Context-sensitive Help and the Answer Wizard

Microsoft's Help is still the best in the industry, for beginners and experienced users alike. Access provides context-sensitive Help; you can press the F1 key whenever you're stuck. Help about the item you're working on appears instantly. Access also has an easy-to-use table of contents, a search facility, a history log, and bookmarks.

In Access 95, Microsoft goes a few steps farther by introducing the Answer Wizard and screen tips. As you can see in Figure 1-4, the *Answer Wizard* responds when you ask for help in plain English. *Screen tips* (also known as What's This?) give you short, on-screen explanations of what something is.

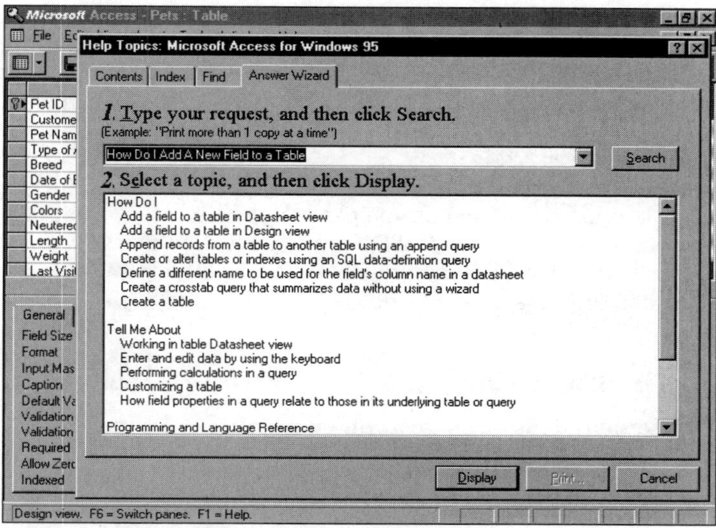

Figure 1-4: The Access 95 Answer Wizard.

Ease-of-use Wizards and Builders

A *Wizard* can turn hours of work into minutes. Wizards ask you questions about content, style, and format; then they build the object for you automatically. Access features nearly 100 Wizards to design databases, applications, tables, forms, reports, graphs, mailing labels, controls, and properties. Figure 1-5 shows a Form Wizard screen. You can even customize Wizards for use in a variety of tasks.

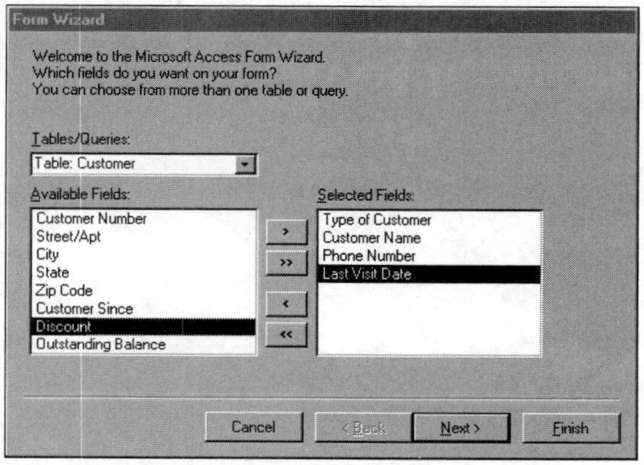

Figure 1-5: A typical Wizard screen.

Importing, exporting, and linking external files

Access lets you import from or export to many common formats, including dBASE, Paradox, FoxPro, Lotus 1-2-3, Excel, SQL Server, Oracle, Btrieve, and many ASCII formats. Importing creates an Access table; exporting an Access table creates a file in the native file format you are exporting to.

Linking (formally known as *attaching*) means you can simply use external data without creating an Access table. You can link to dBASE, Paradox, FoxPro, Excel, ASCII, and SQL data. Linking to external tables and then relating them to other tables is a powerful capability; you can link to Access, FoxPro, dBASE, Paradox, and SQL server.

WYSIWYG forms and reports

The Form and Report Design windows share a common interface and power. Your form or report is designed in a WYSIWYG environment. As you add each control, you see the form take shape as you build your design.

You can add labels, text data fields, option buttons, check boxes, lines, boxes, colors, shading — even pictures, graphs, subforms, or subreports — to your forms and reports. In addition, you have complete control over the style and presentation of data in a form or report, as shown in Figure 1-6. Forms can have multiple pages; reports can have many levels of groupings and totals.

You can view your form or report in a *page preview mode*, zooming out and get a bird's-eye view. You can also view your report with sample data when you're in the design mode, so you don't waste valuable time waiting for a large data file to be processed.

Most important, the report writer is very powerful, allowing up to ten levels of aggregation and sorting. The report writer performs two passes on the data; you can create reports that show the row percentage of a group total which can only be done by having a calculation based on a calculation which requires two passes through the data. You can create many types of reports that include mailing labels and mail-merge reports.

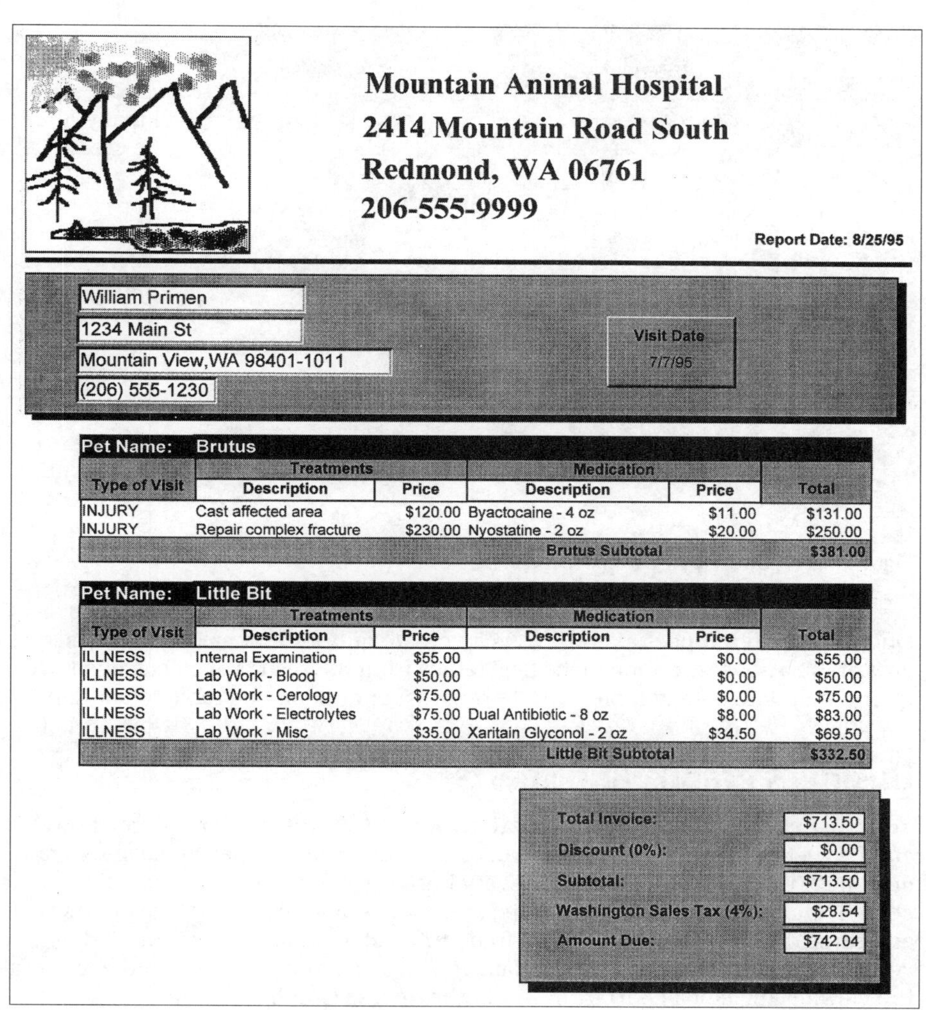

Mountain Animal Hospital
2414 Mountain Road South
Redmond, WA 06761
206-555-9999

Report Date: 8/25/95

William Primen
1234 Main St
Mountain View,WA 98401-1011
(206) 555-1230

Visit Date
7/7/95

Pet Name: Brutus

Type of Visit	Treatments		Medication		Total
	Description	Price	Description	Price	
INJURY	Cast affected area	$120.00	Byactocaine - 4 oz	$11.00	$131.00
INJURY	Repair complex fracture	$230.00	Nyostatine - 2 oz	$20.00	$250.00
			Brutus Subtotal		$381.00

Pet Name: Little Bit

Type of Visit	Treatments		Medication		Total
	Description	Price	Description	Price	
ILLNESS	Internal Examination	$55.00		$0.00	$55.00
ILLNESS	Lab Work - Blood	$50.00		$0.00	$50.00
ILLNESS	Lab Work - Cerology	$75.00		$0.00	$75.00
ILLNESS	Lab Work - Electrolytes	$75.00	Dual Antibiotic - 8 oz	$8.00	$83.00
ILLNESS	Lab Work - Misc	$35.00	Xaritain Glyconol - 2 oz	$34.50	$69.50
			Little Bit Subtotal		$332.50

Total Invoice:	$713.50
Discount (0%):	$0.00
Subtotal:	$713.50
Washington Sales Tax (4%):	$28.54
Amount Due:	$742.04

Figure 1-6: A database-published report.

Multiple-table queries

One of the most powerful features in Access is also the most important. As you can see in Figure 1-7, the Graphical Query by Example (GQBE) window lets you link your tables graphically. You can even link tables of different file types (such as an Access table and a dBASE table); when linked, your tables act as a single entity you can query about your data. You can select specific fields, define sorting orders, create calculated expressions, and enter criteria to select desired records. You can display the results of a query in a datasheet, form, or report.

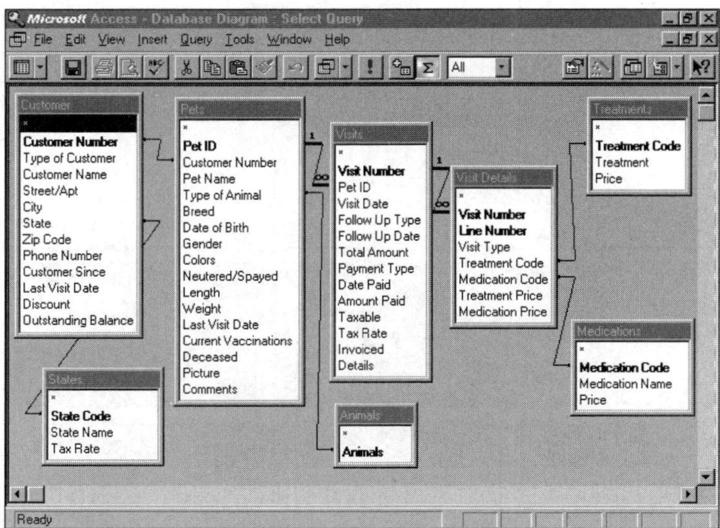

Figure 1-7: A query-by-example window.

Queries have other uses as well. You can create queries that calculate totals, display cross-tabulations, and then make new tables from the results. You can even use a query to update data in tables, delete records, or append one table to another.

Business graphs and charts

You will find the same graph application found in Microsoft Word, Excel, PowerPoint, and Project built into Access. You can create hundreds of types of business graphs and customize the display to meet your every business need. You can create bar charts, column charts, line charts, pie charts, area charts, and high-low-close charts — in two and three dimensions. You can add free-form text, change the gridlines, adjust the color and pattern in a bar, display data values on a bar or pie slice, and even rotate the viewing angle of a chart from within the Access Graph program.

In addition, you can link your graph with a form to get a powerful graphic data display that changes from record to record in the table. Figure 1-8 shows an example.

DDE and OLE capabilities

Through the capabilities of DDE (Dynamic Data Exchange) and OLE (Object Linking and Embedding), you can add exciting new objects to your Access forms and reports. Such objects may be sound, pictures, graphs, even video clips. You can embed OLE objects (such as a bitmap picture) or documents from word processors (such as Word or WordPerfect), or link to a range of cells in an Excel or 1-2-3 spreadsheet. By linking these objects to records in your tables, you can create dynamic database forms and reports and share information between Windows applications.

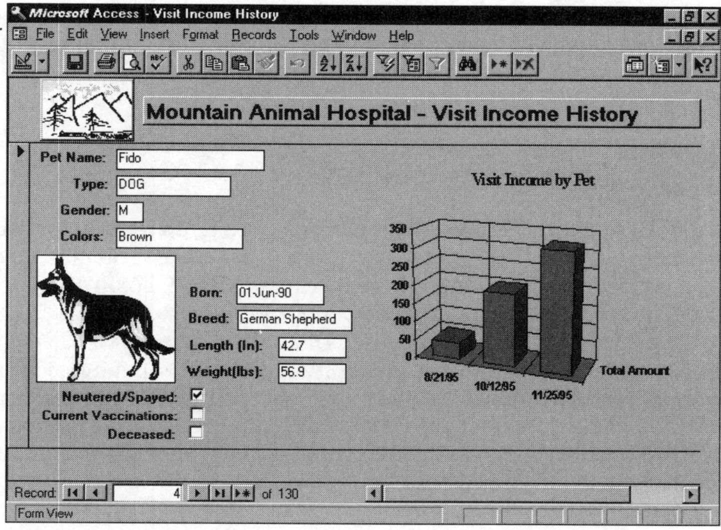

Figure 1-8: A typical form linked to a graph.

Built-in functions

Access contains over one hundred *functions* (built-in small programs that return a value); these perform tasks in a wide variety of categories. Access includes database, mathematics, business, financial, date, time, and string functions. You can use them to create calculated expressions in your forms, reports, and queries.

Macros: programming without programming

For nonprogrammers (or power users who simply don't want to program), there are *macros*. Macros let you perform common tasks without user intervention. Nearly 50 macro actions let you manipulate data, create menus and dialog boxes, open forms and reports, and basically automate any task you can imagine. Macros can probably solve 90 percent of your processing problems.

Modules: Visual Basic for database programming

Access is a serious development environment with a full-featured programming language. The Visual Basic Application edition (VBA for short and formerly known as Access Basic) features an event-driven programming model that lets you do more things than you can do with just forms and reports. VBA Code is a powerful, structured programming language; VBA is also fully extensible, featuring API call routines in any dynamic link library for the Windows 95 and Windows NT operating systems.

A full-featured Development Environment allows multiple windows for color-coded editing and debugging, automatic syntax checking, watchpoints, breakpoints, and single-step execution.

Information for Database Users

If you're already a database user, chances are you're ready to jump right in and start using Access. A word of warning: *This is not your father's Oldsmobile.* You may be an expert in relational database management software such as dBASE, FoxPro, or Paradox, but you may never have used a database under Windows.

You should try to become familiar with Windows software before you jump right in to a database package. Play with Windows Paint; experiment with Word or Excel. Learn how to use the mouse to click, double-click, select, drag, and drop. Create a graph in Excel, use a Wizard, and try the Help system. All these tasks will make your learning experience much faster when you use Access.

You also need to get used to some new terminology. Table 1-1 lists the Access terminology and its dBASE and Paradox equivalents.

Table 1-1
Access, dBASE, and Paradox Terminology

Microsoft Access	***Borland dBASE***	***Borland Paradox***
Database	Catalog	Directory of related files
Table	Database file	Table
Datasheet	BROWSE command	View command
Table Design	MODIFY STRUCTURE	Modify Restructure
Text data type	Character data type	Alphanumeric data type
Primary key	Unique Index	Key field
Index	Index	Tools QuerySpeed
Validation rule	PICTURE/VALID Clause	ValChecks
Query	Query, QBE, View	Query
Form	Screen	Forms
Subform	Multiple File Screen	Multiple-record selection
Open a form	SET FORMAT TO, EDIT	Image PickForm
Find command	LOCATE AND SEEK	Zoom

Microsoft Access	*Borland dBASE*	*Borland Paradox*
Data entry command	APPEND	Modify DataEntry
List box, combo box	Pick list	Lookup
Exclusive/shared access	SET EXCLUSIVE ON/OFF	Edit/Coedit mode
Module	Program file	Script

Information for Spreadsheet Users

If you are an Excel or 1-2-3 expert, you'll find that many things about Access are similar to Excel. First of all, both programs are Windows products, so you should already have experience using the Windows-specific conventions you will use with Access. Access has a spreadsheet view of the data in a table or query, known as a *datasheet*. You'll find you can resize the rows and columns in much the same way as within Excel worksheets. In fact, Access 95 has a data-entry mode exactly like that of Excel. You simply enter data and define column headings; Access will create a table for you automatically.

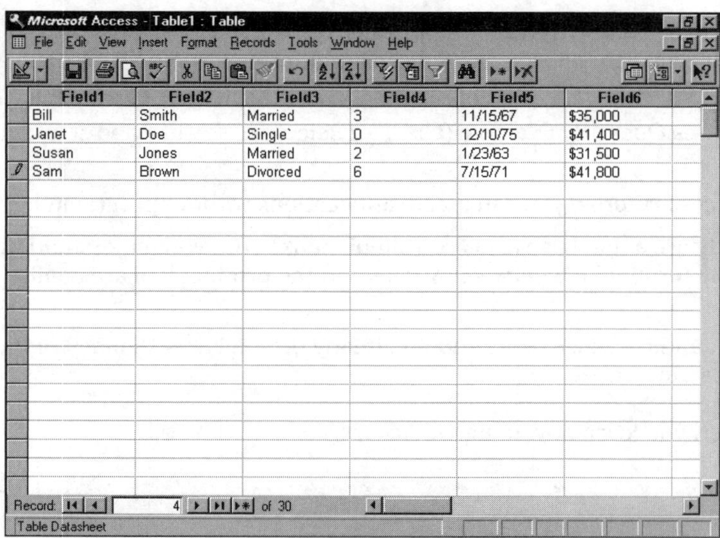

Figure 1-9: Creating a new table using an Access datasheet.

Access has a WYSIWYG drawing capability like that of Excel, and shares the same graph application. Thus you can create the same types of graphs in both programs, and annotate the graphs in the same way. Also, Access uses graph Wizards that you might have used in Excel.

Access 95 contains a Pivot Table Wizard just like Excel's; in fact, it can create Excel pivot tables. You can also drag and drop information from an Access database to an Excel spreadsheet, and link Access databases to Excel spreadsheets. You can query and sort data in both products as well, using a common query interface. (If you've used the Excel menu options for queries and sorting, you already are familiar with these concepts.) You will find Access 95 interoperable with all Microsoft Office products.

Summary

In this chapter, you learned about the capabilities of Access, and got an idea of the types of tasks Access can accomplish. The following points were introduced:

- Access is a database management system (DBMS).
- You can use Access to store and retrieve data, present information, and automate repetitive tasks.
- Using Access, you can develop easy-to-use input forms, process your data, and run powerful reports.
- Access features Query By Example (QBE) for selecting, sorting, and searching data.
- By using Access macros, you can create applications without programming.
- If you already are a database user, you should make sure you understand the differences in terminology between Access and the product you are familiar with.
- Spreadsheet and database users should already be familiar with many of the key concepts used in Access.

In the next chapter, you learn how to install Access.

✦ ✦ ✦

Installing Access for Windows 95

In This Chapter

What hardware and software you need to run Access

How to install Access successfully and run it on your computer

How to install the Access 95 upgrade

How to convert Access 1.x databases

How to handle problems that occur during installation

Access must be installed on your computer before you can use it. The installation is very simple. After you begin the process, you need only to supply the requested disks when prompted. As Access is installed, it displays information about itself on-screen.

Note: Access is installed in a manner similar to other Windows 95 software products. If your company has a special person or team designated to install and troubleshoot software, you may want to have this person or department install Access for you so that your system will be installed like the other systems in your company.

New! If you are installing an upgrade version of Access for Windows 95, Access must already be installed on your machine. New installations of Access for Windows 95 do not require a previous version of Access already installed on your machine.

Determining What You Need

Access requires specific hardware and software to run. Before you install Access, check to see that your computer meets the minimum requirements needed to run it.

Hardware requirements

To use Access for Windows 95 successfully, you'll need an IBM (or compatible) personal computer with an 80486SX-33 or higher processor and 12MB of RAM. To get reasonable performance from Access 95, we recommend an 80486DX-66 computer with at least 16MB of RAM. With more memory, you'll be able to run more applications simultaneously, and overall performance will be increased. A fast video card is also recommended to display pictures and graphs.

You will also need between 15 and 45MB of hard disk space for a typical installation. Keep in mind that you will need additional space to store your database files when you create them. If space is a problem, you can perform a partial installation, or you can delete unwanted files from your hard disk to free up space needed for the installation.

Access needs a VGA monitor as a minimum requirement but I recommend an SVGA (or better) display. This configuration allows you to view more information at one time and to get a sharper resolution.

A mouse or some other compatible pointing device (trackballs and pens will work) is mandatory for you to use Access for Windows 95.

If you're planning to print from Access, you need a printer. Any printer that is supported by Windows 95 works.

Software requirements

Access requires that Microsoft Windows 95 be installed on your computer. Windows 95 does *not* come with Access; it must be purchased separately. If Windows 95 is not currently installed on your computer, install it before you install Access.

Upgrading to Access for Windows 95 from Access 1.x or 2.0

Before you upgrade to Access for Windows 95 from earlier versions of Access, you should consider a few things.

Earlier versions of Access databases must be converted to Access for Windows 95 format before they are usable. After a database is converted to Access for Windows 95 format, it cannot be converted back; it's unusable by Access 1.x or 2.0. As an Access for Windows 95 user, you can open and work with Access 2.0 databases, but you cannot modify any of the objects (forms, reports, queries, and so on) you find in them.

If you are sharing files with people who use older versions of Access, think about leaving the older version of Access on your machine and reinstalling it under Windows 95. Then you can create personal files in Access for Windows 95 but still use Access 2.0 to work with files that are shared with others.

Installing Access

You can now install Access. Insert your CD-ROM into the drive (or Disk 1 into drive A) and then select Run from the Windows 95 Start menu. Windows 95 will display the Run dialog box. Type **A:\SETUP** (or use whatever letter corresponds to the drive containing your installation CD-ROM or disk) into the Command Line box, as shown in Figure 2-1. Select OK to begin the installation. This procedure works for both new installations and upgrades to Access for Windows 95.

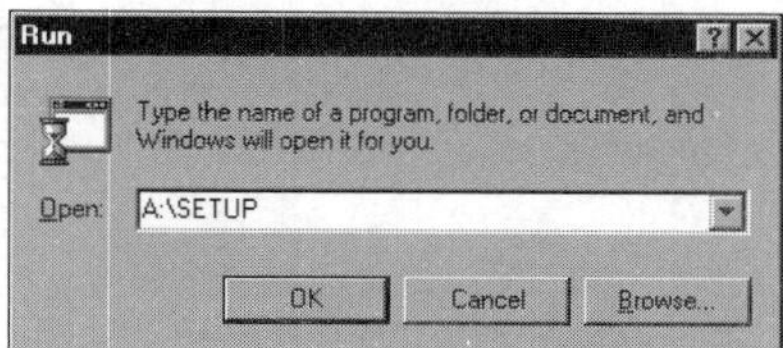

Figure 2-1: The Run dialog box.

Because some Windows 95 programs interfere with the Setup program, Access may warn you to shut down any applications currently running. You can simply click on the Continue button to continue setup or you can click on the Exit Setup button to cancel the installation and shut down your applications (you then can run Setup later).

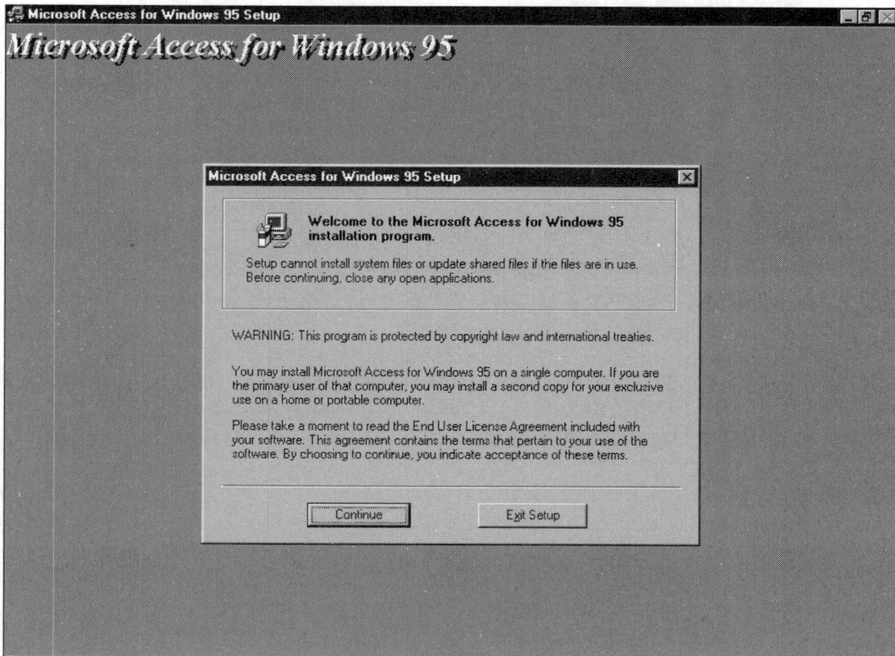

Figure 2-2: The Access 95 Welcome screen.

The Setup program now requires some information from you. If you are installing Access for the first time, you are asked to customize your copy of the program by entering your name and (optionally) a company name.

Next, a screen appears with your product ID number. You should write this number down; you'll need it if you call Microsoft Support for help.

Next, Setup wants to know where you want to install Access (as shown in Figure 2-3). The default is either C:\ACCESS or C:\MSOFFICE\ACCESS if you have Microsoft Office Professional. If this location is satisfactory, select OK to continue with the installation. If you want to change this directory, type in the new drive and directory name. For example, to have Access installed in a subdirectory located on drive D, you would type **D:\ACCESS**. If you type the name of a directory that does not exist, one is created for you.

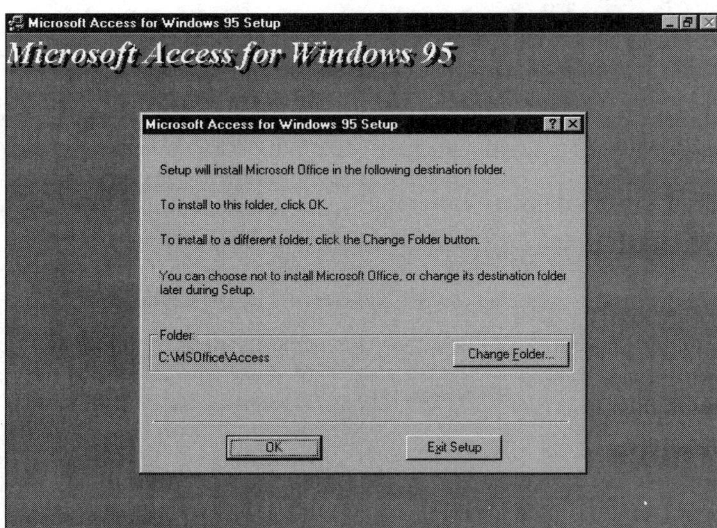

Figure 2-3: Selecting the directory to run Access.

Setup then takes some time to check for available disk space or existing copies of Access files. When this verification step is completed, Setup asks you to choose which type of installation you want, as shown in Figure 2-4. You can choose from the following three options:

Typical	This option installs all the Access files into the directory you specify.
Compact	This option installs the minimum number of files needed to run Access. It's designed for laptop systems with limited hard disk space (or for users who don't need all the options provided with Access).
Custom	This option lets you choose which files you want added. You can install omitted options in the future by rerunning Setup.

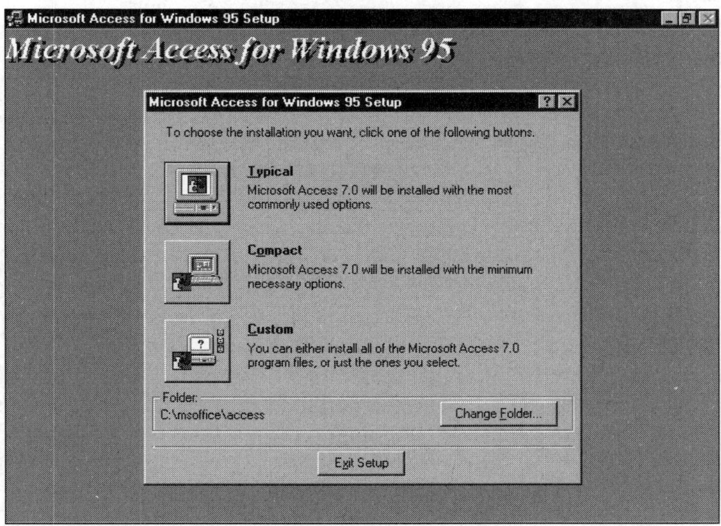

Figure 2-4: Selecting the type of installation.

If you choose Custom installation, you see the screen displayed in Figure 2-5. Setup provides you with a list of options you can install. At this point, all the options are selected to be installed. To deselect one, click on the check box next to the option you do not want installed. The X in the check box will disappear; the option will not be installed.

Setup next determines which disks and files to copy. Depending on the installation type you choose, you may not use all the disks provided.

The installation now proceeds, and you are prompted to insert the required disks as needed. This process will take some time — approximately 30 to 35 minutes for a complete installation.

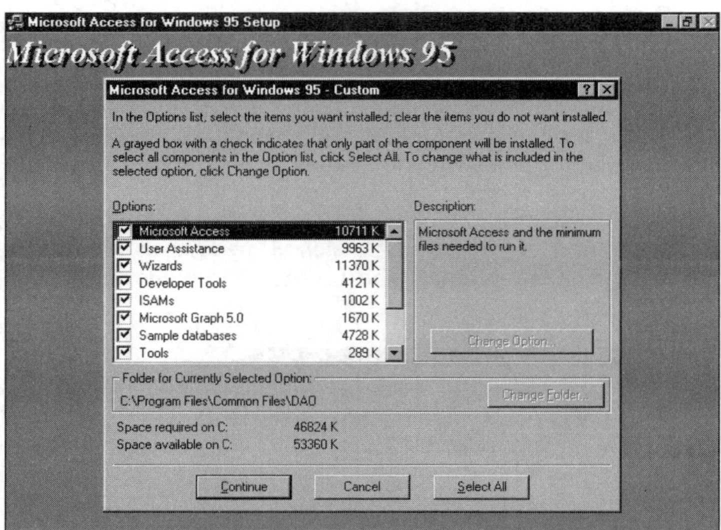

Figure 2-5: Installation Options.

As the installation continues, a series of pictures appears on-screen. These provide some basic information about various features of Access and how you can use them.

Once the installation is complete, you are returned to wherever you were when the installation began. A new program named `Microsoft Access` will be found on your start menu. You can run Access by either choosing Microsoft Access from the Start programs menu or locating the Microsoft Access folder on the desktop or Windows 95 Explorer and then finding the Access icon and double-clicking on it.

Converting Access 1.x and 2.x Files

Access for Windows 95 can convert and read databases created in older versions of Access; you can add, change, and delete data. You can run Access 1.x and 2.x queries, forms, reports, macros, and even Access BASIC modules. Even so, you cannot change any objects (tables, queries, forms, reports, macros, or modules). To redesign an Access 1.x or 2.x object, you must either use Access 1.x or 2.x itself or convert the object to Access for Windows 95.

You convert older Access databases by using Tools➪Database Utilities➪Convert Database in the Access Database window, as shown in Figure 2-6.

Note

No database can be open if you want to see the Convert Database option.

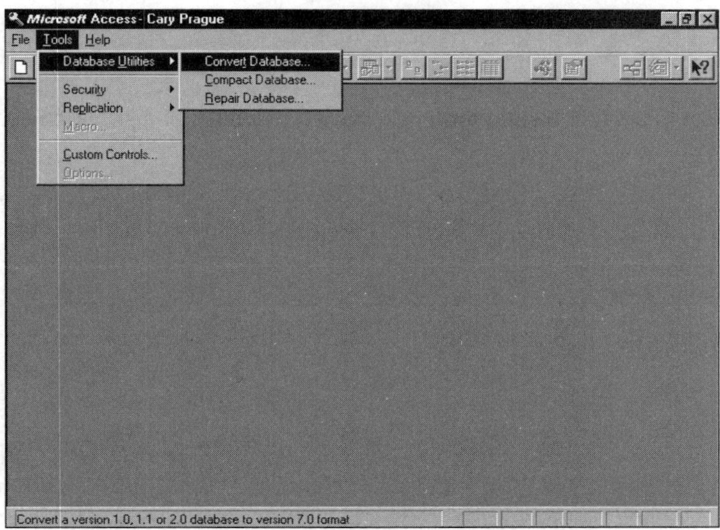

Figure 2-6: Converting an Access database.

A standard Windows 95 file-selector dialog box appears. You select the database to be converted and give it a new name. The database is converted.

Warning If the database is already in Access for Windows 95 format, Access tells you and the database is not converted.

Warning If you try to convert the database and save it to the same path and name, you get an error message; the conversion does not take place.

Before you convert a database, check for a few peculiar things that are not converted correctly by the conversion utility:

✦ If you use Microsoft Access security, you must own the database or be a member of the Admins group that was in effect when the database was created.

✦ After you convert a database to Access for Windows 95, the attachments of its tables into older-version databases are no longer valid. To use the attached tables, you must convert the attaching database as well.

✦ If Access can't find linked tables while converting the linking database, you should use the Linked Table Manager to re-link them.

Troubleshooting

If you run into problems while installing Access, Setup displays a message telling you what the problem may be. Some common problems include lack of disk space and problems reading the floppy disk.

If you receive a message saying that an error has occurred during Setup, you may have run out of disk space. You need to delete some files before proceeding with the installation. You can delete files from the Windows 95 Explorer. Remember to be careful not to delete important files. If you find that you have plenty of available disk space, something else has failed in the installation; you should contact Microsoft Product Support for help.

If your floppy disk drive has problems reading the installation disks, there may be a problem with your floppy disk drive. You may want to contact someone in your company's MIS or tech support department to check the floppy drive for you. Then, if you still receive this message and cannot find the problem, call Microsoft Product Support for help in troubleshooting the problem.

Summary

In this chapter, you learned about the equipment you need to install Access, how to install Access, and how to convert Access 1.x and 2.x databases. The chapter covered the following points:

- You need to have Microsoft Windows 95 installed on your system before you can install Access.
- At least 40MB of free hard disk space is needed to fully install Access for Windows 95.
- If available hard disk space is a problem, you can select Compact or Custom installation to limit the options that are installed. (You can install the omitted options at a later time by rerunning Setup.)
- You must convert older Access databases to work with Access for Windows 95.

Now that you have successfully installed Access, it's time to learn a little bit about how to use this software. Chapter 3 provides information on how to get started using Access.

✦ ✦ ✦

Getting Started with Access

In This Chapter

How you can start Access several different ways

How to add options to the Access command line

How to exit Access

How to get Help

How to use various Help options

Once you've installed Access successfully, you are ready to learn the various ways to start the Access database program. If you haven't installed Access yet, read Chapter 2 before proceeding.

Starting Access

You can start Access in several ways:

- ✦ From the Windows 95 Start menu
- ✦ From an Access shortcut icon
- ✦ From the Access icon in a folder
- ✦ From the Windows Explorer

Starting from the Windows 95 Start menu

When you use Windows 95 to install Access for Windows 95, Windows adds Access to the Start menu's Programs selection automatically. A simple way to start Access for Windows 95 is to click on the Start menu, select the Programs submenu, and then select Microsoft Access. This will start Microsoft Access and display the initial Access screen.

Starting from an Access shortcut icon

If you've gotten the hang of Windows 95, you've probably learned how valuable a *shortcut* can be. Figure 3-1 shows the Windows 95 desktop belonging to one of the authors. The right side of the screen shows a set of shortcuts to the Microsoft Office suite and several other programs. In particular, note the copy of the Access for Windows 95 icon; dragging it to the Windows 95 desktop from the MSOFFICE\ACCESS folder creates a shortcut. You can start Access for Windows 95 quickly by clicking on this icon.

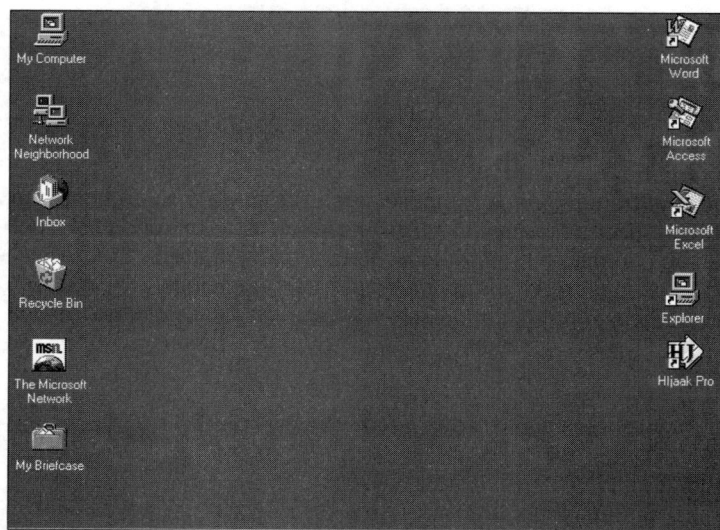

Figure 3-1: The Windows 95 desktop, showing a shortcut to Access.

Starting from an Access icon

If you purchased Access as part of Microsoft Office, then one of your folders in Windows 95 is probably the MSOFFICE folder. Inside that folder you should find a shortcut icon to launch Access for Windows 95. You will also find a folder named `ACCESS` which contains the actual icon for Msaccess.exe, as shown in Figure 3-2. You can start Access by clicking on either one of these icons.

Starting from the Windows Explorer

You can also start Access from the Windows Explorer (which has kind of replaced Program and File Manager) by selecting the database file you want to load. Figure 3-3 shows the Windows Explorer with the file `Mountain Animal Hospital.mdb` selected. This is the name of one the sample database files shipped with this book.

When you find the database file you want to load, double-click on the filename. Windows then starts Access and opens the database you selected. If you are unsure of which file you should choose, check to see that it has a proper file extension. Microsoft Access database files normally have the file extension `MDB`. Since Microsoft Access is a registered application in Windows 95, you will launch Access any time you select a file with the .MDB extension.

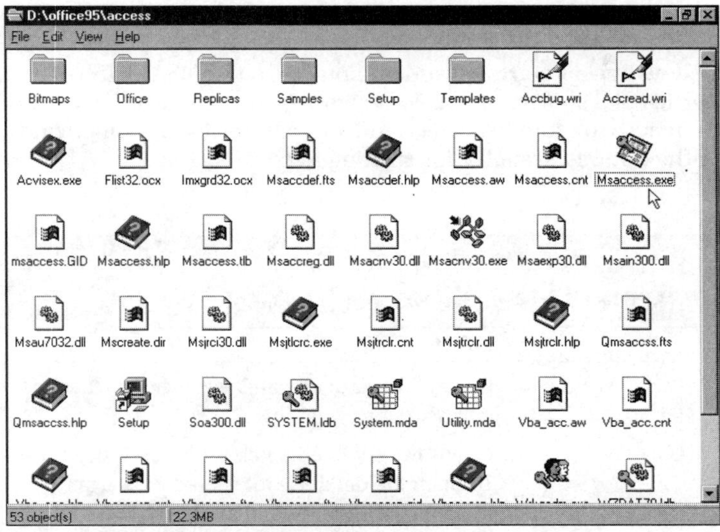

Figure 3-2: The Access for Windows 95 folder.

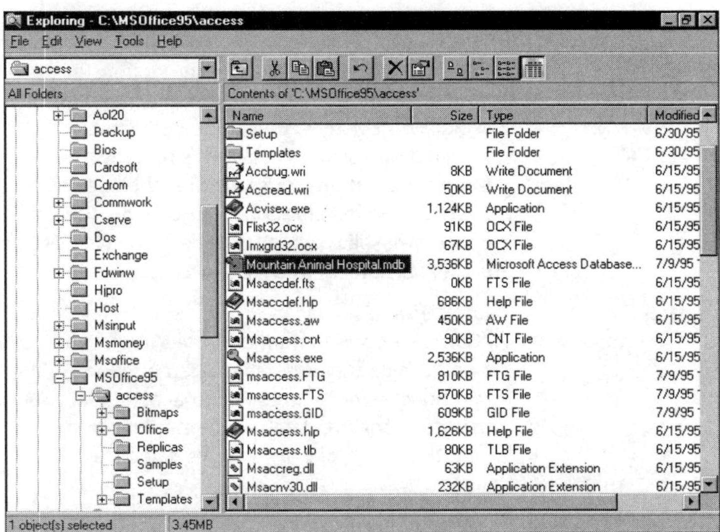

Figure 3-3: Starting a database file in the Windows Explorer.

Note If you already have Access running and you double-click a file in the Windows Explorer, another copy of Access will start, which will load the file you selected. You may want to do this if you want more than one database open at a time. (Access does not let you open more than one database at a time if you are running only one occurrence of Access.)

Options for starting Access

You can customize how Access starts by adding options to the MSACCESS command line from the properties of a shortcut icon. For example, you can have Access open a database, execute a macro, or supply a user name or password — automatically. Table 3-1 identifies the options available for starting Access.

Table 3-1
Command-Line Options for Starting Access

Option	*Effect*
<database>	Opens the specified database. Include a path if necessary.
/Excl	Opens the specified database for exclusive access. To open the database for shared access in a multiuser environment, omit this option.
/RO	Opens the specified database for read-only access.
/User <user name>	Starts Microsoft Access using the specified user name.
/Pwd <password>	Starts Microsoft Access using the specified password.
/Profile <user profile>	Starts Microsoft Access using the options in the specified user profile instead of the standard Windows Registry settings (created when you installed Microsoft Access). This replaces the /ini option used in previous versions of Microsoft Access to specify an initialization file. However, the /ini option will still work for user-defined .INI files from earlier versions of Microsoft Access.
/Compact <target database>	Compacts the database specified before the /Compact option and then closes Microsoft Access. If you omit a target database name following the /Compact option, Access compacts the database using the original database name. To compact to a different name, specify a target database.
/Repair	Repairs the specified database and then closes Microsoft Access.
/Convert <target database>	Converts a database in an earlier version (1.x or 2.0) to a Microsoft Access 95 database with a new name, and then closes Microsoft Access. Specify the source database before using the /Convert option.

Option	*Effect*
/X <macro>	Starts Microsoft Access and runs the specified macro. Another way to run a macro when you open a database is to use an AutoExec macro.
/Cmd	Specifies that what follows on the command line is the value that will be returned by the Command function. This option must be the last option on the command line. You can use a semicolon (;) as an alternative to /Cmd.
/Nostartup	Starts Microsoft Access without displaying the startup dialog box (the second dialog box you see when you start Microsoft Access).
/Runtime	Starts Microsoft Access in run time mode.

Tip

To run a VBA procedure when you open a database, use the RunCode action in a command-line macro or the AutoExec macro, or use the Access 95 Startup dialog. You can also run a VBA procedure when you open a database by creating a form with a VBA procedure defined for its OnOpen event. Designate this as the startup form by using the right mouse button to click in the database window, then click on Startup, and then enter that form in the Display Form box.

For example, to have Access automatically execute a macro called MYMACRO, you would enter the following parameter in the Shortcut Properties section of an Access shortcut. (You may find the command MSACCESS.EXE preceded by its path.)

MSACCESS.EXE /X MYMACRO

You can also use a special option that Access runs automatically when you first open a Microsoft Access database (you will learn more about this in Part V). This is the *Startup form*. You can use it to open certain tables or forms every time you enter a database, or to perform complex processing, change the menus, change the title bar, hide the database window, or do just about anything you can think of.

Note

In Access 2.0, you created a macro named Autoexec to do this. In Access for Windows 95, the startup form is an easier way to run a program automatically when you open a database.

Tip

To prevent a startup form from running automatically, hold down the Shift key as you open the database.

Exiting Access

When you are finished using Access (or any application), you should always exit gracefully. It bears repeating: simply turning off your system is not a good method, and can cause problems. Windows and your applications use many files while they are running, some of which you may not be aware of. Turning off your system can cause these files not to be closed properly, which can result in hard disk problems in the future.

Another reason for exiting gracefully is to ensure that all your data is saved before you exit the application. If you have spent quite a bit of time inputting data and then you turn off your system, accidentally forgetting to save this work, all this unsaved data will be lost! Save yourself time and grief by exiting your applications the correct way.

You can exit Access in several safe ways:

✦ Double-click on the Control icon in the Access title bar.

✦ From the Access menu, select File⇨Exit.

✦ Press Alt+F4.

✦ Display the taskbar and select Microsoft Access. Then right-click and select Close. You can use this method to close Access from within another application.

When you exit Access with one of these methods, you may see a message displayed on-screen that prompts you to save any changes you may have made. You can select Yes to save the changes and exit Access. Selecting No will exit Access without saving the changes you made. Cancel stops Access from closing, and you are returned to Access. You can also choose Help for more information on exiting Access.

Getting Help

Now that you have learned how to start Access, you may need some help in learning how to use the software. Once you have started Access, you can choose from any of the Help options that are available. Some of these include:

✦ Standard Windows 95 Help (Contents, Index, and Find tabs)

✦ Screen Tips

✦ The Answer Wizard

✦ A Visual Introduction to Microsoft Access for Windows 95

✦ The Solutions database

Using Standard Help

When you press F1 to request help, Access presents you with a tabbed dialog box (as shown in Figure 3-4). You can also use the Help menu. This dialog box provides several ways to help you get started using Access. You have four options to choose from:

Contents. As shown in Figure 3-4, the Table of Contents lists major topics grouped by task. When you select a topic, a menu of subtopics appears and leads you to various Help screens.

Index. This displays an alphabetical list of Help topics. You can type the first few letters of the Help topic you are searching for, or scroll through the list.

Find. This feature conducts a finer search than you can do using the Index. First you enter a single keyword. A list of potential topics appears; you select one of these to see a list of Help topics.

Answer Wizard. The Answer Wizard lets you enter questions in English (or whatever language you're using). On the basis of what you type, the Wizard attempts to display a list of Help topics (see Figure 3-6).

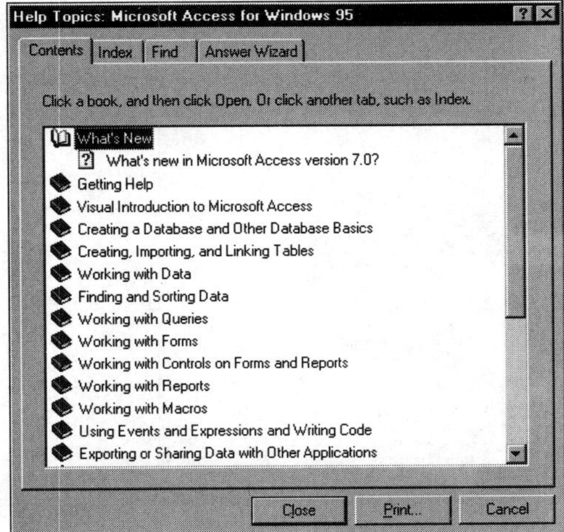

Figure 3-4: The Access for Windows 95 Help dialog box.

If you are have used Access 2.0, the topics under What's New will give you a thorough explanation of the new features in Access for Windows 95.

As you can see in Figure 3-4, the list of Help topics is very general. When you select an option, the icon will appear as an open book indicating a list of subtopics. When you see the icon with a question mark, you can click on it and then the place you want help to display the actual help you need, or another menu of topics.

This is *Small Card Help*, also used to display textual explanations, instructions, and language reference; Figure 3-5 shows a good example. Small Card Help also features an Options menu that lets you annotate, copy the Help text to the Clipboard, print the help you find, and more. (See Table 3-2 for more details.)

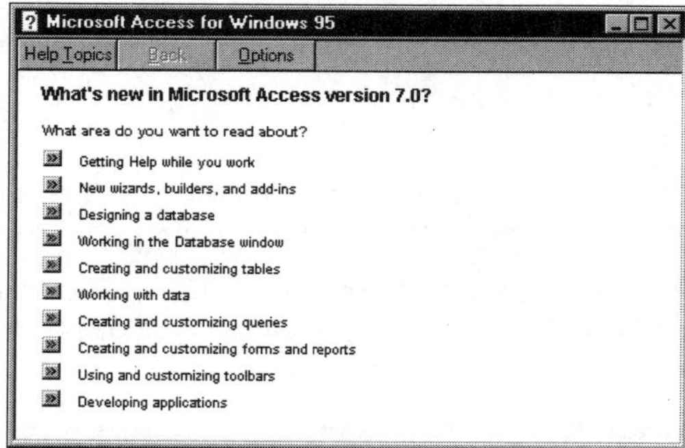

Figure 3-5: An Access for Windows 95 Small Card Help menu.

From Small Card Help menus, you can select any topic and receive more help. A good example of this *Large Card Help* is the option for Getting Help while you work under the What's New Help topics. As you press any of the large buttons, you receive an explanation of the topic (as shown in Figure 3-6). Unlike Small Card Help, Large Card Help is more explanatory and less instructional. There is no Options menu in Large Card Help forms.

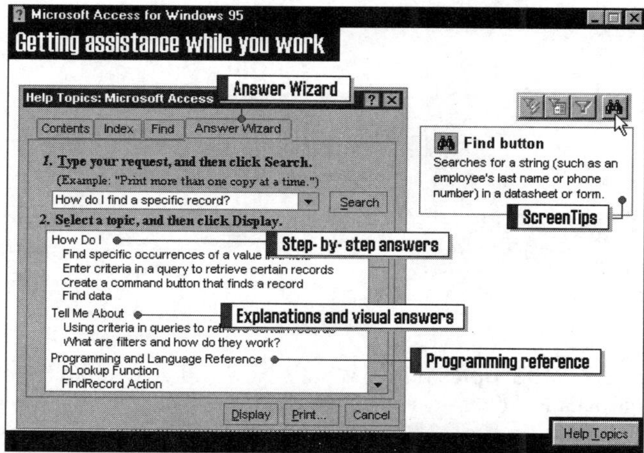

Figure 3-6: Access for Windows 95 Large Card Help display.

Essentials of standard online help

Help in Access is always a keystroke away. There are many easy ways to get help:

✦ Press the F1 key to get standard, context-sensitive help.

✦ Click on the Help button that resembles a cursor arrow and a question mark (on the Access toolbar), and then click on the desired item to get Screen Tip help. You can also press Shift-F1 to display the question-mark cursor. More on Screen Tips later.

✦ Select Help from the Access pull-down menu.

Warning

You can get help at any time in Access, no matter what you are doing. There is help for every aspect of Access — commands, menus, building macros, Access terms and concepts, even programming topics. Figure 3-3 showed the Help Table of Contents window that is displayed when you press F1 (if no activity is in progress).

Often you may not see the Help Table of Contents screen, even when you think you're not performing any activity. Frequently the Databases Help screen appears in the Database window. If a different screen appears after you press F1, simply click on the Contents tab to display the Help Table of Contents screen.

Help is a separate program from Access, and has its own window. Therefore you can move, size, minimize, or close the Help window.

Using Small Card Help options

When Small Card Help is displayed, it shows an Options menu that contains several choices. These appear in Table 3-2.

Table 3-2
Help Menu Options

Option	Description
Annotate	Lets you add text to the current Help topic. Annotations are marked with a paper-clip icon in front of the topic heading. This is a good way to add your own notes to a Help topic for future reference. You can also copy and paste annotations to other Help topics, or into other applications or documents.
Copy	Copies the text of the current Help topic to the Clipboard. From the Clipboard, you can paste the text into another application or document.
Print Topic	Prints the current topic in the Help window. You can print only entire topics.

(continued)

Table 3-2 (continued)

Option	Description
Font	Sets the font size to Small, Normal, or Large.
Keep Help on Top	This option determines whether a Help window is sent to the background when another function is selected in Access. Choices are Default, On Top, and Not On Top.
Use System Colors	This uses the default system colors rather than Access for Windows 95 Help colors.
Version	This selection displays the version, mode, and copyright information about the Windows Help engine.

Screen Tips

Screen Tips are a new type of help found in all Microsoft Office products. They give you short explanations of tasks in the various products. The are text only, generally displayed in a small rectangle. While standard toolbar tooltips display only a word or two, Screen Tips display a paragraph. When you select the Help icon on the toolbar, the cursor changes to an arrow with a question mark. You can then click on various parts of an Access for Windows 95 screen and receive a short explanation of the task or function you clicked on. You can also press Shift-F1 for the same effect. For example, if you press Shift-F1 and then click on the Queries tab in the Database window, you will see a Screen Tip explaining what you can do with a query, as shown in Figure 3-7.

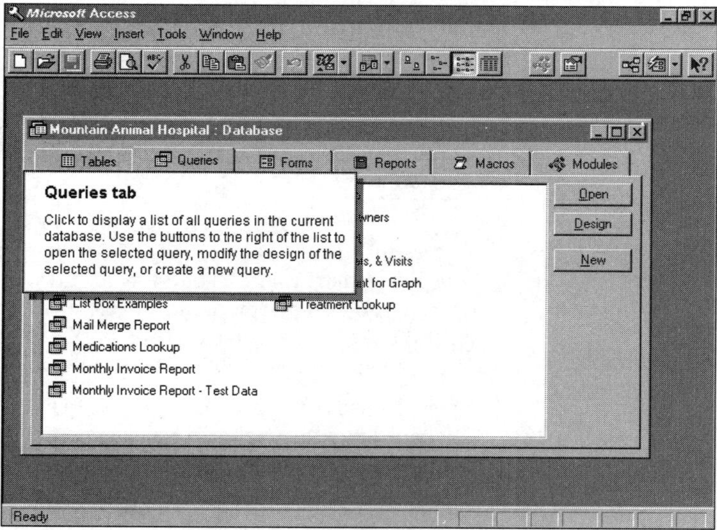

Figure 3-7: An Access for Windows 95 Screen Tip.

Tip

You can create your own Screen Tips in your applications, using the same techniques that create standard Access for Windows 95 Help.

The Access for Windows 95 Answer Wizard

A new type of help in Access for Windows 95 is the *Answer Wizard*. This is the last option on the standard Help screen (as shown earlier in Figure 3-4). The Answer Wizard goes beyond standard Help indexes or keyword searches, allowing you to ask questions in standard terms without having to rely on technical words. As you can see in Figure 3-8, for example, you can type a question such as `How do I display a form?` into the Answer Wizard in layman's terms. Then, when you click on the Search button, Access displays a list of possible topics; you can select a topic or ask a more specific question (for example, `How do I display a form with a graph?`).

Note

You can type questions into the Answer Wizard without worrying about capitalization.

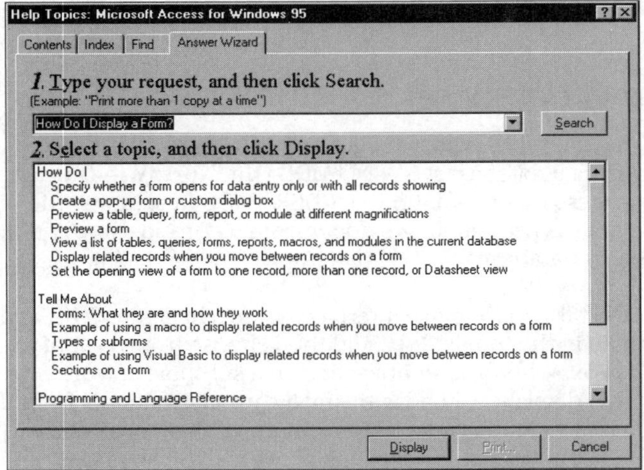

Figure 3-8: Using the Access for Windows 95 Answer Wizard.

Taking a visual tour of Access for Windows 95

In Figure 3-4, you may have noticed one of the options in the Access for Windows 95 Help contents was Visual introduction to Microsoft Access. This is a very basic conceptual introduction to database concepts using Microsoft Access. Using Large Card type help, you have over 50 cards of introductory information. Figure 3-9 shows a typical card from the Visual Introduction. This is a great place to start if you are new to database terminology and techniques. Many of the Large Card Help screens that you can display from various Help options are shared with this Visual Introduction.

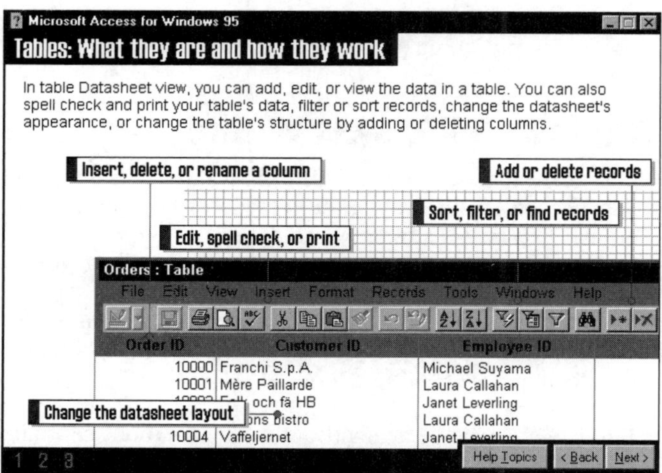

Figure 3-9: A Visual Introduction to Microsoft Access.

Using the Solutions Database

You should be aware of one more place you can get help. The Access SAMPLES directory contains three special databases: NWIND.MDB (the NorthWinds example file used throughout the Access documentation), ORDERS.MDB (a sample order-entry program also used in the Access programmer's documentation), and SOLUTIONS.MDB (a teaching database).

When you open SOLUTIONS.MDB, a Help-like interface (shown in Figure 3-10) appears. You can select a global topic in the top list box, and then choose from a set of specific subtopics in the lower list box. When you double-click on a subtopic, a working example from NorthWinds is displayed along with small card instructional Help. This allows you to work with a real example while learning some of the more complex topics. Unlike the visual introduction which explains concepts, the Solutions database is used to show you how to solve a particular problem using Access.

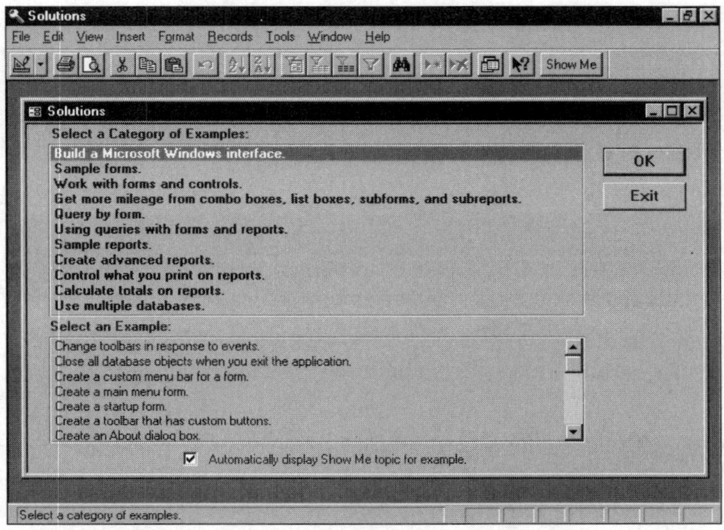

Figure 3-10: The Access for Windows 95 Solutions database.

Summary

In this chapter, you learned various ways to start Access and how to exit the program. You learned about the many ways to use the Access Help system. The following points were covered:

- ✦ You can start Access in various ways; the easiest and most common method is using the Start menu or double-clicking on an Access shortcut icon.
- ✦ You can add options to the Access command line that can automatically open a database, execute a macro, or set a user name or password.
- ✦ You should use one of the suggested ways to exit Access. If you exit by simply turning off your system, the result can be loss of data.
- ✦ There are many types of Help in Access. Small Card Help can provide step-by-step instructions for learning Access; it walks you through the setups needed to create your own database objects.
- ✦ You can press F1 to activate the Help feature, which gives information on how to use Access, or defines various concepts used in Access.
- ✦ Help appears in a window of its own that can be minimized or resized; you can keep it open as you work on your database.
- ✦ Using the Answer Wizard, you can ask questions in plain language and see various Help topics that match your question.
- ✦ The Access Visual Introduction will teach you the fundamental concepts of working with databases using Microsoft Access for Windows 95.

In the next chapter, you review basic database concepts as you begin the journey to understanding database management with Access.

✦ ✦ ✦

A Review of Database Concepts

In This Chapter

What is a database?

What are the differences among databases, tables, records, fields, and values?

Why are multiple tables used in a database?

What are database objects?

Before you begin to use a database software package, you must understand several basic concepts. The most important concept is that the data is stored in a "black box" known as a *table*, and that by using the tools of the database, you can retrieve, display, and report the data in any format you want.

What Is a Database?

Database is a computer term for a collection of information concerning a certain topic or business application. Databases help you organize this related information in a logical fashion for easy access and retrieval.

Figure 4-1 shows a conceptual view of a typical manual filing system that consists of people, papers, and filing cabinets. This lighthearted view of a manual database makes the point that paper is the key to a manual database system. In a real manual database system, you probably have in/out baskets and some type of formal filing method. You access information manually by opening a file cabinet, taking out a file folder, and finding the correct piece of paper. Paper forms are used for input, perhaps with a typewriter. You find information by sorting the papers manually, or by copying desired information from many papers onto another piece of paper (or even into a computer spreadsheet). You might use a calculator or a computer spreadsheet to analyze the data further, or to report it.

Figure 4-1: A typical manual filing system.

A computer database is nothing more than an automated version of the filing-and-retrieval functions of a manual paper filing system. Computer databases store information in a structured format that you define. They can store data in a variety of forms, from simple lines of text (such as name and address) to complex data structures that include pictures, sounds, or video images. Storing data in a precise, known format enables a database management system (DBMS) to turn the data into useful information through many types of output, such as queries and reports.

Figure 4-2 shows a conceptual view of an automated database management system such as Access. The person uses a computer to access the data stored in tables — inputting data to the tables through data-entry forms and retrieving it by using a query. Queries retrieve only the desired data from the tables. Then a report outputs the data to the screen or a printer. Macros and modules allow the user to automate this process, even create new menus and dialog boxes.

Figure 4-2: A computer database system.

A *relational* database management system (RDBMS) such as Access stores data in many related tables. The user can ask complex questions from one or more of these related tables; answers come back to the user as forms and reports.

Databases, Tables, Records, Fields, and Values

In Microsoft Access, the terms database, table, record, field, and Microsoft Access follows traditional database terminology. The terms *database*, *table*, *record*, *field*, and *value* indicate a hierarchy from largest to smallest.

Databases

In Access, a *database* is the overall container for the data and associated objects. Database *objects* include tables, queries, forms, reports, macros, and modules, as shown in Figure 4-2. In some computer software products, the database is the object that holds the actual data; in Access, this is called a *table*.

Access can work with only one database at a time. Within a single Access database, however, you can have hundreds of tables, forms, queries, reports, macros, and modules — all stored in a single file with the file extension .MDB.

Tables

A table is a container for raw data. When you enter data in Access, a table stores it in logical groupings of similar data (the Pets table, for example, contains data about pets); the table's design organizes the information into rows and columns. Figure 4-3 shows a typical Access table design; its *datasheet* (also known as a *browse table* or *table view*) displays multiple lines of data in neat rows and columns.

Records and fields

As shown in Figure 4-3, the datasheet is divided into rows called *records* and columns called *fields*. The data shown in the table has columns of similar information, such as Pet Name, Customer Number, Breed, or Date of Birth; these columns of data items are fields. Each field is identified as a certain type of data (Text, Number, Date, and so on) and has a specified length. Each field has a name that identifies its category of information.

The rows of data within a table are its records. Each row of information is considered a separate entity that can be accessed or sequenced as desired. All the fields of information concerning a certain pet are contained within a specific record.

Values

At the intersection of a row (record) and a column (field) is a *value* — the actual data element. For example, Bobo, the Pet Name of the first record, is one data value. (How do you identify the first record? It's the record with the rabbit. But what if there is more than one rabbit?) Whereas fields are known by the field name, records are usually known by some unique characteristic of the record. In the Pets table, one field is the Pet ID; Pet Name is not unique because there could be two pets named Fido in the table.

Sometimes it takes more than one field to find a unique value. Customer Number and Pet Name could be used, but it's possible for one customer to have two pets with the same name. You could use the fields Customer Number, Pet Name, and Type of Animal. But again, theoretically you could have a customer come in and say, "Hi, my name's Larry — this is my pet snake Darryl, and this is my other pet snake Darryl." Creating a unique identifier (such as Pet ID) helps you tell one record apart from another without having to look through all the values.

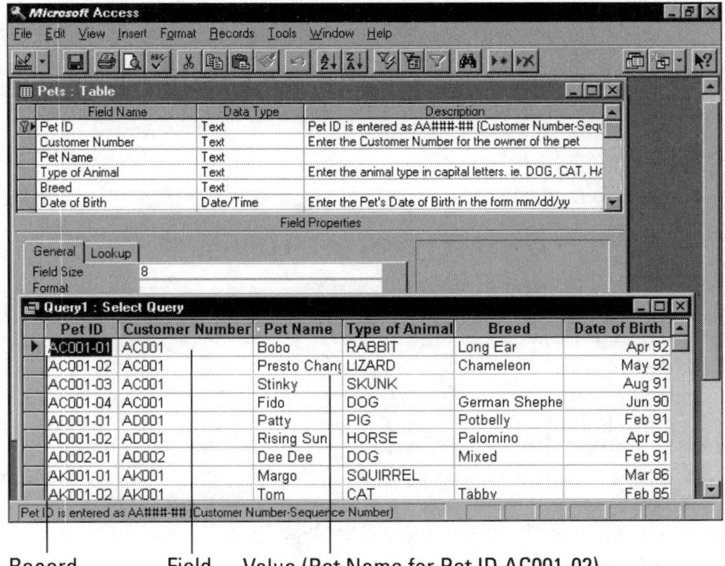

Figure 4-3: A Database table design and datasheet.

Why Use More Than One Table?

A database contains one or more tables (that is, logical groupings of similar data). Most applications that you'll develop in Access have several related tables to present the information efficiently. An application that uses multiple tables can manipulate data more efficiently than it could with one large table.

Multiple tables simplify data entry and reporting by decreasing the input of redundant data. By defining two tables for an application that uses customer information, for example, you don't need to store the customer's name and address every time the customer purchases an item. Figure 4-4 shows a typical table relation: the Customer table related to the Pets table. If there were only one table, the customer name and address would have to be repeated for each pet record. Two tables let the user look up information in the Customer table for each pet by using the common field Customer Number. This way, when a customer changes address (for example), it changes only in one record in the Customer table; when the pet information is on-screen, the correct customer address is always visible.

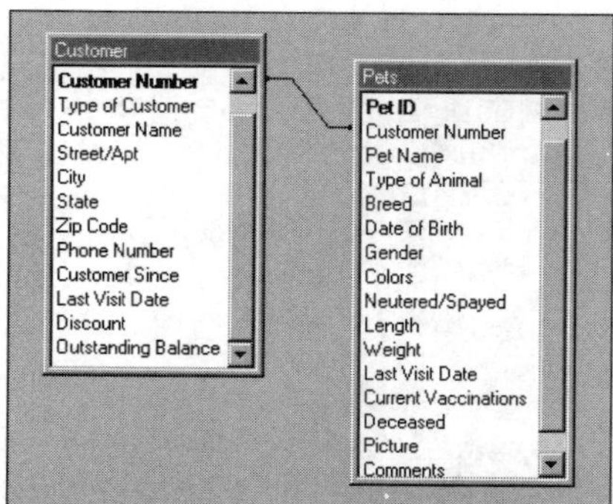

Figure 4-4: Related tables.

By separating your data into multiple tables within your database, you'll find your system is easier to maintain because all records of a given type are within the same table. You will significantly reduce your design and work time if you invest the extra time to segment your data properly into multiple tables.

Tip It is also a good idea to create a separate database for just your tables. By separating your design objects (queries, forms, reports, macros, and modules) and the tables into two different databases, you make it easier to maintain your application.

Later in this book, you will have the opportunity to work through a case study for the Mountain Animal Hospital that consists of eight tables. You will also learn how to use the Access 95 Application Splitter to separate the tables from the design objects.

Database Objects and Views

If you are new to databases (or even an experienced database user), you should understand some key concepts in Access before starting to use the product. The Access database contains six objects; these consist of the data and tools you need to use Access:

Table	Holds the actual data (uses a datasheet to display the raw data)
Query	Lets you search, sort, and retrieve specific data
Form	Lets you enter and display data in a customized format
Report	Lets you display and print formatted data, including calculations and totals
Macro	Gives you easy-to-use commands to automate tasks without programming
Module	Programs written in VBA

Datasheets

Datasheets are one of the many ways you can view data. Although not a database object, a datasheet displays a list of records from your table in a format commonly known as a *browse screen*, or *table view*. A datasheet displays data as a series of rows and columns (comparable to a spreadsheet), as shown in Figure 4-5. A datasheet simply displays the information from a table in its raw form. This spreadsheet format is the default mode for displaying all fields for all records.

You can scroll through the datasheet by using the directional keys on your keyboard. In addition, you can make changes to the displayed data. You should use caution when making any changes or allowing a user to make any modifications in this format. When you change a record in a datasheet, you are actually changing the data in the underlying table.

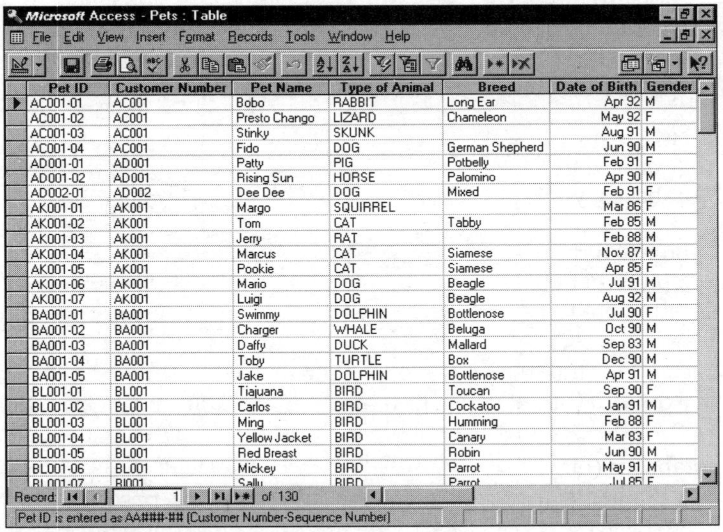

Microsoft Access - Pets : Table

File Edit View Insert Format Records Tools Window Help

Pet ID	Customer Number	Pet Name	Type of Animal	Breed	Date of Birth	Gender
AC001-01	AC001	Bobo	RABBIT	Long Ear	Apr 92	M
AC001-02	AC001	Presto Chango	LIZARD	Chameleon	May 92	F
AC001-03	AC001	Stinky	SKUNK		Aug 91	M
AC001-04	AC001	Fido	DOG	German Shepherd	Jun 90	M
AD001-01	AD001	Patty	PIG	Potbelly	Feb 91	F
AD001-02	AD001	Rising Sun	HORSE	Palomino	Apr 90	M
AD002-01	AD002	Dee Dee	DOG	Mixed	Feb 91	F
AK001-01	AK001	Margo	SQUIRREL		Mar 86	F
AK001-02	AK001	Tom	CAT	Tabby	Feb 85	M
AK001-03	AK001	Jerry	RAT		Feb 88	M
AK001-04	AK001	Marcus	CAT	Siamese	Nov 87	M
AK001-05	AK001	Pookie	CAT	Siamese	Apr 85	F
AK001-06	AK001	Mario	DOG	Beagle	Jul 91	M
AK001-07	AK001	Luigi	DOG	Beagle	Aug 92	M
BA001-01	BA001	Swimmy	DOLPHIN	Bottlenose	Jul 90	F
BA001-02	BA001	Charger	WHALE	Beluga	Oct 90	M
BA001-03	BA001	Daffy	DUCK	Mallard	Sep 83	M
BA001-04	BA001	Toby	TURTLE	Box	Dec 90	M
BA001-05	BA001	Jake	DOLPHIN	Bottlenose	Apr 91	M
BL001-01	BL001	Tiajuana	BIRD	Toucan	Sep 90	F
BL001-02	BL001	Carlos	BIRD	Cockatoo	Jan 91	M
BL001-03	BL001	Ming	BIRD	Humming	Feb 88	F
BL001-04	BL001	Yellow Jacket	BIRD	Canary	Mar 83	F
BL001-05	BL001	Red Breast	BIRD	Robin	Jun 90	M
BL001-06	BL001	Mickey	BIRD	Parrot	May 91	M
BL001-07	BI001	Sally	BIRD	Parrot	Jul 85	F

Record: 1 of 130

Pet ID is entered as AA###-## (Customer Number-Sequence Number)

Figure 4-5: A typical datasheet.

Queries and dynasets

You use a *query* to extract information from a database. A query can select and define a group of records that fulfill a certain condition. You can use queries before printing a report so that only the desired data is printed. Forms can also use a query so that only certain records (that meet the desired criteria) will appear on-screen. You can use queries within procedures that change, add, or delete database records.

An example of a query is when a doctor at Mountain Animal Hospital says, "Show me which of the pets we treat are dogs or cats and are located in Idaho; show them to me sorted by customer name and then by pet name." Instead of asking the question in actual English, the doctor would use a method known as *QBE*, which stands for Query By Example. Figure 4-6 shows a typical query screen that asks the doctor's question.

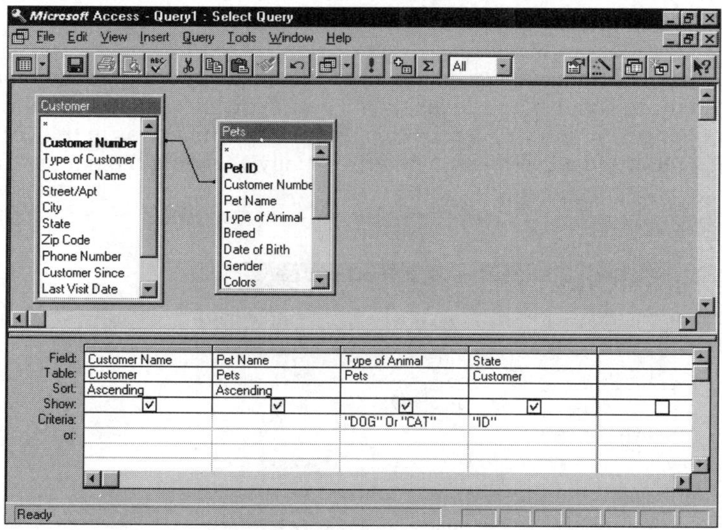

Figure 4-6: A typical query.

When you enter instructions into the QBE window, the query translates them and retrieves the desired data. In this example, first the query combines data from both the Customer and Pets tables, using the related field Customer Number (the common link between the tables). Then it retrieves the fields Customer Name, Pet Name, Type of Animal, and State. Access then filters the records, selecting only those in which the value State is `ID` and the value Type of Animal is `dog` or `cat`. It sorts the resulting records, first by customer name, and then by pet name within the customer names that are alike. Finally the records appear on-screen in a datasheet.

These selected records are known as a *dynaset* — a *dyna*mic *set* of data that can change according to the raw data in the original tables.

After you run a query, you can use the resulting dynaset in a form, which you can display on-screen in a specified format or print on a report. In this way, you can limit user access to only the data that meets the criteria in the dynaset.

Data-entry and display forms

Data-entry forms help users get information into a database table in a quick, easy, and accurate manner. Data-entry and display forms provide a more structured view of the data than does a datasheet. From this structured view, you can view, add, change, or delete database records. Entering data through the data-entry forms is the most common way to get the data into the database table. Figure 4-7 shows a typical form.

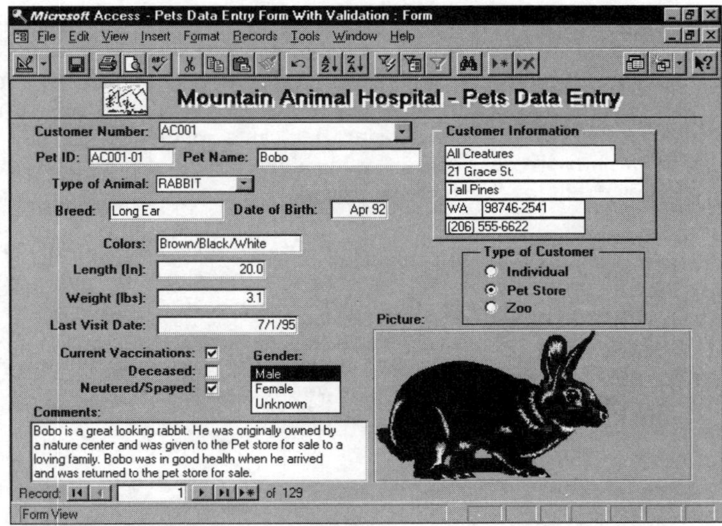

Figure 4-7: A typical data-entry form.

You can use data-entry forms to restrict access to certain fields within the table. You can also use these forms to check the validity of your data before you accept it into the database table.

Most users prefer to enter information into data-entry forms rather than datasheet tables; data-entry forms can be made to resemble familiar paper documents. Forms make data entry self-explanatory by guiding the user through the fields of the table being updated.

Display-only screens and forms are solely for inquiry purposes. These forms allow for the selective display of certain fields within a given table. Displaying some fields and not others means you can limit a user's access to sensitive data while allowing inquiry into other fields.

Reports

Reports present your data in printed format. You can create several different types of reports within a database management system. For example, your report can list all records in a given table, such as a customer table. You can also create a report that lists only the customers who meet a given criterion, such as all those who live in the state of Washington.You do this by incorporating a query into your report design. The query creates a dynaset consisting of the records that contain the state code WA.

Your reports can combine multiple tables to present complex relationships among different sets of data. An example is printing an invoice. You access the customer table to obtain the customer's name and address (and other pertinent data), and the sales table to print the individual line-item information for the products ordered. You can then have Access calculate the totals and print them (in a specific format) on the form. Additionally, you can have Access output records into an *invoice report*, a table that summarizes the invoice. Figure 4-8 shows a typical invoice report.

It is important to keep in mind all the necessary information you want printed when you initially design your database tables. Doing so ensures that the information you require on your various reports is available from within your database tables.

When you design your database tables, keep in mind all the types of information you want printed. Doing so ensures that the information you require on your various reports is available from within your database tables.

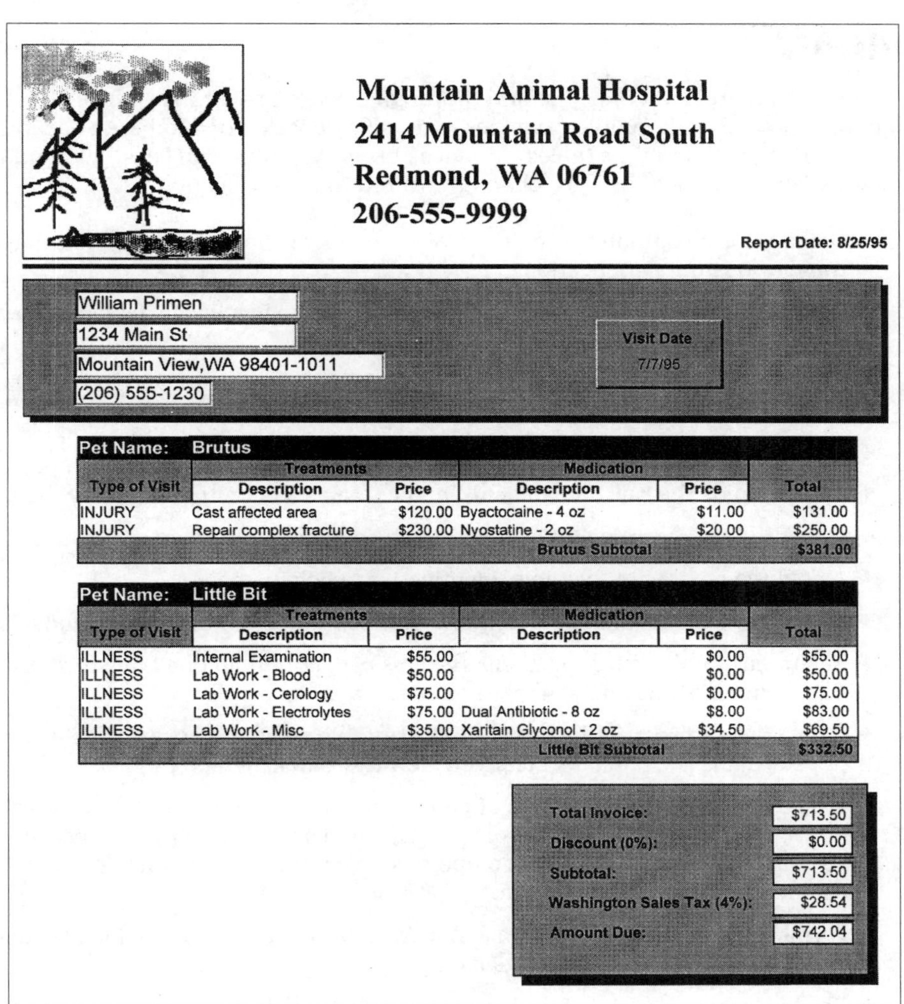

Mountain Animal Hospital
2414 Mountain Road South
Redmond, WA 06761
206-555-9999

Report Date: 8/25/95

William Primen
1234 Main St
Mountain View,WA 98401-1011
(206) 555-1230

Visit Date
7/7/95

Pet Name:	Brutus				
	Treatments		Medication		
Type of Visit	Description	Price	Description	Price	Total
INJURY	Cast affected area	$120.00	Byactocaine - 4 oz	$11.00	$131.00
INJURY	Repair complex fracture	$230.00	Nyostatine - 2 oz	$20.00	$250.00
			Brutus Subtotal		$381.00

Pet Name:	Little Bit				
	Treatments		Medication		
Type of Visit	Description	Price	Description	Price	Total
ILLNESS	Internal Examination	$55.00		$0.00	$55.00
ILLNESS	Lab Work - Blood	$50.00		$0.00	$50.00
ILLNESS	Lab Work - Cerology	$75.00		$0.00	$75.00
ILLNESS	Lab Work - Electrolytes	$75.00	Dual Antibiotic - 8 oz	$8.00	$83.00
ILLNESS	Lab Work - Misc	$35.00	Xaritain Glyconol - 2 oz	$34.50	$69.50
			Little Bit Subtotal		$332.50

Total Invoice:	$713.50
Discount (0%):	$0.00
Subtotal:	$713.50
Washington Sales Tax (4%):	$28.54
Amount Due:	$742.04

Figure 4-8: A typical invoice report.

Summary

You can find more new concepts (and thorough discussions of them) throughout this book. Chapter 12, for example, provides in-depth discussion of database concepts when working with multiple tables, as well as primary and foreign keys, referential integrity, and relationships. This chapter covered the following points:

- ✦ Database is a computer term for a collection of information related to a certain topic or business application.
- ✦ Databases let you organize this related information in a logical fashion for easy access and retrieval.
- ✦ An Access database is a single file with an MDB file extension; it holds all the database objects used in Access.
- ✦ Database objects include tables, queries, forms, reports, macros, and modules.
- ✦ A table holds the raw data in fields, and contains a definition for every field.
- ✦ A record is a row in the table, identified by some unique value.
- ✦ A field is a column in the table, identified by a field name.
- ✦ The value is an element of data found at the intersection of a record and a field.
- ✦ Relational database management systems use more than one table to simplify database reporting and eliminate redundant data.
- ✦ A datasheet (also called a browse table or table view) is a spreadsheet-type view of your data. The datasheet lets you view raw data in a table.
- ✦ A query lets you ask questions of your data; you use the Query By Example (QBE) screen to select fields, sort the data, and select only specific records by specified criteria. The result of a query is a dynaset. This dynamic set of data can be used with a datasheet, form, or report.
- ✦ Forms let you view your data in a more structured format. You can enter data into a form or make the form read-only.
- ✦ Reports are used mainly for calculating and summarizing data, and are frequently printed.

In the next chapter, you take a guided tour through Access and see how some of these objects are used.

✦ ✦ ✦

A Hands-On Tour of Access

✦ ✦ ✦ ✦

In This Chapter

Learning how to navigate the screen by using the mouse, the keyboard, or a combination of the two

Seeing a brief overview of the basic components found on the Access screen

Taking a hands-on tour through a simple Access session, where you learn how to open a database and a table, display a form, create a query, and display a report

✦ ✦ ✦ ✦

To use Access, you need to know how to get around the Access screen. In this chapter, you learn that each task you want to complete in Access can probably be accomplished with several different methods. Some tasks have as many as five ways to accomplish the same thing. It's important to understand that the method using the fewest keystrokes or mouse clicks is usually best.

A Tour of the Screen

In this book, you see many Access windows and shortcut dialog boxes, and you learn many specific terms. It's a good idea to become familiar with these terms. If you've used another database software package before learning Access, you'll need to translate the terms you already know into the words Microsoft Access uses to refer to the same task or action.

Using the mouse and keyboard

You can navigate the Access screen by using the mouse, the keyboard, or a combination of both. The best way to get around in Access is by using a mouse or some other pointing device. You'll find the keyboard useful for entering data and for moving around the various data-entry areas. You'll find it unproductive, however, to try using only the keyboard when designing new forms, queries, or reports. In this book, you learn how to complete tasks by using both the keyboard and mouse. In most cases, using the mouse is preferable.

The Access window

The Access window is the center of activity for everything you do in Access. From here, you can have many windows open, each of which displays a different view of your data. Figure 5-1 shows the Access window with a Database window open inside it.

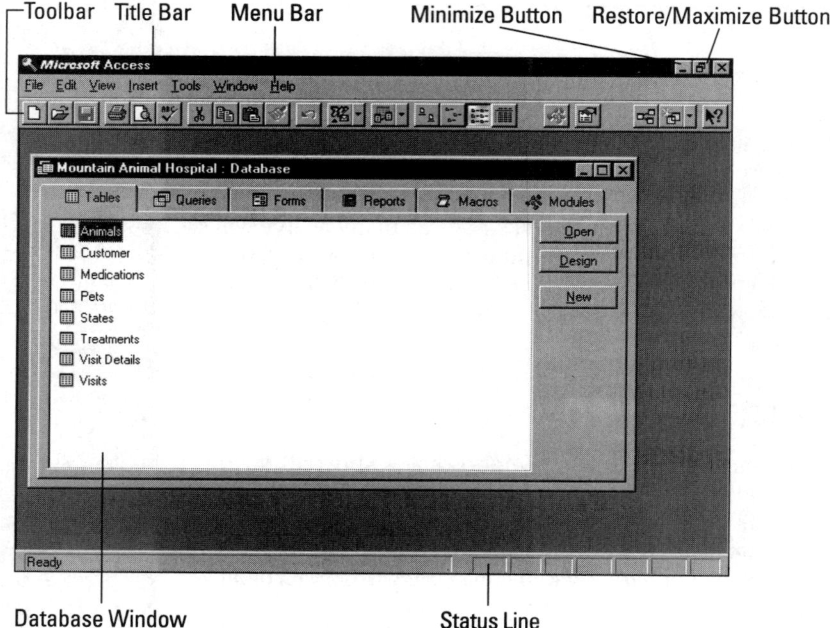

Figure 5-1: The Microsoft Access window.

Following are a number of Access window features you should be familiar with:

Title bar: You know what program is currently active by the name of the program you see displayed in the title bar. The title bar always displays the program name `Microsoft Access`.

Control-menu button: You'll find this button in the upper left corner of nearly every application window. When you click on this button once, a menu appears that lets you do certain tasks, such as move, size, minimize, or close the current application window. When you double-click on the Control button, you exit the application automatically.

Minimize button: Clicking on this button reduces Access to an icon on the Windows 95 taskbar. Access will still be running, and you can reactivate it by clicking on the taskbar.

Restore/Maximize button: You can use this middle button (displayed only when the Access window is maximized) to restore the window to its previous size. The Maximize button (a square with a dark top border) resizes the Access window to a full-screen view. The Maximize button does not appear in Figure 5-1 because Access is already maximized.

Close button: This button with an X on it closes Access when pressed.

Menu bar: The menu bar contains several menu choices. When you click on one, a menu drops down, offering further choices. The items on the menu bar and the choices you find in each menu will vary in Access, depending on what you are working on.

Toolbar: The toolbar is a group of picture buttons just below the menu bar; it provides shortcuts for running commands. The buttons on the toolbar vary, depending on what you are working on at the time. The toolbar can be resized and moved by clicking between buttons and moving it around the screen. You can also select View⇨Toolbars to show, hide, define new, or customize different toolbars; you can use the same command to select large or small buttons, turn off tooltips, and even display monochrome buttons.

Status line: The left side of the status line displays helpful information about what you are doing at the time. In Figure 5-1, the status line simply says `Ready`. The right side of the status line tells you whether certain keyboard settings are active. For example, if you have the Caps Lock on, the word `CAPS` appears in the status line.

Database window: This window appears whenever a database is open; it is the control center of your database. You use the Database window to open the objects contained within a database, including tables, queries, forms, reports, macros, and modules.

Tip

You can change the display in the title bar by changing the Database Startup form. You can display this by selecting Tools⇨Startup⇨Application Title from the Database window.

The Database window

The Database window always displays the name of the open database in the title bar. In Figure 5-1, for example, you see the Mountain Animal Hospital database name in the title bar. The Mountain Animal Hospital database is on the disk that comes with this book; it contains all the tables, forms, and other objects demonstrated.

The Database window has three basic parts to it. You see a set of six object buttons in a horizontal row on top, a set of three command buttons along the right side of the window, and a list of files.

Object buttons: These buttons are located in a horizontal row along the top of the Database window. With these buttons, you can select the type of object you want to work with. For example, selecting the Form button displays a list of forms created for that database. Selecting this button also lets you create a new form or redesign an existing one.

Command buttons: You can use the command buttons, located along the right side of the Database window, to place a database object in a different window or view. These buttons let you create, open, or design a database object.

Object list: This list displays existing files for the database object that you select. You can choose a name from the list to display or redesign the object.

New! You can change the view of the objects in the object list by selecting View from the Database window menu bar. There are four choices:

Large Icons	Displays a large icon with the type of object and the object name
Small Icons	Displays a small icon with the type of object and the object name
List	The default view as shown in Figure 5-1
Details	Lists the object name, date created, and date last modified (see Figure 5-2)

As you can see in Figure 5-2, the Details view shows you more information about each object. Most important is the date last modified. If you are trying to maintain different versions of a database, this gives you a great way to see which database contains your latest version. Of course, you can also use the new Briefcase replication features in Access for Windows 95 to keep multiple databases synchronized.

You can click on the column headers in the database window and re-sort the data by the value in the column. Each time you click on a column you change the order of the sort. For example, clicking on the Name column sorts the data by Name in ascending order. Click on the Name column again and you re-sort the window by descending name. You can sort the details of the database window objects by any of the columns. You can also change a column width by placing your cursor on the divider between column names and then dragging the column cursor that appears to the right to make a column wider or the left to make it narrower.

Tip You can enter a description for an object by right-clicking on the object name and then selecting Properties. You can enter a long description for the object and even hide the object if you want.

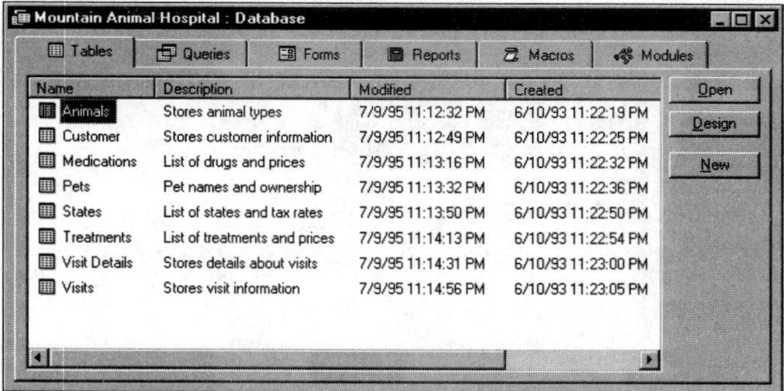

Figure 5-2: Microsoft Access Database window in Details view.

Design windows

The Database window is just one of several windows that you use for your many tasks in Access. Several other windows that you commonly see are the *object design windows*, which let you design such objects as tables, queries, forms, reports, macros, and modules. There are also windows that let you view or edit your data in datasheets, forms, and report previews.

Figure 5-3 shows the Database window, along with the Form Design window and several other windows that assist you in designing forms, and reports. These are generally known as *design windows*. The Form window is shown with several fields displayed. The form that you see in the figure, named Animals, can be used for displaying information about each pet in the Pets table.

In Figure 5-3, you see the most common design windows: the toolbox, foreground color window, field list, special effects window, borders window, and property window. Because the Form window is active, you may also notice that the toolbar is different.

Access for Windows 95 features tear-off windows in the design toolbar. After a window is displayed from the toolbar, it can be dragged anywhere on the desktop and resized.

The toolbox

Figure 5-3 displays the toolbox in the bottom right portion of the screen. You use the toolbox when you design a form or report. The toolbox is similar to a toolbar, but the toolbox is initially vertically arranged and can be moved around. The toolbox shown in the figure contains toggle buttons you can select to add objects to a form or report, such as labels, text boxes, option group boxes, and so on. You can move the toolbox or close it when you don't need it. You can also resize it by clicking and dragging the toolbox border. You can also anchor it as another toolbar by dragging it to an edge of the screen.

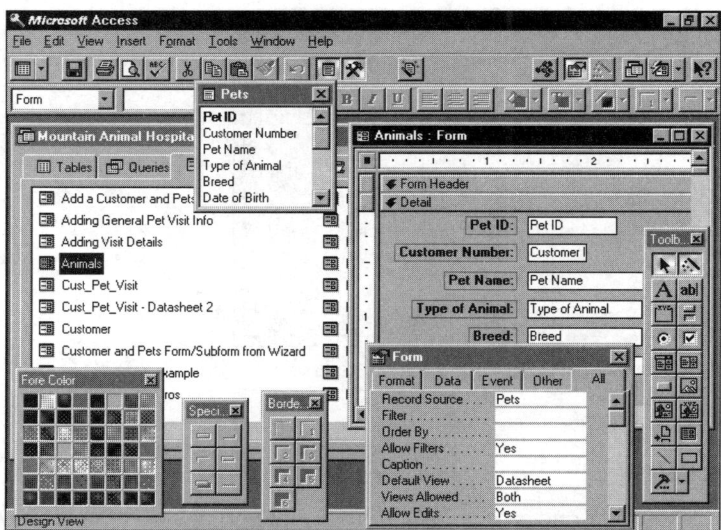

Figure 5-3: Microsoft Access design windows.

Color, special effect, and border windows

The foreground color window is shown in the bottom left corner of the screen in Figure 5-3. There is also a background color window and a border color window. In the figure you can also see the special effects and border widths windows. You can use these windows to change colors of objects such as text (foreground), the background of a control, and the color of the lines, rectangles, and the borders of a control. You can use the special effect window to give their appearance a three-dimensional look (sunken, raised) if desired, add a shadow, or add the Windows 95 chiseled look. Like with the toolbox, the size of the palette is resizable. The border width window lets you change the thickness of lines, rectangles, and control borders.

The Field List window

The Field List window displays a list of fields from the currently open table or query dynaset. Field List windows are used in query, form, and report design windows. You can select fields from this window by double-clicking on them, and you can drag the fields onto a query, form, or report. If you first select a control type in the toolbox and then drag a field from the Field List, a control is created (using the selected control type) which is automatically bound to the data field in the Field List.

The Properties window

In a form or report, each field (called a *control* in Access) has properties that further define the characteristics of the control. The form or report itself and sections of the form or report also have properties. In Figure 5-3 in the lower right-hand area, you see a property window displaying the section properties for a form. Usually, a property window displays only a portion of the properties available for a specific control, so a tabbed dialog box and a vertical scrollbar in the window let you scroll through the complete list. You can also resize a property window and even move it around the screen.

You'll soon see that having many windows open at once, resizing and rearranging them on-screen, helps you use information productively as you create such objects as forms and reports and use the features in Access. Each of the windows is described in detail in the appropriate chapters in this book.

A Simple Access Session

Cross Ref

Now that you are familiar with the Access screen, you can go through a simple Access session even before you know much about Access. Before proceeding, make sure that you are ready to follow along on your own computer. Your computer should be on, and Access should be installed. Chapters 2 and 3 showed you how to install and start Access. You can refer to those chapters for details. If you have not done so already, perform the following steps to get ready for this session:

1. Start your computer. Turn on your computer and start Windows 95 or Windows NT.
2. Start Access for Windows 95. Start Access from the Programs menu or find the Access icon or shortcut and double-click on the icon with the left mouse button to start Access. See Chapter 3 if you need further help starting Access.
3. Remove the New Database window. You will see a window allowing you to choose an existing database or to create a new one. Press the Cancel button (for now) to display the Access window without opening or creating a database.
4. Maximize the Access window. On the upper right corner of the Access window, you might see a gray box containing a square. If the box shows two rectangles, Access is already maximized; you can go on to the next section. If the there is only one square, click on the box to maximize the Access screen. Your screen should now look like the one in Figure 5-4.

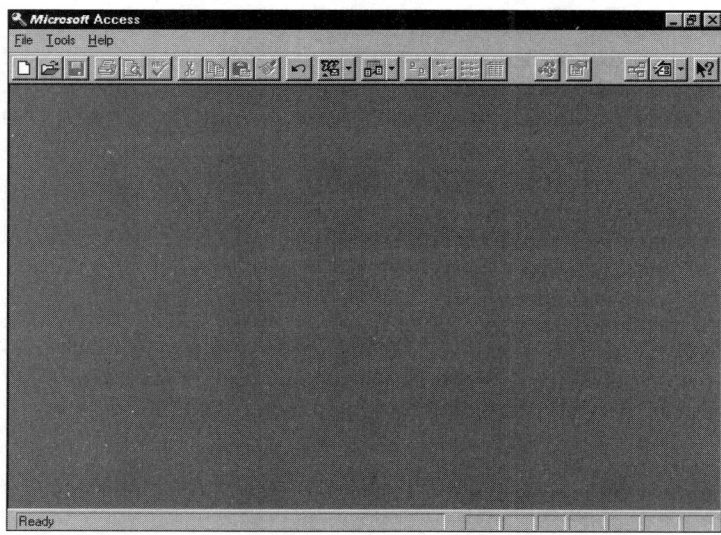

Figure 5-4: The initial Access window.

The Disk in the Back of the Book

In the back of your book is a disk that contains several files. The disk contains several database files that you'll use throughout the book, as well as some dBASE and Paradox files used in Chapter 24. To use this disk, follow the directions in the back of the book on the pages opposite the disk envelope. Following is a description of the two main database files used in this book:

Mountain Animal Hospital MDB
A database containing all the tables, queries, forms, reports, and macros used in this book

Mountain Start.MDB
A file containing tables only

You can use the Mountain Start database file, beginning with Chapter 8, to create your own queries, forms, and reports. You can use the Mountain Animal Hospital database file to see how the final application is created and used.

If you haven't used the disk in your book yet, now is a good time to take it out and copy the disk files to the Access folder or another folder (perhaps named Bible) on your hard disk.

You are now ready to move on. Your goal for this session is to open a database and then perform such simple steps as opening a table, displaying a form, and creating a query. You'll be using the Mountain Animal Hospital database that came with this book (Mountain Animal Hospital.MDB).

Opening a database

The first thing you'll want to do is open the Mountain Animal Hospital database. When you first start Access, you can open an existing database or create a new database. When you press the Cancel button, you see a blank screen, as shown in Figure 5-4. To open the database, follow these steps:

1. Select File⇨Open Database.
2. Select the folder where you placed the files for the book.
3. Click on the name MOUNTAIN ANIMAL HOSPITAL and select OK.

A dialog box similar to the one in Figure 5-5 appears, listing all the databases available in the current folder. If you don't see the MOUNTAIN ANIMAL HOSPITAL database listed, you may have to change the folder Access is looking in. To do so, select the drive and folder in which you stored this database. After you tell Access where to find the database, the name should appear in the File List window of the dialog box.

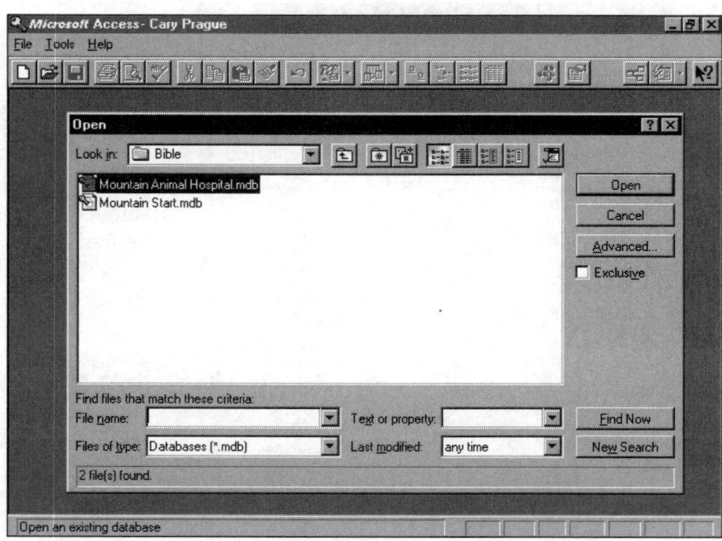

Figure 5-5: The standard Windows 95 Open dialog box.

Access opens the database. You should find the name MOUNTAIN ANIMAL HOSPITAL at the top of the Database window.

Opening a table

Now that you've opened the database, you'll open a table so that you can view some of the data stored in the Mountain Animal Hospital database. You should open the table named Pets. This table contains information about the various pets that are treated at the hospital, including the pet and customer identifications, type of animal, pet name, breed, gender, height, weight, and so forth. Follow these steps to open the Pets table:

1. Click on the Table tab in the Database window if it is not already selected.
2. Select the table called Pets.
3. Select the Open command button found in the right part of the Database window.
4. Maximize the window by selecting the Maximize button in the top right part of the window.

Access now opens the Pets table, and your screen should look like Figure 5-6.

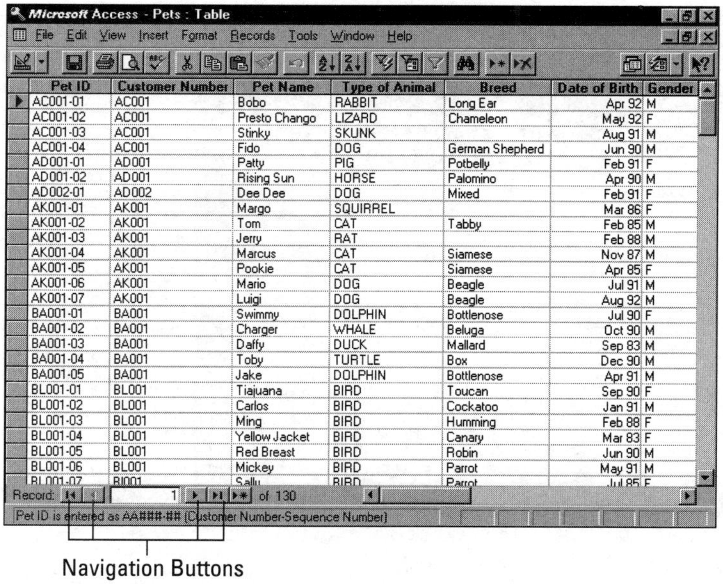

Microsoft Access - Pets : Table

File Edit View Insert Format Records Tools Window Help

Pet ID	Customer Number	Pet Name	Type of Animal	Breed	Date of Birth	Gender
AC001-01	AC001	Bobo	RABBIT	Long Ear	Apr 92	M
AC001-02	AC001	Presto Chango	LIZARD	Chameleon	May 92	F
AC001-03	AC001	Stinky	SKUNK		Aug 91	M
AC001-04	AC001	Fido	DOG	German Shepherd	Jun 90	M
AD001-01	AD001	Patty	PIG	Potbelly	Feb 91	F
AD001-02	AD001	Rising Sun	HORSE	Palomino	Apr 90	M
AD002-01	AD002	Dee Dee	DOG	Mixed	Feb 91	F
AK001-01	AK001	Margo	SQUIRREL		Mar 86	F
AK001-02	AK001	Tom	CAT	Tabby	Feb 85	M
AK001-03	AK001	Jerry	RAT		Feb 88	M
AK001-04	AK001	Marcus	CAT	Siamese	Nov 87	M
AK001-05	AK001	Pookie	CAT	Siamese	Apr 85	F
AK001-06	AK001	Mario	DOG	Beagle	Jul 91	M
AK001-07	AK001	Luigi	DOG	Beagle	Aug 92	M
BA001-01	BA001	Swimmy	DOLPHIN	Bottlenose	Jul 90	F
BA001-02	BA001	Charger	WHALE	Beluga	Oct 90	M
BA001-03	BA001	Daffy	DUCK	Mallard	Sep 83	M
BA001-04	BA001	Toby	TURTLE	Box	Dec 90	M
BA001-05	BA001	Jake	DOLPHIN	Bottlenose	Apr 91	M
BL001-01	BL001	Tiajuana	BIRD	Toucan	Sep 90	F
BL001-02	BL001	Carlos	BIRD	Cockatoo	Jan 91	M
BL001-03	BL001	Ming	BIRD	Humming	Feb 88	F
BL001-04	BL001	Yellow Jacket	BIRD	Canary	Mar 83	F
BL001-05	BL001	Red Breast	BIRD	Robin	Jun 90	M
BL001-06	BL001	Mickey	BIRD	Parrot	May 91	M

Record: 1 of 130

Pet ID is entered as AA###-## (Customer Number-Sequence Number)

Navigation Buttons

Figure 5-6: The Pets Table opened.

Tip

You can also open a table by double-clicking on the table name in the Database window or by clicking the right mouse button while the table name is highlighted. The latter choice displays a shortcut menu, and selecting Open from the shortcut menu opens a table.

Displaying a datasheet

When you open the Pets table, you see a datasheet that contains all the data stored in the Pets table. The data is displayed in a column-and-row format. You can move around the datasheet to view the different types of data stored here. Table 5-1 shows how to move around the table window using the keyboard. You can also use the mouse to navigate throughout the table. Simply click on any cell with the left mouse button to move the cursor to that cell. You can also use the mouse to move the elevators to navigate around the table.

You can also move through the table with the mouse by using the navigation buttons found at the bottom left corner of the datasheet window. (These are sometimes called *VCR buttons.*) The arrows located at the left and right ends with a vertical line next to them move you to the first or last record of the table. The two arrows to the inside of the outer two arrows move you to the preceding or the next record. The right-pointing arrow with the asterisk goes to a new record. Between these arrows is a rectangle that displays the current record number. To the right of the arrows is the number of records. If you know which record you want to move to, you can get there quickly by clicking the mouse on the record number (or by pressing F5), typing the number of the record that you want to move to, and pressing Enter.

Tip

You can also use the GoTo command (found in the Edit menu) to go to the First, Last, Next, Previous, or New record.

Table 5-1
Keyboard Techniques for Moving around the Window

Keyboard Keys	*Action*
Left- and right-arrow keys	Move left or right one column at a time
Up- and down-arrow keys	Move up or down one row at a time
PgUp and PgDn	Move up or down one screen at a time
Ctrl+PgUp and Ctrl+PgDn	Move left or right one screen at a time
Home	Move to the first column of the row the cursor is in
End	Move to the last column of the row the cursor is in
Tab	Move right one column at a time

(continued)

Table 5-1 *(continued)*	
Keyboard Keys	***Action***
Shift+Tab	Move left one column at a time
Ctrl+Home	Move to the first column of the first record in the table
Ctrl+End	Move to the last column of the last record in the table

Viewing a table design

Now that you've seen what kind of information is contained in the Pets table and how to navigate around the datasheet, you can look at the design of the table. You first need to be in the Design view to see the design of the Pets table.

To get to the Design view, click on the Design button in the toolbar; it is the first button on the Access toolbar and shows a triangle, ruler, pencil and has an arrow next to it. When you press the arrow, the icon reveals three icons that represent a set of choices (which include the possible views of the data, such as design and datasheets). When you click on the Design icon, the Pets datasheet will disappear and be replaced by the Design window for the Pets table. Figure 5-7 displays the Pets Design window.

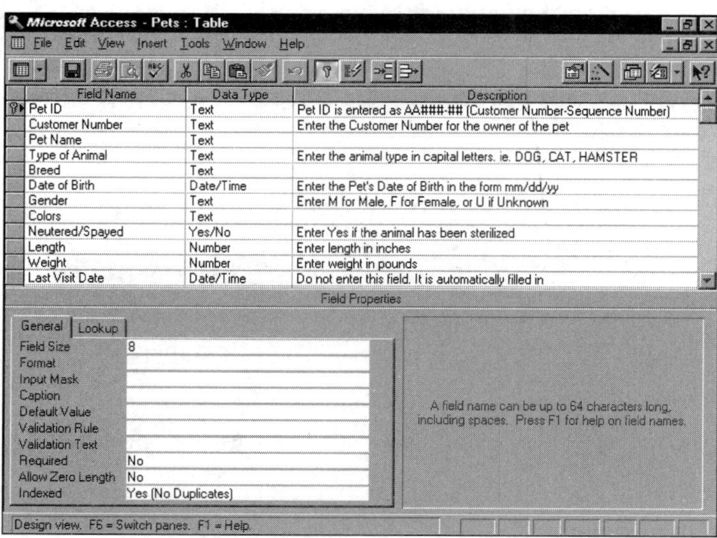

Figure 5-7: Pets Design window.

Here in the Design view is where the fields for the Pets table were set up. When the Pets table was created, fields that were to be included in the table were added here. Depending on the type of information to be entered in each field, a specific data type is given to each field. Some of the data types you can choose are Text, Currency, Date/Time, and Memo. A field is also provided for a description of the type of data the field will contain.

The Design window has two parts. In Figure 5-7, you see that the top half of the window lists the field names and field types and a description for each field of the Pets table. Moving around this window is similar to moving around the Pets datasheet.

The bottom half of the Pets Design window displays the field properties. Different properties can be set up for each field in the table. You can use the mouse or the F6 key to move between the top and bottom panes of the Design window.

The next object you'll display is a form. At this time, you should close the Design window by selecting File⇨Close. This selection closes the Table Design window and returns you to the Database window.

Displaying a form

The steps for displaying a form are similar to the steps for opening a table. In this case, you are opening a different type of database object. Follow these steps for opening the form called Pets:

1. Click on the Forms tab in the Database window.
2. Select the form named Pets.
3. Click on the Open command button on the right of the Database window to open the form.

Tip

You can also double-click on any name to open the form.

The Pets form should look like the one in Figure 5-8.

A form provides another way of displaying or changing data. The Pets form is an example of a simple form. You enter information in each text box just as you would enter information in a table. There are some advantages when using a form instead of a datasheet; in a form, you can view more fields on-screen at once, and you can use many data-entry and validation shortcuts. Also note that you can view the picture of each animal on a form and the contents of the Comments Memo field. You cannot do this when you are using a datasheet.

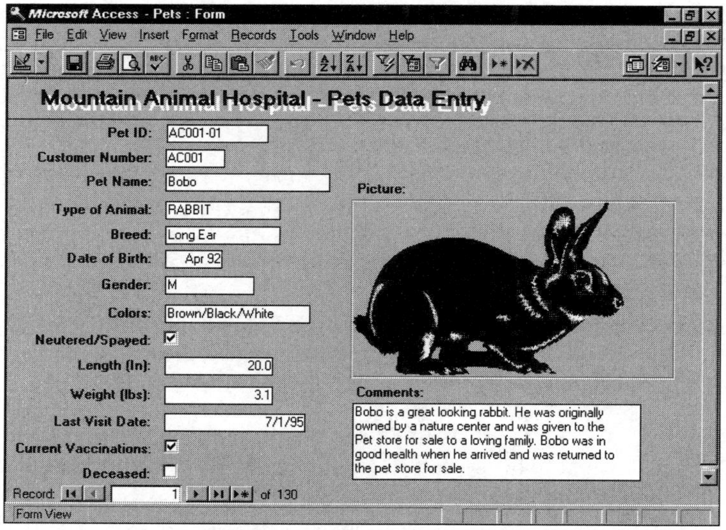

Microsoft Access - Pets : Form
File Edit View Insert Format Records Tools Window Help
Mountain Animal Hospital - Pets Data Entry
Pet ID: AC001-01
Customer Number: AC001
Pet Name: Bobo
Type of Animal: RABBIT
Breed: Long Ear
Date of Birth: Apr 92
Gender: M
Colors: Brown/Black/White
Neutered/Spayed:
Length (In): 20.0
Weight (lbs): 3.1
Last Visit Date: 7/1/95
Current Vaccinations:
Deceased:
Picture:
Comments:
Bobo is a great looking rabbit. He was originally owned by a nature center and was given to the Pet store for sale to a loving family. Bobo was in good health when he arrived and was returned to the pet store for sale.
Record: 1 of 130
Form View

Figure 5-8: The Pets form.

To see how this form was created, click on the Design button located on the Access toolbar (the first button on the left with the triangle, ruler, and pencil). Your form should now look like Figure 5-9.

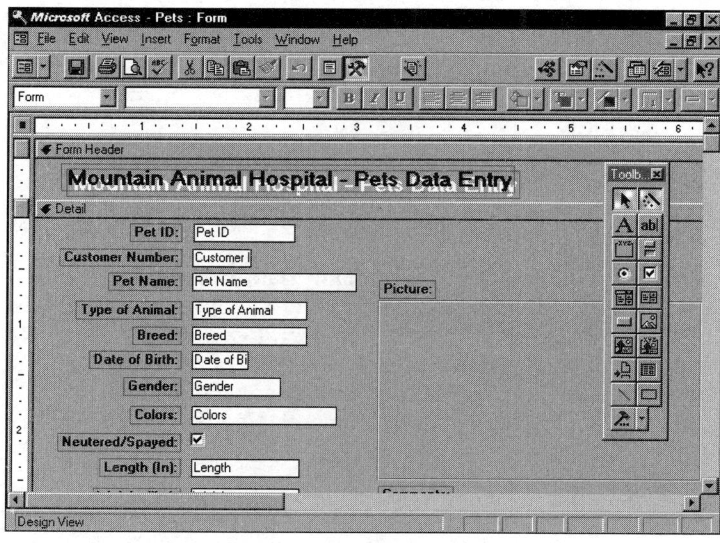

Figure 5-9: The Pets form in Design view.

In Figure 5-9, on the right side of the form is a long, rectangular box containing several buttons. This is the Form Toolbox. You can move the toolbox anywhere on-screen. The toolbox lets you add controls to the form. A control is a graphical object, such as a label, text box, check box, or command button that you can place on a form to display data from a field or enhance the look of the form.

Now that you've seen two different methods of entering data — datasheets and forms — you may have some questions about the data that is stored in the Pets table. You can find the answers to your questions through queries. Before creating a query, you should close the form by selecting File⇨Close. This selection closes both the form and the Form Toolbox and returns you to the Database window. If you made any changes to the form, Access will prompt you to save your changes before closing the form.

Creating a query

A query lets you ask questions about the data stored in your database. The data produced by the query can be saved into its own table for future use or printed out as a report. You next learn how to create a simple query by using the Pets table.

Suppose you want to see only the records in the Pets table in which the type of animal is a dog. You only want to see the pet name, type of animal, and breed. The first step is to create the query and add only the Pets table to it. You can add as many tables as you want to a query, but for this example you add only the Pets table. To create the query and add the Pets table, follow these steps:

1. Select the Query tab from the Database window.
2. Click on New to create a new query. Access displays a list of all Query Wizards available. New Query should be highlighted.
3. Press the OK button to select a New Query in the dialog box. The Show Table window appears showing tables, queries, or both.
4. Select Pets by clicking on the table name in the Show Table dialog box.
5. Select Add.
6. Select Close.

You should now see an empty query window.

The query form consists of two panes. The top pane contains a Field List window of the Pets table fields. You use the Field List window to choose which fields will appear in the query datasheet. The bottom part of the Query screen contains a series of rows and columns. In this pane, you'll ask questions about the fields in your tables. To view the fields Pet Name, Type of Animal, and Breed, and to select only the records where the value of Type of Animal is DOG, follow these steps:

1. Double-click on the Pet Name field from the Field List window to add the field to the query.

2. Add the Type of Animal field to the query.
3. Use the scrollbar to display more fields and add the Breed field to the query.
4. Press F6 to move to the lower pane and place the cursor on the Criteria: row of the Type of Animal column of the query.
5. Type **DOG** in the cell.

Your query should now look like Figure 5-10. You added the three fields to the query that you want to see in your results. In addition, you want to see only the dogs. Placing the word DOG in the criteria range tells Access to find only records where the value of Type of Animal is DOG.

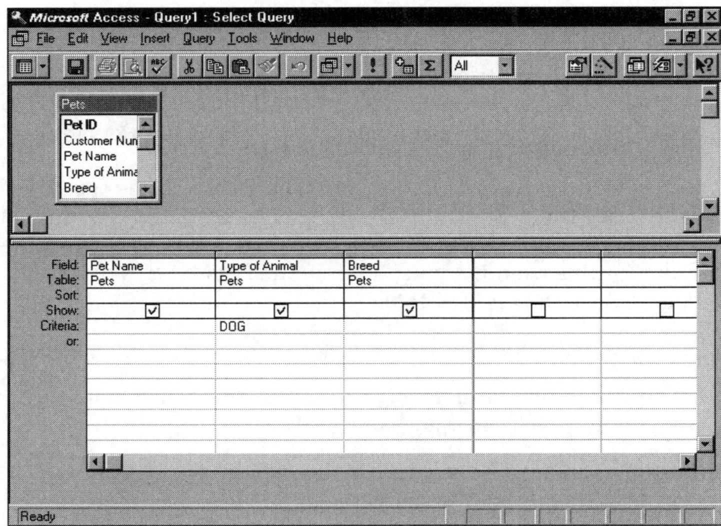

Figure 5-10: The Completed Query Design window.

To run the query, you need to select the Run button. This button shows an exclamation point and is found on the toolbar. After you select this button, Access goes to work to process your query and produce the results in what is called a dynaset. Your dynaset should look like the one in Figure 5-11. The dynaset displays the pet name, type of animal, and breed for each pet that is a dog.

The results from a query can be saved and used for creating a report that you can view or print. The next section explains how to display a report. Select File⇨Close to close the query. Select No because you don't want to save the query.

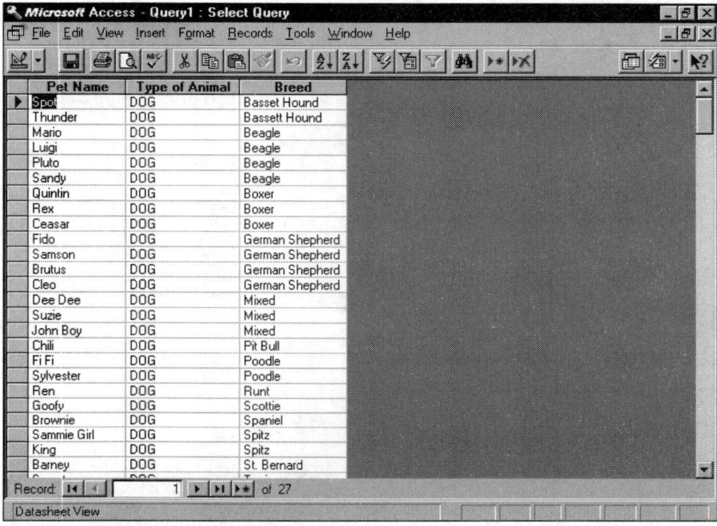

Pet Name	Type of Animal	Breed
Spot	DOG	Basset Hound
Thunder	DOG	Bassett Hound
Mario	DOG	Beagle
Luigi	DOG	Beagle
Pluto	DOG	Beagle
Sandy	DOG	Beagle
Quintin	DOG	Boxer
Rex	DOG	Boxer
Ceasar	DOG	Boxer
Fido	DOG	German Shepherd
Samson	DOG	German Shepherd
Brutus	DOG	German Shepherd
Cleo	DOG	German Shepherd
Dee Dee	DOG	Mixed
Suzie	DOG	Mixed
John Boy	DOG	Mixed
Chili	DOG	Pit Bull
Fi Fi	DOG	Poodle
Sylvester	DOG	Poodle
Ren	DOG	Runt
Goofy	DOG	Scottie
Brownie	DOG	Spaniel
Sammie Girl	DOG	Spitz
King	DOG	Spitz
Barney	DOG	St. Bernard

Figure 5-11: The Query Dynaset.

Displaying a report

Queries or tables can be formatted and placed into a report for output to a printer. Next, you view and print a report that was already created. You'll be using a report of all the pets in the Pets table. Follow these steps for displaying and printing this report:

1. Click on the Reports tab in the Database window.
2. Select Pet Directory from the File List.
3. Select the Preview button (or double-click on the report name).

   The report is displayed in the zoomed preview mode. You can display the entire page by clicking the cursor anywhere on-screen (currently the cursor is shaped like a magnifying glass).
4. Click anywhere on the screen to display the entire page.
5. Click on the two-page icon in the toolbar to display two pages.

The report should look like Figure 5-12.

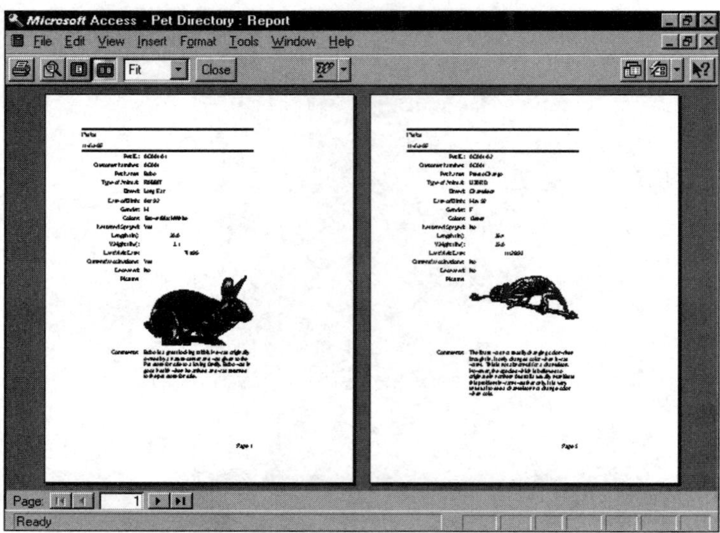

Figure 5-12: The Pets Report in print preview mode.

The Pets Report shows all the fields from the first two records of the Pets table. You can use the PgDn key or the navigation buttons at the bottom left corner of the window to see other pages of the report. The report can also be printed to the Windows printer, or you can return to the Design window to enhance the report.

Select the Close button to return to the Database window.

Ready for More

You now have experienced many of the different capabilities of Access. If you had problems with this chapter, you should start again from the beginning. Make sure that you follow the directions exactly and don't move on to the next steps until you understand what you were supposed to do. Hopefully, this quick view of Access will make you eager to learn how to use Access in detail. Don't be afraid to experiment. You can always reload the files from the disk in the back of the book. You can't hurt Access or your computer.

Now that you have a basic understanding of the various database objects in Access, you are ready to move on to creating your own tables, forms, queries, and reports. But, before moving on to Part II of this book, you should have an understanding of how to design a database system. In Chapter 6, you learn how some of the tables, forms, queries, reports, and macros are designed. Throughout the book, you will see this design implemented.

Summary

In this chapter, you took a quick tour through Access to learn about the windows you can use. You learned some basic terms that you need as you progress through this book, and you now have some hands-on experience in creating and using forms, reports, and queries. The following points were covered:

- ✦ You can navigate through Access by using the mouse or the keyboard.
- ✦ The Access Database window contains several menus and a toolbar.
- ✦ When you open a database, all the database objects that comprise the database are displayed in the Database window.
- ✦ When you open a database table, you see the information stored in the table as a datasheet.
- ✦ You can make your data entry easier by creating a form from an existing table.
- ✦ You can ask questions about data in a table by assembling a query and creating a view known as a dynaset.
- ✦ You can save a query to a report for output to a printer.

✦ ✦ ✦

A Case Study in Database Design

In This Chapter

- Learning the seven-step design method
- Using the Mountain Animal Hospital example
- Creating the overall design of a system
- Learning how to create reports
- Learning how to extract report fields to perform data design
- Designing database tables and relationships
- Learning how to design data-entry rules and validation
- Designing input forms
- Designing menus

The most important lesson to learn as you create a database is good design. Without a good design, you'll be reworking your tables constantly, and you may not be able to extract the information you want from your database. Throughout this book, you learn not only how to use queries, forms, and reports, but also how to design each of these objects before you attempt to create one. A case study of the Mountain Animal Hospital provides examples throughout this book, and specifically in this chapter; although the examples are fictitious, the concepts are not.

Note This chapter is not simple to understand; some of its concepts and ideas are fairly complex. If your goal is to get right into Access, you may want to read this chapter later. If you are fairly familiar with Access but new to designing and creating tables, you may want to read it before you begin the actual process of creating your tables.

Throughout this book, specifically, you learn to design forms and reports that range from simple to complex. You begin by learning to create simple forms and reports with just a few fields from a single table. Then you learn how to create multiple-page forms and reports that use multiple tables. Eventually the forms and reports you create use advanced controls (option buttons, list boxes, combo boxes, and check boxes), and use one-to-many relationships displayed as *subforms* and *subreports*. Finally, you learn how to design customer mailing labels and mail-merge reports. Most importantly, you use the tables in the Mountain Animal Hospital application to learn how to do data design.

The Seven-Step Method for Design

To create database objects such as tables, forms, and reports, you must first complete a series of tasks known as *design*. The better your design, the better your application. The more you think through your design, the faster you can complete any system. Design is not some necessary evil, nor is its intent to produce voluminous amounts of documentation. The sole intent of design is to produce a clear-cut path to follow as you implement it.

Figure 6-1 shows a modified version of this method, designed especially for Access.

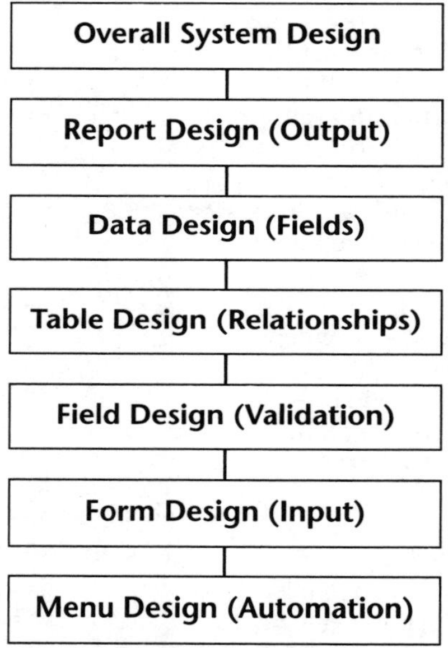

Figure 6-1: The seven-step design flow chart.

These seven design steps, along with the database system illustrated by the examples, will teach you almost all there is to know about Access. You will be able to create and use databases, tables, queries, forms, reports, and macros.

As you read through each step, you'll look at the design in terms of outputs and inputs. Although you see actual components of the system (customers, pets, visits, and visit details), remember that the focus of this chapter is how you design each step. As you watch the Mountain Animal Hospital system being designed, pay attention to the design process, not the actual system.

Step 1: The overall design from concept to reality

All software developers and end users face similar problems. The first set of problems you encounter is with gathering requirements that will meet the needs of the end user (typically your client, your coworker, or yourself). It is important to understand the overall needs the system must meet before you begin to zero in on the details.

The seven-step design method shown in Figure 6-1 can help you create the system you need, at a price (measured in time or dollars) you can afford. The Mountain Animal Hospital, for example, is a medium-size animal hospital that services individuals, pet stores, and zoos across three states. Basically, Mountain Animal Hospital needs to automate several tasks:

- ✦ Entering customer information — name, address, and financial history
- ✦ Entering pet information — pet name, type, breed, length, weight, picture, and comments
- ✦ Entering visit information — details of treatments performed and medications dispensed
- ✦ Asking all types of questions about the information in the database
- ✦ Producing a current Pets and Owners directory
- ✦ Producing a monthly invoice report
- ✦ Producing mailing labels and mail-merge reports

The design process is an *iterative* procedure; as you finish each new step, you'll need to look at all the previous steps again to make sure that nothing in the basic design has changed. If (for example) you are creating a data-entry rule and decide you need another field (not already in the table) to validate a field you've already defined, you have to go back and follow each previous step needed to add the field. You have to be sure to add the new field to each report in which you want to see it. You also have to make sure the new field is on an input form that uses the table the field is in. Only then can you use this new field in your system.

Now that you've defined Mountain Animal Hospital's overall systems in terms of what must be accomplished, you can begin the next step of report design.

Step 2: Report design – placing your fields

Design work should be broken up to the smallest level of detail you know at the time. You should start each new step by reviewing the overall design objectives. In the case of Mountain Animal Hospital, your objectives are to track customers, track pets, keep a record of visits and treatments, produce invoices, create a directory of pets and owners, and produce mailing labels.

Laying out fields in the report

When you look at the reports you create in this section, you may wonder, "What comes first — the duck or the egg?" Does the report layout come first, or do you first determine the data items and text that make up the report? Actually these items are conceived together.

It is not important how you lay out the fields in this conception of a report. The more time you take now, however, the easier it will be when you actually create the report. Some people go so far as to place gridlines on the report so they will know the exact location they want each field to occupy. In this example, you can just do it visually.

The Pets and Owners Directory

Mountain Animal Hospital will begin with the tasks of tracking customers and pets. The first report that must be developed will show important information about pets and their owners, and will be sorted by customer number. Each customer's name and address will appear with a listing of the pets the customer has brought into the Mountain Animal Hospital.

The hospital staff has already decided on some of the fields for the customer file. First, of course, is the customer's name (individual or company), followed by address (the customer's street, city, state, and ZIP code) and phone number.

The last visit date is another field the hospital will maintain on file and use on the report. This field will be used to let Mountain Animal Hospital know when it's time to remove a pet from the Pets table; a pet will be removed if it hasn't been in for a visit in the last three years. The plan is to purge the Pets table each year; recording the last visit is the way to find this information. This field will also alert Mountain Animal Hospital when an animal is due for its yearly checkup so the staff can send out reminder notices.

With that information in mind, the Mountain Animal Hospital people create the report form design shown in Figure 6-2.

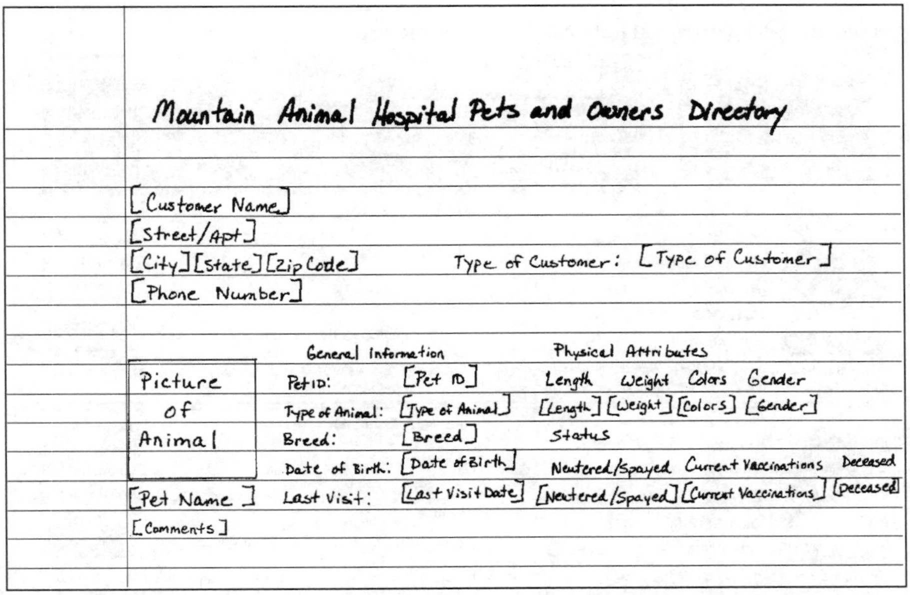

Mountain Animal Hospital Pets and Owners Directory

[Customer Name]
[Street/Apt]
[City][State][Zip Code] Type of Customer: [Type of Customer]
[Phone Number]

General Information Physical Attributes
Picture of Animal
Pet ID: [Pet ID] Length Weight Colors Gender
Type of Animal: [Type of Animal] [Length] [Weight] [Colors] [Gender]
Breed: [Breed] Status
Date of Birth: [Date of Birth] Neutered/Spayed Current Vaccinations Deceased
[Pet Name] Last Visit: [Last Visit Date] [Neutered/Spayed] [Current Vaccinations] [Deceased]
[Comments]

Figure 6-2: The Pets and Owners report design.

Cross Ref If you want to see how to implement this report, Chapter 21 teaches you how to create it. If you want to see how to complete this report with advanced database-publishing enhancements, see Chapter 22.

Figure 6-3 shows the final hard-copy printout of this report; it shows you the capabilities of Access.

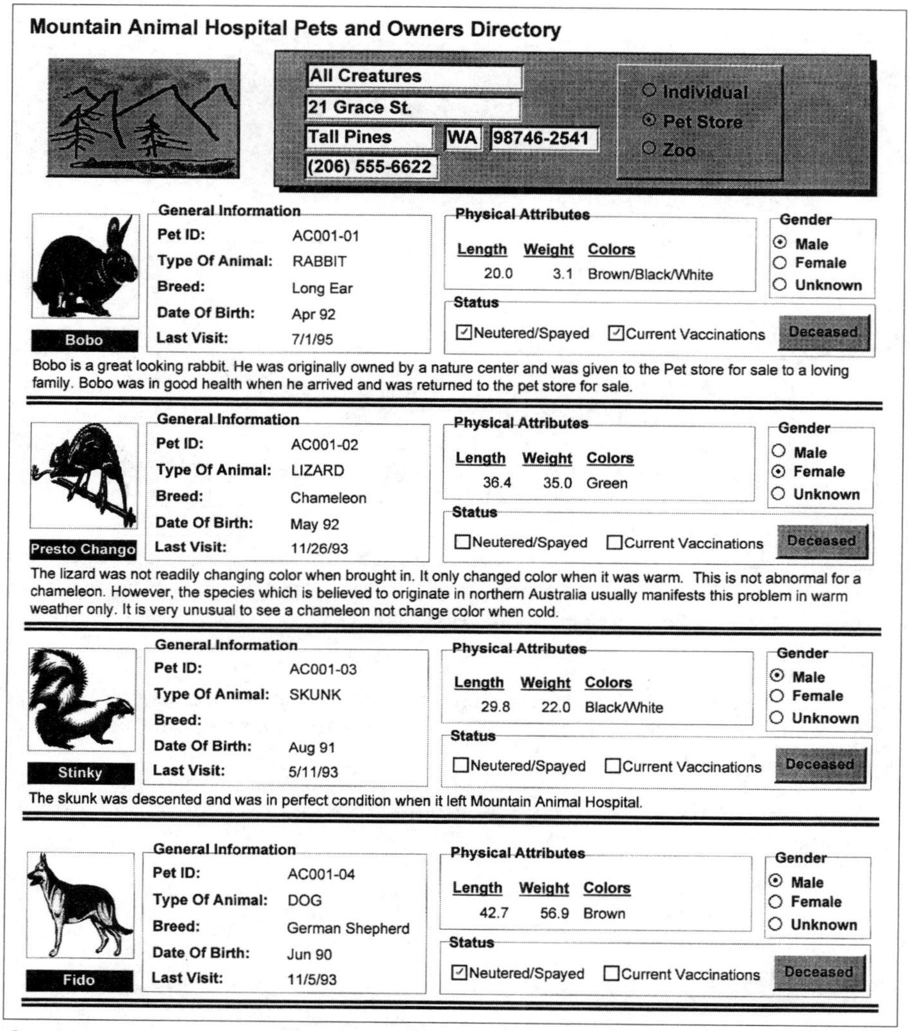

Mountain Animal Hospital Pets and Owners Directory

All Creatures
21 Grace St.
Tall Pines WA 98746-2541
(206) 555-6622

○ Individual ⊙ Pet Store ○ Zoo

Bobo

General Information

Pet ID:	AC001-01
Type Of Animal:	RABBIT
Breed:	Long Ear
Date Of Birth:	Apr 92
Last Visit:	7/1/95

Physical Attributes

Length	Weight	Colors
20.0	3.1	Brown/Black/White

Gender: ⊙ Male ○ Female ○ Unknown

Status: ☑Neutered/Spayed ☑Current Vaccinations Deceased

Bobo is a great looking rabbit. He was originally owned by a nature center and was given to the Pet store for sale to a loving family. Bobo was in good health when he arrived and was returned to the pet store for sale.

Presto Chango

General Information

Pet ID:	AC001-02
Type Of Animal:	LIZARD
Breed:	Chameleon
Date Of Birth:	May 92
Last Visit:	11/26/93

Physical Attributes

Length	Weight	Colors
36.4	35.0	Green

Gender: ○ Male ⊙ Female ○ Unknown

Status: ☐Neutered/Spayed ☐Current Vaccinations Deceased

The lizard was not readily changing color when brought in. It only changed color when it was warm. This is not abnormal for a chameleon. However, the species which is believed to originate in northern Australia usually manifests this problem in warm weather only. It is very unusual to see a chameleon not change color when cold.

Stinky

General Information

Pet ID:	AC001-03
Type Of Animal:	SKUNK
Breed:	
Date Of Birth:	Aug 91
Last Visit:	5/11/93

Physical Attributes

Length	Weight	Colors
29.8	22.0	Black/White

Gender: ⊙ Male ○ Female ○ Unknown

Status: ☐Neutered/Spayed ☐Current Vaccinations Deceased

The skunk was descented and was in perfect condition when it left Mountain Animal Hospital.

Fido

General Information

Pet ID:	AC001-04
Type Of Animal:	DOG
Breed:	German Shepherd
Date Of Birth:	Jun 90
Last Visit:	11/5/93

Physical Attributes

Length	Weight	Colors
42.7	56.9	Brown

Gender: ⊙ Male ○ Female ○ Unknown

Status: ☑Neutered/Spayed ☐Current Vaccinations Deceased

Figure 6-3: The completed Pets and Owners Directory report.

The Monthly Invoice Report

Whereas the Pets and Owners Directory concentrates on information about customers and pets, the Monthly Invoice Report displays information about the individual visits of specific customers and pets. Mountain Animal Hospital needs to produce a monthly report that lists all the daily visits by each customer and the customer's pets. Figure 6-4 shows the design of this report.

Mountain Animal Hospital
2414 Mountain Road South
Redmond, WA 06761
(206) 555-9999

Report Date: [Date]

[Customer Name]
[Street/Apt]
[City, State ZipCode]
[Phone Number]

Visit Date
[Visit Date]

[Pet Name]

	Treatments		Medication		
Type of Visit	Description	Price	Description	Price	Total
[Type of Visit]	[Treatment]	[Treatment Price]	[Medication]	[Medication Price]	[Line Total]
[Type of Visit]	[Treatment]	[Treatment Price]	[Medication]	[Medication Price]	[Line Total]
[Type of Visit]	[Treatment]	[Treatment Price]	[Medication]	[Medication Price]	[Line Total]
[Type of Visit]	[Treatment]	[Treatment Price]	[Medication]	[Medication Price]	[Line Total]
			[Pet Name] Subtotal		Sum[Line Total]

Total Invoice:	Sum[Line Total]
Discount([Discount]%):	[Total Invoice]*[Discount]
Subtotal:	[Total Invoice]-[Discount]
[State] Sales Tax([TaxRate]%):	[Subtotal]*[Tax Rate]
Amount Due:	[Subtotal]-[Sales Tax]

Figure 6-4: The design for the Monthly Invoice Report .

The design of this report shows customer information at the top and data about each visit in the middle. The middle block appears as many times as each customer had visits on the same date. If a customer brings three pets to the hospital on the same day, the report shows the middle block of data three times — once for each pet. The prices are totaled for each line; the sum of these line totals appears at the bottom of the block.

All the data items in the bottom block are summarized and calculated fields. (Because these fields can be calculated whenever necessary, they are not stored in a table.) After subtracting the discount from the subtotal, the report shows a taxable amount. If the customer's visit is subject to tax, the report calculates it at the current tax rate and shows it. Adding the tax to the taxable amount gives the total for the invoice; the customer pays this amount. Figure 6-5 shows final report (created in Chapter 23).

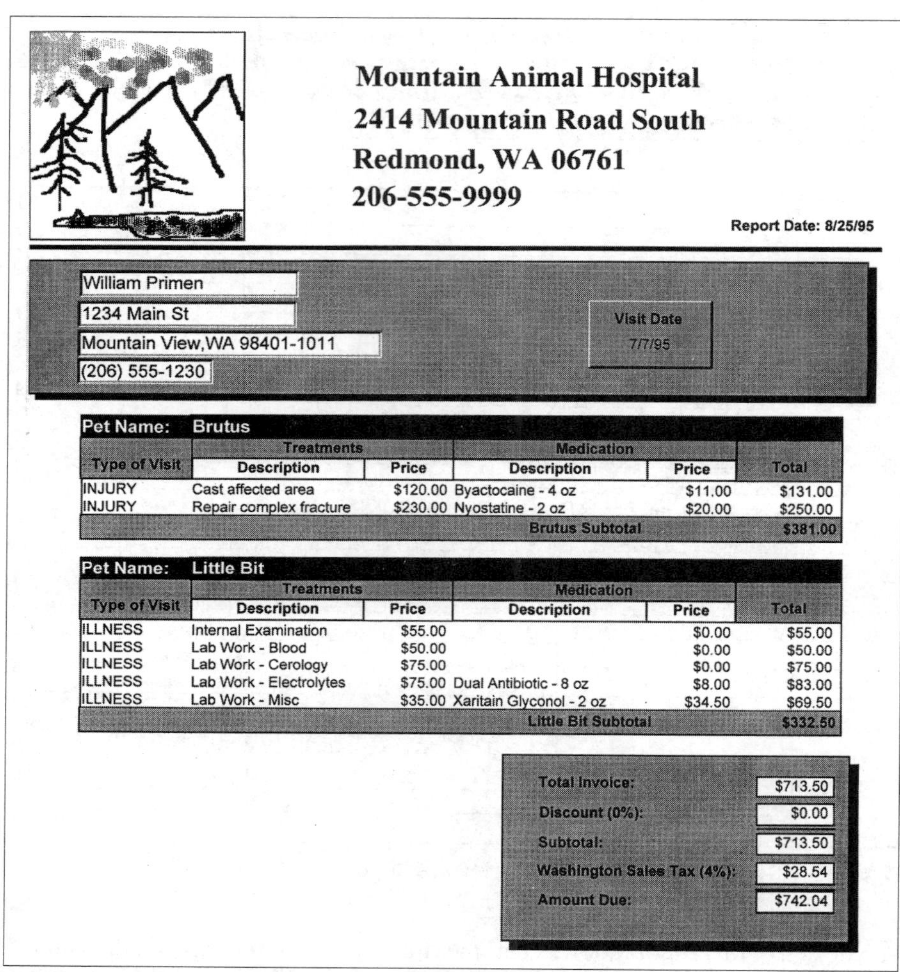

Mountain Animal Hospital
2414 Mountain Road South
Redmond, WA 06761
206-555-9999

Report Date: 8/25/95

William Primen
1234 Main St
Mountain View,WA 98401-1011
(206) 555-1230

Visit Date
7/7/95

Pet Name: Brutus

Type of Visit	Treatments Description	Treatments Price	Medication Description	Medication Price	Total
INJURY	Cast affected area	$120.00	Byactocaine - 4 oz	$11.00	$131.00
INJURY	Repair complex fracture	$230.00	Nyostatine - 2 oz	$20.00	$250.00
			Brutus Subtotal		$381.00

Pet Name: Little Bit

Type of Visit	Treatments Description	Treatments Price	Medication Description	Medication Price	Total
ILLNESS	Internal Examination	$55.00		$0.00	$55.00
ILLNESS	Lab Work - Blood	$50.00		$0.00	$50.00
ILLNESS	Lab Work - Cerology	$75.00		$0.00	$75.00
ILLNESS	Lab Work - Electrolytes	$75.00	Dual Antibiotic - 8 oz	$8.00	$83.00
ILLNESS	Lab Work - Misc	$35.00	Xaritain Glyconol - 2 oz	$34.50	$69.50
			Little Bit Subtotal		$332.50

Total Invoice:	$713.50
Discount (0%):	$0.00
Subtotal:	$713.50
Washington Sales Tax (4%):	$28.54
Amount Due:	$742.04

Figure 6-5: The final Mountain Animal Hospital Invoice Report.

In reality, you'd design many more reports. In the interest of time and pages, however, the preceding two report designs will suffice.

Step 3: Data design – what fields do you have?

Now that you've decided what you want for output, it's time to think about how you'll organize your data into a system to make it available for the reports you've already defined (as well as for any ad hoc queries). The next step in the design phase is to take an inventory of all the data fields you will need to accomplish the output. One of the best methods is to list the data items that are found in each report. As you do so, take careful note of items that are found in more than one report. Make sure that the name for a data item in one report that is the same as a data item in another report is really the same item.

Another step is to see whether you can begin to separate the data items into some logical arrangement. Later, you'll have to group these data items into logical table structures, and then map them onto data-entry screens that make sense. You should enter customer data, for example, as part of a customer table process — not part of a visit entry.

Determining customer information

First you must look at each report. For the Mountain Animal Hospital customer reports, you start with the customer data and list the data items, as shown in Table 6-1.

Table 6-1
Customer-Related Data Items Found in the Customer Reports

Pets and Owners Directory	*Monthly Invoice Report*
Customer Name	Customer Name
Street	Street
City	City
State	State
ZIP Code	ZIP Code
Phone Number	Phone Number
Type of Customer	Discount
Last Visit Date	

As you can see, most of the data fields pertaining to the customer are found in both reports. The table shows only the fields that are used. Fields appearing on both reports appear on the same lines in the table, which allows you to see more easily which items are in which reports. You can look across a row instead of looking for the same names in both reports. Because the related row and the field names are the same, it's easy to make sure you have all the data items. Although locating items easily is not critical for this small database, it becomes very important when you have to deal with large tables.

Determining pet information

After extracting the customer data, you can move on to the pet data. Again, you need to analyze the two reports for data items specific to the pets. Table 6-2 lists the fields in the two reports that contain information about the animals. Notice that only one field in the Monthly Invoice Report contains pet information.

Table 6-2
Pet Data Items Found in the Reports

Pets and Owners Directory	*Monthly Invoice Report*
Pet ID	
Pet Name	Pet Name
Type of Animal	
Breed	
Date of Birth	
Last Visit Date	
Length	
Weight	
Colors	
Gender	
Neutered/Spayed	
Current Vaccinations	
Deceased	
Picture	
Comments	

Determining visit information

Finally, you'll need to extract information about the visits from the Monthly Invoice Report, as shown in Table 6-3. You would use only this report because the Pets and Owners Directory Report does not deal with visit information.

Table 6-3 **Extracting Visit Information**	
Monthly Invoice Report	
Visit Date	Discount
Type of Visit	Tax Rate
Treatment	Total Amount
Treatment Price	Medication Price
Medication	Line Total

The table does not list some of the calculated fields, but you can re-create them easily in the report. Unless a field needs to be specifically stored in a table, you simply recalculate it when you run the report.

Combining the data

Now for the difficult part. You must determine the fields that are needed to create the tables that make up the reports. When you examine the multitude of fields and calculations that make up the many documents you have, you begin to see which fields actually belong to the different tables. (You already did some preliminary work by arranging the fields into logical groups.) For now, include every field you extracted. You will need to add others later (for various reasons), though certain fields will not appear in any table.

After you have used each report to display all the data, it is time to consolidate the data by function — and then compare the data across functions. To do this step, first you look at the customer information and combine all its different fields create one set of data items. Then you do the same thing for the pet information and the visit information. Table 6-4 shows the comparison of data items from these three groups of information.

Table 6-4
Comparing the Data Items from the Three Groups

Customer Data Items	*Pet Data Items*	*Visit Data Items*
Customer Name	Pet ID	Visit Date
Street	Pet Name	Type of Visit
City	Type of Animal	Treatment
State	Breed	Treatment Price
ZIP Code	Date of Birth	Medication
Phone Number	Last Visit Date	Medication Price
Type of Customer	Length	Discount
Last Visit Date	Weight	Tax Rate
Discount	Colors	Total Amount
	Gender	
	Neutered/Spayed	
	Current Vaccinations	
	Deceased	
	Picture	
	Comments	

This is a good way to start creating the table definitions for Mountain Animal Hospital, but there is much more still to do. First, as you learn more about how to perform a data design, you also learn that the information in the visits column must be split into two columns. Some of these items are used only once for the visit; other items are used for each detail line in the visit. This is the part of the design process called *normalization*. One customer (for example) has one pet, which has one visit with many visit details. The customer and pet data items each represent one customer or one pet, but the a visit may require multiple detail lines.

Table 6-5 shows the Visits column broken into two columns. The visit date is no longer a unique field for the second table, which contains multiple items for each visit. You will have to add another field (which you see in Table 6-6).

When you look at Table 6-5, you may wonder how to link these two files together so that Access knows which visit-detail information goes with which visit. A *unique field* (often an identification number or code) can do this job. By adding the same field to each group of information, you can keep like information together. You can create a field called **Visit Number**, for example, and use a consistent methodology to assign it. If you use a numeric sequence of year, the day number of the year, and a sequence number, then the third pet to visit on January 12, 1993, becomes **1993012-03**. The first four digits record the year, the next three digits tell you the number of days since January 1, and then a hyphen separates the date from a sequence number. Once you have added this field to both columns for the Visits and Visit Details tables, you can tie the two files together.

Table 6-5
Dividing the Visits Information

Visits	***Visit Details***
Visit Date	Visit Date
Discount	Type of Visit
Tax Rate	Treatment
Total Amount	Treatment Price
	Medication
	Medication Price

There is one more identification number to assign. The Visit Details table does not have a unique identifier, though it does have a *partially* unique identifier. The Visit Number identifier is unique for an individual visit, but not for a visit that has multiple detail lines. A common practice is simply to assign a sequential number (for example, 001, 002, 003, and so on) for each visit detail.

Cross Ref Commonly, in a one-to-many type of relationship, you need more than one field to make a record unique. See Chapter 12 for a complete discussion of keys and relationships.

Table 6-6 shows a list of the original data items and the reworked items for the Visits and Visit Details tables. The identification fields are shown in bold italics to set them apart.

Table 6-6
A Final Design of Data Items

Customer	*Pets*	*Visits*	*Visit Details*
Customer Number	***Pet ID***	***Visit Number***	***Visit Number***
Customer Name	Pet Name	Visit Date	***Line Number***
Street	Type of Animal	Discount	Type of Visit
City	Breed	Tax Rate	Treatment
State	Date of Birth	Total Amount	Treatment Price
ZIP Code	Last Visit Date		Medication
Phone Number	Length		Medication Price
Type of Customer	Weight		
Last Visit Date	Colors		
Discount	Gender		
	Neutered/Spayed		
	Current Vaccinations		
	Deceased		
	Picture		
	Comments		

These are not the final fields used in the Mountain Animal Hospital database. Actually, many more changes will be made as the design is examined and enhanced.

Step 4: Table design and relationships

After you complete the data design, the next step is the final organization of the data into tables. Figure 6-6 shows the final design for the four tables, an actual database diagram found in Microsoft Access.

Tip

Creating the final set of tables is easy if you have lots of experience. If you don't, that's all right, too, because Access lets you change a table definition after you've created it— without losing any data. In Chapter 7, you'll actually create a table in Access.

In Figure 6-6, you can see the relationships that join one table to another. Notice the relationship between customers and pets, created by adding the Customer Number field to the Pets table. Each pet has a link to its owner, the customer. You can use the same method to establish a relationship between pets and visits. When you add the Pet ID field to the Visits table, each visit itself involves a pet in the Pets table. The Visit Number field establishes a similar relationship between Visits and Visit Details.

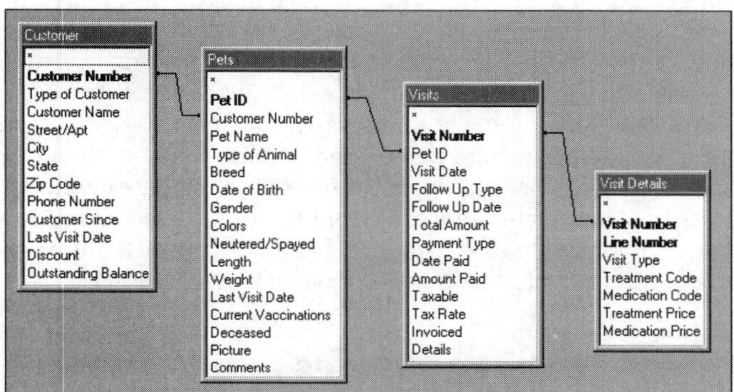

Figure 6-6: The final design, separating the data by function.

Setting relations

Cross Ref

Later, in Chapter 12, you learn all about using multiple tables and how to set relations in Access. For now, a brief discussion of this topic will show you how to design the relations between the various tables you've identified.

Tables are related to each other so that information in one table is accessible to another. Usually, in systems designed with Access, you have several tables that are all related to one another. You establish these *relations* by having fields in the various tables that share a common value. The field names in these tables need not be the same; only the values have to match. In the Pets table, for example, you have the customer number. By relating the customer number in the Pets table to the customer number in the Customer table, you can retrieve all there is to know about the customer.

This saves you from having to store the data in two places, and it is the first reason to have a relation — for a *table lookup*. A field in one table can look up data in another table. Another example: you can use the Pet ID field to create a table-lookup relation from the Visits table to the Pets table. Then, as you enter each item, Access passes data about the item (such as pet name, type of animal, breed, and date of birth) from the Pets table to the Visits table.

There is a second reason to set a relation, however. As you decide how to relate the tables you have already designed, you must also decide how to handle multiple occurrences of data. In this system design, there can be multiple occurrences of visit details for each visit. For example, each treatment or medication is entered on a separate detail line. When this happens, you should split the table into two tables. In this design, you need to place the visit number of the visit in a separate table from the single-occurrence visit. This new Visit Details table is related by the Visit Number field found in the Visits table.

The Visits and Visit Details tables are the central focus of the system. The Visits table needs to be related not only to the Pets table, but also to the Customer table so you can retrieve information from it for the invoice report. Even so, you don't have to link the Visits table directly to the Customer table; you can go through the Pets table to get there. Figure 6-6 shows these *chain link* relationships graphically, in an actual Access screen (the Query window) where you can set relations between tables.

In the course of a visit, the Pet ID field would be entered, linking the pet information to the Visits table. The Pets table uses the Customer Number field to retrieve the customer information (such as name and address) from the Customer table. Although the name and address are not stored in the Visits table itself, this information is needed to confirm that a pet in for a visit belongs to a particular customer.

Step 5: Field design — data-entry rules and validation

The next step is to define your fields and tables in much greater detail. You also need to determine data-validation rules for each field, even define some new tables to help with data validation.

Designing field names, types, and sizes

First, you must name each field. The name should be easy to remember, but descriptive so that you recognize the function of the field by its name. It should be just long enough to describe the field, but not so short that it becomes cryptic. Access allows up to 64 characters (including spaces) for a field name.

You must also decide what type of data each of your fields will hold. In Access, you can choose any of several data types (as shown in Table 6-7).

Table 6-7
Data Types in Access

Data Type	*Type of Data Stored*
Text	Alphanumeric characters; up to 255 characters
Memo	Alphanumeric characters; long strings up to 64,000 characters
Number	Numeric values of many types and formats
Date/Time	Date and time data
Currency	Monetary data
AutoNumber	Automatically incremented numeric counter
Yes/No	Logical values, Yes/No, True/False
OLE object	Pictures, graphs, sound, video, word processing, and spreadsheet files

New! The Lookup Wizard is not actually a data type but a way of storing a field one way but displaying a related value in another table instead. Generally, these are text fields but can also be numeric. For example, you could store 1, 2, or 3 for the Type of Customer and then look up and display the values Individual Pet Store and Zoo instead.

New! The AutoNumber data type was formerly called Counter.

One of these data types must be assigned to each of your fields (the next part of the book explains the data types in more detail). You also must specify the length of the text fields

Designing data-entry rules

The last major design decision concerns *data validation*, which becomes important when data is input. You want to make sure only *good* data gets into your system — data that passes certain tests that you define. There are several types of data validation. You can test for *known individual items*, stipulating (for example) that the Gender field can accept only the values Male, Female, or Unknown. You can test for *ranges* (specifying, for example, that the value of Weight must be between 0 and 1,500 pounds). Finally, you can test for *compound conditions*, such as whether the Type of Customer field indicates an individual (in which case the discount is 0 percent), a pet store (the discount field must show 20 percent), or a zoo (the discount is 50 percent). In the next chapter, you learn where you can enter conditions to perform data validation.

Designing lookup tables

Sometimes you need to design entire tables to perform data validation, or just to make it easier to create your system; these are called *lookup tables*. For example, Mountain Animal Hospital needs a field to determine the customer's tax rate. So you decide to use a lookup table that contains the state code, state name, and state tax rate. This also allows you to enter no more than a two-digit state code in the Customer table, and then look up the state name or tax rate when necessary. The state code then becomes the field that relates the tables. Because the tax rate can change, Access looks up the current tax rate whenever a visit record is created, storing the tax-rate value in the Visits table to capture the tax rate for each visit.

Tip: This is the perfect time to use a Lookup Wizard in the Customer table — to look up and display the state instead of the state code.

Although you can create a field on a data-entry form that limits the entry of valid genders to Male, Female, and Unknown, there are too many allowable animal types to create a field for animal type in a form. Rather, you can create a table with only one field — Type of Animal — and then use the Type of Animal field in the Pets table to link to this field in the Animals lookup table.

Tip: You create a lookup table in exactly the same way as you would any other table, and it behaves in the same way. The only difference is in the way you use the table.

In Figure 6-7, notice that four lookup tables are added to the design. The States lookup table is necessary for determining an individual's tax rate. The Animal lookup table is added to ensure that standard animal types are entered into the Pets table (for the sake of consistency). The Animals lookup table is designed as an alphabetized listing of valid animal types.

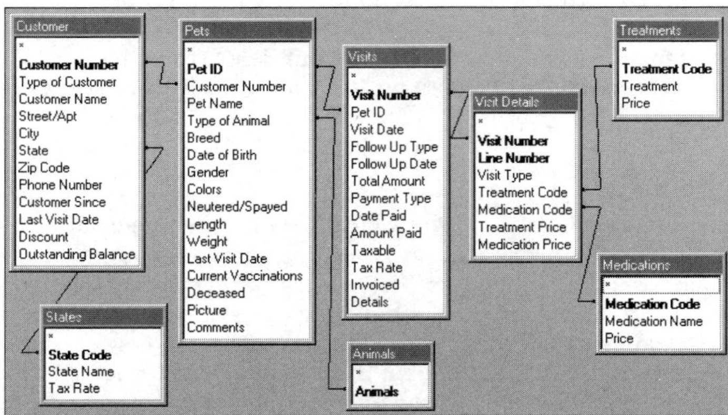

Figure 6-7: The final database diagram, with lookup tables added.

The two tables on the far right, Treatments and Medications, are added for several reasons. The last thing you want is to require that doctor enter a long name to complete the Treatment or Medication fields after an animal's visit. The doctor should be able to choose from a list or enter a simple code. Then the code can be used to look up and retrieve the name of the treatment or medication, along with its current price. In fact, the price that the doctor looks up must be stored in the Visit Details table; prices can change between the time of the visit and the time the invoice is sent out. You would add the Treatments lookup table, then, for storing a list of treatments and their associated prices. Similarly, you would add a Medications table for keeping a list of available medications and their associated prices.

Creating test data

After you define your data-entry rules and how the database should look, it's time to create *test data*. You should prepare this data very scientifically (in order to test many possible conditions), and it should have various purposes. It should let you test the process of data entry — do all the conditions you created generate the proper acceptance or error messages? In addition, you may find some conditions you should test for that you hadn't considered. What happens (for example) when someone enters a blank into a field? How about numbers in a character field? Access automatically traps such things as bad dates or characters in Date and Numeric fields, but you must take care of the rest yourself.

You'll be creating two types of test data. The first is simply data that allows you to *populate*, or fill, the databases with meaningful data. This is the initial *good* data that should end up in the database and then be used to test output. Output will consist mainly of your reports. The second type of test data is for testing data entry. This includes designing data with errors that display every one of your error conditions, along with good data that can test some of your acceptable conditions.

Test data should let you test routine items of the type that you normally find in your data. You should also test for *limits*. Enter data that is only one character long for some fields, and use every field. Create several records that use every position in the database (and thereby every position in the data-entry screen and in the reports).

Create some "bad" test data. Enter data that tests every condition. Try to enter a customer number that already exists. Try to change a customer number that's not in the file. These are a few examples of what to consider when testing your system. Of course, testing your system begins with the test data.

Step 6: Form design – input

Once you've created the data and established table relationships, it is time to design your forms. *Forms* are made up of the fields that can be input or viewed in the edit mode. If at all possible, your screens should look much like the forms you'd use in a manual system. This setup makes for the most user-friendly system.

Designing data-entry screens

When you're designing forms, you will need to place three types of objects on-screen:

- ✦ Labels and text box data-entry fields
- ✦ Special controls (multiple-line text boxes, option buttons, list boxes, check boxes, business graphs, and pictures)
- ✦ Graphic enhancements (color, lines, rectangles, and three-dimensional effects)

You should place your data fields just where you want them on the form. Although normally the cursor moves from top to bottom and left to right when you enter data, you can specify cursor movement from one field to another. You can also specify any size entry you want. As you place the fields, be sure to leave as much space around them as you'll need. A calculated field, such as a total that would be used only for data display, can also be part of a data-entry form.

You can use *labels* to display messages, titles, or captions. *Text boxes* provide an area where you can type or display text or numbers contained in your database. *Check boxes* indicate a condition and are either unchecked or checked (selected). Other types of controls available with Access include list boxes, combo boxes, option buttons, toggle buttons, and option groups.

Cross Ref Chapter 16 covers the various types of controls available in Access. Access also provides a tool called Microsoft Graph that you can use to create a wide variety of graphs. You can also display pictures, using an OLE object stored in a database table.

In this book, you create several basic data-entry forms:

✦ The Customer form

✦ The Pets form

✦ The Visits general information form

✦ The Visit Details form

The Customer form

Cross Ref The Customer Data Entry form shown in Figure 6-8 is the simplest of the data-entry forms you create in this book. It is very straightforward, simply listing the field descriptions on the left and the fields themselves on the right. The unique *key field* is Customer Number. At the top of the form is the main header, a title that identifies this data-entry form by type: the Customer Data Entry Form. You can create this simple form by using a Form Wizard (see Chapter 11 for details).

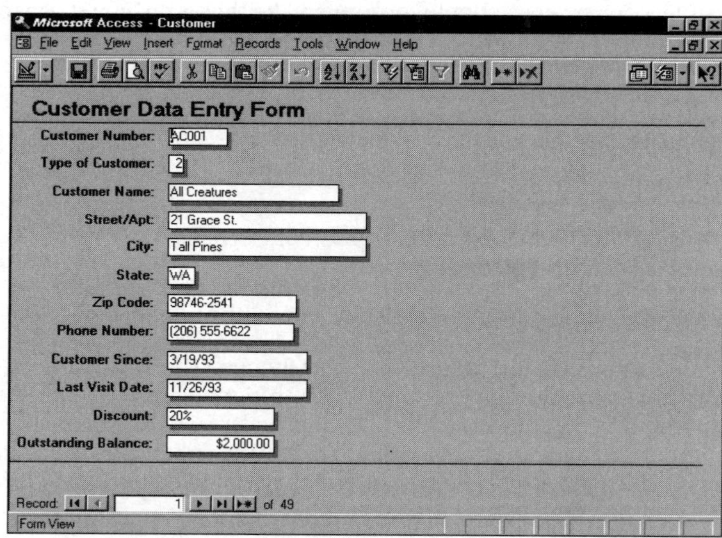

Figure 6-8: The Customer Data Entry form.

The Pets form

Cross Ref

The Pets Data Entry form is more complicated. It contains several types of controls, including option buttons, a list box, several combo boxes, check boxes, a picture, and a memo field. As shown in Figure 6-9, the form contains two sections; one contains pet information, the other contains customer information. You learn how to create this form in Chapter 19.

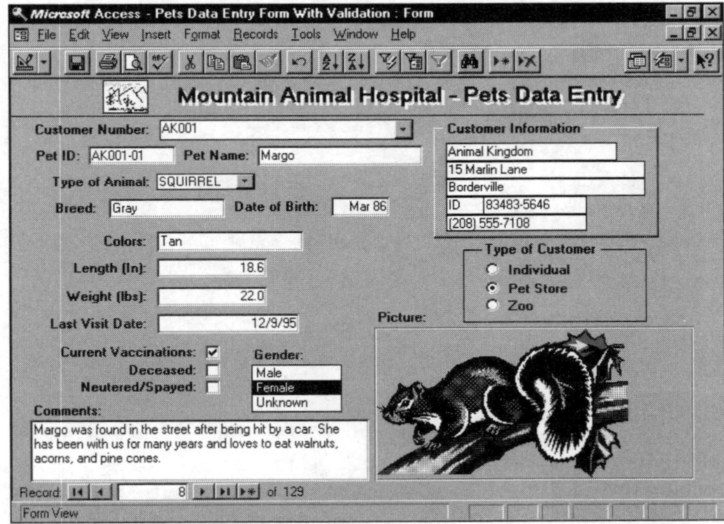

Figure 6-9: The Pets Data Entry form.

The general Visits form

As shown in Figure 6-10, the next data-entry form combines data from several tables to provide general information about visits. This form contains information about customers, pets, and visits; its main purpose is to allow a user to enter such information into the database. Visit Number is the key field for this form.

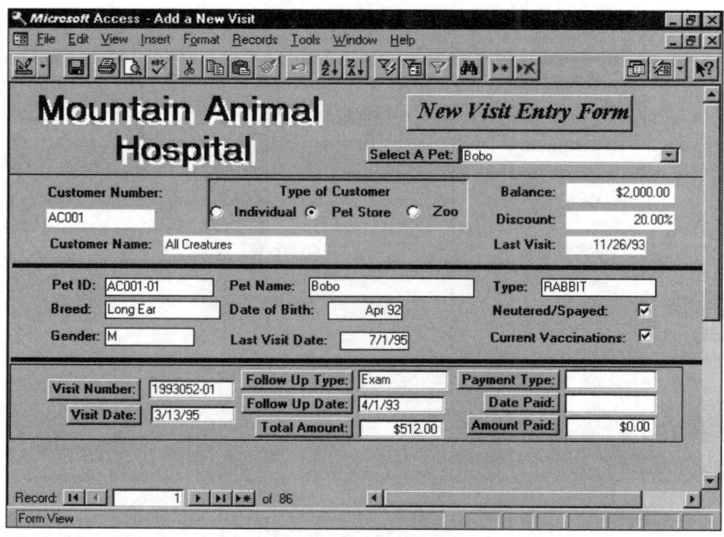

Figure 6-10: The general Visits data-entry form.

The Visit Details form

Cross Ref

The final form you see in this book (shown in Figure 6-11) is for adding the details of individual visits. (You create this form in Chapter 28.) This form contains a *subform* so you can see many visit details at once. Many types of subforms can be linked to a form; you can even have a graph as a subform, as you discover in Chapter 20.

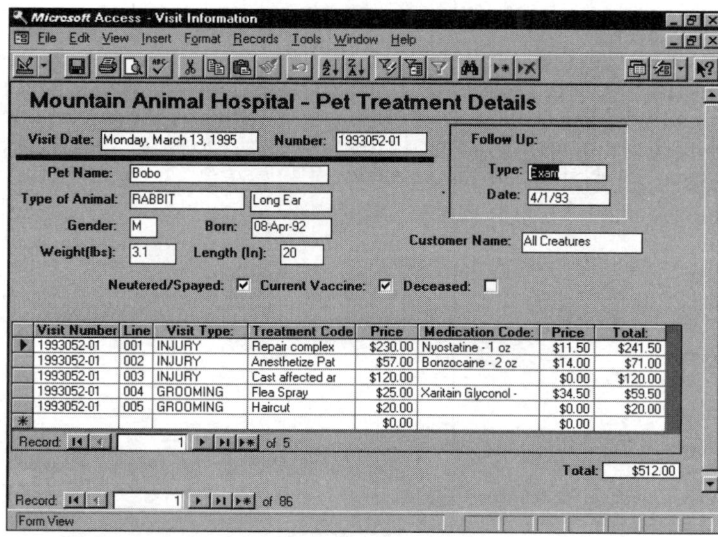

Figure 6-11: The Visit Details data-entry form.

Step 7: Automation design — menus

Once you've created your data, designed your reports, and created your forms, it's time to tie them all together using *switchboards* and *menus*. Figure 6-12 shows a switchboard form that also contains a custom menu bar. Switchboards are graphical menus in the center of a form usually built with command buttons with text or pictures on them. Menus refer to the pull-down menus at the top of a screen. Menus are the key to a good system. The user must be able to follow the system to understand how to move from place to place. Usually each form or report is also a choice on a menu. This means your design must include decisions on how to group the menus. When you examine the overall design and look at all your systems, you begin to see a distinct set of combinations.

Cross Ref You can use Access macros to create a menu at the top menu bar of the switchboard. This menu gives the user the choice of using pull-down menus or switchboard buttons. You create this switchboard, along with the menus and a complicated dialog box, in Chapter 32.

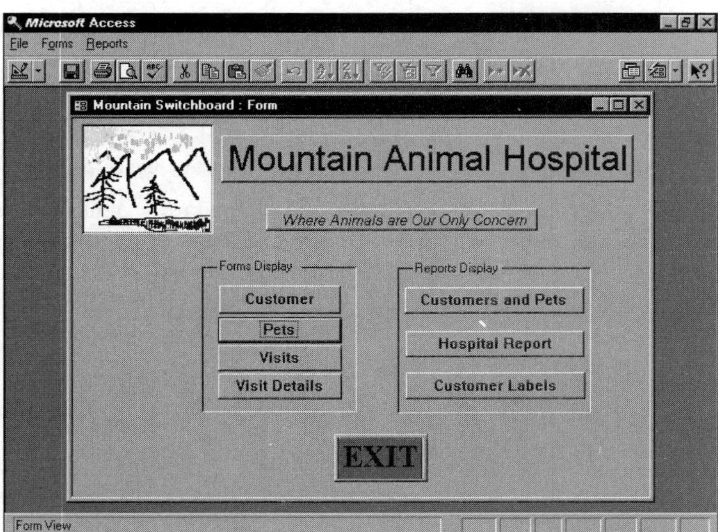

Figure 6-12: A switchboard and menu for Mountain Animal Hospital.

Summary

In this chapter, you learned how to design reports properly and how to extract data items. You learned how to set relations, and saw the design process for the forms and menus that serve as examples in this book. You became acquainted with the Mountain Animal Hospital, a fictitious entity used to illustrate database processing. Mountain Animal Hospital is a medium-size veterinary hospital serving individuals, pet stores, and zoos in three states. The chapter explained the following points:

- ✦ The seven-step method for design includes overall system design, report design, data design, table design, field design, form design, and menu design.
- ✦ The overall design phase helps you think through your system from concept to reality before you touch the keyboard. This makes implementation much more efficient.
- ✦ Report design lets you plan for the output necessary to provide information from your system.
- ✦ In data design, you extract fields from your report in order to group them logically.
- ✦ After you can group your fields logically, you can create tables in which to store your data. You can then define relationships between related tables.
- ✦ During field design, you define the data types of each field and their sizes. You also define data-entry rules to allow only valid data into your system.
- ✦ You can design forms by using the Access Form Design window, which gives you a WYSIWYG view of your data; designing on-screen forms to resemble printed-out forms is the most user-friendly approach.
- ✦ In Access, you can create switchboards and menus to help you navigate through a system.

This chapter completes the first part of this book. In the next part, you learn how to create a table, enter and display data in datasheets, and create simple data-entry forms, queries, and reports. Finally, you learn how to use multiple files.

✦ ✦ ✦

Basic Database Usage

C H A P T E R 7

Creating Database Tables

In This Chapter

Creating a database

Creating a table

Navigating in the Table window

Entering field names and descriptions

Selecting a field data type

Entering field properties

Changing a table design

Creating a primary key

Saving and printing your table design

Renaming, copying, and deleting tables

In this chapter, you learn how to start the process of data base and table creation. You create a database container to hold the tables, queries, forms, reports, and macros that you create as you learn Access. You also create the Pets database table, which stores data about the pets serviced by the Mountain Animal Hospital.

Creating the Pets Table

The Pets table is one of the best examples in the Mountain Animal Hospital database because it illustrates the major field types used by Access. In most tables, you will find that the majority of fields are *text fields*. Most data in the world is either numbers or text. The Pets table contains many text fields to fully describe each animal, but also contains several *numeric fields* to give the animal's length and weight. Another common field type is *date and time*; the Pets table uses a date/time field to record the date of birth. The Pets table also contains several *Yes/No fields* used for making a single choice. Examples of this field are Neutered or Current Vaccination. Large amounts of text are stored in a *memo field* to record notes about the animal, such as special customer preferences or known allergies. Another field type is the *OLE field*, used for storing sound, pictures, or video. In the Pets example, this field will store a picture of the animal.

Before you can create a table, however, you must first create the overall database container.

Creating a Database

The Database window displays all the various object files from your database that you may create while using Access. Actually, a database is a single file. As you create new *object files*, they are stored within the database file. They are not DOS files in themselves; instead, they are stored objects. The database file will start off at about 65,000 bytes and grow as you create new objects — tables, queries, forms, reports, macros, and modules. Adding data to an Access database will also increase the size of the file.

You can create a new database by selecting File⇨New Database from the main Access menu (as shown in Figure 7-1), or by clicking on the first icon in the toolbar.

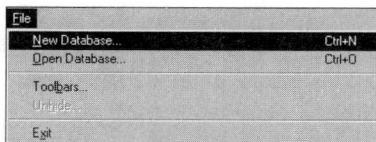

Figure 7-1: Creating a new database by using File⇨New Database.

Tip You can also create a new database by clicking on the New Database icon. This is the first icon in the toolbar.

Create a new database now by clicking on the first toolbar icon.

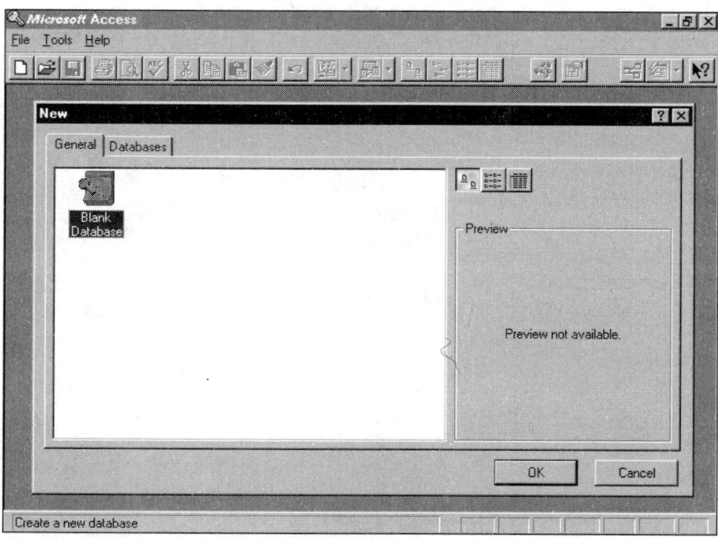

Figure 7-2: The New Database window.

The New Database window appears. There are two tabs — General and Databases. The General section is used for the Database Wizard.

Select the Blank Database icon.

Tip

When you first start Access, the New Database window appears automatically.

Cross Ref

Chapter 33 covers use of the Database Wizard to create instant applications.

After you start the creation process, you must create a name for the database. Figure 7-3 shows a standard Windows 95 file box, which has several areas, including a combo box and a file list. A default name `db1.mdb` appears in the File name combo box. You can simply type the name you want right over the default name. Adding the .MDB file extension is optional; Access adds it automatically when you create the file container. Because the database is a standard Windows 95 file, its filename can be any valid Windows 95 long filename. You can also see the existing .MDB files in the file list part of the window. Although the Save In combo box may be set to the My Documents folder initially, you can change this setting to any folder you have. In this example, that folder is C:\ACCESS95.

Warning

An Access for Windows 95 database cannot be used by previous versions of Access.

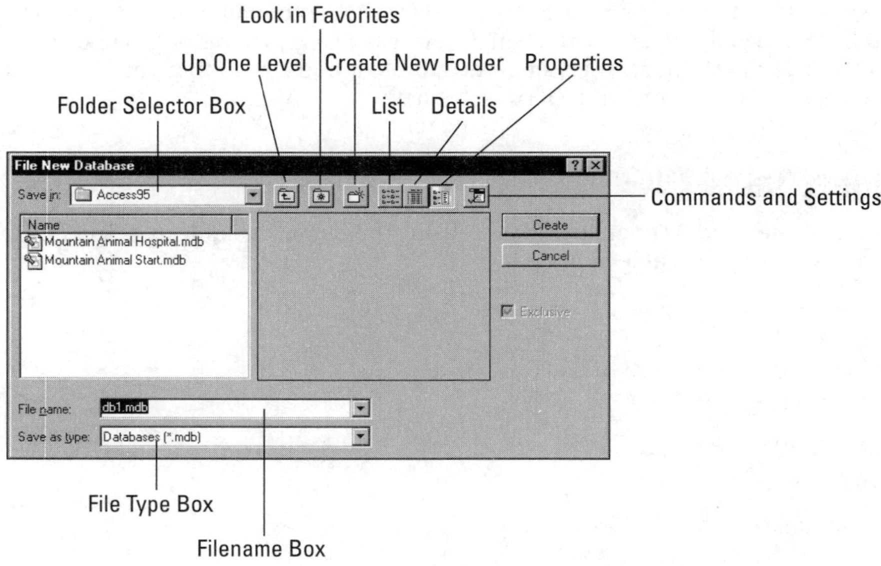

Figure 7-3: Entering a filename for the database container.

Type **My Mountain Animal Hospital** in place of `db1.mdb` as the name for your database. Click on Create to save and open the new database.

Warning If you enter a file extension other than MDB, Access saves the database file but does not display it when you open the database later. By default, Access searches for and displays only those files with an MDB file extension.

The File Selector box displays a list of Access databases in the current subdirectory. The list is for reference only; you use it to see what databases already exist. All the database filenames appear *grayed out*; they are not selectable. You can switch to a different subdirectory or drive to save the new database container by clicking on the arrow to the right of the Save in box and selecting a new folder or drive from the list.

Cross Ref If you are following along with the examples in this book, note that we have chosen the name `My Mountain Animal Hospital` for the name of the database you create as you complete the chapters. This database is for our hypothetical business, the Mountain Animal Hospital. After you enter the filename, Access creates the empty database. The disk that comes with your book contains two database files named `Mountain Animal Hospital Start` (only the database tables), and `Mountain Animal Hospital` (the completed application, including tables, forms, queries, reports, macros, and modules).

The Database Window

The empty Database window is shown in Figure 7-4. After you create or open a database, the look of the screen changes; Access displays additional menus that enable you to perform a variety of tasks. A toolbar appears so that you can quickly create a new query, form, or report, or get help.

Object Tabs

The Database window contains six tabs; using them, you can quickly select any of these six objects available in Access:

✦ Tables

✦ Queries

✦ Forms

✦ Reports

✦ Macros

✦ Modules

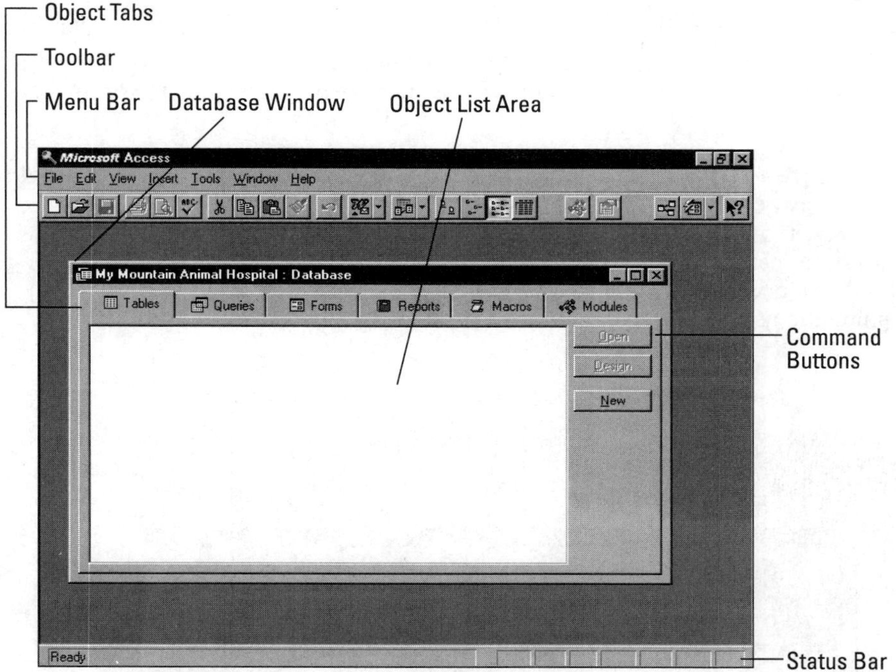

Figure 7-4: The Database window and the empty database.

As you create new object files, the names of the files appear in the Database window. You see only the files for the particular type of object selected. You can select an object type by clicking on one of the object buttons.

The Database window command buttons

The command buttons in the Database window enable you to create a New object or Open an existing object. You can also open an existing object for changes by selecting Design mode. When the button is selected, the appropriate action is taken. Before selecting Open or Design, you should select a filename. When you select New, the type of the new object depends on the object tab that you previously selected. If you chose the Tables tab, a new table is created. Note that when you select some of the other object tabs, the command buttons change. When you select the Reports tab, for example, the three available command buttons are Preview, Design, and New. When you select a macro or module object, the button choices become Run, Design, and New.

The Database window toolbar

The toolbar shown in Figure 7-5 can help you be productive; it enables you to perform tasks quickly without using the menus. (Tools that are not available appear in light gray.)

Tip

If you place the cursor on an icon without clicking, a Help prompt known as a *tooltip* will appear just below the icon, as shown in Figure 7-5. If you want even more help, press Shift+F1, or select the icon at the far right end of the toolbar (it has an arrow and question mark), and then click on any object in the Database window, including any toolbar icon. You will see *What's This* help: a small rectangle with a paragraph explaining the use of the selected object.

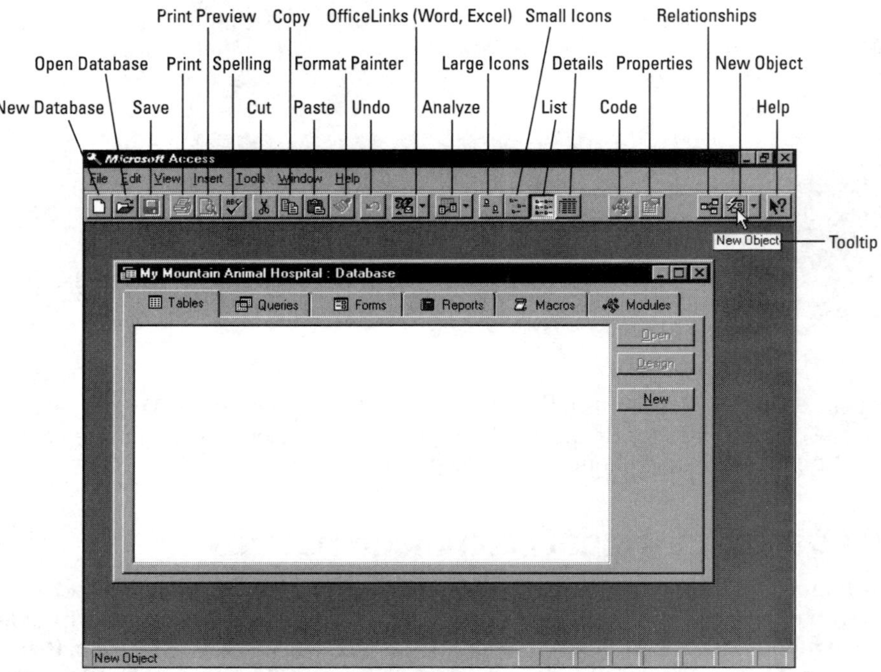

Figure 7-5: The Database window toolbar.

Controlling Access for Windows 95 toolbars

In Access for Windows 95, you have complete control over your toolbars. You can move them, resize them, and even customize them. The toolbar is not anchored to the horizontal area just below the menu bar. You can move the toolbar by placing your cursor in any area between the icons, clicking, and then dragging. As you drag the toolbar around the screen, it changes size and shape. In the middle of the screen, you can size it to any shape you desire; you can also float it over any part of the screen. As you drag it to the borders of the screen, it becomes horizontal across the top or bottom of the screen, or vertical along the left or right sides, anchoring itself to the nearest border.

Normally Access displays only the toolbar that belongs to a design or view screen. The menu item View⇨Toolbars allows you to select from various toolbars (one for each type of screen) and determine which ones to display simultaneously on each screen. Sometimes when every icon is grayed out, it shows that the choice is not appropriate for a specific screen. You can also decide to view toolbar icons as large buttons (great for higher screen resolutions — 1024×768) or in color or black and white. You can also turn off ToolTips by unchecking the Show ToolTips check box.

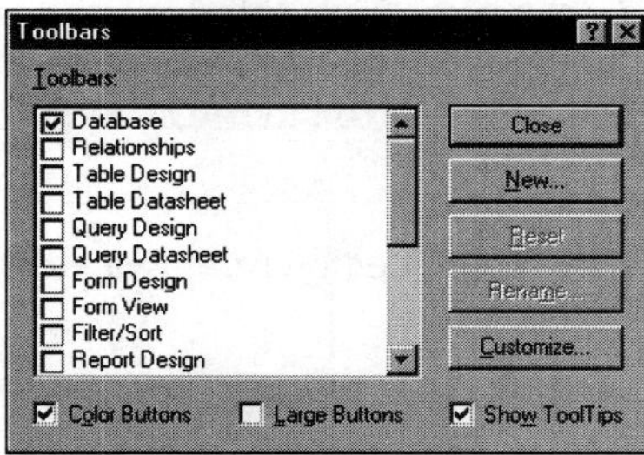

Figure 7-6: Customizing a toolbar.

Figure 7-6 shows the Toolbars customization screen. To add an icon to the toolbar, you would first click on the Customize button to display it on-screen, and then drag the new icon from the customization screen to the toolbar. To remove an icon, you would drag it away from the toolbar and release the mouse button anywhere off the toolbar. (See Chapter 32 for more information on customizing toolbars.)

Creating a New Table

After you design your table on paper, you need to create the table design in Access. Although you can create the table interactively without any forethought, carefully planning out any database system is a good idea. You can make any changes later, but doing so wastes time; generally the result is a system that is harder to maintain than one that is well planned from the beginning. Before you get started, you should understand the table design process.

The table design process

Creating a table design is a multistep process. By following the steps in order, you can create your table design readily and with minimal effort. Follow these steps:

1. Create a new table.
2. Enter each field name, data type, and description.
3. Enter properties for each field you have defined.
4. Set a primary key.
5. Create indexes for necessary fields.
6. Save your design.

You can use any of three methods to create a new table design:

- ✦ You can click on the New command button in the Database window
- ✦ You can select Insert⇨Table from the menus.
- ✦ You can select New Table from the New Object icon in the toolbar.

Tip: If you create a new table by clicking on the New command button in the Database window, make sure that the Table object button is selected first.

Select the New command button in the database window to begin creating a new table.

The New Table dialog box

Figure 7-7 shows the New Table dialog box as Access displays it.

Figure 7-7: The New Table dialog box.

Use this dialog box to select one of five ways to create a new table. These choices are:

Datasheet View	Enter data into a spreadsheet
Design View	Create a table design
Table Wizard	Select a prebuilt table
Import Table Wizard	Import external data formats into a new Access table
Link Table Wizard	Link to an existing external data source

New! Access for Windows 95 provides several ways to create a new table. You can design the structure of the table (such as field names, data types, and size) first, and then add data. Another method is to use the Table Wizard (also found in Access 2.0) to choose from a list of predefined table designs. Access for Windows 95 gives you three new ways to create a new table easily. First, you can enter the data into a spreadsheet-like form known as Datasheet view; Access will create the table for you automatically. You can also use the Import Table Wizard to select an external data source and create a new table containing a copy of the data found in that source; the Wizard takes you through the import process. The Link Table Wizard (the third easy method) is similar to the Import Table Wizard, except the data stays in the original location and Access links to it from the new table.

To create your first table, the Datasheet view is a great method for getting started; then you can use the table's Design view to make any final changes and adjustments.

Cross Ref The Import Table and Link Table Wizards are covered in Chapter 24.

Using the Table Wizard

When you create a new table, you can type in every field name, data type, size, and other table property information, or you can use the Table Wizard (as shown in Figure 7-8) to select from a long list of predefined tables and fields. Unlike the Database Wizard (which creates a complete application), the Table Wizard creates only a table and a simple form.

Wizards can save you a lot of work; they are meant to save you time and make complex tasks much easier. Wizards work by taking you through a series of screens that ask you what you want. You answer these questions by clicking on buttons, selecting fields, entering text, and making yes/no decisions.

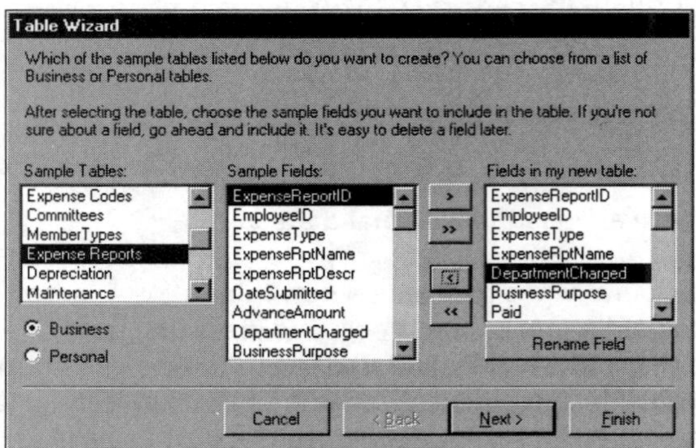

Figure 7-8: A Table Wizard screen.

In the Table Wizard, first you choose between the lists of Business or Personal tables. Some of the Business tables include Mailing List, Contacts, Employees, Products, Orders, Suppliers, Payments, Invoices, Fixed Assets, and Students. The Personal list includes Guests, Recipes, Exercise Log, Plants, Wine List, Photographs, Video Collection, and more.

When you select a table, a list appears and shows you all the fields you might want in the table. Select only the fields you want. Although they are all predefined for data type and size, you can rename a field once it's selected. Once you've chosen your fields, another screen uses input from you to create a primary key automatically. Other screens can then help you link the primary key automatically to another table and establish relationships. Finally, the Wizard can display the table, let you enter records into a datasheet, or even create an automatic form for you. The entire process of creating a simple table and form can take less than one minute! Whenever you need to create a table for an application on the Wizard's list, you can save a lot of time.

Select Datasheet View and click on the OK button to display a blank datasheet with which you can create a new table.

Creating a new table with a datasheet view

The empty datasheet appears, ready for you to enter data and create a new table. You begin by entering a few records into the datasheet. Each column is a field. Each row will become a record in the table. You will learn more about these terms later in this chapter. For now, all you have to do is add data. The more records you add, the more accurately Access can tell what type of data you want for each field, and the approximate size of each data item.

When you first see the datasheet, it's empty. The column headers that will become field names for the table are labeled `Field1`, `Field2`, `Field3`, and so on. You can change the column header names if you want; they become the field names for the table design. You can always change the field names after you have finished creating the table. The table datasheet is initially named `Table` followed by a number. If there are no other tables named Table with a number, Access uses the name `Table1`; the next table would be named Table2, and so forth. You can always change this name when you save the table.

Add the five records as shown in Figure 7-9, and change the column headers to the names shown. You can change a column name by double-clicking on the column name and then editing the value. When you're done, press Enter to save the new column header. If you enter a column header name wider than the default column width, you can adjust the column width by placing the cursor on the line between the column names and then dragging the column line to the right to make it wider or to the left to make it narrower.

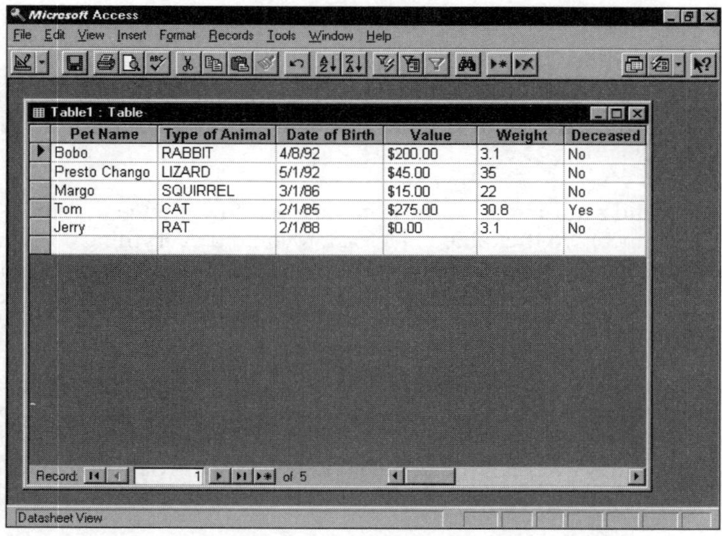

Pet Name	Type of Animal	Date of Birth	Value	Weight	Deceased
Bobo	RABBIT	4/8/92	$200.00	3.1	No
Presto Chango	LIZARD	5/1/92	$45.00	35	No
Margo	SQUIRREL	3/1/86	$15.00	22	No
Tom	CAT	2/1/85	$275.00	30.8	Yes
Jerry	RAT	2/1/88	$0.00	3.1	No

Figure 7-9: A partially completed Datasheet view of the data.

Tip

The Datasheet window works very similarly to a Microsoft Excel spreadsheet. Many techniques are the same for both products; even many menus and toolbar icons are exactly the same.

Once you have finished entering the data, you can save the table and give it a name. To close the table and save the data entered, you can either choose Close from the File menu or click on the Close button in the upper right corner of the Table window (the button with the X on it). You can also click on the Save icon on the toolbar, but this only saves the table; you still have to close it.

Click on the Close button in the window to close the table and save the data entry. A dialog box appears, asking whether you want to save changes to the table named Table1. You can select Yes to save the table and give it a name, No to forget everything, or Cancel to simply return to the table for more data entry.

Select Yes to continue the process to save the table. Another dialog box appears because the table is unnamed (it has the default table name).

Enter Pets and click on OK to continue to save the table. Yet another dialog box appears, asking whether you want to create a primary key — a unique identifier for each record, which you will learn about later in the chapter. For now, just select the No button.

Access saves the table and returns you to the Database window. Notice that the table name `Pets` now appears in the table object list. If you did everything correctly, you have successfully created a table named Pets that has five fields and five records. The next step is to edit the table design and create the final table design you saw in Chapter 6.

To display the Table design window, select the Pets table and click on the Design button. Figure 7-10 shows the Pets Table design window with the design created by the data you entered into the datasheet view. Notice the field names that you created. Also notice the data types that were automatically assigned by the data you entered. In the next part of this chapter, you will learn about these field types.

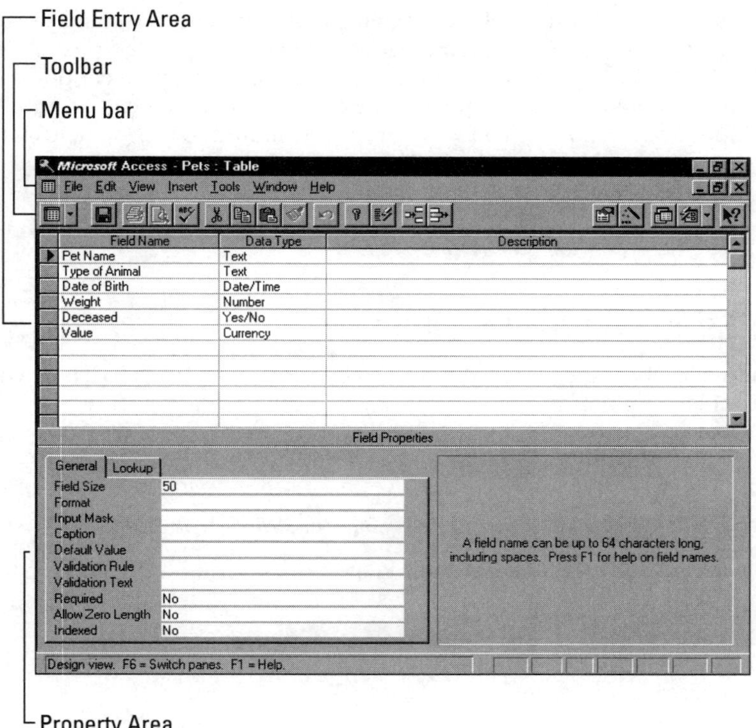

Figure 7-10: The Table design window.

The Table design window

The Table design window consists of two areas:

- ✦ The field entry area
- ✦ The field properties area

The *field entry area* is for entering each field's name and data type; you can also enter an optional description. The *property area* is for entering more options for each field, called *properties*. These include field size, format, input mask, alternate caption for forms, default value, validation rules, validation text, required, zero length for null checking, and index specifications. You will learn more about these properties later in the book.

Tip You can switch between areas (also referred to as *panes*) by clicking the mouse when the pointer is in the desired pane, or by pressing F6.

Using the Table window toolbar

The Table window toolbar, shown in Figure 7-11, contains many icons to assist you in creating a new table definition.

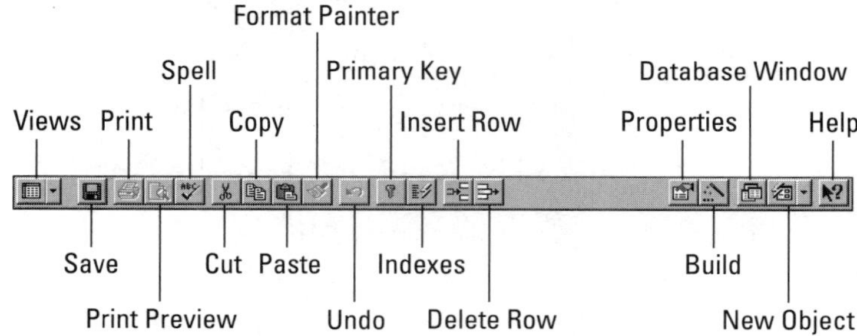

Figure 7-11: The Table window toolbar.

Working with Fields

You create fields by entering a field name and a field data type in each row of the field entry area of the Table window. The *field description* is an option to identify the field's purpose; it appears in the status bar during data entry. After you enter each field's name and data type, you can further specify how each field is used by entering properties in the property area. Before you enter any properties, however, you should enter all your field names and data types for this example. You have already created some of the fields you will need.

Naming a field

A *field name* identifies the field both to you and to Access. Field names should be long enough to identify the purpose of the field, but not overly long. (Later, as you enter validation rules or use the field name in a calculation, you'll want to save yourself from typing long field names.)

To enter a field name, position the pointer in the first row of the Table window under the Field Name column. Then type a valid field name, observing the following rules:

- Field names can be from 1 to 64 characters.
- Field names can include letters, numbers, and many special characters.
- Field names cannot include a period (.), exclamation point (!), brackets ([ ]), or accent grave (`).
- You cannot use low-order ASCII characters, for example ☺ or ☹ (ASCII values 0–31).
- You cannot start with a blank space.

You can enter field names in upper, lower, or mixed case. If you make a mistake while typing the field name, you can simply position the pointer where you want to make a correction, and then type the change. If you spell a field name incorrectly (or simply want to change it later), you can change it at any time — even if it's in a table and the field contains data.

Warning Once you save your table, if you change a field name that is used in queries, forms, or reports, you will have to change it in those objects as well.

Specifying a data type

After you name a field, you must decide what type of data the field will hold. Before you begin entering data, you should have a good grasp of the data types your system will use. Eight basic types of data are shown in Table 7-1; you'll note that some types (such as numbers) have several options.

Table 7-1
Data Types Available in Microsoft Access

Data Type	*Type of Data Stored*	*Storage Size*
Text	Alphanumeric characters	0 – 255 characters
Memo	Alphanumeric characters	0 – 64,000 characters
Number	Numeric values	1, 2, 4, or 8 bytes
Date/Time	Date and time data	8 bytes
Currency	Monetary data	8 bytes
AutoNumber	Automatic number increments	4 bytes
Yes/No	Logical values: Yes/No, True/False	1 bit (0 or –1)
OLE Object	Pictures, graphs, sound, video	Up to 1GB
Lookup Wizard	Displays data from another table	Generally 4 bytes

Figure 7-12 shows the Data Type menu. When you move the pointer into the Data Type column, a down arrow appears in the text-entry box. To open this menu, move the cursor into the Data Type column and click on the down arrow.

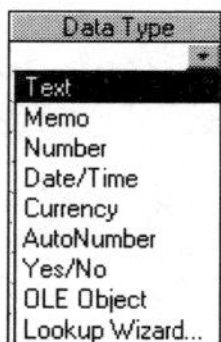

Figure 7-12: The Data Type menu.

Text data is any type of data that is simply characters. Names, addresses, and descriptions are all text data — as are numeric data that are not used in a calculation (such as phone numbers, social security numbers, and ZIP codes). Although you specify the size of each text field in the property area, you can enter no more than 255 characters of data into any text field. Regardless of how many characters you enter into that field later (from 1 to 255), Access will automatically use the number of characters you specify for each record; it uses blanks to fill any remaining positions. Unless you plan to enter the full number of characters you specify into every record, you should probably limit text data to 50 characters. Assume, for example, that you specify a text field as 90 characters, and you find that after you enter 100 records, only 10 of them have used more than 20 of the 90 characters allowed. You can see that a great deal of storage space is going to waste; you should then consider using a Memo data type.

The *Memo* data type holds a variable amount of data, from 0 to 64,000 characters for each record. Therefore, if one record uses 100 characters, another requires only 10, and yet another needs 3,000, you still use only as much space as each record requires. You would therefore cut down considerably on the amount of space your database requires.

The *Number* data type enables you to enter *numeric* data, that is, numbers that will be used in mathematical calculations. (If you have data that will be used in monetary calculations, you should use the *Currency* data type, which enables you to specify many different currency types.)

The *Date/Time* data type can store dates, times, or both types of data at once. Thus, you can enter a date, a time, or a date/time combination. You can specify many types of formats in the property entry area, and then display date and time data as you prefer.

The *AutoNumber* data type stores an integer that Access increments (adds to) automatically as you add new records. You can use the AutoNumber data type as a unique record identification for tables having no other unique value. If, for example, you have no unique identification for a list of names, you can use a AutoNumber field to identify one John Smith from another.

The *Yes/No* data type holds data that has one of two values, and can therefore be expressed as a binary state. Data is actually stored as –1 for yes and 0 for no. You can, however, adjust the format setting to display Yes/No, True/False, or On/Off. When you use a Yes/No data type, you can use many of the form controls especially designed for it.

The *OLE Object* data type provides access for data that can be linked to an OLE server. This type of data includes bitmaps (such as Windows 95 Paint files), audio files (such as WAV files), business graphics (such as those found in Access and Excel), and even full-motion video files. Of course, you can play the video files only if you have the hardware and necessary OLE server software.

The *Lookup Wizard* data type creates a field that lets you use a combo box to choose a value from another table or from a list of values. This is especially useful when you are storing key fields from another table in order to link to data from that table. Choosing this option in the Data Type list starts the Lookup Wizard, with which you define the data type and perform the link to another table. You will learn more about this field type later.

Entering a field description

The *field description* is completely optional; you use it only to help you remember a field's uses or to let another user know its purpose. Often you don't use the description column at all, or you use it only for fields whose purpose is not readily recognizable. If you enter a field description, it appears in the status bar whenever you use that field in Access. The field description can help to clarify a field whose purpose is ambiguous, or give the user a fuller explanation of the values valid for the field during data entry.

Completing the Pets Table

Figure 7-13 shows the completed field entries for the Pets table. If you are following along with the examples, you should modify the table design now for these additional fields. Enter the field names and data types exactly as shown. You will also have to rearrange some of the fields and delete the Value field you created. You may want to study the next few pages in this chapter to understand how to change existing fields (this includes rearranging the field order, changing a field name, and deleting a field).

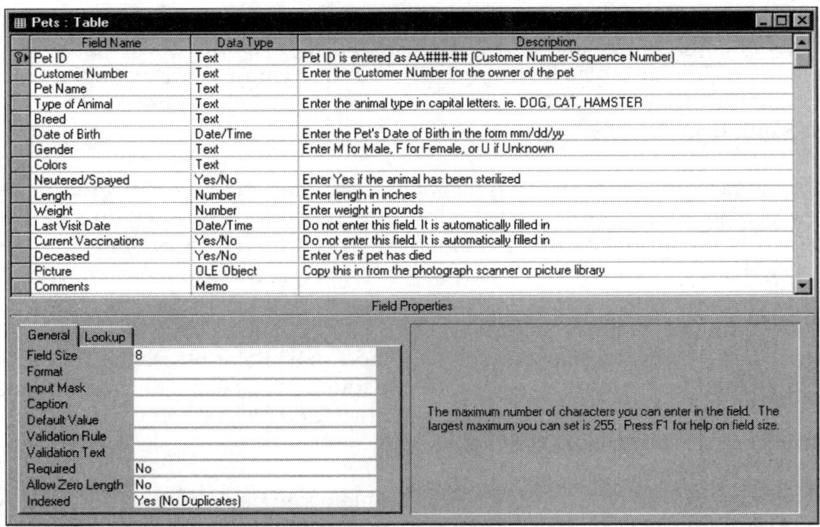

Figure 7-13: The completed Pets table design.

1. Place the pointer in the Field Name column in the row where you want the field to appear.
2. Enter the field name and press Enter (you can also press Tab).
3. In the Data Type column, click on the down arrow and select the data type.
4. Place the pointer in the Description column and type a description (optional).

Repeat each of these steps to complete the Pets data entry for all fields. You can press the down-arrow key to move between rows, or simply use the mouse and click on any row.

Tip You can also type in the name of the data type or the first unique letters. The type will be validated automatically to make sure it's on the drop-down list. A warning message appears for an invalid type.

Changing a Table Design

As you create your table, you should be following a well-planned design. Yet sometimes, changes are necessary, even with a plan. Often you may find you want to add another field, remove a field, change a field name or data type, or simply rearrange the order of the field names. You can make these changes to your table at any time. After you enter data into your table, however, things get a little more complicated. You have to make sure that any changes you make don't affect the data entered previously.

New! In Access 2.0, changes to the table design could be made only in the Table design window. In Access for Windows 95, you can make changes to the table design in a datasheet, including adding fields, deleting fields, and changing field names.

Inserting a new field

To insert a new field, place your cursor on an existing field and select Insert➪Row or click on the Insert Row icon in the toolbar. A new row is added to the table, and any existing fields are pushed down. You can then enter a new field definition. Inserting a field does not disturb other fields or existing data. If you have queries, forms, or reports that use the table, you may need to add the field to those objects as well.

Deleting a field

You can delete a field in one of three ways:

- ✦ Select the field by clicking on the row selector, and then press Delete.
- ✦ Select the field and then choose Edit➪Delete Row.
- ✦ Select the field and then click on the Delete Row icon in the toolbar.

When you delete a field containing data, you'll see a warning that you will lose any data in the table for this field. If the table is empty, you won't care. If your table contains data, however, make sure you want to eliminate the data for that field (column). You will also have to delete the same field from queries, forms, and reports that use the field name.

Tip When you delete a field, you can immediately select the Undo button and return the field to the table. But you must do this step *before* you save the changed table's definition.

If you delete a field, you must also delete all references to that field throughout Access. Because you can use a field name in forms, queries, reports, and even table-data validation, you must examine your system carefully to find any instances where you may have used the specific field name.

Changing a field's location

One of the easiest changes to make is to move a field's location. The order of your fields, as entered, determines the initial display sequence in the datasheet that displays your data. If you decide that your fields should be rearranged, you can simply click on a field selector twice and then drag the field to a new location.

Changing a field name

You can change a field name by simply placing your cursor over an existing field name in the Table design screen and entering a new name; Access updates the table design automatically. As long as you are creating a new table, this process is easy. If you used the field name in any forms, queries, or reports, however, you must also change it in them. (Remember that you can also use a field name in validation rules and calculated fields in queries, as well as in macros and module expressions — all of which must be changed.) As you can see, it's a good idea not to change a field name; it creates more work.

Changing a field size

Making a field size larger is simple in a table design. However, only Text and Number fields can be increased in size. You simply increase the Field Size property for Text fields or specify a different field size for Number fields. You must pay attention to the decimal-point property in Number fields to make sure you don't select a new size that supports fewer decimal places than you currently have.

When you want to make a field size smaller, make sure that none of the data in the table is larger than the new field width (if it is, the existing data will be truncated). Text data types should be made as small as possible to take up less storage space.

Tip

Remember that each text field uses the maximum size of the field, regardless of the value of the data in the field. If your largest data value is 20 bytes long, set the Field Size to 20 and no more.

Changing a field data type

You must be very careful when changing a field's data type if you want to preserve your existing data. Such a change is rare; most data types limit (by definition) what kind of data you can input. Normally, for example, you cannot input a letter into a Numeric field or a Date/Time field.

Some data types do, however, convert readily to others. For example, a Numeric field can be converted to a Text data type, but you lose the understanding of mathematics in the value because you can no longer perform mathematical calculations with the values. Sometimes you might accidentally create a phone number or ZIP code as Numeric and want to redefine the data type correctly as Text. Of course, you also have to remember the other places you've used the field name (for example, queries, forms, or reports).

Warning

The OLE data type cannot be converted to any other format.

You'll need to understand four basic conversion types as you change from one data type to another. The paragraphs that follow describe each of these types.

To Text from other data types

Converting to Text is easiest; you can convert practically any other data type to Text with no problems. Number or Currency data can be converted with no special formatting (dollar signs or commas) if you use the General Number format; the decimal point remains intact. Yes/No data converts as is; Date/Time data also converts as is, if you use the General Date format (mm/dd/yy hh:mm:ss AM/PM).

From Text to Number, Currency, Date/Time, or Yes/No

Only data stored as numeric characters (0, 1, 2, 3, 4, 5, 6, 7, 8, 9) or as periods, commas, and dollar signs can be converted to Number or Currency data from the Text data type. You must also make sure that the maximum length of the text string is not larger than the field size for the type of number or currency field you use in the conversion.

Text data being converted to Date data types must be in a correct date or time format. You can use any legal date or time format (such as, for example, 10/12/95, 12-Oct-95, or October 95), or any of the other date/time formats.

You can convert text fields to either a Yes or No value, depending on the specification in the field. Access recognizes Yes, True, or On as Yes values, and No, False, or Off as No values.

Tip Access can also convert Number data types to Yes/No values. Access interprets Null values or 0 as No, and any nonzero value as Yes.

From Currency to Number

You can convert data from Currency to Number data types as long as the receiving field can handle the size and number of decimal places. Remember that the Field Size property in Numeric fields determines the size (in bytes) of the storage space and the maximum number of decimal places. Anything can be converted to Double, which holds 8 bytes and 15 decimals, whereas Single holds only 4 bytes and 7 decimal places. (For more information, refer to the section "Entering Field Size Properties" earlier in this chapter, and to Table 7-2.)

From Text to Memo

You can always convert from Text to Memo data types because the maximum length of a Text field is 255 characters, whereas a Memo field can hold 64,000 characters. You can convert from Memo to Text, however, only if every value in the Memo fields is less than the Text field size — that is, no more than 255 characters. Values longer than the field size are truncated.

Understanding Field Properties

After you enter the field names, data types, and field descriptions, you may want to go back and further define each field. Every field has properties, and these are different for each data type. In the Pets table, you must enter properties for several data types. Figure 7-14 shows the property area for the field named Length; ten options are available.

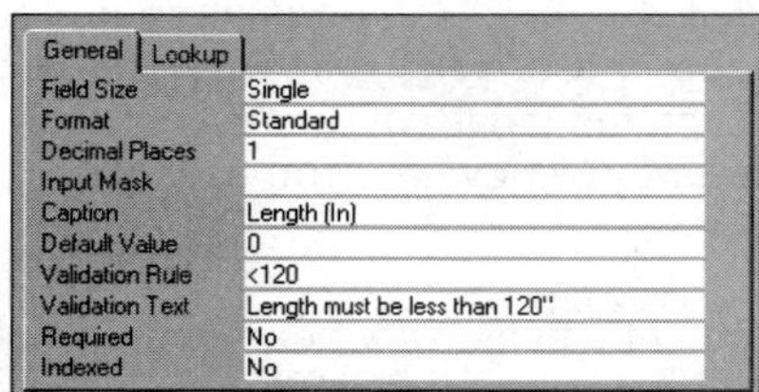

Figure 7-14: Property area for the Length Numeric field.

You can switch between the field entry area and the property area by pressing F6. You can also move between panes simply by clicking on the desired pane. Some properties will display a list of possible values, along with a downward-pointing arrow, when you move the pointer into the field. When you click on the arrow, the values appear in a drop-down list.

Here is a list of all the general properties (note that they may not all be displayed, depending on which data type you chose):

Field Size
Text: limits size of the field to the specified number of characters (1–255); default is 50

Numeric
Allows specification of numeric type

Format
Changes the way data appears after you enter it (uppercase, dates, and so on)

Input Mask
Used for data entry into a predefined and validated format (Phone Numbers, ZIP Codes, Social Security Numbers, Dates, Custom IDs)

Decimal Places
Specifies number of decimal places (Numeric/Currency only)

Caption
Optional label for form and report fields (replacing the field name)

Default Value	The value filled in automatically for new data entry into the field
Validation Rule	Validates data based on rules created through expressions or macros
Validation Text	Displays a message when data fails validation
Required	Specifies whether you must enter a value into a field
Allow Zero Length	Determines whether you may enter the value " " into a text field type to distinguish it from a null value
Indexed	Speeds up data access and (if desired) limits data to unique values

Entering field-size properties

Field Size has two purposes. For Text fields, it simply specifies the storage and display size. For example, the field size for the Pet ID field is 8 bytes. You should enter the size for each field with a text data type. If you don't change the default field size, Access will use a 50-byte size for each text field in every record. You should limit the size to the value equal to the largest number of characters.

For Numeric data types, the field size enables you to further define the type of number, which in turn determines the storage size. Figure 7-14 shows the property area for the Length Numeric field. There are five possible settings in the Numeric Field Size property, as described in Table 7-2.

Table 7-2
Numeric Field Settings

Field Size Setting	*Range*	*Decimal Places*	*Storage Size*
Byte	0 to 255	None	1 byte
Integer	– 32,768 to 32,767	None	2 bytes
Long Integer	– 2,147,483,648 to 2,147,483,647	None	4 bytes
Double	-1.797×10^{308} to 1.797×10^{308}	15	8 bytes
Single	-3.4×10^{38} to 3.4×10^{38}	7	4 bytes
Replication ID	N/A	N/A	16 bytes

You should make the field size the smallest one possible; Access runs faster with smaller field sizes. Note that the first three settings don't use decimal points, but allow increasingly larger positive or negative numbers. The last two choices permit even larger numbers: Single gives you 7 decimal places, and Double allows 15. Use the Double setting when you need many decimal places or very large numbers.

Tip: Remember: Use the Currency data type to define data that stores monetary amounts.

Using formats

Formats allow you to display your data in a form that differs from the actual keystrokes used to enter the data originally. Formats vary, depending on the data type you use. Some data types have predefined formats, others have only user-defined formats, and some types have both. Formats affect only the way your data appears, not how it is actually stored in the table or how it should be entered.

Text and Memo data type formats

Access uses four user-defined format symbols in text and memo data types:

@ Required text character (character or space)

& Text character not required

< Forces all characters to lowercase

> Forces all characters to uppercase

The symbols @ and & work with individual characters you input, but the < and > characters affect the whole entry. If you want to make sure that a name is always displayed as uppercase, for example, you enter > in the Format property. If you want to enter a phone number and allow entry of only the numbers, yet display the data with parentheses and a dash, you enter the following into the Format property: **(@@@)@@@-@@@@**. You can then enter **2035551234** and have the data displayed as `(203)555-1234`.

Number and Currency data type formats

You can choose from six predefined formats for Numeric or Currency formats, and many symbols for creating your own custom formats. The predefined formats are as shown in Table 7-3, along with a column showing how to define custom formats.

Table 7-3
Numeric Format Examples

Format Type	*Number as Entered*	*Number as Displayed*	*Format Defined*
General	987654.321	987654.321	######.###
Currency	987654.321	$987,654.32	$###,##0.00
Fixed	987654.321	987654.321	######.###
Standard	987654.321	987,654.321	###,###.###
Percent	.987	98.7%	###.##%
Scientific	987654.321	9.87654321E+05	#.####E+00

Date/Time data type formats

The Date/Time data formats are the most extensive of all, giving you these seven predefined options:

General Date	(Default) Display depends on the value entered; entering only a date will display only a date; entering only time will result in no date displayed; standard format for date and time is 2/10/93 10:32 PM
Long Date	Taken from Windows Regional Settings Section Long Date setting; example: Wednesday, February 10, 1993
Medium Date	Example: 10-Feb-93
Short Date	Taken from Windows Regional Settings Section Short Date setting; example: 2/10/93
Long Time	Taken from Windows Regional Settings Section Time setting; example: 10:32:15 PM
Medium Time	Example: 10:32 PM
Short Time	Example: 22:32

You can also use a multitude of user-defined date and time settings, including the following:

: (colon)	Time separator; taken from Windows Regional Settings Section Separator setting
/	Date separator
c	Same as General Date format

d, dd	Day of the month — 1 or 2 numerical digits (1 – 31)
ddd	First three letters of the weekday (Sun – Sat)
dddd	Full name of the weekday (Sunday – Saturday)
ddddd	Same as Short Date format
dddddd	Same as Long Date format
w	Day of the week (1 – 7)
ww	Week of the year (1 – 53)
m, mm	Month of the year — 1 or 2 digits (1 – 12)
mmm	First three letters of the month (Jan – Dec)
mmmm	Full name of the month (January – December)
q	Date displayed as quarter of the year (1 – 4)
y	Number of the day of the year (1 – 366)
yy	Last two digits of the year (01 – 99)
yyyy	Full year (0100 – 9999)
h, hh	Hour — 1 or 2 digits (0 – 23)
n, nn	Minute — 1 or 2 digits (0 – 59)
s, ss	Seconds — 1 or 2 digits (0 – 59)
ttttt	Same as Long Time format
AM/PM or A/P	Twelve-hour clock with AM/PM in uppercase as appropriate
am/pm or a/p	Twelve-hour clock with am/pm in lowercase as appropriate
AMPM	Twelve-hour clock with forenoon/afternoon designator, as defined in the Windows Regional Settings Section forenoon/afternoon setting

Yes/No data type formats

Access stores Yes/No data in a manner different from what you might expect. The Yes data is stored as a –1, whereas No data is stored as a 0. You'd expect it to be stored as a 0 for No, with a 1 for Yes, but this simply isn't the case. Without a format setting, you must enter –1 or 0, and it will be stored and displayed that way. With formats, you can store Yes/No data types in a more recognizable manner. The three predefined format settings for Yes/No data types are as follows:

Yes/No	(Default) Displays –1 as Yes, 0 as No
True/False	Stores –1 as True, 0 as False
On/Off	Stores –1 as On, 0 as Off

You can also enter user-defined formats. User-defined Yes/No formats have two to three sections. The first section is always a semicolon (;). Use the second section for the –1 (Yes) values, and the last section for the 0 (No) values. If (for example) you want to use the values `Neutered` for Yes and `Fertile` for No, you enter **";Neutered;Fertile"**. You can also specify a color to display different values. To display the Neutered value in red and the Fertile value in green, you enter **";Neutered[Red];Fertile[Green]"**.

Entering formats

The Pets table uses several formats. Several of the Text fields have a > in the Format property to display the data entry in uppercase. The Date of Birth field has an *mmm yy* display of the date of birth as the short month name, a space, and a two-digit year (`Feb 90`).

Numeric custom formats can vary, based on the value. You can enter a four-part format into the Format property. The first part is for positive numbers, the second for negatives, the third if the value is 0, and the last if the value is null — for example, **#,##0;(#,##0);"– –";"None"**.

Table 7-4, for example, shows several formats.

Table 7-4
Format Examples

Format Specified	*Data as Entered*	*Formatted Data as Displayed*
>	Adam Smith	ADAM SMITH
#,##0;(#,##0);"-0-";"None"	15 -15 0 No Data	15 (15) -0- None
Currency	12345.67	$12,345.67
"Acct No. "0000	3271	Acct No. 3271
mmm yy	9/11/93	Sep 93
Long Date	9/11/93	Friday, September 11, 1993

Entering input masks

Input masks allow you to have more control over data entry by defining data-validation placeholders for each character you enter into a field. For example, if you set the property to **(999)000-0000**, parentheses and hyphens appear as shown, and an underscore (_) appears in place of each 9 or 0 of this phone number template. You would see (___)___-____ in your data entry field. Access will automatically add a \ character before each placeholder; an example would be **\(999\)000\-0000**. You can also enter a multipart input mask, for example **(999)000-0000!;0;" "**. The input mask can contain up to three parts separated by semicolons.

The first part of a multipart mask specifies the input mask itself (for example, (999) 000-0000!). The ! is used to fill the Input Mask from right to left when optional characters are on the left side. The second part specifies whether Microsoft Access stores the literal display characters in the table when you enter data. If you use 0 for this part, all literal display characters (for example, the parentheses and hyphen) are stored with the value; if you enter 1 or leave this part blank, only characters typed into the text box are stored. The third part specifies the character that Microsoft Access displays for spaces in the input mask. You can use any character; the default is an underscore. If you want to display a space, use a space enclosed in quotation marks (" ").

Note When you have defined an input mask and set the Format property for the same data, the Format property takes precedence when Access displays the data. This means that even if you've saved an input mask with data, it is ignored when data is formatted.

Some of the characters that can be used are shown in Table 7-5.

Table 7-5
Input Mask Characters

Character	*Description*
0	Digit (0-9, entry required, plus [+] and minus [–] signs not allowed)
9	Digit or space (entry not required, [+] and [–] not allowed)
#	Digit or space (entry not required, blanks converted to spaces, [+] and [–] allowed)
L	Letter (A-Z, entry required)
?	Letter (A-Z, entry optional)
A	Letter or digit (entry required)
a	Letter or digit (entry optional)
&	Any character or a space (entry required)
C	Any character or a space (entry optional)
<	Causes all characters that follow to be converted to lowercase
>	Causes all characters that follow to be converted to uppercase
!	Causes input mask to fill from right to left, rather than from left to right, when characters on the left side of the input mask are optional. You can include the exclamation point anywhere in the input mask.
\	Causes the character that follows to be displayed as the literal character (for example, \A appears as just A)
.,:;-/	Decimal placeholder, thousands, and date time separator determined by Regional Settings section of the Control Panel

Tip

Setting the Input Mask property to the word **Password** creates a password entry text box. Any character typed in the text box is stored as the character, but appears as an asterisk (*).

The Input Mask Wizard

If you are creating a common input mask, you should use the Input Mask Wizard instead of setting the property to create the mask. When you click on the Input Mask property, the builder button (three periods) appears. You can click on the Build button to start the Wizard.

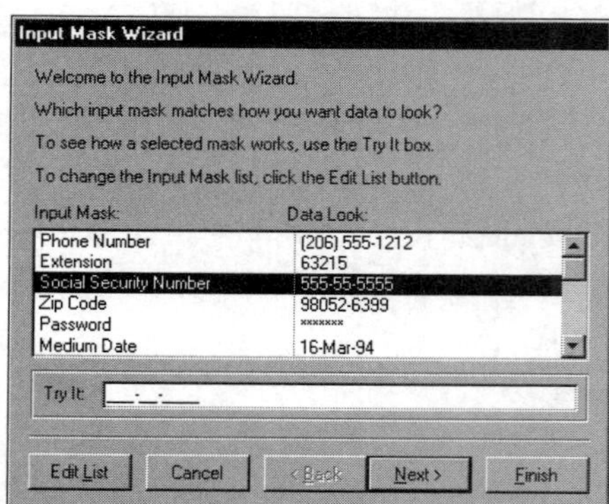

Figure 7-15: The Input Mask Wizard.

Figure 7-15 shows the first screen of the Input Mask Wizard. The Wizard shows not only the name of each predefined input mask, but also an example for each name. You can choose from the list of predefined masks; click on the Try It text box to see how data entry will look. Once you choose an input mask, the next Wizard screen lets you customize it and determine the placeholder symbol. Another Wizard screen lets you decide whether to store any special characters with the data. When you complete the Wizard, Access places the actual input mask characters in the property sheet.

You can also enter as many custom masks as you need, and even determine the international settings so you can work with multiple country masks.

Entering decimal places

Decimal places are valid only for numeric or currency data. The number of decimal places can be from 0 to 15, depending on the field size of the Numeric or Currency field. If the field size is Byte, Integer, or Long Integer, you can have 0 decimal places. If the field size is Single, you can enter from 0 to 7 for the Decimal Places property. If the field size is Double, you can enter from 0 to 15 for the Decimal Places property. If you define a field as Currency (or use one of the predefined formats, such as General, Fixed, or Standard), Access sets the number of decimal places to 2 automatically. You can override this setting by entering a different value into the Decimal Places property.

Creating a caption

You use *captions* when you want to display an alternative to the field name on forms and reports. Normally, the label used to describe a field in a form or a report is the field name. Sometimes, however, you want to call the field name one thing while displaying a more (or less) descriptive label. You should keep field names as short as possible, which makes it easier to use them in calculations. You may then want a longer name to be used for a label in forms or reports. For example, you may use the field name Length but want the label Length (in) on all forms.

Setting a default value

A *default value* is the one Access displays automatically for the field when you add a new record to the table. This value can be any value that matches the data type of the field. A default is no more than an initial value; you can change it during data entry. To enter a default value, simply enter the desired value into the Default Value property setting. A default value can be an expression, as well as a number or a text string. See Chapter 13 to learn how to create expressions.

Note Numeric and Currency data types are set automatically to 0 when you add a new record.

Understanding data validation

Data validation enables you to limit the values that will be accepted into a field. Validation may be automatic, such as the checking of a numeric field for text or a valid date. Validation can also be user-defined. User-defined validation can be as simple as a range of values (such as those found in the Length or Weight fields), or it can be an expression like the one found in the Gender field.

Figure 7-14 (shown earlier) displays the property area for the Length field. Notice the validation options for the Length field. The Validation Rule <120 specifies that the number entered must be less than 120. The Validation Text Length must be less than 120" appears in a warning dialog box (see Figure 7-16) if a user tries to enter a length greater than 120.

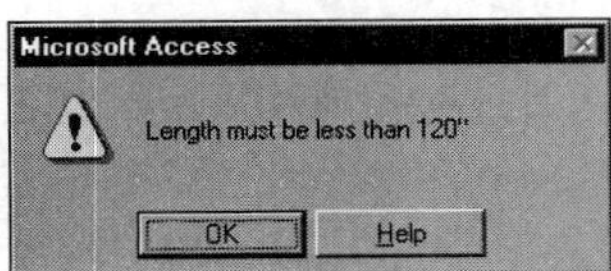

Figure 7-16: A data-validation warning box.

You can also use Date values with Date/Time data types in range validation. Dates are surrounded, or *delimited*, by pound signs when used in data-validation expressions. If you want to limit the Date of Birth data entry to dates between January 1, 1980, and December 31, 1995, you enter **Between #1/1/80# and #12/31/95#**.

If you want to limit the upper end to the current date, you can enter a different set of dates, such as **Between #1/1/80# and Date()**.

The Gender field contains a validation rule based on an expression. The Gender field validation rule is to limit the data entry to three values: M for Male, F for Female, and U for Unknown. The validation rule for this is `InStr("MFU",[Gender])>0`. The expression `InStr` means Access must validate that the entry is in the string specified.

Note Following the design displayed in Figure 7-17, you should now be able to complete all the property areas in the Pets database. You can also find this database (and others you see throughout this book) in the Mountain Animal Start and Mountain Animal Hospital files on the disk that accompanies this book.

Pets Table Properties

Field Name	Field Size	Format	Input Mask	Caption	Default Value	Validation Rule	Validation Text	Required	Allow Zero Length	Index
Pet ID	8		LL000-00;0					Yes		Yes
Customer Number	10							Yes		No
Pet Name	35									No
Type of Animal	20									No
Breed	20									No
Date of Birth		mmm yy				#1/1/70 - DATE()	Date of Birth is Invalid	Yes		No
Gender	7	>@				M, F, U	Value must be M, F, or U			No
Colors	50									No
Neutered Spayed					No					No
Length	Single	Standard 1 decimal		Length(In)	0	< 120	Length must be less than 120"			No
Weight	Single	Standard 1 decimal		Weigth(lbs)	0	0 - 1500	Weight must be less than 1500lbs			No
Last Visit Date										No
Current Vaccinations										No
Deceased										No
Picture										No
Comments										No

Figure 7-17: Properties for the Pets table.

Understanding the Lookup Property window

Figure 7-18 shows the Lookup Property window for a Yes/No field. There is only one property named Display Control. As you can see in the figure, this property has three choices; Text Box, Check Box, and Combo Box. Choosing one of these determines the default control type when a particular field appears on a form. Previous versions of Access created all controls as text boxes; this is still the default. For Yes/No data types, however, you'll probably want to use the Check Box setting. If you know a certain text field can only be one of a few combinations, you may want to use a combo box. When you select the combo-box control type as a default, the properties change to allow you to define a combo box.

Cross Ref You will learn about combo boxes in Chapter 19.

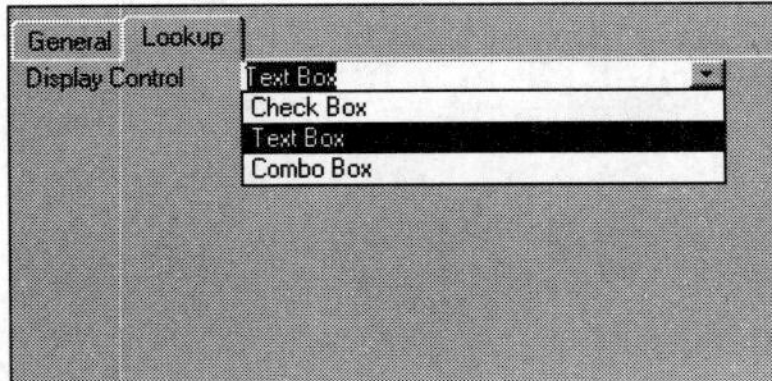

Figure 7-18: The lookup properties for a field.

Note The properties for a lookup field are different. Because a lookup field is really a combo box (you'll learn more about these later), you will see the standard properties for a combo box when you select a lookup field data type.

Determining the Primary Key

Every table should have a *primary key* — one or more fields that make a record unique. (This principle is called *entity integrity* in the world of database management.) In the Pets table, the Pet ID field is the primary key. Each pet has a different Pet ID field so you can tell one from another. If you don't specify a unique value, Access creates one for you.

Creating a unique key

Cross Ref

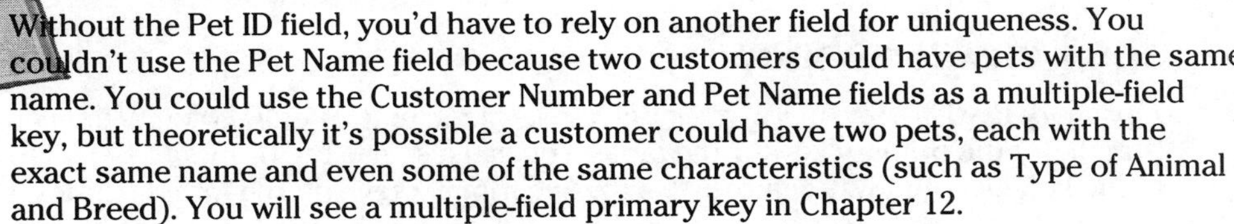

Without the Pet ID field, you'd have to rely on another field for uniqueness. You couldn't use the Pet Name field because two customers could have pets with the same name. You could use the Customer Number and Pet Name fields as a multiple-field key, but theoretically it's possible a customer could have two pets, each with the exact same name and even some of the same characteristics (such as Type of Animal and Breed). You will see a multiple-field primary key in Chapter 12.

If you don't designate a field as a primary key, Access creates a AutoNumber field and adds it to the beginning of the table. This field will contain a unique number for each record in the table, and Access will maintain it automatically. For several reasons, however, you may want to create and maintain your own primary key:

- A primary key is an index.
- Indexes maintain a presorted order of one or more fields that greatly speeds up queries, searches, and sort requests.
- When you add new records to your table, Access checks for duplicate data and doesn't allow any duplicates for the Primary Key field.
- Access will display your data in the order of the primary key.

By designating a field such as Pet ID as the unique primary key, you can see your data in an order you'll understand. In our example, the Pet ID field is made up of the owner's customer number, followed by a dash and a two-digit sequence number. If the Adams family (for example) is the first customer on our list of those whose last name begins with AD, their customer number is AD001. If they have three pets, their Pet IDs will be designated AD001-1, AD001-02, and AD001-03. This way, the Pet ID field shows our data in the alphabetical order of customers by using the first two letters of their last name as a customer number.

Creating the primary key

You can create the primary key in four ways:

- ✦ Select the field to be used as the primary key and choose Edit➪Primary Key.
- ✦ Select the field to be used as the primary key and select the Primary Key button (the key icon) in the toolbar.
- ✦ Right-click the mouse to display the shortcut menu and select Primary Key.
- ✦ Save the table without creating a primary key, and Access will create an AutoNumber field for you.

Before you click on the key icon or select the menu choice, you must click on the gray area in the far left side of the field you want as the primary key. A right-pointing triangle appears. After you select the primary key, a key appears in the gray area to indicate that the primary key has been created.

The Indexes window

A primary key is really an *index*. Notice the key icon in the Pet ID column, indicating that this is the primary key for the table. You can also see the primary key by looking at the Indexes window. (Figure 7-19 shows a primary key entered into the Indexes window.) You can display or remove this sheet from sight by toggling the Indexes button on the toolbar.

You can determine whether an index is a primary key, whether or not it is unique, and whether null values should be ignored.

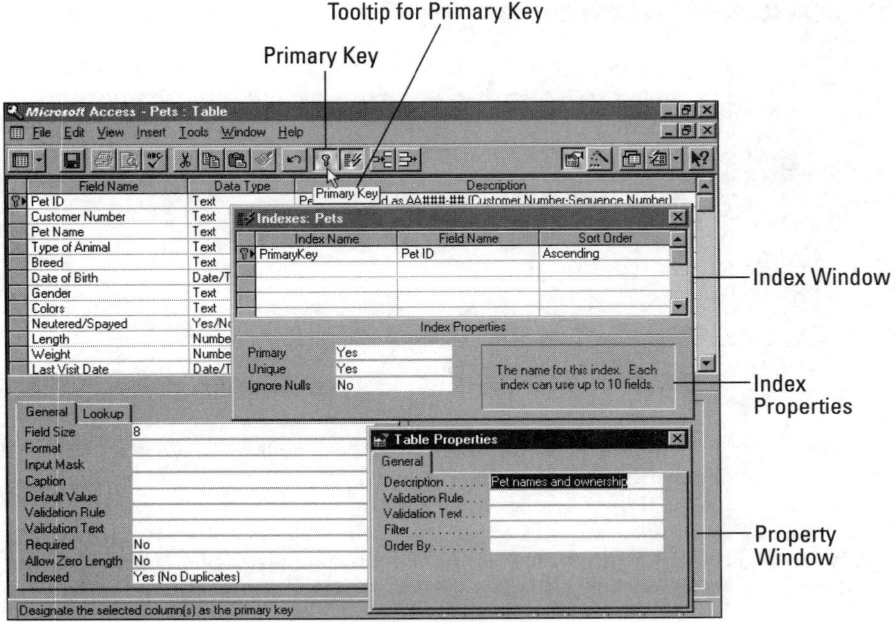

Figure 7-19: Working with indexes and primary keys.

The Table Properties window

Just as each field has a property area, the overall table has one too. Figure 7-19 shows the Table Properties window. Here you can enter a validation rule and message that are applied when you save a record. You can also set up a default sorting order (other than by Primary Key), and even a default filter to only show a subset of the data.

Printing a Table Design

You can print a table design by using Tools➪Analyze➪Documentor. The *Database Documentor* is a tool included with Access for Windows 95 to make it easy to explore your database objects. When you select this menu item, Access shows you a form that lets you select objects to analyze. In this example, there is only one object, the Pets table.

You can also set the various options for printing. When you click on the Options button, a dialog box appears (as shown in Figure 7-20) that lets you select what information from the Table Design to print. You can print the various field names, all their properties, the indexes, and even network permissions.

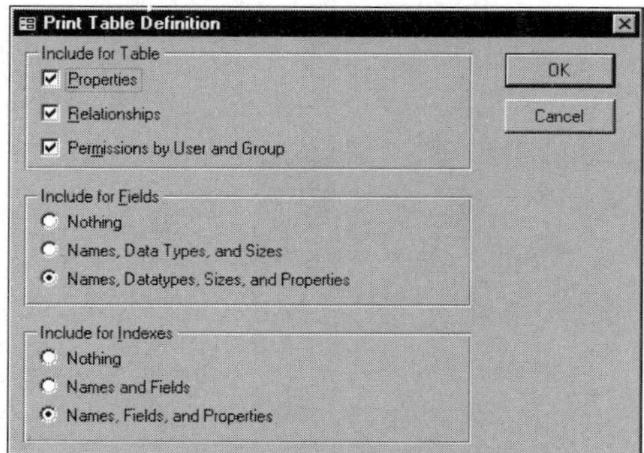

Figure 7-20: The Print Table Definition dialog box.

Once you select which data you want to view, Access generates a report; you can view it in a Print Preview window or send the output to a printer.

Tip

The Database Documentor creates a table of all the objects and object properties you specify. You can use this utility to document such database objects as forms, queries, reports, macros, and modules.

Saving the Completed Table

You can save the completed table design by choosing File➪Save or by clicking on the Save icon in the toolbar. If you are saving the table for the first time, Access will ask you the name of the table; enter it and click on OK. Table names can be up to 64 characters long, and follow standard Access field-naming conventions. If you have saved this table before and want to save it with a different name, choose File➪Save As and enter a different table name. You will create a new table design and still leave the original table with its original name untouched. If you want to delete the old table, select it in the Database window and press Delete. You can also save the table when you close it.

Manipulating Tables in a Database Window

As you create many tables in your database, you may want to use them in other databases or copy them for use as a history file. You may want to copy only the table structure. You can perform many operations on tables in the Database window, including the following:

✦ Renaming tables

✦ Deleting tables

✦ Copying tables in a database

✦ Copying a table from another database

You can perform these tasks both by direct manipulation and by using menu items.

Renaming tables

You can rename a table with the following steps:

1. Select the table name in the Database window.
2. Click once on the table name.
3. Type the name of the new table and press Enter.

You can also rename the table by selecting Edit⇨Rename or by right-clicking on a table and selecting Rename from the shortcut menu. After you change the table name, it appears in the Tables list, which re-sorts the tables in alphabetical order.

Tip

If you rename a table, you must change the table name in any objects where it was previously referenced, including queries, forms, and reports.

Deleting tables

You can delete a table by simply selecting the table name and then pressing the Delete key. Another method is to select the table name and then select Edit⇨Delete or by right-clicking on a table and selecting Delete from the shortcut menu. Like most delete operations, you have to confirm the delete by selecting Yes in a Delete Table dialog box.

Copying tables in a database

By using the Copy and Paste options from the Edit menu or the toolbar icons, you can copy any table in the database. When you paste the table back into the database, you can choose from three option buttons:

✦ Structure Only

✦ Structure and Data

✦ Append Data to Existing Table

Selecting the Structure Only button creates a new table design with no data. This allows you to create an empty table with all the same field names and properties as the original table. You typically use this option to create a temporary table or a history structure to which you can copy old records.

When you select Structure and Data, you create a complete copy of the table design and all its data.

Selecting the button Append Data to Existing Table adds the data of one table to the bottom of another. This option is useful for combining tables, as when you want to add data from a monthly transaction table to a yearly history table.

The following steps show how to copy a table:

1. Select the table name in the Database window.
2. Select Edit⇨Copy.
3. Select Edit⇨Paste.
4. Type the name of the new table.
5. Choose one of the Paste Options.
6. Click on OK to complete the operation.

Figure 7-21 shows the Paste Table As dialog box, where you make these decisions. To paste the data, you have to select the type of paste operation and type the name of the new table. When you are appending data to an existing table, you must type the name of an existing table.

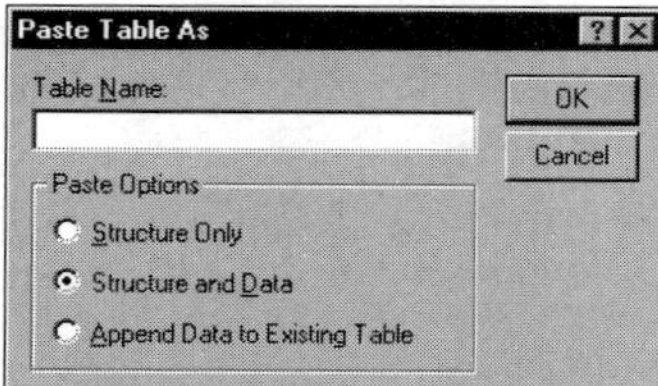

Figure 7-21: Pasting a table.

Copying a table to another database

Just as you can copy a table within a database, you can copy a table to another database. There are many reasons why you may want to do this. Possibly you share a common table among multiple systems, or you may need to create a backup copy of your important tables within the system.

When you copy tables to another database, the relationships between tables are not copied; Access copies only the table design and the data. The method for copying a table to another database is essentially the same as for copying a table within a database. To copy a table to another database, follow these steps:

1. Select the table name in the Database window.
2. Select Edit⇨Copy.
3. Open another database.
4. Select Edit⇨Paste.
5. Type the name of the new table.
6. Choose one of the Paste Options.
7. Click on OK to complete the operation.

Summary

In this chapter, you learned about creating database tables by creating a database window and then examining the types of fields and properties you will typically use in a table. The following points were covered:

- ✦ Databases contain objects, such as tables, queries, forms, reports, macros, and modules.
- ✦ You can create a table by using a Datasheet View, Design View, Table Wizard, Import Table Wizard, or Link Table Wizard.
- ✦ Table designs consist of field names, data types, and descriptions.
- ✦ You can choose from nine basic data types: Text, Number, Currency, AutoNumber, Date/Time, Yes/No, Memo, OLE, and Lookup Wizard.
- ✦ Each field has properties, which are Field Size, Format, Caption, Default Value, Validation Rule, Validation Text, and Indexed.
- ✦ Each table has a primary key field, which is an index and must contain a unique value for each record.
- ✦ When a table design is complete, you can still rearrange, insert, delete, and rename fields.
- ✦ You can rename, delete, or copy and paste tables in the Database window.

The next step is to input data into your table, which you can do in a variety of ways. In the next chapter, you learn how to use a datasheet to input your data.

✦ ✦ ✦

Entering, Changing, Deleting, and Displaying Data

In This Chapter

Displaying a datasheet

Navigating within a Datasheet window

Opening a new datasheet

Adding, changing, and deleting records

Using special data-entry techniques

Finding and replacing specific values

Hiding, freezing, and rearranging datasheet columns

Sorting or filtering records in a database

Saving and printing datasheets

In this chapter, you learn how to use a datasheet to put data into a Microsoft Access table. This method allows you to see many records at once, as well as many of your fields. Using the Pets table created in the preceding chapter, you learn how to add, change, and delete data, and you learn about features for displaying data in a datasheet.

Understanding Datasheets

Using a datasheet is one of the many ways you can view data in Access. Datasheets display a list of records in a format commonly known as a browse screen in dBASE, a table view in Paradox, and a spreadsheet in Excel or 1-2-3. A datasheet is like a table or spreadsheet in that data is displayed as a series of rows and columns. Figure 8-1 shows a typical datasheet view of data. Like a table or spreadsheet, a datasheet displays data as a series of rows and columns. By scrolling the datasheet up or down, you can see records that don't fit on-screen at that moment, and by scrolling left or right, you can see more columns.

Datasheets are completely customizable so you can look at your data in many ways. By changing the font size, you can see more or less of your table on-screen. You can rearrange the order of the records or the fields. You can hide columns, change the displayed column width or row height, and even lock several columns in position so they continue to be displayed as you scroll around other parts of your datasheet.

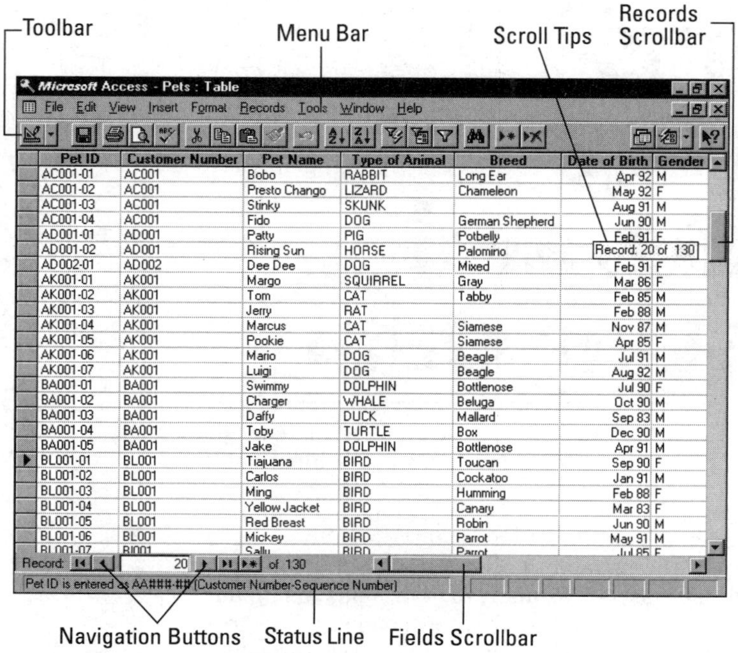

Toolbar | Menu Bar | Scroll Tips | Records Scrollbar

Microsoft Access - Pets : Table

File Edit View Insert Format Records Tools Window Help

Pet ID	Customer Number	Pet Name	Type of Animal	Breed	Date of Birth	Gender
AC001-01	AC001	Bobo	RABBIT	Long Ear	Apr 92	M
AC001-02	AC001	Presto Chango	LIZARD	Chameleon	May 92	F
AC001-03	AC001	Stinky	SKUNK		Aug 91	M
AC001-04	AC001	Fido	DOG	German Shepherd	Jun 90	M
AD001-01	AD001	Patty	PIG	Potbelly	Feb 91	F
AD001-02	AD001	Rising Sun	HORSE	Palomino	Record: 20 of 130	
AD002-01	AD002	Dee Dee	DOG	Mixed	Feb 91	F
AK001-01	AK001	Margo	SQUIRREL	Gray	Mar 86	F
AK001-02	AK001	Tom	CAT	Tabby	Feb 85	M
AK001-03	AK001	Jerry	RAT		Feb 88	M
AK001-04	AK001	Marcus	CAT	Siamese	Nov 87	M
AK001-05	AK001	Pookie	CAT	Siamese	Apr 85	F
AK001-06	AK001	Mario	DOG	Beagle	Jul 91	M
AK001-07	AK001	Luigi	DOG	Beagle	Aug 92	M
BA001-01	BA001	Swimmy	DOLPHIN	Bottlenose	Jul 90	F
BA001-02	BA001	Charger	WHALE	Beluga	Oct 90	M
BA001-03	BA001	Daffy	DUCK	Mallard	Sep 83	M
BA001-04	BA001	Toby	TURTLE	Box	Dec 90	M
BA001-05	BA001	Jake	DOLPHIN	Bottlenose	Apr 91	M
BL001-01	BL001	Tiajuana	BIRD	Toucan	Sep 90	F
BL001-02	BL001	Carlos	BIRD	Cockatoo	Jan 91	M
BL001-03	BL001	Ming	BIRD	Humming	Feb 88	F
BL001-04	BL001	Yellow Jacket	BIRD	Canary	Mar 83	F
BL001-05	BL001	Red Breast	BIRD	Robin	Jun 90	M
BL001-06	BL001	Mickey	BIRD	Parrot	May 91	M
BL001-07	BL001	Sally	BIRD	Parrot	Jul 85	F

Record: 20 of 130

Pet ID is entered as AA###-## (Customer Number-Sequence Number)

Navigation Buttons | Status Line | Fields Scrollbar

Figure 8-1: A typical datasheet.

New! You can sort the datasheet quickly into any order you desire with one toolbar button. You can filter the datasheet for specific records making other records invisible. You can also import records directly to the datasheet, or export formatted records from the datasheet directly to Word, Excel, or other applications that support OLE 2.0.

The Datasheet Window

The Datasheet window is similar to other object windows in Access. At the top of the screen, you see the title bar, menu bar, and toolbar. The center of the screen displays your data in rows and columns. Each record occupies one row; each column, headed by a field name, contains that field's values. The display arranges the records initially by primary key, and the fields by the order of their creation in the table design.

The right side of the window contains a *scrollbar* for moving quickly between records. As you scroll between records, a Scroll Tip (shown in Figure 8-1) tells you precisely where the scrollbar will take you. In Access for Windows 95, the size of the scrollbar *thumb* gives you a proportional look at how many records are being displayed out of the total number of records. In Figure 8-1, the scrollbar thumb takes about 15 percent of the scroll area, always displaying 20 out of 130 records. There is also a proportional scrollbar at the bottom of the screen for moving between fields.

The last line at the bottom of the screen contains a *status bar*. The status bar displays the Field Description you entered for each field in the table design. If there is no Field Description for a specific field, Access displays the words `Datasheet View`. Generally, error messages and warnings appear in dialog boxes in the center of the screen rather than in the status bar. If you need help understanding the meaning of a button in the toolbar, move the mouse over the button and a tooltip appears with a one or two-word explanation while the status bar displays a more comprehensive explanation.

Navigation inside a datasheet

You can move easily around the Datasheet window by using the mouse pointer to indicate where you want to change or add to your data: just click on a field and record location. In addition, the menus, toolbars, scrollbars, and navigation buttons make it easy to move between fields and records. You can think of a datasheet as a spreadsheet without the row numbers and column letters. Instead, your columns have field names, and your rows are unique records that have identifiable values in each cell.

Table 8-1 lists the navigational keys used for moving around within a datasheet.

Table 8-1
Navigating in a Datasheet

Navigational Direction	*Keystrokes*
Next field	Tab
Previous field	Shift+Tab
First field of current record	Home
Last field of current record	End
Next record	Down arrow
Previous record	Up arrow
First field of first record	Ctrl+Home
Last field of last record	Ctrl+End
Scroll up one page	PgUp
Scroll down one page	PgDn
Go to record number box	F5

The navigation buttons

The *navigation buttons* (shown in Figure 8-2) are six controls used to move between records. You can simply click on these buttons to move to the desired record. The two leftmost controls move you to the first record or the previous record in the datasheet (table). The three rightmost controls position you on the next record, last record, or new record in the datasheet (table). If you know the *record number* (the row number of a specific record), you can click on the record number box, enter a record number, and press Enter.

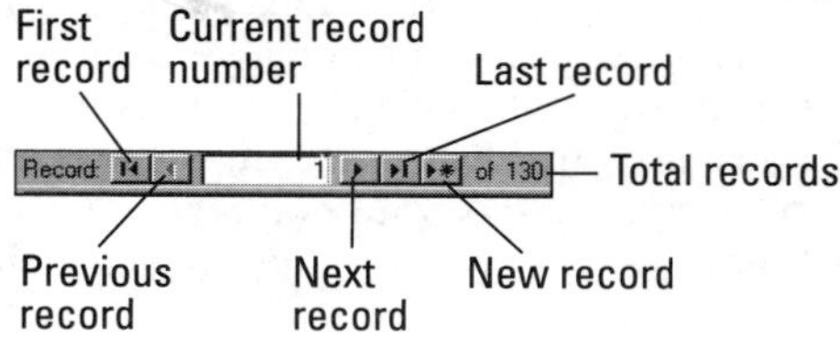

Figure 8-2: Navigation buttons.

If you enter a record number greater than the number of records in the table, an error message appears. The message states that you can't go to the specified record.

The Datasheet toolbar

The Datasheet toolbar (shown in Figure 8-3) provides another way for navigating around the datasheet. The toolbar has many familiar objects on it, as well as some new ones.

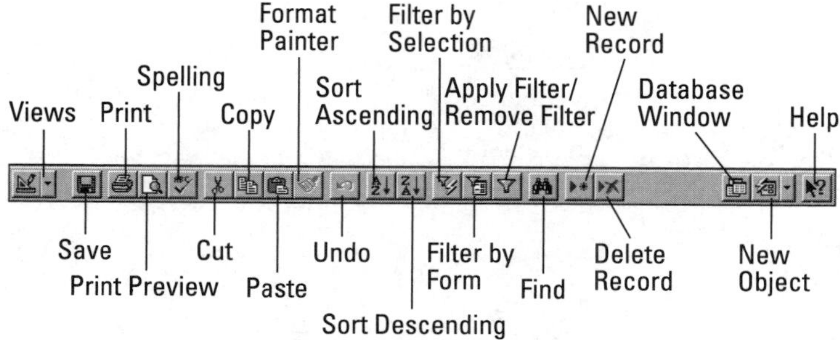

Figure 8-3: The Datasheet toolbar.

The first icon lets you switch between the Table Design and the Datasheet views. By clicking on the Table Design icon, you can make changes to the design of your table. You can then click on the Datasheet icon to return to the datasheet.

Note If you originally displayed a data-entry form, this icon will have three choices: Table Design, Datasheet, and Form.

The next icon, Save, saves any layout changes to the datasheet.

Warning Save does not allow you to roll back changes to the data. As you move from record to record the data is forever changed.

The next set of three icons includes Print (which looks like a printer and sends your datasheet values to your printer) and Print Preview (which looks like a printed-page-with-magnifying-glass and shows you on-screen how your datasheet would look printed). The third icon lets you spell-check your data using the standard Microsoft Office spell-checking feature.

The objects you can paste include a single value, datasheet row, column, or range of values. You can copy and paste objects to and from other programs (such as Microsoft Word or Excel), but the Format Painter is not available in a datasheet.

The next icon lets you Undo a change to a record or (more globaly) undo formatting.

The next two icons are the QuickSort icons. You can select one or more columns and click on one of these buttons to sort the data instantly, in ascending or descending order, using the selected columns as the sorting criteria.

The next three icons in this toolbar look like funnels. They let you determine and display only selected records. The first icon, Filter by Selection, lets you filter records to match a specific highlighted value. Each time you highlight a value, you add the selection to the filter. This additive process continues until you clear the filter. (See the detailed discussion of this filter later in this chapter.) The second icon, Filter by Form, turns each column of data into a *combo box* where you can select a single value from the datasheet and filter for matching records. The last icon in the group turns any filters on or off.

The Find Specified Text icon is a pair of binoculars; you click on it to display a dialog box that lets you search for a specific value in a specific field. Clicking on the Database Window icon displays the Access for Windows 95 Database window. The New Object icons give you pull-down menus so you can create new objects like tables, queries, forms, reports, macros, and modules. The last icon displays Small Card Help.

Opening a Datasheet

You can view your data in a datasheet in many ways. From the Database window, you should follow these steps:

1. Click on the Table tab.

2. Click on the table name you want to open. (In this example, it will be Pets.)
3. Click on Open.

An alternative method for opening the datasheet is to double-click on the Pets table name.

Tip

If you are in any of the design windows, you can click on the Datasheet button and view your data in a datasheet.

Entering New Data

When you open a datasheet, you see all the records in your table; if you just created your table design, you won't see any data in the new datasheet yet. Figure 8-4 shows an empty datasheet. When the datasheet is empty, the record pointer on the first record is displayed as a right-pointing triangle.

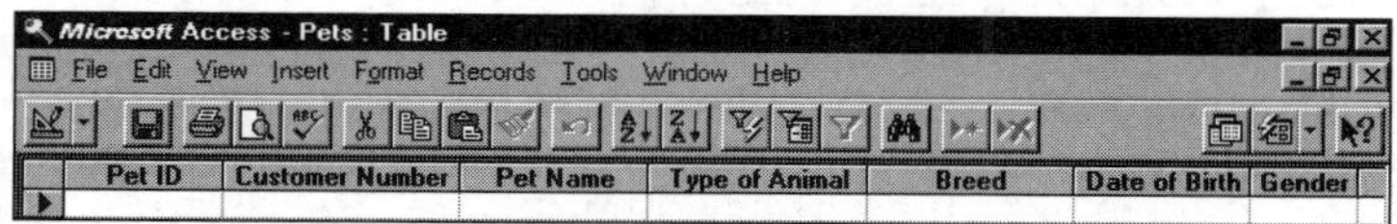

Figure 8-4: An empty datasheet.

You can enter a record into a datasheet field simply by moving the cursor to the field and typing the value. As you begin to edit the record, the record pointer turns into a pencil, indicating that the record is being edited. A second row also appears as you begin to enter the record; this row contains an asterisk in the record-pointer position, indicating a new record. The new-record pointer always appears in the last line of the datasheet; after you enter a record, all new records appear there as well.

The cursor generally starts in the first field of the table for data entry.

If you performed the steps in Chapter 7, you already have five partial records. If not, you have an empty datasheet. To enter or edit the first record in the Pets table, follow these steps. (A portion of the record is shown in Figure 8-5.)

1. Position the cursor in the Pet ID field.
2. Type **AC-001** and press Tab to move to the Customer Number field.
3. Type **AC001-01** and press Tab to move to the Pet Name field.
4. Type **Bobo** and press Tab to move to the Type of Animal field.
5. Type **RABBIT** and press Tab to move to the Breed field.

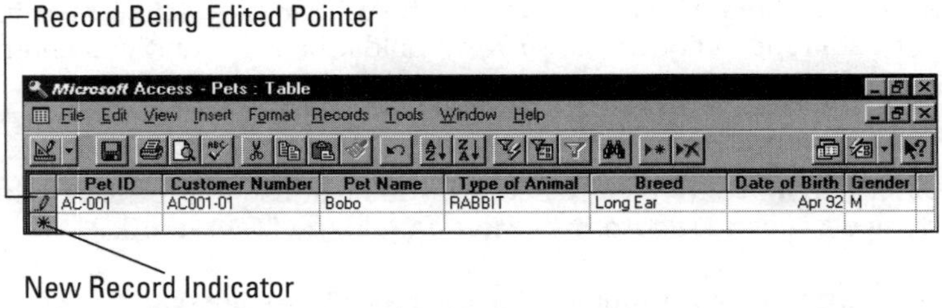

Record Being Edited Pointer

New Record Indicator

Figure 8-5: A record being entered into the datasheet.

6. Type **Long Ear** and press Tab to move to the Date of Birth field.
7. Type **4/8/92** and press Tab to move to the Gender field.
8. Press **M** and press Tab to move to the Colors field.
9. Type **Brown/Black/White** and press Tab to move to the Neutered/Spayed field.
10. Press Tab to move to the Length field (because the default No is acceptable).
11. Type **20.0** and press Tab to move to the Weight field.
12. Type **3.1** and press Tab twice to move to the Current Vaccination field.
13. Type **Yes** (over the default No) and press Tab three times to move to the Comments field.
14. Type **Bobo is a great looking rabbit. He was originally owned by a nature center and was given to the pet store for sale to a loving family. Bobo was in good health when he arrived and was returned to the pet store for sale.**
15. Press Enter to move to the Pet ID field of the second record.

While adding or editing records, you may see four different record pointers:

- ✦ Current record
- ✦ Record being edited
- ✦ Record is locked (multiuser systems)
- ✦ New record

Saving the record

After you enter all the values in the record, normally you move to the next record. This action saves the record. Any time you move to a different record or close the table, the last record you worked with is written to the database. You'll see the record pointer change from a pencil to a right-pointing triangle.

To save a record, you must enter a valid value into the primary key field. The primary key is validated for data type, uniqueness, and any validation rules that you entered into the Validation Rule property.

Tip: The Undo Current Field/Record icon in the toolbar will undo changes to only the current record. After you move to the next record, you must use the regular undo icon. After you change a second record, you cannot undo the first record.

Tip: You can save the record to disk without leaving the record by selecting Records⇨Save Record or by pressing Shift+Enter.

Now that you've seen how to enter a record, you should understand what happened as you entered the first record. Next you learn about how Access validates your data as you make entries into the fields.

Understanding automatic data-type validation

Access validates certain types of data automatically, without any intervention. You don't have to enter any data validation rules for these when you specify table properties. Data types that Access validates automatically include

- Number/Currency
- Date/Time
- Yes/No

Number or Currency fields allow only valid numerics to be entered into the field. Initially, Access will let you enter a letter into a Number field. When you move off the field, however, a dialog box appears with the message `The value you entered isn't appropriate for this data type or field size property for this field`. The same is true of any other inappropriate characters. If you try to enter more than one decimal point, you get the same message. If you enter a number too large for a certain Number data type, you will also get this message.

Date and Time fields are validated for valid date or time values. If you try to enter a date such as 14/45/90, a time such as 37:39:12, or a single letter in a Date/Time field, a dialog box will show you the error message `The value you entered isn't appropriate for this field.`

Yes/No fields require that you enter one of these defined values: Yes, True, One, a number other than 0 for Yes; or No, False, Off, or 0 for No. Of course, you can also define your own acceptable values in the Format property for the field, but generally these are the only acceptable values. If you try to enter an invalid value, the dialog box appears with the usual message to indicate an inappropriate value.

Using various data-entry techniques

Because field types vary, you use different data-entry techniques for each type. You have already learned that some data-type validation is automatic. Designing the Pets table, however, meant entering certain user-defined format and data-validation rules. The following sections examine the types of data entry.

Standard text data entry

The first five fields you entered in the Pets table were Text fields. You simply entered each value and moved on. The Pet-ID field used an *input mask* for data entry. There wasn't any special formatting for the other fields. Note that if you entered a value in lowercase, it is displayed in uppercase. Text can be validated for specific values, and it can be displayed with format properties.

Tip: Sometimes you want to enter a Text field on multiple lines. You can press Ctrl+Enter to add a new line. This is useful (for example) in large text strings for formatting a multiple-line address field. It is also useful in Memo fields for formatting multiple-line entries.

Date/Time data entry

The Date of Birth field is a Date/Time data type, formatted using the *mmm yy* format. Thus, even though you typed **4/8/92**, Access displays the value `Apr 92` when you leave the field. The value 4/8/92 is really stored in the table; you can display it whenever the cursor is in the Date of Birth field. As an alternative choice, you can enter the value in the format specified. You can enter **Apr 92** in the field, and the value `Apr 92` will be stored in the table.

Date of Birth also has the validation rule `Between #1/1/70# And Date()`, which means you can only enter Date of Birth values between January 1, 1970, and the current date.

Cross Ref: The Last Visit Date value is not entered for the Pets table. This is to be filled in when an animal is brought in for a visit and the record is entered in the Visits table. You learn how to do this procedure in Chapter 32.

Tip: Formats affect only the display of the data. They do not change storage of data in the table.

Text data entry with data validation

The Gender field of the Pets table has a data-validation rule entered for it in the Validation Rule property. This rule limits valid entries to M, F, or U. If you try to enter a value other than M, F, or U into the Gender field, a dialog box appears with the message `Value must be M, F, or U`, as shown in Figure 8-6. The message comes from the Validation Text property that was entered into the Pets table Gender field.

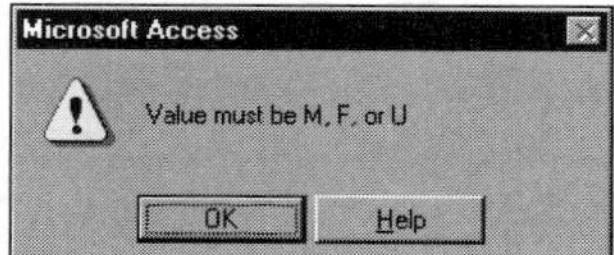

Figure 8-6: Dialog box for a data-validation message.

Numeric data entry with data validation

The Length and Weight fields both have validation rules. The Length field has a Validation Rule property to limit the size of the animal to a realistic length below 10 feet. The Weight field has a Validation Rule property to limit the weight of the animal to below 1,500 pounds. If either of the rules is violated, a dialog box appears with the validation text entered for the field. If an animal arrives that weighs more than 1,500 pounds, or is more than 10 feet long, the validation rule can simply be changed in the table design.

OLE-object data entry

The OLE-data-type field named Picture can be entered into a datasheet, even though you don't see the picture of the animal. An OLE field can be many different items, including the following:

- Bitmap pictures
- Sound files
- Business graphs
- Word or Excel files

Any object an OLE server supports can be stored in an Access OLE field. OLE objects are generally entered into a form so you can see, hear, or use the value. When OLE objects appear in datasheets, you see text that tells what the object is (for example, you might see `Paintbrush Picture` in the OLE field). You can enter OLE objects into a field in two ways:

- Pasting in from the Clipboard
- Inserting into the field from the Insert⇨Object menu dialog box

Cross Ref

For thorough coverage of using and displaying OLE objects, see Chapter 20.

Memo-field data entry

The last field in the table is Comments; it is a Memo data type. This type of field allows up to 64,000 bytes of text for each field. Recall that you entered a long string (about 160 bytes) into the Memo field. As you entered the string, however, you saw only a few characters at a time. The rest of the string scrolled out of sight. By pressing Shift+F2, you can display a *Zoom box* with a scrollbar (see Figure 8-7), which lets you see about 1,000 bytes at a time.

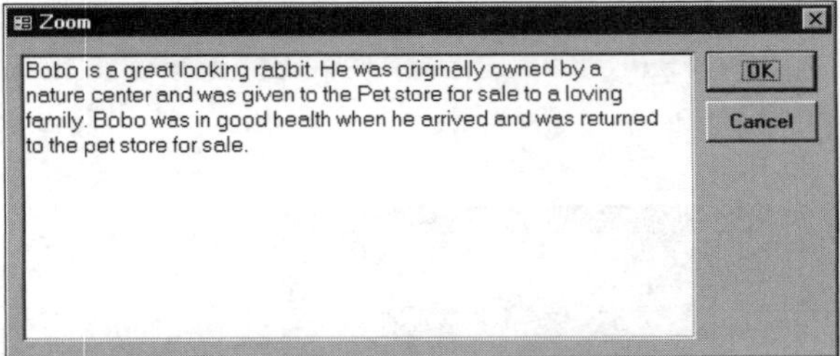

Figure 8-7: The Zoom box for a memo field.

Navigating Records in a Datasheet

Disk

If you are following along with the examples, you may want to use the Mountain Start database file now. For the remainder of this section, you'll work with all the data in the Pets table.

Generally you will want to make changes to records after you enter them. You may want to change records for several reasons:

- ✦ You receive new information that changes existing values.
- ✦ You discover errors that change existing values.
- ✦ You need to add new records.

When you decide to edit data in a table, the first step is to open the table, if it is not open. From the Database window, open the Pets datasheet by double-clicking on Pets in the list of tables.

Note

If you are in any of the Design windows, you can click on the Datasheet button to make changes to your data in a datasheet.

Moving between records

You can move to any record you want by simply scrolling through your records and positioning your cursor on the desired record. When your table is large, however, you probably want to get to a specific record as quickly as possible.

You can use the vertical scrollbar to move between records. The scroll-bar arrows move the record pointer only one record at a time. You must use the scroll-bar elevator to move through many records at a time. You can also click on the area between the scrollbar elevator and the scrollbar arrows to move through many records at once.

The Edit⇨GoTo menu, shown open in Figure 8-8, contains several choices to help you quickly move around the worksheet.

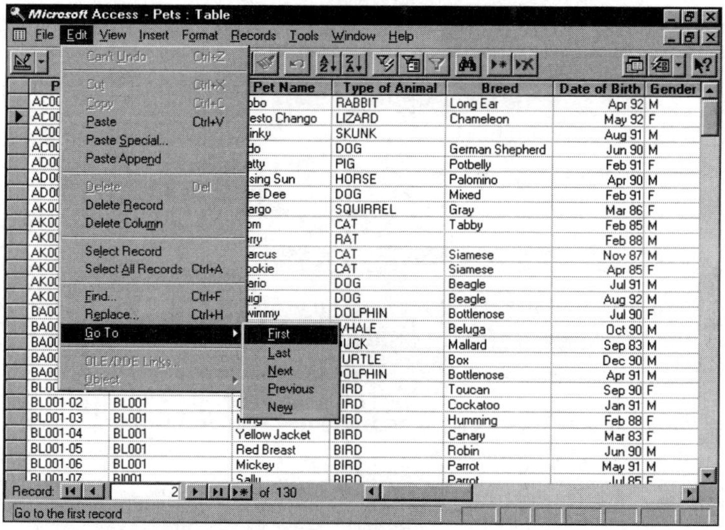

Figure 8-8: Moving between records.

The navigation buttons (also shown in Figure 8-8), are five controls used for moving between records. You can simply click on these buttons to move to the desired record. If you know the record number (row number of a specific record), you can click on the record number box, enter a record number, and press Enter. You can also press F5 to move to the record number box.

Tip

Watch the Scroll Tips when you use scrollbars to move to another area of the datasheet. Access does not update the record number box until you click on a field.

Finding a specific value

Although you can move to a specific record (if you know the record number) or to a specific field in the current record, most of the time you really want to find a certain value in a record. You can use three methods to locate a value in a field:

✦ Select Edit⇨Find

✦ Select the Find Specified Text button in the toolbar (a pair of binoculars).

✦ Press Ctrl+F.

When you choose any of these methods, a dialog box appears (as shown in Figure 8-9). To limit the search to a specific field, make sure your cursor is on the field you want to use in the search before you open the dialog box. Access finds a value in only one specific field at a time unless you select the All Fields option in the dialog box.

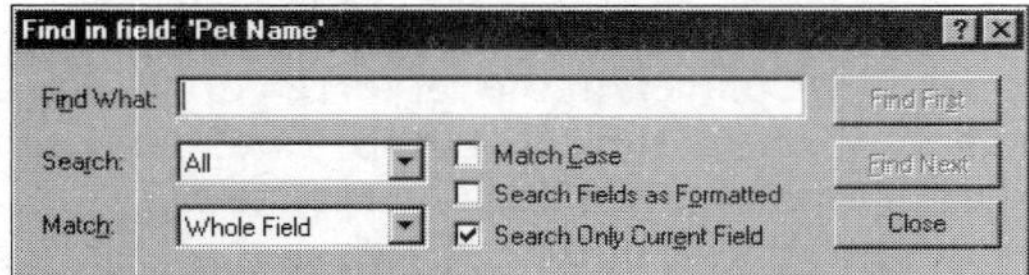

Figure 8-9: The Edit⇨Find dialog box.

The Edit⇨Find dialog box lets you control many aspects of the search. In the Find What text box, you enter the value to be searched for. You can enter the value just as it appears in the field, or you can use three types of wildcards:

*	Any number of characters
?	Any one character
#	Any one number

To look at how these wildcards work, first suppose that you want to find any value beginning with AB; for this, you can enter **AB*.** Then suppose that you want to search for values ending with 001, so you search for ***001**. To search for any value that begins with AB, ends with 001, and contains any two characters in between, you enter **AB??001**. If you want to search for any street number that ends in *th*, you can enter **#th** to find 5th or 8th. To find 5th or 125th, you can use ***th**.

The Match drop-down list contains three choices:

✦ Any Part of Field

✦ Whole Field

✦ Start of Field

The default is Whole Field. This option finds only the whole value you enter. For example, it finds the value SMITH only if the value in the field being searched is exactly SMITH. If you select Any Part of Field, Access searches to see whether the value is contained anywhere in the field; this search finds the value SMITH in the field values SMITHSON, HAVERSMITH, and ASMITHE. A search for SMITH using the Start of Field option searches from the beginning of the field, returning only values like SMITHSON. You can click on one or more of three choices (Up, Down, All) in the Search In combo box.

The choice Search Only Current Field searches only a single field for the value. Unchecking this option searches all fields of the datasheet. Match Case determines whether the search is case-sensitive. The default is not case-sensitive. A search for SMITH finds smith, SMITH, or Smith. If you check the Match Case check box, you must then enter the search string in the exact case of the field value. (Obviously, the data types Number, Currency, and Date/Time do not have any case attributes.) If you have checked Match Case, Access does not use the value Search Fields as Formatted, which limits the search to the actual values displayed in the table. (If you format a field for display in the datasheet, you should check the box.) In the Date of Birth field, for example, you can accomplish a search for an animal born in April 1992 by checking the box and entering **Apr 92**. Without this entry, you must search for the exact date of birth, which may be 4/8/92.

Note

Using Search Fields as Formatted may slow the search process.

When you click on the Find First or Find Next button, the search begins. If Access finds the value, the cursor highlights it in the datasheet. To find the next occurrence of the value, you must click on the Find Next command button on the right side of the dialog box. You can also select Find First to find the first occurrence. The dialog box remains open so you can find multiple occurrences. When you find the value you want, select the Close command button to close the dialog box.

Changing Values in a Datasheet

Usually, you change values by simply moving to the value you want to change or edit. You edit a value for several reasons:

- ✦ Adding a new value
- ✦ Replacing an existing value
- ✦ Changing an existing value

If the field you are in has no value, you can simply type a new value into the field. When you enter any new values into a field, follow the same rules as for a new-record entry.

Replacing an existing value

Generally you enter a field with either no characters selected or the entire value selected. If you use the keyboard to enter a field, normally you select the entire value. (You know that the entire value is selected when it is displayed in reverse video.) You can erase a selected entire value by pressing any key, which replaces the value with that of the pressed key. Pressing Delete simply deletes the value without replacing it. Pressing the Spacebar erases the value and replaces it with a space.

To select the entire value with the mouse, you can use any of these methods:

- ✦ Click just to the left of the value when the cursor is shown as a large plus sign.
- ✦ Select any part of the value and double-click the mouse button. (This works most of the time unless there is a space in the text).
- ✦ Click to the left of the value, hold down the left mouse button and drag the mouse to select the whole value
- ✦ Select any part of the value and press F2.

Tip

You may want to replace an existing value with the default from the Default Value table property. To do so, select the value and press Ctrl+Alt+Spacebar.

If you want to replace an existing value with that of the same field from the preceding record, you can press Ctrl+" [quotation mark].

Warning

Be sure not to press Ctrl+- [hyphen], because the current record will be deleted.

Changing an existing value

If you want to change an existing value instead of replacing the entire value, you can use the mouse and click in front of any character in the field. When you position the mouse pointer in front of an individual character, you activate insert mode; the existing value moves to the right as you type the new value. If you press Insert, your entry changes to overstrike mode; you replace one character at a time as you type. You can use the arrow keys to move between characters without disturbing them. Erase characters to the left by pressing Backspace, or to the right of the cursor by pressing Delete.

Table 8-2 lists various editing techniques.

Table 8-2
Editing Techniques

Editing Operation	*Keystrokes*
Move the insertion point within a field	Press the right- and left-arrow keys
Insert a value within a field	Select the insertion point and type new data
Select the entire field	Press F2 or double-click the mouse button
Replace an existing value with a new value	Select the entire field and type a new value
Replace a value with the value of the previous field	Press Ctrl+'
Replace the current value with the default value	Press Ctrl+Alt+Spacebar
Insert a line break in a Text or Memo field	Press Ctrl+Enter
Save the current record	Press Shift+Enter or move to another record
Insert the current date	Ctrl+; (semicolon)
Insert the current time	Ctrl+: (colon)
Add a new record	Ctrl++ (plus sign)
Delete the current record	Ctrl+– (minus sign)
Toggle values in a check box or option button	Spacebar
Undo a change to the current record	Press Esc or click on the Undo button

Fields that you can't edit

Some fields cannot be edited. These are the individual field types you cannot edit:

AutoNumber fields	Access maintains AutoNumber fields automatically, calculating the values as you create each new record. AutoNumber fields can be used as the primary key.
Calculated fields	Access creates calculated fields in forms or queries; these values are not actually stored in your table.
Locked or disabled fields	You can set certain properties in a form to disallow entry for a specific field. You can lock or disable a field when you designate Form properties.
Fields in multiuser locked records	If another user locks the record, you won't be able to edit any fields in that record.

Using the Undo Features

Often the Undo button is dimmed in Access so it can't be used. As soon as you begin editing a record, you can use this button to undo the typing in the current field. You can also undo a change with the Esc key; pressing Esc cancels either a changed value or the previously changed field. Pressing Esc twice will undo changes to the entire current record.

Several Undo menu commands and variations are available to undo your work. The following list shows how you can undo your work at various stages of completion:

Edit⇨Can't Undo	Cancels the most recent change to your data
Edit⇨Undo Typing	Cancels the most recent change to your data
Edit⇨Undo Current Field/Record	Cancels the most recent change to the current field. Cancels all changes to the current record
Edit⇨Undo Saved Record	Cancels all changes to last saved record

As you are typing a value into a field, you can select Edit⇨Undo or use the toolbar undo buttons to undo changes to that value. After you move to another field, you can undo the change to the preceding field's value by selecting Edit⇨Undo Current Field/Record or by using the Undo button. You can also undo all the changes to a current record that has not been saved by selecting Edit⇨Undo Current Field/Record. After a record is saved, you can still undo the changes by selecting Edit⇨Undo Saved Record. However, after the next record is edited, changes are permanent.

Copying and Pasting Values

Copying or cutting data to the Clipboard is a Microsoft Windows 95 task; it is not actually a specific function of Access. After you cut or copy a value, you can paste it into another field or record by using Edit⇨Paste or the Paste button in the toolbar. Data can be cut, copied, or pasted from any Windows application or from one task to another in Access. Copying or cutting data to the Clipboard is a Microsoft Windows 95 task; it is not actually a specific function of Access. You can copy entire records between tables or even databases, and you can copy datasheet values to and from Microsoft Word and Excel.

Replacing Values Without Typing

Just as you can find a specific value, you can replace one existing value with another. The Edit➪Replace menu choice gives you a dialog box you can use to replace values, as shown in Figure 8-10.

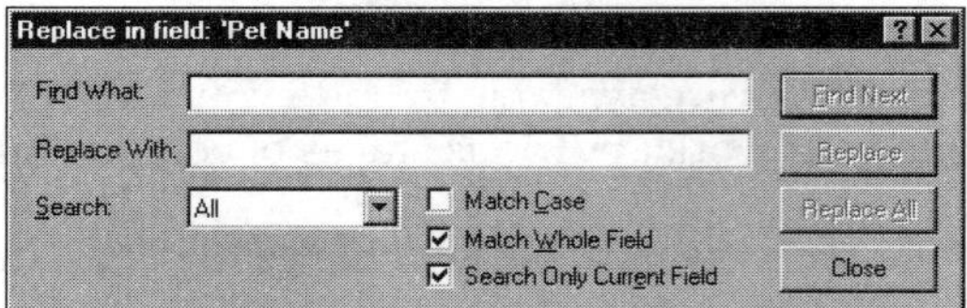

Figure 8-10: The Edit➪Replace dialog box.

The Replace dialog box is very similar to the Find dialog box. In addition to the Find What text box, you see a Replace With text box that lets you enter not only the search string, but also its replacement value. When you press Enter, the search begins. When Access finds the Find What value, the cursor highlights the value. Then you have to select Replace to change the value. If you want to change multiple occurrences, you can select Replace All; Access locates all remaining occurrences and replaces them.

Adding New Records

You add records to the datasheet by positioning the cursor on its last line (where the record pointer is an asterisk) and then entering the new record. There are many ways to go to a new record. You can also select Insert➪Record or you can go directly to a new record by using the new-record button in the toolbar, the navigation button area, or the menu selection Edit➪GoTo➪New. Another way to move quickly to the new record is to go to the last record and press the down-arrow key.

Sometimes you want to add several new records and make all existing records temporarily invisible. The menu item Records➪Data Entry will clear the screen temporarily of all records while you are editing new records. When you want to restore all records, select Records➪Remove Filter/Sort.

Deleting Records

You can delete any number of records by selecting the records and pressing Delete. You can also select the records and choose Edit➪Delete or simply place your cursor in a record and select Edit➪Delete Record. When you press Delete or choose the menu selection, you'll see a dialog box asking you to confirm the deletion (see Figure 8-11). The dialog box forces you to confirm the delete. If you select Yes, the records are deleted. If you select Cancel, no changes are made.

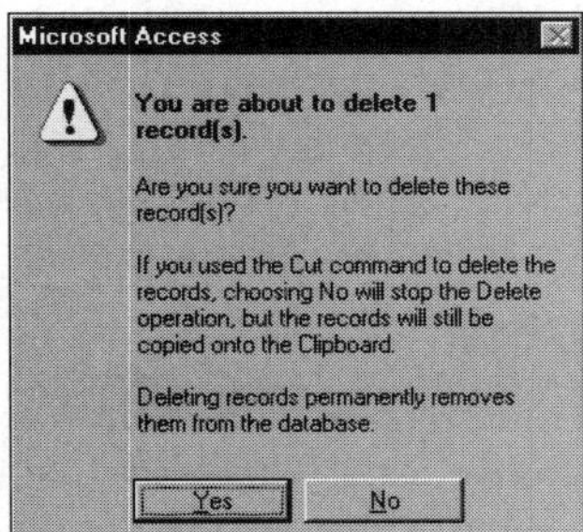

Figure 8-11: The Delete Record dialog box.

You can select multiple contiguous records. To do so, click on the record selector of the first record you want to select, and then drag the record-pointer icon (right-pointing arrow) to the last record you want to select.

Adding, Changing, and Deleting Columns

Warning A new feature in Access for Windows 95 (and a very dangerous one) is the ability to add, delete, and rename columns in a datasheet. This feature actually changes the data design. When you go to the table design screen and make changes, you know you are changing the underlying structure of the data. Within a datasheet, however, you may not realize the consequences of changes you are making. If you are creating applications for others, you should not allow users to use a datasheet to make the changes described in this part of the book.

Deleting a column from a datasheet

You can delete a column from a datasheet by selecting one or more entire columns and then pressing the Delete key, or by placing your cursor in one or more columns and selecting Edit➪Delete Column. When you take this action, a dialog box warns you that you are going to delete all the data in this column, as well as the field itself, from the table design. More importantly, if you have used this field in a data-entry form or a report, you will get an error the next time you use any object that references this field name.

Adding a column to a datasheet

You can add new columns to a datasheet by selecting Insert➪Column, which creates a new column to the right of the column your cursor was in, labeling it `Field1`. You can then add data to the records for the column.

Adding a new column also adds the field to the table design. When you save the datasheet, Access writes the field into the table design, using the characteristics of the data for the field properties. Adding a column uses the same technology as the Datasheet view described in Chapter 7.

Changing a field name (column header)

When adding a new field, you will want to change the column name before you save the datasheet. You can change a column header by double-clicking on the column header and then editing the text in the column header. When you save the datasheet, this column header text is used as a field name for the table design.

Warning When you change a column header, you are changing the field name in the table. If you have used this field name in forms, reports, queries, macros, or modules, they will no longer work until you change them in the other objects. This is a dangerous way to change a field name; only experienced users should use it.

Displaying Records

A number of mouse techniques and menu items can greatly increase your productivity when you're adding or changing records. Either by selecting from the Format menu or by using the mouse, you can change the field order, hide and freeze columns, change row height or column width, change display fonts, and even change the display or remove gridlines.

Changing the field order

By default, Access displays the fields in a datasheet in the same order they would follow in a table or query. Sometimes, however, you need to see certain fields next to each other in order to analyze your data better. To rearrange your fields, select a column (as you see in Figure 8-12) and drag the column to its new location.

You can select and drag columns just one at a time, or you can select multiple columns to drag. Say that you want the fields Pet Name and Type of Animal to appear first in the datasheet. The following steps take you through making this type of change:

1. Position the cursor on the Pet Name field (column) name. The cursor changes to a down arrow.
2. Click to select the column and hold down the mouse button. The entire Pet Name column is now highlighted.
3. Drag the mouse to the right to highlight the Type of Animal column.

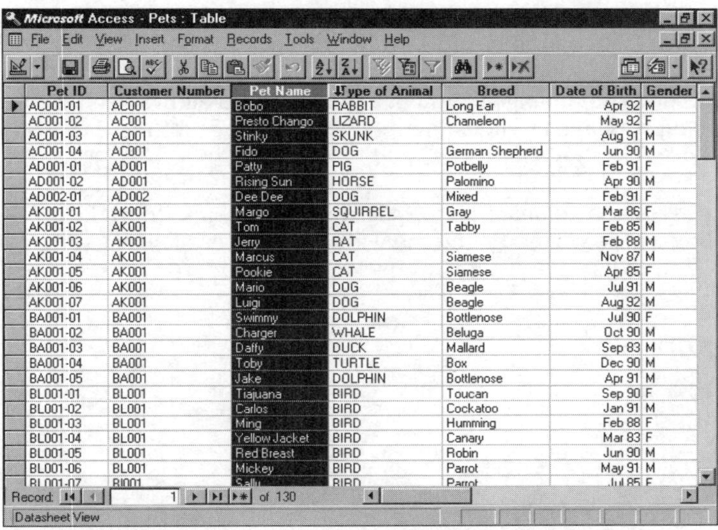

Pet ID	Customer Number	Pet Name	Type of Animal	Breed	Date of Birth	Gender
AC001-01	AC001	Bobo	RABBIT	Long Ear	Apr 92	M
AC001-02	AC001	Presto Chango	LIZARD	Chameleon	May 92	F
AC001-03	AC001	Stinky	SKUNK		Aug 91	M
AC001-04	AC001	Fido	DOG	German Shepherd	Jun 90	M
AD001-01	AD001	Patty	PIG	Potbelly	Feb 91	F
AD001-02	AD001	Rising Sun	HORSE	Palomino	Apr 90	M
AD002-01	AD002	Dee Dee	DOG	Mixed	Feb 91	F
AK001-01	AK001	Margo	SQUIRREL	Gray	Mar 86	F
AK001-02	AK001	Tom	CAT	Tabby	Feb 85	M
AK001-03	AK001	Jerry	RAT		Feb 88	M
AK001-04	AK001	Marcus	CAT	Siamese	Nov 87	M
AK001-05	AK001	Pookie	CAT	Siamese	Apr 85	F
AK001-06	AK001	Mario	DOG	Beagle	Jul 91	M
AK001-07	AK001	Luigi	DOG	Beagle	Aug 92	M
BA001-01	BA001	Swimmy	DOLPHIN	Bottlenose	Jul 90	F
BA001-02	BA001	Charger	WHALE	Beluga	Oct 90	M
BA001-03	BA001	Daffy	DUCK	Mallard	Sep 83	M
BA001-04	BA001	Toby	TURTLE	Box	Dec 90	M
BA001-05	BA001	Jake	DOLPHIN	Bottlenose	Apr 91	M
BL001-01	BL001	Tiajuana	BIRD	Toucan	Sep 90	F
BL001-02	BL001	Carlos	BIRD	Cockatoo	Jan 91	M
BL001-03	BL001	Ming	BIRD	Humming	Feb 88	F
BL001-04	BL001	Yellow Jacket	BIRD	Canary	Mar 83	F
BL001-05	BL001	Red Breast	BIRD	Robin	Jun 90	M
BL001-06	BL001	Mickey	BIRD	Parrot	May 91	M
BL001-07	BL001	Sally	BIRD	Parrot	Jul 85	F

Figure 8-12: Selecting a column to change the field order.

4. Release the mouse button; the two columns should now be highlighted.
5. Click the mouse button again; the pointer changes to an arrow with a box under it.
6. Drag the two columns to the left edge of the datasheet.
7. Release the mouse button; the two columns now move to the beginning of the datasheet.

With this method, you can move any individual field or contiguous field selection. You can move the fields left or right or even past the right or left boundary of the window.

Note

Moving fields in a datasheet does not affect the field order in the table design.

Changing the field display width

You can change the *field display width* (column width) either by specifying the width in a dialog box (in number of characters) or by dragging the column gridline. When you drag a column gridline, the cursor changes to the double-arrow symbol.

To widen a column or to make it narrower, follow these two simple steps:

1. Place the cursor between two column names on the field separator line.
2. Drag the column border to the left to make the column smaller, or to the right to make it bigger.

Tip

You can resize a column instantly to the best fit (based on the longest data value) by double-clicking on the right column border.

Tip

Resizing the column does not change in number of characters allowable in the table's field size. You are simply changing the amount of viewing space for the data contained in the column.

Alternatively, you can resize a column by choosing Format⇨Column Width Figure 8-13 shows the dialog box where you enter column width in number of characters. You can also return the column to its default size by checking the Standard Width check box.

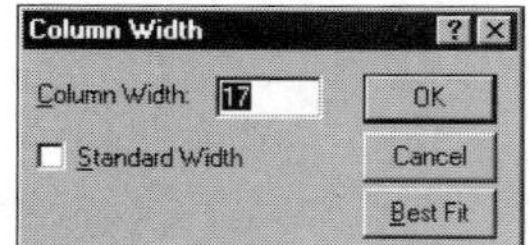

Figure 8-13: The Column Width dialog box.

Warning

If you drag a column gridline to the gridline of the next column to the left, you'll hide the column. This also happens if you set the column width to 0 in the Column Width dialog box. If you do this, you must use Format⇨Unhide Columns to redisplay the columns.

Changing the record display height

You can change the record (that is, row) height of all rows. Drag a row's gridline to make the row height larger or smaller, or select Format⇨Row Height. Sometimes you may need to raise the row height to accommodate larger fonts or text data displays of multiple lines.

When you drag a record's gridline, the cursor changes to the vertical two-headed arrow you see at the left edge of Figure 8-14.

To raise or lower a row's height, follow these steps:

1. Place the cursor between two rows on the record separator line.
2. Drag the row border upward to shrink all row heights. Drag the border downward to increase all row heights.

Note

The procedure for changing row height changes the row size for all rows in the datasheet.

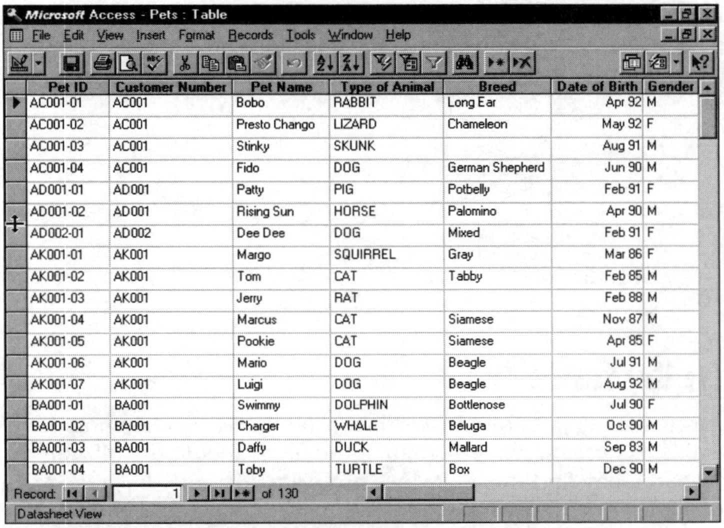

Microsoft Access - Pets : Table

File Edit View Insert Format Records Tools Window Help

Pet ID	Customer Number	Pet Name	Type of Animal	Breed	Date of Birth	Gender
AC001-01	AC001	Bobo	RABBIT	Long Ear	Apr 92	M
AC001-02	AC001	Presto Chango	LIZARD	Chameleon	May 92	F
AC001-03	AC001	Stinky	SKUNK		Aug 91	M
AC001-04	AC001	Fido	DOG	German Shepherd	Jun 90	M
AD001-01	AD001	Patty	PIG	Potbelly	Feb 91	F
AD001-02	AD001	Rising Sun	HORSE	Palomino	Apr 90	M
AD002-01	AD002	Dee Dee	DOG	Mixed	Feb 91	F
AK001-01	AK001	Margo	SQUIRREL	Gray	Mar 86	F
AK001-02	AK001	Tom	CAT	Tabby	Feb 85	M
AK001-03	AK001	Jerry	RAT		Feb 88	M
AK001-04	AK001	Marcus	CAT	Siamese	Nov 87	M
AK001-05	AK001	Pookie	CAT	Siamese	Apr 85	F
AK001-06	AK001	Mario	DOG	Beagle	Jul 91	M
AK001-07	AK001	Luigi	DOG	Beagle	Aug 92	M
BA001-01	BA001	Swimmy	DOLPHIN	Bottlenose	Jul 90	F
BA001-02	BA001	Charger	WHALE	Beluga	Oct 90	M
BA001-03	BA001	Daffy	DUCK	Mallard	Sep 83	M
BA001-04	BA001	Toby	TURTLE	Box	Dec 90	M

Record: 1 of 130

Datasheet View

Figure 8-14: Changing a row's height.

You can also resize all rows by choosing Format⇨Row Height. A dialog box appears so you can enter the row height in point size. You can also return the rows to their default point size by checking the Standard Height check box.

Warning If you drag a record's gridline up to meet the gridline immediately above it in the previous record, you will hide all rows. This also occurs if you set the row height close to 0 (for example, a height of .1) in the Row Height dialog box. In that case, you must select Format⇨Row Height and reset the row height to a larger number to redisplay the rows.

Displaying cell gridlines

Normally gridlines appear between fields (columns) and between records (rows). By selecting Format⇨Cells, you can determine whether to display gridlines, and how they will look. Figure 8-15 shows the Cell Effects dialog box you would use.

New! The Cell Effects dialog box (new in Access for Windows 95) gives you complete control over gridlines. Using the Gridlines Shown check boxes, you can eliminate both Horizontal and Vertical gridlines. If you choose to keep the gridlines, you can change both the Gridline color and the Background color. A sample shows you what the effect you have chosen will look like. You can also determine whether the gridlines are flat (default white background with silver gridlines), Raised (default silver background with gray gridlines), or Sunken (default silver background with white gridlines).

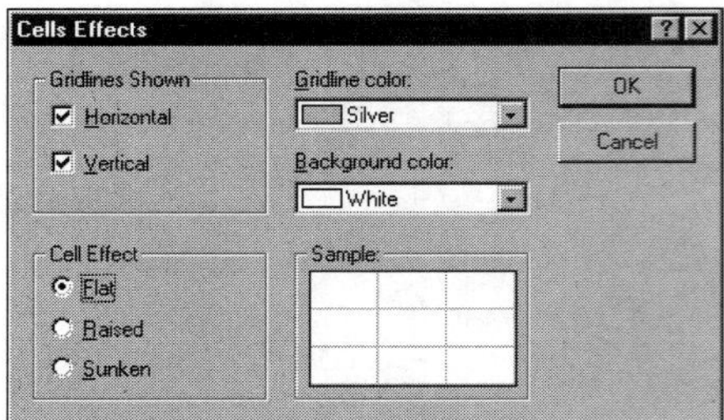

Figure 8-15: Changing cell gridlines.

Changing display fonts

You can resize the row height and column width automatically by changing the *display font*. By default, Access displays all data in the datasheet in the MS Sans Serif 8-point Regular font. You may find this font does not print correctly because MS Sans Serif is only a screen font. Arial 8-point Regular is a good match. If you are using Windows 3.1 with TrueType fonts, you should switch to Arial 8-point. Select Format➪Font to change the font type style, size, and style.

Setting the font display affects the entire datasheet. If you want to see more data on the screen, you can use a very small font (as shown in Figure 8-16). You can also switch to a higher-resolution display size if you have the necessary hardware. If you want to see larger characters, you can increase the font size.

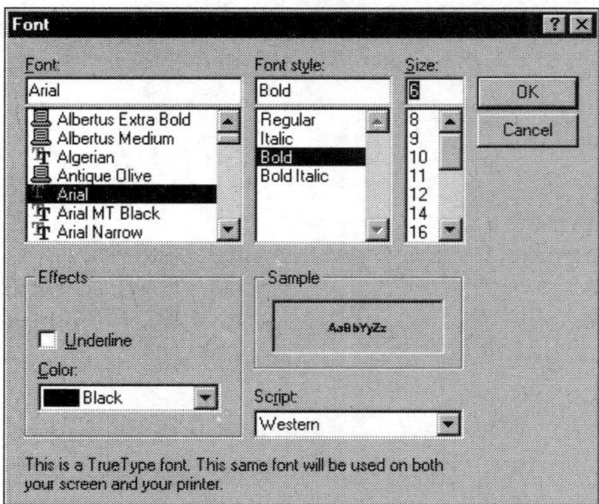

Figure 8-16: Changing to a smaller font size in the datasheet.

To change the font to Arial 6-pt. bold, follow these steps:

1. Select Format⇨Font. A dialog box appears.
2. Select Arial from the Font combo box.
3. Select Bold from the Font style combo box.
4. Enter **6** into the text box area of the Size combo box.
5. Click on OK.

As you change font attributes, a sample appears in the Sample area. This way you can see what changes you are making before you make them. You can also change the font color if you want.

Hiding and unhiding columns

You can hide columns by dragging the column gridline to the preceding field, or by setting the column size to 0. You can also use the Hide Columns dialog box to hide one or more columns. Hide a single column by following these steps:

1. Position the cursor anywhere within the column that you want to hide.
2. Select Format⇨Hide Columns. The column disappears. Actually, the column width is simply set to 0. You can hide multiple columns by first selecting them and selecting Format⇨Hide Columns.

After a column is hidden, you can redisplay it by selecting Format⇨Unhide Columns. This action displays a dialog box that lets you hide or unhide columns selectively by checking off the desired status of each field. When you are finished, click on Close; the datasheet appears, showing the desired fields.

Freezing columns

When you want to scroll among many fields but want to keep certain fields from scrolling out of view, you can use Format⇨Freeze Columns. With this selection, for example, you can keep the Pet ID and Pet Name fields visible while you scroll through the datasheet to find the animals' lengths and weights. The columns you want to keep remain frozen on the far left side of the datasheet; other fields scroll out of sight horizontally. The fields must be contiguous if you want to select more than one at a time to freeze. (Of course, you can first move your fields to place them next to each other.) When you're ready to unfreeze the datasheet columns, simply select Format⇨Unfreeze All Columns.

Saving the changed layout

When you close the datasheet, you save all your data changes, but you lose all your layout changes. As you make all these display changes to your datasheet, you probably won't want to make them again the next time you open the same datasheet. By default, however, Access does not save the datasheet's layout changes. If you want your datasheet to look the same way the next time you open it, you can select File➪Save Layout; this command saves your layout changes with the datasheet.

Disk

If you are following along with the example, do not save the changes to the Pets table.

Saving a record

As you move off a record, Access saves it. You can press Shift+Enter to save a record without moving off it. A third way to save a record is to close the table. Yet another way is to select Records➪Save Record.

Sorting and Filtering Records in a Datasheet

Finding a value lets you display a specific record and work with that record. If you have multiple records that meet a find criteria, however, you may want to display just that specific set of records. Using the Filter and Sort toolbar icons (or the Records menu options Filter and Sort), you can display just the set of records you want to work with. You can also sort selected records instantly into any order you want; use the two QuickSort buttons to sort the entire table, or use the three filter buttons to select only certain records.

Using the QuickSort feature

There may be times when you simply want to sort your records into a desired order. The QuickSort buttons on the toolbar let you sort selected columns into either ascending or descending order. There is a different button on the toolbar for each order. Before you can click on either the Ascending (A–Z) or Descending (Z–A) QuickSort buttons, you must select the fields you want to use for the sort.

You select a field to use in the sort by placing your cursor on the field in any record. Once the cursor is in the column you want to use in the sort, click on the QuickSort button. The data redisplays instantly in the sorted order.

If you want to sort your data on the basis of values in multiple fields, you can highlight more than one column: highlight a column (as previously discussed), hold the Shift key down, and drag the cursor to the right. These steps select multiple contiguous fields. When you select one of the QuickSort buttons, Access sorts the records into major order (by the first highlighted field), and then into orders within orders (based on subsequent fields). If you need to select multiple columns that aren't contiguous (next to each other), you can move them next to each other, as discussed earlier in this chapter.

Tip

If you want to redisplay your records in their original order, use Records⇨Remove Filter/Sort.

Cross Ref

You can learn more about sorting in Chapter 10, "Understanding and Using Simple Queries."

Using Filter by Selection

Filter by Selection is a technology within Access for Windows 95 that lets you select records instantly on the basis of the current value you have selected. For example, suppose you move your cursor to the Type of Animal column and click on the Sort Ascending button. Access sorts the data by type of animal. Now highlight any of the records that contain DOG. When you press the Filter by Selection button, Access selects only the records where the Type of Animal is DOG. In the Pets table, there are 130 records. Once you have selected DOG and pressed the Filter by Selection button you will only see 27 records and all have the value DOG in the Type of Animal field.

You may also notice that the navigation button area tells you the database is currently filtered; in addition, the Apply Filter/Remove Filter icon (third filter icon that looks like a large funnel) is depressed, indicating that a filter is in use. When you toggle this button, it removes all filters or sorts. The filter specification does not go away; it is simply turned off.

Filter by Selection is additive. You can continue to select values, each time pressing the Filter by Selection button. If (for example) you place your cursor in the Gender column in a record where the value of Gender is `M` and press the Filter by Selection button, you will only see 21 records now: the male dogs. If you then place your cursor in the Colors column in a record where the value of Colors is `Brown` and press the Filter by Selection button, you will only see 6 records now: the brown male dogs.

Tip

If you want to specify a selection and then see everything that doesn't match the selection, right-click on the datasheet and select Filter Excluding Selection. This selects everything *but* the 6 currently selected records (an *inverse* selection).

Imagine using this technique to review sales by salespeople for specific time periods or products. Filter by Selection provides incredible opportunities for drill-down into successive layers of data. As you add to Filter by Selection, it continues to add to its own internal query manager (known as Query by Example). Even when you click on the Remove Filter icon to redisplay all the records, Access still stores the query specification in memory. If you click on the icon again (now called Apply Filter) only the six records return. In Chapter 5 you saw a Query by Example (QBE) screen. Figure 8-17 shows this Filter by Selection screen in both a datasheet view and in a query screen. As you can see in Figure 8-17, each of the successive sorts and filters end up in the QBE grid.

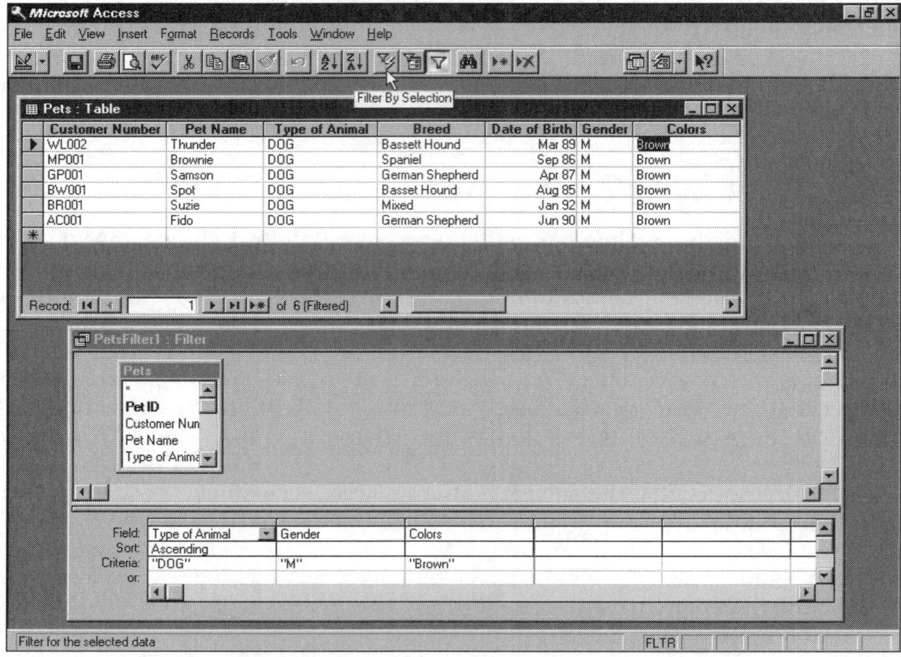

Figure 8-17: Using Filter by Selection.

Filter by Selection has some limitations. Most important, all of the choices are *anded* together. This means that the only operation you can perform is a search for records that meet all of the conditions you specify. Another option, Filter by Form, lets you create more complex analyses.

Tip If you want to start a new query, first select Records➪Filter➪Advanced Filter/Sort When the query screen appears, select Edit➪Clear Grid and then select the Close button.

Using Filter by Form

Filter by Selection is just one way to filter data in Access for Windows 95. Another way is known as Filter by Form. Selecting the second filter icon changes the datasheet to a single record; every field becomes a combo box that allows you to select from a list of all values for that field. As you can see in Figure 8-18, the bottom of the form lets you specify the OR conditions for each group of values you specify.

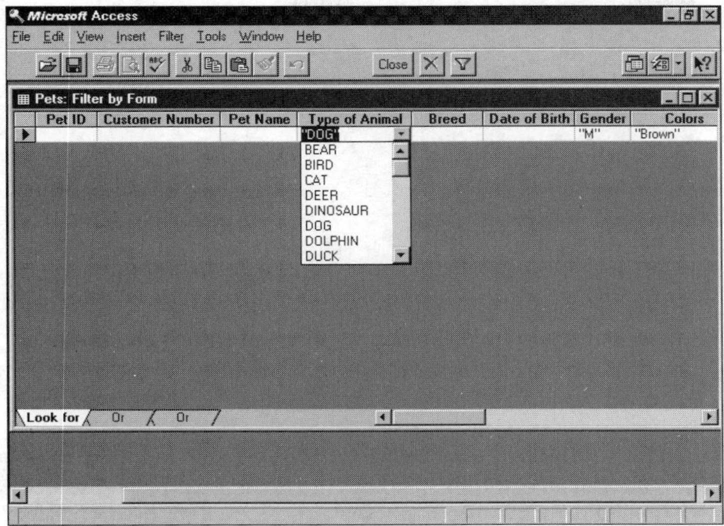

Figure 8-18: Using Filter by Form.

In Figure 8-18, you can see the three conditions created in the Filter by Selection example (described previously in this chapter) in the single line of the Filter by Form screen. If you click on one of the Or tabs, you can enter a second set of conditions. Suppose you want to see brown male dogs or any male ducks. You already have the specification for brown male dogs. You would click on the Or tab and then select DUCKS from the now-empty Type of Animal combo box, and M from the Gender column. When you click on the Apply Filter button (the large funnel), there would now be seven records shown.

You can have as many conditions as you need. If you need even more advanced manipulation of your selections, you can choose Records⇨Filter⇨Advanced Filter/Sort and get an actual QBE screen used to enter more complex queries.

Cross Ref

Later chapters explain more advanced concepts of queries.

Printing Records

You can print all the records in your datasheet in a simple row-and-column layout. Further on, you learn how to produce formatted reports. For now, the simplest way to print is to select File⇨Print or use the Print icon in the toolbar. This selection displays the dialog box shown in Figure 8-19.

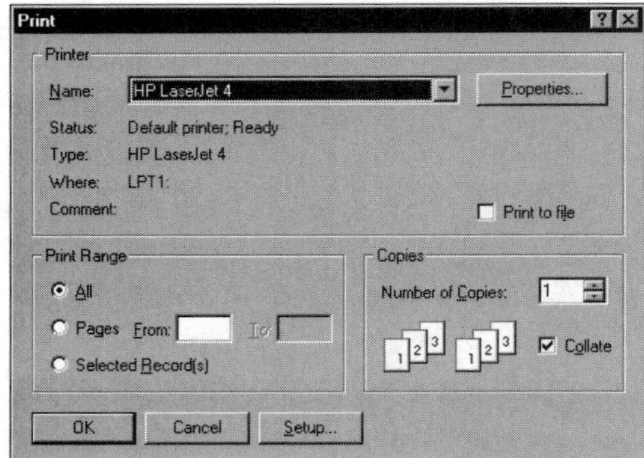

Figure 8-19: The Print dialog box.

Assuming you set up a printer in Microsoft Windows 95, you can select OK to print your datasheet in the font you selected for display (or the nearest printer equivalent). The printout also reflects all layout options that are in effect when the datasheet is printed. Hidden columns do not print. Gridlines print only if the Cell gridline properties are on. The printout reflects the specified row height and column width as well.

Only so many columns and rows can fit on a page; the printout will take up as many pages as required to print all the data. Access breaks up the printout as necessary to fit on each page. As an example, the Pets table printout is four pages long. Two pages across are needed to print all the fields; the records take two pages in length.

Printing the datasheet

You can also control printing from the Print dialog box, selecting from several options:

Print Range	Prints the entire datasheet or only selected pages or records.
Copies	Determines the number of copies to be printed.
Collate	Determines whether multiple copies are collated.

You can also click on the Properties button and set options for the selected printer, or select the printer itself to change the type of printer. The Setup button allows you to set margins and print headings.

Using the Print Preview window

Often, though you may have all the information in the datasheet ready to print, you may be unsure of whether to change the width or height of the columns or rows, or whether to adjust the fonts to improve your printed output. For that matter, you might not want to print out the entire datasheet; you may need printed records only from pages 3 and 4. Before making such adjustments to the datasheet properties, you'll probably want to view the report on-screen.

To preview your print job, you can either click on the Print Preview button on the toolbar (a sheet of paper with a magnifying glass) or select File➪Print Preview. The Print Preview window appears (see Figure 8-20).

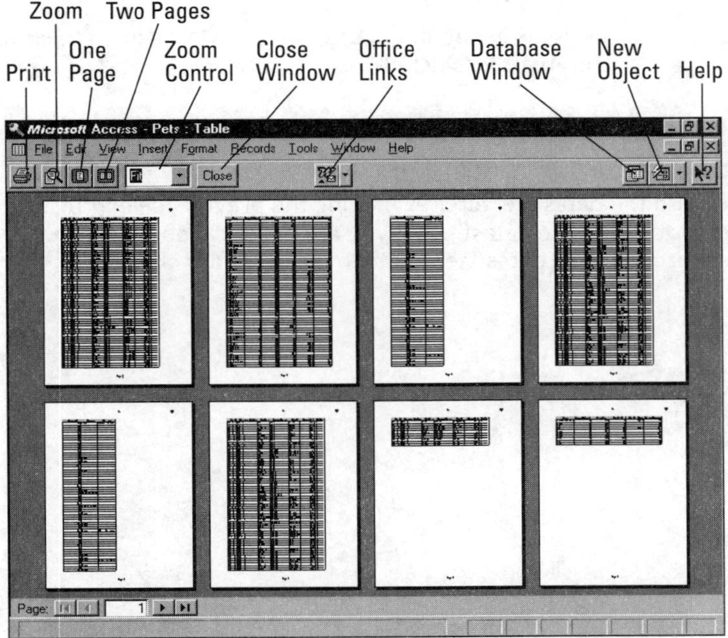

Figure 8-20: Print preview of a datasheet.

After you select the Print Preview button, the screen changes to *print preview mode*. You see a representation of your first printed page; a set of icons appears on the toolbar.

You can use the navigation buttons (located in the lower left section of the Print Preview window), to move between pages, just as you use them to move between records in a datasheet.

The toolbar buttons provide quick access to printing tasks:

Close Window	Returns to Datasheet view
Print	Displays the Print dialog box, accessible when you select File⇨Print from the menu bar
One Page	Toggles in and out to make the print preview show a single page
Two Pages	Shows two pages in the Print Preview
Zoom Control	Zooms in and out of the Print Preview screen to show more or less detail

Tip: You can view more than two pages by selecting View⇨Pages and then selecting 1, 2, 4, 8, or 12.

If you are satisfied with the datasheet after examining the preview, select the Print button on the toolbar to print the datasheet. If you are not satisfied, select the Close button; you'll be returned to the datasheet mode to make further changes to your data or layout.

Summary

In this chapter, you learned about entering data into a datasheet. You learned how to navigate within the datasheet and change the data, as well as how to reposition and resize rows and columns. Then you learned how to preview and print the datasheet. The chapter covered the following points:

- ✦ A datasheet displays data from a table in rows (records) and columns (fields).
- ✦ Using scrollbars, cursor keys, menu options, and the navigation buttons, you can move quickly around the datasheet and position the cursor on any record or field.
- ✦ You can open a datasheet from any Design window by clicking on the Datasheet button (or, from the Database window, by choosing Open with a table selected).
- ✦ Data is entered into a datasheet at the new-record indicator.
- ✦ Access performs automatic data validation for various data types. These are Number, Currency, Date/Time, and Yes/No fields. You can add your own custom data validation at the table or form level.
- ✦ You can paste or insert OLE objects (such as sound, pictures, graphs, Word documents, or video) into OLE fields with Insert➪Object.
- ✦ The navigation buttons enable you to move quickly between records.
- ✦ You can find or replace specific values by using Edit➪Find or Edit➪Replace.
- ✦ You can press Ctrl+Alt+Spacebar to insert the default value into a field, or press Ctrl+' to insert the preceding record's value into a field.
- ✦ Some types of fields can't be edited. These include AutoNumber, calculated, locked, disabled, and record-locked fields, as well as fields from certain types of queries.
- ✦ The Undo feature can undo typing, a field value, the current record, or a saved record.
- ✦ You can delete a record by selecting it and pressing Delete, or by selecting Edit➪Delete.
- ✦ You can change the display of your datasheet by rearranging fields, changing the field display's width or row height, or changing display fonts.
- ✦ You can hide or reshow columns, freeze or unfreeze columns, and remove or show gridlines.
- ✦ You can save any layout changes by using File➪Save Layout.
- ✦ Using the QuickSort buttons, you can instantly change the order the records are displayed in.

- Using Filter by Selection or Filter by Form, you can specify sort orders or filters to limit the record display of a datasheet. This is a limited version of QBE (Query by Example).
- File⇨Print prints your datasheet, File⇨Print Preview previews the pages on the screen.

In the next chapter, you learn how to create a form and how to use a form for data entry.

✦ ✦ ✦

CHAPTER 9

Creating and Using Simple Data-Entry Forms

Forms provide the most flexible way for viewing, adding, editing, and deleting your data. In this chapter, you see how to use Form Wizards as the starting point for your form. You learn about how forms work and the types of forms you can create with Access.

Understanding Data-Entry Forms

Although you can view your data in many ways, a form provides the most flexibility for viewing and entering data. A form lets you view one or more records at a time while viewing all of the fields. A datasheet also lets you view several records at once, but you can see only a limited number of fields. When you use a form, you can see all your fields at once, or at least as many as you can fit on a screen. By rearranging your fields in a form, you can easily get 20, 50, or even 100 fields on one screen. You can also use forms to create multipage screens for each record. Forms are useful for simply viewing data in a formatted display, as well as for entering, changing, or deleting data. You can also print them with all the visual effects you have created.

What types of forms can you create?

You can create six basic types of forms:

- ✦ Columnar (also known as full-screen) forms
- ✦ Tabular forms
- ✦ Datasheets

✦ ✦ ✦ ✦

In This Chapter

The types of forms you can create

The difference between a form and a datasheet

How to create a form with a Form Wizard

How to use the Form window

How to display data with a form

How to enter pictures and data into OLE fields and Memo fields

How to switch into a datasheet from a form

How to find and replace data in a form

How to make simple form design changes

How to save a form

How to print a form

✦ ✦ ✦ ✦

✦ Main/subforms

✦ Pivot table forms

✦ Graphs

Figure 9-1 shows a *columnar form*; you see the fields arranged as columns on-screen. The form can occupy one or more screen pages. Generally you would use this type of form to simulate the hard-copy entry of data; you can arrange the fields any way you want. Most standard Windows controls are available with Access forms, and make data entry more productive and understandable. Lines, boxes, colors, and even special effects (such as shadows or three-dimensional looks) enable you to make great-looking, easy-to-use forms.

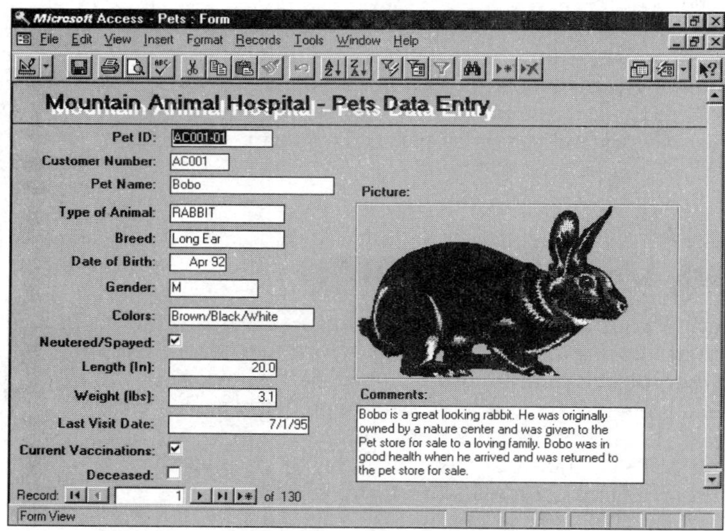

Figure 9-1: A full-screen form.

Figure 9-2 displays a tabular form; note that you can see several records at one time. You can format any part of a tabular form; your column headers can span multiple lines and be formatted separately from the records (unlike datasheets, which do not allow you to customize the column headers). Tabular forms can also have multiple lines per record, and you can add special effects (such as shadows or three-dimensional effects) to the fields. Field controls can also be option buttons or even push buttons.

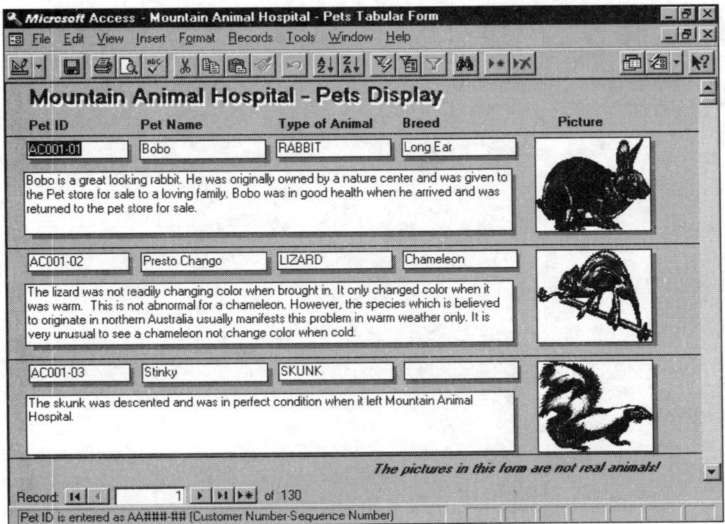

Figure 9-2: A tabular form.

A *main/subform*, shown in Figure 9-3, is a type of form commonly used to display one-to-many relationships. The main form displays the main table; the subform is frequently a datasheet or tabular form that displays the *many* portion of the relationship. For example, each pet's visit information shows up once, while the subform shows many visit detail records. This type of form combines all the benefits of a form and a data-sheet. A subform can show just one record or several records, each on multiple lines.

How do forms differ from datasheets?

With a datasheet, you have very little control over the display of data. Although you can change the type and size of the display font, and rearrange, resize, or hide columns, you cannot significantly alter the appearance of the data. By using forms, you can place each field in an exact specified location, add color or shading to each field, and add text controls to make data entry more efficient.

A form gives you more flexibility in data entry than a datasheet. You can not only add calculated fields to your form, you can also add enhanced data-validation and editing controls (such as option buttons, check boxes, and pop-up list boxes). Adding lines, boxes, colors, and static bitmaps can enhance the look of your data, make your form easier to use, and improve productivity.

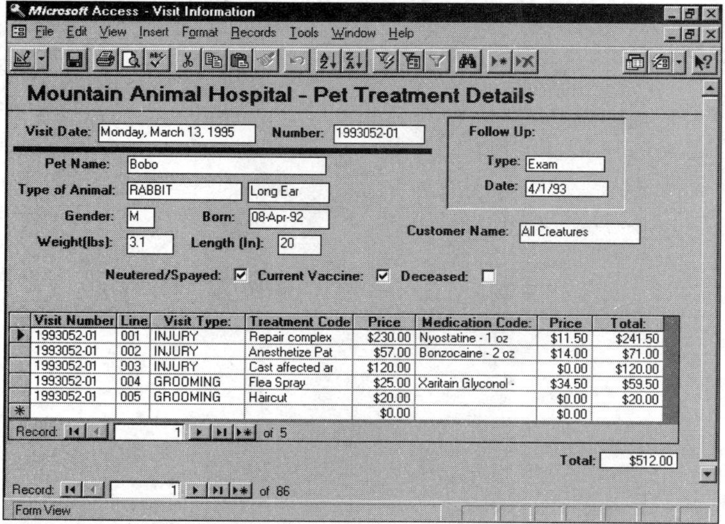

Figure 9-3: A full-screen form.

In addition, OLE objects (such as pictures or graphs) are visible *only* in a form or report. And although you can increase a datasheet's row size to see more of a Memo field, using a form makes it easier to display large amounts of text in a scrollable text box.

Tip Once you create a form with editing controls or enhanced data validation, you can switch into *datasheet mode*, which lets you use data-validation rules and controls such as pop-up lists.

Creating a form with AutoForm

From the Table or query tab in the Database window, a datasheet or nearly any design screen in Access, you can create a form instantly by clicking on the New Object button in the toolbar (a form with a lightning bolt through it) and then choosing one of the AutoForm icons. Another method is to use Insert⇨Form and select one of the AutoForm choices from the dialog box that appears. When you use the AutoForm button, the form appears instantly with no additional work. You can create columnar, tabular, or datasheets with AutoForm. To create a columnar AutoForm using the Pets table, follow these steps:

1. From the Mountain Animal Hospital Database Window, click on the Table tab.
2. Select Pets.

3. Click on the New Object button in the toolbar.
4. Select AutoForm.

The form instantly appears, as shown in Figure 9-4.

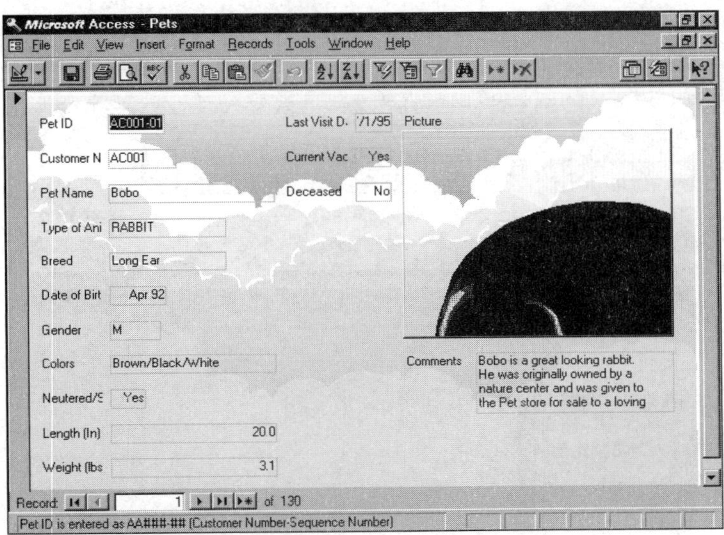

Figure 9-4: The AutoForm form.

If you look at different areas of the form, you can see that some values are not properly displayed. For example, look at the picture of the rabbit (yes, it's the hind quarter of a rabbit) in the first record, you see a portion of the rabbit. Later, you learn how to fix this, as well how to customize the form exactly as you want.

AutoForm is the quickest way to create a form. Generally, however, you want more control over your form creation. Other Form Wizards can help you create a more customized form at the outset.

Creating a Form with Form Wizards

Form Wizards simplify the layout process for your fields. The Form Wizard visually steps you through a series of questions about the type of form you want to create, and then creates it for you automatically. In this chapter, you learn how to create single-column forms with a Form Wizard, using the columnar form as a starting point for creating a full-screen form.

Creating a new form

You can choose from these three methods to create a new form:

- ✦ Select Insert⇨Form from the Database window menu.
- ✦ Select the form tab and then select the New command button from the Database window.
- ✦ Select the New Object button from the Database window, the datasheet, or the Query toolbar, and choose New Form.

Regardless of how you create a new form, the New Form dialog box appears, as you see in Figure 9-5. If you began to create the new form with a table highlighted (or from a datasheet or query), the table or query you are using appears in the text box labeled `Choose the table or query where the object's data comes from.` You can enter the name of a valid table or query (if you are not already using one) before continuing; choose from a list of tables and queries by clicking on the combo box's selection arrow.

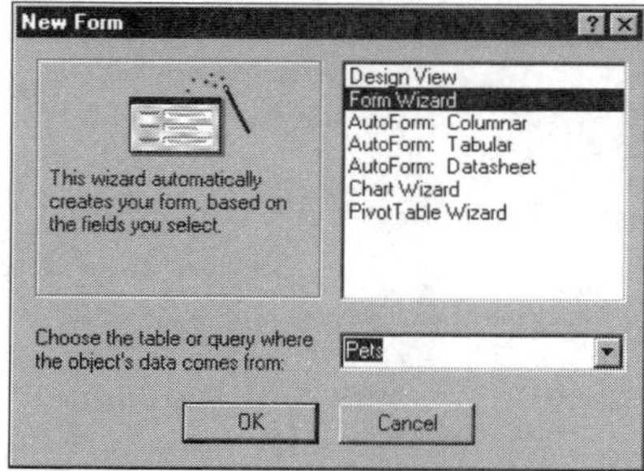

Figure 9-5: The New Form dialog box.

Selecting the New Form type and data source

The New Form dialog box gives you seven choices for creating a form:

Design View	Displays a completely blank form for you to start with in Form design
Form Wizard	Creates a form with one of three default layouts; columnar, tabular, or datasheet, using data fields that you specify in a step-by-step process that lets you customize the form creation process
AutoForm: Columnar	Instantly creates a columnar form

AutoForm: Tabular	Instantly creates a tabular form
AutoForm: Datasheet	Instantly creates a datasheet form
Chart Wizard:	Creates a form with a business graph
PivotTable Wizard:	Creates an Excel Pivot Table

Note As you make selections in a Wizard form, notice how the bitmap picture in the left of the Wizard form changes to show you your selection before you make it.

Disk For this example, choose the Form Wizard option.

Choosing the fields

After you select Form Wizard, you see the field-selection box shown in Figure 9-6. The field-selection dialog box contains three areas where you work. The first area lets you choose fields from multiple tables or queries; you can create many types of forms, including those with subforms. As you select each table or query, the `Available Fields` list will change.

Note If you are an experienced Access 2.0 user, you will find this process very different in Access for Windows 95. There is no longer a separate subform Wizard. Instead, Access for Windows 95 figures out when you have selected data related in a one-to-many relationship, and adds extra screens to create a subform.

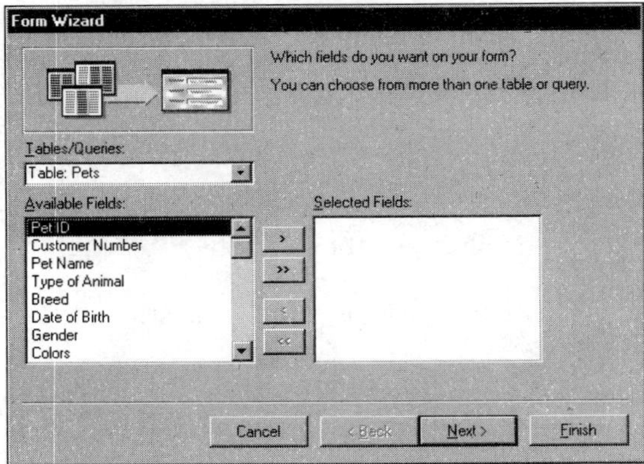

Figure 9-6: Choosing the fields for the form.

The field-selection area consists of two list boxes and four buttons. The `Available Fields:` list box on the left displays all fields from the selected table/query used to create the form. The `Selected Fields:` list box on the right displays the fields you have selected for this form. You can select one field, all the fields, or any combination of fields. The order in which you add the fields to the list box on the right is the order in which the fields will appear in the form. You can use the buttons to place or remove fields in the `Selected Fields:` box. Following is a description of these buttons:

>	Add selected field
>>	Add all fields
<	Remove selected field
<<	Remove all fields

When you highlight a field in the `Available Fields:` list box and select >, the field name appears in the `Selected Fields:` list box. You can add each field you want to the list box. If you add a field by mistake, you can select the field in the `Selected Fields:` list box and select < to remove it from the selection. If you decide to change the order in which your fields will appear in the form, you must remove any fields that are out of order and reselect them in the proper order.

Note You can double-click on any field in the `Available Fields:` list box to add it to the `Selected Fields:` list box.

At the bottom of the form, you find a series of buttons to be used when field selection is completed. The types of buttons available here are common to most Wizard dialog boxes.

Cancel	Cancel form creation and return to the starting point
< Back	Return to the preceding dialog box
Next >	Go to the next dialog box
Finish	Go to the last dialog box (usually the form title)

Tip If you select Next > or Finish without selecting any fields, Access selects all the fields automatically when creating the form.

Disk Select all of the fields by choosing the >> icon. When you are finished, select the Next > button to display the dialog box that lets you choose a form layout.

Choosing the form layout

Once you choose the fields, you have to choose the type of layout. As you can see in Figure 9-7, there are three types of layouts:

Columnar

Tabular

Datasheet

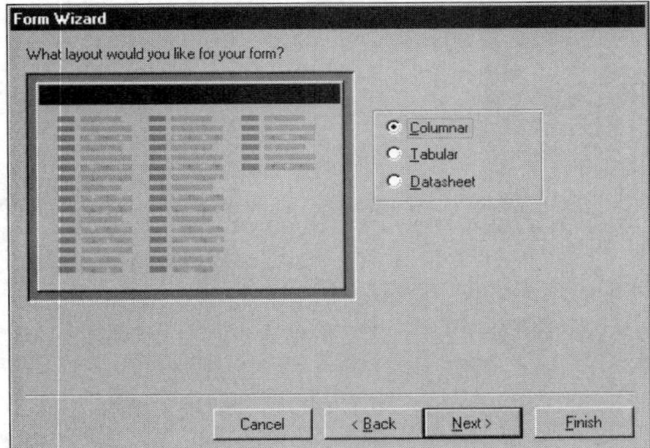

Figure 9-7: Choosing the type of layout for the form.

Disk Select the Columnar layout. Once you choose the type of layout, you can click on the Next> button to display the style of the form.

Choosing the style of the form

After you select all of the fields, you can choose the style for the look of your form from the dialog box shown in Figure 9-8.

You can choose from many different selections by clicking on the desired name in the list box. As you select one of the styles, the display on the left changes to illustrate the special effect used to create the look.

As you can see in Figure 9-8, the default look uses clouds in the background. The last selection Standard is a more traditional look, with a dark gray background and sunken controls. For the first form you create in this chapter, select Clouds. Once you select the style of your form, you are ready to create a title and view the form.

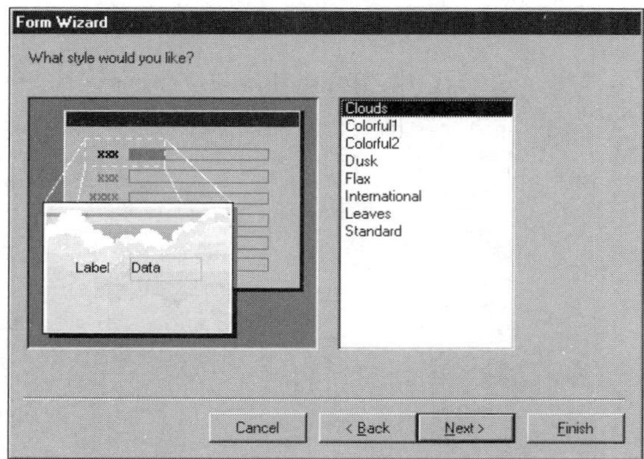

Figure 9-8: Choosing the style of your form.

Warning

The style you select will be used as the default the next time you use the Wizard.

Tip

You can customize the style by changing a form and then using the AutoFormat function in the Form design screen.

Creating a form title

The form-title dialog box is usually the last dialog box in a Form Wizard. It always has a checkered flag to let you know you are at the finish line. By default, the text box for the form title contains the name of the table or query used for the form's data. You can accept the entry for the form title, enter your own, or erase it and have no title. As you can see, the title in Figure 9-9 is `Pets`, the name of the table.

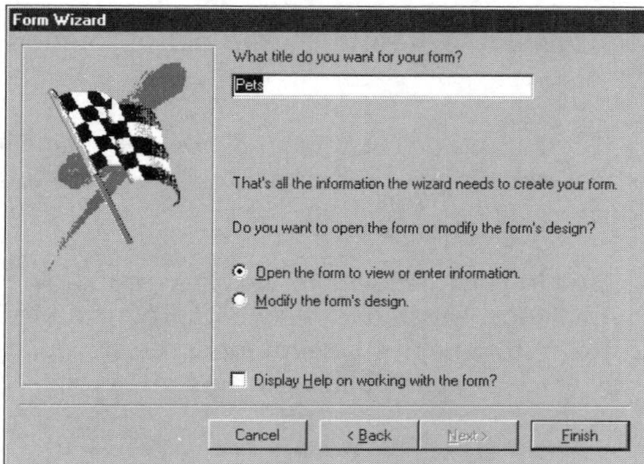

Figure 9-9: Choosing a form title.

Completing the form

After you complete all the steps to design your form, you can open your new form in one of two ways:

✦ Open the form in Form view.

✦ Use the Form design window to make changes to the form.

In this example, you view the form in the Form design window: select the second option button and then select the Finish button.

Once you select the Finish button, the form appears in the Form Design window (as shown in Figure 9-10). Note that you can maximize the window by selecting the Maximize button on the top right corner of the window.

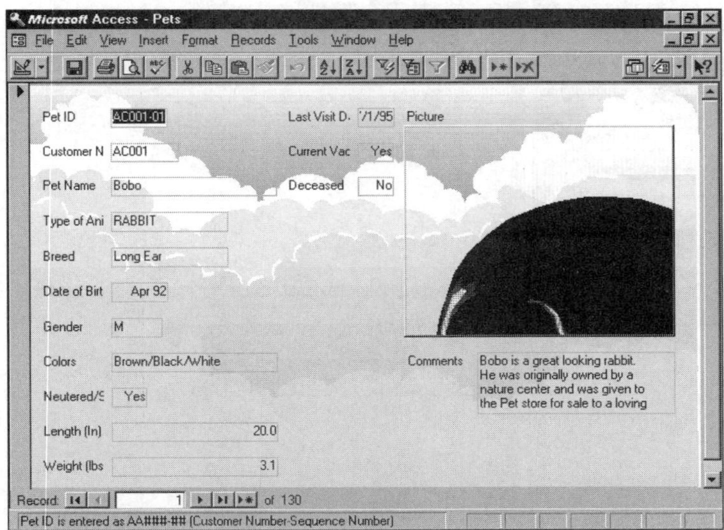

Figure 9-10: A form design created with a Form Wizard.

Changing the Design

As an example of how easy it is to manipulate the field controls, you can change the way the Picture field appears. If you look at Figure 9-10, you see a lovely view of the hind part of the rabbit going over the fence; it would be nice to see the whole rabbit. To fix this, follow these steps:

1. Click on the Picture field (the large empty rectangle under the Picture label).
2. Click on the Property icon in the toolbar (picture of a hand and a sheet of paper).

3. Click on the Size Mode property and change it from Clip to Stretch (as shown in Figure 9-11).

After you complete the move, click on the Form button to redisplay the form. Notice the whole rabbit as shown in Figure 9-12.

Cross Ref

In Chapters 16–20, you learn how to completely customize a form. You learn how to use all the controls in the toolbox, add special effects to forms, create forms with graphs and calculated fields, and add complex data validation to your forms.

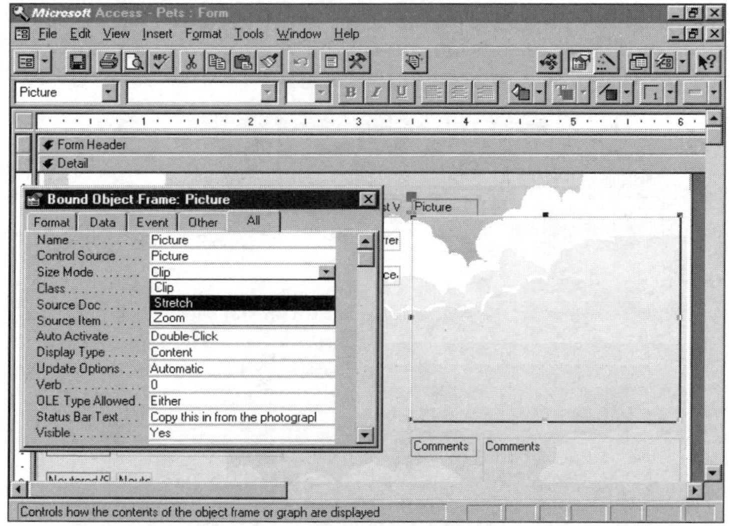

Figure 9-11: Changing a control property.

Using the Form Window

If you look at the Form window, as shown in Figure 9-12, you see that this window is very similar to the Datasheet window. At the top of the screen you will find the title bar, menu bar, and toolbar. The center of the screen displays your data, one record at a time. In this single-column layout, each field occupies one line. If the form contains more fields than will fit on-screen at one time, you can use the vertical scrollbar or press PgDn to see the rest of the record.

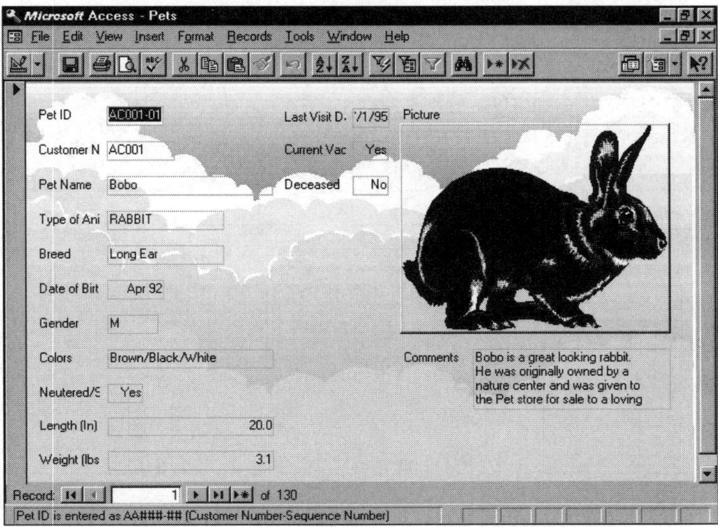

Figure 9-12: The form redisplayed to show the full picture.

The last line at the bottom of the screen contains a status bar. The status bar displays the Field Description you entered into the table design for each field. If there is no Field Description for a specific field, Access displays the words `Form View`. Generally, error messages and warnings appear in dialog boxes in the center of the screen (rather than in the status bar). You can also find the navigation buttons at the bottom of the screen. This feature lets you move quickly from record to record.

The Form toolbar

The Form toolbar, shown in Figure 9-12, is virtually identical to the Datasheet icons with the New buttons missing. One of the few differences is that the first icon contains three selections: Form View, Design View, and Datasheet View.

Navigating between fields

Navigating a form is nearly identical to using a datasheet. You can move around the Form window easily by clicking on the field you want and making changes or additions to your data. Because the Form window displays only as many fields as fit on-screen, you will need to use various navigational aids to move within your form or between records.

Table 9-1 displays the navigational keys used to move between fields within a form.

Table 9-1
Navigating in a Form

Navigational Direction	*Keystrokes*
Next field	Tab, right- or down-arrow key, or Enter
Previous field	Shift+Tab, left-arrow, or up-arrow
First field of current record	Home or Ctrl+Home
Last field of current record	End or Ctrl+End
Next page	PgDn
Previous page	PgUp

If you have a form with more than one page, you see a vertical scrollbar. You can use the scrollbar to move to different pages on the form. You can also use the PgUp and PgDn keys to move between form pages. You can move up or down one field at a time by clicking on the scrollbar arrows. With the elevator, you can move between many fields at once.

Moving between records in a form

Although you generally use a form to display one record at a time, you will still want to move between records. The easiest way to do this is to use the navigation buttons.

The navigation buttons offer the same five controls at the bottom of the screen that you saw in the datasheet. You can click on these buttons to move to the desired record.

Pressing F5 moves you instantly to the record number box.

You can also press Ctrl+PgDn to move to the current field in the next record, or Ctrl+PgUp to move to the current field in the preceding record.

When you're in the first page of a multipage form, pressing PgUp takes you to the current field of the preceding record. When you're in the last page of the multipage form, pressing PgDn takes you to the current field in the next record.

Displaying Your Data with a Form

In Chapter 8, you learned techniques to add, change, and delete data within a datasheet. The techniques you learned there are the same ones that you use within a form. Table 9-2 summarizes these techniques.

Table 9-2
Editing Techniques

Editing Technique	*Keystrokes*
Move insertion point within a field	Press the right- and left-arrow keys
Insert a value within a field	Select the insertion point and type the new data
Select the entire field	Press F2 or double-click the mouse button
Replace an existing value with a new value	Select the entire field and type a new value
Replace value with value of preceding field	Press Ctrl+'
Replace current value with default value	Press Ctrl+Alt+Spacebar
Insert current date into a field	Press Ctrl+;
Insert current time into a field	Press Ctrl+:
Insert a line break in a Text or Memo field	Press Ctrl+Enter
Insert new record	Press Ctrl++
Delete current record	Press Ctrl+–
Save current record	Press Shift+Enter or move to another record
Undo a change to the current record	Press Esc or click on the Undo button

Working with pictures and OLE objects

In a datasheet, you cannot view a picture or any OLE object without accessing the OLE server. In a form, however, you can size the OLE control area large enough to display a picture, business graph, or visual OLE object. You can also size the Memo controls on forms so you can see the data within the field — you don't have to zoom in on the value, as you do with a datasheet field. Figure 9-12 displays both the picture and the Memo data displayed in the form. Each of these controls can be resized.

Recall from Chapter 8 that any object supported by an OLE server can be stored in an Access OLE field. You generally enter OLE objects into a form so you can see, hear, or use the value. As with a datasheet, you have two ways to enter OLE fields into a form:

✦ Paste them in from the Clipboard or the Edit menu.

✦ Insert them into the field from the Insert⇨Object menu.

Cross Ref Chapter 20 covers using and displaying OLE objects in forms in more detail.

Memo field data entry

The last field in the table, `Comments:`, is a Memo data type. This type of field allows for up to 64,000 bytes of text for each field. You can see the first two sentences of data in the Memo field. When you move the cursor into the Memo field, a vertical scrollbar appears. Using this scrollbar, you can view the rest of the data in the field. You can resize the Memo control in the Form Design window if you want to make it larger. You can also press Shift+F2 (as shown in Figure 9-13), and display a Zoom dialog box in the center of the screen, which lets you view about 12 lines at a time.

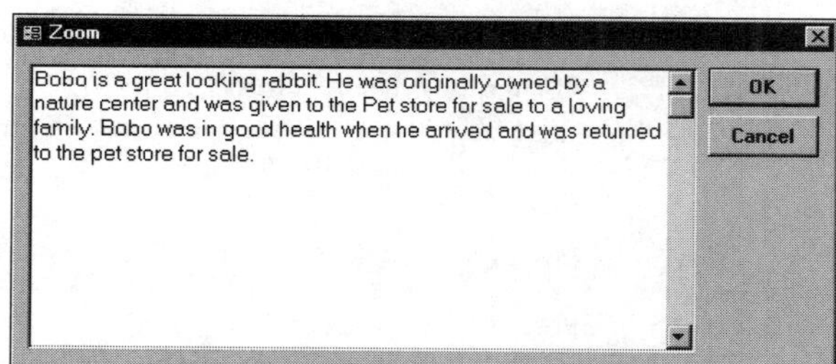

Figure 9-13: Pressing Shift+F2 for a Zoom box view in a Memo field.

Switching to a datasheet

You can display a datasheet view of your data by one of two methods:

✦ Click on the Datasheet button in the toolbar.

✦ Select View⇨Datasheet.

The datasheet is displayed with the cursor on the same field and record it occupied in the form. If you move to another record and field, and then redisplay the form, the form now appears with the cursor on the field and record it last occupied in the datasheet.

To return to the form from a datasheet, you can use either of two methods:

✦ Click on the Form button in the toolbar.

✦ Select View⇨Form.

Sorting and filtering form records

You can use the same techniques to manipulate records in a form as you do in a datasheet (as you learned in the preceding chapter). The only difference is that instead of positioning on a specific record, you display a single record.

Cross Ref

If you need to review the techniques for finding and replacing data or filtering and sorting your records, see the appropriate sections in Chapter 8.

Saving a Record and the Form

As you move off each record, Access saves any changes to the record. You can also press Shift+Enter to save a record without moving off it. The final way to save a record is to save the form. You can save any changes to a form design by selecting Records⇨Save Record. This saves any changes and keeps the form open. When you are ready to close a form and return to the Database window (or to your query or datasheet), you can select File⇨Close. If you made any changes to the form design, you are asked whether you want to save the design.

Printing a Form

You can print one or more records in your form exactly as they look on the screen. (You will learn how to produce formatted reports later in the book.) The simplest way to print is to use the File⇨Print selection or the Print toolbar button. Selecting File⇨Print displays the Print dialog box.

Assuming that you have set up a printer in Windows 95, you can select OK to print your form. Access then prints your form, using the font you selected for display or using the nearest printer equivalent. The printout contains any formatting you specified in the form (including lines, boxes, and shading), and converts colors to gray shades if you are using a monochrome printer.

The printout prints as many pages as necessary to print all the data. If your form is wider than a single printer page, you will need multiple pages to print your form. Access breaks up the printout as necessary to fit on each page.

Using the Print Preview Window

You may find that you have all the information in your form, but you aren't sure whether that information will print on multiple pages or will fit onto one printed page. Maybe you want to see whether the fonts need adjustment, or you need only the printed records from pages 3 and 4. In such cases you will probably want to view the report on-screen before printing to make these adjustments to the form design.

To preview your printout, you can either click on the Print Preview button on the toolbar (a sheet of paper with a magnifying glass on top) or select File⇨Print Preview. Figure 9-14 shows the Print Preview window; it works exactly like the datasheet Print Preview window you learned about in Chapter 8.

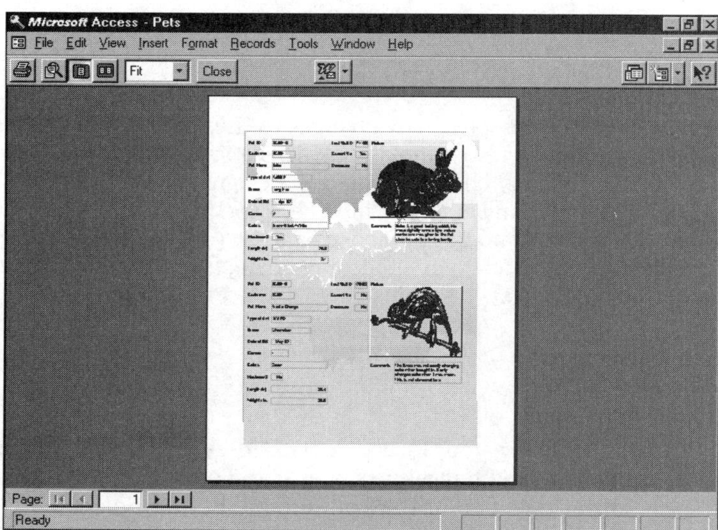

Figure 9-14: The Print Preview window.

If, after examining the preview, you are satisfied with the form, simply select the Print button on the toolbar to print the form. If you are not satisfied, click on the Close window button to return to the form to make further changes to your data or design.

Summary

This chapter examined Form Wizards and how you can use them as the starting point for your form. You learned about how forms work, and encountered the types of forms you can create with Access. The chapter covered these points:

- ✦ Data-entry forms provide the most flexible format for viewing your data; you can arrange your fields in any order you want.
- ✦ Whereas datasheets generally let you view many records at a time, you would use a form to view one record at a time.
- ✦ AutoForm instantly creates a form for you with just one keystroke.
- ✦ Form Wizards simplify form creation by giving you a starting point for form design and stepping you through the process.
- ✦ There are five basic types of forms: full-screen, tabular, main/subforms, pivot tables, and graphs.
- ✦ A Form Wizard lets you specify the type of form, the fields to be used, the type of look you want, and a title.
- ✦ You can specify one or more fields in a Form Wizard.
- ✦ A Form Wizard lets you choose from several types of styles.
- ✦ A form lets you enter data into Picture and Memo fields, and displays the fields as well.
- ✦ You can switch to a datasheet from a form by selecting the Datasheet button.
- ✦ You can print a form with all its formatting, or you can preview it on the screen before printing.

In the next chapter, you learn about simple queries.

✦ ✦ ✦

Understanding and Using Simple Queries

✦ ✦ ✦ ✦

In This Chapter

Understanding the different types of queries

Creating queries

Selecting tables and fields for queries

Displaying information in queries

Sorting information in queries

Selecting specific records in queries

Printing the results of queries

✦ ✦ ✦ ✦

In this chapter, you learn what a query is, and also about the process of creating queries. Using the Pets table, you create several types of queries for the Mountain Animal Hospital database.

Understanding Queries

The primary purpose of any database, manual or automated, is to store and extract information. Information can be obtained from a database immediately after you enter the data or years later. Of course, even with a manually assembled database, obtaining information requires knowledge of how the database is set up.

For example, reports may be filed manually in a cabinet, arranged first by order of year and then by a *sequence number* that indicates when the report was written. To obtain a specific report, you must know its year and sequence number. In a good manual system, you may have a cross-reference book to help you find a specific report. This book may have all reports categorized by type of report (rather than topic) in alphabetical order. Such a book can be helpful, but if you know only the report's topic and approximate date, you still may have to search through all sections of the book to find out where to obtain the report.

Unlike manual databases, computer-automated databases have a distinct advantage; with their tools, you can easily obtain information to meet virtually any criteria you specify.

This is the real power of a database — the capacity for you to examine the data any way *you* want to look at it. Queries, by definition, ask questions about the data stored in the database. After you create a query, you can use its data for reports, forms, and graphs.

What is a query?

The word *query* comes from the Latin word *quærere,* which simply means to ask or inquire. Over the years, the word "query" has become synonymous with quiz, challenge, inquire, or question. Therefore, you can think of a query as a question or inquiry posed to the database about information found in its tables.

A Microsoft Access query is a question you ask about the information stored in your Access tables. The way you ask questions about this information is by using the query *tools*. Your query can be a simple question about information stored in a single table, or it can be a complex question about information stored in several tables. After you ask the question, Microsoft Access returns only the information you requested.

Using queries this way, you can query the Pets database to show you only the dogs that are named within it. To see the dogs' names, you need to retrieve information from the Pets table. Figure 10-1 shows a typical Query screen like the one you saw in Chapter 8. This is the same basic format used behind Filter by Selection or Filter by Form.

After you create and run a query, Microsoft Access can return and display the set of records that you asked for in a datasheet. This set of records is called a *dynaset,* which is simply the set of selected records from a query. As you've seen, a datasheet looks just like a spreadsheet, with its rows of records and columns of fields. The datasheet can display many records simultaneously.

You can query information from a single table. Many database queries, however, require information from several tables.

Suppose, for example, that you want to send a reminder to anyone living in a certain city whose dog or cat is due for an annual vaccination, based on the town license regulations. This type of query requires getting information from two tables: Customer and Pets.

Cross Ref

You may want Access to show you a single datasheet of all customers and their pets that meet your specified criteria. Access can retrieve customer names and cities from the Customer table, and then pet names, animal type, and current vaccination status from the Pets table. Access then takes the information common to your criteria, combines it, and displays all the information in a single datasheet. This datasheet is the result of a query that draws from both the Customer and Pets tables. The database query performed the work of assembling all the information for you. In this chapter, you work only with the Pets table; Part III covers multiple tables.

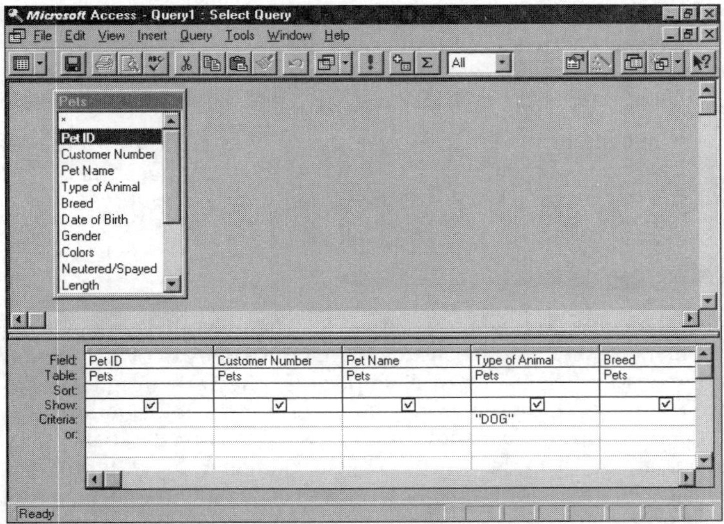

Figure 10-1: A typical select query.

Types of queries

Access supports many different types of queries. They can be grouped into six basic categories:

Select These are the most common. As its name implies, the select query selects information from one or more tables (based on specific criteria), and displays the information in a dynaset you can use to view and analyze specific data; you can make changes to your data in the underlying tables.

Total These are special versions of select queries. Total queries give you the capability to sum or produce totals (such as count) in a select query. When you select this type of query, Access adds the Total row in the QBE pane.

Action These queries let you create new tables (Make Tables) or change data (delete, update, and append) in existing tables. When you make changes to records in a select query, the changes must be made one record at a time. In action queries, changes can be made to many records during a single operation.

Crosstab These queries can display summary data in *cross-tabular* form like a spreadsheet, with the row and column headings based on fields in the table. By definition, the individual cells of the resultant dynaset are tabular — that is, computed or calculated.

SQL There are three SQL query types — *Union*, *Pass-Through*, and *Data Definition*. They are used for advanced SQL database manipulation (for example, working with client/server SQL databases). You can create these queries only by writing specific SQL commands.

Top(n) You can only use this *query limiter* in conjunction with the other five types of queries. It lets you specify a number or percentage of the top records you want to see in any type of query.

Query capabilities

Queries are flexible. They give you the capability of looking at your data in virtually any way you can think of. Most database systems are continually evolving, developing more powerful and necessary tools. The original purpose they are designed for changes over time. You may decide that you want to look at the information stored in the database in a different way. Because information is stored in a database, you should be able to look at it in this new way. Looking at data in a way different from its intended manner is known as performing *ad-hoc* queries. You'll find querying tools are among the most powerful features of your database; querying is indeed very powerful and flexible in Microsoft Access. Here is a sampling of what you can do:

Choose tables You can obtain information from a single table or from many tables that are related by some common data. Suppose you're interested in seeing the customer name along with the type of animals each customer owns. This sample task takes information from the Customer and Pets tables. When using several tables, Access returns the data in a combined single datasheet.

Choose fields You can specify which fields from each table that you want to see in the resultant dynaset. For example, you can look at the customer name, customer ZIP code, animal name, and animal type separated from all the other fields in the Customer or Pets table.

Choose records You can select the records to display in the dynaset by specifying criteria. For example, you may want to see records for dogs only.

Sort records Often you may want to see the dynaset information sorted in a specific order. You may need (for example) to see customers in order by last name and first name.

Perform Calculations You can use queries to perform calculations on your data. You may be interested in performing such calculations as averaging, totaling, or simply counting the fields.

Create tables You may need another database table formed from the combined data resulting from a query. The query can create this new table based on the dynaset.

Create forms and reports based on a query	The dynaset you create from a query may have just the right fields and data you need for a report or form. When you base your form or report on a query, every time you print the report or open the form, your query will retrieve the most current information from your tables.
Create graphs based on queries	You can create graphs from the data in a query, which you can then use in a form or report.
Use a query as a source of data for other queries (subquery)	You can create additional queries based on a set of records you selected in a previous query. This is very useful for performing ad-hoc queries, where you may make small changes to the criteria over and over. The secondary query can be used to change the criteria while the primary query and its data remain intact.
Make changes to tables	Access queries can obtain information from a wide range of sources. You can ask questions about data stored in dBASE, Paradox, Btrieve, and Microsoft SQL Server databases.

How dynasets work

Earlier you learned that Access takes the records that result from a query and displays them in a datasheet, in which the actual records are called a dynaset. Physically a dynaset looks like a table; in fact, it is not. The dynaset is a *dynamic* (or virtual) set of records. *This dynamic set of records is not stored in the database.*

Note When you close a query, the query dynaset is gone; it will no longer exist. But even though the dynaset itself no longer exists, remember that the data that formed the dynaset remains stored in the underlying tables.

When you run a query, Access places the resultant records in the dynaset. When you save the query, the information is *not* saved; only the structure of the query is saved — the tables, fields, sort order, record limitations, query type, and so forth. Consider these benefits of not saving the dynaset to a physical table:

- ✦ The storage device (usually a hard disk) needs less space.
- ✦ The query can use updated versions of any records changed since the query was last run.

Every time the query is executed, it goes out to the underlying tables and re-creates the dynaset. Because dynasets themselves are not stored, a query automatically reflects any changes to the underlying tables made since the last time the query was executed — even in a real-time, multiuser environment.

Creating a Query

After you create your tables and place data in them, you are ready to work with queries. To begin a query, follow these steps:

1. From the Database window, click on the Query tab.
2. Click on the New button.

   The New Query dialog box appears, as shown in Figure 10-2. You can select from the six choices. The first choice displays the Query Design screen.
3. Select New Query and click on the OK button.

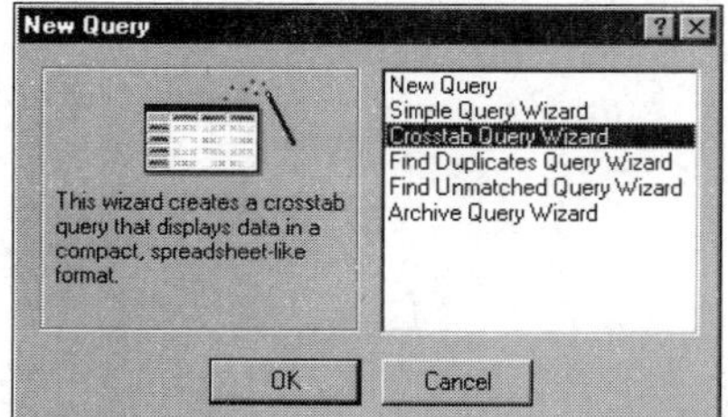

Figure 10-2: The New Query dialog box.

Disk

After you select the new query without first selecting a table, Access opens a window and a dialog box. Figure 10-3 shows both windows. The underlying window is the Query window. The accompanying Show Table dialog box is *nonmodal,* which means simply that you must do something in the dialog box before continuing with the query. Before you continue, you should add tables for the query to work with.

Selecting a table

The Show Table dialog box displays all tables and queries in your database. If you are following along with the examples, you should see one table named `Pets`. If you are using the Mountain Animal Hospital or Mountain Animal Start databases, you should see all the tables in the Mountain Animal Hospital database. You can add the Pets table to the query design with these steps:

1. Click on the Pets table.
2. Select the Add button to add the Pets table to the Query Design window.
3. Select the Close button.

Another method of adding the Pets table to the Design window is simply double-clicking on the Pets table.

You can also begin a new query by selecting the New Query button on the toolbar, or you can select Insert⇨Query from the main Access menu. If you select a table or query before you start a new query, Access will load the selected table or query automatically.

You can activate the Show Table dialog box to add more tables at any time; select Query⇨Show Table from the Query menu.

Tip You can also add tables by moving the mouse to any empty place in the top half of the window (the table/query pane) and clicking the *right* mouse button. By right-clicking, you activate the shortcut menus and select Show Table.

When you want to delete a table from the query pane, you can click on the table name in the query/table entry pane (see Figure 10-4), and either press Delete or select Query⇨Remove Table.

Tip You also can add a table to the query/table pane by selecting the Database window and dragging and dropping a table name from the table window into the Query window.

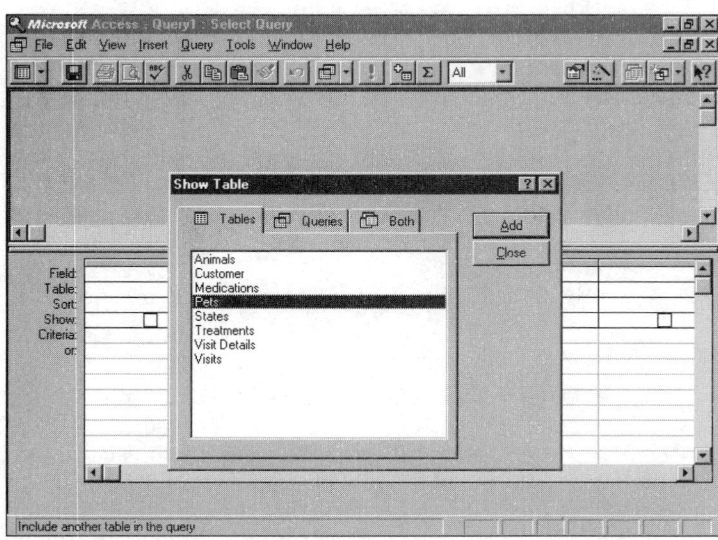

Figure 10-3: The Show Table dialog box in the Query window.

Using the Query window

The Query window has two modes, the *design mode* and the *datasheet mode.* The difference between them is self-explanatory: The design mode is where you create the query, and the datasheet is where you display the query dynaset.

The Query window should now look like Figure 10-4, with the Pets table displayed in the top half of the Query window.

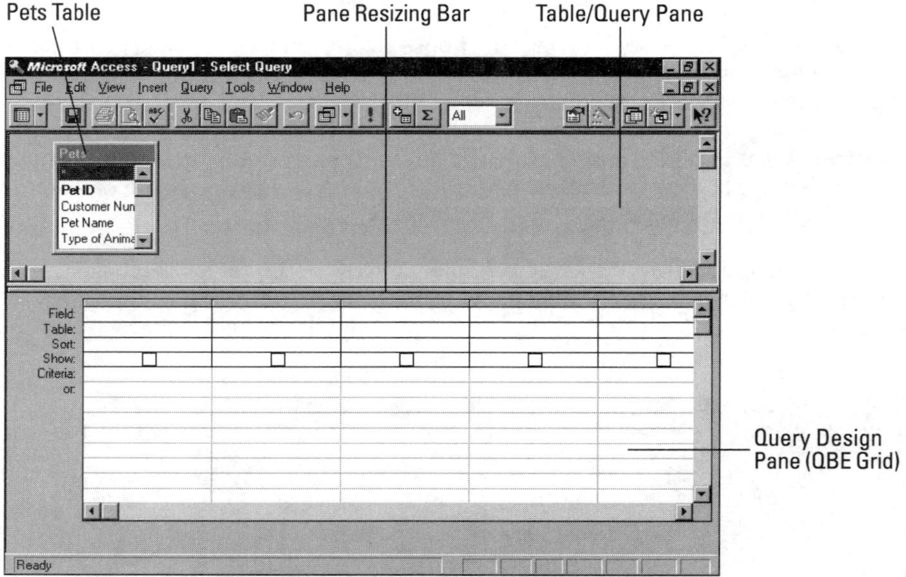

Figure 10-4: The Query window with the Pets table displayed.

The Query window is currently in the design mode; it consists of two panes:

✦ The table/query entry pane

✦ The query by example (QBE) design pane (also called the *QBE grid*)

The *table/query entry pane* is where tables and/or queries and their design structures are displayed. The visual representation of the table lists each field. The *query by example (QBE) pane* is used for the fields and criteria that the query will display in the dynaset. Each column in the QBE design pane contains information about a single field from a table or query in the upper pane.

Navigating the Query Design window

The *title bar* at the top of the Query Design window bears information about a particular window, the type of query, and the query name. Any new query is named Query1. Note that the title bar in Figure 10-4 displays the query type and name as `Query1:Select Query.`

The two window panes are separated horizontally by a *dividing bar*. You'll use this bar to resize the panes: To enlarge the upper pane, click on the bar and then drag it down; drag the bar up to enlarge the lower pane.

You can switch between the upper and lower panes either by clicking on the desired pane or by pressing F6 to move to the other pane. Notice that each pane has scrollbars to help you move around.

Tip

If you resize the Pets design structure vertically, you can see more fields at one time. With horizontal resizing, you can see more field names. To see more fields, first resize the top pane to size the Pets structure vertically.

You can design a query by dragging fields from the upper pane to the lower pane of the Query window. After you place fields on the QBE pane (lower pane), you can set their display order by dragging a field from its current position to a new position in the pane.

Using the Query Design toolbar

The toolbar in the Query Design window contains several buttons specific to building and working with queries, as shown in Figure 10-5.

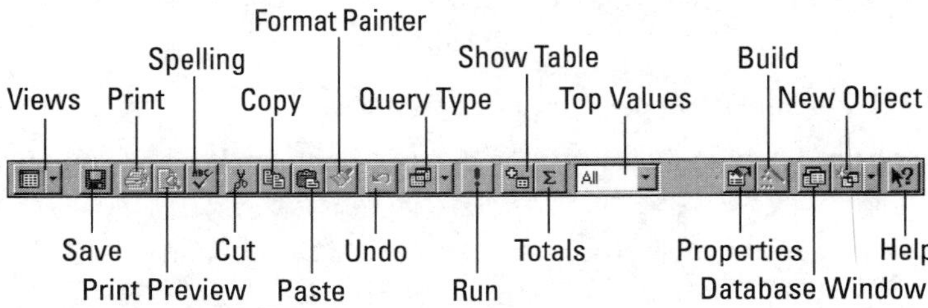

Figure 10-5: The Query Design toolbar.

Using the QBE pane of the Query Design window

Figure 10-4 shows you an empty Query Design pane (QBE grid). You'll see five named rows in this pane:

Field	This is where field names are entered or added.
Sort	This choice lets you enter sort directives for the query.
Show	This check box determines whether to display the field in the resulting dynaset.
Criteria	This is where you enter the first line of criteria to limit the record selection.
Or	This is the first of a number of lines to which you can add multiple values to be used in criteria selection.

You learn more about these rows as you create several sample queries in this chapter.

Selecting Fields

There are several ways to add fields to a query. You can add fields one at a time, select multiple fields, or select all fields. You can use your keyboard or mouse to add the fields.

Adding a single field

You can add a single field in several ways. One method is to double-click on the field name; the field name then appears in the next available column in the Query Design pane. You can also add a field graphically to the Query Design pane by following these steps:

1. Highlight the field name in the table/query entry area.
2. Click on the desired field and drag the Field icon, which appears as you move the mouse.
3. Drop the Field icon in the desired column of the QBE Design pane.

The Field icon looks like a small rectangle when it is inside the Pets table. As the mouse is dragged outside the Pets table, the icon changes to a circle-with-slash ∅ (the international symbol meaning "no"). It means you cannot drop the Field icon in that location. When this icon enters any column in the QBE column, the field name appears in the Field: row. If you drop the field between two other fields, it appears between those fields and pushes all existing fields to the right.

Tip

If you select a field accidentally, you can deselect it by releasing the mouse button while the icon is the No symbol: ∅

To run the query, select the Datasheet button on the toolbar (the first icon from the left). When you are finished, click on the Design button on the toolbar (the first one on the left) to return to design mode.

Another way to add fields to the QBE Design pane is to click on the empty Field: cell in the QBE Design pane and then type the field name in the field cell. Another method is to select the field you want from the drop-down list that appears (see Figure 10-6).

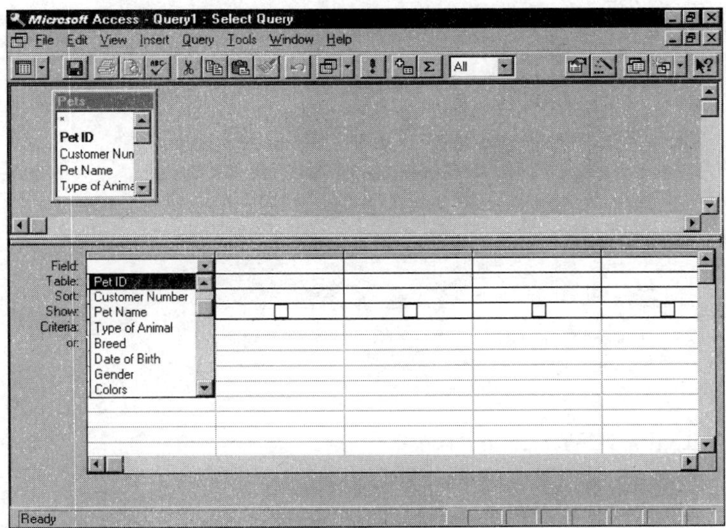

Figure 10-6: Adding a single field in the QBE Design pane (grid).

Adding multiple fields

You can add more than one field at a time by selecting the fields and then dragging the selection to the query pane. For you to add multiple fields from a table simultaneously, the selected fields do not have to be contiguous (one after the other). Figure 10-7 illustrates the process of adding multiple fields.

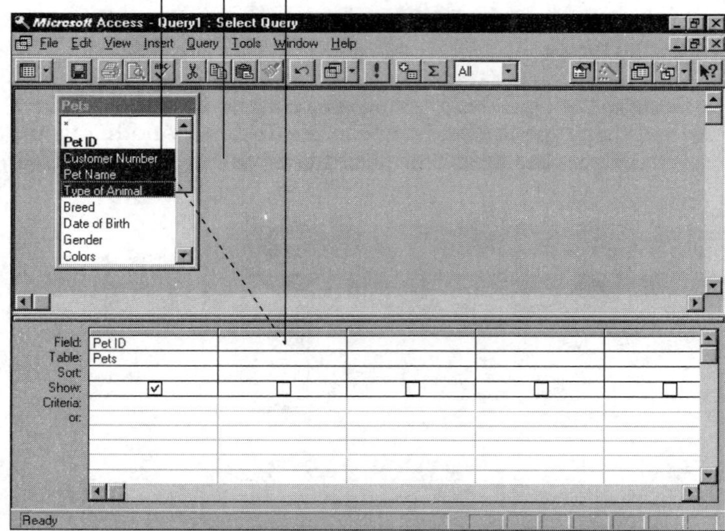

Figure 10-7: Selecting several fields graphically to move to the QBE Design pane.

To add multiple contiguous fields, follow these steps:

1. Remove any existing fields in the QBE pane by selecting Edit⇨Clear Grid from the menu.
2. Highlight the first field name in the table/query entry area that you want to add.
3. Hold the Shift key down and click on the last field that you want to select. (All the fields in-between will be selected as well.)
4. Click on the selected fields and drag the Multiple Field icon, which appears as you move the mouse. The icon appears as a group of three field icons.
5. Drop the Multiple Field icon in the desired column of the QBE Design pane.

To add multiple noncontiguous fields to the query, follow these steps:

1. Remove any existing fields in the QBE pane by selecting Edit➪Clear Grid from the menu.
2. Highlight the first field name in the table/query entry area that you want to add.
3. Hold the Control key down and click on each field you want to select. (Only the fields you select will be highlighted.)
4. Click on the selected fields and drag the Multiple Field icon, which appears as you move the mouse. The icon appears as a group of three field icons.
5. Drop the Multiple Field icon in the desired column of the QBE design pane.

Adding all table fields

Besides adding fields (whether in groups or individually), you can move all the fields to the QBE pane at once. Access gives you two methods for choosing all fields: by dragging all fields as a group, or by selecting the *all-field reference tag* — the asterisk (*).

Dragging all fields as a group

To select all the fields of a table, perform these steps:

1. Remove any existing fields in the QBE pane by selecting Edit➪Clear Grid from the menu.
2. Double-click on the title bar of the table to select all the fields.
3. Point to any of the selected fields with the mouse.
4. Drag the Multiple Field icon down to the QBE pane.

This method fills in each column of the QBE pane automatically. All the fields are added to the QBE pane from left to right, based on their field order in the Pets table. By default, Access displays only the fields that can fit in the window. You can change the column width of each field to display more or fewer columns.

Selecting the all-field reference tag

The first object in the Pets table is an asterisk, which appears at the top of the field list. When you select all fields by using the asterisk, you don't see all the fields moved to the QBE Design pane. You see only that `Pets.*` displayed in the Field: row, indicating that all fields from the table named Pets are now selected. (This example assumes that the QBE Design pane is empty when you drag the asterisk from the Pets table to the QBE Design pane.)

The asterisk places the fields in a single Field: cell. When you dragged multiple fields with the first technique, you dragged actual table field names to the query design pane, thus placing each field in a separate Field: cell across the QBE pane. If you change the design of the table later, you must also change the design of the query. The advantage of using the asterisk for selecting all fields is that you won't have to change the query later if you add, delete, or rename fields in the underlying table or query. (Access will add or remove any fields that change in the underlying table or query, automatically.)

If you are following along with the examples, you need to delete all fields from the query by selecting Edit⇨Clear Grid from the Query Design menu.

Disk Now that you've cleared all the fields, you can select the first nine fields in the Pets table (Pet ID through Neutered/Spayed, inclusively) and move them to the QBE design pane.

To add the all-fields reference tag to the Query Design pane, follow these steps:

1. Click on the asterisk (*) in the Pets table to select this field.
2. Click on the selected field and drag the Field icon to the first cell in the QBE Design pane.

You now have the all-fields reference tag in the QBE pane. When you run this query, all the fields from Pets will be displayed.

Displaying the Dynaset

With multiple fields selected, it is time to display the resultant dynaset. You can switch to the datasheet by either selecting View⇨Datasheet or selecting the Datasheet button on the toolbar. The datasheet should now look like Figure 10-8.

Working with the datasheet

Access displays the dynaset in a datasheet. The techniques for navigating a query datasheet, as well as for changing its field order and working with its columns and rows, are exactly the same as for the other datasheets you worked with in Chapter 8.

New! Unlike Access 2.0, Access for Windows 95 allows you to sort and filter the results of a datasheet created by a query. All data in Access for Windows 95 is editable all the time.

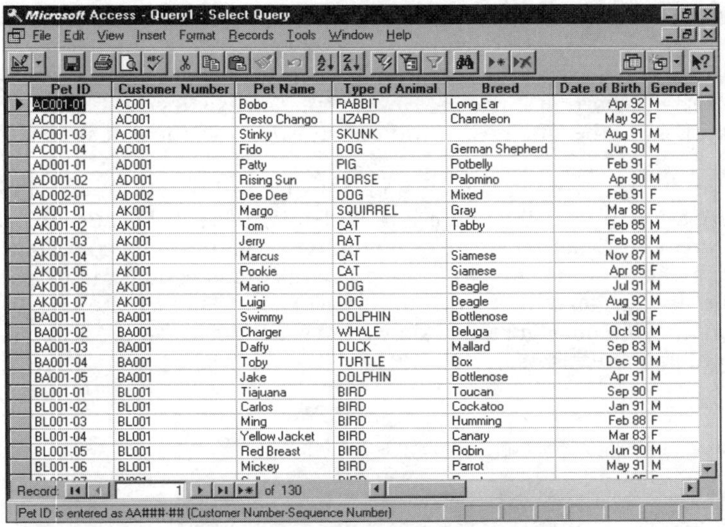

Microsoft Access - Query1 : Select Query

File Edit View Insert Format Records Tools Window Help

Pet ID	Customer Number	Pet Name	Type of Animal	Breed	Date of Birth	Gender
AC001-01	AC001	Bobo	RABBIT	Long Ear	Apr 92	M
AC001-02	AC001	Presto Chango	LIZARD	Chameleon	May 92	F
AC001-03	AC001	Stinky	SKUNK		Aug 91	M
AC001-04	AC001	Fido	DOG	German Shepherd	Jun 90	M
AD001-01	AD001	Patty	PIG	Potbelly	Feb 91	F
AD001-02	AD001	Rising Sun	HORSE	Palomino	Apr 90	M
AD002-01	AD002	Dee Dee	DOG	Mixed	Feb 91	F
AK001-01	AK001	Margo	SQUIRREL	Gray	Mar 86	F
AK001-02	AK001	Tom	CAT	Tabby	Feb 85	M
AK001-03	AK001	Jerry	RAT		Feb 88	M
AK001-04	AK001	Marcus	CAT	Siamese	Nov 87	M
AK001-05	AK001	Pookie	CAT	Siamese	Apr 85	F
AK001-06	AK001	Mario	DOG	Beagle	Jul 91	M
AK001-07	AK001	Luigi	DOG	Beagle	Aug 92	M
BA001-01	BA001	Swimmy	DOLPHIN	Bottlenose	Jul 90	F
BA001-02	BA001	Charger	WHALE	Beluga	Oct 90	M
BA001-03	BA001	Daffy	DUCK	Mallard	Sep 83	M
BA001-04	BA001	Toby	TURTLE	Box	Dec 90	M
BA001-05	BA001	Jake	DOLPHIN	Bottlenose	Apr 91	M
BL001-01	BL001	Tiajuana	BIRD	Toucan	Sep 90	F
BL001-02	BL001	Carlos	BIRD	Cockatoo	Jan 91	M
BL001-03	BL001	Ming	BIRD	Humming	Feb 88	F
BL001-04	BL001	Yellow Jacket	BIRD	Canary	Mar 83	F
BL001-05	BL001	Red Breast	BIRD	Robin	Jun 90	M
BL001-06	BL001	Mickey	BIRD	Parrot	May 91	M

Record: 1 of 130

Pet ID is entered as AA###-## (Customer Number-Sequence Number)

Figure 10-8: The datasheet with several fields.

Changing data in the query datasheet

The query datasheet offers you an easy and convenient way to change data quickly. You can add and change data in the dynaset, and it will be saved to the underlying tables.

When you're adding or changing data in the datasheet, all the table properties defined at table level are in effect. For example, you cannot enter a length value greater than 120 for any animal.

Returning to the query design

To return to the query design mode, select the Design button on the toolbar (the first one from the left).

Tip

You can also toggle between the design and datasheet mode by selecting View⇨Datasheet or View⇨Query Design from the Query menu.

Disk

Clear the query grid by selecting Edit⇨Clear Grid. Next add all the fields to the query grid by first double-clicking on the Pets data structure title bar and then dragging all the selected fields to the query grid.

Working with Fields

There are times when you'll want to work with the fields you've already selected — rearranging their order, inserting a new field, or deleting an existing field. You may even want to add a field to the QBE design without showing it in the datasheet.

The *field selector row* is the narrow gray row above the Field: row. This row is approximately half the size of the others; it's important to identify this row because this is where you select columns, whether single or multiple. Recall that each column represents a field. To select the Pet Name field, move the mouse pointer until a small *selection arrow* (in this case an outlined downward arrow) is visible in the selector row. Then click on the column. Figure 10-9 shows the selection arrow in the next column, and the column after it is selected.

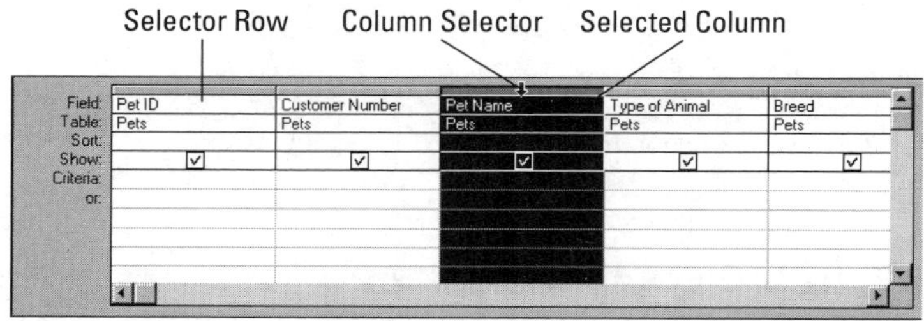

Figure 10-9: Selecting a column in the QBE pane.

If extend mode (F8) is on, the cursor must be in the row whose column you want to select. If the cursor is in an adjacent column and you select a column, you will select the adjacent column (containing the cursor) as well. To deactivate extend mode (EXT), simply press the Escape key.

Changing field order

Several methods are available for changing the order of the fields in the QBE Design pane. One way is to add them in the order you want them to appear in the datasheet, though this method is not always the easiest. You can move fields after they are placed on the QBE design by selecting columns and moving them, just as you learned to move columns in a datasheet. The following steps show you how to move a field:

1. Add several fields to the QBE pane.
2. Select the field you want to move (Breed) by clicking on the field selector above the field name. The column is highlighted.
3. Click on and hold the field selector again; the QBE Field icon, a small graphical box, appears under the arrow.

4. While holding down the left button, drag the column to its new position (to the left of Type of Animal).

Figure 10-10 shows the Breed field highlighted (selected). As you move the selector field to the left, the column separator between the fields Pet Name and Type of Animal changes (gets wider) to show you where Breed will go.

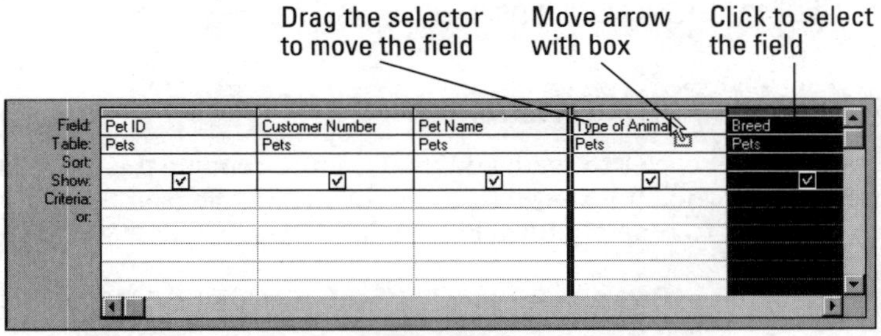

Figure 10-10: Moving the Breed field to between Pet Name and Type of Animal.

Removing a field

You can easily remove a field from the QBE Design pane. Select the field or fields to be deleted in the QBE Design pane, and then press Delete or select Edit⇨Delete. To remove the Customer Number field from the QBE Design pane, follow these steps:

1. Select the Customer Number field (or any other field) by clicking on the field selector above the field name.
2. Press Delete.

Tip If the field is not selected but the cursor is on it, you can select Edit⇨Delete Column. You can delete all the fields in the QBE Design pane in a single operation. Select Edit⇨Clear Grid from the Query Design menu.

Inserting a field

You insert a field from the table/query entry pane in the QBE Design pane by first selecting the field(s) to be inserted from the table/query entry pane. Next, drag your field selection to the QBE Design pane. The following steps show you how to insert the Customer Number field:

1. Select the Customer Number field from the field list in the table/query entry pane.
2. Drag the field from the field list to the column where you want the field to go.
3. Drop the field by releasing the left mouse button.

When you drag a field to the QBE Design pane, it will be inserted wherever you drop the field. If you drop the field on top of another field, it is inserted before that field. If you double-click on the field name in the table/query entry pane, the field is added to the end of the Field: list in the QBE Design pane.

Changing the field display name

To make the query datasheet easier to read, you may want to rename the fields in your query. The new names you choose will become the tag headings in the datasheet of the query. As an example, to rename the field Breed to Lineage, follow these steps:

1. Click to the left of the B in Breed in the Field: row of the QBE design pane.
2. Type **Lineage** and then type a colon (:) between the new name and the old field name.

The heading now reads `Lineage:Breed`. When the datasheet is displayed, you'll see `Lineage` in place of `Breed`.

Note

Renaming the field by changing the datasheet caption changes *only* the name of the heading for that field in the datasheet. It does *not* change the field name in the underlying table.

Showing a field

While performing queries, you may want to show only some of the fields temporarily. Suppose, for example, that you want to show only the fields Pet ID, Pet Name, and Breed. You can delete all other fields (and restore them when you're done with the temporary dynaset), or you can simply indicate which fields you want to see in the datasheet.

When you select fields, Access makes every field a display field automatically. Every Show: property is displayed with a check mark in the box.

To deselect a field's Show: property, simply click on the field's Show: box. The box clears, as you see in Figure 10-11. To reselect the field later, simply click on the Show: box again.

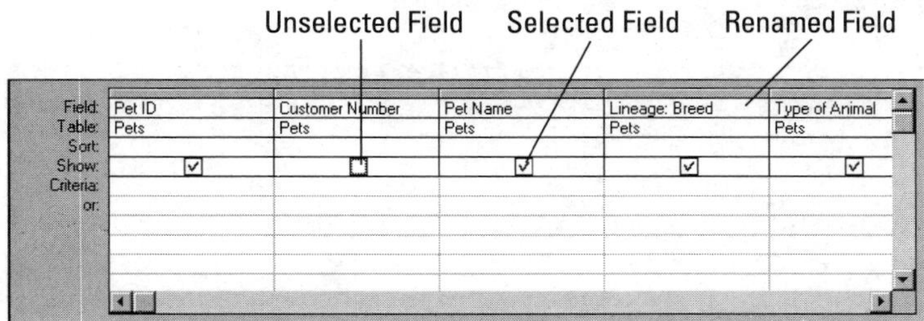

Figure 10-11: The Show: row is checked here only for the fields Pet ID, Pet Name, Breed, and Type of Animal.

Changing the Sort Order

When viewing a dynaset, you may want to display the data in some sorted order. You may want to sort the dynaset to make it easier to analyze the data (for example, to look at all the pets in order by Type of Animal).

Sorting places the records in alphabetical or numeric order. The sort order can be *ascending* (0 – 9 and A – Z) or *descending* (9 – 0 and Z – A).

Just as Access has a Show: property row for fields, there is a Sort: property row for fields in the QBE Design pane. In the following section, you learn how to set this property.

Specifying a sort

To sort the records in the datasheet by Type of Animal in ascending order, perform the following steps:

1. Click on the Sort: cell for the Type of Animal field. An arrow appears in the cell.
2. Click on the down arrow at the right of the cell.
3. Select Ascending from the list.

Figure 10-12 shows the QBE pane with the Type of Animal field selected for sorting by ascending order. Notice that the word `Ascending` appears in the field's Sort: cell.

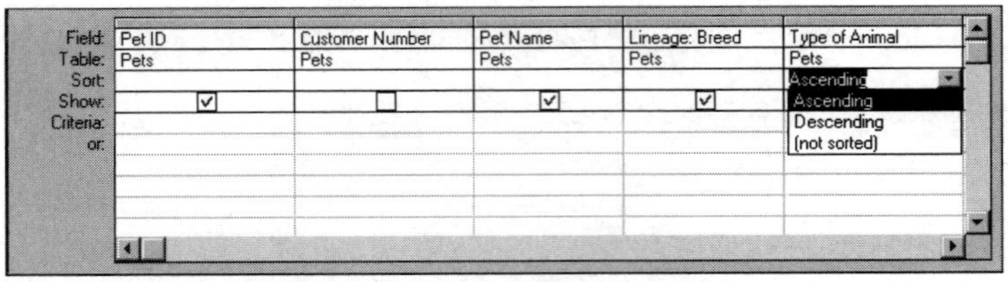

Field:	Pet ID	Customer Number	Pet Name	Lineage: Breed	Type of Animal
Table:	Pets	Pets	Pets	Pets	Pets
Sort:					Ascending
Show:	☑	☐	☑	☑	
Criteria:					
or:					

Ascending
Descending
(not sorted)

Figure 10-12: A field selected for sorting.

If you save a query that has an unused field (its Show box is unchecked), Access eliminates the field from the query pane.

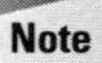

You *cannot* sort on a Memo or an OLE object field.

Sorting on more than one field

Access gives you the capability of sorting on multiple fields. You may, for example, want a primary sort order of Type of Animal and a secondary sort order by Breed. To create this query, start with the query illustrated in Figure 10-12. Then move the Breed field so it is after the Type of Animal field. Finally, add a sort to the Breed field by selecting Ascending in the Sort: cell.

Access *always* sorts the leftmost sort field first. To make sure that Access understands how you want to sort your data, you must arrange the fields in order from left to right according to sort-order precedence. You can easily change the sort order by simply selecting a sort field and moving it relative to another sort field. Access corrects the sort order automatically.

That's all there is to it. Now the dynaset is arranged in order by two different fields. Figure 10-13 shows the multiple-field sort criteria. The sort order is controlled by the order of the fields in the QBE pane (from left to right); therefore, this dynaset is displayed in order first by Type of Animal and then by Breed, as you see in Figure 10-14. Also notice that Breed has been renamed Lineage in the column header of the datasheet in Figure 10-14.

Disk If you are following along with the examples, start a new query and select all the fields before continuing.

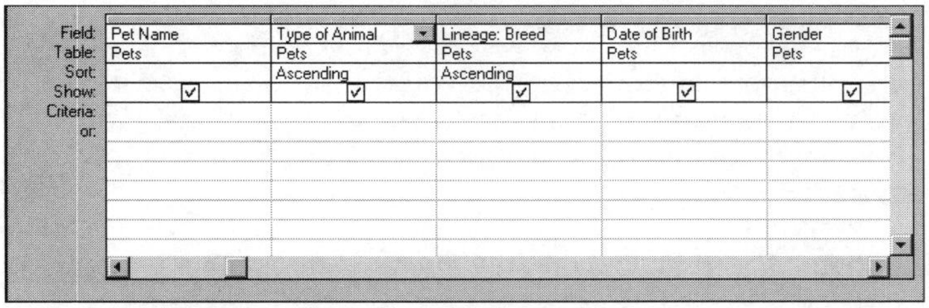

Field:	Pet Name	Type of Animal	Lineage: Breed	Date of Birth	Gender
Table:	Pets	Pets	Pets	Pets	Pets
Sort:		Ascending	Ascending		
Show:	☑	☑	☑	☑	☑
Criteria:					
or:					

Figure 10-13: Multiple-field sort criteria.

Microsoft Access - Query1 : Select Query

File Edit View Insert Format Records Tools Window Help

Pet ID	Customer Number	Pet Name	Type of Animal	Lineage	Date of Birth	Gender
MZ001-01	MZ001	Ben	BEAR	Black	Oct 92	M
RZ001-01	RZ001	Moose	BEAR	Brown	Jan 87	M
ON001-04	ON001	Martin	BEAR	Northern	Apr 86	M
RW001-03	RW001	Pirate	BIRD	Blackbird	Apr 88	M
RW001-01	RW001	Bobby	BIRD	Bobwhite	Apr 86	F
BL001-04	BL001	Yellow Jacket	BIRD	Canary	Mar 83	F
BL001-02	BL001	Carlos	BIRD	Cockatoo	Jan 91	M
WL001-03	WL001	Rosey	BIRD	Cockatoo	Nov 86	F
BL001-03	BL001	Ming	BIRD	Humming	Feb 88	F
WL001-02	WL001	Indigo	BIRD	Parakeet	Oct 89	F
BL001-06	BL001	Mickey	BIRD	Parrot	May 91	M
BL001-07	BI001	Sally	BIRD	Parrot	Jul 85	F
WL001-01	WL001	Tweety	BIRD	Parrot	Dec 87	F
GB001-01	GB001	Strutter	BIRD	Peacock	May 85	M
BL001-05	BL001	Red Breast	BIRD	Robin	Jun 90	M
BL001-01	BL001	Tiajuana	BIRD	Toucan	Sep 90	F
RW001-02	RW001	Tiger	BIRD	Wren	Feb 87	M
IR001-07	IR001	Tiger	CAT	Barn	Feb 88	M
GP001-02	GP001	Delilah	CAT	Burmese	Feb 90	F
WI001-01	WI001	Flower	CAT	Burmese	Apr 89	F
WI002-02	WL002	Lightning	CAT	Burmese	Jul 87	M
IR001-05	IR001	Ceasar	CAT	Domestic	Oct 89	M
WI001-02	WI001	Shadow	CAT	Domestic	May 87	F
CM001-02	CM001	Mule	CAT	House	Sep 89	M
IR001-03	IR001	Stripe	CAT	Long Hair	Mar 87	M

Record: 1 of 130

Pet ID is entered as AA###-## (Customer Number-Sequence Number)

Figure 10-14: A multiple-field sort order displayed.

Displaying Only Selected Records

So far, you've been working with all the records of the Pets table. There are times when you may want to work only with selected records in the Pets table. For example, you may only want to look at records where the value of Type of Animal is DOG. Access makes it easy for you to specify a record's criteria.

Understanding record criteria

Record criteria are simply some rule or rules that you supply for Access. These tell Access which records you want to look at in the dynaset. A typical criterion could be "all male animals," or "only those animals that are not currently vaccinated," or "all animals that were born before January 1990."

In other words, with record criteria, you create *limiting filters* to tell Microsoft Access which records to find and which to leave out of the dynaset.

You specify criteria starting in the Criteria: property row of the QBE pane. Here you designate criteria with an expression. The expression can be simple example data, or can take the form of complicated expressions using predefined functions.

As an example of a simple data criterion, you can type **DOG** in the Criteria: cell of Type of Animal. If you look at the datasheet, you see only records for dogs.

Entering simple character criteria

You would enter character-type criteria into fields that accommodate the Text data type. To use such criteria, you would type in an example of the data contained within the field. To limit the record display to DOG, follow these steps:

1. Click on the Criteria: cell in the Type of Animal column in the QBE design pane.
2. Type **DOG** in the cell.
3. Click on the Datasheet button.

Only the dogs are displayed. Observe that you did *not* enter an equal sign or place quotes around the sample text, yet Access added double quotes around the value. Access, unlike many other applications, automatically makes assumptions about what you want. This is an illustration of its powerful flexibility. You could enter the expression in any of these other ways:

Dog

= Dog

"Dog"

= "Dog"

In Figure 10-15 you see the expression entered under Type of Animal.

Figure 10-15 is an excellent example to demonstrate options for various types of simple character criteria. You could just as well type **Not Dog** in the criteria column, to say the opposite. In this instance, you would be asking to see all records for animals that are not dogs, adding only **Not** before the example text **Dog**.

Generally, when you deal with character data, you enter equalities, inequalities, or a list of values that are acceptable.

With either of these examples, Dog or Not Dog, you entered a simple expression in a Text-type field. Access took your example and interpreted it to show you all records that equal the example data you placed in the Criteria: cell.

This capability is a powerful tool. Consider that you have only to supply an example and Access not only interprets it, but also uses it to create the query dynaset. This is exactly what *query by example* means: You enter an example and let the database build a query based on this data.

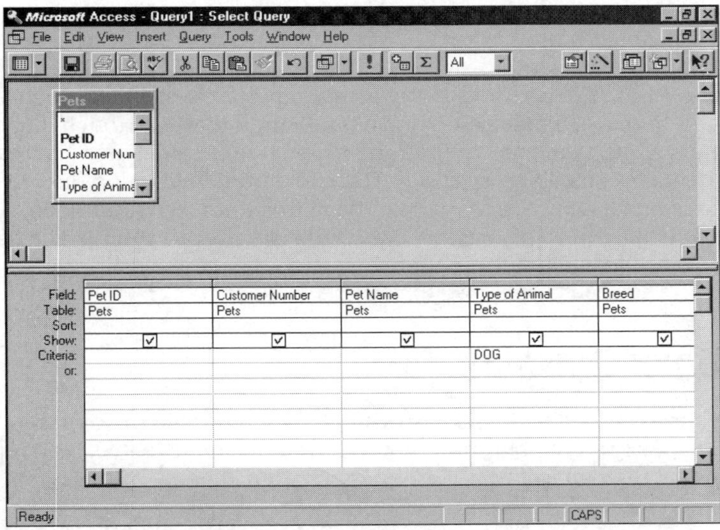

Figure 10-15: Specifying character criteria.

To erase the criteria in the cell, select the contents and press Delete, or select Edit⇨Delete from the Query Design menu.

Disk If you are following along with the examples, delete the criterion in the Type of Animal field before continuing.

Entering other simple criteria

You can also specify criteria for numeric, date, and yes/no fields. Suppose, for example, that you want to look only at records for animals born after 1/1/95. To limit the display to records where the value of Date of Birth is greater than January 1, 1995, follow these steps:

1. Remove any existing fields in the QBE pane by selecting Edit⇨Clear Grid from the menu.
2. Add the Date of Birth field to the QBE grid.
3. Click on the Criteria: cell in the Date of Birth column in the QBE Design pane.
4. Type > **1/1/95** in the cell.
5. Click on the Datasheet button.

Access also compares Date fields to a value by using *comparison operators* such as less than (<), greater than (>), equal to (=), or a combination thereof. Notice that Access adds pound-sign (#) *delimiters* around the date value automatically. Access recognizes these delimiters as differentiating a Date field from Text fields. Just as with entering text data examples, however, you don't have to enter the pound signs; Access understands what you want (based on the type of data you enter in the field), and it converts the entry format for you.

Printing a Query Dynaset

After you create your query, you can quickly print all the records in the dynaset. Although you can't specify a type of report, you can print a simple matrix-type report (rows and columns) of the dynaset that your query created.

You do have some flexibility when printing a dynaset. If you know the datasheet is set up just as you want it, you can specify some options as you follow these steps:

1. Specify your record criteria in the query design mode.
2. Switch to the query datasheet mode by clicking on the Datasheet button on the toolbar.
3. Select File⇨Print from the Query Datasheet menu, or click on the Print button on the toolbar.
4. Specify the print options you want in the Print dialog box.
5. Choose the OK button in the Print dialog box.

Access now prints the dynaset for you. Assuming that you have set up a printer in Microsoft Windows, you can click on OK to print your dataset. Your dataset prints out in the font selected for display, or in the nearest equivalent your printer offers. The printout also reflects all layout options in effect when you print the dataset. Hidden columns do not print; gridlines print only if the Gridlines option is on. The printout reflects the specified row height and column width as well.

Cross Ref Refer to Chapter 8 to review printing fundamentals; that chapter covers printing the datasheet and using the Print Preview functions.

Saving a Query

To save a query while working in design mode, you can follow this procedure:

> Select File➪Save from the Query Design menu, or click on the Save button on the toolbar. If this is the first time you're saving the query, enter a new query name in the Save As dialog box.

To save a query while working in datasheet mode, follow this procedure:

> Select File➪Save from the Datasheet File menu. If this is the first time you're saving the query, enter a new query name in the Save As dialog box.

Tip The F12 key is the Save As key in Access. You can press F12 to save your work and continue working on your query.

Both of these methods will save the query and return you to the mode you were working in. Occasionally, you'll simply want to save and exit the query in a single operation. To do this, select File➪Close from the query or the datasheet and answer Yes to the question `Save changes to Query 'query name'?`. If this is your first time to save the query, you are prompted to supply a query name and whether you want to save the query to the current database or an external file or database.

You can leave the Query window at any time by one of several ways:

- ✦ Selecting File➪Close from the Query menu
- ✦ Selecting Close from the Query window control box
- ✦ Pressing Ctrl+F4 while inside the Query window

All three of these methods activate an Access dialog box that asks, `Save changes to Query 'Query1'?`

Summary

In this chapter, you learned about the types of queries and the basics of how to use them. You had some practice in creating simple queries, and found out about some of the query options Access provides. The chapter covered the following points:

✦ Queries ask questions about your data and return the answers in the form of information.

✦ Types of queries include select, total, crosstab, action, SQL, definition, and Top Values.

✦ Queries let you select tables, fields, sort order, and record criteria.

✦ Queries create a virtual view of the data, known as a dynaset. The data is displayed in a datasheet.

✦ A dynaset is the temporary answer set. Queries save only the instructions and not the data.

✦ The Query window has two panes. The top pane displays the Design view of your tables; the bottom pane is used for entering QBE instructions.

✦ When you add fields with the asterisk button, the query automatically changes if the underlying table changes.

✦ You can display field names differently in the datasheet by adding a new caption with a colon in front of the existing field name.

✦ You can limit records being displayed with record criteria, specifying character, numeric, date/time, and yes/no.

✦ You can use a query's dynaset datasheet just as you would any table — in forms, reports, and other queries.

In the next chapter, you examine how to create and print simple reports.

✦ ✦ ✦

Creating and Printing Simple Reports

✦ ✦ ✦ ✦

In This Chapter

Understanding the types of reports you can create

Knowing the differences between a report and a form

Understanding the process of creating reports

Creating reports with a Report Wizard

Viewing reports on-screen

Printing reports

Saving reports

✦ ✦ ✦ ✦

Reports provide the most flexible way for viewing and printing summarized information. They enable you to display information with the desired level of detail, while letting you view or print your information in almost any format. You can add multilevel totals, statistical comparisons, and even pictures and graphics to a report. In this chapter, you see how to use Report Wizards as a starting point for your report. You see how to create reports, and what types you can create with Access.

Understanding Reports

Reports are used for presenting a customized view of your data. Your report output can be viewed on-screen or printed to a hard-copy device. With reports, you have the ability to control summarization of the information. You can group your data and sort it in any order you want and then present the data in the order of the groupings. You can create totals that add numbers, calculate averages or other statistics, and even display your data graphically. You can print pictures and other graphics as well as Memo fields in a report. If you can think of a report you want, Access can probably create it.

What types of reports can you create?

Four basic types of reports are used in business today:

Tabular reports	These print data in rows and columns with groupings and totals. Variations include summary and group/total reports.
Columnar reports	These print data as a form; can include totals and graphs.
Mail-merge reports	These create form letters.
Mailing labels	These create multicolumn labels or snaked-column reports.

Tabular reports

Tabular reports (also known as *Groups/totals reports*) are generally similar to a table that displays data in neat rows and columns. Tabular reports, unlike forms or datasheets, usually group their data by one or more field values; they calculate and display subtotals or statistical information for numeric fields in each group. Some groups/totals reports also have page totals and grand totals. You can even have *snaked columns* so you can create directories (such as telephone books). As shown in Figure 11-1, reports can use page numbers, report dates, or lines and boxes to separate information. They can have color and shading, and can display pictures, business graphs, and Memo fields, just as forms can. *Summary reports* (a variation of tabular reports in Access) have no detail records.

Columnar reports

Columnar reports (also known as *form reports*) generally display one or more records per page, but do so vertically. Column reports display data very much as a data-entry form does, but the report is used strictly for viewing data and not for entering it. An invoice is a typical example. This type of report can have sections that display only one record, and at the same time have sections that display multiple records from the *many* side of a one-to-many relationship — and even include totals. Figure 11-2 displays a typical column report from the Mountain Animal Hospital database system.

Mailing labels

You can easily create mailing labels, shown in Figure 11-3, by using a report in Access. In fact, you'll want to use the Mailing Label Report Wizard to get you started. The Mailing Label Report Wizard lets you select from a long list of Avery label paper styles, after which Access correctly creates a report design, based on the data you specify to create your label. After the label is created, you can open the report in design mode and customize it as needed. Mailing labels are covered in detail in Chapter 29.

Daily Hospital Report - Friday, July 07, 1995

Customer Name	Pet Name	Type of Animal	Total Amount
George Green			
	Adam	FROG	$86.50
			$86.50
Johnathan Adams			
	Patty	PIG	$150.00
	Rising Sun	HORSE	$225.00
			$375.00
Patricia Irwin			
	C.C.	CAT	$26.00
	Tiger	CAT	$350.00
			$376.00
Stephen Brown			
	Suzie	DOG	$316.00
			$316.00
William Primen			
	Brutus	DOG	$381.00
	Little Bit	CAT	$332.50
			$713.50
		Grand Total :	**$1,867.00**

Figure 11-1: A typical tabular report.

The difference between reports and forms

The main difference between reports and forms is the purpose of the output. Whereas forms are primarily for data entry, reports are for viewing data (either on-screen or in hard-copy form). You can use calculated fields with forms, and generally have these calculate an amount based on the fields in the record. With reports, you calculate on the basis of a common group of records, a page of records, or all the records processed during the report. Anything you can do with a form — except data input — you can duplicate on a report. In fact, you can save a form *as* a report, and then customize the form controls in the Report Design window.

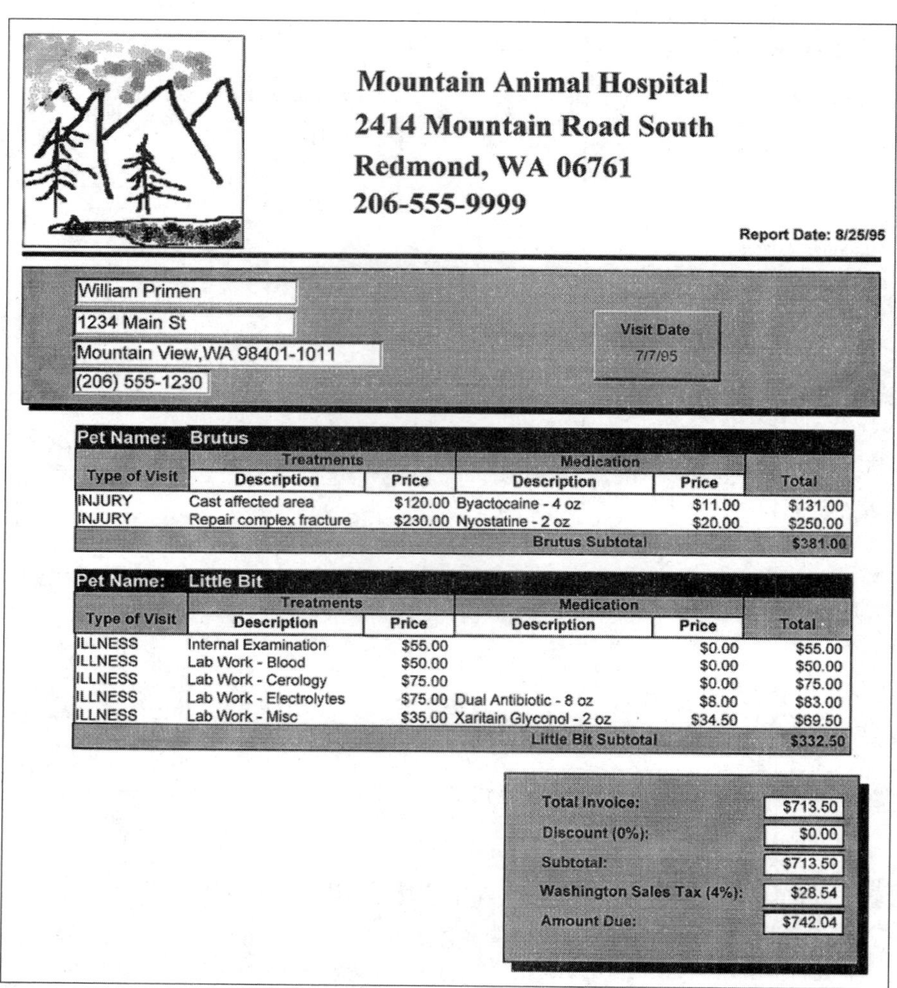

Mountain Animal Hospital
2414 Mountain Road South
Redmond, WA 06761
206-555-9999

Report Date: 8/25/95

William Primen
1234 Main St
Mountain View,WA 98401-1011
(206) 555-1230

Visit Date
7/7/95

Pet Name: Brutus

Type of Visit	Treatments		Medication		Total
	Description	Price	Description	Price	
INJURY	Cast affected area	$120.00	Byactocaine - 4 oz	$11.00	$131.00
INJURY	Repair complex fracture	$230.00	Nyostatine - 2 oz	$20.00	$250.00
			Brutus Subtotal		$381.00

Pet Name: Little Bit

Type of Visit	Treatments		Medication		Total
	Description	Price	Description	Price	
ILLNESS	Internal Examination	$55.00		$0.00	$55.00
ILLNESS	Lab Work - Blood	$50.00		$0.00	$50.00
ILLNESS	Lab Work - Cerology	$75.00		$0.00	$75.00
ILLNESS	Lab Work - Electrolytes	$75.00	Dual Antibiotic - 8 oz	$8.00	$83.00
ILLNESS	Lab Work - Misc	$35.00	Xaritain Glyconol - 2 oz	$34.50	$69.50
			Little Bit Subtotal		$332.50

Total Invoice:	$713.50
Discount (0%):	$0.00
Subtotal:	$713.50
Washington Sales Tax (4%):	$28.54
Amount Due:	$742.04

Figure 11-2: A typical form report.

The process of creating a report

Planning a report begins long before you actually create the report design. The report process begins with your desire to view your data in a table, but in a way that differs from datasheet display. You begin with a design for this view; Access begins with raw data. The purpose of the report is to transform the raw data into a meaningful set of information. The process of creating a report involves several steps:

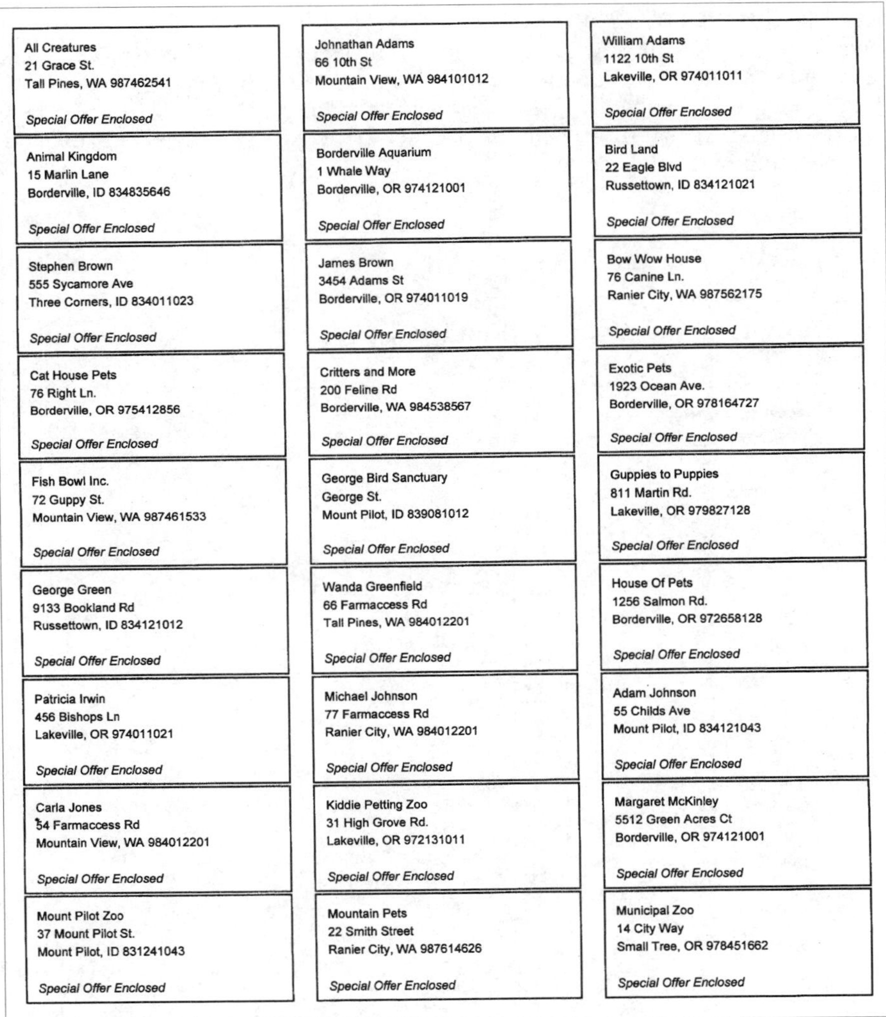
All Creatures
21 Grace St.
Tall Pines, WA 987462541
Special Offer Enclosed

Johnathan Adams
66 10th St
Mountain View, WA 984101012
Special Offer Enclosed

William Adams
1122 10th St
Lakeville, OR 974011011
Special Offer Enclosed

Animal Kingdom
15 Marlin Lane
Borderville, ID 834835646
Special Offer Enclosed

Borderville Aquarium
1 Whale Way
Borderville, OR 974121001
Special Offer Enclosed

Bird Land
22 Eagle Blvd
Russettown, ID 834121021
Special Offer Enclosed

Stephen Brown
555 Sycamore Ave
Three Corners, ID 834011023
Special Offer Enclosed

James Brown
3454 Adams St
Borderville, OR 974011019
Special Offer Enclosed

Bow Wow House
76 Canine Ln.
Ranier City, WA 987562175
Special Offer Enclosed

Cat House Pets
76 Right Ln.
Borderville, OR 975412856
Special Offer Enclosed

Critters and More
200 Feline Rd
Borderville, WA 984538567
Special Offer Enclosed

Exotic Pets
1923 Ocean Ave.
Borderville, OR 978164727
Special Offer Enclosed

Fish Bowl Inc.
72 Guppy St.
Mountain View, WA 987461533
Special Offer Enclosed

George Bird Sanctuary
George St.
Mount Pilot, ID 839081012
Special Offer Enclosed

Guppies to Puppies
811 Martin Rd.
Lakeville, OR 979827128
Special Offer Enclosed

George Green
9133 Bookland Rd
Russettown, ID 834121012
Special Offer Enclosed

Wanda Greenfield
66 Farmaccess Rd
Tall Pines, WA 984012201
Special Offer Enclosed

House Of Pets
1256 Salmon Rd.
Borderville, OR 972658128
Special Offer Enclosed

Patricia Irwin
456 Bishops Ln
Lakeville, OR 974011021
Special Offer Enclosed

Michael Johnson
77 Farmaccess Rd
Ranier City, WA 984012201
Special Offer Enclosed

Adam Johnson
55 Childs Ave
Mount Pilot, ID 834121043
Special Offer Enclosed

Carla Jones
54 Farmaccess Rd
Mountain View, WA 984012201
Special Offer Enclosed

Kiddie Petting Zoo
31 High Grove Rd.
Lakeville, OR 972131011
Special Offer Enclosed

Margaret McKinley
5512 Green Acres Ct
Borderville, OR 974121001
Special Offer Enclosed

Mount Pilot Zoo
37 Mount Pilot St.
Mount Pilot, ID 831241043
Special Offer Enclosed

Mountain Pets
22 Smith Street
Ranier City, WA 987614626
Special Offer Enclosed

Municipal Zoo
14 City Way
Small Tree, OR 978451662
Special Offer Enclosed

Figure 11-3: A typical mailing label report.

- ✦ Defining the report layout
- ✦ Assembling the data
- ✦ Creating the report design using the Access Report Design window
- ✦ Printing or viewing the report

Defining the report layout

You should begin by having a general idea of the layout of your report. You can define the layout in your mind, on paper, or interactively, using the Access Report Design window. Figure 11-4 shows a report layout created in this chapter by using the Access Report Designer. This report is first laid out on paper, showing the fields needed and the placement of the fields.

Daily Hospital Report - **[Visit Date]**

Customer Name	**Pet Name**	**Type of Animal**	**Total Amount**
[~~~~~~~~~~~~]			
	[~~~~~~~~]	[~~~~~~~~~~~~]	[~~~~~~~~~~~~]
	[~~~~~~~~]	[~~~~~~~~~~~~]	[~~~~~~~~~~~~]
	[~~~~~~~~]	[~~~~~~~~~~~~]	[~~~~~~~~~~~~]
		Customer Total:	[~~~~~~~~~~~~]
[~~~~~~~~~~~~]			
	[~~~~~~~~]	[~~~~~~~~~~~~]	[~~~~~~~~~~~~]
	[~~~~~~~~]	[~~~~~~~~~~~~]	[~~~~~~~~~~~~]
	[~~~~~~~~]	[~~~~~~~~~~~~]	[~~~~~~~~~~~~]
		Customer Total:	[~~~~~~~~~~~~]
[~~~~~~~~~~~~]			
	[~~~~~~~~]	[~~~~~~~~~~~~]	[~~~~~~~~~~~~]
	[~~~~~~~~]	[~~~~~~~~~~~~]	[~~~~~~~~~~~~]
	[~~~~~~~~]	[~~~~~~~~~~~~]	[~~~~~~~~~~~~]
		Customer Total:	[~~~~~~~~~~~~]
		Grand Total:	[~~~~~~~~~~~~]

Figure 11-4: A sample report layout.

Assembling the data

After you have a general idea of your report layout, you should assemble the data needed for the report. A report can use data from a single database table, or from the results of a query dynaset. You can link many tables together with a query, then use the result of the query (its dynaset) as the record source for your report. A dynaset appears in Access as if it were a single table. As you've learned, you can select the fields, records, and sort order of the records in a query. Access treats this dynaset data as a single table (for processing purposes) in datasheets, forms, and reports. The dynaset becomes the source of data for the report; Access processes each record to create the report. The data for the report and the report *design* are entirely separate. In the report design, you specify the field names that will be used in the report. Then, when you run the report, Access matches data from the dynaset or table against the fields used in the report, and uses the data available at that moment to produce the report.

Consider the layout shown in Figure 11-4. Here you want to create a report that shows a daily total of all the pets the hospital treated during a specific day. You call this the Daily Hospital Report. Looking at the layout, you can see that you'll need to assemble the following fields:

Visit Date from the Visits table	Used to select the visit date as a criterion in a query
Customer Name from the Customer table	Displays and groups customers on the report
Pet Name from the Customer table	Displays the pet name on the report table
Type of Animal from the Customer table	Displays the type of animal on the report
Total Amount from the Visits table	Displays and calculates totals for amounts charged

You begin the report by creating a query, as shown in Figure 11-5; notice the three tables linked together, and the appropriate fields chosen for the report. The Visit Date field is limited to values of 7/7/95, indicating that this specific view of your data will be limited to customers who visited on July 7, 1995. The Customer Name field is being sorted in ascending sequence, as the report will be grouped by customer name.

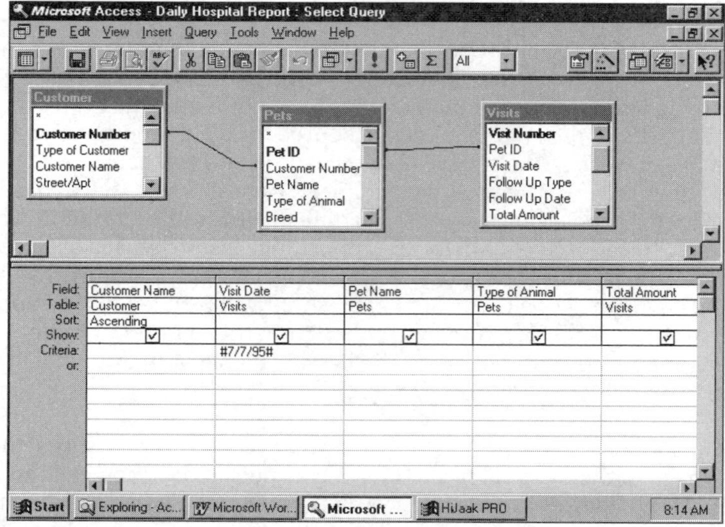

Figure 11-5: Creating a query for a report.

After you assemble the data, you can create the report design. Figure 11-6 shows the results of this query. The datasheet shown in this figure is the dynaset created when you run the Daily Hospital Report query for 7/7/95.

Customer Name	Visit Date	Pet Name	Type of Animal	Total Amount
Johnathan Adams	7/7/95	Rising Sun	HORSE	$225.00
Johnathan Adams	7/7/95	Patty	PIG	$150.00
Patricia Irwin	7/7/95	Tiger	CAT	$350.00
Patricia Irwin	7/7/95	C.C.	CAT	$26.00
Stephen Brown	7/7/95	Suzie	DOG	$316.00
William Primen	7/7/95	Little Bit	CAT	$332.50
William Primen	7/7/95	Brutus	DOG	$381.00

Figure 11-6: The Daily Hospital Report dynaset datasheet.

Creating a Report with Report Wizards

With Access, you can create virtually any type of report. Some reports, however, are more easily created than others; for these, you use a Report Wizard as a starting point. Like Form Wizards, Report Wizards give you a basic layout for your report, which you can then customize.

Report Wizards simplify the layout process of your fields by visually stepping you through a series of questions about the type of report you want to create, and then creating the report for you automatically. In this chapter, you will see both tabular and column reports created by using Report Wizards.

Creating a new report

You can choose from many ways to create a new report, including the following:

✦ Select Insert⇨Report from the Database window menu

✦ Select the Reports tab, and then press the New button in the Database window

✦ Select the New Report object icon from the Database window, the datasheet, or the query toolbar

Regardless of how you create a new report, the New Report dialog box appears; you see it in Figure 11-7.

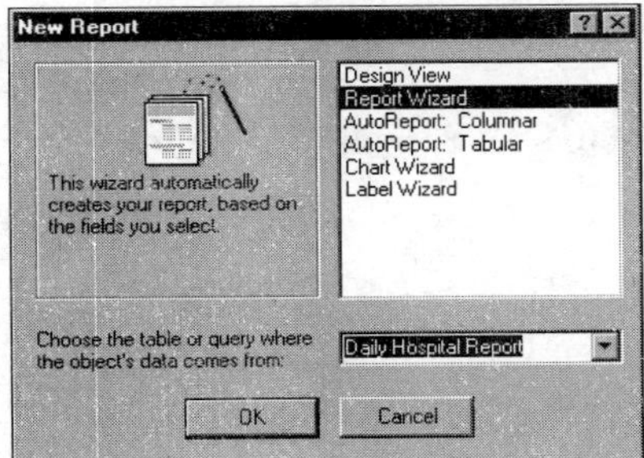

Figure 11-7: The New Report dialog box.

The New Report dialog box lets you choose one of six ways to create a report:

Design View	Displays a completely blank report design window for you to start with
Report Wizard	Helps you create a tabular report by asking you many questions
AutoReport: Columnar	Creates an instant columnar report
AutoReport: Tabular	Creates an instant tabular report
Chart Wizard	Helps you create a business graph
Label Wizard	Helps you create a set of mailing labels

To create a new report using a Report Wizard, follow these steps:

1. Create a new report by selecting a menu, an icon, or a button.
2. Select ReportWizard.
3. Select the query Daily Hospital Report in the New Report dialog box.

Choosing the data source

If you begin creating the report with a highlighted table or from a datasheet or query, you will see the table or query you are using displayed in the `Choose the table or query` text box. Otherwise you can enter the name of a valid table or query before continuing. You can also choose from a list of tables and queries by clicking on the combo-box selection arrow. In this example, you'll use the Daily Hospital Report query you saw in Figure 11-5, which creates data for customer visits on the date 7/7/95.

Tip

If you begin with a blank report, you don't need to specify a table or query before you start.

Cross Ref

Chapter 21 covers creating a new report without using a wizard.

Choosing the fields

After you select the Report Wizard and click on the OK button, a *field selection box* appears. This box is virtually identical to the field selection box used in Form Wizards (see Chapter 9 for detailed information). In this example, you select all the fields except Visit Date, as shown in Figure 11-8.

1. Click on the All Fields button (>>) to place all the fields in the Selected Fields: area.
2. Select the Visit Date field, and then click on the Remove Field button (<) to remove the field.

Tip

You can double-click on any field in the Available Fields list box to add it to Selected Fields: list box. You can also double-click on any field in the Selected Fields: list box to remove it from the box. Access then redisplays the field in the Available fields: box.

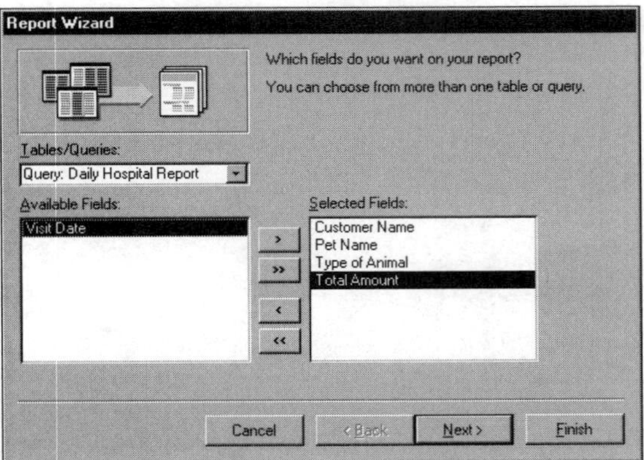

Figure 11-8: Selecting report fields.

New! If you are familiar with Access 2.0, you learned that once you select the table or query to use with the Report Wizard, you were limited to those fields. In Access for Windows 95, you can continue to select other tables or queries by using the Tables/Queries: combo box in this Wizard screen; you can also display fields from additional tables or queries. As long as you have specified valid relationships so Access can link the data, these fields are added to your original selection and you can use them on the report. If you choose fields from tables that don't have a relationship, you will see a dialog box asking you to edit the relationship and join the tables. Or, you can return to the Report Wizard and remove the fields.

Once you have selected your data, click on the Next> button to go to the next Wizard dialog box.

Selecting the view of your data

The next Wizard dialog box lets you set the view of your data, which can include a grouping. (This is a very confusing screen, and will probably be ignored by most people.) The view of your data means how you look at the overall data picture. In this example, you have three tables: Customers, Pets, and Visits. The purpose of this report is to look at visits for pets belonging to a specific customer. The visit, however, is the focus of the data.

If you select to view your report by Visits, notice that all the data appears in the sample page on the right. If you choose to view it by Pets or by Customer, only the Total Amount field is shown on the page; the rest of the fields are shown grouped together. Later, you will group the data by Customer; for now, select to view the report by Visits.

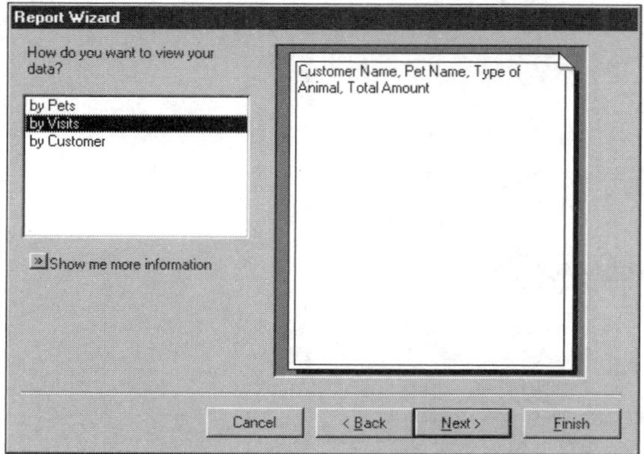

Figure 11-9: Selecting the view of your data.

Selecting the grouping levels

The next dialog box lets you choose which field(s) you want to use for a grouping. In this example, Figure 11-10 shows Customer Name as the only group field. This step designates the field(s) to be used to create group headers and footers. Using the Report Wizard, you can select up to four different group fields for your report; you can change their order by using the Priority buttons. The order you select for the group fields is the order of the grouping hierarchy.

Select the Customer Name field as the grouping field. Notice that the picture changes to graphically show Customer Name as a grouping field.

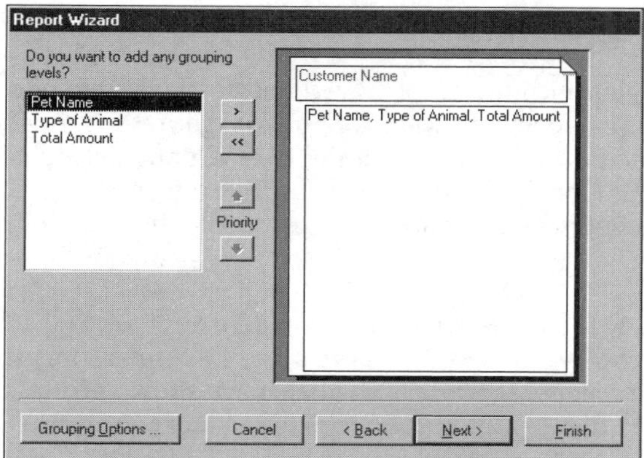

Figure 11-10: Selecting report group fields.

After you select the group field(s), you can click on the Grouping Options button to display the next dialog box, which lets you further define how your report will use the group field.

Defining the group data

The Grouping Options dialog box lets you further define the grouping. This selection can vary in importance, depending on the data type.

You will see different values in the list box for the various data types:

Text	Normal, 1st Letter, 2 Initial Letters, 3 Initial Letters, 4 Initial Letters etc.
Numeric	Normal, 10s, 50s, 100s, 500s, 1000s, 5000s, 10000s, 50000s, 100000s, 500000s
Date	Normal, Year, Quarter, Month, Week, Day, Hour, Minute

Normal means the grouping will be on the entire field. In this example, you'll want to use the entire Customer Name field. By selecting different values of the grouping, you can limit the group values. For example, suppose you are grouping on the Pet ID field. A typical Pet ID value is AP001-01. The first five characters represent the owner; the two after the hyphen represent the pet number for that owner. By choosing the Pet ID field for the grouping and then selecting 5 Initial Letters as the grouping data, you can group the pets by customer instead of by pet.

In this example, the default text field grouping option of Normal is acceptable.

Selecting the sort order

Access sorts the Group record fields automatically in an order that helps the grouping make sense. The additional sorting fields specify fields to be sorted in the detail section. In this example, Access is already sorting the data by Customer Name in the group section. As you can see in Figure 11-11, the data is also going to be sorted by Pet Name so that the pets appear in alphabetical order in the detail section.

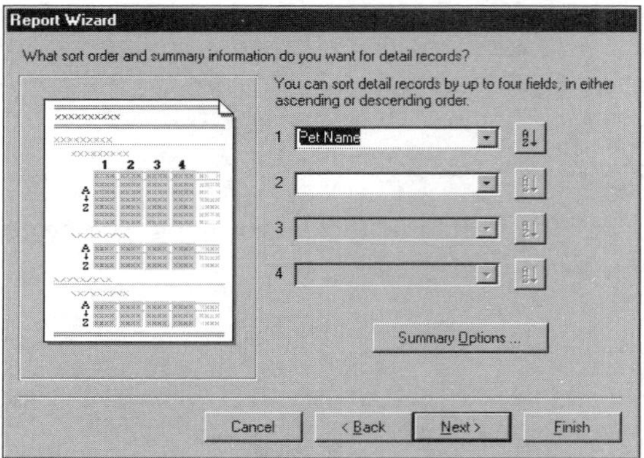

Figure 11-11: Selecting the field sorting order.

You select the sort fields by the same method used for grouping fields in the report. You can select fields you have not already chosen to group, and use these as sorting fields. The fields you choose in this dialog box do not affect grouping; they affect only the sorting order in the detail section fields. You can determine whether the order is ascending or descending by clicking on the toggle button to the right of each sort field.

Selecting Summary Options

At the bottom of the sorting dialog box is a button named Summary Options. Clicking on this button displays the dialog box shown in Figure 11-12. This allows you to determine additional options for numeric fields. As you can see, the field `Total Amount` will be summed. Additionally, you can display averages, minimums, and maximums.

You can also decide whether to show or hide the data in the detail section. If you select Detail and Summary, the report will show the detail data; selecting Summary Only will hide the detail section only showing totals in the report.

Finally, by checking the box labeled `Calculate percent of total for sums`, you can add another number below the total in the group footer. Doing so adds the percentage of the entire report that the total represents. If (for example) you had three customers and their total was 15, 25, and 10, they would show (respectively) 30%, 50%, and 20% below their total (that is, 50) — indicating the percentage of the total sum (100%) represented by their sum .

Clicking on the OK button in this dialog box returns you to the sorting dialog box. There you can click on the Next > button to move onto the next Wizard dialog box.

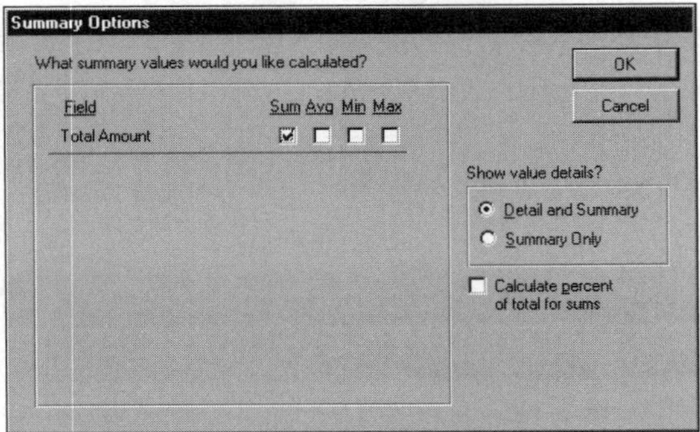

Figure 11-12: Selecting the summary options.

Selecting the Layout

Two more dialog boxes affect the look of your report. The first (shown in Figure 11-13) lets you determine the layout of the data. The Layout area lets you choose one of six different layouts; these tell Access whether to repeat the column headers, whether to indent each grouping, and whether to add lines or boxes between the detail lines. As you select each option, the picture on the left changes to show the effect.

The Orientation area lets you decide whether your report will have a Portrait (up-and-down) or a Landscape (across-the-page) layout. This choice affects how it prints on the paper. Finally, put a check mark next to `Adjust field width so all fields fit on a page`. You can cram a lot of data into a little area. (Magnifying glasses may be necessary!)

For this example, choose Stepped and Portrait, as shown in Figure 11-13.

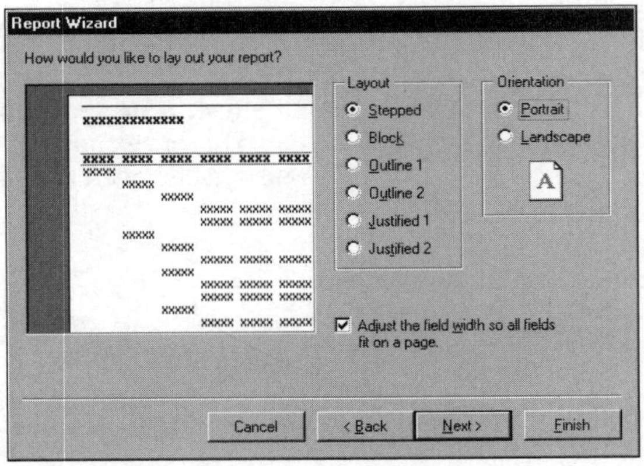

Figure 11-13: Selecting the summary orientation.

Choosing the style

After you choose the layout, you can choose the style of your report from the dialog box shown in Figure 11-14. Each of style has different background shadings, font size, and typeface, and other formatting. As you select each of these, the picture on the left changes to show a preview. For this example, choose Compact (as shown in Figure 11-14).

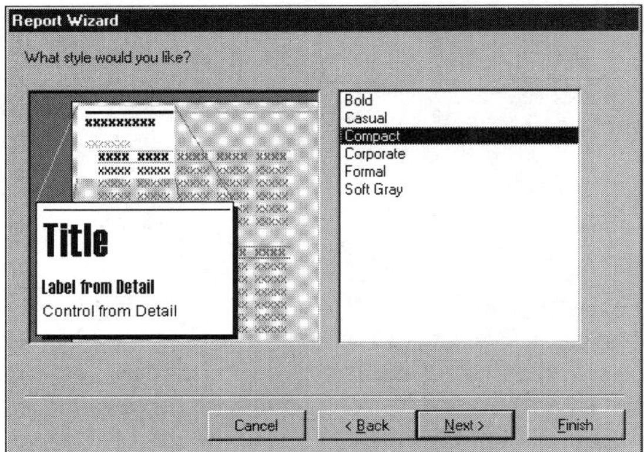

Figure 11-14: Choosing the style of your report.

Tip

You can customize any of the styles, even add your own, by using the AutoFormat menu option from the Format menu of the Reports design screen and choosing Customize.

Opening the report design

Figure 11-15 shows the final Report Wizard dialog box. The checkered flag lets you know you're at the finish line. The first part of the dialog box lets you enter a title for the report. This title will appear once at the beginning of the report, not at the top of each page. The default is the name of the table you used initially. If you used a query, the name will be that of the table used for the view of the data (in this example, it was Visits). As you can see in Figure 11-15, `Daily Hospital Report` has been typed in instead of `Visits`.

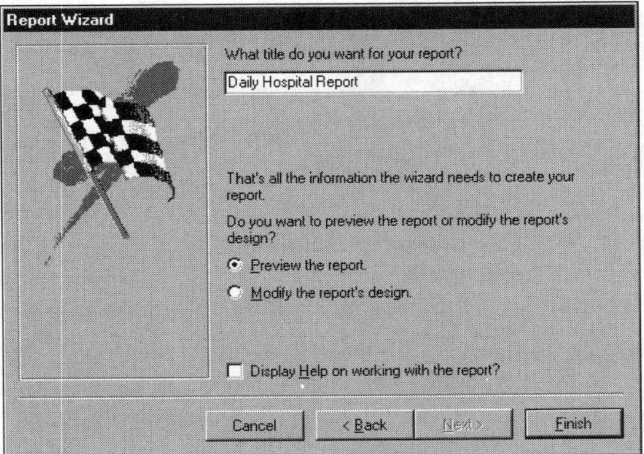

Figure 11-15: The final Report Wizard dialog box.

Next you can choose one of the option buttons at the bottom of the dialog box. You have two choices:

- ✦ Preview the report
- ✦ Modify the report design

For this example, leave the default selection intact to preview the report. When you select the Finish button, you will view your report in the Print Preview window.

Click on Finish to complete the Report Wizard and view the report.

Using the Print Preview window

Figure 11-16 displays the Print Preview window in a zoomed view. This view lets you see your report with the actual fonts, shading, lines, boxes, and data that will be on the printed report. When the print preview mode is in a zoomed view, pressing the mouse button changes the view to a *page preview*, where you can see the entire page.

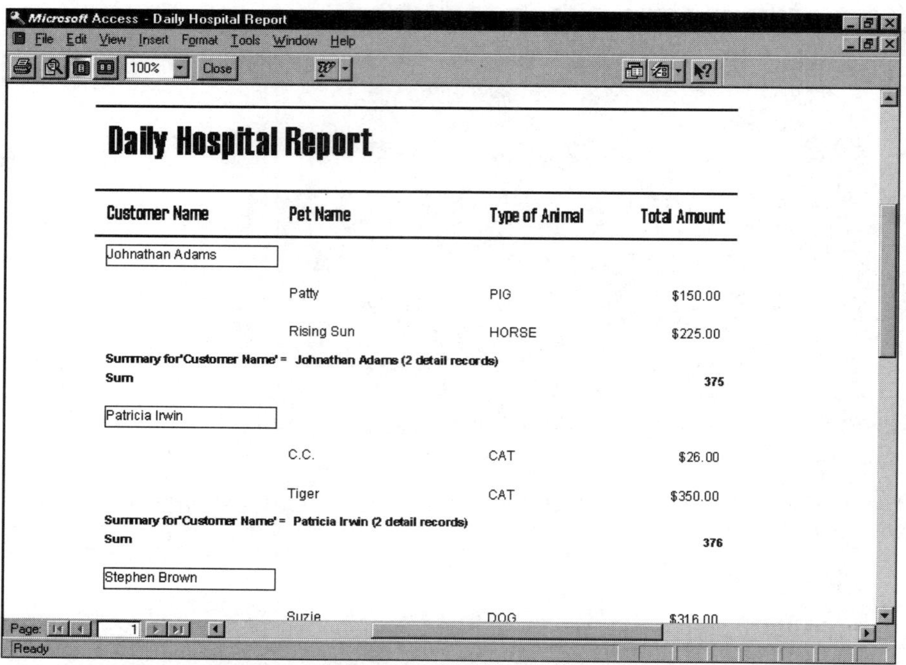

Figure 11-16: Displaying a report in the zoomed preview mode.

You can move around the page by using the horizontal and vertical elevators. Use the Page controls (at the bottom left corner of the window) to move from page to page.

Figure 11-17 shows an entire page of the report, as you would see it in the page preview mode of Print Preview. By using the magnifying-glass cursor here, you can select a portion of the page and then zoom in to that portion for a zoomed view.

In Figure 11-17, you can see a representation of the printed page. Use the navigation buttons (in the lower left section of the Print Preview window) to move between pages, just as you would to move between records in a datasheet. A set of icons appears on the toolbar.

If, after examining the preview, you are satisfied with the report, simply select the Printer icon on the toolbar to print the report. If you are dissatisfied, select the Close button to return to design window; Access takes you to the Report Design window to make further changes.

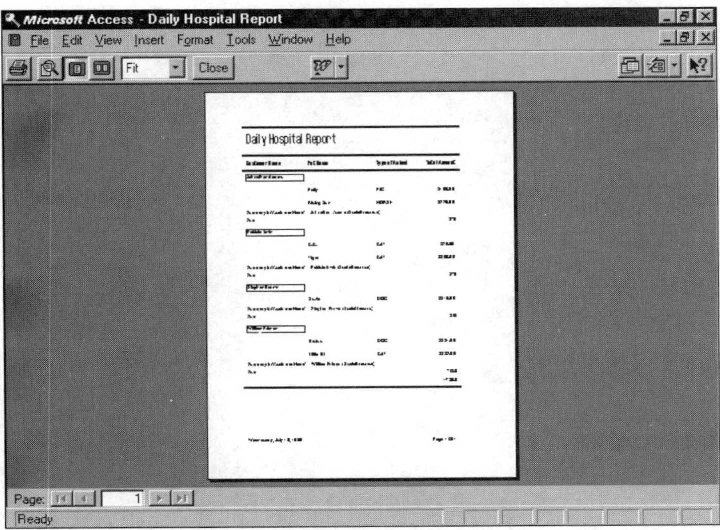

Figure 11-17: Displaying a report in Print Preview's page preview mode.

Viewing the Report Design window

When you select the first icon from the toolbar, Access takes you to the Report Design window, which is similar to the Form Design window. The major difference is in the sections that make up the report design. As you can see in Figure 11-18, the report design reflects the choices you made using the Report Wizard.

Cross Ref You may also see the toolbox, Sorting and Grouping dialog box, property sheet, and Field List window, depending on whether you have pressed the toolbar buttons to see these tools. You learn how to change the design of a report in Chapters 21 and 22.

You can switch back to the print preview mode by selecting the Print Preview icon button on the Report Design toolbar, or by selecting the Print Preview option on the File menu. You can also select Print or Page Setup from the File menu. This menu also provides options for saving your report.

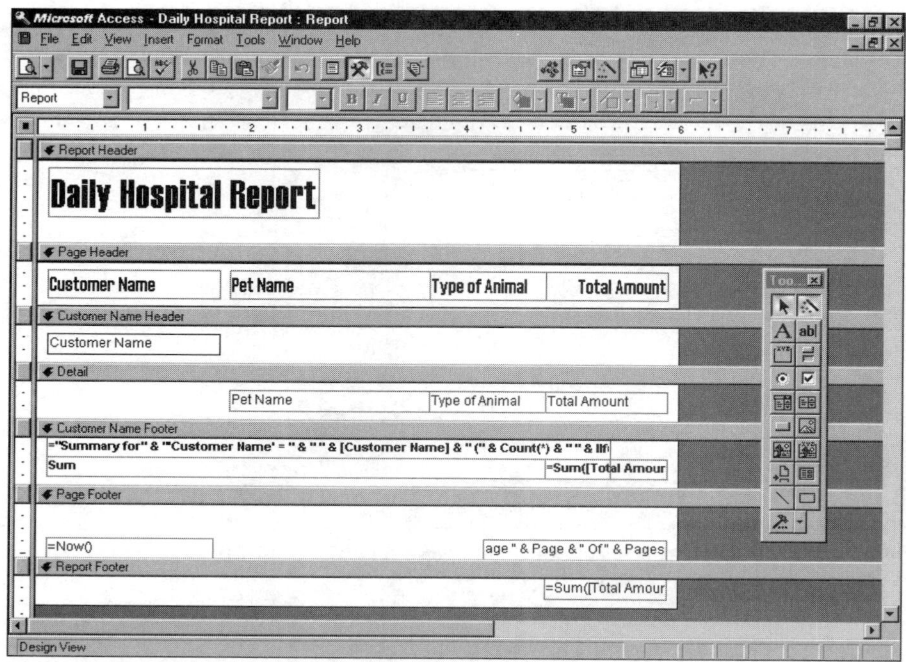

Figure 11-18: The Report Design window.

Printing a Report

You can print one or more records in your report, exactly as they look on-screen, by selecting from any of several places:

- File➪Print in the Report Design window
- Print button in the Preview window
- File➪Print in the Database window (with a report highlighted)

If you select File➪Print, a standard Windows 95 Print dialog box appears. You can select the print range, copies, and print properties. If you click on the Print icon, the report goes immediately to the currently selected printer, without displaying a Print dialog box.

Cross Ref For a complete discussion of printing, see Chapter 22.

Saving the Report

You can save the report design at any time by selecting File⇨Save or File⇨Save As/Export from the Report Design window, or by selecting the Save button on the toolbar. The first time you save a report (or any time you select Save As/Export...), a dialog box lets you select a name. The text box initially displays the default name from the Report Wizard, `Report1`.

Warning Remember that Access saves only the report *design*, not the data or the actual report. You must save your query design separately if you created a query to produce your report. You can re-create the dynaset at any time by running the report which automatically reruns the query.

Creating a Report with AutoReport

From a table, datasheet, form, or nearly any design screen in Access, you can create a report instantly by clicking on the AutoReport button from the New Object icon in the toolbar (it shows a form with a lightning bolt through it) and then selecting from the list of icons that drop down. Another method is to use the Insert⇨Report command, and then click on one of the two AutoReport selections from the dialog box that appears. When you use the AutoReport button, the report appears instantly with no additional work from you. To create an AutoReport using the Pets table, follow these steps:

1. From the Mountain Animal Hospital or Mountain Animal Start Database Containers, click on the Table tab.
2. Select Pets.
3. Click on the New Object button in the toolbar, and then select Auto Report.

The report instantly appears, as shown in Figure 11-19. Actually, the Picture property of the OLE control has been changed to Stretch to show the whole rabbit. (This was done in the Report Design screen, using the techniques you learned in Chapter 9.)

Using AutoReport is the quickest way to create a report. Generally, however, you will want more control over the process. Other Report Wizards are available to help you create more customized reports, as you have seen.

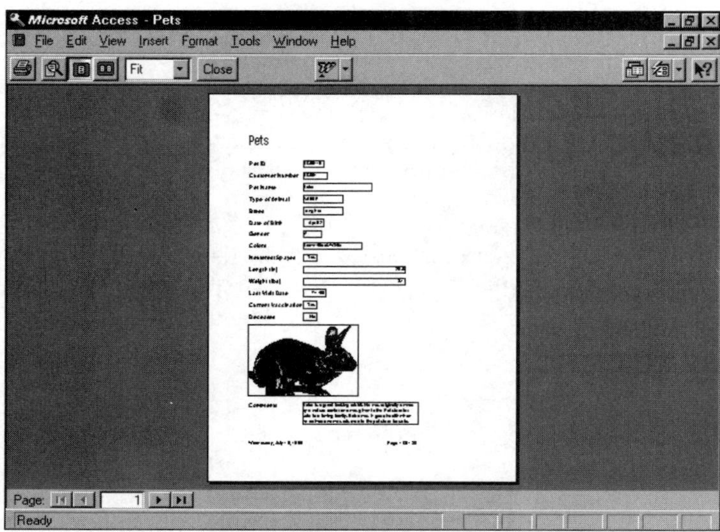

Figure 11-19: The AutoReport report.

Summary

In this chapter, you learned how easily you can create reports in Access. You saw the basic types of reports and how the Report Wizards simplify the process. The chapter covered the following points:

- ✦ The Access report writer lets you create tabular reports, column reports, business graphs, and mailing labels.
- ✦ The process of creating a report consists of defining the layout, assembling the data, creating the report design, and printing or viewing the report.
- ✦ Report Wizards let you create reports by filling in a series of dialog boxes.
- ✦ Reports can be printed or viewed on-screen.
- ✦ You can view reports on-screen in a print preview mode.

In the next chapter, you learn how to manipulate multiple tables with Access objects. You'll see how to relate tables to take full advantage of a relational database's capabilities.

✦ ✦ ✦

Setting Relationships Between Tables

✦ ✦ ✦ ✦

In This Chapter

The tables that make up the Mountain Animal Hospital database

What a key is

The benefits of using primary keys

How to create a multiple-field primary key

What a foreign key is

The types of relations

How referential integrity works

How to create relationships

How to delete relationships

How to use the Table Analyzer Wizard

How to use lookup fields in a table

✦ ✦ ✦ ✦

So far, you have learned how to create a simple table and to enter its data and display it in either a datasheet or a form. Then you learned how to use simple queries and reports. All these techniques were demonstrated, however, with only a single table. The Pets table has been an excellent sample of a single table; it contains many different data types that lend themselves to productive examples.

It's time now to move into the real world of relational database management.

Tables Used in the Mountain Animal Hospital Database

Figure 12-1 diagrams the database of the Mountain Animal Hospital system. You see eight tables in the figure, each of which requires its own table design, complete with field names, data types, descriptions, and properties.

Disk

If you're following along with the examples, either use the Mountain Animal Start files on the disk that accompanies this book, or create these tables yourself. If you want to create each of these tables, you can use Appendix B as a reference for each table's description; then use the steps you learned in Chapter 7 to create each one.

Cross Ref

In the diagram in Figure 12-1, you can see lines joining the tables. These are the *relationship lines* between the tables. Each line indicates a separate relationship between two tables; you establish these at either at the table level (using the *Relationship Builder* feature of Access) or by using a query (Chapter 14 shows you how to establish relationships in a query). In this chapter, you see how to use the Relationship Builder to establish a relationship at the table level.

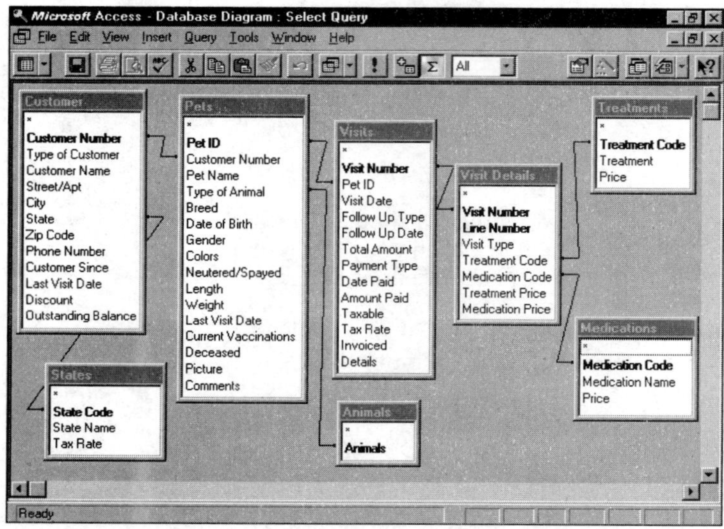

Figure 12-1: The database diagram for the Mountain Animal Hospital system.

Of the eight tables in the database diagram, four actually hold data about Mountain Animal Hospital, and four are used for *lookups*. You can eliminate the lookup tables and still use the system if you want to. These are the four main tables:

Customer	Contains information about each customer
Pets	Contains information about each animal
Visits	Contains information about each visit
Visit Details	Contains multiple records about the details of each visit

Following are the four lookup tables:

States	Used by the Customer table to retrieve state name and tax rate
Animals	Used by the Pets table to retrieve a list of valid animal types

Treatments	Used by the Visit Details table to retrieve treatment name and price
Medications	Used by the Visit Details table to retrieve medication name and price

In order to set relations between tables, you must establish a link between fields that contain common information. The fields themselves do not need to have the same name. The field's data type and length must be the same, however, and (even more importantly) the information contained within both fields for a specific record must be the same in both tables for the link to work. Generally you establish a relationship by linking these *key fields* between tables — the *primary* key in one table to a *foreign* key in another table.

Note In Figure 12-1, each table has one or more fields in bold. These are the fields that define the primary key for each table.

Understanding Keys

Every table should have a *primary key* — one or more fields whose contents are unique to each record. For example, the Customer Number field is the primary key in the Customer table — each record in the table has a different Customer Number (no two records have the same number). This is called *entity integrity* in the world of database management. By having a different primary key in each record (like the Customer Number in the Customer table), you can tell two records (in this case, customers) apart. This is important because you can easily have two individual customers named Fred Smith (or pet stores named Animal Kingdom) in your table.

Theoretically, you could use the customer name plus the customer's address, but two people named Fred Smith could live in the same town and state, or a father and son (Fred David Smith and Fred Daniel Smith) could live at the same address. The goal of setting primary keys is to create individual records in a table that will guarantee uniqueness.

Remember that when creating Access tables, if you don't specify a primary key, Access asks whether you want one. If you say yes, Access will create a primary key for you as an AutoNumber data type. It will place a new sequential number in the primary key field for each record, automatically. Table 12-1 shows a list of tables and their primary keys.

Note In Access, however, you cannot use an AutoNumber data field to enforce referential integrity between tables. Therefore, it is important to specify another data type — like Text or Numeric — for the primary key (more about this topic later in this chapter).

Table 12-1
Tables and Primary Keys

Table	*Primary Key*
Customer	Customer Number
Pets	Pet ID
Visits	Visit Number
Visit Details	Visit Number; Line Number
States	State Code
Animals	Animals
Treatments	Treatment Code
Medications	Medication Code

Deciding on a primary key

Normally a table has a unique field (or combination of fields) — the primary key for that table — that makes each record unique; often it's some sort of ID field that uses the Text data type. To determine the contents of this ID field, usually you specify some simple method for creating the value in the field. Your method can be as simple as using the first letter of the real value you are tracking, along with a sequence number (like A001, A002, B001, B002, and so on). Sometimes your method may rely on a random set of letters and numbers for the field content (as long as each field has a unique value), or you can use a complicated calculation based on information from several fields in the table.

Table 12-2 shows a list of tables and explains how to define the primary key in each one.

As you can see in Table 12-2, it doesn't take a great deal of work (or even much imagination) to create a key. Any rudimentary scheme and a good sequence number, used together, always seem to work. Because Access tells you automatically when you try to enter a duplicate key value, you can simply add the value of 1 to the sequence number. You may think that all these sequence numbers make it hard to look up information in your tables. Just remember that *normally* you never look up information by an ID field. Generally (instead) you look up information according to the *purpose* of the table. In the Customer table, for example, you can look up information by Customer Name. In some cases, the Customer Name is the same, so you can look at other fields in the table (ZIP code, phone number) to find the correct customer. Unless you just happen to know the Customer Number, you'll probably never use it in a search for information.

Table 12-2
Deriving the Primary Key

Table	*Derivation of Primary Key*
Customer	Individuals: first two letters of last name, three-digit sequence number Pet Stores: first letter of first two major words, three-digit sequence number Zoos: first letter of first two major words, three-digit sequence number
Pets	Customer Number, a hyphen (-), and then a sequential number
Visits	Four-digit year and then the Julian day (sequential number)
Visit Details	Visit Number and then another field that holds a three-digit sequence number (Line Number field)
Animals	Type of animal
Treatments	Four-digit unique number (arbitrarily selected)
Medications	Four-digit unique number (arbitrarily selected)

Benefits of a primary key

Have you ever placed an order with a company for the first time and then decided the next day to increase your order? You call the people at the order desk. Sometimes they ask you for your customer number. You tell them you don't know your customer number. This type of thing happens all the time. So they then ask you for some other information — generally, your ZIP code or telephone area code. Then, as they narrow down the list of customers, they ask your name. Then they tell you your customer number (as if you'd care). Some businesses use phone numbers as a unique starting point. When I call for pizza delivery, I give them my phone number, and they proceed to tell me my wife's name, address, and the last ten types of pizza she ordered! Last week, they didn't even ask for my phone number. Now they have Caller ID hooked into their computer screen. Imagine my surprise when they answered the phone with "Good evening, Mrs. Prague." (And I don't even look like my wife!) Their system didn't quite establish the uniqueness of these two customers.

Database systems usually have more than one table, and these tend to be related in some manner. For example, the Customer table and Pets table are related to each other via a Customer Number. The Customer table will always have one record for each customer, and the Pets table will have a record for each pet the customer owns. Because each customer is *one* physical person, you only have one record about the customer in the Customer table. Each customer can own several pets, however, which means you set up another table to hold information about each pet. Again, each pet is *one* physical animal (a dog, a cat, a bird, and so on). So each animal has one record in the Pets table. Of course, you relate the customers' pets in the Pets table to the right customer in the Customer table by using a common field between both tables. In this case, the field is the Customer Number (it is in both tables).

When linking tables, you should link the primary key field from one table (the Customer Number in the Customer table) to a field in the second table that has the same structure and type of data in it (the Customer Number in the Pets table). If the link field in the second table is *not* the primary key field (and usually it isn't), it's known as a *foreign key* field (this topic is discussed later in the chapter).

Besides being a common link field between tables, a primary key field in Access has other advantages:

✦ A primary key field is an index that greatly speeds up queries, searches, and sort requests.

✦ When you add new records, you must enter a value in primary key field(s). Access will not allow you to enter Null values, which guarantees that you'll have only valid records in your table.

✦ When you add new records to a table that has a primary key, Access checks for duplicate data and doesn't let you enter duplicates for the primary key field.

✦ By default, Access displays your data in the order of the primary key.

If you define a primary key based on part of the data in the record, you can have Access automatically place your data in an understandable order. In the example, the Pet ID field is made up of the owner's Customer Number, followed by a hyphen and a two-digit sequence number. If the All Creatures Pet Store is the first customer on the list whose last name begins with AC, the store's customer number is AC001. If someone from this store brings in three pets, the Pet IDs are designated AC001-01, AC001-02, and AC001-03. This way the Pet ID field provides you with data in the order of customers displayed alphabetically.

Tip: Primary key fields should be made as short as possible because they can affect the speed of operations in a database.

Creating a primary key

As discussed in Chapter 7, you create a primary key by selecting the field you want to specify as a primary key and clicking on the Primary Key button on the toolbar (the key). If you are specifying more than one field, you specify the fields you want for the primary key and again click on the Primary Key button. You specify the fields by selecting each field while holding down the Ctrl key.

When specifying multifield primary keys, the order of the selection is important. Therefore, you should check your selection by clicking on the Indexes button on the toolbar and looking at the field order. Figure 12-2 shows the two-field index for the Visit Details table. Notice that the Visit Number is before the Line Number field in the index box.

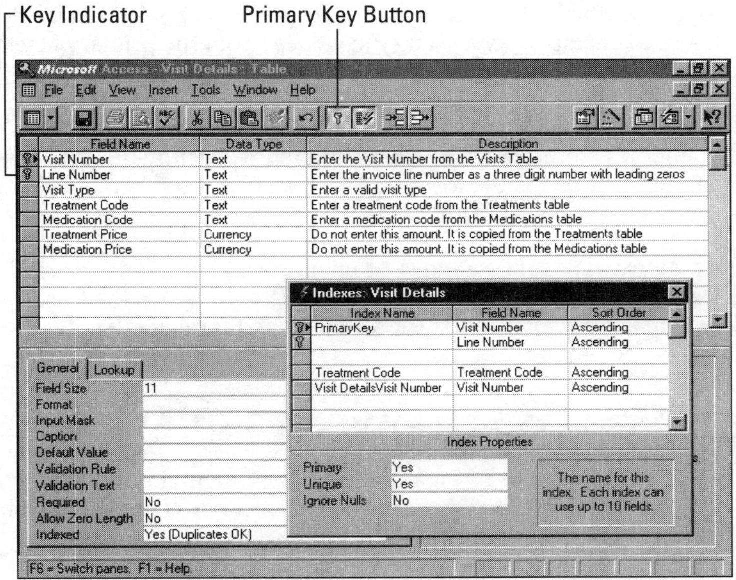

Figure 12-2: The index dialog box showing a two-field primary key.

Note Also notice that there are two additional index names in the index window. These are not keys but indexes used to speed up sorts used in these tables. If you regularly sort data in tables by the same field or fields, you should create an index for that fields. An *index* is an internal table of values that maintains the order of the records. This way, when you need to sort data or find a piece of data instantly, Access can search through the index keys in a known order rather than sequentially through the data.

Warning Creating indexes will slow down data entry; each new record, deleted record, or change to the indexed field will require a change to the index. Use only the index fields you need, which will speed up sorting your application and balance that need with data entry speed.

Understanding foreign keys

Primary keys guarantee uniqueness in a table, and you use the primary key field in one table to link to another. The common link field in the other table may not be (and usually isn't) the primary key in the other table. The *common link field* is a field or fields that hold the same type of data as in the primary key of the link table. The field (or fields) used to link to a primary key field in another table are known as *foreign keys*. Unlike a primary key, which must be created in a special way, a foreign key is any field(s) used in a relationship. By matching the values (from the primary key to the foreign key) in both tables, you can relate two records.

In Figure 12-1, you saw a relationship between the Customer and Pets tables. The primary key of Customer, Customer Number, is related to the Customer Number field in Pets. In Pets, Customer Number is the foreign key because it is the key of a related "foreign" table.

A relation also exists between the States and Customer tables. The primary key of States, State Code, is related to the State field in the Customer table. In the Customer table, State is the foreign key because it is the key of a related foreign table.

Understanding Relations Between Tables

At the beginning of this chapter, you saw eight tables in the Mountain Animal Hospital database, and seven relationships. Before you learn how to create these relationships, it is important that you understand them.

A review of relationships

Relationships established at the table level take precedence over those established at the query level. If you can set a relationship at the table level, it will be recognized automatically when a multiple-table query is created that uses fields from more than one table. Relationships between tables can be grouped into four types:

- One-to-one
- One-to-many
- Many-to-one
- Many-to-many

Understanding the four types of table relationships

When you physically join two tables (by connecting fields with like information), you create a relationship that Access recognizes. Figure 12-3 shows the relationships between all the tables in the Mountain Animal Hospital system.

The relationship that you specify between tables is important. It tells Access how to find and display information from fields in two or more tables. The program needs to know whether it will look for only one record in a table, or several records on the basis of the relationship. The Customer table, for example, has a *one-to-many* relationship to the Pets table. There will *always* be one record in the Customer table for *at least* one record in the Pets table; there could be *many* related records in the Pets table. So Access knows to find only one record in the Customer table, and look for any in the Pets table (one or more) that have the same Customer Number.

The one-to-one relationship

The *one-to-one relationship,* though rarely used in database systems, can be a very useful way to link two tables together. A good example of a one-to-one relationship occurs in most billing systems; a billing file is created to allow additional information necessary to invoice customers at a location other than their listed addresses. This file usually contains the customer number and another set of address fields. Only a few customers would have a separate billing address, so you wouldn't want to add this information to the main customer table. A one-to-one relationship between a customer table and billing table may be established to retrieve the billing address for those customers who want to have a separate address. Although all the information on one table could be added to the other, the tables are maintained separately for efficient use of space.

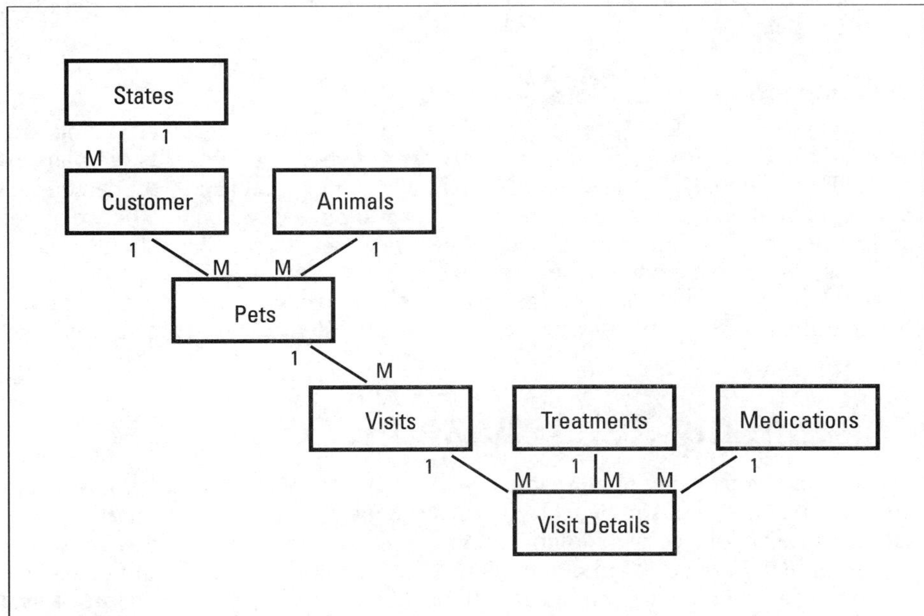

Figure 12-3: The Mountain Animal Hospital relationships.

The one-to-many relationship

The *one-to-many relationship* is used to relate one record in a table with many records in another. Examples are one customer to many pets or one pet to many visits. Both of these examples are one-to-many relationships. The Customer-Pets relationship links the customer number (the primary key of the Customer table) to the customer number in the Pets table (which becomes the foreign key of the Customer table).

The many-to-one relationship

The *many-to-one relationship* (often called the *lookup table* relationship) tells Access that many records in the table will be related to a single record in another table. Normally, many-to-one relationships are *not* based on a primary key field in either table. Mountain Animal Hospital has four lookup tables, each having a many-to-one relationship with the primary table. The States table has a many-to-one relationship with the Customer table; each state record can be used for many customers. Although (in theory) this relationship is one-to-one, it is known as a many-to-one relationship because it does not use a primary key field for the link, and many records from the primary table link to a single record in the other table.

Some one-to-many relationships can be reversed and made into many-to-one relationships. If you set a relationship from Pets to Customers, for example, the relationship becomes many-to-one; many pets can have the same owner. So relationships depend on how you use and interpret the information in your tables. Thus, one-to-many and many-to-one relationships can be considered the same — just viewed from opposite perspectives.

The many-to-many relationship

The *many-to-many relationship* is the hardest for people to understand. Think of it generally as *a pair of one-to-many relationships* between two tables, as happens in the tables Pets and Visits in the Mountain Animal Hospital database. A pet can be serviced at the hospital on many dates, so you see a one-to-many relationship between Pets and Visits. On the other hand, on each date, many pets can be brought into the hospital; this is also a one-to-many relationship. An individual pet may visit the hospital on many dates, and on a given date, many pets visit the hospital. Thus a pair of separate, two-way, one-to-many relationships creates a many-to-many relationship.

Understanding Referential Integrity

In addition to specifying relationships between tables in an Access database, you can also set up some rules that will help in maintaining a degree of accuracy between the tables. For example, you would not want to delete a customer record in your Customer table if there are related pets records in the Pets table. If you did delete a customer record without first deleting the customer's pets, you would have a system that has pets without an owner. This type of problem could be catastrophic.

Imagine being in charge of a bank that tracks loans in a database system. Now imagine that this system has *no* rules that say, "Before deleting a customer's record, make sure that there is no outstanding loan." It would be disastrous! So a database system needs to have rules that specify certain conditions between tables — rules to enforce the integrity of information between the tables. These rules are known as *referential integrity*; they keep the relationships between tables intact in a relational database management system. Referential integrity prohibits you from changing your data in ways that invalidate the links between tables.

Referential integrity operates strictly on the basis of the tables' key fields; it checks each time a key field, whether primary or foreign, is added, changed, or deleted. If a change to a key creates an invalid relationship, it is said to violate referential integrity. You can set up your tables so that referential integrity is enforced automatically.

When tables are linked together, one table is usually called the *parent*, and the other (the table it is linked to) is usually called the *child*. This is known as a *parent-child* relationship between tables. Referential integrity guarantees that there will never be an *orphan*, a child record without a parent record.

Creating Relationships

Unless you have a reason for not wanting your relationships always to be active, you should create your table relationships at the table level using the *Relationship Builder*. If you need to break the table relationships later, you can. For normal data entry and reporting purposes, however, having your relationships defined at the table level makes it much easier to use a system.

Access 95 has a very powerful Relationship Builder. You can add tables, use drag-and-drop methods to link tables, easily specify the type of link, and set any referential integrity between tables.

Using the Relationship Builder tool

You create relationships in the Database window. From this window, you can select the menu item Tools⇨Relationships or click on the Relationships button on the toolbar. The main Relationships window appears, which lets you add tables and create links between them.

The main Relationships window is shown in Figure 12-4. Notice the new toolbar associated with it. When first opened, the Relationships window is a blank surface. You can add tables to the window by using one of several methods :

- ✦ Add the tables before entering the Relationship Builder from the dialog box that's first displayed.
- ✦ Click on the Show Tables button on the toolbar.

- ✦ Select Relationships➪Show Table from the main menu.
- ✦ While in the Relationships window, click the right mouse button (which calls up the shortcut menu), and select Show Table from the menu.

To start the Relationship Builder and add tables to the Relationships window, follow these steps:

1. Click on the Relationships button on the toolbar. Access opens a Show Table dialog box.
2. Select all the tables by double-clicking on them — Customer, Pets, Visits, Visit Details, States, Animals, Medications, and Treatments.
3. Click on the Close button on the Show Table dialog box. Your screen should look like the one in Figure 12-4. Notice that Access has placed each table in the Relationships window. Each table is in its own box; the title of the box is the name of the table. Inside the table box are the names of the fields for each table. Currently, there are no links between the tables. Now you are ready to set relationships between them.

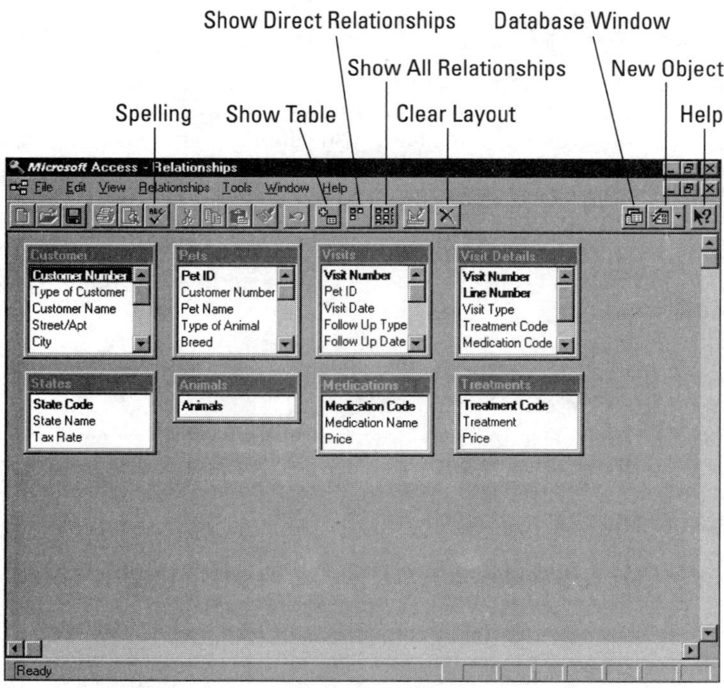

Figure 12-4: The Relationships window with all eight tables added.

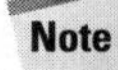

Note If you select a table by mistake, you can remove it from the window by clicking in it and pressing the Delete key.

Tip You can resize each table window to see all the fields, as shown in Figure 12-5.

Creating a link between tables

With the tables in the Relationships window, you are ready to create links between the tables. To create a link between two tables, simply select the common field in one table and drag it over to the field in the table you want to link to, then drop it on the common field.

Follow these steps to create a link between the tables:

1. Click on the Customer Number field of the Customer table.

Note If you select a field for linking in error, simply move the field icon to the window surface and it turns into the international No symbol. While it is displayed as this symbol, release the mouse button and the field linking will stop.

Drag the Customer Number field from Customer and drop it onto the Customer Number field in Pets.

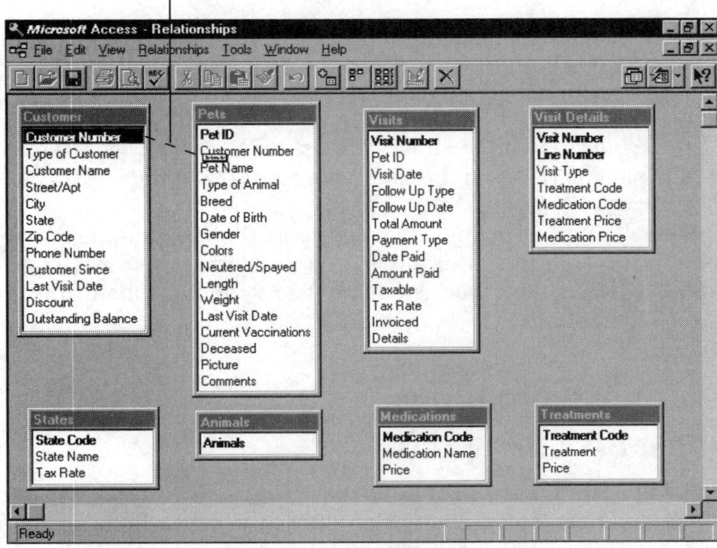

Figure 12-5: Creating relationships (links) between tables.

2. While holding down the mouse button, move the cursor to the Pets table. Notice that Access displays a field select icon.

3. Drag the field select icon to the Customer Number field of the Pets table. Access activates the Relationships dialog box (see Figure 12-6).

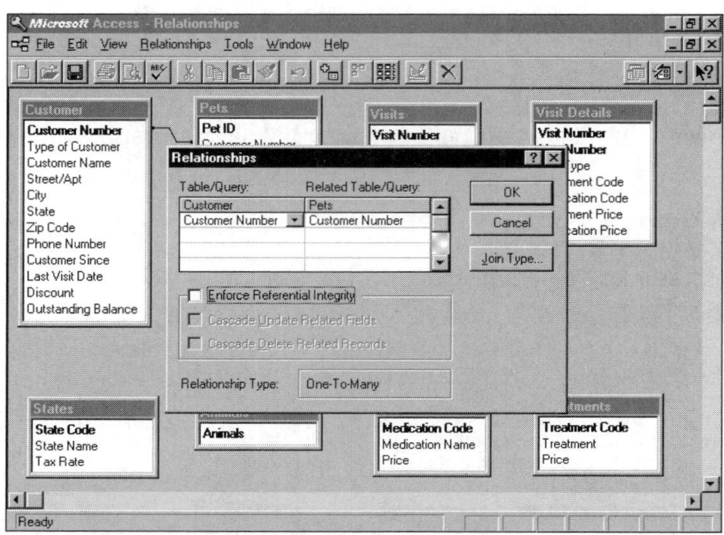

Figure 12-6: The Relationships dialog box.

4. Click on the Create button to create the relationship. Access closes the dialog box and places a join line between the Customer and Pets table.

Note 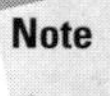

You can reactivate the relationship dialog box for any *join* (link) by double-clicking on the *join line* between the two tables. For example, double-clicking on the join line between the Customer and Pets table will reactivate the relationship dialog box for that link.

Specifying relationship options in the Relationships dialog box

The Relationships dialog box has several options you can specify for your relationship between the Customer and Pets tables. Figure 12-6 shows the dialog box and all the options. The dialog box tells you which table is the Primary table for the link, and whether referential integrity is enforced. The dialog box also tells you the type of relationship (one-to-one or one-to-many) and lets you specify whether you want to allow *cascading* updates and deletes (automatic key changes or deletions in related records) between linked tables when referential integrity is selected.

Disk

For the following sections, you will want to activate the Relationships dialog box for the link between the Customer and Pets tables. To do so, double-click on the join line between the tables.

Specifying the primary table

The top of the dialog box has two table names — Customer on the left and Pets on the right. The Customer table is considered the primary table for this relationship. The dialog box shows the link fields for each table immediately below the table names. Make sure that the correct table name is in both boxes (Customer and Pets) and that the correct link field is specified.

Warning

If you link two tables in the wrong order, simply click on the Cancel button in the dialog box. Access will close the dialog box and erase the join line. Then you can begin again.

Note

If you link two tables by the wrong field, simply select the correct field for each table by using the combo box under each table name.

Enforcing referential integrity

After you specify the link and verify the table and link fields, you can set referential integrity between the tables by clicking on the Enforce Referential Integrity check box below the table information. If you choose not to enforce referential integrity, you can add new records, change key fields, or even delete related records without worrying about referential integrity. You can create tables that are orphans or parents without children. With normal operations (such as data entry or changing information), referential integrity rules should be in force. By setting this option, you can specify several additional options.

Simply click on the check box in front of the option Enforce Referential Integrity. After you do so, Access activates the Cascading choices in the dialog box.

You might find, when you specify Enforce Referential Integrity and click on the Create button (or the OK button if you've re-opened the Relationship Window to create a relationship between tables), that Access will not allow you to. The reason is that you are asking Access to create a relationship supporting referential integrity between two tables that have records that *violate* referential integrity (the child table has orphans in it). In such a case, Access warns you by displaying a dialog box like the one shown in Figure 12-7. The warning happens in this example because there is a Pet record in the database with no Customer record. (There is also a Customer record with no Pet record. You will learn about these instances later in the book.)

Access returns you to the Relationships window after you click on the OK button, and you will need to re-create the relationship. If you are editing an existing join, Access also returns you to the Relationships window by removing the referential integrity option.

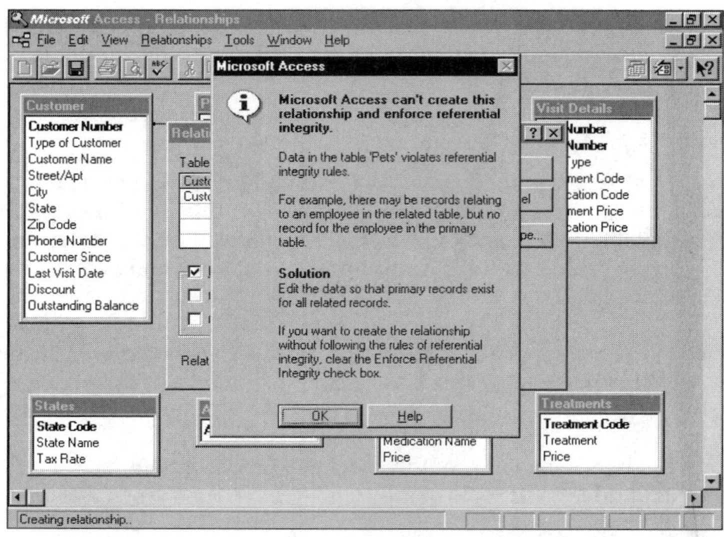

Figure 12-7: A dialog box warning that referential integrity cannot be set between two existing tables.

Note To solve any conflicts between existing tables, you can create a *Find Unmatched Query*, using the Query Wizards to find the records in the *many*-side table that violate referential integrity. Then you can convert the unmatched query to a *delete query* to delete the offending records. You will learn how to do this in Chapter 14.

With the offending records gone, you can go back in and set up referential integrity between the two tables.

Choosing the Cascade Update Related Fields option

If you specify Enforce Referential Integrity in the relationship dialog box, Access lets you select a check box option labeled `Cascade Update Related Fields`. This option tells Access that a user can change the contents of a link field (the primary key field in the primary table — Customer Number, for example).

If the user changes the contents of the primary key field in the primary table, Access will verify that the change is a new number (there cannot be duplicate records in the primary table) and then go through the related records in the other table and change the link field value from the old value to the new one. Suppose you code your customers by the first two letters of their last names, and one of your customers gets married and changes the name that Access knows to look for. You could change the Customer Number and all changes would ripple through other related records in the system.

If this option is not checked, you cannot change the primary key field in the primary table that is used in a link with another table.

Note

If the primary key field in the primary table is a link field between several tables, this option must be checked for all related tables or it will not work.

Choosing the Cascade Delete Related Records option

If you specify Enforce Referential Integrity in the Relationships dialog box, Access activates the `Cascade Delete Related Records` check box. If you select this option, you are telling Access that if a user attempts to delete a record in a primary table that has child records, first it should delete all the related child records and then delete the primary record. This can be a very useful option for deleting a series of related records. For example, if you have chosen Cascade Delete Related Records and you try to delete a particular customer (who moved away from the area) by deleting the Customer record, Access goes out to the related tables — Pets, Visits, and Visit Details — and also deletes all related records for the customer. Access deletes all the records in the Visits Details for each visit for each pet owned by the customer, the visit records, the associated pet records, and the customer record, with one step.

If you do not specify this option, Access will not allow you to delete a record that has related records in another table. In cases like this, you must delete all related records in the Visit Details table first, then related records in the Visits table, then related records in the Pets table, and finally the customer record in the Customer table.

Note

To use this option, you *must* specify Cascade Delete Related Records for *all* the table's relationships in the database. If you do not specify this option for all the tables down the chain of related tables, Access will not allow cascade deleting.

Warning

Use this option with caution! Access does not warn you that it is going to do a cascade delete when you press the Delete key. The program simply does it. Later you may wonder where all your records went. It is generally better to delete records programatically, using macros or Visual Basic for Applications (formerly known as Access Basic).

Saving the relationships between tables

The easiest way to save the relationships you created between the tables is to click on the Save button on the toolbar and then close the window. Another method is to close the window and answer Yes to the Save Relationships dialog box that appears.

Adding another relationship

After you specify all the tables, the fields, and their referential integrity status, you can add additional tables to the Relationships window by clicking on the Relationships button on the toolbar and adding new tables.

Again, if data that violates referential integrity exists in the tables being linked, you must fix the offending table by removing the records before you can set referential integrity between the tables.

Deleting an existing relationship

To delete an existing relationship, simply go into the Relationships window, click on the join line you want to delete, press the Delete key, and answer Yes to the question `Are you sure you want to delete the selected relationship?`.

Join lines in the Relationships window

When you create a relationship between two tables, Access automatically creates a thin join line from one table to another. Figure 12-8 shows the join line between States and Customer.

If you specify that you want to enforce referential integrity, however, Access changes the appearance of the join line. It becomes thicker at each end (alongside the table). It also has either a 1 or the infinity symbol (∞) over the thick bar of the line (on each side of the join line).

Tip: After referential integrity is specified, Access will add the thick lines to the join in any queries that use the tables. This gives you a visual way to know that referential integrity is active between the tables.

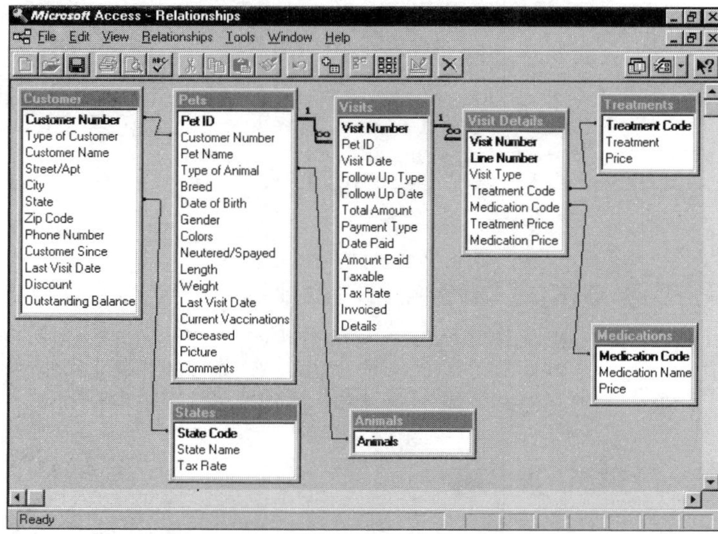

Figure 12-8: The relationships in the Mountain Animal Hospital system.

Creating the relationships for the Mountain Animal Hospital system

Table 12-3 shows how the relationships should be set between all the tables in the system. Notice that referential integrity is set between three of the four primary tables. In addition to having referential integrity, each of the four main tables has the Cascade Delete Related Records option checked.

Table 12-3
Relationships in the Mountain Animal Hospital System

Primary Table / Field	*Related Table / Field*	*Referential Integrity*	*Cascade Delete*
Customer Customer Number	Pets Customer Number	No*	No*
Pets Pet ID	Visits Pet ID	Yes	Yes
Visits Visit Number	Visit Details Visit Number	Yes	Yes
State State Code	Customer State	No	No
Animals Animals	Pets Type of Animal	No	No
Medications Medication Code	Visit Details Medication Code	No	No
Treatments Treatment Code	Visit Details Treatment Code	No	No

*These will be changed in Chapter 14 after you delete orphan records.

Using the Access Table Analyzer

Everything you have read in this chapter assumes that you have already designed your tables and have normalized relationships in the entire database. With many new systems, however (and especially with new developers), this is not the case. Sometimes you might start by importing an Excel spreadsheet file into Access, or by importing a large mainframe file (commonly known as *flat files* because all the data is contained in a single file). When imported into Access, a flat file becomes one single table.

Access for Windows 95 contains a new tool called the Table Analyzer which will analyze a single table and determine whether it is fully normalized. This tool will then make suggestions for splitting up the data into related tables. It will create both primary and foreign keys, search for misspellings of commonly used data, and suggest corrections. If (for example) you have a flat file that contains both sales items and customers in the same table, you might have the customer information (name, address, etc.) repeated over and over. Where the customer name `Animals R Us` is found many times, it might be listed as `Animals R Us Inc.` or `Animals R Us Company` or `Animals are Us` or even misspelled as `Aminals R Us`. The Table Analyzer will not only split your data into two or more tables, but will also suggest corrections to the data.

Disk

To test this tool, you will find an extra table on your Mountain Animal Hospital database named Pets and Customers. This was created by combining several data fields from the Pets and Customers tables into one flat-file table. The customer data is repeated over and over; mistakes were made purposely in the spelling of several customer names. You can use this table to learn how the Table Analyzer tool works.

Starting the Table Analyzer

You can start this tool by selecting Tools➪Analyze➪Table from any design screen. This starts the Table Analyzer Wizard, as shown in Figure 12-9.

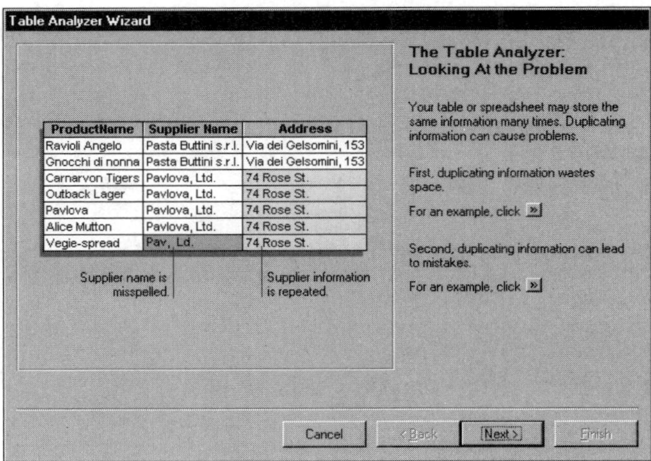

Figure 12-9: Looking At the Problem (the Table Analyzer's first introductory screen).

This first screen shown in Figure 12-9 is actually one of two introductory screens. It has no function other than a help screen. This first screen introduces you to the concepts performed by the Table Analyzer. You can even click on the arrows in the right center of the screen to get a further explanation of why you should not duplicate information in a table.

Once you finish looking at that screen for the first time, you can click on the Next > button to move to the next screen. This screen tells you how the Table Analyzer will solve the potential problems you have in your table. The first screen's title is `Looking At the Problem`; the second screen's title is `Solving the Problem`. Figure 12-10 also shows you some arrows to click on to get even more detailed explanations about data normalization.

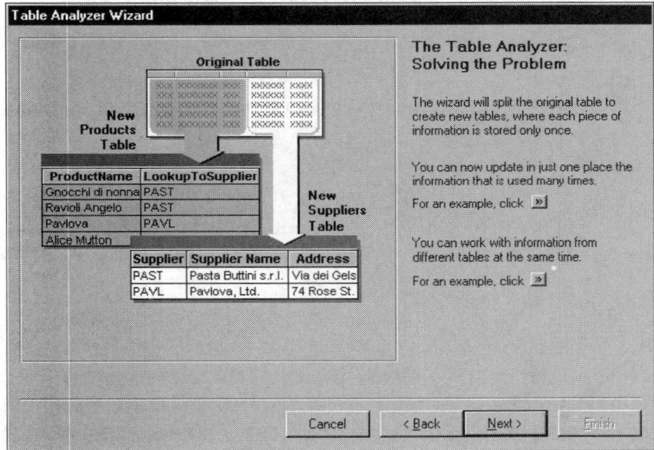

Figure 12-10: Solving the Problem (the Table Analyzer's second introductory screen).

Selecting the table to analyze

After you view the introductory screens, the Table Analyzer displays another screen to let you select the table you want to analyze. If you are following along in this example, select Pets and Customers from the list of tables as shown in Figure 12-11.

Note Only tables can be analyzed, not queries.

Tip You don't have to look at the introductory screens each time you run the Table Analyzer. As you can see in Figure 12-11, there is a check box to eliminate the introductory screens the next time you run the Table Analyzer.

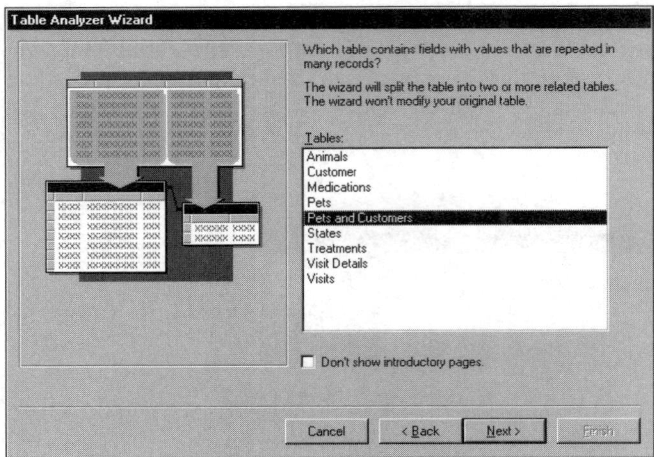

Figure 12-11: Selecting the table to be analyzed.

Analyzing the Table

Once you select the table, (and decide if you want to check the box to not show the introductory screens again) you can click on the Next > button to move on. The next screen simply asks whether you want Access to analyze the tables and make decisions for you, or whether you want to make your own decisions. If you prefer to make your own choices, Access takes you to the Table Analyzer in a special version of the Relationships window. There you can drag and drop fields to create a new table, or drag fields from a related table back into a parent table to undo a relationship. You will learn about this screen next.

When you select Yes, Let the Wizard Decide, the Table Analyzer performs a multi-step analysis of your data, displaying several progress meters on-screen. When the process is completed, the next Wizard screen appears automatically. It shows the proposed structure of the tables, their relationships, and the primary and foreign keys (as shown in Figure 12-12).

As you can see in Figure 12-12, the Table Analyzer has done a great job splitting the flat file into three tables. The first table (named Table1) contains data about the Pet. The second table (named Table2) contains customer information, as well as a primary key for each customer. Table1 also contains a foreign key (currently named Lookup to Table2) which is related to the Primary key.

Analyzing a Flat-File Table

The following figure shows the first data screen of the Pets and Customers table. This data was created by combining the data from the Pets and Customers tables and eliminating the primary and foreign keys and many of the unimportant fields. From the Pets table, you can see the fields Pet Name, Type of Animal, and Breed. From the Customers table, you can see the fields Customer Name, Street/Apt, and City. Out of sight are the State, Zip Code, and Phone Number fields.

If you were to analyze the data, you would see repeating groups. The Customer information is repeated for many records. The Table Analyzer should be able to recognize this repetition and create a separate table for customers. It can do so because all the information is the same for multiple records. Pet information is different for every record (virtually no Pets have the same name). Though there are many Pets of the same type, almost no animals of the same Type have the same breed or name. The Table Analyzer can recognize this piece of data as not being part of a repeating group. When the Table Analyzer looks at the Customer Name, Street/Apt, City, Zip Code, and Phone Number fields, it will find many records with exactly the same data. The seven records for Animal Kingdom, for example, all have the same customer data; Borderville Aquarium has five identical data values in the customer fields.

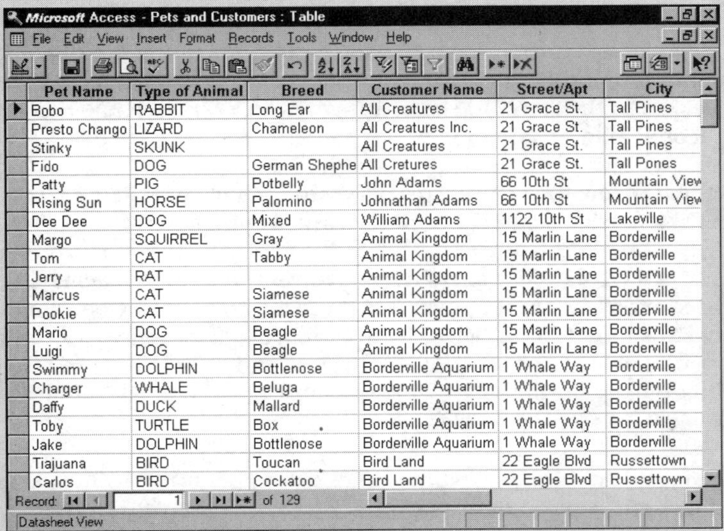

Microsoft Access - Pets and Customers : Table

Pet Name	Type of Animal	Breed	Customer Name	Street/Apt	City
Bobo	RABBIT	Long Ear	All Creatures	21 Grace St.	Tall Pines
Presto Chango	LIZARD	Chameleon	All Creatures Inc.	21 Grace St.	Tall Pines
Stinky	SKUNK		All Creatures	21 Grace St.	Tall Pines
Fido	DOG	German Shephe	All Cretures	21 Grace St.	Tall Pones
Patty	PIG	Potbelly	John Adams	66 10th St	Mountain View
Rising Sun	HORSE	Palomino	Johnathan Adams	66 10th St	Mountain View
Dee Dee	DOG	Mixed	William Adams	1122 10th St	Lakeville
Margo	SQUIRREL	Gray	Animal Kingdom	15 Marlin Lane	Borderville
Tom	CAT	Tabby	Animal Kingdom	15 Marlin Lane	Borderville
Jerry	RAT		Animal Kingdom	15 Marlin Lane	Borderville
Marcus	CAT	Siamese	Animal Kingdom	15 Marlin Lane	Borderville
Pookie	CAT	Siamese	Animal Kingdom	15 Marlin Lane	Borderville
Mario	DOG	Beagle	Animal Kingdom	15 Marlin Lane	Borderville
Luigi	DOG	Beagle	Animal Kingdom	15 Marlin Lane	Borderville
Swimmy	DOLPHIN	Bottlenose	Borderville Aquarium	1 Whale Way	Borderville
Charger	WHALE	Beluga	Borderville Aquarium	1 Whale Way	Borderville
Daffy	DUCK	Mallard	Borderville Aquarium	1 Whale Way	Borderville
Toby	TURTLE	Box	Borderville Aquarium	1 Whale Way	Borderville
Jake	DOLPHIN	Bottlenose	Borderville Aquarium	1 Whale Way	Borderville
Tiajuana	BIRD	Toucan	Bird Land	22 Eagle Blvd	Russettown
Carlos	BIRD	Cockatoo	Bird Land	22 Eagle Blvd	Russettown

Record: 1 of 129

Datasheet View

However, look at the first four data records: The customer name All Creatures has been purposely altered as an example. The first record's Customer Name value is simply `All Creatures`. The second is `All Creatures Inc.` where the fourth record's value is misspelled `All Cretures`. The fourth records city is also misspelled `Tall Pones` instead of the correct Tall Pines. The Access Table Analyzer can ignore such data anomalies as it does its job. Also, the Table Analyzer will usually find some of these misspellings.

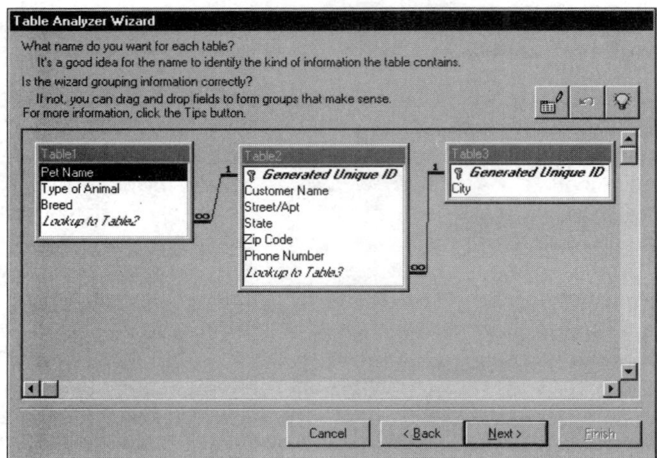

Figure 12-12: The Table Analyzer's Relationships window.

Changing the table and field definitions

You can rename the tables by selecting each table and either clicking on the Rename Table icon button (located in the upper right corner of the Wizard screen) or by double-clicking on the table title bar. Normally you would rename the first table **Pets** and the second table **Customers**.

Tip You can only rename the new key primary and foreign fields in the tables by using the standard Table Design screen after the Wizard is complete.

Although Pets data and Customers data have been well split, placing City by itself is not a great strategy. There are several better ways to do this. One would be simply not to have this third table at all, or have a table of states instead of a table of cities. Another approach would be to move both state and ZIP to the third table, and then use the Zip Code as a primary key of a new City State Zip table, adding Zip Code as a foreign-key lookup in the second table.

You can move a field from one table to another simply by dragging it from one table to another. Likewise, you can drag a field back from one table to another. You can also create a new table by dragging a field from one table to an empty area of the screen. This creates a new table, a primary key for the new table, and a new foreign key in the original table you dragged the field from. You can eliminate a table by dragging all the fields from one table back to other tables. You can also change the order of the fields by selecting one and dragging it above or below other fields in the table.

For this example, you can drag the State and Zip Code fields from Table2 to Table3. You can also rename Table1 to **Pets New**, Table2 to **Customers New**, and Table3 to **Zip Codes**. You can see these changes in Figure 12-13 in the next Wizard screen. Also notice that the foreign-key lookup-field names have changed.

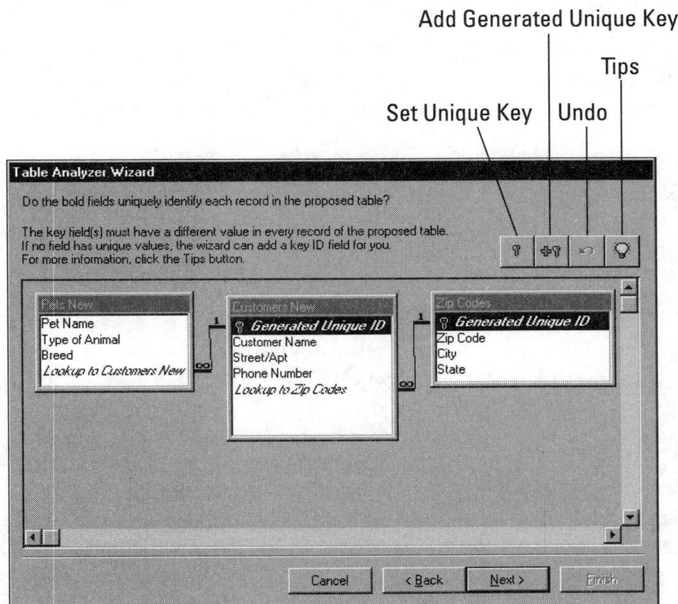

Figure 12-13: The Table Analyzer's Relationships window after changes.

Changing the key fields

Once you complete this Wizard screen, you can click on the Next > button to move to the next Wizard screen. This screen lets you change the key fields that the Table Analyzer has created. Figure 12-13 shows these key fields. The Pets table has no key field at all. You certainly can't use the Pet Name field; many pets can be named Rover or Spot. You will want to create a new key field for this table.

Create a new key field for the New Pets table by clicking on the New Pets table's title bar and then pressing the Add Generated Unique Key icon (the second icon in the group of 4). Access creates a new primary key field.

The Zip Codes table does not need a unique key field; the Zip Code field itself can be used as the unique field (assuming that each ZIP code corresponds to only one city-and-state combination). You can change the Zip Codes table's primary key to the Zip Code field by selecting the Zip Code field and then clicking on the Set Unique Key icon. The Zip Code field becomes the primary key; the original primary key (named Generated Unique ID) disappears.

When you have completed setting all of the primary key fields, you can click on the Next > button to begin a search for aberrant data. Misspellings and inconsistencies in like data are the most common types of problem data the Table Analyzer can find.

When performing the analysis, the Table Analyzer will also check your final field choices for fields that belong together. If the Table Analyzer finds data that doesn't appear to fit the rest of the table's data, you will get a warning message. You can go back and make further changes if you need to.

Searching for typos and duplicate key data

The Table Analyzer will display a series of screens allowing you to correct what it believes are typographical errors. Then it gives you the opportunity to correct the data.

You may see screens that make no sense; the Table Analyzer may make a wrong assumption about what to analyze; it might (for example) do some analysis on duplicate key data. These screens will depend totally on the analysis of your data. In this example, the Table Analyzer misses all the misspelled Cities and Companies as it keys in on the similar phone numbers.

Figure 12-14 shows a typical screen that allows you to make changes to your data. When you click into the Correction column, a list of suggested changes appears. It may not contain the actual value you want. If this is the case, either leave it blank or select Leave As Is.

Completing the Table Analyzer

Once you enter all the corrections you can into the screens for typos or primary-key duplicates, you see the last Table Analyzer screen. This one lets you complete the process. When you're through, Access will display a tiled view of all the new tables; you can see all the data in the new table designs.

Warning One problem the Table Analyzer can cause is to render existing queries, forms, reports, and macros inoperable because all these objects are tied to specific table and field names. When you change the table name or field names within a table, Access will report an error when you try to run the form, report, or macro; they cannot automatically adjust. A solution is to create a new query (with the same name as the original table) that uses the new tables and creates a view identical to the original table.

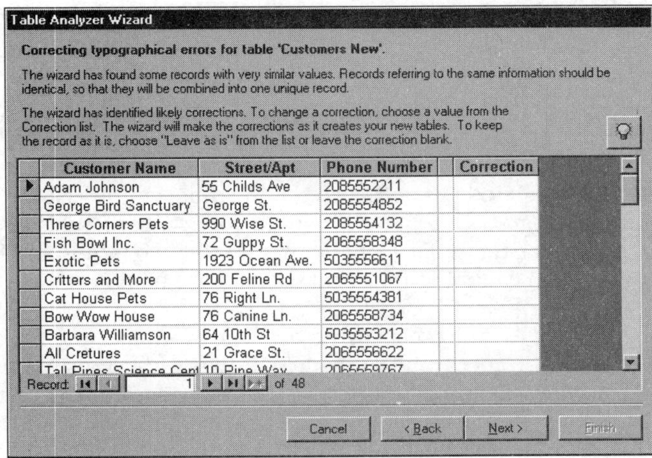

Figure 12-14: Changing typos in the Table Analyzer.

As you can see in Figure 12-15, the Table Analyzer can create a query using the original name of your table, renaming the original table. This way you can continue to use your system, but still take advantage of the relational table structure.

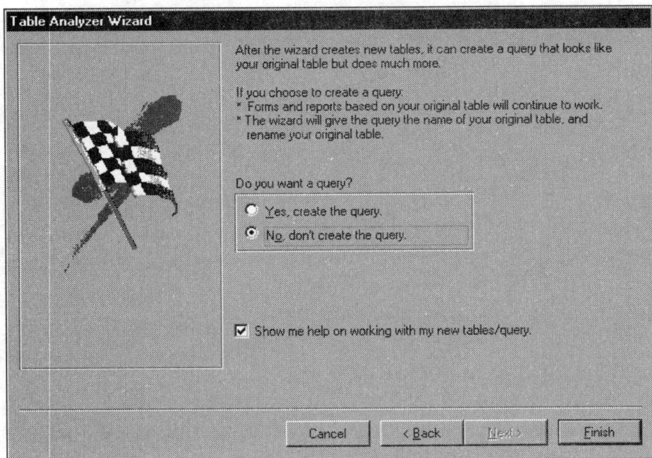

Figure 12-15: Completing the Table Analyzer process.

When you're done, click on the Finish button; the Table Wizard disappears, leaving a tiled view of all the new tables. You can open each table in design view and rename any Foreign Key field names if you want. You may also want to correct data that the Table Analyzer missed, or correct the duplicate keys.

Though the Table Wizard is not perfect, it is an outstanding way to normalize a data table with little effort.

Using the Lookup Wizard in the Table Designer

When you view one table that is related to another, often the table contains a foreign key — generally the primary key of another table. Often the foreign key field is cryptic when you look at it through the related table. Until you relate the two tables and look at the data from a query view, you cannot tell the real value of the field.

For example, Figure 12-16 shows the Pets table sorted by Type of Animal and Breed. Notice the cryptic value in the Customer Number field. In previous versions of Access, the only way to see the Customer Name was to create a query and look at the resulting dynaset. In Access for Windows 95, there is a new way to display the Customer Name in a table that only contains a foreign key lookup to the Customer table.

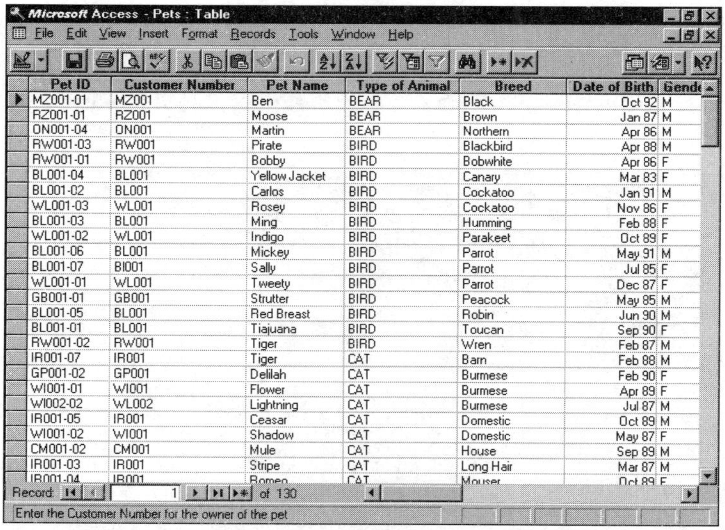

Microsoft Access - Pets : Table

File Edit View Insert Format Records Tools Window Help

Pet ID	Customer Number	Pet Name	Type of Animal	Breed	Date of Birth	Gende
MZ001-01	MZ001	Ben	BEAR	Black	Oct 92	M
RZ001-01	RZ001	Moose	BEAR	Brown	Jan 87	M
ON001-04	ON001	Martin	BEAR	Northern	Apr 86	M
RW001-03	RW001	Pirate	BIRD	Blackbird	Apr 88	M
RW001-01	RW001	Bobby	BIRD	Bobwhite	Apr 86	F
BL001-04	BL001	Yellow Jacket	BIRD	Canary	Mar 83	F
BL001-02	BL001	Carlos	BIRD	Cockatoo	Jan 91	M
WL001-03	WL001	Rosey	BIRD	Cockatoo	Nov 86	F
BL001-03	BL001	Ming	BIRD	Humming	Feb 88	F
WL001-02	WL001	Indigo	BIRD	Parakeet	Oct 89	F
BL001-06	BL001	Mickey	BIRD	Parrot	May 91	M
BL001-07	BI001	Sally	BIRD	Parrot	Jul 85	F
WL001-01	WL001	Tweety	BIRD	Parrot	Dec 87	F
GB001-01	GB001	Strutter	BIRD	Peacock	May 85	M
BL001-05	BL001	Red Breast	BIRD	Robin	Jun 90	M
BL001-01	BL001	Tiajuana	BIRD	Toucan	Sep 90	F
RW001-02	RW001	Tiger	BIRD	Wren	Feb 87	M
IR001-07	IR001	Tiger	CAT	Barn	Feb 88	M
GP001-02	GP001	Delilah	CAT	Burmese	Feb 90	F
WI001-01	WI001	Flower	CAT	Burmese	Apr 89	F
WI002-02	WL002	Lightning	CAT	Burmese	Jul 87	M
IR001-05	IR001	Ceasar	CAT	Domestic	Oct 89	M
WI001-02	WI001	Shadow	CAT	Domestic	May 87	F
CM001-02	CM001	Mule	CAT	House	Sep 89	M
IR001-03	IR001	Stripe	CAT	Long Hair	Mar 87	M
IR001-04	IR001	Romeo	CAT	Mouser	Oct 89	F

Record: 1 of 130

Enter the Customer Number for the owner of the pet

Figure 12-16: A confusing foreign-key value.

You can change the display of this field by redefining the properties of the Customer Number field in the Pets table. To start this process, switch to design view and select the data type of the Customer Number field. Display the data type list. Notice the last item in the list is Lookup Wizard (as shown in Figure 12-17). This is actually not a data type, of course, but rather a way of changing the Lookup properties. Notice that there is only a single property listed in the Lookup properties section. The Lookup Wizard will change this property automatically.

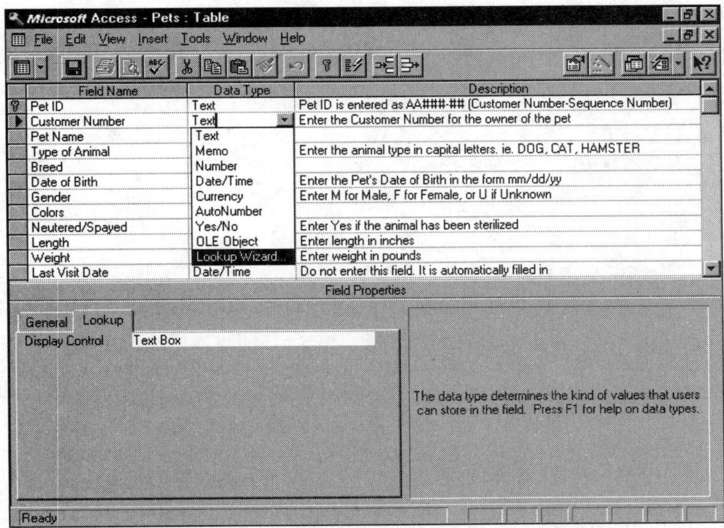

Figure 12-17: Creating a lookup field in a table.

Though you haven't learned about *combo boxes* yet (see Chapters 16 and 19), you have used them. The Data Type list is a combo box. The Lookup Wizard will create the necessary properties for a list box automatically, without requiring you to understand them. Later you will learn how to change them without the Wizard.

In the Customer Number field, select the data type as shown in Figure 12-17, and then select Lookup Wizard. This starts the process to create a lookup to another table instead of displaying the field value itself.

Figure 12-18 shows the first Lookup Wizard screen. There are two choices. The first choice lets you use data from another related table as the displayed value in the field. In this example, you will display the Customer Name from the Customer table in the Customer Number field in the Pets table. Select the first choice, and then click on the Next > button.

The second option lets you type in a list of values. Use this option only when you enter a code such as the Type of Customer field in the Customer table. Later you will learn how to change the Lookup properties of that field to display `Individual` if the code entered is 1, `Pet Store` if the code entered is 2, and `Zoo` if the code entered is 3.

Note Creating a lookup will not change the stored value in the Pets table for the Customer Number field. Only the display of the value is changed.

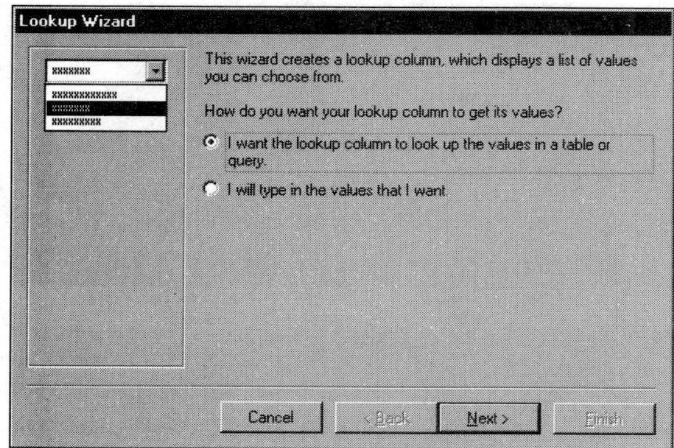

Figure 12-18: Selecting the type of lookup.

The next screen asks `Which table or query contains the fields for the lookup?` and then lets you choose the table to use for the lookup. This is the standard table-selection Wizard screen used in most Wizards. Select the Customer table and click on the Next > button.

The next Wizard screen displays a list of all of the fields in the Customer table, and lets you select the fields you want to use in the lookup. This is also a standard field-selection screen. The method here is to select all the fields in the lookup table that will be used in the display, as well as the field that will hold the actual value. Though you can display more than one field in the table, generally you will display only one field. The second field is stored out of sight and used for the actual value that belongs to the table.

You need to select both the field in the Customer table that will be displayed and the field that matches the foreign key field (Customer Number) in the Pets table. In the Customer table, this Customer Number is the primary key. Select the Customer Name field first, and then the Customer Number field. Remember to click on the > button after you select each field (which copies it from the Available Fields list to the Selected Fields list). After you do this and click on the Next > button, the display and size screen appears (as shown in Figure 12-19).

A list of the data is displayed from the Customer table. In this example, you want to see only the Customer Name field, so you will hide the Customer Number field by changing its display width to 0. You can do this by dragging the field separator on the right of the Customer Number field to meet the Customer Name field. This is the same technique used in a datasheet to hide a field.

After you do this, you should only see the Customer Name field as a single column in the display in the Wizard screen. Click on the Next > button to move to the next Wizard screen.

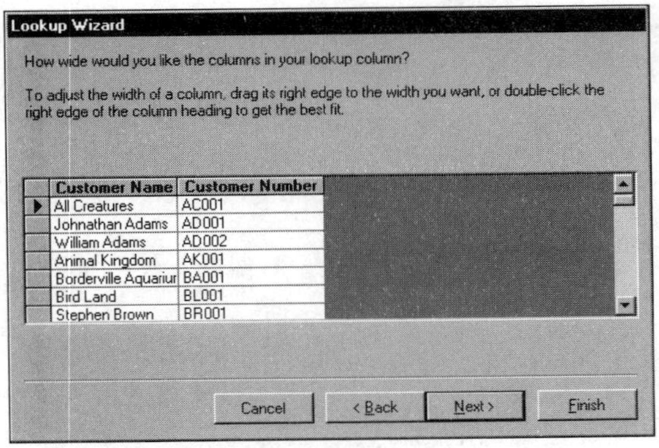

Lookup Wizard

How wide would you like the columns in your lookup column?

To adjust the width of a column, drag its right edge to the width you want, or double-click the right edge of the column heading to get the best fit.

Customer Name	Customer Number
All Creatures	AC001
Johnathan Adams	AD001
William Adams	AD002
Animal Kingdom	AK001
Borderville Aquariur	BA001
Bird Land	BL001
Stephen Brown	BR001

Cancel < Back Next > Finish

Figure 12-19: Sizing the fields.

The next screen asks you which field you want to use to store the actual value in the table. This will be the Customer Number field; select it and click on the Next > button.

The final screen names the column in your table. The default name is the original name of the column. Accept the default name of Customer Number, and then click on the Finish button to complete the Wizard. The choices you made will be used to fill in the properties sheet of the Customer Number field in the Pets table.

Figure 12-20 shows the settings in the Pets table design screen, Notice that the Lookup properties area has changed significantly. The first property tells you that the field will now appear as a combo box whenever displayed in a table, or as a default when placed on a form. Notice, however, that the data type for the Customer Number field is still Text. Even though you chose the Lookup Wizard from the Data Type list, it still creates a Text data type. The Lookup Wizard merely changes the Lookup properties.

The next two Lookup properties define the type of data for the record. In this case, the source of the data in the record is a table or query. Other choices are Value List (you type them into the Row Source property, separated by semicolons) and Field List (a list of fields in a table).

The Row Source displays a statement in SQL (Standard Query Language), an internal language that Access translates all queries into. You can see only a portion of the SQL statement in Figure 12-20. The entire statement is:

```
SELECT DISTINCTROW [Customer].[Customer Name],
       [Customer].[Customer Number] FROM [Customer];
```

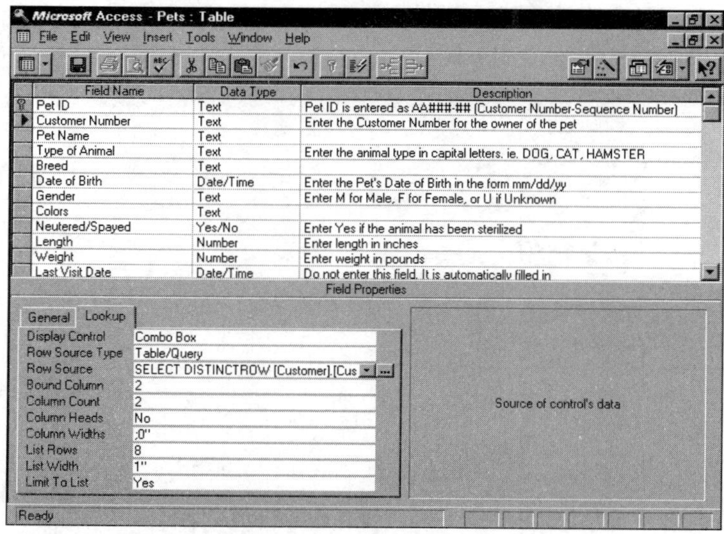

Figure 12-20: Understanding the Lookup properties.

This command simply tells Access to use the Customer Name and Customer Number fields from the Customer table. The next property, Bound Column, is set to 2. This tells Access to use the second column (Customer Number) as the actual value to store in the Customer Number column of the Pets table. The Column Count of 2 tells Access there are two columns in the SQL statement; the Column Heads setting (No) means that when the field list is displayed in the combo box, the name of the column is not displayed. This is only used when multiple columns are displayed.

The column width is set to ;0". This means the first column (Customer Name) is displayed in its default width while the second field's length (Customer Number) is set to 0 and therefore hidden. The List Rows property tells Access to display (in this example) eight rows in the datasheet for the Customer Number field when the combo box is open. Finally, the List Width property determines the width of the open combo box, while the Limit to List property means you can't type a value into the Pets table's Customer Number field if it doesn't already exist in the Customer Number field of the Customers table.

When you display the Pets table in a datasheet view (as shown in Figure 12-21), you now see Customer Name instead of Customer Number in the Customer Number field. Using this method, you can display and limit the selection of any coded field in a table. You can even use fields found in only one table, like the Gender field in the Pets table. Rather than display an M, F, or U, you can select from Male, Female, or Unknown, and still store the correct code in the field.

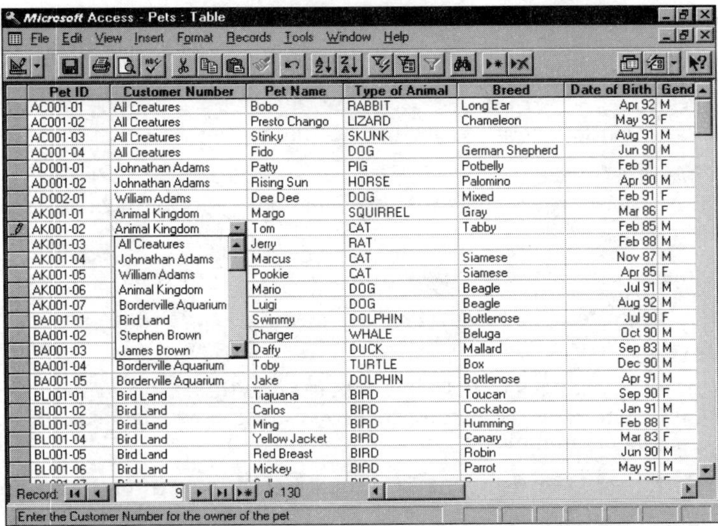

Figure 12-21: Displaying a lookup field in a datasheet.

Summary

Using multiple tables adds far more complexity to a system than working with a single table. Throughout the rest of this book, you learn how to use multiple tables to create more advanced types of forms, reports, and queries. A relational database management system can get quite complicated. By paying attention to details and applying the concepts you learned in this chapter, you should be able to create a system of unlimited complexity with Access. This chapter covered the following points:

- ✦ Eight tables make up the Mountain Animal Hospital example. The four main tables are Customer, Pets, Visits, and Visit Details; the four lookup tables are States, Animals, Treatments, and Medications.
- ✦ A primary key designates one or more fields that make a record unique. This uniqueness is called the entity integrity of a record.
- ✦ A primary key is an index that greatly speeds up searches and query requests.
- ✦ You create primary keys in the Table Design window by clicking on the Primary Key icon after selecting the primary key field.
- ✦ A multiple-field primary key is used when one field is not sufficient to guarantee uniqueness.

- A foreign key is a field that contains a value matching another table's primary key.
- A primary key field and a foreign key field are linked to form a relation.
- The four types of relationships are one-to-one, one-to-many, many-to-one, and many-to-many.
- Referential integrity is a set of rules that prevents data entry if it will result in an invalid relationship.
- When data violates referential integrity, you see an error message.
- In a multiple-table system, you cannot simply delete records without regard to referential integrity.
- Whenever you make changes to key-field data in a multiple-table system, potentially you violate referential integrity. You must follow special steps to change or delete key-field data.
- You create relationships by using the Relationships window from the Database window's Tools menu.
- Using the new Access for Windows 95 Table Analyzer, you can normalize a flat-file table into several related tables automatically.
- Using the new Access for Windows 95 Lookup Wizard, you can place the lookup field properties in a table.

In the next chapter, you learn to use operators, functions, and expressions that are used throughout Access in forms, reports, and queries.

✦ ✦ ✦

Using Access in Your Work

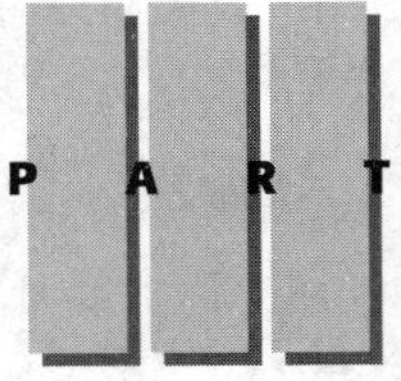

✦ ✦ ✦ ✦

In This Part

✦ ✦ ✦ ✦

CHAPTER

Using Operators, Functions, and Expressions

✦ ✦ ✦ ✦

In This Chapter

What operators, functions, and expressions are, and how they are used

Types of operators

Types of functions

How to create an expression

Special identifier operators and expressions

✦ ✦ ✦ ✦

Operators, functions, and expressions are the fundamental building blocks for Access operations. These operations include entering criteria in queries, creating calculated fields in forms, and creating summary controls in reports.

Operators

Operators let you add numbers, compare values, put text strings together, and create complicated relational expressions. You use operators to inform Access that a specific operation is to be performed against one or more items. Access also uses several special operators for identifying an object.

Types of operators

Following are the types of operators that you learn about in this chapter:

- Mathematical (arithmetic) operators
- Relational operators
- String operators
- Boolean (logical) operators
- Miscellaneous operators

When are operators used?

You use operators all the time. In fact, you use them every time you create an equation. In Access, you use operators to specify data validation rules for table properties, to create calculated fields in forms, or to specify criteria in queries.

Operators indicate that an operation needs to be performed on one or more items. Following are some common examples of operators:

=

&

And

Like

+

Mathematical operators

There are seven basic *mathematical operators*. These are also known as *arithmetic operators* because they are usually used for performing arithmetic calculations:

*	Multiply
+	Add
–	Subtract
/	Divide
\	Integer Divide
^	Exponentiation
Mod	Modulo

By definition, mathematical operators work with numbers. When you work with mathematical operators, numbers can be any numeric data type. The number can be the actual number or one that is represented by a memory variable or a field's contents. Further, the numbers can be used individually or combined to create complex expressions. Some of the examples in this section are quite complex, but don't worry if you don't usually work with sophisticated mathematics.

The * (multiplication) operator

A simple example of when you use the *multiplication operator* is on an invoice entry form. A clerk enters the number of items and the per-item price; a calculated field calculates and displays the total price for that number of items. In this case, the text box contains the formula `[Price] * [Quantity]`. Notice that the field names are enclosed in brackets, which is standard notation for dealing with field names in an expression.

The + (addition) operator

If you want to create a calculated field in the same form, adding the values in fields such as Gross Amount and Tax, you enter the expression **[Gross Amount] + [Tax]**. This simple formula uses the addition operator to add the contents of both fields and place the result in the object that contains the formula.

Besides adding two numbers, the addition operator can be used for concatenating two character strings. For example, you may want to combine the fields First Name and Last Name to display them as a single field. This expression is as follows:

[First Name] + [Last Name]

Warning Although you can *concatenate* (put two strings together) text strings by using the addition operator, you should use the ampersand (&). The reason for this appears in the section "String Operators."

The – (subtraction) operator

An example of using the *subtraction operator* on a form is the calculation of an invoice amount; you might offer a discount to good repeat customers. To determine the Net Amount, you would have a formula that uses the subtraction operator, such as

```
[Gross Amount] - ([Gross Amount]*[Discount]).
```

Note Although parentheses are not mathematical operators, they play an integral part in working with operators, as discussed later in the section "Operator Precedence."

The / (division) operator

You can use the *division operator* to divide two numbers and (as with the previous operators) place the result wherever you need it. Suppose, for example, that a pool of 212 people win the $1,000,000 lottery this week. The formula to determine each individual's payoff is 1,000,000 / 212, resulting in $4,716.98 per person.

The \ (integer division) operator

Should you ever need to take two numbers, round them both to integers, divide the two rounded integers, and receive a nonrounded integer, this operator will do it for you in one step. Here is an example:

Normal Division	*Integer Conversion Division*
100 / 6 = 16.667	100 \ 6 = 16
100.9 / 6.6 = 15.277	100.9 \ 6.6 = 14

Tip Access has no specific function for rounding fractional numbers to whole numbers. You can use this operator to round any number. Simply take the number you want to round, and integer-divide (\) it by 1, as in 125.6 \ 1 = 126.

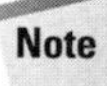

Access rounds numbers based on the greater-than-.5 rule; any number with a decimal value of *x*.5 or less will round down; greater than *x*.5 will round up to the next whole number. This means that 6.5 becomes 6 and 6.6 becomes 7.

The ^ (exponentiation) operator

The *exponentiation operator* (^) raises a number to the power of an exponent. Raising a number simply means indicating the number of times you want to multiply a number by itself. For example, to multiply the value 4 × 4 × 4 (that is, 4 cubed) is the same as entering the formula 4 ^ 3.

Relational operators

There are six basic *relational operators* (also known as *comparison operators*). They compare two values or expressions via an equation. The relational operators include the following:

=	Equal
<>	Not equal
<	Less than
<=	Less than *or* equal
>	Greater than
>=	Greater than *or* equal

What Are Integer Values?

Integers are whole numbers (numbers that contain no decimal places), which in Access are between −32768 and +32767. Examples are 1, 722, 33, −5460, 0, and 22. To determine the integer part of any number, simply drop any decimal values. For example, the integer of 45.123 is 45; for 2.987, the integer is 3; and so forth.

This can be a confusing operator until you understand just what it does. If you enter the following, it should become clear:

? 101 / 6 results in 16.833.

? 101.9 / 6.6 results in 15.439.

? 102 / 7 results in 14.571.

? INT(102 / 7) results in 14.

? 101.9 \ 6.6 results in 14.

The last entry is equivalent to rounding both numbers in the division operation (101.9 = 102 and 6.6 = 7) and then dividing 102 by 7, converting the answer to an integer. In other words, it is equivalent to

INT((101.9 \ 1) / (6.6 \ 1))

The operators always return either a logical value or Null; the value they return says Yes (True), No (not True, that is, False); or it is a Null (unknown/no value).

Note Access actually returns a numeric value for relational operator equations. It returns a –1 (negative 1) for True and a 0 (zero) for False.

If either side of an equation is a Null value, the resultant will always be a Null.

The = (equal) operator

The *equal operator* will return a logical True if the two expressions being compared are the same. Here are two examples of the equal operator in practice:

`[Type of Animal] = "Cat"` will be True if the animal is a cat; False is returned for any other animal.

`[Date of Birth] = Date()` will be True if the date in the Date of Birth field is today.

The <> (not-equal) operator

The *not-equal operator* is exactly the opposite of the equal operator. Here you see the cat example changed to not-equal:

`[Type of Animal] <> "Cat"` will be True if Type of Animal is *anything but* a cat.

The < (less-than) operator

The *less-than operator* returns a logical True if the left side of the equation is less than the right side, as in this example:

`[Weight] < 10` will be True if the Weight field contains a value of less than 10.

The <= (less-than-or-equal-to) operator

The less-than-or-equal-to operator will return a True if the left side of the equation is either less than or equal to the right side, as in this example:

`[Weight] <= 10` will be True if the value of Weight equals 10 or is less than 10.

Note Access is *not* sensitive to the order of the operators. Access accepts either of these forms as the same:

`(<=)` or `(=<)`

The > (greater-than) operator

The *greater-than* operator is the exact opposite of the less-than operator. This operator returns a True whenever the left side of the equation is greater than the right side. Here is an example:

`[Length (In)] > 22` will return True if the value of Length (In) is greater than 22.

The >= (greater-than-or-equal-to) operator

The *greater-than-or-equal-to* operator returns a True if the left side of the equation is either equal to or greater than the right side. Here is an example:

`[Weight (lbs)] >= 100` will return True if the field Weight (lbs) contains a value equal to or greater than 100.

Note Access is *not* sensitive to the order of the operator. Access lets you enter either the form (>=) or (=>).

String operators

Access has two *string operators*. Unlike the other operators you've worked with, these work specifically with the Text data type:

&	Concatenation
Like	Similar to …

The & (concatenation) operator

The *concatenation operator* connects or links (concatenates) two or more objects into a resultant string. This operator works similarly to the addition operator; unlike the addition operator, however, the & operator always forces a string concatenation, as in this example:

`[First Name] & [Last Name]` produces a single string.

However, in the resultant string, no spaces are automatically added. If `[First Name]` equals "Fred" and `[Last Name]` = "Smith," concatenating the field contents yields `FredSmith`. To add a space between the strings, you must concatenate a space string between the two fields. To concatenate a space string between first and last name fields, you enter a formula like

[First Name] & " " & [Last Name]

This operator can easily concatenate a string object with a number- or date-type object. Using the & eliminates the need for special functions to convert a number or date to a string.

Suppose, for example, that you have a Number field, which is House Number, and a Text field, which is Street Name, and that you want to build an expression for a report of both fields. For this, you can enter the following:

[House Number] & " " & [Street Name]

If `House Number` has a value of 1600 and `Street Name` is "Pennsylvania Avenue N.W.," the resultant concatenation of the number and string is

```
"1600 Pennsylvania Avenue N.W."
```

Perhaps you have a calculated field in a report that prints the operator's name and the date and time the report was run. You can accomplish this by using syntax similar to the following:

" This report was printed " & Now() & " by " & [*operator name*]

If the date is March 21, 1996, and the time is 4:45 p.m., this concatenated line will print something like this:

```
This report was printed 3/21/96 4:45:40 PM by Michael R. Irwin
```

Notice the spaces at the end or the beginning of the strings. Knowing how this operator works will make maintenance of your database expressions easier. If you always use the concatenation operator for creating concatenated text strings, you won't have to be concerned with what data type the concatenated objects are. Any formula that uses the & operator converts all the objects being concatenated to a string type for you.

Note Using the & with Nulls: If both objects are Null, the resultant will also be a Null. If only one of the two objects is Null, Access converts the object that is Null to a string type with a length of 0 and builds the concatenation.

The Like (similar to ...) operator

This Like operator compares two string objects by using wildcards. This operator determines whether one object *matches* the pattern of another object. The resultant of the comparison will be a True, False, or Null.

The Like operator uses the following basic syntax:

expression object* Like *pattern object

Like looks for the *expression object* in the *pattern object*; and if it is present, the operation returns a True.

Note

If either object in the Like formula is a Null, the resultant will be a Null.

This operator provides a powerful and flexible tool for string comparisons. The pattern object can use wildcard characters to increase the flexibility (see the sidebar "Using Wildcards").

Tip

If you want to match one of the wildcard characters in the Like operation, the wildcard character must be enclosed by brackets in the pattern object. In the example

```
"AB*Co" Like "AB[*]C*
```

the [*] in the third position of the pattern object will look for the asterisk as the third character of the string.

Following are some further examples using the Like operator:

`[Last Name] Like "M[Cc]*"` will be True for any last name that begins with "Mc" or "MC." "McDonald," "McJamison," "MCWilliams" will all be True; "Irwin" and "Prague" will be False.

`[Answer] Like "[!e-zE-Z]"` will be True if the Answer is A, B, C, D, a, b, c, or d. Any other letter will be False.

`"AB1989" Like "AB####"` will result in True. This string looks for the letters AB and any four numbers after the letters.

`"#10 Circle Drive" Like "[#]*Drive"` will result in True. The first character must be the pound sign, and the last part must be the word *Drive.*

Using Wildcards

Access lets you use these five wildcards with the Like operator:

Character	*Matches*
?	A single character (A to Z, 0 to 9)
F	Any number of characters (0 to *n*)
#	Any single digit (0 to 9)
[*list*]	Any single character in the list
[!*list*]	Any single character *not* in the list

Note that [*list*] and [!*list*] can use the hyphen between two characters to signify a range.

Boolean (logical) operators

Access uses six *Boolean operators*. Also referred to as *logical operators,* these are used for setting conditions in expressions. Many times you'll use Boolean operators to create complex multiple-condition expressions. Like relational operators, these always return either a logical value or a Null. Boolean operators include the following:

And	Logical and
Or	Logical inclusive or
Eqv	Logical equivalence
Imp	Logical implication
Xor	Logical exclusive or
Not	Logical not

The And operator

You use the *And operator* to perform a logical conjunction of two objects; the operator returns the value True if both conditions are true. Following is the general syntax of an And operation:

object expression 1* And *object expression 2

Here is an example:

`[State] = "MN" And [Zip Code] = "12345"` will be True only if *both* conditions are True.

If the conditions on both sides of the And operator are True, the result is a True value. Table 13-1 demonstrates the results.

Table 13-1
And Operator Resultants

Expression 1	*Expression 2*	*Return Resultant*
True	True	True
True	False	False
True	Null	Null
False	True	False
False	False	False

(continued)

Table 13-1 *(continued)*

Expression 1	*Expression 2*	*Return Resultant*
False	Null	False
Null	True	Null
Null	False	False
Null	Null	Null

The Or operator

You use the *Or operator* to perform a logical *disjunction* of two objects; the operator returns the value True if either condition is true. This is the general syntax of an Or operation:

object expression 1* Or *object expression 2

The following two examples show how the Or operator works:

`[Last Name] = "Williams" Or [Last Name] = "Johnson"` will be True if Last Name is either Williams or Johnson.

`[Animal Type] = "Frog" Or [Animal Color] = "Green"` will be True if the animal is a frog or any animal that is green (a snake, bird, and so forth).

If the condition of either side of the Or operator is True, a True value is returned. Table 13-2 demonstrates the results.

Table 13-2
Or Expression Resultants

Expression 1	*Expression 2*	*Return Resultant*
True	True	True
True	False	True
True	Null	True
False	True	True
False	False	False
False	Null	Null
Null	True	True
Null	False	Null
Null	Null	Null

The Not operator

The *Not operator* is used for negating a numeric object; the operator returns the value True if the condition is not true. This operator reverses the logical result of the expression.

Following is the general syntax of a Not operation:

Not *numeric object expression*

The following example shows how to use the Not operator:

`Not [Final Sales Amount] >= 1000` will be true if Final Sales Amount is less than 1000.

If the numeric object is Null, the resulting condition will be Null. Table 13-3 demonstrates the results.

Table 13-3
Not Operator Resultants

Expression	*Return Resultant*
True	False
False	True
Null	Null

Miscellaneous operators

Access has these three miscellaneous operators that can be very useful to you. Their names and what they determine follow:

Between…And	Range
In	List comparison
Is	Reserved word

The Between … And operator

You can use *Between…And* to determine whether an object is within a specific range of values. This is the general syntax:

object expression* Between *value 1* And *value 2

If the value of the object expression is between value 1 and value 2, the result is True; otherwise it is False.

Following is an example of the Between … And operator that uses the IIF function for a calculated control:

```
IIF([Amount Owed] Between 0 And 250, "Due 30 Days," "Due NOW")
```

This displays a 30-day-due notice for values of $250 or less, and due-now notices for values over $250.

The In operator

You use the *In operator* to determine whether an object is equal to any value in a specific list. This is the general syntax:

***object expression* In (*value1, value2, value3, …*)**

If the object expression is found in the list, the result is True; otherwise the result is False.

The IIF function is used again in this example. Here, the In operator is used for a control value in a form:

```
IIF([Animal Type] In ("Cat," "Dog"), "Common Pet," "Unusual Pet")
```

This displays the message `Common Pet` if Animal Type is a cat or dog.

The Is (reserved word) operator

The *Is operator* is used only with the key word Null to determine whether an object has nothing in it. This is the general syntax:

Is Null

This example is a validation-check message in a data-entry form to force entry of a field:

```
IIF([Customer Name] Is Null, "Name Must be Entered,""")
```

Operator precedence

When you work with complex expressions that have many operators, Access must determine which operator to evaluate first, and then which is next, and so forth. To accomplish this task, Access has a built-in predetermined order, known as *operator precedence.* Access always follows this order unless you use parentheses to specify otherwise.

You use parentheses to group parts of an expression and override the default order of precedence. Operations within parentheses are performed before any operations outside of them. Inside the parentheses, Access follows the predetermined operator precedence.

Precedence is determined first according to category of the operator. The following list ranks operators by order of precedence:

1. Mathematical
2. Comparison
3. Boolean

Each of these categories contains its own order of precedence, which is explained next.

The mathematical precedence

Within the general category of mathematical operators, this order of precedence is in effect:

1. Exponentiation
2. Negation
3. Multiplication and/or division (left to right)
4. Integer division
5. Modulo
6. Addition and/or subtraction (left to right)
7. String concatenation

The comparison precedence

Comparison operators observe the following order of precedence:

1. Equal
2. Not-equal
3. Less-than
4. Greater-than
5. Less-than-or-equal-to
6. Greater-than-or-equal-to
7. Like

The Boolean precedence

The third general category, Boolean, follows this order of precedence:

1. Not
2. And
3. Or
4. Xor
5. Eqv
6. Imp

What Are Functions?

Functions are small programs that always, by definition, return a value based on some calculation, comparison, or evaluation that the function performs. The value returned can be string, logic, or numeric, depending on the type of function. Access provides hundreds of common functions that are used in tables, queries, forms, and reports. You can also create your own user-defined functions (UDFs), using the Access Visual Basic language.

Precedence Order

Simple mathematics provide an example of order of precedence. Bear in mind that Access performs operations within parentheses before operations that are not in parentheses. Also remember that multiplication and division come before addition or subtraction.

For example, what is the answer to this simple equation?

X=10+3*4

If your answer is 52, you need a better understanding of precedence in Access. If your answer is 22, you're right. If your answer is anything else, you need a calculator!

Multiplication is performed before addition by the rules of mathematical precedence. Therefore, the equation 10+3*4 is evaluated in this order:

3*4 is performed first, yielding an answer of 12. Then 12 is added to 10, yielding 22.

Look at what happens when you add parentheses to the equation. What is the answer to this simple equation?

X=(10+3)*4

Now the answer is 52. Within parentheses, the values 10 and 3 are added first; then the result of 13 is multiplied by 4, yielding 52.

Using functions in Access

Functions perform specialized operations that enhance the use of Access. Many times, you find yourself using functions as an integral part of Access. The following gives you a feel for the types of tasks you'll use functions to accomplish:

- ✦ Determine a default value in a table
- ✦ Place the current date and time on a report
- ✦ Convert data from one type to another
- ✦ Perform financial operations
- ✦ Display a field in a specific format
- ✦ Look up and return a value based on another
- ✦ Perform an action upon the triggering of an event

Access functions can perform financial, mathematical, comparative, and other operations. Therefore you'll find yourself using functions just about everywhere — in queries, forms, reports, validation rules, and so forth.

Many Access functions evaluate or convert data from one type to another; others perform an action. Some Access functions require use of parameters; others operate without them.

Note A *parameter* is a value you supply to the function when you run it. The value can be an object name, a constant, or a quantity.

Access functions can be quickly identified because they always end with parentheses. If a function uses parameters, the parameters are placed inside the parentheses immediately after the function name.

Following are examples of Access functions:

Now( ) returns the current date and time.

Rnd( ) returns a random number.

Ucase( ) returns the uppercase of an object.

Format( ) returns a user-specified formatted expression.

What Is a Program?

A *program* is a series of defined steps that specify one or more actions that the computer should perform. A program can be created by the user or can already exist in Access; all Access functions are programs that are already created for you. For example, a Ucase() function is a small program. If you employ Ucase () on a string, such as "Michael J. Irwin," Access creates a new string from the existing string, converting each letter to uppercase. The program starts at the leftmost letter, first converting *M* to *M* and then *i* to *I*, and so forth, until the entire string is converted. As it converts each letter, the program concatenates it to a new string.

Types of functions

Access offers several types of functions for you to use. They can be placed in the following general categories:

- ✦ Conversion
- ✦ Date/Time
- ✦ Financial (SQL)
- ✦ Financial (monetary)
- ✦ Mathematical
- ✦ String manipulation
- ✦ Domain

Conversion

Conversion functions change the data type from one type to another. A few common functions are listed here:

Str() returns a numeric as a string:

Str(921.234) returns `"921.234"`.

Val() returns a numeric value from a string:

Val("1234.56") returns `1234.56`.

Val("10 Farmview Ct") returns `10`.

Format() returns an expression according to the user-specified format:

Format("Next,"">") returns `NEXT`.

Format("123456789,""@@@-@@-@@@@") returns `123-45-6789`.

Format(#12/25/93#,"d-mmmm-yyyy") returns `25-December-1993`.

Date/Time

Date/Time functions work with date and time expressions. Following are a couple of common Date/Time functions:

Now() returns the current date and time: `3/4/93 12:22:34 PM`.

Time() returns the current time in 12-hour format: `12:22:34 PM`.

Financial (SQL)

Financial (SQL) functions perform aggregate financial operations on a set of values. The set of values is contained in a field. The field can be in a form, report, or query. Following are two common SQL functions:

Avg() An example is `Avg([Scores])`.

Sum() An example is `Sum([Gross Amount] + [Tax] + [Shipping])`.

Financial (monetary)

Financial (monetary) functions perform financial operations. Following are two monetary functions:

NPV() is the net present value, based on a series of payments and a discount rate. The syntax follows:

NPV(*discount rate, cash flow array*())

DDB() is the double-declining balance method of depreciation return. The syntax follows:

DDB(*initial cost, salvage value, life of product, period of asset depreciation*)

Mathematical

Mathematical functions perform specific calculations. Following are some mathematical functions, with examples of how to use them:

Int( ) determines the integer of a specific value:

Int(1234.55) results in `1234`.

Int(-55.1) results in `-56`.

Fix( ) determines the correct integer for a negative number:

Fix(-1234.55) results in `-1234`.

Sqr( ) determines the square root of a number:

Sqr(9) returns `3`.

Sqr(14) returns `3.742`.

String manipulation

String functions manipulate text-based expressions. Here are several common uses of these functions:

Right( ) returns the rightmost characters of a string:

Right("abcdefg,"4) returns `"defg"`.

Len( ) returns the length of a string:

Len("abcdefgh") results in `8`.

Lcase() returns the lowercase of the string:

Lcase("Michael R. Irwin") returns `michael r. irwin`.

Domain

A *domain* is a set of records contained in a table, a query, or an SQL expression. A query dynaset is an example of a domain. Domain aggregate functions determine specific statistics about a specific domain.

Following are two examples of domain functions:

DAvg( ) returns the arithmetic mean (average) of a set of values:

DAvg("[Total Amount],""Visits") determines the average billing for patients.

DCount( ) returns the number of records specified.

What Are Expressions?

In general, an expression is the means used to explain, or model, something to someone or something. An *expression* in computer terminology is generally defined as a symbol, sign, figure, or set of symbols that present or represent an algebraic fact as a quantity or operation. The expression is a representative object that Access can use to interpret something and, based on that interpretation, to obtain specific information. More simply put, an expression is a *term or series of terms controlled by operators.* Expressions are a fundamental part of Access operations.

You can use expressions in Access to accomplish a variety of tasks. You can use an expression as a property setting in SQL statements, or in queries and filters, even in macros and actions. Expressions can set criteria for a query or filter, or control macros, or perform as arguments in user-defined functions.

Access evaluates an expression each time it is used. If an expression is in a form or report, Access calculates the value every time the form *refreshes* (as with changing records and so forth). This ensures accuracy of the results. If an expression is used as a criterion in a query, Access evaluates the expression every time the query is executed, thereby ensuring that the criteria reflect any changes, additions, or deletions to records since the last execution of the query. If an expression is used in the table design as a validation rule, Access executes the evaluation every time the field is trespassed to determine whether the value is allowed in the field; this expression may be based on another field's value!

Note To give you a better understanding of expressions, consider the various examples that follow — all are examples of expressions:

```
=[Customer First Name] & " " & [Customer Last Name]

=[Total Amount] - ([Total Amount] * [Discount])

<25

[Deceased]=Yes

[Animal Type] = "Cat" And [Gender] = "M"

[Date of Birth] Between 1/88 And 12/91
```

All of these are valid expressions. Access can use them in a variety of ways: as validation rules, query criteria, calculated controls, control sources, and control-source properties.

The parts of an expression

As the many examples in the preceding section demonstrated, expressions can be very simple or quite complex. They can include a combination of operators, object names, functions, literal values, and constants.

Keeping in mind that expressions don't need to contain all these parts, you should have an understanding of each of the following uniquely identifiable portions of an expression:

Operators: `>, =, *, And, Or, Not, Like`, etc.

Operators indicate what type of action (operation) will be performed on one or more elements of an expression.

Object names: `Forms![Add a Customer & Pets], [Customer Address], [Pet Name]`

Object names, also known as *identifiers,* are the actual objects: tables, forms, reports, controls, or fields.

Functions: `Date(), DLookUp(), DateDiff()`

Functions always return a value. The resultant value can be created by a calculation, a conversion of data, or an evaluation. You can use a built-in Access function or a user-defined function (UDF) that you create.

Literal values: `100, Jan. 1, 1988, "Cat," "[A-D]*"`

These are actual values that you supply to the expression. Literal values can be numbers, strings, or dates. Access uses the values exactly as they are entered.

Constants: `Yes, No, Null, True, False`

Constants represent values that do not change.

The following illustration demonstrates the parts of an expression:

```
[Follow Up Date] = Date() + 30
```

`[Follow Up Date]` is an object name, or identifier.

= is an operator.

`Date()` is a function.

+ is an operator.

`30` is a literal.

Creating an expression

Expressions are commonly entered in very property windows, action arguments, and criteria grids. As you create expressions, the area is scrolled so you can continue to enter the expression. Although you can enter an expression in this manner, it is often desirable to see the entire expression as you enter it. This is especially true when you are working with long, complex expressions. Access has a Zoom box you can use to change how much of the expression you see as you enter it. Open this box by clicking where you want to enter your expression and then pressing Shift+F2.

As you enter expressions, Access may insert certain characters for you when you *change focus*. Access will check your syntax and will automatically insert these characters:

- ✦ Brackets ([]) around control names that have no spaces or punctuation in the name
- ✦ Pound Signs (#) around dates that it recognizes
- ✦ Quotation marks (" ") around text that contains no spaces or punctuation in the body

Note: The term *changing focus* refers to the movement of the cursor out of the location where you are entering the expression. You accomplish this by pressing Tab, or by moving the mouse and clicking on another area of the screen.

Warning: Access reports an error when it changes focus under these conditions: Access doesn't understand the date form you enter, the name of the control contains spaces, or a control is not placed in brackets.

Entering object names

You identify object names by placing brackets ([]) around the element. Access requires the use of brackets when the object contains a space or punctuation in its name. If these conditions are not present, you can ignore the brackets — Access inserts them automatically. Therefore, the following expressions are syntactically identical:

```
Breed + [Type of Animal]

[Breed] + [Type of Animal]
```

Notice that in both cases the brackets are placed around Type of Animal because this object name contains spaces.

Although it isn't necessary to enter brackets around objects like Breed in the second example, it is good programming practice always to surround object names with brackets for consistency in entry.

Entering text

You identify text by placing quotation marks around the text element of an expression. Access automatically places the quotation marks for you if you forget to add them.

As an example, you can type **Cat**, **Dog**, and **Frog** into separate criteria cells of a query, and Access automatically adds the quotation marks around each of these three entries. Access recognizes these as objects, and helps you.

Entering date/time values

You identify date/time data by placing the pound signs (#) around the date/time element. Access will evaluate any valid date/time format automatically, and place the pound signs around the element for you.

Expression Builder

Access has added an *Expression Builder* tool that helps you build complex expressions. You can use it anyplace you can build an expression (like when specifying criteria for a query or creating a calculated field on a form or report). You can activate the builder in two ways:

- ✦ Pressing the Build button on the toolbar (the ellipsis).
- ✦ Clicking the *right* mouse button and selecting Build from the shortcut menu.

Special identifier operators and expressions

Access has two special *identifier operators:* the dot (.) and the exclamation point (!). When you work with Access tables, you have a diverse range of ways to display and access objects. You can use fields and their contents; any field object can be used over and over. You can display the field object in numerous forms and reports by using the same reference, the field object name, in every form and report.

For example, the field Pet Name in the Pets table can be used in six or seven different forms. When you want to use the Pet Name field in an expression for a comparison, how do you tell Access which copy of the field Pet Name it should use for the expression? Because Access is a Windows database, it is possible to have several different forms in the same session on the same computer. In fact, it is possible to have multiple copies of Access running the same data and forms.

With all this confusion, there must be a way to specify to Access which Pet Name field object you want the expression to use. That is the purpose of the dot and exclamation point as operator identifiers. These symbols identify and maintain clarity in determining which field to use.

A Few Words About Controls and Properties

When you create a form or report, you place many different objects on the form – fields in text boxes, text labels, buttons, check boxes, combo boxes, lines, rectangles, and so on.

As you select and place these objects on a form, each object is assigned a *control name*. Access supplies it according to predefined rules. For example, control names for fields default to a control-source name of the field name. The field name appears in the text box on the form. The label for the text box is assigned the control name Text, with a sequence number attached to it (for example, Text11 or Text12). The sequence number is added to make each control name unique.

After all objects are placed on the form, you can identify any object on the form (line, button, text box, etc.) by its unique control name. This control name is what you use to reference a specific table field (or field on a form). You can change the name of the control that Access assigned to the object if you want. The only requirement for the new control name is that it must be unique to the form or report that contains it.

Every object on the form (and don't forget that the form itself is an object) has associated *properties*. These are the individual characteristics of each object; as such, they are accessible by a control name. Properties control the appearance of the object (color, size, sunken, alignment, and so forth). They also affect the structure, specifying format, default value, validation rules, and control name. In addition, properties designate the *behavior* of a control – for instance, whether the field can grow or shrink, and whether you can edit it. Behaviors also affect actions specified for the event properties such as On Enter and On Push.

The ! (exclamation) identifier operator

The exclamation mark (!) is a key symbol that is used in conjunction with several reserved words. One such reserve word is *Forms*. When this word is followed by !, you are telling Access that the next object name will be the *form object name* that you want to reference.

As an example, say that you have a Date of Birth field that is in two forms — [Customer & Pets] and [Pet Specifics]. (Note that these two form names are objects; you will need to use brackets to reference them.) You want to refer to the Date of Birth field in the [Pet Specifics] form. The way to specify this form is by use of the ! and the Forms reserved word:

```
Forms![Pet Specifics]
```

Now that the form is specified, you need to further refine the scope to add the field Date of Birth.

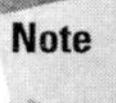
Note Although Chapter 16 covers controls and properties, by this point you should have a partial understanding of what properties and controls are (for a refresher, see the sidebar on form controls and properties).

Actually, what you are specifying is a *control* on the form. That control will use the field you need, which is Date of Birth. The control has the same name as the field. Therefore you access this specific object by using the following expression:

```
Forms![Pet Specifics]![Date of Birth]
```

The second exclamation mark specifies a control on a form — one identified by the reserved word **Forms**.

By following the properties of each object, starting with the object Forms, you can trace the control source object back to a field in the original table.

In summary, the exclamation-point identifier is always followed by an object name. You define this object name by using the name of a form, report, field, or other control name you created in the database. If you don't use the existing name for the desired object, you can change the default value name of the source.

The . (dot) identifier operator

The . (dot) is also a key symbol that is used in conjunction with expression identification operators. Normally it is placed immediately after a user-defined object. Unlike the !, the . (dot) usually identifies a *property* of a specific object. Therefore, if you want to determine the value of the Visible property of the same control you worked with before, you specify it as follows:

```
Forms![Pet Specifics]![Date of Birth].Visible
```

This gives you the value for the Visible property of the specific field on the specific form.

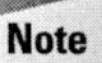
Note Normally the . (dot) identifier is used to obtain a value that corresponds to a property of an object. Sometimes, however, you can use it between a table name and a field name when you are accessing a value associated with a specific field in a specific table, as here:

```
[Pets].[Pet Name]
```

A thorough analysis of the two special identifier operators is beyond the scope of this book. Even so, you'll find that these identifiers enable you to find any object and the values associated with its properties.

Summary

In this chapter, you learned about the building blocks of Access operations: operators, functions, and expressions. The chapter covered the following points:

- ✦ Operators let you add numbers, compare values, put strings together, and create complicated relational expressions.
- ✦ The many types of operators include mathematical, relational, string, Boolean, and a group of miscellaneous operators.
- ✦ The relational operators =, <>, >, >=, <, and <= make comparisons.
- ✦ To concatenate two strings, use the & operator.
- ✦ You can use five pattern-matching wildcards with the Like operator: *, ?, #, [*list*], and [!*list*].
- ✦ The Boolean operators are And, Or, Eqv, Imp, Xor, and Not.
- ✦ Operator precedence determines the order in which Access evaluates the various parts of an expression.
- ✦ Functions are small programs that return a value. Access has hundreds of built-in functions.
- ✦ Functions are classified as conversion, date/time, financial, mathematical, string, or domain.
- ✦ Expressions are used to create a calculation or to model a process.
- ✦ Expressions use operators, object names, functions, literal values, and constants.
- ✦ The Expression Builder can be used to create an expression.
- ✦ Object names are entered in brackets ([]) to identify them. Common objects include field names.
- ✦ The two special identifiers, the exclamation point and the dot, help identify Access objects such as forms, reports, queries, and tables. These identifiers can also identify properties.

In the next chapter, you examine how to create relationships and joins in queries.

✦ ✦ ✦

Creating Relations and Joins in Queries

In This Chapter

Adding more than one table to a query

Manipulating the table/query pane

Determining which table a field is from in a query

Moving and resizing Table Design windows

Creating a database diagram

Adding single fields to a query

Adding multiple fields to a query

Working around query limitations

Understanding types of joins

Changing the type of join

Creating an inner join and an outer join

In previous chapters, you worked with simple queries by using the single table Pets. Using a query to obtain information from a single table is common; often, however, you need to obtain information from several related tables. For example, you may want to obtain a customer's name and the type of pets the customer owns. In this chapter, you learn how to use more than one table to obtain information.

Adding More Than One Table to the Query Window

In Chapter 12, you learned about the different tables in the Mountain Animal Hospital database system. This system is comprised of four primary tables and four lookup tables. You learned about table keys, primary and foreign, and their importance for linking two tables together. You learned how to create relationships between two tables at the table level by using the Tools⇨Relationships menu choice in the Database window. Finally, you learned how referential integrity rules affect data in tables.

After you create the tables for your database and decide how the tables are related to one another, you are ready to begin creating multiple-table queries to obtain information from several tables at the same time.

By adding more than one table to a query and then selecting fields from the tables in the query, you can view information from your database just as though the information from the several tables were in one table. As an example, suppose you need to send a letter to all owners of snakes who brought their pets in for visits in the last two months. For this data, you would need to get the information from three separate tables: Pets, Customer, and Visits. You can do this by using the Pets and Visits tables and creating a query for all animals where the Type of Animal field equals *snake* and where Visit Date falls between today's date and today's date minus two months. Because of the relationship between the Pets and Customer tables, you then have access to the customer information for each snake. You can then create a report form using the related information from the tables Pets, Visits, and Customer.

The first step in creating a multiple-table query is to open each table in the Query window. The following steps show how to open the Pets, Customer, and Visits tables in a single query:

1. Click on the Query tab in the Database window.
2. Click on the New button to create a new query.
3. Select New Query and click on OK in the New Query dialog box.
4. Select the Pets table by double-clicking on the table name.
5. Select the Customer table by double-clicking on the table name.
6. Select the Visits table by double-clicking on the table name.
7. Click on the Close button in the Show Table dialog box.

Note You can also add each table by highlighting the table in the list separately and clicking on Add.

The top pane of the Query Design window is shown in Figure 14-1 with three tables: Pets, Customer, and Visits.

Figure 14-1: The Query Design window with three files added.

Note: You can add more tables by selecting Query⇨Show Table from the Query Design menu or by clicking on the Show Table icon.

Working with the Table/Query Pane

As you can see in Figure 14-1, each table is connected by a single line from the primary key field to the foreign key field. Actually, on your screen it probably looks as if two lines connect Pets to Customer and a single line runs from Customer to Visits. You'll see how to move the table designs so that the lines appear correctly.

The join line

When Access displays each set of related tables, it places a line between the two tables. This line is known as a *join line.* A join line is a graphical line that represents the link between two tables. In this example, the join line goes from the Pets table to the Customer table to connect the two Customer Number fields. A join line also runs from Pets to Visits, connecting the Pet ID fields in these two tables.

This link is created automatically because a relationship was set in the Database window. If Access already knows what the relationship is, it automatically creates the link for you when the tables are added to a query. The relationship is displayed as a join line between two tables.

If Referential Integrity is checked in the relationship between two tables, Access will display a thick portion of the line right at the table window (like the line in Figure 14-2). Notice that the line starts heavy and then becomes thin between Pets and Visits (heavy on both sides). This line variation tells you that Referential Integrity has been set up between the two tables in the Relationship Builder. If a one-to-many relationship exists, the *many* relationship is denoted by an infinity sign (∞).

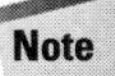

Note: If you have not specified a relationship between two tables and the following conditions are true, Access for Windows 95 will automatically join the tables:

1. The tables have a field in both with the same name.
2. The field with the same name in both tables is the same type (text, numeric, and so on).

The field is a *primary key* field in one of the tables.

Tip: Access for Windows 95 automatically joins the table if a relationship exists. However, you can turn off this property by unchecking the default Enable AutoJoin option from the global options tabbed dialog. To display this option, select Tools⇨Options⇨Tables/Queries and then uncheck the Enable AutoJoin option.

Manipulating the Table Design window

Each Table Design window begins at a fixed size, which shows approximately 4 fields and 12 characters for each field. Each Table Design window is a true window and behaves like one; it can be resized and moved. If you have more fields than will fit in the Table Design window, an elevator is attached to the table design. The elevator lets you scroll through the fields in the Table Design window.

Note After a relationship is created between tables, the join line remains between the two fields. As you move through a table selecting fields, you'll notice that the graphical line will move, relative to the linked fields. For example, if you move the elevator down (toward the bottom of the structure) in the Customer table, you'll notice that the join line moves up with the customer number and eventually stops at the top of the table window.

When you're working with many tables, these join lines can become visually confusing as they cross or overlap. If you move through the table, the line eventually becomes visible, and the field it is linked to will be obvious.

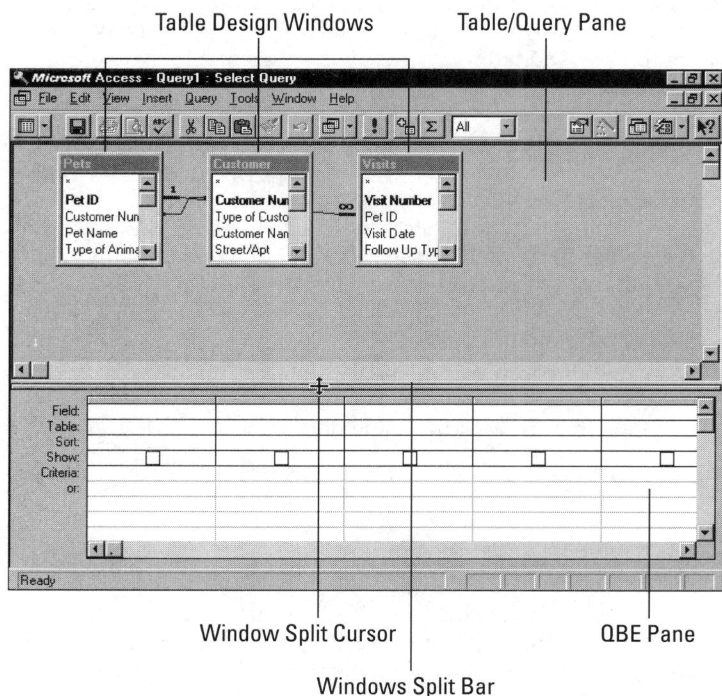

Figure 14-2: Resizing the Query Design panes.

Resizing the table/query pane

When you place table designs on the table/query pane, they appear in a fixed size with little spacing between tables. When you add a table to the top pane, it initially shows you five fields. If more fields are in the table, an elevator bar will be added to the box (right side). The table box may only show part of a long field name (the rest is truncated by the box size). You can move the tables around the pane and even resize them to show more field names and more of the field name. The first step, however, is to resize the pane itself. The Query Design window is made up of two panes. The top pane displays your table designs, whereas the QBE pane below lets you enter fields, sort orders, and criteria. Often the top pane can be larger than the bottom pane; you may want more space for the design and less space for the QBE pane.

You can resize the table/query pane by placing your cursor on the thick line below the elevator. This is the window *split bar.* The cursor changes to a double vertical arrow, as shown in Figure 14-2. You can then drag the split bar up or down. The following steps show how to resize the panes:

1. Place the cursor on the window split bar.
2. Hold down the mouse button and drag the split bar down.
3. Release the bar when it is two lines below the QBE row marked `or:`.

The top pane is now much larger; the bottom pane is smaller but still displays the entire QBE Design area. You now have space to move the table designs around and properly view the table/query pane.

Tip

You can build a database diagram so that you view only the table designs by moving the split bar to the bottom of the screen and then positioning the table designs as you want within the full-screen area.

Moving a table

You can move table designs in the table/query pane by simply placing the cursor on the top of a table design (where the name of the table is) and then dragging the table to a new location. You may want to move the table designs for a better working view or to clean up a confusing database diagram, (like the one shown in Figure 14-2). To move table designs, follow these steps:

1. Place the cursor on the top of the Customer table on the text Customer.
2. Drag the Customer table design straight down until the top of the table design appears where the bottom was when you started.

The screen should now look like Figure 14-3. You can see that each line is now an individual line that goes from one table's primary key to the foreign key in another table.

You can move the table designs anywhere in the top pane. You can spread out the diagram by moving the table designs farther apart. You can also rearrange the table designs. You may want to place the Customer table first, followed by the Pets table and then the Visits table. Remember that, in this example, you are trying to view the snakes that have been in for a visit in the last two months so you can send a letter to the customer. So the sequence of Pets, Customer, and Visits makes sense. You generally want to view your diagram with a particular business purpose in mind. Pets is the main table in this business example and needs to retrieve information from both the Visits and Customer tables.

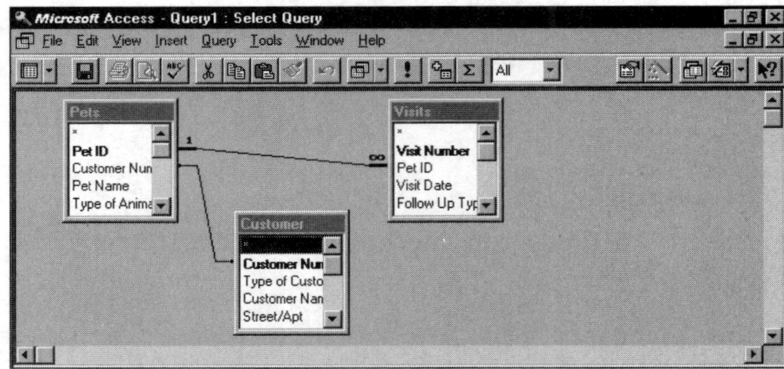

Figure 14-3: A database diagram for the Pets, Customer, and Visits tables.

Removing a table

There are times when you need to remove tables from a query. Any table can be removed from the Query window. Follow these steps to delete the Visits table, bearing in mind that you can restore it later:

1. Select the Visits table in the top pane of the Query window by clicking on either the table or a field in the table.
2. Press the Delete key or select Edit⇨Delete from the Edit menu.

Note: Only one table can be removed from the Query window at a time. The menu choice Edit⇨Clear Grid does *not* remove all tables; this selection is used for removing all fields from the QBE pane. You can also remove a table by right clicking on a table and selecting Remove Table from the shortcut menu.

When you delete a table, any join lines to that table are deleted as well. When you delete a table, there is no warning or confirmation dialog box. The table is simply removed from the screen.

Adding more tables

You may decide to add more tables to a query or you may accidentally delete a table and need to add it back. You can accomplish this task by either selecting Query⇨Show Table from the menu or clicking the *right* mouse button and selecting Show Table from the menu. When you use one of these methods, the Show Table dialog box that appeared when you created the query is redisplayed. To restore the Visits table to the screen, follow these steps:

1. Move the mouse pointer to the top pane (outside of any existing tables) and press the right mouse button. Select Show Table from the menu.
2. Select the Visits table by double-clicking on the table name.
3. Click on the Close button in the Show Table dialog box.

Access returns you to the table/query pane of the Visits table and redisplays the join line.

Resizing a table design

You can also resize each of the table designs by placing the cursor on one of the table design borders. The table design is nothing but a window; thus you can enlarge or reduce it vertically, horizontally, or diagonally by placing the cursor on the appropriate border. When you enlarge the table design vertically, you can see more fields than the default number (five). By making the table design larger horizontally, you can see the complete list of field names. Then, when you resize the table/query pane to take up the entire window, you can create a database diagram.

Creating a database diagram

Figure 14-4 shows a database diagram for these three tables in which you can see all the fields. The more tables and relationships you have, the more important a database diagram becomes in helping you view your data graphically with the proper relationships visible. In upcoming chapters, you'll see many different database diagrams as you use queries to assemble the data for various forms and reports.

In Figure 14-4, the table/query pane is expanded to its full size, so you can't see any of the QBE pane below. You can get to the QBE pane by resizing with the split bar. When you're working with fields in the QBE pane, you should keep the screen split so that you can see both panes.

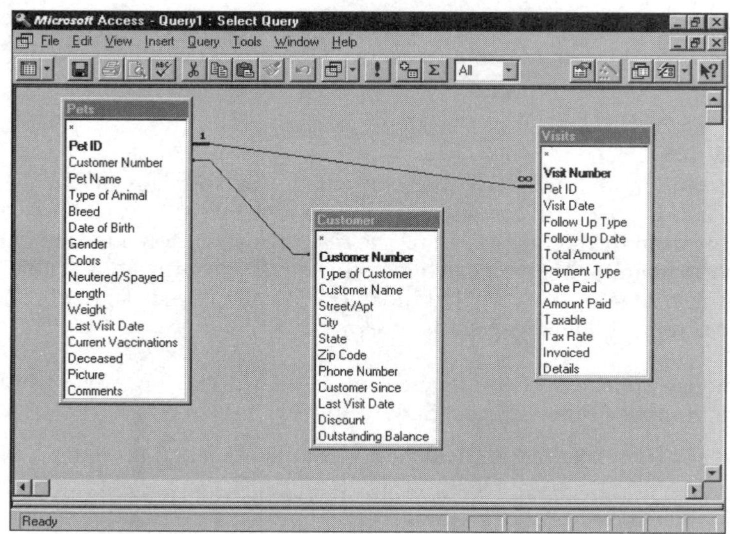

Figure 14-4: A database diagram.

Warning Although you can switch panes by pressing F6, you can't see where the cursor is in the QBE pane while the table/query pane is displayed in full-screen size.

Disk If you are following along on your computer with the examples in this chapter, resize the panes so you can see both the Table Design pane and the QBE pane.

Adding Fields from More Than One Table

You can add fields from more than one table to the query in exactly the same way as when you're working with a single table. You can add fields one at a time, many fields grouped together, or all the fields from one or all tables.

Cross Ref Adding fields from a single table is covered in detail in Chapter 10; this chapter covers the topic in less detail but focuses on the differences between single- and multiple-table field selection.

Adding a single field

You can select a single field from any table by using any of several methods:

- ✦ Double-click on a field name in the table/query pane.
- ✦ Click on a field name in the table/query pane and drag it to the QBE pane.
- ✦ Click on an empty Field: cell in the QBE pane and type a field name.
- ✦ Click on an empty Field: cell and select the field from the drop-down list.

Warning If you type a field name in an empty Field: cell that is in both tables, Access enters the field name from the first table it finds with that field. Access will search the tables, starting from the left side in the top pane.

If you select the field from the drop-down list in the Field: cell, you see the name of the table first, followed by a period and the field name. For example, the field Pet ID in the Pets table is displayed as `Pets.Pet ID`. This helps you to select the right field name. Using this method, you can select a common field name from a specific table.

The easiest way to select fields is still to double-click on the query/table designs. To do so, you may have to resize the table designs to see the fields you want to select. To select Customer Name, Pet Name, Type of Animal, and Visit Date, follow these steps:

1. Double-click on Customer Name in the Customer table.
2. Double-click on Pet Name in the Pets table.
3. Double-click on Type of Animal in the Pets table.
4. Double-click on Visit Date in the Visits table.

Viewing the table names

When you're working with two or more tables, the field names in the QBE pane can become confusing. You may find yourself asking, for example, just which table the field Customer Number is from.

Access automatically maintains the table name that is associated with each field displayed in the QBE pane. The default is to display the table name. To choose not to show the table name in the QBE pane, select View⇨Table Names from the View menu.

This selection controls the display of table names immediately below the corresponding field name in the QBE pane. Figure 14-5 shows the QBE pane with the row Table: below the Field: row. Notice that it contains the name of the table for each field.

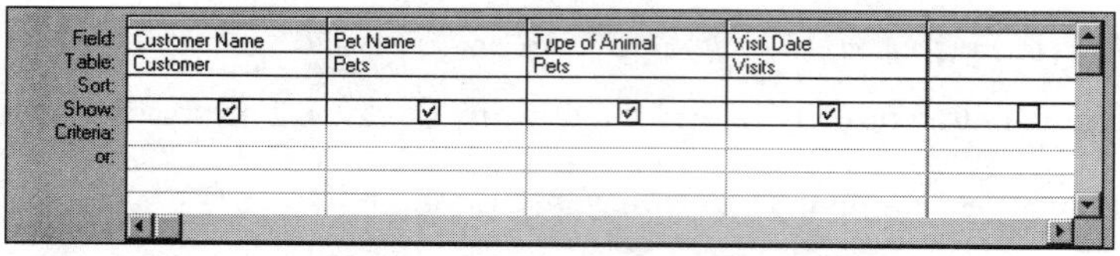

Field:	Customer Name	Pet Name	Type of Animal	Visit Date	
Table:	Customer	Pets	Pets	Visits	
Sort:					
Show:	☑	☑	☑	☑	☐
Criteria:					
or:					

Figure 14-5: The QBE pane with Table names displayed.

The display of the table name is only for your information. Access always maintains the table name associated with the field names.

After you add fields to a query, you can view your data at any time. Although you'll eventually limit the display of data to snakes that have visited you in the last two months, you can view all the data at any time by selecting the Datasheet icon. Figure 14-6 displays the data as currently selected. The fields have been resized to show all the data values.

Adding multiple fields

The process of adding multiple fields is identical to adding multiple fields in a single table query. When you're adding multiple fields from several tables, you must add them from one table at a time. The easiest way to do this task is to select multiple fields and drag them together down to the QBE pane.

You can select multiple fields contiguously by selecting the first field of the list, holding down the Shift key, and using the mouse to go to the last field. You can also select random fields in the list by holding down the Control key (Ctrl) while selecting individual fields with a mouse click.

Adding all-table fields

As with adding multiple fields, when you're adding *all-table fields*, you do it by selecting which table you want to add first, and then selecting the next table. You can select all the fields by either double-clicking on the title bar of the table name or by selecting the Asterisk (*) field. Remember that these two methods produce very different results.

This method automatically fills in each column of the QBE pane. The fields are added in order of their selection in the table, from left to right (based on their field order in the table). By default, Access displays only the first five fields. You can change the column width of each field to display more or fewer columns.

Selecting all fields with the double-clicking method

One method of selecting all the fields is to double-click on the title bar of the table whose fields you want to select.

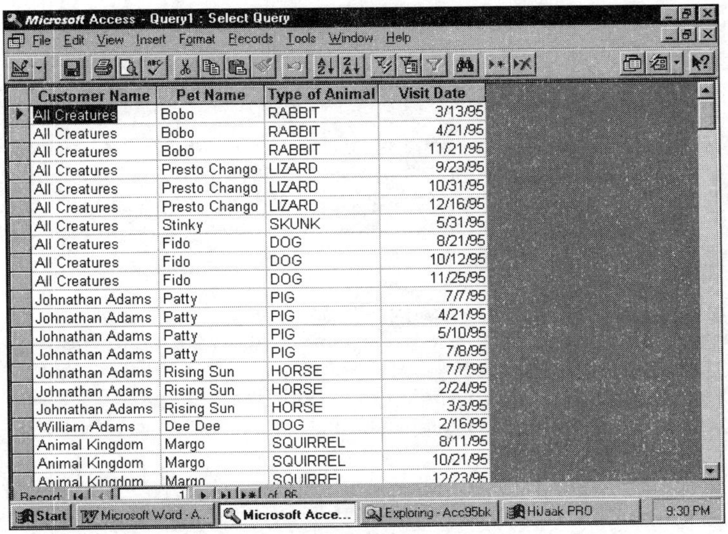

Customer Name	Pet Name	Type of Animal	Visit Date
All Creatures	Bobo	RABBIT	3/13/95
All Creatures	Bobo	RABBIT	4/21/95
All Creatures	Bobo	RABBIT	11/21/95
All Creatures	Presto Chango	LIZARD	9/23/95
All Creatures	Presto Chango	LIZARD	10/31/95
All Creatures	Presto Chango	LIZARD	12/16/95
All Creatures	Stinky	SKUNK	5/31/95
All Creatures	Fido	DOG	8/21/95
All Creatures	Fido	DOG	10/12/95
All Creatures	Fido	DOG	11/25/95
Johnathan Adams	Patty	PIG	7/7/95
Johnathan Adams	Patty	PIG	4/21/95
Johnathan Adams	Patty	PIG	5/10/95
Johnathan Adams	Patty	PIG	7/8/95
Johnathan Adams	Rising Sun	HORSE	7/7/95
Johnathan Adams	Rising Sun	HORSE	2/24/95
Johnathan Adams	Rising Sun	HORSE	3/3/95
William Adams	Dee Dee	DOG	2/16/95
Animal Kingdom	Margo	SQUIRREL	8/11/95
Animal Kingdom	Margo	SQUIRREL	10/21/95
Animal Kingdom	Margo	SQUIRREL	12/23/95

Figure 14-6: Viewing data from multiple tables.

Selecting all fields with the Asterisk (*) method

The first object in each table is an asterisk (at the top of the field list), which is known as the *all-field reference tag.* When you select and drag the asterisk to the QBE pane, all fields in the table are added to the QBE pane, but there is a distinct difference between this method and the double-clicking method. When you add the all-field reference tag (*), the QBE pane shows only one cell with the name of the table and an asterisk. For example, if you select the * in the Pets table, you see `Pets.*` displayed in one field row cell.

Unlike selecting all the fields, the asterisk places reference to all the fields in a single column. When you drag multiple columns, as in the preceding example, you drag actual table field names to the query. If you later change the design of the table, you also have to change the design of the query. The advantage of using the asterisk for selecting all fields is that you won't have to change the query later if you add, delete, or rename fields in the underlying table or query. Changing fields in the underlying table or query will automatically add fields to or remove fields from the query.

Warning Selecting the * has one drawback: You cannot perform criteria conditions on the asterisk column itself. You have to add an individual field from the table and enter the criteria. If you add a field for a criterion (when using the *), the query displays the field twice — once for the * field and a second time for the criteria field. Therefore you may want to uncheck the Show: choice of the criteria field.

Understanding the Limitations of Multiple-Table Queries

When you create a query with multiple files, there are limitations as to what fields can be edited. Generally, you can change data in a query dynaset, and your changes will be saved to the underlying tables. A primary key field normally cannot be edited if referential integrity is in effect and if the field is part of a relationship (unless Cascade Updates is set to Yes).

In order for you to update a table from a query, a value in a specific record in the query must represent a single record in the underlying table. This means you cannot update fields in a Crosstab or Totals query because they both group records together to display grouped information. Instead of displaying the actual underlying table data, they display records of data that are calculated and stored in a virtual (nonreal) table called a *snapshot*.

Updating limitations

In Access version 1.*x*, only the records on the *many* side of a one-to-many relationship were updatable. That has changed in versions 2.0 and 7.0. Table 14-1 shows when a field in a table is updatable. As you can see in Table 14-1, queries based on one-to-many relationships are updatable in both tables (depending on how the query was designed). Any query that creates a *snapshot*, however, is not updatable.

Table 14-1
Updatability Rules for Queries

Type of Query or Field	*Updatable*	*Comments*
One Table	Yes	
One-to-One relationship	Yes	
One-to-Many relationship	Mostly	Restrictions based on design methodology (see text)
Crosstab	No	Creates a *snapshot* of the data
Totals Query (Sum, Avg, etc.)	No	Works with Grouped data creating a *snapshot*
Unique Value property is Yes	No	Shows unique records only in a *snapshot*
SQL-specific queries	No	Union & Pass-through work with ODBC data

Type of Query or Field	*Updatable*	*Comments*
Calculated field	No	Will recalculate automatically
Read-only fields	No	If opened read-only or on read-only drive (CD-ROM)
Permissions denied	No	Insert, Replace, or Delete are not granted
ODBC Tables with no Primary Key	No	A primary key (unique index) must exist
Paradox Table with no Primary Key	No	A primary key file must exist
Locked by another user	No	Cannot be updated while a field is locked by another

Overcoming query limitations

Table 14-1 shows that there are times that queries and fields in tables are not updatable. As a general rule, any query that does aggregate calculations or is an ODBC-based SQL query is not updatable. All others can be updatable. When your query has more than one table, and some of the tables have a one-to-many relationship, there may be fields that are not updatable (depending on the design of the query).

A unique index (primary key) and updatability

If a query uses two tables that have a one-to-many relationship, the *one* side of the join must have a unique (primary key) index on the field that is used for the join. If not, the fields from the *one* side of the query cannot be updated.

Replacing existing data in a query with a one-to-many relationship

Normally, all the fields in the many-side table are updatable in a one-to-many query; the *one*-side table can update all the fields *except* the primary key (join) field. Normally, this is sufficient for most database application purposes. Also normally, you would never change the primary key field in the *one*-side table because it is the link to the records in the joined tables.

At times, however, you may need to change the link-field contents in both tables (make a new primary key in the one table, and have the database program change the link field in all the related records from the *many* table). The new version of Access will let you do this by defining a relationship between the two tables and using referential integrity. If you define a relationship and enforce referential integrity in the Relationship Builder, two check boxes are activated. If you want to allow changes (updates) to the primary key field, check the Cascade Updated Related Fields box, as in Figure 14-7. By checking this option, you can change the primary key field in a relationship; Access will update the link field to the new value, automatically, in all the other related tables.

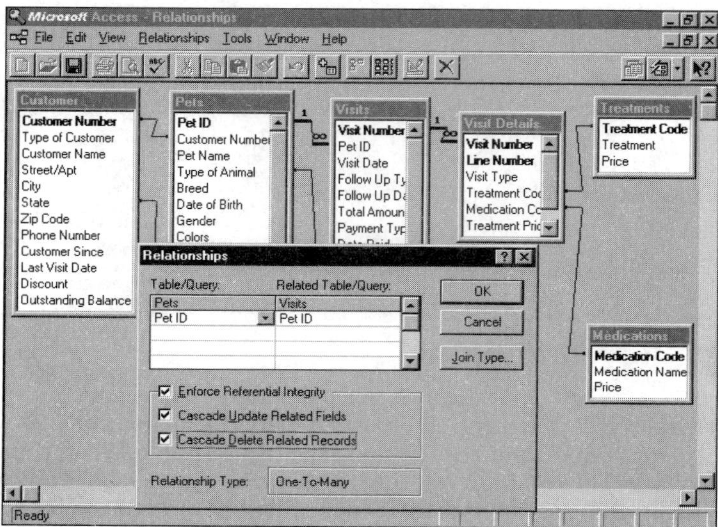

Figure 14-7: The Relationship Builder dialog box, with referential integrity in effect.

Design tips for updating fields in queries

- ✦ If you want to use AutoLookup between forms, be sure to include the join field from the *many* table in your form (instead of the *one* table). Also use a combo or list box to display this field.
- ✦ If you want to add records to both tables of a one-to-many relationship, be sure to include the join field from the *many*-side table, and show the field in the datasheet. Once you've done this, you can add records starting with either table. The *one* side's join field will be copied automatically to the *many* side's join field.
- ✦ If you do not want any fields updatable, set the Allow Edits property of the form to No.
- ✦ If you do not want to update some fields on a form, set the Tab Stop property for the control (field) to No for these fields.
- ✦ If you want to add records to multiple tables in a form, remember to include all (or most) of the fields from both tables. Otherwise you will not have a complete record of data in your form.

Temporary non-updatability in a one-to-many relationship

When updating records on the *one* side of a one-to-many query, you will *not* be able to change the *many*-side *join* field until you save changes to the *one* side. You can quickly save changes to the one side by pressing Shift+Enter or selecting File⇨Save Record from the menu. Once the one side changes are saved, the join field in the *many*-side record can be changed.

Creating Query Joins

You can create joins between tables in the following three ways:

- ✦ By creating relationships between the tables when you design the database (Select Tools⇨Relationships from the Database window menu, or click on the Relationship button on the toolbar)
- ✦ By selecting two tables for the query that have a field that is the same type and name in both, *and* that field is a primary key field in one of the tables
- ✦ By creating joins in the Query window at the time you create a query

The first two methods are automatic. If you create relationships when designing the tables of your database, Access displays join lines based on those relationships automatically when you add the related tables to a query. It also creates an automatic join between two tables that have a common field, provided that field is a primary key in one of the tables.

There may be times when you add tables to a query that are not already related to a specific file, as in these examples:

- ✦ The two tables have a common field, but it is not the same name.
- ✦ A table is not related — and cannot be related to the other table (for example, the Customer table cannot be directly joined to the Treatments table).

If you have two tables that are not automatically joined and you need to relate them, you join them in the Query Design window. Joining tables in the Query Design window does *not* create a permanent join between the tables. Rather, the join (relationship) will apply only to the table for the query that you are working on.

Warning All tables in a query must be joined to at least one other table. If, for example, you place two tables into a query and *do not* join them, Access will create a query based on a *Cartesian product* (also known as the *cross product*) of the two tables. This subject will be discussed later in this chapter. For now, note that a Cartesian product means that if you have five records in table 1 and six records in table 2, then the resulting query will have thirty records (5 × 6) that will probably be useless to you.

Joining tables

Figure 14-8 shows the Pets and Customer tables that are being joined. Tables will not be joined automatically in a query if they are not already joined at the table level, do not have a common named field for a primary key, or have the AutoJoin option turned off.

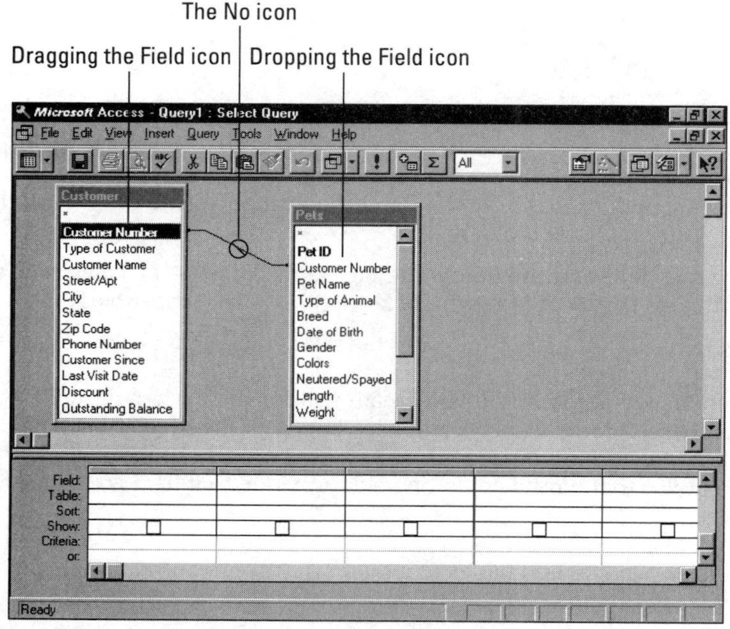

Figure 14-8: Joining tables in the table/query pane.

1. Select the Customer Number field in the Customer Table in the query/table pane.
2. Drag the highlighted field to the Pets table (as you drag the field, the Field icon appears).
3. Drop the Field icon on the Customer Number field in the Pets table.

Figure 14-8 illustrates the process of joining tables. The Field icon first appears in the Customer Number field of the Customer table; then it moves to the Pets table. As it moves between tables, the Field icon changes to the symbol that indicates the icon cannot be dropped in the area between the tables. When the icon is over the Customer Number field, it changes back to the Field icon, indicating you can drop it in that location. When you release the mouse button, the join line appears.

Of course, you can also create joins that make no sense, but when you view the data, you will get less-than-desirable results. If two joined fields have no values in common, you have a datasheet in which no records are selected or a Cartesian product where each and every record is joined with each and every record in the second table. If one table has 100 records and the other has 200 records, the Cartesian join will create a table with 20,000 records. Then, your results will make no sense.

Note

You can select either table first when you create a join.

You would never want to create a meaningless join. For example, you would not want to join the City field from the Customer table to the Date of Birth field in the Pets table. Although Access will let you create this join, the resulting dynaset will have no records in it.

Deleting joins

To delete a join line between two tables, you select the join line and press the Delete key. You can select the join line by placing the cursor on any part of the line and clicking once. For example, create a new query by adding the Customer and Pets table to a query, and then following these steps, you can delete the join line between the Pets and Customer tables:

1. Select the join line between the Customer Number field in the Pets table and the Customer table by placing the cursor on the line and clicking the mouse button.
2. With the join line highlighted, press the Delete key.

After Step 2, the line should disappear. If you delete a join line between two tables that have a relationship set at the database level, the broken join is effective only for the query in which you broke the join. When you exit the query, the relationship between the two tables remains in effect for other operations, including subsequent queries.

Note

You can also delete a join by selecting it and choosing Edit⇨Delete.

Warning

Remember that if you delete a join between two tables, and the tables remain in the Query window unjoined to any other tables, you will get unexpected results in the datasheet. This is due to the Cartesian product that Access creates from the two tables. The Cartesian product will only be effective for this query. The underlying relationship remains intact.

Note

Access enables you to create multiple-field joins between tables (more than one line can be drawn). Remember that the join must be between two fields that have the same data and data type; if not, the query will not find any records to display from the datasheet.

Understanding Types of Table Joins

In Chapter 12, you learned about table relationships. Access understands all types of table and query relations, which include the following:

- ✦ One-to-one
- ✦ One-to-many
- ✦ Many-to-one
- ✦ Many-to-many

When you specify a relationship between two tables, you establish rules for the type of relationship, not for viewing the data based on the relationship.

To view data in two tables, you must join them through a link, which you establish via a common field (or group of fields) between the two tables. The method of linking the tables is known as *joining*. In a query, tables with established relationships are shown already joined. Within a query, you can create new joins or change an existing join line; just as there are different types of relationships, there are different types of joins. In the following sections, you'll learn about these types of joins:

- ✦ Equi-joins (inner joins)
- ✦ Outer joins
- ✦ Self-joins
- ✦ Cross-product joins (Cartesian joins)

Inner joins (equi-joins)

The default join in Access is known as an *equi-join*, or *inner join*. It enables you to tell Access to select all records from both tables that have the same value in the fields that are joined together.

Note

The Access manuals refer to a default join as an *equi-join* (also commonly referred to as an *inner join* in database relational theory). The terms are interchangeable and will be used as such throughout this chapter.

For an example of an equi-join, recall the Customer and Pets tables. Bear in mind that you are looking for all records from these two tables with matching fields. The fields Customer Number are common to both, so the equi-join does not show any records for customers that have no pets or any pets that do not relate to a valid customer number. The rules of referential integrity prevent pet records that are not tied to a customer number. Of course, it's possible to delete all pets from a customer or to create a new customer record with no pet records, but a pet should always be related to a valid customer. Referential integrity should keep a customer number from being deleted or changed if a pet is related to it.

Regardless of how it happens, it's possible to have a customer in the Customer table who has no pets. It's less likely, but still theoretically possible, to have a pet with no owner. If you create a query to show customers and their pets, any record of a customer without pets or a pet record without a matching customer record will not be shown in the resulting dynaset.

It can be important for you to find these *lost* records. One of the features of a query is to perform several types of joins.

Tip Access can help you find *lost* records between tables; use the Query Wizards to build a *Find Unmatched Query*.

Changing join properties

With the Customer and Pets tables joined, certain join behaviors (or *properties*), exist between the tables. The join property is a rule that says to display all records (for the fields you specify) that correspond to the characters found in the Customer Number field of the Customer table and in the corresponding Customer Number field of the Pets table.

To translate this rule into a practical example, this is what happens in the Customer and Pets tables:

- ✦ If a record in the Customer table has a number for a customer not found in the Pets table, then that Customer record will not be shown.
- ✦ If a record in the Pets table has a number for a customer number not in the Customer table, then that Pets record will not be shown.

This makes sense, at least most of the time. You don't want to see records for customers without pets — *or do you?*

A join property is a rule that is operated by Access. This rule tells Access how to interpret any exceptions (possibly errors) between two tables. Should the noncorresponding records be shown?

Access has several types of joins, each with its own characteristics or behaviors. Access lets you change the type of join quickly by changing its properties. You can change join properties by selecting the join line between tables and double-clicking on the line. When you do so, a Join Properties dialog box appears. The dialog box in Figure 14-9 is the result of selecting the join line between the Customer and Pets tables.

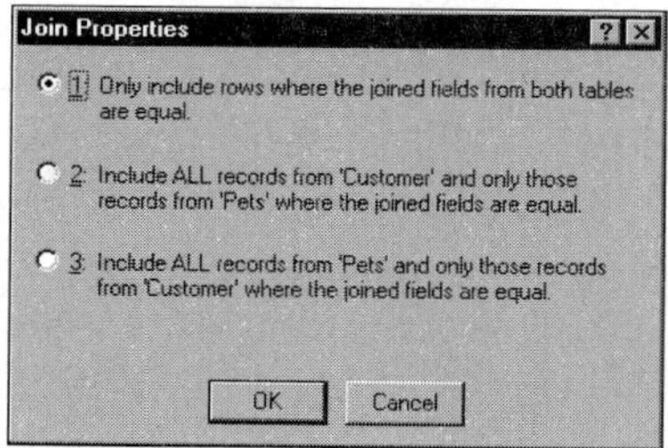

Figure 14-9: The Join Properties dialog box.

The Join Properties dialog box has three option buttons, which are displayed in this manner for the Pets and Customer tables:

1. Only include rows where the joined fields from both tables are equal. *(This is the default.)*
2. Include ALL records from the Customer table and only those records from the Pets table where the joined fields are equal.
3. Include ALL records from the Pets table and only those records from the Customer table where the joined fields are equal.

The first choice is commonly known as an *inner join,* and the other two are known as *outer joins.* These joins control the behavior of Access as it builds the dynaset from the query.

Inner and outer joins

Your Query Design window should presently display two tables in the top pane of the Query window — Pets and Customer. The following sections use these tables as examples to explain how inner and outer joins operate.

Displaying an inner join

To display an inner join, follow this procedure: In the QBE pane, select the fields Customer Number and Customer Name from the Customer table and the fields Pet Name and Type of Animal from the Pets table. Then display the dynaset by selecting the Datasheet button on the toolbar. The datasheet should now look like Figure 14-10, displaying each customer, all the customers' pets, and the type of animal for each pet. Scroll through the records until you reach the bottom of the datasheet.

Notice that each of the 129 records has entries in all four fields. This means every record displayed from the Customer table has a corresponding record or records in the Pets table.

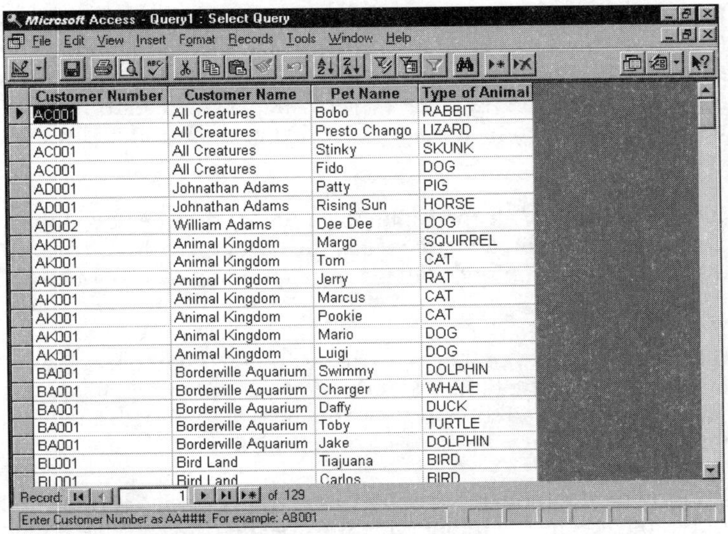

Microsoft Access - Query1 : Select Query

File Edit View Insert Format Records Tools Window Help

Customer Number	Customer Name	Pet Name	Type of Animal
AC001	All Creatures	Bobo	RABBIT
AC001	All Creatures	Presto Chango	LIZARD
AC001	All Creatures	Stinky	SKUNK
AC001	All Creatures	Fido	DOG
AD001	Johnathan Adams	Patty	PIG
AD001	Johnathan Adams	Rising Sun	HORSE
AD002	William Adams	Dee Dee	DOG
AK001	Animal Kingdom	Margo	SQUIRREL
AK001	Animal Kingdom	Tom	CAT
AK001	Animal Kingdom	Jerry	RAT
AK001	Animal Kingdom	Marcus	CAT
AK001	Animal Kingdom	Pookie	CAT
AK001	Animal Kingdom	Mario	DOG
AK001	Animal Kingdom	Luigi	DOG
BA001	Borderville Aquarium	Swimmy	DOLPHIN
BA001	Borderville Aquarium	Charger	WHALE
BA001	Borderville Aquarium	Daffy	DUCK
BA001	Borderville Aquarium	Toby	TURTLE
BA001	Borderville Aquarium	Jake	DOLPHIN
BL001	Bird Land	Tiajuana	BIRD
BL001	Bird Land	Carlos	BIRD

Record: 1 of 129

Enter Customer Number as AA###. For example: AB001

Figure 14-10: The data sheet for an inner join.

Return to query design mode by clicking on the Design icon on the toolbar. When you double-click on the join line between the Customer and Pets tables, you see that the join property for these two tables becomes the first selection shown in the Join Properties dialog box (see Figure 14-9). This is an inner join, or *equi-join*, the most common type. These joins show only the records that have a correspondence between tables.

Creating an outer join

Unlike equi-joins (inner joins), outer joins are used for showing all records in one table while showing common records in the other. An outer join will point graphically to one of the tables. When you look at the join line, it says, "Show all records from the main table (the one missing the arrow) while showing only matching records in the table being pointed to." For a further explanation, follow these instructions:

1. Return to the query design and again double-click on the join line between Customer and Pets.
2. Select the second choice from the Join Properties dialog box, which includes all records from the Customer table and only those records from Pets where the joined fields are equal. Then select the OK button. Notice that the join line now has an arrow at one end, pointing rightward to the Pets table. This is known as a *right outer join* in database terminology.

3. Select the Datasheet button to display this dynaset. Everything looks the same as before. Now move down the page until you can see record number 63. You should see a record for Customer Number JO003, Carla Jones, but no corresponding entry in the field Pet Name or Type of Animal (see Figure 14-11). This record results from selecting the join property that specifies "include all records from Customer ...4."

Note Unlike equi-joins, outer joins show all corresponding records between two tables *and* records that do *not* have a corresponding record in the other table. In the preceding example, you see a record for Carla Jones but no corresponding record for any pets she owns.

If you've changed the display order of the tables since adding them to the Query window, Access does not follow the table order that you set up; rather, it uses the original order in which you selected the tables. As the information is normally the same in either table, it won't make a difference which field is selected first.

Select the Design button on the toolbar to return to the Query Design window. When you created the outer join for the Customer table with the Pets table, Access changed the appearance of the graphical join line to show an arrow at one end. As shown in Figure 14-12, the arrow is pointing toward the Pets table. This tells you that Access has created an outer join and will therefore show you *all* records in the Customer table and *only* those that match in the Pets table.

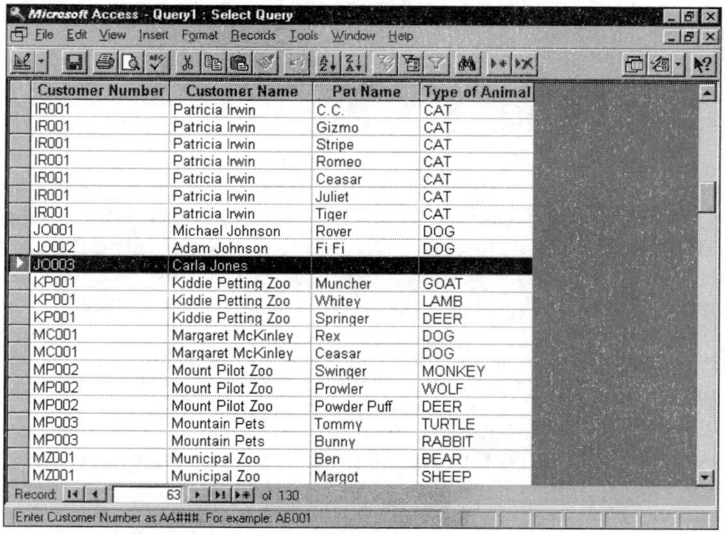

Microsoft Access - Query1 : Select Query

File Edit View Insert Format Records Tools Window Help

Customer Number	Customer Name	Pet Name	Type of Animal
IR001	Patricia Irwin	C.C.	CAT
IR001	Patricia Irwin	Gizmo	CAT
IR001	Patricia Irwin	Stripe	CAT
IR001	Patricia Irwin	Romeo	CAT
IR001	Patricia Irwin	Ceasar	CAT
IR001	Patricia Irwin	Juliet	CAT
IR001	Patricia Irwin	Tiger	CAT
JO001	Michael Johnson	Rover	DOG
JO002	Adam Johnson	Fi Fi	DOG
JO003	Carla Jones		
KP001	Kiddie Petting Zoo	Muncher	GOAT
KP001	Kiddie Petting Zoo	Whitey	LAMB
KP001	Kiddie Petting Zoo	Springer	DEER
MC001	Margaret McKinley	Rex	DOG
MC001	Margaret McKinley	Ceasar	DOG
MP002	Mount Pilot Zoo	Swinger	MONKEY
MP002	Mount Pilot Zoo	Prowler	WOLF
MP002	Mount Pilot Zoo	Powder Puff	DEER
MP003	Mountain Pets	Tommy	TURTLE
MP003	Mountain Pets	Bunny	RABBIT
MZ001	Municipal Zoo	Ben	BEAR
MZ001	Municipal Zoo	Margot	SHEEP

Record: 63 of 130

Enter Customer Number as AA###. For example: AB001

Figure 14-11: A datasheet with a right outer join.

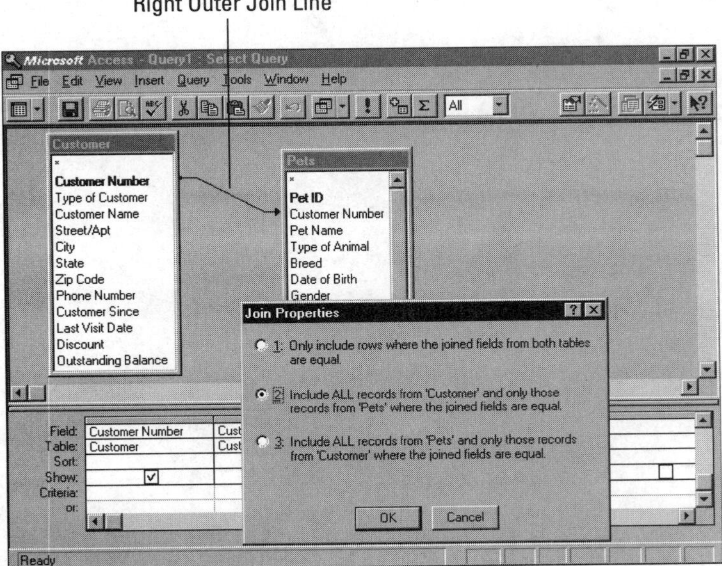

Figure 14-12: The table/query pane showing a right outer join.

Creating another outer join

Return to the query design and again double-click on the join line between the Customer and Pets tables.

Select the third choice from the Join Properties dialog box, which asks to "include all records from Pets. . .". Then click on the OK button. Notice that the join line now has an arrow pointing to the Customer table, as shown in Figure 14-13. This is known as a *left outer join*. (If the arrow is pointing to the right in the top pane, the join is known as a right outer join; when the arrow points to the left, it's a left outer join.)

Select the Datasheet button to display this dynaset. Now move down the page until you can see record number 68, as shown in Figure 14-14. You should see a record with nothing in the field Customer Number or Customer Name. All you see is Animal Name (which is Brownie) and the fact that it's a dog. This record results from selecting the join property to include all records from Pets. This is known as a *left outer join* in database terminology.

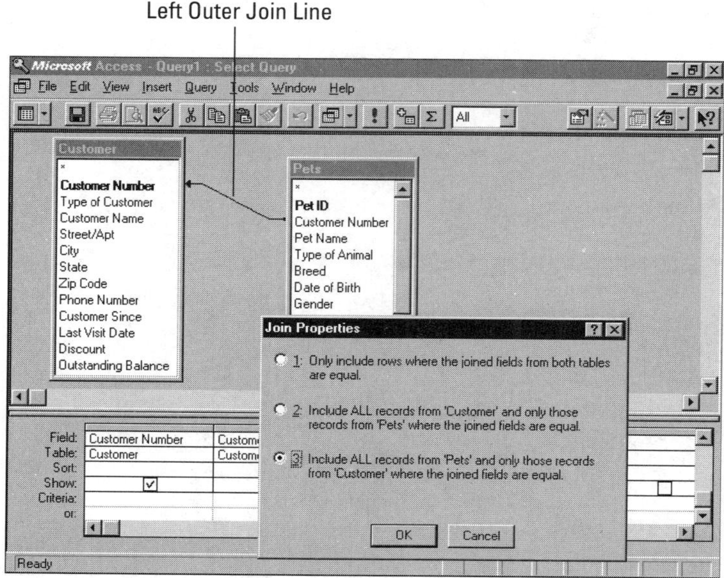

Figure 14-13: The table/query pane showing a left outer join.

Microsoft Access - Query1 : Select Query

File Edit View Insert Format Records Tools Window Help

Customer Number	Customer Name	Pet Name	Type of Animal
KP001	Kiddie Petting Zoo	Whitey	LAMB
KP001	Kiddie Petting Zoo	Springer	DEER
MC001	Margaret McKinley	Rex	DOG
MC001	Margaret McKinley	Ceasar	DOG
		Brownie	DOG
MP002	Mount Pilot Zoo	Swinger	MONKEY
MP002	Mount Pilot Zoo	Prowler	WOLF
MP002	Mount Pilot Zoo	Powder Puff	DEER
MP003	Mountain Pets	Tommy	TURTLE
MP003	Mountain Pets	Bunny	RABBIT
MZ001	Municipal Zoo	Ben	BEAR
MZ001	Municipal Zoo	Margot	SHEEP
ON001	Oregon Nature Center	Thunder	HORSE
ON001	Oregon Nature Center	Flower	SKUNK
ON001	Oregon Nature Center	Swishy	SQUIRREL
ON001	Oregon Nature Center	Martin	BEAR
PC001	Pet City	Sylvester	DOG
PC001	Pet City	Squeeker	GUINEA PIG
PL001	Puppy Love	Pluto	DOG
PL001	Puppy Love	Goofy	DOG
PL001	Puppy Love	Sandy	DOG
PO001	Tyrone Potter	Slither	SNAKE

Record: 68 of 130

Enter Customer Number as AA###. For example: AB001

Figure 14-14: A datasheet with a left outer join.

Creating a Cartesian product

If you add both the Customer and Pets tables to a query and don't specify a join between the tables, Access takes the first Customer record and combines it with all the Pets records; then it takes the second record and also combines it with all the Pets records. This combining of records between tables produces a total of 6,321 records in the resultant dynaset. Combining each record in one table with each record in the other results in a Cartesian product (cross product) of both tables.

Summary

In this chapter, you learned about creating relationships between tables and how to use joins in queries. The chapter covered the following points:

✦ You can add multiple tables to a query, including multiple copies of the same table.

✦ Access creates join lines automatically for any tables that have their relationships set at table level.

✦ You can add fields from multiple-table queries in any order. Multiple-table fields are moved and changed in the same way as fields from single tables.

✦ To view data from two or more tables, you must join them.

✦ You can create joins between two tables by dragging and dropping a field from one table to another. Access draws a graphic join line between the fields.

✦ There are two types of joins — inner joins (equi-joins) and outer joins.

✦ An inner join (also known as an equi-join) displays records that have a common field in both tables with corresponding data in those fields.

✦ An outer join displays all records having corresponding data in both fields, and also displays records from one table that do not have corresponding records in the other table.

✦ The two types of outer joins are left and right. Access displays a pointer in the table/query pane to show the type of outer join that you create.

In the next chapter, you examine how to create select queries.

✦ ✦ ✦

Creating Select Queries

In This Chapter

Creating and using Text expressions as criteria

Using the Like and Not operators and wildcards

Creating and using Memo, Date, and Numeric expressions as criteria

Using the And/Or operators in single-field criteria

Using the In and Between…And operators

Searching for Null data

Using the And/Or operators across several fields

Building complex expressions for queries

Using functions as expressions for criteria

Creating and using a calculated field

Up to this point, you have worked with queries based on criteria against a single field. You also learned how to add multiple tables to a query and how to join tables together. This chapter focuses on extracting information from multiple tables in select queries.

Moving Beyond Simple Queries

Select queries are the most common type of query you will use; they *select* information (based on a specific criterion) from one or more related tables. With these queries, you can ask questions and receive answers about information stored in your database tables. So far, you have worked with queries that pose simple criteria for a single field in a table. You worked with math operators, such as equal (=) and greater-than (>).

Knowing how to specify criteria is critical to designing effective queries. Although queries can be created against a single table for a single criterion, most queries extract information from several tables and more complex criteria. Because of this complexity, your queries retrieve only the data you need, in the order you need it. You may, for example, want to select and display data from the Mountain Animal Hospital database with these limitations:

- ✦ All owners of horses or cows or pigs
- ✦ All animals that were given a specific medication during a specific week last year
- ✦ All owners whose dogs or cats had blood work performed over the past four months
- ✦ Only the first animal of each type you have treated
- ✦ Any animal that has the word *color* in the Memo field Comments

As your database system evolves, you will probably ask questions such as these about the information stored in the system. Although the system was not originally developed specifically for these questions, you can find the information needed to answer them stored in the tables. Because the information is there, you find yourself performing *ad-hoc* queries against the database. The ad-hoc queries you perform by using select queries can be very simple or quite complex.

Select queries are the easiest way to obtain information from several tables without resorting to writing programs.

Using query comparison operators

When you're working with select queries, you may need to specify one or more *criteria* to limit the scope of information you want to see. You accomplish this by using *comparison operators* in equations and calculations. The categories of operators include mathematical, relational, logical, and string operators. In select queries, normally you would use operators in either the Field: or Criteria: cell of the QBE pane.

A good rule of thumb to observe is the following:

> *Use mathematical and string operators for creating calculated fields; use relational and logical operators for specifying scope criteria.*

Cross Ref Calculated fields will be discussed later in this chapter. You can find an in-depth explanation of operators in Chapter 13.

Table 15-1 shows most of the common operators used with select queries.

Table 15-1
Common Operators Used in Select Queries

Mathematical	*Relational*	*Logical*	*String*	*Miscellaneous*
* (multiply)	= (equal)	And	& (concatenate)	Between … And
/ (divide)	<> (not equal)	Or	Like	In
+ (add)	> (greater than)	Not		Is Null
– (subtract)	< (less than)			

Using these operators, you can ferret out such types of records as the following:

- ✦ Pet records that have a picture associated with them
- ✦ A range of records, such as all patients seen between November and January

✦ Records that meet both And *and* Or criteria, such as all pets that are dogs *and* are not either neutered *or* have a current vaccination

✦ All records that do *not* match a value, such as any animal that is *not* a cat

When you supply a criterion to a query, you use the operator with an *example* that you supply. In Figure 15-1, the example entered is `PIG`. The operator is equal (=). Notice that the equal sign is *not* shown in the figure. The equal sign is the default operator for criteria selection.

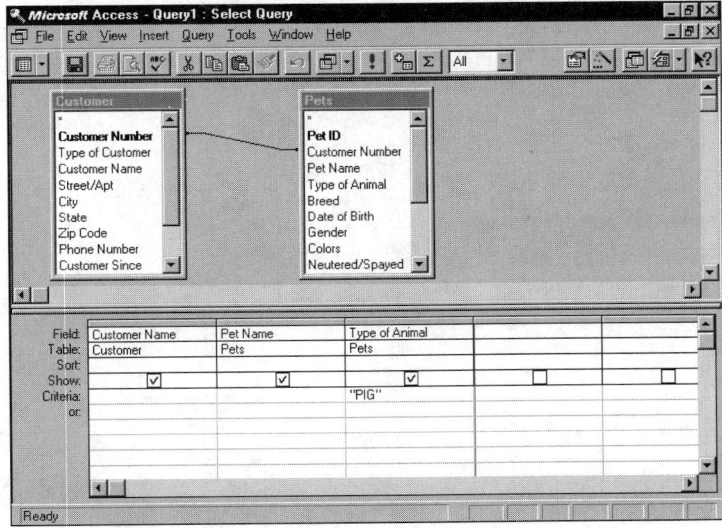

Figure 15-1: The QBE pane with a simple criterion.

Note When working with criteria for select queries, you supply an example of what type of information Access needs to find in the Criteria: cell of the Query By Example (QBE) pane.

Cross Ref Chapter 10 gives an in-depth explanation of working with queries.

Understanding complex criteria selection

As Table 15-1 shows, you can use several operators to build complex criteria. To most people, complex criteria consist of a series of Ands and Ors, as in these examples:

✦ State must be Idaho *or* Oregon

✦ City must be Borderville *and* state must be Washington

✦ State must be Idaho *or* Washington *and* city must be Borderville

These examples demonstrate use of both the logical operators And/Or. Many times, you can create complex criteria by entering example data in different cells of the QBE pane. Figure 15-2 demonstrates how you can create complex And/Or criteria without having to enter the operator key words And/Or at all. This example displays all customers and their pets who satisfy these criteria: *Live in the city of Borderville and live in either the state of Washington or the state of Idaho, and whose pet is not a dog*

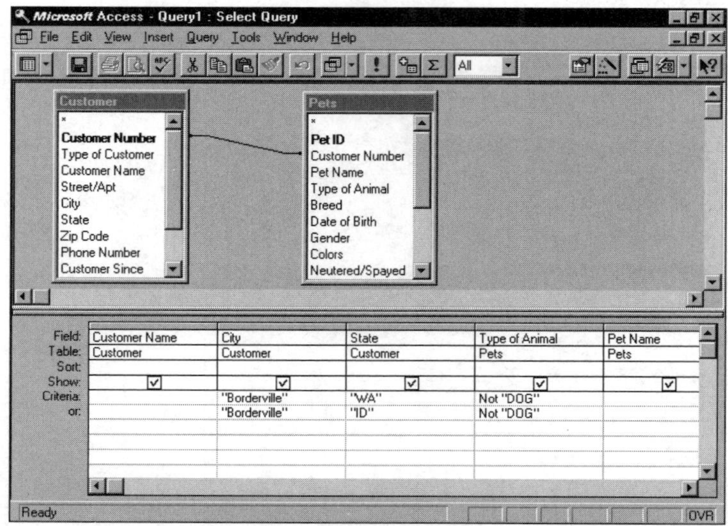

Figure 15-2: Creating complex And/Or criteria by example without using the And/Or operators.

Note Sometimes you see a field name referenced by the table name first and then the field name, with a dot (period) in between the two names. This way, you understand which table a field belongs to. This is especially critical when you're describing two fields that have the same name but come from different tables. In a multiple-table query, you see this format in the field list when you add a field to the QBE pane by clicking an empty column. You can also see this format when you create a multiple table form and use the field list. The general format is *Table Name.Field Name*. Examples are `Pets.Type of Animal` or `Customer.Customer Name`.

If you build a mathematical formula for this query, it will look something like this:

```
((Customer.City="Borderville") AND (Customer.State="WA") AND (Not
      Pets.[Type of Animal]="DOG")) OR
      ((Customer.City="Borderville") AND (Customer.State="ID")
      AND (Not Pets.[Type of Animal]="DOG"))
```

Notice that you must enter the city and pet example for each state line in the QBE pane of Figure 15-2. Later, you use the And/Or operators in a Criteria: cell of the query, eliminating the need for redundant entry of these fields.

Tip

To find records that do *not* match a value, use the Not operator with the value. For example, enter the expression *Not Dog* to find all animals except dogs.

The And/Or operators are the most common when you're working with complex criteria. The operators consider two different formulas (one on each side of the And/Or operators), and then determine individually whether they are True or False. Then they compare the resultants of the two formulas against each other for a logical True/False answer. For example, take the first And statement in the formula just given:

```
(Customer.City="Borderville") AND (Customer.State="WA")
```

The first half of the formula, `Customer.City = "Borderville"`, converts to a True if the city is Borderville (False if a different city; Null if no city was entered in the field).

Then the second half of the formula, Customer.State = "WA", is converted to a True if the state is Washington (False if a different state; Null if no state was entered). Then the And compares the logical True/False from each side against the other to give a resulting True/False answer.

Note

A field has a *Null value* when it has no value at all; it is the lack of entry of information in a field. Null is neither True nor False; nor is it equivalent to all spaces or zero — it has no value. If you never enter a city name in the City field, simply skipping over it, Access leaves the field empty. This state of emptiness is known as Null.

When the resultant of an And/Or is True, the overall condition is True, and the query displays those records meeting the True condition. Table 15-2 gives a quick review of True conditions for each operator.

Table 15-2
Results of Logical Operators And/Or

Left Side Is	*Operator Is*	*Right Side Is*	*Resultant Answer Is*
True	AND	True	True
True	OR	True	True
True	OR	False	True
True	OR	Null	True
False	OR	True	True
Null	OR	True	True

Notice that the And operator is True only when *both* sides of the formula are True, whereas the Or operator is True whenever *either* side of the formula is True. In fact, one side can be a Null value, and the Or operator is still True if the other side is True. This is the distinct difference between And/Or operators.

Cross Ref

Refer to Chapter 13 for further details about logical operators.

Using functions in select queries

When you work with queries, you may want to use built-in Access functions to display information. For example, you may want to display such items as the following:

- ✦ The day of week (Sunday, Monday, and so forth) for visit dates
- ✦ All customer names in uppercase
- ✦ The difference between two date fields

You can display all this information by creating calculated fields for the query. This will be discussed in depth later in this chapter.

Referencing fields in select queries

When you work with a field name in queries, as you do with calculated fields or criteria values, you should enclose the field name in brackets ([]). Access requires brackets around any field name that is in a criterion, and around any field name that contains a space or punctuation. An example of a field name in brackets is the criterion `[Visit Date] + 30`. You will find more examples later in this chapter.

Warning

If you omit the brackets ([]) around a field name in the criterion, Access automatically places quotes around the field name and treats it as text instead of a field name.

Entering Single-Value Field Criteria

Often you may want to limit query records on the basis of a single field criterion, as in these queries:

- ✦ Customer information for customers living in the state of Washington
- ✦ Animals you have treated from the local zoos in the area
- ✦ Customers and animals you treated during the month of January

All three of these queries require a single-value criterion. Simply put, *single-value criterion* is the entry of only one expression in a field. That expression can be example data or a function: `"WA"` or `DatePart("m",[Visit Date])=1` are both examples of single-value criteria.

You can specify criteria expressions for any type of data, whether Text, Numeric, Date/Time, and so forth. Even OLE Object and Counter field types can have criteria specified.

Cross Ref For a full explanation of expressions, operators, identifiers, literals, and functions, see Chapter 13.

Disk All the examples in this chapter rely on several tables: Customer, Pets, and Visits. The majority of these examples use only the Customer and Pets tables. You should create a new query and add the Customer and Pets tables.

As you read each series of steps in this chapter, they tell you which tables and fields make up the query. In most examples, you should clear all previous criteria before going to the next example. Each of the examples focuses on the criteria lines of the QBE pane. You can also view each figure to make sure you understand the correct placement of the criteria in each example. Only a few dynasets are shown; you can follow along and view the data. The Mountain Start database contains only the tables used in this chapter.

Entering character (Text or Memo) criteria

Character criteria are used for Text or Memo data types fields. This is either examples or data about the contents of the field. For example, to create a text criterion to display customers who own birds, follow these steps:

1. Select Customer Name from the Customer table, Pet Name and Type of Animal in the Pets table.
2. Click on the Criteria: cell of Type of Animal.
3. Type **BIRD** in the cell.

Your query should look similar to Figure 15-3. Notice that only two tables are open and only three fields are selected. You can click on the Datasheet button to see the results of this query.

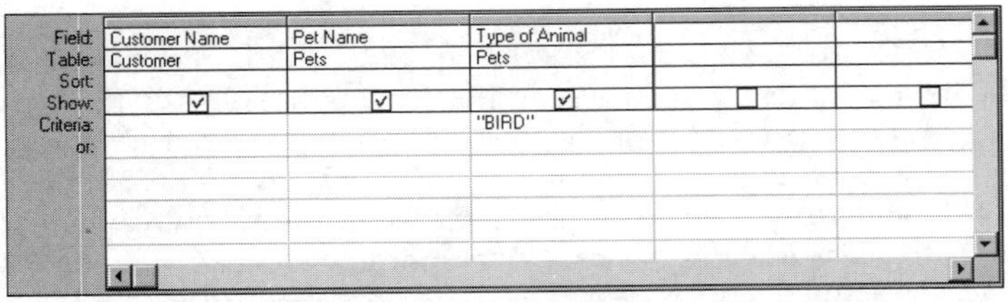

Field:	Customer Name	Pet Name	Type of Animal		
Table:	Customer	Pets	Pets		
Sort:					
Show:	☑	☑	☑	☐	☐
Criteria:			"BIRD"		
or:					

Figure 15-3: The Query Design window, with two files open (and automatically linked).

Tip

When you specify example-type criteria, it is not necessary to match capitalization. Access defaults to case-insensitive when working with queries. You can enter *BIRD*, *bird*, or *BiRd* and receive the same results.

Notice that you didn't have to enter an equal sign before the literal word *bird*. This is because Access uses the equal operator as the default. If you want to see all animals except birds, you use either the <> (not equal) or the Not operator before the word *bird*.

You also didn't have to place quotes around the word *bird*. Access understands that you are talking about the example literal *BIRD*, and places the quotes for you automatically.

In Version 1.*x*, Access places quotation marks (") only around example literals that contain no spaces. If the literal has spaces, you must provide the quotes or Access reports an error on execution. However, in Version 2.0 and for Windows 95, Access automatically places quotation marks around any example data you provide, as long as it is not enclosed in brackets ([ ]).

Tip

You should use the double quotation mark to surround literals. Access normally uses the single quotation mark as a remark character in its programming language. However, when you use the single quotation mark in the Criteria: cell, Access interprets it as a double quotation mark.

The Like operator and wildcards

Up to this point, you've been working with *literal* criteria. You specified the exact field contents for Access to find, which in the example was "Bird." Access used the literal to find the specific records. Sometimes, however, you know only a part of the field contents, or you may want to see a wider range of records on the basis of a pattern. For example, you may want to see all pet visits for pets that begin with the letter *G*; you want to check gerbils, goats, and so forth. Perhaps a more practical example is when you have a customer who owns a pig that was born Siamese. You remember making a note of it in the Comments field; you don't, however, remember which pig it was. This requires using a wildcard search against the Memo field to find any records that contain the word *Siamese*.

Access uses the string operator Like in the Criteria: cell of a field to perform wildcard searches against the field's contents. Access searches for a pattern in the field; you use the question mark (?) to represent a single character or the asterisk (*) for several characters. (This is just like working with filenames at the DOS level.) Besides the two characters, (?) and (*), Access uses three other characters for performing wildcard searches. Table 15-3 lists the wildcards that the Like operator can use.

The question mark (?) stands for any single character located in the same position as the question mark in the example expression. An asterisk (*) stands for any number of characters in the same position in which the asterisk is placed. Unlike the asterisk at

DOS level, Access can use the asterisk any number of times in an example expression. The pound sign (#) stands for any single digit found in the same position as the pound sign. The brackets ([ ]) and the list they enclose stand for any single character that matches any one character of the list located within the brackets. Finally, the exclamation point (!) inside the brackets represents the *Not word* for the list — that is, any single character that does *not* match any character of the list within the brackets.

Table 15-3
Wildcards Used by the Like Operator

Wildcard	*Purpose*
?	A single character (0-9, Aa-Zz)
*	Any number of characters (0 to *n*)
#	Any single digit (0-9)
[*list*]	Any single character in the list
[!list]	Any single character not in the list

These wildcards can be used alone or in conjunction with each other. They can even be used several times within the same expression. The examples in Table 15-4 demonstrate how the wildcards can be used.

To create an example using the Like operator, suppose you want to find that record of the Siamese pig. You know that this fact is referenced in one of the records in the Comments field. To create the query, follow these steps:

1. Remove the criterion field for Type of Animal.
2. Double-click on the Comments field in the Pets table.
3. Click on the Criteria: cell of the Comments field.
4. Type ***Siamese*** in the cell.

Table 15-4
Using Wildcards with the Like Operator

Expression	*Field Used In*	*Results of Criteria*
Like "Re?"	Pets.Pet Name	Finds all records of pets whose names are three letters long and begin with "Re"; examples: Red, Rex, Ren

(continued)

Table 15-4 *(continued)*		
Expression	***Field Used In***	***Results of Criteria***
Like "*Siamese*"	Pets.Comments	Finds all records with the word "Siamese" somewhere within the Comments field
Like "G*"	Pets.Type of Animal	Finds all records for animals of a type that begins with the letter G
Like "1/*/93"	Visits.Visit Date	Finds all records for the month of January 1993
Like "## Main St."	Customer.Street/Apt	Finds all records for houses with house numbers between 10 and 99 inclusively; examples: 10, 22, 33, 51
Like "[RST]*"	Customer.City	Finds all records for customers who live in any city with a name beginning with R, S, or T
Like "[!EFG]*"	Pets.Type of Animal	Finds all records for animals of a types that do not begin with the letters E, F, or G; all other animals are displayed

When you move the cursor, leaving the Criteria: cell, Access automatically adds the operator Like and the quotation marks around the expression. Your query should appear similar to Figure 15-4.

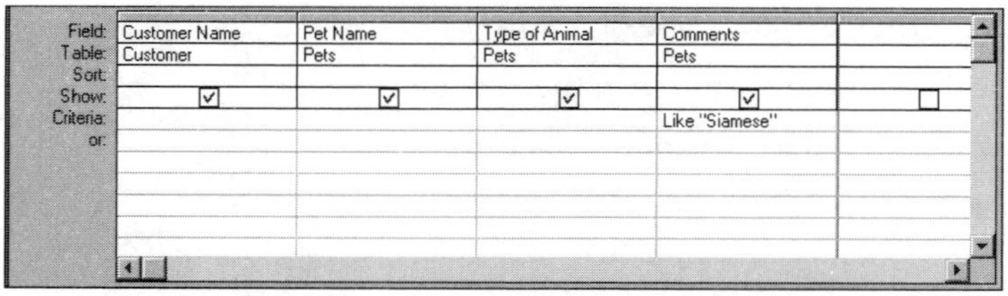

Field:	Customer Name	Pet Name	Type of Animal	Comments	
Table:	Customer	Pets	Pets	Pets	
Sort:					
Show:	☑	☑	☑	☑	☐
Criteria:				Like "Siamese"	
or:					

Figure 15-4: Using the Like operator with a selected query.

Access adds the Like operator and quotation marks for you if you meet the following conditions:

- ✦ There are no spaces in your expression.
- ✦ You use only the wildcards ?, *, and #.
- ✦ You use brackets [ ] inside quotation marks " " .

If you use the brackets without quotation marks, you must supply the operator Like and the quotation marks.

Using the Like operator with wildcards is the best way to perform pattern searches through Memo fields.

Warning The Like operator and its wildcards can be used only against three types of fields: Text, Memo, and Date. Using these with any other type can result in an error.

Specifying nonmatching values

To specify a nonmatching value, you simply use either the Not or the <> operator in front of the expression that you don't want to match. For example, you may want to see all customers and their pets for all states, but you want to exclude Washington. You see how to specify this nonmatching value in the following steps:

1. Start with an empty query, using the Customer and Pets tables.
2. Select the Customer Name and State fields from Customer and Pet Name from Pets.
3. Click on the Criteria: cell of State.
4. Type **Not "WA"** in the cell.

The query should now look similar to Figure 15-5. The query will select all records *except* those for customers who live in the state of Washington.

Note You can use the <> operator instead of Not. In Step 4 of the steps for excluding Washington from the criterion, the resulting dynaset is the same with either operator. These two operators are interchangeable. The exception is with the use of the keyword Is. You cannot say Is <> Null. Rather, you must say Not Is Null.

Field:	Customer Name	State	Pet Name		
Table:	Customer	Customer	Pets		
Sort:					
Show:	☑	☑	☑	☐	☐
Criteria:		Not "WA"			
or:					

Figure 15-5: Using the Not operator in criteria.

Entering numeric (Number, Currency, or Counter) criteria

Numeric criteria are used for Number, Currency, or Counter data type fields. You simply enter the digits and the decimal symbol, if required. For example, you may want to see all animals that weigh over 100 pounds. To create a query like this, follow these steps:

1. Start with a new query, using the Customer and Pets tables.
2. Select the Customer Name in the Customer table, Pet Name, Type of Animal, and Weight in the Pets table.
3. Click on the Criteria: cell of Weight.
4. Type **>100** in the cell.

When you follow these steps, your query looks similar to Figure 15-6. When working with numeric data, Access does not enclose the expression, as it does with string or date criteria.

Numeric fields are generally compared to a value string that uses comparison operators, such as less than (<), greater than (>), or equal to (=). If you want to specify a comparison other than equal, you must enter the operator as well. Remember that Access defaults to equal for all criteria. That is why you needed to specify greater than (>) 100 in the query for animals over 100 pounds.

Working with Currency and counter data in a query is exactly the same as working with numeric data; you specify an operator and a numeric value.

Field:	Customer Name	Pet Name	Type of Animal	Weight	
Table:	Customer	Pets	Pets	Pets	
Sort:					
Show:	☑	☑	☑	☑	☐
Criteria:				>100	
or:					

Figure 15-6: Criteria set for weight of animals.

Entering Yes/No (logic) criteria

Yes/No criteria are used for Yes/No type fields. The example data that you supply in the criteria can be only for Yes or No states. You can use the Not and the <> operators to signify the opposite, but the Yes/No data also has a Null state you may want to check for.

When entering criteria in a Yes/No field, you are not limited to entering a Yes or No expression. Access recognizes several forms of Yes and No. Table 15-5 lists all the positive and negative values you can use.

Thus, instead of typing Yes, you can enter any of the following in the Criteria: cell: **On**, **True**, **Not No**, **<> No**, **<No**, or **–1**.

Note As stated earlier, a Yes/No field can have only three criteria states, Yes, No, and Null. Checking for Is Null will display only records with no value, and checking for Is Not Null will always display all Yes or No records. After a Yes/No field check box is checked (or checked and then unchecked) it can never be null. It will be Yes or No (–1 or 0).

Table 15-5
Positive and Negative Values Used in Yes/No Fields

Yes	True	On	Not No	<> No	<No	–1
No	False	Off	Not Yes	<>Yes	>Yes	0

Entering a criterion for an OLE object

You can even specify a criterion for OLE objects: Is Not Null. As an example, suppose you don't have pictures for all the animals and you want to view only those records that have a picture of the animal — that is, where picture is not Null. You specify the Is Not Null criterion for the Picture field of the Pets table. Once you've done this, Access limits the records to only those that have a picture in them.

Although **Is Not Null** is the correct syntax, you can also type **Not Null** and Access will supply the Is operator for you.

Entering Multiple Criteria in One Field

So far, you've worked with single-condition criteria on a single field at a time. As you learned, single-condition criteria can be specified for any field type. Now you'll work with multiple criteria based on a single field. You may be interested in seeing all records where the type of animal is either a cat or a squirrel for example, or perhaps you want to view the records of all the animals you saw between July 1, 1995, and December 31, 1995.

The QBE pane provides the flexibility for solving these types of problems. You can specify several criteria for one field or for several fields in a select query. Using multiple criteria, for example, you can determine which customers and pets are from Idaho or Washington (`"ID" or "WA"`), or which animals you saw for general examinations in the past 30 days (`Between Date() and Date()-30`).

To specify several criteria for one field, you use the And and the Or operators.

Understanding an Or operation

You use an Or operation in queries when you want a field to meet either of two conditions. For example, you may want to see the customer and pet names of all rabbits and squirrels. In other words, you want to see all records where a customer owns a rabbit *or* a squirrel, *or* both. Following is the general formula for this operation:

```
[Type of Animal] = "Rabbit" Or [Type of Animal] = "Squirrel"
```

If either side of this formula is True, the resulting answer is also True. To clarify this point, consider the following conditions:

- ✦ Customer One owns a rabbit but does not own a squirrel — the formula is True.
- ✦ Customer Two owns a squirrel but does not own a rabbit — the formula is True.
- ✦ Customer Three owns a squirrel and a rabbit — the formula is True.
- ✦ Customer Four does not own a rabbit and does not own a squirrel — the formula is False.

Specifying multiple values for a field using the Or operator

You use the Or operator to specify multiple values for a field. For example, you use the Or operator if you want to see all records of owners of fish or frogs or ducks. To accomplish this task, follow these steps:

1. Create a new query, using the Customer and Pets tables.
2. Select the Customer Name field in the Customer table, Pet Name and Type of Animal in the Pets table.
3. Click on the Criteria: cell of Type of Animal.
4. Type **Fish Or Frog Or Duck** in the cell.

Your QBE pane should resemble Figure 15-7. Notice that Access automatically placed quotation marks around your example data, Fish, Frog, and Duck.

Field:	Customer Name	Pet Name	Type of Animal	
Table:	Customer	Pets	Pets	
Sort:				
Show:	☑	☑	☑	☐
Criteria:			"Fish" Or "Frog" Or "Duck"	
or:				

Figure 15-7: Using the Or operator.

This dynaset can be seen in Figure 15-8. Notice that the only records selected contain `FISH`, `FROG`, or `DUCK` in the Type of Animal column.

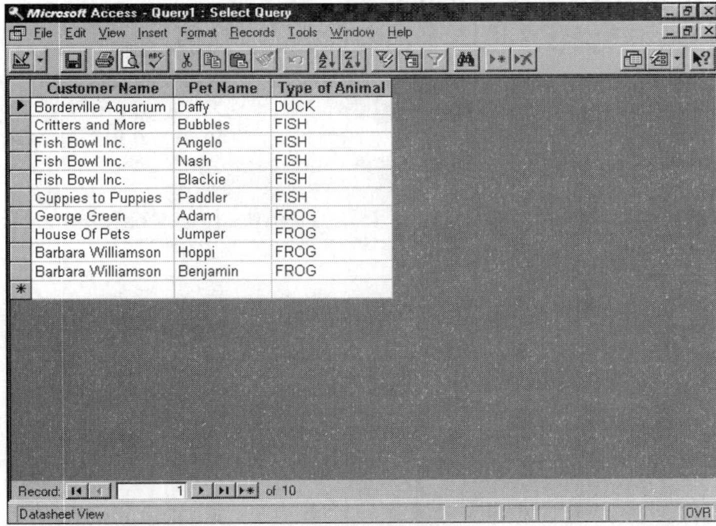

Customer Name	Pet Name	Type of Animal
Borderville Aquarium	Daffy	DUCK
Critters and More	Bubbles	FISH
Fish Bowl Inc.	Angelo	FISH
Fish Bowl Inc.	Nash	FISH
Fish Bowl Inc.	Blackie	FISH
Guppies to Puppies	Paddler	FISH
George Green	Adam	FROG
House Of Pets	Jumper	FROG
Barbara Williamson	Hoppi	FROG
Barbara Williamson	Benjamin	FROG

Figure 15-8: Selecting records with the Or operator.

Using the or cell of the QBE pane

Besides using the literal Or operator, you can supply individual criteria for the field on separate lines of the QBE pane. To do this, you enter the first criterion example in the Criteria: cell of the field, just as you have been. Then you enter the criterion example in the Or: cell of the field. Enter the next criterion in the cell directly beneath the first example; then continue entering examples vertically down the column. This is exactly equivalent to typing the Or operator between examples. Using the example in which you queried for fish, frogs, or ducks, change your QBE pane to look like the one in Figure 15-9. Notice that each type of animal is on a separate line in the query.

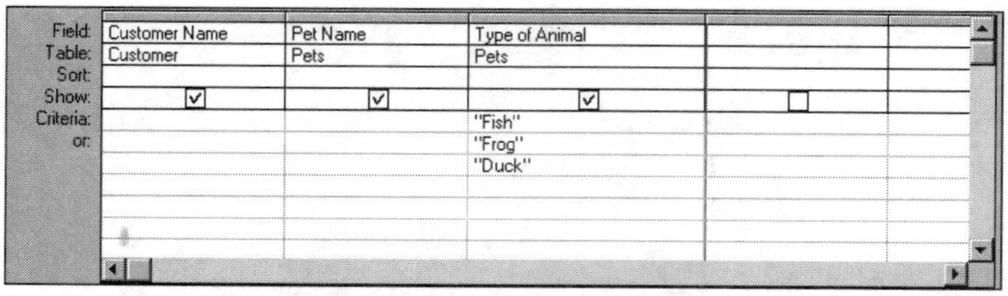

Field:	Customer Name	Pet Name	Type of Animal	
Table:	Customer	Pets	Pets	
Sort:				
Show:	☑	☑	☑	☐
Criteria:			"Fish"	
or:			"Frog"	
			"Duck"	

Figure 15-9: Using the or: cell of the QBE pane.

Access gives you five or: cells for each field. If you need to specify more Or conditions, use the Or operator between conditions (for example: **Cat Or Dog Or Pig**).

Using a list of values with the In operator

You can use another method for expressing the multiple values of a single field. This method uses the operator named *In.* The In operator finds a value that is one of a *list of values.* For example, enter the expression **IN(FISH, FROG, DUCK)** under the Type of Animal field. This action creates a list of values, where any item in the list becomes an example criterion. After you create the query, it should resemble Figure 15-10.

In this example, you can see that quotation marks are automatically entered around Fish, Frog, and Duck.

Note: When you work with the In operator, each value (example data) must be separated from the others by a comma.

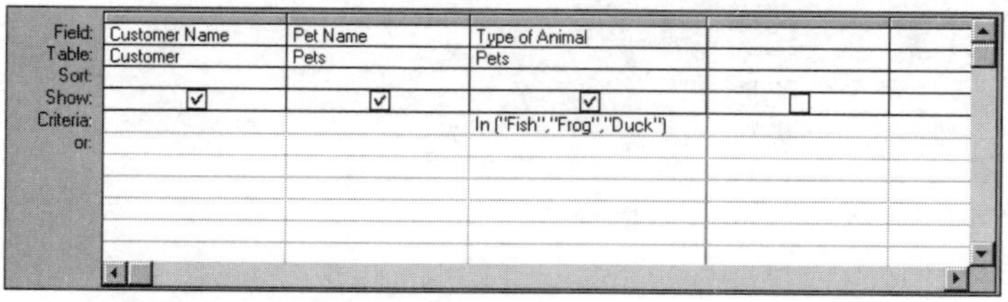

Field:	Customer Name	Pet Name	Type of Animal	
Table:	Customer	Pets	Pets	
Sort:				
Show:	☑	☑	☑	☐
Criteria:			In ("Fish","Frog","Duck")	
or:				

Figure 15-10: Using the In operator.

Understanding an And query

You use And operations in queries when you want a field to meet both of two conditions that you specify. For example, you may want to see records of pets that had a visit date `>= July 1, 1995 And <= December 31, 1995`. In other words, the animal had to be a patient during the last half of the year 1995. The general formula for this example is as follows:

```
[Visit Date] >= 7/1/95 And [Visit Date] <= 12/31/95
```

Unlike the Or operator (which has several conditions under which it is True), the And operator is True only when both sides of the formula are True. When both sides are True, the resulting answer will also be True. To clarify use of the And operator, consider the following conditions:

- ✦ Visit date (6/22/95) is not greater than 7/1/95, but it is less than 12/31/95 — the formula is False.
- ✦ Visit date (4/11/96) is greater than 7/1/95, but it is not less than 12/31/95 — the formula is False.
- ✦ Visit date (11/1/95) is greater than 7/1/95, and it is less than 12/31/95 — the formula is True.

Both sides of the operation must be True for the And operation to be True.

An And operation can be performed in any of several ways against a single field in Access.

Specifying a range using the And operator

You will find And operators used frequently in fields that have Numeric or Date/Time data types. They are seldom used in Text type, although they can be. For instance, you may be interested in viewing all animals whose names start with D, E, or F. You use the And operator here, although the Like operator would be better (`Like"[DEF]*"`). When you use an And operator with a single field, you are using it to set a *range* of acceptable values in the field. Therefore the key purpose of an And operator in a single field is to define a range of records to be viewed. An example of using the And operator to create a range criterion is to display all animals that weigh between 100 and 300 pounds, inclusively. To create this query, follow these steps:

1. Create a new query, using the Customer and Pets tables.
2. Select the Customer Name field in the Customer table, Pet Name, Type of Animal and Weight in the Pets table.
3. Click on the Criteria: cell of Weight.
4. Type **>=100 And <=300** in the cell.

The query should resemble Figure 15-11. Note that you can change the formula to **>99 And <301** with identical results.

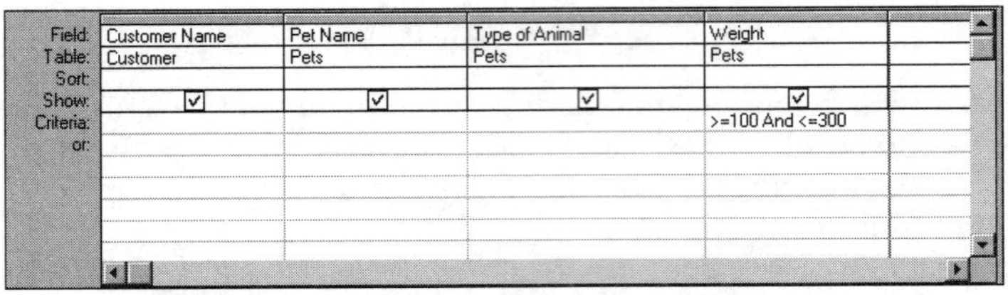

Field:	Customer Name	Pet Name	Type of Animal	Weight
Table:	Customer	Pets	Pets	Pets
Sort:				
Show:	☑	☑	☑	☑
Criteria:				>=100 And <=300
or:				

Figure 15-11: Using the And operator with numeric fields.

Using the Between … And operator

You can use another method for expressing a range of records from a single field. This method uses the operator called *Between … And.* With the Between … And operator, you can find records meeting a range of values — for example, all pets *Between* Dog *And* Pig. Using the example of animals weighing between 100 and 300 pounds, create the query using the Between … And operator, as shown in Figure 15-12.

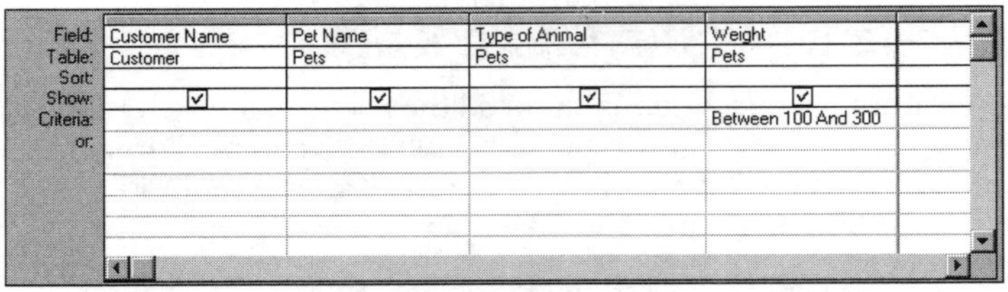

Field:	Customer Name	Pet Name	Type of Animal	Weight
Table:	Customer	Pets	Pets	Pets
Sort:				
Show:	☑	☑	☑	☑
Criteria:				Between 100 And 300
or:				

Figure 15-12: Using the Between … And Operator.

When you use the Between … And operator, each value (example data) is included in the resulting dynaset.

Searching for Null data

A field may have no contents; possibly the value wasn't known at the time of data entry, or the data-entry person simply forgot to enter the information, or the field's information has been removed. Access does nothing with this field; it simply remains an empty field. (You'll recall that a field is said to be *Null* when it's empty.)

Logically, a Null is neither True nor False. A Null is not equivalent to all spaces or to zero. A Null simply has no value.

Access lets you work with Null value fields by means of two special operators:

Is Null

Not Is Null

These operators are used to limit criteria based on Null values of a field. You already worked with a Null value when you queried for animals having a picture on file. In the next example, you look for animal records that don't specify gender. To create this query, follow these steps:

1. Create a new query using the Customer and pets tables.
2. Select the Customer Name field in the Customer table, Pet Name, Type of Animal and Gender field in the Pets table.
3. Click on the Criteria: cell of Gender.
4. Type **Is Null** in the cell.

Your query should now look like Figure 15-13. If you select the Datasheet button, you'll see that there are no records without a gender.

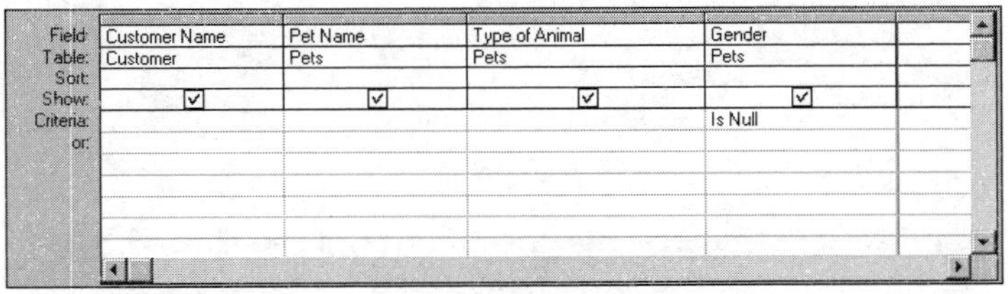

Field:	Customer Name	Pet Name	Type of Animal	Gender
Table:	Customer	Pets	Pets	Pets
Sort:				
Show:	☑	☑	☑	☑
Criteria:				Is Null
or:				

Figure 15-13: Using the Is Null operator.

Entering Criteria in Multiple Fields

You've worked with criteria specified in single fields up to this point. Now you'll work with criteria across several fields. When you want to limit the records based on several field conditions, you do so by setting criteria in each field that will be used for the scope. Say, for example, that you want to search for all dogs or for all animals in Idaho. Or you may want to search for dogs in Idaho or Washington. Again, you may search for all dogs in Washington or all cats in Oregon. Each of these queries requires placing criteria in multiple fields and on multiple lines.

Using And and Or across fields in a query

To use *And* and *Or* across fields, place your example or pattern data in the Criteria: and the Or: cells of one field relative to the placement in another field. When you want to use And between two fields, you place the example or pattern data across the same line. When you want to use Or between two fields, you place the example or pattern data on different lines in the QBE pane. Figure 15-14 shows the QBE pane and a conceptual representation of this placement.

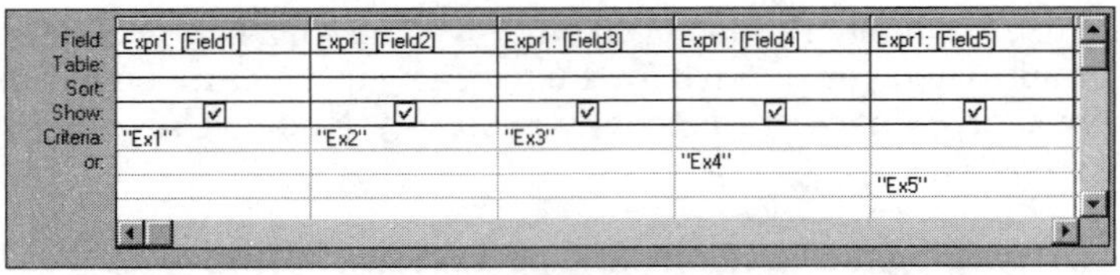

Field:	Expr1: [Field1]	Expr1: [Field2]	Expr1: [Field3]	Expr1: [Field4]	Expr1: [Field5]
Table:					
Sort:					
Show:	☑	☑	☑	☑	☑
Criteria:	"Ex1"	"Ex2"	"Ex3"		
or:				"Ex4"	
					"Ex5"

Figure 15-14: The QBE pane with And/Or criteria between fields.

Looking at Figure 15-14, you see that if the only criteria fields present were Ex1, Ex2, and Ex3 (with Ex4 and Ex5 removed), all three would be Anding between the fields. If only the criteria fields Ex4 and Ex5 were present (with Ex1, Ex2, and Ex3 removed), the two would be Oring between fields. As it is, the selection for this example is (EX1 AND EX2 AND EX3) OR EX4 OR EX5. Therefore this query is True if a value matches any of these criteria:

EX1 AND EX2 AND EX3 or

EX4 or

EX5

As long as one of these three criteria are True, the record will be selected.

Specifying And criteria across fields of a query

The most common type of condition operator between fields is the And operator. Often you will be interested in limiting records on the basis of several field conditions. For example, you may want to view only the records of customers who live in the state of Washington and own rabbits. To create this query, follow these steps:

1. Create a new query, using the Customer and Pets tables.
2. Select the Customer Name and State fields in the Customer table, Pet Name and Type of Animal fields in the Pets table.
3. Click on the Criteria: cell of State.
4. Type **WA** in the cell.
5. Click on the Criteria: cell for Type of Animal.
6. Type **RABBIT** in the cell.

Your query should look like Figure 15-15. Notice that both example data are in the same row.

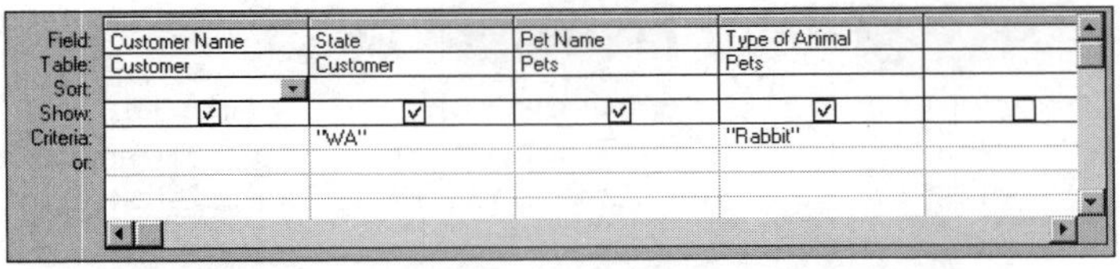

Field:	Customer Name	State	Pet Name	Type of Animal	
Table:	Customer	Customer	Pets	Pets	
Sort:					
Show:	☑	☑	☑	☑	☐
Criteria:		"WA"		"Rabbit"	
or:					

Figure 15-15: An And operator operation across two fields.

Because you placed data for both criteria on the same row, Access interprets this as an And operation.

Specifying Or criteria across fields of a query

Although the Or operator is not used across fields as commonly as the And, occasionally Or is very useful. For example, you may want to see records of any animals in Washington or you may want all rabbits regardless of the state they live in. To create this query, follow these steps:

1. Use the query from the previous example, emptying the two criteria cells.
2. Click on the Criteria: cell of State.
3. Type WA in the cell.
4. Click on the or: cell for Type of Animal.
5. Type **RABBIT** in the cell.

Your query should resemble Figure 15-16. Notice that the criteria entered this time are not in the same row for both fields.

When you place the criterion for one field on a different line from the criterion for another field, Access interprets this as an Or between the fields.

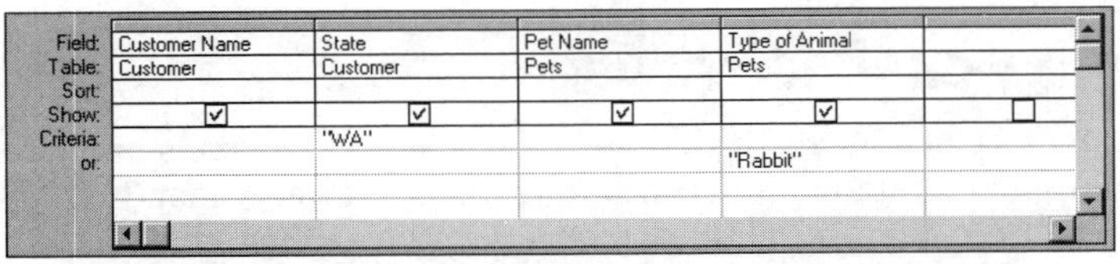

Field:	Customer Name	State	Pet Name	Type of Animal	
Table:	Customer	Customer	Pets	Pets	
Sort:					
Show:	☑	☑	☑	☑	☐
Criteria:		"WA"			
or:				"Rabbit"	

Figure 15-16: Using the Or operator between fields.

Using And and Or together in different fields

Now that you've worked with And and Or separately, you're ready to create a query using And and Or in different fields. In the next example, you want to display information for all skunks in Washington and all rabbits in Idaho. Perform the following steps to create this query:

1. Use the query from the previous example, emptying the two criteria cells.
2. Click on the Criteria: cell of State.
3. Type **WA** in the cell.
4. Click on the or: cell of State.
5. Type **ID** in the cell.
6. Click on the Criteria: cell for Type of Animal.
7. Type **SKUNK** in the cell.
8. Click on the or: cell for Type of Animal.
9. Type **RABBIT** in the cell.

Figure 15-17 shows how the query should look. Notice that `WA` and `SKUNK` are in the same row; `ID` and `RABBIT` are in another row. This query represents two Ands across fields, with an Or in each field.

Field:	Customer Name	State	Pet Name	Type of Animal	
Table:	Customer	Customer	Pets	Pets	
Sort:					
Show:	☑	☑	☑	☑	☐
Criteria:		"WA"		"Skunk"	
or:		"ID"		"Rabbit"	

Figure 15-17: Using Ands and Ors across fields.

A complex query on different lines

Suppose you want to view all records of animals that are either squirrels or cats that were brought in by Animal Kingdom between July 1, 1995, and December 31, 1995. In this example, you use three fields for setting criteria: Customer.Customer Name, Pets.Type of Animal, and Visits.Visit Date. A formula for setting these criteria follows:

```
(Customer.[Customer Name] = "Animal Kingdom" AND (Pets.[Type of
       Animal] = "SQUIRREL" OR Pets.[Type of Animal]="CAT") AND
       (Visits.[Visit Date] >= #7/1/95# AND <= #12/31/95#)
```

You can display this data by creating the query shown in Figure 15-18.

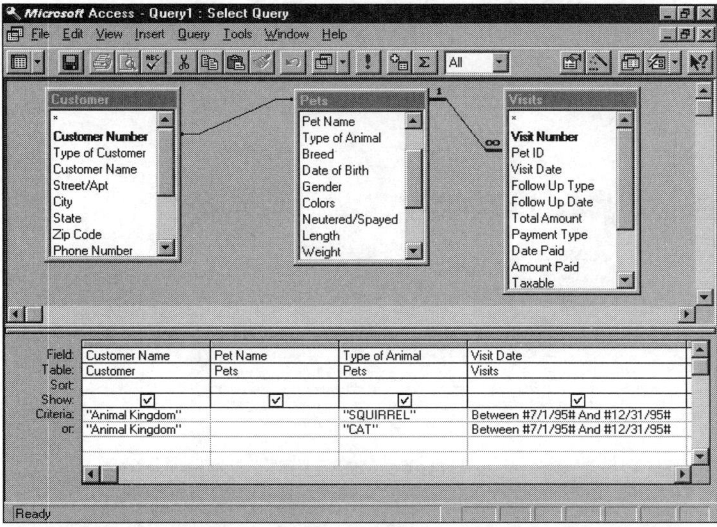

Figure 15-18: Using multiple Ands and Ors across fields.

A complex query on one line

Notice in Figure 15-18 that the Customer Name, `Animal Kingdom`, is repeated on two lines, as is the Visit Date of `Between #7/1/95# And #12/31/95#`. This is necessary because the two lines actually form the query:

```
Animal Kingdom AND SQUIRREL AND Between #7/1/95# And #12/31/95#
       OR
Animal Kingdom AND CAT AND Between #7/1/95# And #12/31/95#
```

You don't have to repeat Animal Kingdom in a query like this. Figure 15-19 shows another approach.

Notice that the criteria in Figure 15-18 have duplicate information in the Or cell of the Customer Name and Visit Date fields. Only the Type of Animal Field has different criteria — `''SQUIRREL''` or `''CAT''`. By combining the Type of Animal information into a single criterion (using the Or), the Customer Name and Visit Date criteria will only have to be entered once, which creates a more efficient query.

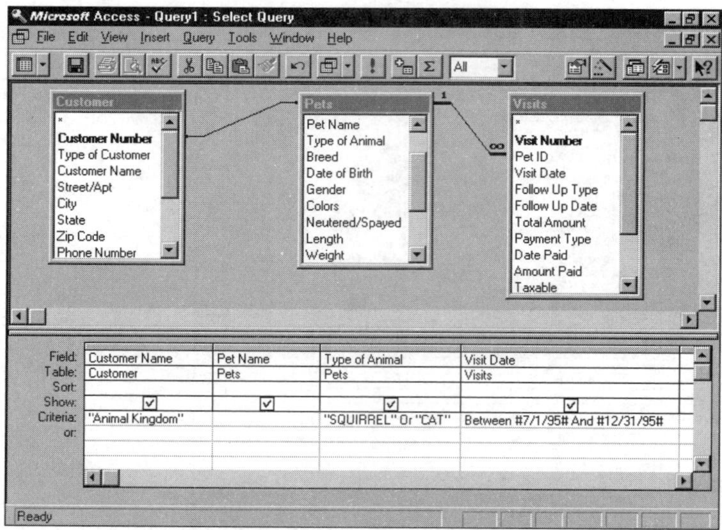

Figure 15-19: Using multiple Ands and Ors across fields on one line.

Creating a New Calculated Field in a Query

When you work with fields in a query, you are not limited to the fields from the tables you use in the query. You can also create *calculated fields* to use in a query — for example, a calculated field named `Discount Amount` that will display an amount by multiplying the value of Discount times Outstanding Balance in the Customer table.

To create this calculated field, follow these steps:

1. Create a new query, using the Customer table.
2. Select the Customer Name, Discount, and Outstanding Balance fields in the Customer table.
3. Click on the empty Field: cell.
4. Type Discount Amount: **[Discount]*[Outstanding Balance]** and move the cursor off of the cell.

If you did this correctly, the cell looks like Figure 15-20. The expression has changed to `Discount Amount:[Discount]*[Outstanding Balance]`. If you didn't add the field name, `Expr1:` would precede the calculation.

Note For two reasons, a calculated field has a name (supplied either by the user or by an Access default). First, a name is needed to supply a label for the datasheet column. Second, the name is necessary for referencing the field in a form, a report, or another query.

Notice that the general format for creating a calculated field is as follows:

Calculated Field Name: *Expression to build calculated field*

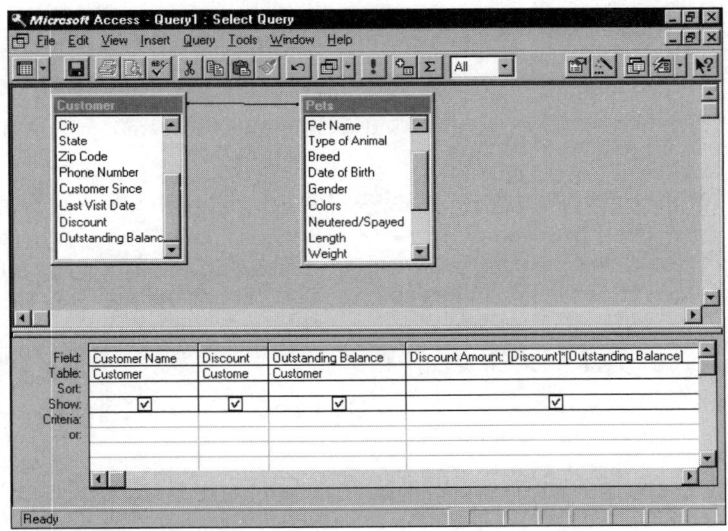

Figure 15-20: A calculated field.

Summary

In this chapter, you learned how to specify criteria to design select queries. You learned about the operators that help you query against fields for the exact information you want. The chapter covered the following points:

✦ With select queries, you select information from tables you can use for datasheets, forms, reports, and other queries.

✦ You can specify record criteria for any type of field.

✦ You can build expressions in the Criteria: cell of a field, based on literal data (examples) or with functions that build the example data.

✦ Access has five distinct wildcards it uses with the Like operator. These are: ?, *, #, [ ], and !. You can use these operators independently or in conjunction with each other.

✦ The Not operator, similar to the <> operator, specifies nonmatching values as criteria.

✦ The And operator forms a True expression only when both sides of a formula are True. An Or operator is True when either side of the formula is True.

✦ With the Or operator, you can specify a list of values for a field. The And operator lets you specify a range of values in a field.

✦ Often you can use the In operator instead of an Or operator; the Between … And operator can be used in place of the And operator.

✦ You can search fields for empty conditions by using the Is Null operator. A Null is the absence of any value in a field.

✦ Calculated fields are created from an expression. The expression can use one or more fields, functions, or other objects.

In the next chapter, you examine controls and properties.

✦ ✦ ✦

Understanding Controls and Properties

In This Chapter

What a control is

How to create a new blank form

The three types of controls: bound, unbound, and calculated

Standards for using controls

How to create a new control

How to use the Field List window

How to use the toolbox

How to select controls

How to manipulate controls

What properties are

How to view the property sheet

This is the first of eight chapters in Part III that examine forms and reports in detail. Controls and properties form the basis of forms and reports. It is critical to understand the fundamental concepts of controls and properties before you begin to apply them to forms and reports.

Disk In this chapter, you use the Pets table in the MOUNTAIN ANIMAL HOSPITAL database. The chapter explains each control by examining one or more fields in the Pets table. To create the first form you need for this chapter, follow these steps:

1. Open the Mountain Animal Hospital or Mountain Animal Start database.
2. Select Insert➪Form.
3. Select Design View from the New Form dialog box.
4. Select the Pets table from the combo box in the New Form dialog box.
5. Click the OK button to display the form design screen.
6. Maximize the form by clicking the maximize button in the top right corner of the window.
7. Expand the light gray area of the form to the full-window size by dragging the bottom right corner of the light gray area to the bottom right corner of the window.

What Is a Control?

A *control* has many definitions in Access. Generally, a control is any object on a form or report, such as a label or text box. You enter values into controls and display them by using a control. A control can be bound to a table field, but it can also be an object, such as a line or rectangle. Calculated fields are also controls, as are pictures, graphs, option buttons, check boxes, and objects. There are also controls that aren't part of Access, but are developed separately; these are *OLE custom controls* (also known as *OCXs*). These extend the base feature set of Microsoft Access.

Cross Ref

OLE Custom Controls are covered in Chapter 20.

Whether you're working with forms or reports, you follow essentially the same process to create and use controls. In this chapter, you see controls explained from the perspective of a form.

The different control types

You find many different control types on a form or report. You can create some of these controls by using the toolbox shown in Figure 16-1. In this book, you learn how to create and use the most-often-used controls (listed in Table 16-1). In this chapter, you learn when to use each control; you also learn how these controls work.

Table 16-1
Controls You Can Create in Access Forms and Reports

Basic Controls	
Label	Literal text is displayed in a label control.
Text box	Data is typed into a text box.
Enhanced Data-Entry and Data-Validation Controls	
Option group	This group holds multiple option buttons, checkboxes, or toggle buttons.
Toggle button	This is a two-state button, up or down, which usually uses pictures or icons.
Option button	Also called *radio buttons,* these buttons are displayed as a circle with a dot when the option is on.
Checkbox	This is another two-state control, shown as a square that contains a check mark if it's on, an empty square if it's off.
Combo box	This box is a pop-up list of values that allows entries not on the list.
List box	This is a list of values that is always displayed on the form or report.
Command button	Also called a *push button,* this button is used to call a macro or run a Basic program to initiate an action.
Subform/Subreport	This control displays another form or report within the original form or report.

Graphic and Picture Controls	
Image	Displays a bitmap picture with very little overhead.
Unbound object frame	This frame holds an OLE object or embedded picture that is not tied to a table field. Includes graphs, pictures, sound files, and video.
Bound object frame	This frame holds an OLE object or embedded picture that is tied to a table field.
Line	This is a single line of variable thickness and color, which is used for separation.
Rectangle	A rectangle can be any color or size, or can be filled in or blank; the rectangle is used for emphasis.
Page break	This is usually used for reports and denotes a physical page break.

Note If the toolbox is not displayed, display it by selecting View⇨Toolbox or clicking on the Toolbox icon.

Tip The toolbox can be moved, resized, and anchored on the window. You can anchor it to any border, grab it, and resize it in the middle of the window.

Figure 16-1 shows the resulting new form.

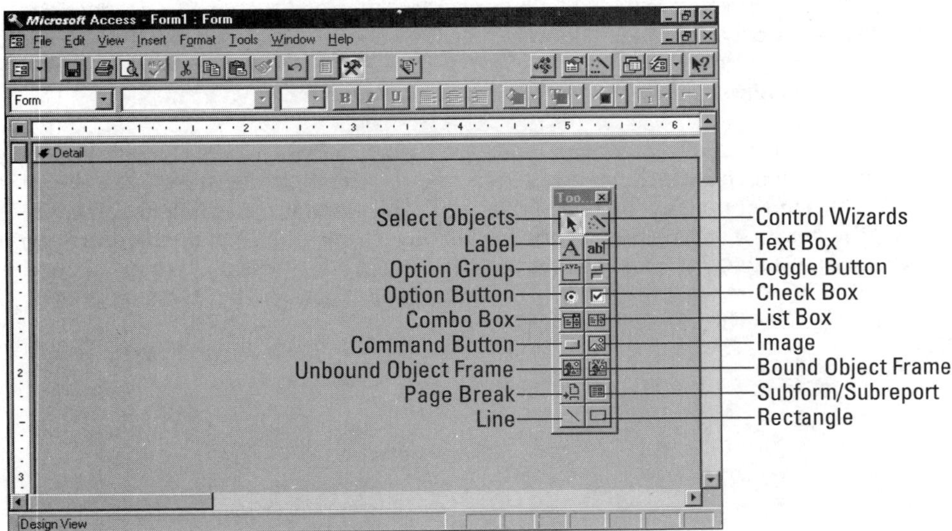

Figure 16-1: A new blank form and the toolbox.

Note The Control Wizard icon does not create a control; rather, it determines whether a Wizard is automatically activated when you create certain controls. The option group, combo box, list box, subform/subreport, object frame, and command button controls all have Wizards that Access starts when you create a new control.

Understanding bound, unbound, and calculated controls

There are three basic types of controls:

- Bound controls
- Unbound controls
- Calculated controls

Bound controls are those that are bound to a table field. When you enter a value into a bound control, Access automatically updates the table field in the current record. Most of the controls that let you enter information can be bound; these include OLE fields. Bound controls can be most data types, including text, dates, numbers, Yes/No, pictures, and memo fields.

Unbound controls retain the value entered but do not update any table fields. You can use these controls for text display, for values to be passed to macros, lines, and rectangles, or for holding OLE objects (such as a bitmap picture) that are not stored in a table but on the form itself. Unbound controls are also known as *variables* or *memory variables.*

Calculated controls are based on expressions, such as functions or calculations. Calculated controls are also unbound, as they do not update table fields. An example of a calculated control is `=[Medication Price] + [Treatment Price]`; this control calculates the total of two table fields for display on a form.

Examples of these three control types are shown in Figure 16-2. The picture of the mountain, which is the company's logo, and the text `Mountain Animal Hospital` are unbound controls. You can find bound controls that contain field names (including the picture) below the text and logo. You also see one calculated control, which is the animal's age. You can see that the function `DateDiff` is used to calculate the number of years from the `Date of Birth` bound control to the function `Now( )`, which returns the current date.

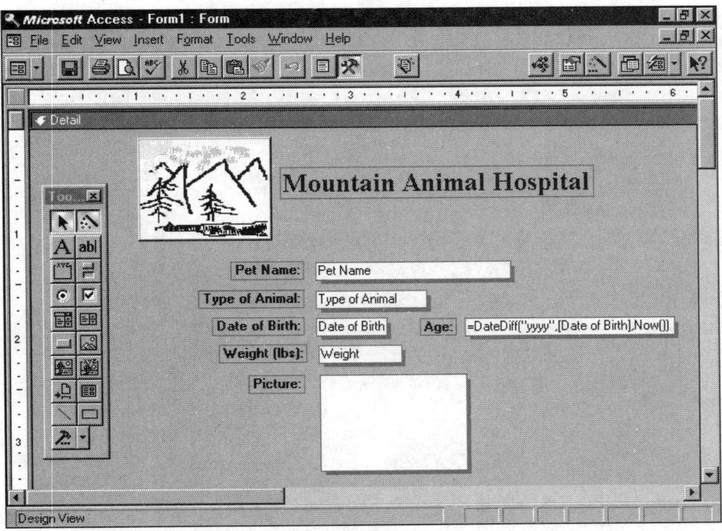

Figure 16-2: The three control types.

Standards for Using Controls

Most of you reading this book have used Microsoft Windows. You probably used other applications in Windows as well, such as word processing applications (Word for Windows, WordPerfect for Windows, or WordPad) or spreadsheet applications (Excel, 1-2-3 for Windows, or Quattro Pro). There is a difference, however, between using a Windows application and designing one.

The controls in Microsoft Access have specific purposes. Their use is not decided by whim or intuition; a scientific method determines which control should be used for each specific situation. Experience will show you that correct screen and report designs lead to more usable applications.

Label controls

A *label control* displays descriptive text (such as a title, a caption, or instructions) on a form or report. Labels can be separate controls, as is common when they are used for titles or data-entry instructions. When labels are used for field captions, often they are attached to the control they describe.

You can display labels on a single line or multiple lines. Labels are unbound controls that accept no input; you use them strictly for one-way communication (they are read and that's all). You can use them on many types of controls. Figure 16-3 shows many uses of labels, including titles, captions, button text, and captions for buttons and boxes. You can use different font styles and sizes for your labels, and you can boldface, italicize, and underline them.

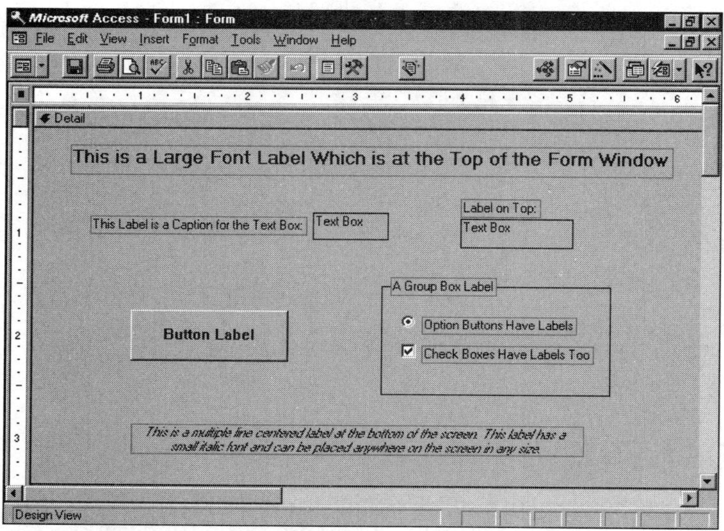

Figure 16-3: Sample label controls.

You should capitalize each word in a label, except for articles and conjunctions, such as *the, an, and, or,* etc. There are several guidelines to follow for label controls when you use them in other controls, as you can see in Figure 16-3. The following list explains some of these guidelines for placement:

Command buttons	Inside the button
Check boxes	To the right of the check box
Option buttons	To the right of the option button
Text box	Above or to the left of the text box
List or combo box	Above or to the left of the box
Group box	On top of and replacing part of the top frame line

Text box controls

Text boxes are controls that display data or ask the user to type information at specific locations. In a text box, you can accept the current text, edit it, delete it, or replace it. Text boxes can accept any type of data, including Text, Number, Date/Time, Yes/No, and Memo, and you can create them as bound or unbound controls. You can use text-box fields from tables or queries, and the text box can also contain calculated expressions. A text box is the most-used control because editing and displaying data are the main purposes of any database system.

Every text box needs an associated label to identify its purpose. Text boxes can contain multiple lines of data, and often do (as when you use one to display Memo field data). Data that is too long for the width of the text field wraps automatically within the field boundaries. Figure 16-4 shows several different text boxes in the Form view. Notice how the different data types vary in their alignment within the text boxes. The Comments text box displays multiple lines in the resized text box, which also has a scrollbar added.

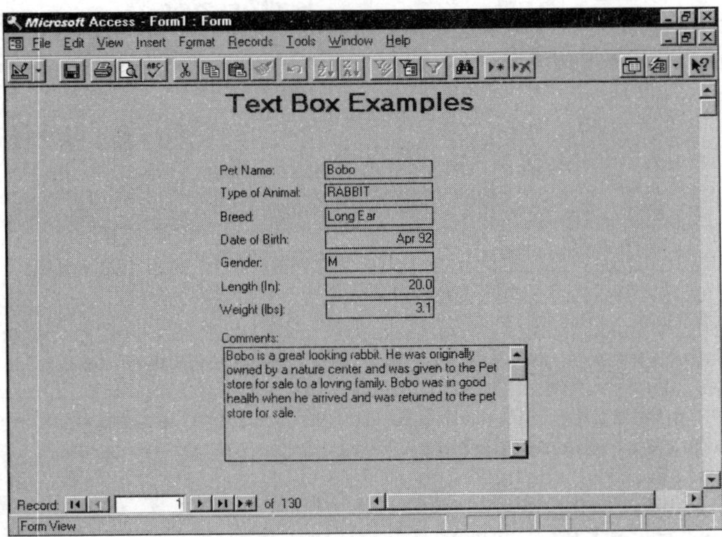

Figure 16-4: Sample text box controls.

Toggle buttons, option buttons, and check boxes

There are three types of buttons that act in the same way, and yet their visual display is very different:

- ✦ Toggle buttons
- ✦ Option buttons (also known as radio buttons)
- ✦ Check boxes

These controls are used with Yes/No data types. Each can be used individually to represent one of two states, whether Yes or No, On or Off, or True or False. Table 16-2 describes the visual representation of these controls.

Table 16-2
Button Control Visual Displays

Button Type	*State*	*Visual Description*
Toggle button	True	Button is sunken
Toggle button	False	Button is raised
Option button	True	Circle with a large solid dot inside
Option button	False	Hollow circle
Checkbox	True	Square with a check in the middle
Checkbox	False	Empty square

Toggle buttons, option buttons, and check boxes return a value of –1 to the bound table field if the button value is Yes, On, or True; they return a value of 0 if the button is No, Off, or False. You can enter a default value to display a specific state. The control is initially displayed in a Null state if no default is entered and no state is selected. The Null state's visual appearance is the same as that of the No state.

Although you can place Yes/No data types in a text box, it is better to use one of these controls. The values that are returned to a text box (–1 and 0) are very confusing, especially because Yes is represented by –1 and No is 0.

Note As you can see in Figure 16-5, you can change the look of the option button or check box by using the special effects options from the Formatting toolbar. See Chapter 18 for more details.

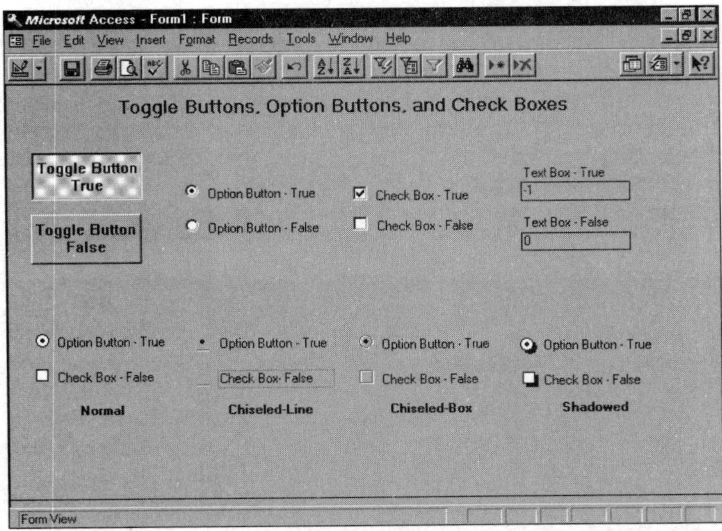

Figure 16-5: Sample toggle buttons, option buttons, and check boxes.

Tip You can format the display of the Yes/No values in the Datasheet or Form view by setting the Format property of the text box control to Yes/No, On/Off, or True/False. If you don't use the Format property, the datasheet will display –1 or 0. Using a default value also speeds up data entry, especially if you set as the default the value selected most often.

Option groups

An *option group* can contain multiple toggle buttons, option buttons, or check boxes. When these controls are inside an option group box, they work together instead of individually. Rather then representing a two-state Yes/No data type, controls within an option group return a number based on the position in the group. Only one control within an option group can be selected at one time; the maximum number of buttons in such a group should be four. If you need to exceed that number, you should switch to a drop-down list box (unless you have plenty of room on your screen).

An option group is generally bound to a single field or expression. Each button inside it passes a different value back to the option group, which in turn passes the single choice to the bound field or expression. The buttons themselves are not bound to any field; instead, they are bound to the option group box.

Figure 16-6 shows three types of buttons; two of these types are shown in option group boxes. In the Toggle Buttons option group, the second choice is selected; the same is true of the Option Buttons option group. Notice, however, that the first and third choices are selected in the Check Boxes rectangle; the check boxes are independent, and not part of an option group. When you make a new selection in an option group, the current selection is deselected. If (for example) you click on Option Button 3 in the option group box in the middle of Figure 16-6, the solid dot will appear to move to the third circle, and the second circle will become hollow.

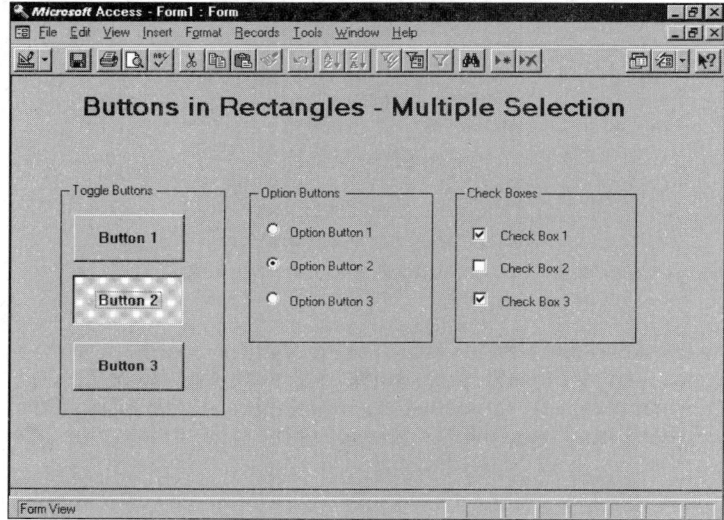

Figure 16-6: Three types of option groups.

Buttons in rectangles

The three types of buttons act very differently, depending on whether they are used individually or in an option group. You can create buttons that look like a group but do not function as a single entity. Figure 16-7 shows a multiple-selection group. Notice that check boxes 2 and 3 are simultaneously selected. This is not an option group; rather, this is a group of controls enclosed in a box. They act totally independently, so they don't have to be in the same box; each control passes either a –1 (True) or a 0 (False) to the field, expression, or control it is bound to. A common use for this type of grouping is to let a user select from a list of nonexclusive options, such as a list of reports or a list of days on which a process should occur.

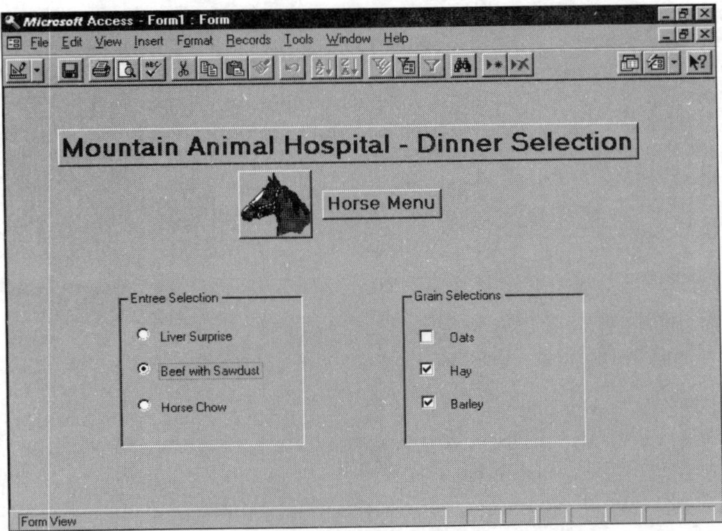

Figure 16-7: Selecting a meal.

Tip

You may want to create groups of buttons that look like option groups but have multiple selections. Rather than using an option button, simply enclose the group of buttons with a rectangle. Each button remains an individual entity instead of becoming part of a group.

List boxes

A *list box* control displays a list of data on-screen just as a pull-down menu does, but the list box is always open. You can highlight an item in the list by moving the cursor to the desired choice and then pressing Enter (or clicking the mouse) to complete the selection. You can also type the first letter of the selection to highlight the desired entry. After you select an item, the item's value is passed back to the bound field.

List boxes can display any number of fields and any number of records. By sizing the list box, you can make it display more or fewer records.

New!

Access for Windows 95 list boxes feature a new *Multi-Select* property that allows you to select more than one item at a time. The results are stored in new properties and have to be used with Visual Basic for Applications.

List boxes are generally used when there is plenty of room on-screen and you want the operator to see the choices without having to click on a drop-down arrow. A vertical — and even horizontal — scrollbar is used to display any records and fields not visible when the list box is in its default size. The highlighted entry will be the one currently selected. If no entries are highlighted, either a selection has not been made or the selected item is not currently in view. Only items in the list can be selected.

You also have a choice of whether to display the column headings on list boxes. Figure 16-8 displays list boxes with three layout schemes.

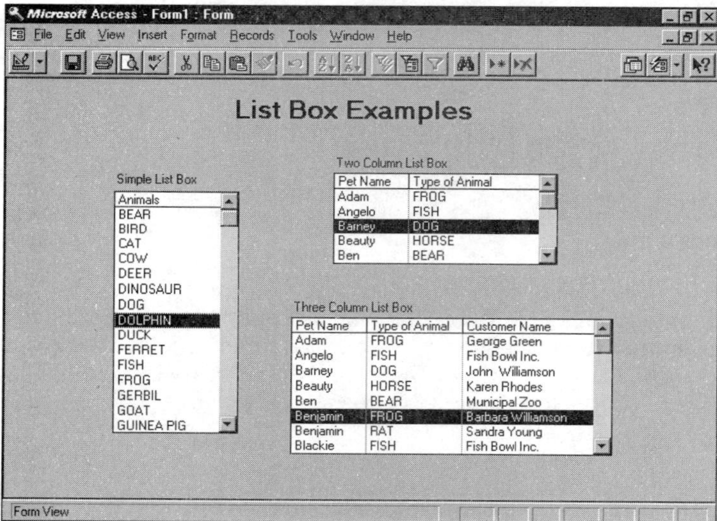

Figure 16-8: Sample list boxes.

Combo boxes

In Access, *combo boxes* differ from list boxes in two ways:

✦ The combo box is initially displayed as a single row with an arrow that lets you open the box to the normal size.

✦ As an option, the combo box lets you enter a value that is not on the list.

You see a list box and a combo box (shown both open and closed) in Figure 16-9.

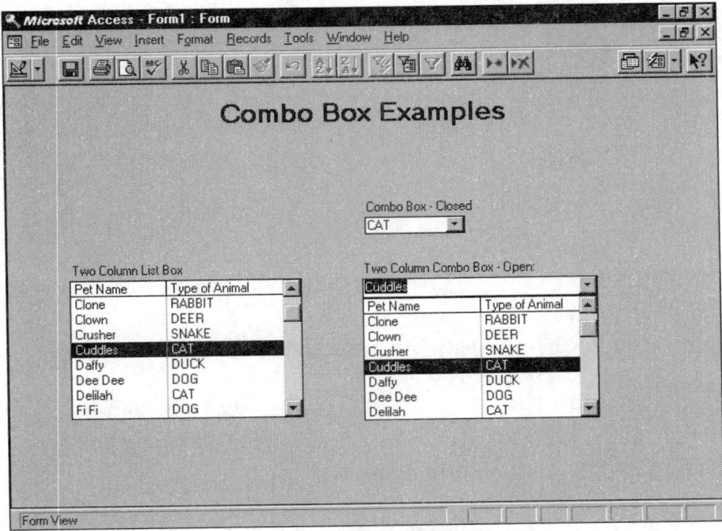

Figure 16-9: Resizing the query design panes.

Creating New Controls

Now that you have learned about the controls that can be used on a form or report, you should learn how to add controls to a form and how to manipulate them in the Form Design window. Although the Form Wizards can quickly place your fields in the Design window, you still may need to add more fields to a form. There are also many times when you simply want to create a report from a completely blank form.

The two ways to create a control

You can create a control in either of two ways:

- ✦ Dragging a field from the Field List window to add a bound control
- ✦ Clicking on a button in the toolbox and then adding a new unbound control to the screen

Using the Field List window

The Field List window shown in Figure 16-10 displays all the fields in the open table/query that was used to create a form. This window is movable and resizable and also displays a vertical scrollbar if there are more fields than will fit in the window.

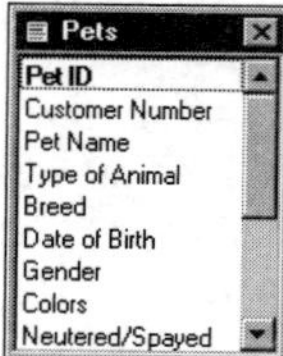

Figure 16-10: The resized Field List window.

You can use one of two methods to display the Field List window:

✦ Click on the Field List button in the toolbar. (This button looks like an Access table).

✦ Select ViewÍField List… from the Form menu bar.

Note: After you resize or move the Field List window, it remains that size for all forms, even if toggled off or if the form is closed. Only if you exit Access is the window set to its default size.

Generally, dragging a field from the Field List window creates a bound text box on the Form Design screen. If you drag an OLE field from the Field List window, you create a bound object frame. Optionally you can select the type of control by first selecting a control from the toolbox and then dragging the field to the Form Design window.

Warning: When you drag fields from the Field List window, the first control is placed where you release the mouse button. Make sure there is enough space to the left of the control for the labels. If there is insufficient space, the labels will slide under the controls.

There are several distinct advantages to dragging a field from the Field List window:

✦ The control is bound automatically to the field that you dragged.

✦ Field properties inherit table-level formats, status-bar text, and data-validation rules and messages.

✦ The label text is created with the field name as the caption.

Using the toolbox

By using the *toolbox buttons* to create a control, you can decide what type of control is to be used for each field. If you don't create the control by dragging it from the Field List window, the field will be unbound and have a default label name such as Field3 or Option11. After you create the control, you can decide what field to bind the control to; you can also enter any text you want for the label, and set any properties you want.

The basic deciding factor for using the field list or the toolbox is simply whether the field exists in the table/query or whether you want to create an unbound or calculated expression. By using the Field List window and the toolbox together, you can create bound controls of nearly any type. You will find, however, that some data types do not allow all the control types found in the toolbox. For example, if you attempt to create a graph from a single field, you simply get a text box.

New! In the new version of Access, you can change the type of control once you create it; then you can set all the properties for the control. For example, suppose you create a field as a text box control and you want to change it to list box. You can use Format⇨Change To and change the control type. Obviously, however, you can change only from some types of controls to others. Anything can be changed to a text box control; option buttons, toggle buttons, and check boxes are interchangeable, as are list and combo boxes.

Dragging a field name from the Field List window

The easiest way to create a text box control is to drag a field from the Field List window. When the Field List window is open, you can click on an individual field and drag it to the Form Design window. This window works exactly in the same way as a Table/Query window in QBE. You can also select multiple fields and then drag them to the screen together. The techniques you would use include the following:

- ✦ Selecting multiple contiguous fields by holding down the Shift key and clicking on the first and last field you want
- ✦ Selecting multiple noncontiguous fields by holding down the Ctrl key and clicking on each field you want
- ✦ Double-clicking on the table/query name in the window's top border to select all the fields

After you select one or more fields, you can drag the selection to the screen.

To drag the Pet Name, Type of Animal, Date of Birth, and Neutered/Spayed fields from the Field List window, follow the next set of steps. If you haven't created a new form, create one first and resize the form as instructed at the beginning of this chapter. When you complete those steps successfully, your screen should look like Figure 16-11.

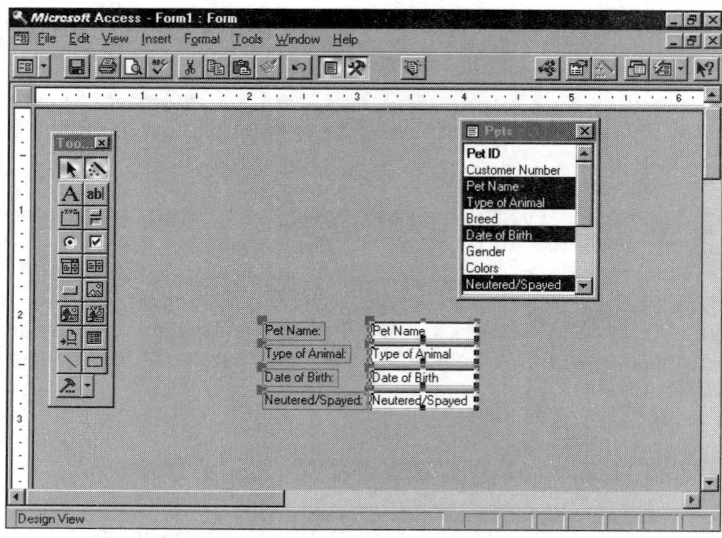

Figure 16-11: Fields dragged from the Field List window.

You can see four controls in the Form Design window, each of them made up of a label control and a text box control (Access attaches the label control to the text box automatically). You can work with these controls as a group or independently, and you can select, move, or delete them. To resize them, you must work with them separately. Notice that each is a text box control, each control has a label with a caption matching the field name, and the text box control displays the bound field name used in the text box.

You can close the Field List window by clicking on the Field List button in the toolbar.

Creating unbound controls with the toolbox

You can create one control at a time by using the toolbox. You can create any of the controls listed in the toolbox. Each control becomes an unbound control that has a default label and a name.

To create three different unbound controls, perform the following steps:

1. Click on the Text Box button in the toolbox (the button appears sunken).
2. Place the cursor in the Form Design window (the cursor has changed to the Text Box button).
3. Click and hold down the mouse button where you want the control to begin, and then drag the mouse to size the control.
4. Click on the Option Button icon in the toolbar (this button appears sunken).

5. Place the cursor in the Form Design window (the cursor has changed to an Option button).
6. Click and hold down the mouse button where you want the control to begin, and then drag the mouse to size the control.
7. Click on the Check Box button in the toolbar (the button appears sunken).
8. Place the cursor in the Form Design window (the cursor has changed to a check box).
9. Click and hold down the mouse button where you want the control to begin, and drag the mouse to size the control.

When you are done, your screen should resemble Figure 16-12.

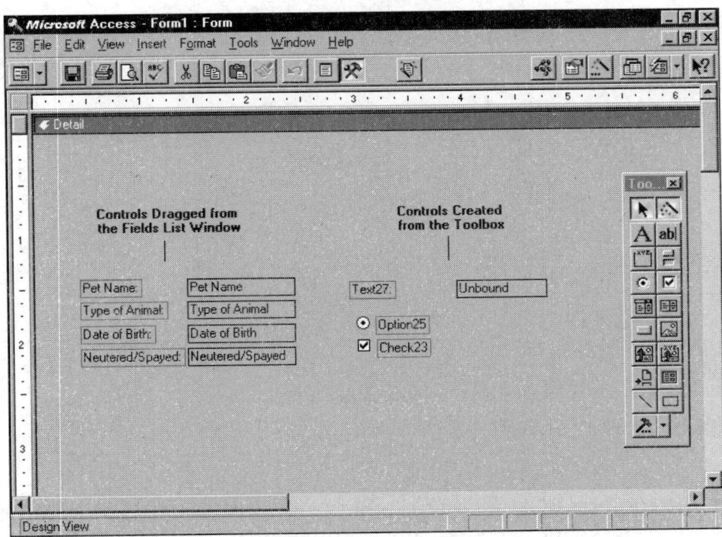

Figure 16-12: Adding three new controls.

Tip

If you just click on the Form Design window, Access will create a default-sized control.

Notice (in Figure 16-12) the difference between the controls that were dragged from the Field List window and the controls that were created from the toolbox. The Field List window controls are bound to a field in the Pets table and are appropriately labeled and named. The controls created from the toolbox are unbound and have default names. Notice that control names are assigned automatically according to the type of control and a number.

Later you learn how to change the control names, captions, and properties. Using properties will speed up the process of naming controls and binding them to specific fields.

Selecting Controls

After you have a control on the Form Design window, you can begin to work with it. The first step is to select one or more controls. Depending on its size, a selected control may show from four to eight *handles* (small squares you can drag) around the control box area at the corners and midway along the sides. The handle in the upper left corner is larger than the other handles; use it to move the control. Use the other handles to size the control. Figure 16-13 displays these controls.

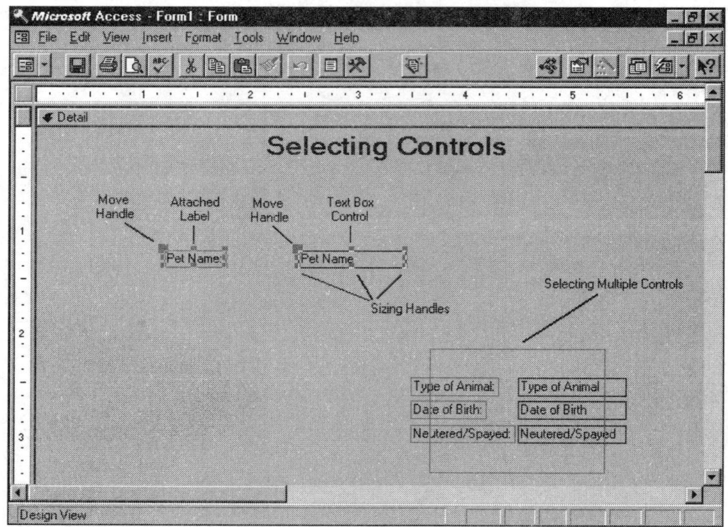

Figure 16-13: A conceptual view of selecting controls.

The pointer tool in the toolbox must be on for you to select a control. The pointer always appears as an arrow pointing diagonally to the upper left corner. If you selected another button in the toolbox and then selected the Lock button in the toolbox, you must click on the pointer again to change the cursor to a selection pointer. If you use the toolbox to create a single control, Access automatically reselects the pointer as the default cursor.

Deselecting selected controls

It is good practice to deselect any selected controls before you select another control. You can deselect a control by simply clicking on an unselected area of the screen that does not contain a control. When you do so, the handles disappear from any selected control.

Selecting a single control

You can select any single control by simply clicking anywhere on the control. When you click on a control, all the handles appear. If the control has an attached label, the handle for moving the label appears as well. If you select a single label control that is part of an attached control, all the handles in the label control are displayed, and only the *Move handle* (the largest handle) is displayed in the attached control.

Selecting multiple controls

You can select multiple controls in these ways:

- Click on each desired control while holding down the Shift key.
- Drag the pointer through the controls you want to select.

The screen in Figure 16-13 shows some of these concepts graphically. When you select multiple controls by dragging the mouse, a light gray rectangle appears as you drag the mouse. When you select multiple controls by dragging the pointer through the controls, be careful to select only the controls you want to select. Any control that is touched by the line or enclosed within it is selected. If you want to select labels only, you must make sure that the selection rectangle encloses only your passes through the labels.

Tip

When you click on a ruler, an arrow appears and a line is displayed across the screen. You can drag the cursor to widen the line. Each control that the line touches is selected.

Tip

If you find that controls are not selected when the rectangle passes through the control, you may have the Selection Behavior global property set to Fully Enclosed. This means that a control will be selected only if the selection rectangle completely encloses the entire control. The normal default for this option is Partially Enclosed. You can change this option by first selecting Tools⇨Options… and then selecting Forms/Reports Category in the Options tabbed dialog box. The option Selection Behavior should be set to Partially Enclosed.

By holding down the Shift key, you can select several noncontiguous controls. This lets you select controls on totally different parts of the screen, cut them, and then paste them together somewhere else on-screen.

Manipulating Controls

Creating a form is generally a multistep process. The next step is to make sure your controls are properly sized and moved into the correct position.

Resizing a control

You can *resize* controls by using any of the smaller handles on the control. The handles in the control corners let you make the field larger or smaller — in both width and height, and at the same time. You use the handles in the middle of the control sides to size the control larger or smaller in one direction only. The top and bottom handles control the height of the control; the handles in the middle change the control width.

When a corner handle is touched by the cursor in a selected control, the cursor becomes a diagonal double arrow. You can then hold down the mouse button and drag the control size handles to the desired size. If the cursor touches a side handle in a selected control, the cursor changes to a horizontal or vertical double-headed arrow. Figure 16-14 shows the Pet Name control after resizing. Notice the double-headed arrow in the corner of the Pet Name control.

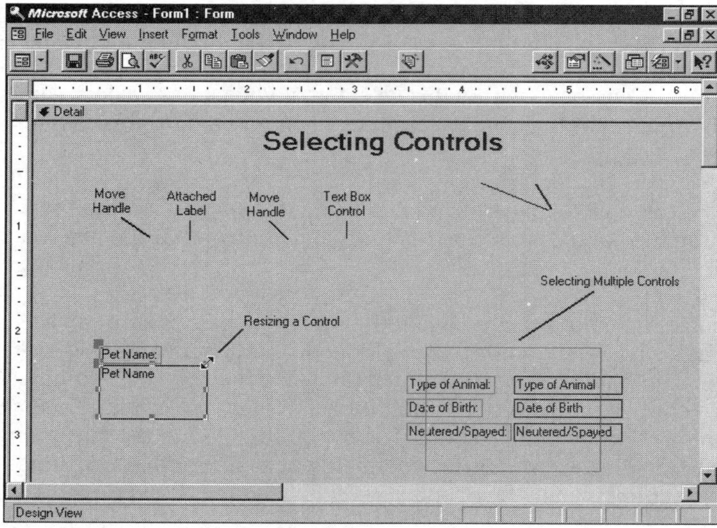

Figure 16-14: Resizing a control.

Tip

You can resize a control in very small increments by using the Shift + arrow keys. This also works with multiple controls selected. They will change by only one pixel at a time.

Moving a control

After you select a control, you can move it. Use either of these methods to move an unselected control:

✦ Click on the control and drag it to a new location.

✦ Select the control and then place your cursor *between* any two Move handles on its border.

If the control has an attached label, you can move both label and control by this method. It doesn't matter whether you click on the control or the label; they are moved together.

You can move a control separately from an attached label simply by grabbing the Move handle of the control and moving it. You can also move the label control separately from the other control by selecting the Move handle of the label control and moving it separately.

Figure 16-15 shows a label control that has been separately moved to the top of the text box control. The Hand button indicates that the controls are ready to be moved together.

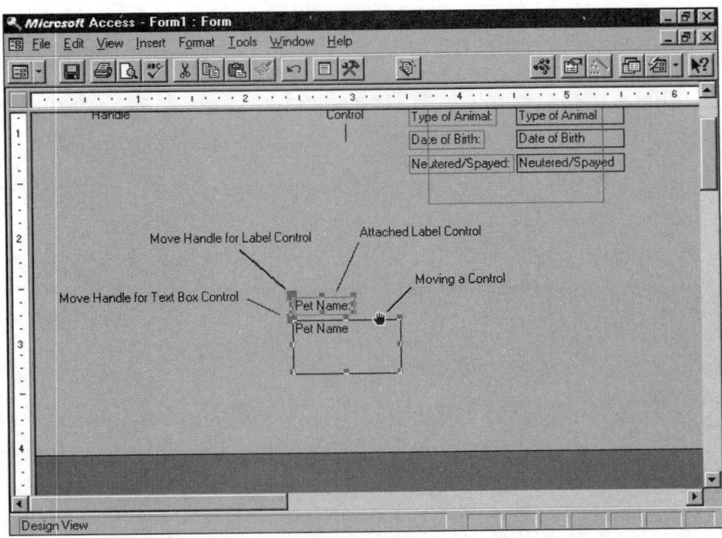

Figure 16-15: Moving a control.

Tip You can move a control in small increments with the keyboard by using Ctrl + arrow keys after you select a control or group of controls.

Tip You can restrict the direction in which a control is moved so that it maintains alignment within a specific row or column. To do so, hold down the Shift key as you press the mouse button to select and move the control. The control will move only in the direction you first move it, whether horizontally or vertically.

Tip

You can cancel a move or a resizing operation by pressing Esc before you release the mouse button. After a move or resizing operation is complete, you can select the Undo button or select Edit➪Undo Move or Edit➪Undo Sizing to undo the changes.

Aligning controls

You may want to move several controls so they are all *aligned* (lined up). The Format➪Align menu has several options, as shown in Figure 16-16 and described in the following list:

Left	Aligns the left edge of the selected controls with that of the leftmost selected control
Right	Aligns the right edge of the selected controls with that of the rightmost selected control
Top	Aligns the top edge of the selected controls with that of the topmost selected control
Bottom	Aligns the bottom edge of the selected controls with that of the bottommost selected control
To Grid	Aligns the top left corners of the selected controls to the nearest grid point

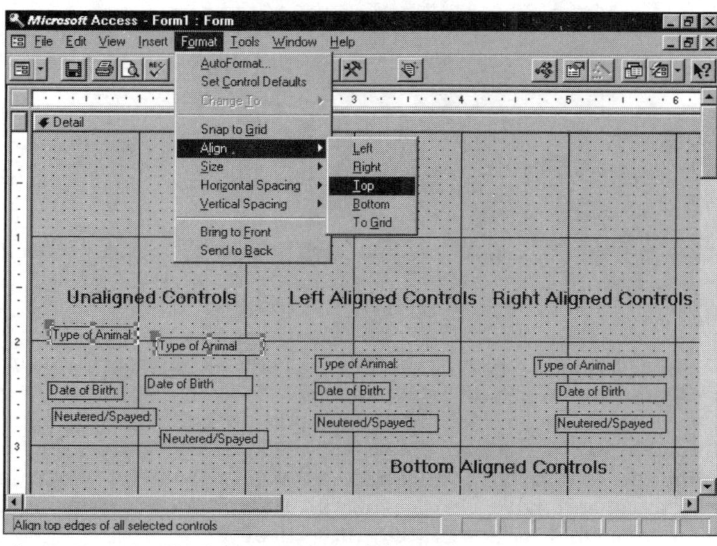

Figure 16-16: Aligning controls and the grid.

By selecting from this menu, you can align any number of controls. When you choose one of the options, Access uses the control that is the closest to the desired selection as the model for the alignment. For example, suppose you have three controls and you want to left-align them. They will be aligned on the basis of the control farthest to the left in the group of the three controls.

Figure 16-16 shows several groups of controls. The first group is not aligned. The label controls in the second group of controls has been left-aligned. The text box controls in the second group have been right-aligned. Each label, along with its attached text box, has been bottom-aligned.

Each type of alignment must be done separately. In this example, you can left-align all of the labels or right-align all of the text boxes at once. However, you would have to align each label and text control bottom separately (three separate alignments).

You may notice a series of dots in the background of Figure 16-16. This is the *grid.* The grid is used to assist you in aligning controls. The grid is displayed by selecting View⇨Grid.

You can use the Format⇨Snap to Grid option to align new controls to the grid as you draw or place them on a form. It also aligns existing controls when you move or resize them.

When Snap to Grid is on and you draw a new control by clicking on and dragging the form, Access aligns all four corners of the control to points on the grid. When you place a new control just by clicking on the form or report, only the upper left corner is aligned.

As you move or resize existing controls, Microsoft Access lets you move only from grid point to grid point. When Snap to Grid is off, Microsoft Access ignores the grid and lets you place a control anywhere on the form or report.

Tip You can turn off Snap to Grid temporarily by holding down the Ctrl key before you create a control (or while you're creating or moving it).

The Size option on the Format menu has several options that assist you in sizing controls based on the value of the data, the grid, or other controls. The options of the size menu are the following:

To Fit	Adjusts the height and width of controls to fit the font of the text they contain
To Grid	Moves all sides of selected controls in or out to meet the nearest points on the grid

To Tallest	Sizes selected controls so they have the same height as the tallest selected control
To Shortest	Sizes selected controls so they have the same height as the shortest selected control
To Widest	Sizes selected controls so they have the same width as the widest selected control
To Narrowest	Sizes selected controls so they have the same width as the narrowest selected control

Tip The grid's *fineness* (number of dots) can be changed from form to form by using the GridX and GridY Form properties. The grid is invisible if its fineness is greater than 16 units per inch horizontally or vertically. (Higher numbers indicate greater fineness.)

Tip There is another pair of alignment options that can make a big difference when you have to align the space between multiple controls. The options Horizontal Spacing and Vertical Spacing change the space between controls on the basis of the space between the first two selected controls. If the controls are across the screen, use the horizontal spacing. If they are down the screen, use the vertical spacing.

Deleting a control

If you find you no longer want a specific control on the Form Design window, you can delete it by selecting the control and pressing Delete. You can also select Edit⇨Delete to delete a selected control or Edit⇨Cut to cut the control to the Clipboard.

You can delete more than one control at a time by selecting multiple controls and pressing one of the Delete key sequences. If you have a control with an attached label, you can delete the label only by clicking on the label itself and then selecting a delete method. If you select the control, both the control and the label will be deleted. To delete only the label of the Pet Name control, follow the next steps. (This example assumes that you have the Pet Name text box control in your Form Design window.)

1. Select the Pet name label control only.
2. Press Delete.

The label control should be removed from the window.

Attaching a label to a control

If you accidentally delete a label from a control, you can reattach it. To create and then reattach a label to a control, follow these steps:

1. Click on the Label button in the toolbox.
2. Place the cursor in the Form Design window (the cursor has become the Text Box button).
3. Click and hold down the mouse button where you want the control to begin; drag the mouse to size the control.
4. Type **Pet Name:** and click outside the control.
5. Select the Pet Name label control.
6. Select Edit➪Cut to cut the label control to the Clipboard.
7. Select the Pet Name text box control.
8. Select Edit➪Paste to attach the label control to the text box control.

Copying a control

You can create copies of any control by duplicating them or by copying them to the Clipboard and then pasting them where you want them. If you have a control for which you entered many properties or specified a certain format, you can copy it and revise only the properties (such as the control name and bound field name) to make it a different control. This capability is also useful when you have a multiple-page form and you want to display the same values on different pages and in different locations.

What Are Properties?

Properties are named attributes of controls, fields, or database objects; you use them to modify the characteristics of the control, field, or object. These attributes can be the size, color, appearance, or name. A property can also modify the behavior of a control, determining (for example) whether the control is editable or visible.

Properties are used extensively in forms and reports for changing the characteristics of controls. Each control has properties; the form itself also has properties, as does each of its sections. The same is true for reports; the report itself has properties, as does each report section and each individual control. The label control also has its own properties, even if it is attached to another control.

Properties are displayed in a *property sheet* (also commonly called a *property window* because it is an actual window). The first column contains the property names; you enter properties in the second column. Figure 16-17 shows a property sheet for the Date of Birth text box.

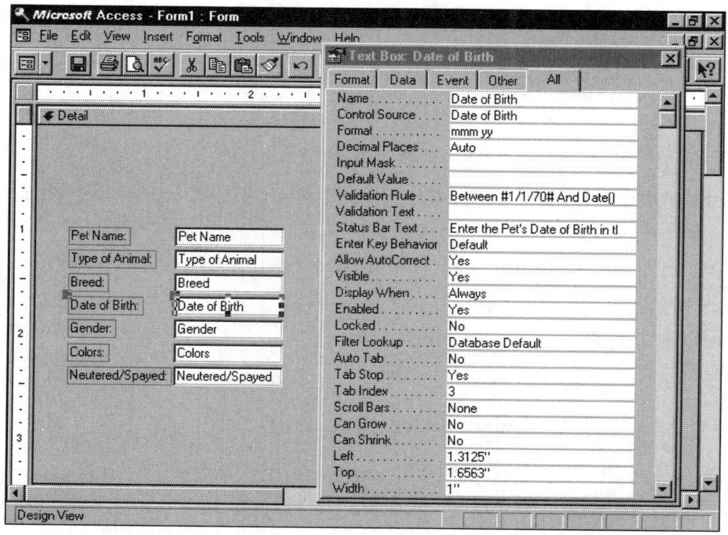

Figure 16-17: The property sheet for the Date of Birth text box.

Viewing a control's properties

There are several ways to view a control's properties:

- ✦ Select View➪Properties from the menu bar.
- ✦ Click on the control and then click on the Properties button in the toolbar.
- ✦ Double-click on any control.

To display the property sheet for the Date of Birth text box control, follow these steps:

1. Create a new blank form, using the Pets table.
2. Drag the fields Pet Name through Neutered/Spayed from the Field List window to the Form Design window.
3. Click on the Date of Birth text box control to select it.
4. Click on the Properties button in the toolbar.

As you can see in Figure 16-17, a partial property sheet is displayed. It has also been resized larger. By widening the property sheet, you can see more of the its values; by increasing the vertical size, you can see more controls at one time. The vertical scrollbar lets you move between various properties. Only the text box control has more properties than can fit on-screen at one time. Because the property sheet is a true window, it can be moved anywhere on-screen and resized to any size. It does not, however, have Maximize or Minimize buttons.

As a tabbed dialog box, the property window lets you see all the properties for a control; you can also limit the view to specific properties. The specific groups of properties include:

Format	These determine how a label or value looks: font, size, color, special effects, borders, scrollbars.
Data	These properties affect how a value is displayed and the control it is bound to: Control source, formats, input masks, validation, default value, and other table-level properties.
Event	Event properties are named events such as a mouse click, adding a record, pressing a key for which you can define a response (in the form of a call to a macro or an Access Basic procedure), and so on.
Other	Other Properties shows additional characteristics of the control, such as the name of the control or the description that appears on the status bar.

Cross Ref The number of properties available in Access has increased greatly since Access 2.0. The most important new properties are described in various chapters of this book. For a discussion of new event properties and event procedures, see Chapters 30-34.

The properties displayed in Figure 16-17 are the specific properties for Date of Birth. The first two properties, Name and Control Source, reflect the field name Date of Birth.

The Name is simply the name of the control itself. You can give the control any name you want. Unbound controls have names such as Field11 or Button13. When a control is bound to a field, it Access names it automatically to match the bound field name.

The Control Source is the name of the table field that the control is bound to. In this example, the Date of Birth field is the name of the field in the Pets table. An unbound control has no control source, whereas the control source of a calculated control is the calculated expression, as in the example `=[Weight] * .65`.

The following properties are always inherited from the table definition of a field for a text box or other type of control. Figure 16-17 shows some of these properties inherited from the Pets table:

- Format
- Decimal Places
- Status Bar Text (from the field Description)
- Input Mask

- ✦ Caption
- ✦ Default Value
- ✦ Validation Rule
- ✦ Validation Text

Changes made to a control's properties don't affect the field properties in the source table.

Each type of control has a different set of properties, as do objects such as forms, reports, and sections within forms or reports. In the next few chapters, you learn about many of these properties as you use each of the control types to create complex forms and reports.

Changing a control property

You can display properties in a property sheet, and you can use many different methods to change the properties. A list of these follows:

- ✦ Entering the desired property in a property sheet
- ✦ Changing a property directly by changing the control itself
- ✦ Using inherited properties from the bound field
- ✦ Using inherited properties from the control's default selections
- ✦ Entering color selections for the control by using the palette
- ✦ Changing text style, size, color, and alignment by using the toolbar buttons

You can change a control's properties simply by clicking on a property and typing the desired value.

Figure 16-17 displays an arrow and a button with three dots to the right of the Control Source property-entry area. Some properties display the arrow in the property-entry area when you click into the area. This tells you that Access provides a pop-up list of values you can choose. If you click on the down arrow in the Control Source property, you find that the choices are a list of all fields in the open table.

Three dots on a button constitute the *Builder button*, used to open one of the many Builders in Access. This includes the Macro Builder, the Expression Builder, and the Module Builder.

Some properties have a list of standard values such as Yes or No; others display varying lists of fields, forms, reports, or macros. The properties of each object are determined by the object itself and what the object is used for.

New! A new feature in Access for Windows 95 is the capability of cycling through property choices by repeatedly double-clicking on the choice. For example, double-clicking on the Display When property will alternately select Always, Print Only, and Screen Only.

Default properties

The properties you see in a specific control's property sheet are for that specific control. You can click on a control to see its properties. You can also create a set of default properties for a specific type of control by clicking on the toolbar button for that control type. For example, to view or change the default properties for a text box in the current form, follow these steps:

1. Make sure that the property sheet is displayed.
2. Click on the Text Box button in the toolbox.

As you can see in Figure 16-18, these are some of the default properties for a text box. You can set these properties; from then on, each new text box you create will have these properties as a starting point. This set of default properties can determine the color and size for new controls, the font used, the distance between the attached label and the control, and most other characteristics.

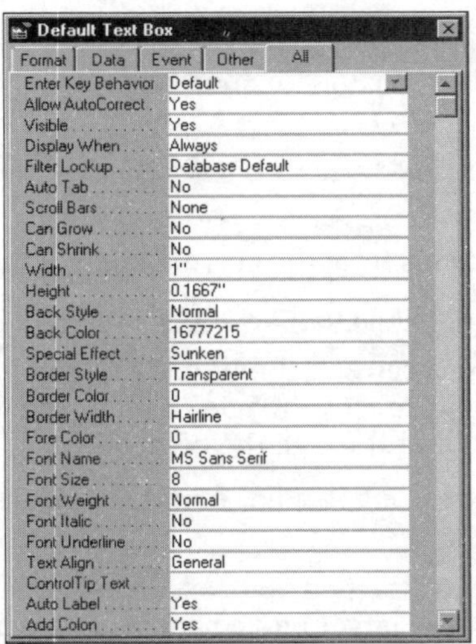

Figure 16-18: Displaying default properties.

By changing the default property settings, you can create customized forms much more quickly than by changing every control.

Access provides many tools for customizing not only your data-entry and display forms, but also reports. In addition, you can apply the default properties to existing controls, and even save a set of default controls as a template. You can then use the template as the basis for a new form. Learning these techniques can save you even more time when you create new forms and reports.

Cross Ref Chapter 18 covers saving control settings and using a tool known as AutoFormat to change settings globally.

Summary

In this chapter, you learned the basic usage of controls and properties for forms and reports. The following points were examined:

- ✦ You can create a new blank form by selecting Insert➪Form Design View.
- ✦ A control is an object on a form or report, such as a label or a text box.
- ✦ There are three types of controls: bound, unbound, and calculated.
- ✦ Text boxes are the most common type of control and let you enter and display data.
- ✦ Controls often have attached label controls to identify the purpose of the control.
- ✦ You can create a new control by dragging a field from the Field List window or by using the toolbox.
- ✦ The Field List window displays a list of all fields from the current table or query.
- ✦ You can drag a field from the Field List window to create a bound control.
- ✦ You can select a control by clicking on it. You can select multiple controls by clicking on them while holding down the Shift key, by dragging a rectangle to enclose the controls, or by dragging the pointer through the controls.
- ✦ You can resize controls by using the small resizing handles found in a selected control.
- ✦ You can move controls by dragging them. An attached control can be moved separately from its attached label by use of the larger move handles in the upper left corner of a selected control.
- ✦ You can align controls by using the Align options of the Format menu. Controls can also be copied, duplicated, and deleted.

- Using the Size options of the Format menu, you can change the size of controls consistently.
- You can space controls evenly by using the Horizontal and Vertical Spacing options in the Format menu.
- Properties are named attributes of controls, fields, or database objects. You can set properties that modify the characteristics of the control, such as size, color, or appearance.
- Properties are displayed in a property sheet. Each type of control has different properties.
- Although an individual control has its own properties, each form maintains a set of default properties for each type of control on the form.

In the next chapter, you learn how to use controls to create a new form.

✦ ✦ ✦

Creating and Customizing Data-Entry Forms

In This Chapter

Creating a multiple-file query to be used for the form

Creating a blank form bound to the query

Learning about form-level properties

Reviewing placement of fields on a form

Modifying controls on a form

Setting the tab order of a form

Creating controls for Memo and OLE fields

Creating a form using two tables

Creating a multiple-page form

Learning how to use form and page headers and footers

Printing a form

Converting a form to a report

In Chapter 16, you learned about all the tools necessary to create and display a form. In this chapter, you use all the skills you learned to create several types of data-entry and display forms.

Disk In this chapter, you use the Customer and Pets tables in the Mountain Animal Start database to create several types of simple forms. Each control will be explained by the use of one or more fields in these tables.

Creating a Standard Data-Entry Form

The first form you create in this chapter is a simple data-entry form that uses two tables. In Chapter 9, you created a simple Pets data-entry form by using a Form Wizard. In this section of the chapter, you create the more complicated form you see in Figure 17-1. This form demonstrates the use of label and text box controls from multiple tables, as well as embedded pictures. You'll continue to modify this form in the next several chapters, adding more complicated controls and emphasis.

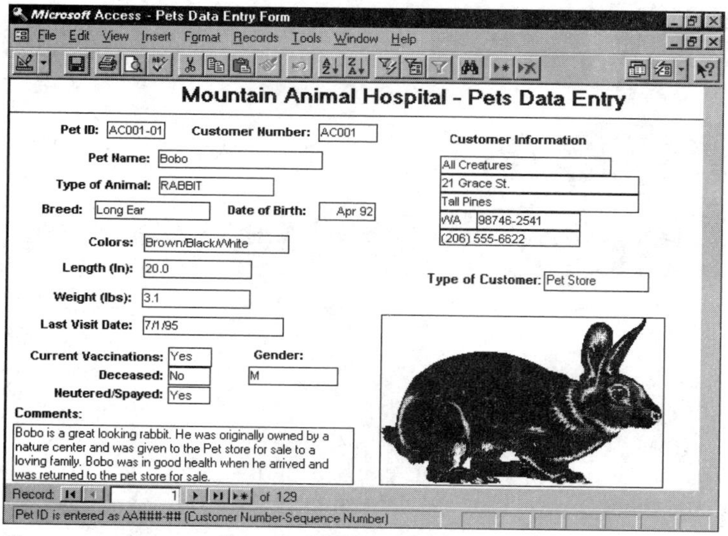

Figure 17-1: A complicated data-entry form.

Assembling the data

With this design in mind, you need to assemble the data. To create this form, you need fields from two tables, Customer and Pets. Table 17-1 lists the necessary fields and their table location.

To assemble this data, you first need to create a query called Pets and Owners, which includes all fields from both tables, even though you aren't going to use all the fields. These extra fields give you the flexibility to add a field later without redoing the query. This can happen, for example, when you see you'll need another field from which to derive a calculated control.

Table 17-1
Fields Needed for the Pets Data-Entry Form

Fields from Pets Table	*Fields from Customer Table*
Pet ID	Customer Name
Customer ID	Street/Apt
Pet Name	City
Type of Animal	State
Breed	ZIP Code

Fields from Pets Table	*Fields from Customer Table*
Date of Birth	Phone Number
Colors	Type of Customer
Length	
Weight	
Last Visit Date	
Current Vaccinations	
Deceased	
Neutered/Spayed	
Gender	
Comments	
Picture	

In this example, you also sort the data by the Pet ID. It's always a good idea to arrange your data into some known order. When you display a form, you see the data in its physical order unless you sort the data.

To create the Pets and Owners query, follow these steps:

1. Click on the query tab in the Database window, and then click on the New button to create a new query.
2. Select New Query in the New Query dialog box and click on OK. The Show Table dialog box appears.
3. Add the Customer table.
4. Add the Pets table.
5. Close the Show Table dialog box.
6. Drag the asterisk (*) from the Customer field list to the first column in the QBE design pane.
7. Drag the asterisk (*) from the Pets field list to the second column in the QBE design pane.
8. Drag the Pet ID field from the Pets field list to the third column in the QBE pane.
9. Click on the Pet ID Show: box to turn it off.
10. Change the Sort to Ascending in the Pet ID field, as shown in Figure 17-2.
11. Select File➪Close, then select Yes, and name the query **Pets and Owners**.

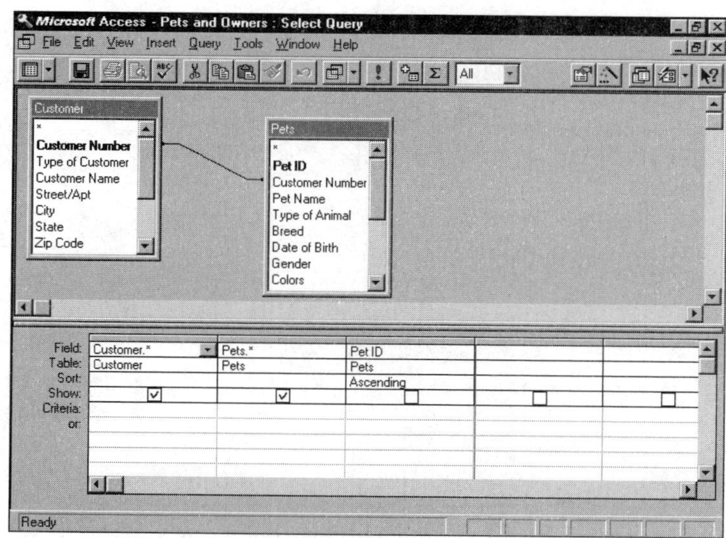

Figure 17-2: The Pets and Owners query.

Note

You use the asterisk (*) to select all fields from each table.

Creating a new form and binding it to a query

Now that you've created the Pets and Owners query, you can create a new form and bind it to the query. Follow these steps to complete this process:

1. Click on the database icon to display the Database window if it is not already displayed.
2. Click on the Forms tab in the Database window and click on the New button.
3. Select Design View in the Wizard list, and then select the Pets and Owners query from the combo box at the bottom of the dialog box.
4. Click on the OK button to create the new form.
5. Maximize the Form window.

You now see a blank Form Design window, as shown in Figure 17-3. The form is bound to the query Pets and Owners, as you can see in the property window on the screen. This means the data from that query will be used when the form is viewed or printed. The fields from the query are available for use in the form design; they will appear in the Field List window.

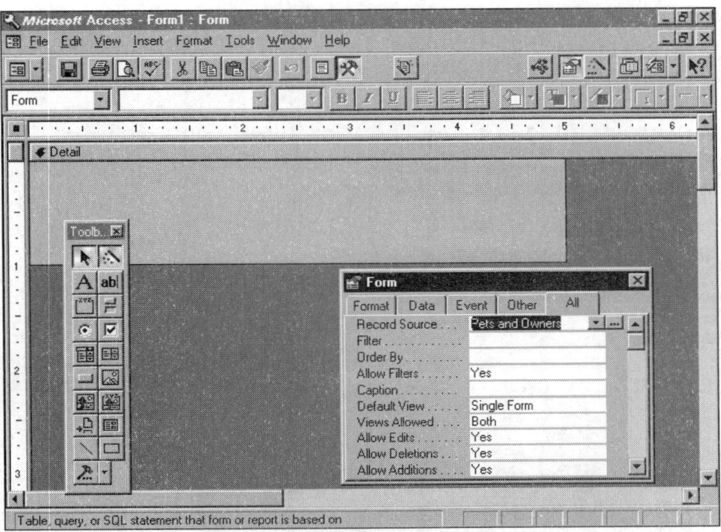

Figure 17-3: The blank Form Design window.

Tip If you need to create a form that contains no field controls, you may want to create a blank form that is not bound to a query. You can do this simply by not selecting a table/query when you select Design View in the New Form dialog box.

Defining the form display size

When you are creating your form, you must resize the workspace of the form. In Figure 17-3, the light gray area in the form is your workspace. If you place controls in the dark gray area outside it, however, the workspace expands automatically until it is larger than the area in which you placed the control. The size of the workspace depends on the size of your form. If you want the form to fill the screen, size it to the size of your screen, which depends on your screen resolution. You can fit more data on-screen if you are using a Super VGA screen size of 800 × 600 or 1024 × 1024 than you can if you are using the standard VGA size of 640 × 480. You never know who may use a form you create; you should stay with the smallest size any anticipated user may have.

A maximized standard VGA screen set to 640 × 480 in Windows 95 can display a full-screen size of approximately 6 1/4 inches by 3 7/8 inches. This includes the space for the title bar, menu bar, and toolbar at the top, the record-pointer column down the left side, the vertical scrollbar areas down the right side, and the navigation buttons/scrollbar and status line at the bottom. You can set form properties to control most of these elements.

The easiest way to set the form size is simply to use your mouse to grab the borders of the light gray area and resize it as you want. If you grab either the top or bottom borders, your cursor turns into a double arrow. If you grab the corner, the cursor becomes a four-headed arrow and you can size both sides at the same time. (You can see this four-headed arrow cursor in Figure 17-4.) For this example, you should set the form size to 6 1/4 inches by 3 7/8 inches, following the next steps, and use Figure 17-4 as a guide. At this size, no form scrollbars should appear.

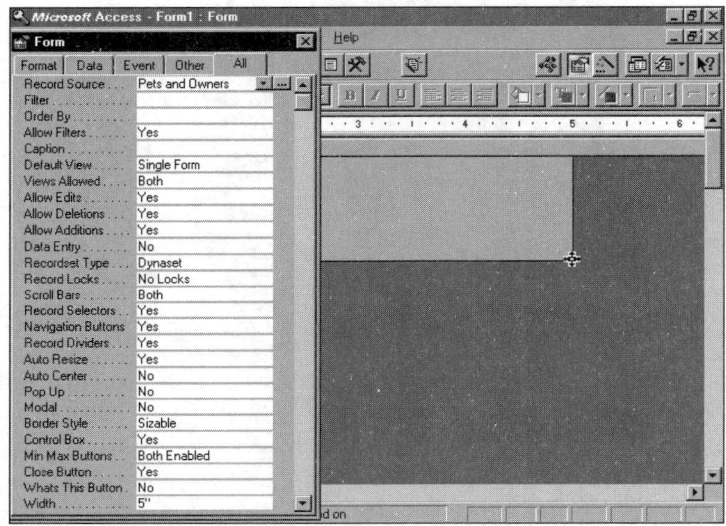

Figure 17-4: Form properties.

Follow these steps to change the form size:

1. Place the cursor at the bottom right corner of the vertical and horizontal borders where the light gray space meets the dark gray area. The cursor should appear as a four-headed arrow.
2. Grab the corner and (pressing the left mouse button) drag the borders until the size is exactly 6 1/4 inches by 3 7/8 inches.

Warning If you add controls beyond the right border, you have to scroll the form to see these controls. This is generally not acceptable in a form. If you add controls beyond the bottom border, you have to scroll the form to see these controls as well; this is acceptable because the form becomes a multiple-page form. Later in this chapter, you learn how to control multiple-page forms.

Changing form properties

You can set many form properties to change the way the entire form is displayed. Table 17-2 (in a later section) discusses some of the most important properties shown in Figure 17-4. Some of them work together, creating certain behaviors in the form that are worth noting in more detail here; other property characteristics are noted later in this chapter.

Embedding a filter or sort in a form

The second and third properties in a form allow you to save an active filter definition and sorted order with a form. When you use Filter by Selection or Filter by Form as you sort your data or select criteria filters, their definitions are copied to the Filter and Order by properties of the form. For example, if you decide to filter the Pets data by only records in the state of Washington and also sort the data by city, you would find `((State)="WA")` in the Filter property and `City` in the Order By property. If the filter is active when you close or save the form, the properties are saved with the form and the filter is reactivated the next time the form is opened.

The next form property, Allow Filters, determines whether the user can create a new filter while using the form. If you change the Allow Filters property to No, the filter buttons are inactive in the form.

Changing the title bar text with the Caption property

Normally the title bar displays the name of the form after it is saved. By changing the Caption property, you can display a different title in the title bar when the form is run. To change the title bar text, follow these steps:

1. Display the property window if it is not already displayed.
2. Click on the Caption property in the property window.
3. Type **Pets Data Entry Form**.
4. Click on any other property or press Enter.

You can display the blank form by selecting the Form button on the toolbar to check the result. The caption you enter here overrides the name of the saved form.

Setting the various views

Two properties determine how your form displays records: Default View and Views Allowed. The Views Allowed property has three settings: Form, Datasheet, and Both. The default setting is Both, which lets the user switch between Form and Datasheet view. If the you set the Views Allowed property to Datasheet, the Form button and the View⇨Form menu selections are not selectable; you can view the data only as a datasheet. If you set the Views Allowed property to Form, the Datasheet button and the View⇨Datasheet menu selections are not selectable; you can view the data only as a form.

The Default View property is different; it determines how the data is displayed when the form is first run. Three settings are possible: Single Form, Continuous Forms, and Datasheet. The first setting, Single Form, displays one record per form page, regardless of form's size. The next setting, Continuous Forms, is the default; it tells Access to display as many detail records as will fit on-screen. Normally you would use this setting to define the height of a very small form, and to display many records at one time. Figure 17-5 shows such a form. The records have a small enough height that you can see a number of them at once. The final Default View setting, Datasheet, displays the form as a standard datasheet when run. You should now change this property to Single Form.

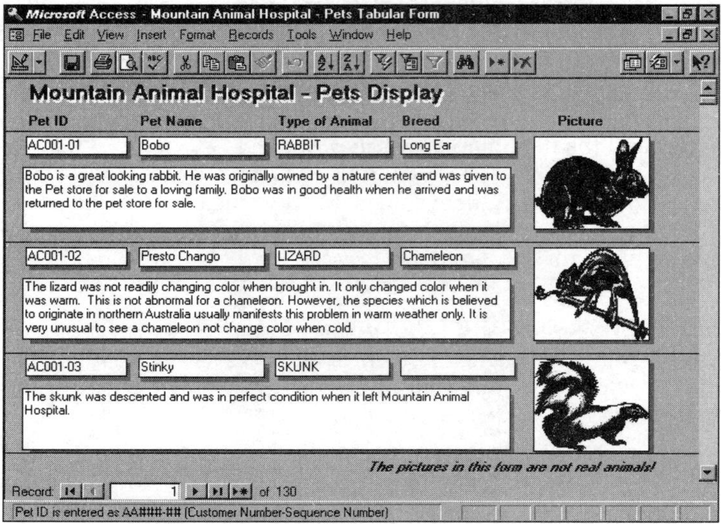

Figure 17-5: Using the Continuous Forms setting of the Default View property.

Eliminating the Record Selector Bar

The Record Selector property determines whether you see the vertical bar on the left side of the form; this bar lets you select the entire record (you see the bar with the editing icon in datasheets). Primarily used in multi-record forms or datasheets, a right-pointing triangle indicates the current record; a pencil icon indicates the record is being changed. Though the record selector bar is important for datasheets, you probably won't want it for a single record form. To eliminate it, simply change the form's Record Selector property to No.

Table 17-2
Form Properties

Property	*Description and Options*	
Caption	Displayed in the title bar of the displayed form	
Default View	Determines the type of view when the form is run	
	Single Form	One record per page
	Continuous Forms	As many records per page as will fit (Default)
	Datasheet	Standard row and column datasheet view
Views Allowed	Determines whether the user can switch between the two views	
	Form	Form view only allowed
	Datasheet	Datasheet view only allowed
	Both	Form or Datasheet view allowed
Allow Edits	Prevents or allows editing of data, making the form read-only for saved records	
	Yes/No	You can/cannot edit saved records
Allow Deletions	Used to prevent records from being deleted	
	Yes/No	You can/cannot delete saved records
Allow Additions	Used to determine whether new records can be added	
	Yes/No	You can/cannot add new records
Data Entry	Used to determine whether form displays saved records	
	Yes/No	Only new records are displayed/All records are displayed
Recordset Type	Used to determine whether multitable forms can be updated; replaces Access 2.0 Allow Updating property	
	Dynaset	Only default table field controls can be edited
	Dynaset (Inconsistent Update)	All tables and fields are editable
	Snapshot	No fields are editable (Read Only in effect)
Record Locks	Used to determine multiuser record locking	
	No Locks	Record is only locked as it is saved
	All Records	Locks entire form records while using the form
	Edited Records	Locks only the current record being edited

(continued)

Table 17-2 *(continued)*

Property	*Description and Options*	
Scrollbars	Determines whether any scrollbars are displayed	
	Neither	No scrollbars are displayed
	Horizontal Only	Displays only the horizontal scrollbar
	Vertical Only	Displays only the vertical scrollbar
	Both	Displays both the horizontal and vertical scrollbars
Record Selectors	Determines whether vertical record selector bar is displayed (Yes/No)	
Navigation Buttons	Determines whether navigation buttons are visible (Yes/No)	
Dividing Lines	Determines whether lines between form sections are visible (Yes/No)	
Auto Resize	Form is opened to display a complete record (Yes/No)	
Auto Center	Centers the form on-screen when it's opened (Yes/No)	
Pop Up	Form is a pop-up that floats above all other objects (Yes/No)	
Modal	For use when you must close the form before doing anything else. Disables other windows. When Pop Up set to Yes, Modal disables menus and toolbar, creating a dialog box (Yes/No)	
Border Style	Determines form's border style	
	None	No border or border elements (scrollbars, navigation buttons)
	Thin	Thin border, not resizeable
	Sizeable	Normal form settings
	Dialog	Thick border, Title bar only, cannot be sized; use for dialog boxes
Control Box	Determines whether Control menu (Restore, Move Size) is available (Yes/No)	
Min Max Buttons		
	None	No buttons displayed in upper right corner of form
	Min Enabled	Minimize Button only is displayed
	Max Enabled	Maximize Button only is displayed
	Both Enabled	Minimize and Maximize buttons are displayed
Close Button	Determines whether to display the Close button in the upper right corner and a Close menu item in the Control menu (Yes/No)	
What's This Button	Determines whether Screen Tips appear when user presses Shift+F1 for Help	

Property	Description and Options	
Width	Displays the value of the width of the form; can be entered, or Access fills it in as you adjust the width of the work area	
Picture	Enter the name of a bitmap file for the background of the entire form	
Picture Size Mode	Options:	
	Clip	Displays the picture at its actual size
	Stretch	Fits picture to the form size (Non-Proportionally)
	Zoom	Fits picture to the form size (Proportionally). This may result in the picture not fitting in one dimension (Height or Width).
Picture Alignment	Options:	
	Top Left	The picture is displayed at the top left corner of the form or report window or image control.
	Top Right	The picture is displayed at the top right corner of the form or report window or image control.
	Center	(Default) The picture is centered in the form or report window or image control.
	Bottom Left	The picture is displayed at the bottom left corner of the form or report window or image control.
	Bottom Right	The picture is displayed at the bottom right corner of the form or report window or image control.
	Form Center	The form's picture is centered horizontally in relation to the width of the form, and vertically in relation to the top most and bottom most controls on the form.
	Picture Tiling	Used when you want to overlay multiple copies of a small bitmap. For example, a single brick can become a wall.
Cycle	Options:	
	All Records	Tabbing from the last field of a record moves to the next record
	Current Record	Tabbing from the last field of a record moves to the first field of that record
	Current Page	Tabbing from the last field of a record moves to the first field of the current page
Menu Bar	Used to specify an alternate menu bar; Builder button lets you create a new menu bar if you want	
Shortcut Menu	Determines whether Shortcut menus are active	

(continued)

Table 17-2 (continued)

Property	*Description and Options*	
Shortcut Menu Bar	Used to specify an alternate Shortcut menu bar	
Grid X	Determines the number of points per inch when the X grid is displayed	
Grid Y	Determines the number of points per inch when the Y grid is displayed	
Layout for Print	Determines whether the form uses screen fonts or printer fonts	
	Yes	Printer Fonts
	No	Screen Fonts
Fast Laser Printing	Prints rules instead of lines and rectangles (Yes/No)	
Help File	Name of the compiled Help file to assign custom help to the form	
Help Context ID	ID of the context-sensitive entry point in the help file to display	

Placing fields on the form

The next step is to place the necessary fields onto the form. When you place a field on a form, it is called a *control,* and is bound to another field (its *control source*). Therefore, you'll see the terms *control* and *field* used interchangeably in this chapter.

As you've learned, the process of placing controls on your form consists of three basic tasks:

- ✦ Displaying the Field List window by clicking on the Field List button in the toolbar
- ✦ Clicking on the desired toolbox control to determine the type of control that is created
- ✦ Selecting each of the fields you want on your form, and then dragging them to the Form Design window

Displaying the field list

To display the Field List window, click on the Field List button on the toolbar. You can resize the Field List window and move it around. The enlarged window (illustrated in Figure 17-6) shows all the fields in the Pets and Owners query dynaset.

Notice, in Figure 17-6, that the fields Customer.Customer Number and Pets.Customer Number, as well as Customer.Last Visit Date and Pets.Last Visit Date, have the table name as a prefix. This prefix distinguishes fields of the same name that come from different tables within a query.

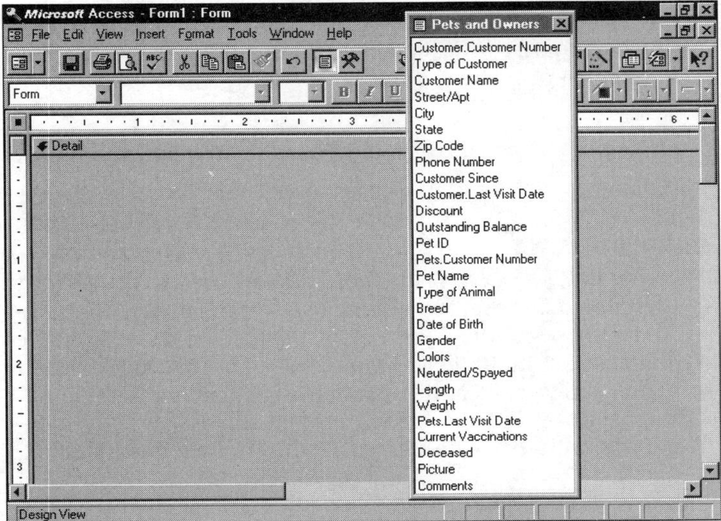

Figure 17-6: The Field List window.

Tip You can move the Field List window simply by clicking on the title bar and dragging it to a new location. You can also select the Move command from the window's Control menu.

Selecting the fields for your form

Selecting a field in the Field List window is the same as selecting that field from a query field list. The easiest way to select a field is simply to click on it, which highlights it; then you can drag it to the Form window.

To highlight *contiguous* (adjacent) fields in the list, click on the first field you want in the field list, and then move the cursor to the last field you want; hold down the Shift key as you click on the last field. The block of fields between the first and last field are displayed in reverse video as you select them. Drag the block to the Form window.

You can highlight noncontiguous fields in the list by clicking on each field while holding down the Ctrl key. Each field is then displayed in reverse video and can be dragged (as part of the group) to the Form design window.

Note One way this method differs from using the query Field List is that you *cannot* double-click on a field to add it to the Form window.

You can begin by selecting the Pets table fields for the detail section. To select the fields you need for the Pets Data Entry form, follow these steps:

1. Click on the Pet ID field.
2. Scroll down the field list until the Comments field is visible.
3. Hold down the Shift key and click on the Deceased field.

The block of fields from Pet ID to Deceased should be highlighted in the Field List window.

Dragging fields onto your form

After you select the proper fields from the Pets table, all you need to do is drag the fields onto the form. Depending on whether you choose one or several fields, the cursor changes to reflect your selection. If you select one field, you see a Field icon (a box containing text). If you select multiple fields, you see a Multiple Field icon instead. These are the cursor icons you've seen in the Query Design screens.

To drag the Pets table fields onto the Form Design window, follow these steps:

1. Click on within the highlighted block of fields in the Field List window.
2. Without releasing the mouse button, drag the cursor onto the form, placing it under the 2-inch mark on the horizontal ruler at the top of the screen and the 1/4-inch mark of the vertical ruler along the left edge.
3. Release the mouse button. The fields now appear in the form, as shown in Figure 17-7.
4. Close the Field List window by clicking on the Field List button on the toolbar.

Notice that there are two controls for each field you dragged onto the form. When you use the drag-and-drop method for placing fields, Access automatically creates a label control that uses the name of the field; it's attached to the text control that the field is bound to. If you followed along with the book in Chapter 14, you changed the Customer Number field in the Pets table to a lookup field. Figure 17-7 shows this field displayed as a combo box (automatically, as it is one of the properties changed in Chapter 14).

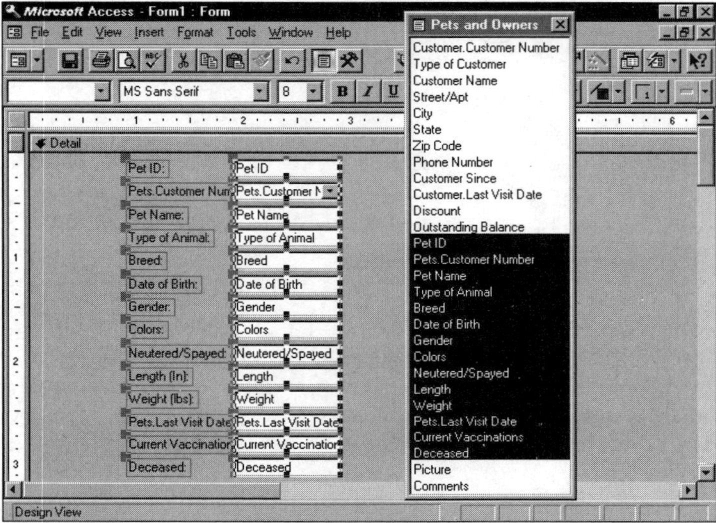

Figure 17-7: Dragging fields to the form.

Working with Label Controls and Text Box Controls

You've already seen how attached label controls are created automatically. With the Text Box button selected in the toolbox, you drag a field from the Field List window to a form; this creates a text box control with an attached label control. Sometimes, however, you want to add text label controls by themselves to create headings or titles for the form.

Creating unattached labels

To create a new, unattached label control, you must use the toolbox unless you copy an existing label. The next task in the example is to add the text header *Mountain Animal Hospital Pets Data Entry* to your form. This task is divided into segments to demonstrate adding and editing text. To create an unattached label control, follow these steps:

1. Display the toolbox.
2. Click on the Label button in the toolbox.

3. Click just to the right of the Pet ID field and drag the cursor to make a small rectangle about 3 inches long and 1/4 inch high.
4. Type **Pets Data**.
5. Press Enter.

Tip: To create a multiple-line label entry, press Ctrl+Enter to force a line break where you want it in the control.

Modifying the text in a label or text control

To modify the text in a control, you need to click on the inside of the label. When you do this, the cursor changes to the standard Windows text cursor, an I-beam. Also notice that the formatting toolbar icons become grayed out and are not selectable. This is because within a label control — or any control — you cannot apply specific formatting to individual characters.

You can now make any edits you want to the text. If you drag across the entire selection so it is highlighted, anything new you type replaces whatever is in this area. Another way to modify the text is to edit it from the control's property window. The second item in the property window is Caption. In the Caption property, you can also edit the contents of a text or label control (for a text control, this property is called *Control Source*) by clicking on the Edit box and typing new text. To edit the label so it contains the proper text, follow these steps:

1. Click in front of the `P` in `Pets Data` in the label control.
2. Type **Mountain Animal Hospital -** before `Pets Data`.
3. Type **Entry** after `Pets Data`.
4. Press Enter.

Tip: If you want to edit or enter a caption that is longer than the space in the property window, the contents will scroll as you type. Or you can press Shift+F2 to open a zoom box that gives you more space to type.

The Formatting Toolbar

Access for Windows 95 features a second toolbar known as the *Formatting toolbar* (described more fully in Chapter 18). Toolbars are really windows. You can move any toolbar by dragging it from its normal location to the middle of a form, and you can change its size and shape. Some toolbars can be *docked* to any edge of the screen (such as the left, right, or bottom). The Formatting toolbar can only be docked at the top or bottom of the screen.

The Formatting toolbar integrates objects from the Access 2.0 Form Design toolbar and the Palette. The first area of the Formatting toolbar (on the left side) selects a control or Form section such as the Form or Page headers or Footers, Detail or the form itself. When you have multiple pages of controls and you want (for example) to select a control that's on page 3 or behind another control, this combo box makes it easy. The next few objects on the Formatting toolbar change text properties. Two more combo boxes let you change the font style and size. (Remember, you may have fonts others do not have. Do not use an exotic font if the user of your form does not have the font.) After the Font Style and Size combo boxes are icons for Bold, Italic and Underlining a text control. Beyond those are alignment icons for Left, Center, and Right text alignment. The last five pull-down icons change color properties, line types and styles, and special effects. See Chapter 18 for more complete descriptions.

Modifying the appearance of text in a control

To modify the appearance of text within a control, select the control by clicking on its border (not in it). You can then select a formatting style you want to apply to the label. Just click on the appropriate button in the toolbar. To add visual emphasis to the title, follow these steps:

1. Click on the form heading label.
2. Click on the Bold button in the formatting toolbar.
3. Click on the drop-down arrow of the Font-Size list box.
4. Select 14 from the Font-Size drop-down list.

The label control still needs to be resized to display all the text.

Sizing a text box control or label control

You can select a control simply by clicking on it. Depending on the size of the control, from three to seven sizing handles appear. One appears on each corner except the upper left, and one appears on each side. When you move the cursor over one of the sizing handles, the cursor changes into a double-headed arrow. When this happens, click on the control and drag it to the size you want. Notice that as you drag, an outline of the new size appears, indicating how large the label will be when you release the mouse button.

Tip

When you double-click on any of the sizing handles, Access usually resizes a control to a *best fit* for the text in the control. This is especially handy if you increase the font size and then notice that the text is cut off, either at the bottom or to the right. For label controls, note that this *best-fit sizing* adjusts the size vertically and horizontally, though text controls are resized only vertically. This is because when Access is in form design mode, it can't predict how much of a field you want to display — the field name and field contents can be radically different. Sometimes, however, label controls are not resized correctly and must be manually adjusted.

You see the text no longer fits within the label control, but you can resize the text control to fit the enhanced font size. To do this, follow these steps:

1. Click on the `Mountain Animal Hospital - Pets Data Entry` label control.
2. Move the cursor over the control. Notice that the cursor changes as it moves over the sizing handles.
3. Double-click one of the sizing handles.

The label control size may still need readjustment. If so, you can place the cursor on the bottom right corner of the control so the diagonal arrow appears; then drag the control until it is the correct size. You will also need to move some of the controls down to make room for the label; you'll want to center it over the form. You can select all the controls and move them down using techniques learned in the previous chapter.

Tip

You can also select Format➪Size➪to Fit to change the size of the label control text automatically.

As you create your form, you should test it constantly by selecting the Form button in the toolbar. Figure 17-8 shows the form in its current state of completion.

Now that you've dragged the Pets fields to the form design and added a form title, you can move the text box controls into the correct position. You then want to size each control to display the information properly within each field.

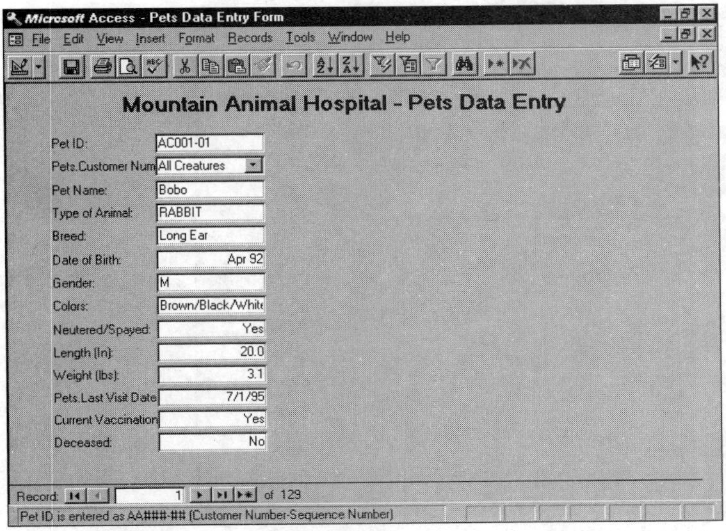

Figure 17-8: A form in progress.

Moving label and text controls

Before you move the label and text controls, it is important to remind you of a few differences between attached and unattached controls. When an attached label is created automatically with a text control, it is called a *compound control* — that is, whenever one control in the set is moved, the other control in the set is also moved.

To move both controls in a compound control, select one of the pair by clicking anywhere on it. Move the cursor over either of the objects. When the cursor turns into a hand, you can click on the controls and drag them to their new location.

Place the controls in their proper position to complete the form design and layout, as shown in Figure 17-9. Notice that the Gender control has its label moved to a position above the text box control. Also notice that some of the text labels are updated. Remember that you can do this by selecting the attached label control and then using the Move handle to move only the label. Also notice that some formatting is added, as you'll do in the next section.

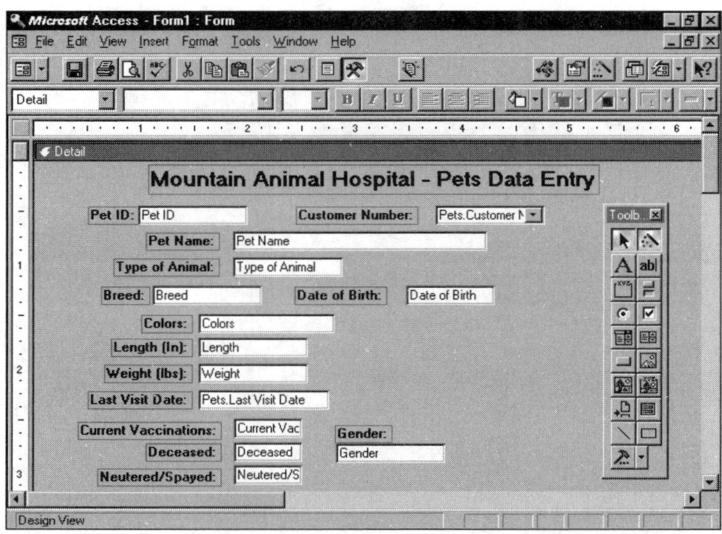

Figure 17-9: Selected and resized label controls in the detail section.

Modifying the appearance of multiple controls

The next step is to make all the label controls in the form bold. This helps you differentiate between label controls and text controls; some of them currently have the same text. The following steps guide you in this process:

1. Select all the attached label controls in the form by clicking on them individually while holding down the Shift key. There are 14 label controls to select, as shown in Figure 17-9.
2. Click on the Bold button on the toolbar.
3. Select Format⇨Size⇨to Fit to resize all the labels.

Note You cannot select the label controls in the steps given here if you use the drag-and-surround method and drag the rectangle through the text boxes. That method also selects all the text boxes; you want to only bold and resize the labels.

If you run the form now, you notice that the Length, Width, and Last Visit Date data items are all right-aligned within the text controls. You want to left-align these controls so values appear left-aligned next to the label. To make this change, follow these steps:

1. Select the Length, Weight, and Pets. Last Visit Date text box controls only; use the cursor to draw a box around the three text box controls.
2. Click on the Left Align button on the toolbar.

Changing the control type

You may notice, in Figure 17-9, that the Customer Number field is a combo box (the default control type you defined in the table using the Lookup Wizard). Though there are times you may want to use a lookup field to display related data, this is not one of those times. In this example, you will need to see the Customer Number for each Pet, not the Customer Name (you'll deal with displaying the Customer information later in this chapter). For now, use these steps to turn the combo box back into a text box control:

1. Select the Customer Number field.
2. Select Format➪Change To➪Text Box to change the control type.

Setting the tab order

Now that you've completed moving all your controls into position, you should test the form again. If you run the form and use Tab to move from field to field, you notice the cursor does not move from field to field in the order you expect. It starts out in the first field, `Pet ID`, and then continues vertically from field to field until it reaches the `Date of Birth` field. Then the cursor jumps down to `Gender`, back up to the `Colors`, and then down again to `Neutered/Spayed`. This route may seem strange, but that is the original order in which the fields were added to the form.

This is called the *tab order* of the form. The form's *default tab order* is always the order in which the fields were added to the form. If you don't plan to move the fields around, this is all right. If you do move the fields around, however, you may want to change the order. After all, though you may make heavy use of the mouse when designing your forms, the average data-entry person still uses the keyboard to move from field to field.

When you need to change the tab order of a form, select the View➪Tab Order. . . menu option in the Design window to change the order to match your layout. To change the tab order of the form, follow the next set of steps. (Make sure you are in the Design window before continuing.)

1. Select View➪Tab Order. . . .
2. Click on the Gender row in the Tab Order dialog box.
3. Click on the gray area in front of the Gender row again; drag the row to the bottom of the dialog box to a point below the Deceased row, as shown in Figure 17-10.
4. Click on the Neutered/Spayed row in the dialog box.
5. Click on the Neutered/Spayed row again; drag the row to the bottom of the dialog box between the Deceased and Gender rows.
6. Click on the OK button to complete the task.

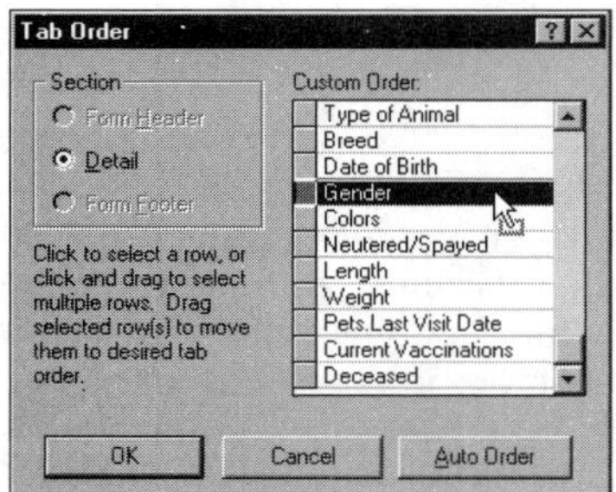

Figure 17-10: The Tab Order dialog box.

The Tab Order dialog box lets you select either one row or multiple rows at a time. You can select multiple contiguous rows by clicking on the first row and then dragging down to select multiple rows. After the rows are highlighted, you can drag the selected rows to their new position.

The Tab Order dialog box has several buttons at the bottom of the box. The Auto Order button places the fields in order from left to right and top to bottom, according to their position in the form. This button is a good place to start when you have significantly rearranged the fields.

Each control has two properties that interact with this screen. The Tab Stop property determines whether pressing the Tab key will land you on the field. The default is Yes; changing the Tab Stop property to No removes the field from the tab order. When you set the tab order, you set the Tab Index property controls. In this example, the first field (`Pet ID`) is set to 1, `Customer Number` is set to 2, etc. Moving around the fields in the Tab Order dialog box will change the Tab Index properties of those (and other) fields.

Adding multiple-line text box controls for Memo fields

Multiple-line text box controls are used for Memo data types such as the Comments field in the Pets table. When you add a Memo field to a form, make sure there is plenty of room in the text box control to enter large amount of text. You have several ways to make certain you've allowed enough space.

The first method is to resize the text box control until it's large enough to accommodate any text you may enter into the Memo field, but this is rarely possible. Usually the reason you create a Memo field is to hold a large amount of text; that text can easily take up more space than the entire form.

One of the options in a text box control is a vertical scrollbar. By adding scrollbars to the your Memo field's text box control, you can allow for any size of data entry. To create a Memo field text box control, follow these steps:

1. Display the Field List window.
2. Drag the Comments field to the bottom left corner of the form below the Neutered/Spayed field.
3. Select the Comments label control and click on the Bold button in the toolbar.
4. Resize the Comments text box control so the bottom of the control is about $^1/_2$ inch high, and put the right side of the control just past the right side of the Gender text box control (as shown in Figure 17-11).
5. Close the Field List window.

The next step (though not mandatory) is to add a vertical scrollbar to the text box control. Adding the scrollbar greatly speeds up your navigation, making it easier to scroll through large amounts of text or move through the data one line at a time when you display the Memo field on the form. If you want to add the scrollbar, follow these steps:

1. Select the Comments text box control.
2. Display the property window.
3. Click on the Scrollbars property and click on the arrow.
4. Select Vertical.

Figure 17-11 shows the added control.

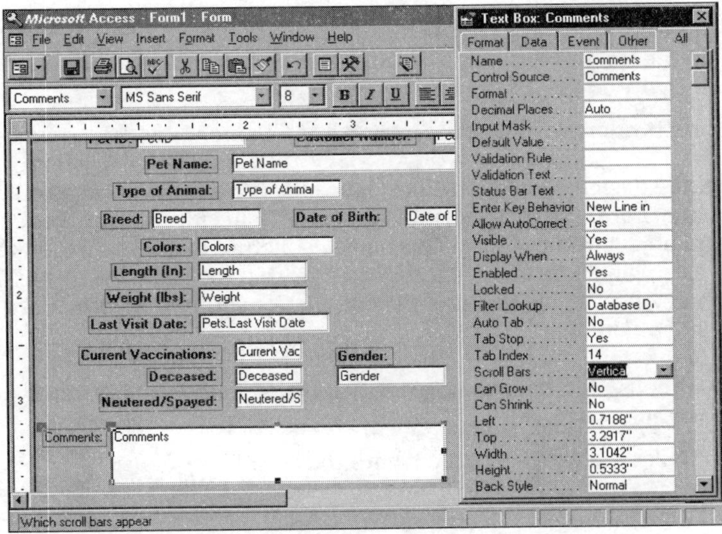

Figure 17-11: Adding a multiple-line text box control.

Note: When you run the form, the scrollbar appears only once when you move into the Comments Memo field.

Adding a bound object frame to the form

When you drag a field that uses the OLE data type to a form, Access creates a bound object frame automatically. You can resize and move this control, just as you can move any control. To add the Picture OLE field to the form, follow these steps:

1. Display the Field List window.
2. Drag the Picture field to the center right area of the form.
3. Select the Picture attached label control.
4. Press Delete to delete the attached label control.
5. Move the left edge of the bound object frame just to the right of the Comments text box.

One problem you may sometimes have when adding controls is that their default size exceeds the form's borders. When this happens, you must resize the control and also resize the border. If you don't resize the border, you'll find the form becomes scrollable outside the normal screen boundaries. This may work, but it doesn't create a well-displayed form. To resize the bound object frame control and the form's border, follow these steps:

1. Select the Picture bound object frame.
2. Resize the control so the right edge is just inside the original form border at 6 1/8 inches on the top border. As you resize the control, you can follow the illustration in Figure 17-12.
3. Resize the form borders to make sure they are at 6 1/4 inches and 3 7/8 inches.

When you're done, the design should look like Figure 17-12. Before you complete the OLE field, there is one more task to perform. The default value for the Size Mode property of a bound object frame is Clip. This means a picture displayed within the frame is shown in its original size and truncated to fit within the frame. In this example, you need to display the picture so it fits completely within the frame. Two property settings let you do this:

Zoom	Keeps picture in its original proportion; may result in extra white space
Stretch	Sizes picture to fit exactly into the frame borders

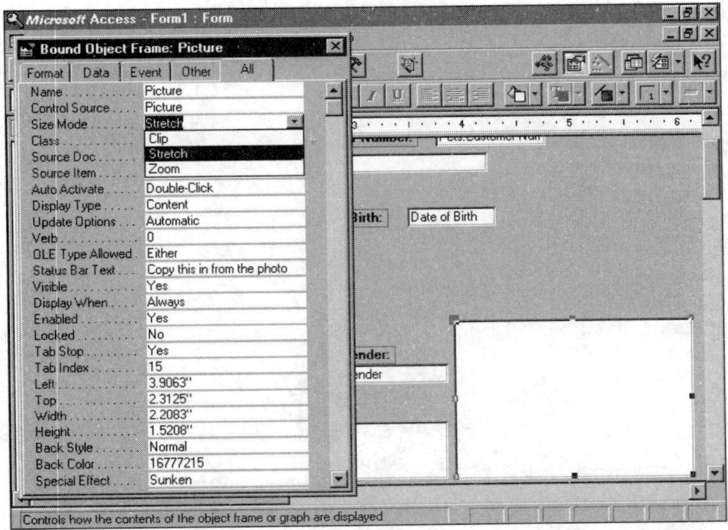

Figure 17-12: Adding an OLE field in a bound object frame control.

Although the Zoom setting displays the picture more correctly, the Stretch setting looks better, unless the picture's proportions are important to viewing the data. To set the Size Mode property of a bound object frame, follow these steps:

1. Select the Picture bound object frame.
2. Display the property window.
3. Select the Size Mode property.
4. Select Stretch.

Figure 17-12 shows the form design as it currently is completed. Notice the property window for the bound object frame control. The Size Mode property is set to Stretch.

When you complete this part of the design, you should save the form and then display it. You can now name this form **Pets Data Entry** if you want. Figure 17-13 shows the form.

So far, you've created a blank form and added several types of controls to the form, but only fields from the Pets table are on the form; originally you created a query that linked the Pets and Customer tables. The Customer table can serve as a lookup table for each Pet record. This allows you to display customer information for each pet.

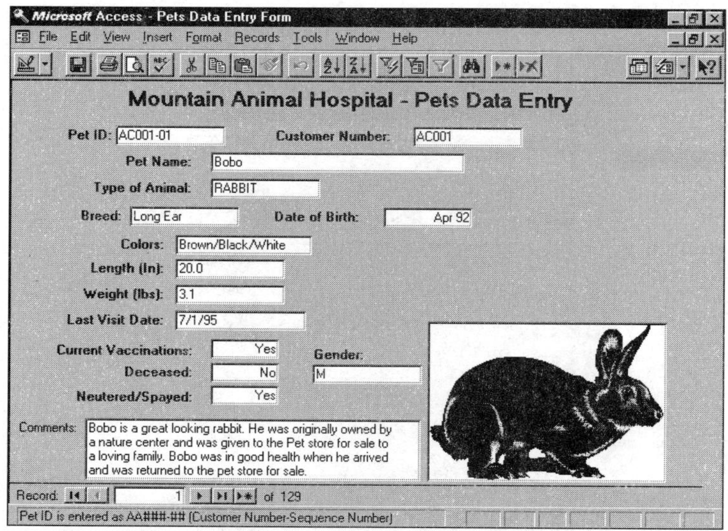

Figure 17-13: The form with a Memo and OLE field.

Creating a Form Using Multiple Tables

When you create a form from a single table, you simply use fields from the one table. When you create a form from multiple tables, normally you use fields from a second table as lookup fields; they let you display additional information. In this section, you learn how to display the customer information.

Adding fields from a second table

You now add the fields from a second table. You want to add the fields to be displayed in the Pets form from the Customer table. These fields will display the customer name and address, along with the Type of Customer field. You place these fields in the upper right portion of the form. Follow these steps to add the customer fields to the form:

1. Display the Field List window.
2. Click on the Type of Customer field.
3. Hold down the Shift key and click on the Phone Number field.
4. Click on within the highlighted block of fields in the Field List window.

5. Without releasing the mouse button, drag the cursor onto the form under the 5-inch mark on the ruler at the top of the screen and the 0.5-inch mark of the ruler along the left edge.

At this point, your form should look like Figure 17-14. You've now placed all of the fields needed for the Pets Data Entry form.

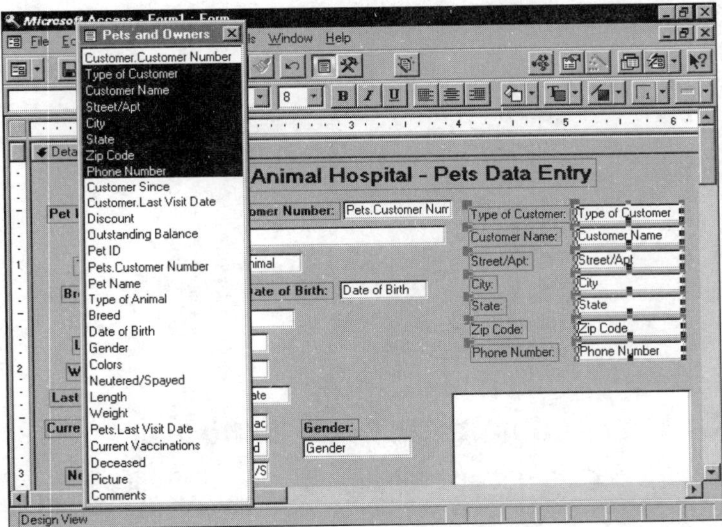

Figure 17-14: Adding the Customer fields.

As you can see in Figure 17-14, the form begins with the Type of Customer field. Actually, you want that field separated from the others (you'll change it to a calculated field later). Use Figure 17-15 as a guide for the final placement of the field.

To move the Type of Customer control below the other customer controls, follow these steps:

1. Deselect all the selected controls by clicking on any empty area of the form.
2. Select just the Type of Customer text box control and its attached label.
3. Move the control just below the Phone Number control so it's just above the Picture bound object frame control.

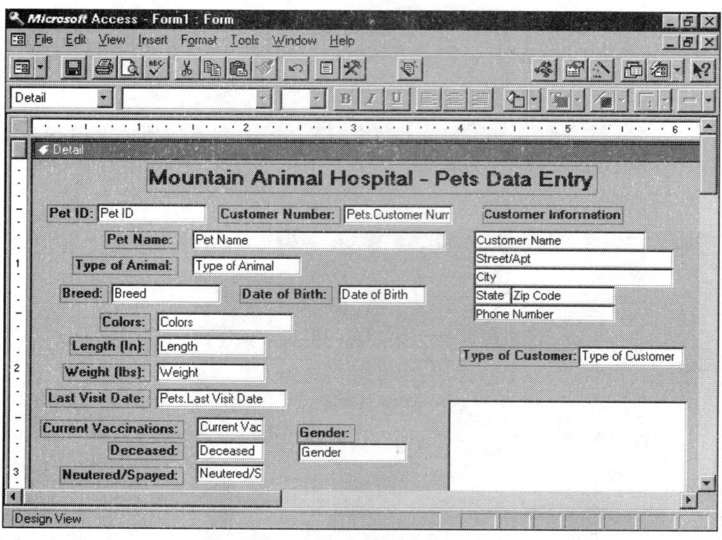

Figure 17-15: Customer fields in the Pets form.

Working with attached label and text controls

As you can see in Figure 17-15, the remaining customer fields will be displayed in a very small area of the screen, with no labels other than the label control Customer Information. It is very easy to delete one or more attached label controls in a form. You simply select the desired label control (or controls) and press Delete. When you delete attached controls, you have two choices:

✦ Delete only the label control.

✦ Delete both the label control and the field control.

If you select the label control and press Delete, only the label control is deleted. If you select the field control and press Delete, both the label control and the field control are deleted. To delete only the Customer label controls (that is, the attached label controls), follow these steps:

1. Draw a box that surrounds only the six label controls from Customer Name through Phone Number.
2. Verify that only the label controls are selected (sizing handles are displayed in all the label controls; only the Move handle is displayed in the text box controls).
3. Press Delete.

Tip

If you want to delete the field control yet keep the attached label control, you can do this by first selecting the label control and choosing Edit⇨Copy. Then select the field control and press Delete to delete both the field control and the label control. Finally, choose Edit⇨Paste to paste the copied label control to the form.

Tip

As you learned in Chapter 16, you can attach a label to an unlabeled control by cutting the unattached label control and then pasting it onto another control.

The final task is to move the customer controls to their final positions and add a label control, as shown in Figure 17-15. Follow these steps to complete this part of the form:

1. Rearrange the controls in the page header to resemble a typical mailing label's address format with State and Zip Code on the same line.
2. Move the Phone Number text box control under the State and Zip Code text box controls.
3. Move the block of name, address, and phone number controls into position so it resembles Figure 17-15. Notice that all the control lines need to touch one another.

Tip

You can use the new Format⇨Vertical Spacing⇨Make Equal option to line up all the controls above each other. If there is still space between them, use the Decrease option.

4. Create a label control with the text **Customer Information**, as shown in Figure 17-15.

Creating a calculated field

The field Type of Customer is a numeric field that displays a 1 if the customer is an individual, 2 if the customer is a pet store, and 3 if the customer is a bird sanctuary, aquarium, or municipal zoo. Rather than having the number displayed, you can transform the value into a more recognizable text expression.

Cross Ref

The easiest way to do this is to replace the original Type of Customer control with a calculated expression. In Chapter 13, you learned about the function called the Immediate IF function (IIf) that lets you transform one value to another. In this example, the expression uses two IIf functions together.

The expression must transform the value of 1 to "Individual," the value of 2 to "Pet Store," and the value of 3 to "Zoo." This is the complete expression:

```
=IIf([Type of Customer]=1,"Individual",IIf([Type of
      Customer]=2,"Pet Store","Zoo"))
```

The first IIf function checks the value of the Type of Customer field; if the value is 1, the value of the calculated control is set to `Individual`. If the value is not 1, another IIf checks to see whether the value of Type of Customer is 2. If the value is 2, the value of the calculated control is set to `Pet Store`. If not 2, the value of the calculated control is set to the only other possibility, which is `Zoo`. To create this new calculated control, follow these steps:

1. Select the Type of Customer text box control.
2. Display the property window.
3. Change the Name to Calculated Type of Customer.
4. Click on the Control Source property and press Shift+F2 to display the zoom box.
5. In the Control Source property, type the following:

   =IIf([Type of Customer]=1,"Individual",IIf([Type of Customer]=2,"Pet Store","Zoo"))
6. Select OK.
7. Close the property window.

New! The new Lookup Wizard for Access helps you create a control to display a different value than the value used in the control. You could use the Lookup Wizard in the Customer table and build a combo box to display `Individual`, `Pet Store` or `Zoo`, but store the values 1, 2, or 3. However, you will create an option group in Chapter 19 so this method is better for now.

Now that the form is complete, you can test it. Run the form and observe that the customer information is now displayed as you see the third record in Figure 17-16.

Changing the updatability of a multiple-table form

If you run the form you just created, you may notice that you can edit the existing pet data or even add new pet records. As you enter a new pet's valid customer number, the customer information is filled in automatically. You can, however, change the customer information. This information is being looked up in the customer table. Since it can affect all records for this customer, you don't want to allow changes to the information fields.

To prevent changes to the customer information fields, use the Locked property. Select all the fields under Customer information. Change the Locked property to Yes.

Warning You must remember that by updating a field such as Customer Name (which is on the *one* side of a one-to-many relationship), you change the one data field in the Customer table that changes a value for all records of pets owned by that customer.

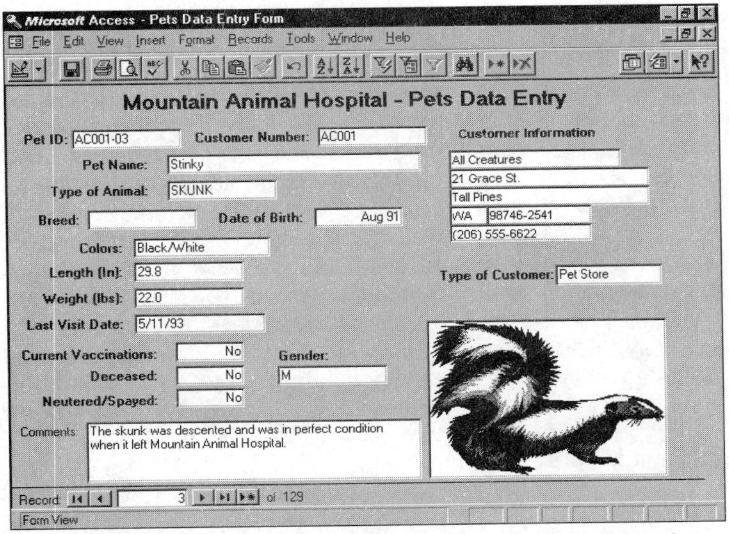

Figure 17-16: The Pets Data Entry form with customer information.

Figure 17-17 shows this property being changed for the Pets Data Entry form.

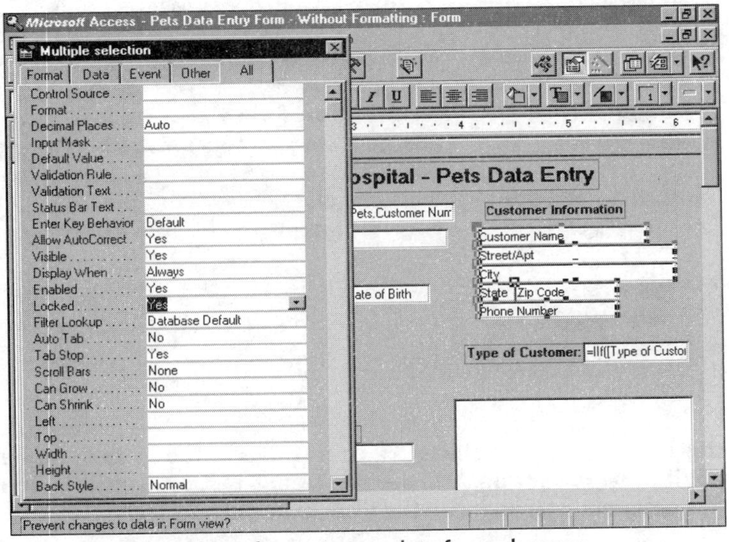

Figure 17-17: Locking the customer data from changes.

Changing Defaults for Attached Label Positioning

Attached label controls are called compound controls because the two controls are *attached*. Sometimes you want to disable this feature, which you can do by changing a default property named AutoLabel. When AutoLabel is set to Yes, a label control is automatically created that bears the name of the field the text control is bound to. With AutoLabel in effect, a label is created automatically every time you drag a field onto a form. Follow these steps to change the AutoLabel default:

1. Display the toolbox if it is not already displayed.
2. Display the property window if it is not already displayed.
3. Click on the Text Box button in the toolbar. The title of the property window should be Default Text Box.
4. Scroll down until you see the AutoLabel property.
5. Click on the AutoLabel text box.
6. Change the contents in the text box to No.

The next property, AutoColon, follows any text in a new label with a colon automatically if the value of the property is set to Yes.

Two properties control where the label appears relative to the control itself. These are the Label X and Label Y properties. Label X controls the horizontal position of the label control relative to the text box control. The default is –1 (to the left of the text box control). As you make the value a smaller negative number, as with .5, you decrease the space from the attached label to the control. If you want the label after the control (as you may for an optionbutton), you use a positive number, such as 1.5, to move the label to the right of the control.

Label Y controls the vertical position of the label control relative to the text box control. The default is 0, which places the label on the same line as the text box control. If you want to place the label above the control, change Label Y to –1 or a larger negative number. The last option, Label Align, lets you control the alignment of the text within the label.

If you changed the AutoLabel default to No, and you now drag fields from the Field List window to the form, you see no label controls attached. The AutoLabel property is in effect only for this form. Because you don't need to add further labeled fields to this form, you can leave the setting of AutoLabel as No.

Disk

You should save this form with all the changes currently made. Name the form **Pets Data Entry Form - Without Formatting**. You use this form later in the chapter and again in the next few chapters, starting with the form in its current state.

Creating a Multiple-Page Form

Suppose you want to add more information to the form. There is little room to add more fields or labels, but you may want to see a larger picture of the animal and to see all the comments at once in the multiple-line text box. Without getting a larger form, you can't do that. You can't just make the screen bigger unless you change to a higher screen resolution, which means getting the necessary hardware. One solution is to create a *multiple-page form*.

Why use multiple-page forms?

You use multiple-page forms when all your information won't fit on one page or when you want to segregate specific information on separate pages. Multiple-page forms allow you to display less information on a page so that a complicated form looks less cluttered. You can also place data items that are not always necessary on the second (or even the third) page, which makes data entry on the first page easier for the user.

You can have as many pages as you need on a form, but the general rule is that more than five pages make the form very tedious. There is also a 22-inch size limitation in the form. You can use a macro to attach other forms to buttons on the form; then you can call up the other pages as you need them by selecting a button.

After you add pages to a form, you can move between them by using the PgUp and PgDn keys or you can use macros or Visual Basic for Applications to program navigation keys.

Note You can create a multiple-page form only when the Default View property of the form is set to Single Form.

Adding a page break

You can add *page breaks* to a form by adding a Page Break control (which you can find near bottom left of the toolbox). Use Figure 17-18 as a guide as you change the Pets Data Entry form to add a separate page for resized Picture and Comments controls.

Follow these steps to add a new page and a page break:

1. Increase the bottom margin of the form to 7 1/2 inches.
2. Move and resize the Comments text box control, as shown in Figure 17-18.
3. Move and resize the Picture text box control.
4. Select the Pet Name text box control in the upper area of the control, and then select Edit⇨Copy.

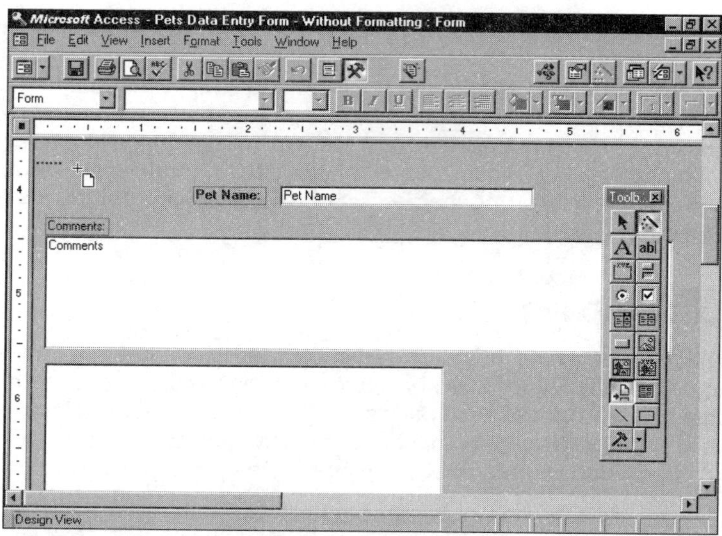

Figure 17-18: Adding a new page and a page break.

5. Select Edit➪Paste and move the copy to the second page of the form.
6. Display the toolbox.
7. Click on the Page Break button in the toolbox.
8. Move the cursor to the left corner of the intersection of the two pages (3³/₄ inches).
9. Click on the mouse to add the page break.

Figure 17-18 shows the completed design.

Notice that you copied `Pet Name` into the second page. This was for display-only purposes. Unless you change the properties of the second Pet Name control, you can also edit its value. When working with forms that require multiple pages, you may want to place controls that are used as headers in a form header section. If you are working with numeric data, you may also want to add a form footer section to display totals.

Figure 17-19 shows the second page of the form for the first record in the table.

Disk You should not save this last set of changes to create a multi-page form. Reopen the form you saved as Pets Data Entry Form - Without Formatting.

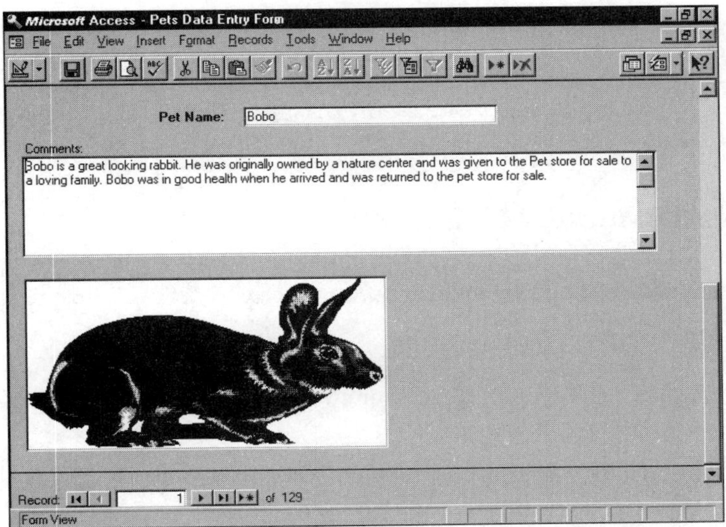

Figure 17-19: The second page of the form.

Using Form and Page Headers and Footers

The most common use of a page or form header is to repeat identification information. In the Pets Data Entry form, for example, the text header is part of the form itself. When you have a second page, you don't see the text header. In Access forms, you can add both form and page sections. Sections include *headers* (which come before the detail controls), and *footers* (which come after the detail controls).

The different types of headers and footers

Several types of headers and footers can appear in a form:

Form header	Displayed at the top of each page when viewed, and at the top when the form is printed
Page header	Displayed only when the form is printed; prints after the form header
Page footer	Appears only when the form is printed; prints before the form footer
Form footer	Displayed at the bottom of each page when viewed, and at the bottom of the form when the form is printed

Form headers and footers are displayed in the form; you can use them optionally in a printed form. *Page headers and footers* are displayed only when a form is printed. Generally, unless you are printing the form as a report, you won't use the page headers or footers. Because you can create reports easily in Access (and even save a form as a report), you won't find much use for page headers and footers.

Creating a form header and footer

You create form headers and footers by selecting View➪Form Header/Footer. When you select this menu option, both the form header and form footer sections are added to the form.

Note

You can add page headers and footers by selecting View➪Page Header/Footer.

To create a form header and move the text header label control into it, follow the next steps:

1. Open the original Pets Data Entry Form - Without Formatting form in design view.
2. Select View➪Form Header/Footer to display the form header and footer.
3. Select the label control `Mountain Animal Hospital - Pets Data Entry`.
4. Move the label control straight up from the detail section to the form header section.
5. Resize the form header to fit the label control properly, as shown in Figure 17-20.
6. Close the form footer area by dragging the Form footer bottom border to meet the top border.

Sometimes, when you display a form with an added header or footer, you lose that much space from the detail section. You must adjust the size of your detail section to compensate for this space.

In this example, you might need to make the height of the detail section smaller because you moved the text label control to the form header section and moved the other controls up in the detail section. You are not using the form footer section; you'll need to close it.

You change the size of a section by placing the cursor on the bottom border of the section, where it turns into a two-headed arrow. Then drag the section border up or down. You can only drag a section up to the bottom of the lowest control in the section.

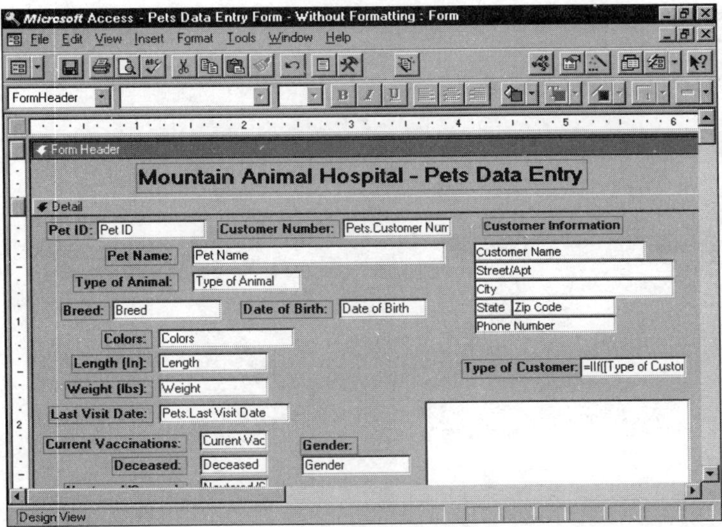

Figure 17-20: Adding a form header.

When you display a form with a header or footer section, you see the sections separated from the detail section by a line. The form headers and footers are literally anchored in place. If you create a scrollable or a multiple-page form, the headers and footers remain where they are while the data in the detail section moves.

Printing a Form

You can print a form by selecting the File➪Print option and entering the desired information in the Print dialog box. Printing a form is like printing anything; you are in a WYSIWYG environment, so what you see on the form is essentially what you get in the printed hard copy. If you added page headers or page footers, you see them at the top or bottom of the printout.

You can also preview the printout by selecting the File➪Print Preview menu option. This displays a preview of the printed page, as shown in Figure 17-21.

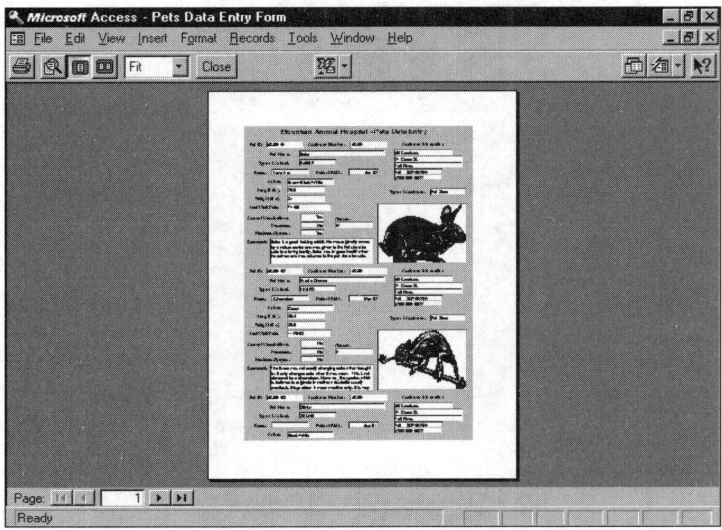

Figure 17-21: A print preview of a form.

Converting a Form to a Report

By right-clicking on a form name in the database window and selecting Save As Report, you can save the form design as a report. The entire form is placed in the report form. If the form has form headers or footers, these are placed in the report header and report footer sections. If the form has page headers or page footers, these are placed in the page header and footer sections in the report. Once the design is in the Report Design window, you can enhance it by using the report design features. This allows you to add group sections and additional totaling in a report without having to re-create a great layout!

Summary

In this chapter, you learned how to create several types of forms without Form Wizards.

- ✦ When you create a form, you can adjust the form size by grabbing the borders and moving them.
- ✦ The Caption form property changes the text on the title bar.
- ✦ The Views Allowed form property lets you determine whether the user can switch to the datasheet view.
- ✦ The Default View form property determines whether the form can display more than one record at a time.
- ✦ The Editing form properties determine whether the form is read-only and whether it allows only new records, records to be added, edited, or deleted.
- ✦ You can place fields on a form by using the Field List window and the toolbox.
- ✦ The tab order determines the direction in which the cursor moves within a data-entry form. You can change this order by selecting View⇨Tab Order....
- ✦ Memo fields are generally displayed by use of multiple-line text box control with a scrollbar.
- ✦ Generally, picture fields (which can be OLE objects or non-OLE bitmaps) are displayed in a bound object frame. The best way to display a picture is to set the Scaling control property to either Stretch or Zoom.
- ✦ The AutoLabel and AutoColumn global properties let you determine where the labels, if any, appear when you create an attached label control.
- ✦ You can create a multiple-page form with the Page Break control.
- ✦ Page headers and footers appear only on the printed form.
- ✦ Form headers and footers appear at the top and bottom of each page in the form.
- ✦ You can print (or preview) a form by using the options in the File menu.
- ✦ You can save a form as a report design and later modify it by right-clicking on a form name in the database window and selecting Save As Report.

In the next chapter, you learn how to add special effects to your forms. These include colors, background shading, and other enhancements such as lines, rectangles, and three-dimensional appearance.

✦ ✦ ✦

CHAPTER 18

Creating Great-Looking Forms

In This Chapter

Enhancing text controls by controlling font size and style

Learning how to apply special display effects to forms

Adding lines and rectangles to a form

Adding color or shading to a form

Adding a background picture to a form

Copying formatting properties between controls

Using AutoFormat and the Format Painter

In Chapter 17, you built a form that started with a blank Form Design screen. That form had no special formatting other than some label and text box controls. The most exciting object on the form was the picture of the rabbit. By using the various formatting windows and the Formatting toolbar, the line and rectangle controls, background pictures, and your own imagination, you can create great-looking forms with a small amount of work.

In this chapter, you learn how to format the data-entry form. You enhance the form you created in the preceding chapter, making it more readable and more presentable.

Making a Good Form Look Great

The Access form designer has the capability to do with a form what any good desktop publishing package can do with words. Just as a desktop publishing package can enhance a word processor's document to make it more readable, the form designer can enhance a database form to make it more usable.

To make your database form more usable, you can draw attention to areas of the form that you want the reader to notice. Just as a headline in a newspaper calls your attention to the news, an enhanced section of the form makes the information it contains stand out.

The Access Form Designer gives you a number of tools to make the form controls and sections visually striking:

- ✦ Lines and rectangles
- ✦ Color and background shading
- ✦ Three-dimensional effects (raised, sunken, etched, chiseled, shadowed)
- ✦ Background pictures
- ✦ Form headers and footers

In this chapter, you enhance the form you created earlier; you add special text features to create shading, shadows, lines, rectangles, and three-dimensional effects. Figure 18-1 shows the form as it appears after some special effects have been added.

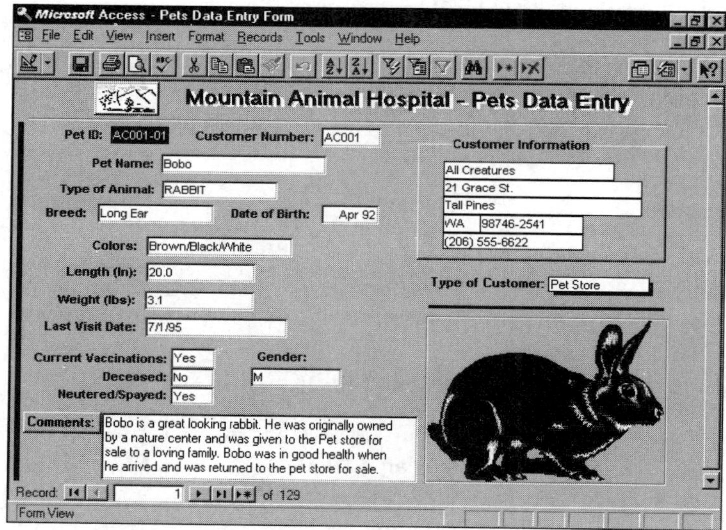

Figure 18-1: An enhanced form.

Understanding WYSIWYG

Access has a WYSIWYG (what-you-see-is-what-you-get) form designer. As you create your controls on-screen, you see instantly what they look like in your form. If you want to see what the data will look like during your form design, the on-screen preview mode lets you see the actual data in your form design without using a hard-copy device.

The Access form designer lets you add color and shading to your form text and controls. You can also display them in reverse video, which shows white letters on a black background. You can even color or shade the background of form sections. As you specify these effects, you see each change instantly on the Design screen.

Using the formatting windows and toolbar

One of the most important controls for enhancing a form is the formatting windows and the Formatting toolbar. There are five formatting windows, including:

- ✦ Background color for shading
- ✦ Foreground color for text
- ✦ Border color for lines, rectangles, and control borders
- ✦ Line thickness for lines, rectangles, and control borders
- ✦ Special effects, such as a raised, sunken, etched, chiseled, or shadowed

Note The Formatting toolbar can be displayed or removed from the screen by selecting View⇨Toolbars and (respectively) either selecting Formatting or right-clicking on the toolbar area and selecting Formatting.

Tip You can tell the currently selected color in the three color icons (background, foreground, and border) by looking in the small square in each picture icon.

You modify the appearance of a control by using a formatting window. To modify the appearance of a control, select it by clicking on it, and then click on one of the formatting windows you'll need in order to change the control's options. Figure 18-2 shows all five formatting windows.

Tip A *formatting window* is a window like the toolbox or the Field List. You can move a formatting window around the screen, but you cannot change its size or anchor it the way you can dock a toolbar to a window border. A formatting window can remain on-screen all the time; you can use it to change the options for one or more controls. To close a formatting window, you click on the Close button or reselect its icon in the Formatting toolbar.

The Fore Color (foreground text) and Back Color (background color) windows are used to change the color of the text or background of a control. You can make a control's background transparent by selecting the Transparent button in the Back Color window. The Border Color window changes the color of control borders, lines, and rectangles. When you click on the Transparent button of the Border Color window, the border on any selected control becomes invisible.

The Border Width window controls the thickness of control borders, lines, and rectangles. A line can be the border of a control or a stand-alone line control. You define the thickness of the line by using the thickness buttons. Available thicknesses (in points) are hairline, 1 point, 2 points, 3 points, 4 points, 5 points, and 6 points.

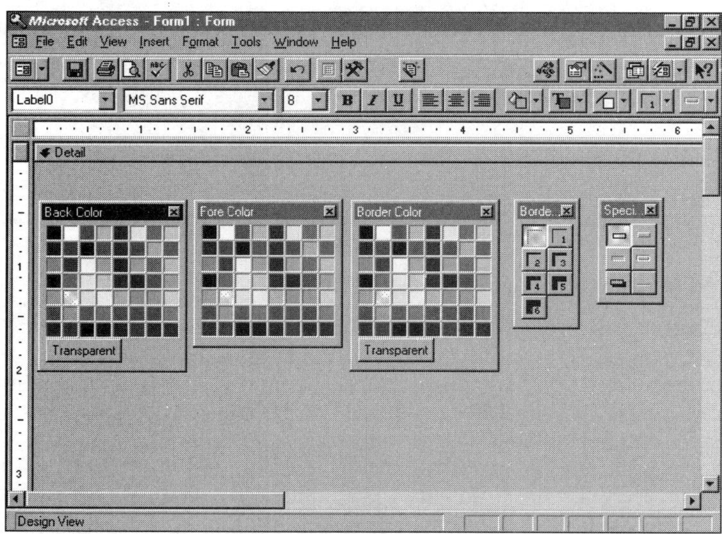

Figure 18-2: The various formatting windows.

There is also a control property to determine the line type; the choices include solid line, dashed line, and dotted line.

Note A *point* (approximately 1/72 inch) is a unit of measurement for character height.

When you're finished with a formatting window, you can close it by clicking on the X in its upper right corner.

Creating special effects

Figure 18-3 shows some of the special effects you can create easily for controls by using the Special Effects formatting window. In the figure, you see that controls with gray as a background color show off special effects much better than those with white. In fact, a form background in gray or a dark color is almost mandatory to make certain special effects easy to see. The next sections describe each of these effects; you'll apply some of them later to modify the Pets Data Entry form.

Special effects can be applied to rectangles, label controls, text box controls, check boxes, option buttons, and option group boxes. Anything that has a box or circle around it can be raised, sunken, etched, chiseled, or shadowed. Figure 16-5 showed special effects applied to check boxes and option buttons.

By simply selecting the control and adding the special effect, you can make your forms look much better and draw attention to their most important areas.

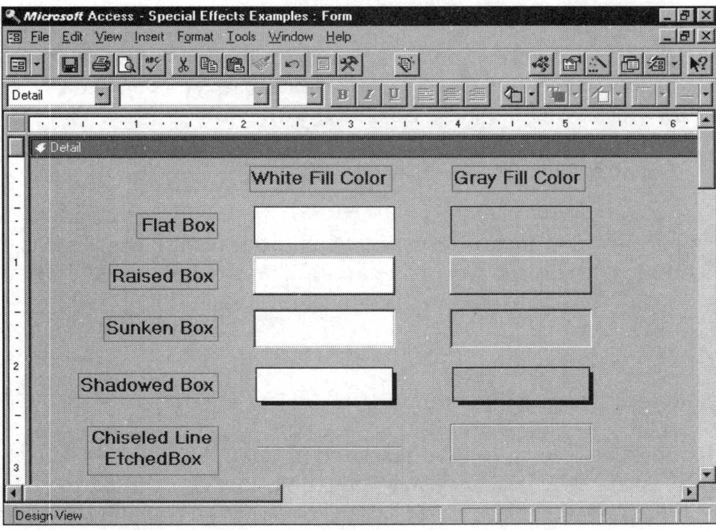

Figure 18-3: Special effects.

Flat

In Figure 18-3, you see a pair of boxes created without any special effect. As you can see in the figure, the flat box stands out better when set against the gray background.

Tip

You can also use the Border Width window to increase the width of the border lines, which makes the box more prominent. The Border Color window lets you change the color of the box. A thick white box also stands out.

Raised

This box is best when used to set off a rectangle that surrounds other controls, or for label controls. The raised box gives the best effect in a dark color against a dark background. As you can see in Figure 18-3, the raised box is difficult to see with a white fill color. By increasing the width of the box, you can give the control an appearance of being higher than the surface of the on-screen background. You achieve the raised three-dimensional effect by contrasting the white left and top borders with the black right and bottom borders.

Sunken

The sunken special effect is the most dramatic and most often used. (This is the standard Windows 95 format in the Form Wizard, and the default control format in the new version of Access.) As you can see in Figure 18-3, either the white or the gray fill color looks very good on a gray form background. You can also increase the width of the border to give the effect of a deeper impression. You achieve the sunken three-dimensional effect with using black left and top borders and white right and bottom borders. The effect works well with check boxes and option buttons.

Shadowed

The shadowed special effect places a solid dark-colored rectangle behind the original control, which is slightly offset to give the shadowed effect. As you can see in Figure 18-3, the black shadow works well behind a box filled with white or gray. You can change the border color to change the shadow color.

Etched

The etched effect is perhaps the most interesting of all the special looks. This is, in effect, a sunken rectangle with no sunken inside area. Windows 95 makes heavy use of etched rectangles.

Chiseled

The chiseled effect adds a chiseled line underneath a selected control.

Disk

In this chapter, you modify the form that you created in Chapter 17 to look like Figure 18-1. If you are using Microsoft Access as you follow the book, you should have the form named `Pets Data Entry Form - Without Formatting` open in the Form Design window.

Changing the form's background color

If you are usually going to view your form on-screen instead of printing it, it may be beneficial to color the background. A light gray background (the Windows 95 default) seems to be the best neutral color in all types of lighting and visual conditions. If you wanted to change the background for the form header and detail sections, you would select the desired section and then select the appropriate background color.

When you change the background color of form sections, you also will want to change the background of individual label controls for a more natural look. Generally, a label control doesn't look good if its background doesn't match the background of the form itself.

Enhancing Text-Based Controls

Generally, it's important to get the label text and data right before you start enhancing display items with shading or special effects. When your enhancements include label and text box control changes, you should begin with them.

Enhancing label and text box controls

You can enhance label and text box controls in several ways:

✦ Changing the text font type style (Arial, Times New Roman, Wingding)

✦ Changing the text font size (4–200)

✦ Changing the text font style (bold, italic, underline)

✦ Changing the text color (using a formatting window)

✦ Adding a shadow

Cross Ref In Chapter 17, you changed the title in the form header. You then changed the text font size and font style. Now you will learn how to add a text shadow to the label control.

Creating a text shadow

Text shadows give text a three-dimensional look by making the text appear to float above the page while its shadow stays on the page. This effect uses the same basic principle as a shadowed box. Use this process to create text shadows:

1. Duplicate the text.
2. Offset the duplicate text from the original text.
3. Change the duplicate text to a different color (usually a lighter shade).
4. Place the duplicate text behind the original text.
5. Change the original text's background color to Clear.

To create a shadow for the title's text, follow these steps:

1. Select the label control that reads `Mountain Animal Hospital - Pets Data Entry`.
2. Select Edit⇨Duplicate.
3. Select the white Fore color (second from the left) to change the duplicate text's color.
4. Drag the duplicate text up and to the right to create the offset from the text below.
5. Select Format⇨Send to Back.

After you complete the shadow, you may have to move the text and its shadow to accommodate the changes you made when you moved the controls. You also may have to move the section border. The text now appears to have a shadow, as shown in Figure 18-4.

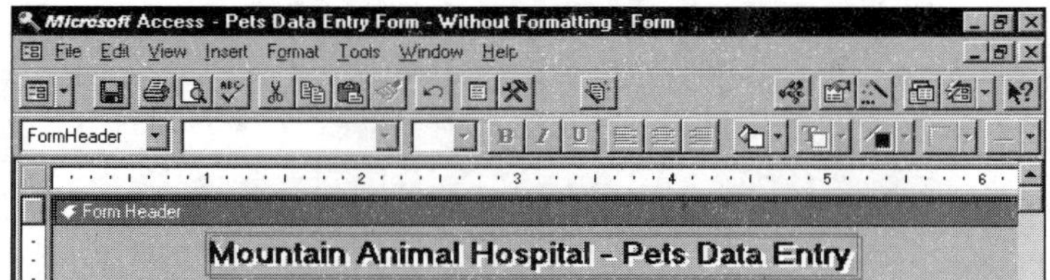

Figure 18-4: Creating text with a shadow and reverse video.

Tip The box around the label control is not visible when the form is printed, because the Transparent button in the Border Color window is depressed.

When you duplicated the original text, the duplicate was offset below the original text automatically. When you place the duplicate text behind the original, it's hidden. You redisplayed it by placing the original text in front. If the offset (distance from the other copy), is too great, the effect will not look like a shadow. You can perfect the shadowed appearance by moving one of the label controls slightly.

Warning Although the shadow appears correctly on-screen and looks great, it won't print correctly on most monochrome printers. What you see normally is two lines of black text; they look horrible. If you plan to print your forms and don't have a printer that prints text in color (or prints many shades of gray by using graphics rather than text fonts), you should avoid using shadowed text on a form.

Changing text to a reverse video display

Text really stands out when you create white text on a black background. This setup is called *reverse video*; it's the opposite of the usual black letters on white. You can convert text in a label control or text box to reverse video by changing the Back Color to black and the Fore Color to white. To change the Pet Name text control to reverse video, follow these steps:

1. Select the Pet ID text box control (not the label control).
2. Select Black from the Back Color formatting window.
3. Select White from the Fore Color formatting window.

Warning If you are using one of the less expensive laser printers, you may not see reverse video if you print your form. The printer drivers may not be able to print it.

Displaying label or text box control properties

As you change values in a label control or text box control by using a formatting window, you are actually changing their properties. Figure 18-5 displays the property window for the text box control in the form header you just modified. As you see in Figure 18-5, many properties can be affected by a formatting window. Table 18-1 shows the various properties (and their possible values) for both label and text box controls.

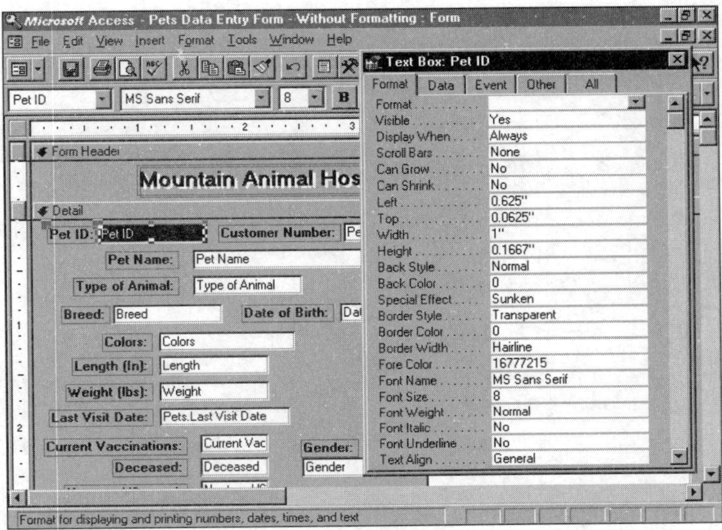

Figure 18-5: Text Box control properties.

Table 18-1
Label or Text Box Format Properties

Property	*Options*	*Description*
Format	Various Numeric, and Date Formats	Determines how the data is displayed
Visible	Yes/No	Yes - Control is displayed normally No - Control is invisible when displayed
Display When	Always, Print Only, Screen Only	Determines when the control is displayed
Scrollbars	None, Vertical, Horizontal, Both	Specifies when scrollbars are displayed
Can Grow	Yes/No	If multiple lines of text are in the control, does the text box get larger?

(continued)

Table 18-1 *(continued)*

Property	***Options***	***Description***
Can Shrink	Yes/No	If fewer lines of text are in the control than in its initial size, does the text box height get smaller?
Left	Position of the left corner of the control in the current measure (include an indicator, such as **cm** or **in**, if you use a different unit of measurement)	Specifies the position of an object on the horizontal axis
Top	Position of the top corner of the control in the current measure	Specifies the position of an object on the vertical axis
Width	The width of the control in the current unit of measure	Specifies the width of a object
Height	The height of the control in the current unit of measure	Specifies the height of an object
Back Style	Transparent, Normal	Determines whether a control's background is opaque or transparent
Back Color	Any available background color	Specifies the color for the interior of the control or section
Special Effect	Flat, Raised, Sunken, Shadowed, Etched, Chiseled	Determines whether a section or control appears flat, raised, sunken, shadowed, etched, or chiseled
Border Style	Transparent or Solid, Dashes, Dots, (Lines/Boxes Only)	Determines whether a control's border is opaque or transparent
Border Color	Any available border color	Specifies the color of a control's border
Border Width	Hairline, 1pt, 2pt, 3pt, 4pt, 5pt, 6pt	Specifies the width of a control's border
Fore Color	Any selection from a formatting window	Specifies the color for text in a control, or the printing and drawing color
Font Name	Any system font name that appears on the toolbar; depends on fonts installed	Specifies the name of the font used for text or a control

Property	Options	Description
Font Size	Any size available for a given font	Specifies the size of the font used for text or a control
Font Weight	Extra Light, Light, Normal, Medium, Semi-Bold, Bold, Extra Bold, Heavy	Specifies the width of the line Windows uses to display and print characters
Font Italic	Yes/No	Italicizes text in a control
Font Underline	Yes/No	Underlines text in a control
Text Align	General (default), Left, Center, Right	Sets the alignment for text in a control

Although you can set many of these controls from the property sheet, you'll find it's much easier initially to drag the control to set the Top, Left, Width, and Height properties or to use a formatting window to set the other properties of the control.

Tip To move the selected control a very small amount, you can press Ctrl+arrow key; the control will move slightly in the direction of the arrow key used.

Displaying Images in Forms

You can display a picture in a form by using *image frames*. This is different from the way a bound OLE control is used. Normally you would store an OLE object (sound, video, Word or Excel document) with a data record, or with an unbound OLE object used specifically for storing OLE objects (those same sound, video, Word or Excel documents) on a form.

New! Image controls are new to Access for Windows 95. These are used only for non-OLE objects such as Paintbrush (.BMP) pictures. Image controls offer a distinct advantage. Unlike OLE objects (which can be edited, but use huge amounts of resources), the image control adds only the size of the bitmap picture to your computer's overhead. Using too many OLE objects in Access causes resource and performance problems. New and existing applications should only use image controls when displaying pictures that don't change or need to be edited within Access.

Tip In Access 2.0, many people learned to select an unbound OLE object picture and then select Edit⇨Save As Picture. This broke the OLE connection but did not fix the resource problem.

You can add an image control to your form by either pasting a bitmap from the Clipboard or embedding a bitmap file that contains a picture. Suppose you have a logo for Mountain Animal Hospital. On the disk that accompanies this book is a bitmap called MTN.BMP. In this section, you add this bitmap to the page header section of the form.

An image object can be displayed in one of three ways:

Clip	Displays picture in its original size
Stretch	Fits the picture into the control regardless of size; often displayed out of proportion
Zoom	Fits the picture into the control (either vertically or horizontally) and maintains proportions; often results in white space on top or right side

To add the logo to the form, follow these steps:

1. Display the toolbox by selecting View⇨Toolbox.
2. Click on the Image button in the Standard toolbox.
3. Click on the left corner below the title; drag the box so it is sized as shown in Figure 18-1. The Insert Picture dialog box appears as shown in Figure 18-6.

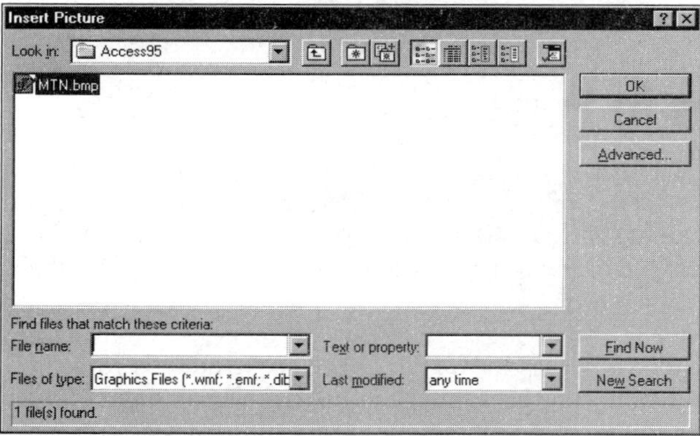

Figure 18-6: Creating an unbound object frame.

From this dialog box, you can select the type of picture object you want to insert into your form. The dialog box supports many picture formats, including .BMP, .TIF, .WMF, .PCX, .ICO, .WPG, .JPG, .PCT, or any picture format your copy of Windows 95 supports.

4. Select MTN.BMP and click on OK.

If the file does not already exist and you want to create a new object (such as a Paintbrush Picture), you must create an unbound OLE frame instead of an image.

After you complete step 5, Access returns you to the Form Design window, where the picture is displayed. You must still change the Size Mode property to Stretch.

5. Display the property sheet.
6. Change the Size Mode property to Stretch.

   Finally, you have to change the Border property so the picture does not simply blend in with the background because there is so much white in it. You can make this modification by changing the border color to black, or you can make the border three-dimensional by selecting the Raised toggle button in the Special Effects formatting window.
7. Display the Special Effects formatting window and click on the Raised toggle button.

The image object frame is complete. Figure 18-6 shows the Insert Picture dialog box.

Working with Lines and Rectangles

You can use lines or rectangles (commonly called *boxes*), to make certain areas of the form stand out and attract attention. In Figure 18-1, you saw several groups of lines and rectangles used for emphasis. In the present example, you still need to add the lines and the rectangle. You can use Figure 18-7 as a guide for this procedure.

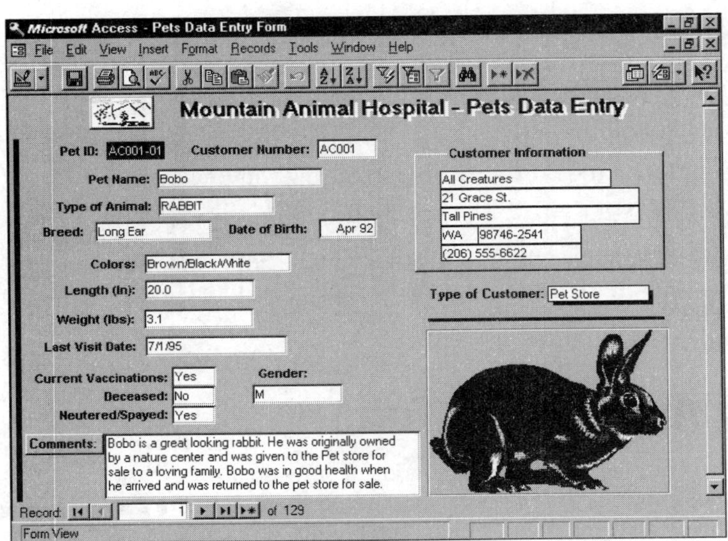

Figure 18-7: Completing the rectangles and lines.

To create the rectangle for the customer information block, follow these steps:

1. Select the Rectangle button in the toolbox.
2. Click to the left of the text Customer Information so the rectangle encompasses the Customer fields and cuts through the middle of the text that reads `Customer Information`.

3. Drag the rectangle around the entire set of Customer text box controls, and then release the mouse button.

4. Select Format⇨Send to Back to redisplay the text boxes.

Tip: You may notice that when you create the rectangle, it blocks out the controls beneath it. By sending the rectangle to the background, you make the controls reappear.

5. Select the gray Background Color in the formatting window.

Tip: You can also redisplay the controls behind the rectangle by checking the Transparent button of the Background Color option in a formatting window. This method, however, does not allow you to add other shading effects. For a rectangle, you should always select Format⇨Send to Back.

You still need to create several lines for the form. You'll still need to add a single horizontal line just below the Type of Customer control, and a thick vertical line down the left side of the form (beginning with Pet ID and ending on the left of the Comments field). To add these lines, complete the following steps (use Figure 18-7 as a guide):

1. Click on the Line button in the toolbox.
2. Create a new horizontal line just above the image picture control.
3. Select the 2 button in the Line Thickness window to make the line thicker.
4. Create a new vertical line, starting just to the left of the Pet ID field. To keep the line vertical, hold down the Shift key as you drag the line to just left of the Comments field (as shown in Figure 18-7).
5. Select the 3 button in the Border Width formatting window to make the line thicker.

Tip: If you hold down the Shift key while creating the line, the line remains perfectly straight, either horizontally or vertically, depending on the initial movement you make when drawing the line.

Emphasizing Areas of the Form

If you really want to emphasize an area of the form, you can add a shadow to any control. The most common types of controls to add a shadow to are rectangles and text boxes. You can create shadows by using the Shadow special effect.

Adding a shadow to a control

If the background is light or white, a dark-colored rectangle is needed. If the background is dark or black, use a light-colored or white rectangle. To create a shadow for the Type of Customer text box, follow these steps:

1. Select the Type of Customer control to receive the shadow.
2. Select the Shadow special-effects button.

To give the form a Windows 95 look and feel, you may want to change some other objects. The first is the rectangle around the bound OLE object (displaying the Rabbit in the first record). A Windows 95 look and feel would have an etched gray rectangle instead of a sunken white one. Figure 18-7 shows this change.

Changing the header dividing line

Form headers are footers are automatically separated from the Detail section by a solid black line. In Access for Windows 95, you can remove this line by changing the Dividing Line form property to No. This removes the line and makes the form appear seamless. This is especially important if you have a background bitmap on the entire form, you're using form headers or footers, and want a single look.

Figure 18-7 shows the form after it has run. Notice the raised rectangle around the Customer information, and the two new lines. Also notice that the Mountain Animal Hospital logo appears in the form header.

Figure 18-8 shows the final form in the Form Design window.

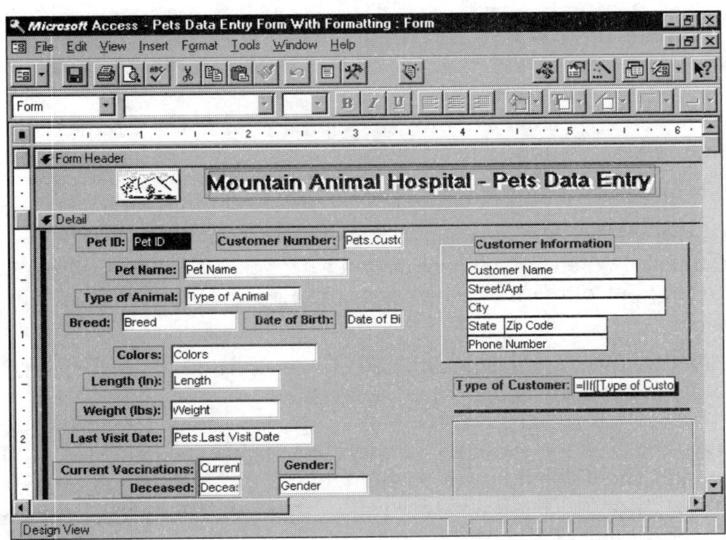

Figure 18-8: The final form.

You'll use this final form in the next chapter, so you should save it now. Select File➪Save As/Export and name the form **Pets Data Entry - With Formatting.**

Adding a Background Bitmap

If you want to emphasize a form even further (or add a really fun effect), you can add a background bitmap to any form, just as you added one control behind another. In Access for Windows 95, you do this by using the form's Picture properties. There are three properties you can work with:

Picture	The name of the bitmap picture. This can be any image-type file.
Picture Size Mode	Clip, Stretch, or Zoom. Clip only displays the picture at its actual size starting at the Picture Alignment property. Stretch and Zoom fill the entire form from the upper left corner of any header to the lower right corner of any footer.
Picture Alignment	Top-Left, Top-Right, Center, Bottom-Left, Bottom-Right, and so on. Use this only used when you use the Clip option in Picture Size mode.
Picture Tiling	Yes/No. When a small bitmap is used with Clip mode, this repeats the bitmap across the entire form. For example, a brick becomes a brick wall.

For this example, you can add the MTN.BMP to the background of the form. Use the following steps to add a background bitmap.

1. Select the Form itself by clicking in the upper left corner of the intersection of the two design rulers.
2. Display the Properties window; click on the Picture property.
3. Enter **C:\ACCESS\MTN.BMP** (or the path to wherever you have placed your bitmap on the disk). When you click to another property, the Mountain Animal Hospital logo (or your bitmap) appears in the upper left corner of the form background.
4. Click on the Picture Size Mode property and change it from Clip to Stretch. The picture will now occupy the entire form background.

If you are following along with the example, you will notice that the field labels still have gray backgrounds, the fields themselves still have white backgrounds, and the bitmap does not show through. If you want it to show through, check the Transparent background color of any control; the background will show through the form.

You can do this by choosing Edit➪Select All to select all the controls and then selecting Transparent from the Back Color formatting window. This produces the effect shown in Figure 18-9. As you can see, the white background of the picture (along with the thick black lines) makes it difficult to see the fields themselves.

Figure 18-9: A bitmap picture behind a form.

Tip

The use of background bitmaps can give you some really interesting capabilities. For example, you can take this process a step farther by incorporating the bitmap into your application. A bitmap can have buttons tied to macros (or Visual Basic for Applications code placed in the right locations). To help the office staff look up a patient, for example, you can create a form that has a map with three states behind it. By adding invisible buttons over each state, you can give the operator the choice of clicking on a state to select the patient records from that state.

You can also scan in a paper form and use that as the form background, placing fields on top of the scanned form itself, without having to spend a lot of time re-creating the form (which gives the phrase *filling out a form* a whole new meaning).

Using AutoFormat

You can change the format of an entire form by using a new feature in Access for Windows 95 known as AutoFormat. This is the first menu option in the Format menu. AutoFormat lets you make global changes to all fonts, colors, borders, background bitmaps, and virtually every property, on a control-by-control type basis. This works instantly and completely, and is totally customizable.

When you select Format⇨AutoFormat a window appears as shown in Figure 18-10. This window lets you select from the standard AutoFormats or any you have created. The figure is shown after you click on the Options >> button. This lets you apply only fonts, colors, or border style properties separately.

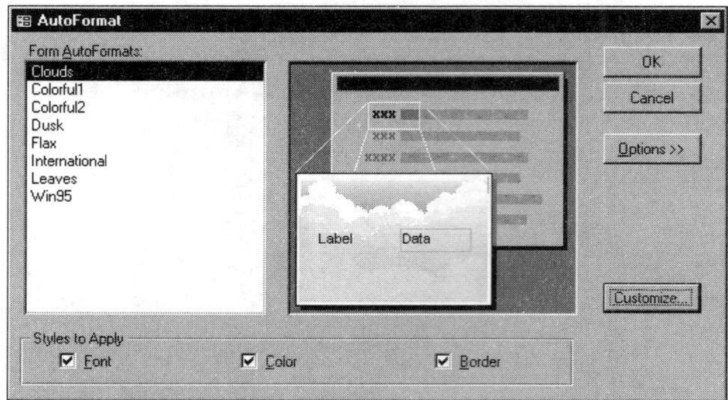

Figure 18-10: Selecting AutoFormat.

In this example, you can choose the Clouds AutoFormat type to change the style of the control fonts and colors, and change the background bitmap as well. As you move between the different AutoFormats you can see an example of the look in the preview area to the right of the selections.

If you are following along in the examples and you choose the Clouds AutoFormat, you will see a series of messages that indicate there is no style set for various objects like lines and rectangles. This is because the Clouds AutoFormat contains only the formatting instructions for label and text controls. You can add the current formatting to the Clouds AutoFormat (actually updating the AutoFormat), or you can leave the current formatting intact for that control type as you go through the process.

When you're done, the controls appear as they do in Figure 18-11.

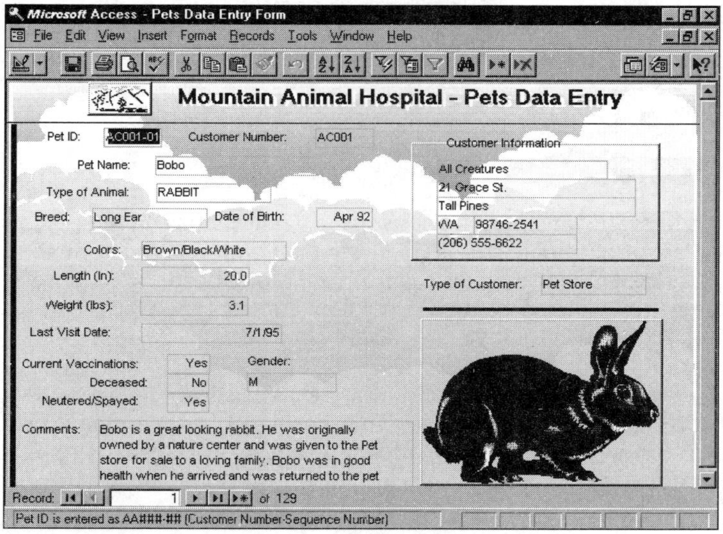

Figure 18-11: Mountain Animal Hospital in the Clouds.

Customizing and adding new AutoFormats

You can modify existing AutoFormats — or define new ones — simply by creating a form, setting various form properties, and starting AutoFormat. Though AutoFormat will change the look of your form totally, it does its job on one control type at a time. This means it can format a label differently from a text box, and differently from a line or rectangle. This capability also lets you define your own formats for every control type, including the background bitmap.

Once you have created a form you want to use as a basis for an AutoFormat, you can select AutoFormat and then click on the Customize button shown in Figure 18-10. Another window appears as shown in Figure 18-12. This allows you to update the currently selected format, add a new format, or delete the currently selected format.

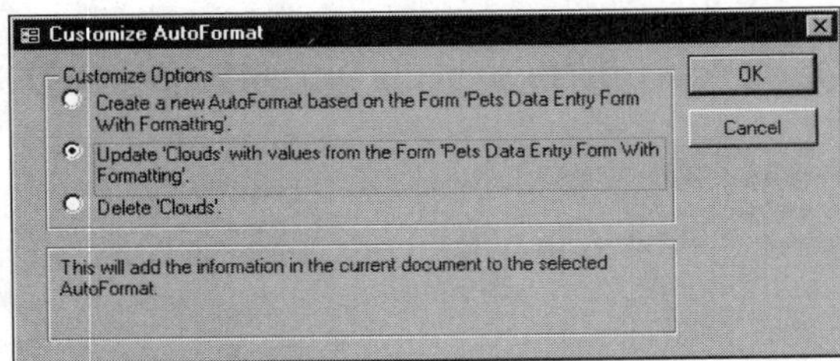

Figure 18-12: Creating your own AutoFormat.

Copying individual formats between controls

A subset of the AutoFormat technology is the Format Painter. This tool allows you to copy formatting properties from one individual control to another. To use the Format Painter, first you select the control whose properties you want to use. Then select the Format Painter icon in the toolbar (a picture of a paintbrush, next to the Paste icon). Your cursor changes to a paintbrush. Click on the control you want to update; Access copies the properties from the control you first selected to the newly selected control.

Summary

No matter what type of form you are creating with the tools in Access, you can get the job done readily and easily. In this chapter, the following points were covered:

- ✦ The Access form designer is a WYSIWYG (what-you-see-is-what-you-get) form tool. What you see in the Design window is what you get when you run the form.
- ✦ A formatting window is a tool in the Form window that lets you set foreground and background colors, control line widths and line types, as well as add three-dimensional effects (such as a raised or sunken appearance) to controls.
- ✦ You can enhance label and text box control text by changing the font type style and size, and by changing the font style to bold or italic. You can specify font color, and even add a shadow by duplicating the text.
- ✦ To display pictures in forms, you can use bound object frames (attached to a data field in the record), or image controls or unbound object frames (which are embedded in the form itself).
- ✦ Lines and rectangles let you separate areas of the form to add emphasis.
- ✦ You can further emphasize areas of the form by adding color, background shading, and three-dimensional effects. You can also use shadows and reverse video for emphasis.
- ✦ The Access for Windows 95 AutoFormat tool lets you change the look of the entire form by applying a set of formatting properties to every control on the form, including the form itself and form selections.
- ✦ You can copy formats between controls by using the Format Painter icon.

In the next chapter, you learn how to add data-validation controls to your form, including list boxes, option buttons, check boxes, combo boxes, and other items.

✦ ✦ ✦

CHAPTER

Adding Data-Validation Controls to Forms

In This Chapter

Creating data-validation expressions

Using the Option Group Wizard

Working with option buttons

Creating Yes/No check boxes

Making visual selections with toggle buttons

Using the List Box Wizard

Working with list boxes

Using the Combo Box Wizard

Working with combo boxes

In the last three chapters, you learned how to create a basic form and how to enhance it by using visual effects to make data entry and display easier. In this chapter, you learn techniques for creating several *data-validation* controls; these will help you make sure the data being entered (and edited) in your forms is as correct as possible.

New! In this chapter, you modify your form from Chapter 18 to look like Figure 19-1. If you are following along with the examples in this book, open either the form you created in Chapter 18 (Pets Data Entry - With Formatting) or the form on the disk that comes with this book (Pets Data Entry Form - Without Validation).

Figure 19-1: The Pets Data Entry form after adding validation controls.

Creating Data-Validation Expressions

You can enter expressions into table design properties (or a form control's property sheet) that will limit input to specific values or ranges of values; the limit will go into effect when a specific control or form is used. In addition, you can display a status line message that advises users how to enter the data properly into the table or form when they move the cursor into a particular field. You can also have Access show an error message if a user makes an invalid entry; you can enter these expressions in a table design or in a form.

Table-level validation

You can enter several types of validation text into a table design, as shown in Table 19-1. When the user of a form or datasheet moves the cursor into the field, messages appear in the status line at the lower left corner of the screen. In your table design, you would enter these messages into the Description column, as shown in Figure 19-2. In this example, the status line message displays `Enter M for Male, F for Female, or U if Unknown` when the cursor moves into the Gender field.

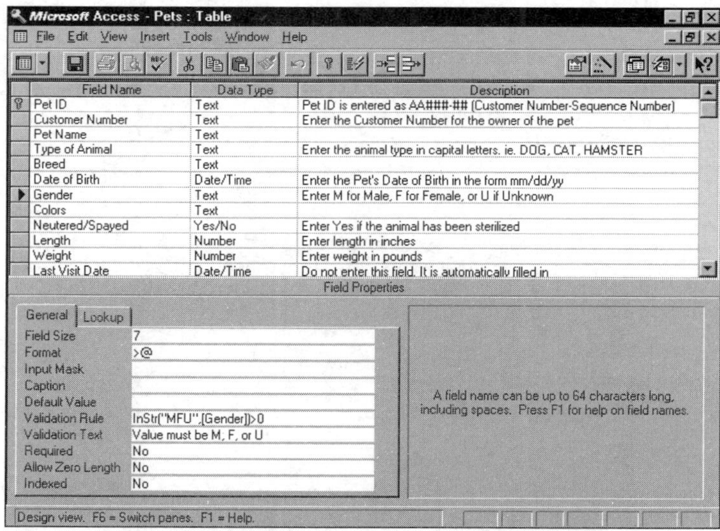

Figure 19-2: The validation properties for the Gender field in the table design.

Table 19-1
Types of Validation Entered into a Table Design

Type of Validation	*Stored in*	*Displayed in Form*
Status line message	Description/Status Bar Text	Status bar
Validation expression	Validation rule	
Error message	Validation text	Dialog box
Input mask	Input mask	Control text box

Validation expressions are the rules the data must follow. Any type of expression can be entered into the Validation Rule property (found in the field properties area of the table design). In Figure 19-2, the expression `InStr("MFU",[Gender])>0` limits the valid entry to the three letters M, F, or U.

You can also display an error message in a dialog box when data entry does not pass the validation rule. This text is entered into the Validation Text property found in the field properties area of the table design. In this example, the dialog box will tell you `Value must be M, F, or U`. Figure 19-2 shows a table design with the Gender field selected in the Pets table. Notice that only the properties are displayed for the highlighted field, though you can see all the descriptions in the upper part of the Table Design window.

Form-level validation

You can enter the same types of validation text into a form's property sheet. When you create a form, the table validation properties are copied into each bound field on the form. This way, if you enter them at the table level, you don't have to enter them for each form. If you want to override them for a particular form, you can do so here by simply entering a new value for any of the properties.

Note Although you enter status bar instructions into a table design's Description column, they appear in the form design's Status Bar Text property.

Entering a validation expression

You can enter a validation expression in a number of different ways for each field in your table or control in your form. For a number field, you can use standard mathematical expressions such as *less than*, *greater than*, or *equal to*, using the appropriate symbols (<, >, =). For example, if you want to limit a numerical field to numbers greater than 100, you enter the following validation expression in the appropriate property box:

> 100

If you want to limit a date field to dates before January 1995, you enter

< #1/1/95#

If you want to limit a numeric or date value to a range, you can enter

Between 0 And 1500

or

Between #1/1/70# And Date()

Cross Ref

You can use a series of the functions included within Access to validate your data. In Figure 19-2, Access interprets the validation expression used to limit the input into the Gender field as "allow only the letters M, F, or U." The Access function `InStr` means *in string.* Access will search the Gender input field and allow only those entries. Chapter 13 details the various functions that are available to you for validation purposes.

Creating Choices with Option Buttons

Sometimes you won't want to allow the user to enter anything at all — only to pick a valid entry from a list. You can limit input on your form this way by using an *option button* (also known as a *radio button*), a control that indicates whether a situation is True or False. The control consists of a string of text and a button that can be turned on or off by clicking the mouse. When you click on the button, a black dot appears in its center, indicating the situation is True; otherwise the situation is False.

Generally, you would use an option button when you want to limit data entry but more than two choices are available. You should, however, limit the number of choices to four when using option buttons. If you have more than four choices, use a list or combo box (described later in this chapter).

By using option buttons, you can increase flexibility in validating data input. For example, the current control for Type of Customer displays a number: 1 means individual, 2 means pet store, and 3 means zoo. It is much more meaningful to a user if all these choices are displayed on-screen. In Figure 19-1 shows the numerical field input changed to an option group box that shows the three choices available to the user.

Only one of the option buttons can be made True for any given record. This approach also ensures that no other possible choices can be entered on the form. In an option group, the option group box itself is bound to a field or expression. Each button inside passes a different value back to the option group box, which in turn passes a single value to the field or expression. Each option button is bound to the option group box rather than to a field or expression.

Warning Only fields with a Numeric data type can be used for an option group in a form. In a report, you can transform nonnumeric data into numeric data types for display-only option buttons (see Chapter 22). You can also display an alternative value by using the Lookup Wizard in the table design screen and displaying a combo box.

To create an option group with option buttons, you must do two things:

- ✦ Create the option group box and bind it to a field.
- ✦ Create each option button and bind each one to the option group box.

Creating option groups

In Access 95, the easiest and most efficient way to create option groups is with the Option Group Wizard. You can use it to create *option groups* with multiple option buttons, toggle buttons, or check boxes. When you're through, all your control's property settings are correctly filled out. This Wizard greatly simplifies the process and allows you to create an option group quickly, but you should still understand a little of the process.

Creating an option group box

When you create a new option group, the Option Group Wizard is triggered automatically. You start this process by clicking on the Option Group icon on the toolbox and then drawing the control box rectangle. Another method is to click on the Option Group button and then drag the appropriate field from the field list window.

Warning To start any of the Wizards that create controls, you must first depress the Control Wizard button on the toolbox.

Before creating an option group for the Type of Customer field, first you must delete the current display of the field: highlight it with your mouse and press the Delete key. You may also want to delete the shadow (the thick line below the control) and narrow the height of the picture so the option group box will fit. Use the completed option group in Figure 19-1 as a guide.

Once you've deleted the existing Type of Customer text box control, you can create the Type of Customer option group box by following these steps:

1. Select the Option Group button from the toolbox.
2. Drag the Type of Customer field from the Field List window to the space under the Customer Information box.

   The first screen of the Option Group Wizard should be displayed (as shown completed in Figure 19-3). In this screen you can enter the text label for each option button, check box, or toggle button that will be in your option group. Enter each entry as you would in a datasheet. You can use the down-arrow key to move to the next choice.

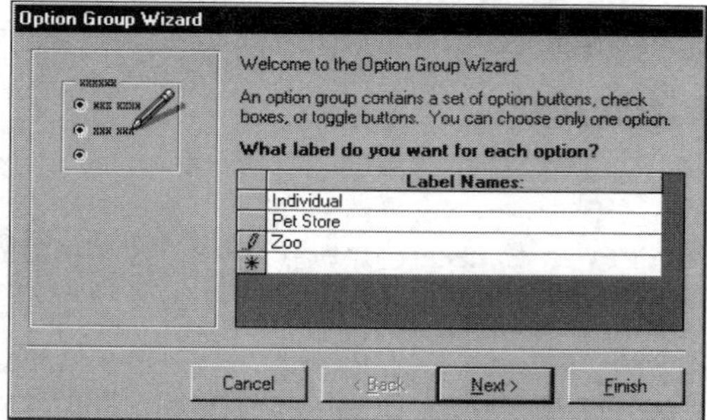

Figure 19-3: Entering the option group choices.

3. Enter **Individual**, **Pet Store**, and **Zoo**, pressing the down-arrow key between choices.
4. Click on the Next > button to move to the default option Wizard screen.

   The next screen lets you select the default control for when the option group is selected. Normally, the first option is the default. If you want to make a different button the default, you would first select the **Yes, the default choice is** option button and then select the default value from the combo box that contains your choices. In this example, the first value will be the default automatically.
5. Click on the Next > button to move to the Wizard screen used for assigning values.

   This screen (shown in Figure 19-4) displays the actual values you entered, along with a default set of numbers that will be used to store the selected value in the bound option group field (in this example, the Type of Customer field). The screen looks like a datasheet with two columns. Your first choice, `Individual`, is automatically assigned a 1, `Pet Store` a 2, and `Zoo` a 3. When Pet Store is selected, a 2 will be stored in the Type of Customer field.

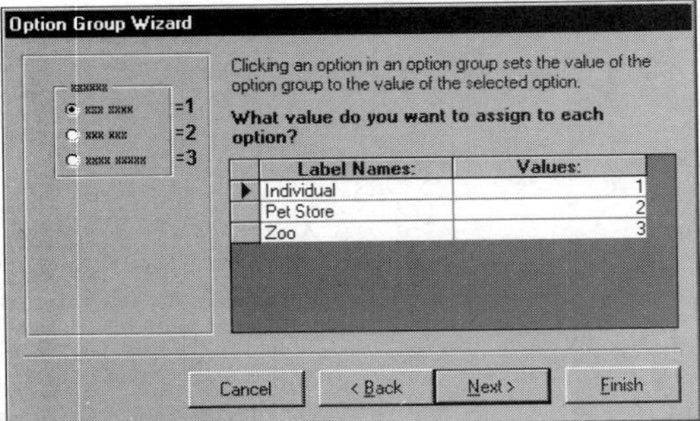

Figure 19-4: Assigning the value of each option button.

In this example, the default values are acceptable. Sometimes, however, you may want to assign values other than 1, 2, 3 . . . You may want to use 100, 200, and 500 for some reason. As long as you use unique numbers, you can assign any values you want.

6. Click on the Next > button to move to the next Wizard screen.

   In this screen, you have to decide whether the option group itself is bound to a form field or unbound. The first choice in the Wizard — `Save the value for later use` — creates an unbound field. If you're going to put the option group in a dialog box that uses the selected value to make a decision, you don't want to store the value in a table field. Thus (in this example) the second value — `Store the value in this field` — is automatically selected because you started with the Type of Customer field. If you want to bind the option group value to a different table field, you can select from a list of all form fields. Again, in this example, the default is acceptable.

7. Click on the Next > button to move to the option group style Wizard screen.

   For this example (as shown in Figure 19-5), select Option buttons and the Etched style. Notice that your actual values are used as a sample. The upper half of this Wizard screen lets you choose what type of buttons you want; the lower half lets you can choose the style for the option group box and the type of group control. The style affects the option group rectangle. If you choose one of the special effects (such as Etched, Shadowed, Raised, or Sunken), that value is applied to the Special Effect property of the option group.

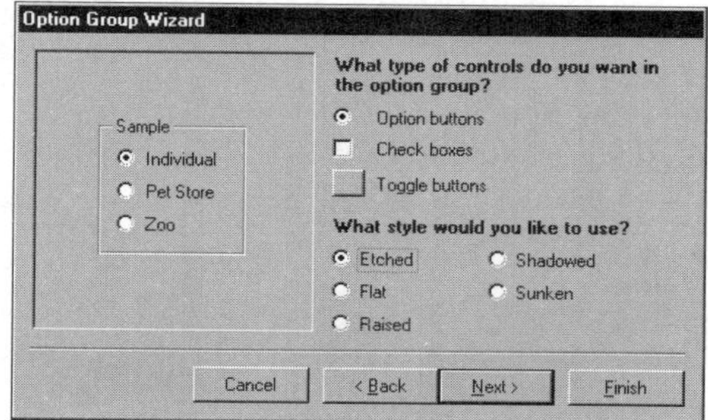

Figure 19-5: Selecting the type and look of your buttons.

Note

As you change your selections, the Sample changes as well.

8. Click on the Next > button to move to the final Option Group Wizard screen.

   This screen lets you give the option group control a label that will appear in the option group border. Then you can add the control to your design and (optionally) display help to customize the control further.

9. Enter **Type of Customer** as your caption for the Option Group.

10. Click on the Finish button to complete the Wizard.

Your Wizard work is now complete. Eight new controls appear on the design screen: the option group, its label, three option buttons, and their labels. Even so, you may still have some work to do. If you refer back to Figure 19-1, you may want to bold the text labels of the option group control and each individual option button. You may want to move the option buttons closer together, or change the shape of the option group box as shown in Figure 19-6. You may want to change the Special Effect property of some controls. As you have learned, you can do this by using the property sheet for the controls.

Figure 19-6 shows the option group controls and the property sheet for the first option button (as automatically created). Notice the Option Value property; it's found only in controls that are part of an option group. You should make all the suggested modifications to make the control look like Figure 19-1.

If you want to create an option group manually, the best advice is *not* to. If you must, however, the steps are the same as for creating any control. First create the option group box, and then create each button inside it manually. You'll have to set all data properties, palette properties, and specific option group or button controls manually.

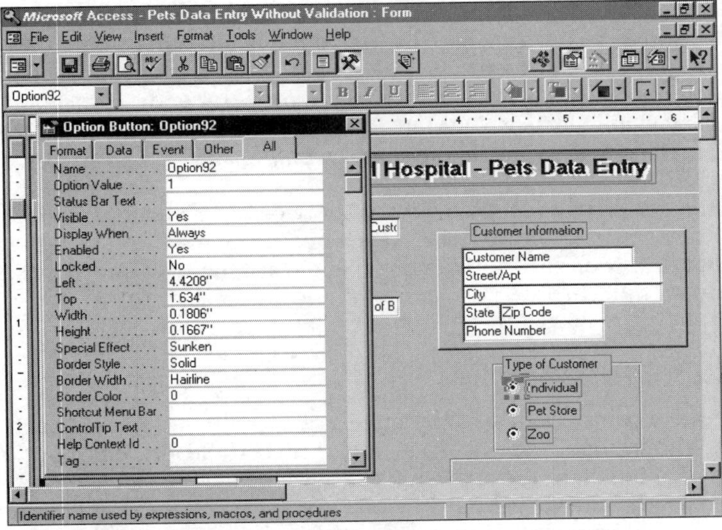

Figure 19-6: The Option Group controls and property sheet.

Warning If you create the option buttons outside the option group box and then drag or copy them into the option group box, they will not work. The reason is that the automatic setting of the Option Value for buttons is left undone, and the option button control has not been bound to the option group box control.

Once this process is complete, you can turn your attention to Yes/No controls.

Creating Yes/No Options

There are three ways to show data properly from Yes/No data types:

- ✦ Display the values `Yes` or `No` in a text box control, using the Yes/No Format property.
- ✦ Use a check box.
- ✦ Use a toggle button.

Although you can place values from Yes/No data types in a text box control and then format the control by using the Yes/No property, it's better to use one of the other controls. Yes/No data types require the values –1 or 0 to be entered into them. An unformatted text box control returns values (–1 and 0) that seem confusing, especially because –1 represents Yes and 0 represents No. Setting the Format property to Yes/No or True/False to display those values will help, but it still requires the user to read the text `Yes/No` or `True/False`. A visual display is much better.

Toggle buttons and check boxes work with these values *behind the scenes* — returning –1 to the field if the button value is on, and 0 if the button is off — but they display these values as a box or button, which is faster to read. You can even display a specific state by entering a default value in the Default property of the form control. The control is displayed initially in a Null state if no default is entered and no state is selected. The Null state appears visually the same as the No state.

The check box is the commonly accepted control for two-state selection. Toggle buttons are nice (they can use pictures instead of a text caption to represent the two states), but not always appropriate. Although you could also use option buttons, they would never be proper as a single Yes/No control.

Creating check boxes

A *check box* is a Yes/No control that acts the same as an option button but is displayed differently. A check box consists of a string of text (to describe the option) and a small square that indicates the answer. If the answer is True, a check mark is displayed in the box. If the answer is False, the box is empty. The user can toggle between the two allowable answers by clicking on the mouse with the pointer in the box.

The Pets Data Entry form contains three fields that have Yes/No data types. These are Current Vaccinations, Deceased, and Neutered/Spayed. The choices are easier to understand if they are shown as a check box (rather than a simple text box control). To change these fields to a check box, you must first delete the original text box controls. The following steps detail how to create a check box for each of the Yes/No fields once you've deleted the original controls.

1. Click on the Check Box icon in the toolbox.
2. While holding down the Ctrl key, select Current Vaccinations, Deceased, and Neutered/Spayed from the Field List window.
3. Using Figure 19-7 as a guide, drag these fields just below the Last Visit Date control. (This process creates each of the check boxes and automatically fills in the Control Source property.)
4. Rearrange the fields so they look like Figure 19-7. (Notice that this example calls for the check boxes to be on the right of the labels.)
5. Select each label control and modify it: change it to the appropriate text, bold it, add a colon to the end of the labels, and then size the controls to fit and align them as necessary.

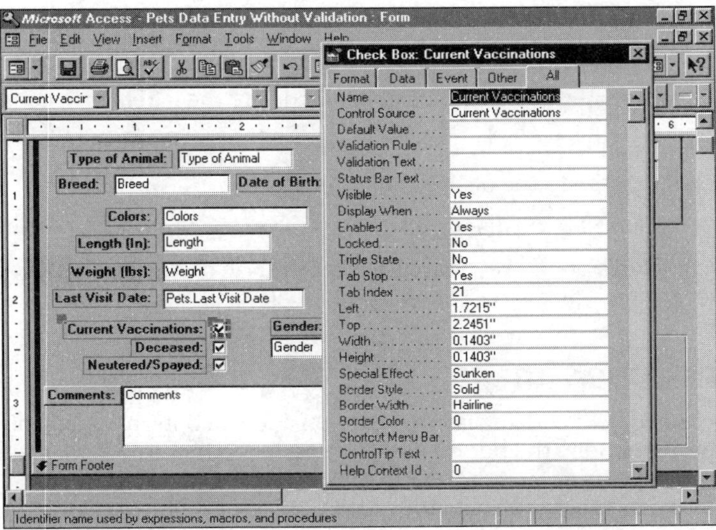

Figure 19-7: Creating check boxes.

Tip

You can set the Display Control option of the Lookup tab in the Table Design to Check Box for any field with a Yes/No data type. Once you've entered this setting, a check box will be created automatically whenever you add this field to a form.

Note

Before creating the check box controls, you could change the Default Check Box Label X property to a negative value; this would automatically place the check boxes to the right of the labels when they are created. The value you would enter depends on the length of the labels. You can change the Add Colon property to Yes to add a colon automatically, and also change the Special Effect property to Sunken. This would save you several steps when creating a group of similar-looking controls.

The completed check boxes appear in Figure 19-7.

Creating visual selections with toggle buttons

A toggle button is another type of True/False control. Toggle buttons act like option buttons and check boxes but are displayed differently. When a toggle button is set to True (in the *pushed* mode), the button appears on-screen as sunken. When it is set to False, the button appears raised.

Toggle buttons provide a capability in addition to what other button controls offer. You can set the size and shape of a toggle button, and you can display text or pictures on the face of the button to illustrate the choice a user can make. This additional capability provides great flexibility in making your form user-friendly.

As an example of how to create a toggle button, you can follow the next steps, using the Deceased Yes/No field (this example is not part of the final form):

1. Select the Deceased check box label control and delete the label.
2. Select the Deceased check box and select Format⇨Change To⇨Toggle Button.
3. Resize the toggle button to the desired size.
4. Type the text **Deceased** to be displayed on the face of the button; press Enter.
5. Using the arrows keys on the keyboard, correct the size of the button to fit the text (or select Format⇨Size⇨to Fit) and move it below the other check boxes.

Adding a bitmapped image to the toggle button

As previously mentioned, you can display a picture on a toggle button instead of displaying text. You can modify the button you just created in the preceding steps, changing it to display a picture (included in the sample files). Using the following steps to add a bitmap to a toggle button, modify the button for the entry field called `Deceased`. (This example assumes you completed the steps to create the toggle button.)

1. Select the toggle button.
2. Open the property sheet and select the Picture property.
3. Click on the Builder button.

   The Picture Builder dialog box appears; in it you can select from over 100 predefined pictures. In this example, you want to select a bitmap named COFFIN.BMP that came with your *Access Bible* disk; it should be on the same directory your Access book files were copied to (the example assumes it's C:\ACCESS95).
4. Click on the Browse button in the Picture Builder dialog box.
5. Select COFFIN.BMP from the C:\ACCESS95 directory; click on the OK button. A sample of the picture appears in the Picture Builder dialog box, as shown in Figure 19-8.
6. Click on the OK button to add the picture to the toggle button. The coffin appears on the toggle button in the design screen. You may need to move it on the screen to make it fit between other controls.

Although option buttons, check boxes, and toggle buttons are great for handling a few choices, they are not a good idea where many choices are possible. Access has other controls that make it easy to pick from a list of values.

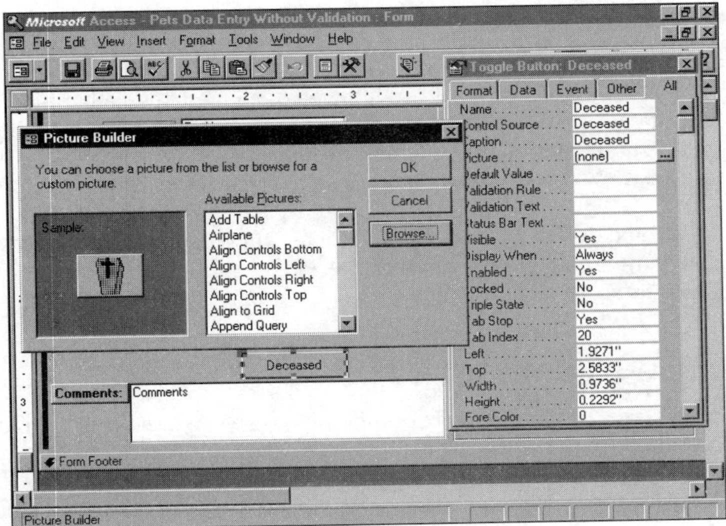

Figure 19-8: The Picture Builder dialog box.

Working with List Boxes and Combo Boxes

Access has two types of controls that let you show lists of data that a user can select from. These controls are *list boxes* and *combo boxes*.

Understanding the differences between list boxes and combo boxes

The basic difference between a list box and a combo box is that the list box is always open, whereas you have to click on the combo box to open the list for selection. In addition, the combo box lets you enter a value that is not on the list.

Cross Ref Chapter 16 contains details on this subject. Review Figures 16-8 and 16-9 if you are not familiar with list boxes and combo boxes.

A closed combo box appears as a single text box field with a downward-pointing arrow on its far right side. A list box, which is always open, can have one or more columns, and from one to as many rows as will fit on-screen, and more than one item to be selected. When open, a combo box displays a single-column text box above the first row, followed by one or more columns and as many rows as you specify in the property sheet. Optionally, a list box or combo box can display column headers in the first row.

Settling real-estate issues

Note

You need to consider the amount of space on the form needed to display either a list box or combo box. If only a few choices are allowed in a given field, a list box is sufficient. If there is not enough room on the form for the choices, use a combo box (a list box is always open but a combo box is initially closed). When you use a list box, the user cannot type any new values but must choose from the selection list.

When you design a list box, decide exactly what choices will be allowed for the given field. You should select an area of your form that has sufficient room for the open list box to display all selections.

Creating a single-column list box

List boxes and combo boxes can be even more difficult to create than option groups, especially when a combo box uses a query as its source and contains multiple columns. The new List Box and Combo Box Wizards in Access make the process much easier. This first example uses the List Box Wizard to create a simple list box for the Gender field.

To create the single-column list box, follow these steps:

1. Delete the existing Gender text box field control and its label.
2. Click on the List Box icon in the toolbox.
3. Display the field list and drag the Gender field to the right of the recently created check boxes.

   The List Box Wizard is starts automatically, as shown in Figure 19-9. The first screen lets you decide whether to type in a list of values, have the values come from a table/query, or create a query-by-form list box that will display all the unique values in the current table. Depending on your answer, you either select the number of columns (and type in the values) or select the fields you want to use from the selected table/query.
4. Select the second option, *I will type in the values that I want,* and click on the Next > button.

   In the next screen, you can choose the number of columns and enter the values you want to use in the List Box. You can also resize the column widths, just like any datasheet. In this example, just enter three values in a single column: **M**, **F**, and **U** (shown completed in Figure 19-10).
5. Enter **1** in the field that specifies Number of columns; then click into the first row under the `Col1:` header.

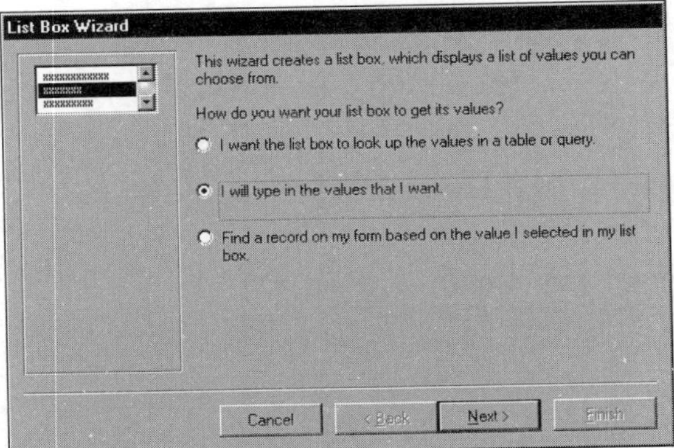

Figure 19-9: Selecting the data source for the list box.

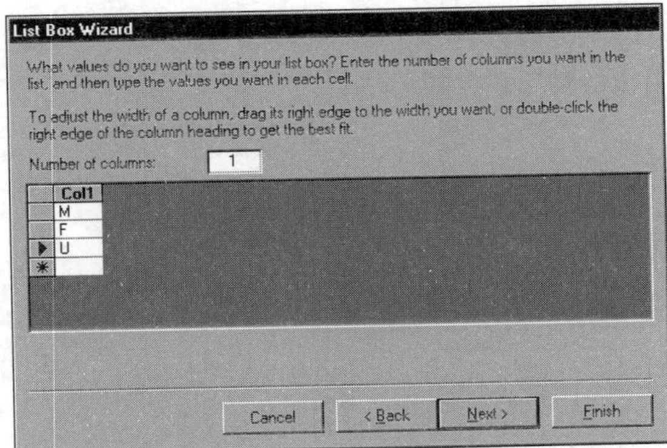

Figure 19-10: Entering the choices for the list box.

6. Enter **M**, press the down arrow, enter **F**, press the down arrow, then enter **U**.
7. Resize the width of the column to match the single-character entry.

Tip: You can double-click on the right side of the column list to size the column automatically.

8. Click on the Next > button to move to the final Wizard screen.

   Use this screen to give the list box control a label that will appear with your list box. When you click on the Finish button, your control is added to your design; optionally you can display Help if you want to continue customizing the control.
9. Click on the Finish button to complete the Wizard.

Your work with the Wizard is now complete, and the control appears on the design screen. You will have to move to label control above the list box control (rather than to its left) and resize the list box rectangle. The Wizard does not do a good job of sizing the box to the number of entries.

Figure 19-11 shows the list box control and the property sheet for the list box.

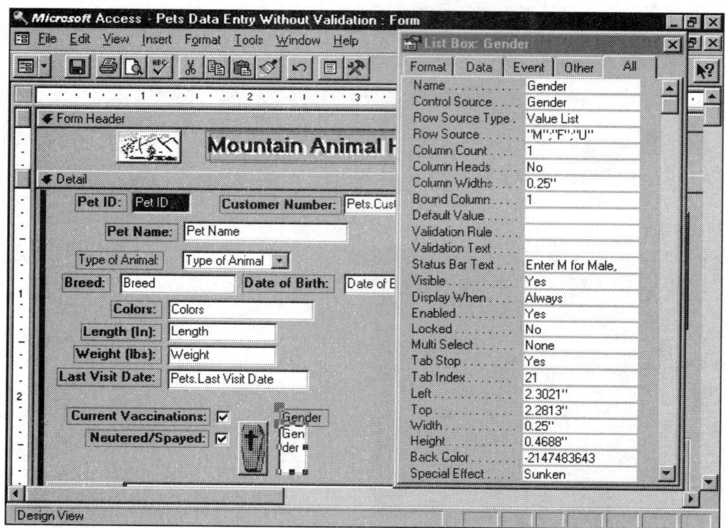

Figure 19-11: The list box control and property sheet.

Understanding list box properties

As you can see in Figure 19-11, several properties define a list box. The Wizard takes care of these (except for the Column Heads property, which adds the name of the column at the top of the list box). Begin by setting the Row Source properties; the first of these is Row Source Type, which specifies the source of the data type.

The Row Source properties are the first two properties you have to set. One of these, Row Source Type, determines the data type. Valid Row Source Type property options are listed in Table 19-2.

Table 19-2
Row Source Type Settings

Row Source Type	*The Source of the Data Type (See below)*
Table/Query	(Default setting) Data is from a table or is the result of a query or SQL statement.
Value List	List of items specified by the Row Source setting.
Field List	List of field names from the Table/Query named by the Row Source setting.
Row Source	Either the Table/Query name or a List of values.

The Row Source property settings depend on the source type specified by Row Source Type.

You use different methods to specify the Row Source property settings, as listed in Table 19-3, depending on the type of source (which you specified by setting the Row Source Type).

Table 19-3
Row Source Property Settings

Row Source Type	*Method of Setting the Row Source Property*
Table/Query	Enter the name of a table, a query, or an SQL statement.
Value List	Enter a list of items separated by semicolons.
Field List	Enter the name of a table or query.

In this example, you entered the values in the Wizard screen. Therefore the Row Source Type is set to Value List, and the Row Source is set to **"M";"F";"U"**. As you can see, the values are entered separated by semicolons.

When you specify Table/Query or Field List as the Row Source Type, you can then pick from a list of tables and queries for the Row Source. The table or query must already exist. The list box will display fields from the table or query according to the order they follow in their source. Settings in the property sheet determine the number of columns, their size, whether there are column headers, and which column is bound to the field's control source.

Tip If you want to use noncontiguous table/query fields in the list box, you should use an SQL statement rather than a list of field names. The Wizard can do this for you automatically. The following is an example of an SQL statement for a two-column list, drawn from the Pets table in the Mountain Animal Hospital database:

```
SELECT [Pet Name], [Type of Animal] FROM [Pets] ORDER BY [Pet ID];
```

These settings include:

Column Count	The number of columns to be displayed.
Column Heads	Yes or No. Yes displays the first set of values or the field names.
Column Width	The width of each column. Each value is separated by semicolons.
Bound Column	The column that passes the value back to the control source field.

For example, suppose you want to list Pet Name, Type of Animal, and Breed, returning Pet Name to the field control. You could enter **Table/Query** in the Row Source Type, and **Pets** in the Row Source. You would then enter **3** for the Column Count and **1.5;1;1** in the Column Width, and **1** for the Bound Column.

These are valid entries for the Row Source property for a list box from the Value List:

For a one-column list with three rows (Column Count = 1):

```
M;F;U
```

For a two-column list with three rows (Column Count = 2):

```
M;Male;F;Female;U;Unknown
```

For a two-column list with five rows of data and a column header (Column Count = 2, Column Heads = Yes):

```
Pet Name;Type of Animal;Bobo;Rabbit;Fido;Dog;Daffy;Duck;Patty;
      Pig;Adam;Frog
```

Creating a multiple-column list box

List boxes are not limited to a single column of data. It's easy to create a list box with multiple columns of data. You could easily go back and run the Wizard again to create a two-column list box, but it's just as easy to modify the list box you already have on the design screen. Follow these next steps to modify the List Box control to change it to a two-column list.

1. Change the Row Source property to **M;Male;F;Female;U;Unknown**.
2. Set the Column Count property to **2**.
3. Enter the Column Widths property as **.25;.75**.
4. Set the Bound Column property to **1**.
5. Resize the List box control to fit the new column widths.

By changing the Number of Columns property to 2 and setting the Column Widths to the size of the data, you can display multiple columns. As you can see in Figure 19-12, there are now multiple columns. The first column's value (specified by the Bound Column property) is passed back to the Gender field.

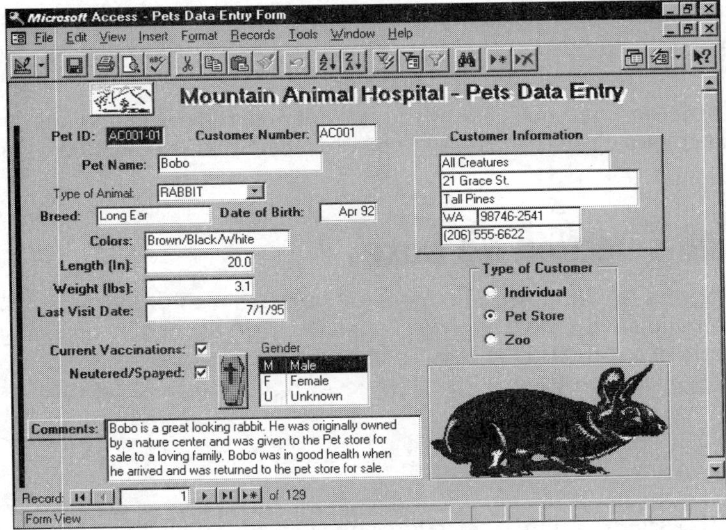

Figure 19-12: Creating a two-column list box.

Note You enter the column widths as decimal numbers; Access adds the abbreviation for inches (`in`) automatically. You can also change it to *cm* or any other unit of measurement.

Warning If you don't size the list box wide enough to match the sum of the column widths, a horizontal scrollbar will appear at the bottom of the control. If you don't size the list box deep enough to display all the items in the list (including the horizontal scrollbar), a vertical scrollbar will appear.

When you look at this list box, you may wonder, "Why display the single-letter code at all?" Your may think you need it to pass the single-letter code back to the Gender field. In fact, that *is* the reason for the first column, but there is no need to display it. Data in hidden *or* displayed columns can be used as a bound column.

Hiding a column in a list box

When you create a multiple-column list box, Access lets you *hide* any column you don't want displayed. This is especially useful when you have a list box bound to a field that you don't want displayed. You can hide the first column in the list box you just created by following these steps:

1. Display the Properties sheet for the list box.
2. Change the Column Widths property to **0;.75**.
3. Resize the List Box Control to the new width.

When you display the list box, you see only the one column; the hidden column is used as the bound column. You can bind a list box to a field that isn't even displayed on-screen.

Creating multi-selection list boxes

A new option for Access for Windows 95 creates list boxes that allow more than one selection. You can build such a *multi-selection* (or *multi-select*) list box by changing the Multi-Select property of a standard list box. To use the multiple selections, however, you have to define a program by using Visual Basic for Applications to capture the selections.

The Multi-Select property has three settings:

None	(Default) Multiple selection isn't allowed.
Extended	Shift+click or Shift+arrow key extends the selection from the previously selected item to the current item. Ctrl+click selects or deselects an item.
Simple	Multiple items are selected or deselected by choosing them with the mouse or pressing the Spacebar.

Cross Ref

Chapter 34 discusses handling multiple selections in a list box.

Creating and Using Combo Boxes

As previously mentioned in this chapter, a *combo box* is very similar to a list; it's a combination of a normal entry field and a list box. The operator can enter a value directly into the text area of the combo box, or else click on the directional arrow (at the right portion of the combo box) to display the list. In addition, the list remains hidden from view unless the arrow is activated, conserving valuable space on the form. A combo box is useful when there are many rows to display; a vertical scrollbar will give the user access to the records that are out of sight.

In this next example, you are going to change the Type of Animal control from a text box to a combo box, using the Combo Box Wizard.

To create a single-column combo box using the Wizard, follow these steps:

1. Delete the existing Type of Animal text box field control and its label.
2. Click on the Combo Box icon in the toolbox.
3. Display the field list and drag the Type of Animal field to the area below `Pet Name`.

   The Combo Box Wizard starts automatically; its first screen is exactly the same as the first list box screen. You decide whether you want to type in a list of values, or whether the values will come from a table or query. In this example, you will get the values from a table.
4. Select the first option, which displays the text `I want the combo box to look up the values in a table or query`; then click on the Next > button.

   As shown in Figure 19-13, this Wizard screen lets you select the table you want to select the values from. By using the row of option buttons under the list of tables, you can view all the Tables, Queries, or Both tables and queries.

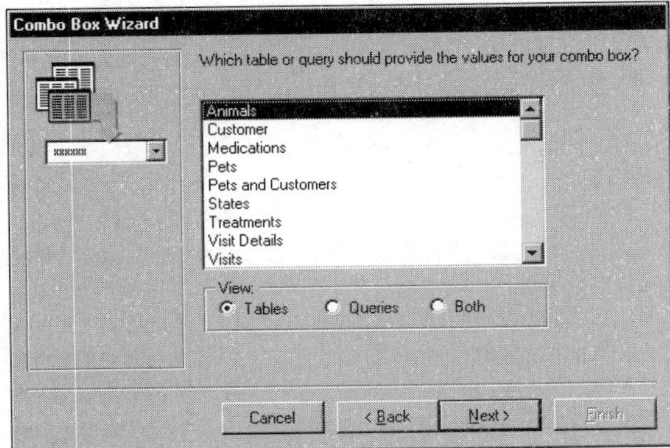

Figure 19-13: Selecting the table for the row source of the combo box.

5. Select the Animals table and click on the Next > button.

   The next screen lets you pick the fields you want to use to populate the combo box. You can pick any field in the table or query and select the fields in any order; Access creates the needed SQL statement for you. In this screen, only one field is shown. The Animals table only has one field (`Animals`), a list of valid animals.

6. Select the Animals field ; click on the > button to add it to the Columns list.

7. Click on the Next > button to move to the next Wizard screen.

   In this screen, a list of the actual values in your selected field appears (as shown in Figure 19-14). Here you can adjust the width of any columns for their actual display.

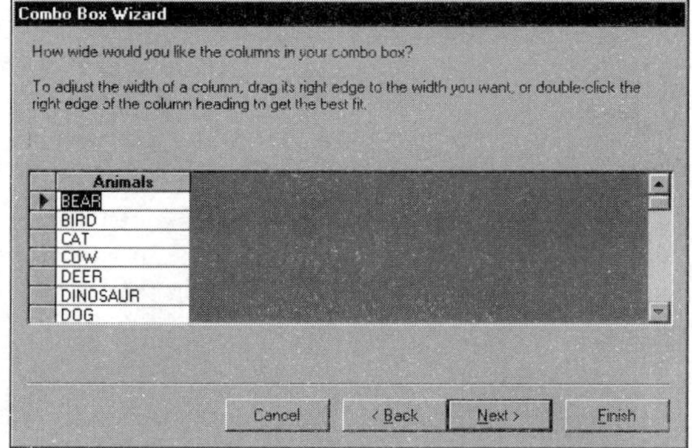

Figure 19-14: Adjusting the column width of the selection.

   The rest of the Wizard screens are like the list box. First, you accept or change the name of the bound field; the last screen lets you enter a label name, and the Wizard creates the combo box.

8. Click on Finish to complete the entries with the default choices.

The control appears on the design screen. Figure 19-15 shows the combo box control and the property sheet for the list box.

The Row Source Type property is set to Table/Query. The Row Source property is set to the SQL statement `Select Distinctrow [Animals] From [Animals]`. This selects the Animal field from the Animals table and limits it to unique values. If you wanted to display the animals in a sorted order, you could do it in one of two ways. Either you would enter the data into the Animals table in a sorted order, or create a simple query to sort the data into the order you want, and then use the query as the basis for the combo box. You can also add sorting directives to the SQL statement by adding **Order By [Animals]**.

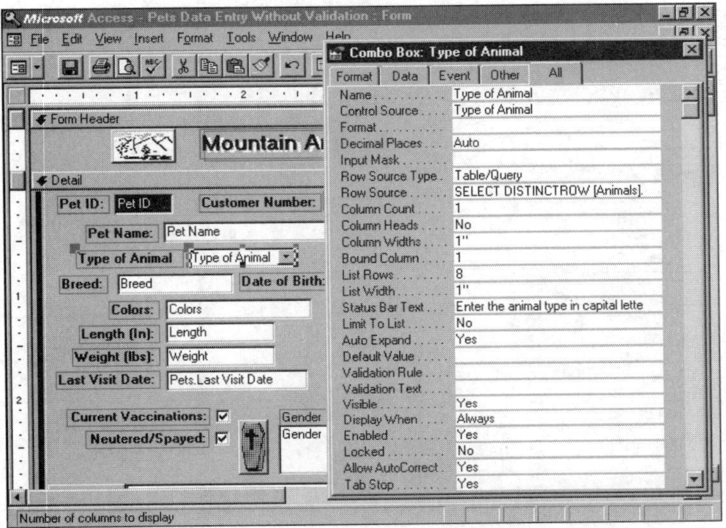

Figure 19-15: The combo box control and property sheet.

The List Rows property sets the number of rows to 8 when the combo box is opened, but the Wizard does not allow you to select this. The last property, Limit To List, determines whether you can enter a value into the Pets table that is not in the list; this is another property the Wizard does not let you select. You must set it directly from the property sheet. The default No value for Limit To List says you can enter new values because you are not limiting the entry to the list.

Tip Setting the AutoExpand property to Yes enables the user to select the combo box value by entering text into the combo box that matches a value in the list. As soon as Access finds a unique match, it displays the value without having to display the list.

Creating a multiple-column combo box from a query

Just as with list boxes, combo boxes may have multiple columns of information. These are displayed when the operator activates the field list. Unless you are extracting fields from a single table — in the order they appear there — you'll probably want to use a query.

Figure 19-16 displays the combo box you will create next. Notice that this combo box displays the Customer Number and Customer Name in the order of the Customer Name. This is accomplished by creating a query. Also notice (in Figure 19-16) that the Customer Number and Customer Name heads are displayed.

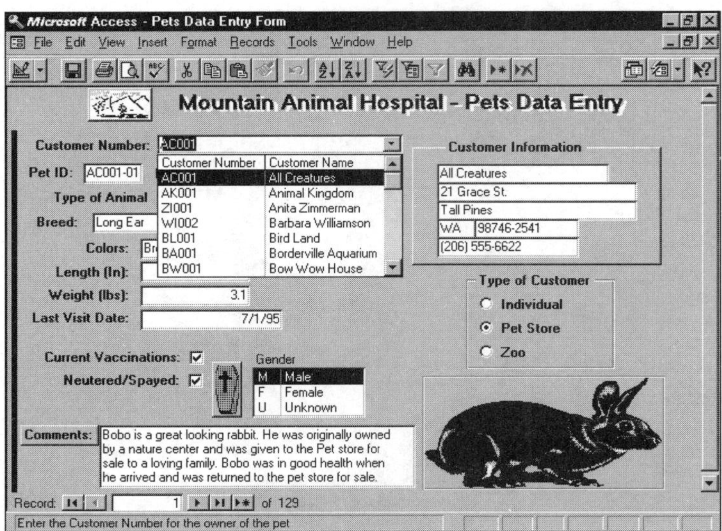

Figure 19-16: Displaying the multi-column combo box.

To understand the selection criteria of a multiple-column combo box, you should first establish the query that will select the proper fields.

Figure 19-17 shows a query called Customer Number Lookup. Note that the Customer table is related to the Pets table; the Customer Name field is selected to be used as the query's sorting field. When used for the combo box, this query will select the Customer Name from the Customer table, match it with the Customer Number in the Customer table, and pass it to the Customer Number in the Pets table. When a Customer is selected, the Customer Number in the Pets table is updated; the correct name is displayed in the Customer area of the form. Thus you can reassign the ownership of a pet, or (more usefully) add a new pet to the system and correctly choose the pet's owner.

The query shown in Figure 19-17 will be the basis for a multiple-column combo box for the field *Pets.Customer Number* on the form. The following steps describe how to create this new combo box without using the Wizard:

1. Delete the original Pets.Customer Number text box control. Select the Pets.Customer Number text box, and then select Format➪Change To➪Combo Box.
2. Move the original Pet ID and Pet Name controls, as shown in Figure 19-18. Also resize the new Customer Number combo box control.

3. Click on the data-entry portion of the new combo box.
4. Enter **Pets.Customer Number** in the Control Source property.
5. Select Table/Query in the Row Source Type property.
6. Set the Row Source property to the query Customer Number Lookup.
7. Enter **2** in the Column Count property.
8. Set the Column Heads property to Yes.
9. Set the Column Widths property to **1;1.25**.
10. Set the Bound Column property to **1**.
11. Set the List Rows property to **8**.
12. Set the List Width property to **Auto**.

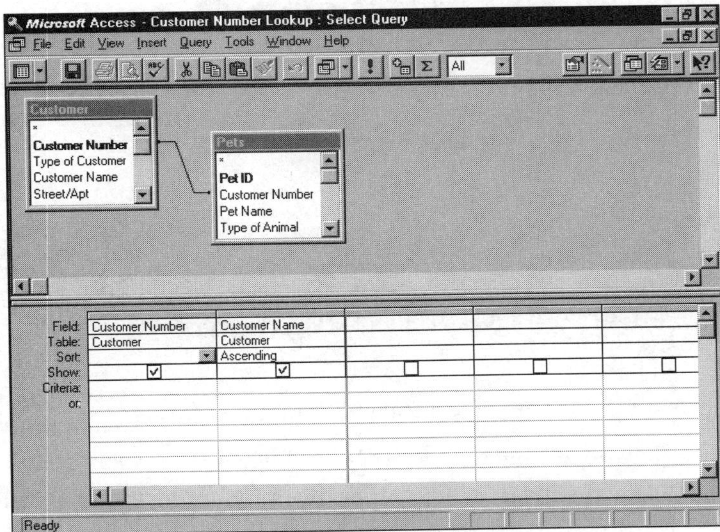

Figure 19-17: Customer Number Lookup query.

If you have followed the preceding steps properly, your screen form design should resemble the form shown in Figure 19-18, while the form view looks like Figure 19-16.

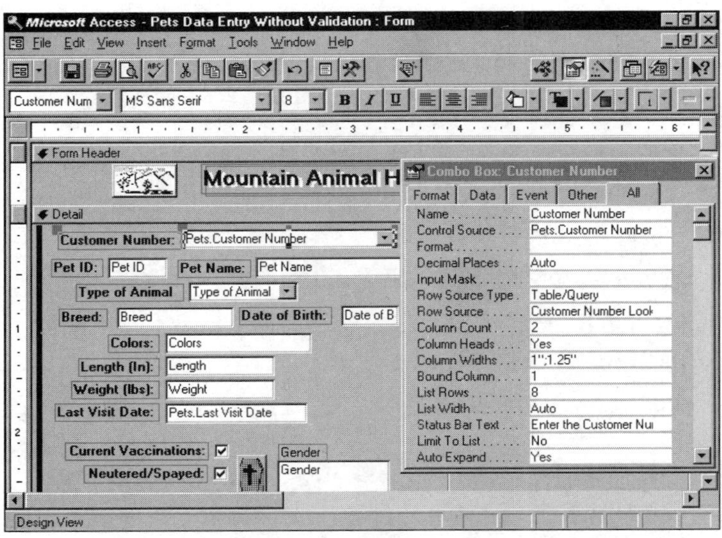

Figure 19-18: A multiple-column combo box.

Summary

In this chapter, you learned many ways to create forms that accept only good data. Validation rules, option buttons, check boxes, list boxes, and combo boxes make it easy. The Control Wizards in Access make it simple. The chapter covered the following points:

- ✦ Data-validation expressions are entered in either tables or forms.
- ✦ The Description column in a table becomes the status-bar text in a form.
- ✦ The Validation Rule and Validation Text properties let you trap for errors and display error messages.
- ✦ You can use option buttons, check boxes, and toggle buttons individually to display a two-state choice, or as part of an option group to display one of several possible choices.
- ✦ An option button (also called a radio button) is the preferred choice for showing three to four choices.
- ✦ Yes/No data is best shown with check boxes.
- ✦ You can also use toggle buttons to display Yes/No data, and you can attach pictures to the face of the button.

- List boxes display choices in an open box.
- Combo boxes display choices in a closed box that the user must select to view the choices.
- List boxes and combo boxes can have one column or many.

In the next chapter, you learn how to link and embed pictures and graphs in your forms and reports.

✦ ✦ ✦

Using OLE Objects, Graphs, and Custom Controls

In This Chapter

Types of objects you can create

Differences between bound and unbound objects

Differences between linking and embedding

Different ways of storing these objects

Modifying an existing OLE object from your form design

Creating a graph and linking it to a form

Using a Form Wizard to create a new graph

Customizing a graph

Using Office Integration in Access for Windows 95, including Spell Checking and AutoCorrect

Creating an Excel Pivot Table

Using custom controls

Access provides many powerful tools for enhancing your forms and Areports. These tools let you add pictures, graphs, sound — even video — to your database application. Chart Wizards make it easy to build business graphs and add them to your forms and reports. OLE Custom Controls (OCXs) extend the power of Access for Windows 95; new features (borrowed from Microsoft Office 95) make using Access forms more productive than ever. In this chapter, you learn the different types of graphical and OLE objects you can add to your system. You also learn how to manipulate them to create professional, productive screen displays and reports. You will also learn how to use some of the new Office 95 tools that work with Access for Windows 95 forms.

Understanding Objects

Access for Windows 95 gives you the capability of embedding pictures, video clips, sound files, business graphs, Excel spreadsheets, and Word documents; you can also link to any OLE (Object Linking and Embedding) object within forms and reports. Access lets you not only use objects in your forms, but also edit them directly from within your form.

Types of objects

As a general rule, Access can add any type of picture or graphic object to a form or report. Access can also interact with any application through DDE (Dynamic Data Exchange) or OLE. You can interact with OLE objects with great flexibility. For example, you can link to entire spreadsheets, ranges of cells, or even an individual cell.

Access can embed and store any binary file within an object frame control. This even includes sound and full-motion video. As long as you have the software driver for the embedded object, you can play or view the contents of the frame.

These objects can be bound to a field in each record (*bound*) or to the form or report itself (*unbound*). Depending on how you want to process the OLE object, you may either place (*embed*) the copy right in the Access database, or tell Access where to find the object (*link*) and place it in the bound or unbound object frame in your form or report. The following sections describe the different ways to process and store both bound and unbound objects by using embedding and linking.

Using bound and unbound objects

A *bound object* is an object displayed (and potentially stored) within a field of a record in a table. Access can display the object in a form or print it on a report. A bound object is bound to an OLE object data type field in the table. If you use a bound object in a form, you can add and edit pictures or documents record by record, the same way you can with values. To display a bound OLE object you use a *bound object frame*. In Figure 20-1, the picture of the pig is a bound object. Each record stores a photograph of the animal in the field named `Picture` in the Pets table. You can enter a different picture for each record.

An *unbound object* is not stored in a table; it is placed on the form or report. An unbound object control is the graphic equivalent of a label control. These are generally used for OLE objects in the form or report itself; they don't belong to any of the record's fields. Unbound objects don't change from record to record.

An *image control* that displays a picture is another example of an unbound object. While an unbound OLE object frame allows you to edit an object by double-clicking on it and launching the source application (PC Paintbrush, Word, Excel, a sound or video editor or recorder), an image control only displays a bitmap picture (usually in .BMP, PCX, or .WMF format) that cannot be edited.

Tip

Always use an image control for unbound pictures; it uses far fewer computer resources than an OLE control, and significantly increases performance.

In Figure 20-1, the picture of the mountain is an image control. The pig is a bound OLE object; the graph is an unbound object. Though the graph is unbound, there is a data link from the graph template to the data on the form. This means the graph is updated each time data in the record changes.

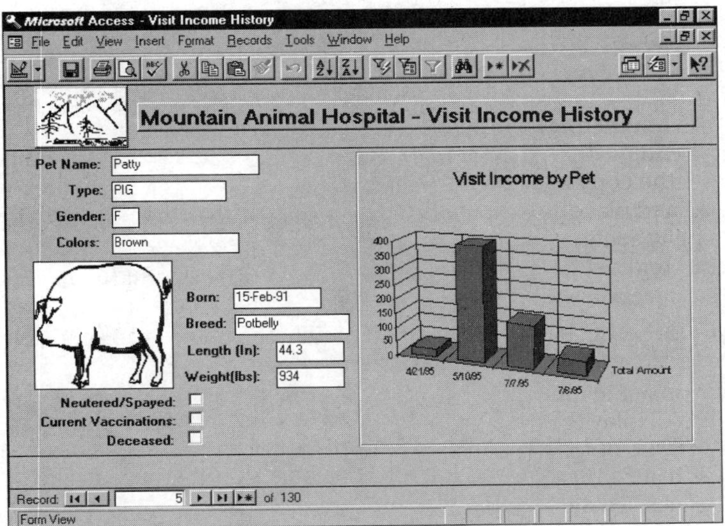

Figure 20-1: Bound and unbound objects.

Linking and embedding

The basic difference between linking and embedding objects within a form or report is that *embedding* the object stores a copy of it within your database. *Linking* an object from another application does not store the object in your database; instead, the external location of the object is stored.

Linking an object gives you two benefits:

- ✦ You can make changes using the external application, even without opening Access.
- ✦ The external file does not use any space in the Access MDB database file.

Warning If the external file is moved to another directory (or if the file is renamed), the link to Access is broken; opening the Access form may result in an error message.

One benefit of embedding is that you don't have to worry about someone changing the location or name of the linked file. Because it is embedded, the file is part of the Access MDB database file. Embedding does have its costs, however. The first is that it takes up space in your database, sometimes a great deal of it (some pictures can take several megabytes). In fact, if you embed an .AVI video clip of just 30 seconds in your database for one record, this can use ten or more megabytes of space. Imagine the space 100 records with video could use.

After the object is embedded or linked, you can use the source application (such as Excel or Paintbrush) to modify the object directly from the form. To make changes to these objects, you need only display the object in Access and double-click on it. This automatically launches the source application and lets you modify the object.

When you save the object, it is saved within Access.

Suppose (for example) you've written a document management system in Access, and have embedded a Word file in an Access form. When you double-click on the image of the Word document, Word is launched automatically and you can edit the document

Note

When the external application is started and you modify the object, the changes are made to the external file, not within your database.

Note

To edit an OLE object, you must have the associated OLE application installed in Windows. If you have embedded an Excel .XLS file but don't own Excel, you can view the spreadsheet (or use its values), but you won't be able to edit it or change it.

Disk

In the next section of this chapter, you use the form shown in Figure 20-2. You can find the form in the Mountain Animal Hospital database file, named `Pet Picture Creation - Empty`.

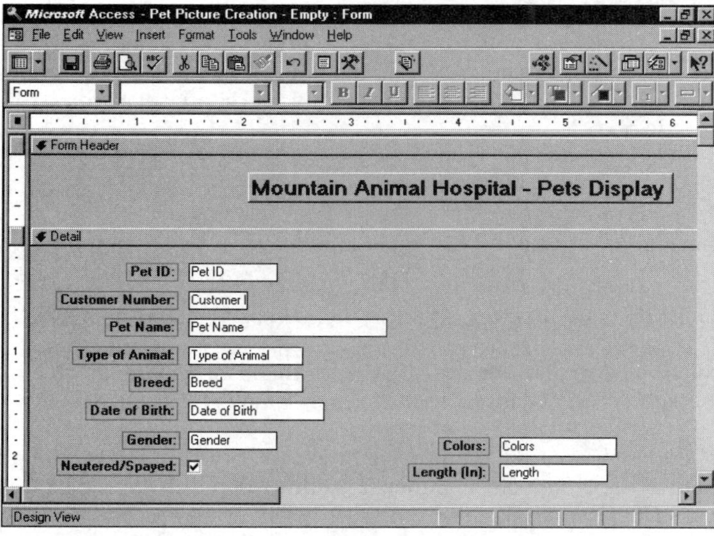

Figure 20-2: The Pet Picture Creation - Empty form.

Embedding Objects

You can embed objects in both unbound and bound object frames, as well as in image frames. Embedding places the object in the Access database, where it is stored in the form, the report design, or a record of a table.

Embedding an unbound object

You can use two methods to embed an unbound object in a form or report:

- ✦ You can simply paste an object onto the form or report; an image or unbound object frame is created that contains the object.
- ✦ You can create an unbound object frame or image frame, and then insert the object or picture into the frame.

Pasting an unbound object

If the object you want to insert is not an OLE object, you *must* paste the object onto the form. As an example, to cut or copy an object and then paste it into an image or unbound object frame, follow these steps:

1. Create or display the object using the external application.
2. Select the object and choose Edit➪Cut or Edit➪Copy.
3. Display the Access form or report and select Edit➪Paste.

This process automatically creates an unbound object frame for an OLE object or an image frame for a picture, and then embeds the pasted object in it.

If the object you paste into a form is an OLE object and you have the OLE application loaded, you can still double-click on the object to edit it. For example, you can highlight a range of cells in an Excel worksheet and paste the highlighted selection into an Access form or report. You can use the same highlight-and-paste approach with a paragraph of text in Word and paste it onto the Access form or report. You can paste both OLE and non-OLE objects onto a form or report with this method, but you'll see that there are other ways to add an OLE object.

Inserting an image-type object

You can also use another method to embed OLE objects or pictures into an unbound object frame or image frame. Suppose you want to embed a file containing a Paintbrush picture. In Figure 20-1, the picture of the mountain appears on the form in the form header; this is an *image frame*. You can embed the picture by either pasting it into the image frame or by inserting the object into the image frame. Follow these steps to create an image frame:

1. Open the form Pet Picture Creation — Empty in Design view.
2. Select the Image Frame button in the toolbar.
3. Create the image frame, using the Image Frame button from the toolbox to draw a rectangle, as shown in Figure 20-3.

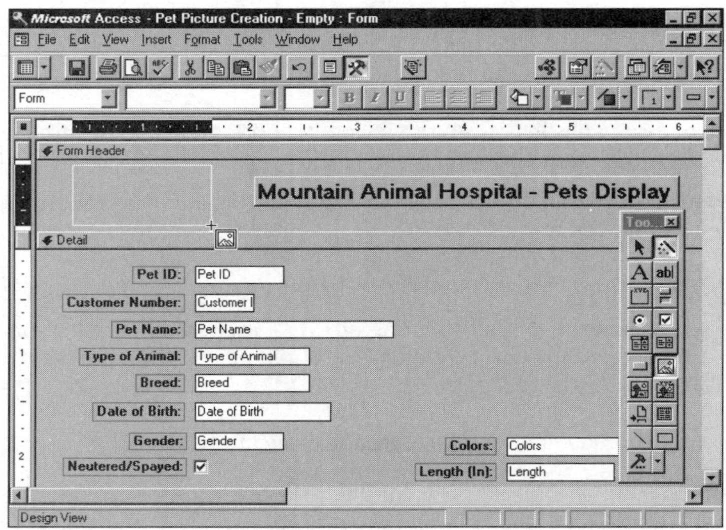

Figure 20-3: Creating an image frame.

When you create an Image frame, the Insert Picture dialog box appears. This dialog box, shown in Figure 20-4, displays the image objects you have on your system.

To embed the existing Paintbrush file MTN.BMP in the image frame, follow these steps:

1. Using the standard file explorer dialog box select MTN.BMP from the folder where your other database files reside. (This file was installed when you installed files from the *Access Bible* disk.)

2. Select OK after the filename appears in the Insert Picture dialog box.

Access embeds and displays the picture in the unbound object frame, as you can see in Figure 20-5. Notice that in this figure the picture of the mountain does not seem to be displayed correctly.

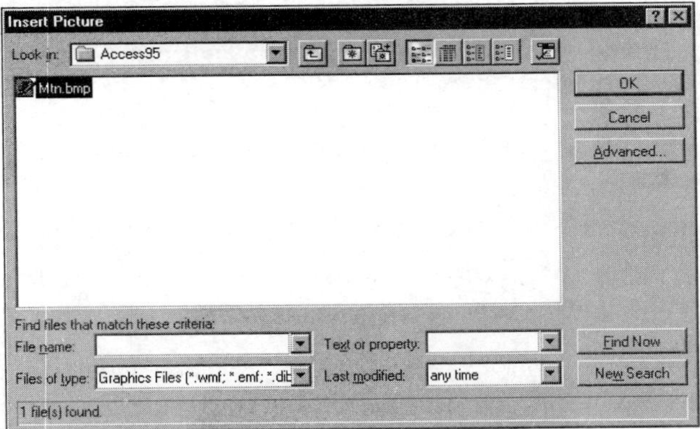

Figure 20-4: The Insert Picture dialog box.

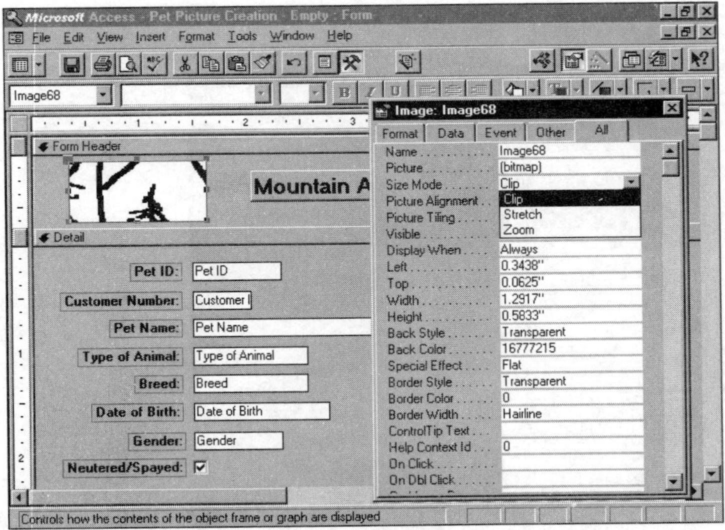

Figure 20-5: The image frame property sheet.

Changing the display of an image

After you add an image to a form or a report, you may want to change the size of the object or the object frame. If you embed a small picture, you may want to adjust the size of the object frame to fit the picture. Similarly, you may want to reduce the size of the picture to fit a specific area on your form or report.

To change the appearance and proportions of the object you embedded, you change the size of the image frame and set the Size Mode property. In Figure 20-6, you see three choices for the Size Mode property:

Clip	Shows the picture using the actual size, truncating both right and bottom
Stretch	Fits the picture within the frame; distorts the picture's proportions
Zoom	Fits the picture proportionally within the frame; may result in extra white space

Use Clip only when the frame is the exact size of the picture, or when you want to crop the picture. Stretch is useful when you have pictures where you can accept a slight amount of distortion. Although using Zoom fits the picture to the frame and maintains the original proportions, it may leave empty space in the frame. Figure 20-6 shows the MTN.BMP file using each of the property selections, as well as the correct view of the picture.

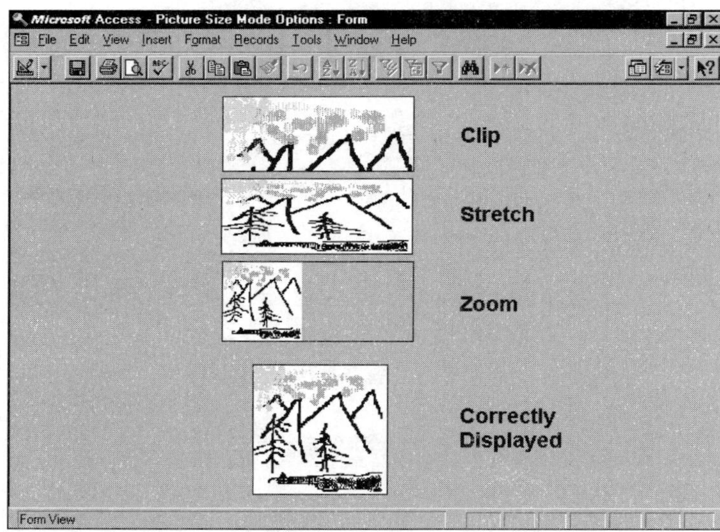

Figure 20-6: Results of using the various scaling options.

To change the Size Mode options for the MTN.BMP file on the Pets form, follow these steps:

1. Select the image frame in the Design view.
2. Display the property sheet.
3. Change the Size Mode setting to Stretch.

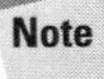

Note If you want to return the selected object to its original size, select it and choose Format⇨Size⇨To Fit.

Embedding bound objects

You can store pictures, spreadsheets, word processing documents, or other objects as data in a table. You can store (for example) a Paintbrush picture, an Excel worksheet, or an object created in any other OLE application.

You store objects in a table by creating a field that uses the OLE Object data type. Once you create a bound object frame, you can bind its Control Source to the OLE object field in the table. You can then use the bound object frame to embed an object into each record of the table.

Note You can also insert objects into a table from the Datasheet view of a form, table, or query, but the objects cannot be displayed in a view other than Form. When you switch to a Datasheet view, you'll see text describing the OLE class of the embedded object. For example, if you insert a .BMP picture into an OLE object field in a table, the text `Picture` or `Paintbrush Picture` appears in the Datasheet view.

Creating a bound OLE object

To create an embedded OLE object in a new bound object frame, follow these steps:

1. Select the Bound Object Frame button from the toolbox.
2. Drag and size the frame as shown in Figure 20-7.
3. Display the properties sheet.
4. Type **Picture** in the Control Source property. This is the name of the OLE field in the Pets table that contains pictures of the animals.
5. Set the Size Mode property to Zoom so the picture will be zoomed proportionally within the area you define.
6. Select and delete the bound object frame label (only).
7. Close and save the changes to this form.

Adding a picture to a bound object frame

After you define the bound object frame control and place it on a form, you can add pictures to it in several ways. You can paste a picture into a record or insert a file object into the frame. You insert the file object for a bound frame in nearly the same way you would insert an unbound object or image frame. The only difference is that where an image frame has a picture inserted in the design screen, a bound object frame has a picture inserted in Form view.

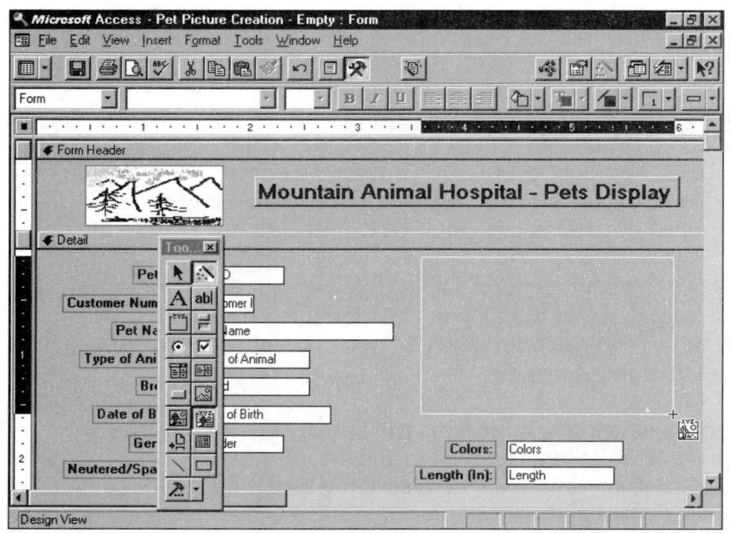

Figure 20-7: Creating a bound object frame.

To insert a picture or other object into a bound object frame, display the form in Form view, move to the correct record (each record can have a different picture or object), select the bound object frame, and then choose Insert➪Object from the Forms menu. The dialog box is a little different. Because you can insert any OLE object (in this example a picture), you first have to select Create from File and then choose the first option, Bitmap Image. You can then select the actual picture. When you're through, the picture or object appears in the space used for the bound object frame in the form.

Note If you create the object (rather than embedding an existing file), some applications display a dialog box asking whether you want to close the connection and update the open object. If you choose Yes, Access embeds the object in the bound object frame, or embeds the object in the datasheet field along with text (such as `Paintbrush Picture`) that describes the object.

After you embed an object, you can start its source application and edit it from your form or report. Simply select the object in Form view and double-click on it.

Editing an embedded object

Once you have an embedded object, you may want to modify the object itself. You can edit an OLE object in several ways. Normally you can just double-click on it and launch the source application; then you can edit the embedded OLE object. As an example, follow these steps to edit the picture of the cat in Windows Paintbrush:

1. Display the form Pets Picture Creation — Empty in Form view.
2. Move to record 12 and select the Picture bound object frame of the cat.
3. Double-click on the picture. The screen changes to an image editing environment with Windows 95 Paint menus and functions available.

Note As you can see in Figure 20-8. Windows 95 supports full in-place editing of OLE objects. Rather than launch a different program, it changes the look of the menus and screen to match Windows 95 Paint, adding that functionality temporarily to Access. Notice the different menus in Figure 20-8.

4. Make any changes you want to the picture.
5. Click on any other control in the form to close Paint.

If you make any changes, you will be prompted to update the embedded object before continuing.

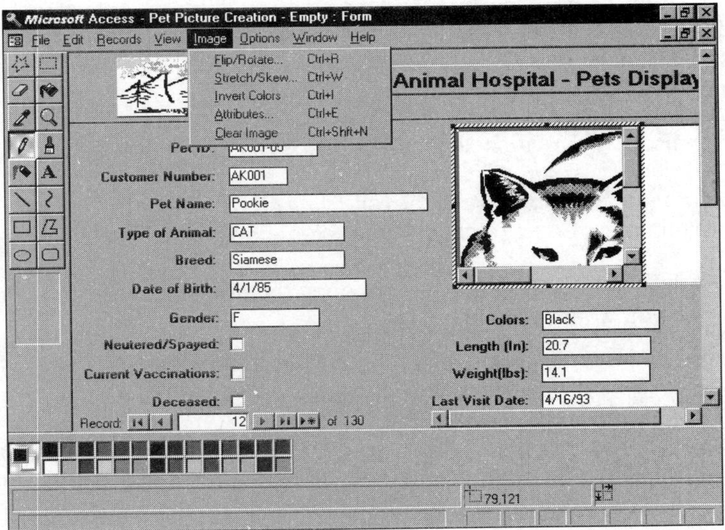

Figure 20-8: Editing the embedded object.

Warning In most cases you can modify an OLE object by double-clicking on it. When you attempt to modify either a sound or video object, however, double-clicking on the object causes it to use the player instead of letting you modify it. For these objects, you must use the Edit menu; select the last option, which changes (according to the OLE Object type) to let you edit or play the object. You can also convert some embedded OLE objects to static images, which breaks all OLE links and simply displays a picture of the object.

Linking Objects

Besides embedding objects, you can link them to external application files in much the same way as you would embed them. The difference is that the object itself is not stored in form, the report, or the database table. Instead, Access stores information about the link in those places, saving valuable space in the MDB file. This feature also allows you to edit the object in its source application without having to go through Access.

Linking a bound object

When you create a link from a file in another application (for example, Microsoft Excel) to a field in a table, the information is still stored in its original file.

Suppose you decide to use the OLE object field to store an Excel file containing additional information about the animal. If the Excel file contains history about the animal, you might want to link the information from the Pet record to this file.

Before linking information in a file to a field, however, you must first create and save the file in the source application.

Disk

On your disk should be a file named PUNKIN.XLS, which is an Excel for Windows 95 worksheet. You can use any spreadsheet or word processing file in this example.

To link information to a bound object, use the following steps. They show you how to use the Picture bound object frame to link a Pets table record to an Excel worksheet:

1. In the source application (Microsoft Excel), open the document that contains the information you want to link to.
2. Select the information you want to link, as shown in Figure 20-9.
3. Select Edit⇨Copy.

   Once you copy the range to the Clipboard, you can paste it into the bound object frame in the Access form by using the Paste Special option of the Edit menu.
4. Switch to Access and open the Pet Picture Creation - Empty form in Form view.
5. Go to record number 32 in the Access form.
6. Select the bound object frame containing the picture of the cat.
7. Select Edit⇨Paste Special.

   The Paste Special dialog box appears as shown in Figure 20-10. When you link a data range to a bound object frame, the link is always manual.
8. Select Paste Link and choose Microsoft Excel worksheet.
9. Click on OK.

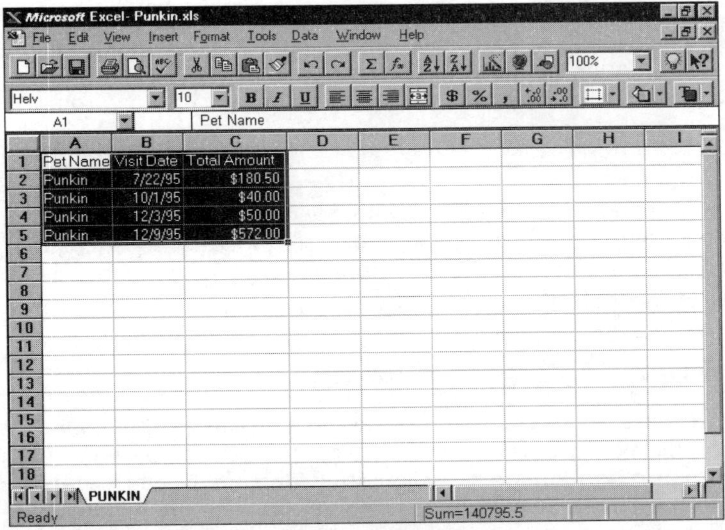

Figure 20-9: Copying a range from Microsoft Excel.

The linked Excel worksheet appears in the bound object frame. Access creates the link and displays the object in the bound object frame or it links the object to the datasheet field, displaying text (such as `Microsoft Excel`) that describes the object. When you double-click on the picture of the worksheet, Excel is launched and you can edit the data.

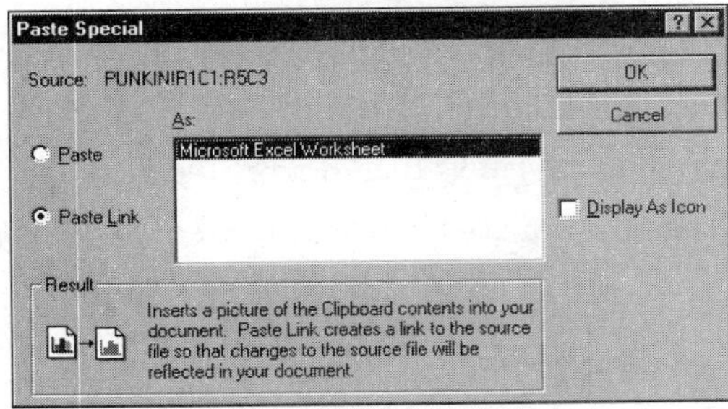

Figure 20-10: Pasting a linked worksheet.

Creating a Graph

Access has the capability of incorporating graphs within a form or report. You can create graphs by using either the Microsoft Graph application (included in your Access package) or any other OLE application. As a general rule, a graph is merely a specialized type of unbound object frame.

You can use Graph to chart data from any of your database tables, or data stored within other applications (such as Microsoft Excel). You can create graphs in a wide variety of styles — bar graphs, pie charts, line charts, and others. Because Graph is an embedded OLE application, it does not work by itself; you have to run it from within Access.

After you embed a graph, you can treat it as any other OLE object. You can modify it from the Design view of your form or report by double-clicking on the graph itself. You can edit it from the Form or Datasheet view of a form. The following sections describe how to build and process graphs that use data from within an Access table, as well as from tables of other OLE applications.

The different ways to create a graph

Access provides two ways to create a graph and place it on a form or a report. Using the Graph form or Report Wizard, you can create a graph as a new form or report, add it to an existing form or report, or add it to an existing form and link it to a table data source. (To use this third method, click on the Unbound Object frame button in the toolbox from the Form Design mode, and then choose Microsoft Graph 5.0 Chart.) Unless you are already an experienced Graph user, familiar with it from previous versions of Access or Excel, you'll find it easier to create a new graph from the toolbox. If you examine the toolbox, however, you will not see a Chart Wizard icon. You must first customize the toolbox so you can add a graph to an existing form by using the Chart Wizard.

As a general rule (for both types of graph creation), before you enter a graph into a form or report that will be based on data from one or more of your tables, you must specify which table or query will supply the data for the graph. You should keep in mind several rules when setting up your query:

- ✦ Make sure you've selected the fields containing the data to be graphed.
- ✦ Be sure to include the fields containing the labels that identify the data.
- ✦ Include any linking fields if you want the data to change from record to record.

Embedding a Graph in a Form

As you learned earlier in this chapter, you can both link and embed objects in your Access tables, and you can create and display objects on your Access forms. Next you create and display a graph based on the Mountain Animal Hospital data, and then display it on a form.

Customizing the toolbox

If you are an experienced Access 2.0 user, you may notice that for the first time, the Chart Wizard button is missing from the Access toolbox. This is now an optional item, left for you to add. Fortunately, as with toolbars, the toolbox can be customized.

The easiest way to customize the toolbox is to right-click on it, display the Shortcut menu, and choose Customize. The Customize Toolbars dialog box appears. You can then select Toolbox from the list of toolbars (as shown in Figure 20-11). Click on the Chart Wizard icon and drag it to the toolbox. This adds the missing icon permanently.

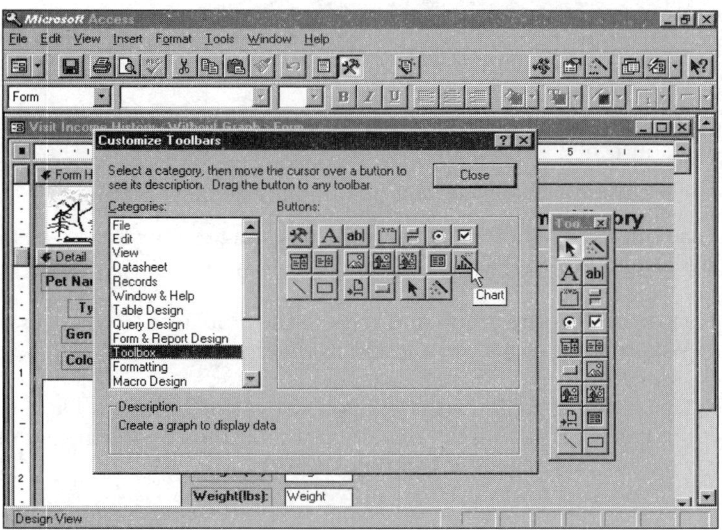

Figure 20-11: Customizing the Toolbox toolbar.

This graph will represent the visits of a pet, showing the visit dates and the dollars received for each visit. When you move through the Pets table, the form recalculates each pet's visits and displays the graph in a graph format. You create the form that Figure 20-1 displays as completed in Form view. You'll use a form that already exists but doesn't contain the graph: Visit Income History - Without Graph.

Disk The form Visit Income History - Without Graph is in the Mountain Animal Hospital.MDB database, along with the final version (called Visit Income History) that contains the completed graph.

Assembling the data

As a first step in embedding a graph, make sure the query associated with the form provides the information you need for the graph. In this example, you need both the Visit Date and the Total Amount fields from the Visits table as the basis of the graph. You also need the Pet ID field from the Visits table to use as a link to the data on the form. This link allows the data in the graph to change from record to record.

Sometimes you'll need to create a query when you need data items from more than one table. In this example, you can select all the data you need right from the Wizard; Access will build the query (actually a SQL statement) for you automatically.

Adding the graph to the form

The following steps detail how to create and place the new graph on the existing form. You should be in the Design view of the form named Visit Income History - Without Graph.

1. Select the Chart button in the toolbox.
2. Position the new cursor at the upper left position for the new graph.
3. Click the mouse button and hold it down while dragging the box to the desired size on the right-hand portion of the form.

Once you size the blank area for the graph and release the mouse button, Access activates the Chart Wizard used to embed a graph in a form.

As shown in Figure 20-12, this Wizard screen lets you select the table or query from which you'll select the values. By using the row of option buttons under the list of tables, you can view all the Tables, all the Queries, or Both.

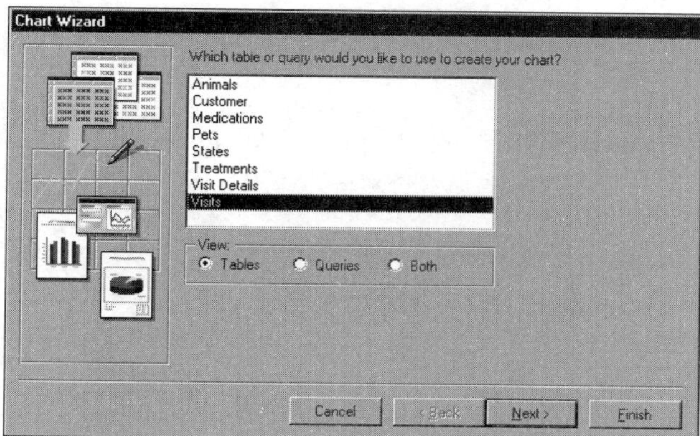

Figure 20-12: Selecting the table for the source of data for the graph.

The following steps take you through the Wizard to create the desired graph and link it to your form:

1. Choose the Visits table as the source for the graph.
2. Click on Next > to go to the next Wizard screen.

   The Chart Wizard lets you select fields to include in your graph.
3. Select the Visit Date and Total Amount Fields by double-clicking on them to move them to the Fields for graph box.
4. Click on Next > to go to the next Wizard screen.

   This screen (Figure 20-13) lets you choose the type of graph you want to create, and determine whether the data series are in rows or columns. In this example, select a column chart; you'll customize it later using the graph options. As you click on each of the graph types, an explanation appears in the box in the lower right corner of the screen.

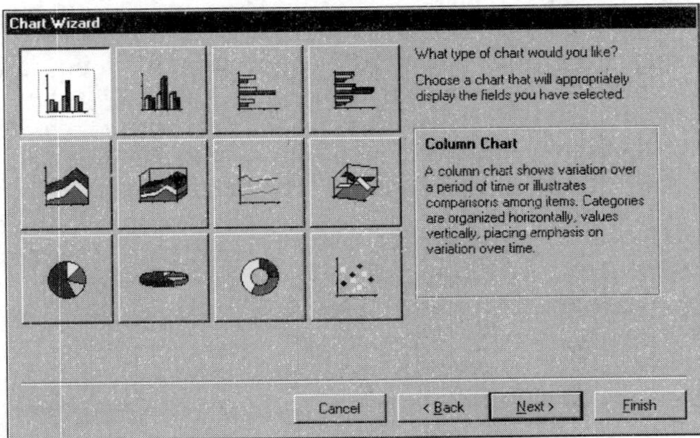

Figure 20-13: Selecting the type of chart.

5. Select the Column Chart (as shown in Figure 20-13), and then click on Next > to go to the next Wizard screen. (The Column Chart is easiest to work with.)

   The next screen (Figure 20-14) makes choices for you automatically and lets you change the assumptions. Figure 20-14 shows that the Visit Date field has been used for the X-axis, while the Total Amount field is used in the y-axis to determine the height of the bars.

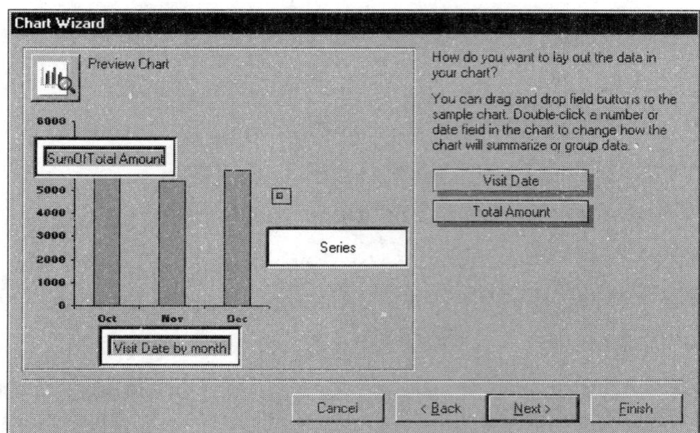

Figure 20-14: Laying out the chart's data elements.

New! This screen is very different from the Access 2 Chart Wizard; it replaces three or four Access 2 Wizard screens with a single screen.

This screen gives you a graphical way to choose the fields you want for your graph; then you can drag them to the simulated graph window. Figure 20-14 shows the Wizard screen divided into two areas. The right side shows the fields you have selected to work with. The left side displays a simulated graph; you can drag fields from the list of fields on the right to the axis area on the left. If you want to change the Visit Date field chosen for you for the x-axis, drag it back from the left side to the right side. Likewise, to make a selection, drag a field name from the right side of the screen to its proper axis on the left side.

Tip If you had several numeric fields, you could drag them (or any multiple fields) to the left side for multiple series; these would appear in a legend. You can also drag the same field to both the x-axis and the Series indicator, as long as you're grouping differently. For example, you could group the Visit Date by month and use it again in the Series grouped by year. Without using the Visit Date field a second time as the series variable, you would have one bar for each month in sequential order — for example, Jan95, Feb95, Mar95, . . . Dec95, Jan96, Feb96 . . . By adding the Visit Date as a series variable and grouping it by year, you could get pairs of bars. Multiple bars for each month, each a different color and representing a different year and a legend for each year.

For this example, the assumptions made by Access are fine. You may notice (in Figure 20-14) that each the field on the left side of the screen is actually a button. When you double-click on one, you can further define how the data is used in the graph.

Generally, the x-axis variable is either a date or a text field. The y-axis field is almost always a number (though it can be a count of values). Only numeric and date fields (such as the y-axis variable Total Amount) can be further defined. If you double-click on the Total Amount field on the left side of the screen, the dialog box shown in Figure

20-15 appears; it lets you define options for summarizing the field. Remember, there may be many records for a given summary; in this example, many Pets may have visits in a specific month.

As you can see in Figure 20-15, Sum has been chosen as the summarization type. You could change it to Average to graph the average amount of a visit, instead of summing all the visit amounts.

Warning You must supply a numeric variable for all of the selections except Count, which can be any data type.

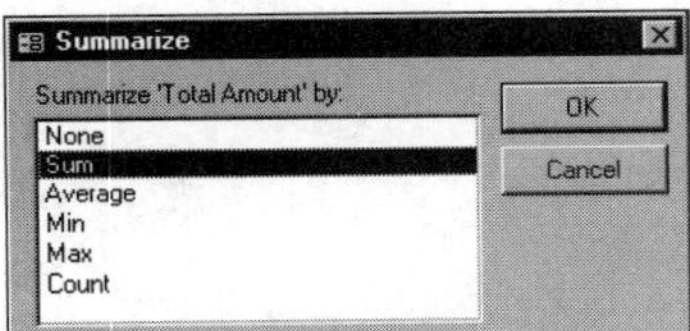

Figure 20-15: Selecting options to summarize the field.

The dialog box shown in Figure 20-16 lets you choose the date hierarchy from larger to smaller rollups. The choices include Year, Quarter, Month, Week, Day, Hour, and Minute. If you have data for many dates within a month and want to roll it up by month, you would choose month. In this example, you want to see all of the detail data. Since the data is in Visits by date (mm/dd/yy), you would select Day to view all the detail records. For this example, change the default selection from Month to Day.

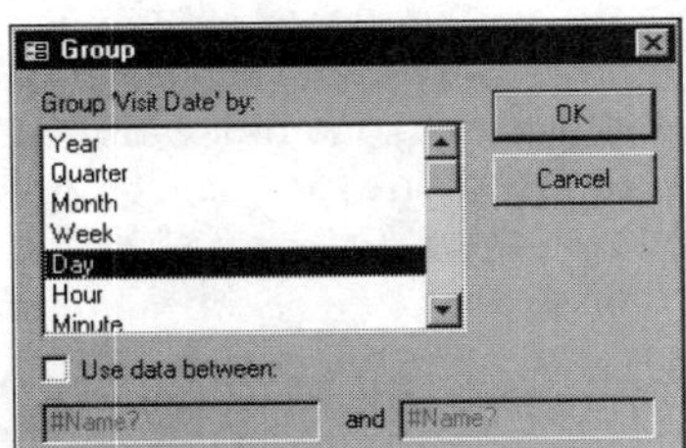

Figure 20-16: Choosing group options for a date field.

You can click on the Preview Chart button at any time to see the results of your choices.

6. Make sure you changed the group options from Month to Day; click on Next> to go to the next Wizard screen.

   Figure 20-17 shows the Field Linking box. If you run the Chart Wizard from inside an existing form, you have the option to link a field in the form to a field in the chart. Even if you don't specify the field when you select the chart fields, you can make the link as long as the field exists in the selected table.

   In this example, Access has correctly selected the Pet ID field from both the Visit Income History form and the Visits table. This way, as you move from record to record (keyed by Pet) in the Visit History form, the graph changes to display only the data for that pet.

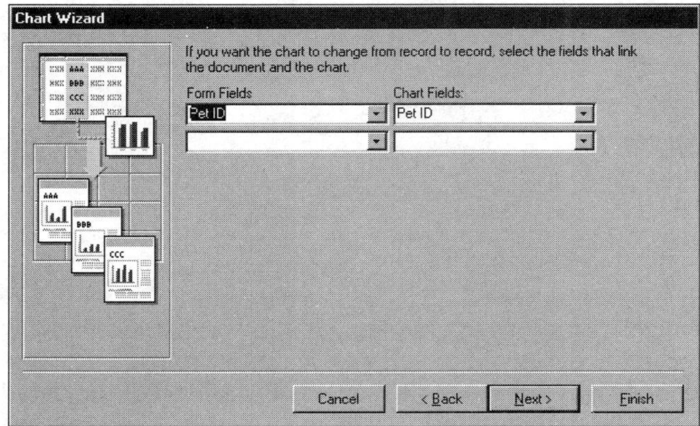

Figure 20-17: Linking fields between the form and the graph.

7. Select Next> to move to the last Wizard screen.

   The last Chart Wizard screen, shown in Figure 20-18, lets you enter a title and determine whether a legend is needed. You won't need one for this example because you have only one data series.

8. Enter **Visit Income History** for the graph title.

9. Select the button next to the text `No, don't display a legend.`

10. Click on Finish to complete the Wizard.

    After you complete all these entries, the sample chart appears in the graph object frame in the design screen (as shown in Figure 20-19). Until you display the form in Form view, the link to the individual pet is not established and the graph is not recalculated to show only the visits for the specific pet's record. In fact, the graph shown is a sample preview; it doesn't use any of your data. If you were worried about where that strange-looking graph came from, don't be.

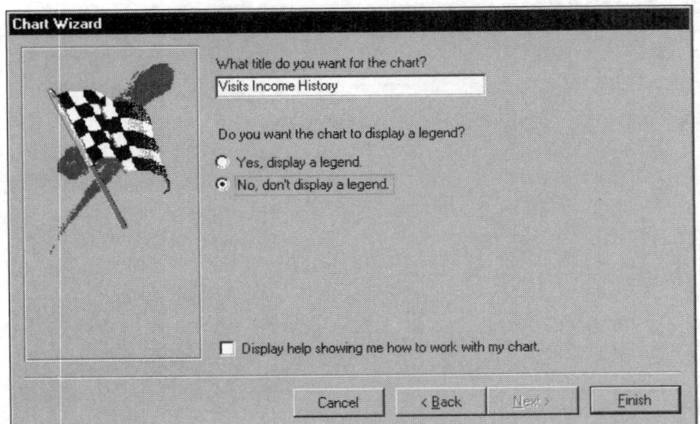

Figure 20-18: Specifying a chart title and legend.

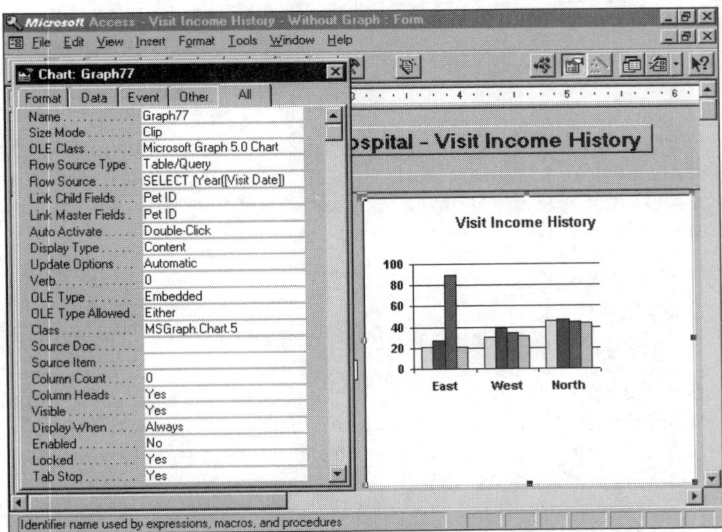

Figure 20-19: The graph in the Form Design window.

11. Click on the Form View button in the toolbar to display the Visit Income History form and recalculate the graph. Figure 20-20 shows the final graph in Form view.

In Figure 20-19, you saw the graph and the property sheet. You display a graph by using a *graph frame*, which shows its data in either Form view or Design view. Take note of some properties in the property sheet. The Size Mode property is set initially to Clip. You can change this to Zoom or Stretch, although the graph should always be displayed proportionally. You can size and move the graph to fit onto your form. When you work with the graph in the Graph window, the size of the graph you create is the same size it will be in the Design window.

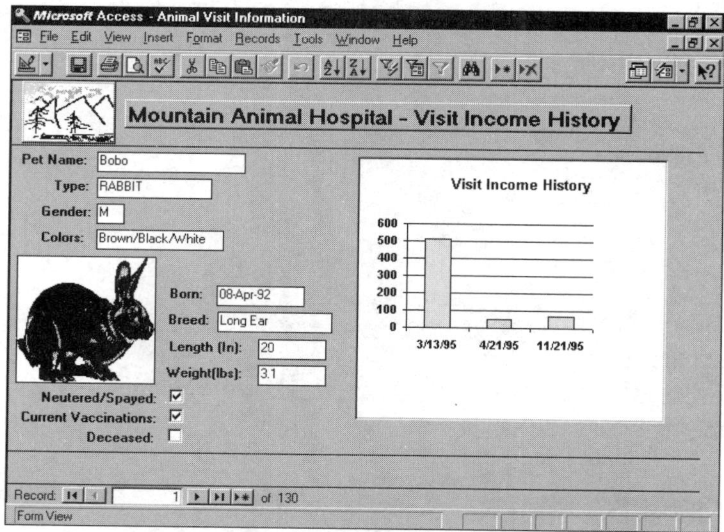

Figure 20-20: Recalculating the graph in form view.

The OLE Class property is Microsoft Graph 5.0 Chart. This is linked automatically by the Chart Wizard. The row source comes from the table of query you used with the graph, but it appears as an SQL statement that is passed to the Graph. The SQL statement (more on this later) created for this graph is:

```
SELECT Format([Visit Date], "DDDDD"), SUM([Visits].[Total
       Amount]) FROM [Visits]
GROUP BY Int([Visit Date]), Format([Visit Date], "DDDDD");
```

The next two properties, Link Child Fields and Link Master Fields, control linking of the data to the form data itself. Using the Link properties, you can link the graph's data to each record in the form. In this example, the Pet ID from the current Pets record is linked to Visit Details records with the same Pet ID.

To change the appearance of the graph, you can double-click on the graph in Design view to open Microsoft Graph. After you make the changes you want, you can select File➪Exit, return to Microsoft Access, and go back to Design view.

Customizing a Graph

Once you create a graph within Access, you can enhance it by using the tools within Microsoft Graph. As demonstrated in the preceding section, just a few mouse clicks will create a basic graph. The following section describes a number of ways to make your graph a powerful presentation and reporting tool.

In many cases, the basic chart you create presents the idea you want to get across. In other cases, however, it may be necessary to create a more illustrative presentation. You can accomplish this by adding any of these enhancements:

- Entering free-form text to the graph to highlight specific areas of the graph
- Changing attached text for a better display of the data being presented
- Annotating the graph with lines and arrows
- Changing certain graphic objects with colors and patterns
- Moving and modifying the legend
- Adding gridlines to reflect the data better
- Manipulating the 3-D view to show your presentation more accurately
- Adding a bitmap to the graph for a more professional presentation
- Changing the graph type to show the data in a different graphic format, such as Bar, Line, or Pie
- Adding or modifying the data in the graph

Once the graph appears in the Graph application, you can begin to modify it.

Understanding the Graph window

The Graph window, shown in Figure 20-21, lets you work with and customize the graph. As you can see, there are actually two windows within the Graph window:

Datasheet	A spreadsheet of the data used in the graph
Chart	The displayed chart of the selected data

Note You can change the look of the graph by resizing the Chart window. Figure 20-21 shows a wider Chart window, which enables you to see labels better.

In the datasheet, you can add, change, or delete data. Any data modify this way is reflected immediately in the graph. After you change the datasheet in the Graph window, you can even tell Access whether to include each row or column when the graph is drawn.

Warning Changing data in a linked record will only change data in the graph for as long as you are on that record. Once you move off it, the changes are discarded.

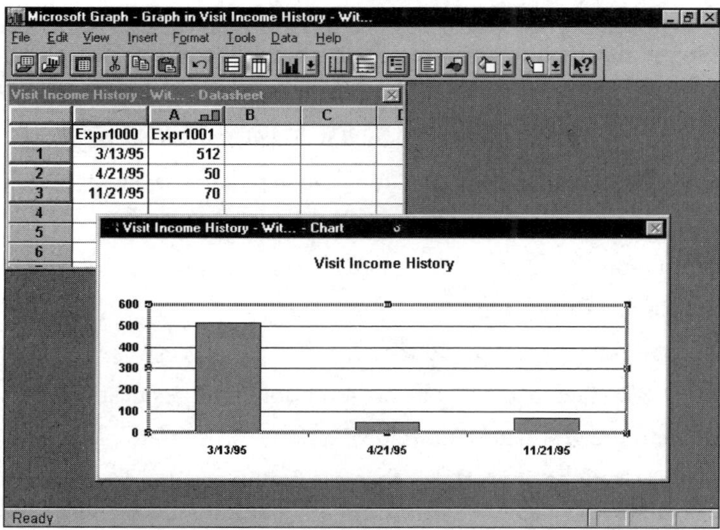

Figure 20-21: The Graph window.

Most importantly, you can use the Chart portion of the Graph window to change the way the graph appears. By clicking on objects such as attached text (or on areas of the graph such as the columns), you can modify these objects. You can customize by double-clicking on an object to display a dialog box, or by making selections from the menus at the top of the window.

Working with attached text

Text generated by the program is called *attached* text. These graph items are attached text:

- ✦ Graph title
- ✦ Value of y-axis
- ✦ Category of x-axis
- ✦ Data series and points
- ✦ Overlay value of y-axis
- ✦ Overlay value of x-axis

Once the initial graph appears, you can change this text. Click on a text object to change the text itself, or double-click on any text item in the preceding list, and then modify its properties.

You can choose from three categories of settings to modify an attached text object:

Patterns	Background and foreground colors, borders, and shading
Fonts	Text font, size, style, and color
Alignment	Alignment and orientation

Note

You can change attributes from the Format menu, too.

The Font options let you change the font assignment for the text within the text object, as shown in Figure 20-22.

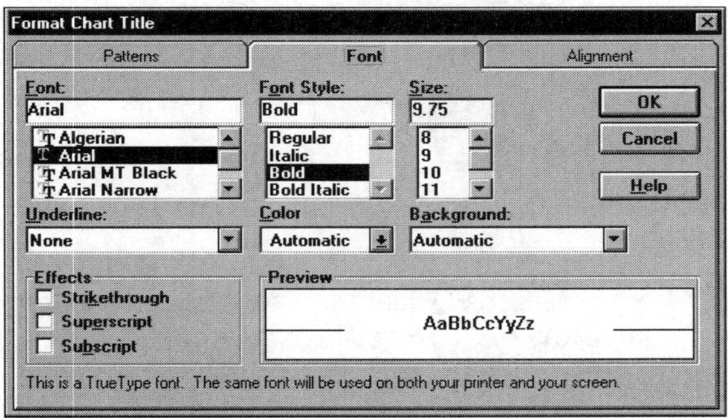

Figure 20-22: The Chart Fonts dialog box.

The Chart Fonts dialog box is a standard Windows font-selector box. Here you can select Font, Size, Font Style, Color, and Background effects. To change the text, follow these steps:

1. Double-click on the chart title `Visit Income History`.
2. Select the Font tab from the Format dialog box.
3. Select Times New Roman in the Font list box.
4. Select Italic in the Font Style list box.
5. Select 12 in the Size list box.
6. Select OK to complete the changes.

As you make the font changes, a sample of each change appears in the Preview box.

The Alignment tab in the dialog box lets you set the horizontal alignment (left, center, right, or justify), the vertical alignment (top, center, bottom or justify), and the orientation (four options will display the text in either horizontal or vertical format). Figure 20-23 shows the Alignment dialog box and the options available.

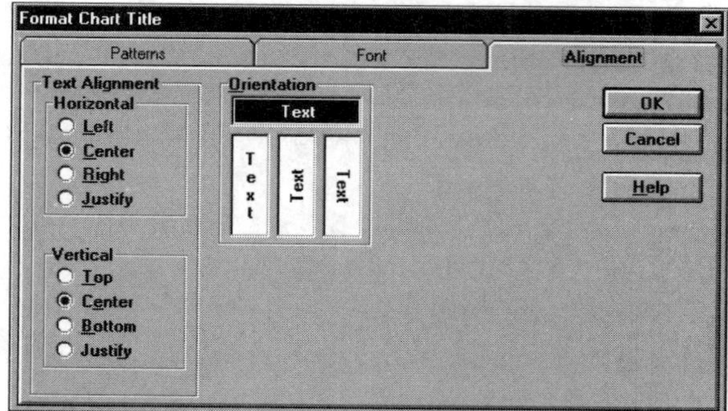

Figure 20-23: The Alignment dialog box.

The most important part of this dialog box is the Orientation setting. Although for some titles it is not important to change any of these settings, it becomes necessary to change them for titles that normally run vertically (such as axis titles).

Sometimes you may need to add text to your graph to present your data better. This text is called *free-form* (or *unattached*) text. You can place it anywhere on your graph and combine it with other objects to illustrate your data as you want. Figure 20-24 shows free-form text being entered on the graph, as well as the changes you previously made to the graph title.

In the next steps, you see how to add free-form text to the graph:

1. Type **For the Period Jan 1-Dec 31, 1995** anywhere on the graph, as shown in Figure 20-24.

   Microsoft Graph positions the text near the middle of the graph. The text is surrounded by handles so you can size and position the text.

2. Drag the text to the bottom left corner of the graph.
3. Right-click on the text, select Format➪Object, and change the font to Times New Roman, 12 point, regular.

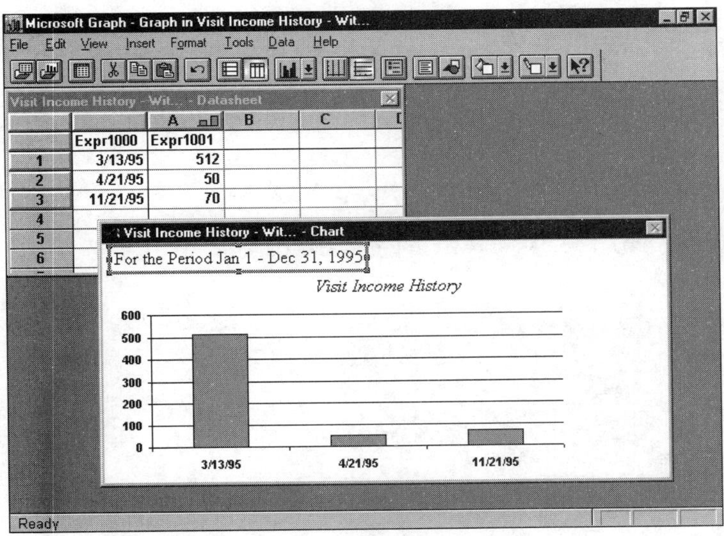

Figure 20-24: Free-form text on a graph.

Changing the graph type

After you create your initial graph, you can experiment with changing the graph type to make sure you selected the type that best reflects your data. Microsoft Graph provides a wide range of graphs to select from; a few mouse clicks can change the type of graph.

The following are the different types of graphs you can select:

Two-Dimensional Charts	*Three-Dimensional Charts*
Area	3-D Area
Bar	3-D Bar
Column	3-D Column
Line	3-D Line
Pie	3-D Pie
Doughnut	3-D Surface
Radar	
XY (Scatter)	

To select a different type of graph, select the Format➪Chart Type menu of the Chart window to display the various chart types. When you select any of the graph options, a window opens (as shown in Figure 20-25) to display all the different graphing options available within the selected graph type. Click on one of them to select your new graph type.

To display some different graph types, follow these steps:

1. Select Format➪Chart Type as shown in Figure 20-25.

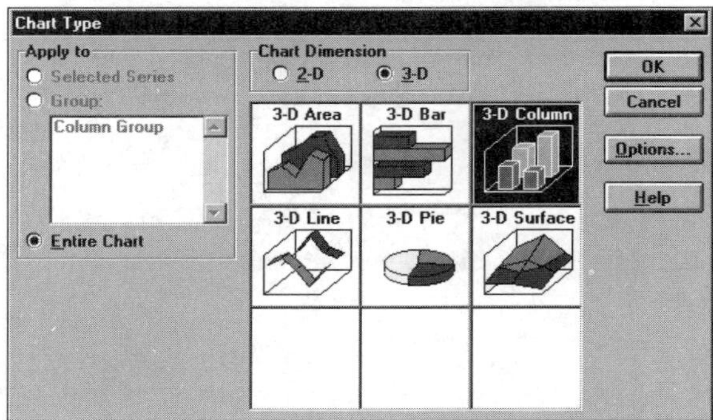

Figure 20-25: The chart types.

2. Change the chart type to 3-D Column.
3. Click on OK to return to the Graph window.

Changing axis labels

You may want to change the text font of the x-axis so you can see all the labels. Follow these steps to change axis labels:

1. Double-click on the x-axis (the bottom axis with the dates on it).
2. Select the Font from the Format Axis dialog box.
3. Change the Size setting to 8 points by entering **8** into the Font Size box.
4. Select OK to return to the chart.

Changing a bar color and pattern

If you are going to print the graph in monochrome, you should always adjust the patterns so they are not all solid colors. You can change the color or pattern of each bar by double-clicking on any bar in the category you want to select.

Modifying gridlines

Gridlines are lines that extend from the axis across the plotting area of the graph to help you read the graph properly. You can add them for the x-axis and y-axis of your graph; if it's three-dimensional, an additional gridline is available for the z-axis. You can add gridlines for any axis on the graph. The *z-axis gridlines* appear along the back and side walls of the plotting area. The *x-* and *y-axis gridlines* appear across the base and up the walls of the graph.

Select Insert⇨Gridlines to begin working with them. On the left wall are the y-axis gridlines; the z-axis gridlines are shown on the back wall, and the x-axis gridlines are shown on the floor. When you double-click on one of these areas, you can change the line type.

Using the Graph AutoFormat

Another option is AutoFormat. If you select the entire chart you can then select Format⇨AutoFormat. Depending on the type of chart you have selected, you'll see from five to twelve different prebuilt formats. When you select one of these, Access makes changes to the graph subtype, formatting of gridlines, styles, and so on. You can also define your own formats and use them. (Figure 20-26 shows AutoFormat being used to create a three-dimensional column chart.)

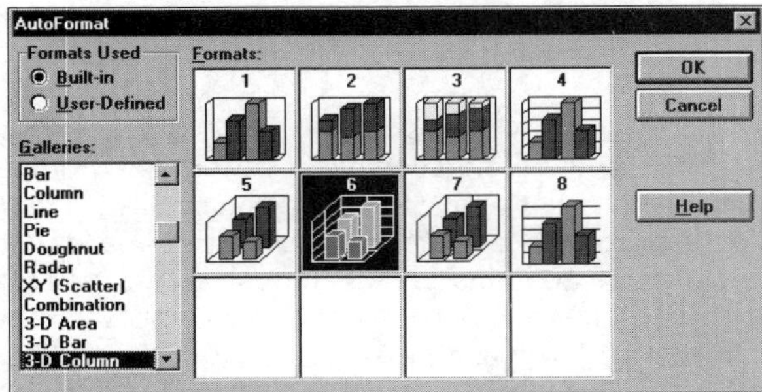

Figure 20-26: Using AutoFormat for a 3-D Column Chart.

Manipulating three-dimensional graphs

In any of the three-dimensional chart options, you can modify the following graph-display characteristics:

- ✦ Elevation
- ✦ Perspective (if Right Angle Axes is turned off)
- ✦ Rotation

✦ Scaling

✦ Angle and height of the axes

You can change the 3-D view by selecting Format➪3-D View. The dialog box shown in Figure 20-27 appears. Then you can enter the values for the various settings, or use the six buttons to rotate the icon of the graph in real time. When you like the view you see, select OK and your chart will change to that perspective.

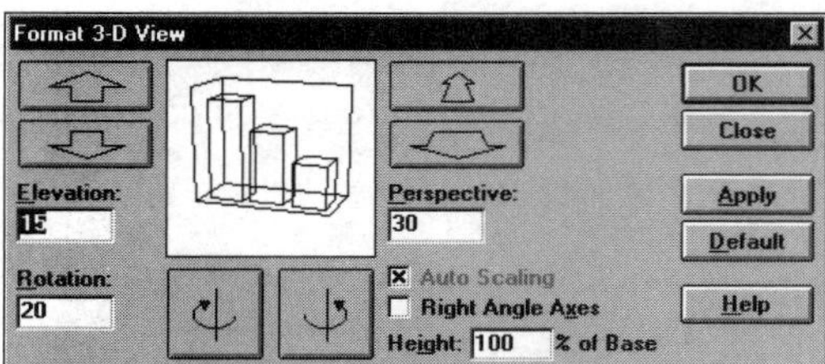

Figure 20-27: The Format 3-D View dialog box.

Note

The Elevation button controls the height at which you view the data. The elevation is measured in degrees; it can range from –90 to 90 degrees.

An elevation of zero displays the graph as if you were level with the center of the graph. An elevation of 90 degrees shows the graph as you would view it from above center. A –90 degree elevation shows the graph as you would view it from below its center.

The Perspective button controls the amount of perspective in your graph. Adding more perspective makes the data markers at the back of the graph smaller than those at the front of the graph. This option provides a sense of distance; the smaller data markers seem farther away. If your graph contains a great amount of data, you may want to use a larger perspective value (the ratio of the front of the graph to the back of the graph). This value can range from 0 to 100. A perspective of 0 makes the back edge of the graph equal in width to the front edge. You can experiment with these settings until you get the effect you need.

The Rotation buttons control the rotation of the entire plotting area. The rotation is measured in degrees, from 0 to 360. A rotation of 0 displays your graph as you view it from directly in front. A rotation of 180 degrees displays the graph as if you were viewing it from the back. (This setting visually reverses the plotting order of your data series.) A rotation of 90 degrees displays your graph as if you were viewing it from the center of the side wall.

The Auto Scaling check box lets you scale a three-dimensional graph so its size is closer to that of the two-dimensional graph using the same data. To activate this option, click on the Auto Scaling check box so that the X appears in the box. When this option is kept activated, Access will scale the graph automatically whenever you switch from a two-dimensional to a three-dimensional graph.

Two options within the Format 3-D View dialog box pertain specifically to display of the axes. The Right Angle Axes check box lets you control the orientation of the axes. If the check box is on, all axes are displayed at right angles to each other.

If the Right Angle Axes check box is selected, you cannot specify the perspective for the three-dimensional view.

The Height entry box contains the height of the z-axis and walls relative to the width of the graph's base. The height is measured as a percentage of the x-axis length. A height of 100 percent makes the height equal to the x-axis. A height of 50 percent makes the height half the x-axis length. You can set this height percentage at over 100 percent; by doing so, you can make the height of the z-axis greater than the length of the x-axis.

If you change the Height setting, your change will not be displayed in the sample graph shown in the 3-D View dialog box.

Once you have made the desired changes, you can select File➪Exit and then select Return to (which will bring you back to the Form Design screen).

You might want to make one more change: a graph frame is really an unbound object frame, and you can change its border type and background (as you can for any unbound object frame). Figure 20-28 shows the final graph after the border has been changed to an etched special effect, and the background colored light gray to match the background of the form. This allows the graph to stand out more than it would if you used a sunken white background.

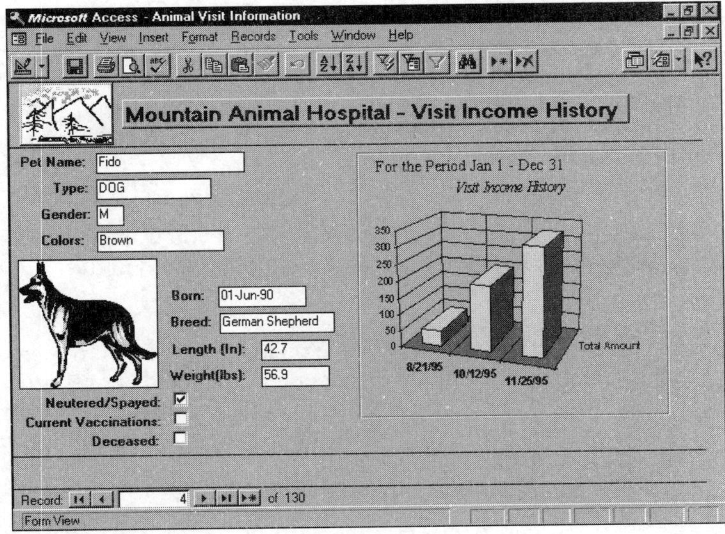

Figure 20-28: The final graph.

Integration with Microsoft Office

Access for Windows 95 is not only integrated with Windows 95, it now shares many major components with Microsoft Office 95. (If you are an Excel for Windows 95 or Word for Windows 95 user, you are going to be especially thrilled.) Access for Windows 95 has an integrated Spell Checker that is used to make sure the data stored in Access for Windows 95 tables and database objects is spelled correctly. The dictionary is shared across all Office 95 applications, including custom words. Access for Windows 95 also shares the Office 95 AutoCorrect features to fix errors while you type.

Checking the spelling of one or more fields and records

You can check the spelling of your data in either form or datasheet view. In Form view, you can only spell-check a single record — and field within the record — at a time. To check the spelling of data in Form view, you would select the field or text whose spelling you want to check, and then click on the Spell Check icon on the toolbar (the icon with the check mark and the small letters `ABC` above it).

When you click on the icon, Access checks the field (or selected text within the field) for spelling, as shown in Figure 20-29.

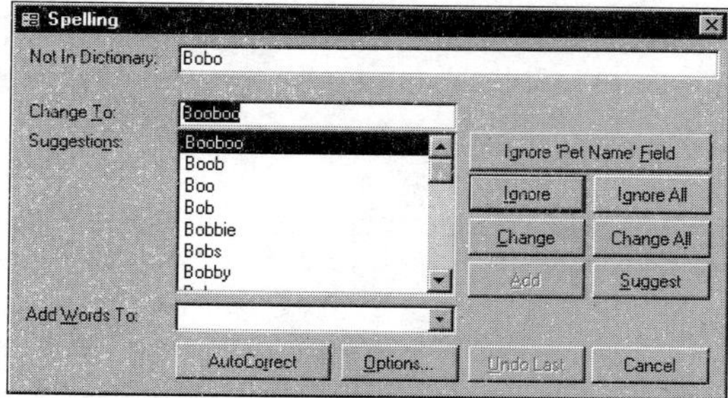

Figure 20-29: Spell-checking in Access.

Tip In the Spelling dialog box that appears, you can click on Add if you want to add the word in the Not In Dictionary: box to the custom dictionary listed in the Add Words To: box.

You can select only one field at a time in Form view. You'll probably want to use only Form view to spell-check selected memo data; to select multiple fields or records, you must switch to Datasheet view. To check the spelling of data in Datasheet view, you would select the records, columns, fields, or text within a field whose spelling you want to check, and then click on the Spell Check icon.

You can also check the spelling in a table, query, or form in the Database window by clicking on the table, query, or form object whose spelling you want to check.

Warning You only spell-check the data inside the objects. Access for Windows 95 cannot spell-check controls.

Correcting your typing automatically when entering data

You can use the AutoCorrect feature to provide automatic corrections to text you frequently mistype, and to replace abbreviations with the long names they stand for (also automatically). For example, you can create an entry "mah" for Mountain Animal Hospital. Whenever you type **mah** followed by a space or punctuation mark, Microsoft Access replaces `mah` with the text `Mountain Animal Hospital`.

You can activate AutoCorrect by selecting Tools⇨AutoCorrect. The dialog box shown in Figure 20-30 appears. You can select the Replace Text As You Type check box. In the Replace box, type the text you want corrected. In the With box, type the corrected text. When you click on Add, the word replacement combination will be added to the AutoCorrect dictionary.

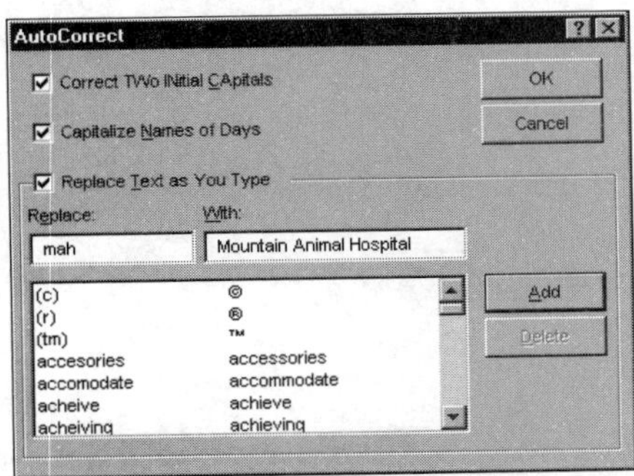

Figure 20-30: Using AutoCorrect in Access for Windows 95.

Warning AutoCorrect won't correct text that was typed before you selected the Replace Text As You Type check box.

Using OLE automation with Office 95

Access for Windows 95 takes advantage of drag-and-drop; you can do it from Datasheet view across Excel and Word. You can instantly create a table in a Word document (or add a table to an Excel spreadsheet) simply by copying and pasting (or dragging and dropping) data from an Access datasheet to a Word document or Excel spreadsheet. (Obviously, you must have Word or Excel to take advantage of these features.)

Access for Windows 95 contains a new Pivot Table Wizard to create Excel pivot tables based on Access tables or queries. A *pivot table* is like a cross-tabulation of your data; you can define the data values for rows, columns, pages and summarization. Figure 20-31 (from the Microsoft Excel 95 Help) shows a conceptual figure of a pivot table. A pivot table can have multiple levels of rows, columns, and even pages. As you can see in the conceptual figure, the center of the table contains numeric data; the rows and columns form a hierarchy of unique data. In this figure, dates and salespeople are the row hierarchies, along with multiple levels of subtotals. The column headers are types of products, while each page of the pivot table is a different region.

Cross Ref A pivot table is like a crosstab query (see Chapter 25), but much more powerful.

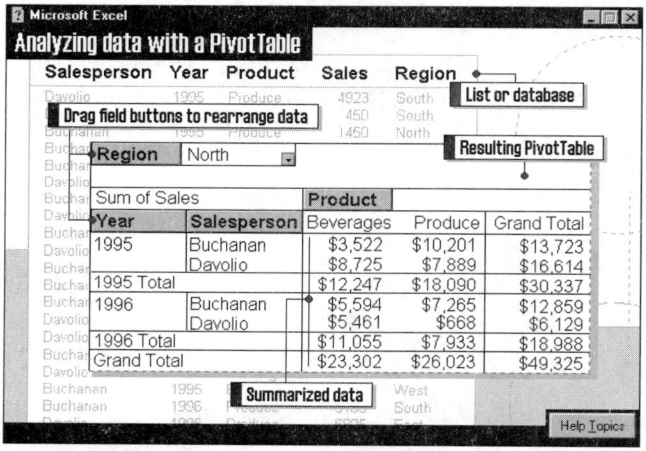

Figure 20-31: A conceptual view of a pivot table.

You start creating a pivot table from the New Form dialog box using one of the standard Wizards you can select. Once you begin the PivotTable Wizard process, you will see the first PivotTable dialog box (shown in Figure 20-32).

This dialog box lets you select the tables or query to use in creating the pivot table. You can select from more than one table, but they must be joined at the database level to create a valid pivot table. In this example, the Pets, Owners, & Visits query is being used. The pivot table will use the Customer and Pets Name fields along with the Visit Date and Total Amount spent.

The next dialog box displayed when you press the Next > button lets you drag the fields to the pivot table (using a technology similar to the Chart Wizard you learned about earlier in this chapter). Unlike the Chart Wizard, it makes no assumptions for you. You must drag each field from the list on the right to the area on the left. As you can see, Customer Name for the Page, Pet Name will be used for the column headers, Visit Date for the row names, and total amount will be summed in the center of the pivot table.

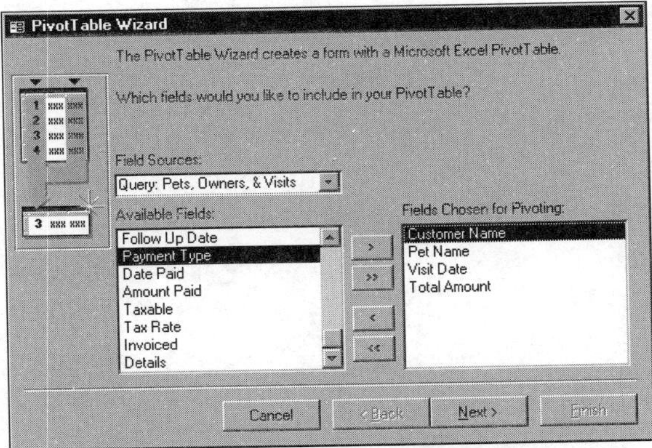

Figure 20-32: Starting the PivotTable Wizard.

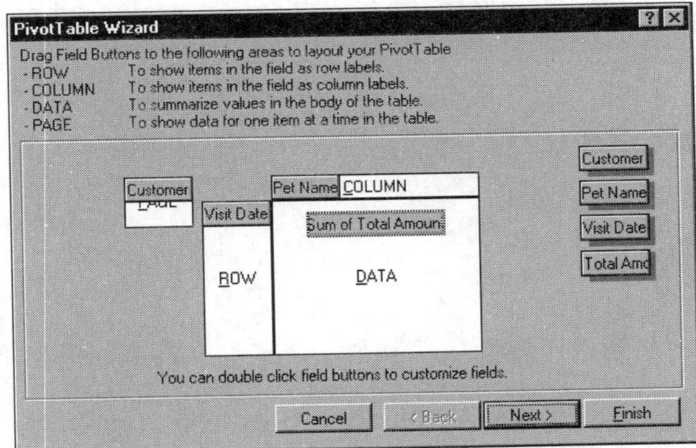

Figure 20-33: Selecting the field locations.

You can double-click on any of the items in the field placement area. You can determine where a field is placed and how subtotals are created for each field (as shown in Figure 20-34). You can see in the figure that you can also change the placement of the field by clicking on the Orientation option buttons. You can also determine how subtotals are created for the field.

Finally, you can choose to hide any of the data items. Although this doesn't make sense for this example, if you were using date data, you could exclude a range of dates; in the case of a few product lines, you could exclude selected products.

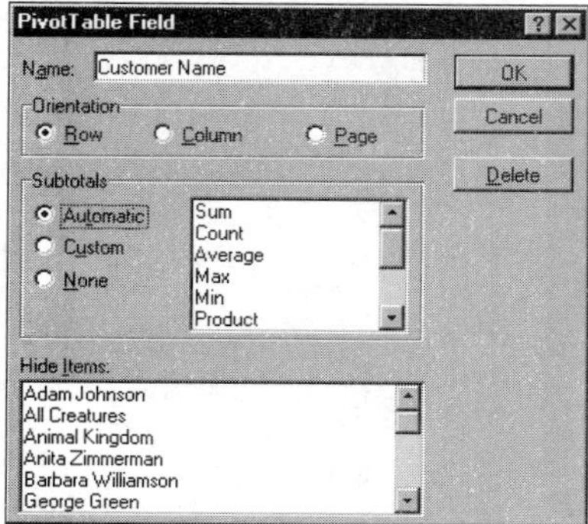

Figure 20-34: Selecting the field locations.

Once you complete this screen, you can complete the last Wizard screen as shown in Figure 20-35.

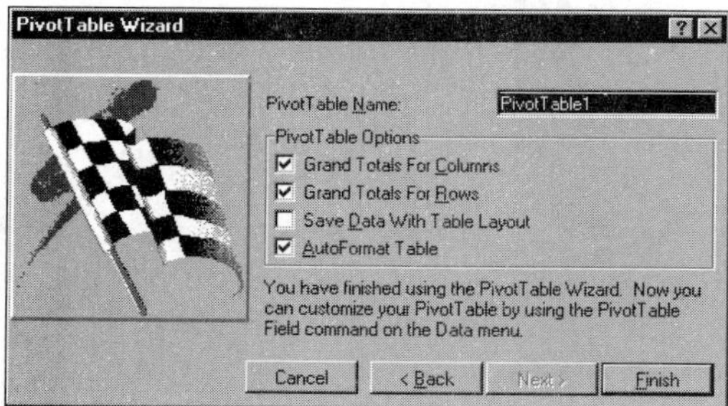

Figure 20-35: Using the final PivotTable Wizard screen.

The final Wizard screen lets you determine whether totals for columns and rows are displayed. You can also determine if the default AutoFormat is used when the pivot table is created. Once you select the Finish button, a new form is created; you can see your results as shown in Figure 20-36.

The pivot table in the figure shows menus and toolbars that are really those of Excel for Windows 95. You must have Excel to use this Wizard. Using the new OLE capabilities, the Excel PivotTable Wizard appears to be integrated with Access; it's really an embedded Excel object. The figure also shows the Excel Data menu open, displaying the various options (including one that changes the pivot table selections). The Query and Pivot toolbar appear in the lower portion of the screen. The page variable `Customer Name` appears as a combo box, initially set to All. This has been changed to show the customer name `All Creatures`. When this selection is made, the data below instantly changes to only show data for pets owned by All Creatures. Notice the row and column totals in the figure.

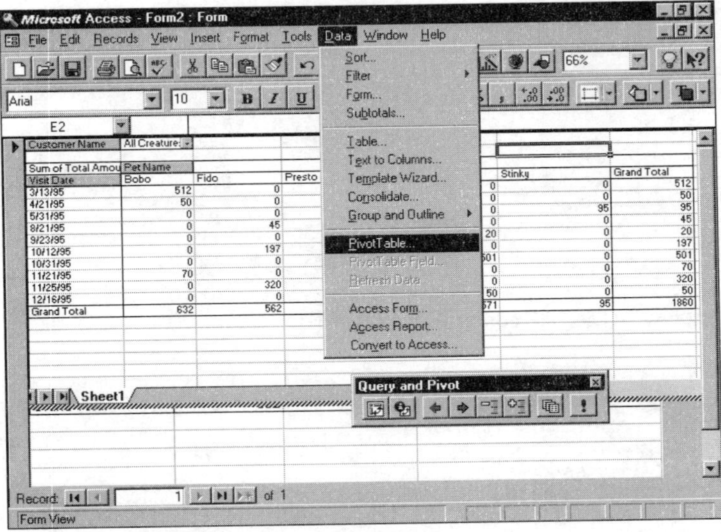

Figure 20-36: The completed pivot table.

Pivot tables are easy to create and provide a much better analysis than crosstabulation queries. When you save the form, the link to Excel remains.

New! Another feature in Excel for Windows 95 lets you create a new Access table directly from an Excel for Windows 95 spreadsheet — automatically — and link them so data changes are made with either product. This is not an Access feature, but an Excel feature you should know; it allows Excel users to update and manipulate Access data without knowing Access.

Using the Calendar OLE Custom Control

OLE Custom Controls (also known as OCXs) are not new to Access. OLE Custom Controls extend the number of controls already found in Access. Some of the more popular controls include a Calendar, Tab Dialog box, Progress Meters, Spin Box, Slider, and many others. Though they existed in Access 2.0 (as 16-bit controls), they were seldom used; they required separate sets of properties and were not totally stable. Access for Windows 95 introduces support for the new 32-bit controls. Figure 20-37 shows a list of the controls that ship with the Access Developer's Toolkit. Only the Calendar control comes with Access.

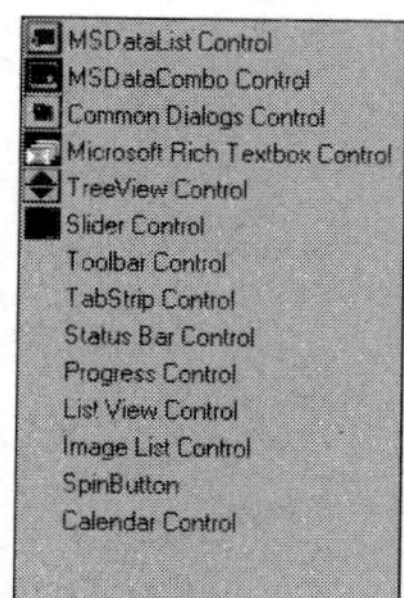

Figure 20-37: A sampling of the OLE custom controls.

The Access Developer's Toolkit is a separate product from Microsoft which allows you to create a runtime application without Access. It also includes the Help compiler, a printed-language reference manual, as well as the Windows Setup Wizard and the OLE controls listed in Figure 20-37.

By selecting Insert➪Custom Control, you can add a custom control to any form or report. If you don't have the Developers Toolkit, you probably will only see the Calendar Control.

You add a custom control as you would to any unbound OLE control. To add a Calendar custom control to a new blank form, follow the steps below:

1. Open a new form in Design view and display the toolbox. Don't select any table in the New Form dialog box.
2. Select Insert➪Custom Control from the menu.
3. Select Calendar Control and click on OK.

The Calendar control appears on the new form. The calendar can be resized like any unbound control, and (of course) it has properties. Figure 20-38 shows the Calendar Control and its properties.

Notice the property window. This window appears showing the properties specific to a Calendar control. These are the properties displayed by the Other tab. With these properties, you can change some of the display characteristics of the Calendar, including the following:

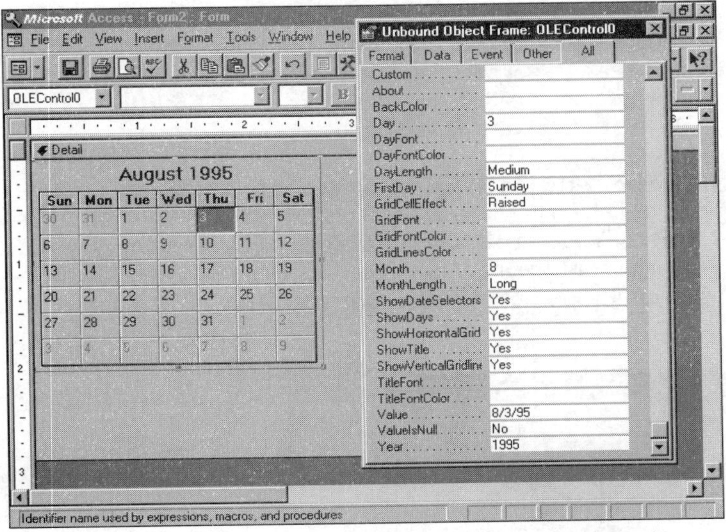

Figure 20-38: The Calendar's controls and its property window.

DayLength	Short(SMTWTFS), Medium (Sun, Mon, Tue, . . .), Long (Sunday, Monday, . . .)
FirstDay	First day of week displayed (default is Sunday)
GridCellEffect	Raised, Sunken, Flat
MonthLength	Long (January, February . . .), Short (Jan, Feb . . .)
ShowDateSelectors	Display a combo box for month and year in form view

Many other properties control various colors and fonts of calendar components. A number of value properties affect the display of the Calendar and the selected date. Four properties change the display of the Calendar data:

Day	The day of the current month (3 in this example)
Month	The month of the current date (8 in this example)
Year	The year being displayed (1995 in this example)
Value	The date displayed (8/3/95 in this example)

Cross Ref The values can be changed in several ways. You can click on a date in the Calendar in Form view, which changes the value property. When the Value property changes, so do the Day, Month, and Year properties. You can also change these properties in the property window, or programmatically from a macro or Visual Basic for Applications. You'll learn how to do this in Chapters 32 and 34.

Another way to change properties in a Custom Control is to display the Control Properties dialog box, as shown in Figure 20-39. This provides combo-box access to certain control properties. You can display this dialog box by selecting Edit⇨Calendar Control Object⇨Properties or by right-clicking on the Calendar control and selecting Calendar Control Object⇨Properties from the shortcut menu.

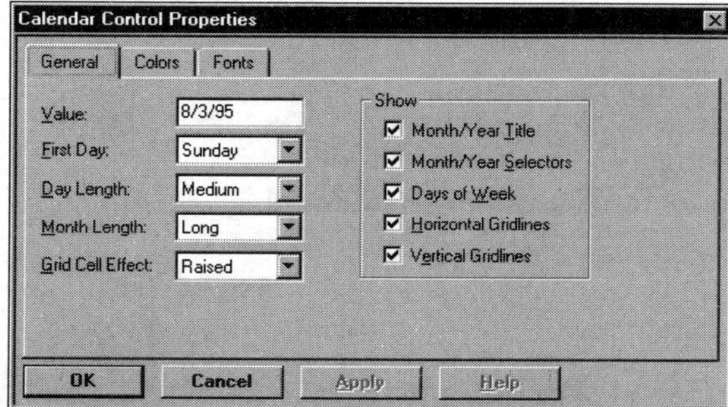

Figure 20-39: The Calendar Control Property dialog box.

When you display the Calendar in Form view, you can also display combo boxes (using the ShowDateSelectors property) to change the month or year, because you can only click on a day in the calendar. These are the Month/Year selectors in the Property dialog box.

The Calendar's real power is that you can link it to a field. When the Calendar is changed, the field value changes. Likewise, if the field value changes, the Calendar display changes. You can easily do this by linking the Calendar to a field by using its Control Source property.

Summary

In this chapter, you learned the differences between linking and embedding graphs and other OLE objects to your forms. You created a graph by using the Chart Wizard, and you used Microsoft Graph to customize the graph to fit your needs. Microsoft Access, because of its Windows compatibility, has the power to share data, pictures, and other objects with any other OLE-compatible products. You also learned that you can embed or link a full range of graphs to your forms with just a few keystrokes. In this chapter, the following points were explained:

- Access adds any type of picture or graphic object to an Access table, including sound and video, a worksheet, or a document.
- A bound object is attached to a specific record, whereas an unbound object is attached only to a form or report.
- Embedded objects are stored in a table, form, or report, but linked objects merely link to an external file.
- You can embed an object by either pasting it into an object frame or inserting the object.
- If the embedded object supports OLE, you can double-click on the object to launch the source application and edit the object.
- The easiest way to create graphs is to use the Chart Wizard in a form.
- Once you create a graph, you can customize the graph by using Microsoft Graph.
- To customize a graph, double-click on it; then you can change the graph type, text, axis labels, legend, gridlines, colors, patterns, and view of the graph.
- You can embed a graph in a form and link it to the data in the form by using the Chart button in the toolbox of the Form or Report Design window; then you follow the steps in the Wizard.
- You can use various Office for Windows 95 features, including spell-checking and AutoCorrect, when you're working with Access data.
- You can create an Excel pivot table to analyze your data by using the PivotTable Wizard.
- Custom Controls extend the functionality of Access forms and reports. The Calendar Custom Control that comes with Access lets you add calendar functions to Access.

In the next chapter, you learn how to create reports.

✦ ✦ ✦

Creating and Customizing Reports

✦ ✦ ✦ ✦

In This Chapter

Learning the eleven tasks necessary to create a great report

Learning how to create a report from a blank form

Learning how to sort and group data

Learning how to add label and text controls to your report

Learning how to modify the appearance of text and label controls

Learning how to add page breaks

Learning how to copy an existing report

✦ ✦ ✦ ✦

In previous chapters, you learned how to create a report from a single table by using a Wizard. You also learned how to create multiple-table queries and work with controls. In this chapter, you combine and build on these concepts. You learn how to create—from scratch—a report that lets you view data from multiple tables, group the data, and sort it in meaningful ways.

Starting with a Blank Form

Cross Ref In Chapter 11, you learned how to create a report by using an Access Report Wizard with a single table as the data source. Wizards are great for creating quick and simple reports, but they are fairly limited and give you little control over field type or placement. Although there are advantages to creating a report with a Wizard and then modifying the report, this chapter focuses on creating a report from a blank form without the help of the Wizards. If you haven't read Chapter 11, now is a good time to read or review it. Chapter 11 covers the basic report concepts that the present chapter assumes you already know. This chapter also assumes that you have read Chapter 16 and are familiar with the basic controls and properties used in forms and reports.

Previous chapters on forms exposed you to all the tools available in the Report Design window. When you create reports, you use some of these tools in a manner slightly different manner from that used to create forms. It is important to review some of the unique menus and toolbar buttons.

You can view a report in three different views: Design, Layout Preview, and Print Preview. You can also print a report to the hard-copy device defined for Windows 95. You've already seen the preview windows in previous chapters. This chapter will focus on the Report Design window.

The Report Design window is where you create and modify reports. The empty Report Design window, shown in Figure 21-1, contains various tools, including the toolbox.

The Design window toolbar

The Report Design View toolbar is shown in Figure 21-2. You can click on the desired button for quick access to such design tasks as displaying different windows, activating Wizards, and utilities. Table 21-1 summarizes what each item on the toolbar does. (The table defines each tool from left to right on the toolbar.)

Note The Report Design toolbar is distinct from the Format toolbar. To make such changes as Font selection and justification, you must first make sure the Format Form/Report Design toolbar is selected.

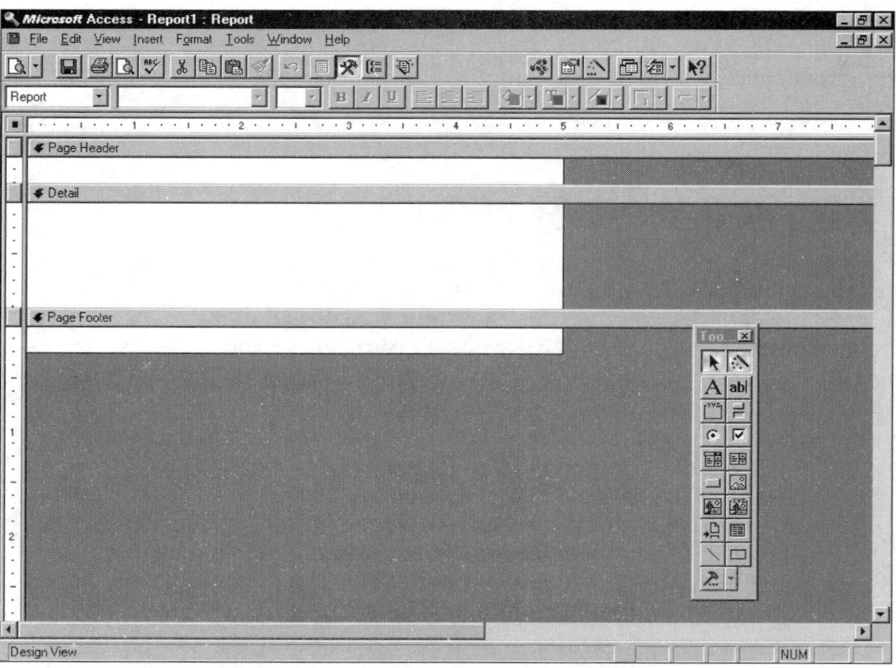

Figure 21-1: The Report Design window, showing the toolbox.

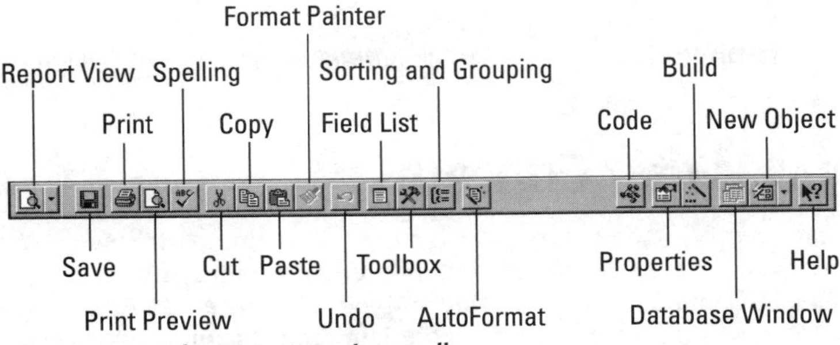

Figure 21-2: The Report Design toolbar.

Table 21-1
The Design View Toolbar

Toolbar Item	*Description*
Report View button	Drop-down box displays the three types of previews available
Save button	Saves the current report design
Print button	Prints form, table, query, or report
Print Preview button	Toggles to print preview mode
Spelling button	Spell-checks current selection or document
Cut button	Removes selection from the document and adds it to the Clipboard
Copy button	Copies the selection to the Clipboard
Paste button	Copies the Clipboard contents to the document
Format Painter button	Copies the style of one control to another
Undo button	Undoes the previous command
Field List button	Displays or hides the Field List window
Toolbox button	Displays or hides the toolbox
Sorting and Grouping button	Displays or hides the Sorting and Grouping box
AutoFormat button	Applies predefined format to form or report
Code button	Displays or hides the module window
Properties button	Displays the properties sheet for the selected item
Build button	Displays Builder or Wizard for selected control or item
Database Window	Displays the Database window
New Object	Creates a new object
Help button	Displays Access Help

The tools in the Report Design screen are virtually identical to the Form Design tools.

Banded Report Writer Concepts

In a report, your data is processed one record at a time. Depending on how you create your report design, each data item is processed differently. Reports are divided into sections, known as *bands* in most report writing software packages. (In Access, these are simply called *sections*.) Access processes each data record from a table or dynaset, processing each section in order and deciding (for each record) whether or not to process fields or text in each section. For example, the report footer section is processed only after the last record is processed in the dynaset.

A report is made up of groups of *details* — for example, all animals Johnathan Adams brought in on a certain day and how much Mr. Adams paid. Each group must have an identifying *group header,* which in this case is customer `Johnathan Adams`. Each group has a footer that calculates the total amount for each customer. For Johnathan Adams, this amount is `$375`. The *page header* contains column descriptions; the *report header* contains the report title. Finally, the *report footer* contains grand totals for the report, and the *page footer* prints the page number.

The Access sections are as follows:

Report header	Prints only at the beginning of the report; used for title page
Page header	Prints at the top of each page
Group header	Prints before the first record of a group is processed
Detail	Prints each record in the table or dynaset
Group footer	Prints after the last record of a group is processed
Page footer	Prints at the bottom of each page
Report footer	Prints only at the end of a report after all records are processed

Figure 21-3 shows these sections superimposed on a report.

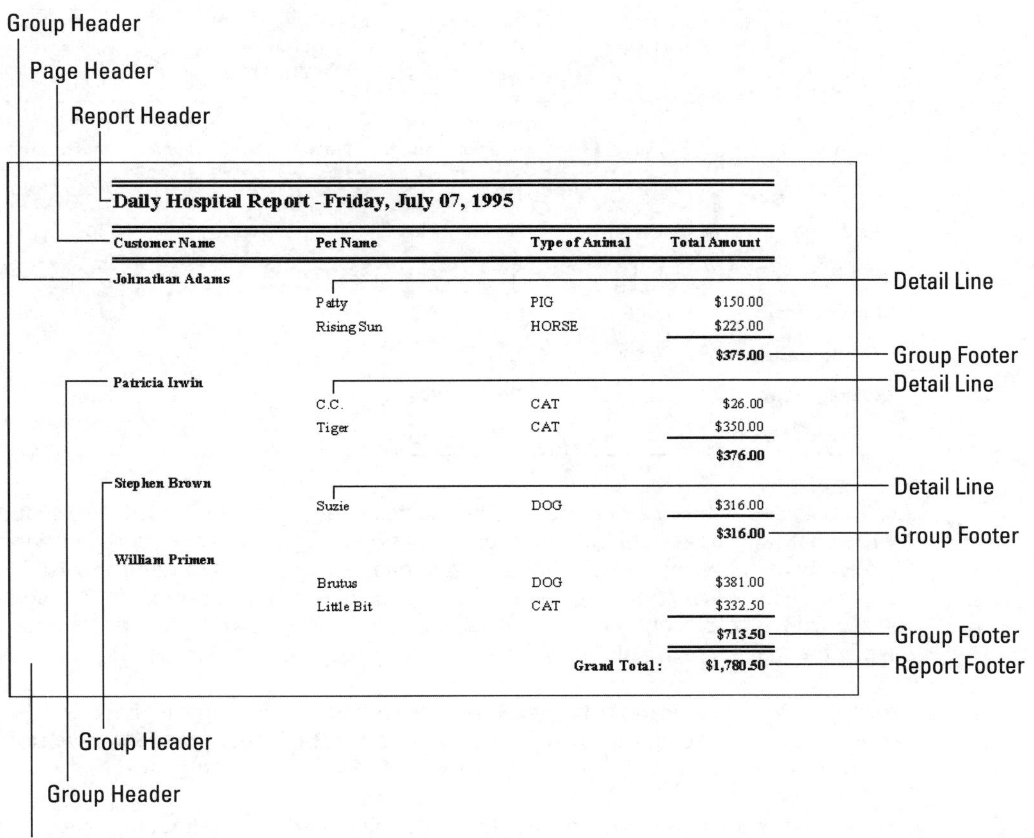

Figure 21-3: Typical Report Writer sections.

How sections process data

Most sections are triggered by the values of the data. Table 21-2 shows the five records that make up the dynaset for the Daily Hospital Report (a Yes indicates that a section is triggered by the data).

Table 21-2
Processing Report Sections

Customer Name	*Pet Name*	*Report Header*	*Page Header*	*Group Header*	*Detail*	*Group Footer*	*Page Footer*	*Report Footer*
Johnathan Adams	Rising Sun	Yes	Yes	Yes	Yes	No	No	No
Johnathan Adams	Patty	No	No	No	Yes	Yes	No	No
Patricia Irwin	C. C.	No	No	Yes	Yes	No	No	No
Patricia Irwin	Tiger	No	No	No	Yes	Yes	No	No
Stephen Brown	Suzie	No	No	Yes	Yes	Yes	No	No
William Primen	Brutus	No	No	No	Yes	No	No	No
William Primen	Little Bit	No	No	Yes	Yes	Yes	Yes	

As you can see, Table 21-2 contains five records. Four groups of records are grouped by the customer name. Johnathan Adams has two records, as does Patricia Irwin; Stephen Brown has one, and William Primen has two records. For each record in the table, there are corresponding columns for each section in the report. A Yes means the record triggers processing in that section; a No means the section is not processed for that record. This report has only one page, so it is very simple.

The report header section is triggered by only the first record in the dynaset. This section is always processed first, regardless of the data. The report footer section is triggered only after the last record is processed, regardless of the data.

For the first record only, Access processes the page header section after the report header section, and then every time a new page of information is started. The page footer section is processed at the bottom of each page and after the report footer section.

Group headers are triggered only by the first record of a group. Group footers are triggered only by the last record in a group. Notice that the Stephen Brown record triggers both a group header and a group footer because it is the only record in a group. If three or more records are in a group, only the first or the last record can trigger a group header or footer; the middle records trigger only the detail section.

Access always processes each record in the detail section (which is always triggered, regardless of the value of the data). Most reports with a great amount of data have many detail records and significantly fewer group header or footer records. In this small report, there are as many group header and footer records as there are detail records.

The Report Writer sections

To get an idea of what a report design looks like in Access, look at Figure 21-4, the Report Design window that produced the Daily Hospital Report. As you can see, the report is divided into sections. One group section displays data grouped by Customer Name, so you see the sections Customer Name Header and Customer Name Footer. Each of the other sections is also named for the type of processing it performs.

You can place any type of text or field controls in any section, but Access processes the data one record at a time. It also takes certain actions (based on the values of the group fields, the location of the page, or placement in the report) to make the bands or sections active. The example in Figure 21-4 is typical of a report with multiple sections. As you've learned, each section in the report has a different purpose and different triggers.

Note Page and report headers and footers must be added as pairs. To establish one without the other, simply resize the section you don't want to a height of zero; then set its Visible property to No.

Warning If you remove a header or footer section, you will lose the controls in those sections as well.

Report header section

Anything in the report header is printed once only at the beginning of the report. In the report header section is a text control that places the words `Daily Hospital Report` in a large font size at the top of the report. Only the first page of the report has this text. You can also see the field control `Visit Date`; it places the value of the visit date from the first record in the report header. In Figure 21-3, you saw that this date is `Friday, July 07, 1995`. This was the value of the Visit Date field for the first record in the dynaset. It has been formatted using the long date format.

The report header section also has a double line placed before the text and field controls. You can place lines, boxes, shading, color, and special effects in any band. (You'll learn more about formatting and special effects in later chapters.)

You can also have anything in the report header section on a separate page. This way, you can create an entire page and include a graphic or picture in the section. A common use of a report header section is as a cover page — or even as a cover letter. Because the header appears only once and doesn't necessarily have to contain any data, a separate page with the report header is a perfect place for a cover page or letter.

Note Only data from the first record can be placed in a report header.

Page header section

Text or field controls in the *page header section* normally print at the top of every page. If there is a report header on the first page that is not on a page of its own, the information in the page header section prints just below the report header information. Typically, page headers serve as column headers in group/total reports; they can also contain a title for the report. In this example, placing the Daily Hospital Report title in the report header section means the title appears only on the first page. You can move it into the page header section if you want it to appear on every page.

The page header section you see in Figure 21-4 also has double lines above and below the text controls. Each of the text controls is separate; each can be moved or sized individually. You can also control special effects (such as color, shading, borders, line thickness, font type, and font size) for each text control.

Note Both the page header and page footer can be set for one of four settings; All Pages, Not with Report Header, Not with Report Footer, Not with Report Header/Footer. This setting can be found in the report's properties.

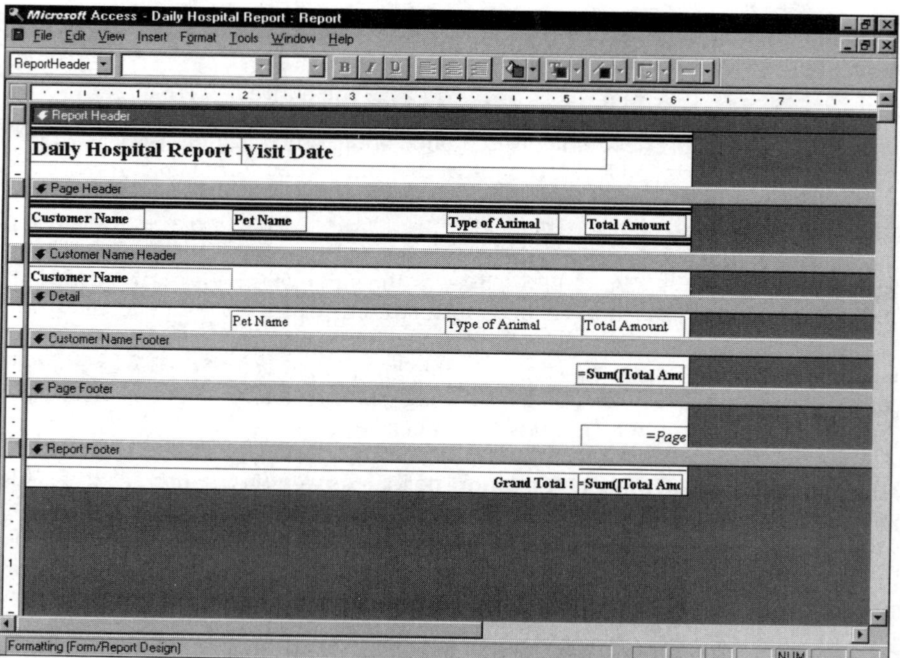

Figure 21-4: The Report Design window.

All Pages	Both the page header and page footer print on every page.
Not with Report Header	Neither the page header or footer print on a page with the report header.
Not with Report Footer	The page header does not print with the report footer. The report footer prints on a new page.
Not with Report Header/Footer	Neither the page header nor the footer prints on a page with either the report header or footer.

Group header

Group headers normally identify a specific value so you know that all the records displayed in a detail section belong to that group. In this example, the detail records are about animals and the cost of their treatments. The group header field control Customer Name tells you these animals are owned by the customer who appears in the group header band. Group header sections immediately precede detail sections.

You may have multiple levels of group headers and footers. In this report, for example, the data is only for July 07, 1995. The detail data is grouped by the field, Customer Name. If you want to see one report for the entire month of July 1995, you can change the query and add a second group section. In this second group section, you can group the data by date — then, within each date, by customer. You can have many levels of groupings, but you should limit the number to between three and six; reports with too many levels become impossible to read. You don't want to defeat the purpose of the report, which is to show information clearly in a summarized format.

Note In order to set group level properties such as Group On, Group Interval, Keep Together, or something other than the default, you must first set the Group Header and Group Footer property (or both of them) to Yes for the selected field or expression.

Detail section

The *detail section* processes *every* record; this is where each value is printed. The detail section frequently contains calculated fields, such as a price extension that multiplies a quantity times a price. In this example, the detail section simply displays the Pet Name, Type of Animal, and Total Amount (which is the cost of the treatments). Each record in the detail section *belongs* to the value in the group header Customer Name.

Tip You can tell Access whether you want to display a section in the report by changing the section's Visible property in the Report Design window. By turning off the display of the detail section (or by excluding selected group sections) you can display a summary report with no detail or with only certain groups displayed.

Group footer

Use the *group footer* to summarize the detail records for that group. In the Daily Hospital Report, the expression `=Sum(Total Amount)` adds the Total Amount fields for a specific customer. In the group for customer Johnathan Adams, this value sums the two Total Amount records ($225.00 and $150.00) and produces the value `$375.00`. This type of field is reset automatically to 0 each time the group changes. (You learn more about expressions and summary fields in later chapters.)

Tip: You can change the way summaries are calculated by changing the Running Sum property of the field box in the Report Design window.

Page footer

The *page footer section* usually contains page numbers or control totals. In very large reports, you may want page totals as well as group totals (as when you have multiple pages of detail records with no summaries). For the Daily Hospital Report, you print the page number by combining the text control `Page:` with the expression `Page:` (which keeps track of the page number in the report).

Report footer

The *report footer section* is printed once at the end of the report after all the detail records and group footer sections are printed. Typically report footers display grand totals or other statistics (such as averages or percentages) for the entire report. The report footer for the Daily Hospital Report uses the expression `=Sum(Total Amount)` to add the Total Amount fields for all treatments. This expression, when used in the report footer, is not reset to 0, as it is in the group footer. The expression is used only for a grand total.

When there is a report footer, the page footer band is printed after the report footer.

The Report Writer in Access is a *two-pass report writer*, capable of preprocessing all records to calculate the totals (such as percentages) needed for statistical reporting. This capability lets you create expressions that calculate percentages as Access processes those records that require foreknowledge of the grand total.

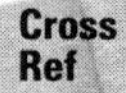

Cross Ref: Chapter 23 covers calculating percentages.

Creating a New Report

Fundamental to all reports is the concept that a report is another way to view the records of one or more tables. It is important to understand that a report is bound either to a single table, or to a query that accesses one or more tables. When you create a report, you must select which fields from a query or table to place in your report. Unless you want to view all the records from a single table in it, you will probably want to bind your report to a query. If you are accessing data from a single table, using a query lets you create your report on the basis of a particular search criterion and sorting order. If you want to access data from multiple tables, you have no choice but to bind your report to a query. In the examples in this chapter, you'll see all the reports bound to a query (even though it is possible to bind a report to a table).

Note

Access lets you create a report without first binding it to a table or object, but you will have no fields on the report. This capability can be used to work out *page templates*, which can serve as models for other reports. You can later add fields by changing the underlying control source of the report.

Throughout this chapter and the next chapter, you learn the tasks needed to create the Mountain Animal Hospital Pets and Owners Directory, of which the first hard-copy page appears in Figure 21-5. In this chapter, you will design the basic report, assemble the data, and place the data in the proper positions. In Chapter 22, you will enhance the report by adding lines, boxes, and shading so that certain areas stand out. You will also add enhanced controls (such as option buttons and check boxes) to make the data more readable.

As with almost every task in Access, there are many ways to create a report without Wizards. It is important, however, to follow some type of methodology; creating a good report involves a fairly scientific approach. You can follow a set of tasks that will result in a good report every time, and then arrange these tasks to create a checklist. As you complete each of the tasks, you can check it off your list. When you are done, you will have a great-looking report. The following section outlines this approach.

Eleven tasks to creating a great report

To create a good report, perform these eleven tasks:

1. Design your report.
2. Assemble the data.
3. Create a new report and bind it to a query.
4. Define your page layout properties.
5. Place the fields on the report, using text controls.
6. Add other label and text controls as necessary.
7. Modify the appearance, size, and location of text, text controls and label controls.
8. Define your sorting and grouping options.
9. Save your report.
10. Enhance your report by using graphics and other control types.
11. Print your report.

Cross Ref

This chapter covers tasks 1 through 9. Chapter 22 discusses using other controls, such as group boxes, option buttons, and Memo fields, as well as methods to enhance your report visually.

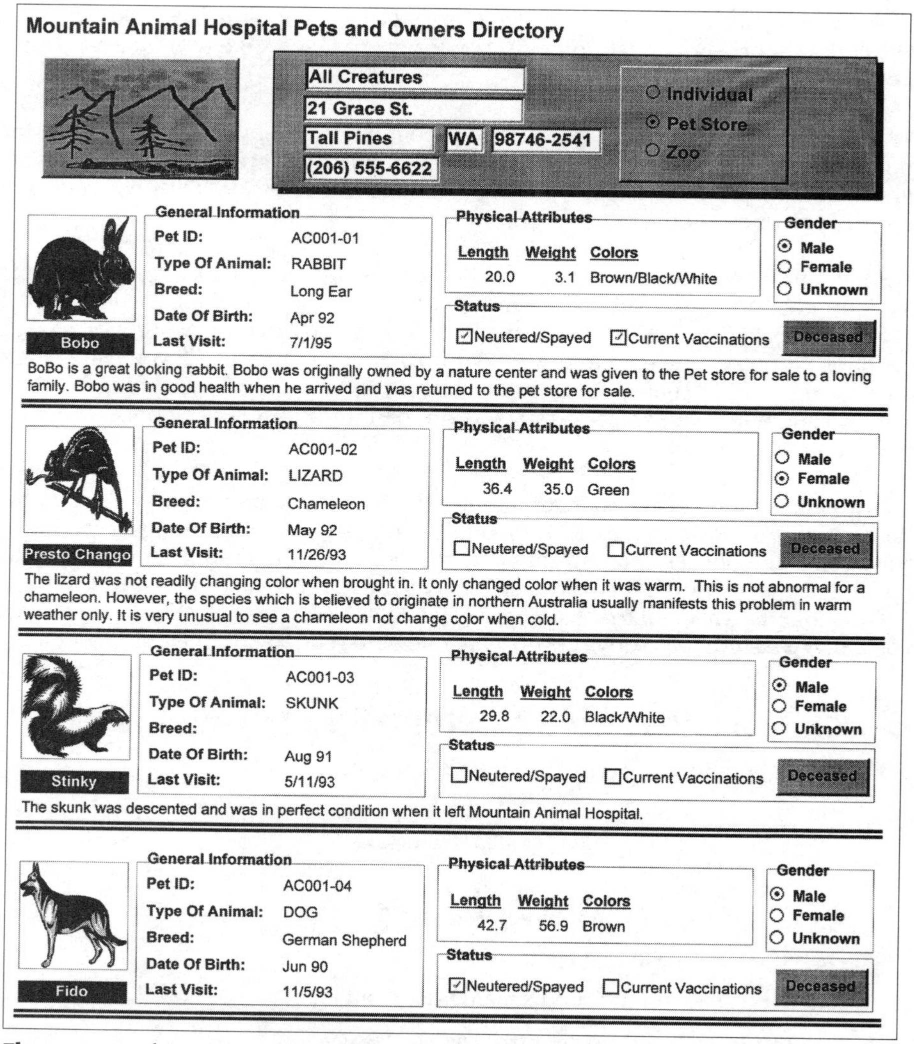

Mountain Animal Hospital Pets and Owners Directory

All Creatures
21 Grace St.
Tall Pines WA 98746-2541
(206) 555-6622

○ Individual
⦿ Pet Store
○ Zoo

Bobo

General Information
Pet ID: AC001-01
Type Of Animal: RABBIT
Breed: Long Ear
Date Of Birth: Apr 92
Last Visit: 7/1/95

Physical Attributes
Length 20.0 Weight 3.1 Colors Brown/Black/White

Gender: ⦿ Male ○ Female ○ Unknown

Status: ☑ Neutered/Spayed ☑ Current Vaccinations Deceased

BoBo is a great looking rabbit. Bobo was originally owned by a nature center and was given to the Pet store for sale to a loving family. Bobo was in good health when he arrived and was returned to the pet store for sale.

Presto Chango

General Information
Pet ID: AC001-02
Type Of Animal: LIZARD
Breed: Chameleon
Date Of Birth: May 92
Last Visit: 11/26/93

Physical Attributes
Length 36.4 Weight 35.0 Colors Green

Gender: ○ Male ⦿ Female ○ Unknown

Status: ☐ Neutered/Spayed ☐ Current Vaccinations Deceased

The lizard was not readily changing color when brought in. It only changed color when it was warm. This is not abnormal for a chameleon. However, the species which is believed to originate in northern Australia usually manifests this problem in warm weather only. It is very unusual to see a chameleon not change color when cold.

Stinky

General Information
Pet ID: AC001-03
Type Of Animal: SKUNK
Breed:
Date Of Birth: Aug 91
Last Visit: 5/11/93

Physical Attributes
Length 29.8 Weight 22.0 Colors Black/White

Gender: ⦿ Male ○ Female ○ Unknown

Status: ☐ Neutered/Spayed ☐ Current Vaccinations Deceased

The skunk was descented and was in perfect condition when it left Mountain Animal Hospital.

Fido

General Information
Pet ID: AC001-04
Type Of Animal: DOG
Breed: German Shepherd
Date Of Birth: Jun 90
Last Visit: 11/5/93

Physical Attributes
Length 42.7 Weight 56.9 Colors Brown

Gender: ⦿ Male ○ Female ○ Unknown

Status: ☑ Neutered/Spayed ☐ Current Vaccinations Deceased

Figure 21-5: The Mountain Animal Hospital Pets and Owners Directory — first page.

Designing the report

The first step in this process is to design the report. By the nature of the report name — Mountain Animal Hospital Pets and Owners Directory — you know you want to create a report that contains detailed information about both the customer and the customer's pets. You want to create a report that lists important customer information at the top of a page, and then lists detailed information about each pet a customer owns, including a picture. You want no more than one customer on a page. If a customer has more than one pet, you want to see as many as possible on the same page. If a customer has more pets than will fit on one page, you want to duplicate the customer details at the top of each page. (The grouping section of this chapter discusses this task.)

Figure 21-6 shows a design of this data. This is not the complete design for the report that you saw in Figure 21-5, but a plan of only the major data items, roughly placed where they will appear in this report. You can sketch this design by hand on a piece of paper, or use any good word processor or drawing tool (such as Micrografx Draw or Word for Windows Draw) to lay out the basic design. Because Access has a WYSIWYG report writer, you can also use that to lay out your report. (Personally, I like the pencil-and-paper approach to good design.)

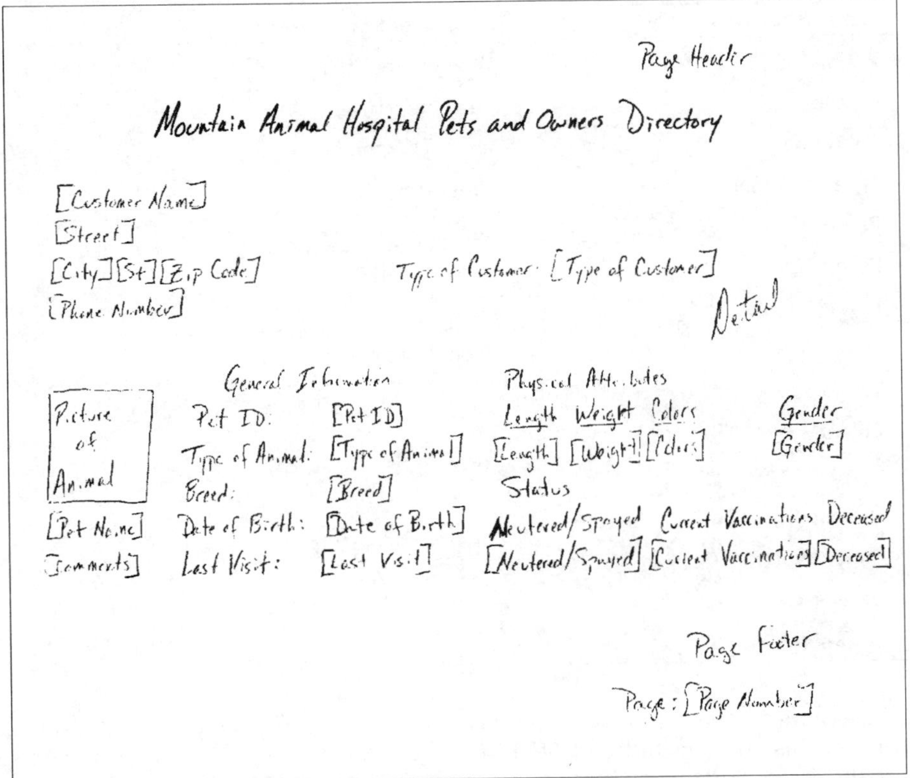

Figure 21-6: The data design for the Mountain Animal Hospital Pets and Owners Directory.

The data design is created only to lay out the basic data elements with no special formatting. Although this design may seem rudimentary, it is nevertheless a good starting point. This layout represents the report you will create in this chapter.

Assembling the data

With this design in mind, you now need to assemble the data. To create this report, you will need fields from two tables, Customer and Pets. Table 21-3 lists the necessary fields and identifies the tables that contain them.

Table 21-3
Tables and Fields Needed for the Pets and Owners Directory

Fields from Pets Table	*Fields from Customer Table*
Pet ID	Customer Number
Picture	Customer Name
Pet Name	Type of Customer
Type of Animal	Street/Apt
Breed	City
Date of Birth	State
Last Visit Date	ZIP Code
Length	Phone Number
Weight	
Colors	
Gender	
Neutered/Spayed	
Current Vaccinations	
Deceased	
Comments	

To assemble this data, first you need to create a query, which you can call Pets and Owners. This query includes *all* fields from both tables, but you aren't going to use all of them. Some of the fields that don't appear on the report itself are used to derive other fields. Some fields are used merely to sort the data, although the fields themselves are not displayed on the report. In this example, you also create a sort by Pet ID. It is always a good idea to arrange your data into some known order. When reports are run, the data is used in its *physical* order unless you sort the data.

To create the Pets and Owners query, follow Figure 21-7.

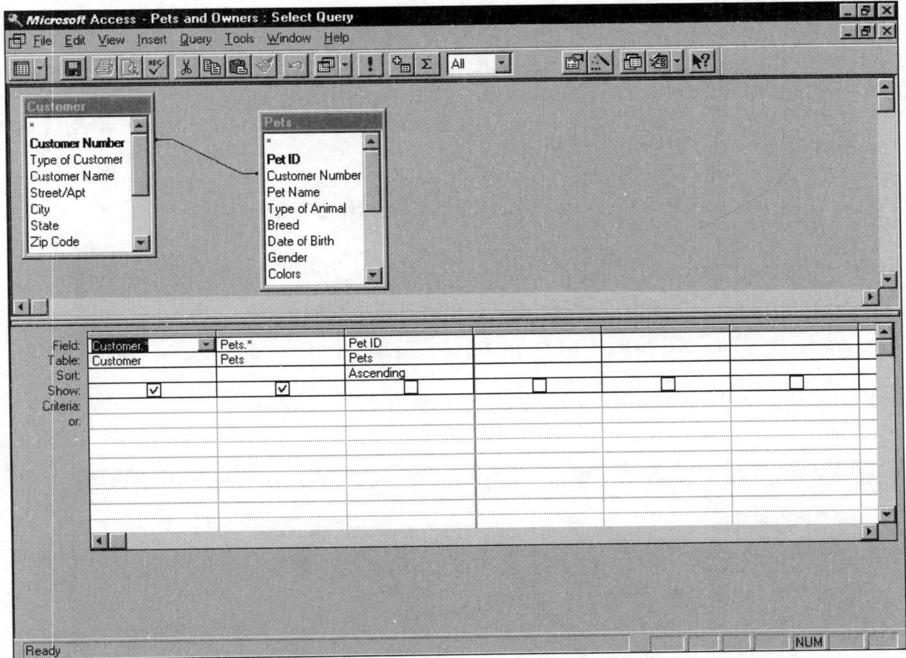

Figure 21-7: The Pets and Owners query.

Note

You use the asterisk (*) to select all fields from each table.

Creating a new report and binding it to a query

Now that you have created the Pets and Owners query, you need to create a new report and bind it to the query. Follow these steps to complete this process:

1. Press F11 to display the Database window if it is not already displayed.
2. Click on the Reports tab.
3. Click on the New command button. The New Report dialog box appears.
4. Select Design View.
5. Click on the combo box labeled `Choose a table or query`. A drop-down list of all tables and queries in the current database appears.
6. Select the Pets and Owners query.

7. Click on OK.

8. Maximize the Report window.

A blank Report Design window appears (see Figure 21-8). Notice the three sections in the screen display: Page Header, Detail, and Page Footer. The report is bound to the query Pets and Owners. This means the data from that query will be used when the report is viewed or printed. The fields from the query are available for use in the report design and will appear in the Field List window.

Note

You can also create a new report by using any of these methods:

- ✦ Clicking on the New Object toolbar button and then selecting New Report
- ✦ Copying, pasting and renaming an existing report
- ✦ Starting a New Report and then selecting one of the AutoReport options

Note

Note that there are two options for the AutoReport: Columnar and Tabular.

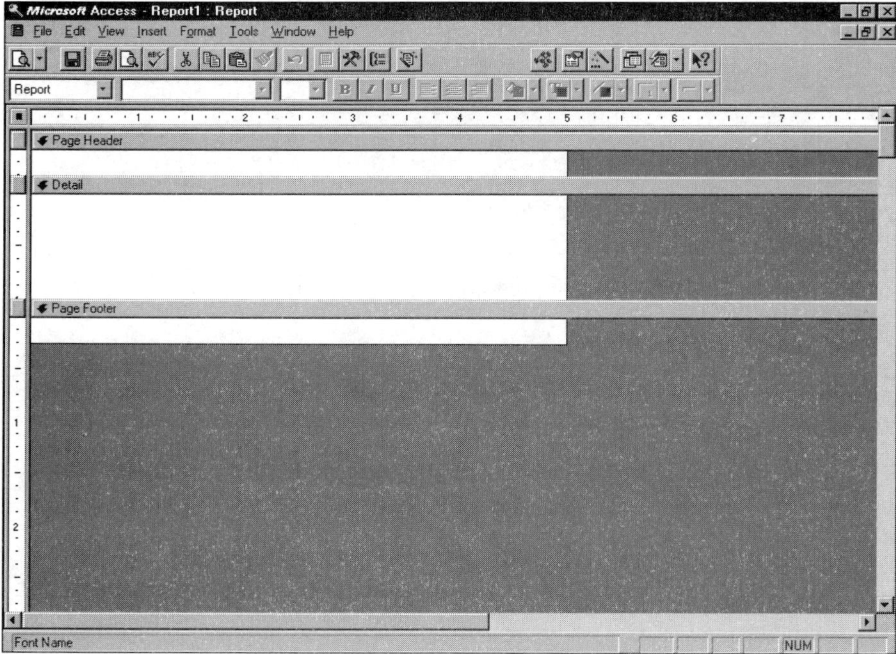

Figure 21-8: A blank Report Design window.

Defining the report page size and layout

As you are planning your report, consider the page layout characteristics as well as the kind of paper and printer you want to use for the output. If you are going to use an Epson dot-matrix printer with a wide-carriage feed, you'll want to design your report with an approach that differs from the one you would use for printing on a Hewlett-Packard LaserJet with 8½-by-11-inch paper. After you make these decisions, you can use several dialog boxes and properties to make adjustments; these work together to create the output you want. You learn how to use these tools in the next several chapters.

Cross Ref First, you need to select the correct printer and page-layout characteristics by selecting File⇨Page Setup. The Page Setup dialog box, shown in Figure 21-9, lets you select your printer and set printer options. Chapter 22 discusses Page Setup options in detail.

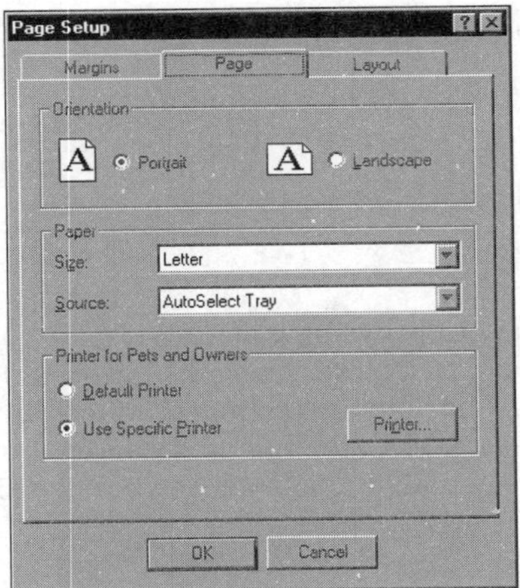

Figure 21-9: The Page Setup dialog box showing the Page tab.

This dialog box is a tab in the Page Setup dialog box. Layout tabs and page margins are also available under the Page Setup dialog box.

The Page dialog box is divided into three sections:

Orientation	Selects the page orientation you want
Paper	Selects the paper size and paper source you want
Printer	Selects the printer you want

Note

Select the Printer button; the Page Setup dialog box for the selected printer appears. Pressing Properties will then bring up a more extensive dialog box with all the applicable options.

For the Pets and Owners report, you'll create a *portrait* report, which is taller than it is wide. The paper you'll use is 8½ × 11 inches; the left, right, top, and bottom margins are all set to 0.250.

Follow these steps to create the proper report setup for the Pets and Owners report:

1. Open the Page Setup dialog box and select the Page tab.
2. Click on the Portrait option button.

   Next to the Orientation buttons are two sheet-of-paper icons with the letter A pictured on them. The picture of the sheet is an indication of its setting.
3. Click on the tab named Margins.
4. Click on the Top margin setting and change the setting to **.250**.
5. Click on the Bottom margin setting and change the setting to **.250**.
6. Click on the Left margin setting and change the setting to **.250**.
7. Click on the Right margin setting and change the setting to **.250**.
8. Click on OK to close the Page Setup dialog box.

Tip

Access displays your reports in the Print Preview view by using the driver of the currently active printer. If you don't have a good quality laser available for printing, install the driver for a PostScript printer so you'll be able to view any graphics you create (and see the report in a high-resolution display). Later you can print to your dot-matrix or other available printer and get the actual hard copy in the best resolution your printer offers.

Warning

In Figure 21-9, you can see the option buttons in the bottom left corner of the Page tab. If you are going to give your database or report to others, you should always select the first option, Default Printer. This way, if you have selected a printer the recipients don't have, the report will use their default printer. If you have selected the second option (Use Specific Printer) and those who run the report don't have that printer, they will get an error message and will not be able to use the report.

After you define your page layout in the Page Setup dialog box, you need to define the size of your report (which is not necessarily the same as the page definition, as you might expect).

To define the report size, place the cursor on the rightmost edge of the report (where the white page meets the gray background). The cursor changes to a two-headed arrow. Drag the cursor to change the width of the report. As you drag the edge, a vertical line appears in the ruler to let you know the exact width if you release the mouse at that point. Be careful not to exceed the width of the page that you defined in the Print Setup dialog box.

When you position the cursor at the bottom of the report, it looks similar to the one for determining width. This cursor determines the height, not of the page length, but of the page footer section or other specified bottom section. (Predefining a page length directly in the report section doesn't really make sense because the detail section will vary in length, based on your groupings.) Keep in mind that the Report Design view is only a representation of the various report sections, not the actual report.

To set the right border for the Pets and Owners report to eight inches, follow these steps:

1. Click on the rightmost edge of the report body (where the white page representation meets the gray background). The cursor changes to a two-headed arrow.
2. Drag the edge to the 8-inch mark.
3. Release the mouse button.

Note

You can also select the Width property in the report's property sheet.

Because the Report Design screen is set to a width of eight inches, you see most of the screen printouts in this chapter taken with a Super VGA Windows screen driver (resolution: 800 × 600) rather than with the standard VGA Windows driver (640 × 480). This higher resolution lets you see almost the entire screen in the screen figures.

Placing fields on the report

As you've seen, Access takes full advantage of the drag-and-drop capabilities of the Windows environment. The method for placing fields on a report is no exception. When you place a field on a report, it is no longer called a field; it is called a *control.* A control has a *control source* (a specific field) that it is bound to, so the terms *control* and *field* are used interchangeably in this chapter.

The process of placing controls on your report consists of three basic tasks:

- ✦ Displaying the Field List window by clicking on the Field List toolbar button
- ✦ Clicking on the desired toolbox control to determine the type of control that will be created
- ✦ Selecting each of the fields you want on your report, and then dragging them to the Report Design window

Displaying the field list

To display the Field List window, click on the Field List button on the toolbar. A small window with a list of all the fields from the underlying query appears. This window is called a *modeless* dialog box because it remains on-screen even while you continue with other work in Access. The Field List window can be resized and moved around the screen. This enlarged window is illustrated in Figure 21-10, showing all the fields in the Pets and Owners query dynaset.

Notice that in Figure 21-10 the fields Customer.Customer Number and Pets.Customer Number, as well as Customer.Last Visit Date and Pets.Last Visit Date, use the table name as a prefix. This setup is necessary to distinguish fields of the same name that come from different tables used in the query.

Tip: You can move the Field List window simply by clicking on the title bar and dragging it to a new location.

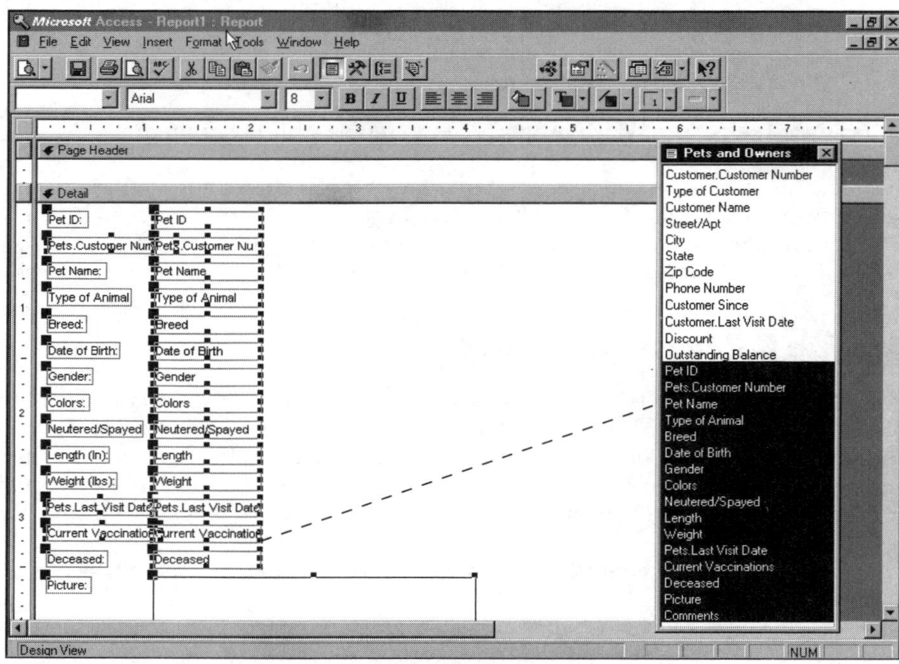

Figure 21-10: Dragging fields to the Design window.

Selecting the fields for your report

Selecting a field in the Report field list is the same as selecting a field in the Query field list. The easiest way to select a field is simply to click on it. As you click on a field, it becomes highlighted. After a field is highlighted, you can drag it to the Report window.

You can highlight *contiguous* (adjacent) fields in the list by following these steps:

1. Click on the first field you want in the field list.
2. Move the cursor to the last field that you want from the list.
3. Hold down the Shift key and click on the last field you want.

The block of fields between the first and last field you selected is displayed in reverse video as it is selected. You can then drag the block of fields to the Report window.

You can highlight noncontiguous fields in the list by clicking on each field while holding down the Ctrl key. Each field will be displayed in reverse video; then you can drag the fields as a group to the Report Design window.

Note: Unlike the Query field list, you *cannot* also double-click on a field to add it to the Report window.

You can begin by selecting the Pets table fields for the detail section. To select the fields needed for the detail section of the Pets and Owners Report, follow these steps:

1. Click on the Pet ID field.
2. Scroll down the field list until the Comments field is visible.
3. Hold down the Shift key and click on the Comments field.

The block of fields from Pet ID to Comments should be highlighted in the Field List window, as shown in Figure 21-10.

Dragging fields onto your report

After you select the proper fields from the Pets table, all you need to do is drag them onto the detail section of your report. Depending on whether you choose one or several fields, the cursor changes to represent your selection. If you select one field, you see a Field icon, which shows a single box with some unreadable text inside. If you select multiple fields, you see a set of three boxes. These are the same icons you saw in the query design screens.

To drag the selected Pet table fields into the detail section of the Report Design window, follow these steps:

1. Click within the highlighted block of fields in the Field List window. You may need to move the horizontal elevator bar back to the left before starting this process.
2. Without releasing the mouse button, drag the cursor into the detail section; place the icon under the 1½-inch mark on the horizontal ruler at the top of the screen and next to the 0-inch mark of the vertical ruler along the left edge of the screen.
3. Release the mouse button.

The fields appear in the detail section of the report, as shown in Figure 21-10. Notice that for each field you dragged onto the report, there are two controls. When you use the drag-and-drop method for placing fields, Access automatically creates a label control (attached to the text control the field is bound to) that uses the name of the field.

Note Notice the OLE (Object Linking and Embedding) control for the field named `Picture`. Access always creates an OLE control for a picture or an OLE-type object. Also notice that the detail section automatically resizes itself to fit all the controls. Below the OLE control is the control for the Memo field Comments.

You also need to place the desired field controls on the report for the customer information you need in the page header section. Before you do this, however, you need to resize the page header frame to leave room for a title you will later add.

Resizing a section

To make room on the report for both the title and the Customer table fields in the page header, you must resize it. You can resize a section by placing the cursor at the bottom of the section you want to resize. The cursor turns into a vertical double-headed arrow; drag the section border up or down to make the section smaller or larger.

To make the page header section larger, resize it by following these steps:

1. Move the cursor between the bottom of the page header section and the top of the detail section.
2. When the cursor is displayed as a double-sided arrow, hold the left mouse button down.
3. Drag the page header section border down until it intersects the detail section's ruler at ½ inch.
4. Release the button to enlarge the page header section.

You can now place the Customer table fields in the page header section by following these steps:

1. Click on the Customer.Customer Number field.
2. Scroll down the field list until the Phone Number field is visible.
3. Hold down the Shift key and click on the Phone Number field.
4. Click within the highlighted block of fields in the Field List window.
5. Without releasing the mouse button, drag the cursor into the page header section; place the icon under the 1½-inch mark on the horizontal ruler at the top of the screen and next to the ⅝-inch mark of the vertical ruler along the left edge of the screen.
6. Release the mouse button; the fields now appear in the page header section of the report, as shown in Figure 21-11.
7. Close the Field List window by clicking on the Field List toolbar button.

Notice that the page header section also expanded to fit the fields that were dragged into the section. At this point, your report should look like Figure 21-11. You have now placed all the fields you need for the Pets and Owners report.

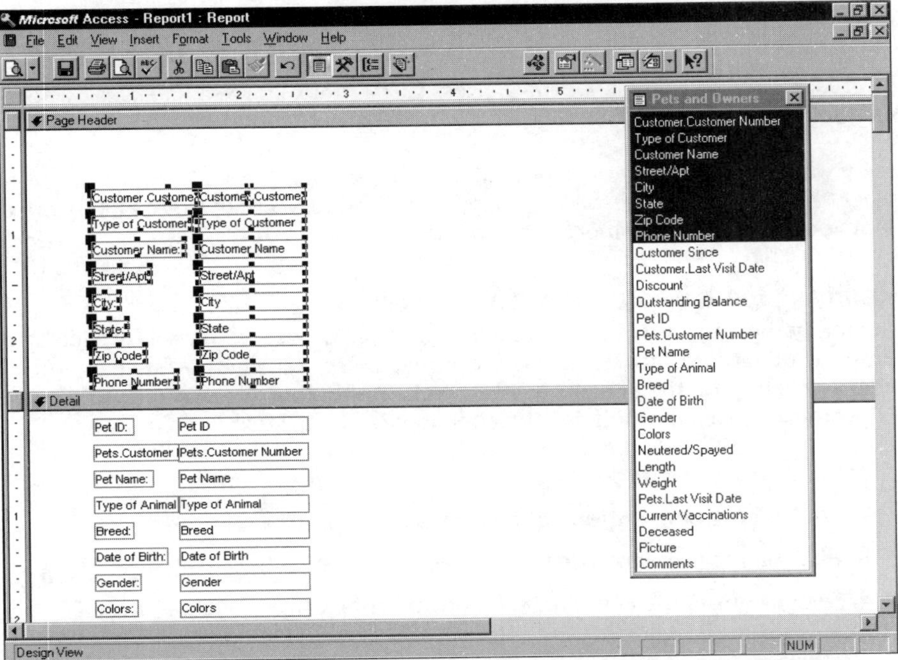

Figure 21-11: The Report Design window for Pets and Owners, with all fields shown.

Working with label controls and text

As you've learned, when you drag a field from the Field List window to a report while the Text Box button is selected in the toolbox, Access creates not only a text box control, but also a label control that is attached to the text box control. There are times you will want to add text label controls by themselves to create headings or titles for the report.

Creating unattached labels

To create a new, unattached label control, you must use the toolbox (unless you copy an existing label). The next task in the present example is to add the text header *Mountain Animal Hospital Pets and Owners Directory* to your report. You will do this task in segments to demonstrate adding and editing text. To begin by creating an unattached label control, follow these steps:

1. Display the toolbox.
2. Click on the Label tool in the toolbox.
3. Click near the top left edge of the page header at about the 1-inch mark on the ruler; then drag the cursor to make a small rectangle about 2 3/4 inches long and 1/4 inch wide.
4. Type **Mountain Animal Hospital Pets and Owners Directory**.
5. Press Enter.

Tip: To create a multiple-line label entry, press Ctrl+Enter to force a line break where you want it in the control.

Tip: If you want to edit or enter a caption that is longer than the space in the property sheet, the contents will scroll as you type. Otherwise, you can press Shift+F2 to open a Zoom box that gives you more space to type.

Modifying the appearance of text in a control

To modify the appearance of the text in a control, select the control by clicking on its border (not in the control itself). You can then select a formatting style to apply to the label by clicking on the appropriate button in the toolbar. To make the title stand out, follow these steps for modifying the appearance of label text:

1. Click on the report heading label.
2. Click on the Bold button on the formatting toolbar.
3. Click on the arrow beside the Font-Size drop-down box.
4. Select 18 from the Font-Size drop-down list box.

The label control appears. You will need to resize it (which you will do later in this chapter) in order to display all of the text.

Working with text boxes and attached label controls

After you enter label controls to define text on the report, you will want to place additive fields on the report.

Adding text box controls

Text box controls serve two purposes in reports. First, they let you display stored data from a particular field in a query or table. Their second purpose is displaying the result of an expression. Expressions can be calculations that use other controls as their operands, or calculations that use Access functions (either built-in or user-defined), or a combination of the two. You've learned how to use a text box control to display data from a field and how to create that control. Next, you learn about text controls that use expressions.

Entering an expression in a text control

Cross Ref

Expressions let you create a value that is not already in a table or query. They can range from simple functions (such as a page number) to complex mathematical computations. Chapter 23 covers expressions in greater detail; for this example, you'll use an expression that is necessary for the report.

A *function* is a process that returns a single value; it can be one of many built-in Access functions, or it can be user-defined. To facilitate page numbering in reports, Access has a function called Page that returns the value of the current report page. The following steps show you how to add a page number to your report:

1. Select the Text Box tool from the toolbox.
2. Scroll down to the page footer section by using the vertical elevator.
3. Select the Properties button in the toolbar.
4. Click in the middle of the page footer section, then create a text box about three quarters of the height of the section and about 3/4 inch wide.
5. Click on the label control to select it.
6. Click on the beginning of the label control text, drag over the default text in the label control, and type **Page:**

7. Click on the text box control (unbound) twice; type **=Page** and press Enter. (Notice that the Control Source property changes on the property sheet to `=Page`, as shown in Figure 21-12.)

8. Click on the Page label control's Move handle (upper left corner); move the label closer to the `=Page` text box control until the right edge of the label control touches the left edge of the text box control. (You will move the entire control to the right side of the page later.)

Tip You can always check your result by clicking on the Print Preview button on the toolbar. You may want to zoom in on the page footer section to check the page number.

Sizing a text box control or label control

You can select a control simply by clicking on it. Depending on the size of the control, from three to seven sizing handles will appear — one on each corner except the upper left, and one on each side. When you move the cursor over one of the sizing handles, the cursor changes into a double-headed arrow. When the cursor changes, click on the control and drag it to the size you want. Notice that, as you drag, an outline appears; it indicates the new size the label control will be when you release the mouse button.

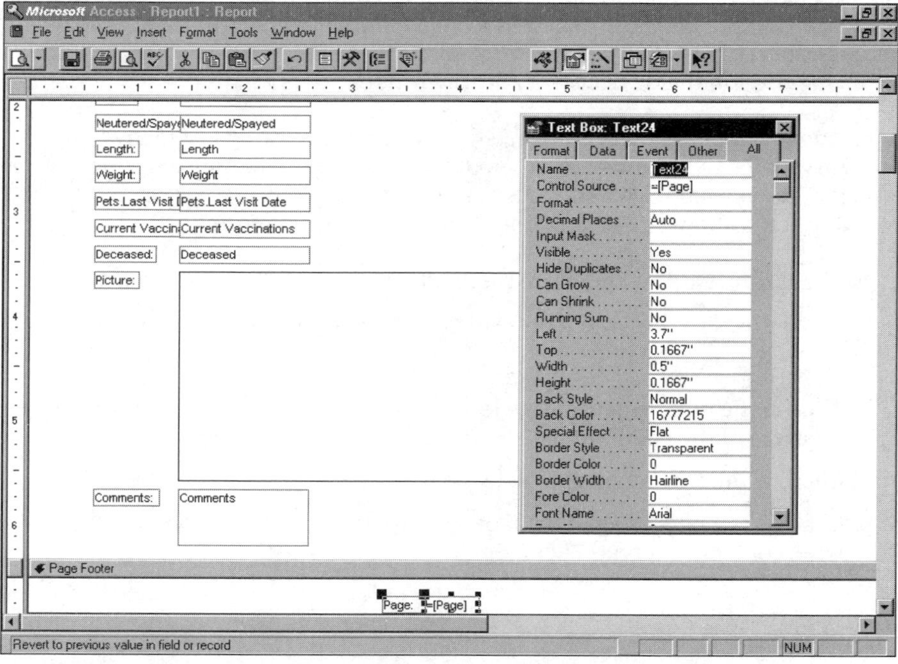

Figure 21-12: Adding a page-number expression in a text box control.

If you double-click on any of the sizing handles, usually Access will resize a control to a best fit for the text in the control. This feature is especially handy if you increase the font size and then notice that the text is cut off, either on the bottom or to the right. Note that for label controls, this *best-fit sizing* resizes both vertically and horizontally, though text controls can only resize vertically. The reason for this difference is that in the report design mode, Access doesn't know how much of a field you want to display; the field name and field contents might be radically different. Sometimes label controls are not resized correctly, however, and have to be adjusted manually.

Changing the size of a label control

Earlier in this chapter (in the steps that modified the appearance of label text), you changed the characteristics of the Pets and Owners label; the text changed, but the label itself did not adjust. Note that the text no longer fits within the label control. You can resize the text control, however, to fit the enhanced font size. Follow these steps:

1. Click on the Mountain Animal Hospital Pets and Owners Directory label control.
2. Move your cursor over the control. Notice how the cursor changes over the sizing handles.
3. Double-click on one of the sizing handles. The label control size may still need to be readjusted.
4. Place the cursor on the bottom right corner of the label control so that the diagonal arrow appears.
5. Hold the left mouse button down and drag the handle to resize the label control's box until it correctly displays all of the text (if it doesn't already).

Tip: You can also select Format➪Size➪to Fit to change the size of the label control text automatically.

Before continuing, you should see how the report is progressing; you should do this frequently as you design a report. You can send a single page to the printer or view the report in a print preview. Figure 21-13 shows a zoomed print preview of how the report currently looks. The customer information is at the top of the page; the Pet information is below that and offset to the left. Notice the title at the top of the page. You can see the page number at the bottom if you click on the magnifying-glass button to zoom out and see the whole page. Only one record per page appears on the report because of the vertical layout. In the next section of this chapter, you move the fields around and create a more horizontal layout.

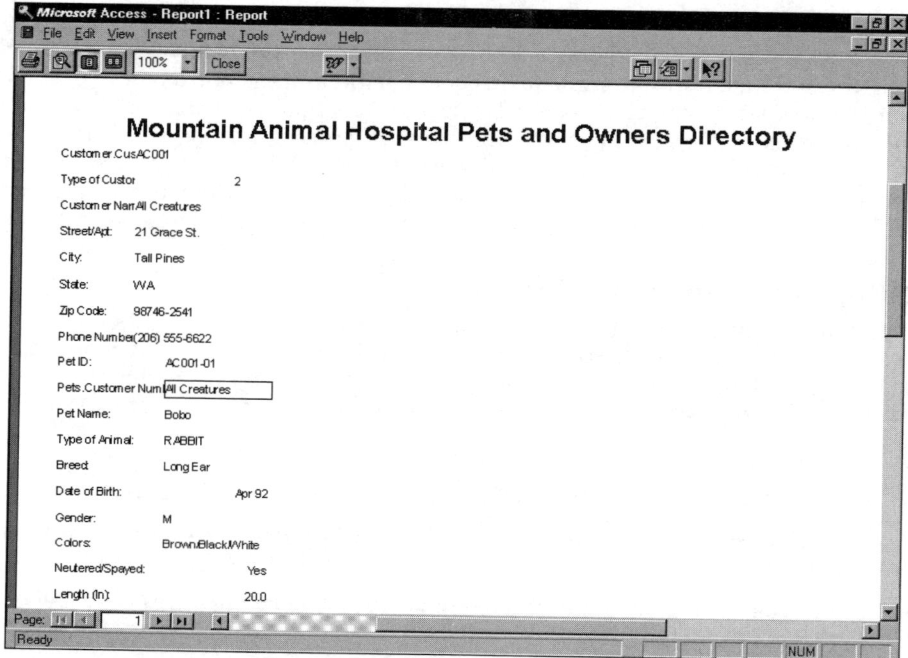

Figure 21-13: A print preview of the report.

Deleting attached label and text controls

As you can see in Figure 21-13, the report begins with the Customer Number field. The original design in Figure 21-6 did not have the Customer Number field on the report. After talking to the report design's architect (who is usually yourself), you find that the Customer Number field is not wanted on the report, either in the page header section or the detail section. It's very easy to delete one or more attached controls in a report. You simply select the desired controls and press Delete. When deleting attached controls, you have two choices:

✦ Delete the label control only.

✦ Delete both the label control and the field control.

If you select the label control and press Delete, only the label control is deleted. If you select the field control and press Delete, both the label control and the field control are deleted. To delete an attached control (in this case, the Customer Number controls and their attached label), follow these steps:

1. Select the Close icon in the toolbar to exit print preview mode. Select the text box control `Customer.Customer (Customer Number)` in the page header.
2. Press Delete.

3. Select the text box control `Pets.Customer Num` in the detail section.
4. Press Delete.

If you accidentally selected the label control that precedes the text box control, the text box control is still visible. You can then simply click on the control and press Delete.

Tip

If you want to delete only the field control and keep the attached label control, you can do so by first selecting the label control and selecting Edit⇨Copy. Next, to delete both the field control and the label control, select the field control and press Delete. Finally, select Edit⇨Paste to paste only the copied label control to the report.

Moving label and text controls

Before discussing how to move label and text controls, it is important to review a few differences between attached and unattached controls. When an attached label is created automatically with a text control, it is called a *compound control.* In a compound control, whenever you move one control in the set, the other control moves as well. With a text control and a label control, whenever you move the text control, the attached label is also moved. Likewise, whenever you move the label control, the text control is also moved.

To move both controls in a compound control, select one of the pair by clicking anywhere on the control. Move the cursor over either of the objects. When the cursor turns into a hand, you can click on the controls and drag them to their new location. Notice that, as you drag, an outline for the compound control moves with your cursor.

Note

The concepts of moving controls are covered visually and in more detail in Chapter 16.

To move only one of the controls in a compound control, you must drag the desired control by its *Move handle* (the large square in the upper left-hand corner of the control). When you click on a compound control, it appears that both controls are selected. If you look closely, you'll see that only one of the two controls is actually selected (as indicated by the presence of both moving and sizing handles). The deselected control displays only a moving handle. A pointing finger indicates that you have selected the Move handles and can now move one control only. To move either control individually, select the control's Move handle and drag it to its new location.

Cross Ref

To move a label that is not attached, simply click on any border (except where there is a handle) and drag it. You can also move groups of controls with the selection techniques you learned in Chapter 16.

To make a group selection, click on the cursor anywhere outside a starting point and drag the cursor through (or around) the controls you want to select. A gray, outlined rectangle is displayed to show the extent of the selection. When you release the mouse button, all the controls that the rectangle surrounds are selected. You can then drag the group of controls to a new location.

Cross Ref The global option Tools⇨Options - Form/Reports - Selection Behavior is a property that controls the enclosure of selections. You can enclose them fully (the rectangle must completely surround the selection) or partially (the rectangle need only to touch the control), which is the default.

In the next steps, you begin to place the controls in their proper position to complete the report design and layout as created (see Figure 21-6). You want this first pass at rearranging the controls to look like Figure 21-14. The steps to move all the controls will be broken up into logical groups. This is the way most reports are created. By making a series of block moves (where many controls are selected) and then refining the positioning, you can complete a report design. Follow these steps to begin placing the controls where they should be:

Roughly positioning the page header controls:

1. Move the Type of Customer control to the right and downward so that the top of the control intersects 1 inch in the vertical ruler and the left edge is under the `P` in `Pets` in the title.
2. In the page header, delete the attached labels (only) from all the text controls except Type of Customer.
3. Rearrange the controls in the page header to resemble a typical mailing-label address format; City, State, and Zip Code should be on the same line.
4. Move the Phone Number text box control under the Zip Code text box control.
5. Move the block of name, address, and phone number controls into position so that the top of the block intersects 1/2 inch in both the vertical and horizontal rulers.
6. Resize the page header section so that it intersects 1 3/4 inches on the left vertical ruler.

Roughly positioning the detail controls:

1. Select the Pet ID, Type of Animal, Breed, Date of Birth, and Last Visit Date controls (and their attached labels) by clicking on each text control while holding down the Shift key.
2. Drag the block of controls to the right so that the left edge intersects 3 inches on the top ruler.
3. Select the Last Visit Date (only) control and its attached label.
4. Drag the Last Visit Date control up so that it is just under the `Date of Birth` control.

5. Select the Gender control and its attached label.
6. Drag the control to the right so that the left edge intersects $5^{1}/_{4}$ inches on the top ruler and $^{1}/_{4}$ inch on the left-side ruler.
7. Select the Colors, Length, and Weight controls and their attached labels by clicking on each text control while holding down the Shift key.
8. Drag the block of controls to the right so the left edge intersects $5^{1}/_{4}$ inches on the top ruler and $^{3}/_{4}$ inch on the left-side ruler.
9. Select the Neutered/Spayed, Current Vaccinations, and Deceased controls and their attached labels by clicking on each text control while holding down the Shift key.
10. Drag the block of controls to the right so they are just under the most recently moved block.
11. Select the Current Vaccinations and Deceased controls and their attached labels by clicking on each text control while holding down the Shift key.
12. Drag the block of controls upward so they are just under the Neutered/Spayed control.
13. Delete the Pet Name label control (only).
14. Delete the Picture label control (only).
15. Delete the Comments label control (only).
16. Select the bottom right handle to resize the Picture control to 1 inch by 1 inch.
17. Move the Picture control to $^{1}/_{8}$ inch by $^{1}/_{8}$ inch on the rulers (top-left corner) of the detail section.
18. Move the Pet Name text box control under the picture so it intersects the left ruler at $1^{1}/_{2}$ inches.
19. Move the Comments text box control under the picture so that it intersects the left ruler at $1^{3}/_{4}$ inches.
20. Resize the Detail section so that it intersects 2 inches on the left ruler.

At this point, you are about half done. The screen should look like Figure 21-14. (If it doesn't, adjust your controls until the screen matches the figure.) Remember that these screen pictures are taken with the Windows screen driver set at 800 × 600. If you are using normal VGA, you'll have to scroll the screen to see the entire report.

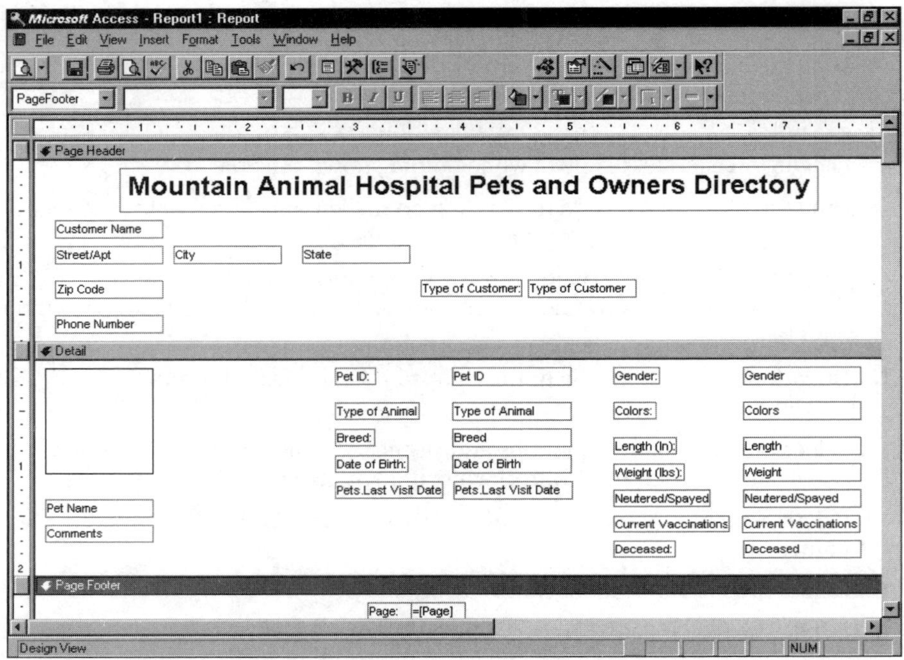

Figure 21-14: Rearranging the controls on the report.

The next step is refining the design to get as close as possible to the design created in Figure 21-6. The page header band is complete for now. Later in this chapter, you'll reformat the controls to change the font size and style. In the next set of steps, you complete the layout of the detail section.

1. Drag the Pet ID attached control to the top of the block of controls containing Type of Animal.
2. Select and drag that block to the right of the Picture OLE control, as shown in Figure 21-15.
3. Drag the controls Neutered/Spayed, Current Vaccinations, and Deceased away from other controls to allow space to move the label controls above the text box controls, as shown in Figure 21-15.
4. Drag each of the label controls to locations above the text box controls by grabbing each Move handle individually and then moving the controls above the text box controls.
5. Select all three label controls and align them by selecting Format⇨Align⇨Bottom.

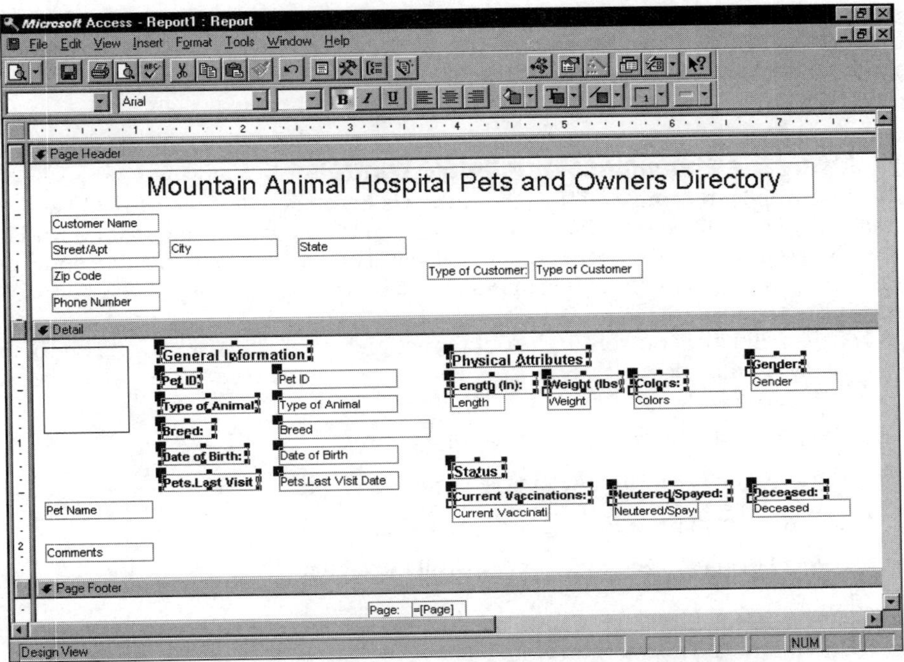

Figure 21-15: The selected and resized label control in the detail section.

6. Repeat Steps 3 and 4 for the Length, Weight, Colors, and Gender controls, moving them into position as shown in Figure 21-15.
7. Move the Comments text box control so it appears below all other controls.

There is still some text to add as label controls. If you compare the design shown in Figure 21-6 to your screen, you can see that you still need to add some label controls to define the groups. To add the label controls, follow these steps:

1. Double-click Label Control button in the toolbox so you can add more than one label control.
2. Create a new label control above the Pet ID field and enter **General Information**. Make sure that you press Enter after entering the text of each label control so the control is sized automatically to fit the text. You still may have to resize the label if it is bigger than the text.
3. Create a new label control above the Length field and enter **Physical Attributes**.
4. Create a new label control above the Neutered/Spayed field and enter **Status**.
5. Click on the Pointer button in the toolbox to unlock the toolbox.

This completes the rough design for this report. There are still properties, fonts, and sizes to change. When you make these changes, you'll have to move fields around again. Use the design in Figure 21-6 only as a guideline. How it looks to *you*, as you refine the look of the report in the Report window, is the real design.

Modifying the appearance of multiple controls

The next step is to change all the label controls in the detail section to bold and 10-point size. This will help to differentiate between label controls and text controls, which currently have the same text formatting. The following steps guide you through modifying the appearance of text in multiple label controls:

1. Select all label controls in the detail section by individually clicking on them while holding down the Shift key. There are 15 label controls to select, as shown in Figure 21-15.
2. Click on the Bold button on the toolbar.
3. Click on the arrow in the Font-Size drop-down box.
4. Select 10 from the Font-Size drop-down list.
5. Select Format⇨Size⇨to Fit to resize all the labels.

Note You cannot select all the label controls in the preceding steps by using the drag-and-surround method. This method would also select all the text boxes; you want only to bold and resize the labels.

You will also need to make all the text box controls bold and increase their font size to 12 points in the page header section. To modify the appearance of text-box controls, follow these steps:

1. Select all the controls except the title in the page header section by clicking on the cursor on the top left corner of the section, and then dragging the cursor to surround all the controls. Include the Type of Customer label control as well.
2. Click on the Bold button on the toolbar.
3. Click on the Font-Size box drop-down arrow.
4. Select 12 from the Font-Size drop-down list.
5. Select Format⇨Size⇨to Fit to resize all the text box controls.

Notice that the text box controls do not display the entire field name. Remember that sizing to fit works only on the vertical height of a control. It is impossible to know how wide a field's value will be — you'll have to adjust these values manually. You can use the Print Preview window (shown in Figure 21-16) to check on your progress.

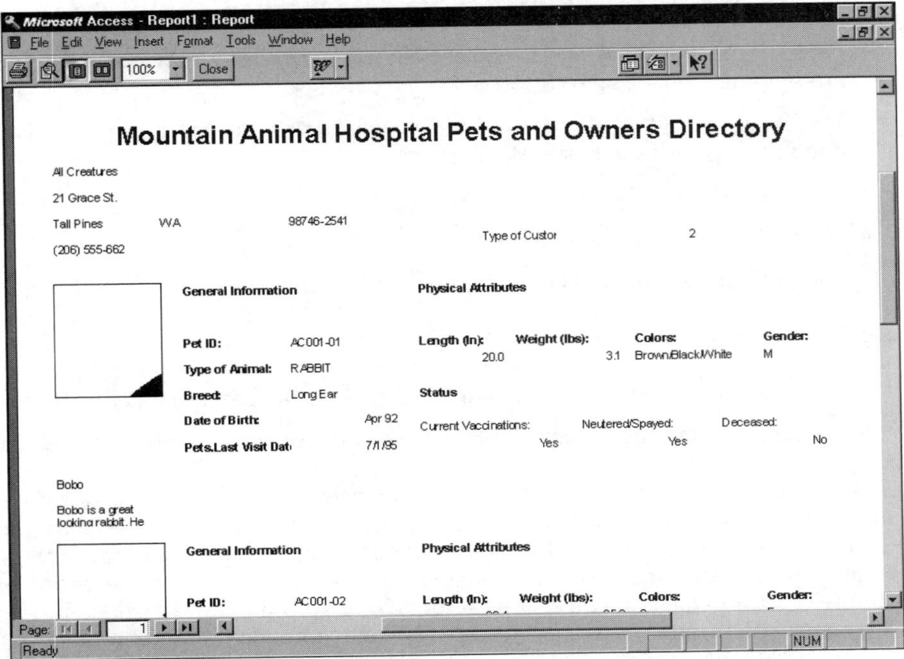

Figure 21-16: Previewing the report.

Looking at the print preview reveals many problems. These include the following:

Page header section:

- ✦ The Customer Name text box is not wide enough.
- ✦ There is too much space after the State text box before the ZIP Code.
- ✦ The Phone Number text box is not wide enough.
- ✦ The Type of Customer label needs to be longer.
- ✦ The Type of Customer text box value needs to be left-aligned.

Detail section:

- ✦ None of the text boxes in the detail section is 10-point; all are 8-point.
- ✦ The Pet Name needs to be bolded, centered, and moved closer to the picture.
- ✦ The data under General Information is not lined up properly.

- The Pets.Last Visit Date label needs to have the prefix Pets deleted.
- Pet ID, Type of Animal, and Breed are left-aligned, whereas the other two values are right-aligned.
- The Length and Weight values under Physical Attributes are right-aligned and don't line up with the labels above them.
- The Gender control doesn't quite fit.
- The Picture OLE control is not correctly displayed.
- The Comments memo field displays only the first few words.

Page footer section:

- The Page Number control needs to be moved to the right edge of the page.
- The page number needs to be left-aligned; both controls should be italicized.

Tip

Remember that you may have only looked at the data for one record. Make sure you look at data for many records before completing the report design, and watch the maximum sizes of your data fields. Another suggestion is to create a dummy record to use only for testing; it should contain values that use each position of the field. For example, a great name to test a 24-character field is `Fred Rumpelstiltskin III`. (Of course, with proportional fonts, you really can't count characters because an *i* uses less space than an *m*.)

The problems just noted will have to be fixed before this report is considered complete. You can fix many of them easily with the techniques you've already performed. Complete the changes as outlined in the list on the previous pages. When you're through, your screen should look like Figure 21-17.

Once you make the final modifications, you are finished, except for fixing the picture. To do this, you'll need to change properties, which you do in the next section. This may seem an enormous number of steps, as the procedure were designed to show you how laying out a report design can be a slow process. Remember, however, that when you are clicking away with the mouse, you don't realize how many steps you are doing as you design the report layout visually. With a WYSIWYG layout like that of the Access report designer, you may need to perform many tasks, but it's still easier and faster than programming. Figure 21-17 shows the final version of the design layout as you'll see it in this chapter. In the next chapter, you will continue to improve this report layout.

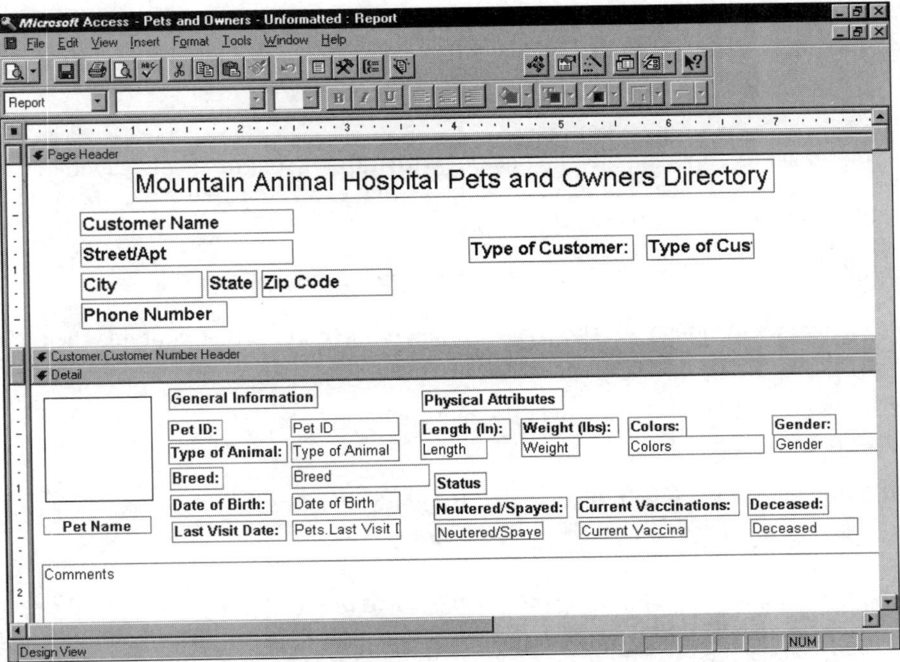

Figure 21-17: The final design layout.

Changing label and text-box control properties

To change the properties of a text or label control, you need to display the control's property sheet. If it is not already displayed, perform one of these actions:

- ✦ Double-click on the border of the control (anywhere but a sizing handle or Move handle).
- ✦ Click on the Properties button on the toolbar.
- ✦ Select View➪Properties.
- ✦ Right-click the mouse and select Properties.

The *property sheet* lets you look at a control's property settings and gives you an easy way to edit the settings. When you use tools such as the formatting windows and text-formatting buttons on the Formatting toolbar, you are changing the property settings of a control. When you click on the Bold button, for example, you are really setting the Font Weight property to Bold. It is usually much more intuitive to use the toolbar (or even the menus), but some properties are not accessible this way. Sometimes, in fact, objects have more options available through the property sheet.

The Size Mode property of an OLE object (bound object frame), with its options of Clip, Stretch, and Zoom, is a good example of a property available only through the property sheet.

The Image control, which is a bound object frame, presently has its Size Mode property set to Clip, which is the default. With Clip, the picture is displayed in its original size. For this example, change the setting to Stretch so the picture is sized automatically to fit the picture frame.

Cross Ref Chapter 20 covers the use of pictures, OLE objects, and graphs.

To change the property for the bound object frame control that contains the picture, follow these steps:

1. Click on the frame control of the picture bound object.
2. Click on the Size Mode property.
3. Click on the arrow to display the drop-down list box.
4. Select Stretch.

This completes the changes to your form. A print preview of a single record appears in Figure 21-18. Notice how the picture is now properly displayed; the Comments field now appears across the bottom of the detail section.

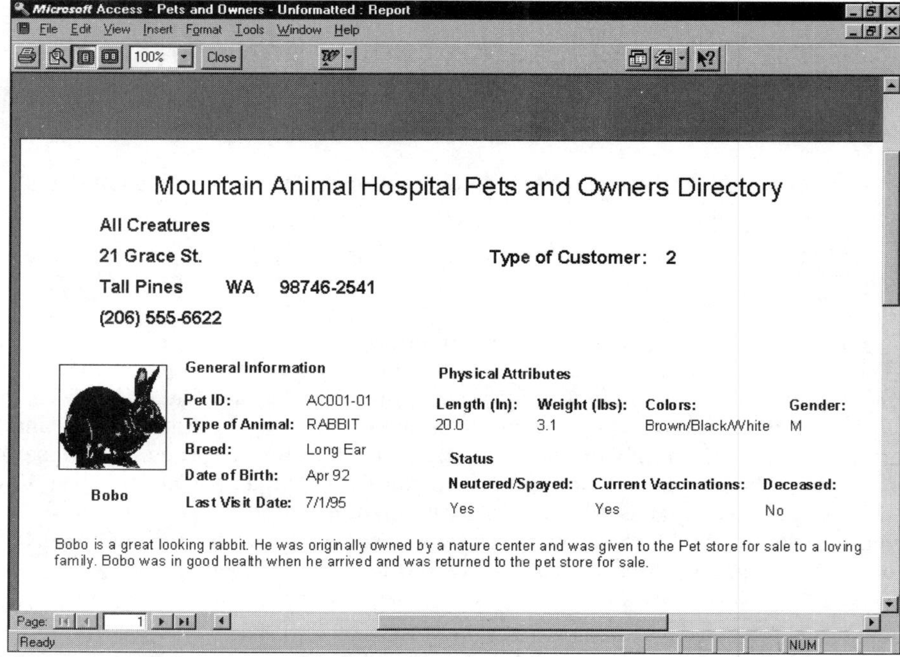

Figure 21-18: The final report print preview.

Formatting the display of text controls

With the formatting toolbar, you can change the appearance of a control and its text. For example, you can make a control's value bold or change its font size. You can make further changes by using the property sheet. Depending on the type of field a text box is bound to — or on whether it contains an expression — you can use various types of format masks. You can type the character > to capitalize all letters, or you can create an input mask to add parentheses and hyphens to a phone number. For numeric and date-formatting properties, you can select from a drop-down list box, which lets you add dollar signs to a number or format a date in a more readable way.

Growing and shrinking text box controls

When you print or print-preview fields that can have variable text lengths, Access provides options for enabling a control to grow or shrink vertically, depending on the exact contents of a record. The option Can Grow determines whether a text control will add lines to fit additional text if the record contains more lines of text than the control can display. The option Can Shrink determines whether a control will delete blank lines if the record's contents use fewer lines than the control can display. Although you can use this property for any text field, it is especially helpful for Memo field controls.

An explanation of the acceptable values for these two properties appears in Table 21-4.

Table 21-4
Text Control Values for Can Grow and Can Shrink

Property	*Value*	*Description*
Can Grow	Yes	If the data in a record uses more lines than the control is defined to display, the control resizes to accommodate additional lines.
Can Grow	No	If the data in a record uses more lines than the control is defined to display, the control does not resize; it truncates the data display.
Can Shrink	Yes	If the data in a record uses fewer lines than the control is defined to display, the control resizes to eliminate blank lines.
Can Shrink	No	If the data in a record uses fewer lines than the control is defined to display, the control does not resize to eliminate blank lines.

To change the Can Grow settings for a text control, follow these steps:

1. Select the Comments text control.
2. Display the property sheet.
3. Click on the Can Grow property; then click on the arrow and select Yes.

Note The Can Grow and Can Shrink properties are also available for report sections. Use a section's property sheet to modify these values.

As you near completion of testing of your report design, you should also test the printing of your report. Figure 21-19 shows a hard copy of the first page of the Customer and Pets report. You can see three pet records displayed for the Customer named All Creatures.

Mountain Animal Hospital Pets and Owners Directory

All Creatures
21 Grace St.
Tall Pines WA 98746-2541
(206) 555-6622

Type of Customer: 2

Bobo

General Information

Pet ID: AC001-01
Type of Animal: RABBIT
Breed: Long Ear
Date of Birth: Apr 92
Last Visit Date: 7/1/95

Physical Attributes

Length (In):	Weight (lbs):	Colors:	Gender:
20.0	3.1	Brown/Black/White	M

Status

Neutered/Spayed:	Current Vaccinations:	Deceased:
Yes	Yes	No

BoBo is a great looking rabbit. Bobo was originally owned by a nature center and was given to the Pet store for sale to a loving family. Bobo was in good health when he arrived and was returned to the pet store for sale.

Presto Chango

General Information

Pet ID: AC001-02
Type of Animal: LIZARD
Breed: Chameleon
Date of Birth: May 92
Last Visit Date: 11/26/93

Physical Attributes

Length (In):	Weight (lbs):	Colors:	Gender:
36.4	35.0	Green	F

Status

Neutered/Spayed:	Current Vaccinations:	Deceased:
No	No	No

The lizard was not readily changing color when brought in. It only changed color when it was warm. This is not abnormal for a chameleon. However, the species which is believed to originate in northern Australia usually manifests this problem in warm weather only. It is very unusual to see a chameleon not change color when cold.

Stinky

General Information

Pet ID: AC001-03
Type of Animal: SKUNK
Breed:
Date of Birth: Aug 91
Last Visit Date: 5/11/93

Physical Attributes

Length (In):	Weight (lbs):	Colors:	Gender:
29.8	22.0	Black/White	M

Status

Neutered/Spayed:	Current Vaccinations:	Deceased:
No	No	No

The skunk was descented and was in perfect condition when it left Mountain Animal Hospital.

Figure 21-19: The final report hard-copy printout.

You should, however, print several pages of the report. When you get to page 2, you may see a problem: the animals owned by Johnathan Adams are listed on the page for All Creatures, a pet store. What's wrong? The problem is that you haven't told Access how to group your data. Figure 21-19 displays three records on a page, but All Creatures brought in four pets. The next page begins again with All Creatures in the page header. Then the first record is Fido, the dog belonging to All Creatures. But the next record is Patty the Pig, belonging to Johnathan Adams. This record needs to trigger a page break because the Customer record has changed (later in this chapter, you learn how to do this). You may also notice on page 2 that the Breed field is not fully displayed. You should expand the text box to display the entire text `German Shepherd`.

Warning If every even-numbered page is blank, you accidentally widened the report past the 8-inch mark. If you move a control to brush up against the right page-margin border or exceed it, the right page margin increases automatically. Once it is past the 8-inch mark, it can't display the entire page on one physical piece of paper. The blank page you get is actually the right side of the preceding page. To correct this, make sure all your controls are within the 8-inch right margin; then drag the right page margin back to 8 inches.

Sorting and grouping data

So far, you've completely designed the layout of your report. You may think you're done, but some tasks still remain; one of these is sorting.

Sorting lets you determine the order in which you view the records in a datasheet, form, or report, based on the values in one or more fields. This is important when you want to view the data in your tables in a sequence other than that of your input. For example, new customers are added to the Customer table as they become clients of the hospital; the physical order of the database reflects the date and time a customer is added. Yet when you think of the customer list, you probably expect it to be in *alphabetical* order, and you want to sort it by Customer Number or Customer Name. By sorting in the report itself, you don't have to worry about what order the data is in. Although you can sort the data in the query, it is more advantageous to do it in the report. This way, if you change the query, the report is still in the correct order.

The Customer Name and Customer Number fields

You may have noticed that the Customer Name field is not in last name/first name order, but the Customer Number is generally in a sorted order by the customer's last name. The Customer Number field begins with the first two characters of a customer's last name if the customer is an individual (Type of Customer = 1). If the customer is a pet store (Type of Customer = 2) or zoo (Type of Customer = 3), the Customer Number field begins with the first two logical characters of the pet store or zoo name.

For an illustration, examine the following list, which shows Type of Customer, Customer Name, and Customer Number for the first five records in the Customer table:

Type of Customer	Customer Name	Customer Number
2 - Pet Store	**A**ll **C**reatures	AC001
1 - Individual	Johnathan **Ad**ams	AD001
1 - Individual	William **Ad**ams	AD002
2 - Pet Store	**A**nimal **K**ingdom	AK001
3 - Zoo	**B**orderville **A**quarium	BA001

You can take this report concept even further by *grouping* — breaking related records into groups. Suppose, for example, you want to list your customers first by Customer Name and then by Pet Name within each Customer Name group. To do this, you must use the Customer Number field to sort the data. Groupings that can create group headers and footers are sometimes called *control breaks* because changes in data trigger the report groups.

Before you can add a grouping, however, you must first define a *sort order* for at least one field in the report. You do this by using the Sorting and Grouping box, which is shown completed in Figure 21-20. In this example, you will use the Customer.Customer Number field to sort on first and then the Pet ID field, which you will use as the secondary sort.

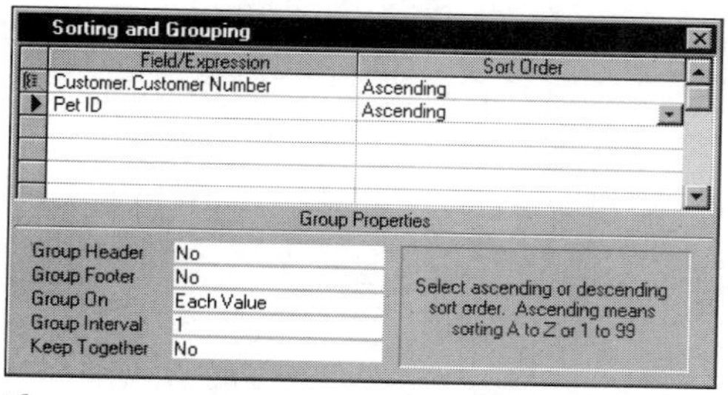

Figure 21-20: The Sorting and Grouping box.

To define a sort order based on Customer Number and Pet ID, follow these steps:

1. Click on the Sorting and Grouping button on the toolbar to display the Sorting and Grouping box.
2. Click on the cursor in the first row of the Field/Expression column of the Sorting and Grouping box. A downward-pointing arrow appears.
3. Click on the arrow to display a list of fields in the Pets and Owners query.
4. Click on the Customer.Customer Number field in the field list. Notice that Sort Order defaults to Ascending.
5. Click on the cursor in the second row of the Field/Expression column.
6. Click on the arrow to display a list of fields in the Pets and Owners query.
7. Scroll down to find the Pet ID field in the field list and then select Pet ID. The Sort Order defaults to Ascending.

Tip

To see more of the Field/Expression column, you can drag the border between the Field/Expression and Sort order columns to the right (as in Figure 21-20).

Note

You can drag a field from the Field List into the Sorting and Grouping box Field/Expression column instead of entering a field or choosing one from the field list in the Sorting and Grouping box Field/Expression column.

Although in this example you used a field, you can alternatively sort (and group) by using an expression. To enter an expression, click in the desired row of the Field/Expression column and enter any valid Access expression, making sure you start it with an equal sign, as in `=[Length]*[Weight]`.

Note

To change the sort order for fields that you placed in the Field/Expression column, simply click on the Sort Order column and click on the down arrow to display the Sort Order list; then select Descending.

Creating a group header or footer

In this example, you'll need to sort by the Customer Number and Pet ID. You will also need to create a group header for Customer Number in order to force a new page break before each new customer page. This way, a customer page will display pet records only for that customer; customers who have more pets than will fit on one page will continue to generate new pages, with only the customer information and pets for that customer. You don't need a group footer in this example, as there are no totals by customer number or other reasons to use a group footer.

To create a group header that lets you sort and group by customer number, follow these steps:

1. Click on the Sorting and Grouping button on the toolbar if the Sorting and Grouping box is not displayed. The field Customer.Customer Number should be displayed in the first row of the Sorting and Grouping box; it should indicate that it is being used as a sort in Ascending order.
2. Click on Customer.Customer Number in the Field/Expression column.
3. Click on the Group Header property in the bottom pane; an arrow appears.
4. Click on the arrow in the right-hand side of the edit box; a drop-down list appears.
5. Select Yes from the list.
6. Press Enter.

After you define a header or footer, the row pointer changes to the grouping symbol shown in Figure 21-21. This is the same symbol you see in the Sorting and Grouping button in the toolbar. In Figure 21-21, you can see not only the grouping row pointer, but also a newly created section. The Customer.Customer Number header section

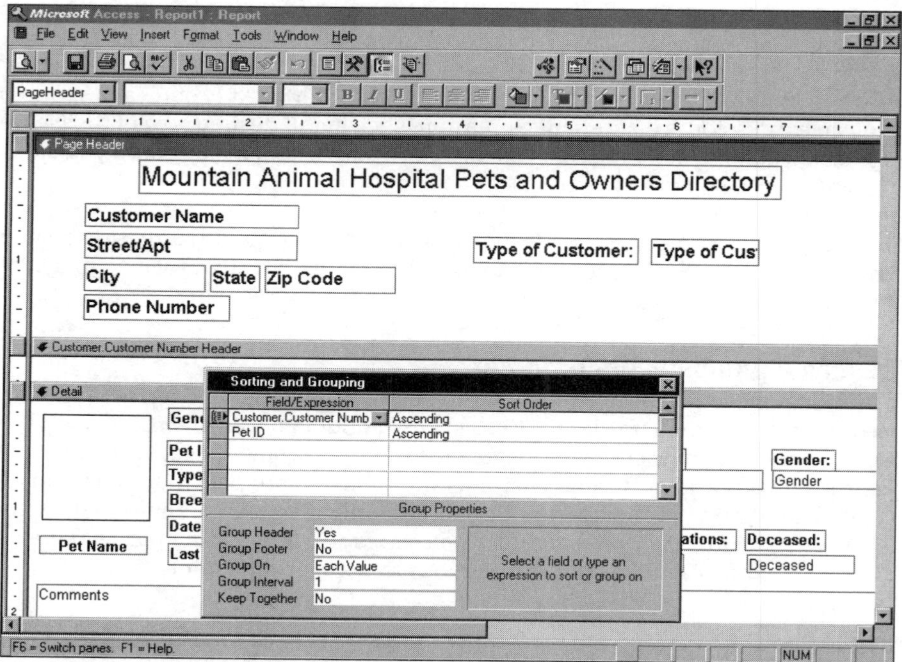

Figure 21-21: The group header definition.

appears between the page header and detail sections. If you define a group footer, it appears below the detail section. If there are multiple groupings in a report, each subsequent group becomes the one closest to the detail section. The groups defined first will be farthest from the detail section.

The Group Properties pane (displayed at the bottom of the Sorting and Grouping box) contains the following properties:

Group Header	Yes creates a group header. No removes the group header.
Group Footer	Yes creates a group footer. No removes the group footer.
Group On	Specifies how you want the values grouped. The options you see in the drop-down list box depend on the data type of the field on which you're grouping. If you group on an expression, you see all the options. Group On has more choices to make:

For Text data types, you have two choices:

Each Value	The same value in the field or expression
Prefix Characters	The same first *n* number of characters in the field

For Date/Time data types, you have further options:

Each Value	The same value in the field or expression
Year	Dates in the same calendar year
Qtr	Dates in the same calendar quarter
Month	Dates in the same month
Week	Dates in the same week
Day	Dates on the same date
Hour	Times in the same hour
Minute	Times in the same minute

With AutoNumber, Currency, or Number data types, you have two options:

Each Value	The same value in the field or expression
Interval	Values falling within the interval you specify

Group Interval		Specifies any interval that is valid for the values in the field or expression you're grouping on.
Keep Together	Whole Group	Prints header detail and group footer on one page.
	With First Detail	Prevents the contents of the group header from printing without any following data or records on a page.
	No	Doesn't Keep Together

Disk

After you create the Customer Number group header, you are done with the Sorting and Grouping box for this report. You may need to make further changes to groupings as you change the way a report looks; the following three topics detail how to make these changes. You should not make any of these changes, however, if you are following along with the examples. If you want to practice these skills, you can save the report before practicing, and then retrieve the original copy of the report that you saved. After the next three sections, you will have to size the group header section and change its properties.

Changing the group order

Access lets you easily change the Sorting and Grouping order without moving all the individual controls in the associated headers and footers. Here are the steps to change the sorting/grouping order:

1. Click on the selector of the field or expression you want to move in the Sorting and Grouping window.
2. Click on the Selector again and hold down the left mouse button.
3. Drag the row to a new location.
4. Release the mouse button.

Removing a group header or footer

To remove a page or report header/footer section, use the View⇨Page Header/Footer and View⇨Report Header/Footer toggles as detailed earlier in this chapter. To remove a group header or footer but leave the sorting intact, follow these steps:

1. In the Sorting and Grouping window, click on the selector of the field or expression you want to remove from the grouping.
2. Click on the Group Header edit box.
3. Change the value to **No**.
4. Press Enter.

To remove a group footer, follow the same steps but click on Group Footer in Step 2.

To permanently remove both the sorting and grouping for a particular field (and thereby remove the group header and footer sections), follow these steps:

1. Click on the selector of the field or expression you want to delete.
2. Press Delete. A dialog box appears, asking you to confirm the deletion.
3. Click on OK.

Hiding a section

Access also lets you hide headers and footers so you can break data into groups without having to view information about the group itself. You can also hide the detail section so you get only a summary report. To hide a section, follow these steps:

1. Click on the section that you want to hide.
2. Display the section property sheet.
3. Click on the Visible property's edit box.
4. Click on the drop-down list arrow on the right side of the edit box.
5. Select No from the drop-down list box.

Note: Sections are not the only objects in a report that can be hidden; controls also have a Visible property. This property can be useful for expressions that trigger other expressions.

Disk: If you are following along in the examples, you should complete the next steps.

Sizing a section

Now that you've created the group header, you must decide what to do with it. Its only purpose in this example is to trigger a page break before a new customer record is displayed. (You learn how to do this later in this chapter.) For this example, you don't need to place any controls within the section. Unless you want to see the empty space on the report from the height of the group header section, close the section. You can do this by resizing the section height to 0.

To modify the height of a section, drag the border of the section below it. If (for example) you have a report with a page header, detail section, and page footer, change the height of the detail section by dragging the top of the page footer section's border. You can make a section larger or smaller by dragging the bottom border of the section. For this example, change the height of the group header section to zero with these steps:

1. Move your cursor over the section borders. Notice that the cursor changes to a horizontal line split by two vertical arrows.
2. Select the top of the detail section border.
3. Drag the selected border until it meets the bottom of the header Customer.Customer Number. Notice the gray line that indicates where the top of the border will be when you release the mouse button.
4. Release the mouse button.

Adding page breaks

Access lets you add page breaks based on group breaks; you can also insert forced breaks within sections, except in page header/footer sections.

In some report designs, it's best to have each new group start on a different page. In the Pets and Owners report you created in this chapter, one of the design criteria is that no more than one customer will appear on a page (though a customer can appear on more than one page). You can achieve this effect easily by using the Force New Page property of a group section, which lets you force a page break every time the group value changes.

The four Force New Page settings are as follows:

None	No forced page break (the default)
Before Section	Starts printing the current section at the top of a new page every time there is a new group
After Section	Starts printing the next section at the top of a new page every time there is a new group
Before & After	Combines the effects of Before Section and After Section

To create the report you want, you must force a page break before the Customer Number group by using the Force New Page property in the Customer Number header. To change the Force New Page property on the basis of groupings, follow these steps:

1. Click anywhere in the Customer.Customer Number header.
2. Display the property sheet.
3. Select the Force New Page property.
4. Click on the drop-down list arrow on the right side of the edit box.
5. Select Before Section from the drop-down list box.

Figure 21-22 shows this property sheet.

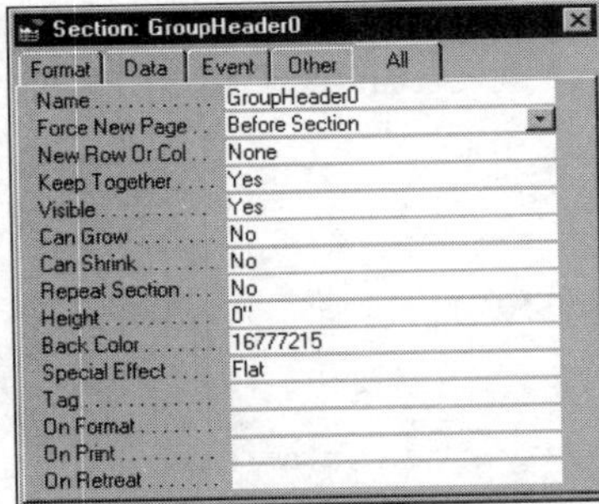

Figure 21-22: Forcing a page break in a group header.

If you run the report now, you'll see that page 2 has correctly printed only the last record from All Creatures. Page 3 now contains the two pets owned by Johnathan Adams.

Tip: Alternatively, you can create a Customer Number footer and set its Force New Page property to After Section.

Sometimes you don't want to force a page break on the basis of a grouping, but still want to force a page break. For example, you may want to split a report title across several pages. The solution is to use the Page Break tool from the toolbox; the steps follow.

1. Display the toolbox.
2. Click on the Page Break tool.
3. Click in the section where you want the page break to occur.
4. Test the results by using Print Preview.

Note: Be careful not to split the data in a control. Place page breaks above or below controls; do not overlap them.

Saving your report

After all the time you spent creating your report, you'll want to save it. As a matter of fact, even though it is covered toward the end of this chapter, it is good practice to save your reports frequently, starting as soon as you create them. This prevents the frustration of losing your work due to a power failure or human error. Save the report as follows:

1. Select File⇨Save. If this is the first time you've saved the report, the Save As dialog box appears.
2. Type in a valid Access name. For this example, type **Pets and Owners - Unformatted**.
3. Select OK.

If you already saved your report, Access silently (or not so silently, depending on your disk drive) saves your file, with no message about what it is up to.

Summary

In this chapter, you learned the basic operations involved in creating a report. Concepts covered include the following:

✦ A report gives you a different way of viewing data in one or more tables.

✦ Because of the advanced capabilities of Access, you are limited only by your imagination and your printer in the types of reports you can create.

✦ In the Report Design window, Access provides you with powerful but easy-to-use tools. These tools are the toolbars, the Properties window, the Sorting and Grouping box, and the Field List.

✦ The Report Design View toolbar gives you quick access to such design tasks as displaying various windows and applying formatting styles.

✦ With the toolbox, you can create, place, or select the controls on a report.

✦ The Field List window displays all fields available to a report from the query or table the report is bound to.

✦ Properties for a control can be viewed and edited from the control's property sheet.

✦ The Sorting and Grouping box lets you create group or summary sections on the report, and define sort orders.

✦ You can place fields on a report by displaying the field list, selecting your fields, and then dragging the fields onto your report.

✦ You can edit control properties by direct manipulation (through the various tools of the Report Design window) or you can edit these properties from the property sheet.

✦ You can create a summary report by hiding the detail section.

✦ Sorting lets you organize your data in a different order from the order you used during input.

✦ Grouping lets you organize your data in related groups that make the data easier to understand.

In the next chapter, you learn how to publish your reports using Access database publishing features.

✦ ✦ ✦

Database Publishing and Printing

In This Chapter

Understanding the terms *database publishing* and *WYSIWYG*

Enhancing text controls by controlling font size and style

Working with multiline text controls

Applying special display effects to reports

Using a set of option buttons instead of a text box control

Using check boxes and toggle buttons to display Yes/No fields

Adding lines and rectangles to a report

Adding color or shading to a report

Adding three-dimensional effects to a report

Reviewing the Print and Print Setup dialog boxes

In Chapter 21, you built a report from a blank form. That report was fairly simple. You worked only with label and text box controls, and the report had no special formatting. There were no lines or boxes, and no shading to emphasize any areas of the report. Although the report displays all the necessary data, you can make the data more readable by using *check boxes,* option buttons, and toggle buttons to display certain fields.

In this chapter, you see how to complete the formatting of the report you created in the preceding chapter, enhancing it to make it more readable and presentable.

Note Because the Report Design window is set to a width of eight inches, most of the screen printouts in this chapter appear as if an 800 × 600-resolution Super VGA Windows screen driver is used rather than the standard 640 × 480 VGA Windows driver. This lets you see almost the entire screen in the figures.

Database Publishing with Access

The term *database publishing* generally refers to the process of enhancing a report from a database by using special effects that desktop publishing packages provide. The Access Report Writer can accomplish with data, reports, and forms what any good desktop publishing package can do with words. Just as a desktop publishing application can enhance a word processing document to make it more readable, a database publisher can enhance a database report to make it more usable.

You can, for example, draw attention to areas of the report that you want the reader to notice. Just as a headline in a newspaper screams out the news, an enhanced section of the report screams out the information.

Cross Ref

You accomplish database publishing in reports with a variety of controls and by enhancing the controls with color, shading, or other means of emphasis. In Chapters 18, 19, and 20, you learned how to add to a form to many of the controls you work with in this chapter. You use a somewhat different process to add and enhance these controls in a report. One major difference is the ultimate viewing medium. Because the output of these controls is usually viewed on paper, you have design concerns that differ from those of creating a design to be viewed on-screen. Another difference is the use of each data control. In a form, you input or edit the data; in a report, you just view it.

Figure 22-1 shows the hard copy of the final report you create in this chapter. Notice that it has been significantly enhanced by adding special effects and more control types than mere labels or text boxes. Important information, such as the type of customer, gender, and current vaccinations, is easily understood at a glance; readers need only look at an option button (⦿ /❍) or check box (☐/☑) rather than a numeric code or text.

The Access Report Writer offers you a number of tools to make the report controls and sections stand out visually. These tools enable you to create such special effects as

✦ Lines and rectangles

✦ Color and background shading

✦ Three-dimensional effects (raised, sunken, and shadowed, flattened, etched, and chiseled)

In this chapter, you use all of these features as you change many of the text box controls into option buttons, toggle buttons, and check boxes. You also enhance the report with special text options: shading, shadows, lines, rectangles, and three-dimensional effects.

Warning

When you add shading to a report, you can increase printing time dramatically. Also, avoid adding colors unless you plan to print to a color printer.

Understanding WYSIWYG printing

Access has a *WYSIWYG* (what-you-see-is-what-you-get) report writer. As you create controls on-screen, you see instantly how they will look in your report. If you want to see how the data will look, you can take advantage of several types of on-screen preview modes. These modes enable you to see the actual data without involving a hard-copy device.

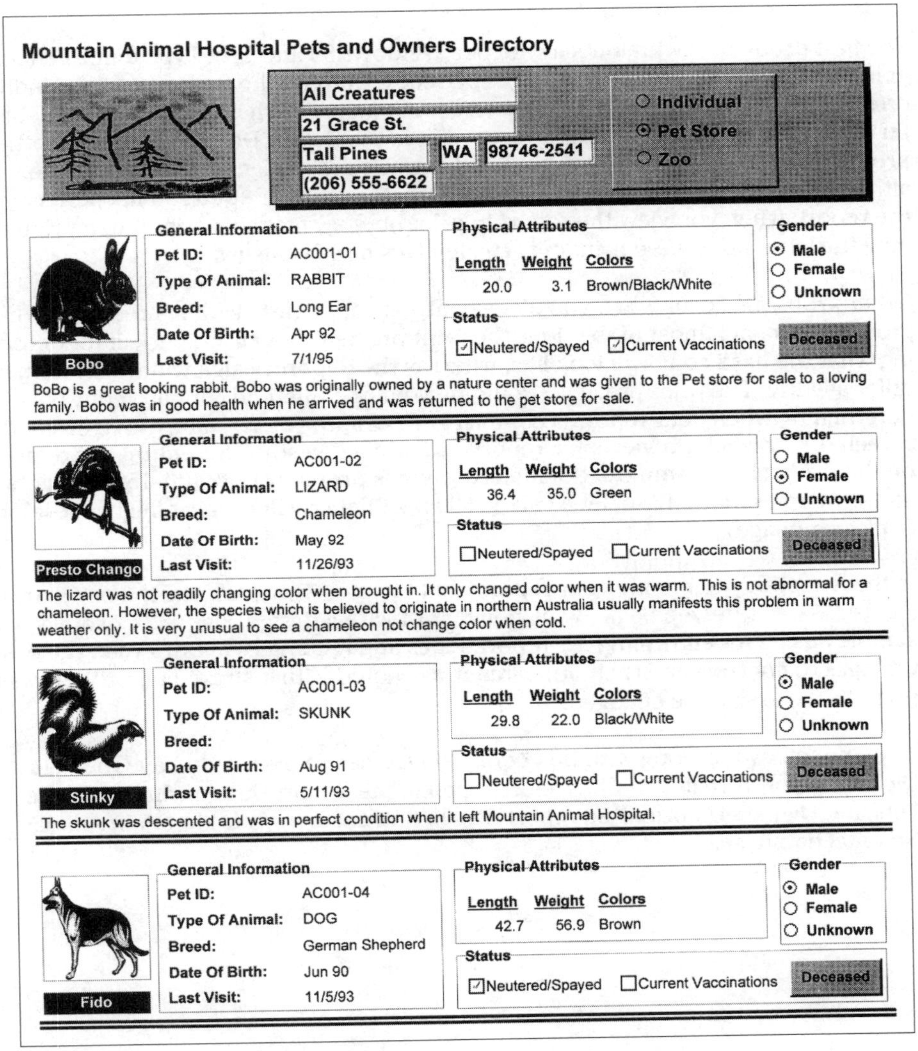

Mountain Animal Hospital Pets and Owners Directory

All Creatures
21 Grace St.
Tall Pines WA 98746-2541
(206) 555-6622

○ Individual
⊙ Pet Store
○ Zoo

Bobo

General Information
Pet ID: AC001-01
Type Of Animal: RABBIT
Breed: Long Ear
Date Of Birth: Apr 92
Last Visit: 7/1/95

Physical Attributes
Length 20.0 Weight 3.1 Colors Brown/Black/White

Gender
⊙ Male
○ Female
○ Unknown

Status
☑Neutered/Spayed ☑Current Vaccinations Deceased

BoBo is a great looking rabbit. Bobo was originally owned by a nature center and was given to the Pet store for sale to a loving family. Bobo was in good health when he arrived and was returned to the pet store for sale.

Presto Chango

General Information
Pet ID: AC001-02
Type Of Animal: LIZARD
Breed: Chameleon
Date Of Birth: May 92
Last Visit: 11/26/93

Physical Attributes
Length 36.4 Weight 35.0 Colors Green

Gender
○ Male
⊙ Female
○ Unknown

Status
☐Neutered/Spayed ☐Current Vaccinations Deceased

The lizard was not readily changing color when brought in. It only changed color when it was warm. This is not abnormal for a chameleon. However, the species which is believed to originate in northern Australia usually manifests this problem in warm weather only. It is very unusual to see a chameleon not change color when cold.

Stinky

General Information
Pet ID: AC001-03
Type Of Animal: SKUNK
Breed:
Date Of Birth: Aug 91
Last Visit: 5/11/93

Physical Attributes
Length 29.8 Weight 22.0 Colors Black/White

Gender
⊙ Male
○ Female
○ Unknown

Status
☐Neutered/Spayed ☐Current Vaccinations Deceased

The skunk was descented and was in perfect condition when it left Mountain Animal Hospital.

Fido

General Information
Pet ID: AC001-04
Type Of Animal: DOG
Breed: German Shepherd
Date Of Birth: Jun 90
Last Visit: 11/5/93

Physical Attributes
Length 42.7 Weight 56.9 Colors Brown

Gender
⊙ Male
○ Female
○ Unknown

Status
☑Neutered/Spayed ☐Current Vaccinations Deceased

Figure 22-1: An enhanced report.

The Access Report Writer lets you add color, shading, or reverse video (white letters on a black background) to your report text and controls. You can even color or shade the background of report sections; you see the effect immediately. Although what you see on the Report Design screen *seems* exactly what you'll get when you print, you should be aware of some factors that affect just how close what you see is to what you really get.

The first problem is with fonts. If you use Windows 95 and TrueType fonts, generally about 95 percent of your fonts appear perfectly, both on the Report Design window on-screen and in the hard-copy report. A common problem is that letters don't all fit on the report even though they appear to fit in the Report Design window. Another problem is that controls shift very slightly from perfect alignment. For example, although the Report Design window shows that the word `Deceased` fits perfectly in the report, when you view the report in print preview mode or print it to a printer, only the letters `Decease` print out. The final *d* simply vanishes.

Other problems occur when you place controls very tightly within a rectangle or group box. In fact, most of the time, the print preview modes are perfect for determining what the hard copy will look like, whereas the Report Design window view may differ slightly. The print preview should be your only method (or hard copy) of determining when your report is complete. Make sure you're using the right Windows screen driver when previewing a report; you can get vastly different results depending on the driver. For example, a dot-matrix driver is probably only 100–150 dpi (dots per inch), whereas an HP LaserJet 4 can be 600 dpi; higher values mean higher resolution (a clearer image).

Disk

In this chapter, you modify your report from Chapter 21 to look like the one shown in Figure 22-1. Before you begin, you should start with a design. Figure 22-2 shows a sample design for enhancing the report. Lines and rectangles are drawn in the design. Changes to controls and their appearance are noted with instructions and arrows that point to the area to be changed.

If you are following along with this book using Access, you should have the Pets and Owners report (created in Chapter 21) open in the Report Design window or the Pets and Owners-Unformatted report design that came in your Mountain Animal Hospital database.

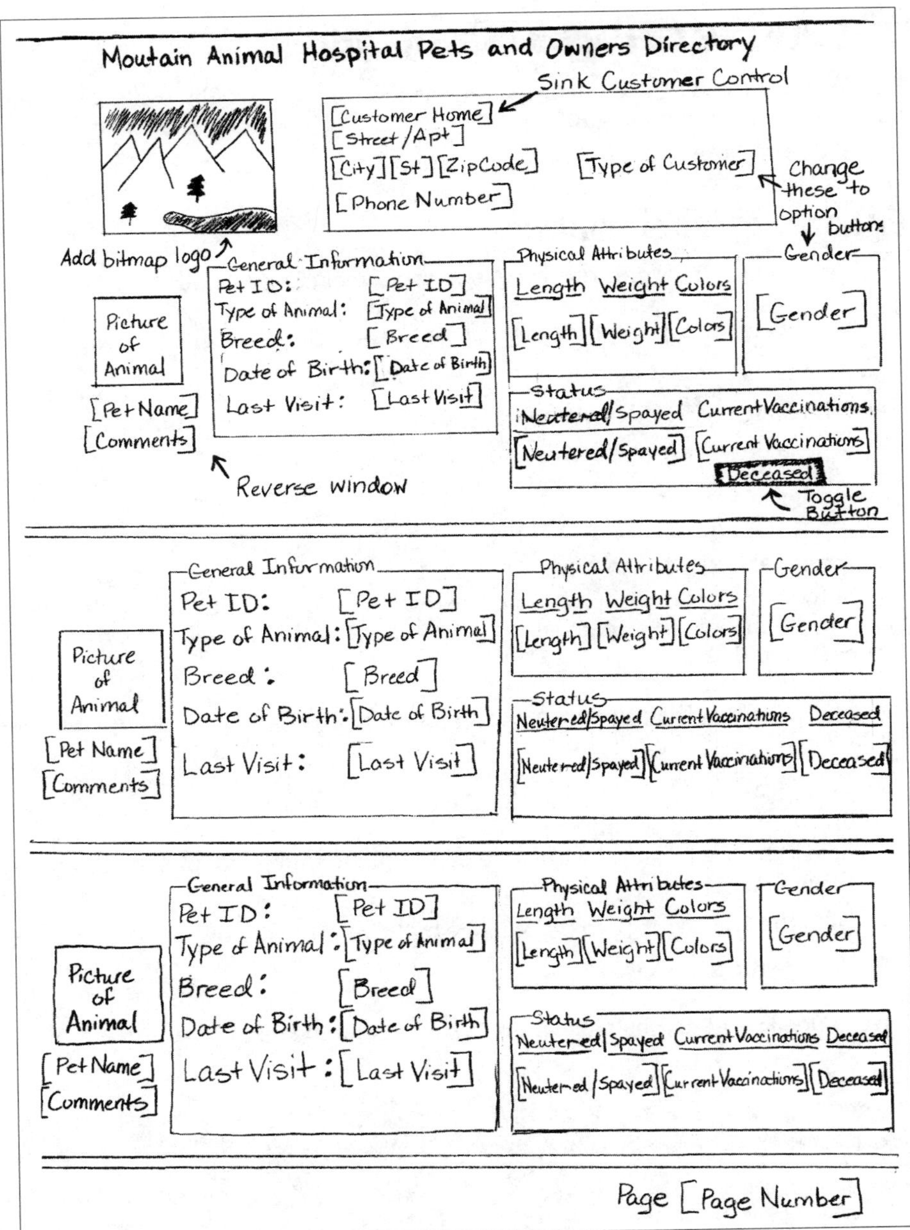

Figure 22-2: A design for report enhancements.

Enhancing Text-Based Controls

Before you start using such display items as shading or three-dimensional effects, it's important to get the data right. If your enhancements include control changes, start with these changes.

Enhancing label controls

You can enhance label controls in several ways, including the following:

- ✦ Changing the type style of the text font (Arial, Times New Roman, Wingdings)
- ✦ Changing the text font size (4 to 200 points)
- ✦ Changing the text font style (bold, italic, underline)
- ✦ Changing the text color (using the Fore color button)
- ✦ Adding a shadow

Changing text fonts and size

In Chapter 21, you learned how to change the text font type, size, and style. Now you learn how to make further changes as you change the title to match the design in Figures 22-1 and 22-2.

These figures show that the text needs to be left-justified on the page and made one size smaller.

To change the font placement and size, follow these steps:

1. Select the label control with the text Mountain Animal Hospital Pets and Owners Directory.
2. Drag the label control to the left side of the Report window.
3. Change the font size to **16**.

You will need to adjust the Label frame to display all the text.

Using the AutoFormat button

Access has an AutoFormat button that can assign predefined styles to a report and its controls. To use the AutoFormat functions, click on the AutoFormat button in the toolbar when you're in a report design. Access shows the AutoFormat dialog box for reports (Figure 22-3). Select the desired AutoFormat and click on OK to complete the formatting. All your controls (and the overall look of the form) will be changed as shown in the AutoFormat preview.

Figure 22-3: The AutoFormat dialog box.

Creating a text shadow

Text shadows create a three-dimensional look. They make the text appear to float above the page while shadows stay on the page. You can create text shadows using these techniques:

- ✦ Duplicating the text
- ✦ Offsetting the duplicate text from the original text
- ✦ Changing the duplicate text to a different color (usually a lighter shade)
- ✦ Placing the duplicate text behind the original text
- ✦ Changing the original text Back Color Transparent button

Note Microsoft Access has a shadow effect in the Special Effects button under the Formatting toolbar. This effect creates a shadow only on boxes or on the text box, not on the text itself. Compare the Mountain Animal Hospital Pets and Owners Directory of Figure 22-4 and Figure 22-5.

To create a shadow for the title's text, follow these steps:

1. Select the label control with the text `Mountain Animal Hospital Pets and Owners Directory`.
2. Select Edit⇨Duplicate.
3. Select light gray from the Foreground color window to change the duplicate text color.
4. Drag the duplicate text slightly to the right and upward to lessen the offset from the original text below.
5. Select Format⇨Send to Back.
6. Select the original copy of the text (the one now in front).
7. Click on the Transparent button in the Back Color window.

The text now appears to have a shadow, as you see in Figure 22-5. The box around the label control will not be visible when the report is printed.

Warning Although the on-screen shadow looks great, it does not print correctly on most monochrome printers. Normally you just get two lines of black text that look horrible. Unless you have a printer that prints text in shades of gray (using graphics rather than text fonts) or a color printer that prints gray, avoid using shadowed text on a report.

Displaying label or text-box control properties

As you use the formatting to change values in a label or text box control, you actually change their properties. Figure 22-4 displays the property sheet for the label control you just created. As you can see in the figure, many properties (described in Chapter 18) can be affected by the formatting windows.

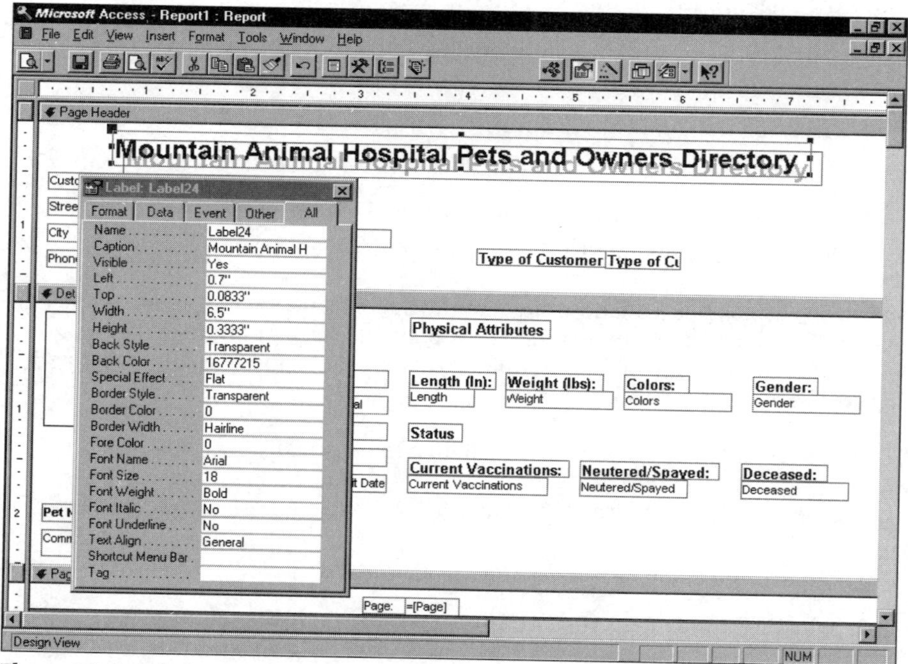

Figure 22-4: Label control properties.

Although you can set many of these controls from the property sheet, it's much easier to drag the control to set the Top, Left, Width, and Height, and to use the Formatting toolbar to set the other properties of the control.

Tip

Access (like other Microsoft Office products) has a Format Painter in the standard toolbar. This excellent and convenient tool allows you to copy styles from one selection to the next. Simply click on the item whose style you want to copy; then click on the Format Painter icon, and then on the item that needs the style change.

Tip

A better idea than to shadow the text is to shadow the label box. You can easily do this by deleting the duplicate text label, selecting the original label, and changing the special effect to Shadowed. This displays a cleaner look, as shown in Figure 22-5.

Working with multiple-line text box controls

There are two reasons to use a multiple-line text box:

- ✦ To display a Text data type on multiple lines
- ✦ To display large amounts of text in a Memo data type

Displaying multiple lines of text using a text box

In the sample report, the Street/Apt text box control in the page header sometimes contains data that takes up more than one line. The way the text box control is sized, you can only see the first line of data. There are generally two ways to see multiple lines of text in a text box control.

- ✦ Resize the control vertically to allow more lines to be displayed.
- ✦ Change the Can Grow or Can Shrink properties.

When you resize a control by making it larger vertically, it uses as much space as you allow for it — more space than necessary if the value does not occupy the entire space. For example, most of the values of the Street/Apt text box control use one line; some use two. If you resize the Street/Apt text box control to display two lines, the control displays two lines for *every* customer. This leaves a blank line between the Street/Apt control and the City control whenever the Street/Apt value uses only one line.

One solution to this problem is to use the Can Grow or Can Shrink properties of the text box control rather than resizing the control. If you change the value of the Can Grow property to Yes, the control grows vertically if there are more lines than can be displayed in the default control. Another solution is to resize the control so it's larger, and then use the Can Shrink property to remove any blank lines if the value of the data does not use the full size of the control.

When you set the Can Grow property in a text box control to Yes, this also sets the property for the detail, group header, and group footer, or report header or footer sections.

Displaying Memo fields in multiple-line text box controls

The Memo data type fields generally use large amounts of text. You can display these fields on a report simply by placing the text box in the desired section (usually the detail section) and resizing it to the desired width and height.

In a form, you can add *scrollbars* to display any text that doesn't fit the space allotted. In a report, you don't have that option; to display text properly, use the Can Grow and Can Shrink properties. In Chapter 21, you created a large text box control to accommodate several lines of memo text, but you never set the Can Grow and Can Shrink properties. If you have a record with more than four lines of text, you won't see the other lines. Similarly, any records without Memo field data display only four empty lines. Therefore you should set the Can Grow and Can Shrink properties to Yes for the Comments text box control that uses the Memo data type. To do so, follow these steps:

1. Select the Properties button in the toolbar to display the property sheet.
2. Select the Comments text box control.
3. Change the height of the control to one line to fit the Comments caption.
4. Change the Can Grow property to Yes.
5. Change the Can Shrink property to Yes.
6. Shrink the detail section height by dragging the page footer border upward until it's just below the Comments control.

To see the effect of the Can Grow and Can Shrink properties, display the report in the Print Preview window. Notice the Comment line and the shadowed line in Figure 22-5, which shows the Print Preview window. If you look at the print preview in zoom mode, you'll see that the spaces between the records are the same, regardless of the size of the Comments field. If no comment text is present, the next record begins immediately below the preceding record's information.

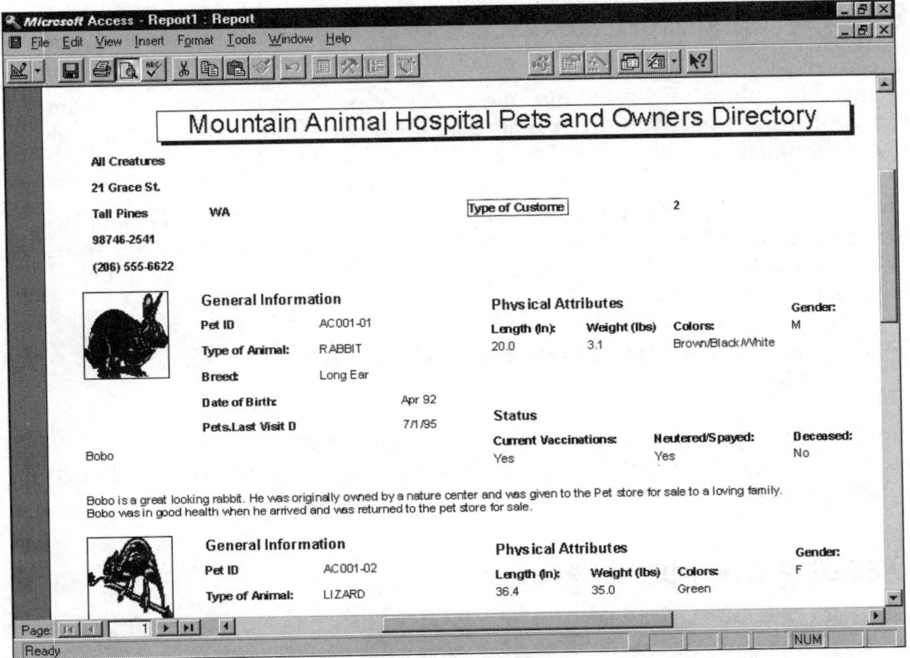

Figure 22-5: Displaying the Print Preview window.

Adding New Controls

You can change many data types to control types other than text boxes. These data types include Text, Number, and Yes/No. The other control types you can use are:

- ✦ Option buttons
- ✦ Check boxes
- ✦ Toggle buttons

Note Microsoft Access lets you change some control types from one to another. Generally, text box controls can become combo box or list box controls; check boxes, option buttons, and toggle buttons are interchangeable.

Displaying values with option groups and option buttons

In your design, as shown in Figure 22-2, you see two text box controls that should be changed to option buttons within an option group. These text box controls are the Type of Customer field in the page header section and the Gender field in the detail section.

An option group is generally bound to a single field or expression. Each button in the group passes a different value to the option group, which in turn passes the single choice to the bound field or expression. The buttons themselves are not bound to a field, only to the option group box.

Cross Ref If you haven't used an option button or option group yet, read Chapter 16 before continuing.

You can use only numeric data values to create an option button within an option group. The Type of Customer field is relatively easy to change to an option group; its values are already numeric, expressed as customer types 1, 2, or 3.

Creating the option group

To create the option group for the Type of Customer control, you must first delete the existing Type of Customer control. Then you can create a new option group and use the Option Group Wizard to create the option buttons.

Cross Ref Chapter 19 offers a more complete example of creating an option group and option buttons with the Option Group Wizard.

Follow these steps to create an option group using the Option Group Wizard:

1. Delete the existing Type of Customer control.
2. Select the option group button from the toolbox.
3. Drag the Type of Customer field to the space in the Page Header section.

   The first screen of the Option Group Wizard should be visible (as shown completed in Figure 22-6). Enter the text label for each option button that will be in your option group, just as you would do in a datasheet. You can use the down-arrow key to move to the next choice.

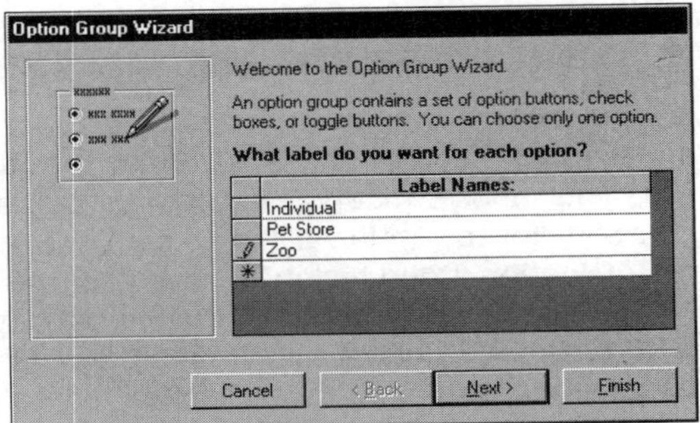

Figure 22-6: Entering the option group choices.

4. Enter **Individual**, **Pet Store**, and **Zoo**, pressing the down-arrow key between choices.
5. Click on the Next > button to move to the default option Wizard screen.

   The next screen lets you select the default control for when the option group is selected. Normally the first option is the default. If you want to make a different button the default, you would first select the Yes option button, and then select the new default value from the combo box that shows your choices. In this example, the first value will be the default automatically.
6. Click on the Next > button to move to the Assigning Values screen of the Wizard.

   The next Wizard screen displays the actual values you entered, along with a default set of numbers that will be used to store the selected value in the bound option group field. The screen looks like a datasheet with two columns. In this example, this is the Type of Customer field. Your first choice, Individual, is automatically assigned a 1, Pet Store a 2, and Zoo a 3. When Pet Store is selected, a 2 will be stored in the Type of Customer field.

   In this example, the default values are acceptable. Sometimes, you may want to assign values other than 1, 2, 3 . . . . You might want to use 100, 200, and 500 for some reason. As long as you use unique numbers, you can assign any values you want.
7. Click on the Next > button to move to the next Wizard screen.

   In this Wizard screen, you have to decide whether to bind the option group itself to a form field or to leave it unbound. The first choice in the Wizard, `Save the value for later use`, creates an unbound field. When you are using the option group in a dialog box that uses the selected value to make a decision, you don't want to store the value in a table field. In this example, the second value, `Store the value in this field`, is automatically selected because you started with the Type of Customer field. If you want to bind the option group value to a different table field, you can select from a list of all form fields. Again, in this example, the default is acceptable.

8. Click on the Next > button to move to Wizard screen that sets the option group style.

   Again, as shown in Figure 22-7, for this example, the defaults are acceptable. Notice that your actual values are used as a sample. In this Wizard screen, the lower half of the Wizard screen lets you choose what type of buttons you want. The upper half lets you choose the style for the option group box and the type of group control. The style affects the option group rectangle. If you choose Raised, Sunken, Etched, or Shadowed that value is applied to the Special Effect property of the option group. Additionally, for Option Buttons and Check Boxes, if you choose any of the special effects, the property for each option button or check box is set to the special effect.

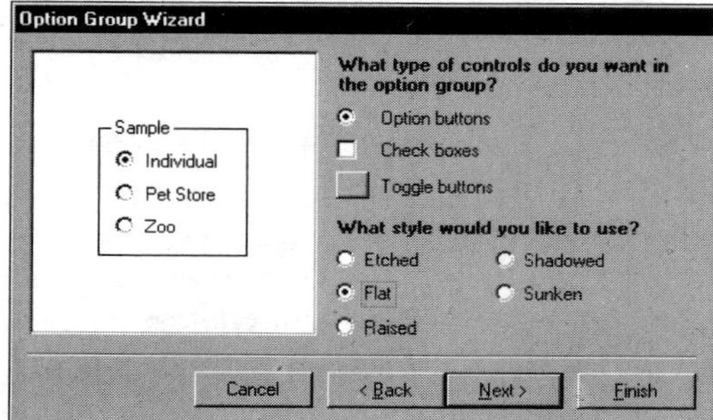

Figure 22-7: Selecting the type and look of your buttons.

As you change your selections, the Sample changes as well.

9. Click on the Next > button to move to the final option group Wizard screen.

   The final screen lets you give the option group control a label that will appear in the option group border. You can then add the control to your design and optionally display help.

10. Enter Type of Customer as your label for the Option Group.

11. Click on the Finish button to complete the Wizard.

    Your Wizard work is now complete, and the controls appear on the design screen. Eight controls have been created: the option group, its label, three option buttons, and their labels. In this example, you don't want the option group label.

12. Select the option group label `Type of Customer`, and click on the Delete key.

Creating an option group with a calculated control

You also want to display the Gender field as a set of option buttons. There is one problem, however. The Gender field is a Text field with the values of M, F, and U. You can create option buttons only with a Numeric field. You can do this easily with the Type of Customer field, which is numeric. How can you solve this problem with the Gender field? The solution is to create a new calculated control that contains an expression. The expression must transform the values M to 1, F to 2, and U to 3. You create this calculation by using the Immediate IF function (IIf), with this expression:

=IIf([Gender]="M","1",IIf([Gender]="F","2","3"))

The first IIf function checks the value of Gender; if the value is "M", the value of the calculated control is set to 1. If the value is not "M", another IIf checks for a Gender value of "F". If the value is "F", the calculated control value is set to 2. If the value is not "F", the value of the calculated control is set to 3. To create this new calculated control, follow these steps:

1. Create a new text box control under the Pet Name control, as shown in Figure 22-8.
2. Delete the attached label control.
3. Display the property sheet for the text box control.
4. Change the Control Name property to **Gender Number**.
5. Type **=IIf([Gender]="M","1",IIf([Gender]="F","2","3"))** in the Control Source property.
6. Change the Visible property to **No**.

Because you change the Visible property of the calculated control to No, the control is not displayed when you produce the report. Once you create the calculated control, you can use it as the control source for an option group. Figure 22-8 shows this new calculated control.

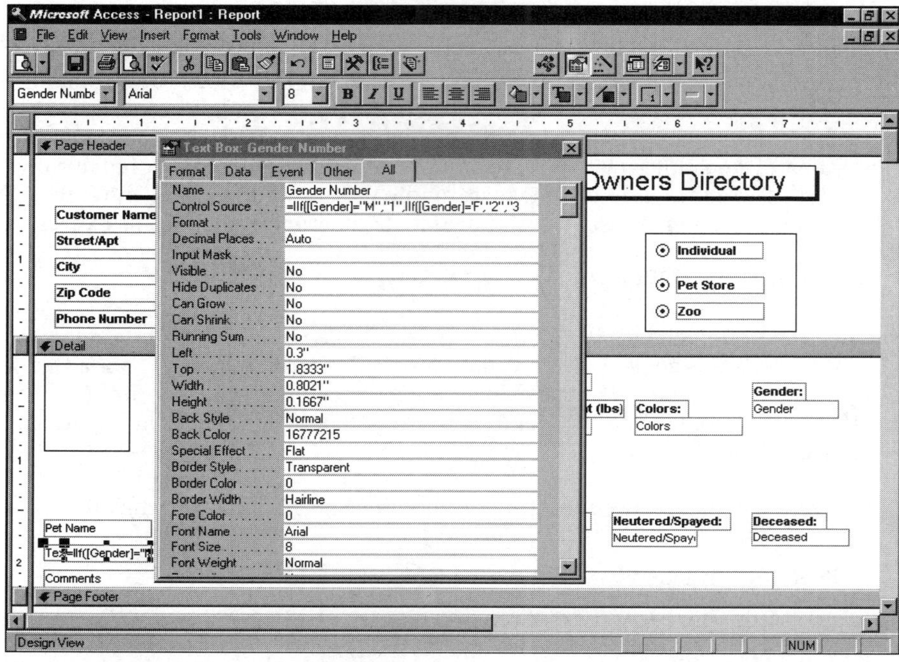

Figure 22-8: Creating a calculated control.

To create the option group for Gender (based on this calculated control), follow these steps:

1. Delete the existing Gender text box and label control in the detail section.
2. Select the Option Group button from the toolbox.
3. Drag the Option Group rectangle to the space in the detail section.
   The first screen of the Option Group Wizard should be displayed.
4. Enter **Male**, **Female**, and **Unknown**, pressing the down-arrow key between choices.
5. Click on the Next > button three times to move to the Control Source screen.

   In this Wizard screen, you have to decide whether the option group itself will be bound to a form field or unbound. In this example, you will use the first choice in the Wizard, `Save the value for later use`, which creates an unbound field. You cannot select a calculated field in the Wizard; after completing it, you will change the control source of the option group.

6. Click on the Next > button to move to the option group style Wizard screen.

   Again, for this example, the defaults are acceptable. Notice that your actual values are used as a sample.

7. Click on the Next > button to move to the final option group Wizard screen.

8. Enter **Gender**.

9. Click on the Finish button to complete the Wizard.

   Your Wizard work is now complete, and the controls appear on the design screen. Currently, as an unbound control, the Control Source property is blank. You must set this to the calculated control Gender Number.

10. Select the option group control and change the Control Source property to **=[Gender Number]**, as shown in Figure 22-9.

11. Name the control Gender by changing the Name property to **Gender**.

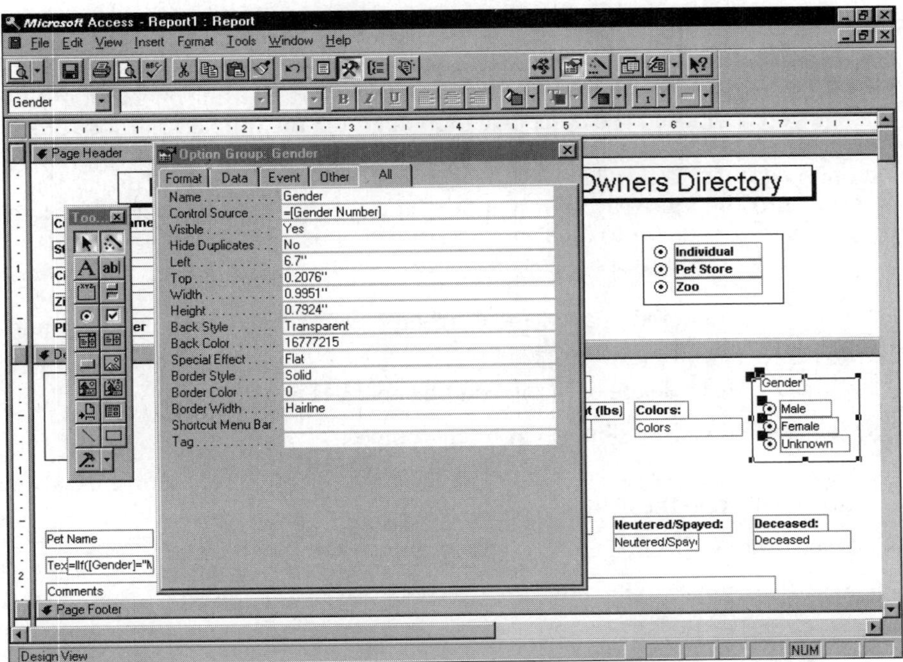

Figure 22-9: Completing an option group for a calculated control.

You may need to change the size of the rectangle to fit within the 8-inch margin. If you have to make it smaller, remember to change the margin (which may be larger than 8 inches now).

12. Resize the option group rectangle and reset the right margin to **8** inches.

The last task is to enhance all the text on the control buttons to 12-point bold. To accomplish this, follow these steps:

1. Select the entire Gender option group box, all the buttons, and their attached labels.
2. Click on the Bold button in the toolbar.
3. Select Format➪Size➪to Fit to resize the label control boxes.

You may still need to align the labels before your task is complete. The final design for the option buttons is shown in Figure 22-9, including the option button properties.

Displaying Yes/No values with check boxes

You can make Yes/No values more readable on a report by using check boxes. Although you could also use them in an option group, the primary purpose of a check box is to display one of two states for a single value; check boxes are easier to create than option groups. You will now change the Neutered/Spayed and Current Vaccination fields into check boxes. As with option button controls, you must first delete the existing text box controls to create a check box that uses the fields. To create the check boxes, follow these steps, using Figure 22-10 as a guide:

1. Select the Neutered/Spayed and Current Vaccination text box controls (and their associated labels) in the detail section.
2. Press Delete to delete both the text box controls and the attached label controls.
3. Select the Check Box button from the toolbox.
4. Using Figure 22-10 as a guide, drag the Neutered/Spayed and Current Vaccination fields from the field list to create two new check boxes.
5. Select both check box controls; change the font size to **10**.
6. Size the controls to fit; move them as necessary.

The completed check boxes are shown in Figure 22-10.

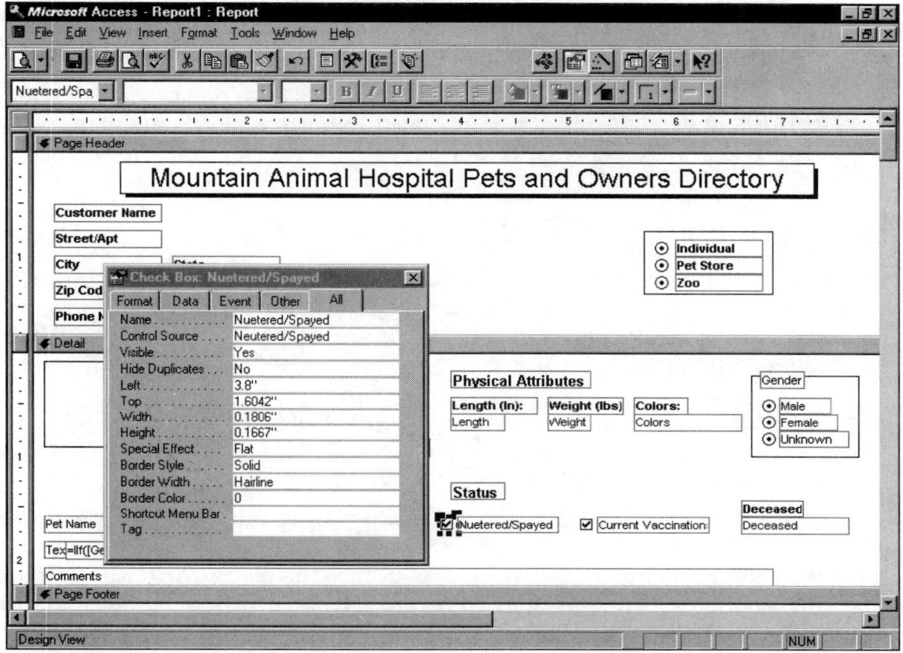

Figure 22-10: The completed check boxes.

Displaying values as toggle buttons

You can use toggle buttons as another way to make Yes/No data type easier to read. A toggle button appears to sit above the screen if the value of the Yes/No data type is No. If the value is Yes, the button appears to be pressed in the screen. To create a toggle button for the Deceased field, follow these steps:

1. Select the Deceased text box control (and its associated label) in the detail section.
2. Press Delete to delete both the text box control and the attached label control.
3. Select the Toggle Button icon from the toolbox.
4. Using Figure 22-11 as a guide, create a new toggle button by dragging the Deceased field from the field list.
5. Double-click on the toggle button and type **Deceased**.
6. Select Format⇨Size⇨to Fit to fit the button around the caption text.

The toggle button is displayed with the caption centered within the control.

You can also display a picture on the face of the toggle button instead of text by entering the filename of a bitmap image in the Picture property of the toggle button.

Remember, Access allows you to change some controls from one type to another; first you select the control, right-clicking to display the shortcut menu, and then select the new control style from the Change To option.

Displaying bound OLE objects in reports

In the report you are creating in this chapter, a picture of each animal is shown in the detail section. Some of the animals are displayed as they look, but others appear stretched out of proportion. Presto Chango (who is not really a hunchbacked lizard) illustrates this distortion.

Pictures are stored in OLE controls. The two types of OLE controls are as follows:

Bound object frames	Pictures are stored in a record.
Image frames	Pictures are embedded or linked to a report section itself.

In this report, there is already a bound object frame. The picture field is an OLE data type that has bitmaps embedded in each record. The Picture bound object control gets its values from the Picture field in the Pets table.

Displaying an image in a report

You can also add an image object to your report. Do this by pasting a bitmap from the Clipboard, or by either embedding or linking a bitmap file that contains a picture. Suppose you have a logo for the Mountain Animal Hospital. On the disk that accompanies this book is a bitmap called MTN.BMP. In this section, you can add this bitmap to the page header section (provided you copied it to your Access directory).

Using Figure 22-11 as a guide, you will move the customer information to the right side of the page header section, and then add the bitmap to the left side after creating the image frame. To add an unbound object frame, follow these steps.

1. Select the customer information in the Page Header section and move it to the right, as shown in Figure 22-11.
2. Click on the Image Frame button in the toolbox.

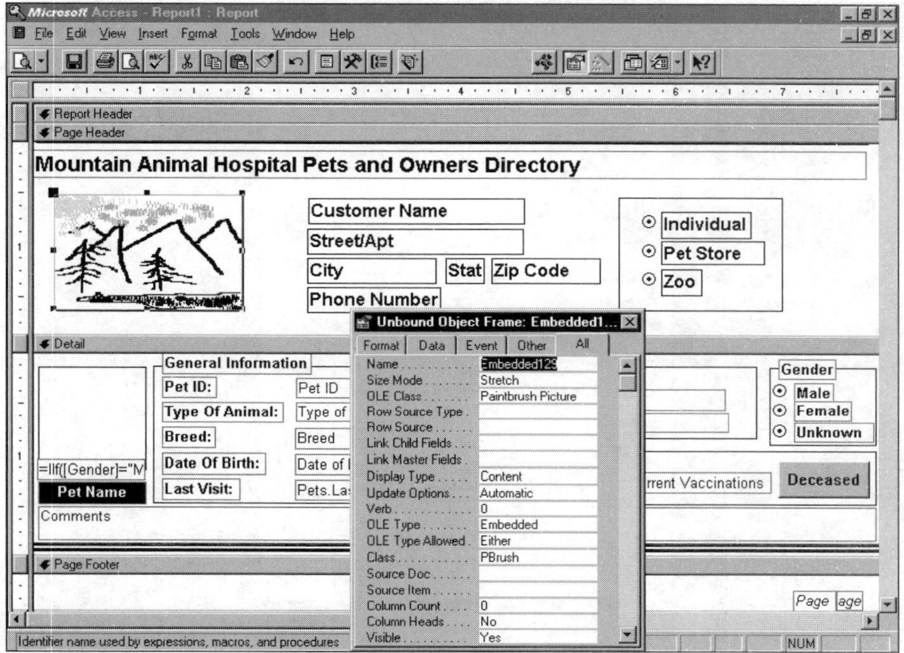

Figure 22-11: Creating toggle buttons.

3. Click on the left corner below the title; drag the box so it's sized as shown in Figure 22-11. The Insert Picture dialog box appears.

   From this dialog box, you can select the picture file name you want to insert into your report.

4. Select MTN.BMP from your Access directory (or wherever you copied the files for the book) and click on OK.
5. Display the property sheet.
6. Change the Size Mode property to Stretch.

   Finally, change the Border property so the picture does not simply blend into the background (there is too much white in the picture); change the border color to black or make the border three-dimensional (as shown in the next step).

7. Click on the Raised button in the Special Effects formatting window.

The image frame is now complete. This is a good time to view the report in the Print Preview window. Figure 22-12 shows the report in print preview mode.

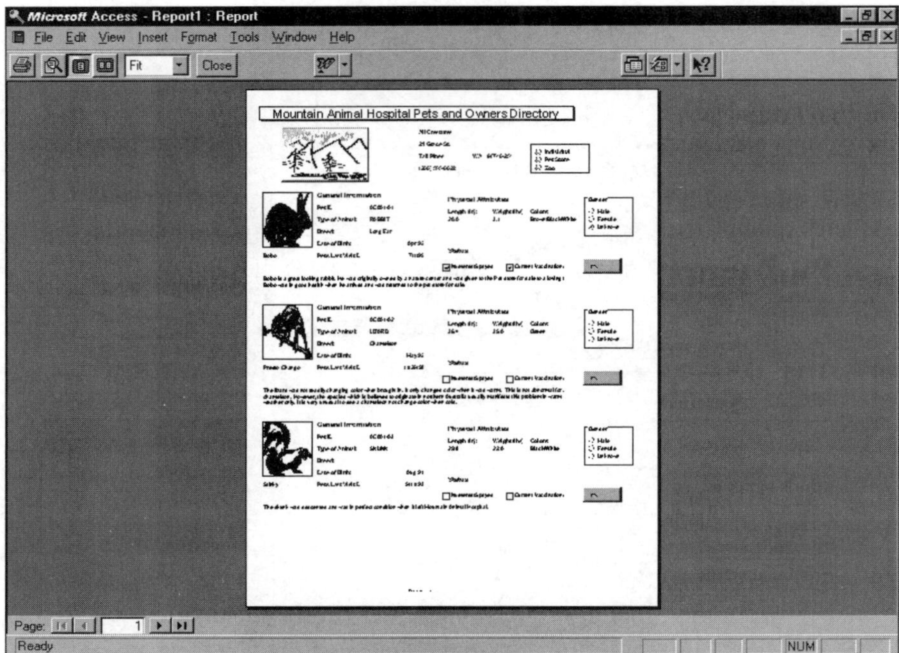

Figure 22-12: Previewing the report.

Note You can see that the toggle button does not display the text correctly in the button. At this size, no text font can display text correctly (in the previewed size) in a button. When the report is printed, however, the text will appear correctly.

Working with Lines and Rectangles

You can use lines and rectangles (commonly called boxes) to make certain areas of the report stand out or to bring attention to desired areas of the report. In Figure 22-1, you saw several groups of lines and rectangles that were used to emphasize data in the report. You need four rectangles and two different lines to complete the lines and boxes in this report.

To create the rectangle for the page header, follow these steps, using Figure 22-13 as a guide:

1. Select the Rectangle button in the toolbox.
2. Click on the upper-left part of the page header section to the right of the picture and just below the title.

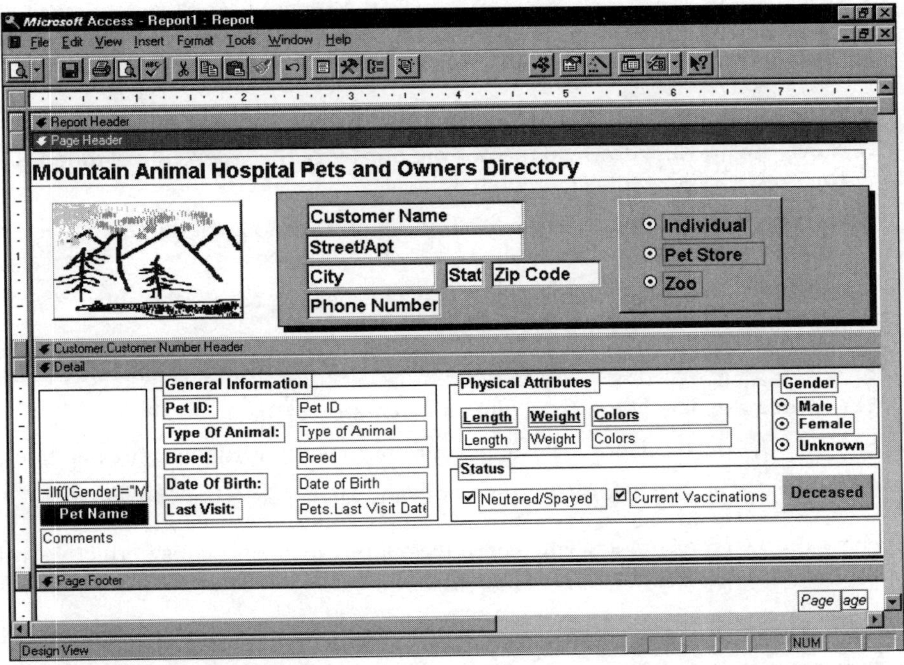

Figure 22-13: The final report.

3. Drag the rectangle around the entire set of customer text boxes and option buttons.
4. Select Format⇨Send to Back to redisplay the text boxes and option buttons.

Tip You may notice that when you create the rectangle, it blocks out the controls beneath it. By sending the rectangle to the background, you make the controls reappear.

You can also redisplay the controls by changing the Transparent button of the Back Color. This option, however, does not let you add other shading effects. For a rectangle, you should always select Send to Back.

The next three rectangles are in the detail section. You can create the rectangles by following the same steps you used to create the rectangle in the page header section. As you create them, you may find yourself rearranging some of the controls to fit better within the rectangles. You'll also want to change the label controls for Length, Weight, and Colors, as shown in Figure 22-13.

You also need several lines for the report. A single line needs to be added to the top of the report above the title, and two lines need to be added below the Comments text box. To add these lines, complete the next set of steps, using Figure 22-13 as a guide. You can also take this opportunity to remove the shadow on the title if you added it earlier.

1. If you didn't change it earlier, select the gray title line of text (`Mountain Animal Hospital Pets and Owners Directory`) used to create the shadow.
2. Delete the label control of the shadow only.
3. Move the title line down so the bottom border of the label control touches the top border of its enclosing rectangle.
4. Click on the Line button in the toolbox. If you wish to Lock the toolbar selection, double-click on it. To release the selection, press Esc.
5. Create a new line above the title in the page header, across the entire width of the report.
6. Select the third selection in the Border Width window to make the line thicker.
7. Create a new line below the Comments text box in the detail section.
8. Select the third selection in the Border Width window to make the line thicker.
9. Duplicate the line below the comments and align it with the line above.

Tip: If you hold down the Shift key while creating a line, the line remains perfectly straight, either horizontally or vertically, depending on the initial movement of drawing the line.

Emphasizing Areas of the Report

The report is now almost complete, but several tasks remain. According to the original printout and design shown in Figures 22-1 and 22-2, you still need to shade the rectangle in the page header, add a shadow to the rectangle, sink the Customer text box controls, raise the Type of Customer option group box, and change Pet Name to reverse video.

Adding background shade

You can add a background shade to any control. Adding background shading to a rectangle shades any controls contained within the rectangle. You can, however, add background shading to all controls that are selected at one time. To add background shading to the rectangle in the page header section, follow these steps:

1. Select the Rectangle control in the page header section.
2. Select the light gray Back Color.

Sinking controls

Generally, in a report, you cannot sink controls; they don't look sunken on a white background. You can, however, use a gray background to enhance the depth of a control; both sunken and raised controls stand out on a gray background. Because you just added a gray background to the rectangle in the page header, you can sink or raise controls within the rectangle. To give the Customer text box controls a sunken appearance, follow these steps:

1. Select each of the Customer text box controls in the page header section.
2. Click on the Sunken selection from the Special Effects button.

Raising controls

Just as you can sink a control, you can raise one. Raised controls, like sunken controls, look much better on a gray or dark background. To raise the Type of Customer option group control, follow these steps:

1. Select the Type of Customer option group control.
2. Click on the Raised selection from the Special Effects button.

Tip

If you sink or raise a check box, Access uses a different, smaller check box that has the appearance of depth.

Creating a shadow on a rectangle

If you want to emphasize an area of the report, you can add a shadow to any control. Most commonly, rectangles and text boxes are the types of controls given this effect. You create the shadows by adding a solid-color rectangle that is slightly offset and behind the original control. If the background is light or white, you need a dark-colored rectangle. If the background is dark or black, you need a light-colored or white rectangle. To create a shadow for the page header rectangle, follow these steps:

1. Select the rectangle in the page header.
2. Click on the Special Effect button in the Format toolbar.
3. Select Shadow from the window.

Changing text to a reverse video display

Text really stands out when you create white text on a black background. This is called *reverse video*; it's the opposite of the usual black-on-white. You can convert text in a label control or text box to reverse video by changing the fill color to black and the text color to white. To change the Pet Name text control to reverse video, follow these steps:

1. Select the Pet Name text control (not the label control).
2. Click on the black Back Color button.
3. Click on the white Fore Color button.

Figure 22-13 shows the final report in the Report Design window.

Seeing Your Output in Different Ways

You can see your output from a report in several ways:

- Print previewing (to multiple pages)
- Printing to hard copy
- Printing to a file
- Printing the report definition

Using the Print Preview window

Throughout this chapter, you used the Print Preview window to view your report. Figure 22-5 displayed your report in the Print Preview window in a zoomed view. This lets you see your report with the actual fonts, shading, lines, boxes, and data that will be on the printed report. When the print preview mode is in a zoomed view, you can press the mouse button to change the view to a page preview (where you can see the entire page).

You can use the horizontal and vertical elevators to move around the page, or move from page to page by using the page controls at the bottom left corner of the window.

The *page preview mode* of the Print Preview window displays an entire page of the report, as shown in Figure 22-14. The cursor is shaped like a magnifying glass in Print Preview windows; using this cursor during page preview lets you select a portion of the page and then zoom in to that portion for a detailed view.

In Figure 22-14, you see a representation of the printed page. You can use the navigation buttons (located in the lower left section of the Print Preview window) to move between pages, just as you would use them to move between records in a datasheet.

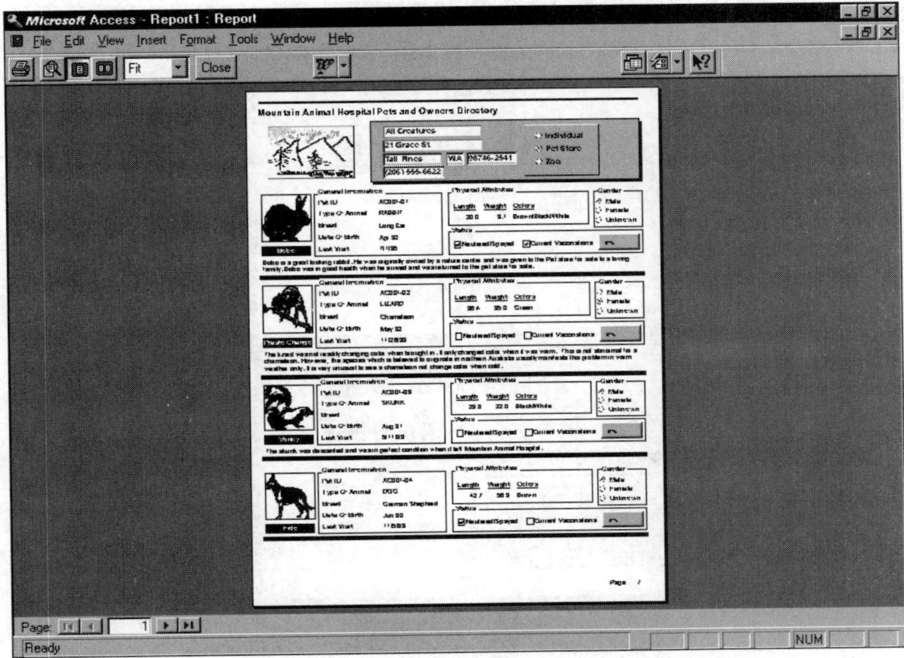

Figure 22-14: Displaying a report in page preview mode in Print Preview.

The first six buttons displayed on the toolbar provide quick access to printing tasks:

Print	Displays the Print dialog box
Zoom	Toggles in and out of Page Preview and Zoomed view
One Page	Displays a single page in Print Preview
Two Pages	Displays two pages in Print Preview
Zoom Control	Select Percent of Size to Zoom (200%, 150%, 100%, 75%, 50%, 25%, 10%, Fit)
Close Window	Returns to Design view

You are not limited to a one- or two-page preview; Access for Windows 95 lets you view up to 12 pages on a single screen. As you can see in Figure 22-15, the View⇨Pages menu lets you select 1, 2, 4, 8, or 12 pages to preview. In Figure 22-15, eight pages have been selected and are visible. You can also right-click on the Print Preview page and select pages or the Zoom percentage. When you use the shortcut menus, you can select up to 20 pages to preview at a time; you can also determine their arrangement in rows and columns (2 × 4, 5 × 4, 3 × 4, and so on).

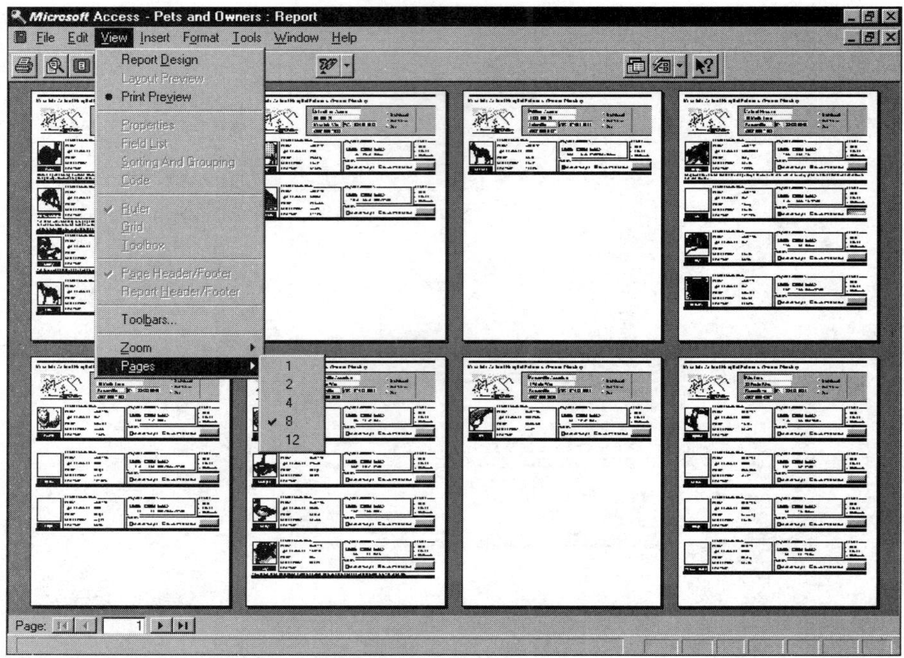

Figure 22-15: Multi-page Print Preview mode.

If you are satisfied with the report after examining the preview, simply select the Print button on the toolbar and print it. If you are not satisfied with your report, select the Close button to return to the Report Design window and make further changes.

Using layout previews

Layout preview is different from a print preview. A print preview uses a query's dynaset; layout preview displays sample data (ignoring criteria) or joins in an underlying query.

The purpose of a layout preview is strictly to show you the field placement and formatting. Thus you can create a report design without having to assemble your data properly; in a large query, this can save considerable time. You can see a sample preview by one of two methods: select View➪Layout Preview, or click on the Report

View button and then select the Layout Preview icon (the bottom one) in the Report Design toolbar. You can switch back to the Report Design window by selecting the Close Window button if you entered the Print Preview from the Report Design window. If you entered from the Database window, you are returned there.

Note You can also zoom in to a layout page preview on the sample data, or print the sample report from the Layout Preview window.

Printing a report

You can print one or more records in your form (exactly as they look on-screen) from several places:

- Select File⇨Print in the Report Design window.
- Select the Print button in the Preview window.
- Select File⇨Print in the Database window with a report highlighted.

Note If you are in the Print Preview window, your actual data prints. If you are in the Layout Preview window, only sample data prints.

The Print dialog box

Once you decide to print your report, the Print dialog box is displayed, as shown in Figure 22-16. The Print dialog box lets you control several items by giving you the following choices:

Name	Lets you select the printer
Print Range	Prints the entire report or selected pages
Copies	Selects the number of copies
Collate	Selects whether or not to collate copies
Print to File	Prints to a file rather than the printer

The Print dialog box that is displayed is specific to your printer and based on your setup in Microsoft Windows. Although each printer is different, the dialog box is essentially the same. Generally, dot-matrix or impact printers have a few more options for controlling quality than do laser printers.

Assuming you set up a printer in Microsoft Windows 95, you can select OK to print your form. Your form is printed using the font you selected for display (or the nearest printer equivalent). The printout contains any formatting in the form, including lines, boxes, and shading. Colors are converted to shades on a monochrome printer.

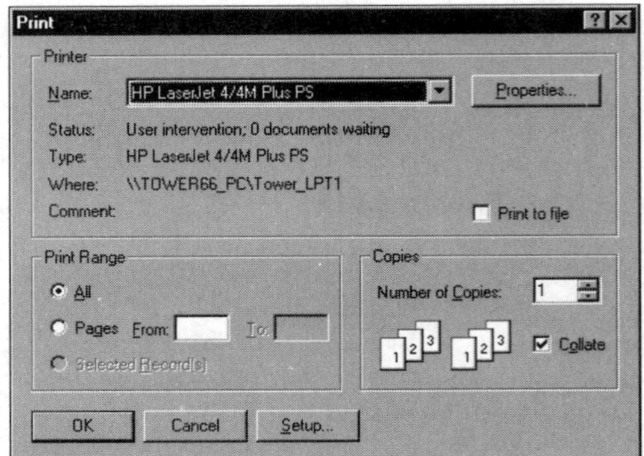

Figure 22-16: The Print dialog box.

If you need to further set up your Windows printer options, you can choose the Properties button in the Print dialog box. This dialog box sets up your printer, not your report. If you want to fine-tune the setup of your report, use the Setup button (which provides more options).

You can display print setup options in other ways as well, including the following:

- ✦ Selecting File➪Page Setup from the Report Design window
- ✦ Selecting File➪Page Setup from the Database window

The Page Setup dialog box

The Page Setup dialog box, shown in Figure 22-17, is divided into three tabbed dialog boxes: Margins, Page, and Layout. (You will use the Layout tab in Chapter 29 when you work with labels and multi-column reports.)

Margins	Sets the page margins. Also has option for Print Data Only.
Page	Selects page orientation, paper size and source, and printer device.
Layout	Select grid settings, item size, and layout items.

In the Page tab, you can control the Orientation of the report. There are two choices: Portrait and Landscape. Clicking on the Portrait button changes the report so the page is taller than it's wide. Clicking on the Landscape button changes the report orientation so the page is wider than it's tall.

Tip

A good way to remember the difference between landscape and portrait is to think of paintings. Portraits of people are usually taller than wide; landscapes of the outdoors are usually wider than tall. When you click on either button, the page icon (letter A) changes to show your choice graphically.

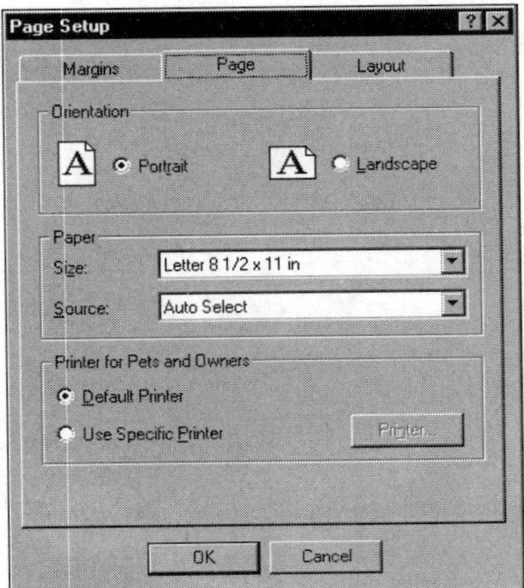

Figure 22-17: The Page tab in the Page Setup dialog box.

The Paper section indicates the size of the paper you want to use, as well as the paper source (for printers that have more than one source available). Clicking on Source displays a drop-down list of paper sources available for the printer you selected. Depending on the printer selected, you may have one or more paper trays or manual feed available. Click on the source you want to use.

Clicking on Size displays a drop-down box showing all the paper sizes available for the printer (and paper source) you selected. Click on the size you want to use.

If you click on the Data Only check box in the Margins tab, Access prints only the data from your report and does not print any graphics. (This feature is handy if you use preprinted forms.) Also, printing complex graphics slows down all but the most capable printers; not printing them saves time.

The Margins section shown in Figure 22-18 displays (and allows you to edit) the left, right, top, and bottom margins. To edit one or more of these settings, click on the appropriate text box and type in a new number.

Tip Page Setup settings are stored with each report. It's therefore possible to use several different printers for various reports, as long as you don't use the default Windows printer. This can also be a problem, though, because if you exchange files with another user who doesn't have the same printer installed, the other user must modify the Page Setup settings.

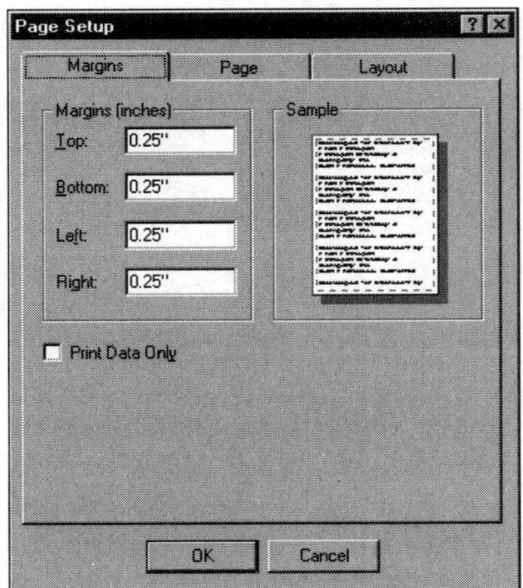

Figure 22-18: The Margins tab in the Page Setup dialog box.

Someone may send you a report you can't view or print because a Windows printer driver you don't have was used. If the report was created with a driver not installed on your system, Access will display a dialog box and let you print with your default printer.

Summary

In this chapter, you learned how to enhance your reports and how to print them. The chapter covered the following points:

- ✦ *Database publishing* is a term that generally describes report formatting from a database application that offers lines, boxes, shading, and other types of desktop publishing enhancements.
- ✦ The Access Report Writer is a WYSIWYG (what-you-see-is-what-you-get) report writer. What you see in the Design window is generally what you get on the hard-copy report.
- ✦ The form/report formatting buttons in the Report window let you set text and fill colors, control line widths, and add three-dimensional effects to controls, such as a raised or sunken appearance.
- ✦ You can enhance the text of label and text box controls by changing the font type style, font size, and such font style attributes as bold, italic, or font color. You can even add a shadow by duplicating the text or selecting the special effects.

- Multiple-line text box controls can display large amounts of text. To avoid leaving blank lines, you can set the Can Grow and Can Shrink properties to control the precise amount of space needed.
- Controls such as option buttons, check boxes, and toggle buttons make it easier to view your data. You must delete an existing control before you can create one of these controls using the same data field.
- When any of these controls are placed inside an option group, they act together instead of separately, and only one is active at a time.
- Option buttons are generally used to let a user select only one of a group, whereas check boxes and toggle buttons represent a two-state selection from Yes/No data types.
- You can display pictures in reports by using object frames. The two types of object frames are bound (the objects are attached to a data field in each record), and unbound (the objects are embedded in the report itself).
- Lines and rectangles let you separate areas of the report to add emphasis.
- You can further emphasize areas of the report by adding color, background shading, three-dimensional effects, shadows, and reverse video.
- You can view your report by previewing it or by printing it to a hard-copy device.
- You can view up to 20 pages at a time in Print Preview on one screen.
- Two types of print previews are available: print preview and layout preview. With print preview, you see your actual data; a layout preview uses only portions of your table data, but is very fast.
- You can set printing selections from the Page Setup dialog box.

In the next chapter, you learn how to create reports with totals and summaries.

✦ ✦ ✦

Creating Calculations and Summaries in Reports

In the last two chapters, you learned how to design and build reports from a blank form, as well as how to create striking and effective output by using many of the advanced features in Access. In this chapter, you learn how to use expressions to calculate results.

Disk: If you don't want to build the reports created in this chapter, they are included on your sample disk in the Reports tab. The reports are named Monthly Invoice Report - No Cover, Monthly Invoice Report, Monthly Invoice Report - Percentages, and Monthly Invoice Report - Running Sum.

Note: Because the Report Design window is set to a width of eight inches, you see most of the screen printouts in this chapter taken with an 800×600 resolution Super VGA Windows screen driver (rather than the standard 640×480 VGA Windows driver), which lets you see almost the entire screen in the figures.

✦ ✦ ✦ ✦

In This Chapter

Designing a report with multiple group totals

Creating several levels of sorting and grouping totals

Entering and using expressions and functions in text boxes

Using concatenation in text expressions

Calculating sums for each group

Calculating running sums

Calculating percentages based on group totals

Creating a report cover page

✦ ✦ ✦ ✦

Creating a Multilevel Grouping Report with Totals

You now create a report that displays information about visits to the hospital for each customer's pets on specific days. This report displays data in an invoice format that lists the type of visit, treatments given, medication dispensed, and the cost of each of these items. The data is totaled for each line item and summarized for each visit. The report can display multiple pets for the same customer on the same day. Finally, totals are shown for each visit by a customer, including the total amount spent, any discounts, and tax. A sample hard-copy page of the report is shown in Figure 23-1. Later in this chapter, you see how to enhance this report to display individual line-item percentages and cumulative running totals.

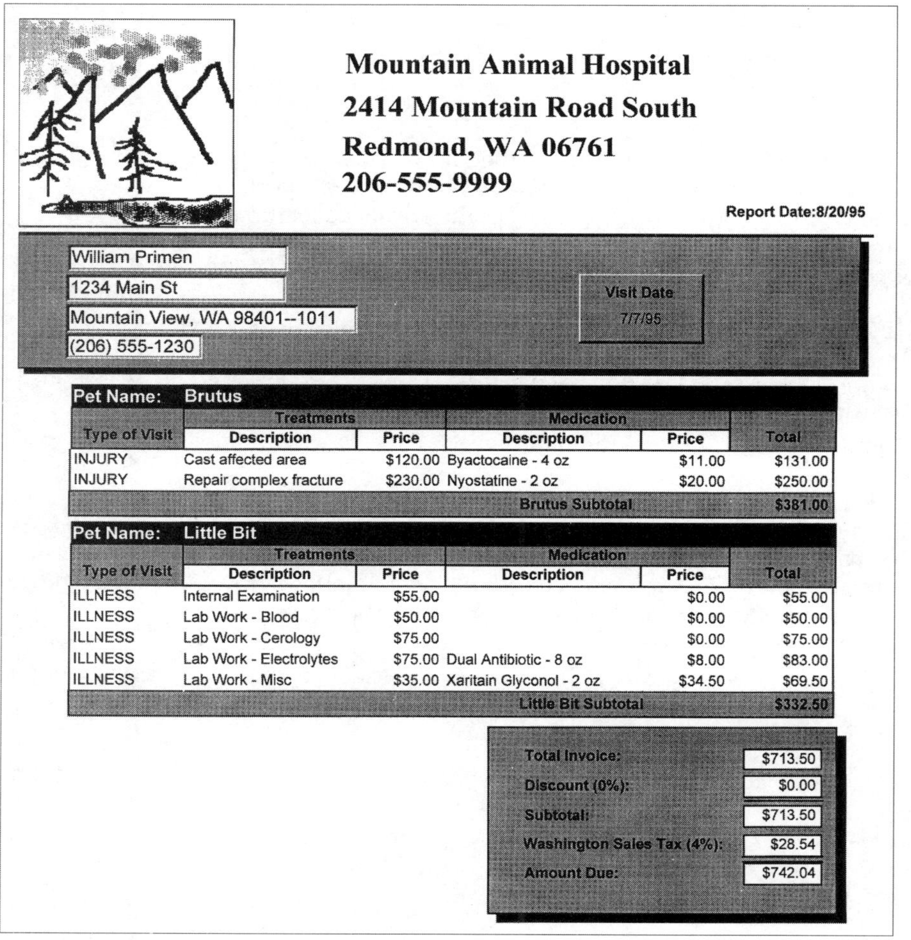

Mountain Animal Hospital
2414 Mountain Road South
Redmond, WA 06761
206-555-9999

Report Date:8/20/95

William Primen
1234 Main St
Mountain View, WA 98401--1011
(206) 555-1230

Visit Date
7/7/95

Pet Name: Brutus

Type of Visit	Treatments		Medication		Total
	Description	Price	Description	Price	
INJURY	Cast affected area	$120.00	Byactocaine - 4 oz	$11.00	$131.00
INJURY	Repair complex fracture	$230.00	Nyostatine - 2 oz	$20.00	$250.00
			Brutus Subtotal		$381.00

Pet Name: Little Bit

Type of Visit	Treatments		Medication		Total
	Description	Price	Description	Price	
ILLNESS	Internal Examination	$55.00		$0.00	$55.00
ILLNESS	Lab Work - Blood	$50.00		$0.00	$50.00
ILLNESS	Lab Work - Cerology	$75.00		$0.00	$75.00
ILLNESS	Lab Work - Electrolytes	$75.00	Dual Antibiotic - 8 oz	$8.00	$83.00
ILLNESS	Lab Work - Misc	$35.00	Xaritain Glyconol - 2 oz	$34.50	$69.50
			Little Bit Subtotal		$332.50

Total Invoice:	$713.50
Discount (0%):	$0.00
Subtotal:	$713.50
Washington Sales Tax (4%):	$28.54
Amount Due:	$742.04

Figure 23-1: The sample Invoice Report page.

Designing the Invoice Report

The Invoice Report is an excellent example for showing the types of tasks necessary to create common types of reports. It uses many of the advanced report-writing features in Access — sorting and grouping, group summaries, text expressions, and graphical objects. Following is a summary of what the Invoice Report's design includes:

- The Mountain Animal Hospital name, address, phone number, and logo on the top of every page
- Owner detail information (customer name, street/apt., city, state, Zip code, and telephone)
- Visit date
- Pet name
- Visit detail information for each pet (including type of visit, treatment, treatment price, medication, medication price, and total cost)
- A subtotal that summarizes each pet's visit details (total cost subtotal for the pet)
- A subtotal that summarizes the total cost for each pet on a visit date for a particular owner, and then calculates a total that lists and incorporates the owner's discount and proper state sales tax

The report design also must be shaped according to the following considerations:

- The report must be sorted by the fields Visit Date, then Customer Number, and then Pet ID.
- No more than one visit date per printed page should appear.
- No more than one customer per printed page should appear.
- One or more pets belonging to the same owner can appear on each printed page.
- If there is more than one pet per invoice, the pets should be listed in Pet ID order.

The design for this report is shown in Figure 23-2. As you can see, each section is labeled, and each control displays either the field name control or the calculated control contents. With the exception of the Mountain Animal Hospital logo (an unbound object frame) and several lines and rectangles, the report consists primarily of text box controls.

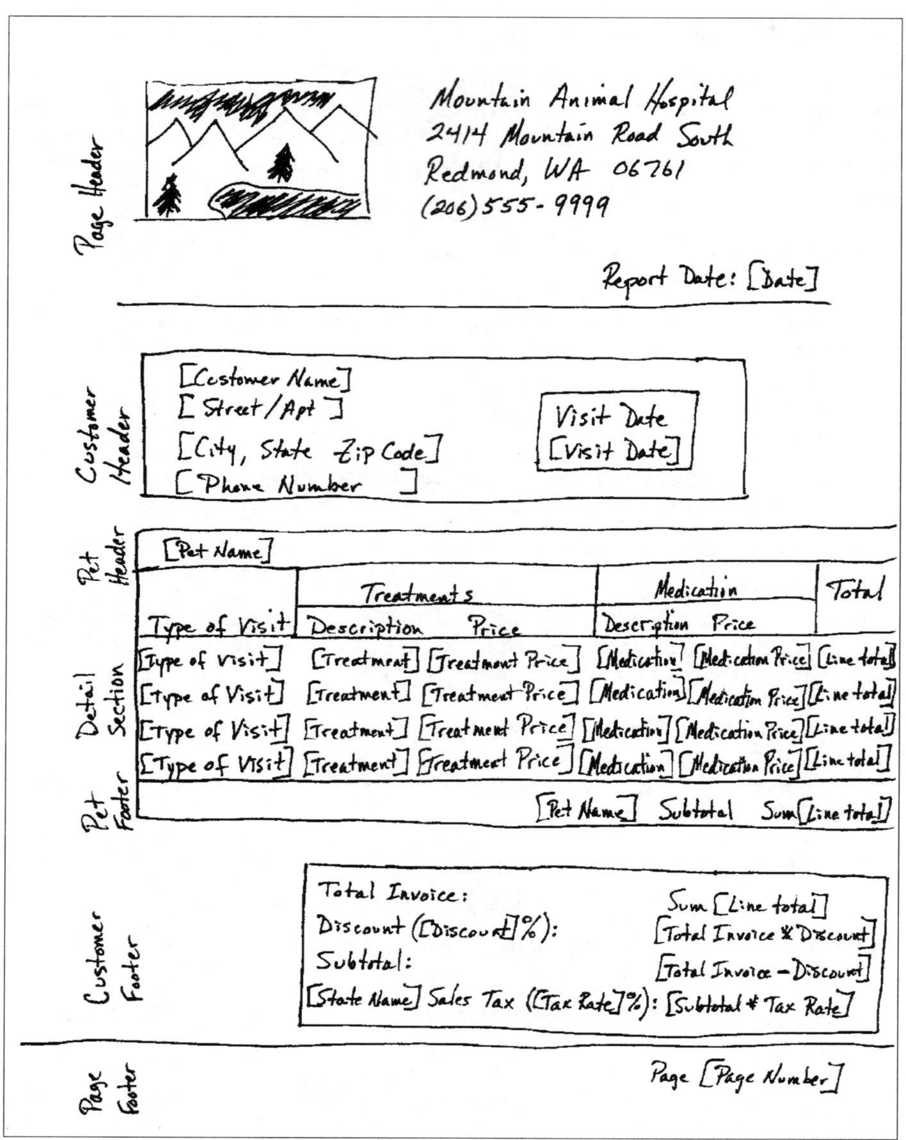

Figure 23-2: A design for the Invoice Report.

Designing and creating the query for the report

The Invoice Report uses fields in practically every table you've seen in the Mountain Animal Hospital database. Although the design in Figure 23-2 shows the approximate position and use of each control, it is equally important to perform a data design that lists each table field or calculated control. This data design should include the purpose of the field or control and the table in which the field originates. Using such a design plan, you can be sure to build a query that contains all the fields you may need. Table 23-1 lists these controls, the section in the report where they are used, and the originating table. Important: Do this type of data design *before* creating the query to build your report from.

Table 23-1
The Data Design for the Invoice Report

Report Section	*Control Purpose*	*Type of Control*	*Table Field/ Calculation*	*Table*
Page header	Logo	Unbound object frame		
Page header	Name and address	Label controls (4)		
Page header	Report date	Calculated text box	Date Function	
Customer header	Customer name	Bound text box	Customer Name	Customer
Customer header	Street and Apt.	Bound text box	Street/Apt	Customer
Customer header	City	Bound text box	City	Customer
Customer header	State	Bound text box	State	Customer
Customer header	ZIP Code	Bound text box	Zip Code	Customer
Customer header	Phone Number	Bound text box	Phone Number	Customer
Customer header	Visit date	Bound text box	Visit Date	Visits
Pet header	Pet name	Bound text box	Pet Name	Pets
Pet header	Text labels	Label controls (8)		
Detail	Type of visit	Bound text box	Visit Type Visit	Details
Detail	Treatment	Bound text box	Treatment	Treatments
Detail	Treatment price	Bound text box	Treatment Price	Visit Details
Detail	Medication	Bound text box	Medication Name	Medications
Detail	Medication price	Bound text box	Medication Price	Visit Details
Detail	Line total	Calculated text box	Treatment Price + Medication Price	

(continued)

Table 23-1 *(continued)*

Report Section	*Control Purpose*	*Type of Control*	*Table Field/ Calculation*	*Table*
Pet footer	Pet name	Calculated text box	Pet Name + Text	Pets
Pet footer	Line total sum	Calculated text box	Sum(Line Total)	
Customer footer	Text labels	Label controls (3)	Lines 1, 3, 5	
Customer footer	Discount label	Calculated text box	Text + Discount	Customer
Customer footer	State sales tax	Calculated text box	State Name + Tax Rate	States/Visits
Customer footer	Total invoice	Calculated text box	Sum(Line Total)	
Customer footer	Discount amount	Calculated text box	Total Invoice * Discount	
Customer footer	Subtotal	Calculated text box	Total Invoice - Discount	
Customer footer	Sales tax	Calculated text box	Subtotal * Tax Rate	Visits
Customer footer	Amount due	Calculated text box	Subtotal + Sales Tax	
Page footer	Page number	Calculated text box	Text + Page Number	

After you complete the data design for a report, you can scan the Table column to determine the tables necessary for the report. When you create the query, you may not want to select each field individually; if not, use the asterisk (*) field to select all the fields in each table. This way, if a field changes in the table, the query can still work with your report.

Warning Remember that if a table field name changes in your query, you'll need to change your report design. If you see a dialog box asking for the value of a specific field when you run your report — or the text `#Error` in place of one of your values after you run it — chances are a table field has changed.

After examining Table 23-1, you may notice that every table in the Mountain Animal Hospital database is needed for the report — with the exception of the Animals lookup table. You may wonder why you need *any* of the four lookup tables. The States, Animals, Treatments, and Medications tables are mainly to be used as lookup tables for data validation when you're adding data to forms, but you can also use them to look up data when printing in reports.

In the Invoice Report, the State Name field from the States table is used for looking up the full state name for the sales tax label in the Customer footer. The Tax Rate field can also be found in the States table, but at the time of the visit, the current tax rate is copied to the Visits table for that record. Only the codes are stored in the Visit Details table, so Access looks up the Treatment and Medication Name fields from their respective tables.

These seven tables are all joined together using the Monthly Invoice Report query, as illustrated in Figure 23-3.

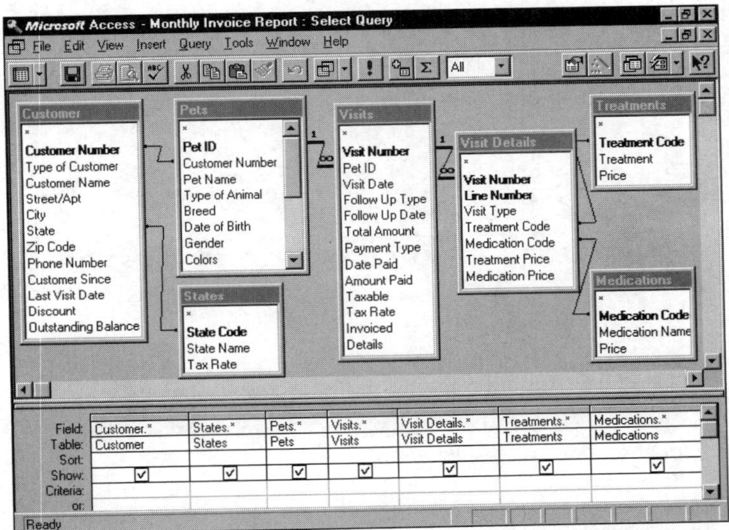

Figure 23-3: The Query Design window for the Monthly Invoice Report query.

After your query is completed, you can create your report.

Cross Ref Chapter 21 contains a detailed explanation of creating a new report from a blank form; it also shows you how to set page size and layout properly. If you are unfamiliar with these topics, read Chapter 21 before continuing. The present chapter focuses mainly on multiple-level groupings, calculated and summarized fields, and expressions.

Designing test data

One of the biggest mistakes you can make when designing and creating complex reports is not checking the results your report displays. Before you create your complete report, you should have a good understanding of your data. One way is to create a query using the same sorting order the report will use, and create any detail line calculations. You can then check the query's datasheet results, using these to check the report's results. When you are sure the report is using the correct data, you can be sure it will always produce great results. Figure 23-4 shows a simple query (the Monthly Invoice Report - Test Data) to use for checking the report you create in this chapter.

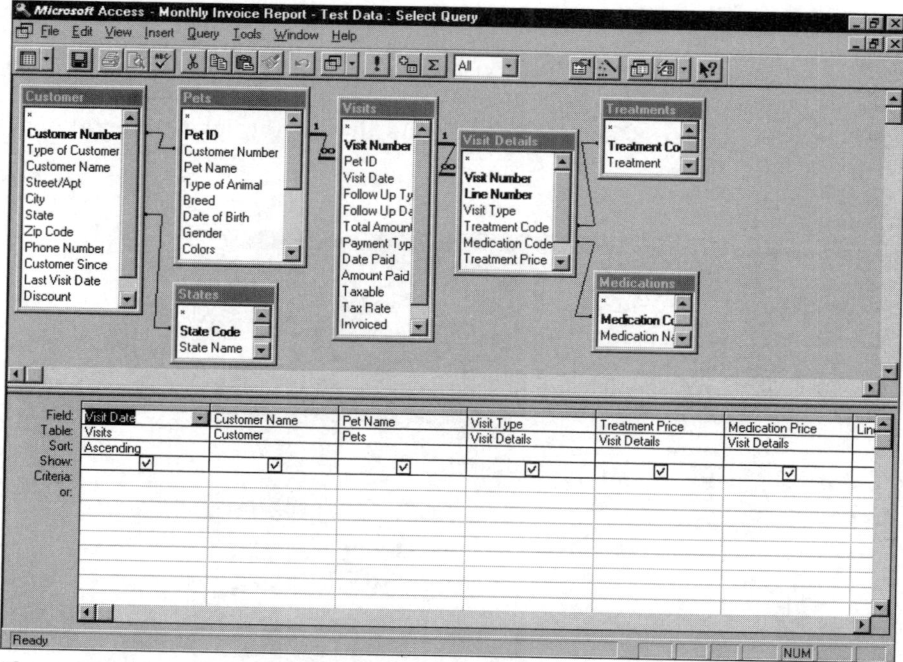

Figure 23-4: A query for checking data results.

Normally you can make a copy of the report query, adding the sorting orders and using only the detail fields you need to check totals. You can then add the numbers manually, or convert the query to a Total query to check group totals. Figure 23-5 shows the datasheet produced by this query; you can compare the results of each task in the report design to this datasheet.

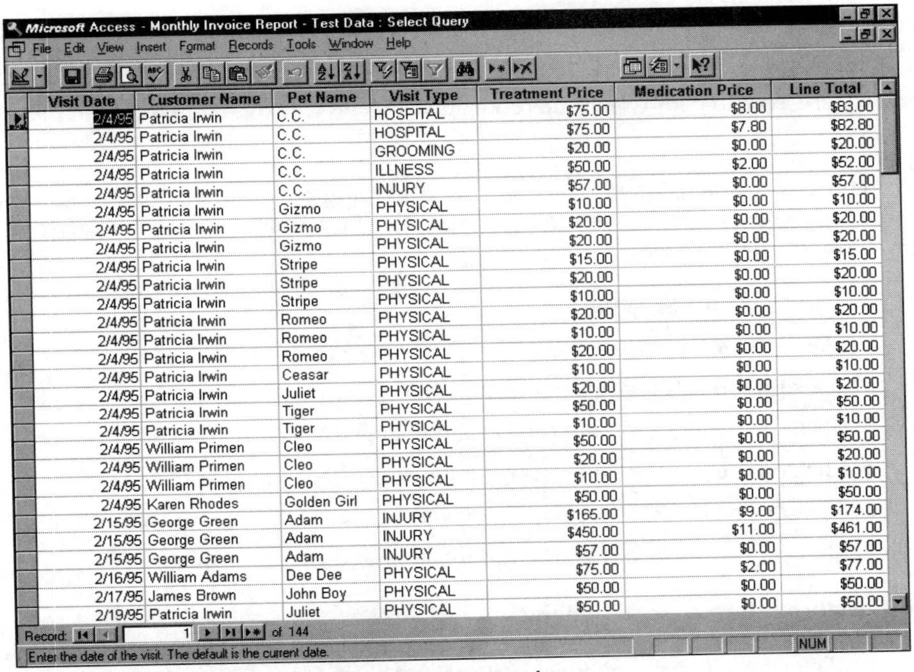

Microsoft Access - Monthly Invoice Report - Test Data : Select Query

File Edit View Insert Format Records Tools Window Help

Visit Date	Customer Name	Pet Name	Visit Type	Treatment Price	Medication Price	Line Total
2/4/95	Patricia Irwin	C.C.	HOSPITAL	$75.00	$8.00	$83.00
2/4/95	Patricia Irwin	C.C.	HOSPITAL	$75.00	$7.80	$82.80
2/4/95	Patricia Irwin	C.C.	GROOMING	$20.00	$0.00	$20.00
2/4/95	Patricia Irwin	C.C.	ILLNESS	$50.00	$2.00	$52.00
2/4/95	Patricia Irwin	C.C.	INJURY	$57.00	$0.00	$57.00
2/4/95	Patricia Irwin	Gizmo	PHYSICAL	$10.00	$0.00	$10.00
2/4/95	Patricia Irwin	Gizmo	PHYSICAL	$20.00	$0.00	$20.00
2/4/95	Patricia Irwin	Gizmo	PHYSICAL	$20.00	$0.00	$20.00
2/4/95	Patricia Irwin	Stripe	PHYSICAL	$15.00	$0.00	$15.00
2/4/95	Patricia Irwin	Stripe	PHYSICAL	$20.00	$0.00	$20.00
2/4/95	Patricia Irwin	Stripe	PHYSICAL	$10.00	$0.00	$10.00
2/4/95	Patricia Irwin	Romeo	PHYSICAL	$20.00	$0.00	$20.00
2/4/95	Patricia Irwin	Romeo	PHYSICAL	$10.00	$0.00	$10.00
2/4/95	Patricia Irwin	Romeo	PHYSICAL	$20.00	$0.00	$20.00
2/4/95	Patricia Irwin	Ceasar	PHYSICAL	$10.00	$0.00	$10.00
2/4/95	Patricia Irwin	Juliet	PHYSICAL	$20.00	$0.00	$20.00
2/4/95	Patricia Irwin	Tiger	PHYSICAL	$50.00	$0.00	$50.00
2/4/95	Patricia Irwin	Tiger	PHYSICAL	$10.00	$0.00	$10.00
2/4/95	William Primen	Cleo	PHYSICAL	$50.00	$0.00	$50.00
2/4/95	William Primen	Cleo	PHYSICAL	$20.00	$0.00	$20.00
2/4/95	William Primen	Cleo	PHYSICAL	$10.00	$0.00	$10.00
2/4/95	Karen Rhodes	Golden Girl	PHYSICAL	$50.00	$0.00	$50.00
2/15/95	George Green	Adam	INJURY	$165.00	$9.00	$174.00
2/15/95	George Green	Adam	INJURY	$450.00	$11.00	$461.00
2/15/95	George Green	Adam	INJURY	$57.00	$0.00	$57.00
2/16/95	William Adams	Dee Dee	PHYSICAL	$75.00	$2.00	$77.00
2/17/95	James Brown	John Boy	PHYSICAL	$50.00	$0.00	$50.00
2/19/95	Patricia Irwin	Juliet	PHYSICAL	$50.00	$0.00	$50.00

Record: 1 of 144

Enter the date of the visit. The default is the current date.

NUM

Figure 23-5: The datasheet for checking data results.

Creating a new report

With the report planning and data testing completed, it's time to create the new report. In Chapter 21, you learned how to create a report from a blank form. The steps to create a new report (and binding it to a query) are repeated for you here:

1. Press F11 to display the Database window if it is not already displayed.
2. Click on the Report tab.
3. Click on the New command button. The New Report dialog box appears.
4. Select Design View.
5. Select the Monthly Invoice Report query.
6. Click on OK.
7. Maximize the Report window.

A blank Report Design window appears, showing three sections (Page Header, Detail, and Page Footer). The report is bound to the query Monthly Invoice Report; data from that query will be used when the report is viewed or printed. The fields from the query are available for use in the report design, and will appear in the Field List window.

You must also change the Printer Setup settings and resize the Report Design window area for the report (see Chapter 21 for details). The steps for specifying Page Setup settings are shown again here:

1. Select File⇨Page Setup.
2. Select the Margins tab.
3. Click on the Left Margin setting and change the setting to **.250**.
4. Click on the Right Margin setting and change the setting to **.250**.
5. Click on the Top Margin setting and change the setting to **.250**.
6. Click on the Bottom Margin setting and change the setting to **.250**.
7. Click on OK to close the Print Setup window.

Follow these steps to set the report width:

1. Click on the rightmost edge of the report body (where the white area meets the gray).
2. Drag the edge to the 8-inch mark on the ruler.
3. Release the mouse button.

These steps should complete the initial setup for the report. Next you create the report's sorting order.

Creating the sorting orders

In a query, you can specify sorting fields; you designated three of them in the query you created to display test data. In a report, however, you must also specify the sorting order when you create groups; Access ignores the underlying query sorting. In the underlying query for this report, no sorting is specified because it must be entered here as well.

In this report design, there are three sorting levels: Visit Date, Customer Number, and Pet ID. You'll need to use all these levels to define group headers, and you need the latter two for group footers. If you look back at the original design in Figure 23-2, you see that Visit Date is not shown as a group. Later, as you create your report, you'll see why a grouping to use the Visit Date header section is necessary.

Before you can add a grouping, you must first define the sort order for the report. You've learned to do this task with the Sorting and Grouping box (shown completed on the blank Report Design window in Figure 23-6).

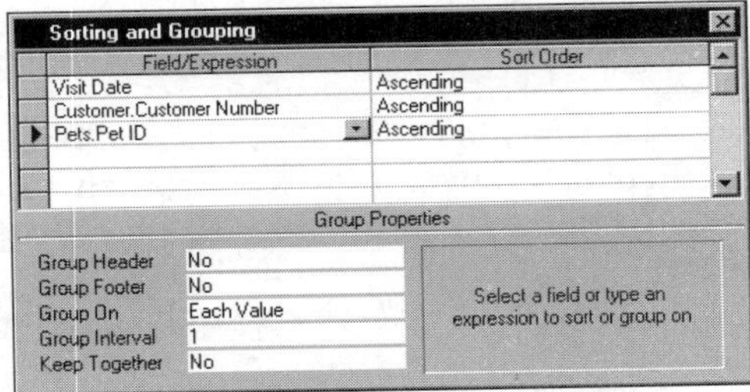

Figure 23-6: Creating the sorting orders.

To complete the sorting orders as shown in Figure 23-6, follow these steps:

1. Click on the Sorting and Grouping button on the toolbar to display the Sorting and Grouping box.
2. Click on the cursor on the first row of the Field/Expression column of the Sorting and Grouping box. A downward-pointing arrow appears.
3. Click on the arrow to display a list of fields in the Monthly Invoice Report query.
4. Click on the Visit Date field in the field list. Notice that Sort Order defaults to Ascending.
5. Click on the cursor on the second row of the Field/Expression column.
6. Click on the arrow to display a list of fields in the Mountain Invoice Report query.
7. Click on the Customer.Customer Number field in the field list. Notice that Sort Order defaults to Ascending.
8. Click on the cursor on the third row of the Field/Expression column.
9. Click on the arrow to display a list of fields in the Mountain Invoice Report query.
10. Click on the `Pets.Pet ID` field in the field list. Notice that Sort Order defaults to Ascending.

Tip To see more of the Field/Expression column, you can drag the border between the Field/Expression and Sort Order columns to the right (as in Figure 23-6).

You next see how the detail section is created for this report. Because this chapter's intent is to focus on expressions and summaries, be sure you've read Chapters 21 and 22, and that you understand how to create and enhance the labels and text boxes in a report.

Creating the detail section

The detail section is shown completed in its entirety in Figure 23-7. The section has been completed and resized. Notice that there is no space above or below any of the controls, which allows multiple detail records to be displayed as one comprehensive section on a report. This section must fit snugly between the Pet header and Pet footer, as shown in Figures 23-1 and 23-2, and so it has been resized to the exact size of the controls.

Creating the detail section controls

The detail section has five unlabeled bound text box controls, two line controls, and one calculated control. The bound text box controls are as follows:

- ✦ Visit Details.Visit Type
- ✦ Treatments.Treatment
- ✦ Visit Details.Treatment Price
- ✦ Medications.Medication Name
- ✦ Visit Details.Medication Price

You need to drag each of these bound text box controls from the Report window field list onto the detail section and then properly size the controls. The default text box property Auto Label should be set to No.

The two line controls are vertical lines. One is on the left side of the detail section under the left edge of the Type of Visit text box control. The other is on the right side of the detail section under the right edge of the calculated control.

The last control is a calculated text box control. This control calculates the total of the Treatment Price and the Medication Price for each detail line. You need to enter the formula into a new unlabeled text box: **=[Treatment Price]+[Medication Price].** A calculated control always starts with an equal sign (=), and each field name must be placed in brackets. Figure 23-7 also shows the property sheet for this calculated text box control, which is named Pet Line Visit Total. The Pet Line Visit Total control is also formatted with the Currency format property so that the dollar signs appear. If any of the totals is over $1,000.00, the comma also appears. The Decimal Place property is set to Auto, which is automatically set to 2 for the Currency format.

Creating calculated controls

You can use any valid Access expression in any text control. Expressions can contain operators, constants, functions, field names, and literal values. Some examples of expressions are shown next:

`=Date()`	Date function
`=[Customer Subtotal]*[Tax Rate]`	A control name multiplied by a field name
`=Now()+30`	A literal value added to the result of a function

The control (Control Source property) shown in Figure 23-7 calculates the total for each individual line in the detail section. To create this calculated control, follow these steps:

1. Create a new text control in the detail section, as shown in Figure 23-7.
2. Display the property sheet for the new text box control.

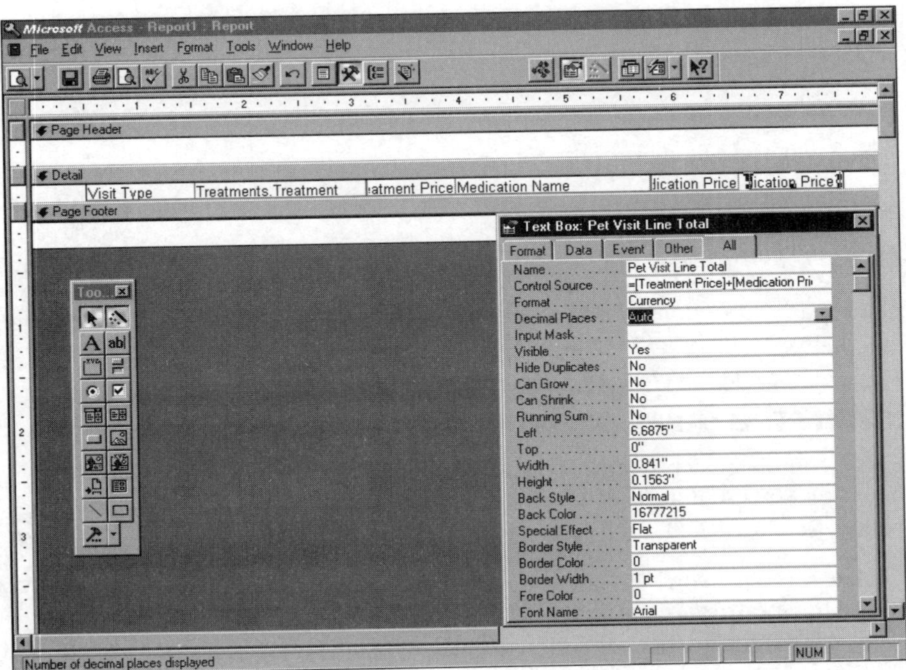

Figure 23-7: The detail section.

3. Enter **=[Treatment Price]+[Medication Price]** in the Control Source property cell.
4. Set the Format property to Currency.

Naming controls used in calculations

Every time you create a control, Access inserts a name for it into the Control Name property of the control's property sheet automatically. The name is really a description that defines what kind of control it is; for example, text controls show the name `Field`, and label controls show the name `Text`. Each name is followed by a sequential number. An example of a complete name is `Field13`. If the next control you create is a label, it is named `Text15`. These names can be replaced with user-defined names, such as Report Date, Sales Tax, or any other valid Access name, which lets you reference other controls easily (especially those containing expressions).

For example, if you have the fields Tax Rate and Subtotal and want to calculate Amount of Tax Due, you enter the expression **=[Tax Rate]*[Subtotal]** and call it Amount of Tax Due. You can then calculate Total Amount Due by entering the expression **=[Subtotal]+[Amount of Tax Due]**. This lets you change an expression in a calculated field without having to change all other references to that expression. To change the name of the control for Treatment Price + Medication Price Total, follow these steps:

1. Select the calculated control (=[Treatment Price]+[Medication Price]).
2. Display the property sheet.
3. Select the Name property.
4. Replace the default with **Pet Visit Line Total.**

Warning Later, you learn you cannot use a calculated control name in a *summary* calculation. You'll learn you must summarize the original calculation. For example, instead of creating an expression such as =Sum(Pet Visit Line Total), you must enter the summary expression **=Sum([Treatment Price]+[Medication Price])**.

Testing the detail section

As you complete each section, you should compare the results against the test datasheet you created, as displayed in Figure 23-5. The easiest way to view your results is either to select the Print Preview button on the toolbar (and view the report on-screen) or to print the first few pages of the report. Figure 23-8 displays the Print Preview screen. If you compare the results to the test data in Figure 23-5, you'll see that all the records are correctly displayed. You may notice, however, that the records are not exactly in the right order. This is acceptable as long as groups of the same visit date for the same customer and pet are together. In Figure 23-5, the first five total amounts are $83.00, $82.80, $20.00, $52.00, and $57.00. In Figure 23-8, the first five totals are $83.00, $82.80, $20.00, $52.00, and $57.00. Because the data is not also sorted by the line number in the Visit Details table, the final sort is not precise.

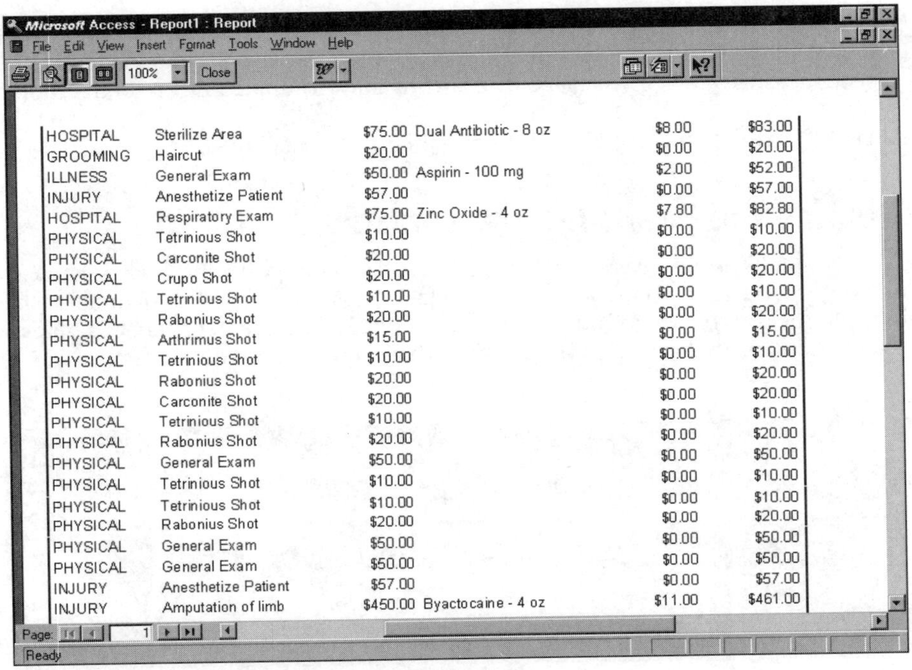

Microsoft Access - Report1 : Report

File Edit View Insert Format Tools Window Help

100% Close

HOSPITAL	Sterilize Area	$75.00	Dual Antibiotic - 8 oz	$8.00	$83.00
GROOMING	Haircut	$20.00		$0.00	$20.00
ILLNESS	General Exam	$50.00	Aspirin - 100 mg	$2.00	$52.00
INJURY	Anesthetize Patient	$57.00		$0.00	$57.00
HOSPITAL	Respiratory Exam	$75.00	Zinc Oxide - 4 oz	$7.80	$82.80
PHYSICAL	Tetrinious Shot	$10.00		$0.00	$10.00
PHYSICAL	Carconite Shot	$20.00		$0.00	$20.00
PHYSICAL	Crupo Shot	$20.00		$0.00	$20.00
PHYSICAL	Tetrinious Shot	$10.00		$0.00	$10.00
PHYSICAL	Rabonius Shot	$20.00		$0.00	$20.00
PHYSICAL	Arthrimus Shot	$15.00		$0.00	$15.00
PHYSICAL	Tetrinious Shot	$10.00		$0.00	$10.00
PHYSICAL	Rabonius Shot	$20.00		$0.00	$20.00
PHYSICAL	Carconite Shot	$20.00		$0.00	$20.00
PHYSICAL	Tetrinious Shot	$10.00		$0.00	$10.00
PHYSICAL	Rabonius Shot	$20.00		$0.00	$20.00
PHYSICAL	General Exam	$50.00		$0.00	$50.00
PHYSICAL	Tetrinious Shot	$10.00		$0.00	$10.00
PHYSICAL	Tetrinious Shot	$10.00		$0.00	$10.00
PHYSICAL	Rabonius Shot	$20.00		$0.00	$20.00
PHYSICAL	General Exam	$50.00		$0.00	$50.00
PHYSICAL	General Exam	$50.00		$0.00	$50.00
INJURY	Anesthetize Patient	$57.00		$0.00	$57.00
INJURY	Amputation of limb	$450.00	Byactocaine - 4 oz	$11.00	$461.00

Page: 1

Ready

Figure 23-8: A print preview of the detail section.

Notice that the calculated control correctly calculates the sum of the two numeric price text box controls and displays them in the Currency format.

Creating the Pet ID header and footer sections

When the detail section is complete, you can move *outward* to create the inner group headers and footers. The innermost group is the Pet ID group. You need to create both a header and a footer for this section.

As you've learned, to create group headers and footers for the Pet ID sort you already created, you need only change the Group Header and Group Footer properties of the Pets.Pet ID Field/Expression to Yes (as shown in Figure 23-9). To display the group headers and footers to make this change, follow these steps:

1. Display the Sorting and Grouping box if it is not displayed.
2. Click on the Pets.Pet ID row in the window.
3. Click on the Group Header property and change it to **Yes**.
4. Click on the Group Footer property and change it to **Yes**.

Note After a group header or footer is defined, the first column of the Sorting and Grouping box for the field you created in the header or footer displays a grouping icon (the same icon you see when you select the Sorting and Grouping button on the toolbar).

The Pet ID header and footer sections should now be displayed.

Creating the Pet ID header controls

The Pets.Pet ID group header, shown in Figure 23-9 along with the Sorting and Grouping box, creates a group break on Pet ID, which causes each pet's individual visit details to be grouped together. This is the section where the pet's name is displayed, as well as labels that describe the controls that appear in the detail section.

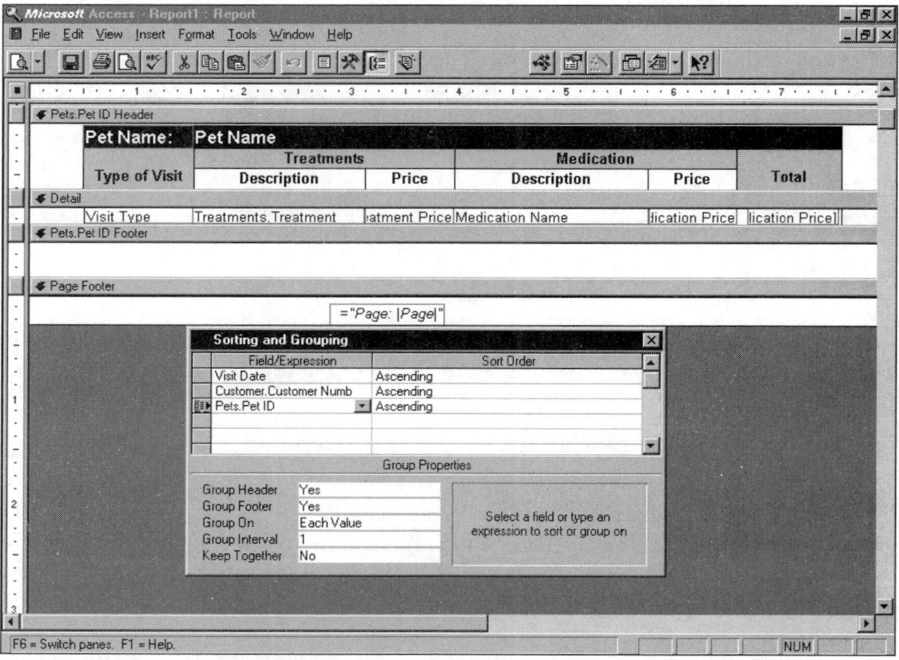

Figure 23-9: The Report Design window for the Pets.Pet ID group header.

There are no calculated controls in this header. There are no lines or rectangles. In fact, with the exception of the pet name itself, all controls are label controls. Each label control is stretched so the borders make perfect rectangles on the desired areas and the text is centered where appropriate. The Fore Color and Back Color buttons are then used for coloring the background and the text.

Notice the use of reverse video in the Pet Name label and text control. Also notice that the Type of Visit, Treatments, Medication, and Total label controls display black text on a light gray background. This setup, along with the borders, creates a visually appealing section. Notice there is no room between the bottom of the controls and the bottom of the section. This (along with the lack of space in the detail section) creates the illusion that several sections are really one. You create the label controls Type of Visit and Total by pressing Ctrl+Enter before you enter the text, which makes it use two lines.

Creating the Pet ID footer controls

The Pets.Pet ID group footer, shown in Figure 23-10, is where you subtotal all the visit detail information for each pet. Thus, if a pet has more than one treatment or medication per visit, the report summarizes the visit detail line items in this section. In fact, even if there is only one detail record for a pet, a summary is displayed.

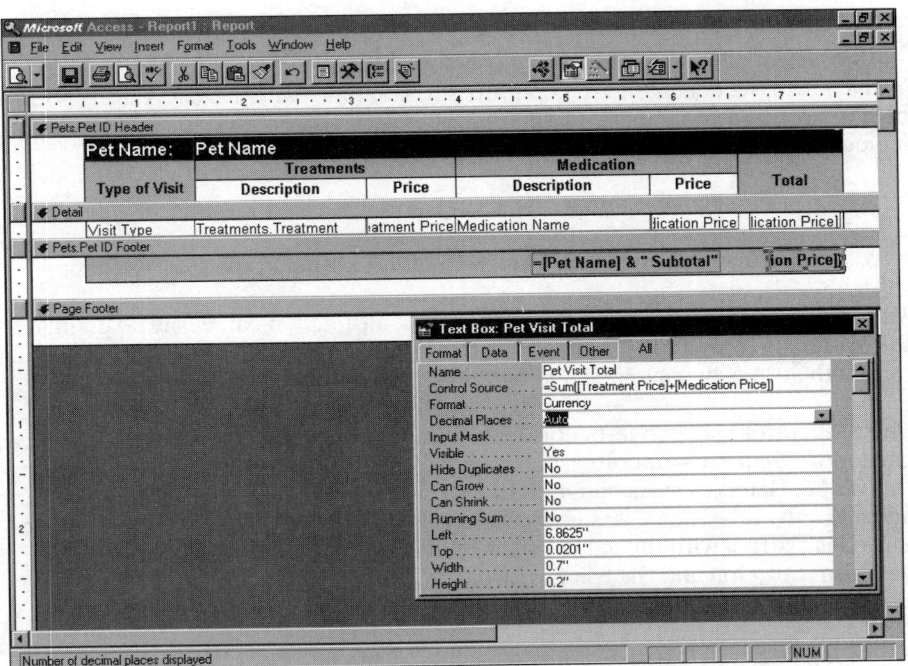

Figure 23-10: Creating a group summary control.

The Pets.Pet ID footer section contains three controls:

Rectangle	Displays the boundaries of the section and is shaded in light gray
Label control	Displays Pet Name and the text `Subtotal`
Summary text box control	Displays the total of all Pet Visit line totals for each pet

The rectangle completes the area displayed under the detail section; it serves as a *bottom cap* on the previous two sections. Notice there is no space between the top of the controls and the top of the section. Notice also how the edges line up, setting the entire section (Pet ID header, detail section, Pet ID footer) apart from other areas of the report.

The first control combines the Pet Name field with the text Subtotal. You use a process known as *concatenation.*

Using concatenation to join text and fields

You can use the concatenation operators to combine two strings. (A *string* is either a field or an expression.) Several different operators can be used for concatenation, including the following:

+	Joins two Text data type strings
&	Joins two strings; also converts non-Text data types to Text data

The + operator is standard in many languages, although it can easily be confused with the arithmetic operator used to add two numbers together. The + operator requires that both strings being joined are Text data types.

The & operator also converts nonstring data types to string data types; therefore it is used more than the + operator. If, for example, you enter the expression **="Today's Date Is:" & Date()**, Access converts the result of the date function into a string and adds it to the text `Today's Date Is:`. If the date is August 2, 1995, the result returned is a string with the value `Today's Date Is:8/2/95`. The lack of space between the colon and the 8 is no error; if you want to add a space between two joined strings, you must add one.

Access can join any data type to any data type using this method. If you want to create the control for the Pet Name and the text Subtotal using this method, you enter the expression **=[Pet Name] & "Subtotal"**, which appends the contents of the Pet Name field to the text Subtotal. No conversion occurs because the contents of Pet Name and the literal value `Subtotal` are both already text. Notice that there is a space between the first double quotation mark and the text Subtotal.

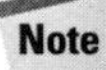

Note: If you use the + operator for concatenation, you must convert any nonstring data types; an example would be by using the CStr( ) function to return a date with the Date( ) function to a string data type. If you want to display the system date with some text, you have to create a text control with the following contents:

="Today's Date Is:" +cstr(Date())

You can insert the contents of a field directly into a text expression by using the ampersand (&) character. The syntax is

="Text String "&[Field or Control Name]&" additional text string"

or:

[Field or Control Name]&" Text String"

You can use this method to create the control for the Pet Name text box control; follow these steps:

1. Create a new text control in the Pets.Pet ID Footer section.
2. Enter the expression = **[Pet Name]&" Subtotal"** (as shown in Figure 23-10).

Calculating group summaries

Creating a sum of numeric data within a group is very simple. Following is the general procedure for summarizing group totals for bound text controls:

- ✦ Create a new text control in the group footer (or header).
- ✦ Enter the expression =**Sum([Control Name])** where *Control Name* is a valid field name in the underlying query or the name of a control in the report.

If, however, the control name is for a calculated control, you will have to repeat the control expression. Suppose, for example, that in the Pets.Pet ID footer you want to enter the following expression into the text box control to display the total of the detail line:

```
=Sum([Pets Line Visit Total])
```

If you try this, it won't work; that is simply a limitation of Microsoft Access. To create a sum for the totals in the detail section, you have to enter

=Sum([Treatment Price]+[Medication Price])

This is how the summary shown in Figure 23-10 was created.

New! Access knows to sum the detail lines for the Pet ID summary because you put the summary control in the Pets.Pet ID section. Each time the value of the Pet ID changes, Access resets the summary control automatically. Later, when you create this same summary control in the Customer ID footer section, Access will reset the total only when the value of Customer ID changes.

You can use expressions in a report in two ways. The first is to enter the expression directly in a text control. For example, enter

[Treatment Price]+[Medication Price]

The second way is to create the expression in the underlying query, as you saw in Figure 23-4, where you created a field named Line Total in the query itself. You can then use the calculated field of the query in a text control on the report. The advantage of the former method is you have the flexibility to create your expressions *on the fly,* as well as being able to reference other report objects, such as text controls with expressions. The disadvantage is that you cannot use summary expressions on calculated controls.

If you add a calculated field to your underlying query, you can then refer to this field in the detail section or in any group section. The syntax you would use is

=Sum([Calculated Field Name])

If you want to create the detail section Line Total and Pet ID Subtotal by using the calculation from the query, first you create the query's calculated field as

Line Total: [Treatment Price]+[Medication Price]

Then you create the summary control in the report as

=Sum([Line Total])

Either method works; either is acceptable.

You can use the Print Preview window to check the progress of your report. Figure 23-11 displays the report created so far; notice how the three sections come together to form one area.

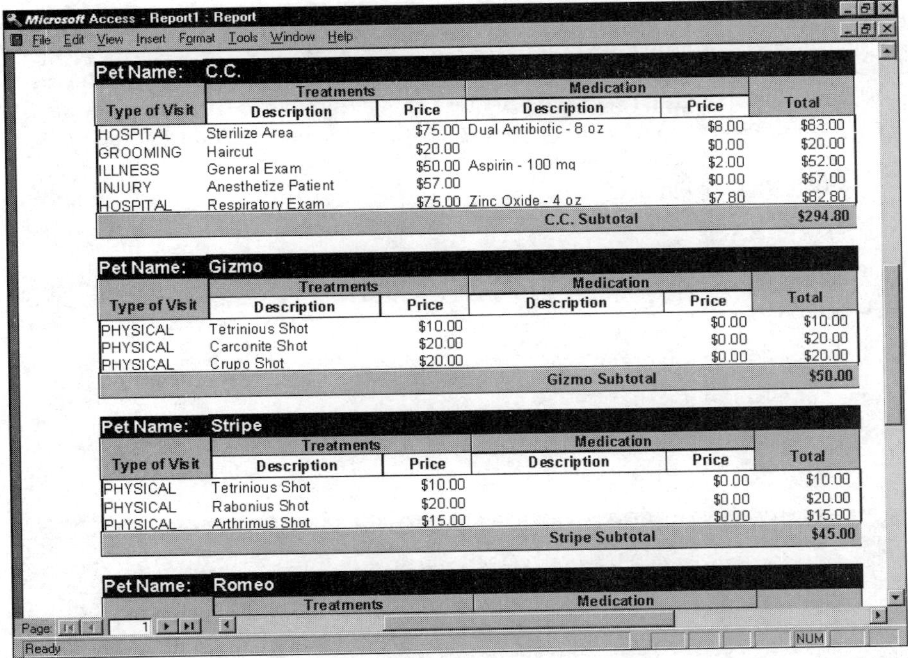

Microsoft Access - Report1 : Report

File Edit View Insert Format Tools Window Help

Pet Name: C.C.

Type of Visit	Treatments Description	Treatments Price	Medication Description	Medication Price	Total
HOSPITAL	Sterilize Area	$75.00	Dual Antibiotic - 8 oz	$8.00	$83.00
GROOMING	Haircut	$20.00		$0.00	$20.00
ILLNESS	General Exam	$50.00	Aspirin - 100 mg	$2.00	$52.00
INJURY	Anesthetize Patient	$57.00		$0.00	$57.00
HOSPITAL	Respiratory Exam	$75.00	Zinc Oxide - 4 oz	$7.80	$82.80
			C.C. Subtotal		$294.80

Pet Name: Gizmo

Type of Visit	Treatments Description	Treatments Price	Medication Description	Medication Price	Total
PHYSICAL	Tetrinious Shot	$10.00		$0.00	$10.00
PHYSICAL	Carconite Shot	$20.00		$0.00	$20.00
PHYSICAL	Crupo Shot	$20.00		$0.00	$20.00
			Gizmo Subtotal		$50.00

Pet Name: Stripe

Type of Visit	Treatments Description	Treatments Price	Medication Description	Medication Price	Total
PHYSICAL	Tetrinious Shot	$10.00		$0.00	$10.00
PHYSICAL	Rabonius Shot	$20.00		$0.00	$20.00
PHYSICAL	Arthrimus Shot	$15.00		$0.00	$15.00
			Stripe Subtotal		$45.00

Pet Name: Romeo

Treatments Medication

Page: 1

Ready NUM

Figure 23-11: The Print Preview window of a report's group header and the detail and group footer sections.

Creating the Customer Number header and footer sections

When the Pet ID sections are complete, you can move *outward* again to create the next outer group header and footer. The next group as you move outward is Customer Number; you can create a header and footer for this section by following these steps:

1. Display the Sorting and Grouping box if it is not already displayed.
2. Click on the Customer.Customer Number row in the window.
3. Click on the Group Header property and change it to Yes.
4. Click on the Group Footer property and change it to Yes.

There is one task left to do: each new customer for a specific date should be displayed on a separate page. If you view the report as it currently exists, you notice there are no specific page breaks. You can create a page break every time the customer number changes by setting the Force New Page property of the Customer.Customer Number header to Before Section. Doing so will ensure that each customer's information is printed on a separate page.

Creating the Customer Number header controls

Cross Ref

The Customer.Customer Number group header is shown completed (at the top of the report design) in Figure 23-12. This section is very similar to the Customer section created in Chapters 21 and 22. There are seven fields used in this section:

- ✦ Customer Name
- ✦ Street/Apt
- ✦ City
- ✦ State
- ✦ Zip Code
- ✦ Phone Number
- ✦ Visit Date

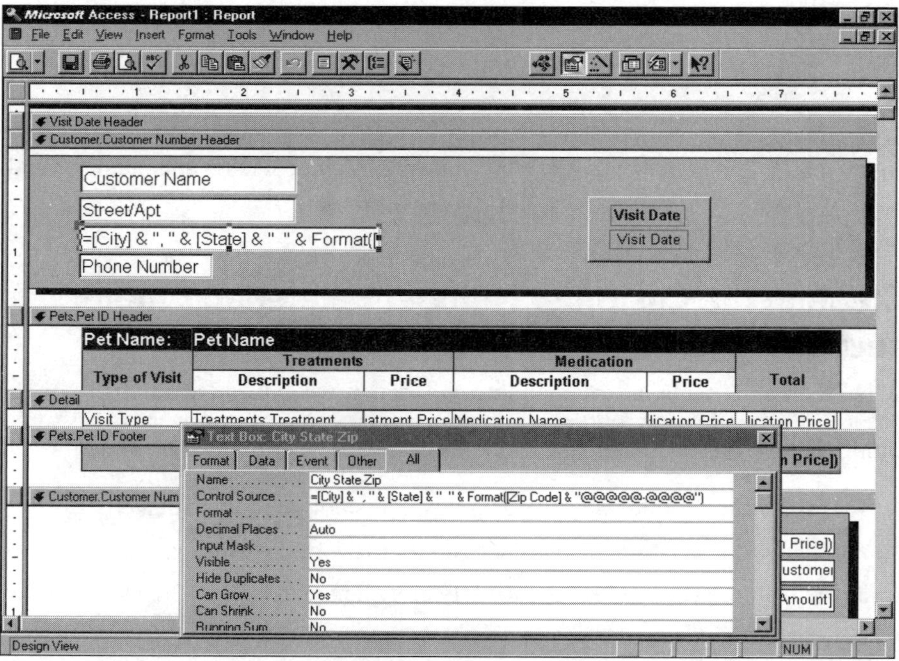

Figure 23-12: The Report Design window for the Customer.Customer Number group header.

Cross Ref

The first six controls are from the Customer table; the Visit Date control is from the Visits table. The entire section is surrounded by a gray shaded rectangle and a shadow box. (Chapter 22 explains how to create this effect.) The Visit Date control has an attached label and is surrounded by a transparent rectangle (which you create by setting the Back Color window's Transparent button). The control uses the Raised appearance option; the Customer controls are sunken (a three-dimensional effect created by selecting the Sunken button in the Special Effects window).

One change you can make is to rearrange the display of the City, State, and Zip Code fields. Instead of displaying these fields as three separate controls, you can concatenate them to appear together. You can save space by compressing any trailing spaces in the city name, adding a comma after city, and also by compressing the space between State and Zip Code. You can make the changes by creating a concatenated text box control. Follow these steps:

1. Delete the City, State, and Zip Code controls in the Customer Number header.
2. Create a new unlabeled text box control.
3. Enter **=[City]&", "&[State]&" "&[Zip Code]** in the Control Source property of the text box control.

The only problem with this expression is that the Zip code is formatted in the Zip Code table field, using the @@@@@-@@@@ format to add a hyphen between the first five and last four characters. As currently entered, the control may display the following value when run: `Lakeville, OR 974011021`.

You still need to format the Zip Code field. Normally, the function Format( ) is used for formatting an expression. In this example, the function should be written as

Format([Zip Code],"@@@@@-@@@@")

You can add this to the concatenation expression, substituting the Format expression in place of the Zip Code field. To complete this example, change the control to

```
=[City]&", "&[State]&" "&Format([Zip Code],"@@@@@-@@@@")
```

To check the Customer Number group heading, you can view the report in the Print Preview window, as shown in Figure 23-13.

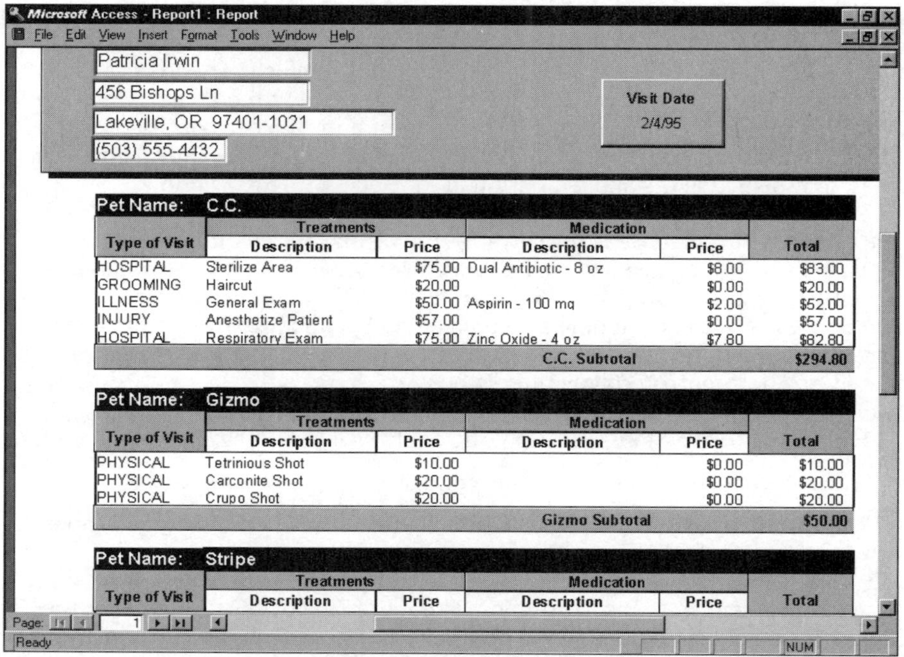

Figure 23-13: Viewing the report in the Print Preview window.

Creating the Customer Number footer controls

The Customer.Customer Number footer section contains ten controls: five label controls and five text box controls. The text box control expressions (and their associated labels) appear in Table 23-2.

Each of the concatenated label controls uses the same standard notation you learned in this chapter; each of the text box controls is a simple expression. Notice that Customer Total uses exactly the same expression as the Pet ID total, except now it resets the total by Customer Number.

Table 23-2
Expressions in the Customer Number Footer

Expression Name	*Label Control*	*Text Box Control*
Customer Total	Total Invoice:	=Sum([Treatment Price]+[Medication Price])
Discount Amount	="Discount	=[Customer Total] *[Discount] ("&[Discount] *100&"%):"
Customer Subtotal	Subtotal:	=[Customer Total]-[Discount Amount]
State Sales Tax	=[State Name]&"	=[Customer Subtotal] *[Visits.Tax Rate] Sales Tax ("&[Visits. Tax Rate]*100&"%):"
Amount Due	Amount Due:	=[Customer Subtotal]+[State Sales Tax]

The Customer.Customer Number footer, (shown in Figure 23-14) is where you create and summarize the line-item totals for each pet for a particular owner for a particular visit. You also want to display a customer's discount rate, the amount of the discount in dollars, the customer's state, the state sales tax as a percentage, the state sales tax in dollars, and (finally) a total for the amount due. All this information will appear in separate boxes with shadows; you create these by using the shadow special effect on the rectangle. If you are following along with this example, the steps for each of the controls follow.

Because the first group has many pets and visit detail lines, you'll have to look at page 3 to see the first customer number footer. To create the label for Total Invoice (and for the text box controls), follow these steps:

1. Create a new label control.
2. Change the Caption property to **Total Invoice:**.
3. Create a new text box control.
4. Change the Name property to **Customer Total**.
5. Change the Control Source property to

   `=Sum([Treatment Price]+[Medication Price]).`

Follow these steps to create the Discount Amount label and text box controls:

1. Create a new label control.
2. Change the Control Source property to `="Discount ("&[Discount]*100&"%):"` which concatenates the word `Discount` with the customer's discount rate, and then multiplies by 100 to give a percentage.

3. Create a new text box control.
4. Change the Name to **Discount Amount.**
5. Change the Control Source to **=[Customer Total]*[Discount]**, which multiplies the customer's discount rate by the amount calculated in the Customer Total control.

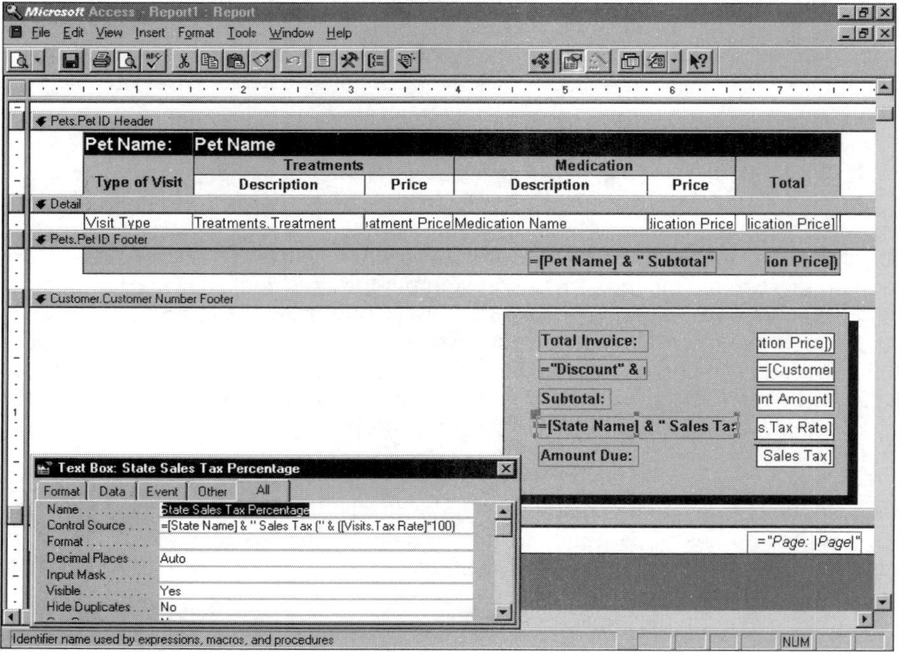

Figure 23-14: The Report Design window for the Customer.Customer Number group footer.

To check the Customer Number group heading, you can view the report in the Print Preview window, as shown in Figure 23-15.

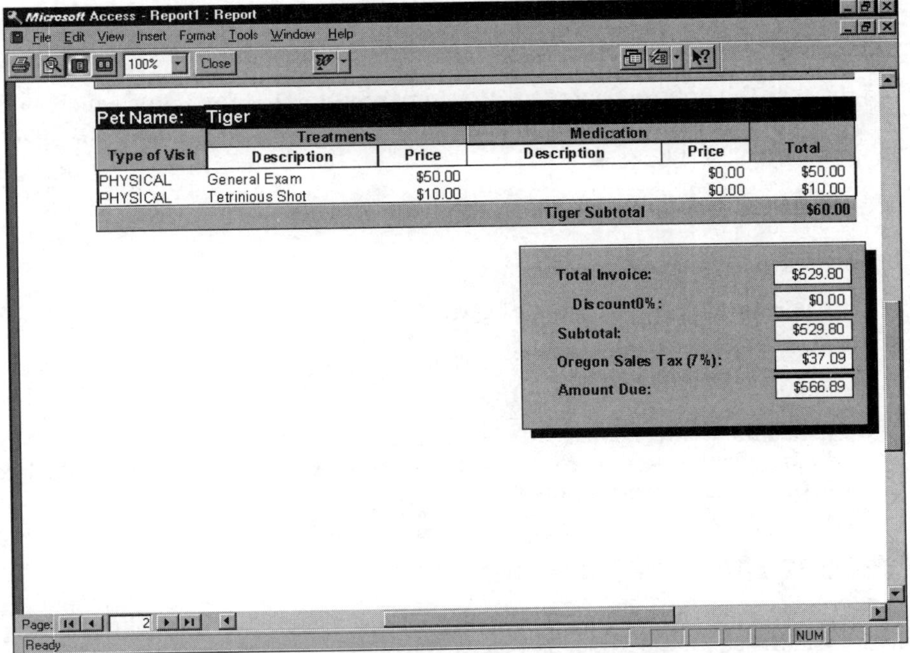

Figure 23-15: Viewing the report in the Print Preview window.

To create the Customer Subtotal label and text box controls, follow these steps:

1. Create a new label control.
2. Change the caption to **Subtotal:**.
3. Create a new text box control.
4. Change the Name to **Customer Subtotal**.
5. Change the Control Source to **=[Customer Total]-[Discount Amount]**, which subtracts the amount calculated in the Discount Amount control from the sum calculated in the Customer Total control.

Create the State Sales Tax label and text box controls with these steps:

1. Create a new label control.
2. Change the Control Source to `=[State Name]&" Sales Tax ("&[Visits.Tax Rate]*100&"%):"` which concatenates the customer's state name (full spelling) and the words `Tax Rate` with the customer's tax rate, and then multiplies by 100 to give a percentage.

3. Create a new text box control.
4. Change the Name to **State Sales Tax**.
5. Change the Control Source to **=[Customer Subtotal]*[Tax Rate]**, which multiplies the customer's state tax rate by the amount calculated in the Customer Subtotal control.

Next, create the Amount Due label and text box controls:

1. Create a new label control.
2. Change the Caption to **Amount Due:**.
3. Create a new text box control.
4. Change the Name to **Amount Due**.
5. Change the Control Source to `=[Customer Subtotal]+[State Sales Tax]` which adds the customer's calculated state sales tax to the amount calculated in the Customer Subtotal control.

Creating the Visit Date header

You have one more group header to create — Visit Date — but it won't display anything in the section. The section has a height of 0; essentially, it's *closed*. The purpose of the Visit Date header is to force a page break whenever the Visit Date changes. Without this section, if you were to have two customer records for the same customer on different dates that appear consecutively in the report's dynaset, the records will appear on the same page. The only forced page break you created so far was for Customer Number; by adding one for Visit Date, you complete the report groupings. To create the Visit Date grouping for the header and add the page break, follow these steps:

1. Display the Sorting and Grouping box if it is not already displayed.
2. Click on the Visit Date row Field/Expression column.
3. Click on the Group Header property.
4. Click on the arrow and select Yes from the drop-down list.
5. Double-click on the section to display its property sheet.
6. Change the Height property to **0**.
7. Change the Visible property to No.
8. Change the Force New Page property to Before Section.

Creating the page header controls

The page header appears at the top of every page in the Invoice Report. The page header and footer controls are not controlled by the Sorting and Grouping box; you have to select View⇨Page Header/Footer. In this report, the page header has been open all the time. This section contains a small version of the Mountain Animal Hospital logo in the upper left-hand corner, as well as the name, address, and phone number for the hospital. The section also contains the report date and a horizontal line at the bottom to visually separate it from the rest of the page. By default, the page header and footer are created and displayed automatically when a new report is created. All you have to do is change the height and add the proper controls.

Cross Ref In Chapter 22, you learned how to add the unbound bitmap MTN.BMP to the report. The label controls that display the Mountain Animal Hospital page header are four separate controls. The only control that needs explanation is the Report Date control.

Access offers several built-in functions that let you display and manipulate date and time information. The easiest to start with is the Date() function, which returns the current system date when the report is printed or previewed. To add a text control to the report header that displays the date when the report is printed, follow these steps:

1. Create a new text control in the page header, as shown in Figure 23-16.
2. Display the control's property sheet.
3. In the Control Source property cell, type **="Report Date: "&Date()**.

This process concatenates the text Report Date with the current system date.

Another date function Access offers is DatePart(), which returns a numeric value for the specified portion of a date. The syntax for the function is

DatePart(*interval,date,firstweekday,firstweek*)

where *interval* is a string expression for the interval of time you want returned, and *date* is the date you want to apply the function to.

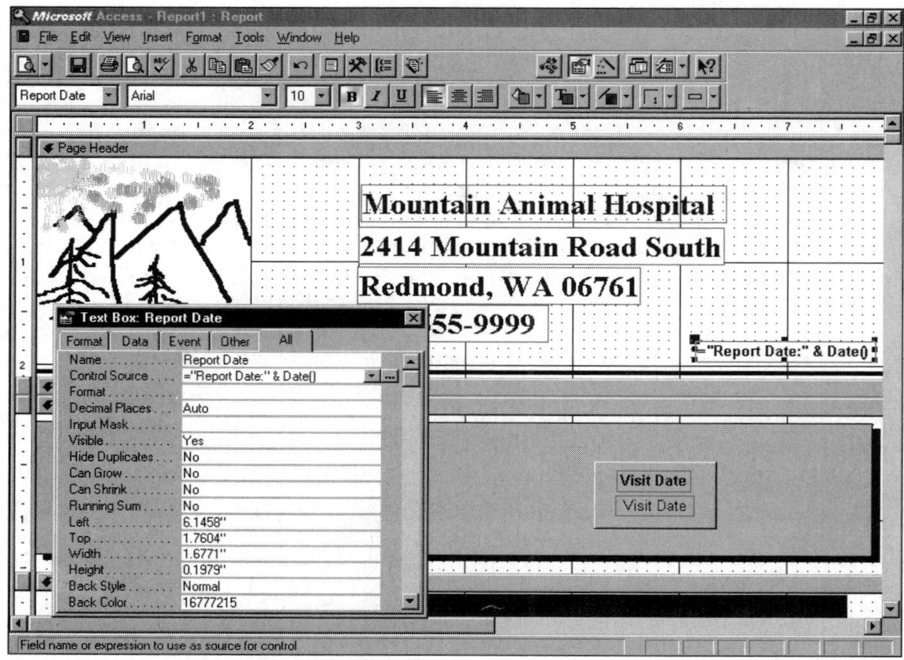

Figure 23-16: The page header.

Table 23-3 lists some valid intervals and the time periods they represent.

Table 23-3
DatePart( ) Intervals

Interval	*Time Period*
yyyy	Year
q	Quarter
m	Month
y	Day of year
d	Day
w	Weekday
ww	Week
h	Hour
n	Minute
s	Second

Expression	*Result*
=DatePart("yyyy",25-Dec-1992)	1992 (the year)
=DatePart("m",25-Dec-1992)	12 (the month)
=DatePart("d",25-Dec-1992)	25 (the day of the month)
=DatePart("w",25-Dec-1992)	6 (the weekday; Sunday=1, Monday=2 . . .)
=DatePart("q",25-Dec-1992)	4 (the quarter)

The date can be a literal date (such as `1-Jan-1993`), or a field name that references a field containing a valid date.

Creating the page footer controls

Normally you would use the page footer to place page number or to hold page totals. For this report, the footer's only purpose is to display a thick horizontal line at the bottom of every page, followed by the page number in the right bottom corner.

To number the pages in your report, Access provides the Page function. You access it by using it in an expression in a text control that returns the current page of the report. As with all expressions, one that has the Page property in it must be preceded by an equal sign (=). To create a footer with a page number, follow these steps:

1. Create a new text control in the lower right-hand section of the page footer.
2. Display the control's property sheet.
3. In the Control Source property cell, type **="Page: "&Page**.
4. Select the Italics button in the toolbar.

Although it makes the most sense to put the page number in the page header or page footer, you can place a control with the Page property in any section of your report. You can also use the Page property as part of an expression. For example, the expression `=Page*10` will display the result of multiplying the actual page number by ten.

You have now completed the Monthly Invoice Report. Compare your report design with the one shown originally in Figure 23-2 and then with the final output in Figure 23-17. Figure 23-17 shows page 14 of the report, a good example of displaying all the sections on one page. (Look back at Figure 23-1 to see a hard copy of the report page.)

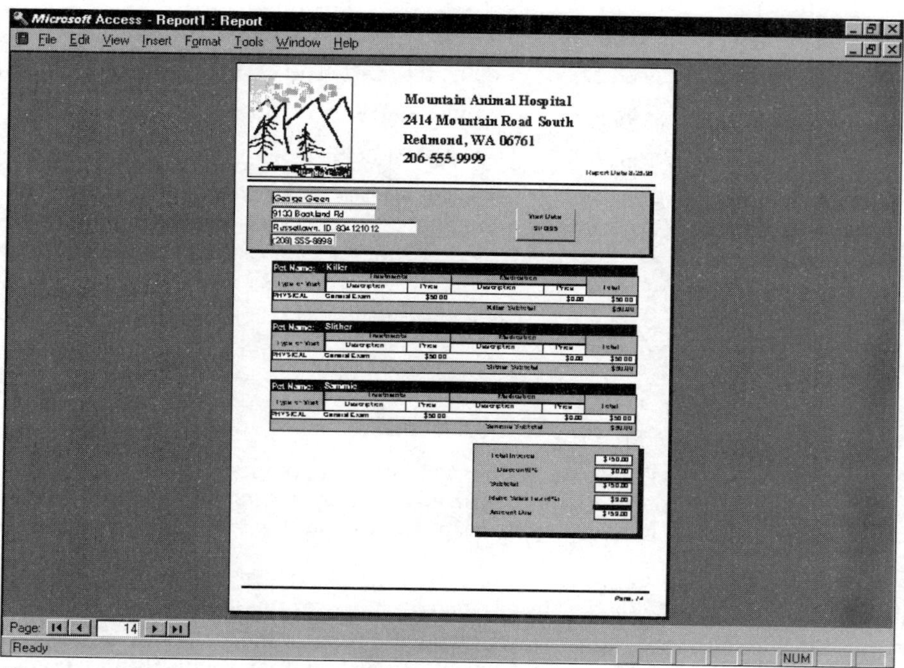

Figure 23-17: The report design output on-screen.

Before moving on, you need to create a few more controls. You can create controls based on knowledge of the final report because Access features a *two-pass report writer* that makes it possible. For example, you can create a control that displays the percentage of one total to a grand total, or create a cumulative total to display cumulative totals.

Calculating percentages using totals

You can calculate a line percentage to determine what percent of the total cost for a pet's visit each line is. By comparing the line item to the total, you can calculate the percentage of a particular item to a whole. To do so, you'll need to move all the controls for the Pet ID header and footer and the detail section to the far left side of the report. To create a new control that displays what percentage of the whole (Mountain Animal Hospital Charges) is for each pet, follow these steps:

1. Duplicate the Pet Visit Line Total control.
2. Position the duplicate to the right of the original.
3. Change the Control Source to `=[Pet Visit Line Total]/[Pet Visit Total]`.
4. Change the Format property to **Percent**.
5. Create a new label control with the caption Percent above it, as shown in Figure 23-18.

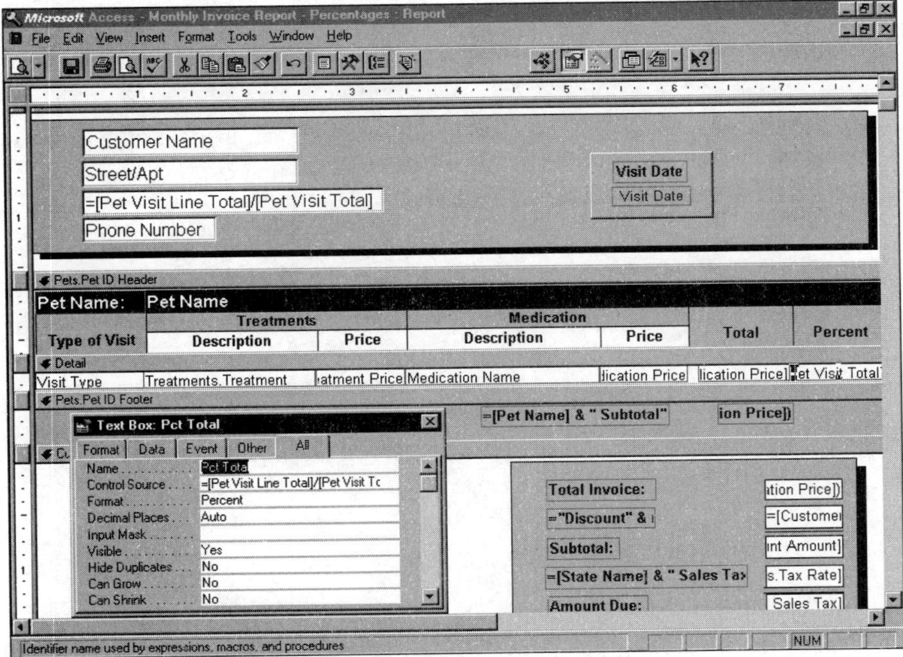

Figure 23-18: Creating a percentage control.

The calculation takes the individual line total control [Pet Visit Line Total] in the detail section and divides it by the summary control [Pet Visit Total] in the page header section. The Percent format automatically handles the conversion and displays a percentage.

Calculating running sums

Access also lets you calculate *running sums* (also known as *cumulative totals*) easily; simply change the Running Sum property for a control. If you want (for example) to create a running total of how much is spent as each pet's charges are totaled, follow these steps:

1. Duplicate the rectangle and its controls in the Pets.Pet ID footer section.
2. Display the new rectangle just below the existing one, as shown in Figure 23-19.

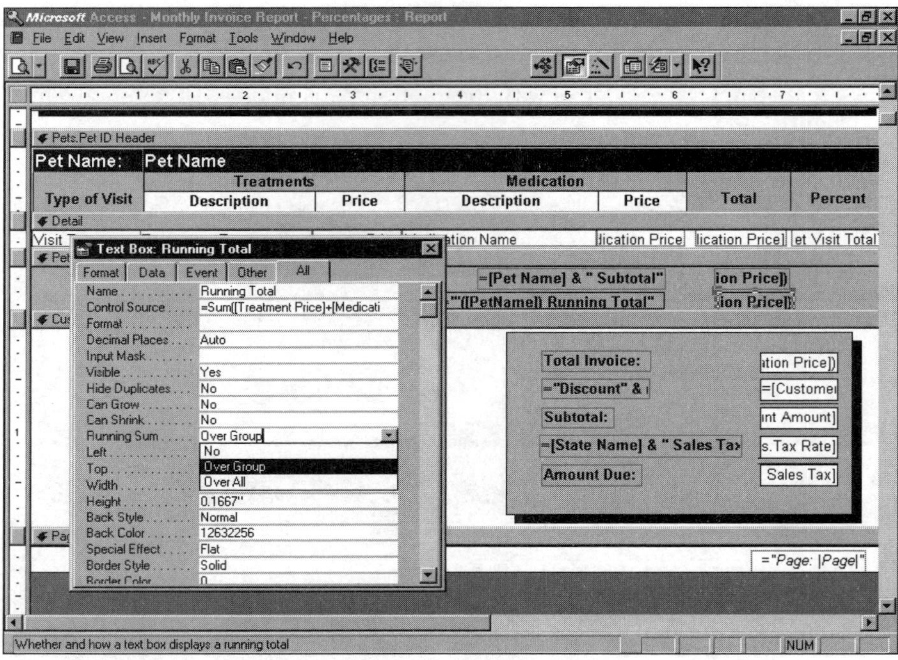

Figure 23-19: Creating a running sum control.

3. Select the label control and change the caption to **=[Pet Name]&" Running Total"**.
4. Select the new control with the expression **=Sum([Treatment Price]+[Medication Price])**.
5. Display the control's property sheet.
6. Change the Name to **Running Total**.
7. Click on the Running Sum property.
8. Select Over Group from the drop-down list shown in Figure 23-19.

Access will now add the current subtotal to all previous subtotals for each owner. Alternatively, you can create a running sum across all values in a report. This is useful if you want to present an overall summary in the report's footer section.

You can display the percentages and the running total by performing a print preview, as shown in Figure 23-20.

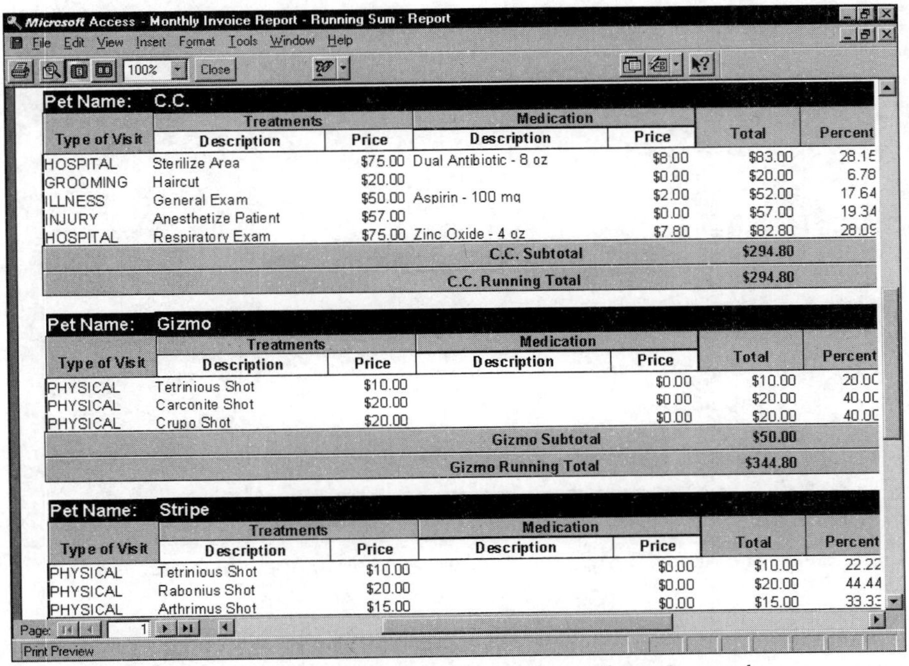

Microsoft Access - Monthly Invoice Report - Running Sum : Report

File Edit View Insert Format Tools Window Help

100% Close

Pet Name: C.C.

Type of Visit	Treatments: Description	Treatments: Price	Medication: Description	Medication: Price	Total	Percent
HOSPITAL	Sterilize Area	$75.00	Dual Antibiotic - 8 oz	$8.00	$83.00	28.15
GROOMING	Haircut	$20.00		$0.00	$20.00	6.78
ILLNESS	General Exam	$50.00	Aspirin - 100 mg	$2.00	$52.00	17.64
INJURY	Anesthetize Patient	$57.00		$0.00	$57.00	19.34
HOSPITAL	Respiratory Exam	$75.00	Zinc Oxide - 4 oz	$7.80	$82.80	28.09
			C.C. Subtotal		$294.80	
			C.C. Running Total		$294.80	

Pet Name: Gizmo

Type of Visit	Treatments: Description	Treatments: Price	Medication: Description	Medication: Price	Total	Percent
PHYSICAL	Tetrinious Shot	$10.00		$0.00	$10.00	20.00
PHYSICAL	Carconite Shot	$20.00		$0.00	$20.00	40.00
PHYSICAL	Crupo Shot	$20.00		$0.00	$20.00	40.00
			Gizmo Subtotal		$50.00	
			Gizmo Running Total		$344.80	

Pet Name: Stripe

Type of Visit	Treatments: Description	Treatments: Price	Medication: Description	Medication: Price	Total	Percent
PHYSICAL	Tetrinious Shot	$10.00		$0.00	$10.00	22.22
PHYSICAL	Rabonius Shot	$20.00		$0.00	$20.00	44.44
PHYSICAL	Arthrimus Shot	$15.00		$0.00	$15.00	33.33

Page: 1

Print Preview

Figure 23-20: A print preview displaying percentages and running totals.

Creating a title page in a report header

The main purpose of the report header (illustrated in Figure 23-21) is to provide a separate title page. From the report description given earlier, you know that the report header must contain Mountain Animal Hospital's logo, name, address, and phone, as well as a report title. In the sample Monthly Invoice Report file, all these controls are created for you.

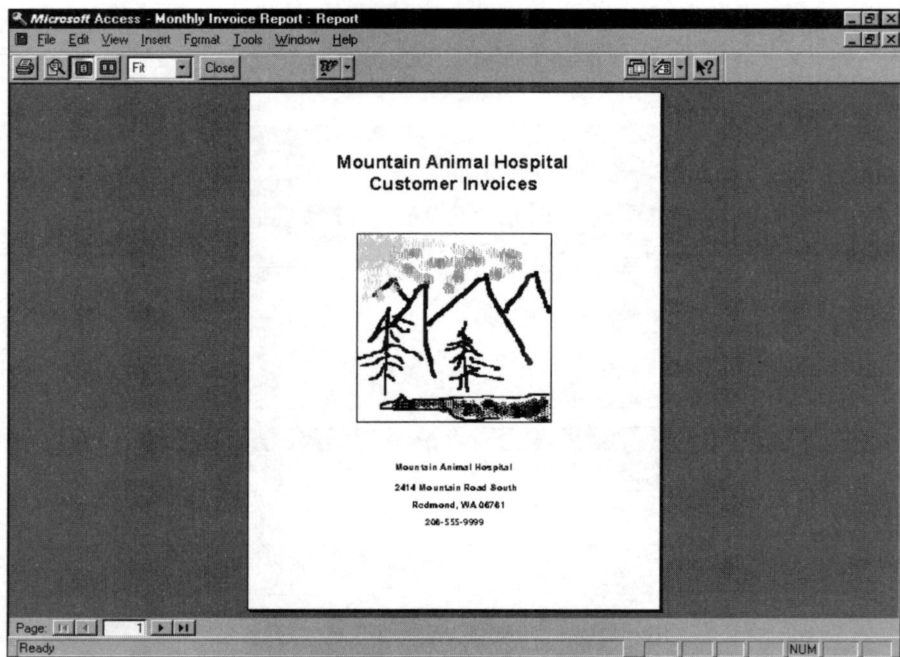

Figure 23-21: The Report Design Print Preview window for the report header.

If you created the report from scratch, you can follow these steps to create a report header:

1. Click on the report header section and then open its Properties sheet.
2. Resize the height of the report header section to about 9 1/2 inches.
3. Set the Force New Page property of the report header section to After Section so a page break occurs after the report header.
4. Create label controls for the report title, name, address, and phone.
5. Create an image picture control (using MTN.BMP) and change the Size Mode property to Stretch.

Using the report footer

The report footer is not actually used in this report; it's displayed because the report header cannot be displayed in Design view without it. The normal use of the report footer is for grand totals that occur once in the report. You can also use it in an accounting type of report, or in a letter concerning the totals for an audit trail.

Summary

In this chapter you learned how to create multilevel reports as well as subreports. The following points were covered:

- ✦ Access lets you easily create multilevel grouping reports.
- ✦ A calculated control contains mathematical expressions.
- ✦ Text box controls can contain field names or expressions.
- ✦ Text expressions use the concatenation operators +, or &| to combine text strings and/or text strings and other data types.
- ✦ The Date( ) function returns the current system date.
- ✦ The DatePart( ) function returns a numeric value for the specified portion of a date.
- ✦ Controls can, and should be, named. You can then reference them in other controls.
- ✦ When you use the =Sum( ) function in a group header or footer (or page or report header or footer), it summarizes all the values of a field within that group.
- ✦ Access can use summary totals to calculate line-item or group-total percentages.
- ✦ Access can perform running sums within a group, as well as across groups.

In the next chapter, you learn how to link to external data by attaching, importing, and exporting.

✦ ✦ ✦

Advanced Database Features

✦ ✦ ✦ ✦

In This Part

✦ ✦ ✦ ✦

Working with External Data

◆ ◆ ◆ ◆

In This Chapter

Linking to external data

Splitting an Access database into separate programs and data

Working with Linked tables

Importing from external data

Creating import/export specifications

Exporting to external tables and files

◆ ◆ ◆ ◆

So far, you've only worked with data in Access tables. In this chapter, you explore using data from other types of files. You learn to work with data from database, spreasdsheet, and text-based files.

Access and External Data

Exchanging information between Access and another program is an essential capability in today's database world. Information is usually stored in a wide variety of application programs and data formats. Access (like many other products) has its own native file format, designed to support referential integrity and provide support for such rich data types as OLE objects. Most of the time, this format is sufficient; occasionally, however, you need to move data from one Access database file to another, or even to a different software program's format.

Types of external data

Access has the capability to use and exchange data among a wide range of applications. For example, you may need to get data from other database files (such as FoxPro, dBASE or Paradox files) or obtain information from an SQL Server, Oracle, or network Btrieve file. Access can move data among several categories of applications:

- ✦ Other Windows applications
- ✦ Spreadsheets

- PC database management systems
- Btrieve files
- Server-based database systems (ODBC)
- Text or mainframe files

Methods of working with external data

Often you will need to move data from one application or file into your Access database. You may need to obtain information that you already have in an external spreadsheet file. You can re-enter all the information by hand — or have it *imported* into your database. Perhaps you need to put information from your Access tables into Paradox files. Again, you can re-enter all the information into Paradox by hand, or have the information *exported* to the Paradox table. Access has tools that allow you to move data from a database table to another table or file. It could be a table in Access, dBASE, or Paradox; it could be a Lotus 1-2-3 spreadsheet file. In fact, Access can exchange data with over 14 different file types, including the following:

- Access database objects (all types)
- dBASE (III+, IV, and 5)
- FoxPro (2.*x* and 3.0)
- Paradox 3.*x*, 4.*x*, and 5.0
- Text files (ANSI and ASCII; DOS or OS/2; delimited and fixed-length)
- Lotus 1-2-3, 2.*x* and 3.*x*
- Btrieve 5.1*x*, 6.0
- Excel 2.*x* and greater
- ODBC (Microsoft SQL Server, Sybase server, and Oracle server)

Access can work with these external data sources in several ways; Table 24-1 shows how, and to what purpose.

Table 24-1
Methods of Working with External Data

Method	*Purpose*
Link	Create a link to a table in another Access database or use the data from a different database format.
Import	Copy data *from* a text file, another Access database, or another applications format into an Access table.
Export	Copy data from an Access table *to* a text file, another Access database, or another applications format.

Should you import or Link data?

As Table 24-1 shows, you can work with data from other sources in two ways: Linking or importing. Both methods allow you to work with the external data.

There is a distinct difference between the two methods:

- ✦ Importing makes a copy of the external data and brings the copy into the Access table.
- ✦ Linking uses the data in its current file format (such as dBASE or Paradox file).

There are clear advantages and disadvantages to each method.

New!

Linking in Access for Windows 95 was called *attaching* in Access 2.0 and 1.*x*

When to import external data

Access cannot Link to certain file formats; these include text files and 1-2-3 spreadsheet files. If you need to work with data from these formats, you must import it. You can, however, Link to Excel files in Access for Windows 95.

Of course, importing data means you've doubled the storage space required for that particular data, because it now resides in two different files on the storage device.

Working with other Access databases

Access can open only one database at a time; therefore you can't work directly with a table in a different database. Even so, if you need to work with tables or other Access objects (such as forms and queries) from another Access database, you don't have to close the current one. Instead, simply import or Link the object in the other database to your current database. You'll be able to view or edit data in more than one database table directly.

Warning

Because importing makes another copy of the data, you may want to erase the old file once you import the copy into Access. Sometimes, however, you won't want to erase it. For example, the data may be sales figures from a spreadsheet still in use. In cases like this, simply maintain the duplicate data and accept that storing it will require more space.

One of the principal reasons to import data is to customize it to meet your needs. You can specify a primary key, change field names (up to 64 characters), and set other field properties. With Linked tables, on the other hand, you are restricted to setting very limited field properties. For example, you cannot specify a primary key, which means you can't enforce integrity against the Linked table.

Note

When you Link to another Access database, you can do everything you can do with tables in the primary database. This includes defining primary keys and enforcing referential integrity.

When to Link to external data

If you leave data in another database format, Access can actually make changes to the table while the original application is still using it. This capability is useful when you want to work with data in Access that other programs also need to work with. For example, you might need to obtain updated personnel data from a dBASE file (maintained in an existing networked dBASE application) so you can print out a monthly report in Access. Another example is when you use Access as a front end for your SQL database; you can Link to an SQL table and update the data directly to the server, without having to batch-upload it later.

The biggest disadvantage of working with Linked tables is that you lose Access's internal capability to enforce referential integrity between tables (*unless* you are linked to an Access database).

Linking External Data

Access can directly Link to several Database Management System (DBMS) tables individually or simultaneously. Once an external file is Linked, Access builds and stores a link to the table.

Database connectivity

As the database market continues to grow, the need to obtain information from many different sources will escalate. If you have information captured in an SQL server table or a Paradox table, you don't want to reenter the information from these tables into Access. Ideally, you want to open the table and use the information in its native format, without having to copy it or write a translation program to access it. For many companies today, this capability of accessing information from one database format while working in another is a primary goal.

Copying or translating data from one application format to another is both time-consuming and costly. The time it takes can be the difference between success and failure. Therefore you want a *heterogeneous* environment between your DBMSs and its data. Access provides this environment through Linking tables.

Types of Database Management Systems

Access lets you connect, or *Link,* to several different DBMSs, directly accessing information stored in them. Following are the database systems that Access supports:

✦ Other Access database tables

✦ dBASE (versions III, IV, and 5)

✦ FoxPro (versions 2.*x* and 3.0)

✦ Paradox (versions 3.0, 4.*x*, and 5.0)

✦ Btrieve (versions 5.1*x*, and 6.0)

✦ Microsoft SQL Server, Sybase Server, Oracle or any ODBC-aware database

You can Link to any of these table types, individually or mixed together. If you Link to an external file, Access displays the filename in the Database Table window (just as it does for other Access tables), but the icon Linked with the table will be different. It starts with an arrow pointing from left to right and points to an icon. A table icon tells you it's an Access table, a dB icon tells you it's a dBASE table, and so on. Figure 24-1 shows several Linked tables at the top of the list, which are all external tables. These tables are Linked to the current database. Notice that all the Linked tables have an icon with an arrow. (The icon clues you in to the type of file Linked).

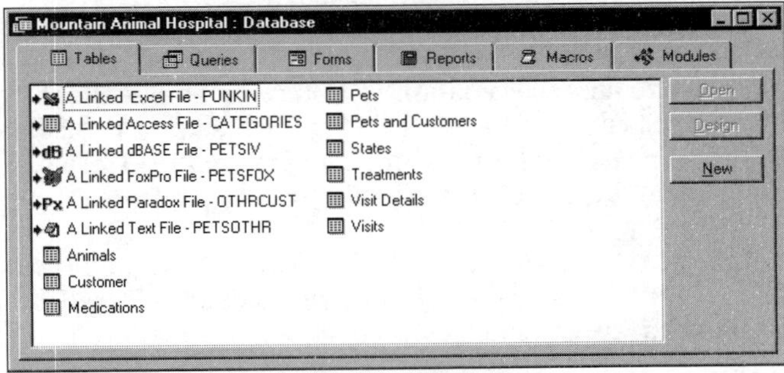

Figure 24-1: Linked tables in the database.

In Figure 24-1, OTHRCUST is a Paradox table, and PETSIV is a dBASE table (composed of a database [DBF] and memo [DBT] file). Notice the arrow on the left side of the icon, pointing to the table icon.

Once you Link a table to your Access database, you can use it as you would any other table. You can query against it, link another table to it, and so forth. For example, Figure 24-2 shows a query design and dynaset using the linked tables `Customer` (from Access) and `PETSIV` (from dBASE). You don't have to use an Access table; you can just as easily link the Paradox and dBASE tables.

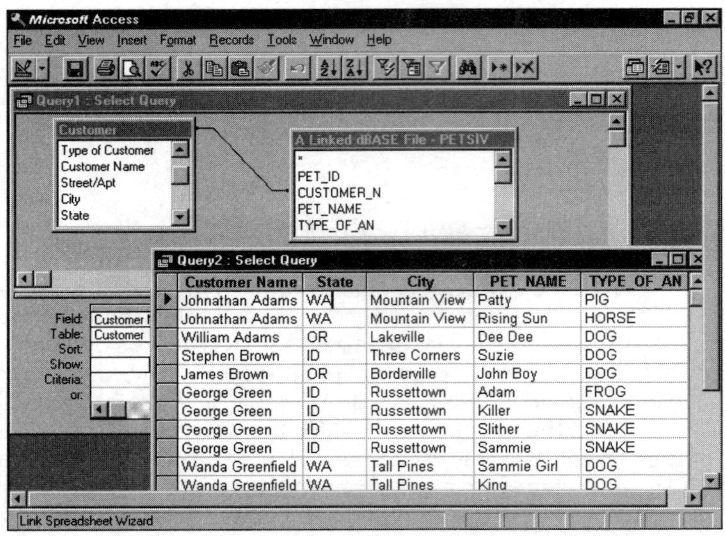

Figure 24-2: A query design and dynaset of an Access table and a Linked dBASE IV table.

Warning After you Link an external table to an Access database, you *cannot* move the table to another drive or directory. Access does not actually bring the file into the MDB file; it maintains the link via the filename *and* the drive:path. If you move the external table, you have to update the link using the Linked Table Manager.

Disk The examples in this chapter use the database ATCIMPEX.MDB. This database is included on your disk, along with several different types of DBMS files: Paradox, dBASE IV, dBASE III+, and FoxPro 2.*x* with indexes.

Linking to other Access database tables

When you work with an Access database, normally you create every table you want to use in it. If the table exists in another Access database, however, you can Link to this other Access database and use the table (rather than re-creating it and duplicating its data).

You may, for example, want to Link to another Access table that is on a network. Once you Link to another Access table, you use it just like another table in the open database. To Link to the Visits table in the Mountain Animal Hospital Access database from the ATCIMPEX database file, follow these steps:

1. Open the ATCIMPEX database.
2. Select File➪Get External Data➪Link Tables. . .4 (as shown in Figure 24-3). Access opens the Link dialog box (a standard Windows 95 File dialog box).

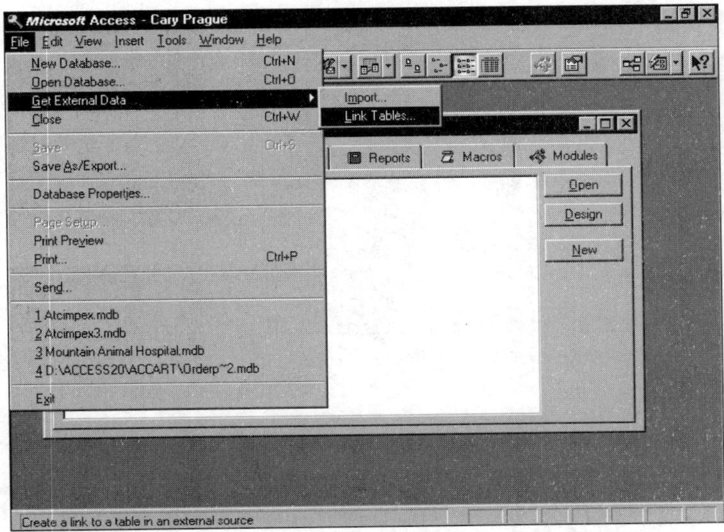

Figure 24-3: Selecting the File➪Get External Data➪Link Tables. . .4 menu commands.

You can select the .MDB file you want to link to. You can also change the type of files displayed in the Link dialog box; it can link to any type of external data. Though the default is to show only Access files (.MDB), you can link to any of the supported file types.

3. Find and select the Mountain Animal Hospital.MDB file in the dialog box. You may have to search for a different drive or directory.

4. Double-click on the Mountain Animal Hospital.MDB file (or select it and click on the Link button). Access closes the dialog box and displays the Link Tables dialog box.

5. Select Visits and click on OK.

After you Link the Visits table from the Mountain Animal Hospital database, Access returns to the Database window and shows you that the Visits table is now Linked to your database. Figure 24-4 shows the Visits table Linked to the current database. Notice the arrow on the Visits table's icon; it shows the table has been Linked from another source.

Tip You can link more than one table at a time by selecting each table before you click on the OK button. You can also use the Select All button to select all of the tables.

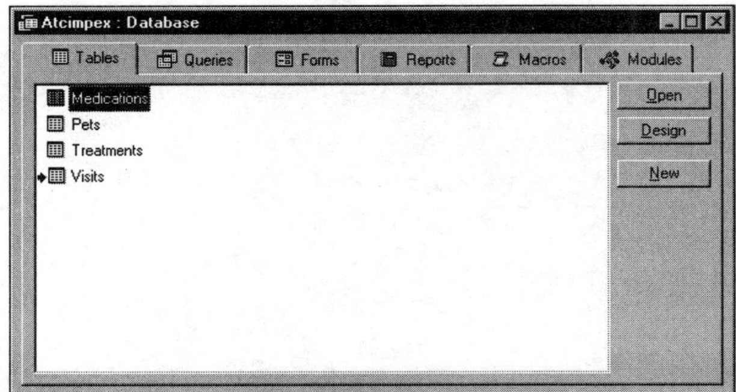

Figure 24-4: The Database window with Visits table added.

Splitting an Access database into multiple linked databases

Generally you split an Access application into two databases. One contains only your tables; the other contains all your queries, forms, reports, macros and modules. This is extremely important when moving an application to a multiuser environment. While the database with the queries, forms, reports, macros, and modules go on each client machine, the database with the tables goes on the server. This has several major benefits:

- ✦ Everyone on the network shares one common set of data.
- ✦ Many people can update data at the same time.
- ✦ When you want to update the forms, reports, macros, or modules, you don't have to interrupt processing or worry about data corruption.

If you start with your database split when you create a new application, you'll find it's easier to complete your application later. Some things you just can't do with a linked table without a little extra work; these include finding records and importing data. By using different techniques with linked tables, however, you can do anything you can do with a single database.

If you're starting from scratch, you first create a database with just the tables for your application. You then create another new database and link the tables from the first database to the second (as you learned in the previous section of this chapter).

Once you have built a system with all your objects (including the tables) in one database file, however, it's a little more difficult to split your tables. One method is to duplicate your database file in Windows by copying and pasting it. In one version, you delete everything but the tables from the duplicate database file. In the other version, you delete only the tables. Then you use the database file without the tables as a starting point, and link to all the tables in the database.

Access for Windows 95 features a Wizard that can do this for you automatically. Using the Mountain Animal Hospital database, for example, you can split out all the tables into a separate database file. Later, you can import all those tables into the original database if you want, or continue to use the split database file.

You start the Database Splitter Wizard by selecting Tools⇨Add-ins⇨Database Splitter. This displays a set of Wizard screens to help you split a single database into two. The first Wizard screen simply confirms you want to split the databases, as shown in Figure 24-5.

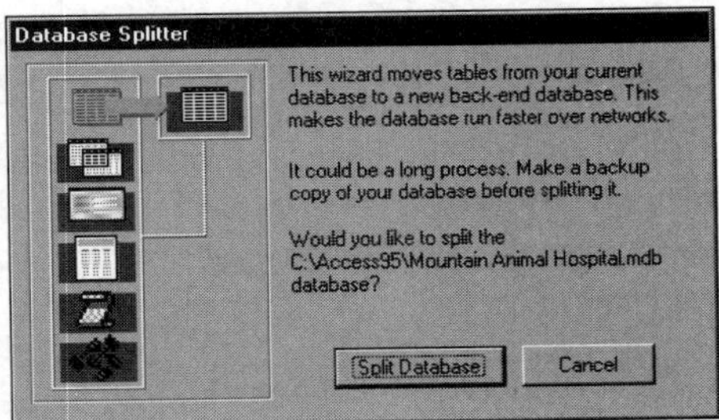

Figure 24-5: The Database Splitter Wizard.

When you click on the Split Database button, you are presented with the standard Windows 95 File Save dialog box (named the Database Splitter window). Here you can enter the name of the new database you want Access to create with just the tables. When you're ready for Access to split the tables, click on the Split button.

Access creates the new database, copies all the tables from the original database to the new database, and then links to them. When the process is done, you see a message that tells you the database was successfully split. Figure 24-6 shows the original database file with linked tables.

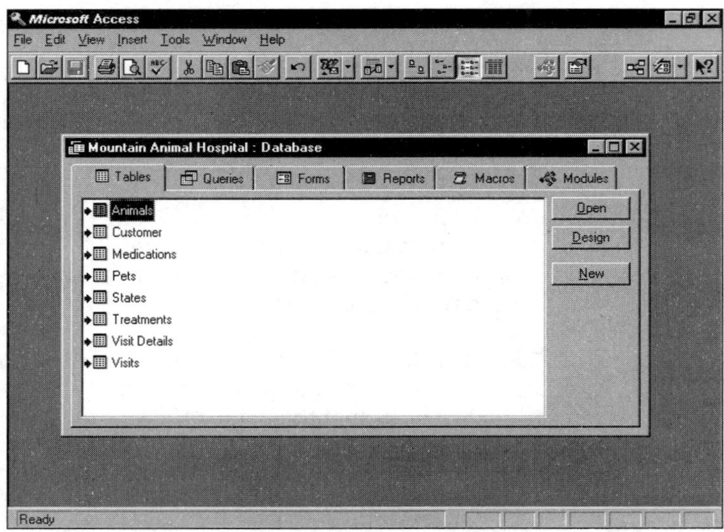

Figure 24-6: Linked tables in the Mountain Animal Hospital database.

Linking to dBASE and FoxPro databases (tables)

You can Link to DBF files in either dBASE or FoxPro format. As with other Access database tables, once an *x*BASE (dBASE or FoxPro) file is Linked, you can view and edit data in the DBF format.

dBASE and FoxPro save tables in individual files with the extension DBF. In *x*BASE, these DBF files are called databases. In Access, however, a *table* is equivalent to an *x*BASE *database*. (Access considers a *database* a complete collection of all tables and other related objects.) To maintain consistency in terminology, this book will consider *x*BASE databases to mean the same thing as dBASE or FoxPro tables.

Access and dBASE/FoxPro indexes

When you Link a dBASE or FoxPro file, you can also tell Access to use one or more index files (NDX and MDX for dBASE, and IDX and CDX for FoxPro). Use of these indexes will improve performance of the link between *x*BASE and Access.

If you inform Access of the associated index files, Access will update the indexes every time it changes the DBF file. By Linking a DBF file and its associated indexes, Access can link to DBFs in real time in a network environment. Access recognizes and enforces the automatic record-locking feature of dBASE and FoxPro, as well as the file and record locks placed with *x*BASE commands and functions.

Tip: You should always tell Access about any indexes associated with the database. If you don't, it will not update them; dBASE or FoxPro will have unexpected problems if their associated index files are not updated.

When you tell Access to use one or more associated indexes (NDX, MDX, IDX, or CDX) of a dBASE or FoxPro file, Access maintains information about the fields used in the index tags in a special information file. This file has the same name as the dBASE or FoxPro file with an extension of INF.

Warning: If you Link a dBASE or FoxPro file and associated indexes, Access must have access to the index files in order to Link the table. If you delete or move the index files or the Access INF file, you will not be able to open the Linked DBF file.

Linking to dBASE IV tables

To Link the dBASE IV table PETSIV.DBF and its associated memo file (DBT), follow these steps:

1. Open the ATCIMPEX database and select File⇨Get External Data⇨Link Tables. . .4
2. In the Link dialog box, select Files of type: dBASE IV. Access displays just the dBASE IV DBF files.
3. Double-click on PETSIV.DBF in the Select Index Files list box. (The memo file PETSIV.DBT is Linked automatically and given the DBF extension.) Access activates the Select Index Files box and displays all NDX and MDX files.
4. Click on the Cancel button (there are no related indexes for this table). Access closes the Select Index Files box and displays a dialog box to indicate the link was successful.

   Note: If there are any indexes to associate with this table, you select them here.
5. Click on the OK button. Access re-displays the Select File dialog box.
6. Click on the Close button to finish Linking dBASE files. Access displays the Database window with the file PETSIV Linked.

Note: You can cancel Linking at any time by clicking on the Cancel button in the Select File dialog box before you select a table.

Linking to dBASE III tables with an index

You Link to dBASE III or FoxPro tables in exactly the same way you Linked to the PETSIV.DBF. You can, for example, Link to a dBASE III table named VISITDTL.DBF and an associated index named VISITDTL.NDX. When you Link this table, you'll need to specify the index file. Refer to Step 4 of the process (just given) that Links to a dBASE table; here you select the File Name — VISITDTL.NDX — in the dialog box. Access will inform you when it has added the index file.

When you add index files, Access automatically creates and updates an Access information file. This file contains information about the index and associated dBASE or FoxPro file, has the same name, and ends in the extension INF.

Linking to Paradox tables

You can Link DB files in either Paradox 3.x or Paradox 4.x format. As with other Access database tables, once a Paradox file is Linked, you can view and edit data in the DB format.

Access and Paradox index files

If a Paradox table has a primary key defined, it maintains the index information in a file that ends in the extension PX. When you Link a Paradox table that has a primary key defined, Access Links the associated PX file automatically.

If you Link a Paradox table that has a primary key, Access needs the PX file to open the table. If you move or delete the PX file, you will not be able to open the Linked table.

If you Link a Paradox table to Access that does not have a primary key defined, you will not be able to use Access to update data in the table; you can only view it.

Access can Link to DBs in real time in a network environment. Access recognizes and enforces the file- and record-locking feature of Paradox.

Working with Linked Tables

After you Link to an external table from another database, you can use it just as you would another Access table.

Once Linked, external tables can be used with forms, reports, and queries. When working with external tables, you can modify many of their features; for example, you can rename the table, set view properties, and set links between tables in queries.

Setting view properties

Although an external table can be used like another Access table, you cannot change the structure (that is, delete, add, or rearrange fields) of an external table. You can, however, set several table properties for the fields in a Linked table:

- ✦ Format
- ✦ Decimal Places
- ✦ Caption
- ✦ Input Mask

Setting relationships

Access does not let you set permanent relations at the table level between non-Access external tables and Access tables. If you need to set a relationship between an external table and another Access table, you must do it in a query. Then you can use the query in a form, another query, or a report.

Setting links between external tables

To set a link between an external table and another Access table, simply create a query and use the drag-and-drop method of setting links. Once a link is set, you can change the join properties from equi-join (inner join) to external join by double-clicking on the link.

Using external tables in queries

When using a query, you can join the external table with another table, internal or external. This gives you powerful flexibility when working with queries. Figure 24-7 shows a query using several different database sources:

- ✦ An Access tables
- ✦ A Paradox table
- ✦ A dBASE IV table

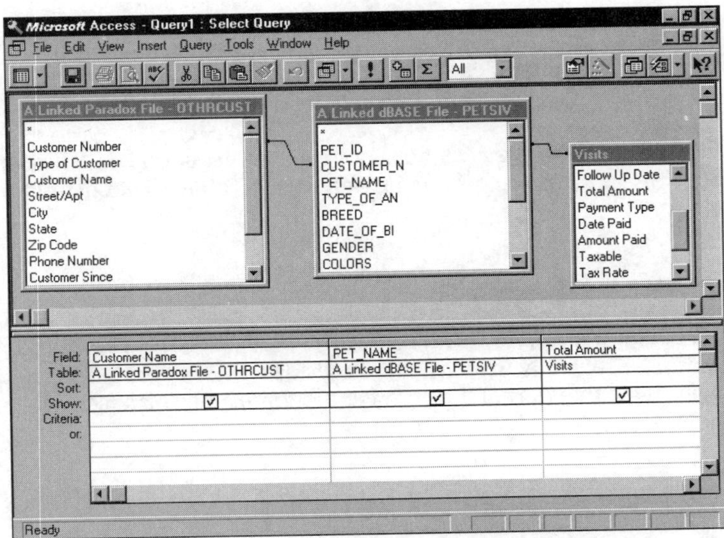

Figure 24-7: A query using several external database tables.

Notice that the query in Figure 24-7 has joins between all tables. This query will obtain information from all the tables and display a datasheet similar to the one in Figure 24-8.

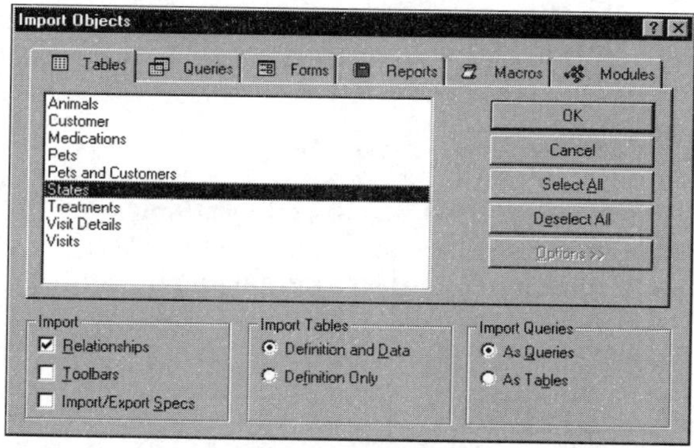

Figure 24-8: A datasheet display of the dynaset created by the query in Figure 24-7.

Renaming tables

You can rename a Linked external table. Because Access lets you name a table with up to 64 characters (including spaces), you may want to rename a Linked table to be more descriptive. For example, you may want to rename the dBASE table called PETSIV to Pets Table from dBASE.

To rename a file you can select Edit⇨Rename... from the Database menu. Another (quicker) method is clicking on the filename, clicking on it again, and entering a new name.

Note When you rename an external file, Access does not rename the actual DOS filename or SQL server table name. It uses the new name only in the Table object list of the Access database.

Optimizing Linked tables

When working with Linked tables, Access has to retrieve records from another file. This process takes time, especially when the table resides on a network or in an SQL database. When working with external data, you can optimize performance by observing these points:

✦ *Avoid using functions in query criteria.* This is especially true for aggregate functions like DTotal or Dcount, which retrieve all records from the Linked table automatically and then perform the query.

✦ *Limit the number of external records to view.* Create a query specifying a criterion that limits the number of records from an external table. This query can then be used by other queries, forms, or reports.

✦ *Avoid excessive movement in datasheets.* View only the data you need to in a datasheet. Avoid paging up and down and jumping to the last or first record in very large tables. (The exception is when adding records to the external table.)

✦ *If you add records to external Linked tables, create a form to add records and set the Default Editing property to Data Entry.* This makes the form an entry form that starts with a blank record every time it's executed.

✦ *When working with tables in a multiuser environment, minimize locking records.* This will free up records for other users.

Deleting a Linked table reference

To delete a Linked table from the Database window, follow these steps:

1. In the Database window, select the Linked table you want to delete.
2. Either press the Delete key or select Edit⇨Delete from the Database menu.
3. Select OK in the Access dialog box to delete the file.

Note Deleting an external table will delete only its name from the database object list. The actual file will not be deleted at the DOS level.

Viewing or changing information for Linked tables

Once a table is Linked, it or its associated indexes shouldn't be moved. If they are, Access will not be able to find them. You can use the Linked Table Manager to re-establish Linked files.

If you move, rename, or modify tables or indexes associated with a Linked table, you can use the Linked Table Manager to update the links. To use this tool, select Tools⇨Add-Ins⇨Linked Table Manager. Access will display a dialog box similar to the one in Figure 24-9. Select the Linked table that needs the information changed; Access will verify that the file cannot be found, and will prompt you for the new information.

	A	B	C	D	E	F	G
1	Customer Numl	Type of Cus	Customer Name	Street/Apt	City	State	Zip Code
2	AC001	P	All Creatures	21 Grace St.	Tall Pines	Wa	987462541
3	AD001	I	Johnathan Adams	66 10th St	Mountain \	WA	984101012
4	AD002	I	William Adams	1122 10th St	Lakeville	OR	974011011
5	AK001	P	Animal Kingdom	15 Marlin Lane	Borderville	ID	834835646
6	BA001	Z	Borderville Aquarium	1 Whale Way	Borderville	Or	974121001
7	BL001	P	Bird Land	22 Eagle Blvd	Russettow	Id	834121021
8	BR001	I	Stephen Brown	555 Sycamore /	Three Cor	ID	834011023
9	BR002	I	James Brown	3454 Adams St	Borderville	OR	974011019
10	BW001	P	Bow Wow House	76 Canine Ln.	Ranier City	Wa	987562175
11	CH001	P	Cat House Pets	76 Right Ln.	Borderville	Or	975412856
12	CM001	P	Critters and More	200 Feline Rd	Borderville	WA	984538567
13	EP001	P	Exotic Pets	1923 Ocean Ave	Borderville	Or	978164727
14	FB001	P	Fish Bowl Inc.	72 Guppy St.	Mountain \	WA	987461533
15	GB001	Z	George Bird Sanctuar	George St.	Mount Pilo	ID	839081012
16	GP001	P	Guppies to Puppies	811 Martin Rd.	Lakeville	Or	979827128
17	GR001	I	George Green	9133 Bookland	Russettow	ID	834121012
18	GR002	I	Wanda Greenfield	66 Farmaccess	Tall Pines	WA	984012201

Figure 24-9: The Linked Table Manager.

Importing External Data

When you import a file (unlike when you Link tables), you copy the contents from an external file into an Access table. You can import external file information from several different sources:

- ✦ Microsoft Access (other unopened databases)
- ✦ Paradox 3.*x*, 4.*x*, and 5.0
- ✦ FoxPro (2.*x* and 3.0)
- ✦ dBASE (III, IV, and 5)
- ✦ SQL databases (Microsoft SQL server, Sybase server, and Oracle server)
- ✦ Delimited text files (fields separated by a delimiter)
- ✦ Fixed-width text files (specific widths for each field)
- ✦ Microsoft Excel (all versions)
- ✦ Lotus 1-2-3 and 1-2-3 for Windows (versions WKS, WK1, and WK3)

You can import information either to new tables or existing tables, depending on the type of data being imported. All data types can be imported to new tables, but only spreadsheet and text files can be imported to existing tables.

When Access imports data from an external file, it does not erase or destroy the external file. Therefore, you will have two copies of the data — the original file (in the original format) and the new Access table.

Note If the filename of the importing file exists already in an Access table, Access adds a chronological number (1, 2, 3, and so on) to the filename until it has a unique table name. If an importing spreadsheet name is Customer.XLS (for example) and there is an Access table named Customer, the imported table name becomes Customer1. If Customer and Customer1 tables already exist, Access creates a table named Customer2.

Importing other Access objects

You can import other Access database tables, or any other object in another database. This means you can import an existing table, query, form, report, macro, or module from another Access database. As an example, use these steps to import the States table from the MTNANHSP Access database:

1. Open the ATCIMPEX database and select File⇨Get External Data⇨Import.
2. In the Import dialog box, select Files of type: Microsoft Access.
3. Double-click on Mountain Animal Hospital.MDB in the File Name list box. Access closes the selection box and opens the Import Objects dialog box as shown in Figure 24-10. At the bottom of this figure you can see the options displayed when you click on the Options>> button.
4. In the Mountain Animal Hospital.MDB list box, double-click on States.

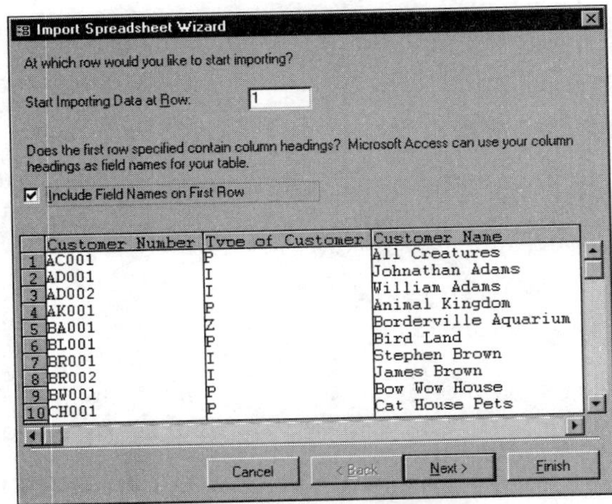

Figure 24-10: The Import Objects dialog box.

Access imports the States table into the ACTIMPEX database and closes the Import Objects dialog box. You can select more than one item at a time, using the Select All and Deselect All buttons to select or deselect all the objects in a specific category. The Options button lets you further define how to import Access data.

You can choose to import relationships, custom toolbars, and import/export specifications from an Access database. You can determine whether the tables you import come in with just the table design or the data as well. Finally, the last set of options lets you decide whether queries you import come in as queries or run as Make-Table action queries to import a new table. (See Chapter 26 for details on Make-Table queries.)

The States table appears in the Database window display without a Link symbol in the icon. Unlike Linking the table, you have copied the States table and added it to the current database. Therefore, because it's not linked but an actual part of the database, it occupies space like the original Access table.

Besides adding tables from other Access databases, you can also add other objects (including queries, forms, reports, macros, or modules) by clicking on each of the tabs in the Import Objects dialog box. You can select objects from each and then import them all at once.

Importing PC-based database tables

When importing data from personal-computer-based databases, you have two basic categories of database file types you can import:

- ✦ xBASE (dBASE, FoxPro)
- ✦ Paradox

Each type of database can be imported directly into an Access table. The native data types are converted to Access data types during the conversion.

Importing a PC-based database

You can import any Paradox, dBASE III, dBASE IV, dBASE V, FoxPro, or Visual FoxPro database table into Access. To import one of these, simply select the correct database type in the Files of type: box during the import process.

After selecting the type of PC-based database, you select which file you want to import; Access imports the file for you automatically.

If you try to import a Paradox table that is encrypted, Access prompts you for the password after you select the table in the Select File dialog box . Enter the password and select the OK button to import an encrypted Paradox table.

When Access imports xBASE fields, it converts them from their current data type into an Access data type. Table 24-2 lists how the data types are converted.

When importing any xBASE database file in a multiuser environment, you must have exclusive use of the file. If other people are using it, you will not be able to import it.

Table 24-2
Conversion of Data Types from xBASE to Access

xBASE Data Type	*Access Data Type*
Character	Text
Numeric	Number (property of Double)
Float	Number (property of Double)
Logical	Yes/No
Date	Date/Time
Memo	Memo

As with xBASE tables, when Access imports Paradox fields, the Paradox fields are converted from their current data type into an Access data type. Table 24-3 lists how the data types are converted.

Table 24-3
Conversion of Data Types from Paradox to Access

Paradox Data Type	*Access Data Type*
Alphanumeric	Text
Number	Number (property of Double)
Short Number	Number (property of Integer)
Currency	Number (property of Double)
Date	Date/Time
Memo	Memo
Blob (Binary)	OLE

Importing spreadsheet data

You can import data from Excel or Lotus 1-2-3 spreadsheets to a new or existing table. The key to importing spreadsheet data is that it must be arranged in tabular (columnar) format. Each cell of data in a spreadsheet column must contain the same type of data. Table 24-4 demonstrates correct and incorrect columnar-format data.

Table 24-4
Spreadsheet Cells with Contents

	A	B	C	D	E	F
1	TYPE	WEIGHT	BDATE		JUNK	GARBAGE
2	DOG	122	12/02/92		123	YES
3	CAT	56	02/04/89		22	134.2
4	BIRD	55	05/30/90		01/01/91	DR SMITH
5	FROG	12	02/22/88		TEST	$345.35
6	FISH	21	01/04/93		═══════	
7	RAT	3	02/28/93		$555.00	<== TOTAL

Table 24-4 represents cells in a spreadsheet, in the range A1 through F7. Notice that the data in columns A, B, and C and rows 2 through 7 is the same type. Row 1 contains field names. These columns can be imported into an Access table. Column D is empty, and cannot be used. Columns E and F do *not* have the same type of data in each of their cells; they may cause problems when you try to import them into an Access table.

Figure 24-11 shows an Excel spreadsheet named MORECUST.XLS (actually a spreadsheet with some of the same fields and data as other Mountain Animal Hospital tables).

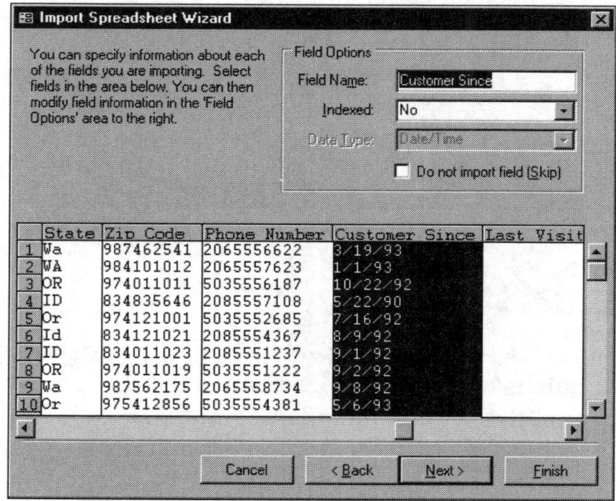

Figure 24-11: An Excel spreadsheet.

To import the Excel spreadsheet named MORECUST.XLS, follow these steps:

1. Open the ATCIMPEX database and select File➪Get External Data➪Import.
2. In the Import dialog box, select Files of type: Microsoft Excel (*.xls). Access closes the Import box and displays the first Spreadsheet Import Wizard screen.
3. Double-click on MORECUST.XLS in the File Name list box. Access opens the first Import Spreadsheet Wizard screen for the table MORECUST.XLS; the screen resembles the one in Figure 24-12.

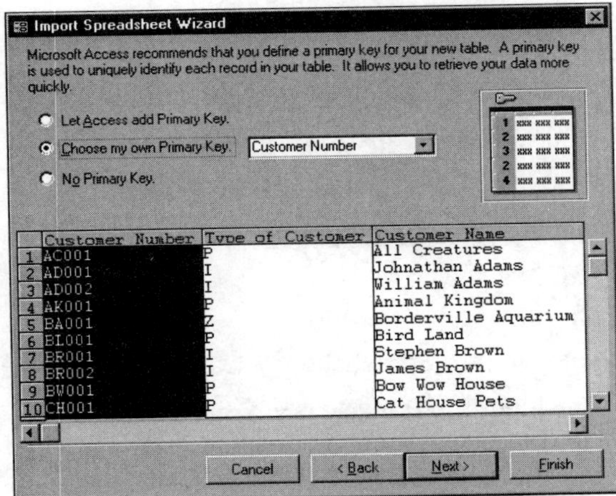

Figure 24-12: The first Import Spreadsheet Wizard screen.

This screen displays a sample of the first few rows and columns of the spreadsheet. You can scroll the display to see all the rows and columns if you need to. Enter the starting row number to import the data. To use the first row of the spreadsheet to name fields in the table, use the check box.

4. Click on Include Field Names on First Row. The display changes.
5. Click on Next> to display the second Import Spreadsheet Wizard screen.

   This screen (shown in Figure 24-13) lets you click on each column of the spreadsheet to accept the field name, change it, and decide whether it will be indexed; the Wizard determines the data type automatically. You can also choose to skip each column if you want.

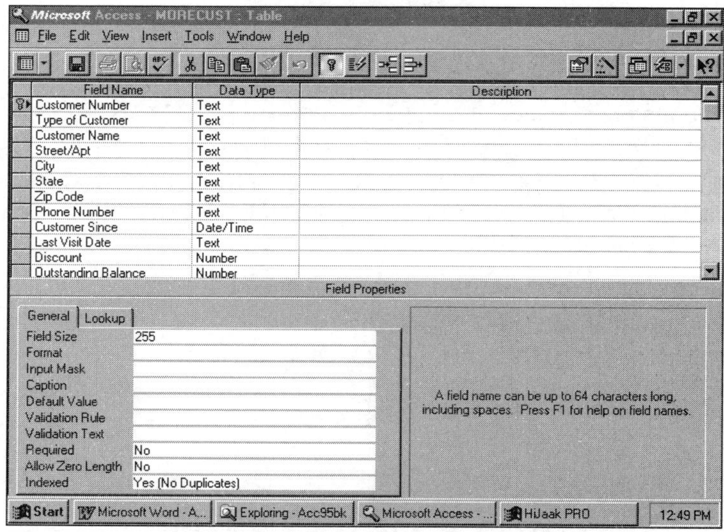

Figure 24-13: Determining the field names and data types.

6. Click on Next> to display the next Import Spreadsheet Wizard screen.

   This screen lets you choose a field for the Primary key. You can let Access create a new AutoNumber field (by choosing Let Access add Primary Key), enter your own (by selecting Choose my own Primary Key and selecting one of the columns), or have no primary key. Figure 24-14 shows these options.

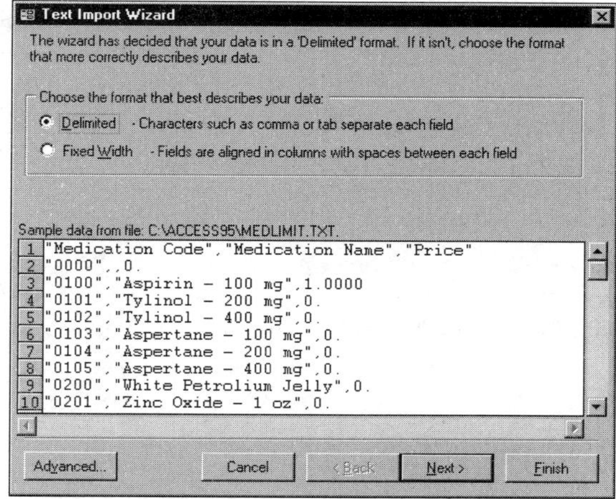

Figure 24-14: Determining the primary key.

7. Select Choose my own Primary Key and select the Customer Number field.
8. Click on Next> to display the last Import Spreadsheet Wizard screen.

   The last screen lets you enter the name for the imported table and (optionally) run the Table Analyzer Wizard.
9. Click on Finish> to import the spreadsheet file.

The filename appears in the Access database window. Figure 24-15 shows the MORECUST table in design view. Notice that a standard Access table has been created from the original spreadsheet file.

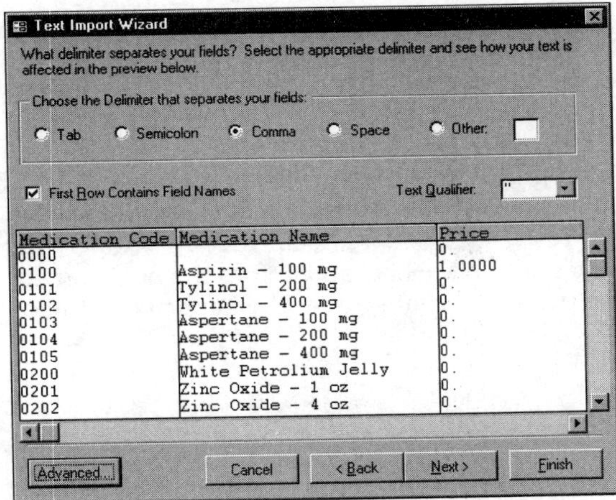

Figure 24-15: The MORECUST Access table.

Importing from word processing files

Access does not offer a specific way to import data from word processing files. If you need to import data from a word processing file into Access, convert the word processing file to a simple text file first and then import it as a text file. Most word processors have the ability to convert their formatted text to text files or ASCII files.

Importing text file data

You can import from two different types of text files, *delimited* and *fixed-width*. These types of files use, in turn, an *import/export specification* file (optional for delimited, mandatory for fixed-width). Unformatted mainframe data is generally transferred from the mainframe to a personal computer as a text file.

Delimited text files

Delimited text files are sometimes known as *CSV* (for *comma-separated values*) files; each record is on a separate line in the text file. The fields on the line contain no trailing spaces, normally use commas as field separators, and require certain fields to be enclosed in a *delimiter* (such as single or double quotation marks). Usually the text fields are also enclosed in quotation marks or some other delimiter, as in these examples:

```
"Irwin","Michael","Michael Irwin Consulting",05/12/72
"Prague","Cary","Cary Prague Books and Software",02/22/86
"Zimmerman-Schneider","Audrie","IBM",01/01/59
```

Notice that the file has three records (rows of text) and four fields. Each field is separated by a comma, and the text fields are delimited with double quotation marks. The starting position of each field, after the first one, is different. Each record has a different length because the field lengths are different.

Tip

You can import records from a delimited text file that has fields with no values. To specify a field with no value, place delimiters where the field value would be, putting no value in between (for example, `"Irwin","Michael",,05/12/72`). Notice that there are two commas after the field content ~~Michael~~ and before the field content `05/12/72`. The field between these two has no value; it will be imported with no value into an Access file.

Fixed-width text files

Fixed-width text files also place each record on a separate line. However, the fields in each record are of a fixed length. If the field contents are not long enough, trailing spaces are added to the field. The following material demonstrates this:

```
Irwin          Michael     Michael Irwin Consulting         05/12/82
Prague         Cary        Cary Prague Books and Software   02/22/86
Zimmerman      Audrie      IBM                              01/01/59
-Schneider
```

Notice that the fields are not separated by delimiters. Rather, they start at exactly the same position in each record. Each record has exactly the same length. If a field is not long enough, trailing spaces are added to fill the field.

You can import either a delimited or a fixed-width text file to a new table or existing Access table. If you decide to append the imported file to an existing table, the file's structure must match that of the Access table you're importing to.

Note

If the Access table being imported has a key field, the text file cannot have any duplicate key values or the import will report an error.

Importing delimited text files

To import a delimited text file named MEDLIMIT.TXT, follow these steps:

1. Open the ATCIMPEX database and select File➪Get External Data➪Import.
2. In the Import dialog box, select Files of type: Text files (*.txt,*.csv,*.tab,*.asc).
3. Double-click on MEDLIMIT.TXT in the File Name list box. Access opens an Import Text Options dialog box for the table MEDLIMIT.TXT. The dialog box resembles the one in Figure 24-16.

   This screen displays the data in the text file and guesses whether the text file is Delimited or Fixed Width. As you can see, the Wizard has determined correctly that the file is Delimited.

Note Notice at the bottom of the screen there is a button marked Advanced. Click on it to further define the import specifications. You will learn more about this option in the upcoming section on fixed-width text files. Generally, it's not needed for Delimited files.

4. Click on the Next> button to display the next Text Import Wizard screen.

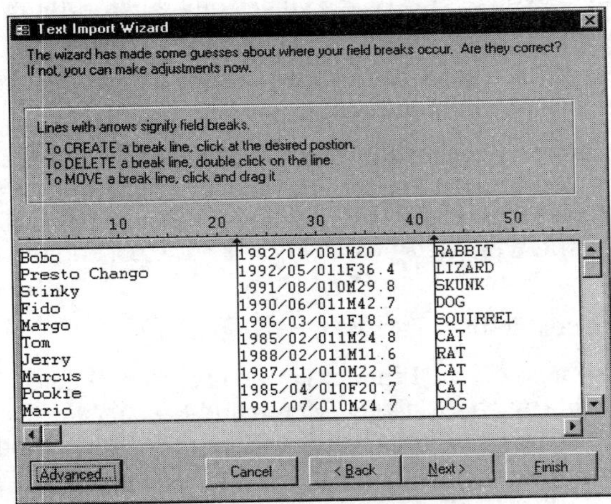

Figure 24-16: The first Text Import Wizard screen.

As you can see in Figure 24-17, this screen lets you determine what type of separator to use in the delimited text file. Generally this is a comma, but you could use a tab, semicolon, space, or other character (such as an asterisk), which you would enter in the box next to the Other option button. You can also decide whether to use text from the first row as field names for the imported table.

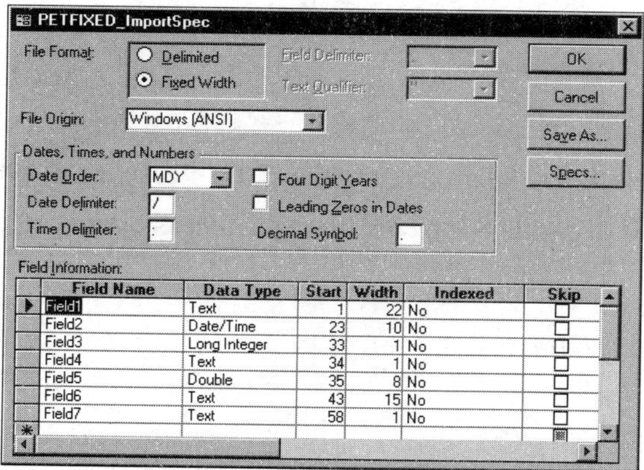

Figure 24-17: The second Text Import Wizard screen.

5. Click on the Next> button to display the next Import Text Wizard screen.

   This screen lets you determine whether you're storing the imported data in a new table or an existing table. If you decide to use an existing table, you have to choose it from a list.

   The next few screens are exactly the same as the Spreadsheet Import Wizard screens you saw in the previous part of this chapter.

6. Click on the Next> button to display the next Import Text Wizard screen, which lets you click on each column of the Text Import grid, accept or change the field name, decide whether it will be indexed, and set the data type (which is also automatically determined by the Wizard). You can choose to skip a column if you want.

7. Click on Next> to display the next Import Text Wizard screen.

   This screen lets you choose a field for the Primary key. You can let Access create a new AutoNumber field (by choosing Let Access add Primary Key), enter your own (by selecting Choose my own Primary Key and selecting one of the columns), or have no primary key.

8. Click on Next> to display the last Import Text Wizard screen.

   The last screen lets you enter the name for the imported table and (optionally) run the Table Analyzer Wizard.

9. Click on Finish> to import the delimited text file.

Access creates a new table, using the same name as the text file's name. The filename appears in the Access Database window, where Access has added the table MEDLIMIT.

Importing fixed-width text files

In *fixed-width* text files, each field in the file has a specific width and position. Files downloaded from mainframes are the most common fixed-width text files. As you import or export this type of file, you must specify an import/export setup specification. You create this setup file by using the Advanced options of the Import Table Wizard.

To import a fixed-width text file, follow these steps:

1. Open the ATCIMPEX database and select File⇨Get External Data⇨Import.
2. In the Import dialog box, select Files of type: Text files (*.txt,*.csv,*.tab,*.asc).
3. Double-click on PETFIXED.TXT in the File Name list box. Access opens an Import Text Options dialog box for the table PETFIXED.TXT. (The dialog box resembles the one shown earlier in Figure 24-16.)

   This screen displays the data in the text file and guesses whether the type of text file is Delimited or Fixed Width. As you can see, the Wizard has correctly determined that it's a Fixed Width file.
4. Click on Next> to display the next Import Text Wizard screen.

   This screen makes a guess about where columns begin and end in the file, basing the guess on the spaces in the file.

Figure 24-18 shows that Access has not done a good job in this file. It has recognized the first field correctly, but the second three fields have been lumped together. You'll need to add field break lines at positions 32, 33, and 34. The idea is to show the end of the Date field, the beginning and end of the Type of Animal field (1, 2, 3), the Gender field (M, F), and the beginning of the Weight field.

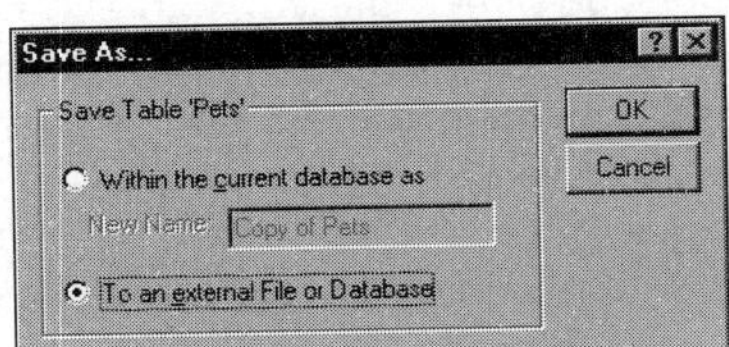

Figure 24-18: Selecting the export function.

As you can see in Figure 24-18, you can drag a field break line, add one, or delete one to tell Access where the fields really are. As you do so, you're actually completing an internal data table known as the Import/Export Specifications. When you click on the Advanced button at the bottom of the import screens, you see this data screen.

Figure 24-19 shows the Import Specification screen.

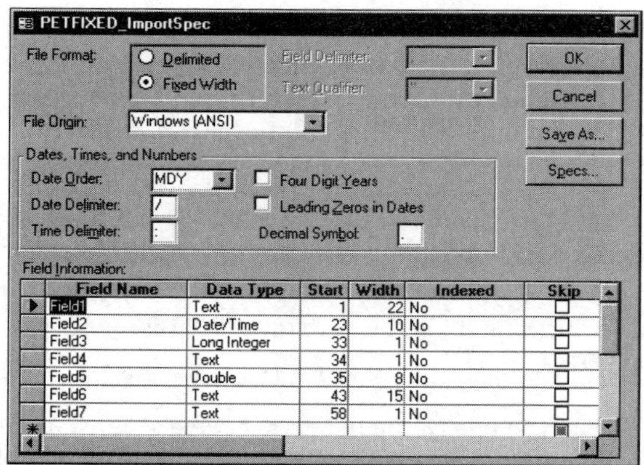

Figure 24-19: The Import Specification screen for fixed-width text files.

Using the Import Specification screen

Access offers several options for importing and exporting text files. These options differ based on the operation and type of file being worked with. The different text file formats that Access can work with are as follows:

- ✦ Delimited text (separated by commas, tabs, none, or user-specified)
- ✦ Fixed-width text (each field has the same length with filler of blanks)

Each type of text file has records and fields. The records are specified by rows or lines of text. The fields are contained from left to right in a row of text.

Each setting (attribute or option) can be independently set. These settings, such as date formats, give you the flexibility to fine-tune the type of text file you can export or import. This eliminates the need to receive a restrictively formatted type of text file from another source. Once you create the settings, however, you must save them in a specification file.

You use the File Origin option to specify a Windows text file or a DOS or an OS/2 text file. Access offers three pull-down choices:

- ✦ Windows (ANSI)
- ✦ DOS or OS/2 (PC-8)
- ✦ Macintosh

The default value is the Windows text file. If the type of file you're importing is a DOS or OS/2 text file, you select the DOS or OS/2 (PC-8) choice. You can also take a file from a Macintosh by selecting this option.

Use the Field Delimiter option only for delimited text files; they separate the fields by use of a special character such as a comma or semicolon. Three field-separator choices are available in this combo box:

;	Semicolon
{tab}	Tabulation mark
{space}	Single space
,	Comma

You can specify your own field separator directly in this combo box.

Use the Text Qualifier option only for delimited text files. It specifies the type of delimiter to be used when you're working with Text-type fields. Normally the text fields in a delimited file are enclosed by specified delimiters (such as quotation marks). This is useful for specifying Number-type data (like Social Security numbers) as Text type rather than Number type (it won't be used in a calculation). There are three list box choices:

{none}	No delimiter
"	Double quotation mark
'	Single quotation mark

The default value is a double quotation mark. This list box is actually a combo box; you can enter your own delimiter. If the one you want is not among these three choices, you can specify a different text delimiter by entering a new one directly into the combo box — for example, the caret symbol (^).

Tip

If you use CSV files, you should set the text qualifier to the double quotation mark (") and the field delimiter to a comma (,).

Warning

If you specify your own delimiter, it must be the same on both sides of the text. For example, you can't use both of the curly braces ({})as user-specified delimiters; you can only specify one character. If you specify the left curly brace, Access looks only for the left curly brace as a delimiter — on both sides of the text:

{This is Text data enclosed in braces{

Notice that only the left brace is used.

As it imports or exports data, Access converts dates to a specific format (such as MMDDYY). In the example MMDDYY, Access converts all dates to two digits for each portion of the date — month, day, and year — separating each by a specified delimiter. Thus January 19, 1995 would be converted to 1/19/95. Six choices are available in the Date Order combo box:

- DMY
- DYM
- MDY
- MYD
- YDM
- YMD

These choices specify the order for each portion of a date. The *D* is the day of month (1–31), *M* is the calendar month (1–12), and *Y* is the year. The default date order is set to the American format of month, day, and year. When you work with European dates, the order must changed to day, month, and year.

You use the Date Delimiter option to specify the date delimiter. This option tells Access what type of delimiter to use between the parts of date fields. The default is a forward slash (/), but this can be changed to any user-specified delimiter. In Europe, for example, date parts are separated by periods, as in 22.10.95.

Warning When you import text files with date type data, you must have a separator between the month, day, and year, or Access reports an error if the field is specified as a Date/Time type. When you're exporting date fields, the separator is not needed.

With the Time Delimiter option, you can specify a separator between the segments of time values in a text file. The default value is the colon (:). In the example 12:55, the colon separates the hours from the minutes. To change the separator, simply enter another in the Time Delimiter box.

You use the Four Digit Years check box when you want to specify that the year value in date fields will be formatted with four digits. By checking this box, you can export dates that include the century (as in 1881 or 1993). The default is to exclude the century (as when a year is expressed as 93).

The Leading Zeros in Dates option is a check box where you specify that date values include leading zeros. You can specify, for example, that date formats include leading zeros (as in 02/04/93). To specify leading zeros, check this box. The default is without leading zeros (as in 2/4/93).

You use the Decimal Symbol option to specify the character that separates the whole number from the fractional portion of a number. The default value is a period (as in the number 1234.56).

As the option name specifies, the Field Information option is used only with fixed-width text files. You must create a specification file for importing or exporting fixed-width text files. At a minimum, you must enter information about each field you want to import or export. Following is a list of the type of information you need to specify:

Field Name	The Access field name in the Access table
Data Type	The data type of the field, such as Text, Date/Time, Yes/No, and so on
Start	The field's starting position (column) in the text file
Width	The width of the individual field
Indexed	Whether to index the field for faster searches
Skip	Whether to include the field in the new table

Each of these columns must be specified for each field you import or export.

Tip When you export data to a fixed-width text file, you need only specify field information for the Access fields you want to export to the text file. You are not required to specify all the fields in an Access table.

Warning If you're importing fixed-width text files into an existing table, you must supply field information for each field in the correct order of the fields for the Access table. If you don't specify each field, Access may report an error.

In addition to all its options, the Import Specifications dialog box includes command buttons. Table 24-5 shows each button and explains its purpose.

Table 24-5
Setup Buttons and Purpose

Button Name	*Purpose*
OK	Leave and save changes in dialog box.
Cancel	Abandon changes and leave dialog box.
Save As	Prompt for specification filename to save options to.
Specs	Display a list of current specification names. You can open or delete one.

You can accept the values you see in this dialog box, basing your choices on the fields you selected in the previous Wizard screen.

You can click on OK to return to the Import Fixed Text Wizard screen, and then complete the rest of the screens (exactly the same as those for delimited or spreadsheet files).

Modifying imported table elements

Once you import a file, you can refine the table in the design view. The following list itemizes and discusses some of the primary changes you may want to make to improve your table:

- ✦ Add field names or descriptions. You may want to change the names of the fields you specified when you imported the file. For example, xBASE databases allow no more than ten characters in names.
- ✦ Change data types. Access may have guessed the wrong data type when it imported several of the fields. You can change these fields to reflect a more descriptive data type (such as Currency instead of Number, or Text instead of Number).
- ✦ Set field properties You can set field properties to enhance the way your tables work. For example, you may want to specify a format or default value for the table.
- ✦ Set the field size to something more realistic than the 255 bytes Access allocates for each imported text field.
- ✦ Define a primary key. Access works best with tables that have a primary key. You may want to set a primary key for the imported table.

Troubleshooting import errors

When you import an external file, Access may not be able to import one or more records, in which case it reports an error when trying to import them. When Access encounters errors, it creates an Access table named Import Errors (with the user's name Linked to the table name). The Import Errors table contains one record for each record that causes an error.

Once errors have occurred and Access has created the Import Errors table, you can open the table to view the error descriptions.

Import errors for new tables

Access may not be able to import records into a new table for the following reasons:

- ✦ A row in a text file or spreadsheet may contain more fields than are present in the first row.

✦ Data in the field cannot be stored in the data type Access chose for the field.

✦ On the basis of the first row's contents, Access automatically chose the incorrect data type for a field. The first row is OK, but the remaining rows are blank.

Import errors for existing tables

Access may not be able to append records into an existing table for the following reasons:

✦ The data is not consistent between the text file and the existing Access table.

✦ Numeric data being entered is too large for the field size of the Access table.

✦ A row in a text file or spreadsheet may contain more fields than the Access table.

✦ The records being imported have duplicate primary key values.

The Import Errors table

When errors occur, Access creates an Import Errors table you can use to determine which data caused the errors.

Open the Import Errors table and try to determine why Access couldn't import all the records. If the problem is with the external data, edit it. If you're appending records to an existing table, the problem may be with the existing table; it may need modifications (such as changing the data types and rearranging the field locations). After you solve the problem, erase the Import Errors file and import the data again.

Note: Access attempts to import all records that do not cause an error. If you reimport the data, you may need to clean up the external table or the Access table before reimporting. If you don't, you may have duplicate data in your table.

Tip: If importing a text file seems to take an unexpectedly long time, it may be because of too many errors. You can cancel importing by pressing Ctrl+Break.

Exporting to External Formats

You can copy data from an Access table or query into a new external file. This process of copying Access tables to an external file is called *exporting*. You can export tables to several different sources:

✦ Microsoft Access (other unopened databases)

✦ Delimited text files (fields separated by a delimiter)

✦ Fixed-width text files (specific widths for each field)

- Microsoft Excel (all versions)
- Lotus 1-2-3 and 1-2-3 for Windows (versions WKS, WK1, and WK3)
- Paradox 3.x, 4.x, and 5.0.
- FoxPro 2.*x* and Visual FoxPro 3.0
- dBASE III, dBASE IV, and dBASE 5
- Rich text formats (RTF)
- Word Mail Merge (.txt)
- ODBC Data Sources SQL databases (Microsoft SQL Server, Sybase server, and Oracle server)

When Access exports data from an Access table to an external file, the Access table isn't erased or destroyed. This means you will have two copies of the data: the original Access file and the external data file.

Exporting objects to other Access databases

You can export objects from the current database to another, unopened Access database. The objects you export can be tables, queries, forms, reports, macros, or modules. To export an object to another Access database, follow these steps:

1. Open the database that has the object you want to export and select File➪Save As/Export from the Database menu as shown in Figure 24-20.

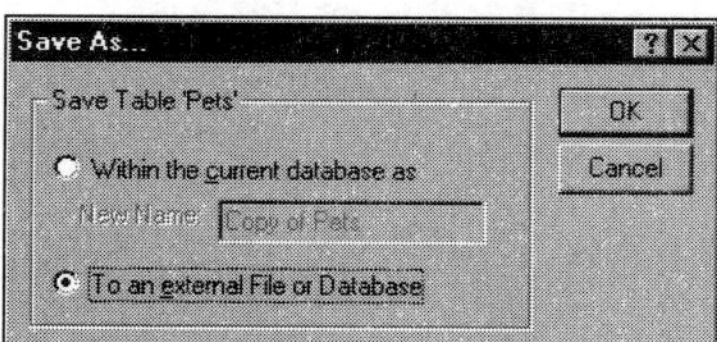

Figure 24-20: The Save As/Export dialog box.

2. In the Export dialog box, select To an external file or database. Click on OK.

   Access opens the standard Save As dialog box — the same one that appears whenever you save an object to another name. The difference is that you can specify a different format (Save as type). When you open the combo box, a list of formats appears. Select the one you want; Access will save the data to that format.

When this process is complete, Access copies the object you specified to the other database and immediately returns you to the Database window in Access.

If you attempt to export an object to another Access database that has an object of the same type and name, Access warns you before copying. You then have the option to cancel or overwrite.

Summary

This chapter explored using data from other types of files. You worked with data from database, spreadsheet and text-based files. This chapter covered the following points:

- ✦ Access can work with various types of external data, including spreadsheets, PC-based databases, Btrieve tables, SQL server tables, and text files.
- ✦ Access can Link to other Access tables, *x*BASE (dBASE and FoxPro) databases, Paradox tables, and Btrieve and SQL server tables. When you Link to these tables through Access, you can view and edit the files in their native formats.
- ✦ You should always split your Access application into two databases: one with tables and one with all the other objects. You then link the tables from the second database to the first (the one that has only the tables). This approach makes multiuser systems more efficient.
- ✦ You can use Linked tables for queries, forms, and reports. You can set relations between Linked tables and Access tables. You can even rename a Linked table for better clarity.
- ✦ When you're working with text files (delimited and fixed length), you have extensive flexibility for importing and exporting them by using the import/export specifications setup file.
- ✦ When you create an import/export setup file, you can set several options, such as a specific delimiter, the format of date fields, and so forth.
- ✦ You can import data from other Access objects, dBASE databases, FoxPro databases, Paradox tables, Btrieve tables, SQL server tables, Excel spreadsheets, Lotus 1-2-3 spreadsheets, and text files. All these file types can be imported to new tables.
- ✦ Spreadsheets and text files can also be appended to existing Access tables.
- ✦ You can export Access table data to several different external files: dBASE databases, FoxPro databases, Paradox tables, Btrieve tables, SQL server tables, Excel spreadsheets, Lotus 1-2-3 spreadsheets, and text files.

In the next chapter, you examine advanced select queries.

✦ ✦ ✦

Advanced Select Queries

In this chapter, you work with advanced select queries. So far, you've worked with relatively simple select queries, where you selected specific records from one or more tables based on some criteria. This chapter shows you queries that display totals, create cross tabulations, and obtain criteria from the user at run time.

Your queries have specified criteria for single or multiple fields (including calculated fields) using multiple tables. You also worked with wildcard characters and fields not having a value (Is Null). You are already accustomed to using functions in queries to specify record criteria or to create calculated fields. Finally, you've realized that Access queries are a great tool for performing ad-hoc "what-ifs."

This chapter focuses on three specialized types of advanced select queries:

- ✦ Total
- ✦ Crosstab
- ✦ Parameter

Using these queries, you can calculate totals for records, summarize data in row-and-column format, and run a query that obtains criteria by prompting the operator of the query.

✦ ✦ ✦ ✦

In This Chapter

Creating queries that calculate totals

Performing totals on groups of records

Using different types of queries that total

Specifying criteria for queries that total

Creating crosstab queries

Specifying criteria for crosstab queries

Specifying fixed column headings for crosstab queries

Creating a parameter query

Running a parameter query

Using the Parameter Query dialog box

✦ ✦ ✦ ✦

Creating Queries That Calculate Totals

Many times, you want to find information in your tables based on total-type data. For example, you may want to find the total number of animals you've treated or the total amount of money each customer spent on animals last year. Access supplies the tools to accomplish these queries without the need for programming.

Access performs calculation totals by using nine aggregate functions that let you determine a specific value based on the contents of a field. For example, you can determine the average weight of all cats, the maximum and minimum length of all animals you have treated, or the total count of all records in which the type of animal is either a duck or fish. Performing each of these examples as a query results in a dynaset of answer fields based on the mathematical calculations you requested.

To create a total query, you use a new row in the QBE pane — the Total: row.

Displaying the Total: row in the QBE pane

To create a query that performs a total calculation, you create a select query and then activate the Total: row of the QBE pane. You can activate the Total: row by either of these two selection methods below.

First open a new query using the Pets table.

- ✦ Select View⇨Totals from the Design menu.
- ✦ Select the Totals button (the Greek sigma symbol button, Σ, which is to the right of the midway mark) on the toolbar.

Figure 25-1 shows the Total: row after it is added in the QBE pane. Notice that the Totals button is selected on the toolbar and the Total: row is placed in the QBE pane between the Table: and Sort: rows.

Note If the toolbar is not visible, select View⇨Toolbars. . . from the Query menu. Then select Query Design and then close the dialog box.

If the Table: row is not present on your screen, the Total: row will be between the Field: and Sort: rows. You can activate the Table: row by selecting View⇨Table Names from the Design menu.

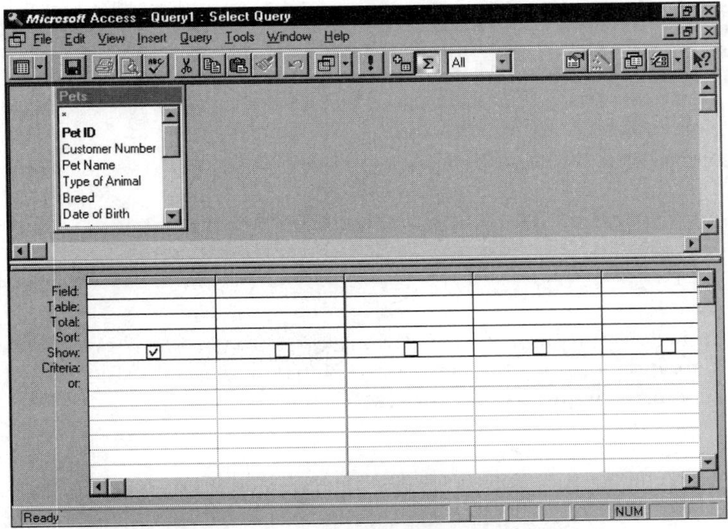

Figure 25-1: Activating the Total: row of the QBE pane.

Removing the Total: row from the QBE pane

To deactivate the Total: row in the QBE pane, simply reselect either activation method (with the Totals button or the menu choice). The Totals button is a toggle that alternately turns the Total: row on and off.

The Total: row options

You can perform total calculations against all records or groups of records in one or more tables. To perform a calculation, you must select one of the options from the drop-down list box in the Total: row for every field you include in the query, including any hidden fields (with the Show: option turned off). Figure 25-2 shows the drop-down list box active in the Total: row of the field Pet ID.

What is an aggregate function?

The word *aggregate* implies gathering together a mass (group or series) of things and working on this mass as a whole — a total. Therefore, an aggregate function is a function that takes a group of records and performs some mathematical function against the entire group. The function can be a simple *count* or a complex *expression* that you specify, based on a series of mathematical functions.

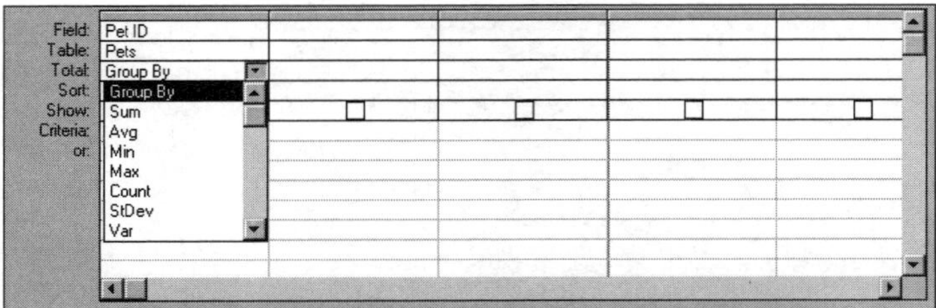

Figure 25-2: The drop-down list box of the Total: row.

Although you see only 8 options in Figure 25-2, there are actually 12 to choose from. You can view the remaining options by using the elevator on the right side of the box. The 12 options can be broken into 4 distinct categories:

- ✦ Group By
- ✦ Aggregate
- ✦ Expression
- ✦ Total Field Record Limit

Table 25-1 lists each category, its number of Total options, and its purpose.

Table 25-1
Four Categories of Total Options

Category	*Number of Options*	*Purpose of Operator*
Group By	1	Groups common records together against which Access performs aggregate calculations
Aggregate	9	Specifies a mathematical or selection operation to perform against a field
Expression	1	Groups several total operators together and performs the group totals
Total Field Record Limit	1	Limits records before record limit performing a total calculation against a field

Notice that the Aggregate category has nine options. Its options are used by the other three categories.

Group By category

This category has one option, the Group By option. You use this option to specify that a certain field in the QBE pane is to be used as a grouping field. For example, if you select the field Type of Animal, the Group By option tells Access to group all cat records together, all dog records together, and so on. This is the default option for all Total: cells; when you drag a field to the QBE pane, Access automatically selects this option. Figure 25-2 shows that this is also the first choice in the drop-down list box. These groups of records will be used for performing some aggregate calculation against another field in the query. This will be discussed later in further detail.

Expression category

Like the Group By category, the Expression category has only one option — Expression. This is the second-from-last choice in the drop-down list box. You use this option to tell Access that you will create a calculated field using one or more aggregate calculations in the Field: cell of the QBE pane. For example, you may want to create a query that shows each customer and how much money the customer saved, based on the individual's discount rate. This requires creating a calculated field that uses a sum aggregate against the Total Amount field in the Visits table, which is then multiplied by the Discount field in the Customer table. This type of calculation is discussed in detail later.

Total Field Record Limit category

The Total Field Record Limit category is the third category that has a single option — the Where option. This option is the last choice in the drop-down list box. When you select this option, you tell Access that you want to specify a limiting criteria against an aggregate type field, as opposed to a Group By or an Expression field. The limiting criteria will be performed *before* the aggregate options are executed. For example, you may want to create a query that will count all pets by types of animals that weigh less than 100 pounds. Because the Weight field is not to be used for a grouping, as is Type of Animal, and won't be used to perform an aggregate calculation, you specify the Where option. By specifying the Where option, you are telling Access to use this field only as a limiting criteria field — before it performs the aggregate calculation (counting types of animals). This type of operation is also discussed in detail later in this chapter.

Aggregate category

The Aggregate category, unlike the others, has nine options: Sum, Avg, Min, Max, Count, StDev, Var, First, and Last. These options appear as the second through tenth options of the drop-down list box. Each of these options performs some operation. Seven of the options perform mathematical operations, whereas two perform simple selection operations. When each option is executed, it finds — calculates or determines — some answer or value and supplies it to a cell in the resulting dynaset. For example, you may want to determine the maximum (Max) and minimum (Min) weight of each animal in the Type of Animal field in the Pets table. On the other hand, you may want the total number (Count) of animals in the Pets table. You use these aggregate options to solve such types of queries.

Options such as these are what most people think about when they hear the words *total query.* Each of the options performs a calculation against a field in the QBE pane of the query and returns a single answer in the dynaset. As an example, there can only be one maximum weight for all the animals. Several animals may have the same maximum weight, but only one weight is the heaviest of all.

The other three categories of options can be used against any type of Access field (Text, Memo, Yes/No, etc.). However, some of the aggregate options can be performed only against specific field types. For example, you cannot perform a Sum option against Text type data, and you cannot use a Max option against an OLE object.

Table 25-2 lists each option, what it does, and what field types you can use with the option.

Performing totals on all records

You can use total queries to perform calculations against all records in a table or query. For example, you can find the total number of animals in the Pets table, their average weight, and the maximum weight of the animals. To create this query, follow these steps:

1. Select the Pets table.
2. Click on the Totals button in the toolbar to turn it on.
3. Double-click on the Pet ID field in the Pets table.
4. Double-click on the Weight field in the Pets table.
5. Double-click on the Weight field in the Pets table again.
6. In the Total: cell of Pet ID, select Count.
7. In the Total: cell of Weight, select Avg.
8. In the second Total: cell of Weight, select Max.

Your query should look similar to Figure 25-3.

This query calculates the total number of pet records in the Pets table, as well as the average weight of all animals and the heaviest weight of all the animals.

Warning The Count option of the Total: cell can be performed against any field in the table (or query). However, Count will eliminate any records that have a Null value in the field you select. Therefore, you may want to select the primary key field on which to perform the Count total, because this field cannot have any Null values, thus assuring an accurate record count.

Table 25-2
Aggregate Options of the Total: Row

Option	*Finds*	*Field Type Support*
Count	The number of non-Null values in a field	AutoNumber, Number, Currency, Date/Time, Yes/No, Text, Memo, OLE object
Sum	The total of values in a field	AutoNumber, Number, Currency, Date/Time, Yes/No
Avg	The average of values in a field	AutoNumber, Number, Currency, Date/Time, Yes/No
Max	The highest value in a field	AutoNumber, Number, Currency, Date/Time, Yes/No, Text
Min	The lowest value in a field	AutoNumber, Number, Currency, Date/Time, Yes/No, Text
StDev	The standard deviation of values in a field	AutoNumber, Number, Currency, Date/Time, Yes/No
Var	The population variance of values in a field	AutoNumber, Number, Currency, Date/Time, Yes/No
First	The field value from the *first* record in a table or query	AutoNumber, Number, Currency, Date/Time, Yes/No, Text, Memo, OLE object
Last	The field value from the *last* record in a table or query	AutoNumber, Number, Currency, Date/Time, Yes/No, Text, Memo, OLE object

If you select the Datasheet button on the toolbar, you should now see a query similar to Figure 25-4. Notice that the dynaset has only one record. When performing calculations against *all records* of a table or query, the resulting dynaset will have only *one* record.

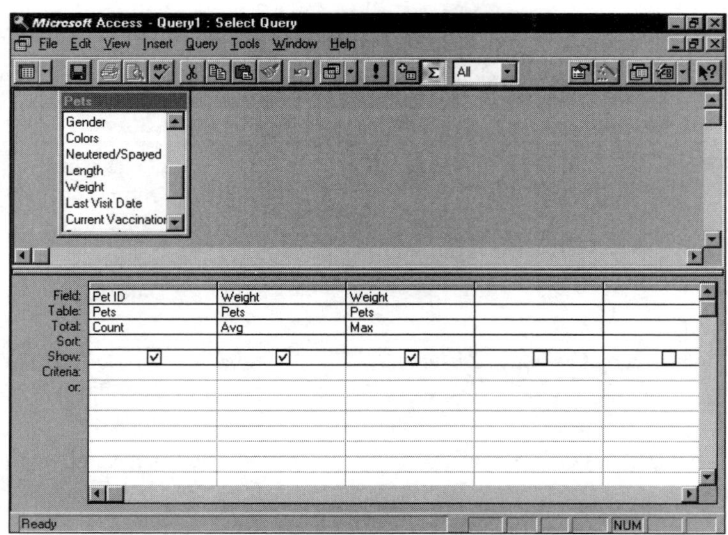

Figure 25-3: A query against all records in the Pets table.

Note Access creates a default column heading for all total fields in a totals datasheet, such as the one you see in Figure 25-4. The heading name is a product of the name of the total option and the field name. Thus, you see in the figure that the heading names are CountOfPet ID, AvgOfWeight, and MaxOfWeight. You can change the column heading name to something more appropriate by renaming the field in the QBE pane of the Design window. As you do with any other field you want to rename, simply place the cursor at the beginning of the field cell you want to rename (to the left of the field name). After you place the cursor at the beginning, type the name you want to display, followed by a colon.

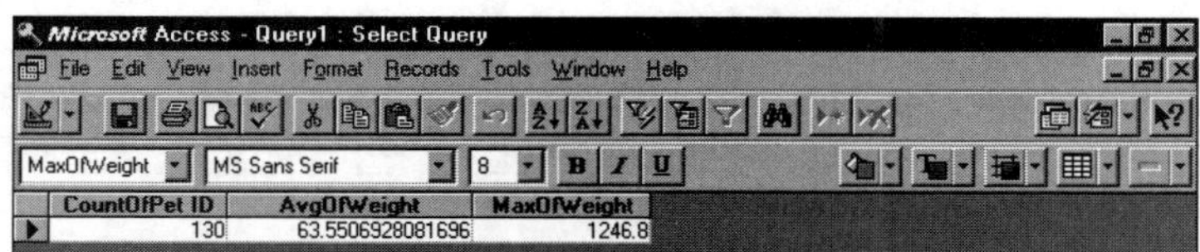

Figure 25-4: This datasheet of a dynaset was created from a total query against all records in a table.

Performing totals on groups of records

Most of the time, you need to perform totals on a group of records rather than on all records. For example, you may need to calculate the total number of animals that you've treated for each type of animal. In other words, you want to create a group for each type of animal — bear, cat, dog, and so on — and then perform the total calculation against each of these groups. In database parlance, this is known as *control break* totaling.

Calculating totals for a single group

When you create your query, you specify which field or fields to use for grouping the totals and which fields to perform the totals against. Using the preceding example, to group the Type of Animal field, you select the Group By option of the Total: cell. Follow these steps to create the query:

1. Open a new query and select the Pets table.
2. Click on the Totals button, the Σ, on the toolbar to turn it on.
3. Double-click on the Type of Animal field in the Pets table.
4. Double-click on the Pet ID field in the Pets table.
5. In the Total: cell of Type of Animal, select Group By.
6. In the Total: cell of Pet ID, select Count.

The query in Figure 25-5 groups all like animals together and then performs the count total for each type of animal. Unlike performing totals against all records, this query produces a dynaset of many records — one record for each type of animal. Figure 25-6 demonstrates how the datasheet looks if you select the Datasheet button on the toolbar.

Field:	Type of Animal	Pet ID			
Table:	Pets	Pets			
Total:	Group By	Count			
Sort:					
Show:	☑	☑	☐	☐	☐
Criteria:					
or:					

Figure 25-5: Totals against a group of records.

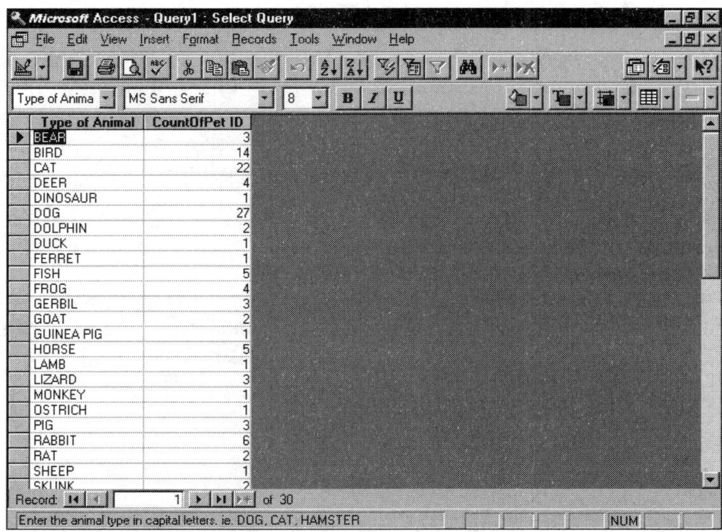

Figure 25-6: Datasheet of totals against the group Type of Animal field.

The dynaset in Figure 25-6 has a single record for each type of animal. Notice that the count was performed against each type of animal; there are 3 bears, 14 birds, and so on. Also notice that the Group By field displays one record for each unique value in that field. The Type of Animal field is specified as the Group By field and displays a single record for each type of animal, showing Bear, Bird, Cat, Dog, and so on. Each of these records is shown as a row heading for the datasheet, indicating a unique record for each type of animal specified that begins with the Group By field content (bear, bird, etc.). In this case, each unique record is easy to identify by the single-field row heading under Type of Animal.

Calculating totals for several groups

You can perform group totals against multiple fields and multiple tables as easily as with a single field in a single table. For example, you may want to group by both customer and type of animal to determine the number of animals each customer owns by animal type. To create a total query for this example, you specify **Group By** in both Total fields (Customer Name and Type of Animal).

This query, shown in Figure 25-7, uses two tables and also groups by two fields to perform the count total. First, the query groups by Customer Name and then by Type of Animal. When you select the Datasheet button on the toolbar, you see a datasheet similar to the one in Figure 25-8.

Field:	Customer Name	Type of Animal	Pet ID		
Table:	Customer	Pets	Pets		
Total:	Group By	Group By	Count		
Sort:					
Show:	☑	☑	☑	☐	☐
Criteria:					
or:					

Figure 25-7: A multiple-table, multiple-field Group By total query.

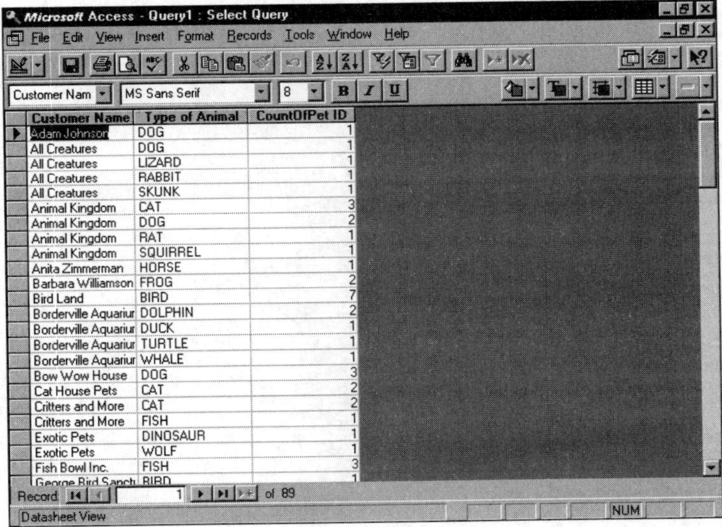

Customer Name	Type of Animal	CountOfPet ID
Adam Johnson	DOG	1
All Creatures	DOG	1
All Creatures	LIZARD	1
All Creatures	RABBIT	1
All Creatures	SKUNK	1
Animal Kingdom	CAT	3
Animal Kingdom	DOG	2
Animal Kingdom	RAT	1
Animal Kingdom	SQUIRREL	1
Anita Zimmerman	HORSE	1
Barbara Williamson	FROG	2
Bird Land	BIRD	7
Borderville Aquariur	DOLPHIN	2
Borderville Aquariur	DUCK	1
Borderville Aquariur	TURTLE	1
Borderville Aquariur	WHALE	1
Bow Wow House	DOG	3
Cat House Pets	CAT	2
Critters and More	CAT	2
Critters and More	FISH	1
Exotic Pets	DINOSAUR	1
Exotic Pets	WOLF	1
Fish Bowl Inc.	FISH	3
George Bird Sancti	BIRD	1

Figure 25-8: Datasheet of a multiple-field Group By query.

The datasheet in Figure 25-8 shows several records for the customer Animal Kingdom. This customer has three cats, two dogs, one rat, and one squirrel. This datasheet has a unique record based on two Group By fields — Customer Name and Type of Animal. Therefore, the unique row headings for this datasheet are created by combining both fields — first the Customer Name and then the Type of Animal.

Note: You can think of the Group By field(s) in a total query as fields that specify the row headings of the datasheet.

Tip Access groups records based on the order of the Group By fields in the QBE pane (from left to right). Therefore, you should pay attention to the order of Group By fields. Although the order doesn't change the aggregate totals of the fields, the order of Group By fields does determine how you see the results in the datasheet. If you place the Type of Animal field before the Customer Name field, the resulting datasheet shows the records in order by animal first and then customer. Figure 25-9 demonstrates this setup, showing the bear records and their owners (with the total number) and then the bird records and their owners, and so on.

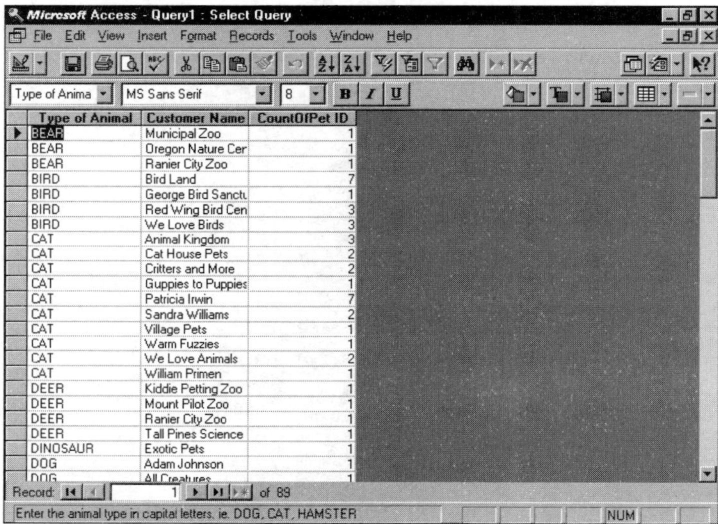

Figure 25-9: Changing the order of Group By fields.

By changing the order of the Group By fields in a totals query, you can look at your data in new and creative ways.

Specifying criteria for a total query

Besides grouping records for total queries, you can also specify criteria to limit the records that will be processed or displayed in a total calculation. When you're specifying record criteria in total queries, you have several options available to you. You can create a criterion against any of these three fields:

- ✦ A Group By field
- ✦ An Aggregate Total field
- ✦ A Non-Aggregate Total field

Using any one or all three of these criteria types, you can easily limit the scope of your total query to a finite criteria.

Specifying criteria for a Group By field

To limit the scope of records that will be used in a grouping, you specify a criteria in the Group By fields. For example, you may want to calculate the average length and weight of only three animals — bears, deer, and wolves. Doing so requires specifying a criteria on the Group By field Type of Animal. Such a query looks like Figure 25-10.

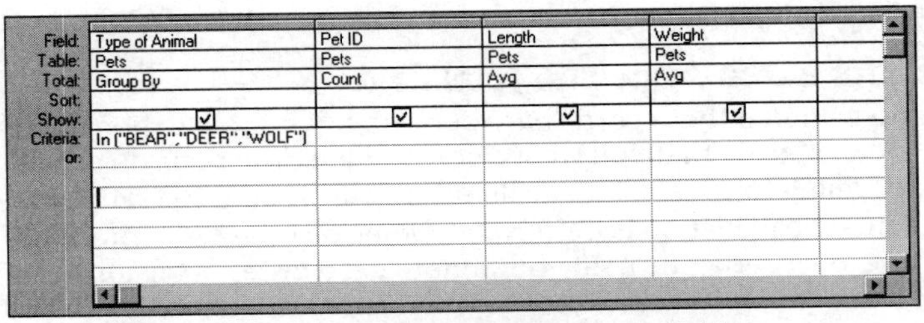

Field:	Type of Animal	Pet ID	Length	Weight
Table:	Pets	Pets	Pets	Pets
Total:	Group By	Count	Avg	Avg
Sort:				
Show:	☑	☑	☑	☑
Criteria:	In ("BEAR","DEER","WOLF")			
or:				

Figure 25-10: Specifying a criteria in a Group By field.

By specifying a criteria in the Group By field, only those records that meet the Group By criteria will have the aggregate calculations performed. In this example, the count, average length, and average weight will be performed only for animals that are bears, deer, and wolves. This results in a three-record dynaset, with one for each animal.

Specifying criteria for an Aggregate Total field

There are times when you want a query to calculate aggregate totals first and then display only those totals from the aggregate calculations that meet a specified criteria. In other words, you want Access to determine all totals for each Group By field and then take the totals field and perform the criteria against the totals before creating the resulting dynaset.

For example, you may want a query to find the average length of all animals, grouped by type of animal, where the average length of any animal is greater than 20 inches. This query should look like Figure 25-11. Notice that the criterion >20 is placed in the Aggregate Total field, Length. This query calculates the average length of all animals grouped by type of animal. Then the query determines whether the calculated totals for each record are greater than 20. Records greater than 20 are added to the resulting dynaset, and records less than or equal to 20 are discarded. Note that the criterion is performed *after* the aggregate calculations are performed.

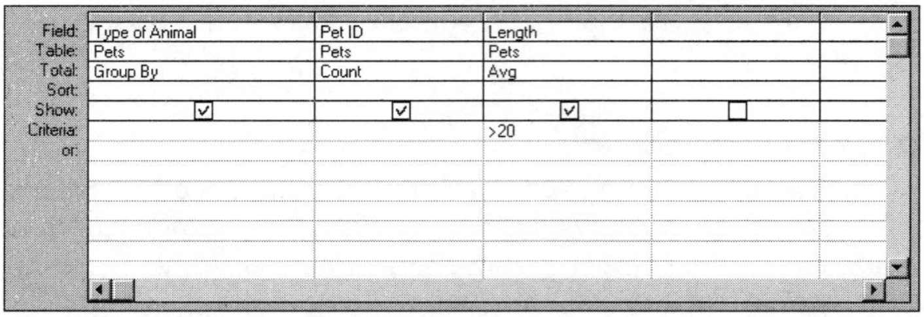

Field:	Type of Animal	Pet ID	Length	
Table:	Pets	Pets	Pets	
Total:	Group By	Count	Avg	
Sort:				
Show:	☑	☑	☑	☐
Criteria:			>20	
or:				

Figure 25-11: A query with a criteria set against an Aggregate Total field.

Specifying criteria for a Non-Aggregate Total field

The preceding example limited the records *after* performing the calculations against total fields. You also can specify that you want Access to limit the records based on a total field *before* performing total calculations. In other words, limit the range of records against which the calculation is performed. Doing so creates a criterion similar to the first type of criteria; the field you want to set a criterion against is not a Group By field.

For example, you may want to display the total amount of money charged for each animal during the first half of 1995 after February 9. You want to use the Visit Date field to specify criteria, but you don't want to perform any calculations against this field or to use it to group by. In fact, you don't even want to show the field in the resulting datasheet.

Figure 25-12 shows how the query should look. Notice that Access automatically turned the Show: cell off in the Visit Date field.

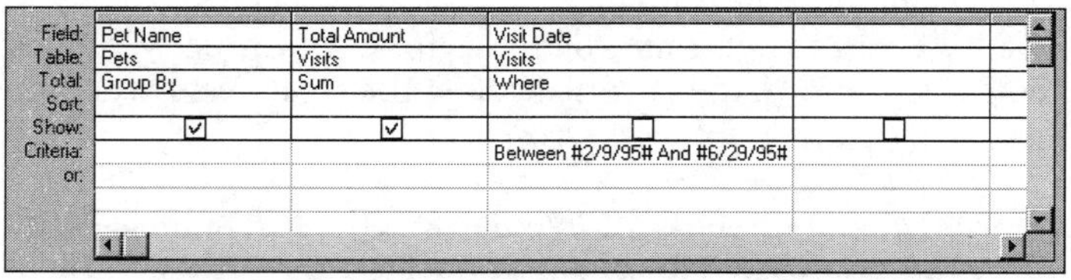

Field:	Pet Name	Total Amount	Visit Date	
Table:	Pets	Visits	Visits	
Total:	Group By	Sum	Where	
Sort:				
Show:	☑	☑	☐	☐
Criteria:			Between #2/9/95# And #6/29/95#	
or:				

Figure 25-12: Specifying a criteria for a Non-Aggregate field.

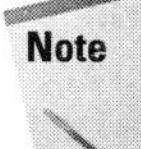

Access automatically turns off the Show: cell whenever it encounters a Where option in the Total: cell of a field. Access understands that you are using the field only to specify criteria so you don't want to see it.

In the query that you just completed, Access displays only those records for pets that have visited the hospital from February 9 to June 29, 1995. All other records are discarded.

Warning When you specify a Where option in a Total: cell, you cannot show the field. The reason is that Access uses the field to evaluate the Where criteria before performing the calculation. Therefore, the contents are useful only for the limiting criteria. If you try to turn on the Show: cell, Access will display an error message.

Creating expressions for totals

Besides choosing one of the Access totals from the drop-down list box, you can create your own total expression. You can base your total expression on several types of totals in an expression, such as when you use Avg and Sum or multiple Sums together. Or you can base your expression on a calculated field comprised of several functions — or a calculated field based on several fields from different tables. Suppose, for example, that you want a query that shows the total amount of money each customer owed before discount. Then you want to see the amount of money these customers saved based on their discount. You want the information to be grouped by customer. Follow these steps to create this query:

1. Start a new query and select the Customer, Pets, and Visits tables.
2. Click on the Totals button, Σ, on the toolbar to turn it on.
3. Double-click on the Customer Name field in the Customer table.
4. Double-click on the Total Amount field in the Visits table.
5. In the Total: cell of Customer Name, select Group By.
6. In the Total: cell of Total Amount, select Sum.
7. Click on an empty Field: cell of the QBE pane.
8. Type **Total Saved:Sum([Visits].[Total Amount]*[Customer]![Discount])** in the cell.

Access generally places the total option Expression in the Total: cell of the calculated field Total Saved: (if it doesn't, place the total option Expression in the Total: cell).

Note Your query should be similar to Figure 25-13. Notice that the query uses two fields from different tables to create the Total Saved: calculated field. You had to specify both the table and the field name for each field that the Sum function used.

If you click on the Datasheet button on the toolbar, your dynaset should be similar to Figure 25-14.

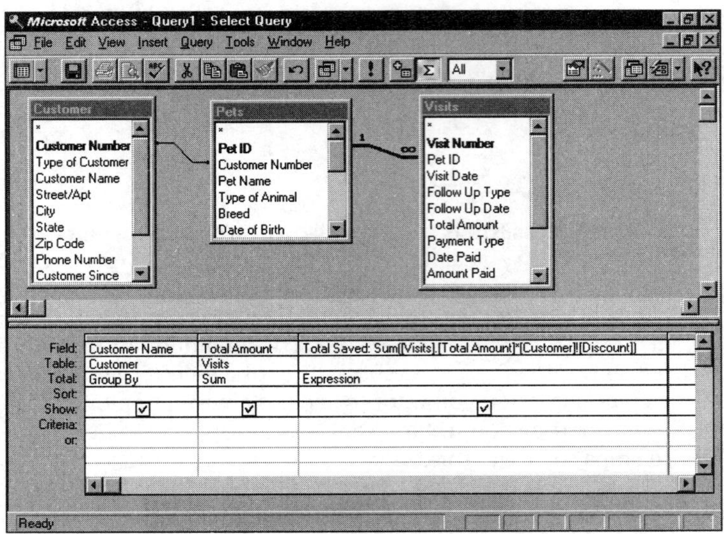

Figure 25-13: A query using an Expression total.

Customer Name	SumOfTotal Amount	Total Saved
Adam Johnson	$167.80	0
All Creatures	$1,860.00	372.000005543232
Animal Kingdom	$1,223.00	244.600003644824
Anita Zimmerman	$50.00	
Barbara Williamson	$100.00	0
George Green	$1,389.50	0
James Brown	$100.00	10.0000001490116
Johnathan Adams	$936.00	46.8000006973743
Karen Rhodes	$281.00	0
Margaret McKinley	$60.00	0
Michael Johnson	$70.00	0
Patricia Irwin	$1,340.80	0
Sandra Williams	$643.00	0
Sandra Young	$234.00	0
Stephen Brown	$316.00	0
Tyrone Potter	$106.00	0
Wanda Greenfield	$30.00	0
William Adams	$77.00	3.85000005736947
William Price	$385.00	0
William Primen	$843.50	0

Record: 1 of 20

Datasheet View

Figure 25-14: A datasheet created by an Expression total.

Tip

Notice in the datasheet in Figure 25-14 that the calculated field Total Saved shows up to 12 decimal places. You can limit the decimal places by using the Format( ) function around the Sum( ) function. To do so, add the following to the existing criteria formula in the calculated Field: cell:.

Total Saved:Format(Sum([Visits].[Total Amount]*[Customer]![Discount]),"Standard")

Creating Crosstab Queries

With Access, you can use a specialized type of total query, the crosstab, to display summarized data in a compact and readable format. A crosstab query summarizes the data in the fields from your tables and presents the resulting dynaset in a row-and-column format.

Understanding the crosstab query

Simply put, a crosstab query is a two-dimensional summary matrix that is created from your tables. This query presents summary data in a spreadsheetlike format that you create from fields you specify. This is a specialized type of total query in which the Total: row in the QBE pane is always active. The Total: row cannot be toggled off in a crosstab query!

In addition, the Total: row of the QBE pane is used for specifying a Group By total option for both the row and the column headings. Like other total queries, the Group By option specifies the row headings for the query datasheet and comes from the actual contents of the field. However, unlike other total queries, the crosstab query also obtains its column headings from the value in a field (table or calculated) instead of from the field names themselves.

Warning

The fields used as rows and columns must always have Group By in the Total: row. Otherwise, Access reports an error when you attempt to display or run the query.

For example, you may want to create a query that will display the Type of Animal field as the row heading and the owner's state as the column heading, with each cell containing a total for each type of animal in each state. Table 25-3 demonstrates how you want the query to look.

In Table 25-3, the row headings are specified by Type of Animal: Bear, Bird, and so on. The column headings are specified by the state: ID, OR, and WA. The cell content in the intersection of any row and column is a summary of records that meets both conditions. For example, the Bear row that intersects the OR column shows that the clinic treats two bears in the state of Oregon. The Dog row that intersects with the WA column shows that the clinic treats 13 dogs in the state of Washington.

Table 25-3
A Typical Crosstab Query Format

Type of Animal	*ID*	*OR*	*WA*
Bear	0	2	1
Bird	11	0	3
Cat	4	12	6
Dog	6	7	13
Pig	0	0	3

This table shows a very simple crosstab query that is created from the fields Type of Animal and State, with the intersecting cell contents determined by a Count total on any field in the Pets table.

Creating the crosstab query

Now that you have a conceptual understanding of a crosstab query, it is time to create one. To create a crosstab query like the one described in Table 25-3, follow these steps:

1. Start a new query and select the Customer and Pets tables.
2. Double-click in the Type of Animal field in the Pets table.
3. Double-click in the State field in the Customer table.
4. Double-click in the Pet ID field in the Pets table.
5. Select Query➪Crosstab in the Query menu or press the Query Type button on the toolbar (this will bring down a drop box listing the types of queries).
6. In the Crosstab: cell of Type of Animal, select Row Heading.
7. In the Crosstab: cell of State, select Column Heading.
8. In the Crosstab: cell of Pet ID, select Value.
9. In the Total: cell of Pet ID, select Count.

Your query should look similar to Figure 25-15. Notice that Access inserted a new row named Crosstab: between the Total: and Sort: rows in the QBE pane.

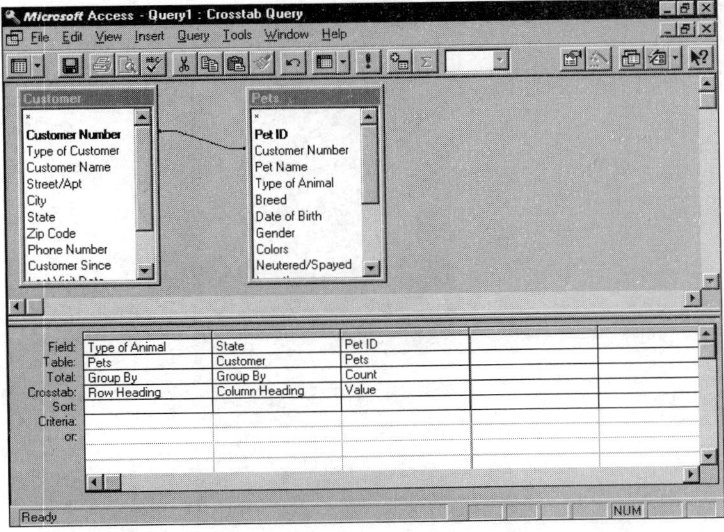

Figure 25-15: Creating a crosstab query.

As Figure 25-15 demonstrates, you *must* specify a minimum of three items for crosstab queries:

- ✦ The Row Heading field
- ✦ The Column Heading field
- ✦ The summary Value field

These three items are specified in the appropriate Crosstab: cells of the fields. After you specify the contents for the three Crosstab: cells, you specify Group By in the Total: cell of both the Row Heading and the Column Heading fields and an aggregate Total: cell operator (such as Count) for the Value field.

If you have done this procedure correctly, selecting the Datasheet button on the toolbar reveals a datasheet similar to the one in Figure 25-16.

Notice that the dynaset is comprised of distinct (nonrepeating) rows of animals, three columns (one for each state), and summary cell contents for each animal against each state; that is, the clinic treats no bears in the state of Idaho but it does treat two in Oregon and one in Washington.

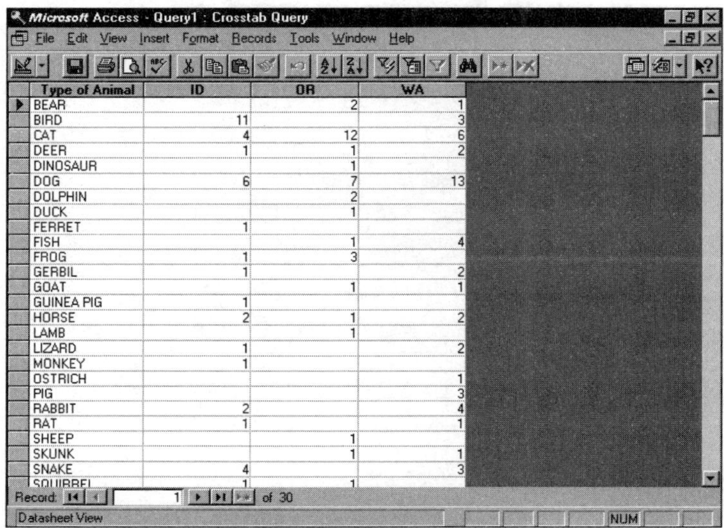

Type of Animal	ID	OR	WA
BEAR		2	1
BIRD	11		3
CAT	4	12	6
DEER	1	1	2
DINOSAUR		1	
DOG	6	7	13
DOLPHIN		2	
DUCK		1	
FERRET	1		
FISH		1	4
FROG	1	3	
GERBIL	1		2
GOAT		1	1
GUINEA PIG	1		
HORSE	2	1	2
LAMB		1	
LIZARD	1		2
MONKEY	1		
OSTRICH			1
PIG			3
RABBIT	2		4
RAT	1		1
SHEEP		1	
SKUNK		1	1
SNAKE	4		3
SQUIRREL	1	1	

Figure 25-16: Datasheet of a crosstab query.

Entering multiple-field row headings

When you're working with crosstab queries, you can specify only one summary Value field and one Column Heading field. You can, however, add more than one Row Heading field. By adding multiple Row Heading fields, you can further refine the type of data you want presented in the crosstab query.

For example, suppose that you're interested in seeing the types of animals from the last crosstab query further refined to the level of city. In other words, you want to see how many of each type of animal you have from each city within each state. Such a query is shown in Figure 25-17. Notice that there are two Crosstab: cells that show Row Heading for the fields State and City. Access groups the Crosstab: rows first by the State and then by the City. Access specifies the group order from left to right.

Field:	State	City	Type of Animal	Pet ID	
Table:	Customer	Customer	Pets	Pets	
Total:	Group By	Group By	Group By	Count	
Crosstab:	Row Heading	Row Heading	Column Heading	Value	
Sort:					
Criteria:					
or:					

Figure 25-17: Crosstab query using two fields for the row heading.

If you select the Datasheet button on the toolbar, Access presents a datasheet similar to the one in Figure 25-18. Notice that the row heading depends on both the State and City fields. The dynaset is displayed in order, first by state (ID, OR, WA) and then by city within the state (Borderville, Mount Pilot, Russettown, and so forth).

Microsoft Access - Query1 : Crosstab Query

File Edit View Insert Format Records Tools Window Help

State	City	BEAR	BIRD	CAT	DEER	DINOSAUR
ID	Borderville			3		
ID	Mount Pilot		1		1	
ID	Russettown		7	1		
ID	Three Corners		3			
OR	Borderville			2		
OR	Lakeville	1		10	1	
OR	Small Tree	1				
WA	Borderville			2		
WA	Mountain View			3	1	
WA	Ranier City	1		1	1	
WA	Tall Pines		3			

Figure 25-18: Datasheet with multiple-field row headings of a crosstab query.

Tip

A crosstab query can have several row headings but only one column heading. If you want to display a several-field column heading and a single-field row heading, simply reverse your heading types. Change the multiple-field column headings to multiple-field row headings and change the single-row heading to a single-column heading.

Specifying criteria for a crosstab query

When you work with crosstab queries, you may want to specify record criteria for the crosstab. Criteria can be specified in a crosstab query against any of these fields:

- ✦ A new field
- ✦ A Row Heading field
- ✦ A Column Heading field

Specifying criteria in a new field

You can add criteria based on a new field that will not be displayed in the crosstab query itself. For example, you may want to create the crosstab query that you see in Figure 25-17, where the two fields, State and City, are used as the row heading. However, you only want to see records where the type of customer is an individual (or the contents equal the number 1). To specify criteria, simply follow these additional steps:

1. Start with the crosstab query in Figure 25-17.
2. Double-click in the Type of Customer field in the Customer table.
3. Select the Criteria: cell of Type of Customer.
4. Type **1** in the cell.

Note The Crosstab: cell of the Type of Customer field should be blank. If it is not, select `(not shown)` to blank the cell.

Your query should now resemble the one in Figure 25-19. Notice that you added a criterion in a field that will not be displayed in the crosstab query.

Field:	State	City	Type of Animal	Pet ID	Type of Customer
Table:	Customer	Customer	Pets	Pets	Customer
Total:	Group By	Group By	Group By	Count	Group By
Crosstab:	Row Heading	Row Heading	Column Heading	Value	
Sort:					
Criteria:					1
or:					

Figure 25-19: Specifying criterion in a crosstab query on a new field.

Now that the new criterion is specified, you can click on the Datasheet button of the toolbar to see a datasheet similar to the one portrayed in Figure 25-20.

Microsoft Access - Query1 : Crosstab Query

File Edit View Insert Format Records Tools Window Help

State	City	CAT	DOG	FROG	GERBIL	HORSE
ID	Mount Pilot		1			
ID	Russettown			1		
ID	Three Corners		1			
OR	Borderville		3			
OR	Lakeville	7	1	2		
WA	Mountain View	3	2			
WA	Ranier City		1			
WA	Tall Pines		3		2	

Figure 25-20: The datasheet after specifying criterion on a new field.

Notice that the datasheet in Figure 25-20 shows only columns where at least one of the intersecting row cells has a value. For example, only two gerbils appear in the Gerbil column. Several types of animal columns are gone. Bears, birds, deer, and others are missing because none of these types is owned by an individual.

Specifying criteria in a Row Heading field

Not only can you specify criteria for a new field, you can specify criteria for a field that is being used for a Row Heading. When you specify a criteria for a Row Heading, Access excludes any rows that do not meet the criteria specified.

For example, you may want to view a crosstab query for all animals where the state is Idaho (ID). To create this query, start with the crosstab query shown in Figure 25-17. If you created the last query, simply remove the Type of Customer column from the QBE pane. To create this query, make the QBE pane look like Figure 25-21. When you view this query, you see only records from Idaho.

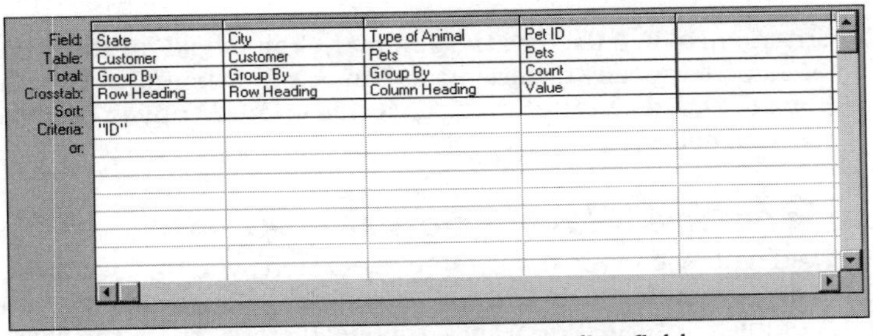

Field:	State	City	Type of Animal	Pet ID	
Table:	Customer	Customer	Pets	Pets	
Total:	Group By	Group By	Group By	Count	
Crosstab:	Row Heading	Row Heading	Column Heading	Value	
Sort:					
Criteria:	"ID"				
or:					

Figure 25-21: Criteria set against a Row Heading field.

You can specify criteria against any field that is used as a Row Heading field. You can even specify criteria for multiple Row Heading fields to create a finely focused crosstab query.

Specifying criteria in a Column Heading field

You also can specify criteria for the field being used as the column heading. When you specify the criteria for a column heading, Access excludes any columns that don't meet the specified criteria. In the next example, you want a crosstab query for any animal that is either a cat or a dog. To create this query, again start with the crosstab query shown in Figure 25-17. If you created the last query, simply remove the criteria for the State field from the QBE pane. The QBE pane should look similar to the one in Figure 25-22.

Notice that the specified criterion is placed in the Criteria: cell of the Column Heading field Type of Animal. If you now select the Datasheet button on the toolbar, you should see a datasheet that has only two column headings, Cat and Dog. The other headings have been eliminated.

Field:	State	City	Type of Animal	Pet ID	
Table:	Customer	Customer	Pets	Pets	
Total:	Group By	Group By	Group By	Count	
Crosstab:	Row Heading	Row Heading	Column Heading	Value	
Sort:					
Criteria:			"CAT" Or "DOG"		
or:					

Figure 25-22: A criterion specified against the Column Heading field.

Tip You cannot specify criteria in a field used as the summary Value field for the crosstab query. However, if you need to specify criteria based on this field, simply drag the field again to the QBE pane and set a criterion against this second copy of the field, while keeping the Crosstab: cell empty.

Specifying criteria in multiple fields of a crosstab query

Now that you've worked with each type of criterion separately, you may want to specify criteria based on several fields. In the next example, you see how to create a crosstab query with complex criteria. You want a row heading based on the Type of Animal field and a column heading based on the Month value of the Visit Date field. The Value cells are based on the Sum of Total Amount.

Finally, you want to limit the months to part of 1995. To create this complex crosstab query, make the QBE pane look like Figure 25-23. This is clearly the most complex crosstab query you have created. Notice that you specified a column heading based on a calculated field.

Field:	Type of Animal	Total Amount	Expr1: Format([Visit Date],"mmm")	Expr2: Year([Visit Date])
Table:	Pets	Visits		
Total:	Group By	Sum	Group By	Expression
Crosstab:	Row Heading	Value	Column Heading	
Sort:				
Criteria:			"Feb" Or "Mar" Or "Apr" Or "May"	1995
or:				

Figure 25-23: A complex crosstab query.

This query should display a datasheet in which the columns are Feb, Mar, Apr, or May for the year 1995. When you select the Datasheet button on the toolbar, you should see a datasheet similar to the one in Figure 25-24. Notice that the datasheet has only four columns; the order of the columns is alphabetical, not the chronological, by-month order that you entered in the Criteria: cell of the field. The next section of this chapter shows you how to fix the column order.

Type of Animal	Apr	Feb	Mar	May
CAT		$629.80	$310.00	$335.00
DOG		$257.00	$257.80	$70.00
FROG	$130.00	$692.00	$50.00	$70.00
GERBIL			$109.00	
HORSE		$70.00	$69.00	$50.00
PIG	$25.00		$50.00	$662.00
RABBIT	$50.00		$512.00	
RAT			$174.00	$109.00
SKUNK				$95.00
SNAKE			$206.00	

Figure 25-24: The datasheet of very complex crosstab criteria.

Note As the preceding crosstab query shows, you can set criteria in the QBE pane for a number of fields, including calculated fields. Because you have the ability to set complex, or focused, criteria, you can create very specific crosstab queries.

Specifying fixed column headings

There are times when you want more control over the appearance of the column headings. By default, Access sorts column headings in alphabetical or numeric order. This can be a problem, as you saw in the preceding example and illustrated in Figure 25-24. Your columns will be more readable if the columns are in chronological order instead of alphabetical. You can use the option `Column Headings` in the Query Properties box to solve this problem. This option lets you make these choices:

- ✦ Specify an exact order for the appearance of the column headings
- ✦ Specify fixed column headings for reports and forms that use crosstab queries

To specify fixed column headings, follow these steps:

1. Begin with the crosstab query shown in Figure 25-23. Move the pointer to the top half of the query screen and click on it once.
2. Click on the Properties button (a hand holding a piece of paper) on the toolbar or select View⇨Properties... from the Query Design menu.

3. Select the Column Headings text box entry area.
4. Type **Feb, Mar, Apr, May** in the box.

The Query Properties dialog box should look like the one in Figure 25-25. When you move to another entry area, Access converts your text into "Feb", "Mar", "Apr", "May" in the Query Properties dialog box.

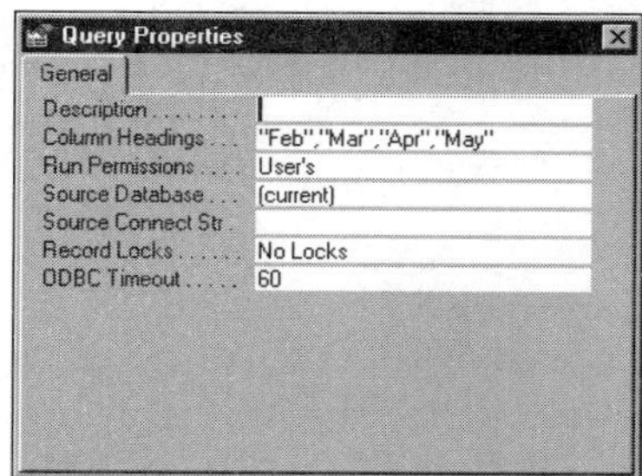

Figure 25-25: The Query Properties dialog box.

If you look at the datasheet, you see that it now looks like Figure 25-26. The order for the column headings is now chronological.

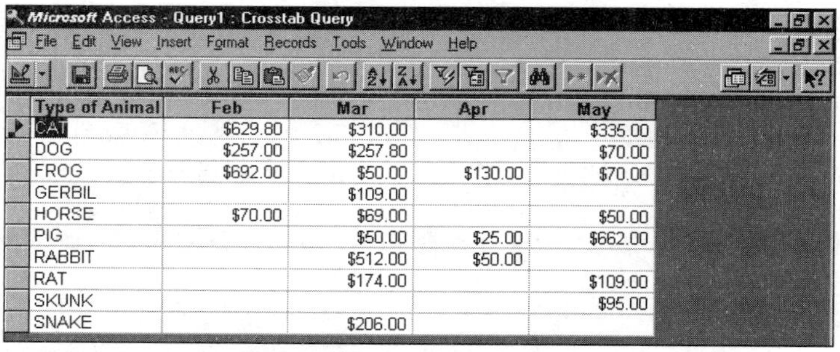

Microsoft Access - Query1 : Crosstab Query

Type of Animal	Feb	Mar	Apr	May
CAT	$629.80	$310.00		$335.00
DOG	$257.00	$257.80		$70.00
FROG	$692.00	$50.00	$130.00	$70.00
GERBIL		$109.00		
HORSE	$70.00	$69.00		$50.00
PIG		$50.00	$25.00	$662.00
RABBIT		$512.00	$50.00	
RAT		$174.00		$109.00
SKUNK				$95.00
SNAKE		$206.00		

Figure 25-26: The datasheet with the specified column order.

Note The column names that you enter *must* match the query headings exactly. If you enter February instead of Feb, Access will accept the heading without reporting an error. But when you display the query, no records for that column will appear.

You can enter column names without separating them by semicolons. To do so, enter each name on a new line (press Ctrl+Enter to move to a new line).

Crosstab Query Wizard

Access for Windows 95 employs several Query Wizards, helpful additions to the query design surface. One such Wizard, the Crosstab Query Wizard (Figure 25-27), is an excellent tool to help you create a crosstab query quickly.

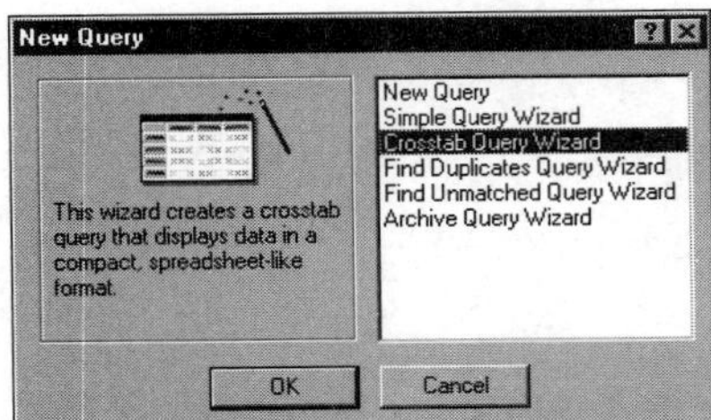

Figure 25-27: The Access Query Wizard.

There are some limitations, however:

✦ If you need to use more than one table for the crosstab query, you need to create a separate query that has the tables you need for the crosstab query. For example, you may have a Group By Row Heading from the Pets table (Type of Animal) and a Group By Column Heading from the Customer table (State). The Crosstab Query Wizard allows you to select only one table or query for the Row and Column heading.

The workaround: Create a query of the Customer and Pets tables, selecting the all fields reference for each, and then save this intermediate query. Then use this intermediate query as the record source for the Wizard.

✦ You cannot specify the limiting criteria for the Wizard's query.

The workaround: Make the Wizard do the query and then go in and set the limiting criteria.

✦ You cannot specify column headings or column orders.

The workaround: Again, have the Wizard create the query and then modify it.

To use the crosstab query, simply click on the New button and then select the Crosstab Wizard (third down from the top) in the dialog box. Click on OK and then follow the prompts that Access asks for:

✦ The table or query name for the source

✦ The fields for the row headings

✦ The fields for the column headings

✦ The field for the body

✦ The title

After you specify these things, Access creates your crosstab query and then runs it for you.

Creating a Parameter Query

You can automate the process of changing criteria for queries that you run on a regular basis by creating *parameter queries.*

Understanding the parameter query

As the name *parameter* suggests, a parameter query is one that you create that prompts the user for a quantity or a constant value every time the query is executed. Specifically, a parameter query prompts the user for criteria every time it is run, thereby eliminating the need to open the query in design mode to change the criteria manually.

Parameter queries are also very useful with forms or reports because you can have Access prompt the user for the criteria when the form or report is opened.

Creating a single-parameter query

You may have queries that require minor modifications to the criteria of a field every time they are run. Suppose you have a query that displays all pets for a specific customer. If you run the query often, you can design a parameter query to prompt the user for a customer number whenever the query runs. To create the query, follow these steps:

1. Starting with a select query, select the Customer and Pets tables.
2. Double-click in the Customer Number field in the Customer table.
3. Double-click on the Customer Name in the Customer table.
4. Double-click in the Pet Name field in the Pets table.
5. Click on the Criteria: cell for Customer Number.
6. Type **[Enter a Customer Number]** in the cell.
7. Deselect the Show: cell of Customer Number if you don't want this field to show in the datasheet. It has been left in the upcoming example figure.

That's all there is to creating a single-parameter query. Your query should resemble Figure 25-28.

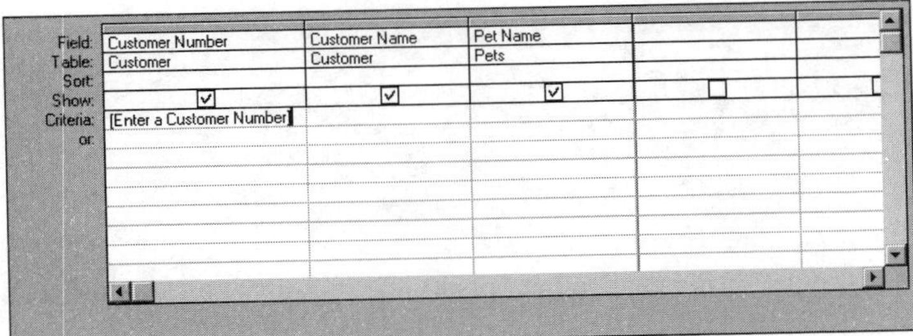

Figure 25-28: A single-parameter query.

In the preceding example, you created a parameter query that prompts the user for a customer number by displaying the message Enter a Customer Number every time the query is run. Access will convert the user's entry to an equals criteria for the field Customer Number. If a valid number is entered, Access will find the correct records.

Warning When you specify a prompt message for the parameter, you should make the message meaningful, yet brief. When the parameter query is run, Access will display up to approximately 50 characters of any prompt message. If the message is longer than 50 characters, it will be truncated to approximately the first 50 characters.

Running a parameter query

To run a parameter query, select either the Run button or the Datasheet button on the toolbar. A parameter dialog box appears on-screen, such as the one in Figure 25-29, prompting the user for a value.

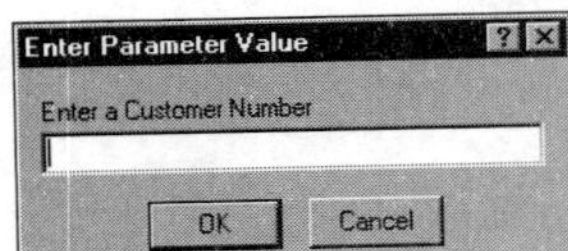

Figure 25-29: The Enter Parameter Value dialog box.

After the user enters a value or presses Enter, Access runs the query, based on the criteria entered. If the criteria is valid, the datasheet will show records matching the criteria; otherwise, the datasheet displays no records.

If the user types **GR001** in the parameter dialog box, Access will display a datasheet similar to the one in Figure 25-30.

Notice that the records displayed in Figure 25-30 are only those for George Green, whose customer number is GR001.

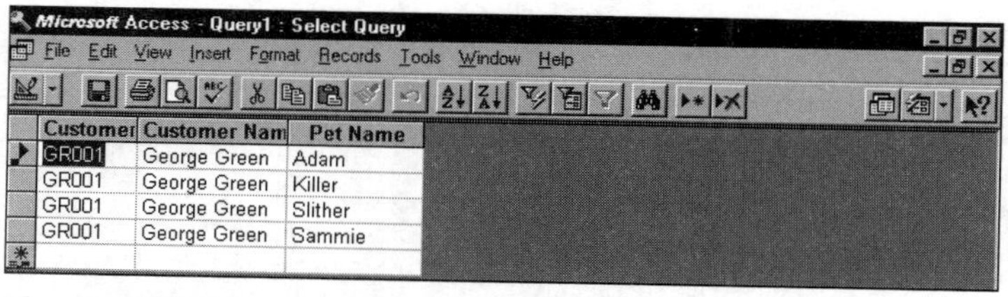

Customer	Customer Nam	Pet Name
GR001	George Green	Adam
GR001	George Green	Killer
GR001	George Green	Slither
GR001	George Green	Sammie

Figure 25-30: Datasheet of records specified by a parameter query.

Creating a multiple-parameter query

You are not limited to creating a query with a single parameter. You can create a query that asks for multiple criteria. For example, you may want a query that displays all pet and visit information based on a type of animal and a range of visit dates. You can design this multiple-parameter query as simply as you did the single-parameter query. To create this query, follow these steps:

1. Select the Pets and Visits tables.
2. Double-click in the Pet Name field in the Pets table.
3. Double-click in the Type of Animal field in the Pets table.
4. Double-click in the Visit Date field in the Visits table.
5. Click on the Criteria: cell for Type of Animal.
6. Type **[Enter an Animal Type]** in the cell.
7. Click on the Criteria: cell for Visit Date.
8. Type **Between [Start Date] And [End Date]** in the cell.

Steps 6 and 8 contain the prompt messages that you specify for the prompt criteria. This query will display three parameter query prompts. Your query should resemble the one in Figure 25-31.

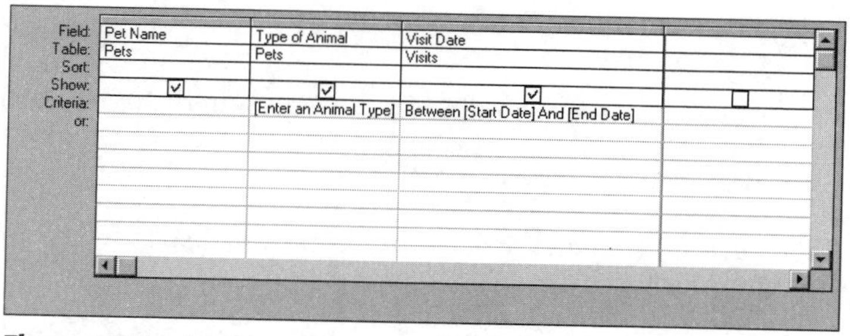

Field:	Pet Name	Type of Animal	Visit Date	
Table:	Pets	Pets	Visits	
Sort:				
Show:	☑	☑	☑	☐
Criteria:		[Enter an Animal Type]	Between [Start Date] And [End Date]	
or:				

Figure 25-31: A parameter query with three criteria specified.

When you run this query, Access prompts the user for the three criteria in this order:

- ✦ Enter an Animal Type
- ✦ Start Date
- ✦ End Date

Like the single-parameter example, the user must enter valid criteria. If the user enters valid criteria in all three dialog boxes, Access displays all records meeting the specified criteria. Otherwise, it will display no records.

Tip You can create parameter queries using any valid operator, including the Like operator with wild cards. An example is the query with the parameter Like [Enter a State Abbr or Enter for all States] & *. This parameter lets the user run the query for a single state or for all states.

Viewing the parameter dialog box

Access defaults the prompt order to left to right, based on the position of the fields and their parameters. However, you can override the prompt order by selecting the Query⇨Parameters...Query menu choice and specifying an order.

To specify a specific prompt order, enter the criteria on the QBE pane just as you have until now. For example, to specify a prompt order of Start Date, End Date, and Animal Type, follow these steps:

1. Start with the query in Figure 25-31.
2. Select Query⇨Parameters...from the Query menu.
3. Type **[Start Date]** in the first cell under the Parameter column.
4. Press Tab to move to the Data Type column.
5. Type **Date/Time** or select the Date/Time type from the drop-down list box.
6. Press Tab to move to the Parameter column.
7. Type **[End Date]** in the first cell under the Parameter column.
8. Press Tab to move to the Data Type column.
9. Type **Date/Time** or select the Date/Time type from the drop-down list box.
10. Press Tab to move to the Parameter column.
11. Type **[Enter an Animal Type]** in the first cell under the Parameter column.
12. Press Tab to move to the Data Type column.
13. Enter **Text** or select the Text type from the drop-down list box.
14. Press Enter or select the OK button to leave the dialog box.

Your Query Parameters dialog box should look like the one in Figure 25-32.

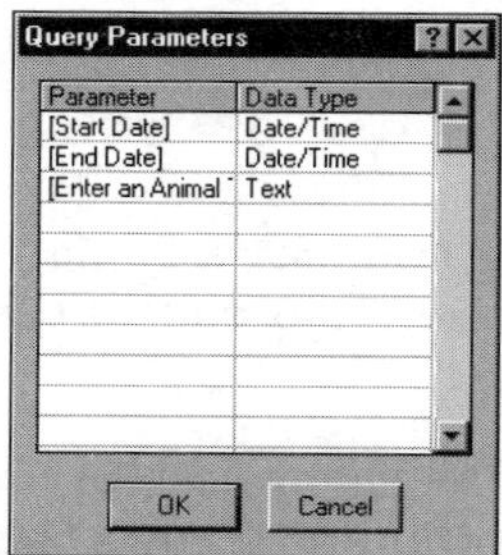

Figure 25-32: The Query Parameters dialog box.

Notice that the message prompt in the Parameter column must exactly match the message prompt in each of the Criteria: cells of the QBE pane. If the prompt message does not match, the query will not work correctly.

Warning When you specify a parameter order, you must specify the correct data type for each parameter in the Query Parameters dialog box, or Access will report a data type mismatch error.

Summary

In this chapter, you learned how to work with complex select queries. You learned how to use totals, crosstab, and parameter queries. The following points were discussed:

- ✦ The three specialized select query types are totals, crosstab, and parameter.
- ✦ The Total: row of the QBE pane can be broken into four distinct total categories: Group By, Expression, Total Field Record Limit, and Aggregate.
- ✦ Access has nine Aggregate Total options. These operators perform mathematical or selection operations.
- ✦ Total queries can perform calculations against all records of a table or against groups of records in a table.
- ✦ Total queries can be used to specify criteria that limit the records that can be processed. These criteria can be against a Group By field, an Aggregate Total field after totaling is performed, or a Non-Aggregate Total field before totaling is performed.
- ✦ You can create a total query based on an expression that uses one or more of the Aggregate Total options and/or a series of Access functions.
- ✦ A crosstab query is a two-dimensional summary matrix that has field contents specified for both the row and column headings. Each intersecting cell between the row and column heading has a Value content (usually an Aggregate Total option).
- ✦ Crosstab queries can have multiple fields for specifying row headings but can have only one field for specifying column headings and one for specifying the total operation against the Value cell.
- ✦ You can specify the order of the column headings in a crosstab query in the Query Properties box by specifying the order in the Column Headings box.
- ✦ The new Crosstab Query Wizard simplifies creating a crosstab query.
- ✦ A parameter query is used for obtaining user-specified criteria when the query is run. This eliminates the need to redesign the query every time the user runs it.
- ✦ A parameter query can prompt the user for more than one parameter. If the user wants the order of prompting to be different from the default, it must be specified in the Query Parameter dialog box.

In the next chapter, you work with action queries. You make tables, perform global updates, and delete records using queries.

✦ ✦ ✦

Creating Action Queries

In This Chapter

What action queries are

How action queries work

Creating an action query

Creating an update action query

Creating new tables with a make-table query

Creating an append query

Creating a delete query

Running action queries

Troubleshooting action queries

As you've seen, queries are tools that let you question or request information from your database. In this chapter, you learn about a special type, called the *action query,* that lets you *change* the field values in your records. For example, you can change a medications field to increase all prices by 10 percent or delete all information from the records of a deceased animal.

What Is an Action Query?

The name *action query,* as you can guess, defines a query that does something more than simply select a specific group of records and present them to you in a dynaset. The word *action* suggests performing some operation — doing, influencing, or affecting something. The word is synonymous with operation, performance, and work. This is exactly what an action query does: some specific operation or work.

An action query can be considered a select query that is given a *duty* to perform against a specified group of records in the dynaset.

When you create any query, Access creates it as a select query automatically. You can specify a different type (such as action) from the Query Design menu. From this menu, you can choose from several types of action queries. (The menu's selections are Make Table, Update, Append, and Delete.)

Like select queries, action queries create a dynaset you can view in a datasheet. To see the dynaset, you simply click on the Datasheet button on the toolbar. Unlike select queries, action queries perform an action — specified in the QBE pane of the query design — when you click on the Run button (the button with the exclamation point) on the toolbar.

You can quickly identify action queries in the Database window by the special exclamation-point icons that sit beside their names. There are four different types of action queries (see Figure 26-1); each has a different icon.

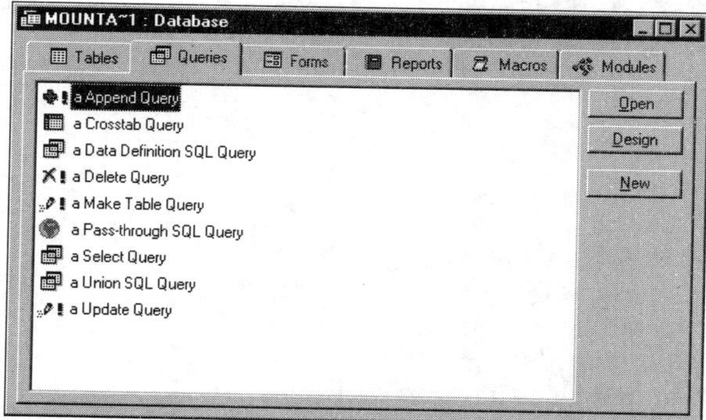

Figure 26-1: The query container of the Database window, showing select and action queries.

Uses of Action Queries

You can use action queries to accomplish the following tasks:

- ✦ Delete specified records from a table or group of tables
- ✦ Append records from one table to another
- ✦ Update information in a group of records
- ✦ Create a new table from specified records in a query

The following examples describe some practical uses for action queries:

- ✦ You want to create history tables and then copy all inactive records to them. (You consider a record inactive if the customer hasn't brought a pet to the office in over three years.) You decide to remove the inactive records from your active database tables.

  What to do? Use a make-table query to create the history tables and a delete query to remove the unwanted records.

- ✦ One of your old clients, whom you haven't seen in over four years, comes in with a new puppy; you need to bring the old information back into the active file from the backup files.

  What to do? Use an append query to add records from your backup tables to your active tables.

Warning Action queries change, add, or delete data. As a result, it's a good idea to observe the following rules:

- ✦ Always back up your table *before* performing the query.
- ✦ Always create and view the action query (use the Datasheet button on the toolbar) *before performing it.*

The Process of Action Queries

Because action queries are irreversible, you should consider following this four-step process when working with them:

1. Create the action query specifying the fields and the criteria.
2. View the records selected in the action query by clicking on the Datasheet button of the toolbar.
3. Run the action query by clicking on the Run button of the toolbar.
4. Check the changes in the tables by clicking on the Datasheet button of the toolbar.

If you follow the preceding steps, you should be able to use action queries in relative safety.

Viewing the Results of an Action Query

Action queries perform a specific task — many times a destructive task. Be very careful when using them. It's important to view the changes that they will make before you run the action query, and to verify afterward that they made the changes you anticipated. Before you learn how to create and run an action query, it's important to review the process for seeing what your changes will look like *before* you change a table permanently.

Viewing the query before using update and delete queries

You can click on the Datasheet View button to see with which set of data the action query will work. Meanwhile, when you're updating or deleting records with an action query, the actions take place on the underlying tables of the query currently in use. Therefore, to view the results of an update or a delete query, you can click on the Datasheet button to see whether the records were updated or deleted.

If your update query made changes to the fields you used for selecting the records, you may have to look at the underlying table or change the selection query to see the changes. For example, if you deleted a set of records with an action button, the resulting select dynaset of the same record criteria will show that no records exist. By removing the delete criteria, you can view the table and verify that all the records specified have been deleted.

Switching to the result table of a make-table or append query

Unlike the update or delete queries, make-table and append queries copy resultant records to another table. After specifying the fields and the criteria in the QBE pane of the Query Design window, the make-table and the append queries copy the specified fields and records to *another* table. When you run the queries, the results take place in another table, not the current table.

Pressing the Datasheet button shows you a dynaset of only the criteria and fields that were specified, not the actual table that contains the new or added records. To view the results of a make-table or append query, you need to open the new table and view the contents to verify that the make-table or append query worked correctly. If you won't be using the action query again, do *not* save it. Delete it.

Reversing action queries

Action queries copy or change data in underlying tables. After an action query is executed, it cannot be reversed. Therefore, when you're working with action queries, you should consider creating a select query first to make sure the record criteria and selection are correct for the action query.

Warning Action queries are destructive; before you perform one, you should always make a backup of the underlying tables.

Creating an Action Query

Creating an action query is very similar to creating a select query. You specify the fields for the query and any *scoping criteria.*

Besides specifying the fields and criteria, you specify an action-specific property — Append to, Make new table, Update to, or Delete where.

Scoping criteria

Action queries can use any expression comprised of fields, functions, and operators to specify any limiting condition you need to place on the query. Scoping criteria are one form of record criteria. Normally the record criteria serve as a filter to tell Access which records to find and/or leave out of the dynaset. Because action queries do not create a dynaset, you use *scoping criteria* to specify a set of records for Access to operate on.

Creating an Update Action Query to Change Values

In this section, you see how to handle an event that requires you to change many records.

Suppose that the city of Mountain View has passed an ordinance that requires horses within its borders to receive a new type of vaccination, starting this year. To create this query, you work with the Customer and Pets tables. First, change the existing status of the Current Vaccinations field in the Pets table from Yes to No wherever the field shows a current vaccination status. Then enter **horse** in the Criteria: row for Type of Animal and **Mountain View** in the Criteria: row for the City field.

It's possible to update each record in the table individually by using a form or a datasheet. Using a select query dynaset to make these changes, however, takes a very long time. The method is not only time-consuming, it's inefficient — especially if you have many records to change. In addition, this method also lends itself to typing errors as you enter new text into fields.

The best way to handle this type of event is to use an *update* action query to make many changes in just one operation. You save time and eliminate many of those typos that crop up in manually edited records.

To create an update query that performs these tasks, follow a two-phase process:

1. Create a select query. View the data you want to update by pressing the Datasheet button.
2. Convert the select query to an update query. Then run the update query after you're satisfied that it will affect only the records you want to affect.

Creating a select query before an update action

The first step in making an update query is to create a select query. In this particular case, the query is for all customers who live in Mountain View and own horses. Perform the following steps to create this query:

1. Create a new query using the Customer and Pets tables.
2. Select the City field from the Customer table and Type of Animal and Current Vaccination from the Pets table.
3. Specify a criterion of **"Mountain View"** in the City field and **"Horse"** in the Type of Animal field.

   The Select Query Design window should now resemble the one in Figure 26-2. Notice that the QBE pane shows all three fields, but shows criteria only in the fields `City` and `Type of Animal`.
4. Examine the datasheet to make sure it has only the records you want to change. Return to the design surface when you're finished.

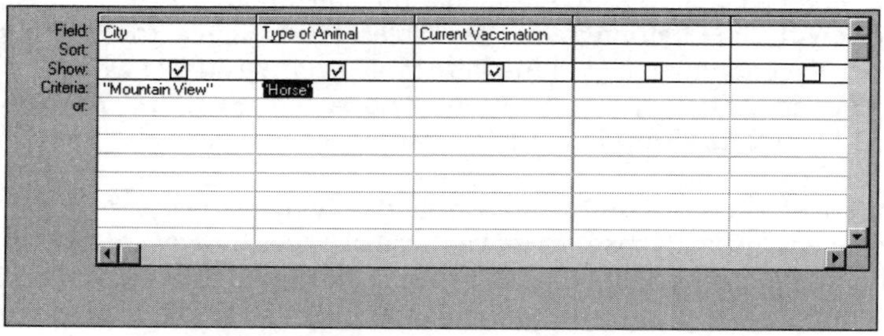

Figure 26-2: Entering a select query.

The select query datasheet should resemble the one shown in Figure 26-3. Notice that only the records for horses whose owners reside in Mountain View appear in the dynaset.

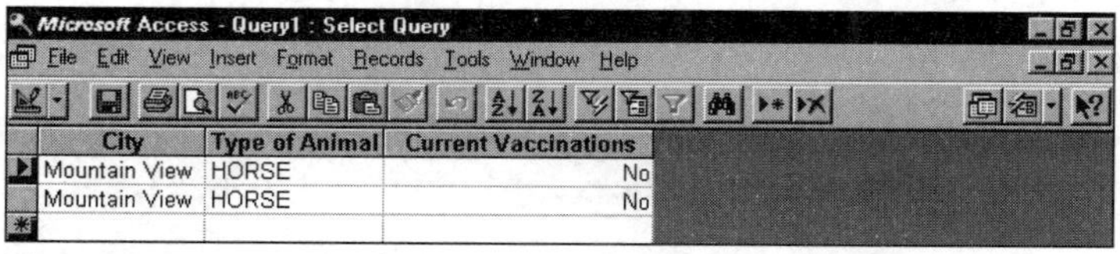

Figure 26-3: Dynaset showing only the records for horses whose owners live in Mountain View.

You are now ready to convert the select query to an update query.

Converting a select query to an update query

After you create a select query and verify the selection of records, it's time to create the update query. To convert the select query to an update query, follow these steps:

1. Select Update Query from the Query Type button on the toolbar or select Query➪Update from the menu.

   Access changes the title of the Query window from `Query1: Select Query` to `Query1: Update Query`. Access also adds the `Update To:` property row to the QBE pane, as shown in Figure 26-4.

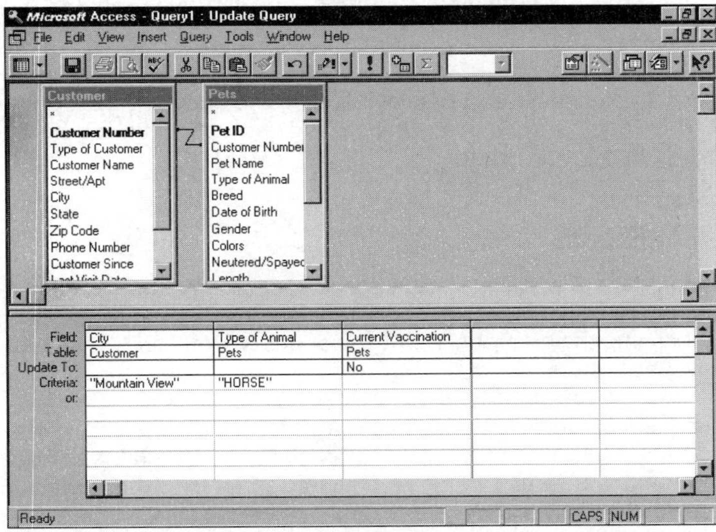

Figure 26-4: The design pane for the update query.

2. In the Update to: cell of Current Vaccination, enter **No**.
3. Click on the Run button on the toolbar (or select Query➪Run from the menu).

   Access displays the dialog box shown in Figure 26-5. This dialog box displays a message: `You are about to update x row[s]. Once you click Yes, you can't use the Undo command to reverse the changes. Are you sure you want to update these records?` Two buttons are presented, Yes and No.

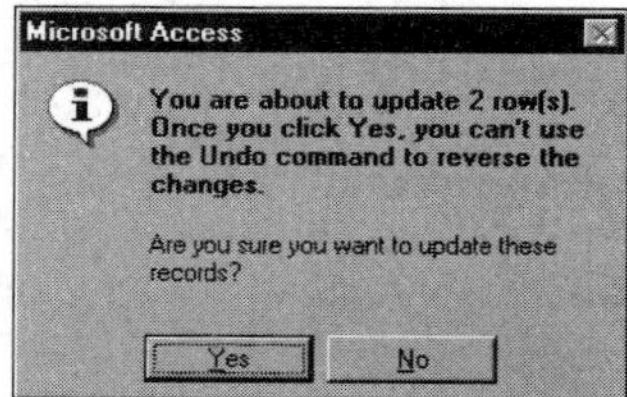

Figure 26-5: The dialog box for updating records.

4. Click on the Yes button to complete the query and update the records. Selecting No stops the procedure (no records are updated).

Note If you're changing tables that are attached to another database, you *cannot* cancel the query.

Tip You can change more than one field at a time by filling in the Update To: section of any field you want to change. You can even change field contents of fields you used for limiting the records that is, the criteria.

Checking your results

After completing the update query, you should check your results. You can do so by changing the update query back to a select query (click on the Select Query button on the toolbar). After changing the query back to a select query, you can review the changes in the datasheet.

The update made *permanent* changes to the field Current Vaccination for all horses whose owners live in Mountain View. If you did not back up the Pets table before running the update query, you cannot easily restore the contents to their original Yes or No settings. Hope you have a good memory.

Note If you update a field that was used for a limiting criterion, you must change the criterion in the select query to the new value in order to verify the changes.

Creating a New Table Using a Make-Table Query

You can use an action query to create new tables based on scoping criteria. To make a new table, you create a *make-table* query. Consider the following situation that might give rise to this particular task, and for which you would create a make-table query.

A local pet food company has approached you for a mailing list of customers who own dogs or cats. This company wants to send these customers a coupon for a free four-pound bag of food for each animal they own. The pet food company plans to create the mailing labels and send the form letters if you supply a table of customer information, pet names, and type of animal. The company also stipulates that, because this is a trial mailing, only those customers you've seen in the past six months should receive letters.

You've decided to send the company the requested table of information, so now you need to create a new table from the Customer and Pets tables. To accomplish this task, you create a make-table query that will perform these actions.

Creating the make-table query

You decide to create a make-table query for all customers who own dogs or cats and who have visited you in the past six months. (For this example, assume that six months ago was February 1, 1995.) Perform the following steps to create this query:

1. Create a new query using the Customer and Pets tables.
2. Select Make Table from the Query Type button on the toolbar.

   Access displays the Make Table dialog box, shown in Figure 26-6.
3. Type **Mailing List for Coupons** in the Table Name: field; press Enter or click on OK. Notice that the name of the window changes from `Query1: Select Query` to `Query1: Make Table Query`.
4. Select the mailing information fields (customer name through ZIP code) from the Customer table and the fields Pet Name, Type of Animal, and Last Visit Date from the Pets table.
5. Specify the criteria **In("CAT","DOG")** in the Type of Animal field and **>#2/1/95#** in the Last Visit Date field.

   The Query Design window should resemble the one in Figure 26-7. Notice that the fields are resized so that they all appear in the QBE pane. Two fields (Type of Animal and Last Visit Date) contain criteria.

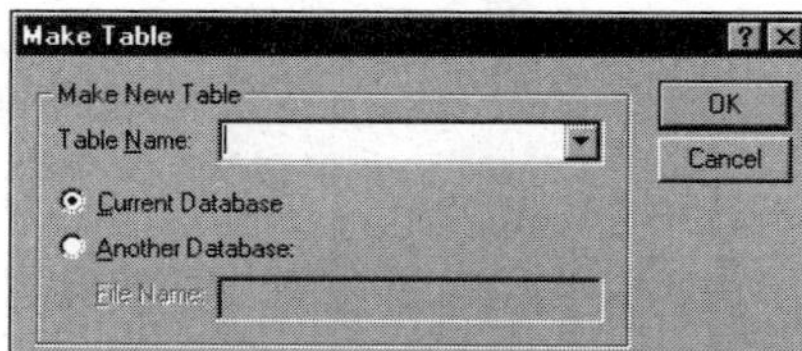

Figure 26-6: The Make Table dialog box.

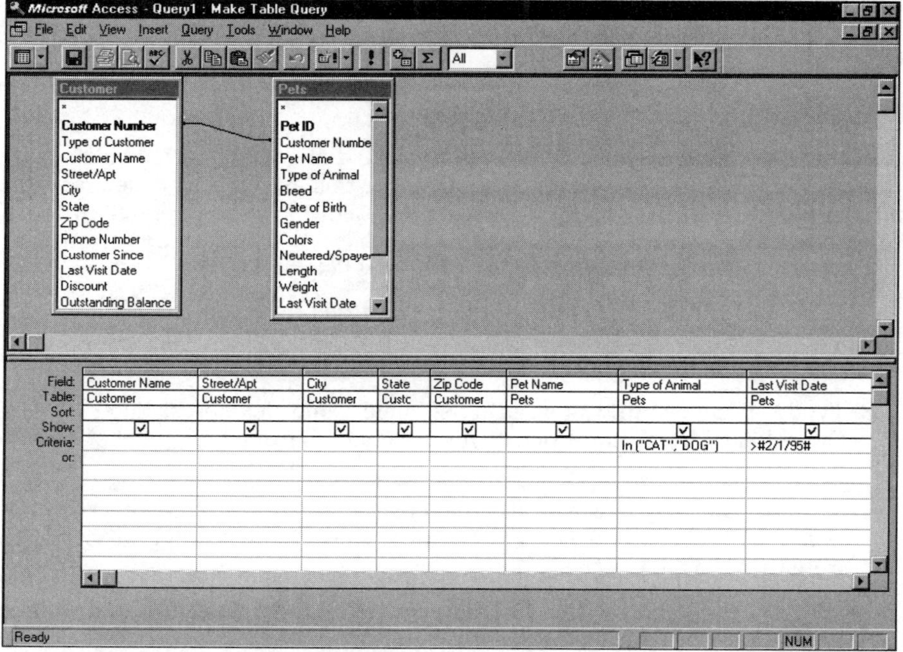

Figure 26-7: The Customer and Pets tables are in the top pane; the fields Customer Name, Street/Apt, City, State, Zip Code, Pet Name, Type of Animal, and Last Visit Date are in the bottom pane.

6. Click on the Datasheet View button on the toolbar to view the dynaset (see Figure 26-8).
7. Make sure that the dynaset has only the records you specified.
8. Click on the Design button to switch back to the Query Design view.
9. Deselect the Show: property of the field `Last Visit Date`.

Customer Name	Street/Apt	City	State	Zip Code	Pet Name	Type of Animal	Last Visit Date
All Creatures	21 Grace St.	Tall Pines	WA	98746-2541	Fido	DOG	11/5/95
Animal Kingdom	15 Marlin Lane	Borderville	ID	83483-5646	Tom	CAT	10/11/95
Animal Kingdom	15 Marlin Lane	Borderville	ID	83483-5646	Marcus	CAT	2/28/95
Animal Kingdom	15 Marlin Lane	Borderville	ID	83483-5646	Pookie	CAT	4/16/95
Animal Kingdom	15 Marlin Lane	Borderville	ID	83483-5646	Mario	DOG	10/15/95
Animal Kingdom	15 Marlin Lane	Borderville	ID	83483-5646	Luigi	DOG	8/3/95
James Brown	3454 Adams St	Borderville	OR	97401-1019	John Boy	DOG	2/3/95
Bow Wow House	76 Canine Ln.	Ranier City	WA	98756-2175	Sweety	DOG	6/17/95
Bow Wow House	76 Canine Ln.	Ranier City	WA	98756-2175	Quintin	DOG	8/15/95
Cat House Pets	76 Right Ln.	Borderville	OR	97541-2856	Silly	CAT	4/14/95
Critters and More	200 Feline Rd	Borderville	WA	98453-8567	Mule	CAT	9/3/95
Wanda Greenfield	66 Farmaccess Rd	Tall Pines	WA	98401-2201	Sammie Girl	DOG	2/23/95
Cat House Pets	76 Right Ln.	Borderville	OR	97541-2856	C.C.	CAT	6/17/95
Patricia Irwin	456 Bishops Ln	Lakeville	OR	97401-1021	Gizmo	CAT	4/22/95
Patricia Irwin	456 Bishops Ln	Lakeville	OR	97401-1021	Stripe	CAT	5/4/95
Patricia Irwin	456 Bishops Ln	Lakeville	OR	97401-1021	Romeo	CAT	5/4/95
Patricia Irwin	456 Bishops Ln	Lakeville	OR	97401-1021	Ceasar	CAT	5/4/95
Patricia Irwin	456 Bishops Ln	Lakeville	OR	97401-1021	Juliet	CAT	5/5/95
Patricia Irwin	456 Bishops Ln	Lakeville	OR	97401-1021	Tiger	CAT	6/17/95
Michael Johnson	77 Farmaccess Rd	Ranier City	WA	98401-2201	Rover	DOG	4/23/95
Adam Johnson	55 Childs Ave	Mount Pilot	ID	83412-1043	Fi Fi	DOG	3/7/95
Margaret McKinley	5512 Green Acres Ct	Borderville	OR	97412-1001	Rex	DOG	3/9/95
Margaret McKinley	5512 Green Acres Ct	Borderville	OR	97412-1001	Ceasar	DOG	3/9/95
Pet City	91 Main St.	Mount Pilot	ID	83187-5638	Sylvester	DOG	6/18/95
William Primen	1234 Main St	Mountain View	WA	98401-1011	Brutus	DOG	5/19/95
Village Pets	30 Murphy St.	Russettown	ID	83019-8573	Ren	DOG	6/28/95
Sandra Williams	2211 Main St	Mountain View	WA	98401-1021	Flower	CAT	6/1/95
Sandra Williams	2211 Main St	Mountain View	WA	98401-1021	Shadow	CAT	6/18/95

Figure 26-8: The dynaset of cats and dogs seen since February 1, 1995.

You do not want to copy this field to the new table Mailing List for Coupons. Only those fields selected with an X in the check box of the Show: row are copied to the new table. By deselecting a field with a criteria set, you can base the scoping criteria on fields that will *not* be copied to the new table.

10. Click on the Run button on the toolbar or select Query⇨Run from the menu.

Access indicates how many records it will copy to the new table (see Figure 26-9).

11. Click on the Yes button to complete the query and make the new table. Selecting No stops the procedure (no records are copied).

When you're creating numerous make-table queries, you need to select Make Table Query from the Query Type button on the toolbar, or select Query⇨Make Table... from the menu; this command renames the make-table query each time. Access assumes you want to overwrite the existing table if you don't reselect the make-table option. Access warns you about overwriting before performing the new make-table query; as an alternative, you could change the Destination table name in the Property sheet.

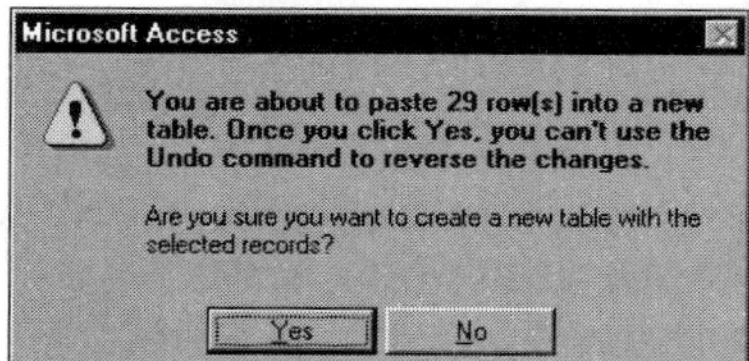

Figure 26-9: The dialog box for copying records.

Checking your results

After you complete the make-table query, you should check your results. You can do so by opening the new table Mailing List for Coupons, which has been added to the database container (see Figure 26-10).

Customer Name	Street/Apt	City	State	Zip Code	Pet Name	Type
All Creatures	21 Grace St.	Tall Pines	WA	98746-2541	Fido	DOG
Animal Kingdom	15 Marlin Lane	Borderville	ID	83483-5646	Tom	CAT
Animal Kingdom	15 Marlin Lane	Borderville	ID	83483-5646	Marcus	CAT
Animal Kingdom	15 Marlin Lane	Borderville	ID	83483-5646	Pookie	CAT
Animal Kingdom	15 Marlin Lane	Borderville	ID	83483-5646	Mario	DOG
Animal Kingdom	15 Marlin Lane	Borderville	ID	83483-5646	Luigi	DOG
James Brown	3454 Adams St	Borderville	OR	97401-1019	John Boy	DOG
Bow Wow House	76 Canine Ln.	Ranier City	WA	98756-2175	Sweety	DOG
Bow Wow House	76 Canine Ln.	Ranier City	WA	98756-2175	Quintin	DOG
Cat House Pets	76 Right Ln.	Borderville	OR	97541-2856	Silly	CAT
Critters and More	200 Feline Rd	Borderville	WA	98453-8567	Mule	CAT
Wanda Greenfield	66 Farmaccess Rd	Tall Pines	WA	98401-2201	Sammie Girl	DOG
Cat House Pets	76 Right Ln.	Borderville	OR	97541-2856	C.C.	CAT
Patricia Irwin	456 Bishops Ln	Lakeville	OR	97401-1021	Gizmo	CAT
Patricia Irwin	456 Bishops Ln	Lakeville	OR	97401-1021	Stripe	CAT
Patricia Irwin	456 Bishops Ln	Lakeville	OR	97401-1021	Romeo	CAT
Patricia Irwin	456 Bishops Ln	Lakeville	OR	97401-1021	Ceasar	CAT
Patricia Irwin	456 Bishops Ln	Lakeville	OR	97401-1021	Juliet	CAT
Patricia Irwin	456 Bishops Ln	Lakeville	OR	97401-1021	Tiger	CAT
Michael Johnson	77 Farmaccess Rd	Ranier City	WA	98401-2201	Rover	DOG
Adam Johnson	55 Childs Ave	Mount Pilot	ID	83412-1043	Fi Fi	DOG

Figure 26-10: The new table Mailing List for Coupons.

Note When you create a table from a make-table query, the fields in the new table inherit the data type and field size from the fields in the query's underlying tables; however, no other field or table properties are transferred. If you want to define a primary key or other properties, you need to edit the design of the new table.

Tip: You can also use a make-table action query to create a backup of your tables before you create action queries that change the contents of the tables. Backing up with this method *does not* copy the table's properties or primary key to the new table.

To copy any database object (table, query, form, or other object) while you're in the Database window, follow these steps:

1. Highlight the object you need to copy.
2. Press Ctrl+C (or select Edit⇨Copy) to copy the object to the Clipboard.
3. Press Ctrl+V (or select Edit⇨Paste) to paste the object from the Clipboard.
4. Enter the new object name (table, form, and so forth) and select the OK button in the dialog box. If the object is a table, you also can specify Structure with or without the data and append it to an existing table.

Creating a Query to Append Records

As the word *append* suggests, an append query attaches or adds records to a specified table. An append query adds records from the table you're using to another table. The table you want to add records to must already exist. You can append records to a table in the same database or in another Access database.

Append queries are very useful for adding information to another table on the basis of some scoping criteria. Even so, append queries are not always the fastest way of adding records to another database. If you need (for example) to append all fields and all records from one table to a new table, the append query is *not* the best way to do it. Instead, use the Copy and Paste options of the Edit menu when you're working with the table in a datasheet or form.

Tip: You can add records to an open table. You don't have to close the table before adding records. However, Access does not automatically refresh the view of the table that has records added to it. To refresh the table, press Shift+F9. This action requeries the table so you can see the appended records.

When you're working with append queries, you need to be aware of the following rules:

1. If the table you're appending records to has a primary-key field, the records you add cannot have Null values or duplicate primary-key values. If they do, Access will not append the records.
2. If you add records to another database table, you must know the location and name of the database.

3. If you use the asterisk (*) field in a QBE row, you cannot also use individual fields from the same table. Access assumes you're trying to add field contents twice to the same record, and will not append the records.

4. If you append records with a AutoNumber field (an Access-specified primary key), do not include the AutoNumber field if the table you're appending to also has the field and record contents (this causes the problem specified in rule 1). Also, if you're adding to an empty table and you want the new table to have a new AutoNumber number (that is, order number) based on the criteria, do not use the AutoNumber field.

If you follow these simple rules, your append query will perform as expected and become a very useful tool.

Here's an example that will help illustrate the use of append queries: Every February, you archive all records of animals that died in the preceding year. To archive the records, you perform two steps. First, you append them to existing backup files. Second, you delete the records from the active database.

In this case, you want to add records to the backup tables for deceased animals in your active tables. In other words, you will copy records to three tables — Pets, Visits, and Visit Details. You need three backup files to perform this exercise. To create the backup files, perform the following steps:

1. Press F11 or Alt+F1 to display the Database window.
2. Click on the Tables tab to display the list of tables.
3. Click on the Pets table to highlight it.
4. Press Ctrl+C (or select Edit⇨Copy) to copy the object Pets table to the Clipboard.
5. Press Ctrl+V (or select Edit⇨Paste) to display the Paste Table As dialog box.
6. Click on Structure Only in the Paste Options section of the dialog box (or tab to the Paste Options section and click on S).
7. Click on the Table Name: box and type **Pets Backup**.
8. Click on the OK button (or press Enter after typing the filename).
9. Open the Pets Backup table (it should be empty); then close the table.

Repeat this process for both the Visits and Visit Details tables, naming them **Visits Backup** and **Visit Details Backup**, respectively.

To create an append query that copies the deceased animals' records, follow a two-step process:

1. Create a select query to verify that only the records you want to append are copied.
2. Convert the select query to an append query and run it.

Note

When you're using the append query, only fields with names that match in the two tables are copied. For example, you may have a small table with six fields and another with nine. The table with nine fields has only five of the six field names that match fields in the smaller table. If you append records from the smaller table to the larger table, only the five matching fields are appended. The other four fields remain blank.

Creating the select query for an append query

To create a select query for all pets that died last year, along with their visit histories, follow these steps:

1. Create a new query using the Pets, Visits, and Visit Details tables.
2. Select the Deceased field from the Pets table.
3. Specify a criterion of Yes in the Deceased field.

   You may want to select some additional fields from each table, such as Pet Name, Visit Date, Visit Type, Treatment Code, and so forth. The Select Query Design window should resemble the one in Figure 26-11. Notice that all the fields are resized to appear in the QBE pane. The only field and criterion that must be in this select query is the first field, Deceased. If you add any other fields, make sure you remove them before converting this query to an append query.
4. Go to the datasheet and make sure that all the Deceased field contents say `Yes`. (See Figure 26-12.)
5. Return to design mode. With the select query created correctly, you are ready to convert the select query to an append query.

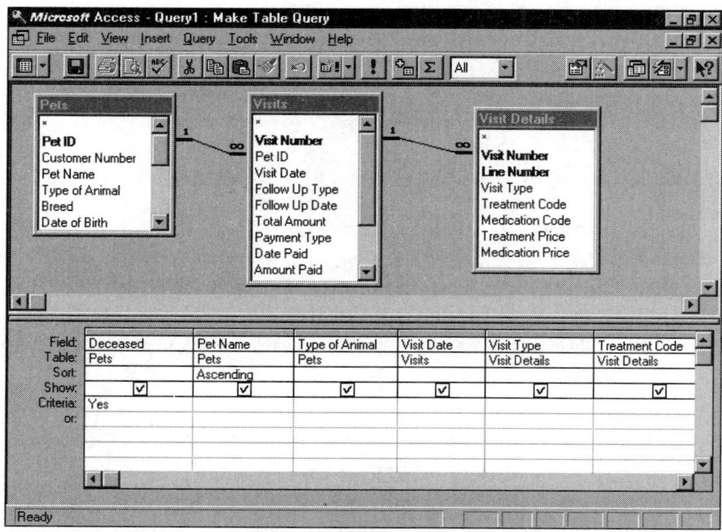

Figure 26-11: The tables Pets, Visits, and Visit Details are in the top pane, and selected fields are in the QBE pane.

Microsoft Access - Query1 : Make Table Query

File Edit View Insert Format Records Tools Window Help

Deceased	Pet Name	Type of Animal	Visit Date	Visit Type	Treatment Coc
Yes	Golden Girl	HORSE	2/4/95	PHYSICAL	0300
Yes	Golden Girl	HORSE	7/5/95	ROUTINE	0400
Yes	John Boy	DOG	2/23/95	PHYSICAL	0300
Yes	John Boy	DOG	2/17/95	PHYSICAL	0300
Yes	Romeo	CAT	2/4/95	PHYSICAL	0101
Yes	Romeo	CAT	2/4/95	PHYSICAL	0102
Yes	Romeo	CAT	5/24/95	PHYSICAL	0100
Yes	Romeo	CAT	2/4/95	PHYSICAL	0100
Yes	Tiger	CAT	2/4/95	PHYSICAL	0300
Yes	Tiger	CAT	2/4/95	PHYSICAL	0100
Yes	Tiger	CAT	7/7/95	OTHER	0900
Yes	Tiger	CAT	7/7/95	OTHER	0901
Yes	Tom	CAT	7/11/95	PHYSICAL	0300
Yes	Tom	CAT	10/31/95	GROOMING	2004
Yes	Tom	CAT	10/31/95	GROOMING	2001
Yes	Tom	CAT	10/31/95	PHYSICAL	0300
Yes	Tom	CAT	8/4/95	PHYSICAL	0303
Yes	Tom	CAT	7/11/95	GROOMING	2002
Yes	Tom	CAT	7/11/95	PHYSICAL	0102

Figure 26-12: A dynaset of records for all deceased animals.

Converting to an append query

After you create the select query and verify that it is correct, you'll need to create the append query (actually, three different append queries — one each for the tables Visit Details, Visits, and Pets — because append queries work with only one table at a time). For this example, first copy all fields from the Visits Detail table. Then copy all the fields from the Visits table. Finally, copy all the fields from the Pets table.

To convert the select query to an append query and run it, perform the following steps:

1. Deselect the Show: property of the Deceased field.
2. Select Append from the Query Type button on the toolbar, or select Query⇨Append... from the Design menu.

   Access displays the Append dialog box, shown in Figure 26-13.

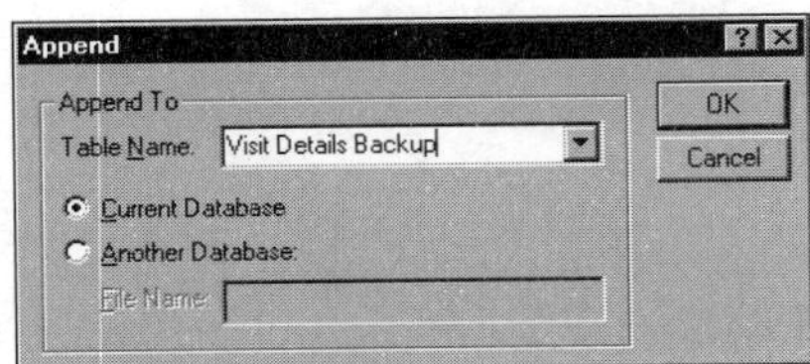

Figure 26-13: The Append dialog box.

3. Type **Visit Details Backup** in the Table Name: field and either press Enter with the cursor in the field or click on OK with the cursor in the dialog box.
4. Drag the asterisk (*) field from the Visit Details table to the QBE pane to select all fields.

   The QBE pane should look like Figure 26-14. Access automatically fills in the Append To: field under the `All` field-selector column.
5. Click on the Run button on the toolbar (or select Query⇨Run from the menu).

   Access displays a dialog box that displays a message: `You are about to append x row[s]`. Then it presents two buttons (Yes and No). Once you click on Yes, you can't use the Undo command to reverse the changes.

6. Click on the Yes button to complete the query and copy (append) the records to the backup table. Selecting No stops the procedure (no records are copied).

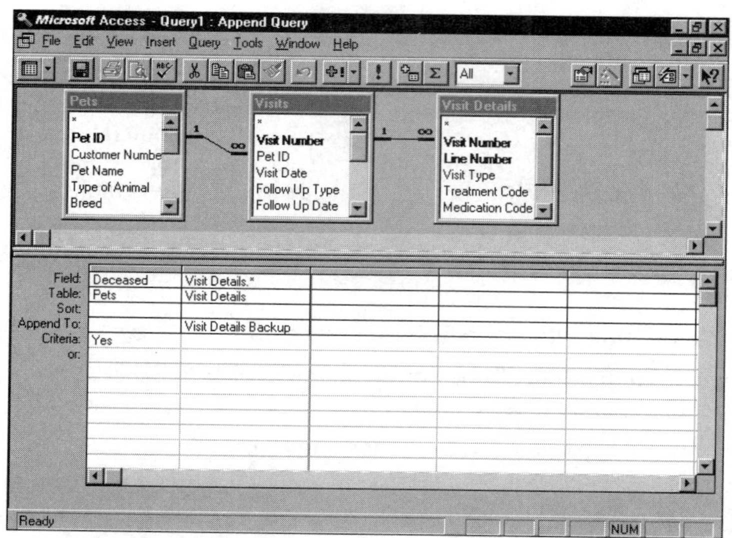

Figure 26-14: The QBE pane for an appended query.

Note Once the Visit Details records for deceased animals are backed up, repeat Steps 2 through 5 for the Visits and Pets tables. Before you append fields from these other tables, however, you must remove the previous All selector field `[Visit Details.*]` from the QBE pane.

Warning If you create an append query by using the asterisk (*) field and you also use a field from the same table as the asterisk to specify a criterion, you must take the criteria field out of the Append To: row. If you don't, Access reports an error. Remember, the field for the criterion is already included in the asterisk field. If you leave the Show on, it tries to append the field twice, repeating an error. Then Access halts the append query, appending no records to the table.

Checking your results

After you complete the three append table queries, check your results. To do so, go to the Database window and select each of the three tables to be appended to (Pets Backup, Visits Backup, and Visit Details Backup); view the new records.

Creating a Query to Delete Records

Of all the action queries, the *delete query* is the most dangerous. Unlike the other types of queries you've worked with, delete queries wipe out records from tables permanently and *irreversibly.*

Like other action queries, delete queries act on a group of records on the basis of scoping criteria.

A delete action query can work with multiple tables to delete records. If you intend to delete related records from multiple tables, however, you must do the following:

- ✦ Define relationships between the tables in the Relationships Builder.
- ✦ Check the Enforce Referential Integrity option for the join between tables.
- ✦ Check the Cascade Delete Related Fields option for the join between tables.

Figure 26-15 shows the Relationships dialog box for the join line between tables. Notice that the options Enforce Referential Integrity and Cascade Delete Related Records are selected.

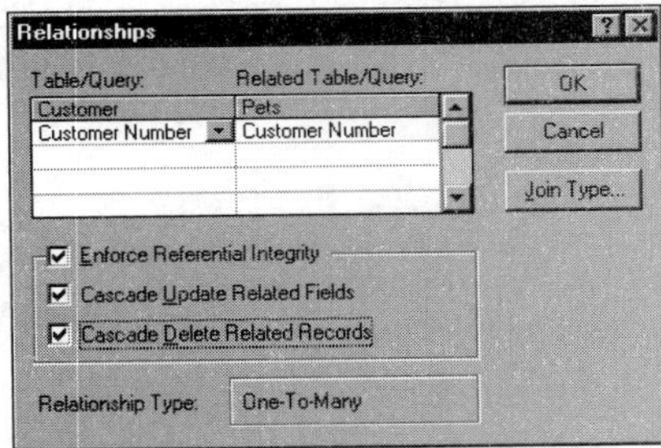

Figure 26-15: The Relationships dialog box.

When working with one-to-many relationships without defining relationships and putting Cascade Delete on, Access deletes records from only one table at a time. Specifically, Access deletes the *many* side of the relationship first. Then you must remove the *many* table from the query and delete the records from the *one* side of the query.

This method is time-consuming and awkward. Therefore, when deleting related records from one-to-many relationship tables, make sure you define relationships between the tables and check the Cascade Delete box in the Relationships dialog box.

Warning Because of the permanently destructive action of a delete query, you should always make backup copies of your tables before working with them.

The following example will help illustrate the use of Access action queries. In this case, you have a large number of records to delete.

In this situation, you are going to delete all records of deceased animals. Recall that you already copied all deceased pet records to backup tables in the append query section. The tables you're dealing with have these relationships:

✦ One pet has many visits

✦ One visit has many visit details

These are both one-to-many relationships. As a result, if you don't define permanent relationships between the tables and have turned on Cascade Delete, you'll need to create three separate delete queries. (You would need to delete from the Visit Details, Visits, and Pets tables — in that order.)

With relations set and Cascade Delete on, however, you need only delete the records from the Pets table; Access automatically deletes all related records. Assume for this example you have already appended the records to another table — or you made a new table of the records that you're about to delete, you've set up permanent relationships among the three tables, and you've turned on Cascade Delete for both relationships (that is, between Pets and Visits and between Visits and Visit Details).

Creating a cascading delete query

To create a *cascading delete query* for all pets that died last year, along with their visit histories, perform the following steps:

1. Create a new query using the Pets, Visits, and Visit Details tables.
2. Select Query⇨Delete from the Design menu.

   Notice that the name of the window changes from `Select Query:Query1` to `Delete Query:Query1`.
3. Select the Deceased field from the Pets table.
4. Specify the criterion **Yes** in the Deceased field.

   The Delete Query Design window is shown in Figure 26-16. The only field and criteria that must appear in this delete query is the first field, Deceased.
5. Go to the datasheet and verify that only records that say `Yes` are there.
6. Return to the Design window.
7. Click on the Run button on the toolbar (or select Query⇨Run from the menu).

Figure 26-16: The delete query's QBE pane.

Access displays a dialog box with a message: `You are about to delete x row[s] from the specified table (Pets). Once you click Yes, you can't use the Undo command to reverse the changes. Are you sure you want to delete the selected records?` Access does not specify how many rows will be deleted from the other tables that may be linked to the table you selected.

8. Click on the Yes button to complete the query. The records are removed from all three tables. When you click on the Yes button, Access deletes the records in the Pets table and then automatically deletes the related records in the Visits and Visit Details tables. Selecting No stops the procedure (no records are copied).

Remember that a delete query permanently and irreversibly removes the records from the table(s). Therefore it is important to back up the records you want to delete *before* you delete them.

Checking your results

After completing the delete query, you can check your results by simply pressing the Datasheet button on the toolbar. If the delete query worked correctly, you will see no records in the datasheet.

You have now deleted all records of deceased animals from the database tables Pets, Visits, and Visit Details.

Note Delete queries remove entire records, not just the data in specific fields. If you need to delete only values in specific fields, use an update query to change the values to empty values.

Creating Other Queries Using the Query Wizards

In the preceding chapter, we described how to use a Query Wizard to create a crosstab query. Access has three other Wizards that can help you maintain your databases:

✦ Find Duplicate Records Wizard: Shows any duplicate records in a single table, on the basis of a field in the table.

✦ Find Unmatched Records Wizard: Shows all records that do not have a corresponding record in another table (for example, a customer with no pets or a pet with no owner).

✦ Archive Wizard: Lets you back up records in a single table and then optionally delete the records you just backed up.

Both the Find Duplicate Records Wizard and Archive Wizard work on a single table. The Find Unmatched Records Wizard compares records from one table to another.

These Wizards (along with all the others, such as the Crosstab Wizard) are listed when you first start a new query.

Find Duplicate Records Wizard

This Wizard helps you create a query that reports which records in a table are duplicated using some field(s) in the table as a basis. Access asks which field(s) you want to use for checking duplication, and then prompts you to enter some other field(s) you may want to see in the query. Finally, Access asks for a title; then it creates and displays the query.

This type of Wizard query can help you find duplicate key violations, a valuable trick when you want to take an existing table and make a unique key field with existing data. If you try to create a unique key field and Access reports an error, you know you have either nulls in the field or duplicate records. Then the query helps you find the duplicates.

Find Unmatched Records Wizard

This Wizard helps you create a query that reports any orphan or widow records between two tables.

An *orphan* is a record in a *many*-side table that has no corresponding record in the *one*-side table. For example, say you have a pet in the Pets table that does not have an owner in the Customers table (the pet is an orphan).

A *widow* is a record in the *one* side of a one-to-many or one-to-one that does not have a corresponding record in the other table. For example, say you have a Customer who has no animals in the Pets table.

Access asks for the names of the two tables you want to compare; it also asks for the link field name between the tables. Access prompts you for the fields you want to see in the first table and for a title. Then it creates the query.

This type of query can help you find records that have no corresponding records in other tables. If you create a relationship between tables and try to set Referential Integrity, but Access reports it cannot activate that feature, some records are violating integrity. This query helps you find them quickly.

Archive Records Wizard

This Wizard helps you create a query that will back up records for a specific criterion and then delete the records from the current table (if the user so requests). The query, created by the Wizard, will actually perform two queries, one after the other — a make-table query and a delete query. Even so, this query works with only one table at a time, and is based on a single-field criterion (that is, based on one field in the table).

Access prompts you for the table you want to archive, and then for a single-field criterion you want to archive for. Then Access reports the number of records to be archived and shows them to you for verification, asking whether you want to delete them after archiving. Finally Access prompts you for a title and runs the query. As it runs, Access again prompts you to verify that you want to archive the records. If you answer Yes, Access copies the records to a table by the same name, adding `Arc` (for archive) to the name.

The Archive Records type of query is an excellent way to back up any table in your application. However, the delete Archived records option should be used with caution, because it permanently removes the records from the tables. When working with related tables, this query should back up all child tables first, and then parent tables. For instance, the Pet table should be backed up before the Customer table. This should be done because the Archive Records query works with only one table at a time. Working from the bottom of the hierarchy up will assure that you have archived all tables. When working with lookup tables and nonrelated tables, this query offers an excellent way to create a working backup.

Saving an Action Query

Saving an action query is just like saving any other query. From the design mode, you can save the query and continue working by clicking on the Save button of the toolbar (or by selecting File➪Save from the Query menu). If this is the first time you're saving the query, Access prompts you for a name in the Save As dialog box.

You can also save the query and exit, either by selecting File➪Close from the menu or by double-clicking on the Window menu button (top left corner of the Query window) and answering Yes to this dialog box question: `Save changes to the design of '<query name>'`? You also can save the query by pressing F12.

Running an Action Query

After you save an action query, you can run it by simply double-clicking on its name. Access will warn you that an action query is about to be executed, and ask you to confirm before it continues with the query.

Troubleshooting Action Queries

When you're working with action queries, you need to be aware of several potential problems. While you're running the query, any of several messages may appear, including messages that several records were lost due to *key violations,* or that records were *locked* during the execution of the query. This section discusses some of these problems and how to avoid them.

Data-type errors in appending and updating

If you attempt to enter a value that is not appropriate for the specified field, Access doesn't enter the value; it simply ignores the incorrect values and converts the fields to Null values. When you're working with append queries, this means that Access will append the records, but the fields may be blank!

Key violations in action queries

When you attempt to append records to another database that has a primary key, Access will not append records that contain the same primary-key value.

Access does not let you update a record and change a primary-key value to an existing value. You can change a primary-key value to another value under these conditions:

- ✦ The new primary-key value does not already exist.
- ✦ The field value you're attempting to change is not related to fields in other tables.

Access does not let you delete a field on the *one* side of a one-to-many relationship without first deleting the records from the *many* side.

Access does not let you append or update a field value that will duplicate a value in a *unique index field* — one that has the Index property set to Yes (No Duplicates).

Record-locked fields in multiuser environments

Access will not perform an action query on records locked by another user. When you're performing an update or append query, you can choose to continue and change all other values. But remember that if you allow Access to continue with an action query, you won't be able to determine which records were left unchanged!

Text fields

When appending or updating to a Text field that is smaller than the current field, Access will truncate any text data that doesn't fit in the new field. Access will *not* warn you that it truncated the information.

Summary

In this chapter, you learned how to create and use a special type of query called the action query. This type of query goes beyond performing searches; the query can make changes to the data. The chapter covered the following points:

- ✦ Action queries perform some operation on the tables you're using. The operation can be deleting records, changing the contents of records, adding records to another table, or making new tables.
- ✦ The various types of action queries include make-table, append, update, and delete.
- ✦ Action queries do not create a dynaset. To view the results of an action query, you must convert it to a select query (if it's a delete or update query) or view the affected table.
- ✦ Always back up your tables before you work with action queries.
- ✦ When you create an action query, it's best to create a select query first to make sure the action is going to affect the correct records.
- ✦ Append action queries can work with only one table at a time.
- ✦ Append action queries must already have an existing table to append to. The query does not create a table for you if one doesn't already exist.
- ✦ The append query is not the best method for appending all records from one table to another. It's better to copy the table to the Clipboard and paste it to the other table.
- ✦ Make-table action queries can take fields from one or many tables and combine them into a single table.
- ✦ Delete action queries can delete records from multiple tables that have a one-to-one relationship.
- ✦ Delete action queries for tables with one-to-many relationships require deleting the *many*-side records first; then the *one* side can be deleted.
- ✦ Unless an action query is going to be executed over and over, do not save it.
- ✦ Access enforces all referential rules when performing action queries. If an action query attempts to perform an operation that violates referential integrity, Access halts the operation.

In the next chapter, you examine advanced query topics.

✦ ✦ ✦

Advanced Query Topics

In This Chapter

Using calculated fields

Hiding fields and columns

Understanding what happens when queries are saved

Sorting fields and using existing indexes

Setting query design options

Setting query properties

Viewing and using SQL statements

In this chapter, you work with queries in more detail and complexity than in earlier chapters. So far, you have worked with all types of queries: select, action, crosstab, and parameter. You have not, however, worked with all the options you can use with these types of queries.

This chapter focuses on a wide range of advanced query topics. You will read about several topics explained in other chapters; this chapter will address them in more detail. A firm understanding of advanced queries can solve unexpected problems for you later.

Using Lookup Tables and Joins

You can use a *lookup table* to validate the entry of data or find additional information based on a key value. Such a table uses, by definition, a many-to-one relationship; many records in the primary table can reference information from one record in the lookup table. A lookup table can be permanent or transient:

Permanent	Created solely for lookup purposes
Transient	Used as either a lookup table or a primary table

The Mountain Animal Hospital database has four permanent lookup tables: States, Pets, Treatments, and Medications.

The Customer table is an example of a *transient lookup table*. When you're working with a form to add pet personal information (name, type, and so on), the Customer table becomes a lookup table based on the customer number. Although the Customer table is a primary table of the database, in this case it may become a lookup table for the Pets table.

Working with lookup tables in queries does require an understanding of joins and how they work. For example, you may be interested in displaying visit details along with the specific treatment and medication given for each visit. Treatment and medication information will come from the lookup tables — in this case, Treatments and Medications. To create this query, follow these steps:

1. Select the Visit Details, Treatments, and Medications tables and join them if they are not already joined.
2. Double-click on the Visit Number field in the Visit Details table.
3. Double-click on the Visit Type field in the Visit Details table.
4. Double-click on the Treatment field of the Treatments table.
5. Double-click on the Medication Name field of the Medications table.

Your query should look like Figure 27-1. Notice that Visit Details uses both Treatments and Medications as lookup tables.

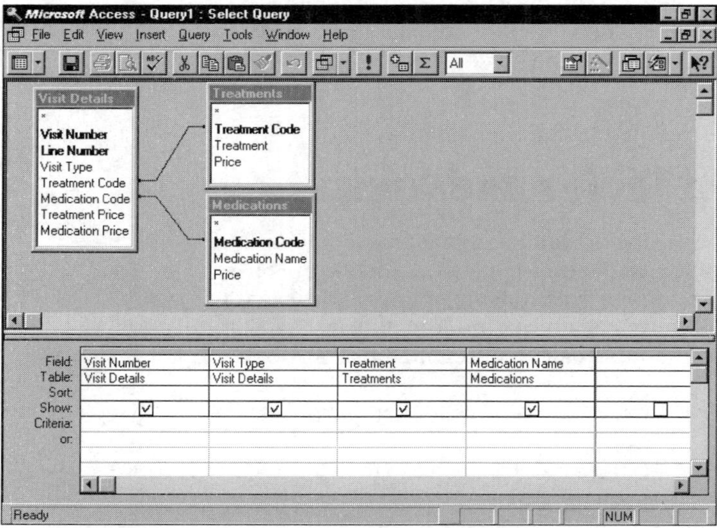

Figure 27-1: Creating a query with two lookup tables.

After you create the query, you can select the Datasheet option from the Query View button on the toolbar to display a dynaset similar to the one in Figure 27-2 (clicking once will toggle you back and forth between the Design View and the Datasheet. Clicking on the drop-down box will show all three options: Query View, Datasheet, and SQL.

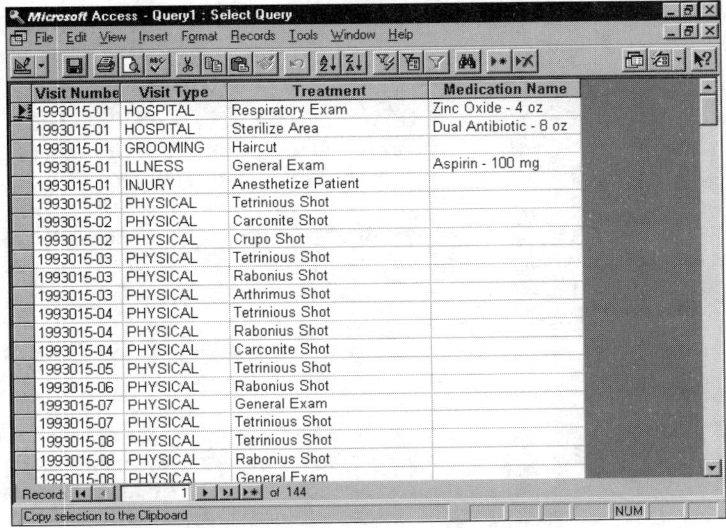

Visit Numbe	Visit Type	Treatment	Medication Name
1993015-01	HOSPITAL	Respiratory Exam	Zinc Oxide - 4 oz
1993015-01	HOSPITAL	Sterilize Area	Dual Antibiotic - 8 oz
1993015-01	GROOMING	Haircut	
1993015-01	ILLNESS	General Exam	Aspirin - 100 mg
1993015-01	INJURY	Anesthetize Patient	
1993015-02	PHYSICAL	Tetrinious Shot	
1993015-02	PHYSICAL	Carconite Shot	
1993015-02	PHYSICAL	Crupo Shot	
1993015-03	PHYSICAL	Tetrinious Shot	
1993015-03	PHYSICAL	Rabonius Shot	
1993015-03	PHYSICAL	Arthrimus Shot	
1993015-04	PHYSICAL	Tetrinious Shot	
1993015-04	PHYSICAL	Rabonius Shot	
1993015-04	PHYSICAL	Carconite Shot	
1993015-05	PHYSICAL	Tetrinious Shot	
1993015-06	PHYSICAL	Rabonius Shot	
1993015-07	PHYSICAL	General Exam	
1993015-07	PHYSICAL	Tetrinious Shot	
1993015-08	PHYSICAL	Tetrinious Shot	
1993015-08	PHYSICAL	Rabonius Shot	
1993015-08	PHYSICAL	General Exam	

Figure 27-2: Datasheet of a query with two lookup tables.

Using the DLookUp( ) function for lookup tables

Another way to find specific lookup information based on a field is to create a calculated field using the DLookUp( ) function. You use DLookUp( ) to find information in a table that is not currently open. The general syntax for this function is as follows:

DLookUp("[*Field to display*]", "[*Lookup Table*]", "<*Criteria for Search*>")

"[*Field to display*]" in quotation marks is the field in the lookup table you want to find.

"[*Lookup Table*]" in quotation marks is the table containing the field you want to display.

"<*Criteria for Search*>" in quotation marks signifies criteria used by the lookup function.

Access suggests that *Criteria for Search* is not necessary, but if you want to use a different criterion for each record, it is essential. When you use DLookUp( ), the format of your criteria is critical. The syntax of *Criteria for Search* is as follows:

"[Field in Lookup Table]='< Example Data>' "

You can replace the equal operator with any valid Access operator.

'<*Example Data*>' in single quotation marks is usually a literal, such as 'DOG' or 'AC001'. If the data is a field in the current table, you must use the following syntax:

" & [Field in This Table] & "

(continued)

(continued)

Notice that the field is surrounded with double quotation marks (") and ampersands (&).

Although using the DLookUp( ) function to build a calculated field seems complex, it can be a simple way to create a query for use by a form or report. To create a query that finds the medication name and treatment in the Treatments and Medications tables, follow these steps:

1. Select the Visit Details table.
2. Double-click on the Visit Type field in the Visit Details table.
3. In an empty field in the QBE pane, type **TreatmentType:DLookUp("[Treatment]","[Treatments]","[Treatment Code] = '"&[TreatmentCode]&"'")**.
4. In another empty field in the QBE pane, type **MedicationType:DLookUp("[MedicationName]","[Medications]", "[Medication Code]='"&[Medication Code]&"'")**.

When you enter the field name of the current table in the criteria for the DLookUp() function, you must not use spaces. After the equal sign, you type the entry in this format:

single quote — double quote — ampersand — [*field name*] — ampersand — double quote — single quote — double quote

No spaces can be entered between the quotation marks (single or double).

Figure 27-3 shows how the query looks after you enter the calculated fields Treatment Type and Medication Type. Notice that you don't see the entire formula you entered.

If you're having problems typing in Steps 3 or 4, press Shift+F2 to activate the Zoom window. After you activate the window, the entire contents will be highlighted; press F2 again to deselect the contents and move to the end of them.

If you now select the Datasheet option in the Query View button on the toolbar, you see a datasheet similar to Figure 27-4. Notice that several records have no medication name.

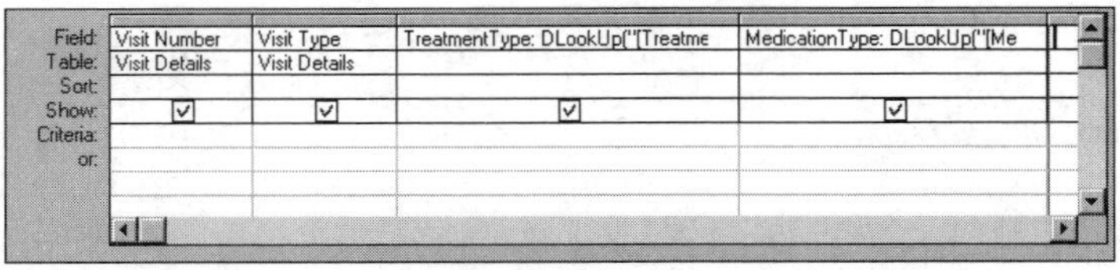

Field:	Visit Number	Visit Type	TreatmentType: DLookUp("[Treatme	MedicationType: DLookUp("[Me
Table:	Visit Details	Visit Details		
Sort:				
Show:	☑	☑	☑	☑
Criteria:				
or:				

Figure 27-3: The QBE pane showing two calculated fields using the DLookUp( ) function.

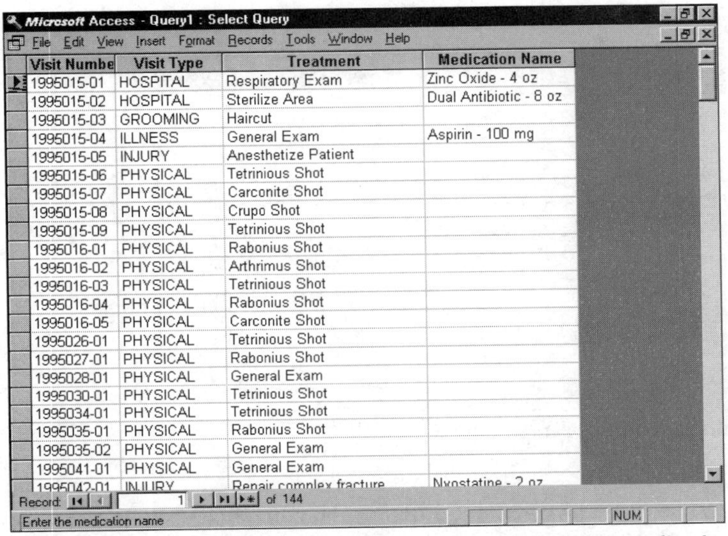

Microsoft Access - Query1 : Select Query

File Edit View Insert Format Records Tools Window Help

Visit Numbe	Visit Type	Treatment	Medication Name
1995015-01	HOSPITAL	Respiratory Exam	Zinc Oxide - 4 oz
1995015-02	HOSPITAL	Sterilize Area	Dual Antibiotic - 8 oz
1995015-03	GROOMING	Haircut	
1995015-04	ILLNESS	General Exam	Aspirin - 100 mg
1995015-05	INJURY	Anesthetize Patient	
1995015-06	PHYSICAL	Tetrinious Shot	
1995015-07	PHYSICAL	Carconite Shot	
1995015-08	PHYSICAL	Crupo Shot	
1995015-09	PHYSICAL	Tetrinious Shot	
1995016-01	PHYSICAL	Rabonius Shot	
1995016-02	PHYSICAL	Arthrimus Shot	
1995016-03	PHYSICAL	Tetrinious Shot	
1995016-04	PHYSICAL	Rabonius Shot	
1995016-05	PHYSICAL	Carconite Shot	
1995026-01	PHYSICAL	Tetrinious Shot	
1995027-01	PHYSICAL	Rabonius Shot	
1995028-01	PHYSICAL	General Exam	
1995030-01	PHYSICAL	Tetrinious Shot	
1995034-01	PHYSICAL	Tetrinious Shot	
1995035-01	PHYSICAL	Rabonius Shot	
1995035-02	PHYSICAL	General Exam	
1995041-01	PHYSICAL	General Exam	
1995042-01	INJURY	Repair complex fracture	Nystatine - 2 oz

Record: 1 of 144

Enter the medication name NUM

Figure 27-4: A datasheet with some of the records for the Medication Name field left blank.

Using Calculated Fields

Queries are not limited to actual fields from tables; you can also use *calculated fields* (created by performing some calculation). A calculated field can be created in many different ways, for example:

✦ Concatenating two Text type fields using the ampersand (&)

✦ Performing a mathematical calculation on two Number type fields

✦ Using an Access function to create a field based on the function

In the next example, you create a simple calculated field, Total Due, from the Outstanding Balance and Discount fields in the Customer table. Follow these steps:

1. Create a new query by using the Customer table.
2. Select the Outstanding Balance and Discount fields from the Customer table.
3. Click on an empty Field: cell of the QBE pane.
4. Press Shift+F2 to activate the Zoom box.
5. Type **Total Due: [Outstanding Balance]-[Outstanding Balance]*[Discount]**.
6. Select the OK button in the Zoom box (or press Enter).

Once you complete these steps, your query should look like Figure 27-5. `Total Due` is the calculated field name for the expression `[Outstanding Balance] - [Outstanding Balance] * [Discount]`. The field name and expression are separated by a colon.

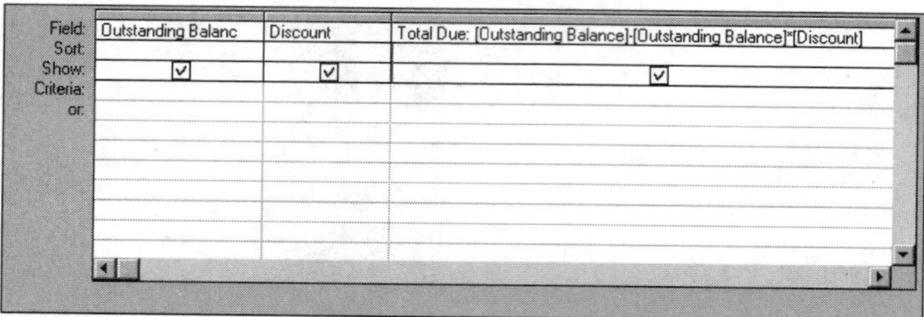

Figure 27-5: Creating a simple calculated field.

Access for Windows 95 has an Expression Builder you can use to help you create any expression — for example, a complex calculated field for a query. In the following example, you create a calculated field named Next Visit Date that displays a date six months later. You can use this date for a letter report you plan to send to all customers; the date is based on the Last Visit Date field of the Pets table. To create this calculated field, follow these steps:

1. Create a new query by using the Pets table.
2. Select the Pet Name, Type of Animal, and Last Visit Date fields from the Pets table.
3. Click on an empty Field: cell in the QBE pane.
4. Activate the Expression Builder by clicking on the Build button on the toolbar (wand). Another method: *right*-click to display the shortcut menu and select Build.

   Access displays the Expression Builder dialog box, as shown in Figure 27-6.

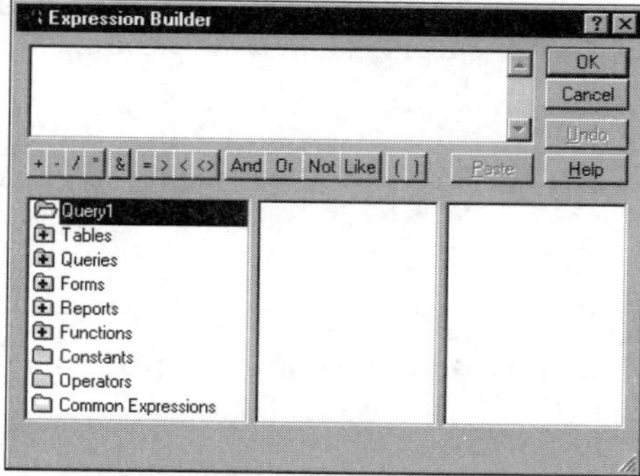

Figure 27-6: The Expression Builder dialog box.

Now build the expression **DateAdd("m",6,[Pets]![Last Visit Date])** for the calculated field.

5. Go to the bottom left window of the Expression Builder dialog box and expand the Functions tree (double click on it).

6. Select the Built-in Functions choice (double-click on it).

Access places information into the two windows to the right of the one you're in (see Figure 27-7).

7. Go to the third window (which lists all the functions).

8. Select the DateAdd function (double-click on it).

Access places the Function in the top left window, with information about the necessary parameters.

9. Go to the top left window and click on the parameter <interval>.

10. Type **"m"**.

11. Click on <number> and replace it with **6**.

12. Click on <date> and highlight it.

The function should look like the one in Figure 27-7.

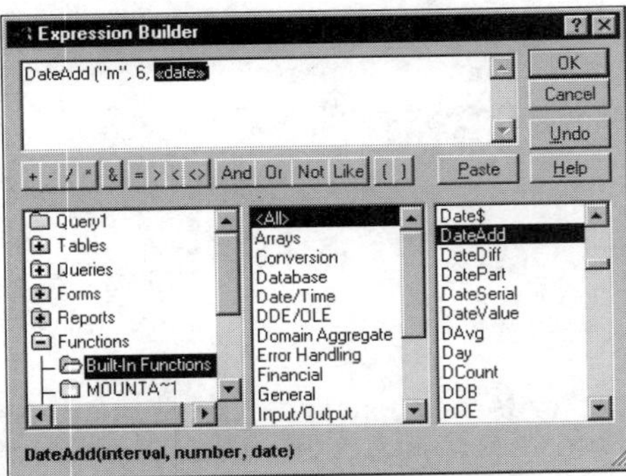

Figure 27-7: Creating a calculated field.

13. Go back to the bottom left window; double click on Tables.

14. Select the Pets table (click on it).

15. Select [Last Visit Date] from the middle window on the bottom (double-click on it).

Access places the table and field name in the last part of the DateAdd function.

16. Select the OK button in the Expression Builder.

    Access returns you to the QBE pane and places the expression in the cell for you.

17. Access assigns a name for the expression automatically, labeling it `Expr1`. Should your field now show this name, change it from `Expr1` to **Next Visit Date** by simply overwriting it.

If you perform these steps correctly, the cell looks like Figure 27-8. The DateAdd( ) function lets you add six months to Pets.Last Visit Date. The *m* signifies you are working with months rather than days or years.

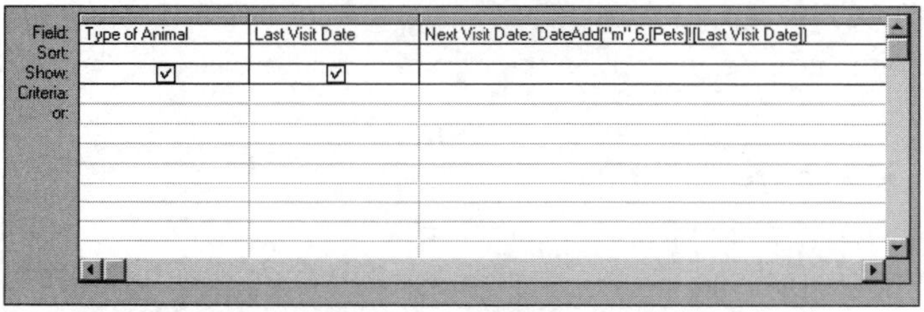

Field:	Type of Animal	Last Visit Date	Next Visit Date: DateAdd("m",6,[Pets]![Last Visit Date])
Sort:			
Show:	☑	☑	
Criteria:			
or:			

Figure 27-8: A calculated field named Next Visit Date.

Of course, you could type in the calculated field, but the Expression Builder is a valuable tool when you're creating complex, hard-to-remember expressions.

Finding the Number of Records in a Table or Query

To determine quickly the total number of records in an existing table or query, use the Count(*) function. This is a special use of the Count( ) function. For example, to determine the total number of records in the Pets table, follow these steps:

1. Start a new query using the Pets table.
2. Click on the first empty Field: cell in the QBE pane.
3. Type **Count(*)** in the cell.

Access adds the calculated field name `Expr1` to the cell in front of the Count( ) function. Your query should now look like Figure 27-9.

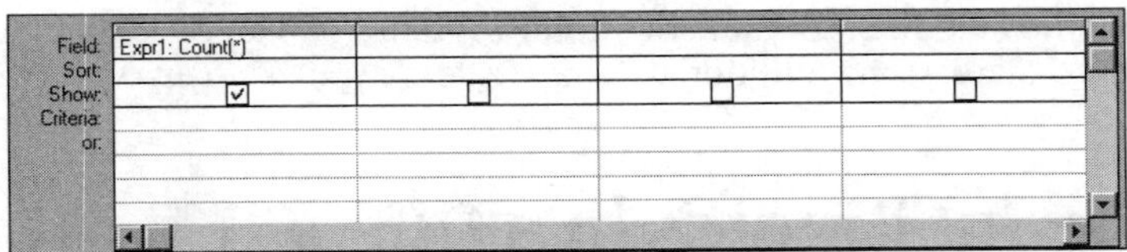

Figure 27-9: Using the Count(*) function.

When you look at the datasheet, you'll see a single cell that shows the number of records for the Pets table. The datasheet should look like the one in Figure 27-10.

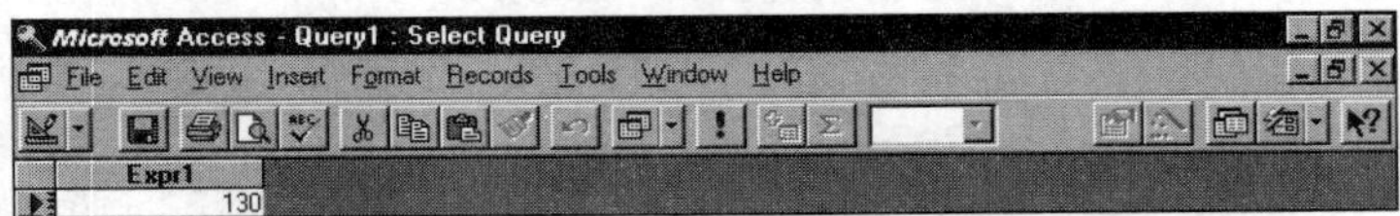

Figure 27-10: The datasheet of a Count(*) function.

If you use this function with the asterisk wild card (*), this is the only field that can be shown in the datasheet. That is why you entered the expression Count(*) in an empty QBE pane.

You can also use the Count(*) function to determine the total number of records that match a specific criterion. For example, you may want to know how many cats you have in the Pets table. Follow these steps to ascertain the number of cats in the table:

1. Start a new query and select the Pets table.
2. Click on the first empty Field: cell in the QBE pane.
3. Type **Count(*)** in the cell.
4. Double-click on the Type of Animal field of the Pets table.
5. Deselect the Show: cell for Type of Animal.
6. Type **"CAT"** in the Criteria: cell for Type of Animal.

Figure 27-11 shows how the query should look. If you select the Datasheet option from the Query View button on the toolbar, Access will again display only one cell in the datasheet; it contains the number of cats in the Pets table.

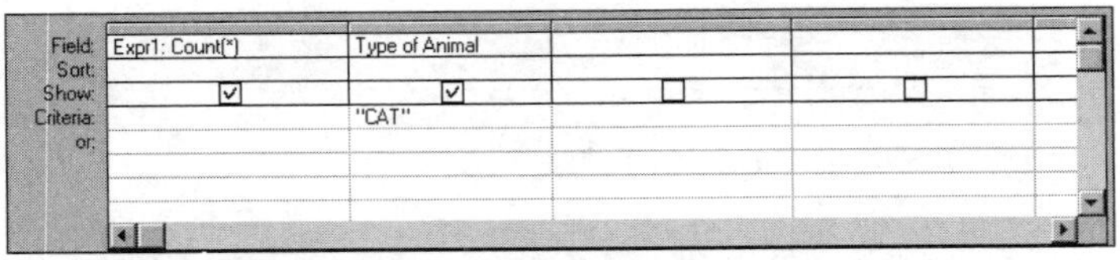

Figure 27-11: The query to show the number of cats.

Remember that only the field that contains the Count(*) function can be shown in the datasheet. If you try to display any additional fields, Access reports an error.

Finding the Top (*n*) Records in a Query

Access for Windows 95 not only enables you to find the number of records in an existing table or query, it also provides you with the capability of finding the query's first *(n)* records (that is, a set number or percentage of its records).

Suppose you want to identify the top ten animals you have treated — in other words, for which animal has which owner paid the most to your business? To determine the top ten animals and their owners, follow these steps:

1. Create a new query using the Customer, Pets, and Visits tables.
2. Select Customer Name from the Customer Table, Type of Animal and Pet Name from the Pets table, and Total Amount from the Visits table.
3. Click on the Totals button, Σ, on the toolbar.
4. Change Group By (under the Total Amount field) to **Sum**.
5. Sort the Total Amount field in Descending order.

   The resulting query should look like the one in Figure 27-12.

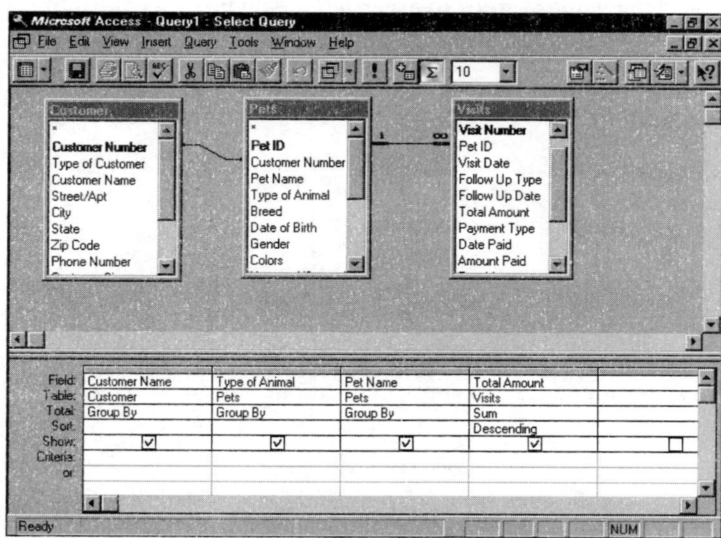

Figure 27-12: A total query with three Group By fields.

6. Click on the combo box next to the Σ button on the toolbar.
7. Select from the combo box or enter **10** in the Top Values property cell, as shown in Figure 27-12.

You are ready to run your query. When you click on the Query View button on the toolbar, you should see the top ten money-producing records in the dynaset, which should look like Figure 27-13.

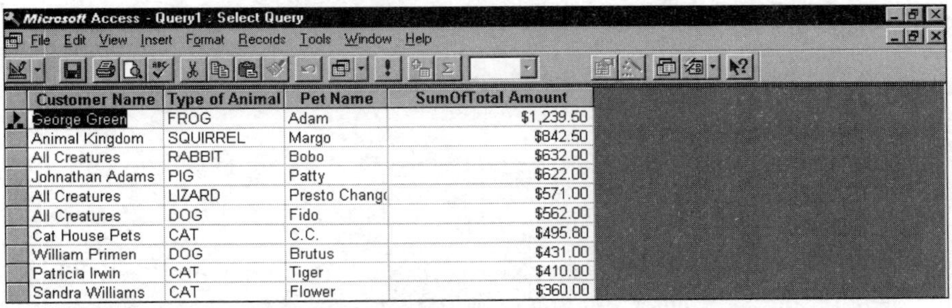

Customer Name	Type of Animal	Pet Name	SumOfTotal Amount
George Green	FROG	Adam	$1,239.50
Animal Kingdom	SQUIRREL	Margo	$842.50
All Creatures	RABBIT	Bobo	$632.00
Johnathan Adams	PIG	Patty	$622.00
All Creatures	LIZARD	Presto Chang(	$571.00
All Creatures	DOG	Fido	$562.00
Cat House Pets	CAT	C.C.	$495.80
William Primen	DOG	Brutus	$431.00
Patricia Irwin	CAT	Tiger	$410.00
Sandra Williams	CAT	Flower	$360.00

Figure 27-13: Dynaset of the top ten records in a query.

SQL-Specific Queries

Access for Windows 95 has added three query types that cannot be created by using the QBE pane; instead, you type the appropriate SQL statement directly into the SQL view window. These new *SQL-specific* queries are

✦ Union query: Combines common fields from more than one table or query into one recordset.

✦ Pass-through query: Allows you to send SQL commands directly to any SQL database server in the SQL database server's SQL syntax.

✦ Data definition query: Lets you create or alter database objects in Access databases directly.

To create any of these queries, select the type you want to create from the Query➪SQL Specific menu. (There is no applicable button available on the toolbar.)

Creating union queries

Union queries let you quickly combine several tables that have common fields. The resultant *snapshot* (like a dynaset) is not updatable.

For example, a competing veterinarian retires, and gives you all the client records from her practice. You decide to create a union query to combine the data from both practices. Figure 27-14 shows a union query that returns the Customer name and city in order (by city).

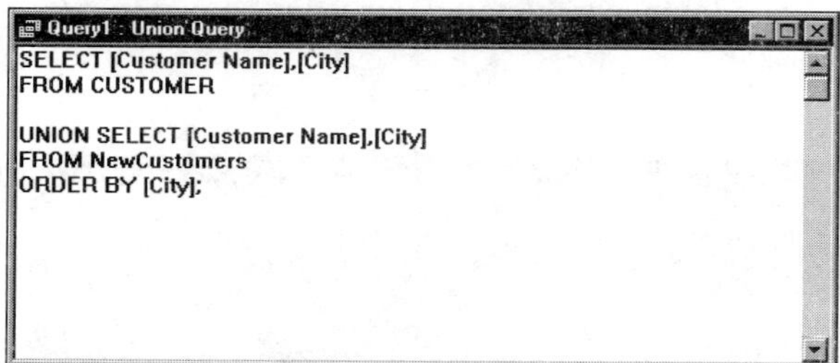

Figure 27-14: An SQL union query.

Notice that a union query has two or more SQL SELECT statements. Each SELECT statement requires the same number of fields, in the same order.

Creating pass-through queries

A *pass-through query* sends SQL commands directly to an SQL database server (such as Microsoft SQL Server, Oracle, and so on). You send the command by using the syntax required by the particular server. Be sure to consult the documentation for the appropriate SQL database server.

Figure 27-15 shows a pass-through query for a Microsoft SQL Server that creates a new table named Payroll and defines the fields in the table.

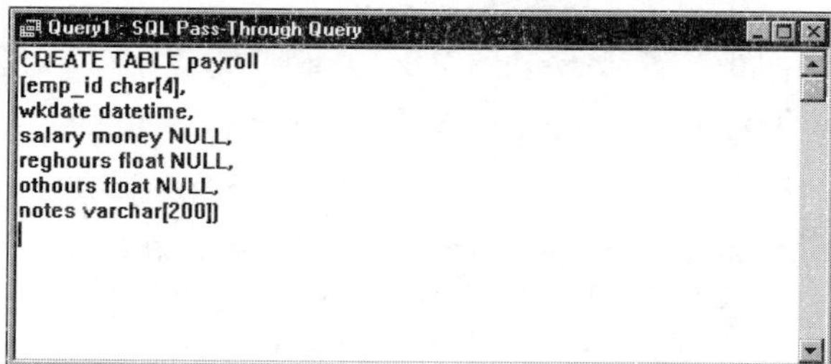

Figure 27-15: A pass-through query for SQL Server.

Warning: Never attempt to convert a pass-through query to another type of query. If you do, Access erases the entire SQL statement you typed in.

Warning: When working with pass-through queries, you should not perform operations that change the state of the connection. Halting a transaction in the middle (for example) may cause unexpected results.

Creating data definition queries

Of these three SQL-specific queries, the *data definition query* is the least useful. Everything you can do with it, you can also do using the design tools in Access. The data definition query is, however, an efficient way to create or change database objects. With a data definition query, you can use any of the following SQL statements:

- CREATE TABLE
- ALTER TABLE
- DROP TABLE
- CREATE INDEX
- DROP INDEX

How Queries Save Field Selections

When you open a query design, you may notice that the design has changed since you last saved the query. When you save a query, Access rearranges (even eliminates) fields on the basis of several rules. The following list summarizes these rules:

- If a field does not have the Show: box checked, but has criteria specified, Access moves it to the rightmost columns in the QBE pane.
- If a field does not have the Show: box checked, Access eliminates it from the QBE pane column unless it has sorting directives or criteria.
- If you create a totalling expression with the Sum operator in a total query, Access changes it to an expression using the Sum function.

Because of these rules, your query may look very different after you save and reopen it. In this section of the chapter, you learn how this happens (and some ways to prevent it).

Hiding (not showing) fields

Sometimes you won't want certain fields in the QBE pane to show in the actual dynaset of the datasheet. For example, you may want to use a field such as Customer Number to specify a criterion or a sort without showing the actual field.

To *hide,* or exclude, a field from the dynaset, you simply click off the Show: box under the field you want to hide. Figure 27-16 demonstrates this procedure. Notice that the field Type of Customer is used to specify a criteria of displaying only individuals ("1"). You don't want the Type of Customer field in the actual datasheet, so you click off the Show: cell for the Type of Customer field.

Field:	Type of Customer	Customer Name	Pet Name	Type of Animal
Table:	Customer	Customer	Pets	Pets
Sort:				
Show:	☐	☑	☑	☑
Criteria:	1			
or:				

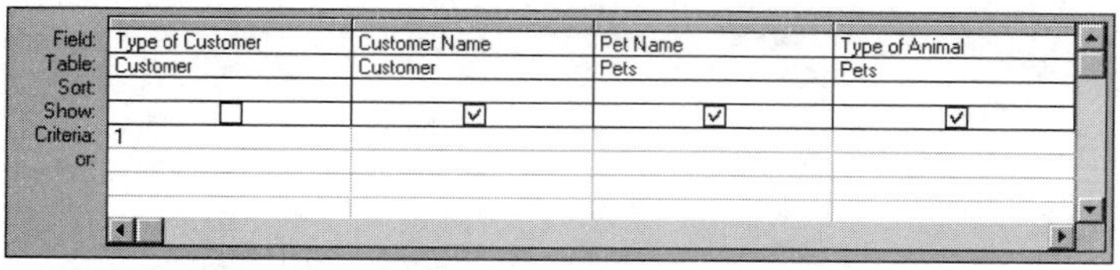

Figure 27-16: Hiding a field.

Any fields that have the Show: cell turned off (and for which you entered criteria) are placed at the end of the QBE pane when you save the query. Figure 27-17 shows the same query as Figure 27-16 after it is saved and brought back into the Design screen. Notice that the field `Type of Customer` has been moved to the end (extreme right) of the QBE pane. The location of a hidden field will not change the dynaset. Because the field is not displayed, its location in the QBE pane is unimportant. You always get the same results, even if you've placed a hidden field in the QBE pane.

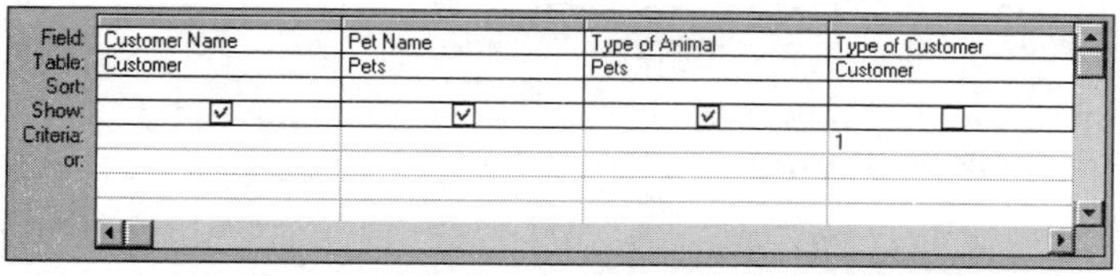

Field:	Customer Name	Pet Name	Type of Animal	Type of Customer
Table:	Customer	Pets	Pets	Customer
Sort:				
Show:	☑	☑	☑	☐
Criteria:				1
or:				

Figure 27-17: A query that has been saved with a hidden field.

Note

If you hide any fields in the QBE pane that are not used for sorts or criteria, Access eliminates them from the query automatically when you save it. If you want to use these fields and need to show them later, you'll have to add them back to the QBE pane.

Warning If you're creating a query to be used by a form or report, *you must show any fields it will use,* including any field to which you want to bind a control.

Renaming Fields in Queries

When working with queries, you can rename a field to describe the field's contents more clearly or accurately. For example, you may want to rename the Customer Name field to Owner Name. This is useful for working with calculated fields or calculating totals; Access automatically assigns nondescript names such as Expr1 or AvgOfWeight, but it's easy to rename fields in Access queries. To change the display name of the Customer Name field, for example, follow these steps:

1. Select the Customer table.
2. Double-click on the Customer Name field.
3. Place the cursor in front of the first letter of `Customer Name` in the Field: cell.
4. Type **Owner Name:** (be sure to include a colon).

Figure 27-18 shows the query field renamed. Notice that the field has both the display name, which is `Owner Name`, and the actual field name, which is `Customer Name`.

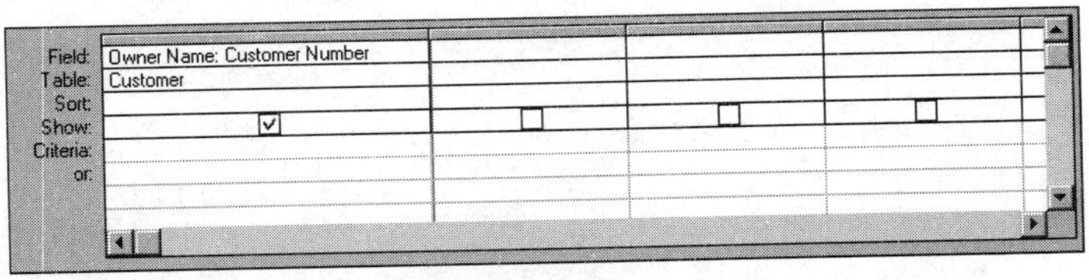

Field:	Owner Name: Customer Number			
Table:	Customer			
Sort:				
Show:	☑	☐	☐	☐
Criteria:				
or:				

Figure 27-18: Renaming a query field.

Note When naming a query field, you should delete any names assigned by Access (on the left of the colon). For example, remove the name `Expr1` when you name the calculated field.

If you rename a field, Access uses only the new name for the heading of the query datasheet; it does the same with the control source in any form or report that uses the query. Any new forms or reports you create on the basis of the query will use the new field name. (Access does not change the actual field name in the underlying table.)

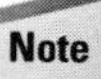

Note: If you *only* want to change the name that appears on the datasheet, change the Captions property of the Field: cell, typing the new name in this cell. This new name will then appear only when you view the datasheet; it will not show up in the query's design view.

When working with renamed fields, you can use an *expression name* (the new name you specified) in another expression within the same query. For example, you may have a calculated field called First Name that uses several Access functions to separate an individual's first name from the last name. For this calculated field, you can use the field called Owner Name you created earlier.

Warning: When you work with referenced expression names, you cannot have any criteria specified against the field you're referencing. For example, you cannot have a criterion specified for Owner Name if you reference Owner Name in the First Name calculation. If you do, Access will not display the contents for the expression field Owner Name in the datasheet.

Hiding and Unhiding Columns in the QBE Pane

Sometimes you may want to hide specific fields in the QBE pane. This is not the same as hiding a field by clicking on the Show box. Hiding a column in the QBE pane is similar to hiding a datasheet column, which is easy: You simply resize a column (from right to left) until it has no visible width. Figure 27-19 shows several fields in the QBE pane; in the next example, you hide one of its columns.

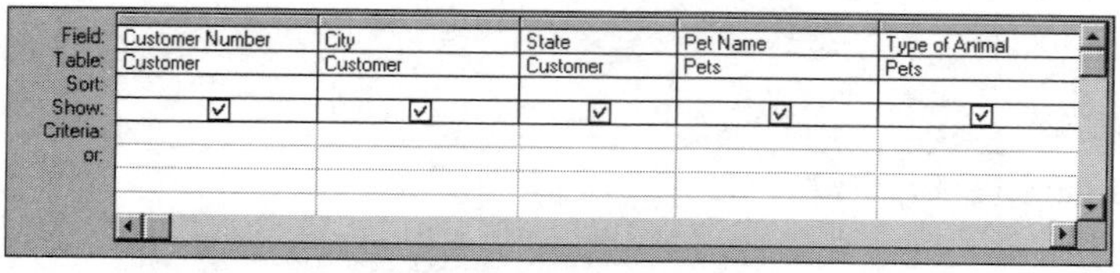

Field:	Customer Number	City	State	Pet Name	Type of Animal
Table:	Customer	Customer	Customer	Pets	Pets
Sort:					
Show:	☑	☑	☑	☑	☑
Criteria:					
or:					

Figure 27-19: A typical QBE pane.

Follow these steps to hide the City column:

1. Move the mouse pointer to the right side of the City field on the *field selector* (a small, thick bar icon with arrows on both sides).
2. Click on the right side of the City field, and drag it toward the Customer Name field until it totally disappears.

Figure 27-20 shows the QBE pane with the City field hidden.

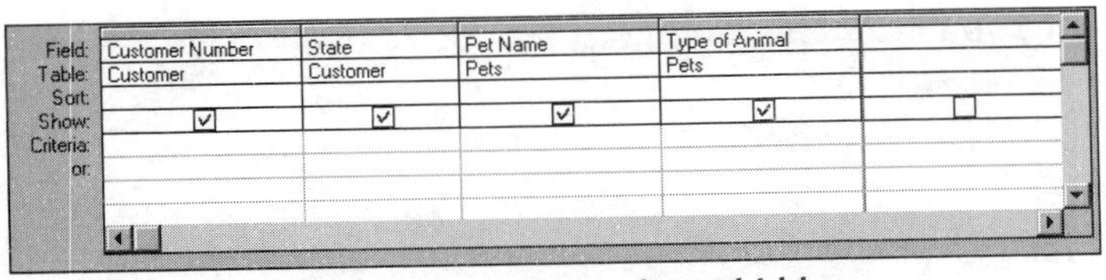

Figure 27-20: The QBE pane with a column hidden.

After you hide a field, you can *unhide* it by reversing the process. If you want to unhide the City column, follow these steps:

1. Move the mouse pointer to the left side of the field State on the selector bar (the bar with arrows appears). Make sure you are to the right of the divider between `Customer Name` and `State`.
2. Click on the left side of `State` and drag it toward the `Pet Name` field until you size the column to the correct length.
3. Release the button; the field name `City` will appear in the column you unhide.

Query Design Options

There are three default options you can specify when you work with a query design. You can view and set these options by selecting Tools⇨Options from the main Query menu, and then selecting the Tables/Queries tab. Figure 27-21 shows this Options dialog box.

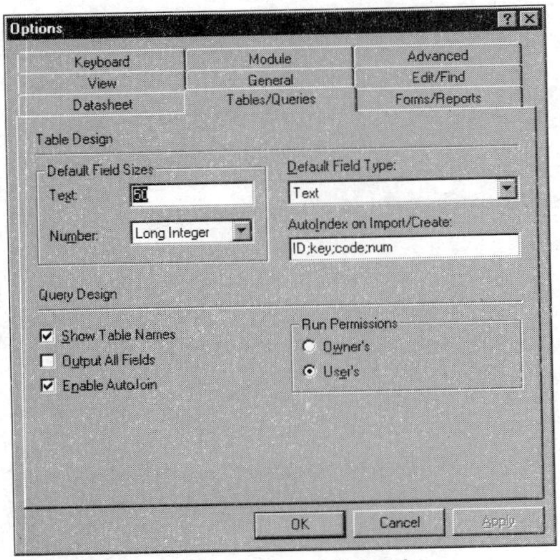

Figure 27-21: The Options dialog box.

Notice these four items you can set for queries:

✦ Output All Fields

✦ Run Permissions

✦ Show Table Names

✦ Enable AutoJoin

Generally the default for Show Table Names and Output All fields is No. Run Permissions offers you a choice of either the Owner's permission or the User's (the default). Finally, Enable AutoJoin controls whether Access will use common field names to perform an automatic join between tables that have no relationships set. Table 27-1 describes each option and its purpose.

Note: When you set query design options, they specify actions for new queries only; they do not affect the current query. To show table names in the current query, select View⇨Table Names from the main Query menu. To specify the other two options for the current query, select View⇨Properties....

Table 27-1
Query Design Options

Option	*Purpose*
Output All Fields	Shows all fields in the underlying tables, or only the fields displayed in the QBE pane
Run Permissions	Restricts use in a multiuser environment; a user restricted from viewing the underlying tables can still view the data from the query
Enable AutoJoin	Uses common field names to perform an automatic join between tables that have no relationships set
Show Table Names	Shows the Table: row in the QBE pane when set to Yes; hides the Table: row if set to No.

Setting Query Properties

To set query properties, either click on the Properties button on the toolbar, *right*-click on Properties and choose it from the shortcut menu, or select View⇨Properties from the main Query menu. Access displays a Query Properties dialog box. Your options depend on the query type and on the table or field with which you're working. Table 27-2 shows the Query-Level properties you can set.

You can use the Query-Level properties, just as you would the properties in forms, reports, and tables. *Query-Level properties* displayed when you click depend on the type of query being created.

Table 27-2
Query-Level Properties

Property	***Description***	***Query***					
		Select	***Crosstab***	***Update***	***Delete***	***Make-Table***	***Append***
Description	Text describing the table or query	X	X	X	X	X	X
Output All Fields	Show all fields from the underlying tables in the query	X				X	X
Top Values	Number of highest or lowest values to be returned	X				X	X
Unique Values	Return only unique field values in the dynaset	X				X	X
Unique Records	Return only unique records for the dynaset	X	X	X	X		X
Run Permissions	Establish permissions for the specified user	X	X	X	X	X	X
Source Database	External database name for all tables/queries in the query	X	X	X	X	X	X

(continued)

Table 27-2 (continued)

Property	***Description***	***Query***					
		Select	***Crosstab***	***Update***	***Delete***	***Make-Table***	***Append***
Source Connect Str	Name of application used to connect to external database	X	X	X	X	X	X
Record Locks	Records locked while query runs (usually action queries)	X	X	X	X	X	X
ODBC Timeout	Number of seconds before reporting error for opening DB	X	X	X	X	X	X
Filter	Filter name loaded automatically with query	X	X	X	X	X	X
Order By	Sort loaded automatically with query	X	X	X	X	X	X

An SQL Primer

When you use graphical Query By Example, Access converts what you create into a *Structured Query Language (SQL)* statement. This SQL statement is what Access actually executes when the query runs.

Many relational databases use SQL as a standardized language to query and update tables. It is relatively simple to learn and use. Even so, Access does not require you know it or use it — though Access uses it, you won't ever have to know it's there.

Viewing SQL Statements in Queries

If you're familiar with SQL, you can view and/or edit an SQL statement. If you make changes to an SQL statement, Access reflects them automatically in the QBE pane.

To view an SQL statement that Access creates, select View⇨SQL … from the Query menu. Figure 27-22 shows a typical SQL statement that will display the fields Customer Name and State for dogs in Idaho or Oregon.

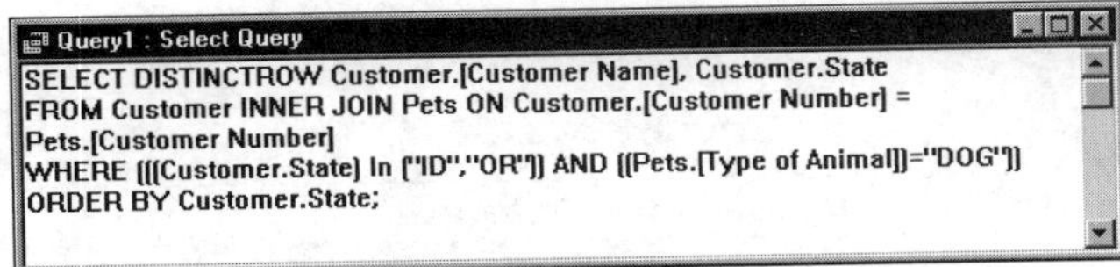
```
Query1 : Select Query
SELECT DISTINCTROW Customer.[Customer Name], Customer.State
FROM Customer INNER JOIN Pets ON Customer.[Customer Number] =
Pets.[Customer Number]
WHERE (((Customer.State) In ("ID","OR")) AND ((Pets.[Type of Animal])="DOG"))
ORDER BY Customer.State;
```

Figure 27-22: An SQL statement in Access.

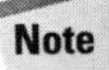

Note If you want to modify an existing SQL statement or create your own, enter changes directly into the SQL dialog box. To add new lines in the dialog box, press Ctrl+Enter.

You can use SQL statements directly in expressions, macros, forms, and reports. You might use one, for example, in the RowSource or RecordSource properties of a form or report. Even so, you don't have to "know the language" to use SQL statements directly. You can simply create the needed statement (for such purposes as selecting specific records) in the Query window. Then you activate the SQL dialog box and copy (Ctrl+C) the entire SQL statement you created. Switch to where you want to use the statement, and then paste it (Ctrl+V) where you need it (for example, the RowSource property of the property sheet).

Tip You can create SQL statements in the SQL dialog box. Whether you write your own statement or edit one, Access updates the Query window when you leave the dialog box. Tables are added to the top portion; fields and criteria are added to the QBE pane.

An SQL primer

Up until now, you have created queries using the query designer of Access. You have even been told you can examine the SQL statement Access builds selecting View➪SQL from the menu.

As you already know, one way to learn SQL statements is to build a query graphically and then view the corresponding SQL statement. Earlier, for example, Figure 27-22 showed the following SQL statement:

```
SELECT DISTINCTROW Customer.[Customer Name], Customer.State
FROM Customer
INNER JOIN Pets ON Customer.[Customer Number] = Pets.[Customer
      Number]
WHERE (((Customer.State) In ("ID","OR"))
AND ((Pets.[Type of Animal])="DOG"))
ORDER BY Customer.State;
```

Four common SQL commands

This statement uses the four most common SQL commands. Table 27-3 shows each command and explains its purpose.

Table 27-3
Four Common SQL Keywords

Command	*Purpose in SQL Statement*
SELECT	This command/keyword starts an SQL statement. It is followed by the names of the fields that will be *selected* from the table or tables (if more than one is specified in the FROM clause/command). This is a *required* keyword.
FROM	This clause/keyword specifies the name(s) of the table(s) containing the fields specified in the SELECT command. This is a *required* keyword.
WHERE	This command specifies any condition used to filter (limit) the records that will be viewed. This keyword is used only when you want to limit the records to a specific group on the basis of the condition.
ORDER BY	This command specifies the order in which you want the resulting dataset (the selected records that were found and returned) to appear.

Using these four basic commands, you can build very powerful SQL statements to use in your Access forms and reports.

Note

The DISTINCTROW keyword

The DISTINCTROW keyword in the preceding SQL statement is an *optional* predicate keyword. Access uses it as a *restricter keyword* to specify which records should be returned. This predicate keyword is not used by other SQL database languages. In Access, it limits the display of duplicate records, basing its restrictions on the values of the entire duplicate record. It works like the DISTINCT predicate of other SQL languages, except DISTINCT works against duplicate fields within the SELECT statement. DISTINCTROW works against their records (even fields that are not in the SELECT statement). This is covered in more detail later.

The SELECT command

The SELECT command (or *clause*) is the first word found in two query types; in a select query or make-table query, the SELECT clause specifies the field(s) you want displayed in the Results table.

After specifying the keyword SELECT, you need to specify the fields you want to display (for more than one, use a comma between the fields). The general syntax is:

SELECT *Field_one, Field_two, Field_three …*

where *Field_one*, *Field_two*, etc. are replaced with the name of the table fields.

Notice that commas separate each field in the list from the others. For instance, if you want to specify customer name and city using fields from the Customer table, you would specify the following:

```
SELECT [Customer Name], City
```

If you need to view fields from more than one table, you should specify the name of the tables in which to find the fields. If you want to select fields from both the Customer and Pets table, for example, the SELECT clause would look like this:

```
SELECT Customer.[Customer Name], Customer.City,
Pets.[Type of Animal], Pets.[Pet Name]
```

When you build a query in Access, it places the table name before the field name automatically. In reality, you need only specify the table name if more than one table in the SQL statement have fields with the same name. For instance, a field named `[Customer Number]` appears in both the Customer table and the Pets table. If you want to SELECT a `[Customer Number]` field in your SQL statement, you *must* specify which of these to use — the one in Customer or the one in Pets.

The following SQL SELECT clause demonstrates the syntax:

```
SELECT Customer.[Customer Number], [Customer Name], City,
[Type of Animal], [Pet Name]
```

Tip Although table names are *not* required for nonduplicate fields in an SQL statement, it's a good idea to use them anyway for clarity.

Tip You can use the asterisk wild card (*) to specify that all fields should be selected. If you're going to select all fields from more than one table, specify the table, a period (.), and then the name of the field — in this case, the asterisk.

Using the brackets around field names

Notice that the SELECT clause just described uses brackets around the field name Customer Name. Any field name that has spaces within it requires the use of brackets.

Specifying SELECT Predicates

When you create a SELECT SQL statement, several predicates can be associated with the SELECT clause. These are:

- ALL
- DISTINCT
- DISTINCTROW
- TOP

Use them to restrict the number of records returned. They can work in conjunction with the WHERE clause of an SQL statement.

The ALL predicate is the default. It selects all records that meet the WHERE condition specified in the SQL statement. Selecting it is optional (it's the default value).

Use the DISTINCT predicate when you want to omit records that contain duplicate data in the fields specified in the SELECT clause. For instance, if you create a query and want to look at both the Customer Name and the Type of Animal the customer owns, *without* considering the number of animals of a given type, the SELECT statement would be:

```
SELECT DISTINCT [Customer name], [Type of Animal]
```

If a customer owns two dogs — that is, has two Dog records (one named Bubba and one named Killer) in the Pets table — only one record will appear in the resulting datasheet. The DISTINCT predicate tells Access to show only one record if the values in the selected fields are duplicates (that is, same customer number and same type of animal). Even though there are two different records in the Pets table, only one is shown. DISTINCT eliminates duplicates on the basis of the fields selected to view.

The DISTINCTROW predicate is unique to Access. It works much like DISTINCT, with one big difference: It looks for duplicates on the basis of *all* fields in the table(s), not just the selected fields. For instance, if a customer has two different Dog records in the Pets table, and uses the predicate DISTINCTROW (replacing DISTINCT) in the SQL statement just described, *both* records will be displayed. DISTINCTROW looks for duplicates in all the fields of the Customer and Pets tables. If any field is different (in this case, the name of the pet), then both records are displayed in the datasheet.

The TOP predicate is also unique to Access. It lets you restrict the number of displayed records, basing the restriction on the WHERE condition to the TOP <number> of values. For instance, TOP 10 will display only the first 10 records that match the WHERE condition. You can use TOP to display the top five customers who have spent money on your services. For instance, the following SELECT clause will display the top five records:

```
SELECT TOP 5 [Customer Name]
```

The TOP predicate has an optional keyword, PERCENT, that displays the top number of records on the basis of a percentage rather than a number. To see the top 2 percent of your customers, you would use a SELECT clause like this one:

```
SELECT TOP 2 PERCENT [Customer Name]
```

The FROM clause of an SQL statement

As the name suggests, the FROM clause (command) specifies the tables (or queries) that hold the fields named in the SELECT clause. This clause is required; it tells SQL where to find the records.

When you're working with one table (as in the original example), the FROM clause simply specifies the table name:

```
SELECT [Customer Name], City,

FROM Customer
```

When you are working with more than one table, you can supply a TableExpression to the FROM clause to specify which data will be retrieved. The FROM clause is where you set the relationship between two or more tables for the SELECT statement. This link will be used to display the data in the resulting data sheet.

The TableExpression can be one of three types:

- ✦ INNER JOIN … ON
- ✦ RIGHT JOIN … ON
- ✦ LEFT JOIN …ON

Use INNER JOIN … ON to specify the traditional equi-join of Access. For instance, to join Customers to Pets via the Customer Number field in the FROM clause, the command would be

```
SELECT  Customer.[Type of Customer], pets.[Type of Animal]
FROM Customer INNER JOIN pets ON Customer.[Customer Number] =
      pets.[Customer Number]
```

Notice that the FROM clause specifies the main table to use (Customer). Then the INNER JOIN portion of the FROM clause specifies the second table to use (Pets). Finally, the ON portion of the FROM clause specifies which fields will be used to join the table together.

The LEFT JOIN and RIGHT JOIN work exactly the same, except they specify an outer join instead of an inner join (equi-join).

The WHERE clause of an SQL statement

Use the WHERE clause (command) of the SQL statement only when you want to specify a condition. (This clause is optional, unlike the SELECT/DELETE … and FROM.)

The original SQL statement we started with (for example) specified the following WHERE clause:

```
WHERE (Customer.[Type of Customer]=2)
```

The WHERE condition can be any valid expression. It can be a simple, one-condition expression (such as the one just given) or a complex expression based on several criteria.

Note: If you use the WHERE clause, it *must* follow the FROM clause of the SQL statement.

The ORDER BY clause

Use the ORDER BY clause to specify a sort order. It will sort the displayed data by the field(s) you specify after the clause, in ascending or descending order. In the original example, you specified a sort order by Customer Number:

```
ORDER BY Customer.[Customer Name];
```

Specifying the end of an SQL statement

Since an SQL statement can be as long as 64,000 characters, you need a way to tell the database language that you've finished creating the statement. End an SQL statement with a semicolon (;).

Tip: Access is very forgiving about the ending semicolon. If you forget to place one at the end of an SQL statement, Access will assume it should be there, and run the SQL statement as if it were there.

Warning: If you place a semicolon *inside* an SQL statement accidentally, Access will report an error and attempt to tell you where it occurred.

Using SELECT, FROM, WHERE, and SORT BY, you can create some very powerful SQL statements to display and view data from your tables.

For instance, build an SQL statement that will do the following:

1. Select the Customer's Name and City, Pet Name and Type of Animal fields.
2. Join FROM the Customer and Pets tables, where the Customer and Pets table are linked ON the Customer number.
3. Display only records where the Customer is a pet store (type = 2).
4. Sort the data in order by the Customer number.

The SQL statement could be:

```
SELECT [Customer Name], City, [Pet Name], [Type of Animal]
FROM Customer INNER JOIN Pets ON Customer.[Customer Number] =
      Pets.[Customer Number]
WHERE [Type of Customer] = 2
ORDER BY Customer.[Customer number];
```

This is simply a quick overview of SQL statements and how to create them in Access for Windows 95; various other clauses (commands) can be used with SQL statements. SQL is relatively easy to understand and work with. It offers several benefits and power over creating graphical queries and using queries.

Summary

In this chapter, you worked with queries in great detail. The chapter covered the following points:

- ✦ When you're working with lookup tables, always set an outer join that points to the lookup table. An alternative is to use the DLookUp( ) function.
- ✦ When using tables in queries, open (use) only the tables whose fields you will use. Because Access creates equi-joins automatically, you may not see all the records unless you set outer joins.
- ✦ You can create calculated fields for display, set criteria against them, and even sort on them in a query.
- ✦ If you hide a field and save the query, Access moves the hidden field to the end of the display. If you don't use a hidden field for a criterion or sort and you save the query, Access deletes the hidden field from the QBE pane.
- ✦ Columns in the QBE pane can be hidden and unhidden by clicking on the side of the field on the selector bar and dragging it until the field disappears.
- ✦ Query properties are optional for all queries except make-table and append queries.
- ✦ SQL statements can be viewed and modified. If you modify an SQL statement, Access updates the QBE pane automatically to reflect the changes.
- ✦ You can use SQL statements in expressions, macros, forms, and reports by copying and pasting them where you need them.

In the following chapter, you learn how to create multiple-table forms.

✦ ✦ ✦

Creating and Using Subforms

In This Chapter

What is a subform?

How to create a subform with a Wizard

How to create a subform by dragging a form from the Database window to a form

How to add validation to a subform

How to add totals to a subform

Subforms give you great flexibility in displaying and entering data with multiple tables. You can still edit all the fields without worrying about integrity problems. With a subform, you can even enter data into a one-to-many form relationship.

What Is a Subform?

Simply put, a *subform* is a form within a form. It lets you use data from more than one table in a form; you can display data from one table in one format while using a different format for data from the other table. You can, for example, display one customer record in a form while displaying several pet records in a datasheet subform.

Although you can edit multiple tables on a typical form, using a subform gives you the flexibility to display data from several tables or queries at once.

As you may recall, you can display data on a form in several ways:

Form	Display one record on a form
Continuous	Display multiple records on a form
Datasheet	Display multiple records using one line per record

Including a subform on your form enables you to display your data in multiple formats, as in Figure 28-1. This figure shows a form for entering visit details. It shows data from a query that lists information from the Customer, Pets, and Visits tables at the top, in a form view. At the bottom is a subform that displays information from the Visit Details table. Notice that both the form and the subform have record selectors; each acts independently.

The subform actually contains data from three tables. In addition to its data from Visit Details, the subform shows descriptions of each treatment from the Treatments table, and medication listings from the Medications table. As you'll learn when you create this form later in the chapter, a drop-down list box appears when you select either of these latter fields in the datasheet. Each one is actually a combo box that lets you select a description from the Treatments or Medications table; then it will store the appropriate code in the Visit Details table for you.

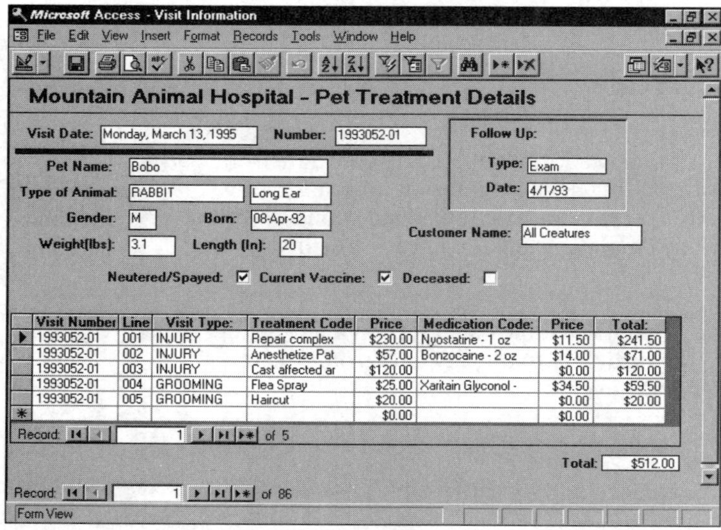

Figure 28-1: The form for adding visit details.

When you create a subform, you link the main form to it by a common field of expression. The subform will then display only records that are related to the main form. The greatest advantage of subforms is their ability to show the one-to-many relationship. The main form represents the *one* part of the relationship; the subform represents the *many* side.

You can create a subform in several ways:

- ✦ Using the Form Wizard as you create a new form
- ✦ Using the Subform Wizard in a existing form

✦ Using the Subform button in the toolbox and modifying control properties

✦ Dragging a form from the Database window to another form

Creating Subforms with the Form Wizard

The Access Form Wizard can create a form with an embedded subform if you choose more than one table (or use a query with more than one table). If you don't use the Wizard, you have to create both the form and subform separately; then you embed the subform and link it to the main form.

Creating the form and selecting the Form Wizard

Both the form and the subform are created automatically by the Form Wizard when you specify more than one table in a one-to-many relationship. In this example, you create a form that displays information from the Customer table in the main form; the subform shows information from the Pets table. To create the form, follow these steps:

1. Create a new form by selecting the Forms tab in the Database window and clicking on the New button.
2. Select Form Wizard in the New Form dialog box; select the Customer table from the Tables/Queries combo box. (See Figure 28-2.)

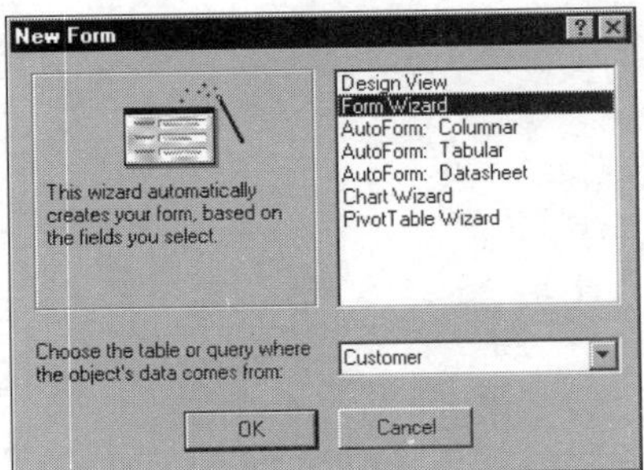

Figure 28-2: Selecting the Form Wizard.

New! Access 2.0 users should note that there is no Main/Subform Wizard in Access for Windows 95. The standard Form Wizard handles the process of creating a new form with a subform automatically.

Note Selecting the Customer table when you begin the Wizard is a mere convenience. You can select a different table in the next dialog box.

After you select the Form Wizard, you need to select the fields for the main part of the form.

Choosing the fields for the main form

You now select each of the fields you want in the main form. The Customer table will be used for the these fields. Figure 28-3 shows the completed field selection. To select the fields for this example, follow these steps:

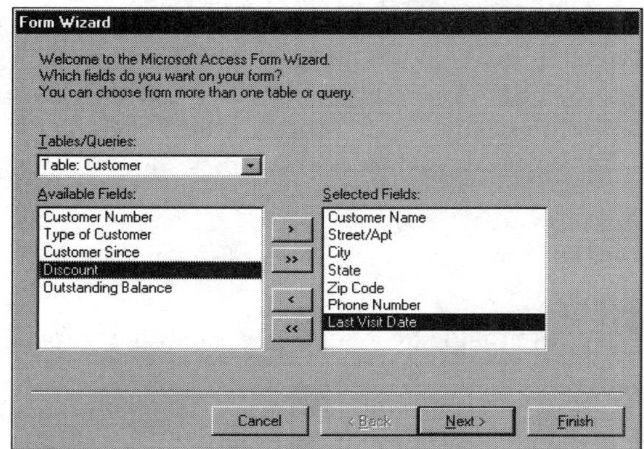

Figure 28-3: Selecting the fields for the main form.

1. Select Customer Name and select the > button.
2. Select Street/Apt and select the > button.
3. Select City and select the > button.
4. Select State and select the > button.
5. Select Zip Code and select the > button.
6. Select Phone Number and select the > button.
7. Select Last Visit Date and select the > button.

Selecting the subform table or query

Because a subform uses a data source separate from the form, you have to select the table or query to be used with the subform. To select the subform table/query, select the Pets table from the list box, as shown in Figure 28-4.

You will notice after a few seconds that the field list below in the Available Fields list box changes to display fields in the Pets table. The fields already selected from the Customer table in the Selected Fields list box remain.

Choosing the fields for the subform

Fields for the subform are selected in exactly the same way as fields for the main form. Those you select from the Pets table will be added to the list of fields already selected from the Customer table.

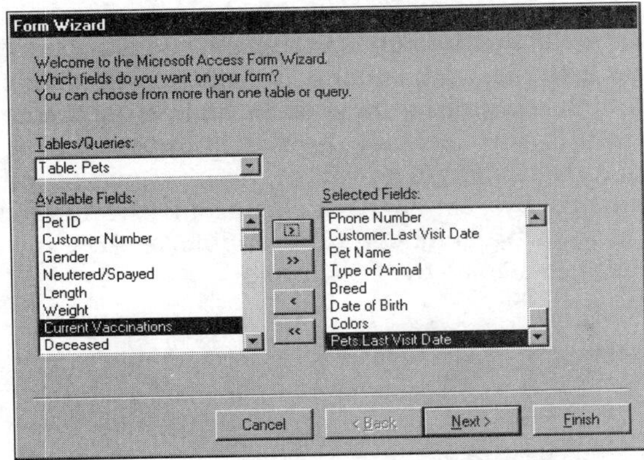

Figure 28-4: Selecting the fields for the subform.

To select the fields for the subform, follow these steps:

1. Select Pet Name and select the > button.
2. Select Type of Animal and select the > button.
3. Select Breed and select the > button.
4. Select Date of Birth and select the > button.
5. Select Colors and select the > button.
6. Select Pets Last Visit Date and select the > button.
7. Select the Next > button to move to the next dialog box.

Note Notice the Pets Last Visit Date field in the Selected Fields list box. Because both tables have a field named Last Visit Date, a prefix is added from the table that uniquely identifies the field.

After you select the fields for the subform, you can move to the next Wizard screen to decide how the linkage between forms will be built and how the data on the form will look.

Selecting the Form Data Layout

The next dialog box is shown as part of conceptual diagram in Figure 28-5. A multi-table relationship gives you many ways to lay out the data. The top part of the figure shows an automatic decision Access makes on the basis of the one-to-many relationship between Customer and Pets. The data is viewed by Customer, with a subform with the Pets data.

In the left side of the dialog box, you can choose how you want to view your form. Below the field view diagram, you can select whether you want to see your data as a Form with subform(s) or as Linked forms.

In the top part of the figure that shows the entire Form Wizard dialog box, you can see the form with a subform: Customer fields are in the main form, and Pets fields are in the subform. The bottom left part of the diagram shows conceptually what the data would look like if you viewed the data by Pets instead. The data from both tables would be placed in a single form. The bottom right part of the figure shows how it would look if you chose to view the data by Customer but chose Linked forms instead. Rather than creating a Customer form with an embedded Pets subform, Access would create a Customer form with a button to display the Pets form.

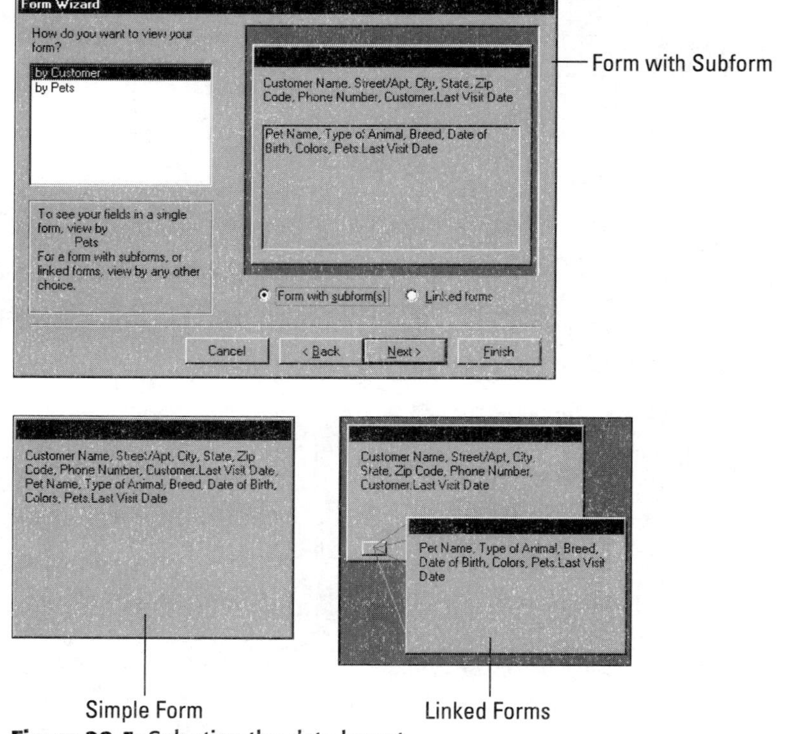

Figure 28-5: Selecting the data layout.

Once you select the type of form you want (the data is viewed `by Customer`, with a `Form with subform(s)` with the Pets data) you can click on the Next> button to move to the subform layout screen.

Selecting the Subform Layout

When you create a form with an embedded subform, you must decide what type of layout to use for the subform. The two possibilities are *tabular* and *datasheet*. The datasheet is the default, but it may not be the choice you want to accept. Datasheets are rigid by nature; you can't change certain characteristics (such as adding multiline column headers or precisely controlling the location of the fields below). You can choose a tabular layout for added flexibility. Where a datasheet combines the headers and data into a single control type (the datasheet itself), a tabular form places the column headers in a form header section, placing the field controls in the form's detail section.

Select the Datasheet layout as shown in Figure 28-6.

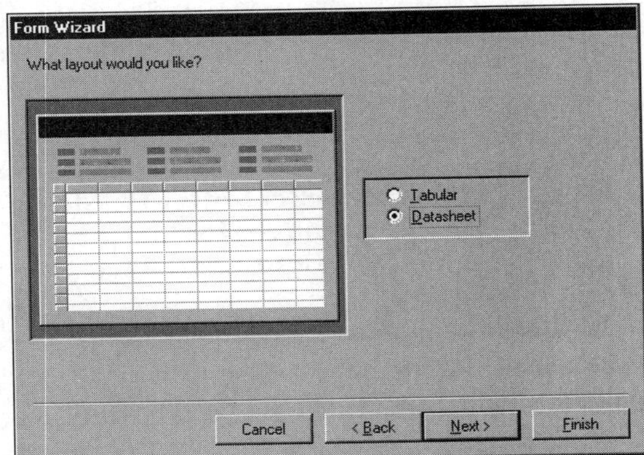

Figure 28-6: Selecting the subform layout.

Selecting the form style

As with other Form Wizards, you can determine how the form will look by selecting one of the AutoFormat choices. The style applies to the main form. The subform, displayed as either a separate tabular form or a datasheet, has the same look.

Cross Ref Chapter 9 explains determining a form's look, and Form Wizards in general, in more detail.

The final dialog box lets you select the title for the form and the subform.

Selecting the form title

You can accept the default titles (the table names Access gives the main form and subform), or you can enter a custom title. The text you enter appears in the form header section of the main form. (See Figure 28-7.)

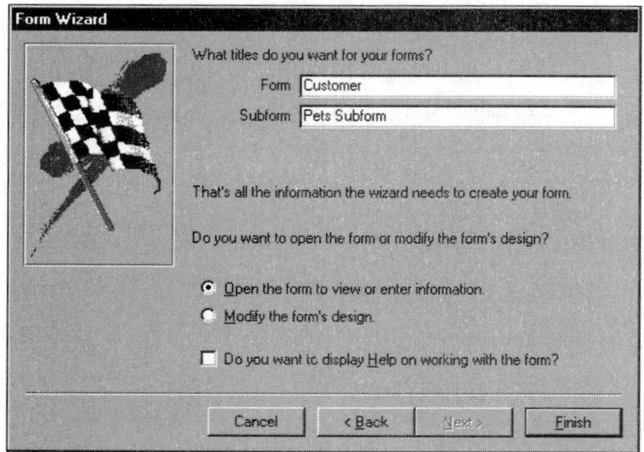

Figure 28-7: Selecting titles for the form and subform.

When you accept the names (or enter a name of your choice), the subform is saved as a form; it will appear in the Database window when you select Forms. You should try to name your forms and subforms something similar so you can tell that they go together. After you complete this step, you can view your form or its design.

Displaying the form

After the subform is named, the screen displays either the form or its design, depending on the option button you choose. In this example, you see the form as shown in Figure 28-8.

The tabular form layout was chosen for the subform. Whether you create your subform through a Wizard, by dragging one to the form, or by using the toolbox, Access creates either a datasheet or tabular (continuous) form. You can change it by changing the Default View property to either Single Form, Continuous Form (Tabular), or Datasheet.

You can change the look of the subform by moving to Design View and double-clicking on the subform control. This displays the subform's main form; there you change the subform all you like. You can move fields around, adjust the column widths, change the formatting, modify the distance between rows, and rearrange the columns. When you make these changes, you'll see them in effect the next time you view the subform. If you scroll down to the bottom of the subform, you'll notice that the asterisk (*) appears in the record selector column. As with any continuous form or datasheet, you can add new records by using this row.

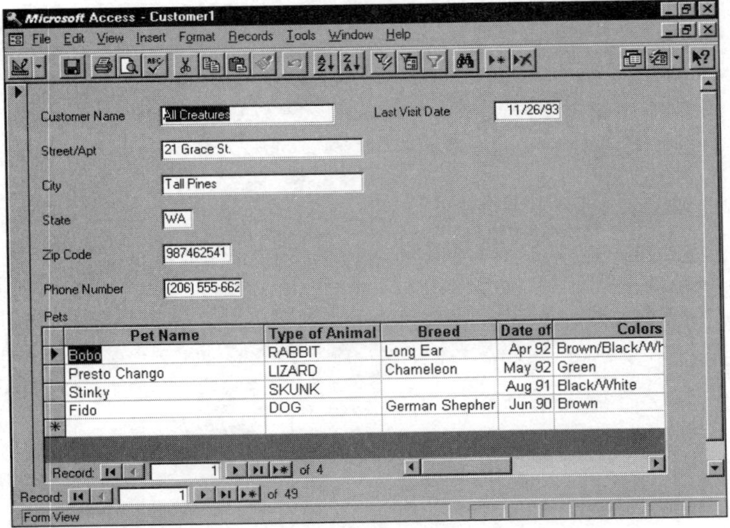

Figure 28-8: The Customer and Pets form.

Both the main form and the subform have record selectors because they are actually separate forms. As you use the outer record selector in the main form, you move from one customer record to another, and the link automatically changes which pets are displayed. This way, when you look at the record for All Creatures, you see pets for All Creatures. When you switch to Animal Kingdom, its pets are displayed.

When you use the inner record selector of the subform, you can scroll the records within the tabular form or datasheet. This is especially important if there are more records in the subform than can be displayed in the subform area. You can use the scrollbar too.

Displaying the main form design

To understand how the forms are actually linked from main form to subform, view the main form in Design View, as in Figure 28-9.

The design for the main form shows the fields from the Customer table at the top and the subform control at the bottom. The subform control is similar to other controls (such as the unbound object control). It stores the name of the subform, however, rather than storing the names of the fields in the form. When you run the form, Access retrieves the subform, displaying the fields in the subform.

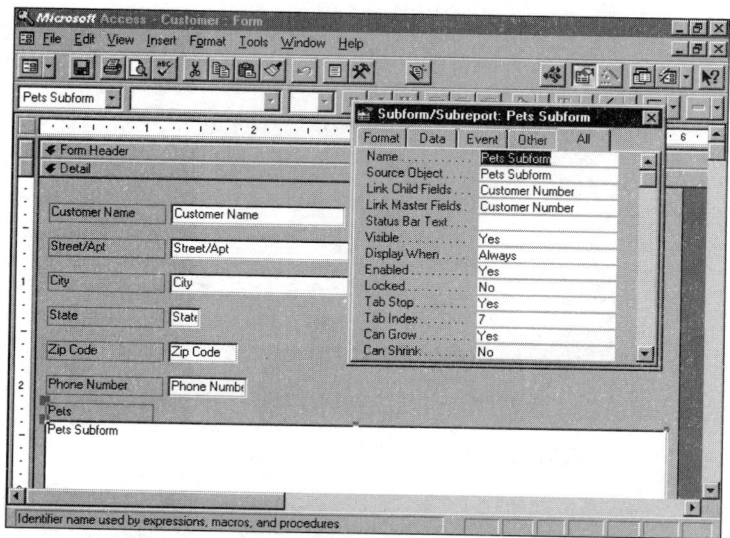

Figure 28-9: The Customer and Pets main form design.

Warning You must always create first the form you intend to use as a subform; the main form will not be usable until the subform form is created.

The Subform control property sheet is also shown. Notice the two properties Link Child Fields and Link Master Fields; these determine the link between the main form and the subform. The field name from the main table/query is entered in the Link Master Fields property. The field name from the subform table/query is entered in the Link Child Fields property. When the form is run, the link determines which records from the child form are displayed in the subform.

Note This control is used for both subforms and subreports.

Displaying the subform design

To understand how the subform is actually built, view the subform in Design View (as shown in Figure 28-10). A subform is simply another form; it can be run by itself without a main form. In fact, you should always test your subform by itself before running it as part of another form.

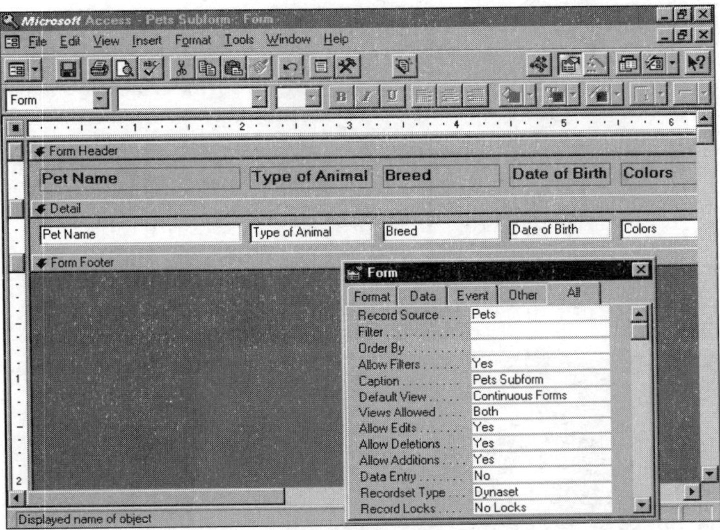

Figure 28-10: The Pets subform design.

Tip

A subform that will be viewed as a datasheet needs only to have its fields added in the order you want them to appear in the datasheet. Remember that you can rearrange the fields in the datasheet.

In Figure 28-10, you can see that all the fields are from the Pets table. You can also create a subform design with fields from multiple tables by using a query as the data source.

Notice that in the Form property sheet for the Pets subform, the Default View property is set to Continuous Forms. This means the subform is displayed as a continuous form, whether run by itself or used in a form. You can change it to datasheet if you want, or create a multiple-line form (which would then display its multiple lines in a subform).

Tip

You can use the form footer of a subform to calculate totals or averages, and then use the results on the main form. You learn how to do this later in the chapter.

The Form Wizard is a great place to start when creating a form with a subform. In the next section, however, you learn to create a subform without using a Form Wizard. Then you customize the subform to add combo box selections for some of the fields, as well as calculating both row and column totals.

Creating a Simple Subform Without Wizards

As mentioned earlier, there are several ways to create a subform without Wizards. You can drag a form from the Database window to a form, or you can use the Subform tool in the toolbox. The most desirable way is to drag the form from the Database window, because Access will try to create the links for you.

Disk

In this section, you create the form shown in Figure 28-11. The entire form is on your disk in the Mountain Animal Hospital database, and is called Adding Visit Details. The completed subform is called Data for Subform Example.

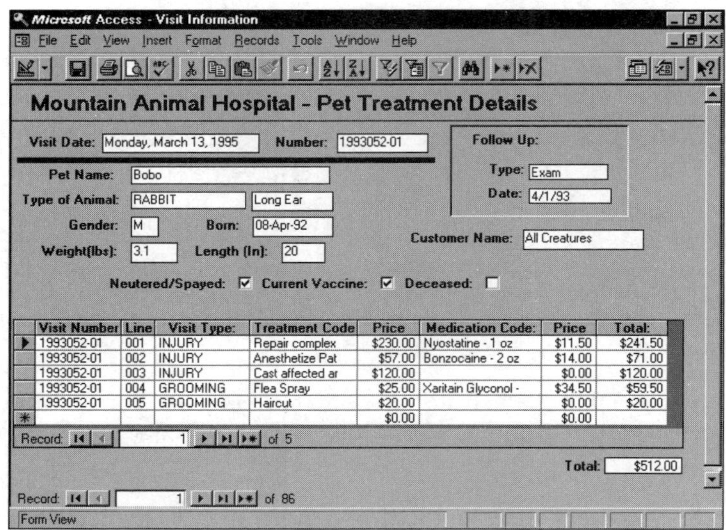

Figure 28-11: The Adding Visit Details form.

In this chapter, you'll work only with the Adding Visit Details form as a main form; you create and embed the Data for Subform Example form as a subform. (You may want to copy the Adding Visit Details form from the example disk and then delete the subform and subform totals box. You can use that copy to create the main form for this section of the chapter, and save yourself a great deal of work.)

The Adding Visit Details form is divided into several sections. The top half uses the query Pets, Owners, and Visits to display data from the Pets, Customer, and Visits tables. The Adding Visit Details form's only purpose is to let you add or review details about an existing visit. The middle of the form contains the subform that displays information about the visit details in a datasheet. Data in this subform comes from the query Data for Subform Example. Finally, there is a total for the data in the subform displayed in a text box control in the main form.

Creating a form for a subform

The first step in creating an embedded subform is to create the form to be used as the subform. Of course, this begins with a plan and a query. The *plan* is what you see in Figure 28-11. This datasheet, however, is not just a few fields displayed as a datasheet. The field Visit Type is a combo box that uses a Value List; you create that layer in this section. The fields Treatment Code and Medication Code do not display codes at all; instead, they display the treatment description and the medication description. The Price fields actually come from the Treatments table and Medications table by way of links. Finally, Total is a calculated field.

To create this datasheet, you start at the beginning. Figure 28-12 shows the query used for the subform.

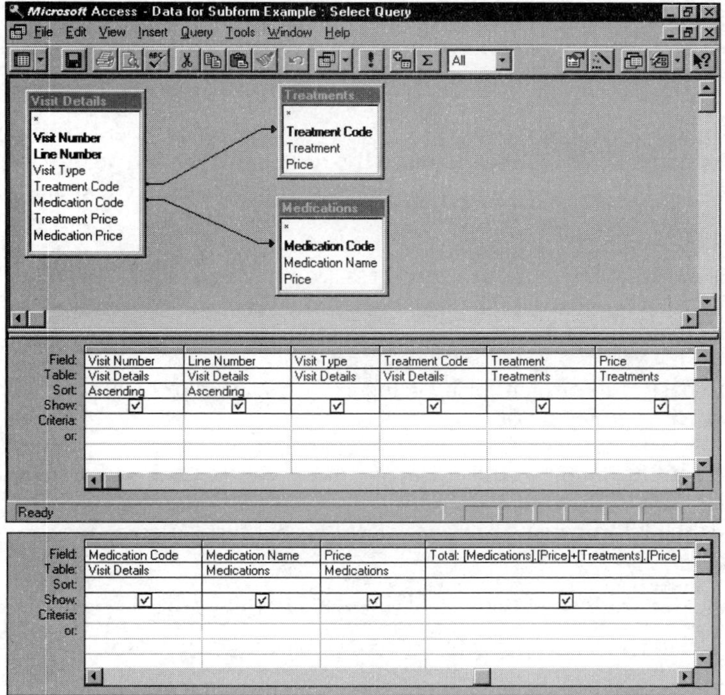

Figure 28-12: A composite figure showing the subform query.

Note: This figure is actually a composite of two screen shots to show all the fields selected in the query.

At the top of the query, you can see the three tables needed. Notice that the Visit Details table is joined to both the Treatments and Medications tables using a right outer join. You learned about this in Chapter 14. This is necessary so that if a Visit Detail record has either no treatment or no medication, it will not appear because of referential integrity.

Cross Ref: Chapter 12 discusses the implications of referential integrity on a system using lookup tables.

The bottom pane of the query shows the fields that can be used for the datasheet. These include the Visit Number, Line Number, Visit Type, Treatment Code, and Medication Code fields from the Visit Details table. The fields Treatment and Price (from the Treatments table) and the fields Medication Name and Price (from the Medications table) can be used to display the actual data they name instead of the codes. This can be further enhanced by using the combo boxes, as you'll soon see.

The final field in the query, `Total: [Medications].[Price]+[Treatments].[Price]`, names the field Total and sets the calculation to the total of both Price fields — the one in the Medications table and the one in the Treatments table. This field displays the line totals for each record in the datasheet.

Creating a *subform datasheet* is an iterative process; you have to see how many fields can fit across the screen at once. If your goal is not to use a horizontal scrollbar, you'll have to use only as many fields as you can fit across the screen.

You can create the basic subform either by using a Form Wizard or by creating a new form and placing all the needed fields in it.

To create the initial subform, follow these steps:

1. Create a new blank form, using the query Data for Subform Example as the Record Source.
2. Open the Field List window and drag all the fields to the form.
3. Change the Default View property to Datasheet, as shown in Figure 28-13.
4. Display the form as a datasheet to check the results.

When you display the datasheet, you see that the fields don't even come close to fitting. There simply isn't enough room to display all of them. There are two solutions: Use a scrollbar or get creative. By now, you've learned enough to get creative!

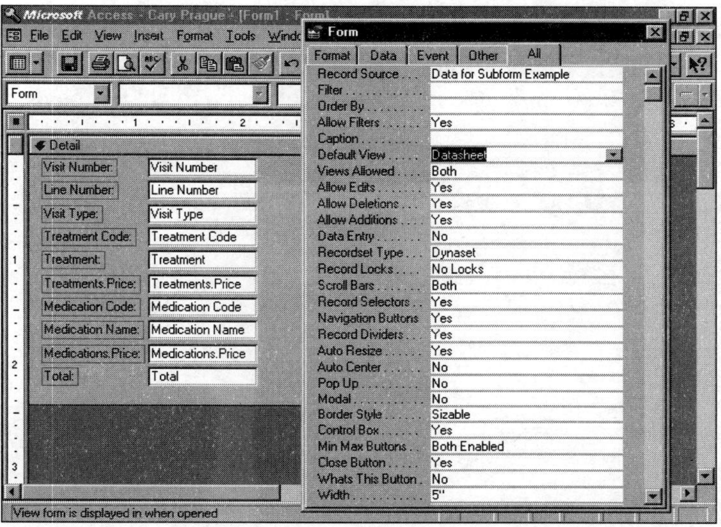

Figure 28-13: Creating the subform.

First of all, what fields are absolutely necessary to the entry of data, and which are strictly lookup fields? The first necessary field is Visit Number; it's used to link to the main form, and must be included. Next is Line Number, the second field that makes up the multiple-field key in Visit Details. You must enter a Visit Type for each record, so that field needs to stay. Next come the details themselves. To enter a treatment, you must enter a treatment code and a medication code (if any). The codes themselves are used to look up the description and price. Therefore, you only need Treatment Code and Medication Code. Even so, you also want to display the prices and the line total. So the only fields you can eliminate are Treatment and Medication Name — and even then the datasheet doesn't fit across the page. To make it all fit, follow these steps:

1. Switch to Form Design view.
2. Delete the fields Treatment and Medication Name.
3. Change the labels for Treatments.Price and Medications.Price to simply **Price**.
4. Switch back to Datasheet view.
5. The fields still don't fit. But by changing the column widths, you can fix that. Adjust the column widths, as shown in Figure 28-14.
6. Save the form as **Data for Subform Example**.

This is usually a good starting point. Notice that in Figure 28-14 some extra space shows on the right side. Because this datasheet will be placed in the center of another form, you must take into consideration the space the record selector column and scrollbar of the main form will use. After you view the datasheet in the main form, you can make final adjustments. You may also wonder why so much space was left for the Treatment Code and Medication Code columns. Later, when you change these into combo boxes, you'll need this amount of space. (Normally, you might not have realized this yet.)

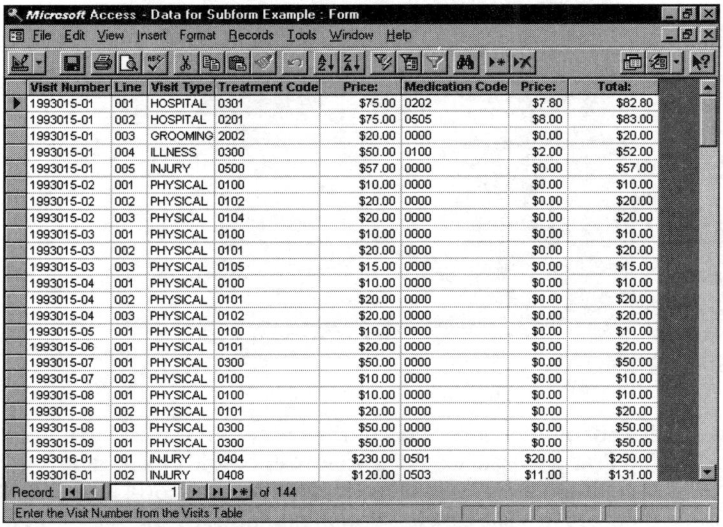

Microsoft Access - Data for Subform Example : Form

File Edit View Insert Format Records Tools Window Help

Visit Number	Line	Visit Type	Treatment Code	Price:	Medication Code	Price:	Total:
1993015-01	001	HOSPITAL	0301	$75.00	0202	$7.80	$82.80
1993015-01	002	HOSPITAL	0201	$75.00	0505	$8.00	$83.00
1993015-01	003	GROOMING	2002	$20.00	0000	$0.00	$20.00
1993015-01	004	ILLNESS	0300	$50.00	0100	$2.00	$52.00
1993015-01	005	INJURY	0500	$57.00	0000	$0.00	$57.00
1993015-02	001	PHYSICAL	0100	$10.00	0000	$0.00	$10.00
1993015-02	002	PHYSICAL	0102	$20.00	0000	$0.00	$20.00
1993015-02	003	PHYSICAL	0104	$20.00	0000	$0.00	$20.00
1993015-03	001	PHYSICAL	0100	$10.00	0000	$0.00	$10.00
1993015-03	002	PHYSICAL	0101	$20.00	0000	$0.00	$20.00
1993015-03	003	PHYSICAL	0105	$15.00	0000	$0.00	$15.00
1993015-04	001	PHYSICAL	0100	$10.00	0000	$0.00	$10.00
1993015-04	002	PHYSICAL	0101	$20.00	0000	$0.00	$20.00
1993015-04	003	PHYSICAL	0102	$20.00	0000	$0.00	$20.00
1993015-05	001	PHYSICAL	0100	$10.00	0000	$0.00	$10.00
1993015-06	001	PHYSICAL	0101	$20.00	0000	$0.00	$20.00
1993015-07	001	PHYSICAL	0300	$50.00	0000	$0.00	$50.00
1993015-07	002	PHYSICAL	0100	$10.00	0000	$0.00	$10.00
1993015-08	001	PHYSICAL	0100	$10.00	0000	$0.00	$10.00
1993015-08	002	PHYSICAL	0101	$20.00	0000	$0.00	$20.00
1993015-08	003	PHYSICAL	0300	$50.00	0000	$0.00	$50.00
1993015-09	001	PHYSICAL	0300	$50.00	0000	$0.00	$50.00
1993016-01	001	INJURY	0404	$230.00	0501	$20.00	$250.00
1993016-01	002	INJURY	0408	$120.00	0503	$11.00	$131.00

Record: 1 of 144

Enter the Visit Number from the Visits Table

Figure 28-14: Adjusting the subform datasheet.

Adding the subform to the main form

After the subform is complete, you can add it to the main form. The easiest way is to display the main form in a window and then drag the subform to the main form. This creates the subform object control automatically, and potentially links the two forms.

To add the Data for Subform Example to the Adding Visit Details form you're using as the main form, follow these steps:

1. Display the Adding Visit Details form in a window in Design View so you can also see the Database window.
2. Display the form objects in the Database window.
3. Click on the form name Data for Subform Example and drag it to the Adding Visit Details form, as depicted in Figure 28-15.
4. Maximize the Form window.
5. Resize the subform so that it fits on-screen below the three check boxes.
6. Delete the subform label control.
7. Display the property sheet for the subform control to verify the link.

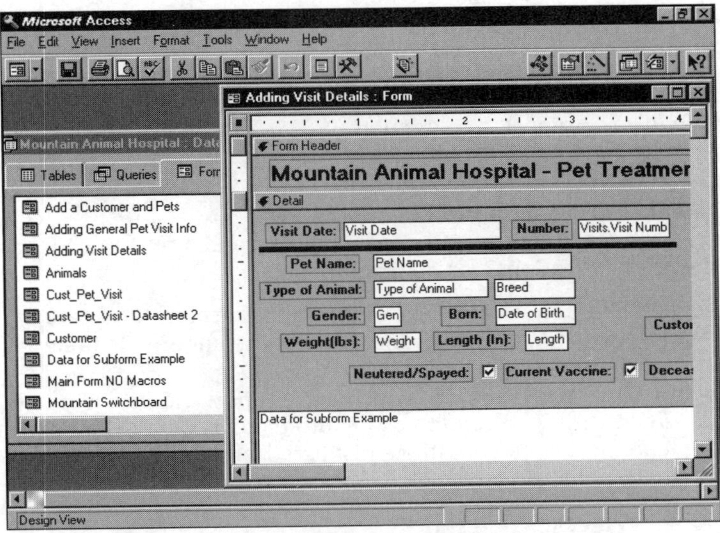

Figure 28-15: The form for Adding Visit Details.

The form should look like Figure 28-16, except that the Link Child Fields and Link Master Fields sections will not be filled in. This means the main form (Master) and the subform (Child) are not linked. This is because the primary key for the Visit Details table is a multiple-field key. Access cannot automatically link this type of primary key.

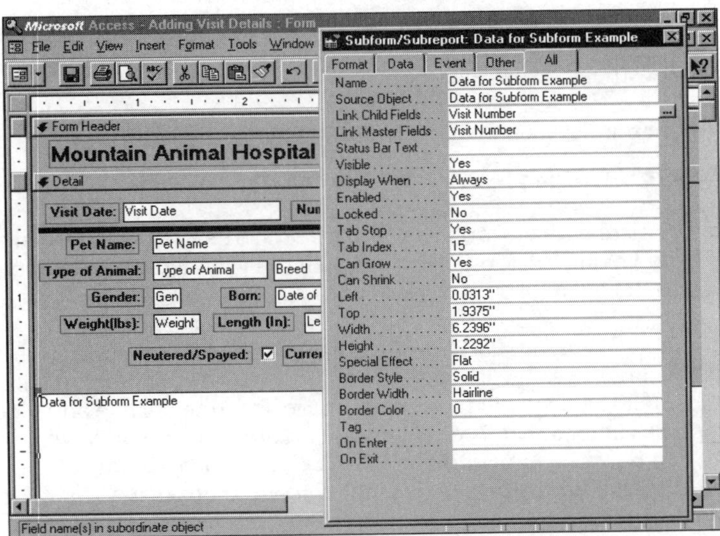

Figure 28-16: The subform in the main form.

Linking the form and subform

When you drag a form from the Database window onto another form to create a subform, Access tries automatically to establish a link between the forms. This is also true when you drag a form or report onto a report.

Access establishes a link under these conditions:

- Both the main form and subform are based on tables, and a relationship has been defined with the Relationships command.
- The main form and subform contain fields with the same name and data type, and the field on the main form is the primary key of the underlying table.

If Access finds a relationship or a match, these properties show the field names that define the link. You should verify the validity of an automatic link. If the main form is based on a query, or if neither of the conditions just listed is true, Access cannot match the fields automatically to create a link.

The Link Child Fields and Link Master Fields property settings must have the same number of fields and must represent data of the same type. For example, if the Customer table and the Pets table both have Customer ID fields (one each) that contain the same type of data, you enter **Customer ID** for both properties. The subform automatically displays all the pets found for the customer identified in the main form's Customer ID field.

Although the data must match, the names of the fields can differ. For example, the Customer ID field from the Customer table can be linked to the Customer Number field from the Pets table.

To create the link, follow these steps:

1. Enter **Visit Number** in the Link Child Fields property.
2. Enter **Visit Number** in the Link Master Fields property.

Without the link, if you display the form, you see all the records in the Visit Details table in the subform. By linking the forms, you see only the visit details for the specific visit being displayed in the main form.

Display the form, as shown in Figure 28-17. Notice that the only visit numbers displayed in the datasheet are the same as the visit numbers in the main form. In Figure 28-17, you may notice that the user will have to enter the Treatment Code and Medication Code. In the type of systems that Access lets you create, you should never have to enter a code that can be looked up automatically. You can change some of the fields in the datasheet to use lookup tables by creating combo boxes in the subform.

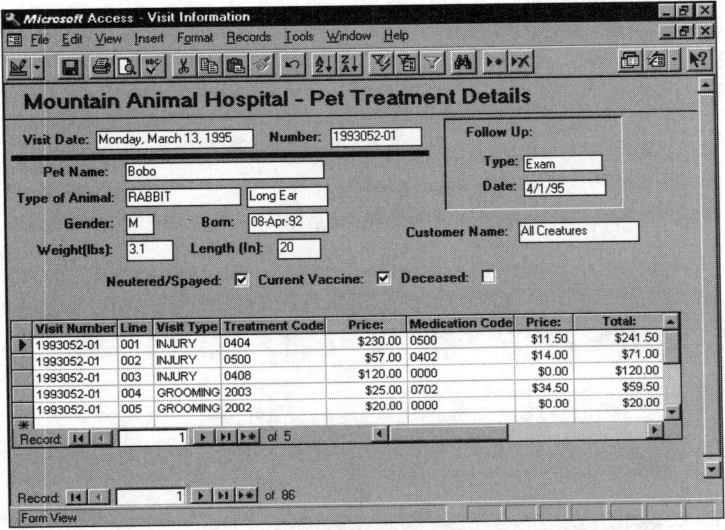

Figure 28-17: Displaying the main form and the subform.

Adding lookup tables to the subform fields

You can change the way the data is displayed in a subform of a main form by changing the design of the subform itself. You now make three changes:

- ✦ Display the Visit Type field as a Value List combo box.
- ✦ Display the Treatment Code as a combo box showing the Treatment Name, letting Access enter the Treatment Code automatically.
- ✦ Display the Medication Code as a combo box showing the Medication Name, letting Access enter the Medication Code automatically.

Cross Ref Combo boxes are discussed in detail in Chapter 19.

By changing a field in a subform to a combo box, when you click on the field in the datasheet of the subform, the list will drop down and you can select from the list.

The first control to change is the Visit Type field. To create a value list combo box without using the Wizard, follow these steps:

1. Display the subform in the Design View.
2. Select the existing Visit Type text box control.
3. From the menu bar, select Format⇨Change To⇨Combo Box.
4. With the Visit Type combo box selected, display the property sheet.
5. Select Value List for the Row Source Type property.

6. Enter **INJURY;PHYSICAL;GROOMING;HOSPITAL** in the Row Source property.
7. Set the Column Count property to **1** and the Column Widths to **1"**.
8. Set the Bound Column property to **1** and the List Rows property to **8**.
9. Set the Limit To List property to **No** to allow an alternative treatment type to be added.

This combo box and property sheet are shown in Figure 28-18.

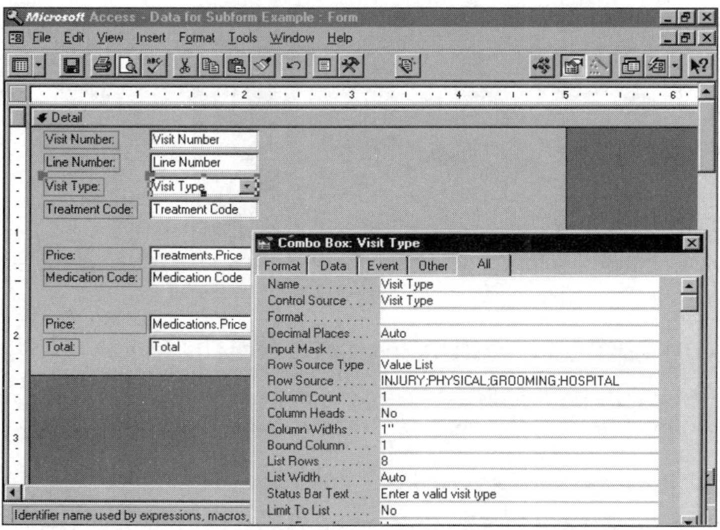

Figure 28-18: Creating a value list combo box for the Visit Type field.

Note You can also display fields in a datasheet as check boxes or as individual option buttons. You cannot display an option button group, a list box, or a toggle button in a datasheet.

When the user clicks on the Visit Type field in the datasheet, the combo box appears. When the user selects the arrow, the list box is displayed with the values `INJURY`; `PHYSICAL`; `GROOMING`; or `HOSPITAL`. Because the Limit To List property is set to No, the user can also add new values to the Visit Details table.

The next two combo boxes are very similar. You want to create two combo boxes. The first allows you to see the treatment descriptions instead of the treatment codes. When you select a treatment description, the code is entered automatically. The second combo box is the same, except it uses the Medications table instead of the Treatments table.

In order to create these combo boxes, you need to create several queries. Figure 28-19 shows the query for the Treatment Code combo box.

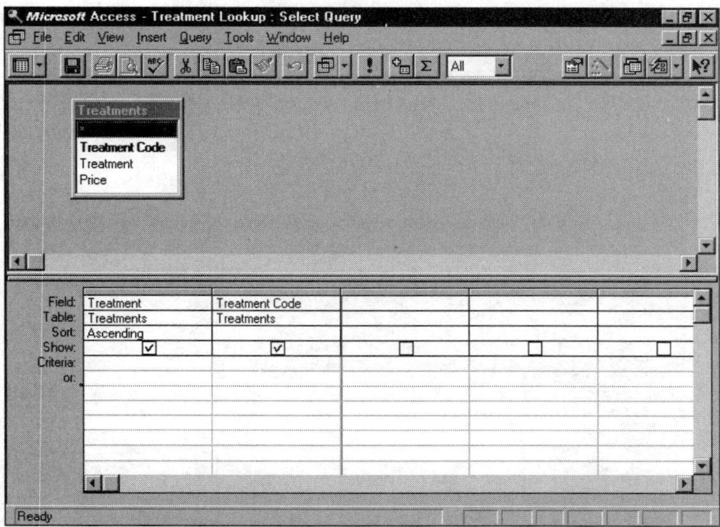

Figure 28-19: The query for the Treatment Code combo box.

As you can see, all fields come from the Treatments table. The fields appear in the combo box in order of the value of Treatment. This is the treatment name. This is an alphabetical listing because the field is a Text field data type. Notice that two fields are used in the query. The treatment code will actually be hidden so that only the treatment name is displayed.

After you create the query, you can create the combo box. To create the combo box for the treatment code, follow these steps:

1. Display the subform in the Design View.
2. Select the existing Treatment Code text box control.
3. From the menu bar, select Format⇨Change To⇨Combo Box.
4. With the Treatment Code combo box selected, display the property sheet.
5. Select Table/Query for the Row Source Type property.
6. Enter **Treatment Lookup** in the Row Source property.
7. Set the Column Count property to **2** and the Column Heads property to **Yes**.
8. Set the Column Widths property to **2";0"**.
9. Set the Bound Column property to **2** and the List Rows property to **4**.
10. Set the List Width property to **2"**.
11. Set the Limit To List property to **Yes** so the user must select from the list.

Figure 28-20 shows this combo box completed. When the form is run and the user selects the Treatment Code field, the list of valid treatment codes is shown. Because the Bound Column is 2 (the hidden Treatment Code column), Access places the value of the Treatment Code in the Treatment Code field in the Visit Details table.

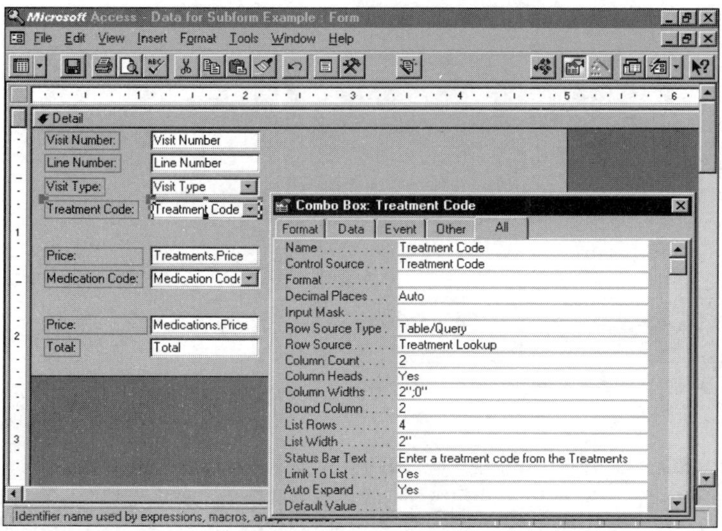

Figure 28-20: Creating a combo box for the Treatment Code.

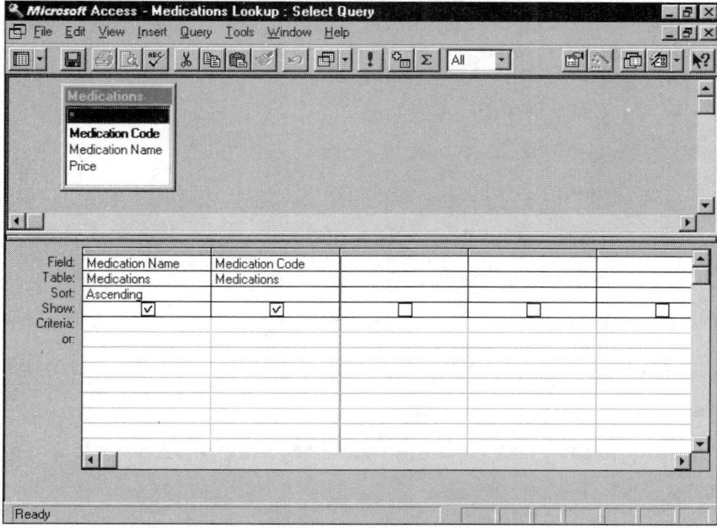

Figure 28-21: The query for the Medication Code combo box.

The Medication Code lookup table is virtually identical to the Treatment Code lookup table; only the field name is different. To create this combo box, you also need to create a query. Figure 28-21 shows the query for the Medication Code combo box.

As you can see, all these fields come from the Medications table. They appear in the combo box in order of the value of the Medication Name (an alphabetical listing because the uses the Text data type). Notice that two fields are used in the query. The Medication Code is actually hidden; only the Medication name is displayed.

After you create the query, you can create the combo box. To create the combo box for the Medication Code, follow these steps:

1. Display the subform in the Design View.
2. Select the existing Medication Code text box control.
3. From the menu bar, select Format➪Change To➪Combo Box.
4. With the Medication Code combo box selected, display the property sheet.
5. Select Table/Query for the Row Source Type property.
6. Enter **Medications Lookup** in the Row Source property.
7. Set the Column Count property to **2** and the Column Heads property to **Yes**.
8. Set the Column Widths property to **2";0"**.
9. Set the Bound Column property to **2** and the List Rows property to **4**.
10. Set the List Width property to **2"**.
11. Set the Limit To List property to **Yes** so the user must select from the list.

Figure 28-22 shows this combo box completed. When the form is run and the user selects the Medication Code field, the list of valid treatment codes is shown. Because the Bound Column is 2 (the hidden Medication Code column), Access places the value of the Medication Code in the Medication Code field in the Visit Details table.

After you make these changes, you can test your changes. You may want first to display the form as a datasheet in the Form view of the subform. You can also close the form and display the subform in the main form. Close the subform and run the main form named Adding Visit Details.

First, you can test the combo boxes. Click on the Visit Type field. An arrow should appear. When you click on the arrow, the list of valid visit types is displayed. You can then select the desired visit type or enter a new one in the combo box. When the combo box is closed, Access enters this data into the Visit Type field of the Visit Details table.

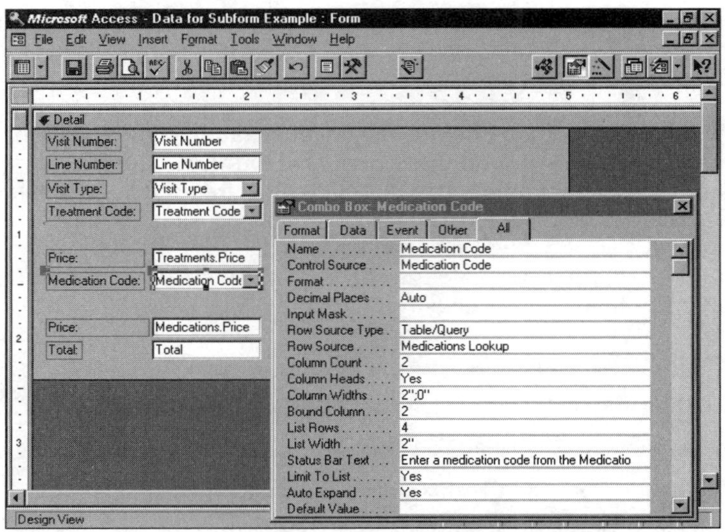

Figure 28-22: Creating a combo box for the Medication Code.

When you select the Treatment Code field and select the arrow, a combo box is also displayed, as shown in Figure 28-23. The combo box displays only three columns because the List Rows property is set to 4 and the Column Heads property is set to Yes.

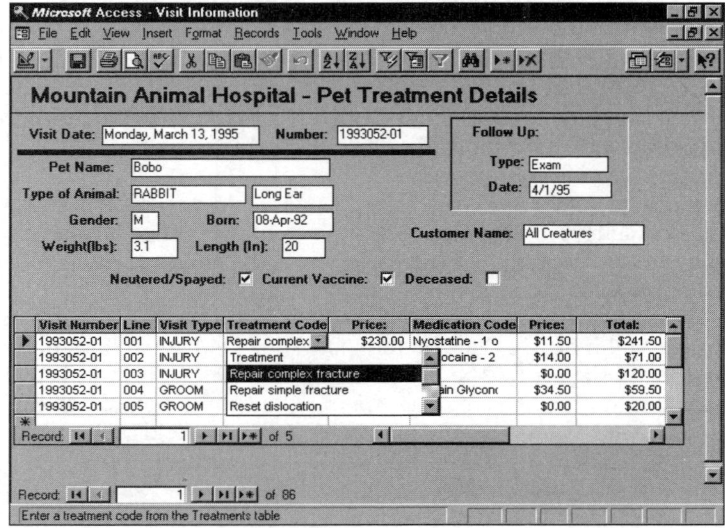

Figure 28-23: Displaying the subform.

The treatment description is shown in its entirety, even though the Treatment Code field entry area is smaller. This is controlled by setting the List Width property to 2. If you leave this property set to the default (Auto), you may find your data truncated (or displayed with too much white space after the values) because the list width will be the size of the actual combo box control on the subform. When you select the desired treatment, Access automatically enters the hidden value of the treatment code in the Treatments table into the Treatment Code field in Visit Details.

The Medication Code field works in exactly the same way. Notice that as you select various treatments, the price is updated automatically in each line to reflect the selection. As either Treatment Price or Medication Price changes, the Total field is also updated.

The last change to make to the form is to create a field to display totals of all the line items in the datasheet.

Creating totals in subforms

To create a total of the line items in the subform, you have to create an additional calculated field in the form you're using as a subform. Figure 28-24 shows a new field being created in the form footer in this form.

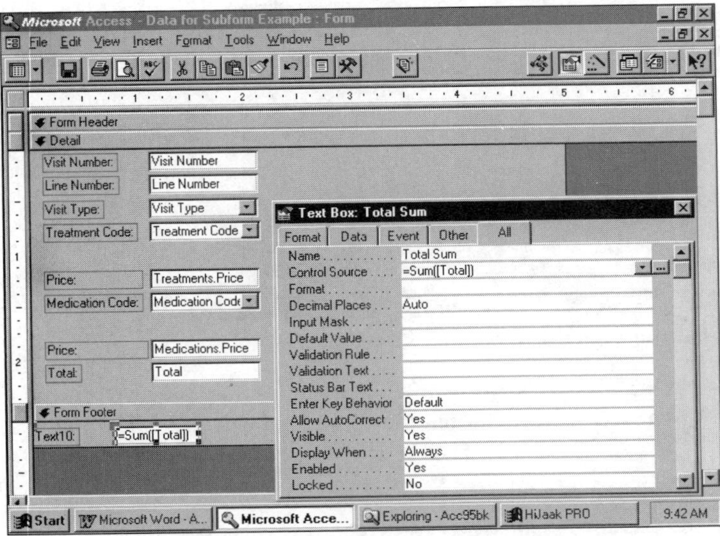

Figure 28-24: Creating a summary calculation.

Just as you can create summaries in reports, you can create them in forms. Use the form footer; that way the calculation occurs after all the detail records are processed. When the form is displayed in single-form view, this total is always equal to the detail record. In continuous-form or datasheet view, however, this calculation is the sum of the processed record.

As shown in Figure 28-24, the text box Control Source property is the expression `=Sum([Total])`. This is the sum of all the values found in the Total field. To display the data as a dollar amount, the field's Format property should be set to Currency and the number of decimal places is set to 2.

Although the text box control was created in the subform, it's actually displayed by a text box control (which references the subform control) placed in the main form. This control is shown in Figure 28-25.

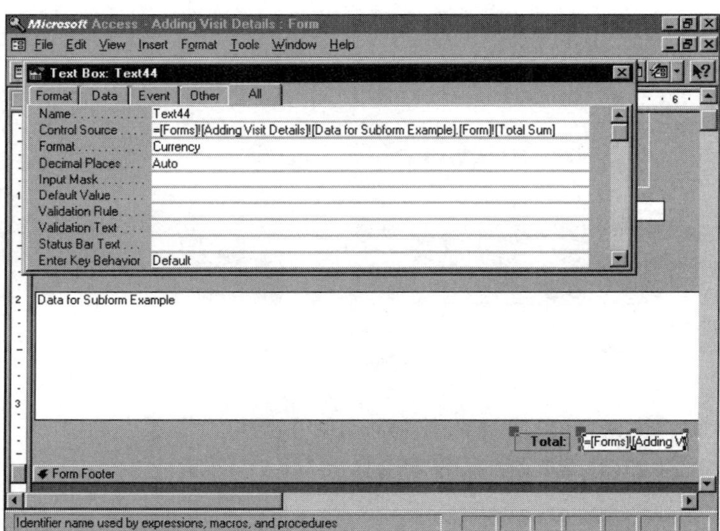

Figure 28-25: Referencing a control in another form.

Because the field is in another form, it must be referenced with the fully qualified terminology `(Object type![Form name]![Subform name].Form![Subform field name])`.

As you can see in the property sheet, the Control Source property is as follows:

```
=[Forms]![Adding Visit Details]![Data for Subform Example].[Form]!
[Total Sum]
```

The first part of the reference specifies the name of the form; `Form` tells Access that it's the name of a form. By using the ! character, you tell Access that the next part is a lower hierarchy. The control name `[Total Sum]` actually contains the value to be displayed.

Warning If you are an experienced Access 2.0 user, you may find that many of the field reference calculations you type in no longer work; they just display the `#Name? Symbol` message in your calculated or referenced text boxes. A major change was made in Access for Windows 95 that makes it mandatory to fully qualify all references. In Access 2.0, you could leave off the first part of the reference (`Forms![`*`formname`*`]`). In the example just given, you could have just used the subform name first, leaving out the `Forms![Adding Visit Details]` part.

The final form, including the total for the subform, is shown in Figure 28-26.

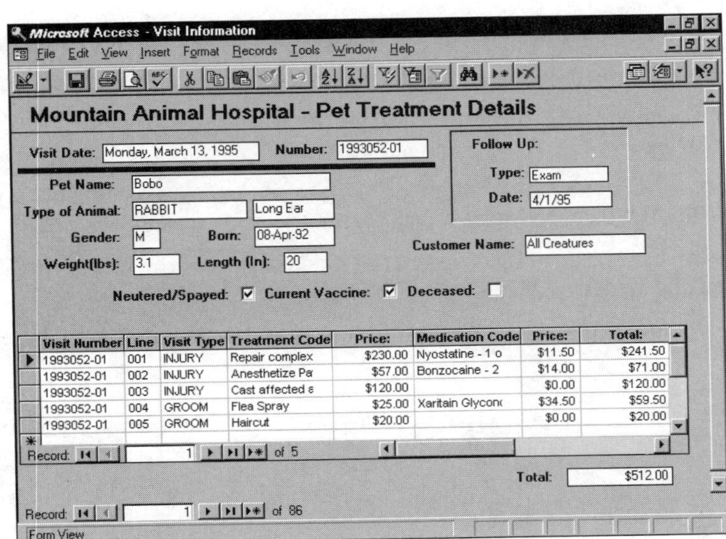

Figure 28-26: Displaying the totals.

Summary

In this chapter, you learned how to use subforms to make displaying data from multiple tables easier. You learned how to create a subform with a Wizard, as well as how to create subforms by dragging the form from the Database window to another form. You also learned how to change the display of the subform. The chapter covered the following points:

- A subform is simply a form within a form.
- There are several ways to create a subform:

  Use the Form Wizard

  Drag a form from the Database window to another form

  Use the toolbox and the Form Wizard
- A subform can be displayed as a single form, a continuous form, or a datasheet.
- Before adding a subform to an existing form, you must create the subform.
- By using the Form Wizard, you can create a form with an embedded subform datasheet.
- When you create a subform by dragging a form from the Database window, you may have to link the form to the subform manually.
- You link a form and subform by entering the field names for the link in the Link Master Fields and Link Child Fields properties.
- You can add lookup tables and even combo boxes to the datasheet used in a subform.

In the next chapter, you learn how to create mailing labels, snaked column reports, and mail-merge reports.

✦ ✦ ✦

Creating Mailing Labels and Mail Merge Reports

✦ ✦ ✦ ✦

In This Chapter

Using the Mailing Label Report Wizard

Modifying mailing label reports

Using the expanded Page Setup dialog box

Understanding snaked column reports

Creating a snaked column report

Creating a mail merge letter in Access

Using the Access to Word Mail Merge Wizard

✦ ✦ ✦ ✦

For correspondence, you often need to create mailing labels and form letters, commonly known as *mail merges.* The Access report writer helps you create these types of reports, as well as the reports with multiple columns known as *snaked column reports*.

Creating Mailing Labels

You create mailing labels in Access by using a report. You can create the basic label by starting from a blank form, or you can use the Mailing Label Report Wizard. The Mailing Label Report Wizard is much easier and saves you a great deal of time and effort.

There is no special report for creating mailing labels. Like any other, the report for a mailing label is made up of controls; the secret to the mailing label is using the margin settings and the Page Setup screen. In previous chapters, you learned how to use the Page Setup dialog box to change your margins. One of the tabs in the dialog box is Layout. When you select this tab, the Layout dialog box expands to reveal additional choices you use to control the number of labels across the report, as well as how the data is placed on the report. You learn how to use this dialog box later in this chapter.

The best way to create mailing labels is to use the Mailing Label Report Wizard.

Creating the new report with the Label Wizard

You create a new report to be used for a mailing label just as you create any other report. To create a new report for a mailing label, follow these steps:

1. From the Database window, select the Reports tab
2. Select New to create a new report.
3. Select Label Wizard.
4. Select Customer from the table/query combo box.
5. Click on OK.

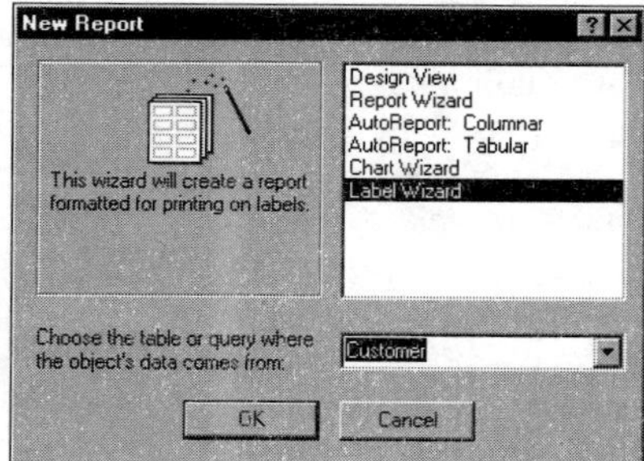

Figure 29-1: Choosing the Label Wizard.

The Label Size dialog box should now be displayed.

Selecting the label size

The first Wizard dialog box you see will ask you to select a label size. You can select the type of label stock you want to print to. Nearly a hundred Avery label stock forms are listed. (Avery is the world's largest producer of label paper.)

You can find nearly every type of paper Avery makes in these lists. You can select from lists of English or Metric labels. You can also select sheet feed for laser printers or continuous for tractor-fed printers. Select between the two from the option buttons below the label sizes.

The list box shown in Figure 29-2 contains three columns:

Avery number	The model number found on the Avery label box
Dimensions	The height and width of the label in either inches or millimeters
Number across	The number of labels that are physically across the page

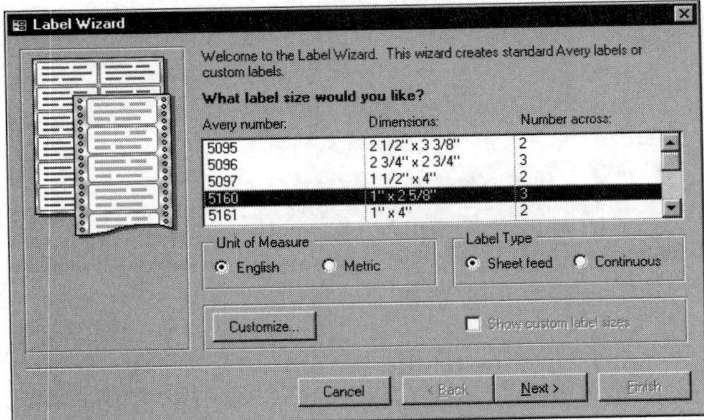

Figure 29-2: Selecting the label size.

When you select a label size, you're actually setting the Page Setup parameters, as you learn later in this chapter.

Select Avery number: 5160, as shown in Figure 29-2. Notice that there are three labels across, and the size is shown as `1" x 2 5/8"`. You'll see these values again when you examine the Page Setup dialog box. After you select the label size, you can again select the Next > button to go to the next dialog box.

Note You can also select the Customize button to create your own specific label specifications if the labels you're using are not a standard Avery label.

Selecting the font and color

The next dialog box (shown in Figure 29-3) displays a set of combo boxes to let you select various attributes about the font and color of the text used in the mailing label. For this example, click on the Italic check box (if it is checked) to turn off the italic effect. Notice the sample text changes to reflect the difference. Change the font size to **8** so it fits all of the mailing label text onto the label. The remaining choices are Arial, Bold, and black text. Click on the Next > button to move to the next dialog box.

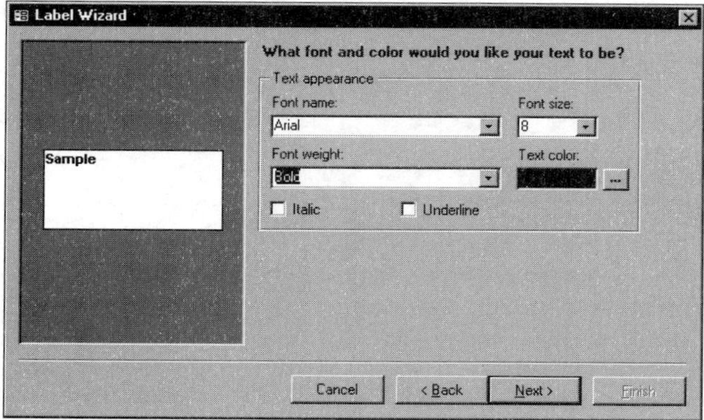

Figure 29-3: Selecting the font type, size, and color.

Creating the mailing label text and fields

This dialog box lets you choose the fields from the table or query to appear in the label. You can also add spaces, unbound text, blank lines, and even punctuation.

The dialog box is divided into two areas. The left area, titled `Available fields:`, lists all the fields in the query or table. Figure 29-4, shown completed, displays the fields from the Customer table. The right area, titled `Prototype label:`, shows the fields used for the label and displays a rough idea of how the mailing label will look when it's completed.

The fields or text you use in this dialog box serve only as a starting point for the label. You can make additional changes later in the Report Design window.

You can select a field either by double-clicking on the field name in the Available fields: area, or by selecting the field name and then clicking on the > command button between the two areas. You can remove a field by highlighting it and then pressing Delete on your keyboard. You move to the next line by pressing the Tab key.

You may enter text at any point simply by placing your cursor where you want to insert the text and typing it in. This includes spaces and punctuation marks as well.

If you add a new line to the label and leave it blank, it will appear only as a blank line in the label (provided you've also changed the Can Shrink property manually to No for the unbound text box control you created to display that blank line). The default property for this control is Yes; the blank line is not displayed, and the lines above and below the blank line appear together.

To create the label as shown completed in Figure 29-4, follow these steps:

1. Double-click on the Customer Name field in the Available fields: list.
2. Press the Tab key to go to the next line.
3. Double-click on the Street/Apt field in the Available fields: list.
4. Press the Tab key to go to the next line.
5. Double-click on the City field in the Available fields: list.
6. Position your cursor after the City field and type a comma (,) to add a comma to the label.
7. Press the Spacebar to add a blank space to the label after the comma.
8. Double-click on the State field in the Available fields: list.
9. Press the Spacebar to add a blank space to the label after the State field.
10. Double-click on the Zip Code field in the Available fields: list.
11. Click on the Next > button to go to the next dialog box.

The completed label is displayed in Figure 29-4.

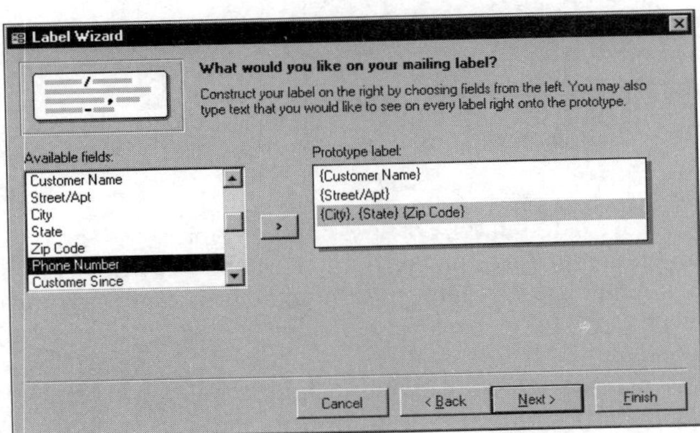

Figure 29-4: The completed label in the Label Wizard.

Sorting the mailing labels

The next dialog box will prompt you to select a field on which to sort by, as shown in Figure 29-5. Depending on how you have your database set up (and on how you want to organize your information) you may sort it by one or more fields. The dialog box consists of two sections; one lists the available fields, the other the selected sort fields. To select a field, double-click on it (it will appear on the right-side column labeled `Sort by:`) or use the arrow buttons (> and >>). The single > means that only the highlighted field will be selected; the double >> means every field showing in the column will be selected. In this example, you will select Customer Name as the field to sort by. When you're done, click on Next to bring up the final dialog box.

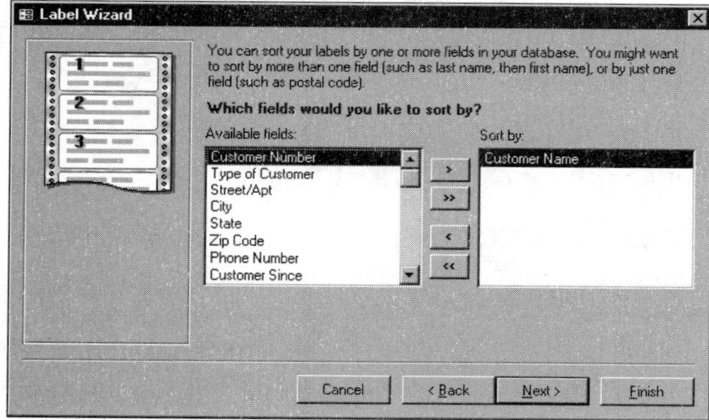

Figure 29-5: The Label Wizard's Sort By dialog box.

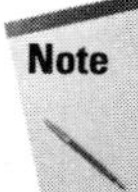

The order in which the fields are listed in the Sort by: column represents the order in which they will be sorted, top-down. If you have a database set up in which you have first and last name, you can select the last name and then the first name as the sort order.

The last dialog box in the Mailing Label Report Wizard sequence lets you decide whether to view the labels in the Print Preview window or to modify the report design in the Report Design window. The default name is the word `Label` followed by the table name. In this example, that is `Labels Customer`. Change it to a more meaningful name like `Customer Mailing Labels`. This final dialog box is shown in Figure 29-6.

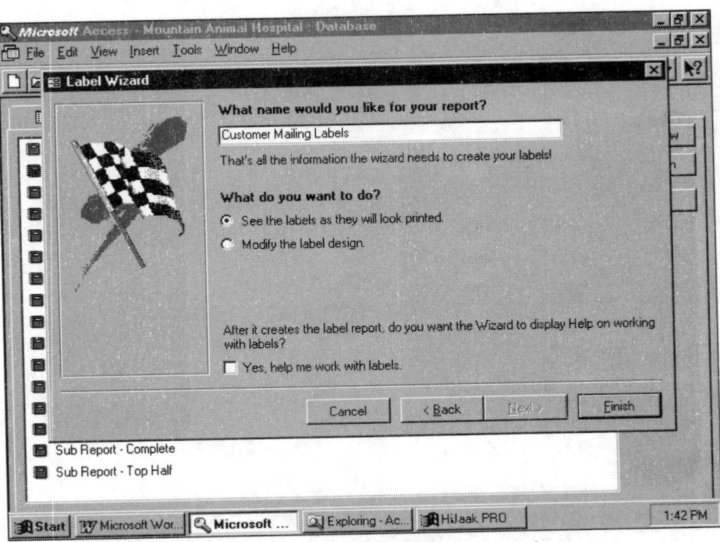

Figure 29-6: The final mailing Label Wizard dialog box.

Displaying the labels in the Print Preview window

When you click on the Finish button, you are taken directly to the Print Preview window (as shown in Figure 29-7). This is the normal Print Preview window for a report. By using the magnifying-glass cursor, you can switch to a page view to see an entire page of labels at once, or you can zoom in to any quadrant of the report. By using the navigation buttons at the bottom left corner of the window, you can display other pages of your mailing label report.

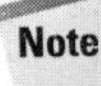

Note Remember that a mailing label is simply a report; it behaves as a report normally behaves.

You can print the labels directly from the Print Preview window, or you can select the first icon in the toolbar to display the Report Design window.

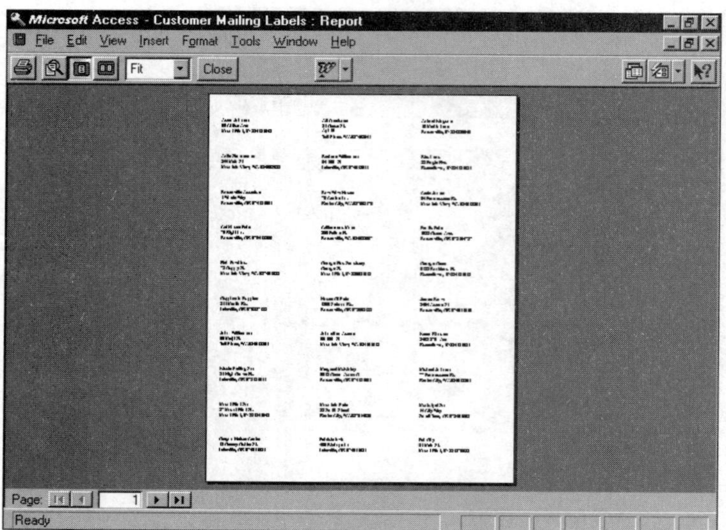

Figure 29-7: Viewing labels in the Print Preview window.

Modifying the label design in the Report Design window

When you select the Close Window icon, the label design is displayed in the Report Design window, as shown in Figure 29-8. Notice that the height of the Detail band is set at 1 inch, and the right margin of the report is set at 2 5/8 inches. This gives you the measurement you defined when you chose the label size of `1" x 2 5/8"`.

If you look at the report print preview, you notice that the first record's ZIP code value is `834121043`. As you learned in Chapter 23, the Zip Code field is normally formatted using the @@@@@-@@@@ format. This format displays the stored sequence of nine numbers with a hyphen placed where it properly goes.

The control source was originally

```
=[City] & ", " & [State] & " " & [Zip Code]
```

The Mailing Label Report Wizard uses the ampersand (&) type of concatenation when working with text strings; any formatting is missing. In the property sheet for the third line text box, you must change the control source to

```
=[City] & ", " & [State] & " " & Format([Zip Code],"@@@@@-@@@@").
```

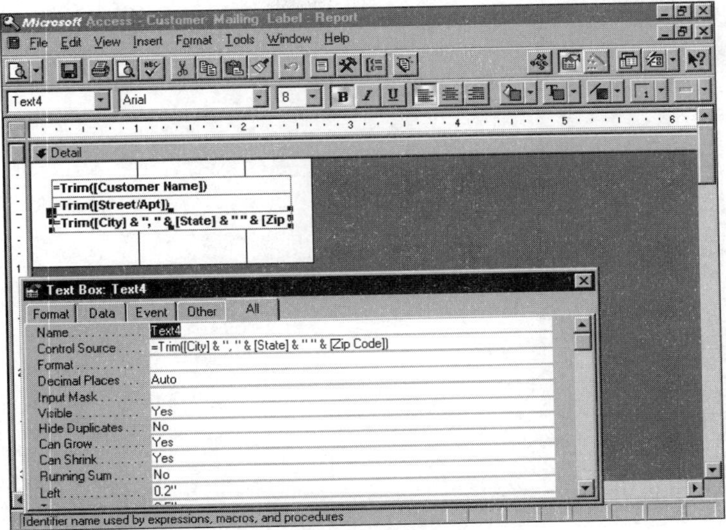

Figure 29-8: The Report Design window.

This control source correctly displays the ZIP code as `83412-1043` when it's printed or displayed. You can make this change by simply selecting the control and adding the Format( ) function.

Another change you could make is to the font size. In this example, Arial (the Helvetica TrueType font) with a point size of 8 is used. Suppose you want to increase the text size to 10 points. You select all the controls and then click on the Font Size drop-down list box and change the font size to 10 points. The text inside the controls becomes larger, but the control itself does not change size. As long as the text is not truncated or cut off on the bottom, you can make the font size larger.

You can also change the font style of any text. For example, suppose you want the Customer Name text to appear in italics. You need only select the text box control and select the Italics button on the toolbar.

Now you've changed your text as you want, it's time to print the labels. Before you do, however, you should examine the Page Setup window.

To display the Page Setup window, select File⇨Page Setup. The Page Setup window appears. Here you can select the printer, change the Orientation to Portrait or Landscape option (have you *ever* seen landscape label paper?), change the Paper Size or Source settings, and set the margins. The margin setting controls the margins for the entire page. These affect the report itself, not just the individual labels.

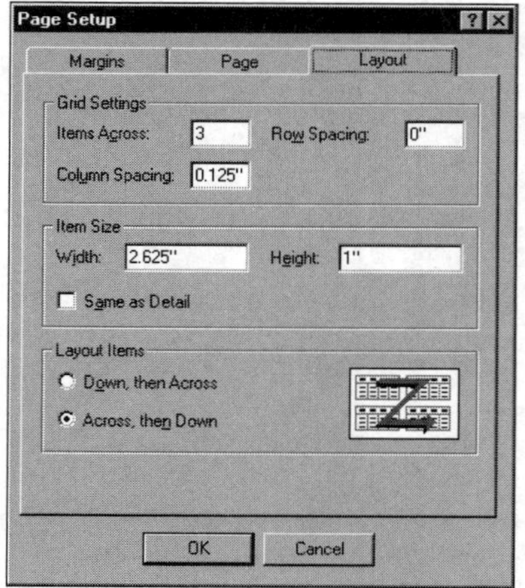

Figure 29-9: The Layout tabbed dialog page from the Page Setup window.

To change the settings of each label and determine the size and number of labels across the page, you need to select the Layout tabbed dialog box. The window then displays additional options, as shown in Figure 29-9.

Several items appear in the Layout dialog box. The first three items (under the Grid Settings) determine the spacing of the labels on the page:

Items Across	Number of columns in the output
Row Spacing	Space between the rows of output
Column Spacing	Amount of space between each column (this property is not available unless you enter a value greater than 1 for the Items Across property)

The Item Size settings determine the size of the label itself:

Width	Sets the width of each label
Height	Sets the height of each label
Same as Detail	Sets the Width and Height properties to the same width and height as the detail section of your report

The Layout Items section determines in which direction the records are printed:

Down, then Across	Prints consecutive labels in the first column and then starts in the second column when the first column is full
Across, then Down	Prints consecutive labels across the page and then moves down a row when there is no more room

After the settings are completed, you can print the labels.

Printing labels

After you create the labels, change any controls as you want, and check the Page Setup settings, you can print the labels. It's always a good idea to preview the labels one last time. Figure 29-10 shows the final labels in the Print Preview window. The ZIP code is correctly displayed.

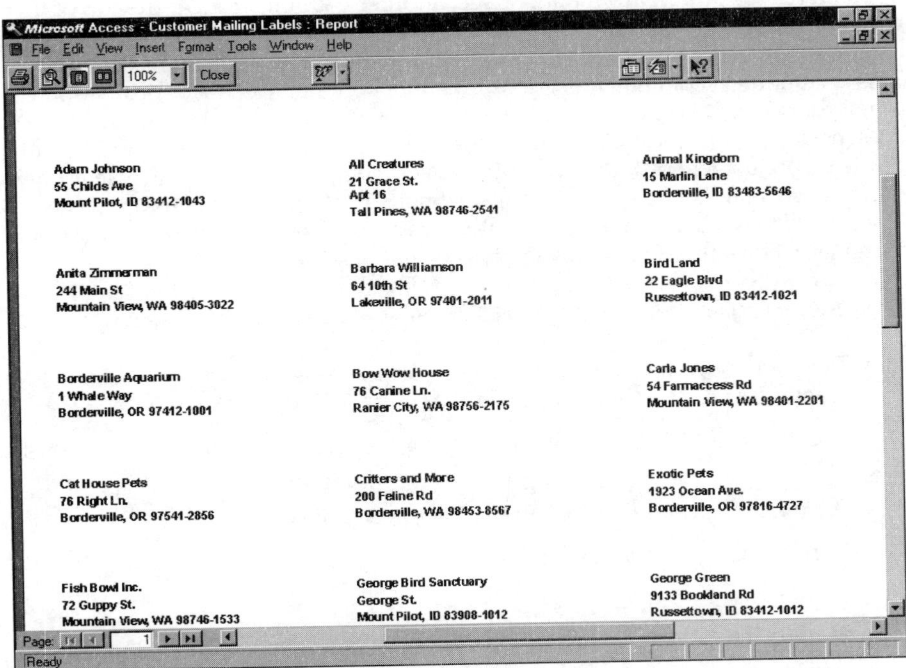

Figure 29-10: The final report print preview.

You can print the labels simply by selecting the Print button in the toolbar and then selecting OK in the Print dialog box. You can also print the labels directly from the Report Design window by selecting File➪Print.

Of course, you must insert your label paper first. If you don't have any #5160 label paper, you can use regular paper. The labels will simply be printed in consecutive format like a telephone directory. In fact, that's actually another feature of Access reports — the capability to create what is known as a *snaked column report*.

Creating Snaked Column Reports

All the reports discussed in this book so far are either form-based (that is, free-form) or single-column lists. (*Single column* means each column for each field appears only once on each page.) Often this is not the best way to present your data. Access gives you another option: *snaking columns*. This option lets you define the sections of a report so they fit in an area that is less than half the width of the printed page. When the data reaches the bottom of the page, another column starts at the top of the page; when there is no more room on the page for another column, a new page starts.

This technique is commonly used for text in telephone directories or newspapers and other periodicals. An example of a database use is a report that prints several addresses, side by side, for a page of adhesive mailing labels you feed through your laser printer. You just learned how to create labels for mailing. Now you will learn how to apply these same techniques to a report. Snaked column reports have a major difference from mailing labels: they often have group sections, page headers, and footers; mailing labels have only data in the detail section.

The general process for creating a snaked column report is as follows:

- ✦ Decide how you want your data to be displayed — how many columns do you want? How wide should each column be?
- ✦ Create a report that has detail and group section controls no wider than the width of one column.
- ✦ Set the appropriate options in the Page Setup dialog box.
- ✦ Verify your results by using a print preview.

Creating the report

You create a snaked column report in the same way you create any report. You start out with a blank Report Design window. Then you drag field controls to the report design and add label controls, lines, and rectangles. Next you add any shading or special effects you want. Then you're ready to print your report. The major difference is the placement of controls and the use of the Page Setup window.

Figure 29-11 shows a completed design for the Customers by State (3 Snaking Columns) report. The report displays a label control and the date in the page header, along with some solid black lines to set the title apart from the directory details. The detail section contains information that lists the customer number, customer name, address, and phone number. Then, within this section, you see three information fields about the customer's history with Mountain Animal Hospital. The page footer section contains another solid black line and a page number control.

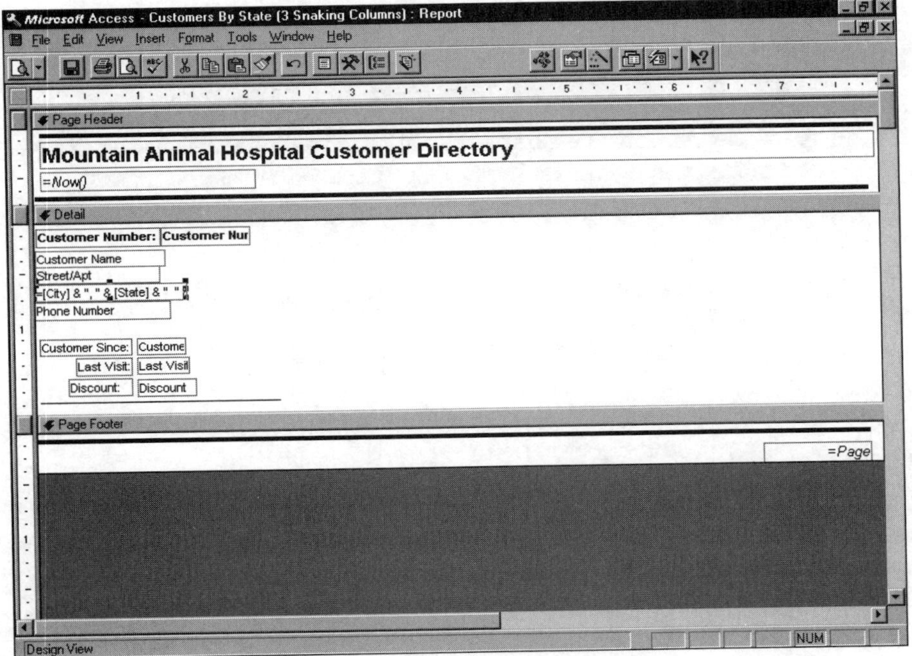

Figure 29-11: Defining a snaked column report design.

What's important here is to make sure the controls in the detail section use no more space for their height or width than you want for each occurrence of the information. Because you're going to be printing or displaying multiple detail records per page in a snaked-column fashion, you must note the size. In this example, you can see that the detail section data is about 1¾ inches high and about 2 inches wide. This is the size of the item you will define in the Layout dialog box.

Defining the page setup

You learned in the "Creating Mailing Labels" section of this chapter how to enter values for Page Setup settings. Next you learn some other ways to enter these values. Figure 29-12 shows the Layout dialog box and the settings used to produce the Customer Directory report. Notice the Items Across setting: 3. This means you want three customer listings across the page.

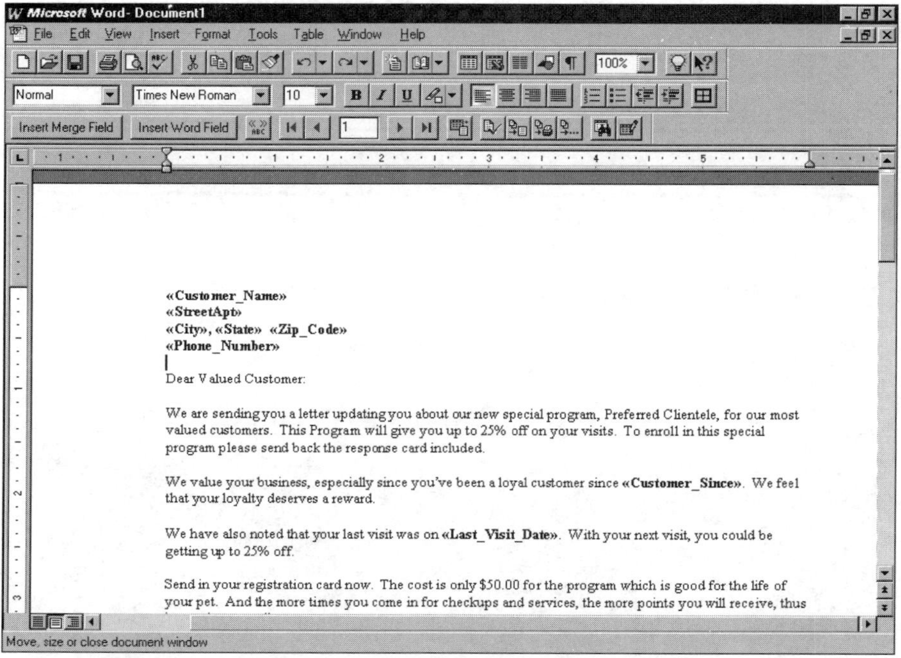

Figure 29-12: Defining the layout setup for a snaked column report.

The next groups of settings to change are the Item Size and Row and Column spacing. These settings actually work together. As you learned in the section on mailing labels, these controls set the size of each data group and the spacing between groups of data. You don't have to define the Item Size to exactly match the size of the data.

In this example, the data is 1 3/4 inches high and about 2 inches wide in the detail section. You can define Width as **2 in** and Height as **1.75 in**. You can then define the Row Spacing to be **.5 in** and the Column Spacing to be **.75 in**. This is one way to set up the multiple columns and allow enough space between both the rows and the columns.

In this example, however, you set the Row Spacing and Column Spacing to **0** and increase the Width and Height settings to include the row and column spacing needs. Setting the Width for 2.75 inches is the same as having the Width set to 2 inches and the Column Spacing set to .75 inches. The same is true for the Height and Row Spacing. There is no difference between setting the Height to 1.75 inches and the Row Spacing to .3 inches and setting the Height to 2.05 inches and the Row Spacing to 0 inches.

Notice that the Layout Items setting is Down, then Across. The icon under `Item Layout` shows the columns going up and down. You saw in Figure 29-9 that when the setting is Across, then Down, the icon shows rows of labels going across. In this customer directory, you want to fill an entire column of names first before moving to the right to fill another column. Therefore you select the Down, then Across setting.

Printing the snaked column report

After the expanded Page Setup dialog box settings are completed, you can print your report. Figure 29-13 shows the first page of the final snaked column report. The data is sorted by state and customer number. Notice that the data snakes down the page. The first record is for Customer Number AK001, in Idaho. Below that is customer BL001. There are five customers in the first column. After the fifth customer (Customer Number GR001), the next customer is found at the top of the middle column. Notice that the last record in the last column of the first page starts the Oregon customers.

Mountain Animal Hospital Customer Directory

Sunday, August 06, 1995

Customer Number: AK001
Animal Kingdom
15 Marlin Lane
Borderville, ID 83483-5646
(208) 555-7108

Customer Since: 5/22/90
Last Visit: 12/9/93
Discount: 20%

Customer Number: BL001
Bird Land
22 Eagle Blvd
Russettown, ID 83412-1021
(208) 555-4367

Customer Since: 8/9/92
Last Visit:
Discount: 20%

Customer Number: BR001
Stephen Brown
555 Sycamore Ave
Three Corners, ID 83401-1
(208) 555-1237

Customer Since: 9/1/92
Last Visit: 1/16/93
Discount: 0%

Customer Number: GB001
George Bird Sanctuary
George St.
Mount Pilot, ID 83908-1012
(208) 555-4852

Customer Since: 4/20/93
Last Visit:
Discount: 50%

Customer Number: GR001
George Green
9133 Bookland Rd
Russettown, ID 83412-1012
(208) 555-8898

Customer Since: 12/4/92
Last Visit: 6/17/93
Discount: 0%

Customer Number: JO002
Adam Johnson
55 Childs Ave
Mount Pilot, ID 83412-1043
(208) 555-2211

Customer Since: 4/1/93
Last Visit: 3/7/93
Discount: 0%

Customer Number: MP002
Mount Pilot Zoo
37 Mount Pilot St.
Mount Pilot, ID 83124-1043
(208) 555-9000

Customer Since: 3/15/92
Last Visit:
Discount: 50%

Customer Number: PC001
Pet City
91 Main St.
Mount Pilot, ID 83187-5638
(208) 555-1765

Customer Since: 12/24/9
Last Visit: 6/18/93
Discount: 20%

Customer Number: PO001
Tyrone Potter
9133 Bookland Rd
Three Corners, ID 83412-1
(208) 555-1199

Customer Since: 3/11/93
Last Visit: 6/15/93
Discount: 0%

Customer Number: RH001
Karen Rhodes
3403 37th Ave
Russettown, ID 83412-1021
(208) 555-9113

Customer Since: 11/11/9
Last Visit: 6/15/93
Discount: 0%

Customer Number: RN001
Rocky Nature Center
2234 Pine St.
Russettown, ID 83124-5145
(208) 555-0983

Customer Since: 2/10/93
Last Visit:
Discount: 50%

Customer Number: TC001
Three Corners Pets
990 Wise St.
Three Corners, ID 83985-7
(208) 555-4132

Customer Since: 6/27/92
Last Visit:
Discount: 20%

Customer Number: VP001
Village Pets
30 Murphy St.
Russettown, ID 83019-8573
(208) 555-1234

Customer Since: 7/5/92
Last Visit: 6/28/93
Discount: 20%

Customer Number: WL001
We Love Birds
1434 Pauly St.
Three Corners, ID 83412-1
(208) 555-7763

Customer Since: 9/6/93
Last Visit:
Discount: 20%

Customer Number: AD002
William Adams
1122 10th St
Lakeville, OR 97401-1011
(503) 555-6187

Customer Since: 10/22/9
Last Visit: 1/27/93
Discount: 5%

Figure 29-13: A snaked column report.

Creating Mail Merge Reports

Now you've learned how to create snaked column reports and mailing labels (actually, they are the same thing), there is one more type of report to create — the *mail merge report* (these are also known as *form letters*). A mail merge report is simply a report containing large amounts of text that have embedded database fields. For example, a letter may contain the amount owed by a customer and the name of a pet within the body of the text.

The problem is to control the *word wrap*. This means that the text may take more than one line, depending on the length of the text and the embedded field values. Different records may have different length values in their embedded fields. One record may use two lines in the report, another may use three, yet another may require only one.

New! Access for Windows 95 contains a Report Wizard that exports your data to Word and launches Word's Print Merge feature. Why would you want to use a word processor, however, when you're in a database? What happens if you don't use Microsoft Word? Most word processors can perform mail merges using database data. Access itself does not have a specific capability to perform mail merging. Even so, as you see in this section, Access can indeed perform mail merge capabilities with nearly the same precision as any Windows word processor!

In the first section of this chapter, you created mailing labels that indicated a special offer. You can use these labels to address the envelopes for the mail merge letter you now create. Suppose you need to send a letter to all your customers who have an outstanding balance. You need to let them know you need payment now.

Figure 29-14 shows a letter created with Access. Many of the data fields embedded in this letter come from an Access query. The letter itself was created entirely with the Access Report Writer, as were its embedded fields.

Mountain Animal Hospital
2414 Mountain Road South
Redmond, WA 06761
(206) 555-9999

August 06, 1995

All Creatures
21 Grace St.
Tall Pines, WA 98746-2541

Dear All Creatures:

It has come to our attention that you have an outstanding balance of $2,000.00. We must have payment within 10 days or we will have to turn this account over to our lawyers. We give great service to your pets. In fact, according to our records, we have helped care for your animals since March 1993.

The entire staff is very fond of your animals. They especially like Bobo, and they would be very upset if your pet was no longer cared for by us. Since your last visit date on November 26, 1993, we have tried to contact you several times without success. Therefore, we are giving you 10 days to pay at least half of the outstanding balance, which comes to $1,000.00.

In advance, thank you, and we look forward to hearing from you and receiving your payment by August 16, 1995.

Sincerely,

Fred G. Rizzley

President
Mountain Animal Hospital

Figure 29-14: A letter created with the Access Report Writer.

Assembling data for a mail merge report

You can use data from either a table or a query for a report. A mail merge report is no different from any other report. As long as you specify a table or query as the control source for the report, the report can be created. Figure 29-15 displays a typical query used for the letter.

Table 29-1 shows the fields or functions embedded in the text blocks used to create the letter. Compare the values found in each line of the letter (shown in Figure 29-14) to the fields shown in the table. Later in this chapter, you'll see how each field or function is embedded in the text.

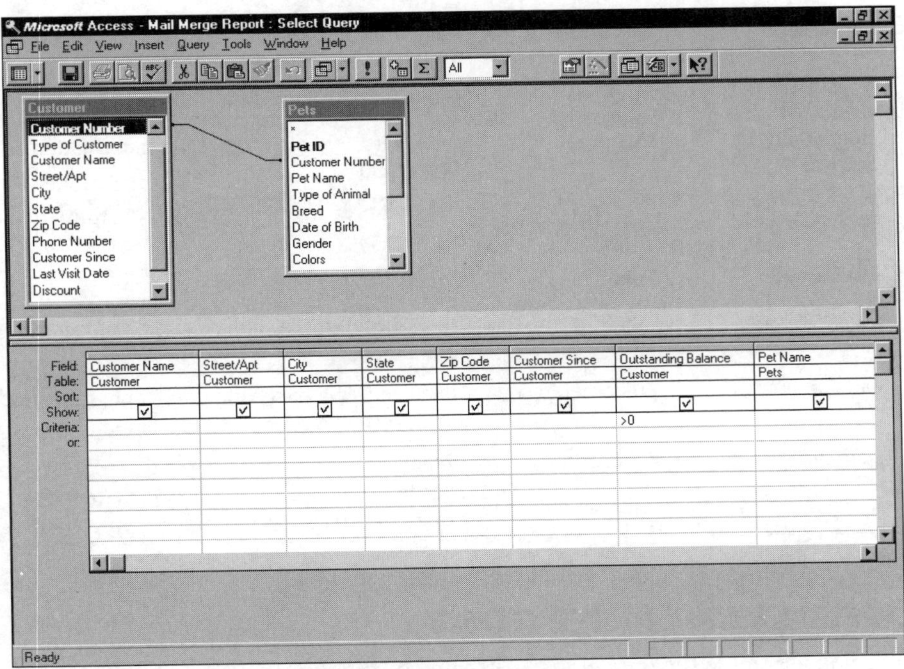

Figure 29-15: A typical query for a mail merge report.

Table 29-1
Fields Used in the Mail Merge Report

Field Name	*Table*	*Usage in Report*
Date()	Function	Page header; displays current date; formatted as mmmm dd, yyyy
Customer Name	Customer	Page header; displays customer name
Street/Apt	Customer	Page header; displays street in the address block
City	Customer	Page header; part of city, state, ZIP code block
State	Customer	Page header; part of city, state, ZIP code block
ZIP Code	Customer	Page header; part of city, state, ZIP code block; formatted as @@@@@-@@@@
Customer Name	Customer	Detail; part of salutation
Outstanding Balance	Customer	Detail; first line of first paragraph; formatted as $#,##0.00
Customer Since	Customer	Detail; fourth line of first paragraph; formatted as mmmm yyyy
Pet Name	Pets	Detail; first line of second paragraph
Last Visit Date	Customer	Detail; second/third line of second paragraph; formatted as mmm dd, yyyy
Outstanding	Customer/	Detail; fifth line of second paragraph; formatted as $#,##0.00 Balance *.5 Calculation
Date Add();	Function;	Detail; second line of third paragraph; Date Add adds ten days Now() Function to system date Now(); formatted as mmmm dd, yyyy

Creating a mail merge report

After you assemble the data, you can create your report. Creating a mail merge report is much like creating other reports. Frequently a mail merge has only a page header and a detail section. You can, however, use sorting and grouping sections to enhance the mail merge report (although normally form letters are fairly consistent in their content).

Usually the best way to begin is with a blank report. The Report Wizards don't really help you create a mail merge report. After you create the blank report, you can begin to add your controls to it.

Creating the page header area

Generally a form letter has a top part that includes your company's name, address, and possibly a logo. You can print on preprinted forms that contain this information, or you can scan in the header and embed it in an unbound object frame. Usually the top part of a form letter also contains the current date, along with the name and address of the person or company you're sending the letter to.

Figure 29-16 shows the page header section of the mail merge report. In this example, an unbound bitmap picture is inserted that contains Mountain Animal Hospital's logo. The text for the company information is created with individual label controls. As you can see in the top half of the page header section, the current date is also displayed along with a line to separate the top of the header from the body of the letter. You can see the calculated text box control's properties at the bottom of Figure 29-16. The Format( ) and Date( ) functions are used to display the date with the full text for month, followed by the day, a comma, a space, and the four-digit year.

The date expression is entered as

=Format(Date(),"mmmm dd, yyyy")

and then automatically changed to

```
=Format(Date(),"mmmm dd"",""yyyy")
```

This expression takes the system date of 08/03/95 and formats the date as August 3, 1995.

The customer name and address fields are also displayed in the page header. The standard concatenated expression is used to display the city, state, and ZIP code fields:

```
=[City] & ", " & [State] & " " & Format([Zip Code],"@@@@@-@@@@")
```

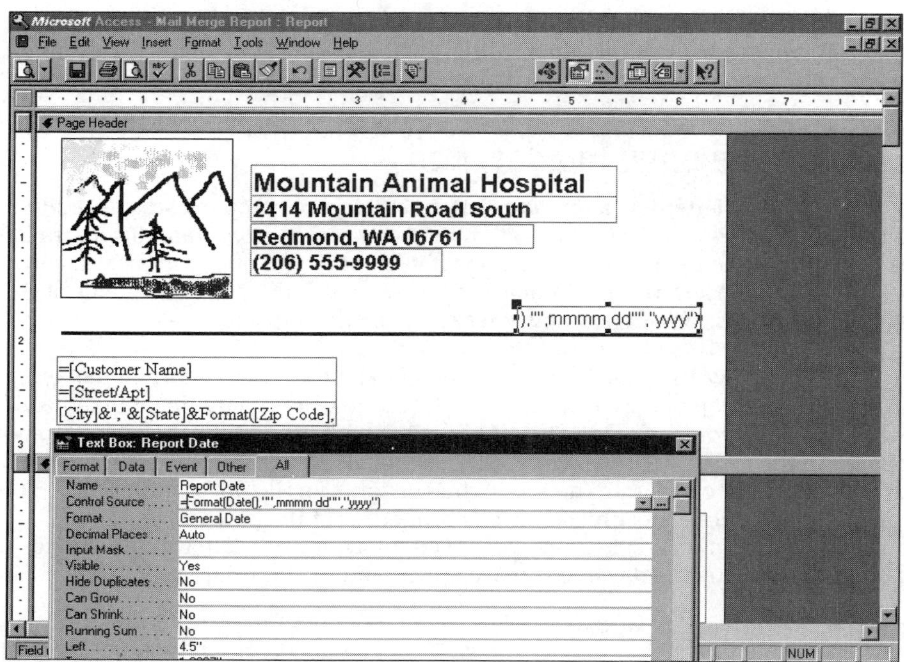

Figure 29-16: The page header section of a mail merge report.

Working with embedded fields in text

The body of the letter is shown in Figure 29-17. Each paragraph is one large block of text. A standard text box control is used to display each paragraph. The text box control's Can Grow and Can Shrink properties are set to Yes. This allows the text to take up only as much space as needed.

Embedded in each text block are fields from the query or expressions that use the fields from the query. In the page header section, the & method is used to concatenate the city, state, and ZIP code. Although this method works for single concatenated lines, it does not allow word wrapping, which is critical to creating a mail merge report. If you use this method in large blocks of text, you get only a single truncated line of text.

Cross Ref

As you learned in Chapter 23, the & method of concatenation handles word wrap within the defined width of the text box. When the text reaches the right margin of a text box, it shifts down to the next line. Because the Can Grow property is turned on, the text box can have any number of lines. It's best to convert nontext data to text when you concatenate with the & method. Although this isn't mandatory, it displays the embedded fields more correctly when they are correctly converted and formatted.

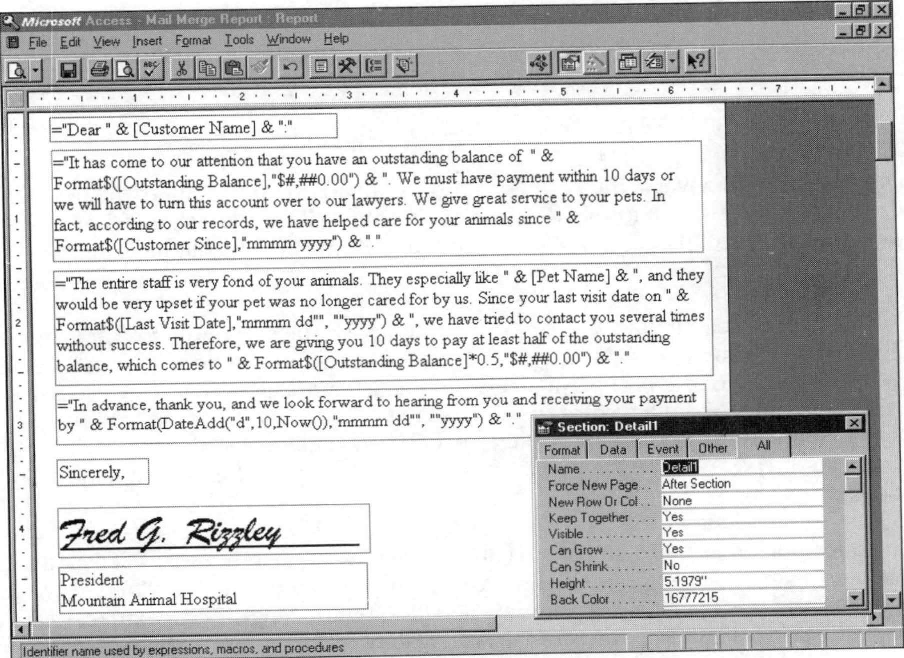

Figure 29-17: The body of the letter in the Report Design window.

The first text block is a single-line text box control that concatenates the text `"Dear"` with the field `Customer Name`. Notice that there are some special symbols within the first text box control. Remember that each text box is made up of smaller groups of text and expressions. By using the & character, you can concatenate them.

The expression **="Dear" & [Customer Name] & ":"** begins with an equal sign and a double quote. Because the first item is text, it's surrounded by " characters. [Customer Name] needs to be enclosed in brackets because it's a field name; it should also be surrounded by & characters for concatenation. The colon at the end of the expression appears in the letter; it too is text, and must be surrounded by double quotes.

The next control produces the first paragraph of the letter. Notice there are five lines in the text box control, but only four lines in the first paragraph of the letter (as shown in Figure 29-14). If you compare the two figures carefully, however, you'll see that the text box for the date is on the fifth line of the paragraph in the text control, whereas it's in the fourth line of the paragraph in the printed letter. This is a good example of word wrap. The lines shrank to fit the data.

The first line of the text control simply displays a text string. Notice the text string is both enclosed in double quotes *and* concatenated to the next expression by the & character. The second line begins with an expression:

```
Format$([Outstanding Balance],"$#,##0.00") & "."
```

The expression converts the numeric expression to text, and formats the field Outstanding Balance so it shows a dollar sign, a comma (if the value is 1,000 or more), and two displayed decimal places. Without the format, the field would have simply displayed `381` for the first record rather than `$381.00`.

The rest of the second line of the paragraph through the end of the fourth is one long text string. It's simply enclosed in double quotes and concatenated by the & character. The last line of the first paragraph contains an expression that formats and converts a date field. The expression `Format$([Customer Since],"mmmm yyyy")` formats the date value to display only the full month name and the year. (The date format in the page header demonstrated how to display the full month name, day, and year.)

Warning The maximum length of a single concatenated expression in Access is 254 characters between a single set of quotes. To get around this limitation, just end one expression, add an **&** character, and start another. The limit on the length of an expression in a single text box is 2,048 characters (almost 40 lines)!

The last line of the second paragraph formats a numeric expression, but it also calculates a value within the format function. This is a good example of an expression within a function. The calculation **[Outstanding Balance] * .5** is then formatted to display dollar signs, and a comma if the number is 1,000 or more.

The last paragraph contains one text string and one expression. The expression advances the current date Now() by 10 days by using the expression **DateAdd("d",10,Now())**.

The bottom of the letter is produced using the label controls as shown in Figure 29-17. These label controls display the closing, the signature, and the owners title. The signature of Fred G. Rizzley is created here by using the Script font. Normally you would scan in the signature and then use an unbound frame object control to display the bitmap picture that contains the signature.

One thing you must do is set the Force New Page property of the detail section to After Section so there is always a page break after each letter.

Printing the mail merge report

You print a mail merge report in exactly the same way you would any report. From the Print Preview window, you can simply select the Print button. From the Report Design window, you can select File⇨Print. The report is printed out like any other report.

Using the Access Mail Merge Wizard for Word for Windows 6.0 or 95

Another feature in Access 95 is a Wizard to open Word automatically and start the Print Merge feature. The table or query you specify when you create the new report is used as the data source for the Word for Windows 6.0 or Word for Windows 95 print merge.

Warning You must have either Word 6.0 for Windows 3.1, Word for Windows 95 Version 7.0, or the Word in Office 95 to use the Mail Merge Wizard in Access for Windows 95.

1. From the Database container window, select either the Table or Query Tab.
2. Select the table or query you would like to merge with Word for Windows.
3. Click on the OfficeLinks drop-down button in the toolbar.
4. Click on Merge It to start the Mailmerge Report Wizard as shown in Figure 29-18.

   After you select the MS Word Mail Merge Wizard, Access displays the Microsoft Word Mail Merge Wizard screen as shown in Figure 29-19.

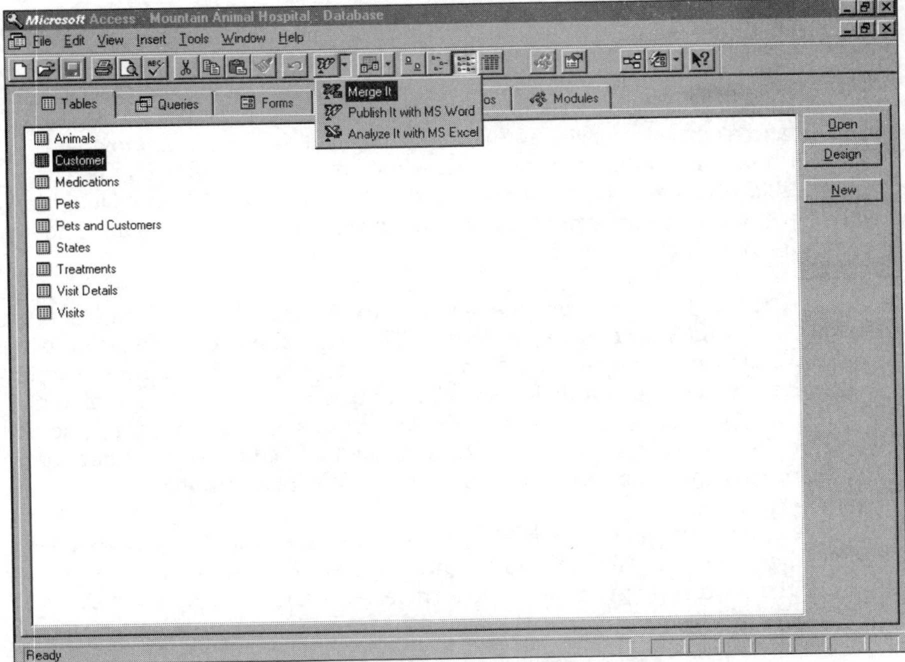

Figure 29-18: Selecting the MS Word Mail Merge Wizard.

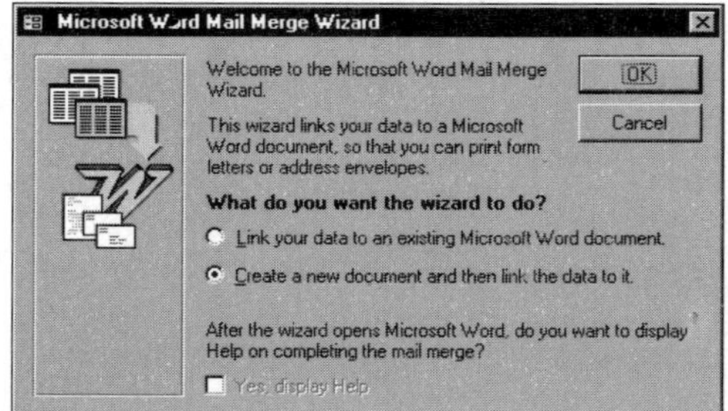

Figure 29-19: The Microsoft Word Mail Merge Wizard screen.

This screen lets you decide whether to start Word for Windows 6.0 or 7.0 with a new document, and whether Word should open an existing document. If you select the option that says to Link your data to an existing Microsoft Word document, Access displays a standard Windows file selection box that lets you select an existing document. The document is retrieved, Word is displayed, and the Print Merge feature is active. You can then modify your existing document.

In this example, you will start with a new document.

5. Select the option to Create a new document and then link the data to it.
6. Click on OK to launch Word and display the Print Merge toolbar.

You may also get a dialog box asking for the field and record delimiter, usually a quote (") and a comma (,), with some type of merged data. You can now create your document, adding merge fields where you want them. As shown in Figure 29-20, you simply type your text and click on the Insert Merge Field button whenever you want to display a field list from your Access table or query. The fields appear with a pair of carets around them.

When you're through, you can use the Mailmerge command button to merge the actual data and print your mail merge letters. There are some advantages to using the Microsoft Word print merge facility to create your letters. You have the availability of a spell checker, you can properly justify your paragraphs, and you can individually change the font type, size, or weight of individual words or characters. The negatives are that you have to use a word processor, you can't format numeric or date data, and you can't embed other Access objects such as datasheets or graphs.

An example of a document created using the Mailmerge feature is shown in Figure 29-21. The merged fields have been highlighted in bold to make them stand out. An example of the hard-copy printout of the form letter is shown in Figure 29-22.

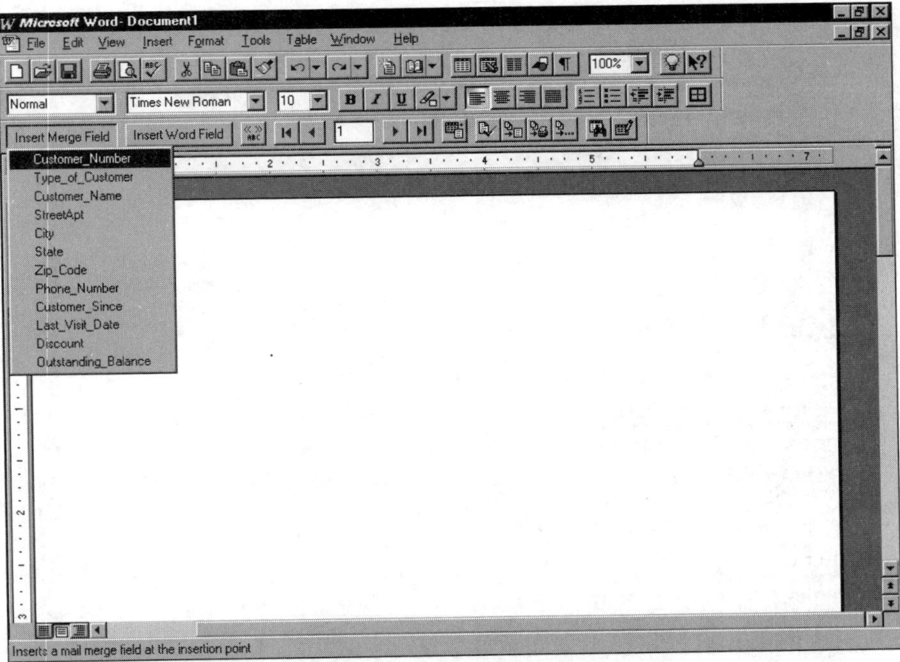

Figure 29-20: The Word for Windows Print Merge screen.

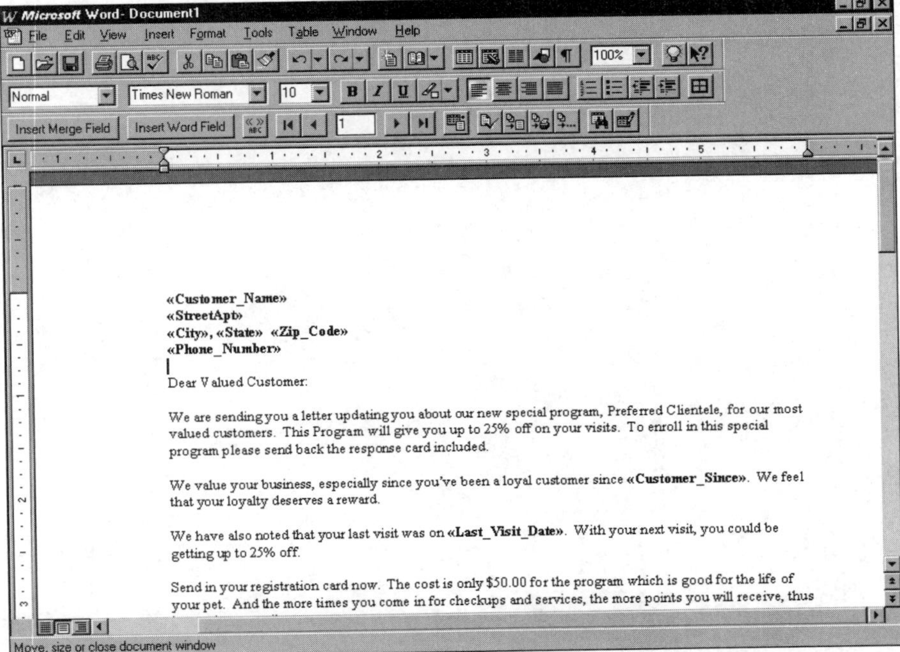

Figure 29-21: An example of a document created with the Mailmerge feature.

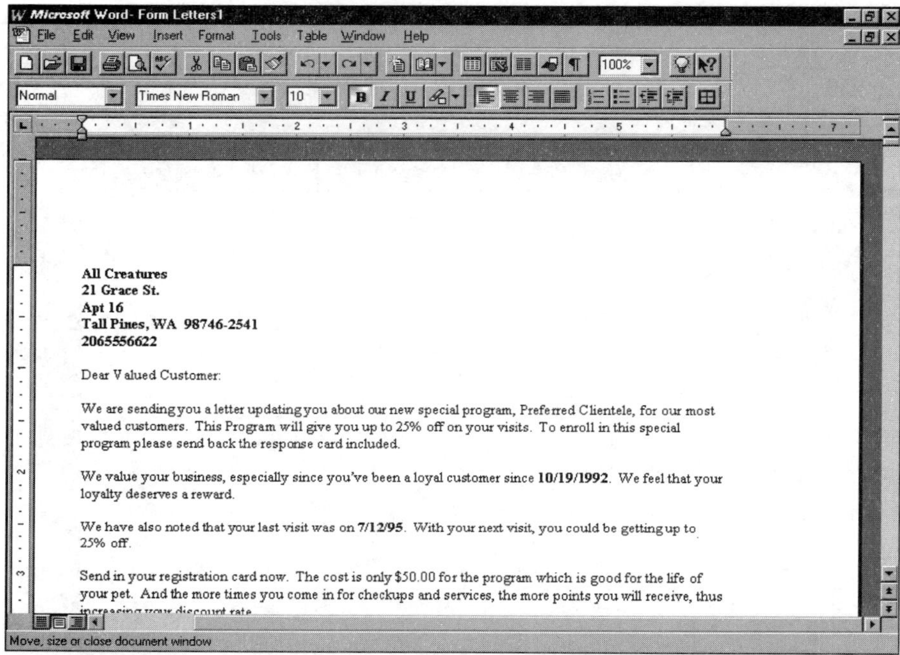

All Creatures
21 Grace St.
Apt 16
Tall Pines, WA 98746-2541
2065556622

Dear Valued Customer:

We are sending you a letter updating you about our new special program, Preferred Clientele, for our most valued customers. This Program will give you up to 25% off on your visits. To enroll in this special program please send back the response card included.

We value your business, especially since you've been a loyal customer since **10/19/1992**. We feel that your loyalty deserves a reward.

We have also noted that your last visit was on **7/12/95**. With your next visit, you could be getting up to 25% off.

Send in your registration card now. The cost is only $50.00 for the program which is good for the life of your pet. And the more times you come in for checkups and services, the more points you will receive, thus

Figure 29-22: Printout of the form letter using the Mailmerge function.

When you're through editing and printing your letter, you can return to Access by selecting File➪Close or File➪Exit.

Summary

In this chapter, you learned how to create mailing labels, snaked column reports, and mail merge reports. The following concepts were discussed:

- ✦ Mailing labels are most easily created using the Access Mailing Label Report Wizard.
- ✦ The Report Wizard lets you select the fields for the mailing label and also select from over 100 Avery mailing label forms.
- ✦ Using the Report Design window, you can customize the mailing label further.
- ✦ The secret to mailing labels is changing the settings in the expanded Page Setup dialog box.
- ✦ Snaked column reports can be snaked vertically or horizontally.
- ✦ Snaked column reports are essentially large labels on paper; they are used for such things as customer directories.
- ✦ You can create mail merge reports with the Access Report Writer.
- ✦ By using concatenated text boxes, you can create paragraphs of text with embedded fields that word-wrap to create form letters.
- ✦ You can use the Format( ) function to reformat numeric and date fields in a mail merge report.
- ✦ The Word for Windows 6.0 or 95 Mail Merge Wizard makes exported Access data easy to use with the Print Merge feature in Word 6.0 or Word for Windows 95.

This completes Part IV of the book, which deals with advanced Access query, form, and report topics. The next section covers the use of Access macros you can use to automate tasks without programming.

✦ ✦ ✦

Applications in Access

✦ ✦ ✦ ✦

In This Part

✦ ✦ ✦ ✦

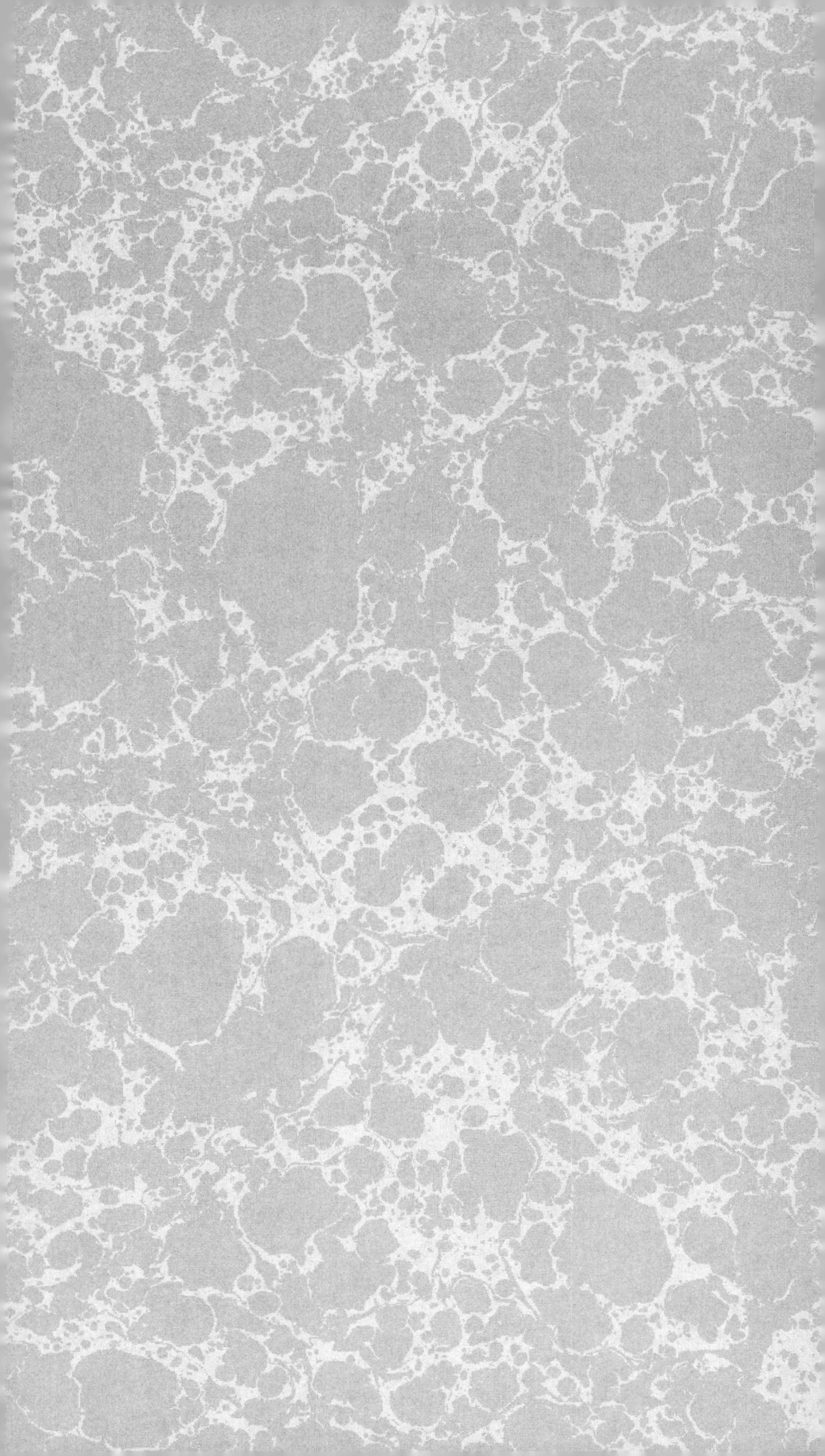

An Introduction to Macros and Events

In This Chapter

How macros work

The various components of the Macro window

How to create and run a macro

How to edit, delete, and rename macros

How to create macro groups

How to create a macro that starts automatically

How to supply conditions to macros

How to troubleshoot macros

How events work

How events are triggered

When you work with your database system, you may perform the same tasks over and over. Instead of doing the same steps every time, you can automate the process by using macros.

Database management systems continually grow as you add records in a form, perform *ad-hoc* queries, and print new reports. As the system grows, you save many of the objects for later use — for a weekly report, a monthly update query, and so on. You tend to create and perform many tasks repetitively. Every time you add customer records, for example, you open the same form; you print the same form letter for customers whose pets are overdue for their annual shots.

You can create Access *macros* to perform these tasks. After you've created these small programs, you may want certain macros to take effect whenever a user performs some action (such as pressing a button or opening a form). Access uses *events* to trigger a macro automatically.

Understanding Macros

Access macros automate many repetitive tasks without writing complex programs or subroutines. In the example of the form letter for customers whose pets are overdue for annual shots, a macro can perform a query and print the results for all such customers.

What is a macro?

A *macro* is an object like other Access objects (tables, queries, forms, and reports), except you create it to automate a particular task (or series of tasks). Think of each task as the result of one or more steps, each step being an action not found in the Access menu but in the Visual Basic or VBA language. You can also use Access macros to simulate menu choices or mouse movements.

Unlike macros in spreadsheets, normally Access macros are not used to duplicate individual keystrokes or mouse movements. They perform specific, user-specified tasks, such as opening a form or running a report.

Every task you want Access to perform is called an *action*. Access provides 49 actions you can select and perform in your macros. For example, you may have a macro that performs the four actions shown in Figure 30-1:

- ✦ Place the hourglass on the screen
- ✦ Automatically open a form
- ✦ Maximize the form after opening it
- ✦ Display a message box that says the macro is complete

Macro actions are created in a Macro Design window. The macros are run by entering the macro name in the Event properties of a form or report.

When to use a macro

You can use macros for any repetitive task you do in Access, so you save time and energy. In addition, because the macro performs the actions in the same way every time, macros add accuracy and efficiency to your database. You can use macros to perform such tasks as

- ✦ Link and run queries and reports together
- ✦ Open multiple forms and/or reports together
- ✦ Check for data accuracy on validation forms
- ✦ Move data between tables
- ✦ Perform actions when a command button is selected

As an example, a macro can find and filter records for a report. You can add a button to a form that makes a macro perform a user-specified search. Macros can be used throughout the Access database system.

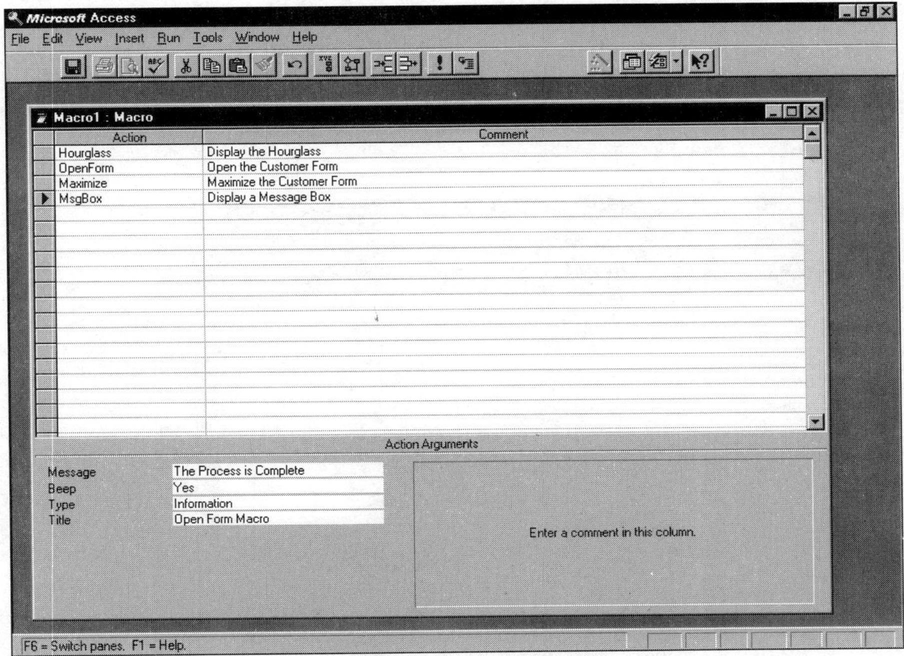

Figure 30-1: A macro designed with four actions (tasks).

The Macro Window

As with other Access objects, you create a macro in a graphical design window. To open a new Macro window, follow these steps:

1. In an open database, press F11 (or Alt+F1) to select the Database window.
2. Click on the Macros tab.
3. Click on the New command button in the Database window.

After you complete these steps, Access displays an empty Design window similar to the one in Figure 30-2. Notice the different parts of the window in this figure.

As Figure 30-2 shows, the Macro Design window has four parts: a menu and a toolbar above the Design window, and these two window panes:

✦ Action pane (top portion of the window)

✦ Argument pane (bottom portion of the window)

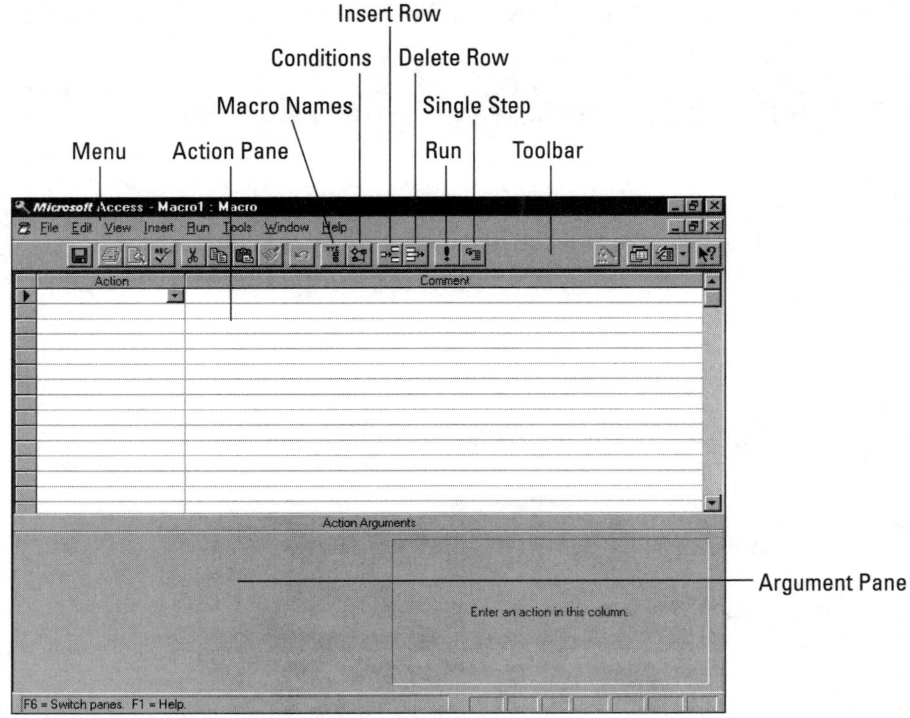

Figure 30-2: The empty Macro Design window.

The Action pane

By default, when you open a new Macro Design window, as in Figure 30-2, Access displays two columns in the Action pane (top pane). These are the Action and Comment columns. Two more columns, Macro Name and Condition, can be displayed in the Action pane by selecting View⇨Macro Names and View⇨Conditions or by selecting the equivalent icons ion the toolbar.

Note If you want to change the default so that all four columns are open, select Tools⇨Options and then select the View tab and place a check mark in both the Show in Macro Design items.

Each macro can have one or many actions (individual tasks you want Access to perform). You add individual actions in the Action column, and you can add a description of each action in the Comment column. Access ignores the comments when the macro is run.

The Argument pane

The lower portion of the window is the *Argument pane*. This is where you supply the specific *arguments* (properties) needed for the selected action. Most actions need additional information to carry out the action, such as which object should be used. For example, Figure 30-3 shows the action arguments for a typical action named OpenForm, which opens a specific form and has six different arguments that can be specified:

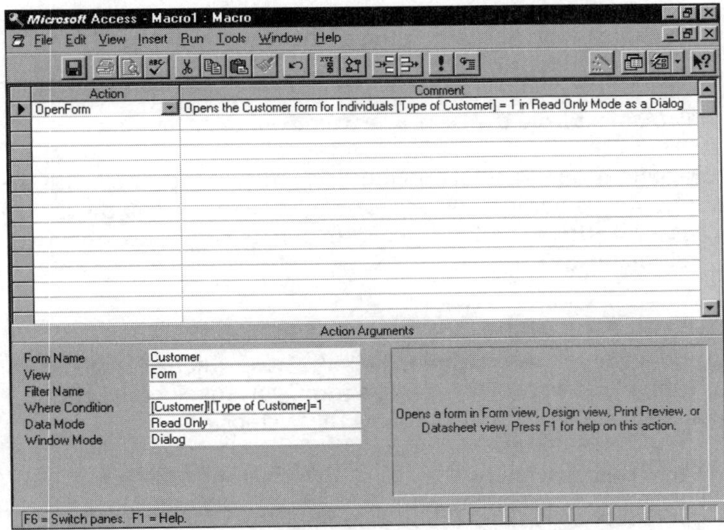

Figure 30-3: Arguments displayed for the OpenForm action.

Form Name	Specifies the Access form to open
View	Specifies the view mode to activate: Form, Design, Print Preview, Datasheet
Filter Name	Applies the specified filter, or query
Where Condition	Limits the records displayed
Data Mode	Specifies a data-entry mode: Add, Edit, or Read Only
Window Mode	Specifies a window mode: Normal, Hidden, Icon, Dialog

Note Some actions, such as Beep and Maximize, have no arguments; most require at least one argument.

Creating a macro

To create a macro, you use both panes of the Macro window — Action and Argument. After you supply actions and associated arguments, you can save the macro for later use.

Entering actions and arguments

You can add actions to a macro in any of several ways:

✦ Enter the action name in the Action column of the Macro window.

✦ Select actions from the pull-down list box of actions (in the Action column).

✦ Drag and drop an object from the Database window into an action cell.

The last method, drag-and-drop, is useful for common actions associated with the database. For example, you can drag a specific form to an action cell in the macro Action column; Access will add the action OpenForm and its known arguments (such as the form name) automatically.

Selecting actions from the combo box list

The easiest way to add an action is by using the combo box, which you can access in any action cell. For example, if you want to open a form, you specify the action OpenForm. To create the OpenForm action, follow these steps:

1. Open a new Macro Design window.
2. Click on the first empty cell in the Action column.
3. Click on the arrow that appears in the action cell.
4. Select the OpenForm action from the combo box.

u don't have to add comments to the macro, but it's a good idea to document the ason for each macro action (as well as a description of the entire macro).

Specifying arguments for actions

After entering the OpenForm action, you can enter the arguments into the bottom pane. You'll recall that Figure 30-3, which displays the completed arguments, shows that the bottom pane has six action arguments associated with this specific action. The arguments View, Data Mode, and Window Mode have default values. Because Access does not know which form you want to open, you must at least enter a form name. To open the form named Customer as a dialog in read-only mode, you enter the three arguments Form Name, Data Mode, and Window Mode, as shown earlier in Figure 30-3.

To add the arguments, follow these steps:

1. Click in the Form Name cell (or press F6 to switch to the Argument pane).
2. Select the Customer form from the pull-down list box (or type the name).
3. Click in the Data Mode cell.
4. Select the Read Only choice from the pull-down list (or type the choice).
5. Click in the Window Mode cell.
6. Select the Dialog choice from the pull-down list (or type the choice).

Your macro should now resemble the one in Figure 30-3. Notice that the Form Name is now specified and the default values of the Data Mode and Window Mode cells are changed.

Selecting actions by dragging and dropping objects

You can also specify actions by dragging and dropping objects from the Database window. When you add actions in this manner, Access adds the appropriate arguments automatically. To add the same form (Customer) to an empty Macro window, follow these steps:

1. Start with an empty Macro Design window.
2. Select Window⇨Tile Vertically from the Design menu. Access places the Macro and Database windows side by side.
3. Click on the Forms tab in the Database window. Access displays all the forms, as in Figure 30-4.
4. Click on and drag the form Customer from the Database window. Access displays a Form icon as it moves into the Macro window.
5. Continue to drag and drop the Form icon in any empty action cell of the Macro window.

Access displays the correct action and arguments automatically.

Note After using the drag-and-drop method to select actions, you may need to modify the action arguments to further refine them from their default values. Recall that in the last example, you changed Data Mode and Window Mode for the form.

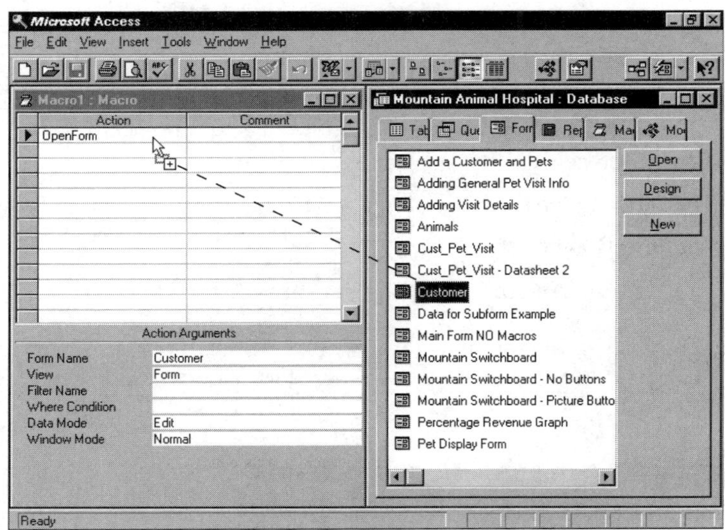

Figure 30-4: The Macro and Database windows are tiled side by side.

Adding multiple actions to a macro

You are not limited to adding a single action in a macro. You can have multiple actions assigned to a macro. For example, you may want to display an hourglass and then, while it's displayed, open two forms. Then you can have the computer beep for the user after completing the macro. To accomplish these multiple actions, follow these steps:

1. Open a new Macro Design window.
2. Click on the first empty cell in the Action column.
3. Select the Hourglass action from the pull-down list box or type it.
4. Click in the comment cell alongside the Hourglass action.
5. Type **Display the hourglass while the macro is running**.
6. Click on the next empty cell in the Action column.
7. Select the OpenForm action from the pull-down list box, or type the name of the action.
8. Click in the argument cell Form Name.
9. Select the Add a Customer and Pets form.

10. Click in the comment cell alongside the OpenForm action.
11. Type **Open the Add a Customer and Pets form**.
12. Click in the next empty cell in the Action column.
13. Select the OpenForm action from the pull-down list box or type the action.
14. Click in the argument cell Form Name.
15. Select the Adding Visit Details form.
16. Click in the comment cell alongside the OpenForm action.
17. Type **Open the Adding Visit Details form**.
18. Click in the next empty cell in the Action column.
19. Select the Beep action from the pull-down list box or type the action.

Your macro design should now look similar to Figure 30-5. Notice that this macro will open both forms as it displays the hourglass. After both forms are open, the macro beeps to signal that it is finished.

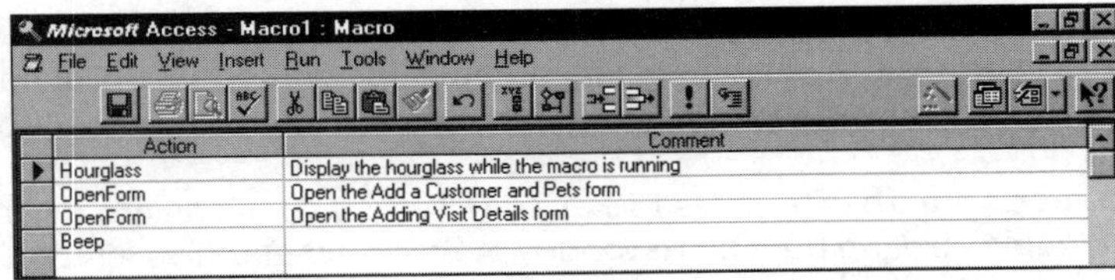

Figure 30-5: Adding multiple actions to a single macro.

Tip When you're adding more than one action, you can specify each action, one after the other, with several rows of spaces in between. These blank rows can contain additional lines of comments for each macro action.

Rearranging macro actions

When you work with multiple actions in a macro, you may change your mind about the order of the actions. For example, you may decide that the macro created in Figure 30-5 should have the Beep action come first in the macro. To move the action, follow these steps:

1. Select the action by clicking on the row selector to the left of the action name.
2. Click on the highlighted row again and drag it to the top row.

Deleting macro actions

If you placed an action in a macro you no longer need, you can delete the action. In the example of the macro shown in Figure 30-5, you may decide you don't want to open the form Adding Visit Details. To delete the action, follow these steps:

1. Select the action by clicking on the row selector to the left of the action's name.
2. Press Delete or select Edit⇨Delete Row from the menu.

Tip: You can also delete a row by using the right-click shortcut menu — select the row to delete, press the *right* mouse button, and select Delete Row.

Saving macros

Before you can run a macro, it must be saved. After you save a macro, it becomes another database object you can open and run from the Database window. To save a macro, follow these steps:

1. Select File⇨Save from the Macro Design menu or click on the Save button on the toolbar.
2. If the macro has not been saved, you must enter a name in the Save As dialog box. Press Enter or choose OK when you're through.

Tip: The fastest way to save a macro is to press F12 or Alt+F2 and give the macro a name. Another way is to double-click on the Macro window's Control menu (top left corner) and answer the appropriate dialog box questions.

Editing existing macros

After you create a macro, you can edit it by following these steps:

1. In the Database window, select the Macro tab.
2. Highlight the macro you want to edit.
3. Click on the Design button in the Database window.

Copying entire macros

To copy a macro, follow these steps:

1. Click on the Macro tab in the Database window.
2. Select the macro you want to copy.

3. Press Ctrl+C or choose Edit⇨Copy to copy the macro to the Clipboard.
4. Press Ctrl+V or choose Edit⇨Paste to paste the macro from the Clipboard.
5. In the Paste As dialog box, type the new name.

Renaming macros

Sometimes you need to rename a macro because you changed the event property in the form or report property. To rename a macro, follow these steps:

1. Select the Database window by pressing F11 or Alt+F1.
2. Click on the Macro tab to display all the macro names.
3. Highlight the macro whose name you want to change.
4. Choose Edit⇨Rename from the Database menu or click the *right* mouse button and choose Rename from the shortcut menu.
5. Enter the new name.

Running Macros

After a macro is created, you can run it yourself from several locations within Access:

✦ A Macro window

✦ A Database window

✦ Other object windows

✦ Another macro

Running a macro from the Macro window

You can run a macro directly from the Macro Design window by clicking on the toolbar's Run button (the exclamation mark) or by choosing Run from the Design menu.

Running a macro from the Database window

You can run a macro from the Database window by following these steps:

1. Click on the macro tab in the Database window.
2. Select the macro you want to run.
3. Either double-click on the macro or choose the Run button.

Running a macro from any window in the database

To run a macro from any window in the database, follow these steps:

1. Select Tools⇨Macro from the menu.
2. In the Macro dialog box, enter the name or select it from the pull-down list box.
3. Click on the OK button or press Enter.

Running a macro from another macro

To run a macro from another macro, follow these steps:

1. Add the action **RunMacro** to your macro.
2. Enter the name of the macro you want to run in the Macro Name argument.

Automatically running a macro when you open a database

You can instruct Access to run a macro automatically every time a database is opened; there are two ways to do this. Access recognizes a special macro name: *AutoExec.* If Access finds it in a database, it executes this macro automatically every time the database is opened. For example, you may want to open some forms and queries automatically and immediately upon opening the database.

To run a macro automatically when a database is opened, follow these steps:

1. Create a macro with the actions you want to run when the database is opened.
2. Save the macro and name it **AutoExec.**

If you close that database and reopen it, Access runs the AutoExec macro automatically.

Tip

If you have a macro named AutoExec but you *don't* want to run it when you open a database, hold down the Shift key as you select the database in the Open Database dialog box.

New!

In Access for Windows 95, databases have an option for setting Startup properties. Here, as shown in Figure 30-6, you can enter the name of a form you want to start when Access is opened. This form can contain the name of a macro to run when the form is loaded (more about form events later). You display the Startup Properties window by selecting Tools⇨Startup from any window. Options you set in the Startup Properties window are in effect as long as the Access database is open. You can set many options from the Startup Properties window; for instance, you can change the title bar of all windows, specify the name of an icon file to use when Access is minimized, and affect many Access custom menus and toolbars.

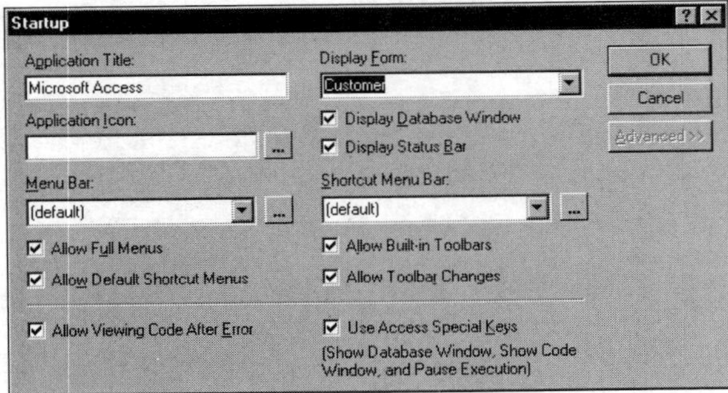

Figure 30-6: Using the Startup properties.

Macro Groups

As you create macros, you may want to group a series of related macros into one large macro. To do this, you need some way of uniquely identifying the individual macros within the group. Access lets you create a *macro group* (a macro file that contains one or more macros).

Creating macro groups

Like individual macros, macro groups are database objects. When you look in the macro object list of the Database window, you see only the macro group's name. Inside the group, each macro has a unique name you assign (along with the actions for each macro).

You may, for example, want to create a macro group of all macros that will open forms. To create this type of macro, follow these steps:

1. In the Database window, select the Macro tab.
2. Click on the New command button in the Database window. Access opens the Macro Design window.

3. Select View⇨Macro Names or select the Macro Names button on the toolbar. Access adds the Macro Name column to the Action pane.
4. In the Macro Name column, enter a name for the macro.
5. In the Action column, next to the macro name you just entered, enter an action for the macro.
6. Select the Action column under the action you just entered so you can enter the next action.
7. Enter the next action (if the macro has more than one) in the Action column. Continue to enter actions until all are specified for that specific macro. To add another macro to the group, repeat Steps 4 through 7.
8. Save the macro group, naming it **Open and Close Forms**.

Figure 30-7 shows how a macro group will look. Notice that there are five separate macros within it.

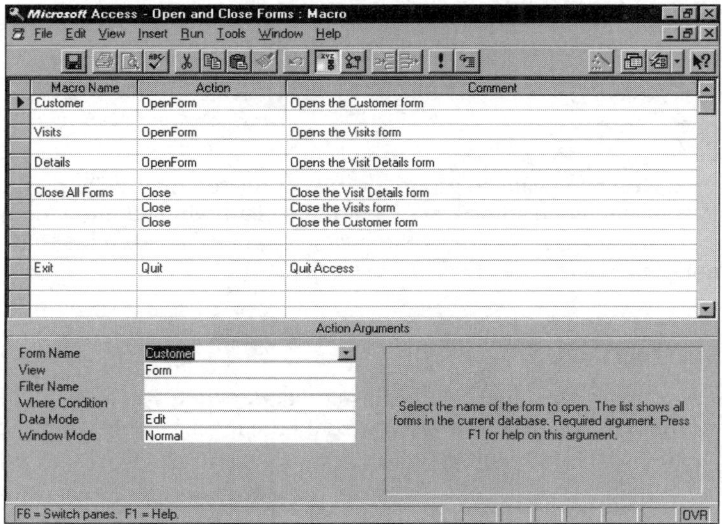

Figure 30-7: A macro group.

The macro group in Figure 30-7 shows five macros: Customer, Visits, Details, Close All Forms, and Exit.

The Arguments pane shows only the arguments for the highlighted macro name.

Tip Although not necessary, it's a good idea to leave a blank line between macros to improve readability and clarity.

Running a macro in a macro group

After you create a macro group, you'll want to run each macro inside the group. To run one, you must specify both the group name and the macro name.

Cross Ref Later in this chapter, you will learn how to use the events that run macros.

To specify both group and macro names, you will have to enter the group name, a period, and then the macro name. If you type **Open and Close Forms.Visits**, for example, you specify the macro Visits in the group macro named Open and Close Forms.

Warning If you run a group macro from the Macro Design window or from the Database window, you cannot specify a macro name inside the macro group. Access will run only the first macro or set of actions specified in the group macro. Access stops executing actions when it reaches a new macro name in the Macro Name column.

To run a macro inside a group macro — using the other windows in the database or another macro — you simply enter both the macro group name and macro name, placing a period between the two names.

Tip You also can run a macro by selecting Macro from the Tools menu and typing the group and macro name.

Supplying Conditions for Actions

In some cases, you may want to run some action or actions in a macro only when a certain condition is true. For example, you may want to display a message if there are no records available for a report, and then stop execution of the macro. In such a case, you can use a condition to control the flow of the macro.

What is a condition?

Simply put, a *condition* is a logical expression; it can only be True or False. The macro will follow one of two paths, depending on the condition of the expression. If the expression is True, the macro follows the True path; otherwise it follows the False path. Table 30-1 shows several conditions and the True/False results.

Table 30-1
Conditions and Their Results

Condition	*True Result*	*False Result*
Forms!Customer!State="WA"	If the state is Washington	Any state except Washington
IsNull(Gender)	If there is no gender specified	Gender is male or female (not Null)
Length <= 10	If length is less than or equal to 10 inches	If the length is greater than 10 inches
Reports![Pet Directory]! [Type animal] = "CAT" OR Reports! [Pet Directory]! [Type of Animal] = "DOG	If type of animal is a cat or dog	Any animal other than cat or dog

Activating the Condition column in a macro

As Table 30-1 demonstrates, a condition is an expression that results in a logical answer of Yes or No. The answer must be either True or False. You can specify a condition in a macro by following these steps:

1. Enter the Macro Design window by creating a new macro or editing an existing one.
2. Select View➪Conditions or select the Conditions button on the toolbar. The Condition column is inserted to the left of the Action column. If the Macro Name column is visible, the Condition column is between the Macro Name and the Action columns (see Figure 30-8).

Referring to control names in expressions

When working with macros, you may need to refer to the value of a control in a form or report. To refer to a control in a form or report, use the following syntax:

```
Forms!form-name!control-name
Reports!report-name!control-
name
```

If a space occurs within the name of a form, report, or control, you must enclose the name in brackets. For example, Forms![Add a Customer and Pets]!State refers to the State control (field on form) on the currently open form called Add a Customer and Pets.

If you run a macro from the same form or report that contains the control, you can shorten this syntax to the control name.

Note: To reference a control name on a form or report, first make sure the form or report is open.

With the Condition column visible, you can specify conditions for one or many actions within a macro.

Tip

In Figure 30-8, you can see that the Condition and Comment columns are wider than the Action column. You can widen or shrink columns by positioning the cursor on the column border and dragging the column line.

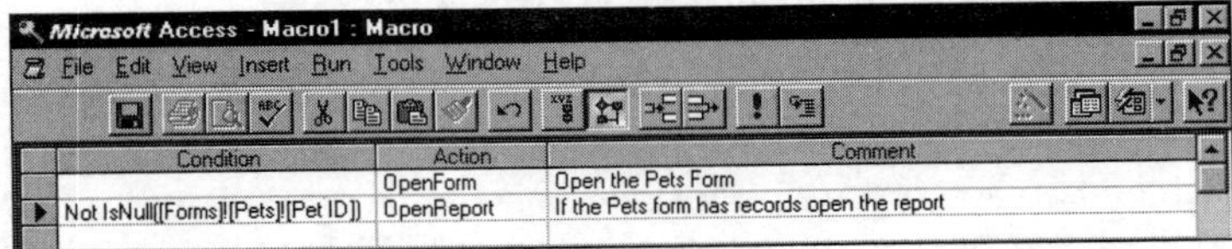

Figure 30-8: The Condition column added to the Macro Design window.

Specifying a condition for a single action

You may want to specify a condition for a single action. An example of this is activating the report Pet Directory only when there are records in the form Pets, based on a query named Only Cats and Dogs. If there are no records present, you want the macro to skip activation of the report. To have the macro specify this condition, as shown in Figure 30-8, follow these steps:

1. In the Macro window, click on the Conditions button on the toolbar.
2. In the first action cell of the Action pane, select OpenForm.
3. In the Form Name cell of the Argument pane, select Pets.
4. In the next action cell of the Action pane, select OpenReport.
5. In the Report Name cell of the Argument pane, select Pet Directory.
6. Click on the condition cell next to the action OpenReport.
7. Type **Not IsNull(Forms![Pets]![Pet ID])**.

At the completion of these steps, your macro should resemble the one in Figure 30-8.

In this example, the condition specified is True if there are no records (the first Pet ID is Null) in the open form Pets. If the condition is True, when the macro is run, the action OpenReport is not performed; otherwise the report is opened in print preview mode.

Warning When you specify conditions in a macro and reference a control name (field name), the source (form or report) of the control name must already be open.

Specifying a condition for multiple actions

Besides specifying a condition for a single action, you can specify a condition that will be effective for multiple actions. That is, a single condition will cause several actions to occur. In this way, you can also create an If-Then-Else condition.

If you want Access to perform more than one action, add the other actions below the first one. In the Condition column, place an ellipsis (...) beside each action. Figure 30-9 shows a macro in which two actions are performed based on a single condition. Notice that the condition has been changed to IsNull from Not IsNull.

In Figure 30-9, the condition IsNull(Forms![Pets]![Pet ID]) performs the two actions MsgBox and StopMacro if the condition is True. Notice the ellipsis (...) in the cell immediately under the specified condition, which is the condition cell for the action StopMacro.

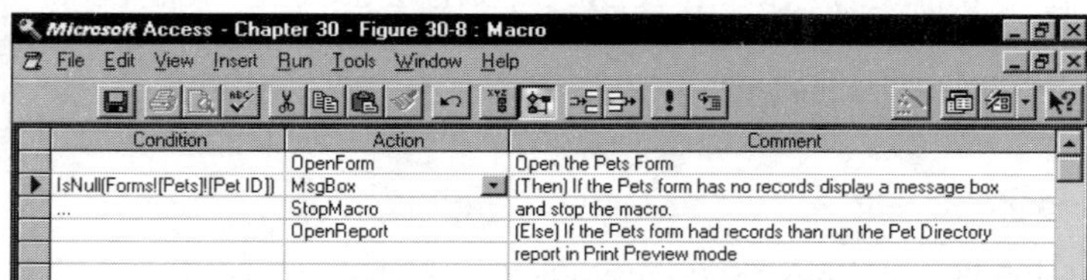

Condition	Action	Comment
	OpenForm	Open the Pets Form
IsNull(Forms![Pets]![Pet ID])	MsgBox	(Then) If the Pets form has no records display a message box
...	StopMacro	and stop the macro.
	OpenReport	(Else) If the Pets form had records than run the Pet Directory
		report in Print Preview mode

Figure 30-9: This macro shows two actions based on a single condition.

When you run the macro, Access evaluates the expression in the condition cell. If the expression is True, Access performs the action beside the expression, and then all the following actions that have an ellipsis in the Condition column. Access continues the True actions until it comes to another condition (using the new condition from that point on).

If the expression is False, Access ignores the action(s) and moves to the next action row that does not have an ellipsis.

Warning If Access reaches a blank cell in the Condition column, it performs the action in that row regardless of the conditional expression. The only way to avoid this is to control the flow of actions by use of a *redirection action* such as RunMacro or StopMacro. For example, if the second conditional action (StopMacro) is not after the MsgBox action, the OpenReport action is executed regardless of whether the conditional expression is True or False. On the other hand, the MsgBox action takes effect only if the field Pet ID is Null (True).

Controlling the flow of actions

By using conditional expressions, you can control the flow of action in the macro. The macro in Figure 30-9 uses the action StopMacro to stop execution of the macro if the field is Null; thus it avoids opening the report Pet Directory if the table is empty.

Several macro actions can be used to change or control the flow of actions based on a condition. The two most common are the actions StopMacro and RunMacro; they also control the flow of actions within a macro.

Troubleshooting Macros

Access has two tools to help you find problems in your macros:

- ✦ The single-step mode
- ✦ The Action Failed dialog box

The single-step mode

If, while running a macro, you receive unexpected results, you can use the *single-step mode* to move through the macro one action at a time, pausing between actions. By single-stepping, you can observe the result of each action and isolate the action or actions that caused the incorrect results.

To use single-stepping, click on the Single-Step button on the toolbar. To use this feature on the macro in Figure 30-9, follow these steps:

1. Edit the macro, bringing it into the Macro Design window.
2. Click on the Single-Step button on toolbar or select Run⇨Single Step.
3. Run the macro as you normally do or by clicking on the Run button on the toolbar.

Access displays the Macro Single Step dialog box, showing the macro name, the action name, and the arguments for the action. Figure 30-10 shows a typical Macro Single Step dialog box.

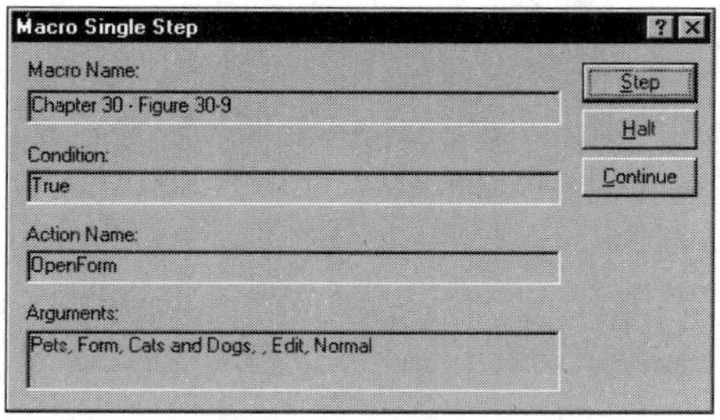

Figure 30-10: The Macro Single Step dialog box.

Table 30-2
Macro Single-Step Button Options

Button	*Purpose*
Step	Runs the action in the dialog box. If no error is reported, the next action appears in the dialog box.
Halt	Stops the execution of the macro and closes the dialog box.
Continue	Turns off the single-step mode and runs the remainder of the macro.

The Action Failed dialog box

If a macro action causes an error (either during single-step mode or when running normally), Access opens a dialog box that looks exactly like the Macro Single Step dialog box, except the only available button is the Halt button.

To correct the problem, choose Halt, return to the Macro Design window, and correct the problem.

Understanding Events

With the actions stored in macros, you can run the macro either via a menu choice or by naming the macro **AutoExec**. The AutoExec macro runs automatically every time you open the database. Access also offers another method to activate a macro: basing it on a user action.

For example, the user can select a command button to activate a macro or by the action of opening a form. To accomplish this, Access takes advantage of something known as an *event.*

What is an event?

An Access event is the result or consequence of some user action. An Access event can occur when a user moves from one record to another in a form, closes a report, or selects a command button on a form.

Your Access applications are *event-driven*. Objects in Access respond to many types of events. Access responds to events with behaviors that are built-in for each object. Access events can be recognized by specific object properties. For example, if a user presses the mouse button with the pointer in a check box, the property OnMouseDown recognizes that the mouse button was pressed. You can have this property run a macro when the user presses the mouse button.

Events in Access for Windows 95 can be categorized into seven groups:

- **Windows (Form, Report) events:** opening, closing, resizing, and so on
- **Data events:** making current, deleting, after updating, and so on
- **Focus events:** activating, entering, exiting, and so on
- **Keyboard events:** pressing a key, releasing a key, and so on
- **Mouse events:** clicking, pressing a mouse button down, and so on
- **Print events:** formatting, printing, and so on
- **Error and Timing events:** happen after some time, or on an error

In all, nearly fifty events can be checked in Forms and Reports to specify some action upon their taking place.

How do events trigger actions?

You can have Access run a macro when a user performs any one of the 50 events that Access recognizes. Access can recognize an event through use of special properties for forms, controls (fields), and reports.

For example, Figure 30-11 shows the property sheet for a form. This form has many properties, which may be used to respond to corresponding events. Forms themselves aren't the only objects to have events; so do form sections (page header, form header, detail, page footer, form footer) and every control on the form (labels, text boxes, check boxes, option buttons, etc.).

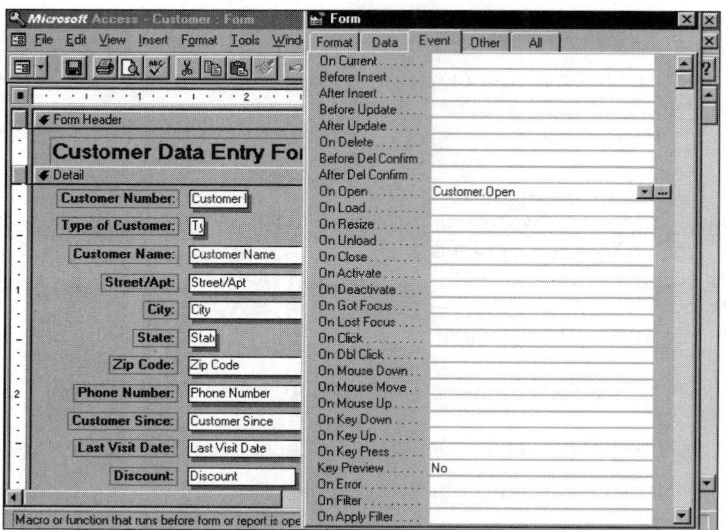

Figure 30-11: The property sheet for a form, showing the On Open property entered.

Where to trigger macros

In Access, you can run event-driven macros by using properties in forms and reports. There are no event properties for tables or queries.

Even so, when you work with forms, you can run macros based on Access switchboards (full screen button type menus), command buttons, and pull-down menus. These features make event-driven macros very powerful and easy to use. In the next few chapters, you will learn about many events and the macro actions that events can use.

Summary

In this chapter, you learned the basics of macros and events:

✦ An Access macro is a database object that lets you automate tasks without writing complex programs. Macros should be used to automate repetitive tasks. In Access, the tasks you perform are known as *actions*.

✦ Two panes comprise the Macro Design window: Action and Argument. In the Action pane, you specify Access actions. You can add them from a pull-down list box or by dragging and dropping common objects.

✦ Access requires arguments (variables) in order to perform actions.

✦ Macros can be saved, renamed, edited, and copied just like any other Access object.

✦ Access has a special macro called AutoExec that runs automatically when the database is opened. You can deactivate the AutoExec macro by holding down the Shift key when you open the database.

✦ You can use the Startup window to control many options in an Access database when it's first opened

✦ When you create macros, you can consolidate them into a group macro. Group macros use a column in the Action pane called the Macro Name column.

✦ When you work with macros, you can specify a condition for one or more actions. If the condition is True, the action is performed; if False, the action is skipped.

✦ Access offers two methods for troubleshooting macros: single-stepping and using the Action Failed dialog box. With these tools, you can trace any errors in your macros or halt a faulty macro.

✦ You can use an *event* (a result or consequence of some action performed by the user) to run a macro. In Access, events are recognized by use of special properties. The only objects in which Access recognizes events are forms and reports.

In the next chapter, you see many uses of macros and how they are generally run from triggered events. In Chapter 32, you learn how to create menu-based systems using events and macros.

✦ ✦ ✦

Using Macros in Forms and Reports

In This Chapter

How to respond to events in forms and reports

How to use macros in forms

How to use macros in reports

How to filter records with a macro

How to validate data with a macro

How to create accelerator keys (hot keys).

At this point, you should know how to create and run macros, and you should know how to automatically start a macro when opening a database. In addition, you should be able to create and specify conditions for macros.

Now you're going to learn how to use macros in real examples by using tables, forms, queries, and reports that you created in previous chapters.

Types of Macros

Cross Ref

In Chapter 30, you learned how to create macros, and you learned how to associate a macro with a form or report property. *Macros* are Access objects consisting of one or more actions. Macros can open a dialog box, run a report, or even find a record.

Usually you create macros to perform redundant tasks or do a series of required actions after some initial action. For example, macros can synchronize two forms while a user moves from record to record. They can also validate new data after it is entered by a user.

Before activating a macro, you need to decide where and how you will use it. For example, you may have a macro that opens the Customer form, and you want Access to run the macro every time a user opens the Pets form. In this case, you place the name of the macro in the On Open property of the Pets form. Then, every time the user opens the Pets form, the On Open property will trigger the macro opening the Customer form.

Or you may want to trigger another macro every time a user presses an accelerator key (also known as a *hot key*). For example, if you want an Import dialog box to be activated when the user presses Ctrl+I, you should attach the macro to the key combination Ctrl+I in a hot-key macro file.

Although the second macro performs some tasks or actions, it is different from the first one. The second macro is activated by a user action (pressing a hot key); the first one is activated when a user performs some specific action that is recognized by a form property.

Macros can be grouped together based on their usage. The four basic groups follow:

✦ Form

✦ Report

✦ Import/Export

✦ Accelerator Keys

Macros used in forms and reports are the most common. Using macros in these objects lets you build intelligence into each form and report. Macros are also used for importing or exporting data to and from other data sources. And, finally, macros can be activated by the use of hot keys.

Review of events and properties

Simply put, an *event* is some user action. The event can be an action such as opening a form or report, changing data in a record, selecting a button, closing a form or report, and so forth. Access recognizes nearly 50 events in forms and reports.

To recognize one of these events, Access uses form or report *properties*. Each event has an associated form or report property. For example, the On Open property is associated with the event of opening a form or report.

You trigger a macro by specifying the macro name. The name is specified as a parameter for the event property you want to have the macro run against. For example, if you want to run a macro named OpenPets every time the user opens the Customer form, you place the macro name in the parameter field alongside of the property On Open in the form named Customer.

Macros for forms

You can create macros that respond to *form events*. These events are triggered by some user action, which may be opening a form or selecting a control button on a form. Access knows when the user triggers an event through its recognition of event-specific form properties. Forms let you set properties for field controls. These properties can be quite useful during the design phase of a form, as when you use a property to set a format or validation rule.

However, macros give you added power by letting you specify actions to be performed automatically based on a user-initiated event. The event is recognized by Access by use of event properties such as Before Update, On Delete, or On Enter. Unlike a simple format or field-level validation rule, a macro can perform multiple-step actions based on the user event. For example, after a user presses the Delete key to delete a record but before the deleted record is removed from the table, you can have a macro that automatically runs asking the user to verify that the record should be deleted. In this case, you use the On Delete property to trigger execution of the macro.

Macros for forms can respond both to *form events* and *control events*. Form events take effect at the form level; control events take effect at the individual control level. Form events include deleting a record, opening a form, or updating a record. These events work at the form and record levels. Control events, on the other hand, work at the level of the individual control. These controls are the ones you specify when you create your form and include such items as a field (text box), a toggle button, an option button — even a command button. Each control has its own event properties that can trigger a macro. These events include selecting a command button, double-clicking on a control, or selecting a control.

By specifying a macro at the control level, you can activate a customer form when the user double-clicks on a field object or its label object. For example, you may have a form that identifies the customer by name but gives no further customer information. When the user double-clicks on the customer's name, your macro can activate a customer form that shows all the customer information. To accomplish this, you use the field object property On Dbl Click to specify a macro that opens the customer form. Then the macro will run and open the Customer form every time the user double-clicks on the Customer field.

Figure 31-1 shows a form with a label named Customer Name; note the field containing the name `All Creatures`. When the user double-clicks on either the label (Customer Name) or the name (All Creatures), the Customer form opens.

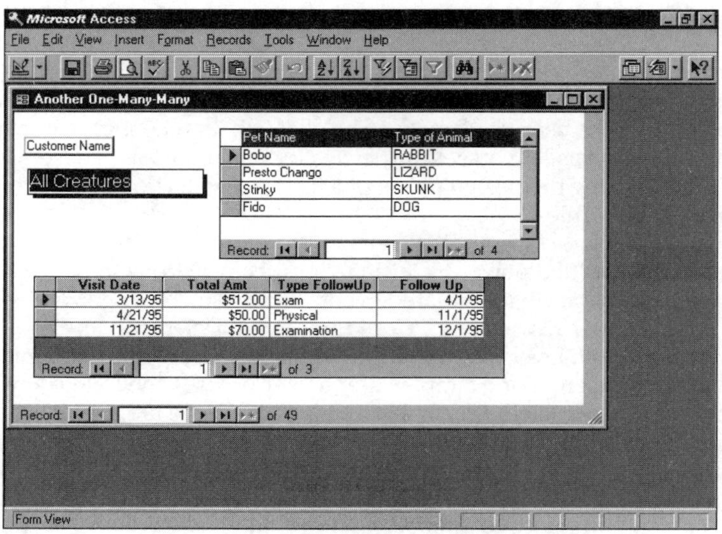

Figure 31-1: A typical form with labels and controls (fields).

Notice that the form in Figure 31-1 does not display any outward sign that the user can initiate a macro by double-clicking the label or field. However, the On Dbl Click property is set for the field to automatically execute the macro that opens the Customer form. In Figure 31-2, you can see the macro is being specified in the On Dbl Click property. The macro group name is Update Form and the specific macro name is ShowCustomer in the group.

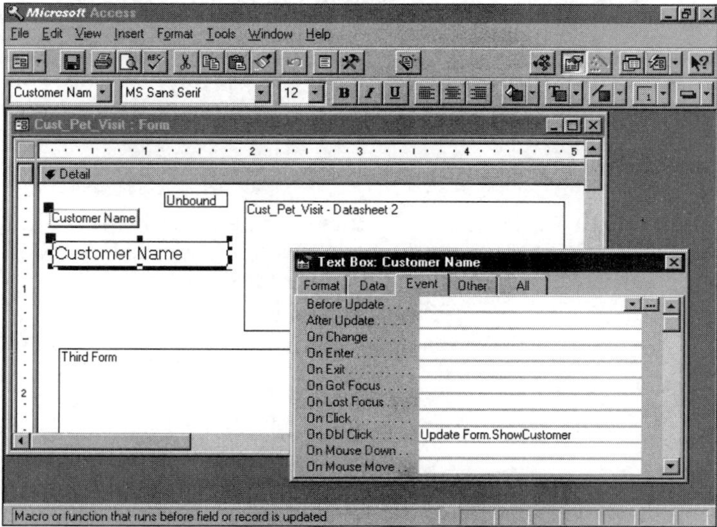

Figure 31-2: Using a form event to call a macro.

Tip By using the properties of text boxes, the event will be triggered when it occurs on the text box (field) or its associated label.

Macros for reports

Just as with forms, macros can also enhance the use of the reports. You may, for example, want to prompt the user for a range of records to be printed before printing the report. You may want to display a message on the report whenever a certain condition is met. You may even want to underline or highlight a field on the basis of its value, as when the value is too small or too great. Macros give you this type of refined control in reports.

Macros for reports can respond both to *report events* and *report section events*. Report events take effect at the report level; report section events take effect at the section level of the report.

Macros for accelerator keys

You can also associate a macro with a specific key or combination of keys. By assigning a macro to a key combination, it can be activated by a user pressing the key or key combination. For example, you may assign the key combination Ctrl+P to print the current record displayed on-screen. Another example is assigning the key combination Ctrl+N to skip to the next record in the report or form. Creating hot keys gives you additional capabilities in your forms and reports without requiring you to write complicated programs.

You use most hot-key macros when you work with forms and reports, although hot-key macros can be used in queries or other Access objects.

Form-Level Event Macros

When you work with forms, you can specify macros based on events at the form level, the section level, or the control level. If you attach a macro to a form-level event, whenever the event occurs, the action takes effect against the form as a whole (as when you change the record pointer or leave the form).

Attaching macros to forms

To have your form respond to an event, you write a macro and attach the macro to the event property in the form that recognizes the event. Many properties can be used to trigger macros at the form level. Table 31-1 shows each property, the event it recognizes, and how the property works.

As Table 31-1 shows, there are many form-level events that can trigger a macro. These events work only at the level of forms or records. They take effect when the pointer is changed from one record to another or when a form is being opened or closed. Control at a level of finer detail (such as the field level) can be obtained by using the control-level events covered later in this chapter.

Table 31-1
The Form-Level Events and Associated Properties

Event Property	*When the Macro Is Triggered*
On Current	When you move to a different record and make it the current record
Before Insert	After data is first entered into a new record but before the record is actually created
After Insert	After the new record is added to the table
Before Update	Before changed data is actually updated in the record
After Update	After changed data updates a record
On Delete	When a record is deleted but *before* the deletion takes place
Before Del Confirm	Just before Access displays the Confirm Delete dialog box
After Del Confirm	After the Delete Confirm dialog box closes and confirmation has happened
On Open	When a form is opened, but the first record is not displayed yet
On Load	When a form is loaded into memory but not yet opened
On Resize	When the size of a form changes
On Unload	When a form is closed and the records unload, before the form is removed from the screen
On Close	When a form is closed and removed from the screen
On Activate	When an open form receives the focus, becoming the active window
On Deactivate	When a different window becomes the active window, but before it loses focus
On Got Focus	When a form with no active or enabled controls receives the focus
On Lost Focus	When a form loses the focus

Event Property	***When the Macro Is Triggered***
On Click	When you press and release (click) the left mouse button on a control in a form
On Dbl Click	When you press and release (click) the left mouse button twice on a control/label in a form
On Mouse Down	When you press the mouse button while the pointer is on a form
On Mouse Move	When you move the mouse pointer over an area of a form
On Mouse Up	When you release a pressed mouse button while the pointer is on a form
On Key Down	When you press any key on the keyboard when a form has focus; when you use a SendKeys macro
On Key Up	When you release a pressed key or immediately after the SendKeys macro
On Key Press	When you press and release a key on a form that has the focus; when you use SendKeys macro
On Error	When a run-time error is produced
On Filter	When a filter has been specified but before it is applied
On Apply Filter	After a filter is applied to a form
On Timer	When a specified time interval passes

Opening a form with a macro

Sometimes you may want to open a form with a macro. For example, every time you open the Pet Display form, you may also want to open the Customer form. This will enable a user to click on either form to see information from both at once.

To accomplish this, you create a macro named OpenCust and attach it to the On Open property of the Pet Display form.

To create the macro, follow these steps:

1. Select the Macros tab in the Database window to select the Macro Object list.
2. Click on the New button to display the Macro Design window.
3. Click on the first empty Action cell.
4. Select the OpenForm action from the pull-down menu of the Action cell.
5. Click in the Form Name cell of the Action Arguments (bottom part of window).
6. Select or type **Customer**.
7. Save the macro by clicking on the Save button on the toolbar and naming it **OpenCust**.

Notice that in Figure 31-3 the OpenCust macro has only one action — OpenForm, with the action argument Form Name of Customer.

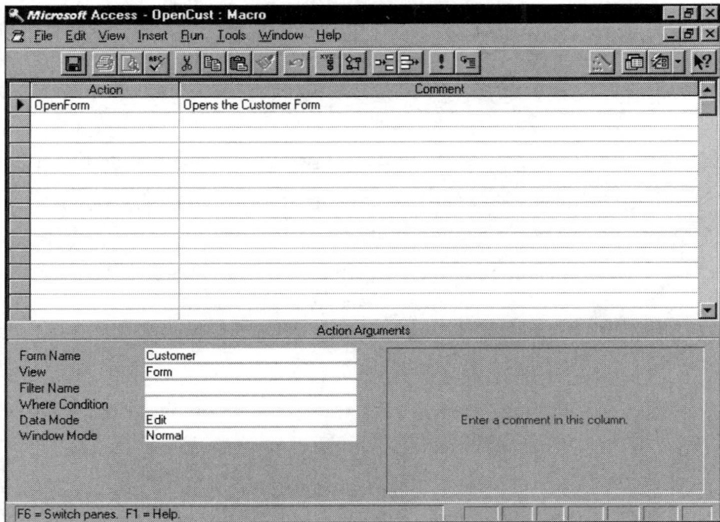

Figure 31-3: A macro to open a form.

The macro in Figure 31-3 has only a single action associated with it, which is the OpenForm action. This action has six possible arguments, although you only entered the form name `Customer` in the example. You accepted the default values of the other arguments. This action opens the specified form (Customer) for you automatically.

With the OpenCust macro created, you will need to enter design mode for the Pet Display form; attach the macro OpenCust to the form property On Open.

Attaching a macro to a form

With the OpenForm macro saved, you are now ready to *associate*, or *attach*, it with the On Open property of the form Add a Customer and Pets. To attach the OpenCust macro to the form, follow these steps:

1. Select the Forms tab in the Database window to select the Form List.
2. Select the form named Pets Display form and bring it into the design mode.
3. Display the property sheet by clicking the Properties button on the toolbar.

The title of the Property window dialog box should be `Form`. If it isn't, select the form by clicking on the gray box in the top left corner of the form (where the rulers intersect).

4. Select the Event tab from the tabs at the top of the Properties window.

5. Move to the On Open property in the Form property window. Select or type the macro name **OpenCust** in the On Open property cell.

   The property sheet should look similar to the one in Figure 31-4. Notice that the macro name OpenCust is placed in the property area of the On Open property.

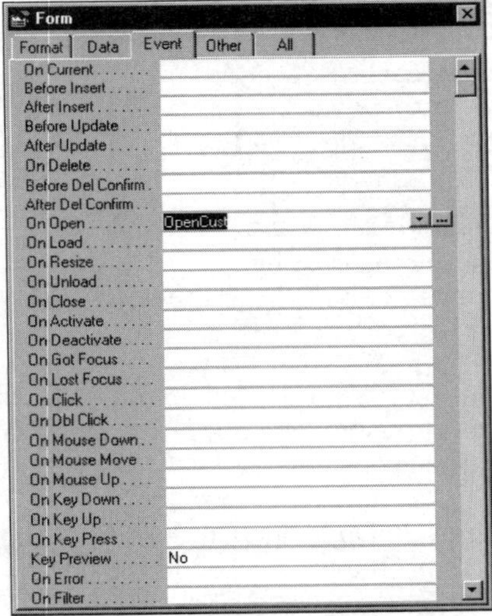

Figure 31-4: Entering a macro in the On Open property of a form.

6. Save the form and return to the Database window.

With the OpenCust macro attached to the form Pets, you are ready to try running it. Open the Pets Display Form. Notice that Access automatically opens the Customer form for you, placing it behind the Pet Display Form. Now you can use either form by clicking on it to look at the individual records. Figure 31-5 shows both forms open.

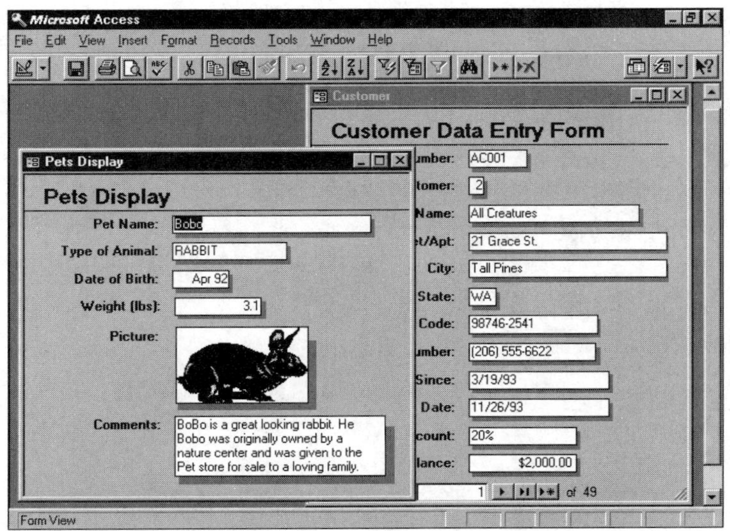

Figure 31-5: Two forms open; one form is opened automatically by a macro attached to the On Open property of the other form.

The only problem with these two forms is that they are not related. Every time you change the pet, it would be nice if the Customer form showed you the correct owner of the pet.

Of all the form-level events, the most common are On Open and On Current. Although the others are available for use, these two events probably are used for 80 percent of all form-level macros.

Synchronizing two forms with On Current

Notice that the forms in Figure 31-5 are independent of each other. This means that when you skip through the Pet Display Form, the Customer form is not automatically updated to display the related owner information for the pet. To make these two forms work together, you can synchronize them by relating the data between the forms with the On Current property.

You can use the same macro you used before (OpenCust) but now you must specify a Where Condition for the OpenForm action. The condition on which to synchronize these two forms occurs when the Customer Number is the same in both forms. To specify the synchronizing condition between these two forms, follow these steps:

1. Open the macro OpenCust in design mode.
2. Click on the Where Condition box of the Action Arguments.
3. Type **[Customer Number] = Forms![Pet Display Form]![Customer Number]**.
4. Resave the OpenCust macro.

Note: Notice in Step 3 that you typed **[Customer Number]**, which is the control name for the Customer Number field in the Customer form. You typed this on the left side of the expression without reference to the form name. The left side of the Where expression in an OpenForm action uses the form specified in the Form Name action argument (three lines above). The right side of the expression requires the keyword *Forms*, the form name, and the control name.

Warning: If you specify an unopened form in the Where Condition box, you will get an error message at run time, but not as you create the macro.

Now that you have modified the macro, you need to set the On Current property of the Pet Display Form.

To add the OpenCust macro to the form, follow these steps:

1. Remove the macro from the On Open property of the form and add it to the On Current property.
2. Open the Pets Display form in design mode.
3. Move to the On Current property of the property window.
4. Type **OpenCust** in the On Current parameter box.
5. Save the changes to the form.

Now, when you open the Pets form and a pet record is displayed, the Customer form also opens and displays the correct owner for that pet. As you change pets, the Customer form automatically displays the new owner information. These two forms are now synchronized.

Note: Even though the two forms are synchronized on the basis of the On Current property, you must still close both forms separately. Closing one form does not automatically close the other. If you want to close both forms at the same time automatically, you need to specify another macro for the On Close property.

To see how these two forms work together, open the Pets form and then click on the Datasheet button on the toolbar. The Customer form becomes active and is moved to the front of the Pets form. If you click a different pet record in the Pets datasheet, the Customer form is automatically updated to reflect the new owner. Figure 31-6 demonstrates how this works.

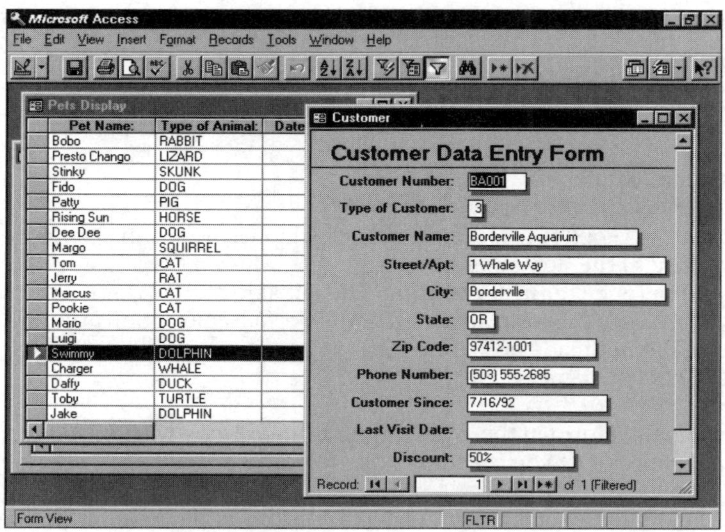

Figure 31-6: Two forms synchronized.

As Figure 31-6 demonstrates, you are not limited to a single-record view when synchronizing forms. The Pets form has been set to Datasheet; as you click on different records in the datasheet, the Customer form is updated automatically to reflect the new owner.

The On Current property of the Pets form triggers the OpenCust macro every time the record changes. If you click on the next navigation button, you see that the Customer form shows only one record—the owner record that is related to the current individual pet record in the Pets form. Notice that in the bottom of the Customer form in Figure 31-6, the record number shows `Record 1 of 1 (Filtered)`. The Where condition in the macro acts as a filter to the Customer form.

If you know this, you can easily understand the use of the On Current property: It activates a macro that performs actions based on the specific record indicated by the form that is using the On Current property. In this case, the current Pet record triggers the macro that finds the correct owner in the Customer form. Every time the Pet record changes, the On Current property is activated and the next owner is found.

Running a macro when closing a form

There are times when you'll want to perform some action when you close or leave a form. For example, you may want Access to keep an automatic log of the names of everyone using the form. Using the two forms from the previous examples, you may want to close the Customer form automatically every time the user closes the Pets form.

To automatically close the Customer form every time the Pets form is closed, you need to create a new macro to perform the actions. Then you need to attach the macro to the On Close property of the Pet Display Form.

To create a macro that closes a form, follow these steps:

1. Select the OpenCust macro and enter the design mode.
2. Activate the Macro Name column by clicking on the Macro Name button on the toolbar. This lets you create a macro group.
3. Select a blank Macro Name cell below the OpenForm action.
4. In the empty Macro Name cell, type **Close Customer**.
5. Select the empty Action cell alongside the Close Customer macro name.
6. Select the Close action from the pull-down menu.
7. Select the action argument Object Type.
8. Type (or select) **Form**.
9. Select the action argument Object Name.
10. Type (or select) the form name **Customer**. The macro should now look similar to Figure 31-7.
11. Resave the macro with the new changes.

Figure 31-7 shows the new macro ClosCust added to the macro OpenCust. Until now, the OpenCust macro has been a single-purpose macro. Adding another macro has made it into a group macro of two macros. The first macro is the default macro, which opens a form, and the second is a macro named Close Customer.

Cross Ref Macro groups are covered in Chapter 30.

Notice that the Close Customer macro has only one action: Close. This action has two arguments, both of which you must enter. The first argument is the Object Type, which specifies the type of object you want to close (form or report, and so on). The second argument is the Object Name, which specifies by name the object you want to close (in this case, the form named Customer).

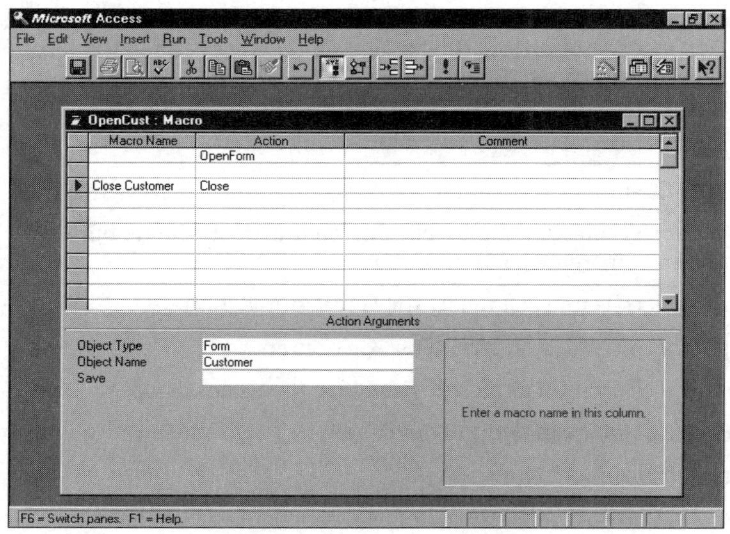

Figure 31-7: Adding a Close action macro to a macro group.

Now that you've created the Close Customer macro, you can attach it to the form named Pet Display Form by following these steps:

1. Select the Pet Display Form and click Design.
2. Activate the property sheet for the form.
3. Select the On Close property in the property sheet.
4. Type **OpenCust.Close Customer** in the On Close property parameter box. The property sheet should look like Figure 31-8.
5. Save the form with the new changes.

Note Notice in Figure 31-8 that when you type the macro name in the On Close parameter box, you specify the macro group name. Then you type a period; finally you type the name of the macro.

Opening the Pet Display Form continues to maintain the current owner information in the Customer form because you left the macro with its On Current property set. Now, however, the On Close property is also set. Because you specified On Close with the Pets form, the Customer form closes automatically for you when you close the Pets form.

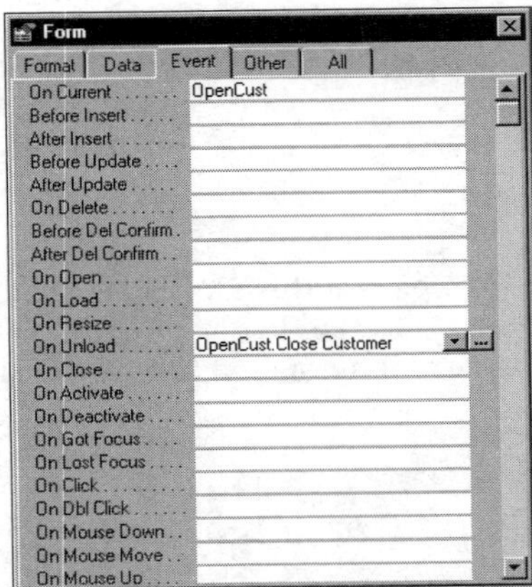

Figure 31-8: The property sheet with the On Close property set.

New! The macro attached to the On Close property simply closes the Customer form. If the user accidentally closes the Customer form and then the Pets form, Access does not report an error. Therefore, you don't have to specify an On Close for the Customer form to allow closing only via the Pets form. Using this principle, you can have one form that specifies the closing of many forms. If the forms are open, Access will close them; otherwise Access will issue the Close command with no harm done.

Confirming a delete with On Delete

The On Delete property can be used to execute a macro that displays a message and confirms that the user wants to delete a record. For example, to create a macro named ConfirmDelete, follow these steps:

1. Enter the macro design mode, create a new macro, and click on the Condition column.
2. Select the first Condition cell.
3. Type **MsgBox("Do you Want to Delete this Record?", 273, "Delete")<>1**.
4. Select the Action cell next to the Condition box.
5. Select or type the **CancelEvent** action.
6. Select the next Condition cell.
7. Type an ellipsis, which is three periods (**...**).
8. Select the Action cell next to the Condition box.
9. Select or type the **StopMacro** action.
10. Select the next Action cell.

11. Select or type the **SendKeys** action.
12. Select the Keystrokes action argument.
13. Type **{Enter}**.
14. Save the macro to the name **ConfirmDelete**.

The macro should look like the one in Figure 31-9. Notice that this macro also uses the CancelEvent action. The condition for this macro uses the MsgBox( ) function (see the sidebar "Using the MsgBox( ) Function" in this chapter for a detailed explanation).

Macro Name	Condition	Action	Comment
	MsgBox("Do You Want to Delete this Record",273,"Delete")<>1	CancelEvent	
	...	StopMacro	
		SendKeys	

Figure 31-9: A macro to delete a record.

The macro in Figure 31-9 shows the use of another new action—SendKeys. This action lets you send prearranged keystrokes to Access or another active application. The passed keystrokes are processed just as if you pressed them while working in an application. In this case, Access displays a message box like the one in Figure 31-10. Notice that the message box has two buttons—OK and Cancel. Access displays the box and waits for a keystroke. When the user selects the Cancel button, the macro cancels the delete event and stops the macro.

If the user selects the OK button in the message box, the macro performs the SendKeys action. In this case, the macro sends the Enter keystroke. If the user does not take this action, Access displays its Delete message dialog box, forcing the user to verify again that the record should be deleted. Using SendKeys sends the Enter keystroke to the Access Delete message box, telling it to accept the deletion.

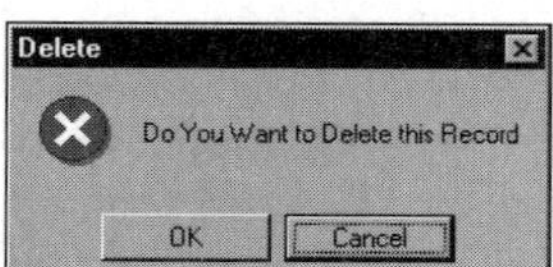

Figure 31-10: A message box for the delete macro.

Warning This macro does not bypass referential integrity between tables. If you have referential integrity set between the Customer table and the Pets table and have not authorized Cascade Delete through the entire application, the macro fails. To override this, either set up cascade deletes through all the tables or expand the macro to perform a cascade delete by creating an SQL statement and running the SQL statement (use the RunSQL action).

With the delete macro ConfirmDelete completed, you next attach it to the Pets Display form by placing the macro name in the entry box of the On Delete property of the form. Figure 31-11 shows the property sheet for the Pets Display form with the On Delete property set.

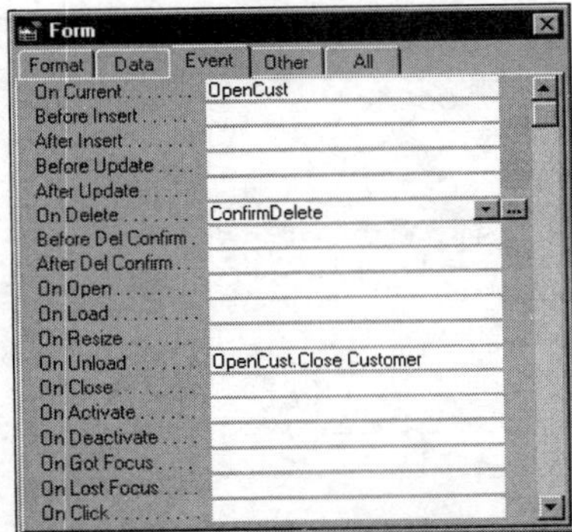

Figure 31-11: Setting an On Delete property.

To see how this macro and the On Delete property work, follow these steps:

1. Display the first record in the Pets Display Form.
2. Select Edit⇨Delete Record from the main menu.

   Access responds with the message box you saw in Figure 31-10. In this message box, the Cancel button is the default.
3. Select the Cancel button to not delete this record.

Control Event Macros

So far, you've worked with event macros at the form level. You can also trigger macros at the control level, using an event as a basis. When you attach a macro at the control level, the macro takes effect against the control. For example, you can immediately verify complex data validation at the field level (instead of when the record is exited) by using the field's Before Update property instead of the property at the form level.

Using the MsgBox() function

The MsgBox() function is a very powerful function that can be used to display a message in a dialog box, wait for a user response, and then return a value based on the user's choice. The function has three arguments:

MsgBox(*"message"* [, *type of msg* [, *box title*]])

The *message* here is the string displayed in the dialog box as a message.

The *type of msg* is the numeric expression controlling the buttons and icons in the dialog box.

The *box title* is the string displayed in the title bar of the dialog box.

Only the message is required. If you don't specify *type of msg* or *box title,* Access displays one button – OK. There is no icon and no title.

Access offers a wide range of type of message numbers. The type of message number specifies three message parts: (1) number and type of buttons, (2) icon style, and (3) default button. The following list describes each:

Number and Button Type

Value	*Display Button*
0	OK
1	OK, Cancel
2	Abort, Retry, Ignore
3	Yes, No, Cancel
4	Yes, No
5	Retry, Cancel

Icon Style

Value	*Display*	*Icon*
0	None	
16	x Critical	X in a circle
32	? Warning	Question mark in a balloon
48	! Warning	Exclamation sign in a triangle
64	i	Informational in a balloon

Default Button

Value	*Button*
0	First
256	Second
512	Third

Using the preceding table, you specify the second parameter of the MsgBox() function by summing the three option values. For example, you can have a message box show three buttons (Yes, No, and Cancel [3]), use the Question mark (?) [32], and make the Cancel button the default [512]. Just add the three values (512+32+3) to get the second parameter number, which is 548.

If you omit *type of msg* in the function, MsgBox displays a single OK button and makes it the default button with no icon displayed.

Besides displaying the message box with all the options, the MsgBox() function also returns a value that indicates which button the user selects. The number it returns depends on the type of button selected. The following table shows each button and the value that MsgBox() returns:

Button Selected	*Value Returned*
OK	1
Cancel	2
Abort	3
Retry	4
Ignore	5
Yes	6
No	7

If the dialog box displays a Cancel button, pressing the Esc key is the same as selecting the Cancel button.

Attaching macros to controls

To have a control respond to an event, you write a macro and attach the macro to the property in the control that recognizes the event. There are several properties that can be polled to trigger macros at the control level. Table 31-2 shows each property, the event it recognizes, and how it works.

As Table 31-2 demonstrates, you can use any of the control-level events to trigger a macro. One of these, On Click, works only with command buttons.

Table 31-2
The Control-Level Events and Associated Properties

Event Property	*When the Macro Is Triggered*
Before Update	Before changed data in the control is updated to the table
After Update	After changed data is updated in the control to the data
On Change	When contents of a text box or combo box's text changes
On Updated	When an OLE object's data has been modified
On Not In List	When a value that isn't in the list is entered into a combo box
On Enter	Before a control actually receives the focus from another control
On Exit	Just before the control loses focus to another control
On Got Focus	A nonactive or enabled control receives the focus
On Lost Focus	A control loses the focus
On Click	Press and release (click) the left mouse button on a control
On Dbl Click	Press and release (click) the left mouse button twice on a control/label
On Mouse Down	Pressing a mouse button while the pointer is on a control
On Mouse Move	Moving the mouse pointer over a control
On Mouse Up	Releasing a pressed mouse button while the pointer is on a control
On Key Down	Pressing any key on the keyboard when a control has the focus or using the SendKeys macro
On Key Press	Press and release a key on a control that has the focus or use SendKeys macro
On Key Up	Releasing a pressed key or immediately after the SendKeys macro

Forms have several different types of objects on them — Labels, Text boxes, OLE, Subforms, Command buttons, check boxes, and so on. Each of these has several event properties associated with it. You can attach a macro, an expression, or Access Basic code to any of them. To see any objects event properties, simply activate the Properties dialog box and select event properties while working with the object.

Working with Macros on Forms

You can group macros for forms in six categories according to their function:

- ✦ Validating data
- ✦ Setting values
- ✦ Navigating between forms and records
- ✦ Filtering records
- ✦ Finding records
- ✦ Printing records

Each category uses specific macro actions to perform its job.

Validating data

You already worked with macros to validate data at both the form level and control level. When validating data, you worked with several macro actions: MsgBox, CancelEvent, StopMacro, and GoToControl.

The most common event properties that trigger validation macros are the On Delete and Before Update properties, although any property can be used.

Displaying a message

To display a message, you use the MsgBox action. This action has four arguments:

Message	Specifies the user message in a dialog box
Beep	Sounds a computer beep when the dialog box is opened
Type	Specifies the type of icon displayed in the dialog box, such as the stop sign, a question mark, and so on
Title	Specifies a user-entered title for the box

Canceling events

To cancel an event, you use the CancelEvent action. This action has no arguments — it simply cancels the event that triggers the macro to run. For example, if the macro is attached to the Before Update property of a form, the update is canceled.

Stopping a macro

To stop execution of a macro, use the StopMacro action. This action stops execution of the macro immediately and returns the user to the calling form. This action is useful for stopping a macro based on a condition specified in the macro.

Going to a specific control

If you need to return to a specific control (field) in a form, use the GoToControl action. This action has one argument, the control name. If you supply a control name, this action takes you to that control. You normally use this action just before the StopMacro action.

Setting values

By setting control, field, and property values with macros, you can make data entry easier and more accurate. Besides these advantages, you can link several forms, databases, and reports to make them work together more intelligently.

Setting values with a macro can accomplish these tasks:

- ✦ Hide or display a control on the basis of a value in the form (Visible property)
- ✦ Disable or lock a control on the basis of a value in the form (Enable and Locked properties)
- ✦ Update a field in the form on the basis of the value of another control
- ✦ Set the value of a control in a form on the basis of the control of another form

The SetValue action is used to set values with a macro. This action has two arguments:

Item	The name of the control or property
Expression	The expression used to set the value

Tip If you use the SetValue action to change the value of a control (field) being validated, do not attach it to the Before Update property. Access cannot change the value of a control while it is being validated; it can only change the value after it has been saved. Therefore you should use the After Update property instead.

Warning You cannot use the SetValue macro action on bound or calculated controls on reports; the same is true for calculated controls on forms.

Converting a field to uppercase

If you allow entry of a field in either uppercase or lowercase, you may want to store it in uppercase. To accomplish this, create a macro that uses the SetValue action to set the value of the field for you. In the Item argument box, enter the name of the field you want to convert to uppercase. In the Expression argument box, enter the function **UCase()** with the name of the field to be converted. The function Ucase( ) must already exist. Figure 31-12 shows the arguments for converting the field Customer Name to uppercase.

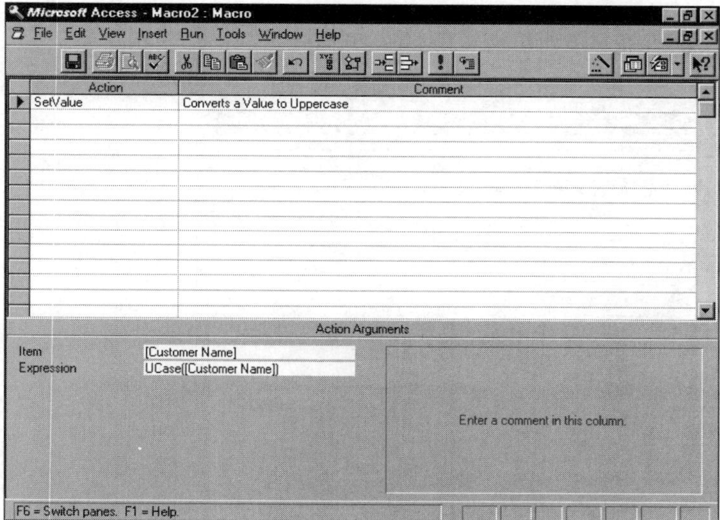

Figure 31-12: Converting a field to uppercase.

After you create the macro, place the macro name in the After Update property sheet.

If the user enters a customer name in lowercase or mixed case, Access automatically runs the macro and converts the field to uppercase when the user completes the update.

Assigning values to new records

When you add new records to a form, it is often convenient to have values automatically filled in for fields using values from another open form. SetValue is also used to do this.

For example, after adding a new customer in the Customer form, you may immediately want to add a Pet record in another form and have the Customer Number automatically filled in.

For example, the Customer form's after update event can be programmed to add a Pet record after the Customer record's Pet Name value is changed. A macro opens the Pet form in the Add Data Mode using the OpenForm action. The next macro action, SetValue, automatically sets the value of Customer Number in the Pets form to the Customer Number in the Customer form. Figure 31-13 shows the arguments for this macro.

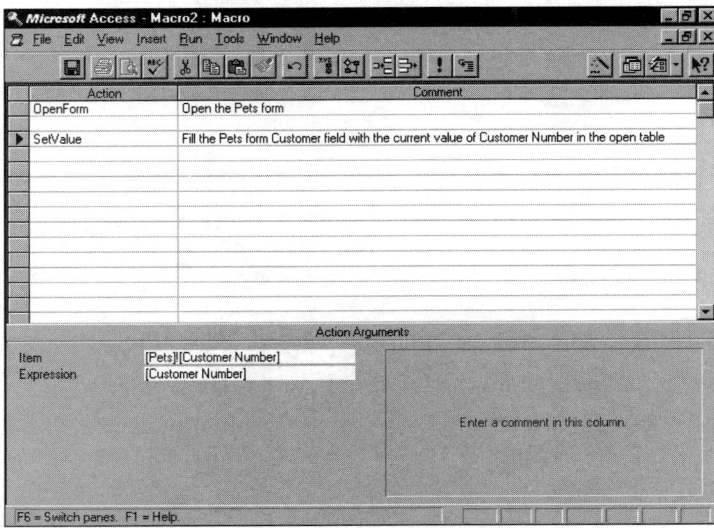

Figure 31-13: Macro arguments to set a field value in another form on the basis of a value in the current form.

Tip The Item argument can also use its full syntax rather than the abbreviation shown in Figure 31-13. The syntax is:

```
Forms![Pets]![Customer Number]
```

The Expression argument references the Customer Number in the currently open form, which is the Customer form. When working with the SetValue action in this way, you must specify the entire syntax for the name of the field being replaced in the Item box.

Navigating in forms and records

Whenever you need to move to a specific control (field), record, or page in a form, you use also use the GoTo*XXXX* actions, where *XXXX* represents the control, record, or page.

Moving to a specific control

To move to a specific control, use the GoToControl action. This action has one argument, which is Control Name. To move to a specific field, simply supply the control name in this argument.

Moving to a specific record

To move to a specific record in a table, query, or form, use the GoToRecord action. This action has four arguments:

Object Type	Type of object (form, table, or query)
Object Name	Name of the object specified in Object Type
Record	Specifies which record to go to (previous, next, new, first, last, and so on)
Offset	The number of records to offset from (if 10, go back 10 records)

Using this action, you can move to any record in a form, query, or table.

Moving to a specific page

To move to a specific page and place focus in the first control of the page, use the GoToPage action. This action has three arguments:

Page Number	Specifies the page number you want to move to
Right	The upper left-hand corner of page (horizontal position)
Down	The upper left-hand corner of page (vertical position)

This action is useful for working with multiple-page forms.

Filtering records

You can create a macro or series of macros to filter records in a form. For example, you may want to have a Customer form with four buttons to limit the form's records to a single state or allow all states. (Even though you haven't learned about buttons yet, you can learn how they would interact with a group of macros.) The form will look similar to Figure 31-14. Notice that there are four buttons in the box named Filter Records.

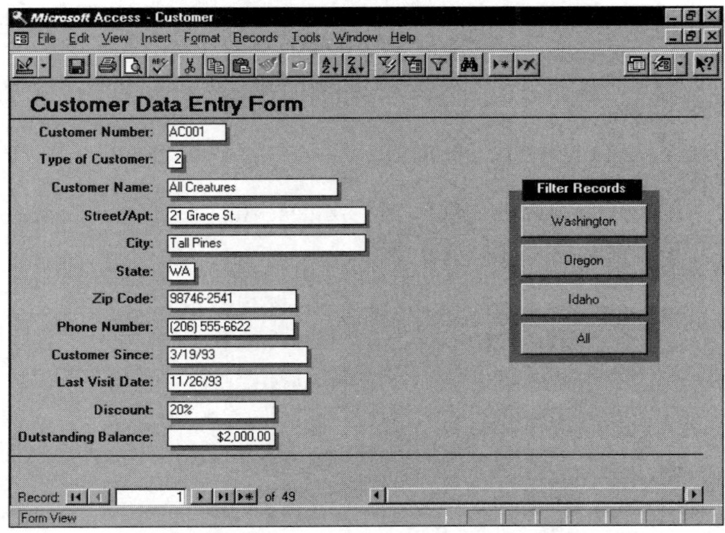

Figure 31-14: A form with buttons used to activate filter macros.

Each button in Figure 31-14 is attached to a different macro. Three of the macros use the ApplyFilter action, and one uses the ShowAllRecords action.

Using the ApplyFilter action

To set a filter condition in a macro, use the ApplyFilter action. This action has two arguments: Filter Name and the Where Condition. You can use either one, but you should only use one unless you pre-define a filter and want to filter the filter. For this example, you use the Where Condition argument. To create a macro named StateFilter.WA, follow these steps:

1. Enter the Macro Design window.
2. Enter the macro name **WA** into the group macro StateFilter.
3. Select or type **ApplyFilter** for the action.
4. Type **[State] = "WA"** in the Where Condition argument box.

After you create this macro, you create two more next. One macro is named StateFilter.ID; the other is named StateFilter.OR. These set a condition equal to the individual state.

Using the ShowAllRecords action

When you create filter conditions with macros, you should always create another macro that uses the ShowAllRecords action. This action removes an existing filter set by another macro. This action has no arguments. For the next example, create a macro named StateFilter.All with the ShowAllRecords action.

When you complete this process, all four macros should look like the ones in Figure 31-15.

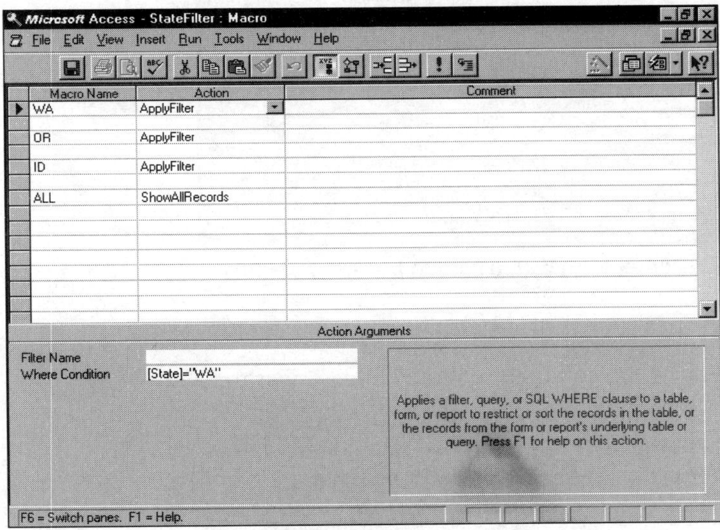

Figure 31-15: A macro group with four filter macros.

Running filter macros

To run a filter macro, simply attach the macro name to the On Push property of the appropriate command button. Then the macro will execute and implement the filter condition every time the button is selected.

Finding Records

One of the most powerful ways of using macros is to locate user-specified records. This type of macro uses two macro actions: GoToControl and FindRecord. For example, you can add a search routine to the Customer form, as shown in Figure 31-16. You can create an unbound combo box; as you can see in Figure 31-17, it is named CustomerSelect.

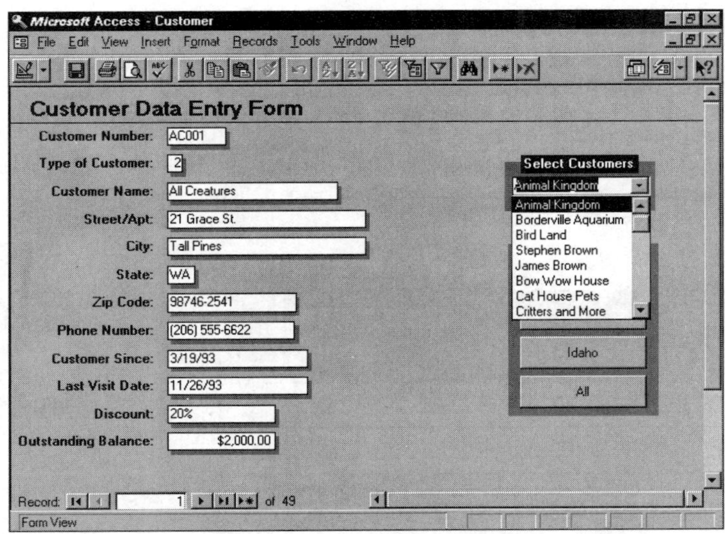

Figure 31-16: The Customer form with a combo box used to find records.

Your property sheet for the combo box should look similar to Figure 31-17.

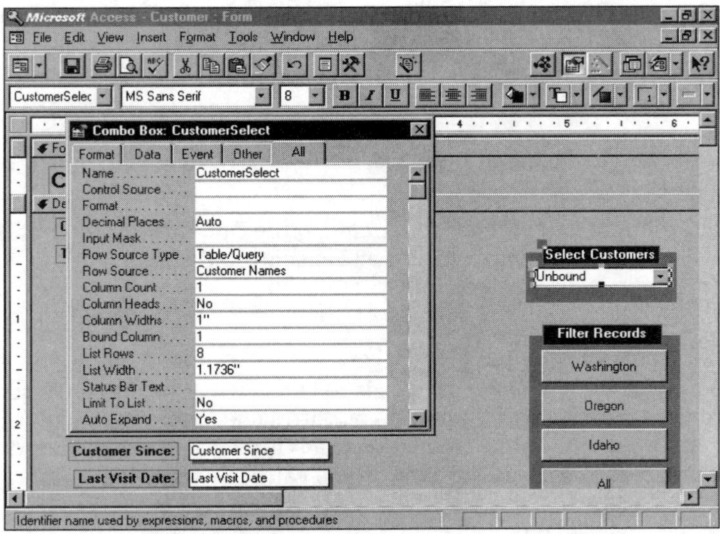

Figure 31-17: The property sheet for the unbound combo box.

Beyond completion of these steps, you can beautify the label and combo box area (as a look back at Figure 31-16 shows). These enhancements aren't required.

After you create the unbound combo box, you are ready to create the FindRecord macro to find the Customer record by the Customer Name field. To create the macro, follow these steps:

1. Select or type **GoToControl** in the first empty Action cell.
2. Type **[Customer Name]** in the Control Name argument cell.
3. Select or type **FindRecord** in the next empty Action cell.
4. Type **=[CustomerSelect]** in the FindWhat argument box.
5. Save the macro, naming it **FindRecord**.

That's it! Your macro should now resemble the one in Figure 31-18.

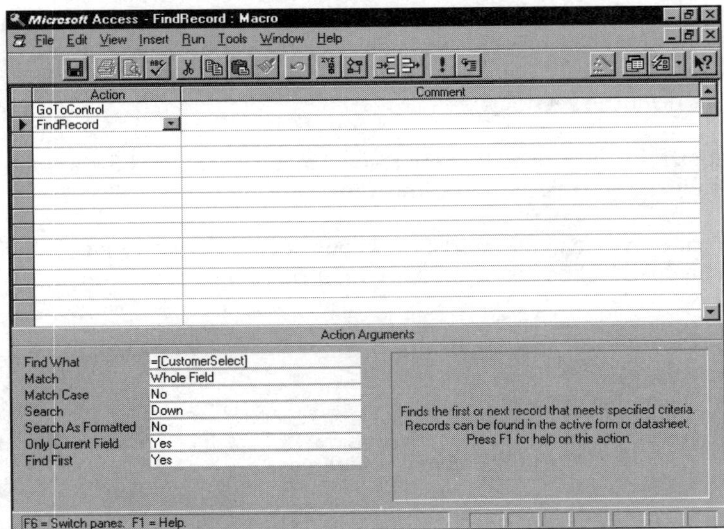

Figure 31-18: A macro to find a record, based on the customer's name.

In the GoToControl argument, you placed the form control name [Customer Name], which is the same as the field name, to limit the scope of the search to the current field (Customer Name). Then in the FindRecord argument Find What, you placed the control name for the unbound combo box. By placing the unbound combo box in the Find What box, you specify that the macro will find the name via the combo box but update the record on the basis of the Customer Name.

Warning: Note that you entered an equal sign before the control name CustomerSelect in the Find What argument box. If you don't enter the equal sign, the macro will not work.

Now that you've created the macro, you're ready to attach it to the After Update property for the unbound combo box. To attach the macro, follow these steps:

1. Move to the After Update property of the CustomerSelect control (unbound combo box).
2. Type **FindRecord** in the Action Arguments cell (the name of the macro).

The form now uses the combo box to find any Customer!

Report Event Macros

Just as with forms, reports can also use macros that perform actions based on events that you specify. You can work with macros at the report level or the section level. If you attach a macro at the report level, it takes effect when the event occurs against the report as a whole, such as when you open or close the report. If you attach the macro at the section level, it takes effect when the event occurs within a section (as when you format or print the section).

Several event properties can be used for report-level macros. Table 31-3 shows each property, the event it recognizes, and how it works.

As Table 31-3 illustrates, you can use any of the report-level events to trigger a macro. These events can be used just as you use their counterparts in forms.

Table 31-3
The Report-Level Events and Associated Properties

Event Property	*When the Macro Is Triggered*
On Open	When a report is opened but before it prints
On Close	When a report is closed and removed from the screen
On Activate	When a report receives the focus, becomes the active window
On Deactive	When a different window becomes the active window
On No Data	When the report has no data passed to it from the active table or query
On Page	When the report changes pages
On Error	When a run-time error is produced in Access

Opening a report with a macro

You may want to use the On Open property of a report to run a macro that prompts the user to identify the records to print. The macro can use a filter or use the ApplyFilter action.

For example, you may want to activate a form or dialog box that prompts the user to identify a state or to print the report Customer Mailing Labels. To accomplish this task, you create a filter macro similar to the one in the section on forms and attach it to the On Open property of the report.

Report Section Macros

Besides the report-level properties, Access offers three event properties you can use at the section level for a report macro. Table 31-4 shows each property, the event it recognizes, and how it works.

Table 31-4
The Report Section-Level Events and Associated Properties

Event Property	*Event*	*When the Macro is Triggered*
On Format	Format	When Access knows what data goes in a section (but prior to laying the data out for printing)
On Print	Print	After Access lays out the data in a section for printing (but prior to actually printing the section)
On Retreat	Retreat	After the Format event but before the Print event; occurs when Access has to "back up" past other sections on a page to perform multiple formatting passes

Using On Format

You use the On Format property when a user's response can affect page layout or when the macro contains calculations that use data from sections you don't intend to print. The macro will run before Access lays out the section (following your other property settings for the report, such as Keep Together, Visible, or Can Grow).

You can set the On Format and On Print properties for any section of the report. However, the On Retreat is not available for the Page Header or Page Footer sections.

For example, you may want to highlight some data on the form, based on a certain condition that the macro determines. If the condition is met, the macro uses the SetValue action to change a control's Visible property to Yes.

Using On Print

You use the On Print property when no user's response affects page layout or when the macro depends on what page it finds the records to be printed. For example, you may want to have a total calculation placed in either the header or footer of each page.

Report Properties

When you work with macros that use the On Print and On Format properties of report sections, you may need to use two special conditional printer properties:

- Format Count
- Print Count

These two conditional printer properties are used in the Condition Expression column of a macro. Both are read-only properties; Access sets their values. Therefore you can check these properties, but you cannot change their values. These properties determine when an event occurs twice.

Using Format Count

The Format Count property is used as a macro condition to determine the number of times the On Format property setting is evaluated for the current line on the report.

It is possible for a line to be formatted more than once. For example, when printing labels, the last label may not fit on a page; there may be room for only one line of a two-line label. If the label won't fit on the page, Access prints it on the next page. The Format Count for any lines moved from the bottom of the page to the top of the next page is set to 2 because the lines are formatted twice.

If you are accumulating a count of the number of labels being printed, you use the Format Count property in the Condition box of the macro to disregard counting the label a second time.

Using Print Count

Like the Format Count property, the Print Count property is used as a macro condition. This property determines the number of times the On Print setting is evaluated for the current line of the report.

It is possible for part of a record to be printed on one page and the remainder to be printed on the next page. When that occurs, the On Print event occurs twice, so the Print Property is incremented to 2. When this occurs, you don't want to have the macro perform its action twice; therefore you check to see whether the Format Count has changed, and then you stop the macro action.

To understand how this works, suppose you have a macro that counts the number of records being printed on a page. The record number is placed in the page footer section of each page of the report. If a record is printed across two pages, you want the records counted on only one of the pages.

Working with macros in reports

Like form macros, report macros can be triggered at two levels — report and section. A macro triggered at report level can prompt a user for a range of records to print before doing anything with the report.

On the other hand, a section-level macro can be used for printing messages on a report when a condition is met. For example, if a customer has not paid on his or her bill in 30 days, the report may print a reminder line that a partial payment is overdue.

Report-level macros can be executed before or after a report is printed or previewed. Section-level macros can be executed before or after a section of the report is printed or previewed. Thus section-level macros tend to be used for more-refined actions, such as including conditional lines of text in the report.

Underlining data in a report with a macro

You can use a macro to underline or highlight data dynamically in a report. This is accomplished by hiding or displaying controls and sections.

For example, suppose that you print the Monthly Invoice Report and you want to underline the Amount Due control if the total amount is over $500.00. You can do this by adding a control to the group footer named Customer.Customer Number Footer and creating a macro that toggles the Visible property for the control.

Figure 31-19 shows a line added below the Amount Due control. This control is named AmtDueLine.

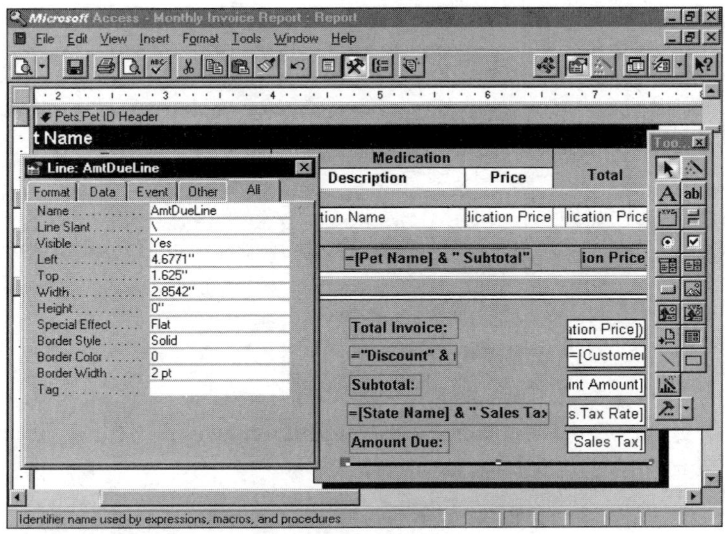

Figure 31-19: A report form with a line added.

In Figure 31-19, notice that the Visible property is currently set to Yes in the property sheet for the control AmtDueLine.

With the control (line) placed on the report, create a macro that sets the Visible property for this control. This macro requires two conditions—one for [Amount Due]>500 and the other for not being greater than this amount. To create the macro, follow these steps:

1. Create a macro named PrtLine.
2. Select an empty cell in the Condition column.
3. Type **[Amount Due]>500** in the Condition cell.
4. Select the associated Action cell.
5. Select or type **SetValue**.
6. Select the Item argument.
7. Type **[AmtDueLine].Visible**.
8. Select the Expression argument.
9. Type **Yes**.
10. Select another empty Condition cell.
11. Type **Not [Amount Due]>500**.

12. Select the associated Action cell.
13. Select or type **SetValue**.
14. Select the Item argument.
15. Type **[AmtDueLine].Visible**.
16. Select the Expression argument.
17. Type **No**.
18. Save the macro.

The macro should look similar to the one in Figure 31-20. Notice that the macro in this figure has a separate condition to turn the Visible property on (set to Yes) and off.

Now that the macro is created, you will need to attach it to the group section named Customer.Customer Number Footer in the Monthly Invoice Report. The macro is attached to the On Format property of the section. Figure 31-21 shows the property sheet with the macro added to the On Format property.

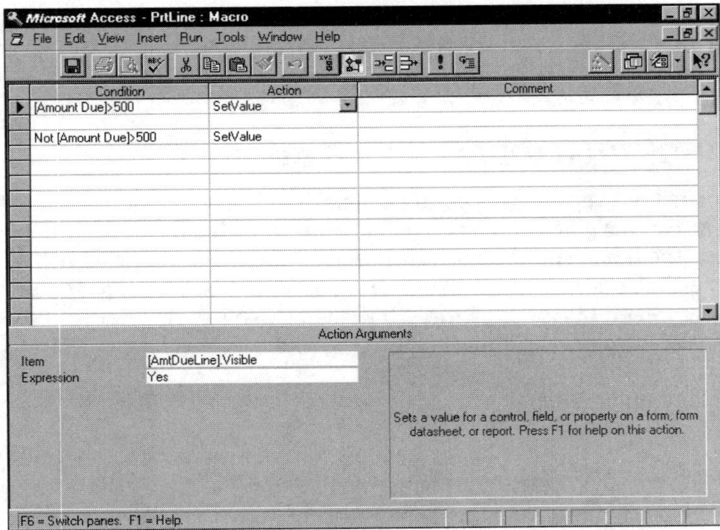

Figure 31-20: A macro to turn the Visible property of a control on or off.

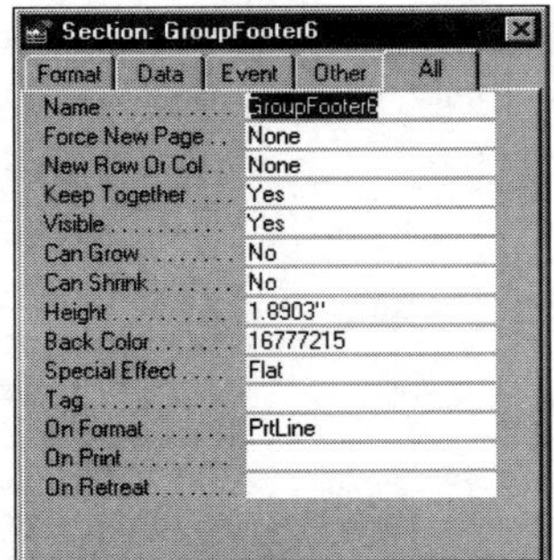

Figure 31-21: A property sheet with a macro name in the On Format property.

Hiding data in a report with a macro

You can hide data in a report with the same method you just used to display or hide a line. You simply set the Visible property to Yes or No in a macro. After you set the property to Yes or No in a macro, attach the macro to the On Format property of the section where the data resides.

Filtering records for a report with a macro

You can filter records for a report by creating a macro and attaching it to the On Open property of the report. This gives you a consistent way of asking for criteria. The On Open property runs the macro no matter how the user opens the report. For example, the user can double-click on the report name, choose a command from a custom menu, or select a command button on a form. If the On Open property is used to trigger the macro, you have only to run the dialog box against this single property.

Cross Ref

Chapter 32 shows a menu and dialog box that perform this type of filtering.

Importing and Exporting Macros

You can easily use data from other formats in Access. You can import, export, and attach tables via commands on the File menu in the Database window. However, if you consistently transfer the same data, you may want to automate the process in a macro.

Using command buttons to import or export

If you create a macro to transfer data, you can activate the macro by use of a command button and the On Click property of the button.

When you create the macro, Access provides three actions to help you transfer the data:

✦ TransferDatabase

✦ TransferSpreadsheet

✦ TransferText

By using these actions and their arguments, you can create very powerful (but simple) transfer-data macros.

Creating Accelerator Keys (Hot Keys)

You can assign a macro to a specific key or combination of keys, such as Ctrl+P. Once you assign a macro to a key, the key is known as a *hot key.* By assigning hot keys, you can create one macro to perform an action no matter what form, view, or table you're in. For example, the Ctrl+P key combination can be used to print the current record.

You can assign macros to any number of hot keys. All hot key macros are stored in a single group macro that Access uses. That group macro is known as a *key assignment* macro. When you open a database, Access looks for a macro name that is specified in the Options dialog box of the View menu. If the macro exists, it runs automatically, assigning macros to hot keys. Figure 31-22 shows several hot key assignments in an AutoKeys macro.

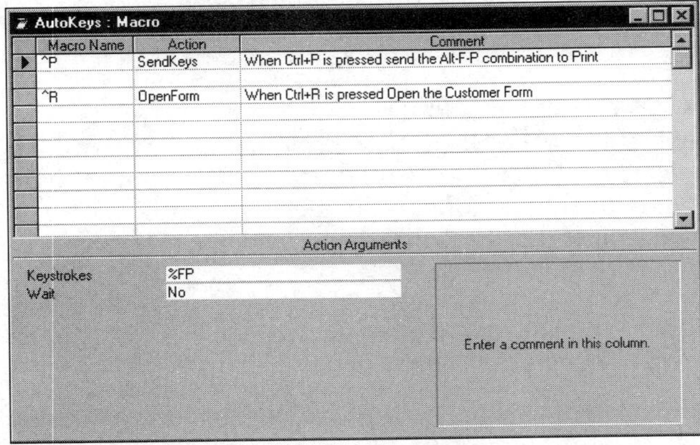

Figure 31-22: A macro to assign hot keys.

Changing the default key assignment macro

You specify the name of the macro for the hot keys in the Options dialog box of the View menu choice in the Database window. The default name for this macro is AutoKeys, but you can give it any name you want. To specify a different hot-key macro name (default key assignment), follow these steps:

1. Select Tools⇨Options… from the Database window menu.
2. Select the Keyboard tab.
3. In the Key Assignment Macro box, replace the default AutoKeys macro name with the name of the macro group that contains the key assignments you want to use.
4. Click on Apply to apply the settings immediately without closing the dialog box; click on OK to apply the settings and close the dialog box. Enter the new name of the hot-key macro in the Key Assignment Macro box of the Items.

You can have several different key assignment macros, each under a different name. To change from one hot-key macro to another, simply enter the new name in the Options box. Then close and reopen the database to make the new key assignment macro active.

Creating a hot-key combination

To create a hot-key combination and assign actions to it requires creating a macro named AutoKeys and using macro names based on the key combination you want to use to specify an action. The macro names can be based on a specific Access syntax called SendKeys syntax: Otherwise they can use the typical macro actions.

Using SendKeys syntax for key assignments

When you enter a key combination in the Macro Name column, you specify the key combination by using a specific syntax known as SendKeys syntax. Table 31-5 shows several key combinations and their corresponding SendKeys syntax. When you assign actions to a key combination, you enter the SendKeys syntax in the Macro Name column.

Using Table 31-5 as a reference, you see that to assign some macro actions to the Tab key, you name a macro **{TAB}** in the group macro Autokeys.

Creating a hot key

To create a hot key, follow these steps:

1. Create a macro named AutoKeys.
2. Type the key combination in the Macro Name column.
3. Type the set of actions you want to associate with the key combination.
4. Repeat Steps 2 and 3 for every hotkey you want to assign actions to.
5. Save the macro.

Table 31-5
SendKeys Syntax

Key Combo	*SendKeys Syntax*	*Key Combo*	*SendKeys Syntax*
Backspace	{BKSP} or {BS}	F2	{F2}
Caps Lock	{CAPSLOCK}	Ctrl+A	^A
Enter	{ENTER} or ~	Ctrl+F10	^{F10}
Insert	{INSERT}	Ctrl+2	^2
Left arrow	{LEFT}	Shift+F5	+{F5}
Home	{HOME}	Shift+Delete	+{DEL}
PgDn	{PGDN}	Shift+End	+{END}
Escape	{ESC}	Alt+F10	%{F10}
PrintScreen	{PRTSC}	Alt+Up arrow	%{UP}
Scroll Lock	{SCROLLLOCK}	Left arrow 10 times	{LEFT 10}
Tab	{TAB}	Shift+BA together	+(BA)

Access makes the key assignment immediate. When you press the key combination, Access runs the macro actions. In the preceding steps, you can also make several key assignments, creating a macro for each key combination. Just remember to name the macro group **AutoKeys** (or whatever name you specified in the Options dialog box).

Summary

This chapter provided an in-depth explanation of macro usage. You learned how to use macros in forms and reports and how to create hot keys. The following topics were covered:

- ✦ An event is some user action. The action may be opening a form, changing data in a record, or selecting a command button.
- ✦ Access recognizes user events by using a corresponding property of a form or report. For example, the On Open property is associated with the event of opening a form.
- ✦ You can attach form macros to the form or to individual controls. Forms can use form-level events and control-level events.
- ✦ Form-level macros can display messages, open a form, synchronize two forms, and validate data entry.
- ✦ The two most common form properties for validating data at the form level are On Delete and Before Update.
- ✦ With the MsgBox( ) function, you can specify conditions in macros. It is a very powerful function that displays messages and command buttons to obtain user input.
- ✦ Control-event macros can be triggered when the user enters or exits a control, clicks on a button, or double-clicks on a control.
- ✦ You use the SetValue action in macros to hide a control, update a field on the basis of another field value, or disable a control.
- ✦ Report macros can be triggered at report level or at the report section level. Only two event properties are used at the report level; two are used at the report section level.
- ✦ By using macros in reports, you can apply a filter to a report, hide or print a line, or hide some other object on a report, basing the macro on a condition.
- ✦ You can assign macro actions to combinations of keys by using a key assignment macro and macro names based on the SendKeys syntax of Access.

In the next chapter, you work with macros in menus, switchboards, and dialog boxes to further automate your database system.

✦ ✦ ✦

Creating Switchboards, Menus, Toolbars, and Dialog Boxes

In This Chapter

How to create a switchboard by using a form and command buttons

How to use the Command Button Wizard

How to use the Picture Builder

How to add a custom menu to a form or report

How to use the Menu Builder

How to create Shortcut Menus

How to create custom Toolbars

How to create Control Tips

How to create a print dialog box

Until this chapter, you created individual Access objects: tables, queries, forms, reports, and macros. You worked with each of these objects interactively in Access, selecting the Database window and using the assorted objects.

In this chapter, you tie these objects together into a single database application — without having to write or know how to use a complex database program. Rather, you automate the application through the use of switchboards, dialog boxes, and menus. These objects make your system easier to use; they hide the Access interface from the final user.

What Is a Switchboard?

A *switchboard* is fundamentally a form. The switchboard form is a customized application menu that contains user-defined command buttons. With these command buttons, you can run macros that automatically select such actions as opening forms or printing reports.

Using a switchboard button, you replace many interactive user steps with a single button selection (or *click*). For example, if you want to open the form Add a Customer and Pets interactively, you must perform three actions: Switch to the Database window, select the Forms tab, and open the form. If you use a switchboard button to perform the same task, you simply select the button. Figure 32-1 shows the switchboard window with several buttons. Each command button triggers a macro that performs a series of steps, such as opening the Customer form or running the Hospital Report.

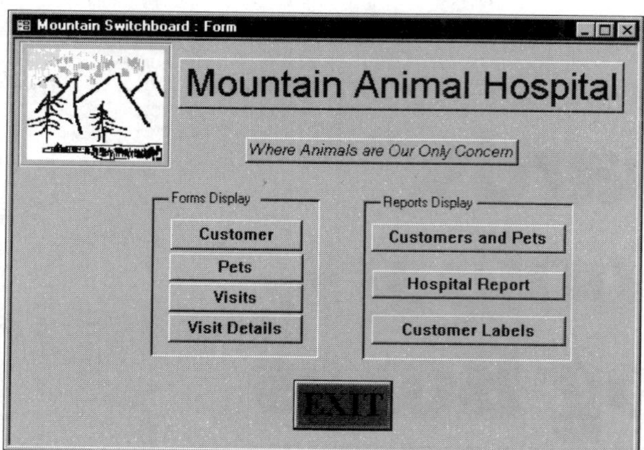

Figure 32-1: A switchboard with several command buttons for forms and reports.

By using a switchboard and other objects covered in this chapter, you can tie your database objects together in a single database application. Rather than the Access interactive interface, the application will have a user interface you create. A primary component of that user-defined interface is the switchboard you create.

Using a switchboard

A switchboard's primary use is as an application interface menu. The switchboard in Figure 32-1 is the application interface menu for the Mountain Animal Hospital database. As you see in the figure, the switchboard contains several command buttons. When the user clicks on any switchboard button, a macro is triggered that performs some action or a series of actions.

Creating the basic form for a switchboard

You create a switchboard by adding command buttons to an existing Access form. The form in Figure 32-1 is a basic display form.

Because switchboard forms are used as application menus, they tend to use a limited number of form controls. Typically you find command buttons, labels, object frames (OLE objects such as pictures), lines, and rectangles. Normally switchboards lack the other types of form controls such as text boxes (bound to fields), list and combo boxes, graphs, subforms, and page breaks.

To create a basic switchboard form, you place labels like titles and group headings on the form. In addition to the labels, you may also want to place lines, rectangles, and pictures on the form to make it aesthetically appealing. You create the basic switchboard form by using the techniques you already learned in chapters covering form objects.

Consider, for example, the switchboard in Figure 32-1. Minus the command buttons, this is a typical Access application form. Its major components are a title and two group sections. The title is comprised of three parts:

✦ The main text title, Mountain Animal Hospital

✦ A picture logo showing mountains and trees

✦ A text logo: Where Animals Are Our Only Concern

Below the title are two sunken rectangles. On the top border of each rectangle is a label; the rectangle to the left is labeled `Forms Display`, and the rectangle to the right is labeled `Reports Display`. Each rectangle now appears in a *sunken* state, contains several command buttons when the switchboard form is completed.

Working with command buttons

Command buttons are the type of form control you use to run macros. Command buttons are the simplest type of form controls, with the single purpose of executing a macro.

Command buttons run macros that perform a multitude of tasks in Access:

✦ Opening and displaying other forms

✦ Opening a pop-up form, or dialog box, to collect additional information

✦ Opening and printing reports

✦ Activating a search or displaying a filter

✦ Exiting Access

Disk On your disk in the Mountain Animal Hospital database is a form named `Mountain Switchboard-No Buttons`. You can use that as a starting point to create your switchboard, as shown in Figure 32-2.

Figure 32-2 shows a command button named Button01 and its property sheet. In this property sheet, you see the event properties available for a command button.

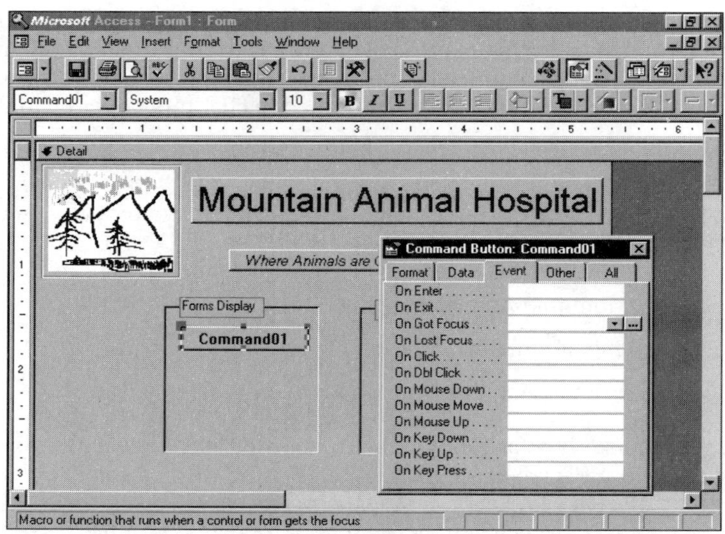

Figure 32-2: A single-button switchboard form with its open property sheet.

Each event property can trigger a macro. For example, to trigger a macro named OpenCust when the user clicks on the button, place the macro name OpenCust in the parameter box for the On Click property. The keyword *On* identifies an event property. The property identifies the user event that must occur to trigger an action.

Warning On Click and On Dbl Click are mutually compatible. If you activate both the On Click property (giving it a macro name) and the On Dbl Click property, Access follows this order of precedence for the mouse clicking and trapping:

1. On Click (single click)
2. On Dbl Click (double-click)
3. On Click (single click)

In other words, Access processes an On Click first and then an On Dbl Click and, finally, an On Click *again.* So Access *always* processes the On Click if it is defined. To prevent the second On Click macro from running, place a CancelEvent action in the On Dbl Click macro.

In addition, if the macro you call from an On Click opens a dialog box (message box, pop-up form, and so forth), the second click is lost and the On Dbl Click is never reached! If you use On Click and On Dbl Click, the On Click should not open a dialog box if you need to capture the On Dbl Click.

What is focus?

To understand the terminology associated with command buttons, you need to know the term *focus*. The two command button properties On Enter and On Exit gain or lose focus. In other words, the focus represents the next item of input from the user. For example, if you tab from one button to another, you lose the focus on the first button as you leave it, and you gain the focus on the second as you enter it. In a form with several command buttons, you can tell which button has focus by the dotted box around the label of the button. Focus does not denote the state of input, as when you press a button; rather, focus is the object that is currently active and awaiting some user action.

The focus for mouse input always coincides with the button down, or pointer, location. Because focus occurs at the moment of clicking on a command button, the property On Enter is not triggered. The reason is that On Enter occurs just before the focus is gained; that state is not realized when you selecting a command button by us a mouse. The On Enter state never occurs. Rather, the focus and On Click occur simultaneously, bypassing the On Enter state.

Creating command buttons

A command button's primary purpose is to activate, or run, a macro. Access gives you two ways to create a command button:

✦ Click on the Command Button icon in the Form toolbox

✦ Drag a macro name from the database container to the form

In this chapter, you will see both of these methods at least once as you learn how to create the eight command buttons shown in Figure 32-1 (four buttons to display a form, three to display a report, and one to exit the application). In this first example, you see how to create the first form button by using the Command Button Wizard.

When using the Command Button Wizard, you not only create a command button, but you also can automatically embed a picture on the button. And, more important, you can create a VBA module to perform a task, including Record Navigation (Next, Previous, First, Last, Find), Record Operations (Save, Delete, Print, New, Duplicate), Form Operations (Open, Close, Print, Filter), Report Operations (Print, Preview, Mail), Applications (Run Application, Quit, Notepad, Word, Excel), and Miscellaneous (Print Table, Run Query, Run Macro, AutoDialer).

To create the Customer button by using the Command Button Wizard, follow these steps:

1. Open the form Mountain Switchboard - No Buttons in design mode.
2. Make sure that the Control Wizard icon is toggled on.
3. Select the Command Button icon in the toolbox.
4. Place the cursor on the form in the upper left corner of the Form Display rectangle and draw a small rectangle.

Note Command buttons have no control source. If you try to create a button by dragging a field from the Field List, a text box control (not a command button) is created. You must draw the rectangle or drag a macro to create a command button.

The Command Button Wizard displays the dialog box shown in Figure 32-3. You can select from several categories of tasks. As you choose each category, the list of actions under the header `When button is pressed` changes. In addition, the sample picture changes as you move from action to action. In Figure 32-3, the specified category is Form Operations, and the desired action is Open Form.

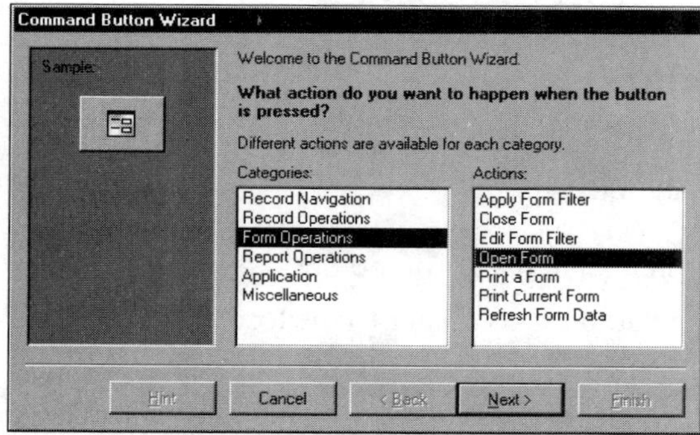

Figure 32-3: The Command Button Wizard's Categories and Actions dialog box.

5. Choose the Form Operations category and the Open Form action.
6. Press the Next > button to move to the next screen.

   The Wizard displays a list of the Mountain Animal Hospital database's forms.
7. Select the Customer form and press the Next > button to move to the next Wizard screen.

   The next screen is a specific dialog box for this button. Because you have chosen the Open Form action, Access uses built-in logic to now ask you what you want to do now with this form. As you can see in Figure 32-4, Access can automatically write a VBA program behind the button to open the form and show all records; if necessary, it can let you specify fields to search for specific values after the form is opened.

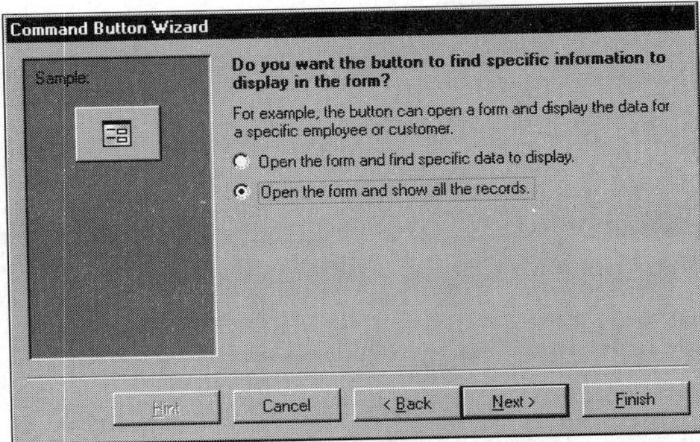

Figure 32-4: The Command Button Wizard Open Form With Specific Data Question.

8. Select Open the form and show all the records and press Next > to move on.

   The next screen lets you decide what you want to appear on the button. You can display text or a picture on the button. The button can be resized to accommodate any size text. The default is to place a picture on the button. You can choose from the default button for the selected action or you can click in the Show all pictures check box to select from over 100 pictures. You also can press the Browse button to select an icon (.ICO) or bitmap (.BMP) file from your disk. For this example, simply display the text Customer on the button.

9. Select the Text option button and type **Customer** into the text box.

   The sample button displays the text instead of the picture (see Figure 32-5).

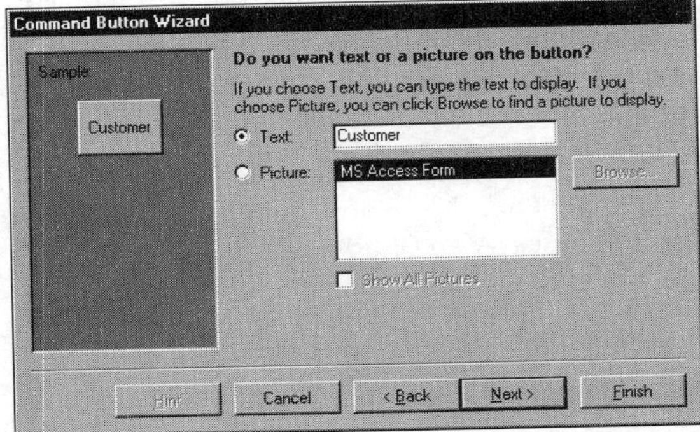

Figure 32-5: Selecting a picture or text for the button.

10. Press the Next > button to move to the final Wizard screen, which lets you enter a name for the button and then display the button on the form.

11. Enter **Customer** as the name of the button. Press Finish. The button appears on the Form Design screen as shown in Figure 32-6.

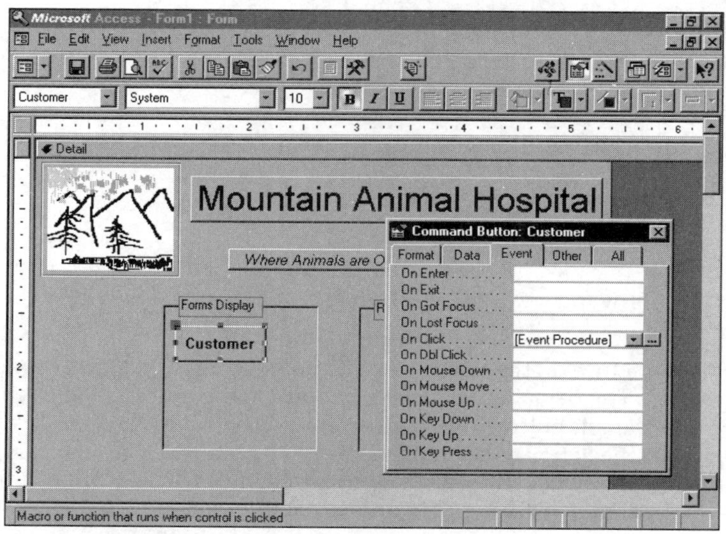

Figure 32-6: Adding a button to the form design.

Notice the property sheet displayed in Figure 32-6. The On Click property displays Event Procedure, which means that a module is stored *behind* the form. You can see this VBA module library is to press the Builder button (three dots) next to the `[Event Procedure]` text. When the Customer button is clicked, the VBA program is run and the Customer form is opened.

A module window appears with the specific VBA program code that's necessary to open the Customer form (see Figure 32-7). There is no need to look at this code unless you plan to change the program. This is covered in Chapter 33.

You can create a command button and attach a macro very easily—or attach pictures—without using the Wizard. If you want to dabble in VBA, the Command Button Wizard is a great place to start.

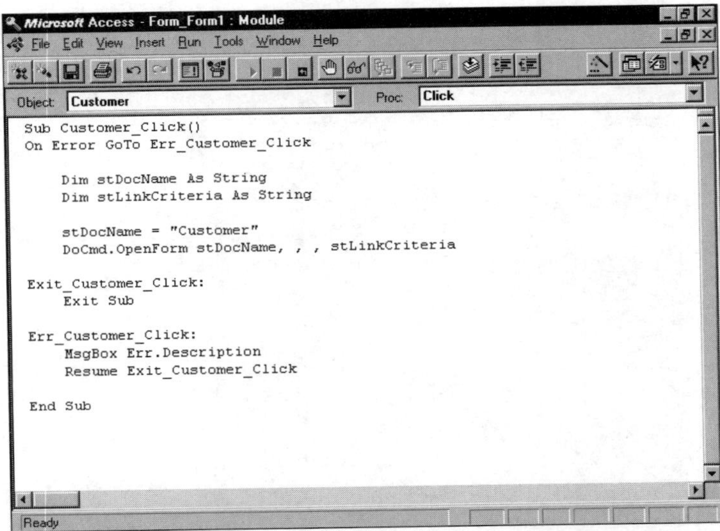

Figure 32-7: The Event Procedure Module for opening the Customer form.

To change the caption of a command button follow these steps:

1. Display the form Mountain Switchboard - No Buttons in design view.
2. Make sure that the Control Wizard icon is toggled off.
3. Select the Command Button icon in the toolbox.
4. Place the cursor on the form under the Customer button in the Form Display rectangle and draw a small rectangle.

   The command button appears with a name inside (begins with `Command`) and a number. Access also deselects Command button in the toolbox and highlights the selection pointer.
5. Double-click on the button and change the caption name from Command# to **Pets**.
6. Repeat Steps 2 through 5 for the form buttons Visits and Visit Details.
7. Repeat Steps 2 through 5 for the report buttons Customers and Pets, Hospital Report, and Customer Labels.

With all the buttons displayed, your screen should look like Figure 32-8.

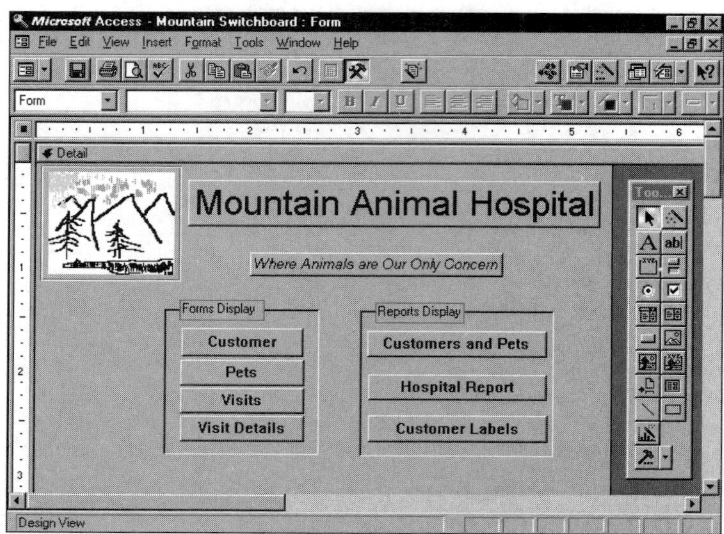

Figure 32-8: All buttons on-screen.

Linking a command button to a macro

As soon as you create a command button in the Design window, it is already active. You can click on it, although it doesn't perform any action unless you created it with the wizard. If you switch to the Form window by selecting the Form button on the toolbar, you'll see the switchboard. You can push any of the seven buttons you created in the design mode.

Every time you select a button, it graphically pushes down, showing that it has been selected. Except for the Customer button, however, nothing else occurs; only the button movement happens. By switching back to the design mode and selecting the Design button on the toolbar, you can link a macro to the button.

To link a command button to a macro, you enter the macro name into the property cell of one of the command button's event properties. To see the property sheet for a command button, follow these steps:

1. In design mode, select the Pets command button by clicking it.
2. Click on the Properties button on the toolbar or select View⇨Properties on.

A property sheet similar to the one in Figure 32-2 should be visible on your screen. Notice the event properties that begin with the word *On* in the property sheet.

The property most commonly used to link a command button to a macro is On Click. This property runs a macro whenever a user selects the button. When the button is selected, the On Click property becomes True and the specified macro is run. To associate the macro named Pets in the macro group Mountain Switchboard, follow these steps:

1. Click on the Pets command button.
2. Click on the On Click property cell in the property sheet for the command button.
3. Type **Mountain Switchboard.Pets** in the cell and press Enter.

Make sure that you type both the macro group name and then the macro name separated by a period.

Tip When you enter a macro name, the macro does not have to exist. You can enter the name of a macro that you create later. In this way, you can create the switchboard first and the macros later. If the macro name you enter in the On Click cell does not exist when you open the form and select the button, Access displays an error message.

Using these methods, you can now complete all seven buttons properties, assigning a macro for each button on the basis of the On Click property. Table 32-1 shows each button name and the macro it will call.

Table 32-1
The Seven Buttons and Their Macro Names

In Rectangle	*Button Name*	*Macro for On Click*
Form	Customer	Event Property (created by Button Wizard)
Form	Pets	Mountain Switchboard.Pets
Form	Visits	Mountain Switchboard.Visits
Form	Visit Details	Mountain Switchboard.Visit Details
Report	Customer and Pets	Mountain Switchboard.Customer and Pets
Report	Hospital Report	Mountain Switchboard.Hospital Report
Report	Customer Labels	Mountain Switchboard.Customer Labels

The macros for the Mountain Switchboard

In this example, each command button opens either a form or a report by using the OpenForm or OpenReport macro actions. The Exit button closes the form with the Quit macro action.

You can create each of the macros and its actions by following these general steps:

1. Enter a macro name in the Macro Name column.
2. Enter a macro action in the Action column (such as OpenForm, OpenReport, or Close) or select the macro action from the drop-down list box.
3. Enter a macro argument (name of form or report) for each action.
4. Optionally, enter a remark (as a reminder) in the Comment Column.

New! Another way to add a macro action and argument is to drag the form or report from the Database window to the macro's Action column. Access automatically adds the correct action in the Action column, which is OpenForm or OpenReport. Access also adds the correct argument in the Name cell of the arguments.

If you want to create the group macro for this chapter, you can follow Table 32-2. This table shows each macro name, the action for each macro, and the form or report name. (These are shown in Figure 32-9.) The macro Mountain Switchboard should already exist in the macro object list of the Database window.

Table 32-2
Macros Used in the Group Macro

Macro Name	*Action*	*Argument Name (Form, Report, Object)*
Pets	OpenForm	Pets
Visits	OpenForm	Adding General Pet Visit Info
Visit Details	OpenForm	Adding Visit Details
Customer and Pets	OpenReport	Pets & Owners
Hospital Report	OpenReport	Invoices
Customer Label	OpenReport	Customer By State (three snaking columns)
Exit	Close	Mountain Switchboard

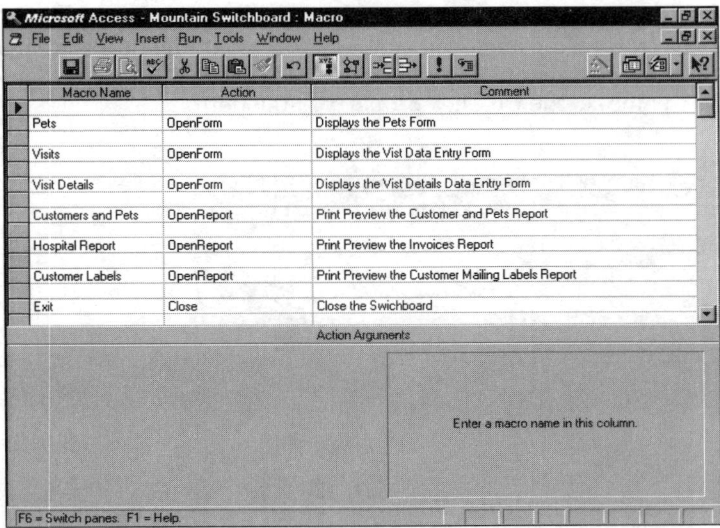

Figure 32-9: The seven macros used for Mountain Switchboard.

Notice that Table 32-2 shows that the action Close will close the form named Mountain Switchboard. These macros work with the actual form named Mountain Switchboard. The Exit command button will be created next.

Dragging a macro to the form to create a button

The form Mountain Switchboard does not have an Exit command button. You already learned one way to add a command button in the Form Design window. Another way to create a command button is by dragging and dropping a macro name from the macro Database window to a position on the switchboard.

For example, to create an Exit command button for the form Mountain Switchboard by using the drag-and-drop method, follow these steps:

1. Enter the design mode for the form Mountain Switchboard - No Buttons
2. Activate the Database window by pressing F11 or Alt+F1.
3. In the Database window, select the Macro object button to display all macros.
4. Highlight the Mountain Switchboard in the Macro Object list.
5. Click on the macro Mountain Switchboard; drag and drop it onto the form below the rectangles.
6. Click the button name and change it to **Exit**
7. Click in the cell of the On Click property of the Exit button.
8. Move to the end of the macro group name and type **.Exit**

Your screen should now look similar to Figure 32-10. Notice that when you added the macro to the form by the drag-and-drop method, Access automatically created a command button, named it the same as the macro, and placed the macro name (in this case, a group name) in the On Click property of the button.

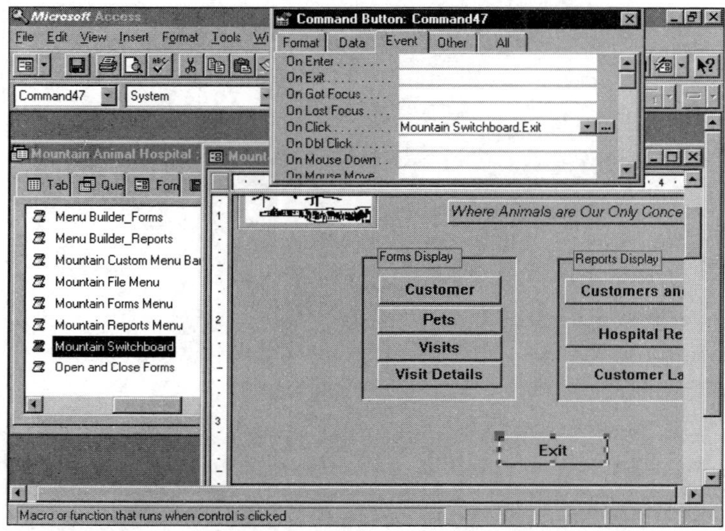

Figure 32-10: The new button created by dragging and dropping a macro onto the form.

When you added the macro name to the On Click property, you did not have to add the macro group name. Rather, you moved to the end and placed a period after the group name and then the macro name. Access automatically brought the group name into the On Click property for you.

Tip If you drag and drop a macro that is not a group macro, Access correctly places the macro name in the On Click property and names the button the same as the macro.

Warning If you drag a macro group, as you did in this example, and do not add a macro name to the On Click property, Access runs the first macro in the macro group.

Adding a picture to a command button

Disk All the command buttons you have created contained text in the caption property of the button. However, you can have the button display a picture instead. For example, the disk in the back of the book contains a file named EXIT.BMP, which is a bitmap of an exit sign. You can have the Exit command button show the picture EXIT.BMP rather than the word *Exit*.

To change a command button to a picture button, you can use one of these methods:

- ✦ Type the name of the bitmap (.BMP) containing the picture into the Picture property of the button.
- ✦ Use the Picture Builder to select from an icon list that comes with Access.
- ✦ Specify the name of an icon or bitmap file.

To change the Exit command button to the picture button, EXIT.BMP, follow these steps:

1. In the Mountain Switchboard form, select the Exit command button.
2. Display the property window.
3. Click on the *Picture* property for the Exit button.
4. Click on the Builder button (three dots on a little button).

   The Picture Builder dialog box appears. No picture appears because the button you are modifying has none. Because you are adding a picture for an exit button, you may want to see if there is an Exit button in Access. You can scroll down the list of Available Pictures, as shown in Figure 32-11. Access has an Exit picture, but it may not be what you want. You can select any bitmap or icon file on your disk.

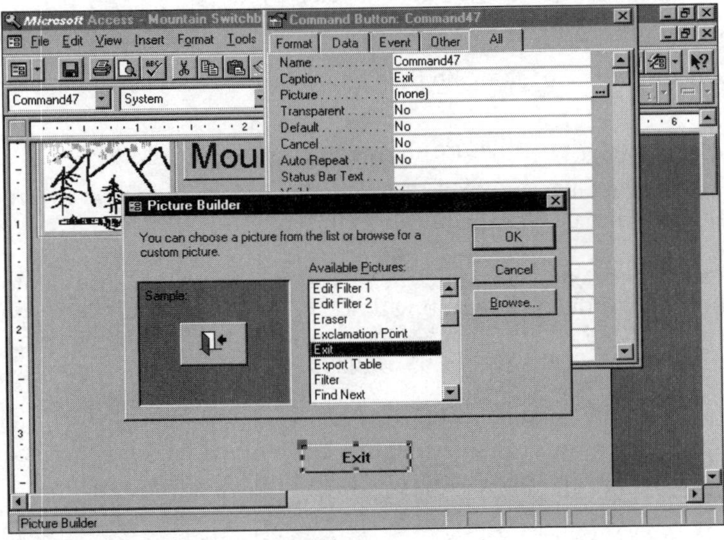

Figure 32-11: The Picture Builder.

5. Click on the Browse button.

   The Select Bitmap dialog box shows a standard Windows directory list. Select the directory that contains your file (as shown in Figure 32-12).

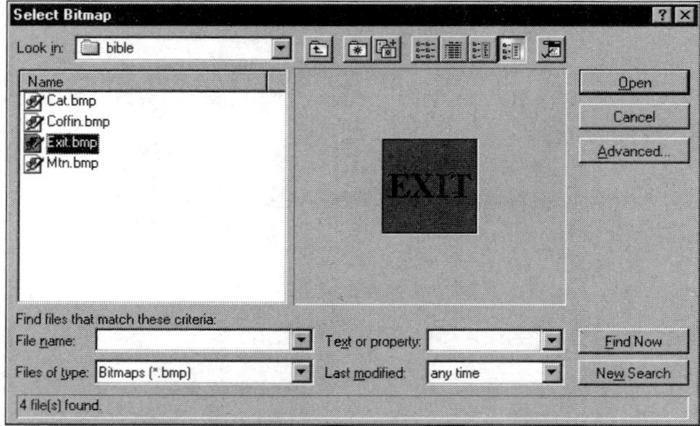

Figure 32-12: The Picture Builder.

6. Select the directory that contains the file EXIT.BMP, select the file, and press Open. The bitmap appears in the sample area. Although it doesn't fit in the sample, it should fit on the button when it is displayed.

7. Press OK to accept the bitmap.

   Access places the word `(bitmap)` in the Picture property of the command button.

8. Resize the button so that the picture shows only the word Exit.

   Your form should look like Figure 32-13. Notice that Access added the word (bitmap) to the Picture cell for the button Exit.

Tip You also can directly type the filename into the Picture property. If Access cannot find the picture file, it displays a dialog box stating that it couldn't find your file. If you know the drive and directory where the file is located, enter them in the picture cell with the filename (for example, C:\ACCESS95\BIBLE\EXIT.BMP).

This action completes the Mountain Switchboard. Save your switchboard. The next task is to customize the menu bar to correspond to the buttons on the switchboard so that the choices can be made from the menu or the buttons.

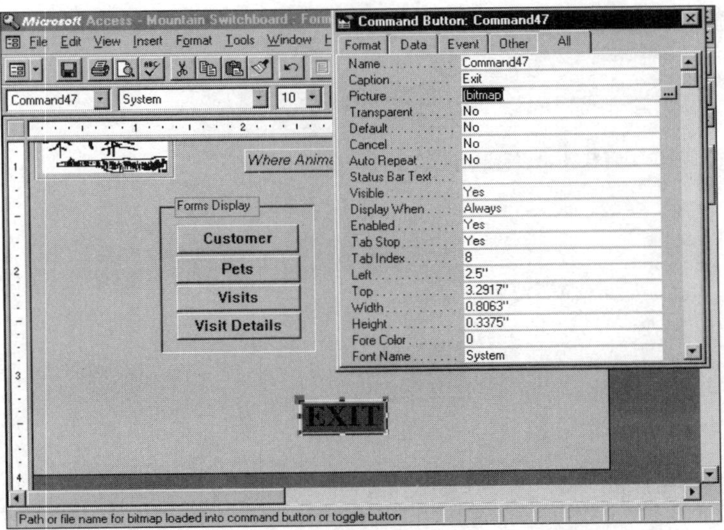

Figure 32-13: The final form with a picture button added.

Creating Customized Menu Bars

Besides creating switchboards with Access, you can create a custom drop-down menu bar that adds functionality to your system. You can add commands to this menu that are appropriate for your application. These commands may be the actions specified in your switchboard command buttons. When you create a custom drop-down menu bar, the new bar will replace the Access menu bar.

Tip The menu bar is referenced only by a form; you can create a single menu bar and use it for several forms.

Figure 32-14 shows the Mountain Switchboard with a custom drop-down menu bar attached. Notice that each of the three choices on the bar menu, File, Forms, and Reports, has a drop-down menu attached.

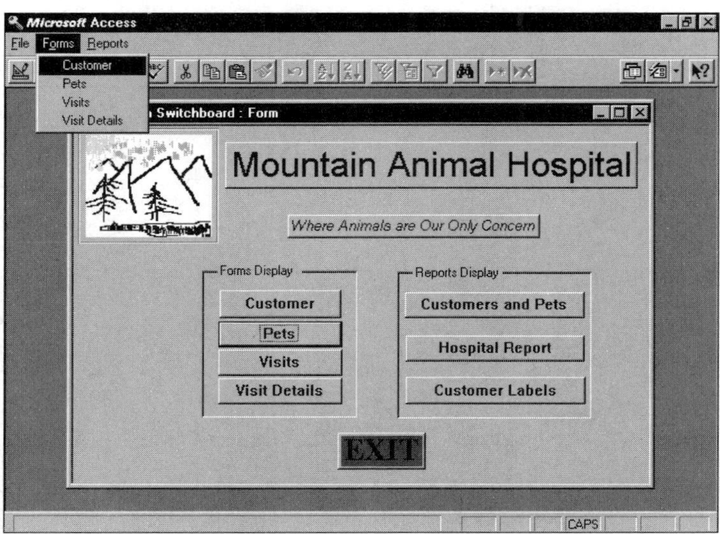

Figure 32-14: The custom drop-down menu bar.

You can use Access macros to create a menu bar and its attached drop-down menus. To create a drop-down menu bar, you follow these three basic steps:

1. Define each drop-down menu choice and its commands (actions) in a macro group.
2. Create the menu bar in a macro by using the AddMenu action.
3. Attach the menu bar to a form by setting the On Menu property for the form.

Another way to create a menu bar is to use the Menu Builder, which we cover later in this chapter.

Defining the drop-down menus

To create a drop-down menu, you must create a separate macro group for the menu. This macro will contain a separate macro name for each command (choice) in the menu. Access uses the macro name for the command name in the menu.

Defining a single-bar drop-down menu

To create a drop-down menu for the menu bar prompt File (which has the single command Exit), follow these steps:

1. Create a new macro.
2. Activate the Macro Name column by selecting the Macro Names button on the toolbar.
3. Type **Exit** in the first empty Macro Name cell.
4. Type **Close** in the Action cell or select the Close action from the pull-down menu.
5. Type **Form** in the Object Type action argument for the Close action or select Form from the pull-down menu.
6. Select Mountain Switchboard from the pull-down list in the Object Name action argument.
7. Select Yes from the pull-down list in the Save action argument.

At the completion of these steps, your macro should look like the one in Figure 32-15.

The macro in Figure 32-15 can now be saved to a macro file. For this example, save it to a macro file named **Mountain File Menu**.

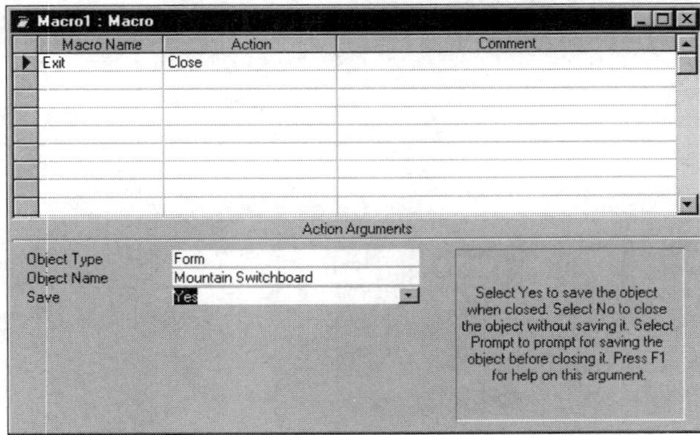

Figure 32-15: A group macro with a single macro to be used as a drop-down menu.

Defining a multiple-bar drop-down menu

To create a drop-down menu with multiple bars, you also create a group macro. However, instead of creating a single macro in the macro group, you create a macro for each menu command (choice) of the drop-down menu. For example, to create the four-command drop-down menu for the menu-bar prompt called Forms, follow these steps:

1. Create a new macro and activate the Macro Name column.
2. Type **Customer** in the first empty Macro Name cell.
3. Type **OpenForm** in the Action cell or select the OpenForm action from the pull-down menu.
4. Type **Customer** in the Form Name action argument or select Customer from the pull-down menu.
5. Type **Pets** in the next empty Macro Name cell.
6. Type **OpenForm** in the Action cell or select the OpenForm action from the pull-down menu.
7. Type **Pets** in the Form Name action argument or select Pets from the pull-down menu.

Repeat Steps 5 through 7 for the macro named Visits and the form named Adding General Pet Visit Info. Then repeat these steps for the macro named Visit Details and the form named Adding Visit Details. At the completion of these steps, your macro should look like the one in Figure 32-16.

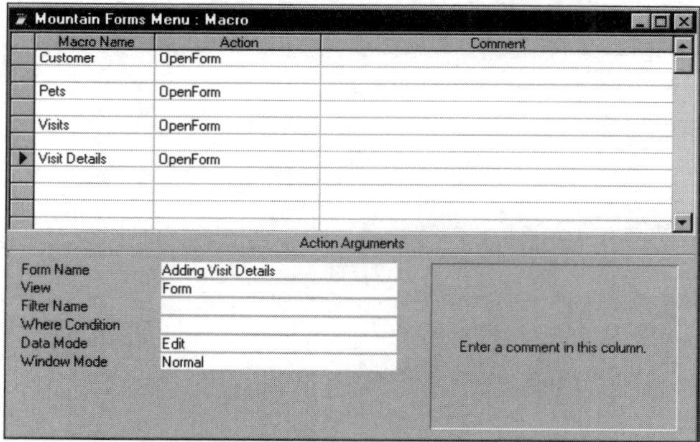

Figure 32-16: A group macro for a drop-down menu.

Save the macro you just created and give it the name **Mountain Forms Menu**. You can now create the macro named Mountain Reports Menu, which will be used for the Reports prompt.

Adding options to a drop-down menu

As you work with macros for use in your custom drop-down menus, you'll want to take advantage of the special options for these menus. Access offers these two options for your drop-down menu:

Separator lines	A single hyphen	Lines separating the menu choices
User-defined access keys	&letter	Hot-key characters you can assign

With the first of these options, you can place a line between two menu commands. The second option lets you define a letter from the menu prompt name that you select to access the menu. A typical example of this is the use of F to access the File menu in the Windows menu system. (Note that the Windows method for identifying this key is to underline the letter within the menu name.)

Next you create a drop-down menu for the menu bar prompt named Reports. You will add an access key for each prompt, and then add a line to separate the first command from the second. Follow these steps to complete this menu:

1. Create a new macro and activate the Macro Name column.
2. Type **&Customers and Pets** in the first empty Macro Name cell.
3. Type **OpenReport** in the Action cell or select the OpenReport action from the pull-down menu.
4. Type **All Customers and Pets** in the Report Name action argument or select All Customers and Pets from the pull-down menu.
5. Type **-** (a hyphen) in the next empty Macro Name cell.
6. Type **&Hospital Report** in the next empty Macro Name cell.
7. Type **OpenReport** in the Action cell or select the OpenReport action from the pull-down menu.
8. Type **Invoices** in the Report Name action argument or select Invoices from the pull-down menu.
9. Type **Customer &Labels** in the next empty Macro Name cell.
10. Type **OpenReport** in the Action cell or select the OpenReport action from the pull-down menu.
11. Type **Customer Mailing Labels** in the Report Name action argument or select Customer Labels from the pull-down menu.

If you followed all eleven steps, your macro should look similar to the one in Figure 32-17. You should save this macro to a macro file named Mountain Reports Menu.

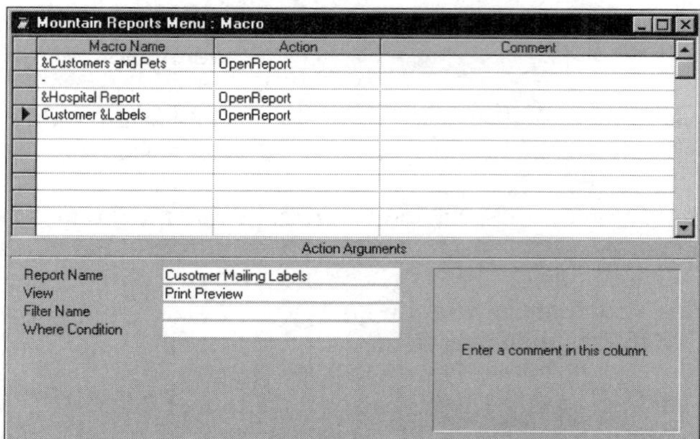

Figure 32-17: Creating a macro that will display a menu, separating lines and access keys.

The macro group in Figure 32-17 will create a drop-down menu that should look similar to Figure 32-18. Notice that in this figure the letter C is underlined in the menu command Customers and Pets. Also notice that the top choice is separated by a line from the next choice.

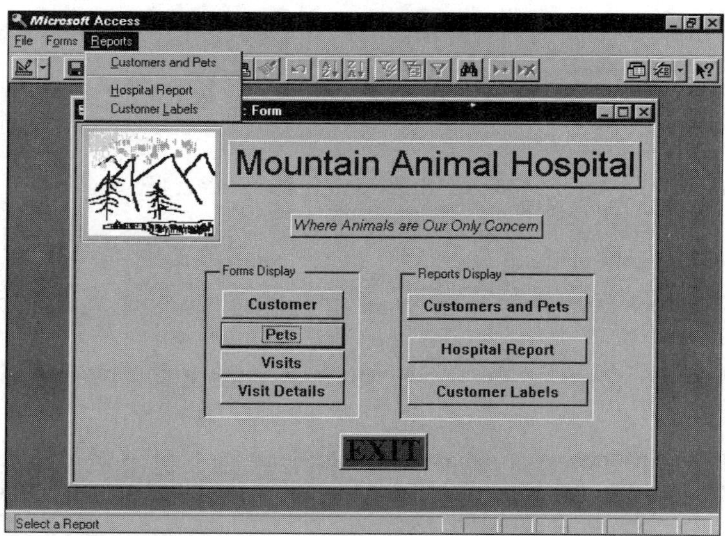

Figure 32-18: The drop-down menu with the options of separator lines and access keys.

When you created the macro names in the preceding steps, you specified a letter as the access key by placing the ampersand (&) before the letter. Step 9 shows that the access key will be the letter *L* because the ampersand is immediately in front of this letter. To specify that you want a line between menu commands, you placed a hyphen (-) in the Macro Name cell in Step 5.

You can go back and add separator lines or access keys to your other menu commands by using these techniques.

Defining a menu bar

Now that you've created the drop-down menus, you are ready to create a macro that will be the menu bar. This menu macro will have an action for each drop-down menu macro. To create a menu bar with the three choices File, Forms, and Reports, follow these steps:

1. Create a new macro.
2. Type **AddMenu** in the Action cell or select the AddMenu action from the pull-down menu.
3. Type **&File** in the Menu Name cell in the action arguments pane.
4. Select the Mountain File Menu macro from the pull-down menu in the Menu Macro Name cell in the action arguments pane.
5. Type **Select the Exit Choice to Close the Switchboard** in the Status Bar Text cell of the action arguments pane.

Repeat Steps 2 through 5 first for F&orms (macro name Mountain Forms Menu) and &Reports (macro name Mountain Reports Menu).

At the completion of these steps, your macro should look similar to Figure 32-19.

Notice that the macro in Figure 32-19 has three actions, one for each drop-down menu. Also notice that the action AddMenu is the same for all three choices. This action is used for building an Access menu bar.

Tip

You can also specify an access key for menu prompts. The user can select this access key all menu *hot keys* are selected — by pressing the Alt key with the access key. For example, pressing Alt+F activates the File menu.

Save the macro you just created under the name **Mountain Custom Menu Bar**.

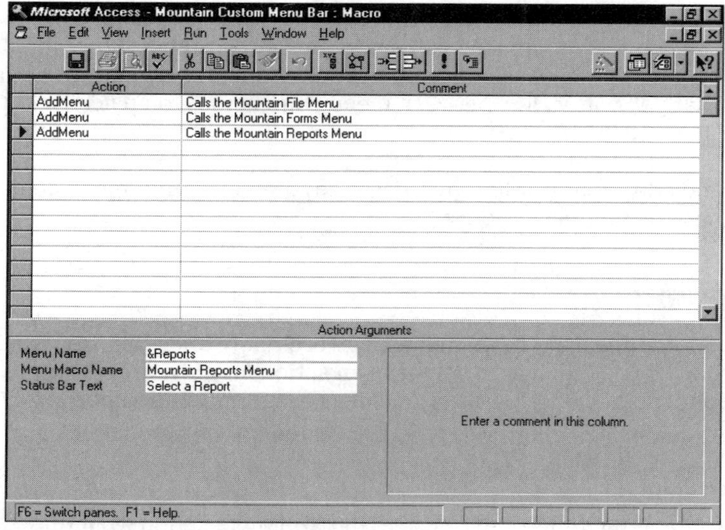

Figure 32-19: The macro for a menu bar.

Attaching the menu bar to a form

You have now completed the drop-down menus and the menu bar named Mountain Custom Menu Bar to attach the drop-down menus to. You are now ready to attach the menu bar to a form.

To attach a menu bar to a form, open the form in design mode and set the Menu Bar property of the form to the menu bar macro name. To attach the menu bar named Mountain Custom Menu Bar to the switchboard form Mountain Switchboard, follow these steps:

1. Open the form Mountain Switchboard in design mode.
2. Activate the property sheet by selecting the Properties button on the toolbar.
3. Click in the small blank box to the left of the ruler (immediately below the toolbar).

   Access displays the title `Form` for the property sheet.
4. Click in the Menu Bar property of the property window.
5. Select the Mountain Customer Menu Bar from the pull-down menu (or type the menu bar name).

By following these steps, you have just attached the menu bar named Mountain Customer Menu Bar with its drop-down menus to the form. You should have a design screen similar to the one in Figure 32-20.

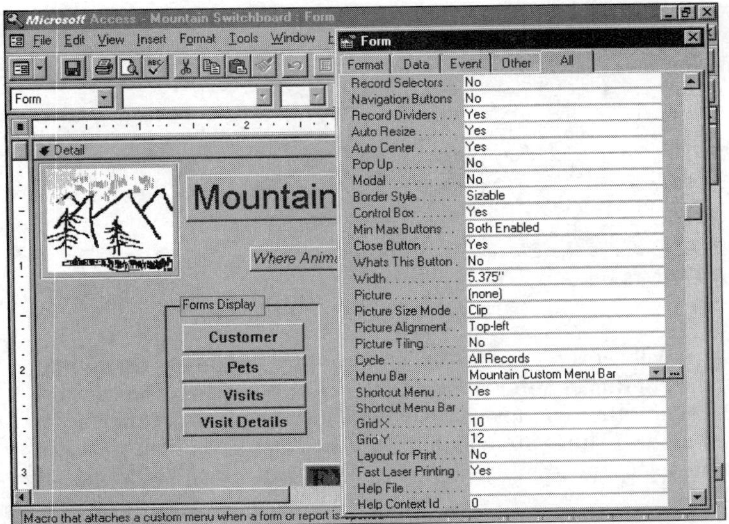

Figure 32-20: Attaching a menu bar to the form using the On Menu property.

You are now ready to save the form and open it to see how the menus tie together.

The Access Menu Builder

Until now, you have created the menu by hand. Access for Windows 95, however, has a Menu Builder that can help you create menus, drop-down menus, write (and save) the underlying macros, and attach the menu to a form. If you need to create a menu and attach it to a form, the Menu Builder enables you to do so automatically.

To run the Menu Builder and create a new menu (or start from an existing menu) select Tools⇨Add-Ins⇨Menu Builder to start the Menu Builder. The first menu builder window is shown in figure 32-21. This window shows you a list of all macro libraries. Since only macros can be used for menus, all of your existing menus are shown.

Tip You can modify existing menus using the Menu Builder but they must rigidly adhere to using three actions—Run Macro, Run Code, and DoMenuItem. Since few menus are created using only these actions, once you create a new menu with the Menu Builder and modify it in the Macro window, you will not be able to use the Menu Builder again for the same purpose.

You have the choice of editing an existing menu bar, creating a new one, or deleting a menu (which actually deletes the macro library).

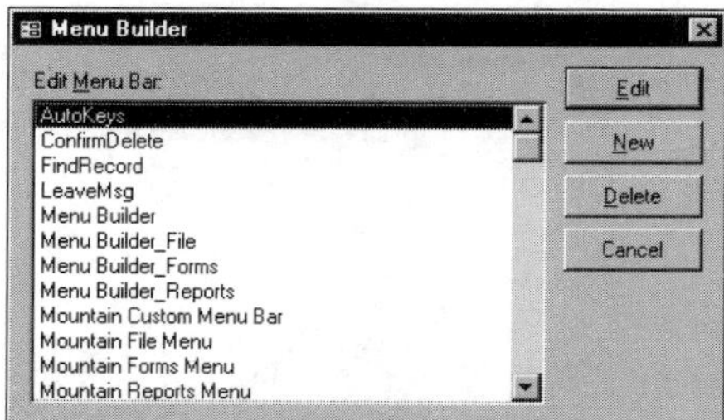

Figure 32-21: Using the Menu Builder.

For this example, you will see a new menu created that looks like the menu you created in the last part of this chapter. When you choose New from the window shown in Figure 32-21, another window is displayed, letting you select from one of the existing Access menu bars. These are called *menu templates* and are stored within Access. You can also select the <Empty Menu Bar> option to create a brand new menu.

You can modify or add to existing menu bars in Access or create completely new menu bars for your custom applications. When you edit existing Access menus, the changes are displayed in the default menus. You can add your own menu items and even delete or change standard Access menu items. Imagine adding a menu item to open the Pets or Customer forms from the Tools menu.

You can define the text for each pull-down menu and even define submenus or dialog box calls. You create each menu as a hierarchy. For this example, you can select the <Empty Menu Bar> option to create a new menu. As you define each menu item, you enter the text for the menu in the Caption text box. To designate hot keys, precede the appropriate letter with an ampersand (&); the letter will appear underlined in the menu.

Using the arrow buttons, you can rearrange or change the menu level. In other words, you can create various levels of pull-down submenus or top-level bar menu items. You can even enter a line separator by entering a single hyphen (-) on a line. Figure 32-22 shows the menu bar you just created, typed into the Menu Builder.

In the Action text box, you enter the type of action, such as DoMenuItem, RunCode, or RunMacro. The DoMenuItem has several arguments that, when entered, help determine which menu item to run when an item is selected: You pick the standard Access menu bar and the submenu command. When you want Access to perform an action other than dropping down a subordinate menu (which requires no action) or enacting a menu item, you code it in a module or enter it in a macro. (You simply enter the macro name as you would in any event property.)

When you are finished, the Menu Builder creates a series of macros: one for the menu bar and a separate macro for each pull-down menu in the menu-bar hierarchy. Figure 32-23 shows the database container displaying these macros and the Forms macro open.

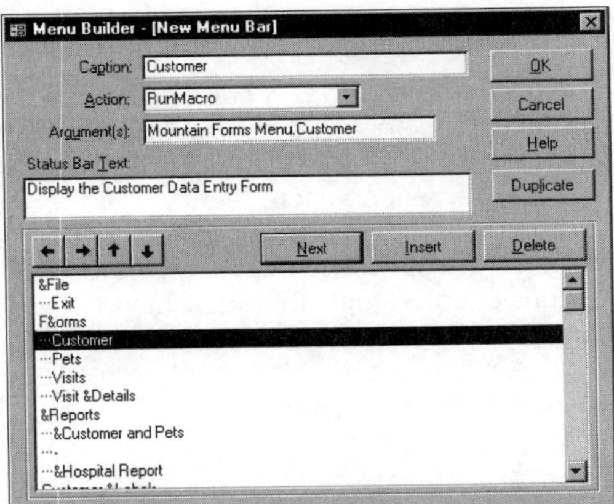

Figure 32-22: The Menu Builder screen with the Mountain Menu.

New! Access for Windows 95 contains a new macro action called SetMenuItem that can be used to gray out menu items that are not selectable; it is based on a context-sensitive action. You can also add a check mark in front of a menu item. For example, by using the SetMenuItem action, you could add a check mark when a form is opened in Mountain Switchboard and remove the check mark when it is closed. See the SetMenuItem action for details.

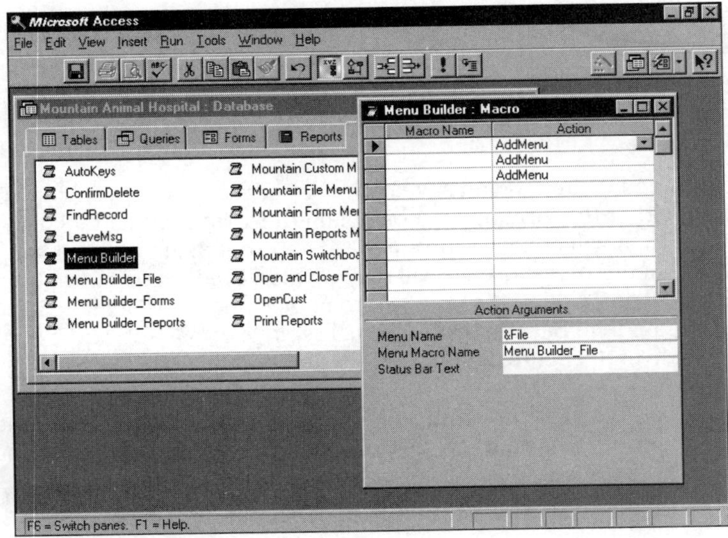

Figure 32-23: The final macros.

Creating shortcut menus

Access for Windows 95 allows you to create *custom shortcut menus* that open when the right mouse button is clicked these can replace the standard shortcut menus in Access for Windows 95. You can define shortcut menus for the form itself or for any control on the form. Each control can have a different shortcut menu.

A shortcut menu is created similarly to the way drop-down menus are created in a standard menu bar. The shortcut menu consists of a single first-level menu place holder; the real menu items are stored in the second-level items. A typical definition in the Menu Builder is shown in Figure 32-24. You can use the Menu Builder to create shortcut menus or you can simply create two macros to do this job.

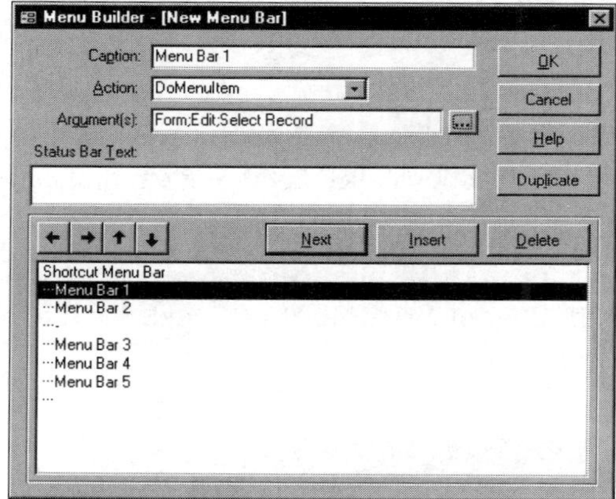

Figure 32-24: A typical shortcut menu definition in the Menu Builder.

Once you create the menu definition and save it for the shortcut menu, you can attach the shortcut menu to either the form or any control on the form. If you attach the shortcut menu to a form, it will override the standard shortcut menu for the form. If you attach a shortcut menu to a control, it will only be displayed when you right-click while on that control. Figure 32-25 shows the macro named Shortcut Menu being attached to the Shortcut Menu Bar property of Pets Display Forms. Notice the macro window in the right side of the figure; it shows the generated macro.

You may also notice that the Shortcut Menu property is set to Yes. This is for either the default shortcut menus or shortcut menus that you create. If it is set to No, you will not see any shortcut menus when you right-click.

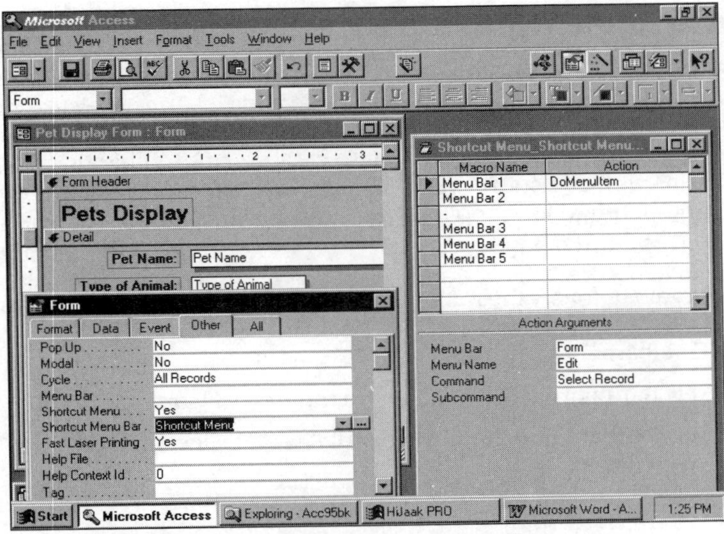

Figure 32-25: Adding the shortcut menu to the form.

Figure 32-26 shows the shortcut menu on the Pets Display form. The menu will be displayed to the right of wherever the mouse was clicked, even if it extends beyond the window. You can then select the desired menu item; the actions listed in the menu macro are run.

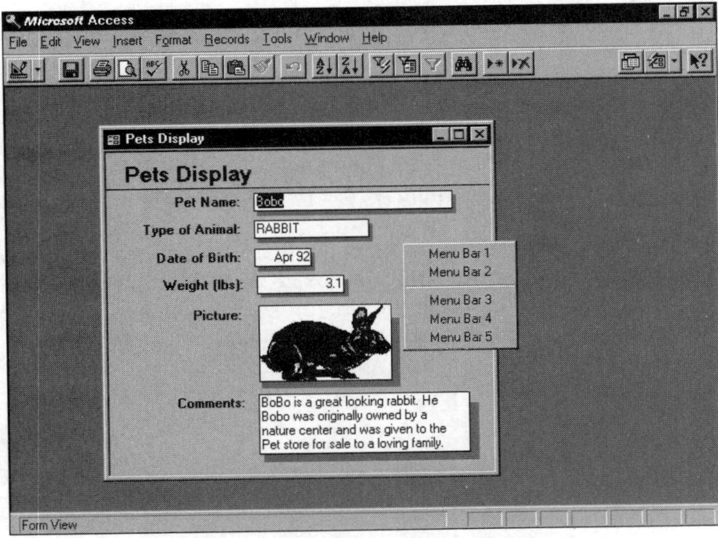

Figure 32-26: Viewing the form with the shortcut menu.

Creating and using custom toolbars

Access has always let you define new toolbars for your application and customize existing toolbars. However, Access for Windows 95 also adds features like customizing the pictures on the buttons (known as button faces). For example, suppose that when you display the Mountain Switchboard, you want to create a new toolbar that lets you open the various forms with one button push. You can create a new toolbar or even add some icons to the standard form toolbar. For this example, you will create a new toolbar.

To create a custom toolbar, follow these steps:

1. Select View⇨Toolbars…
2. Click on the New button from the Toolbars window (see Figure 32-27).
3. Enter **Mountain Toolbar** in the New Toolbar dialog and click on OK.
4. Select Customize…

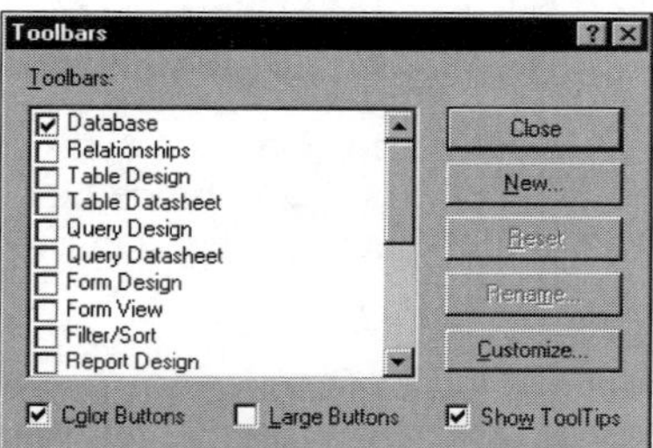

Figure 32-27: The Toolbars window.

After you name the new toolbar, it appears at the bottom of the Toolbars window. Currently this toolbar contains no buttons. You can customize it by adding buttons to it, assigning actions to the buttons, and changing the picture on the button.

When you create a new toolbar, all you see is a small square (the empty toolbar) and the Customize Toolbars window as shown in Figure 32-28. You add buttons to the new toolbar by displaying the desired function in the Customize Toolbars window and dragging each button to the new toolbar. You can mix and match as much as you need to.

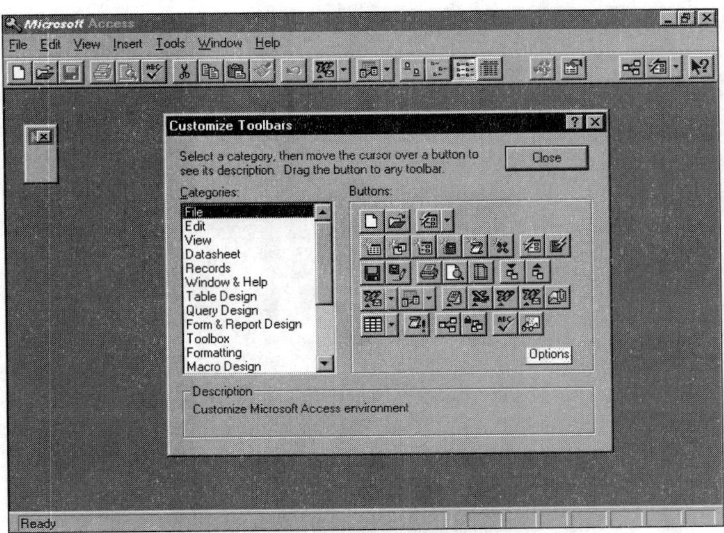

Figure 32-28: The Customize toolbars window.

As you select from each of the standard toolbars, you see a list of the icons representing the various methods. Each icon—besides having a different picture—performs a different task and also contains a different tooltip, as you can see in Figure 32-28. As you move from one definition to another, you will see the pictures change, indicating different sets of tools.

In this example, you want to create a toolbar that launches the various forms and reports you added to the menu. Rather than add buttons that perform tasks normally found in design windows, you simply want to open forms and reports. You can do this by scrolling down to the functions named All Forms or All Reports. You can drag the names of the forms and reports to the toolbars and then change the standard icons tooltip text. To add functions to the Mountain Switchboard, follow these steps below:

1. Display the function All Forms in the Customize Toolbars window.
2. From the Forms list, drag Customer to the small square that represents the switchboard, as shown in Figure 32-29.

   A form icon appears in the toolbar square. This represents the Customer form and contains code to open the Customer form automatically when pressed. It also contains a tooltip that you will learn how to change. If you pass your mouse over this button now, the tooltip Open form 'Customer' is displayed.

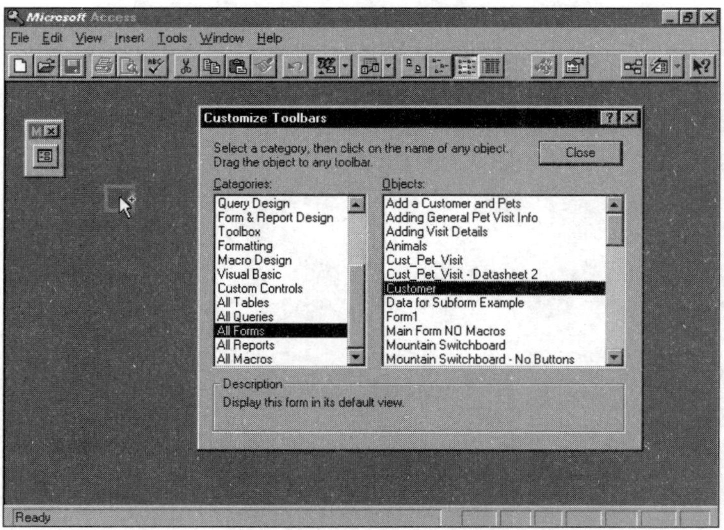

Figure 32-29: Dragging a New Icon to the Toolbar

3. From the forms list, drag Pets just to the right of the Customer icon but inside the new toolbar. You should have two form icons.

Warning If you release the dragged icon outside the toolbar, a new toolbar is created. Just delete the new toolbar by clicking on the Close button (or deleting the Toolbar1 text in the Functions list) if you accidentally save the unwanted toolbar.

4. From the Forms list, drag Adding General Pet Visit Info just to the right of the Pets icon but inside the new toolbar. You should have three form icons.
5. From the Forms list, drag Adding Visit Details just to the right of the third icon but inside the new toolbar. You should have four form icons.
6. Display the function All Reports in the Customize Toolbars window.
7. From the Reports list, drag Pets and Owners just to the right of the of the last form icon but inside the new toolbar. You should have a report icon.
8. From the Reports list, drag Invoices just to the right of the of the report icon but inside the new toolbar. You should have two report icons.
9. From the Reports list, drag Customer Mailing Labels just to the right of the of the last report icon but inside the new toolbar. You should have three report icons.

Tip You can add a space between icons by dragging them one at a time to the right or left, starting with the first or last icon. The icon window will also resize and the icons will no longer be on the same line. Resize the window wider and the icons will again line up along with a space between the desired icons. You have to move one icon at a time.

The Mountain toolbar should look like figure 32-30. The next step is to change the button-face pictures and edit the tooltips.

Note Once you create a button, you cannot change what the button does. Its function is stored internally within Access and attached when you select the button from the Customize Toolbars window. You can do more, however, than just run the standard Access functions in the default toolbars. You can drag a button from any existing query, form, report, or macro. Since you can program a macro to do almost anything (including run a VBA program), you can create a button to launch any query, form, report, or function you need. You can also change the macro at any time, which changes the function of the button.

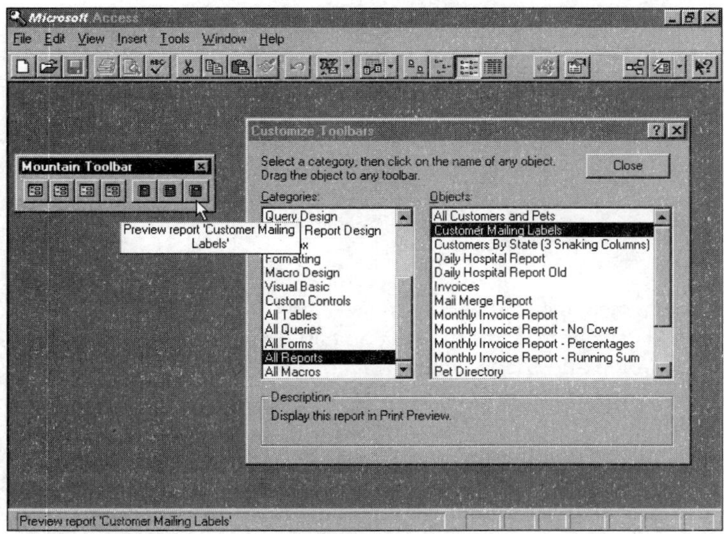

Figure 32-30: Form and report icons on the toolbar.

You can make changes to toolbar buttons by right-clicking on each button and making a selection from the menu that is displayed, as shown in Figure 32-31.

Warning If you close the Customize Toolbars window, the toolbar will still be active but you cannot display the shortcut menu to customize the button face or tooltips.

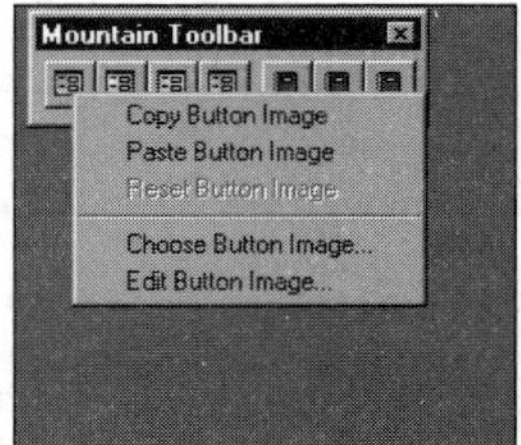

Figure 32-31: Changing a toolbar icon.

The shortcut menu contains five options:

Copy Button Image	Copies the current button face image to the Clipboard
Paste Button Image	Copies the current picture in the Clipboard to the button face
Reset Button Image	Changes the button face image to the default image
Choose Button Image	Changes the button-face image from a list of images stored in Access
Edit Button Image	Use a minibutton image editor to change an image

There are several ways to change the button image. The easiest is to select from a set of button images that Access stores internally. You can do this by selecting Choose Button Image from the menu and then clicking on a picture in the Choose Button Image window that appears (as shown in Figure 32-32). When you choose a picture and press OK the button image changes.

You can also change the tooltip from the Choose Button Image window by changing the default text at the bottom of the window. Currently, as shown in Figure 32-32, the default text for one of the reports is `Preview report 'invoices'`. The default tooltip for custom buttons is generally the operation performed by the button with the name of the query, form, or report. You can change it by simply editing the text in the Description box.

Tip: You can also change a button face to only text by clicking in the Text check box and entering the text you want on the button.

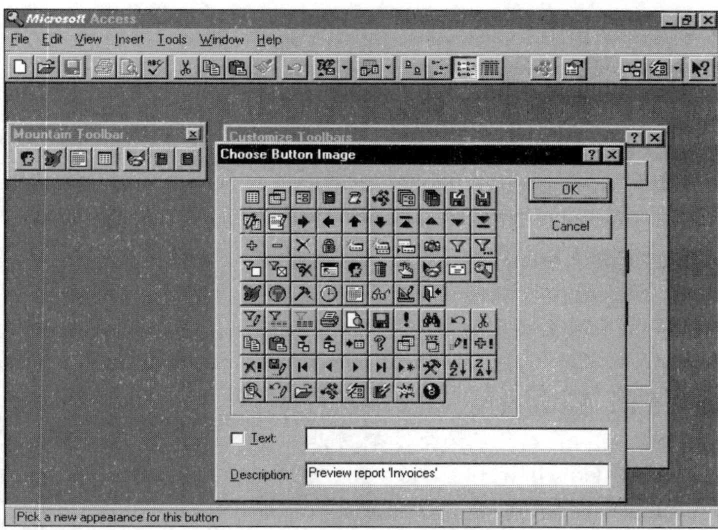

Figure 32-32: Choosing a toolbar button face image.

As you can see in Figure 32-32, there are not too many pictures to choose from. You can, however, create your own and copy them to the Clipboard. Once you have an image on the Clipboard, you can use the Paste Button image option of the shortcut menu to add the image to the button. The image must be sized to fit the button. You can also use the Edit Button Image to change the image once it is on the button face. Figure 32-33 shows the Button Editor.

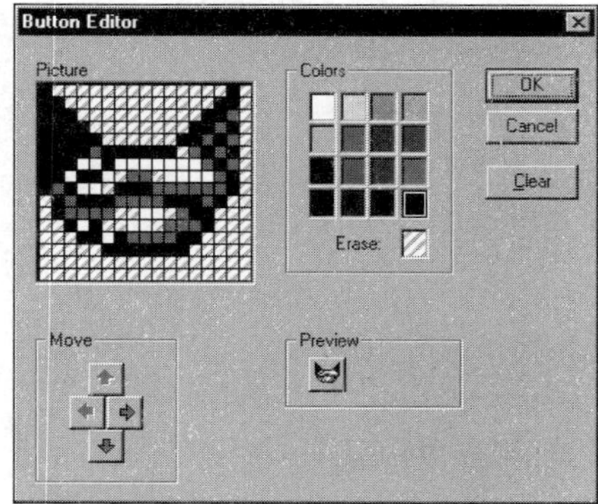

Figure 32-33: Editing a toolbar button face image.

You can edit the button face by moving the image around and changing individual pixels of color.

Tip Cary Prague Books and Software offers a library of 1,500 pictures for use in custom toolbars and button faces. The Picture Builder add-on picture pack for Access 2.0 and the Toolbar Customization Pack for Access for Windows 95 is available for $99.95 by calling (800) 277-3117 or (203) 644-5891. You can also request a free catalog of Access add-ons by calling or faxing at (203) 648-4710.

Once you have completed creating all of the buttons on your toolbar and have customized the button faces and tooltips, you can close the button customization window and close the toolbar you've created. The next step is to add the toolbar to a custom form.

If you are adding your toolbar to a form, you should do it when the form opens. The general procedure is to use a macro to display the custom toolbar; use the macro action Show Toolbar. You also will want to turn off the standard Access form toolbar. Figure 32-34 shows the macro changes you would need to make this happen. A new macro action in the Mountain Switchboard named Display Mountain Toolbar has been created.

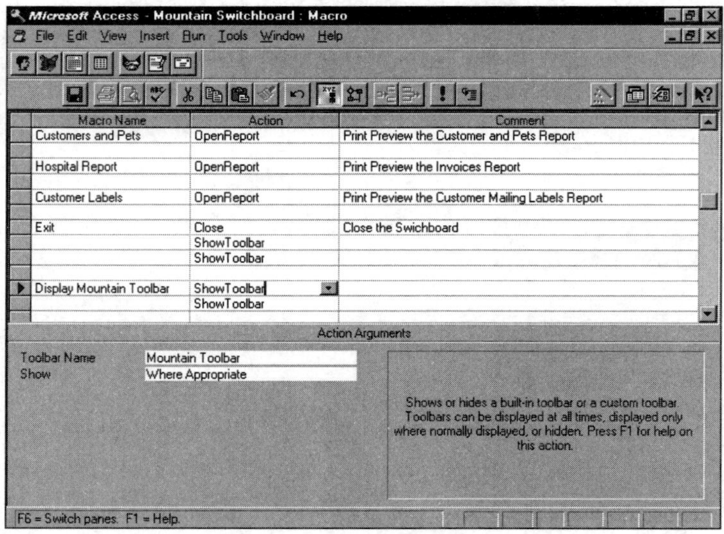

Figure 32-34: Creating a macro to show the toolbar.

The new macro Display Mountain Toolbar contains two actions. The first (pictured at the bottom of Figure 32-34) opens the Mountain Toolbar. The Show option has three choices:

Yes	Displays Mountain Toolbar on all objects
No	Turns off the display of the toolbar (if it is currently displayed)
Where Appropriate	Displays the toolbar when it makes sense to do so (usually just in forms)

In this example, the Mountain Toolbar is turned on where appropriate. The second Show Toolbar action in the Display Mountain Toolbar macro is used to turn off the Form View toolbar.

Also shown in Figure 32-34 are two macro actions that have been added to the Exit macro. The first turns off the Mountain Toolbar; the other turns back on the Form View toolbar.

Once you have made these changes, you can display the Mountain Switchboard, as shown in Figure 32-35. Note the Mountain toolbar on the screen and the tooltip (showing for one of the reports).

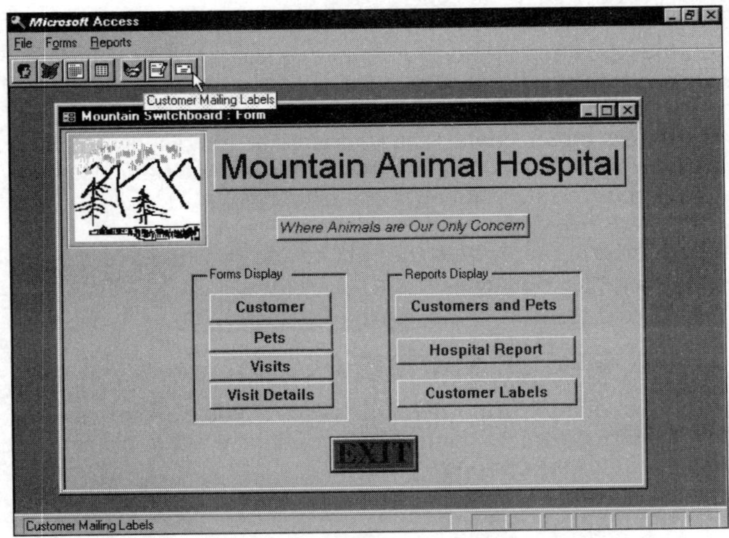

Figure 32-35: Displaying a custom toolbar in a form.

Adding control tips to a form

Although tool tips must be added using the toolbar customization windows, you can add a tooltip known as a *control tip* to any control. When you place your cursor on a control, textual help resembling a tooltip is displayed with a yellow background. You can create a control tip by entering text into the ControlTip Text property. Whatever you enter into this property is displayed when you place the cursor on a control and leave it there for about a second.

Running a macro automatically when you start Access

After you create the switchboard, a menu bar, and the associated drop-down menu, you may want Access to open the form automatically every time you open the database. You can do this in one of two ways. The recommended way is to create a macro named AutoExec that performs the necessary actions. To create an AutoExec macro to open the switchboard automatically, follow these steps:

1. Create a new macro (you'll name it AutoExec later).
2. Type **Hourglass** (or select the action) in the first empty Action cell.
3. Type **Minimize** (or select the action) in the next empty Action cell.
4. Type **OpenForm** (or select the action) in the next empty Action cell.
5. Type **Mountain Switchboard** (or select the switchboard form name) in the Form name cell in the action arguments pane.

Save the macro with the name AutoExec. After you save do so, Access will run the macro automatically every time you open the database.

The AutoExec macro shows three actions. The Hourglass action displays an hourglass while the macro is processing. The Minimize action minimizes the Database window. The OpenForm action opens the switchboard.

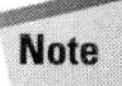

Note To bypass an AutoExec macro, simply hold the Shift key down while selecting the database name from the Access File menu.

Controlling options when starting Access

Rather than run a macro to open a form when Access starts you can use the new Access for Windows 95 startup form to control many options when you start Access. This includes setting the following options:

✦ Changing the text on the title bar

✦ Specifying an icon to use when Access is minimized

- ✦ Global custom menu bar
- ✦ Global custom shortcut menu bar
- ✦ Global Custom Toolbar
- ✦ Display a form on startup (for example, AutoExec macros)
- ✦ Control display of default menus, toolbars, the Database window, and status bar

Figure 32-36 Shows the Access startup window. You can display this by selecting Tools⇨Startup or by right-clicking on the border of the Database Window and selecting Startup.

When you press the Advanced> button, you can set additional options. These include the following:

- ✦ Whether to display a code screen after untrapped VBA errors
- ✦ Whether the special Access keys are enabled to view the Database or Code windows
- ✦ Whether the special Access keys are enabled to pause execution of a VBA program

Note This button replaces both the AutoExec macros and items formerly used in the Access 2.0 INI file.

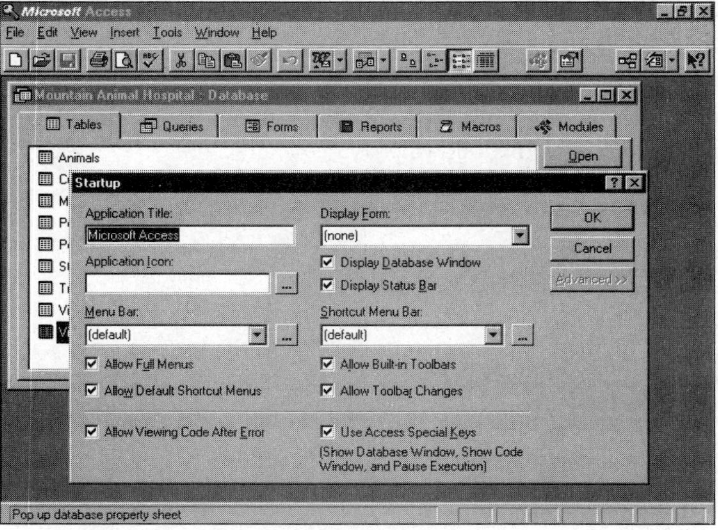

Figure 32-36: The Startup Options window.

Creating a Print Report Dialog Box Form and Macros

A dialog box is also a form, but it is unlike a switchboard; the dialog box usually displays information, captures a user entry, or lets the user interact with the system. In this section, you create a complex dialog box that prints reports and labels.

By using a form and some macros, you can create a dialog box that controls printing of your reports. This dialog box can even display a list of pets and their owners (see Figure 32-37), so you can print only a single page of the Pets Directory without having to change the query.

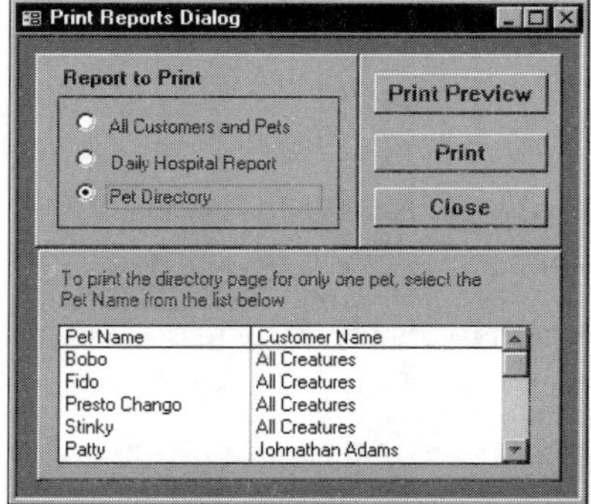

Figure 32-37: A Print Reports dialog box.

Although this dialog box is more complex than a switchboard, it uses the same types of Access objects, which include the following:

- ✦ A form
- ✦ Form controls and properties
- ✦ Macros

Creating a form for a macro

The form you use in this example displays the various controls. There are three basic sections to the form.

The upper left corner of the form contains three option buttons, which are placed within an option group. The option buttons let you select one of the three listed reports. Each of the reports is already created and can be seen in the Database window. If you select All Customers and Pets or the Daily Hospital Report, you can print or print-preview that report. If you select Pet Directory, as shown in Figure 32-37, you see a list box of pets and their owners. You can then choose a pet name for a printout from the Pet Directory report for only that one pet. If you don't choose a pet name, records for all pets are printed from the Pet Directory report.

The upper right corner of the form contains three buttons. Each button runs a different macro in the Print Report macro library. The first option button, Print Preview, runs a macro that opens the selected report in a Print Preview window. The second option button, Print, runs a macro that will print the selected report to the default printer. The last button, Close, simply closes the form without printing any reports.

To create a form for your macro, first create a blank form and size it properly. Follow these steps:

1. Create a new blank form unbound to any table or query.
2. Resize the form to $3^1/_2$ inches × 3 inches.
3. Change the Back color to dark gray.

Three rectangles are placed on the form to give it a distinctive look. You can create the three rectangles (as shown in Figure 32-37) by following these steps:

1. Select the Rectangle button on the toolbox
2. Using Figure 32-37 as a guide, create three separate rectangles.

   Each rectangle in this example is shown with the Raised special effect. To create this effect, follow these steps:
3. Select a rectangle.
4. Change the Back color to light gray.
5. Click on the Raised special-effect button in the Special Effect window.
6. Click on the Transparent button in the Border Color window.
7. Repeat Steps 3 through 6 for the second and third rectangles.

   Finally, to enhance the Raised special effect, drag each rectangle away from the adjacent rectangles so that the darker background of the form shows between the rectangle borders. You may need to resize one of the rectangles to line up the edges.

Creating the option group

After you create the form and the special effects, you can then create the necessary controls. The first set of controls is the option group. In Chapter 19, you learned how to use the Option Group Wizard to create option buttons. To create the option group and option buttons, follow the steps given here and use Figure 32-37 as a guide. In this example, the option group buttons are not bound to a field; they are used for the dialog box selection, not to enter data.

1. Select the Option Group button from the toolbox, making sure that the Control Wizard icon is on.
2. Draw an option-group rectangle within the upper left rectangle, as shown in Figure 32-38.

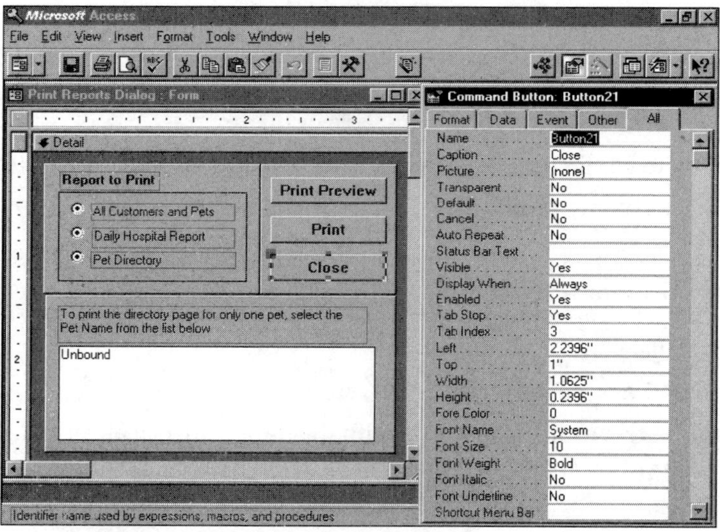

Figure 32-38: The Print dialog box in design view.

3. Enter **All Customers and Pets**, **Daily Hospital Report**, and **Pet Directory** as three separate labels in the first Option Group Wizard.
4. Click the Finish button to go to the last wizard screen.

   Your option buttons and the option group appear in the first rectangle. You may need to move or resize the option group's box to fit properly (see Figure 32-38).

Creating command buttons

After you complete the option group and the option buttons, you can create the command buttons. These pushbuttons trigger the actions for your dialog box. As you can see in Figure 32-38, there are three buttons:

Print Preview	Displays the selected report in the Print Preview window
Print	Prints the selected report to the default print device
Close	Closes the dialog box

To create each command button, follow the next steps. Because each button will be the same size, you will duplicate the second and third buttons from the first.

1. Turn the Wizard off; then select the Command Button in the toolbox.
2. Create the first command button as shown in Figure 32-38.
3. Select Edit⇨Duplicate to duplicate the first command button.
4. Move the button as shown in Figure 32-38.
5. Select Edit⇨Duplicate to duplicate the second command button.
6. You may need to move the button into position as shown in Figure 32-38.

   You now need to change the command button captions. The remaining steps show how to make these changes.
7. Select the first command button and change the Caption property to **Print Preview.**
8. Select the second command button and change the Caption property to **Print**.
9. Select the third command button and change the Caption property to **Close**.

Creating a list box on the print report form

The last control you need in the dialog box is the list box that displays the pet name and customer name when the Pet Directory option button is selected. To create the list box, follow these steps, using Figure 32-39 as a guide. In this example, you'll create the list box without using the Wizard.

1. Select the List Box button from the toolbox. Make sure the Control Wizard icon is off.
2. Using Figure 32-39 as a guide, create the list box rectangle.
3. Move the label control to a position above the list box.

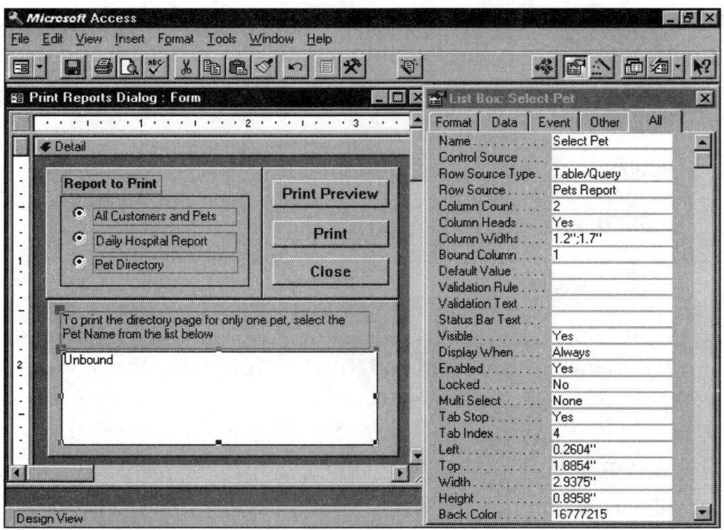

Figure 32-39: The list box definition on the form.

4. Resize the label control so the bottom right corner is just above the list box, as shown in Figure 32-39.
5. Using the formatting windows, change the Back color of the label to light gray to match the background of the bottom rectangle.
6. Change the Caption property for the list box by clicking on the label of the field (the caption in the label itself) and typing **To print the directory page for only one pet, select the Pet Name from the list below**. The text in the label will word wrap automatically as you type.

After the list box and label are created, you must define the columns of the list box. To define the columns and data source for the list box, follow these steps, using Figure 32-39 as a guide:

1. Change the Name property to **Select Pet**.
2. Make sure that the Row Source Type indicates Table/Query.
3. Change the Row Source to Pets Report.
4. Change the Column Count to 2.

Note

The Pets Report must be created before you try to run this form. The Pets Report is a simple query that requires an interesting technique to create (see the sidebar "The Pets Report query for the Print Reports form list box" for more information).

5. Change Column Heads to Yes.
6. Change the Column Widths to 1.2, 1.7.
7. Make sure that the Bound Column property indicates **1**.

Before continuing, you should save the form. Save the file but leave the form on-screen by selecting the menu option File⇨Save. Name the form **Print Reports Dialog Box**.

When the form is completed, you are half done. The next task is to create each of the macros you need and create the macro library. When you complete that task, you can add the macros to the correct event properties in the form.

Creating the print macros

As you've learned, macros are attached to the events of controls or objects. These events include entering, exiting, updating, or selecting a control. In this example, macros are attached to several controls and objects. Table 32-3 shows the macros that you create for this example and how they will run.

Table 32-3
Macros for the Print Reports Form

Macro Name	*Attached to Control/Object*	*Attached to Property*	*Description*
Show List	Form	On Open	Displays list box if the third option button is on
Show List	Option group	After Update	Displays list box if the third button is selected
Print Preview	Print preview	On Click	Displays selected report in print-button preview mode when Print Preview button is selected
Print	Print button	On Click	Prints selected report if Print button is selected
Close	Close button	On Click	Closes form if Close button is selected

The Pets Report query for the Print Reports form list box

The Pets Report is a simple query that has the Customer and Pets tables related by the Customer Number field. The query has two fields displayed: Pet Name from the Pets table and Customer Name from the Customer table. The data is sorted first by Customer Number and second by Pet Name. Figure 32-40 shows the partial datasheet for this list box.

You can see in Figure 32-40 that the Pet Name field is in the first column and the Customer Name field is in the second column. The data is sorted first by the customer number and second by the pet name. As you learned previously, to sort data by two fields, you must place the fields in the Query Design window in the order you want the two fields sorted in. To sort by the customer number first and then by the pet name, you must place the Customer Number field first in the query but not select it. You then place the Customer Name field third in the query and select it. The query would place Customer Name first in the datasheet. The query design after it is saved and reopened is shown in Figure 32-41. Remember, Access will rearrange fields when a field is not selected to be viewed by unchecking the Show check box.

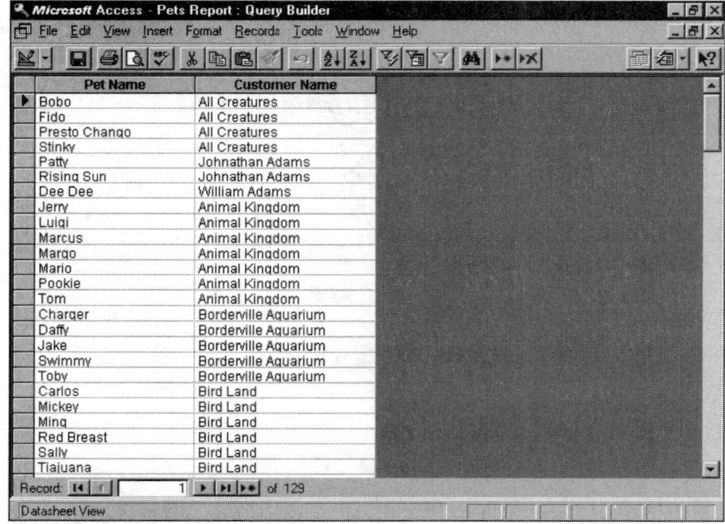

Pet Name	Customer Name
Bobo	All Creatures
Fido	All Creatures
Presto Chango	All Creatures
Stinky	All Creatures
Patty	Johnathan Adams
Rising Sun	Johnathan Adams
Dee Dee	William Adams
Jerry	Animal Kingdom
Luigi	Animal Kingdom
Marcus	Animal Kingdom
Margo	Animal Kingdom
Mario	Animal Kingdom
Pookie	Animal Kingdom
Tom	Animal Kingdom
Charger	Borderville Aquarium
Daffy	Borderville Aquarium
Jake	Borderville Aquarium
Swimmy	Borderville Aquarium
Toby	Borderville Aquarium
Carlos	Bird Land
Mickey	Bird Land
Ming	Bird Land
Red Breast	Bird Land
Sally	Bird Land
Tiajuana	Bird Land

Figure 32-40: The partial datasheet for the Pets Report query.

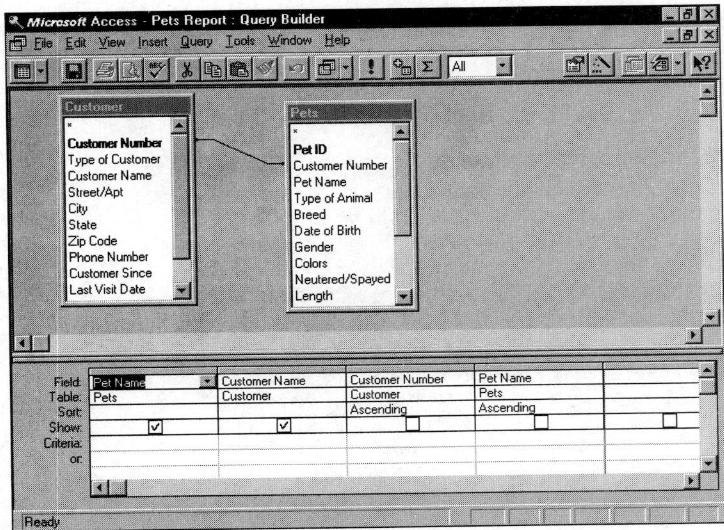

Figure 32-41: The query design for the Pets Report list box.

Creating the Print Macro Library

In the last two chapters, you learned that creating a macro library is the same as creating any macro. You can create this macro library by following these steps:

1. From the Form window toolbar, select the New Object icon and select New Macro to create a new macro.
2. Select View⇨Macro Names or select the Macro Names button in the toolbar, to display the Macro Names column.
3. Select View⇨Conditions or select the Conditions button in the toolbar to display the Condition column.

As you may recall, the Macro Names and Conditions menu options add two columns to the basic Macro window. You will use these columns to enter more parameters into the macro. The Macro Name column is used for creating the individual macro entry points in a macro library. The Condition column determines whether the action in the Action column should be run (on the basis of the conditions). To create the macro, follow these steps:

1. In the third row of the Macro Name column, type **Show List**.
2. In the sixth row of the Macro Name column, type **Print Preview**.
3. In the ninth row of the Macro Name column, type **Print**.
4. In the twelfth row of the Macro Name column, type **Close**.
5. Select File➪Save As/Export and name the macro **Print Reports**.

You can see these macros correctly created in Figure 32-42.

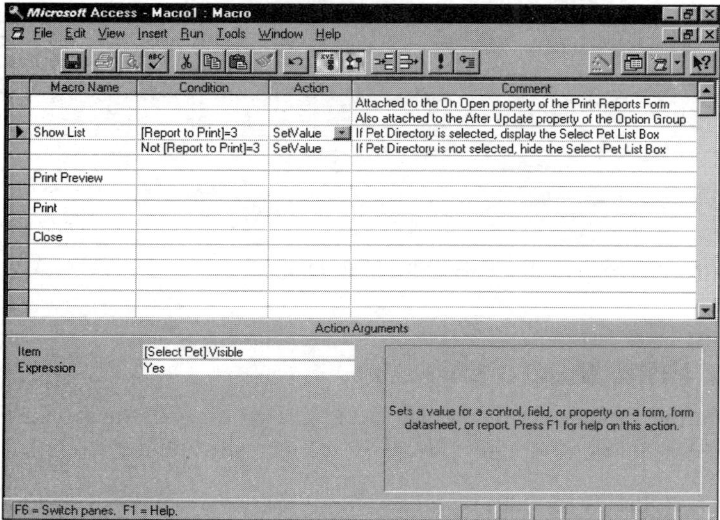

Figure 32-42: Creating the Show List macro and the Print Reports macro group.

Creating the Show List macro

The Show List macro either displays or hides the list box that lists the pet names and customer names. This macro uses the SetValue macro command to run from either the form object and the option group control. The SetValue macro command lets you set a property of a control in the form. In this example, the list box is named Select Pet. The Visible action argument is set to Yes to display the list box or No to hide the list box.

There will need to be two conditions for the Show List macro. The first condition holds if the third option button has been selected; the second condition holds if it has not been selected. The Macro Name column has already been set to Show List.

In the first line of the Show List macro, you will set the Condition column to [Report to Print]=3 to reflect the third option button being chosen from the option group. This line will display the list box, so the action of the macro is set to SetValue, the Item action argument is set to [Select Pet].Visible, and the Expression action argument is set to Yes. Figure 32-42 displays these settings.

You can also see the second line of the Show List macro and comments in Figure 32-42. Notice in the second line that the Condition column indicates that the third option button in the option group not chosen and is therefore set to Not [Report to Print]=3. This line will hide the list box, so the action of the macro is SetValue, the Item property is set to [Select Pet].Visible, and the Expression property is set to No. To create the macro, follow these steps:

1. Type the first two lines in the Comment column, as shown at the top of Figure 32-42.
2. Move the cursor to the first line of the Show List macro row.
3. Place the cursor in the Condition column and type **[Report to Print]=3**.
4. Place the cursor in the Action column and either select or type **SetValue**.
5. Press F6 to move to the Item property in the Action Arguments pane and type **[Select Pet].Visible**.
6. Move to the Expression property and type **Yes**.
7. Press F6 to return to the Action column and then move to the Comments column.
8. Enter the comments in the Comment column, as shown in Figure 32-42.
9. Move your cursor to the second line of the Show List macro row.
10. In the Condition column, type **Not [Report to Print]=3**.
11. In the Action column, type (or select) **SetValue**.
12. Press F6 to move to the Item box in the Action Arguments pane and type **[Select Pet].Visible**.
13. Move to the Expression property and type **No**.
14. Press F6 to return to the Action column and then move to the Comments column.
15. Enter the comments in the Comment column, as shown in Figure 32-42.

When you complete the Show List macro, you can enter the calls to the macro in the form events properties. After this task is completed, you can test the macro. Before continuing, select File⇨Save to save the Print Reports macro library and leave it open on-screen.

Entering the Show List macro calls

You are now ready to enter the macro calls for the Show List macro. This macro is called from two places:

- ✦ The On Open property of the form object
- ✦ The After Update property of the option group control

As you've learned, these properties are found in the property sheet of the form. To enter the two macro calls, follow these steps:

1. From the Print Reports Macro window, select Window➪2 Print Reports Dialog: Form.
2. Make sure that the property window is displayed. If not, click on the Properties button in the toolbar.
3. Display the form's property window by clicking on the gray square next to the intersection of both form ruler's.
4. Enter **Print Reports.Show List** into the On Open property of the Form property sheet.
5. Click on the Option Group control.
6. Enter **Print Reports.Show List** in the After Update property of the Option Group property sheet, as shown in Figure 32-43.

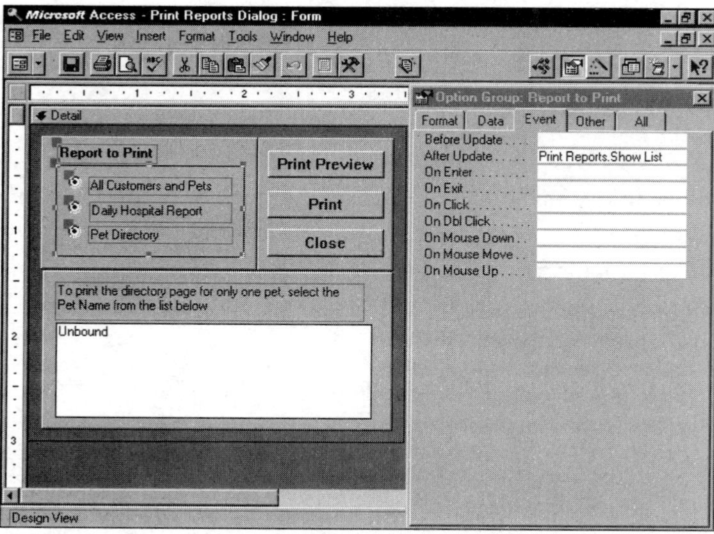

Figure 32-43: Entering the macro call.

You can test this macro by clicking on the Form View button on the toolbar. As you click on the first and second option buttons, the list box should become invisible. When you select the third option button, the list box should appear. Return to the Design window before continuing.

Creating the Print Preview macro

The Print Preview macro is the next macro you need to create. You can switch to the Macro window by selecting Window➪3 Print Reports:Macro. This macro is fairly complicated, although it uses only three different macro commands. As you enter the macro commands, you may need to add more lines to the Macro window. Select Insert➪Row whenever you need to add a new row to the Macro window.

Note You must first select a row to add a new row.

Figure 32-44 shows the completed Print Preview, Print, and Close macros in the Macro window. You can enter all the comments and create the first macro row by following these steps:

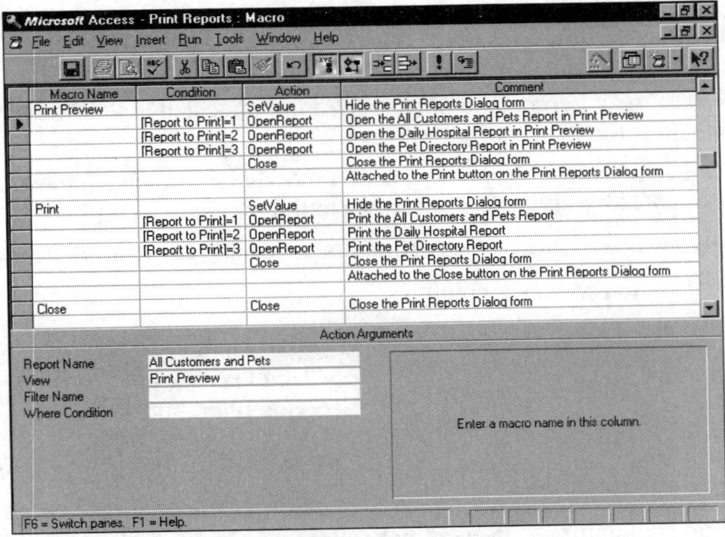

Figure 32-44: Creating the Print Preview macro.

1. Type all the lines in the Comment column, as shown in Figure 32-44.
2. Move the cursor to the first line of the Print Preview macro row.
3. In the Action column, type (or select) **SetValue**.
4. Press F6 to move to the Item property of the Action Arguments pane and type **Visible**.
5. Move to the Expression box in the Action Arguments pane and type **No**.

Because no control is specified, it defaults to the form itself. This will hide the entire Form window when the Print Reports macro is started.

The next three lines of the macro determine the actions to be taken when the Print Preview button is selected for each of the possible option button choices. The first two choices simply display the selected report in a print preview mode. The third choice displays a report by selecting the pet name chosen from the list box. To create the next row, follow these steps:

1. Move your cursor to the second row of the Print Preview macro.
2. In the Condition column, type **[Report to Print]=1**.
3. In the Action column, type (or select) **OpenReport**.

   The OpenReport macro command opens the report specified in the Action Arguments pane of the Macro window.
4. Press F6 to move to the Report Name box in the Action Arguments pane of the Print Preview macro and type **All Customers and Pets**.
5. Move to the View box in the Action Arguments pane and type **Print Preview**.
6. Press F6 to return to the Action column.

These action arguments specify to open the report named All Customers and Pets in a Print Preview window. The second Print row of the Print Preview macro is very similar to the first, except you must reference the second option button being selected. To create the next row, follow these steps:

1. Move the cursor to the third row of the Print Preview macro.
2. In the Condition column, type **[Report to Print]=2**.
3. In the Action column, type (or select) **OpenReport**.
4. Press F6 to move to the Report Name box in the Action Arguments pane and type **Daily Hospital Report**.
5. Move to the View box in the Action Arguments pane and type **Print Preview**.
6. Press F6 to return to the Action column.

The third OpenReport row contains an extra action argument that the first two rows do not use. The Pet Directory report must use the results of the List Box selection to determine whether to print the entire Pets Directory report or print only the report for the specific pet selected. To create the next row, follow these steps:

1. Move the cursor to the fourth row of the Print Preview macro and insert a row.
2. In the Condition column, type **[Report to Print]=3**.
3. In the Action column, type (or select) **OpenReport**.
4. Press F6 to move to the Report Name box in the Action Arguments pane and type **Pet Directory**.
5. Move to the View box in the Action Arguments pane and type **Print Preview**.
6. Move to the Where Condition and type the following:

   =IIF(Forms![Print Reports Dialog]![Select Pet]Is Null,"","[Pet Name] = Forms![Print Reports Dialog]![Select Pet]").

The Where Condition specifies the condition when the pet name is selected. The condition has two parts. The first part of the IIF function handles the condition when no pet name is selected, and it forms the object hierarchy. The hierarchy is as follows:

Object	Forms
Form name	Print Reports Dialog
Control name	Select Pet (the list box)
Selection	Is Null

Note

Each of the hierarchy objects is separated with an exclamation mark (!).

If there is no selection, all the pet records are used. The second half of the IIF function is used when a pet name is selected. The second half of the function sets the value of Pet Name to the value chosen in the list box control.

Creating the Print macro

You can create all the macro code for the Print macro by copying each line from the Print Preview macro. Then substitute **Print** for Print Preview in the View box of the Action Arguments pane for each Open Report action.

Creating the Close macro

The Close macro simply uses Close for the action. Enter **Form** for the Object Type and **Print Reports Dialog** for the Action Arguments object name.

Entering the Print Preview, Print, and Close macro calls

You use the command buttons to trigger an action. Each uses the On Click property. To enter the three macro calls, follow these steps:

1. From the Print Reports Macro window, select Window➪2 Form: Print Reports Dialog.
2. Make sure that the property sheet is displayed. If not, click on the Properties button on the toolbar.
3. Display the Print Preview command button property by clicking on the Print Preview button.
4. Enter **Print Reports.Print Preview** in the On Click on property of the button's property sheet, as shown in Figure 32-45.

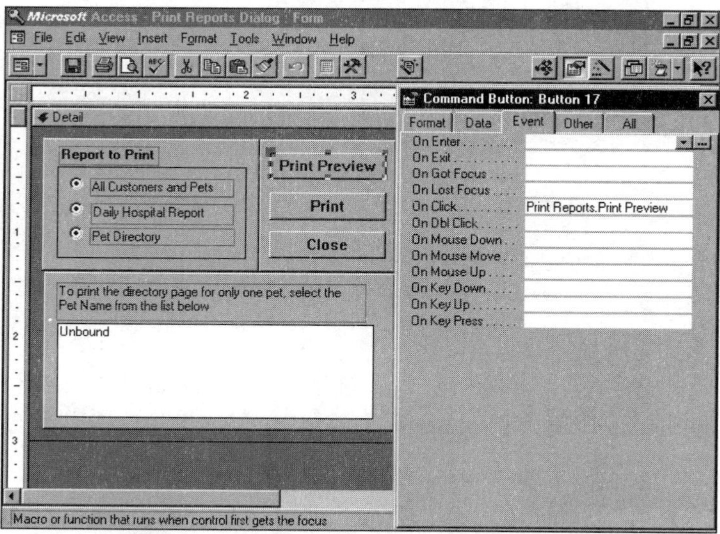

Figure 32-45: Entering the Print Preview macro call into the command button's property sheet.

5. Display the Print command button property sheet by clicking on the Print button.
6. Enter **Print Reports.Print** in the On Click property of the button's property sheet.
7. Display the Close command button property sheet by clicking on the Close button.
8. Enter **Print Reports.Close** into the On Click property of the button's property sheet.

Sizing the dialog and changing form properties

The last step in creating a dialog box is to change the Form window properties and size and place the window. You need to set several form properties. Properties and their explanations are listed in Table 32-4.

Table 32-4
Properties for a Form Dialog Box

Property	*Value*	*Description*
Default View	Single Form	Displays the form as a single form; necessary for forms that take up less than half a page
Views Allowed	Form	User cannot switch into datasheet mode
Scroll Bars	Neither	(Scroll bars should be omitted in a dialog box.)
Navigation Buttons	No	Record navigation buttons are not displayed
Record Selectors	No	Does not display the standard record selectors at the bottom left of the form
Auto Resize	Yes	Automatically resizes the form when opened
Auto Center	Yes	Automatically centers the form when opened
Border Style	Dialog	Makes border nonsizable
Pop Up	Yes	Allows the form to be displayed on top of other windows as a pop-up dialog box
Modal	Yes	User must make a choice before leaving the dialog box

You should set the Pop Up property to No if the dialog box will call any other windows. If this property is set to Yes, the dialog box is always displayed on top; you can't get to other windows without first closing the dialog box.

Summary

In this chapter, you learned how to create switchboards and dialog boxes by using an Access form. You also learned how to create your own custom menu. The following points were discussed:

- ✦ Switchboards are forms that usually contain command buttons.
- ✦ Switchboards are used as menus to help you navigate within your system.
- ✦ You can create command buttons by using the toolbox, by dragging a macro onto a form, or by using the Command Button Wizard.
- ✦ Command buttons trigger macros through several properties.
- ✦ The best way to create multiple command buttons that are all the same size is by duplicating the first button you created.
- ✦ You link a command button to a macro by entering the macro name in the proper event (On) property.
- ✦ You can create macro actions by entering them into the Macro window, by selecting them from the Action pull-down menu, or by dragging a form or report into a macro's Action cell.
- ✦ You can have a command button display a picture instead of a text caption by entering the bitmap name into the command button's Picture property or by using the Picture Builder.
- ✦ Access lets you create custom bar menus through the use of macros.
- ✦ Each drop-down menu must be a separate macro. You can specify bar separators and hot keys in a menu.
- ✦ You can activate a custom bar menu by entering a macro name in the On Menu property of a form or report.
- ✦ The Access Menu Builder simplifies creating a menu.
- ✦ You can create shortcut menus using the Menu Builder
- ✦ You can create a macro that runs automatically when you open a database by naming the macro AutoExec.
- ✦ You can bypass a macro that runs automatically by holding down the Shift key when you open the Database window.

- ✦ You can control startup properties by changing options in the Startup window.
- ✦ You can create and customize toolbars and use them with Access forms.
- ✦ You can create control tips that work like tooltips but can be used with any controls.
- ✦ A dialog box is nothing more than a form that is used as a pop-up window; usually it contains various controls, such as option buttons, list boxes, and command buttons.
- ✦ A dialog box's pop-up property should be set to No if you are going to open any other windows from the dialog box.

As you have seen in the last few chapters, macros provide powerful alternatives to programming. In the final two chapters of this book, you will get a quick introduction to modules and VBA.

✦ ✦ ✦

Introduction to Applications with VBA

In This Chapter

Using the Database Wizard to create instant applications

Understanding the basics of VBA

Creating a new module

Using the Module window

Using the Command Button Wizard to create VBA code

Converting macros to VBA

You've learned how to create macros to automate operations. You can, however, program Access in other ways. Writing VBA modules is the best way to create applications. Adding error routines, setting up repetitive looping, and adding procedures that macros simply can't perform give you more control of application development. In this chapter, you learn what a module is and how to begin to use VBA.

Instant Applications: Using the Access for Windows 95 Database Wizard

It's 3 p.m. on a Friday. A potential new client just called and said he hears that you do great work. The client wants a custom system to do whatever — and wants to see a prototype of what you can do by Monday morning at 10 a.m. Do you cancel the weekend picnic with the family? Do you reschedule your golf or tennis match and order plenty of Jolt Cola? No. There's a new way to get started: the Access for Windows 95 Database Wizard!

Table Wizards in Access for Windows 95 allow you to choose business and personal table definitions — employees, orders, video library, household inventory, and so on — from a list. Some definitions contain multiple tables, such as Orders and Items. After you select your table(s), Access displays a set of fields and allows you to choose which ones to include. The program then builds the table for you. Optionally, you can also have a simple AutoForm created. Although this feature is a real time-saver, it pales in comparison with the next generation of Access.

The Access for Windows 95 Database Wizard takes the concept of Table Wizards to a new dimension by combining the best features of Access Wizards with the amazing power of an application generator. *Application generators* have been popular for many years in some products. These products enable you to create a custom table design, create a form or report, and then automatically generate code to tie everything together.

The Access for Windows 95 Database Wizard doesn't require you to define a table design first; it doesn't make you create a form or report; it simply builds a complete, customizable application, including tables, forms, modules, reports, and a user-modifiable switchboard. The wizard doesn't build just one table or form. The Database Wizard builds groups of tables; adds the table relationships; builds forms for each table, including one-to-many forms, where appropriate; and even adds critical reports for the type of application that you are building. This process means that the Wizard creates an entire ready-to-run application. As you go through the Wizard process, you determine which fields from each table definition are used; some fields are mandatory, and some are optional. You can always make changes after the application is built.

The order-entry application that you build in this chapter creates 10 tables, 14 forms, and 8 reports, including customer reports, sales reports, and even an aged-receivables statement — everything you need to start a basic order-entry system.

You start the Database Wizard by choosing File⇨New Database. Access for Windows 95 displays a window that contains the Blank Database icon for creating a new database. select the Database tab, as shown in Figure 33-1. Each icon represents a different application the Database Wizard can create. When you create an application, that application is created in its own database container.

The Database Wizard allows you to choose among 22 applications, as follows:

Address Book	Music Collection
Asset Tracking	Order Entry
Book Collection	Picture Library
Contact Management	Recipes
Donations	Resource Scheduling
Event Management	Service Call Mangement
Expenses	Students and Classes
Household Inventory	Time and Billing
Inventory Control	Video
Ledger	Wine List
Membership	Workout

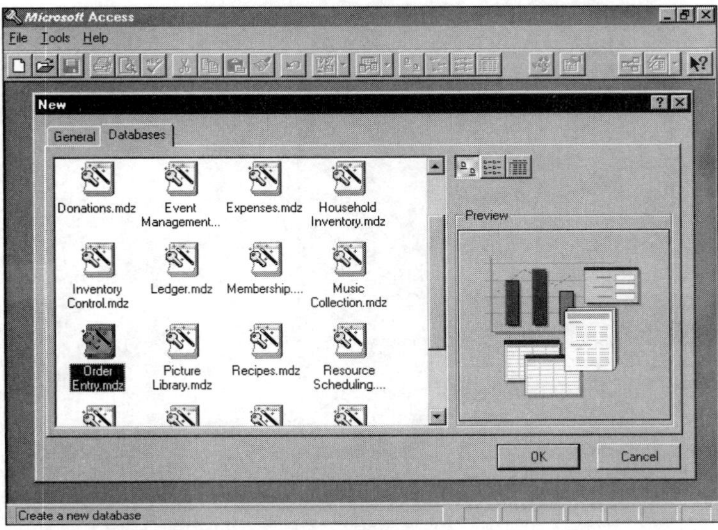

Figure 33-1: Starting the Database Wizard.

When you decide which application is closest to the one that you want to create, double-click on it to start defining your own application. For the example in this chapter, choose the Order Entry application.

Getting started

When you choose the Order Entry application, a dialog box appears. enter a name for the database. This dialog box is a standard File Explorer-type dialog box that allows you to select the drive, directory, and database name. The default name is the name of the application. In this example, the name is Order Entry1.mdb. You can make the name anything you want, and you can change it later by renaming the database with the Windows 95 Explorer. Press the Create button to create the new database.

When the Wizard starts, the dialog box shown in Figure 33-2 appears, showing a pictorial representation of the system. In this example, the dialog box tells you that six basic functions will be created: Customer information, Order information, Order Details, Payment information, Product information, and My company information. These functions generally are tables or forms. After you view this introductory dialog box, you can click on the standard Next> button to go to the next dialog box.

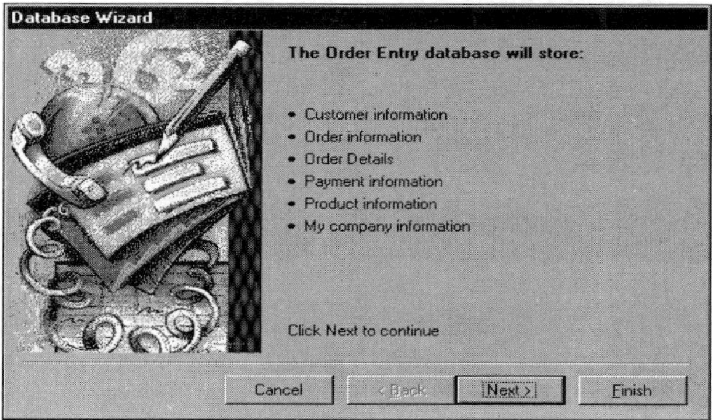

Figure 33-2: Learning what the database will create for you.

Working with tables and fields

The next Wizard screen (see Figure 33-3) enables you to work with the tables and fields of the database. Most of the fields and tables are mandatory, but you also can select optional fields for each table. The tables are listed on the left side of the dialog box, and the fields that make up the table are on the right side of the dialog box.

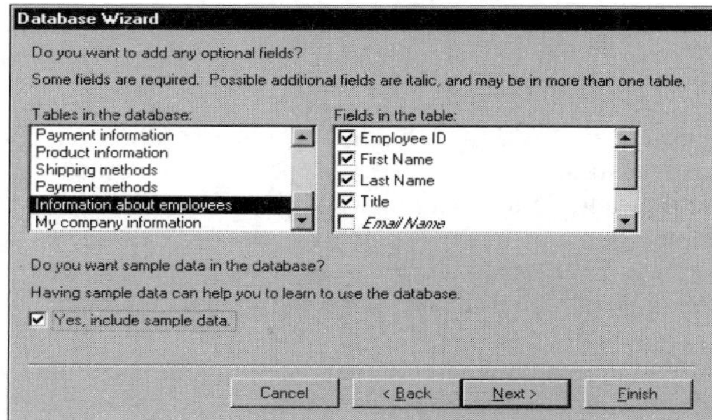

Figure 33-3: Working with tables and fields.

As you select each table, the list of fields changes. Fields that are optional appear italicized. When you check the fields, the Wizard includes them in the table design. You also have the option to specify that the Database Wizard include sample fictitious data to get you started.

Selecting AutoFormat styles

After you make your selections, you can move to the next Wizard screen, which allows you to select the style for your forms. You can choose any of the AutoFormat options. If you created your own AutoFormats, they are listed here, too. After you select the style of your forms, you can do the same for reports. The next Wizard screen (see Figure 33-4) allows you to select an AutoFormat style for the printed report. You can add your own formats for each of the reports that the Wizard creates.

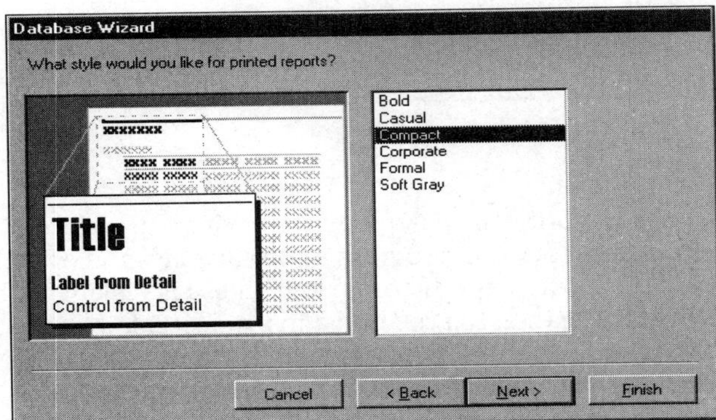

Figure 33-4: Selecting an AutoFormat for a report.

Customize by selection

After you select the style of forms and reports, you see a wizard screen that enables you to give your application a title and even a bitmap picture. In Figure 33-5, the standard title of Order Entry has been changed to Mountain Scenes Order Entry System, and the client's logo (a small sun rising over a mountain, the same one as Mountain Animal Hospital) has been included. You can scan a logo or select any standard Windows 95 image file for inclusion in the application. When you click on the Picture button, the Database Wizard displays a dialog box that you can search to find the desired picture. The picture appears in the main switchboard and in all the reports.

When you complete this Wizard screen and click the Next > button, the last Database Wizard screen appears. This Wizard screen, which displays a checkered flag, asks whether you want to learn how to use a database (developers never ask for help, do they?) and whether you want to start the application after it is built. Clicking on the Finish button clears the screen and builds the application.

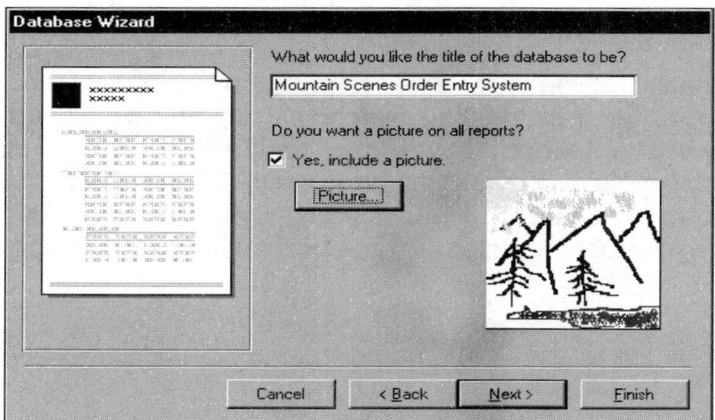

Figure 33-5: Renaming the application and adding a picture.

As the creation process progresses, you see a dialog box displaying the Wizard's magic wand and two progress meters. The top progress meter displays the overall progress. The bottom progress meter displays the progress Access is making with creating each object — first the tables; then the relationships, queries, forms, switchboards, reports, and even database properties. Below this dialog box, you can see the Database window magically filling with names as each new object is created.

Note

If this is the first time you are using the Database Wizard, you will be asked for your company name, address, and related information. After you complete this screen, the switchboard is displayed.

Using the switchboard system

If you elected to start the application in the last Wizard screen, the main switchboard appears (as shown in Figure 33-6), and the Database window is minimized. Otherwise, the Database window is displayed.

The main switchboard is your gateway to the system functions. As you see in Figure 33-6, the switchboard displays five main items. The first item — Enter/View Orders by Customer — displays the one-to-many orders form (see Figure 33-7), where you can review or edit all the orders sorted by your customer's name. The next item — Enter/View Other Information — displays another switchboard screen that allows you to display all the peripheral forms for editing all the support tables. In this example, those tables include Employees, Company Information, Products, Payment methods, and Shipping methods. At the bottom of each switchboard screen (other than the main switchboard) is the option *Return to Main Switchboard.*

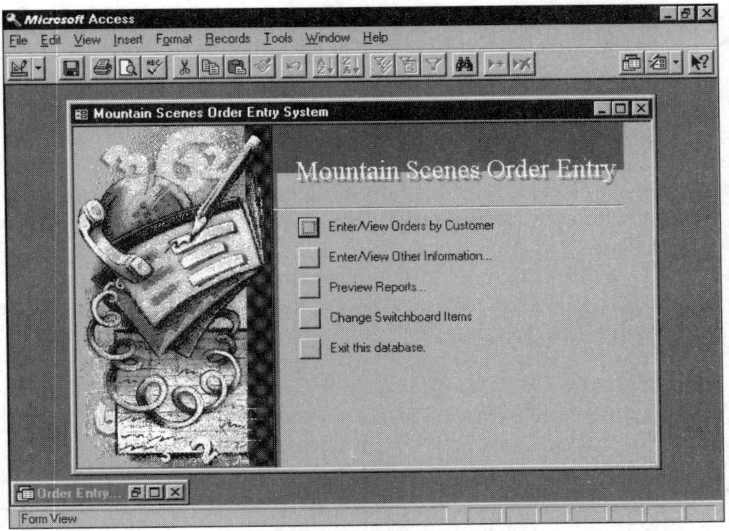

Figure 33-6: The main switchboard.

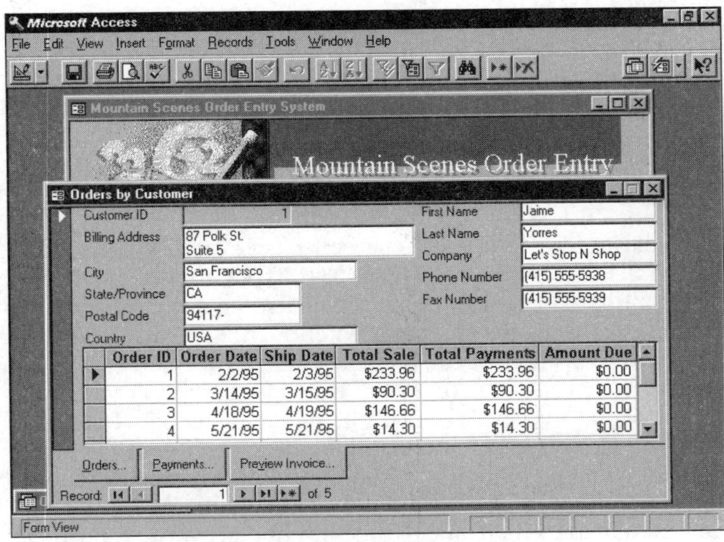

Figure 33-7: A typical one-to-many form.

In Figure 33-7, you see a form that actually is a summary of a specific customer's orders. At the bottom of the form are several buttons for displaying an order, displaying a payment, or printing an invoice for the customer. If you look at the order form itself, you see that it has several supporting tables, such as products, employees, payment methods, and shipping methods. The form has embedded subforms that allow you to select data from these lookup tables. From the data-entry switchboard screen, you can even set various global company options, such as company name and address, payment terms, and other information used for invoices and other reports.

Besides the data-entry switchboard, a switchboard is available for viewing and printing your reports. For the Order Processing example, the reports include Customer Listing; Invoice; Receivables Aging Report; and Sales by Customer, Employee, or Product. The company name and logo (if specified) appear at the top of each report.

Although the forms and reports are simplistic, they serve as a great starting point for creating more robust applications. Obviously, the Wizard decides the choices of forms and reports, but you can create your own forms and reports and then add them to the Order Entry switchboard. One of the options in the main switchboard allows you to customize the switchboards themselves.

Customizing the switchboards

The Database Wizard contains a series of hierarchical screens (similar to the Menu Builder) that allow you to create and maintain switchboard items. Unfortunately, this technology works only in the Database Wizard. If you are creative, you can copy the switchboards and the supporting tables to other applications, but you must have access to the Access for Windows 95 wizard libraries, because some of the code resides in the common areas.

Figure 33-8 shows one of the screens used to customize the switchboards. This screen shows the switchboard definition shown in Figure 33-6. To customize a switchboard, you start with the Switchboard Page definitions, which list the switchboard's name. In Figure 33-8, this switchboard is named Opening Switchboard Page. Each page contains the items shown in Figure 33-8, and you can edit each item. When you edit an item, you enter the item name (text) and the command, which is similar to the macro commands but more explanatory. There are only eight commands: GoTo Switchboard, Open Form in Add Mode, Open Form in Edit Mode, Open Report, Design Application, Exit Application, Run Macro, and Run Code. With these eight commands, you can do almost anything. Based on which of the eight commands you select, the last entry area changes to display the name of the switchboard, form, report, macro, or VBA function.

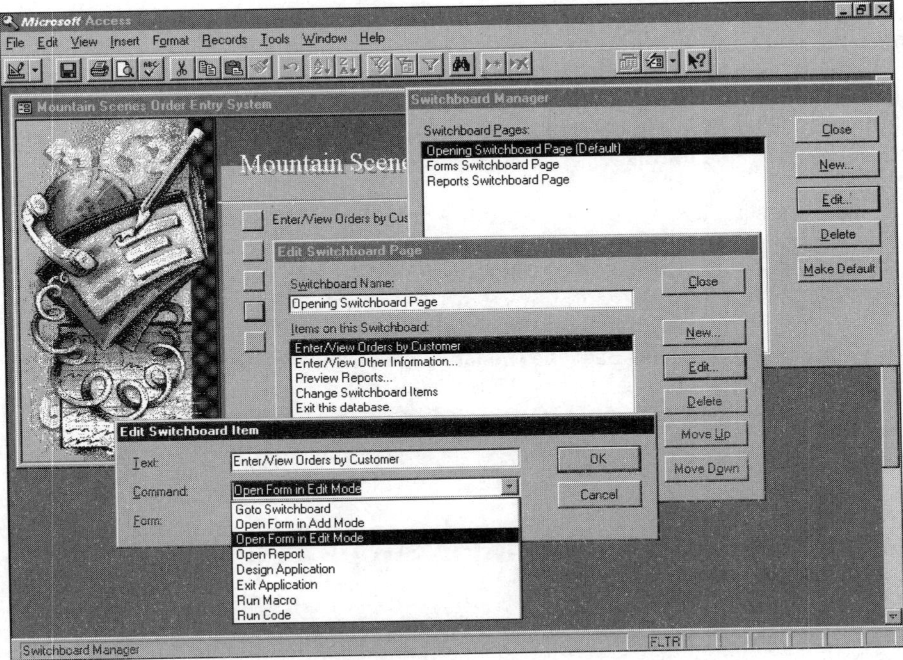

Figure 33-8: Modifying a switchboard.

Although the Database Wizard allows you to create instant applications, these applications are very simple — good only for the most basic business or personal applications. As a starting point, though, they are excellent for new users and even for developers who need to prototype a system fast. Because you can customize everything (especially the switchboards), you can develop a custom solution quickly to get started or impress your customers.

Building Applications from Scratch

Access has an excellent variety of tools that allow you to work with databases and their tables, queries, forms, and reports without ever having to write a single line of code. At some point, you may begin building more sophisticated applications. You may want to make your applications more "bulletproof" by providing more intensive data-entry validation or implementing better error handling.

Some operations cannot be accomplished through the user interface, even with macros. You may find yourself saying, "I wish I had a function that would ..." or "There just has to be a function that will let me ..." At other times, you find that you are continually putting the same formula or expression in a query or filter. You may find yourself saying, "I'm tired of typing this formula into ..." or "Doggone it, I typed the wrong formula in this ..."

For situations such as these, you need the horsepower of a structured programming language. Access provides a programming language called Visual Basic, Applications Edition, which most often is referred to as *VBA*. VBA extends the capabilities of Access, offering power beyond the scope of macros.

Note VBA has replaced Access Basic as the language within Access for Windows 95. Although VBA is similar to Access Basic, some major changes were made.

Getting started with programming in Access requires an understanding of its event-driven environment.

Understanding events and event procedures

In Access, unlike traditional *procedural* programming environments, the user controls the actions and flow of the application. The user determines what to do and when to do it, such as changing information in a field or clicking a command button.

Using macros and event procedures, you implement the responses to these actions. Access provides event properties for each of the controls that you place on the form. When you attach a macro or event procedure to a control's event property, you do not have to worry about the order of actions that a user may take on a particular form.

In an event-driven environment such as Access, the objects — forms, reports, and controls — respond to events. Basically, an event procedure is program code that executes when an event occurs. The code is directly attached to the form or report that contains the event that is being processed. An Exit command button, for example, exits the form when the user clicks that button. Clicking on the command button triggers its On Click event. The event procedure is the program code (or macro) that you create and attach to the On Click event. Every time the user clicks on the command button, the event procedure runs automatically.

Up to this point, you have used macros to respond to an object's events. In addition to macros, Access provides a built-in programming language for creating procedures.

Creating programs in Visual Basic, Applications Edition

Before Access for Windows 95, Access used its own Basic language, called Access Basic. Access for Windows 95 abandoned Access Basic, replacing it with Microsoft's Visual Basic for Applications (*VBA*). Although VBA is similar to Visual Basic, distinct differences exist.

VBA will become the common language for all Microsoft applications. Currently, VBA is in Access, Visual Basic, Excel, and Project; it is planned for the next version of Word as well. VBA is a modern, structured programming language that offers many of the programming structures that programmers are accustomed to: If. . .Then. . .Else, Select Case, and so on. VBA allows a programmer to work with functions and subroutines in an Englishlike language. The language also is extensible, being capable of calling Windows 95 API routines, and can interact through DAO (Data Access Objects) with any Access or Visual Basic data type.

Using the Module window, you can create and edit VBA code or procedures. Each procedure is a series of code statements that performs an operation or calculation.

Note

A *procedure* is simply some code, written in a programming language, that follows a series of logical steps in performing some action. You could, for example, create a Beep procedure that makes the computer beep as a warning or notification that something has happened in your program.

There are two types of procedures:

- ✦ Sub procedures
- ✦ Functions

Sub procedures

A *sub procedure* is program code that does not return a value. Because it does not return a value, a sub procedure cannot be used in an expression or be called by assigning it to a variable. A sub procedure typically runs as a separate program called by an event in a form or report.

You can use a subroutine (known as a *sub*) to perform actions when you don't want to return a value. In fact, because you cannot assign a value to a control's event properties, you can only create sub procedures for an event.

You can call subs and pass a data value known as a *parameter*. Subs can call other subs. Subs also can call function procedures.

The code statements that are inside the sub procedure are lines of Visual Basic statements. (Remember that this statement refers to the language Visual Basic, not to the product.) These statements make up the code that you want to run every time the procedure is executed. The following example shows the Exit command button's sub procedure:

```
Sub Button_Click ()
 DoCmd.Close
End Sub
```

The Button_Click () sub procedure is attached to the Exit command button's On Click event. When the user clicks the Exit command button, the command DoCmd Close executes to close the form.

Function procedures

A *function procedure* returns a value. The value can be Null, but the procedure always returns a value. You can use functions in expressions or assign a function to a variable.

Like subs, functions can be called by other functions or by subs. You also can pass parameters to a function.

You assign the return value of a function to the procedure name itself. You then can use the value that is returned as part of a larger expression. The following function procedure calculates the square footage of a room:

```
Function nSquareFeet (dblHeight As Double, dblWidth As Double) As
      Double
 nSquareFeet = dblHeight * dblWidth
End Function
```

This function receives two parameters for the height and width of the room. The function returns the results to the procedure that called it by assigning the result of the calculation to the *procedure name* (nSquareFeet).

To call this function, you could use code like this:

```
dblAnswer = nSquareFeet(xHeight, xWidth)
```

Sub and function procedures are grouped and stored in modules. The Modules tab in the Database window stores the common procedures that any of your forms can access. You can store all your procedures in a single module. Realistically, though, you'll probably want to group your procedures into separate modules, categorizing them by the nature of the operations that they perform. An Update module, for example, might include procedures for adding and deleting records from a table.

Creating a new module

To create a new module, follow these steps:

1. Click on the Module tab in the Database window.
2. Click on the New button.

Access opens a new module, named Module1, in a Module window. This new module should look like the one shown in Figure 33-9. In this figure, notice that Access places a line of text in the first line in the window, beginning with Option Compare Database.

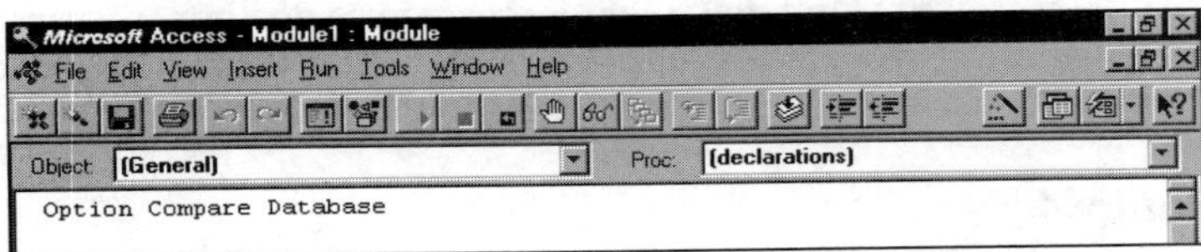

Figure 33-9: The newly opened module window.

Notice that the Module window in Figure 33-9 displays the tools for the Module editor. Also notice the section in the toolbar titled `Proc`, with a pull-down combo box alongside it. This combo box displays `declarations` because you currently are in the declarations part of the module.

Each module includes two or more sections:

✦ A single declarations section

✦ A section for each procedure

Note Is there a difference between a module and a procedure? *Modules* are the containers that are used to organize your code. You can think of a module as being a library of procedures. You can create many modules for an Access database.

Note Each form has its own module. Every form or report you create in your database contains a built-in form module or report module. This module is known as *code-behind-form*, or CBF (the same for reports). This form or report module is an integral part of each form or report; it is used as a container for the event procedures that you create for the form or report. The module is a convenient way to place a form's event procedures in a single collection. Generally, if the module will be used only by a single form or report object, it should go behind the form or report. If the module will be needed more globally or will be used by common menus or toolbar definitions, it should be placed in a *global module*.

The declaration section

You can use the declaration section to *declare* (define) variables that you want to use in procedures. You can declare variables that will be used only by the procedures in a module or by all procedures across all modules within a database.

You are not required to declare variables in this section, because variables can also be declared in the individual procedures. In fact, you don't have to declare a variable at all. Access allows *implicit* variable declarations — that is, declarations created on the fly. If you enter a variable name in an expression, and the variable hasn't been declared, Access accepts and declares it for you.

Tip Entering the declaration statement Option Explicit forces you to declare any variables that you will use when creating procedures for the module. Although this procedure involves a little more work, it speeds execution of module code by Access.

Creating a new procedure

After you complete any declarations for the module, you are ready to create a procedure. Follow these steps to create a procedure called BeepWarning:

1. Go to any empty line in the Module window.
2. Type **Sub BeepWarning** to name the module. The module window should look similar to Figure 33-10.
3. Press Enter.

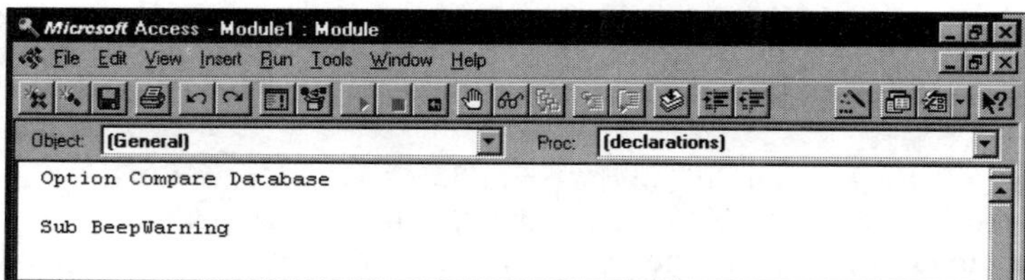

Figure 33-10: Entering a new procedure in the Module window.

If you enter the name of a function that you previously created in this module (or in another module within the database), Access informs you that the function already exists. Access does not allow you to create another procedure with the same name.

Your Module window should look like Figure 33-11.

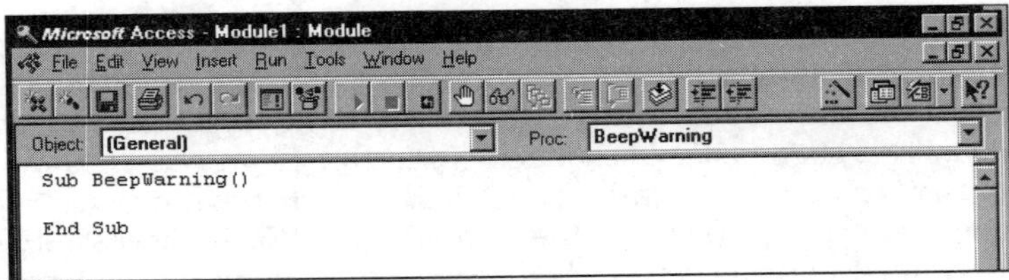
Microsoft Access - Module1 : Module
File Edit View Insert Run Tools Window Help
Object: (General)
Proc: BeepWarning
Sub BeepWarning()
End Sub

Figure 33-11: The Module window, displaying a new procedure.

Notice that when you pressed Enter, Access did two things automatically:

- ✦ Placed the procedure named BeepWarning in the Procedure combo box in the toolbar
- ✦ Placed parentheses at the end of the procedure name
- ✦ Added the End Sub statement to the procedure

You are no longer in the declarations section of the module; you are now in an actual procedure.

Now you can enter the lines of code needed for your procedure. In this example, you are passing a variable with an integer data type to the procedure as a parameter, so you need to place a parameter name between the parentheses on the procedure name line. Your completed function should look like the one shown in Figure 33-12.

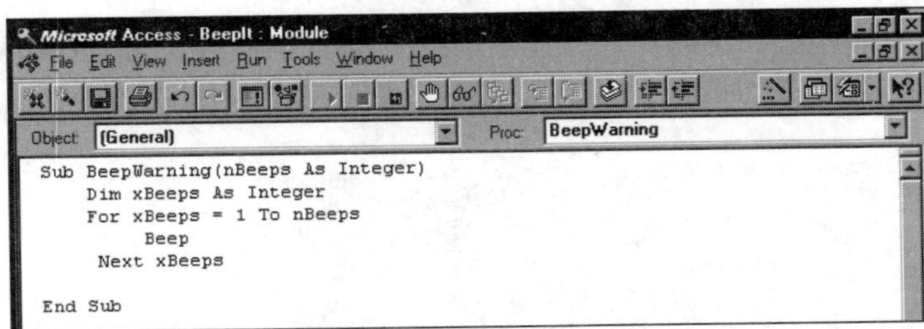
Microsoft Access - BeepIt : Module
File Edit View Insert Run Tools Window Help
Object: (General)
Proc: BeepWarning
Sub BeepWarning(nBeeps As Integer)
Dim xBeeps As Integer
For xBeeps = 1 To nBeeps
Beep
Next xBeeps
End Sub

Figure 33-12: The BeepWarning procedure completed.

When BeepWarning runs, it beeps for the number of times specified. To run the BeepWarning procedure and make it beep five times, you would add the following statement to a procedure (or call it as a function from a form event):

BeepWarning 5

Compiling procedures

After you create all the procedures, you should compile them by choosing Run ➪ Compile All Modules from the module menu or by clicking the Compile All Modules button in the toolbar. This action checks your code for errors (a procedure known as *syntax checking*; *syntax* is computer grammar) and also converts the programs to a form that your computer can understand. If the compile operation is successful, the Compile button is dimmed, and you can't click it again. If the compile operation is not successful, an error window appears.

Note: Access compiles all uncompiled procedures, not just the current procedure.

Saving a module

When you finish creating your procedures, you should save them by saving the module. As you do any other Access object, you can save the module by choosing File➪Save or they will be saved automatically when you close the window. You should consider saving the module every time you complete a procedure.

Creating procedures in the form or report design window

All forms, reports, and their controls can have event procedures associated with their events. While you are in the design window for the form or report, you can add an event procedure quickly in one of three ways:

- ✦ Choosing Build Event from the shortcut menu (see Figure 33-13)
- ✦ Choosing Code Builder in the Choose Builder dialog box when you click on the ellipsis button to the right of an event in the Property dialog box
- ✦ Enter the text **Event Procedure**, or select it from the top of the event combo box (see Figure 33-14)

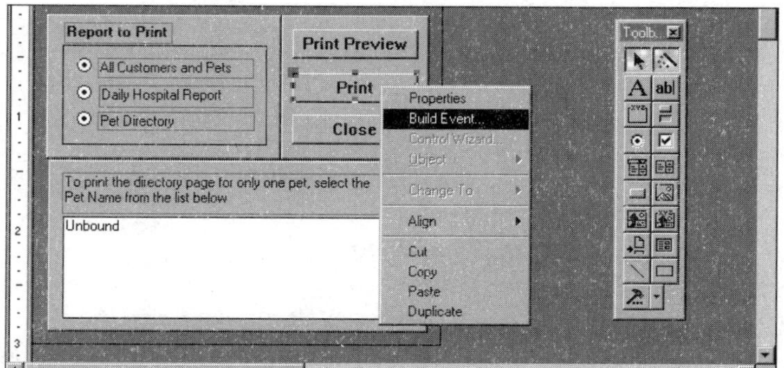

Figure 33-13: Shortcut menu for a control on the design surface of a form.

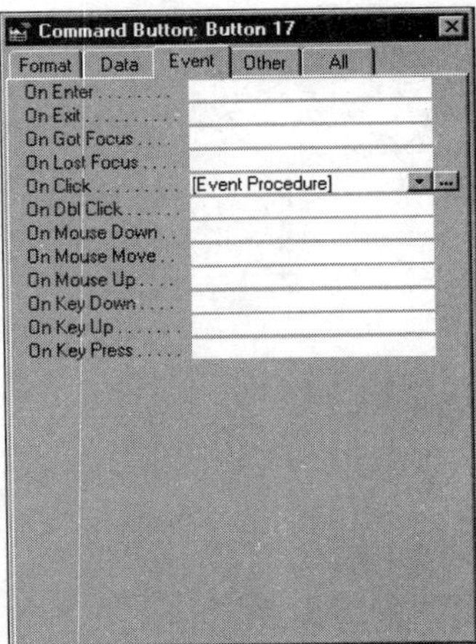

Figure 33-14: Properties dialog box for the Form Designer.

Whether you choose the Build Event from the shortcut menu choice or click the ellipsis button in the Property dialog box, the Choose Builder dialog box appears. Choosing the Code Builder item displays the Module window, as shown in Figure 33-15. If you click on the Form Design window, the menu and toolbar change to the form's menu and toolbar. This way, you can toggle back and forth between the form designer and the Module window.

Note If an event procedure is already attached to the control, the text [Event Procedure] is displayed in the event area. Clicking on the Builder button instantly displays the procedure for the event in a Module window, hence the name Event Procedure.

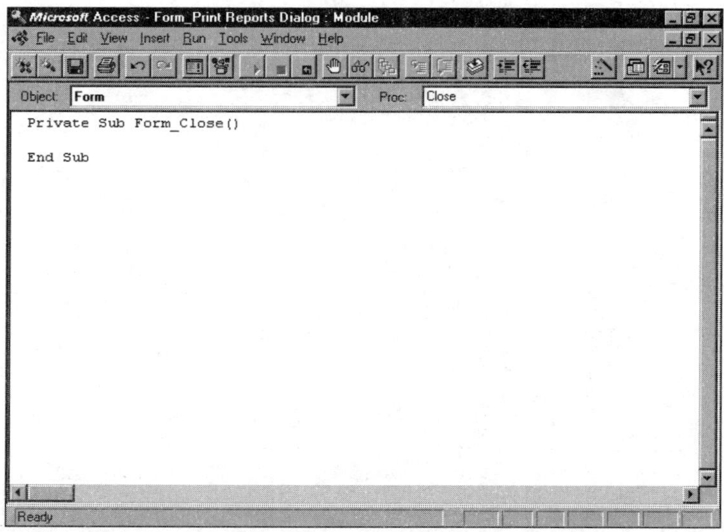

Figure 33-15: This is a form module open in the Form Designer.

Editing an Existing Procedure

To edit an existing procedure, follow these steps:

1. Click on the Module button in the Database window.
2. Double-click on the module name that contains the procedure. The declaration portion of the module appears.
3. Find the procedure you want and select it from the Proc pull-down menu.

Tip After you are in a module, you can select any procedure in another module quickly by pressing F2 or choosing View➪Object Browser. Access displays the Object Browser dialog box, shown in Figure 33-16. Highlight a different module name in the Modules section of the View Procedures dialog box to see the names of all procedures in the new module. When you select a module, you then can select a method and display the function call, as shown in figure 33-16.

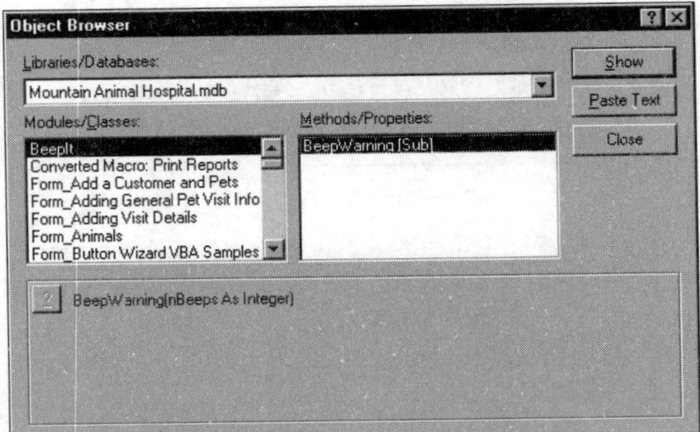

Figure 33-16: Selecting a procedure to edit.

Working in the Module window

Whenever you create Visual Basic procedures for your Access applications, you write that code in a Module window. Although the Module window is confusing at first, it is easy to understand and use.

Parts of the Module window

When you enter the Design mode of a module — whether it is via a form or report module or the module object (Database window) — the module window and its associated menu and toolbar open to allow you to create or edit your procedures.

When you open a module from the Modules tab of the Database window, the Module window has the same features as the Module window for a form or report design window. The only difference between the two is that for a form (or report) module, the Object and Procedure combo boxes in the toolbar list the form's objects and events. You can select these objects and events to create or edit event procedures for the form. The object combo box for a module that you open from the Database window displays only one choice: General. The Procedure combo box contains only the names of existing procedures.

The Module window has three basic areas:

- ✦ Menu bar
- ✦ Toolbar
- ✦ Code window

The menu bar of the Module window has eight menus: File, Edit, View, Insert, Run, Tools, Window, and Help. Table 33-1 describes the items in each menu.

Table 33-1
List of menu items in Module window

Menu	*Menu Item*	*Purpose*
File	Save	Saves the procedures in the module.
	Save As Text	Activates a dialog box, allowing you to save the currently open module to a text file (.txt)
Edit	Indent	Shifts the selected code or the line at the insertion point four spaces to the right, by default. Use this command to format and align blocks of code. To change the default shift, change the Tab Width in the Module section of the Options dialog box.
	Outdent	Shifts the selected code or the line at the insertion point four spaces to the left, by default. Use this command to format and align blocks of code. To change the default shift, change the Tab Width in the Module section of the Options dialog box.
View	Object Browser	Displays all methods and properties in the current database, in other available databases, and in available applications that support Visual Basic. Use this command to display and insert code templates of a selected method or property.
	Debug Window	Displays the Debug window so that you can test and debug code.
Insert	Insert Procedure	Inserts a procedure declaration statement after the current insertion point in the active module or at the end of a procedure, if the insertion point is inside a procedure. You can specify the procedure name, type, scope, and whether or not the procedure is static.
	Module	Displays the Module window so that you can create a new module
	File	Inserts code from a text file into the current module above the line that contains the insertion point.

Menu	Menu Item	Purpose
Run	Continue	Used to continue code execution after it has been suspended.
	End	Terminates execution of Visual Basic procedures and clears all private variables, but preserves all public variables. When you change procedures in a module, use this command to reinitialize those procedures before rerunning them.
	Reset	Stops execution of a procedure, clearing all variables.
	Step Into	Used to execute one statement at a time in a procedure file. When it comes to a called procedure, the module continues in the new procedure one line at a time.
	Step Over	Used to execute one statement at a time. The command treats any called procedure as a single line, however.
	Step to Cursor	Runs the procedure from the current executable statement to the selected line or location of the insertion point (which must be within the same procedure) and then reenters Break mode. Use this command to avoid stepping through each line of code unnecessarily .
	Toggle Breakpoint	Sets or removes a breakpoint in your code while debugging it.
	Clear All Breakpoints	Clears all breakpoints within your code.
	Set Next Statement	Used to change the execution sequence of your code, starting at the insertion point that you specify.
	Show Next Statement	Shows the next executable statement of the procedure.
	Compile Loaded Modules	Compiles all the procedures in the currently active module.
	Compile All Modules	Compiles all procedures in all modules in the current database, whether the module is loaded or not.

(continued)

Table 33-1 *(continued)*

Menu	Menu Item	Purpose
Tools	Add Watch	Creates a watch expression at the selected expression (such as a variable, property, or function call) in the Module window, so that you can examine its values in the Watch pane of the Debug window.
	Edit Watch	Modifies or deletes a watch expression at the selected expression (such as a variable, property, or function call). In the Watch pane of the Debug window, you also can double-click on the selected expression.
	Instant Watch	Displays the value of a selected expression (such as a variable, property, or function call). Optionally, you can add the expression to the Watch pane of the Debug window to continue examining its value.
	Calls	Displays a list of active procedure calls, starting with the most recently called, so that you can trace the calling sequence. Access enables this button or command only when the Module window or the Debug window is open and when code execution is suspended.
	Custom Controls	Registers or unregisters custom controls in the Windows registration database (which is used for tracking information about applications, such as filename and path). Registration determines whether custom controls are available.
	References	Displays a list of available references from object libraries and databases. Use this command to make procedures in other databases callable from the current database or to change the order in which Access searches object libraries and databases to resolve differences.
Window	Split Window	Splits the code window into two windows so that you can edit multiple procedures simultaneously.

As Table 33-1 shows, many of the menu items are used for debugging your code.

The Module toolbar

The Module window's toolbar (refer to Figure 33-15) helps you create new modules and their procedures quickly. The toolbar contains buttons for the most common actions you use to create, modify, and debug modules.

The Code window

The code window — the most important area of the Module window — is where you create and modify the VBA code for your procedures.

The code window has the standard Windows features that enable you to resize, minimize, maximize, and move the window. You also can split the window into two areas. At times, you want to edit two procedures at the same time; perhaps you need to copy part of one procedure to another. To work on two procedures simultaneously, simply choose Window⇨Split Window. You can resize the window by moving the split bar up and down. Now you can work with both procedures at the same time. To switch between windows, press the F6 key or click the other window.

The Debug window

When you write code for a procedure, you may want to try the procedure while you are in the module, or you may need to check the results of an expression. The Debug window allows you to try your procedures without leaving the module. You can run the module and check variables. You could, for example, type **?**.

To view the Debug window, choose View⇨Debug Window. Figure 33-17 shows the Immediate pane of the Debug window.

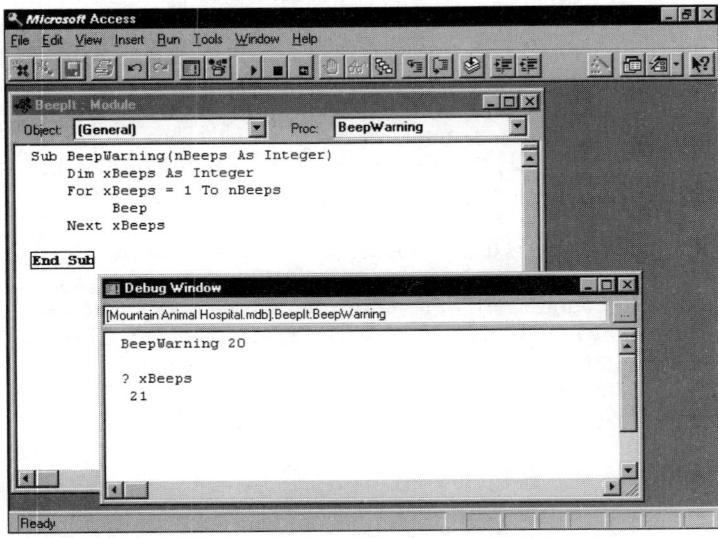
Microsoft Access
File Edit View Insert Run Tools Window Help
BeepIt : Module
Object: (General)
Proc: BeepWarning
Sub BeepWarning(nBeeps As Integer)
Dim xBeeps As Integer
For xBeeps = 1 To nBeeps
Beep
Next xBeeps
End Sub
Debug Window
[Mountain Animal Hospital.mdb].BeepIt.BeepWarning
BeepWarning 20
? xBeeps
21
Ready

Figure 33-17: The Debug window.

Before Access for Windows 95, the Immediate window was independent of the Module window. In Access for Windows 95, the Immediate window is part of the Debug window.

After you create a sub procedure, you can run it to see whether it works as expected. You can test it with supplied arguments.

To run the BeepWarning Sub with arguments, follow these steps:

1. Activate the Immediate pane by selecting it from the Debug window.
2. Type **BeepWarning 20,** and press Enter. The BeepWarning sub runs with the argument 20.

You may have heard 20 beeps or (if you have a really fast machine) only a few beeps because the interval between beeps is short.

Figure 33-17, earlier in this section, shows this command, along with an additional check of the value of the variable named xBeeps, which should be 21. This value is 21 because it increments 1 beyond the number that you give it when you run the module.

Migrating from Macros to VBA

Because you can accomplish many tasks by using macros or the user interface, without the need for programming, should you now concentrate on using Visual Basic for your applications? The answer depends on what you are trying to accomplish. The fact that Access for Windows 95 includes VBA does not mean that Access macros are no longer useful. Access developers will want to learn VBA and add it to their arsenal of tools for creating Access applications.

VBA is not always the answer. Although VBA enables you to create programs that can eliminate the need for most macros, macros are appropriate in some cases. Some tasks, such as assigning global key assignments, can be accomplished only via macros. You can perform some actions more easily and effectively by using a macro.

Depending on the task that you need to accomplish, a Visual Basic procedure can offer better performance. But the opposite also is true: a VBA procedure may run at the same speed as a macro counterpart, or even slower. Simply deciding to use VBA for performance proves to be ineffective in most cases. In fact, most people may find that the time needed to create an application actually increases when they rely on using VBA to code everything in their application.

When to use macros and procedures

In Access, you will want to continue to use macros at times, because they offer an ideal way to take care of many details, such as running reports and forms. Because the arguments for the macro actions are displayed with the macro (in the bottom portion of the Macro window), you can develop applications and assign actions faster. You won't have to remember complex or difficult syntax. Some macros that do simple things such as opening forms or reports are significantly faster than their VBA counterparts.

Four actions in Access can be accomplished only via macros; no Visual Basic equivalents or methods exist. These actions are:

- ✦ Making global key assignments
- ✦ Creating a custom menu bar
- ✦ Running macros/procedures from a toolbar button
- ✦ Carrying out an action or series of actions when a database first opens

Tip You cannot attach a Visual Basic procedure directly to a toolbar button; you can attach only a macro. If you need to run a VBA procedure from a toolbar, however, you can use the RunCode macro action in a macro attached to the toolbar.

Several actions that you can accomplish via VBA are better suited for macros. The following actions tend to be more efficient when they are run from macros:

- ✦ Using macros against an entire set of records — for example, to manipulate multiple records in a table or across tables (such as updating field values or deleting records)
- ✦ Opening and closing forms
- ✦ Running reports
- ✦ Working with toolbars (such as hiding or showing them)

Note Visual Basic supplies a DoCmd Object that you can use to accomplish most macro actions. This object actually runs the macro task. You could, for example, specify DoCmd.Close to run the close macro, closing the current active form. But even this method has flaws. DoCmd cannot perform at least eight macro actions: AddMenu, MsgBox, RunApp, RunCode, SendKeys, SetValue, StopAllMacros, and StopMacro. Some of these actions have VBA equivalents.

Although macros sometimes prove to be the solution of choice, VBA is the tool of choice at other times. You probably will want to use Visual Basic, rather than macros, when you want to perform any of the following tasks:

✦ *Creating and using your own functions.* In addition to using the built-in functions in Access, you can create and work with your own functions by using VBA.

✦ *Creating your own error routines and messages.* You can create error routines that detect an error and decide what action to take. These routines bypass the cryptic Access error messages.

✦ *Using OLE and DDE to communicate with other Windows applications or to run system-level actions.* You can write code to see whether a file exists before you take some action, or you can communicate with another Windows application (such as a spreadsheet), passing data back and forth.

✦ *Using existing functions in external Windows DLLs.* Macros don't allow you to call functions in other Windows Dynamic Link Libraries.

✦ *Working with records one at a time.* If you need to step through records or to move values from a record to variables for manipulation, code is the answer.

✦ *Maintaining the application.* Unlike macros, code can be built into a form or report, making maintaining the code more efficient. Additionally, if you move a form or report from one database to another, the event procedures built into the form or report move with it.

✦ *Creating or manipulating objects.* In most cases, you'll find that it's easiest to create and modify an object in that object's Design view. In some situations, however, you may want to manipulate the definition of an object in code. Using Visual Basic, you can manipulate all the objects in a database, including the database itself.

✦ *Passing arguments to your Visual Basic procedures.* You can set arguments for macro actions in the bottom part of the Macro window when you create the macro, but you can't change arguments when the macro is running. With Visual Basic, however, you can pass arguments to your code at the time it's run or use variables for arguments — something you can't do with macros. This capability gives you a great deal of flexibility in the way your Visual Basic procedures run.

Tip If you create a form or report that will be copied to other databases, it is a good idea to create your event procedures for that form or report in Visual Basic, rather than use macros. Because macros are stored as separate objects in the database, you have to remember which ones are associated with the form or report you are copying. On the other hand, because Visual Basic code can be attached to the form or report, copying the form automatically copies the VBA event procedures that are associated with it.

Converting existing macros to Visual Basic

After you become comfortable with writing VBA code, you may want to rewrite some of your application macros as Visual Basic procedures. As you set off on this process, you quickly realize how mentally challenging the effort can be as you review every macro in your various macro libraries. You cannot merely cut the macro from the Macro window and paste it into a Module window. For each condition, action, and action argument for a macro, you must analyze the task that it accomplishes and then write the equivalent statements of VBA code in your procedure.

Fortunately, Access provides a feature that converts macros to VBA code automatically. One of the options in the Save As dialog box is Save As Visual Basic Module; you can use this option when a macro file is highlighted in the Macros tab of the Database Window. This option allows you to convert an entire macro library to a module in seconds. To start this process, choose File⇨Save As/Export, as shown in Figure 33-18.

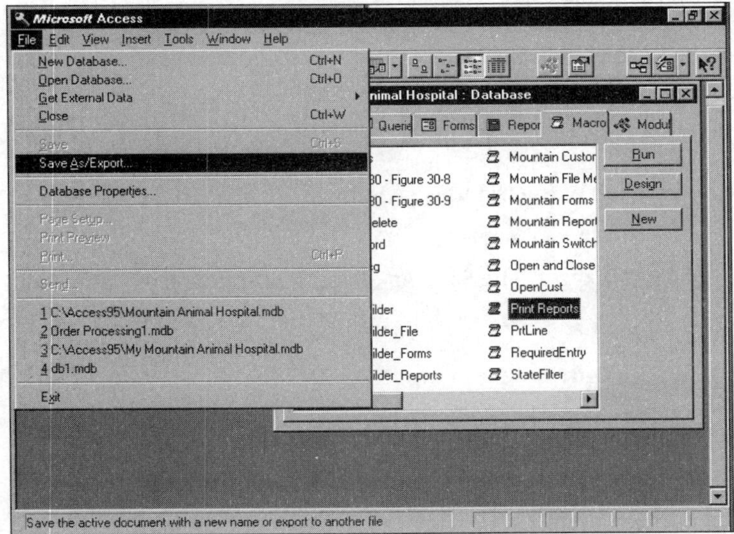

Figure 33-18: Choosing File⇨Save As/Export.

To try the conversion process, you can convert the Print Reports macros in the Mountain Animal Hospital database. Figure 33-19 displays the macros for the Print Reports macro library.

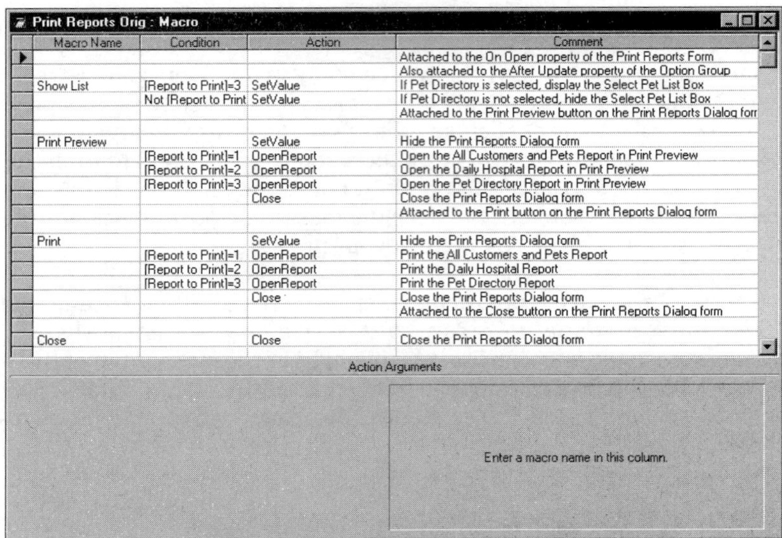

Macro Name	Condition	Action	Comment
			Attached to the On Open property of the Print Reports Form
			Also attached to the After Update property of the Option Group
Show List	[Report to Print]=3	SetValue	If Pet Directory is selected, display the Select Pet List Box
	Not [Report to Print	SetValue	If Pet Directory is not selected, hide the Select Pet List Box
			Attached to the Print Preview button on the Print Reports Dialog forr
Print Preview		SetValue	Hide the Print Reports Dialog form
	[Report to Print]=1	OpenReport	Open the All Customers and Pets Report in Print Preview
	[Report to Print]=2	OpenReport	Open the Daily Hospital Report in Print Preview
	[Report to Print]=3	OpenReport	Open the Pet Directory Report in Print Preview
		Close	Close the Print Reports Dialog form
			Attached to the Print button on the Print Reports Dialog form
Print		SetValue	Hide the Print Reports Dialog form
	[Report to Print]=1	OpenReport	Print the All Customers and Pets Report
	[Report to Print]=2	OpenReport	Print the Daily Hospital Report
	[Report to Print]=3	OpenReport	Print the Pet Directory Report
		Close	Close the Print Reports Dialog form
			Attached to the Close button on the Print Reports Dialog form
Close		Close	Close the Print Reports Dialog form

Figure 33-19: The Print Reports macro library.

Follow these steps to run the conversion process:

1. Click on the Macros tab of the Database window.
2. Select the Print Reports macro library.
3. Choose File➪Save As/Export. The Save As dialog box appears, as shown in Figure 33-20.

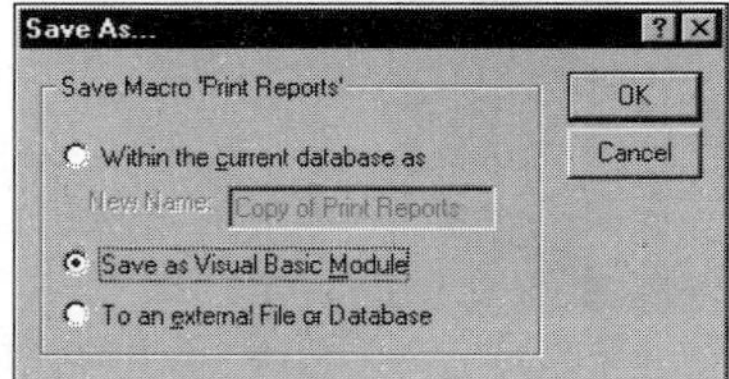

Figure 33-20: The Save As Visual Basic Module dialog box.

4. Choose Save as Visual Basic Module, and click on OK. The Convert Macro dialog box appears, as shown in Figure 33-21.

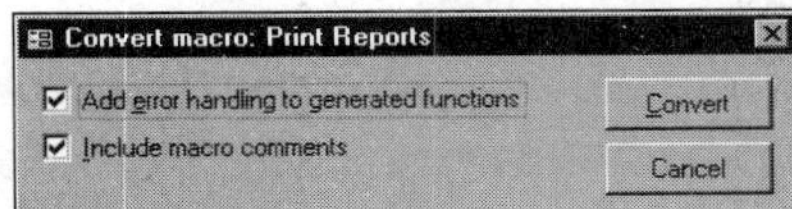

Figure 33-21: The Convert Macro dialog box.

5. Select the options that include error handling and comments, and click on Convert.

   Access briefly displays each new procedure as it is converted. When the conversion process completes, the Conversion Finished message box appears.

6. Click on OK to remove the message box.
7. Access displays the Modules tab of the Database window, as shown in Figure 33-22. Access names the new module Converted Macro: Print Reports.

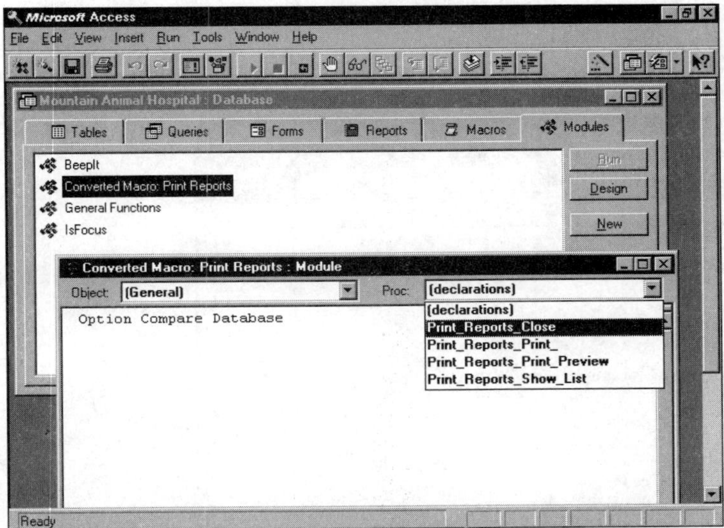

Figure 33-22: The newly converted module.

When you open the Module window for the new module, you can view the procedures created from the macros. As you can see in Figure 33-22, Access created four functions from the Print Reports macro: Print_Reports_Close, Print_Reports_Print, Print_Reports_Print_Preview, and Print_Reports_Show_List. Figures 33-23 and 33-24 show samples of the new procedures.

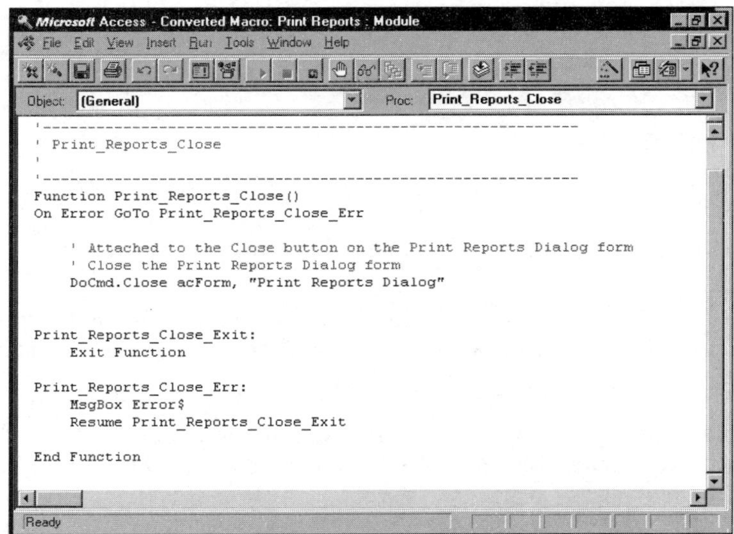

Figure 33-23: The Print_Reports_Close function.

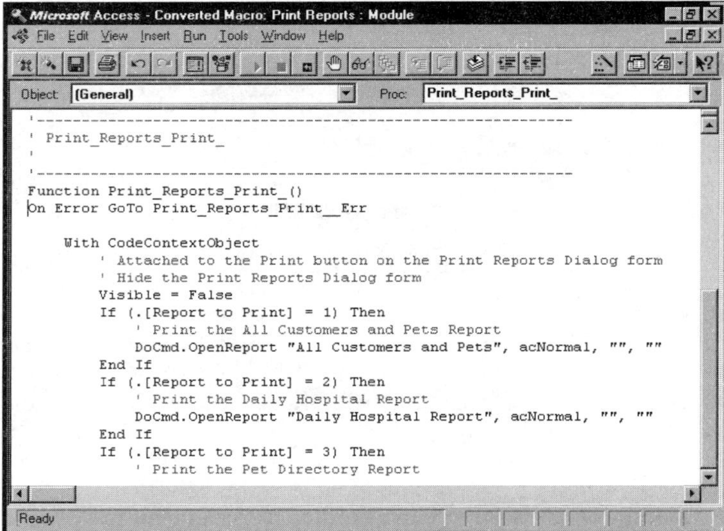

Figure 33-24: The Print_Reports_Print function.

At the top of each function, Access inserts four comment lines for the name of the function. The Function statement follows the comment lines. Access names the functions, using the macro library's name as a prefix (Print_Reports); the macro name (if one is supplied) for the suffix; and Close for the Close function.

When you specify that you want Access to include error processing for the conversion, Access automatically inserts the OnError statement as the first command in the procedure. The OnError statement tells Access to branch to other statements that display an appropriate message and then exit the function. Error processing is covered in more detail in Chapter 34.

The statement beginning with DoCmd is the actual code that Access created from the macro. The DoCmd methods run Access actions from Visual Basic. An action performs important tasks, such as closing windows, opening forms, and setting the value of controls. In the Close macro, for example, Close Print Reports Dialog closes the Print Reports dialog box. Access converts the Close macro action arguments to the properly formatted parameters for the DoCmd methods.

In the Print_Reports_Print function, the group of statements beginning with the With command retrieves the settings of some of the controls in the Print Reports dialog box. The DoCmd action prints various reports based on the value of the settings in the dialog box. Chapter 34 covers conditional structures, such as the If. . .End If statements that you see in these functions.

Tip You also can convert macros that are used in a form by choosing Tools⇨Macros⇨Convert Form's Macros to Visual Basic in Forms Design view.

Using the Command Button Wizard to create VBA code

A good way to learn how to write event procedures is to use the Command Button Wizard, which was covered in Chapter 32. When Access creates a command button with a Wizard, it creates an event procedure and attaches it to the button. You can open the event procedure to see how it works and then modify it to fit your needs. The Wizard speeds the process of creating a command button, because it does all the basic work for you. When you use the Wizard, Access prompts you for information and creates a command button based on your answers.

You can create more than 30 types of command buttons by using the Command Button Wizard. You can create a command button that finds a record, prints a record, or applies a form filter, for example. You can run this Wizard by creating a new command button on a form. Figure 33-25 shows a command button being created in the Record Operations category, with the Delete Record action.

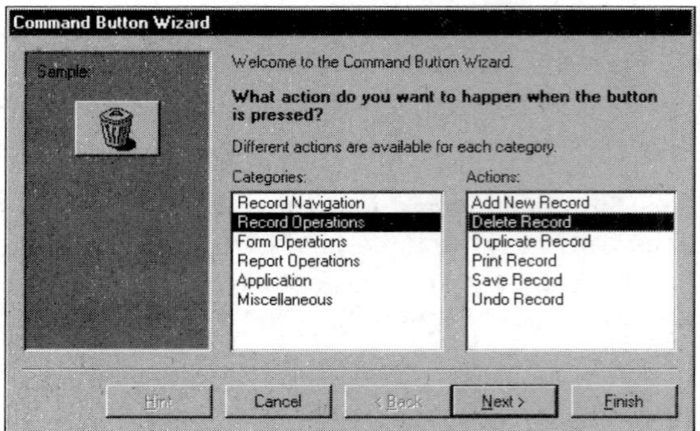

Figure 33-25: The Command Button Wizard.

Note In the Mountain Animal Hospital database is a form named Button Wizard VBA Samples. This form, shown in Figure 33-26 in Design mode, contains the result of running the Button Wizard with several selections. The Button Wizard VBA Samples form contains a dozen command buttons created with the Command Button Wizard. You can review the procedures for each command button on the form to see how powerful Visual Basic code can be.

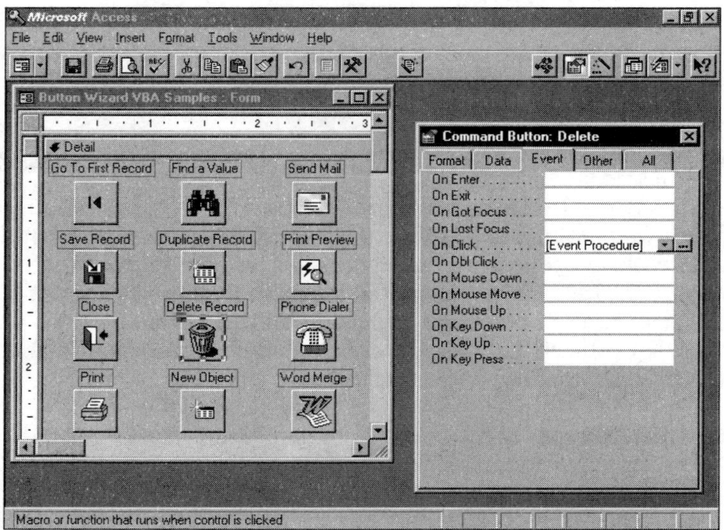

Figure 33-26: Examples of Command Button Wizard buttons.

To view the sample code, follow these steps:

1. Display the Button Wizard VBA Samples form in Design view.
2. Display the Property window for the desired button.
3. Click on the Builder button (. . .) for the On Click event property to display the command button's Module window, with the procedure.

Figure 33-27 shows the code for the Delete Record command button.

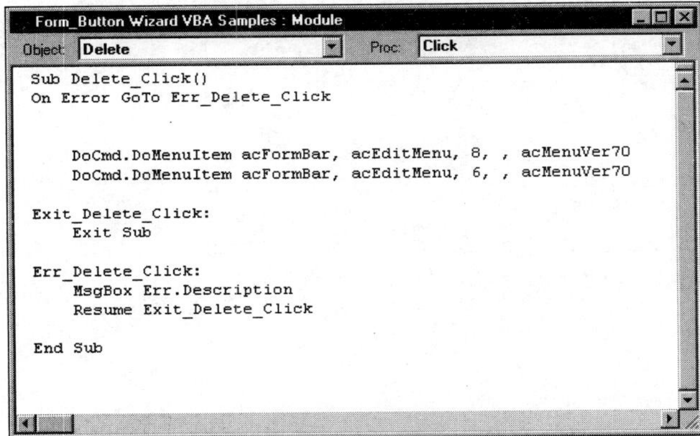

Figure 33-27: The On Delete button's On Click procedure.

Figure 33-28 shows the code for a Dialer command button. The Dialer_Click procedure retrieves the text in the current field and then passes the text to a utility that dials the telephone.

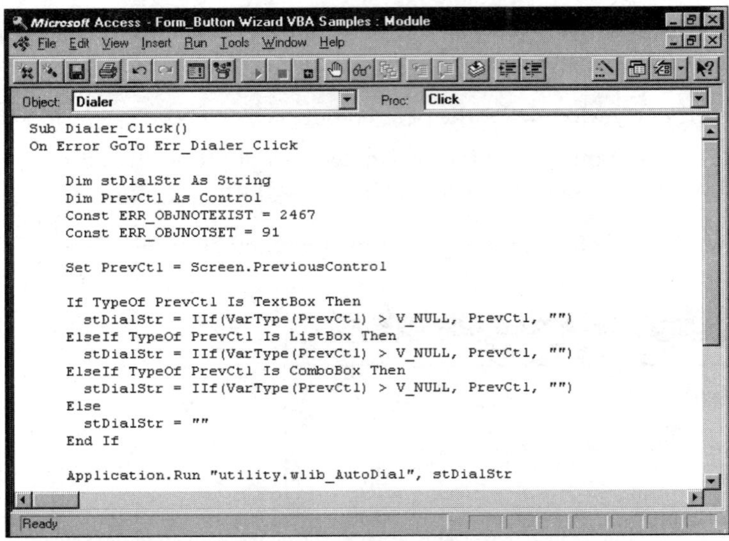

Figure 33-28: The Dialer command button's On Click procedure.

Summary

In this chapter, you learned how to create instant applications, use the Module window and convert macros to VBA code. The following topics were covered:

- ✦ You can use the Database Wizard to create an application by clicking on an icon and answering a few questions.
- ✦ The Database Wizard features a customizable switchboard for adding new forms and reports to the application that the Wizard creates for you.
- ✦ Module code can be created in a global module container or can be stored behind a form or report.
- ✦ Sub procedures are called from events. Functions also are called from events or expressions and are used to return a value.
- ✦ You can use the Immediate pane of the Debug window to test your program or check variables as you run your program.
- ✦ The Command Button Wizard enables you to create more than 30 types of buttons by selecting options from a list.
- ✦ You can convert a macro group to a VBA module library by selecting the macro and then choosing File⇨Save As/Export.

In the next chapter, you learn how to create modules, add variables, use logical constructs (If Then, While, Case), add error checking, and use recordset manipulation.

✦ ✦ ✦

The Access 95 Programming Environment

✦ ✦ ✦ ✦

In This Chapter

Creating modules

Capabilities of the VBA language

Filtering records with a procedure

Working with combo boxes and list boxes with procedures

Manipulating data using DAO

✦ ✦ ✦ ✦

The Visual Basic language offers a full array of powerful commands for manipulating records in a table, controls on a form, or just about anything else. This chapter continues Chapter 33's discussion of working with procedures in forms, reports, and standard modules.

Understanding Modules

In the preceding chapter, you created a few procedures and became somewhat familiar with the VBA programming environment. You probably are a little uncomfortable with modules and procedures, however, as well as unsure when and how to create them.

Modules and their procedures are the principal objects of the VBA programming environment. The programming code that you write is placed in procedures that are contained in a module. The procedures can be independent procedures, unrelated to a specific form or report, or they can be integral parts of specific forms and reports.

Two basic categories of modules can be stored in a database:

✦ Standard Modules	(Stored in the Module Object)
✦ Form/Report	(CBF - Code Behind Form/CBR - Code Behind Report)

As you create Visual Basic procedures for your Access applications, you use both types of modules.

Form and report modules

All forms, reports, and their controls can associate event procedures to their events. These event procedures can be macros or Visual Basic code. Every form or report that you create in your database contains a form module or report module. This form or report module is an integral part of the form or report, and is used as a container for the event procedures that you create for the form or report. This method is a convenient way to place all of a form's event procedures in a single collection.

Creating Visual Basic event procedures in a form module can be very powerful and efficient. When an event procedure is attached to a form, it becomes part of the form. When you need to copy the form, the event procedures go with it. If you need to modify one of the form's events, you simply click on the ellipsis button for the event, and the form module window for the procedure appears. Figure 34-1 illustrates accessing the event procedure of the First Record button's On Click event shown in the form named Button Wizard VBA Samples. Notice that in the On Click property is the text `[Event Procedure]`. When you click on the Builder button next to [Event Procedure], you will see the module window for that form (and specifically the On Click event for that button control).

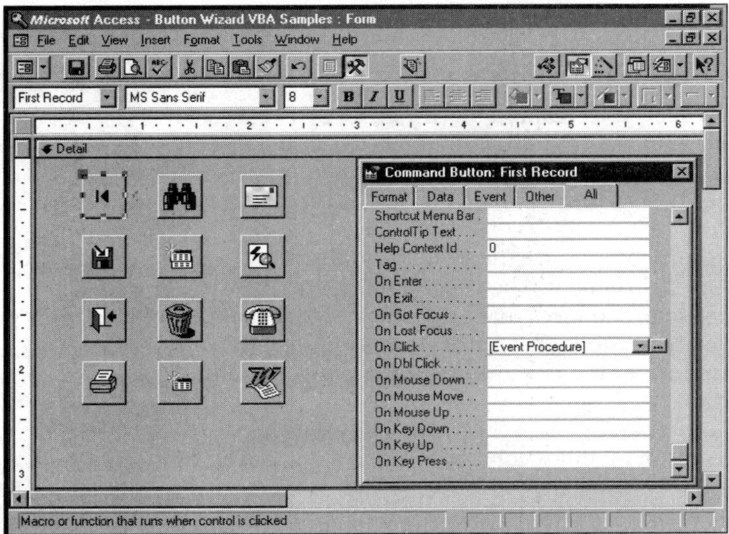

Figure 34-1: Accessing a control's event procedure.

Cross Ref You learned about the Button Wizard VBA Samples form in Chapter 33.

Standard modules

Standard modules are independent from form and report objects. These modules can be used to store code, in the form of procedures, that can be used from anywhere within your application. In previous versions of Access (1.0 through 2.0), standard modules were known as *global modules*.

You can use standard procedures throughout your application for expressions, macros, event procedures, and even other procedures. To use a standard procedure, you simply call it from a control as a function or an event based on an event procedure, based on the type of procedure that it is. Remember that two basic types of procedures are stored in modules:

- ✦ Subs, which perform actions without returning a value
- ✦ Functions, which always return a value

Procedures run — modules contain

A procedure is executed; it performs some action. You create the procedures that your application will use. Modules, on the other hand, simply act like containers, grouping procedures and declarations together. A module cannot be run; rather, you run the procedures that are contained in the module. These procedures can respond to events or can be called from expressions, macros, and even other procedures.

You use the Modules container of the database to store your standard procedures. The module container is the section of the database that has a tab labeled Modules.

Although you can place any type of procedure in any module, you should group your procedures into categories. Most modules contain procedures that are related in some way. Figure 34-2 shows a standard module called Calendar. The Calendar module contains some procedures for working with dates, called DayOfWeek and Due28Day.

Event procedures that work with a single form or report belong in the module of the form or report. A specific form's module should contain only the declarations and event procedures needed for that form and its controls (command buttons, check boxes, text labels, text boxes, combo boxes, and so on). Placing another form's or report's event procedures in this form's module doesn't make sense.

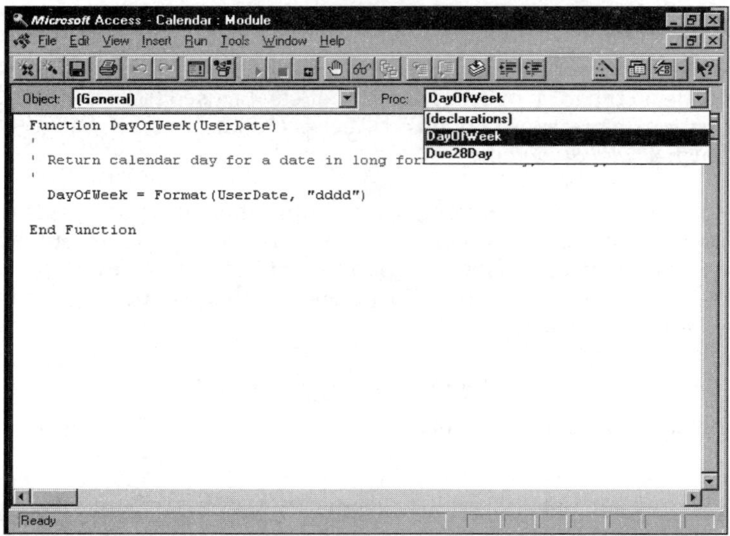

Figure 34-2: A standard module containing date-manipulation procedures.

To begin creating more sophisticated procedures with Visual Basic, you need to understand some of VBA's fundamental programming elements. These basic elements include the following:

- ✦ Variables and how they interact with data
- ✦ Data types
- ✦ Programming syntax for logical constructs

Although this book is not a how-to programming book, it attempts to explain the concepts of the Visual Basic environment in Access and how you can use it to manipulate Access objects.

Using Variables

One of the most powerful concepts in programming is the variable. A *variable* is a temporary storage location for some value and is given a name. You can use a variable to store the result of a calculation, or you can create a variable to make the value of a control available to another procedure.

To refer to the result of an expression, you create a *name* to store the result. The named result is the variable. To assign an expression's result to a variable, you use the = operator. Following are some examples of calculations that create variables:

```
counter = 1
counter = counter + 1
today = Date()
```

Naming variables

Every programming language has its own rules for naming variables. In Visual Basic, a variable name must meet the following conditions:

- Must begin with an alphabetical character
- Can't contain an embedded period or type-declaration character
- Must have a unique name; the name cannot be used elsewhere in the procedure or in modules that use the variables
- Must be no longer than 255 characters

Although you can make up almost any name for a variable, most programmers adopt a standard convention for naming variables. Some common practices include:

- Using uppercase and lowercase characters, as in TotalCost.
- Using all lowercase characters, as in counter.
- Preceding the name with the data type of the value. A variable that stores a number might be called nCounter.

When you need to see or use the contents of a variable, you simply use its name. When you specify the variable's name, the computer program goes into memory, finds the variable, and gets its contents for you. This procedure means, of course, that you need to be able to remember the name of the variable.

Visual Basic, like many other programming languages, allows you to create variables on the fly. In the Counter = 1 example, the Counter variable was not *declared* before the value 1 was assigned to it.

Declaring variables

Declaring a variable before assigning anything to it sets up a location in the computer's memory for storing a value for the variable ahead of time. The amount of storage allocated for the variable depends on the type of data that you plan to store in the variable. More space is allocated for a variable that will hold a currency amount (such as $1,000,000) than for a variable that never will hold a value greater than, say, 255.

Even though Visual Basic does not require you to declare your variables before using them, it does provide various declaration commands. Getting into the habit of declaring your variables is good practice. Declaring a variable assures that you can assign only a certain type of value to it — always a number or always characters, for example. In addition, you can attain real performance gains in most languages by predeclaring variables. For purposes of maintenance, most programmers like to declare their variables at the top of the procedure.

Warning Although Visual Basic does not require initial declaration of variables, you should avoid using undeclared variables. If you do not declare a variable, the code may expect one type of value in the variable when another is actually there. If, in your procedure, you set the variable TodayIs to *Monday* and later change the value for TodayIs to a number (such as TodayIs = 2), the program generates an error when it runs.

The Dim statement

To declare a variable, you use the Dim statement. When you use the Dim statement, you must supply the variable name that you assign to the variable. The format for the Dim statement is:

Dim *variable name* [As *type*]

Figure 34-3 shows the Dim statement for the variable xBeeps. Notice that the variable name follows the Dim statement. In addition to naming the variable, you can use the optional As clause to specify data type for the variable. The data type is the kind of information that will be stored in the variable: String, Integer, Currency, and so on. The default data type is known as *variant*. A variant data type can hold any type of data.

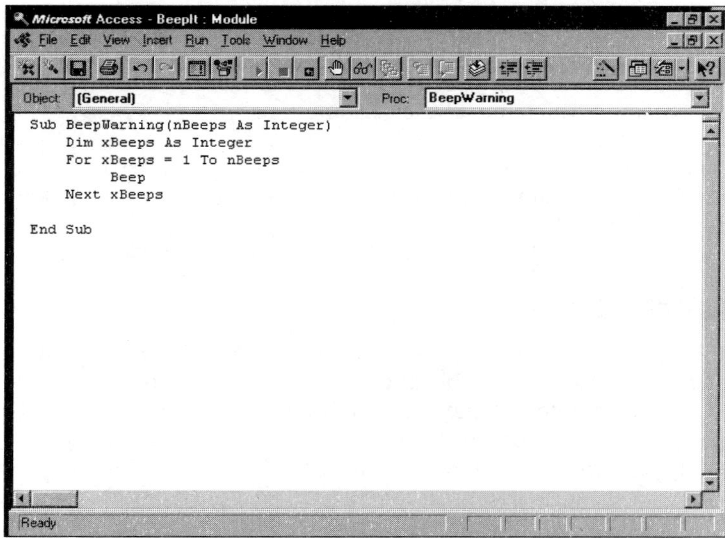
Microsoft Access - BeepIt : Module
File Edit View Insert Run Tools Window Help
Object: (General)
Proc: BeepWarning
Sub BeepWarning(nBeeps As Integer)
Dim xBeeps As Integer
For xBeeps = 1 To nBeeps
Beep
Next xBeeps
End Sub
Ready

Figure 34-3: Using the Dim statement to declare a variable.

Tip When creating variables, you can use uppercase, lowercase, or mixed-case characters to specify the variable or call it later. Visual Basic variables are not case-sensitive. This fact means that you can use the TodayIs variable later without having to worry about the case that you used for the name when you created it; TODAYIS, todayis, and tOdAyIs all reference the same variable. Visual Basic automatically changes any explicitly declared variables to the case that was used in the declaration statement (Dim statement).

When you use the Dim statement to declare a variable in a procedure, you can refer to that variable only within that procedure. Other procedures, even if they are stored in the same module, do not know anything about the variable. This is known as a *private* variable because it was declared in a procedure and is only known in the procedure where it was declared and used.

Variables can also be declared in the *declarations* section of a module. Then, all the procedures in the module can access the variable. Procedures outside the module in which you declared the variable however, cannot read or use the variable.

To declare a variable for use by procedures in different modules, you use the Public statement.

The Public statement

To make a variable available to all modules in the application, use the Public keyword when you declare the variable. Figure 34-4 illustrates using the Public keyword to declare a variable. Notice that the statement is in the declarations section of the module. Public variables must be declared in the declarations section of the module.

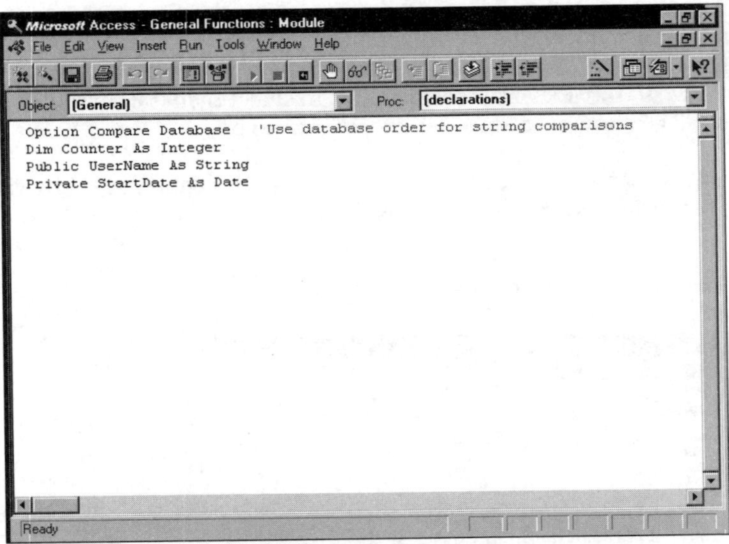

Figure 34-4: Declaring a public variable.

Although you can declare a public variable in any module, it seems logical to declare public variables only within the module that will use them the most. The exceptions to this rule are true global variables that you want to make available to all procedures across modules and that are not specifically related to a single module. You should declare global variables in a single standard module so you can find them easily.

Warning: You cannot declare a variable public within a procedure. It must be declared in the declarations section of a module. If you attempt to declare a variable public, you receive an error message.

Tip: In a standard, report, or form module, you can refer to a public variable from a different form or report module. To access the value of a public variable from another module, you must qualify the variable reference, using the name of the form or report object. Employee_MainForm.MyVariable, for example, accesses a form named Employee_MainForm and obtains the value of the variable MyVariable.

The Private statement

The declarations section in Figure 34-4, earlier in this chapter, shows the use of the Dim and Private statements to declare variables. Technically, there is no difference between Private and Dim, but using Private at the module level to declare variables that are available to all procedures is a good idea. Declaring private variables does the following things:

- ✦ Contrasts with Dim, which must be used at the procedure level, distinguishing where the variable is declared and its scope (Module versus Procedure)
- ✦ Contrasts with Public, the other method of declaring variables in modules, making understanding your code easier

Tip: You can go to the declarations section of a module while you are creating an event procedure in a form by selecting declarations from the Procedure combo box. Another way to move to the declarations section is to select (general) in the Object combo box. Figure 34-5 shows the Module window combo boxes.

When you declare a variable, you use the AS clause to assign a data type to the variable. Data types for variables are similar to data types in a database table definition.

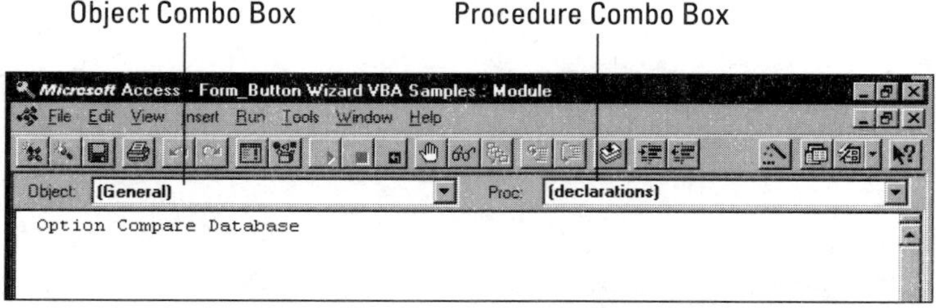

Figure 34-5: Accessing a module's declarations section.

Working with Data Types

When you declare a variable, you also can specify the data type for the variable. All variables have a data type. The type of variable determines what kind of information can be stored in the variable.

A *string variable* — a variable with a data type of string — can hold any values ranging from A–Z, a–z, and 0–1, as well as formatting characters (#, -, !, and so on). Once created, a string variable can be used in many ways: comparing its contents with another string, pulling parts of information out of the string, and so on. If you have a variable defined as a string, however, you cannot use it to do mathematical calculations. Conversely, you cannot assign a number to a variable declared as a string.

Table 34-1 describes the 11 data types that Visual Basic supports.

Table 34-1
Data Types Used in Visual Basic

Type	*Range*	*Description*
Boolean	True or false	2 bytes
Byte	0 to 255	1 byte binary data
Currency	–922,337,203,685,477,5808 to 922,337,203,685,477,5807	8-byte number with fixed decimal point
Date	01 Jan 100 to 31 Dec 9999	8-byte date/time value
Double	–1.79769313486231E308 to –4.94065645841247E–324	8-byte floating-point number
Integer	–32,768 to 32,767	2-byte integer
Long	–2,147,483,648 to2,147,483,647	4-byte integer
Object	Any object reference	4 bytes
Single	negative values: –3.402823E38 to –1.401298E – 45 positive values: 1.401298E –45 to 3.402823E38	4-byte floating-point number
String	0 to approximately 65,400 characters	String of characters
Variant	Same as Date, Double, and String; also can contain Error or Null values 16 bytes, plus 1 byte for each character, if variable is a string. It can be any of these types: Date/Time, floating-point number, integer, string, or object.	

Most of the time you use the string, date, integer, and currency or double data types. If a variable always contains whole numbers between –32,768 and 32,768, you can save bytes of memory and gain speed in arithmetic operations if you declare the variable an integer type.

When you want to assign the value of an Access field to a variable, you need to make sure that the type of the variable can hold the data type of the field. Table 34-2 shows the corresponding Visual Basic data types for Access field types.

Table 34-2
Comparative Data Types of Access and VBA

Access Field Data Type	*Visual Basic Data Type*
AutoNumber (Long Integer)	Long
AutoNumber (Replication ID)	—
Currency	Currency
Computed	—
Date/Time	Date
Memo	String
Number (Byte)	Byte
Number (Integer)	Integer
Number (Long Integer)	Long
Number (Single)	Single
Number (Double)	Double
Number (Replication ID)	—
OLE object	Array of bytes
Text	String
Yes/No	Boolean

Note If a variable may have to hold a value of Null, it must be declared as variant. Variant is the only data type that can accept Null values.

Now that you understand variables and their data types, you're ready to learn how to use them in writing procedures.

Understanding VBA Logical Constructs

One of the real powers of a programming language is the capability to have a program make a decision based on some condition. Often, a program in VBA performs different tasks based on some value. If the condition is True, the code performs one action. If the condition is False, the code performs a different action. This procedure is similar to walking down a path and coming to a fork in the path; you can go to the left or to the right. If a sign at the fork points left for home and right for work, you can decide which way to go. If you need to go to work, you go to the right; if you need to go home, you go to the left. Conditional processing of code works the same way. A program looks at the value of some variable and decides which set of code should be processed.

When writing code, you need to be able to control which actions execute. You may want to write some statements that execute only if a certain condition is True.

Conditional processing

An application's capability to look at a value and, based on that value, decide which code to run is known as *conditional processing.*

Visual Basic offers two sets of conditional processing statements:

✦ If. . .Then. . .Else. . .End If

✦ Select Case

The If. . .Then. . .Else. . .End If statement

The If. . .Then and If. . .Then. . .Else statements allow you to check a condition and, based on the evaluation, perform a single action. The condition must evaluate to True or False. If the condition is True, the program moves to the next statement in the procedure. If the condition is False, the program skips to the statement following the End If statement.

In Figure 34-6, the Print Reports dialog box displays an option group, called Report to Print, that displays three reports. When you choose the Pet Directory report, a list of pets appears at the bottom of the dialog box. When you choose either of the other two reports, the list of pets disappears. Figure 34-7 shows the dialog box with the All Customers and Pets report option selected and nothing displayed in the now-invisible list box.

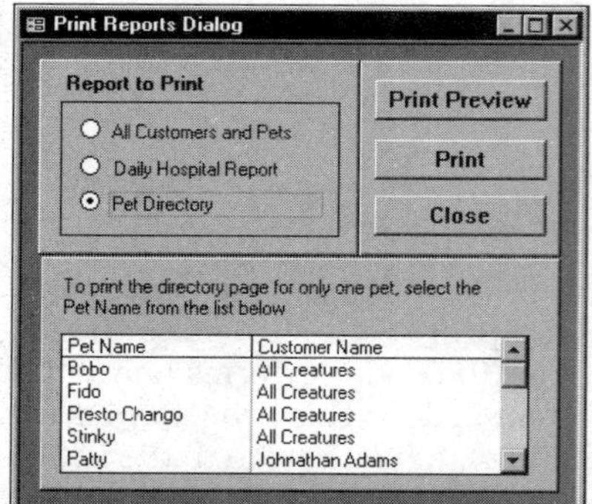

Figure 34-6: Choosing the Pet Directory report in the Print Reports dialog box.

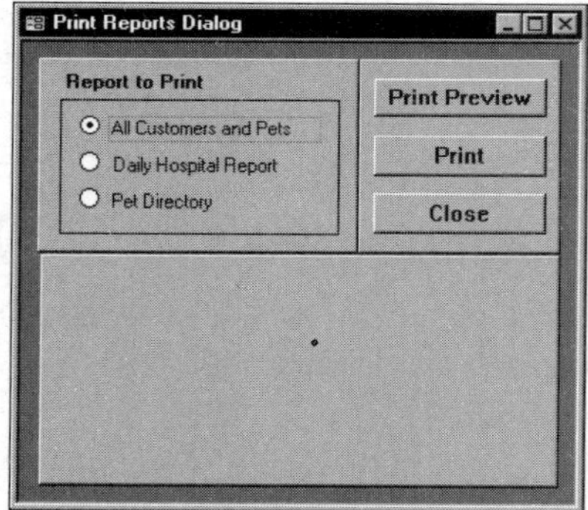

Figure 34-7: Choosing the All Customers and Pets report in the Print Reports dialog box.

In Chapter 32, you learned how make the Select Pet list box visible and invisible in the Print Reports dialog box. Figure 34-8 illustrates the Show List macro for the Print Reports dialog box. The two condition statements determine which SetValue action to use to set the Select Pet list box's Visible property to Yes when the Pet Directory option is selected and to No when another report option is selected.

You can write a procedure to perform the same actions as the Show List macro. Figure 34-9 shows the Print_Reports_Show_List procedure. Notice that the If. . .Then. . .End If construct replaces the Condition statement used in the macro.

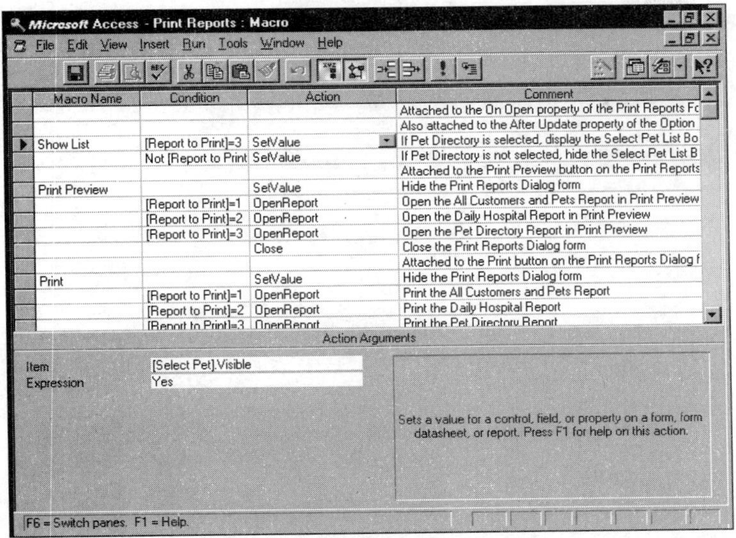

Figure 34-8: Using a macro to make a control visible.

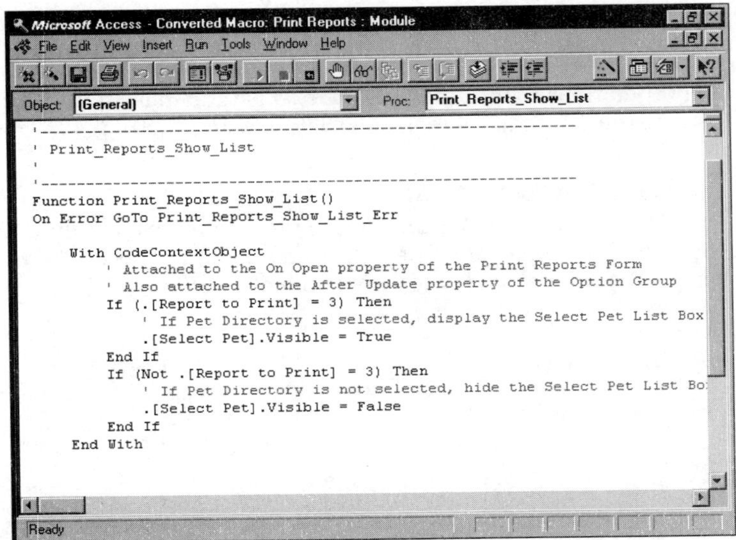

Figure 34-9: Using the If. . .Then. . .End If statement.

The Else statement is optional. You can use Else to test for a second condition when the If statement evaluates to False. When the If statement is True, the program executes the statements between the If statement and the Else statement. When the If statement evaluates to False, the program skips to the Else statement, if it is present. Then, if the Else statement is True, the program executes the following statement. If the Else statement is False, the program skips to the statement following the End If statement.

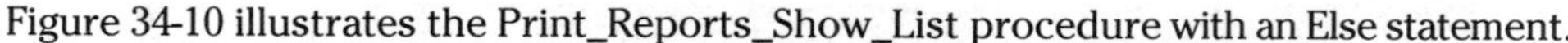

Figure 34-10 illustrates the Print_Reports_Show_List procedure with an Else statement.

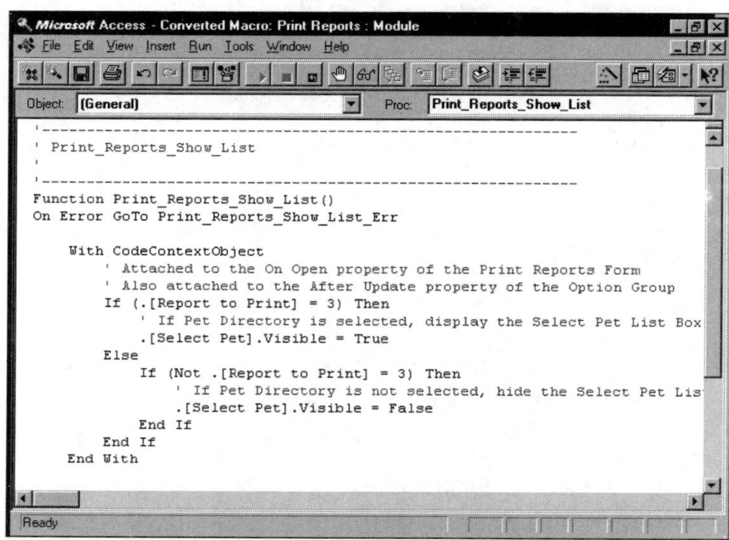

Figure 34-10: Using the Else statement.

When you have many conditions to test, the If. . .Then. . .Else statements can get rather complicated. A better approach is to use the Select Case construct.

The Select Case. . .End Select statement

In addition to the If. . .Then statements, Visual Basic offers a command for checking more than one condition. You can use the Select Case statement to check for multiple conditions. Following is the general syntax of the statement:

```
Select Case test_expression
   Case expression value1
        code statements here (test expression = value1)
   Case expression value2
        code statements here (test expression = value2) ...
   Case Else
        code statements (test expression = none of the values)
End Select
```

Notice that the syntax is similar to that of the If. . .Then statement. Instead of a condition in the Select Case statement, however, VBA uses a test expression. Then each Case statement inside the Select Case statement tests its value against the test expression's value. When a Case statement matches the test value, the program executes the next line or lines of code until it reaches another Case statement or the End Select statement. Visual Basic executes the code for only one matching Case statement.

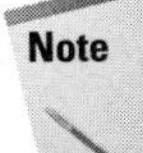

Note If more than one Case statement matches the value of the test expression, only the code for the first match executes. If other matching Case statements appear after the first match, Visual Basic ignores them.

The Print Reports dialog box prints a different report for each of the three Report to Print options. Figure 34-11 shows the Print command button's Print macro. The three condition statements determine which OpenReport action is used to print the appropriate report.

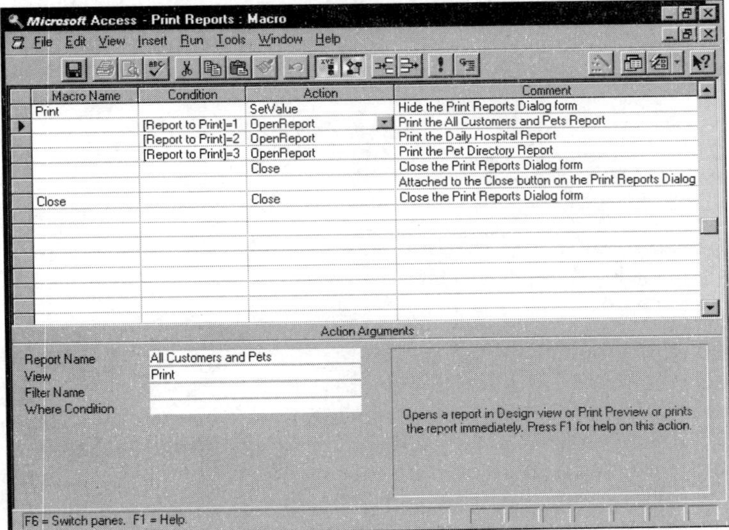

Figure 34-11: Using a macro to print a report.

The Print_Reports_Print procedure, illustrated in Figure 34-12, performs the same actions as the Print macro. Notice that the procedure replaces each of the macro's Condition statements with a Case statement.

The Select Case statement looks at the value of the control Report to Print and then checks each Case condition. If the value of Report to Print is 1 (All Customers and Pets), the Case 1 statement evaluates to True, and the All Customers and Pets report prints. If Report to Print is not 1, Visual Basic goes to the next Case statement to see whether Report to Print matches that value. Each Case statement is evaluated until a match occurs or the program reaches the End Select statement.

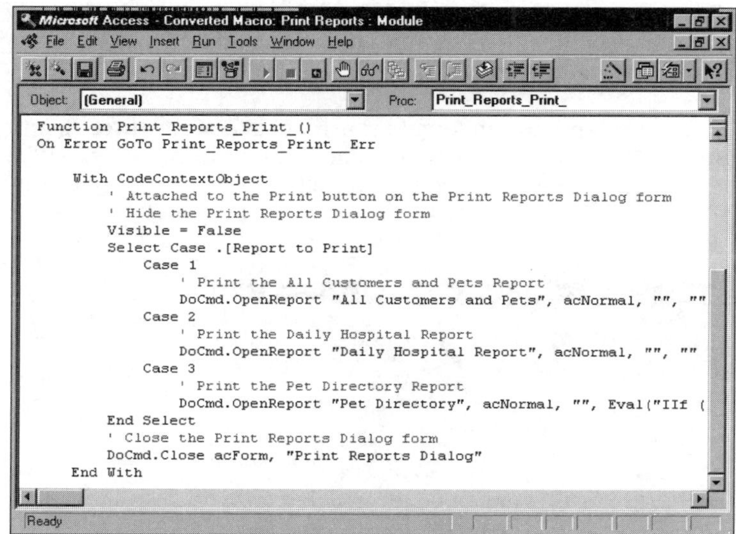

Figure 34-12: Using the Select Case statement.

The Case Else statement is optional. The Case Else clause always is the last Case statement of Select Case. You use this statement to perform some action when none of the Case values matches the test value of the Select Case statement.

In some procedures, you may want to execute a group of statements more than one time. Visual Basic provides some constructs for repeating a group of statements.

Repetitive looping

The capability to determine conditions and then process a statement or group of statements based on the answer can be very powerful.

Another very powerful process that VBA offers is *repetitive looping* — the capability to process some series of code over and over. The statement or group of statements is processed continually until some condition is met.

Visual Basic offers two types of repetitive-looping constructs:

- ✦ Do. . .Loop
- ✦ For. . .Next

The Do. . .Loop statement

The Do. . .Loop statement is used to repeat a group of statements while a condition is true or until a condition is true. This statement is one of the most common commands that can perform repetitive processes.

Following is the format of the Do. . .Loop statement:

```
DO [While | Until condition]
      code statements [for condition = TRUE]
       [Exit DO]
      code statements [for condition = TRUE]
LOOP [While | Until condition]
```

Notice that the Do. . .Loop statement has several optional clauses. The two While clauses tell the program to execute the code inside Do. . .Loop as long as the test condition is True. When the condition evaluates to False, the program skips to the next statement following the Loop statement. The two Until clauses work in just the opposite way; they execute the code within Do. . .Loop as long as the condition is False. Where you place the While or Until clause determines whether the code inside Do. . .Loop executes.

The Exit Do clause is used to terminate Do. . .Loop immediately. The program then skips to the next statement following the Loop statement.

The Print_Reports_Print2 procedure, illustrated in Figure 34-13, prints multiple copies of the report, based on the value of the Number of Copies control on the form. Notice that the procedure declares a Counter variable. The program increments the Counter variable each time the report prints. When Counter is greater than Number of Copies, Do. . .Loop stops printing copies of the report.

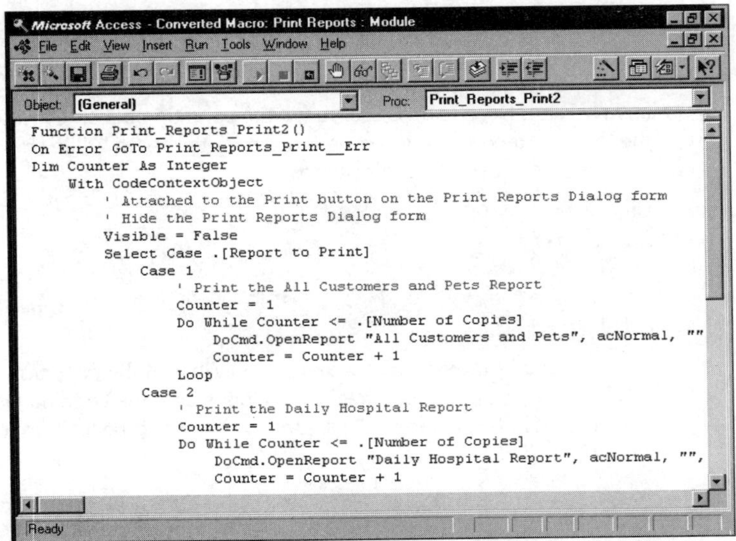


```
Function Print_Reports_Print2()
On Error GoTo Print_Reports_Print__Err
Dim Counter As Integer
    With CodeContextObject
        ' Attached to the Print button on the Print Reports Dialog form
        ' Hide the Print Reports Dialog form
        Visible = False
        Select Case .[Report to Print]
            Case 1
                ' Print the All Customers and Pets Report
                Counter = 1
                Do While Counter <= .[Number of Copies]
                    DoCmd.OpenReport "All Customers and Pets", acNormal, ""
                    Counter = Counter + 1
                Loop
            Case 2
                ' Print the Daily Hospital Report
                Counter = 1
                Do While Counter <= .[Number of Copies]
                    DoCmd.OpenReport "Daily Hospital Report", acNormal, "",
                    Counter = Counter + 1
```

Figure 34-13: Using the Do. . .Loop statement.

The While and Until clauses provide powerful flexibility for processing Do. . .Loop in your code. Table 34-3 describes the various alternatives for using the While and Until clauses and how they affect the processing of code:

Table 34-3
Repetitive Looping, Using Do. . .Loop with the While and Until Clauses

Pseudo Code	***Purpose of Do. . .Loop***

Do	*Code starts here*
	If *condition* Then
	Exit Do
	End If

Loop	The code always runs. The code has some conditional statement (If. . .Then) that, if True, runs the Exit Do statement. The Exit Do statement allows the user to get out of Do. . .Loop. If that statement were missing, the code inside the loop would run forever.
Do	While *condition* *code starts here for the condition on the Do While line being TRUE*
Loop	The code inside the Do While loop runs only if the condition is True. The code runs down to the Loop statement and then goes back to the top to see whether the condition is still True. If the condition is initially False, Do. . .Loop is skipped; if the condition becomes False, the loop is exited when the code loops back to the Do While line. Exit Do is not needed for this purpose.
Do	Until *condition* *code starts here for the condition on the Do Until line being FALSE*
Loop	This code works the opposite way from Do While. If the condition is False (not True), the code begins and loops until the condition is True; then it leaves the loop. Again, the loop and its code are skipped if the Until condition is True.
Do	*Code starts here for the condition on the Do While line being TRUE*

Pseudo Code	***Purpose of Do. . .Loop***
Loop While *condition*	This code always runs at least one time. First, the code is executed and reaches the Loop While line. If the condition is True, the code loops back up to process the code again; if not, the code loop ends.
Do	*Code starts here for the condition on the Do Until line being FALSE*
Loop Until *condition*	This code works similarly to the preceding one. The code always runs at least one time. When the code reaches the Loop Until line, it checks to see whether the condition is True. If the condition is True, the code drops out of the loop. If the condition is False, the code loops back up to redo the code.

The second repetitive-looping construct is the For. . .Next statement.

The For. . .Next statement

For. . .Next is a shortcut method for the Do. . .Loop construct. You can use For. . .Next when you want to repeat a statement for a set number of times. The Step clause followed by an increment lets you process the loop in a nonsingle step amount. For example, if start number was 1 and end number was 100 and you wanted to increment the counter by 10 each time you would use Step 10. Though the loop would only be executed 10 times (or is it 11?) the value of the counter would be 1, 11, 21, and so on, instead of 1, 2, 3, and so on.

Following is the general syntax of the For. . .Next statement:

```
For counter variable name  = start number  To end number
[Step increment]
code statements begin here and continue to Next If condition code
[Exit For]
End If code can continue here after the Exit for
Next [counter]
```

You can code the Print_Reports_Print2 procedure by using the For. . .Next construct. In Figure 34-14, notice that the For. . .Next statements replace the Do While. . .Loop statements of the Print_Reports_Print3 procedure. Notice also that the statement Counter = Counter + 1 is omitted.

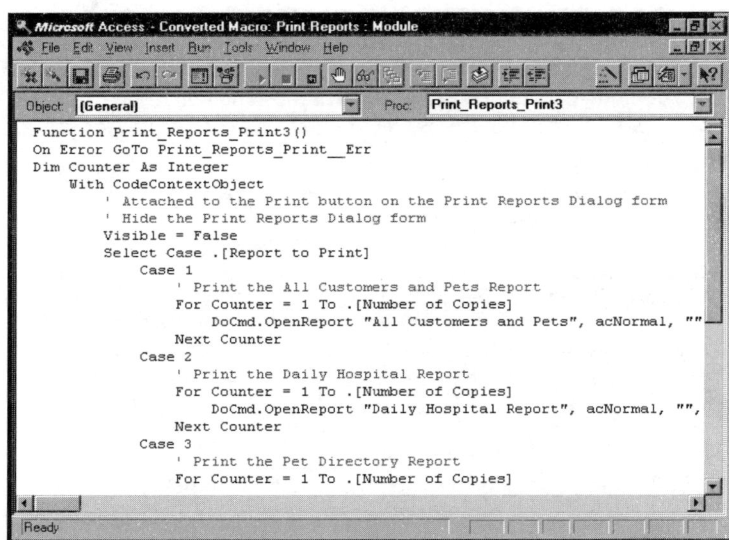

Figure 34-14: Using the For. . .Next loop.

At the start of the For. . .Next loop, the program initializes Counter to 1; then it moves on and executes the DoCmd statement. Whenever the program encounters the Next statement, it automatically increments Counter by 1 and returns to the For statement. The program compares the value of Counter with the value in the Number of Copies control. If the test is True, the DoCmd executes again; otherwise, the program exits the loop.

Whenever you write your own procedures, it is a good idea to plan for any error conditions that may occur when your procedure runs.

Planning for Runtime Errors

If an error occurs when you run a procedure, Access displays an error message and stops executing the program. When the procedure terminates, your application can end up in a state of flux, depending on the nature of the error.

Chapter 33 covered compiling procedures to make sure that the syntax of your code is correct. Running the procedure yourself to make sure that it does what you expect it to is good practice. Even though the syntax of your procedure may be exactly right, you may have omitted a necessary statement or misnamed a reference to some control on your form.

Even though you may have tested and retested the procedures in your application, things still can go wrong. Reports and forms can be deleted, and tables can become corrupted. When you write your procedures, you cannot alleviate situations like these. You can, however, provide a means of recovering from errors gracefully.

The Print_Reports_Close procedure, illustrated in Figure 34-15, closes the Print Reports dialog box. If the Print Reports dialog box is missing when the procedure runs, an error occurs. The On Error statement at the top of the procedure provides a way to recover from errors.

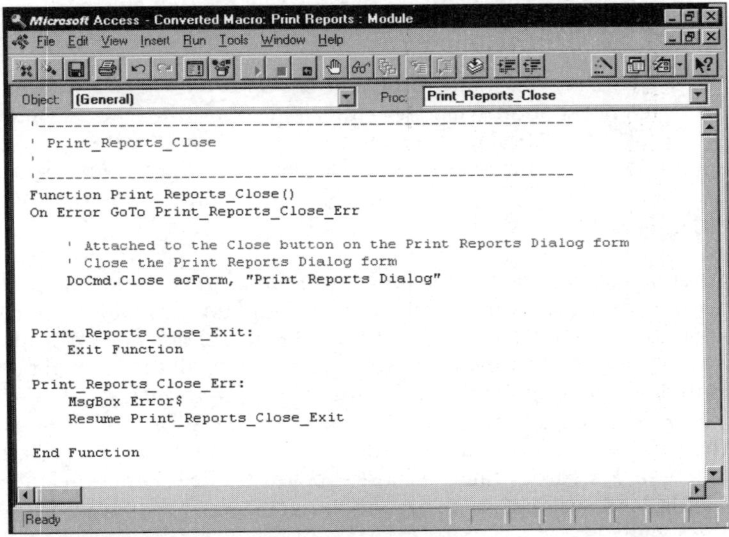

Figure 34-15: Planning for runtime errors.

Adding an On Error subroutine to a procedure

If any error occurs when you run your procedure, and you did not include an On Error statement, Access displays a message and stops running the procedure. Adding an On Error statement to a procedure allows the procedure to keep running even if an error occurs.

Following is the syntax for the On Error statements:

```
On Error GoTo labelname
On Error Resume Next
```

Using the On Error GoTo statement signals Access that you want it to perform some special instructions if an error occurs anywhere in the procedure. The GoTo *labelname* clause tells Access where to look for the special instructions. You replace the keyword *labelname* with a label name.

On Error Resume Next tells Access that you want to ignore the error and go on to the next statemment. This can be dangerous if the statement that gets ignored because of an error contained an important instruction like to multiply two numbers. With the calculation not performed, all sorts of things can begin to go wrong. You should only use On Error Resume Next in procedures where this can't happen.

A label name is used to identify a special section of code somewhere in your procedure. A label name can be any combination of characters that start with a letter and end with a colon. In Figure 34-15, earlier in this chapter, the On Error statement for the Print_Reports_Close function points to the line label Print_Reports_Close_Err. At the bottom of the function, you see Print_Reports_Close_Err:. If an error occurs when Print_Reports_Close runs, Access looks for the section of code that starts with Print_Reports_Close_Err: and executes the statements that follow.

The lines of code that follow a label name are called a *subroutine*. A subroutine is like a procedure within a procedure. The commands in a subroutine can be executed multiple times by the sub or function that contains the commands; or they may not execute at all, depending on the purpose of the error-handling routine. An error-handling subroutine, such as Print_Reports_Close_Err, runs only if an error occurs in the Print_Reports_Close function.

You can add subroutines anywhere in your procedure. Usually, you add subroutines to the bottom of your procedure, somewhere after the Exit Sub (or Exit Function) statement and before the End Sub (or End Function). Be careful of where you add subroutines to your procedure, however, because Access runs all the lines of code in your procedure until it reaches an Exit or End statement. Even though you have labeled a section of code, Access skips line labels and runs the subroutine's lines of code as though they are part of the main procedure. In the example in Figure 34-15, the Print_Reports_Close_Err subroutine was added below the Exit Function statement because the subroutine is to run only if an error occurs.

A subroutine can branch to another subroutine within a procedure. Notice that the Print_Reports_Close_Err subroutine calls the Print_Reports_Close_Exit subroutine, using the Resume command. The Print_Reports_Close_Exit subroutine simply exits the function.

The Resume command tells Access to exit the error subroutine and continue running the code in the main procedure. You must tell Access when to end an error-handling subroutine by using a Resume statement or an Exit Sub (or Exit Function) statement. If you do not end your subroutine appropriately, Access assumes that any statements in the rest of the procedure are part of the subroutine and continues running the lines of code in the procedure until it reaches the End statement. If Access encounters an End Sub (or End Function) statement during an error-handling subroutine, an error occurs.

In the Print_Reports_Close function, the Print_ Reports_Close_Exit subroutine contains the Exit Function statement. If no error occurs when the procedure runs, Access automatically runs the Print_Reports_Close_Exit subroutine and exits the function. If an error occurs, Access runs the Print_Reports_Close_Err subroutine and then branches to Print_Reports_Close_Exit.

Including only one Exit statement in your procedure is good programming practice. Instead of branching to another subroutine, you could just as easily have added the statement Exit Function to Print_Reports_Close_Err. By using a subroutine to exit the function, you can exit from anywhere in the procedure without inserting multiple Exit statements.

In addition to providing a means of recovering from runtime errors, you may want to notify the user that an error occurred.

Displaying meaningful runtime error messages

Even though recovery from most errors that occur in your application is possible, it is important to notify the user any time an error occurs. That way, if what the user sees next on-screen seems to be abnormal, he or she has some idea why. If an error occurs in retrieving data from a table, for example, and the next screen displays empty controls, the error message alerts the user that something has gone wrong with the application.

When you notify the user that an error has occurred, you also should supply an appropriate message that gives the user some idea what the problem is. You can determine the cause of any error condition by using the built-in error-trapping mechanism in Access. Access has a code and message assigned for any possible error situation that could occur. You can retrieve this information to display a meaningful message in a message box.

To retrieve the message for an error, use the Err.Description command. As shown in Figure 34-16, the error subroutine for the Find_Next_Click sub uses the Msgbox command to display a message box whenever an error occurs in the procedure. The Err.Description command tells the message box to retrieve and display the text of the error.

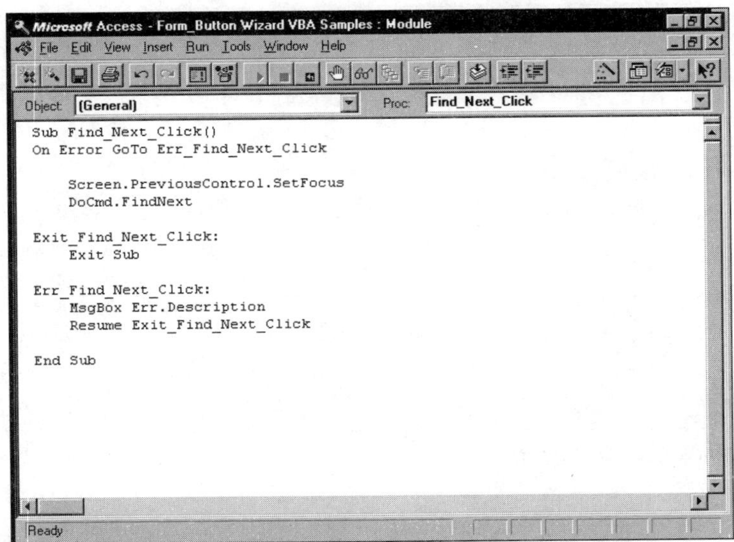

Figure 34-16: Displaying a runtime error message.

Note In previous versions of Access, the Error$ statement returned the description for an error code. VBA includes Error$ so that Access 95 can be compatible with code from earlier versions of Access. Even though Error$ is a valid command, you should use Err.Description in any new procedures that you write.

Sometimes, for certain error conditions, you may want to display your own message text instead of using the messages built into Access.

Trapping for specific error codes

Even though Access supplies a complete set of generic message codes and descriptions, you sometimes want to be even more specific about the error condition. You can test for a specific error code and then display your own message whenever that error occurs. For other errors, you may want to use the generic message descriptions.

In Figure 34-17, the RoundIt_Err subroutine first checks the value of the error code. For Error Code 13, a more meaningful message than the generic message `Type mismatch` appears. For any error code other than 13, the Err.Description command displays the generic message text.

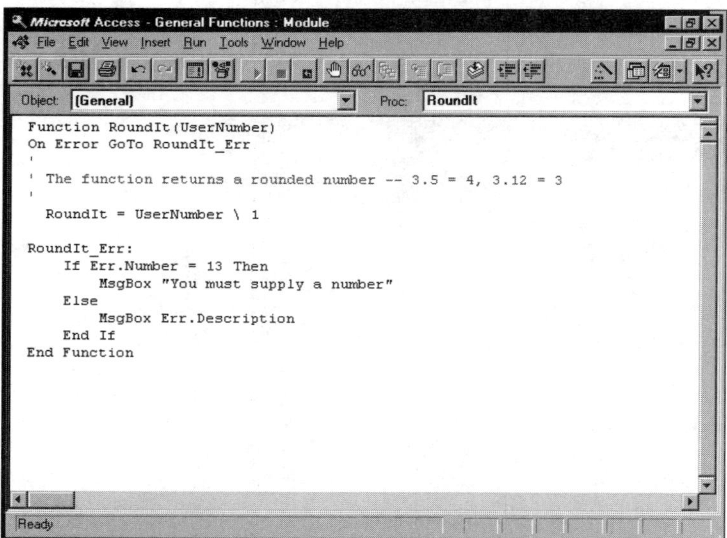

Figure 34-17: Trapping a specific error.

One of the most common features you will want to provide in your applications is the capability to locate data quickly. Having multiple ways to search for a specific record quickly is important and productive.

Filtering Records in Procedures

You can create intelligent search dialog boxes to locate and display or print records, using different search types. In this section, you learn how you can use VBA code to locate and display or print a specific record or a set of records, using search criteria.

Displaying a dialog box for selecting a record

You can add a Find button to the Customers form to display the Search for Customer dialog box, shown in Figure 34-18. This dialog box provides two ways of searching for a customer. Each method displays a list of customers. The contents of the list box change, depending on the type of search that you select. When you select a customer in the list box (by clicking an entry in the list box and then clicking the OK button, or by double-clicking an entry in the list box), the Search for Customer dialog box closes, and the Customers form displays the selected customer record.

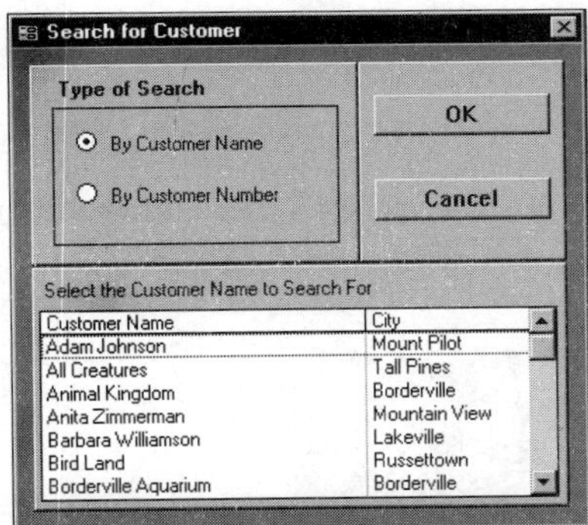

Figure 34-18: Searching for a customer.

Refreshing the items for a list box

This form uses an option group that contains two option buttons, a list box, and two command buttons. The secret to changing the contents of the list box is manipulating its Row Source property each time you click on an option button. When you click on one of the option buttons, a simple procedure updates the contents of the list box at the bottom of the form.

The bottom rectangle of the form is a list box. When you click on an option button in the Type of Search option group, the list box displays the customer list, using a different set of fields and in different order.

Figure 34-19 illustrates Design view for the dialog box, showing the properties for the By Search Type list box. The Row Source property is a select query instead of a table. You can build a select query by using the standard query screen. When you select the Row Source property and click on the ellipsis button (. . .), the SQL statement translates back to its query equivalent, and the query design screen appears.

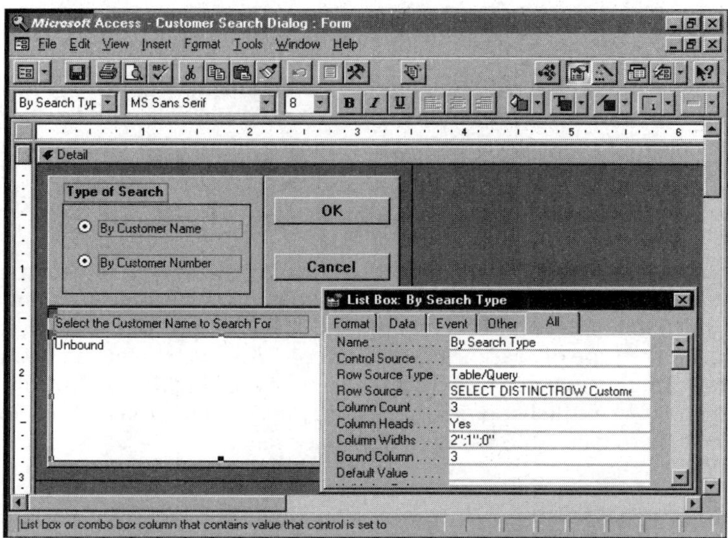

Figure 34-19: Designing a list box for search criteria.

Figure 34-20 shows the Query Builder window for the By Search Type list box default query.

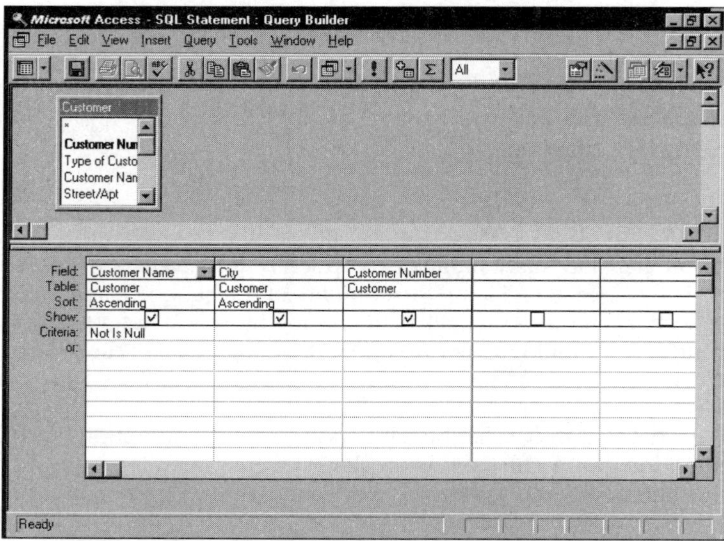

Figure 34-20: Using the Query Builder to generate an SQL statement.

Tip

Notice in Figure 34-19 that the Bound Column property is set to 3 and that the list box displays only two columns. The third column is the Customer Number field. The Customer Number is used in the search procedure. Even though the Customer Number is not visible in the dialog box, you can access its value along with the other visible fields in the selected list box row.

If you want to view the SQL statement that Access creates for you, choose View ➪ SQL in the Query Builder window. The SQL statement window, shown in Figure 34-21, appears when you choose View ➪ SQL.

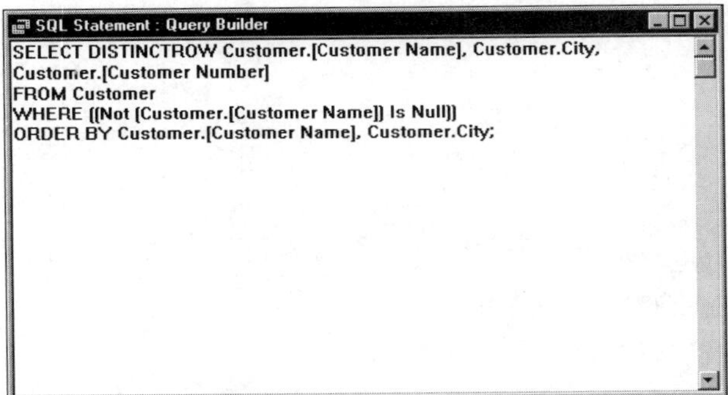

Figure 34-21: Viewing the SQL statement for a query.

The Type of Search option group has an associated After Update event procedure that changes the Row Source query each time the option button changes. Figure 34-22 shows the Type_of_Search_AfterUpdate procedure.

The Type_of_Search_AfterUpdate procedure displays the Customer Name and City fields when the By Customer Name option button (Type of Search.Value = 1) is selected. The By Customer Number option (Type of Search.Value = 2) displays the Customer fields Customer Number and Customer Name in the list box, in Customer Number order. The procedure sets the Row Source property to the appropriate select query for each Type of Search option.

Tip

One secret to this method of updating the contents of the list box is to initially set the Row Source property to Null. Because Access reruns the query as you specify each property setting, the Row Source property must be set to Null; otherwise, the query is run as each property is changed. This method speeds the query by preventing Access from unnecessarily retrieving the query results for each property setting in the procedure.

Another way to make the list box display itself faster is to store the queries as actual queries. You can create and name the queries by using the Queries tab of the Database window. Instead of typing the SQL statement in the procedure, you set the Row Source property to the query name. This method runs the query 10 percent to 40 percent faster.

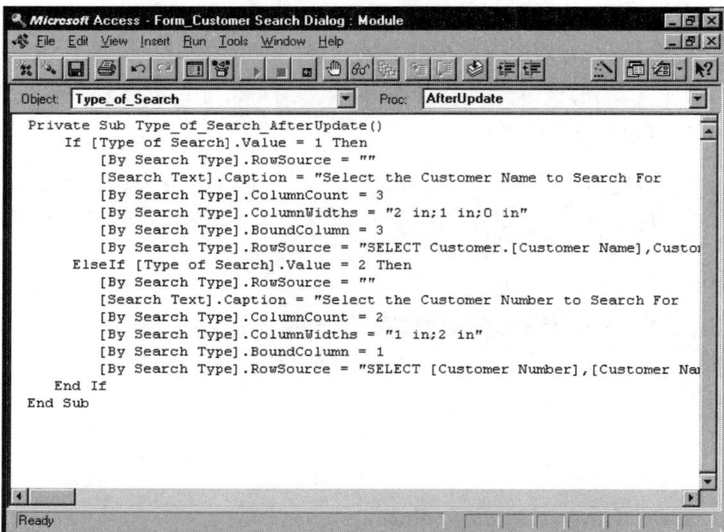

Figure 34-22: Updating the properties of a list box.

Finding the selected record

The OK command button in the Customer Search dialog box runs a simple VBA program that locates the record that you selected in the list box and displays the record in the associated form. Figure 34-23 shows the OK_Click procedure for the OK button.

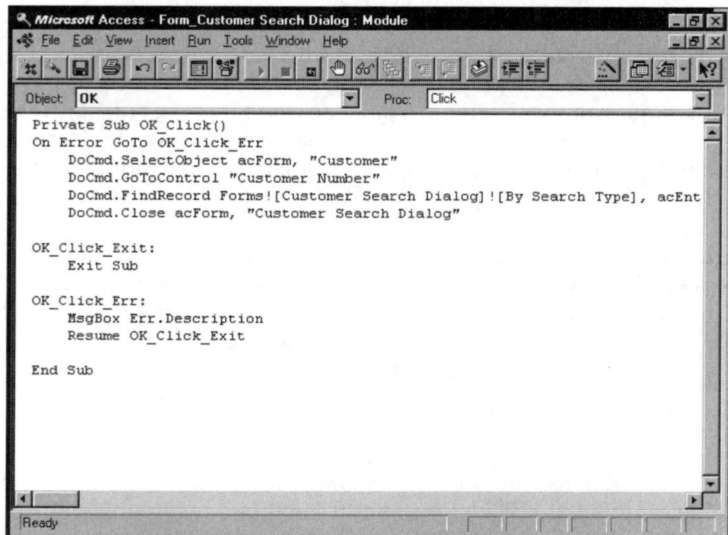

Figure 34-23: Using a VBA program to find a record.

The OK_Click procedure uses the FindRecord action to locate a record. The FindRecord action works just like the Find command (Edit menu), and its arguments are the same as the fields in the Find dialog box. Table 34-4 lists the argument settings for the FindRecord action.

Table 34-4
Using the FindRecord Action

Argument	*Setting*	*Description*
Find What	Forms![Customer Search Dialog]![By Search Type]	The selected row in the By Search Type list box
Where	acEntire	Match whole field
Match Case	False	Case-insensitive
Direction	acDown	Search forward in the table
Search As Formatted	False	Search for data as it is stored in the database
Search In	acCurrent	Search in the current field (Customer Number)

Before running the FindRecord action, you must set the focus to the field to be searched. The SelectObject action — the first statement in the procedure — sets the focus to the Customer form. After you set the focus to the appropriate form, you need to set the focus to the appropriate control. The GoToControl action sets the focus to a control. The second statement in the procedure sets the focus to the Customer Number field. The key field in your form is always the control to which you want to set focus before you run the FindRecord action.

Using *intelligent search* dialog boxes, you can easily provide your user a multitude of ways to search for a record. You can have as many intelligent search dialog boxes in an application as you need, each dialog box working with a different form and a different set of tables and fields.

Another useful feature in professional applications is the capability to print reports quickly and easily, without having to sit in front of a computer and select one report after another. You can create an intelligent Print dialog box to print reports, envelopes, and mailing labels for one record or for a set of records.

Selecting a set of records to print

You can add a Print button to a form to display the Print dialog box, shown in Figure 34-24. This Print dialog box can print up to three reports at the same time and also provides three methods of selecting the records to be printed. Different options for filtering records appear, depending on the type of criteria you select. When you click on the OK button, the Print dialog box closes, and the report or reports print for the selected customers.

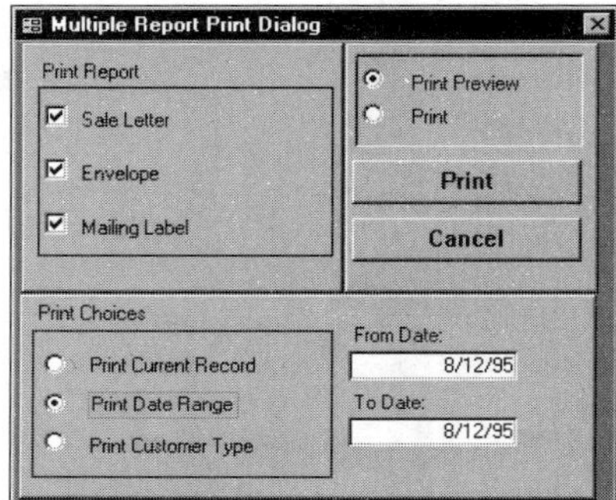

Figure 34-24: Selecting records to print.

This form uses a group of check boxes, two option groups, and two command buttons. You use the check boxes — named Sale Letter, Envelope, and Mailing Label — to select the report or reports to be printed. You can select one or more reports to print at the same time. The three reports are called Customer Sale Letter, Customer Envelope, and Customer Mailing Label. You can view the reports from the Database container.

Using VBA to display and hide controls

The Print Choices option group, named Print Criteria, runs a VBA procedure that displays and removes form controls, based on the selected option button. When the dialog box opens, the From Date, To Date, and Customer Type controls are hidden. Figure 34-25 shows the dialog box in Design view, showing the position of the Customer Type combo box.

The VBA procedure for the Print Choices option group is shown in Figure 34-26. When you select the Print Current Record option, the procedure hides the From Date, To Date, and Customer Type controls. The report or reports print only for the current record. When you select the Print Date Range option (Print Criteria = 2), the From Date and To Date text boxes appear. You then specify a beginning date and ending date to print all customers whose Last Visit Date falls between the two dates. When you select the Print Customer Type option (Print Criteria = 3), the Customer Type combo box appears, allowing you to print the selected reports for all customers whose Customer Type matches the type you selected. Notice that the procedure sets the Visible property for the controls to either True or False, which displays or hides them.

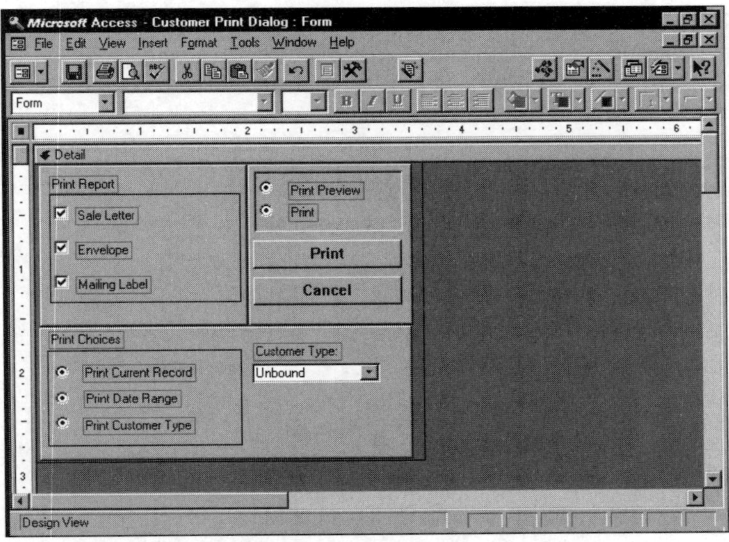

Figure 34-25: Displaying and hiding controls on a form.

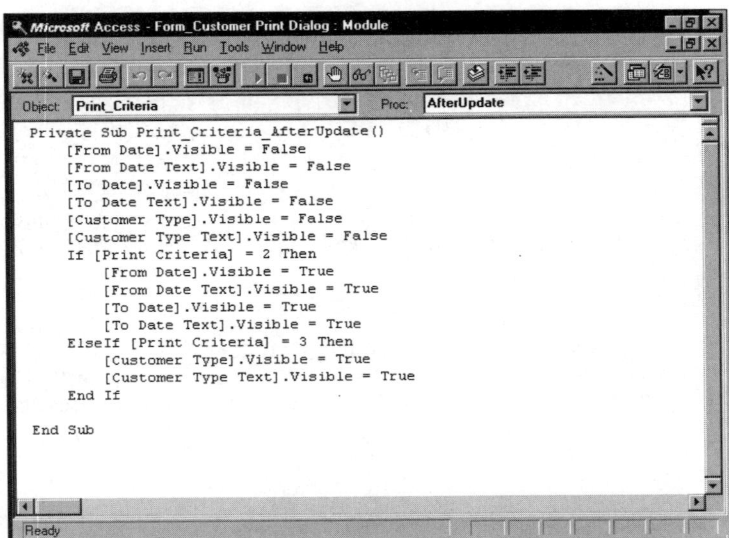

Figure 34-26: Using a procedure to display and hide controls on a form.

Printing records by using selection criteria

The Print command button in the dialog box runs the Print_Customers_Click procedure. Figure 34-27 shows the procedure, which is triggered by the command button's On Click event property.

```
Private Sub Print_Reports_Click()
   'Hide the Customer Multiple Report Print Dialog
    Forms![Customer Print Dialog].Visible = False
   ' Destination is Print Preview
    If Forms![Customer Print Dialog]![Type of Output] = 1 Then
        ReportDest = acPreview
    Else        ' Destination is printer
        ReportDest = acNormal
    End If
   ' Determine Print Criteria selected
    Select Case [Print Criteria]
        Case 1    ' Current Customer
           ' Print Sale Letter
            If Forms![Customer Print Dialog]![Sale Letter] = -1 Then
                DoCmd.OpenReport "Customer Sale Letter", ReportDest, ,
                "[Customer]![Customer Number]=Forms![Customer]![Customer
                Number]"
            End If
           ' Print Envelope
            If Forms![Customer Print Dialog]![Envelope] = -1 Then
                DoCmd.OpenReport "Customer Envelope", ReportDest, ,
                "[Customer]![Customer Number]=Forms![Customer]![Customer
                Number]"
            End If
           ' Print Mailing Label
            If Forms![Customer Print Dialog]![Mailing Label] = -1 Then
                DoCmd.OpenReport "Customer Mailing Labels", ReportDest, ,
                "[Customer]![Customer Number]=Forms![Customer]![Customer
                Number]"
            End If
        Case 2      ' Date Range
            If Forms![Customer Print Dialog]![Sale Letter] = -1 Then
                DoCmd.OpenReport "Customer Sale Letter", ReportDest, ,
                "[Customer]![Last Visit Date] Between Forms![Customer
                Print Dialog]![From Date] and Forms![Customer Print
                Dialog]![To Date]"
            End If
           ' Print Envelope
            If Forms![Customer Print Dialog]![Envelope] = -1 Then
                DoCmd.OpenReport "Customer Envelope", ReportDest, ,
                "[Customer]![Last Visit Date] Between Forms![Customer
                Print Dialog]![From Date] and Forms![Customer Print
                Dialog]![To Date]"
            End If
```

(continued)

```
            ' Print Mailing Label
            If Forms![Customer Print Dialog]![Mailing Label] = -1 Then
                DoCmd.OpenReport "Customer Mailing Labels", ReportDest, ,
                "[Customer]![Last Visit Date] Between Forms![Customer
                Print Dialog]![From Date] and Forms![Customer Print
                Dialog]![To Date]"
            End If
        Case 3      ' Customer Type
            ' Print Sale Letter
            If Forms![Customer Print Dialog]![Sale Letter] = -1 Then
                DoCmd.OpenReport "Customer Sale Letter", ReportDest, ,
                "[Customer]![Type of Customer]=Forms![Customer Print
                Dialog]![Customer Type]"
            End If
            ' Print Envelope
            If Forms![Customer Print Dialog]![Envelope] = -1 Then
                DoCmd.OpenReport "Customer Envelope", ReportDest, ,
                "[Customer]![Type of Customer]=Forms![Customer Print
                Dialog]![Customer Type]"
            End If
            ' Print Mailing Label
            If Forms![Customer Print Dialog]![Mailing Label] = -1 Then
                DoCmd.OpenReport "Customer Mailing Labels", ReportDest, ,
                "[Customer]![Type of Customer]=Forms![Customer Print
                Dialog]![Customer Type]"
            End If
    End Select
End Sub
```

Figure 34-27: Opening a report by using a procedure.

Notice that the Print_Reports_Click procedure uses the Select Case structure to test the value of the Print Criteria option group. Each Case statement includes three sets of If. . .End If statements for testing which of the reports is selected. Separate If. . .End If statements were used instead of a single If. . .Else. . .End If structure, because you can select multiple reports to print.

Working with Combo-Box and List-Box Controls

You have seen in previous examples how combo boxes and list boxes provide an effective method of validating data entry in a form. These boxes can display a list of values that the user can choose so that the user does not have to memorize customer numbers, for example, or remember the spelling of a customer's name.

Figure 34-28 shows the Select a Pet combo box for the Add a New Visit Entry form. In the Mountain Animal Hospital database, the name of the form is Adding Visits for New Pets.

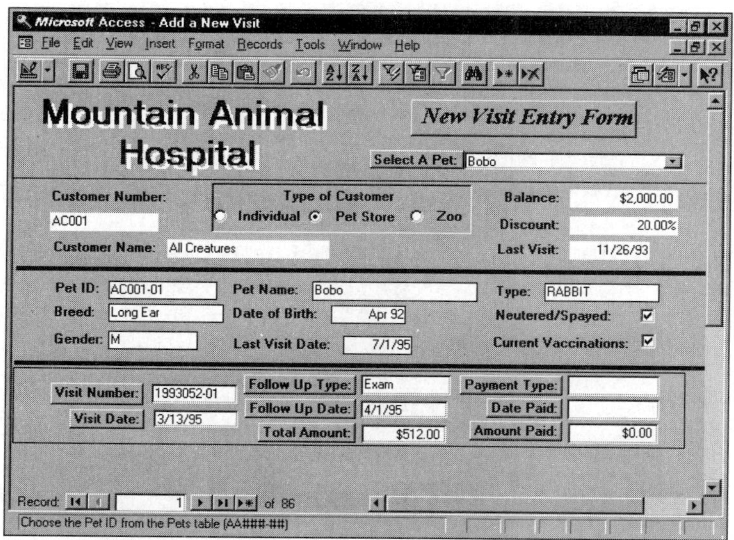

Figure 34-28: Using a combo box to validate data entry.

Handling a combo-box entry that is not in the list

As an option, you can set up a combo box to accept a value that is not in the list. Suppose that a customer brings in a new pet for a visit. The Select a Pet combo box in the New Visit Entry form displays only pets that have visited Mountain Animal Hospital before. Instead of making the user exit the New Visit Entry form and enter the new-patient pet in the Pets form, you can allow the user to type the name of the pet in the combo box. When the user types in the combo box a value that is not in the list of values, the Pets Data Entry form automatically appears. When the user completes the information for the pet and closes the Pets Data Entry form, the New Visit Entry form appears, and the combo box displays the pet in the list.

Entering in the combo box an item that is not in the list of valid values triggers the NotInList event. Figures 34-29 and 34-30 show the properties for the Select a Pet combo box. By connecting an event procedure to the NotInList event, you can override the normal `Not in list` error that is built into Access and allow the user to add the new value to the list. Notice that you also must set the LimitToList property to Yes.

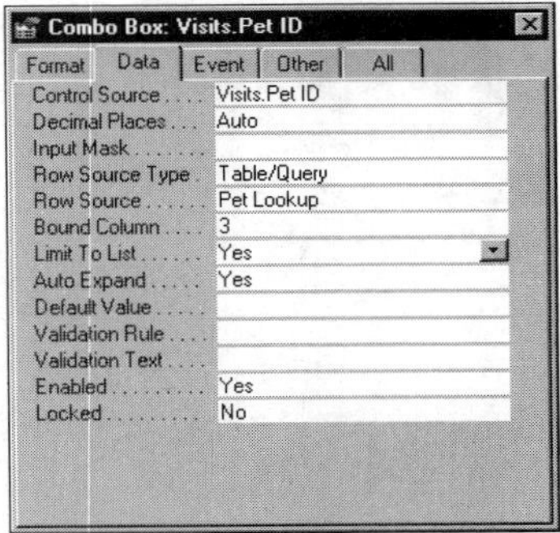

Figure 34-29: Limiting combo-box values to items in the list.

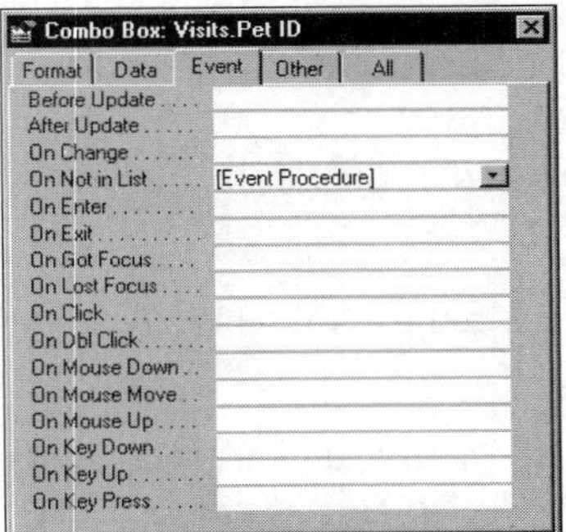

Figure 34-30: Handling combo-box values that are not in the list.

The LimitToList property determines how Access responds to entries that do not match any of the list items. When you set LimitToList to No, Access accepts anything that the user enters, as long as the entry conforms to the ValidationRule property, if one exists. When you set LimitToList to Yes and the user enters an invalid value, Access checks to see whether an event procedure exists for the NotInList event property. If no procedure is attached, Access displays the standard `Item Not In List` error message; otherwise, Access does not display the error message and runs the procedure instead. Figure 34-31 shows the NotInList procedure, called Visits_Pet_ID_NotInList, for the Select a Pet combo box.

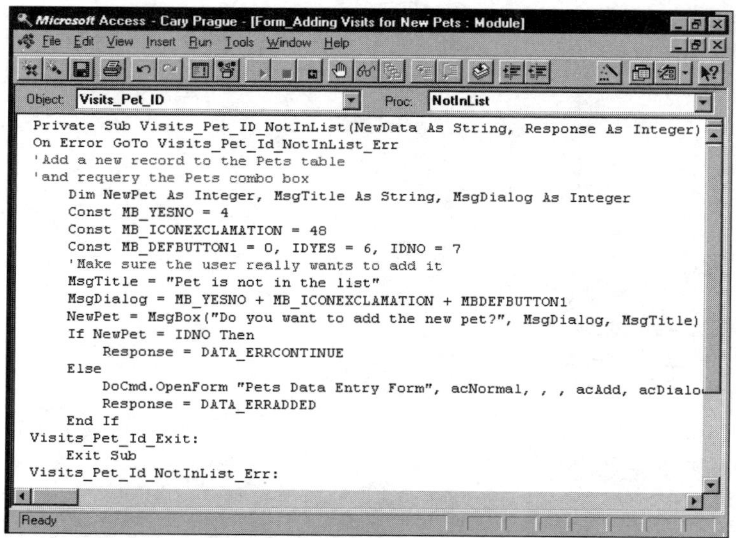

Figure 34-31: A procedure for combo-box values that are not in the list.

Warning Make sure that you change the Limit To List property in the combo box to No before using the On Not in List event

The Const declarations at the top of the Visits_Pet_ID_NotInList procedure are called symbolic constants. *Constants* are variables whose values do not change during execution of the procedure, and *symbolic constants* are names for certain constants. The constants used in this procedure are used as the arguments for the MsgBox function. Instead of using numbers such as 52 and 0 as the arguments, you can create a meaningful name that makes it easier to understand what your code is doing. Use all-uppercase characters to name symbolic constants.

Symbolic constants are names for certain values that are available anywhere in your VBA procedures. The actual values may be 0, 1, or 2, but providing a meaningful name makes it easier to understand what your code is doing. Symbolic constants are named using all uppercase.

This procedure first displays a confirmation message to make sure that the user really wants to add the new item. If the user chooses No (they do not want to add the item), the procedure ends. The user then must choose a valid item from the list. Before exiting a NotInList procedure, you must set the Response variable to one of three values. The Response variable tells Access what to do with the invalid item.

The three values for the Response variable are represented by symbolic constants. These symbolic constants are built into Access and are available to any of your VBA programs. The following table describes the three Response values:

Value	*Description*
DATA_ERRDISPLAY	Displays the standard error message and does not add the item to the list
DATA_ERRCONTINUE	Does not display the standard error message and does not add the item to the list
DATA_ERRADDED	Does not display the standard error message and reruns the query for the RecordSource

Tip If you use DATA_ERRCONTINUE or DATA_ERRADDED as Response values, you need to make sure that you display a message to the user at some point in your procedure. Otherwise, the user will not be able to leave the field and will not know why.

If the user does want to add the new item to the combo box, the Visits_Pet_ID_NotInList procedure displays a blank Pets Data Entry form. When the user closes the Pets Data Entry form, Visits_Pet_ID_NotInList sets the value for the Response variable before exiting. Setting Response to DATA_ERRADDED tells Access to query the list of items for the combo box again. When Access requeries the Select a Pet combo box list, it retrieves the newly added pet from the Pets table.

Handling MultiSelect list boxes

Sometimes, it makes sense for a field to have more than one value at a time. With MultiSelect list boxes, you can provide a list of values for a field and allow the user to select one or more items.

In the Pet Vaccinations List Box Example form, shown in Figure 34-32, you can select one or more vaccination types in the list box on the left. When you click the Add button, the selected items appear in the Current Vaccinations list box on the right. When you select one or more items in this list box and click on the Remove button, the selected items disappear from the Current Vaccinations list box.

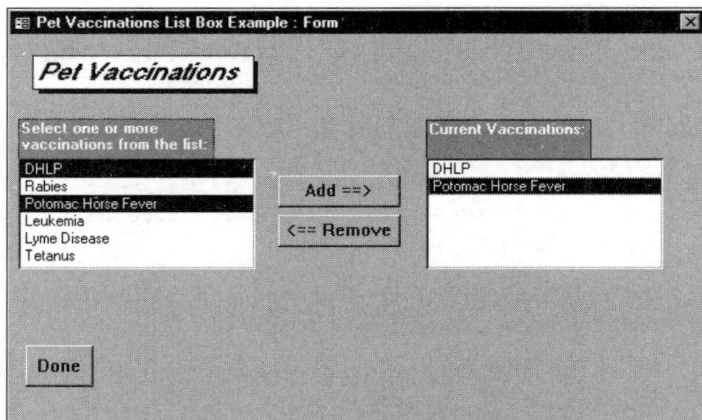

Figure 34-32: Making multiple selections in a list box.

You use the MultiSelect property of a list box to specify whether, and how, a user can make multiple selections in a list box. Figure 34-33 shows the properties of the Vaccinations list box for the Pet Vaccinations form. Notice that the MultiSelect property is set to Simple.

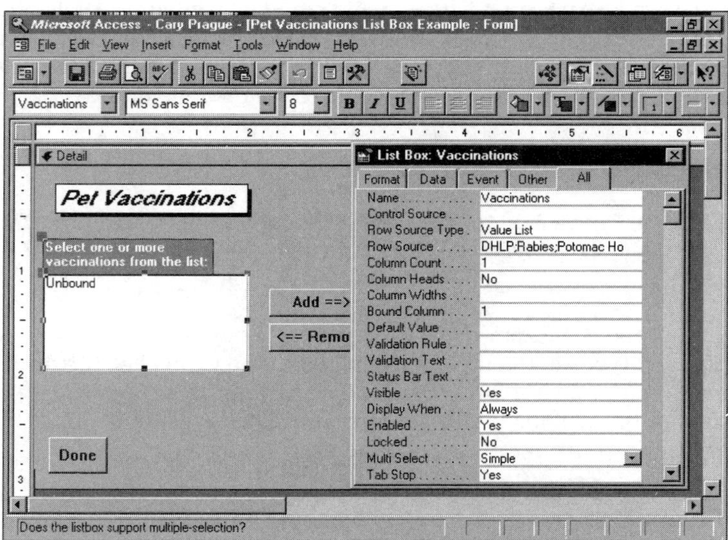

Figure 34-33: Setting the properties for a MultiSelect list box.

Setting MultiSelect to Simple or Extended allows the user to select multiple items. If you want to use the normal single-selection list box, set MultiSelect to None. The following table lists the MultiSelect property settings:

Setting	*Description*	*Visual Basic*
None	(Default) Multiple selection isn't allowed.	0
Extended	Shift+click or Shift+arrow key extends the selection from the previously selected item to the current item. Ctrl+click selects or deselects an item.	1
Simple	Multiple items are selected or deselected by clicking them with the mouse or pressing the spacebar.	2

The Add command button in the Pet Vaccinations form runs the Add_Button_Click procedure, shown in Figure 34-34. The procedure is triggered by the command button's On Click event.

```
Private Sub Add_Button_Click()
    Dim VaxListCounter As Integer, VaxCurrentCounter As Integer
    Dim VaxListItems As Integer, VaxCurrentItems As Integer
    Dim ListStr As String, FoundInList As Integer
    VaxListItems = [Vaccinations].ListCount - 1
    VaxCurrentItems = [Current Vaccinations].ListCount - 1
    For VaxListCounter = 0 To VaxListItems
        If [Vaccinations].Selected(VaxListCounter) = True Then
            If IsNull([Current Vaccinations].RowSource) Then
                ListStr = [Vaccinations].Column(0,
                 VaxListCounter) & ";"
                [Current Vaccinations].RowSource = ListStr
            Else
                FoundInList = False
                For VaxCurrentCounter = 0 To VaxCurrentItems
                    If [Current Vaccinations].Column(0,
                     VaxCurrentCounter) = [Vaccinations].Column(0,
                     VaxListCounter) Then
                        FoundInList = True
                    End If
                Next VaxCurrentCounter
                If Not FoundInList Then
                    ListStr = [Current Vaccinations].RowSource &
                     [Vaccinations].Column(0, VaxListCounter) &
                     ";"
                    [Current Vaccinations].RowSource = ""
                    [Current Vaccinations].RowSource = ListStr
                End If
            End If
        End If
    Next VaxListCounter
End Sub
```

Figure 34-34: Processing the selected items in a MultiSelect list box.

The Add_Button_Click procedure checks each item in the Vaccinations list box to see whether the item is selected. The list box's ListCount property tells you how many items are in the list. To refer to an individual item in the list, you refer to its numbered position in the list. The position numbers start at 0, so the first item is 0, the second is 1, and so on. An item is selected when its Selected property is True and unselected when the Selected property is False. To find out whether the first item in the Vaccinations list is selected, for example, you use the following statement:

```
If [Vaccinations].Selected(0) = True Then
```

The parentheses following the Selected property indicate which items in the list you are interrogating.

If a Vaccinations item is selected, the procedure copies it to the Current Vaccinations list box. If the item is already in the Current Vaccinations list box, however, it cannot be copied again. The OK_Button_Click procedure checks each item in the Current Vaccinations list to see whether it matches the selected item in the Vaccinations list. To refer to the items listed in a list box, you use the Column property. When you use the Column property, you supply a column number and a row number. Column numbers and row numbers also start at 0. The Current Vaccinations list box uses only one column (0). To refer to the second item in the Current Vaccinations list, you use the following syntax:

```
[Current Vaccinations].Column(0, 1)
```

If the selected Vaccinations item is in the Current Vaccinations list, the procedure does not add it to the Current Vaccinations list. The procedure loops back to the top and checks the next Vaccinations item.

If the selected Vaccinations item is not in the Current Vaccinations list, the procedure adds the item to the Current Vaccinations list box. To add an item to a list box, you concatenate it to the RowSource property. Because the RowSource property and the list box item are strings, you add them together, using the & operator. To delimit one list-box item from another, you also must add a semicolon (;) to the end of the string.

The Remove button on the Pet Vaccinations form runs the Remove_Button_Click procedure. The procedure is shown in Figure 34-35.

The Remove_Button_Click procedure removes items from the Current Vaccinations list box. Basically, the procedure adds all the unselected items to a string variable, ignoring any selected items; then it assigns the string variable to the RowSource property of the Current Vaccinations list box.

In previous chapters, you saw how to update data in a table by using a form. Using VBA and some special data-access tools built into Access, you can update data in a table that is not part of a form.

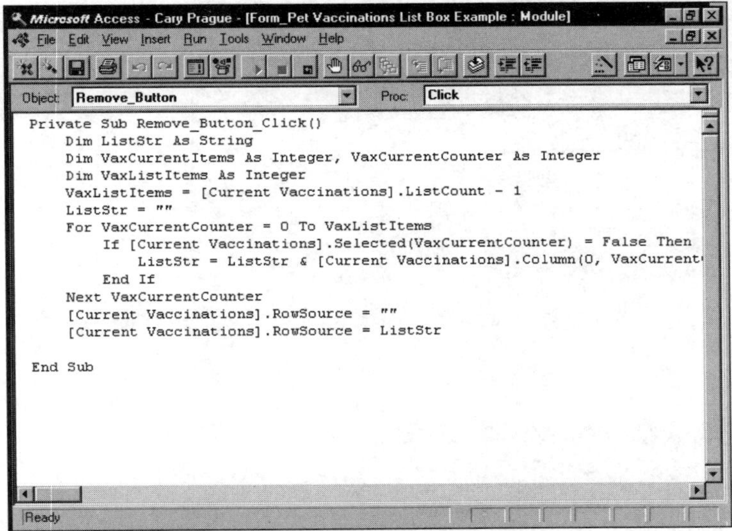

Figure 34-35: Removing items from a list box.

Creating Programs to Update a Table

Updating data in a table by using a form is easy; you simply place controls on the form for the fields of the table that you want to update. Figure 34-36 shows the Visit Information form. The name of the form for this example is Adding Visit Details and Updating Customer. The fields that you see on the form update the Pets, Customer, and Visits tables.

Sometimes, however, you want to update a field in a table that you do not want to display on the form. When information is entered in the Visit Information form, for example, the Last Visit Date field in the Customer table should be updated to reflect the most recent date on which the Customer visited the animal hospital. When you enter a new visit, the value for the Last Visit Date field is the value of the Visit Date field on the Visit Information form.

Because the Last Visit Date field can be derived from the Visit Date field, you do not want the user to have to enter it. Theoretically, you could place the Last Visit Date field as a calculated field that is updated after the user enters the Visit Date field. Displaying this field, however, could be confusing and really has nothing to do with the current visit.

The best way to handle updating the Last Visit Date field is to use a VBA procedure.

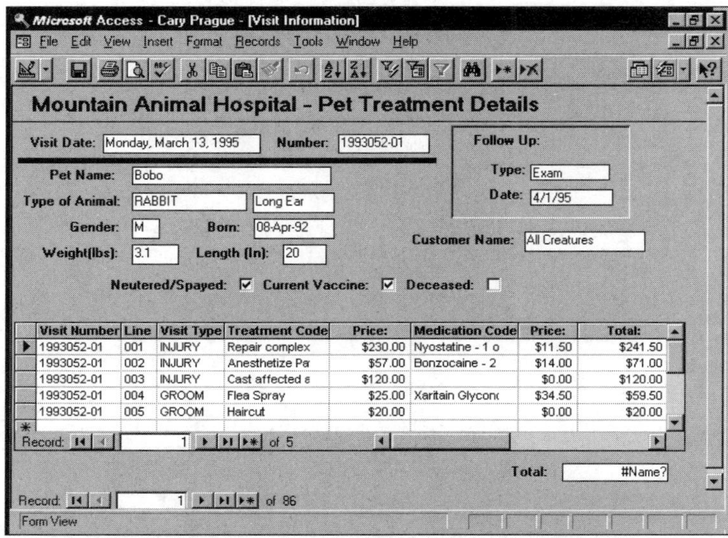

Figure 34-36: Using a form to update data in tables.

Updating a record

You can create a VBA procedure to update a field in a table. The AfterUpdate event for the Visit Information form runs a procedure to update the Customer table. The procedure is shown in Figure 34-37.

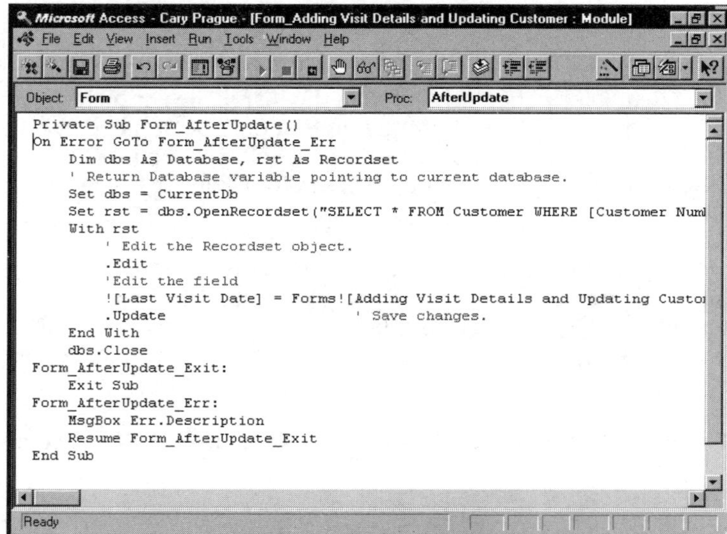

Figure 34-37: Using a procedure to update a table.

The Form_AfterUpdate procedure for the Visit Information form updates the Last Visit Date in the Customer table. This procedure uses special programming language to operate directly on a table in the Mountain Animal Hospital database.

The programming language used to access and manipulate the data in a database is called *Data Access Objects*, or DAO. When you update data by using a form, Access itself uses an entire system of programs, written in DAO, to access and update the database.

The system of DAO programs built into Access is called the Microsoft Jet database engine, or Jet. Jet, which stands between your application and the data on disk, manages data-access management, including querying, updating, data-type conversion, indexing, locking, validation, and transaction management.

As you can see in the Form_AfterUpdate procedure, you can write your own procedures to talk to Jet. When you write these procedures, you combine VBA code with methods and functions from DAO.

To use DAO to work with a table, you first declare DAO variables, using the Dim and Set statements. The Dim statement in this example declares DAO variables for the name of the database (dbs) and the recordset that the procedure wants to access (rst). A *recordset* is simply a set of records from a database table or the set of records that result from running a query. The Set statement assigns a value to a DAO variable. The variable dbs is assigned to the current database — Mountain Animal Hospital, in this example. You use CurrentDb to refer to the currently active database. You use the OpenRecordset function to tell Jet what recordset you want to work with.

When you use data access objects, you interact with data almost entirely by using Recordset objects. Recordset objects are composed of rows and columns, just like database tables.

The first argument for the OpenRecordset function is the table name, query name, or an SQL statement. In Chapter 27, you learned about writing SQL statements to retrieve data from a table. The example in this section uses an SQL statement to retrieve the Customer record for the customer referred to in the Visit Information form.

You can choose the type of Recordset object that you want to create by using the second argument of the OpenRecordset method. The following table describes the three types of Recordset objects:

Recordset Type	*Description*
Table-type Recordset	A representation, in code, of a base table that you can use to add, change, or delete records in a single database table.
Dynaset-type Recordset	The result of a query that can have updatable records. A dynaset-type Recordset is a dynamic set of records that can use to add, change, or delete records in an underlying database table or tables. A dynaset-type Recordset can contain fields from one or more tables in a database.
Snapshot-type Recordset	A static copy of a set of records that you can use to find data or generate reports. A snapshot-type Recordset can contain fields from one or more tables in a database but cannot be updated.

If you don't specify a type, the Microsoft Jet database engine attempts to create a table-type Recordset. The table recordset type usually is the fastest of the three types, because you are opening the table directly and don't require the overhead of filtering records. When the source for the Recordset is a query or SQL statement, as in the example, you cannot use the Table type. The Dynaset type makes the most efficient use of memory, because it loads only the unique key values from the table.

When the Recordset has been opened, you can begin working with the values in its rows and columns. The statements between the With and End With commands apply to the Rst object — the Recordset of data from the Customer table.

Before you can modify any of the data in a Recordset, you need to tell Jet ahead of time, using the DAO command Edit. The Edit command copies the current record to a buffer so you can change any of the fields in the record.

Before you enter the Edit command, however, you need to make sure you are in the record you want to edit. When a Recordset opens, the current record is the first record. Because the SQL statement in the example in this section is based on the table's unique key, you know that the first record in the Recordset is the only record.

To update a field in the current record of the Recordset, you simply assign a new value to the name of the field. In this example, you assign the value of the Visit Date field on the Visit Information form to the Last Visit Date field in the Recordset.

After you make the desired changes in the record, use DAO's Update method to save your changes. The Update method copies the data from the buffer to the Recordset, overwriting the original record.

Warning: If you edit a record and then perform any operation that moves to another record without first using Update, you lose your changes without warning. In addition, if you close a recordset or end the procedure that declares the recordset or the parent Database object, your edited record is discarded without warning.

The Close statement at the end of the Form_AfterUpdate procedure closes the Recordset. Closing recordsets when you finish using them is good practice.

You can use DAO to add a record to a table just as easily as you can update a record.

Adding a new record

To use DAO to add a new record to a table, you use the AddNew command. Figure 34-38 shows the procedure for adding a new customer to the Customer table.

```
Private Sub New_Customer_Click()
On Error GoTo New_Customer_Click_Err
    Dim dbs As Database, rst As Recordset
   ' Return Database variable pointing to current database.
    Set dbs = CurrentDb
    Set rst = dbs.OpenRecordset("Customer", dbOpenDynaset)
    With rst
        ' Add new record to end of Recordset object.
        .AddNew
        ![Customer Number] = "JN-001"
        ![Customer Name] = "Jacob Nottingham"    ' Add data.
        .Update                        ' Save changes.
End With
    dbs.Close
New_Customer_Click_Exit:
    Exit Sub
New_Customer_Click_Err:
    MsgBox Err.Description
    Resume New_Customer_Click_Exit
End Sub
```

Figure 34-38: Adding a new record to a table.

As you see in this example, using the AddNew method is very similar to using the Edit method. The AddNew method creates a buffer for a new record. After entering the AddNew command, you simply assign values to the fields. When you enter the Update command, the new record buffer is added to the end of the Recordset.

As you might imagine, you also can use DAO methods to delete a record.

Deleting a record

To remove a record from a table, you use the DAO method Delete. Figure 34-39 shows the procedure for deleting a record from the Customer table.

```
Private Sub Delete_Customer_Click()
On Error GoTo Delete_Customer_Click_Err
    Dim dbs As Database, rst As Recordset
   ' Return Database variable pointing to current database.
    Set dbs = CurrentDb
    Set rst = dbs.OpenRecordset("SELECT * FROM Customer WHERE [Customer
       Number] ='" & Forms![Adding Visit Details and Updating
       Customer]![Customer.Customer Number] & "'", dbOpenDynaset)
    With rst
       ' Delete the record.
        .Delete
    End With
    dbs.Close
Delete_Customer_Click_Exit:
    Exit Sub
Delete_Customer_Click_Err:
    MsgBox Err.Description
    Resume Delete_Customer_Click_Exit
End Sub
```

Figure 34-39: Deleting a record from a table.

Notice that you need to code only one statement to delete a record. You do not precede the Delete method with Edit or follow it with Update. As soon as the Delete method executes, the record is removed from the Recordset permanently.

Using DAO to manipulate data in your database can be very powerful. Figure 34-40 shows a more complex example of the capabilities of DAO. The Clone_Customer_Click procedure creates a new record from an existing record.

This procedure uses a record from the Customer table as a template to create a new Customer record. The procedure first copies the Customer record to a new table called New Customer. The New Customer table is created by using a query called Clone Customer. You create queries in your procedures by using the CreateQueryDef function. You define the SQL statement for the query by setting the SQL property to an SQL string. When you enter the Execute command, the new query is added to the Queries tab of the Database window.

The procedure opens a Recordset on the New Customer table to update the fields that will make it a unique row in the Customer table later. Finally, the procedure updates the SQL statement for the Clone Customer query to an SQL Insert command to copy the New Customer record to the Customer table.

```
Private Sub Clone_Customer_Click()
On Error GoTo Clone_Customer_Click_Err
    Dim dbs As Database, rst As Recordset, myQuery As QueryDef
   ' Return Database variable pointing to current database.
    Set dbs = CurrentDb
    Set myQuery = dbs.CreateQueryDef("Clone Customer")
    myQuery.SQL = "SELECT * INTO [New Customer] FROM Customer WHERE
        [Customer Number] ='" & Forms![Add a New Customer]![Customer
        Number] & "';"
    myQuery.Execute
    Set rst = dbs.OpenRecordset("SELECT * FROM [New Customer]",
        dbOpenDynaset)
    With rst
       ' Add new record to end of Recordset object.
        .Edit
        ![Customer Number] = "JN-001"
        ![Customer Name] = "Jacob Nottingham"   ' Add data.
        ![Phone Number] = "(413)555-3322"
        .Update                         ' Save changes.
    End With
    rst.Close
    myQuery.SQL = "INSERT INTO Customer SELECT [New Customer].* FROM [New
        Customer];"
    myQuery.Execute
    dbs.QueryDefs.Delete "Clone Customer"
    dbs.Close
Clone_Customer_Click_Exit:
    Exit Sub
Clone_Customer_Click_Err:
    MsgBox Err.Description
    Resume Clone_Customer_Click_Exit
End Sub
```

Figure 34-40: Cloning a record.

Summary

This chapter provided an in-depth explanation of programming in Access. You learned how to create procedures to select and update data by using VBA and DAO. The chapter covered the following topics:

- Modules are the principal objects of the VBA programming environment. Form-level modules contain the procedures that apply only to a specific form. Standard modules are available throughout the application.
- You use the Dim statement to declare a variable. Declaring variables makes your programs more bugproof.
- When you declare a variable, you also specify its data type. VBA data types are similar to Access field types.
- Conditional processing and repetitive looping allow your programs to execute code on the basis of certain conditions.
- By using the On Error statement, you can plan for runtime errors.
- You set the RowSource property in a procedure to change the contents of a list box on a form. The list box displays faster if you set the RowSource property to null before updating any of the other list-box properties.
- You set a control's Visible property in a procedure to display or hide the control.
- The LimitToList and NotInList properties of a combo box allow you to use a procedure to add an item to the combo-box list.
- You use the ListCount property in a procedure to count the number of items in a list box and the Selected property to see whether an item is selected.
- Using VBA and DAO, you can update data that is not displayed on an active form.

✦ ✦ ✦

Microsoft Access for Windows 95 Specifications

This appendix shows the limits of Microsoft Access databases, tables, queries, forms, reports, and macros.

Databases

Attribute	*Maximum*
MDB file size	1GB for Access for Windows 95, 2.0, and 1.1; 128MB for Access 1.0 (Because your database can include attached tables in multiple files, its total size is limited only by available storage capacity.)
Number of objects in a database	32,768
Number of characters in object names	64
Number of characters in a password	14
Number of characters in a user name or group name	20
Number of concurrent users	255

Tables	
Attribute	***Maximum***
Number of characters in a table name	64
Number of characters in a field name	64
Number of fields in a record or table	255
Table size	1GB
Number of characters in a Text field	255
Number of characters in a Memo field	65,535
Size of OLE object field	1GB
Number of indexes in a record or table	32
Number of fields in an index	10
Number of characters in a validation message	255
Number of characters in a table description	255
Number of characters in a field description	255

Queries	
Attribute	***Maximum***
Number of tables in a query	32
Number of fields in a dynaset	255
Dynaset size	1GB
Number of sorted fields in a query	10
Number of levels of nested queries	50

Forms and Reports

Attribute	*Maximum*
Number of characters in a label	2,048
Number of characters in a text box	65,535
Form or report width	22 inches (55.87 cm)
Section height	22 inches (55.87 cm)
Height of all sections plus section headers (Design view)	200 inches (508 cm)
Number of levels of nested forms or reports	3 (form-subform-subform)
Number of fields/expressions you can sort or group on (reports only)	10
Number of headers and footers in a report	1 report header/footer; 1 page header/footer; 10 group headers/footers
Number of printed pages in a report	65,536

Macros

Attribute	*Maximum*
Number of actions in a macro	999
Number of characters in a comment	255
Number of characters in an action argument	255

Mountain Animal Hospital Tables

The Mountain Animal Hospital Database file is made up of eight tables. There are four main tables and four lookup tables. The main tables are Customer, Pets, Visits, and Visit Details. The four lookup tables are States, Animals, Treatments, and Medications. This appendix displays a database diagram of all eight tables and the relations between them. Screen figures of each of the eight tables are shown in the Table Design window.

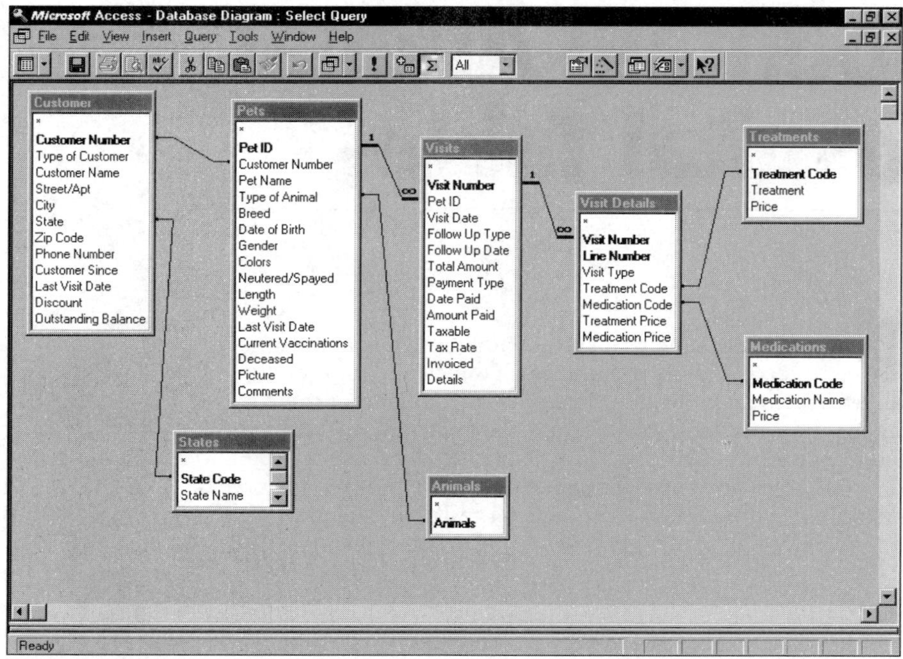

Figure B-1: The database diagram.

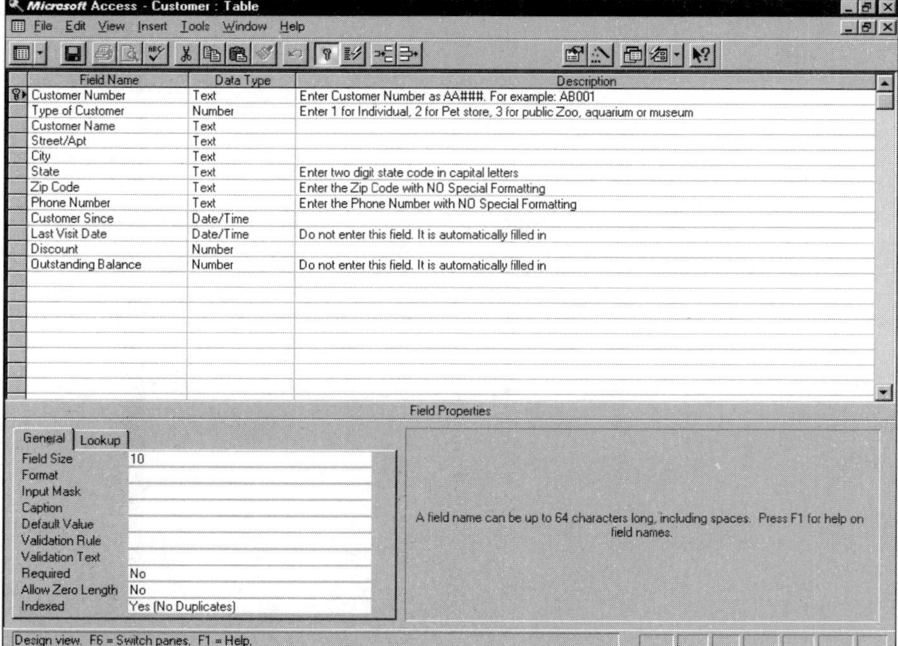

Figure B-2: The Customer Table.

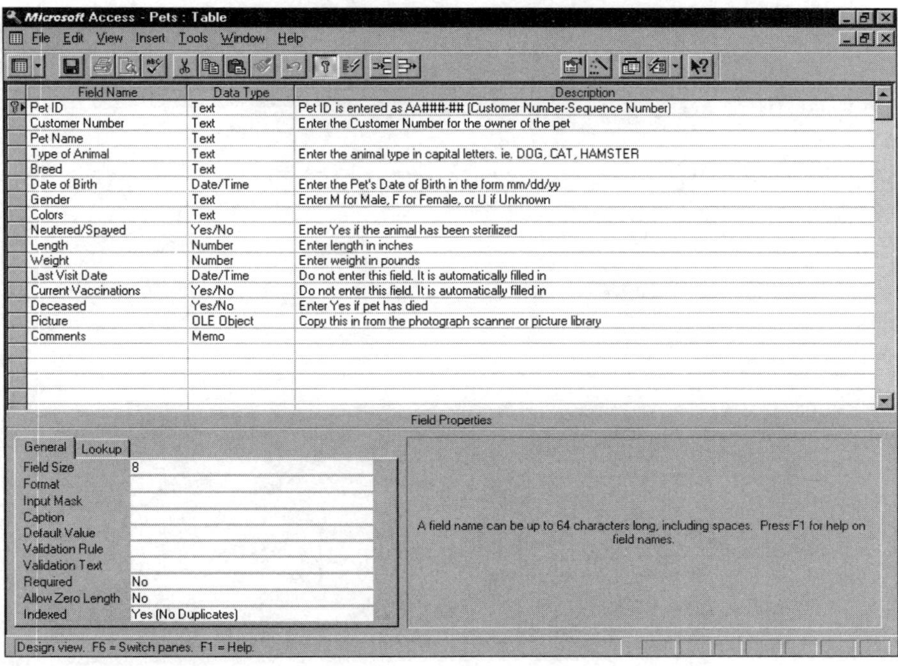

Figure B-3: The Pets Table.

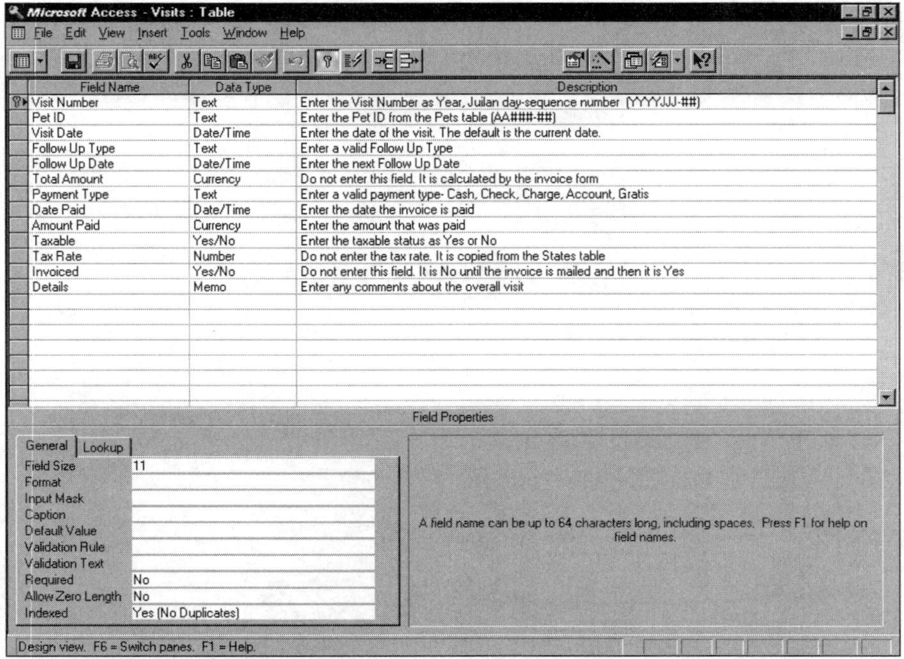

Figure B-4: The Visits Table.

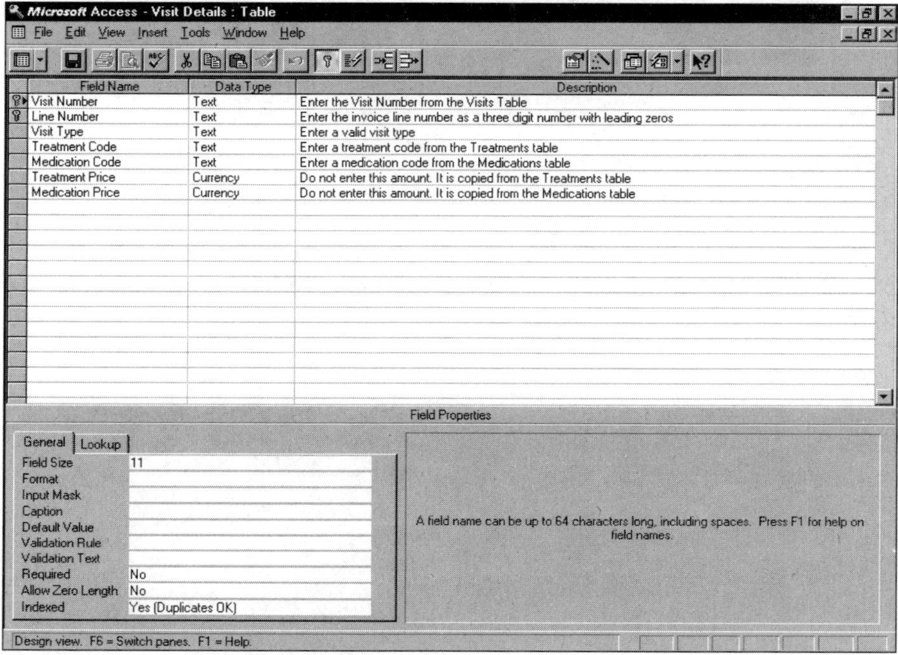

Figure B-5: The Visit Details Table.

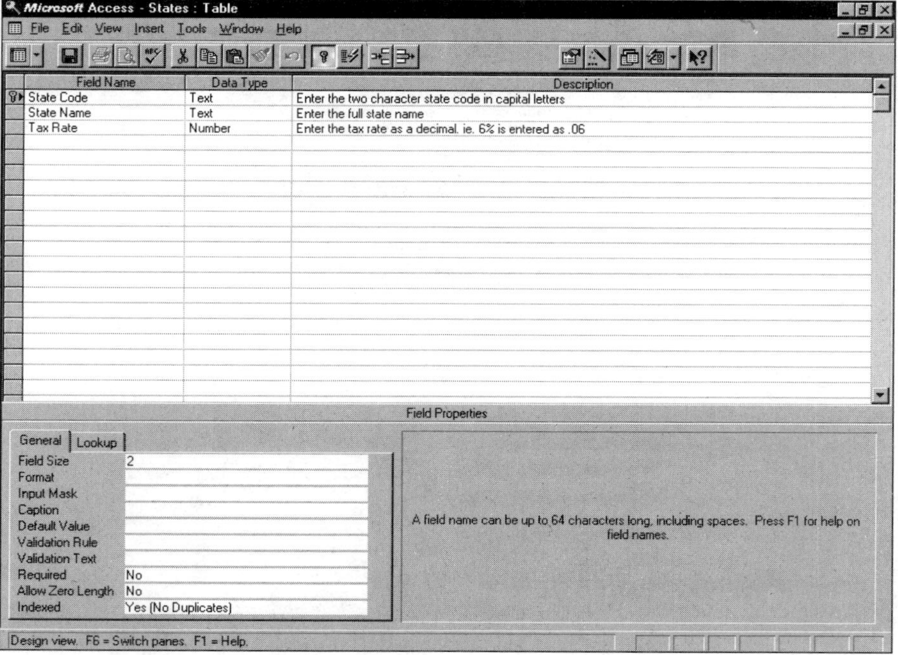

Figure B-6: The States Table.

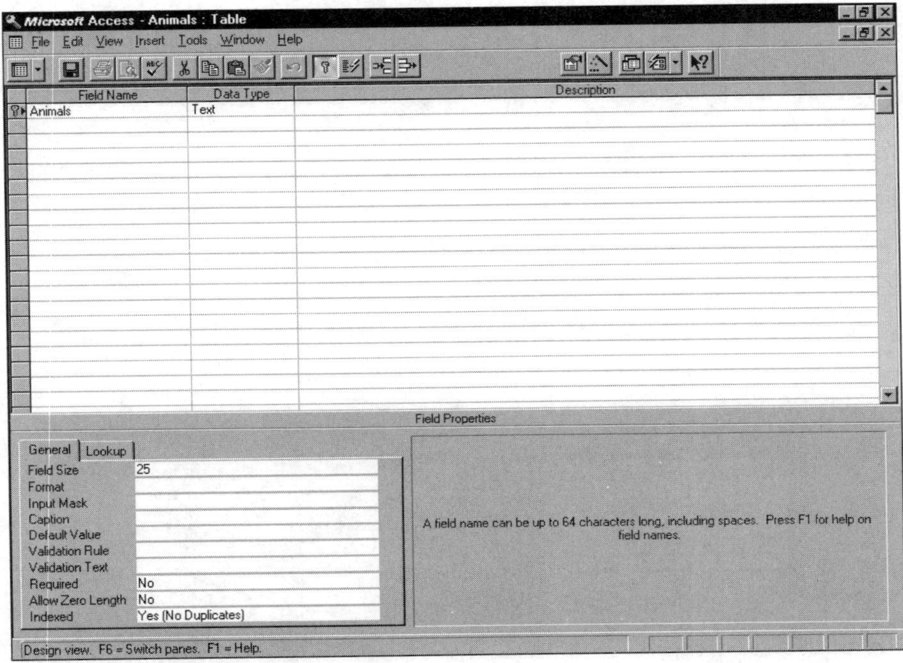

Figure B-7: The Animals Table.

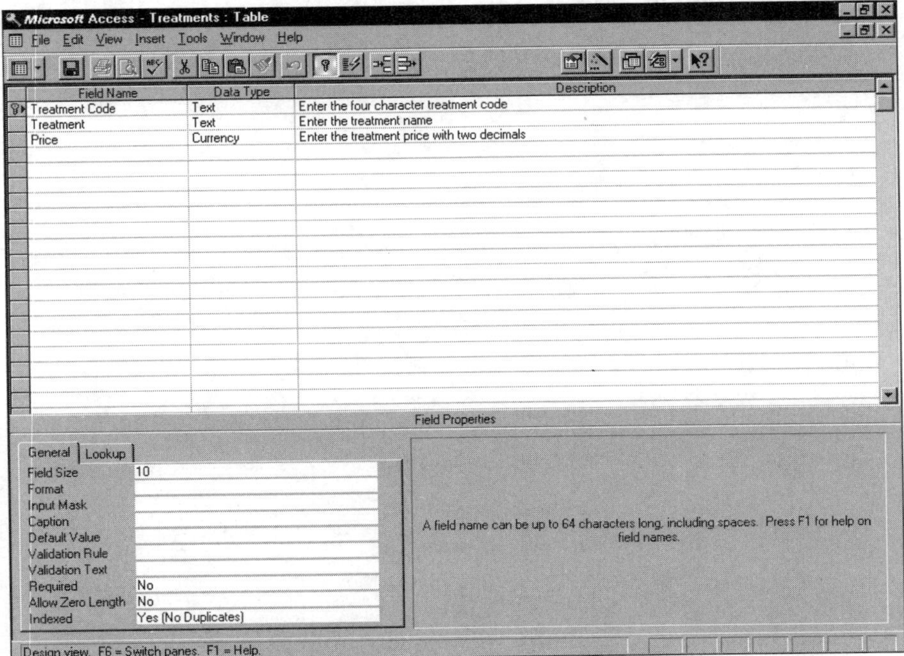

Figure B-8: The Treatments Table.

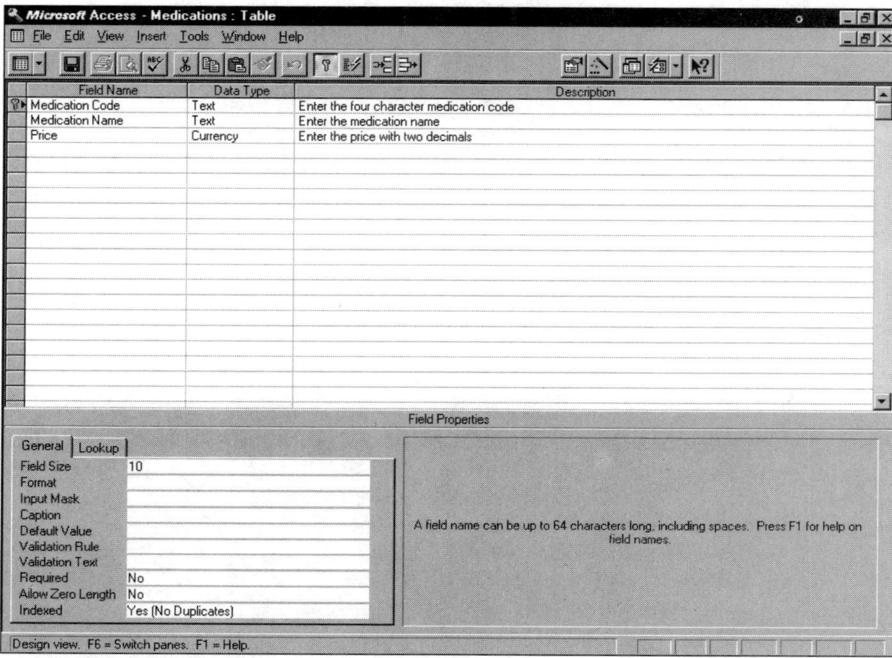

Figure B-9: The Medications Table.

Index

Symbols

A

(continued)

B

(continued)

C

D

E

(continued)

G

H

I

J

K

L

M

(continued)

N

O

P

(continued)

Q

(continued)

R

(continued)

S

T

(continued)

U

V

W

X

Y

Z

(continued)

Notes

Notes

Notes

Notes

Notes

Notes

Notes

Notes

The Fun & Easy Way™ to learn about computers and more!

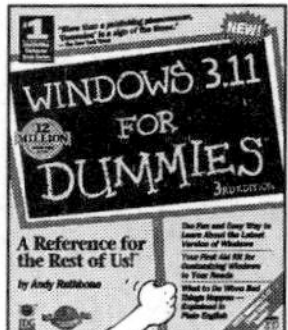

WINDOWS 3.11
FOR
DUMMIES
A Reference for the Rest of Us!

Windows® 3.11 For Dummies®, 3rd Edition
by Andy Rathbone
ISBN: 1-56884-370-4
$16.95 USA/
$22.95 Canada
SUPER STAR

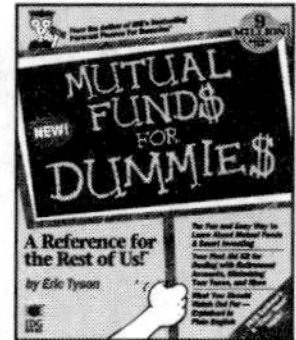

Mutual Funds For Dummies™
by Eric Tyson
ISBN: 1-56884-226-0
$16.99 USA/
$22.99 Canada
SUPER STAR

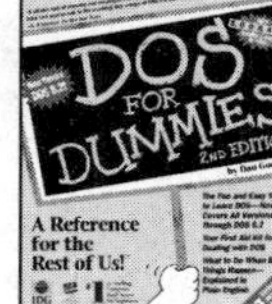

DOS
FOR
DUMMIES
2ND EDITION
A Reference for the Rest of Us!

DOS For Dummies®, 2nd Edition
by Dan Gookin
ISBN: 1-878058-75-4
$16.95 USA/
$22.95 Canada

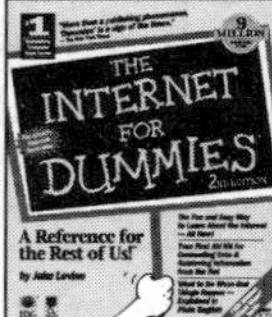

THE INTERNET
FOR
DUMMIES
A Reference for the Rest of Us!

The Internet For Dummies®, 2nd Edition
by John Levine & Carol Baroudi
ISBN: 1-56884-222-
$19.99 USA/
$26.99 Canada
VIII FINALIST

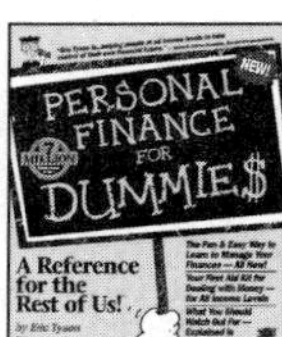

PERSONAL FINANCE
FOR
DUMMIE$
A Reference for the Rest of Us!

Personal Finance For Dummies™
by Eric Tyson
ISBN: 1-56884-150-7
$16.95 USA/
$22.95 Canada
SUPER STAR

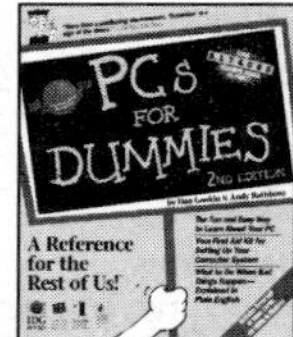

PCs
FOR
DUMMIES
A Reference for the Rest of Us!

PCs For Dummies®, 3rd Edition
by Dan Gookin & Andy Rathbone
ISBN: 1-56884-904-4
$16.99 USA/
$22.99 Canada
VIII FINALIST

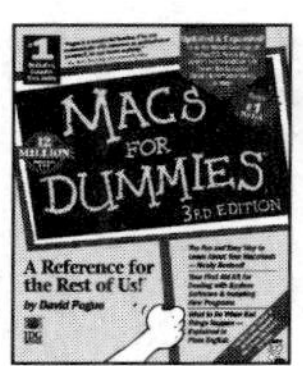

MACS
FOR
DUMMIES
3RD EDITION
A Reference for the Rest of Us!

Macs® For Dummies®, 3rd Edition
by David Pogue
ISBN: 1-56884-239-2
$19.99 USA/
$26.99 Canada
SUPER STAR

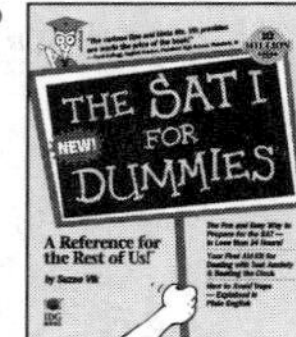

THE SAT I
FOR
DUMMIES
A Reference for the Rest of Us!

The SAT® I For Dummies™
by Suzee Vlk
ISBN: 1-56884-213-
$14.99 USA/
$20.99 Canada
SUPER ST

Here's a complete listing of IDG Books' *...For Dummies®* titles

Title	Author	ISBN	Price
DATABASE			
Access 2 For Dummies®	by Scott Palmer	ISBN: 1-56884-090-X	$19.95 USA/$26.95 Canada
Access Programming For Dummies®	by Rob Krumm	ISBN: 1-56884-091-8	$19.95 USA/$26.95 Canada
Approach 3 For Windows® For Dummies®	by Doug Lowe	ISBN: 1-56884-233-3	$19.99 USA/$26.99 Canada
dBASE For DOS For Dummies®	by Scott Palmer & Michael Stabler	ISBN: 1-56884-188-4	$19.95 USA/$26.95 Canada
dBASE For Windows® For Dummies®	by Scott Palmer	ISBN: 1-56884-179-5	$19.95 USA/$26.95 Canada
dBASE 5 For Windows® Programming For Dummies®	by Ted Coombs & Jason Coombs	ISBN: 1-56884-215-5	$19.99 USA/$26.99 Canada
FoxPro 2.6 For Windows® For Dummies®	by John Kaufeld	ISBN: 1-56884-187-6	$19.95 USA/$26.95 Canada
Paradox 5 For Windows® For Dummies®	by John Kaufeld	ISBN: 1-56884-185-X	$19.95 USA/$26.95 Canada
DESKTOP PUBLISHING/ILLUSTRATION/GRAPHICS			
CorelDRAW! 5 For Dummies®	by Deke McClelland	ISBN: 1-56884-157-4	$19.95 USA/$26.95 Canada
CorelDRAW! For Dummies®	by Deke McClelland	ISBN: 1-56884-042-X	$19.95 USA/$26.95 Canada
Desktop Publishing & Design For Dummies®	by Roger C. Parker	ISBN: 1-56884-234-1	$19.99 USA/$26.99 Canada
Harvard Graphics 2 For Windows® For Dummies®	by Roger C. Parker	ISBN: 1-56884-092-6	$19.95 USA/$26.95 Canada
PageMaker 5 For Macs® For Dummies®	by Galen Gruman & Deke McClelland	ISBN: 1-56884-178-7	$19.95 USA/$26.95 Canada
PageMaker 5 For Windows® For Dummies®	by Deke McClelland & Galen Gruman	ISBN: 1-56884-160-4	$19.95 USA/$26.95 Canada
Photoshop 3 For Macs® For Dummies®	by Deke McClelland	ISBN: 1-56884-208-2	$19.99 USA/$26.99 Canada
QuarkXPress 3.3 For Dummies®	by Galen Gruman & Barbara Assadi	ISBN: 1-56884-217-1	$19.99 USA/$26.99 Canada
FINANCE/PERSONAL FINANCE/TEST TAKING REFERENCE			
Everyday Math For Dummies™	by Charles Seiter	ISBN: 1-56884-248-1	$14.99 USA/$22.99 Canada
Personal Finance For Dummies™ For Canadians	by Eric Tyson & Tony Martin	ISBN: 1-56884-378-X	$18.99 USA/$24.99 Canada
QuickBooks 3 For Dummies®	by Stephen L. Nelson	ISBN: 1-56884-227-9	$19.99 USA/$26.99 Canada
Quicken 8 For DOS For Dummies®, 2nd Edition	by Stephen L. Nelson	ISBN: 1-56884-210-4	$19.95 USA/$26.95 Canada
Quicken 5 For Macs® For Dummies®	by Stephen L. Nelson	ISBN: 1-56884-211-2	$19.95 USA/$26.95 Canada
Quicken 4 For Windows® For Dummies®, 2nd Edition	by Stephen L. Nelson	ISBN: 1-56884-209-0	$19.95 USA/$26.95 Canada
Taxes For Dummies™, 1995 Edition	by Eric Tyson & David J. Silverman	ISBN: 1-56884-220-1	$14.99 USA/$20.99 Canada
The GMAT® For Dummies™	by Suzee Vlk, Series Editor	ISBN: 1-56884-376-3	$14.99 USA/$20.99 Canada
The GRE® For Dummies™	by Suzee Vlk, Series Editor	ISBN: 1-56884-375-5	$14.99 USA/$20.99 Canada
Time Management For Dummies™	by Jeffrey J. Mayer	ISBN: 1-56884-360-7	$16.99 USA/$22.99 Canada
TurboTax For Windows® For Dummies®	by Gail A. Helsel, CPA	ISBN: 1-56884-228-7	$19.99 USA/$26.99 Canada
GROUPWARE/INTEGRATED			
ClarisWorks For Macs® For Dummies®	by Frank Higgins	ISBN: 1-56884-363-1	$19.99 USA/$26.99 Canada
Lotus Notes For Dummies®	by Pat Freeland & Stephen Londergan	ISBN: 1-56884-212-0	$19.95 USA/$26.95 Canada
Microsoft® Office 4 For Windows® For Dummies®	by Roger C. Parker	ISBN: 1-56884-183-3	$19.95 USA/$26.95 Canada
Microsoft® Works 3 For Windows® For Dummies®	by David C. Kay	ISBN: 1-56884-214-7	$19.99 USA/$26.99 Canada
SmartSuite 3 For Dummies®	by Jan Weingarten & John Weingarten	ISBN: 1-56884-367-4	$19.99 USA/$26.99 Canada
INTERNET/COMMUNICATIONS/NETWORKING			
America Online® For Dummies®, 2nd Edition	by John Kaufeld	ISBN: 1-56884-933-8	$19.99 USA/$26.99 Canada
CompuServe For Dummies®, 2nd Edition	by Wallace Wang	ISBN: 1-56884-937-0	$19.99 USA/$26.99 Canada
Modems For Dummies®, 2nd Edition	by Tina Rathbone	ISBN: 1-56884-223-6	$19.99 USA/$26.99 Canada
MORE Internet For Dummies®	by John R. Levine & Margaret Levine Young	ISBN: 1-56884-164-7	$19.95 USA/$26.95 Canada
MORE Modems & On-line Services For Dummies®	by Tina Rathbone	ISBN: 1-56884-365-8	$19.99 USA/$26.99 Canada
Mosaic For Dummies®, Windows Edition	by David Angell & Brent Heslop	ISBN: 1-56884-242-2	$19.99 USA/$26.99 Canada
NetWare For Dummies®, 2nd Edition	by Ed Tittel, Deni Connor & Earl Follis	ISBN: 1-56884-369-0	$19.99 USA/$26.99 Canada
Networking For Dummies®	by Doug Lowe	ISBN: 1-56884-079-9	$19.95 USA/$26.95 Canada
PROCOMM PLUS 2 For Windows® For Dummies®	by Wallace Wang	ISBN: 1-56884-219-8	$19.99 USA/$26.99 Canada
TCP/IP For Dummies®	by Marshall Wilensky & Candace Leiden	ISBN: 1-56884-241-4	$19.99 USA/$26.99 Canada

For scholastic requests & educational orders please call Educational Sales at 1. 800. 434. 2086

FOR MORE INFO OR TO ORDER, PLEASE CALL ▸ 800 762 2974

For volume discounts & special orders please call Tony Real, Special Sales, at 415. 655. 3048

9/19/95

Title	Author	ISBN	Price
The Internet For Macs® For Dummies®, 2nd Edition	by Charles Seiter	ISBN: 1-56884-371-2	$19.99 USA/$26.99 Canada
The Internet For Macs® For Dummies® Starter Kit	by Charles Seiter	ISBN: 1-56884-244-9	$29.99 USA/$39.99 Canada
The Internet For Macs® For Dummies® Starter Kit Bestseller Edition	by Charles Seiter	ISBN: 1-56884-245-7	$39.99 USA/$54.99 Canada
The Internet For Windows® For Dummies® Starter Kit	by John R. Levine & Margaret Levine Young	ISBN: 1-56884-237-6	$34.99 USA/$44.99 Canada
The Internet For Windows® For Dummies® Starter Kit, Bestseller Edition	by John R. Levine & Margaret Levine Young	ISBN: 1-56884-246-5	$39.99 USA/$54.99 Canada

MACINTOSH

Title	Author	ISBN	Price
Mac® Programming For Dummies®	by Dan Parks Sydow	ISBN: 1-56884-173-6	$19.95 USA/$26.95 Canada
Macintosh® System 7.5 For Dummies®	by Bob LeVitus	ISBN: 1-56884-197-3	$19.95 USA/$26.95 Canada
MORE Macs® For Dummies®	by David Pogue	ISBN: 1-56884-087-X	$19.95 USA/$26.95 Canada
PageMaker 5 For Macs® For Dummies®	by Galen Gruman & Deke McClelland	ISBN: 1-56884-178-7	$19.95 USA/$26.95 Canada
QuarkXPress 3.3 For Dummies®	by Galen Gruman & Barbara Assadi	ISBN: 1-56884-217-1	$19.99 USA/$26.99 Canada
Upgrading and Fixing Macs® For Dummies®	by Kearney Rietmann & Frank Higgins	ISBN: 1-56884-189-2	$19.95 USA/$26.95 Canada

MULTIMEDIA

Title	Author	ISBN	Price
Multimedia & CD-ROMs For Dummies®, 2nd Edition	by Andy Rathbone	ISBN: 1-56884-907-9	$19.99 USA/$26.99 Canada
Multimedia & CD-ROMs For Dummies®, Interactive Multimedia Value Pack, 2nd Edition	by Andy Rathbone	ISBN: 1-56884-909-5	$29.99 USA/$39.99 Canada

OPERATING SYSTEMS:

DOS

Title	Author	ISBN	Price
MORE DOS For Dummies®	by Dan Gookin	ISBN: 1-56884-046-2	$19.95 USA/$26.95 Canada
OS/2® Warp For Dummies®, 2nd Edition	by Andy Rathbone	ISBN: 1-56884-205-8	$19.99 USA/$26.99 Canada

UNIX

Title	Author	ISBN	Price
MORE UNIX® For Dummies®	by John R. Levine & Margaret Levine Young	ISBN: 1-56884-361-5	$19.99 USA/$26.99 Canada
UNIX® For Dummies®	by John R. Levine & Margaret Levine Young	ISBN: 1-878058-58-4	$19.95 USA/$26.95 Canada

WINDOWS

Title	Author	ISBN	Price
MORE Windows® For Dummies®, 2nd Edition	by Andy Rathbone	ISBN: 1-56884-048-9	$19.95 USA/$26.95 Canada
Windows® 95 For Dummies®	by Andy Rathbone	ISBN: 1-56884-240-6	$19.99 USA/$26.99 Canada

PCS/HARDWARE

Title	Author	ISBN	Price
Illustrated Computer Dictionary For Dummies®, 2nd Edition	by Dan Gookin & Wallace Wang	ISBN: 1-56884-218-X	$12.95 USA/$16.95 Canada
Upgrading and Fixing PCs For Dummies®, 2nd Edition	by Andy Rathbone	ISBN: 1-56884-903-6	$19.99 USA/$26.99 Canada

PRESENTATION/AUTOCAD

Title	Author	ISBN	Price
AutoCAD For Dummies®	by Bud Smith	ISBN: 1-56884-191-4	$19.95 USA/$26.95 Canada
PowerPoint 4 For Windows® For Dummies®	by Doug Lowe	ISBN: 1-56884-161-2	$16.99 USA/$22.99 Canada

PROGRAMMING

Title	Author	ISBN	Price
Borland C++ For Dummies®	by Michael Hyman	ISBN: 1-56884-162-0	$19.95 USA/$26.95 Canada
C For Dummies®, Volume 1	by Dan Gookin	ISBN: 1-878058-78-9	$19.95 USA/$26.95 Canada
C++ For Dummies®	by Stephen R. Davis	ISBN: 1-56884-163-9	$19.95 USA/$26.95 Canada
Delphi Programming For Dummies®	by Neil Rubenking	ISBN: 1-56884-200-7	$19.99 USA/$26.99 Canada
Mac® Programming For Dummies®	by Dan Parks Sydow	ISBN: 1-56884-173-6	$19.95 USA/$26.95 Canada
PowerBuilder 4 Programming For Dummies®	by Ted Coombs & Jason Coombs	ISBN: 1-56884-325-9	$19.99 USA/$26.99 Canada
QBasic Programming For Dummies®	by Douglas Hergert	ISBN: 1-56884-093-4	$19.95 USA/$26.95 Canada
Visual Basic 3 For Dummies®	by Wallace Wang	ISBN: 1-56884-076-4	$19.95 USA/$26.95 Canada
Visual Basic "X" For Dummies®	by Wallace Wang	ISBN: 1-56884-230-9	$19.99 USA/$26.99 Canada
Visual C++ 2 For Dummies®	by Michael Hyman & Bob Arnson	ISBN: 1-56884-328-3	$19.99 USA/$26.99 Canada
Windows® 95 Programming For Dummies®	by S. Randy Davis	ISBN: 1-56884-327-5	$19.99 USA/$26.99 Canada

SPREADSHEET

Title	Author	ISBN	Price
1-2-3 For Dummies®	by Greg Harvey	ISBN: 1-878058-60-6	$16.95 USA/$22.95 Canada
1-2-3 For Windows® 5 For Dummies®, 2nd Edition	by John Walkenbach	ISBN: 1-56884-216-3	$16.95 USA/$22.95 Canada
Excel 5 For Macs® For Dummies®	by Greg Harvey	ISBN: 1-56884-186-8	$19.95 USA/$26.95 Canada
Excel For Dummies®, 2nd Edition	by Greg Harvey	ISBN: 1-56884-050-0	$16.95 USA/$22.95 Canada
MORE 1-2-3 For DOS For Dummies®	by John Weingarten	ISBN: 1-56884-224-4	$19.99 USA/$26.99 Canada
MORE Excel 5 For Windows® For Dummies®	by Greg Harvey	ISBN: 1-56884-207-4	$19.95 USA/$26.95 Canada
Quattro Pro 6 For Windows® For Dummies®	by John Walkenbach	ISBN: 1-56884-174-4	$19.95 USA/$26.95 Canada
Quattro Pro For DOS For Dummies®	by John Walkenbach	ISBN: 1-56884-023-3	$16.95 USA/$22.95 Canada

UTILITIES

Title	Author	ISBN	Price
Norton Utilities 8 For Dummies®	by Beth Slick	ISBN: 1-56884-166-3	$19.95 USA/$26.95 Canada

VCRS/CAMCORDERS

Title	Author	ISBN	Price
VCRs & Camcorders For Dummies™	by Gordon McComb & Andy Rathbone	ISBN: 1-56884-229-5	$14.99 USA/$20.99 Canada

WORD PROCESSING

Title	Author	ISBN	Price
Ami Pro For Dummies®	by Jim Meade	ISBN: 1-56884-049-7	$19.95 USA/$26.95 Canada
MORE Word For Windows® 6 For Dummies®	by Doug Lowe	ISBN: 1-56884-165-5	$19.95 USA/$26.95 Canada
MORE WordPerfect® 6 For Windows® For Dummies®	by Margaret Levine Young & David C. Kay	ISBN: 1-56884-206-6	$19.95 USA/$26.95 Canada
MORE WordPerfect® 6 For DOS For Dummies®	by Wallace Wang, edited by Dan Gookin	ISBN: 1-56884-047-0	$19.95 USA/$26.95 Canada
Word 6 For Macs® For Dummies®	by Dan Gookin	ISBN: 1-56884-190-6	$19.95 USA/$26.95 Canada
Word For Windows® 6 For Dummies®	by Dan Gookin	ISBN: 1-56884-075-6	$16.95 USA/$22.95 Canada
Word For Windows® For Dummies®	by Dan Gookin & Ray Werner	ISBN: 1-878058-86-X	$16.95 USA/$22.95 Canada
WordPerfect® 6 For DOS For Dummies®	by Dan Gookin	ISBN: 1-878058-77-0	$16.95 USA/$22.95 Canada
WordPerfect® 6.1 For Windows® For Dummies®, 2nd Edition	by Margaret Levine Young & David Kay	ISBN: 1-56884-243-0	$16.95 USA/$22.95 Canada
WordPerfect® For Dummies®	by Dan Gookin	ISBN: 1-878058-52-5	$16.95 USA/$22.95 Canada

scholastic requests & educational orders please Educational Sales at 1. 800. 434. 2086

FOR MORE INFO OR TO ORDER, PLEASE CALL ▸ 800 762 2974

For volume discounts & special orders please call Tony Real, Special Sales, at 415. 655. 3048

Fun, Fast, & Cheap!™

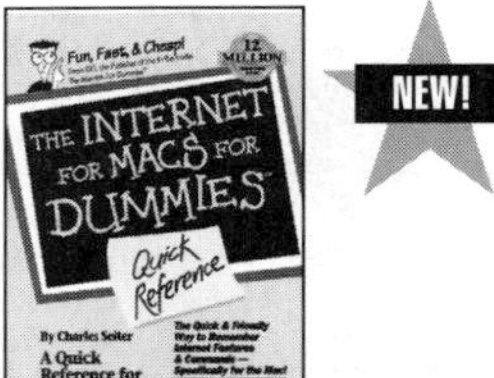

The Internet For Macs® For Dummies® Quick Reference
by Charles Seiter

ISBN:1-56884-967-2
$9.99 USA/$12.99 Canada

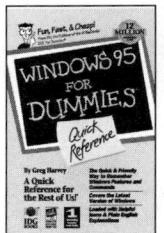

Windows® 95 For Dummies® Quick Reference
by Greg Harvey

ISBN: 1-56884-964-8
$9.99 USA/$12.99 Canada

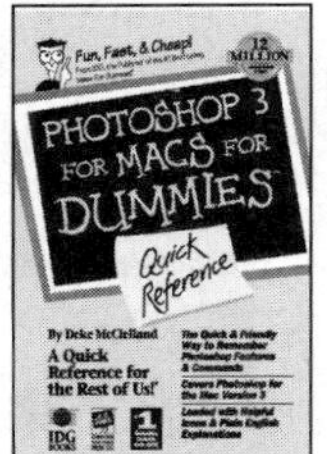

Photoshop 3 For Macs® For Dummies® Quick Reference
by Deke McClelland

ISBN: 1-56884-968-0
$9.99 USA/$12.99 Canada

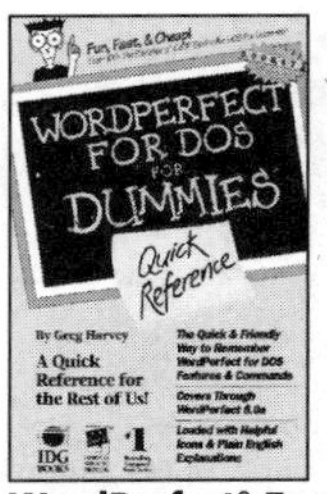

WordPerfect® For DOS For Dummies® Quick Reference
by Greg Harvey

ISBN: 1-56884-009-8
$8.95 USA/$12.95 Canada

Title	Author	ISBN	Price
DATABASE			
Access 2 For Dummies® Quick Reference	by Stuart J. Stuple	ISBN: 1-56884-167-1	$8.95 USA/$11.95 Canada
dBASE 5 For DOS For Dummies® Quick Reference	by Barrie Sosinsky	ISBN: 1-56884-954-0	$9.99 USA/$12.99 Canada
dBASE 5 For Windows® For Dummies® Quick Reference	by Stuart J. Stuple	ISBN: 1-56884-953-2	$9.99 USA/$12.99 Canada
Paradox 5 For Windows® For Dummies® Quick Reference	by Scott Palmer	ISBN: 1-56884-960-5	$9.99 USA/$12.99 Canada
DESKTOP PUBLISHING/ILLUSTRATION/GRAPHICS			
CorelDRAW! 5 For Dummies® Quick Reference	by Raymond E. Werner	ISBN: 1-56884-952-4	$9.99 USA/$12.99 Canada
Harvard Graphics For Windows® For Dummies® Quick Reference	by Raymond E. Werner	ISBN: 1-56884-962-1	$9.99 USA/$12.99 Canada
Photoshop 3 For Macs® For Dummies® Quick Reference	by Deke McClelland	ISBN: 1-56884-968-0	$9.99 USA/$12.99 Canada
FINANCE/PERSONAL FINANCE			
Quicken 4 For Windows® For Dummies® Quick Reference	by Stephen L. Nelson	ISBN: 1-56884-950-8	$9.95 USA/$12.95 Canada
GROUPWARE/INTEGRATED			
Microsoft® Office 4 For Windows® For Dummies® Quick Reference	by Doug Lowe	ISBN: 1-56884-958-3	$9.99 USA/$12.99 Canada
Microsoft® Works 3 For Windows® For Dummies® Quick Reference	by Michael Partington	ISBN: 1-56884-959-1	$9.99 USA/$12.99 Canada
INTERNET/COMMUNICATIONS/NETWORKING			
The Internet For Dummies® Quick Reference	by John R. Levine & Margaret Levine Young	ISBN: 1-56884-168-X	$8.95 USA/$11.95 Canada
MACINTOSH			
Macintosh® System 7.5 For Dummies® Quick Reference	by Stuart J. Stuple	ISBN: 1-56884-956-7	$9.99 USA/$12.99 Canada
OPERATING SYSTEMS:			
DOS			
DOS For Dummies® Quick Reference	by Greg Harvey	ISBN: 1-56884-007-1	$8.95 USA/$11.95 Canada
UNIX			
UNIX® For Dummies® Quick Reference	By John R. Levine & Margaret Levine Young	ISBN: 1-56884-094-2	$8.95 USA/$11.95 Canada
WINDOWS			
Windows® 3.1 For Dummies® Quick Reference, 2nd Edition	by Greg Harvey	ISBN: 1-56884-951-6	$8.95 USA/$11.95 Canada
PCs/HARDWARE			
Memory Management For Dummies® Quick Reference	Doug Lowe	ISBN: 1-56884-362-3	$9.99 USA/$12.99 Canada
PRESENTATION/AUTOCAD			
AutoCAD For Dummies® Quick Reference	by Ellen Finkelstein	ISBN: 1-56884-198-1	$9.95 USA/$12.95 Canada
SPREADSHEET			
1-2-3 For Dummies® Quick Reference	by John Walkenbach	ISBN: 1-56884-027-6	$8.95 USA/$11.95 Canada
1-2-3 For Windows® 5 For Dummies® Quick Reference	by John Walkenbach	ISBN: 1-56884-957-5	$9.95 USA/$12.95 Canada
Excel For Windows® For Dummies® Quick Reference, 2nd Edition	by John Walkenbach	ISBN: 1-56884-096-9	$8.95 USA/$11.95 Canada
Quattro Pro 6 For Windows® For Dummies® Quick Reference	by Stuart J. Stuple	ISBN: 1-56884-172-8	$9.95 USA/$12.95 Canada
WORD PROCESSING			
Word For Windows® 6 For Dummies® Quick Reference	by George Lynch	ISBN: 1-56884-095-0	$8.95 USA/$11.95 Canada
Word For Windows® For Dummies® Quick Reference	by George Lynch	ISBN: 1-56884-029-2	$8.95 USA/$11.95 Canada
WordPerfect® 6.1 For Windows® For Dummies® Quick Reference, 2nd Edition	by Greg Harvey	ISBN: 1-56884-966-4	$9.99 USA/$12.99/Canada

For scholastic requests & educational orders please call Educational Sales at 1. 800. 434. 2086

FOR MORE INFO OR TO ORDER, PLEASE CALL ▸ 800 762 2974

For volume discounts & special orders please call Tony Real, Special Sales, at 415. 655. 3048

9/19/95

Windows® 3.1 SECRETS™
by Brian Livingston

ISBN: 1-878058-43-6
$39.95 USA/$52.95 Canada
Includes software.

MORE Windows® 3.1 SECRETS™
by Brian Livingston

ISBN: 1-56884-019-5
$39.95 USA/$52.95 Canada
Includes software.

Windows® GIZMOS™
by Brian Livingston & Margie Livingston

ISBN: 1-878058-66-5
$39.95 USA/$52.95 Canada
Includes software.

Windows® 3.1 Connectivity SECRETS™
by Runnoe Connally, David Rorabaugh, & Sheldon Hall

ISBN: 1-56884-030-6
$49.95 USA/$64.95 Canada
Includes software.

Windows® 3.1 Configuration SECRETS™
by Valda Hilley & James Blakely

ISBN: 1-56884-026-8
$49.95 USA/$64.95 Canada
Includes software.

Internet SECRETS™
by John Levine & Carol Baroudi

ISBN: 1-56884-452-2
$39.99 USA/$54.99 Canada
Includes software.

Internet GIZMOS™ For Windows®
by Joel Diamond, Howard Sobel, & Valda Hilley

ISBN: 1-56884-451-4
$39.99 USA/$54.99 Canada
Includes software.

Network Security SECRETS™
by David Stang & Sylvia Moon

ISBN: 1-56884-021-7
Int'l. ISBN: 1-56884-151-5
$49.95 USA/$64.95 Canada
Includes software.

PC SECRETS™
by Caroline M. Halliday

ISBN: 1-878058-49-5
$39.95 USA/$52.95 Canada
Includes software.

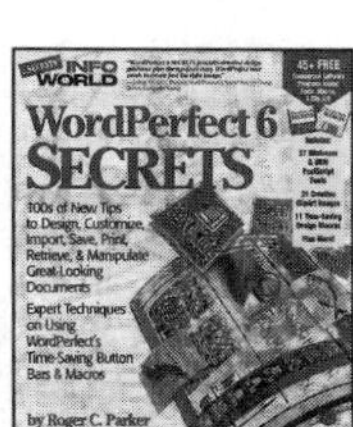

WordPerfect® 6 SECRETS™
by Roger C. Parker & David A. Holzgang

ISBN: 1-56884-040-3
$39.95 USA/$52.95 Canada
Includes software.

DOS 6 SECRETS™
by Robert D. Ainsbury

ISBN: 1-878058-70-3
$39.95 USA/$52.95 Canada
Includes software.

Paradox 4 Power Programming SECRETS,™ 2nd Edition
by Gregory B. Salcedo & Martin W. Rudy

ISBN: 1-878058-54-1
$44.95 USA/$59.95 Canada
Includes software.

Paradox 5 For Windows® Power Programming SECRETS™
by Gregory B. Salcedo & Martin W. Rudy

ISBN: 1-56884-085-3
$44.95 USA/$59.95 Canada
Includes software.

Hard Disk SECRETS™
by John M. Goodman, Ph.D.

ISBN: 1-878058-64-9
$39.95 USA/$52.95 Canada
Includes software.

WordPerfect® 6 For Windows® Tips & Techniques Revealed
by David A. Holzgang & Roger C. Parker

ISBN: 1-56884-202-3
$39.95 USA/$52.95 Canada
Includes software.

Excel 5 For Windows® Power Programming Techniques
by John Walkenbach

ISBN: 1-56884-303-8
$39.95 USA/$52.95 Canada
Includes software.

scholastic requests & educational orders please call Educational Sales, at 1. 800. 434. 2086

FOR MORE INFO OR TO ORDER, PLEASE CALL ▸ 800. 762. 2974

For volume discounts & special orders please call Tony Real, Special Sales, at 415. 655. 3048

9/19/95

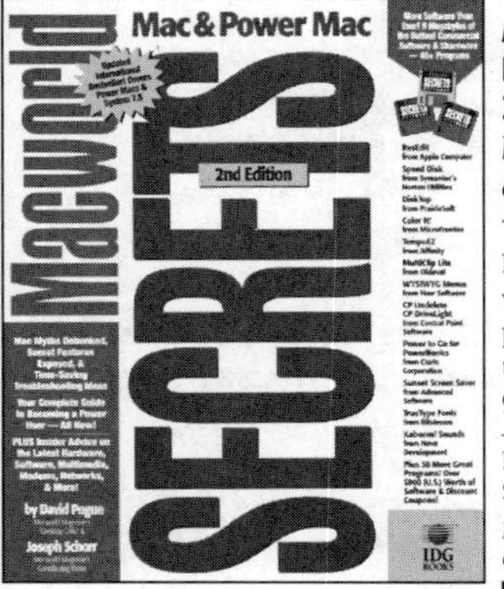

Macworld® Mac® & Power Mac SECRETS,™ 2nd Edition
by David Pogue & Joseph Schorr

HOT!

This is the definitive Mac reference for those who want to become power users! Includes three disks with 9MB of software!

WINNERS 1994-95 TECHNICAL PUBLICATIONS AND ART COMPETITIONS OF THE SOCIETY FOR TECHNICAL COMMUNICATION

ISBN: 1-56884-175-2
$39.95 USA/$54.95 Canada

Includes 3 disks chock full of software.

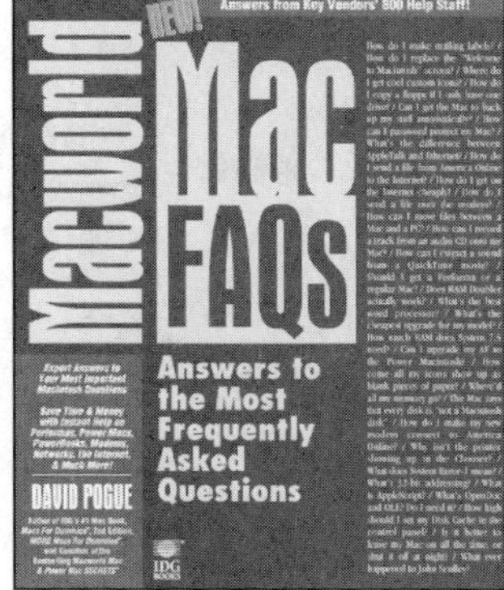

Macworld® Mac® FAQs™
by David Pogue

HOT!

Written by the hottest Macintosh author around, David Pogue, *Macworld Mac FAQs* gives users the ultimate Mac reference. Hundreds of Mac questions and answers side-by-side, right at your fingertips, and organized into six easy-to-reference sections with lots of sidebars and diagrams.

ISBN: 1-56884-480-8
$19.99 USA/$26.99 Canada

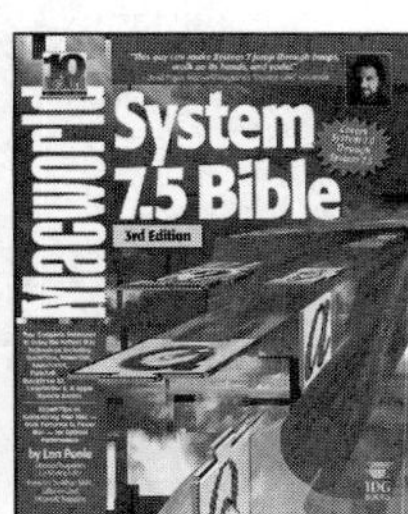

Macworld® System 7.5 Bible, 3rd Edition
by Lon Poole

ISBN: 1-56884-098-5
$29.95 USA/$39.95 Canada

Macworld® ClarisWorks 3.0 Companion, 3rd Edition
by Steven A. Schwartz

ISBN: 1-56884-481-6
$24.99 USA/$34.99 Canada

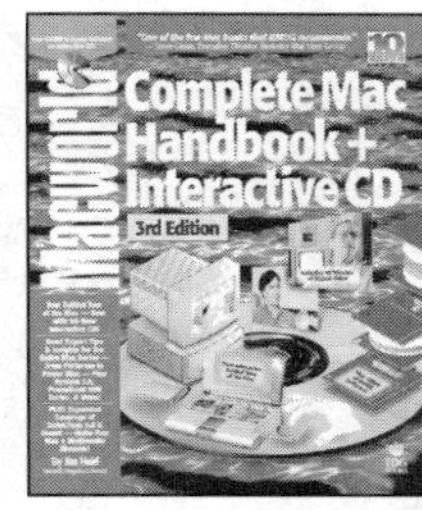

BMUG SPRING 1995 CHOICE PRODUCT

Macworld® Complete Mac® Handbook Plus Interactive CD, 3rd Edition
by Jim Heid

ISBN: 1-56884-192-2
$39.95 USA/$54.95 Canada

Includes an interactive CD-ROM.

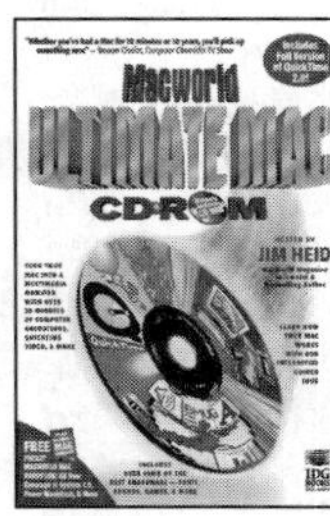

Macworld® Ultimate Mac® CD-ROM
by Jim Heid

ISBN: 1-56884-477-8
$19.99 USA/$26.99 Canada

CD-ROM includes version 2.0 of QuickTime, and over 65 MB of the best shareware, freeware, fonts, sounds, and more!

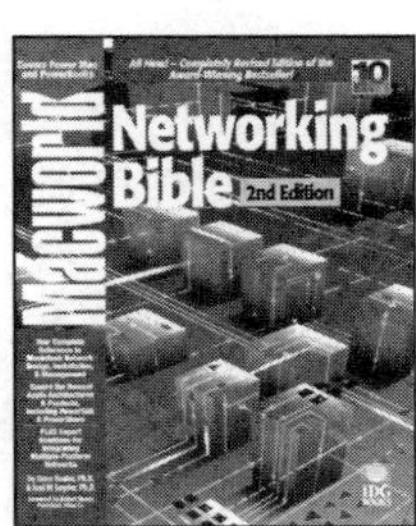

Macworld® Networking Bible, 2nd Edition
by Dave Kosiur & Joel M. Snyder

ISBN: 1-56884-194-9
$29.95 USA/$39.95 Canada

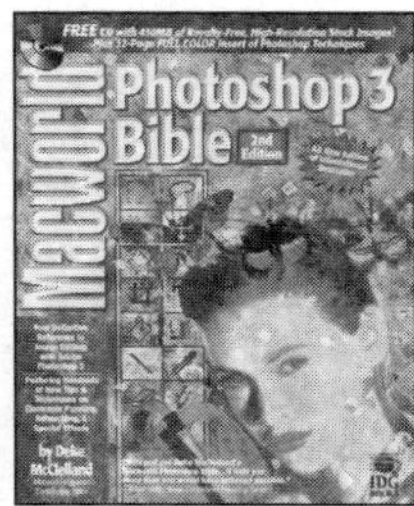

Macworld® Photoshop 3 Bible, 2nd Edition
by Deke McClelland

ISBN: 1-56884-158-2
$39.95 USA/$54.95 Canada

Includes stunning CD-ROM with add-ons, digitized photos and more.

NEW!

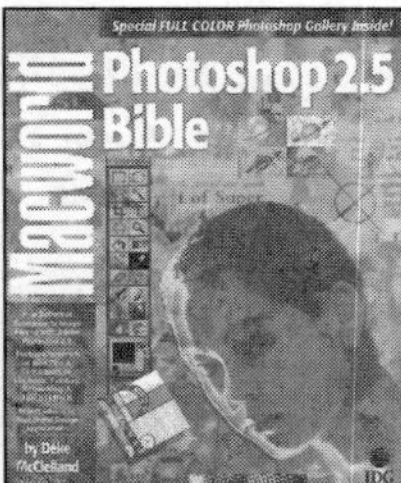

Macworld® Photoshop 2.5 Bible
by Deke McClelland

ISBN: 1-56884-022-5
$29.95 USA/$39.95 Canada

Macworld® FreeHand 4 Bible
by Deke McClelland

ISBN: 1-56884-170-1
$29.95 USA/$39.95 Canada

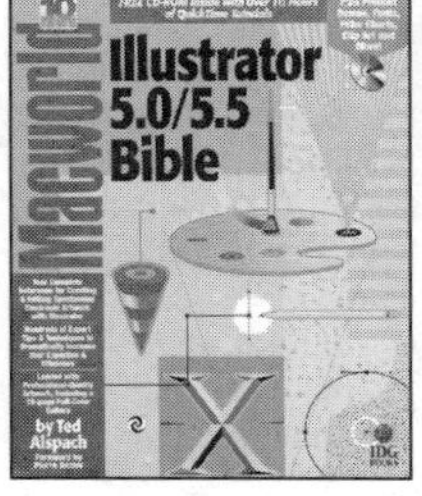

Macworld® Illustrator 5.0/5.5 Bible
by Ted Alspach

ISBN: 1-56884-097-7
$39.95 USA/$54.95 Canada

Includes CD-ROM with QuickTime tutorials.

: scholastic requests & educational orders please
Educational Sales, at 1. 800. 434. 2086

FOR MORE INFO OR TO ORDER, PLEASE CALL 800 762 2974

For volume discounts & special orders please call
Tony Real, Special Sales, at 415. 655. 3048

"*Macworld Complete Mac Handbook Plus CD* covered everything I could think of and more!"

Peter Tsakiris, New York, NY

"Very useful for PageMaker beginners and veterans alike—contains a wealth of tips and tricks to make you a faster, more powerful PageMaker user."

Paul Brainerd, President and founder,
Aldus Corporation

"Thanks for the best computer book I've ever read—*Photoshop 2.5 Bible*. Best $30 I ever spent. I *love* the detailed index....Yours blows them all out of the water. This is a great book. We must enlighten the masses!"

Kevin Lisankie, Chicago, Illinois

"*Macworld Guide to ClarisWorks 2* is the easiest computer book to read that I have ever found!"

Steven Hanson, Lutz, FL

"...thanks to the *Macworld Excel 5 Companion*, 2nd Edition occupying a permanent position next to my computer, I'll be able to tap more of Excel's power."

Lauren Black, Lab Director,
Macworld Magazine

Macworld® QuarkXPress 3.2/3.3 Bible
by Barbara Assadi & Galen Gruman

ISBN: 1-878058-85-1
$39.95 USA/$52.95 Canada

Includes disk with QuarkXPress XTensions and scripts.

Macworld® PageMaker 5 Bible
by Craig Danuloff

ISBN: 1-878058-84-3
$39.95 USA/$52.95 Canada

Includes 2 disks with PageMaker utilities, clip art, and more.

Macworld® FileMaker Pro 2.0/2.1 Bible
by Steven A. Schwartz

ISBN: 1-56884-201-5
$34.95 USA/$46.95 Canada

Includes disk with ready-to-run data bases.

Macworld® Word 6 Companion, 2nd Edition
by Jim Heid

ISBN: 1-56884-082-9
$24.95 USA/$34.95 Canada

Macworld® Guide To Microsoft® Word 5/5.1
by Jim Heid

ISBN: 1-878058-39-8
$22.95 USA/$29.95 Canada

Macworld® ClarisWorks 2.0/2.1 Companion, 2nd Edition
by Steven A. Schwartz

ISBN: 1-56884-180-9
$24.95 USA/$34.95 Canada

Macworld® Guide To Microsoft® Works 3
by Barrie Sosinsky

ISBN: 1-878058-42-8
$22.95 USA/$29.95 Canada

Macworld® Excel 5 Companion, 2nd Edition
by Chris Van Buren & David Maguiness

ISBN: 1-56884-081-0
$24.95 USA/$34.95 Canada

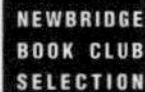

Macworld® Guide To Microsoft® Excel 4
by David Maguiness

ISBN: 1-878058-40-1
$22.95 USA/$29.95 Canada

For scholastic requests & educational orders please call Educational Sales, at 1. 800. 434. 2086

FOR MORE INFO OR TO ORDER, PLEASE CALL 800 762 2974

For volume discounts & special orders please Tony Real, Special Sales, at 415. 655. 3048

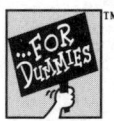

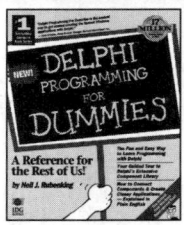

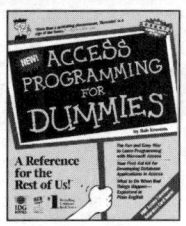

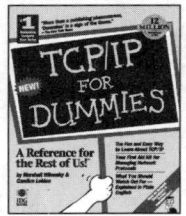

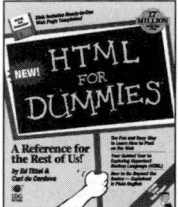

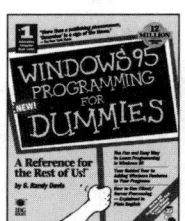

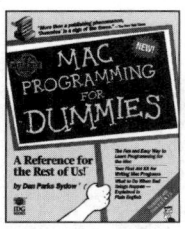

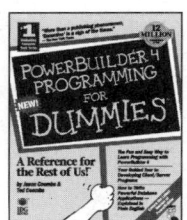

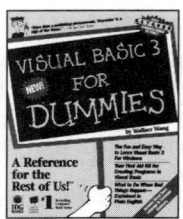

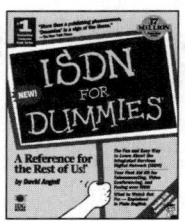

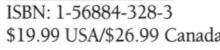

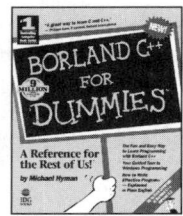

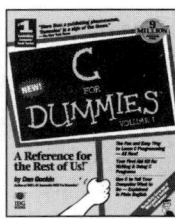

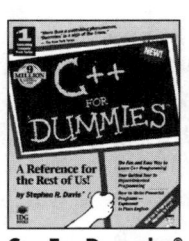

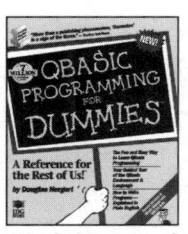

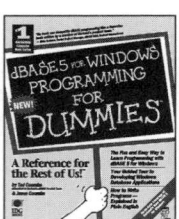

9/19/95

Official Hayes Modem Communications Companion
by Caroline M. Halliday

ISBN: 1-56884-072-1
$29.95 USA/$39.95 Canada
Includes software.

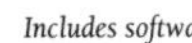

1,001 Komputer Answers from Kim Komando
by Kim Komando

ISBN: 1-56884-460-3
$29.99 USA/$39.99 Canada
Includes software.

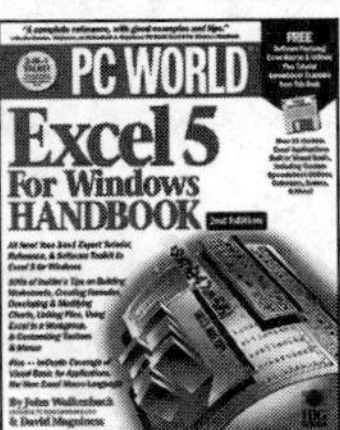

PC World Excel 5 For Windows® Handbook, 2nd Edition
by John Walkenbach & Dave Maguiness

ISBN: 1-56884-056-X
$34.95 USA/$44.95 Canada
Includes software

PC World WordPerfect® 6 Handbook
by Greg Harvey

ISBN: 1-878058-80-0
$34.95 USA/$44.95 Canada
Includes software.

PC World DOS 6 Command Reference and Problem Solver
by John Socha & Devra Hall

NATIONAL BESTSELLER!

ISBN: 1-56884-055-1
$24.95 USA/$32.95 Canada

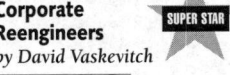

Client/Server Strategies™: A Survival Guide for Corporate Reengineers
by David Vaskevitch

SUPER STAR

ISBN: 1-56884-064-0

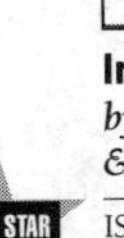

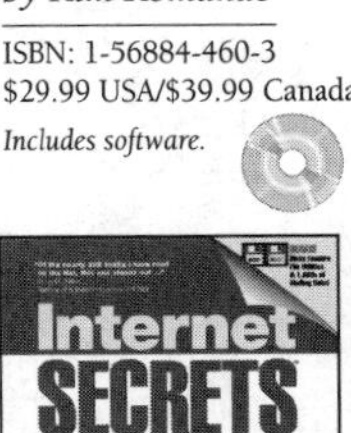

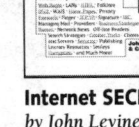

Internet SECRETS™
by John Levine & Carol Baroudi

ISBN: 1-56884-452-2
$39.99 USA/$54.99 Canada
Includes software.

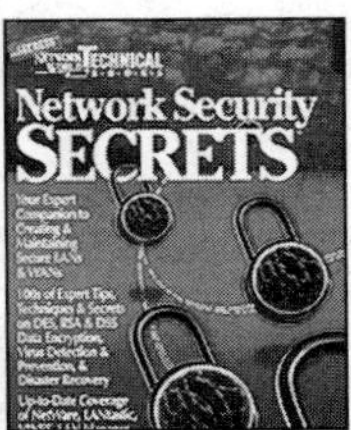

Network Security SECRETS™
by David Stang & Sylvia Moon

ISBN: 1-56884-021-7
Int'l. ISBN: 1-56884-151-5
$49.95 USA/$64.95 Canada
Includes software.

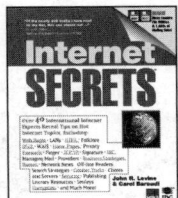

PC SECRETS™
by Caroline M. Halliday

ISBN: 1-878058-49-5
$39.95 USA/$52.95 Canada
Includes software.

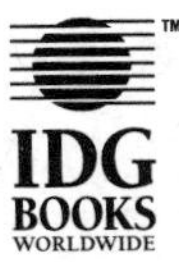

Here's a complete listing of PC Press Titles

Title	Author	ISBN	Price
BBS SECRETS™	by Ray Werner	ISBN: 1-56884-491-3	$39.99 USA/$54.99 Canada
Creating Cool Web Pages with HTML	by Dave Taylor	ISBN: 1-56884-454-9	$19.99 USA/$26.99 Canada
DOS 6 SECRETS™	by Robert D. Ainsbury	ISBN: 1-878058-70-3	$39.95 USA/$52.95 Canada
Excel 5 For Windows® Power Programming Techniques	by John Walkenbach	ISBN: 1-56884-303-8	$39.95 USA/$52.95 Canada
Hard Disk SECRETS™	by John M. Goodman, Ph.D.	ISBN: 1-878058-64-9	$39.95 USA/$52.95 Canada
Internet GIZMOS™ For Windows®	by Joel Diamond, Howard Sobel, & Valda Hilley	ISBN: 1-56884-451-4	$39.99 USA/$54.99 Canada
Making Multimedia Work	by Michael Goodwin	ISBN: 1-56884-468-9	$19.99 USA/$26.99 Canada
MORE Windows® 3.1 SECRETS™	by Brian Livingston	ISBN: 1-56884-019-5	$39.95 USA/$52.95 Canada
Official XTree Companion 3rd Edition	by Beth Slick	ISBN: 1-878058-57-6	$19.95 USA/$26.95 Canada
Paradox 4 Power Programming SECRETS,™ 2nd Edition	by Gregory B. Salcedo & Martin W. Rudy	ISBN: 1-878058-54-1	$44.95 USA/$59.95 Canada
Paradox 5 For Windows® Power Programming SECRETS™	by Gregory B. Salcedo & Martin W. Rudy	ISBN: 1-56884-085-3	$44.95 USA/$59.95 Canada
PC World DOS 6 Handbook, 2nd Edition	by John Socha, Clint Hicks & Devra Hall	ISBN: 1-878058-79-7	$34.95 USA/$44.95 Canada
PC World Microsoft® Access 2 Bible, 2nd Edition	by Cary N. Prague & Michael R. Irwin	ISBN: 1-56884-086-1	$39.95 USA/$52.95 Canada
PC World Word For Windows® 6 Handbook	by Brent Heslop & David Angell	ISBN: 1-56884-054-3	$34.95 USA/$44.95 Canada
QuarkXPress For Windows® Designer Handbook	by Barbara Assadi & Galen Gruman	ISBN: 1-878058-45-2	$29.95 USA/$39.95 Canada
Windows® 3.1 Configuration SECRETS™	by Valda Hilley & James Blakely	ISBN: 1-56884-026-8	$49.95 USA/$64.95 Canada
Windows® 3.1 Connectivity SECRETS™	by Runnoe Connally, David Rorabaugh & Sheldon Hall	ISBN: 1-56884-030-6	$49.95 USA/$64.95 Canada
Windows® 3.1 SECRETS™	by Brian Livingston	ISBN: 1-878058-43-6	$39.95 USA/$52.95 Canada
Windows® 95 A.S.A.P.	by Dan Gookin	ISBN: 1-56884-483-2	$24.99 USA/$34.99 Canada
Windows® 95 Bible	by Alan Simpson	ISBN: 1-56884-074-8	$29.99 USA/$39.99 Canada
Windows® 95 SECRETS™	by Brian Livingston	ISBN: 1-56884-453-0	$39.99 USA/$54.99 Canada
Windows® GIZMOS™	by Brian Livingston & Margie Livingston	ISBN: 1-878058-66-5	$39.95 USA/$52.95 Canada
WordPerfect® 6 For Windows® Tips & Techniques Revealed	by David A. Holzgang & Roger C. Parker	ISBN: 1-56884-202-3	$39.95 USA/$52.95 Canada
WordPerfect® 6 SECRETS™	by Roger C. Parker & David A. Holzgang	ISBN: 1-56884-040-3	$39.95 USA/$52.95 Canada

ɔr scholastic requests & educational orders please
ıll Educational Sales, at 1. 800. 434. 2086

FOR MORE INFO OR TO ORDER, PLEASE CALL ▶ 800 762 2974

For volume discounts & special orders please call
Tony Real, Special Sales, at 415. 655. 3048

9/19/95

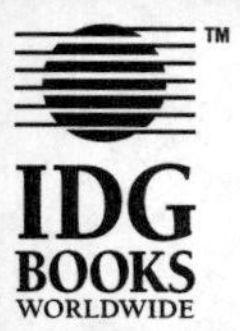

Order Center: **(800) 762-2974** (8 a.m.–6 p.m., EST, weekdays)

Quantity	ISBN	Title	Price	Total

Shipping & Handling Charges

	Description	First book	Each additional book	Total
Domestic	Normal	$4.50	$1.50	$
	Two Day Air	$8.50	$2.50	$
	Overnight	$18.00	$3.00	$
International	Surface	$8.00	$8.00	$
	Airmail	$16.00	$16.00	$
	DHL Air	$17.00	$17.00	$

*For large quantities call for shipping & handling charges.
**Prices are subject to change without notice.

Ship to:

Name ____________________

Company ____________________

Address ____________________

City/State/Zip ____________________

Daytime Phone ____________________

Payment: ☐ Check to IDG Books Worldwide (US Funds Only)
☐ VISA ☐ MasterCard ☐ American Express

Card # ____________________ Expires ____________

Signature ____________________

Subtotal ____________

CA residents add applicable sales tax ____________

IN, MA, and MD residents add 5% sales tax ____________

IL residents add 6.25% sales tax ____________

RI residents add 7% sales tax ____________

TX residents add 8.25% sales tax ____________

Shipping ____________

Total ____________

Please send this order form to:

IDG Books Worldwide, Inc.
7260 Shadeland Station, Suite 100
Indianapolis, IN 46256

Allow up to 3 weeks for delivery. Thank you!

IDG BOOKS WORLDWIDE LICENSE AGREEMENT

Important — read carefully before opening the software packet. This is a legal agreement between you (either an individual or an entity) and IDG Books Worldwide, Inc. (IDG). By opening the accompanying sealed packet containing the software disk, you acknowledge that you have read and accept the following IDG License Agreement. If you do not agree and do not want to be bound by the terms of this Agreement, promptly return the book and the unopened software packet(s) to the place you obtained them for a full refund.

1. **License.** This License Agreement (Agreement) permits you to use one copy of the enclosed Software program(s) on a single computer. The Software is in "use" on a computer when it is loaded into temporary memory (i.e., RAM) or installed into permanent memory (e.g., hard disk, CD-ROM, or other storage device) of that computer.

2. **Copyright.** The entire contents of this disk and the compilation of the Software are copyrighted and protected by both United States copyright laws and international treaty provisions. You may only (a) make one copy of the Software for backup or archival purposes, or (b) transfer the Software to a single hard disk, provided that you keep the original for backup or archival purposes. The individual programs on the disk are copyrighted by the authors of each program respectively. Each program has its own use permissions and limitations. To use each program, you must follow the individual requirements and restrictions detailed in each. Do not use a program if you do not want to follow its Licensing Agreement. None of the material on this disk or listed in this Book may ever be distributed, in original or modified form, for commercial purposes.

3. **Other Restrictions.** You may not rent or lease the Software. You may transfer the Software and user documentation on a permanent basis provided you retain no copies and the recipient agrees to the terms of this Agreement. You may not reverse-engineer, decompile, or disassemble the Software except to the extent that the foregoing restriction is expressly prohibited by applicable law. If the Software is an update or has been updated, any transfer must include the most recent update and all prior versions. Each shareware program has its own use permissions and limitations. These limitations are contained in the individual license agreements that are on the software disk. The restrictions include a requirement that after using the program for a period of time specified in its text, the user must pay a registration fee or discontinue use. By opening the package which contains the software disk, you will be agreeing to abide by the licenses and restrictions for these programs. Do not open the software package unless you agree to be bound by the license agreements.

4. **Limited Warranty.** IDG Warrants that the Software and disk are free from defects in materials and workmanship for a period of sixty (60) days from the date of purchase of this Book. If IDG receives notification within the warranty period of defects in material or workmanship, IDG will replace the defective disk. IDG's entire liability and your exclusive remedy shall be limited to replacement of the Software, which is returned to IDG with a copy of your receipt. This Limited Warranty is void if failure of the Software has resulted from accident, abuse, or misapplication. Any replacement Software will be warranted for the remainder of the original warranty period or thirty (30) days, whichever is longer.

5. **No Other Warranties.** To the maximum extent permitted by applicable law, IDG and the author disclaim all other warranties, express or implied, including but not limited to implied warranties of merchantability and fitness for a particular purpose, with respect to the Software, the programs, the source code contained therein, and/or the techniques described in this Book. This limited warranty gives you specific legal rights. You may have others which vary from state/jurisdiction to state/jurisdiction.

6. **No Liability For Consequential Damages.** To the extent permitted by applicable law, in no event shall IDG or the author be liable for any damages whatsoever (including without limitation, damages for loss of business profits, business interruption, loss of business information, or any other pecuniary loss) arising out of the use of or inability to use the Book or the Software, even if IDG has been advised of the possibility of such damages. Because some states/jurisdictions do not allow the exclusion or limitation of liability for consequential or incidental damages, the above limitation may not apply to you.

7. **U.S.Government Restricted Rights.** Use, duplication, or disclosure of the Software by the U.S. Government is subject to restrictions stated in paragraph (c) (1) (ii) of the Rights in Technical Data and Computer Software clause of DFARS 252.227-7013, and in subparagraphs (a) through (d) of the Commercial Computer — Restricted Rights clause at FAR 52.227-19, and in similar clauses in the NASA FAR supplement, when applicable.

Installing the *Microsoft Access for Windows 95 Bible*, 3nd Edition Companion Disk

Warning: *Before installing any of the files from the companion disk, read the Disclaimer and Copyright Notice on the preceding page.*

The companion disk contains the example files that are used and created in this book. The files appear in their completed form so you can avoid a lot of typing if you only want to see how certain forms, reports, or queries work. Also included are files that were created as starting points for some of the more complicated examples in the chapters. There are three Access database files (.mdb extension) used specifically for the book; there are also many external files. The other database files are full working versions of our best-selling Access for Windows 95 products for you to use, royalty free, and incorporate into your applications.

The three Access for Windows 95 database files containing the book examples are

MTNSTART.MDB	Contains only the tables used in the examples in the book
MOUNTAIN.MDB	Contains all completed tables, queries, forms, reports, macros, and modules
ATCIMPEX.MDB	Contains several tables for learning linking, importing, and exporting external files

Warning: After running the setup, you must rename the first two files as explained in the installation notes on the next page. The other files described below should be used after you have mastered Microsoft Access for Windows 95.

CHECK95.MDB	Fully functional Check Writer including a Check Register and Check Reconciliation module
BUSFORMS.MDB	Contains three forms from the highly acclaimed add-on product The Access Business Forms Library

The external files included on the disk include Paintbrush bitmaps, Excel, dBASE, Paradox, and text files used in various chapters throughout this book.

One file on the disk, SETUP.EXE, is a standard Windows 95 setup. When used as described in the following instructions, SETUP.EXE creates a directory that you name (or defaults to C:\BIBLE95) and copies all of the Access database files to it; the external files are also copied to this new directory. We strongly recommend that you select a directory other that the main Access 95 or Office 95 directory. It is assumed that Access for Windows 95 is already installed.

The disk is in $3^1/_2$-inch HD format and contains approximately 1.4MB of data. When the files are installed, they will use approximately 7MB on your hard disk.

The instructions for installing the companion disk follow.

1. Insert the disk into your $3^1/_2$-inch HD floppy-disk drive.
2. Select Run... from the Windows 95 Start menu.
3. Type **A:\SETUP** into the Open dialog box.
4. Press the OK button.

Setup will ask you where you want to copy the sample files. The default directory is C:\BIBLE95. You can change the default location to any valid drive or directory on your system.

After you install the files, you need to rename two of the .MDB files to correspond to the long file names used in the book. Due to the unavailability of installation programs that support long file names, we had to rename our database files to create the installation routines. Please rename the following files:

Mountain.mdb	Rename to Mountain Animal Hospital.mdb
MtnStart.mdb	Rename to Mountain Animal Start.mdb

The other .MDB files can be used with their present names. All of the .MDB files are Microsoft Access for Windows 95 files. They only work in Microsoft Access for Windows 95 and do not work in Microsoft Access 2.0, 1.1, or 1.0.

There is also a file on your disk that is not installed by the SETUP routine. BUTTONS.EXE is a self-extracting file; use Windows Explorer to copy it to a directory on your hard drive, then open the directory and double-click on BUTTONS or BUTTONS.EXE. The button files with the .BMP file extension are the commonly available 32 × 32 pixel size (also known as icon size). These are for our command buttons. The files with the .B24 extension are 24 × 23 size which is the new Microsoft Office toolbar size buttons. As described in our book, you use these to customize a toolbar; they automatically will shrink to the correct 17 × 15 small size when used on a toolbar.

Besides the sample files used by the book, including the Mountain Animal Hospital examples, the disk contains several files from Cary Prague Books and Software, the world's largest Microsoft Access add-on vendor.

These are fully working applications which you can use and customize:

Check95.mdb	Fully functional Check Writer including a Check Register and Check Reconciliation
BusForms.mdb	Access Business Forms Library Sampler

Both are given to you free of charge for your own use. These are both standard Access database files. To use either of them, simply open the database file; a program will automatically display the library.

Check95.mdb is an upgrade to our award winning Check Writer for Microsoft Access 2.0. This product won the Microsoft Network award in August 1995 for best Access software product. You are free to use it in your applications and modify it any way you want.

Busforms.mdb is a sample of our Business Forms Library (a collection of 35 forms and reports). These contain some really innovative techniques that have never been seen anywhere else. The entire library contains tables, forms, reports, and macros for each of the forms and reports. You can integrate them into your own applications, thereby saving you hundreds of hours of work. Microsoft liked these forms so much they distributed this sampler in the Microsoft Access Welcome Kit with Microsoft Access 2.0.

IDG BOOKS WORLDWIDE REGISTRATION CARD

RETURN THIS REGISTRATION CARD FOR FREE CATALOG

Title of this book: Access 95 Bible, 3E

My overall rating of this book: ❑ Very good [1] ❑ Good [2] ❑ Satisfactory [3] ❑ Fair [4] ❑ Poor [5]

How I first heard about this book:

❑ Found in bookstore; name: [6]

❑ Book review: [7]

❑ Advertisement: [8]

❑ Catalog: [9]

❑ Word of mouth; heard about book from friend, co-worker, etc.: [10]

❑ Other: [11]

What I liked most about this book:

What I would change, add, delete, etc., in future editions of this book:

Other comments:

Number of computer books I purchase in a year: ❑ 1 [12] ❑ 2-5 [13] ❑ 6-10 [14] ❑ More than 10 [15]

I would characterize my computer skills as: ❑ Beginner [16] ❑ Intermediate [17] ❑ Advanced [18] ❑ Professional [19]

I use ❑ DOS [20] ❑ Windows [21] ❑ OS/2 [22] ❑ Unix [23] ❑ Macintosh [24] ❑ Other: [25] ____________ (please specify)

I would be interested in new books on the following subjects:
(please check all that apply, and use the spaces provided to identify specific software)

❑ Word processing: [26]

❑ Spreadsheets: [27]

❑ Data bases: [28]

❑ Desktop publishing: [29]

❑ File Utilities: [30]

❑ Money management: [31]

❑ Networking: [32]

❑ Programming languages: [33]

❑ Other: [34]

I use a PC at (please check all that apply): ❑ home [35] ❑ work [36] ❑ school [37] ❑ other: [38] ____________

The disks I prefer to use are ❑ 5.25 [39] ❑ 3.5 [40] ❑ other: [41] ____________

I have a CD ROM: ❑ yes [42] ❑ no [43]

I plan to buy or upgrade computer hardware this year: ❑ yes [44] ❑ no [45]

I plan to buy or upgrade computer software this year: ❑ yes [46] ❑ no [47]

Name: Business title: [48] Type of Business: [49]

Address (❑ home [50] ❑ work [51]/Company name:)

Street/Suite#

City [52]/State [53]/Zipcode [54]: Country [55]

❑ **I liked this book!** You may quote me by name in future IDG Books Worldwide promotional materials.

My daytime phone number is ____________

IDG BOOKS®
THE WORLD OF COMPUTER KNOWLEDGE

YES!

Please keep me informed about IDG's World of Computer Knowledge. Send me the latest IDG Books catalog.

NO POSTAGE NECESSARY IF MAILED IN THE UNITED STATES

BUSINESS REPLY MAIL

FIRST CLASS MAIL PERMIT NO. 2605 FOSTER CITY, CALIFORNIA

IDG Books Worldwide
919 E Hillsdale Blvd, STE 400
Foster City, CA 94404-9691

DER NEUE PAULY

Altertum Band 5 Gru–Iug

DER NEUE PAULY

(DNP)

DER NEUE PAULY
Enzyklopädie der Antike

Herausgegeben
von Hubert Cancik und
Helmuth Schneider

Altertum

Band 5 Gru–Iug

Verlag J. B. Metzler
Stuttgart · Weimar

Die Deutsche Bibliothek – CIP-Einheitsaufnahme

Der neue Pauly : Enzyklopädie der Antike/hrsg. von Hubert Cancik und Helmuth Schneider. – Stuttgart ; Weimar : Metzler, 1998
ISBN 3-476-01470-3
NE: Cancik, Hubert [Hrsg.]

Bd. 5. Gru-Iug – 1998
ISBN 3-476-01475-4

Gedruckt auf chlorfrei gebleichtem, säurefreiem und alterungsbeständigem Papier

ISBN 3-476-01470-3 (Gesamtwerk)
ISBN 3-476-01475-4 (Band 5 Gru-Iug)

Typographie und Ausstattung:
Brigitte und Hans Peter Willberg
Grafik und Typographie der Karten:
Richard Szydlak
Abbildungen: Günter Müller
Satz: pagina GmbH, Tübingen
Gesamtfertigung: Franz Spiegel Buch GmbH, Ulm
Printed in Germany

Verlag J. B. Metzler Stuttgart · Weimar

Inhaltsverzeichnis

Redaktion

Jochen Derlien
Dr. Brigitte Egger
Susanne Fischer
Christa Frateantonio
Dietrich Frauer
Mareile Haase
Dr. Ingrid Hitzl
Heike Kunz
Michael Mohr
Vera Sauer
Dorothea Sigel
Anne-Maria Wittke

BAND 5

Autoren VIII, 6 Graziano **Arrighetti** Pisa *GR. A.*
VIII, nach 44 füge ein: *Lucia* ***Galli*** *Florenz* *L. G.*
X, 5 Ekkehard W. **Stegemann** *Basel*

Hadrumetum 64, 48 C. G. *PICARD*, Catalogue

Hebryzelmis [1] 220, 49 Die Münzen der thrak. Dynasten, *1997*

Herakleia [7] 366, 10 **[7] H.** ***Pontike*** (Heraclea Pontica)

Hermeneutik 425, 10 der ant. Gramm. *vorbehalten*

Herodotos 475, 3 f. The Historical Method of Herodotus, *1989*
475, 34 KOMM.: D. *ASHERI* u. a.
475, 50 *J.* GOULD, Herodotus
475, 52 *D. BOEDEKER (Hrsg.),* Herodotus and

Hormisdas [3] 728, 30 älterer Bruder *Adarnarses*

Hydra [2] 774, 41 *Antoninus* Liberalis 12

Hypatia 799, 41 (gest. 415 *n. Chr.*)

Hypatios [4] 801, 15 Konstantinopel am *18.*1. gegen

Hypatos [1] 802, 2 byzantines des *IX*[e] et Xe siècles

Ignatios [2] Magister 925, 58 Graeca I, *1829*, 436–444

Imagines maiorum 946, 28 f. (so zuletzt [5. *2, 38*])

Intestatus 1048, 45 Recht (bis *1899*) galt

Iohannes [4] Chrysostomos 1059, 34 ff. Seit 372 *ein asketisches Leben führend, kehrte I. 378 – gesundheitlich angeschlagen – nach Antiocheia zurück,* wurde

Iohannes [22] 1065, 18 **[22]** ***I. Diaconus.*** Verf. einer

Iohannes [23] 1065, 21 **[23]** ***I. Diaconus.*** Verf eines

Ionisch 1081, 21 f. κούρη *Δεινοδίκεω* τοῦ

Iran 1101, 49 Meder (→ *Medoi*; Anfang 7. bis

Ischys 1119, 24 (*Ἴσχυς*)

Italien, Alphabetschriften 1164, 38 → *Iguvium*; Tabulae Iguvinae

Hinweise für die Benutzung

Anordnung der Stichwörter

Die Stichwörter sind in der Reihenfolge des deutschen Alphabetes angeordnet. I und J werden gleich behandelt; ä ist wie ae, ö wie oe, ü wie ue einsortiert. Wenn es zu einem Stichwort (Lemma) Varianten gibt, wird von der alternativen Schreibweise auf den gewählten Eintrag verwiesen. Bei zweigliedrigen Stichwörtern muß daher unter beiden Bestandteilen gesucht werden (z. B. *a commentariis* oder *commentariis, a*).

Informationen, die nicht als Lemma gefaßt worden sind, können mit Hilfe des Registerbandes aufgefunden werden.

Gleichlautende Stichworte sind durch Numerierung unterschieden. Gleichlautende griechische und orientalische Personennamen werden nach ihrer Chronologie angeordnet. Beinamen sind hier nicht berücksichtigt.

Römische Personennamen (auch Frauennamen) sind dem Alphabet entsprechend eingeordnet, und zwar nach dem *nomen gentile*, dem »Familiennamen«. Bei umfangreicheren Homonymen-Einträgen werden *Republik* und *Kaiserzeit* gesondert angeordnet. Für die Namensfolge bei Personen aus der Zeit der Republik ist – dem Beispiel der RE und der 3. Auflage des OCD folgend – das *nomen gentile* maßgeblich; auf dieses folgen *cognomen* und *praenomen* (z.B. erscheint *M. Aemilius Scaurus* unter dem Lemma *Aemilius* als *Ae. Scaurus, M.*). Die hohe politische Gestaltungskraft der *gentes* in der Republik macht diese Anfangsstellung des Gentilnomens sinnvoll.

Da die strikte Dreiteilung der Personennamen in der Kaiserzeit nicht mehr eingehalten wurde, ist eine Anordnung nach oben genanntem System problematisch. Kaiserzeitliche Personennamen (ab der Entstehung des Prinzipats unter Augustus) werden deshalb ab dem dritten Band in der Reihenfolge aufgeführt, die sich auch in der »Prosopographia Imperii Romani« (PIR) und in der »Prosopography of the Later Roman Empire« (PLRE) eingebürgert und allgemein durchgesetzt hat und die sich an der antik bezeugten Namenfolge orientiert (z.B. *L. Vibullius Hipparchus Ti. C. Atticus Herodes* unter dem Lemma *Claudius*). Die Methodik – eine zunächst am Gentilnomen orientierte Suche – ändert sich dabei nicht.

Nur antike Autoren und römische Kaiser sind ausnahmsweise nicht unter dem Gentilnomen zu finden: *Cicero*, nicht *Tullius*; *Catullus*, nicht *Valerius*.

Schreibweise von Stichwörtern

Die Schreibweise antiker Wörter und Namen richtet sich im allgemeinen nach der vollständigen antiken Schreibweise.

Toponyme (Städte, Flüsse, Berge etc.), auch Länder- und Provinzbezeichnungen erscheinen in ihrer antiken Schreibung (*Asia, Bithynia*). Die entsprechenden modernen Namen sind im Registerband aufzufinden.

Orientalische Eigennamen werden in der Regel nach den Vorgaben des »Tübinger Atlas des Vorderen Orients« (TAVO) geschrieben. Daneben werden auch abweichende, aber im deutschen Sprachgebrauch übliche und bekannte Schreibweisen beibehalten, um das Auffinden zu erleichtern.

In den Karten sind topographische Bezeichnungen überwiegend in der vollständigen antiken Schreibung wiedergegeben.

Die Verschiedenheit der im Deutschen üblichen Schreibweisen für antike Worte und Namen (*Äschylus, Aeschylus, Aischylos*) kann gelegentlich zu erhöhtem Aufwand bei der Suche führen; dies gilt auch für *Ö / Oe / Oi* und *C / Z / K*.

Transkriptionen

Zu den im NEUEN PAULY verwendeten Transkriptionen vgl. Bd. 3, S. VIIIf.

Abkürzungen

Abkürzungen sind im erweiterten Abkürzungsverzeichnis am Anfang des dritten Bandes aufgelöst.

Sammlungen von Inschriften, Münzen, Papyri sind unter ihrer Sigle im zweiten Teil (Bibliographische Abkürzungen) des Abkürzungsverzeichnisses aufgeführt.

Anmerkungen

Die Anmerkungen enthalten lediglich bibliographische Angaben. Im Text der Artikel wird auf sie unter Verwendung eckiger Klammern verwiesen (Beispiel: die Angabe [1. 5[23]] bezieht sich auf den ersten numerierten Titel der Bibliographie, Seite 5, Anmerkung 23).

Verweise

Die Verbindung der Artikel untereinander wird durch Querverweise hergestellt. Dies geschieht im Text eines Artikels durch einen Pfeil (→) vor dem Wort / Lemma, auf das verwiesen wird; wird auf homonyme Lemmata verwiesen, ist meist auch die laufende Nummer beigefügt.

Querverweise auf verwandte Lemmata sind am Schluß eines Artikels, ggf. vor den bibliographischen Anmerkungen, angegeben.

Verweise auf Stichworte des zweiten, rezeptions- und wissenschaftsgeschichtlichen Teiles des NEUEN PAULY werden in Kapitälchen gegeben (→ ELEGIE).

Karten und Abbildungen

Texte, Abbildungen und Karten stehen in der Regel in engem Konnex, erläutern sich gegenseitig. In einigen Fällen ergänzen Karten und Abbildungen die Texte durch die Behandlung von Fragestellungen, die im Text nicht angesprochen werden können. Die Autoren der Karten und Abbildungen werden im Verzeichnis auf S. VIff. genannt.

Karten- und Abbildungsverzeichnis

NZ: Neuzeichnung, Angabe des Autors und/oder der zugrunde liegenden Vorlage/Literatur
RP: Reproduktion (mit kleinen Veränderungen) nach der angegebenen Vorlage

Lemma
Titel
Autor/Literatur

Gymnasion
Das Gymnasium nach Vitruv
NZ nach: R. Förtsch, Arch. Komm. zu den Villenbriefen des jüngeren Plinius, 1993, Taf. 75, 1.
Olympia, Gymnasion und Palaistra
NZ nach: Ch. Wacker, Das Gymnasion in Olympia. Geschichte und Funktion, 1996, Abb. 3.

Haartracht
I. Griechische Frauenfrisuren
NZ nach: H. Blanck, Einführung in das Privatleben der Griechen und Römer, 1976, 62, Abb. 14.
II. Römische Frauenfrisuren
NZ nach: H. Blanck, Einführung in das Privatleben der Griechen und Römer, 1976, 74, Abb. 17.

Ḥâḍra-Vasen
Verbreitung der Ḥâḍra-Vasen (zwischen ca. 260–197 v. Chr.)
NZ: R.F. Docter (nach A. Enklaar, Chronologie et peintres des hydries de Hadra, in: BABesch 60, 1985, 106–151, bes. 146 Abb. 23)

Handel
Handelswege in der römischen Kaiserzeit nach Auskunft antiker Quellen (1.–3. Jh. n. Chr.)
NZ: Redaktion/H.-J. Drexhage/H. Schneider

Haruspices
Terminologie antiker Leberschau
NZ: M. Haase

Hasmonäer
Das Hasmonäerreich in Judäa und Peripherie zur Zeit des Königs Alexandros Iannaios (103–76 v. Chr.)
NZ: W. Eder/Redaktion
Stemma
NZ nach: C. Colpe, s.v. H., KlP 2, 1979, 249f.

Ḫattusa
Ḫattusa: Archäologischer Lageplan der Großreichszeit
NZ: J. Seeher (nach P. Neve, Die Ausgrabungen in Bogazköy/Hattusa 1993, in: AA 1994, 290 Abb. 1)
Übersicht zu den hethitischen Königen und Königinnen
NZ nach Vorlagen von F. Starke
Politische Karte des hethitischen Großreiches: »Ḫattusa« (13. Jh. v. Chr.)
NZ: F. Starke

Haus
Babylon, spätbabylonisches Wohnhaus
NZ nach: E. Heinrich, s.v. Haus, B. Archäologisch, RLA 4, 1972–75, Abb. 18.
Ägyptisches Haus, Amarna
NZ nach: D. Arnold, Lexikon der ägypt. Baukunst, 1994, 101, Abb. B.
Olynthos, Pastas-Haus
NZ nach: W. Hoepfner, E.L. Schwandner, Haus und Stadt im klass. Griechenland, 1986, 44, Abb. 29.
Peiraieus, Prostas-Haus
NZ nach: W. Hoepfner, E.L. Schwandner, Haus und Stadt im klass. Griechenland, 1986, 15, Abb. 10.
Orraon (Ammotopos)
NZ nach: W. Hoepfner, E.L. Schwandner, Haus und Stadt im klass. Griechenland, 1986, 270, Abb. 266 (Erd- und Obergeschoß).
Eretria, sog. Mosaikenhaus
NZ nach: E. Walter-Karydi, Die Nobilitierung des griech. Wohnhauses in der spätklass. Zeit, in: W. Hoepfner, G. Brands (Hrsg.), Basileia. Die Paläste der Hellenistischen Könige, 1996, 3, Abb. 1.
Rom, Palatin, etrusk. Patrizierhaus
NZ nach: M. Cristofani (Hrsg.), La grande Roma dei Tarquini, Ausstellungskatalog, 1990, 98.
Atriumhaus
NZ nach: W. Müller, G. Vogel, dtv-Atlas zur Baukunst I, 1974, 222.
Pompeji, Casa dei Capitelli figurati
NZ nach: W. Müller, G. Vogel, dtv-Atlas zur Baukunst I, 1974, 222.
Pompeji, Casa del Fauno
NZ nach: W. Müller, G. Vogel, dtv-Atlas zur Baukunst I, 1974, 222.
Ostia, Mietshaus
NZ nach: E. Brödner, Wohnen in der Antike, ^{2}1993, 59, Abb. 14a.

Hebegeräte
Kran vom Hateriergrab
NZ nach: F. Sinn, K.S. Freyberger, Vatikan. Museen. Museo Gregoriano Profano ex Lateranse. Die Grabdenkmäler 2. Die Ausstattung des Hateriergrabes, 1993, 136.

Heiligtum
Das Herculesheiligtum in Ostia zu Beginn des 2. Jh. n. Chr. mit Benennung der Tempel- und Nebenräume in antiker Terminologie
NZ: U. Egelhaaf-Gaiser/M. Haase (nach: R. Mar, El santuario de Hércules y la urbanistica de Ostia, in: Archivo español de arqueología 63, 1990, 157, Abb. 6)

Heizung
Hypokaustanlage
NZ nach Vorlage von H.-O. Lamprecht

Hellenistische Staatenwelt
Die hellenistische Staatenwelt im 3. Jh. v. Chr.
NZ: W. Eder/Redaktion (nach: H. Waldmann, Vorderer Orient. Die hell. Staatenwelt im 3. Jh. v. Chr., TAVO B V 3, 1983. © Dr. Ludwig Reichert Verlag, Wiesbaden)
Die hellenistische Staatenwelt im 2. Jh. v. Chr.
NZ: W. Eder/Redaktion (nach: H. Waldmann, Vorderer Orient. Die hell. Staatenwelt im 2. Jh. v. Chr., TAVO B V 4, 1985. © Dr. Ludwig Reichert Verlag, Wiesbaden)

Autoren

Luciana **Aigner-Foresti** Wien L. A.-F.
Maria Grazia **Albiani** Bologna M. G. A.
Annemarie **Ambühl** Basel A. A.
Walter **Ameling** Würzburg W. A.
Graziano **Arrighetti** Pisa A. GR.
Ernst **Badian** Cambridge E. B.
Balbina **Bäbler** Bern B. BÄ.
Jürgen **Bär** Berlin J. BÄ.
Matthias **Baltes** Münster M. BA.
Pedro **Barceló** Potsdam P. B.
Dorothea **Baudy** Konstanz D. B.
Gerhard **Baudy** Konstanz G. B.
Hans **Beck** Köln HA. BE.
K. **Belke** Wien K. BE.
Andreas **Bendlin** Oxford A. BEN.
Albrecht **Berger** Berlin AL. B.
Gábor **Betegh** Budapest G. BE.
Klaus **Bieberstein** Fribourg K. B.
Gebhard **Bieg** Tübingen GE. BI.
Gerhard **Binder** Bochum G. BI.
Vera **Binder** Tübingen V. BI.
A. R. **Birley** Düsseldorf A. B.
Bruno **Bleckmann** Strasbourg B. BL.
René **Bloch** Basel R. B.
Horst-Dieter **Blume** Münster H.-D. B.
Christfried **Böttrich** Leipzig CHR. B.
Ewen **Bowie** Oxford E. BO.
Jan N. **Bremmer** Groningen J. B.
Burchard **Brentjes** Berlin B. B.
Christoph **Briese** Randers CH. B.
Klaus **Bringmann** Frankfurt/Main K. BR.
Luc **Brisson** Paris L. BR.
Sebastian P. **Brock** Oxford S. BR.
Kai **Brodersen** Mannheim K. BRO.
Marco **Buonocore** Rom M. BU.
Christoph **Burchard** Göttingen CH. BU.
Leonhard **Burckhardt** Basel LE. BU.
Alison **Burford-Cooper** Ashville A. B.-C.
Jan **Burian** Prag J. BU.
Pierre **Cabanes** Clermont-Ferrand PI. CA.
Gualtiero **Calboli** Bologna G. C.
Ursula **Calmeyer-Seidl** Berlin U. SE.
Giorgio **Camassa** Udine G. CA.
J. Brian **Campbell** Belfast J. CA.
Eva **Cancik-Kirschbaum** Berlin E. C.-K.
Calum M. **Carmichael** Ithaca C. M. C.
Paul A. **Cartledge** Cambridge P. C.
Heinrich **Chantraine** Mannheim HE. C.
Eckhard **Christmann** Heidelberg E. C.
Justus **Cobet** Essen J. CO.
Gudrun **Colbow** Lüttich G. CO.
Carsten **Colpe** Berlin C. C.
Edward **Courtney** Charlottesville, ED. C.
Giovanna **Daverio Rocchi** Mailand G. D. R.
Giuliana **De Francesco** Rom G. d. F.
Loretana **de Libero** Hamburg L. d. L.
Philip **de Souza** Twickenham P. d. S.
Wolfgang **Decker** Köln W. D.
Jan **den Boeft** Leiderdorp J. d. B.
Massimo **Di Marco** Fondi (Latina) M. D. MA.
Karlheinz **Dietz** Würzburg K. DI.
Roald Fritjof **Docter** Amsterdam R. D.
Klaus **Döring** Bamberg K. D.
Yvonne **Domhardt** Zürich Y. D.
Alice **Donohue** Bryn Mawr A. A. D.
Tiziano **Dorandi** Paris T. D.
Anne-Marie **Doyen-Higuet** Ciney A. D.-H.
Paul **Dräger** Trier P. D.
Thomas **Drew-Bear** Lyon T. D.-B.
Hans-Joachim **Drexhage** Marburg H.-J. D.
Boris **Dreyer** Göttingen BO. D.
Constanze **Ebner** Innsbruck C. E.
Werner **Eck** Köln W. E.
Walter **Eder** Bochum W. ED.
Ulrike **Egelhaaf-Gaiser** Potsdam UL. EG.-G.
Beate **Ego** Tübingen B. E.
Ulrich **Eigler** Freiburg U. E.
Paolo **Eleuteri** Venedig P. E.
Karl-Ludwig **Elvers** Bochum K.-L. E.
Johannes **Engels** Köln J. E.
Robert K. **Englund** Berlin R. K. E.
Michael **Erler** Würzburg M. ER.
Malcolm **Errington** Marburg MA. ER.
Marion **Euskirchen** Bonn M. E.
Giulia **Falco** Athen GI. F.
Marco **Fantuzzi** Florenz M. FA.
Heinz **Felber** Leipzig HE. FE.
Martin **Fell** Münster M. FE.
Menso **Folkerts** München M. F.
Nikolaus **Forgó** Wien N. F.
Sotera **Fornaro** Heidelberg S. FO.
Bernhard **Forssman** Erlangen B. F.
Thomas **Franke** Dortmund T. F.
Christa **Frateantonio** Gießen C. F.
Klaus **Freitag** Münster K. F.
Jörg **Frey** Stuttgart J. FR.
Helmut **Freydank** Potsdam H. FR.
Thomas **Frigo** Bonn T. FR.
Roland **Fröhlich** Tübingen RO. F.
Andreas **Fuchs** Jena A. F.
Jörg **Fündling** Bonn JÖ. F.
Therese **Fuhrer** Zürich T. FU.
Peter **Funke** Münster P. F.
William D. **Furley** Heidelberg W. D. F.
Massimo **Fusillo** Rom M. FU.
Hartmut **Galsterer** Köln H. GA.
Hannes **Galter** Graz HA. G.
Richard **Gamauf** Wien R. GA.
José Luis **García-Ramón** Köln J. G.-R.
Hans-Joachim **Gehrke** Freiburg H.-J. G.
Karin **Geppert** Tübingen KA. GE.
Jörg **Gerber** München J. G.
Tomasz **Giaro** Frankfurt/Main T. G.
Christian **Gizewski** Berlin C. G.
Susanne **Gödde** Münster S. G.
Herwig **Görgemanns** Heidelberg H. GÖ.
Hans **Gottschalk** Leeds H. G.
Marie-Odile **Goulet-Cazé** Antony M. G.-C.
Fritz **Graf** Basel F. G.
Herbert **Graßl** Salzburg H. GR.
Reinhard **Grieshammer** Heidelberg R. GR.
Kirsten **Groß-Albenhausen** Frankfurt/Main K. G.-A.
Fritz **Gschnitzer** Heidelberg F. GSCH.
Linda-Marie **Günther** München L.-M. G.

Maria Ida **Gulletta** Pisa M. I. G.
Hans Georg **Gundel** Gießen H. G. G.
Beate **Gundert** London, Ontario BE. GU.
Andreas **Gutsfeld** Berlin A. G.
Mareile **Haase** Tübingen M. HAA.
Richard **Haase** Leonberg RI. H.
Ilsetraut **Hadot** Limours I. H.
Pierre **Hadot** Limours P. HA.
Claus **Haebler** Münster C. H.
Verena Tiziana **Halbwachs** Wien V. T. H.
Klaus **Hallof** Berlin K.H.
Ruth E. **Harder** Zürich R. HA.
Elke **Hartmann** Berlin E. HA.
Stefan R. **Hauser** Berlin S. HA.
Hartwig **Heckel** Bochum H. H.
Nils **Heeßel** Heidelberg NI. HE.
Ulrich **Heider** Köln U. HE.
Martin **Heimgartner** Basel M. HE.
Theodor **Heinze** Genf T. H.
Joachim **Hengstl** Lahntal-Grossfelden JO. HE.
Peter **Herz** Regensburg P. H.
Bernhard **Herzhoff** Trier B. HE.
Stephen **Heyworth** Oxford S. H.
Thomas **Hidber** Bern T. HI.
Friedrich **Hild** Wien F. H.
Christoph **Höcker** Hamburg C. HÖ.
Olaf **Höckmann** Mainz O. H.
Peter **Högemann** Tübingen PE. HÖ.
Nicola **Hoesch** München N. H.
Martin **Hose** München MA. HO.
Wolfgang **Hübner** Münster W. H.
Christian **Hünemörder** Hamburg C. HÜ.
Hermann **Hunger** Wien H. HU.
Richard **Hunter** Cambridge R. HU.
Rolf **Hurschmann** Hamburg R. H.
Werner **Huß** Bamberg W. HU.
Brad **Inwood** Toronto B. I.
Karl **Jansen-Winkeln** Berlin K. J.-W.
Klaus-Peter **Johne** Berlin K. P. J.
Sarah Iles **Johnston** Columbus S. I. J.
Lutz **Käppel** Tübingen L. K.
Jochem **Kahl** Münster J. KA.
Hansjörg **Kalcyk** Petershausen H. KAL.
Hans **Kaletsch** Regensburg H. KA.
Klaus **Karttunen** Espoo K. K.
Helen **Kaufmann** Basel HE. KA.
Peter **Kehne** Hannover P. KE.
Karlheinz **Kessler** Emskirchen K. KE.
Wilhelm **Kierdorf** Köln W. K.
Helen **King** Reading H. K.
Jörg **Klinger** Bochum J. KL.
Claudia **Klodt** Hamburg CL. K.
Dietrich **Klose** München DI. K.
Ernst Axel **Knauf** Zumikon E. A. K.
Heiner **Knell** Darmstadt H. KN.
Matthias **Köckert** Berlin M. K.
Christoph **Kohler** Tübingen C. KO.
Herwig **Kramolisch** Eppelheim HE. KR.
Jens-Uwe **Krause** Heidelberg J. K.
Rolf **Krauss** Berlin R. K.
Ludolf **Kuchenbuch** Hagen LU. KU.
Hartmut **Kühne** Berlin H. KÜ.
Amélie **Kuhrt** London A. KU.
Heike **Kunz** Tübingen HE. K.
Bernhard **Kytzler** Durban B. KY.
Yves **Lafond** Bochum Y. L.
Marie-Luise **Lakmann** Münster M.-L. L.
Heinz-Otto **Lamprecht** Köln H.-O. L.
Joachim **Latacz** Basel J. L.
Yann **Le Bohec** Lyon Y. L. B.
Thomas **Leisten** Tübingen T. L.
Jürgen **Leonhardt** Bad Doberan J. LE.
Hartmut **Leppin** Hannover H. L.
Anne **Ley** Xanten A. L.
Wolf-Lüder **Liebermann** Bielefeld W.-L. L.
Rüdiger **Liwak** Berlin R. L.
Hans **Lohmann** Bochum H. LO.
Mario **Lombardo** Lecce M. L.
Volker **Losemann** Marburg V. L.
Michael **Maaß** Karlsruhe MI. MA.
Giacomo **Manganaro** Sant' Agata li Battiata GI. MA.
Ulrich **Manthe** Passau U. M.
Christian **Marek** Zürich C. MA.
Christoph **Markschies** Jena C. M.
A. **Mastrocinque** Verona A. MAS.
Andreas **Mehl** Halle/Saale A. ME.
Mischa **Meier** Bochum M. MEI.
Gerhard **Meiser** Halle/Saale GE. ME.
Franz-Stefan **Meissel** Wien F. ME.
Burkhard **Meißner** Halle/Saale B. M.
Klaus **Meister** Berlin K. MEI.
Piero **Meloni** Cagliari P. M.
Giovanna **Menci** Florenz G. M.
Stefan **Meyer-Schwelling** Tübingen S. M.-S.
Simone **Michel** Hamburg S. MI.
Martin **Miller** Berlin M. M.
Franco **Montanari** Pisa F. M.
Ornella **Montanari** Bologna O. M.
Glenn W. **Most** Heidelberg G. W. M.
Claire **Muckensturm-Poulle** Besançon C. M.-P.
Christian **Müller** Hagen C. MÜ.
Stefan **Müller** Hagen S. MÜ.
Walter W. **Müller** Marburg W. W. M.
Christa **Müller-Kessler** Emskirchen C. K.
Peter **Nadig** Duisburg P. N.
Michel **Narcy** Paris MI. NA.
Heinz-Günther **Nesselrath** Bern H.-G. NE.
Richard **Neudecker** Rom R. N.
Günter **Neumann** Würzburg G. N.
Johannes **Niehoff** Freiburg J. N.
Herbert **Niehr** Rottenburg H. NI.
Hans Georg **Niemeyer** Hamburg H. G. N.
Hans Jörg **Nissen** Berlin H. J. N.
René **Nünlist** Basel RE. N.
Vivian **Nutton** London V. N.
John H. **Oakley** Williamsburg J. O.
Joachim **Oelsner** Leipzig J. OE.
Norbert **Oettinger** Augsburg N. O.
Eckart **Olshausen** Stuttgart E. O.
Robin **Osborne** Oxford R. O.
Jürgen **Osing** Berlin J. OS.
Renate **Oswald** Graz R. OS.
Johannes **Pahlitzsch** Berlin J. P.
Umberto **Pappalardo** Neapel U. PA.
Barbara **Patzek** Wiesbaden B. P.
Christoph Georg **Paulus** Berlin C. PA.

Anneliese **Peschlow-Bindokat** Berlin A. PE.
Ulrike **Peter** Berlin U. P.
Volker **Pingel** Bochum V. P.
Robert **Plath** Erlangen R. P.
Annegret **Plontke-Lüning** Jena A. P.-L.
Thomas **Podella** Lübeck TH. PO.
Werner **Portmann** Berlin W. P.
Paul **Potter** London, Ontario P. PO.
Friedhelm **Prayon** Tübingen F. PR.
Francesca **Prescendi** Basel FR. P.
Frank **Pressler** Heidelberg F. P.
Fritz **Raber** Innsbruck FR. R.
Dominic **Rathbone** London D. R.
Michael **Redies** Berlin M. R.
Johannes **Renger** Berlin J. RE.
Peter J. **Rhodes** Durham P. J. R.
John A. **Richmond** Blackrock J. A. R.
Christoph **Riedweg** Zürich C. RI.
Jörg **Rieker** Freiburg JÖ. RI.
Josef **Rist** Würzburg J. RI.
Emmet **Robbins** Toronto E. R.
Michael **Roberts** Middletown M. RO.
Wolfgang **Röllig** Tübingen W. R.
Veit **Rosenberger** Augsburg V. RO.
Christoph **Rottler** Tübingen C. R.
Jörg **Rüpke** Potsdam J. R.
David T. **Runia** Leiden D. T. R.
Walther **Sallaberger** Leipzig WA. SA.
Klaus **Sallmann** Mainz KL. SA.
Eleonora **Salomone Gaggero** Genua E. S. G.
Helen **Sancisi-Weerdenburg** Utrecht H. S.-W.
Luigi **Santi Amantini** Genua L. S. A.
Marjeta **Šašel Kos** Ljubljana M. Š. K.
Kyriakos **Savvidis** Witten K. SA.
Brigitte **Schaffner** Basel B. SCH.
Bernd **Schaller** Göttingen BE. SCH.
Dietmar **Schanbacher** Dresden D. SCH.
Ingeborg **Scheibler** Krefeld I. S.
Johannes **Scherf** Tübingen JO. S.
Gottfried **Schiemann** Tübingen G. S.
Peter L. **Schmidt** Konstanz P. L. S.
Pauline **Schmitt-Pantel** Paris P. S.- P.
Winfried **Schmitz** Bielefeld W. S.
Ulrich **Schmitzer** Erlangen U. SCH.
Helmuth **Schneider** Kassel H. SCHN.
Franz **Schön** Regensburg F. SCH.
Hanne **Schönig** Mainz H. SCHÖ.
Martin **Schottky** Pretzfeld M. SCH.
Peter **Schreiner** Köln P. S.
Jörg **Schulte-Altedorneburg** Marburg J. S.-A.
Heinz-Joachim **Schulzki** Mannheim H.-J. S.
Elmar **Schwertheim** Münster E. SCH.
Jürgen **Seeher** Istanbul J. SE.
Stephan Johannes **Seidlmayer** Berlin S. S.
Reinhard **Senff** Bochum R. SE.
Anne Viola **Siebert** Münster A. V. S.
Uwe **Sievertsen** Berlin U. S.
Dietrich **Simon** Jena DI. S.
Holger **Sonnabend** Stuttgart H. SO.
Wolfgang **Spickermann** Bochum W. SP.
Günter **Spitzbart** Herscheid G. SP.
Karl-Heinz **Stanzel** Tübingen K.-H. S.
Frank **Starke** München/Tübingen F. S.
Ekkehard W. **Stegemann** Bern E. STE.
Elke **Stein-Hölkeskamp** Köln E. S.-H.
Dieter **Steinbauer** Regensburg D. ST.
Matthias **Steinhart** Lahr M. ST.
Magdalene **Stoevesandt** Basel MA. ST.
Marten **Stol** Leiden MA. S.
Helmut **Storch** Tübingen H. ST.
Daniel **Strauch** Berlin D. S.
Karl **Strobel** Trier K. ST.
Meret **Strothmann** Bochum ME. STR.
Gerd **Stumpf** München GE. S.
Thomas A. **Szlezák** Tübingen T. A. S.
Sarolta A. **Takacs** Harvard S. TA.
Michel **Tardieu** Joigny MI. TA.
Gerhard **Thür** Graz G. T.
Franz **Tinnefeld** München F. T.
Malcolm **Todd** Durham M. TO.
Kurt **Tomaschitz** Wien K. T.
Isabel **Toral-Niehoff** Freiburg I. T.-N.
Renzo **Tosi** Bologna R. T.
Alain **Touwaide** Madrid A. TO.
Hans **Treidler** Berlin H. T.
Giovanni **Uggeri** Florenz G. U.
Jürgen **Untermann** Pulheim J. U.
Marc **van de Mieroop** New York M. v. M.
Edzard **Visser** Basel E. V.
Artur **Völkl** Innsbruck A. VÖ.
Iris **von Bredow** Bietigheim-Bissingen I. v. B.
Jürgen **von Ungern-Sternberg** Basel J. v. U.-S.
Rudolf **Wachter** Basel R. WA.
Christine **Walde** Basel C. W.
Katharina **Waldner** Berlin K. WA.
Gerold **Walser** Basel G. W.
Uwe **Walter** Köln U. WAL.
Irina **Wandrey** Berlin I. WA.
Ralf-B. **Wartke** Berlin R. W.
Peter **Weiß** Kiel P. W.
Michael **Weißenberger** Düsseldorf M. W.
Karl-Wilhelm **Welwei** Bochum K.-W. WEL.
Rainer **Wiegels** Buchenbach RA. WI.
Lothar **Wierschowski** Oldenburg L. WI.
Josef **Wiesehöfer** Kiel J. W.
Gernot **Wilhelm** Würzburg GE. W.
Wolfgang **Will** Bonn W. W.
Andreas **Willi** Basel AN. W.
Nigel **Wilson** Oxford N. W.
Aloys **Winterling** Bielefeld A. WI.
Eckhard **Wirbelauer** Freiburg E. W.
T. P. **Wiseman** Exeter T. W.
Anne-Maria **Wittke** Tübingen A. W.
Frieder **Zaminer** Berlin F. Z.
Leonid **Zhmud** St. Petersburg L. ZH.
Bernhard **Zimmermann** Freiburg B. Z.
Reto **Zingg** Basel RE. ZI.

Übersetzer

A. Beuchel	A. BE.
J. Derlien	J. DE.
H. Dietrich	H. D.
P. Eleuteri	P. E.
S. Felkl	S. F.
A. Heckmann	A. H.
T. Heinze	T. H.
H. Helting	H. H.
H. Kaufmann	H. K.
R. P. Lalli	R. P. L.
J. W. Mayer	J. W. M.
M. Mohr	M. MO.
S. Paulus	S. P.
P. Plieger	P. P.
C. Pöthig	C. P.
F. Prescendi	F. P.
B. v. Reibnitz	B. v. R.
L. v. Reppert-Bismarck	L. v. R.-B.
U. Rüpke	U. R.
J. Salewski	J. S.
I. Sauer	I. S.
V. Sauer	V. S.
B. Schaffner	B. S.
R. Schaub	R. SCH.
M. A. Söllner	M. A. S.
L. Strehl	L. S.
C. Strobel	C. ST.
R. Struß-Höcker	R. S.-H.
A. Thorspecken	A. T.
A. Wittenburg	A. WI.
S. Zimmermann	S. Z.

Mitarbeiter in den Fachgebietsredaktionen

Alte Geschichte: Anne Krahn, Mischa Meier, Meret Strothmann

Griechische Philologie: Anna Korth, Raphael Sobotta

Historische Geographie: Dorothea Gaier, Vera Sauer M. A.

Kulturgeschichte: Hartwig Heckel, Judith Hendricks, Maren Saiko

Lateinische Philologie, Rhetorik: Martina Dürkop, Bärbel Geyer, Guido Greschke

Orientalistik: Helga Vogel

Philosophie: Vanessa Kucinska

Religion und Mythologie: Alexandra Frey, Helen Kaufmann, Raphael Michel

Sozial- und Wirtschaftsgeschichte: Kathrin Umbach

Sprachwissenschaft: Christel Kindermann, Dr. Robert Plath

Gründer s. Ktistes

Grumentum. Stadt in → Lucania, wo die Sora (h. Sciaura) in den Akiris (h. Agri) mündet (vgl. Strab. 6,1,3; Ptol. 3,1,70); Ruinen 1,5 km östl. von Grumento. Hart umkämpft im 2. Punischen Krieg (Liv. 23,37,10; 27,41,3) und im Bundesgenossenkrieg (vgl. App. civ. 1,41). *Municipium, tribus Pomptina* (*regio III*). Vom guten Lagariner-Wein bei G. spricht Plinius (nat. 14,69).

E.O.

Grundbuch. Im rechtlichen Sinn kann man von einem G. sprechen, wenn ein lückenloses, entweder alle Einwohner (Personalfoliensystem) oder alle Grundstücke eines Bezirkes (Realfoliensystem) umfassendes Register von Grundstücken »öffentlichen Glauben« genießt, und dadurch dem eingetragenen Erwerber das Eigentumsrecht garantiert ist. In der Ant. gab es zahlreiche schlichte Grundstücksregister (→ Kataster), die jedoch meistens als Grundlage für die Steuererhebung dienten (Beispiele und Lit. [1]).

Allein aus dem ptolemäischen und röm. Ägypten sind Einrichtungen zur Kontrolle von Rechtsgeschäften über Grundstücke (und auch Sklaven) bekannt, die den Wirkungen eines modernen G. nahekommen könnten, doch erfüllten sie eine derartige Funktion nur zum Teil. Die καταγραφή (*katagraphḗ*, »Niederschreibung«, Registrierung) der ptol. Zeit ist die Eintragung von Urkunden über Grundstücks-, Haus- und Sklavenkäufe in ein Sonderregister, um jene Geschäfte evident zu halten. Erst in röm. Zeit eingeführt und durch ein Edikt des *praefectus Aegypti* M. Mettius Rufus 89 n. Chr. neu bekräftigt wurde der Betrieb der βιβλιοθήκη ἐγκτήσεων (*bibliothḗkē enktḗseōn*, Register des Liegenschaftsvermögens). Auf einem Personalfolium waren die einer Person gehörenden Grundstücke und → Hypotheken registriert. Jeder Erwerber hatte seine Erwerbsurkunde zur ἀναγραφή (*anagraphḗ*, Registrierung) einzureichen, nachdem der Registerführer (βιβλιοφύλαξ, *bibliophýlax*) anhand des Registerblattes des Veräußerers dessen Verfügungsmacht kontrolliert hatte. Doch war diese Formalität weder für die Wirksamkeit des Eigentumserwerbs nötig, noch konnte sich ein Dritter auf die Richtigkeit der Eintragung berufen. Immerhin war dadurch im Liegenschaftsverkehr ein hoher Standard an Sicherheit erreicht.

→ Kataster

1 F. M. Heichelheim, s. v. Grundbuch, KlP 2, 879.

Wolff, 184–255 • H.-A. Rupprecht, Einführung in die Papyruskunde, 1994, 140 f.

G.T.

Grundeigentum s. Wirtschaft

G

Grundherrschaft. G. ist kein durch zeitgenössische Quellen belegter, sondern ein erst im Übergang zur Moderne entstandener Ordnungsbegriff der Agrar- und Sozialverfassung, der ein für das europ. MA und das Ancien Régime typisches Konglomerat rententragender Verfügungsgewalt über »Land und Leute« meint [7]. Insofern sind alle Übertragungen dieses Begriffs – auch auf die röm. Ant. – eher irreführend. Klass. bleibt M. Webers [10] klare Abgrenzung der G. von der ant. bzw. neuzeitlichen Plantage und der Gutsherrschaft im Rahmen seiner Idealtypologie des Herreneigentums.

Zur Entstehung der G. haben soziale und wirtschaftliche Gegebenheiten der Spätant. wesentlich beigetragen, so etwa das Besitzrecht der Kirche, der → Colonat (ergänzt durch das Weiterleben vorrömischer Formen ländlicher Abhängigkeit), das ländliche → Patrocinium senatorischer Großgrundbesitzer gegenüber Schutzbedürftigen und die → Emphyteuse. Hinzu kam dann die Konfiskation der kaiserlichen Ländereien durch die Herrscher der germanischen *regna*, die sonst wenig änderten, sich vielmehr mit den röm. Großgrundbesitzern arrangierten, die Steuerorganisation übernahmen, aber im Bereich der landwirtschaftlichen Produktion die Ackersklaverei bevorzugten.

Die formative Phase der G. setzte erst im 7. Jh. im merowingischen Gallien ein, wo die röm. Steuerverfassung für die Herrschenden schrittweise ihre Verbindlichkeit verloren hatte. Nach heutiger Auffassung ging das karolingische Königtum zusammen mit dem Adel, den Bischöfen und den Benediktinerabteien dazu über, die großen Herrenländereien in den Gegenden mit leichten, fruchtbaren Böden statt von Sklaven (*mancipia*) durch Tagesfrondienste neu angesiedelter *servi* oder durch Stückfronden integrierter *ingenui* bestellen zu lassen. Einer zweigeteilten Organisation (frz. domaine bipartite, engl. manor, dt. Fronhofsverfassung, Villikation) in Herrenland und Hufenland wurde dabei der Vorzug gegeben. Die *mansus*- bzw. Hufen-Betriebe blieben selbständig und abgabepflichtig. Diese »Betriebsgrundherrschaft« breitete sich auch durch systematische Rodung sowie durch gezielte örtliche Siedlungsverlagerung in den karolingischen Kernlanden zwischen Loire und Rhein aus und erscheint in der Überlieferung seit dem späten 8. Jh. als die bestimmende Form. Dieses Bild trügt aber insofern, als jede Großgrundherrschaft ein räumlich lockeres Konglomerat aus sklavistisch bestimmten Großhöfen, bipartiten Domänen, nur abgabepflichtigen oder schutzhörigen Kleinbetrieben und leiherechtlich Assoziierten darstellt. Die großräumige Durchsetzung der G. ist deshalb bis heute ein umstrittenes Phänomen geblieben – die mediterranen Agrarverhältnisse werden vielfach als noch ant. Kombination von Ackersklaverei und Freibauern [1], die ostrheinischen als kleinformatige, von hofhörigen Sklaven bestimmte Vorstufen der Bipartition bzw.

persönlicher Abgabenherrschaft [8] gedeutet. Die Lehre vom »german.« Ursprung der ma. G. kann als definitiv überholt gelten.

1 P. Bonnassie, From Slavery to Feudalism in South-Western Europe, 1991 **2** J.-P. Devroey, Etudes sur le grand domaine carolingien, 1993 **3** R. Kaiser, Das röm. Erbe und das Merowingerreich, 1997 **4** L. Kuchenbuch, Die Klostergrundherrschaft im Frühma., in: F. Prinz (Hrsg.), Herrschaft und Kirche, 1988, 297–343 **5** Ders., G. im früheren MA, 1991 **6** J. Percival, Seigneurial Aspects of Late Roman Estate Management, in: English Historical Review 84, 1969, 449–473 **7** K. Schreiner, »G.«. Entstehung und Bedeutungswandel eines geschichtswiss. Ordnungs- und Erklärungsbegriffs, in: H. Patze (Hrsg.), G. im späten MA, 2 Bde., 1983, Bd. 1, 11–75 **8** A. Verhulst, Rural and Urban Aspects of Early Medieval Northwest Europe, 1992 **9** Ders. (Hrsg.), Die G. im frühen MA, 1985 **10** M. Weber, Wirtschaftsgesch., 1923 **11** C. R. Whittaker, Rural Labour in Three Roman Provinces, in: P. Garnsey (Hrsg.), Non-Slave Labour in the Greek-Roman World, 1980, 73–99 **12** Ders., Circe's Pigs. From Slavery to Serfdom in the Later Roman World, in: M. L. Finley (Hrsg.), Classical Slavery, 1987, 88–120.

LU.KU.

Grundstrich s. Schriftstile

Gruppe R. Eine Gruppe att. Lekythen mit wgr. polychromer Mattfarbenbemalung aus der Zeit zw. 420 und 410 v. Chr. Nach Gefäßform, Ornamentik, Maltechnik und Farbigkeit (rote Konturlinien, schwarzgraue Ornamentzeichnung) kommen sie aus der gleichen Werkstatt wie die Lekythen des Schilfmalers, sind aber größer als diese und in der Zeichnung der Figuren wesentlich qualitätvoller. Sie wurden deshalb von Beazley von den Lekythen des Schilfmalers getrennt und unter dem Hilfsnamen Group R = Group of the R(eed painter) vereinigt. Die Zuordnung zur Gruppe bedeutet jedoch nicht, daß alle diese Lekythen von einem Maler stammen müssen, nur die beiden berühmtesten (Athen, NM, Inv.Nr. 1816/1817) sind sicher von einer Hand.

Charakteristisch für die Bilder der Gruppe sind: Dreifiguren-Kompositionen (meistens Grabszenen), eine äußerst sorgfältige und subtile Umrißzeichnung, ein mittels bewegtem Kontur und Körperdrehung erreichtes plastisches Volumen der Figuren und ein Ausdruck von Schwermut und sorgenvollem Ernst, der sowohl über den oft in Dreiviertelansicht gegebenen Gesichtern liegt als auch ihre Körperhaltung prägt. In der Forschung werden die Bilder der G.R mit dem Maler → Parrhasios in Verbindung gebracht und als Reflexe seiner Kunst gedeutet.

Beazley, ARV², 1383–1384, Nr. 1–22; 1692 • Beazley, Addenda², 371–372 • D. C. Kurtz, Athenian White Lekythoi-Patterns and Painters, 1975, 58–68, Taf. 49–50 • A. Rumpf, Parrhasios, in: AJA 55, 1951, 1–12, Abb. 1.3–4. • I. Wehgartner, Att. wgr. Keramik, 1983, 29.

J.d.B.

Gruß. I. Grussgebärden II. Verbale Grussformeln

I. Grussgebärden
A. Handreichung B. Kuss und Umarmung
C. Erheben der rechten Hand
D. Ehrerbietungen gegenüber Älteren und Ranghöheren

A. Handreichung

Nach griech. und röm. Sitte gab man Gastfreunden, Familienmitgliedern, Vertrauten oder Freunden die rechte Hand und drückte sie fest (Hom. Il. 10,542 u.ö.; Xen. Kyr. 3,2,14; Aristoph. Nub. 81; Plut. Cicero 879; Plut. Antonius 952; Plut. de amicorum multitudine 94b), sowohl bei der Begrüßung (bei Plut. Caesar 708 schon eher Leutseligkeit) wie auch beim Abschied. Der Handschlag galt als Zeichen der Freundschaft und des Vertrauens (Xen. Kyr. 3,2,14; Liv. 30,12,18); er wurde bes. Menschen gewährt, mit denen man sich innig verbunden fühlte und deren unerwartete Wiederkehr (aus Krieg oder von einer Reise) Freude erregte (Hom. Il. 10,542; Hom. Od. 24,409; Aischyl. Ag. 34f.; Ov. met. 7,495f.). Diese Form des G. konnte so weit gehen, daß man den Ankommenden an der Hand ins Haus bzw. an seinen Sitzplatz führte (Hom. Od. 1,119–121). Ebenso gab man sich die Hand bei einem Abschied auf längere Zeit (Xen. Kyr. 3,2,14) bzw. in Erwartung des Todes (Eur. Alc. 193; Plut. Themistokles 127; Plut. Brutus 1008). Bei Tac. hist. 2,49 küssen die Soldaten dem toten Kaiser Otho sogar die Hand: Hier ist der Gedanke der Ehrerbietung und Trauer mit einzubeziehen. Entsprechend der Bed. der Handreichung galten infolgedessen Menschen, die ohne ersichtlichen Grund die Hand eines anderen ergriffen, als Schmeichler (Hor. sat. 1,9,4; Plaut. Aul. 115f.).

B. Kuss und Umarmung

Zu der Begrüßung gehörte mitunter auch die Umarmung (ἀσπασμός, *aspasmós*; lat. *complexus*) und der → Kuß (φίλημα, *phílēma*; lat. *osculum*, Hom. Od. 17,38f.), hierbei nicht selten der Kuß auf Haupt und Schultern bzw. der Handkuß (Hom. Od. 24,397; → Gebärden; → *salutatio*); mit Kuß und Umarmung verabschiedete man sich auch voneinander, vor allem vor dem Tod (Lukian. verae historiae 1,30 mit einer bes. phantasievollen Erzählung). Der Kuß als Begrüßungsform, eine persische Sitte (Hdt. 1,134), war über den griech. Osten vorgedrungen und hatte sich während des Hell. verbreitet; zu Beginn der röm. Kaiserzeit hatte er sich bereits bei den unterschiedlichsten Anlässen etabliert (bei einem Besuch, bei der Rückkehr von einer Reise etc.). Plin. nat. 26,2f. führt einen zu seiner Zeit häufigen Gesichtsausschlag (die Flechte, eine von ihm *mentagra* genannte Krankheit) auf das Küssen bei Begrüßung oder Abschied zurück, und Tac. ann. 4,57 erwähnt die Abneigung – vielleicht aus diesem Grund – des Tiberius gegen den Kuß; derselbe Kaiser versuchte vergeblich, das überhand nehmende Küssen zu verbieten (Suet. Tib. 34,2), dem man sogar bei der Begegnung auf der Straße ausgesetzt war, worüber sich Mart. 2,10; 2,12; 10,22; 11,95; 11,98 u.ö. polemisch ausließ.

C. ERHEBEN DER RECHTEN HAND

Eine weitere G.-Gebärde war das Erheben der rechten Hand (→ Gebärden; vgl. das Schulszenenrelief in Trier [1]), gelegentlich auch gegenüber der Gottheit bei Gebet oder Opfer. Mitunter erhob man den Zeigefinger der rechten Hand zum G. (Aristain. 2,14; Suet. Aug. 80, daher *digitus salutaris* genannt).

D. EHRERBIETUNGEN GEGENÜBER ÄLTEREN UND RANGHÖHEREN

Es war verpönt, den Kopf bei der Begrüßung zu neigen (Hor. sat. 2,5,91 f.; vgl. SHA Alex. 18,1 f.), da dies als Zeichen der Unfreiheit galt. Allerdings verlangten Höflichkeit und Ehrerbietung bei Griechen und Römern, daß Jüngere sich vor Älteren erhoben oder ihnen Platz machten und daß man vor dem Ranghöheren aufstand (Hom. Il. 1,533 f.; Hdt. 2,80; Iuv. 13,55). Dementsprechend erhob man sich auch im Theater beim Eintritt des Kaisers (Suet. Aug. 53; 56; → *acclamatio*; → Beifall), ja sogar vor den Lehrern (Lukian. convivium 7). Hierher – in den Bereich der Ehrerbietung oder Schmeichelei – gehört auch das Entblößen des Hauptes vor dem Ranghöheren.

II. VERBALE GRUSSFORMELN

Zu diesen G.-Gebärden traten verbale G.-Formeln, wobei der Grieche »sei gegrüßt« (χαῖρε, *chaíre*; Amphora Rom, VM [2]; vgl. [3]) bei Begrüßung und Abschied, der Römer entsprechend *salve* (vgl. Lukian. pro lapsu 13) oder *ave* bzw. *have* bei der Begrüßung sagte (vgl. den Gladiatoren-G. *Ave, imperator, morituri te salutant*, welcher mit *Avete, vos* beantwortet wurde, Suet. Claud. 21,6) und sich mit »leb' wohl« (*vale*, auch *ave*) verabschiedete; *vale* konnte auch am Abend als Begrüßungsform verwandt werden. Es handelt sich ausnahmslos um urspr. Segenswünsche. Dabei nannten Griechen wie Römer zusätzlich noch den Namen bzw. den Titel des zu Grüßenden. Üblich war auch bei den Römern die Anrede »Herr« (*domine*, vgl. Suet. Aug. 53; Mart. 5,57). Schon bei Hom. Od. 24,402 wird Sorge um das gesundheitliche Wohl des zu Grüßenden getragen; dies wird auch weiterhin beibehalten, so daß der G. um die Frage nach dem Wohlbefinden oder den Wunsch einer guten Gesundheit für den Angesprochenen erweitert wurde (πῶς ἔχετε, »wie geht's«; ὑγίαινε, etwa »laß dir's gut geh'n«; ähnlich εὖ πράττειν und καλῶς ἔχε, im Sinne von »alles Gute!«, auch bei Kranken, Lukian. pro lapsu 4; Lukian. de saltatione 76; vgl. Ps.-Platon epist. 3,315a–c). Nach Lukian. pro lapsu (1; 2; 14; vgl. 8) wurde *chaíre*, *chaírete* bei der ersten Begrüßung und am Morgen angewandt. Nicht unerwähnt sollen die *chaíre*-G.-Formeln auf den att. Trinkschalen bleiben, die häufig mit Zusätzen wie ›und trinke gut‹ [4] o.ä. versehen sind, oder die Epigramme der Grabdenkmäler mit G. und Gegen-G. des Verstorbenen und der Vorbeikommenden [5]. Entsprechendes gilt dann auch im Röm. [5; 6]; auch der Läufer Philippides soll gegrüßt haben, bevor er die Siegesmeldung der Marathonschlacht überbrachte (Lukian. pro lapsu 3). Bei den Römern sind die G.-Formeln entsprechend ausgeprägt: Man erweiterte – dies ist u.a. aus den Komödien zu entnehmen – die höfliche Begrüßung *salve* mit einem *di te bene ament* (etwa: »die Götter seien dir gnädig!«: Plaut. Capt. 138), dazu konnte die Frage *quid fit, quid agitur?* (etwa: »wie geht's, wie steht's?«) gestellt werden, die mit *recte* (etwa: »danke, gut!« oder »ganz gut!«: vgl. Ter. Ad. 883 f.) beantwortet wurde.

Mitunter flöteten abgerichtete Vögel den Ankommenden den G. entgegen (Mart. 14,73; Pers. pr. 8; vgl. Petron. 28), oder man schrieb die Begrüßung auf den Boden (vgl. den Bürgersteig vor der Casa del Fauno [7]).
→ Gebärden; Gebet; Gestus; Trauer

1 R. SCHINDLER, Führer durch das Landesmuseum Trier, 1977, Abb. 141 **2** JHS 30, 1910, Taf. **3** J.D. BEAZLEY, The Kleophrades-Painter, 1974, 14, Nr.2 **4** W. HORNBOSTEL, Aus der Glanzzeit Athens, 1986, 50, Nr. 13 **5** G. PFOHL, Griech. Inschr., [2]1980, Nr. 20,28 **6** H. GEIST, Röm. Grabinschr., 1969, 25–28, bes. Nr. 25 **7** E. PERNICE, Pavimente und figürliche Mosaiken, in: Die hell. Kunst in Pompeji VI, 1938, 90, Taf. 42,1.

K. BOGEN, Gesten in Begrüßungsszenen auf att. Vasen, 1969 • E. BRANDT, Gruß und Gebet, 1965 • C. SITTL, Die Gebärden der Griechen und Römer, 1890 • A.B. SPIESS, Der Kriegerabschied auf att. Vasen der archa. Zeit, 1992 • D. STUTZINGER, Der Adventus des Kaisers und der Einzug Christi in Jerusalem, in: H. BECK, C. BOL (Hrsg.), Spätant. und frühes Christentum, Ausstellung Frankfurt a. M. 1983–1984, 1983, 284–307 • P. VEYNE, Les saluts aux dieux, in: RA, 1985, 47–61. R.H.

Grylloi. Laut Plinius (nat. 35,114) die Benennung für karikierende Darstellungen in der Malerei, seitdem Antiphilos [4] aus Alexandreia einen gewissen Gryllus derart dargestellt habe. Urspr. handelte es sich um Tänzer mit grotesken Körperproportionen und Verrenkungen. Da *gryllographeín* und *grylloeidḗs* später allg. auf lächerlich proportionierte Körper bezogen werden, lassen sich auch kleinformatige rundplastische Darstellungen als *g.* bezeichnen. Eine Zuweisung des gesamten Genres an die alexandrinische Kunst wird heute nicht mehr aufrechterhalten. Zumindest fragwürdig ist auch die Einbeziehung sämtlicher Tierkarikaturen und monströser Figuren und der in der pompejanischen Wandmalerei überlieferten Götterparodien zu den *g.* Andererseits wird die antiquarische Identifizierung der ant. *g.* zunehmend abgelöst durch kultursoziologische Deutungen aller Arten von Darstellungen mißgestalteter und lächerlicher Menschen (→ Karikaturen; Realismus als Ausdrucksmittel).

K. LATTE, G., in: Glotta 34, 1955, 190–192 • W. BINSFELD, G., 1956 • G. BECATTI, s.v. G., EAA 3, 1960, 1065–1066 • J.P. CÈBE, La caricature et la parodie dans le monde romain antique des origines à Juvénal, 1966 • N. HIMMELMANN, Alexandria und der Realismus in der griech. Kunst, 1983 • L. GIULIANI, Die seligen Krüppel. Zur Deutung von

Mißgestalten in der hell. Kleinkunst, in: AA 1987, 701–721 • H. Wrede, Die tanzenden Musikanten von Mahdia und der alexandrinische Götter- und Heroenkult, in: MDAI(R) 95, 1988, 97–114. R.N.

Gryllos (Γρύλλος).

[1] Athener; Vater → Xenophons. Traill, PAA 281935.

[2] Sohn → Xenophons, geb. nach 399 v. Chr. G. wurde mit seinem Bruder Diodoros in Sparta erzogen. 362 kämpften beide im athenischen Heer als Verbündete Spartas; G. fiel als Reiter in einem Gefecht vor der Schlacht von Mantineia und wurde deswegen hoch geehrt (Xen. hell. 7,5,15–17; Diog. Laert. 2,52–55; Paus. 8,9,5). In Athen zeigte ein Gemälde der Schlacht G. und den boiot. Feldherrn → Epameinondas (Paus. 1,3,4; 8,11,6). Traill, PAA 281945.

J. K. Anderson, Xenophon, 1974, 193–195. W.S.

Gryn(e)ion (Γρύν(ε)ιον). Aiol. Stadt im Norden von Kyme. Nach Herodot gehörte G. zu den 11 alten aiol. Städten (1,149). Weitere Belege: Ἀχαιῶν λιμήν (»Achaierhafen«), Skyl. 98; vgl. *portus Grynia*, Plin. nat. 5,121. Als Mitglied des → Attisch-Delischen Seebundes zahlte G. ⅓ Talent. E. 5. Jh. v. Chr. herrschte hier und in Myrina Gongylos von Eretria, dem Dareios die Stadt als Dynastensitz geschenkt hatte (Xen. hell. 3,1,6). 335 v. Chr. eroberte Parmenion G. und verkaufte die Bewohner in die Sklaverei (Diod. 17,7,9). Doch existierte die Stadt, wie die eigene Mz.-Prägung im 3. Jh. zeigt, auch weiterhin; z.Z. Strabons gehörte G. schon zum Territorium von Myrina (13,3,5). Von überregionaler Bed. war offensichtlich das Heiligtum des Apollon, das schon Mitte 3. Jh. v. Chr. erwähnt wird und das noch der Rhetor Aristeides im 2. Jh. n. Chr. besuchte. Der Tempel soll ganz in weißem Marmor gestaltet gewesen sein (Strab. 13,3,5). Zum Heiligtum gehörte auch ein Orakel (Verg. Aen. 4,345).

W. Kroll, L. Bürchner, s. v. G., RE 7, 1900 f. • O. Jessen, s. v. Gryneios, RE 7, 1901 f. E.SCH.

Gryps s. Greif

Gubla s. Byblos

Gürtel I. Keltisch-Germanisch
II. Griechisch-Römisch

I. Keltisch-Germanisch

Seit dem E. des Neolithikums (3. Jt. v. Chr.) sind in Mitteleuropa G. im arch. Fundgut (meist Grabbeigaben) durchgängig nachgewiesen. Die G. selbst waren aus organischem Material (Leder usw.) und sind nicht erh., dagegen aber die (metallenen) Besatzstücke als Verschluß (G.-Haken/-Ringe) bzw. zur Verzierung (G.-Bleche). Aus der Frühphase (E. 3. Jt. v. Chr.) sind auch G.-Haken aus Knochen bekannt. In der Brz. (2. Jt. v. Chr.) wurden die G.-Teile meist aus Bronze gegossen, bzw. aus Draht oder Blech gearbeitet; sie sind gleichermaßen von Männern und Frauen getragen worden.

Bis in die → Hallstatt-Kultur (8.–6. Jh. v. Chr.) sind G.-Haken verschiedener Form und G.-Bleche (z. T. reich verziert) üblich. Mit Beginn der → Latène-Zeit (ab 5. Jh. v. Chr.) ändert sich die G.-Tracht: G.-Bleche verschwinden und G.-Haken (auch aus Eisen) unterschiedlichster Formen und versehen mit kelt. Ornamenten dominieren. Im 4. u. 3. Jh. v. Chr. enthalten die Männergräber (eiserne) Schwertgurtketten, und den Frauen sind bronzene, reich verzierte G.-Ketten beigegeben. Die german. → Jastorf-Kultur (5.–1. Jh. v. Chr.) kennt ebenfalls G.-Haken (meist aus Eisen). Mit Beginn der Kontakte zum Röm. Reich sind bei den german. Gruppen von der älteren Kaiserzeit an (ab 1. Jh. n. Chr.) G.-Schnallen und Riemenzungen üblich.

Die G. haben zweifellos neben der praktischen Funktion als Kleidungsbestandteil für die Träger auch magische Kräfte gehabt und belegten zudem ihren (Sozial-)Status.

→ Germanische Archäologie; Keltische Archäologie; Kleidung; Schwert

A. Haffner, Zum G. der Latènezeit, in: R. Cordie-Hackenberg u. a. (Hrsg.), Hundert Meisterwerke kelt. Kunst, 1992, 151–158 • I. Kilian-Dirlmeier, Die hallstattzeitlichen Gürtelbleche und Blechgürtel Mitteleuropas (Prähistor. Bronzefunde XII,1), 1972 • Dies., Gürtelhaken, Gürtelbbleche und Blechgürtel der Brz. Mitteleuropas (Prähistor. Bronzefunde XII,2), 1975 • R. Madyda-Legutko, Die Gürtelschnallen der Röm. Kaiserzeit und der frühen Völkerwanderungszeit im mitteleurop. Barbaricum, 1986. V.P.

II. Griechisch-Römisch

(ζώνη, *zṓnē*; ζωστήρ, *zōstḗr*; lat. *cingulum*; ζῶμ(μ)α bei Alk. 74D). In der griech. Tracht sind es v.a der → Peplos und der → Chiton, die – außer bei Kindern und Priestern – stets einmal oder zweimal gegürtet wurden, wobei der G. durch den Bausch verdeckt werden konnte. Mäntel wurden dagegen nicht gegürtet. Ebenso bildete der G. einen Teil der etr. und röm. → Kleidung. Hier ist es die → Tunica der Frau, die durch G. gehalten wurde. Der G. gehörte zu den Dingen, die Mädchen bei ihrer Hochzeit weihten (Paus. 2,33,1; Anth. Pal. 5,159) oder Wöchnerinnen an Artemis weihten (Anth. Pal. 6,210; 272). Da das griech. Frauengewand vom G. zusammengehalten wurde, öffnete es sich, sowie man ihn löste, womit das Sich-Ausziehen, z. B. in der Hochzeitsnacht, eingeleitet werden konnte (Alk. 74D; Anth. Pal. 7,182; Hom. h. Aphr. 164). Von Bed. war der G. der Aphrodite, der *kestós* (Hom. Il. 14,214–217, vgl. die Kanne in Paestum, Mus. Inv.Nr. 20295 [1]). G. oder Teile davon, wie Schließen und Beschläge, haben sich – soweit sie aus Metallen gefertigt waren – seit der Frühzeit erhalten. Prachtvolle Verzierungen mit figürlichem und ornamentalem Dekor weisen vielfach die brn. ital. G. auf, wie z. B. die Schließen oder Beschläge am *cingulum militare* der röm. Soldaten.

→ Artemis; Eileithyia; Kleidung

1 Trendall, Pästum, 239, Nr. 964, Taf. 146.

H. Cüppers, Ziegel mit Abdrücken von Gürtelbeschlägen, in: Blessa I., FS J. Schaub, 1993, 259–262 • C. A. Faraone, Aphrodite's ΚΕΣΤΟΣ and Apples for Atalanta. Aphrodisiacs in Early Greek Myth and Ritual, in: Phoenix 44, 1990, 219–243 • W. Fuchs, Ein selinuntischer Frauen-G. des Strengen Stils, in: Numismatica e Antichità classiche 17, 1988, 81–84 • Ders., Ein selinuntischer Frauen-G. des Strengen Stils, in: FS N. Himmelmann, 1989, 227–229 • M. Junkelmann, Die Legionen des Augustus. Der röm. Soldat im arch. Experiment, 1986, 161 f. • Ders., Die Reiter Roms, III: Zubehör, Reitweise, Bewaffnung, 1992, 129 f. • E. G. D. Robinson, South Italian Bronze Armour, in: Ders., A. Cambitoglou, Classical Art in the Nicholson Museum, Sydney, 1995, 145 f., 149–153 • R. Rolle (Hrsg.), Gold der Steppe, Arch. der Ukraine. Austellung Arch. Landesmus. Schleswig, 1991 • E. M. Ruprechtsberger, Zu spätant. Gürtelbeschlägen aus Salzburg-Maxlan, in: Die Römer in den Alpen, 1989, 175–195 • W. Speyer, s. v. G., RAC 12, 1232–1266 • M. Suano, Sabellian-Samnite Bronze Belts in the Brit. Mus., in: Brit. Mus. Occasional Papers No. 57, 1986. R. H.

Gulussa. Zweiter Sohn des → Massinissa; Gesandter in Rom (Liv. 42,23–24; 43,3,5–7; Liv. per. 48) [3. 429 f.; 433]. 150 v. Chr. Gesandter → Massinissas an Karthago, wobei der Angriff auf Gesandte zum Krieg führte (App. Lib. 317–319; 336–339; Liv. per. 49) [2. 54; 3. 434]. Bei Erbteilung 149 v. Chr. mil. Kommandeur; im 3. Pun. Krieg auf Roms Seite (App. Lib. 500–527; 596–604; Liv. per. 50) [3. 447 ff.; 454]. Verhandlung mit Hasdrubal; bekannt mit Scipio und Polybios (Pol. 34,16; 38,7–8; Diod. 32,22) [1. 638; 677; 695–699]. Tod vor 118 v. Chr. Sein Sohn: Massiva (Sall. Iug. 5; 35,1).
→ Afrika; Mauretania; Numidia

1 F. W. Walbank, A Historical Commentary on Polybius, Bd. 3, 1979 2 M.-R. Alföldi, Die Gesch. des numidischen Königreiches und seiner Nachfolger, in: H. G. Horn, C. B. Rüger (Hrsg.), Die Numider, 1979, 43–74 3 Huss. B. M.

Gummi. Als Lehnwort aus dem Ägypt. tritt κόμμι (*kómmi*) zuerst bei Hdt. 2,86 als Klebstoff für die Leinwandbinden um die einbalsamierten Leichen auf. Es wurde vom sog. ägypt. Schotendorn Acacia arabica = nilotica (→ Akazie) gewonnen, den schon Theophr. h.plant. 4,2,8 beschreibt (vgl. *spina nigra*, Plin. nat. 13,63). Weitere G.-Lieferanten nennt Plin. nat. 13,66. Dioskurides 1,133 p. 1, 205 Wellmann = 1,160 p. 225 Berendes kennt G. vom Sonnenwirbel, Chondrilla iuncea L. (Compositae). Die medizinische Bed. verschiedener *cummi*, u. a. für die Augen und Wunden, stellt Plin. nat. 24,105 zusammen. C. HÜ.

Gundericus (Gunderich). G. wurde nach dem Tod seines Vaters → Godigiselus 406 n. Chr. zum König der vandalischen Hasdingen gewählt, vereinigte seine Scharen mit den Alanen unter Respendial (Greg. Tur. Franc. 2,9), besiegte die Franken und überschritt Ende 406 den Rhein. Ohne auf organisierten Widerstand zu treffen, plünderte er Gallien (Oros. 7,40,3; Chron. min. 1,299; 465 Mommsen; Zos. 6,3), zog 409 über die Pyrenäen (Chron. min. 2,17; Soz. 9,12; Greg. Tur. Franc. 2,2) und sicherte sich 411 den Osten der Provinz Gallaecia (Chron. min. 2,18). 418 unterstellten sich ihm die vandalischen Silingen und die Alanen. Er kämpfte 418/9 erfolgreich gegen Sueben und dehnte seinen Machtbereich in Spanien trotz röm. Widerstandes erheblich aus (Chron. min. 1,469; 2,18 ff.; Salv. gub. 7,66). Er starb 428 während der Plünderung Sevillas; sein Nachfolger wurde sein Halbbruder → Geisericus (Chron. min. 2,21).

PLRE 2, 522 • F. Clover, The Late Roman West and the Vandals, 1993 • Chr. Courtois, Les vandales et l'afrique, 1955, bes. 393 • H.-J. Diesner, Das Vandalenreich, 1966, 24 ff. M. MEI. u. ME. STR.

Gundeschapur (*Ǧundīsābūr*, »Platz der Armee Šāpūrs«; mpers. *Veh-Andiyōk-Šābūr*, »besser als Antiocheia [hat] Šāpūr [diese Stadt gemacht]«; syr. *Bēṯ Lāpāṭ*). Etwa 30 km östl. von Susa gelegene Stadt, in der der Sāsānide Šāpur (→ Sapor) I. im 3. Jh. n. Chr. aus Syrien deportierte Handwerker und Spezialisten ansiedelte. Der Ort entwickelte sich bald zu einem kulturellen und wiss. Zentrum mit eigener »Hochschule« (wichtig v. a. auf dem Gebiet der Medizin), zu einem Hauptstandort der pers. Seidenmanufaktur und einem Zentrum der Christenheit Ḫūzistāns. Im sāsān. Gefängnis von G. starb der Religionsstifter → Mani.

J. Wiesehöfer, Das ant. Persien, 1994, s. v. Ǧundaisābūr. J. W.

Gundestrup. In dem Moor G., Amt Ålborg in Nordjütland, wurde 1891 ein großer demontierter Kessel aus 13 teilweise vergoldeten Silberplatten und einem Rahmengestell gefunden (Dm fast 70 cm, Gewicht ca. 9 kg). Auf den Platten sind in einer charakteristischen Darstellungsweise in Treibtechnik zahlreiche Abbildungen von Göttern, Opferszenen, Fabelwesen usw. angebracht. Die Fragen nach Datierung, Herkunft und Funktion des G.-Kessels werden seit der Auffindung bis h. kontrovers diskutiert. Unstrittig ist der kult. Charakter ebenso wie die Deponierung im german. Norden. Herstellung und Nutzung werden aber sowohl in Gallien (sei es im Norden, sei es im hellenisierten Süden) gesehen, ferner im südosteurop. Raum (wiederum wechselnd zw. Thrakern/Dakern und den eher kelt. → Scordisci), als auch (h. kaum noch vertreten) im german. Norden. Die Herstellungszeit wird meist in der 2. H. des 1. Jh. v. Chr. angesetzt; aber auch hier schwankt die Datierung zw. dem 2. Jh. v. Chr. und frühgesch. Zeit. Der G.-Kessel gibt vielfältige Einblicke in die Kunst und Religion der kelt. Welt und deren südöstl. Nachbarn.
→ Dakoi; Keltische Archäologie; Thrakes

R. Hachmann, G.-Studien, in: BRGK 71, 1990 (1991), 565–903 • F. Kaul, G.-kedlen, 1991 • G.S. Olmstedt, The G. Cauldron, 1979 • R. Pittioni, Wer hat wann und wo den Silberkessel von G. angefertigt?, 1984. V. P.

Gundicharius (Gundahar, Gundihar, Guntiar). In der Überlieferung Sohn des Gibica; König der Burgunden. G. erhob 411 n. Chr. mit dem Alanenkönig Goar den gallischen Senator → Iovinus in Mainz zum Kaiser (Olympiodoros FHG 4, 61 fr. 17). Nach dessen Tod 417 schloß er ein → *foedus* mit → Honorius (Chron. min. 1,467; 2,155 MOMMSEN), fiel aber dennoch 435 in die Provinz Belgica I ein, wo → Aetius [2] ihn niederrang (Sidon. carm. 7,234 f.). 436 fand G. bei einem vielleicht von Aetius lancierten Überfall der Hunnen mit angeblich 20000 Burgunden den Tod (Chron. min. 1,475; 660; 2,22 f.; 156). Dies bildet den histor. Kern der burgundischen Heldensage und ist auch im Nibelungenlied verarbeitet (dort G. = Gunther) [2].

1 PLRE 2, 523 2 A. HEUSLER, Nibelungensage und Nibelungenlied, 61965 3 STEIN, Spätröm. R., 400; 480 f.

M. MEI.

Gundiok (Gundovech). König der Burgunden 457–470 n. Chr., aus der Familie des → Athanarich [1. 44], verheiratet mit einer Schwester Ricimers (Malalas 374–75; Iohannes Antiochenus fr. 209), seine Söhne sind Gundobad, Godigisclus, Chilperich und Godomer (Greg. Tur. Franc. 2,28). Als Verbündeter Theoderichs II. zog er mit seinem Bruder Chilperich I. 455 gegen die Sueben in Gallien und siedelte dort nach dem Sieg Theoderichs 457. Im J. 463 *magister utriusque militiae (per Gallias)*; im selben Jahr informierte er Papst Hilarius über die unrechtmäßige Amtsführung des Bischofs von Vienna (Hilarius epist. 9 THIEL). PLRE 2,523 f. (Gundiocus).

1 H. WOLFRAM, Die Goten, 31990.

M. MEI. u. ME. STR.

Gundobad. Sohn des Gundiok, Burgundenkönig 474–516 n. Chr., Arianer. Auf der Seite des → Ricimer tötete er als *magister utriusque militiae* 472 Anthemios [2] (Chron. min. 1,306 MOMMSEN), verwaltete das Westreich und erhob 473 Glycerius zum *Augustus* (Chron. min. 1,664). 474 kehrte er, inzwischen *comes* und *patricius*, nach Gallien zurück und trat in Vienna die Nachfolge Ricimers an. Er besiegte die Alamannen und fiel um 490 in Ligurien ein (Ennod. 80). Den Sohn Sigismundus verheiratete er 496 mit Areagni, einer Tochter Theoderichs. Seinen Bruder Godigisclus, der sich 500 im Streit um die Herrschaft mit → Chlodovechus verbündet hatte, schlug er 501 und übernahm die Alleinherrschaft (Iohannes Antiochenus fr. 209,2; Greg. Tur. Franc. 2,32 f.). Die Kämpfe gegen die West- und dann die Ostgoten 507–9 endeten mit großen, auch territorialen Verlusten. G. suchte nun die Annäherung an die Katholiken (vgl. den Streit mit Avitus, dem Bischof von Vienna, Avitus epist. 4 und 5; MGH AA 7). G. starb 516 (Greg. Tur. Franc. 3,5; Chron. min. 2,234).

Auf ihn geht die *lex Burgundionum* (*lex Gundobada*) zurück, eine Sammlung älterer Gesetze mit *Novellae* des G. (MGH leges 1,1,1).

PLRE 2, 524 f. • A. DEMANDT, Die Spätantike, 1989, Index s. v. • H. WOLFRAM, Die Goten 31990, 311 f.

M. MEI. u. ME. STR.

Guneus (Γουνεύς). Anführer des 28. im homer. Schiffskatalog beschriebenen Kontingents (Hom. Il. 2,748–755). Sein Herrschaftsgebiet, umrissen durch die Ortsnamen Kyphos und Dodona sowie die Stammesnamen der Ainianer und Peraiber, umfaßt etwa das Zentrum des Pindosmassivs und verbindet Thessalien mit Epeiros. Im ep. Kyklos taucht G. danach nur noch in den → Nostoi wieder auf; hier war von einem Schiffbruch vor Kap Kaphereus, vielleicht auch von einer Auswanderung nach Libyen die Rede. Demnach spielte G. im vorhomer. Mythos offensichtlich keine Rolle; sein Name dürfte vielmehr aus dem der thessal. Stadt → Gonnos abgeleitet und sein großes Herrschaftsgebiet erst im Schiffskatalog festgelegt worden sein.

E. VISSER, Homers Kat. der Schiffe, 1997, 721–735.

E. V.

Gunthamundus. Sohn des Gentunis, Vandalenkönig 484–496 n. Chr. (Iord. Get. 170; Prok. BV 1,8,6 f.), kämpfte erfolgreich gegen die Mauren. 491 scheiterte sein Versuch, Sizilien zurückzuerobern (Ennod. panegyricus 70). Gegenüber den Katholiken zeigte er sich nach anfänglicher Verfolgung tolerant. PLRE 2, 525 f.

H.-J. DIESNER, Das Vandalenreich, 1966, 84–88.

M. MEI. u. ME. STR.

Guntharith (Guntharis, Gundarus, Gontharis). *Bucellarius* des → Solomon I., *magister militum* und *dux Numidiae* seit 545 n. Chr. (Iord. de origine actibusque Romanorum 384). G., den Solomon mit einem Heer gegen die Mauren nach Bagai am Fluß Abigas vorausgeschickt hatte, entging nur durch dessen rasche Hilfe einer Niederlage (Prok. BV 2,19,6–16). In einem geheimen Bund mit dem Maurenfürsten Antalas beschloß G. 546 die Beseitigung des → Areobindus [3], was auch gelang (Prok. BV 2,25,1–28). G. besetzte Karthago und wurde nach nur 36 Tagen Herrschaft (Prok. BV 2,27–28) von → Artabannes [2] erstochen (Iohannes Antiochenus FHG 4,232–237).

PLRE 3, 574–76 (Guntharis 2) • J. A. S. EVANS, The Age of Justinian, 1996, 152, 170, 189 • RUBIN, Bd. 2, 1995, 41, 47–49.

M. MEI. u. ME. STR.

Gunther s. Gundicharius

Gunugu (neupun. *Gngn*). Pun. oder pun. beeinflußter Handelsplatz westl. von Caesarea, h. Sidi Brahim bei Gouraya. Unter Augustus stieg G. zur *colonia* auf, deren Bürger der *tribus Quirina* zugeteilt wurden. Belegstellen: Plin. nat. 5,20; Ptol. 4,2,5 (Κανουκκίς); Itin. Anton. 15,1 (*Gunugus*); Geogr. Rav. p. 40,45 (*Gunubus*); 88,10 (*Gunagus*); 132,19 (*Cunagus*). In der *Notitia episcopatuum Mauretaniae Caesariensis* (111a) ist für das J. 484 ein *episcopus Gunugitanus* erwähnt. Inschr.: Répertoire d'épigraphie sémitique III 1979–2000; CIL VIII 2, 9071; 9423; Suppl. 3, 21447–21452; AE 1976, 235 Nr. 751.

S. LANCEL, E. LIPIŃSKI, s. v. G., DCPP, 202.

W. HU.

Guraios (Γουραῖος, Arr. an. 4,25,7; Γαροίας, Arr. Ind. 4,11, nach Megasthenes; altind. Gaurī). Im »Ind. Kaukasos« (Hindukusch) entspringender, in den Kophen (h. Kābul) mündender Fluß (h. Panǧkorā), in einer tiefen Klamm, den → Alexandros [4] d.Gr. auf seinem Feldzug überquerte. Im G.-Gebiet lebten die Viehzucht treibenden *Guraíoi* (Γουραῖοι, Arr. an. 4,23,1; 25,6), deren Land nach Ptolemaios *Gōryaía* (Γωρυαία, 7,1,42) mit der Stadt *Gōrýa* (Γωρύα, 7,1,43) hieß, vielleicht das h. Ǧalālābād.

TAVO B V 1. A.P.-L.

Gurgenes. Bei Prokopios (BP 1,12,4ff.) König des kaukasischen Iberien, der Iustinus I. um Hilfe gegen die von Kavad I. geforderte Einführung des Feuerkults bat und vor den Persern in das lazische Bergland floh. TOUMANOFF [1] hält ihn für den legendären Vaḫtang Gorgasal der georg. und armen. Überl., was MARTIN-HISARD [2] ablehnt.

1 C. TOUMANOFF, Studies in Christian Caucasian History, 1963, 362–378 2 B. MARTIN-HISARD, Le roi Vaxtang Gorgasal, in: Temps, mémoire, tradition au Moyen Âge: Aix-en-Provence, 4–5 juin 1982 (Actes du 13ᵉ congrès de la Société des Historiens Médiévistes ...), 1983, 207–242.

A.P.-L.

Gurges. Röm. Cognomen (»Kehle«, pejorativ »Verschwender«, Macr. sat. 3,13,7; vgl. *gurgulio*), in der republikanischen Zeit in der Familie der Fabii.

KAJANTO, Cognomina 269 · WALDE/HOFMANN 1, 627f.

K.-L.E.

Gurke. Die großen, einjährigen Arten der meist tropischen Familie der Cucurbitaceae mit beachtlichen Beerenfrüchten stammen alle aus Vorderasien. Die verschiedenen Arten wurden in der Ant. oft miteinander verwechselt. Die eigentliche G. Cucumis sativus L. (σίκυς, σίκυος, ἀγγούριον, lat. *cucumis*) begegnet bei Plin. nat. 19,64–66 als ein für Tiberius in Treibhäusern (*intra specularium munimenta*) immer frisch gezogenes Gemüse. Das Verfahren, die Samen vor dem Aussäen zwei Tage lang in Milchmet (*lac mulsum*) zu legen, damit sie süßer würden, beschreibt Theophr. h. plant. 7,1,6. Die kleinen grünen G. in It. werden von der großen grünen, gelben und schwarzen (Artzugehörigkeit unbekannt!) »Fleisch-G.« unterschieden. Die G. wächst in jeder Form (nach Theophr. h. plant. 7,3,5) und zum Wasser hin. Die medizinischen Anwendungen der einzelnen Arten, v.a. als Augenheilmittel, beschreibt Plin. nat. 20,3–12.

Die Griechen kannten nach Plin. nat. 19,68 drei Sorten, die spartanische, skytalische (walzenartige) und die böotische, doch bezieht dessen Quelle (Theophr. h.plant. 7,4,6) diese Angaben auf die Honigmelone, Cucumis melo L. Diese beschreibt Plin. nat. 19,67 als angeblich in Kampanien entstandene goldgelbe »G.« unter dem Namen *melopepo* (μηλοπέπων).

Von Plinius ebenfalls als G. angesehen wird die h. häufiger im Süden angebaute Wassermelone, Citrullus vulgaris Schrad. (nat. 19,65 unter dem Namen *pepo*, πέπων; vgl. Plin. nat. 20,11, Theophr. h. plant. 7,3,5 und Dioskurides 2,135 p. 1,206 WELLMANN = 2,163 p. 226f. BERENDES). Die Spritz-G. Ecballium elaterium L. tritt bei Plin. nat. 19,74 und 20,3–6 (als Lieferant des z.B. gegen Trübung der Augen verwendeten Mittels Elaterium; vgl. auch Dioskurides 4,150 p. 2, 292–296 WELLMANN = 4,152 und 155 p. 449–451 BERENDES) als *cucumis silvestris* auf. Wie diese hat auch die Koloquinthe, Citrullus colocynthis, giftige Früchte. Wahrscheinlich wird noch der Flaschenkürbis (die Kalebasse), aus dem Vorratsgefäße hergestellt wurden, als σικύα Ἰνδική (κολοκύντη bei Athen. 2,58f bzw. *cucurbita* bei Plin. nat. 19,69–71 u.ö.) erwähnt. Der eigentliche Gartenkürbis, Cucurbita pepo L., ist erst im 16. Jh. aus Amerika eingeführt worden. C.HÜ.

Gurza. Stadt in der *Africa Byzacena*, 12 km nordwestl. von → Hadrumetum, h. Kalaa Kebira (zur Lage vgl. Tab. Peut. 6,2: *Gurra*). G. war pun. beeinflußt. Patronatsurkunden sind aus den J. 12 v.Chr. (CIL VIII 1,68) und 65 n.Chr. (CIL VIII 1,69) erhalten. Inschr.: CIL VI 4,2, 32757; 36277; VIII 1, 68–72; Suppl. 4, 23021. Der bei Pol. 1,74,13 bezeugte Ort Γόρζα/Gorza lag wohl nicht allzu weit von Utica entfernt [1. 258].
→ Patronat

1 HUSS.

E. LIPIŃSKI, s.v. G./Gorza, DCPP, 202. W.HU.

Gustatio s. Cena

Gutta. Röm. Cognomen (Gentilname?) einer sonst unbekannten Familie.
[1] G. aus Capua, unterstützte als Feldherr 82 v.Chr. die Marianer im Bürgerkrieg gegen Sulla (App. civ. 1,416).
[2] G. (evtl. Spitzname?), um 55 v.Chr. Praetor und zusammen mit T. Annius [I 14] Milo Bewerber um das Consulat für 52 v.Chr. (Cic. ad Q. fr. 3,6,6; MRR 3,100). K.-L.E.

Guttae. Lat. für Tropfen (Pl.); in architektonischem Sinne einzig bei Vitruv (4,1,2 und 4,3,6) belegter ant. t.t. für die tropfenartigen zylindrischen Gebilde, die sich an Teilen des steinernen Gebälks der dor. Bauordnung finden und die als imitierte Nägel bzw. Nagelköpfe die anachronistische Transformation der einstigen Holzbauform in den kanonischen dor. Steintempel bezeugen [1. 53–55; 3. 10–13]. G. finden sich in (meist) drei parallelen Sechser-Reihen am → Mutulus des → Geison sowie am Architrav als unterer Abschluß der → Regula [2. 112–120].

1 CH. HÖCKER, Architektur als Metapher. Überlegungen zur Bed. des dor. Ringhallentempels, in: Hephaistos 14, 1996, 45–79 2 W. MÜLLER-WIENER, Griech. Bauwesen in der Ant., 1988 3 B. WESENBERG, Griech. Säulen- und Gebälkformen in der lit. Überlieferung, in: DiskAB 6, 1997, 1–15. C.HÖ.

Gutturale. Der nlat. *terminus technicus* G. (»Kehllaute«) für eine Konsonantenklasse ist traditionell (Nomina, die vor den Endungen ein g, k/c oder χ haben, heißen Gutturalstämme). Heute bevorzugt die Forsch. den angemesseneren Begriff »Tektale«, da bei der Hervorbringung dieser Kons. der Zungenrücken gegen das Munddach (lat. *tectum*) gedrückt wird, um den Luftstrom durch Enge bzw. Verschluß zu hindern, wodurch das für G. typische Geräusch erzeugt wird. Dem Uridg. spricht man neun oder zehn tektale Phoneme zu. Die g. Verschlußlaute verteilen sich nach dem jeweiligen Artikulationsort auf drei Reihen: am vorderen Gaumen (lat. *palatum*) werden die Palatale $\hat{k}$, $\hat{g}$, $\hat{g}^h$ gebildet, am hinteren Gaumen(segel, lat. *velum*) die Velare *k*, *g*, g^h, und ebenda mit gleichzeitiger Lippenrundung die → Labiovelare k^w, g^w, g^{wh}. Nach der Artikulationsart unterscheidet man stimmlose (= Tenues, *k* usw.), stimmhafte (= Mediae, *g* usw.) und stimmhaft behauchte (= Mediae aspiratae, g^h usw.). Der → Laryngal h_2 dürfte ein tektaler Reibelaut /*x*/ gewesen sein. Die auffällig große Anzahl uridg. G. ist in allen histor. idg. Sprachen reduziert. Der Zusammenfall der palatalen und velaren Reihe (*$\hat{k}$, **k* > *k* ~ griech. κ, lat. *c*) charakterisiert die → Kentumsprachen, zu denen auch Griech. und Lat. gehören.
→ Indogermanische Sprachen; Lautlehre; Satemsprache

W. COWGILL, M. MAYRHOFER, Idg. Gramm. I 1/2, 1986, 102–109, 121 f. • LEUMANN, 146–153 • RIX, HGG, 82–97. D.ST.

Guttus s. Gefäßformen

Gyaros (Γύαρος). 17 km² große, h. unbewohnte Insel (Glimmerschiefer) der nordwestl. Kykladen, h. Jura oder Gioura. An der Ostseite finden sich Spuren alter Terrassenkulturen, nahe einer Quelle und einer alten Mole Reste des ant. Ortes G., der im 3. Jh. v. Chr. eigene Kupfer-Mz. prägte; z.Z. Strabons war G. nur noch ein armes Fischerdorf, in der Kaiserzeit ein gefürchteter Verbannungsort (Tac. ann. 3,68; 4,30; Plut. mor. 602c.; Iuv. 1,73; 10,170; Lukian. Toxaris 17f.; Philostr. Ap. 7,16,2; Strab. 10,5,3; Plin. nat. 4,69; 8,104; 222; IG XII 5, 651; XII Suppl., 117). 1573–1617 lag G. im Herzogtum Naxos und geriet dann unter türk. Herrschaft. Unter Papadopoulos Verbannungsort für Regimegegner (1967–1974).

HN, 486 • LAUFFER, Griechenland, 241 • PHILIPPSON/KIRSTEN 4, 81 • IG XII 5, S. XXXI. H.KAL.

Gyas
[1] Gefährte des → Aeneas (Verg. Aen. 1,222; 1,612; 12,460). Als Schiffsführer nimmt er an der Regatta zu Anchises' Ehren teil (Verg. Aen. 5,114f.; Hyg. fab. 273). Das patrizische Geschlecht der Geganii hat sich nach Servius (Aen. 5,117) von ihm abgeleitet, was aber wohl eine spätere Konstruktion ist.
[2] Latiner, ein Riese mit Keule, Sohn des Melampus, der seinerseits mit Hercules nach Italien gekommen sein soll. Sein Bruder Cisseus und er werden von Aeneas in der Schlacht getötet (Verg. Aen. 10,317). RE.ZI.

Gye (γύη, γύης) wird als Mehrfaches eines Feldmaßes bei Homer (Il. 9,579, Od. 7,113; 18,374) erwähnt. Die genaue Größe des Maßes ist nicht zu ermitteln, da sich in späteren Kommentaren (Eust.) und Lexika (Hesych.) verschiedene Angaben finden. So wäre *g.* einmal mit ½ → *pléthron* bzw. auch 1 röm. → *iugerum* oder 1 *pléthron* gleichzusetzen. Bei Il. 9,579 und Od. 18,374 entspricht sie wohl etwa dem *pléthron*, bei Od. 7,113 mindestens 12 *pléthra*. In Unteritalien kommt eine *g.* mit 50 *pléthra* vor.

F. HULTSCH, Griech. und röm. Metrologie, ²1882, 40–42; 668–669. GE.S.

Gyenos (Γυηνός). Stadt in der → Kolchis (Ps.-Skyl. 81). Jetzt verbunden mit der 1935/6 beim Hafenbau entdeckten ant. Siedlung (6. Jh. v. Chr. – 6. Jh. n. Chr.) bei Očamčire an der georg. Pontosküste. Der arch. Befund zeigt auf drei künstlichen, von Gräben umgebenen Hügeln Reste von Holzarchitektur mit gestampftem Lehmboden; neben kolchischer Keramik fanden sich auch Frg. archa.-ion. und att.-rf. sowie schwarzglasierter Keramik. Als jüngster Bau ist eine Saalkirche mit Pastophorien (*opus mixtum*) aus dem 6. Jh. n. Chr. zu nennen.

D. KAČARAVA, G. KVIRKVELIA, Goroda i poselenija Pričernomor'ja antičnoj epochi, 1991, 76 ff. A.P.-L.

Gyes (Γύης). Nach den Hss. [1] wohl die verschriebene Form von Gyges, einem der → Hekatoncheiren.

1 M. L. WEST, Hesiod, Theogony, 1966, 210. RE.ZI.

Gygaia/-e limne (Γυγαίη λίμνη). See in Lydia nördl. des → Hermos und von → Sardeis, an den im Süden die lyd. Königsnekropole (h. Bintepe, »Tausend Hügel«) mit den Grabtumuli des → Alyattes, → Gyges und anderer Fürsten (Hipponax fr. 42 MASSON) anschließt; evtl. nach dem gleichnamigen Vorfahren des → Gyges (Nikolaos von Damaskos FGrH 90 F 46) oder einer Sagengestalt benannt. G.l. wird schon bei Homer erwähnt (Hom. Il. 20,390f.; vgl. 2,865), mythographische Fabeleien finden sich bei Lykophr. Alexandra 1353 (»Typhons Lager«) und Prop. 3,11,17 (»Omphales Bad«). Der See war ganzjährig gefüllt (Hdt. 1,93,5) und wurde als (angeblich künstlich angelegtes) Rückhaltebecken gegen die Hochwasser in der flüssereichen Hermosebene genutzt (Strab. 13,4,7); später wurde er auch Koloë-See (Κολόη λίμνη) nach dem nahegelegenen Tempel der Artemis Koloëne gen. (Strab. 13,4,5); z. T. war er verlandet (*Gygaeum stagnum*, Plin. nat. 5,110). H. als Marmara gölü (»Marmorsee«) bezeichnet.

Am Südufer befinden sich (auf dem Ahlatlı tepecik) Begräbnisplätze einer prähistor. Siedlung mit neolithischen und frühbrz. Funden (Pithos- und Kistengräber, 3. Jt.), die auch in lyd. Zeit (7./6. Jh. v. Chr.) bewohnt war.

G. M. A. HANFMANN, Letters from Sardis, 1972, Index • Ders., Sardis und Lydien, in: AAWM 1960, 6 • Ders., The seventh campaign at Sardis (1964), in: BASO 177, 1965, 2–37 • Ders., The ninth campaign at Sardis (1966), in: BASO

186, 1967, 40–42 • D.G. MITTEN, in: BASO 191, 1969, 7–10 • J.G. PEADLEY, Ancient Literary Sources on Sardis (Archaeological Exploration of Sardis, Monograph 2), 1972, 69f. und Index • L.ROBERT, Documents d'Asie Mineure, 1987, 296–321, 341f. H.KA.

Gyges (Γύγης).
[1] Lyd. König (ca. 680–644 v.Chr.) und Begründer der Mermnaden-Dynastie, soll nach Herodot (1,12) die Frau des von ihm ermordeten Vorgängers → Kandaules geheiratet und (so) die Herrschaft in Sardeis errungen haben. Woher die Lyd. sprechenden Mermnaden stammten, ist ungewiß (aus Maionien/Mysien?). Jedenfalls dürften sie erst im 1.Jt. in Sardeis sein. Ihr Verhältnis zu den luwisch-sprachigen ([1. 384,10] → Luwisch, → Lydisch) Vorbewohnern (Herakleidai?, Hdt. 1,7) war wohl eher feindlich. Für uns beginnt die lyd. Geschichte von Sardeis und dem Land, das die Assyrer *māt Luddi* (7. Jh.), die Ionier (6./5. Jh.) *Lydíē* (→ Lydia) nannten, mit G. Sein Name geht wohl auf ein verkürztes luwisches PN-Kompositum mit *ḫūḫa-*, »Großvater«, zurück. G. wird als *týrannos* bezeichnet (vgl. *tyrannís* Archil. fr. 19 WEST), das bei Hesychios lyd. **laila* glossiert ist, was wiederum mit heth. *laḫḫijala-*, »Kriegsheld«, genetisch verwandt ist. Er lebte in der Tat vom Kampf: Gegen ion. Städte wie Milet veranstaltete er Razzien (Hdt. 1,14) und an Psammetichos I. verschacherte er ionische und karische Untertanen als Söldner (Assurbanipal Prisma A II 111ff.; Diod. 1,66, vgl. Hdt. 2,152). G. wurde dadurch sprichwörtlich reich (»Goldprotz«: Archil. fr. 19 WEST, vgl. Hdt. 1,14). Der Kampf wurde ihm aber auch zum Schicksal: Unter dem Druck der Kimmerier, idg. Reitervölker, denen die lyd. Dynasten noch mit dem Streitwagen, ihre ion. Söldner in der Phalanx entgegentraten (Sappho fr. 16 VOIGT), wandte G. sich an → Assurbanipal, unterwarf sich, zahlte Tribut (Assurbanipal Prisma E) und konnte so die Kimmerier-Gefahr bannen. Doch warf G. dann das Joch Assurbanipals vorschnell ab, woraufhin die Kimmerier ihren Druck massiv verstärkten. Sardeis wurde schließlich von ihnen erobert (Strab. 14,1,40 zitierend Kall. fr. 3 G.-P.), G. fand einen grausamen Tod (Assurbanipal Prisma A II 16ff.). Die Dynastie blieb an der Macht, doch konnte G.' Sohn Ardys den Thron zwar besteigen (Hdt. 1,15), aber wegen der Kimmerier nur als Vasall der Assyrer die Herrschaft ausüben (Assurbanipal Prisma A II 18ff.).

1 F.STARKE, Sprachen und Schriften ..., in: B.PONGRATZ-LEISTEN u.a. (Hrsg.), FS RÖLLIG, 1997, 381–395.

M.COGAN, H. TADMOR, Gyges and Ashurbanipal, in: Orientalia 46, 1977, 65–85 • H.GELZER, Das Zeitalter des G., in: RhM 30, 1875, 230–268 • E.LIPIŃSKI, Gygès et Lygdamis, in: Orientalia Lovaniensia Periodica 24, 1993, 65–71 • G.RADET, Lydie, 1893. PE.HÖ.

[2] Urweltwesen s. Hekatoncheiren

Gylippos (Γύλιππος). Spartiat, Sohn des Kleandridas. Seine Erziehung (→ *agōgḗ*) wurde vielleicht (zeitweise?) durch einen wohlhabenden Spartaner ermöglicht, da Ailianos (var. 12,43) ihn als *Mothax* (»Bastard«) bezeichnet [1. 434]. Als Syrakus von Sparta Hilfe gegen die Athener erbat, wurde er nach Sizilien gesandt (Thuk. 6,93; 104), gelangte im Sommer 414 v.Chr. mit kleiner Streitmacht nach Himera, verstärkte dort sein Heer erheblich, brach nach Syrakus durch, organisierte den Widerstand und verhinderte die Einschließung der Stadt (Thuk. 7,1–7). Nach vorentscheidenden Kämpfen im Hafen und auf der Hochebene von Epipolai zwang er mit im Sommer 413 in Sizilien gewonnenen Verstärkungen (Thuk. 7,46) die Athener nach weiteren Schlachten im Hafen zum Rückzug ins Innere der Insel (Thuk. 7,51–87), den er angeblich tolerierte (Thuk. 7,81,1). Als die athenische Streitmacht kapituliert hatte, bemühte er sich vergebens, die Hinrichtung der athenischen Strategen Demosthenes [1] und Nikias zu verhindern (Thuk. 7,86,2; Plut. Nikias 27f.). Übertrieben ist wohl der bei Plutarch (comparatio Timoleonis et Aemilii 2) aus Timaios übernommene Vorwurf unersättlicher Habgier, der angeblich gegen den wenig beliebten G. in Syrakus erhoben wurde. Er könnte auf Nachrichten zurückgehen, die von einem Prozeß gegen seinen Vater 446 wegen Bestechlichkeit (Plut. Perikles 22) und von der Unterschlagung von Beutegeldern berichten, die G. im Auftrag Lysanders 404 von Athen nach Sparta bringen sollte (Plut. Lysandros 16–17,1). Es bleibt offen, ob G. nach Aufdeckung des Skandals Selbstmord beging (Athen. 6,234a) oder aus Sparta floh und zum Tode verurteilt wurde (Diod. 13,106,8–10).

1 D.LOTZE, Μόθακες, in: Historia 11, 1962.

D.KAGAN, The Peace of Nicias and the Sicilian Expedition, 1981, Index s.v. K.-W.WEL.

Gylis (Γῦλις). Spartiat, 394 v.Chr. Polemarchos, übernahm nach der Schlacht bei Koroneia das Heer des Agesilaos [2] II. und stieß nach Lokris vor. Er fiel auf dem Rückzug (Xen. Ag. 2,15; hell. 4,3,21–23). K.-W.WEL.

Gylon (Γύλων). Athener, soll Ende des 5. Jh. v.Chr. das Athen gehörige nordpontische → Nymphaion den ›Feinden übergeben‹ und dafür die Todesstrafe erhalten haben (Aischin. Ctes. 171); wahrscheinlich war sein Vergehen weniger schwer (Demosth. or. 28,3). G. erhielt von den bosporanischen Herrschern den Ort Kepoi mit seinem Territorium zugewiesen, aus dem er reiche Abgaben einzog. Er heiratete eine reiche Skythin und kehrte mit ihr nach Athen zurück. Eine seiner Töchter war Mutter des → Demosthenes [2] (TRAILL, PAA 282005).

V.F. GAJDUKEVIČ, Das Bosporanische Reich, 1971, 189f.
I.v.B.

Gymnasiarchie (γυμνασιαρχία). Aufsicht über ein → Gymnasion durch einen Gymnasiarchos, dessen Funktionen nach Umfang und Bedeutung örtlich und zeitlich variierten. In Athen war im 5. und 4. Jh. v. Chr. die G. eine einjährige → *leitūrgía* (λειτουργία; And. 1,132; Demosth. or. 20,21) mit der Aufgabe, für Fakkelwettläufe an den Großen Panathenäen, Hephaistien, Promethien und Festen des Pan eine bestimmte Zahl von Läufern zu trainieren und mit allem Nötigen zu versorgen. Ende des 4. Jh. wurde hier die G. eine Art Amt, das iteriert werden konnte. Auch außerhalb Athens betrug ihre Dauer ein Jahr mit vielfältigen und wechselnden Verpflichtungen für Gymnasien, die in der klass. Epoche breiteren Kreisen aristokratische Wertvorstellungen vermittelten und in hell. und röm. Zeit neben athletischen Trainingsstätten vor allem für Griechen in der Diaspora im Vorderen Orient und in Ägypten Zentren ihres kulturellen und geselligen Lebens waren.

W. Decker, Zum Gymnasiarchengesetz im antiken Griechenland, in: S. Yaldai u. a. (Hrsg.), Menschen im Sport. FS H.-E. Rösch, 1997, 12–19 • Ph. Gauthier, M. B. Hatzopoulos, La loi gymnasiarchique de Beroia, 1993 • H. W. Pleket, Sport und Leibesübungen in der griech. Welt des hell.-röm. Zeitalters, in: H. Überhorst (Hrsg.), Geschichte der Leibesübungen, Bd. 2, 1978, 280–311 • P. J. Sijpesteijn, Liste des gymnasiarques de métropoles de l'Égypte romaine, 1967 • I. Weiler, Der Sport bei den Völkern der Alten Welt, 1981, 91 ff.

K.-W. WEL.

Gymnasiarchos s. Gymnasiarchie

Gymnasion (γυμνάσιον).
I. Bautyp II. Das hellenistische Gymnasion

I. Bautyp

Öffentliche Anlage für sportliche und musische Freizeitaktivitäten in der griech. Polis; der Begriff leitet sich von γυμνός/*gymnós* (nackt) her und bezieht sich auf die → Nacktheit bei sportlichen Übungen und Wettkämpfen. Synonym zu G. findet sich für die Zeit seit dem 4. Jh. v. Chr. in ant. Schriftquellen wie in moderner Fachlit. der Begriff der → Palaistra (vgl. Vitruv 5,11). Diese bezeichnet als »Ringerschule« urspr. lediglich einen funktional bestimmten baulichen Teilbereich des G., nämlich den großen Peristylhof mit einem Sandplatz für die Ringer in der Mitte, der jedoch in der architektonischen Ausgestaltung des G. seit etwa 400 v. Chr. zum optisch prägenden und regelmäßig besterhaltenen Element dieser Anlagen wird.

Das G. des 6. Jh. v. Chr. war zunächst ein architektonisch wenig ausgestalteter Platz, meist in einem durch Bäume verschatteten Hain, bei dem die langgestreckte Laufbahn (*drómos*) dominierte; dieses G. wurde etwa ab

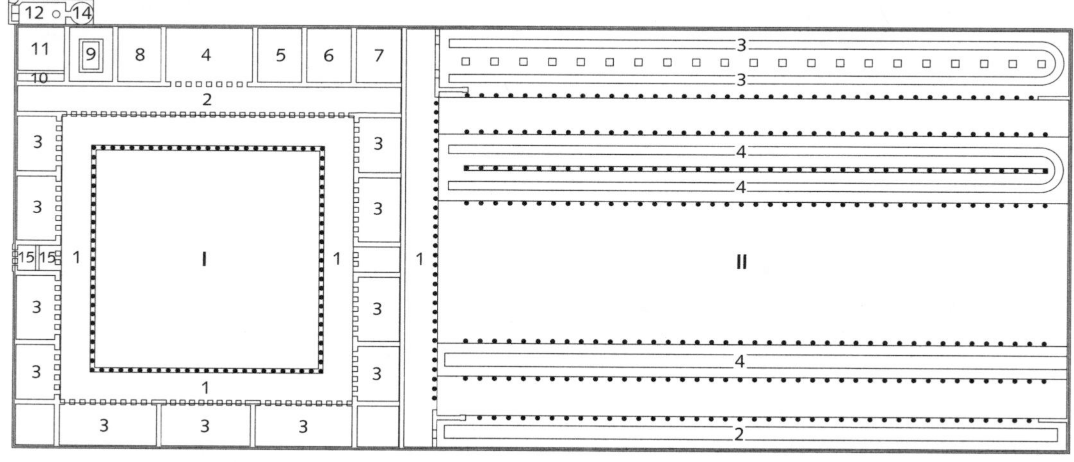

Das Gymnasium nach Vitruv (5,11).

I. Palaestra
1./2. Peristylon (1. Porticus simplices 2. Porticus duplex)
3. Exedrae
4. Ephebeum
5. Coryceum
6. Conisterium
7. Lutron
8. Elaeothesium
9. Frigidarium
10. Iter in propnigeum
11. Propnigeum
12. Sudatio
13. Calida Lavatio
14. Laconicum
15. Torbau

II. Eigentliches Gymnasium
1. Porticus
2. Xystus
3. Porticus (Xystus) duplex
4. Paradromides

Peristylon	Umfang	2 Stadien
Ephebeum	Breite : Tiefe	3 : 2
Xystus	Länge der Bahn	1 Stadium
	Lichte Breite	10+12+10= 32 Fuß

0 20 m

der Jahrhundertmitte durch eine niedrige Mauer umfaßt und damit als auch baulich markierter Ort faßbar (Athen). Im 5. Jh. v. Chr. bildete sich als Teil des G. die Palaistra als großer, meist annähernd quadratischer Peristylhof aus; diese Struktur wurde zum markantesten Teil der G.-Architektur, wie sie seit dem 4. Jh. v. Chr. in zahlreichen griech. Poleis und Heiligtümern entstand (frühe Beispiele: Thera, Nemea, Delphi).

Das G. als funktional zusammengehöriges Konglomerat verschiedener architektonischer Elemente avancierte in Spätklassik und Hell. zu einem der größten Bau-»Typen« der griech. Welt; nicht selten beanspruchte es ein Areal von über zwei Hektar. Um einen großen Freiplatz herum gruppierten sich die einzelnen Bauelemente: eine offene, meist ein → Stadion lange Rennbahn (*drómos*), eine überdachte Laufbahn (→ *xystós*) und lange Säulenhallen, in denen die verschiedenen Übungs- und Unterrichtsräume angesiedelt waren: das Umkleidezimmer (*apodytḗrion*), ein Salbraum (*elaiothḗsion*), das Waschzimmer (*lutrón*), Kalt- und Warmbäder (Bäder als frühe Ausprägungen öffentlicher → Thermen), ein Herdraum (*pyriatḗrion*), → Latrinen sowie die verschiedenen Räume für die Vorbereitungen zu sportlichen Wettkämpfen; dann, außerhalb der Säulenhallen, → Exedren für Aufenthalt und Unterricht, bisweilen ein Ballspielplatz (Delphi) und kleine Heiligtümer (meist für Hermes, Herakles oder die Musen). Die Palaistra mit ihrem in der Regel annähernd quadratischen Peristylhof bildete oft einen Annex dieser Anlage (z. B. Olympia) und war an allen vier Seiten mit Raumgruppen umgeben, die zur speziellen Vorbereitung der Kampfsportarten dienten.

Das G. wurde im Hell. zu einer zentralen öffentlichen Bauaufgabe und damit zugleich zu einem beliebten Repräsentationsgegenstand der jeweiligen Bauträger (→ Bauwesen). Aufwendige Propylon-Bauten markierten die Zugänge zur G.-Anlage sowie zur nun vermehrt baulich davon separierten Palaistra (Olympia); Säulenhallen und Peristyle wurden aus kostbaren Baumaterialien errichtet und reich mit → Bauplastik verziert. Die kleinasiatischen »Prunk-Gymnasien« von Priene, Milet oder Ephesos zeigten in diesem Sinne einen erheblichen Bauluxus, erstreckten sich bisweilen auf riesiger Grundfläche und ergänzten das G. um neue Bereiche (→ Bibliothek, → Theater, z. B. die G. von Pergamon oder Rhodos).

Anders als die aus dem urspr. Bauzusammenhang des G. isolierte Palaistra erfuhr das G. als eigenständiges Baukonglomerat in der röm. Architektur keine Tradierung, sondern wurde als multifunktionale Sport- und Freizeitarchitektur ersetzt von den → Thermen, die alle Aufgaben des G. adaptierten, sie zugleich aber im Sinne der Bedürfnisse der röm. Kultur umgewichteten. Eine Ausnahme bildeten Restaurierungen und Erweiterungen bestehender, traditioneller Anlagen im griech.-kleinasiatischen Kulturraum (z. B. das Eudemos.-G. in Milet) sowie vereinzelte Neubauten, die in ihrer Prachtentfaltung den Thermen in nichts nachstanden

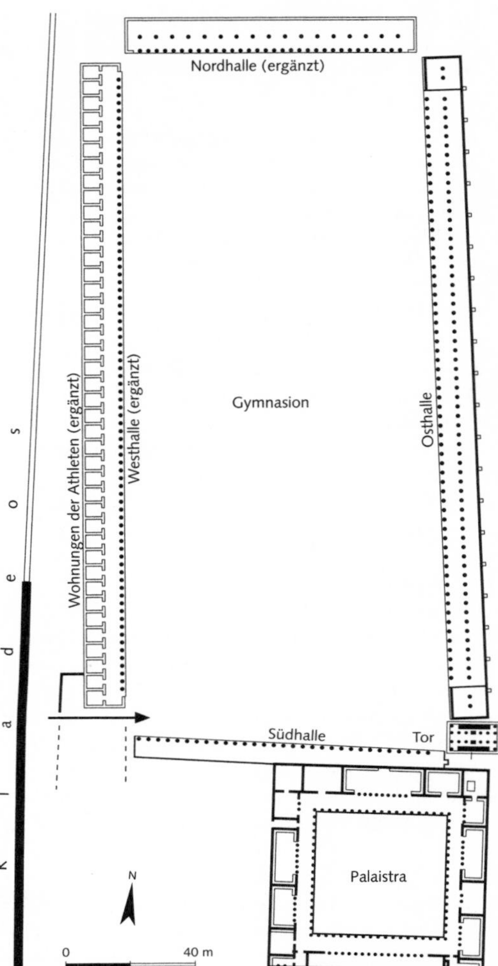

Olympia, Gymnasion und Palaistra (rekonstruierter Grundriß).

und zu einer Anspielung auf die als vorbildhaft verstandene griech. Kulturtradition wurden (z. B. das Hafen-G. in Ephesos; vgl. dagegen aber Vitr. 5,11).

Aus dem Wandel der drei auf das 6. Jh. v. Chr. zurückgehenden großen G. in Athen – Akademie (→ Akademeia), Kynosarges und Lykeion – zu Philosophenschulen des Platon, Antisthenes und Aristoteles erwuchs in der Moderne das humanistische Verständnis vom G. als einer hochstehenden Bildungseinrichtung der gesellschaftlichen Elite.

J. Delorme, Gymnasion, 1960 • P. Gauthier, Notes sur le rôle du gymnasion dans les cités helléniques, in: M. Wörrle, P. Zanker (Hrsg.), Stadtbild und Bürgerbild im Hell., Kongr. München 1993, 1995, 1–11 • S. L. Glass, Palaistra and G. in Greek Architecture, 1981 • Ders., The Greek G. Some Problems, in: The Archaeology of the Olympics, Kongr. Los Angeles 1984, 1988, 155–173 • H.v. Hesberg, Das griech. G. im 2. Jh. v. Chr., in: M. Wörrle, P. Zanker

(Hrsg.), Stadtbild und Bürgerbild im Hell., Kongr. München 1993, 1995, 13–27 • H. LAUTER, Die Architektur des Hell., 1986, 132–148 • M. MAASS, Das ant. Delphi, 1993, 62–67 • A. MALLWITZ, Olympia und seine Bauten, 1972, 268–289 • W. MARTINI, Das G. von Samos (Samos 16), 1984 • W. MÜLLER-WIENER, Griech. Bauwesen in der Ant., 1988, 166–170 • W. RADT, Pergamon, 1988, 131–146 • P. SCHAZMANN, Altertümer von Pergamon VI, Das G., 1923 • TRAVLOS, Athen, 42–51, 340f., 345–347 • CH. WACKER, Das G. in Olympia. Gesch. und Funktion, 1996 • W. ZSCHIETZSCHMANN, Wettkampf- und Übungsstätten in Griechenland, Bd. 2: Palästra-Gymnasium, 1961. C.HÖ.

II. Das Hellenistische Gymnasion

A. Allgemeines B. Sonderfälle
C. Die Bedeutung für die Kulte
D. Das Gymnasion als Sitz von Vereinen
E. Historische Entwicklung
F. Kulturelle Auswirkungen des Gymnasions auf die beherrschten Völker

A. Allgemeines

Das griech. G. diente in klass. Zeit vor allem der körperlichen Ertüchtigung und vormil. Übungen (→ Ephebeia). Zeugnisse, die darüber hinausweisen könnten (→ Schule), sind spärlich [3. 1–16]. Erst in hell. Zeit entwickelte sich das G. zunehmend zu einer Unterrichtsanstalt, die auch Fertigkeiten in Musik (Instrumentenspiel und Gesang) und lit. Grundkenntnisse vermittelte, nicht aber in den mathematischen Fächern wie Geom., Astronomie und Arithmetik [1; 2; 3]. Der im Neuplatonismus entstandene Zyklus der »sieben freien Künste« (Gramm., Rhet., Dialektik, Geom., Arithmetik, Astronomie, theoretische Musik) hat weder im Hell. noch in der Kaiserzeit die Grundlage des allg. Jugendunterrichts abgegeben [1; 2]. Die G. als Universitäten zu bezeichnen [4. 316] und ihnen damit pauschal ein hohes Bildungsniveau zuzuschreiben, ist unangemessen und kann allenfalls für Athen, das eine Sonderstellung einnimmt, zutreffen. Die griech. Städte der Oikumene wiesen kein einheitliches Bildungssystem auf. Jede Stadt sorgte für die Jugenderziehung der Freigeborenen, und nur für diese, nach Maßgabe ihrer finanziellen Mittel [3. 40, 42, 60]. Häufig verdankten die G. ihre Gründung und ihren Unterhalt privaten Stiftungen (vgl. z. B. die Stiftungsurkunde von Koressos auf Keos: Syll.[3] 958; die Knabenschulstiftungen des Polythrus in Teos: Syll.[3] 578), wurden aber stets öffentlich von der Stadt verwaltet. Die Lehrer wie die Gymnasiarchen wurden von der Volksversammlung jährlich für ein Jahr gewählt. Die Höhe des Bildungsniveaus hing von der Dauer und Qualität des in den G. vermittelten Unterrichts ab. Manche Städte konnten es sich leisten, gesonderte G. für Knaben (*paídes*, παῖδες), Heranwachsende (Epheben [*éphēboi*, ἔφηβοι]: Jungen vom Eintritt der Pubertät, also etwa von 15 bis 18 J.) und für junge Männer (*néoi*, νέοι = 18- bis 19-Jährige) einzurichten [vgl. 3. 34–42], und der sich somit auf etwa acht Jahre erstreckende Unterricht muß sehr erfolgreich gewesen sein. Ärmere Städte konnten im allg. nur ein G., das der Epheben, unterhalten, bisweilen auch keines (Paus. 10,4,1). In diesen Fällen mußte Lesen und Schreiben privat erlernt werden [3. 28, 40, 42]; für Äg. [5. 17f.]. Die kurze Zeit des öffentlichen Unterrichts von etwa 3 Jahren konnte für sich allein keinen hohen Bildungsstand erzielen. In jeder noch so kleinen griech. Stadt gab es für Begüterte Privatunterricht bei Wanderlehrern, die gelegentlich auch zu Gastvorträgen ins G. eingeladen wurden [3. 50–51; 1. 304], die auch von Außenstehenden besucht werden konnten. In vielen Städten entstanden vom 2. Jh. v. Chr. an zusätzlich private Institute von häufig hohem Niveau, die Unterricht in Gramm. (= griech. Lit.) und Rhet. erteilten. In den Städten, in denen sich ein Philosoph niedergelassen hatte, konnten im Rahmen dieses Unterrichts auch Kenntnisse in den mathematischen Wissenschaften erworben werden, die sonst nur zur Berufsausbildung z. B. der Architekten und Geometer gehörten [1. 41–44].

B. Sonderfälle

Abweichend von der bereits genannten Einteilung in Altersgruppen traten in Äg. die Epheben ein Jahr früher in das G. ein – vorher war der Unterricht privat –, was mit den besonderen steuerlichen Verhältnissen in diesem Land zusammenhing [3. 90f.]. Außerdem scheint dieser (wahrscheinlich nur Sport-) Unterricht im G. nur ein Jahr gedauert zu haben [3. 91].

In Athen betraf die Epheheninstitution ausnahmsweise die jungen Männer zw. 18 und 19 Jahren, und dieser einzige städtisch organisierte Unterricht dauerte nur ein Jahr [3. 34]. Außerdem wurde der Leiter dieser Anstalt nicht *gymnasíarchos* (γυμνασίαρχος) genannt wie in den meisten griech. Städten, sondern *kosmētḗs* (κοσμητής) (4. Jh. v. Chr.: IG II 478; 3. Jh. v. Chr.: IG II 1350–1352; 2. Jh. v. Chr.: IG II[2] 900; 930; 991; 1006; 1008; 1027 etc.; 1. Jh. v. Chr.: IG II[2] 1028–1030; 1039–1043 etc.). Dem Alter der jungen Männer entsprechend war das Unterrichtsprogramm anspruchsvoll. Sie hörten Vorlesungen in Philos., Gramm. und Rhet. Diese Institution erlangte hohes Ansehen, und die Söhne reicher Eltern kamen von weither angereist, um in sie aufgenommen zu werden ([3. 26]; vgl. IG II I[2] 1028 (100/99 v. Chr.) und IG II[2] 2097 (169/70)), was die Rolle Athens als griech. Kulturzentrum bestätigt.

Eine Sonderstellung nahm auch das G. in Teos, dem Sitz der dionysischen → Techniten, ein; denn die von dort stammenden Siegerlisten (CIG II 3088) erwähnen u. a. Unterrichtsfächer (Rhythmographie, Melographie, Komödie, Trag.), die sonst nirgends vorkommen und wohl speziell auf die Ausbildung zum Schauspieler ausgerichtet waren.

C. Die Bedeutung für die Kulte

Das G. war auch Kultstätte. Der Gott der Wissenschaften, Hermes, sowie Herakles, häufig auch die Musen, wurden in den G. als Schutzgötter verehrt und hatten dort Altäre [4. 453ff.]. Auch der → Heroenkult spielte in den G. eine recht bedeutende Rolle. Im G.

wurden u.a. Stifter und hervorragende Schüler bestattet, denen somit der Rang von Heroen und entsprechende kult. Verehrung zuteil wurde [3. 64–71; 4. 448–449]. In zunehmendem Maße schmückten aber auch, bes. seit dem Ende der röm. Republik, profane Götterstatuen als reine Kunstgegenstände (*ornamenta* γυμνασιώδη, vgl. Cic. Att. 1,6) das G. Die Schuljugend wurde regelmäßig zu städtischen Götterfesten und Herrscherkulten herangezogen; sie stellte die Chöre, die die Hymnen sangen, was musikalische Schulung voraussetzte [6. 115, 214–216, 380–382]. Auch an den zahlreichen Prozessionen hatte sie teilzunehmen [3. 67–71] und war somit stark in das öffentliche Leben eingebunden. Wettkämpfe und die damit verbundenen Siegerehrungen spielten im G. ebenfalls eine große Rolle. Das hell. G. kannte keine Examina, dafür aber Wettbewerbe (vor Publikum) in allen Unterrichtsfächern: mil. Übungen, Dauerlauf, Stadionlauf, Doppellauf, Ringkampf, Faustkampf, Allkampf (Pankration), Zitherspiel, Gesang, Lesen, Rezitation epischer Gedichte. Es gab auch Preise für gutes Betragen. Die Namen der Sieger wurden öffentlich vom Stadtschreiber angeschlagen oder sogar inschr. festgehalten (Syll.^{3} 958, bes. 40f.). Hauptsächlich geben die leider sehr spärlichen inschr. erhaltenen Siegerlisten (u.a. aus Koressos auf Kos, 3. Jh. v. Chr.: Syll.^{3} 958; aus Chios: Syll.^{3} 959) sowie die Ehrendekrete für den Leiter der G., meist Gymnasiarch (gelegentlich Ephebarch/ἐφήβαρχος oder Kosmet) genannt, Auskunft über den Schulbetrieb. Der Gymnasiarch hatte neben der Aufsicht über den Lehrbetrieb auch für einen großen Teil der Betriebskosten aufzukommen. Wir besitzen auch Nachrichten über Paidonomen (παιδονόμοι), die gegebenenfalls die Knabenschulen unter sich hatten.

D. Das Gymnasion als Sitz von Vereinen

Auch Schülervereine, denen der Erwachsenen nachgebildet, hatten im G. ihren Sitz. Sie faßten Ehrenbeschlüsse für bes. verdiente Lehrer oder sonstige Persönlichkeiten oder bemühten sich um das Andenken toter Kameraden; letzteres kann als Teil des Heroenkultes angesehen werden [3. 75–78].

E. Historische Entwicklung

Allmählich, bes. unter röm. Herrschaft, büßte das G. seine Rolle als Bildungsstätte ein. Die täglichen Leibesübungen kamen aus der Mode: Die Römer lehnten den Nacktsport, der damit verbundenen Pädophilie wegen (vgl. Cic. rep. 4,4,4; Tusc. 4,70), und die musikalische Unterweisung ab [2], und auch bei den meisten fremden Völkern (Ägyptern, Syrern) hatte der Sport keinen hohen Stellenwert. G. wurden zu → Thermen. Dazu trug der sich immer stärker etablierende Berufssport ebenfalls bei. Das öffentliche Unterrichtswesen (Elementarunterricht, Unterricht in Gramm., Rhet. und – sehr selten – Philos.) wurde in der Kaiserzeit (die ersten Anzeichen finden sich schon im 1. Jh. v. Chr.) von den einzelnen Städten unabhängig vom G. organisiert. Diese Entwicklung ist Anf. des 2. Jh. n. Chr. abgeschlossen [1. 215–261].

F. Kulturelle Auswirkungen des Gymnasions auf die beherrschten Völker

Das hell. G. spielte zumal in den von Alexandros [4] eroberten und nach ihm von seinen maked. Generälen und ihren Nachfolgern beherrschten Gebieten (von Kleinasien bis hin nach Baktrien und Persien, Mesopotamien und Äg.) eine große kulturelle Rolle. Die von den Seleukiden und den Lagiden gegr. oder eroberten Städte wurden zu Zentren griech. Kultur, wobei das G. zum Sinnbild und Wahrer nationaler Identität wurde. Die Griechen interessierten sich bekanntlich nicht für Sprache und Kultur der von ihnen beherrschten Völker – in den G. wurde weder die Sprache noch die Gesch. des unterworfenen Volkes auch nur ansatzweise gelehrt; es lag an den Unterworfenen, sich ihnen kulturell anzunähern, Verwaltungssprache war das Griech. Ob oder wieweit das griech. G. wenigstens den »Kulturgriechen« offenstand, ist eine umstrittene Frage, die aber wohl im großen und ganzen negativ zu beantworten ist. Gelegentliche Aufnahmen Fremder in griech. G. dürften wohl, wie die seltene Teilnahme von Nichthellenen an den panhellenischen Spielen, damit zu erklären sein, daß die betreffenden Kulturgriechen oder ganze Städte den auf der griech. Myth. beruhenden Nachweis ihres Griechentums zu erbringen sich bemüht hatten. Rom leitete z.B. seine Herkunft von Troja ab (Aeneas), und die phöniz. Stadt Sidon von Argos [7]. Die führenden Einwohner solcher Städte, die sich noch dazu nachweislich an die griech. Kultur assimiliert hatten, galten in den Augen der Griechen dann nicht mehr als Fremde.

Die → Hellenisierung der Oberschicht der fremden Völker gelang mit unterschiedlichem Erfolg. Die phöniz. Küstenstädte wie Arados, Tyros, Sidon und Byblos, die schon seit langem mit den Griechen Handelsverbindungen unterhalten hatten und unter griech. Herrschaft nicht umbenannt worden waren, wurden wohl am schnellsten und am vollständigsten hellenisiert, wenn auch das Bewußtsein ihrer eigenen Kultur dort stets lebendig blieb [8]. Wahrscheinlich war auch einigen phöniz. Städten das Recht zugebilligt worden, G. nach griech. Vorbild (mit griech. Sprache und griech. Lit.) zu gründen und zu unterhalten. Eine zweisprachige, phöniz.-griech. Inschr. (IGLS VII, Nr. 4001) vom Jahre 25/24 v. Chr. legt dies nahe. Ihr Auftraggeber ist Phönizier, bezeichnet sich als Gymnasiarchen, und die für das griech. G. typischen Schutzgötter Hermes und Herakles/Melqart werden erwähnt. Auch die aram. sprechenden Syrer hatten von den Seleukidenkönigen ähnliche Rechte erhalten [9. 64]; darauf weist auch die kritische Bemerkung (Athen. 5,210f) des aus Apameia stammenden stoischen Philosophen Poseidonios (ca. 135–51 v. Chr.) hin, daß die Syrer die G. hauptsächlich dazu benutzten, sich zu baden, zu ölen, zu parfümieren und dort Gelage zu veranstalten, so als handle es sich um ihre Privathäuser. Es ist kaum vorstellbar, daß die Griechen einen solchen Mißbrauch ihrer eigenen G. geduldet hätten. Wenn man dem 2. Makkabäerbuch (4,9ff.) glaubt (was überwiegend der Fall ist), so hatte eine Faktion hellenisierter Juden unter ihrem Hohepriester Josua, der sich bezeichnenderweise in Jason umbenannte, 175/174 v. Chr. vom Seleukidenkönig Antiochos IV. das Recht erwirkt, Jerusalem in eine griech. Polis mit dem Namen Antiocheia umzugestalten, den Tempel (das Zentrum des ant. Judentums) dem Zeus Olympios zu weihen und ein G. einzurichten (anders [10.103 f.]). Daß die Bibel ins Griech. übersetzt werden mußte (Septuaginta), zeugt zudem von der Tatsache, daß die Juden der Diaspora weitgehend hellenisiert waren und Hebräisch nicht mehr lesen konnten. In Äg. scheint die Hellenisierung nicht so durchgehend gewesen zu sein, was wohl u.a. darauf zurückzuführen ist, daß dieses Land längst nicht in dem Maße »verstädtert« war wie Kleinasien und Syrien. Wieweit die zahlreichen dortigen Papyrus- und Scherbenfunde, die u.a. griech. Grammatik- und Schreibübungen enthalten, auf den Unterricht der griech. G. oder auf Privatunterricht zurückzuführen sind, ist in den meisten Fällen nicht zu entscheiden [5].

Das griech. G. übte also auf den Hellenisierungsprozeß in den von den Griechen unterworfenen Gebieten keinen unmittelbaren Einfluß aus, der darin bestanden hätte, daß sein Unterricht möglichst vielen Einheimischen offenstand (das Gegenteil war der Fall), sondern mittelbar dadurch, daß seine Unterrichtsgegenstände in dem Streben nach sozialem Aufstieg bei den fremden Völkern in privatem Rahmen und in den G. für Nichtgriechen verbreitete Nachahmung fanden.
→ Hellenisierung

1 I. Hadot, Arts libéraux et philosophie dans la pensée antique, 1984 2 Dies., Geschichte der Bildung. Artes liberales, in: F. Graf (Hrsg.), Einleitung in die lat. Philol., 1997 3 M.P. Nilsson, Die hell. Schule, 1955
4 J. Delorme, Gymnasion. Étude sur les monuments consacrés à l'éducation en Grèce, 1960 5 R. Criboire, Teachers and Students in Graeco-Roman Egypt, 1996
6 L. Robert, J. Robert, La Carie, Bd. 2, 1954
7 E. Bikermann, Sur une inscription grecque de Sidon, in: Mélanges Syriens offerts à R. Dussaud, 1939, 91–99
8 F. Millar, The Phoenician Cities. A Case-Study of Hellenisation, in: PCPhS 209, 1983, 55–71 9 A. Mehl, Erziehung zum Hellenen – Erziehung zum Weltbürger, in: Nikephoros 5, 1992, 43–73 10 A. Momigliano, Sagesses barbares. Les limites de l'hellénisation, 1980 (umstritten).

I. H.

Gymnastik s. Sport

Gymnetes (γυμνῆτες). Leichtbewaffnete. Pollux (3,83) bezeichnet die niedere Bevölkerung in Argos als *g.* und vergleicht diese mit den → Heloten in Sparta, den → Penestai in Thessalien und den → Korynephoroi in Sikyon. Es handelte sich jedoch in Argos (wie in Sikyon) eher um Abhängige als um Sklaven, und Stephanos von Byzantion (s.v. χίος) nennt sie wahrscheinlich richtig *gymnésioi*. Der Irrtum des Pollux ist vielleicht damit zu erklären, daß die Heloten oft als Leichtbewaffnete kämpften (*psíloi*, Hdt. 9,29), für die im Griech. der Begriff *g.* verwendet wurde. Die *g.* und *gymnomáchoi* werden zuerst bei Tyrtaios erwähnt (fr. 11,35–8; P.Oxy. 3316,14); sie waren wahrscheinlich ärmere Spartaner, die hinter den schützenden Schilden der → Hopliten standen. In der Schlacht bei Plataiai (479 v. Chr.) stellten die Heloten die leichtbewaffneten Truppen Spartas, die 35 000 Mann stark gewesen sein sollen (Hdt. 9,29). Die *g.* kämpften auf beiden Seiten in der Schlacht von Delion im Jahre 424 v. Chr. (Thuk. 4,90,4; 4,93,3); zu diesem Zeitpunkt wurden sie bei der Reiterei an den Flügeln aufgestellt. In all diesen Fällen hatte der Einsatz der *g.* wohl aus polit. und sozialen Gründen nur eine zweitrangige Bedeutung. Allein in Syrakus hat das leichtbewaffnete Fußvolk (ἡ γυμνητεία, *gymnēteía*; Thuk. 7,37,2) unter Führung des Spartaners Gylippos 414 v. Chr. eine wichtige Rolle gespielt, vielleicht als Folge der bes. Situation der Belagerung der Stadt durch die Athener oder aufgrund des demokratischen Systems. Die *g.* sind auch für die Anfangsjahre des → Korinthischen Krieges belegt (Xen. hell. 4,2,14); unter den leichtbewaffneten Truppen haben dann allerdings bald die → Peltasten, zuerst unter dem Befehl des Iphikrates, an Bedeutung gewonnen (Xen. hell. 4,5,13–17; Nep. 11). In der Kriegführung der hell. Zeit wurde der Einsatz der leichtbewaffneten Söldnertruppen aufgrund polit., aber auch strategischer und wirtschaftlicher Faktoren begünstigt.

1 P. Cartledge, Hopliten und Helden: Spartas Beitrag zur Technik der ant. Kriegskunst, in: K. Christ (Hrsg.), Sparta, 1986, 387–425, 470 2 O. Lippelt, Die griech. Leichtbewaffneten bis auf Alexander den Großen, 1910
3 D. Lotze, Μεταξὺ Ἐλευθέρων καὶ Δούλων, 1959
4 L. Thommen, Lakedaimonion Politeia, 1996.

P.C./Ü: A.BE.

Gymnias (Γυμνιάς, Xen. an. 4,7,19). Große, volkreiche und wohlhabende Stadt der *Skythēnoí* am linken Ufer des Harpasos (h. Çoruh su), an der Stelle oder in der Nähe des h. Bayburt.

O. Lendle, Komm. zu Xenophons Anabasis, 1995, 270–272.

A.P.-L.

Gymnosophisten (γυμνοσοφισταί). Wörtlich: »die nackten Weisen«; das Wort erscheint erstmals im Pap. Berol. 13044 (1. Jh. v. Chr.) zur Bezeichnung der zehn indischen Weisen, mit denen Alexander d. Gr. ein – ganz sicher legendäres [3] – Gespräch geführt haben soll [1]. Die ersten neun dieser Weisen mußten je eine von Alexander gestellte Frage naturwiss. oder metaphysischen Inhalts beantworten, während der zehnte Weise den Wert dieser Antworten zu beurteilen hatte. (Plut. Alexander 64; 65,1; Clem. Al. strom. 6,4,38; Ps.-Kallisthenes 3,5–7 Kroll). Laut einigen kaiserzeitlichen Alexander-Biographen begaben sich schon zuvor griech. Weise zu den G. in die Lehre, namentlich Lykurg, Pythagoras, Demokrit, Sokrates und Platon; auch Philosophen späterer Zeit, insbes. Pyrrhon und Plotin, wollten angeblich mit den G. in Kontakt treten.

Die Lebensart der G. zeichnet sich nach den genannten Quellen aus durch Ehrfurcht vor der Natur und Ablehnung der Errungenschaften der Zivilisation. Die Lehre der G. ist um so schwerer zu umreißen, als sie uns nur über den Umweg der griech. – bes. der kynischen – Philos. zugänglich ist, die hier als Filter gewirkt haben mag [3]. In zahlreichen Texten der röm. Zeit erscheinen die indischen G. lediglich als Muster von Mut und Frömmigkeit (Phil. De Abrahamo 1,82; Proklos in Tim. 1,208 Diehl) oder als Beispiele für ein einfaches, naturnahes Leben (Phil. De Somniis 2,56). In den stereotypen Verzeichnissen der barbarischen Weisen oder in den Diskussionen über den griech. oder fremden Ursprung der Philos. erscheint nur der blanke Name »G.« (Diog. Laert. 1,1 und 6; Clem. Al. strom. 6,7,57). Seltener als die indischen treten in den Quellen die äthiopischen G. auf. In den *Aithiopiká* des Heliodoros erscheinen die G. als eine Kaste von weisen Priestern. In Philostr. Ap. 6 werden sie als weniger begabte Doppelgänger der indischen Brahmanen dargestellt [4].

1 U. Wilcken, Alexander der Große und die indischen Gymnosophisten, in: SPrAW 1923, philol.-histor. Klasse, 150–183 **2** H. van Thiel, Alexanders Gespräch mit den Gymnosophisten, in: Hermes 100, 1972, 343–358
3 C. Muckensturm, Les Gymnosophistes étaient-ils des cyniques modèles?, in: Dies., Le cynisme ancien et ses prolongements, 1993, 225–239 **4** P. Robiano, Les gymnosophistes éthiopiens chez Philostrate et chez Héliodore, in: REA 94, 1992, 3–4, 413–428. C.M.-P.

Gynäkologie A. Spezialgebiet bei den Hippokratikern B. Behandlungsmethoden C. Fertilität und Schwangerschaft D. Entwicklung gynäkologischer Theorien ab Herophilos

A. Spezialgebiet bei den Hippokratikern

Die Frage, ob G. als ein medizinisches Spezialgebiet zu betrachten ist, wurde in der Ant. kontrovers behandelt. Diese Debatte, die sich in ihren Grundzügen rekonstruieren läßt, kann auf Hesiod zurückgeführt werden, der die Nachfahren → Pandoras, der ersten Frau, programmatisch als eine eigene »Rasse« darstellt (γένος γυναικῶν; theog. 585–590). *Gynaikeía* (was weibliche Sexualorgane, Menstruation, aber auch Behandlung von Frauenkrankheiten bezeichnen kann) ist der griech. Titel der beiden langen Texte aus dem Corpus Hippocraticum, die sich ausschließlich mit Frauenkrankheiten beschäftigen (Hippokr. *De mulierum affectibus* 1 und 2 = Mul.; zu den Abkürzungen der Werktitel des Corpus Hippocraticum s. → Hippokrates). In Mul. 1,62 (8,126 L.) wird davor gewarnt, kranke Frauen wie Männer zu behandeln; der Autor versichert vielmehr, daß sich die Heilung von Frauenkrankheiten erheblich von der von Männerkrankheiten unterscheidet, und begründet damit nach [1. 154] erst eigentlich die griech. G. Das Corpus Hippocraticum enthält zudem eine Abhandlung über das Problem der Unfruchtbarkeit (*De sterilibus*), eine abweichende Redaktion von Material aus Mul. 1 und 2 (*De natura muliebri*), Texte über Empfängnis und Wachstum des Fötus (*De genitura, De natura pueri*), eine Diskussion über die Risiken einer Frühgeburt (*De octimestri partu* = Oct.), die Beschreibung der Entfernung eines abgestorbenen Fötus aus der Gebärmutter (*De exsectione foetus*) sowie einen kurzen Traktat über Krankheiten junger Mädchen (*De virginum morbis*). All diese Abhandlungen lassen die Ansicht erkennen, daß sich Frauen von Männern in einem Maße unterscheiden, das einen eigenen medizinischen Ansatz rechtfertigt; allerdings heißt es in Texten wie Oct. auch, daß dieselben prognostischen und therapeutischen Grundsätze, die sich auf Krankheit, Gesundheit und Tod aller Menschen beziehen, wie z.B. die Lehre von den »kritischen Tagen«, der zufolge bestimmte Tage während einer Phase besonders entscheidend sind, sich ebensogut auf Empfängnis, Fehlgeburt und Geburt bei Frauen anwenden lassen (Oct. 9 = 7,446 L.).

Worin aber besteht nun die Andersartigkeit der Frau? Die hippokratischen Schriften verweisen bei der Beantwortung dieser Frage keineswegs nur auf die Funktion des Gebärens und die dazu erforderlichen Organe, sondern sehen das wichtigste Unterscheidungskriterium in der Textur des Körperfleisches. Frauen seien feucht und schwammig, das Fleisch des Mannes dagegen trockener und fester. Zur Illustration dieses Hauptunterschieds diente der Vergleich von weiblichem Fleisch mit Wolle einerseits und männlichem mit einem dicht gewebten Kleidungsstück andererseits (Mul. 1,1 = 8,10–14 L.; Gland. 16 = 8,572 L.); dahinter steht die Vorstellung von der Frau als Rohstoff und dem Mann als fertigem Produkt in einem handwerklichen Herstellungsverfahren. Wegen der loseren Textur ihres Fleisches entnähmen Frauen ihrer Nahrung mehr Flüssigkeit, deren angesammelten Überschuß sie mit Hilfe der Menstruation wieder ausscheiden müßten. Wenn die Menstruation ausbleibe, steige das überschüssige Blut weiterhin im Körper an und übe Druck auf verschiedene Organe aus, bis der Tod eintrete. In diesem Modell ist sogar denkbar, daß die durch die anhaltende Ansammlung von Menstrualblut entstehende Hitze zu einer Geschlechtsumwandlung führt, bevor der Tod eintritt; in einer Krankengeschichte in den hippokratischen Büchern *Epidemiarum* (= Epid.) wird erzählt, daß bei Phaethusa von Abdera nach der Abreise ihres Mannes die Regel aussetzte und sie daraufhin Haarwuchs am Körper und eine tiefe Stimme entwickelte (Epid. 6,8,32 = 5,356 L.).

Krankengeschichten von Patientinnen finden sich in allen sieben Büchern *Epidemiarum*, während andere hippokratische Schriften, die von Krankheit im allg. handeln, Frauenkrankheiten ein eigenes Kapitel widmen (z.B. Aph. 5, Coac. 503–544 = 5,700–708 L. und der letzte Teil von Loc. Hom.). Während in Mul. 1 und 2 das Ausbleiben der Menstruation als Hauptursache für eine ganze Reihe von Krankheitssymptomen bei Frauen gilt, werden in Loc. Hom. 47 (6,344 L.) v.a. die Bewegungen der Gebärmutter für Frauenkrankheiten verantwortlich gemacht. Dabei gilt eine Bewegung nach vorn als besonders schwerwiegend, nicht nur wegen der dadurch verursachten Schmerzen, sondern auch wegen der Blockade des Menstrualflusses; eine Aufwärtsbewegung kann bis in den Kopf hinein Körperorgane in Mitleidenschaft ziehen. Die Gebärmutter stellte man sich als krugförmig vor, und so wurde sie in der Mustio-Handschrift aus dem 9. Jh. bildlich dargestellt.

Übermäßiger oder unzeitiger Menstrualfluß galt gleichermaßen als ungesund (Aph. 5.57 = 4,552 L.). Da man von Verbindungen zw. der Gebärmutter und der weiblichen Brust ausging (Gland. 16 = 8,572 L.), so daß Muttermilch ›die Schwester der Monatsblutung‹ (Epid. 2,3,17 = 3,118 L.) genannt werden konnte, wurde versucht, heftige Regelblutungen durch Aufsetzen von Schröpfgläsern auf die Brust zum Stillstand zu bringen (Aph. 5.50 = 4,550 L.). Aristoteles, demzufolge Frauen »kalt« und Männer »warm« waren, entwickelte diese Argumentationslinie weiter; er behauptete, Regelblut, Muttermilch und Samen seien aufeinanderfolgende Veredelungsprodukte einer einzigen Substanz, wobei nur der männliche Teil einer Spezies über genügend Hitze verfüge, um das Endstadium des Umwandlungsprozesses, d. h. den Samen, bilden zu können (z. B. Aristot. part.an. 650a8 ff.; gen.an. 774a1).

Der Bereich der medizinischen Versorgung von Frauen weckte bei den unterschiedlichsten Praktikern Interesse. In hippokratischen Texten werden eine ›heilende Frau‹ (ἡ ἰητρεύουσα, Mul. 1,68 = 8,144 L.) und ›weibliche Heiler‹ (αἱ ἀκεστρίδες, Carn. 19 = 8,614 L.) als Geburtshelferinnen genannt, doch dürften sie aller Wahrscheinlichkeit nach – neben Hilfsdiensten an der Seite hippokratischer Ärzte – auch selbständig Frauen mit Gesundheitsproblemen geholfen haben. Frauen konnten sich darüber hinaus bei Familienmitgliedern oder in der Nachbarschaft beraten lassen oder auf der Suche nach Heilung zu einem Tempel gehen. Angesichts der im Corpus Hippocraticum überlieferten Heilmittel wurde die Vermutung geäußert, sie zeugten für eine unter Frauen gepflegte mündliche Heiltradition (→ Frau; Geburt).

B. Behandlungsmethoden

Die Behandlung von Frauenkrankheiten bestand hauptsächlich darin, die Intensität der Blutproduktion durch diätetische Maßnahmen zu beeinflussen, zurückgehaltenes Blut zu entfernen oder die Gebärmutter von einem ungeeigneten Ort – etwa der Leber, zu der sie auf der Suche nach zusätzlicher Feuchtigkeit gewandert sei – zurückzubewegen. In der Regel entschied man sich für eine Kombination von Maßnahmen. Eine Flüssigkeit entziehende Diät wurde Frauen mit schleimhaltigen Regelblutungen verordnet, darüber hinaus aber auch Dampfbäder, Brechmittel und reinigende Gebärmuttereinlagen (Mul. 1,11 = 8,44–46 L.). Die hippokratische G. kannte eine große Palette von pharmakologischen Substanzen, darunter Stoffe wie Schwefel, Asphalt, Meerzwiebel und Lorbeer, aber auch Tierexkremente, die allesamt in Reinigungsritualen (→ Kathartik) Verwendung fanden [2]. Wohlriechenden Substanzen wie z. B. Myrrhe sprach man wärmende Eigenschaften zu (sie entziehen etwa zurückgehaltenes Blut dem Körper), und verabreichte sie mit Hilfe von heißen Umschlägen, Dampfbädern und Tampons. Bei einem Verfahren, das man Räucherung nannte, wurden Dämpfe durch den Gebärmutterhals in den Uterus eingeleitet, um ihn zu öffnen, ihn, falls er sich fortbewegt hatte, an seinen angestammten anatomischen Ort zurückzubringen, oder Stoffe, die – wie z. B. verhaltenes Menstrualblut – Krankheiten verursachten, auszutreiben. Die Gebärmutter konnte durch süße, an der Vagina aufsteigende Düfte abwärts gelockt werden, wobei über die Nase inhalierte üble Gerüche den Descensus noch beförderten (z. B. Mul. 2,123 = 8,266 L.; 2,154 = 8,330 L.); bei einem Gebärmuttervorfall wurden die über Nase und Vagina wirkenden Duftstoffe vertauscht (z. B. Mul. 2,125 = 8,268 L.). Erbrechen oder Niesen konnten ebenfalls dazu dienen, der Gebärmutter einen Stoß zu versetzen (Mul. 2,142 = 8,314 L.); vgl. auch → Hysterie.

Explizit wurden der obere und der untere Teil des weiblichen Körpers in Beziehung zueinander gesetzt, nicht nur in der Terminologie, was sich noch in unserem heutigen Sprachgebrauch spiegelt (vgl. »Gebärmutterhals« und »Schamlippen«), sondern auch in theoretischer Hinsicht; Ps.-Aristoteles behauptete, die Gebärmutter »atme« den Samen ebenso »ein«, wie Mund und Nase Stoffe einatmeten, und der Bereich von der Vulva bis ins Innere der Gebärmutter ähnele dem zwischen Nasenlöchern und Kehlkopf (Steril. 643b 35; 636b 17–18; 637a 21–35). Auch die Überzeugung griech. und röm. Autoren, der Verlust der Jungfräulichkeit lasse sich daran erkennen, daß das Mädchen eine tiefere Stimme bekäme, läßt sich auf diese Vorstellung zurückführen [3].

C. Fertilität und Schwangerschaft

Die potentielle Fruchtbarkeit einer Frau wurde mit Hilfe von Duftstoffen getestet, wobei es herauszufinden galt, ob sich die Düfte frei im Körper ausbreiten konnten (Aph. 5,59 = 4,554 L.). Als Hindernis für eine Geburt galt eine extrem dichte, heiße, kalte, trockene oder feuchte Gebärmutter (Aph. 5,62 = 4,554 L.), da in solchem Milieu der Samen nicht überleben könne. Fettleibigkeit, von der man glaubte, sie verenge den Muttermund und versperre dem männlichen Samen den Eintritt, galt als ein weiteres Geburtshindernis (Aph. 5,46 = 4,548 L.). Aristoteles zufolge menstruierten fettleibige Frauen nicht, weil das ganze überschüssige Blut vom Körper aufgezehrt werde (Aristot. gen.an. 746b27–29). Ausbleiben der Menstruation in Verbindung mit Übelkeit war als Schwangerschaftszeichen bekannt (Aph. 5,61 = 4,554 L.), was sich durch Verabreichung von Honigwasser bestätigen ließ; bekam die Frau daraufhin eine Kolik, war sicher, daß sie ein Kind bekam (Aph. 5,41 = 4,546 L.). Man glaubte, daß sich der Muttermund während der Schwangerschaft schließe (Aph. 5,51 = 4,550 L.). Das → Geschlecht des ungeborenen Kindes konnte man aus der Gesichtsfarbe der Mutter folgern: Blässe ließ auf ein Mädchen schließen (Aph. 5,42 = 4,546 L. und Steril. 216 = 8,416 L.).

D. Entwicklung gynäkologischer Theorien ab Herophilos

Im Kontext der alexandrinischen Anatomie, die v.a. mit dem Namen → Herophilos verbunden ist, wurden Frauen eher als »verkehrte« Männer denn als eigene »Rasse« gesehen. Was an Zeugungsorganen beim Mann außen liege, existiere analog im Inneren des weiblichen Körpers. Herophilos entdeckte die Eierstöcke (fr. 61 von Staden), wenn ihm auch ihre Funktion verborgen blieb. Ein Zweig der ant. G. beschreibt die Frau als Behälter, in dem der männliche Samen aufgehen konnte, während andere Texte davon ausgehen, daß Männer wie Frauen Samen zur Zeugung des Fötus beisteuern (z.B. *De genitura, De natura pueri*). Auch wenn Herophilos die Eileiter gesehen hatte, kannte er doch nicht deren Aufgabe und glaubte, sie verliefen zur Blase; anscheinend entdeckte erst → Galenos, daß sie in die Gebärmutter inserieren (De uteri diss. 9 = CMG 5,2,1,48). Herophilos beschrieb die Haltebänder der Gebärmutter, die die enorme Beweglichkeit der Gebärmutter, wie sie die hippokratische G. vertrat, zu einer technischen Unmöglichkeit werden ließen (fr. 114 von Staden); die Theorie vom »Wanderuterus« wurde jedoch lediglich im Sinne einer Sympathienlehre zwischen den oberen und unteren Körperregionen umformuliert, wonach letztere in ersteren Symptome verursachen konnten. Was die Therapie betrifft, so ergaben sich aus den anatomischen Fortschritten in Alexandreia kaum Neuerungen; daß hippokratische Rezepturen gegen Frauenkrankheiten weiterhin überliefert wurden, wenn auch, je nach Verfügbarkeit, mit leichten Veränderungen in bezug auf die Inhaltsstoffe, belegen Papyri. Die Dufttherapie des »Wanderuterus« wurde von einigen Autoren nun anders gedeutet; Celsus beispielsweise, der einsah, daß die Gebärmutter an den Darmbeinen befestigt ist (5,1,12), meinte, der Sinn der Dufttherapie bestehe darin, die bewußtlose Patientin aufzuwecken (4,27,1).

→ Soranos stellte die Frage, ob Frauen Zustände erleben, die einzig ihrem Geschlecht vorbehalten sind (Gyn. 3,1), und faßte die Positionen seiner Vorläufer zu dieser Frage zusammen: Autoren wie der im frühen 4. Jh. v. Chr. wirkende Diokles [6] von Karystos (fr. 169 Wellmann) und die Schule der Empiriker hatten geglaubt, es gebe frauenspezifische körperliche Zustände, während Erasistratos und Herophilos im 3. Jh. v. Chr. sowie die Schule der Methodiker diese These verwarfen. Die Methodiker glaubten vielmehr, daß, da Männer und Frauen aus demselben Stoff bestünden und denselben Regeln entsprechend reagierten, auch alle Krankheiten von denselben Gesetzmäßigkeiten bestimmt würden. Soranos selbst behauptete, die Gebärmutter bestehe aus demselben Stoff wie der übrige Körper, auch wenn sie frauenspezifisch sei und eigene Funktionen erfülle; obwohl also einige Zustände wie Schwangerschaft und Laktation frauenspezifisch seien, unterschieden sich ihre Krankheiten nicht grundsätzlich von denen der Männer. → Aretaios vertrat einen ähnlichen Standpunkt (2,11 = CMG 2,34), auch wenn er einräumte, daß die Beweglichkeit der Gebärmutter zu gewissen Gesundheitsstörungen wie hysterischen Erstickungsanfällen, Gebärmuttervorfall und Ausfluß führe, die Frauen nicht mit Männern teilten.

Die galenische G. (→ Galenos) unterscheidet sich von der hippokratischen insofern, als nun nicht mehr das Menstrualblut, sondern der »weibliche Samen« als diejenige Flüssigkeit gilt, deren Zurückhaltung die größte Gefahr für den Körper darstellt (Loc. Aff. 6,5 = 8,420–424, 432 K.). Während die Hippokratiker den seßhaften Lebensstil und die feuchte und schwammige Natur der Frau als Faktoren betrachteten, die zur Blutverhaltung beitragen und auf diesem Wege zur Menstruation, war Galen der Meinung, eine Veränderung des Lebensstils in Kombination mit klimatischen Einflüssen könne theoretisch männlich-weibliche Normen auf den Kopf stellen: In de caus. puls. 3,2 (9,109–110 K.) lesen wir, daß der Puls einer warm-trockenen Frau, die in Ägypten lebe und unter freiem Himmel arbeite, stärker sei als der eines kalt-feuchten Mannes, der untätig in Pontos lebe.

Im griech. Osten überlebte das gynäkologische Gedankengut des Soranos durch seine Aufnahme und Anpassung im Werk der Enzyklopädisten Oreibasios, Aëtios [3] und Paulos von Aigina. Ein unabhängiger griech. Text, das Buch der → Metrodora, ist in einer Hs. aus dem 9. Jh. erhalten. Im lat. Westen legte im späten 4. und frühen 5. Jh. Caelius [II 11] Aurelianus seinem Werk Soranos zugrunde. Ein im *Liber ad Soteris* festgehaltener Dialog zwischen Soranos und einer Hebamme wurde ebenfalls überl., möglicherweise als Katechismus für Geburtshilfe. Im Westen scheint das Augenmerk eher auf praktische Unterweisung in der Heilkunst als auf Medizintheorie gerichtet gewesen zu sein [4].

→ Frau; Geburt; Geschlechterrollen; Hippokrates (mit Abkürzungsliste der Werktitel)

1 P. Manuli, Donne mascoline, femmine sterili, vergini perpetue, in: S. Campese, P. Manuli, G. Sissa (Hrsg.), Madre Materia, 1983, 147–192 **2** H. von Staden, Women and dirt, in: Helios 19, 1990, 7–30 **3** A.E. Hanson, D. Armstrong, Vox virginis, in: BICS 33, 1986, 97–100 **4** A.E. Hanson, M.H. Green, Soranus of Ephesus: Methodicorum Princeps, in: ANRW II 37.2, 1994, 1042–1061.

L.A. Dean-Jones, Women's Bodies in Classical Greek Science, 1994 • N. Demand, Birth, Death, and Motherhood in Classical Greece, 1994 • P. Diepgen, Die Frauenheilkunde der alten Welt, 1937 • D. Gourevitch, Le mal d'être femme, 1984 • H. Grensemann, Hippokratische Gynäkologie, 1982 • A.E. Hanson, Hippocrates: Diseases of Women I, in: Signs 1, 1975, 567–584 • G.E.R. Lloyd, Science, Folklore and Ideology, 1983 • A. Rousselle, Images médicales du corps. Observation féminine et idéologie masculine: le corps de la femme d'après les médecins grecs, in: Annales: économies, sociétés, civilisations 35, 1980, 1089–1115 • H. von Staden, Apud nos foediora verba: Celsus' reluctant construction of the female body, in: G. Sabbah (Hrsg.), Le Latin médical, 1991, 271–296.

H.K./Ü: L.v.R.-B.

Gynaikokratie (γυναικοκρατία). Der Begriff G. (»Frauenherrschaft«, von griech. γυνή/*gynḗ*, »Frau« und κρατεῖν/*kratein*, »herrschen«; vgl. *gynaikokrateisthai*, »von Frauen beherrscht werden«) ist zuerst in philos. Texten des 4. Jh. v. Chr. belegt. Die Verwendung erfolgt fast immer polemisch. Bei Aristoteles wird die G. im Kontext der Kritik an der *politeía* (Verfassung) der Spartaner thematisiert und als Voraussetzung von Habgier und einer extrem ungleichen Verteilung des Bodens gesehen (Aristot. pol. 1269b 12–1270a 31; vgl. auch Plut. Lykurgos 14,1). Für Aristoteles besteht kein Unterschied, ob die Frauen selbst herrschen oder die führenden Politiker von Frauen beherrscht werden (καίτοι τί διαφέρει γυναῖκας ἄρχειν ἢ τοὺς ἄρχοντας ὑπὸ τῶν γυναικῶν ἄρχεσθαι: pol. 1269b 23–34); im Abschnitt über die Tyrannis spricht er von der G. innerhalb des Hauses, die auch für die vollendete Demokratie charakteristisch sei (pol. 1313b 32–35). Der Topos des von seiner Frau beherrschten Mannes soll auf einen Ausspruch des Themistokles zurückgehen; später soll Cato sich ähnlich geäußert haben (Plut. Themistokles 18; Cato maior 8,2–3); in der Spätant. erscheint der Begriff G. in den kritischen Bemerkungen des Prokopios über Belisarios (Prok. HA 5,26). Auch in der Komödie wurde die G. thematisiert; eine Komödie des Amphis trug den Titel »G.« (Athen. 336c). Auch bei Aristophanes (*Lysistrate*, *Ekklesiazusai*, spätes 5./frühes 4. Jh. v. Chr.) wird dargestellt, wie Frauen polit. Macht auszuüben versuchen (vgl. bes. Eccl. 105–109), und auf diese Weise werden die Geschlechterrollen und ihre Verkehrung problematisiert. Nach einer späten, Varro zugeschriebenen Version der Erzählung vom Streit zwischen Athene und Poseidon waren im frühen Athen die Frauen an den Abstimmungen beteiligt und trugen Kinder die Namen ihrer Mütter (Aug. civ. 18,9). Von den Lydern berichtet der Aristoteles-Schüler Klearchos, daß es → Omphale gelungen sei, als Frau eine Tyrannenherrschaft über die effeminierten Männer, die sich zunehmend wie Frauen verhielten, zu errichten (Athen. 515d–516a). Auch von fremden, meist an den Randzonen der bekannten Welt lebenden Völkern wurde erzählt, daß Frauen die Männer beherrschten oder zumindest genauso viel Macht wie diese besäßen (Hdt. 4,26,2 über die Issedonen). Die Auffassung, daß die Völker des Ostens von Frauen regiert würden, begegnet noch in der spätant. Lit. (SHA trig. tyr. 30,1; Claudianus, in Eutropium 1,321–323).

Neben solchen Vorstellungen über die Herrschaft von Frauen in der Frühzeit oder bei fernen Völkern finden sich in der griech. Lit. auch Hinweise auf matrilineare Familienstrukturen. So nimmt Herodot wahr, daß bei den Lykiern der Brauch bestand, die Herkunft von der Mutter und den weiblichen Vorfahren abzuleiten; der Rechtsstatus eines Kindes hing dementsprechend von dem der Mutter, nicht dem des Vaters ab (Hdt. 1,173,4–5; vgl. Plut. mor. 248d). Ebenso fand die Betonung der Herkunft aristokratischer Familien von Frauen im unteritalischen Lokroi Epizephyrioi Beachtung (Pol. 12,5–6).

→ Amazones; Frau; Geschlechterrollen; Matriarchat

A. S. Bradford, Gynaikokratoumenoi: Did Spartan Women Rule Spartan Men?, in: Ancient World 14, 1986, 13–18 · M. H. Dettenhofer, Die Frauen von Sparta. Ökonomische Kompetenz und polit. Relevanz, in: Dies. (Hrsg.), Reine Männersache? Frauen in Männerdomänen der ant. Welt, 1994, 15–40 · B. Wagner-Hasel (Hrsg.), Matriarchatstheorien der Altertumswissenschaft, 1992.

H. SCHN.

Gynaikonitis (γυναικωνῖτις). Im Gegensatz zum → *andrṓn* [4] bezeichnet *g.* den introvertierten Frauentrakt im griech. → Haus, der in der Regel von dem eher extrovertierten Bereich der Männerwelt abgeschlossen im Obergeschoß des Gebäudes lag und auch die Werkzeuge der wirtschaftlichen Produktion der Frau (Webstuhl, Spinnrad etc.) barg; die mindere Stellung der → Frau in der patriarchalischen Gesellschaft Griechenlands kam in dieser Hierarchisierung der baulichen Verhältnisse zum Ausdruck.

W. Hoepfner, E. L. Schwandner, Haus und Stadt im klass. Griechenland, 1986, 290.

C. HÖ.

Gynaikonomoi (γυναικονόμοι). Als G. (»Frauenaufseher«) wurden in verschiedenen griech. Städten die Beamten bezeichnet, die für die Einhaltung von Gesetzen zum Verhalten von Frauen, speziell an Festen und bei Begräbnissen, verantwortlich waren. Aristoteles betrachtete dieses Amt als weder demokratisch noch oligarchisch, sondern als aristokratisch (pol. 4, 1300a4–8; 6, 1323a3–6). Tatsächlich finden sich *g.* aber in Staaten verschiedener Prägung, etwa in Thasos ([2. Nr. 141, 154–155]; 4.–3.Jh v. Chr.), Gambrea (Syll.[3] 1219; 3. Jh. v. Chr.) oder Sparta (IG V 1, 170; 3. Jh. n. Chr.), sogar in Ägypten, wo sie anscheinend eine Rolle bei der Registrierung männlicher Bürger spielen (PHibeh II 196; 3. Jh. v. Chr.). Für Athen erwähnt Philochoros *g.* (FGrH 328 F 65): Das Amt war vermutlich von Demetrios [4] von Phaleron eingeführt worden.

1 D. Ogden, Greek Bastardy, 1996, 352–353 (Ägypten), 363–375 (allgemein) 2 J. Pouilloux, Recherches sur l'histoire et les cultes de Thasos, Bd. 1, 1954 3 C. Wehrli, Les gynéconomes, in: MH 19, 1962, 33–38.

P. J. R.

Gyndes (Γύνδης). Nach Herodot (1,189; 202; 5,52) mesopot. Flußname. Der Perserkönig Kyros soll vor der Einnahme Babylons 539 v. Chr. das Wasser des G. in 360 Kanäle abgeleitet haben. Herodot bezeichnet, geogr. unhaltbar, als Quellgebiet des G. den → Araxes und die pers. Region → Matiane. Wegen der Anmarschrichtung des Kyros ist eine Verknüpfung mit der Diyālā (babylon. *Turan/Turnat*; lat. *Tornadotus*, Plin. nat. 6,132) bzw. dem Kanalsystem zw. Diyālā und → Tigris am wahrscheinlichsten.

M. Streck, s. v. G., RE 6, 2091 f.

K. KE.

Gyrton(e) (Γυρτών[η]). Sowohl in der Argonautensage (→ Argonautai; Apoll. Rhod. 1,57) als auch in der *Ilias* (Hom. Il. 2,738) erscheinen Lapithai aus G. Die Stadt gehörte urspr. zu Perrhaibia, war aber in histor. Zeit ein bed. Ort der thessal. Pelasgiotis. 431 v. Chr. befand sich bei den thessal. Hilfstruppen für Athen auch ein Kontingent aus G. (Thuk. 2,22). Im J. 215 wurden auf Geheiß Philippos' V. mindestens 60 Gyrtonier im benachbarten → Larisa eingebürgert (IG IX 2, 517). 191 und 171 widerstand die Stadt den Belagerungen Antiochos' [5] III. bzw. des Perseus (Liv. 36,10; 42,54). Bis ins 1. Jh. v. Chr. stellte G. öfter den thessal. Bundesstrategen. Für die Kaiserzeit ist der Ort nicht mehr bezeugt. G. lag nordöstl. von Larisa, im Gebiet des Erimon-Bergzuges am rechten Peneios-Ufer. Die genaue Lage von G. ist jedoch nicht gesichert, die Zuweisung des Namens an das moderne Dorf Bakraina geht auf STÄHLIN zurück, der dies später selbst anzweifelte (→ Mopsion, → Dotion).

H. KRAMOLISCH, Die Strategen des Thessal. Bundes, 1978, 32f. • PHILIPPSON/KIRSTEN 1, 271 Anm. 1 • F. STÄHLIN, Das hellenische Thessalien, 1924, 91 f. HE.KR.

Gyth(e)ion (Γύθ(ε)ιον). Lakonische Perioikenstadt an der nordwestl. Küste des innersten Lakon. Golfs in verhältnismäßig geschützter Lage mit guten Verkehrsverbindungen. In histor. Zeit Haupthafen → Spartas (ca. 45 km von G. entfernt), befestigt, mit Schiffswerften und künstlich angelegtem Hafen (in der Brz. waren die Flottenstützpunkte der Region Las und Helos). Belegstellen: Skyl. 46; Xen. hell. 1,4,11; 6,5,32; Pol. 5,19,6; Strab. 8,3,12; 5,2; Ptol. 3,14,32; Paus. 3,21,6–9. Davor liegt die Insel Kranae (h. Marathonisi, durch Damm mit dem Festland verbunden), auf der Paris das erste Mal der Helena beiwohnte (Hom. Il. 3,445; Paus. 3,22,1; Steph. Byz. s. v. G.) und von der die ältesten ant. Reste stammen. Nach der Einnahme 369 v. Chr. durch die Thebaner (Xen. hell. 6,5,32) fiel G. kurz vor 362 wieder in die Hand der Spartaner (Polyain. 2,9). Die Stadt wurde 192 v. Chr. von Nabis eingenommen, dann blieb sie bis 146 unter achaischer Kontrolle. In röm. Zeit gehörte G. zum Bund der → Eleutherolakones und erlebte die größte Blüte: G. war der natürliche Süd-Ausgang der Eurotas-Ebene, und der Marmorabbau in Lakonia durch Rom mußte die Bed. der Stadt noch steigern. Aus der Kaiserzeit stammen der größte Teil der zahlreichen Inschr., die Mz. und die meisten der ausgedehnten, aber unbed. Ruinen nördl. des h. G., am ansehnlichsten das Theater an den Hängen der Akropolis. In der Spätant. wird G. nicht mehr erwähnt.

W. CAVANAGH et al., The Laconia Survey, in: ABSA Suppl. 27, 1996, 296f. • H. EDGERTON, N. SKOUPHOPOULOS, Sonar search at Gytheion harbor, in: AAA 5, 1972, 202–206 • E. S. FORSTER, Gythium and Northwestern Coast of the Laconian Gulf, in: ABSA 13, 1906–1907, 219–237 • C. LE ROY, s. v. G., PE, 369 • Ders., Richesse et exploitation en Laconie au Ier siècle av. J.-C., in: Ktema 3, 1978, 261–266 • D. MUSTI, M. TORELLI, Pausania. Guida della Grecia. III, 1991, 262–266. Y.L.

H

H (sprachwissenschaftlich)

A. SCHRIFTGESCHICHTLICHES
B. VORKOMMEN VON /H/ C. HERKUNFT VON /H/

A. SCHRIFTGESCHICHTLICHES

Dem achten Buchstaben des griech. Alphabets liegt der semit. Kons.-Buchstabe *ḥet* zugrunde. Folglich bezeichnete ⟨H⟩ in mehreren griech. Lokalalphabeten das kons. Phonem /h/, z. B. in altatt. HOPOΣ = ὅρος; daher rührt auch die Verwendung des lat. ⟨H⟩. In anderen griech. Alphabeten, z. B. dem von Milet (wo /h-/ geschwunden war), diente ⟨H⟩ dagegen für e-Vokale. Gelegentlich ist ⟨H⟩ in der Frühzeit auch Silbenzeichen für /hē/ oder /he/; so in der naxischen Nikandre-Inschr. CEG I 403 [1. 124f.], in der vier verschiedene Verwendungen von ⟨H⟩ zu erkennen sind. Schließlich setzte sich mit dem Standardalphabet von Milet die Verwendung von ⟨H⟩ für /ē̜/ durch. Da nunmehr aber ein Buchstabe für das weiterhin gesprochene /h/ fehlte, wurde aus ⟨H⟩ ein neues Zeichen ⊢ = /h/ geschaffen, das in der Buchschrift als »Spiritus-asper«-Zeichen über Vokalbuchstaben und ρ gesetzt wurde.

B. VORKOMMEN VON /H/

Im Griech. kommt /h/ vor allem wortanlautend vor, dazu – in der Buchschrift gewöhnlich vernachlässigt – hinter Kompositionsfuge (»Interaspiration«: P Oxy. 2442 fr. 105,10 παρέδρος; lat. *synhodus*); Interjektionen wie εὐάν sind vereinzelt. Ähnlich im Lat.: *habēre ad-hibēre, hērēs ex-hērēdāre*; dazu Interjektionen wie *āh, prōh*, aber auch weitere Einzelfälle wie *ahēnus, mihi, uehere*.

In beiden Sprachen wurde /h/ schwächer als andere Kons. gesprochen; im → Sandhi übte es – außer bei der Aspiration im Griech. (ἀφ' οὗ) – keine kons. Wirkung aus: *maior honos* –⏑⏑– (Ov. met. 13,96). Demzufolge war /h/ von Anfang an vom Schwund bedroht. In lat. Inschr. fehlt es häufig oder ist falsch gesetzt: *ostes hocidit* (CIL III 3800) = *hostis occīdit*. Schließlich war das griech. und lat. /h/ allgemein beseitigt.

C. HERKUNFT VON /H/

Die Herkunft des /h/ in griech. Erbwörtern ist von der in lat. durchaus verschieden. Während das lat. *h* gewöhnlich eine Media aspirata *gh* fortsetzt, kann griech. *h* auf *s, i̯, u̯, su̯* oder auf die Aspiration eines anlautenden *u-* (*u-* > *hu-*) zurückgeführt werden: ἑπτά < **septm̥*; ὅς (Relativpron.) < **i̯os*; ἕσται »ist gekleidet« < **u̯estai̯*; ὅς (Possessivpron.) < **su̯os*; ὕδωρ < **udōr*. Dagegen: lat.

ueh-ere < **u̯eǵh-*; *hostis* < **ghostis* (vgl. nhd. *be-weg-en*; *Gast*).
→ E (sprachwissenschaftlich); Itazismus; Psilose

1 HEUBECK.

LEUMANN, 173–175 · LSAG, 28f., 427 · ALFRED SCHMITT, Der Buchstabe H im Griech., 1952 (= Ders., KS, 477–522) · SCHWYZER, Gramm., 145–147, 218–222, 303–306 · ThLL 6,3, 2389–2391. B.F.

Haarnadel s. Nadel

Haarnetz s. Phenake

Haaropfer s. Opfer

Haarstrich s. Schriftstile

Haartracht I. ALTER ORIENT
II. GRIECHENLAND UND ITALIEN

I. ALTER ORIENT

Unterschiede bestanden im Alten Orient nicht nur zw. männlichen und weiblichen, sondern auch zw. Menschen- und Götterfrisuren. Die altoriental. H. basierten gewöhnlich auf langem Haar. Mit Ausnahme von Göttinnen, die *en face* mit langen Locken abgebildet werden konnten, trug man bis zum 1. Jt. meist Flechtfrisuren. Männer bevorzugten Knoten-, Frauen Kranzfrisuren. Form und Größe der Knoten bzw. Kränze bildeten ein Unterscheidungsmerkmal zw. Götter- und Menschenfiguren. Kahlköpfigkeit ist als bes. Form der H. oft im Kult bezeugt. Vom 1. Jt. an wurde das Haar häufig offen mit einem Lockenbausch als Abschluß getragen. Die H. war der Mode unterworfen und konnte sich von Generation zu Generation ändern. Männer- und Frauenfrisuren sind in neuassyr. Zeit nicht mehr voneinander zu unterscheiden. Funde von Perücken beweisen, daß man auch künstliche H. kannte. Der Festigung und dem Schmuck dienten Haarnadeln und Bänder. Bes. Frisuren oder eine außergewöhnliche Haarfülle dienten als Charakteristikum bei der Benennung mancher Dämonen und einiger Frauenklassen.

J. BÖRKER-KLÄHN, s. v. H., RLA 4, 1–22. G.CO.

II. GRIECHENLAND UND ITALIEN
A. ALLGEMEINES B. GRIECHENLAND C. ETRURIEN D. ROM

A. ALLGEMEINES

Bei den Völkern der Ant. galt das Haar als ein bes. Sitz des Lebens und der Kraft, den es zu pflegen und zu schützen galt (→ Phenake, → Nadel). Der Verlust des Haares symbolisierte Alter oder Krankheit, ein Kürzen oder Abschneiden Unfreiheit und Knechtschaft. Andererseits war ein freiwilliges Scheren des Haares Zeichen für Selbstaufgabe z. B. für den Dienst an einer Gottheit. Die Leben und Kraft spendende Funktion des Haares oder einzelner Locken überliefern verschiedene Mythen, von denen die Samson-Delilah-Geschichte die bekannteste ist; im griech. Bereich ist diese Symbolik ebenfalls verbreitet: Nisos-Skylla und Pterelaos-Komaitho sind hier zu nennen, ebenso die Haare der → Gorgo, die → Athena dem → Kepheus gab. Das Haar war auch Objekt von → Magie und Aberglaube: Haaropfer und -weihung bei Gelübde, in Buß- und Trauerzeiten, bei Hochzeit oder Geschlechtsreife waren geläufig und z. B. am Grab oder zu Ehren der Götter eine unabdingbare Verpflichtung eines Versprechens oder Gelübdes. Ferner hielt man immer wieder auffällige Haartrachten für etwas bes. Erwähnenswertes, z. B. die H. der Abantes, Maxyges oder Pramnai; auch wurden Besonderheiten oder der Zustand des Haares bzw. seiner Farbe auf histor. Personen als Name, in Rom auch als Gentil- und Beiname, übertragen: Calvus, Chrysa, Cincinnatus, Crispinus, Flav(i)us, Hirtius, Helva, Pyrrha/Pyrrhos, Rufus, Rutilus usw.

B. GRIECHENLAND

Bei den Männern des min. Kreta war halblanges Haar, oft in Strähnen unterteilt, üblich; über der Nasenwurzel hing dazu eine einzelne, verlängerte Strähne; daneben war auch welliges, schulterlanges oder kurzes Haupthaar beliebt. Die min. Frauen hatten langes Haar, das sich in massige Strähnen unterteilte, die auf Schultern und Oberarmen auflagen und bis zur Taille reichten. Sie trugen die Haare auch zu Schleifen, in Form des einfachen Drehers oder Knotens, und zu Zöpfen gelegt. Bei den kret. und myk. H. wurden vielfach Schmuckbänder in das Haar der Frauen und Männer mit eingedreht (Hom. Il. 12,52 [1]), wie auch Schläfenschmuck die Wangen der Frauen verzierte. Die komplizierte min. Frauen-H. mit Querscheitelung, offenen Locken oder Knoten wurde von den Damen der myk. Palastzeit übernommen. Zur Zeit der »→ Dunklen Jahrhunderte« wurden Kurz- und Lang-H. ebenso getragen wie ungebundenes oder zu Zöpfen geflochtenes Haar.

Ab der 2. H. des 8. Jh. ist die »Etagenperücke« belegt, bei der das bislang gleichförmig herabhängende Haar in einer kompakten Masse vom Kopf absteht und horizontal mittels Stoff- oder Metallbändern gegliedert ist [2]. Bei der Dame von Auxerre ist als Variante diese H. in Strähnen geteilt, wodurch eine karo-artige Wirkung erzielt wird. Die »Etagenperücke« entstand in Anlehnung an die ägypt. Kopftracht auf Kreta und breitete sich von dort über die gesamte griech. Welt aus. Späte Belege dafür sind noch im 6. Jh. anzutreffen. Um 600 v. Chr. wurde bei Männern und Frauen das füllige, mitunter wellig herabhängende, oftmals durch Bänder geteilte (z. B. Sappho 98 a D) oder zu einzelnen Strähnen geformte Haar bevorzugt: Haarspiralen, die sich vielfach erhalten haben, geben den Frisuren den nötigen Halt. Einzelne Strähnen können dabei frei an den Schläfen oder auf den Rücken herabhängen. Mittels Reifen oder Schmuckbändern wird das Haupthaar über der Stirn, auf die dann wellige Locken hereinragen, gehalten. Bei der »Perlfrisur« werden die einzelnen Strähnen noch zusätzlich durch Bänder oder Ringe unterteilt (z. B. bei den archa. Kuros-Figuren); die Stirn wird von Buckellocken gerahmt. Im späten 6. Jh. wurde der Gebrauch von → Phenake und Haarteilen üblich, wodurch sich komplizierter angeordnete Haartrachten ergaben [3]. Auch wurden Spiral- und Zickzacklocken Mode. Um die Mitte des 6. Jh. wurde als Neuerung das lange Haar im Nacken zusammengefaßt und unter einer Kopfbinde eingesteckt (→ Krobylos); die Haarenden hingen frei herunter (Abb. I A). Bei einer zweiten H. wurde das Haar zu einem Zopf eingedreht und mit einer Spirale (→ Tettix) zusammengehalten oder zu einem Knoten eingeschnürt.

Im letzten Drittel des 6. Jh. v. Chr. begann bei den Männern, wohl als Ausdruck einer bürgerlichen Reaktion auf die adligen Lang-H., die Zeit der Kurz-H. (auch »Athletenfrisur« genannt); hierbei schließt das Haar in Nackenhöhe ab und kann lockig, in kurzen Strähnen oder straff auf dem Kopf aufliegen. Lange Haare behielten vorwiegend die Bildnisse der männlichen Götter oder die vornehmen Adligen. Allerdings setzte sich die Kurz-H. bei den Männern spätestens mit der 2. H. des 5. Jh. endgültig durch. Die Frauen bevorzugten nach wie vor das lange Kopfhaar: Es wird, wie Darstellungen zeigen, mit Binden, Haarnetzen, Haarnadeln (→ Nadel) zusammengehalten und eingebunden (Abb. I B). Das gescheitelte Haar bedeckt in lockeren, welligen Strähnen die Stirn oder ist straff in den Nacken geführt. In der zweiten H. des 5. Jh. kam die »Lampadionfrisur« (Fackel-H.) auf: Bei ihr ist das Haar hochgebunden und endet über dem Scheitel in einer Spitze, die an das Züngeln von Flammen erinnert (Abb. I C). Ebenfalls beliebt war die »Pferdeschwanzfrisur«.

Noch vor Beginn des 4. Jh. wurde die »Melonenfrisur« eingeführt, die sich bis ans Ende der Antike hielt: Hierbei wird das Haar in Segmente geteilt, die dann entweder straff oder gedreht zum Hinterkopf geführt und zu einem Haarkranz oder (Rund-)Knoten geformt werden (Abb. I D). Ebenfalls zu Beginn des 4. Jh. v. Chr. wurde die Haarschleife üblich. Das gescheitelte Haar wird auf den Kopf geführt und mittels eines Bandes zusammengefaßt, die Haarenden hängen dann frei auf den Kopf. Diese Frisur war – wie auch die Melonenfrisur – ein Merkmal von Jugendlichkeit und wird von jugendlichen Gottheiten (Apoll, Artemis, Aphrodite) gern getragen. Neben diesen H. tauchten in den letzten Jh. eine Fülle weiterer H. auf. Zu den beliebtesten zählten: das gescheitelte Haar mit hochgesetztem Knoten, Melonenfrisur mit hochsitzendem Knoten, die Nakkenrolle mit straff zum Nacken geführtem Haar, Mittelscheitelfrisur mit Schläfenrolle und Haarknoten (Abb. I E). Von diesen H. zu trennen sind die H. der Philosophen, Kinder (ab dem 4. Jh. z. T. mit Scheitelzopf), Sklaven und Handwerker.

Auch die H. Alexanders d.Gr. (→ Alexandros [4]) mit den emporstehenden Stirnhaaren (ἀναστολή, *anastolē*), die vielfach Nachahmung fand (z. B. → Pompeius), soll als Besonderheit erwähnt werden; sie hat bei → Satyrn bereits einige Vorläufer, ist für Alexander aber aus der Heroenikonographie (→ Achilleus) entlehnt. Die durch die ἀναστολή hervorgerufene Wirkung der scheinbar aufgewühlten Haare, oft im Verbund mit strähnigem, aus dem Haarwirbel zur Stirn geführtem Haupthaar und mit langem Nackenhaar, war bei ihm nachfolgenden Herrschern beabsichtigt und sollte alexandergleiche Kraft und Aktivität symbolisieren.

C. Etrurien

Die H. der Etrusker unterscheiden sich kaum von denen der Griechen; man bevorzugte allg. langes Haar, das entweder ungebunden herabhing, zu Zöpfen geflochten oder im Perlhaarstil angeordnet war. Auch rahmen oftmals Buckellocken die Stirn der Dargestellten. Anders als in Griechenland konnten jedoch Frauen auch eine Kurz-H. tragen, bei der das Haar in Locken gelegt um den Kopf geführt wurde. Im 5. und 4. Jh. v. Chr. waren die Haartrachten meist denen der Griechen angepaßt. Frauen trugen z. B. die Melonenfrisur, und Männer die Kurz-H. Oft ist dabei das Haar in Strähnen vom Wirbel aus nach vorne gekämmt und liegt in schweren, flammenähnlichen Kommalocken auf der Stirn. Aus dem frühen 1. Jh. v. Chr. zeigt die Statue des »Arringatore« (Florenz, AM) die Kurz-H. mit flach auf dem Kopf liegenden, in Reihen übereinander geschichteten Lokkenbündeln; im Haarwirbel sind sie radial angeordnet.

D. Rom

In der frühen Zeit trug der Mann eine Lang-H. (vgl. Varro rust. 2,11,10), die sich im Aussehen wohl kaum von der griech. oder etr. unterschieden haben dürfte. Entsprechend erfolgte vermutlich im 5. Jh. v. Chr. ein Wandel zur Kurz-H. Für das frühe 2. Jh. v. Chr. läßt das Münzbild des T. Quinctius → Flamininus eine Angleichung an hell. Herrscher-H. erkennen. Während der späten Republik wurde das Haar der Männer zumeist ungescheitelt in lockeren, glatten Strähnen vom Haarwirbel in die Stirn und weit in den Nacken gekämmt. In der röm. Kaiserzeit wurde die H. ganz wesentlich vom Herrscherhaus bestimmt. Die verschiedenen H. der Kaiser und Kaiserinnen wurden durch Porträt- und Münzkunst verbreitet und von Bürgern und Provinzialen mit zahlreichen Varianten adaptiert. Allg. war es bis zum frühen 2. Jh. n. Chr. für Männer Mode, das Haar kurz, ungescheitelt und in die Stirn gekämmt zu tragen. Daneben zeigen Bildnisse Neros, Domitians u. a. das Haar in sichelförmigen, gewellten Locken, die in mehreren Reihen übereinander gelegt sind (*coma in gradus formata*, Suet. Nero 51). Zukunftsweisend insbes. für die Mitglieder seiner Familie war die H. des → Augustus, der mit der markanten Gabel-Zangen-Einteilung des Stirnhaares eine charakteristische H. schuf, die später von Kaiser Traian noch einmal wiederholt wurde, während das Haar ansonsten glatt in die Stirn gekämmt wurde. Ein Wechsel der H. trat mit Hadrian ein: Dessen Kopfhaar ist eher flach, das Stirnhaar aber besteht aus bewegten Locken oder wulstartigen Rollen (→ Bart). Diese H. veränderte sich bei seinen Nachfolgern insofern, als die ganze Haarmasse zu vielen kleinen Löck-

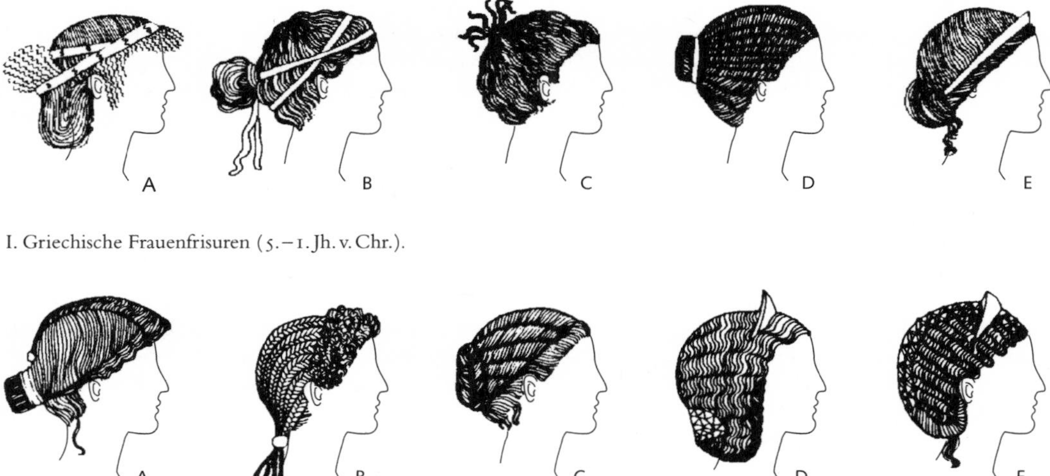

I. Griechische Frauenfrisuren (5.–1. Jh. v. Chr.).

II. Römische Frauenfrisuren (1. Jh. v. Chr.–4. Jh. n. Chr.).

chen aufgetürmt wurde. Mit den Soldatenkaisern des 3. Jh. n. Chr. wurde kurzes Haar getragen, in konstantinischer Zeit jedoch ließ man das Haar wieder länger wachsen: Es wird vom Haarwirbel in die Stirn gekämmt, wobei es diese in einem sanften Bogen umschreibt; auch kann das Haar auf der Stirn in einer Welle aufliegen und die Ohren bedecken.

Ungleich komplizierter und vielfältiger sind die Haartrachten der röm. Frauen (Ov. ars 3, 151 f., vgl. Ov. ars 3,133–149 mit Hinweisen, welche H. zu welchem Gesicht paßt). Hatte in der republ. Zeit die Römerin das Haar schlicht zurückgekämmt bzw. an griech. Vorbildern orientierte getragen, so wurde die H. am Ende der Republik um komplizierte Elemente wie Stirnhaarschlaufen und Zöpfe auf der Kalotte bereichert. In frühaugust. Zeit war die »Octavia-H.« Mode: Bei ihr wird das Haar straff in den Nacken geführt und zu einem Knoten geformt, während eine zweite Strähne über den Scheitel nach vorne gezogen in einem flachen Knoten endet (Ov. ars 3,139 f.; Abb. II A). In der Nachfolge erschien ein Nackenzopf, der um die Mitte des 1. Jh. n. Chr. durch ein Lockenbukett bereichert wurde, das sich zum Ende des Jh. zu einem runden, hohen Wulst erweiterte (s. Iuv. 6,502 f.; Mart. 2,66), für den zu errichten → Phenake und Haarteile nötig waren (Abb. II B).

Mit dem Beginn des 2. Jh. erfolgte ein Wechsel zu einer schlichteren H., bei der Frauen die zu geflochtenen Zöpfen zusammengefaßten Haare mehrfach um den Kopf führten. Die hadrian.-antonin. Zeit bevorzugte onduliertes, in Schlaufen gestaffeltes oder zu einer flachen Rolle zusammengedrücktes Stirnhaar: Die Haarmasse wurde gewellt oder mit Knoten oder Haarnest auf dem Hinterkopf in Art der Melonenfrisur nach hinten geführt [4] (Abb. II C). Ein völliger Wechsel erfolgte mit Iulia Domna (→ Phenake): Ihre H. ist eine kompakte Haarmasse, die in waagerechten abfallenden Wellen gefaßt ist, und häufig auf einen Mittelscheitel verzichtet (Abb. II D). Die Stirn umrahmen mitunter kleine Korkenzieherlöckchen. Die typische H. seit dem 1. Drittel des 3. Jh. n. Chr. war die Scheitelzopffrisur: Die Haare sind beiderseits des Mittelscheitels nach hinten gekämmt; im Nacken wird das Haar in einer breiten Bahn umgeschlagen und hochgenommen. Diese Bahn wird über den Scheitelpunkt vorgezogen und festgesteckt (Abb. II E). Gegen Ende des Jh. konnte aus dem Scheitelzopf auch eine Schlinge auf der Stirn werden, wobei dann auch das Stirnhaar melonenartig unterteilt wurde [5].

→ Bart; Trauer

1 H. Reusch, Die zeichnerische Rekonstruktion des Frauenfrieses im boiot. Theben, 1956, Taf. 15
2 C. Davaras, Die Statue von Astritsi, in: AK 8. Beih., 1972, 24–25, 58. 3 Richter, Korai, Abb. 411–419 4 M. Wegner, Datier. röm. Haartrachten, in: AA 1938, 276–325
5 K. Wessel, Röm. Frauenfrisuren von der severischen bis zur konstantinischen Zeit, in: AA 1946/7, 62–76.

L. Bonfante, The Etruscan Dress, 1975, 67–80 • R. Brilliant, Hairiness. A Matter of Style and Substance in Roman Portraits, in: FS F. E. Brown, 1993, 302–312 • L. Byvanck-Quarles van Ufford, La coiffure des jeunes dames d'Athènes au second quart du 5ème siècle av. J. C., in: FS J. M. Hemelrijk, 1986, 135–140 • E. David, Sparta's social hair, in: Eranos 90, 1992, 11–21 • W. H. Gross, s. v. Haartracht, Haarschmuck, in: KlP 2, 1967, 897–899 • E. B. Harrison, Greek Sculptured Coiffures and Ritual Haircuts, in: R. Hägg (Hrsg.), Early Greek Cult Practise, 1988, 247–254 • S. A. H. Kennell, Women's Hair and the Law. Two Cases from Late Antiquity, in: Klio 73, 1991, 526–536 • A. Klein, Child Life in Greek Art, 1932, 36 f. • J. H. Krause, Plotina oder die Kostüme des Haupthaares bei den Völkern der alten Welt mit Berücksichtigung einiger Kostüme neuerer Völker …, 1858 • I. Jenkins, D. Wil-

LIAMS, Sprang Hair Nets. Their Manufacture and Use in Ancient Greece, in: AJA 89, 1985, 411–418 • H. P. LAUBSCHER, Fischer und Landleute. Stud. zur hell. Genreplastik, 1982, 44, 51–53 • S. MARINATOS, Haar- und Barttracht, (ArchHom Bd. 1 B), 1967 • J. MEISCHNER, Das Frauenporträt der Severerzeit, 1964 • A. ONASSOGLOU, Ein Klappspiegel aus einem Grab in der Ostlokris, in: AA 1988, 439–459 • K. POLASCHEK, Stud. zu einem Frauenkopf im Landesmuseum Trier und zur weibl. Haartracht der iulisch-claudischen Zeit, in: TZ 35, 1972, 141–210 • H. RÜHFEL, Das Kind in der griech. Kunst, 1984 • A. V. SIEBERT, Quellenanalytische Bemerkungen zu Haartracht und Kopfschmuck röm. Priesterinnen, in: Boreas 18, 1995, 77–92. R. H.

Habicht. Es ist fast unmöglich, genau zu unterscheiden, ob ἱέραξ/*hiérax*, homer. ἴρηξ, im speziellen Fall den H. (Accipiter gentilis), den Sperber (A. nisus) oder eine Falkenart bezeichnet. Synonym wurde κίρκος/*kírkos* verwendet (z. B. Hom. Il. 22,139). Bei Hom. Il. 15,237 ist mit dem Taubentöter φασσοφόνος/*phassophónos* offenbar der H., mit *írēx* jedoch der Sperber gemeint. Der lat. Name *accipiter* (*acceptor* bei Lucil. 1130) leitete sich volksetym. von *accipere* her (Isid. orig. 12,7,55, vgl. Plaut. Persa 406 f.).

Aristot. hist.an. 8(9),3,592b 2f. unterscheidet nach der Größe zw. dem φαβοτύπος/*phabotýpos* und σπιζίας/*spizías*. Bei Aristot. hist.an. 8(9),36,620a 17–b 5 erscheinen diese unter 11 Greifvogelarten, bei Plin. nat. 10,21 f. unter 16. Typisch für den H. und verwandte Greifvögel ist seine Wendigkeit und Geschwindigkeit (Hom. Il. 13,62 und 819; 15,237; 16,582; 18,616; Od. 13,86; vgl. Paus. 7,12,2), sowie seine Raubvogelnatur (z. B. Plat. Phaid. 82a; Lucr. 4,1009; Ov. ars 2,147; Sen. dial. 4,16,1). Er jagt v. a. kleinere Vögel bis zur Taubengröße (Hom. Il. 13,62–64; 15,237 f.; 16,582 f.; 21,493 f.; 22,139 f.; Eur. Andr. 1141; Alkm. frg. 15 D.; Aristot. hist.an. 8(9),11, 615 a 6; Varro Men. 289, rust. 3,7,6; Verg. Aen. 11,721 f.; Hor. carm. 1,37,17 f.; Ov. met. 11,344 f., trist. 1,1,75; Sen. Oed. 903; Dionysios 1,6 [1. 6 f.]), manchmal aber auch Mäuse (Batrachomyomachia 49) und andere Tiere. Fabulös ist, daß der H. kein Vogelherz frißt (Aristot. hist.an. 8(9),11,615a 5; Plin. nat. 10,24), in den einzelnen Jahreszeiten unterschiedlich schreit (Lucr. 5,1079–81), sein Schrei Hühnereier absterben läßt (Plin. nat. 10,152), er sich manchmal in einen Kuckuck (Aristot. hist.an. 6,7,563b 14–28; Plin. nat. 10,25) oder einen Wiedehopf (Geop. 15,1,22) verwandelt und von anderen Greifvögeln sowie dem Chamäleon verfolgt wird (Paul. Fest. 32; Plin. nat. 10,109; 28,113; Gell. 10,12,2).

Da der H. eine Gefahr für die Geflügelzucht darstellte, fing man ihn mit Netzen oder Leimruten (Ter. Phorm. 330; Varro rust. 3,7,7; Hor. epist. 1,16,50 f.). Auch die älteste griech. Fabel zeigt ihn als Räuber (Hes. erg. 203 ff.; vgl. Aisop. 4 HAUSRATH; Plut. mor. 158 b), als Symbol dafür erscheint er bei Platon (Phaid. 82a) und Plautus (Persa 409), in Paradoxien z. B. bei Lukrez (3,752: *accipiter fugiens veniente columba*) und Ovid (fast. 2,90: *accipitri iuncta columba*). Der Eigenname Hierax begegnet doppelsinnig bei Aristoph. Equ. 1052 für Kleon. Wegen seines guten Sehvermögens (Polemon von Laodikeia, Physiognomia 1,184,10 FOERSTER u. a.) sollte aus dem in Schweineschmalz gekochten H. eine Augensalbe hergestellt werden (Gal. 14,243; vgl. Marcellus, De medicamentis 8,66) und nach Plin. nat. 29,125 nicht nur sein in Rosenöl gekochtes Fleisch, sondern auch der veraschte Kot mit att. Honig bei Augenkrankheiten helfen.

In der Beizjagd begegnen in der Ant. nur Falken, so bei Ktesias frg. 11 mit Bezug auf Indien und Aristot. hist.an. 8(9),3,6,620a 30 ff. (vgl. Antigonos von Karystos, Rerum mirabilium collectio 28; Plin. nat. 10,23; Ail. nat. 2,42) für Thrakien. Insgesamt spielte die Beizjagd bis zum 5. Jh. n. Chr. nur eine geringe Rolle [2. Bd. 2, 24 f.]. Wie weit sich die angebliche Heiligkeit dem Apollon (Aristoph. Av. 516) oder dem Mars (Serv. Aen. 11,721) sowie die Bed. in der Mantik (Iambl. de myst. 6,3 p.243 PARTHEY; Cic. nat. deor. 3,19; Obseq. 58; Sil. 4,104; Stat. Theb. 3,503) nicht nur auf den Falken, sondern auch auf den H. bezieht, ist unklar. Jedenfalls beziehen sich die meisten derartigen Hinweise auf Ägypten. (etwa Hdt. 2,65; Ail. nat. 10,14 und 12,4; Hekat. 73 B 6 D.-K.; Strab. 17,1,40,812 und 17,1,47,817; Diod. 1,87,8) und somit auf den → Horus-Falken [3. 117 f.]. Dafür spricht auch die Angabe des Aristoteles (hist.an. 7(8),28,606a 21–24), daß dort kleinere Vertreter der Art lebten. Daß in der Traumdeutung der Vogel Diebstahl bzw. Raub bedeute (Artem. 2,20 p.137 und 4,56 p.279 PACK), bezieht sich wieder auf den H.

1 A. GARZYA (ed.), Dionysii Ixeuticon libri, 1963 2 KELLER 3 D'ARCY W. THOMPSON, A Glossary of Greek Birds, 1936, Ndr. 1966. C. HÜ.

Habitancum. Römisches Lager beim h. Risingham (Northumberland), einer der Vorposten nördl. des Hadrianswalls im Tal des Rede. Die frühen Phasen der Besetzung liegen im Dunkeln; es gibt keinen Beweis dafür, daß das Fort zur selben Zeit wie der hadrianische Grenzwall gebaut wurde. Ein Lager existierte sicher in den 140er J.; in severischer Zeit war es ein Hauptstützpunkt der Besetzung des Nordens. Die Garnison von H. war im 2. Jh. die *cohors IIII Gallorum*, im 3. Jh. die *cohors I Vangionum*, begleitet von einem *numerus exploratorum* und einer *vexillatio Raetorum Gaesatorum*. Im Inneren des Lagers sind *principia* (Kommandatur) und ein Badehaus nachgewiesen [1. 235–40].

1 E. BIRLEY, Research on Hadrian's Wall, 1961.

M. TO./Ü: I. S.

Habitatio bedeutet zunächst Wohnung, z. B. als Gegenstand von Kauf und Verkauf (→ *locatio conductio*; Dig. 2,14,4; 19,2,5) oder Schutzobjekt der *lex Cornelia de iniuriis* (Dig. 47,10,5,5). Weiter bedeutet *h.* das Wohnrecht, welches u. a. durch Vermächtnis (→ *legatum*) begründet wird (Dig. 7,8,10 pr.). Das Verhältnis der *h.* zum → *usus* und zum → *usus fructus* (Nießbrauch) war zweifelhaft. In der Wirkung (*effectu quidem*) deckte sich die *h. legata* »beinahe« (*paene*) mit dem *usus legatus* (Papin./Ulp. Dig. 7,8,10 pr.). Die röm. Juristen beschäftigten sich mit Fragen wie: Wie ist das Vermächtnis einer χρῆσις (→ *chrēsis*) zu verstehen? Wie das eines *usus* oder *usus fructus habitandi causa* (Wohnungsnießbrauch)? Auf wie lange sollte eine *h.* zugewandt sein? (eine Streitfrage der *veteres*; für eine Zuwendung auf Lebenszeit ist P. Rutilius Rufus, Dig. 7,8,10 pr.–3). Die *h.* ist Teil der *alimenta legata* (Versorgungsvermächtnisse, Dig. 34,1,6). Die vermachte *h.* konnte Gegenstand eines Vergleichs (→ *transactio*) sein (Dig. 2,15,8,1; 12,13,25). Justinian trennt die *h.* von *usus* und *usus fructus* und entscheidet gewisse Zweifelsfragen (Inst. Iust. 2,5,5; Cod. Iust. 3,33,13). Zum Vorbehalt beim Verkauf eines Hauses Dig. 19,1,21,6, bei der Übereignung Dig. 7,1,32.

HONSELL/MAYER-MALY/SELB, 188 • KASER, RPR I, 454; II 306. D.SCH.

Habitus. Röm. Cognomen in der Familie der Cluentii (→ Cluentius [2]) u.a. K.-L.E.

Habron (Ἅβρων). Griech. Grammatiker, Sklave phrygischen Ursprungs, lehrte (und studierte vielleicht auch) zuerst auf Rhodos, dann in Rom in der 1. H. des 1. Jh. n. Chr (Suda α 97 ADLER). Er war Schüler des Aristarcheers → Tryphon und behandelte die gleichen Themen wie dieser, bezog dabei jedoch eine andere Position und kritisierte die Lehre des Aristarchos [4] von Samothrake auch im Hinblick auf die Pronomina (vgl. [1. 1520; 7. 91]). Neun Zitate aus seinem Werk Περὶ ἀντωνυμίας (›Über das Pronomen‹) werden von Apollonios [11] Dyskolos (vgl. Syntaxis 245,6 Anm. UHLIG) angeführt; fast alle Fragmente der Schrift Περὶ παρωνύμων (›Über Nominalableitungen‹; vgl. [10]) hängen dagegen von Ailios → Herodianos ab. In den Scholien zur *Téchnē* des → Dionysios [17] Thrax (371,7–9 und 532,33–36 HILGARD) gibt es ein Werk Περὶ κτητικῶν (*Über Possessivpronomina*: Der Begriff wurde schon von Tryphon benutzt, vgl. Apollonios Dyskolos GG II/1, De pronominibus 16,14–18 und [3. 192]). H. beschäftigte sich auch mit Dialektformen (vgl. ebd. 51,9–16), Etym. und Wortbildung. H. scheint zusammen mit → Tryphon eine entscheidende Funktion in der Systematisierung der griech. Grammatik vor Apollonios Dyskolos ausgeübt zu haben, vor allem, wenn man die *Téchnē* des Dionysios Thrax als unecht ansieht: [3; 4; 8].

1 R. BERNDT, Die Fragmente des Gramm. H., in: Berliner philologische Wochenschrift 1915, 1451–1455, 1483–1488, 1514–1520 2 J. CHRISTES, Sklaven und Freigelassene als Grammatiker und Philologen im ant. Rom, 1979, 92–93
3 V. DI BENEDETTO, Dionisio Trace e la techne a lui attribuita, in: ASNP 27, 1958, 169–210 und 28, 1959, 87–118
4 P.M. FRASER, Ptolemaic Alexandria, 1972, 475, 810
5 H. FUNAIOLI, s.v. H., RE 7, 2155–2156 6 A. HILLSCHER, Hominum Litteratorum Graecorum, 1891, 386–387
7 F.W. HOUSEHOLDER, The Syntax of Apollonius Dyscolus, 1981, 5 und u.ö. 8 J. PINBORG, Current Trends in Linguistics 13, 1975, 115 9 A. DE VELSEN, Tryphonis ... fragmenta, 1853 (Ndr. 1965), 2 10 C. WENDEL, s.v. Tryphon, RE 8A, 732–733. S.FO./Ü: T.H.

Habronichos (Ἁβρώνιχος, auch Ἀβρώνιχος). Sohn des Lysikles, Athener aus dem Demos Lamptrai (zur Namensform [1]). Er überbrachte der griech. Flotte bei Artemision im J. 480 v. Chr. die Nachricht von der Niederlage des → Leonidas bei den Thermopylen (Hdt. 8,21). Im J. 479 wurde er mit → Aristeides [1] nach Sparta geschickt, um dort den → Themistokles über den Fortgang des Mauerbaus zu unterrichten (Thuk. 1,91,3). Später war H. ein potentieller Kandidat für den → Ostrakismos, sein Name (mit Demotikon) begegnet auf einigen Ostraka (ML 21).

1 A.E. RAUBITSCHEK, (H)abronichos, in: CR 70, 1956, 199–200.

DAVIES 20 • TRAILL, PAA 101650. HA.BE.

Ḫabur (akkad. *Ḫābūr*, griech. Χαβώρας; nicht identisch mit Araxes [1. 43]). Linksseitiger größter Nebenfluß des → Euphrates in NO-Syrien. Wird aus Karstquellen gespeist, die in 13 Töpfen bei Rāʾs al-ʿAin (Rēšʿainā) an die Oberfläche treten. Zunächst verläuft der Ḫ. südöstl. bis Hassaka (Oberlauf), dann wird die Fließrichtung nach Süden durch den Vulkan Kaukab (Unterlauf) abgedrängt, die Mündung liegt nahe dem Ort Buṣaira (Kirkesion). Das Ḫ.-Einzugsgebiet (»Ḫ.-Dreieck«) entwässert das südl. Taurus-Vorland (Mardin, Ṭūr ʿAbdīn). Der Verlauf der Regenfeldbaugrenze südl. von Hassaka bestimmt die Siedlungs- und Wirtschaftsweise: im Ḫ.-Dreieck ist reiche, seßhafte Agrarwirtschaft möglich, entlang des Unterlaufes dagegen Weidewirtschaft mit Transhumanz.

Der obere Ḫ. ist arch. noch nicht systematisch erforscht, der untere Ḫ. wurde von H. KÜHNE und W. RÖLLIG 1975 und 1977 begangen (TAVO). Erste Siedlungsspuren stammen bereits aus dem mittleren Paläolithikum (Moustérien) am unteren Ḫ. Vereinzelte Siedlungen sind aus dem akeramischen (8.–7. Jt. v. Chr.) und keramischen Neolithikum (ca. 6000–4500 v. Chr., Ḫalaf-Zeit) sowie aus dem Chalkolithikum (ca. 4500–3000 v. Chr., Ubaid- u. Uruk-Zeit) belegt. Zur Zeit der Urbanisierung (3. Jt. v. Chr.) wurden im gesamten Flußgebiet nur kleine und mittelgroße Siedlungen angelegt; die großen Zentren dagegen liegen in der Steppe und im Ḫ.-Dreieck. Erste Keilschriftzeugnisse (2. H. 3. Jt.) lassen die Bildung eines ḫurrit. Reiches von Urkiš (Tall Mūzān) und Nawar (Tall Birāk) erkennen (→ Ḫurriter). In die gleiche Zeit fällt die Okkupation durch die Akkader. In der altbabylon. Zeit ist die Abhängigkeit des unteren Ḫ. vom Königreich → Mari belegt, während das Ḫ.-Dreieck zum altassyr. Königreich gehörte (19./18. Jh. v. Chr.). Die noch nicht wiederentdeckte Hauptstadt des → Mittani-Reiches (1550–1350 v. Chr.), Waššukanni, ist vielleicht in Tall Faḫarīya am oberen Ḫ. zu lokalisieren. Im mittelassyr. Reich (1350–932

v. Chr.) wurde das bed. Provinzzentrum Dūr-Katlimmu am unteren Ḫ. eingerichtet, von dem die Steppenbereiche und das Westreich kontrolliert wurden. Während der obere Ḫ. und der mittlere Euphrat in die Hände der eindringenden → Aramäer fielen, blieb der untere Ḫ. unter assyr. Kontrolle. Zur Zeit des assyr. »Weltreiches« (932–612 v. Chr.) gehörte der Ḫ. zum Kern des Reichsgebietes. Im Achämenidenreich (→ Achaimenidai) und im Reich Alexanders (→ Alexandros [4], mit Karte) verlor die Region an Bedeutung. Die seleukidische Zeit ist noch kaum faßbar. Vom 2. Jh. v. Chr. bis zum 2. Jh. n. Chr. gehörte das Ḫ.-Gebiet zum parth. Reich. Vom 2. Jh. an verlief die Ostgrenze des röm. Reiches am Ḫ. Die Region war bis zur Eroberung Syriens durch die Araber (632 n. Chr.) Zankapfel zw. Byzanz und den pers. Sāsāniden.

1 O. LENDLE, Komm. zu Xenophons Anabasis, 1995
2 TAVO, Karten B I 16, B I 17, B II 7, B II 8, B II 12, B III 7, B IV 10, B IV 13, B V 3, B V 4, B V 6, B V 7, B V 8, B V 13, B VI 5, B VII 2. H. KÜ.

Hacke. Selbst wenn Getreide wie gewöhnlich in Pflugkultur angebaut wurde, machte das Hacken einen beträchtlichen Teil der gesamten Jahresarbeit aus (Colum. 2,11; 2,12,1 ff.); es war oft Aufgabe von gefesselten Sklaven (*servi vincti*) und wurde im Getreidebau im Winter und ein zweites Mal im Frühjahr durchgeführt. Die H. wurde dabei in verschiedenen Funktionen verwendet: Anstelle des Pfluges wurde sie zum Umbrechen (κατεργασία, *subigere*) im Garten, in Obst- und Weinkulturen, auf stadtnahem Feld, im Feldbau der Kleinbauern (»Pflug des armen Mannes«; vgl. zu Apulia Varro rust. 1,29,2) oder im Gebirge eingesetzt. Mit der H. konnten aber nur kleine Flächen bearbeitet werden. Außerdem hat man Dünger oder Samen mit der H. in die Erde eingearbeitet. Eine weitere wichtige Aufgabe des Hackens war die Herstellung der Feinkrume v. a. durch Zerschlagung der Schollen nach dem Pflügen (*occare*, → Egge) und durch Lockerung der Erde (*sarire*). Ferner wurde die H. zur Beseitigung des Unkrauts (*purgare, runcare*) gebraucht.

Für die Bodenbearbeitung nahm man eine schwere H. mit breitem Blatt und langem Stiel (μάκελλα, *ligo*, vgl. Colum. 2,15,5; eine leichtere Form: *marra*, Colum. 10,89). Zum Umbrechen, Wenden und Wurzelroden wurde die *dolabra*, eine schwere, zweiseitige Kreuz- oder Pickel-H. verwendet (Colum. 2,2,28; schon minoisch belegt). Daneben gab es weitere Typen der H., die für verschiedene Funktionen geeignet waren. Die H. mit kleinerem, spitzen Blatt (*sarculum*: Colum. 2,11,1; 2,15,2; 2,17,4) wurde auch anstelle des Pfluges im Gebirge (Plin. nat. 18,178: *montanae gentes sarculis arant*) und zur Lockerung des Bodens sowie zur Unkrautbekämpfung in Feld und Garten (Plin. nat. 18,241: *sarculo levi purgare*) eingesetzt. Die H. mit zwei Zinken (δίκελλα, *bidens*) diente für die *subactio* im Weinberg (Colum. 3,13,3; 4,5,1) und auch für *pulveratio* und *ablaqueatio*; daneben war die eiserne Harke mit mehreren Zinken bekannt (*rastrum*: Plin. nat. 18,180). Die zweiseitige, leichte Gartenhaue der Gegenwart (mit zwei Zinken) ist seit der Spätant. belegt (vielleicht unter dem Begriff *ascia*).

→ Egge

1 M.-C. AMOURETTI, Le pain et l'huile dans la Grèce antique, 1986, 93–100 2 G. COMET, Le paysan et son outil, 1992, 118–137 3 W. GAITZSCH, Werkzeug und Handwerk in Pompeji, in: AW 14, 1983, 3, 3–11 4 W. SCHIERING, Landwirtschaftliche Geräte, in: ArchHom 2, 1990, H 152–154 5 K. D. WHITE, Agricultural Implements of the Roman World, 1967, 36–68. E. C.

Hadad (der Name ist etym. vielleicht mit arab. *hadda* »brechen, schlagen«, *haddat*, »Donner«, zu verbinden). Belegstellen: Ios. ant. Iud. 9,93 (Ἄδαδος); Phil. Bybl. FGH 3, 569, 24 (Ἄδωδος); Plin. nat. 37,186 (*Adadu*); Macr. Sat. 1,23,17 (*Adad*). Westsemit. Name des → Wettergottes, der akkad. als Adad, keilschriftlichluw. und hethit. als Tarhu(a)n(t) seit der Mitte des 3. Jt. in zahlreichen lokalen Ausprägungen (bes. als Ḫadda von Ḫalab/Aleppo [1]) kult. Verehrung genoß. Ikonographisch erscheint er als Stier oder in Verbindung mit Stier(en) und (zwei) Berg(en) [2] sowie mit Donnerkeule oder Axt und zwei- bzw. dreizackigem Blitzsymbol in den Händen [3]. In den Bewässerungskulturen Mesopotamiens wurde er als »Deichgraf des Himmels«, aber auch als Sturmgott mit zerstörerischer Kraft (Cod. Ḫammurapi 47,64–80, TUAT 1), in den Regenfeldbaukulturen Nordmesopotamiens, Anatoliens und Syriens v. a. als die Vegetation fördernder Regenbringer erfahren; außerdem vereinte er kosmische und chthonische Aspekte [4].

Adad begegnet in (den Onomastika von) Māri, Ebla, Alalaḫ und Emar [5]. In → Ugarit erscheint der Wettergott in den myth. Texten hauptsächlich unter dem zum Eigennamen verfestigten Titel → Baal. Namen von ugaritischen Königen, aber auch aus dem südsyr.-palästin. Raum (s. die PN in den → Amarna-Briefen [6]) mit dem theophoren Element (*h*)*addu* zeigen, daß H. auch dort verehrt wurde.

In den aram. Inschr. der 1. H. des 1. Jt. spielt H. eine Rolle an der Spitze lokaler Panthea ([7]; KAI Nr. 214; 215,22; 216,5 u.ö.) und im Totenkult für den verstorbenen König (KAI Nr. 215 [8]).

In hell.-röm. Zeit wurde H. häufig mit → Zeus (Keraunios, z. B. CIG 4520) und → Iuppiter Optimus Maximus gleichgesetzt. In → Baalbek weist die Ikonographie (Macr. Sat. 1,23,12 und [9]) den Iuppiter → Heliopolitanus als solarisierten H. aus. In der Gestalt des Iuppiter Optimus Maximus ist H. bis nach Rom gelangt (CIL VI 117; 399). Noch größere Verbreitung hat H. von Doliche als Iuppiter → Dolichenus durch die röm. Soldaten in severischer Zeit gefunden [10].

1 H. KLENGEL, Der Wettergott von Halab, in: JCS 19, 1965, 87–93 2 K. KOCH, Hazzi-Safôn-Kasion. Die Gesch. eines Berges und seiner Gottheiten, in: B. JANOWSKI, K. KOCH, G. WILHELM (Hrsg.), Religionsgesch. Beziehungen zw.

Kleinasien, Nordsyrien und dem AT, 1993, 171–224 **3** A. Abou Assaf, Die Ikonographie des altbabylon. Wettergottes, in: BaM 14, 1983, 43–66 **4** N. Wyatt, The Relationship of the Deities Dagan and Hadad, in: Ugarit-Forsch. 12, 1980, 377 **5** H. B. Huffmon, Amorite Personal Names in the Mari Texts, 1965 • M. Krebernik, Die Personennamen der Ebla-Texte, 1988 **6** R. S. Hess, Amarna Personal Names, 1993 **7** J. Tropper, Die Inschriften von Zincirli, 1993 **8** H. Niehr, Zum Totenkult der Könige von Samʾol im 9. und 8. Jh. v. Chr., in: Studi epigrafici e linguistici 11, 1994, 57–73 **9** Y. Hajjar, La triade d'Héliopolis-Baalbek, 1977 • **10** M. Hörig, Jupiter Dolichenus, in: ANRW II.17/4, 1984, 2136–2179.

H. Gese, Die Religionen Altsyriens, 1970, 1–232 • J. C. Greenfield, Aspects of Aramean Religion, in: P. D. Miller (Hrsg.), Ancient Israelite Religion. FS Cross, 1987, 67–78 • V. Haas, Gesch. der hethit. Rel., 1994 • P. W. Haider, M. Hutter, S. Kreuzer (Hrsg.), Religionsgesch. Syriens von der Frühzeit bis zur Gegenwart, 1996 • J. Teixidor, The Pagan God. Popular Religion in the Graeco-Roman Near East, 1977.

M. K.

Hades (Ἅιδης). Griech. Bezeichnung für die Unterwelt und deren Herrscher. Verschiedene Schreibweisen sind belegt: Aides, Ais und Aidoneus bei Homer, H. (aspiriert) nur in Attika. Die Etym. ist unklar; der neueste Vorschlag ist, H. auf *a-wid »unsichtbar« zurückzuführen [1. 575 f.], vgl. aber [2. 302]. Außerhalb von Attika, etwa bei Homer (Il. 23,244; Od. 11,623), kann das Wort auch die → Unterwelt bezeichnen, deren Tore vom Höllenhund → Kerberos bewacht werden (Il. 5,646; 8,368). Bei Homer liegt H. unter der Welt, aber man erreicht ihn auch, wenn man ans W-Ende der Erde fährt, d. h. hier treffen verschiedene Unterweltsvorstellungen zusammen [3. 60]. Ein Fluß trennt diesen »unerfreulichen Ort« (Hom. Od. 11,94; Hes. erg. 152 ff.) von der Welt der Lebenden (Hom. Il. 23,70–101; Od. 11,51 ff.); die Gestalt des Fährmannes → Charon ist allerdings erst eine nach-homer. Erfindung [3. 303–361]. Ohne Bestattung konnten die Toten H. nicht betreten (Hom. Il. 23,71 ff.; Eur. Hec. 28–54).

Gemäß Hom. Il. 5,395 ff. wird H. ›in Pylos unter den Toten‹ von → Herakles verwundet. Dieser dunkle Mythos gehört wahrscheinlich zu Herakles' Rolle als »Herr der Tiere« [4. 86] und deutet darauf hin, daß H. schon in der Bronzezeit personifiziert wurde. Auf jeden Fall war H. in Griechenland ein schattenhafter Gott, der wenig Mythen und noch weniger Riten hatte; seine Abb. auf archa. Vasen läßt sich nicht mit Sicherheit nachweisen [5. 389]. Nach Hom. Il. 15,187–193 erhält er die Unterwelt, als er mit seinen Brüdern Zeus und Poseidon lost; diese Stelle läßt sich wohl letztlich auf das akkad. Epos → *Atrahasis* zurückführen [6. 90 f.]. Zwar herrscht H. schon bei Homer über die Unterwelt, erscheint aber erst in nach-homer. Zeit als Totenrichter (Aischyl. Suppl. 228–231; Eum. 273 ff.), eine Funktion, die später auf Minos, Aiakos und Rhadamanthys übertragen wurde (Plat. apol. 41a; Plat. Gorg. 523e–24a; Demosth. or. 18,127). Obwohl dies in der bildenden Kunst nicht ersichtlich ist [5. 367–406], macht seine Verbindung zur Unterwelt H. »verhaßt« (Il. 8,368), »unversöhnlich« und »unbeugsam« (Il. 9,158); dieser Aspekt geht bes. aus den späteren Fluchtäfelchen hervor [7. 53; 84; 89; 110; 134]. Oft wurde er indirekt als »Zeus der Unterwelt« (Hom. Il. 9,457), »König der unter der Erde Lebenden« (Aischyl. Pers. 629) oder »Unterweltsgott« (Soph. Ai. 571) bezeichnet. Da der Tod keine Ausnahme macht, wurde er auch als *polydégmōn*, »viel-aufnehmend« (Hom. h. 2,17), *pasiánax*, »Herr über alles« [8. Nr. 43 f.] und *hagēsílaos*, »Anführer des Volkes« (Aischyl. fr. 406 TrGF) beschrieben. Er war sogar der personifizierte Tod schlechthin (Semonides 1,14 IEG; Pind. P. 5,96; N. 10,67; I. 6,15).

Paradoxerweise hielt man ihn auch für einen »guten und klugen Gott« (Plat. Phaid. 80d7), der den Menschen von unten gute Dinge heraufschickte (Aristoph. fr. 504 PCG; Plat. Krat. 403a3–5). Dieser Glaube führte im 5. Jh. v. Chr. zu seinem Beinamen → Pluton (Soph. fr. 273; 283 TrGF [9. 105–113], der mit den eleusinischen Kultfiguren → Plutos [9. 49–55] und Eubuleus [9. 56–59] in Verbindung stand. Trotz der Verbindung mit »Wohlstand« ging die Assoziation mit der Unterwelt nicht verloren, und später wurden die Eingänge der Unterwelt *plutṓnia* genannt (Strab. 5,4,5). Da H. so schwer zu fassen und nicht auf eine Funktion einzugrenzen war, hatte er keinen Kult (Soph. Ant. 777–780); man glaubte auch, er sei Gebeten und Gaben gegenüber gleichgültig eingestellt (Aischyl. fr. 161 TrGF; Eur. Alc. 424). In Griechenland scheint es nur in Elis einen H.-Tempel gegeben zu haben, der bezeichnenderweise nur einmal im Jahr offen war (Strab. 8,3,14; Paus. 6,25,2).

Der berühmteste H.-Mythos ist seine Entführung der → Persephone; diese Gesch. wurde an verschiedenen Orten in der griech. Welt lokalisiert [10. 74–78]. Da Persephone mit Liebe und Hochzeit verbunden war [11. 147–188] und eine Entführung zum spartanischen Hochzeitsritus gehörte, war der Mythos wohl urspr. eine narrative Darstellung vorhochzeitlicher Mädchenriten. Die Vereinigung von H. und Persephone wurde zu einem Emblem für Hochzeit überhaupt, so daß Mädchen, die unverheiratet starben, »H.-Bräute« genannt wurden [3. 250]. Aufgrund von H.' »höllischem« Wesen ist es keine Überraschung, daß das Paar kinderlos blieb (Apollod. FGrH 244 F 102a2). Die beiden wurden weithin zusammen verehrt, gewöhnlich als Pluton und → Kore (IG II[3] 1620c); in Eleusis sogar als die Götter par excellence, Theos und Thea, [9. 114 f.]. Erst ein späterer Mythos erzählt von H.' Geliebter → Minthe, die von Persephone in die Minze verwandelt wird (Strab. 8,3,14; Ov. met. 10,728 ff.).

H. verlor seine Bed. als allg. Bestimmungsort im 5. Jh. v. Chr., als die Vorstellung von Seelen aufkam, die sich in die obere Luftschicht begeben, während die Körper von der Erde aufgenommen werden (CEG 1. 10,6 f.); dieser Glaube ist schon in den Trag. des Euripides ersichtlich und bezieht sich dort auf Sterbliche (Eur. Suppl. 531–534; Eur. Hel. 1013–1016) und ver-

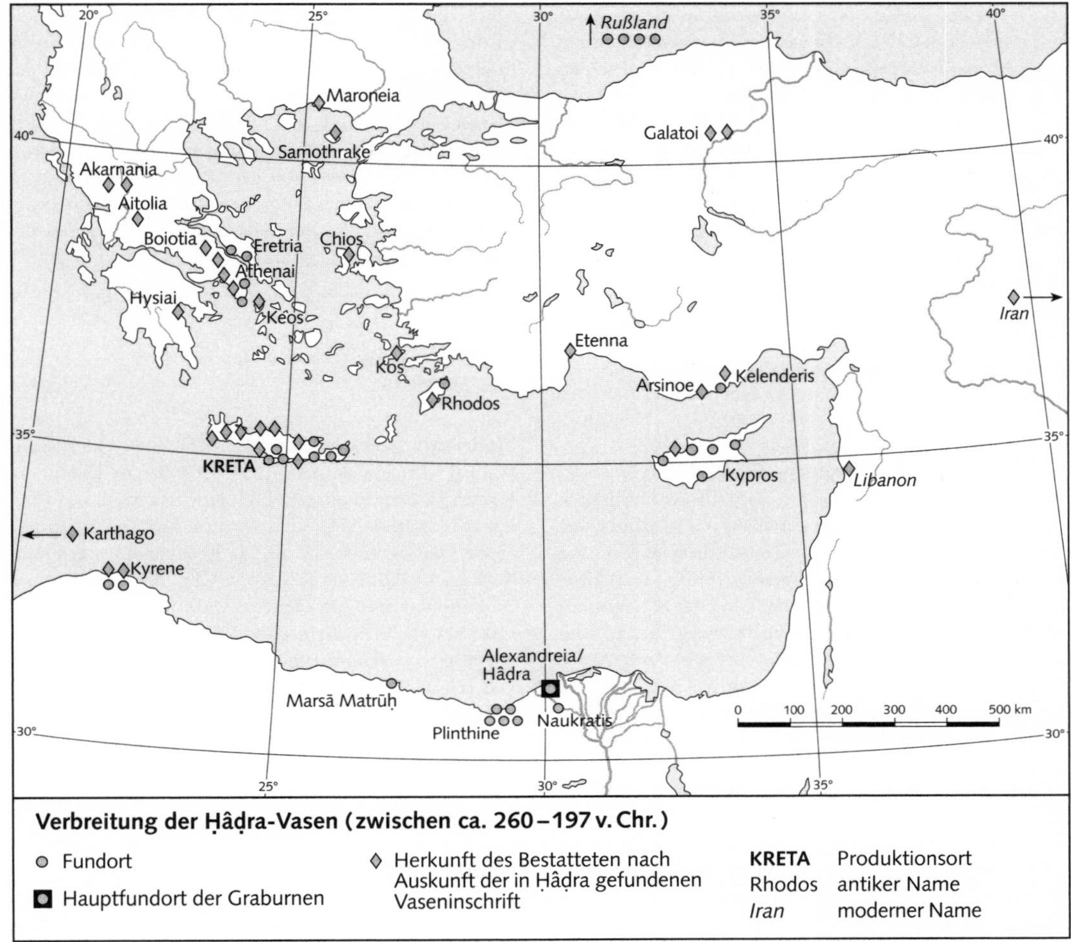

Verbreitung der Ḥâḍra-Vasen (zwischen ca. 260–197 v. Chr.)

göttlichte Sterbliche (Eur. Erechtheus fr. 65, 71 f. Austin). Auf spät- und nachklass. apulischen Vasen wird H. oft mit → Orpheus verbunden, was vielleicht als Zeichen für eine veränderte Rolle in den rel. Vorstellungen in S-It. aufgefaßt werden kann [5. 394].

→ Jenseitsvorstellungen

1 C.J. Ruijgh, Scripta Minora I, 1991 **2** Burkert
3 C. Sourvinou-Inwood, ›Reading‹ Greek Death to the End of the Classical Period, 1995 **4** W. Burkert, Structure and History in Greek Mythology and Ritual, 1979
5 S.F. Dalinger et al., s.v. H., LIMC 4.1 **6** W. Burkert, The Orientalizing Revolution, 1992 **7** J. Gager, Curse Tablets and Binding Spells from the Ancient World, 1992
8 A. Audollent, Defixionum Tabellae, 1904
9 K. Clinton, Myth and Cult. The Iconography of the Eleusinian Mysteries, 1992 **10** N.J. Richardson, The Homeric Hymn to Demeter, 1973
11 C. Sourvinou-Inwood, ›Reading‹ Greek Culture, 1991.

A. Henrichs, s.v. H., OCD, [3]1996, 661 f.

J.B./Ü: H.K.

Ḥâḍra-Vasen. Moderner t.t., der die hell. bemalten → Hydrien bezeichnet, die hauptsächlich zw. 270 und 180 v. Chr. hergestellt wurden; benannt nach dem ägyptischen Fundort Ḥâḍra bei → Alexandreia, wo die Mehrheit der etwa 300 bekannten Exemplare zutage kam. H. leiten sich von den weißgrundigen Hydrien ab, die früher ebenfalls zu dieser Gattung gerechnet wurden. Ihre Herkunft aus Zentral-Kreta gilt heute aufgrund naturwiss. Analysen als gesichert. Mit unbemalten Exemplaren setzt die Produktion sich hier bis ins 1. Jh. v. Chr. fort.

Aufgrund der Bemalung werden vier Hauptgruppen (Werkstätten) unterschieden, von denen die »Lorbeergruppe« mit 14 Vasenmalern am besten erforscht ist. Innerhalb der »Delphinengruppe« werden acht Vasenmaler unterschieden. Eine dritte Gruppe wird nach ihrer anspruchslosen Bemalung als »einfache Gruppe« bezeichnet und als die älteste betrachtet. Alexandreia kannte zw. 240 und 120 v. Chr. schließlich eine eigene Produktion der H. (»Gruppe der zweiglosen Lorbeerblätter«) mit mindestens zwei Vasenmalern.

Auf Kreta wurden H. vorwiegend im Haushaltsbereich verwendet. Die Mehrzahl der H. wurde allerdings nach Alexandreia exportiert, wo sie als Aschenurnen im Totenkult Verwendung fanden. Unter diesen zeichnen sich etwa 30 H. aus durch Angabe des Namens des Verstorbenen mit Rang und Herkunft, des Namens des ptolem. Beamten, der mit der Beerdigung beauftragt war, und des Datums. Bei den Verstorbenen handelt es sich entweder um Gesandte oder Führer der Söldnertruppen, die in Alexandreia starben und ein Staatsbegräbnis bekamen.

L. Guerrini, Vasi di Hadra, Tentativo di sistemazione cronologica di una classe ceramica, 1964 · A. Enklaar, Chronologie et peintres des hydries de Hadra, in: BABesch 60, 1985, 106–151 · Ders., Les hydries de Hadra II: Formes et ateliers, in: BABesch 61, 1986, 41–65. R.D.

Hadramaut (arab. Ḥaḍramaut, Ḥaḍramōt, Ḥaḍramūt; Ἀδραμύτα, Theophr. h. plant. 9,4). Altsüdarab. Reich mit der im Westen gelegenen Hauptstadt Sabota, d.i. Šabwa(t); seine Bewohner sind das östlichste Volk von Arabia Felix, die sog. *Chadramōtítai* (Strab. 16,4) bzw. *Atramitae* (Plin. nat. 6,155). In der Ant. war H. nicht nur das gleichnamige Tal mit seinen Einzugsgebieten, sondern umfaßte die gesamte Region bis zum Arab. Meer. Das Königreich H. ist seit dem 7. Jh. v. Chr. in altsüdarab. Inschr. bezeugt, zuerst als Vasall von → Saba. Durch Einnahme des im Osten angrenzenden Weihrauchlandes erlangte H. auch wirtschaftliche Bed. (Verbindung mit dem Händlervolk der Minäer). Seine größte Ausdehnung brachte im 2. Jh. n. Chr. die Einbeziehung der Reste von Qatabān im Westen. Ende des 3. Jh. eroberten die himjarischen Könige H., einigten Südarabien zu einem großen Reich und titulierten sich auch Könige von H.

→ Altsüdarabisch

H. v. Wissmann, Zur Arch. und ant. Geogr. von Südarabien. Ḥaḍramaut, Qatabān und das ʿAden-Gebiet in der Ant., 1968 · P.A. Grjaznecič, A.V. Sedov (Hrsg.), Chadramaut. Archeologičeskie, ėtnografičeskie i istoriko-kul'tuniye issledovanija, Bd. 1, 1995 · Hadramawt, la vallée inspirée. Saba, Arabie méridionale 3–4, 1997. W.W.M.

Hadria (h. Atri). Erst Hatria, später H., Stadt 7 km westl. der Adria-Küste im Süden des Picenum (*regio V*) zw. dem Vomanus (h. Vomano; Sil. 8,438) und dem Matrinus (h. Piomba). Von Siculi und Liburni gegr., von Piceni eingenommen. Nach deren Unterwerfung wurde hier eine *colonia Latina* gegr. (289 v. Chr.; Liv. per. 11), die Mz. mit der Legende *HAT(ria)* prägte (vgl. Steph. Byz. s. v. Ἀτρία). *Municipium, tribus Maecia* [1. 64], von Sulla oder Augustus rekolonisiert. Berühmt waren die Amphoren aus H. (Plin. nat. 35,161). Hadrianus ließ hier Restaurierungsmaßnahmen vornehmen (familiäre Beziehungen: SHA Hadr. 1; 19). Es lassen sich Siedlungsspuren aus dem 6. Jh. v. Chr. erkennen (picenische Nekropolen auf dem Colle di Giustizia und in Pretara). Die Ruinen der röm. Stadt liegen unter der modernen, in deren Grundriß die Straßen der regelmäßigen röm. Stadtanlage, *insulae* (1 *actus*). Die Mauern bestehen aus *opus quadratum* aus Flintkonglomerat. Die viereckige Zisterne mit Pilastern im Gebiet der Thermen bildet h. die Krypta der Kathedrale; eine weitere Zisterne befindet sich beim Forum unter dem Palazzo Acquaviva. Im NO befinden sich ein Heiligtum und ein Theater; weiterhin sind eine *villa suburbana* und Brennöfen für Keramik und Terracotta erhalten.

1 W. Kubitschek, Imperium Romanum tributim discriptum, 1889.

G. Azzena, Atri, forma e urbanistica, 1987 · L. Sorricchio, H., 1911. G.U./Ü: H.D.

Hadrianis (Ἁδριανίς). Letzte der fünf nachkleisthenischen → Phylen Attikas, 127/8 n. Chr. zu Ehren des Kaisers Hadrianus eingerichtet. Jede der damals 12 Phylen (10 kleisthenische sowie Ptolemais und Attalis) gab einen Demos an die H. ab, zu denen als 13. nach dem Tod des → Antinoos [2] 130 n. Chr. der neue Demos → Antinoeis trat. Die Trittyes spielen bei der Formierung der nachkleisthenischen Phylen keine Rolle. Die proportionale Repräsentation der Demen in den Phylen war schon 201/200 v. Chr. aufgegeben. Daher zeigen kaiserzeitliche Buleutenlisten für die einzelnen Demen ein uneinheitliches Bild.

→ Antigonis; Demetrias; Ptolemais

W.K. Pritchett, The Five Attic Tribes After Kleisthenes, 1943 · Traill, Attica, 25 ff., bes. 31, 34, Tab. 15. H.LO.

Hadrianopolis (Ἁδριανόπολις).

[1] Kaisareia (Καισάρεια). Stadt in Paphlagonia im Bekken von Eskipazar (früher Viranşehir), nahe der Burg von Semail, dem Mittelpunkt der paphlagon. Landschaft Sanisene [2]. Diese wurde mit Potamia und Marmolitis 6/5 v. Chr. als *regio attributa* [1. 116 ff.] ein Teil der paphlagon. *eparchía* der Prov. Galatia, der bald als *pólis* H. (urspr. Καισαρεῖς Προσειλημμενεῖται [1. Nr. 1]) organisiert wurde. Vor 305/6 n. Chr. wurde H. zur Prov. Paphlagonia, 384/387 zur Honorias ([1. Nr. 10], 6. Jh.) geschlagen; von 451 bis ins 12. Jh. als Bistum belegt.

1 C. Marek, Stadt, Ära und Territorium in Pontus-Bithynia und Nord-Galatia, 1993, 100–125, 187–210 2 K. Strobel, Galatien und seine Grenzregionen, in: E. Schwertheim (Hrsg.), Forsch. in Galatien (Asia Minor Stud. 12), 1994, 29–65.

K. Belke, Paphlagonien und Honorias, 1996, 63, 155 f. K.ST.

[2] Von Kaiser Hadrian wohl zur Förderung der Urbanisierung gegr. Ort [1]. In der Ant. teils Phrygia, teils Lykaonia zugerechnet, in frühbyz. Zeit in der Prov. Pisidia. Lokalisierung an einer direkten Straße von → Philomelion (Akşehir) nach → Ikonion eher bei h. Koçaş (24 km südöstl. von Philomelion) als beim 20 km südöstl. gelegenen Adaras [2. 456f.]. Mz. nennen einen Fluß Karmeios [3. 74], wohl den h. Koçaş (auch Ağık oder Adıyan) Çayı. H. war Bistum (Suffragan des pisidischen → Antiocheia [5]) seit (spätestens) 325 n. Chr. [4. 47, 134] bis ins 11./12. Jh. Zahlreiche Inschr. [5].

1 MAGIE 1, 622; 2, 1484. 2 W. M. CALDER, Inscriptions of Southern Galatia, in: AJA 36, 1932, 452–464 3 J. TISCHLER, Kleinasiat. Hydronymie, 1977 4 E. HONIGMANN, La liste originale des pères de Nicée, in: Byzantion 14, 1939, 17–76 5 MAMA 7, 30–37.

K. BELKE, N. MERSICH, Phrygien und Pisidien (TIB 7), 79, 145f., 171. K. BE.

[3] Stadt in Thrakien, am Zusammenfluß von Tuntza und Maritza (= Hebros), die ab hier schiffbar ist, h. Edirne (Türkei). Von Kaiser Hadrian gegr. unter Einbeziehung einer Vorgängersiedlung, für die thrak. (*Uscudama*) und griech. Namen (Ὀρεστίας u. a., nach [5. 161f.] archaisierender Gebrauch) überl. sind. An der Straße von Serdica nach Byzantion gelegen (Itin. Anton. 175,6; 322,8; Tab. Peut. 7,3 WEBER), besaß H. vor allem mil. Bed.: als Hauptort der Provinz Haemimontus, Zentrum der Waffenproduktion sowie als Ort zweier Entscheidungsschlachten um die Kaiserherrschaft – im J. 313 n. Chr. (Sieg des Licinius über Maximinus Daia bei Tzirallum [5. 63; 6. 14]) und 324 (Sieg des Constantinus über Licinius [6. 18]) – und der schon von Amm. 31,12–16 als epochal bewerteten Niederlage Kaiser Valens' gegen die Goten im J. 378 ([6. 35–37, 116, 166] mit weiteren Hinweisen).

Die strategische Lage am Weg nach Konstantinopel machte H. einerseits zum Angriffsziel von Avaro-Slaven (6./7. Jh.), Bulgaren (bes. 9./10. Jh., aber auch später) und Kreuzfahrern (11.–13. Jh.), andererseits bis zur Eroberung durch die Türken (um 1370) zu einem zentralen Ort der byz. Militärordnung (Einzelheiten bei [5. 162–165]). Bischöfe sind nachgewiesen seit dem 4. Jh. [2. 1453ff.], doch war H. trotz der Stellung als Metropolis von Haemimontus in der byz. Kirchenordnung nachrangig. Von der ant. Stadt sind kaum noch Reste erh., aus byz. Zeit nur wenige, v. a. der Befestigungen und einiger Kirchen [3. 167; 4. 23; 5. 165f.].

1 E. OBERHUMMER, s. v. H., RE 7, 2174f. 2 D. STIERNON s. v. H., DHGE 22, 1442–1466 3 J. GRUBER, G. WEISS, K. KREISER, s. v. Adrianopel, LMA 1, 167f. 4 T. E. GREGORY, N. PATTERSON ŠEVČENKO, A. KAZHDAN, s. v. Adrianople, s. v. Adrianople, battle of, ODB 1, 23f. 5 SOUSTAL, Thrakien (TIB 6, 161–167 (weitere Lit.) 6 J. MARTIN, Spätant. und Völkerwanderung, ³1995. E. W.

Hadrianos (Ἁδριανός).

[1] Sophist aus Tyros, mit 18 Jahren ein Lieblingsschüler des → Herodes Atticus (Philostr. soph. 2,10,585–586). Mit → Flavius Boëthos (ebenfalls aus Phönizien) besuchte er 162–166 n. Chr. die Anatomievorlesungen von → Galenos in Rom (Gal. 14,627; 629 KUHN). Vielleicht war er Ziel des Spotts in Lukians *Pseudologístēs* [1]. Er lehrte in Ephesos (Philostr. soph. 2,23,605) und ehrte dort (163–169) [2] seinen Patron, den Consular Cn. → Claudius [II 64] Severus, mit einer Statue und einem Gedicht [3; 4]. Spätestens ab 176 hatte er den kaiserlichen Lehrstuhl in Athen inne [5], wo er das Bürgerrecht besaß und die Grabrede auf Herodes hielt (177/8). Seit den ersten Jahren nach 180 hatte er den Lehrstuhl in Rom inne, wo seine Stimme sogar diejenigen anzog, die des Griech. nicht mächtig waren (Philostr. soph. 2,10,589). Eine Rede veranlaßte Kaiser Marcus Aurelius zu Ehrungen und Geschenken; kurz vor seinem Tod mit ca. 80 Jahren übertrug ihm Commodus das Amt des *ab → epistulis Graecis* (Philostr. soph. 590). Werke: Suda α 528 ADLER nennt ›Metamorphosen‹ (7 B.); zwei Werke zur rhet. Technik (3 und 5 B.); *Phalaris*; Briefe; Reden; eine *consolatio* für Celer (den Lehrer von Marcus Aurelius und Verus?, SHA Aur. 2,4 und *ab epistulis Graecis*, Philostr. soph. 1,22,524; Aristeid. 50,57). Eine kurze (fragmentarische?) Rede ist erh. [6], die die Verbrennung einer Frau beantragt, die eine Hexe verbrannt hatte. Libanios (or. 64,41) kennt eine Grabrede für einen Schauspieler namens Maximinos.
→ Philostratos; Zweite Sophistik

1 C. P. JONES, Two Enemies of Lucian, in: GRBS 13, 1972, 478–86 2 R. SYME, The Ummidii, in: Roman Papers 2, 1979, 690 3 IK 15, 1539 4 FGE 566–8 5 I. AVOTINS, Holders of the Chairs of Rhetoric at Athens, in: HSPh 79, 1975, 320–321 6 H. HINCK, Polemonis declamationes, 1873, 44f. (Ed.).

G. W. BOWERSOCK, Greek Sophists in the Roman Empire, 1969, 55–63; 82–4; 91–2 • PIR H 4. E. BO./Ü: L. S.

[2] Ein vermutlich in Syrien lebender Grieche, vielleicht identisch mit einem Mönch, an den → Neilos drei Briefe richtete (epist. 2,60; 3,118; 3,266), schrieb vor 440 n. Chr. eine knappe ›Einführung in die Heiligen Schriften‹ (*Eisagōgḗ*), das erste so betitelte Werk. Es war auch im Westen bekannt (Cassiod. inst. 1,10); sein Ziel ist es, figürliche Redeweisen v. a. des AT zu erläutern: Sinn-, Wort- und Satzfiguren. Die Schrift versucht, auf der Basis des griech. Bibeltextes charakteristische Eigenarten der hebr. Sprache zu erklären (§ 1) und schließt mit knappen Bemerkungen zur allg. Hermeneutik (§ 132–134). Dabei folgt sie Grundsätzen der → Antiochenischen Schule, insbes. → Theodoros von Mopsuestia, → Iohannes Chrysostomos und → Theodoretos von Kyrrhos. Da zahlreiche, bei [3] nicht berücksichtigte Katenenfragmente erh. sind [1. 6527; 2. 24, 28, 39, 48, 53f., 324], bedarf der Text einer neuen Edition. Möglicherweise wurde bisher nur die Epitome oder lediglich ein Teil eines umfangreicheren Werkes ediert.

1 CPG 3 2 G. KARO, H. LIETZMANN, Catenarum Graecarum Catalogus, 1901 3 F. GOESSLING (ed.), Adrians ΕΙΣΑΓΩΓΗ ΕΙΣ ΤΑΣ ΘΕΙΑΣ ΓΡΑΦΑΣ aus neu aufgefundenen Handschriften, 1887 4 L. DIESTEL, Gesch. des Alten Testamentes in der christl. Kirche, 1869, 110 5 G. MERCATI, Pro Adriano, in: RBi 11, 1914, 246–255 (= Ders., Opere Minore 3, Studi e Testi 78, 1937, 383–392). C. M.

Hadrianus A. Herkunft und senatorische Laufbahn B. Die Herrschaftsübernahme C. Grenzkonzeption und militärische Unternehmungen D. Die Sorge um das Reich – die Reisen E. Die Administration F. Nachfolgeregelung

A. Herkunft und senatorische Laufbahn

Röm. Kaiser 117–138 n. Chr. Sohn des Senators P. Aelius Hadrianus Afer und einer Domitia Paulina; seine Heimat war → Italica in der spanischen Provinz Baetica. Geb. am 24. Jan. 76 wohl in Rom als P. Aelius Hadrianus. Im 10. Lebensjahr verlor er den Vater, der praetorischen Rang erreicht hatte. Seine Vormünder wurden der Ritter Acilius Attianus und der Senator M. Ulpius Traianus, der spätere Kaiser, sein Großonkel (s. Stemma bei [1. 308]), beide ebenfalls aus Italica stammend. Frühzeitig wurde H. mit griech. Literatur und Kultur vertraut gemacht. Vor Aufnahme der senatorischen Laufbahn lebte er nur für kurze Zeit in Italica.

Um 94 begann er seine Karriere als *decemvir stlitibus iudicandis, praefectus urbi feriarum Latinarum* und *sevir*. Anschließend war er senatorischer Militärtribun bei drei Legionen: bei der *legio II Adiutrix* in Pannonien, der *V Macedonica* in Moesia inferior im J. 96/7. Als Traianus, damals Statthalter von Germania superior, von Nerva adoptiert und zum Nachfolger bestimmt wurde, überbrachte H. die Glückwünsche des niedermoesischen Heeres. Anschließend war er Tribun bei der *legio XXII Primigenia* in Mainz. Anf. Febr. 98 beim Tod Nervas eilte er zu Traianus nach Köln, um ihm als erster die Nachricht zu überbringen; angeblich versuchte H.' Schwager Iulius Servianus, Legat von Germania superior, das zu verhindern. Von da an war H. stets in der Nähe des Traianus als nächster männlicher Verwandter; außerdem heiratete er im J. 100 Sabina, die Großnichte des Traianus. H.' senatorische Laufbahn (ILS 308; HA Hadr. 3,1–10) unter Traianus zeigte kaum Auffälligkeiten: Teilnahme am 1. Dakerkrieg als *quaestor* des Kaisers, Volkstribun, 104 *praetor*; Teilnahme am 2. Dakerkrieg 105 als Legat der *legio I Minervia* (in beiden Kriegen wurde er mit *dona militaria* ausgezeichnet); 106–108 praetorischer Statthalter von Pannonia inferior. Im Mai 108 wurde er *cos. suff.* mit 32 Jahren – außergewöhnlich für einen Nichtpatrizier. Damals wurde ihm angeblich eröffnet, daß Traianus ihn adoptieren wolle, doch kein außergewöhnliches öffentliches Zeichen folgte. In dieser Zeit hielt er sich in Griechenland auf und war 112 Archon in Athen.

B. Die Herrschaftsübernahme

H. nahm am Partherkrieg als *comes* des Traianus teil; spätestens in der ersten Jahreshälfte 117 wurde er zum Statthalter von Syrien ernannt; ob er wirklich zum *cos. II* für 118 designiert wurde, ist unsicher. Da Traianus erkrankte, war aber die Statthalterschaft H.' in Syrien eine deutliche Botschaft, wen Traianus als seinen Nachfolger wollte; doch eine Adoption erfolgte erst in Selinus in Kilikien, wo Traianus am 7. (?) Aug. 117 starb. H. erhielt die Nachricht in Syrien am 9. Aug. Angeblich soll der Brief des Traianus durch seine Frau Plotina, die H. seit langem förderte, und den *praefectus praetorio* Acilius [II 1] Attianus erst nach dem Tod des Kaisers gefälscht worden sein. Was wirklich im Detail geschah, ist heute nicht mehr zu klären. Doch alle sozialen und politischen Faktoren deuten darauf hin, daß Traianus H. als seinen Nachfolger wollte. Am 11. Aug. wurde H. durch die Truppen in Syrien als Kaiser akklamiert (*dies imperii*). Sein Name lautete jetzt: Imperator Caesar Traianus Hadrianus Augustus. Das *nomen gentile* des Traianus, Ulpius, übernahm er nicht, weshalb Neubürger und Freigelassene den Namen P. Aelius trugen.

H.' Regierungsbeginn war schwierig: Der Mißerfolg des Traianus gegen die Parther wurde durch Aufgabe auch des letzten Restes der Eroberungen anerkannt, dem von Traianus eingesetzten abhängigen Partherkönig die Unterstützung entzogen. In Dakien und an der mittleren Donau, in Britannien und Mauretanien brachen Aufstände aus; Marcius Turbo, der *praefectus praetorio*, erhielt im Donauraum dafür ein spezielles Kommando (RMD I 21). Die Reste der Erhebung der Juden im Osten, in Ägypten und der Cyrenaica wurden niedergeschlagen. Angeblich verschworen sich vier Consulare: Avidius Nigrinus, Cornelius Palma, Publilius Celsus und schließlich Lusius Quietus aus Mauretanien, den Traianus 116/7 in Iudaea eingesetzt hatte; alle vier wurden auf Befehl des *praefectus praetorio* nach Verurteilung durch den Senat hingerichtet; das Verhältnis H.' zum Senat war so zeitlebens belastet. Vermutlich waren sie alle zwar Gegner der neuen Politik H.' an den Reichsgrenzen, nicht jedoch Verschwörer.

Nach der Rückkehr H.' in die Hauptstadt am 9. Juli 118 entwickelte er ein besonderes Bemühen um Senat und Volk von Rom: Erlaß der Schulden an den *fiscus* für die Jahre 104–118 von insgesamt 900 Millionen Sesterzen; die Szene ist auf den *Anaglypha Traiani* dargestellt. Das Vermögen von Verurteilten sollte ins → *aerarium*, nicht in das → *patrimonium* des Kaisers gehen. Verarmte Senatoren erhielten finanzielle Unterstützung; für die Empfänger von → *alimenta* in Italien wurden die Bedingungen verbessert. Nur insgesamt zweimal übernahm H. noch den Consulat (118 und 119, also insgesamt nur *cos. III*) – ein Zeichen von *moderatio*. Die Siegertitel des Traianus, die ihm übertragen wurden, wies er generell zurück, auch den Titel *pater patriae*; erst im J. 128 akzeptierte er ihn. Äußerlich verbesserte sich so das Klima; aber bei der Mehrheit der Senatoren blieben Ressentiments bis über H.' Tod hinaus.

C. Grenzkonzeption und militärische Unternehmungen

H. gab der röm. Reichspolitik eine entscheidende Wendung gegenüber der Zeit des Traianus. Auf mil. Expansion wurde betont verzichtet, einige durch Traianus erworbene Gebiete dagegen aufgegeben: im Osten alle parth. Territorien, sodann der östliche Teil des durch H. neugeordneten Dakien (h. Südost-Rumänien und Moldawien), eine Folge heftiger Angriffe der Roxolanen und Sarmaten, während derer der Statthalter C. Iulius Quadratus Bassus fiel. Manche senatorischen Kreise haben gegen die Aufgabe der eroberten Gebiete opponiert. Der Ausbau der Grenzanlagen in Obergermanien und Rätien, in Nordafrika und besonders in Britannien (Hadrianswall) konnte als Zeichen für mil. Zurückhaltung nach außen verstanden werden. Kein expansionistischer Krieg wurde unter H. geführt. Dennoch vernachlässigte Hadrian das Heer nicht; bei seinen Reisen durch die Provinzen kontrollierte er die Truppen, wovon vor allem die Manöverkritik von Lambaesis sowie die Einrichtung des Kultes der Disciplina zeugen (ILS 2487; 9133–5), ebenso aber auch Münzen, auf denen sein Besuch bei den Provinzheeren verewigt ist. Wenn nötig, setzte er das Heer auch als Drohung ein, so 123 gegenüber den Parthern, doch wurde die Krise durch eine Unterredung mit dem Partherkönig am Euphrat gelöst. H.' mil. Zurückhaltung ist auch am Verzicht auf Imperatorenakklamationen erkennbar. Die einzige Ausnahme ist die Annahme des Titels *imperator II* nach dem langwierigen → Bar Kochba-Krieg, wohl erst im Frühjahr 136. Diese Revolte, ausgelöst wohl durch die Gründung der Kolonie Aelia Capitolina anstelle von Jerusalem und möglicherweise durch das Verbot der Beschneidung, verursachte gewaltige Verluste unter den röm. Truppen. Erst durch den Einsatz der Heere von Iudaea, Arabia und Syrien und weiterer abkommandierter Einheiten konnte der Guerillakrieg Bar Kochbas nach etwa vier Jahren siegreich beendet werden. H. verlieh Triumphalornamenta an Sex. Iulius Severus, T. Haterius Nepos und C. Publicius Marcellus (ILS 1056; IGR III 175; ILS 1058); für ihn selbst errichtete wohl der Senat einen Triumphbogen im südlichen Galiläa bei Tel Shalem (unpublizierte Inschr.).

D. Die Sorge um das Reich – Die Reisen

Der Nachdruck der Politik H.' lag auf der inneren Entwicklung des Reiches. Mittel dazu war seine ausgedehnte Reisetätigkeit durch fast alle Provinzen [4. 188 ff.]. Die erste Reise, begonnen nach dem 21.4.121, führte über Gallien, Germania superior, Raetien, Noricum und Germania inferior nach Britannien, wo er den Bau des *vallum Hadriani* zwischen Ituna und Tina durch den Statthalter Platorius Nepos veranlaßte. Die Rückkehr führte ihn bis nach Tarraco, ohne daß er seine Heimatprovinz Baetica besucht zu haben scheint. Spätestens im Frühjahr 123 reiste er wegen der Partherkrise nach dem Osten. Von Syrien zog er über Kappadokien ans Schwarze Meer und verbrachte die Zeit von Ende 123 bis Herbst 124 in Bithynien, sodann vor allem in Asien. Von Oktober 124 bis Sommer 125 in Griechenland, vor allem Athen; Rückkehr nach Rom über Sizilien im Sommer 125. Eine Reise durch Italien begann am 3. März 127 (Vidman, FO[2] 49; vgl. [12. II 695; VI 349]: möglicherweise nur Norditalien); Anf. August 127 in Rom zurück. Im Frühsommer 128 Aufbruch nach Nordafrika mit Besuch bei der *legio III Augusta*, sodann über Rom nach Griechenland, wo er den Winter 128/9 erneut in Athen verbrachte. Im Frühjahr 129 nach Ephesos, Zug durch Kleinasien nach Antiocheia in Syrien, Palmyra; Winter 129/130 in Syrien. Besuch in Arabia und Iudaea; Sommer 130 nach Ägypten, wo im Okt. sein Liebling → Antinoos [2] im Nil ertrank. Im Frühjahr 131 Abreise aus Alexandreia nach Syrien, über Thrakien und Moesien nach Athen mit Winteraufenthalt 131/2. Ob er dann nach Rom zurückkehrte oder sich nochmals nach dem Osten, u. a. in das aufständische Iudaea begab, ist umstritten.

Die Reisen verschafften H. breiteste Kenntnis über die lokalen und überregionalen Probleme des Reiches. Er stärkte das Selbstbewußtsein der Provinzen, die als eigenständige Einheiten auf den Reichsmünzen erschienen und damit gegenüber It. aufgewertet wurden; dort setzte H. dagegen vier *legati Augusti pro praetore* als dezentrale Amtsträger ein, die faktisch die Funktion von Provinzstatthaltern hatten (Antoninus Pius hob diese Regelung wieder auf [13]). Vor allem das Städtewesen wurde gefördert: durch Neugründung von Städten wie z. B. der Poleis Hadrianutherae, Hadriani und Hadriania in Asien, das Municipium Choba in Mauretanien, die Erhebung von Italica in der Baetica und Mursa in Pannonien zu *coloniae* oder die Gründung von Antinoopolis als Gedenkort für Antinoos in Ägypten, das in außergewöhnlichem Maß privilegiert wurde; durch Finanzierung von zahllosen Bauten, z. B. in Gabii (CIL XIV 2747), Ostia (CIL XIV 95), Athen [1. 219], Alexandreia Troas (Philostr. soph. 2,1,8) oder Caesarea Maritima (z. B. AE 1928, 136; 137); durch Vergabe des umfassenderen *ius Latii maius*, wodurch alle Dekurionen einer latinischen Gemeinde das röm. Bürgerrecht erhielten. Gerade die zahlreichen auf uns gekommenen Briefe an Städte zeigen die Intensität seines Bemühens [14].

Obwohl sich H.' Fürsorge auf alle Regionen des Reiches bezog, profitierten die östlichen, meist griech.-sprachigen Provinzen am meisten. Das griech. Element erhielt durch die Gründung des Panhellenion in Athen ein neues Zentrum. Mitglieder waren griech. Städte aus dem gesamten Reich; Mittelpunkt wurde der gigantische Tempel des panhellenischen Zeus, der jetzt endlich nach vielen vorausgegangenen Versuchen vollendet wurde. Die Inauguration des Tempels erfolgte in Anwesenheit H.' 131/2. H. selbst wurde im Osten Olympios (seit 128/9), Panhellenios (seit 132) und Panionios genannt, wodurch ein Kern seines politischen Handelns gekennzeichnet wird. Auch die Einweihung in die Eleusinischen Mysterien gehört in diesen Zusammenhang. Allerdings hat nicht erst er den Anteil der Senatoren aus dem griech. Osten beträchtlich erhöht, das war vielmehr schon seit den Flaviern geschehen. Nur der erste Consul aus dem griech. Mutterland findet sich erst unter H.: Ti. Claudius Atticus Herodes, ca. 132/3. Dennoch vernachlässigte er den Westen, vor allem aber Rom, nicht. Zahlreiche Bauten wurden von ihm dort finanziert, ein Tempel für seine »Eltern« Traianus und Plotina, das → Pantheon, der Doppeltempel von Venus und Roma, deren Kult damit auch in der Reichshauptstadt etabliert wurde.

Frühzeitig hatte H. begonnen, bei Tivoli eine Residenz ganz eigenen Charakters zu errichten, die sich über 1,5 qkm hinzog, die sog. *villa Hadriana* (→ Villa, → Tibur). Daß er Erinnerungen an seine Reisen dort Gestalt werden ließ, ist unbestreitbar.

E. Die Administration

Das Besondere an H.' Regierungsstil waren seine Reisen; doch die ihm häufig zugeschriebene Systematisierung der Administration des Reiches, vor allem der von Rittern geleiteten Bereiche, ist nicht sein Werk; vielmehr ergänzte er nur in geringem Umfang die Maßnahmen seiner Vorgänger Domitianus und Traianus. Möglicherweise wurde die Aufgabe eines *advocatus fisci* von ihm eingeführt; der erste bekannte Träger aber hatte, entgegen HA Hadr. 20,6, vorher eine mil. Aufgabe übernommen (AE 1975, 408). Die angebliche Reorganisation des kaiserlichen Rates, des *consilium principis*, ist eine spätant. Erfindung. Bedeutsam aber wurde, wenn auch nur zeichenhaft, die Fixierung der praetorischen Ediktsammlung (→ *Edictum* [2] *perpetuum*), die H. Salvius Iulianus übertrug (ILS 8973); die Konzentration der Weiterbildung des Rechtes durch den Kaiser wird dadurch dokumentiert. Auf dem Feld der institutionalisierten Reichsorganisation blieb H. ansonsten in den Bahnen seiner Vorgänger.

F. Nachfolgeregelung

Aus der Ehe mit Sabina hatte H. keine Kinder. Sein Verhältnis zu ihr soll auch sehr gespannt gewesen sein; ob dies zutrifft oder nur Hofklatsch wiedergibt, ist kaum zu entscheiden. Doch dürften H.' pädophile Neigungen, vor allem seine Beziehungen zu Antinoos [2], das Verhältnis beeinträchtigt haben. Nach der Rückkehr von der großen letzten Reise stellte sich für H., der zunehmend unter Krankheiten litt, die Frage der Nachfolge. Im J. 136 adoptierte er einen der Consuln des Jahres, L. Ceionius Commodus, der den Namen L. Aelius Caesar annahm. Die Wahl wirkt überraschend, zumal der Erwählte an Tuberkulose litt; der Grund ist trotz vieler Spekulationen unbekannt. Die Wahl erregte Widerstand bei H.' Verwandten, L. Iulius Ursus Servianus, *cos. III* im J. 134, und Pedanius Fuscus, H.' Großneffen; eine »Revolte« gegen H. wurde aufgedeckt, die »Verschwörer« hingerichtet. Doch auch Aelius Caesar starb am 31.12.137. Am 24.1.138 benannte H. den 51-jährigen Senator T. Aurelius Fulvus Boionius Arrius Antoninus (Antoninus [1] Pius) als seinen Nachfolger; die Adoption wurde am 25.2. vollzogen. Antoninus mußte seinerseits den Sohn des verstorbenen Aelius Caesar, den späteren Lucius Verus, und den jungen Marcus Aurelius, den H. als Verissimus bezeichnete und hochschätzte, adoptieren, wodurch die Weiterführung der Herrschaft über zwei Generationen gesichert war. Am 10.7.138 starb H. nach einer langen Krankheit in Baiae. Die Asche wurde später in seinem Mausoleum (h. Engelsburg) jenseits des Tiber beigesetzt. Die Divinisierung durch den Senat erfolgte erst, als Antoninus Pius dies mit der Drohung erzwang, andernfalls sei auch seine Adoption hinfällig. Es war die letzte Folge der latent immer vorhandenen Spannung zwischen H. und dem Senat.

Münzen: RIC II 314ff.
Porträts: Fittschen/Zanker Katalog I Nr. 46ff. • M. Bergmann, Zu den Porträts des Traian und Hadrian, in: A. Caballos, P. León (Hrsg.), Itálica MMCC, 1997, 137ff.
Lit.: **1** A. R. Birley, Hadrian. The Restless Emperor, 1997 (mit ausführlicher Bibliographie) **2** Ders., Hadrian and Greek Senators, in: ZPE 116, 1997, 209ff. **3** E. Champlin, Hadrian's Heir, in: ZPE 21, 1976, 79ff. **4** H. Halfmann, Itinera principum, 1986 **5** C. P. Jones, The Panhellenion, in: Chiron 26, 1996, 29ff. **6** O. Lenel, Edictum perpetuum, ³1927 **7** R. Syme, Hadrian, the Intellectual, in: Ders., RP VI 103ff. **8** Ders., Hadrian as Philhellene. Neglected Aspects, in: Ders., RP V 546ff. **9** M. Tagliaferro Boatwright, Hadrian and the City of Rome, 1990 **10** D. Willers, Hadrians panhellenisches Programm, 1990 **11** M. Zahrnt, Hadrian, in: M. Clauss (Hrsg.), Die röm. Kaiser, 1997, 124ff. **12** Syme, RP **13** W. Eck, Die Verwaltung des röm. Reiches 1, 1995, 315ff. **14** J. H. Oliver, Greek Constitutions, 1989, 150ff.

W. E.

Hadrumetum (Ἀδρύμης). Phöniz. Handelsplatz an der tunes. Ostküste, h. Sousse. Belegstellen: Ps.-Skyl. 110 (GGM I 88); Sall. Iug. 19,1; Solin. 27,9. Aus pun. bzw. neupun. Zeit stammen der Tofet (mit bedeutsamen Stelen), eine Nekropole (mit verschiedenen Grabbeigaben) und über 60 Inschr. 310 v. Chr. trat H. auf die Seite des → Agathokles [2] (Diod. 20,17,3–5). 203 v. Chr. wählte → Hannibal H. zu seiner Basis; nach der Niederlage von Naraggara kehrte er dorthin zurück (Pol. 15,5,3; 15,3; Nep. Hann. 6,3 f.; Liv. 30,29,1; 35,4; App. Lib. 33, 139; 47,206). Zu Beginn des 3. Pun. Krieges schloß H. ein Bündnis mit den Römern und erhielt daher nach Kriegsende den Status eines *populus liber* (App. Lib. 94,446). In caesarischer Zeit verlor die Stadt ihre Freiheit, gewann sie aber bereits 36 v. Chr. wieder (Plin. nat. 5,25). Traianus erhob sie zur *colonia* (CIL VI 1, 1687). Noch im 2. Jh. wurde H. der Sitz des *procurator regionis Hadrumetinae*. Strittig ist, ob H. auch der Sitz eines *legatus proconsulis Africae* war. Die Blütezeit der Stadt fiel in severische Zeit. Unter Diocletianus stieg H. zur Hauptstadt der neuen *provincia Valeria Byzacena* auf. Die erh. arch. Monumente sind bed. Inschr.: CIL VIII 1, 59–67; 2, 10503–10510; Suppl. 1, 11137–11150; Suppl. 4, 22909–23020; AE 1977, 258 Nr. 863; 1989, 285 Nr. 879; 287 Nr. 885; 290 Nr. 893; 1991, 461 Nr. 1639.

L. Foucher, H., 1964 • S. Lancel, E. Lipiński, s. v. Hadrumète, DCPP, 203 f. • C. G. Piccard, Catalogue du Musée Alaoui. Nouvelle série. Bd. I 1, o.J., 298–300 • K. Vössing, Unt. zur röm. Schule, Bildung, Schulbildung im Nordafrika der Kaiserzeit, 1991, 92–102.

W. HU.

Hadylion (Ἀδύλιον, Ἡδύλε[ι]ον). Gebirgszug (h. Vetritza) mit einer durchschnittlichen Kammhöhe von 300–400 m (höchster Punkt: 543 m) an der Nordgrenze zw. Phokis und Boiotia; im Westen bei Parapotamioi durch den Kephisos vom → Parnassos getrennt; im

Osten und SO an die Berge Palaiovuna (ant. Hyphanteion?) und Akontion angrenzend. Belegstellen: Demosth. or. 19,148 (mit schol.); Theop. FGrH 115 F 157; Strab. 9,3,16; Plin. nat. 4,25; Plut. Sulla 16f.

PHILIPPSON/KIRSTEN, I,2, 425. P.F.

Haedui. Mächtiges, reiches Volk der *Gallia Celtica* (nachmals Lugdunensis; → Gallia). Im Westen war das Gebiet der H. im wesentlichen von Doubs und Saône begrenzt; im Norden waren → Senones, → Mandubii und → Lingones Nachbarn der H. Bündnisse mit den → Bituriges im Westen und den Senones, → Parisii und → Bellovaci im Norden ermöglichten den H. die Kontrolle des Handels vom Mittelmeer zum Ärmelkanal; enge Beziehungen zu den → Boii öffneten ihnen den Zugang zu den reichen Kelten Zentraleuropas. Nach Liv. 5,34 nahmen die H. im 6. Jh. v. Chr. an der gall. Wanderung nach Oberit. teil. Diese Tradition erklärt vermutlich, daß von allen gall. Völkern die H. als einzige sowohl im Landesinneren wie auch in ihren Grenzgebieten eine große Vielfalt an untergeordneten ethnischen Gruppen aufwiesen (Caes. Gall. 1,11,4; 2,14,2; 6,4,2; 7,5,2; 7,75,2). Früh schlossen sie sich den Römern an und wurden von diesen »Brüder und Blutsverwandte«, *fratres consanguineique* genannt (Caes. Gall. 1,33,2). Nach langer Vorherrschaft wurden sie von den → Sequani unterworfen, doch setzte Caesar sie wieder in ihre frühere Stellung ein. Sie empörten sich evtl. schon 54, sicher aber 52 v. Chr. und 21 n. Chr. gegen Rom. Zur Zeit der augusteischen Neuordnung bildeten die H. zusammen mit den → Segusiavi und → Ambarri das Bindeglied zw. der Prov. Lugdunensis im Norden der Rhône mit der Prov. Narbonensis. Als Kaiser Claudius den Galliern das *ius honorum* erteilte, gelangten sie als erste in den Senat (Tac. ann. 11,25). In karolingischer Zeit gründete die *civitas Aeduorum* drei Diözesen mit Sitzen in Autun, Chalon und Mâcon.
→ Augustodunum; Bibracte

C. GOUDINEAU, C. PEYRE, Bibracte et les Eduens, 1993 • M. PINETTE et al., Autun-Augustodunum, 1987 • E. THÉVENOT, Les Eduens n'ont pas trahi, 1960. Y.L.

Haemimontus. Eine der sechs Prov. der *dioecesis* Thracia mit der Hauptstadt → Hadrianopolis [3]. Sie umfaßte das Territorium an der Donau zw. der Mündung des Flusses Vit bis zum Delta, die westl. Pontosküste bis Konstantinopolis (ohne die Stadt selbst), die Propontis und die nördl. Ägäis bis zur Mündung des Nestos.

V. VELKOV, Cities in Thrace and Dacia in Late Antiquity, 1977, 61 • SOUSTAL, Thrakien. I.v.B.

Hängende Gärten. Bauwerk der → Semiramis (9./8. Jh. v. Chr.) in → Babylon (oder in Niniveh [2]), eines der Sieben → Weltwunder, weder in der keilschriftlichen Überl. noch in der Stadtbeschreibung Herodots (1,178 ff.) erwähnt; die Überl. dazu setzt erst im 4. Jh. v. Chr. ein [1. 48 f.]. Der Auffassung, die Königin Semiramis habe sie errichten lassen, widerspricht Diodoros (3,10,1 ff.); Iosephos (ant. Iud. 10,11,225 f.) nennt Nebukadnezar II. (605–562 v. Chr.) als Erbauer. Als Weltwunder galten sie wegen der Größe, der Bauweise und der Bewässerungstechnik, beschrieben von den ant. Autoren als hohe, mehrfach gestufte, quadratische Terrassenanlage, die auf Gewölben ruhe (Strab. 16,1,5). Zum Aussehen und zur Lokalisierung der H. G. wurden mehrere Rekonstruktionen vorgeschlagen [3. 44 ff.; 4. 19 ff.]; eindeutige arch. Befunde fehlen bislang.
→ Bīsutūn; Gartenanlagen; SIEBEN WELTWUNDER

1 K. BRODERSEN, Die Sieben Weltwunder, ²1997
2 S. DALLEY, Niniveh, Babylon and the Hanging Gardens: Cuneiform and Classical Sources Reconciled, in: Iraq 56, 1994, 48–58 3 W. EKSCHMITT, Die Sieben Weltwunder, ¹⁰1995 4 W. NAGEL, Wo lagen die H. G. von Babylon?, in: MDOG 110, 1978, 19–28. J.BÄ.

Häresie I. CHRISTLICH II. ISLAMISCH

I. CHRISTLICH

Begriff zur ausgrenzenden Bezeichnung einer unerwünschten, von der Orthodoxie abweichenden religiösen Lehrmeinung. Der griech. Terminus → *haíresis* (αἵρεσις, lat. *haeresis* [5]) ist im vor- und nicht-christl. Kontext noch ausnahmslos wertneutral verwendet: Aus der Grundbed. »Nehmen«, »Wählen« kommt es zur Bed. »rel. oder philos. Schulmeinung«, »Schulrichtung« sowie schließlich »Angehörige einer Schulrichtung«, »Partei(ung)«, »Sekte«, vgl. z. B. die Titel bei Lukian, *Hermótimos ē̓ perí hairéseōn*; Antipater von Tarsos, *Katá tō̓n hairéseōn*; Varro, *Perí hairéseōn* (menippeische Satire); vgl. ferner Lukian. Hermotimus 48; convivium 10; vita Demonacis 13; Plot. 2,9,6; Diog. Laert. 1,18–21; 2,87 f.; Diod. 2,29,6; Epikt. 2,19,20 f.; Pol. 5,93,8 etc.; S. Emp. P. H. 1,16 f. 34. 185. 212. 236 f. 241; 2,6; 3,218 [1. 6]. Iosephos verwendet den Terminus zur Bezeichnung der drei (inner-)jüd. Religionsgruppen (der Sadduzäer, Pharisäer und Essener), vgl. Ios. ant. Iud. 7,347; 13,171. 288. 293; Ios. bell. Iud. 2,118. 122. 137. 142. 162; Eus. HE 10,5,2 (vgl. Ios. bell. Iud. 2,119. 124. 141 *hairetistḗs*, »Anhänger einer Partei«) [7].

Im NT erscheint das Subst. *haíresis* neunmal: In der Apg steht es ausschließlich für (inner-)jüd. Gruppen (5,17: Sadduzäer; 15,5; 26,5: Pharisäer; 24,5. 14; 28,22: aber auch »Nazoräer« = Christen); für die Apg war das Christentum also sowohl noch eine jüd. *haíresis* als auch christl. »orthodox«; aus jüd. Mund hat das Wort *haíresis* freilich bereits einen pejorativen Klang (Apg 24,5). Bei Paulus kündigt sich dann die spätere Bed. an: In Gal 5,20 und 1 Kor 11,18 f. ist von divergierenden christl. innergemeindlichen *hairéseis* die Rede, die hier bereits als unerwünschte Tendenz gebrandmarkt werden. In der nachapostolischen Zeit bezeichnet das Wort *haíresis* in der Regel die von der vermeintlich »rechten« Lehre des jeweiligen Autors abweichende »Irrlehre« (Tit 3,10; vgl. 2 Petr 2,1 etc.); vom 2. Jh. n. Chr. an ist es im negativen Sinn fest etabliert (Ignatius an die Epheser 6,2; Ders. an die Trallianer 6,1; Iust. Mart. apol. 1,26,8; Iust. Mart. dial. 35,3; 51,2 etc.), als häresiologischer t. t. begegnet er schließlich durchgängig ab → Eirenaios und → Tertullian [1. 2. 3. 4.].

Ein gesch. Abriß der christl. H. ist aus prinzipiellen Erwägungen unmöglich: Während der innerchristl. Auseinandersetzungen um die wahre Lehre trifft der Vorwurf der H. stets den Gegner. Eine wiss. H.-Geschichte, die selbst nicht christl. → Häresiologie betreiben will, müßte von vornherein einen bestimmten Überlieferungsstrang als orthodox voraussetzen. Die moderne kirchengesch. Forsch. operiert daher mit der »gesch. Erfolglosigkeit« einer Lehrmeinung als Bestimmungskriterium [8. 318]. Von den ant. Häresiologen behandelte Häretiker sind u. a. → Simon Magus, → Markion, → Valentinos, → Areios [3]. Augustinus setzt sich v. a. mit folgenden H. auseinander: → Gnosis; → Manichäismus; Donatismus; Pelagianismus (→ Pelagios) [8. 320–326].

Mit der konstantinischen Wende und der daraus resultierenden Einheit der Kirche setzte die staatliche Bekämpfung von Häretikern ein: Verbannung, Bücherverbrennungen, Versammlungsverbot waren übliche Strafen ab dem 4. Jh.; die Todesstrafe blieb die Ausnahme. Ab dem 13. Jh. verschärfte sich die staatliche Gewaltanwendung gegen Häretiker (Inquisition). Mit der Reformation bildete sich schließlich eine Entwicklung zur Toleranz heraus, die bis heute andauert (vgl. [8. 326–341]).

→ Häresiologie; Kanon; Häresie

1 LSJ s. v. αἵρεσις B II. 2 2 Bauer/Aland, s. v. αἵρεσις 3 H. Schlier, s. v. αἱρέομαι etc., ThWB 1, 179–184 4 G. Baumbach, s. v. αἵρεσις, Exegetisches Wörterbuch zum Neuen Testament 1, 1978, 96f. 5 ThlL 6, 3, 250f. 6 J. Glucker, Antiochos and the Late Academy, 1978 7 M. Simon, From Greek Hairesis to Christian Heresy: Early Christian Literature and the Classical Intellectual Tradition, in: FS R. M. Grant, 1979, 101–116 = Ders., Le christianisme antique et son contexte religieux, Scripta varia II, 1981, 821–836 8 A. Schindler, s. v. H. II, TRE 14, 318–341.

W. Bauer, Rechtgläubigkeit und Ketzerei im älteren Christentum, hrsg. von G. Strecker, ²1964 • M. Desjardins, Bauer and Beyond: On Recent Scholarly Discussion of Hairesis in the Early Christian Era, in: The Second Century 8, 1991, 68–82. L. K.

II. Islamisch

H. (*zandaqa*) wird im frühen Islam den Manichäern vorgeworfen [2]. Der Terminus – es gibt keine genau entsprechende arab. Übers. für H. [1. 51–63] – erfährt aber bald eine Bedeutungserweiterung und meint jegliche Art der Ketzerei, rel. Haltungen und Verhaltensweisen, die von der (orthodoxen) Norm abweichen und dadurch eine Gefahr für den islamischen Staat beinhalten, schließlich jedes Freidenkertum. Der anfängliche Vorwurf der H. gegenüber bestimmten Literaten mündete ab der 2. H. des 8. Jh. in inquisitorische Verfolgung und Brandmarkung der Beschuldigten. H. wurde z. T. mit der Todesstrafe geahndet.

→ Kalam; Mani

1 B. Lewis, Some Observations on the Significance of Heresy in the History of Islam, in: Studia Islamica 1, 1953, 43–63 2 G. Vajda, Les zindîqs en pays d'islam au début de la période abbaside, in: Rivista degli Studi Orientali 17, 1938, 173–229.

L. Massignon, s. v. zindīḳ, EI 4, 1228a–1229a. H. Schö.

Häresiologie. Als Häresiologen bezeichnet man verschiedene frühchristl. Autoren, die in einer oder mehreren ihrer Schriften vergangene und zeitgenössische → Häresien aufzählen, inhaltlich beschreiben oder zu widerlegen versuchen. Schwerpunkte dieses sog. antihäretischen Schrifttums (zur Problematik des Häresie-Begriffs vgl. [1. 290–295]) liegen in den ersten drei Jh. auf der Auseinandersetzung mit → Gnosis, → Montanismus sowie judenchristl. Gruppierungen.

Eine erste Zusammenstellung verschiedener Häresien und ihrer sukzessiv auf Simon Magus zurückgeführten Ursprünge verdankt sich → Iustinus (*Sýntagma*; verloren, Rekonstruktion des Inhalts bei [3. 21–30]). Grundlegend für alle späteren Autoren wird die v. a. gegen die valentinianische Gnosis gerichtete Schrift *Adversus haereses* des Irenaeus von Lyon (→ Eirenaios [2]). Ausgehend von der geschichtlichen Entwicklung des Gnostizismus bietet sie um 180 in fünf Büchern, auf reichem Quellenmaterial basierend, eine systematische, auf kirchlicher Theologie beruhende Widerlegung seiner Lehren. Weitere Traktate gehen auf → Hippolytos von Rom (*Refutatio omnium haeresium*) und → Tertullianus (Grundlagenwerk: *De praescriptione haereticorum*; Einzelschriften: *Adversus Marcionem* u. a.) zurück.

Auf diese aufbauend, sind spätere H. geprägt von der Tendenz zur schematisierenden Zusammenstellung der Glaubensirrtümer und ihrer Urheber (»Ketzerkataloge«). Einen Höhepunkt bildet → Epiphanios [1] von Salamis (gest. 403), der in seinem *Panárion* (›Arzneikasten‹) 80 Arten von Häresie, davon 20 vorchristl. Formen, darstellt. Weitere Autoren mit einschlägigen Schriften sind (in Auswahl): → Theodoretos von Kyrrhos (*Haereticarum fabularum compendium*), Philastrius von Brescia (*Diversarum haereseon liber*), → Augustinus (*De haeresibus*, unvollendet), → Iohannes von Damaskos (*Perí hairéseōn* als zweiter Teil seines Hauptwerkes *Pēgḗ gnṓseōs*).

→ Apologien; Polemik

1 N. Brox, s. v. Häresie, RAC 13, 248–297 2 Eresia ed eresiologia nella Chiesa antica: XIII Incontro di Studiosi dell'Antichità Cristiana, 1985 (Augustinianum 25/3, 583–903) 3 A. Hilgenfeld, Die Ketzergesch. des Urchristentums, urkundlich dargestellt, 1884 (Ndr. 1963) 4 A. Schindler, s. v. Häresie II., TRE 14, 318–341, bes. 322–326. J. Ri.

Hafen, Hafenanlagen A. Allgemeines B. Griechenland und Hellenismus C. Rom D. Wirtschaftliche Bedeutung von Häfen E. Häfen in der Literatur

A. Allgemeines

Hafenanlagen waren landfeste Bauten (Molen, Wellenbrecher und Hafenbecken), die dem Schutz von Schiffen vor Brandung und Sturm dienten und gleichzeitig den Ladebetrieb sowie die Lagerung der Fracht (Speicher) erleichtern sollten. In den Schiffshäusern (νεώσοικοι, *navalia*) der ant. Kriegshäfen wurden die Kriegsschiffe zw. den Einsätzen gelagert. Ant. Handelshäfen waren der Standort von Annona- und Zollbehörden, von Vereinigungen der Schiffseigner, Kaufleute und Hafenarbeiter, von Seegerichten, Geldwechslern, Heiligtümern, Gaststätten und Bordellen.

H. waren im Mittelmeerraum, in dem der überregionale Güteraustausch auf die Seewege angewiesen war, bedeutende Wirtschaftszentren und für die Versorgung von Städten und Heiligtümern mit Lebensmitteln, Baumaterial, Rohstoffen und Holz sowie für den Reiseverkehr notwendig. Spätestens seit dem 6. Jh. v. Chr. gewannen sie außerdem an Bedeutung als Stützpunkte der Kriegsflotten. Voraussetzung für die Entstehung von H. und Hafenanlagen war einerseits die Küstenform, etwa das Fehlen von natürlichen H., andererseits der Bau von größeren Schiffen. Strandhäfen blieben bis ins 1. Jt. v. Chr. durchaus verbreitet – möglichst an beiden Seiten einer Halbinsel, um bei jeder Wetterlage Schutz vor Sturm und Brandung zu haben (vgl. etwa Hom. Od. 6,263 ff.).

B. Griechenland und Hellenismus

Der älteste arch. nachgewiesene H., ein Becken in Theben-West (Birkat Habu) am Nil aus dem 2. Jt. v. Chr., zeigt ebenso wie Hafendarstellungen, daß die Nilschiffahrt im Alten Ägypten H. erforderte. Im 2. Jt. v. Chr. schufen phönikische Städte H., wie sie jetzt erstmals auf Kreta nachgewiesen wurden (z. B. in Amnissos und Kommos). Für diese Zeit bezeugen die Wracks von Ulu Burun und von Kap Gelidonya in Lykien die Schiffahrt im östl. Mittelmeerraum. Der in der Bronzezeit bereits hochentwickelte Seeverkehr im östl. Mittelmeer brach um 1200 v. Chr. zusammen und hatte erst nach dem 8. Jh. v. Chr. wieder ein Niveau, das H. erforderte. Eine imponierende bautechnische Leistung war im 6. Jh. v. Chr. der Bau des Hafens von → Samos mit einer ca. 300 m langen Mole und mit Schiffshäusern für die Kriegsflotte des Polykrates (Hdt. 3,45; 3,60); dieser H. war bereits in die Stadtbefestigung integriert. Die beiden H. von Korinth wurden wahrscheinlich im 6. Jh. v. Chr. durch den Diolkos, einen Schleppweg, über den Isthmos miteinander verbunden.

Der H. von Athen lag bis zum frühen 5. Jh. v. Chr. an der flachen Bucht von Phaleron. Auf Initiative des Themistokles befestigten die Athener in der Zeit der Perserkriege den → Peiraieus, der drei als H. geeignete Buchten besaß, und bauten die Halbinsel zum Handels- und Krieghafen aus (Hdt. 6,116; Thuk. 1,93,3; Paus. 1,1,2; Plut. Themistokles 19,3). Unter Kimon wurden die »Langen Mauern« (μακρὰ τείχη) begonnen, die Athen und den Peiraieus miteinander verbanden. Athen und sein H. stellten somit eine einzige Festung dar, die auf dem Seeweg versorgt werden konnte (Plut. Kimon 13,6; Thuk. 1,107,1; 1,108,3; 2,13,6f.; 7,28,1; Strab. 9,1,15). In klass. Zeit dienten die beiden kleineren Buchten im Osten als Stützpunkt der Kriegsflotte (H. von Munychia und von Zea); hier befanden sich mehr als 250 Schiffshäuser und die Skeuothek des Philon (nach 350 v. Chr.), eine langgestreckte Halle, in der die Ruder und andere Ausrüstungsgegenstände der Trieren gelagert wurden (vgl. Syll.[3] 969). Der Kantharos-Hafen im Westen war der Handelshafen von Athen, der durch die Halbinsel Eetioneia vom offenen Meer getrennt war. In unmittelbarer Nähe lagen eine große Stoa (Thuk. 8,90,5), die wahrscheinlich als Getreidespeicher diente, und das Deigma (Xen. hell. 5,1,21), ein Handelszentrum. Das Emporion an der Ostseite des Kantharos-H. war durch eine Mauer von der Stadt abgegrenzt. Megara war ebenfalls mit dem H. Nisaia durch »lange Mauern« verbunden, die im 1. Peloponnesischen Krieg von den Athenern errichtet worden waren (Thuk. 1,103,4). Welche Bedeutung im 5. Jh. v. Chr. einem günstigen H. beigemessen wurde, zeigt vor allem der Synoikismos der Städte auf der Insel Rhodos 411–408 v. Chr. (Diod. 13,75,1); die neue Stadt → Rhodos wurde nach dem Vorbild des Peiraieus (Strab. 14,2,9) an der Nordspitze der Insel erbaut, wo es möglich war, zwei H. anzulegen; der größere H. war vor dem Meer durch eine Mole geschützt, die während der Belagerung durch Demetrios Poliorketes 305 v. Chr. heftig umkämpft war (Diod. 20,85,4–88,8).

Im Hell. wurden mit großem technischem Aufwand künstliche H. angelegt. Herausragendes Beispiel hierfür ist → Alexandreia, wo durch einen sieben Stadien langen Damm (Heptastadion) zw. dem Festland und der vorgelagerten Pharos-Insel zwei geschützte H. geschaffen wurden, im Osten der »Große H.«, im Westen der Eunostos-H.; hier wurde ein weiteres Hafenbecken ausgeschachtet (Kibotos-H.). Weitere Hafenanlagen gehörten zu den königlichen Palästen auf der Lochias-Halbinsel. Das Emporion und die Schiffshäuser erstreckten sich im »Großen Hafen« von der Mole des Antonius bis zum Heptastadion. Der zu Beginn des 3. Jh. v. Chr. errichtete Leuchtturm stand am östl. Ende der Insel → Pharos, nach der er auch seinen Namen erhielt (Strab. 17,1,6–10; Plin. nat. 36,83). Der Pharos wurde in der Ant. Vorbild aller späteren Leuchttürme.

Die von den Karthagern angelegten H. waren oft ausgeschachtete, mit Steinblöcken eingefaßte Becken, die durch einen Kanal mit dem Meer verbunden waren (κώθων); solche H. sind für Motye auf Sizilien und für Karthago selbst arch. belegt. In Karthago handelt es sich um ein rechteckiges Becken, das als Handelshafen diente, und um den dahinter liegenden, kreisförmigen Kriegshafen mit einer runden Insel in der Mitte und über 200 Schiffshäusern an beiden Seiten; wahrscheinlich stammt diese Anlage aus dem 4. Jh. v. Chr. (Strab. 17,3,14).

C. Rom

Das Wachstum der Stadt Rom erforderte schon früh den Ausbau von H. und Hafenanlagen, wobei die Bauaktivitäten sich nach dem 2. Pun. Krieg zunächst auf das Emporium am Tiber in unmittelbarer Nähe der Stadt konzentrierten (Liv. 35,10,12; 35,41,10). Die Censoren ließen 179 und 174 v. Chr. das Emporium vor der Porta Trigemina erweitern und dort Portiken errichten (Liv. 40,51,6; 41,27,8); zu diesen Bauten gehörte auch die *porticus Aemilia*, die mit dem großen Speicherkomplex südlich des Aventin identifiziert wird. Allerdings verfügte Rom in der Zeit der Republik nicht über einen für Getreideschiffe geeigneten Seehafen an der Tibermündung. Das Getreide aus den Provinzen wurde nach → Puteoli gebracht, dessen H. in augusteischer Zeit durch den Bau einer 370 m langen und 15 m breiten Mole erweitert wurde; die Mole von Puteoli war kein Steindamm, sondern bestand aus 15 durch Bögen miteinander verbundenen Pfeilern. Als Baumaterial wurde Gußmörtel (*opus caementicium*) verwendet, der unter Wasser erhärtet (Strab. 5,4,6; Vitr. 2,6; 5,12; Plin. nat. 35,166; Cass. Dio 48,51,4). Erst Claudius veranlaßte nach einer Hungerrevolte in Rom den Bau eines monumentalen Molenhafens an der Tibermündung. Als Fundament für die Molen und den Leuchtturm dienten Frachtschiffe, die versenkt wurden; dazu zählte auch jenes Schiff, das unter Gaius zum Transport eines Obelisken von Ägypten nach Rom eingesetzt worden war (Tac. ann. 12,43; Suet. Claud. 18; 20; Plin. nat. 16,201 f.; 36,70; Cass. Dio 60,11,1–5). Das Projekt Neros, einen Kanal von Puteoli nach Rom zu bauen und auf diese Weise einen sicheren Binnenschiffahrtsweg für die Getreideversorgung zu schaffen, mußte hingegen aufgegeben werden (Tac. ann. 15,42,2). Traianus ergänzte den unter Claudius angelegten H. später landeinwärts durch ein ausgeschachtetes sechseckiges Becken. Portus (»der H.«) wurde mit seinen zahlreichen Lagerhallen und Verwaltungsbauten zum Zentrum der Annona. Das Getreide wurde in Portus auf Treidelkähne (*caudicariae*) umgeladen und auf dem Tiber nach Rom transportiert, wo der Flußhafen in der Prinzipatszeit weiter ausgebaut wurde.

Die Bautätigkeit röm. Magistrate oder der Principes beschränkte sich keineswegs auf die Stadt Rom, sondern galt auch It. und den Provinzen. 179 v. Chr. ließ der Censor M. Aemilius Lepidus bei Tarracina eine Mole errichten (Liv. 40,51,2), und Nero sorgte dafür, daß sein Geburtsort Antium einen großzügigen H. erhielt (Suet. Nero 9). Unter Traianus wurden die H. von Centumcellae (Plin. epist. 6,31,15–17) und Ancona ausgebaut. Zahlreiche Hafenbauten und insbes. Leuchttürme wie die von La Coruña (Brigantium; vgl. Oros. 1,2,71) oder von Dover sind Zeugnisse für die röm. Bautätigkeit in den Provinzen: Zu den Bauten des Septimius Severus, die → Leptis Magna ein neues Gesicht verliehen, gehörte ein Hafenbecken mit Lagerhallen und einem Leuchtturm. Die Einfahrt röm. H. konnte mit Ketten versperrt werden, wofür man mechanische Geräte (*machinae*) einsetzte (Vitr. 5,12,1). Klientelkönige folgten dem röm. Vorbild; so ordnete König Herodes ca. 20 v. Chr. den Bau des Hafens von Caesarea Maritima an; an offener Küste wurde durch Molen ein geschütztes Hafenbecken geschaffen, wobei bereits die Gußmörteltechnik angewendet wurde, ein Beleg dafür, wie schnell *opus caementicium* als Baustoff im Mittelmeerraum eine weite Verbreitung fand (vgl. Ios. bell. Iud. 1,408–415).

Die Binnenschiffahrt auf den großen Flüssen in den nordwestl. Provinzen war ebenfalls auf Anlegestellen und H. angewiesen. Gerade an Rhein und Donau sind eine Vielzahl von Kaianlagen arch. nachgewiesen. In Köln befand sich der röm. H. gut geschützt zw. der Stadt und der vorgelagerten Rheininsel. Für derartige Kaianlagen wurden häufig Eichenstämme verwendet, so etwa in Xanten oder in London. In der Spätant. wurden an Grenzflüssen Anlegestellen oft landseits durch Mauern geschützt, während am feindlichen Ufer eine Turmfestung errichtet wurde. In der Prinzipatszeit waren die röm. Flotten nicht in den großen Handelshäfen stationiert, sondern verfügten über eigene Stützpunkte in Misenum (Strab. 5,4,5 f.; Cass. Dio 48,50) und Ravenna.

H. wurden oft durch Denkmäler oder aufwendige Bauten repräsentativ ausgestaltet; wahrscheinlich stand die monumentale Statue des Helios von Rhodos am Eingang des Hafens und vermittelte so einen Eindruck von dem Reichtum der Stadt. Auf jeder Seite der Hafeneinfahrt von Caesarea Maritima wurden drei Kolosse aufgestellt (Ios. bell. Iud. 1,413). In röm. H. – etwa in Ancona – verwiesen Ehrenbogen und Inschr. auf den Auftraggeber, wobei auch der Zweck des Baus genannt wird (*quod accessum Italiae hoc etiam addito ex pecunia sua portu tutiorem navigantibus reddiderit*; CIL IX 5894 = ILS 298). Die Fertigstellung der H. an der Tibermündung wurde im Münzbild gefeiert. Der Bau von Hafenanlagen fand durchaus Beachtung und Bewunderung in der Öffentlichkeit; so wurde etwa die Mole von Puteoli in Epigrammen gerühmt (Anth. Gr. 7,379; 9,708).

Es bestand in den von den Meeresströmungen abgeschlossenen Hafenbecken immer die Gefahr der Versandung. Aus diesem Grund ruhte die Mole von Puteoli auf großen Pfeilern, um so die Wasserströmung zu erhalten; in Cosa führten Kanäle strömendes Wasser in den H., und die H. an der Tibermündung waren durch einen Kanal mit dem Fluß verbunden. Für Ephesos sind wiederholte Versuche, den H. offen zu halten, belegt (Tac. ann. 16,23,1; IEph I a 23).

D. Wirtschaftliche Bedeutung von Häfen

Während die H. von Athen und Rom primär die Funktion hatten, die Versorgung der städtischen Bevölkerung zu sichern, gab es auch Hafenstädte, die vorrangig Güter aus dem Hinterland exportierten. Gades etwa, das durch Cornelius Balbus einen neuen H. erhalten hatte, war für den Export von Getreide, Wein und Öl aus der Provinz Baetica nach Rom wichtig (Strab. 3,2,4–6; 3,5,3); Alexandreia soll mehr Güter exportiert als importiert haben (Strab. 17,1,7). Andere Hafenstädte waren Zentren des Handels mit Regionen außerhalb des Imperium Romanum; dies gilt etwa für Aquileia, das im Austausch mit dem Donauraum eine entscheidende Rolle spielte (Strab. 5,1,8); Ausgangspunkt des Indienhandels war die Hafenstadt Myos Hormos am Roten Meer (peripl. maris Erythraei 1; Strab. 2,5,12; 17,1,45). Welchen Umfang der Güteraustausch in den H. annahm, geht aus der Höhe der Hafenzölle hervor, die Anfang des 4. Jh. v. Chr. im Peiraieus für 36 Talente (216000 Drachmen; And. 1,133 ff.) verpachtet wurden: demnach belief sich der Wert der im Peiraieus importierten oder exportierten Güter auf ca. 1800 Talente (10,8 Mio. Drachmen). Die Hafenzölle trugen erheblich zu den Einnahmen ant. Städte bei; sie werden in diesem Zusammenhang bei Ps.-Aristoteles ausdrücklich erwähnt ([Ps.]Aristot. oec. 1346a). Bevor Delos von den Römern zum Freihafen erklärt wurde, stammte der größte Teil der öffentlichen Einnahmen von Rhodos aus solchen Zöllen (1 Mio. Drachmen; Pol. 31,7,10).

E. Häfen in der Literatur

In der polit. Theorie wurde die Frage, ob die Nähe zum Meer und zu einem H. vorteilhaft für eine Polis sei, unterschiedlich beurteilt. Während Platon die mit einem H. verbundenen Handelsaktivitäten und Geldgeschäfte als eine Gefahr für die Stadt sieht und folgerichtig Beschränkungen für Import und Export empfiehlt (Plat. leg. 704d–705b; 847b–e), hält Aristoteles eine Verbindung zum Meer eher für günstig, da nur so alle wichtigen Güter leicht beschafft werden könnten (Aristot. pol. 1327a). Cicero schließlich zählt Ausgaben für *navalia* und *portus* zu den sinnvollen Aufwendungen für die *res publica* (Cic. off. 2,60). Zur Topik ant. Lobreden gehört auch der Hinweis auf den H. und die Vielfalt der angebotenen Waren (Peiraieus: Isokr. or. 4,42; Portus: Aristeid. 26,11–13; vgl. zu Antiocheia auch Lib. or. 11,34–41). Plinius führt im Panegyrikos den Bau von H. unter den Verdiensten des Herrschers auf (Plin. paneg. 29,2). Vor allem bautechnische Aspekte der Anlage von H. behandelt Vitruvius in seiner Architekturtheorie (Vitr. 5,12). Unter den bildlichen Darstellungen röm. H. sind neben den Münzen das Relief im Museo Torlonia (Portus, ca. 200 n. Chr.) und ein Wandgemälde aus Stabiae (H. von Puteoli, 1. Jh. n. Chr., jetzt Neapel, NM) zu nennen.

→ Alexandreia; Binnenschiffahrt; Caesarea Maritima; Horrea; Karthago; Leptis Magna (mit Abb.); Ostia (mit Abb.); Peiraieus; Portus; Puteoli; Rhodos

1 R. Bartoccini, Il porto romano di Leptis Magna, 1958 **2** D. J. Blackman, Ancient Harbours in the Mediterranean, in: International Journ. of Nautical Archaeology 11, 1982, 79–104; 185–211 **3** Casson, Ships, 361–370 **4** L. Casson, Harbour and River Boats of ancient Rome, in: JRS 55, 1965, 31–39 **5** F. Castagnoli, Installazioni portuali a Roma, in: D'Arms/Kopff, 35–42 **6** A. M. Colini, Il porto fluviale del Foro Boario a Roma, in: D'Arms/Kopff, 43–53 **7** O. Höckmann, Ant. Seefahrt, 1985, 144–156 **8** G. W. Houston, Ports in Perspective: Some Comparative Materials on Roman Merchant Ships and Ports, in: AJA 92, 1988, 553–564 **9** J. Le Gall, Le Tibre fleuve de Rome dans l'antiquité, 1953 **10** K. Lehmann-Hartleben, Die ant. Hafenanlagen des Mittelmeeres, 1923 **11** A. M. McCann, J. Bourgeois, E. K. Gazda, The Roman port and fishery of Cosa, 1987 **12** R. Meiggs, Roman Ostia, ²1973 **13** G. Milne, The Port of Roman London, 1985 **14** J. P. Oleson, G. Branton, The Technology of King Herod's harbour, in: R. L. Vann (Hrsg.), Caesarea Papers, JRA Suppl. 5, 1992, 49–67 **15** A. Raban (Hrsg.), Harbour Archaeology, British Archaeological Reports, International Series 257, 1985 **16** J. W. Shaw, Bronze age Aegean harboursides, in: D. A. Hardy (Hrsg.), Thera and the Aegean World, 3, 1990, 420–436 **17** J. W. Shaw, Greek and Roman harbourworks, in: G. F. Bass (Hrsg.), A History of Seafaring Based on Underwater Archaeology, 1972, 87–112 **18** O. Testaguzza, Portus, 1970 **19** Travlos, Attica, 258–287; 340–363 **20** White, Technology, 104–110.

O.H.

Hafer. Der wilde und der kultivierte H. (Avena sativa L., βρόμος/*brómos*, *avena*) fand in der Ant. im Gegensatz zur Gerste (→ Getreide) in der Ernährung nur gelegentlich, etwa als Mehl für Graupen und diätetischen Brei (Hippokr. De victu 2,7(= 43) und Plin. nat. 22,137), meist jedoch als Viehfutter (grün oder in Form von Heu: Colum. 2,10,32) Verwendung. Dioskurides (mit guter Beschreibung 2,94 p. 1, 172 f. Wellmann = 2,116 p. 203 Berendes) empfiehlt den Brei gegen Durchfall und den Schleim daraus gegen Husten. Meistens gilt er, anders als bei den daraus ihren H.-Brei bereitenden Germanen (vgl. Plin. nat. 18,149 f.), nur als Unkraut (Theophr. h. plant. 8,9,2; Verg. georg. 1,154).

→ Getreide C.HÜ.

Hagesarchos aus Megalopolis, Vater des kyprischen Strategen Ptolemaios (PP 6,14778), selbst ptolem. *stratēgós epí Kariās* (στρατηγὸς ἐπὶ Καρίας) unter Ptolemaios III., war auch für Samos zuständig; 225/4 v. Chr. als eponymer Offizier einer Militäreinheit belegt.

K. Hallof, Ch. Mileta, Samos und Ptolemaios III., in: Chiron 27, 1997, 255–283, bes. 268 ff. W.A.

Haggada. Der Terminus *H.* (abgeleitet vom *Hif'il* der hebr. Wz. *ngd* – »sagen, erzählen«) bzw. dessen aram. Äquivalent *Aggada* bezeichnet sämtliche nicht-halakhischen Überlieferungen der rabbinischen Lit. und ist somit ein Sammelbegriff für alle im weitesten Sinne narrativen Stoffe dieses umfangreichen Literaturcorpus. Eine solch negative Definition des Begriffes findet sich bereits im MA bei Šmuel ha-Nagid (993–1055): ›Haggada ist jede Auslegung im Talmud, zu jedwedem Thema, das nicht Gebot ist.‹ Dabei kommt wesensmäßig der Schriftauslegung, die ihrerseits wiederum auf ganz spezifischen hermeneutischen und methodischen Prämissen basiert (vgl. die sog. 32 Middot des Rabbi Eliezer), ganz bes. Bed. zu. Zu den zentralen Themen dieser Aus-

legungen, die den Text der biblischen Erzählungen – oft bis hin zu einzelnen Worten, auffälligen Ausdrücken und Schreibweisen – narrativ ausschmücken und ausdeuten, zählen die a) Einheit und Einzigkeit Gottes, b) die Bed. der Tora als einer Offenbarung Gottes an sein Volk, c) die Liebe Gottes zu Israel, die in der Vorstellung von der *sympátheia theú* ihren sinnfälligsten Ausdruck findet, d) Israels baldige Befreiung von der verhaßten röm. Fremdherrschaft sowie e) der Glaube an eine gerechte Weltordnung, die – trotz aller anders erscheinenden Wirklichkeit – dem Frommen seinen Lohn nicht versagen wird. Neben diese Kommentarlit. treten aber auch andere lit. Gattungen wie Erzählungen, Anekdoten, Märchen, Fabeln, Sprichwörter usw., die unter diesem Begriff subsumiert werden. Dabei ergänzen sich Paränese und Paraklese in komplementärer Art und Weise: Das Studium und das Befolgen der Tora sowie die Praxis des Gebetes und Taten der Nächstenliebe werden eingeschärft, gleichzeitig wird eine Zukunft verheißen, in der Israel in unmittelbarer Gottesgemeinschaft ohne Not und Unterdrückung leben kann. Als wichtigste H.-Sammlungen sind die verschiedenen Midraš-Werke zu nennen wie u. a. der Midraš Rabba (zum Pentateuch und den Megillot), die Pesiqta Rabbati, die Pesiqta de Rav Kahana oder Midraš Tanchuma, deren Überlieferungen im Zeitraum vom 4. Jh. n. Chr. bis ins frühe MA zusammengestellt wurde. Aber auch die beiden Talmude, der palästinische und v. a. der babylon. Talmud, enthalten zahlreiche haggadische Überlieferungen.
→ Halakha; Midraš; Mišna; Talmud; Tosefta

H. Bietenhard, s. v. H., TRE 30 (30), 351–354 • L. Ginzberg, The Legends of the Jews, 1909–1938 • G. Stemberger, Der Talmud. Einführung, Texte, Erläuterungen, 1982, 158–285. B. E.

Hagia Irini A. Lage B. Archäologische Reste

A. Lage
Beim h. Dorf H. I. an der NW-Küste Zyperns (→ Kypros) finden sich Reste einer ant. Hafenstadt, besiedelt von der späten Bronze- bis in die mittlere Kaiserzeit. Am Altar eines extraurbanen Heiligtums wurde eine große Zahl von Tonvotiven *in situ* gefunden.

E. Gjerstadt et al., Ajia Irini, in: The Swedish Cyprus Expedition, Bd. 2, 1935, 642–824 • L. Quilici et al., Rapporti di scavo ad Aghia Irini. Studi ciprioti e rapporti di scavo 1, 1971, 9–170 • S. Törnquist, Arms, Armour and Dress of the Terracotta Sculpture from Ajia Irini, Cyprus, in: Medelhavsmuseet Bulletin 6, 1972, 7–55. R. SE.

B. Archäologische Reste
Das Heiligtum (Fruchtbarkeitskult) von H. I. stammt vom Ende der Spät-Brz. und wurde mit Umbauten der kypro-geom. Zeit bis um 500 v. Chr. genutzt; Wiederbelebung des Kults in hell. Zeit. Schwedische Grabungen (1929/1930) erbrachten neben Architekturresten eine Fülle von Skulptur (meist aus → Terrakotta) versch. Größe aus allen Epochen (u. a. phöniz. *ex votos*, Belege für kypro-ägypt. Stil und ion. Einflüsse). Abseits des Heiligtums Reste der städtischen Siedlung ab kypro-archa. Zeit. Ital. Grabungen (seit 1970) in der Küstennekropole Palaiokastro legten viele Gräber der Spät-Brz., mit Wiederbenutzung in archa. Zeit, frei (reiche Keramikfunde, u. a. myk., griech. und ost-griech. Importe, phöniz. Inschr.). Weitere Nekropolen mit protogeom. Keramik und syro-palästin. Einfluß.

V. Karageorghis, Archaeology in Cyprus 1960–1985, The Cyprus Dept. of Antiquities 1935–1983, 1985. A. W.

Hagia Sophia. Bedeutendste Kirche Konstantinopels. Sie wurde am Ort der 532 n. Chr. in einem Aufstand zerstörten Kirche Μεγάλη Ἐκκλησία (*Megálē Ekklēsía*; 1. H. 4. Jh.) auf Betreiben und Kosten Iustinians nach Entwürfen der Architekten Anthemios von Tralles und → Isidoros [9] von Milet als riesig dimensionierte Kombination von Langhaus und → Zentralbau errichtet. Die gewaltige Kuppel lastet auf vier in den Fels gegründeten Pfeilern. Am 27. 12. 537 im Beisein des Kaisers geweiht (Prok. aed. 1,1,20–78; Malalas 479 B), stürzte die Kuppel im Frühsommer 558 ein, wobei von der arch. Forsch. häufig ein Zusammenhang mit dem Erdbeben vom Dezember 557 vermutet wurde. Der Bau einer → Kuppel beruhte indessen weiterhin nicht auf statischer Berechnung, sondern auf einem »Trial and Error«-Verfahren, und die markanten Veränderungen im Profil des Kuppelneubaus geben Grund für die Annahme, der Kuppeleinsturz sei eher durch eine zu flache Einwölbung und die dadurch entstandenen zu hohen Schubkräfte verursacht gewesen.

Der Wiederaufbau der Kuppel unter Leitung des jüngeren → Isidoros [10] sorgte bei einem Durchmesser von ca. 33 m (der Kuppel-Grundriß weicht dabei markant von der Kreisform ab) für ein um nahezu 7 m steileres Profil über einer zusätzlich verstärkten Tragkonstruktion. Die Gestalt der Kirche ist aus einem anläßlich der Neueinweihung (24. 12. 563) verfaßten, den Bau ausführlich beschreibenden Gedicht des → Paulos Silentiarios bis in Details hinein bekannt; die reiche Ausstattung der Spätant. mit Mosaiken, Fresken und → Inkrustationen ist jedoch wegen der zahlreichen späteren Veränderungen und Erweiterungen an Architektur und Dekoration, die sich bis ins 12. Jh. erstreckten, nur noch zu kleinen Teilen erhalten.

Während der westl. Eroberung im Zuge des Vierten Kreuzzuges (1204) geplündert und anschließend latinisiert, wurde der Bau nach der Rückgewinnung der Stadt 1261 wieder für den orthodoxen Ritus hergerichtet; unmittelbar nach der islamischen Eroberung Konstantinopels durch Mehmet II. (29. 5. 1453) wurde die H. S. zur Hauptmoschee der Stadt umfunktioniert.

C. Fossati, U. Peschlow, Die H. S.: nach dem Tafelwerk von 1852, 1980 • H. Kähler, Die H. S., 1967 • A. Kleinert, Die Inkrustationen der H. S., 1979 • W. Kleiss, Beobachtungen zur H. S. in Istanbul, in: MDAI (Ist) 15, 1965, 168–185 • R. Mark, A. S. Cakmak (Hrsg.),

H. S. from the Age of Justinian to the Present, 1992 • W. Müller-Wiener, Bildlex. zur Top. Istanbuls, 1977, 84–96 • O. Veh, W. Pülhorn (edd.), Prokop, Bauten. Paulos Silentiarios, Beschreibung der H. S., 1977. C. HÖ.

Hagia Thekla (Ἁγία Θέκλα), h. Ayatekla, Meriamlik. Bedeutende, stadtartig ausgebaute Wallfahrtsstätte mit Stadtmauer, Zisternen, einem Aquädukt und mehreren monumentalen Kirchen (Klöstern) südl. von Seleukeia am Kalykadnos in West-Kilikia mit Kulttradition zu älteren Heiligtümern des Apollon Sarpedonios, der Athene und der Artemis (als πότνια Θηρῶν, »Herrin der Tiere«). Neben den apokryphen Akten (*Pauli et*) *Theclae* sind Vita und Miracula der Hl. Thekla aus der Mitte des 4. Jh. erh. [1]. Gregorios von Nazianzos weilte hier 376–379, die Nonne Egeria 384. Kaiser Zenon ließ nach 476 eine neue Kirche für die Hl. Thekla (über deren Grabhöhle?) bauen. Mit dem Ende der christl.-armen. Herrschaft in Kilikien (1375) verlor sich die Erinnerung an die Heilige. Der ON *Meriamlik* bedeutet »Ort der Hl. Maria«.

1 G. Dagron, Vie et miracles de Sainte Thècle, 1978.

F. Hild, H. Hellenkemper, Kilikien und Isaurien, TIB 5, 441–443 • H. Hellenkemper, Frühe christl. Wallfahrtsstätten in Kleinasien, in: Akt. XII. Int. Kongr. für christl. Arch. (JbAC Erg. Bd. 20,1, 1995), 262–264. F. H.

Hagiographie
s. Acta Sanctorum; Literatur (christlich)

Hagnias (Ἁγνίας). Vater des → Tiphys, des Steuermanns der → Argo, rekonstruiert aus dem Patronymikon Hagniades (Apoll. Rhod. 1,105; 560; Orph. Arg. 122; 542; 690; Apollod. 1,111). J. S.-A.

Hagnon (Ἅγνων).
[1] Vater des Theramenes [1. 191], 440 v. Chr. *stratēgós* im Krieg Athens gegen das aufständische Samos (Thuk. 1,117,2). H. gründete 437/6 Amphipolis (Thuk. 4,102,3; 5,11,1). Zu Beginn des Peloponnesischen Krieges übte er 431/0 und 429/8 erneut das Strategenamt aus (Thuk. 2,58,1; 6,31,2; 2,95,3 [2. 117, 121]). Nach Plutarch (Perikles 32) zählte er zu den Gegnern des → Perikles. Im April 421 unterzeichnete er neben anderen den Friedensvertrag (sog. Nikias-Frieden) zwischen Athen und Sparta (Thuk. 5,19,2; 24,1). Nach der sizilischen Katastrophe wurde H. in einen Rat aus älteren Männern gewählt (Lys. 12,65), die ›jeweils nach dem Gebot der Stunde wichtige Angelegenheiten vorberaten sollten‹ (Thuk. 8,1,3). Traill, PAA 107380.

1 S. Hornblower, Commentary on Thucydides, 1, 1991
2 Develin. W. W.

[2] aus Teos, einer der → Hetairoi von → Alexandros [4]. Die Quellen berichten von ihm hauptsächlich Luxus und Schmeichelei. Für Kriegsdienst war er kaum tauglich.

Berve 2, Nr. 17. E. B.

[3] aus Tarsos. Einer der wohl älteren Schüler des → Karneades, der für einen beträchtlichen Teil der Vorlesungsmitschriften seines Lehrers verantwortlich zeichnet (Philod. index Academicorum XXIII 4); Cic. ac. 2,16 hält ihn für gleichrangig mit Kleitomachos. In der bei Quint. 2,17,15 bezeugten Anklageschrift gegen die Rhet. spiegelt sich die zu dieser Zeit in der Akademie verbreitete rhetorikkritische Haltung. In welchem wiss.-systematischen Zusammenhang einzelne wohl H. zuzuweisende Äußerungen (Athen. 13,602d; Plut. De sollertia animalium 12,968d und Schol. Hom. Il. 4,101) stehen, läßt sich nicht mehr angeben. K.-H. S.

Hagnonides (Ἁγνωνίδης). Sohn des Nikoxenos aus Pergase. 325/4 v. Chr. Antragsteller in einer Seeurkunde (IG II2 1629a 14f.); wurde im Verlauf der Harpalos-Affäre von Deinarchos (Hyp. in Demosthenem 40; Dion. Hal. de Dinarcho, 10f.) angeklagt. Nach der Niederlage Athens 322 konnte der verbannte H. auf Vermittlung Phokions auf der Peloponnes bleiben. H. betrieb allerdings später dessen Hinrichtung (Mai 318; Plut. Phokion 33–37; Nepos Phocion 3,3). Noch 318/7 als Antragsteller belegt (IG II2 448B Z. 39), wurde er nach 317 zum Tode verurteilt (Plut. Phokion 38). (Evtl. der Ankläger des Philosophen Theophrast?, s. Diog. Laert. 5,37). PA 176; Traill, PAA 107455.

Habicht 58ff. BO. D.

Hagnus (Ἁγνοῦς, urspr. Ἀγνοῦς). Att. Mesogeia-Demos der Phyle Akamantis, ab 307/6 v. Chr. der Demetrias, ab 200/199 v. Chr. der Attalis; er stellte fünf → *buleutaí*. Früher bei Dankla östl. Markopulo lokalisiert [1. 48], jetzt südwestl. bei Dardiste [2. 132] aufgrund des FO des Demendekrets IG II² 1083, das in dieser Sammlung irrtümlich Myrrhinus zugeschrieben ist. Leon, der Theseus den Hinterhalt der Pallantiden bei Gargettos verraten hatte, erhielt in H. Kult (Steph. Byz. s. v. Ἀ.) [3. 12]. Der alte Zwist galt als ursächlich für das Heiratsverbot mit Pallene (Plut. Theseus 13,2f.) [3. 224[5]].

1 Traill, Attica 9, 48, 67, 110 Nr. 48, Tab. 5, 12, 14 2 Ders., Demos and Trittys, 1986, 132 3 Whitehead, Index s. v. H. H. LO.

Hahn s. Huhn

Hahnenkampf A. Verbreitung und Beliebtheit B. Organisation und Ablauf

A. Verbreitung und Beliebtheit
H. sind belegt vom 5. Jh. v. Chr. bis in die röm. Kaiserzeit (frühester Beleg bei Pind. O. 12,14, spätester bei Herodian. 3,10,3). Sie waren bes. bei den Griechen beliebt [1. 117; 2. 82–92]: Kampfhähne galten als Musterbeispiel für Siegeswillen (Ail. var. 2,28); in dieser Funktion sind sie auf den panathenäischen Preisamphoren abgebildet [3. 34] (→ Panathenäische Amphoren), bei

Aischyl. Eum. 861 symbolisieren sie die Kriegswut (Hahn als »Vogel des Ares« bei Aristoph. Av. 835), ihre Aggressivität war sprichwörtlich (H.-Metaphern bei Aristoph. Ach. 166; Equ. 494). Aristophanes ließ in der ersten Fassung der ›Wolken‹ die beiden streitenden »Reden« (*lógoi*) als Kampfhähne verkleidet gegeneinander antreten [4. 90–93; 5]. Die Römer mochten H. weniger; sie galten als typisch griech. und als Kinderspiel (Colum. 8,2,5) [1. 122].

B. Organisation und Ablauf

In Athen fanden seit dem Ende der Perserkriege im Dionysostheater gesetzlich festgeschriebene H. statt (Ail. var. 2,28), bei denen alle wehrfähigen jungen Männer zuschauen mußten (Lukian. Anacharsis 37); daneben waren H. ein beliebtes Freizeitvergnügen. Sie wurden in Spielhallen (Aischin. Tim. 53), Kneipen oder auf freien Plätzen, bes. in Gymnasien, ausgetragen. Man züchtete spezielle Kampfhähne; als bes. kampflustig galten solche aus Tanagra (Plin. nat. 10,48). Kampfhähne wurden stundenlang spazierengetragen, weil man glaubte, durch Erschütterungen die Kraft der Tiere zu erhöhen (Plat. leg. 7,789b-d), und mit Knoblauch gefüttert (oder eingerieben: Hesych. s. v. σκοροδίσαι), um ihre Aggressivität zu steigern (Xen. symp. 4,9; schol. zu Aristoph. Ach. 166 und Equ. 494). Zum Kampf wurden die Hähne mit eisernen Sporen (πλῆκτρον) ausgerüstet (schol. zu Aristoph. Av. 759), auf Tische oder Plattformen gesetzt und aufeinander gehetzt. Manchmal starb der unterlegene Hahn (Demosth. or. 54,9); wenn er überlebte, gehörte er dem Sieger (Theokr. 22,71; Aristoph. Av. 70f. mit schol.). Später gab es auch Geldpreise und Wetten, es entstand der Beruf des Trainers für Kampfhähne (Colum. 8,2,5: *rix<i>osarum avium lanista, cuius patrimonium, pignus aleae, victor gallinaceus abstulit* [1. 119f.]).

1 M. Gwyn Morgan, Three non-Roman blood sports, in: CQ 25, 1975, 117–122 2 E. Paraskevaidis, Τὰ παίγνια τῶν ἀρχαίων Ἑλλήνων, in: Platon 41, 1989, 68–92 3 D. G. Kyle, Athletics in Ancient Athens, 1987 4 K. J. Dover, Aristophanes' Clouds, 1968 5 O. Taplin, Phallology, phylakes, iconography and Aristophanes, in: PCPhS 33, 1987, 92–104.

J. Dumont, Les combats de coqs furent-ils un sport?, in: Pallas 34, 1988, 33–44 • H. Hoffmann, H. in Athen, in: RA 1974, 195–220 • K. Schneider, s. v. Hahnenkämpfe, RE 7, 2210–2215 • G. R. Scott, History of Cockfighting, 1957 • D. W. Thompson, A glossary of Greek birds, 1936, 33–37.

S. MÜ.

Hai. Zu dieser Ordnung der Knorpelfische (σελάχη, σελάχια, χονδράκοντα, vgl. Aristot. hist.an. 1,2, 489b 6; Ail. nat. 11,37) bieten die Quellen keine saubere Unterscheidungsmöglichkeit, sondern unterschiedliche Bezeichnungen. Aristoteles kannte zwar die wichtigsten Arten: 1) den Hunds- oder Schweine-H. (κύων, γαλεὸς νεβρίας), 2) den glatten Marder-H. (γαλεὸς λεῖος, Mustelus laevis), 3) den Fuchs-H. oder Meerfuchs (ἀλωπεκίας), 4) den Katzen-H. (σκύλλιον, *scyllium*), 5) den Dorn-H. (ἀκανθίας), 6) den Stern-H. (ἀστερίας, Mustelus vulgaris) und 7) den Blau-H. (καρχαρίας, vielleicht mit πρηστίς, *pristis, pistis* identisch). Doch rechnet Aristot. hist.an. 6,10,565a 14–6,11,566a 19 alle bis auf die haiartigen Nr. 3 und Nr. 1 (γαλεώδη: hist.an. 6,11,566a 31) zu den echten H.; hist.an. 8(9),37,621b 16 unterscheidet aber Nr. 5 von den *galeoí*. Bei Ail. nat. 1,55 gibt es drei Arten von Nr. 1: a) die größten (Blauhai?), b) die mit Flecken (κατεστιγμένοι) und c) die mit Dornen (κεντρίναι = Nr. 5). Man muß daraus schließen, daß *kýōn* (Hund) eine volkstümliche allg. Bezeichnung war wie bei Hom. Od. 12,95f. Ihre Fortpflanzung beschreibt Aristot. 6,10,565 a 15ff.: sie legen Eier, die dann im Mutterleib ausgebrütet werden (vgl. auch Ail. nat. 11,37; Unglaubwürdiges zur Jagd: 1,55).

Nach Paus. 2,34,2 waren sie für Schwimmer gefährlich, Plin. nat. 9,110 sieht nur die *scyllia* als Gefahr für Perlenfischer. Bei Athen. 7,306d erscheint der Hai in Listen von Küchenartikeln bei Komikern (καρχαρίας: 7,294c-e; ἀλωπεκία: 8,356c, aber auch γαλεός oder κύων). Heute ißt man nur noch Nr. 5 (den Dornhai) in Form der geräucherten »Schillerlocken«. Obwohl Erfahrungen mit Haien die Entstehung der Sagen von → Andromeda und → Hesione begünstigt haben, ist das Ungeheuer (κῆτος/*kḗtos*) selten haiähnlich. Die Berliner Hydria Nr. 3238 [3. Bd. 3.2, 2053] weist entsprechende Flossen und Zähne auf.

Als Sensation galt die Wiederentdeckung des seit 1673 nicht mehr beobachteten glatten Marderhais des Aristoteles durch den deutschen Anatomen und Physiologen Johannes Müller (1801–1858) in Material aus dem Mittelmeer im Frühjahr 1840 [1; 2].

1 J. Müller, Über den glatten H. des Aristoteles und über die Verschiedenheiten unter den H. und Rochen in der Entwicklung der Eier, in: Physikalische Abh. 1840, 1842, 187–259 2 W. Haberling, Der glatte H. des Aristoteles. Briefe J. Müllers über seine Wiederauffindung an W. H. Peters 1839–1840, in: Archiv für Gesch. der Naturwiss. und Technik 10, 1928, 166–184 3 Roscher.

C. HÜ.

Haimatites. Dieser »Blutstein« (αἱματίτης, *haematites*) wird heute als eine Form des roten Eisenoxidsteines angesehen. Schon Theophrast (de lapidibus 37, [1. 70]) leitet seinen Namen von dem Aussehen nach trockenem geronnenen Blut (*haíma*) ab. In den alten Reichen des Orients schätzte man ihn als Edelstein. Plinius empfiehlt ihn u. a. zur Behandlung blutunterlaufener Augen (nat. 36,144–148), zur Stillung des Blutflusses bei Schwindsüchtigen und Frauen. Im Anschluß an Sotakos, einen griech. Steinkundigen des 4. Jh. v. Chr., unterscheidet er fünf Arten; unter Berufung auf einen Zachalias berichtet er über Zauber-Praktiken babylonischer Magier mit *h.* (37,169). Durch Dioskurides (5,126, Wellmann 3,94f. = 5,143, Berendes 545), Isidorus (orig. 16,8,5) und die Steinbücher (*Lithica*), etwa das des Marbod von Rennes (11. Jh. n. Chr., V. 467–486 [2. 70ff.]), wurde H. dem MA sehr bekannt (z. B. Thomas v. Cantimpré 14,27 [3. 361]). Auch im Kitāb al-Muršid des at-Tamīmī

(10. Jh. n. Chr.), c. 14 wird er ausführlich besprochen [4. 65–70].
→ Edelsteine

1 D. E. Eichholz (ed.), Theophrastus de lapidibus, 1965 2 J. M. Riddle (ed.), Marbode of Rennes' De lapidibus, 1977 3 H. Boese (ed.), Thomas Cantimpratensis, Liber de natura rerum, 1973 4 J. Schönfeld, Über die Steine. Das 14. Kap. aus dem »K. a. M« ..., 1976 (Islamkundliche Untersuchungen 38). C. HÜ.

Haimon (Αἵμων, »kundig«), Heroenname.
[1] Eponymos der thessal. Haimones, Sohn des → Pelasgos, Vater des → Thessalos (Rhianos von Bene, FGrH 265 F 30), oder Sohn des Zeus und der Melia (IG IX 2, 582: 1. Jh. v. Chr., Larisa [1]), oder Sohn des Ares (Schol. Apoll. Rhod. 2,527e).
[2] Sohn des → Lykaon, Gründer von Haimoniai in Arkadien (Paus. 8,44,1; Apollod. 3,97).
[3] Anführer der Pylier, Gefährte des → Nestor (Hom. Il. 4,296).
[4] Thebaner, Vater des → Maion (Hom. Il. 4,394 ff.).
[5] Thebaner, Sohn des → Kreon, im alten Mythos Opfer der → Sphinx (Apollod. 3,54; → *Oidipodeia* fr. 1 PEG I [2. 7; 17]). Daher kann gegen Bethe [3] die Liebe H.s zu → Antigone nicht der alten Sage angehören; erst Sophokles macht H. zu ihrem Verlobten und erfindet so den Vater-Sohn-Konflikt, in dessen Verlauf H. sich bei der Leiche seiner Braut tötet (Soph. Ant. 1234 ff.). Bei Eur. Antigone, fr. 157–178 TGF [4] heiratet H. die wohl durch Dionysos von der Todesstrafe befreite Antigone und zeugt mit ihr → Maion; bei Eur. Phoen. 1672–1682 dagegen verzichtet Kreon auf die Heirat erst nach Antigones Drohung, H. in der Hochzeitsnacht zu ermorden. Nach Hyg. fab. 72 versteckt H. seine ihm zur Tötung übergebene Braut und hat mit ihr einen Sohn, nach dessen Ermordung durch Kreon H. sich und Antigone tötet.

1 Wilamowitz 1, 186 mit Anm. 2 2 E. Bethe, Thebanische Heldenlieder, 1891 3 Ders., s. v. Antigone (3), RE 1, 2403 4 A. Lesky, Die tragische Dichtung der Hellenen, ³1972, 328 f.

O. Kern, s. v. H. (1)–(12), RE 7, 2217 f. • I. Krauskopf, s. v. Antigone, LIMC 1.1, 818–828 • Dies., s. v. H., LIMC 4.1, 406 • Ch. Zimmermann, Der Antigone-Mythos in der ant. Lit. und Kunst, 1993. P. D.

[6] Ein östl. von Chaironeia in den Kephisos mündender, teilweise auch mit dem Thermodon gleichgesetzter Bach (Plut. Demosthenes 19; Plut. Theseus 27); die genaue Lokalisierung bleibt unsicher [1].

1 F. Bölte, s. v. H. 13), RE 7, 2218 f. P. F.

Haimos (Αἶμος). Gebirgszug in Thrakien, das Balkangebirge (türk. Balkan, bulg. Stara planiná; der Name ist wohl thrak.). Der H. erstreckt sich vom Timacus bis zum Pontos und stellt eine ausgeprägte Wasserscheide dar. Nach ant. Ansicht begann der H. schon an der Adria (Strab. 7, fr. 10). Da er zwar nicht sehr hoch, aber doch schwer zu überqueren ist, war er oftmals auch eine ethnische und polit. Grenze. Erste Erwähnung findet sich bei Hekataios (FGrH 1 F 169). Zahlreiche Mythen sind mit dem H. verbunden (Apollod. 1,6,3; Ps.-Plut. de fluviis 11,3; Serv. Aen. 1,317; 321; Steph. Byz. s. v. Αἶ.). I. v. B.

Ovid liefert das Aition des Gebirges (met. 6,88): H. und Rhodope, die Kinder von Boreas und Oreithyia, wurden ein Paar und nannten sich Zeus und Hera. Zur Strafe für diesen Frevel wurden sie in Gebirge verwandelt. C. W.

In der Ant. führten die Straßen von Oescus nach Philippopolis und von der Donau nach Kabyle und Ainos über den H.; z.Z. des Hdt. lebten südl. des H. verschiedene thrak. Stämme, nördl. die Getai. Erst die Odrysai eroberten nördl. davon gelegene Territorien. Auch → Alexandros [4] d.Gr. überquerte den H. auf seinen Eroberungszügen gegen die Getai und Triballoi. Im H. gab es Erzvorkommen, dichte Wälder und gute Weidegebiete; der H. bot zudem Schutz gegen Angreifer. Das führte zu einem recht hohen wirtschaftlichen und kulturellen Standard der einheimischen Stämme v. a. in hell. Zeit, was viele arch. Stätten bezeugen. In röm. Zeit wurden an den Pässen des H. Festungen errichtet, die nach dem 3. Jh. zu einer zweiten Verteidigungslinie (hinter dem Donau-Limes) ausgebaut wurden. Der H. war lange Zeit Grenze zw. dem byz. Reich und den über die Donau einfallenden Stämmen, später dem bulgar.-slav. Reich.

Ch. Danoff, Zu den histor. Umrissen Altthrakiens I, 1944. I. v. B.

Hain (ἄλσος/*álsos*, lat. *lucus*). In Griechenland und Italien ein sakraler Bezirk, der durch seinen Baumbestand gekennzeichnet war (vgl. Strab. 9,2,33); auch wenn *lucus* urspr. »Lichtung« meinte. Zum H. gehörte mindestens ein Altar, meistens auch Weihgeschenke; oft konnte ein H. auch Teil einer größeren sakralen Anlage mit einem Tempel sein: so im Apollonheiligtum von → Didyma (Strab. 14,1,5), dem samischen Heraion (LSCG, Suppl. 18) oder im röm. H. der → Dea Dia. Sakralisiert war der H., weil er als Aufenthaltsort einer Gottheit galt; prägnant drücken dies röm. Autoren wie Verg. Aen. 8,352 oder Sen. epist. 41,3 aus, die aus der Erscheinungsform des H. auf eine (unbekannte) Gottheit schließen. Dabei sind in Rom Differenzierungen der Grammatiker zu fassen, die in den griech. Quellen keine Entsprechungen haben [1. 14–20]: *lucus* wird von *nemus* (einem Ort mit kultiviertem Baumbestand) und von *silva* (dem menschlicher Pflege entzogenen Wald) als sakral abgehoben (Serv. auct. 1,310). Der H. als Ort »sakralisierter Natur« war gelegentlich eine Stätte bes. intensiver Begegnung mit dem Göttlichen; deswegen besaßen Orakelheiligtümer oft H. (Dodona: Soph. Trach. 171; zu Didyma, Klaros und Gryneion [1. 23–29]; Myra in Lykien: Athen. 8,8,333d-e), ebenso inkubatorische Heilheiligtümer (Kos: LSCG 150 und [2] ED 181). Der H. war Besitz der Gottheit; entsprechend konnte es verboten sein, in ihm Tiere weiden zu lassen, vor allem aber, Holz in ihm zu fällen (etwa Korope: LSCG 84; Kos: LSCG 150; Rom: CIL I 366); Zuwiderhandlung zog göttl. Strafe nach sich [3. Nr. 7]. In Rom machte jeder Eingriff in den Baumbestand ein Sühneopfer erforderlich (Cato agr. 139; Dea Dia [4. 95–172]). Saubere Kategorisierung ist aber weder in Griechenland noch in Rom möglich. H. konnten außerhalb der Städte (in einem *nemus* der H. der → Diana Nemorensis von Aricia: Cato orig. 58; in einer *silva* etwa Liv. 24,3,4) liegen, aber auch in einer Stadt (H. um das Hephaisteion von Athen [5], in Rom H. z.B. von → Bellona, → Mefitis, → Strenae und → Vesta). H. waren nicht an bestimmte Gottheiten gebunden – auch wenn Apollo und Artemis/Diana oft erscheinen – und nicht mit bestimmten Bäumen bepflanzt (oft ist der Lorbeer genannt; Liste bei [1. 41]). Im Gefolge der Romantik ist der H. in der Forsch. immer wieder mit dem → Baumkult verbunden worden (nicht zuletzt von FRAZER). Dies ist jedoch nicht haltbar: Die Bäume eines H. waren an sich heilig und unverletzlich, weil sie in Besitz einer Gottheit standen [1. 15–18, 171–180].

→ Heiligtum

1 DE CAZANOVE, J. SCHEID (Hrsg.), Les bois sacrés, 1993 **2** M. SEGRE, Iscrizioni di Cos (hrsg. von D. PEPAS-DELMOUSOU, M. A. RIZZA), 1994 **3** G. PETZL, Die Beichtinschr. Westkleinasiens, 1994 **4** J. SCHEID, Romulus et ses frères. Le collège des frères arvales, modèle du culte public dans la Rome des empereurs, 1990 **5** J. M. Camp, The Athenian Agora, 1986, 87.

D. E. BIRGE, Sacred groves in the ancient Greek world, Diss. Berkeley 1982 • B. JORDAN, J. PERLIN, On the protection of sacred groves, in: Studies presented to St. Dow, 1984, 153–159 • D. BIRGE, Sacred groves and the nature of Apollo, in: J. SOLOMON (Hrsg.), Apollo. Origins and Influences, 1994, 9–18. F.G.

Hairesis (αἵρεσις). Wichtiger Begriff der ant. Philos.- und Medizingeschichtsschreibung, später der christl. Dogmengeschichte. Seine urspr. Bedeutung ist »Auswahl«, entweder konkret (z.B. »Wahl« eines Beamten), oder eher abstrakt (z.B. »Entscheidung«). *H.* bedeutet in einer ersten Bedeutungserweiterung »Veranlagung« oder »Neigung«, die auf wiederholten Entscheidungen oder Wahlen beruht; In einer zweiten Bedeutungserweiterung heißt *h.* »Denkrichtung« oder »-schule« und spielt eine bedeutende Rolle in der ant. Philosophiegeschichtsschreibung. Entsprechende lat. Begriffe sind *disciplina* oder *secta*. Die ant. griech. und lat. Begriffe sind eher abstrakten Inhalts und bezeichnen keine Institution an sich. Der für *h.* oft verwendete moderne Begriff »Sekte«, der für eine streng definierte Personengruppe gebraucht wird, ist daher irreführend (→ Häresie).

Im Vorwort zu seiner Philosophiegeschichte stellt → Diogenes Laertios fest, es habe zehn *hairéseis* in der ethischen Philos. gegeben: Akademiker, Kyrenaiker, Eleaten, Megariker, Kyniker, Ereträer, Dialektiker, Peripatetiker, Stoiker und Epikureer (1,18). In seiner (auf → Hippobotos zurückgehenden) Liste weiterer neun *hairéseis* merkt er an, daß die Bezeichnung der Pyrrhoneer als *h.* umstritten sei, da diese keine eindeutige Lehrmeinung (*asapheía*) besäßen, und fügt hinzu, es sei kürzlich eine neue eklektische *h.* durch → Potamon von Alexandria gegründet worden.

Offenbar werden nur nachsokratische Schulen als *h.* bezeichnet. Von entscheidender Bedeutung hierfür ist die hell. Lit. »Über die Schulen« (Περὶ αἱρέσεων) mit ihrer systematischen Darstellung der Lehren der verschiedenen Schulen oder eher deren Gründern ([2]; → Doxographie). Für die nachsokratische Philos. bietet Diogenes Laertios bezeichnenderweise nur einen Abriß der Lehren des Gründers jeder *h.* (vgl. 7,38). Die bedeutendsten *hairéseis* um das 2. Jh. n. Chr. sind die Platoniker (als Nachfolger der Akademie), Peripatetiker, Stoiker, Epikureer und (Neu-)Pythagoreer. Man erwartete von einem Philosophen Treue zu einer der *hairéseis*, was in der Praxis bedeutete, daß man die Schriften der Gründer und der Mitglieder in deren Nachfolge (διαδοχή, *diadochḗ*) gründlich studierte [3].

Auch in der ant. Medizin findet sich der Begriff *h.*: Um das 1. Jh. v. Chr. bekunden die Ärzte ihre Zugehörigkeit zu drei »Schulen«, den Dogmatikern, den Empirikern und den Methodikern (vgl. → Galenos, ›Über die *hairéseis* für Anfänger‹), die man hauptsächlich nach ihren Diagnose- und Therapiemethoden unterschied ([4]; → Medizin).

In seiner Beschreibung des zeitgenössischen Judentums stellt → Iosephos fest, daß es drei *hairéseis* gebe, Pharisäer, Sadduzäer und Essener, und stellt deren zentrale Eigenschaften dar (bell. Iud. 2,119–162). Analog dazu wird im NT die christl. Bewegung von ihren Gegnern ›die *h.* der Nazarener‹ genannt (Apg 24,5, vgl. 14). In beiden Fällen ist der Begriff, wie schon in der griech. Philos. und Medizin, noch grundsätzlich neutral verwendet. Im 2. Jh. bezeichnen die beiden frühen christl. Theologen → Iustinus und → Eirenaios mit *h.* solche »Denkrichtungen«, die von der kirchlichen Lehre abweichen, wie sie in der apostolischen Nachfolge formuliert ist. Diese negative Deutung wird bei → Clemens [3] und → Origenes weiterentwickelt und wird zum Ausgangspunkt für den wichtigen ideologischen Begriff der → Häresie machen. Griech. Hairesiographie wird so zur christl. → Häresiologie (z.B. → Hippolytos, *Refutatio omnium haeresium*, ›Widerlegung aller *hairéseis*‹), und Anhänger einer *h.* werden zu Häretikern (vgl. z.B. → Tertullianus, *De praescriptione haereticorum*).

1 J. GLUCKER, Antiochus and the Late Academy, 1978, 166–206 **2** J. MEJER, Diogenes Laërtius and his Hellenistic Background, 1978, 75–81 **3** D. SEDLEY, Philosophical Allegiance in the Greco-Roman World, in: M. GRIFFIN, J. BARNES (Hrsg.), Philosophia Togata: Essays on Philosophy and Roman Society, 1989, 97–119 **4** H. VON STADEN, H. and Heresy: The Case of the *haireseis iatrikai*, in: B. F. MEYER, E. P. SANDERS (Hrsg.), Jewish and Christian Self-Definition, vol 3: Self-Definition in the Greco-Roman World, 1982, 76–100 **5** A. LE BOULLUEC, La notion d' hérésie dans la littérature grecque, IIe-IIIe siècles, Tome I: De Justin à Irénée, Tome II: Clément d' Alexandrie et Origène, 1985.

H. Brox, s. v. Häresie, RAC 13, 248–297. D.T.R./Ü: J.DE.

Hakoris. Sohn des Herieus, Vater des Euphron (griech. Übersetzung von Herieus) (OGIS 94; PKöln 4,186). Befehligte 187 v. Chr. unter Komanos Truppen gegen Anchwennefer, wohl als Stratege des Hermopolites oder Kynopolites. Eponym des Ortes Akoris [1].

W. Clarysse, Hakoris, in: AncSoc 22, 1991, 235 ff. W.A.

Halai (Ἁλαί). »Salzpfannen«, Name mehrerer Ortschaften, in Attika zweier Demen.

[1] H. Aixonides (Ἁλαὶ Αἰξωνίδες), att. Demos, der mit Aixone die Paralia-Trittys der Phyle Kekropis bildete. Daher (bloß administrativ? [3. 148[476]]) durch »Aixonides« von H. [2] an der Ostküste Attikas unterschieden. H. stellte sechs (zehn) → *buleutaí*. H. (h. Vula und Vuliagmeni [7. 466 Abb. 588]) grenzte im Norden an Aixone (h. Glyphada), im Osten an Anagyrus (h. Vari) (Strab. 9,1,21). Seine Ostgrenze markierten Horos-Inschr. auf der Kaminia [1; 2; 3. 63 ff. Taf. 35].

Dekrete von H. bezeugen u.a. eine → Agora (IG II^{2} 1174 Z. 13–15), einen → *dēmarchos [3]* [8. 58[84], 410 f. Nr. 15 f.], *tamíai* [8. 143] sowie einen *euthynos* ([8. 117 f.]; Näheres s. [8. 380 f. Nr. 50–58 und Index s. v. H. Aixonides]; → *euthynai*). Das Dekret IG II^{2} 1175 (ca. 360 v. Chr.) reagiert auf einen internen (rel.?) Skandal [8. 97, 182 f., 380 Nr. 53].

Für H. sind mehrere Kulte bezeugt [8. 206]: Apollon Zoster [8. 380 f. Nr. 55], Aphrodite (IG II^{2} 2820), Artemis, Athena (Paus. 1,31,1), Dionysos Anthios (IG II^{2} 1356 Z. 9 f.), Poseidon? (Athen. 297e *Halai* [8. 208]).

Ant. Reste: An mehreren Stellen finden sich prähistor. Siedlungsreste und Gräber [3. 66 f.], myk. Gräber (SH III A-C) nahe Glyphada [7. 467 Abb. 589–594]. Im Bereich Vula/Ano Vula sind zwei dörflich verdichtete Habitate aus klass. Zeit [3. 27–70 Taf. 34; 5. 129 ff. Abb. 16–18 Taf. 88,3.4, 89, 90; 7. 467, 474 ff. Abb. 595–597] sowie zahlreiche Einzelgehöfte und Gräber erhalten. Das Heiligtum von Zoster (Steph. Byz. s. v. Ζωστήρ) mit dem archa. Apollon-Tempel [3. 58; 7. 467, 477 Abb. 599 f.], das Apollon, Artemis, Leto und Athena geweiht war (Paus. 1,31,1), liegt auf der h. transgredierten [5. 14 f.] Landenge nördl. des Kaps. Das spätklass.(!) »Priesterhaus« nordöstl. deutet Lauter als »Villa« [3. 59 ff.]. Im → Chremonideïschen Krieg (267–262 v. Chr.) entstanden eine Befestigung über einer prähistor. Siedlung auf Kap Zoster [3. 68; 6] sowie das frühhell. Kastro Vuliagmenis am Westende des Defilees von Vari [4. 95 ff. Abb. 3]. Seit frühhell. Zeit [3. 67; 8. 360] geht die Besiedlung drastisch zurück.

1 H.R. Goette, Neue att. Felsinschr., in: Klio 76, 1994, 120–134 2 H. Lauter, Zwei Horosinschr. bei Vari, in: AA 1982, 299–315 3 Ders., Att. Landgemeinden in klass. Zeit, in: MarbWPr 1991, 1–161 4 H. Lauter-Bufé, Die Festung auf Koroni und die Bucht von Porto Raphti, in: MarbWPr 1988, 67–102 5 H. Lohmann, Atene, 1993 6 J.R. McCredie, Fortified Military Camps in Attica (Hesperia Suppl. 11), 1966, 30 ff. 7 Travlos, Attika, 466–479 Abb. 588–602 8 Whitehead.

C.W.J. Eliot, Coastal Demes, 1962 · Traill, Attica, 20, 50, 59, 67, 110 Nr. 49, 124 Tab. 7 · Whitehead, Index s. v. H. Aixonides. H.LO.

[2] H. Araphenides (Ἁλαὶ Ἀραφενίδες). Att. Paralia-Demos der Phyle Aigeis; stellte fünf (neun) → *buleutaí*. Bei Lutsa an der Ostküste Attikas zw. Brauron im Süden (Strab. 9,1,22; Steph. Byz. s. v. Ἁ.) und Araphen im Norden gelegen [2]. Daher (nur administrativ?) durch »Araphenides« von H. [1] unterschieden. Drei Demendekrete [5. 381 Nr. 59–61] bezeugen diverse Funktionsträger sowie (indirekt) ein Theater, in dem an den ländl. Dionysia Agone stattfanden [4. 211; 5. 123[12], 141[118], 212, 220[263], 222]. Überregionale Bed. besaßen Kult (Aition: Eur. Iph. T. 1449 ff.) und Tempel [2; 3] der Artemis Tauropolos und die Tauropolia (Hesych. s. v. T.; Men. Epitr. 234, 255, 260, 300, 479, 685; [1–3; 4. 211]). Athen. 297e bezeugt für H. einen Poseidonkult. Die verlorene Komödie des Menandros *Halaieís* (Ἁλαιεῖς) spielte in H. [5. 338[76], 341[81]].

1 L. Deubner, Att. Feste, ^{3}1969, 208 f. 2 C.W.J. Eliot, s. v. H. Araphenides, PE, 373 f. 3 H. Knell, Der Tempel der Artemis Tauropolos in Lutsa, in: AA 1983, 39–43 4 Travlos, Attika 5 Whitehead.

Traill, Attica, 16, 40, 59, 67, 110 Nr. 50, 124 Tab. 2 · Travlos, Attika, 211–215 Abb. 264–268 · Whitehead, Index s. v. H. Araphenides. H.LO.

[3] Ursprünglich zum opuntischen Lokris gehörig, war H. seit ca. 270 v. Chr. nördlichster boiot. Hafenort am Golf von Euboia (Strab. 9,2,13; 4,2; Paus. 9,24,5; Steph. Byz. s. v. Ἁ.). Siedlungsspuren des im Ostteil der Bucht von Opus (h. Atalanti) nordwestl. des h. Theologos unmittelbar am Meer gelegenen Orts reichen von neolithischer bis in byz. Zeit. Die Stadtbefestigung aus der Zeit um 600 v. Chr. wurde 426/5 durch Erdbeben zerstört, im 4. Jh. erneuert und erweitert; auch nach der Zerstörung durch die Truppen Sullas 86/5 v. Chr. erfolgte eine sehr rasche Wiederbesiedlung (Plut. Sulla 26). In Teilen noch gut erh. sind Stadtmauern, Innenbebauung (u. a. Tempel der Athena Poliuchos mit drei Bauphasen aus archa. und klass. Zeit; spätröm. Thermen) und Nekropolen.

J.E. Coleman, Excavations at H., 1990–1991, in: Hesperia 61, 1992, 265–289 · Lauffer, Griechenland, 253 · N.D. Papachatzis, Παυσανίου Ἑλλάδος Περιήγησις 5, ^{2}1981, 167 f. · P. Roesch, Thespies et la confédération béotienne, 1965, 66 f. · Schachter, Bd. 1, 114 f.; Bd. 3, 100, 161 f. · P.W. Wallace, Strabo's description of Boiotia, 1979, 59 f. P.F.

Halakha. Der Terminus *H.* (abgeleitet von der hebr. Wz. *hlk* – »gehen«) bezeichnet sowohl eine einzelne jüd. Gesetzesbestimmung oder feststehende Regel als auch das gesamte System der gesetzlichen Bestimmungen der jüd. Tradition. Die Grundlagen dieser Bestimmungen, die nach traditioneller Auffassung als »mündliche Tora« (*Tora she-be-al-pä*) und als Mose am Sinai offenbart gelten, bilden die Gesetzescorpora des Pentateuch (z. B. das sog. »Bundesbuch« Ex 20,22–23,19), deuteronomisches Gesetz (Dt 12,1–26,15) oder Heiligkeitsgesetz (Lv 17–26). Deren Einzelbestimmungen wurden nach der Kanonisierung des Pentateuch in nachexilischer und frühjüd. Zeit vereinheitlicht, aktualisiert und ergänzt, wobei es in den unterschiedlichen Gruppierungen des Frühjudentums wie Sadduzäern, Pharisäern oder Essenern zu ganz unterschiedlichen Meinungen und Auffassungen kommen konnte (vgl. z. B. 4Q Ma'aseh Miqzat ha-Tora). Die früheste nachbiblische autoritative Gesetzessammlung bildet die Mišna, die – wiederum auf älteren Traditionen beruhend – ca. um 200 n. Chr. von dem Patriarchen Jehuda ha Nasi kodifiziert wurde. In sechs verschiedenen Ordnungen (hebr. *sedarīm*) mit insgesamt 63 Traktaten (hebr. *peraqīm*) enthält sie Gesetzesbestimmungen zu Ritual, Reinheit und Kult (speziell auch zu landwirtschaftlichen Abgaben), zu Festzeiten und Festbräuchen sowie zu Kalenderfragen, zum Umgang mit Armen, zum Familien- und Schadensrecht und deckt damit alle Bereiche des menschlichen Lebens ab.

Als weitere frühe jüd. Zusammenstellungen halakhischen Inhalts sind die Tosefta sowie die sog. halakhischen Midrašim Mekhilta de Rabbi Yischmaʿel (zu Ex), Sifra (zu Lv) und Sifre Numeri bzw. Sifre Deuteronomium zu nennen. Die Mišna bildet die Grundlage für weitere halakhische Konkretionen, Ergänzungen und Diskussionen, die dann in den beiden Talmudīm, dem palästinischen (Endredaktion ca. Ende 5. Jh. n. Chr.) und dem babylon. (Endredaktion ca. 6. Jh.), zusammengestellt wurden. Grundlage der *H.* ist die biblische Überl., die mit einem ganz bestimmten methodischen und hermeneutischen Instrumentarium (den sog. sieben Middot oder Regeln des Hillel, die ihrerseits deutliche Einflüsse der ant. Rhet. aufweisen) ausgelegt werden. Im Hinblick auf eine Aktualisierung der *H.* erlassen rabbinische Autoritäten aber auch ganz neue Bestimmungen, die z. T. eine radikale Uminterpretation des bestehenden biblischen Rechtes darstellen (sog. *Taqqanot*). Schließlich können auch seit langem bestehende Bräuche als bindendes Recht gelten und sogar ältere *Halakhot* verdrängen (*Minhag*).

Neben der Notwendigkeit einer Aktualisierung führte auch die Tendenz, die Einhaltung der Tora durch zusätzliche Vorschriften immer mehr abzusichern (vgl. mAv 1,1: ›Machet einen Zaun um die Tora‹) zum Ausdruck kommt, zu einem ständigen Anwachsen des Traditionsstoffes. Aufgrund der bed. Rolle, die das babylon. Judentum in der Spätant. und im frühen MA spielte, wurde der babylon. Talmud zur höchsten halakhischen Instanz. Da das Material aber eher unsystematisch vorliegt und somit unübersichtlich erscheint, empfand man schon bald das Bedürfnis und die Notwendigkeit einer klaren Zusammenfassung der Einzelbestimmungen (vgl. u. a. das Gesetzbuch des Isaak Alfasi [1013–1103], *Mishne Tora* des Maimonides [1135–1204] oder den *Šulchan Aruch* des Josef Karo [1488–1575]). Zudem bestand seit dem frühen MA die Praxis, in schwierigen Fällen bei Fachgelehrten Einzelentscheide, sog. Responsen, einzuholen. Bereits seit der Ant. wird die Frage nach einer Begründung der oft rational nicht nachzuvollziehbaren gesetzlichen Bestimmungen diskutiert, ohne daß darauf eine eindeutige Antwort gefunden werden könnte. Insgesamt wird darauf verwiesen, daß Gott die Tora mit ihren halakhischen Bestimmungen nur deshalb gegeben habe, damit sich Israel Verdienst erwerben könnte; gleichzeitig wird aber auch davor gewarnt, die *H.* gleichsam berechnend und in der Hoffnung auf Lohn durchzuführen; Israel soll vielmehr sein ›wie Knechte, die ihrem Herrn aus Liebe dienen‹ (mAv 1,3). Abgesehen von der praktischen Funktion der *H.* kommt auch ihrem theoretischen Studium höchste Bed. zu, da es als eine Art Gottesdienst angesehen wird, bei dem Gott mit seiner Gegenwart (*Šekhina*) anwesend ist (vgl. u. a. bBer 17a). So ist es letztlich auch die Beschäftigung mit der H., die nach der Zerstörung des Tempels noch direkten Kontakt zu Gott gewährt.

→ Haggada; Rabbinische Literatur; Talmud; Tosefta

L. Jacobs, s. v. Halacha, TRE 30 (30), 384–388 • L. Jacob, J. und B. De-Vries, s. v. Halakhah, Encyclopaedia Judaica 2, 1156–1166 • G. Stemberger, Der Talmud. Einführung, Texte, Erläuterungen, 1982, 71–158 • G. Stemberger, Das klass. Judentum, 1979, 126–160. B. E.

Halbgott s. Heroenkult; Herakles

Halbkursive s. Kursive

Halbsäule s. Säule

Hales (h. Alento). Fluß in Lucania, an dessen Mündung der allmählich versandende Ankerplatz von Elea lag (Strab. 6,1,1; Cic. Att. 16,7,5; [2]), wohl benannt nach einer einheimischen Gottheit [1].

1 L. Ronconi, La ninfa Hyele, in: Atti e Memorie dell'Accademia Patavina 95, 1982/3, 65–72 2 G. Schmiedt, Contributo alla recostruzione della situazione geotopografica di Velia nell'antichità, in: PdP 25, 1970, 65–92.

D. Musti, Le fonti per la storia di Velia, in: PdP 21, 1966, 318–335, bes. 321. M. I. G./Ü: V. S.

Halesus (meist Halaesus geschrieben). Ital. Heros, Gefährte oder unehelicher Sohn → Agamemnons, der nach It. floh (Serv. Aen. 7,723). Er gilt als Gründer von → Falerii und eponymer Heros der → Falisci und brachte den dortigen Iuno-Kult aus Argos mit (Ov. am. 3,13,31–35; fast. 4,73 f.; Verbindung von Falerii mit Argos: Cato fr. 47 HRR), oder als Gründer von Alsium (Sil. 8,474). Im ersten Fall ist der faliskische Lautwandel *f* > *h* [1], im zweiten die Namensform **Alesus* vorausgesetzt. – Bei Vergil führt H., der Begleiter Agamemnons (Aen. 7,723), dem Turnus »tausend Völker« aus dem nördl. Kampanien zu (Aurunker, Sidiciner, Osker usw., Aen. 7,725–730; 10,352f. [2]). Sein Vater, ein Wahrsager, hat H. im Wald versteckt gehalten, um ihn am Kriegszug zu hindern (Aen. 10,417, möglicherweise eine Erfindung Vergils). – H., den Sohn des → Neptun, besingen die Veientaner in ihrem lokalen Salierlied (Serv. Aen. 8,285). – Die Vielfalt der Traditionen ist meist durch verschiedene Versuche italischer Orte zu erklären, sich homerische Ahnen zu geben, teilweise wohl auch durch dichterische Erfindung.

1 A. NEHRING, Lat. Gramm., in: Glotta 14, 1925, 233–275
2 J. PERRET, H. ou Messapus (A propos d'Aeneis VII 641–871), in: Mélanges de philosophie, de littérature et d'histoire ancienne offerts à Pierre Boyancé, 1974, 557–568.

G. GARBUGINO, s.v. H., EV 1,90. F.G.

Halex (Ἅληξ). Fluß im südl. Bruttium, h. Alice. Nach Timaios (FGrH 566 F 43b) und Strabon (6,1,9) Grenzfluß zw. Rhegion und Lokroi (nach Paus. 6,6,4 dagegen Kaikinos). Im Peloponnesischen Krieg (426 v. Chr.) Schauplatz einer athen. Expedition gegen Lokroi (Thuk. 3,99).

NISSEN 2, 955. H.SO.

Halia (Ἁλία, Ἁλίη), »die zum Meer Gehörige« [1].

[1] → Nereide in den Kat. [2] bei Hom. Il. 18,40, Hes. theog. 245 (θ' Ἁλίη [3]; aber Θαλίη [4]) und Apollod. 1,11. Eine Frauenfigur auf einem att. rf. Lekanisdeckel trägt die Beischrift H. [5].

[2] Nach einem rhodischen Mythos bei Diod. 5,55 Schwester der → Telchinen, bei denen Poseidon aufwuchs. Dieser zeugt mit H. sechs Söhne und eine Tochter, Rhodos. Die von Aphrodite zur Strafe für ihre Hybris in Wahnsinn versetzten Söhne vergewaltigen ihre Mutter H., worauf sie sich ins Meer stürzt und seitdem unter dem Namen → Leukothea göttl. Verehrung erfährt.

1 KAMPTZ, 268 2 R. WACHTER, Nereiden und Neoanalyse: ein Blick hinter die Ilias, in: WJA, 1990, 19–31 3 Hesiodi Theogonia, Opera et dies, Scutum, ed. F. SOLMSEN, [3]1990 4 Hesiod, Theogony, ed. M. L. WEST, 1966, mit Komm. zur Stelle 5 R. VOLLKOMMER, s.v. H., LIMC 4.1, 407f. A.A.

Haliakmon (Ἁλιάκμων). Größter südmaked. Fluß, durchfließt die Landschaften Orestis, Elimeia und Pieria und mündet in den Thermaiischen Golf. Durch das untere H.-Tal verlief eine wichtige Route nach Thessalia.

E. MEYER, s.v. H. (2), RE Suppl. 11, 674f. MA.ER.

Haliartos (Ἁλίαρτος, Ἀρίαρτος, Ἀρίαρτος [1. 483]). Boiot. Stadt am Südrand des Kopais-Sees 20 km westl. von Thebai. Die Akropolis mit archa. Athena-Heiligtum befindet sich auf dem vom MH bis in röm. Zeit besiedelten Hügel Kastri Mazíou, an den sich die befestigte Unterstadt anschließt. Im 6. Jh. v. Chr. prägte das von Homer (Il. 2,503) erwähnte H. Mz. mit dem Bundesemblem, dem »Schild der Boioter« [2. 345]. Im Territorium lag das Bundesheiligtum des Poseidon von Onchestos. Ab 446 (?) bildete H. mit Koroneia und Lebadeia einen Distrikt des Boiot. Bundes (Hell. Oxyrh. 19,3,392). Der Spartaner Lysandros fiel 394 in der Schlacht bei H. (Xen. hell. 3,5,17f.). Im 3. Maked. Krieg auf Seiten der Feinde Roms, wurde H. 172 v. Chr. von den Römern zerstört, das Land Athen übereignet (Pol. 27,1,5; 30,21; Liv. 42,44,1; 46,9f.; 56,3–5; 63,3). Athen entsandte Siedler und verwaltete das Gebiet (Strab. 9,2,30) durch *epimelētaí* [3. 168–171]. Vgl. zu H. auch Herakleides Kritikos 1,25 und Paus. 9,32f.

1 W. SPOERRI, s.v. H., LFE 1 2 HN 3 P. ROESCH, Études Béotiennes, 1982.

FOSSEY, 301–308. K.F.

Halieis (Ἁλιεῖς, Ἁλιαί). Hafenstadt an der Bucht von Portocheli in der Argolis, auf Betreiben von Hermione von Exulanten aus → Tiryns kurz nach 479 v. Chr. gegr. (Hdt. 7,137). Reste der ant. Stadt, teilweise im Meer versunken, wurden gegenüber der h. Stadt auf einem kleinen, den Hafeneingang beherrschenden Kap gefunden. Wohl E. des 4. Jh. v. Chr. wurde H. zerstört. Belegstellen: Skyl. 52; Strab. 8,6,11; Paus. 2,36,1 (Ἁλίκη).

B. BERGQUIST, Primary or secondary temple function: the case of H., in: OpAth 18, 1990, 23–37 • M. H. JAMESON, s.v. H., EAA[2], 21–23 • M. H. MCALLISTER, The Fortifications of Ancient H., 1973. Y.L.

Halieuticon. Plin. nat. 32,11. 152 erwähnt ein Werk mit dem Titel *H.* (›Fischerei‹, wahrscheinlich ein Gen. Pl., Ἁλιευτικῶν), welches → Ovid, wie er sagt, im Exil ›begann‹. Plinius' Zitate scheinen die gut 130 *Versus Ovidi de piscibus et feris* zu paraphrasieren, die durch zwei Hss. des 8./9. und 10. Jh. überliefert sind. Das kurze Fr. kann aus stilistischen, sprachlichen und metr. Gründen nicht Ovid zugeschrieben werden, doch scheint nach-plinianische Fälschung sehr unwahrscheinlich zu sein. Es schöpft letztlich aus der ant. zoologischen Trad.

ED.: E. DE SAINT-DENIS, Ovide, Halieutiques, 1975.
LIT.: J. RICHMOND, Chapters on Greek Fish-Lore, 1973 • Ders., The authorship of the H. ascribed to Ovid, in: Philologus 120, 1976, 92–106. J.A.R./Ü: M.MO.

Halikarnassos (Ἁλικαρνασσός).

I. LAGE II. HISTORISCHE ENTWICKLUNG
III. ARCHÄOLOGISCHER BEFUND
IV. LITERARISCHE PERSÖNLICHKEITEN

I. LAGE

Küstenstadt im Süden von → Karia am Golf von Keramos, h. Bodrum. Die Stadtanlage (Strab. 14,2,16; Steph. Byz. s.v. Ἁ.; Vitr. 2,8,10–14) glich dem Zuschauerrund eines Theaters: eine kreisrunde Hafenbucht, der ›geschlossene Hafen‹ (λιμὴν κλειστός, Ps.-Skyl. 98a), beiderseits von felsigen erhöhten Landvorsprüngen eingerahmt, im Osten vom Zephyrion (urspr.

eine Insel, Plin. nat. 2,204), im Westen von der Salmakis (Arr. an. 1,23,3), im Hintergrund stufenartig ansteigend die Stadt. Bis ins 4. Jh. v. Chr. konzentrierte sich die Besiedlung auf Zephyrion und Salmakis, das Zentrum der Maussollos-Stadt war noch Nekropolengebiet (bes. im Bereich des → Maussolleion).

II. Historische Entwicklung
A. Frühgeschichte B. Griechische und römische Zeit C. Byzantinische Zeit

A. Frühgeschichte

Die uralte kar. Stadt erhielt angeblich schon im 12. Jh. v. Chr. (1175: Tac. ann. 4,55) aus der Argolis (Troizen: Hdt. 7,99; Paus. 2,30,8; Argos: Vitr. 12,8,12; Mela 1,16,3) griech. Siedler, wahrscheinlich aber erst im 11./10. Jh. im Rahmen der »Ion. Kolonisation« (→ Ionische Wanderung). Als vorgriech. Bevölkerung werden neben Kares nördl. und westl. von H., bes. auf der nach Westen bis → Myndos sich erstreckenden »Halbinsel von H.« Leleges genannt, die vermutlich frühe Kontakte mit myk. Griechen (Nekropole von Müskebi) hatten und sich bis in → Maussollos' Zeit gegen H. behaupteten. Die älteste griech. Niederlassung in H. befand sich wohl auf Zephyrion; mit Salmakis bzw. mit der gleichnamigen Quelle scheint (in mythisch-aitiologischer Fabel, Vitr. 2,8,11 f.; Strab. 14,2,16; vgl. Ov. met. 4,285 ff.) das binnenwärts verdrängte kar. Substrat verbunden. Noch Mitte 5. Jh. war in H. nach Ausweis der PN der kar.-stämmige Anteil der Bevölkerung stark, wenngleich weitgehend hellenisiert; das dor. Element (Hdt. 7,99,3) blieb trotz noch im 4. Jh. lebendiger Tradition (Oikist Anthes aus Troizen mit gemischt-griech. Kolonisten, Strab. 14,2,16; Paus. 2,30,10) und dor. Institutionen allezeit schwach; Umgangs- und Urkundensprache war das ion. Griechisch.

B. Griechische und römische Zeit

Aus der dor. Hexapolis früh ausgestoßen (Hdt. 1,145), kam H. vermutlich nach 560 v. Chr. unter die Herrschaft des Kroisos, 546 unter die der Perser (Hdt. 1,174 f.; 2,178; 3,4; 3,11) und wurde Sitz der kar.-griech. Dynastenfamilie des Lygdamis, dessen Tochter die von Herodot gerühmte → Artemisia [1] war. Vermutlich um 468, z.Z. von Kimons südkleinasiat. Expedition, wurde H. Mitglied des → Attisch-Delischen Seebunds. Nach fehlgeschlagener Erhebung gegen den gleichnamigen (Ur-?)Enkel Lygdamis (gegen Mitte 5. Jh.) flüchtete → Herodot aus H. nach Samos (Suda s. v. Herodotos); danach gelang die Beseitigung der Tyrannis. Ein Gesetz dieser Zeit über umstrittenen Grund- und Hausbesitz (ML 32; histor. griech. Inschr. in Übersetzungen 1, 1992, 52) nennt Lygdamis noch neben den Verfassungsorganen von H. und der damals noch halbwegs autonomen Gemeinde Salmakis. Gegen E. des Peloponnesischen Krieges fiel H. erneut unter pers. Oberhoheit, gehörte aber vor 390 zur neugeschaffenen Satrapie Karia unter den Dynasten von → Mylasa. Phormion aus H., 392 Olympionike im Boxen, wurde 388 mit zwei weiteren Boxern wegen Bestechung zu einer schweren Buße in Olympia verurteilt (Paus. 5,21,3). Gegen die 389 von Thrasybulos den wiedergewonnenen Bundesgenossen Athens auferlegte Zollabgabe legte H. erfolgreich Beschwerde ein (Lys. 28,12; 17), die erneute Hinwendung zu Athen blieb Episode. Nach dem Königsfrieden 386 unterstand H. der Kontrolle des Hekatomnos von Mylasa.

H. gewann erst Bed., als dessen Sohn → Maussollos H. anstelle von Mylasa zur Hauptstadt erhob (Diod. 15,90,3) und – unter Heranführung von Bevölkerung aus sechs Städtchen der Leleges aufgrund eines Synoikismos (Kallisthenes FGrH 124 F 25; Strab. 13,1,58 f.) – H. zur Großstadt mit Seegeltung ausbaute: Das Hanggelände zw. Zephyrion und Salmakis wurde nach hippodamischem Schema bebaut; nahe dem Hafen die Agora, oberhalb im terrassierten Stadtgebiet eine querlaufende, von hangaufwärts strebenden Nebenstraßen geschnittene Hauptstraße (Vitr. 2,8,11) angelegt, in deren Mitte sich das Grabmal des Maussollos erhob. Dieses liegt exakt im Zentrum eines Kreises, dessen Durchmesser der Länge der Hauptstraße zw. den beiden Stadttoren entspricht (10 Stadien, ca. 1,76 km) und der das gesamte Areal vom Hafen bis zu den Höhen nördl. der Stadt umschreibt – die ganze Stadt gleichsam ein Denkmal ihres Neugründers. Auf Zephyrion, wo im 5. Jh. vermutlich der Apollontempel der Stadt stand, erhob sich der Palast des Maussollos (Vitr. 2,8,10; Plin. nat. 36,47); hinter den Mauern versteckt am »Isthmos« zum Festland befand sich der Kriegshafen (*portus secretus*, Vitr. 2,8,13 f.) mit Zugang zum Palast (dieser vielleicht auch nördl. des Isthmos auf dem Festland gelegen?) und Kanal zur Außenbucht.

Den Versuch von Rhodos, sich nach Maussollos' Tod 353 im Handstreich der Stadt und ihres Hafens zu bemächtigen, wußte Artemisia [2] zu vereiteln (Vitr. 2,8,14). Im J. 334 wurde die durch Memnon von Rhodos verteidigte Stadt von Alexander d.Gr. nach kurzer Belagerung erobert und zerstört (Arr. an. 1,20,5–23,6; Diod. 17,23,4–27,6). Am Kampf beteiligte sich auf Alexanders Seite die Dynastin → Ada mit eigenen Truppen und nahm eine der beiden Akropolen von H. ein (Strab. 14,2,17; Zephyrion oder Salmakis oder Bergfestungen im Mauerring?). In hell. Zeit stand H. anfangs zumeist unter ptolem. Einfluß, war 192 v. Chr. frei und auf Seiten Roms (Liv. 37,10,16); 88 v. Chr. geriet die Stadt unter die Herrschaft Mithradates' VI. (App. Mithr. 21); 80/79 wurde sie Opfer der Raffgier des Verres, damals Legat des Statthalters von Cilicia (Cic. Verr. 2,1,49); 62–58 von Seeräubern heimgesucht, erholte sich H. dank der Fürsorge des Q. Tullius Cicero, des Statthalters von Asia (Cic. ad Q. fr. 1,1,25); 58 v. Chr. wurde H. der röm. Prov. eingegliedert. Die Bitte um Verleihung einer → Neokorie 26 n. Chr. beschied Tiberius abschlägig (Tac. ann. 4,55). Der Judengemeinde in H. war freie Kultausübung garantiert (Ios. ant. Iud. 14,10,23).

C. Byzantinische Zeit

395 n. Chr. wurde H. Stadt des oström. Reiches; im 13. Jh. gelangte H. unter die Herrschaft der Seldschuken-Emire Menteşe von Milâs (Mylasa), 1402 wurde die Stadt von den Johanniterrittern von Rhodos übernommen: Erbauung der Festung S. Pietro, »Petronion«, auf Zephyrion durch den Deutschen Heinrich Schlegelholt. Bei deren Verstärkung 1495 wurde nochmals dem → Maussolleion Steinmaterial entnommen, so daß dieses, durch Erdbeben ruiniert, nunmehr bis zum Grund (Aufdeckung der Grabkammer) abgetragen wurde. Im MA ein Flecken namens Mese (Μέση) oder Tabia (»inmitten Liegende«, »Verschanzung«), kam H. 1523 nach Abzug der Johanniter endgültig unter türk. Herrschaft.

III. Archäologischer Befund

Unter den im 19. Jh. von Newton (1856–1858) u. a. bestimmten und z. T. freigelegten ant. Bauten sind noch vorhanden zuoberst am Osthang des Göktepe eine große Plattform für einen Ares- bzw. Marstempel (röm.), in dem einst eine akrolithe Kolossalstatue von Leochares oder Timotheos stand (Vitr. 2,8,11; Plin. nat. 36,4); am Südhang des Göktepe befindet sich das Theater (3. Jh.? mit kaiserzeitlichen Umbauten) für 13 000 Zuschauer; im Westen der Stadt wurde ein röm. Haus mit Mosaikböden gefunden, ebensolche wurden auch im südl. Teil des Peribolos des Maussolleions aufgedeckt. Der Wiederauffindung bzw. systematischer Ausgrabung harren im Ostteil der Stadt eine röm. Stoa (auf großer Terrasse, 30 Säulen), eine hell. Stoa, ein Gymnasion (?), ein Demeter-Persephone-Tempel. Wahrscheinlich bei der Salmakisquelle oberhalb des türk. Arsenals unweit einer Türbe – wohl nicht auf dem weiter südl. gelegenen Kaplan kalesi (»Tigerschloß«), der nur prähistor. Lesefunde aufwies –, wurde ein Heiligtum von Aphrodite und Hermes (bzw. des Hermaphroditos) vermutet. An mehreren Stellen erh. ist die über 6 km lange Stadtmauer, die die Stadtberge im Norden umzog (oberhalb des Theaters in den Gipfelfelsen zahllose Kammergräber meist hell.-röm. Zeit); im Osten ist das Tor nach Mylasa zu erkennen (Arr. an. 1,20,4; 21,1; h. zerstört), im Westen, wo die Straße nach Myndos beginnt, das Tripylon mit vorgelegtem, tiefem Graben; an dieser schwächsten Stelle gelang Alexander der Einbruch (Arr. an. 1,20,8; 22,4–7). Der ant. Hauptachse zw. den Toren folgt noch h. die Turgut-Reis-Straße, an deren Südseite das Grabungsfeld des → Maussolleion (h. mit Museum) liegt. H. ist h. aus arch. Sicht eine skandinavische Domäne: Forschungen, Grabungen und Surveys der Dänen und Schweden werden seit den 1980er Jahren durchgeführt.

IV. Literarische Persönlichkeiten

An lit. Persönlichkeiten stammen außer dem »Vater der Geschichtsschreibung« Herodot aus H. (Cic. leg. 1,1,5) in der 2. H. des 1. Jh. v. Chr. der Historiker → Dionysios [18], sowie in hadrianischer Zeit der Musikwissenschaftler → Dionysios [20] Musikos, evtl. identisch mit dem Lexikographen Ailios → Dionysios [21]. H. KA.

G. E. Bean, J. M. Cook, The H. Peninsula, in: ABSA 50, 1955, 85–108 • G. Bockisch, Die Karer und ihre Dynasten, in: Klio 51, 1969, 117–175 • L. Bürchner, s. v. H., RE 7, 2253–2264 • W. Hoepfner, H., die Hauptstadt des Maussollos, in: Ant. Welt 18/4, 1987, 51–54 • Ders., Haus und Stadt im klass. Griechenland, 1994, 226–234 • S. Hornblower, Mausolus, 1982 • J. Isager (Hrsg.), Hecatomnid Caria and the Ionian Renaissance (Kongr. Odense 1991), 1994 • W. Judeich, Kleinasiat. Studien, 1892 • G. Jürgens, De rebus Halicarnassensium 1, 1877 • T. Linders (Hrsg.), Architecture and Society in Hecatomnid Caria (Kongr. Upsala 1987), 1989 • Magie 2, 909 ff. • Ch. Th. Newton, A History of Discoveries at H., Cnidus, and Branchidae, 1862 • P. Pedersen, The Fortifications of H., in: REA 96, 1994, 215–235 • L. Rocchetti, EAA 1, 251–253. H. KA. u. C. HÖ.

Halikyai (Ἁλικύαι). Stadt der → Elymoi zw. Lilybaion und → Entella [1. 168–171] im karthagischen Einflußbereich. Im Peloponnesischen Krieg mit Athen verbündet (Thuk. 7,32,1; IG I², 20), 278/7 von Pyrrhos, 263 von den Römern erobert (Diod. 22,10,2; 23,5). Cicero rechnet die *Halicyenses* zu den *civitates immunes ac liberae* (Cic. Verr. 3,13; 91; 5,15), Plinius zu den *stipendiarii* (Plin. nat. 91).

1 BTCGI 3.

G. Bejor, Città di Sicilia, in: ASNP 12/3, 1982, 838 f. • G. Manganaro, La Sicilia da Sesto Pompeo a Diocleziano, in: ANRW II 11.1, 1988, 78 Anm. 429. GI. MA./Ü: H. D.

Halimus (Ἁλιμοῦς). Att. Asty-Demos der Phyle Leontis, mit drei → *buleutaí* (zur Bevölkerungsgröße [4. 286]), nach Strab. 9,1,21 an der Westküste Attikas zw. Phaleron und Aixone 35 Stadien (= 6,2 km) von der Stadt (Demosth. or. 57,10) entfernt zu lokalisieren. H., das im Osten an Euonymon grenzte, lag beim h. Halimos und Hagios Kosmas, dem ant. Kap → Kolias mit dem Heiligtum der Demeter Thesmophoros und der Kore (Paus. 1,31,1; Hesych. s. v. Κωλιάς; [1–3]; prähistor. Siedlung: [5]). Für H. sind Thesmophoria bezeugt (schol. Aristoph. Thesm. 80 [6. 80]) sowie folgende Kulte [6. 207[172]]: Herakles (Demosth. or. 57, 46–48; 62 [6. 114[147], 181 f.]), Hestia (SEG 21, 813), Dionysos (SEG 2, 7 Z. 23 [2; 6. 204[172], 221[268]]). Den Kult der Aphrodite Kolias lokalisiert Strabon (9,1,21) fälschlich in Anaphlystos [6. 207[172]]. Fünf → *dḗmarchoi* sind namentlich bekannt [6. 411 f. Nr. 18–22]. Der Historiker → Thukydides stammte aus H. Demosthenes behandelt einen Justizskandal in H. (or. 57; [6. 105 ff. 296 ff.]).

1 J. Day, Cape Colias, Phalerum and the Phaleric Wall, in: AJA 36, 1932, 1–11 2 J. J. Hondius, A new inscription of the deme Halimous, in: ABSA 24, 1919/21, 151–160
3 G. Karo, Arch. Funde, in: AA 1930, 100 4 H. Lohmann, Atene, 1993 5 G. Mylonas, Agios Kosmas, 1959
6 Whitehead.

Traill, Attica, 43, 62, 68, 110 Nr. 51, Tab. 4 • J. S. Traill, Demos and Trittys, 1986, 130 • Whitehead, Index s. v. H.
H. LO.

Halios geron (ἅλιος γέρων, »Meergreis«). Alte Meeresgottheit, urspr. ohne Eigennamen, dann mit → Nereus, → Proteus, → Phorkys und → Glaukos identifiziert, mit denen er die Wesenszüge des Greisenalters, der Weissagekunst und der Verwandlungsfähigkeit teilt [1; 2]. In der *Ilias* tritt der *H.g.* als Vater der → Thetis und der → Nereiden auf (Hom. Il. 1,358; 538 = 556; 18,141; 20,107; 24,562; Hom. Od. 24,58), wird aber erst bei Hesiod explizit mit Nereus gleichgesetzt (theog. 234; 1003; vgl. schol. Pind. P. 9,164 DRACHMANN und Cornutus, De natura deorum 23). In Hom. Od. 4,365; 384 erhält Proteus, in 13,96 (345) Phorkys den Beinamen *H.g.* Der Kult eines *H.g.*, d.h. wohl jeweils lokaler Gottheiten, ist vereinzelt belegt: im lakonischen Gythion (Paus. 3,21,9: Nereus), bei den Iberern (schol. Apoll. Rhod. 2,767: Glaukos; vgl. Avien. 263) und am Bosporos (Dionysios Byzantios 49 p. 20 GÜNGERICH: Nereus, Phorkys, Proteus oder der Vater der Nymphe Semystra). Zwei bildliche Darstellungen mit Beischrift sind erhalten, wovon eine den *H.g.* (Nereus) mit Fischschwanz im Kampf gegen Herakles zeigt [3; 4].

1 NILSSON, GGR, 240–244 **2** A. LESKY, Thalatta, 1947, 112f. **3** R. GLYNN, s.v. H.G., LIMC 4.1, 409–410 **4** E. BUSCHOR, Meermänner, 1941. A.A.

Halipedon (Ἁλίπεδον, Ἁλαί). Sumpfige Ebene (Hesych. s.v. Ἀ.) nördl. des Haupthafens des Peiraieus [1; 2], 403 v. Chr. Schauplatz einer Niederlage des Thrasybulos gegen den Spartanerkönig Pausanias (Xen. hell. 2,4,30–34).

1 W. JUDEICH, Top. von Athen, ^{2}1931, 425, 426 Anm. 1 **2** W. KOLBE, s.v. H., RE 7, 2268 **3** TRAVLOS, Athen 3, 164 Abb. 213 (Neophaliron). H.LO.

Halirrhothios (Ἁλιρρόθιος). Attischer Heros, Sohn von Poseidon und einer Nymphe, dessen Tod Gegenstand des ersten Prozesses vor dem Areopag (→ Areios pagos) bildete. In der geläufigsten Mythenform, welche die Rolle des Areopags als Blutgericht erklärt, vergewaltigt er die Tochter von Ares und Aglauros, Alkippe, und wird von Ares erschlagen; Ort beider Taten ist die Quelle im späteren Asklepieion über dem Dionysostheater. Poseidon klagt Ares an, das Gericht der zwölf Götter spricht ihn frei (Eur. El. 1258–1262; Apollod. 3,180; Paus. 1,21,4; Demosth. or. 23,66; Marmor Parium FGrH 239,3; Aristeid. Panathenaikos 46).

Eine andere Erzählung verbindet ihn mit der Aufgabe des Areopag, die attischen Ölbäume zu schützen: Um seinen Vater an Athena zu rächen, versucht H., Athenas Ölbäume (μορίαι) umzuschlagen. Er tötet sich dabei versehentlich selbst mit der Axt, und Poseidon klagt Ares als den Herrn des Eisens an (Serv. georg. 1,18; schol. Aristoph. Nub. 1005). Vielleicht gehört dazu die Bestrafung des Ares zum Knechtsdienst bei einem Sterblichen (vgl. Apollon bei Admetos, Panyassis fr. 16 EpGF). F.G.

Halisarna (Ἁλίσαρνα).

[1] Kleine Stadt, Dynastensitz im Grenzgebiet der Landschaften Mysia und Troas. Bei Xenophon (hell. 3,1,6; an. 7,8,17) wird H. im Zusammenhang mit dem Spartanisch-Persischen Krieg 400–396 v. Chr. erwähnt. Der dort gen. Dynast Prokles ist Nachkomme des Anf. des 5. Jh. v. Chr. hierher verbannten Spartanerkönigs Damaratos, der H. neben Pergamon und Teuthrania von Dareios. I. geschenkt bekommen hatte (Paus. 3,7,8). Genaue Lage, weitere Gesch. unbekannt.

L. BÜRCHNER, s.v. H. (1), RE 7, 2270. E.SCH.

[2] Ortschaft im SO von Kos (Strab. 14,2,19), in der Gegend von Kardamena.

PHILIPPSON/KIRSTEN 4, 297. H.SO.

Halitherses (Ἁλιθέρσης), »auf dem Meere Mut habend« [1; 2].

[1] Sohn des → Ankaios [2] und der Samia (Asios EpGF fr. 7; PEG I).

[2] Seher in der ›Odyssee‹, Sohn des Mastor (2,157f.), Gefährte des Odysseus und des Telemachos (2,253; 17,68), der unter Berufung auf eine frühere Prophezeiung die Freier aufgrund eines Vogelzeichens vergeblich vor der Rückkehr des Odysseus warnt (2,161ff.) und nach dem Freiermord vom Bürgerkrieg abrät (24,451ff.) [3; 4].

1 KAMPTZ, 88; **2** E. RISCH, Wortbildung der homerischen Sprache, ^{2}1974, 78 **3** ST. WEST, in: A Commentary on Homer's Odyssey, Bd. 1, 1988, 142; **4** A. HEUBECK, ebenda, Bd. 3, 1992, 409f. A.A.

Halkyone s. Alkyone

Halkyoneus (Ἁλκυονεύς bzw. Ἀλκυονεύς). Sohn des → Antigonos [2] Gonatas, dem er in Argos 272 v. Chr. den Kopf des gefallenen Erzrivalen → Pyrrhos brachte; vom Vater als Barbar getadelt, behandelte H. Pyrrhos' Sohn Helenos ehrenvoll (Plut. Pyrrhos 34; Plut. mor. 119C; Ail. var. 3,5). L.-M.G.

Hallstatt-Kultur. Die ältere Eisenzeit in Mitteleuropa wird als H. bezeichnet, nach dem Ort Hallstatt im Salzkammergut. Dort fand man um die M. des 19. Jh. ein großes Gräberfeld (über 1 000 Bestattungen) mit reichhaltigem Fundmaterial, das als typisch angesehen wurde und noch im 19. Jh. zur Definition der H. führte. Der Fundplatz hat eine ganz besondere Bedeutung, da es sich um ein schon in der Eisenzeit intensiv abgebautes Salzbergwerk handelt [5; 11. 67–79].

Die H. umfaßt die Zeit von der M. des 8. Jh. bis zur M. des 5. Jh. v. Chr. Eine Frühphase (= ältere H.) dauert bis zum E. des 7. Jh., danach folgt die späte H. (= jüngere H.) [4; 10; 12. 35–64]. Das Hauptverbreitungsgebiet der H. reicht von Zentralfrankreich bis nach Westungarn und Slovenien und von den Alpen bis in die Mittelgebirgszone. Auf Grund unterschied. Entwicklung und arch. Formen wird eine östl. von einer westl. H. geschieden [1; 3; 6; 10; 11. 80–116; 12. 65–158].

Die H. entwickelt sich aus der brz. → Urnenfelder-Kultur und ist u. a. durch die Herausbildung der Eisentechnologie geprägt. Im Zusammenhang damit stehen offensichtlich gesellschaftliche, wirtschaftliche und auch religiöse Umstellungen, die einen aufwendigen Grabkult (Hügel, Kammerbau, bevorzugte Körperbestattung), eine Differenzierung der Bevölkerungsstruktur (reiche Gräber, erste Importfunde usw.) und ein Zurückgehen der Hortfundsitte bewirken. Insgesamt ist die H. bäuerlich geprägt, wobei aber zunehmend Handel, Handwerk und differenzierte Siedlungsformen hinzukommen [1; 10; 11. 389–398].

In der Ost-H. sind bereits in der älteren Phase deutlich Elemente der von Osten vordringenden Reiternomaden (→ Kimmerier, → Skythen usw.) in Gräbern mit entsprechenden Pferdegeschirr-Ausstattungen faßbar, dazu kommen → Helme (italische Formen) und Beile als charakteristische Grabbeigaben, die vereinzelt auch mit Bronzegefäßen und mächtigen Grabhügelbauten kombiniert sind und den Status von → Fürstengräbern erreichen (z. B. Klein Klein in der Steiermark) [6; 11. 29–137; 12. 185–204]. Ein wichtiges Zentrum der östl. H. bildet auch Krain, ebenfalls mit besonders reichen Gräbern [1; 6; 12. 241–260]. Weitere Formen der Grabausstattungen (Schmuck, Tracht, Keramik) charakterisieren die verschiedenen regionalen Gruppen im gesamten Bereich der H.

Eine grundsätzlich ähnliche Entwicklung hin zu reichen Grabhügelbestattungen ist in der westl. H. zu beobachten, hier vor allem durch die Beigabe von vierrädrigen Wagen und Langschwertern aus Bronze oder Eisen ausgezeichnet. Vereinzelt taucht in den Gräbern der älteren H. auch schon Bronzegeschirr (z. T. etr. Import) auf [1; 3; 4; 9].

Der Höhepunkt dieser Entwicklung liegt aber in der späten H. des 6./5. Jh. v. Chr., in der die → Fürstengräber (s. dort auch Karte) von SW-Deutschland bis Burgund das Bild bestimmen. In der späten H. sind auch Veränderungen in anderen Bereichen erkennbar, so z. B. bei der Waffenausstattung, in der das Schwert durch den Dolch ersetzt wird, oder bei den Fibelformen, der Keramik usw. [3; 4; 10]. Ein typischer Krieger der späten H. ist in der Steinskulptur von → Hirschlanden überliefert. In der H. gewinnt die figürliche Darstellung (Plastik, Toreutik, Keramik) an Bedeutung, was auf mediterrane Anregungen und Vermittlung oberit. Gruppen (Situlen-Kreis) zurückzuführen ist. Hier mischen sich Darstellungen griech./etr. Elemente (Fabelwesen usw.) mit solchen der H. (Bewaffnung usw.) auf Bronzegefäßen (Situlen), Gürteln usw. [2; 12. 261–298].

Zumindest in der Ost-H. sind befestigte Siedlungen auf Höhen mit Holz-Stein-Erde-Mauern häufiger zu finden (z. B. Sticna/Slovenien), die bereits in der älteren H. einsetzen und erst mit deren E. verlassen werden [6; 8; 12]. In der westl. H. sind solche Höhenbefestigungen erst in dem späten Abschnitt bekannt; sie haben ihre markantesten Vertreter in den z. T. mediterran geprägten → Fürstensitzen [3; 8; 10]. In diesen Siedlungen zeigt sich auf vielen Gebieten ein intensiver Kontakt (Handel u. a.) mit dem Mittelmeerraum (Etrurien, griech. Kolonien), der Lebensweise (Luxusgüter, Wein, Textilien usw.), Technologie (→ Drehscheiben- und → Drehbank-Kenntnis) und Siedlungsweise (Lehmziegel, Bastionen, Bebauungsstruktur) bestimmt. In Süddeutschland (Bayern) sind sogen. ›Herrenhöfe‹ (Wall-Graben-umhegte Vierecke) als Großgehöfte anzusehen und Ausdruck eines bäuerlichen Adels [7].

Die späte West-H. wird mit Bezug auf griech. Nachrichten mit frühen → Kelten identifiziert. Nachbargebiete der H. sind hingegen kaum ethnisch zu benennen, wenn man vom Ostflügel (Kimmeriern/Skythen) und dem Süden (→ Etrusker, andere ital. Stämme, Illyrer usw.) absieht [3; 6]. Im Westen und Norden der H. bestehen nachlebende Bronzezeitkulturen weiter, denen die Eisentechnologie noch fremd ist; in Norddeutschland sind dies evtl. Vorläufer der german. → Jastorf-Kultur [1; 12. 297–332]. Im 5. Jh. v. Chr. wird die H. von der → Latène-Kultur abgelöst; wie, wo und warum dieser Prozeß erfolgte, läßt sich bisher kaum fassen [3; 10].

→ Befestigungswesen; Dürrnberg; Etrusci (mit Karte); Germanische Archäologie; Handel; Heuneburg (mit Karte); Hochdorf; Hortfund; Illyricum; Keltische Archäologie (mit Karte); Salz; Vix

1 M. Egg, C. Pare, Die Metallzeiten in Europa und im Vorderen Orient, in: Die Abteilung Vorgeschichte im Röm.-German. Zentralmuseum, 1995, 160–192 **2** O.-H. Frey, Die Entstehung der Situlenkunst, in: Röm.-German. Forsch. 31, 1969 **3** W. Kimmig, Die griech. Kolonisation im westl. Mittelmeergebiet und ihre Wirkung auf die Landschaften des westl. Mitteleuropa, in: JRGZ 30, 1983, 5–78 **4** G. Kossack, Südbayern während der Hallstattzeit, in: Röm.-German. Forsch. 24, 1959 **5** K. Kromer, Das Gräberfeld von Hallstatt, 1959 **6** Ders., Das östl. Mitteleuropa in der frühen Eisenzeit (7.–5. Jh. v. Chr.), in: JRGZ 33, 1986, 3–93 **7** K. Leidorf, Herrenhöfe, Bauernhöfe und Tempelbezirke der frühen Eisenzeit, in: H. Becker (Hrsg.), Arch. Prospektion, 1996, 143–154 **8** E. Lessing, Hallstatt: Bilder aus der Frühzeit Europas, 1980 **9** C. Pare, Wagons and Wagon-Graves of the Early Iron Age in Central Europe, 1992 **10** K. Spindler, Die frühen Kelten, 1983 **11** Die Hallstattkultur: Frühform europäischer Einheit. Internationale Ausst., Steyr, 1980 (ohne Hrsg.) **12** Die Hallstattkultur. Ber. über das Symposium in Steyr, 1981 (ohne Hrsg.). V. P.

Halonnesos (Ἁλόννησος). Die Insel der nördl. Ägäis (Strab. 9,5,16; Mela 2,106; Harpokr. s. v.), h. Hag. Eustratios, Hagistrati oder Strati, war Objekt eines Konflikts zw. Philippos II. und Athen: Demosth. 7 hypoth.; 7,2; 12,12; 18,69; Aisch. 3,83; Plut. Demosthenes 9,5; Dion. Hal. Demosthenes 9; 13; Athen. 6,223d–224b. Die Athen gehörige Insel war von Seeräubern besetzt; Philippos II. vertrieb diese, gab die Insel aber den Athenern nicht zurück. Ant. Siedlungsspuren.

L. Bürchner, H. (2), in: RE Suppl. 3, 880–883 • IG XII 8, S. 17f. • Kirsten-Kraiker, 807. H. KAL.

Halos (Ἅλος). Die Reste von H. liegen am Südende des Κρόκιον πεδίον (Krokische Ebene) auf und am Nordfuß eines Othrys-Ausläufers, wo der Übergang vom Malischen Golf zum Golf von Pagasai leicht zu sperren war, da die Küste nur einige 100 m entfernt war (h. ca. 2 km). Den Namen verdankt H. der reichen salzhaltigen Quelle des Amphrysos am Fuß des Stadtberges. Schon im Schiffskatalog der Ilias gen. (Hom. Il. 2,682), war es ein wichtiger thessal. Hafen während der Perserkriege (Hdt. 7,173); aus dem 4. Jh. v. Chr. sind Bronzemünzen bekannt (HN 295); 346 zerstörte Philippos II. H. und gab das Stadtgebiet an Pharsalos (Strab. 9,5). In frühhell. Zeit erfolgte in der Ebene eine Neugründung, wohl als Hafenstadt für Achaia Phtiotis. Aus der Mitte des 2. Jh. ist ein Grenzabkommen mit Thebai im Norden bekannt (IG IX 2 add. ult. 205). Für die Kaiserzeit gibt es keine Nachrichten, in frühbyz. Zeit ist der Name aber belegt (Steph. Byz. s. v.). Die Nachfolgesiedlung Halmyros (ca. 6 km nördl. von H.) spielte in der Kreuzfahrerzeit eine wichtige Rolle.

H. hatte einen altertümlichen Kult des Zeus Laphystios (Hdt. 7,197: Menschenopfer in Dürrezeiten), außerdem einen Tempel der Artemis Panachaia (IG IX 2, add. ult. 205). Die Mauern auf dem Stadtberg über der Quelle sind nach h. Stand nicht STÄHLINS »Althalos«, sondern eine byz. Festung und eine kleine Akropolis der hell. Stadt in der Ebene. Diese selbst, mit fast quadratischer Stadtmauer (ca. 750 m) und rechtwinkligem Straßensystem, weist nur einen Siedlungshorizont auf und war bereits um 260 v. Chr. zerstört (evtl. durch Erdbeben). Der Hafen von H. (und damit wohl die kontinuierlich bewohnte Siedlung) ist weiter zum Meer hin zu vermuten, beim ehemaligen Dorf Tsengeli, dessen Gebiet h. mil. Sperrzone ist.

BCH 114, 1990, 773 (Grabungsbericht) • P. PANTOS, R. REINDERS, in: Αρχαιολογία 3, 1982, 94 (Grabungsbericht) • R. REINDERS, Earthquakes in the Almirós Plain and the Abandonment of New Halos, in: E. OLSHAUSEN, H. SONNABEND (Hrsg.), Stuttgarter Kolloquium zur Histor. Geographie des Altertums 6, 1996. Naturkatastrophen in der ant. Welt (Geographica Historica 10), 1998 • F. STÄHLIN, Das hell. Thessalien, 1924, 177ff. • TIB 1, 1976, 170f. s. v. Halmyros. HE. KR.

Halosydne (Ἁλοσύδνη).

[1] Name des Meeres oder einer Meeresgöttin (der → Amphitrite laut schol. ad loc.) in Hom. Od. 4,404, wo die Robben als »Sprößlinge der H.« erscheinen.

[2] Epitheton der → Thetis (Hom. Il. 20,207) und der → Nereiden insgesamt (Apoll. Rhod. 4,1599). Die Etym. war in der Ant. umstritten (u. a. »Meerestochter«; vgl. Hesych. s. v. ὕδναι); h. erkl. man H. als »Meereswoge« (mit Gen. ἅλός und *n*-Stamm von ὕδωρ) [1; 2; 3]. Vielleicht auch schon myk. belegt (PY Ta 642 a_2-ro-u-do-pi /halos hudo^h^phi/: »mit Aquamarinen«) [4].

1 FRISK, s. v. 2 CHANTRAINE, s. v. 3 E. RISCH, Wortbildung der homerischen Sprache, ²1974, 219, 228
4 VENTRIS/CHADWICK, 339f. A. A.

Halotus. Eunuch, der Vorkoster des → Claudius [III 1] war und ihm auf Befehl → Agrippinas [3] das Gift gegeben haben soll, an dem er starb. Obwohl er sich unter Nero schuldig machte, schützte ihn Galba und übertrug ihm eine finanziell einträgliche Prokuratur. PIR² H 11.

W. E.

Halsschmuck

A. GRIECHENLAND B. ETRURIEN UND ROM

A. GRIECHENLAND

Neben dem bekannten Mythos der → Eriphyle spielt H. eine ähnliche Rolle bei → Skylla (Aischyl. Choeph. 613–622); daneben sei die Komödie *Plókion* des Menander (vgl. Plut. mor. 2,141d; Gell. 2,23,6) erwähnt. Bei Aristain. 1,1 sind die Steine des H. so angeordnet, daß sie den Namen der Laïs ergeben. H. (ἁλύσιον, κάθημα, μάννος, μανιάκης, ὅρμος, πλόκιον) hat sich als Kette oder Reif, mit und ohne Anhänger seit der Frühzeit im gesamten Mittelmeergebiet in großer Anzahl erhalten, wobei Farb- und Schmucksteine, Metalle, Ton u. a. als Materialien dienten und in verschiedensten Formen und Kombinationen verarbeitet wurden. Bereits der H. der vormyk., myk. und min. Zeit (Ägina-Schatz, London, BM; »Priamosschatz«, ehemals Berlin) erreichte eine hohe technische und künstlerische Qualität (z. T. mit Granulation und Filigran), wobei sich die Fuchsschwanzkette aus achtförmigen und umgebogenen Doppelschlaufen als Leitform bis in die Moderne entwickelte. In der archa. Zeit sind Halsketten und eng um den Hals gelegte Stoffbänder mit einem oder mehreren Anhängern (u. a. Eichel- und Tierkopfanhänger) vertreten, die mit T-förmigen Ösen an einer Kette befestigt sind. Noch vor der Mitte des 5. Jh. v. Chr. tritt als Neuerung der bewegliche Anhänger auf, der nicht mehr starr an der Kette hängt, sondern bei den Bewegungen der Trägerin mitschwingt. Bestimmend für das 4. Jh. v. Chr. sind das flache, wie geflochten wirkende und aus vielen Schlaufen in der Technik der Fuchsschwanzkette zusammengesetzte Halsband (wohl das πλόκιον, *plókion*) und der in der Zukunft sehr beliebte Speerspitzenanhänger (ὅρμος λογχωτός, *hórmos lonchōtós*). Anzufügen sind kordelartige Fuchsschwanzketten. Nach der Mitte des 4. Jh. v. Chr. wird der H. nicht mehr mit Schnüren im Nacken befestigt, sondern weist einen Haken- und Ösenverschluß auf, der von Löwenköpfen überdeckt wird und vorn in der Halskuhle liegt (→ *torques*); als Dekor des Verschlusses wählt man dann auch den Heraklesknoten. Zu diesen unterschiedlichen Formen des H. treten noch Amulettanhänger (*periderídia*), Ketten mit halbmondförmigen Anhängern, Tierkopfketten mit Delphin-, Löwen-, Antilopen- oder Luchsverschluß, ferner die Bandelierketten. Ketten trug die Frau im Hell. nicht nur um den Hals, sondern auch auf dem Gewand von den Schultern herabhängend.

B. ETRURIEN UND ROM

Auch der etr. und röm. H. (*monile, monilia*, seltener *collaria*) weist eine hohe Qualität in Technik (Fuchs-

schwanzketten, aus Golddraht geflochtene Ketten, Gliederketten) und Material auf; dies zeigen bereits frühe Exemplare (z. B. aus der Tomba Regolini Galassi in Cerveteri). Wie in Griechenland ist auch bei etr. Männern in der frühen Zeit H. anzutreffen, wozu bei Kindern noch Amulett-H. kommt. In der röm. Zeit ist H. dann nur noch bei Frauen üblich (Quint. 11,3.; Apul. met. 5,8.; Suet. Galba 18). Beliebt war auch der eng um den Hals gelegte H., der vielfach mit den als Amulett dienenden mondsichelförmigen *lunulae* (dazu z. B. Plin. nat. 37,44) und einem radförmigen Ornament am Verschluß ausgestattet ist. Großer Wertschätzung erfreuten sich auch die *catellae* oder *catenae* (Hor. epist. 1,17,55; Isid. orig. 19,31,11) genannten Halsketten, die bis zu den Hüften herabhingen, bzw. die *lineae* mit den aufgereihten Perlen oder durchbohrten Edelsteinen. Darstellungen des H. sind aus zahlreichen Denkmälern bekannt, worunter u. a. nicht nur Wandgemälde, sondern auch die → Mumienporträts Auskunft geben. Hinzu treten die vielen Funde aus den Vesuvstädten und den Grabstätten Italiens und der Provinzen.
→ Schmuck

I. Blanck, Stud. zum griech. Halsschmuck der arch. und klass. Zeit, 1974 • H. Büsing, Ein goldenes Halsband mit Amphoren-Anhängern, in: Ant. Welt 23, 1992, 123–128 • I. G. Damm u. a. (Hrsg.), Goldschmuck der röm. Frau, Ausstellung Köln 1993 • A. D'Amicis, Collane, in: E. M. de Juliis (Hrsg.), Gli ori di Taranto in Età Ellenistica, Ausstellung Hamburg 1989, 193–224 • B. Deppert-Lippitz, Griech. Goldschmuck, 1985 • A.-M. Manière-Lévêque, L'évolution des bijoux »aristocratiques« féminins à travers les trésors protobyzantins d'orfèvrerie, in: RA 1997, 79–106 • B. Pfeiler, Röm. Goldschmuck des ersten und zweiten Jh. n. Chr. nach datierten Funden, 1970 • M. Pfrommer, Unt. zur Chronologie früh- und hochhell. Goldschmucks, IstForsch 37, 1990.
R. H.

Haluntium, Halontion (Ἀλόντιον). Stadt an der Nordküste von Sicilia (Dion. Hal. ant. 1,51; Cic. Verr. 2,3,103; 2,4,51; Plin. nat. 3,90; 14,80: Weinbau), h. San Marco d'Anunzio. Zum Gymnasion von H. vgl. SEG 26, 1060 (Revision bei [1]). Zur Mz.-Produktion vgl. [2. 5–16].

1 G. Manganaro, Sikelika, 1988 2 F. Bianco, Archeologia Storica di Messina, 1993.
GI. MA./Ü: H. D.

Halykos (Ἅλυκος). Fluß (84 km lang) an der sizilischen SW-Küste, mündet nordwestl. von Capo Bianco bei Herakleia Minoa ins Meer, h. Plátani. Der H. wird in den Verträgen zw. Dionysios. I. (376 oder 374 v. Chr.: StV 2, Nr. 261) bzw. Timoleon (339 v. Chr.: StV 2, Nr. 344) und den Karthagern als Demarkationslinie zw. den beiden Machtbereichen genannt. E. O.

Halys (Ἅλυς). Längster Fluß Kleinasiens (über 900 km), h. Kızıl İrmak (»roter Fluß«). Die Quellflüsse in der Landschaft Kamisene (östl. von Sivas) aufnehmend, fließt der H. in weit nach Süden ausholendem Bogen durch Kappadokia, wendet sich östl. des Tuz Gölü (»Salzsee«) nach Norden, streift Galatia (in älterer Zeit Phrygia) und durchbricht als Grenzfluß der Landschaften Paphlagonia und Pontos das Gebirge zur Mündung ins Schwarze Meer. Die griech. Namensform wurde mit Salzlagern der Landschaft Ximene in Verbindung gebracht; vorgriech. Namen sind unbekannt, und die Bestimmung der Sprache, auf die der Flußname zurückgeht, ist umstritten [1. 60]. Erstmals bei Aischyl. Pers. 865 gen., findet der H. oft Erwähnung im ant. Schrifttum (bes. Hdt. 1,6; 5,52; Strab. 12,3,12; Plin. nat. 6,6); berühmt geworden sind die Gesch. um die H.-Überschreitung des lyd. Königs → Kroisos (Hdt. 1,75; Aristot. rhet. 3,5).

1 J. Tischler, Kleinasiat. Hydronomie, 1977.

D. J. Georgacas, From the river systems in Anatolia, in: Journ. of the American Name Society 12, 1964, 197–214.
C. MA.

Ham (hebr.: *cham*, etwa »heiß«). Neben Sem (→ Semiten) und Japhet einer der drei Söhne → Noahs und gemäß Gn 10 der Stammvater der vier Nationen Kusch, Miṣrayīm, Put und Kanaan, die später als Hamiten bezeichnet wurden. Die Gesch. Hams, der nach Gn 9,22 ff. seinen Vater Noah beschämt hatte, wurde in unterschiedlicher Weise im nachbiblischen rabbinisch-haggadischen Schrifttum verarbeitet. Y. D.

Hamadryaden (ἁμαδρυάδες; lat. *hamadryades*; später auch: ἀδρυάδες, ἀδρυάδες, *adryades*), Baumnymphen. Im Unterschied zu den im Bereich von Bäumen sich aufhaltenden Dryaden sind die H. mit dem Baum (δρῦς, *drys*), in dem sie leben, aufs engste verbunden: Mit ihm zugleich (ἅμα, *hama*) entstehen und vergehen sie (schol. Apoll. Rhod. 2,477; Serv. ecl. 10,62, vgl. Pind. fr. 165). Der Begriff ist zuerst belegt bei Apoll. Rhod. 2,477 (bzw. Anth. Pal. 9,823,6), die Vorstellung bereits in Hom. h. 5,256 ff. Das Konzept der H. geht vielleicht zurück auf die bei Hesiod genannten Eschennymphen (Μελίαι, → *Melíai*, Hes. theog. 187; vgl. Hes. erg. 145) [1. 186]. Das sympathetische Verhältnis der Nymphen zu ihren Bäumen kommt bes. bei Kall. h. 4,79 ff. und in Erzählungen über Baumfrevel (z. B. Erysichthon) zum Ausdruck (Kall. h. 6,31 ff.; Ov. met. 8,725 ff.). Im Motiv des blutenden Baumes (Ov. met. 8,762 ff.; 9,325 ff.) läßt sich möglicherweise der Reflex eines alten Glaubens an beseelte Bäume fassen (vgl. [2. 92]). Animistische Deutungen, wie sie etwa Mannhardt [3] auf die H. angewandt hat, werden der griech.-röm. Vorstellung einer anthropomorphen Natur jedoch nicht gerecht (so [4. 249]; dagegen [5. 187; 6]). Anders als für Nymphen im allg. ist kultische Verehrung für die H. kaum bezeugt (vgl. aber Apoll. Rhod. 2,477 ff. und Nonn. Dion. 44,88 f.). In späterer Zeit wurde die Verbindung zwischen den H. und ihrem Baum als weniger symbiotisch angesehen – so in einigen Verwandlungssagen (Ov. met. 1,690: Syrinx; Nonn. Dion. 2,98: Daphne). In den *Dionysiaká* des Nonnos, die das häufigste Vorkommen des

Begriffs aufweisen, verlassen die H. ihre Bäume und leben nach deren Tod weiter (z.B. 37,20). Bereits bei Properz (1,20) und Ovid (fast. 4,231) werden die H. nicht mehr streng von anderen Nymphen unterschieden. Eine für die H. spezifische Ikonographie läßt sich nicht belegen.
→ Baumkult; Erysichthon; Nymphai

1 WILAMOWITZ, 1, 184–187 2 A. HENRICHS, »Thou shalt not kill a tree«: Greek, Manichaean and Indian tales, in: Bulletin of the American Society of Papyrologists 16, 1979, 85–108 3 W. MANNHARDT, Ant. Wald- und Feldkulte, 1877, Bd. 2, 1–38 4 NILSSON, GGR 1, 244–255 5 C. BOETTICHER, Der Baumkultus der Hellenen, 1856 6 L. MALTEN, Motivgesch. Untersuchungen zur Sagenforsch., in: Hermes 74, 1939, 200ff. S.G.

Hamaxanteia (Ἁμαξάντεια). Att. Paralia?-Demos der Phyle Hippothontis, stellte einen → *buleutés*. Lage unbekannt.

TRAILL, Attica, 51, 68, 110 Nr. 52, Tab. 8 • J.S. TRAILL, Demos and Trittys, 1986, 138 • WHITEHEAD, 372 Anm. 6. H.LO.

Hamaxia (Ἁμαξία, Stadiasmus maris magni 208). Ort in der westl. Kilikia, mit Sinekkales (6 km westl. von Korakesion) zu identifizieren [1. 78f.]; der Name ist wohl von ἅμαξα (»Holzfuhrwerk«) abzuleiten [2. 250f.]. H. gehörte zu den Schenkungen des Antonius an Kleopatra (Strab. 14,5,3). Es existiert kein sicherer Beleg für einen Polis-Status [1. 79]. Arch.: gut erh., ummauerte Siedlung mit Torbau im Süden, dreischiffiger Kirche im Westen, Nekropole im NW.

1 G.E. BEAN, T.B. MITFORD, Journeys in Rough Cilicia 1964–1968, 1970, 78ff. 2 J. NOLLÉ, Pamphylische Studien 6–10, in: Chiron 17, 1987, 235–276. K.T.

Hamaxitos (Ἁμαξιτός). Kleine Stadt in der Troas, nach COOK ([1. 231ff.], dort auch die älteren Lokalisierungen) im Bereich des nordwestl. vom h. Gülpınar an der Küste gelegenen Beşik Tepesı. Vermutlich von den Achaioi gegr., wurde H. von kilikischen Bewohnern von Chrysa besiedelt (Strab. 13,1,63). Nach 427 v.Chr. war H. wohl von Mytilene abhängig, wurde in den att. Tributquotenlisten mit 4 Talenten Phoros zu den aktaiischen Poleis gezählt. Etwa 400 v.Chr. stand H. unter der Herrschaft der Dynastin Mania, bevor Derkylidas H. 399 v.Chr. kampflos übernahm (Xen. hell. 3,1,15f.). Durch → Antigonos [1] Monophthalmos wurde H. in einem Synoikismos mit Alexandreia Troas vereint. Aufgegeben wurde H. aber nicht: Der Hafen H. wird noch in dem Zollgesetz aus Ephesos [2. 61] erwähnt, ebenso bei Plinius (nat. 5,124). Berühmt war der Tempel des Apollon Smintheios/Smintheus, dessen aus röm. Zeit stammende Ruinen noch h. in Gülpınar zu sehen sind. Die göttl. Verehrung der Mäuse in H. ist dagegen älter (vgl. Ail. var. 12,4; Strab. 13,1,63).

1 J.M. COOK, The Troad, 1973, 227ff. 2 H. ENGELMANN, D. KNIBBE (Hrsg.), Das Zollgesetz der Prov. Asia, in: EA 14, 1989.

W. LEAF, Strabo on the Troad, 1923, 227ff. E.SCH.

Hamilkar (Karthagischer Name Hmlk = »Gnade ist mlk«, Ἀμίλκας).

[1] Sohn des Hanno und einer Syrakusanerin (Hdt. 7,165), Enkel des → Mago [1. 36,183f.], Vater des → Geskon [1]; karthagischer Feldherr ca. 500–480 v.Chr., dessen Rolle beim Sardinienfeldzug seines Bruders Hasdrubal unklar ist (Iust. 19,1,6f.) [1. 37]. Heftig umstritten ist H.s Königs- bzw. Sufetenamt [2. 459–461; 3. 70f., 90–97]. Im J. 480 unternahm H. einen Kriegszug gegen das von → Theron eroberte und mit Hilfe des → Gelon [1] verteidigte → Himera, dessen vormaliger Stadtherr → Terillos, ein Gastfreund H.s, gemeinsam mit → Anaxilaos [1] um Waffenhilfe gebeten hatte (Hdt. 7,165). Das Unternehmen endete mit der karthagischen Niederlage, H. fand den Tod im Selbstopferritual (Hdt. 7,167) [3. 51–64]. Die Legende, die Schlacht bei Himera habe parallel zum griech. Sieg bei Salamis stattgefunden (Hdt. 7,166), steht ebenso wie der Bericht, H. habe im Auftrag des → Xerxes die Griechen Siziliens angegriffen (Diod. 11,1,4f.; 20; StV 2,129) [1. 38; 2. 97f.] im Dienst sikeliotischer Propaganda [3. 15–48].

[2] Karthagischer Stratege für West-Sizilien, der 318 und 315 v.Chr. zugunsten oligarchischer Exulanten um → Deinokrates [1] in den syrakusanischen Bürgerkrieg gegen → Agathokles [2] eingriff (Iust. 22,2,2–4) [2. 178f.; 4. 55]. Daß H. 318 insgeheim auf Agathokles' künftige Hilfe bei seinem eigenen Staatsstreich gehofft habe (Iust. 22,2,5f.), ist ein Gerücht [1. 44; 4. 56]. Nachdem H. 314/3 einen Frieden im sikeliotischen Krieg vermittelt hatte, durch den die Hegemonie des Tyrannen von Syrakus bestätigt wurde (Diod. 19,65; 71,6f.; StV 3,424), führten Exilsyrakusaner in Karthago Beschwerde über H.: Er wurde abgesetzt und verurteilt, starb unterdessen aber in Sizilien (Iust. 22,3) [1. 43f.; 2. 181–183; 4. 55–57].

[3] H. Barkas (»der Blitz«). Begründer der → Barkiden, Vater von → Hannibal [4], → Hasdrubal [3] und → Mago; genialer karthagischer Feldherr. Im 1. Punischen Krieg überfiel H., seit 247 Nauarch als Nachfolger des → Karthalo [2], in Partisanenmanier bruttisches und lukanisches Küstengebiet sowie röm. Stellungen auf Sizilien und verschanzte sich selbst an der sizilischen Nordküste nahe Panormos am → Heirkte (h. Monte Castellaccio?); 244 eroberte er die Stadt → Eryx und führte gegen das röm. → Drepanon [4] einen zähen, entbehrungsreichen Kleinkrieg (Pol. 1,56; 58; Diod. 24,6; 8f.; Zon. 8,16). Nach dem Verlust der Flotte des → Hanno [5] handelte H. als bevollmächtigter Stratege im Frühjahr 241 die Friedenspräliminarien, u.a. den eigenen freien und ehrenhaften Abzug, aus und legte dann in Lilybaion sein Kommando nieder. Die Demobilisierung des Söldnerheeres überließ er dem → Geskon [3] (Pol. 1,62f.; 66; 68,12; 3,9,7; 27; StV 3,493) [1. 51f.; 2. 246–252; 5. 9–12].

H.s Motive für den Amtsverzicht sind ebenso unklar wie seine Rolle am Vorabend des sog. Söldnerkrieges. In dessen Verlauf erhielt H. im J. 240 den Oberbefehl gegen die Aufständischen und operierte trotz diverser Kompetenzstreitigkeiten mit → Hanno [6], dem Strategen für Libyen, erfolgreich: Er entsetzte → Utica, besiegte mehrfach → Spendius, u.a. in der spektakulären Schlacht bei Prion (was ihm nicht zuletzt durch die Unterstützung des Numiderfürsten Naravas, mit dem H. sich verschwägerte, möglich war) und überwältigte schließlich auch (gemeinsam mit Hanno) den Führer des Aufstandes, → Mathos (Pol. 1,75–78; 81f.; 84–88; Zon. 8,17,8) [1. 52–54; 2. 252–266; 5. 13–23]. Indessen annektierten die Römer Sardinien [2. 266–268; 5. 23f.], was den weiteren Lebensweg H.s insofern bestimmte, als er, seit 238 Stratege für Libyen auf Lebenszeit(!), für Karthago nach dem Verlust der Seemacht einen neuen Weg zu ökonomischer und politischer Stabilität finden wollte und daher 237 mitsamt Heer und Familie nach Gades (h. Cadiz) übersetzte, um im eisen- und silbererzreichen Südspanien Karthagos direkte Herrschaft zu etablieren. Mit einer Reihe energischer Feldzüge gegen tartessische und keltiberische Stammesfürsten erreichte H., der im J. 229 gegen die Orisser fiel, sein hochgestecktes Ziel, denn er hinterließ seinem Nachfolger → Hasdrubal [2] eine gefestigte Herrschaft, deren neues Zentrum das neugegründete Leuke Akra (= Alicante?) war (Pol. 2,1,7; Diod. 25,10; Liv. 21,1f.) [1. 56–58; 2. 270–274; 5. 25–39].

[4] Karthagischer Offizier des → Hasdrubal [3] (?, vgl. Liv. 31,11,5) [1. 62, 360], der in Oberitalien auf eigene Faust noch 200 v.Chr. einen Aufstand der → Cenomanni [3] und → Insubres organisierte, daraufhin nach einer röm. Demarche in Karthago zwar exiliert wurde, aber erst im J. 197 von C. → Cornelius [I 11] Cethegus besiegt werden konnte (Liv. 31,10f.; 19) [1. 62f.].

[5] Karthagischer Gesandter, der 149 v.Chr. mit → Geskon [5] und → Mago das karthagische Deditionsangebot nach Rom brachte (Pol. 36,3,7f.) [1. 65].

[6] H. Phameas (Pol. 36,8,1) irrtümlich für → Himilkon [5] Phameas [1. 64, 371].

1 Geus 2 Huss 3 W. Ameling, Karthago, 1993 4 L. M. Hans, Die Göttin mit der Tiara, in: SNR 66, 1987, 45–58 5 J. Seibert, Hannibal, 1993. L.-M. G.

Hamiten, Hamitisch s. Afroasiatisch

Hammon s. Ammon

Ḫammurapi (Ḫammurabi). Bedeutendster Herrscher der 1. Dyn. von → Babylon, regierte von 1792–1750 v.Chr. Nach langen Kämpfen mit rivalisierenden mesopot. Mächten, aber auch mit den Herrschern → Elams, die Souveränität über die Staaten Mesopotamiens beanspruchten, hat Ḫ. seit 1755 v.Chr. ganz Mesopotamien von Mari am mittleren Euphrat und der Gegend um das h. Mossul bis an den pers. Golf beherrscht. Mehr als 200 von ihm stammende Briefe und zahlreiche Berichte der Abgesandten eines seiner Verbündeten und späteren Rivalen, Zimrilim von Mari, erhellen wie selten bei einer Herrschergestalt des Alt. deren Handeln und Verhalten in vielen Details. Ḫ.s Ruhm als großer Herrscher hat in Mesopot. bis ins 1. Jt. fortgelebt (→ Amulett). Dies beruht v.a. auf der von ihm veranlaßten Sammlung von Rechtsnormen, die auf einer 1902 in → Susa gefundenen Stele verzeichnet sind, die im 13. Jh. v.Chr. dorthin verschleppt wurde (Übers.: [1]). Die Stele ist eines der ältesten und mit über 280 Paragraphen umfangreichsten »Rechtsbücher«. Für die Rechtsgesch. Mesopotamiens und des Altertums ist sie deswegen von großer Bedeutung.

→ Keilschriftrechte

1 TUAT 1, 39–80.

H. Klengel, König Ḫ. und der Alltag Babylons, 1991 • J. Renger, Noch einmal: Was war der »Kodex« Ḫ. – ein erlassenes Gesetz oder ein Rechtsbuch?, in: H.-J. Gehrke (Hrsg.), Rechtskodifikation und soziale Normen, 1994, 27–59 (mit Lit.). J. RE.

Hampsicora. Vornehmer Sarde, im J. 215 v.Chr. mit seinem Sohn Hostus Organisator und mil. Führer des Aufstandes sardischer Stämme gegen die röm. Herrschaft. H. erhielt unzureichende karthagische Unterstützung durch → Hasdrubal [4] und tötete sich nach einer vernichtenden Niederlage gegen T. → Manlius Torquatus (Liv. 23,32,7–10; 40,3–41,6).

Huss, 348f. L.-M. G.

Hamster. Der nur nördlich der Alpen an Getreidefeldern vorkommende H. (Cricetus cricetus) war weder Griechen noch Römern bekannt. Der früher mit dem H. gleichgesetzte [1] Winterschlaf haltende μυωξός/ *myōxós* bei Opp. kyn. 2,574 und 585 bezeichnet jedoch den Siebenschläfer (*glis*). Der *crichetus* bei Thomas von Cantimpré 4,26 (nach dem bisher unentdeckten *Liber rerum*) wird zwar recht gut beschrieben, doch passen die Beschreibung seiner Größe (wie ein Eichhörnchen) und des Lebensraumes (*Apulea*) nicht dazu. Albertus Magnus, De animalibus 22,47 [3. 1375] sichert durch die Glosse *hamester Germanice* die Bestimmung als *cricetus*.

1 Lamer, s.v. H., RE Suppl. 3, 885 2 H. Boese (ed.), Thomas Cantimpratensis, Liber de natura rerum, 1973 3 H. Stadler (ed.), Albertus Magnus, De animalibus, 2, 1921. C. HÜ.

Handel I. Alter Orient II. Phönizien III. Etrurien IV. Griechenland V. Rom VI. Byzanz VII. Frühes Mittelalter

I. Alter Orient (Ägypten, Vorderasien, Indien)

Fern- oder Überland-H. – im Gegensatz zu Austausch und Allokation von Gütern des tägl. Bedarfs auf lokaler Ebene –, im Alten Orient arch. seit dem Neolithikum, in Texten seit dem 3. Jt. v. Chr. belegt, beruhte auf der Notwendigkeit, die Versorgung mit sog. strategischen Gütern (Metallen, Bauholz) sicherzustellen, die im eigenen Territorium nicht vorhanden waren, sowie auf dem Bedürfnis nach Luxus- und Prestigegütern bzw. den dafür benötigten Materialien.

In histor. Zeit lag die Organisation des H. in der Regel in der Hand zentraler Institutionen (Palast, Tempel; Ausnahme: Zinn-H. Assurs mit Anatolien, → Kaneš), die prakt. Durchführung in der Hand von Handelsagenten. Vielfach belegt sind Handelsniederlassungen, z. T. mit Warendepots, in entfernten Orten (z. B. Händler aus Assur in Kaneš, aus Mari in Ḫalab/Aleppo, aus Babylonien in Dilmun, aus Palmyra in → Charax Spasinu, aus Griechenland in → Naukratis). → Staatsverträge schützten die Händler vor der Willkür lokaler Herrscher. Der Tauschwert der Waren hing oft von außer-ökonomischen Faktoren ab. Neben dem friedlichen H. spielten mil. organisierte Expeditionen (z. B. von Äg. nilaufwärts nach Nubien auf der Suche nach Gold) oder systemat. Eroberungen mit dem Ziel, sich die benötigten Materialien als Beute und Tribut zu sichern (z. B. Assyrien im 1. Jt. v. Chr. – Metalle und Pferde für die Kriegsführung, Luxusgüter), eine Rolle. Das fast einzige Exportgut Mesopot. waren Textilien, für andere Materialien war Mesopot. lediglich Umschlagplatz. Äg. exportierte hauptsächlich Gold, aber auch Stoffe und hochwertige Handwerkserzeugnisse.

Die nach Mesopot. gebrachten Güter kamen meist über Zwischenstationen ins Land. Im pers. Golf war → Dilmun Drehscheibe des Überseeh-H.s mit Oman (dort sind Kupferlagerstätten und Verhüttung arch. nachzuweisen) und den → Indus-Kulturen (Holz, Schmuckstein, v. a. Karneol). Kupfer stammte auch aus Zypern und Anatolien. Zinn kam auf dem Landweg über den Iran nach Susa, Ešnunna an der Dijāla und von da über die Euphrat-Route nach Mari und weiter nach Nord- und Mittelsyrien bzw. über die Pässe im Gebiet des h. Suleimanie nach → Assur und weiter nach Anatolien (Kaneš). Bauholz wurde in großem Umfang aus Syrien und dem Libanon auf dem Euphrat nach Babylonien geflößt. Die damit verbundenen Erfahrungen sind im → Gilgamesch-Epos reflektiert, die Handelsbeziehungen zum iran. Plateau in sumer. Epen. Syrien und der Libanon lieferten außerdem Elfenbeinschnitzereien, Purpurstoffe/-gewänder und Wein. Über lange Distanz gehender Transport von Getreide war nur per Schiff möglich und erfolgte daher nur in Notsituationen. Sklaven bezog Äg. v. a. aus Syrien, Babylonien aus dem NO des h. Iraq.

Zu den Luxusgütern, die nach Äg., Syrien, Anatolien und Mesopot. gelangten, gehörten v. a. Kosmetika, wohlriechende Öle, Harze und andere Duftstoffe, Gewürze, die aus weit entfernten Regionen im Umkreis des Vorderen Orients stammten. Über die Herkunft von Silber und Gold schweigen die Quellen weitgehend. Gold bezogen die Ägypter aus Nubien, Silber stammte u. a. aus Anatolien; aus dem Osten Irans und Afghanistan kam → Lapis Lazuli. Der H. mit Prestigegütern spielte sich weitgehend in Form von Geschenkaustausch zw. Herrschern ab (u. a. belegt in den → Amarna-Briefen; Gold nach Babylonien).

Im 2. und 1. Jt. v. Chr. spielten vor allem Emporien (→ Emporion) und Stadtstaaten (u. a. → Al-Mīnā, → Arados [1], → Berytos, Byblos [1], → Ioppe, → Sidon, → Tyros, → Ugarit) an der Mittelmeerküste eine wichtige Rolle in der Verbindung des Orients mit der Ägäis. Im syr.-mesopot. Raum erfüllten verschiedene Orte im Grenzbereich zu anderen Staaten oder an den Schnittpunkten wichtiger Handelswege zu unterschiedl. Zeiten eine entsprechende Funktion: → Karkemiš am oberen Euphrat, → Ebla in der Ebene von Aleppo mit Verbindung zu Emar und Mari am Euphrat; Assur (im 20./19. Jh. Zinn-H. mit Anatolien); in Babylonien waren wichtige Schaltstellen für den Überland-H. Ešnunna (zum iran. Plateau im 20.–18. Jh.) und Sippar (Euphratroute nach NW – Mari und Emar – und SO – Pers. Golf, Elam im 19.–17. Jh.). Für den Ost-West-Verkehr durch die syr. Steppe waren → Palmyra seit frühgesch. Zeit und Ḫatra vom 1. bis 3. Jh. n. Chr. wichtige Stützpunkte. Verschiedentlich haben sich Orte am Schnittpunkt wichtiger Handelswege auch zu bedeutenden staatlichen Zentren entwickelt, die z. T. weite Territorien beherrschten (Mari im 19./18. Jh.; Palmyra seit d. 1. Jh. v. Chr.).

Der Überland-H. im Nahen Osten geschah bis ins 1. Jt. mittels Eselskarawanen (Kamele wurden erst nach dem 2. Jt. v. Chr. eingesetzt). Als Transportwege hatten Nil, Euphrat, Tigris und Indus für Äg., Mespot. und Indien fundamentale Bedeutung. Der H. zwischen Äg. und Levante (→ Byblos [1]) geschah seit dem AR durch seegängige Schiffe, zw. der Ägäis und Äg. im 2. Jt. über das kretische Hierapetra und zu Land entlang der libyschen Küste zum Nildelta (→ Ägäische Koine). Im 6. Jh. v. Chr. wurde die Seeroute um die Arab. Halbinsel herum von Äg. aus beherrscht, nachdem zuvor schon der Seeweg durch das Rote Meer nach Äthiopien (Punt) befahren wurde. Von → Necho veranlaßt, umfuhren phönik. Seefahrer Afrika (Hdt. 2,158). Die Route von Südarabien entlang der Westküste Arabiens ist erstmals unter Salomo für die Königin von Saba bezeugt (→ Weihrauchstraße), und von da weiter über den → Königsweg nach Syrien. Von Äg. lief der Landweg über Raphia und Hazor, die beide als Umschlagplätze nach Mittel- und Nordsyrien dienten. Der See-H. zw. Indien und Mesopot. lief bis ins 2. Jt. über Dilmun im Pers. Golf; seit dem 3. Jh. v. Chr. spielte → Arabien eine bedeutende Rolle im Indienhandel.

→ Barabara; Elfenbein(schnitzerei); Merv; Patala

1 W. Helck, s. v. H., LÄ 3, 944–48 2 H. Klengel, H. und Händler, 1969 3 C. Lamberg-Karlowsky, Trade Mechanisms in Indo-Mesopot. Relations, in: Journal of the American Oriental Society 92, 1972, 222–229. J.RE.

II. Phönizien

Die phöniz. Präsenz und Expansion im Mittelmeerraum war neben anderen Faktoren und Ursachen vornehmlich mit dem Fern-H. verbunden, mit der Zufuhr von Rohstoffen und Agrarprodukten einerseits sowie mit dem Absatz von Bauholz aus dem Libanon und veredelten Fertigprodukten andererseits. Vom Beginn der Eisenzeit am E. des 11. Jh. bis in das 6. Jh. v. Chr. hinein war die Organisation des von den phöniz. Städten Tyros, Sidon und Byblos betriebenen mediterranen H. der polit. Exekutive mit ihrem wirtschaftlichen Schutz unterstellt, ein stabiles und in den folgenden Jh. nicht wesentlich verändertes System, dessen Ursprung in alten und soliden brz. Strukturen des Vorderen Orients lag. Der Bericht des ägypt. Gesandten Wen-Amun (1085–1060 v. Chr.) am Hofe Zakar Baals, des Königs von Byblos, sowie die im AT enthaltenen Nachrichten (2 Sam 5; 1 Kg 5–7, 9–10; 2 Chr 8–9, 20 [969–930 v. Chr.]; Jes 23 [E. 8./Anf. 7. Jh. v. Chr.]; Ez 26–28 [586 v. Chr.]) sind wertvolle, zugleich aber spärliche Überlieferungen dieser Zeit. Wegen ihres teils ungeklärten Ursprungs und hinsichtlich ihrer Datier. und Aussagekraft für das Verständnis des phöniz. H. sind sie umstritten.

Der König verfügte über die notwendige Verwaltungsstruktur und über das Monopol zur Gewinnung und Beschaffung der besonderen und reichlich vorhandenen Rohstoffe dieser Region sowie des H. mit diesen. Ihm standen hervorragende Handwerker mit weithin gerühmten Kenntnissen und Fertigkeiten zur Verfügung, und er besaß die legale und fiskalische Hoheit der Seehäfen und der territorialen Gewässer. Unabhängig in ihrer Organisation, doch in enger Verbindung und Zusammenarbeit mit dem Haus des Königs und dessen H.-Flotte, bildeten komplementär dazu Konsortien kapitalkräftiger und einflußreicher privater Kaufleute und Schiffseigner – H.-Dynastien mit verzweigten und weitreichenden H.-Kontakten und H.-Partnern – das Rückgrat für ausgedehnte, über die Mittelmeerregion weit hinausreichende Unternehmungen, mit denen sich ebenso große Profite wie Verluste erzielen ließen. Sie besaßen bedeutende Flotten oder rüsteten diese aus und boten wirksamen finanziellen Schutz gegen die mit dem H. verbundenen Risiken und Gefahren. Das Phänomen des »Geschenk-H.« mit und des »Austausches« von Luxusgegenständen und Pretiosen war eine Voraussetzung professionellen H., die die gegenseitigen Verbindungen förderte und in Geschäften mit H.-Partnern als Form von finanziellem Vorschuß gehandhabt wurde. Das enge Zusammenspiel zwischen phöniz. Rel., Staat und Monarchie erwies sich in der Instrumentalisierung des Tempels als polit. und merkantile Einrichtung, die dem H. auch die finanzielle Unterstützung ermöglichte.

Die Stadt → Tyros war berühmt wegen ihrer Seemacht, ihrer internationalen Bedeutung im mediterranen Fern-H. und ihres Reichtums. Glanz, Herrlichkeit und Arroganz galten gleichsam als Syn. für das heraufbeschworene Elend nach ihrem Untergang, und beides war Anlaß dramatischer Weissagungen at. Propheten. Während des 9.–8. Jh. v. Chr., der Zeit der Blüte und größten Ausdehnung des tyrischen H. nach Osten, operierten Agenten für die tyrischen H.-Organisationen auf drei wirtschaftlich kontrollierten Rohstoffmärkten, um die Versorgung der Stadt und ihres Handwerks zu gewährleisten – in Israel, Arabien und Ophir, Nordsyrien und Kilikien sowie Zypern und dem westl. Mittelmeerraum. Tyros kaufte Weizen, Feigen, Honig, Öl und Harz in Juda und Israel; Wolle und Wein in Damaskus; Schafe und Ziegen in Arabien und Kedar; Pferde und Maultiere in Togarma; Reitdecken in Dedan; Malachit, Rubine, Purpur, Stoffe, Leinen, Stickereien und Korallen in Edom; Textilien, Teppiche und Tauwerk in Harran, Kanna, Eden, Saba, Assur, Medien und Kulmer; Sklaven, Br.-Gefäße, Eisen, Gewürze und Kalmus in Jawan, Tubal und Meschech; Gold, Silber, Eisen, Zinn, Blei, Elfenbein, Affen und Pfauen in Tarsis; Parfumöle, Edelsteine und Gold in Saba und Ragma; Eisen und Gewürze in Uzal; Elfenbein und Ebenholz in Rhodos (Ez 27,12–24). Überraschend, wenn auch histor. erklärbar, werden Zypern als Bundesgenosse von Tyros und der H. mit Kupfer an dieser Stelle nicht erwähnt.

Bei Homer (Il. 23,740–751; Od. 4,613–619; 13,272–286; 14,287–300; 15,414–483), für den der H. mit dem Konzept der griech. Aristokratie unvereinbar und daher verachtet ist (Od. 8,158–164), sind die Phönizier, die »Sidonier«, das h.-treibende Volk *par excellence* – im guten wie im schlechten Sinne. Sie sind kühne, ausgezeichnete Seeleute, haben das Monopol über den See-H. und besegeln die damals bekannte Welt, sie besitzen ihre eigenen Schiffe und sind immerwährend präsent in den Häfen der Ägäis, des ion. Meeres und der nordafrikan. Küste (Lemnos, Syros, Kreta, Pylos, Ithaka, Libyen, Ägypten), sind zugleich aber auch seßhaft und haben Haus und Land daheim. Ihre Handwerkskunst ist ausnahmslos berühmt, bewundert und begehrt. Gelegenheits-H. geringen Umfangs und ohne Bed. läßt Homer die Phönizier betreiben, eine idyllische Vorstellung, die zudem durch Feindseligkeit, Rassismus und Konkurrenzangst belastet ist: Ein Jahr bringen sie damit zu, eine Schiffsfracht Schund zu verhökern, während sie allein profitorientiert jede sich bietende Gelegenheit zu ihrem Vorteil und Geschäft ausnutzen. Sie sind Piraten, entführen Menschen und rauben Kinder, handeln mit Sklaven, aber auch mit Getreide und Wein. Faktoreien, dauerhafte Siedlungen oder Kolonien der Phönizier kennt Homer nicht.

→ Kypros; Phönizische Archäologie

R. D. Barnett, Ezekiel and Tyre, in: Eretz Israel 9, 1969, 6–13 • J. D. Muhly, Homer and the Phoenicians, in: Berytus 19, 1970, 19–64 • G. Bunnens, Commerce et diplomatie phéniciens au temps de Hiram I de Tyr, in: Journ. of the Economic and Social History of the Orient 19, 1976, 1–31 • Ders., La mission d'Ounamun en Phénicie. Point de vue d'un non-égyptologue, in: Riv. di Stud. Fenici 6, 1978, 1–16 • Ders., L'expansion phénicienne en Méditerranée (Inst. Belge de Rome 18), 1979 • S. F. Bondi,

Note sull'economia fenicia I: Impresa privata e ruolo dello stato, in: Egitto e Vicino Oriente 1, 1978, 139–149 • H. G. NIEMEYER, Die Phönizier und die Mittelmeerwelt im Zeitalter Homers, in: JRGZ 31, 1984, 3–29 • E. LIPIŃSKI, Products and brokers of Tyre according to Ezekiel 27, in: Stud. Phoenicia 3, 1985, 213–220 • M. GRAS, P. ROUILLARD, J. TEIXIDOR, L'univers phénicien, 1989, bes. 79–127 • M. E. AUBET, The Phoenicians and the West, 1996, bes. 77–118. CH. B.

III. ETRURIEN

Etruskische Objekte finden sich von Spanien bis in das Schwarzmeergebiet und von Polen bis nach Karthago [5. 24 f., 64 f.]. Nur in wenigen Fällen waren dabei die Etr. selbst die Überbringer der Gegenstände aus Gold, Bronze und Ton.

Die etr. Städte waren polit. unabhängig, entsprechend ist von einer unterschiedlichen Ausrichtung des H. der einzelnen Stadtstaaten auszugehen. Bes. frühe Kontakte besaßen die zur Küste ausgerichteten Siedlungen → Populonia, → Vetulonia, Vulci (→ Volcae), → Tarquinii, Cerveteri (→ Caere) und → Veii. Die Küstenlinie in der etr. Zeit unterschied sich von der heutigen durch stärkere Gliederung und Lagunen, die zunehmend verlandeten, so daß etwa Vetulonia später keinen direkten Zugang zum Meer hatte. Nach den Funden zu urteilen, bestanden bereits frühe Kontakte mit den Völkern nördl. der Alpen [1. 1031 ff.] und mit Griechenland [10] (präkolonialer H.). Der See-H. setzte, belegt durch Funde auf → Corsica, → Sardinia und → Sicilia sowie in → Karthago, schon im 7. Jh. v. Chr. ein [6]. Problematisch bleiben die Br.-Funde des 8. Jh. v. Chr. bes. im Heiligtum von Olympia, die wahrscheinlich eher Weihungen von aus dem Westen zurückkehrenden Griechen als von Etr. selbst darstellen [10]. Ein lit. Topos ist die Verurteilung der etr. Piraterie durch griech. Quellen, was ein zusätzliches Licht auf die Konkurrenz mit griech. Seefahrern wirft [12]. Eine besondere Bed. in den frühen Beziehungen kam Cerveteri zu, dessen starke Ausrichtung zum Meer hin die drei Seehäfen → Alsium, Pyrgi und Punicum anzeigen. Pyrgi (→ Pyrgoi) spielte hierbei im Hinblick auf den H. mit Karthago eine wichtige Rolle, ein weiterer Beleg für die engen Beziehungen zu Karthago ist der Name Punicum. Ebenfalls über einen wichtigen Hafen verfügte Tarquinia, das mit → Graviscae ein stark griech. geprägtes → Emporion besaß. Regisvilla (Regae), der Seehafen von Vulci (mit einer großen Anzahl importierter att. Keramik und bedeutender Br.-Industrie), ist bislang nur wenig untersucht worden.

Die bes. häufig auftretenden etr. Bucchero-Kantharoi wurden vermutlich von griech. Händlern in die Ägäis gebracht [9]. Die Verbreitung des → Bucchero und der etr.-korinth. Keramik sowie der Br.-Geräte vermittelt ein Bild des See-H. nach Südfrankreich mit der um 600 v. Chr. gegründeten phokäischen Kolonie → Massalia, die den Zwischen-H. zu den kelt. Stämmen kontrollierte. Im Hintergrund standen hier die wichtigen Zinnminen in Cornwall. Mit der zunehmenden Bed. und dem Aufschwung der inneretr. Siedlungen gerieten Nord-It. und das kelt. Gebiet nördl. der Alpen in den Blickpunkt [1]. Die im späten 6. Jh. v. Chr. in der Poebene gegründeten etr. Kolonien → Atria und → Spina hatten neben Felsina (Bologna) beste Beziehungen nach Athen und gehörten zu den Vermittlern griech. Objekte bis in das kelt. Kernland [13; 14].

Die Vielzahl von att. und anderen Vasen in den etr. Gräbern (→ Etrusci) ermöglicht eine Einschätzung des H.-Umfangs zu unterschiedlichen Zeiten [13]. Die wenigsten der einstmals verhandelten Objekte sind im arch. Befund nachweisbar. Das Interesse der phöniz. und griech. H.-Partner beruhte auf dem Metallreichtum (v. a. Eisen) der Insel Elba (→ Ilva), der → Tolfaberge und der Colline Metallifere. Daneben gab es auch H. mit Wein und Ölen, wie die Funde von etr. Amphoren in Siedlungen und Schiffswracks an der Südküste Frankreichs und anderswo beweisen [2]. Ebenfalls wichtige Rohstoffe wie → Holz, → Elfenbein sowie → Glas, ferner Farbstoffe zur Textilveredlung, sind nur selten überliefert. Das gilt auch für das → Salz, das bei der Konservierung der Lebensmittel und der Viehzucht eine große Rolle spielte. Nachweise anderer Lebensmittel wie Getreide, das die südetr. Städte noch im 3. Jh. v. Chr. für den Kriegszug des Scipio Africanus liefern mußten (Liv. 28,45), fehlen nahezu völlig im arch. Befund. Die Erzeugnisse der etr. Br.-Werkstätten und hier bes. der Vulcenter Handwerker im 6. und 5. Jh. v. Chr. sind von großer Wichtigkeit für die Beurteilung des etr. Fern-H. und spielen eine große Rolle als eine der Grundlagen für die kelt. Chronologie [14]. In der Spätzeit der etr. Stadtstaaten, die unter dem Schatten der röm. Expansion stand, waren die H.-Beziehungen überwiegend auf kleinräumigen H. und Warentausch reduziert, nur wenige einheimische Produkte gelangten über den etr. Kernraum hinaus.

→ Etrusci, Etruria (mit Karten)

1 L. AIGNER-FORESTI (Hrsg.), Etrusker nördl. von Etrurien. Etr. Präsenz in Nordit. sowie ihre Einflüsse auf die einheim. Kulturen, Akt. des Symposiums Wien 1989, 1992
2 M. CRISTOFANI, P. PELAGATTI (Hrsg.), Il commercio etrusco arcaico. Atti dell'incontro di studio, 1983, 1985
3 M. CRISTOFANI, Economia e società, in: G. PUGLIESE CARRATELLI (Hrsg.), Rasenna. Storia e civiltà degli Etruschi, 1986, 79–156, bes. 124–156 **4** M. CRISTOFANI, Gli Etruschi del mare, ²1989 **5** Die Etrusker und Europa. Ausstellungs-Kat. Berlin, 1992 **6** M. GRAS, Trafics tyrrhéniens archaïques, 1985 **7** Ders., La Méditerranée archaïque, 1995, 134–163 **8** F.-W. VON HASE, Etrurien und das Gebiet nordwärts der Alpen in der ausgehenden Urnenfelder- und frühen Hallstattzeit, in: Atti del secondo congr. internazionale Etrusco, Florenz 1985, 1989, Bd. 2, 1031–1062 **9** Ders., Der etr. Bucchero aus Karthago. Ein Beitr. zu den frühen H.-Beziehungen im westl. Mittelmeergebiet, in: JRGZ 36, 1989, 327–410 **10** Ders., Présences étrusques et italiques dans les sanctuaires grecs (VIIIe–VIIe siècle av. J.-C.), in: D. BRIQUEL, F. GAULTIER (Hrsg.), Les Étrusques, les plus religieux des hommes. Actes du colloque international Paris 1992, 1997, 293–323
11 Ders., Ägäische, griech. und vorderoriental. Einflüsse auf

das tyrrhen. It., in: Beitr. zur Urnenfelderzeit nördl. und südl. der Alpen, Monographien des Röm.-German. Zentralmus. Mainz, 1995, 239–286 **12** J.-R. JANNOT, Les navires étrusques, instruments d'une thalassokratie?, in: CRAI 1995, 743–778 **13** P. KRACHT, Stud. zu den griech.-etr. H.-Beziehungen vom 7. bis 4. Jh. v. Chr., 1991 **14** D. VORLAUF, Die etr. Bronzeschnabelkannen: eine Unt. anhand der technolog.-typolog. Methode, 1994. GE. BI.

IV. GRIECHENLAND

A. ALLGEMEIN B. FERNHANDEL C. MARKTPLÄTZE UND HANDELSZENTREN D. FUNKTION VON GELD UND DARLEHEN

A. ALLGEMEIN

Im ant. Griechenland wurde in allen Epochen auf lokaler und überregionaler Ebene regelmäßig H. mit Gebrauchsgütern wie Nahrungsmitteln, Handwerkserzeugnissen oder Tieren und mit Luxusartikeln wie Parfüm, Edelmetallen und kostbaren Textilien, aber auch mit Sklaven betrieben. In der myk. Epoche reichten die Handelsverbindungen der Griechen über den gesamten Mittelmeerraum, nach ca. 1200 v. Chr. scheint die Beteiligung der Griechen am Fernhandel jedoch dramatisch zurüchgegangen zu sein; erst im 8. Jh. v. Chr. blühte der griech. Fernhandel wieder auf, als griech. Händler neben Phöniziern, Syrern und Etruskern an Orten wie → Al-Mīnā und → Pithekussai tätig waren. Außerdem bestanden auch enge Beziehungen zu Äg., wo griech. Händler in → Naukratis ihre Niederlassungen hatten. Zu den wichtigen Exportgütern der archa. Zeit gehörten Wein und Olivenöl. So verkaufte Charaxos, der Bruder der → Sappho, Wein aus Lesbos in Äg. (Strab. 17,1,33). Hohe Gewinne wurden auch bei Handelsfahrten nach Spanien erzielt (Hdt. 4,152). Schon zu Beginn des 5. Jh. gewannen daneben die Getreideimporte für die griech. Städte zunehmend an Bedeutung (Hdt. 7,147,2; Demosth. or. 20,30–33). Seit dem 6. Jh. v. Chr. waren Schiffe mit breitem Rumpf üblich, die ein großes Rahsegel besaßen, gesegelt wurden und über einen beträchtlichen Laderaum verfügten.

Der arch. Nachweis griech. H. erfolgt zumeist aufgrund von Keramikfunden, die die Präsenz von Händlern aus Griechenland oder von solchen Händlern erkennen lassen, die in engem Kontakt mit den Griechen standen. Keramik stellt jedoch gewöhnlich nicht die wichtigste Handelsware dar; Keramikgefäße dienten vor allem als Behälter für Massengüter wie Wein oder Fischsoße. Mit Vasenbildern verzierte Qualitätsware, die oft zusammen mit Massengütern oder Luxusartikeln transportiert wurde, hatte eher geringen Wert.

B. FERNHANDEL

Der Fernhandel wurde zumeist im kleinen Rahmen von professionellen Händlern (ἔμποροι) betrieben; diese *émporoi* erhielten die Waren von den Herstellern im Austausch gegen Geld oder andere Güter und gaben sie dann an die Verbraucher weiter, die wiederum mit Geld oder anderen Gütern bezahlten. Ein solcher H. war mit erheblichen geschäftlichen Risiken verbunden, und die Händler mußten oft mehrere Häfen aufsuchen, um ihre Ware verkaufen zu können. In lit. Quellen wird der typische Händler als eine freie Person von bescheidenem Vermögen dargestellt, die von einem Markt zum anderen zieht und dabei verschiedenartige Güter in kleinen Mengen verkauft. Ein Händler konnte auch ein eigenes Schiff besitzen, aber die meisten Händler gingen befristete Partnerschaften mit Schiffsbesitzern (ναύκληροι, → *naúklēroi*) ein. Dieses Bild wird partiell von Schiffswracks (wie dem Giglio- oder Kyrenia-Wrack) bestätigt, deren Frachten aus einer Vielzahl unterschiedlicher Produkte bestanden.

H. wurde mit einer Vielzahl von Austauschmechanismen betrieben, darunter Kauf und Verkauf, Tauschhandel (z. B. Getreide gegen Holz, Sklaven gegen Wein) sowie Austausch von Geschenken. Ein Transfer von Gütern ohne Austausch, ganz gleich, ob er durch Krieg, → Seeraub, einseitige Gaben von Geschenken oder durch Raub verursacht war, hat ebenfalls als Charakteristikum wirtschaftlicher Aktivität in Griechenland zu gelten. So waren viele der Sklaven, die in Griechenland auf den Sklavenmärkten verkauft wurden, Kriegsgefangene oder Opfer der Piraterie.

Im allgemeinen besaßen Händler ein nur geringes Ansehen, besonders im Vergleich mit Grundbesitzern, die ihren Lebensunterhalt aus dem Ertrag des Bodens gewannen (Hom. Od. 8,159–164; Hes. erg. 618–694; Aristot. pol. 1255b 40–1259a 36). Die Figur des nicht vertrauenswürdigen fremdländischen Händlers war seit Homer ein Gemeinplatz in der griech. Lit. (Hom. Od. 15,415–484).

Die Beteiligung von Frauen am H. war aufgrund von Gesetz oder Gewohnheit eingeschränkt, sie waren normalerweise von Geschäften in größerem Rahmen ohne männliche Kontrolle ausgeschlossen. Am häufigsten betrieben Frauen H. mit Nahrungsmitteln, billigen Textilien und besonders mit Parfüm. In der hell. Epoche, als mehr Frauen unabhängig über ihr Vermögen verfügen konnten, sind auf Inschriften gelegentlich Frauen belegt, die im großen Stil, oft durch Bevollmächtigte, im Geschäftsleben aktiv waren. Sklaven und Freigelassene waren häufig im Kleinhandel engagiert, oft in Abhängigkeit von Bürgern und Metoiken.

C. MARKTPLÄTZE UND HANDELSZENTREN

Der Austausch konnte in Läden, auf Marktplätzen, in Häfen und in Heiligtümern stattfinden. Die Handelsplätze unterschieden sich erheblich hinsichtlich ihrer Größe und Bedeutung; so gab es auf der einen Seite die kleine → Agora einer eher unbedeutenden Polis, auf der anderen Seite die Vielzahl von Märkten an Orten wie Athen, Milet, Delos, Alexandreia und Rhodos. In solchen Städten gab es auch spezialisierte Marktplätze wie den Fischmarkt von Athen (Aristoph. Vesp. 790). Die meisten Küstenstädte bauten Handelshäfen mit entsprechenden Einrichtungen an den Kais wie etwa Lagerhäusern und Kontoren für die Kaufleute und Amtsstuben für die Magistrate (→ Hafenanlagen).

Einige Städte waren auf bestimmte Produkte spezialisiert (z. B. Kos auf feine Textilien, Athen auf Öl oder Städte am Schwarzen Meer auf Fisch). Derartige spezialisierte Märkte entstanden aufgrund ihrer Lage an den Handelswegen oder in der Nähe der Produktions- und Verbraucherzentren sowie aufgrund günstiger polit. Verhältnisse. So war Korinth seit frühester Zeit ein Zentrum des H. zwischen der Peloponnes und dem übrigen Griechenland, Athen wurde in der klass. Zeit ein wichtiges Handelszentrum, und das hell. Rhodos profitierte von seiner Lage zwischen Syrien und der Ägäis sowie von seinen engen Verbindungen zu Äg., wodurch es zu einem bedeutenden Getreideumschlagplatz avancierte. Delos, das 166 v. Chr. den Status eines Freihandelshafens erhielt, war ein wichtiges Zentrum des Sklavenhandels. Die Griechen waren außerdem mit weitverzweigten Handelsnetzen in Mitteleuropa und Asien verbunden.

Gesetze, die den H. regulieren und begrenzen sollten, reichen mindestens bis in das 6. Jh. v. Chr. zurück (Plut. Solon 24). Marktplätze waren gewöhnlich der Besteuerung und Regulierung unterworfen und unterstanden der Aufsicht von Beamten. Im klass. Athen sowie im Peiraieus beaufsichtigten zehn → *agoranómoi* (ἀγορανόμοι) die Märkte, unterstützt von zehn *metronómoi* (μετρονόμοι), die Maße und Gewichte überwachten, zehn Beamten, die den Außenhandel kontrollierten (ἐπιμεληταί ἐμπορίου, *epimelētaí emporíu*) und bis zu 35 *sitophýlakes* (σιτοφύλακες), die das Angebot und die Preise auf dem Getreidemarkt überwachten (Lys. 22,8 f.); diese Beamten wurden durch Los bestimmt (Aristot. Ath. pol. 51). Außerdem gab es im 4. Jh. v. Chr. Gerichte, die für Streitfälle bei Handelsgeschäften zuständig waren (Aristot. Ath. pol. 59,5).

D. Funktion von Geld und Darlehen

Münzgeld war in der griech. Welt seit dem 6. Jh. v. Chr. gebräuchlich. Obwohl seine primäre Funktion nicht die eines Tauschmittels war, spielte es schließlich im H. eine äußerst wichtige Rolle. Kleine Silbermünzen wurden im alltäglichen Austausch vor allem dort verwendet, wo die Polis durch die ständige Bezahlung von Soldaten, Amtsträgern oder Handwerkern dafür sorgte, daß stets genügend Geld im Umlauf war. In klass. und hell. Zeit wurde der Wert der meisten gehandelten Güter in Geld ausgedrückt.

Der H. wurde darüber hinaus durch die Bereitstellung von → Krediten für Käufer oder Verkäufer erleichtert. Vielen Händlern fehlten die finanziellen Mittel, um die Waren sofort selbst bezahlen zu können; sie waren daher auf → Darlehen angewiesen. Gegen Ende des 5. Jh. v. Chr. hatten die Athener eine spezielle Form des → Seedarlehens zur Finanzierung vor allem des Fernhandels mit Getreide oder Wein entwickelt. Der Händler oder Schiffseigner lieh Geld zu einem hohen Zinssatz für die Bezahlung der Fracht, die, manchmal zusammen mit dem Schiff, als Sicherheit für das Darlehen fungierte. Das Darlehen und die Zinsen wurden zu einem festgesetzten Termin zurückgezahlt, wobei jedoch Seeräuberei, Schiffbruch oder die Beschlagnahmung des Schiffes bzw. der Fracht die Verpflichtung zur Rückzahlung des Darlehens aufhob. Das hohe Risiko wurde im 4. Jh. v. Chr. durch Zinssätze von bis zu 30 % ausgeglichen. Derartige Vereinbarungen sind für Athen vor allem durch Gerichtsreden bezeugt (Demosth. or. 32,20; 33,4; 34; 35,10 ff.; 35,51; 56,1; Lys. 32,6).

→ Geld, Geldwirtschaft; Getreidehandel, Getreideimport; Markt; Sklavenhandel

1 J. Boardman, The Greek Overseas, [3]1980 2 Finley, Ancient Economy 3 F. Meijer, O. v. Nijf, Trade, Transport and Society in Ancient Greece: A Sourcebook, 1992 4 Millett 5 P. Millett, Maritime Loans and the Structure of Credit in Fourth-Century Athens, in: Garnsey/Hopkins/Whittaker, 36–52 6 C. Mossé, The World of the Emporium in the Private Speeches of Demosthenes, in: Garnsey/Hopkins/Whittaker, 53–63 7 A. J. Parker, Ancient Shipwrecks of the Mediterranean and the Roman Provinces, 1992 8 H. Parkins, C. Smith (Hrsg.), Trade, Traders and the Ancient City, 1998 9 Rostovtzeff, Hellenistic World 10 D. Schaps, The Economic Rights of Women in Ancient Greece, 1979 11 S. v. Reden, Exchange in Ancient Greece, 1995.

P. d. S./Ü: A. H.

V. Rom

A. Republik B. Prinzipat C. Spätantike

A. Republik

Der H. spielte gegenüber der Landwirtschaft bis zum 3. Jh. v. Chr. in der Wirtschaft Mittelitaliens eine deutlich untergeordnete Rolle. Erst die im 3. Jh. v. Chr. einsetzende Münzprägung (→ Münzwesen) und die zunehmenden Kontakte zum hell. Wirtschaftsraum haben einen grundlegenden Wandel der rückständigen Wirtschaftsstruktur Roms bewirkt. Allerdings hat die etr. Oberschicht schon vom späten 7. Jh. v. Chr. an hochwertige griech. Keramikprodukte nach Mittel- und Norditalien importiert; die Goldtäfelchen von Pyrgi sind ein Indiz für die Präsenz der Karthager an der etrurischen Küste.

Im westl. Mittelmeer war der Seehandel zunächst eine Domäne griech., etr. und vor allem karthagischer Händler. Die röm.-karthagischen Verträge (Pol. 3,21–26) spiegeln karthagische Interessen wider, lassen aber erkennen, daß die Position Roms im westl. Mittelmeerraum stärker wurde. In der Zeit des 1. und 2. Pun. Krieges wurde Rom nicht nur zu einer Seemacht, sondern röm. Händler folgten den Legionen nach Afrika, um von den Feldzügen und der Beute zu profitieren (Pol. 1,83,7; 14,7,2 f.). Spätestens seit der *lex Claudia de nave senatorum* (218 v. Chr.; Liv. 21,63,3) – einem Gesetz, das Senatoren und ihren Söhnen den Besitz von Schiffen mit einer Ladekapazität von mehr als 300 Amphoren untersagte – wurde H. mit Einsatz erheblicher finanzieller Mittel betrieben. In diesem Zusammenhang sind die *societates publicorum* (→ *Publicani*) zu sehen, die Steuern und Zölle pachteten und zeitweise für die Versorgung der in Spanien kämpfenden Legionen tätig waren (Liv. 23,48,9–23,49,3). Mit der Zerstörung → Karthagos 146

v. Chr. war Rom im westl. Mittelmeerraum zur führenden Handelsmacht geworden. Der inneritał. H. wurde in diesem Zeitraum wahrscheinlich durch den röm. Straßenbau begünstigt.

Bereits im 3. Jh. v. Chr. waren ital. Kaufleute im östl. Mittelmeerraum, zunächst in der Adria, aktiv; um sie zu schützen, führte Rom Krieg gegen die Illyrer (Pol. 2,8–12). In Ambrakia an der östl. Adriaküste wurden schon 189 v. Chr. röm. und ital. Kaufleute durch einen Senatsbeschluß von den Hafenzöllen befreit (Liv. 38,44,4); im Norden der Adria entwickelte Aquileia [1] sich zu einer bedeutenden Hafenstadt (Strab. 5,1,8). Nach dem 3. Makedonischen Krieg erklärten die Römer → Delos zum Freihandelshafen und machten die Insel so zum wichtigsten Handelszentrum des östl. Mittelmeerraumes, während Rhodos seine vorherrschende Position im H. verlor (Pol. 31,7; Strab. 10,5,4).

Den griech. Händlern waren die ital. Kaufleute durch ihre Organisationsform überlegen. Sie waren in den Prov., aber auch außerhalb der röm. Gebiete im H. tätig. So verteidigten ital. Kaufleute um 114 v. Chr. Cirta gegen → Iugurtha (Sall. Iug. 21,2; 26,1 ff.); für Kleinasien und Delos ist die Präsenz röm. und ital. Kaufleute durch die von Mithradates befohlenen Massaker belegt (App. Mithr. 22 f.; Paus. 3,23,3 ff.; vgl. außerdem Cic. ad Q. fr. 1,1,6). Röm. → *negotiatores* werden außerdem für Gallia Narbonensis und später für die von Caesar eroberten Gebiete erwähnt (Cic. Font. 11 f.; Cenabum: Caes. Gall. 7,3,1). Die Interessen dieser Kaufleute wurden von Rom durchaus mit mil. Mitteln verteidigt (Cic. Manil. 11).

Die ostentative Lebensführung der röm. Oberschicht führte in der späten Republik zu umfangreichen Luxusimporten aus dem Osten nach Rom. Neben dem H. mit Agrarprodukten, die aus dem gesamten Mittelmeerraum nach Rom strömten, verdient der Export von Wein aus It. nach Gallien besondere Erwähnung; gerade die Amphoren mit dem Stempel SES des Landbesitzers Sestius aus Cosa belegen den erheblichen Umfang dieses H. Große wirtschaftliche Bedeutung besaß auch der → Sklavenhandel während des 2. und 1. Jh. v. Chr.: Vor allem Gallier verkauften Kriegsgefangene oder Schuldsklaven in großer Zahl nach It., und aus dem östl. Mittelmeerraum gelangten viele Menschen – teilweise als Opfer der Piraterie – auf den Sklavenmarkt (Strab. 14,5,2). Die Wirtschaftsethik der röm. Oberschichten schloß ein direktes Engagement von Senatoren im H. aus (Cato agr. praef.); bei Cicero wird der Kleinhandel als schmutzig bezeichnet, der Großhandel hingegen positiv beurteilt (Cic. off. 1,151).

B. Prinzipat

Mit der Entstehung des Prinzipats und mit der *Pax Augusta*, der inneren Befriedung des Imperium Romanum, begann für den röm. H. eine neue Epoche; der Güteraustausch erhielt durch die Sicherheit der Verkehrswege, besonders der Schiffahrtswege, und durch den Ausbau der → Infrastruktur, etwa den Bau von Häfen, neue Impulse. Dabei blieb die Versorgung der großen Städte mit Lebensmitteln für den überregionalen H. von zentraler Bedeutung. Die Versorgung von Rom wurde durch die → *cura annonae* organisiert, wobei Getreide von den Prov. Africa und Aegyptus, Öl, Wein und Garum von den spanischen Prov. geliefert wurden. Daneben bestand aber ein freier Getreidemarkt in Rom. Die → Heeresversorgung, an deren Wegen und Zielorten sich auch der freie H. orientierte, unterstand ebenfalls der zentralen Verwaltung. Die Kaufkraft röm. Soldaten stellte zudem selbst an entfernten Standorten einen Anreiz für den lokalen und überregionalen H. dar.

Die zunehmende Urbanisierung sowie der vielfach vermutete Bevölkerungsanstieg im 1. und 2. Jh. n. Chr. wirkten sich ebenfalls auf den H. aus. Luxusgüter aus dem fernen Osten, besonders aus Indien, gelangten zu Lande etwa über Palmyra in den Mittelmeerraum oder wurden auf dem Seeweg zu den Häfen am Roten Meer und dann über den Nil nach Alexandreia gebracht (Strab. 17,1,45; → Indienhandel). Geringeren Umfang hatte hingegen der Güteraustausch mit dem freien Germanien und Nordeuropa; wichtige Importgüter waren z. B. Sklaven, Felle und Bernstein. Obgleich Händler oft ihre Waren – gerade auch Getreide – dort verkauften, wo sie möglichst hohe Gewinne erzielen konnten (Cic. dom. 11; Philostr. Ap. 4,32; Manil. 4,165 ff.), haben viele von ihnen regelmäßig H. mit bestimmten Regionen getrieben, so etwa Flavius Zeuxis aus Hierapolis, der zweiundsiebzigmal nach It. fuhr (IGR 4,841). Der Fernhandel war weitgehend auf die Seewege angewiesen, da die Kosten des Landtransports wesentlich höher waren als die der Schiffahrt; es bestand zwischen Schiffahrt, Binnenschiffahrt und Landtransport eine Kostenrelation von etwa 1:4,9:28. Unter diesen Umständen waren gerade Häfen und Hafenstädte wie Gades (Strab. 3,5,3), Puteoli (Strab. 5,4,6) oder Alexandreia (Strab. 17,1,7; 17,1,13) Wirtschaftszentren von überregionaler Bedeutung.

So beeindruckend der Fernhandel im Imperium Romanum auch war, es sollte nicht übersehen werden, daß sich der größte Teil des insgesamt nicht quantifizierbaren H. in überschaubaren regionalen Räumen abspielte. Der Produzenten-H. (landwirtschaftlich wie gewerblich) befriedigte zu großen Teilen wechselseitig die jeweiligen Bedürfnisse von Stadt und ländlichem Territorium. Die Einrichtung und Organisation unzähliger städtischer und ländlicher Märkte (*nundinae*; vgl. Plin. epist. 5,4; 5,13; 9,39; → Markt) unterstützte den mehr oder weniger regelmäßigen Warenfluß, der von spezialisierten Händlern getragen wurde. Solche lokalen Märkte fanden teilweise nur in großen zeitlichen Abständen und in Verbindung mit Festen oder Gerichtsverhandlungen statt (Dion Chrys. 35,15 ff.). Die Preise waren von Stadt zu Stadt oft extrem unterschiedlich, besonders nach Mißernten, die zu einem Steigen der Getreidepreise führten (Dion Chrys. 46,10).

Der Einfluß des Steuer- und Zollwesens (→ Steuern; → Zölle) auf den H. ist schwer abzuschätzen. Die zen-

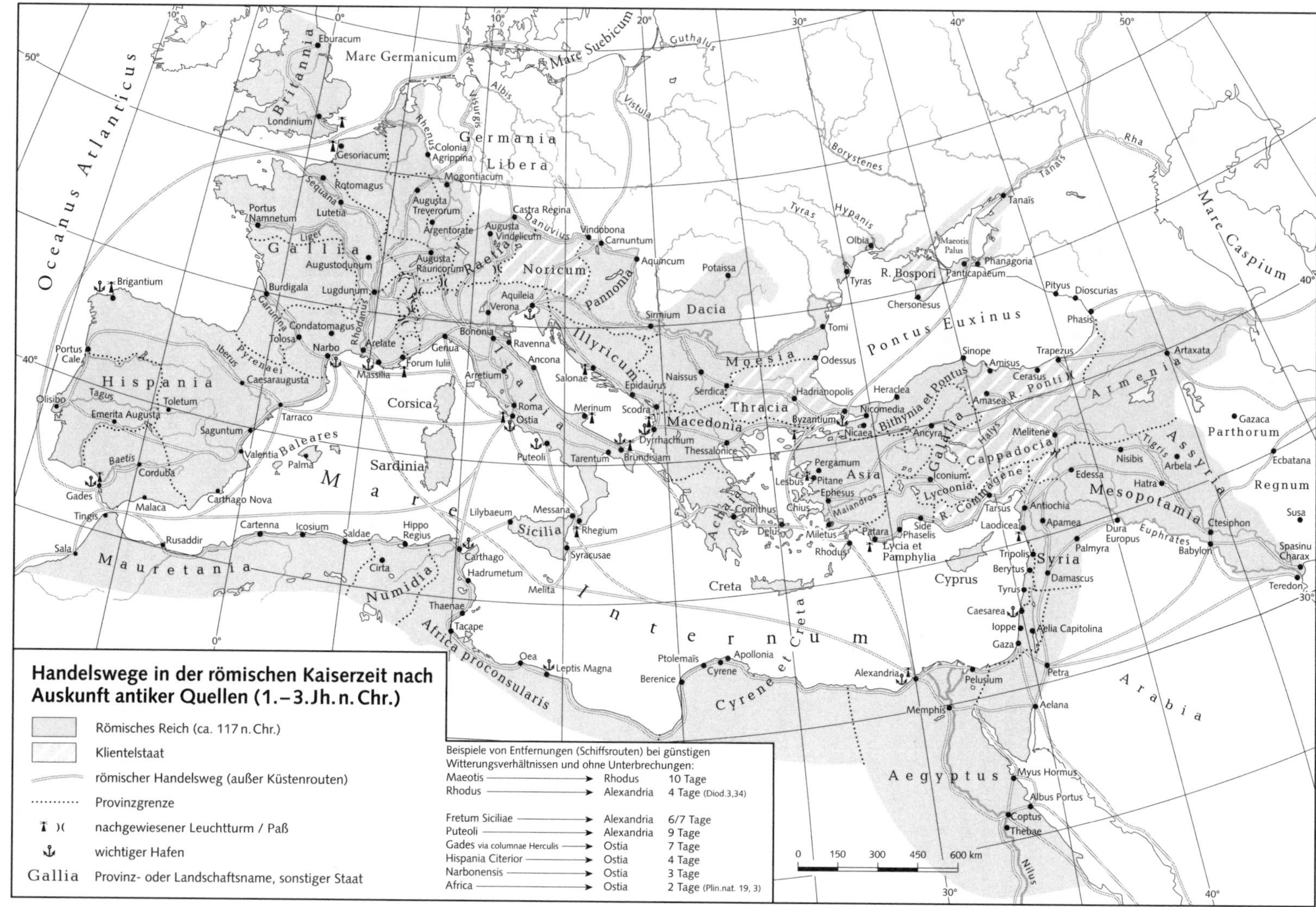

Handelswege in der römischen Kaiserzeit nach Auskunft antiker Quellen (1.–3. Jh. n. Chr.)

trale Aussage des »Steuer-Handel-Modells« von K. Hopkins [14] jedoch ist anregend: Die steuerexportierenden Prov. (z. B. Asia, Gallia) müssen Produkte in die steuerempfangenden Regionen (z. B. Grenzprovinzen mit hohem Militärpotential) ausführen, um das für die nächsten Steuererhebungen nötige Münzgeld zu erwirtschaften. Das röm. Zollwesen scheint für den H. insgesamt keine ausgesprochene Belastung dargestellt zu haben. Das Imperium verfügte damit über ein Instrumentarium, das sowohl seinem Abschöpfungsbegehren genügte, als auch durch Privilegien, zeitweise Begünstigungen, grundsätzliche Zollbefreiung usw. fördernde Impulse geben konnte. Hohe Zolltarife wurden an den Grenzen erhoben (bis zu 25 % des Warenwertes an der Ostgrenze). Das tat dem Warenverkehr aber insofern keinen Abbruch, als in der Regel Luxusgüter die Grenzen in das Reich passierten.

Über die Einkünfte von Händlern können keine konkreten Aussagen gemacht werden; keine Quelle verrät uns irgendeine Kalkulation. Lediglich die Tatsache, daß Waren über weite Räume transportiert worden sind, belegt den finanziellen Erfolg händlerischen Engagements. Die großen Vermögen wurden in der Regel nicht durch den H. erwirtschaftet, wenngleich auch Angehörige der röm. Oberschicht einen Teil ihres Reichtums aus der mittelbaren Beteiligung an diesem Wirtschaftszweig bezogen. Einige Mitglieder überregionaler bzw. interprovinzieller Handelsorganisationen dürften ebenfalls zu beträchtlichem Reichtum gekommen sein, wie etwa *negotiatores* des *corpus/collegium cisalpinorum et transalpinorum* oder Angehörige der *collegia nautarum*. Die seltenen Preisangaben gewähren kaum Aufschlüsse über die Gewinne der Händler, da sie keine Informationen über die Differenz von Einkaufs- und Verkaufspreis bieten.

C. Spätantike

Im Laufe des 3. Jh. n. Chr. änderten sich die Bedingungen für den H. deutlich. Vor allem die Grenzkonflikte im Norden und Osten, die Zerstörungen in vielen Teilen des Imperium Romanum zur Folge hatten, machten einen kontinuierlichen H. zumindest zeitweise unmöglich. Die Forsch. ist sich zudem einig, daß mit diesen Entwicklungen ein deutlicher Bevölkerungsrückgang verbunden war. Der Zusammenbruch des Geldsystems – insbesondere der Rückgang des Silbergehaltes in den Denarprägungen (→ Geldentwertung) und die Preissteigerungen (→ Preis) – wird als Indikator des wirtschaftlichen Niedergangs gesehen. Andererseits darf nicht angenommen werden, daß diese wirtschaftlichen Veränderungen in gleicher Weise alle Regionen des Imperium Romanum und den H. insgesamt betrafen. In einigen Städten und Regionen ist durchaus wirtschaftliche Prosperität feststellbar; hier sei nur auf die Städte Side und Perge an der kleinasiatischen Südküste, weiterhin blühende Landstriche in Äg. und das röm. Britannien hingewiesen, für das gerade zu Beginn des 3. Jh. n. Chr. eine lange Friedensperiode begann. Die Konsolidierung der Grenzen, tiefgreifende Reformen des Verwaltungs-, Steuer- und Währungswesens verbunden mit Versuchen der Preis- und Lohnbindung haben seit der Zeit des Diocletianus dem H. allerdings einen veränderten Rahmen gegeben.

→ Geld, Geldwirtschaft; Import – Export; Handel

1 W. Ameling, Karthago, 1993, 147–151 **2** E. Badian, Publicans and Sinners, 1972, 67–81 **3** J. M. Blázquez, J. Remesal, E. Rodríguez, Excavaciones arqueológicas en el Monte Testaccio (Roma), 1994 **4** P. A. Brunt, The Equites in the Late Republic, in: Ders., The Fall of the Roman Republic, 1988, 144–193 **5** D'Arms **6** D'Arms/Kopff **7** H.-J. Drexhage, Preise, Mieten/Pachten, Kosten und Löhne im röm. Ägypten, 1991 **8** ESAR **9** J. M. Frayn, Markets and Fairs in Roman Italy, 1993 **10** P. Garnsey, C. R. Whittaker (Hrsg.), Trade and Famine in Classical Antiquity, 1983 **11** K. Greene, The Archaeology of the Roman Economy, 1986 **12** J. Hatzfeld, Les trafiquants italiens dans l'orient hellénique, 1919 **13** P. Herz, Studien zur röm. Wirtschaftsgesetzgebung. Die Lebensmittelversorgung, 1988 **14** K. Hopkins, Taxes and Trade in the Roman Empire, in: JRS 70, 1980, 101–125 **15** G. Jacobsen, Primitiver Austausch oder freier Markt? Unters. zum H. in den gallisch-germanischen Prov., 1995, 48–64 **16** Jones, Economy **17** Jones, LRE, 824–872 **18** L. De Ligt, Fairs and Markets in the Roman Empire, 1993 **19** F. De Martino, Wirtschaftsgesch. des alten Rom, 1985 **20** F. Meijer, O. von Nijf, Trade, Transport, and Society in the Ancient World, 1992 **21** J. Nollé, Nundinas instituere et habere, 1982 **22** G. Reger, Regionalism and Change in the Economy of Independent Delos, 314–167 B. C., 1994 **23** J. Remesal, Heeresversorgung und die wirtschaftlichen Beziehungen zwischen der Baetica und Germanien, 1997 **24** Rostovtzeff, Roman Empire **25** E. Sidebotham, Roman Economic Policy in the Erythra Thalassa 30 B. C. – A. D. 217, 1986 **26** B. Sirks, Food for Rome, 1991 **27** A. Tchernia, Italian wine in Gaul at the end of the Republic, in: Garnsey/Hopkins/Whittaker, 87–104.

Karten-Lit.:
T. Frank, An Economic Survey of Ancient Rome, Bde. I–VI, ND 1975 • F. de Martino, Wirtschaftsgesch. des alten Rom, 1985 • F. Vittinghoff (Hrsg.), Europäische Wirtschafts- und Sozialgesch. in der röm. Kaiserzeit, 1990, bes. 20–160; 375–752.

H.-J. D.

VI. Byzanz

A. Literatur und Quellenlage B. Zeitliche Gliederung C. Gesamtwirtschaftlicher Hintergrund des Handels
D. Formen des Handels und Typologie der Kaufleute E. Haupthandelsprodukte
F. Einnahmen

A. Literatur und Quellenlage

Eine Gesamtuntersuchung des byz. H. existiert nicht. Für den vorliegenden Zeitabschnitt fehlen urkundliche Quellen fast gänzlich. Geschichtswerke aus der Zeit nach 600 n. Chr. bringen nur sehr vereinzelte Hinweise. Wichtige Quellen sind trotz methodischer Probleme die Heiligenviten (→ *vitae sanctorum*) und die Siegel der Kommerkiarier (Zollbeauftragte). Unsere Kenntnisse bleiben daher sehr punktuell und zufällig.

B. ZEITLICHE GLIEDERUNG

Der H. in den Grenzen der ant. Welt erreichte mit der Wiederherstellung des Gesamtimperiums unter Iustinianus einen letzten Höhepunkt, der sich freilich überwiegend auf den Mittelmeerraum beschränkte, während der Asien- und → Indienhandel weitgehend in den Händen der → Sāsāniden lag; für den H. nördl. der Alpen und Pyrenäen waren die Byzantiner allenfalls Zulieferer. Die Kriege auf dem Balkan gegen Avaren und Slaven und in Kleinasien gegen die Sāsāniden führten schon seit 570 zu schweren Behinderungen auf den Landwegen, doch erst das Vordringen der Araber bis in die Ägäis seit der Mitte des 7. Jh. brachte eine erhebliche Einschränkung auch des Seehandels mit sich und stellt so in diesem Bereich eine deutlich markierte Zeitgrenze dar.

C. GESAMTWIRTSCHAFTLICHER HINTERGRUND DES HANDELS

Im Reich des Iustinianus bestand der schon aus früheren Jh. bekannte Handelsschwerpunkt im Osten, bedingt durch die hier endenden Handelswege aus Afrika und Asien, die Dichte des Städtenetzes und die Zahl der dort lebenden Menschen, zumal zahlreiche Gebiete noch nicht dem h. bekannten Wüstungs- und Verödungsprozeß durch Klimaveränderungen ausgesetzt waren. Die Stadt als Umschlagplatz des Binnen- und Fernhandels verlor im Balkanraum innerhalb von 30 Jahren (570–600) vollständig ihre Bed., in Kleinasien durch das Vordringen der Araber bis um 650. Kriegerische Einwirkungen, aber auch Seuchen und Erdbeben ließen rasch die Einwohnerzahlen in Stadt und Land sinken. Weitgehend unbekannt bleibt die Bed. des Schwarzen Meeres (Pelze, Fische, der für Byzanz offensichtlich nicht bes. wichtige Bernstein). Immer mehr entwickelte sich Konstantinopel in diesem Zeitraum im Schutze seiner unüberwindlichen Mauern zu einer Drehscheibe des See- und Landhandels. Der H. profitierte vom ausgezeichneten röm. Straßensystem, das einer eigenen byz. Behörde unterstand und sorgsam instandgehalten wurde. Die Zusammenstellung des sog. Rhodischen Seegesetzes im Verlaufe des 8. Jh. zeigt, daß die Seeschiffahrt trotz arab. Präsenz vor allem im lokalen H. nicht völlig zum Erliegen gekommen war. Eine wichtige Rolle im H. spielte hierbei auch das weitgehend »neutrale« Zypern. Soweit der H. auf der Basis des Geld-Warenverkehrs beruhte, besaß er dank des Goldsolidus eine auch in Asien und Afrika akzeptierte, sichere Grundlage.

D. FORMEN DES HANDELS UND TYPOLOGIE DER KAUFLEUTE

Die Bed. des H. in Byzanz beruhte in erster Linie auf den seit der röm. Spätant. weiter bestehenden Fernkontakten, die auch der polit. Zusammenbruch des iustinianischen Imperiums nur wenig beeinträchtigte. So berichten Quellen Anf. des 7. Jh. vom Handelsverkehr zw. Alexandreia und den Britischen Inseln. Der Ceylon-Bericht bei Kosmas (erst später als »Indienfahrer« bezeichnet, → Kosmas Indikopleustes) erwähnt für das 6. Jh. die byz.-sāsānidische Konkurrenz im Ostasien-H. Mz.-Funde im Verlauf der → Seidenstraße belegen eine direkte oder indirekte byz. Präsenz. Chroniken sprechen von kurz- oder längerfristigen Handelsabkommen mit den Avaren, den Turkvölkern Zentralasiens, den Sāsāniden und später auch den Arabern. Es scheint allerdings, daß die Byzantiner seit dem späten 6. Jh. immer seltener selbst als Fernhändler wirkten, sondern an bestimmten Punkten im Reich (bes. in Konstantinopel oder grenznahen Städten) die Waren entgegennahmen und den Zwischenhandel organisierten. Araber (bzw. Angehörige des islamischen Glaubens) errichteten schon im 8. Jh. eine Moschee in Konstantinopel, was auf eine regelmäßige Handelstätigkeit schließen läßt. Eine nicht geringe Rolle spielte im 7. und 8. Jh. der mit den sog. Kommerkiariern (Zoll- und Steuerbeauftragten) in Verbindung stehende H., der in der Forschung noch kontrovers diskutiert wird, am ehesten aber mit dem staatlich überwachten Naturalhandel in Krisenlagen und zur Versorgung des Heeres in Verbindung steht.

Neben dem Geld-Warenverkehr erhielt ganz allgemein gesehen der Tausch-H. mit Naturalien seit dem 7. Jh. zunehmende Bedeutung auch im byz. Reich. Bedeutsam für den schwer greifbaren frühen Binnen-H. war das Aufkommen von Handelsmessen (Jahrmärkten) in Verbindung mit Kirchenfesten (Ephesos, Trimithos auf Zypern).

E. HAUPTHANDELSPRODUKTE

Getreide stand hinsichtlich Bed. und Umfang immer an erster Stelle, bes. zur Versorgung der Großstadt Konstantinopel (zunächst aus Äg., später aus Thrakien und dem Schwarzmeerraum). Für diesen H. war das polit. Motiv entscheidend, im Zentrum des Reiches Hungerrevolten zu verhindern.

Öl diente nicht nur der Versorgung der Bevölkerung als Nahrungsmittel, sondern war auch unerläßlich für die Beleuchtung der Kirchen. Fisch und Fischprodukte (Trockenfisch, Fischeier) stellten in den meernahen Regionen ein Grundnahrungsmittel dar. Wein, besonders Süßwein, war ein Exportprodukt, wovon Amphoren (→ Transportamphoren) in Schiffswracks Zeugnis ablegen. Zu den Exportwaren zählten auch Käse und Trockenfleisch. Wichtige Produkte des regionalen Binnenmarktes (schon früh für Konstantinopel belegt) waren Gemüse und Obst. Dem H. mit Holz kam bes. in diesen Jh. wegen des Baus von Kriegsschiffen eine besondere Bed. zu; Eisen war wichtig für die nicht ausschließlich staatliche Waffenherstellung sowie zur Weitergabe an auswärtige Völkerschaften, die Byzanz gegen dessen Feinde unterstützten. Das byz. Reich, im besonderen aber Konstantinopel, war Sammelpunkt von Luxusprodukten, sei es für die eigene Verwendung am Hof (und durch die damit verbundenen Schichten) oder zum Weiterverkauf. In erster Linie fielen die verschiedenen Arten von Seide (d. h. Seide aus China bzw. Mittelasien und seit dem 6. Jh. auch in Byzanz hergestellte Seide) darunter. Auch wurde der gesamte Bedarf an Gewürzen im Westen und Norden Europas durch den

Import aus Byzanz gedeckt. In Byzanz selbst fanden im Zeitraum bis 800 auch Edelhölzer (u. a. aus Afrika) Verwendung, doch ist ein Weiterverkauf noch kaum anzunehmen. Überhaupt gibt es für die meisten Produkte, bei denen seit dem 10. Jh. Byzanz als Herkunftsland erscheint, bis zum 8./9. Jh. im Westen noch keinen Nachweis, oder man hatte bereits die Möglichkeit eines direkten Bezuges ohne die byz. Vermittlung.

F. Einnahmen

Die steuerlichen Gewinne aus dem H. waren für den byz. Staat (trotz der weit verbreiteten gegenteiligen Meinung) weitaus geringer als jene aus dem Landbesitz und beliefen sich auf kaum mehr als 5–10 % der Gesamtsteuereinnahmen. Der Handelszoll im vorliegenden Zeitraum hatte die Bezeichnung *octava* und betrug etwa 12,5 % des Wertes, doch unterliegen diese Angaben noch einer kontroversen Beurteilung.

→ Geld, Geldwirtschaft; Handel

1 G. F. Bass, E. H. van Doorninck, Yassi Ada. A Seventh Century Byzantine Shipwreck, 1982 **2** D. Claude, Der H. im westl. Mittelmeer während des Frühmittelalters, 1985 **3** J. Ferluga, Mercati e mercanti fra Mar Nero e Adriatico: il commercio nei Balcani dal VII al XI secolo, in: Mercati e mercanti nell'alto medioevo, 1993, 443–489 **4** M. F. Hendy, Studies in the Byzantine Monetary Economy c. 300–1450, 1985 **5** J. Koder, Gemüse in Byzanz, 1993 **6** A. E. Laiou, s. v. Commerce and Trace, ODB I, 489–491 **7** D. G. Letsios, Νόμος Ῥοδίων ναυτικός. Das Seegesetz der Rhodier, 1996 **8** M. Lombard, Les métaux dans l'ancien monde du Ve au XIe siècle, 1974 **9** R. S. Lopez, The Role of the Trade in the Economic Readjustment of Byzantium in the Seventh Century, in: Dumbarton Oaks Papers 13, 1959, 69–85 **10** H. Magoulias, The Lives of the Saints as Sources of Data for the History of Commerce in the Byzantine Empire in the Sixth and Seventh Centuries, in: Kleronomia 3, 1971, 303–330 **11** N. Oikonomides, Silk trade and production in Byzantium from the sixth to the ninth century: the seals of the Kommerkiarioi, in: Dumbarton Oaks Papers 40, 1986, 33–53 **12** A. P. Rudakov, Ocherki vizantijskoj kul'tury po dannym grecheskoy agiografii, (Ndr.) 1970, 138–174 **13** P. Schreiner, s. v. H. (in Byzanz), LMA 4, 1898–1903 **14** Ders., Zivilschiffahrt und Handelsschiffahrt in Byzanz, in: R. Ragosta (Hrsg.), Le genti del Mare Mediterraneo, Bd. 1, 1981, 9–25 **15** J. L. Teall, The Grain Supply of the Byzantine Empire 330–1025, in: Dumbarton Oaks Papers 13, 1959, 87–139.

P. S.

VII. Frühes Mittelalter

Die von H. Pirenne [7] 1937 formulierte These, daß erst die muslimischen Eroberungen mit ihren den Mittelmeer- und Orienthandel abschnürenden Wirkungen den Kollaps der ant. Wirtschaftsstrukturen und damit zugleich die Ruralisierung des NW, bes. des Karolingerreiches, bewirkt hätten, ist h. zugunsten von Vorstellungen allmählichen strukturellen Wandels und räumlicher Verlagerungen seit dem 5. Jh. n. Chr. modifiziert worden. Dazu haben Forsch. auf verschiedenen Gebieten beigetragen: die Arch. mit ihren Flächengrabungen von Handelsplätzen (Haitabu, Birka, Dorestad, Hamwih), die Numismatik durch Verfeinerung ihrer Methodik handelsgesch. Interpretation des enorm vergrößerten Fundmaterials, die Wirtschaftsgesch. mit neuen Erkenntnissen zur Rolle des grundherrlich gebundenen H. und schließlich die Orientierung an anthropologischen Theorien zum frühen H. und Austausch sowie an Zentralitätslehren der Geographie.

Während der Jh. des Übergangs von der Spätant. zum frühen MA diktierten die großen polit. und kirchlichen Umformungsprozesse im Westen des Imperiums bzw. in dessen Nachfolgereichen und deren Nachbarregionen in hohem Maße Form und Wirkung des H., der hier als profaner Gütertausch in Abgrenzung von Gaben auf Gegenseitigkeit und Zeremonialtausch verstanden wird. Neben der Zentrierung der westl. Christenheit auf Rom und der fränkischen Großreichsbildung bildeten zwei Vorgänge wichtige Voraussetzungen für den allmählichen kommerziellen Strukturwandel: die Ausbreitung der Avaren und Slaven in Osteuropa (seit dem 6. Jh.), die den Fernhandel zwischen Ostsee und Schwarzem Meer, Balkan und Adria beeinträchtigte und eine Umorientierung auf den Seeweg zur Rheinmündung und die Flußwege durch Gallien nach Marseille zur Folge hatte, sowie die arab. Eroberung der Mittelmeerküsten von Äg. bis Spanien (7./8. Jh.) und die folgende Blockade der Seewege durch Byzanz. Aus dieser neuen Konstellation resultierte langfristig eine Angleichung der Austauschverhältnisse in den Regionen diesseits und jenseits der nordalpinen imperialen Grenzen sowie eine Verlagerung der Seehandelsaktivitäten auf die Kanalküste und die Nordsee mit Anschluß zum skandinavischen NO und zum mediterranen Süden.

Im einzelnen zeichneten sich bereits im 6. Jh. Bindungen der jüd., griech. und syr. Fernhändler an die neuen regionalen Herrschaftsträger (Schutz, Zollbefreiung) und ebenso neue Außenhandelsverbindungen über den Kanal und nach Osten ab. Diese Tendenzen verstärkten sich in den Umbruchjahrzehnten seit dem späten 7. Jh. Die intensiver werdenden Austauschbeziehungen mit der Küste Britanniens sowie den Nord- und Ostseeanrainern wurden im wesentlichen von Friesen und Angelsachsen, aber auch von Franken getragen. Neben den traditionellen Gütern (Sklaven, Wein, Öl, Gewürzen) wurden zunehmend gewerbliche Roh- und Fertigerzeugnisse aus dem eigenen Hinterland (Keramik, Mühlsteine, Tuche, Waffen, Glas) gehandelt. Die gentilen Herrschaftsträger, deren Interesse an der Intensivierung des markt- und geldvermittelten Austauschs immer klarer zutage tritt, haben diesen H. nachdrücklich gefördert.

Trotz der sachlich breit gestreuten Regelungen, die besonders die Kapitularien der früheren Karolinger bezeugen (Ordnung des östlichen Grenz- und des Küstenhandels, Brücken- und Straßenbau, Zollwesen, Märkteförderung und Marktkontrolle, Münzreformen, Maß- und Gewichtsordnung, Ausfuhrverbot, Wucherkritik, Notstandspreise), ist keine den H. systematisch erfassende Normgebung erkennbar; gänzlich ausgespart blieb die rechtliche Ausgestaltung der Handelsgeschäfte selbst (Kauf, Preis, Kredit). Dies ändert jedoch nichts daran, daß mit der Entstehung des nw Küstenhandelsraums und dessen enger Verbundenheit mit Flußschiffahrt und gewerblichem Hinterland ein Grundstein (neben Italien) zum säkularen Aufstieg des ma. Städtewesens gelegt wurde.

1 H. Adam, Das Zollwesen im fränkischen Reich und das spätkarolingische Wirtschaftsleben, 1996 (VSWG Beih. 126)
2 P. Contamine u.a., L'économie médiévale, 1997, 41–80
3 H.-J. Drexhage, s.v. H., RAC 13, 519–574
4 P. Grierson, Commerce in the Dark Ages: a Critique of the Evidence, in: Transactions of the Royal Hist. Soc., 5th ser., V/8, 1959, 123–140 5 R. Hodges, Dark Age Economics, 1982 6 Mercati e mercanti nell'alto medioevo, 1993 7 H. Pirenne, Mahomet et Charlemagne, 1937
8 H. Siems, H. und Wucher im Spiegel frühma. Rechtsquellen, 1992 9 Untersuchungen zu H. und Verkehr der vor- und frühgesch. Zeit in Mittel- und Nordeuropa, Bd. 1–6, 1985–1989 (AAWG) 10 A. Verhulst, Der H. im Merowingerreich: Gesamtdarstellung nach schriftlichen Quellen, in: Antikvariskt arkiv 39, 1970, 2–54. LU.KU.

Handelsamphoren s. Transportamphoren

Handschriften A. Bestimmung B. Beschaffenheit C. Verbreitung

A. Bestimmung 1. Begriff
2. Überlieferungsgeschichtliche Bedeutung

1. Begriff

Das handgeschriebene Buch ist die Quelle unserer Kenntnis fast der gesamten ant. Lit. Die ganz wenigen Ausnahmen sind die Inschr., z.B. der *Res Gestae Divi Augusti* (→ Augustus) an einer Tempelwand in Ankara oder das philos. Manifest des → Diogenes [18] von Oinoanda [14. 199–202]. Gewöhnlich wird nicht ganz korrekt zw. denjenigen in der ant. Welt geschriebenen Büchern unterschieden, die generell, aber nicht ganz zu Recht als → Papyri bekannt sind, und denjenigen, die später produziert wurden, als die Papyrusrolle (→ Rolle) dem → Codex als Standardformat eines Buches gewichen war.

2. Überlieferungsgeschichtliche Bedeutung

Für den Herausgeber eines klass. Texts sind die H. von Interesse, insofern sie bei der Rekonstruktion des genauen Wortlauts eines ant. Autors behilflich sind. Ein Text ist oft in einer großen Anzahl von Abschriften überliefert, von denen aber nur eine oder wenige für den Herausgeber brauchbar sind. Man hat daher relativ junge H. lange Zeit unterbewertet, wenn Textzeugen aus dem frühen MA vorhanden waren. Inzw. hat man jedoch erkannt, daß jüngere H. in einigen Fällen wertvolle Lesarten liefern, die sich des öfteren auf ältere ant. Vorlagen zurückführen lassen. Es hat sich auch gezeigt, daß in einigen jungen H. notwendige Textverbesserungen von ma. oder Renaissance-Gelehrten vorgenommen wurden. Neben ihrem Interesse für die Textkonstitution haben H. jedoch auch eine sozial- und geistesgesch. Bed.: Der Aufwand, der für die Herstellung eines handgeschriebenen Buches nötig war, zeigt ein Bedürfnis an, einen klass. Text zu lesen. Die Erkenntnisse in der griech. und vor allem in der lat. Paläographie erlauben den Gelehrten in einer zunehmenden Anzahl von Fällen, den urspr. Besitzer oder das kulturelle Umfeld zu identifizieren, für den bzw. für das ein Buch angefertigt wurde.

B. Beschaffenheit 1. Varianten
2. Marginalien 3. Abschnittsmarkierungen
4. Datierung und Herkunftsermittlung
5. Textinhalt

1. Varianten

Leser waren sich immer über die Fehleranfälligkeit handgeschriebener Texte im klaren; in den H. sind daher wechselseitige Überprüfungen, vor allem gegen die Vorlage selbst, nachweisbar. Die ant. → Subskriptionen lenken die Aufmerksamkeit auf diesen Vorgang, der aber im MA selten erwähnt wird [3. 66]. Manchmal wurde der Originaltext dadurch verändert, daß man einfach über ihn schrieb oder ihn zuvor ausradierte (ein gutes Pergamentblatt ist dick genug, um das Entfernen einer Oberflächenschicht auszuhalten). Varianten wurden auch am Rand oder im Zeilenzwischenraum eingetragen, manchmal mit einem Hinweis auf ihre Quelle (jedoch selten wünschenswert eindeutig), wie z.B. *u.c.* für *uetus codex*, öfters einfach durch *a(liter)* oder *uel* oder γρ(άφεται). Aber mitunter sieht es so aus, als ob solche Markierungen Lesarten begleiten, die von ihrem Urheber selbst konjiziert wurden; und einige Schreiber versuchten, den Text beim Kopieren zu verbessern (→ Interpolation) – nicht aus »Unredlichkeit« des Schreibers, sondern als Versuch, den vorliegenden Text zu verstehen. Eine detaillierte Unt. der Überlieferungs-Gesch. ist erst durch die Erfindungen der letzten Jh., des Buchdrucks, der Photographie sowie der Mobilität der Wissenschaftler möglich, und erst hier wurde die strikte Bewahrung des Überlieferten gegen die Lesbarkeit zur Kardinaltugend einer H. erhoben.

2. Marginalien

Die meisten Texte sind mit großzügigen Rändern geschrieben; das mag teils ästhetische Gründe gehabt haben, bot jedoch auch Platz für Randbemerkungen. Z.B. können hier Anmerkungen zu Schwierigkeiten beim Lesen der Vorlage stehen. Die älteste H. des → Propertius (Wolfenbüttel, Cod. Gud. lat. 224) weist eine Reihe von Buchstaben am Rand auf, welche die Aufmerksamkeit auf Sentenzen leiten sowie auf andere Verse, die man sich vielleicht eigens herausschreiben wollte; an einigen Stellen sind diese Markierungszeichen unsinnig (z.B. *uuta*, für *nota*?) und müssen von einer Vorlage abgeschrieben worden sein. An anderen Stellen weisen die Komm. größeren Bezug zum Textinhalt auf (z.B. *uere ais poeta* und *modeste* jeweils neben Prop. 4,1,54 und 58 im Florentinus Laurentianus S. Marco 690, eine H., die ca. 1400–1405 für Niccolò Niccoli kopiert und später als Palimpsest verwendet wurde). Die Komm. können auch zur Erläuterung von Schwierigkeiten im Text beitragen, wobei Glossen zu Eigennamen bes. häufig sind. Wörter über der Zeile oder am Rand waren oft nicht eindeutig als Glosse oder Variante erkennbar: dies führte zu einer fehlerhaften Abschrift. In einigen Fällen ist der Komm. gründlich, und der Anmerkungsteil einer Seite kann umfangreicher als der eigentliche Text sein (z. B. in der großen Ilias-H. Venedig, Marcianus Graecus 454 oder auf der Seite der Vergil-H., Bern 165 [4. Abb. Nr. LXVIII]. Häufig verwendeten die Schreiber für die Randeintragungen eine andere Schrift, bei der sie von Ligaturen und Abkürzungen freieren Gebrauch machten, um Platz zu sparen.

3. Abschnittsmarkierungen

Als Lesehilfen wurden Abschnitte zw. und innerhalb von Werken auf unterschiedliche Weise markiert (→ Gedichttrennung), dazu fügte man (oft selbst erfundene) Überschriften ein, um einen Eindruck vom Inhalt zu vermitteln (z. B. im sogenannten Oblongus von → Lucretius). In zahlreichen Hss. der ›Metamorphosen‹ des → Ovidius stehen nach den Überschriften Kurzzusammenfassungen des folgenden Mythos; H. der ›Fasten‹ führen im Anhang eine tabellenartige Liste. In der frühesten Periode der griech. Überlieferungsgesch. scheint das griech. Drama keine regelmäßigen Bezeichnungen der Sprecher aufzuweisen, diese wird aber im Laufe der Zeit zunehmend hinzugefügt; die gelegentlich überlieferten → Regieanweisungen im Text des → Aristophanes [1] (z. B. Aristoph. Thesm. 277) sind fast sicher spätere Einfügungen.

4. Datierung und Herkunftsermittlung

H. enthalten verschiedene Merkmale, die für den Kodikologen sowie für den Erforscher der Textgesch. von Interesse sind. Physische Eigenschaften wie → Tinte, → Pergament oder → Papier (das oft durch die Wasserzeichen datierbar ist) und Buchbindung können wesentliche Informationen geben, ebenso Aspekte der Herstellung, wie der Aufbau der Lagen (→ Lagenzählung), die → Linierung und natürlich die → Schrift selbst sowie die Interpunktion (→ Lesezeichen; auch durch andere Details, wie die Verwendung eines Superskriptes auf dem »o« (ó), um lat. Vokative zu bezeichnen). Von Bed. ist auch der Buchschmuck: Dieser reicht von einem kurzen Schnörkel, der einen Zwischenraum ausfüllen soll, bis zu den Kunstwerken der »illuminierten« H. Schon die ant. Vergil-H. enthalten Bilder, die den folgenden Text illustrieren (siehe [3. 244 ff] mit Illustrationen). Vorsatzblätter vor und nach den Textseiten wurden oft für Federproben verwendet, und da diese unabhängig vom Textinhalt waren, können auch sie sehr hilfreich bei der Rekonstruktion der Gesch. einer H. sein.

5. Textinhalt

Der Inhalt eines einzelnen Cod. kann einheitlich sein (z. B. die gesammelten Werke eines einzigen Autors); andere H. bieten sehr uneinheitliche Sammlungen verschiedenster Texte. Ein klass. Beispiel hierfür ist der wichtige Cod. Bern. 363 (letztes Viertel des 9. Jh.), der den halben → Servius-Komm. zu → Vergil, verschiedene Abh. über die Rhet., Auszüge aus → Horatius und (etwas kürzere) aus den ›Metamorphosen‹ des Ovid, das Geschichtswerk des Beda Venerabilis und schließlich verschiedene ma. Gedichte enthält (Faksimile [10]). Der für das Griech. wichtige Cod. Laurentianus 32,9 enthält die sieben erh. Werke des → Aischylos und des → Sophokles, sowie die *Argonautica* des → Apollonios [2] Rhodios.

C. Verbreitung 1. Sammlungen
2. Handschriften in antiken Bibliotheken
3. Mittelalter und Renaissance

1. Sammlungen

Griech. und lat. H. wurden bis in die 2. H. des 16. Jh. geschrieben; die Gesamtzahl der bis heute überlieferten ist beachtenswert: bis zu 45000 griech. und erheblich mehr lat. H. Die überwiegende Mehrzahl gehört heute den großen öffentlichen Bibliotheken in Europa und Nordamerika. Keine der ant. Bibliotheken hat bis in die Neuzeit überlebt, aber einige Klöster und frühe weltliche Bibliotheken besitzen immer noch für die urspr. Sammlung eigens angefertigte ma. Bücher. Ihr sehr geringer Prozentsatz resultiert nicht nur aus Diebstahl oder nicht erfolgter Rückgabe ausgeliehener Exemplare: Bücher wurden zu allen Zeiten häufig auf Reisen mitgenommen.

2. Handschriften in antiken Bibliotheken

Im röm. Reich gab es eine Vielzahl von privaten und öffentlichen → Bibliotheken; einige der letzteren waren sehr gut bestückt. Sie haben in der Regel nicht so überlebt, daß sie heute noch *in situ* aufzufinden wären. Die wenigen Ausnahmen sind erwähnenswert: die koptischen Codices, die 1945 in Nag Hammadi gefunden wurden, und die große Slg. von beinahe 600 Rollen, die in der 4. Höhle bei → Qumran entdeckt wurden; es ist aber nicht sicher, daß die Höhle als Bibliothek gedacht war [9. 192–193]. Dies trifft eher für den sogenannten Dišnā-Fund zu (vgl. [9. 172–174] zur Entdeckung im J. 1952; vgl. auch [15]), eine Bibliothek von teilweise griech., teilweise kopt. Texten, die in dem Pachomius-Kloster (im oberen Ägypten) ab dem 4. Jh. aufgebaut und während des 7. Jh. begraben wurde. Ein weiteres Beispiel einer ant. Bibliothek, die teilweise *in situ* geborgen wurde, ist der Papyrusrollen-Fund von 1941 in Tura; aus ihm gingen acht Codices mit Werken von → Origenes und → Didymos [5] dem Blinden hervor. Das Musterbeispiel einer ant. Bibliothek ist die Sammlung von verkohlten Rollen, die 1752 in einer Villa in Herculaneum gefunden wurden, die den Pisones gehörte (→ Herculanensische Papyri). Diese Bibliothek bestand aus vornehmlich griech. Titeln zur epikureischen Philos.; ganz anders als die lit. Papyri, die in Ägypten gefunden wurden. Letztere stammen im wesentlichen aus Privatbibliotheken, die sich im einzelnen nicht mehr identifizieren lassen.

3. Mittelalter und Renaissance

a) Der Übergang von der antiken zur mittelalterlichen Buchproduktion

In der Spätant. und in den folgenden »dunklen Jh.« wurden Bibliotheken in allen Gebieten des röm. Reiches entweder zerstört oder stark dezimiert, und die den weltlichen und kirchlichen Autoritäten zur Verfügung stehenden Mittel glichen den Verlust nur teilweise aus. Die Stiftung des → Cassiodorus in seinem Vivarium überlebte nicht, aber das Kloster von Bobbio bewahrte einen Teil des alten Bestandes. Sowohl im westl. Europa als auch in Byzanz läßt sich seit ca. 800 n. Chr. eine Renaissance beobachten (→ Makedonische Renaissance). In beiden Gebieten hängt dies mit der Übernahme einer neuen → Minuskel-Schrift zusammen. Seit den letzten zwei oder drei Jh. war die Produktion teilweise durch die Verknappung der Papyrusvorräte behindert (Papyrus war das normale Schreibmaterial des Alt.). → Pergament als Alternative war zwar haltbarer, aber teurer. Die neue Minuskel-Schrift erlaubte eine ökonomischere Verwendung des Schreibmaterials. Im byz. Gebiet wurde die Produktion von H. auch durch die Gründung von Papierfabriken (→ Papier) in verschiedenen arabischen Ländern gefördert; die Byzantiner nützten diese neue Erfindung seit dem 11. Jh. Die meisten Gebiete des westlichen Europas hatten erst später dazu Zugang. Obwohl um 1147 bei Xátiva, einer Gegend südlich von Valencia, unter arab. Einfluß Papierproduktion bezeugt ist [17. 133f], breitete sie sich in größerem Maße erst im 13. Jh. oder noch später in andere Länder aus.

Auch in Byzanz war die Knappheit des Schreibmaterials bisweilen ein Problem: Pergament war ein Saisonprodukt, das vom Fleischverbrauch abhängig war [18. 1–15]. So entstanden Palimpseste, die den Originaltext zerstörten, um Platz für bedeutsamere Texte zu machen (Beispiele in [14. 192–195]).

Nach der Herstellung der Bücher in neuen Schriftarten wurden unzählige alte Vorlagen, von denen manche bis in die Spätant. zurückdatierten, weggeworfen; man hat errechnet, daß heute mehr als 6700 lat. H. in der neuen Karolingischen → Minuskel überliefert sind; aus der Zeit vor ca. 800 sind nur ungefähr 1865 vollständig oder fragmentarisch erhalten [16; 47].

b) Bibliotheken und Handschriftensammlungen

Meist lag – wie auch in der Ant. – die Buchherstellung bei Personen, die entweder für sich selbst abschrieben oder als professionelle Schreiber tätig waren. Viele Klöster, sowohl im Westen als auch in Byzanz, waren Zentren der Buchproduktion. Ab dem 9. Jh. läßt sich die Existenz einiger privater und institutioneller Bibliotheken verfolgen. Die wichtigste im Westen wurde für Karl den Großen in seinem Palast errichtet; wahrscheinlich gab es Entsprechendes im Palast des byz. Kaisers, aber über die Bibliotheken im byz. Reich ist weitaus weniger bekannt. Der Buchbestand wurde allmählich vergrößert, insbes. im Westen während des 12. Jh. Einige Universitäten entwickelten das sogenannte → Peciasystem: Mustervorlagen von grundlegenden Texten wurden in kleinere Abschnitte aufgeteilt und von Buchhändlern an Studenten ausgeliehen [6; 2]. Dieses System ist für Byzanz nicht nachweisbar; dort gab es von vielen Texten wahrscheinlich noch weitaus häufiger als im Westen nur eine einzige Abschrift. Auch Rückschläge sind zu vermerken, wie z. B. die Verwüstung im byz. Reich durch den vierten Kreuzzug 1204–1205.

Einige Bestandslisten der größeren Bibliotheken sind überliefert [5]. Das beste Beispiel aus der byz. Welt stammt aus dem St. Johannes-Kloster auf Patmos; ein Katalog aus dem J. 1200 weist knapp über 300 Bände auf (eine genaue Berechnung ist schwierig); ein Fünftel davon war aus Papier, der Rest aus Pergament ([1. 15–30 mit 6 Abb.] bietet den neuesten Forschungsstand). Aus dem Westen sind mehr Kataloge überliefert; im 13. Jh. erreichte ein Orden ein ungewöhnlich hohes Organisationsniveau: Die engl. Franziskaner erstellten einen Einheitskatalog für die Bestände ihrer Niederlassungen im ganzen Land (erh. in den Hss. Bodleian Library, Tanner 165 und Cambridge, Peterhouse 169). In einigen Fällen konnte eine Privatsammlung durchaus mit einer öffentlichen Bibliothek konkurrieren, wie z. B. jene Richards von Fournival (um 1250), der bei Amiens einen Besitz von rund 300 Exemplaren zusammenstellte, die kurz nach seinem Tod zur Grundlage der Bibliothek der Sorbonne wurden.

Auch die Päpste hatten eine reiche und bed. Sammlung. Nachdem ihre alte Lateran-Bibliothek verschwunden war, wurde im 13. Jh. eine neue erstellt (hiervon gibt es einen Katalog aus dem Jahre 1295) und eine dritte mußte während des Exils in Avignon 1309–77 angelegt werden; nur ein kleiner Teil hiervon fand seinen Weg nach Rom zurück [13].

Die Anzahl von wichtigen Slgg. wurde in der Renaissance langsam größer. Zu den großen privaten Sammlern zählen Petrarca, Coluccio, Salutati und Niccolò Niccoli; die päpstliche Bibliothek machte einen großen Schritt unter Nikolaus V. (1447–1455) vorwärts, und die Medici sorgten dafür, daß ihre Bibliothek den kulturellen Ambitionen von Florenz angemessen war.

Was das Griech. anbelangt, so stimulierte das neue Bewußtsein der Vorteile, die das Studium des Lateinischen mit sich brachte, ab ca. 1400 die Suche nach H. in den erreichbaren Gebieten des ehemaligen byz. Reiches; die hervorragenden Slgg. waren jene der Medici, Nikolaus' V. und des Kardinals Bessarion, der 1468 seine Bücher Venedig überließ, wo sie immer noch den Kern der Biblioteca Marciana ausmachen (bezüglich dieser Bibliotheken siehe [8; 7; 11]). Humanisten, die erkannten, daß der Buchbestand der lat. Lit. vermehrt werden konnte, retteten auch eine große Anzahl von lat. H. aus vernachlässigten Klosterbibliotheken. Beachtenswerte Funde machte Petrarca (1304–1374), Boccaccio (1313–1375) hatte Schätze in Montecassino ans Licht gebracht, eine Generation später war Poggio, der in Deutschland und in der Schweiz suchte, noch erfolgreicher.

Die Suche nach griech. Büchern ging auch nach der Renaissance weiter: Noch im 18. und 19. Jh. wurde eine ansehnliche Menge davon nach Westeuropa gebracht. Die Ortsveränderungen, denen griech. H. aus der Zeit vor ca. 1600 ausgesetzt waren, waren so groß, daß nur wenige in ihrem Herstellungsland verblieben; den lat. H. ging es diesbezüglich etwas besser.

Daß H. in ein anderes Land kamen, war üblich; doch auch innerhalb desselben Landes wechselten H. häufig die Bibliothek, insbes. aufgrund von Konfiszierungen des Kircheneigentums im England des 16. Jh. und in der napoleonischen Zeit in Frankreich und anderen europäischen Ländern. Der Prozeß des Verlustes und Wiederaufbaus sowie auch die Zirkulation von Büchern führten dazu, daß nur wenige Bibliotheken Sammlungen über lange Zeit hindurch intakt bewahren konnten. Die Patmos-Bibliothek z. B. besitzt heute nurmehr etwa 100 von den 300 Büchern, die im Jahre 1200 angegeben waren. Einige der größeren Bibliotheken, die in der Renaissance gegründet wurden, waren in unterschiedlichem Grade bei der Wahrung ihres Bestandes erfolgreich und haben bis heute überlebt (Informationen zur Gesch. einiger der größeren Sammlungen griech. H. bietet [12. 1–13]).

→ Kodikologie; Paläographie; Papyri; Codex

1 C. Astruc, Travaux et mémoires 8, 1981
2 I. J. Bataillon, R. H. Rouse (Hrsg.) La production du livre universitaire au moyen âge: exemplar et pecia, 1988
3 B. Bischoff, Paläographie des röm. Alt. und des abendländischen MA, 1979 **4** É. Chatelain, Paléographie des classiques latins (2 Bände), 1884–92 **5** A. Derolez, Les catalogues de bibliothèques, 1979 **6** J. Destrez, La pecia dans les manuscrits universitaires du xiiie et du xive siècle, 1935 **7** R. Devreese, Le fonds grec de la Bibliothèque Vaticane des origines à Paul V (Studi e Testi 244), 1965
8 E. B. Fryde, Greek manuscripts in the private library of the Medici 1469–1510, 1996 **9** H. Y. Gamble, Books and Readers in the Early Church, 1995 **10** H. Hagen, Augustinus Beda Horatius Ovidius Servius alii: Cod. Bernensis 363 phototypice editus, 1897 **11** L. Labowsky, Bessarion's library and the Bibliotheca Marciana, 1979
12 G. Laurion, Les principales collections de manuscrits grecs, in: Phoenix 15, 1961, 1–13 **13** F. Milkau, G. Leyh, Hdb. der Bibliothekswiss. 3/1, ²1955 **14** L. D. Reynolds, N. G. Wilson, Scribes and Scholars, ³1991 **15** J. M. Robinson, The Pachomian monastic library at the Chester Beatty Library and the Bibliothèque Bodmer, o. J. **16** R. H. Rouse, in: R. Jenkyns, The Legacy of Rome: A New Appraisal, 1992 **17** O. Valls i Subirà, The History of Paper-Making in Spain I, 1978 **18** N. G. Wilson, in: (o. Hrsg.), Byzantine Books and Bookmen (Dumbarton Oaks Colloquium), 1975.

P. Ganz (Hrsg.), The role of the book in medieval culture, Bibliologia 3–4, 1986 • M. B. Parkes, Pause & effect: an introduction to the history of punctuation in the West, 1992 • C. Questa, R. Raffaelli (Hrsg.), Il libro e il testo, 1984 • L. D. Reynolds (Hrsg.), Texts and transmission, 1983, xiii–xliii • E. G. Turner, Greek manuscripts of the Ancient World, ²1987.

N. W. u. S. H./Ü: H. H.

Handwerk I. Alter Orient und Ägypten II. Iran III. Keltisch-germanischer Bereich IV. Etrurien V. Klassische Antike VI. Byzanz VII. Frühes Mittelalter

I. Alter Orient und Ägypten

Das H. in Äg., in Syrien-Palästina und in Mesopot. läßt sich am besten anhand der verwendeten Materialien kategorisieren: Stein, Knochen und andere tierische Produkte, Ton und Glas, Metalle, Holz, Wolle und Flachs, Leder sowie Rohr und Pflanzenfasern. Daraus verfertigte man Gegenstände verschiedenster Art, vom Kochtopf bis zum fein gearbeiteten Schmuckstück. Für das Bau-H. waren Stein, Ton, Rohr und Holz wichtig. Für die Untersuchung verschiedener Formen des H. lassen sich drei Arten von Quellen mit unterschiedlicher Aussagekraft heranziehen: konkrete arch. Funde, bildliche Darstellungen von Gegenständen und Handwerkern sowie schriftliche Nachrichten.

Der Erhaltungszustand der arch. Funde hängt vom Material und der Region ab. Alle H.-Produkte sind in der äg. Wüste besser erh. als im Niltal oder generell im asiat. Teil des Nahen Ostens. Bes. eindrucksvoll ist der Erhaltungszustand von Leder, Rohr, Tau und Leinen. Keramik ist in der gesamten Region gut belegt. Gefäße, Statuen und andere Objekte aus Stein, die eher in Äg. und Syrien-Palästina als in Mesopot. üblich waren, sind gut erhalten. Kostbare Funde wie Goldschmuck wurden nur in Gräbern und unter ungewöhnlichen Bedingungen gemacht. Funde wie die intakte Grabstelle des Tutenchamun (14. Jh. v. Chr.), der Königsfriedhof von Ur (Mitte 3. Jt. v. Chr.) und die Gräber der neuassyrischen Königinnen aus Kalḫu (9. Jh. v. Chr.) zeigen neben den technischen Fähigkeiten der Handwerker auch, welches Vermögen für persönliche Repräsentationszwecke aufgebracht wurde. Eine große Zahl dieser Kostbarkeiten wurde schon in der Ant. geraubt, teilweise sogar schon kurz nach der Grablegung. In Äg. findet sich hauptsächlich Steinarchitektur. Gebäude aus nicht gebrannten Lehmziegeln sind – anders als in Mesopot. – nicht erhalten. Belege für Werkzeug sind in Äg. häufig, andernorts dagegen selten. Nur eine geringe Anzahl an Werkstätten ist arch. genau untersucht worden.

Ikonographisches Fundmaterial mit Motiven von handwerklichen Produkten oder Handwerkern bei der Arbeit gibt es in Äg., wo seit jeher Gräber mit Szenen aus dem Alltagsleben ausgeschmückt wurden, in Fülle [1]. Zwar existieren mesopot. Abbildungen z. B. von Textilarbeitern oder Töpfern, doch lassen sich ihnen keine nennenswerten technischen Informationen entnehmen. Auch der syro-palästin. ikonographische Befund ist eher spärlich.

Über geschäftliche Transaktionen mit selbständigen Handwerkern oder Werkstätten in Mesopot. liegen viele schriftliche Zeugnisse vor; sie geben Auskunft über die Quantität der importierten Rohmaterialien und die fertiggestellten Exportprodukte, woraus sich beispielsweise Informationen über die Materialien gewinnen lassen, die man für die Herstellung eines Streitwagens benötigte. Belege über den Verkauf von H.-Produkten in Äg. sind zwar vorhanden, jedoch bedauerlicherweise nicht aus zusammenhängenden Archiven einzelner Werkstätten. Die Untersuchung dieser Quellen befindet sich noch in den Anfängen. Die Beleglage für das syro-palästin. Gebiet ist wie im ikonographischen Bereich schlecht, obwohl die ausgezeichneten Fähigkeiten z. B. der Phönizier in der Textilweberei, dem Zimmerhandwerk oder der Metallarbeit aus Texten bekannt sind.

Die für den Grundbedarf benötigten Gegenstände wurden hauptsächlich in privaten Haushalten hergestellt; Institutionen wie Paläste oder Tempel waren für die Deckung ihres Bedarfs auf ganze Werkstätten angewiesen. Wie es aussieht, produzierten in Mesopot. die mit Tempel oder Palast verbundenen Handwerker auch für Privatkunden, wogegen die Belege für äg. Handwerker auf eine Bindung an einen Privathaushalt oder den Staat hindeuten. Privatwirtschaftliche Nebentätigkeiten dieser Handwerker sind auch schon damals wahrscheinlich. Eine große Anzahl von Handwerkern war an den gigantischen Bauprojekten in polit. Blütezeiten beteiligt. Der Bau und die Ausschmückung von völlig neuen Hauptstädten, wie Achet-Aton (→ Amarna) in Äg. oder Dūr-Šarrukīn in Assyrien, muß die Arbeitskräfte tausender gelernter Arbeiter in Anspruch genommen haben; dazu kommt eine Vielzahl ungelernter Arbeitskräfte für Hilfstätigkeiten. Leider ist keines dieser Projekte in den Textquellen dokumentiert.

Die technischen Fähigkeiten der Handwerker im Nahen Osten galten bereits in der Antike als sehr hoch. H.-Produkte wurden im Handel mit den umliegenden Gegenden gegen Rohstoffe eingetauscht. Dieser Handel schuf die Voraussetzungen für die Beeinflussung der griechischen Welt durch nahöstliche H.-Stile und Techniken, v.a. in der Mitte des 2. Jt. und im 8. Jh. v. Chr.

1 R. Drenkhahn, Die Handwerker und ihre Tätigkeiten im alten Äg., 1976 2 A. Lukas, Ancient Egyptian Materials and Industries, [4]1989 3 P. R. S. Moorey, Ancient Mesopotamian Materials and Industries: The Archeological Evidence, 1994. M. v. M./Ü: S. Z.

II. Iran

Der in relativ kurzer Zeit entwickelte einheitliche achäm. Hofkunststil verdankt sich einem großköniglichen Programm, das zum Zwecke der Betonung der *pax achaemenidica* in einem polyethnischen Großreich viele disparate Kunstelemente aus »eines Herren Ländern« zu einem Ganzen zusammenfügen ließ. Handwerker sind nicht nur aus den Objekten zu erschließen, sondern auch in Dareios' [1] I. »Burgbau-Inschrift« aus Susa [3. DSf] und den elam. Schatzhaustäfelchen aus Persepolis [1; 2] erwähnt. Unter den pers. Waren und Kunstobjekten, die in den Westen gelangten, waren Glas, Textilien, Gefäße aus Metall, Schmuck und Möbel bes. begehrt; sie setzen entsprechendes H. in Iran voraus. Aus sāsānidischer Zeit kennen wir die gewaltsame Ansiedlung von (kriegsgefangenen) Facharbeitern im Reich und die Einrichtung königlicher Werkstätten unter bes. Aufsicht. In der Hierarchie der städtischen Bevölkerung nahm nach Ausweis der nestorianischen Synode von 544 aus → Gundeschapur der »Vorsteher der (königlichen) Handwerker« die erste Stelle unter den Laien ein, noch vor den Vorstehern der Korporationen der freien Handwerker, die »gildenartig« organisiert waren. Bekannte Gewerbe waren das Textil- und Baugewerbe sowie Toreutik, Teppich- und Schmuckherstellung.

1 G. G. Cameron, Persepolis Treasury Tablets, 1948
2 R. T. Hallock, Persepolis Fortification Tablets, 1969
3 R. G. Kent, Old Persian, 1953 4 M. C. Miller, Athens and Persia in the Fifth Century B. C., 1997
5 N. Pigulevskaja, Les villes de l'état iranien aux époques parthe et sassanide, 1963, 116ff., 159ff. 6 A. Tafazzoli, A List of Trades and Crafts in the Sassanian Period, in: AMI 7, 1974, 191–196 7 J. Wiesehöfer, Das ant. Persien, 1994, Index s. v. 8 H. E. Wulff, The Traditional Crafts of Persia, 1966. J. W.

III. Keltisch-germanischer Bereich

Zum kelt.-german. H. stehen fast nur arch. Quellen zur Verfügung, um Einblicke in einzelne H.-Zweige, Materialien und auch Fertigungsverfahren zu erhalten; Struktur, Organisation, Sozialstellung usw. der H. sind bisher kaum faßbar.

Von der Brz. an und besonders in der kelt. Eisenzeit (→ Hallstatt- und → Latène-Kultur) sind Werkstattplätze, H.-Bezirke in Siedlungen und vereinzelt auch Handwerker-Gräber bekannt, die sich durch Baustrukturen und aufwendige und spezialisierte Einrichtungen (Öfen, Herde, Drehscheiben usw.), durch Abfälle (Knochenreste, Keramikfehlbrände, Schlacken etc.), durch Produkte und v. a. durch spezielle Werkzeuge ausweisen. Es lassen sich Töpfer, Schmiede für Br., Eisen und Edelmetalle, holzverarbeitende Handwerker (Stellmacher, Böttcher, Zimmerleute, Schiffsbauer, Drechsler), Knochenschnitzer (Nadeln, Kämme), Textil- u. Leder-Handwerker, Glas-, Bernstein- und Gagatverarbeiter nachweisen. Im kelt. Bereich sind vielfach Kontakte mit dem Süden faßbar, wie z. B. Bau-H. mit Kenntnis der Lehmziegelbauweise auf der → Heuneburg oder Granulationstechnik bei Goldschmieden. Im german. Raum ist eher ein einfaches H. im dörflichen Rahmen anzunehmen, das z. T. durch Einflüsse kelt. H. geprägt ist und auch bis in die Kaiserzeit der ersten Jh. n. Chr. erh. bleibt.

→ Germanische Archäologie; Keltische Archäologie; Ziegel

Ch. Eluère (Hrsg.), Outils et ateliers d'orfèvres des temps anciens, 1993 • J.-P. Guillaumet, L'artisanat chez les Gaulois, 1996 • G. Jacobi, Werkzeug und Gerät aus dem Oppidum von Manching, 1974 • H. Jankuhn u. a. (Hrsg.), Das H. in vor- und frühgesch. Zeit, 2 Bde., 1981/3 • S. Sievers, Die Kleinfunde der Heuneburg, 1984. V. P.

IV. Etrurien

Das etr. H. bietet nach den erh. Denkmälern ein sehr komplexes Bild. Die wenigen Schriftquellen wie Plinius (nat. 35,152), der von dem korinth. Adligen → Demaratos [1] berichtet, der Handwerker mit nach Tarquinia brachte, sind spät. Einen gewissen Ruf hatten etr. Br.-Geräte für das Haus (Kritias bei Athen. 1,28b; Pherekrates bei Athen. 15,700c). Nur wenige etr. Künstler sind mit ihrem Namen bekannt. Vulca von Veii, der im späten 6. Jh. v. Chr. als Auftragsarbeit das Kultbild des kapitolinischen Iuppiter in Rom schuf, gehört zu den wenigen Ausnahmen (Plin. nat. 34,34). Bei den Pretiosen der → Fürstengräber handelt es sich um Auftragsarbeiten. Mit dem Erstarken der Mittelschicht im 6. Jh. v. Chr. sind erste Anzeichen für eine breite Produktion zu erkennen. Alle H.-Richtungen erfuhren einen Aufschwung mit dem Beginn der griech. Kolonisation. Immer wieder sind, durch griech. oder phönik. Einfluß vermittelt, in bestimmten H.-Zweigen Neuansätze zu erkennen.

Ab dem 8. Jh. wurde die schnell drehende Töpferscheibe genutzt. Die Gefäße im etr.-geom. Stil lehnen sich stark an importierte griech. Keramik an. Dies gilt auch für die zeitlich folgenden Vasenstile. Zum Teil ist von eingewanderten Handwerkern auszugehen (z. B. → Caeretaner Hydrien). Die Maler der Grabfresken standen in enger Verbindung zu den Vasenmalern. Die typisch etr. → Buccherokeramik wurde in Anlehnung an Metallarbeiten zuerst in Cerveteri entwickelt (2. Viertel 7. Jh.) und hielt sich in degenerierter Form (*Bucchero grigio*) bis ins 4. Jh. v. Chr. Andere etr. Städte wie Chiusi und Orvieto sind ab dem 6. Jh. v. Chr. führend in der Herstellung des stempelverzierten *Bucchero pesante*. Die in Athen nur begrenzt eingesetzte *Sixtechnik* wirkte in der etr. *Sovradipinta*-Technik noch länger fort (→ Rotfigurige Vasenmalerei). Die *Vernice-nera*-Keramik hatte ihre Zentren der Herstellung mehr im Süden der it. Halbinsel. Bemerkenswert ist die verzinnte Keramik hell. Zeit aus dem Bereich Orvieto-Bolsena, die Metallgefäße imitiert und für den Grabbereich hergestellt wurde.

Von großer Bed. war die von den Phönikern erlernte Goldschmiedekunst in der hochentwickelten Technik des Filigran und der Granulation.

Etr. Toreuten waren hervorragende Vertreter ihres Standes. Ihre Produktpalette umfaßte eine große Anzahl verschiedenster Geräte (bes. Handspiegel), vom Möbel- und Wagenbeschlag bis zu Gefäßen, die z. T. bereits in Serien gefertigt wurden (Schnabelkannen). Ebenso bedeutend waren seit dem 8. Jh. v. Chr. die Waffenwerkstätten, die noch zur Zeit des Scipio Africanus (Liv. 28,45) das röm. Heer mit Ausrüstung versorgten (namentlich aus → Arretium/Arezzo).

Die Arbeiten der Tischler, Wagen- und Schiffsbauer sind nur über Bildquellen zu beurteilen. Die Darstellungen von Möbeln auf Wandmalereien, Vasen etc. vermitteln das Bild eines H., das in Anlehnung an griech. Formen → Möbel für den gehobenen Bedarf herstellte. Sowohl Transport- als auch Streitwagen sind im Fundbestand nachzuweisen.

Eine bes. Stellung nahmen die Koroplasten ein, da die in Etr. üblicherweise hölzernen Tempeldächer als Witterungsschutz mit reliefverzierten Tonplatten und vollplastischen Figuren aus Ton versehen waren (→ Terrakotta). Zu den Werken der Koroplastik (u. a. »Ehepaar-Sarkophage«, Statuen) treten jene aus Stein, v. a. Grabplastik in Tarquinia, Vulci und Chiusi in archa. Zeit und später in Volterra (Alabaster) mit herausragenden Werkstätten. Von zentraler Bed. sind auch die unterirdischen → Hypogaeen mit reicher aus dem Tuffstein gemeißelter Innenarchitektur (bes. Cerveteri und Chiusi). Ab der Mitte des 6. Jh. v. Chr. setzte die etr. Glyptik ein, die bes. Bohrtechniken voraussetzte. Von der Textil- und Lederverarbeitung, die wahrscheinlich zumeist häuslichen Charakter besaß, wissen wir wenig.
→ Etrusci, Etruria

L. Bonfante, Etruscan Dress, 1975 · M. Bonghi Jovino (Hrsg.), Produzione artigianale ed esportazione nel mondo antico. Il Bucchero etrusco, Atti Milano 1990, 1993 · G. Colonna, Il maestro dell'Ercole e della Minerva. Nuova luce sull'attività dell'officina veiente, in: OpRom 16, 1987, 7–41 · M. Cristofani, I bronzi degli Etruschi, 1985 · M. Cristofani, M. Martelli (Hrsg.), L'oro degli Etruschi, 1985 · M. Egg, Ital. Helme. Stud. zu den ältereisenzeitl. Helmen It.s und der Alpen, 1986 · U. Fischer-Graf, Spiegelwerkstätten in Vulci, 1980 · E. Formigli, G. Nestler, Etr. Granulation. Eine ant. Goldschmiedetechnik, 1993 · F.-W. von Hase, Früheisenzeitl. Kammhelme aus It., in: Ant. Helme. Slg. Lipperheide und andere Bestände des Antikenmus. Berlin, 1988, 195–211 · S. Haynes, Etruscan Bronzes, 1985 · Y. Huls, Ivoires d'Etrurie, 1957 · M. Martelli, La ceramica degli Etruschi. La pittura vascolare, 1987 · A. Naso, Architetture dipinte. Decorazioni parietali non figurate nelle tombe a camera dell'Etruria meridionale (VII–V sec. a. C.), 1996 · F. Prayon, Frühetr. Grab- und Hausarchitektur, 1975 · G. M. A. Richter, Engraved Gems of the Greeks and the Etruscans, 1968, bes. 173–213 · E. Rystedt, C. Wikander, Ö. Wikander, Deliciae Fictiles. Proc. of the First International Conference on Central Italic Architectural Terracottas at the Swedish Institute in Rome 1990, 1993 · S. Steingräber, Etr. Möbel, 1979 · Ders. (Hrsg.), Etr. Wandmalerei, 1985 · P. Zazoff, Etr. Skarabäen, 1968.

GE. BI.

V. Klassische Antike

A. Allgemeines B. Kultur und Wirtschaft C. Ausbildung und Arbeitsbedingungen im Handwerk D. Standort und technische Ausstattung der Werkstätten E. Handwerker und Auftraggeber F. Löhne G. Sozialer Status H. Literatur und Philosophie

A. Allgemeines

Obgleich die polit. Strukturen sich im Verlauf der Ant. grundlegend gewandelt haben, blieben die Arbeitsbedingungen im H. und die soziale Lage der Handwerker im wesentlichen unverändert: Für die Produktion von Gebrauchsgütern und die Hervorbringung von Kunstwerken war die Handarbeit von entscheidender Bed., mechanische Instrumente wurden nur in geringem Umfang verwendet, und es gab in vielen Zweigen des H. keine bahnbrechenden technischen Neuerungen. Die Öffentlichkeit verachtete den Handwerker, schätzte aber seine Produkte (Plut. Perikles 2,1). Eine klare Unterscheidung zwischen Handwerker und Künstler im heutigen Sinne existierte nicht; die Begriffe τέχνη (*téchnē*) und *ars* bezeichnen sowohl die handwerkliche als auch die künstlerische Tätigkeit. Neben den lit. Texten und den Inschr., die nicht in gleicher Weise alle Aspekte des ant. H. beleuchten, sind außerdem die zahlreichen Werkstattbilder auf att. Vasen und die röm. Grabreliefs (v.a. aus It. und Gallien) als wichtige Zeugnisse heranzuziehen.

B. Kultur und Wirtschaft

Abgesehen von isolierten und daher autarken Haushalten konnte die Eigenproduktion den Bedarf an H.-Erzeugnissen nicht vollständig decken. Obwohl die Eigenproduktion im Haushalt in allen Epochen der Ant. fortbestand (Werkzeuge und Geräte: Hom. Il. 23,831ff.; Cato agr. 5,6; 31; 37,3; Textilherstellung: Hes. erg. 536ff.; Verg. georg. 1,293f.; 1,390ff.; Suet. Aug. 73; Colum. 12,3,6), war das H. von der archa. Zeit bis zur Spätant. für Wirtschaft und Ges. lebenswichtig; einerseits war die Bevölkerung der Städte auf Gebrauchsgüter wie Gefäße, Textilien und Möbel oder auf Nahrungsmittel wie Brot angewiesen, andererseits fanden viele Menschen der urbanen Zentren im H. Arbeit und Auskommen. Die Landwirtschaft wiederum benötigte in großem Umfang die Kompetenz von Handwerkern (vgl. Hes. erg. 430; Cato agr. 14; 16) oder Erzeugnisse des H. (Cato agr. 22; 135; Varro rust. 1,16,3). Der Handel spielte für die Versorgung mit Produkten des H. zunächst nur eine untergeordnete Rolle, denn normalerweise verkaufte ein Handwerker seine Erzeugnisse in der Werkstatt direkt an den Kunden. In vielen Regionen haben kleine Werkstätten für den lokalen Bedarf produziert, obgleich auch Produktionszentren von überregionaler Bed. entstanden – in der Keramikherstellung während der archa. und klass. Zeit etwa bei Korinth und Athen oder in röm. Zeit bei → Arretium sowie in Süd- und Mittelgallien.

In der homer. Ges. gehörten Handwerker zu den wenigen Fremden, die in einem Gemeinwesen willkommen waren, weil sie über spezielle Fähigkeiten verfügten (Hom. Od. 17,381ff.); nur spezialisierte Wanderhandwerker konnten repräsentative Gegenstände für die Oberschicht herstellen. Kultstatuen, Weihgaben und Skulpturen, Gold- und Silbergeschirr, Tempel oder Wandgemälde wurden oft nicht nur in kleinen, ländlichen Siedlungen, sondern auch in Städten, in denen viele Handwerker tätig waren, von Fremden geschaffen. Die Mobilität dieser Handwerker war mit der Entstehung eines städtischen H. nicht verschwunden, sondern weiterhin kennzeichnend für Arbeit und Leben vieler Bildhauer, Baumeister und Bergleute. Wirtschaftskrisen, die Veränderung des allg. Geschmacks, aber auch gesetzliche Maßnahmen wie etwa das von → Demetrios [4] von Phaleron erlassene Verbot, in Athen aufwendige Grabdenkmäler aufzustellen (Cic. leg. 2,66), konnten die Auftragslage dieser Handwerker abrupt verschlechtern. Umgekehrt erforderte die Durchführung größerer Bauprojekte die Rekrutierung einer entsprechenden Zahl gut ausgebildeter Arbeitskräfte; Bauvorhaben mußten sich so am Arbeitskräftepotential orientieren. Das röm. Heer, das für die Herstellung von Rüstungen, Waffen und Belagerungsgerät sowie für den Bau von Unterkünften und Nachschubwegen ebenfalls auf Handwerker und Techniker (→ *fabri*) angewiesen war, besaß in republikanischer Zeit eigene Einheiten von Handwerkern unter dem Befehl des *praefectus fabrum* (Veg. mil. 2,11). Um die Versorgung der Bevölkerung zu sichern, wurde Handwerkern in der Spätant. untersagt, ihren Beruf zu wechseln oder ihre Werkstatt aufzugeben; einige Berufe wurden erblich, so daß Söhne gezwungen waren, die Tätigkeit ihres Vaters zu übernehmen. Zahlreiche Erlasse betrafen gerade die Bäcker in Rom, die dem *corpus pistorum* (Vereinigung der Bäcker) angehörten und Brot für die Verteilung an die Bevölkerung zu liefern hatten (Cod. Theod. 14,3). In anderen Städten richteten sich die Zwangsmaßnahmen der Verwaltung ebenfalls v.a. gegen die Bäcker (Antiocheia: Lib. or. 1,205–210; 1,226f.).

Aufgrund der Struktur der ant. Wirtschaft konnte eine steigende Produktion bestimmter Güter zu einem Verfall der Preise und damit auch zu einer Abwanderung von Handwerkern führen (vgl. Xen. vect. 4,6). Die Einkünfte der Handwerker sowie Qualität und Preis ihrer Erzeugnisse waren durch das Marktgeschehen weitgehend geschützt; es fehlten allerdings Zusammenschlüsse von Handwerkern mit dem Ziel, Produktion und Verkauf der Erzeugnisse effizient zu organisieren. Erst in der Spätant. wurden *corpora* gebildet, die v.a. die Beziehungen zwischen der Verwaltung und den einzelnen Handwerkern regeln sollten.

Für einfache Handwerker war eine gewisse Vielseitigkeit notwendig, denn die meisten Herstellungsprozesse (Hausbau, Möbelherstellung) erforderten die Bearbeitung verschiedenartiger Materialien. Handwerker in kleineren Städten waren bisweilen gezwungen, unterschiedliche Erzeugnisse – etwa eiserne Pflugscharen, Sicheln, Messer, Nägel und Schlüssel – herzustellen, um genügend Aufträge für ihre Werkstatt zu erhalten. Das Element des Wettbewerbs, das auch in anderen Bereichen des ant. Lebens anzutreffen war, trug zur Qualität im H. und zum wirtschaftlichen Erfolg der Handwerker bei. So sprach Hesiod davon, daß ein Töpfer dem Töpfer, dem Zimmermann ein Zimmermann mißgünstig sei (κεραμεὺς κεραμεῖ κοτέει καὶ τέκτονι τέκτων; Hes. erg. 25), und Städte richteten Wettbewerbe für Töpfer aus, wie die Grabinschr. des Bakchios bezeugt, der mehrere Kränze gewonnen hat (IG II^2 11387). Es gibt zudem einzelne Hinweise auf eine wirtschaftliche Konkurrenz zwischen Handwerkern verschiedener Städte; nach

Athenaios versuchten Handwerker in Rhodos, preisgünstigere Metallgefäße als die Athener herzustellen und so neue Käuferschichten zu erreichen (Athen. 469b).

Auf die kulturelle Entwicklung haben Handwerker durch die Gestaltung von Gebrauchsgütern einen kaum übersehbaren Einfluß ausgeübt. Die att. Keramik war ein wichtiger Bildträger; die Töpfer und Vasenmaler haben auf diese Weise die visuellen Welten der Griechen gestaltet und einen grundlegenden Beitrag zur Interpretation trad. Mythen oder alltäglicher sozialer Konstellationen geleistet. Darüber hinaus war die Werkstatt in den Dörfern und Städten auch ein Ort sozialer Kommunikation; Sokrates soll viele seiner Gespräche in der Werkstatt des Schusters Simon an der Agora von Athen geführt haben (Diog. Laert. 2,122; vgl. Xen. mem. 4,2,1; Hes. erg. 492f.).

C. Ausbildung und Arbeitsbedingungen im Handwerk

Die Ausbildung im H. erfolgte durch einen erfahrenen Handwerker, oft durch den Vater oder einen anderen Verwandten (Plat. Prot. 328a). Nicht nur der Mythos des → Daidalos [1] (Apollod. 3,15,8), sondern auch zahlreiche Inschr. und lit. Zeugnisse weisen darauf hin, daß ein H. innerhalb einer Familie trad. und eine Werkstatt oft vom Sohn übernommen wurde. Wie aus Werkstattszenen auf att. Vasen hervorgeht, war Kinderarbeit ohne Zweifel häufig. Hatte ein Handwerker keine Söhne, so konnte er einen Jungen adoptieren oder ein unfreies Kind kaufen. Die Praxis, nicht zur Familie gehörende Kinder oder Sklaven in einem H. auszubilden, ist nur für das ptolemaiische und röm. Ägypten gut belegt (vgl. etwa POxy. 275; 725); es ist aber – aufgrund von Hinweisen auf das Lehrer-Schüler-Verhältnis im Bereich der Bildhauerei und Malerei (Plat. Men. 91d; Plin. nat. 36,16f.) – anzunehmen, daß dies auch in anderen Regionen und Epochen praktiziert wurde.

Die Dauer der Ausbildung hing zum einen von der individuellen Lernfähigkeit, zum anderen aber auch von den Erwartungen des Meisters ab. Die Ausbildung begann mit unbedeutenden Aufgaben. In der Töpferei etwa drehte ein Knabe die Töpferscheibe, während der Meister das Gefäß formte; sprichwörtlich galt es als unsinnig, das Töpfern mit dem → Pithos zu beginnen (Plat. Gorg. 514e). Obgleich ein vollständig ausgebildeter Architekt, Töpfer, Bildhauer, Maler, Schmied oder Schuhmacher alle Arbeitsschritte seines H. beherrschte, ist in den Werkstätten doch eine Spezialisierung einzelner Gehilfen auf bestimmte Arbeitsprozesse feststellbar. Die zunehmende Verwendung spezieller Bezeichnungen für bestimmte Handwerker bedeutet aber nicht, daß ganze Werkstätten sich in entsprechender Weise spezialisiert hätten. Ohne Zweifel herrschte eine strenge Disziplin im H., um eine Beschädigung von Werkzeug und Material sowie Verletzungen zu vermeiden; dies galt bes. dann, wenn Feuer, schwere Gewichte oder scharfe Werkzeuge bei der Ausübung des H. gebraucht wurden.

Ein gut ausgebildeter Sklave konnte mit seiner Freilassung rechnen und hatte dann auch die Möglichkeit, seinerseits freie Arbeiter zu beschäftigen oder gar Sklaven zu besitzen. Statusunterschiede waren angesichts der Anforderungen des H. fast bedeutungslos; zwischen der Arbeit von freien Handwerkern und von Sklaven kann etwa im östl. Säulengang des Erechtheion kein Unterschied festgestellt werden. Frauen (Ehefrauen, Töchter, Sklavinnen) wurden vielleicht in größerer Zahl im H. beschäftigt, als die wenigen Zeugnisse andeuten (vgl. Xen. mem. 2,7 sowie eine Vasenmalerin: rf. Hydria, Beazley ARV 571,73).

Die Arbeitszeit für Tätigkeiten außerhalb des Hauses richtete sich wahrscheinlich nach der Länge des Tages; viele Tätigkeiten konnten auch bei künstlichem Licht ausgeführt werden. Zahlreiche Handwerker arbeiteten in einer engen und ungesunden Umgebung; ihre Arbeitsbelastung konnte zu Krankheiten und körperlichen Deformierungen führen. Im Bau-H. war es trotz des Einsatzes von großen Kränen und Flaschenzügen sowie von schweren Wagen für den Transport der Steinblöcke noch immer die Aufgabe der Handwerker, Baumaterial mit Muskelkraft zu bewegen, zumal die Schubkarre noch unbekannt war.

D. Standort und technische Ausstattung der Werkstätten

Die antike Werkstatt umfaßte normalerweise die für die Produktion notwendigen Menschen, Werkzeuge und Materialien. Der Standort der Werkstatt – und damit auch das Gebäude selbst – war nur von zweitrangiger Bed.; je nach der aktuellen Aufgabe konnte ein Handwerker seine Werkstatt an einen anderen Ort verlegen. In einigen Handwerkszweigen war der Standort der Werkstätten von den Rohstoff- oder Brennstoffvorkommen abhängig. Guter, für die Keramikherstellung geeigneter Ton wurde in der Nähe von Korinth und Athen gefunden und war Voraussetzung für die Keramikproduktion in diesen Städten; auch bei Arretium wurden die lokalen Tonvorkommen genutzt. Metallhaltige Erze wurden in vielen Fällen in entlegenen Regionen abgebaut und verhüttet (→ Bergbau); hier entstanden dann Siedlungen für die Bergleute, so etwa im Laureion-Gebiet in Attika oder in Vipasca im röm. Spanien (CIL II 5181 = ILS 6891). Zentren der Metallverarbeitung befanden sich außerdem in Hafenstädten; Eisenerz aus Elba wurde nach Puteoli gebracht und dort verarbeitet (Diod. 5,13,1f.). In der Textilproduktion ist ebenfalls eine Konzentration von Werkstätten in solchen Regionen zu beobachten, in denen hochwertige Rohstoffe gewonnen wurden (Wolle: Patavium, Strab. 5,1,7; 5,1,12; Leinen: Tarsos, Dion Chrys. 34,21–23; Byssos: Patrai, Paus. 7,21,14). In vielen größeren Städten waren die meisten Handwerkszweige vertreten; in Athen waren im H.-Distrikt in der Nähe der Agora Töpfer, die Terrakottafiguren herstellten, Schuhmacher, Bronzeschmiede und Steinmetze, die Marmor bearbeiteten, ansässig, in Pompeii lebten und arbeiteten über die ganze Stadt verteilt Bäcker, Weber, Walker,

Schmiede, Töpfer und Bauhandwerker. Inschr. belegen, daß dies auch für Rom gilt.

Die ant. Werkstätten waren unterschiedlich groß: Schmiede, Juweliere oder Weber arbeiteten wohl allein oder nur mit wenigen Gehilfen, wie att. Vasenbilder und röm. Grabreliefs aus It. und Gallien zeigen; die Werkstatt war oft direkt mit der Wohnung des Handwerkers verbunden und diente gleichzeitig auch als Laden. In einer Töpferei oder einer Bronzegießerei konnten hingegen durchaus sechs oder mehr Handwerker arbeiten. Größere Werkstätten sind für das klass. Griechenland nur selten belegt (Lys. 12,8; 12,19: 120 Schildmacher; Demosth. or. 27,9: 2 → *ergastḗria* mit 32 und 20 Sklaven; vgl. Demosth. or. 36,4), waren aber in einigen Zweigen des röm. Gewerbes wie den großen Ziegeleien üblich.

Das ant. H. war seinem Wesen nach stark traditionsverhaftet. Es gab keine technischen Fortschritte, die den Arbeitsprozeß grundlegend hätten verändern können. Dennoch entstanden immer wieder neue handwerkliche Techniken wie beispielsweise die Herstellung reliefverzierter Keramik mit Hilfe von Formschüsseln im Hell., das Glasblasen im 1. Jh. v. Chr. oder das Ziegelbrennen im frühen Prinzipat. Auch innerhalb fest etablierter Handwerkstrad. gab es Möglichkeiten für Innovationen, wie sie bes. für die Verarbeitung von → Glas belegt sind. Im Bereich der Bronzeverarbeitung muß das Hohlgußverfahren als ein wesentlicher Fortschritt gewertet werden, der überhaupt erst die Verfertigung lebensgroßer Bronzestatuen möglich machte. Das qualifizierte H. beruhte wesentlich auf Erfindungsreichtum, Kenntnis und manueller Geschicklichkeit, nicht auf einer aufwendigen technischen Ausstattung. Eine steigende Nachfrage führte nicht zu technischen Veränderungen und zur Etablierung von Großbetrieben, sondern zur Einrichtung neuer Werkstätten, in denen mit der trad. Technik gearbeitet wurde. Bisweilen haben allerdings mehrere Handwerker gemeinsam Installationen von hoher Kapazität genutzt; in Gallien ließen mehrere Töpfer ihre Tonware in einem Töpferofen brennen. Immer wieder hat man aus den kurzen Bemerkungen Xenophons (Xen. Kyr. 8,2,5 f.) auf Massenproduktion durch erhöhte Spezialisierung geschlossen, doch das eigentliche Ziel handwerklicher Spezialisierung war nicht die Erhöhung der Produktivität, sondern die Qualitätssteigerung. Nach Augustinus lag ein weiterer Vorteil der Spezialisierung in der Verkürzung der Ausbildungszeit (Aug. civ. 7,4).

E. Handwerker und Auftraggeber

Handwerker arbeiteten nicht allein für den Verkauf an anonyme Kunden, sondern oftmals für Auftraggeber, was gerade für die Skulptur und das Bauwesen gilt; in diesem Bereich spielten öffentliche Aufträge eine wichtige Rolle. Die Handwerker hatten in solchen Fällen die Vorstellungen der Auftraggeber zu berücksichtigen. Wie ein Werkstattbild zeigt, wurde die Fertigstellung von Statuen durch die Auftraggeber kontrolliert (rf. Schale, Berlin SM, Beazley ARV 400,1). Die Mitglieder von Baukommissionen waren wahrscheinlich in der Lage, über architektonische Entwürfe kompetent zu urteilen; daher sollte ihr Einfluß auf die öffentliche Bautätigkeit nicht unterschätzt werden.

Bei der Vergabe von Aufträgen einigten sich Handwerker und Auftraggeber über Material, Größe, Stil, Preis und Termin der Fertigstellung (vgl. etwa CIL I[2] 698 = ILS 5317); der Handwerker haftete für jeglichen Schaden am gelieferten Material oder für dessen Verschwendung (Dig. 9,2,27,29). Für das 5. Jh. v. Chr. sind Verträge zwischen privaten Auftraggebern und Handwerkern nur selten erwähnt; so behauptet Andokides, Alkibiades habe den Maler → Agatharchos gezwungen, für ihn zu arbeiten, obgleich er Verträge mit anderen Auftraggebern zu erfüllen hatte (And. 4,17). Für das klass. Griechenland zeigen Rechenschaftsber., daß die Auftragnehmer streng an die Vertragsbedingungen gebunden waren; es waren neben allen Details eines Bauwerkes auch die Länge des Arbeitstages, die Zahl der Handwerker, ihr Lohn, die Beilegung von Konflikten zwischen den einzelnen Gruppen von Handwerkern sowie Maßnahmen bei Überschreitung der Termine genau festgelegt. Die Handwerker, die bei großen Bauprojekten die Aufsicht hatten und die Vielzahl verschiedener Arbeitsschritte koordinierten, wurden als *architéktōnes* (ἀρχιτέκτωνες, »Architekten«) bezeichnet, ein Titel, der nur für das Bau-H. belegt ist und auf die herausragende Stellung des Zimmermanns (τέκτων, *téktōn*) im ant. Bau-H. hinweist. Wenn das Gemeinwesen direkt Arbeiten vergab und wie in Athen im 5. Jh. v. Chr. pro Tag (oder pro Stück) bezahlte, hing die Weiterbeschäftigung des einzelnen Handwerkers v. a. von der Zustimmung des verantwortlichen Architekten ab; angesichts dieser Situation konnten die Handwerker in Konfliktfällen allenfalls damit drohen, die Arbeit nicht mehr fortzuführen. Für das ptolemaiische und das röm. Ägypten sowie Kleinasien sind Arbeitsniederlegungen belegt, die auf mangelnde Lieferung von Material oder Lebensmitteln oder auf das Ausbleiben der Löhne zurückzuführen sind.

F. Löhne

Die Quellenlage für die Bezahlung der H.-Arbeit ist unzureichend. Der Tageslohn war in Athen während des 5. Jh. v. Chr. für einen nicht voll ausgebildeten Handwerker etwas niedriger, für einen qualifizierten Handwerker etwas höher als der Sold eines Hopliten. Für die Steinbrüche und Minen der *principes* galt ein Lohntarif, der sich eher nach dem Alter des Arbeiters als nach der Art der Arbeit richtete, wobei der Höchstlohn dem Sold eines röm. Soldaten entsprach. Das → *Edictum Diocletiani* (7,1–63) zeigt zwar, welche Relationen zwischen den Löhnen in den verschiedenen Handwerkszweigen bestanden, aber es ist aufgrund der Quellenlage kein Vergleich mit dem Sold der Soldaten im Jahre 301 möglich. Handwerker verdienten normalerweise genügend, um sich einen angemessenen Lebensstandard zu sichern, sie konnten aber keinen Reichtum erwerben. Die Leineweber in Tarsos waren nicht einmal in der Lage, die für den Erwerb des Bürgerrechts notwendigen 500 Drachmen aufzubringen (Dion Chrys. 34,23); immerhin zeigen aber einige bei Plinius überlieferte Anekdoten (Plin. nat. 34,37; 35,62; 35,88) sowie Weihgaben und Grabmonumente, daß einzelne Handwerker – darunter vornehmlich qualifizierte Bildhauer und Maler – reich wurden und ihren Wohlstand auch demonstrativ zur Schau stellten. Ein Beispiel hierfür ist das große Grabdenkmal des Bäckers Eurysaces an der Porta Maggiore in Rom mit den Reliefs, die die Arbeit in einer Bäckerei anschaulich darstellen.

G. Sozialer Status

In der Ant. bestand ein ausgeprägtes Vorurteil gegenüber Menschen, die körperlich arbeiteten (βάναυσοι, *bánausoi* oder *sordidi*); wiederholt werden in der ant. Lit. die Deformierung des Körpers, Krankheit und früher Tod aufgrund der Anstrengungen der unablässigen Arbeit, die keine Muße ließ für eine öffentliche oder musische Tätigkeit, sowie die wirtschaftliche und soziale Abhängigkeit als charakteristisch für das Leben von Handwerkern genannt (Xen. mem. 2,8; oik. 4,2f.; vgl. Aristot. pol. 1278a; 1337b). Die Geringschätzung der *bánausoi* war nirgends so stark ausgeprägt wie in Sparta (Xen. Lak. pol. 7,1f.) und im demokratischen Athen, wo Politikern eine Beziehung zum H. zum Vorwurf gemacht werden konnte; in Korinth sollen die Handwerker nach Herodot am wenigsten verachtet worden sein (Hdt. 2,167). Auch in Rom war die soziale Ablehnung körperlicher, abhängiger Arbeit und des H. weit verbreitet: Nach Cicero übten alle Handwerker ein schmutziges Gewerbe aus, da eine Werkstatt nichts Freies haben könne (*Opificesque omnes in sordida arte versantur; nec enim quicquam ingenuum habere potest officina*; Cic. off. 2,150; vgl. Dion Chrys. 7,110ff.). Dennoch nannten in röm. Zeit viele Handwerker ihren Beruf auf Grabinschr., was aber auch darauf zurückzuführen ist, daß es in Rom anders als in Griechenland üblich war, den sozialen Status eines Verstorbenen genau anzugeben. Es existieren viele weitere Anzeichen dafür, daß Handwerker auf die Verachtung durch die Öffentlichkeit mit einem Selbstbewußtsein reagierten, das auf ihrem handwerklichen Können beruhte. Hier sind bes. die Signaturen zu nennen, die zwar auch zur Kennzeichnung von Handelsware dienten, oft aber den Stolz des Handwerkers auf seine Leistung demonstrieren. Gerade att. Weihreliefs und Vasenbilder zeigen gut das Selbstverständnis der Töpfer und Vasenmaler: Auf einem Gefäß sind Vasenmaler bei der Arbeit dargestellt, die von Göttinnen bekränzt werden (rf. Hydria, um 470 v. Chr., Beazley ARV 571,73). Wenn auch nur wenige Handwerker ein öffentliches Amt innehatten, so bot ihnen doch eine Mitgliedschaft in Kultvereinen oder in Berufsvereinen die Möglichkeit, ihre sozialen und polit. Ambitionen zu verwirklichen. In der Öffentlichkeit traten Handwerker im frühen Prinzipat durchaus als Kollektiv auf: Die *fullones* (→ Walker) von Pompeii errichteten der Eumachia eine Statue und nannten sich selbst in der zugehörigen Inschr. (CIL X 813 = ILS 6368).

H. Literatur und Philosophie

Die frühgriech. Lit. bietet zahlreiche Beschreibungen handwerklicher Tätigkeit und nennt viele Handwerker mit Namen; bei Homer spielt handwerkliche Geschicklichkeit für die Handlung der Epen eine entscheidende Rolle (vgl. Hom. Il. 18,368–617; Od. 5,243–261; 8,492f.; 23,183–204); auch in den Gleichnissen erscheinen handwerkliche Techniken (Hom. Od. 9,384–394; vgl. Hes. theog. 862–866). Hephaistos und Athene lehren die Menschen ihre *téchnē* (Hom. Il. 15,410ff.; Od. 7,109ff.; 23,160). Die Würde technischen Handelns resultiert aus der Herkunft der *téchnai* von den Göttern. Gleichzeitig beruht die Ambivalenz des H. auf der Einsicht, daß das Tun des Handwerkers für die Menschen nachteilig zu sein vermag (Hes. erg. 60–75) oder der Täuschung und Überwindung eines Stärkeren dient (Hom. Od. 8,266–332). In der Ant. existierte keine theoretische Analyse handwerklicher Produktion, in verschiedenen Kontexten haben Philosophen aber die Arbeit des Handwerkers thematisiert. Platon begründet im ›Protagoras‹ unter Rekurs auf den Prometheus-Mythos die Notwendigkeit handwerklicher Arbeit mit der natürlichen Ausstattung des Menschen, der ›nackt, unbeschuht, unbedeckt und unbewaffnet‹ der *téchnai* bedarf, um überleben zu können (Plat. Prot. 320d–322d). In Zusammenhang mit einer sprachtheoretischen Fragestellung wird der Werkzeuggebrauch eingehend untersucht (Plat. Krat. 387a–390d; vgl. auch polit. 279a–283a zur Textilherstellung). Aristoteles diskutiert in seinen Ausführungen über die verschiedenen Formen des Wissens bzw. über die zentrale Frage des Werdens den Akt des Herstellens (ποίησις, *poíēsis*; Aristot. eth. Nic. 1140a; metaph. 1032a–1033b), der wesentlich darin besteht, daß eine vorgedachte Form (εἶδος, *eídos*) auf einen vorhandenen Stoff (ὕλη, *hýlē*) übertragen wird. Diese Position dient in den zoologischen Schriften dazu, das Phänomen der Konzeption zu erklären (Aristot. gen. an. 729b–730b; vgl. 735a; 740b), wobei hier die auf das Werkzeug übertragene und damit auf den Arbeitsgegenstand wirkende Bewegung der Hand als grundlegend für den Herstellungsprozeß erachtet wird. In der polit. Theorie findet das geringe Ansehen der Handwerker seinen Ausdruck in der Auffassung, daß diese nicht zur Bürgerschaft einer Polis gehören sollten (Plat. leg. 846a–847b; Aristot. pol. 1328b).

1 O. Behrends, Die Rechtsformen des röm. H., in: H. Jankuhn (Hrsg.), Das H. in vor- und frühgesch. Zeit (AAWG 122), 1981, 141–203 **2** Blümner, Techn.
3 A. Burford, Craftsmen in Greek and Roman Society, 1972 **4** Dies., The Greek Temple Builders at Epidauros, 1969 **5** J. Crook, Law and Life of Rome, 1967
6 H. Cuvigny, The Amount of Wages Paid to the Quarryworkers at Mons Claudianus, in: JRS 86, 1996, 139–145 **7** R. Duncan-Jones, The Economy of the Roman Empire, [2]1982 **8** P. Garnsey (Hrsg.), Non-Slave Labour in the Greco-Roman World, 1980 **9** B. Gralfs, Metallverarbeitende Produktionsstätten in Pompeji, 1988
10 W. V. Harris, The Organisation of the Roman Terracotta Lamp Industry, in: JRS 70, 1980, 126–145 **11** J. F.

HEALY, Mining and Metallurgy in the Greek and Roman World, 1978 **12** H. JANKUHN (Hrsg.), Das H. in vor- und frühgesch. Zeit (AAWG 122), 1981 **13** JONES, LRE, 858–864 **14** N. KAMPEN, Image and Status: Roman Working Women in Ostia, 1981 **15** H. LOANE, Industry and Commerce of the City of Rome 50 B. C.-A. D. 200, 1938 **16** B. MAYESKE, Bakeries, Bakers, and Bread at Pompeii, PhD Diss. University of Maryland, 1972 **17** D. P. S. PEACOCK, Pottery in the Roman World, 1982 **18** H. v. PETRIKOVITS, Die Spezialisierung des röm. H., in: H. JANKUHN (Hrsg.), Das H. in vor- und frühgesch. Zeit (AAWG 122), 1981, 63–132 **19** G. PRACHNER, Die Sklaven und Freigelassenen im arretinischen Sigillatagewerbe, 1980 **20** R. H. RANDALL JR., The Erechtheum Workers, in: AJA 57, 1953, 199–210 **21** F. DE ROBERTIS, Lavori e lavorati nel mondo romano, 1963 **22** E. SCHLESIER, Ethnologische Aspekte zu den Begriffen »H.« und »Handwerker«, in: H. JANKUHN (Hrsg.), Das H. in vor- und frühgesch. Zeit (AAWG 122), 1981, 9–35 **23** A. STEWART, Greek Sculpture, 1990 **24** STRONG/BROWN **25** J. M. C. TOYNBEE, Death and Burial in the Roman World, 1971 **26** S. TREGGIARI, Roman Freedmen during the Late Republic, 1969 **27** Dies., Urban Labour in Rome: Mercennarii and Tabernarii, in: P. GARNSEY (Hrsg.), Non-slave Labour in the Greco-Roman World, 1980, 48–64 **28** A. WALLACE-HADRILL, Houses and Society in Pompeii and Herculaneum, 1994 **29** J. B. WARD-PERKINS, Marble in Antiquity, 1992 **30** R. S. YOUNG, A working-class district, in: Hesperia 20, 1951, 135–288 **31** G. ZIMMER, Griech. Bronzegußwerkstätten, 1990 **32** ZIMMER.

A. B.-C./Ü: A. BE.

VI. BYZANZ

A. QUELLENLAGE UND LITERATUR
B. DAS HANDWERK IM RAHMEN DER WIRTSCHAFTLICHEN ENTWICKLUNG
C. ORGANISATIONSFORMEN DER HANDWERKER

A. QUELLENLAGE UND LITERATUR

Die Quellenlage bereitet einer Darstellung des H. Schwierigkeiten. Dies trifft bes. auf Angaben über Art und Verbreitung der einzelnen H.-Zweige zu. Allein aus den äg. Papyrusdokumenten verfügen wir bis ins 7. Jh. über ausreichende Hinweise, doch sind diese auf die übrigen Reichsteile nicht übertragbar. Eher sporadische Angaben bringen die Heiligenviten (→ *vitae sanctorum*) und der Chronist → Theophanes.

B. DAS HANDWERK IM RAHMEN DER WIRTSCHAFTLICHEN ENTWICKLUNG

Es ist zu unterscheiden zwischen privaten Einzelhandwerkern (τεχνίτης, *technítēs*), die vielfach auch Verkäufer ihrer Ware, also Kaufleute waren, und den (teilweise unfreien) Handwerkern in den staatlichen Monopolbetrieben (Seidengewerbe, Waffenherstellung, Arsenale, Edelmetallverarbeitung in den Münzstätten), die in den großen Städten, bes. Konstantinopel, angesiedelt waren. Die rege Bautätigkeit (→ Bauwesen) unter Iustinianus, bes. die Neugestaltung Konstantinopels, stellt einen Höhepunkt für alle H.-Zweige dar (Prok. aed.).

Der Niedergang des Städtewesens seit der 2. H. des 6. Jh. brachte auch einen entscheidenden Einbruch in die Vielfalt handwerklicher Tätigkeiten. Wenig berührt davon war allein Konstantinopel, doch lebte auch in jenen Siedlungen, die auf Kastra zusammengeschrumpft waren, die zur Versorgung der Bevölkerung nötige Anzahl von Handwerkern weiter. Wichtig waren dabei bes. die Bauhandwerker für die Errichtung und Ausbesserung von Verteidigungsanlagen, aber auch die Bestellung der Äcker war ohne spezialisiertes Schmiede-H. nicht möglich. Alle konkreten Benennungen von H.-Berufen (z. B. in den Briefen des → Theodoros Studites, 8./9. Jh.) beziehen sich mit großer Wahrscheinlichkeit allein auf Konstantinopel.

C. ORGANISATIONSFORMEN DER HANDWERKER

Die spätant. Handwerkerkorporationen werden bis in die Zeit des Iustinianus genannt (Digesten, Prok. HA, Inschriften aus Korykos). Die nächste ausdrückliche Erwähnung von Organisationen findet sich erst wieder im Eparchenbuch → Leons VI. aus dem Jahr 911/912. Dieser lange Zeitraum ließ die Frage aufkommen, ob die Korporationen des 10. Jh. die spätant. Berufsgenossenschaften fortführten und ob es im 7. und 8. Jh. überhaupt Handwerkerverbände gab. Das Problem ist wohl überhaupt nur für die Hauptstadt Konstantinopel relevant, da in den meisten der übrigen kastellartigen Siedlungen Handwerker zwar nötig, aber aufgrund ihrer geringen Zahl keine Organisationsformen erforderlich waren. Die Struktur der Berufsverbände des 10. Jh. weist gegenüber der Spätant. auch keine so grundlegenden Unterschiede auf, daß ein völliger Neubeginn wahrscheinlich wäre. Gegen eine völlige Unterbrechung sprechen auch Hinweise bei Chronisten, denen zufolge die Kaiser sich bei verschiedenen Staatsangelegenheiten der Unterstützung der Handwerker versicherten. Bes. bemerkenswert ist dabei die schriftliche und mündliche Eidesleistung bei der Ernennung von Konstantin VI. zum Mitkaiser (776), an der auch οἱ τῶν ἐργαστηριακῶν (Theophanes 449,25–450,7 DE BOOR) teilnahmen. Dies setzt, auch von der sprachlichen Ausdrucksweise her, Berufsverbände voraus.

1 W. BRANDES, Die Städte Kleinasiens im 7. und 8. Jahrhundert, 1989, bes. 149–152 **2** H. MAGOULIAS, Trades and Crafts in the Sixth and Seventh Centuries as Viewed in the Lives of the Saints, in: Byzantinoslavica 37, 1976, 11–35 **3** A. I. ROMANCUK, Chersonesos und sein ländliches Territorium im 8./9. Jahrhundert, in: H. KÖPSTEIN, F. WINCKELMANN, Studien zum 8. und 9. Jahrhundert in Byzanz, 1983, 35–45 **4** P. SCHREINER, Die Organisation byz. Kaufleute und Handwerker, in: Untersuchungen zu Handel und Verkehr 6 (AAWG), 1989, 44–61 **5** A. STÖCKLE, Spätröm. und byz. Zünfte, 1911.

P. S.

VII. FRÜHES MITTELALTER

Vier Tendenzen sind es, die die Träger, Felder und Formen handwerklicher Tätigkeit vom 6.–9. Jh. n. Chr. charakterisieren: die Verlagerung des Schwergewichts von den *civitates* zu präurbanen bzw. ruralen Herrschaftszentren (→ Domänen, Pfalzen, Burgen, Bischofskirchen, Klöster; dazu Markt- bzw. Handelsplätzen), die einsetzende Angleichung der Regionen diesseits und jenseits der ehemaligen röm. Reichsgrenzen, der Rückgang bestimmter handwerklicher Standards (→ Glas) einerseits, die Elaborierung und Verbreitung anderer Techniken (Wassermühlen, Waffen) andererseits sowie Ansätze zu neuen gewerblichen Zentren (friesisch-flandrische Tuche, badorfer Keramik, Basaltmühlsteine in der Vulkaneifel u.a.). Neuere Siedlungs- und montanarch., linguistische sowie rechts-, wirtschafts-, technik- und kunsthistor. Forsch. haben zu diesem Bild beigetragen. Ihm fehlt aber noch eine begriffliche Abrundung, die aus leitenden Gegenbegriffen wie etwa Autarkie-Markt, Stadt-Land, Hauswerk-Handwerk, Lohnwerk-Preiswerk, Abgabe-Dienst, Freiheit-Knechtschaft, wandernd-seßhaft, Gebrauchsgut-Kunstwerk herausführt und damit der Vielfalt der Erscheinungen gerecht wird.

Das H. des frühen MA ist allerdings nur schemenhaft greifbar. Die wenigen, aus Schriftquellen oder Bodenfunden des 6.–9. Jh. stammenden Informationen reichen weder in ihrer Anzahl noch in ihrer Bandbreite aus, um das handwerkliche Feld insgesamt abzudecken oder soziale bzw. betriebliche Zuordnungen, geschweige denn urbane bzw. regionale Profilierungen zu gestatten.

Als Ausgangspunkt gewerblicher Belebungen dienten neue regnale, kirchliche und adlige Herrschaftssitze (über 500 steinerne Großbauten im 8.–9. Jh. im Frankenreich; Waffen-, Manuskript-, Liturgicawerkstätten), Küsten- bzw. Flußhandelsplätze (mit saisonal präsenten Veredelungswerkern) sowie villikale Einrichtungen gewerblicher Weiterverarbeitung und Materialgewinnung (Getreidemühlen, Malzdarren/Brauhäuser, Schmieden, Web- und Spinnhäuser (*genitia*), Töpfereien, Schmelzöfen, Salzsiedereien). Damit läßt sich ein Muster herrschaftsabhängiger, d.h. unfreier gewerblicher Dienstbarkeiten (*ministeria, servientes*) erkennen, das vom Schreibermönch über den klosterinternen *aurifaber*, der als begehrter Leihsklave die Runde macht, bis zum Erzgräber im Bergwald und zum Fährmann an der Furt reicht, die von ihrer servilen Hufe lebten. Auch wenn in der Karolingerzeit die Belege für einen gezielten Absatz an (hochrangige) Kunden oder auf lokalen, regionalen und Fernhandelmärkten zunehmen, scheint es nur selten zu betrieblichen Abschichtungen von seßhaften Gewerben im Sinne doppelt freien Marktbezugs (Ankauf der Materialien und Verkauf der Erzeugnisse) gekommen zu sein.

Im frühmittelalterlichen Überlieferungs- und Umbildungsprozeß des antiken *mechanicae*-Kanons fehlt, trotz zunehmender Wirklichkeitsbezüge und monastischen *opus manuum*-Gebots, jedes Anzeichen dafür, daß handwerkliche Tätigkeiten als vom Landbau, Haushalt und Handel distinkte *opera* oder *artes* begriffen und bestimmte von ihnen höher eingeschätzt wurden. Für das Bezeichnungsverhalten blieben Einzel-*opera*, Herrschaftsnähe und Dienstebene bestimmend. Auf dieselbe Weise wirkte die aristokratisch-kirchliche, von einer Ambivalenz von Verachtung und Bewunderung geprägte Einstellung gegenüber dem H. sich auf den einzelnen *artifex/faber* aus. Der besonderen Kunstfertigkeit wurde besondere Anerkennung als Einzelleistung nicht zuteil; maßgebend ist der Platz des anonymen Werkstücks im kirchlichen Kult- bzw. adligen Prunkgefüge; selbst subtil dekoriertes Schmuck- bzw. Schatzgut wird bei Bedarf arglos eingeschmolzen. Die Vorstellung, die seit dem 8./9. Jh. bestehenden *geldoniae* – von der Kirche bekämpfte örtliche Schwurbünde zur Abwehr aktueller Gefahren – gingen auf die spätant. → *collegia* oder german. Opferkulte zurück, sollte aufgegeben werden. Seit dem frühen 11. Jh. sind es Händler (*mercatores*), nicht Handwerker (*artifices*), die anfangen, sich als Berufsgruppen zu korporieren.

1 Artigianato e tecnica nella società dell'alto medioevo occidentale, Bd. 1–2, 1971 **2** H. JANKUHN (Hrsg.), Das H. in vor- und frühgesch. Zeit, Bd. 1–2, 1981/83 (AAWG) **3** U. KOCH (Hrsg.), Die Franken, Wegbereiter Europas, Bd. 2, 1996 **4** A. DOPSCH, Wirtschaftsentwicklung der Karolingerzeit, Bd. 2, 1922, 137–186 **5** K. EBERLEIN, Miniatur und Arbeit, 1995 **6** D. HÄGERMANN, Technik im frühen Mittelalter, in: W. KÖNIG (Hrsg.), Propyläen Technikgeschichte 1, 1991, 315–505 **7** H. ROTH, Kunst und Kunsthandwerk im frühen MA, 1986 **8** F. SCHWIND, Zu karolingerzeitlichen Klöstern als Wirtschaftsorganismen und Stätten handwerklicher Tätigkeit, in: L. FENSKE (Hrsg.), Institutionen, Kultur und Gesellschaft im MA (FS J. Fleckenstein), 1984, 101–123.

LU.KU.

Hanf. Die zweihäusige (mit kleinerer männlicher Form) 2–4 m hoch wachsende Faserpflanze Cannabis sativa L. (κάνναβις/-ος, *cannabis/-us*) aus der Familie der Urticaceae mit ihren fingerförmigen langgestielten Blättern. Der H. wuchs vor 500 v. Chr. wohl im Bereich vom Kaspischen Meer bis nach China. Die Skythen sollen den Samen des dort wildwachsenden und angebauten Krautes für rituelle Schwitzbäder und ekstatischen Rausch verwendet haben (Hdt. 4,74 f.), was für den aus der Unterart Cannabis indica gewonnenen »Haschisch« spricht (vgl. Hesych. s.v. κάνναβις). Die Thraker dagegen sollen die Bastfasern zu linnenähnlichen Stoffen verarbeitet haben. Der H.-Anbau kam später nach Griechenland (z.B. nach Elis, Paus. 6,26,6); Pers. 5,146 und Gell. 17,3,4 erwähnen den Anbau in Italien. Hieron II. von Syrakus importierte im 3. Jh. v.Chr. von der Rhône Schiffstaue aus H. (Athen. 5,206 f), dies ist auch für die Stadt Athen belegt (Xen. Ath. pol. 2). H.-Stricke kannte bereits der röm. Satiriker Lucilius (fr. 1325 M.; vgl. Varro, rust. 1,23,6).

Der H. wird im Garten ab Ende Februar auf gut gedüngtem Boden gesät (Colum. 2,10,21; Pall. agric. 3,5); Plin. nat. 19,173 f. beschreibt die Behandlung der reifen Samen und der Faser bei verschiedenen Sorten nach der Ernte im Herbst. Seile, die unter Wasser verwendbar waren, wurden dagegen aus dem span. Halfagras (*spartum*) hergestellt (Plin. nat. 19,29). Man glaubte, der ölreiche Samen des wilden (bei Dioskurides 3,148 WELLMANN = 3,155 BERENDES des angebauten) H. mache zeugungsunfähig, der Saft daraus vertreibe Würmer und andere Tiere aus den Ohren, die gekochte Wurzel helfe äußerlich gegen Gicht und Brandwunden (Plin. nat. 20,259). Verwechselt wurde der H. u. a. bei Dioskurides (3,149 WELLMANN = 3,156 BERENDES) mit dem Hanfblättrigen Eibisch (Malvaceae; Althaea cannabina L.). → Lein

1 V. HEHN, O. SCHRADER, Kulturpflanzen und Haustiere, [8]1911, Ndr. 1963, 190–193 2 F. ORTH, s. v. H., RE 7, 2313–2316.

C. HÜ.

Hannas (NT Ἄννας, Ios. Ἄνανος, rabbinisches Schrifttum *Elḥanan, Ḥanin*).

[1] Jüd. Hoherpriester 6–15 n. Chr., der als erster in dieses Amt von den Römern eingesetzt wurde (Ios. ant. Iud. 18,26). Auch nach seiner Absetzung (ebd. 18,34) besaß er, als ehemaliger Hoherpriester Mitglied des → Synhedrion, großen polit. Einfluß. Mit seinem Schwiegersohn Kaiphas war er entscheidend am Prozeß gegen Jesus (Jo 18,13; 24; vgl. [1]) wie gegen die Apostel Petrus und Johannes (Apg 4,6) beteiligt. Er war das Haupt eines der mächtigsten, aber auch bes. verrufenen (babylon. Talmud Pesaḥim 57a; Siphre Dt 14,22 § 105) nichtzadoqitischen Hohenpriestergeschlechter. Von seinen Nachkommen amtierten fünf Söhne und ein Enkel als Hohepriester (Ios. ant. Iud. 20,197; 223).

[2] Sohn von H. [1]. Amtierte 62 n. Chr. für drei Monate als Hoherpriester (Ios. ant. Iud. 20,197). Er wurde abgesetzt (ebd. 20,203), da er die Abwesenheit des Prokurators Albinus ausgenutzt hatte, um durch das → Synhedrion ihm mißliebige Leute, darunter Jakobus, den Bruder Jesu, wegen Gesetzlosigkeit zum Tode verurteilen zu lassen (ebd. 20,200; dieser Bericht ist kaum christl. Interpolation, vgl. [2]). Im jüd. Krieg spielte H. eine führende Rolle in Jerusalem (Ios. bell. Iud. 2,563; 647). Sein Versuch, die Diktatur der Zeloten zu beseitigen und den Aufstand in gemäßigtere Bahnen zu lenken, scheiterte nach anfänglichen Erfolgen (ebd. 4,151–313). H. fiel 68 n. Chr. in Jerusalem bei Kämpfen mit den von den Zeloten herbeigerufenen Idumäern (ebd. 4,315–316).

1 J. BLINZLER, Der Prozeß Jesu, [3]1960, 85–94
2 M. DIBELIUS, Der Brief des Jakobus, [8]1956, 12–14.

SCHÜRER 1, [3/4]1901, 581–583; 2, [4]1907, 256, 270–275 • J. JEREMIAS, Jerusalem z.Z. Jesu, [3]1962, 216–223 u.ö.

BE. SCH.

Hannibal (*Ḥnbʿl* = »Gnade des Bʿl«; Ἀννίβας).

[1] Erfolgreicher karthagischer Feldherr, Sohn des Magoniden → Geskon [1], u. a. im Exil in Selinunt aufgewachsen, etablierte die punische »Provinz« in West-Sizilien (»Epikratie«) durch die Feldzüge 410/09 und 406/05 v. Chr., wobei das Hilfegesuch von Segesta der Anlaß, die hegemoniale Expansion von Syrakus die tiefere Ursache für die von H. inaugurierte karthagische Interventionspolitik war [1. 107–114; 2. 37, 41, 119]. Wegen der gnadenlosen Belagerungen von Selinunt, Himera und Akragas (Diod. 13,43 f.; 54–62), vor allem wegen der Opferung von 3000 Gefangenen bei Himera als Rache für die Niederlage des → Hamilkar [1] vom J. 480 (Diod. 13,62,4 f.) gilt H. als »Griechenhasser« [vgl. aber 1. 109, 112; 3. 69, 409], dem sogar unterstellt wird, er habe mit dem Feldzug von 406 ganz Sizilien unterwerfen wollen (Diod. 13,79 f.; 85 f.) [3. 68]. Zur weitsichtigen Diplomatie H.s gehörten Verhandlungen mit Athen (SEG 10,136 = StV 2,208) [1. 117 f.]. Beim Tode H.s vor Akragas (406) übernahm sein Mitfeldherr und Verwandter → Himilkon [1] den Oberbefehl [1. 119; 3. 69].

[2] Karthagischer Nauarch und Stratege ca. 269–258 v. Chr., Vater (?) seines Amtskollegen → Hanno [4]; H. sicherte im J. 269 Messana gegen → Hieron [2] durch eine Besatzung, die am Vorabend (?) des 1. Pun. Krieges von den → Mamertini vertrieben wurde (Pol. 1,10 f.; Diod. 22,13,7 f.) [2. 102, 112]. H. verteidigte dann bis Anfang 261 Akragas gegen die Römer, räumte die Stadt nach einer schweren Niederlage des Hanno (Pol. 1,17–19) [3. 70, 414 und S. 112] und operierte danach mit seiner Flotte in tyrrhenischen Gewässern (Zon. 8,10). Im J. 260 brachte H.s Offizier Bodo den röm. Konsul L. → Cornelius [I 74] Scipio Asina auf (Pol. 1,21,6–8) [vgl. 3. 15], doch wurde H. selbst wenig später bei Mylai von C. → Duilius [1] vernichtend geschlagen (Pol. 1,23). Der nun von seinem Kommando abberufene H. (Vir. ill. 38,2 f.; Zon. 8,11) wurde 258 mit der Verteidigung Sardiniens betraut, bezahlte aber seine glücklose Niederlage gegen C. Sulpicius Paterculus mit dem Tod (Pol. 1,24,5–7; Zon. 8,12) [3. 71, 422].

[3] H. »der Rhodier« [3. 221, 1297]. Vornehmer karthagischer Besitzer einer extrem schnellen (Piraten-?) Pentere, brach auf eigene Faust 250/49 v. Chr. wiederholt die röm. Seeblockade von Lilybaion; als H. gefaßt wurde, bauten die Römer nach dem Modell seines Schiffes eine neue Flotte (Pol. 1,46,4–47,10; 59,8) [3. 73; 4. 134–137].

1 HUSS 2 L. M. HANS, Karthago und Sizilien, 1983 3 GEUS 4 W. AMELING, Karthago, 1993.

L.-M. G.

[4] Sohn des → Barkiden → Hamilkar [3] Barkas, 247/46–183 v. Chr., berühmtester Karthager, genialer Feldherr und zeitlebens Gegner Roms, nach dem der 2. Pun. Krieg H.-Krieg genannt wird. H. soll im J. 237, als er seinen Vater nach Iberien begleitete, unerbittlichen Römerhaß geschworen haben (Liv. 35,19; App. Ib. 9,34). Bis 224 scheint H. teils in Spanien, teils in Karthago gelebt zu haben; dann wurde er Unterfeldherr seines Schwagers → Hasdrubal [2] (Liv. 21,3,2–4,2), nach dessen Tod (221) die Truppen H. zum nachfolgenden Strategen für Libyen und Iberien ausriefen, was auch in Karthago bestätigt wurde (Pol. 3,13,3 f.; Liv. 21,3,1; Diod. 25,15; App. Ib. 8,29). Nach erfolgreichen Feldzügen gegen keltiberische Stämme (→ Carpetani, → Olkades, → Vaccaei) wollte H. den Widerstand von Saguntum brechen, was eine röm. Demarche 220/19 in Carthago Nova und anschließend in Karthago zu verhindern suchte (Pol. 3,13–15; Liv. 21,5–6; 9,3). Der karthagische Senat wies die Römer ab und gab H. freie Hand (App. Ib. 10,37); aus dem Konflikt um die von H. nach achtmonatiger Belagerung eroberte Stadt (Pol. 3,17) erwuchs der 2. Pun. Krieg (218–201 v. Chr.): Nachdem die Römer in Karthago die Auslieferung H.s, der im Frühjahr 218 das Gebiet nördl. des Ebro eroberte, vergeblich gefordert und daraufhin den Krieg erklärt hatten, durchkreuzte H. die röm. strategischen Planungen mit dem raschen und kühnen Vormarsch über Pyrenäen und Alpen nach Oberitalien, wo er im Oktober eintraf; die verlustreiche Überquerung der Alpen mit 38000 Mann, 8000 Reitern und Elefanten ist in topographischen Details vieldiskutiert. Der Siegeszug H.s, den die röm. Niederlagen des P. → Cornelius [I 68] Scipio am Ticinus und des Ti. Sempronius Longus an der Trebia (218), sodann des C. → Flaminius [1] am Trasimener See (217) und des L. → Aemilius [I 31] Paullus bei Cannae (216) markieren, mündete jedoch in Süditalien in einen ruhmlosen Stellungskrieg, da die Römer nicht zu Verhandlungen, H. nicht zur Belagerung Roms bereit war. H., der gehofft hatte, mit der Freiheitsparole das röm. Bundesgenossensystem demontieren zu können, gewann 216–213 zwar Städte wie Capua, Lokroi, Tarent und schloß auch Bündnisse mit dem Makedonenkönig → Philippos V. und mit Syrakus (StV 3,524; 525; 527–529; 531), blieb aber letztlich polit. erfolglos. Die Römer gewannen seit der Rückeroberung von Syrakus, Capua etc. (212–209) sowie mit dem Sieg über → Hasdrubal [3] (207) und den Erfolgen des P. → Cornelius [I 71] Scipio in Spanien (209–206) eindeutig die Oberhand. Im J. 203 kehrte H. zwar unbesiegt nach Nordafrika zurück, um als bevollmächtigter Stratege nunmehr gegen die seit 204 erfolgreichen und mit → Massinissa verbündeten röm. Invasionstruppen des Scipio zu kämpfen, doch hatte H.s Niederlage bei Zama (Herbst 202) die Kapitulation Karthagos zur Folge (StV 3,548).

H., im J. 200/199 auf röm. Drängen von seinem Oberbefehl abberufen, trat erst wieder 196 hervor, als er, zum Sufeten gewählt, mit einer Verfassungsreform die Mitgliedschaft im Gerichtshof der Einhundertvier beschnitt und durch strenge Kontrolle der Steuereinziehung die Staatseinnahmen stabilisierte (Liv. 33,45,6–47,3). Daraufhin animierten seine polit. Gegner die Römer zum Eingreifen in die inneren Angelegenheiten Karthagos, indem H. einer antiröm. Konspiration mit → Antiochos [5] III. dem Großen verdächtigt wurde; H. entzog sich einer röm. Untersuchungsgesandtschaft im J. 195 durch Flucht ins Seleukidenreich, während er in Karthago geächtet und sein Haus zerstört wurde (Liv. 33,47–49; Nep. Hann. 7; Iust. 31,1–2). Obgleich H. in Ephesos als kompetenter Informant am Vorabend des Krieges gegen die Römer Zugang zum königlichen Kronrat fand, galt er nicht als ernsthafter Berater; in dem ihm überlassenen kleinen Flottenkommando in der südl. Ägäis operierte H. dann glücklos (Liv. 37,23–24; App. Syr. 22,108–109; Iust. 31,6,7–10). Da die Römer 189/88 von dem besiegten Antiochos die Auslieferung H.s verlangten, floh der Exilkarthager via Kreta und Armenien, wo er die Gründung von Artaxata organisiert haben soll, nach Bithynien (Nep. Hann. 9–10; Plut. Lucullus 31,4–5; Iust. 32,4–5). Dort diente H. dem König → Prusias I. im Krieg gegen den Romfreund → Eumenes [3] II. (186–183) von Pergamon als Admiral sowie bei der Gründung von Prusa (Plin. nat. 5,148). Als zu Kriegsende eine röm. Gesandtschaft unter Ti. → Quinctius Flamininus von Prusias die Auslieferung H.s forderte, tötete er sich in → Libyssa mit Gift (Pol. 23,5,1; App. Syr. 11,43; Plut. Flamininus 20; Liv. 39,51; Nep. Hann. 12). Sein Grabmal nahe dem Sterbeort am Astakenischen Golf wurde um 200 n. Chr. von Septimius Severus, dem röm. Kaiser aus Nord-Afrika, monumental gestaltet (Herodian. 4,8,5); in jüngerer Zeit ließ Atatürk oberhalb der Küste bei Gebze eine Gedenkstätte für H. errichten.

Persönlichkeit und mil.-polit. Leistung H.s haben schon die Historiographen → Silenos und → Sosylos, die H.s Heer begleiteten und aus deren nicht erhaltenen Werken spätere Autoren (z. B. Polybios, Livius, Nepos) schöpften, geschildert. Das antike Bild von H. als genialem Feldherrn mit Zügen Alexanders des Großen sowie als Inkarnation des ewig romfeindlichen Karthago wird in jüngerer Zeit differenziert. Ungeachtet der fortgesetzten Diskussion, inwieweit H. als Staatsmann dort versagt hat, wo er hätte aus seinen Siegen polit. Konsequenzen ziehen müssen, bzw. inwieweit H. nicht primär loyaler Repräsentant Karthagos, sondern nach dem Muster hell. Herrscher eine selbständige polit. Potenz war, liegt H.s histor. Bedeutung darin, Zeitgenossen und späteren Generationen die für Roms Gegner fatale Unbeirrbarkeit röm. Bündnis- und Expansionspolitik vor Augen geführt zu haben.

→ Punische Kriege (mit Karte)

Geus 75–94 • E. Groag, Hannibal als Politiker, 1929 • L. M. Günther, Hannibal im Exil, in: H. Devijver, E. Lipiński (Hrsg.), Punic Wars, 1989, 241–250 • W. Hoffmann, Hannibal, 1962 • Huss • D. A. Kukofka, Süditalien im Zweiten Punischen Krieg, 1990 • T. Schmitt, Hannibals Siegeszug, 1991 • K. H. Schwarte, Der Ausbruch des Zweiten Punischen Krieges, 1983 • J. Seibert, Der Alpenübergang Hannibals, in: Gymnasium 95, 1988, 21–73 • Ders., Hannibal. Feldherr und Staatsmann, 1993 • Ders., Forschungen zu Hannibal, 1993 • Ders., Hannibal, 1997.

L.-M. G.

Hannibalianus

[1] Afranius H. Offizier aus dem Stab des Probus (HA Probus 22,3), 285 n. Chr. mit Asclepiodotos *praefectus praetorio*, 292 ebenfalls mit Asclepiodotos *consul ordinarius*, 297–8 *praefectus urbi*. Vielleicht war H. der Vater der Stieftochter Maximians, → Theodora.

[2] Halbbruder des → Constantinus [1] († 337 n. Chr.) aus der Ehe des Constantius [1] mit Theodora, der im Unterschied zu seinen Brüdern Dalmatius [1] und Iulius Constantius [4] in der ausgehenden Regierungszeit des Constantinus keine Rolle spielt, vermutlich weil er damals schon verstorben war.

[3] Flavius H. Sohn des Dalmatius [1], Neffe des → Constantinus [1]. 335 n. Chr. in die Mehrherrschafts- und Nachfolgeordnung des Constantinus einbezogen. Er wurde mit Constantina verheiratet und sollte als von Rom abhängiger *rex regum* Armenien und die angrenzenden Kaukasus-Monarchien beherrschen (RIC VII 589, Nr. 145, Anon. Vales. 35; Ps.-Aur. Vict. epit. Caes. 41,20). 337 wurde er wie andere Angehörige der Nebenlinie des constantinischen Kaiserhauses umgebracht.

B.BL.

Hanno

[1] »König« (Sufet) von Karthago wohl im frühen 5. Jh. v. Chr., bekannt nur durch seine Schiffsexpedition entlang der Westküste Afrikas, die zwecks Anlage bzw. Sicherung karthagischer Kolonien von den »Säulen des Herakles« (Straße von Gibraltar) bis zur Insel Kerne (h. vor Mauretanien?) und zwecks Erkundung der Fahrtmöglichkeiten weiter bis zur Bucht Notu Keras (»Horn des Südwinds«, h. Kamerun?) führte.

Erwähnt wird H.s Fahrt seit dem 3. Jh. v. Chr. (Aristot. mir. 833a 11), v. a. bei Mela (3,90; 93), Plinius (nat. 2,169; 5,8) und Arrianos (Ind. 43,11f.); dazu tritt ein kurzer Text mit dem Titel *Ánnōnos Karchēdoníōn basileōs períplus* (›Des Karthagerkönigs Hanno Umfahrt‹) im Cod. Palatinus graecus 398 (9. Jh.), der zu unbekannter Zeit wohl aus dem pun. Original ins Griech. übers. wurde. V. a. diese erstmals 1533 von S. Gelenius edierte, an wundersamen Details reiche Schrift verursachte den Nachruhm H.s; so führte die Erwähnung von als γορίλλαι (*gorillai*) bezeichneten Wilden (§ 18) zu der neuzeitlichen Bezeichnung einer Menschenaffenart. → Forschungsreisen

GGM 1, 1–14 • J. BLOMQUIST, The Date and Origin of the Greek Version of Hanno's Periplus, 1979 • K. BAYER, in: G. WINKLER, R. KÖNIG (Hrsg.), C. Plinius Secundus d. Ä., Naturkunde B. 5, 1993, 337–353 (Ed., Übers., Komm.; Lit. ebd. 360–363).

K.BRO.

[2] H. Sabellus. Soll als karthagischer Feldherr um 500 v. Chr. (?) Nordafrika unterworfen haben (Pomp. Trog. prol. 19) [1. 97]; H. wird häufig irrtümlich identifiziert mit → H. [1] und mit H., dem Sohn des Magoniden → Hamilkar [1] [1. 97f., 556–558 und 105, 609].

[3] H. »der Große« (pun. *rb*) [1. 223]. Karthagischer Stratege 368–362 (?) v. Chr. auf Sizilien, führte bei Eryx einen überraschenden Schlag gegen die Flotte des → Dionysios [1] (Diod. 15,73,4; Iust. 20,5,11) und war danach auch in Nordafrika mil. erfolgreich (Pomp. Trog. prol. 20) [1. 106f.]; oft irrtümlich identifiziert mit H., dem »Hochverräter« [1. 107, 618], der Mitte 4. Jh. die Vergiftung des karthagischen Senats geplant haben soll (Iust. 21,4).

[4] Karthagischer Stratege im 1. Pun. Krieg auf Sizilien 264–261, wohl Sohn des → Hannibal [2]; H., der das verbündete Akragas zum Bollwerk ausbauen ließ, Messana gemeinsam mit dem für eine Allianz gewonnenen → Hieron [2] belagerte, 263 nach röm. Teilerfolgen in die westsizilische Epikratie abzog, wo er erfolgreich operierte (Pol. 1,11; Diod. 22,13,9) [2. 223f.], erlitt Anfang 261 vor dem belagerten Akragas eine schwere Niederlage und erhielt dafür in Karthago eine Geldstrafe von 6000 Goldstücken (Pol. 1,12; 15; 18; Diod. 23,3; 5; 8; 9,2; Zon. 8,9) [2. 228]. H. erhielt wohl schon 258 wieder ein (Flotten-) Kommando, das er bei Sardinien erfolgreich führte [1. 113, 648], begegnet 256 als glückloser Nauarch in der Niederlage am Eknomon (Pol. 1,27f.) und kämpfte danach gegen die röm. Invasionstruppen in Nordafrika, wo er bei Clupea auch Landtruppen befehligte (Pol. 1,36,10–12; Oros. 4,9,7; Zon. 8,12; 14) [1. 113, 654].

[5] Karthagischer Nauarch im 1. Pun. Krieg; seine Versorgungsflotte für die Truppen des → Hamilkar [3] Barkas am Eryx wurde im März 241 v. Chr. bei der westlichsten Aegatischen Insel [1. 119, 681] von C. Lutatius Catulus aufgebracht und besiegt, H. dafür hingerichtet (Pol. 1,60f.; Zon. 8,17,1–3) [2. 248f.]. Eine Identifizierung mit H. [4] ist falsch [1. 119, 679].

[6] H. »der Große« (pun. *rb*) [1. 116, 662]. Prominenter karthagischer Politiker der 2. Hälfte 3. Jh., der als Stratege für Libyen um 247 Theveste (h. Tébessa) erobert hatte (Diod. 24,10) [2. 246, 232] und bei Ausbruch des sog. Söldnerkrieges nach seinen gescheiterten Verhandlungen in Sicca (h. El Kef) 241 den Oberbefehl zur Niederwerfung des Libyschen Aufstandes erhielt (Pol. 1,66f.; 73) [2. 254, 257f.]. Infolge glückloser Kriegführung mußte H. im J. 240 das Kommando über das karthagische Heer an → Hamilkar [3] Barkas abgeben; es kam trotz wiederholter Differenzen zwischen den beiden Strategen 238 zum gemeinsamen entscheidenden Sieg über → Mathos (Pol. 1,74; 82; 87f.) [1. 116f.]. Als nach dem Ende dieses Krieges die Strategie für Libyen H.s Rivalen übertragen wurde, stellte sich H. an die Spitze der polit. Kritik an den → Barkiden [vgl. 1. 117f.] und begegnet in der Überlieferung zum 2. Pun. Krieg als Gegenspieler → Hannibals [4], dessen Auslieferung an die Römer H. im J. 219 ebenso verlangt haben soll wie einen raschen Frieden 216 nach dem Sieg bei Cannae (Liv. 21,10; 23,12,6–13,6) [3. 216]. H. ging 202 gemeinsam mit → Hasdrubal [6], mit dem er bereits 203 eine röm. Gesandtschaft in Karthago beschirmt hatte, als Friedensunterhändler zu den Römern (App. Lib. 34,145; 49,213).

[7] H., bzw. richtiger (?): Banno [1. 120], karthagischer Offizier im 2. Pun. Krieg, 218 v. Chr. als Statthalter → Hannibals [4] im neueroberten Gebiet zwischen Ebro und Pyrenäen von Cn. → Cornelius [I 77] Scipio gefangengenommen (Pol. 3,35,4f.; 76,5f.; Liv. 21,60, 5–9; Zon. 8,25,1) [1. 12f.].

[8] Karthagischer Besatzungskommandant von → Capua 212–211 v. Chr., der in einem flehentlichen Schreiben → Hannibal [4] um Hilfe gegen die röm. Belagerung gebeten haben soll; nach dem Fall der Stadt wurde H. als Gefangener nach Rom gebracht (Liv. 26,5,6; 12,10–19; App. Hann. 36,153; 43,185) [1. 125f.].

[9] Karthagischer Stratege für Sizilien 212–210 als Nachfolger → Himilkons [4]; erlitt am Himeras eine schwere Niederlage gegen M. → Claudius [I 11] Marcellus im J. 212, weil er dünkelhaft (?) auf die numidische Reiterei unter dem Libyphoiniker → Myttones verzichtet hatte; aus dem 211/10 belagerten Akragas konnte H. nach Nordafrika entkommen, als Myttones, dem H. inzwischen das Kavalleriekommando entzogen hatte, die Stadt an M. → Valerius Laevinus verriet (Liv. 25,40f.; 26,40) [1. 124f.; 3. 317, 335f.].
[10] Karthagischer Stratege im 2. Pun. Krieg, 208/07 v. Chr. Nachfolger des → Hasdrubal [3] in Spanien, wo er mit 9000 keltiberischen Rekruten überraschend dem M. → Iunius [I 31] Silanus unterlag; als Gefangener wurde H. nach Rom gebracht (Liv. 28,1,4; 2,11; 4,4) [1. 126].
[11] Offizier (*praefectus*) des → Mago, der 206 v. Chr. am Baetis (h. Guadalquivir) dem röm. Legaten L. → Marcius Septimus unterlag, aber einer Gefangennahme entging (Liv. 28,30,1; vgl. App. Ib. 31,121–126) [1. 126f.].
[12] Karthagischer *nobilis iuvenis*, Kavallerieoffizier bei → Hasdrubal [5], warb 204 v. Chr. in Numidien einige tausend Reiter für den Widerstand gegen die röm. Invasionstruppen an; H. eroberte die Stadt Salaeca (h. Henchir el Bey?), wurde dann aber in einer Falle von P. → Cornelius [I 71] Scipio und → Massinissa besiegt (Liv. 29,28f.; 34); ob H. dabei getötet wurde oder als vornehmer Gefangener gegen die von Hasdrubal festgehaltene Mutter Massinissas ausgetauscht wurde (App. Lib. 14,60; Zon. 9,12), ist unklar [1. 127f.].

1 Geus 2 Huss 3 J. Seibert, Hannibal, 1993. L.-M. G.

Haoma s. Zoroastres

Haplologie s. Lautlehre

Harappa s. Indus-Kultur

Harem (*ḥarīm*). Geheiligter, unverletzlicher, verbotener Ort, d. h. die Teile des Hauses, in dem die Frauen (Mutter, Ehefrau/en, Töchter, unverheiratete Schwestern; Konkubinen) einer Familie leben und die nur von männlichen Familienmitgliedern betreten werden dürfen, die in einem bestimmten Verwandtschaftsverhältnis stehen. Auch Bezeichnung der weiblichen Mitglieder einer Familie. Die Geschlechtersegregation wird an koranischen Aussagen festgemacht (Sure 33,53–59). In Europa herrschte lange eine erotisch-exotische Vorstellung vom H., beeinflußt v. a. durch die Schilderungen in ›1001 Nacht‹, Gemälde und Reiseberichte, geprägt von der Kenntnis über den H. im osmanischen Sultanspalast.

EI 3, s. v. Ḥarīm, 209a-b · N. M. Penzer, The Ḥarēm, [2]1966 (über den Sultanspalast in Istanbul). H. SCHÖ.

Haremhab (Ἅρμαις). Als Generalissimus unter Tutanchamun und Eje diente H. den letzten Amarna-Herrschern. Als König verfolgte er das Andenken aller Amarna-Herrscher, bes. Echnatons und Ejes, während er Tutanchamuns Grab schonte [2]. In der pseudo-manethon. Überl. gilt H. als → Danaos (Ios. c. Ap. 1,26).

1 J. v. Beckerath, s. v. H., LÄ 2, 962–4 2 M. Eaton-Krauss, Tutankhamun at Karnak, in: MDAI(K) 44, 1988, 10f. R. K.

Harii. Neben → Helvecones, Manimi, Halisiones und Nahanarvali mächtiger Teilstamm der Vandali-Lugii (Tac. Germ. 43,2). Unsicher ist die Identifizierung mit den Charini (Plin. nat. 4,99) [1]; die alte Konjektur von hsl. *alii* (Tac. Germ. 43,4) zu *(H)arii* ist aufzugeben: Damit entfallen die Folgerungen zum angeblichen *ferialis exercitus* (»Gespensterheer«, »Totenheer«) der H. [2].

1 G. Neumann, s. v. Charini, RGA 4, 371f. 2 A. A. Lund, Kritischer Forsch.-Ber. zur *Germania* des Tacitus, in: ANRW II 33.3, 1989–2222, bes. 2171f.

D. Timpe, Romano-Germanica, 1995, 127–129. K. DI.

Harioli. Etym. und Bed. des Begriffs H. sind unklar: H. ist entweder eine Diminutivbildung von *haruspex* (→ *haruspices*) oder leitet sich von lat. *ara* (»Altar«) her [1. 886]. Als H. wurden im ant. Rom Personen bezeichnet, die sich in verschiedenen Formen der → Divination auskannten und für Privatpersonen wahrsagten. Da der Terminus durchweg abwertend gebraucht wird (z. B. Cato agr. 5,4; Catull. 90,2; in der Komödie u. a. Plaut. Cist. 746; Plaut. Men. 76; Plaut. Most. 571 und 791; Plaut. Rud. 326, 347, 377, 1139ff.; Ter. Phorm. 492, 708 u. ö.), liegt die Vermutung nahe, daß man den H. keine spezifischen Fähigkeiten oder Funktionen zuweisen kann, sondern es sich lediglich um ein »Schimpfwort« handelte. Dieser Befund ist insofern bemerkenswert, als sich daran zeigt, daß man in der röm. Ant. außerhalb der offiziell sanktionierten Divination offenbar keinen – d. h. auch keinen sprachlichen – Bereich für private Wahrsagung (positiv) definierte.

1 G. Thiele, s. v. Harioli, RE Suppl. 3, 886–888.

S. Montero, Mántica inspirada y demonologica. Los »harioli«, in: AC 62, 1993, 115–129. C. F.

Harma (Ἅρμα). Bereits im homer. Schiffskatalog (Hom. Il. 2,499; Strab. 9,2,26) genannter boiot. Ort an der Straße Thebai – Chalkis [1] zw. Teumessos und Mykalessos; mit dem Verschwinden des → Amphiaraos bzw. der Rettung des → Adrastos [1] (Strab. 9,2,11; Paus. 1,34,2; 9,19,4) in Verbindung gebracht. Zeitweise bildete H. gemeinsam mit Eleon, Mykalessos und Pharai einen von Tanagra abhängigen Dorfverband; in röm. Zeit war der Ort verlassen (Strab. 9,2,11; 14). H. wird mit dem h. Kastron (polygonaler Mauerring; FH bis hell. Funde) auf dem südöstl. Ende des Lykovouni genannten südöstl. Ausläufers des Messapion-Gebirges ca. 4 km nördl. des h. Harma identifiziert.

Fossey, 85–89 · J. M. Fossey, Η αρχαία τοπογραφία της Βοιωτίας, in: Ders., Papers in Boiotian Topography and

History, 1990, 16–18 • LAUFFER, Griechenland, 258 • N. D. PAPACHATZIS, Παυσανίου Ἑλλάδος Περιήγησις 5, [2]1981, 126–128 • P. W. WALLACE, Strabo's Description of Boiotia, 1979, 49f. P. F.

Harmachis (ägypt. *Ḥrw-m-3ḫ.t*, »Horus im Horizont«).
[1] Name, unter dem die große → Sphinx von → Giza seit Anf. des NR (ca. 1500 v. Chr.) als Verkörperung des Sonnengottes verehrt wurde. Viele Votivstelen dokumentieren die Popularität des Kultes bei Privatleuten wie bei Königen.

J. ASSMANN, s. v. H., LÄ2, 992–996. S. S.

[2] Sohn des Anemhor, Vater des Nesysti III.; hoher Priester des Ptah von Memphis (ca. 260 – nach 194/3 v. Chr.); manchmal identifiziert mit dem Rebellenkönig → Harwennefer, was aber aus chronologischen Gründen unwahrscheinlich ist.

PP 3,5358. • J. QUAEGEBEUR, The Genealogy of the Memphite High Priest Family in the Hellenistic Period, in: D. J. CRAWFORD (Hrsg.), Studies on Ptolemaic Memphis, 1980, 43–81, bes. 67f., Nr. 16; 81.

[3] Agent des Oikonomos Horos im Süden des Herakleopolites; sein Amtsarchiv belegt Transaktionen vom April 215 – Febr. 214 v. Chr.

W. CLARYSSE, Harmachis, Agent of the Oikonomos, in: AncSoc 7, 1976, 185–207. W. A.

[4] Aufständischer einheimisch-äg. Herrscher im südl. Oberäg. z.Z. Ptolemaios' V. (210–180 v. Chr.).

J. ASSMANN, s. v. H., LÄ 2, 992–996. S. S.

Harmodios (Ἁρμόδιος).
[1] H. aus Athen, verschwor sich mit → Aristogeiton [1] und anderen, um die Tyrannen → Hippias [1] und → Hipparchos [1] bei den Panathenäen 514 v. Chr. zu ermorden. Es gelang ihnen jedoch nur, Hipparchos zu töten. H. fand bei dem Attentat den Tod (Hdt. 5,55–58; Thuk. 1,20; 6,54–59; Aristot. Ath. pol. 18). Für Thukydides war die Verschwörung ausschließlich persönlich motiviert: H. und seine Schwester hätten Demütigungen hinnehmen müssen, nachdem H. die homoerotische Werbung des Hipparchos abgewiesen hatte. In Athen wurden H. und Aristogeiton bald nach dem Sturz des Hippias 511/10 als Freiheitskämpfer und Begründer der Demokratie gefeiert und mit der Aufstellung einer Statue des → Antenor [2] auf der Agora geehrt.

H. BERVE, Die Tyrannis bei den Griechen 1, 1967, 68–74 • DAVIES 12267, III • B. FEHR, Die Tyrannentöter, 1984 • TRAILL, PAA 203425. E. S.-H.

[2] H. aus Tarsos (TrGF I 156), Sohn eines Asklepiades; siegte im 1. Jh. v. Chr. mit dem Satyrspiel ›Protesilaos‹ an den Romaia in Magnesia am Mäander (TrGF I: DID A 13,4). B. Z.

Harmonia (Ἁρμονία). Tochter des Ares und der Aphrodite, Ehefrau des → Kadmos, Mutter von → Ino, → Semele, → Agaue, → Autonoe und → Polydoros (Hes. theog. 933–937; 975–978; Apollod. 3,25). Die Hochzeit von Kadmos und H., zu der die Götter reiche Geschenke (u. a. ein von Hephaistos hergestelltes Halsband und einen → Peplos, bei Alkmaion [1], Amphiaraos) bringen, war ein beliebtes Thema (Pind. P. 3,88–92; Paus. 3,18,12; Apollod. 3,25). Das Brautlied wird von den Musen gesungen (Thgn. 15–18). Kadmos und H. werden am Ende ihres Lebens auf die Insel der Seligen versetzt (Eur. Bacch. 1338f.; Pind. O. 2,78), nach einigen (zuvor) in Schlangen verwandelt (Eur. Bacch. 1330–1332; Ov. met. 4,563–603). In Theben zeigte man den Thalamos (»Brautgemach«) der H. und den Ort des Musengesangs (Paus. 9,12,3) sowie drei von H. gestiftete *xóana* (→ Xoanon) der Aphrodite (Paus. 9,16,3). Zusammen mit den Charites, Horai, Hebe, Aphrodite u. a. ist H. auch die Verkörperung der durch ihren Namen bezeichneten Eigenschaft (Hom. h. 3,194–196; Aischyl. Suppl. 1039–1042). Sie erscheint auch als Tochter des Zeus (Aischyl. Prom. 551) und Mutter der Musen (Eur. Med. 831f.). Seit dem 5. Jh. v. Chr. wurde H. mit dem Mysterienkult in Samothrake verbunden, wo sie als Tochter des Zeus und der → Elektra (bzw. der → Elektryone) gilt und nach ihrer Entführung durch Kadmos von der Mutter gesucht wird wie → Kore/Persephone von → Demeter (Hellanikos FGrH 4 F 23; Ephoros FGrH 70 F 120; Diod. 5,48–49).

E. PARIBENI, s. v. H., LIMC 4.1, 412–414 • M. ROCCHI, Kadmos e H.: Un matrimonio problematico, 1989. K. WA.

Harmostai (ἁρμοσταί, ion. ἁρμοστῆρες: Xen. hell. 4,8,39).
[1] Spartanische Militärbefehlshaber zur Beaufsichtigung bestimmter Gebiete. Die in den Scholien zu Pindar (O. 6,154) erwähnten 20 H. der Lakedaimonier können nicht mehr sicher als Aufsichtsbeamte über Perioikenpoleis identifiziert werden und sind eher als »Gouverneure« außerhalb des spartanischen Polisgebietes zu verstehen [1. 11f.; 2. 62f.]. Der im frühen 4. Jh. für Kythera belegte *harmostḗs* (IG V 1,937) bildete wohl eine Ausnahme aus mil. Gründen. Nach dem Peloponnesischen Krieg wurden von H. geführte Garnisonen an gefährdeten Stellen des auswärtigen Machtbereichs Spartas eingesetzt (Xen. hell. 1,1,32; 1,2,18; 1,3,5; 1,3,15; 2,3,14; 4,8,3 ff.), z. T. auf Initiative des → Lysandros, der die oligarchischen → Dekadarchiai [1] in abhängigen Poleis zu stützen suchte [3. 66ff.; 4. 152f.].
[2] Befehlshaber thebanischer Garnisonen, die zuerst während des 2. Peloponnesfeldzuges des → Epameinondas 369 v. Chr. in Sikyon (Xen. hell. 7,2,11; 7,3,4 und 9), dann 366 auf Beschluß des Boiotischen Bundes in achaiischen Poleis zur Vertreibung von Oligarchen eingesetzt wurden, aber die erneute Machtergreifung der Exulanten nicht verhindern konnten (Xen. hell. 7,1,43) [5. 191ff.; 6. 61].
[3] Ein *harmostḗs* aus Sinope war um 400 v. Chr. Besatzungskommandant in Kytyora (Xen. an. 5,5,19).

1 St. Link, Der Kosmos Sparta, 1994 2 L. Thommen, Lakedaimonion Politeia, 1996 3 D. Lotze, Lysander und der Peloponnesische Krieg, 1964 4 J.-P. Bommelaer, Lysandre de Sparte, 1981 5 J. Buckler, The Theban Hegemony 371–362 BC, 1980 6 H. Beck, Polis und Koinon, 1997. K.-W. WEL.

Harmozike (Ἁρμοζική Strab. 11,3,5; Ἀρμάκτικα Ptol. 5,11,3; 8,19,4; *Hermastis iuxta Cyrum* Plin. nat. 6,29; *Armastika* Geogr. Rav. 2,8; georg. *Armazˁiḫe*, »Festung des Armazi«).

Residenz der Könige des kaukasischen → Iberia auf dem Bagineti-Hügel im h. Mccheta südl. gegenüber der Mündung des → Aragos in den → Kyros; 65 v. Chr. von Pompeius erobert.

Grabungen seit 1937 erbrachten Bauten der hell. u. röm. Zeit: Festungsmauer (Lehmziegelmauer auf Quaderfundament), quergelagerter »Säulensaal« (Quadermauerwerk, Holzsäulen mit Steinbasen und -kapitellen), zwei Thermenbauten (röm. Provinzialtypus, Bruchsteinmauerwerk), Kult(?)komplex mit Architekturgliedern ungewöhnlicher Form und Dekoration sowie eine Nekropole röm. Zeit mit reichen Gräbern: u. a. eine Silberschale mit Porträt Marc Aurels, bzw. mit Pferd vor einem Altar, Goldschmuck mit polychromer Inkrustation, Silberbeschläge für Möbelfüße (vgl. Plut. Pompeius 34). Gegenüber, am Nordufer des Kyros, lag → Mestleta, die Hauptstadt Iberias.

A. Apakidze (Hrsg.), Mccheta. Archeologičeskie raskopki, 1958 ff. • O. Lordkipanidse, Archäologie, 1991, 159 f. • W. Tomaschek, s. v. Armastika, RE 2, 1177. A. P.-L.

Harpagos (Ἅρπαγος).
[1] Meder, kämpfte als Feldherr ab ca. 550 v. Chr. im Dienst des Kyros gegen Lyder, Ionier, Karer und Lykier (Hdt. 1,80; 162–169; 171–176). Gegen die ionischen Städte warf er Dämme auf (Hdt. 1,162) und setzte bei ihrer Eroberung die ersten Katapulte der Geschichte ein, so nachweislich gegen Phokaia.
[2] Persischer Feldherr, nahm im → Ionischen Aufstand (499–497 v. Chr.) Histiaios in Milet gefangen, der dann von dem Satrapen Artaphernes [2] von Sardeis gekreuzigt wurde (Hdt. 6,28–30).

P. Briant, L'histoire de l'empire Perse, 1996, 111–113 • J. Cobet, Milet 1994–1995, in: AA 1997, 249–284, bes. 260. PE. HÖ.

Harpalos (Ἅρπαλος). Sohn des Machatas, Neffe von → Derdas [3] und → Phila aus dem Königshaus von → Elimeia (Athen. 13,557c), Jugendfreund von → Alexandros [4] d. Gr. und mit den anderen 337 v. Chr. von → Philippos II. verbannt. Zum Kriegsdienst körperlich untauglich, wurde er Alexandros' Schatzmeister (Arr. an. 3,6,6). Ende 334 floh er aus unbekannten Gründen nach Megara, doch gab ihm Alexandros im Frühjahr 331 seinen alten Posten zurück. 330 blieb er zur Überwachung der von Persepolis transportierten Beute in → Ekbatana und war wohl mit seinem Landsmann → Kleandros an der Ermordung → Parmenions beteiligt. Nach Babylon, wo der Hauptteil des Reichsschatzes deponiert war, abkommandiert, residierte er im Palast und wurde durch seine Ausschweifungen auf Kosten des Schatzes berüchtigt, vor allem durch seine athenischen → Hetairai → Pythionike und → Glykera [1], die er mit Ehrungen und Kostbarkeiten überschüttete. Für den Nachschub sorgte er gewissenhaft und erfüllte Alexandros' persönliche Wünsche (Curt. 9,3,21; Plut. Alexandros 8,3). Nach Athen schickte er Getreide und wurde mit dem Bürgerrecht belohnt.

Als nach Alexandros' Rückkehr aus Indien Kleandros der Säuberung zum Opfer fiel, floh H. mit 30 Schiffen, 6000 Söldnern und 3000 Talenten Silber und forderte Mitte 324 in Athen Einlaß. Aus Furcht vor dem Heer abgewiesen, ließ er Heer und Flotte in → Tainaron und wurde als gefährdeter Bürger mit drei Schiffen und 700 Talenten aufgenommen. Als Alexandros seine Auslieferung forderte, wurde er in Haft gesetzt und sein Silber beschlagnahmt. Er entkam aber bald, was in Athen zur Verurteilung von → Demosthenes [2] und anderen prominenten Politikern führte. Bei der Sammlung seiner Streitkräfte auf Kreta wurde er von → Thibron ermordet; sonst wäre er wohl der erste der Diadochen (→ Diadochen und Epigonen) geworden.

E. Badian, Harpalus, in: JHS 81, 1961, 16–43 • Berve 2, Nr. 143 • Heckel, 213–221 • S. Jaschinski, Alexander und Griechenland unter dem Eindruck der Flucht des Harpalos, 1981. E. B.

Harpalyke (Ἁρπαλύκη).
[1] Tochter des thrak. Königs Harpalykos, der sie nach dem Tode ihrer Mutter mit Kuh- und Stutenmilch aufzieht und zur Kriegerin ausbildet. Nach seinem Tod lebt sie als Viehdiebin und Jägerin, bis sie in einem Netz gefangen und getötet wird. An ihrem Grab fanden rituelle Kämpfe statt (Serv. auct. Aen. 1,317; Hyg. fab. 193). Die älteste Erwähnung findet sich bei Vergil (Aen. 1,317), dem H. wahrscheinlich als Vorbild für → Camilla diente (Verg. Aen. 11,532–915).
[2] Tochter der Epikaste und des arkad. Klymenos, der sie in einem inzestuösen Verhältnis sexuell mißbraucht (Euphorion fr. 24a v. Groningen; Parthenios 13). Als er ihre Ehe mit Alastor verhindert, tötet sie aus Rache ihren jüngeren Bruder (Euphorion; Parthenios), nach anderen ihren von Klymenos gezeugten Sohn (Lact. Placidus; Stat. Theb. 5,120; Hyg. fab. 206) und setzt ihn dem Vater zum Mahl vor. H. wird in einen Vogel namens χαλκίς (*chalkís*) verwandelt (Parthenios) oder von ihrem Vater getötet (Hyg. fab. 206), der anschließend Selbstmord begeht. Auffällig ist die Parallele zum Mythos von → Tereus.
[3] Nach Athen. 14,619e eine Jungfrau, die aus Trauer stirbt, weil ihre Liebe zu einem Iphis nicht erwidert wird. Zur Erinnerung an sie heißt ein Wettgesang, der von jungen Frauen ausgeführt wird, *harpalýkē*.

O. Crusius, s. v. H., Roscher 1, 1835–1841 • J. Eitrem, s. v. H., RE 7, 2401–2404. K. WA.

Harpalykos (Ἁρπάλυκος).
[1] Thrak. König, Vater der → Harpalyke.
[2] Aus Panopeus. Sohn des → Hermes, Lehrer des → Herakles im Ringkampf, Boxen und Pankration (Theokr. 24,111–118).
[3] Trojaner, von → Camilla mit der Lanze getötet (Verg. Aen. 11,675).
[4] Sohn des → Lykaon (Apollod. 3,97). Nach [1] mit dem Giganten Harpolykos zu vergleichen.

1 A. S. F. Gow (ed.), Theocritus, 1952, zu 24,115 f. 2 K. J. Dover, Theocritus, 1971, zu 24,116; 2,16. T. H.

Harpasos (Ἅρπασος).
[1] Südl. Nebenfluß des Maiandros in Karia (Plin. nat. 2,210; 5,109; Ptol. 5,2,15; Q. Smyrn. 10,141–146; Steph. Byz. s. v. H.), h. Akçay, am Mittellauf cañonartig verengt, weiter südl. h. gestaut (Kemer-Talsperre). Altes ion. Siedlungsgebiet, in Ufernähe Ruinen ant. Siedlungen (z. B. Neapolis, Harpasa, h. Arpaz bei Esenköy). Im Sommer 228 v. Chr. besiegte → Attalos [4] I. am H. Antiochos → Hierax, 189 machte Cn. Manlius Vulso am H. Station (Liv. 38,13,2 ff.). Inschr. und Mz. bis in die Kaiserzeit.

W. M. Calder, G. E. Bean, A classical map of Asia Minor, 1958 · Reisekarte Türkiye-Türkei, Türk. Verteidigungsministerium/Kartograph. Vlg. Ryborsch, Obertshausen bei Frankfurt/M. 1994, Bl. 2 · W. M. Ramsay, The Historical Geography of Asia Minor, 1890, 423 · Magie 2, 738 f. · L. Robert, A travers l'Asie Mineure, 1980, 355–362. H. KA.

[2] Fluß in der → Kolchis (Xen. an. 7,18; Ἄψαρος, Arr. per. p. E. 9r45 Diller), h. Čoroḫi (türk. Çoruh Nehri), entspringt am Karakaban Dağı/Türkei und mündet südl. von Batʿumi/Georgien ins Schwarze Meer. Mit leichten Schiffen war der H. befahrbar. An seinem Oberlauf lag → Gymnias (Xen. an. 7,19; h. Bayburt), eine Station der Karawanenstraße nach Trapezus. Die Ebene des H. war sehr fruchtbar, für Ackerbau und Viehzucht gut geeignet. Reiche brz. Funde (Pitšwnari). In histor. Zeit siedelten Chalybes und Taochen am rechten und Skythenen am linken Ufer. Die Römer befestigten die H.-Mündung (Apsaros) gegen Piraten. Später waren dort fünf Kohorten, darunter die *cohors II Claudiana* (CIL X 1202), stationiert.

M. I. Maksimova, Antičnye goroda jugovostočnogo Pricernomor'a [Ant. Städte an der südl. Schwarzmeerküste], 1956 · O. Lendle, Komm. zu Xen. an., 1995, 270–273. I. v. B.

Harpaston (ἁρπαστόν, *harpastum*). Bezeichnung für einen kleinen, festen Ball, dann auch für ein Fangballspiel mit diesem (Poll. 9,105; Athen. 1,14 f.), dem → *phainínda* ähnlich (vgl. Clem. Al. 3,10,50 [und schol.]). Im zweiten Fall handelte es sich um ein körperbetontes Kampfspiel; Einzelheiten zum Spielverlauf sind nicht bekannt. Eine Spielpartei attackiert den gegnerischen, ballführenden Spieler und versucht, ihm den Ball abzunehmen (ἁρπάζειν, »[hastig] greifen«, »raffen«, »rauben«). Dieser ist bestrebt, seine eigenen Mitspieler anzuspielen, die ihrerseits von den Angreifern am Fangen des Balles gehindert werden. Die ballführende Partei versucht, den Mittelteil des Spielfeldes zu behaupten, die gegnerische Partei, in Ballbesitz zu gelangen und ihrerseits in den Mittelteil vorzudringen. Hierbei kam es zu Behinderungen durch Wegstoßen, Beinstellen oder Tritte und zu einem Ringen um den Ball, bei dem offenbar alle Griffe erlaubt waren (Sen. epist. 80,1–3; Epikt. 2,5,16; Mart. 4,19,6; 7,32,10; 14,48). Das *h.* erforderte hohe Geschicklichkeit und körperliche Gewandtheit.
→ Ballspiele; Spiel

E. Wagner, Kritische Bemerkungen zum Harpastum-Spiel, in: Gymnasium 70, 1963, 356–366 · I. Weiler, Der Sport bei den Völkern der Alten Welt, 1981, 212. R. H.

Harpocras. Freigelassener des Claudius, der ihn dadurch geehrt hat, daß er ihm in Rom den Gebrauch einer Sänfte und die Abhaltung von Spielen, was üblicherweise nur Magistraten gestattet war, erlaubt haben soll. PIR² H 16. W. E.

Harpokration (Ἁρποκρατίων).
[1] Platonischer Philosoph aus Argos, 2. Jh. n. Chr., Schüler des → Attikos, von Proklos ›Spitzenplatoniker‹ (Πλατωνικῶν κορυφαῖος) genannt [1. 18]. Bedeutend waren sein Komm. zu Platon (24 B.) [1. 28, 152, 180 ff., 191, 194, 197, 206, 216 f.], und sein Platon-Lex. (2 B.) [1. 28, 235]. H. vertrat wie Attikos und Plutarch ein Entstehen der Welt in einem einmaligen (zeitlichen) Akt, lehnte sich aber in seiner Auffassung vom → Demiurgos [3] und der Unsterblichkeit aller Seelen stark an → Numenios an. Das Böse in der Seele stammt nach H. aus den sichtbaren Körpern [2. 190, 512].

1 Dörrie/Baltes, III, 1993 2 Dies., IV, 1996.

Frg.: J. Dillon, H.'s Commentary on Plato, in: Californian Studies in Classical Antiquity 4, 1971, 125–146.
Lit.: Ders., The Middle Platonists, 1977, 258–262.
M. BA. u. M.-L. L.

[2] (Valerius) H. Griech. Rhetor und Lexikograph aus Alexandreia, 2. Jh. n. Chr.
A. Person B. Werke

A. Person
Sein Lebenslauf ist kaum bekannt; die Suda erwähnt nur seine Herkunft, seinen Namen und die Titel zweier Werke: ›Lexikon zu den zehn Rednern‹ (Λέξεις τῶν δέκα ῥητόρων) und ›Sammlung »blühender« Ausdrücke‹ (Ἀνθηρῶν συναγωγή) (Suda α 4014). Die Datierung ist durch POxy. 2192, col. II 28–38 (2. Jh. n. Chr.) gesichert: Der Brief erwähnt H. bei der Suche nach Buchrollen; SHA Verus 2,5 nennt einen H. als Lehrer des Kaisers L. Verus. H. lebte also in einer kulturell interessierten Umgebung, zu der auch Pollio und der Sohn Diodoros gehörten.

B. Werke

Die ›Sammlung der Glanzstücke‹ muß der (durch → Apuleius bekannten) Gattung der *Florida* angehört haben; hiervon sind nicht einmal Fragmente erhalten. Das ›Lexikon‹ enthält die Glossen der zehn Redner des hell. Kanons und ist, neben → Galenos' Lexikon zu Hippokrates, das erste lexikographische Werk in recht streng alphabetischer Reihenfolge (die von diesen abweichenden 10 % der Lemmata darf man wohl der späteren Überlieferung zuschreiben). Die ausführlichen Erklärungen zu den Glossen enthalten zahlreiche Zitate auch anderer att. Autoren, z.B. des Aristophanes und der »kleineren« Komödiendichter sowie des Aristoteles (auf die *Athenaíōn politeía* verweist H. oft und überliefert zudem sonst unbekannte Fragmente); aus dem Werk lassen sich wichtige Informationen z.B. zur Überlieferung der *Hellēniká* und der *Anábasis* des Xenophon ableiten. Es handelt sich um ein Lex., das für die Autorenlektüre und nicht zur Vorgabe attizistischer Normen erstellt worden war; seine Quellen stammen aus dem Hell. (z.B. Aristophanes [4] von Byzanz und Aristarchos [4] von Samothrake) und der Kaiserzeit (z.B. Didymos [1] von Alexandria), aber einige Nachrichten gehen auch auf frühere Autoren zurück (Hekataios, Hellanikos, Theopompos, Istros). Das ›Lexikon‹ ist in zwei Bearbeitungen erhalten: Die Epitome wurde noch vor Photios angefertigt und steht in enger Beziehung zu dessen Lexika und der Suda. Sie ist durch vier Hss. (unter denen der Cod. Parisinus Graecus 2552 aus dem Jahr 1496 Eigentümlichkeiten aufweist, die auf eine Kontamination mit einer anderen Redaktion hindeuten) sowie durch Exzerpte im Cod. Baroccianus 50 dokumentiert (vgl. [3]). Die vollständigere Bearbeitung ist in zahlreichen Hss. überliefert, unter denen der Cod. Marcianus Gr. 444 (14. Jh.) mit 71 Glossen, die sich nicht in der übrigen Überlieferung finden, und der Cod. Ricciard. 12 (15. Jh.), der von Keaney als der 1491/92 von I. Laskaris für Lorenzo de' Medici erworbene Cod. identifiziert wurde, hervorzuheben sind. Das Lex. wurde aber höchstwahrscheinlich im 13.–14. Jh. interpoliert, vielleicht von Manuel Moschopoulos. Ein Papyrus-Bruchstück ist ebenfalls erhalten (PRylands 532 = Pack[2] 458, Ende 2., Anf. 3. Jh. n.Chr.).

→ Glossographie; Lexikographie

Ed.: 1 G. Dindorf (Ed.), Harpocrationis Lexicon in decem oratores Atticos, I–II, 1853 2 J.J. Keaney (Ed.), Harpocration. Lexeis of the Ten Orators, 1991.
Lit.: 3 J.A. Cramer, Anecdota Graeca e codd. manuscriptis bibliothecarum Oxoniensium I–IV, 1835–37, in: AO 2, 488–500 4 B. Hemmerdinger, Les papyrus et la datation d'Harpocration, in: REG 72, 1959, 107–109 5 J.J. Keaney, Moschopoulos and Harpocration, in: TAPhA 100, 1969, 201–207 6 Ders., Alphabetization in Harpocration's Lexicon, in: GRBS 14, 1973, 415–423 7 Ders., John Lascaris and Harpocration, in: GRBS 23, 1982, 93–95 8 R. Otranto, Rec. Harpocration, ed. Keaney, in: Quaderni di Storia 38, 1993, 225–231. R.T./Ü: T.H.

[3] Alexandrinischer Verf. von Schriften über Astrologie und magische Heilkräfte von Pflanzen, Tieren und Steinen, 2.–3. Jh. n.Chr. Manches findet sich übereinstimmend in den Kyraniden und im Corpus Hermeticum. Einige Hss. seines Werkes enthalten einen Widmungsbrief an einen Kaiser, in dem der Verf. davon spricht, Gramm. in Kleinasien unterrichtet zu haben, bevor er nach Alexandreia gekommen sei, doch scheint dieser Brief urspr. zu einem heute verlorenen Werk gehört zu haben und unter Umständen nicht einmal von H. verfaßt worden zu sein.

→ Corpus Hermeticum V.N./Ü: L.v.R.-B.

Harpyien (Ἅρπυιαι, lat. *Harpyiae*). Weibl. Ungeheuer der griech. Myth., die als Töchter von Thaumas und Elektra (Apollod. 1,2,6) einer älteren Generation von Göttern angehören. Diese »Greifer« (< ἁρπάζω, *harpázō* = »packen«, »rauben«), die nirgendwo detailliert beschrieben werden, sind Personifikationen der dämonischen Kräfte von Stürmen und werden immer als geflügelte Frauen dargestellt. Homer verwendet sie, um das spurlose Verschwinden des Odysseus (Hom. Od. 1,241; 14,371) oder den plötzlichen Tod der Töchter des → Pandareos (Od. 20,66–78) zu erklären. Ihre Namen – Podarge (Hom. Il. 16,149–151) oder Aello und Okypete (Hes. theog. 267) – weisen auf ihre Geschwindigkeit hin. Meist sind es wie bei Hesiod nur zwei H., spätere Quellen erwähnen jedoch (eventuell vom Theater beeinflußt) drei oder lassen die Zahl unbestimmt. Iris, die schnelle Götterbotin, ist ihre Schwester (Apollod. 1,2,6). Ihre wichtigste myth. Rolle spielen die H. in der Argonautensage: Sie quälen den thrak. König → Phineus, indem sie sein Essen wegschnappen, bis sie schließlich von den Söhnen des Boreas verjagt werden (schon bei Hes. fr. 150–156 M-W; Aischyl. Eum. 50f.; bes. beliebt im Hell.: detailliert dargestellt bei Apoll. Rhod. 2,234–434). Bei Vergil, der die eine H. erstmals Celaeno nennt, spielen sie eine Rolle in Aeneas' Abenteuer auf den Inseln der Strophades (Verg. Aen. 3,209–277) [1].

1 R.J. Rabel, The Harpyiae in the Aeneid, in: CJ 80, 1984–5, 317–325.

L. Kahil, s.v. H., LIMC 4.1, 445–450. J.B./Ü: B.S.

Ḥarran. Siedlung 40 km sö von Edessa, altorient. Ḫarrān(u), griech. Κάρραι, lat. Carrhae, aram. Ḥrn, mod. Harran, wichtiges Handelszentrum und bedeutender Kultort des Mondgottes → Sin; belegt seit Mitte des 3. Jt. v.Chr., assyr. Provinzhauptort und 611/10 v.Chr. Residenz des letzten neuassyr. Königs; Tempelneubau unter → Nabonid (Stelenfunde). In biblischer Trad. war Ḥ. Aufenthaltsort Abrahams (Gn 11,31). Maked. Siedler von Ḥ. unterstützten die gegen die Parther vordringenden Römer (Cass. Dio 37,5,5), doch 53 v.Chr. kam es zur Niederlage und zum Tod des Crassus bei Ḥ. (Plut. Crassus 17–29; Cass. Dio 40,17–27). Die Folgen der Schlacht, die Gefangennahme der Soldaten und bes. der

Verlust der röm. Feldzeichen prägten die röm. Partherpolitik bis zur diplomatisch erreichten Rückführung unter Augustus. Ḥ. blieb parth. als Teil des Königreiches Osrhoëne (→ Edessa [2]), ab 214 n. Chr. röm. *colonia* und *Metropolis Mesopotamiae*.

Caracalla plante einen Besuch des Tempels des Mondgottes, dessen Kult (Sekte der Sabier) noch im MA existierte (Cass. Dio 79,5,4); auch Kaiser Iulianus opferte im Tempel (Amm. 23,3,2). Syr. Quellen (Doctrina Addai, Acta Šarbel, Jakobos v. Sarug) kennen Ḥ. als multiethnisches Zentrum des Paganismus; neben Sin und dessen Gemahlin Nikkal bestanden u. a. Kulte der Atargatis und der Tyche (aram. Gad, arab. Allat).

W. Cramer, s. v. Ḥ., RAC 15, 634–50 · H. J. W. Drivers, Cults and Beliefs at Edessa, 1980 · J. N. Postgate, s. v. Ḥ., RLA 4, 1972–75, 122–124 · F. H. Weissbach, s. v. Κάρραι, RE 10, 2009–21. K. KE.

Harsiesis. Sohn des Paious (?), etablierte sich während des Bürgerkrieges (132–124 v. Chr.) als Gegenpharao und war der letzte Ägypter, der den Titel »Pharao« trug. Wurde vermutlich von der thebanischen Priesterschaft unterstützt; zwischen dem 26. Juni und Nov. 131 v. Chr. wurde in Theben nach ihm datiert, aber schon am 10. Nov. wurde er dort nicht mehr anerkannt. Er flüchtete nach Norden, wo seine Rebellion vor dem 15. Sept. 130 ein Ende fand.

K. Vandorpe, City of Many a Gate, in: S. P. Vleeming (Hrsg.), Hundred-Gated Thebes, 1995, 203–239, bes. 233 ff. · B. C. McGing, Revolt Egyptian Style, in: APF 43, 1997, 273–314, bes. 295 f. W. A.

Harun al-Raschid (*Hārūn ar-Rašīd*). Fünfter abbasidischer (→ Abbasiden) → Kalif (786–809 n. Chr.). Populär durch die Erzählungen aus ›1001 Nacht‹. Seine Regierungszeit war gekennzeichnet durch polit. Unruhen in den arab. Ländern von Nordafrika bis zum Jemen, Schwierigkeiten der Konsolidierung des → Islam im östl. Herrschaftsbereich sowie Kriege gegen Byzanz. Sein Verdienst im kulturellen Bereich ist v. a. die Förderung der Übers. griech. naturwiss. und philos. Lit. ins Arabische.

F. Omar, s. v. Hārūn al-Rashīd, EI 3, 232b–234b. H. SCHÖ.

Haruspices. I. Alter Orient s. Divination.
II. A. Einleitung und Definition
B. Lateinische Belege
C. Etruskische Belege

A. Einleitung und Definition

H. ist die lat. Bezeichnung für Eingeweidebeschauer und -deuter (bei Tieren) verschiedener ant. Kulturkreise, v. a. aus Etrurien (Cic. div. 1,3). Die Etym. des ersten Wortgliedes ist ungeklärt; man hat u. a. ⟨*hira* (»Gedärm«) und *hostia* (von *haruga*, »Opfertier«) angenommen [1. 45]. Die Eingeweideschau (*haruspicina*) galt in republikanischer Zeit in Rom als *ars*, eine auf Beobachtung beruhende »Erfahrungswiss.« (Cic. div. 1,24 f.), deren Beherrschung und Pflege verschiedene Poleis, Familien und Völker zur → Divination befähigte (Cic. div. 1,91 f.: Telmessos in Karien, Geschlechter der Iamiden und Klutiden in Elis/Peloponnes, Etrusker).

B. Lateinische Belege 1. Etruskische Haruspices 2. Römische Haruspices

1. Etruskische Haruspices

Die ant. lit. Nachrichten, welche über die etr. H. vorliegen, sind fast ausschließlich durch röm. bzw. lat. schreibende Autoren überliefert. Livius berichtet (1,56,4), die H. seien bereits in der Königszeit zur Beratung und Entsühnung von Vorzeichen, → *prodigia* (*publica*), herangezogen worden; wahrscheinlicher ist nach MacBain, daß man die H. erst seit dem 3. Jh. v. Chr. (280/278), nachdem die Römer die Mehrzahl der etr. Städte als polit. Verbündete in den Punischen Kriegen gewonnen hatten, regelmäßig befragte [3. 43 ff.]: Nach Aufforderung durch den röm. Senat gaben sie *responsa* (»Gutachten«) ab, in denen sowohl diejenigen Gottheiten, die in Zusammenhang mit dem Vorzeichen gebracht wurden, genannt waren, als auch Mittel zur Entsühnung. Die Auslegung und Umsetzung der *responsa* oblag jedoch den Angehörigen des Senats und den röm. Priestern (Cic. har. resp. 20 ff., 34 f.; Cic. div. 2,21). Ob der in republikanischer Zeit inschr. und lit. bezeugte *ordo* (*LX haruspicum*) der H. auf Veranlassung der Römer gegr. war oder die Etrusker sich selbst organisiert hatten, ist nicht geklärt; diskutiert wird auch, ob sein Hauptsitz in Rom war (vgl. CIL VI 2161) oder nur ein »Büro« (zu den strittigen Fragen [3. 47 ff.; 4. 10 f.]).

Wie lange die Haruspizin nur von etr. H. in Rom ausgeübt wurde, ist unklar; die röm. Kaiser scheinen bis ins 1. Jh. n. Chr. etr. »Leib«-H. bevorzugt zu haben [5. 2441]. Daneben gab es (wohl ebenfalls etr.) herumziehende H., die für Privatpersonen tätig waren (Plin. nat. 8,102; Herodian. 8,3,7).

2. Römische Haruspices

Seit der Übers. der (ps.-)tagetischen (→ Tages) Schriften waren die Römer theoretisch in der Lage, die Haruspizin selbst auszuüben. Belege für solche röm. H. sind aus verschiedenen, v. a. nordwestl. Prov. stammende Inschr. und die *lex coloniae* der Stadt Urso (CIL II 5439, Kap. 62). Jedoch geben weder Inschr. noch die Stadtverfassung von Urso Aufschluß über die Tätigkeit der H.; die in der Verfassung gen. H. werden lediglich als Subalternbeamte der städt. Magistrate (*aediles, duoviri*) qualifiziert.

Seit dem 3. Jh. n. Chr. erscheinen auf Inschr. auch sog. »Legions-H.« (z. B. CIL VIII 2567; 2586; 2809; Nordafrika), zu deren Aufgaben möglicherweise die Eingeweideschau vor mil. Einsätzen zählte. Ob es sich bei den in der *Historia Augusta* häufiger erwähnten H. um Römer handelte, ist ungewiß (SHA Alex. 13,2; 27,6; 44,4; SHA Maximini Duo 30,2; SHA Tac. 15,2 und 4). C. F.

Terminologie antiker Leberschau

Schafsleber *(facies visceralis)*

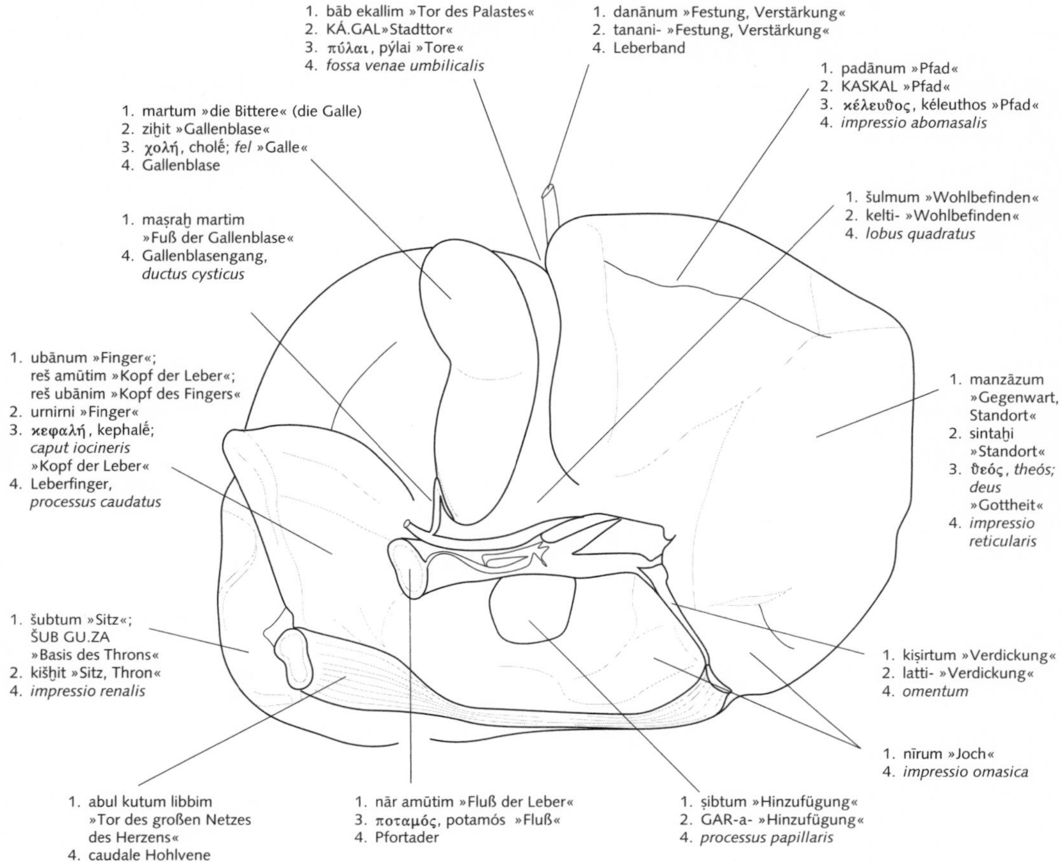

Standort des Leberschauers

Angegeben sind, soweit bekannt: 1. die in akkadischen Texten gebräuchlichen Termini 2. die in hethitischen Texten gebräuchlichen Termini 3. griech./lat. Termini 4. die moderne medizinische Bezeichnung.

M. HAA.

C. Etruskische Belege 1. Inschriften und Bilder 2. Lebermodelle – etruskische und altorientalische Haruspizin

1. Inschriften und Bilder

Das mögliche etr. Wort für H. kommt als Name oder Amtsbezeichnung [6. 139, 274f.] in Grab-Inschr. im nördl. Etrurien bzw. in Umbrien vor. In der Bilingue von Pesaro (Ende 1. Jh. v. Chr.; CIL XI 6363; ET Um 1.7; [7. 105]; vgl. ET Cl 1.1036, Ta 1.17) korrespondiert etr. *netsvis trutnvt frontac* mit lat. *haruspex fulguriator*; dabei gibt *netsvis* wohl eines oder beide Wortglieder von *haruspex* wieder [6. 274; 8. 190f.]. Die H. waren also Spezialisten nicht nur für Innereien-, sondern auch für Blitzschau und wohl überhaupt für Zeichendeutung. Wenn *natis* auf einem Skarabäus (ET Vt G.1; vgl. ET AS 1.314, Cl 1.1461) des 4./3. Jh. v. Chr. [9. 52; vgl. aber 10. 278, 305] mit *netsvis* zusammenhängt [1. 117], ist dies der wohl früheste inschr. Nachweis.

Mögliche etr. Abb. von H. finden sich von ca. 500 bis 100 v. Chr. auf Urnen, Sarkophagen, Spiegeln, Skarabäen, Münzen, Gefäßen aus Bronze und Ton sowie als Votivstatuetten [9; 11; 12]. Als Kennzeichen gelten die Kleidung (hohe Kopfbedeckung, Mantel mit Spange), das Gerät (→ *lituus*, → *liber linteus*), die spezifische Körperhaltung (gebeugter Oberkörper, aufgestütztes Bein). Die Identifizierung ist nicht immer sicher, zumal bildliche, inschr. und lit. Belege sich selten direkt verbinden lassen (aber → Umbricius Melior).

2. Lebermodelle – etruskische und altorientalische Haruspizin

Während das Br.-Modell von Piacenza (um 100 v. Chr.; [13]) durch Verbreitung oriental. Mantik in hell.

Zeit erklärbar ist [14. 109f.], würde eine Verwendung der etr. Tonleber aus Falerii (vor 241 v. Chr.; [7. 146 Nr. 194]) durch etr. H. die Kenntnis oriental. Lebermodelle des 2. Jt. v. Chr. [14. 107f., 110] und der zugehörigen Zeichensysteme voraussetzen. Myk. Funde [15] weisen Italien seit Mitte des 2. Jt. als Einflußgebiet der → Ägäischen Koine aus: Man darf vermuten, daß die etr. Haruspizin diese älteren Kulturschichten bewahrt; dafür könnten auch Äquivalenzen der Zeichenterminologie sprechen; vgl. ferner [11] zur »frühgesch.« H.-Tracht. Die Überlieferung könnte (mit [14]; anders z.B. [16. 642–645; 17. 46–53]: oriental. »Einflüsse« im 8./7. Jh. v. Chr. bzw. in hell. Zeit) von der babylon. über die hurrit. [18] zur hethit. oder SW-anatol. und so – nach 1200 v. Chr. – zur etr. Haruspizin führen.
→ Divination; Etrusci, Etruria III M. HAA.

1 Pfiffig 2 O. Thulin, s. v. Etrusca disciplina, RE 6, 725–730 3 B. MacBain, Prodigy and Expiation: A Study in Religion and Politics in Republican Rome, 1982
4 S. Montero, Política y adivinación en el Bajo Imperio Romano. Emperadores y harúspices (193 D. C.- 408 D. C.), 1991 5 O. Thulin, s. v. H., RE 7, 2431–2468 6 H. Rix, Das etr. Cognomen, 1963 7 Die Etrusker und Europa, Kat. Berlin, 1993 8 M. Hano, Le témoignage des inscriptions latines sur les h., in: La divination dans le monde étrusco-italique 6, 1995, 184–199 9 L. B. van der Meer, Iecur Placentinum..., in: BABesch 54, 1979, 49–64
10 Zazoff, AG 11 F. Roncalli, Die Tracht des H. ..., in: Die Aufnahme fremder Kultureinflüsse in Etrurien..., Kongr. Mannheim 1981, 124–132 12 A. Maggiani, Immagini di aruspici, in: 2° Congr. Internazionale Etrusco III, 1989, 1557–1563 13 A. Maggiani, Qualche osservazione sul fegato di Piacenza, in: SE 50, 1982, 53–88
14 J. W. Meyer, Zur Herkunft der etr. Lebermodelle, in: Phoenicia and Its Neighbours, Kongr. Brüssel, 1985, 105–120 15 L. Vagnetti, Primi contatti..., in: I Greci in Occidente, Kat. Venedig 1996, 109–116 16 Dumézil
17 W. Burkert, The Orientalizing Revolution, 1992
18 M. Schuol, Die Terminologie des hethit. SU-Orakels, in: Altoriental. Forsch. 21, 1994, 73–124; 247–304.

R. Bloch, Réflexions sur le destin et la divination haruspicinale en Grèce et en Étrurie, in: Iconographie classique et identités régionales, 1986, 77–83 • La divination dans le monde étrusco-italique, 1–7 = Caesarodunum Suppl. 52, 1985; 54, 1986; 56, 1986; 61, 1991; 63, 1993; 64, 1995; 65, 1996. C. F. u. M. HAA.

Abb.-Lit.: C. Thulin, Die etr. Disziplin II. Die Haruspicin, 1906, Ndr. 1968, 46f.; 50–54 • R. D. Biggs, G.-W. Meyer, s. v. Lebermodelle, RLA 6, 1980–3, 518–527 • Ch. Guittard, Haruspicine et *devotio*: »Caput iocineris a familiari parte caesum« (Tite-Live 8,9,1), in: La divination dans le monde étr.-italique 3, Caesarodunum Suppl. 56, 1986, 49–67 • W. Burkert, The Orientalizing Revolution, 1992, 49f. mit Anm. 21. M. HAA.

Harwennefer (= *Haronnophris*, griech. *Hurgonaphor*). Anführer einer einheimischen Revolte, der Okt./Nov. 205 v. Chr. in Theben zum Pharao gekrönt wurde; seine Herrschaft schloß Abydos und Pathyris mit ein; aus Abydos (und Ptolemais) verdrängte ihn eine ptolem. Offensive erst 201/0. Im Sommer 199 ist → Anchwennefer als Nachfolger bezeugt.

P. W. Pestman, Haronnophris and Chaonnophris, in: S. P. Vleeming (Hrsg.), Hundred-Gated Thebes, 1995, 101–134 • B. C. McGing, in: APF 43, 1997, 285ff. W. A.

Hasaitisch (Hasäisch), frühnordarab. Dial. (→ Arabisch). Seine Inschr., in einem leicht abgewandelten altsüdarab. → Alphabet geschrieben, sind vorwiegend Grabinschr., darunter zwei hasait.-aram. → Bilinguen, aus dem nö Saudiarabien (ca. zw. 5. u. 2. Jh. v. Chr.).
→ Altsüdarabisch; Semitische Sprachen

W. W. Müller, Das Altarab. und das klass. Arabisch, Hasaitisch, in: W.-D. Fischer (Hrsg.), Grundriß der arab. Philol., 1982, 25–26. C. K.

Hasdrubal (*ʿzrbʿl* = »Hilfe ist Bʿl«; Ἀσδρούβας).
[1] Karthagischer Feldherr im 1. Pun. Krieg, der 256 v. Chr. mit → Bostar [1] den röm. Invasionstruppen des Konsuls M. → Atilius [I 21] Regulus bei Adys unterlag, 255 wohl unter → Xanthippos am Sieg bei Tynes mitwirkte (Pol. 1,30; 32; Diod. 23,11) [1. 48, 264 und 132, 751] und seit 251 u. a. mit 140 Elefanten auf Sizilien operierte, bis er bei Panormos vom röm. Konsul L. → Caecilius [I 11] Metellus vernichtend geschlagen wurde (Pol. 1,38; 40; Diod. 23,21). In Karthago wurde H. für sein Versagen hingerichtet (Zon. 8,14,12) [2. 241].
[2] Prominenter karthagischer Politiker und Stratege (vgl. Liv. 21,2,3–7), evtl. Vater des → Mago [1. 188, 1115], Schwiegersohn und als Stratege für Afrika und Iberien Nachfolger des → Hamilkar [3] Barkas (Pol. 2,1,9), den H. 237 v. Chr. nach Gades begleitete, nachdem er ihm als Exponent der »Volkspartei« bereits 240 Beistand geleistet hatte (App. Ib. 4,16–5,17). Nach Nordafrika entsandt zur Wiederherstellung der numidischen Gefolgschaft (Diod. 25,10,3) [1. 133; 2. 272, 274], kehrte H. erst im J. 229 nach Spanien zurück, als Hamilkar gefallen war, zu dessen Nachfolger die Truppen H. wählten, was auch in Karthago bestätigt wurde (App. Ib. 6,22; Liv. 21,2,4) [1. 133f.]. Bis zu seiner Ermordung im J. 221 (Pol. 2,36,1; App. Hann. 2,8) konsolidierte H. mit mil. und diplomatischen Mitteln, u. a. durch Heirat einer iberischen Fürstin, die Stellung Spaniens als karthagische Provinz, wobei die Herrschaft der → Barkiden monarchisches Profil annahm [3. 149; 4. 40–42], z. B. mit der Gründung der Residenzstadt → Carthago Nova (h. Cartagena) im J. 227 (?) [3. 134; 4. 43f.]. Als historisch unzuverlässig sind nicht nur Berichte über H.s Homosexualität (Liv. 21,2,4; 3,4) und separatistisch-umstürzlerische Bestrebungen (Pol. 3,8; 10,10,9) zurückzuweisen [1. 135; 2. 275f., 56; 4. 41f.], sondern wohl auch die Überlieferung des sog. Ebrovertrages, den H. 226 mit Rom geschlossen haben soll (StV 3,503) [4. 44–47].
[3] Sohn des → Hamilkar [3] Barkas, berühmter karthagischer Stratege neben seinem Bruder → Hannibal [4] (vgl. Pol. 11,2), kämpfte 218–216 v. Chr. als Oberbe-

fehlshaber in Spanien (Liv. 21,22) eher glücklos gegen aufständische Keltiberer (Liv. 22,21,5–8) und gegen Cn. → Cornelius [I 77] Scipio bei Ibera, Sagunt, Iliturgi und Intibili (Liv. 22,19f.; 23,26–29; 49,5–14) [1. 137f.; 4. 250f.]. Nachdem H. im J. 214 in Numidien den abtrünnigen → Syphax besiegt hatte (App. Ib. 15,58–16,60) [2. 357; 4. 284[84]], gelang H. 211 mit → Mago und → Hasdrubal [5] auch die Rückeroberung Spaniens [1. 138f.], 208 nach dem Verlust von → Carthago Nova an P. → Cornelius [I 71] Scipio der Übergang nach Gallien [4. 369–373]. Im Frühjahr 207 drang H. mit einem großen, von Kelten verstärkten Heer bis nach Umbrien vor, wo dann seine vernichtende Niederlage am → Metaurus gegen M. → Livius Salinator das Kriegsglück endgültig wendete (Liv. 27,43–49) [1. 140–142; 4. 385–390].

[4] H. »der Kahle« (*Calvus*: Liv. 23,34,16) [1. 225]. Karthagischer Feldherr im 2. Pun. Krieg, geriet 215 auf Sardinien in röm. Gefangenschaft, als sein Heer, das den → Hampsicora stärken sollte, aber wegen Seesturmschäden verspätet eingetroffen war, von T. → Manlius Torquatus aufgerieben wurde (Liv. 23,40f.; Zon. 9,4) [1. 148f.; 2. 348f.].

[5] Sohn des → Geskon [3], renommierter karthagischer Feldherr im 2. Pun. Krieg in Spanien und Afrika. Nach gemeinsamen Erfolgen mit Hasdrubal [3] und → Mago in Iberien im J. 211 (Liv. 25,32; 34–36; App. Ib. 16) [2. 373f.; 4. 319f.] unterlag H. als Oberfeldherr 206 bei → Ilipa dem P. → Cornelius [I 71] Scipio (Pol. 11,20–24; Liv. 28,12–16; App. Ib. 27). H. vermittelte dann in Afrika die karthagisch-numidische Allianz und verheiratete seine Tochter → Sophoniba mit → Syphax, mit dem gemeinsam er nach gelegentlichen Erfolgen gegen die röm. Invasionstruppen unter P. Cornelius Scipio im J. 204 im Medjerdatal (»auf den Großen Feldern«) unterlag (Pol. 14,6; 8; Liv. 29,35; 30,4–8; App. Lib. 18–24) [1. 146f.; 4. 433–442]. Die weiteren Nachrichten über den abgesetzten und zum Tod verurteilten (?) H. bis zu seinem Freitod im J. 202 sind unzuverlässig [1. 147; 2. 411, 56].

[6] H. »der Bock« (ἔριφος, *haedus*) [1. 225, 1317], innenpolit. Gegner der → Barkiden (vgl. Liv. 30,44) [1. 150; 2. 242, 166], der gemeinsam mit → Hanno [6] im J. 202 als Friedensunterhändler zu P. → Cornelius [I 71] Scipio und nach Rom reiste (App. Lib. 49,213–53,229; Liv. 30,42,12–19).

[7] Karthagischer Feldherr im 3. Pun. Krieg; gemeinsam mit → Karthalo Boetharch gegen → Massinissa, wurde H. nach der Niederlage vom J. 150 zum Tode verurteilt (Pol. 36,16,12; Diod. 32,3; App. Lib. 70,319–74,341) [2. 439], dann aber, nachdem er mit einer Privatarmee Karthago belagerte, zu Beginn des Krieges gegen Rom zum Strategen ernannt (App. Lib. 80,374; 93,439) [1. 153f.; 2. 443f.]. Nach wechselvollen Kämpfen und intriganter Beseitigung seines Kollegen Hasdrubal, Enkel des Massinissa, erlangte H. das alleinige Kommando, das er in despotischer Weise ausübte (vgl. Pol. 38,7) [1. 154f.]. Nachdem H. durch → Gulussa die Kapitulationsverhandlungen eröffnet hatte, setzte er sich zuletzt noch zu P. Cornelius [I 70] Scipio ab und starb später in röm. Ehrenhaft (Zon. 9,30) [2. 456].

1 Geus 2 Huss 3 P. Barceló, Karthago und die Iberische Halbinsel vor den Barkiden, 1988 4 J. Seibert, Hannibal, 1993.

L.-M. G.

Hase (Lepus europaeus Pallas). Der H. ist von Mitteleuropa bis Vorderasien und Südafrika in der Kultursteppe und im Wald verbreitet. Name: λαγωός (homer.), λαγώς, λαγῶς/*lagōs* (att.), λαγός (ion., dor.), λέπορις (aiol., sizil.: Varro rust. 3,12,6), lat. *lepus* bzw. die Ableitungen davon λαγίον, λαγίδιον, λαγιδεύς, ferner Sonderbezeichnungen nach charakterischen Merkmalen wie »Ducker« (πτώξ; Hom. Il. 17,676; Aischyl. Eum. 326; Theophr. h. plant. 4,3,5; Theokrit 1,110), »Rauhfuß« (δασύπους; in der Komödie, bei Xen. und Aristot.), »der Schnelle« (ταχίνας; lakon. nach Ail. nat. 7,47) und »der Springer« (κέκην, kret. nach Hesych.).

Im Mittelmeergebiet kam der H. fast überall vor, sogar auf Inseln, mit Ausnahme von Ithaka (Aristot. hist. an. 7(8),28, 606a 2–5; Plin. nat. 8,226), Kyrnos (Korsika; Pol. 12,3,10 gegen den Historiker Timaios) u.a. In Attika war er vielleicht seltener (Nausikrates comicus bei Athen. 9,399 f = CAF 2,296). Das Erscheinen auf manchen Inseln ist z.T. histor. bezeugt, für Astypalaia durch Hegesandros von Delphi (Athen. 9,400 d) und Sizilien durch Aristoteles (res publica Rheginensium 1565a 7). Lokale Arten wurden unterschieden, z.B. für Makedonien (Aristot. hist. an. 2,17,507a 16–19; vgl. Plin. nat. 11,190), Äg. (Aristot. ebd. 7(8),28,606a 24), Skythien (Aristot. hist. an. 8(9),33,619b 15), Krastonien (Aristot. mir. 122, 842a 15f.) und Sizilien (mir. 82, 836b 19) sowie It. (Varro rust. 3,12,5). Der Schnee-H. der Alpen wird von Varro rust. 3,12,5 und Plin. nat. 11,190 erwähnt, aber, abgesehen von der weißen Winterfärbung, ohne besondere Kennzeichnung. Xenophon (kyn. 5) beschreibt ähnlich wie Ailianos (Ail. nat. 13,14f.) hervorragend die beiden H.-Arten (die größere = maked., die kleinere = ital., letztere wahrscheinlich identisch mit dem χελιδόνειος λαγωός bei Diphilos Frg. 1, vgl. Athen. 9,401a, der ihn mit dem Kaninchen identifiziert), einschließlich ihres Verhaltens.

Zoologisch wurden viele Besonderheiten dieser doppelzähnigen (ἀμφόδοντες, *amphódontes* bei Aristot. hist. an. 3,1,511a 30f.; 3,21, 522b 9) Nagetiere beachtet: die Schnelligkeit und das Vorsetzen der wesentlich längeren Hinterbeine beim Laufen (Hom. Il. 17,676; Hes. scut. 302; Xen. kyn. 5; Ail. nat. 13,14f), die starken, weichen Haare sogar im Maul und unter den Füßen (Aristot. hist. an. 3,12, 519a 22f.; gen. an. 4,5,774a 35; Xen. kyn. 5; Plin. nat. 11,229: hier wird dieses Merkmal von Trogus auf ihre Geilheit zurückgeführt), die unvollkommene Blutgerinnung wegen des Fehlens des Fibrins (ἶνες, Aristot. hist. an. 3,6,515b 35–516a 5), das angebl. Vorkommen von Saugwarzen im Uterus des Weibchens (3,11,511a 29–31), in manchen Verbreitungsgebieten eine zweiteilige Leber (2,17,507a 16–19,

Plin. nat. 11,190; Ail. nat. 5,27 und 11,40; Gell. 16,115), das Vorhandensein des Lab-Ferments im Magen wie bei den Wiederkäuern (3,21,522b 8 f.; Plin. nat. 11,239) sowie die gewaltige Fruchtbarkeit (Aristot. hist. an. 6,33,579b 30–580a 5; Hor. sat. 2,4,44). Sogar die inzwischen nachgewiesene Nachbefruchtung (Superfecundatio [1. 156]) war bekannt (Hdt. 3,108,3; Aristot. hist. an. 5,9,542b 30f.; gen. an. 4,5,774a 30–32; Plin. nat. 8,219), aber eine von Archelaos bei Plin. nat. 8,218 behauptete Jungfernzeugung und die Bildung von Embryonen im Männchen (Ail. nat. 13,12) sind frei erfunden. Das angebliche Schlafen mit offenen Augen wurde oft wiederholt (Xen. kyn. 5,11; Plin. nat. 11,147; Ail. nat. 2,12 und 13,13). Die schlaue Feigheit des H. war geradezu sprichwörtlich (vgl. Hdt. 3,108; Aristot. hist. an. 1,1,488b 15; Xen. kyn. 5; Ail. nat. 7,19): ›feiger als ein phrygischer H.‹ (δειλότερον λαγὼ Φρυγός, Strab. 1,36) und ›ein (zum Schein) schlafender Hase‹ (λαγώς καθεύδων, Zenob. 4,84). Die Fabel stellt ihn als dumm und feige dar (Aisop. 143; 169 und 254; Syntipas 10 Hausrath). Antisthenes bei Aristot. Pol. 3,15,1284a 15f. bezeichnet die Forderung der H. nach Gleichberechtigung aller Tiere als absurd.

Viele Feinde stellten dem H. nach, etwa der Adler (Hom. Il. 17,676 und 22,310; Aisop. 3 und 273; Aristot. hist. an. 8(9),33,619b 9), Hunde (Hom. Il. 10,360–2; Hom. Od. 17,295; Aisop. 139), der Löwe (Aisop. 153, vgl. H.-Jagd mit Löwen im röm. Zirkus bei Ov. fast. 5,371 f.) und Füchse (Ail. nat. 13,11; vgl. Aisop. 169). Sein größter Feind aber war der Mensch, der ihn zum Verzehr des mageren Fleisches immer jagte (Rezepte bei Athen. 9,399d f. mit Komikerzitaten; über Jagdmosaiken z.B. in Piazza Armerina [2. Abb. 102–104]). Angeblich sollte der Verzehr für mehrere Tage schön machen (Plin. nat. 28,260; Mart. 5,29 und 13,92; vgl. ein Scherzgedicht auf Alexander Severus, SHA Alex. 19) und gegen zahlreiche Krankheiten nahezu aller Körperteile helfen (vgl. Plin. nat. 28,166; 178f; 199; 215 u.ö.) bzw. magisch wirken. Ein H. kostete deshalb im Edictum Diocletiani bis 150 Denare, ein Kaninchen nur 40. Man versteht daher die schon in der röm. Republik beliebte Haltung von H. zusammen mit anderem Wild in großen Gehegen (*leporaria*, Varro rust. 3,3,2 und 3,12,1–7; Colum. 9,1,8 f.; Gell. 2,20). Nach Xenophon (kyn. 5) jagte man ein einzelnes oder viele Tiere auf einer Treibjagd mit großen Stellnetzen (δίκτυον, πάναγρον) oder Weg- bzw. Fallnetzen (ἐνόδιον, ἄρκυς) oder nur mit Hunden (vgl. Verg. georg. 1,308). Die Eumeniden nennen (Aischyl. Eum. 326) den von ihnen gejagten Orestes folglich H. (πτώξ). Die gefangenen Tiere tötete man mit dem Schlagstock (καλαῦροψ, homer.; λαγωβόλον).

Sein ruhiges Verhalten, aber auch seine erotische Natur empfahl ihn wie den Sperling u.a. als Spieltier, z.B. bei Melagros (Anth. Pal. 7,207), wie viele Abb. (z.B. auf röm. Wandgemälden [2. 190] in Gesellschaft des Bakchos) von Eroten und Mädchen nahelegen. Plautus (Cas. 138) verwendet *lepus* neben *columba* (»Haustaube«) und *passer* (»Sperling«) als Kosewort. Eine kult. Bed. bei Griechen und Römern ist nicht nachweisbar, im AT wird er als unrein betrachtet (Lv 11,6; Dt 14,7).

Das Kaninchen (Oryctolagus cuniculus Lilljeborg; vgl. ein Wandgemälde aus Herculaneum [2. 192 und Abb. 105]) mit dem von den Römern übernommenen iberischen Namen *cuniculus* stammt aus Spanien und wurde von Pol. 12,3,10, Poseidonios sowie Theopompos bei Athen. 9,400 f–401 a als κ(ο)ύνικλος/*kúniklos* bezeichnet. Strabo (3,144: λαγιδεύς) nennt es massilisch λεβηρίς und (γεώρυχος) λαγιδεύς oder auch δασύπους (trotz der richtigen Identifizierung mit dem H. bei Aristot. hist. an. 7(8),28, 606a 24), was Plin. nat. 8,219 fälschlich übernimmt. Die Römer registrierten nicht nur seine Herkunft (Catull. 37,18: *cuniculosa Celtiberia*), sondern auch seine Ausbreitung nach Gallien, den Balearen und Inseln westlich It. Die Quellen (u.a. Varro rust. 3,12,6; vgl. Mart. 13,60) nennen es eine andere H.-Art, ähnlich der ital., aber kleiner, und erwähnen seine verzweigten und ganze Städte unterhöhlenden (Plin. nat. 8,217f.) Gänge (iber. *cuniculi*). Eine Massenvermehrung auf den Balearen unter Augustus führte zu einer Hungersnot, welche von Staats wegen u.a. durch die starke Bejagung mit eingeführten → Frettchen (*viverra*; Strab. 3,144: γαλῆ ἀγρία aus Libyen) eingedämmt wurde (Plin. nat. 8,218). Der fast ausgetragene Fötus (iberisch *laurex* bei Plin. nat. 8,217) war bis ins MA eine Delikatesse (vgl. Gregor von Tours, historia Francorum 5,4). Eine Zucht hat es offenbar in der Ant. nicht gegeben.

→ Jagd

1 J. Niethammer, Säugetiere, 1979 2 Toynbee, Tierwelt.

H. Gossen, s. v. H., RE 7, 2477 • Ders., s. v. Kaninchen, RE 10, 1867 • Keller 1, 210–218 • F. Orth, s. v. Jagd, RE 9,558 • Ders., s. v. Leporarium, RE 12, 2068 • Ders., s. v. Lepus, RE 12, 2079.

C.HÜ.

Hasel. Die Gattung Corylus L. der Betulaceae ist in Europa v.a. durch den weit verbreiteten, Gebüsche bildenden (vgl. Verg. ecl. 1,14) Strauch-H. Corylus avellana (*abellana* schon bei Cato agr. 8,2; *corylus*: H.-Holz für den Kelterdeckel ebd. 18,9; *corulus* Colum. 7,9,6) vertreten. Im Mittelmeerraum wachsen ferner der von Vorderasien bis in den Balkan verbreitete, bis zu 20 m hohe Baum-H. C. colurna L., die Byz. oder Zeller-Nuß C. pontica Koch und die Bart-, Lombard- oder Lambertsnuß C. maxima Mill. (= tubulosa Willdenow; vielleicht = *nuces calvae*, Cato agr. 8,2 = *galbae* Plin. nat. 15,90). Diese drei Arten faßt Theophr. h. plant. 3,15,1 f. als *Hērakleōtikḗ karýa* zusammen. Seit der Ant. finden sich die von Dioskurides (1,125,3 Wellmann = 1,179 Berendes) *kárya Pontikḗ* (= Plin. nat. 15,88, vgl. Macr. Sat. 3,18,6) genannten H. in mehreren Sorten in Kultur am Schwarzen Meer und wurden von dort nach Südit. (bes. nach Abella/Avellino in Kampanien), nach Frankreich und Süddeutschland gebracht. Der lat. Name *nux* *abellana* bei Plin. nat. 15,88 deutet wie die griech. Bezeichnungen auf eine vielfältige Nutzung der ölreichen Nüsse hin, z.B. trotz ihrer diätetisch negativen Beurteilung (Dioskurides ebd. = Plin. nat. 23,150) zur Ernährung sowie in der Medizin gegen Husten und Katarrh. Für Verg. georg. 2,299 (mit Servius z. St.) galt der H. als Feind des Weinstocks. Die Germanen, Kelten und Slaven bevorzugten die Nüsse, verwendeten aber auch die Ruten des wilden H. zur Wassersuche und als Symbol des Lebens. Von *coruletum, columum* u.ä. bzw. vom ahd. *hasal* sind viele Ortsnamen wie Coleri, Glurns, Haseldorf oder Haslach abgeleitet.

→ Walnuß C.HÜ.

Hasmonäer. Jüdische Priesterfamilie aus Modeïn, der Priesterklasse Joarib zugehörig; der Name, nur bei Iosephos und im Talmud überliefert, bezieht sich auf einen nicht genau identifizierbaren Ḥašmōn (nach Ios. bell. Iud. 1,36 Vater, nach Ios. ant. Iud. 12,265 Urgroßvater des Mattathias). Mit Mattathias begann 167 v. Chr. der bewaffnete Widerstand gegen den von → Antiochos [6] IV. verhängten Glaubenszwang. Seinem Sohn → Iudas Makkabaios gelang 165 die Rückeroberung und Wiedereinweihung des Tempels von Jerusalem. Nachdem → Antiochos [7] V. im J. 163 die jüdische Theokratie unter dem Hohenpriester Alkimos restituiert hatte, gewannen die H. trotz Niederlagen allmählich die Kontrolle über Iudaea und annektierten unter Ausnutzung der dynastischen Kämpfe und der außenpolit. Schwierigkeiten der seleukidischen Oberherren große Teile der Peripherie des jüdischen Siedlungsgebietes (größte Ausdehnung unter → Alexandros [16] Iannaios, s. Karte Sp. 179f.). Der seleukid. Thronprätendent → Alexandros [13] Balas ernannte Ionathan 152 zum Hohenpriester, und nach Gewinnung der Freiheit, d.h. dem Ende der Tributpflicht, und der Eroberung der seleukid. Zitadelle in Jerusalem (143/2) übertrug das Volk 141 die erbliche Hohepriesterwürde an Simon.

Vielleicht schon Aristobulos I., mit Sicherheit Alexandros Iannaios nahm den Königstitel an. Die damit auch äußerlich dokumentierte Nähe zum hell. Königtum führte zu schweren inneren Konflikten. Schon nach Wiederherstellung der Theokratie unter Antiochos V. hatte sich die Vereinigung frommer Schriftgelehrter vom Bündnis mit den H. losgesagt. Unter Alexandros Iannaios kam es zum offenen Bürgerkrieg mit den → Pharisaioi. Nach dem Tod der → Alexandra Salome brach zwischen Aristobulos [2] II. und → Hyrkanos [3] II. ein dynastischer Konflikt aus, der eine entscheidende Voraussetzung für die Unterstellung des verkleinerten jüd. Staates unter die röm. Statthalter von Syrien seit dem J. 63 war. Hyrkanos II. wurde der Königstitel aberkannt, und die eigentliche Macht fiel an den Vertrauensmann der Römer, an → Antipatros [4], den Vater → Herodes' [1] I. Im Zuge der parth. Invasion und der röm. Rückeroberung des Orients (40–37) wurde die Herrschaft der H. beseitigt. Quellen: 1 und 2 Makk; Ios. bell. Iud. 1,36–437; ant. Iud. 12,265–15,56.

→ Judentum

1 Schürer, Bd. 1 2 J. Wellhausen, Israelitische und jüdische Geschichte, [8]1921 3 E. Bickermann, Der Gott der Makkabäer, 1937 4 Ders., From Ezra to the Last of the Maccabees, 1962 5 F.-M. Abel, Histoire de la Palestine 1, 1952 6 K. Bringmann, Hell. Reform und Religionsverfolgung in Judäa, 1983. K.BR.

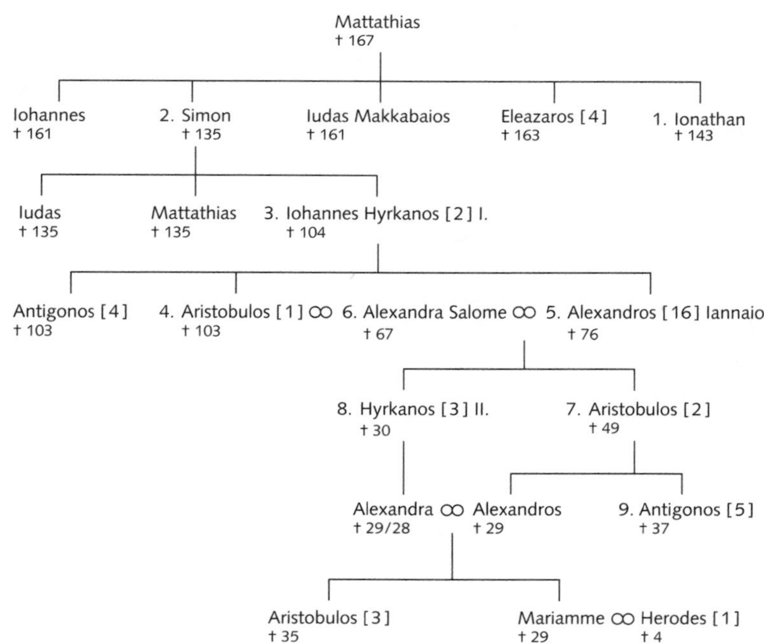

Personen, die als Hohepriester bzw. als Könige und Hohepriester die Herrschaft ausübten, sind in der Reihenfolge ihrer Regentschaften durchnumeriert; s. zu ihnen die Einzelartikel.

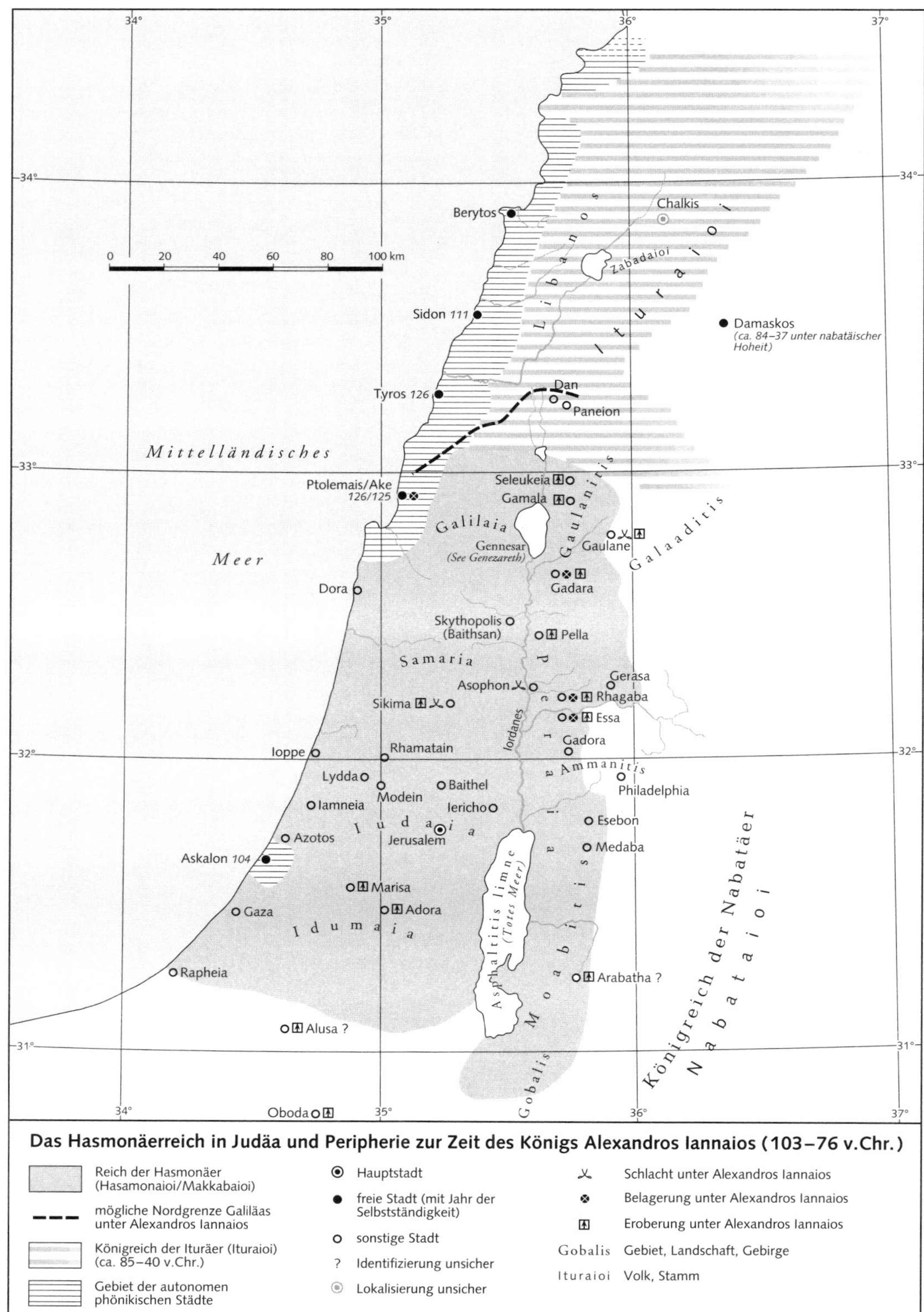

Das Hasmonäerreich in Judäa und Peripherie zur Zeit des Königs Alexandros Iannaios (103–76 v.Chr.)

Reich der Hasmonäer (Hasamonaioi/Makkabaioi)
mögliche Nordgrenze Galiläas unter Alexandros Iannaios
Königreich der Ituräer (Ituraioi) (ca. 85–40 v.Chr.)
Gebiet der autonomen phönikischen Städte
Hauptstadt
freie Stadt (mit Jahr der Selbstständigkeit)
sonstige Stadt
? Identifizierung unsicher
Lokalisierung unsicher
Schlacht unter Alexandros Iannaios
Belagerung unter Alexandros Iannaios
Eroberung unter Alexandros Iannaios
Gobalis Gebiet, Landschaft, Gebirge
Ituraioi Volk, Stamm

KARTEN-LIT.: H. WALDMANN, Syrien und Palästina in hell. Zeit. TAVO B V 16.2. Die Makkabäer und die Hasmonäer (167–37 v. Chr.), 1987.

Hassan (*Ḥasan*). Enkel des Propheten → Mohammed, Sohn seiner Tochter → Fatima und seines Vetters → Ali, Bruder des → Husain, 624/5 bis nach 670 n. Chr. Nach der Ermordung Alis verzichtete H. nach Verhandlungen auf das Kalifat zugunsten des → Omajjaden (Umayyaden) → Muʿāwiya (661) und blieb fortan polit. unbedeutend. Für die → Schiiten ist er der zweite → Imam nach seinem Vater Ali.

L. VECCIA VAGLIERI, s. v. Ḥasan b. ʿAlī b. Abī Ṭālib, EI 3, 240b–243b. H. SCHÖ.

Hasta

[1] Hasta, hastati. Die *hasta* diente im röm. Heer während der mittleren Republik vor allem als Stoßlanze für den Nahkampf, obwohl sie auch geworfen werden konnte; sie hatte einen hölzernen Schaft und eine Eisenspitze. Die *h.* war der Kampfweise der → Phalanx angepaßt, blieb aber im Gebrauch, als die Römer im 4. Jh. v. Chr. zur flexibleren Aufstellung in Manipeln (→ *manipulus*) übergingen. Nach Livius (Liv. 8,8,5–13), dessen Darstellung allerdings nicht unproblematisch ist, bestand das röm. Heer 340 v. Chr. aus drei Schlachtreihen, den *hastati*, den *principes* und den *triarii*. Die *triarii* waren mit der *h.* bewaffnet; es ist anzunehmen, daß die *hastati* ebenfalls mit der *h.* ausgerüstet waren. Der Wurfspeer (→ *pilum*) hingegen wird an dieser Stelle nicht erwähnt. Polybios nennt in seiner Beschreibung des röm. Heeres, die wohl die Situation im 2. Jh. v. Chr. widerspiegelt, als Kriterien für die Aufstellung der Soldaten Besitz und Alter: Die *hastati*, jüngere Männer, trugen eine volle Rüstung und standen in der ersten Schlachtreihe, die *principes* in der zweiten Reihe, während die älteren und kampferprobten Soldaten als *triarii* in der dritten Reihe aufgestellt wurden (Pol. 6,21–23). Die *hastati* und *principes* waren mit einem ovalen Schild, einem Schwert und wahrscheinlich zwei *pila* ausgerüstet und trugen bronzene Brustpanzer und Beinschienen; die *hastati* hatten Bronzehelme mit langen Federn, die sie größer erscheinen ließen. Nur noch die *triarii* waren mit der *h.* bewaffnet; die *h.* der Leichtbewaffneten (*velites*) wurde mit einer Wurfschlinge versehen und war so zum Wurf geeignet (*h. amentata*; Cic. Brut. 271). Trotz dieser Veränderungen behielten die *hastati* ihren Namen bei.

Hastati und *principes* einer Legion waren jeweils in zehn Manipel zu je 120 Mann unterteilt, während die zehn Manipel der *triarii* je 60 Mann stark waren. In der Schlacht begannen die *hastati* den Nahkampf und zogen sich, falls sie zurückgeschlagen wurden, durch die Reihen der *principes* zurück. Die *hastati* besaßen im Legionslager (→ *castra*) einen festen Platz an der *via quintana* und bildeten auf dem Marsch eine eigene Kolonne (Pol. 6,28 f.; 6,40).

Obgleich die Manipel bis zur Zeit Caesars durch die *cohortes* (→ *cohors*) ersetzt wurden, bestanden die Namen der alten Schlachtreihen in den Titeln der *centuriones* weiter (*hastatus prior* und *hastatus posterior*). Seit dieser Neuordnung wurde die *h.* nicht mehr verwendet, alle Soldaten waren fortan mit dem *pilum* bewaffnet. Im Prinzipat verwendete man den Begriff *h.* für verschiedene Speere der → *auxilia*. Die *h. pura* gehörte zu den militärischen Auszeichnungen (→ *dona militaria*) der Offiziere aus dem *ordo equester* und dem *ordo senatorius*.

1 M. C. BISHOP, J. C. N. COULSTON, Roman Military Equipment, 1993, 52–53; 69 2 L. KEPPIE, The Making of the Roman Army, 1984, 14–67. J. CA./Ü: A. BE.

[2] Im rechtlichen Sinne ist *h.* laut Gai. inst. 4,16 gleichbedeutend mit *festuca*. Bei der → *legis actio sacramento in rem* erscheinen beide als Symbole des von den Parteien geltend gemachten Herrschaftsanspruchs *iusti dominii* (des rechtlich begründeten Eigentums) über die streitgegenständliche Sache. Daraus erklärt sich, daß in dem für die → *vindicatio* zuständigen Centumviralgericht eine *h.* aufgestellt war (Dig. 1,2,2,29). Die *h.* stellte späterhin insgesamt das Symbol für staatlich initiierte Veräußerungen dar (Cic. Phil. 2,64).

M. KASER, K. HACKL, Das röm. Zivilprozeßrecht, [2]1997, 14, 97. C. PA.

[3] Hölzernes Ritualinstrument mit Eisenspitze, verbranntem und blutigem Schaft, das die → *fetiales* im alten röm. Ritus der Kriegserklärung in das Feindesgebiet schleuderten oder mit dem sie den symbolischen Akt vor dem Bellona-Tempel (vgl. *hastiferi* = Anhänger des Bellona-Kultes [1]) in Rom vollzogen. Die *h.* galt auch als Symbol für den Gott → Mars (*h. Martis*, die im Sacrarium der Regia aufbewahrt wurde: Serv. Aen. 8,3) oder als Attribut der → Salii (Dion. Hal. ant. 2,70: λόγχη) [2]. Unsicher ist hingegen die Zuschreibung als Attribut für das Flaminat (anders: [3]).

1 AE 48,8; 48,29 2 A. V. SIEBERT, Instrumenta sacra, im Druck 3 TH. SCHÄFER, Flaminat und h., in: Scritti in ricordo di G. Massari Gaballo e di U. Tocchetti Pollini (Comune di Milano, Ripartizione Cultura, Raccolte Archeologiche Numismatiche), 1986, 129f. mit Anm. 42.

F. KLINGMÜLLER, s. v. H. (1), RE 7, 2502. A. V. S.

[4] *Oppidum* am Tanaro in Liguria, *municipium II virale* oder *colonia* (Ptol. 3,1,45) der *regio IX*, *tribus Pollia*, an der *via Fulvia* (Tab. Peut. 3,5), h. Asti/Piemont; *dioecesis*, langobardisches Herzogtum. Berühmt für Keramik (Plin. nat. 35,160; Anth. Pal. 11,27,3). 402 n. Chr. leistete H. Alaricus [2] Widerstand (Claud. carm. 27f., 203), 480 Überfall der Burgundiones, 534 n. Chr. unterstützt von den Ostgoten (Cassiod. var. 11,15,2). Erh. sind Torre Rosso, Thermen, Theater, *domus*, Nekropolen. An der ligur. Küste und in Etruria zwei *mansiones* gleichen Namens (Tab. Peut. 3,5; 4,3; Geogr. Rav. 4,32; 5,2).

S. GIORCELLI BERSANI, Alla periferia dell'impero, 1994, 45–76 • M. SOMÀ, Note topografiche su Asti romana, in: Bollettino storico-bibliografico subalpino 93, 1995, 219–243 • E. ZANDA, A. CROSETTO, L. PEJRANI, Asti. Interventi archeologici e ricerche in centro storico (1981–1986), in: Quaderni della Soprintendenza Archeologica del Piemonte 5, 1986, 67–121.

E.S.G./Ü: H.D.

[5] Stadt in der Baetica (Plin. nat. 3,1; Strab. 3,1,9; Liv. 39,21), Überreste auf dem Hügel Mesa de Asta 25 km nördl. von Puerto San Maria. Älteste Erwähnung 189 v. Chr. (CIL II 5041). 187 v. Chr. von C. → Atinius [2] erobert (Liv. 39,21), von Caesar 45 v. Chr. als *colonia Hasta Regia* (auf Br.-Mz.: *Felix*) konstituiert (vgl. Plin. nat. 3,11). Zuletzt erwähnt in den Märtyrerakten des Marcellus; in arab. Zeit zerstört.

M. ESTEVE GUERRERO, Miscellanea arqueologica Jerezana, 1979 • M. FERRERO, Apuntes para una interpretación estadística de la cerámica aparecida en Asta Regia, in: Boletín del Museo de Cádiz 2, 1979–1980, 37–44 • P. PIERNAVEJA, Sobre Marcial y un pretendido Romanus, in: Archivo Español de Arqueología 48, 1975, 181 f. • TOVAR 2, 148–150.

M.F.P.L.u.P.B./Ü: H.D.

Haterius

[1] Von Cic. fam. 9,18,3 im J. 46 v. Chr. erwähnt; vielleicht identisch mit dem gleichnamigen Proskribierten bei App. civ. 4,29.

[2] Q. H. Vielleicht Nachkomme von H. [1], aus senatorischer Familie. Wenn er 26 n. Chr. fast 90jährig gestorben ist, muß er ca. 65 v. Chr. geboren sein. Mit dem Haus des Augustus war er über seine Frau verwandtschaftlich verbunden. *Cos. suff.* 5 v. Chr., also schon in hohem Alter. Öfter von Tac. bei Senatsverhandlungen unter Tiberius erwähnt. Er erscheint als ein Muster von unüberlegtem Freimut und Schmeichelei (Tac. ann. 1,13,4; 3,57; 59). Wegen seiner impulsiven Beredsamkeit war er berühmt (PIR² H 24). Vielleicht ist ihm das Grab zuzuweisen, das an der via Nomentana stand [1. Bd. 2, 340]. Dann ist CIL VI 1426 (vgl. Additamenta CIL VI pars VIII ad 1426) auf ihn zu beziehen. Die erwähnten Ämter dürften nur eine Auswahl darstellen, doch sind sie möglicherweise auf einen Sohn zu beziehen.

[3] D. H. Agrippa. Sohn oder Enkel von H. [2]. Im J. 15 n. Chr. *tr. pl.*, 17 als Praetor nachgewählt, dabei von Germanicus und Drusus unterstützt. Als *cos. des.* beantragte er die Todesstrafe gegen Clutorius Priscus. Im J. 22 *cos. ord.* Im J. 32 erfolglose Anklage gegen die Konsuln des J. 31. PIR² H 25.

[4] Q. H. Antoninus. Wohl Sohn von H. [3]. *Cos. ord.* 53 n. Chr. Nero gewährte ihm jährlich eine finanzielle Unterstützung, weil er das väterliche Vermögen verschwendet hatte. PIR² H 26.

[5] T. H. Nepos. Ritter, Vater von H. [6]. Von 119–124 n. Chr. war er *praefectus Aegypti* [2. 284]. Ihm wird üblicherweise der ritterliche Cursus in CIL XI 5213 = ILS 1338 aus Fulginiae zugewiesen (PFLAUM I 217 ff., PIR² H 29). Dann hätte er jedoch von 114–119 fünf hohe ritterliche Amtsstellungen übernehmen müssen. Wahrscheinlicher handelt es sich um einen unbekannten Ritter [cf. 3. 485 f.].

[6] T. H. Nepos Atinas Probus Publicius Matenianus. Sohn von H. [5], aus Fulginiae stammend. *Frater Arvalis* wohl seit 118 n. Chr.; praetorischer Legat von Arabia ca. 130 bis mindestens 133, vielleicht bis 135 [4. 23, 25, 26]. *Cos. suff.* 134; konsularer Statthalter von Pannonia superior ca. 137–140. Letzter bekannter Senator, der die *ornamenta triumphalia* erhielt, vermutlich am Ende seiner Statthalterschaft in Arabien im Kampf mit den aufständischen Juden unter Bar Kochba.

CIL XI 5212 = ILS 1058 • W. ECK, in: Chiron 13, 1983, 167 ff., 182 ff. • PIR² H 30.

[7] Ti. H. Saturninus. Praetor. Statthalter von Pannonia inferior ca. 161–164 n. Chr. (THOMASSON Lat. I 113); *cos. suff.* 164 (CIL XVI 185; RMD I 64). PIR² H 32.

1 NASH 2 G. BASTIANINI, in: ZPE 17, 1975 3 R. SABLAYROLLES, Libertinus miles, 1996 4 N. LEWIS (Hrsg.), The Documents from the Bar Kokhba Period in the Cave of Letters, 1989, Nr. 23, 25, 26.

W.E.

Ḥatra

[1] Handelszentrum in Nordmesopot., Mitte 1. Jh. n. Chr. gegründet. Mitte 2. Jh. Ausbau zur befestigten Rundstadt (ca. 2 km Dm). H. war ein bed. Heiligtum des Sonnengottes → Šamaš und ab ca. 166 Hauptstadt eines »Königreichs der Araber«, gleichzeitig arsakidische Grenzprovinz. Die Stadt wurde vergeblich belagert von Traian (116 n. Chr.) und Septimius Severus (196 und 198). Nach Ende der Arsakiden-Dyn. war sie kurzzeitig mit Rom gegen die Sāsāniden verbündet, wurde aber 240/241 n. Chr. erobert, danach aufgegeben.

H. J. DRIJVERS, H., Palmyra und Edessa, in: ANRW II 8, 799–906 • S. R. HAUSER, H. und das Königreich der Araber, in: J. WIESEHÖFER (Hrsg.), Das Partherreich und seine Zeugnisse (Historia Einzelschriften 122), 1998, 493–528.

S.HA.

[2] Die Sprache von Ḥ. gehört zur östl. Dialektgruppe des → Aramäischen und ist durch einige hundert Inschr. (1. – 3. Jh. n. Chr.) überliefert. Sprache und Schriftduktus ähneln dem der gleichzeitigen Inschr. aus → Assur und finden sich auch an anderen Orten zw. Euphrat, Tigris und Ḫābūr (Ǧadala, aṣ-Ṣaʿadiya, Takrīt, → Dura-Europos, Tall Šaiḫ Ḥamad). Aus den überwiegend kurzen, selten datierten Gedenk-, Votiv- und Grabinschr. sowie Graffiti läßt sich das Stadtpantheon mit → Šamaš, der Triade Maran, Martan und Barmaren, sowie Bēl (→ Baal) und Nišar rekonstruieren. Das Onomastikon ist neben vielen arabischen und einigen iranischen PN überwiegend aramäisch.

→ Palmyrenisch

S. ABBADI, Die PN der Inschr. aus Ḥ, 1983 • B. AGGOULA, Inventaire des Inscriptions Hatréennes, 1991 • R. BERTOLINO, La Cronologia di H., 1995 • F. VATTIONI, H., 1994.

C.K.

Hatti s. Ḫattusa

Hattisch. Das noch weitgehend enigmatische H. ist erst in Grundzügen seiner agglutinierenden, wohl nicht-ergativischen Sprachstruktur verständlich; erkannt sind u. a. die extreme Präfigierung des Verbums, eine stark reduzierte Kasusmorphologie des Nomens, die Unterscheidung zweier Genera (mask. und fem.), die Funktion versch. Partikeln. Der überwiegende Teil der Lexeme ist unbekannt, weshalb die einsprachigen Texte weitgehend dunkel bleiben. Unter den wenigen und zudem meist nur mangelhaft erhaltenen hatt.-hethit. → Bilinguen dominieren Mythologeme, die noch fester Bestandteil von Ritualen sind, sich also noch nicht verselbständigt haben. Die Hattier, urspr. in Zentralanatolien und nördl. bis zum Schwarzen Meer hin ansässig, waren in vielen Bereichen prägend für die sich im Laufe der 1. H. d. 2. Jt. herausbildende hethit. Kultur, so daß eine Reihe von Begriffen hatt. Ursprungs Eingang in das Hethit. fand; exemplarisch sei hier auf die Titel *tabarna*, *tawananna* und *tuhkanti* verwiesen, die der regierende hethit. König, seine Gattin sowie der designierte Thronfolger trugen.

Der überwiegende Teil der hatt. Texte dürfte dem kult.-rel. Bereich zuzuordnen sein, wofür auch die Rezitationen und Lieder innerhalb hethit.-sprachiger Ritualbeschreibungen sprechen. Schon im Laufe der hethit. Gesch. ging die Kenntnis des H. offenbar verloren, so daß sich die Texte in jüngeren Abschriften oft als fehlerhaft erweisen.

→ Anatolische Sprachen; Ḫattusa

J. Klinger, Untersuchungen zur Rekonstruktion der hattischen Kultschicht, 1996. J. KL.

Ḫattusa I. Stadt, archäologisch
II. Staat und Grossreich der Hethiter

I. Stadt, archäologisch

Hauptstadt der Hethiter in Zentralkleinasien bei Boğazkale (früher Boğazköy), Prov. Çorum, ca. 150 km östl. von Ankara/Türkei. Sporadisch seit dem Chalkolithikum (6. Jt. v. Chr.) besiedelt, war Ḫ. im 19./18. Jh. v. Chr. Standort einer assyr. Handelskolonie (*kārum*; → Kaneš) neben einer einheimischen hattischen Siedlung. Um 1700 v. Chr. wurde die Stadt zerstört; seit Ḫattusili I. (um 1600 v. Chr.) war sie Sitz der hethit. Könige und Reichshauptstadt. Unter Ḫattusili III. und seinen Söhnen Tudḫalija IV. und Suppiluliuma II. erfolgte eine Neugestaltung des Stadtbildes von Ḫ. und der Ausbau als zentraler Kultort: Neubau der Residenz auf Büyükkale, Errichtung des Großen Tempels, gleichzeitig Erweiterung der Stadt auf mehr als das Doppelte durch Einbeziehung der südl. Oberstadt; dort Anlage eines Tempelviertels (29 Tempelbauten identifiziert, vgl. Lageplan Sp. 187f.); Ausgestaltung des Felsheiligtums von → Yazılıkaya. Kurz nach 1200 v. Chr. wurde die Stadt erneut zerstört (Untergang des hethit. Großreichs). Ḫ. ist FO großer Archive von → Keilschrift-Tafeln.

Nach einem »Dunklen Zeitalter« läßt sich eine ausgedehnte phryg. Besiedlung vom 9. bis 5. Jh. v. Chr. nachweisen; vereinzelt sind ostgriech. und achäm. Einflüsse erkennbar. Die Identifizierung des Orts mit dem von Herodot (1,76; 79) gen. Pteria der Meder wird neuerdings in Frage gestellt zugunsten des rund 60 km sö gelegenen Kerkenes Dağı. Siedlungsspuren stammen aus der galatisch-hell. Zeit und der röm. Kaiserzeit, v. a. im Gebiet der ehemaligen hethit. Altstadt. Eine erneute Befestigung von Büyükkale (2 km östl. der röm. Straße Tavium – Amaseia) ist festzustellen. Aus früh- und mittelbyz. Zeit fanden sich bäuerliche Anwesen und Kirchen- und Klosteranlagen. Auf die nachfolgende Siedlungslücke folgte Ende des 17. Jh. die Ansiedlung einer Turkmenengruppe der Dulkadiroğlu.

K. Bittel, Ḫ., Hauptstadt der Hethiter, 1983 • P. Neve, Ḫ., Stadt der Götter und Tempel, [2]1996 • Ders., Die Ausgrabungen in Boğazköy/Ḫattuša 1993, in: AA 1994, 290 Abb. 1 (Stadtplan). J. SE.

II. Staat und Grossreich der Hethiter
A. Einleitung B. Grundzüge der politischen Geschichte C. Staatsverfassung D. Staat und Religion

A. Einleitung

Ḫattusa (nach der gleichnamigen Hauptstadt) bzw. vollständiger »Land Ḫ.« (*Ḫattusas utnē*; akkadograph. KUR [URU]*ḪATTI* [1. 96[1]]) ist seit dem 16. Jh. v. Chr. die hethit. Benennung des sich bereits E. des 18. Jh. in Zentralkleinasien formierenden Staates der Hethiter wie auch des vom 14. Jh. bis kurz nach 1200 bestehenden, letztlich fast ganz Kleinasien, Nord-Syrien sowie einen Teil Nord-Mesopot. umfassenden hethit. Großreiches, das sich als bundesgenössisch organisierter Staatenstaat (hethit. Kernstaat und vertraglich gebundene Vasallenstaaten) darstellt.

Die in der Sekundärlit. häufig noch anzutreffende Benennung »Ḫatti« beruht auf der in hethit. Texten als Logogramm für *Ḫattusa-* dienenden akkad. Namensform *Ḫatti*. Diese fand allerdings in alle nichtanatolischen Sprachen des Alten Orients Eingang und wurde nach dem Zusammenbruch des hethit. Reiches auch als zusammenfassende Bezeichnung für die (luw.-sprachigen) hethitischen Nachfolgestaaten Kleinasiens und Nord-Syriens des 1. Jt. v. Chr. verwendet, die selbst den Namen *Ḫatti* nie benutzt haben [2]. Entsprechend beziehen sich neuassyr. *Ḫattû/Ḫattaja*, hebr. *Ḥittîm* »Hethiter« auf die Bewohner dieser Nachfolgestaaten, während hethit. *Ḫattusumen-* »Hethiter« für die Mitglieder der staats-/reichstragenden königlichen Sippe (kö. Si.) steht, der im 14./13. Jh. auch Vasallenkönige angehörten. Die hethit. Staatsangehörigkeit wird durch »Mann/Leute/Prinz (u. ä.) des Landes Ḫ.« bezeichnet.

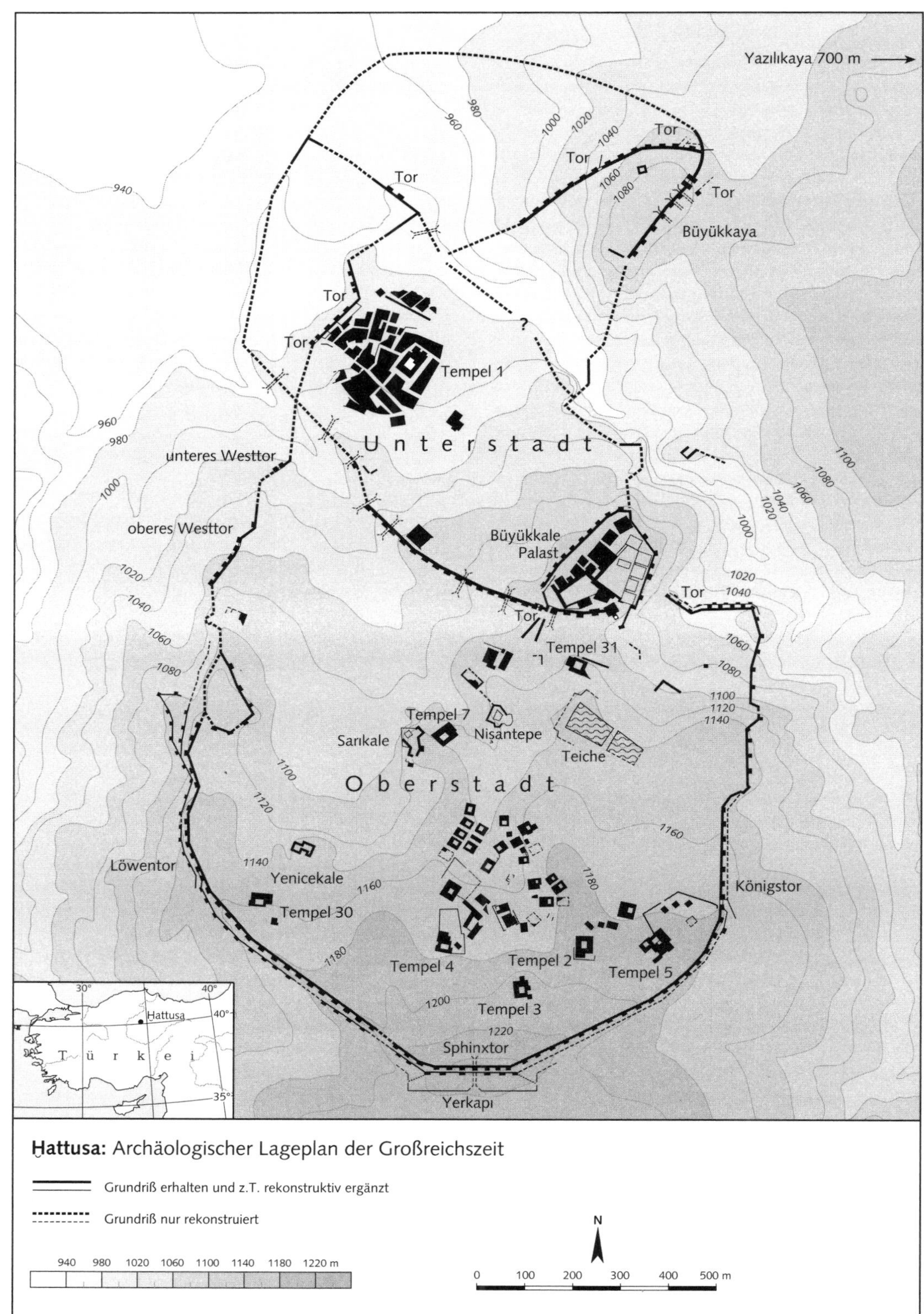

Ḫattusa: Archäologischer Lageplan der Großreichszeit

B. Grundzüge der politischen Geschichte

1. Vorgeschichte und Anfänge des hethitischen Staates (3. Jt. – 18. Jh.)

Von den schon im 3. Jt. in Kleinasien ansässigen idg.-anatolischen Sprachträgern (→ anatol. Sprachen) hatten sich die Hethiter innerhalb des Halys-Bogens niedergelassen, wo sie auf eine autochthone Bevölkerung trafen, deren eigene Sprache (→ Hattisch) allerdings spätestens im 18.–16. Jh. durch das → Hethitische verdrängt wurde.

Als die Assyrer zu Anf. des 2. Jt. ihre Handelsniederlassungen mit dem Zentrum Kaneš (hethit. *Nēsa-*) in Kleinasien errichteten, war dieses Gebiet polit. in rivalisierende Kleinkönigtümer aufgesplittert. Ende des 18. Jh. gelang es jedoch dem (auch in altassyr. Texten bezeugten) König Anitta (dessen Vater Pitḫāna, König von Kussara, Nēsa erobert und zu seiner Residenz gemacht hatte) nach eigenem, in einer Abschrift des 16. Jh. überlieferten Bericht [3], von Nēsa aus durch Niederringung insbes. der bedeutenden Königtümer Zalpa, Ḫ. und Purusḫanda das Großkönigtum zu gewinnen und somit einen zentralanatolischen, von der Schwarzmeer- bis zur Mittelmeerküste reichenden Territorialstaat zu bilden (vgl. dazu [4. § 1–4], wo mit dem vermeintlichen PN Labarna [5. 111] als Staatsgründer eigentlich nur Anitta gemeint sein kann). Für diesen Staat war bereits die spezifisch hethit. Herrschaftsorganisation, bei der König und kö. Si. gleichermaßen polit. Verantwortung tragen, kennzeichnend [6. 81–83, 114]. Er dürfte ungeachtet des nach Anitta einsetzenden Überlieferungshiats von ca. 130 J. im wesentl. bis ins 16. Jh. fortbestanden haben.

2. Ḫattusa im 16.–14. Jh.

Ḫattusili I. (ca. 1565–1540), unter dem nunmehr der Ort Ḫ. als Hauptstadt bezeugt ist und die hethit. Überlieferung einsetzt, stammte, obgleich wohl nicht direkter Nachkomme Anittas, nach seiner Selbstbezeichnung als »Kussaräer« und als »Neffe der *taṷannanna-* (regierenden Königin)« gewiß aus dem engeren Kreis der alten kö. Si. Unter ihm wurde die hethit. Expansionspolitik wiederaufgenommen, die sich jetzt gegen West-Kleinasien (→ Arzawa) sowie insbes., zur Gewinnung der Vormachtstellung in Syrien, gegen das Großkönigtum Ḫalpa (→ Aleppo) richtete und unter Mursili I. in der Eroberung Ḫalpas und schließlich sogar Babylons (1531 [mittlere Chronologie: 1595]; E. der Ḫammurapi-Dyn.) gipfelte.

Ein – nach ersten Spannungen in der kö. Si. schon z.Z. Ḫattusilis I. – mit der Ermordung Mursilis I. offen ausbrechender, bis ca. 1500 andauernder blutiger innerdynastischer Machtkampf führte indes nicht nur zum alsbaldigen Verlust aller eroberten Gebiete, wodurch → Mittani (hethit. *Mittanna-*) der Weg zur Vormachtstellung in Nord-Syrien bereitet wurde, sondern begünstigte auch den Einfall der → Kaskäer (z.Z. Ḫantilis I.) in die pontische Region, woraus dem hethit. Kerngebiet und der Hauptstadt eine bis ins 13. Jh. fortdauernde Bedrohung erwuchs.

Das E. dieses innen- wie außenpolit. Niedergangs markiert die unter Telibinu (ab ca. 1500) fixierte, an die alten polit. Grundwerte der kö. Si. (Loyalität, Einigkeit, Verantwortungsbewußtsein) anknüpfende formelle Verfassung [4], die u.a. Thronfolge sowie Kompetenzen von König und kö. Si. regelte und Ausgangspunkt zahlreicher, Administration, Kult- und Militärwesen betreffender gesetzgeberischer Maßnahmen (»Dienstanweisungen«/»Instruktionen«; bis in die Zeit Arnuwandas I., ca. 1400–1375) wurde. Außenpolit. kennzeichnen die seit Telibinu geschlossenen → Staatsverträge (zuerst mit → Kizzuwatna) den Wechsel von der bisherigen bloßen Eroberungs- und Inkorporations- zur fortan bestimmend werdenden Bundesgenossenpolitik – ein Gebot der Staatsklugheit, da die kö. Si. auch personell kaum in der Lage gewesen war, alle eroberten Gebiete selbst zu verwalten.

Unter Tudḫalija I. (ca. 1420–1400) wurde der Kampf mit Mittani um die Rückgewinnung der Vormachtstellung in Syrien aufgenommen (Feldzug nach → Isuwa, Zerstörung von Ḫalpa). Gleichzeitig trat durch das Erstarken Arzawas im 15. Jh. ganz West-Kleinasien in das Blickfeld hethit. Politik (Feldzüge bis nach Āssuwa/Mysien) [7; 8. 455–456]; doch zwang die Zuspitzung der Kaskäer-Gefahr z.Z. Arnuwandas I. und bes. Tudḫalijas II. (ca. 1375–1355, Plünderung der Stadt Ḫ.) dazu, die Kräfte zunächst vor allem auf die Sicherung des Kerngebietes zu konzentrieren [9; 10].

3. Das Grossreich Ḫattusa (14.–13. Jh.)

Der Aufstieg Ḫ. zum Großreich und zur dritten Großmacht Vorderasiens neben Äg. und Babylonien erfolgte unter Suppiluliuma I. (ca.1355–1320), dem es, durch Thronstreitigkeiten in Mittani und durch die außenpolit. Untätigkeit Äg. (Amenophis III./IV.) in Syrien begünstigt, in einem einzigen Feldzug gelang, zuerst Isuwa, dann alle von Mittani kontrollierten Kleinstaaten zwischen Euphratbogen und Mittelmeer (u.a. → Alalaḫ (hethit. *Alalḫa-*), → Ugarit (hethit. *Ugaritta-*), Nuḫašše (hethit. *Nuḫassa-*) sowie im äg. Hoheitsbereich insbes. → Amurru (hethit. *Amurra-*) zu erobern bzw. kampflos auf seine Seite zu ziehen. Wie zuvor schon Azzi-Ḫajasa in NO-Kleinasien konnte er diese Kleinstaaten und letztlich auch den polit. zusammengebrochenen Kernstaat Mittani selbst als (im Innern selbständige) Vasallenstaaten vertraglich an Ḫ. binden. Zur Festigung dieses Systems indirekter Herrschaft wurden ferner die Sekundogenituren Ḫalpa und – als polit. Zentrum für alle syr. Angelegenheiten weit bedeutender – Karkamis (hethit. *Karkamissa-*; → Karkemiš) eingerichtet.

Durch die Zerschlagung Arzawas, das seit Anf. des 14. Jh. infolge mehrerer Vorstöße ins »Untere Land« (*Katteran utnē*) eine ernste Bedrohung Ḫ. dargestellt hatte, sowie durch die Bildung der arzawischen Vasallenstaaten → Mirā (Kerngebiet Arzawas mit der Hauptstadt Abasa/Ephesos), Ḫaballa und Sēḫa konnte dann Mursili II. (ca. 1318–1290) das Reichsgebiet bis zur ägäischen Küste (einschließlich Lazba/Lesbos und anderer vorge-

Übersicht zu den hethitischen Königen und Königinnen

Daten	Könige	Königinnen
E. 18. Jh.	a) Könige von Nēsa	
	Pitḫāna von Kussara	
	Anitta [Sohn Pitḫānas], Großkönig	
	(Nach Anitta Überlieferungslücke von ca. 130 Jahren)	
	b) Großkönige von Ḫattusa	
ca. 1565–1540	1. Ḫattusili I. [»Kussaräer«, »Neffe der *tau̯annanna*«]	Kaddusi
ca. 1540–1530	2. Mursili I. [Sohn von 1.]	Kali
nach ca. 1530	3. Ḫantili I. [Schwager von 2.]	Ḫarapsegi
	4. Zidanta I. [Schwiegersohn von 3.]	?
	5. Ammuna [Sohn von 4.]	?
	6. Ḫuzzija I. [verwandtschaftliche Stellung unklar]	?
nach ca. 1500	7. Telibinu [Sohn von 5.?, Schwager von 6.]	Istabarija
	8. Taḫurwaili [Position 8. unsicher, verwandtschaftliche Stellung unklar]	
	9. Alluwamna [Schwiegersohn von 7.]	Ḫarapsili
	10. Ḫantili II. [wahrscheinlich Sohn von 9.]	?
	11. Zidanta II. [wahrscheinlich Sohn von 10.]	Ijaja
	12. Ḫuzzija II. [wahrscheinlich Sohn von 11.]	Summiri
		Katteshabi
	13. Muwattalli I. [Sohn/Bruder von 12?]	Katteshabi?
ca. 1420–1400	14. Tudḫalija I. [Sohn von 12.]	Nigalmadi
ca. 1400–1375	15. Arnuwanda I. [Schwieger- und Adoptivsohn von 14.]	Asmunigal
ca. 1375–1355	16. Tudḫalija II. [Sohn von 15.]	Taduḫeba
ca. 1355–1320	17. Suppiluliuma I. [Sohn von 16.]	Taduḫeba
		Ḫenti
		Malnigal
ca. 1320–1318	18. Arnuwanda II. [Sohn von 17.]	Malnigal
ca. 1318–1290	19. Mursili II. [Sohn von 17.]	Malnigal
		Gassulawija
		Tanuḫeba
ca. 1290–1272	20. Muwattalli II. [Sohn von 19.]	Tanuḫeba
ca. 1272–1265	21. Mursili III. – Urḫitesub [Sohn von 20.] (noch 1245 im äg. Exil bezeugt)	Tanuḫeba
ca. 1265–1240	22. Ḫattusili II. (= bisher »III.« !) [Sohn von 19.]	Puduḫeba
ca. 1240–1215	23. Tudḫalija III. (= bisher »IV.« !) [Sohn von 22.]	Puduḫeba
ca. 1220–?	24. Kurunta von Tarḫuntassa [Sohn von 20.]	?
nach ca. 1215	25. Arnuwanda III. [Sohn von 23.]	?
	26. Suppiluliuma II. [Sohn von 23.]	?
	Die ersten Könige der aus dem hethit. Reich hervorgehenden Großkönigtümer	
um 1200	a. *Sekundogenitur Karkamis:* Kuzitesub [Ururenkel von 17.], Großkönig	
	b. *Sekundogenitur Tarḫuntassa:* Ḫartapu [Sohn Mursilis = wahrscheinlich 21.], Großkönig	
	c. *Vasallenstaat Mirā:* Masḫuitta [Ururenkel Masḫuiluwas von Arzawa/Mirā und der Tochter von 17.], Großkönig	

lagerter Inseln) ausdehnen. So befand sich, nachdem z.Z. Muwattallis II. auch Wilusa (Troas) den arzawischen Vasallenstaaten angeschlossen war, im 13. Jh. – abgesehen von Māsa, → Lukkā und das seit dem 14. Jh. zu → Achijawa (Griechenland) gehörige Millawa(n)da (→ Miletos) – ganz West-Kleinasien in hethit. Hand [8. 450–455]. Unter Muwattalli II. wurde die schon von Suppiluliuma I. und bes. von Mursili II. betriebene Rückeroberung des Kaskäer-Gebietes zwischen Plā und »Oberem Land« (*Srazzi utnē*) wohl weitgehend vollendet (Rückgewinnung der Kultstadt Nerikka), in Syrien die Expansionspolitik Ramses II. (vorübergehender Abfall Amurrus zu Äg.) in der Schlacht von → Qadesch (Kadeš; heth. *Kinza-*) im J. 1275 erfolgreich gestoppt.

Innenpolit. evozierten allerdings die einseitig (bis hin zur Abtretung von Hoheitsrechten) geförderte Karriere von Muwattallis Bruder Ḫattusili sowie umstrittene Entscheidungen (wie die zeitweilige Verlegung der

Hauptstadt nach Tarḫuntassa) erste Spannungen und Parteiungen innerhalb der kö. Si. [11], die unter Mursili III.-Urḫitesub zur Thronusurpation Ḫattusilis II. (»III.«) führten (Flucht Urḫitesubs ins äg. Exil). Doch konnte die drohende Spaltung der kö. Si. zunächst abgewendet werden durch die Schaffung der Sekundogenitur Tarḫuntassa für Kurunta (den zweiten, von Ḫattusili II. adoptierten Sohn Muwattallis II., der nach Urḫitesub eigentlicher Anspruchsberechtigter auf den hethit. Thron war) sowie durch den Friedensvertrag mit Ramses II. (1259; Anerkennung der Dyn.-Linie Ḫattusilis II. [12. § 10]), der eine fortan enge äg.-hethit. Freundschaft (dynast. Verbindung 1246) begründete [13]. Den guten Beziehungen zu Äg. (und Babylonien) z.Z. Ḫattusilis II. stand indes ein sich zunehmend verschlechterndes Verhältnis zu den in Richtung Nord-Mesopot. (Mittani, assyr. Ḫanigalbat) und Euphrat expandierenden Assyrern (Salmanassar I.) gegenüber. Im Westen führten die gegen Mirā und Sēḫa gerichteten polit.-mil. Aktionen des von Millawanda aus operierenden arzawischen Prinzen Pijamaradu [8. 453–454] zum diplomat. Notenwechsel mit Achijawa (Tawaglawa-Brief) sowie zu Feldzügen nach Lukkā und Millawanda.

Für Tudḫalija III. (»IV.«, ca. 1240–1215; vgl. die biograph. Skizze [14]), der unter Zurücksetzung eines »älteren Bruders« (wohl Kurunta) zur Thronfolge bestimmt worden war, stellte sich beim Regierungsantritt verschärft das Problem der Spaltung der kö. Si. Indes konnten Konzessionen an die Sekundogenitur Tarḫuntassa (bes. protokollarische Gleichstellung Kuruntas mit dem König von Karkamis als Drittem im Reich nach Großkönig und Kronprinz) [15] und nachdrückliche Appelle an Loyalität und Geschlossenheit der kö. Si. einen zumindest vorübergehend erfolgreichen Staatsstreich Kuruntas nicht verhindern [16. 62]. Zusätzliche Belastungen erwuchsen dem Reich u.a. aus der mil. Konfrontation mit Assyrien (Tukulti-Ninurta I.; hethit. Niederlage bei Niḫirija).

4. Der Zusammenbruch des Grossreichs und seine Nachfolge

Nach nur kurzer Regierung Arnuwandas III. (nach 1215) wurde Suppiluliuma II. unter dem Vorzeichen größter innenpolit. Nervosität letzter hethit. Großkönig. Abgesehen von Feldzügen nach Māsa und Lukkā (in Verbindung mit einer Seeschlacht bei → Alaschia, hethit. *Alasija-*) weist ein mil. Unternehmen gegen Tarḫuntassa auf den ausgebrochenen »Bürgerkrieg« [16. 57–65]. Auch wenn der endgültige Zusammenbruch des Reiches noch nicht in allen Einzelheiten klar ist, steht h. fest, daß er nicht durch hereinbrechende → Seevölker, sondern von innen her erfolgte und daß Anf. des 12. Jh. im Osten und Süden die Sekundogenituren Karkamis bzw. Tarḫuntassa als Großkönigtümer das Erbe unmittelbar antraten [16. 64; 17]. Überdies scheint im Westen der bedeutendste arzawische Vasallenstaat, Mirā, noch z.Z. Suppiluliumas II. das Großkönigtum erlangt zu haben [18]. Diese neuen Großkönigtümer bildeten zugleich die Voraussetzung für eine h. den Begriff »Dunkle Jahrhunderte« für Kleinasien relativierende histor. Kontinuität bis ins 8./7. Jh., die im Süden und SO Kleinasiens (einschl. Nord-Syriens) direkt zu verfolgen ist und im Westen wohl ansatzweise greifbar wird (→ Kleinasien).

C. Staatsverfassung

Seit seinen Anfängen verstand sich der hethit. Staat, dessen Verfassung wohl am ehesten als aristokratisch mit monarchischer Spitze charakterisiert werden kann, als eine polit. Körperschaft (*ḫassuu̯as tuu̯ekka-*, »Körper des Königs«, d.h. der öffentliche bzw. Staatskörper) mit dem König als Haupt und den Angehörigen der (im 14./13. Jh. weit verzweigten) kö. Si., den »Herren«, als deren maßgebenden Gliedern (zur personellen Zusammensetzung im 13. Jh. [19]). Der kö. Si. oblag die ethische Verpflichtung, das Land Ḫ., das dem Wettergott gehörte und dem König zur Verwaltung anvertraut war, zu erhalten, zu erweitern und seinen Wohlstand zu mehren.

Die kö. Si., der man durch Geburt oder (z.B. im Falle der Vasallenkönige) durch Einheirat angehörte, bildete als polit. Organ den *bangu-* (»Gemeinschaft [des Staates/Reiches]«), den der König in allen grundlegenden polit. Fragen zur »Versammlung« (*tulii̯a-*) einberief. Der innere Kreis der kö. Si., die Angehörigen der Königsfamilie (»Prinzen«), auch soweit sie aus den Sekundogenituren stammten, stellte die »Großen« (im 13. Jh.: »Vorrangigen«), die Inhaber der höchsten Hofämter (»Großer der Leibgardisten/Schreiber/Mundschenke« etc.), die als Berater und ausführende Organe (Gesandte, Heereskommandeure) gemeinsam mit dem König die Regierung bildeten [20]. Prinzen verwalteten auch als »Landesherren« (*utnii̯asḫes*) die »inneren (inkorporierten) Länder« des Kernstaates (»auswärtige Länder« = Vasallenstaaten).

Der König mußte sich, auch wenn er im rechtlichen Sinne regierte, bei seinen Entscheidungen weitgehend der Zustimmung der kö. Si. versichern, von deren Mitgliedern wiederum loyales Verhalten gegenüber dem König und dem Land Ḫ. erwartet wurde (Treueide). Pragmatismus, Betonung der Verantwortung jedes einzelnen für Staat bzw. Reich, argumentative Auseinandersetzung mit dem Standpunkt der Gegenseite und Überzeugungskraft waren daher wesentliche Elemente polit. Denkens und Handelns, die bes. in → Geschichtsschreibung und Staatsverträgen der Hethiter sichtbar werden. Das Königtum war erblich, doch konnte bei fehlender männl. Nachkommenschaft ersten und (von einer Nebenfrau) zweiten Ranges die Dyn.-Linie auch über den (adoptierten) Ehemann einer erstrangigen Prinzessin (z.B. Arnuwanda I.) fortgesetzt werden; der vom König bestimmte Thronfolger bedurfte der Anerkennung durch den *bangu-*, der dann seinerseits einen Treueid auf den desiginierten Thronfolger leistete [21].

Neben dem Königtum stand ein institutionalisiertes, auf Lebenszeit verliehenes Königinnentum, das die Hauptgemahlin des Königs, zunächst Kronprinzessin, erst beim Tod der Vorgängerin übernahm. Die Königin

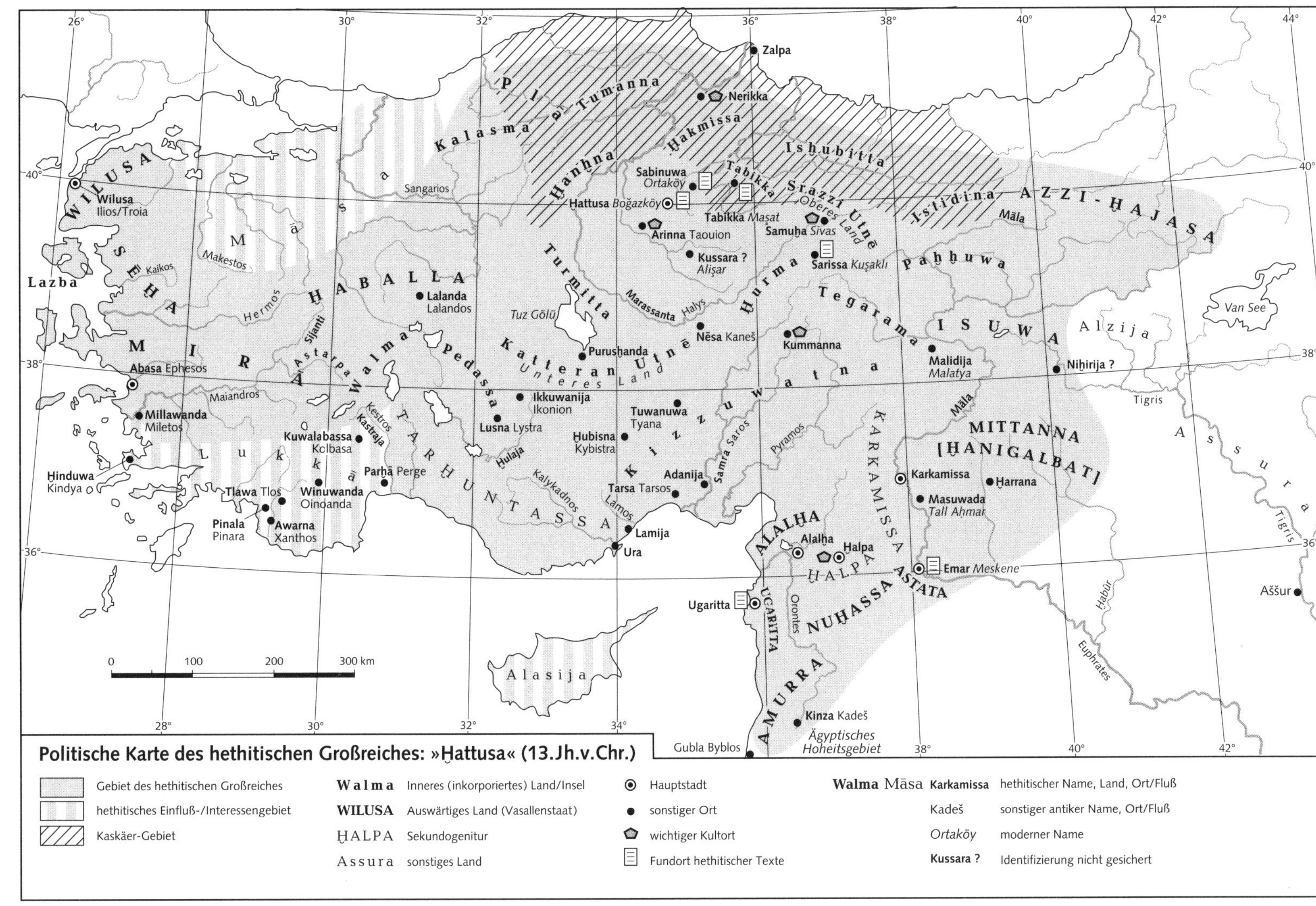
Zalpa
Nerikka
Kalasma
Pala
Tumanna
Ḫakmissa
Ḫanḫana
Isḫupitta
Sabinuwa Ortaköy
Tabikka Maşat
Ḫattusa Boğazköy
Arinna Taouion
Samuḫa Sivas
Srazzi Utnē
Oberes Land
Istitina
AZZI-ḪAJASA
Māla
Kussara ? Alişar
Sarissa Kuşaklı
Paḫḫuwa
WILUSA
Wilusa Ilios/Troia
Lazba
SEḪA
Kaikos
Makestos
Māsa
Sangarios
ḪABALLA
Lalanda Lalandos
Hermos
Turmitta
Tuz Gölü
Marassanta
Halys
Ḫurma
Tegarama
Nēsa Kaneš
Kummanna
ISUWA
Alzija
Van See
MIRĀ
Abasa Ephesos
Sijanti
Astarpa
Walma
Pedassa
Katteran Utnē
Unteres Land
Purusḫanda
Malidija Malatya
Niḫirija ?
Tigris
Maiandros
Millawanda Miletos
Ikkuwanija Ikonion
Lusna Lystra
Tuwanuwa Tyana
Kizzuwatna
Ḫubisna Kybistra
Kestros
Kastraja
Kuwalabassa Kolbasa
Lukkā
TARḪUNTASSA
Ḫulaja
Kalykadnos
Samra Saros
Pyramos
Ḫinduwa Kindya
Tlawa Tlos
Winuwanda Oinoanda
Parḫā Perge
Pinala Pinara
Awarna Xanthos
Tarsa Tarsos
Adanija
Lamos
Lamija
Ura
MITTANNA
[ḪANIGALBAT]
Karkamissa
Ḫarrana
Masuwada Tall Aḥmar
KARKAMISSA
Assura
ALALḪA
Alalḫa
Halpa
ḪALPA
Emar Meskene
ASTATA
Ugaritta
UGARITTA
Orontes
NUḪASSA
Ḫabur
Euphrates
Aššur
Alasija
AMURRA
Kinza Kadeš
Ägyptisches Hoheitsgebiet
Gubla Byblos
0 100 200 300 km
Politische Karte des hethitischen Großreiches: »Ḫattusa« (13.Jh.v.Chr.)
Gebiet des hethitischen Großreiches
hethitisches Einfluß-/Interessengebiet
Kaskäer-Gebiet
Walma Inneres (inkorporiertes) Land/Insel
WILUSA Auswärtiges Land (Vasallenstaat)
ḪALPA Sekundogenitur
Assura sonstiges Land
Hauptstadt
sonstiger Ort
wichtiger Kultort
Fundort hethitischer Texte
Walma Māsa Karkamissa hethitischer Name, Land, Ort/Fluß
Kadeš sonstiger antiker Name, Ort/Fluß
Ortaköy moderner Name
Kussara ? Identifizierung nicht gesichert

wirkte aktiv am polit. Leben mit, wie dies bes. für Puduḫeba, die Gemahlin Ḫattusilis II. (»III.«), bezeugt ist [22].

D. Staat und Religion

Die in der ethischen Verantwortung gegenüber den Göttern, bes. → Wettergott und Sonnengöttin, begründete Interdependenz von Staat und Religion, die u. a. in den zumeist königlichen Gebeten (ab 15. Jh.) als Ort polit. Reflexion greifbar wird [23], fand ihren wichtigsten öffentlichen Ausdruck in den im Jahresverlauf an verschiedenen Kultorten abgehaltenen, oft mehrtägigen und von einer komplexen Liturgie (Opfer, Kultmahl, Rezitation, Musik, Gesang, Tanz, szenischen Darbietungen) begleiteten Festen. Hier nahmen König und Königin als oberste Priester sowie die Mitglieder der kö. Si., zumal als Träger von Hofämtern, ihre bis ins Detail festgelegten kult. Funktionen wahr. Der Staatskult, in den auch die Götter eroberter Gebiete aufgenommen wurden, stand anfänglich unter hattischem, im 15.–13. Jh. zunehmend unter hurrit. Einfluß (→ Hurriter, → Yazılıkaya). Der Wille der Götter in polit. und mil. Fragen wurde mit verschiedenen Orakeltechniken ermittelt (→ Divination). Die staatliche Tätigkeit im zivilen und mil. Bereich erforderte, um mit dem Willen der Götter im Einklang zu stehen, die Durchführung zahlreicher, zumeist kathartischer Rituale (zu den mil. Ritualen s. [24]). Diese dienten auch der Abwehr von Zauberei, die ungeachtet des Verbots in der Telibinu-Verfassung [4. § 50] eine in der innenpolit. Auseinandersetzung bes. von weiblichen Mitgliedern der kö. Si. oft eingesetzte Waffe war [25] (→ Magie).

Auf einer im Alten Orient einzigartigen Unterscheidung zwischen dem König als natürlicher Person (*body natural*) und als Repräsentant des Königtums, der nie stirbt, sondern ›Gott wird‹ (*body politic*), beruht das königliche (auch für Königinnen durchgeführte) Totenritual, bei dem der *body natural* sofort verbrannt und der anschließende 13tägige *rite de passage* an einer Figur des/der Verstorbenen vollzogen wurde, ebenso die vergleichsweise bescheidene Bestattung des *body natural* einerseits sowie die kult. Verehrung des unsterblichen *body politic* andererseits, dem im 13. Jh. ferner ein Memorial (*ḫēgur*, zu seiner polit. Bedeutung [26. 27–35]) errichtet wurde [20. 174[145], 181[164]; 27]; s. auch → Totenkult.

→ Hethitisches Recht; Kleinasien; Literatur (Hethiter); Siegel; Hethitologie

1 A. Goetze, Kleinasien, [2]1957 **2** J. D. Hawkins, s. v. Ḫatti, RLA 4, 152–159 **3** E. Neu, Der Anitta-Text, 1974
4 I. Hoffmann, Der Erlaß Telipinus, 1984 **5** F. Starke, Der Erlaß Telipinus, in: WO 16, 1985, 100–113 **6** Ders., Ḫalmašuit im Anitta-Text und die hethit. Ideologie vom Königtum, in: ZA 69, 1979, 47–120 **7** St. De Martino, L'Anatolia occidentale nel Medio Regno ittita (Eothen 5), 1996 **8** F. Starke, Troia im Kontext des histor.-polit. und sprachlichen Umfeldes Kleinasiens im 2. Jt., in: Studia Troica 7, 1997, 447–487 **9** S. Alp, Hethit. Briefe aus Maşat-Höyük, 1991 **10** J. Klinger, Das Corpus der Maşat-Briefe und seine Beziehungen zu den Texten aus Ḫattuša, in: ZA 85, 1995, 74–108 **11** Ph. Houwink Ten Cate, Urhi-Tessub revisited, in: Bibliotheca Orientalis 51, 1994, 234–260 **12** E. Edel, Der Vertrag zw. Ramses II. von Äg. und Hattusili III. von Hatti, 1997 **13** Ders., Die äg.-hethit. Korrespondenz aus Boghazköi, 1994
14 H. Klengel, Tutḫalija IV. von Ḫatti, in: Altoriental. Forsch. 18, 1991, 224–238 **15** H. Otten, Die Bronzetafel aus Boğazköy, Ein Staatsvertrag Tutḫalijas IV., 1988 **16** J. D. Hawkins, The Hieroglyphic Inscription of the Sacred Pool Complex at Hattusa, 1995 **17** D. Sürenhagen, Polit. Niedergang und kulturelles Nachleben des hethit. Großreiches, in: U. Magen, M. Rashad (Hrsg.), FS Th. Beran, 1996, 283–293 **18** J. D. Hawkins, Tarkasnawa King of Mira, »Tarkondemos«, Karabel, and Boğazköy Sealings, in: Anatolian Studies 48, 1998 (im Druck) **19** Th. van den Hout, Der Ulmitešub-Vertrag, 1995 **20** F. Starke, Zur »Regierung« des hethit. Staates, in: Zschr. für Altoriental. und Biblische Rechtsgesch. 2, 1996, 140–182
21 G. Beckman, Inheritance and Royal Succession Among the Hittites, in: H. A. Hoffner, G. M. Beckman (Hrsg.), FS H. G. Güterbock, 1986, 13–31 **22** H. Otten, Puduḫepa, 1975 **23** R. Lebrun, Hymnes et prières hittites, 1980
24 R. H. Beal, Hittite Military Rituals, in: M. Meyer, P. Mirecki (Hrsg.), Ancient Magic and Ritual Power, 1995, 63–92 **25** M. Hutter, Bemerkungen zur Verwendung mag. Rituale in mittelhethit. Zeit, in: Altoriental. Forsch. 18, 1991, 32–43 **26** H. Otten, Die 1986 in Boğazköy gefundene Bronzetafel, 1989 **27** Th. van den Hout, Death as a Privilege, The Hittite Royal Funerary Ritual, in: J. M. Bremer et al. (Hrsg.), Hidden Futures, 1994, 37–75.

R. H. Beal, The Organization of the Hittite Military, 1992 • T. Bryce, The Kingdom of the Hittites, 1998 • V. Haas, Gesch. der hethit. Rel., 1994 • E. v. Schuler, Die Kaškäer, 1965 • G. Walser (Hrsg.), Neuere Hethiterforsch., 1964.
Kartenliteratur: O. Gurney, Hittite Geography, in: H. Otten et al. (Hrsg.), FS S. Alp, 1992, 213–221 • F. Starke, Troia im Kontext des histor.-polit. und sprachlichen Umfeldes Kleinasiens im 2. Jt., in: Studia Troica 7, 1997, Abb. 1. • TAVO B III 6.

F. S.

Haus

I. Vorderer Orient und Ägypten
II. Griechenland, Etrurien, Rom

I. Vorderer Orient und Ägypten

Der Wohnhausgrundriß ist im Vorderen Orient üblicherweise in Rechteckbauweise und mehrzellig gestaltet. Wichtigstes Baumaterial sind in Mesopot. Lehmziegel; in Iran, Syrien und Kleinasien findet sich daneben eine stärkere Verwendung von Stein. Das typische babylon. Wohn-H. besteht aus Räumen um einen zentralen Hof. Es besitzt meist nur einen Eingang, der Hauptsaal liegt im Süden, der Mittagssonne abgewandt. Das neuassyr. Wohn-H. ist demgegenüber zweigeteilt in einen Vorhof mit Wirtschaftsräumen und einen inneren Hof mit Wohnquartieren, verbunden durch den Empfangsraum. Die H.-Größe und Ausstattung waren variabel. Auch Mehrgeschossigkeit kam vor, sie ist jedoch im Grabungsbefund schwer nachzuweisen. Da die gleichen Räume häufig für verschiedene Zwecke genutzt werden konnten, etwa im jahreszeitlichen Wech-

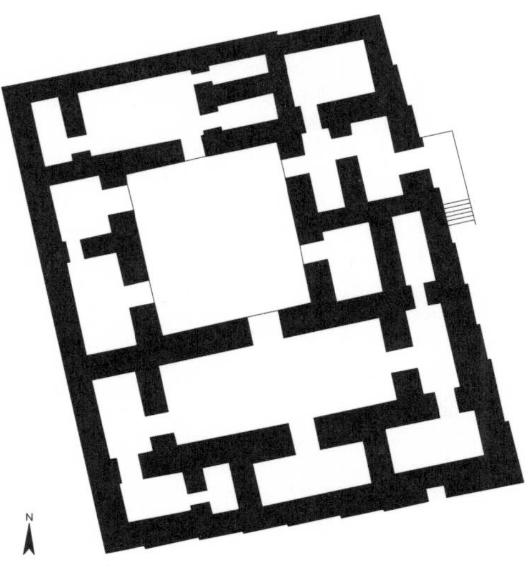

Babylon, spätbabylonisches Wohnhaus (Grundriß).

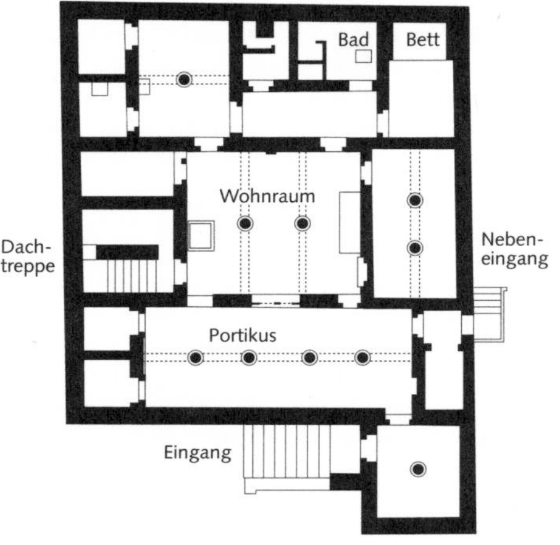

Amarna, Haus Q 46/1, 18. Dynastie (Grundriß).

sel, ist es vielfach nicht möglich, scharf umrissene Raumfunktionen zu benennen. Jüngere Unt. im Bereich der H.-Forschung zielen vermehrt darauf ab, Einblick in die soziale Organisation der H.-Bewohner (Familienstrukturen) und ggf. Statusunterschiede zu gewinnen.

Gängiger H.-Typ war auch in Äg. das mehrräumige Hofhaus aus Lehmziegeln. Bereits das gut ausgestattete Mittelklasse-H. setzte streng geschiedene Bereiche für Öffentlichkeitsverkehr, hausgemeinschaftliches Leben und Privatsphäre des H.-Besitzers und seiner Familie voraus. Bei reicheren H. des NR bestand ein zentrales Element in einem überdeckten Mittelraum bzw. einer Säulenhalle. Daran schlossen sich Privatquartiere mit Schlafzimmer, Bad und Toilette an. Neben freistehenden Land-H. mit offenen Küchenbereichen, Ställen und Gärten kennt man ebenfalls dicht gedrängte Stadt-H., die bisweilen mehrere Stockwerke besaßen. → Architektur; Bautechnik

D. Arnold, s. v. H., Lex. der ägypt. Baukunst, 1994, 99–102 • C. Castel, Habitat urbain néo-assyrien et néo-babylonien, 1992 • E. Heinrich, s. v. H. (B. Arch.), RLA 4, 1972–1975, 176–220 • Ders., Architektur von der alt- bis zur spätbabylon. Zeit, in: PropKg 14, 1975, 241–287 • M. Krafeld-Daugherty, Wohnen im Alten Orient (Altertumskunde des Vorderen Orients 3), 1994 • G. Leick, s. v. House, A Dictionary of Near Eastern Architecture, 1988, 95–100 • P. A. Miglus, Das Wohngebiet von Assur (WVDOG 93), 1996 • K. R. Veenhof (Hrsg.), Houses and Households in Ancient Mesopotamia, 1996. U.S.

II. Griechenland, Etrurien, Rom

A. Allgemeines B. Das griechische Haus
C. Frühitalische und etruskische Häuser
D. Römische Häuser

A. Allgemeines

In der griech., etr. und röm. Kultur ist das H. als Nutz- und Schutzarchitektur, als Repräsentationsobjekt und zugleich als Zentrum der hauswirtschaftlich geprägten Ökonomie der Mittelpunkt der → Familie, in der etr.-röm. Kultur auch Mittelpunkt rel. Handlungen (H.- und Schutzgottheiten). Hier schneiden sich die Sphären von → Privatheit und Öffentlichkeit, indem das H. zum einen den intimen Rückzugsort der weiblichen Mitglieder der Hausgemeinschaft bildet, zum anderen den Rahmen gesellschaftlicher und beruflicher (Rom) Verpflichtungen des Mannes. Spätestens die seit dem 6. Jh. v. Chr. entwickelten Bauformen ant. Häuser sowohl im griech. wie auch im etr.-röm. Kulturkreis zeigen diese Ambivalenz durch eine markante Kombination von Abschottung gegenüber der Außenwelt (etwa durch die Verlagerung der → Gynaikonitis in das für Fremde unzugängliche Obergeschoß) und der Anlage quasi-öffentlicher Repräsentationstrakte innerhalb des Hauses, z. B. das → Andron [4] für das Symposion (→ Gastmahl) oder das → Atrium als Raum für den Empfang der Klientel (→ *cliens*).

Jede Verbreiterung des Nutzungsspektrums manifestierte sich dabei unmittelbar in der Bauform, die für jeweils benötigte Funktionen eigene Trakte oder Räumlichkeiten ausprägte; schon an der Wende zum 1. Jt. v. Chr. wird das bis dahin vorherrschende universell genutzte Einraumhaus immer öfter durch spezialisierte Mehrraum-Architekturen ersetzt, die je nach Bedarf Wohn-, Wirtschafts-, Kult- und Repräsentationsbereiche voneinander trennten. Der bauliche Aufwand für das H. blieb bis in das späte 5. Jh. v. Chr. hinein grundsätzlich eher zweckgebunden und somit wenig repräsentativ (vorherrschend waren Architekturen aus Lehmziegeln, Bruchstein und Holz über einem Feldsteinsockel, was den insgesamt schlechten Erhaltungszustand und den damit unmittelbar verknüpften geringen mod. Kenntnisstand begründet, vgl. → Architektur). Dies änderte sich im Laufe des 4. Jh. v. Chr.: Der im Zuge der Entpolitisierung und des Zerfalls der griech. Polis-Ges. entstandene Rückzug der Bürger in den Privatbereich artikuliert sich in rapide wachsendem Bau-, Material- und Ausstattungsluxus der H.-Architekturen; typologisch sind dabei weder der hell. → Palast noch später die röm. → Villa als luxuriöse, herrschaftliche und repräsentative Wohnformen letztlich von den allg. Erscheinungsformen des H. zu trennen.

Innerhalb einzelner Siedlungen bildeten H. entweder untereinander baulich verbundene Raum-Agglomerationen (frühe Beispiele der nachmyk. bzw. der nachminoischen Zeit: Dreros und Karphi auf Kreta; Zagora auf Andros) oder formten als Ensemble eine mehr oder weniger dicht bebaute Streusiedlung (Antissa, Athen, Lefkandi, Alt-Smyrna, Nichoria); eine regelmäßige, größerflächige Hausbebauung in einem Zug entstand erst im Kontext der Gründung der griech. Koloniestädte im späten 8. und frühen 7. Jh. v. Chr., wie etwa in → Megara Hyblaea auf Sizilien (→ *insula*; → Städtebau) sowie bei großflächigen Stadtanlagen in Etrurien (→ Marzabotto, 6. Jh. v. Chr.). Inwieweit städtische Neuplanungen innerhalb des griech. Kulturraums mit normierten »Typenhäusern« (in Reihe gebauten H. mit immer gleichem, nur wenig variiertem Grund- und Aufriß) bebaut wurden, wird kontrovers beurteilt; ein arch. Nachweis wird regelmäßig durch den Umstand erschwert, daß in den Befunden niemals der Neubau-Zustand, sondern immer nur das im Laufe der Zeit entstandene Ergebnis mannigfacher baulicher Veränderungen faßbar wird. Zumindest für die Bebauung des Peiraieus hat es den Anschein, als seien die gleichgroßen Grundstücke innerhalb einer *insula* nicht durch zentral organisierte Einzelbebauung erschlossen worden, ähnlich den trotz gleichförmiger Landeinteilung recht individuell bebauten etr. und röm.-latinischen Städtegründungen (z. B. Cosa).

Nicht nur der Bau einer Siedlung, auch der Bau eines einzelnen H. setzt Rücksichtnahme auf geologische und geophysische Rahmenbedingungen voraus; Vitruvs (in Details von der Forsch. weiterhin diskutierte) Darstellung des griech. Privathauses im 6. B. von *De architectura* macht unabhängig von Details den Stellenwert einer Berücksichtigung klimatischer Verhältnisse, der Sonnenstände und Himmelsrichtungen, aber auch die Relevanz eines Einbezugs eventueller Probleme der Infrastruktur (→ Latrinen; → Kanal/Kanalisation; → Wasserversorgung) hinreichend deutlich (vgl. zur Ausnutzung der Sonnenenergie auch Xen. mem. 3,8).

B. Das griechische Haus

Auch wenn der Denkmälerbestand von Hausarchitekturen der geom. Zeit (10.–8. Jh. v. Chr.) durch neue Funde und Ausgrabungen (u. a. Lefkandi, Nichoria, Antissa/Lesbos, Zagora/Andros) in den vergangenen 20 Jahren erheblich vermehrt werden konnte, ist die Frage nach der Existenz und der Qualität einer baulich-typologischen Trad. zu den Architekturformen der myk.-minoischen Welt weiterhin in der Diskussion; allein das freistehende Herdhaus, wie es sich in einigen späten Exemplaren z. B. in Emporio/Chios (7. Jh. v. Chr.) gefunden hat, scheint mit Vorbehalt als bautypologisches Kontinuum faßbar (→ Megaron). Üblich sind in geom. Zeit langgestreckte H. mit Apsis (Athen, Thermos, Olympia) oder in ovaler, an beiden Schmalseiten gerundeter Form (Alt-Smyrna), die z. T. in mehrere Trakte untergliedert waren (Antissa; → Apsis mit Abb.) und eine Länge von 5 m (Alt-Smyrna) bis zu 14 m (Nichoria) aufweisen konnten; eine Ausnahme bildet hier allein der Toumba-Bau aus Lefkandi mit seiner Gesamtlänge von nahezu 45 m (vgl. → Tempel). Daneben finden sich Anten- und Rechteckhäuser, z. T. bereits mit mehrräumiger Binnengliederung (Thorikos, Asine, Athen, Tsikkalario), denen dabei die Axialität und Symmetrie der zeitgleichen ital.-etr. H. fehlt. Über die Gestalt dieser Bauten, von denen sich meist nur geringe Spuren der Fundamentierung sowie seit der Mitte des 7. Jh. v. Chr. vereinzelt Dachziegel erhalten haben, besteht weiterhin wenig Kenntnis; die zahlreich erh. Hausmodelle aus Ton erlauben insgesamt nur bedingt Rückschlüsse auf die aufgehenden Teile der real gebauten frühgriech. Architektur.

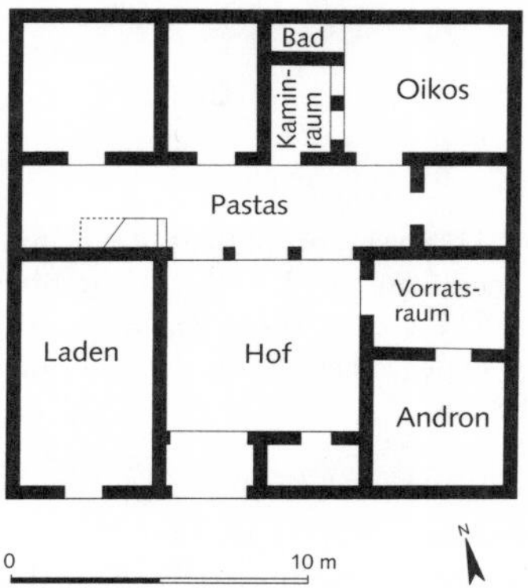

Olynthos, Pastas-Haus, 1. H. 4. Jh. v. Chr. (Grundriß).

Ab dem 7. Jh. v. Chr. wird der Hof zum prägenden Element der mehrgliedrigen griech. H., wobei sich im 6./5. Jh. v. Chr. zwei Grundtypen des H. herausbilden, das Pastas-Haus und das Prostas-Haus.

1. Das Pastas-Haus

Das Pastas-H. ist als annähernd quadratisches Konglomerat nach Süden, zur Mittagssonne hin orientiert und weist hier den meist zweigeschossigen Wohntrakt auf, der sich über eine quergelagerte, korridorähnliche, zum Hof hin offene Vorhalle (*pastás*) erschließt; → Andron [4], Xenon (Fremdenzimmer), Küche, Oikos (Wohnraum), → Bäder, → Thalamoi (Schlafräume) und Tameion (Raum für Wertsachen) sowie die Treppe zum Obergeschoß mit der → Gynaikonitis sind gleichermaßen über die Vorhalle zugänglich. Um den Hof herum gruppiert finden sich einstöckig erbaute Wirtschaftstrakte, Speicher, Werkstätten und zur Straße hin orientierte Läden. Der Haustyp findet sich in seiner

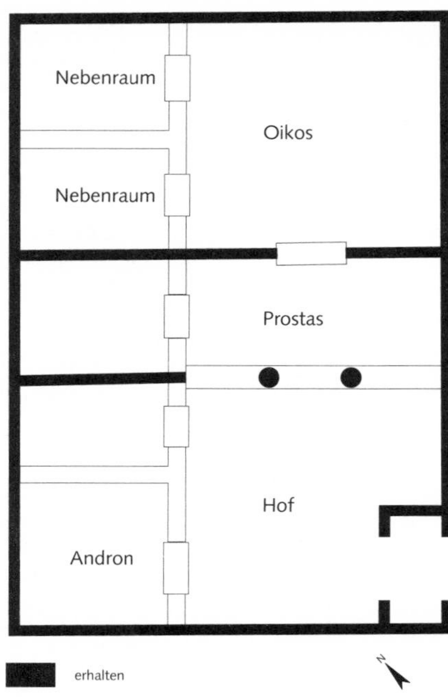

Peiraieus, Prostas-Haus, 1. H. 5. Jh. v. Chr. (Grundriß).

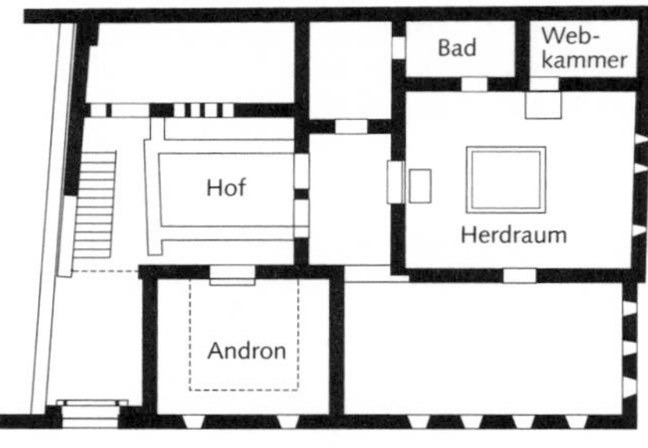

Erdgeschoß

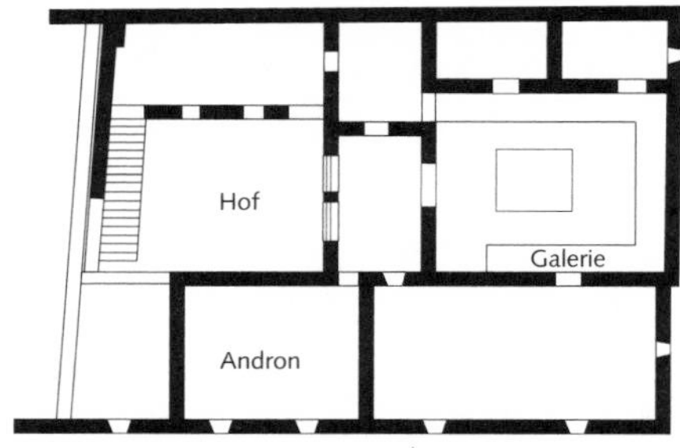

Obergeschoß

Orraon (Ammotopos), Haus 1, 4. Jh. v. Chr. (Erd- und Obergeschoß).

Frühform in Megara Hyblaea (dort ist die Entwicklung vom kolonialen Einraumhaus, 2. H. 8. Jh. v. Chr., über das Zweiraumhaus, 7. Jh. v. Chr., bis zu den archa. »Pastas-H.« faßbar), in »typenreiner« Form dann bei den frühen H. in → Olynthos.

2. Das Prostas-Haus

Das Prostas-H. wird überwiegend als eine Weiterentwicklung des Einraum-Megaron-H. verstanden; einen Beleg findet eine solche Ableitung vielleicht in den wohl ältere Bauten in ihrer Struktur tradierenden Prostas-H. von Kolophon (4. Jh. v. Chr.) sowie in einem megaron-ähnlichen ländlichen H. bei Ano Saphi/Böotien. Das als Raumkonglomerat langrechteckige Gebilde mit einem quer darin eingeschobenen Hof reduziert die Korridor-Halle des Pastas-H. auf einen nur auf den Oikos bezogenen, zum Hof hin offenen Vorraum; Andron und Vorraum verfügen über einen separaten, vom Hof aus zu erreichenden Zugang. Der zweistöckige Wohntrakt ist ebenfalls nach Süden orientiert; an die Gegenseite des Hofes grenzen, meist in Form separater Baukomplexe, einstöckige Wirtschaftsräume. Das Prostas-H. findet sich in »typenreiner« Form erstmals in der neukonzipierten Stadtanlage von Peiraieus (1. H. des 5. Jh. v. Chr.; → Hippodamos von Milet), danach in Priene, Abdera und zahlreichen weiteren Stadtanlagen des späteren 5. und 4. Jh. v. Chr.

3. Das Herdraum-Haus

Inwieweit das Herdraum-H. nordwestgriech. Prägung einen eigenen Typus oder aber eine weitere Variante des Megaron-Hauses repräsentiert, ist unsicher; die bis zum Dachansatz erh. Stein-H. von Orraon/Ammotopos nahe Ambrakia/Arta (und möglicherweise verschiedene mit diesen analoge Bauten in Kassope, jeweils 4. Jh. v. Chr.) zeigen einen von einem Korridor abzweigenden, über diesen Verteiler mit dem Hof verbundenen, jedoch zwei Geschosse hohen, lichten Oikos mit Herd im Zentrum und einer oberen Galerie mit Nebenräumen.

4. Das Peristyl-Haus

Eine Neuerung des frühen 4. Jh. v. Chr. und zugleich ein deutlicher Indikator veränderter Ansprüche an Hausbau, Ausstattung (→ Inkrustationen; → Mosaik; → Wandmalerei) und Wohnumfeld ist das Peristyl-H. Die Herkunft der Form ist umstritten; einerseits kann im Peristyl eine Umfunktionierung des urspr. dem Wirtschaftsbereich zugehörigen Hofs in eine Repräsentationsanlage mit innerer Säulenstellung gesehen werden (wie dies arch. gut dokumentierte Befunde in Olynth nahelegen, wo im Laufe des 4. Jh. v. Chr. zahlreiche Pastas-H. in Peristyl-H. umgebaut wurden); andererseits lassen sich als Vorläufer des Peristyl-H. verschiedene Bankett-H. in Heiligtümern (Argos, Troizen) oder andere Festarchitekturen wie das Pompeion am Kerameikos in Athen anführen, deren innere Säulenstellung kaum derart erklärt werden kann. Von diesem Peristyl zweigen die verschiedenen Raumgruppen des H. ab. Frühe Beispiele sind einige H. von → Eretria. Das im Vergleich zu den H. klass. Zeit (Größe ca. 300 m^2) exorbitante Anwachsen der Baugrößen bis hin zu 2000 m^2 Fläche zeigen hell. Peristyl-H. auf Delos oder in Pella, die sich bisweilen nur noch graduell hinsichtlich Größe, Ausstattung und durch die wenig exponierte Lage, nicht aber im Grundsätzlichen von den Palästen hell. Herrscher unterschieden.

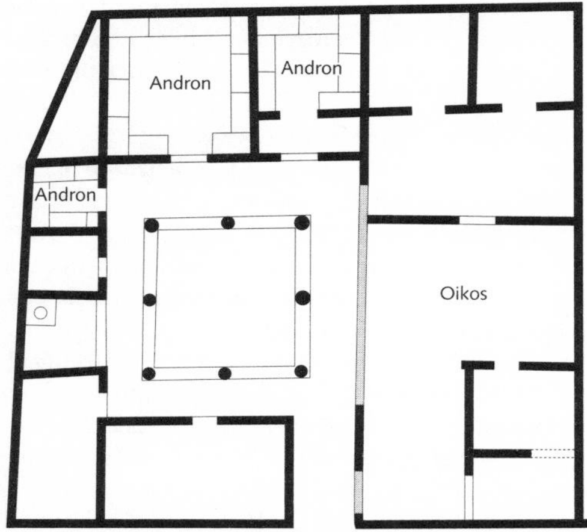

Eretria, sog. Mosaikenhaus, 4. Jh. v. Chr. (Grundriß).

5. Kosten

Die Erstellungs- und Unterhaltungskosten griech. H. variierten von Ort zu Ort, bisweilen sogar innerhalb eines Ortes erheblich. Inschr. aus Olynth nennen eine Preisspanne von 900 bis 5300 Drachmen; der durchschnittliche Kaufwert eines H. wird bei 1000 bis 2000 Drachmen gelegen haben (bei 1 Drachme Tageslohn). Aktuelle Besitzverhältnisse und Grundschulden waren Gegenstand kommunaler Archivtätigkeit. Vermietung war immer vertraglich geregelt und, wie Inschr. aus Delos überliefern, relativ preiswert (50 Drachmen Jahresmiete). Immobilien wurden häufig ohne Tür und Dachziegel zur Miete oder zum Kauf angeboten; beide Elemente waren kostbar, mehrfach wiederverwendbar und zählten deshalb zu den beweglichen Gütern (→ Hausrat).

C. Frühitalische und etruskische Häuser

Aus zunächst meist einräumigen Rund- und Ovalhütten mit Walm- und kleinem Vordach (z.B. Hütten auf dem Palatin in Rom, 8. Jh. v. Chr.) bzw. einfachen Rechteckstrukturen aus Lehm und Flechtwerk (S. Giovenale, 7. Jh. v. Chr.), deren Aufbau überwiegend vermittels hausförmiger Tonurnen rekonstruiert wird, entwickelten sich in der etr. Kultur bald komplexere H.-Typen mit verschiedenen, funktional voneinander geschiedenen Räumen und Gebäudetrakten. Die schlecht erh. Fundamentreste der dicht bebauten, orthogonal strukturierten *insulae* von → Marzabotto (um 500 v. Chr.) lassen kaum Rückschlüsse auf die Grundrißorganisation einzelner H. zu; die etr. Grab-Architektur spiegelt jedoch bis in konstruktive Details hinein den H.-Bau (→ Grabbauten). Großflächige, repräsentative Adels-H. des 6. Jh. v. Chr. wie der »Palast« von → Murlo (Abmessungen ca. 60 × 60 m) oder der »Bau F« in → Acquarossa zeigen neben erheblichem Prunk der Ausstattung (Säulenhallen, reich bemalte Terrakotta-Verkleidungen) eine Dreiteilung in Wohnbereich, Räumlichkeiten für Feste und Gelage sowie für sakrale Veranstaltungen; die im späteren röm. H. allgegenwärtige Verehrung von Haus- und Schutzgottheiten als ein wichtiger Teilbereich des Wohnens hat hier ihre Ursprünge. Die etr. Herkunft ital.-röm. H.-Architektur zeigen wichtige H. in Rom, z.B. die im 6. Jh. v. Chr. erbaute *regia* am Forum Romanum (die nicht vom griech. Megaron-Typ herzuleiten ist), ebenso wie das im ital. Hausbau seit dem 4. Jh. v. Chr. weit verbreitete → Atrium, das seine ältesten bislang bekannten Belege in etr. H. auf dem Palatin in Rom und in den um einen Mittelhof gruppierten H. in Marzabotto (jeweils 6. Jh. v. Chr.) findet.

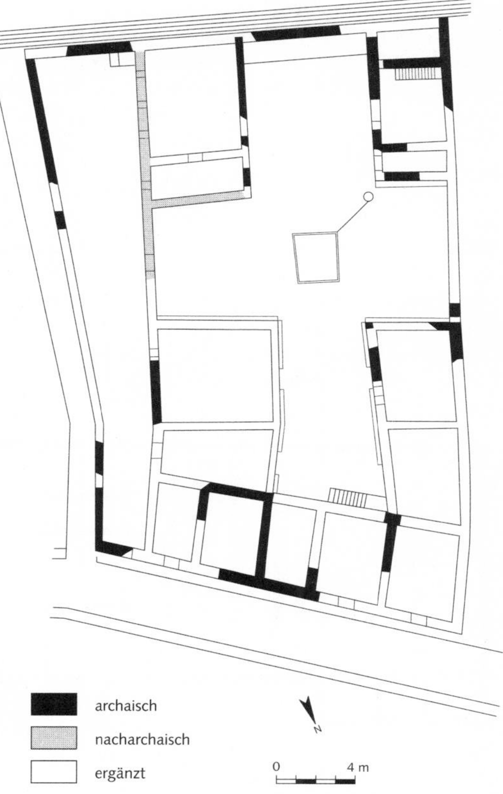

Rom, Palatin, Patrizierhaus, Ende des 6. Jhs. v. Chr.

D. Römische Häuser

1. Das Atrium-Haus

Wichtigste Form des ital. H. der republikanischen Zeit ist das *Atrium-H.*, das als ein Bautyp der etr.-ital. H.-Architektur zunächst nicht nur als Privat-H. (Rom, Palatin, 6. Jh. v. Chr.), sondern – in erheblicher Baugröße – auch als öffentliches Gebäude in Erscheinung tritt

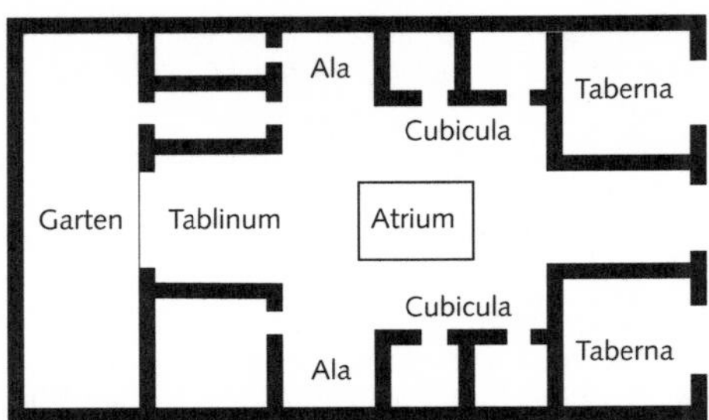

Atriumhaus, Schema, 4. Jh. v. Chr. (Grundriß).

(z. B. das *atrium publicum* am Forum in Cosa) und seit dem 4. Jh. v. Chr. rapide Verbreitung findet. Die langrechteckige, klappsymmetrisch, auf eine Durchblicksachse angelegte Struktur mit einem offenen, verschieden geformten Lichthof (→ Compluvium; → Atrium) als Zentrum kombiniert Wirtschafts-, Wohn-, Hallen- bzw. Korridorbereich und Garten; von der Straße erschließt sich, zwischen zwei oder mehreren nur nach außen geöffneten, ansonsten mit dem Innenraum des H. unverbundenen Wirtschaftsräumen (*tabernae*) hindurchführend, ein oft zweiteiliger Flur (→ *vestibulum*; *fauces*), der auf das Atrium mit dem → Impluvium (→ Zisterne) in der Mitte stößt. An das Atrium grenzen die Schlafräume (*cubicula*); den hinteren Teil des Atriums bilden die *alae* (türlose, in ganzer Höhe offene Seitenräume für verschiedene Funktionen, z. B. als Abstell- oder Speiseraum oder als Raum für die Ahnenbilder, → *ala* [1]) sowie das → *tablinum*, das wiederum den Durchgang zum Garten (*hortus*) ermöglicht, der – als schmale, hofartig hochummauerte Fläche – den hinteren Abschluß des Atrium-H. bildet. Nicht alle ital. H. waren Atrium-H.; in ital.-röm. Städten findet sich bis ins 1. Jh. v. Chr. hinein daneben ein vergleichsweise asymmetrisch organisierter H.-Typ, der auf das Atrium ebenso wie auf *tabernae* (und damit auf jedweden wirtschaftlichen Funktionsbereich) verzichtet und verschiedene *cubicula* um ein überdachtes *tablinum* herum gruppiert, das über eine Küche auf den Garten hinführt (Cosa).

Das Prinzip des Atrium-H. erwies sich als hinreichend flexibel, auch höheren Ansprüchen an Repräsentation zu genügen. Bes. in der Kombination mit dem aus der hell. H.-Architektur entnommenen Peristyl konnten seit dem 2. Jh. v. Chr. z. T. großformatige und prestigeträchtige Baukomplexe entstehen, wie sie etwa aus Pompeii bekannt sind. Die *Casa dei Capitelli Figurati* vewendet dabei den Standard-Typus des Atrium-H., erweitert diesen jedoch anstelle des Gartens um ein raumgreifendes Garten-Peristyl. In der *Casa del Fauno* finden sich gleich zwei Atrien mit nun ebenfalls zwei Peristylen (einem Wohn- und einem Gartenperistyl) zu einer schon fast villenartigen Wohnanlage verschmolzen, die jedoch gleichwohl den Charakter eines in eine *insula* eingefügten Stadt-H. bewahrt. Nicht selten finden sich im kaiserzeitlichen It. schließlich auch repräsentative Peristyl-H. ohne ein Atrium (Ostia).

2. Mietshäuser

Ein wichtiger Faktor der röm. Stadt ist das mehrstöckige Mehrfamilien- oder Miets-H., das sich nicht nur in den Metropolen, sondern, in bescheideneren Formaten, auch in ländlichen Städten findet (mehrgeschossige, z. T. extra für Vermietung umgebaute Atrium-H. in Herculaneum, z. B. die *Casa Sannitica*

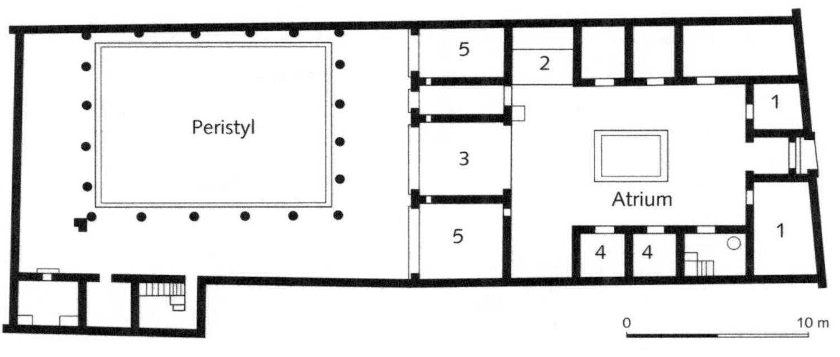

Pompeji, Peristylhaus, »Casa dei Capitelli figurati«, 2. Jh. v. Chr. (Grundriß).

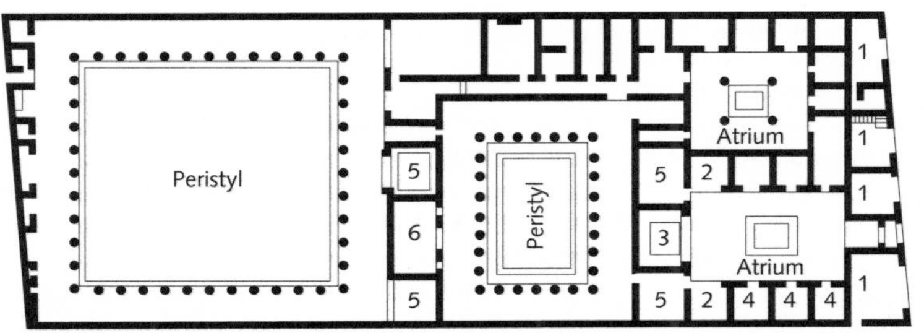

Pompeji, Haus mit Doppelperistyl, »Casa del Fauno«, 2. Jh. v. Chr. (Grundriß).

oder die *Casa a Graticcio*, wo das Atrium zum Lichthof mutiert und die → *cenacula*, die Mietwohnungen im zweiten Stock, z.T. mit einer separaten Treppe erschlossen werden). In besonderer städtischer Siedlungsverdichtung (Rom, Ostia, Puteoli) fanden sich bis zu sechsgeschossige, um einen engen Lichthof herumgebaute Hochhäuser, die als eine ganze *insula* bedeckende Baukomplexe meist schnell und billig von Privatunternehmen erbaute Spekulationsobjekte waren und den Bauvorschriften (→ Baurecht) wohl oft nicht entsprachen (vgl. u.a. Iuv. 3,188–310). Sie waren im Erdgeschoß von einer Porticus umgeben und mit Ladengeschäften bestückt, wiesen im ersten Stock eine Art *piano nobile* auf, darüber dann niedrigere und schlichter ausgestattete Geschosse; die Wohnqualität und damit auch der Mietzins nahmen von unten nach oben ab. Die einzelnen Appartements waren meist nur in Leichtbauweise voneinander separiert; die einzelnen Stockwerke erschlossen sich über Treppen und verwinkelte Korridore. Es fehlten → Heizung, Sanitäreinrichtungen (vgl. → Körperpflege; → Latrinen) und Küchen. Das Hantieren mit offenem Feuer und den tragbaren Öfen und Herden in den Wohnungen führte dabei oft zu verheerenden Brandkatastrophen. Luxuriöses Wohnen in städtischen Mietshäusern war eher selten; die *Casa dei Dipinti* in Ostia mit ihren großzügigen Wohnungen, die sich jeweils über mehrere Etagen erstreckten, bildete eine Ausnahme, auch wenn generell die Mietshäuser von Ostia in ihren Ausstattungen einen gegenüber der → *Subura* Roms sehr gehobenen Standard repräsentierten.

Außerhalb It. finden sich in städtisch-urbanen Kontexten neben den mit bescheidenen zwei- oder dreiräumigen, meist nur im Fundament erh. und deshalb in der Grundrißorganisation und der Funktionsdifferenzierung schwer zu rekonstruierenden H. dicht bebauten *insulae* (Augusta Raurica) verschiedene Varianten des Hof- und Atrium-H. (z.B. in Volubilis oft mit einem zweiten, *atriolum* gen. Hof). Über das gesamte Imperium Romanum verbreitet war das Peristyl-H. So erheben sich etwa die mehrstöckigen, reich ausgestatteten Hang-H. über unregelmäßigem Grundriß mit zentralem Peristyl entlang der Kureten-Straße in → Ephesos (2. Jh. n. Chr.); auch in den Nord-West-Prov. fanden sich zahlreiche Peristyl- und Hof-H., wobei etwa im gallo-röm. Bereich, aber auch in Hispanien eine Vermischung einheimisch-traditioneller und importierter Formen zu konstatieren ist.

E. Akurgal, Alt-Smyrna I. Wohnschichten und Athenatempel, 1983 • T.F.C. Blagg, First-Century Roman Houses in Gaul and Britain, 1990 • E. Brödner, Wohnen in der Ant., 1989 • V.J. Bruno, R.T. Scott, Cosa 4. The Houses, 1993 • J.R. Clarke, The Houses of Roman Italy, 100 B.C. – A.D. 250, 1991 • M. Cristofani (Hrsg.), La Grande Roma dei Tarquini, Ausstellungs-Kat. Rom, 1990, 97–99 • H. Drerup, Griech. Baukunst in geom. Zeit, ArchHom O, 1969 • S. Ellis, La casa, in: A. Guillou (Hrsg.), La civiltà bizantina, 1993, 167–226 •

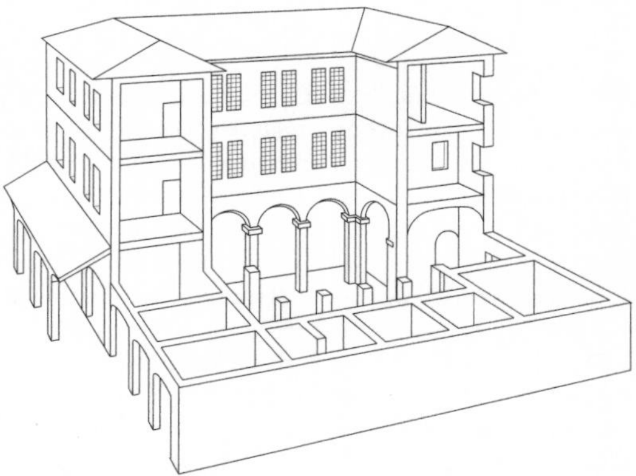

Ostia, Schnitt durch ein Mietshaus der mittleren Kaiserzeit.

K. Fagerström, Greek Iron Age Architecture, 1988 • D. Fusaro, Note di architettura domestica greca nel periodo tardo-geometrico e arcaico, in: Dialoghi di archeologia 4, 1982, 5–30 • H. von Hesberg, Privatheit und Öffentlichkeit in der frühhell. Hofarchitektur, in: W. Hoepfner, G. Brands (Hrsg.), Basileia. Die Paläste der hell. Könige, 1996, 84–96 • W. Hoepfner, E.L. Schwandner, H. und Stadt im klass. Griechenland, [2]1994 • W. Hoepfner, Zum Typus der Basileia und der königlichen Andrones, in: W. Hoepfner, G. Brands (Hrsg.), Basileia. Die Paläste der hell. Könige, 1996, 1–43 • A. Kalpaxis, Früharcha. Baukunst in Griechenland und Kleinasien, 1976 • M. Kiderlen, Megale Oikia. Unt. zur Entwicklung aufwendiger griech. Stadthausarchitektur von der Früharchaik bis ins 3. Jh. v. Ch., 1995 • M. Kreeb, Unt. zur figürlichen Ausstattung delischer Privathäuser, 1988 • La casa urbana hispanorromana, Kongr. Zaragoza (1988), 1991 • C. Lang-Auinger, Hanghaus 1 in Ephesos – Der Baubefund, FiE 8/3, 1996 • F. Lang, Archa. Siedlungen in Griechenland, 1996, 78–117 • H. Lauter, Architektur des Hell., 1986, 223–227 • H. Maehler, H. und ihre Bewohner im Fayum in der Kaiserzeit, in: G. Grimm (Hrsg.), Das röm.-byz. Ägypt., 1983, 119–137 • A.G. McKay, Röm. H., Villen und Paläste, 1980 • W. Müller-Wiener, Griech. Bauwesen in der Ant., 1986, 176–179 • Palast und Hütte. Beitr. zum Bauen und Wohnen im Alt. Kongr. Bonn (1979), 1982 • F. Pesando, Oikos e ktesis. La casa greca in età classica, 1987 • F. Prayon, Frühetr. Grab- und Hausarchitektur (22. Ergh. MDAI(R)), 1975 • J. Raeder, Vitruv, De architectura VI 7 und die hell. Wohnungs- und Palastarchitektur, in: Gymnasium 95, 1988, 316–368 • K. Reber, Aedificia Graecorum. Zu Vitruvs Beschreibung des griech. H., in: AA 1988, 653–666 • Th. Schattner, Griech. Hausmodelle. Unt. zur frühgriech. Architektur (15. Beih. MDAI(A)), 1990 • S. Sinos, Die vorklass. Hausformen in der Ägäis, 1971 • A. Streily, Alt-Smyrna, Graben H: Zur griech. H.-Architektur des 9. und 8. Jh. v. Chr., in: Thetis 4, 1997, 63–84 • A. Wallace-Hadrill, Houses and Society in Pompeii and Herculaneum, 1994 • E. Walter-Karydi, Die Nobilitierung des griech. Wohnhauses in der spätklass. Zeit, in: W. Hoepfner, G. Brands (Hrsg.), Basileia. Die Paläste der hell. Könige, 1996, 56–61 • Wohnungsbau im Alt., Kongr. Berlin (= DiskAB 3), 1978.

C.HÖ.

Hausgrab s. Grabbauten

Hausrat (griech. τὰ ἔπιπλα, ἡ σκευή; lat. *supellex, instrumentum*). H. umfaßt die Gegenstände, die man zum täglichen Leben braucht und die den Hauptteil der beweglichen Habe ausmachen; dazu gehören in erster Linie → Möbel, Koch- und Küchengeschirr, Beleuchtungsgerät, → Teppiche, → Decken, im weiteren Sinn auch → Schmuck und → Kleidung, ferner nach heutigem Verständnis Teile aus dem Bereich der Immobilien, z. B. die Türen und Dachziegel des → Hauses. Daneben sind diejenigen Gegenstände als H. anzuführen, die die Eigenständigkeit der griech. und röm. Hauswirtschaft ausmachen, wie Webstühle, Webgewichte, Webkämme oder Handpressen und -mühlen (*trapetum*), → Mörser und Mörserkeulen für Öl und Getreide und im weiteren Sinne auch Acker- und Gartengerät (versammelt z. B. bei Anth. Pal. 6,297), nicht zuletzt auch die für die Haushaltung benötigte Sklaven- und Dienerschaft. Hinzu kommen Küchengegenstände wie Käsereiben (κνῆστις, Hom. Il. 11,640, oder τυρόκνηστις, Aristoph. Vesp. 963, Av. 1579), Bratpfannen, Bratrost (*craticula*), Kochtöpfe, Dreifüße für Töpfe, die ἐσχάρα (flache Siedepfanne), Teller, Servierplatte (→ *repositorium*, → Tafelausstattung), Rührlöffel (→ *rudis*), Schöpfkelle (κύαθος, *simpulum*), Salzfäßchen (ἁλία, *concha, salinum*), Töpfe, Bestecke wie Tranchiermesser, Gabel und Löffel (*ligula, cochlear*), Siedekessel für → Seife, → Filter aus Stoff, Ton und anderen Materialien zum Durchseihen von Öl, Wasser, Wein etc. und nicht zuletzt die Vorratsgefäße für Wein, Öl, Mehl, Honig etc., ferner Körbe und Säcke zum Transport von Nahrungsmitteln, Kleidern usw. Neben den metallenen Prunkgefäßen (vgl. z. B. Iuv. 12,43–48), die aus Grab-, Hort- oder Siedlungsfunden bekannt sind (Schatzfunde von Boscoreale, Hildesheim, Kaiseraugst u. a.), benutzte man als → Eßgeschirr auch in den sozial höher gestellten Schichten aus Gründen des besseren Geschmacks tönernes Geschirr (Vitr. 8,6,11, vgl. Cic. Att. 6,1,13). Dem Holzgeschirr, das sich wegen der Vergänglichkeit des Materials nur selten erh. hat, kam natürlich in allen sozialen Schichten eine herausragende Bed. zu.

Weitere H.-Gegenstände dienten der → Beleuchtung (Kandelaber, Lampen, Fackelhalter etc.) oder förderten die Bequemlichkeit, wie Teppiche (z. B. Mart. 1,49,31), tragbare Kohlebecken (*foculus*) mit dem πνιγεύς (*pnigeús*), einem Deckel, der zum Ersticken der Flammen diente, und dem *rutabulum* (Schürhaken); ferner → Kissen und Polster (die mit *plumae*, Flaumfedern von Gänsen oder Schwänen, aber auch mit Stroh, Heu, Schilf oder Seegras gefüllt waren), Überzüge aus Leinen, Wollstoffen oder Leder und für den Ausgang → Sänfte und → Schirme.

Unentbehrlich waren auch Gerätschaften für die tägliche Körperpflege, wie die Badewanne (→ Bäder) oder tragbare (Anth. Pal. 11,74,7; Hor. sat. 1,6, 109) Aborte (ἀμίς, *matella* für die Männer, σκάφιον, *scaphium* für die Frauen, Petron. 41,9; 47,5), bzw. das λάσανον (*lásanon*) als → Nachttopf; für die hierbei anfallende Reinigung nutzte man Wasser und den Schwamm (Aristoph. Ran. 487), der auch an einem Holzstab befestigt sein konnte (Mart. 12,48,7). Den tragbaren Abort pflegte man beim Gelage zu benutzen und ebenso im Schlafzimmer (Poll. 10,44). Der Sklave, den man mit einem Fingerschnippen mit dem tragbaren Abort herbeirief (→ Gebärden), hieß *lasanophóros*. Festinstallierte Aborte (ἄφοδος, κοπρών, ἰπνός, vgl. Aristoph. Ach. 81; Poll. 10,44) waren noch im 4. Jh. v. Chr. selten (→ Latrinen; s. z. B. Syll.[3] 1261,11, vgl. Athen. 10,417d). Einen goldenen Abort erwähnt Mart. 1,37. Der Reinlichkeit dienten ferner Badewanne (ἀσάμινθος, *labrum, solium*), Fuß- und Handwaschbecken (ποδανιπτήρ, λεκανίς, *pelvis, gutturnium*), Abtrockentücher, → Kamm, → Spiegel, → Schere, Pinzette, Ohrlöffel, Zahnstocher, Schminktöpfe etc. (→ Körperpflege), und nicht zuletzt hauseigene → Bäder in den Häusern der Oberschicht.

Zur Reinigung des Hauses bzw. H. hatte man für die Fußböden den Besen (κάλλυντρον, κόρηθρον, κόρημα, σάρωτρον, σάρον, *scopae*), der aus Ulmen-, Tamarisken- oder Myrtenzweigen gefertigt war. Um den Unrat, der z. B. nach Regengüssen im Haushof oder nach Gastmählern anfiel, besser wegfegen zu können, bestreute man den Boden mit Sägespänen (Iuv. 14,60–67; Hor. sat. 2,4,81; Petron. 68); zur Reinigung der Möbel nahm man den Staubwedel (→ *peniculus*) zu Hilfe. Mit → Schwamm und Öl reinigte man seine Schuhe (Aristoph. Vesp. 600 [1]). Zum H. zu rechnen sind auch → Schreibmaterial (→ Griffel, Schreibtafel, Tintenfaß etc.) und verschiedenes Bildungsgut (Buchrollen, Musikinstrumente). An der Wand brachten Römer den → *pluteus* (Regal, Brett) an für Büsten, Schriftgut u. a. m. Auch das Spielzeug für die Kinder (→ Kinderspiel) sei hier genannt. Anzufügen sind noch verschiedene Kultgeräte (Räucherwaren, → Thymiaterion, Altar, Arula, Sarkophag, Urnen) für den Haus- bzw. Grabkult.

Zum H. zählten ferner Nutztiere (Pferd, Schaf, Ziege, Huhn usw.) wie auch Schoßtiere (Schlange, Fuchs, Hund, Grille, Hase, Affe, Hauskatze). Vögel – diese hielt man in Vogelkäfigen, sofern man nicht mit ihnen spielte oder sie im Raum fliegen ließ – waren v. a. bei den Römern sehr beliebt (vgl. Plin. epist. 4,2); erinnert sei an den Spatz oder Dompfaff der Lesbia (Catull. 2,3), den Papagei der Corinna (Ov. am. 2,6) oder den sprechenden Star des Britannicus und Nero (Plin. nat. 10,120; Plut. mor. 972f); hinzu kamen noch Eulen und Elstern und weitere Katzentiere wie Löwe, Tiger, Gepard. Von praktischer Bed. waren auch Haustiere, die zur Vertilgung von Ungeziefer, Käfern oder Wanzen (κόρις, vgl. Aristoph. Ran. 114, [2]) im Haus dienten (z. B. Reiher, Igel, Katze). Mäusen rückte man mit Hilfe von Fallen, Gift, Katzen oder Wieseln zu Leibe. Wanzen, Läuse (φθείρ, Kopf- oder Kleiderlaus) oder Flöhe (ψύλλος) bekämpfte man auf unterschiedliche Weise (vgl. Plin. nat. 33,17f.). Gegen → Fliegen kam die Klatsche (*muscarium*, vgl. Mart. 3,82,2) zum Einsatz oder in der Nacht das Mückennetz (ἀμφίβληστρον, *canopium*). Gegen Motten half »Ölschaum« (Plin. nat. 15,33).

Listen, die den H. eines Haushaltes en détail und in seinen Wertrelationen erfassen, sind verschiedentlich überl., z.B. in den öffentlichen Versteigerungen des H. von → Alkibiades (414/3 v.Chr.; vgl. Tod 80), der Erbschaft des Demosthenes (Demosth. or. 27,10, woraus sich der Wert des H. als das Dreifache des Wertes des Hauses ermitteln läßt); in den Komödien des Aristophanes (z.B. Eccl. 730–747, vgl. Plaut. Aul. 94f.) werden eine Fülle von Gegenständen genannt, ebenso in den Komödienfr. des Nikostratos (4. Jh. v. Chr.) und im PLond. 3,191,15 (113–117 n.Chr.); weitere Hinweise ergeben sich aus verschiedentlich überl. → Eheverträgen. Sie offenbaren den Umfang an verschiedenen Lagerpolstern, (Kopf-)Kissen, Decken, Matten, Tüchern, Leibwäsche, Bezügen, Tafelgeschirr, Gerätschaften aus Metall (Leuchter, Kessel, Spiegel etc.).

Darstellungen von angesammeltem H. sind recht häufig ([3], att. Grabrelief, Vasen): z.B. zeigen Vasenbilder Frauen am Webstuhl und bei anderen Tätigkeiten, wie auch Terrakotten Frauen, Kinder und Männer bei der Speisezubereitung am Mörser, beim Teigkneten, an Backöfen, am Grill, bei Waffen- oder Werkzeugherstellung [4] usw. agieren lassen; daneben haben sich reale Kochöfen, Pfannen, Wärmeöfen, Bratspieße, Feuerböcke, Bestecke usw. zahlreich erh. Die Bed. von H.-Gegenständen mag sich darin äußern, daß die Braut diese (insbes. Kleidung und Schmuck) bei der Überführung vom Elternhaus in das des Bräutigams erhielt, was gleichermaßen für griech. wie röm. → Hochzeitsbräuche gilt (Eust. zu Hom. Il. 24,29), wie auch in der Sitte, seinen Gastfreunden als Geschenke Bücher, Salbgefäße, Decken, Gürtel u.a. mitzubringen (Suet. Vesp. 19; schol. Iuv. 6,203; Suet. Aug. 75; Mart. 7,53; Petron. 56,8; 60,4). Von dem H. des röm. Hauses geben nicht nur die lit. Quellen, sondern v.a. die zahlreichen Funde aus den Vesuv-Städten und die Grabinventare It. und der nördl. Provinzen gute Auskunft.

1 R. Hurschmann, Symposienszenen auf unterital. Vasen, 1985, Taf. 22 A 34 **2** V.M. Strocka (Hrsg.), Frühe Zeichner 1500 bis 500 v.Chr., Ausst.-Kat. Freiburg, 1992, 74 Nr. 75 **3** Trendall, Paestum, 84 Nr. 127 Taf. 46 (und öfter) **4** B.A. Sparkes, L. Talcott, Pots and Pans of Classical Athens, 1958.

B.A. Ault, Classical houses and households: an architectural and artifactural case study from Halieis, Greece, 1994 • F. Baratte, Röm. Silbergeschirr in den gall. und german. Prov., Limesmuseum Aalen 32, 1984 • J. Boersma, Private latrines in Ostia: a case study, in: BABesch 71, 1996, 151–160 • E. Brödner, Wohnen in der Ant., 1989 • G. Bruns, Küchenwesen und Mahlzeiten, ArchHom Q, 1970 • H.A. Cahn, A. Kaufmann-Heinimann, Der spätröm. Silberschatz von Kaiseraugst, 1984 • M. Cremeo, Venuskunkeln aus Kleinasien, in: AA 1996, 135f. • D.C. Drummond, R.M. und J.J. Janssen, An ancient Egyptian rat trap, in: MDAI(K) 46, 1990, 90–98 • L. Foxhall, Household, gender and property in Classical Athens, in: CQ 39, 1989, 22–44 • A.R. Furger, Der Inhalt eines Geschirr- oder Vorratsschrankes aus dem 3. Jh. von Kaiseraugst-Schmidmatt, in: Jahresberichte aus Augst und Kaiseraugst 10, 1989, 213–268 • W. Gaitzsch, Ant. Korb- und Seilerwaren, 1986 • J.F. Gardner (Hrsg.), The Roman Household. A Sourcebook, 1991 • W. Hilgers, Lat. Gefäßnamen, 31. Beih. BJ, 1969 • D.W. Hobson, House and Household in Roman Egypt, in: YClS 28, 1985, 211–229 • H.J. Kellner, G. Zahlhaas, Der Röm. Tempelschatz von Weißenburg in Bayern, 1993, 111–125 • R. Neudecker, Die Pracht der Latrine, 1994 • R. Noll, Das Inventar des Dolichenusheiligtums von Mauer an der Url (Noricum), 1980 • R. Petrovsky, Stud. zu röm. Bronzegefäßen mit Meisterstempeln, 1993 • Pompeji wiederentdeckt, Ausst. Hamburg 1993, 1993 • T.L. Shear Jr., The Persian destruction of Athens, in: Hesperia 62, 1993, 429–480 • B.A. Sparkes, The Greek kitchen, in: JHS 82, 1962, 121–137 • D.B. Thompson, An ancient shopping center, 1971 • Toynbee, Tierwelt • S. Treggiari, Jobs in the household of Livia, in: PBSR 43, 1975, 18–27 • E. Trinkl, Ein Set aus Spindel, Spinnwirtel und Rocken aus einem Sarkophag in Ephesos, in: Österr. Jb. für Arch. 63, 1994, Beibl., 81–92 • G. Wickert-Micknat, Die Frau, ArchHom R, 1982, 38–80 • M. Vallerin, Pelvis estampillés de Bassit, in: Syria 71, 1994, 171–185. R.H.

Heba (Magliano). Die röm., im 3. oder 2. Jh. v.Chr. eingerichtete Kolonie H. lag auf einem Hügel südöstl. von Magliano. Die Gleichsetzung mit dem bei Ptol. 3,1,43 und Plin. nat. 3,52 erwähnten H. ist aufgrund einer Inschr. auf einem → Cippus gesichert. Eine etr. Vorgängersiedlung ist nur wegen der im späten 7. Jh. v.Chr. einsetzenden und im 6. Jh. bes. reichen Nekropolen vorauszusetzen. Wichtig ist eine im ant. Stadtgebiet gefundene Bleiplatte des 5.–4. Jh. v.Chr., auf der spiralförmig ein etr. Text über Opfervorschriften eingeritzt ist.

M. Michelucci, Caltra, Καλουσιον, H. Indagini sugli insediamenti etruschi nella bassa valle dell'Albegna, in: Studi di antichità in onore di G. Maetzke, 1984, 377–392 • A. Minto, Per la topografia di Heba etrusca nel territorio di Magliano in Toscana, in: SE 9, 1935, 11–59. M.M.

Hebamme

I. Alter Orient II. Griechenland III. Rom

I. Alter Orient

H. sind in Babylonien und Äg. nur aus Anspielungen in lit. Texten bekannt. Im → Atraḫasis-Mythos öffnet die Muttergöttin die Gebärmutter, läßt die Frau auf dem »Ziegel« gebären (vgl. Ex 1,16) und bestimmt beim Abschneiden der Nabelschnur das Geschick des Kindes.

E. Brunner-Traut, s.v. H., LÄ 2, 1074f. • M. Stol, Zwangerschap en geboorte bij de Babyloniërs en in de Bijbel, 1983, 84–86. MA.S.

II. Griechenland

Die Gesch. von der ersten H. mit Namen Agnodike (Hyg. fab. 274), die angeblich als Mann verkleidet am Unterricht eines gewissen Herophilos teilnahm, ist offensichtlich ein Gründungsmythos für den Beruf der H. [3. 52–85]. Es ist jedoch davon auszugehen, daß Frauen schon immer anderen Frauen bei der Geburt geholfen haben, so daß es nicht verwundert, wenn sie in dieser Rolle im *Corpus Hippocraticum* begegnen (Carn. 19 = 8,614 L.; zu den Abkürzungen der Schriften des *Corpus Hippocraticum* s. die Tabelle bei → Hippokrates). Der Legende zufolge fungierte Athena bei Leto als H. und gab später ihr ganzes Wissen an Artemis, die Göttin der Geburten, weiter (Aristeid. 37,18). Die H. war wahrscheinlich u.a. für das Durchtrennen der Nabelschnur verantwortlich (Aristot. hist. an. 587a9), woher der ion. Begriff für H., *omphalētómos*, stammt (Hippokr. Mul. 1,46 = 8,106 L.; Hipponax fr. 19 WEST). Sokrates, der behauptet, selbst Sohn einer H. zu sein (Plat. Tht. 149b-e), beschreibt die H. (*maía*) als ältere Frau, die mit Zauberformeln und -gesängen, aber auch mit Medikamenten die Wehen einleitet und eine erfolgreiche Geburt sicherstellt. H. dürften auch Rezeptbücher geschrieben haben, in denen u.a. Fragen der Empfängnis behandelt wurden (Plin. nat. 28,23). Die Bezeichnung der Phanostrate aus dem 4. Jh. v. Chr. als H. und Ärztin (IG II/III,3²,6873) könnte darauf schließen lassen, daß die Zuständigkeiten von H. und Ärztinnen getrennt waren und sich die *maíai* ausschließlich auf die Geburtshilfe beschränkten, während die Ärztinnen ein weiteres Betätigungsfeld hatten, doch ist diese Folgerung keineswegs gesichert [1. 275–290; 5]. Ärzte traten bei der Geburt ebenfalls auf (z.B. Hippokr. Foet. Exsect. 15 = 8,484 L.; siehe auch die männlichen H. auf Paros im 1. Jh. n. Chr., IG 12,5,199), dabei arbeiteten häufig männliche und weibliche Heilkundige zusammen [1. 212f.]. Die gynäkologischen Schriften aus dem *Corpus Hippocraticum* wenden sich, wie auch spätere einschlägige Texte, an eine männliche Leserschaft.

III. ROM

Soranos' ›Gynäkologie‹ aus dem 2. Jh. n. Chr., die bedeutendste ant. Schrift über die Geburt, charakterisiert eine gute H. u.a. als nüchtern, verschwiegen, nicht abergläubisch, arbeitsam, belesen und in Diätetik, Chirurgie und Arzneimittelkunde ausgebildet. Die 25 Geburtshelferinnen, die im CIL genannt werden, sind zumeist Sklavinnen oder Freigelassene [4; 5. 515–518]; lit. Quellen lassen eine große Vielfalt in bezug auf Sozialstatus und Sachverstand erkennen. Galen lobt die H., die der Frau des Consul Boethus beistanden, in den höchsten Tönen (De praecogn. 8, CMG 5,8,1,110); er hätte solches Lob sicher nicht für die Kellnerin gefunden, die Eunapios zufolge (vit. soph. 463) auch als örtliche H. fungierte. Doch legen histor. Vergleichsdaten nahe, daß letztere die typische H. verkörpert, die medizinische und andere Betätigungen miteinander zu verbinden verstand.

→ Geburt; Gynäkologie; Soranos

1 L.A. DEAN-JONES, Women's Bodies in Classical Greek Science, 1994 2 N. DEMAND, Monuments, midwives, and gynecology, in: P.J. VAN DER EIJK u.a., Ancient Medicine in its Socio-cultural Context, 1995, 275–290 3 H. KING, Agnodike and the profession of medicine, in: PCPhS 12, 1986, 53–75 4 J. KORPELA, Das Medizinpersonal im ant. Rom, 1987 5 D. NICKEL, Berufsvorstellungen über weibliche Medizinalpersonen in der Ant., in: Klio 61, 1979, 515–518.

V.N./Ü: L.v.R.-B.

Hebdomas s. Woche

Hebe (Ἥβη) bedeutet dem Namen nach »Jugend«, Personifikation der Jugendschönheit. Ihr waren Kulte in Mantineia (Paus. 8,9,3), in Kos zusammen mit Herakles (Cornutus 31) und bes. in Argos mit Hera (Paus. 2,17,5) gewidmet. In der myth. Dichtung ist sie als Tochter von Zeus und Hera besser faßbar als im Kult (Hes. theog. 922; 950–952; Apollod. 1,13). Sie wird → Herakles nach seinem Tod zur Braut gegeben (Pind. N. 1,69–72). Unter Göttern tritt sie als Helferin (Hom. Il. 4,2; 5,722; 905) auf, im Chor als Tänzerin (Hom. h. 3,195). Ikonographie: die (nicht erh.) Statue des Naukydes zu Argos; in der Vasenmalerei häufig als Mundschenkin abgebildet [1]. In Rom vgl. → Iuventas(us).

1 A.F. LAURENS, s.v. H. 1, LIMC 4.1, 458–464.

RE.ZI.

Hebegeräte. Seitdem in Griechenland große → Tempel aus Stein errichtet wurden (frühes 6. Jh. v. Chr.), standen die Architekten vor dem Problem, schwere Quadersteine für die Wände oder den Architrav und Säulentrommeln soweit zu heben, wie der Bauplan es notwendig machte. Dabei waren oft Lasten von einem beträchtlichen Gewicht zu bewältigen, denn immerhin wiegt Stein etwa 2,25 t/m³ und Marmor ca. 2,75 t/m³. In archa. Zeit hatten Blöcke für den Architrav ein Gewicht zwischen 10 und 40 t. Die Steine wurden zunächst über eine Rampe an ihren Platz gebracht, wie dies für den Bau des Artemistempels in Ephesos belegt ist (Plin. nat. 36,95). Nach etwa 525 v. Chr. ging man zu dem Einsatz von H. über; dies geht aus dem geringeren Gewicht der Blöcke und aus der Einarbeitung von Seilkanälen an den Quadersteinen hervor, wodurch ein Anlegen der Seile möglich wurde.

Grundlegendes Instrument für alle H. der Ant. war die Rolle, deren Wirkung bereits in den *Mechanika* des Aristoteles beschrieben wurde; die Verwendung einer Rolle, über die ein Seil läuft, ist allerdings noch keineswegs kraftsparend, aber die Richtung, in der die Kraft wirken muß, hat sich so geändert, daß die Arbeit erleichtert wird. Aristoteles war bereits bekannt, daß mit Hilfe einer Kombination von zwei Rollen schwere Lasten mit einer vergleichsweise geringen Kraft gehoben werden können (Aristot. mechanika 852a; 853a-b). Es gehörte dann zu den bedeutenden Aufgaben der späteren → Mechanik, durch eine Kombination verschiedener mechanischer Instrumente möglichst leistungsfähige H. zu konstruieren und deren Wirkung auch exakt zu erfassen. → Heron legt schließlich dar, daß bei Verwendung einer größeren Zahl von Rollen einerseits entsprechend weniger Kraft benötigt wird, um ein bestimmtes Gewicht zu heben, andererseits aber bei der Arbeit ein Verzögerungseffekt eintritt (Heron, mechanika 2,23). Es werden H. mit ein, zwei, drei oder vier senkrechten Stützen und mit einer Rolle oder einer

Kombination von Rollen (Flaschenzug) beschrieben (Heron, mechanika 3,2–5).

Die auf röm. Baustellen eingesetzten Krane werden bei → Vitruvius dargestellt: Es handelt sich um zwei an ihrer Spitze miteinander verbundene, schräg aufgestellte Stämme, die durch Halteseile in ihrer Lage gehalten wurden. Das Tragseil wurde über drei Rollen geführt, von denen die beiden oberen in einem an der Spitze befestigten Kloben angebracht waren, die untere Rolle sich an dem Kloben befand, an dem auch die Greifzange festgemacht war, mit der die Last gehoben wurde; entsprechend der Verwendung von drei Rollen wird dieser Kran als *Trispastos* (»Dreizug«) bezeichnet, bei Verwendung von fünf Rollen als *Pentaspastos* (»Fünfzug«). Bemerkenswert ist die Tatsache, daß das Seil an einer Haspel befestigt war, die mit langen Hebelstangen gedreht wurde.

Neben der Rolle wurde auch der Hebel als kraftsparendes mechanisches Prinzip genutzt. Für das Heben schwerer Lasten empfiehlt Vitruvius, statt der Haspel ein großes Trommelrad zu verwenden, das von Männern getreten wurde. Beweglicher war nach Vitruvius ein Kran, der nur aus einem einzigen Mast bestand, aber auch erfahrene Arbeitskräfte zur Bedienung verlangte. Die bei Vitruvius verwendete griech. Terminologie zeigt, daß die Römer Kran und Flaschenzug von den Griechen übernommen haben (Vitr. 10,2,1–10; vgl. Lucr. 4,905 f.). Derartige H. sind auf röm. Reliefs mehrmals abgebildet; am bekanntesten ist das Relief vom Grab der Haterii (Rom, VM; vgl. außerdem das Relief in Capua (vgl. [1. 48]).

→ Deus ex machina

1 J. P. Adam, La construction romaine, 1984, 44–53
2 Blümner, Techn. 3, 111–129 **3** J. J. Coulton, Ancient Greek Architects at Work, 1977 **4** Ders., Lifting in Early Greek Architecture, in: JHS 94, 1974, 1–19 **5** J. G. Landels, Engineering in the Ancient World, 1978, 84–98
6 W. Müller-Wiener, Griech. Bauwesen in der Ant., 1988
7 White, Technology, 78–82.

H. SCHN.

Kran vom Hateriergrab; Vatikan. Museen, Museum Gregoriano Profano (Inv. 9998), 120 n. Chr. (Zeichnung nach Relief mit Ergänzungen).

Hebräisch. Der Begriff H. leitet sich vom Gentiliz »Hebräer« ab und gehört zur → kanaanäischen Sprachgruppe des Semitischen. Das 22 Zeichen umfassende alt-hebr. Schriftsystem der Inschr. entwickelte sich aus dem protokanaanäischen → Alphabet. Die spätere sogenannte hebr. → Quadratschrift fand nur als Buchschrift Verwendung. Das H. umfaßt verschiedene Sprachstufen, gesprochenes klass. H., auch als Alt-H. definiert, das in Inschr. (10.–6. Jh. v. Chr.) auf Stein, Ostraka, Papyri, Metall und in den ältesten Teilen des AT (11.–6. Jh. v. Chr.) wie Ri 5, Gn, Ex, Lv, Nm, Dt, Jos, Sam und Kg überliefert ist. Es folgt die exilische (Jes, Jer, Ez sowie »kleine Propheten«) und nachexilische Periode der späten at. Bücher (Dan, Esr, Est, HL, Prd, Neh, Chr) und der Apokryphen (6.–2. Jh. v. Chr.), welche durch die biblischen und nichtbiblischen Schriften aus → Qumran und Iudaea (1. Jh. v.– 2. Jh. n. Chr.) beendet wird. Daran schließt das Mittel-H. (2.–3. Jh. n. Chr.) der Mischna (Gesetzesteil des Talmuds) und anderer → rabbinischer Literatur (Tosefta, halakhische Midraschim) an, die stark von aram., griech. und lat. Wörtern durchsetzt ist. Das Neu-H. wurde nur als Schulsprache der späten Schriftgelehrten gebraucht. Aus diesem künstlichen Zweig wurde im 19. Jh. das heutige Ivrit geschaffen (offizielle Sprache des Staates Israel seit 1948).

→ Bibel; Inschriften; Judentum

C. BROCKELMANN, Das Hebräische (HbdOr III,1), 1953, 59–132 • J. RENZ, W. RÖLLIG, Hdb. der Althebr. Epigraphik, 1–3, 1995. C.K.

Hebron, kanaan. *ḥæbrōn* (»Bündnisort« oder »Verkehrsknotenpunkt«, die gleiche Semantik liegt dem jüngeren(!) Namen *Qiryat ʿArbaʿ*, »Vierstadt«, sc. der vier in 1 Sam 25,3; 27,10; 30,26–31 genannten Sippen bzw. Stämme, zugrunde); griech. Χεβρων (LXX), Ἑβρών, Γιβρών, Ναβρόν, Χεβρών u.ä. (Ios. passim); *ha-barûk* (»der Gesegnete« = Abraham, Gn 14,19) in → Qumran (DJD III 298, DJD II 160); arab. *al-Ḫalīl ar-Raḥmān* (»der Freund [= Abraham, s. z.B. Jes 41,8] des Erbarmers [= Allah]«). Zentralort des judäischen Gebirges, 30 km südl. von Jerusalem an der alten Straße von Bethel nach Beeršeba, bzw. an den alten Transitverbindungen nach Ägypten und Arabien. Die Lage an der Grenze zw. fruchtbarem Ackerland und dem Steppengebiet des Negeb machte H. zu einem Umschlagplatz für Bauern und Viehzüchter.

Bedeutend im 18. – 16. Jh. v. Chr. (mit zyklopischer Stadtmauer, Nm 13,22; 28; 33), wurde die Stadt im 15. – 13. Jh. zugunsten von → Jerusalem aufgelassen. Einen neuen Siedlungsaufschwung erlebte H. seit dem 12. Jh. v. Chr., als es zum Zentrum der Kalibbiter wurde (Jos 14,12–15; 15,13 f.; Ri 1,20). Etwa gleichzeitig muß sich auch die Abraham-Sippe bei H. niedergelassen haben, die laut Gn 18 von den Göttern von H. begrüßt wird. In der ersten Hälfte des 10. Jh. v. Chr. wurde H. für 7 Jahre Hauptstadt des judäischen Stammeskönigtums, das der philistäische Vasall → David [1] aus Judäern, Kenitern und Jerachmeelitern zu Lasten der Kalibbiter (Kriegsbericht 2 Sam 2,1–4) gegründet hatte und von wo aus er das Königtum über Israel erwarb (2 Sam 5, 1–5). Noch unter David wurde H. erneut zugunsten von Jerusalem verlassen, doch nicht ohne Widerstand (1 Sam 15,7; 9). Literatursoziologische Überlegungen lassen in H. das Zentrum der landjudäischen Opposition gegen die Hauptstadt Jerusalem vermuten.

Zw. 597 und 582 verlor Juda die Kontrolle über H. und die Stadt wurde edomitisch/idumäisch. Im 6./5. Jh. v. Chr. gab es offenbar am Abraham-Heiligtum, das sich von → Mamre nach H. zu verlagern im Begriff war (Gn 23), einen jüd.-idumäisch-arab. Simultankult (Gn 25,9; 35,29), wie auch nach Sozomenos im 4./5. Jh. n. Chr. in Mamre (*Ramet al-Ḫalīl*, »Höhle des Freundes«). Dort ließ schon Herodes d. Gr. auf den Resten eines hasmonäischen Baus einen Temenos errichten, dessen Trümmer Hadrian für ein Heiligtum für Hermes-Mercur wiederverwenden ließ; im Osten des Temenos finden sich noch Reste einer konstantinischen Basilika (vgl. Eus. vita Const. 3,51 ff.), die den Sāsānideneinfall 614 n. Chr. nicht überlebt hat. Eine jüd. Siedlung im idumäischen H. belegt auch Neh 11,25. Nachdem 129/128 v. Chr. die Idumäer zwangsjudaisiert wurden und in der Folge ein Idumäer, Herodes d.Gr., den neuerrichteten Thron in Jerusalem bestieg (37–34 v. Chr.), baute er die Patriarchengräber (Höhle Machpela), lokalisiert auf dem Osthügel im *Ḥaram al-Ḫalīl*, monumental aus (Umfassungsmauer erh.). Die Gräber wurden unter byz., früharab., Kreuzfahrer- und Ayyubiden-Herrschaft weiter ausgebaut und waren in byz. Zeit für Juden und Christen, seit der arab. Eroberung 639 auch für Muslime ein wichtiger Wallfahrtsort. Im NW des Ḥaram ließ Iustinian eine Basilika errichten; im SO liegt eine zur Moschee umgebaute Kirche aus der Kreuzfahrerzeit. 1165 n. Chr. wurde H. unter dem Namen St. Abraham Bischofssitz.

→ Edom; Juda und Israel

O. KEEL, M. KÜCHLER, Orte und Landschaften der Bibel 2, 1982, 670–696 • E. A. KNAUF, Die Umwelt des AT, 1994, 235–237 • A. Ofer, NEAEHL 2, 606–609. M.K. u. E.A.K.

Hebros (Ἕβρος). Südthrak. Fluß, h. bulgar. Marica, byz./ngr. Εὖρος, nach der Donau längster Fluß auf der Balkanhalbinsel. Nach Ps.-Plutarchos (De fluviis 3) soll sein früherer Name Rhombos gewesen sein. Sein Quellgebiet liegt im Rila-Gebirge (Thuk. 2,96,4). Von dort aus fließt er in östl. Richtung durch die fruchtbare thrak. Ebene bis → Hadrianopolis, wo er den Tonzos aufnimmt, sich dann nach Süden wendet und bei Ainos mit zwei Armen in die Ägäis mündet (Strab. 7, fr. 52). Am Unterlauf waren die Ufer sumpfig (Aristeid. 24,59B). Ab Hadrianopolis wurde der H. schiffbar; nach Strab. 7, fr. 48 konnten leichte Schiffe bis nach Philippopolis fahren. Damit war er einer der wichtigsten Verkehrswege ins Innere von → Thrakia. An seinem Lauf lagen neben Philippopolis und Hadrianopolis eine Reihe weiterer Städte, z. B. Kypsela, Ainos und Doriskos (Traianopolis), teilweise an Orten älterer Hallstattsiedlungen. Wichtige Straßen kreuzten den H.: bei Kypsela die *via Egnatia*, bei Philippopolis und Hadrianopolis die Straße Singidunum – Naissos – Serdica – Byzantion. Auf den Mz.-Bildern dieser Städte erscheint oft die Darstellung des Flußgottes H.

G. KAZAROV, Antični izvestija za reka Marica, in: FS Mitropolit Maxim, 1931, 81–86 • C. DANOV, Zu den histor. Umrissen Altthrakiens 1, 1944. I.v.B.

Hebryzelmis (Ἑβρύζελμις).

[1] Auf Münzen ΕΒΡΥΤΕΛΜΙΟΣ bzw. ΕΒΡΥ. König der Odrysen in den 80er Jahren des 4. Jh. v. Chr. (IG II/III^{2} 31; Syll.^{3} 1,138; TOD 117) [1. 18]; vielleicht ein Sohn von Seuthes II. [4]. Einige Wissenschaftler identifizieren H. mit Ἀβροζέλμης, dem Dolmetscher Seuthes' II., der mit Xenophon (an. 7,6,43) verhandelte [5]. H. prägte mehrere Typen von Bronzemünzen [2. 106–112].

1 C. L. LAWTON, Attic Document Reliefs, 1995 2 U. PETER, Die Münzen der thrak. Dynasten, 1996 3 A. HÖCK, Der Odrysenkönig Hebrytelmis, in: Hermes 26, 1891, 453–462 4 V. VELKOV, Der thrakische König Hebryzelmis und seine Herkunft, in: Thracia 11, 1995, 299 f. 5 K. VLAHOV, Zur Frage der Gräzisierung thrakischer Personennamen, in: Živa antika 15/1, 1965, 39–44. U.P.

[2] Einer der vier Söhne von Seuthes III. und Berenike (IGBulg 3,1731). U.P.

Hecht. Dieser mitteleurop. Raubfisch (Esox lucius L.) mit reich bezahntem breiten Maul war den Griechen unbekannt. Auson. Mos. 120–124 dagegen erwähnt den H. (*lucius*) als in Teichen zw. Algen lauernden Feind der Frösche, der in der Küche nicht geschätzt werde. Der griech. Arzt → Anthimos [1] (De observatione ciborum 40; [1. 18]) teilt dagegen ein german. Kochrezept mit. Bei Thomas von Cantimpré 7,48 [2. 264f.] wird er nach einer zeitgenössischen Quelle des 13. Jh. (*Liber rerum*, vgl. Alexander Neckam 2,32 [3. 147]) mit dem *lupus marinus* identifiziert und als bes. grausamer Verfolger sogar der eigenen Brut bezeichnet (vgl. Albertus Magnus, de animalibus 24,40, [4. 1537]). Den kristallähnlichen angeblichen Stein im Kopf des *lupus* erwähnt neben Thomas auch Plinius (nat. 9,57).

1 H. GOSSEN, s.v. H., RE 7, 2591 2 H. BOESE (ed.), Thomas Cantimpratensis, Liber de natura rerum, 1973 3 TH. WRIGHT (ed.), Alexander Neckam, De naturis rerum, 1857, Ndr. 1967 4 H. STADLER (ed.), Albertus Magnus, De animalibus, Bd. 2, 1920. C. HÜ.

Hedna (ἕδνα, ep. ἐέδνα). Nur im kollektiven Plural gebräuchlich, sind *h.* bei Homer → Geschenke des Bräutigams an den Vater der Braut (Idee der »Kaufehe«) oder an die Braut selbst (ähnlich dem german. Wittum), doch abweichend Hom. Od. 1,277 und 2,196: Ausstattung der Braut durch ihren Vater (verwandt mit den → *parápherna* oder der → *pherné*), manchmal auch als »Mitgift« zu deuten (→ *proíx*), nicht eindeutig zu klären: Od. 2,53 (Verbum); Il. 13,382 (Nomen hiervon). Vermutlich liegt den *h.* der archa. Gedanke zugrunde, soziale Beziehungen durch Gaben und Gegengaben zu vermitteln.

R. KÖSTLER, Raub- und Kaufehe bei den Hellenen, in: Ders., Homer. Recht, 1950, 29–48 • Ders., H., ebd. 49–64 • M. SCHMIDT, s.v. H., LFE 2, 1991, 396f. G. T.

Hedone s. Lust

Hedschra (*hiǧra*). Auswanderung, Übersiedlung des Propheten → Mohammed (Muḥammad) und einiger seiner Anhänger von → Mekka nach → Medina 622 n. Chr. nach tribalen Schwierigkeiten (Aufkündigung des Clan-Schutzes seitens seines Stammes Quraiš); Beginn der islamischen Zeitrechnung. Erst mit der H. begannen Mohammeds Wirken auch als Staatsmann sowie die eigentliche Ausbreitung des → Islam (zunächst durch Bündnispolitik).

A. NOTH, Die Hiǧra, in: U. HAARMANN (Hrsg.), Gesch. der arab. Welt, 1987, 11–57. H. SCHÖ.

Hedyle (Ἡδύλη). Nach Athen. 297a die Tochter der att. Iambendichterin Moschine und die Mutter von → Hedylos; also schrieb sie im frühen 3. Jh. v. Chr. [1]. Athenaios weist H. fünf elegische Verse (und ein Wort eines sechsten) zu, die aus einem Gedicht mit dem Titel *Skýlla* stammen. Darin bringt → Glaukos [2] in Sizilien oder Südit. seiner geliebten → Skylla maritime Geschenke, vermutlich vor ihrer monströsen Metamorphose (vgl. Ov. met. 13, 904ff.; Hyg. fab. 199).

1 GA I,2, 289.

SH 456 • U. v. WILAMOWITZ-MOELLENDORFF, Lesefrüchte, in: Hermes 60, 1925, 302 (= Ders., KS 4, 390). E. BO./Ü: J. S.

Hedylos (Ἥδυλος). Epigrammdichter des Kranzes des Meleagros (Anth. Pal. 4,1,45), Sohn der Elegikerin → Hedyle, lebte auf Samos und unter Ptolemaios II. in Alexandreia (283/2–243 v. Chr.). Von seinen Gedichten (Weih-, Grab-, epideiktische, sympotische und Spott-Epigramme) sind acht bei Athenaios und fünf in der *Anthologia Palatina* überliefert (unecht wahrscheinlich Anth. Pal. 11,123 und 414; von → Asklepiades [1] ist vielleicht 5,161; zu anderen möglichen Werken in Vers und Prosa vgl. Athen. 7,297a; Strab. 14,683; Etym. m. 72,16). Diese wenigen Epigramme genügen, um eine Dichterpersönlichkeit ersten Ranges zu erkennen, die eine intensive Bindung zw. Leben und Inspiration fühlt (vgl. Epigramme 5 und 6 GOW-PAGE). Wahrscheinlich gab es eine von H. zusammengestellte Anthologie des Asklepiades, des Poseidippos und seiner selbst (vgl. → Anthologie).

SH 457–460 • GA I,1, 100–103; I,2, 289–298 • I. G. GALLI CALDERINI, Su alcuni epigrammi dell' Anthologia Palatina..., in: Atti dell' Accademia Pontiana N. S. 31, 1982, 239–280 • Ders., Edilo epigrammista, in: ebd. N. S. 32, 1983, 363–376 • Ders., Gli epigrammi di Edilo..., in: ebd. N. S. 33, 1985, 79–118. M. G. A./Ü: M. A. S.

Heeresversorgung I. GRIECHENLAND II. RÖMISCHE REPUBLIK III. PRINZIPAT

I. GRIECHENLAND

Das Problem der Versorgung großer Heere wurde bereits im 5. Jh. v. Chr. wahrgenommen: Herodot schildert nicht nur die Lage der Griechen, die dem persischen Heer 480 v. Chr. Lebensmittel liefern mußten (Hdt. 7,118f.), sondern berechnet auch dessen Tagesbedarf auf insgesamt 110340 Medimnen (ca. 4400 t; Hdt. 7,187; vgl. 9,41,2); Thukydides nimmt an, daß sich die Griechen vor Troia aus Mangel an mitgeführten Lebensmitteln durch Anbau von Getreide und Seeraub ernährten (Thuk. 1,11; vgl. Hom. Il. 1,125; 7,466ff.). Der Einsatz der → Phalanx brachte eine Systematisierung der H. mit sich: Stellung der Ausrüstung und Selbstverpflegung – in Athen für drei Tage – wurden Pflicht (IG I^3 1 = Syll.^{3} 13; Aristoph. Ach. 197; Vesp. 243; Pax 312; 1181ff.). Bei längeren Feldzügen versorgten die *póleis* die Soldaten mit Nahrungsmitteln, die jedoch bezahlt werden mußten. Oftmals wurden Versorgungsgüter in großen Konvois zum Heer gebracht (Hdt. 9,39; Diod. 11,80,3f.). Die → Trierarchie in Athen schloß vielleicht auch die Verpflegung der Ruderer ein (Thuk. 6,31,3; Plut. mor. 349a). Zur athenischen Flotte gehörten 415 v. Chr. 30 Versorgungsschiffe mit Getreide sowie Handelsschiffe (Thuk. 6,44). Plünderungen und das Abernten der Felder im Feindesland waren gängige Methoden der H. (Xen. Kyr. 3,3,16: θρεψόμεθα ἐκ τῆς πολεμίας).

Die seit dem 4. Jh. v. Chr. häufig eingesetzten Söldner hatten sich selbst auszurüsten und zu versorgen. Es war üblich, daß die Soldaten ihren Bedarf auf lokalen Märkten oder bei Kaufleuten, die im Troß des Heeres mitzogen, deckten (Xen. an. 1,5,6; 1,5,10; 3,2,20f.; 4,8,23; Kyr. 6,2,38; vgl. Aristot. oec. 2,23). Xenophon maß der Versorgung der Soldaten eine entscheidende Bedeutung für den Erfolg von Feldzügen bei (Xen. Kyr. 1,6,9f.; 6,2,25–39). Welche Probleme dabei zu bewältigen waren, wird am Beispiel der Armee Alexanders d.Gr. deutlich: Für 65 000 Menschen, 6100 Pferde und ca. 2420 Trag- und Zugtiere wurden wahrscheinlich mehr als 100 t Getreide pro Tag benötigt.

II. Römische Republik

Das ursprüngliche Prinzip der röm. H. hat Cato prägnant formuliert: *Bellum se ipsum alet* (›der Krieg wird sich selbst ernähren‹, Liv. 34,9,12; 195 v. Chr.). Nach Möglichkeit sollte die H. durch Plünderungen, Requisitionen, Tributerhebungen und Einquartierungen auf Gegner, Unterworfene und Bundesgenossen abgewälzt werden. Die Grünfuttergewinnung für die Tiere war die tägliche Aufgabe der *pabulatores* (vgl. Frontin. strat. 2,5,31; 2,13,6). In den Prov. kämpfende Legionen und die Flotte wurden seit 215 v. Chr. teilweise durch *societates* (*redemptores*; → *societas*) von It. aus mit Kleidung und Getreide versorgt (Liv. 23,48,4–23,49,3; vgl. 34,9,12). Den Soldaten wurden die Kosten für die Kleidung und das Getreide vom Sold abgezogen (Pol. 6,39), seit C. → Sempronius Gracchus (2. H. 2. Jh. v. Chr.) erhielten sie aber die Kleidung ohne einen solchen Abzug (Plut. C. Gracchus 5). Getreide wurde oft von Verbündeten geliefert; im 2. Jh. v. Chr. schickten die Numider den Legionen in Makedonien große Mengen Getreide, und das Heer des Pompeius war im Krieg gegen Sertorius auf Lieferungen aus Gallien angewiesen (Liv. 44,16,1 ff.; 45,13,13 ff.; Sall. hist. 2,98,9). Caesar bereitete seine Feldzüge in Gallien logistisch gut vor und zog wiederholt gallische Stämme zu Getreidelieferungen heran, woraus sich mehrmals Konflikte ergaben (Caes. Gall. 2,2,6; 3,7,3 f.; 3,20,2; 7,3,1; 7,10,1; 7,10,3). Daneben wird die Beschaffung von Schiffsausrüstungen oder der Kauf von Pferden in Spanien und It. erwähnt (Caes. Gall. 5,1,4; 7,55,2).

III. Prinzipat

Gleichzeitig mit der Stationierung der Legionen an den Grenzen setzte in augusteischer Zeit auch die systematische H. ein. So wurden die Truppen in Germanien aus den Einnahmen der zivilen *annona* (→ *cura annonae*) mit Öl aus der Baetica versorgt. Die H. gehörte zum Aufgabenbereich der Statthalter und der Prokuratoren des Princeps (Strab. 3,4,20). In den Legionen wurden die Versorgungsgüter durch die Verwaltung sorgfältig erfaßt (Veg. mil. 2,19). Grundlage der H. waren die Steuern aus den Provinzen, wobei je nach Bedarf und Leistungsfähigkeit Naturalien oder Geld gefordert wurden (Strab. 4,5,3; Tac. hist. 4,74,1; Tac. Agr. 19,4; BGU 1564; Dig. 50,16,27: *tributum*). Auch in der Prinzipatszeit wurden Verpflegung, Unterkunft und Kleidung mit dem Sold verrechnet (PGen.Lat. 1 [1]). Die Ausgaben für die Legionen und die Kaufkraft der Soldaten begünstigten die Bildung von *canabae* und *vici* (→ *vicus*) in der Nähe der Legions- und Auxiliarlager und hatten damit Einfluß auf die wirtschaftl. Entwicklung der Grenzprov. Diese *canabae* waren Siedlungen von Händlern und unterstanden der mil. Aufsicht; so ist etwa ein *magister canabensium* belegt (vgl. CIL III 6166 = ILS 2474; CIL III 7474 = ILS 2475). Da sie bei Auflassung eines Lagers ebenfalls aufgegeben wurden, konnten aus *canabae* keine dauerhaften Siedlungen entstehen. Für die H. hatte das *territorium legionis* nur eine geringe Bed. Die *prata legionum* und *cohortium* dienten als Weideland für die Reit- und Lasttiere der Armee. Die *fabricae* (→ *fabrica*) in den Lagern waren Werkstätten für Reparatur- und Instandhaltungsarbeiten. Zur Erstausstattung einer Legion wurden 38 t Roheisen für Waffen und 54 000 Kalbshäute für die Zelte benötigt. Für die insgesamt 300 000 Soldaten mußten im Jahr etwa 1 Mio. t Weizen (4 *modii* im Monat = ca. 316 kg pro Soldat im Jahr) bereitgestellt werden. Nicht geringer war der Bedarf an Futter (auch Gerste) für die Pferde und Lasttiere. Angesichts solcher Zahlen ist die Auffassung des Vegetius (um 400 v. Chr.) verständlich, daß zu große Heere wegen der Versorgungsschwierigkeiten abzulehnen seien. Dezidiert stellt Vegetius fest, Heere seien öfter durch Hunger als in der Schlacht vernichtet worden, weswegen es erforderlich sei, die notwendigen Vorräte rechtzeitig anzulegen (Veg. mil. 3,1; 3,3).

Unter den Severern wurde die *annona militaris* zur Verwaltung jener Naturalsteuern eingerichtet, die für das Heer bestimmt waren. Außerdem wurde das Amt des *actuarius* (→ *actarius*) geschaffen, der in der röm. Armee diese Mittel verwaltete (Amm. 25,10,7; Aur. Vict. Caes. 33,13); die *actuarii* haben diese Position oft für ihre eigenen Interessen mißbraucht, weswegen in der Spätantike der Versuch unternommen wurde, sie einer effizienten Kontrolle zu unterwerfen (Cod. Theod. 8,1,14). Waffen und Rüstungen wurden seit dem 4. Jh. n. Chr. in den *fabricae* hergestellt, die zunächst dem → *praefectus praetorio* und später dem *magister officiorum* unterstanden. Die Rationen der Soldaten bestanden im 4. Jh. n. Chr. aus Fleisch, Brot und Wein; es war verboten, diese Lieferungen in Geldforderungen umzuwandeln (Cod. Theod. 7,4,6; 7,4,18; 7,4,20). Die kaiserlichen Edikte zur H. sind im Cod. Theod. 7,4 und 7,6 (Kleidung) zusammengestellt.

1 J. Nicole, C. Morel (ed.), Archives militaires du 1er siècle. Texte inédit du papyrus latin de Genève No. 1, 1900 (Ndr. 1985).

J. P. Adams, Logistics of the Roman Imperial Army: Major Campaigns on the Eastern Front in the First Three Centuries A. D., 1979 • D. van Berchem, L'annone militaire de l'imperium Romanum, in: Mémoires de la Société nationale des antiquaires de France, Ser. 8, Bd. 10, 1937, 117–202 • R.W. Davies, The Supply of Animals to the Roman Army and the Remount System, in: Latomus 28, 1969, 429–459 • D.W. Engels, Alexander the Great and the Logistics of the Macedonian Army, 1978 • P. Erdkamp, The Corn Supply of the Roman Armies during the Third and Second Century B. C., in: Historia 44, 1995, 168–191 • W. Hansson, L. Keppie (Hrsg.), Roman Frontier Studies, 1980 • Jones, LRE, 623–630 • Th.D. Kissel, Untersuchungen zur Logistik des röm. Heeres in den Provinzen des griech. Ostens (27 v. Chr. – 235 n. Chr.), 1995 • A. Labisch, Frumentum commeatusque. Die Nahrungsmittelversorgung der Heere Caesars, 1975 • A. Mócsy, Das Problem der militärischen Territorien im Donauraum, in: Acta Antiqua 20, 1972, 133–168 • W.K. Pritchett, The Greek State at War I, 1971 • J. Remesal Rodriguez, Heeresversorgung und die wirtschaftlichen Beziehungen zwischen der Baetica und Germanien, 1997 • L. Wierschowski, Heer und Wirtschaft. Das röm. Heer der Prinzipatszeit als Wirtschaftsfaktor, 1984. L. WI.

Heerlager s. Castra

Heerwesen
I. Alter Orient II. Griechenland III. Rom

I. Alter Orient
A. Allgemein B. Quellen
C. Waffengattungen

A. Allgemein
Der Vielzahl der Staaten und Kulturen des Vorderen Orients und Ägyptens in der Zeit vom 3. bis zum 1. Jt. v. Chr. mit jeweils ganz eigenen Voraussetzungen entspricht die unterschiedliche Rekrutierung, Zusammensetzung, Organisation, Kampfesweise und Größe ihrer Heere.

B. Quellen
Der Alte Orient hat kein militärtheoretisches Schrifttum hervorgebracht. Erzählende Quellen dienen ausschließlich der Überhöhung des Herrschers und seiner Siege, gewähren daher nur selten Einblick in die Abläufe. Quellen aus dem Bereich der Administration beleuchten jeweils nur kleine Teile der vermutlichen Gesamtorganisation. Allg. bestehen noch erhebliche lexikalische Defizite im Bereich des mil. Fachvokabulars. Über Ausrüstung und Bewaffnung informieren erh. Originale und das in einigen Epochen umfangreiche Bildmaterial (u. a. äg. Wandmalereien des NR und mesopot. Reliefs aus dem 3. bzw. 1. Jt. v. Chr.).

C. Waffengattungen
Erstmals ist um die Mitte des 3. Jt. v. Chr. für sumer. Stadtstaaten eine Kombination unterschiedlicher Waffensysteme zu belegen: Neben einer tiefgestaffelten Formation mit Lanze und großem Schild (erinnernd an die griech. Hoplitenphalanx) steht ein anderer Teil des sumer. Fußvolkes mit Wurfspeer ohne Schild. Eine dritte Gruppe bilden die vierrädrigen Streitwagen, deren Besatzung Wurfspeere bereit hält. Beginnend mit dem Akkad. Reich (etwa 2350 v. Chr.) setzen sich beweglichere Gefechtsformen durch. Der Bogen wird zur wichtigsten Fernwaffe, die Ausrüstung für den Nahkampf besteht aus Schild und Speer bzw. Axt oder Kolben (im 2. Jt. v. Chr. auch mit Sichelschwert). Mit der → Domestikation des Pferdes erlebt der → Streitwagen um die Mitte des 2. Jt. v. Chr. einen Aufstieg in allen Staaten des Vorderen Orients. Zunächst von zwei Pferden gezogen und mit einem Bogenschützen – der zugleich Kommandant des Wagens ist – und dem Wagenlenker besetzt, wird im Laufe der Zeit die Besatzung um einen (erstmals im 13. Jh. v. Chr.), im 7. Jh. v. Chr. um einen weiteren Schildträger vermehrt, wie auch die Zahl der Zugpferde von zwei auf vier steigt (8. Jh. v. Chr.). Seit dem 9. Jh. v. Chr. erwähnen die Quellen regelmäßig auch mit Bogen oder Lanze bewaffnete Reiterei. Zur Einnahme befestigter Orte waren Belagerungstürme, Sturmböcke und das Anlegen von Dämmen, Rampen und Minen in Gebrauch, doch entwickelte der Alte Orient keinerlei Artillerie. Die Verwendung des Eisens seit dem frühen 1. Jt. v. Chr. hat sicherlich die Ausrüstung der Heere verbilligt, Auswirkungen auf die Kampfesweise sind bislang aber nicht erkennbar.

R. Drews, The End of the Bronze Age, 1993 • W. Helck, s. v. Militär, LÄ 4, 128–134 • W. Mayer, Politik und Kriegskunst der Assyrer, 1995, 419–482 (Bibliogr. 525–545) • M. de Odorico, The Use of Numbers and Quantifications in Assyrian Royal Inscriptions (State Archives of Assyria Stud. 3), 1995, 107–112. A. F.

II. Griechenland
A. Geometrische und archaische Zeit
B. Klassische Zeit C. Die Zeit Philipps II. und Alexanders D. Hellenismus

A. Geometrische und archaische Zeit
Kriege organisierter Heere von Gemeinwesen sind in Griechenland erst im 8. Jh. v. Chr. faßbar. Frühere Formen von Kämpfen beschränkten sich auf Beutezüge, Piraterie oder Auseinandersetzungen unter Nachbarn, die von Adligen und ihrem Anhang ausgetragen wurden; Erinnerungen daran sind in Homers Epen noch greifbar (Hom. Il. 11,670 ff.; Hom. Od. 14,229 ff.). Mit der Herausbildung der → Polis, ihrem wirtschaftlichen Erstarken, mit dem Bevölkerungswachstum und der Kolonisation veränderten sich Dimension und Art der Kriege. Sie wurden nun um weite Landstriche und um die Existenz einzelner Poleis geführt; diese stützten sich auf die landbesitzenden Bauern als Fußkämpfer, deren Bewaffnung sich langsam vereinheitlichte. Bis etwa 650 v. Chr. bildete sich in den meisten Gebieten allmählich die → Phalanx, deren Frühformen bei Homer kenntlich werden (Il. 13,126–135; 16,211–217; vgl. Tyrtaios 11,29–34), als die normale Kampfformation heraus. Abgesehen von Bergregionen wie Aetolien und Akarnanien und von Thessalien, das sich vorrangig auf Reitertruppen stützte, waren

in Griechenland Bürgerhopliten (→ *hoplítai*), die sich selbst ausrüsteten, das Rückgrat des Heeres. Es gab nur wenige Reiter, und Leichtbewaffnete spielten eine geringe Rolle. Über nennenswerte Flotten verfügten vornehmlich die Inselgriechen sowie Korinth und Milet. Kriege waren zwar häufig, in Dauer und Auswirkung aber meist begrenzt; sie waren oft nach einer Feldschlacht, die auf ebenem Gelände nach fast rituell festgelegten Regeln ausgetragen wurde, beendet. Entsprechend gering waren die taktischen Möglichkeiten der Feldherren: Sie hatten Kampfplatz, Zeitpunkt und Aufstellung zu wählen, die Moral ihrer Truppen zu stärken und im Kampf Vorbild zu sein.

B. Klassische Zeit

Die Phalanx blieb bis in die → Diadochen-Zeit (spätes 4./frühes 3. Jh. v. Chr.) Grundlage griech. Armeen, von denen nur diejenigen Spartas und Athens besser bekannt sind. In Athen wurden die 20- bis 59jährigen Bürger der obersten drei Zensusklassen als Hopliten eingezogen, → Theten wurden seit den Perserkriegen als Ruderer oder seltener als Leichtbewaffnete und in der Spätphase des Peloponnesischen Krieges sogar als Hopliten eingesetzt, die auf Kosten der Polis ausgerüstet wurden. Die 18- und 19jährigen Männer leisteten als → Epheben Militärdienst (Aristot. Ath. Pol. 42). → Metoiken konnten für Wachdienst und in Notsituationen herangezogen werden. Die → Reiterei bestand seit Perikles aus 1000 Mann der reichsten Schicht. Der Heerbann war in zehn → Phylen oder Taxeis (→ *táxis*; 1000–1300 Mann im 5. Jh., ca. 600 im 4. Jh.) unterteilt, die ihrerseits in Lochen (→ *lóchos*) zerfielen. Wie wohl in allen übrigen Poleis beruhte die Heeresordnung auf der sozialen Gliederung der Bürgerschaft. Die Taxeis wurden von Taxiarchen, die Lochen von Lochagen geführt. Nach der Neuordnung von 501/500 v. Chr. kommandierten zehn Strategen (→ *stratēgós*), die alljährlich von den einzelnen Phylen gewählt wurden, gleichberechtigt die Streitkräfte; die Volksversammlung ordnete die Mobilisierungen an und legte gleichzeitig die Strategie der Feldzüge fest.

Sparta wurde im 6. Jh. v. Chr. dank seines Bevölkerungspotentials und aufgrund der Organisation des Peloponnesischen Bundes die führende griech. Landmacht. Mit der Eroberung Messenes waren auch die wirtschaftlichen Voraussetzungen für eine im Vergleich zu anderen griech. Städten verstärkte Hinwendung zum Militärischen gegeben. Der spartanische Heerbann bestand zunächst aus den Vollbürgern, den → Spartiaten; spätestens nach den Bevölkerungsverlusten im 5. Jh. v. Chr. durch die Perserkriege, Erdbeben und die Kriege mit Athen kamen minderberechtigte Gruppen, besonders die Perioiken, dazu. Damit wurde vermutlich auch die alte Gliederung der Armee nach den lokalen Strukturen in Phylen (*phylaí*) und Oben (*ōbaí*) aufgegeben. Eine Aufteilung in relativ kleine Einheiten und eine klare Kommandostruktur machten das spartanische Heer außerordentlich manövrierfähig. Aufgrund der Quellenlage ist es aber unmöglich, Sicherheit über seine Gliederung zu erlangen. Die kleinste Einheit im 5. (Hdt. 1,65,5) wie im 4. Jh. v. Chr. (Xen. Lak. pol. 11,4) war die → *enōmotía*, die wohl 32, später 36 (Xen. hell. 6,4,12) Mann Sollstärke umfaßte. Ihre Zahl wie ihr Verhältnis zu den größeren Einheiten, den Pentekostyen, Lochen oder Moren (→ *mõra*; Xen. Lak. pol. 11,4 kennt 6 Moren Hopliten und Reiter, Thuk. 5,68,3 erwähnt nur Lochen und Pentekostyen), ist strittig. Dienstpflicht bestand bis zum 60. Lebensjahr. Heerführer war jeweils einer der Könige, der im Feld von 300 → *híppeis* als Leibgarde begleitet wurde, oder ein *ad hoc* bestimmter Beamter.

Während dieses Krieges und in der folgenden Zeit kam es im griech. Militärwesen zu folgenreichen Wandlungen, unter denen vor allem das Aufkommen der ursprünglich aus Thrakien stammenden, leichtbewaffneten → Peltasten, die beweglicher als Hopliten waren, die Schaffung von Elitetruppen (Theben, Arkadien), der vermehrte Einsatz von → Söldnern, die Einführung der schiefen Schlachtordnung durch den Thebaner → Epameinondas sowie die Fortschritte der Belagerungstechnik (Aristot. pol. 1330b f.; Diod. 14,42; 14,51 f.) zu nennen sind. Diese Neuerungen stellten höhere Anforderungen an die mil. Führung; dementsprechend wurden seit Beginn des 4. Jh. v. Chr. Schriften zur mil. → Taktik verfaßt (Aineias [2] Taktikos). Einzelne Schriften Xenophons behandeln ebenfalls diesen Themenbereich (Xen. hipp.).

C. Die Zeit Philipps II. und Alexanders

Seit der Vereinigung ganz Makedoniens verfügte Philipp II. über das größte mil. Machtpotential im Balkanraum; durch permanente Reformen im H. (Demosth. or. 9,49f.; Diod. 16,3) konnte er die mil. Überlegenheit über Griechenland erlangen. Er stützte sich auf die schwere, neu mit der Sarissa (einem Langspieß) und einem leichten Schild ausgerüstete Phalanx (organisiert auf territorialer Basis in Taxeis à 1500 Mann), eine schlagkräftige, in einer Keilformation kämpfende Reiterei, eine gut entwickelte Belagerungstechnik und verbündete Truppen, die er in sein Heeresaufgebot integrierte. Fußsoldaten wie Reiter waren in königliche Garde (*pezhétairoi* bzw. → *hétairoi*) und normale Einheiten gegliedert. Alexander d.Gr. hatte auf seinem Feldzug 12000 Mann maked. Fußtruppen, 3000 Mann Hetairenreiterei, thessalische Reiter, griech. Söldner, Bogenschützen und andere Leichtbewaffnete bei sich. Dieses Heer wurde gegen Ende von Alexanders Herrschaft auch durch Einheiten von Persern und anderen unterworfenen Völkern verstärkt, wobei die Phalanx ihren maked. Charakter behielt. Die verschiedenen Truppengattungen wurden meist kombiniert eingesetzt.

D. Hellenismus

Die hell. Reiche, die *de facto* Militärmonarchien waren, verfügten über Berufsheere, die der Armee Alexanders nachgebildet waren. Unter den → Diadochen erreichten die Heereszahlen den höchsten Stand der griech. Geschichte. Wesentliche Neuerungen waren die Schaffung von griech.-maked. Militärsiedlungen, die als

Rekrutierungsbasis dienten, die Verwendung von Kriegselefanten und der Bau von technisch aufwendigen Belagerungsgeräten (→ Poliorketik). Zunehmend wurden Soldaten aus dem jeweiligen Herrschaftsbereich eines Königs rekrutiert, mit Ausnahme Makedoniens ging das maked. und griech. Element nach 200 v. Chr. in den hell. Armeen zurück.
→ Flottenwesen; Heeresversorgung

1 F. E. ADCOCK, The Greek and Macedonian Art of War, 1957 **2** J. K. ANDERSON, Military Theory and Practice in The Age of Xenophon, 1974 **3** B. BAR-KOCHBA, The Seleucid Army, 1976 **4** J. BLEICKEN, Die athenische Demokratie, [2]1994, 199ff., 489ff. **5** L. BURCKHARDT, Bürger und Soldaten, 1996 **6** P. DUCREY, Guerre et guerriers dans la Grèce antique, 1985 **7** HM II, 405ff. **8** J. HACKETT (Hrsg.), Warfare in the Ancient World, 1989 **9** N. G. L. HAMMOND, The Macedonian State, 1989, 100–136 **10** KROMAYER/VEITH **11** J. LATACZ, Kampfparänese, Kampfdarstellung und Kampfwirklichkeit in der Ilias, bei Kallinos und Tyrtaios, 1977 **12** M. LAUNEY, Recherches sur les armées hellénistiques, 1949 **13** J. F. LAZENBY, The Spartan Army, 1985 **14** R. LONIS, La guerre en Grèce. Quinze années de recherche, 1968–1983, in: REG 98, 1985, 321–379 **15** W. K. PRITCHETT, The Greek State at War 1–5, 1971–1991 **16** J. RICH, G. SHIPLEY (Hrsg.), War and Society in the Greek World, 1993 **17** I. G. SPENCE, The Cavalry of Classical Greece, 1993 **18** H. VAN WEES, The Homeric way of war. The »Iliad« and the Hoplite Phalanx, in: G&R 41, 1994, 1–18.

LE. BU.

III. ROM
A. DIE ZEIT DER REPUBLIK B. PRINZIPAT
C. SPÄTANTIKE

A. DIE ZEIT DER REPUBLIK

Die urspr. Struktur des röm. Heeres ist weitgehend unbekannt, und der Historiker kann sich nur auf die spätere historiographische Überl. stützen. Eine Legion war nach dem Vorbild der Bürgerschaft gegliedert: Sie bestand aus 3000 Mann, wobei jede der drei → *tribus* (*Titienses*, *Ramnes* und *Luceres*) 1000 Mann stellen mußte. Jeder dieser Truppenteile von 1000 Mann Stärke war in zehn Centurien (→ *centuria*) unterteilt, die jeweils einer *curia* (→ *curiae*) entsprachen (Varro ling. 5,89; 5,91; Liv. 10,6,7). Die mil. Führung hatten normalerweise drei Militärtribunen und 30 Centurionen inne. Die Reiter (*celeres*) vervollständigten das Heeresaufgebot. Die Soldaten mußten ihre Ausrüstung selbst stellen. Nach Einführung des → *census* und der Einteilung der Bürgerschaft in fünf *classes* und 193 *centuriae* hatte die → Reiterei eine Stärke von 18 *centuriae* (Liv. 1,43; Dion. Hal. ant. 4,16ff.). Allein die Soldaten der drei ersten *classes* hatten die Rüstung und Bewaffnung von Hopliten (→ *hoplítai*). Die Heeresordnung Roms beruhte auf dem *census* und war von ihrer Struktur her timokratisch. Taktik und Bewaffnung folgten dem griech. Vorbild der → Phalanx.

Mit dem Bevölkerungswachstum, der Vergrößerung des *ager Romanus* (röm. Territorium), der Gewährung des röm. Bürgerrechtes an zahlreiche Italiker und der inneren polit. Entwicklung wurde die Truppenstärke auf zwei Legionen mit jeweils 4000 Fußsoldaten und 300 Reitern erhöht (Pol. 3,107). Die beiden Legionen wurden von den Consuln befehligt. In einer Krisensituation wurde die Einheit der mil. Führung durch die Ernennung eines Dictators gesichert. In den Kriegen des 5. und 4. Jh. v. Chr. entstand eine neue, seit Beginn des 3. Jh. v. Chr. belegte Schlachtordnung: Die Legion wurde seitdem in drei Schlachtreihen aufgestellt, um so die Taktik der Manipel (→ *manipulus*) anwenden zu können (15 Manipel der *hastati*, → *hasta* [1], in der ersten Schlachtreihe, 15 Manipel der *principes* in der mittleren und 15 Manipel der → *triarii* in der letzten; Liv. 8,8). Die Manipel operierten getrennt voneinander, was ihnen bes. in unebenem Gelände große Beweglichkeit verlieh; die Soldaten kämpften nicht mehr Schulter an Schulter und konnten somit besser fechten. Diese Aufstellung wurde von den Leichtbewaffneten (→ *velites*), die vor der ersten Schlachtreihe standen, und den Reitern auf den Flügeln ergänzt. Die Bundesgenossen oder → *socii* verstärkten die Fußtruppen, stellten überdies Reiter und Eliteeinheiten, die → *extraordinarii*. In dieser Zeit wurde die Bewaffnung mit → Schwert (*gladius*) und Wurfspeer (→ *pilum*) eingeführt, die für lange Zeit Gültigkeit behielt (Pol. 6,19–42).

Die röm. Expansion im Zeitalter der Pun. Kriege ermöglichte eine deutliche Erhöhung der Truppenstärke. So haben in der Schlacht von Cannae 216 v. Chr. acht Legionen und *socii* unter dem Befehl beider Consuln gekämpft, nach Polybios insgesamt etwa 80000 Fußsoldaten und 6000 Reiter (Pol. 3,107; 3,113). Die Entstehung der Prov. brachte neue mil. Aufgaben mit sich: Den Provinzstatthaltern wurden für die Kriegführung in benachbarten Gebieten Truppen zugewiesen. Gleichzeitig wandelte sich auch die Taktik: Ohne Zweifel legte Scipio in Spanien vor der Schlacht bei Ilipa (206 v. Chr.) jeweils drei seiner Manipel zu einer Kohorte (→ *cohors*) zusammen (Pol. 11,23). → Marius scheint den Einsatz der Kohorte geregelt zu haben; dieser herausragende General (dem sicherlich zu viele Veränderungen im röm. H. zugeschrieben wurden) hatte außerdem die Idee, jeder Legion einen Adler als → Feldzeichen zu geben; 107 v. Chr. ließ er auch → *capite censi* in die röm. Legionen aufnehmen (Sall. Iug. 86,2 f.). Bereits im Bundesgenossenkrieg (91–88 v. Chr.) wurde deutlich, daß die Kohorte als mil. Einheit erheblich an Bedeutung gewonnen hatte.

B. PRINZIPAT

Augustus hat das röm. H. umfassend reformiert. Er schuf eine Garnison in Rom: Diese umfaßte neun Praetorianerkohorten (die Elitetruppen des Princeps), deren Standort zunächst aber nicht Rom, sondern benachbarte kleinere Städte waren. Außerdem wurden drei *cohortes urbanae* und sieben *cohortes vigiles* aufgestellt, die als Polizei bzw. Feuerwehr dienten. Der größte Teil des Heeres war in den Prov. stationiert. Ungefähr 25 Legionen bildeten den Kern der Streitkräfte (Tac. ann. 4,5; Ios. bell. Iud. 3,70–107). Die Legionen, die 5000 Mann stark waren, wurden von den *legati Augusti pro praetore* mit Hilfe von sechs *tribuni militum*, einem *praefectus castrorum* (→ *legatus*; → *tribunus*; → *praefectus*) und 59 Centurionen (→ *centurio*) kommandiert. Jede Legion hatte 59 Centurien und war gleichzeitig in 10 Kohorten unterteilt, von denen die erste nur fünf Centurien umfaßte, die aber doppelte Mannschaftsstärke besaßen. Zu den 125 000 röm. Soldaten kamen noch fast ebensoviele Soldaten der *socii* hinzu; diese dienten als → *auxilia* in Einheiten mit einer Mannschaftsstärke von 500 (*cohors quingenaria*) oder 1000 Soldaten (*cohors milliaria*). Man unterschied zwischen einfachen Kohorten (Fußtruppen), gemischten Kohorten (*equitatae*, Fußtruppen und Reiterei) und den *alae* (Reiterei, → *ala*). Seit Beginn des 2. Jh. wurden einige barbarische Völker als Bogenschützen oder Reiter in *numeri* eingesetzt. Schließlich wurde eine wirkliche Kriegsmarine mit zwei großen Stützpunkten in Italien (Misenum und Ravenna) geschaffen; hinzu kamen in den Prov. stationierte Flotten (→ Flottenwesen).

In den Grenzgebieten – die in der neueren Forschung oft fälschlich als »Limes« bezeichnet wurden, also mit einem in der Antike kaum verwendeten Begriff – entstanden neben natürlichen Hindernissen wie Flüssen Befestigungen wie Wallanlagen, Türme und kleinere Militärlager und zudem ein Straßennetz. Das Wort *limes* implizierte das Fehlen natürlicher Hindernisse und steht so im Gegensatz zum Begriff *ripa* (»Ufer«), der auf die Existenz eines Flusses hinwies. Diese Grenze erfüllte verschiedene mil. Funktionen: Sie war ein Hindernis für potentielle Feinde und ermöglichte es, Räuberbanden innerhalb des Reiches zu kontrollieren. Darüber hinaus hatte sie komplexe ökonomische, kulturelle und rel. Funktionen; an der Grenze wurden Zölle erhoben, und sie trennte die röm. Welt vom Gebiet der → Barbaren.

C. Spätantike

Die Krise des 3. Jh. machte einen Wandel des röm. H. nötig, der allerdings schwer zu analysieren ist, da für das 3. Jh. Quellen weitgehend fehlen. Es ist durchaus anzunehmen, daß Diocletianus und Constantinus viele Reformen durchführten, auch wenn nicht alle Neuerungen auf sie zurückgingen. Unter Diocletianus wurde die Zahl der röm. Soldaten stark erhöht. Wichtiger noch waren aber die strukturellen Veränderungen: Nach Auflösung der Praetorianerkohorten wurde eine neue Garde geschaffen, die *protectores*, *domestici* und die fünf *scholae palatinae* (Reiterei) umfaßte. Die Mannschaftsstärke der Legionen wurde an die der Einheiten der *auxilia*, nämlich der *alae*, *vexillationes* der Reiterei, *cohortes* und *numeri*, angepaßt und belief sich normalerweise auf etwa 1000 Soldaten. Immer häufiger rekrutierte das Imperium Barbaren, die aufgrund eines *foedus* (Vertrag) im röm. Heer dienten. Auch die Armeeführung erhielt eine neue Struktur: Die Gardetruppen unterstanden dem *magister officiorum*; der *magister equitum* befehligte die Reiterei, der *magister peditum* die Fußtruppen. Neben diesen beiden *magistri militum* wurden auch die Stellungen eines *magister militum per Orientem*, eines *mag. mil. per Gallias* und eines *mag. mil. per Illyricum* besetzt. Die Truppen in den einzelnen Prov. unterstanden den *duces* (→ *dux*), während die höherrangigen *comites militares* (→ *comes*) die Befehlsgewalt über mehrere Prov. ausübten. Auch in der Führung des Heeres gab es seit Mitte des 4. Jh. zunehmend Barbaren; so bekleideten germanische Heerführer oft das Amt des *magister militum*. Der Gegensatz zwischen den Grenztruppen (→ *limitanei*) und den mobilen Einheiten (→ *comitatenses*) war wahrscheinlich weniger ausgeprägt, als oft behauptet wurde. Tatsächlich waren einige Einheiten der *comitatenses* an der Grenze stationiert, und Einheiten der *limitanei* standen im Hinterland. Die *comitatenses*, die kaum so mobil waren, wie angenommen wurde, nahmen im röm. Heer nicht unbedingt eine zentrale Position ein.

Gegen Ende des 4. Jh. kam es zu einer tiefgreifenden Krise des röm. H. im Westen; die röm. Truppen konnten die Barbaren 406 nicht an der Überschreitung des Rheins und 410 nicht an der Einnahme Roms hindern. Während der röm. Westen zum barbarischen Westen wurde, wandelte der röm. Orient sich zum byzantinischen Reich.

→ Militärtechnik

1 G. Brizzi, Studi militari romani, 1983 **2** A. Demandt, Die Spätantike, 1989, 255–272 **3** J. Harmand, L'armée et le soldat, 1967 **4** Jones, LRE, 607–686 **5** L. Keppie, The Making of the Roman Army, 1984 **6** Kromayer/ Veith **7** Le Bohec **8** Ders., Guerres puniques, 1995 **9** G. R. Watson, Roman Soldier, [2]1985 **10** G. Webster, The Roman Imperial Army, [2]1974. Y. L. B./Ü: C. P.

Hegelochos (Ἡγέλοχος).

[1] Sohn des Hippostratos, Offizier unter → Alexandros [4]. Anfangs Kommandeur der Vorhutkavallerie, wurde er im Sommer 333 v. Chr. beauftragt, aus von griech. Städten gesammelten Schiffen eine maked. Flotte zu bilden (Arr. an. 2,2,3; ungenau Curt. 3,1,19f.; Amphoteros war ihm unter- und nicht beigeordnet). Nach dem Tod von → Memnon beherrschte seine Flotte den Hellespont, wo er u. a. eine athenische Getreideflotte aufhielt (Ps.-Demosth. or. 17,20). Er eroberte Tenedos, Chios, Lesbos und Kos. Der persische Admiral → Pharnabazos wurde gefangengenommen, entkam aber. Die gefangenen Perserfreunde aus den Inseln übergab H. in Ägypten dem Alexandros. Er fiel bei → Gaugamela (Curt. 6,11,22), wo er Ilarch (→ Reiterei) der → Hetairoi war (Arr. an. 3,11,8). Nach → Philotas' Angabe beim Folterverhör soll er sich mit Philotas und → Parmenion gegen Alexandros verschworen haben (Curt. 6,11,21–33). Das wird von Curtius bezweifelt und ist eine Erfindung zur Rechtfertigung der Ermordung Parmenions.

J. E. Atkinson, A Commentary on Q. Curtius Rufus... Books 5–7,2, 1994, 242–244 (zur »Verschwörung«) • Berve 1, 160f.; 2, Nr. 341. E. B.

[2] Nach Diodoros (34/5,20) Stratege, der eher für Ptolemaios' VIII. (124 v. Chr.) als für Ptolemaios IX. (110/108) eine Armee der Alexandriner besiegte.

PP 1, 151; 2, 2162 • F. WALTON, Notes on Diodorus, in: AJPh 77, 1956, 408–414, bes. 409ff. W.A.

Hegemon (Ἡγέμων).

[1] von Thasos. Dichter der Alten Komödie (erh. ein Fragment der *Philínna*, vgl. PCG V 547) und erster professioneller Parodist (παρῳδός, Aristot. poet. 1448a 12f.). Mit ihm wurde die parodisierende Dichtung zur lit. Gattung, zum lustigen Anhang bei den Rhapsodenwettkämpfen, ebenso wie das Satyrspiel bei den Tragödienagonen (vgl. [1]). Im einzigen erh. Fragment ruft H., bekannt unter dem Spottnamen »Linse« (φακῆ), humorvoll die schwierigen Anfänge seiner eigenen Karriere in Erinnerung (42–44 BRANDT). Später, 415 v. Chr., hatte er einen glänzenden Erfolg mit der *Gigantomachía* (Chamaileon fr. 44 WEHRLI). Vom einem ebenso hexametrischen *Deípnon* (dem evtl. frühesten Beispiel → gastronomischer Dichtung) ist nur der Titel erh. An nicht nur hexametrische Parodien läßt vielleicht Append. Peor. Bodl. II 65 denken.

1 E. DEGANI, Studi su Ipponatte, 1984, 187f.

P. BRANDT, Corpusculum poesis epicae Graecae ludibundae I, 1888, 37–49 • E. DEGANI, Poesia parodica greca, 1983, 17–24 • R. GLEI, Aristoteles über Linsenbrei, in: Philologus 136, 1992, 42–54 • V. TAMMARO, Note al frammento parodico di Egemone, in: Mousa. Scritti in onore di G. Morelli, 1997, 123–126. O.M./Ü: M.A.S.

[2] Autor eines aus dem Kranz des Meleagros stammenden Grabepigramms, das das Heldentum der bei den → Thermopylen gefallenen Spartanern – ohne dem Feind den Rücken zu kehren (ἀστρεπτεί, ein *hapax legomenon*) – rühmt (Anth. Pal. 7,436; zum Philolakonismus bes. des hell. Epigramms, vgl. → Epigramm E.). Unwahrscheinlich ist die Identifikation des Epigrammatikers mit dem Epiker H. aus Alexandreia (Ἡγήμων), der die Niederlage der Spartaner bei Leuktra (371 v. Chr.) besang.

GA I,1, 103; I,2,298f. M.G.A./Ü: M.A.S.

Hegemonia (ἡγεμονία, »Führungsposition«). Ein wichtiger Grundzug zwischenstaatlicher Beziehungen in Griechenland war die Bildung von Bündnissen, in denen eines der Mitglieder eine hervorgehobene Stellung als *hēgemṓn* (»Führer«) einnahm. Das früheste Beispiel bildet eine Gruppe von Bündnisverträgen, mit deren Hilfe Sparta im 6. Jh. v. Chr. seine Position auf der Peloponnes sicherte und die sich, nach mod. wiss. Sprachgebrauch, zum → Peloponnesischen Bund verdichteten: Kleomenes I. konnte so 506 ›ein Heer aus der ganzen Peloponnes sammeln‹ (Hdt. 5,74,1), und 432 faßten die Spartaner den Kriegsbeschluß gegen Athen, bevor sie ihre Verbündeten zu einem Kongreß einberiefen, um darüber abzustimmen (Thuk. 1,87,4; 118,3). Vermutlich bestand die formelle Verpflichtung der Bündner ›zu folgen, wohin immer Sparta sie führen (*hēgeísthai*) mochte‹ ([1. 108–110]; vgl. SEG 28, 408 = ML [1988] 67 *bis*). Sparta war auch der *hēgemṓn* der Griechen, die sich zum Widerstand gegen die persische Invasion von 480 zusammenschlossen. Argos und Syrakus hielten sich angeblich dem Bündnis fern, weil ihnen keine Beteiligung an der *h.* zugestanden wurde (Hdt. 7,148–152; 157–162). Nach dem Perserkrieg führte die Unbeliebtheit des Pausanias zur ›Übernahme der *h.*‹ durch die Athener und zur Gründung des → Attisch-Delischen Seebunds (Thuk. 1,95f.), in dem sie nicht nur die mil. Führer stellten, sondern auch die Schatzmeister (*hellēnotamíai*) und andere Funktionsträger. Im → Korinthischen Bund, den Philipp II. nach der Schlacht bei Chaironeia 338 v. Chr. errichtete, führte er den Titel *hēgemṓn* (IG II[2] 236 = TOD 177). Später gebrauchten die Antigoniden (→ Antigonos) diese Bezeichnung auch in den von ihnen begründeten Bundesorganisationen (302: Plut. Demetrios 25,3; 224: Pol. 2,54,4).

1 G. E. M. DE STE. CROIX, The Origins of the Peloponnesian War, 1972 2 V. EHRENBERG, Der Staat der Griechen, [2]1965, 137–147. P.J.R.

Hegemonios. Sonst unbekannter, vorgeblicher Verf. einer wirkmächtigen, vollständig nur in lat. Übers. überlieferten und als *Acta Archelai* (CPG 3570) bekannten antimanichäischen (→ Mani, Manichäismus) Streitschrift.

Trotz eines Hinweises auf eine syr. Quellenschrift (Hier. vir. ill. 72), dürfte die Grundlage der noch in der 1. H. des 5. Jh. gefertigten lat. Übers. ein zw. 330 und 348 entstandenes griech. Original gewesen sein [1. 136–140]. Zweifelsfreie Angaben zu Autor – H. nennt als Verf. sich selbst (Acta 68: *ego scripsi*; im Sinne von »Schreiber«, »Redaktor«?) – und Entstehungsort lassen sich nicht machen.

Eingebettet in eine fiktive Rahmenhandlung – mehrfache Begegnung zw. dem mesopot. Bischof Archelaos und Mani – versuchen die *Acta*, die zentralen Lehren des Manichäismus, bes. seine Christenpolemik, zu widerlegen. Im Gang der Erzählung wird gegen Mani dreifach vorgegangen: Nach einer vorausgehenden Befragung des Turbo, eines Boten des Mani, über diesen und seine Lehre (Kap. 7–13) besiegt Archelaos den von ihm nach Carchar (wohl Carrhae bzw. Ḥarrān, vgl. [1. 140–145]) Eingeladenen zweimal in öffentlicher Disputation vor »heidnischen« Vertretern der Stadt (Kap. 43 und 61), um schließlich in einer dritten Konfrontation Person und Lehren des selbsternannten Parakleten endgültig der Lächerlichkeit preiszugeben (Kap. 61–66). Manis Flucht und Tod in Persien vollenden den christl. Triumph.

Unter Berücksichtigung ihrer polemischen, verzeichnenden Grundtendenz bieten die bis ins 19. Jh. als Hauptquelle zum Manichäismus geltenden *Acta* ein in groben Zügen verläßliches Bild zeitgenössischer manichäischer Mission und Propaganda [1. 152], gerade auch bei den Mani betreffenden biographischen Angaben (Kap. 62–66, Übers. [2. 220–223]). Ein den *Acta* angefügter Ketzerkatalog dürfte um 400 in Rom verfaßt worden sein (Ps.-H.: CCL 9, 325–329).

ED.: CH.H. BEESON (ed.), GCS 16, 1906.
LIT.: 1 S.N.C. LIEU, Fact and Fiction in the *Acta Archelai*, in: Ders., Manichaeism in Mesopotamia and the Roman East, 1994, 132–152 2 M. SCOPELLO, Vérités et contre-vérités: la vie de Mani selon les *Actes Archelai*, in: Apocryha 6, 1995, 203–234. J.RI.

Hegesandros

[1] Athenischer Rhetor, Sohn des Hegesias aus dem Demos Sunion und Bruder des → Hegesippos [1], 361/0 v. Chr. Schatzmeister (Aischin. Tim. 55f.; 95) des Strategen Timomachos und trotz dessen Verurteilung wegen Bestechung wenig später → Tamias der Athene (Aischin. Tim. 110f. und schol.), gehörte also zu den Reichsten. Im Timokratesprozeß warf ihm wohl verleumderisch → Aischines [2] illegale Bereicherung vor. H. galt als Gegner des Aristophon von Azenia, Freund des Diopeithes [3] (Aischin. Tim. 63f.) und Anhänger des → Demosthenes [2]. 357/6 beantragte er im Bundesgenossenkrieg ein Dekret (IG II² 123 = TOD, 156) über die Garnison auf Andros und verteidigte Timarchos 345 gegen Aischines (Aischin. Tim. 64; 71).
→ Rhetorik

DAVIES, 209 • DEVELIN, Nr. 1350 • PA 6307 • TRAILL, PAA 480930. J.E.

[2] H. aus Delphi [1], 2. Jh. n. Chr., Verf. von *Hypomnḗmata* in mindestens sechs Büchern, einer Slg. von unterhaltsamen und pikanten Kuriositäten und Anekdoten mit ges. Hintergrund, wahrscheinlich nach inhaltlichen Kriterien angeordnet (ein Buch Περὶ ἀνδριάντων καὶ ἀγαλμάτων, ›Über Statuen und Götterbilder‹) scheint ein systematisch angelegter Katalog von Votivgegenständen in Delphi gewesen zu sein), mit Spitzen gegen Athen und Interesse am maked. Herrscherhaus [4]; H. schöpft aus Anekdotensammlungen desselben Typs, aber auch aus histor. Werken (→ Mnesiptolemos; → Pythermos). Hauptquelle für die (in [2] gesammelten) Frg. ist Athenaios, der ihn eigenhändig exzerpiert hat [3].

1 G. DAUX, Notes de lecture, in: BCH 81, 1957, 391 2 FHG IV, 412–422 3 F. JACOBY, s. v. H., RE 7, 2600–2602 4 L. PRANDI, Perché »guerra cremonidea«? Egesandro di Delfi (FGH, IV, p. 415, frg. 9) e la fortuna di un nome, in: Aevum 12, 1989, 24–29 5 F. SUSEMIHL, Gesch. der griech. Litt. in der Alexandrinerzeit, I, 1891, 489–491. S.FO./Ü: T.H.

Hegesaretos (Ἡγησάρετος). Thessalier aus Larissa, von Cicero in einem Empfehlungsschreiben aus dem Jahr 46 v. Chr. als *princeps civitatis* bezeichnet (fam. 13,25). Führer der pompeianischen *factio* in Thessalien (Caes. civ. 3,35,2). Von Caesar vermutlich begnadigt. W.W.

Hegesianax aus Alexandreia (Troas). Lebte unter Antiochos III. von Antiocheia (222–187 v. Chr.) und wurde, als er dem König seine Gedichte schenkte, dessen »Freund« (*phílos*, SH 464). 197 und 193 war er seleukidischer Botschafter beim röm. Senat, 196 bei T. Quinctius Flamininus in Korinth. Grammatiker, Verf. des Werkes ›Über den Stil des Demokritos‹ und ›Über den poetischen Stil‹ sowie astronomisch-myth. Gedichte (*Phainómena*, SH fr. 465–467; insgesamt fünf Hexameter sind überliefert, doch ist die Zuweisung unsicher; vgl. [7. 734[70]], mit Lit.). H. ist der älteste bekannte Verf. von ›Troischen Gesch.‹ (*Trōïká*), die, vielleicht auch unter dem Namen *Historíai* zitiert (vgl. aber [6. 48–49] mit weiterer Lit.), unter dem fiktiven Namen Kephalon (oder Kephalion) von Gergis veröffentlicht wurden – eines der ersten Werke, die die homer. Erzählungen in Gestalt eines myth. Romans auf der Grundlage vorgeblicher epigraphischer oder lit. Dokumente historisierten. H. zeigt sich Rom gegenüber freundlich; zu den polit. Intentionen des Werks und den möglichen Beziehungen zur diplomatischen Tätigkeit des Autors vgl. [7] mit reicher Bibliogr.; [5].

1 SH 464–470 2 FGrH I A: 45 3 CollAlex 8–9 4 I.C. CUNNINGHAM, The Hexameter of Fragmentary Hellenistic Poets, in: Quaderni urbinati di cultura classica 25, 1977, 95–100 5 J.G. FARROW, Aeneas and Rome: pseudoepigrapha and politics, in: CJ 87, 1991–1992, 339–359 6 S. MERKLE, Die Ephemeris belli Troiani des Dictys von Kreta, 1989, 48–49 (mit Lit.) 7 E. PACK, Antiochia, in: G. CAMBIANO, L. CANFORA, D. LANZA (Hrsg.), Lo spazio letterario della Grecia antica I/2, 1993, 733–736 8 F. SUSEMIHL, Gesch. der griech. Litt. in der Alexandrinerzeit 2, 1892, 31–33. S.FO./Ü: T.H.

Hegesias (Ἡγησίας).

[1] → Kyrenaïker, lebte in den Jahrzehnten vor und nach 300 v. Chr. Wegen der Modifikationen, die er (vermutlich in Auseinandersetzung mit → Epikuros) an der urspr. kyrenaïschen Lustlehre vornahm, ließen manche ant. Philosophiehistoriker mit ihm eine neue Phase in der Gesch. der Kyrenaïker beginnen. H. schätzte die Aussicht, daß es einem gelinge, sich → Lust zu verschaffen und Schmerz zu meiden, erheblich pessimistischer ein als die urspr. Kyrenaïker. Er begründete dies mit den zahlreichen Leiden, von denen der Körper heimgesucht werde, und den Zufälligkeiten des Lebens. Worauf es in erster Linie ankomme, sei daher, Schmerzempfindungen zu vermeiden. Demgemäß setzte er als Ziel (*télos*) nicht wie die urspr. Kyrenaïker die Lust (*hēdonḗ*), sondern das Freisein von körperlichen und seelischen Schmerzen an. Diese Anschauungen und die aus ihnen hergeleitete, daß dem Leben kein eigener Wert zukomme, legte H. in einer Schrift mit dem Titel ›Der Hungerselbstmörder‹ (Ἀποκαρτερῶν) dar. Seine pessimistische Weltsicht brachte H. den Beinamen Πεισιθάνατος (*Peisithánatos*, »der zum Tod überredet«) ein. Ptolemaios I. Soter soll H. verboten haben, seine Lehren zu verbreiten, weil sich durch sie zahlreiche Menschen zum Selbstmord verleiten ließen. Wichtigste Quellen: Diog. Laert. 2,85–86; 93–96 und Cic. Tusc. 1,83–84.

SSR IV F • K. DÖRING, s. v. H., in: GGPh² 2.1, 1998, § 19 B. K.D.

[2] Griech. Rhetor und Historiker des 4. und 3. Jh. v. Chr. aus Magnesia am Sipylos; von seinen epideiktischen Reden (→ Epideixis) und seiner Alexander-Gesch. (FGrH 142) sind einige Fr. überl., meist in polemischem Kontext zit. (z. B. Dion. Hal. comp. 18,125–27 USENER-RADERMACHER; ohne Wertung: Strab. 9,1,16): H. verstand sich zwar selbst als Fortsetzer der att. Redekunst (Cic. Brut. 286), galt aber seit dem 1. Jh. v. Chr. als Hauptrepräsentant des mehr und mehr verpönten → Asianismus (Cic. orat. 226; 230; Ps.-Longinus, de sublimitate 3,2); sein von kurzen, stark rhythmisierten Kola und kühnen Metaphern geprägter, mit Paronomasien und Homoioteleuta überladener Stil, den Cicero parodiert (Att. 12,6,1), wurde aber von (dem ebenfalls für seinen Stil getadelten: Quint. inst. 10,1,95; Aug. civ. 6,2) Varro bewundert (Cic. Att. 12,6,1).

G. KENNEDY, The art of persuasion in Greece, 1963, 301–303 • NORDEN, Kunstprosa Bd. 1, 134–139 • L. PIOTROWICZ, De Hegesia Magnete rerum gestarum scriptore, 1915 • E. SPINELLI, Il racconto di un racconto, in: Vichiana 18, 1989, 333–340 • A. TRAGLIA, Elementi stilistici nel De lingua Latina di Varrone, in: ASNP 12, 1982, 481–511. M. W.

Hegesidamos (Ἡγησίδαμος). In der Suda s. v. Ἱππίας als Lehrer des → Hippias von Elis genannt. M. MEI.

Hegesikles s. Agesikles

Hegesileos (Ἡγησίλεως). Verwandter des Eubulos von Probalinthos (Demosth. or. 19,290), → Strategos der athenischen Truppen in der Schlacht von Mantineia 362 v. Chr. (Xen. vect. 3,7; Ephoros FGrH 70 F 85; Diod. 15,84,2) und wahrscheinlich 349/8 erneut Stratege der athenischen Hilfstruppen für den Tyrannen Plutarchos aus Eretria. Im Einvernehmen mit diesem wurde er in einem → Eisangelia-Verfahren wegen Täuschung des Demos verurteilt (Demosth. or. 19,290 mit schol.).

DEVELIN, Nr. 1358 • PA 6339 • TRAILL, PAA 481385. J. E.

Hegesilochos (Ἡγεσίλοχος).

[1] Rhodier, nutzte 356/5 v. Chr. den Konflikt zwischen Rhodos und Athen (→ Bundesgenossenkriege [1]) aus, um mit Unterstützung des → Maussollos von Karien an der Spitze einer oligarchischen Clique die Macht in Rhodos zu übernehmen.

R. M. BERTHOLD, Rhodes in the Hellenistic Age, 1984, 31, mit Anm. 41 (Quellen und Lit.). M. MEI.

[2] (auch: Ἀγησίλοχος/Hagesilochos). Sohn des Hagesias, Rhodier, gemäßigter Römerfreund, der sich als Prytane (172/1 v. Chr.) und als Gesandter (im Sommer 169 nach Rom) im Frühjahr 168 zu L. → Aemilius [I 32] Paullus für die Unterstützung Roms gegen → Perseus einsetzte (Pol. 27,3,3; 28,2; 16; Liv. 42,45) [1. 139f., 144f.; 2. 185–190].

1 H. H. SCHMITT, Rom und Rhodos, 1957 2 J. DEININGER, Der polit. Widerstand gegen Rom in Griechenland, 1971. L.-M. G.

Hegesinus (Ἡγησίνους).

[1] H. aus Pergamon, 1. Hälfte 2. Jh. v. Chr., wohl identisch mit Hegesilaos bei Clem. Al. strom. 1,64,1. Er übernahm die Leitung der Akademie von Euandros (Diog. Laert. 4,60). H., der letzte Vertreter der Mittleren Akademie (Galen hist. phil. 3 = DIELS, DG 599f.; Clem. Al. ebd.), war der Lehrer des Karneades (Cic. ac. 2,16), seines späteren (vor 155 v. Chr.) Nachfolgers im Scholarchat. Der Name H. taucht nur in Sukzessionslisten auf, über die Namensnennung hinausgehende Nachrichten fehlen.

→ Akademeia K.-H. S.

[2] Epiker, aus dessen Werk *Atthís* Paus. 9,29,1 vier Hexameter über die Gründung von Askra durch Oioklos zitiert [1]. Pausanias' Quelle ist → Kallippos von Korinth, der den Namen H. wahrscheinlich erfunden hat

1 J. ZWICKER, s. v. Oioklos, RE 17, 2283.

PEG I, 143–144 (mit Lit.) • EpGF 166 • FGrH III B: 331 (Komm.: 609–610). S. FO./Ü: T. H.

Hegesippos (Ἡγήσιππος).

[1] Sohn des Hegesias aus Sunion, athenischer Rhetor und Gesandter aus reicher Familie. 357/6 v. Chr. beantragte er in der Ekklesia Hilfe für Eretria (IG II² 125 = TOD, 154), 356/5 die athenische Symmachie mit Phokis (Aischin. Ctes. 118; Demosth. or. 19,72–74 mit schol.) und zwischen 346 und 340 weitere Dekrete zur Außenpolitik (Demosth. or. 18,75). Im J. 345 verteidigte er mit seinem Bruder Hegesandros [1] den Timarchos gegen → Aischines [2] (Aischin. Tim. 71). Er opponierte bei der Gesandtschaft Pythons gegen eine Revision des Philokratesfriedens, blieb selbst als Gesandter zu → Philippos II. im Streit über Halonessos erfolglos (vgl. die Rede des H.: Ps.-Demosth. or. 7) und versuchte 343/2 mit → Demosthenes [2], Polyeuktos und Lykurgos auf der Peloponnes, dem Einfluß Philipps entgegenzuwirken (Demosth. or. 9,72). 338/7 beantragte er Dekrete zu Ehren der Akarnanen und über Phormion und Karphinas (IG II² 237 = TOD, 178), ca. 333/2 hielt er vielleicht die Rede ›Über die Verträge mit Alexander‹ (schol. zu Demosth. or. 17 p. 195 DILTS). Eine 341/0 geleistete Bürgschaft für Trieren bei der Expedition nach Chalkis löste er 325/4 ein (IG II² 1623, 185 und 1629, 543), die letzte Nachricht aus seinem Leben.

→ Rhetorik

DAVIES, 209f. • DEVELIN, Nr. 1360 • PA 6351 • TRAILL, PAA 481555. J. E.

[2] Dichter der Neuen Komödie. Athenaios zitiert 30 Verse aus den ›Brüdern‹ (Ἀδελφοί) mit der prahlerischen Selbstanpreisung eines Kochs (fr. 1), sowie sechs Verse aus den ›Die die Gefährten lieben‹ (Φιλέταιροι) mit einem Dialogfragment, in dem Sprecher B die von Sprecher A wiedergegebene Maxime des → Epikuros (Ἐπίκουρος ὁ σοφός), das höchste Gut sei die Lust (ἡδονή), freudig auf das Essen bezieht. Auf Grund dieses

Zitates ist H. wohl in das 3. Jh. (evtl. nach dem Tod des Philosophen 271/0 v. Chr.) zu datieren.

1 PCG V, 548–551. T. HI.

[3] Epigrammdichter im Kranz des Meleagros, der seine Muse als μαινὰς βότρυς (»rasende Weintraube«) bezeichnet (Anth. Pal. 4,1,25), doch haben die acht überlieferten Gedichte (Weih- und Grab-Epigramme) eigentlich nichts »Rasendes« an sich: sie sind (nicht wortwörtliche) Imitationen v. a. von Anyte, Nikias, Kallimachos und Leonidas von Tarent (Anth. Pal. 7,276, jedoch sehr unsicher). Die metrische Kombination zweier Epigramme (ebd. 6,266 und 13,12), die für das 3. Jh. v. Chr. nachweisbar erscheint, legt die Lebenszeit des H. um die Mitte dieses Jh. nahe.

GA I,1, 104–106; I,2, 299–304 • A. CAMERON, The Greek Anthology from Meleager to Planudes, 1993, 3 f. M. G. A./Ü: M. A. S.

[4] H. aus Mekyberna bei Olynth, Verf. von *Pallēniaká*, wohl um 300 v. Chr. Einzige bekannte ältere Lokalgesch. chalkidischer Städte in Thrakien, daraus einige auf die Sagenzeit bezügliche Fr. erhalten. Die angeblichen *Milēsiaká* des H. beruhen wohl auf einer Korruptel.

ED.: FGrH 391.
LIT.: F. JACOBY, s. v. H. (4), RE 7,2, 2610 f. K. MEI.

[5] H. wird von → Eusebios [7] zwar als ›einer der ersten Nachfolger der Apostel‹ bezeichnet (Eus. HE 2,23,3), dürfte aber nach Ausweis eines Fragmentes, das Eusebios selbst überliefert (HE 4,22,3), eher in der Zeit zw. 174 und 189 n. Chr. schriftstellerisch tätig gewesen sein. Er schrieb fünf B. *Hypomnḗmata* (Eus. HE 4,22,1), von denen Fr. hauptsächlich bei Eusebios, aber auch bei Philippos Sidetes und dem Florilegienautor Stephanos Gobaros (6. Jh., Photios, Bibliotheke cod. 232 p. 288b 10–16) überl. sind (CPG 1, 1302; möglicherweise existierten allerdings bis ins 17. Jh. noch Hss. des Textes). Themen sind: Iakobos, der Bruder Jesu (Eus. HE 2,23,3–19), die Jerusalemer Bischöfe (HE 3,11 und 32,1–8 sowie 4,22,4), palästinische Lokaltrad. über die Familie Jesu (HE 3,20,1–6) und eine Genealogie der Häresien (HE 4,22,5–6). H. ist nicht der erste Zeuge für das Theologumenon einer personalen Kontinuität der Weitergabe bes. Geistesgaben von Lehrautorität und Kirchenleitung (»apostolische Sukzession«); vielmehr interpretiert Eusebios eine Passage des H. über die ungebrochene Lehrkontinuität der röm. Gemeinde im apostolischen Glauben (HE 4,22,3) im Lichte dieser erst später aufgekommenen und erstmals bei → Eirenaios [2] von Lyon bezeugten Vorstellung (vgl. HE 4,11,7). Eusebios hat aus der Tatsache, daß H. aus aram. und hebr. Texten zitierte, geschlossen, er sei vom Judentum zum Christentum übergetreten; auch referiere er aus der ›ungeschriebenen jüd. Trad.‹ (HE 4,22,8), was u. U. auf eine Ausbildung als Schriftgelehrter hinweisen könne. Die Zuordnung des H. zum Judenchristentum ist ebenso umstritten wie diese Kategorie selbst; für sie spricht u. a. sein bes. Interesse an der Jerusalemer Urgemeinde und ihrem Bischof Jakobos sowie der Antipaulinismus des bei Photius überl. Fragmentes. H. selbst erwähnt eine Romreise (Eus. HE 4,22,2).

ED.: TH. ZAHN, Apostel und Apostelschüler in der Provinz Asien (Forsch. zur Gesch. des nt. Kanons 6/1), 1900, 228–249 • L. ABRAMOWSKI, ΔΙΑΔΟΧΗ und ὈΡΘΟΣ ΛΟΓΟΣ bei Hegesipp, in: ZKG 87, 1976, 321–327 • E. CASPAR, Die älteste röm. Bischofsliste (Schriften der Königsberger Gelehrten Ges., Geisteswiss. Klasse 4), 1926 (Ndr. 1975), 447–451 • A. v. HARNACK, Die Chronologie der altchristl. Litteratur 1, 1897, 311–313 • N. HYLDAHL, Hegesipps Hypomnemata, in: Studia Theologica 14, 1960, 70–113. C. M.

[6] H. von Tarent s. Kochbücher

Hegesipyle (Ἡγησιπύλη). Tochter des Königs Oloros von Thrakien. Heiratete ca. 515–513 v. Chr. → Miltiades und gebar ihm → Kimon (Hdt. 6,39,2; Plut. Kimon 4,1).

C. FERETTO, Milziade ed Egesipile. Un matrimonio d'interesse, in: Serta Historica Antiqua [1], 1986, 77–83. U. P.

Hegesistratos (Ἡγησίστρατος).
[1] Sohn des → Peisistratos und der Argeierin Timonassa (Hdt. 5,94; Aristot. Ath. pol. 17,3). Von seinem Vater um 530 v. Chr. als Tyrann von Sigeion eingesetzt, verteidigte er die Stadt als »Kolonie« der Peisistratiden gegen die Mytilenäer (Hdt. a.O.).
→ Tyrannis

DAVIES 11793,VI (B) • M. STAHL, Aristokraten und Tyrannen, 1987, 220 f. • TRAILL, PAA 481600.

[2] H. aus Elis, Sohn des Tellias. Floh aus der spartanischen Gefangenschaft und wurde Seher im Heer des → Mardonios. Nach der Schlacht von Plataiai (479 v. Chr.) fiel H. den Spartanern erneut in die Hände und wurde hingerichtet (Hdt. 9,37 f.).

[3] Samier, Sohn des Aristagoras, im 4. Jh. v. Chr. Anführer einer Gesandtschaft zum spartanischen König → Leotychidas, den H. angesichts des Rückzuges der Phoiniker von Samos zum Vorgehen gegen die Perser in Ionien aufforderte (Hdt. 9,90–92).

J. HEINRICHS, Ionien nach Salamis, 1989, 46–55. HA. BE.

[4] Unter → Dareios [3] 334 v. Chr. Kommandant von Miletos, wollte die Stadt zuerst an → Alexandros [4] übergeben, verteidigte sie aber dann und fiel wahrscheinlich bei ihrer Erstürmung (Arr. an. 1,18,4; 19,4). E. B.

[5] Überbrachte 262/1 v. Chr. als Gesandter des Ptolemaios II. einen Brief an Milet, ohne konkrete Zusagen machen zu können (IMilet I 3, 139). Die Stadt fiel wenig später von Ptolemaios ab. W. A.

Hegetor. Alexandrinischer Arzt, zeitlich zw. Herophilos (330/320–260/250 v. Chr.), dessen Nachfolger er war, und Apollonios (1. Jh. v. Chr.), von dem er zitiert wird; gemeinhin wird er wegen seiner Polemik gegen die → Empiriker hinsichtlich der Aitiologie ins 2. Jh. v. Chr. gesetzt.

Von seinem Werk sind nur indirekte Zit. erhalten, von denen drei mit seinem Namen versehen sind und das letzte (Gal. Def. med. 220 = 19,448 f. K.) ihm nur zugewiesen wurde [1. 73 Anm. 44; 137 Anm. 183; 2]. Das fr. 3 stammt aus einer Schrift *Perí aitíōn* (›Über die Ursprünge‹), in dem H. den aitiologischen Nihilismus der Empiriker widerlegt; er verteidigt jene Forsch. nach den Ursachen der pathologischen Fakten, die anatomische Studien und klinische Unt. verbindet, und trägt damit zur Definition einer rationalistisch geprägten Epistemologie bei. Die fr. 1 und 2 betreffen die Sphygmologie und enthalten eine Definition und Theorie des Pulses. Das fr. 4 betrifft den Herzrhythmus und nimmt die von dem Herophileer → Zenon (1. H. des 2. Jh. v. Chr.) vorgeschlagene Definition wieder auf, wobei der Begriff *schésis* durch den der *táxis* ersetzt wird.

All diese Elemente weisen darauf hin, daß H. die Lehre des Herophilos, wie sie aus anderen Quellen bekannt ist, fortsetzte.

1 J. Kollesch, Unt. zu den pseudogalenischen Definitiones medicae, 1973 2 Staden A. TO./Ü: T. H.

Hegetorides (Ἡγητορίδης). Angesehener Bürger aus Kos. Die Gesch. seiner Tochter, die von Persern verschleppt und nach der Schlacht bei Plataiai (479 v. Chr.) als Schutzflehende vom spartanischen Regenten → Pausanias befreit worden sein soll, ist eines von Herodots Beispielen für die moralische Überlegenheit der Griechen (Hdt. 9,76; vgl. Paus. 3,4,9). E. S.-H.

Hegias (Ἡγίας).

[1] Bildhauer, signierte auf der Basis einer verlorenen Bronzestatue auf der Akropolis von Athen, die um 490–480 v. Chr. zu datieren ist. Als spätarcha. Künstler, Zeitgenosse von → Kritios und Nesiotes, → Onatas, → Ageladas und → Kalon sowie als Lehrer des → Pheidias erwähnen ihn Pausanias (8,42,10), Plinius (nat. 34,49) und Dion Chrysostomos (55,1). Quintilian (inst. 12,10,7) und Lukian (Rhetorum praeceptor 9) beschreiben seinen Stil als noch archa. und nennen ihn mit vollem Namen Hegesias. Plinius (nat. 34,78) sah von ihm in Rom Dioskuren und eine Athena, schuf aber Verwirrung, indem er ihm auch einen *Pyrrhus rex* und *pueri celetizontes* zuwies und ihn außerdem (nat. 34,49) in die 83. Olympiade (448–444 v. Chr) datierte. Für jene Sujets einen späteren, gleichnamigen Künstler zu erschließen, besteht kein Zwang, da die ›reitenden Knaben‹ uns unbekannt sind und zudem wahrscheinlich ein Versehen des Plinius vorliegt, der an anderer Stelle (nat. 34,80) eine Hygieia und Minerva des Bildhauers → Pyrrhus nennt.

H. Brunn, Gesch. der griech. Künstler 1, 1857, 101–102 • Lippold, 108 • P. Orlandini, s. v. H. (1), EAA 3, 1960, 1128–1130 • Overbeck, Nr. 420, 422, 452–456 (Quellen) • A. E. Raubitschek, Dedications from the Athenian Agora, 1949, Nr. 94 • B. S. Ridgway, The Severe Style in Greek Sculpture, 1970, 89. R. N.

[2] Konnte 190 v. Chr. als römerfreundliches Mitglied einer teilweise seleukidenfreundlichen Gesandtschaft seiner Heimatstadt Phokaia nicht erreichen, daß der sich Phokaia nähernde Seleukos, Sohn Antiochos' III., deren einstweilige Neutralität anerkannte (Pol. 21,6,2 ff.). A. ME.

[3] Bildhauer der frühen Kaiserzeit aus Athen. Er signierte gemeinsam mit Philathenaios die Statue des Claudius als Zeus, die für den Kaiserkult im Metroon von Olympia aufgestellt war.

K. Hitzl, Die kaiserzeitliche Statuenausstattung des Metroon, in: OlF 19, 1991 • Loewy, Nr. 332. R. N.

[4] Sohn der Asklepigeneia (Tochter des Achiadas und der Plutarche) und des Theagenes, Mitglied der Familie des → Plutarchos von Athen. H. wurde trotz seiner Jugend von dem Neuplatoniker Proklos (412–485 n. Chr.) zu seinen Lehrveranstaltungen über die *Oracula Chaldaica* zugelassen (Marinus, vita Procli 26; Damaskios, vita Isidori 351 Zintzen), doch war er auch Schüler des → Isidoros [4] von Alexandreia (Damaskios, vita Isidori 230 Zintzen). Er wurde Lehrer an der neuplatonischen Schule (→ Neuplatonismus), interessierte sich jedoch mehr für die → Theurgie als für philos. Überlegungen und brachte dadurch die Schule in Verruf (ebd. 221). Sein Lehrer Isidoros versuchte ihn ständig zur Vernunft zu bringen (ebd. 227). Als fanatischer Paganer schuf er sich Feinde unter den Christen (ebd. 351). Seine beiden Söhne Eupeithios und Archiadas hatten an der Philos. kein Interesse (Suda s. v. Ἡγίας, 2,550,3–24 Adler; s. v. Εὐπείθιος καὶ Ἀρχιάδας, 2,464,20–465,9). L. BR./Ü: J. DE.

Heidelberg-Maler s. Kleinmeisterschalen

Heilgötter, Heilkult

I. Einleitung II. Mesopotamien und Syrien III. Ägypten IV. Griechenland und Rom

I. Einleitung

Heilung von Krankheiten kann zwar grundsätzlich in den Bereich jeder Gottheit oder jedes Heroen als Inhabers übermenschlicher Kraft zur Hilfeleistung fallen, doch in der Realität des Kultes hat sich die Funktion des Heilens auf einige bes. wirkkräftige Gottheiten und Heroen konzentriert [1].

1 W. A. Jayne, The Healing Gods of Ancient Civilizations, 1925. F. G.

II. Mesopotamien und Syrien

Durch Namen, Epitheta und Erwähnungen in medizinischen Texten wurde in Mesopot. eine Reihe von Gottheiten mit Heilkräften assoziiert, wobei die Bed. der Heilgöttinnen ungleich größer war als die der H. Die verschiedenen, schon seit der Fara-Zeit (Mitte 3. Jt.) belegten Heilgöttinnen sind spätestens seit der altbabylon. Zeit (1. H. 2. Jt.) in der Gestalt der Gula zusammengefallen [1. 101–106]. Ihr Hauptkultort war die Stadt Isin [3]. Auch den großen Göttern → Marduk und Ea wurden in Epitheta Funktionen als H. zugewiesen.

In Syrien sind seit der Mitte des 1. Jt. v. Chr. → Ešmūn, der mit Asklepios gleichgesetzt wurde, und Šadrapa (etymologisiert als *šd-rp'* »Šed heilend«) als H. belegt [2. 286f.]. In Kleinasien haben H. nur eine unbed. Rolle gespielt.

1 H. Avalos, Illness and Health Care in the Ancient Near East, 1995, 99–231 2 H. W. Haussig (Hrsg.), WB der Myth., 1. Abt., Bd. 1: Götter und Mythen im Vorderen Orient, 1965 3 B. Hrouda, Isin 1, 1977. NI. HE.

III. Ägypten

Alle äg. Gottheiten können grundsätzlich auch als H. angerufen werden. So werden z. B. → Amun oder → Min in Gebeten als Ärzte bezeichnet; → Thot oder → Horus gelten u. a. als Ärzte der Götter. Horus erscheint auch als Kindgott auf den in der Spätzeit häufigen magischen Statuen (»Horusstelen«), die v. a. gegen Schlangenbisse und Skorpionstiche helfen sollen. → Isis ist als Herrin des Zaubers bes. geeignet, Kranke zu heilen; als Mutter des Horus ist sie speziell für Kinderkrankheiten zuständig. Götter, die als Verursacher von Krankheiten bekannt sind, wie die Skorpiongöttin → Selkis oder Sachmet, die durch ihre Pfeile und »Boten« Seuchen verbreitet, sind auch für deren Heilung zuständig und gelten als Schutzpatrone der Ärzte. In der Spätzeit, v. a. in ptolem. und röm. Zeit, werden die vergöttlichten Gelehrten und Baumeister Imhotep (→ Imuthes) und Amenhotep als Nothelfer und H. verehrt. Der Kult des Amenhotep ist auf Theben beschränkt, aber Imhotep wird als »Sohn des Ptah« in das äg. Pantheon eingebunden und seit ptolem. Zeit landesweit angebetet. Von den Griechen wird er mit → Asklepios gleichgesetzt.

H. Brunner, s. v. Götter, Heil-, LÄ 2, 645–647 · D. Wildung, Imhotep und Amenhotep, 1977. K. J.-W.

IV. Griechenland und Rom

A. Die Gottheiten B. Der Kult

A. Die Gottheiten 1. Frühes Griechenland 2. Griechenland und Rom seit dem 5. Jh. 3. Spätere Entwicklungen

Es ist zwischen den Inhabern bes. handwerklicher Kunstfertigkeit und denen bes. Heilkraft zu unterscheiden; entsprechend der Ambivalenz göttlicher und heroischer Wirkung können letztere auch Sender von Krankheiten sein. Mit dem Fortschreiten medizinischer Kenntnisse und der Erfolge der wiss. Medizin schränkt sich die Funktion von H. immer stärker auf nicht erfolgreich medizinisch behandelbare Krankheiten und somatische Dysfunktionen ein, unter denen Schwierigkeiten im Sexual- und Fortpflanzungsbereich nach Ausweis der anatomischen Votive (→ Weihung) besonders prominent sind. Als weitere Folge der Verwissenschaftlichung großer Teile der Medizin werden rituelle Heilungen, wenn sie außerhalb der institutionellen Heilkulte stattfinden, in die Heilmagie (→ Magie) abgedrängt; dabei ist allerdings die ant. Wahrnehmung, die oft durch die Konkurrenzsituation zwischen Ärzten und rituellen Heilern geprägt ist, in weit weniger Fällen diskriminierend, als die mod. Forsch. wahrhaben will.

1. Frühes Griechenland

Im frühen Griechentum ist der vornehmlichste H. → Apollon, der im 1. Buch der *Ilias* die große Pest erst mit seinen Pestpfeilen (ein altoriental. Motiv) sendet und sie nach der rituellen Besänftigung durch die Griechen wieder heilt; diese Doppelfunktion Apollons hält sich bis in die Kaiserzeit, wo das klarische (→ Klaros) Orakel mehreren kleinasiatischen Städten die Aufstellung eines pfeilschießenden Apollon zur Abwehr der großen Pest von 165/166 n. Chr. empfahl, wohl auch im Rückgriff auf das homer. Bild [1]. Verbreitete Epiklese des Heilers Apollon in nachhomer. Zeit ist → Paian, auch Name des rituellen Gesangs und Tanzes, mit dem der Gott schon in Hom. Il. 1,467–474 versöhnt wird. Diese Epiklese nimmt den Namen eines myk. Kultempfängers auf, *Paiawon* (Knossos: [2. 164f.]), der auch bei Homer als Wundheiler und Kenner von Heilmitteln erscheint (Hom. Il. 5,401; Od. 4,232), wo aber die Identifikation mit Apollon unsicher ist. Später ist bes. die Funktionsepiklese *Iatrós*, »Arzt«, verbreitet, aus welcher der Kult des Apollo Medicus wohl anläßlich eines Seuchenzugs in Rom übernommen und wegen einer Pest im J. 433 v. Chr. mit einem Tempel ausgestattet wird (Liv. 4,25,3. 29,7).

Neben dem Gott, der die medizinisch unheilbare Seuche heilen kann, steht bei Homer der Heilheros → Machaon, der Sohn des → Asklepios, dessen handwerkliche Kunst die Wunden der Krieger heilt (Hom. Il. 5,193–219), der aber auch seinerseits ein tüchtiger Kämpfer ist (Hom. Il. 11,504–520); im Kyklos kommt in derselben Rolle sein Bruder → Podaleirios dazu (Q. Smyrn. 4,396–404): In der fiktionalen Welt des Epos entsprechen sie den histor. Wundärzten, nachhomer. werden sie nicht nur innerhalb der Kultgruppe des Asklepios, sondern auch allein oder zu zweit als Heilheroen kult. verehrt (Machaons Grab und Heiligtum in Gerenia, Paus. 3,26,9; sein Sohn Polemokrates in Eua, Paus. 2,38,6; seine Söhne in Pharai, Paus. 4,30,3; Heroon des Podaleirios bei den Daunern, Strab. 6,3,9). Erste Hilfe leisten auch andere epische Helden: in der *Odyssee* benutzen die Onkel des Odysseus einen wirkkräftigen Spruch, *epaiodḗ*, um das Blut einer Schenkelwunde zu stillen (Hom. Od. 19,457f.) – ein Problem, das bis in die Neuzeit immer wieder die Domäne der »magischen« Medizin gewesen ist.

2. Griechenland und Rom seit dem 5. Jh.

In klass. und nachklass. Zeit stellen die Votive, insbes. die anatomischen Votive, die zentrale Zeugnisgruppe für Heilkulte dar, sowohl in Griechenland [3] wie in Italien [4; 5]. Sie zeigen, welche Gottheiten als Heiler verehrt wurden und welche Probleme für welches Geschlecht bes. drängend waren, und sie geben Einblick in die medizinische Pathologie [6]. In der griech. Welt erweisen sich dadurch (neben dem weit verbreiteten → Asklepios) zum einen → Herakles und → Zeus (allerdings bes. der kaiserzeitl., oriental. Zeus → Hypsistos auf der athenischen Pnyx), zum anderen eine Reihe von Frauengottheiten (→ Demeter, → Eileithyia, → Artemis) als bes. wichtig. Bei Herakles ist es Folge der weit verbreiteten und bes. in der späteren Ant. sehr wichtigen Schutz- und Hilfsfunktion des Heros (mit der sehr verbreiteten Epiklese *Alexíkakos*, »Übelabwehrer«), bei den Frauengottheiten erwächst die Heilfunktion aus ihrer weitergehenden Sorge für → Geburt und Kinderpflege (→ Kurotrophos); ein Sonderbereich ist Demeters Heilung von Augenkrankheiten, die vielleicht aus der Rolle des Sehens in den eleusin. Mysterien herausgewachsen ist [7]. Daneben stehen die zahlreichen, bes. für Attika gut belegten → Heroenkulte [8], etwa derjenige des mehrfach bezeugten → Iatros, des → Amynos (»Abwehrer«) und des Pankrates (»Allmächtiger«), der zusammen mit Herakles oder als eine Form desselben verehrt wurde [9].

Weiter gestreut, doch in manchen Fällen nicht mehr identifizierbar sind die durch die anatomischen Votive für die republikan. Zeit belegten ital. H., unter denen die Frauenkulte wiederum eine bes. große Rolle spielen; die Befunde von Latium unterscheiden sich nicht grundsätzlich von denen Etruriens, außer daß die etr., allein durch Funddeposite belegten H. grundsätzlich anonym bleiben [10]. Wichtig und gut bezeugt ist die Heilkraft der → Quellen und der mit ihnen verbundenen Gottheiten (Frontin. aqu. 1,4). Neben dem seit dem mittleren Hellenismus in Mittelitalien belegten → Aesculapius (großes Heiligtum in Fregellae, architektonisch dem von Kos nachgebaut [11]), der seit seiner Einführung in Rom im J. 293 v. Chr. Apollo Medicus allmählich zurückdrängte, steht insbes. → Minerva, die seit dem 3. Jh. v. Chr. in Lavinium und als Minerva Medica in Rom in einem Tempel auf dem Esquilin verehrt wurde (Cic. div. 2,123; Ov. fast. 3,827f.; CIL VI 10133), daneben auch → Iuno (Lucina) und die Quell- und Geburtsgöttin → Carmentis. In Griechenland wie in It. wird seit späthell. Zeit → Isis als H. wichtig; dies nimmt eine schon ägypt. Funktion auf, gehört aber zugleich zu ihrer zunehmend bedeutsamen Rolle als allmächtige Beschützerin ihrer Verehrer und läßt sich nicht auf einen spezifischen Bereich beschränken (Diod. 1,25,2–5); in ihren Kreis gehören auch die Heiler Hermes-Thot und Imuthes-Asklepios [12. 199–209].

3. Spätere Entwicklungen

Eine große Rolle spielen → Quellgottheiten, insbes. von Thermalquellen, im kelt. Bereich; viele von ihnen werden in röm. Zeit mit Apollo (weit verbreitet Apollo → Grannus), die Göttin Sul im britischen Bath mit Minerva identifiziert [13; 14]. In nt. Trad. ist Christus selbst Heiler von sonst hoffnungslosen Krankheiten (Besessenheit, Blutfluß); deswegen benutzen → Exorzismen zur Heilung von Besessenheit ebenso wie Amulette gegen Krankheiten seinen Namen. Die eigentliche Nachfolge der paganen H. und Heilheroen treten zahlreiche Heilige an, in deren Viten die Heilungswunder in der Nachfolge Jesu eine bedeutende Rolle spielen und den Kult und die Erwartungen an den Heiligen mitformen.

B. Der Kult

1. Einzelne Kultformen

Ebenso unterschiedlich wie die H. sind die Formen des Heilkultes. Heilung kann durch die üblichen Formen des ant. Kults, also durch Gebet und Opfer, gesucht werden. Schon die Griechen der *Ilias* veranstalten ein großes Opferfest mit gemeinsamem Mahl und anschließendem Tanzen und Singen des Paian, um der Pest Einhalt zu gebieten. Die sehr zahlreichen Votive sind das Resultat eines Gebets, welches das Gelübde enthielt, im Falle der Heilung das entsprechende Votiv darzubringen. Im Falle von Krankheiten, die als Besessenheit oder als Strafe verstanden werden, etwa → Epilepsie oder psychische Störungen (*manía*, »Wahnsinn«), wendet man kathartische Riten an, deren Natur sich an der die Krankheit verursachenden Gottheit ausrichtet (Hippokr. De morbo sacro 2f.; Plat. rep. 2,364bd).

Einen Sonderbereich bilden die sog. Beicht-Inschr., eine umfassende Gruppe von Inschr.-Stelen aus Nordwest-Lydien, die mit einer Inschr. in einem lokalen Heiligtum (bes. des Men und der Meter) aufgestellt wurden, welche ein (wissentlich oder unwissentlich begangenes) rel. Vergehen mitsamt der dadurch als Strafe erhaltenen, sonst unerklärbaren Krankheit darstellte; das öffentliche und durch die Inschr. permanent gemachte Bekenntnis bringt dem Bekenner die Gesundheit zurück [15].

2. Inkubation

Das verbreitetste rituelle Mittel zur Heiligung freilich ist der Tempelschlaf, die → Inkubation; er ist ein rituelles Mittel, um mit der Gottheit in direkten Kontakt zu kommen und an ihrem überragenden Wissen teilzuhaben. Inkubation ist nicht nur im Kult des → Asklepios und demjenigen der ohnehin meist im Traum helfenden Isis institutionalisiert, sondern findet sich in einer Vielzahl von Heilkulten, wobei die Inhalte der Traumforderung und Traumsendung entsprechend der allgemein divinatorischen Funktion des Traumes nirgends nur auf Heilung beschränkt sind (→ Traumdeutung); ebenso setzt sie sich im christl. → Heiligenkult bis in die Neuzeit fort [16]. Was mod. als »magische« Medizin bezeichnet wird [17], benutzt in Griechenland und Rom die seit Homer belegten Sprüche (*epoidaí*, *carmina*) zusammen mit oft seltsamen Ingredienzien und Riten, um medizin. nicht oder nur schwer faßbare Leiden (Kopf- und Zahnschmerzen, aber auch Luxationen, Cato agr. 160; Plin. nat. 28,21) zu behandeln; wie bedeutend wenigstens für die spätere Zeit die Heilung für die Magie ist, belegt deren von Plin. nat. 30,1 skizzierte Gesch., in der die Medizin eine der Quellen für Magie ist. Diese Funktion zeigt sich auch in den Rezepten der graeco-ägypt. → Zauberpapyri, die zusätzlich die magische Traumforderung als nicht-institutionalisierte Form der Inkubation zur Heilung benutzen.

→ Heroenkult; Inkubation; Medizin; Magie; Weihung

1 H. W. Parke, The Oracles of Apollo in Asia Minor, 1985, 150–158 **2** M. Gérard-Rousseau, Les mentions religieuses dans les tablettes mycéniennes, 1968 **3** B. Forsén, Griech. Gliederweihungen. Eine Unt. zu ihrer Typologie und ihrer religions- und sozialgesch. Bed., 1996 **4** M. Tabanelli, Gli ex-voto poliviscerali etruschi e romani. Storia, ritrovamento, interpretazione, 1962 **5** A. Comella, Tipologia e diffusione dei complessi votivi in Italia in epoca medio- e tardo-repubblicana, in: MEFRA 93, 1981, 717–810 **6** J. M. Turfa, Anatomical Votives and Italian Medical Tradition, in: J. P. Small, R. D. De Puma (Hrsg.), Murlo and the Etruscans. Art and society in ancient Etruria, 1994, 224–240 **7** O. Rubensohn, Demeter als Heilgottheit, in: MDAI(A) 20, 1895, 360–367 **8** F. Kutsch, Attische Heilgötter und Heilheroen, 1913 **9** E. Vikela, Die Weihreliefs aus dem Athener Pankrates-Heiligtum am Ilissos. Religionsgesch. Bed. und Typologie, 1994 **10** Pfiffig, 269–271 **11** F. Coarelli (Hrsg.), Fregellae 2. Il santuario di Esculapio, 1986 **12** R. Merkelbach, Isis Regina – Zeus Sarapis. Die griech.-ägypt. Rel. nach den Quellen dargestellt, 1995 **13** C. Landes (Hrsg.), Dieux Guérisseurs en Gaule romaine, 1992 **14** A. Rouselle, Croire et guérir. La foi en Gaule dans l'antiquité tardive, 1990 **15** G. Petzl, Die Beichtinschr. Westkleinasiens, 1994 **16** M. F. G. Parmentier, Incubatie in de antieke hagiografie, in: A. Hilhorst (Hrsg.), De heiligenverering in de eerste eeuwen van het christendom, 1988, 27–40 **17** G. Lanata, Medicina magica e religione popolare in Grecia fino all'età di Ippocrate, 1967. F.G.

Heilige, Heiligenverehrung

A. Jüdisch-alttestamentliche Tradition
B. Die frühe Kirche
C. Hellenistisch-römische Einflüsse

Mit der Entwicklung des Christentums setzte bald auch die Heiligenverehrung ein. H.(r) ist in der kathol. Kirche ein (seit 1234) vom Papst verliehener Titel, der die liturg. Verehrung in der Gesamtkirche gestattet. Voraussetzung für die Heiligsprechung sind das »heiligmäßige Leben« des Betreffenden und wenigstens zwei Gebetserhörungen wunderbaren Charakters (zur Verfahrensordnung im »Kanonisationsprozeß« s. die Apostol. Konstitution *Divinus perfectionis magister*: [1]). Zeitlich voraus geht die »Seligsprechung«: Sie gestattet die öffentliche Verehrung (*cultus publicus*) in einer bestimmten Region oder innerhalb eines Teils der kirchlichen Gemeinschaft (z. B. in einem Orden). – In den Ostkirchen bestimmt die für das Gebiet des Wirkungskreises des H. zuständige kirchliche Obrigkeit über seine liturg. Verehrung.

A. Jüdisch-alttestamentliche Tradition

Die Verschiedenartigkeit der at. Schriften sowie ihr Entstehungsraum von etwa 1000 Jahren gestatten nur unter großer Vorsicht, einige Grundlinien hervorzuheben. Eine H.-Verehrung im heutigen Sinn ist dem AT fremd. Im Mittelpunkt des Interesses steht gewöhnlich nicht die Frömmmigkeit des einzelnen, sondern das Geschehen zwischen Gott und seinem Volk. Ihm, dem von Gott auserwählten, steht auch der Titel »heilig« zu (Ex 19,6) – wie allem, dem eine besondere Nähe zu Gott, dem allein heiligen (*kadoš*, 1 Sam 2,2), eigen ist: dem Tempel (Ps 11,4), der Priesterschaft (Lv 21,15), den Opfergaben (Lv 22,10), den Orten, an denen Gott gesprochen hat (Ex 3,5). Der Israelit, der nach dem Gesetz lebt, wird als »Gerechter« bezeichnet, nicht als Anerkennung einer außergewöhnlichen Leistung, sondern er darf mit der bes. Hilfe Gottes rechnen (Ps 34,16ff.). Auch die »Propheten« entsprechen nicht den traditionellen H. Auserwählt von Gott schon im Mutterleib (Jer 1,5), erfüllen sie einen Auftrag, von dem gelöst ihre Person und ihr Schicksal unwichtig werden.

Am ehesten kann man in der Bed. der Grabstätten von Patriarchen (bekannt waren die Grabmäler von Abraham, Isaak und Jakob und deren Frauen) und von Propheten (vgl. Mt 23,29; Lk 11,47) einen Ansatz von H.-Verehrung sehen. Doch fehlt hier jede Erwartung, durch Wunder oder Gebetserhörung private Not zu wenden. Erst in den beiden letzten vorchristl. Jh. tauchen Elemente auf, die in der späteren H.-Verehrung ihre Entfaltung finden. Bei Philon von Alexandreia (20 v. Chr. – ca. 54 n. Chr.), der jüd. und platon. Gedankengut miteinander verbindet, treten die Seelen der Väter bei Gott mit Gebeten für ihre Söhne und Töchter ein; Abraham, Jakob, Mose werden bei der endzeitlichen Sammlung des Volkes als *paráklētoi* zur Versöhnung mit Gott beitragen (Philon, De praemiis et poenis 166f.; vgl. auch Lk 9,30ff.). Man kann hier unschwer erkennen, wie die zunehmende Beschäftigung mit der Frage des Weiterlebens nach dem Tod bzw. der Auferstehung (vgl. Mk 12,18–27; Apg 23,6) zu einer neuen Rolle der Verstorbenen führt. Auch das Buch der Weisheit (2. H. des 1. Jh. v. Chr.) kennt das Fortleben der Seelen der Gerechten, die am Ende die Völker richten werden (Weish 3–5).

B. Die frühe Kirche

Da die ersten Christen durchweg Juden waren, die sich von ihren Mitbürgern anfangs nur dadurch unterschieden, daß sie sich zu Jesus als Messias bekannten, läßt sich zunächst keine die jüd. Trad. sprengende H.-Verehrung erkennen. Die Mitglieder der christl. Gemeinden werden als »H.« bezeichnet (Röm 1,7; Phil 4,21f.), nicht aufgrund bes. Tugendhaftigkeit, sondern als von Gott »Auserwählte«, die ›durch den Glauben Gottes Söhne (sind) in Christus Jesus‹ (Gal 3,26). Die Aufmerksamkeit der Christen richtet sich auf die baldige Wiederkehr des Herrn, die einige noch zu ihren Lebzeiten erfahren werden (Mt 24,34; 1 Kor 15,51); dennoch kann man auf Ansätze späterer H.-Verehrung verweisen. Wenn die Gemeinde fürbittend für die Herrscher und für alle Menschen eintritt (1 Tim 2,1–3), warum sollte sie das nicht auch nach deren Tode tun?

Wenn Paulus daran erinnert, daß Gott ›uns nicht dazu berufen hat, unrein zu leben, sondern heilig zu sein‹ (1 Thess 4,7), also neben die bereits bestehende, ontische Heiligkeit eine noch zu erlangende, ethische stellt, dann ist eine Grundlage dafür gegeben, auf Vorbilder zu verweisen und sich an ihnen zu orientieren.

Der ausdrückliche Beginn von H.-Verehrung wird allg. in der → Märtyrer-Verehrung gesehen. Dabei wird vor allem auf den Bericht vom Martyrium des Bischofs Polykarpos von Smyrna (um 160) verwiesen. Darin findet sich die Überzeugung, daß der Märtyrer seit dem Augenblick seines Todes bei Gott ist, die Ermunterung, ihn zum Vorbild zu nehmen, der Eifer, sich seiner körperlichen Überreste, ›die wertvoller sind als Edelstein und Gold‹ (Martyrium Polycarpi 18,2 MUSURILLO), zu versichern, die Aufforderung an die Gemeinde, sich jährlich am Todestag an seinem Grab zu versammeln.

Die fürbittende Funktion, die Philon von Alexandreia den Vätern Israels zuweist (s.o.), findet sich bei Origenes (185–254) ausdrücklich auf die Märtyrer ausgedehnt (Eís martýrion protreptikós 37 [2]). Die Ehrung und Verehrung der Märtyrer nimmt im 3. Jh. rasch zu, es werden kalendarische Verzeichnisse (Martyrologien) angelegt, das Grab der Märtyrer wird zum Kultzentrum und, seit dem 4. Jh., zum Ziel von → Wallfahrten (bes. die Gräber von Petrus und Paulus in Rom). Bald beschränkt sich die gewöhnlich mit einer Eucharistiefeier verbundene liturg. Verehrung nicht mehr nur auf Märtyrer. Es treten (seit dem 3. Jh., vgl. Cypr. epist. 12) die »Bekenner« (*confessores*) hinzu, die für ihren Glauben viel erlitten haben, jedoch nicht den Tod (gelegentlich werden auch sie als »Märtyrer« bezeichnet), bald auch die »Asketen«, deren freiwillige Entsagung als eine Art Martyrium verstanden wurde (Athanasius, Vita Antonii 47,1; ebenso in der *Vita Martini* des Sulpicius Severus). Bes. Beachtung findet ein Märtyrer oder Asket, wenn er zugleich Bischof war: das bischöfliche Amt wird bald selbst zum Feld der Bewährung für Heiligkeit (so Paulinus von Mailand 422 in seiner *Vita Ambrosii*).

Seit Anfang des 5. Jh., als sowohl die bleibende Jungfräulichkeit wie auch der Titel »Mutter Gottes« (*Dei genitrix*) anerkannt waren, setzt auch die Marienverehrung ein.

C. HELLENISTISCH-RÖMISCHE EINFLÜSSE

Da erwartet werden kann, daß rel. Ausdrucksformen neben der eigenen Trad. auch dem kulturellen Umfeld entnommen wurden, interessiert hier die Frage, wie weit das Christentum griech.-röm. Praktiken aufgriff. Zu Anfang dieses Jh. glaubte man, in den (ersten) H. eine Übernahme ant. Göttergestalten zu erkennen [3]. Eingehendere Unt. zeigten, daß pagane Kulte zwar vereinzelt durch christl. ersetzt wurden (so will Kyrillos von Alexandreia an die Stelle des Isiskultes in Menuthis die Verehrung der Märtyrer Cyrus und Johannes setzen: vgl. [4]), daß aber die H.-Verehrung nicht durch eine umgekehrte Stoßrichtung verstanden werden kann (vgl. [5]); das gilt im ganzen auch für den ant. → Heroenkult. Zahlreiche seiner Elemente finden sich allerdings in der H.-Verehrung wieder: die Errichtung von Kapellen und Tempeln am Grab, die Gedächtnismähler, der jährlich wiederkehrende Festtag, die Wallfahrt zum Grab, um Heilung zu erlangen. Vor allem aber teilt der H. mit dem Heros die Lokalbindung: das Grab des H. wie dasjenige des Heros fokussiert zuerst einmal die kult. Verehrung.

Der alten Kirche war die Nähe der H.-Verehrung zum Heroenkult durchaus einsehbar. Um sich radikal davon abzusetzen, bezog sie H.-Verehrung in ihrer theolog. Begründung direkt auf Christus: nicht der H., Christus allein ist der Retter und Vermittler zu Gott. In Christus selbst wird nicht ein ant. Heros erkannt, er wird vielmehr im Rahmen eines (modifizierten) jüd. Glaubensverständnisses gedeutet; er kämpft siegreich gegen den Teufel (*diábolos*), Vergleiche werden dem zeitgenössischen Umfeld entnommen, dem Soldatentum (Eph 6,10–20) und dem sportlichen Wettkampf (1 Kor 9,25; 2 Tim 2,5. 4,7f.). Der H. kämpft nicht seinerseits gegen den Teufel, er nimmt vielmehr an Christi Kampf teil, dessen Sieg gegen den zum Glaubensabfall drängenden Satan gerade im Märtyrer sichtbar geworden ist. Der H. hat deutlich hinter Christus zurückzustehen: so setzt sich die Gemeinde von Smyrna mit dem Argument auseinander, die Verehrung Polykarps könne Christus in den Hintergrund drängen (Martyrium Polycarpi 17,2f. MUSURILLO).

Dieselbe Deutung der Glaubensexistenz als Kampf mit dem Teufel findet sich auch bei den in der Wüste lebenden Asketen (z.B. Athanasius, Vita Antonii 7,1; 34,1; 47,1). H.-Verehrung erweist sich somit als in der jüd.-christl. Glaubenstrad. angelegt. Wie weit und in welcher Form sie allerdings Gestalt gewinnt, hängt sowohl von theologisch-spirituellen Akzentsetzungen ab wie auch von den Bedürfnissen und Traditionen der jeweiligen kulturellen Epoche.

→ HEILIGE

1 Acta Apostolicae Sedis 75, 1983, 349–355 **2** GCS Bd. 1, 35, Z. 21–25 **3** TH. BAUMEISTER, Martyr invictus. Der Martyrer als Sinnbild der Erlösung in der Legende und im Kult der frühen koptischen Kirche (Forschungen zur Volkskunde 46), 1972, 14f. **4** R. HERZOG, Der Kampf um den Kult von Menuthis, in: Pisciculi, FS Fr.J. Dölger, 1939, 117–124 **5** F. GRAUS, Volk, Herrscher und Heiliger im Reich der Merowinger, 1965, 171–196.

TH. BAUMEISTER, s.v. Heiligenverehrung I, RAC 14, 96–150 • P. MCPARTLAN, s.v. Sainteté, Dictionnaire critique de théologie, hrsg. von J.-Y. LACOSTE, 1998, 1043–1047 • TH. BAUMEISTER, G.L. MÜLLER, A. ANGENENDT et al., s.v. Heiligenverehrung, LThK[3] 4, 1296–1304 • A. ANGENENDT, H. und Reliquien, 1994 ([2]1997) • P. BROWN, The Cult of Saints, 1981 (dt.: Die Heiligenverehrung, 1991) • N. JOHANSSON, Parakletoi. Vorstellungen von Fürsprechern für die Menschen vor Gott in der at. Rel., im Spätjudentum und Urchristentum, 1944 • TH. KLAUSER, Christl. Märtyrerkult, heidnischer Heroenkult und spätjüd. Heiligenverehrung, 1960 • B. KÖTTING, Heiligkeit und Heiligentypen in den ersten christl. Jahrhunderten, in: Diözesanpriester I, 1949, 12–27 • H. MUSURILLO (Hrsg.), The Acts of the Christian Martyrs, 1972.

RO.F.

Heilige Kriege (ἱεροὶ πόλεμοι). Als Begriff begegnet *hierós pólemos* erst im späten 5. Jh. v. Chr. und bedeutet nach Aristophanes (Av. 554ff., speziell 556 mit schol. = Philochoros FGrH 328 F 34 b) »Krieg gegen die Gottheit«, während Thukydides (1,112,5; mit dem Zusatz καλούμενος ›der sogenannte‹) hiermit die Intervention der Spartaner 448 in Delphi, vorgeblich zum Schutz des Apollonheiligtums [1. 1–14], bezeichnet. Die Vorstellung eines Glaubenskampfes für eine Gottheit gab es hiernach nicht [2. 67–87]. Auch galt nicht jeder Krieg um Delphi als »heilig«, insonderheit nicht der heute als »Erster« gezählte, dessen Geschichtlichkeit (im frühen 6. Jh.) in der Forschung umstritten ist [3. 242–246; 4. 34–47, 161–166]. Vermutlich wollte damals die → Amphiktyonia von Thermopylai die Schutzherrschaft über Delphi gewinnen, wenn auch das angebliche Motiv der Sicherung des Heiligtums vor dem Zugriff der Krisaier (Plut. Solon 11,1; Aischin. Tim. 3,107f.; Paus. 10,37,6) spätere Propaganda ist. Jedenfalls tagten nach der Zerstörung Krisas die Amphiktyonen jährlich zweimal in Delphi. Der 2. h.K. entstand im Kontext des athenisch-spartanischen Dualismus. Die Spartaner entrissen 448 trotz des 451 mit Athen geschlossenen Waffenstillstandes den phokischen Verbündeten der Athener die Kontrolle über Delphi und nahmen das Risiko eines Krieges in Kauf, um Stärke und Handlungsfreiheit zu demonstrieren. Da sie aber nicht längere Zeit Truppen in Delphi halten konnten, übergab ein athenischer Verband unter Perikles das Heiligtum wieder den Phokern (Thuk. 1,112,5; Plut. Perikles 21), die jedoch nach der athenischen Niederlage bei Koroneia bald erneut in Abhängigkeit von Sparta gerieten. Verheerende Folgen hatte der 3. h.K., den die Phoker provozierten, als sie im Sommer 356 Delphi besetzten (Aischin. leg. 130–136; Diod. 16,24,2;3–25,1; 28,2; 30,1–2; Paus. 3,10,4; 10,2,3). Anlaß war die Verurteilung führender Phoker zu einer unerschwinglichen Geldsumme wegen angeblicher Tempelfrevel. Mit den Tempelschätzen warb Philomelos ca. 10000 Söldner an, so daß die Phoker die stärkste griech. Landmacht wurden. Ihr Ziel, Mittelgriechenland zu beherrschen und nach Thessalien auszugreifen, veranlaßte Philipp II. von Makedonien, der Archon (Tagos) des Thessalischen Bundes war, einem Hilfegesuch der Aleuaden von Larissa zu folgen. Nach langen Kämpfen besetzte er 346 die Thermopylen (Demosth. or. 19,53ff.; Diod. 16,59,1ff.) und zwang die Phoker zur Kapitulation. Sie wurden von den Amphiktyonen zur Zahlung von 10000 Talenten verurteilt und gezwungen, fortan in Dörfern zu siedeln [5. 125ff.; 6. 114f.]. Ihre beiden Stimmen im Amphiktyonenrat erhielt Philipp II., der damit das Kräftefeld in der griech. Staatenwelt entschieden zu seinen Gunsten verschoben hatte. Der in der Forschung als 4. h.K. gezählte, in den Quellen indes als ›Krieg um Amphissa‹ (ἐν Ἀμφίσσῃ πόλεμος) bezeichnete Konflikt 339/8 wurde von den Amphiktyonen bereits auf Drängen Philipps beschlossen [7. 239–260] und hatte zur Folge, daß Philipp die Thermopylensperre umgehen und den Hellenenbund bei → Chaironeia 338 entscheidend schlagen konnte.

1 K. Brodersen, Heiliger Krieg und Heiliger Friede in der frühen griech. Geschichte, in: Gymnasium 98, 1991, 1–14 2 W. Burkert, Krieg, Sieg und die Olympischen Götter, in: F. Stolz (Hrsg.), Religion zu Krieg und Frieden, 1986 3 G. A. Lehmann, Der »Erste Heilige Krieg« – eine Fiktion, in: Historia 29, 1980, 242–246 4 K. Tausend, Amphiktyonie und Symmachie, 1992 5 M. Jehne, Koine Eirene, 1994 6 H. Beck, Polis und Koinon (Historia Einzelschriften 14), 1997 7 P. Londey, The Outbreak of the 4th Sacred War, in: Chiron 20, 1990, 239–260.

J. Buckler, Philip II and the Sacred War, 1989. K.-W. WEL.

Heiligtum I. Generelles
II. Antike Terminologie

I. Generelles

Dt. Sammelbegriff für unterschiedlichste Arten von Kultstätten; nicht sprachverwandt mit den aus dem lat. *sanctus* (»eingehegt«) hergeleiteten mitteleurop. Begriffen *sanctuaire*, *santuario* und *sanctuary*: der dt. Begriff H. geht auf das german. Adj. **heila-*, **heilu-* (»heil«, »ganz«) zurück [1. 78]. In der dt.-sprachigen religionswiss. Forsch. des 20. Jh. wird H. mittlerweile synonym zu den o. gen. von *sanctus* abgeleiteten Termini gebraucht. Dies steht u.a. in Zusammenhang mit den arch. und lit. Belegen für die tatsächliche Ab- oder Begrenzung der ant. H. von der Umgebung durch Mauern, Bäume, Felsen etc. [2. 142ff.].

Die Forsch. hat sich daher in den vergangenen Jahren bemüht, v.a. durch die Unt. der verschiedenen Funktionen von H. und ihrer einzelnen Komponenten die ant. Verhältnisse präziser zu erfassen, so etwa, indem u.a. auf die Verflechtung der H. mit dem → Mythos [3. 100ff.] und neben ihrer rel. Bed. auf ihre Rolle als regionale, ökonom. und polit. Zentren verwiesen wurde [4; 5. 37ff.]; → Tempel. Grundsätzlich ist jedoch zu betonen, daß die Morphologie der H. trotz einigen Gemeinsamkeiten – wie z.B. abgegrenztem Areal, »Allerheiligstem«, Altar, Vorkommen privater und öffentlicher H. in verschiedenen ant. Ges. – erhebliche kulturell bedingte Unterschiede aufweist: In das Spektrum gehören u.a. agrar. Berg-H. (vor allem Nordwesteuropas), Orakel-H. (→ Delphoi) und städt. H. des Mittelmeerraumes und Vorderen Orients sowie die dort ebenfalls nachweisbaren Sonnen- und Zelt-H.; zudem zeigen die Formen der H.-Gründungen (→ Weihung) deutliche Differenzen untereinander, die bereits in der Ant. bewußt waren (vgl. Plin. epist. 10,49).

In Israel setzt sich gegenüber einer Vielzahl von H. Jerusalem als einziger Kultort durch (2 Kg 23; Dt 12; noch heute im Judentum Gebetsrichtung nach Jerusalem, vgl. Mekka im Islam). Im Christentum spielt Jerusalem nach der Zerstörung des Tempels 70 n. Chr. eine nur geringe Rolle (Gebetsrichtung nach Osten seit dem 2. Jh.), gewinnt neue Bed. als Wallfahrtsort nach dem Fund der Kreuzreliquie und dem Bau der Grabeskirche unter Constantin d. Gr. (Weihe 335). Wichtigstes christl. H. im Westen ist das seit dem 2. Jh. verehrte Petrusgrab (Peterskirche) in Rom.

→ Asylon; Consecratio; Delubrum; Tempel

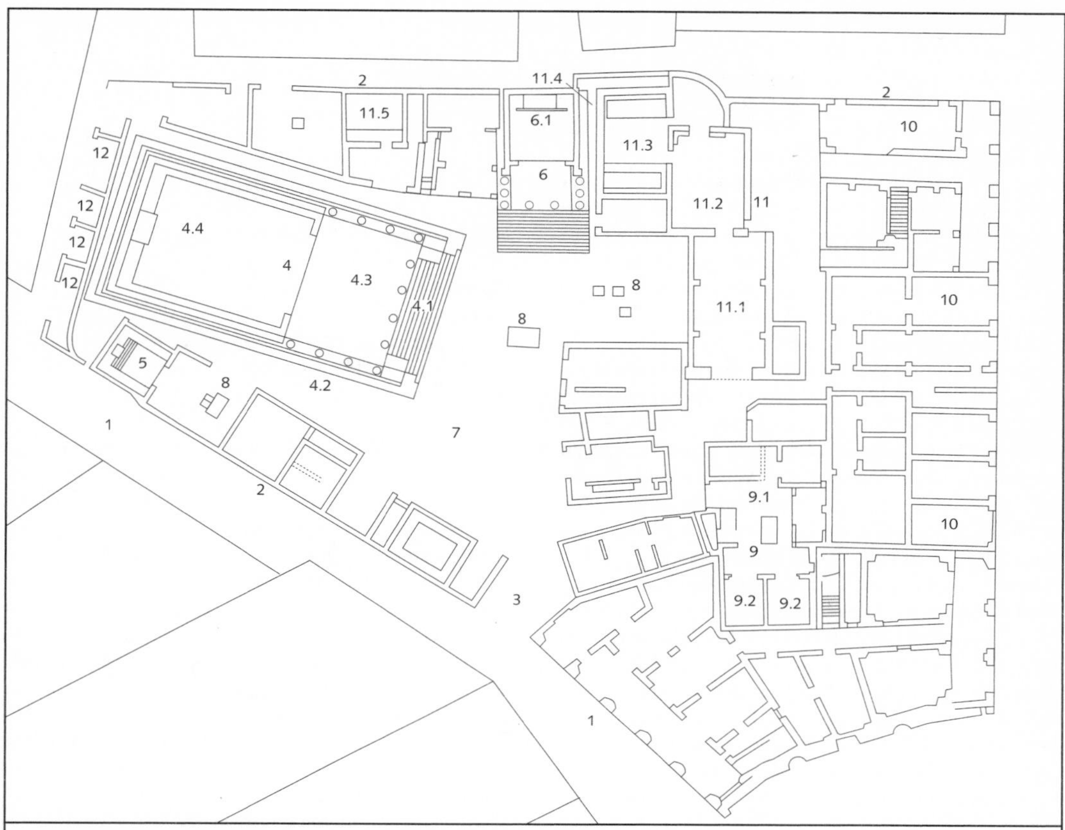

Das Herculesheiligtum in Ostia zu Beginn des 2. Jh. n. Chr. mit Benennung der Tempel- und Nebenräume in antiker Terminologie

Die Terminologie ist aus anderweitigen inschriftlichen und literarischen Belegen rekonstruiert.
Die Nebenräume wurden möglicherweise zur Finanzierung des Heiligtums und seines Kultvereins genutzt.

1 Straße *(via)*
2 Umfassungsmauer *(murus, maceria, consaeptum)*
3 Haupteingang *(ianua, ostium)*
4 Herculestempel *(aedes)*
4.1 Treppe *(gradus)*
4.2 Podium *(podium)*
4.3 Pronaos *(pronaus)*
4.4 Tempelcella *(cella)*
5 »Tempel des Rundaltars«
6 tetrastyler Tempel *(tetrastylos)*
6.1 Springbrunnen *(fons, saliens)*
7 Innenhof *(area)*
8 Altäre *(ara)*
9 Vereinshaus? *(schola)*
9.1 Atrium *(atrium)*
9.2 Speiseräume? *(triclinium)*
10 Mietshäuser *(aedes conductae, meritorium)*
11 »Thermen des Butticosus« *(balneum, thermae)*
11.1 *frigidarium*
11.2 *tepidarium*
11.3 *caldarium*
11.4 Dienstleistungskorridor
11.5 Zisterne mit Wasserrad *(cisterna)*
12 Läden *(taberna)*

1 C. Colpe, s.v. Heilig, HrwG 3, 74–80 **2** Burkert **3** F. Graf, Griech. Myth., 1987 **4** U. Sinn, Aphaia und die »Aigineten«. Zur Rolle des Aphaia-H. im rel. und ges. Leben der Insel Aigina, in: MDAI(A) 102, 1987, 131–167 **5** J. Bremmer, Götter, Mythen und H. im ant. Griechenland, 1996.

H. Busse, G. Kretschmar, Jerusalemer H.-Trad. in altkirchlicher und frühislam. Zeit, 1987 • Dies., L'espace sacrificiel dans les civilisations méditerranéennes de l'antiquité, 1991 • F. Graf, H. und Ritual. Das Beispiel der griech.-röm. Asklepieia, in: A. Schachter (Hrsg.), Le sanctuaire grec, 1992, 159–199.

C.F.

II. Antike Terminologie

Häufigster Terminus ist griech. → *témenos*, lat. *templum*, der »ausgeschnittene« bzw. von den Auguren abgegrenzte Raum. Das Tempelhaus (*naós*, *aedes*) gewinnt innerhalb des Altarbezirks unter freiem Himmel (→ *fanum*, → *sacellum*, → *delubrum*) zunehmend an repräsentativer Bed. Eine Begriffsscheidung ist v. a. bei den Antiquaren gewahrt (Liv. 10,37,15; Fest. 318; Non. p. 494): In der Lit. bezeichnet *fanum* dagegen (ähnlich *hierón*) den Kultbezirk samt seinen Gebäuden (Cic. Verr. 2,4,96), *sacellum* (neben → *aedicula*) häufig die Larenkapelle (Liv. 4,30,10). *ántron* (Hom. Od. 13,103) und *spḗlaion* übertragen röm. Inschr. von der Höhle auf die künstlich angelegten Mithräen (→ Mithras) (CIL VI 733; [1. Bd. 1, Nr. 407]). *Sacrarium*, laut Ulp. Dig. 1,8,9,2

Aufbewahrungsort hl. Gegenstände in privaten wie öffentlichen Gebäuden, beziehen die lit. Quellen oft auf die Mysterienkulte (Liv. 39,9,4; Apul. met. 6,2,5). Selten begegnet *sanctuarium* (ILS 5412, 5413).

Minimalausstattung des H. sind die natürliche oder künstliche Begrenzung – Ufer, Mauern (*toíchos; maceria, murus*) oder Steine (*hóros, terminus*) – und eine Opferstätte: Altar (*bōmós, ara*) oder Votiv- und Depositgruben (*bóthros, favissa*). Oft finden sich natürliche oder künstlich gefaßte Quellen (*pēgḗ, krḗnē; fons*). Schon früh übernehmen H. als (über)regionale Versammlungsorte polit. (z.B. Bundes-H. des → Apollon auf → Delos, der → Diana am Nemi-See und auf dem Aventin) und wirtschaftliche Funktionen (Märkte beim Hercules-H. am Forum Boarium) und entwickeln sich bes. seit dem Hell. durch Einrichtung von Spielen, Museen, Bibliotheken zu kulturellen Zentren (z.B. Apollontempel auf dem Palatin). Im Zuge der allg. Verstädterung werden auch die ländlichen und vorstädtischen H. und hl. → Haine (*álsos, lucus*) zunehmend verbaut und durch zahlreiche Zweckräume (*ta synkýronta* OGIS 1,52) – Portiken (*stoá, porticus*), Speisesäle (*hestiatórion, triclinium*), Herbergen (*katagṓgion, hospitium*), und Bäder (*lutrón, balneum*) – architektonisch bereichert (z.B. die Kur- und Pilger-H. in → Kos und → Epidauros, der Hain der → Dea Dia in Rom, das Hercules-H. in Ostia, vgl. die Abb.). Eine ähnliche Entwicklung zur Allzweckeinrichtung ist bei den Diasporasynagogen (*proseuchḗ*) feststellbar. Die reiche Terminologie dieser Nebenräume in Kultanlagen ist bisher nur in Ansätzen erforscht.

Neben den Kirchen (z.B. *basilica*) mit Taufkapelle (*baptisterium*), Märtyrergrab (*memoria*) und Friedhof (*coemeterium*) sind in frühchristl. und byz. Zeit v.a. die Klöster (*monastḗrion*) den ant. H. in ihrer Multifunktionalität und komplexen Raumgliederung vergleichbar: Das Typikon des 1136 eröffneten Pantokratorklosters in Konstantinopel erwähnt u.a. Mönchszellen (*kellíon*), ein Gästehaus (*xenṓn*) und Hospiz (*gērokomeíon*), Bad (*lutrón*), Bäckerei (*mankipeíon*) und Mühle (*myliká ergastḗria*) sowie eine Begräbnisstätte (*tópos*) mit Oratorium (*euktḗrion*) [2].

→ Altar; Synagoge; Tempel

1 M.J. Vermaseren, Corpus Inscriptionum et Monumentorum Religionis Mithriacae, 2 Bd., 1956–1960
2 P. Gautier, Le typikon du Christ Sauveur Pantocrator, in: REByz 32, 1974, 1–145.

S. Alcock, R. Osborne (Hrsg.), Placing the Gods. Sanctuaries and Sacred Space in Ancient Greece 1994 • Les Bois Sacrés: actes du colloque international organisé par le Centre Jean Bérard 23–25 Nov. 1989, 1993 • F. Coarelli, I Santuari del Latio in età repubblicana, 1989 • I.E. Edlund, The Gods and the Place. Location and Function of Sanctuaries in the Countryside of Etruria and Magna Graecia (700–400 B.C.), 1987 • A. Fridh, Sacellum, Sacrarium, Fanum and Related Terms, in: S.-T. Teodorsson (Hrsg.), Greek and Latin Studies in Memory of Cajus Fabricius, 1990, 173–187 • R. Hägg, N. Marinatos, G.C. Nordquist (Hrsg.), Early Greek Cult Practice: Proc. of the Fifth International Symposium at the Swedish Institute at Athens 26–29 Jun. 1986, 1988 • M.-C. Hellmann, Recherches sur le vocabulaire de l'architecture grecque, d'après les inscriptions de Délos, 1992 • H. Jordan, Über die Ausdrücke aedes templum fanum delubrum, in: Hermes 14, 1879, 567–583 • N. Marinatos, R. Hägg (Hrsg.), Greek Sanctuaries, 1993. UL.EG.-G.

Heimarmene s. Schicksal

Heirat s. Ehe

Heiratsalter I. Forschungsgegenstand und Methode II. Heiratsalter in Griechenland III. Heiratsalter im Imperium Romanum

I. Forschungsgegenstand und Methode

Das H. von Mann und Frau bei der ersten Heirat bestimmte in vorindustriellen Gesellschaften – neben Mortalität und Menopause – den für die Kinderzeugung zur Verfügung stehenden Zeitraum. Normalerweise bedingt eine Verlängerung dieses Zeitraumes eine proportional ansteigende Fertilität. Das H. des Mannes ist zugleich bedeutsam für die Größe des Generationenabstandes und die sozialen und rechtlichen Beziehungen innerhalb von → *oíkos* und *familia*. Zur Ermittlung des H. hat die althistor. Forsch. eine Reihe von methodischen Ansätzen entwickelt, die sich hinsichtlich der ausgewerteten Quellen sowie deren Gewichtung unterscheiden.

Alle Bestimmungen des H. in der Ant. skizzieren zunächst einmal eine gesellschaftliche Erwartungshaltung gegenüber einer angemessenen H.-Spanne. Die methodischen Probleme und die in den Unt. eingeräumte Notwendigkeit zeitlicher, räumlicher und sozialer Differenzierung decken sich im übrigen mit den Fragen bzw. Ergebnissen komparatistischer Demographie für andere Epochen.

II. Heiratsalter in Griechenland

Der Schwerpunkt von Unt. zum H. in Griechenland liegt bislang auf den lit. Zeugnissen (Gerichtsreden sowie medizinischen, philos. und historiographischen Texten), weniger auf inschr. und anthropologischem Material. Dabei geht man von einem üblichen ersten H. von 14–15 J. für Mädchen und von knapp 30 J. für Männer aus. Es ist jedoch mit einer großen Variationsbreite je nach Polis, Region, Zeitraum und sozialer Schicht zu rechnen. Einen ungefähren Anhaltspunkt bieten gerade die Empfehlungen zum H. in der Dichtung und der polit. Theorie; so sollte nach Hesiod ein Mann im Alter von etwa 30 J. heiraten und die Frau fünf Jahre erwachsen sein (Hes. erg. 695–698); Platon, der mehrmals auf die Frage des H. eingeht, nennt 25–35 J. für den Mann, 16–20 J. für die Frau (Plat. leg. 721b; 772d; 785b). Der Altersunterschied zwischen dem Vater und seinen Kindern sowie die Gesundheit der Kinder und der Frauen sind für Aristoteles in diesem Zusammenhang entscheidende Argumente: Der Vater sollte nicht zu jung sein, weil er dann wenig Autorität besitze, die Frau, weil frühe Geburten ihr Leben gefährdeten; ein Alter von 37 J. für den Mann und 18 J. für die Frau ist nach Aristoteles angemessen für die Heirat (Aristot. pol. 1334b 29–1335a 35).

III. Heiratsalter im Imperium Romanum

Nach röm. Recht lag das gesetzliche Mindestalter für eine legitime Heirat bei 12 (Mädchen) bzw. 14 J. (Knaben; vgl. Cod. Iust. 5,4,24). Allerdings haben kulturvergleichende Unt. gezeigt, daß eine beträchtliche Spanne zwischen einer gesetzl. Untergrenze und dem Zeitpunkt der tatsächlich erfolgten Eheschließung liegen kann; zudem handelt es sich bei der genannten Vorschrift um eine *lex imperfecta*, bei der man im Falle einer Zuwiderhandlung nicht bestraft wurde, sondern lediglich nicht in den Genuß der mit der Bestimmung verbundenen Vorzüge kam. Setzte die Gesetzgebung des Augustus einen *terminus ante quem* mit der Verfügung, daß Frauen und Männer spätestens bis zum 20. bzw. 25. Lebensjahr ein Kind haben sollten (Ulp. reg. 16,1; FIRA 2,278), so legten die Bestimmungen des Hadrianus für Alimentarstiftungen möglicherweise einen solchen *terminus post quem* mit dem Auslaufen der Unterstützung nach dem 14. (Mädchen) bzw. 18. Lebensjahr (Jungen) fest (Dig. 34,1,14,1). Aus der lit. Überl. ergibt sich ein ähnlich breiter Spielraum (ca. 12–18 J. für Mädchen, 20–30 J. für Männer), wobei allerdings solche Zahlenangaben kaum unkritisch übernommen werden können; vor allem bleibt unklar, inwieweit diese Zeugnisse tatsächlich repräsentativ sind. Medizinische Schriften bieten keineswegs übereinstimmende Informationen zum Eintritt der Geschlechtsreife, die einer Verheiratung vorauszugehen pflegte; für Mädchen wird meist (etwa bei Soranos) ein Alter von 14 J. angegeben. Für Frauen ergibt sich damit ein Zeitraum der Empfängnisfähigkeit zwischen 15 und 40 J. (Soran. 1,20; 1,33 f.).

Es ist aber keineswegs sicher, daß solche vereinzelten Angaben verallgemeinert werden können, und fraglich ist zudem, welche Faktoren in der Ant. die Menarche beeinflußt haben. Sind präpubertäre Heiraten auch keinesfalls auszuschließen, so scheinen Kinderehen doch kaum üblich gewesen zu sein. Eine Auswertung von röm. Inschr. (vor allem Grabinschr.), die das H. errechnen lassen, ergab ein durchschnittliches H. bei Mädchen von 15 und bei Männern von 23–24 J. [7]. In der neueren Forsch. wurde diese Studie vor allem wegen der geringen Zahl der ausgewerteten Inschr. und wegen des starken Übergewichts von stadtröm. Zeugnissen kritisiert und für Angehörige unterer sozialer Schichten ein etwas höheres H. von Frau und Mann (kurz vor 20 bzw. Ende 20) postuliert. Die errechnete späte Heirat von Männern in Verbindung mit ihrer hohen Mortalität im Alter von über 50 J. führte auch zu einer Neubewertung der → *patria potestas* und des Vater-Sohn-Verhältnisses in der *familia* [11]. Allerdings wurde der Quellenwert des epigraphischen Materials grundsätzlich durch den Hinweis darauf, daß Grabinschr. immer aus dem Kontext des Todes, nicht dem des Lebens bzw. der Hochzeit stammen, in Frage gestellt [13].

Aus äg. Verträgen und Haushaltsdeklarationen der Prinzipatszeit kann das H. zumeist indirekt erschlossen werden. Dabei liegt der Median in den Zensusdeklarationen bei 17,5 (Frauen) und über 25 J. (Männer); für die Verträge postuliert man ein übliches weibliches H. von 17–19 J.; allerdings können die Abweichungen von diesem Muster beträchtlich sein.

→ Ehe; Familie; Frau

1 R. S. Bagnall, B. W. Frier, The Demography of Roman Egypt, 1994 **2** M. Durry, Le mariage des filles impubères, in: CRAI 1955, 84–90 **3** Ders., Le mariage des filles impubères dans la Rome antique, in: RIDA 2, 1955, 263–273 **4** Ders., Sur le mariage romain, in: RIDA 3, 1956, 227–243 **5** E. Eyben, Geschlechtsreife und Ehe im griech.-röm. Altertum und im frühen Christentum, in: E. W. Müller (Hrsg.), Geschlechtsreife und Legitimation zur Zeugung, 1985, 403–478 **6** D. Gourevitch, Le mal d'être femme, 1984 **7** K. Hopkins, The Age of Roman Girls at Marriage, in: Population Studies 18, 1965, 309–327 **8** J.-U. Krause, Witwen und Waisen im röm. Reich I: Verwitwung und Wiederverheiratung, 1994 **9** S. B. Pomeroy, Families in Classical and Hellenistic Greece, 1997 **10** R. P. Saller, Men's Age at Marriage and Its Consequences in the Roman Family, in: CPh 82, 1987, 21–34 **11** Ders., Patriarchy, Property and Death in the Roman Family, 1994 **12** Ders., D. I. Kertzer (Hrsg.), The Family in Italy from Antiquity to the Present, 1991 **13** B. D. Shaw, The Age of Roman Girls at Marriage. Some Reconsiderations, in: JRS 77, 1987, 30–46.

J. W.

Heirkte (Εἱρκτή, Pol. 1,56,3; Ἑρκτή, Diod. 22,10,4). Ausgedehntes, schwer zugängliches Bergmassiv bei Panormos, 278/7 v. Chr. von Pyrrhos den Karthagern abgenommen, 248 von diesen wiedergewonnen und drei J. lang gegen röm. Angriffe verteidigt (Pol. 1,56 f.; Diod. 33,20). Es handelt sich offenbar um den Monte Pellegrino (606 m) nördl. von Palermo.

BTCGI 7, 1989, 343.

GI. MA.

Heius. Lat. Eigenname (Schulze 459).

H., C. Um 75 v. Chr. angesehener und reicher Bürger der sizilischen Stadt Messana. Aus seinem Besitz raubte → Verres vier berühmte griech. Statuen und wertvolle Teppiche (Cic. Verr. 2,4,3–19; 27). Trotzdem trat er 70 im Auftrag seiner Gemeinde als Entlastungszeuge für Verres in Rom auf, belastete ihn jedoch im Kreuzverhör Ciceros (Verr. 2,2,13; 4,15–19; 150; 5,47). K.-L. E.

Heizung A. Allgemein B. Heizungsarten C. Heizwirkung

A. Allgemein

In allen Mittelmeerländern treten im Winter auch Frosttemperaturen auf (durchschnittl. Minimal-Temperatur: Rom –9° C; Zentraltürkei –18° C; Südfrankreich –11° C; Sizilien –3° C; Nord-Algerien –2° C). Als Wärmequelle für Wohnungen kamen urspr. das Herdfeuer, metallene Holz- oder Holzkohlebecken verschiedener Art, in der griech. Ant. aber nur vereinzelt auch festinstallierte, bisweilen kaminähnliche Feuer-stellen in Frage (z. B. Kassope, »Marktbau«, [2. 128]). Hierbei mußte stets für einen Abzug der teilweise giftigen Rauchgase gesorgt und ein kalter Fußboden in Kauf genommen werden. Andererseits waren diese Heizarten leicht regulierbar; warmes Wasser wurde auf dem → Herd sowie in den → Bädern mit Hilfe von Metallbehältern oder Steinbecken über Holz- oder Holzkohlefeuer bereitet.

Ein Entwicklungssprung vollzog sich durch die Erfindung des Prinzips der zentralbeheizten Raumerwärmung vom Fußboden her (Unterflur-Heizung, griech. ὑπόκαυστον, lat. *hypocaustum*, [3. 161 f.]). Als »Erfinder« der Hypokaust-H. um 80 v. Chr. gilt im Anschluß an Plin. nat. 9,168 und Val. Max. 9,1,1 C. Sergius Orata aus Puteoli, der, um das Wachstum seiner Fisch- und Schalentierzucht zu beschleunigen, Wasserbecken über einem Hohlraum bauen ließ, was eine Beheizung von unten ermöglichte. Indessen ist aber sicher, daß mindestens die Bäder in → Gortys bereits im 3. Jh. v. Chr. mit ähnlich angelegten, unterirdischen Raumheizungssystemen versehen waren (→ Bäder, mit Abb.). In den riesigen → Thermen der röm. Kaiserzeit wuchsen beheizbare Wasserbecken dann ins Gigantische; die Barbarathermen in Trier (→ Augusta [6] Treverorum) enthielten zwei beheizte Becken von je 13 × 23 m Fläche; die Augustus-Thermen in Ankara eines von ca. 50 m Länge. Auch im Haus- und Villenbau verbreitete sich diese Form der H. seit dem späten 1. Jh. v. Chr. über den gesamten Raum des Imperium Romanum.

Behagliches Wohnen ist abhängig von der Luft- und Wandtemperatur, von der Luftbewegung, -feuchtigkeit und -reinheit. Wärmeübertragungen konnten durch Strahlung (mod. Beispiel: Fußbodenheizung) und Konvektion (Luft erwärmt sich an heißen Medien; mod. Beispiel: Heizkörper) erfolgen. Eine Strahlungsheizung erzeugt keine Zugluft und wird daher im Empfinden der Konvektionsheizung immer vorgezogen. Ant. Heiz-Systeme wirkten zu ca. ⅔ durch Strahlungswärme; h. überwiegt bei weitem die Konvektionsheizung. Als Heizmaterial diente v. a. → Holz, das bes. in der röm. Ant. für den Betrieb der zahlreichen Thermenanlagen in großen Mengen notwendig war (was zu großflächigen, bis heute existenten Erosionszonen rund um das Mittelmeer geführt hat); effektiver, aber teurer war der Betrieb einer H. mit Holzkohle.

B. Heizungsarten

1. Hypokaust-Verfahren (ab 3./2. Jh. v. Chr.): In einer von außen zu bedienende Heizkammer (*praefurnium*) wurde Luft erhitzt und strömte in Hohlräume zwischen kleinen Pfeilern (meist aus quadratischen oder runden Ziegelplatten, mit Ton oder Kalkmörtel aufgemauert), auf denen die Fußbodenplatten auflagen. Die Luft erwärmte die Pfeiler sowie den Fußboden und zog dann über senkrechte Abzugskanäle (meist) in den Ecken der Räume nach oben sowie anschließend ins Freie. Vitruv (5,10) gab im 1. Jh. v. Chr. eine detaillierte Beschreibung dieser Form der H.

2. Hypokaust-Wand-H. (ab 1. Jh. n. Chr.): Eine deutlich verbesserte Heizwirkung ergab sich, wenn in die Wände zusätzlich Stränge aus Hohlziegeln (*tubuli*) eingebaut wurden. So konnte die heiße Luft auch die Wände erwärmen und danach meist über einen oberen Heizkanal ins Freie entweichen.

3. Luft-H. (ab 1. Jh. n. Chr.): Beide vorgenannten Konstruktionen wurden auch für eine Luft.-H. herangezogen. Hierbei nutzte man das Wärmespeichervermögen möglichst massiver Pfeiler sowie dicker Fußböden, Wände und Decken aus. Nach Erwärmung dieser Bauteile ließ man das Feuer erlöschen, den Rauch abziehen und Frischluft durch die Heizkammer in die Räume einströmen. Mod. Brennversuche zeigten, daß Rauchgasreste nur eine geringe Belästigung für den Menschen mit sich brachten, v. a. im Vergleich zum offenen Feuer.

4. Kanal-H. (ab 2. Jh. n. Chr.): Man verwendete sie v. a. als »Spar-Bauweise« in den kalten Nordprov. des röm. Reiches; sie bestand meist aus einem gedeckten, horizontalen Heizkanal unter dem Fußboden, der von außen erwärmt wurde und in die Raummitte führte. Von hier aus liefen Kanäle in die vier Ecken und mündeten in senkrechten Hohlziegel-Strängen oben ins Freie. Vorteile waren der geringe bauliche Aufwand und eine leichte Bedienbarkeit, ein Nachteil jedoch die geringe Effektivität, die sich jedoch durch Kombination mit einer kleinen Hypokaust-Anlage ausgleichen ließ.

C. Heizwirkung

An rekonstruierten röm. → Thermen in Deutschland wurden mehrfach Heizversuche bei winterlichen Temperaturen durchgeführt [1]. Auf den Fußböden zeigten sich dabei Temperaturen zwischen 20° und 50° C sowie an den Wänden zwischen 18° und 30° C. Als üblich ließen sich für das *caldarium* einer Therme, den Warmbaderaum, Lufttemperaturen von ca. 32° C, eine Luftfeuchtigkeit von 100 %, eine Lufttemperatur im *sudatorium* von sogar 37° ermitteln sowie eine Wassertemperatur am Einlauf von ca. 48° C (das warme Wasser mußte hier mit kaltem Wasser gemischt werden). Die negative Energiebilanz ant. Hypokaust-H. wurde durch den Umstand ihrer schlechten Regulierbarkeit noch gesteigert; größere Anlagen waren durchgehend (24 Stunden am Tag) in Betrieb.

1 D. Baatz, Heizversuch an einer rekonstruierten Kanal-H. in der Saalburg, in: Saalburg-Jb. 36, 1979, 31–44
2 W. Hoepfner, E. L. Schwandner, Haus und Stadt im klass. Griechenland, ²1994 **3** I. Nielsen, Thermae et Balnea, ²1993.

J. Becker et al. (Hrsg.), Gesundes Wohnen, 1986, 36–104 • E. W. Black, Hypocaust Heating in Domestic Rooms in Roman Britain, in: Oxford Journal of Archaeology 4, 1985, 77–92 • E. Brödner, Die röm. Thermen und das ant. Badewesen, 1983, 155–162 • E. Brödner, Wohnen in der Ant., 1989, 119–124 • H. in der röm. Architektur. Berichte zum 3. Augster Symposion 1980, Jahresber. aus Augst und Kaiseraugst 3, 1983 • H.-O. Lamprecht, Opus Caementitium, ⁵1996, 126–137 • W. Müller-Wiener,

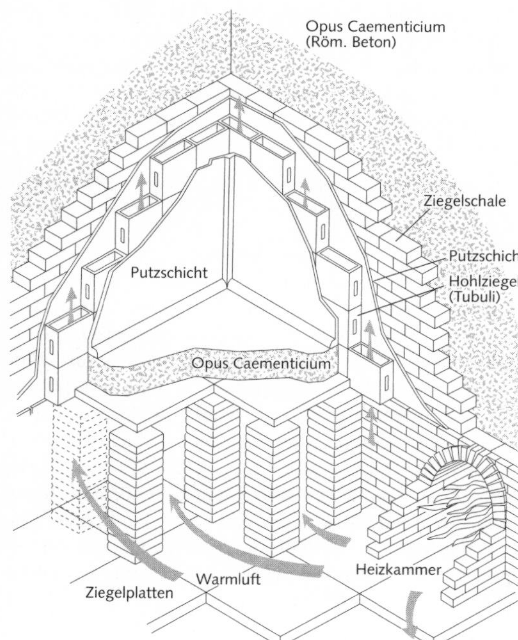

Schema einer Hypokaustanlage mit Wandheizung.

Griech. Bauwesen in der Ant., 1986, 169–170 • H.J. SCHALLES et al. (Hrsg.), Colonia Ulpia Traiana: Die röm. Bäder, 1989, 21–42. H.-O.L.

Hekabe (Ἑκάβη, lat. Hecuba). Gattin des troianischen Königs → Priamos, Mutter zahlreicher Kinder (Hom. Il. 24,496; Eur. Hec. 421), unter ihnen → Hektor, → Paris/Alexandros, → Kassandra, → Polyxene und → Troilos. Über ihre Eltern herrscht Unklarheit, bei Hom. Il. 16,718f. ist sie Tochter des Königs → Dymas [1], bei Eur. Hec. 3 des Königs Kisseus (vgl. auch Hyg. fab. 91; 111; 243), Apollod. 3,148 nennt als dritten Namen Sangarios. Über ihre Mutter berichtet Suet. Tib. 70,3. Bei Homer unternimmt sie auf Hektors Wunsch hin mit einem → Peplos einen Bittgang zu Athena (Hom. Il. 6,269–311) und versucht, ihn vom Kampf mit → Achilleus abzuhalten (Hom. Il. 22,79–83). Später bereitet sie für Priamos eine Libation an Zeus vor, als er trotz ihres Einspruchs Achilleus um die Herausgabe der Leiche Hektors bitten will (Hom. Il. 24,193–216; 283–321). H. führt die Totenklage um Hektor an (Hom. Il. 22,430; 24,747–760). Der Traum der H. vor der Geburt des Paris/Alexandros, daß sie eine Fackel gebäre, und die Aussetzung des Neugeborenen sind wohl schon ein Motiv der → *Kypria* (Pind. paian fr. 8a 17–20, mit Variationen Apollod. 3,148; Enn. scaen. 35–46). Bei der Eroberung Troias wird H. nach Stesich. fr. 198 PMG von Apollon nach Lykien entrückt, was sich wohl mit der Mythenversion verbinden läßt, daß Hektor ein Sohn der H. und des Apollon sei (Stesich. fr. 224 PMG; Ibykos fr. 295 PMG).

Lyriker und Tragiker geben H. eine prominente Rolle bei der Darstellung des Schicksals der Besiegten: Sie erlebt die Ermordung ihres Gatten und ihrer Tochter Polyxene mit (Soph. Polyxena; Eur. Hec. 518–570; Eur. Tro. 482f.), ist in Trauer um ihre toten Angehörigen versunken (Eur. Tro. 1250), versucht vergeblich, → Menelaos zur Bestrafung der → Helene zu überreden (Eur. Tro. 890) und rächt schließlich die Ermordung ihres Sohnes Polydoros an dessen Mörder Polymestor, indem sie ihn blendet und seine Kinder tötet (Eur. Hec. 1116–1121); hier baut Euripides entweder einen Lokalmythos in seine Trag. ein, oder aber er hat die Figur des Polymestor neu erschaffen und mit ihr das Schicksal des Polydoros verbunden. Dem Los, als Sklavin ihrem Erzfeind → Odysseus dienen zu müssen (Eur. Tro. 277), entgeht H., indem sie sich bei der thrak. Chersones von einem der griech. Schiffe ins Meer stürzt, dabei in einen Hund verwandelt wird, worauf ihr an Land ein Grabmal errichtet wird (κυνὸς σῆμα, *kynós sḗma*; Eur. Hec. 1265), das den Seeleuten als Orientierungspunkt dient (Strab. 13,1,28; Diod. 13,40,6; Ov. met. 13,565–575; Sen. Ag. 705–709; Suda s.v. H.). Hierbei handelt es sich wohl ebenfalls um eine Lokalsage, die für die Polymestor-Gesch. nutzbar gemacht wird. Nach einigen Autoren verwandelt sich H. bereits in Troia in einen Hund (Q. Smyrn. 14,346–351; Triphiodoros, Ilii excidium 401f.), oder dies geschieht nach ihrer Steinigung durch die Griechen (Lykophr. 330–334). Diese Verwandlung weist auf die Göttin → Hekate hin, der der Hund zugeordnet ist und mit der H. durch ihre Rache an Polymestor für seinen Mißbrauch der Gastfreundschaft in Verbindung gebracht werden kann [1. 154–155]. Euripides hat mit H. eine der eindrucksvollsten Frauenfiguren seiner Tragödien geschaffen, die von den röm. Tragikern und Epikern aufgenommen wurde (Ennius, Accius: *Hecuba*; Pacuvius, *Iliona*; Verg. Aen. 2,524–558; Seneca, *Troades*). In der bildlichen Darstellung ist H. ein Beispiel für das kollektive Schicksal der troianischen Königsfamilie, ihre Rache an Polymestor wird kaum dargestellt. Sie erscheint bei der Peplos-Übergabe der Troianerinnen an Athene, als Zuschauerin beim Kampf zw. Achilleus und Hektor, bei Hektors Begräbnis und als prominentes Opfer bei der Eroberung Troias durch die Griechen. Zu späteren Darstellungen in Lit. und Kunst vgl. [2].

1 D. LYONS, Gender and Immortality. Heroines in Ancient Greek Myth and Cult, 1997 2 HUNGER, Mythologie, 149–150.

LIT.: R.E. HARDER, Die Frauenrollen bei Euripides, 1993 • A.-F. LAURENS, s.v. H., LIMC 4.1, 473–474 • N. LORAUX, Matrem nudam. Quelques versions grecques, in: L' Ecrit du Temps 11, 1986, 90–102 • J. MOSSMAN, Wild justice. A study of Euripides' Hecuba, 1995 • CH. SEGAL, Euripides and the poetics of sorrow: Art, gender, and commemoration in Alcestis, Hippolytus and Hecuba, 1993, 157–213 • E. SITTIG, s.v. H., RE 7, 2652–2662 • F. ZEITLIN, Euripides' Hecuba and the somatics of Dionysiac drama, in: Ramus 20, 1991, 53–94.

ABB.: A.-F. LAURENS, s.v. H., LIMC 4.2, 280–283. R.HA.

Hekademos s. Akademos

Hekaerge (Ἑκαέργη).
[1] Beiname der → Artemis (Clem. Al. strom. 5,8,48,4 f.; EpGr 460,6).
[2] Ein im Kult der → Artemis tätiges mythisches Mädchen der Stadt Melite in Thessalien namens Aspalis Ameilete H. Weil sie sich erhängt hatte, um einer Vergewaltigung durch den Tyrannen Tartaros zu entgehen, opferten ihr die Mädchen jährlich eine junge Ziege, indem sie sie aufhängten (Nikandros bei Antoninus Liberalis 13).
[3] Eine der → Kydippe analoge, aus einem Artemistempel entführte, im Kindbett verstorbene Kore der Insel Keos, die unter den Namen Aphrodite Ktesylla und Ktesylla H. kultisch verehrt wurde (Nikandros bei Antoninus Liberalis 1).

NILSSON, Feste, 207 ff. • O. JESSEN, E. NEUSTADT, s. v. H. (1–3), RE 7, 2662 f. G. B.

[4] Eine der Hyperboreerinnen (→ Hyperboreioi), deren Gräber auf → Delos kult. verehrt wurden. Ihr Name ist von den Epiklesen der Artemis (s. unter [1]) und des Apollon (→ Hekaergos) abgeleitet. H. erscheint als Variante zu Arge, die laut Hdt. 4,35 mit → Opis als erste von den Hyperboreern ›zusammen mit den Göttern‹ nach Delos kam und in einem Hymnos des → Olen besungen wurde. Paus. 5,7,8 erwähnt einen Hymnos des Melanopos auf Opis und H. Bei Kall. h. 4,292 f. treten Upis, H., und → Loxo, Töchter des → Boreas, als Überbringerinnen der ersten Opfergaben und Empfängerinnen von Haaropfern der delischen Mädchen vor der Hochzeit auf (vgl. Paus. 1,43,4), Funktionen, die urspr. dem zweiten Hyperboreerinnen-Paar Hyperoche und Laodike (Hdt. 4,33 f.) zukamen. Nach Plat. Ax. 371a hätten Opis und H. (oder Hekaergos; vgl. Serv. Aen. 11,532; 858) eherne Tafeln myst. Inhalts mitgebracht. Später zählt H. zu den Begleiterinnen der Artemis (Claud. carm. 24,253; Nonn. Dion. 5,491; 48,332).

W. SALE, The Hyperborean Maidens on Delos, in: Harvard Theological Review 54, 1961, 75–89. A. A.

Hekaergos (Ἑκάεργος). Beiwort des → Apollon und der → Artemis (→ Hekaerge), meist gedeutet als *ϝέκα (vgl. ἑκών) + ϝέργον, »aus freien Stücken handelnd«, von den Dichtern jedoch mit ἑκάς, ἕκαθεν verbunden: »aus der Distanz handelnd«.

W. BECK, s. v. H., LFE 2, 493–494. RE. N.

Hekale (Ἑκάλη).
[1] Heroine des gleichnamigen att. Demos am Pentelikon, die → Theseus, der auf dem Weg zum Kampf mit dem marathonischen Stier von einem Sturm überrascht wird, trotz ihrer Armut sehr gastfreundlich aufnimmt. Als er nach seinem Sieg zurückkehrt, findet er sie tot und stiftet ihr und → Zeus Hekal(ei)os aus Dankbarkeit einen Kult, zu dem die umliegenden Demen für ein Jahresopfer zusammenkommen. Auf ältere Atthidographen greifen → Kallimachos (Hekale fr. 230–377) und Plut. Theseus 14,6b-c (= Philochoros FGrH 328 F 109) in ihren Darstellungen zurück. Kallimachos wiederum beeinflußte die Ausgestaltung einzelner Motive bei späteren Autoren (z. B. die Gastfreundschaft: Ov. met. 8,626–724; Nonn. Dion. 17,32–86).

LIT.: P. FRIEDLÄNDER, s. v. H., RE 7, 2665 f. • A. S. HOLLIS, Callimachus, H., 1990, 5–10, 26–35, 341–354 • E. SIMON, s. v. H., LIMC 4.1, 481.
ABB.: E. SIMON, s. v. H., LIMC 4.2, 283. R. HA.

[2] Att. Mesogeia-Demos der Phyle Leontis, ab 224/3 v. Chr. der Ptolemaïs, mit einem *buleutḗs*. Für seine genaue Lage am Weg von Athen nach Marathon (Plut. Theseus 14 nach Philochoros, FGrH 328 F 109; [1]) beweisen zusammengetragene Funde am Kloster Kukunar(t)i (u. a. Kultkalender des Demos Marathon: IG II[2] 1258 [2; 3. 128[44], 173, 185, 384 Nr. 76]) oder an der frühchristl. Kirche von Mygdaleza (= Anakaia? [2]) wenig. Das Frg. eines Dekrets ebd. weist H. [3. 386 f. Nr. 97] Plotheia zu. Am Kult des Zeus Hekaleios, der explizit in H. lokalisiert wird, waren mehrere Demen »um« H. beteiligt [3. 210 f.].

1 D. M. LEWIS, Cleisthenes and Attica, in: Historia 12, 1963, 22–40 2 J. S. TRAILL, Demos and Trittys, 1986, 131 mit Anm. 24 3 WHITEHEAD, Index s. v. H.

E. SIMON, s. v. H., LIMC 4.1, 481 • TRAILL, Attica, 6, 8, 19, 46, 62, 69, 110 Nr. 53, Tab. 4, 13. H. LO.

Hekamede (Ἑκαμήδη). Tochter des Arsinoos von Tenedos. H. wurde von → Achilleus, der Tenedos zerstörte, als Beute mitgenommen und später dem Nestor als Ehrengeschenk übergeben (Hom. Il. 11,624; 14,6; Suda, s. v.).

H. W. STOLL, s. v. H., Roscher 1, 1885. K. WA.

Hekataios (Ἑκαταῖος).
[1] Tyrann von → Kardia, von → Alexandros [4] im Amt belassen, obwohl sich → Eumenes [1] um die Befreiung der Stadt bemühte (Plut. Eumenes 3). Im Lamischen Krieg unterstützte er → Antipatros [1] (Diod. 18,14,4).
[2] Einer der → Hetairoi von Alexandros [4], von ihm 336 v. Chr. mit der Kaltstellung von → Attalos [1] beauftragt, den er ermordete (Diod. 17,2,5; 5,2).

BERVE 2, Nr. 292 (nicht mit Nr. 293 identisch). E. B.

[3] H. aus Milet. Sohn des Hegesandros, ca. 560–480 v. Chr., erster »Logograph« (nach der seit FR. CREUTZER gängigen, aber schiefen Bezeichnung für die Prosaschriftsteller vor Herodot), von dem zahlreiche Fragmente erhalten sind (ca. 370 in der Sammlung der FGrH 1). H. ist von größter Bedeutung für die Entwicklung der griech. Geogr. und Geschichtsschreibung. Nach ant. Überl. (T 3 bei Strab. 14,1,7) war er Schüler des → Anaximandros. Dies ist chronologisch kaum möglich, jedenfalls beeinflußte Anaximandros H. nachhaltig: Seine Kosmogonie, seine Darstellung der Entwicklung der Lebewesen und der Menschen sowie die von ihm geschaffene Erdkarte inspirierten H. zu Werken, in denen er oftmals die Anschauungen und Vorstellungen des Vorgängers berichtigte und ergänzte (dazu bes. [1. 409ff.]). Im J. 500 riet H. unter Hinweis auf die Größe des Perserreiches und das Militärpotential des Großkönigs vergeblich vom → Ionischen Aufstand ab, auch sein Vorschlag zum Flottenbau fand kein Gehör (Hdt. 5,36). Nach dem Scheitern der Revolte setzte er sich angeblich bei dem Satrapen Artaphernes für eine milde Behandlung der Ionier ein (Diod. 10,25,4). Inwieweit er die Perserkriege noch erlebte, ist unsicher. H. war ein ›weitgereister Mann‹ (Agatharchides geogr. 1,1) und hielt sich u. a. längere Zeit in Ägypten auf (Hdt. 2,143).

Werke: 1. ›Erdkarte‹ (FGrH F 36). H. verbesserte die Erdkarte des Anaximandros ›in bewundernswerter Weise‹ (T 12a). Eine Vorstellung von dieser Karte liefert die anonyme Kritik Herodots (4,36), die sich nach allgemeiner Überzeugung gegen H. richtet (vgl. F 36b): Demnach betrachtete H. die Erde als kreisrunde Scheibe, rings vom Ozean umflossen und zwei gleich große Erdteile umfassend, nämlich Europa und Asien. Die Grenze zwischen beiden bildete eine vom Mittel- zum Schwarzen Meer laufende Ost-West-Linie, die zusammen mit einer von der Donau zum Nil reichenden Nord-Südlinie die Erde in vier gleich große Quadranten teilte. Auch die einzelnen Länder hatten nach H. die Form geometrischer Figuren, z.B. von Kreisen, Quadraten, Rechtecken und Trapezen. Weiter unterschied er als erster Zonen und Gürtel und wurde so zum Vorläufer des → Eudoxos von Knidos, der die Einteilung in Längen- und Breitengrade schuf.

2. *Periḗgēsis* oder *Períodos gē̃s*, ›Erdbeschreibung‹ (F 37–369). Die Erdbeschreibung kommentierte und illustrierte die Erdkarte und umfaßte 2 B. mit dem Titel ›Europa‹ bzw. ›Asien‹ (letzteres von Kallimachos irrtümlich für unecht erklärt, vgl. T 15). Inhaltlich und formal an die → Periplus-Literatur anknüpfend, folgte H. im allgemeinen dem Küstenverlauf, drang aber gelegentlich ins Binnenland, manchmal sogar bis zum Erdrand vor. Von Spanien ausgehend, beschrieb er Europa, Asien, Ägypten und Libyen und kehrte dann zu den »Säulen des Herakles« zurück. Das materialreiche, lit. anspruchslose Werk gab ein aktualisiertes Gesamtbild des Wissens von der Erde und ihren Bewohnern, jedoch ohne die Absicht unmittelbarer praktischer Verwendung wie bei den Periploi. Aufgeführt waren Völker, Stämme, Grenzen, Städte, Flüsse, Gebirge etc. Durch Angabe von Entfernungen und Himmelsrichtungen wurde häufig die relative Lage der Örtlichkeiten zueinander bestimmt (vgl. z.B. F 100, 108, 144, 207). Es fehlte nicht an Hinweisen auf das Brauchtum der Bewohner (F 154, 287, 323, 358), die Natur des Landes (F 291, 292, 299) sowie Fauna und Flora (F 291). Auch myth. Angaben und Gründungssagen waren nicht selten (F 31, 32, 119, 120, 140, 302), dagegen blieben histor. Anmerkungen die Ausnahme (F 74, 119).

Von den ca. 330 erhaltenen Frg. stammen fast 80 % aus dem geogr. Lexikon des Stephanos von Byzanz (6. Jh. n. Chr.) und enthalten daher zumeist nur die nüchterne Aufzählung von Städten nebst knappen Lageangaben (vgl. etwa F 38–101). Zusätzliches Material des H. läßt sich aus Herodot gewinnen: Er zitierte H. als einzige seiner Vorlagen namentlich (2,143,1; 6,137,1) und entlehnte nach ant. Urteil (F 324a) im ägypt. Logos u. a. die Angaben über den Vogel Phönix (2,73), das Flußpferd (2,71) und die Krokodiljagd (2,70) aus H. (vgl. F 324b = Hdt. 2,70–73); vgl. auch die Konkordanz zwischen Hdt. 2,156,1 und F 305. Auch der libysche Logos Herodots (4,168–199) beruht, wie [2. 2728ff.] auf Grund der Übereinstimmung von 4,186,1 und 4,191,1 mit F 335 gezeigt hat, im wesentlichen auf H.

3. *Genealogíai* = ›Genealogien‹ (auch als *Historíai* oder *Hērōología*) zitiert (F 1–35). Zentrale Thematik des 4 B. umfassenden Werkes war die *Hērōología*, d.h. die »Geschichte« der Heroen und Halbgötter. Erh. ist der programmatische Einleitungssatz (F 1a bei Demetrios, de elocutione 12): ›Hekataios von Milet verkündet folgendes: Dies schreibe ich, wie es mir wahr zu sein scheint. Denn die Erzählungen der Griechen sind viele und lächerliche, wie sie mir jedenfalls vorkommen.‹ H. suchte entsprechend die ›vielen‹, d.h. ungeordneten und zusammenhanglosen Erzählungen der Heroenzeit zu systematisieren, miteinander zu vernetzen und in ein chronologisches System einzubinden, ähnlich wie es Hesiod in der ›Theogonie‹ bereits für die Götterwelt getan hatte (die entsprechend bei H. keine Berücksichtigung fand). Die Chronologie nahm ihren Ausgang mit Herakles und beruhte auf der Generationenrechnung [1. 70]. Ferner unterzog er die ›lächerlichen‹ Geschichten des Mythos einer rationalistischen Kritik und entkleidete sie des Phantastischen und Übernatürlichen. Besonders instruktive Beispiele hierfür sind F 1, 6, 19, 26. Die konsequente Anwendung dieses Prinzips wird von [3. 418,10a] unterschätzt, von [1. 48ff.] dagegen überbewertet [vgl. 4. 23].

In der Forschung warf man H. oft Kritik ›am untauglichen Objekt und mit untauglicher Methode vor‹ (W. Spoerri). In Wirklichkeit darf seine kritische Einstellung zur Überl. als ›Keimzelle der griech. Historiographie‹ [5] gelten. H. schrieb in einem archaischen Stil von liebenswürdiger Einfachheit (vgl. T 16–20).

1 K. von Fritz, Griech. Geschichtsschreibung 1, 1967
2 F. Jacoby, s. v. H. (3), RE 7, 2667–2750
3 H. Strasburger, Die Entdeckung der polit. Gesch. durch Thukydides, in: H. Herter (Hrsg.), Thukydides, 1968, 412–476 **4** K. Meister, Die griech. Geschichtsschreibung, 1990 **5** O. Lendle, Einführung in die griech. Geschichtsschreibung, 1992, 10ff.

Fr.: FGrH 1 • G. Nenci, Hecataei Milesii Fragmenta, 1954.
Lit.: T. S. Brown, The Greek Historians, 1973, 7ff. • F. Jacoby, Griech. Historiker, 1956, 186–237 (grundlegend, erstmals: vgl. Anm. 2) • E. Moscarelli, Ecateo: verifiche e proposte, in: Atti dell' accademia Pontaniana 42, 1993, 129–146 • L. Pearson, Early Ionian Historians, 1939, Kap.

2 • P. Tozzi, Studi su Ecateo di Mileto I–V, in: Athenaeum 41–45, 1963–67 • B. Uhde, Die Krise der Gegensätze, in: Tijdschrift voor Philosophie 33, 1971, 559–571 • St. West, Herodotus' portrait of Hecataeus, in: JHS 111, 1991, 144–160. K. MEI.

[4] H. von Abdera. 4. Jh. v. Chr.; geb. in Abdera oder Teos; Philosoph und Historiker, der zur Zeit Alexanders d.Gr. und Ptolemaios I. lebte (Ios. c. Ap. 1,22). Er war Schüler des Skeptikers Pyrrhon und bekleidete vermutlich ein offizielles Amt unter → Ptolemaios I. Soter, das ihn nach Sparta führte (Plut. Lykurgos 20,2). H.' Werke sind nur in Fragmenten erhalten: ›Über die Hyperboräer‹ (Περὶ Ὑπερβορέων; Diod. 2,47) und eine Geschichte Ägyptens (Αἰγυπτιακά, [6. 61–78], Diod. 1). In der Suda wird außerdem ein Werk über Homer und Hesiod (Περὶ τῆς ποιήσεως Ὁμήρου καὶ Ἡσιόδου) genannt, das nicht erhalten ist und auch sonst keine Erwähnung findet. In der ›Geschichte Ägyptens‹ werden die Juden in nicht-polemischer Weise beschrieben. Dieser Tatsache verdankt sich die Zuschreibung des Werkes ›Über die Juden‹ (Περὶ Ἰουδαίων) an H. Dieses pseudepigraphische Werk (Pseudo-Hekataios I) wurde vermutlich von einem hellenisierten Juden verfaßt; Zitate finden sich bei Ios. (c. Ap. 1, 183–214; 2, 43) und eine Erwähnung bei Origenes (contra Celsum 1,15) [1; 7. 146–148; 6. 78–91]. Bei dem Werk ›Über Abraham und die Ägypter‹ (Κατ' Ἄβραμον καὶ τοὺς Αἰγυπτίους; Titel bei Clem. Al. strom. 5,113) handelt es sich um eine weitere Zuschreibung an H. (Ps.-Hekataios II), es stammt aber vermutlich von einem dritten Autor [7. 149151].

Ed.: 1 FGrH 264, F 1–14; F 21–24 2 M. Stern, Greek and Latin Authors on Jews and Judaism, Bd. 1, 22–24; 26–44 (Ps.-H.).
Lit.: 3 B. Schaller, H. von Abdera, Über die Juden. Zur Frage der Echtheit und der Datierung, in: ZNTW 54, 1963, 15–31 4 Schürer, 671–677 5 W. Spoerri, s. v. H. von Abdera, RAC 14, 1988, 275–310 6 G. E. Sterling, Historiography and Self-Definition. Josephos, Luke-Acts and Apologetic Historiography, 1992, 55–91 7 N. Walter, Fragmente jüd.-hell. Historiker, 1976, 144–153. I. WA.

[5] H. von Thasos (Ἑκαταῖος Θάσιος). Epigrammatiker; sonst unbekannt. Ihm (oder dem Dioskurides) weist die *Anthologia Palatina* ein Grabepigramm auf eine 18jährige zu, die bei der Geburt ihres Kindes starb, das selbst nur 20 Tage gelebt hat (7,167). Die Zugehörigkeit zum Kranz des Meleagros ist ungewiß.

GA I,2,270. M. G. A./Ü: M. A. S.

Hekate (Ἑκάτη). Bis in die Neuzeit ist die Göttin H. als Gespensterherrin, als dämonische Mittlerin par excellence zwischen Unten und Oben bekannt. In dieser Funktion ist sie eng mit der → Magie verbunden, in der die »Benutzung« von Totengeistern eine wichtige Rolle spielt (Eur. Med. 397; Hor. sat. 1,8,33). H. stammt wohl aus Karien und kam etwa in archa. Zeit nach Griechenland, von wo aus sich ihre Verehrung in der ganzen griech.-röm. Welt ausbreitete. Ihr Kult in Karien (vor allem Lagina) und an anderen kleinasiat. Orten blieb bis in die Kaiserzeit bedeutend [5. 11–56, 166–168; 6; 7. 257–259]. Der mythische Stammbaum der gewöhnlich als Jungfrau dargestellten H. bleibt unscharf: Die wichtigste Quelle, Hesiod (theog. 409–411), macht sie zur Tochter der Titanen → Asteria [2] und → Perses und damit zur Cousine von → Artemis und → Apollon (vgl. schol. Apoll. Rhod. 3,467). Ihr Name ist wohl mit Apollons Epiklesen Hekatos und Hekatobolos verwandt; eine überzeugende Etym. freilich fehlt. H.s Rolle als Gespensterherrin hebt die Lit. seit der klass. Zeit hervor (Adespota 375 TrGF; Eur. Hel. 569 f.). Bes. in der späteren Ant. wird sie selbst als angsteinflößende, gespensterhafte Gestalt aufgefaßt (PGM P4, 2520–2611).

Andere Quellen zeigen jedoch, daß sie immer auch als normale, gar gütige Gottheit verstanden werden konnte. Der H.-Hymnus bei Hesiod (theog. 404–492) preist sie als mächtige Göttin, die verschiedenen Gruppen – unter diesen Müttern, Königen und Fischern – beistehen konnte. Pindar beschreibt sie als »freundliche Jungfrau« (Paian 2,73–77). Die Ikonographie stellt sie – außer auf spätant. magischen Gemmen und Bleitäfelchen [4. 1010 f., Nr. 291–322] – ohne jede erschreckenden Züge dar: eine att. Votivstatuette des späten 6. Jh. v. Chr. zeigt sie sitzend, nicht anders gewandet als andere Göttinnen auch ([4. Nr. 105], mit IG I 2, 836); att. Vasenbilder, auf denen sie an Hochzeiten Fackeln trägt, zeichnen sie als mädchenhafte Gestalt in einem → Peplos [4. 993, Nr. 44–46 mit Komm.].

H.s Bezug zu Geisterwesen läßt sich zum einen aus ihrer Funktion in vorehelichen Übergangsriten der Frauen ableiten (Hes. theog. 450; 452; Aischyl. Suppl. 676; Eur. Tro. 323; Vita Homeri 30; schol. Aristoph. Vesp. 804; mehr dazu [1. Kap. 6]): Mädchen, die unverheiratet, und Frauen, die kinderlos und somit nach griech. Vorstellung erfolglos starben, konnten zu drohenden Geistern werden, die im Gefolge von H. umgingen, wohl weil diese für ihr Los verantwortlich war. In diesem Kontext ist auch ihre Identifikation mit → Iphigeneia zu sehen (Hes. fr. 23b; Prokl. summ. Cypr. 55–64; [1. Kap. 6]). Ein anderer wichtiger Mythos, der möglicherweise auf Euripides zurückzuführen ist, verbindet H. mit → Persephone, die als Jungfrau in die Unterwelt gelangte (Hom. h. 2,24 f.; 52–59; 438–440 mit Komm. von [8]; Kall. fr. 466; Orph. fr. 41; [4. 989–991; 1013, Nr. 1–17]).

Zum anderen trug zum Bild der Geisterherrin H. ihre Rolle als Hüterin von Eingängen und anderen liminalen öffentlichen und privaten Orten, an denen man sich Geister vorstellte, bei ([1. Kap. 6; 3]; Aischyl. fr. 388; Aristoph. Vesp. 802–804). Schreine oder Statuetten von H. (*hekataía*) beschützten Eingänge und Wegkreuzungen (»Dreiwege«, *tríodoi*); Mahlzeiten (*deípna*) wurden für H. und die Gespenster, vor allem in der Neumondsnacht an den Dreiwegen niedergelegt (Aristoph. Plut. 594 mit schol.; Demosth. or. 54,39; Plut. mor.

708 f; Apollod. FGrH 244 F 110). Dort deponierte man auch die nicht mit den H.-Mählern zu verwechselnden Überbleibsel [3] häuslicher Reinigungsriten (Plut. mor. 280c; 290d; Lukian. Dialogi mortuorum 1,1; Suda, Phot. und Etym. m. s. v. κάθαρμα). H.s enger Bezug zu den Wegkreuzungen spiegelt sich in der griech. Epiklese Trioditis, dem röm. Namen Trivia und der seit klass. Zeit häufigen plastischen Darstellung als Göttin mit drei Köpfen oder überhaupt als drei Göttinnen [4. 998–1004, Nr. 112–215; 5. 84–165] wider. Im Laufe der Zeit kamen andere Epiklesen zum Ausdruck der Dreigestalt dazu; Charikleides (fr. 1) gibt eine nicht ganz ernstgemeinte Sammlung.

H.s Verbindung mit dem Hund und Hundeopfern (Eur. fr. 968 TGF; Aristoph. fr. 608 PCG; schol. Aristoph. Pax 276) resultiert wohl einerseits aus ihrer Rolle als Geburtsgöttin (→ Eileithyia, → Genita Mana, → Genetyllis), andererseits verband man den Hund am Ende der klass. Zeit mit H.s Auftreten als Gespensterherrin, die von Rudeln heulender Hunde, die man als Totenseelen verstand, bei ihren nächtlichen Umgängen begleitet oder deren Kommen von Hundegeheul angekündigt wurde (Theokr. 2,12 f.; 35 f.; Verg. Aen. 6,255–258 [2. Kap. 9]). Die Totenseelen in H.s Gefolge verursachten Wahnsinn oder nächtlichen Schrecken (Hippokr. De morbo sacro 6 p. 342 LITTRÉ), was H.s Rolle in Mysterienkulten erklärt, welche u. a. die Heilung von Wahnsinn versprachen (Aristoph. Vesp. 122; Paus. 2,30,2; Dion Chrys. or. 4,90; Aristot. mir. 173; [1. Kap. 4]).

In Kult, Mythos und Ikonographie wurde H. mit verschiedenen Göttinnen identifiziert, vor allem mit → Artemis (Aischyl. Suppl. 676; IG XIII 383,125–127; [4; 5. 11–23; 7. 228–231]), mit der sie das Interesse an Mädcheninitiationen und Geburten sowie die Darstellung mit zwei Fackeln teilt; ferner mit → Selene (Plut. mor. 416e-f, [2. 29–38]) und mit Enodia, einer thessal. Göttin (Soph. fr. 535), die ebenfalls mit Geburten und mit dem Schutz von Eingängen in Zusammenhang gebracht wird (IG IX 2, 575; 577; [1. Kap. 6; 5. 57–83]). In den → Zauberpapyri wird H. oft mit → Kore/Persephone (etwa PGM PIV, 1403–1405; 2745–2747) und mit Ereschkigal, der sumer. Unterweltsherrin, zusammengestellt (etwa PGM P4 1417; LXX 4–25). In der Spätant. führte ihre Verbindung mit Geburten und mit dem Schutz liminaler Orte auch zu ihrer Rolle als Schutzgottheit der → Theurgie, wo sie mit der platon. kosmischen Seele identifiziert wurde, welche die (irdische) Welt der Materie von der (himmlischen) Welt des *nus* trennt; sie ermöglicht die Passage einzelner Seelen hinab in die Einkörperung und hinauf zur Vereinigung mit dem Göttlichen [2].

→ Ahoros; Apollon; Artemis; Dämonen; Eileithyia; Genetyllis; Genita Mana; Hekabe; Iphigeneia; Kore/Persephone; Lagina; Magie; Nekydaimon; Selene; Theurgie; Zauberpapyri

1 S. I. JOHNSTON, Restless Dead, 1999 **2** Dies., H. Soteira, 1990 **3** Dies., Crossroads, in: ZPE 88, 1991, 217–224 **4** H. SARIEN, s. v. H., LIMC 6.1, 985–1018 **5** TH. KRAUS, H., 1960 **6** A. LAUMONIER, Les cults indigènes en Carie, 1958, 344–425 **7** GRAF **8** N. J. RICHARDSON, The Homeric Hymn to Demeter, 1974.

J. HECKENBACH, s. v. H., RE 7, 2769 • NILSSON, Feste 394–401 • M. L. WEST, Hesiod Theogony, 1966, 276–290.

S. I. J.

Hekatombaion (Ἑκατόμβαιον). Heiligtum bei → Dyme [1], bei dem Kleomenes III. 226 v. Chr. einen Sieg über die Achaioi errang (Pol. 2,51,3; Plut. Kleomenes 14,2, Aratos 39,1). Genaue Lage unbekannt; die Lokalisierung ist abhängig von der Interpretation der Marschroute des Kleomenes.

M. OSANNA, Santuari e culti dell'Acaia antica, 1996, 42 f.

Y. L.

Hekatombe s. Opfer

Hekatomnos (Ἑκατόμνως). Karischer Dynast aus Mylasa (Syll.[3] 167; 168). Sohn des Hyssaldomos. 392/1 v. Chr. von Artaxerxes II. zum Satrapen über die neugegründete Satrapie Karia bestellt (Diod. 14,98,3). H. sollte zusammen mit dem Satrapen Autophradates von Lydien den Krieg gegen den abtrünnigen → Euagoras [1] I. von Salamis auf Kypros führen (115 Theopompos FGrH F 103). Der Krieg zur See lief 391 an, erfolglos, denn H. unterstützte Euagoras heimlich mit Geld (Diod. 14,98,3 mit 15,2,3). H. plante wohl seinerseits einen Abfall (Isokr. or. 4,162), führte ihn aber nicht aus. Tod des H. und Akzession seines Sohnes → Maussollos 377/6 (errechnet nach Diod. 16,36,2).

S. HORNBLOWER, Mausolus, 1982, 29–39. PE. HÖ.

Hekatompedos (Ἑκατόμπεδος). Vermutlich eine ca. 32 m breite Straße in Syrakusai nahe dem Hexapyla-Tor (Plut. Dion 45,5, vgl. Diod. 16,20,2. GI. MA./Ü: V. S.

Hekatompylos. Nach Appianos (Syr. 57,298, Ἑκατόμπολις) Neugründung Seleukos' I. in der Komisene, nach Plinius (nat. 6,17,44) 133 Meilen von den Kaspischen Toren entfernt. Wohl das h. Šahr-e Qūmes bei → Damghan. Wurde nach vorübergehender arsakidischer Besetzung zu Beginn des 2. Jh. v. Chr. parth. Residenzstadt. Bei Ausgrabungen kamen zahlreiche Zeugnisse aus parth. Zeit zum Vorschein, darunter – neben Palastarchitektur, Keramik und Siegelabdrücken – auch zwei parth. Ostraka mit Namenslisten, deren zweites wohl in das Jahr 170 arsakidischer Ära = 78 v. Chr. zu datieren ist.

A. D. H. BIVAR, The Second Parthian Ostracon from Qūmis, in: Iran 19, 1981, 81–84 • M. A. R. COLLEDGE, Parthian Art, 1977, s. v. H. J. W.

Hekaton von Rhodos. Schüler des → Panaitios und einflußreicher Stoiker des 1. Jh. v. Chr. → Diogenes [17] Laertios hat H.s Schriften für seine Darstellung der stoischen Ethik benutzt. Die von ihm angeführten Auf-

fassungen des H. entsprechen altstoischer Orthodoxie. Unter den von Diogenes oft zitierten (meist umfangreichen) Werken finden sich die *Chreíai* (die er als Quelle biographischer und anekdotischer Informationen über Stoiker und Kyniker heranzieht), und die Abh. ›Über das Lebensziel‹, ›Über die Tugenden‹, ›Über die Güter‹, ›Über die Affekte‹, ›Über die stoischen Paradoxa‹. Cicero erwähnt mindestens 6 B. ›Über die Pflicht‹ (περὶ καθήκοντος), die dem Quintus Aelius Tubero gewidmet waren (off. 3,63 und 89). Auch Seneca benutzte Schriften des H. in *De beneficiis* und in seinen Briefen. In seiner Behandlung der Tugenden unterscheidet H. zw. Qualitäten, die auf theoretischer Überlegung gründen (wie Klugheit/*phrónēsis*, Selbstbeherrschung und Gerechtigkeit) und solchen, die nicht intellektuell begründet sind (wie Stärke und Gesundheit); darin folgt er der orthodoxen stoischen und sokratischen Auffassung, nach der moralische Tugenden Formen des Wissens sind. Cicero zufolge (off. 3,63,89 ff.) legte H. bei der Entscheidung, wie man in schwierigen Fällen die angemessene Handlungsweise finden solle, beträchtliches Gewicht auf das Eigeninteresse. Darin gab er dem Ansatz des → Diogenes [15] von Babylon den Vorzug vor dem des → Antipatros [10] von Tarsos (off. 3,51–55).
→ Panaitios

H. Gomoll, Der stoische Philosoph H., 1933 • M. Pohlenz, Die Stoa, 1955, 123–4. B.I./Ü: B.v.R.

Hekatoncheires (Ἑκατόγχειρες, *centimani* = »Hundert-Händer«). Briareos (auch Aigaion genannt: Hom. Il. 1,403 f.), Kottos und Gy(g)es (zur Namensform [1]) sind von → Uranos und → Gaia stammende, kräftige Monsterwesen (hundert Arme, fünfzig Köpfe: Hes. theog. 147 ff.), die von ihrem Vater gefesselt und in den Tartaros geworfen werden (617 ff.). Zeus befreit sie und macht sie wegen ihrer hundert Arme zu Kampfgefährten gegen die → Titanen (626 ff.). Daß die H. anschließend die besiegten Titanen im Tartaros bewachen (Apollod. 1,2,7), geht wohl auf eine Fehlinterpretation von Hes. theog. 734 f. zurück.

Gelegentlich treten die H. auch einzeln in Erscheinung (die Gruppenbezeichnung »H.« findet sich erst bei den späten Mythographen): Mit Briareos' Unterstützung vereitelt → Thetis einen Anschlag gegen Zeus (Hom. Il. 1,401 ff.). Nach Eumelos (Titanomachie fr. 3 Bernabé) nimmt Briareos allein an der → Titanomachie teil, aber auf seiten der Titanen (vgl. Verg. Aen. 10,565 ff.).

Die ähnliche äußere Erscheinung als Urwesen dürfte die Ursache dafür sein, daß einzelne H. gelegentlich als → Giganten bezeichnet werden (z.B. Kall. h. 4,142). Entsprechend schwierig ist ihre Identifikation auf bildl. Darstellungen [2].

1 M.L. West, Hesiod. Theogony, 1966, 209 2 E. Simon, s.v. H., LIMC 4.1, 481–482. RE.N.

Hekatonnesoi (Ἑκατόννησοι). Inselgruppe im Norden der östl. Meeresstraße, die Lesbos vom kleinasiat. Festland trennt, h. Moschonisia; ihre größte Insel war Pordoselene oder Nasos, h. Moschonisi. Die Bewohner nannte man *Nēsiṓtai* (Hdt. 1,151; Diod. 13,77; Strab. 13,2,5; Plin. nat. 5,137; Ptol. 5,2,5; Ail. nat. 2,6; Hesych. s.v. H.; Steph. Byz. s.v. Ἑκατόννησοι und Σελήνης πόλις). Die Stadt *Selēnēs pólis* war wohl wie Mytilene eine aiol. Gründung, von dem sie lange kulturell und polit. abhängig war. H. war Mitglied im → Attisch-Delischen Seebund. Mz. ΠΟΡΔΟΣΙΛ vom 5.–3. Jh. v. Chr., ΠΟΡΟΣΕΛΗΝΕΙΤΩΝ in der röm. Kaiserzeit.

HN 563 • Kirsten/Kraiker, 532. H.KAL.

Hekatoste (ἑκατοστή). Als H. wurden in der Ant. → Steuern in Höhe von 1 % bezeichnet:

1. In Athen gab es zahlreiche Formen der H. (Aristoph. Vesp. 658), so die bei Ps.-Xen. Ath. pol. 1,17 genannte ἑκατοστὴ ἡ ἐν Πειραιεῖ (*hekatostḗ hē en Peiraieí*) und der in IG I³ 182 Z.15 belegte Hafenzoll. Nach Theophrast (F 650 Fortenbaugh; Stob. 44,20 Wachsmuth-Hense) mußte bei Grundstücksverkäufen der Käufer eine einprozentige Verkaufssteuer erlegen. Auch die ant. und byz. Lexika zählen zu den Verkaufssteuern (ἐπώνια) »gewisse H.« (Anecd. Bekk. I 255,1). Drei frg. erhaltene Inschriftstellen aus der Zeit um 330–310 v. Chr. belegen eine einprozentige Verkaufssteuer bei Immobilien, die der Verkäufer bzw. Verpächter zu entrichten hatte (IG II² 1594–1603; SEG 42,130 bis). Diese H. floß in die Kasse der Schatzmeister der Athena (vgl. IG II² 1471 Z.10–13; SEG 38,138).

2. In Chalkedon ist eine H. als Zuschlag zum Verkaufspreis für ein Priesteramt belegt (Syll.³ 1009,19: um 200 v. Chr.).

3. In Chios wurde im 4. Jh. v. Chr. eine H. auf Ernteerträge, im karischen Pidasa im 2. Jh. v. Chr. auf die Getreideernte erhoben.

4. Im ptolem. Äg. ist H. als Hafenzoll, Zoll auf Weinhandel und Steuern beim Landverkauf nachgewiesen, im kaiserzeitlichen Äg. als zusätzliche Gebühr bei Getreidelieferungen, als Torzoll und Verkaufssteuer sowie als Steuer bei Vermögen über 20 000 Sesterzen.

5. In Berytos ist inschriftlich eine H. als Marktsteuer für das 5.–7. Jh. n. Chr. bezeugt (SEG 39,1575–1577).

1 Busolt/Swoboda 2 M. Corsaro, Tassazione regia e tassazione cittadina dagli Achemenidi ai re ellenistici, in: REA 87, 1985, 73–95 3 M. Faraguna, Atene nell' età di Alessandro, in: Atti della accademia nazionale dei Lincei 389. Memorie 9,2,2, 1992, 167–445 4 K. Hallof, Der Verkauf konfiszierten Vermögens vor den Poleten in Athen, in: Klio 72, 1990, 402–426 5 B.R. MacDonald, The Phanosthenes Decree, in: Hesperia 50, 1981, 141–146 6 Préaux, 186; 334 f.; 379 7 V.J. Rosivach, The rationes centesimarum, in: Eirene 28, 1992, 49–61 8 Rostovtzeff, Hellenistic World 9 S.L. Wallace, Taxation in Egypt from Augustus to Diocletian, 1938, 39; 231 f.; 268 ff.; 278. W.S.

Hekebolos (Ἑκηβόλος). Ep. Epitheton für → Apollon in seiner Funktion als Bogenschütze (Hom. Il. 1,14 u.ö.), für → Artemis in frühgriech. Texten nur in der Nikandre-Inschr. (SEG 19, 507 5) belegt; später mit erheblich erweitertem Bezugsfeld. In der Ant. als »fernhin treffend« (zu ἑκάς und βάλλειν) aufgefaßt (schol. T zu Hom. Il. 1,14; vgl. Aischyl. Eum. 628: τόξοις ἑκηβόλοισιν), wahrscheinlicher ist eine Ableitung zu ἑκών (etwa: »nach Belieben treffend«).

FRISK, s.v. H. • CHANTRAINE, s.v. H. E.V.

Hekhalot-Literatur. Die H., zu der als wichtigste Makroformen *Hekhalot Rabbati* (›Die großen Paläste‹), *Hekhalot zuṭarti* (›Die kleinen Paläste‹), *Maʿase Merkaba* (›Das Werk des Thronwagens‹), *Merkaba Rabba* (›Der große Thronwagen‹), *Reʾuyyot Yeḥeqkel* (›Die Visionen des Ezechiel‹), *Massekhet Hekhalot* (›Traktat der Paläste‹) und der 3. Henoch gehören, ist ein Zeugnis der frühen jüd. Mystik, für die ein ›experimentelles, durch lebendige Erfahrung gewonnenes Wissen von Gott‹ [4. 4] konstitutiv ist. Eines der bedeutendsten Motive ist die Himmelsreise eines Frommen: Nach gefahrvollen Auseinandersetzungen mit Gottes Engeln, die keinem Menschen den Zutritt in die himmlische Welt gestatten wollen (»Gefährdungsmotiv«), durchquert der Fromme mit Hilfe göttlichen Schutzes die sieben himmlischen Paläste (hebr. *Hekhalot*), in deren Innern Gott auf seinem Thronwagen (*Merkaba*) als König der Welt residiert, und kann schließlich an dem dort stattfindenden Gottesdienst und am Lobpreis der Engel teilnehmen. In diesem Gesamtkontext spielen Beschwörungen, die die zerstörerische Kraft der Engel bannen sollen, sowie hochpoetische Hymnen, mit denen Gott von seinem Hofstaat gepriesen wird, eine wichtige Rolle. Die Überlieferungen der H. enthalten auch magische Formeln, mit Hilfe derer sich der Eingeweihte die volle Kenntnis der Tora aneignen bzw. sich vor dem Vergessen der Tora schützen kann. Damit steht der Mystiker in direktem Gegensatz zum Ideal des rabbinischen Judentums, das die Erkenntnis Gottes und die Deutung der Welt durch das beständige, oft mühevolle Lernen der Tora sich zu erschließen versucht. Die H. ist wohl in spät- oder nachtalmudischer Zeit (ca. 6.–7. Jh. n. Chr.) in Aufnahme älterer Trad. entstanden. Im Hinblick auf die Darstellung des himmlischen Gottesdienstes lassen sich aber bemerkenswerte Parallelen zu Texten aus → Qumran (vgl. v.a. die Sabbatopferlieder, 4Q Shirot ʿOlat-ha-Shabbat) sowie zum NT (vgl. 2 Kor 12,1–4; Hebr 13,22; Apk 4) aufzeigen. Vermutlich schöpfen diese unterschiedlichen Überl. aus gemeinsamen Quellen.

1 J. DAN, The Ancient Jewish Mysticism, 1993
2 P. SCHÄFER, Der verborgene und offenbare Gott. Hauptthemen der frühen jüd. Mystik, 1991 3 Ders. (Hrsg.), Übers. der H. 1–4, 1987–1994 4 G. SCHOLEM, Die jüd. Mystik in ihren Hauptströmungen, 1967, 43–78. B.E.

Hekte (ἕκτη). Griech. Bezeichnung für das Sechstel einer Einheit. Nominalbezeichnung der aus einer Gold-Silber-Legierung hergestellten Elektronstatere (→ Stater) von Kyzikos (inschr. IG I² 199; 203), Mytilene und Phokaia. Daneben finden sich Serien des 7. bis 5. Jh. v. Chr. aus unbestimmten kleinasiat. Münzstätten, die nach dem milesischen, phokäischen und samisch-euböischen Standard ausgebracht sind [3. 7–17]. Die im Gold-Silber-Verhältnis von 1:13 ⅓ [1. 55] als Gemeinschaftsprägungen nach dem Münzvertrag von 394 v. Chr. [2. 29] hergestellten Münzen von Mytilene und Phokaia entsprechen als Sechstelstatere (Durchschnittsgewicht 2,55 g) 4 att. → Drachmen bzw. 20 äginet. → Obolen [1. 56]. An Teilstücken kommen Hemi-H. (1/12 Stater), Obolos (1/24 Stater), Hemiobolos (1/48 Stater) und Tartemorion (1/96 Stater) vor.
→ Elektron

1 F. BODENSTEDT, Phokäisches Elektron-Geld von 600–326 v. Chr., 1976 2 Ders., Die Elektronmünzen von Phokaia und Mytilene, 1981 3 Monnaies Grecques de Haute Epoque – Collection Jonathan P. Rosen. Venté Publique Monnaies et Medailles S. A. Bâle No. 72, 1987.

H. CHANTRAINE, s.v. H., KlP 2, 986 • L. WEIDAUER, Probleme der frühen Elektronprägung, 1975 • N. M. WAGGONER, Early Greek Coins from the Jonathan P. Rosen Collection, 1983. H.-J.S.

Hektemoroi (ἑκτήμοροι) waren Landpächter in Attika; ihre Verarmung war eine der wichtigsten Erscheinungen der sozialen und wirtschaftlichen Krise, die → Solon als Schlichter (διαλλακτής, *diallaktḗs*) und Archon beilegen sollte. Die Schreibweise des Begriffs (ἑκτήμορος bei Aristot. Ath. pol. 2,2 sowie bei den meisten Lexikographen; ἑκτημόριος bei Plutarch) wurde in der Ant. ebenso diskutiert wie seine Bedeutung. Nach Plutarch (Solon 13,4 f.) behielten die *h.* fünf Sechstel der Erträge des von ihnen bearbeiteten Landes und mußten ein Sechstel als Pacht abgeben, während der byz. Gelehrte Eustathios (*Commentarius ad Homeri Odysseam* 19,28) behauptet, daß die *h.* fünf Sechstel abzugeben hatten. In der mod. Forschung werden Abgaben in Höhe von einem Sechstel der Erträge für wahrscheinlicher gehalten. Bei einer so geringen Belastung hätte aber eine derart schwere wirtschaftliche Krise nur von einem Bevölkerungswachstum oder von einem Rückgang der Fruchtbarkeit des Bodens in einem völlig unwahrscheinlichen Ausmaß verursacht werden können; aus diesem Grund ist anzunehmen, daß die entschiedene Ablehnung sozialer Abhängigkeitsverhältnisse ein ebenso wichtiger Faktor der Krise war wie die wirtschaftliche Not.

Obwohl *h.* später ausschließlich mit den Reformen Solons in Verbindung gebracht wurden, kann der Begriff *h.* in keinem Text Solons nachgewiesen werden; es bleibt daher auch unklar, ob Solon den Status der *h.* offiziell abgeschafft hat oder ob dieser, bedingt durch die anderen Reformmaßnahmen, allmählich verschwand. Solon selbst hat sich gerühmt, die → *hóroi*

(Grenzsteine), die ›die schwarze Erde zur Sklavin gemacht‹ hätten, beseitigt zu haben (Aristot. Ath. pol. 12,4), und es ist durchaus wahrscheinlich, daß von dieser Aufhebung der auf dem Boden ruhenden Schuldlast auch der Status der *h.* betroffen war. Unter welchen Umständen und zu welchem Zeitpunkt die Abgabepflicht der *h.* in Attika entstand und geregelt wurde, ist gegenwärtig nicht zu erkennen; ebenso bleibt unklar, ein wie großer Teil der Bevölkerung Athens im 7. Jh. v. Chr. zu den *h.* gehörte. Arch. Grabungen in Attika konnten bisher keinen grundsätzlichen Wandel in der Siedlungsstruktur um 600 v. Chr. feststellen.
→ Seisachtheia

1 RHODES, 90–97. R. O./Ü: A. BE.

Hekteus (ἑκτευς). Griech. Bezeichnung für ein Trokkenmaß, hauptsächlich für Getreide, im Volumen ⅙ → Medimnos, entsprechend 8 → Choinikes und 32 → Kotylai. Nach [1] beträgt der H. je nach Landschaft 8,75 l (Attika) oder 12,12 l (Ägina) [1. 504–506]. In ptolemäischer Zeit entspricht der H. 13,13 l [1. 623]. Nach [3] durchlief der att. H. die Stufen 4,56, 5,84, 6,56, 8,75, 10,21, 10,94 l, der äginet.-lakon. H. entsprach 9,12 l. Bei [6] beträgt der solon. H. 8,64 l, der jüngere att. 9,82 l, der äginet. 12,33 l, der sizil. 8,73 l. [7] setzt den att. H. mit 7,248 l, den sizil. mit 9,06 l und den ptolem. mit 10,87 l an.
→ Hohlmaße (Griechenland und Rom)

1 F. HULTSCH, Griech. und röm. Metrologie, [2]1882
2 H. CHANTRAINE, s. v. H., KlP 2, 987 3 O. VIEDEBANTT, s. v. H., RE 7, 2803–2806 4 Ders., Forsch. zur Metrologie des Alt., 1917, Ndr. 1974 5 Ders., in: H. v. PETRIKOVITS (Hrsg.), FS für A. Oxé, 1938, 135–146 6 H. NISSEN, Griech. und röm. Metrologie, HdbA I[2], 842 f. 7 A. OXÉ, in: BJ 147, 1942, 91–216. H.-J. S.

Hektor (Ἕκτωρ; lat. Hector). Sohn des troianischen Königspaars → Priamos und → Hekabe, Ehemann der → Andromache und Vater des → Astyanax. Als kampfstärkster Priamos-Sohn ist H. (und nicht der Kriegsverursacher Paris) in der *Ilias* für die Verteidigung der belagerten Stadt verantwortlich. Am erfolgreichsten ist er am dritten Kampftag: Nach Agamemnons Verwundung (Hom. Il. 11,200ff.) durchbricht H. die Schutzmauer der Achaier (12,445ff.), drängt diese – trotz eines Rückschlags (14,409ff.) – bis zu ihren Schiffen zurück und steckt eines davon in Brand (16,112ff.); den an → Achilleus' Stelle zu Hilfe eilenden → Patroklos tötet er (16,787ff.) und nimmt ihm Achilleus' Rüstung ab (17,122). Damit veranlaßt H. Achilleus zur Aufgabe des Kampfboykotts. Am vierten Kampftag unterliegt H. Achilleus im Zweikampf (B. 22). Sein Leichnam wird von diesem mißhandelt und schließlich nur auf göttliche Intervention dem greisen Priamos ausgehändigt (B. 24). Mit der Bestattung von H.s Leichnam endet die *Ilias*.

Das Kämpferische ist H.s eine Seite, ebenso wichtig ist sein von Liebe, Fürsorge und Verantwortungsbewußtsein geprägtes Verhältnis zu Eltern, Frau und Sohn (bes. deutlich in der berühmten Abschiedsszene Hom. Il. 6,392ff. [1]). Charakterisiert wird er weiter durch: a) seine mehrfach geäußerten Begründungen, daß er – trotz düsterer Aussichten – aus Verantwortung für die Gemeinschaft gar nicht anders könne, als die Stadt zu verteidigen (z. B. 6,441ff.; 22,99ff.); b) seine wiederholten Hinweise auf die Beurteilung seiner Taten durch die Nachwelt (6,461f.; 6,479; 7,87–91; 7,300–302; 22,106f.); c) die gelegentlich zu optimistische Einschätzung der Lage (z. B. »überhört« er in Zeus' Prophezeiung seines Erfolgs, daß dieser auf den dritten Kampftag beschränkt ist: 11,208f. gegen 18,293f.); in die gleiche Richtung geht seine Mißachtung von Warnungen, v. a. jene des am gleichen Tag wie er geborenen → Polydamas (12,210ff.; 18,243ff.; vgl. auch 13,725ff.), der mit seiner pessimistischeren Lagebeurteilung recht behält, wie H. zu spät erkennen muß (22,100–103); ähnlich abweisend verhält er sich gegenüber Patroklos' Ankündigung, daß ihm der Tod von Achilleus' Hand unmittelbar bevorstehe (16,844–862). H. ist im Unterschied zu Achilleus menschlicher Abkunft (von den griechenfreundlichen Göttern stets betont, z. B. 24,56ff.). Gerade diese »Menschlichkeit« trägt nicht unwesentlich dazu bei, daß H. trotz (oder vielleicht sogar wegen) seiner Fehler eine Identifikationsfigur ist. Überhaupt erscheint in Homers Darstellung der Troianer (d. h. Kriegsgegner!) H. als Figur, der offensichtlich die Sympathien von Dichter und Publikum in nicht geringem Maß gelten.

Nach einer plausiblen Vermutung hat Homer die Bed. H.s innerhalb der Troia-Erzählung aufgewertet und ihn zum eigentlichen Gegenspieler Achilleus' entwickelt (daß er ihn erfunden hat, ist dagegen nicht beweisbar [2. 182–185]). H. repräsentiert die (im Epos wohl traditionelle) Figur des Verteidigers einer belagerten Stadt. Der Name H. ist bereits im Mykenischen bezeugt [3] und ist sprechend (zu ἔχειν, urspr. wohl »Bezwinger«, »Sieger« [4]; von Homer als »Halter«, »Verteidiger« gedeutet: Il. 24,730).

Die H.-Darstellung Homers ist für die gesamte spätere Lit. prägend und wird nur noch in Einzelheiten ergänzt oder modifiziert [5. 476–480]: Stesichoros (fr. 224 PMGF), Ibykos (fr. 295 PMGF), Euphorion (fr. 56 POWELL) und Lykophron (Alexandra 265) machen ihn zum Sohn Apollons (wohl aufgrund einer Fehldeutung von Hom. Il. 24,258–259). Sappho (fr. 44 VOIGT) schildert die Hochzeit von H. und Andromache. Der Troianer, der den ersten an Land springenden Griechen (Protesilaos) tötet, bleibt bei Homer (Il. 2,701) anonym; bezeichnenderweise füllen die *Kypria* (argumentum p. 42 BERNABÉ) diese »Lücke« und identifizieren ihn mit H. (vgl. Soph. fr. 497 RADT).

Der dominierende Einfluß der *Ilias* wird auch an den bildlichen H.-Darstellungen klar ersichtlich [5. 480; 6]. Sie zeigen H. v. a. a) in Wappnungsszenen, b) beim Abschied, c) in Kampfszenen; dann d) die Mißhandlung und e) die Herausgabe seines Leichnams.

1 W. Schadewaldt, Von Homers Welt und Werk, 41965, 207–233 2 W. Kullmann, Die Quellen der Ilias, 1960 3 DMic s. v. e-ko-to 4 M. Meier, ἔχω und seine Bedeutung im Frühgriech., in: MH 33, 1976, 180–181 5 P. Wathelet, Dictionnaire des Troyens de l'Iliade 1, 1988, 466–506 6 O. Touchefeu, s. v. H., LIMC 4.1, 482–498.

W. Schadewaldt, H. in der Ilias, in: WS 69, 1956, 5–25 • H. Erbse, H. in der Ilias, in: Ders., Ausgewählte Schriften zur Klass. Philol., 1979, 1–18 • J. Redfield, Nature and Culture in the Iliad, 21994 • J. de Romilly, Hector, 1997.
RE. N.

Hektoridas. Bildhauer, wird in den Abrechnungen für die Skulpturen eines Giebels des Asklepiostempels in → Epidauros angeführt, der um 370 v. Chr. fertiggestellt war. Ihm sind daher die als *Iliupersis* zu ergänzenden Frg. zuzuschreiben, die als eigenständige Arbeit gelten müssen und nicht – wie vielfach vermutet – als Kopien nach Modellen des → Timotheos. Außerdem legte H. Modelle für die Bemalung von Löwenkopfwasserspeiern vor. Seine Signatur findet sich auf der Basis einer verlorenen Statue ebenfalls in Epidauros.

A. Burford, The Greek temple builders at Epidauros, 1969 • Lippold, 220 • N. Yalouris, Die Skulpturen des Asklepiostempels in Epidauros, 1992.
R. N.

Heleios (Ἕλειος). Jüngster Sohn des → Perseus (Apollod. 2,49; Paus. 3,20,6); Eponym der Stadt Helos in Lakonien, die er nach der Teilnahme am Taphierfeldzug gegründet haben soll (Apollod. 2,59; Strab. 8,5,2).
J. S.-A.

Helellum (Tab. Peut. 3,4; *Alaia*, Geogr. Rav. 26). Röm. *vicus* der Triboci im Oberelsaß (nicht identisch mit → Helvetum) an der Route Argentovaria – Argentoratus am Übergang der Ill beim h. Ehl-Benfeld, Dep. Bas-Rhin [1]; einer spätlatènezeitlichen Siedlung folgte in augusteischer Zeit der gallo-röm. *vicus*, der sich schließlich ca. 100 m beiderseits der Hauptstraße auf einer L von ca. 1000 m entwickelte. Eine Nekropole (3./4. Jh. n. Chr.) befindet sich im Süden von H. Trotz kleinerer Handwerksbetriebe war H. v. a. Handelszentrum. Der *vicus*, der durch eine Benefiziarierstation gesichert wurde, blieb trotz mehrfacher Zerstörung bis ins 4. Jh. bewohnt.

1 H. Steger, **Regula*/Riegel am Kaiserstuhl – Helvetum?, in: Römer und Alamannen im Breisgau (Arch. und Gesch. 6), 1994, 233–361.

E. Kern, Benfeld-Ehl (Bas-Rhin), in: Atlas des agglomérations secondaires de la Gaule, 1994, 148 f. • F. Petry, Observations sur les vici explorés en Alsace, in: Caesarodunum 11, 1976, 273–295.
F. SCH.

Helena

[1] s. Helene [1]

[2] Frau bzw. Konkubine des → Constantius [1], Mutter des Constantinus [1] (→ Constantinus [1] mit Stemma). Die Umbenennung von Drepana in → Helenopolis in constantinischer Zeit erklärt sich durch ihre besondere Verehrung für den Märtyrer Lukianos und ist kein Hinweis auf einen bithynischen Ursprung. Vermutlich stammte sie aus dem Balkanraum, vielleicht aus Naissus, dem Geburtsort des Constantinus. Ihre Rolle am Hof ihres Sohnes ist in den ersten Jahren seiner Regierung kaum bestimmbar, offensichtlich wurde sie durch ihn zum Christentum geführt (Eus. vita Const. 3,47,2). Im November 324 n. Chr. wurde sie zusammen mit → Fausta zur Augusta erhoben. Damit waren einige Ehrenrechte (z. B. das Ausbringen von Goldprägungen für H., vgl. Eus. a.O. 3,47,2) verbunden, sowie die Möglichkeit, für Maßnahmen der Kirchenbauförderung im Heiligen Land auf den kaiserlichen Schatz zurückzugreifen (Eus. a.O. 3,47,3), ohne daß H. deshalb als Mitregentin bezeichnet werden kann. Eine besondere Rolle weist ihr die spätere Legende bei der Auffindung des »Wahren Kreuzes« zu, wegen der sie in der orthodoxen Kirche zusammen mit Constantinus als Heilige verehrt wird (Fest am 21. Mai). Authentischer Kern dieser Legende ist die im Pilgerbetrieb (→ Pilgerschaft) dieser Zeit übliche Bemühung um Reliquien, die tatsächlich bereits in constantinischer Zeit zur vermeintlichen Entdeckung des »Wahren Kreuzes« geführt haben dürfte.

J. W. Drijvers, Helena Augusta, 1992.

[3] Tochter des Constantinus [1], heiratete 355 n. Chr. auf Veranlassung Constantius' [2] II. ihren Cousin, den neu erhobenen Caesar → Iulianus [5]. Sie starb 360/1 und wurde an der Via Nomentana bestattet (Amm. 21,1,5).
B. BL.

Helene (Ἑλένη, Helena).

[1] Göttin, die an verschiedenen Kultplätzen in und um Sparta verehrt wurde, vor allem im Menelaion in → Therapne (Hdt. 6,61; Paus. 3,15,3; Hesych. s. v. Ἑλένεια, [1]). Auf → Rhodos hatte sie einen Kult als H. Dendritis (Paus. 3,19,10), in → Kenchreai und auf → Chios ist sie als Quellgottheit belegt (Paus. 2,2,3; Steph. Byz. s. v. Ἑλένη). Für ihren Namen gibt es keine vollständig gesicherte Etym. [2. 63–80]. Zu den Zeugnissen über ihren Kult in histor. Zeit vgl. [1]; zu den Riten, die Theokr. 18 beschreibt, und der Funktion, die sie beim Erwachsenwerden der Frauen haben, vgl. [3. Bd. 1, 281–285, 333–350]. Mit den → Dioskuroi wird H. durch Zeugnisse verbunden, die beschreiben, daß sie Seeleuten als positiv oder negativ zu deutendes Flämmchen erscheint (Eur. Or. 1637; Plin. nat. 2,37,101; zu einem gemeinsamen Kult in Athen vgl. Eust. 1425,62–63 ad Hom. Od. 1,399; Interpretationsversuche bei [2. 48–53] und [4. 190–193]). Später spielte H. in der Gnostik (→ Gnosis) eine bedeutende Rolle [5. 345–355].

In der ep. Tradition gilt → Zeus als H.s Vater (Hom. Il. 3,418; Od. 4,184; 219; 227), während als Mutter → Nemesis (Kypria fr. 9,1 PEG I) genannt wird, die ein Ei gebiert, das zu → Leda, der Gattin des Tyndareos, gebracht wird, oder das sie findet und aus dem H. auf die Welt kommt (Sappho fr. 166f. VOIGT; Kratinos fr. 115 PCG IV = Athen. 9,373e; Hyg. astr. 2,8; Apollod. 3,127–128). Leda als Mutter nennt zuerst Eur. Hel. 18f. (dann Paus. 3,16,1). Die Dioskuren gelten als ihre Brüder (Hom. Il. 3,236–238). Bei Hes. cat. fr. 24 ist H. die Tochter des → Okeanos. → Theseus raubt H. zusammen mit → Peirithoos und bringt sie nach Aphidna, von wo sie die Dioskuren wieder zurückbringen. Wie alt H. zu diesem Zeitpunkt ist, ist unklar (Alkm. fr. 21 PMG; Hellanikos FGrH 4 F 168b; Hyg. fab. 79). Nach einigen Quellen soll H. dem Theseus → Iphigeneia geboren haben (Stesich. fr. 191 PMG = Paus. 2,22,7). Als Tyndareos H. verheiraten will, läßt er die zahlreichen Freier (Hes. cat. fr. 196–200; 202; 204; Hyg. fab. 81) einen Eid schwören, den künftigen Gatten der H. bei Kämpfen um sie zu unterstützen (Stesich. fr. 190 PMG). Mit ihrem Gatten → Menelaos hat sie die Tochter → Hermione (Hom. Od. 4,12–14; Eur. Or. 107–112).

Die übergroße Schönheit der H. wird gepriesen und ist schon in der Ant. ein Topos (z.B. Hom. Il. 3,154–158; in Ov. met. 15,232f. klagt die gealterte H. über den Verlust ihrer Schönheit). Aphrodite (Hom. Il. 3,399–420) oder → Paris (Hom. Il. 13,626f.), der sie nach Troia entführt, wird das Parisurteil zur Last gelegt, das den troianischen Krieg auslöst (Sappho fr. 16 VOIGT; Alk. fr. 283 VOIGT; Alkm. fr. 77 PMG; Hyg. fab. 92). Nach Paris' Tod heiratet H. → Deiphobos, den Menelaos nach der Eroberung Troias erschlägt (Hom. Od. 8,517; Ilias parva fr. 4 PEG I; Apollod. epit. 5,22). Nach dem Fall Troias vergibt ihr Menelaos und kehrt mit ihr nach Griechenland zurück (Ilias parva fr. 19 PEG I; Iliupersis argumentum PEG I).

Schon früh ist Kritik an H. und ihrer Rolle als Auslöserin des troian. Kriegs greifbar (Alk. fr. 42 VOIGT); Stesichoros (fr. 192 PMG) widerrief seine negative Darstellung, indem er nur ein *eídōlon* (»Trugbild«) H.s mit Paris nach Troia ziehen läßt, während H. selbst nach Ägypten entrückt wird (Hdt. 2,113–115 mit leichter Variation), wo sie lebt, bis Menelaos sie auf seiner Rückkehr von Troia dort findet und nach Griechenland zurückbringt (Eur. Hel.). Auch Gorgias (*Enkōmion Helénēs*, ›Lob der Helena‹) und Isokrates (or. 10) verteidigen H. Im Drama ist sie eine sehr beliebte Figur (Aischyl. Ag. 403–408; 737–749; Soph. fr. 176–184 TrGF; Kratinos fr. 39–51 PCG IV), wobei die Schönheit der H. zu einem wichtigen Thema wird (Eur. Tro. 991f.; Eur. Andr. 627–631; Aristoph. Lys. 155f.). In Eur. Or. 1625–1642 wird sie von → Orestes überfallen, worauf Apollon sie entrückt. Eine andere Mythenvariante läßt sie nach ihrem Tod die Gattin des → Achilleus auf der Insel Leuke werden (Paus. 3,19,11; 13). In der lat. Lit. wird sie mehrheitlich negativ gezeichnet (Verg. Aen. 2,567–587; 6,494–530; Hor. epod. 17,42; sat. 1,3,107; Sen. Tro.; Dares Phrygius; Dictys, Ephemeris belli Troiani; Ov. epist. 16, 17 setzt sich davon ab und schildert H.s moralische Bedenken beim Erwägen der Beziehung zu Paris). In der bildlichen Darstellung der H. dominieren wenige Szenen aus ihrem Leben: Ihre Geburt, ihre Entführungen und das erneute Zusammentreffen mit Menelaos. Zu ihrem Nachleben in Lit. und Kunst vgl. die Zusammenstellung bei [6].

1 H.W. CATLING, H. CAVANAGH, Two inscribed bronzes from the Menelaion, Sparta, in: Kadmos 15.2, 1976, 145–157 2 L.L. CLADER, H. The evolution from divine to heroic in Greek epic tradition, 1976 3 C. CALAME, Les chœurs de jeunes filles en Grèce archaïque, 2 Bd., 1977 4 O. SKUTSCH, H., her name and nature, in: JHS 107, 1987, 188–193 5 J. FOSSUM, G. QUISPEL, s.v. H. (1), RAC 14, 338–355 6 HUNGER, Mythologie, 154–156.

LIT.: N. AUSTIN, H. of Troy and her Shameless Phantom, 1994 • K. BASSI, H. and the discourse of denial in Stesichorus' Palinodie, in: Arethusa 26, 1993, 51–75 • E. BETHE, s.v. H., RE 7, 2824–2835 • L. BRAUN, Die schöne H., wie Gorgias und Isokrates sie sehen, in: Hermes 110, 1982, 158–174 • O. CARBONERO, La figura di Elena di Troia nei poeti latini da Lucrezio a Ovidio, in: Orpheus 10, 1989, 378–391 • F. CHARPOUTHIER, Les Dioscures au service d'une déesse, 1935 • L. KAHIL, Les enlèvements et le retour d'H. dans les textes et les documents figurés, 1955 • Dies., N. ICARD, s.v. H., LIMC 4.1, 498–563 • D. LYONS, Gender and Immortality, Heroines in Ancient Greek Myth and Cult, 1997, 134–135, 138–141, 148–149, 158–159, 161–162 • H. PELLICCIA, Sappho 16, Gorgias' H. and the preface to Herodotus' Histories, in: YClS 29, 1992, 63–84 • J.I. PORTER, The seductions of Gorgias, in: Classical Antiquity 12, 1993, 267–293 • G.B. SCHMID, Die Beurteilung der H. in der frühgriech. Lit., 1982 • M. SUZUKI, Metamorphoses of H. Authority, Difference, and the Epic, 1989.

ABB.: L. KAHIL, N. ICARD, s.v. H., LIMC 4.2, 291–358.

R.HA.

[2] Malerin aus Ägypt. (Alexandreia?); ihr Vater Timon war ebenfalls Maler (Phot. 190,481). Ihre Tätigkeit ist in die 2. H. des 4. Jh. v.Chr. zu datieren, da sie ein zeitgenössisches, nicht erh. Gemälde der Alexanderschlacht bei Issos geschaffen haben soll, das zur Regierungszeit Vespasians im *templum pacis* in Rom ausgestellt war. Die Forsch. diskutierte H. zuweilen im Zusammenhang mit der in Pompeji überlieferten Mosaikkopie des Gemäldes (→ Alexandermosaik); eine Urheberschaft wurde unter Hinweis auf die Unfähigkeit von Frauen zu ›Kunstleistungen von dieser Höhe‹ (sic!), nicht etwa mangels anderer Belege verworfen [1. 2837].

1 E. Pfuhl, s.v. H. (7), RE 7.

A. COHEN, The Alexandermosaic, 1996, 139–143 • L. FORTI, s.v. H., EAA 3, 1134f.

N.H.

[3] Schmale Felsinsel von ca. 12 km L (H 281 m ü.M.) vor der Ostküste von Attika (Strab. 9,1,22; 9,5,3), auch *Mákris* (Μάκρις, Steph. Byz. s.v. Ἑ.; Eur. Hel. 1673ff.; Mela 2,7,10; Plin. nat. 4,62; [1; 2]). Prähistor. Funde: [3; 4; 5].

1 W. Kolbe, L. Bürchner, s. v. H. (1), RE 7, 2823 f. 2 L. Bürchner, s. v. Μάκρις, ἡ, RE 14, 814 3 N. Lambert, Vestiges préhistoriques dans l'île de Makronissos, in: BCH 96, 1972, 873–881 4 Dies., Vestiges préhistoriques dans l'île de Macronisos, in: AAA 6, 1973, 1–12 5 P. Spitaels, Provatsa on Makronissos, in: AAA 15, 1982, 155–158.

H.LO.

Helenion (ἑλένιον, *helenium*). Der Name ist laut Plin. nat. 21,59 und 159 von den Tränen der Helena (etwas anders Ail. nat. 9,21) abgeleitet. Röm. Autoren meinten mit der *(h)enula* oder *inula* im allg. den Alant (Inula helenium L.), eine große in Westasien und Osteuropa wachsende Composite. Sie wurde seit der Spätant. als Heilpflanze in Gärten kultiviert (vgl. Colum. 11,3,17 und 35). Bes. die bittere Wurzel (Beschreibung des Einmachens mit süßen Zusätzen: Colum. 12,48,1–5; Plin. nat. 19,91; Hor. sat. 2,8,51) sollte (Dioskurides 1,28 Wellmann = 1,27 Berendes; Plin. nat. 20,38) u.a. gegen Blähungen, Husten, Krämpfe, Magenstörungen (Plin. nat. 19,92; Hor. sat. 2,2,44) und den Biß wilder Tiere helfen. *H.* galt für Plin. nat. 21,159 als weibliches Schönheitsmittel. Theophrast (h. plant. 2,1,3; 6,6,2) und andere bezeichneten damit aber auch Labiaten wie Calamintha incana oder Satureia thymbra L. (wohl = *tragoríganos* bei Dioskurides 3,30 Wellmann = 3,32 Berendes). Im 17. Jh. ging der Name auf amerikanische Compositen der Gattung Helianthus L. (Helenium indicum C. Bauhin, Sonnenblume) und Helenium L. über.

R. Stadler, s. v. H., RE 7, 2838–2840.

C.HÜ.

Helenius Acron. Röm. Grammatiker, zumal Kommentator. Sein Teilkomm. zu Terenz (*Adelphoe* und *Eunuchus*) ist in der gramm. Trad. berücksichtigt; von seinem berühmteren Horaz-Komm. ([3. 1,3] setzt ihn über Porphyrio und Modestus) finden sich Spuren in den verschiedenen Rezensionen der Schol., bes. bei → Porphyrio. Da Gellius H. nicht zu kennen scheint, H. andererseits von Porphyrio (zu Hor. sat. 1,8,25) und Iulius Romanus (Char. p. 250,11 ff. Barwick) benutzt wird, liegt eine Datier. in das spätere 2. Jh. n. Chr. nahe. H. als Verf.-Name eines humanistischen Strangs der Horaz-Schol. [3; 6] ist ohne jede Gewähr.

Frg.: 1 P. Wessner, Aemilius Asper, 1905, 16 ff.
2 A. Langenhorst, De scholiis Horatianis quae Acronis nomine feruntur quaestiones selectae, 1908, 6 ff.
Ed.: 3 Pseudacronis schol. in Hor. vetustiora, ed. O. Keller, 2 Bde., 1902–1904.
Lit.: 4 P. Graffunder, Entstehungszeit ... der akronischen Horazschol., in: RhM 60, 1905, 128–143
5 G. Noske, Quaestiones Pseudacroneae, 1969, 220 ff.; 236 ff. 6 C. Villa, I manoscritti di Orazio III, in: Aevum 68, 1994, 129–134 7 P. L. Schmidt, in: HLL, § 444.

P.L.S.

Helenopolis. Ort am Ausgang des Golfs von Astakos in Bithynia, urspr. Drepanon, h. Altinova. Geburtsort der → Helena [2], ihr zu Ehren von Constantinus [1] zur Stadt erhoben, von Iustinianus ausgebaut (Amm. 26,8,1; Prok. aed. 5,2).

R. Janin, Les églises et les monastères des grands centres byzantins, 1975, 97 f. • W. Ruge, s. v. Drepanon (4), RE 5, 1687.

K.ST.

Helenos (Ἕλενος).

[1] Einer der frühen großen Seher, im ep. Kyklos wichtiger als bei Homer; Sohn des → Priamos und der → Hekabe (Hom. Il. 6,76; 7,44; Soph. Phil. 605 f.; Apollod. 3,151; POxy. 56,3829), Zwillingsbruder der → Kassandra (Antikleides FGrH 140 F 17; POxy. 56,3830). Einer wahrscheinlich archa. Trad. nach erhält H. bereits als Kind seine Sehergabe im Tempel des Apollon Thymbraios, wo er und Kassandra eingeschlafen sind. Als die Eltern am nächsten Morgen zurückkommen, sehen sie, wie die hl. Schlangen die ›Zugänge zu ihren Sinnesorganen‹ mit den Zungen reinigen (Antikleides l.c.; rationalisiert in Arrianos FGrH 156 F 102); diese Verbindung mit Apollon ist auch auf einem apulischen Volutenkrater von ca. 330 v. Chr. zu sehen, wo H. mit Lorbeerkranz und -zweig in der Hand dargestellt ist [1]. Bei Homer berät und ermutigt H. Hektor, da er »der bei weitem beste Vogelflugdeuter« ist (Hom. Il. 6,76) und »die Stimme der Götter« hört (Hom. Il. 7,53). Wie andere archa. griech. Seher [2] kämpft er auf dem Schlachtfeld (Hom. Il. 12,94 f.; 13,576–600) und gehört zur höchsten Aristokratie [3. add. PKöln VI, 245].

Gemäß den *Kypria* prophezeit H. Unglück, bevor → Paris nach Sparta zieht. Später nimmt er an den Leichenspielen nach dessen angeblichem Tod teil (Hyg. fab. 273,12) und bewirbt sich mit Deiphobos um die Hand der »Witwe« → Helene [1]. Nach seiner Niederlage zieht er sich zum Idagebirge zurück. Dort nimmt ihn Odysseus in einem Hinterhalt gefangen; H. weissagt ihm, daß Troia mit Hilfe von Herakles' Bogen, den er → Philoktetes übergeben hat, eingenommen werden könne (Ilias Parva; Bakchyl. fr. 7; Soph. Phil. 604–616; 1337–1341; POxy. 27,2455 fr. 17,254–259 = Hypothesis von Euripides' *Philoktetes*); spätere Quellen geben als fatale »Talismane« für Troia → Pelops' Knochen (Apollod. 5,9; Tzetz. schol. Lykophr. 911), das Troianische Pferd oder den Erwerb des → Palladions an (Konon FGrH 26 F 1,34; Q. Smyrn. 10,343–361). Nach anderen späten Quellen läuft H. freiwillig zu den Griechen über (Triphiodoros 45–50) oder bittet Priamos, zu den Molossern gehen zu dürfen (Dion Chrys. 11,137; 142), eine Version, die klar von Euripides' *Andromache* beeinflußt ist (1233–45; Verg. Aen. 3,295–297); er soll mit → Andromache sogar ein Kind, Kestrinos, gehabt haben (Paus. 1,11,1).

1 N. Icard-Gianolto, s. v. H., LIMC 8.1, 613 f., Nr. 1
2 J. N. Bremmer, The Status and Symbolic Capital of the Seer, in: R. Hägg (ed.), The Role of Rel. in the Early Greek Polis, 1996, 97–109 3 P. Wathelet, Dictionnaire des Troyens de l'Iliade, 1988, Nr. 109.

J.B./Ü: H.K.

[2] Sohn des Apollonios (?) aus Kyrene; Vater der Thaubarion (PP 3/9, 5139). 134 v. Chr. als Beauftragter des Königs in Diospolis; seit ca. 120 in verschiedenen Funk-

tionen auf Zypern tätig (vgl. auch SEG 41, 1479), von 117/6 bis zur Ernennung Ptolemaios' IX. Stratege der Insel (συγγενής, στρατηγὸς καὶ ἀρχιερεὺς καὶ ἀρχικυνηγός, *syngenḗs, stratēgós kai archiereús kai archikynēgós*), zwischen 116 und 114/3 τροφεύς (*tropheús*) Ptolemaios' X. Alexander. Nach dessen Königsproklamation wurde er von 114 bis 106/5 unter ihm *stratēgós* von Zypern; seit 107/6 ist H. auch Admiral und γραμματεὺς τοῦ ναυτικοῦ (*grammateús tu nautikú*; nicht auf Zypern beschränkt); in diesem Jahr ist er als Priester Kleopatras III. auf Lebenszeit bezeugt.
→ Hoftitel

PP 3/9, 5112; 6, 15041 • E. VAN'T DACK, Apollodôros et Helenos, in: Sacris erudiri 31, 1989/90, 429–441, bes. 431 ff. W.A.

Helenus. Freigelassener Octavians griech. Herkunft. Er besetzte 40 v.Chr. Sardinien für Octavian, wurde aber dort von Menodoros verdrängt (App. civ. 5,277), gefangen und an Octavian zurückgeschickt (Cass. Dio 48,30,1; 48,45,5). Zu seinen Ehren ILS 6267 (= CIL X 5808). ME.STR.

Helepolis. Die *h.* (ἑλέπολις, wörtl. »Städtenehmer«) war ein großer, mit Rädern versehener, bewegbarer Belagerungsturm, der Soldaten und Katapulte an die Mauern einer belagerten Stadt heranführen sollte. Der Begriff ist erst für einen von Poseidonios für Alexander d.Gr. gebauten Turm belegt (Biton 52 f. WESCHER; vgl. zur Belagerung von Tyros Arr. an. 2,18–24), *helepóleis* wurden aber wohl schon von → Dionysios [1] I. von Syrakus benutzt (Diod. 14,51,1). Sie sind evtl. oriental. oder karthagischer Herkunft (Diod. 13,55). Schon in der Antike berühmte *h.* verwendete → Demetrios [2] Poliorketes bei den Belagerungen von Salamis auf Zypern im Jahr 307 v.Chr. (Diod. 20,48,2 f.) und Rhodos 304 v.Chr. (Diod. 20,91,2 f.; Plut. Demetrios 21,1 f.). Letztere erbaute Epimachos aus Athen (Athenaios Mechanicus 27W, → Athenaios [5]; Vitr. 10,16,4). Sie hatte 9 Etagen, eine Seitenlänge von über 20 m und eine Höhe von etwa 50 m. *H.* waren schwerfällig und als Holzbauten trotz Schutzverkleidung aus Metall oder Leder leicht zu beschädigen; überdies brauchten sie glatten und festen Boden für den Einsatz.
→ Poliorketik

1 KROMAYER/VEITH, 70, 219, 226, 236 2 O. LENDLE, Texte und Untersuchungen zum technischen Bereich der antiken Poliorketik, 1983, 36–106 3 E.W. MARSDEN, Greek and Roman Artillery. Technical treatises, 1971, 84 f. LE.BU.

Heliadai (Ἡλιάδαι). Die Söhne des → Helios und der Rhodos (Rhode: Hellanikos FGrH 4 F 137; schol. Hom. Od. 17,208 mit Klymene, Mutter der Heliades, verwechselt [1]): Ochimos, Kerkaphos, Aktis, Makar(os) (Makareus), Kandalos, Triopas und Phaethon (= Tenages: Pind. O. 7,71–73; vgl. schol. 131a-c, 132a). Nach einem rhod. Lokalmythos bei Pind. O. 7,34–55 [2. 2849] rät Helios den H., der Athene nach ihrer Geburt als erste zu opfern. In der Hast vergessen sie jedoch beim Opfer das Feuer (ἄπυρα ἱερά: Aition für einen rhod. Brauch, Pind. O. schol. 71b; 73; Diod. 5,56). Nach Zenon FGrH 523 F 1 bringen vier der Brüder Tenages aus Eifersucht um und wandern deshalb aus: Makar nach Lesbos, Kandalos nach Kos, Aktis nach Ägypten, Triopas nach Karien. Die Heroen sind jedoch offenbar von dort übernommen.

1 U. VON WILAMOWITZ-MÖLLENDORFF, Phaethon, in: Ders., KS, Bd. I, 1935, 110–148 2 L. MALTEN, s.v. H., RE 7, 2849–2852. T.H.

Heliades (Ἡλιάδης).
[1] Offizier des → Alexandros [13] Balas, den er nach seiner Niederlage, die er 145 v.Chr. am Oinoparas durch Ptolemaios VI. und → Demetrios [8] II. erlitt (Ios. ant. Iud. 13,4,8), mit einem anderen Offizier und einem nordsyr. Beduinenscheich zugunsten von durch die Sieger angebotenen Sicherheiten verriet und mitermordete (Diod. 32,10,1). C.C.
[2] s. Helios

Heliaia (ἡλιαία). 1. Abgeleitet von ἁλίζω (*halízō*, »versammeln«) bedeutet *h.* urspr. schlicht »Versammlung«. Im dor. Gebiet erhielt sich dieser Ausdruck für die Volksversammlung [1. 32 ff.] und in Arkadien für ein vermutlich 50köpfiges Gremium, das polit. und gerichtliche Entscheidungen traf (IG V 2,6A 24 und 27; 3,20 = IPArk Nr. 2 und 3, beide aus Tegea [2. 36 f]).

2. In Athen führte nach Aristot. Ath. Pol. 9,1 (vgl. dazu [3. 160]) Solon gegen gerichtliche Entscheidungen der Archonten die → *éphesis* an die *h.* ein, damals entweder die gesamte Volksversammlung als Gerichtsgemeinde [3. 160] oder ein durch Los ermittelter kleinerer Gerichtshof [4. 30], wofür auch die Parallele aus Tegea spricht. In den späteren Quellen ist die *h.* jedenfalls ein Gerichtshof, synonym mit → *dikastḗrion*, im 4. Jh. v.Chr. bemannt mit mindestens 1000 Geschworenen [4. 191]. *H.* war wie *dikastḗrion* Schlagwort für das System der Geschworenengerichtsbarkeit des demokratischen Athen [5. 4], jeder → *dikastḗs* hatte den »heliastischen Eid« zu schwören [4. 182 f.].

3. *H.* bezeichnete in Athen schließlich als Gerichtsstätte jenen Ort, an dem die *h.* tagte. Er ist auf der Agora zu lokalisieren. Folgende Hypothese wird geäußert [5]: Im 5. Jh. war *h.* (auch *Mētiocheíon* oder *Meízon* genannt) der rechteckige Peribolos an der Südwestecke der Agora, im 4. Jh. Gebäude A der Vorläufer des quadratischen Peristylbaues im Nordosten der Agora, der zur Zeit von Aristoteles' *Athenaion politeia* als Gesamtkomplex die *dikastḗria* mitsamt der *h.* beherbergte.

1 M. WÖRRLE, Unt. zur Verfassungsgesch. von Argos, 1964 2 G. THÜR, H. TAEUBER, Prozeßrechtliche Inschr. der griech. Poleis. Arkadien, 1994 3 RHODES 4 M.H. HANSEN, The Athenian Democracy in the Age of Demosthenes, 1991 5 A.L. BOEGEHOLD, The Lawcourts at Athens (Ath. Agora vol. XXVIII), 1995. G.T.

Helikaon (Ἑλικάων). Sohn → Antenors [1], Gatte der Priamos-Tochter Laodike (Hom. Il. 3,123). Bei der Eroberung von Troia rettet ihn Odysseus (Paus. 10,26,8). Mit Antenor (Verg. Aen. 1,247) und seinem Bruder Polydamas (Serv. Aen. 1,242) gründet H. Patavium (Mart. 10,93). RE. ZI.

Helike (Ἑλίκη).

[1] Stadt in der Ebene von Aigion in Achaia zw. den Mündungen von Selinus und Kerynitis (h. Buphusia) mit dem berühmten Heiligtum des Poseidon Helikonios. H. beteiligte sich an der ion. und der großgriech. Kolonisation (Gründung von Sybaris, Strab. 6,1,13–15), war in klass. Zeit Hauptsitz des Achaiischen Bundes mit dem Bundesheiligtum Homarion. 373 v. Chr. wurde H. durch ein nächtliches Erdbeben mit Flutwelle zerstört und versank im Meer. Die genaue Lage von H. ist unbekannt. Belegstellen: Hom. Il. 2,575; Hdt. 1,145; Pol. 2,41,7; Diod. 15,48 f.; Strab. 8,7,2; Paus. 7,24,5–25,4.

Y. LAFOND, Die Katastrophe von 373 v. Chr. und das Verschwinden der Stadt H. in Achaia, in: E. OLSHAUSEN, H. SONNABEND (Hrsg.), Naturkatastrophen in der ant. Welt (Geographica Historica 10), 1998, 118–123. Y. L.

[2] s. Sternbilder

Helikon (Ἑλικών).

[1] Gebirge in Mittelgriechenland, trennt das Kopais-Becken und das obere Kephissos-Tal vom Golf von Korinth (vgl. Strab. 9,2,25; Paus. 9,28,1–31,7). Der westl. Teil des H. gehörte zu Phokis, der östl. zu Boiotia. Höchste Erhebung ist der Gipfel des Palaiovouno (1748 m). Nur wenige Pässe führen über den quellen- und waldreichen H., der wegen seiner Kräuter gerühmt wurde. Der H. verfügt über große Flächen, die in der Ant. für die Landwirtschaft und Weideviehhaltung genutzt werden konnten. Bekannt war der H. für seine Kulte. An seinen Ostausläufern befanden sich auf dem Gipfel des Zagora ein Zeusheiligtum und darunter die → Hippokrene. In einem Bachtal lag südl. von Askra die zu Thespiai gehörende Kultstätte der Musen. Ob der in Hom. h. ad Venerem 22,3 bezeugte Kult des Poseidon Helikonios auf den H. bezogen werden kann, ist unsicher.

A. HURST, A. SCHACHTER (Hrsg.), La montagne des Muses (Recherches et rencontres 7), 1996. K. F.

[2] H. von Kyzikos. Mathematiker und Astronom aus dem Kreise des Platon, → Eudoxos [1] und → Isokrates. H. sagte die Sonnenfinsternis vom 12. Mai 361 v. Chr. voraus (Plut. Dion 19) und war mit Eudoxos an der Lösung des Problems der → Würfelverdoppelung beteiligt (Plut. mor. 579C).

F. BOLL, s. v. H. (2), RE 8, 7–8. M. F.

[3] H. und sein Vater Akesas galten nach Athen. 2,48b als berühmte Weber aus dem kyprischen Salamis. Beide sollen angeblich den ersten panathenäischen → Peplos der Athena Polias geschaffen haben. Als Werk H.s galt ein Mantel, den später die Rhodier Alexander d. Gr. schenkten und den dieser in der Schlacht von Gaugamela getragen haben soll (Plut. Alexandros 32). Ein Epigramm nennt H. und Akesas zusammen als Schöpfer eines Werkes in Delphi (Athen. 2,48b). Der Ausdruck Ἀκέσεως καὶ Ἑλικῶνος ἔργα (»Ein Werk wie von Akesas und Helikon«) galt sprichwörtlich für bes. bewundernswürdige Webarbeiten (→ Textilkunst).

G. CRESSEDI, s. v. H., EAA 3, 1135. R. H.

[4] s. Musik

Helikonios (Ἑλικώνιος). Aus Byzanz, Chronist, ausschließlich aus der Suda bekannt, verfaßte eine χρονικὴ ἐπιτομή (*chronikḗ epitomḗ*) von Adam bis auf Kaiser Theodosius I. (Suda E 851). Die Suda (A 3215 und 3868) zitiert je eine Notiz aus der Chronik über das Leben Apions und Arrians.

PLRE 1, 411 [Heliconius] · G. WIRTH, Helikonios der Sophist, in: Historia 13, 1964, 506–509. F. T.

Heliodoros (Ἡλιόδωρος).

[1] Sohn des Aischylos aus Antiocheia am Orontes, wurde gemeinsam mit Seleukos IV. erzogen und war unter diesem 187–175 v. Chr. Höfling (τῶν περὶ τὴν αὐλήν) und vielgeehrter Kanzler (ὁ ἐπὶ τῶν πραγμάτων τεταγμένος) (IG XI 4,1112–1114, bzw. OGIS 247; App. Syr. 45). Als die Finanznot nach der Niederlage von Seleukos' Vater Antiochos III. gegen die Römer (190/188) in Verbindung mit innerjüdischen Intrigen zu besonderen Abgabenforderungen an die Juden geführt hatte und H. bei deren Eintreibung im Auftrag seines Königs auf Opposition gestoßen war, ermordete er Seleukos IV. im J. 175 und übernahm die Vormundschaft über dessen Sohn Antiochos. Doch wurde er alsbald vom Bruder des Ermordeten und neuen König, Antiochos IV., und dessen Helfern Eumenes II. und Attalos II. vertrieben (2 Makk 3,4 ff.; App. Syr. 45; Hieron. in Dan 11,20, ohne Nennungs H.s). Wie JACOBY gezeigt hat, läßt sich aus FGrH 373 F 8 die Abfassung eines Memoirenwerks durch H. nicht erschließen.

A. BOUCHÉ-LECLERCQ, Histoire de Séleucides (323–64 avant J.-C.), 1913/1914, 238–242, 580–582, 627 · GRUEN, Rome, 646 f. · O. MØRKHOLM, Antiochus IV of Syria, 1966, Index s. v. · H. H. SCHMITT, Untersuchungen zur Geschichte Antiochos' d. Gr. und seiner Zeit, 1964, 20 · WILL, 33, 36, 41, 44, 46 f., 49, 104, 136 f. A. ME.

[2] Perieget; eine Erwähnung des Antiochos [6] Epiphanes (reg. 175–164 v. Chr.) in einem überzeugend zugewiesenen (Athenaios 2,45C) Fr. gibt für H. einen datierenden *terminus post quem*. Plinius (nat. 1,34,35) schreibt ihm eine Abhandlung über die *anathḗmata* der Athener zu; Harpokration (s. v. Νίκη Ἀθηνᾶ) und Athenaios (9,406D) bezeichnen H. als ὁ Περιηγητής (»der Perieget«), Athenaios (6,229E) nennt ihn ferner einen Athener und erwähnt eine Schrift Περὶ Ἀκροπόλεως (›Über die Akropolis‹) in 15 B. Harpokration überl. einmal (s. v. Προπύλαια ταῦτα) den erweiterten Titel Περὶ τῆς Ἀθήνησιν ἀκροπόλεως (›Über die Akropolis in Athen‹) und zitiert, ebenfalls einmalig (s. v. Ὀνήτωρ), περὶ τῶν Ἀθήνησιν τριπόδων (›Über die Dreifüße in Athen‹), letzteres üblicherweise als Ausschnitt eines größeren Werkes gedeutet. Die wenigen Fr. legen eine topographische Organisation und eine Darstellung in erheblicher Ausführlichkeit nahe.

FGrH 373. A.A.D.

[3] Bildhauer aus Rhodos. Plinius (nat. 36,35) benennt ein berühmtes Symplegma von H., das in Rom in der Porticus Octaviae stand, fälschlich als ›Pan und Olympus‹. Die Identifizierung mit einer oft kopierten Gruppe des Pan und des Daphnis gilt als gesichert. Fraglich ist, ob H. mit einem in Halikarnassos und Rhodos im späten 2. Jh. v. Chr bezeugten H. identisch ist oder mit einem H., den Plinius im Katalog nat. 34,91 aufnahm. Stilistisch wird das Werk in die Zeit um 100 v. Chr. datiert.

M. Bieber, The sculpture of the Hellenistic age, 1961, 147, Abb. 628 · Lippold, 323–324 · Loewy, Nr. 403 · N. Marquardt, Pan in der hell. und kaiserzeitlichen Plastik, 1995, 195–206 · Overbeck, Nr. 2096, 2097 (Quellen). R.N.

[4] H. aus Athen (TrGF I 209); sonst unbekannter, bei Galen (De antidotis XIV p. 144 Kühn) erwähnter Tragiker, wohl auch Verf. einer in der Paradoxographen-Tradition stehenden Schrift *Apolytiká* (›Heilmittel‹).

A. A. M. Esser, Zur Frage der Lebenszeit Heliodors von Athen, in: Gymnasium 54/55, 1943/4, 114–117. B.Z.

[5] Griech. Chirurg aus Äg. (?). Seine Lebenszeit wird aus einer Erwähnung bei Iuvenal (sat. 6,370–373) erschlossen; man sah ihn daher als Zeitgenossen des Satirikers an, datierte ihn aber auch in hell. Zeit. Er soll in Rom praktiziert haben und wurde als Pneumatist angesehen.

Vier Abh. sind uns bekannt: eine ›Chirurgie‹ in 5 B., die chirurgische Eingriffe in der Anordnung *a capite ad calcem* darstellte und von der Bemühung um sichere Behandlungsmethoden zeugt [1. 114–116, 121]; ›Über Luxationen‹; ›Über die Gelenke‹; ›Über Verbände‹. Erh. sind nur Fr. der erstgenannten Schrift, direkt durch einen einzigen Pap. [1; 2] und indirekt durch Zitate bei Oreibasios.

Unter H.' Namen zirkulierten mehrere griech. [3] und lat. [4] Schriften, darunter die *Cirurgia Eliodori*, die lat. Übers. eines Fragebogens aus hell. Zeit [5]. Mehrere Pap.-Texte sind ihm zugewiesen worden [6; 7; 8; 9. 164 f.]), ohne Zweifel wegen des hohen Ansehens, das H. von der Ant. bis in die Renaissance genoß [9. 165].

→ Pneumatische Schule

1 M.-H. Marganne, Un témoignage unique sur l'incontinence intestinale: P. Monac. 2. 23, in: D. Gourevitch (Hrsg.), FS M.D. Grmek, 1992, 109–121 2 D. Manetti, P.Coln. inv. 339, in: A. Carile, Die Pap. der Bayerischen Staatsbibliothek München, 1986, 19–25 3 H. Diels, ADAW 1906, 41 f. 4 G. Sabbah u. a., Bibliogr. des textes médicaux latins, 1987, 93 f. 5 M.-H. Marganne, La Cirurgia Eliodori et le P. Genève inv. 111, in: Etudes de Lettres 1968/1, 65–73 6 Marganne, Nr. 75, 77, 87, 103, 153, 168 7 I. Andorlini-Marcone, L'apporto dei papiri alla conoscenza della scienza medica antica, in: ANRW II 37.1, Nr. 9, 54, 57, 70, 75, 98 8 D. Fausti (Ed.), P. Strasb. inv. gr. 1187, in: Annali della Facoltà di Lettere e Filosofia di Siena 10, 1989, 157–169 9 M.-H. Marganne, L'ophtalmologie dans l'Egypte gréco-romaine d'après les papyrus littéraires grecs, 1994.

M.-H. Marganne, Le chirurgien Héliodore. Trad. directe et indirecte, in: Etudes de médecine romaine, 1989, 107–111. A.TO./Ü: T.H.

[6] Metriker des 1. Jh. n. Chr., Lehrer des → Eirenaios [1], Verf. einer Ausgabe der Komödien des Aristophanes, in der der Text in *stíchoi* und *kōla* eingeteilt war. Kolometrische Zeichen machten auf rhythmische und metrische Phänomene aufmerksam und verwiesen auf einen fortlaufenden Komm., der fast ausschließlich metrische Fragen behandelte. Die Einträge unterschieden die Verse nach ihrer Länge (ἐν ἐκθέσει/ἐν εἰσθέσει). Die im Corpus der Aristophanesscholien überlieferten Fragmente sind in [7], dann in [8. 396–421] gesammelt worden. Zur kritischen Terminologie des H. vgl. [5]. H. wandte ein bereits bekanntes herausgeberisches Verfahren auf Aristophanes an [1]. Er schrieb auch eine Abh. über Metrik ›für diejenigen, die über die Hauptbegriffe der metrischen Theorie verfügen wollen‹ (Choiroboskos bei Heph. 181, 9–11 Consbruch), die nach Longinos (bei Heph. 81,13 C.) mit der ›Definition der Metren‹ (ἀπὸ τοῦ μέτρων ὅρου) begann; gegen den elementaren Charakter der Darstellung polemisierte Hephaistion [2. 49].

H. war ein Verfechter der Lehre von den (ihm zufolge acht) »urspr. Metra« (μέτρα πρωτότυπα, → Hephaistion; → Philoxenos; → Verskunst) und zog auch die Theorie der Bildung neuer Metren durch die Auslassung und Hinzufügung einer oder mehrerer Silben zu Beginn des Kolons heran (ἐπιπλοκή/*epiplokḗ*; vgl. [2. 97–99]). → Iuba von Mauretanien benutzte ihn als Quelle.

→ Verskunst

1 C. Questa, L'antichissima edizione dei cantica di Plauto, in: RFIC 102, 1974, 183–186 2 B. M. Palumbo Stracca, La teoria antica degli asinarteti, 1979 3 O. Hense, Heliodoreische Unt., 1870 4 Ders., s. v. H. (16), RE 8, 28–40 5 D. Holwerda, De Heliodori commentario metrico in Aristophanem, in: Mnemosyne 17, 1964, 113–139 und 20, 1967, 247–272 6 R. Pfeiffer, History of Classical Scholarship, 1968, 189, 196 7 O. Thiemann, Heliodori colometriae Aristophaneae quantum superest, 1864 8 J. W. White, The Verse of Greek Comedy, 1912 (Ndr. 1969), 384–395. S.FO./Ü: T.H.

[7] H. Arabios. Sophist, um 210–235 n. Chr., laut Philostratos aus Arabien (Philostr. soph. 2,32), kaum identisch mit T. Aurelius H. aus Palmyra (IGR 1,43–45) oder dem Romanautor H. [8] aus Emesa. Als er 213 als Gesandter allein die Interessen seines Vaterlandes vertreten mußte, erlaubte ihm Kaiser Caracalla beeindruckt, aus dem Stegreif vorzutragen und ernannte ihn zum *advocatus fisci* sowie ihn und seine Söhne zu Rittern (*equites equo publico*). Nach dem Tod des Caracalla wurde H. verbannt, später von einer Mordanklage freigesprochen; er lebte zur Schaffenszeit des Philostratos in Rom. → Philostratos; Zweite Sophistik

F. G. B. Millar, The Emperor in the Roman World, 1977, 234; 281 f. • PIR H 54. E.BO./Ü: L.S.

[8] Autor des Romans *Aithiopiká*. Die einzige sichere Nachricht über sein Leben ergibt sich aus einer *sphragís* an einer Stelle des Romans, die man heute als »Paratext« bezeichnen würde: H. bezeichnet sich als ›Phönizier aus der Stadt Emesa, aus dem Geschlecht der Nachfahren des Helios, als Sohn des Theodosios, Heliodoros‹. Der Name H. mag ein passendes Pseudonym für einen Autor sein, dessen Werk den Gott Helios rühmt, doch dürfte die Selbstaussage zweifellos richtig sein. Die Chronologie ist umstritten: Rohde datiert das Werk in die Regierungszeit des Kaisers Aurelian (270–275 n. Chr.), der den Kult des Sol zur Staatsreligion erklärte [1. 496–7], andere früher, aber nicht vor dem Tod des (aus Emesa stammenden) Elagabal, und setzen H. mit dem arab. Sophisten H. [7] gleich, der 240 starb und von Philostratos (soph. 2,32) erwähnt wird [2]; diese mögliche Datierung stellt eine Verbindung zu dessen ›Leben des Apollonios von Tyana‹ und dem neupythagoreischen Kreis der → Iulia Domna her. Eine weitere Datierung ins 4. Jh. n. Chr. beruht auf der Ähnlichkeit zw. der Syene-Episode im 9. Buch der *Aithiopiká* und der Erzählung der Belagerung von Nisibis im Jahre 350 durch den späteren Kaiser → Iulianus (Iul. or. 1 und 3) [3]: Es ist jedoch nicht ausgeschlossen, daß dieser, ein notorischer Romanleser, hier H. imitiert (das Problem wird durch die Existenz weiterer griech. und syr. Quellen verschärft) [4]. Diese letzte Datierung läßt sich mit den Aussagen des Historikers Sokrates in Einklang bringen, dem zufolge H. Bischof von Trikka war und die *Aithiopiká* in seiner Jugend schrieb (Sokr. 5,22)

Welche Datierung auch immer die richtige ist, die *Aithiopiká* sind der späteste ant. griech. Roman. H. arbeitet in einer beliebten Gattung, die er durch eine komplexe narrative Architektur veredelt und in philos. Ton erneuert (was sich zu dem ironischen Pastiche des → Achilleus Tatios [1] spiegelbildlich verhält). Mit einer direkten Anleihe bei der Odyssee – Beginn *medias in res* und Nachholen der Vorgesch. in der Binnenerzählung – wird die typische Struktur des griech. Romans umgeformt. Die übrigen Romane erzählen in linearer Form eine zirkuläre Gesch., die in der Heimatstadt der Protagonisten beginnt und endet, die *Aithiopiká* dagegen in zirkulärer Form eine lineare Gesch.: die Rückkehr der äthiopischen Prinzessin Charikleia in ihre Heimat. Die mysteriöse Eingangsszene des Romans ähnelt einer Filmeinstellung: Eine romantypische Entführung wird aus der Perspektive einer Räuberbande erzählt, die das Geschehen nicht verstehen. Langsam begreift der Leser, daß die beiden Protagonisten Charikleia und Theagenes die Opfer sind; sie werden dem Knemon, einem jungen Mann aus Athen, übergeben, der ihnen seine Lebensgesch. erzählt – eine novellistische Variante des Phaidra-Mythos (I). Erst nach dem Scheintod Charikleias und der Trennung der drei erfährt Knemon die Vorgesch. des Paares von dem ägypt. Priester Kalasiris (II): wie sie sich in Delphi verliebten (III), wie Charikleias Herkunft durch den auf eine Binde geschriebene Bericht ihrer Mutter, der äthiop. Königin Persinna, bekannt wird, wie das Paar aus Delphi flieht (IV) und mit Piraten und Rivalen kämpft (V). An dieser Stelle greift der außerhalb der Handlung stehende Haupterzähler wieder ein und läßt Kalasiris und Charikleia, als Bettler verkleidet, Theagenes suchen (VI); darauf folgt eine lange, in Memphis spielende »persische« Episode, in der Kalasiris stirbt, nachdem er seine Kinder wiedergefunden hat, und Theagenes das Objekt der Begierde der Arsake, der Schwester des Großkönigs, wird (VII–VIII). Der Roman schließt mit dem Sieg des äthiop. König Hydaspes über die Perser bei Syene (IX); das Königspaar erkennt schließlich seine Tochter Charikleia wieder, weiht die beiden Protagonisten dem Helios und der Selene und schafft damit auch die Menschenopfer ab (X).

Die raffinierte Erzähltechnik des H. hat immer eine thematische Funktion. Der spannungsreiche Anfang zeigt bereits das den Roman durchziehende Thema: die Entschlüsselung der Wahrheit und des Göttlichen als Indizienprozeß, in welchem die Leser und die Romanfiguren mit schwer zu deutenden Zeichen konfrontiert werden [5]. Auch die metadiegetische Erzählung wird zu einem metalit. Verfahren; zw. Erzähler und Adressat der Erzählung entwickelt sich eine quasi maieutische Beziehung: Kalasiris (der die Rolle des Autors widerspiegelt) drängt Knemon (der seinerseits den typischen Leser von Liebesromanen repräsentiert) dazu, die tiefere Bedeutung der Gesch. zu erfassen; die naive »Lesereaktion« Knemons, dem Abschweifungen und spektakuläre Beschreibungen bes. gut gefallen, ist jedoch nur partiell. Durch die narrative Polyphonie werden verschiedene Kulturen in einer Steigerung ins Blickfeld gerückt, die in der Weisheit der → Gymnosophisten kulminiert. Ein einheitliches theologisches System ist nicht erkennbar (trotz der schon ant. Versuche allegorischer Interpretation); der neuplatonische Einfluß ist stark (z. B. beim Motiv der Liebe auf den ersten Blick, das dem platonischen ›Phaidros‹ nachempfunden ist). Die gegenseitige Liebe der beiden Protagonisten hat für H. sakralen Wert und ist der erotischen Promiskuität der Hetäre Thisbe und der Arsake entgegengesetzt (auch wenn letztere zur Leseridentifikation einlädt [6. 3 f.]. Die Jungfräulichkeit wird (anders als bei Achilleus Tatios) auch bei Männern in fast christl. anmutenden Tönen gepriesen (die Vorstellung von Sexualität als Sünde ist dem Roman jedoch fremd). Die Gleichrangigkeit des Paares wird betont, doch hinterläßt die Romanheldin den zweifellos stärkeren Eindruck, nicht nur wegen ihrer Schönheit und Reinheit, sondern auch wegen ihrer pragmatischen Fähigkeiten, deren exquisit odysseischer Charakter unverkennbar ist.

In byz. Zeit war der Roman sehr beliebt und wurde u.a. von Theodoros Prodromos nachgeahmt. In der Renaissance tauchte er wieder auf (*editio princeps*: Basel 1534) und hatte aufgrund einer Übereinstimmung mit der Poetik der Zeit seinen größten Erfolg im Barock: Die *Aithiopiká* wurden in alle wesentlichen Sprachen übersetzt und von den Trattatisten gleichrangig neben Homer und Vergil gestellt, vielfach imitiert und rezipiert (u.a. von Cervantes in den *Trabajos de Persiles y Sigismonda*, Racine und Shakespeare). Calderón und andere dramatisierten ihn, Basile legte im *Teagene* eine freie Versfassung vor. Das letzte Echo seines reichen Nachlebens dürfte Verdis Oper *Aida* sein [7].

→ Roman; ROMAN

1 E. ROHDE, Der griech. Roman und seine Vorläufer, ^{2}1914 2 F. ALTHEIM, Helios und H. von Emesa, 1942 3 M. VAN DER WALK, Remarques sur la date des Éthiopiques, in: Mnemosyne 9, 1941, 97–100 4 T. SZEPESSY, Die Neudatierung des Heliodoros und die Belagerung von Nisibis, in: Acta XII Eirene 1975, 279–87 5 J. WINKLER, The Mendacity of Kalasiris and the Narrative Strategy of Heliodoros's ›Aithiopika‹, in: YClS 27, 1982, 93–158 6 M. FUSILLO, Il romanzo greco, 1989 7 O. WEINREICH, Der griech. Liebesroman, 1962.

J. R. Morgan, H., in: G. SCHMELING (Hrsg.), The Novel in the Ancient World, 1996 · P. PAULSEN, Inszenierung des Schicksals, 1992 · S. SANDY, Heliodorus, 1982 · S. SZEPESSY, Die Aithiopika des Heliodoros und der griech. sophistische Liebesroman, in: H. GÄRTNER (Hrsg.), Beiträge zum griech. Liebesroman, 1984, 432–450.

M.FU./Ü: T.H.

[9] 7. Jh. n. Chr.; Verf. eines Komm. zur *Téchnē grammatikḗ* des → Dionysios [17] Thrax [2], der auch in den Scholien zu diesem herangezogen wird; von dem anon. überlieferten Werk fehlt im Cod. Oxoniensis Barroccianus 116 (14. Jh.) der Anfang; die Auszüge des Georgios → Choiroboskos liefern den *terminus ante quem* für die Datierung.

ED.: 1 GG I,3, 67–106.
LIT.: 2 A. HILGARD, Praefatio in GG I,3, XIV-XVIII (mit älterer Lit.) 3 R. R. H. ROBINS, The Byzantine Grammarians, 1993, 77–86 4 J. E. SANDYS, A History of Classical Scholarship I, 1958, 139. S.FO./Ü: T.H.

Heliogabalus s. Elagabal

Heliokles (gen. *Díkaios*, mittelind. *Heliyakriya*). Griech. König Baktriens im 2. Jh. v. Chr., nur durch seine Mz. belegt. Nach TARN [1] Sohn des Eukratides I. und der letzte griech. König Baktriens, 141/128 von Nomaden gestürzt. NARAIN [2] und BOPEARACHCHI [3] unterscheiden aus numismat. Gründen zwischen zwei H. Der zweite sei ein Sohn des ersten und habe im Süden des Hindukusch geherrscht.

1 W. W. TARN, The Greeks in Bactria and India, ^{2}1951 2 A. K. NARAIN, The Indo-Greeks, 1958 3 BOPEARACHCHI, 74–76, 222–225 (H. I.), 97–99, 281–285 (H. II.). K.K.

Helion. *Comes* und *magister officiorum* 414–427 n. Chr. Sein Wirken ist durch zahlreiche Gesetze im Codex Theodosianus belegt. 422 schloß er im Auftrag Theodosius' II. Frieden mit den Persern (Sokr. 7,20), 425 überbrachte er Valentinian III. die Nachricht seiner Erhebung zum Caesar (Olympiodoros fr. 43 BLOCKLEY).

M.R.

Heliopolis, Heliupolis

[1] Äg. *Jwnw*, hebr. *ʾôn*, h. Matarije. Stadt am Ostrand der Südspitze des Nildeltas (h. Stadtteil Kairos), Metropole des 13. unteräg. Gaues und seit dem AR wichtigster Kultort des Sonnengottes in seinen Formen → Aton und Re-Harachte (→ Re). Für einen Schöpfungsmythos, der in dem Generationenmodell der »Neunheit von H.« (Aton – Geb – Nut – Schu – Tefnut – Osiris – Isis – Seth – Nephthys) von der Sonne ausgehend die Entstehung von Welt und Götterwelt parallelisiert, war H. von zentraler theolog. Bedeutung. In griech.-röm. Zeit wurde H. als Zentrum alter Weisheit von Reisenden aufgesucht (Hdt. 2,3; Strab. 17,1,29), doch die Bed. des Ortes ging zurück und seine Denkmäler (Obelisken) wurden in andere Städte des Deltas und bis nach It. abtransportiert. H. ist arch. noch kaum erschlossen; am Ort steht ein Obelisk Sesostris' I. *in situ*.

[2] s. Baalbek.

D. RAUE, Prosopographie von H. im NR, 1998. S.S.

Heliopolitanus. Der Hauptgott der Biqāʿ-Ebene, in der sich seit dem 2. Jh. v. Chr. das arab. Reich der Ituräer (→ Ituraea) konstituiert hatte, war seit vorarab. Zeit der »Herr der Biqāʿ« (*bʿl bqʿ*). Unter dem Namen Zeus Helios oder Iuppiter (Optimus Maximus) H. wurde er in röm. Zeit in → Baalbek (= Heliopolis) verehrt, wo sein Haupttempel auf älteren Resten errichtet wurde. Seine Solarisierung dürfte auf ptolem. Einfluß beruhen. Der ikonographisch und inschr. gut bezeugte Gott ist → Wettergott, Regenspender, Herr der Quellen, Orakelgott, höchster Gott und Kosmokrator. Bildliche Darstellungen zeigen ihn als jungen Mann auf einem von zwei Stieren flankierten Sockel. In der Rechten hält er ein Ährenbündel und in der Linken eine Peitsche. Auf dem z. T. mit Strahlenkranz umgebenen Kopf trägt er einen → Kalathos oder eine äg. Krone. Sein Gewand ist mit Astralsymbolen verziert. Die gängige Auffassung, derzufolge der Hauptgott von Baalbek zusammen mit Venus und Mercur als Triade verehrt worden sei, wird in der neueren Forschung stark in Frage gestellt [4].

1 P. HAISER et al. (Hrsg.), Religionsgesch. Syriens, 1996, 198–210 2 Y. HAJJAR, Baalbek, grand centre religieux sous l'Empire, in: ANRW II 18.4, 2458–2508 3 G. H. HALSBERGHE, The Cult of Sol Invictus, 1972 4 MILLAR, Near East, 281–285. H.NI.

Helios s. Sol

Helisson (Ἑλισσών).
[1] Zu allen Jahreszeiten wasserreicher Fluß in Arkadia, Nebenfluß des Alpheios [1], entspringt im NW-Abhang des Mainalon, fließt zunächst nach Süden, durchbricht dann, sich nach Westen wendend, in enger Schlucht das aus Kalken aufgebaute arkad. Zentralgebirge, fließt durch das Becken von Megalopolis und mündet westl. davon in den Alpheios (Paus. 5,7,1; 8,29,5; 30,1 f.). Durch das obere Tal des H. verläuft eine wichtige Verkehrsverbindung nach Nord-Arkadia (h. die Straße Tripolis – Vitina).

Philippson/Kirsten 3, 261 ff.

[2] Fluß im Westen von Sikyon, der bei Kiato in den Golf von Korinthos mündet (Paus. 2,12,2; Stat. Theb. 4,52).

Philippson/Kirsten 3, 161. C.L.u.E.O.

[3] Ortschaft der Mainalioi im Quellgebiet des gleichnamigen Flusses H. [1] bei Mantineia, aber durch das Mainalon-Gebirge getrennt. Anf. des 4. Jh. v. Chr. *kṓmē* von Mantineia, später mit der ganzen Landschaft Megalopolis einverleibt. Belegstellen: Diod. 16,39,5; Paus. 8,3,3; 27,3; 27,7; 30,1.

M. Jost, Villages de l'Arcadie antique, in: Ktema 11, 1986 (1990), 150–155. Y.L.

Heliupolis s. Heliopolis

Helixos (Ἕλιξος). Stratege aus Megara. H. führte 411 v. Chr. ein Flottenkontingent des → Peloponnesischen Bundes, das Byzantion zum Abfall von Athen brachte (Thuk. 8,80). Als die Stadt später von den Athenern belagert wurde, verteidigte H. sie bis zu ihrer Kapitulation im Winter 409/8 (Xen. hell. 1,3,15; 17; 21).
E.S.-H.

Helkias
[1] Verwandter und Freund des Königs → Herodes [1] Agrippa I. (Ios. ant. Iud. 19,9,1; 20,7,1), 40 n. Chr. Mitglied der Deputation an den syr. Statthalter P. Petronius (ebd. 18,8,4), welche erreichte, daß Caligulas Statue nicht im Tempel aufgestellt wurde; danach hat er wohl die Stelle eines Oberbefehlshabers des Heeres von einem Silas (ebd. 19,6,3; 7,1) übernommen, den er nach Agrippas Tod 44 n. Chr. umbringen ließ (ebd. 19,8,3).
[2] Tempelschatzmeister (γαζοφύλαξ) in Jerusalem, kam als Mitglied einer Deputation des → Synhedrions 61 oder 62 n. Chr. nach Rom, wo von Nero erreicht wurde, daß eine Mauer stehenbleiben durfte, die dem Agrippa II. den Blick in den Tempel versperrte. Die spätere Kaiserin Poppaea Sabina behielt H. in Rom (Ios. ant. Iud. 20,8,11), wohl um sich von ihm in der jüd. Rel. unterweisen zu lassen. C.C.

Helladios (Ἑλλάδιος).
[1] H. aus Antinupolis in Ägypten. Grammatiker des 4. Jh. n. Chr., Verf. einer *Chrēstomatheía* (»Wissenswerte Dinge«) in iambischen Trimetern. Photios, die einzige biographische Quelle, exzerpierte sie (cod. 279, 529b 25–536a 22), kannte aber auch eine Prosaepitome (vgl. [4. 99; 6. 16]). Das enzyklopädische Werk bietet gramm., etym., histor., myth. usw. Informationen; zur lit. Gattung vgl. [6. 24–26]. Weder Anordnungskriterium noch Vorlage des Komm. sind erkennbar – jedenfalls ist Phrynichos nicht als Hauptquelle anzusehen (so [6], dagegen [2]). Eine Abhängigkeit von Aristophanes von Byzanz ist auszuschließen [3]. Photios überliefert auch Titel anderer verlorener Werke in iambischen Trimetern.

1 A. Cameron, Pap. Ant. III 115 and the iambic prologue, in: CQ 20, 1970, 120 2 E. Fischer, Die Ekloge des Phrynichos (SGLG 1), 1974, 48 3 W.J. Slater, Aristophanis Byz. Fragmenta (SGLG 6), 1986, XVIII und 19, Anm. 4 A. Gudeman, s. v. H. (2), RE 8, 98–102 5 M. Haupt, Opuscula II, 1876, 421–427 6 H. Heimannsfeld, De Helladii Chrestomathia quaestiones selectae, 1911 7 Ders., Zum Text des H. bei Photius (cod. 279), in: RhM 69, 1914, 570–574 8 R.A. Kaster, Guardians of Language, 1988, 411–412 9 P. Maas, Rez. von [6], in: ByzZ 21, 1912, 269–270 10 E. Orth, Photiana, 1928, 68–69.
S.FO./Ü: T.H.

[2] H. aus Alexandreia. Grammatiker, Zeuspriester in Alexandreia, floh 391 n. Chr. nach Konstantinopel (Sokr. 5,16,1–14). Er war unter Theodosios II. (404–450) tätig (Suda ε 732) und erhielt wahrscheinlich am 15. März 425 die *comitiva primi ordinis* (Cod. Theod. 6,21,1; vgl. [1]). Auf dieses Ereignis könnte sich die Lobrede auf Theodosios beziehen, die die Suda zusammen mit anderen Titeln von epideiktischen Reden oder vielleicht Gedichten zitiert. H. war außerdem Verf. eines 7 B. umfassenden Lex. (Λεξικὸν κατὰ στοιχεῖον), dessen alphabetische Anordnung sich auf die erste Silbe beschränkte – es war ›das umfangreichste‹ der dem Photios bekannten Lexika (cod. 145,98b 40–99a 12) und ist von der Suda (praef.) als eine ihrer Quellen genannt.

1 A. Cameron, The Empress and the Poet, in: YClS 27, 1982, 286.

A. Cameron, Wandering Poets, in: Historia 14, 1965, 470–509 (Ndr. s. [1]) 3 A. Gudeman, s. v. H. (3), RE 8, 102–103 4 R.A. Kaster, Guardians of Language, 1988, 411–412 5 O. Seeck, s. v. H. (8), RE 8, 103. S.FO./Ü: T.H.

[3] Sonst nicht bekannter Autor eines kurzen Spottepigramms (Anth. Pal. 11,423), das einen Färber (βαφεύς) aufs Korn nimmt, der die Fähigkeit besitzt, durch Farben die eigene Armut in Reichtum zu verwandeln. Es gehört wahrscheinlich zur Epigrammsammlung des Diogenianos [2] von Herakleia; daher läßt sich H. ungefähr in die Zeit Hadrians (1. Hälfte 2. Jh. n. Chr.) datieren. M.G.A./Ü: M.A.S.

Hellana. Straßenstation in Etruria an der *via Cassia* zw. Florentia (ca. 27 km entfernt) und Pistoriae (ca. 9 km entfernt; Tab. Peut. 4,2; Geogr. Rav. 4,36); 848 n. Chr. als Alina belegt (MGH, Diplomata Karolina 3,242, Nr. 102) und daher mit Agliana (Pistoia) zu identifizieren.

S. PIERI, Toponomastica della Valle dell'Arno, 1919, 114 · M. LOPES PEGNA, Itineraria Etruriae, in: SE 21, 1950/1, 407–443, bes. 426. G.U./Ü: J.W.M.

Hellanikos (Ἑλλάνικος).

[1] H. aus Mytilene (T 1). War entgegen der ant. Trad., die sein Geburtsdatum teils ins ausgehende 6. Jh. (T 4), teils an den Anfang des 5. Jh. (T 3), teils ins Jahr 480/479 v. Chr. setzt (T 1 und 6), eher jüngerer als älterer Zeitgenosse des → Herodotos: Die datierbaren Werke gehören jedenfalls ins letzte Drittel des 5. Jh.

H. zerlegte das herodoteische Themenbündel durch eine Reihe von Monographien in einzelne Bestandteile und fügte im Rückgriff auf → Hekataios [3] sogar neue Themen hinzu: Auf diese Weise entstanden Schriften zur Mythographie, Ethnographie und Chronologie, die weniger auf eigenständiger Forsch. als auf früheren Autoren beruhten, z. B. Hekataios, Akusilaos von Argos (T 18), Herodot (F 72) und Damastes von Sigeion (F 72), und nicht selten kompilatorischen Charakter hatten. H. ist der erste »Vielschreiber« der griech. Lit. Überliefert sind die Titel von 23 Werken, die jedoch bis auf ca. 200 Fr. verloren sind.

In seinen mythographischen Werken *Deukaliōneía, Phoronís, Asōpís und Atlantís* (jeweils zwei B. umfassend, mit Ausnahme der einbändigen *Asōpís*) reduzierte H. die Genealogien der griech. Frühgesch. auf vier Urväter, systematisierte und vernetzte sie durch Synchronismen, Konstruktionen und Spekulationen und formte sie so zu einem einheitlichen Ganzen. Die meisten der behandelten Genealogien fanden Eingang in die *Trōiká*. Auf diese Weise entstand ›ein in sich geschlossenes Gesamtbild der griech. Frühgesch.‹ [1].

Ethnographische Werke: H. schrieb allgemeine Darstellungen, z. B. zu ›Sitten von Barbaren‹, ›Gründungsgesch. von Völkern und Städten‹, ›Über Völker‹, ›Völkerbenennungen‹ (die drei zuletzt genannten Titel bezeichnen vielleicht ein und dasselbe Werk). Ferner verfaßte er Monographien über ausländische Völker, u. a. *Aigyptiaká, Lydiaká, Persiká, Skythiká*, sowie über griech. Stämme und Landschaften, z. B. *Aioliká, Lesbiká, Argoliká, Boiōtiká, Thessaliká*. In diese Reihe gehört auch die zwei B. umfassende *Atthís* (F 163–172), die nach 407/6 erschienen ist (F 171 und 172) und den Beginn der Atthidographie (→ Atthis) bezeichnet. H. schilderte die athenische Gesch. von den myth. Anf. bis in die Zeit des Peloponnesischen Krieges. Zu diesem Zweck erstellte er eine Liste der athenischen Könige und ergänzte die Archontenliste so weit nach oben, daß er den Anschluß an die Königszeit fand. Thukydides (1,97,2) kritisiert die ungenaue Chronologie der → Pentekontaetie bei H.

Chronographische Werke: Zwei Schriften des H. bezeichnen den Beginn der griech. Chronographie, nämlich die ›Herapriesterinnen von Argos‹ (F 74–84) und die *Karneoníkai* = ›Sieger an den Karneen‹ (F 85 f.). Hier wurde der Versuch gemacht, mit Hilfe der Regierungsdauer der argivischen Priesterinnen bzw. der Sieger des spartanischen Festes ein tragendes chronologisches Gerüst für die gesamte griech. Gesch. zu errichten (vgl. F 79, 84).

In der Forsch. gilt H., der in archaisierendem Stil schrieb, gemeinhin als ›Abschluß der älteren griech. Geschichtsschreibung‹ [2]; in Wirklichkeit markiert er auch einen Neubeginn, vor allem als ›erster griech. Universalhistoriker‹ [1] und kühner Innovator auf chronologischem Gebiet.

1 O. LENDLE, Einführung in die griech. Geschichtsschreibung, 1992, 63 ff. 2 F. JACOBY, s. v. H. (7), RE 8.1, 104–153 (grundlegend).

FR.: FGrH 4, 323a, 608a · F. JACOBY, FGrH III C, Fasc. I · CH.W. FORNARA, Commentary on Nos. 608a–608, 1994 · J.J. CAEROLS PÉREZ (Hrsg. und Übers.), Hélanico de Lesbos. Fragmentos, 1991.

LIT.: D. AMBAGLIO, Per la cronologia di Ellanico di Lesbo, in: RAL 32, 1977, 389–398 · Ders., L'opera storiografica di Ellanico di Lesbo, in: Ricerche di storiografia antica 2, 1980, 9–192 · R. DREWS, The Greek Accounts of Eastern History, 1973, 97 ff. · K. VON FRITZ, Die griech. Geschichtsschreibung 1, 1967, 476 ff. · F. JACOBY, Atthis, 1949 · R.J. LENARDON, Thucydides and Hellanicus, in: Classical Contributions. Studies in Honour of M. F. McGregor, 1981, 59–70 · K. MEISTER, Die griech. Geschichtsschreibung, 1990, 41 f. · J. H. SCHREINER, Historical Methods, Hellanikos and the Era of Kimon, in: Opuscula Atheniensia 15, 1984, 169–171 · Ders., Hellanikos, Thucydides and the Era of Kimon, 1997 · J. D. SMART, Thucydides and Hellanicus, in: J. S. MOXON, J. D. SMART, A. J. WOODMAN (Hrsg.), Past Perspectives, 1986, 19–35. K. MEI.

[2] Alexandrinischer Grammatiker um 200 v. Chr. (vgl. Suda s. v. Πτολεμαῖος ὁ Ἐπιθέτης), einer der wichtigsten Vertreter der → Chorizontes (Prokl. vita Homeri, p. 102,3 ALLEN). Seine Lehren sind nur in geringen Resten über die kritischen Anmerkungen des → Aristarchos [4] von Samothrake und seiner Schüler in den Homerscholien (schol. Hom. Il. 5,269; 15,651; 19,90; schol. Hom. Od. 2,185) kenntlich. Auch mit Herodot scheint er sich beschäftigt zu haben (schol. Soph. Phil. 201). → Xenon

F. MONTANARI, H., in: SGLG 7, 1988, 43–73 · Ders., Un misconosciuto frammento di Ellanico di Lesbo (e piccole note su frammenti meno dubbi), in: Studi Classici e Orientali 37, 1987, 183–189. F. M.

Hellanodikai (Ἑλλανοδίκαι, auch Ἑλληνοδίκαι). Die Aufseher und Kampfrichter bei den Wettkämpfen von Olympia, Nemea (IG IV 587) und den Asklepieia in Epidauros (IG IV 946; 1508). Die H. der olympischen Spiele wurden in Elis aus lokalem Adel für je ein Fest bestimmt. Das Amt (Amtseid: Paus. 5,24,10), dessen sakrale Komponente sich noch in einem Reinigungsritual der H. spiegelt (Paus. 5,16,8), beinhaltete wahrscheinlich hohe finanzielle Aufwendungen. Die Zahl der H. war zunächst auf einen bis zwei beschränkt, spätestens seit Mitte des 4. Jh. v. Chr. wurden zehn die Regel, doch sind zeitweilig bis zu zwölf H. bezeugt (Paus.

5,9,4–6; Philostr. Ap. 3,30; schol. Pind. O. 3,22). Ihnen kam bei den Spielen eine nahezu unumschränkte Autorität zu, symbolisiert durch ein Purpurgewand (Etym. m. s.v. H.). Nachdem sie zehn Monate lang von Nomophylakes in die Regeln eingewiesen wurden (Paus. 6,24,3), oblag ihnen die Prüfung der Teilnahmeberechtigungen und Qualifikationen der Athleten, die schiedsrichterliche Gewalt, die Zuerkennung von Preisen und die Führung der Siegerlisten; allerdings durften sie nicht in das Regelwerk eingreifen. Überdies besaßen sie Straf- und Züchtigungsrecht über die Athleten [1. 111–120]. Ein Amtshaus der H. (*Hellanodikaiṓn*) bezeugt Pausanias (6,24,1–3).

Ein Amt der H. mit richterlicher Funktion in Sparta erwähnt Xenophon (Lak. pol. 13,11).

1 M.I. Finley, H.W. Pleket, Die olympischen Spiele der Antike, 1976. M.MEI.

Hellas

[1] H., Hellenes (Ἑλλάς, Ἕλληνες). Die Hellenes (homer. Ἕλλανες, ion.-att. Ἕλληνες) waren in homer. Zeit ein Stamm in Südthessalien i.e.S. oder allenfalls im Spercheios-Gebiet, das nach ihnen benannte Land Hellas (Ἑλλάς) der Landschaft Phthia benachbart (Hom. Il. 2,683 f.; 9,395, 447, 478; 16,595; Hom. Od. 11,496). Ant. und moderne Spekulationen, die Hellenes hätten urspr. um → Dodona gesiedelt, beruhen auf der unbeweisbaren Annahme eines Zusammenhangs mit den Hellopes (→ Hellopia) und dem dodonaiischen Priestergeschlecht der Helloi oder Selloi (Hom. Il. 16,234).

Im Schiffskatalog der *Ilias* und in der *Odyssee* begegnen zweigliedrige Ausdrücke zur Bezeichnung aller Griechen und ganz Griechenlands, in denen sich *Hellás* und *Pan-héllēnes* (»die Hellenen insgesamt«) offenbar auf das festländische Griechenland, *Árgos* und *Achaioí* auf die Peloponnes beziehen (Hom. Il. 2,530; Hom. Od. 1,344; 4,726, 816; 15,80). Die H. dürften also in Nord- und Mittelgriechenland zeitweise eine führende Stellung eingenommen haben, von der wir sonst nichts wissen. Durch Reduktion des zweigliedrigen Ausdrucks auf das erste Glied wurde dann seit Hesiod der Hellenenname zur üblichen Bezeichnung aller Griechen. Der Landesname H. konnte zunächst auf alle von Griechen bewohnten Gebiete, auch auf die Kolonien, bezogen werden, wurde dann aber im allg. Sprachgebrauch auf einen in sich geschlossenen geogr. Raum, das griech. Mutterland, eingeschränkt, gelegentlich sogar auf das Festland unter Ausschluß auch der Peloponnes (Demosth. or. 19,303; Plin. nat. 4,23; Ptol. 3,14,1). Die Nordgrenze Griechenlands zog man im allg., ohne Rücksicht auf die sprachlichen Verhältnisse, vom Ambrakischen Golf über den Pindos zum Olympos und zum Tempetal: so schon die *Ilias*, so auch im 5. Jh. der Geograph Phileas von Athen (bei Dionysios Kalliphontos 31 ff., GGM I p. 239), so noch Strabon (1. Jh. v./1. Jh. n. Chr.) im 8.–10. Buch. Die Völker jenseits dieser Grenze, Epeirotai (→ Epeiros) und Makedones, galten bis in die klass. Zeit als Barbaren, später als Griechen.

Als im Gefolge der großen Hellenisierungsprozesse (→ Hellenisierung) die äußeren Grenzen des Griechentums unscharf wurden und die Griechen unter der röm. Herrschaft ihr polit. Eigenleben nach und nach einbüßten, als sie sich schließlich als Träger des auf den Osten reduzierten Reiches, als »Römer« fühlten, verlor der Hellenenname allmählich seine klass. Bed., zumal er durch die jüd.-christl. Sonderbed. »Heiden« belastet war. Die Griechen im Byz. und Osman. Reich hießen *Rhōmaíoi* bzw. *Rūmī*. Die Befreiungs- und Erneuerungsbewegung seit dem 18. Jh. signalisierte mit der Wiederbelebung der Namen *Héllēnes* und *Hellás* die Rückwendung zu den großen Traditionen des Alt.

W. Will, H. Klein, s.v. Hellenen, RAC 14, 375–445 (mit Lit.). F.GSCH.

[2] Frau des Gongylos von Eretria, Mutter Gongylos' III., nahm Xenophon 399 v. Chr. bei seiner Rückkehr aus Vorderasien in Pergamon gastfreundlich auf (Xen. an. 7,8,8).

G. Fogazza, Sui Gongilidi di Eretria, in: PdP 27, 1972, 129 f. PE.HÖ.

Helle (Ἕλλη). Tochter des → Athamas und der → Nephele, flieht mit ihrem Bruder → Phrixos auf einem goldenen Widder vor ihrer Stiefmutter Ino und ertrinkt im Meer, das danach → Hellespont (Pind. fr. 189; Aischyl. Pers. 69 f.) heißt (Apollod. 180–182; Ov. fast. 3,851–876; Hyg. fab. 1–3; ihr Grab auf der Chersonesos: Hdt. 7,58,2). Valerius Flaccus (5,476 ff.; 2,611) bindet H. und Phrixos enger an die → Argonauten, indem er Athamas vom Bruder zum Sohn des → Kretheus und damit Phrixos und H. zu dessen Enkeln macht; gleichfalls seine Erfindung ist, daß auch H. dem → Pelias im Traum erscheint und während der Fahrt der Argo als Nereide aus dem Meer auftaucht (1,50; 2,587 ff. [1. 333 ff.]). H. ist vielleicht durch den Märchentyp »Brüderchen und Schwesterchen« in den Mythos gekommen.

1 P. Dräger, Argo pasimelousa I, 1993.

Ph. Bruneau, s.v. Phrixos et H., LIMC 7.1, 398–404 · P. Friedländer, s.v. H., RE 8, 159–163 · U. v. Wilamowitz-Moellendorf, Hell. Dichtung, [2]1962, 2, 244 Anm. 1. P.D.

Hellebic(h)us. Träger eines germanischen Namens; als *comes et magister utriusque militiae per Orientem* von 383 bis 387 n. Chr. bezeugt; in Antiocheia euergetisch tätig. Leitete zusammen mit → Caesarius [3] 387 die Untersuchungen nach dem Antiochener Statuenaufstand. → Libanios dankte ihm mit einem Panegyrikos dafür, daß er ein mildes Verfahren erreicht habe (or. 22). H. korrespondierte mit Libanios (epist. 2; 868; 884; 898; 925) und → Gregorios [3] von Nazianzos (epist. 225). Wohl Christ [1]. (PLRE 1,277 f.).

1 v. Haehling 265–267. H.L.

Helleborus (ἐλλέβορος, *helleborus*, dt. Nieswurz). Der Name bezieht sich auf Giftpflanzen verschiedener Familien: 1) die Ranunculacee Helleborus L. (ἐλλέβορος μέλας bei Theophr. h. plant. 9,14,4 u.ö. = H. cyclophyllus Boissier, nicht H. niger L., die Christrose; Dioskurides 4,162 WELLMANN = 4,149 BERENDES; Paus. 10,36,7). Insbes. die Wurzel wurde als Abführmittel verwendet (Plin. nat. 25,48). 2) die Liliacee Veratrum album L. (ἐλλέβορος λευκός, Helleborus candidus, der weiße Germer: Hippokr. de victu 1,35 [1. 292]; Theophr. h. plant. 9,10,1–4 mit vielen Lokalformen; Dioskurides 4,148 WELLMANN und BERENDES). Diese ist ein schwer dosierbares diätetisches Brech- und Abtreibemittel (Paus. 10,36,7). In Phokis soll Herakles mit schwarzem H. vom Wahnsinn befreit worden sein. Trotz schlechter Beschreibung bei Plinius (nat. 13,114 und 27,76) wurde die *helleborínē* oder *epipaktís* des Dioskurides (4,108 WELLMANN = 4,107 BERENDES), die man gegen Gifte und Leberleiden innerlich anwendete, als die Orchideengattung Helleborine Miller bzw. das Kahle Bruchkraut Herniaria glabra L. gedeutet.

1 W.H.S. JONES (ed.), Hippocrates, De victu, vol. 4, 1931, Ndr. 1992, 292. C.HÜ.

Hellen (Ἕλλην). Eponymer Stammvater der Hellenen, damit der Gesamtheit aller Bewohner Griechenlands; die einzelnen Stämme haben ihre Namen nach H.s Söhnen und Enkeln → Doros, → Xuthos (Vater des → Ion und des → Achaios [1]) und → Aiolos [1]. Als Eltern des H. werden → Pyrrha und entweder → Deukalion (Hes. fr. 2; schol. Hes. erg. 158a; Thuk. 1,3,12; Diod. 4,60,2) oder Zeus (schol. Plat. symp. 208d; Apollod. 1,49) genannt. Im homer. Schiffskatalog bewohnen die Hellenen nur ein kleines Gebiet Griechenlands (Spercheios-Gebiet); demnach ist hier die Konstruktion Reflex eines älteren Zustands, während bei den nachhomer. Belegen der Stand des 7. Jh. v. Chr. (H. als Vorvater *aller* Griechen) zugrunde liegt.
→ Hellas

G.A. CADUFF, Ant. Sintflutsagen, 1986, 84–87 · E. VISSER, Homers Katalog der Schiffe, 1997, 650–659. E.V.

Hellenika Oxyrhynchia. Zwei Reihen von Papyrusfragmenten, beide 2. Jh. n. Chr.: POxy. 842 = PLond., Fundjahr 1906, hrsg. von GRENFELL und HUNT (die den anonymen Autor P. = Papyrus nannten) und PSI 1304 = PFlor., Fundjahr 1942, ein und demselben Geschichtswerk aus der ersten Hälfte des 4. Jh. v. Chr. angehörend und insgesamt ca. 20 Seiten griech. Gesch. (mit Lükken!) umfassend. Dazu kommt vielleicht ein neues Fr., vgl. [1].

Inhalt: Ereignisse des ionisch-dekeleischen Krieges (→ Dekeleia), bes. Seeschlacht von Notion 407/6 (= PFlor.). Polit. Stimmung in Griechenland 397/6, Seekrieg zwischen Athenern unter → Konon und Spartanern, thebanisch-phokische Auseinandersetzungen (mit Exkurs über die Verfassung des boiotischen Bundes), Feldzüge des → Agesilaos [2] in Kleinasien (= PLond.).

Die H.O. bilden eine wertvolle und unabhängige Parallelüberlieferung zu Xen., hell. B. 1 und 2, und liegen über Ephoros der Darstellung Diodoros' in B. 13 und 14 zugrunde. Der Verf. steht den geschilderten Ereignissen zeitlich nahe und arbeitet auf der Basis von Autopsie und eigener Erkundung. Die Darstellung ist sachlich, der Stil unprätentiös, ohne direkte Reden, aber mit häufigen Exkursen. Der Verf. disponiert wie Thukydides (zitiert in Kap. 2 des PFlor.) nach Sommern und Wintern und benützt wie dieser ein Epochenjahr, nämlich 403/2 (= Übernahme der Hegemonie durch die Spartaner). Demnach war er wohl ein Fortsetzer des Thukydides für die Zeit von 411 bis mindestens 395, der nach dem Königsfrieden 387/6 (vgl. 11,2) und vor dem Ende des Heiligen Krieges 346 (13,3) schrieb.

Verfasserfrage: Zahlreiche Untersuchungen führten zu folgenden Identifizierungen: Ephoros (WALKER, GELZER), Theopompos (ED. MEYER, LAQUEUR, RUSCHENBUSCH, LEHMANN, REBUFFAT), Androtion (MOMIGLIANO, CANFORA), Daimachos (JACOBY), Kratippos (BREITENBACH, ACCAME, HARDING); genaue Literaturnachweise bei [2. 65 ff.].

Gegen diese These spricht jedoch, daß Ephoros und Theopomp keine Primärquellen sind. Ephoros schreibt zudem *katá génos* (»nach Sachgebieten«), ferner ist der Verf. offenbar kein Universalhistoriker. Stil, Ethos und Darstellung dürften Theopomp ausschließen. Der Autor war auch kein Atthidograph: Androtion disponiert nach Archonten. Der boiot. Lokalschriftsteller Daimachos scheidet deshalb aus, weil der Verf. ohne Sympathie für die Politik Thebens ist (vgl. 12,4–5, auch wenn er gute Kenntnisse über Boiotien und den boiot. Bund besitzt). Detailkenntnisse der Verhältnisse in Athen, Sympathie für Konon und enger Anschluß an Thukydides deuten auf einen athenischen Autor und – entsprechend dem oben Gesagten – auf einen Fortsetzer des Thukydides: Am ehesten kommt → Kratippos von Athen (FGrH 64) in Frage, der zu Unrecht von JACOBY als ›später Schwindelautor‹ bezeichnet wurde, vielmehr ein bedeutender Historiker war: Besonders die Übereinstimmung der Inhaltsangabe und Grundtendenz von Kratippos' Werk bei Plutarch (mor. 345C–E) mit Ephoros bei Diodor (B. 13 und 14) legt diese Identifizierung nahe [vgl. 3].
→ Kratippos (weitere Lit.)

1 G.A. LEHMANN, Ein neues Frg. der H.O., in: ZPE 26, 1977, 181–191 2 K. MEISTER, Die griech. Geschichtsschreibung, 1990 3 S. ACCAME, Ricerche sulle Elleniche di Ossirinco, in: Miscellanea greca e romana 6, 1978, 125–183.

FR.: FGrH 66 · M. CHAMBERS (Hrsg.), H.O., 1993 (nach V. BARTOLETTI, 1959) · P.R. MCKECHNIE, S.J. KERN (Hrsg., Übers., Komm.), H.O., 1988 · J.A. BRUCE, A Historical Commentary on the H.O., 1967.
LIT.: G. BONAMENTE, Studi sulle Elleniche di Ossirinco, 1973 · H.R. BREITENBACH, s.v. H.O., RE Suppl. 12, 383–426 (grundlegend) · P. HARDING, The Authorship of the H.O., in: The Ancient History Bull. 1, 1987, 101–110 ·

E. REBUFFAT, Teopompo e le Elleniche di Ossirinco, in: Orpheus 14, 1993, 109–124. K.MEI.

Hellenisierung I. GESCHICHTE II. SPRACHE

I. GESCHICHTE
A. BEGRIFF B. HISTORISCHE ENTWICKLUNG
C. KUNST UND ARCHITEKTUR
D. ZUSAMMENFASSUNG

A. BEGRIFF

Unter H. wird im folgenden ein komplexes Akkulturationsphänomen verstanden, das sich aus verschiedenen, auf mehreren Ebenen ablaufenden Prozessen zusammensetzte. Neben dem sprachlich-lit. Bereich wurden auch in Architektur, bildender Kunst sowie in Religion und Kult griech. Vorstellungen und Ausdrucksformen rezipiert; es wurden auch nichtgriech. Muster soziopolit. Organisation in solche griech. Prägung umgeformt (Polisstaat, Formen des Vereinswesens, → Gymnasion). All diese Veränderungen hatten oft weitreichende Auswirkungen auf die kulturell-ethnische Identität der betreffenden Ges. Die H. führte in unterschiedlichem Grad zum Bruch mit der Vergangenheit, wobei aber nicht nur zw. den Kulturen, sondern innerhalb jedes Kulturraumes auch nach sozialen Gruppen unterschieden werden muß. Sonderfälle der H. waren diejenigen Ges., in denen die einheimischen Kulturmuster weithin bestimmten, was an griech. Kulturfertigkeiten als brauchbar für die eigenen Zwekke oder ungefährlich für die eigene Identität übernommen wurden, u.a. Rom, das Judentum, der parth.-sāsānid. Iran und Karthago, wo sich trotz umfangreicher H.-Prozesse die einheimische Identität in ungebrochener Traditionslinie behaupten konnte, zwar gewandelt, aber auch gestärkt. Der Rekurs auf eine – reale oder idealisierte – vorgriech. Vergangenheit diente hier auch bewußt der Abgrenzung vom nähergerückten Griechentum.

Berücksichtigt werden hier diejenigen v.a. ostmediterranen und nahöstl. Kulturräume, die im Zeitraum zw. Alexanderzug und arab.-islam. Eroberung unter der polit. Kontrolle griech. oder dem Hell. kulturell-mental nahestehender Machtzentren standen und dauerhaft unter die Herrschaft Roms kamen. Zu fragen ist auch nach den Ursachen und Faktoren der Akkulturationsprozesse, ob aus den Charakteristika des Griechentums selbst erklärbar, aus dem einheimischen Wunsch nach Selbst-H. oder gar aus dem Druck griech. oder philhellenischer Machteliten. Zwei Gesichtspunkte treten hinzu: Die griech. Kultur war selbst eine histor. veränderbare Größe, d.h. der bei der Beschreibung von H. anzulegende Maßstab bleibt also nicht der gleiche. Außerdem begannen seit der Kaiserzeit mit der → Romanisierung und der Christianisierung zwei weitere Akkulturationsprozesse sich mit der H. zu überlappen, teils fördernd, teils hemmend.

B. HISTORISCHE ENTWICKLUNG
1. VORHELLENISTISCHE ZEIT 2. HELLENISMUS
3. KAISERZEIT 4. SPÄTANTIKE

1. VORHELLENISTISCHE ZEIT

Mit Ausnahme Etruriens war die kulturelle Ausstrahlung der früheren griech. Kolonien primär auf das unmittelbare Hinterland beschränkt. Erst seit dem 5. Jh. v.Chr. waren griech. Kulturfertigkeiten und Spezialisten in stärkerem Maße bei Nichtgriechen gefragt (Kunsttstile, Münzprägung, Kriegstechnik u.a. bei Persern, Phöniziern und Etruskern). Weiterreichende Folgen ergaben sich im Laufe des 4. Jh. in einigen küstennahen Regionen Kleinasiens (Karien, Lykien, Pamphylien). Neben der Rezeption griech. Kunst und Architektur begann dort die Umwandlung einheimischer Siedlungszentren und polit. Einheiten nach dem Muster des griech. Gemeindestaates (→ Polis). In Karien spielten dabei die sich philhellenisch gebenden Fürsten der Hekatomnidendynastie (v.a. → Maussollos, 377–353 v.Chr.) eine führende Rolle, in Lykien und Pamphylien lag die Initiative wohl mehr bei den polit. Gemeinschaften selbst. Ähnliches spielte sich im Westen bei den Sikulern auf Sizilien ab. Einen Grenzfall bildeten die nördl. Landschaften Makedonien und Epeiros: Trotz großer Nähe zum Griechentum konnten deren Bewohner als »Barbaren« eingeordnet werden, bes. wegen der andersartigen polit.-sozialen Strukturen (zentrale Rolle des Königtums und seiner Adelsgefolgschaft). Nur die Herrscherfamilien stellten zunächst Anspruch auf Anerkennung ihrer griech. Identität und rezipierten massiv Elemente der griech. Kultur. Einen weiteren Sonderfall bildete Zypern, wo Griechen und Phönizier nebeneinander siedelten und sich gegenseitig beeinflußten; so ist die im Rahmen der griech. Gesch. ungewöhnliche Rolle stabiler Stadtfürstentümer in den zypr. Poleis kaum ohne den Hinweis auf den engen Kontakt mit den phöniz. Nachbarn zu erklären.

2. HELLENISMUS

Durch Alexanderzug (→ Alexandros [4], mit Karte) und Diadochenkriege (→ Diadochen) gelangten erstmalig zahlreiche Griechen und Makedonen auch in entlegenere Räume nichtgriech. Bevölkerung und Kultur. Die Neuankömmlinge besetzten den Kern der Machtapparate der sich ausbildenden hell. Monarchien in Heer und Verwaltung oder dienten als Geschäftsleute, Kaufleute, Künstler und Handwerker den Interessen der Verwaltung bzw. befriedigten die Bedürfnisse ihrer Landsleute in fremder Umgebung. Die maked. Herrscher selbst organisierten ihre engere Umgebung – die Hofges. – nach heimatlichem Muster als Adelsgefolgschaft (→ *hetairía*, → *hetaíroi*; → Hof) mit den damit verbundenen Ausdrucksformen (z.B. Symposion, → Gastmahl). Alexanders Versuch, die den König von seiner Umgebung stärker abgrenzenden Strukturen des pers. Hofes zum Vorbild zu nehmen, fand keine Nachahmung. Schwerpunkte der griech.-maked. Ansiedlung waren Lydien, Karien, Teile Phrygiens und Kilikiens, in der Levante Nordsyrien (sog. → »Tetrapolis«: Antiocheia [1], Seleukeia, Apameia [3] und Laodikeia) und das Gebiet der späteren → Dekapolis im Ostjordanland, im Osten der nw-iranische Raum im Hinterland der Metropole Seleukeia am Tigris, in Äg. Alexandreia und das mitteläg. → Fajum. Im Herrschaftsgebiet der Seleukiden dominierte die geschlossene Ansiedlung in Poleis oder polisähnlichen Militärsiedlungen (Katoikien, → *kátoikos*), im ptolem. Äg. ließen sich die Militärsiedler (Kleruchen, → *klērúchoi*) oft innerhalb einheimischer Dörfer nieder.

Das aufgrund all dieser Siedlungsvorgänge beträchtlich gewachsene H.-Potential blieb aber in der eigentlichen hell. Epoche zu großen Teilen ungenutzt, wobei zwei Faktoren als Hemmschuh wirkten: Zum einen hatten die Herrscher selbst nur geringes Interesse an der Förderung von H.-Vorgängen in den einheimischen Bevölkerungen und zeigten nur wenig Bereitschaft, Assimilierte als gleichberechtigte Neuaufsteiger in die ethnisch-kulturell abgegrenzte Machtelite aufzunehmen. Dies galt bes. im 3. Jh. v. Chr., blieb aber bis z.Z. der röm. Herrschaft weiter bestimmend. Die Anzahl von führenden Männern nichtgriech. Herkunft in der nächsten Umgebung der Könige (v. a. Iraner) ging nach den ersten Jahrzehnten stark zurück. Auf der unteren Ebene waren gerade die Einheimischen in der Nähe der griech. und maked. Siedler meist in deutlich hierarchischer Form an die als Rentiers lebenden Herren gebunden, eine Aufnahme in den privilegierten Personenverband anfangs schwierig.

Der fehlenden Förderung von H. entsprach zum anderen die gezielte Unterstützung traditioneller, einheimischer Organisationsformen und Kulturmuster auf den mittleren und unteren Ebenen der Herrschaftsausübung. Dadurch war Assimilation der lokalen Eliten an die Kultur der neuen Herrscher zwecks Machterhalt unnötig. Hintergrund war die v. a. in pers. Tradition stehende Organisationsstruktur der hell. Reiche. Wie zuvor unterstand der größte Teil des Herrschaftsgebietes in regional unterschiedlicher Dichte königlichen Amtsträgern; die unterste Ebene bildeten lokale Einheiten jeweils einheimischer Prägung, die in verschiedenen Graden von der Zentrale abhängig sein konnten: Einzelne Dorfgemeinschaften oder -gruppen, »private« und königliche Domänen, Tempelfürstentümer, tribal organisierte Bergvölker, in Palaestina der jüd. Tempelstaat unter Leitung der Hohenpriester, die phöniz. Stadtstaaten unter Führung ihrer Könige und Aristokratien, in Babylonien die von Priesterschaft, Gemeindeversammlung und einheimischen Stadtoberen gemeinsam geführten Städte. Die griech.-maked. Siedlungen bildeten mitsamt des von ihnen direkt kontrollierten Umlandes nur Inseln innerhalb einer andersartigen territorialen Struktur. Sie waren also nicht die einzigen Verwaltungs- und Organisationszentren, vielmehr dienten sie wohl primär als Versorgungs- und Rekrutierungsbasis für die Kernbereiche der königlichen Herrschaftsapparate.

Symptomatisch für die Begrenztheit der H. ist die relativ geringe Anzahl einheimischer Gemeinwesen ohne griech. Siedlerkern, die im Laufe des Hellenismus zu Poleis wurden bzw. diesen Status bestätigt bekamen. Das dieser Regel widersprechende Verhalten → Antiochos [6] IV. Epiphanes (175–164 v. Chr.) läßt sich eher auf fiskalische Interessen als auf kulturelles Sendungsbewußtsein zurückführen; seine auf eine Umwandlung des jüd. Kultes zielende Politik ist wohl nur von dem spezifisch lokalen Zusammenhang her verständlich. Es waren v. a. nichtgriech., »philhellenisch« orientierte Fürsten, die einheimische Gemeinwesen in griech. Poleis umwandelten: die bithyn. und kappadok. Könige, die Könige von Kommagene, am Ende der Epoche die jüd. Herrscher der herodianischen Dyn. (→ Herodes). Die griech. Kultur diente hierbei als Statussymbol, um so mit den maked. Herrschern gleichziehen zu können.

Aktive Selbst-H. einheimischer Bevölkerungen gab es daneben in denjenigen Gebieten des westl., südwestl. und südl. Kleinasiens, wo diese Veränderungen schon vor dem Hell. begonnen hatten: In Karien, Lykien und Pamphylien wurde der Prozeß der Polisbildung zu Ende geführt, Neuland eroberte die griech. Kultur nur in Teilen Lydiens und Pisidiens. In der Levante taten sich die phöniz. Stadtstaaten hervor: In der 1. H. des 3. Jh. endeten die alten Stadtkönigtümer, zunächst gefolgt von einer in einheimischer Trad. stehenden Organisationsform unter der Leitung sog. Schofeten (»Richter«). Charakteristischerweise fiel die endgültige Poliswerdung der phöniz. Städte in die Zeit der Schwächung des seleukidischen Königtums seit der Mitte des 2. Jh. v. Chr. Dazu kam als Ausweis der neuen ethnisch-kulturellen Zuordnung die Teilnahme von Bürgern an der griech. → Festkultur und die Interpretation der eigenen Vorgesch. im Rahmen der griech. Myth. (Mythos von → Kadmos). Das Gleiche gilt für die Phönizier auf Zypern, wo andererseits die Griechen jetzt dem *mainstream* der griech. Kulturentwicklung beitraten (u. a. Aufgabe der Stadtfürstentümer und der alten Silbenschrift, → Kyprominoische Schriften). Die wachsende merkantile Ausrichtung der Phönizier auf den ägäischen Raum scheint bei diesen Transformationen ein zentraler Faktor gewesen zu sein. Damit traten die städtischen Zentren der Levanteküste zusammen mit den erwähnten Teilen Kleinasiens und den oben aufgezählten Bereichen der frühell. Ansiedlung als neue Zentren des Griechentums neben die alten griech. Siedlungsgebiete, ebenso wie die jetzt unstrittig als Griechen betrachteten und in Poleis lebenden Bewohner des Epeiros und Makedoniens.

Doch blieb solch eine umfassende Form der H. mit Folgen für die lokale Identität bis zur Ankunft Roms im Osten die Ausnahme. Bes. in Babylonien, Äg. und Iudaea existierte die einheimische kulturelle, rel. und polit. Überl. teils nur wenig verändert fort. Die letztgen. Gebiete bieten auch das deutlichste Beispiel kontinuierlicher einheimischer Schriftlichkeit und Lit.-Produktion in der Landessprache.

3. KAISERZEIT

a) ADMINISTRATION

Mit der Ausdehnung des röm. Provinzialsystems im östl. Mittelmeerraum seit dem letzten Drittel des 2. Jh. v. Chr. war es ausgerechnet eine nichtgriech. Macht, die die bisherigen Hemmnisse einer umfassenderen H. beseitigte. Die neue Vormacht Rom war selbst aus einem Gemeindestaat hervorgegangen und blieb in der Kaiserzeit in mancher Hinsicht von dieser Trad. geprägt. Kaiser, Senat und Statthalter waren aus It. den Umgang mit lokalen Einheiten gewohnt, die sich auf ein städtisches Zentrum und sein Umland beschränkten, gebildet von einer Bürgergemeinde, die unter der Führung einer stadtsässigen Grundbesitzerelite analog der röm. Senatsaristokratie stand. Dieser Erwartungshaltung entsprach im Osten die griech. Polis am besten. Daneben war den Römern eine Reihe zentraler griech. Kulturmuster vertraut, die sie selbst adaptiert hatten und als eigene betrachteten. Schon die Republik hatte in den von ihr annektierten Gebieten die Zwischenebene der königlichen Territorialverwaltung aufgelöst oder verfallen lassen, der röm. Statthalter trat so mit den ihm untergebenen lokalen Einheiten der Städte, Stämme, Heiligtümer und Dörfer direkt in Verbindung. Dabei war eine mögliche Vereinheitlichung der Organisation dieser Einheiten nach dem vertrauten Vorbild der Polis auch praktisch von Vorteil. Diesem strukturell bedingt größeren Wohlwollen der neuen Macht gegenüber einheimischen H.-Wünschen entsprach ein gewachsenes Interesse gerade der lokalen Eliten. Zum einen bewirkte die Fixierung Roms auf das Polis-Modell und die damit verbundenen Kommunikationsformen ein verstärktes Streben nach Erlangen dieses Rechtsstatus, da die Untertanen den bestmöglichen Kontakt mit ihren Herren wollten. Zum anderen wurden auch im Osten seit dem letzten Drittel des 1. Jh. n. Chr. in größerer Zahl Angehörige der lokalen Oberschichten in die Reichsaristokratie des Senatoren- und Ritterstandes aufgenommen. Die griech. Kultur und Bildung wurde dabei zum Eintrittsbillett.

Durch diese Kombination aus Förderung von oben und Wunsch nach Selbst-H. der Provinzialen wurde ein Prozeß grundlegender territorialer und struktureller Umwandlung in Gang gesetzt. An seinem Ende, im frühen 4. Jh. n. Chr., bestand der östl. Teil des röm. Reiches vorwiegend aus den Territorien von Poleis, die jetzt ein durchgehendes administratives Netz bildeten, dazwischen vereinzelt kaiserliche Domänen, private Gutsbezirke und direkt dem Statthalter unterstellte Dorfgemeinden. Die Situation des Hell. hatte sich somit umgekehrt. Nur in Äg. wurde die ptolem. Trad. einer bis in die Dörfer hinunterreichenden königlichen Verwaltung zunächst weitergeführt, allerdings wurde die Organisation der Hauptorte der äg. Gaue (*nomoi*) zunehmend dem Bild griech. Poleis angeglichen, bis die Situation sich im 4. Jh. auch hier nur noch wenig von der anderer Reichsteile unterschied.

b) KULTUR

Diese administrativ-polit. Veränderungen waren Rahmen und Voraussetzung für weitergehende kulturelle und mentale Prozesse. Die Ausdehnung der Polisorganisation brachte die umfassende H. der lokalen Eliten; damit brach die »hochkulturelle« Variante der jeweiligen Regionalkulturen weg: Die zentralen Heiligtümer wurden per → *interpretatio Graeca* »umgewidmet«, griech. Kunst und Architektur bestimmten das Bild, Lit.-Produktion gab es nur noch auf Griech. und in griech. Formen; man legte sich Gründungsmythen zu, die der eigenen Stadt eine »griech.« Vorgesch. gaben. Zudem wandelte sich die Kommunikation zw. Elite und einfacher Bevölkerung (→ Euergetismus, Festkultur, → Theater und → Schauspiele, → Rhetorik). Selbst die Landbevölkerung wurde davon erfaßt: Zwar lebten vielerorts vorgriech. Trad. der Volkskultur bes. im rel. Bereich weiter und in ausgedehnten Gebieten dominierte weiterhin die einheimische Umgangssprache, doch fanden seit Beginn der Kaiserzeit griech. Formen der Gemeinschaftsbildung verstärkt ihren Weg auf die Dörfer: Dorfgemeinden waren bes. in Syrien und Kleinasien oft nach dem Muster der Polis verfaßt, mit eigenen Kassen sowie Magistraturen und einer stiftenden dörflichen Oberschicht. In vielen ländlichen Gebieten tauchte eine griech. Inschriftenkultur auf, verbunden mit einer neuen Monumentalisierung ländlicher Architektur nach dem Vorbild städtischer griech. Formen. Ungebrochene Kontinuität vorgriech. Trad. war nicht mehr möglich.

c) AUSNAHMEN

Partielle Ausnahme – neben dem Judentum – bildete wieder Äg., wo in vielen Tempeln die alten Kulttrad. gepflegt wurden und Priester und Schreiber bis ins 3. Jh. n. Chr. eine Lit.-Produktion in demot. Schrift und äg. Sprache aufrecht erhielten. Eine interessante Abweichung stellten die Kulturräume dar, die seit dem Ende des 2. Jh. v. Chr. in den Grenzgebieten der syr.-mesopot. Wüstensteppe entstanden waren (→ Nabataioi, → Palmyra, → Edessa, → Ḥatra). Sie zeichneten sich durch eine jeweils individuelle Synthese aus griech. und nichtgriech. Elementen aus, sowie durch eine aram. Schriftlichkeit. Es handelte sich aber nicht einfach um Fortführung alter Trad., sondern um Neuentwicklungen, Ergebnisse der zunehmenden Seßhaftwerdung nomadischer Bevölkerungsgruppen an den Rändern des Kulturlandes. Dabei gerieten diese Gruppen zugleich in den Ausstrahlungsbereich der bäuerlichen Volkskultur ihrer altseßhaften Nachbarn und in den der hellenisierten Zentren.

d) ROMANISIERTER HELLENISMUS

Neben der H. gab es auch im Osten ansatzweise das Phänomen der Romanisierung. Zwar war die Ausstrahlungskraft der wenigen röm. Siedlungskolonien gering – ihr röm.-lat. Charakter überlebte das 3. Jh. nicht – doch strömten röm. Kulturmuster zunehmend indirekt ein. Gerade der Aufstieg von Angehörigen der städtischen Eliten in die Reichsaristokratie hatte eine Annäherung der griech. an die röm. Stadtkultur zur Folge (Bauformen und -techniken, Klientelstrukturen, Namensformen, LW aus dem Lat., Gladiatorenspiele und Tierhetzen, → *munera*, städt. Ämter und Institutionen). In beschränkterem Umfang wirkte die z. T. massive Präsenz der Armee in den Grenzgebieten seit dem 2. Jh. n. Chr. in diese Richtung. Ein romanisierter Hell. war das Ergebnis.

4. SPÄTANTIKE

Die Zeit vom frühen 4. bis zum späten 6. Jh. n. Chr. war im Osten grundsätzlich durch Kontinuität in Hinblick auf die H. geprägt. Noch existierende Lücken im territorialen Verteilungsmuster griech. geprägter Städte wurden geschlossen, die griech. Inschr.- und Monumentekultur auf dem Lande breitete sich bes. in Syrien weiter aus, in Kleinasien wurden die einheimischen Sprachen auch im anatol. Hochland nur noch von Minderheiten gesprochen. Andererseits tauchten neue Widersprüche auf. Wichtig wurde dabei die Christianisierung der Mehrzahl der Reichsbewohner bis zum 6. Jh. Das → Christentum hatte sich zunächst in den griech.-hell. Zentren des östl. Mittelmeerraumes entwickelt und war somit stark von griech. Einflüssen geprägt. Andererseits betrachteten sich die Christen als »neues Volk«, weder Griechen noch Barbaren, und neigten dazu, den Begriff »Hellenen« (Ἕλληνες) mit »Heidentum« gleichzusetzen. Dies führte zusammen mit der Verbreitung einer Reichsidentität besonders bei der Oberschicht im 5. Jh. zum Identitätsbruch bei gleichzeitiger Kulturkontinuität: Anstatt »Grieche« war die übliche Selbstbezeichnung jetzt »Christ« oder »Römer« oder beides.

Zudem war das Christentum als auf kanonischen Texten aufbauende Offenbarungs- und Verkündigungsreligion auf die Wiedergabe seiner Botschaft auch in den nichtgriech. Umgangssprachen angewiesen. Dies führte im 4. Jh. in Äg. und Mesopot. zur Entstehung einer christl. Lit. in kopt. (äg.) bzw. syr. (aram.) Sprache. Es handelte sich aber dabei nicht um eine bewußte Gegenbewegung gegen die griech. Kultur als solche: Zum einen blieb der Wirkungskreis beider Lit. vor der islam. Eroberung beschränkt; in Äg. dominierte immer noch das griech. Schrifttum, die sog. syr. Lit. konnte westl. des Euphrat kaum Fuß fassen, im röm. Kleinasien gab es überhaupt nichts Entsprechendes. Zum anderen waren die beiden Lit. in Form und Inhalt stark von der griech. christl. Lit. abhängig. Auch fehlte ein positiver Rückbezug auf die jeweilige »eigene« vorhell. Vergangenheit, die ja zugleich eine vorchristl. war. Die auf das kollektive Selbst bezogene lit. Erinnerung an eine Vorzeit vor dem Alexanderzug war ganz heilsgeschichtlich, orientiert an der israelitisch-jüd. Gesch. So konnten weder Pharaonen noch altaram. Könige Ansatzpunkte für etwaiges »antigriech.« oder »antiimperiales« Sonderbewußtsein bieten. Polemik gegen das »Griechentum« war hier Ablehnung des »Heidentums«, auch wenn letzteres nichtgriech. Züge aufwies.

Auch verwischten zw. dem 4. und dem 6. Jh. umfangreiche Veränderungen im polit. und sozialen Bereich den Unterschied zw. griech. und nichtgriech. Organisationsformen zunehmend: z. B. die Auflösung der Polis als Bürgergemeinde, was im 6. Jh. in ein von den Bischöfen, kaiserlichen Beamten und lokalen Notabeln geprägtes Städtewesen mündete, und die wachsende soziale Autorität charismatischer, als eng mit dem Göttlichen verbunden gedachter Außenseitergruppen (Mönche, Asketen) in Stadt und Land, bei Griechen und Nichtgriechen.

C. KUNST UND ARCHITEKTUR

Seit der Archaik waren es die ästhetischen Ausdrucksformen der griech. Kultur gewesen, die am bereitwilligsten von Nichtgriechen rezipiert wurden. Dies war schon im 6. Jh. v. Chr. in Etrurien der Fall gewesen, im 5. und 4. Jh. dann in Karien und Lykien, wo die einheimischen Dynasten griech. Formen bes. im Bereich der Grabrepräsentation verwandten (→ Grabbauten). Im Hell. wirkte die griech. Kunst auch in Milieus, die in struktureller Hinsicht kaum von der H. erfaßt wurden. So entstanden bes. im iran. Raum eigenwillige Synthesen aus einheimischer und griech. Kunst und Architektur. Die neuen griech.-maked. Siedlungen besaßen natürlich überall primär Monumente in unvermischt griech. Stil, wobei aber gerade die Hauptzentren Alexandreia, Antiocheia am Orontes und Seleukeia am Tigris für uns bislang kaum faßbar werden. Aber bes. in Äg. und Babylonien existierte daneben die einheimische Bau- und Kunsttrad. fast unverändert weiter. Die Kaiserzeit brachte auch in diesem Bereich Ausdehnung und Standardisierung: Das Kunstschaffen in rein einheimischer Trad. wurde in Äg. selten, überall setzte sich seit dem 2. Jh. n. Chr. eine einheitlichere, durch westl. Einflüsse erweiterte griech. »Reichskunst« durch, Mischformen wurden zurüchgedrängt. Nur in den neuentstandenen Kulturbereichen der syr.-mesopot. Wüstensteppe existierten sie bis ins 3. Jh. Die Spätant. setzte einerseits den Trend zur Homogenität fort, andererseits entwickelten sich wieder stärker lokale Besonderheiten, allerdings jetzt auf einheitlicher Basis und ohne daß dabei das Band mit der von den großen Zentren geprägten Reichskunst irgendwo gelöst worden wäre.

D. ZUSAMMENFASSUNG

Die oft wiederholte Beurteilung der H. des Vorderen Orients von Alexander bis → Mohammed als eine oberflächliche, nur von kleinen Eliten getragene Kulturdecke über einem tiefen Untergrund vorhell. Kontinuitäten trifft die Komplexität des Phänomens nicht. Vielmehr stand am Ende einer tausendjährigen Entwicklung im oströn. Reich eine in Grundzügen überall ähnliche Provinzialkultur, die je nach regionaler Schattierung unterschiedliche Anteile griech., röm. und vorgriech. Herkunft verarbeitet hatte. Die griech. Kulturformen boten dabei eine Art akzeptierter »Gemeinsprache« für den Ausdruck auch regionaler Identitäten und für den Zweck der Kommunikation zw. den einzelnen Reichsteilen und mit dem Zentrum. Wirklich ungebrochene vorgriech. Trad. gab es nicht mehr. Im äußersten Falle war ein völliger Identitätsbruch erfolgt, war man in Fremd- und Eigenwahrnehmung zu Griechen geworden, fungierten Überreste des vorgriech. Kulturzusammenhanges als »Lokalkolorit«. Diese Situation kann man wohl für den größeren Teil der Stadtbevölkerungen annehmen, sowie für viele Landgebiete Kleinasiens, in Teilen auch Syriens, Phöniziens und Palaestinas. Fließend war der Übergang zu derjenigen Situation, wo nur die Elite von diesem radikalen Bruch betroffen war, aber eine vorwiegend mündlich und über Kultformen tradierte einheimische Volkskultur weiterbestand. Allerdings war auch diese von den Veränderungen der H. und dem Wegfall ihrer »hochkulturellen« Variante nicht unberührt geblieben. Dies galt wohl in der Spätant. für die größten Teile des ländlichen Raumes in Syrien-Palaestina und Äg. Schließlich finden wir auch die Ausbildung einer neuen kulturellen Synthese aus dem Bruch heraus (Bereiche der kopt. und syr. Lit.). Die frühislam. Kultur war Erbin dieses komplexen kulturellen Gemenges. Sie führte damit auch zentrale griech. Trad. weiter und stellte somit nicht einfach den Abschluß eines oft fälschlich sog. Prozesses der »Reorientalisierung« dar.

→ Hellenismus; Hellenistische Staatenwelt; Romanisierung

R.S. Bagnall, Egypt in Late Antiquity, 1993 • G.W. Bowersock, Hellenism in Late Antiquity, 1990 • A.K. Bowman, Egypt after the Pharaohs, 1986 • P. Bilde u.a. (Hrsg.), Religion and Religious Practice in the Seleucid Kingdom, 1990 • J.-M. Dentzer, W. Ortmann, Archéologie et histoire de la Syrie II, 1989 • B. Funck (Hrsg.), Hellenismus. Beitr. zur Erforschung von Akkulturation und polit. Ordnung in den Staaten des hell. Zeitalters. Akten des Internat. Hellenismus-Kolloquiums 9.–14. März 1994 in Berlin, 1996 • A.H.M. Jones, The Cities of the Eastern Roman Provinces 2, 1971 (Ndr. 1983) • A. Kuhrt, S. Sherwin-White (Hrsg.), Hellenism in the East. The Interaction of Greek and non-Greek Civilizations from Syria to Central Asia after Alexander, 1987 • H. Lauter, Die Architektur des Hellenismus, 1986 • F.G.B. Millar, The Phoenician cities: a case-study of hellenisation, in: PCPhS 209, 1983, 55–71 • Ders., Empire, community and culture in the Roman Near East: Greeks, Syrians, Jews and Arabs, in: Journal of Jewish Studies 38/2, 1987, 143–164 • Ders., The Roman Near East. 31 BC-AD 337, 1993 • M. Sartre, L'orient romain. Provinces et sociétés provinciales en Méditerranée orientale d'Auguste aux Sévères (31 avant J.-C.–235 après J.-C.), 1991 • Ders., L'Asie mineure et l'Anatolie d'Alexandre à Diocletien, 1996 • D. Schlumberger, Der hellenisierte Orient. Die griech. und nachgriech. Kunst außerhalb des Mittelmeerraumes, 1969 • F.R. Trombley, Hellenic Religion and Christianization c. 370–529, 2 Bde., 1993.

J.G.

II. Sprache

A. Allgemein B. Ägypten, Kleinasien, Syrien
C. Hellenisierung und Latein

A. Allgemein

Schon mit den griech. Kolonisierungen (→ Kolonisation) entstanden griech. Sprachinseln außerhalb des »Mutterlandes«, u.a. in Nordafrika (Kyrene), Unterit., Sizilien und Südfrankreich, deren sprachlicher Einfluß z.T. heute noch spürbar ist; eines der folgenreichsten Ereignisse der griech. Sprachgesch. aber war die Entscheidung Philipps, das Griech. zur Sprache (= Spr.) der maked. Hofkanzlei zu machen, denn mit den Eroberungen → Alexandros' [4] d.Gr. (mit Karte) und den Diadochenreichen (→ Diadochen, mit Karte) breitete sich die griech. Spr. in der Gestalt der *Koinḗ* weit über das urspr. griech. Sprachgebiet hinaus aus. Einheimische Spr. verloren dabei teilweise zuerst ihren schriftsprachlichen Status (sofern sie ihn gehabt hatten) und starben aus, andere unterlagen griech. Spracheinfluß v.a. im Wortschatz, wieder andere verloren ihren Rang als Amtsspr., blieben aber erh., so z.B. das Aram. Eine Spr. kann aber noch lange nach dem Ende ihrer inschr. Dokumentation als gesprochene Spr. weiterleben: so gibt es nach dem 4. Jh. v.Chr. keine lyk. Inschr. mehr, aber dennoch wurde es nach dem Zeugnis Apg 14,11 mind. bis ins 1. Jh. n.Chr. in Lystra noch gesprochen.

Mit der Etablierung v.a. des Ptolemäer- und des Seleukidenreiches und der Gründung griech. Städte trat das Griech. mit verschiedenen Spr. in Kontakt, was nur selten zur Aufnahme fremden Wortguts im Griech. führte (z.B. βάιον »Palmzweig« aus dem Äg. *bꜥj*, vgl. neugriech. τα βάγια »Palmsonntag«; die semit. LW im Griech. datieren meist aus viel früherer Zeit, sind z.T. sogar bereits myk. nachweisbar wie etwa χιτών), häufiger zur Entlehnung griech. Wörter in andere Spr. (wegen des Prestiges des Griech. als Spr. der Herrscher).

Griech. Inschr. finden sich bis in den ind. Sprachraum hinein (eine Inschr. Aśokas in Qandahār ist griech. und aram. abgefaßt); die Seleukiden bedienten sich gleichfalls des Griech., in Fortsetzung des achäm. Gebrauchs des Aram. (z.B. existiert ein zweispr. griech.-aram. Meilenstein von ca. 280 v.Chr. aus Pasargadai). Am Hofe des Partherkönigs Hyrodes wurden Euripidestragödien (Plut. Crassus 33) aufgeführt; noch unter den ersten Sāsāniden wurden mittelpers. Inschr. griech. Fassungen beigegeben.

B. Ägypten, Kleinasien, Syrien

Im Ptolem. Reich war das Griech. Amts- und Verwaltungsspr., in mehrspr. Inschr. ist die griech. Version das Original. Da Äg. das einzige Land ist, aus dem griech. → Papyri in größerer Anzahl erh. sind, sind sie die wichtigste nichtlit. Quelle für das hell. und kaiserzeitliche Griech. Die sprachlichen Eigenheiten der Papyri lassen sich meist aus der griech. Sprachgesch. erklären, ohne daß man kopt. Substrateinfluß zu bemühen hätte. In Alexandreia findet sich außerdem ein hellenisiertes Judentum (oft werden hebr. Namen ins

Griech. umgesetzt, bes. beliebt sind zufällig in beiden Spr. gleich oder ähnlich lautende Namen wie Simeon/Simon oder Josua/Iason), auf dessen Initiative die Entstehung der → Septuaginta zurückgeht, die aber auch in Palaestina rasch maßgeblich wurde.

Was Kleinasien angeht, so hielt die karische Königin → Artemisia [2] bereits im J. 353 v. Chr. einen griech. Rhetorik-Agon ab. Einheimische Spr. überlebten aber bis in die Spätant. hinein: neuphryg. Inschr. (in griech. Alphabet, oft zweispr.) reichen bis ins 4. Jh. n. Chr., und nach einer Aussage des Hieronymus wurde zu seiner Zeit in Kleinasien noch Kelt. gesprochen. Wie stark sich hier griech. Spracheinfluß z. B. auf den Wortschatz auswirkte, läßt sich mangels Dokumentation nicht abschätzen. Man kann davon ausgehen, daß in byz. Zeit Kleinasien ein geschlossenes griech. Sprachgebiet gewesen ist und die Verhältnisse sich erst mit der Einwanderung von Turkvölkern änderten.

Auch in Syrien und Palaestina sind griech. sprachlicher Einfluß und griech. Inschr.-Funde in jüd. Kontext erheblich, ein hellenisiertes Judentum hat es auch dort gegeben – schließlich sind die Evangelien ja auf Griech. verfaßt, und zwar *nicht* in einem spezifisch jüd. Griech. (die Semitismushypothese hat sich weitgehend erledigt). Selbst → Bar Kochba schrieb seine Briefe teilweise auf Griech. Gerade diese Region hat spezifisch griech. Schriftsteller hervorgebracht (→ Lukianos von Samosata, → Iamblichos).

C. Hellenisierung und Latein

Bes. gut erforscht ist die Hellenisierung des Lat.: Die lat. Lit. beginnt mit einer Übers. aus dem Griech. (→ Livius Andronikos), röm. lit. Genera haben griech. Vorbilder (Ausnahme: → Satire), und das Lat. kennt viele griech. LW, wobei es sich nicht nur um »Bildungswortschatz« wie etwa *philosophia* handelt, sondern um Alltagswortschatz, Bezeichnungen für Handelsgüter (alt ist z. B. *ampulla* zu griech. ἀμφορεύς), für Pflanzen (*malum* < dor. μᾶλον) und sogar Schimpfwörter (*malacus*, Plaut. < griech. μαλακός); eine ganze Reihe griech. Wörter im Lat. war auch volkssprachlich (vgl. frz. *jambe* < griech. καμπή). Beim lat.-griech. Sprachkontakt handelt es sich um einen Sonderfall, da es dem Lat. als Spr. des Röm. Reiches gelang, auch das Griech. zu beeinflussen, was sich u. a. in einer großen Anzahl lat. Wörter im Griech. widerspiegelt, die nicht nur aus den Bereichen Verwaltung, Militär und Rechtswesen stammen und sich bis h. im Neugriech. nachweisen lassen (neugriech. σπίτι »Haus« < lat. *hospitium*). In lit. ambitionierten Texten werden lat. Wörter aber gemieden. Die wechselseitige Beeinflussung reichte aber so weit, daß sprachliche Entwicklungen vom Lat. zu den roman. Spr. einerseits, vom Alt- zum Neugriech. andererseits parallel verlaufen, so daß von einem lat.-griech. Sprachbund (Kramer) gesprochen werden kann.

Die Römer betrieben kaum eine aktive Sprachpolitik, sondern behielten das Griech. als Amtsspr. im Osten bei (lat. LW z. B. im Aram., Hebr., Arab., Syr., Kopt. wurden durch das Griech. vermittelt). Das führte dazu, daß die sprachliche H. im Osten auch in röm. Zeit weiterlief und sogar mit der Christianisierung neuen Auftrieb bekam (die südlichste griech. Inschr. ist die des Nubierkönigs Silko aus der Mitte des 6. Jh. n. Chr.); im lat. Sprachraum sind christl. Termini häufig griech. Ursprungs (frz. *église* < ἐκκλησία), und über das Lat. gelangten sie in andere Spr. wie z. B. das Deutsche. Allerdings führte die Christianisierung auch dazu, daß eine Reihe von Spr. neu oder erstmals verschriftet wurden (erste Texte sind meist Übers. nt. Schriften) wie etwa das Syr., das Kopt., das Äthiop., das Got., das Armen. und das Georg. Die Tatsache, daß diese Spr. früh zu geschriebenen Spr. des Christentums wurden, hat wohl zu ihrem Überleben beigetragen: Kopt. erlag erst dem Arab., und bis h. existiert in Syrien eine aram. Sprachinsel. Got. überlebte auf der Krim bis ins 16. Jh. n. Chr. In allen diesen Spr. lassen sich griech. Spracheinflüsse nachweisen; so wird etwa der Anteil griech. LW im Kopt. auf etwa 20 % geschätzt (auch Partikel wie ἀλλά oder γάρ). Auch im Armen. und Georg. sind viele griech. Wörter erh., aber an lat. Wörtern nur solche, die auch im Griech. belegt sind.

F. Altheim, Die Weltgeltung der griech. Spr., in: E. C. Welskopf (ed.), Neue Beitr. zur Gesch. der Alten Welt. I: Alter Orient und Griechenland, 1964, 315–332 • F. Biville, Les emprunts du latin au grec. Approche phonétique, 1990 • A. Böhlig, Die griech. LW im sahidischen und bohairischen NT (= Stud. zur Erforschung des christl. Äg. 2), 1953 • R. Browning, Medieval and Modern Greek, [2]1983 • S. Daris, Il lessico latino nel greco d'Egitto [2]1991 • A. Debrunner, A. Scherer, Gesch. der griech. Spr. II. Grundfragen und Grundzüge des nachklass. Griech., 1969 • G. Deeters, Die kaukasischen Spr. III – Wortschatz, in: G. Deeters, G. Solta, V. Inglisi (ed.), Armenisch und kaukasische Spr. (HbdOr I.7), 1963, 33–46 • W. Dietrich, Griech. und Romanisch. Parallelen und Divergenzen in Entwicklung, Variation und Strukturen (= Münstersche Beitr. zur Roman. Philol. 11), 1995 • H. Hübschmann, Armenische Grammatik. 1. Teil Armenische Etym., 1897 (Ndr. 1962) • A. Jefferey, The Foreign Vocabulary of the Qur'ān, 1935 • S. Kapsomenos, Das Griech. in Äg., in: MH 10, 1953, 247–262 • G. Narr (ed.), Griech. und Romanisch (= Tübinger Beitr. zur Linguistik 16), 1971 • G. Neumann, J. Untermann (ed.), Die Spr. im röm. Reich der Kaiserzeit (Kolloquium vom 8.–10. April 1974), 1980 • A. Thumb, Die griech. Spr. im Zeitalter des Hell., 1901 • J. Kramer, Der kaiserzeitliche griech.-lat. Sprachbund, in: N. Reiter (ed.), Ziele und Wege der Balkanlinguistik (Beitr. zur Tagung vom 2.–6. März 1981 in Berlin), 1983, 115–131 (= Balkanologische Veröffentlichungen 8) • R. Schmitt, Die Sprachverhältnisse in den östl. Provinzen des röm. Reiches, in: ANRW II 29.2, 554–586 • D. Sperber, A Dictionary of Greek and Latin Legal Terms in Rabbinic Literature, 1984 • W. von Wartburg, Die griech. Kolonisation in Südgallien und ihre sprachlichen Zeugen im Westroman., in: Zschr. für roman. Philol. 68, 1952, 1–48.

V.BI.

Hellenismus (*hellēnismós*). Dient in der Antike wohl schon seit Aristoteles bzw. dessen Schüler → Theophrastos als Bezeichnung für den korrekten Gebrauch der griech. Sprache (*hellēnízein* = »griech. sprechen«), ist als Begriff jedoch erst im 2. Jh. v. Chr. belegt (2 Makk 4,13) und bezeichnet dort die aus jüdischer Sicht abgelehnte griech. Art und Lebensweise. Ausgehend von der etwa gleichzeitig bei alexandrinischen Gelehrten entstehenden Bed. von H. als »griech. Geisteswelt«, verwenden dann christl. Schriftsteller H. im Sinne von »Heidentum« und in der Spätant. auch zur Bezeichnung häretischer Strömungen innerhalb des Christentums [1. 5–22] (→ Häresie). Als Bezeichnung einer zeitlich abgrenzbaren histor. Epoche findet sich H. in der Ant. nicht.

Seit dem 17. Jh. bezeichnet das Adjektiv »hellenistisch« die besondere, mit ungriech. Elementen versetzte Sprache des Bibelgriechischen, das Substantiv H. aber bis in den Beginn des 19. Jh. die griech. Lebensweise und Geisteswelt als Ausdruck des griech. »Genius«. In dieser Bed. hat sich H. bis heute im Frz. erhalten, während im angelsächsischen Sprachraum die intensive Beschäftigung mit griech. Sprache und Kultur ebenfalls als H. gilt (*Hellenist* als »Berufsbezeichnung« für »Gräzisten«).

Daneben erhielt ausgehend von Deutschland unter dem Eindruck des Werkes von J. G. DROYSEN [2] und seiner Nachfolger der Begriff H. den Charakter eines Epochenbegriffs. Das entscheidende Kriterium für die Qualifizierung des Zeitraums etwa zwischen Alexander d. Gr. und Augustus als histor. Epoche ist für DROYSEN die Verschmelzung der griech. Zivilisation mit der Kultur oriental. Völker (bei eindeutiger Dominanz des Griech.), die letztlich die Entstehung des Christentums ermöglichte. Da der H.-Begriff bei DROYSEN jedoch auch von anderen Kriterien geprägt wird (etwa der Entwicklung des rationalen Geistes innerhalb des Griechentums oder der Veränderung der polit. Struktur der Griechen durch die »Hellenistische Monarchie«), ist eine klare zeitliche und räumliche Eingrenzung des H. im Gefolge DROYSENS nicht möglich, zumal er einerseits erst in der 2. Auflage [3] den H. mit Alexander beginnen läßt und in einem großangelegten Plan einer Geschichte des H. bis zur Entstehung des Islam gehen will [1. 91 f.] und andererseits in seiner Definition des H. den ostmediterranen Raum und Vorderasien im Blick hat, aber in seine Darstellung Karthago, Sizilien und Rom miteinbezieht. Die noch übliche Eingrenzung des H. von Alexander (334 v. Chr.) bis Augustus beruht deshalb auf einer durchaus gut begründeten Konvention [4. 1–3, 129–131], die jedoch z. T. mit ebenfalls guten Gründen häufig durchbrochen wird (Beginn 360 v. Chr.: [5. 299]) und neuerdings eine starke Tendenz zeigt, die Epoche des H. erst nach dem Tode Alexanders 323 v. Chr. beginnen zu lassen (etwa [6], [7], [8], [9]). Das Ende des H. wird (entgegen DROYSEN, der letztlich bis Caesar gehen wollte [1. 91 f.]), heute fast allgemein mit dem Sieg des Augustus über Antonius und Kleopatra bei Aktium (31 v. Chr.) bzw. der Einziehung Ägyptens in das röm. Reich (30 v. Chr.) gleichgesetzt.

→ Periodisierung; EPOCHENBEGRIFFE; HELLENISMUS

1 R. BICHLER, »H.«, 1983 **2** J. G. DROYSEN, Gesch. des H. 1. Theil, Gesch. der Nachfolger Alexanders, 1836 **3** Ders., Gesch. des H., 1. Theil, Gesch. Alexanders d. Gr., ²1877 **4** H. J. GEHRKE, Gesch. des H., 1990 **5** H. BENGTSON, Griech. Gesch., ⁵1977 **6** C. PRÉAUX, Le monde héllenistique, 1978 **7** WILL **8** CAH 7.1, 1984 **9** P. GREEN, From Alexander to Actium, 1990.

W. ED.

Hellenistische Dichtung A. ALLGEMEINES B. DRAMATISCHE DICHTUNG C. SATIRISCHE UND IAMBISCHE DICHTUNG D. HEXAMETER UND ELEGISCHES DISTICHON

A. ALLGEMEINES

Die griech. Dichtung aus der Zeit zw. Alexanders Tod 323 v. Chr. und Octavians Sieg über Kleopatra 31 v. Chr. ist durch große Themenvielfalt und hohen Formenreichtum gekennzeichnet; leider ist nur sehr wenig von der Dichtung des späten 2. und frühen 1. Jh. v. Chr. bekannt, die für die röm. → Neoteriker wichtig gewesen sein muß. Während das 5. Jh. von der att. Komödie und Trag. dominiert wurde, brachten andere Gegenden schon im 4. Jh., bes. in der Ägäis und im Osten, bedeutende Dichter hervor (→ Antimachos [3] aus Kolophon, → Erinna, → Philitas), deren Werke wichtige Merkmale der h.D. vorwegnehmen und zu einem großen Teil eher in ion. als in att. Tradition standen. Die Veränderungen der polit. Lage im 4. und 3. Jh. führten zur Konzentration großer Macht in der Hand weniger bed. Herrscherhäuser (der Ptolemäer in Alexandreia, der Antigoniden in Pella, der Seleukiden in Antiocheia) und damit auch zu einem ausgeprägten Mäzenatentum; ein großer Teil h.D. stand in Zusammenhang mit einem dieser Höfe (→ Hellenistische Staatenwelt; Hof).

Die ersten Ptolemäer schufen Institutionen, in denen philol. Gelehrsamkeit entstehen konnte (das → Museion, die königliche → Bibliothek), und Antiochos III. zog nach. Einige Dichter waren zugleich bedeutende Gelehrte (→ Aratos [4], → Kallimachos, → Eratosthenes [2], → Euphorion [3], → Philetas), was ihre Dichtungen prägte (→ Philologie). Weit wichtiger ist jedoch, daß die Verbreitung von Texten in Buchform, die Trennung dichterischer Texte von den Aufführungskontexten, für die sie urspr. bestimmt waren (vgl. unten), und die graduelle Trennung einer Elite- von einer Volkskultur dazu führte, daß die Dichter jetzt für ein lesendes Publikum schrieben; die Gestalt der Dichtung wurde dadurch stark beeinflußt. Die Entstehung von → Gedichtbüchern, die später für die röm. Dichter so bedeutsam werden sollten, geht wohl auf das 3. Jh. zurück. Daß man sich immer wieder Neubearbeitungen früherer Dichtung, bes. der homer., und der Gesch. und Aitiologie griech. Kulte und Institutionen zuwandte, ist nicht einfach Zeichen der Gelehrsamkeit der hell. Dichter, sondern reflektiert auch ihr Interesse an einer Kontinuität des griech. Kulturerbes; darin kommt die Anerkennung eines Bruchs und Wandels zum Ausdruck.

B. DRAMATISCHE DICHTUNG

Tragödien und Satyrspiele schrieb man auch weiterhin, und die Dionysostechniten (»Künstler des Dionysos«) inszenierten Stücke in der ganzen griech. Welt. Beide Gattungen florierten in Alexandreia (zumindest einige aus der sog. »Pleiade« trag. Dichter schrieben dort), doch wahrscheinlich waren viele Tragödien schon reine Buchdichtung (und weisen damit vielleicht schon den Weg zu → Seneca). Behandelt wurden traditionelle wie auch weniger konventionelle Themen einschl. der zeitgenössischen Gesch., doch in Inszenierung und Kostümierung unterschied sich die Trag. weiterhin von den anderen dramat. Formen und entfernte sich immer mehr von ihnen; auch in der Metrik kennzeichnet die Vermeidung der Auflösung im iambischen Trimeter die Trag. als der Umgangssprache fernstehend (so auch → Lykophrons ›Alexandra‹). Die Komödie breitete sich über Athen hinaus aus und wurde zu einem wichtigen Bestandteil hell. Kultur. Die Neue Komödie, zu deren drei größten Dichtern man → Menandros, → Diphilos und → Philemon zählte, behandelte das Privatleben wohlhabender Bürger und ihrer Abhängigen; sie war nicht mehr an das öffentl. Leben von Athen gebunden, wie es für die Alte Kom. der Fall gewesen war. Sie wurde fast ganz gesprochen, der → Chor spielte in dem Stück selbst keine Rolle mehr, sondern diente nur noch zur Teilung in fünf Akte. Der moralisierende Charakter der Neuen Kom. hat wahrscheinlich die populäre Ethik der hell. Zeit mitgeprägt.

Trag. wie Kom. beeinflußten andere poetische Formen, die nicht im strikten Sinne dramatisch waren. Lykophrons ›Alexandra‹ ist eine lange, an Priamos gerichtete Erzählung über Kassandras Prophezeiungen, bei Machons *Chreíai* handelt es sich um eine iambische Version der im 4. Jh. weitverbreiteten anekdotischen Literatur. Von bes. Bed. war die Trad. des volkstümlichen → Mimos; nur spärliche Pap.-Reste der »Drehbücher« dieser oft obszönen Darbietungen sind erhalten. Lit. Übernahmen dieser volkstümlichen Formen kann man bei → Theokritos (Eidyllien 2; 3; 14; 15) und in den choliambischen Mimiamben des → Hero(n)das sehen.

C. SATIRISCHE UND IAMBISCHE DICHTUNG

Die aggressiven Trad. des archa. Iambus und der att. Alten Kom. wurden in einer bemerkenswerten Bandbreite poetischer Formen fortgesetzt. Wie Herodas bezog sich auch → Kallimachos in seiner vermischten Sammlung von 13 iambischen und lyrischen *Íamboi* auf Hipponax als Autorität. → Timon machte sich in seinen gelehrten, hexametrischen *Sílloi* (›Schielende Verse‹) über Eifer und Ehrgeiz von Philosophen lustig. Spott über mächtige polit. Persönlichkeiten wird, abgesehen von → Sotades aus Maroneia, selten in formellen Versen zum Ausdruck gebracht. Der moralisierende Charakter der h.D.läßt sich auch in den »kynischen« *Melíamboi* des → Kerkidas von Megalopolis (kurzen lyrischen Gedichten, die Gier und Anmaßung anprangern) und den Choliamben des → Phoinix von Kolophon beobachten.

D. HEXAMETER UND ELEGISCHES DISTICHON

Die Dominanz des sog. Epos als metrischer Form (worunter sowohl der Hexameter als auch das elegische Distichon zu verstehen ist), gehört zu den augenfälligsten Merkmalen der hell. Lit. Das heroisch-monumentale Epos in homer. Trad. lebt fort, wenngleich es in seinen Formen und Inhalten (einschließlich der Konzeption des Heroentums) zumindest seit → Apollonios [2] Rhodios und vielleicht schon seit → Rhianos an erneuert wurde; über die myth. Epen einiger anderer, schwer datierbarer Autoren läßt sich jedoch nichts sagen, und genausowenig darf man einfach davon ausgehen, daß ihre Werke monumentale Dimensionen hatten. In hell. Zeit florierten das histor. bzw. myth.-histor. → Epos ebenso wie auch das enkomiastische Epos. Wie umfangreich die enkomiastischen »Epen« waren, ist schwierig abzuschätzen, doch sind die besser bekannten allesamt recht kurz und besitzen höchstens den Umfang archa. Hymnen (an deren Traditionen sie anknüpfen).

Die hell. Hexameterhymnen wie Kallimachos' Hymnen und Theokrit 22 weisen eine stärkere aitiologische Komponente auf als die »homer.« Hymnen, aber letztere hatten die Aitiologie mehr als jede andere Gattung der archa. Dichtung in den Vordergrund gestellt (→ Aitiologie); die starke mimetische Komponente, die vor allem Kall. h. 2, 5 und 6 auszeichnet, verwirklicht vielleicht in hexametr. Form eine Möglichkeit, die schon der lyrische → Hymnos und die anderen hieratischen Gattungen der Lyrik ausführlich realisiert hatten. Andere hell. Hymnen, die tatsächlich für sakrale Funktionen bestimmt waren, bewahren die lyrischen Metren der archa. hieratischen Hymnen (→ Aristonus [4] von Korinth, → Isyllos von Epidauros, Philodamos von Skarpheia). Mit dem Metrum experimentieren dagegen – ganz ausdrücklich (SH 310,3 und 677) – die Hymnen des → Philikos von Korkyra und des → Kastorion von Soloi.

Das didaktische Epos des Hell. kann zuweilen auch in hesiodeischer Tradition universalistische Ansprüche erheben (→ Aratos [4]), wählt aber gewöhnlich sehr technische Gegenstände, in denen der Verf. nicht unbedingt kompetent sein muß (meistens versifiziert er sogar bereits vorliegende Prosalehrbücher). Weitere Gedichte über Astronomie: → Aratos [4]; Paradoxographie: Philostephanos von Kyrene und Archelaos von Chersonesos; Geographie: Kallimachos d.J.; Fischfang: → Numenios von Herakleia, → Nikandros; Landwirtschaft und Bienenzucht: Nikandros; Medizin: Aratos, Heliodoros von Athen, Philon von Tarsos. Die metrische Innovation eines → Lehrgedichts in iambischen Trimetern scheint auf Apollodoros [7] von Athen (Chronographie) zurückzugehen und setzt sich bes. zwischen dem 2. und 1. Jh. v. Chr. in Werken der beschreibenden Geographie durch (Skymnos, Dionysios [26], Sohn des Kalliphon; Apollodoros).

Die myth. Kataloge in Hexametern gehen zumindest auf → Hesiodos (›Frauenkatalog‹) zurück, in elegischer Form hatte wenigstens Antimachos [3] (*Lýdē*) schon solche verfaßt. Die *Aítia* des Kallimachos wählen z.B. aus der vorausgehenden myth. Trad. (aus derjenigen der in Prosa schreibenden Lokalhistoriker des 4. Jh. weit mehr als aus derjenigen früherer Dichter) genau den Aspekt (die Aitiologie) und die Qualität (»kleine« Mythen) aus, die dem neuen ästhetischen Geschmack am ehesten entsprechen. → Hermesianax' Gedicht *Leóntion* und der Frauenkatalog des Nikainetos von Samos stellen myth. Liebesgeschichten in hesiodeischer Trad. dar – aber darüber hinaus auch, zumindest Hermesianax, Liebesgesch. von histor. Persönlichkeiten wie Sokrates; weitere Neuheiten sind die *Érōtes ē kaloí* (›Liebesgeschichten‹ oder ›Schöne Knaben‹) des → Phanokles und die *Ehoîoi* des Sostratos bzw. Sosikrates von Phanagoreia, die myth. Gesch. von homosexueller Liebe behandeln. Eine spezifische Form des Katalogs sind solche von *Araí* (»Flüchen«; → *defixiones*; vgl. Moiro, Pap. Brux. II,22; Kall. *Íbis*; Euphorion von Chalkis, *Poteriokléptēs*/›Becherdieb‹, *Chiliádes*).

Auch der → bukolischen Dichtung des → Theokritos liegt die Mentalität eines primitivistischen Eskapismus und einer Idealisierung des Landlebens zugrunde, die wahrscheinlich mit dem Alltagsleben in der neuen städtischen Wirklichkeit zu verbinden ist.

Das → Epyllion ist im Hinblick auf die iliadisch-odysseische Tradition des Epos eine Neuerung, hat aber in der ps.-hesiodeischen *Aspís* und den narrativen Kernen des hymnischen oder katalogischen Epos der Archaik Vorläufer.

→ Epos; Hellenismus; Katalogdichtung; Komödie; Lehrgedicht; Mäzenatentum; Satyrspiel; Tragödie

P. Bing, The Well-Read Muse: Present and Past in Callimachus and the Hellenistic Poets, 1988 · A. Cameron, Callimachus and his Critics, 1995 · G. Cambiano, L. Canfora, D. Lanza (Hrsg.), Lo spazio letterario della Grecia antica, 1.2, 1993 · B. Effe, Dichtung und Lehre: Unt. zur Typologie des ant. Lehrgedichts, 1977 · P.M. Fraser, Ptolemaic Alexandria, 1972 · R. Hunter, The New Comedy of Greece and Rome, 1985 · Ders., Theocritus and the Archaeology of Greek Poetry, 1996 · G.O. Hutchinson, Hellenistic Poetry, 1988 · R. Kassel, Die Abgrenzung des Hell. in der griech. Literaturgesch., 1987 · A. Körte, P. Händel, Die hell. Dichtung, [2]1960 · F. Susemihl, Gesch. der griech. Lit. in der Alexandrinerzeit, 1891–92 · G. Weber, Dichtung und höfische Ges., 1993 · U. von Wilamowitz-Moellendorff, Hell. Dichtung in der Zeit des Kallimachos, 1924 · K. Ziegler, Das hell. Epos, [2]1966 (ital. Übers. 1988, mit einem Überblick über die Testimonien zu den Epici minores) · G. Zanker, Realism in Alexandrian Poetry, 1987. M.FA. u. R.HU./Ü: T.H.

Hellenistische Staatenwelt

A. Historische Entwicklung
B. Zwischenstaatliche Beziehungen
C. Innerstaatliche Organisation

A. Historische Entwicklung

Die h.S. entstand aus dem Zerfall des Reiches → Alexandros' [4] d.Gr im östl. Mittelmeerraum und Vorderasien und durch die Imitation hell. Staats- und Verwaltungsformen durch einzelne Herrscher in Sizilien und Süditalien (→ Agathokles [2], → Hieron II.). Nach dem Tod des 32jähr. Alexander, der weder einen regierungsfähigen Erben noch eine feste Reichsverwaltung hinterließ, war die Einheit des Reiches gefährdet, da dessen Teile ausschließlich an die Person Alexanders gebunden waren (König der Makedonen, Führer des → Korinthischen Bundes, Großkönig der Perser, Pharao in Ägypten) und sich mit ihm eine neue Legitimation des hell. Königtums, gegründet auf Eroberung (»Speererwerb«), entwickelt hatte, die bald auch von seinen Generälen genutzt wurde. In den → Diadochenkriegen bildeten sich seit 305 v.Chr. selbständige königl. Dynastien in Ägypten (Ptolemaios), Thrakien und Kleinasien (Lysimachos) sowie in Nordsyrien und Babylonien (Seleukos) heraus, die nach dem Tod des Antigonos [1] in der Schlacht bei Ipsos (301 v.Chr.) bestätigt wurden und sich nach der Niederlage des Lysimachos (bei Kurupedion, 281) endgültig verfestigten. Nachdem sich in Makedonien nach chaotischen Jahrzehnten Antigonos [2] Gonatas 276 nach einem Abwehrsieg über die Kelten als König etablieren konnte, war die Aufteilung des Alexanderreiches im Kern abgeschlossen und blieb mit geringen Veränderungen etwa 200 Jahre erhalten:

a) Das Reich der Ptolemaier (Lagiden; → Ptolemaios) mit dem Kernland Ägypten (Zentrum: → Alexandreia) und umfangreichen (aber schwankenden) Außenbesitzungen in Kyrene, Koilesyrien und Palästina, Zypern, der Ägäis und dem westl. Kleinasien. Trotz starkem röm. Einfluß seit Beginn des 2. Jh. v.Chr. blieb das Reich auch nach Verlust der Außenbesitzungen selbständig, bis es nach dem Sieg des Octavian (→ Augustus) über Antonius [I 9] und Kleopatra 30 v.Chr. als »persönliche Provinz« des Kaisers in das röm. Reich eingegliedert wurde.

b) Das Reich der → Seleukiden mit dem Kernland Nordsyrien und Babylonien (mehrere Zentren: u.a. Antiocheia am Orontes, Sardes, Seleukeia am Tigris) mit stark schwankendem Umfang, der um 303 vom Ostrand des Mittelmeers bis nach Indien reichte, seit der Mitte des 3. Jh. durch Loslösung Baktriens, Erstarkung der Parther, Streit innerhalb der Dynastie und Kriege mit Ägypten und Rom ständig abnahm und seit 129 auf Nordsyrien beschränkt war; im Jahr 63 v.Chr. wurde es von Pompeius zur röm. Provinz Syria gemacht.

c) Das Reich der Antigoniden (→ Antigonos) im alten Kernland Makedonien (Zentrum: Pella) mit Thrakien, Thessalien und Teilen Griechenlands, das sich von Beginn an gegen die Einmischung der Ptolemaier und später Seleukiden in Griechenland zu wehren hatte. Durch eine zurückhaltende Politik gegenüber den auf Autonomie bedachten griech. Poleis, gepaart mit mil. Druck, der von den »Fußfesseln Griechenlands« Demetrias, Chalkis und Korinth ausging, gelang es den Antigoniden trotz der Expansionsversuche Spartas (→ Agis [4]) sowie des Achaiischen und des Aitolischen

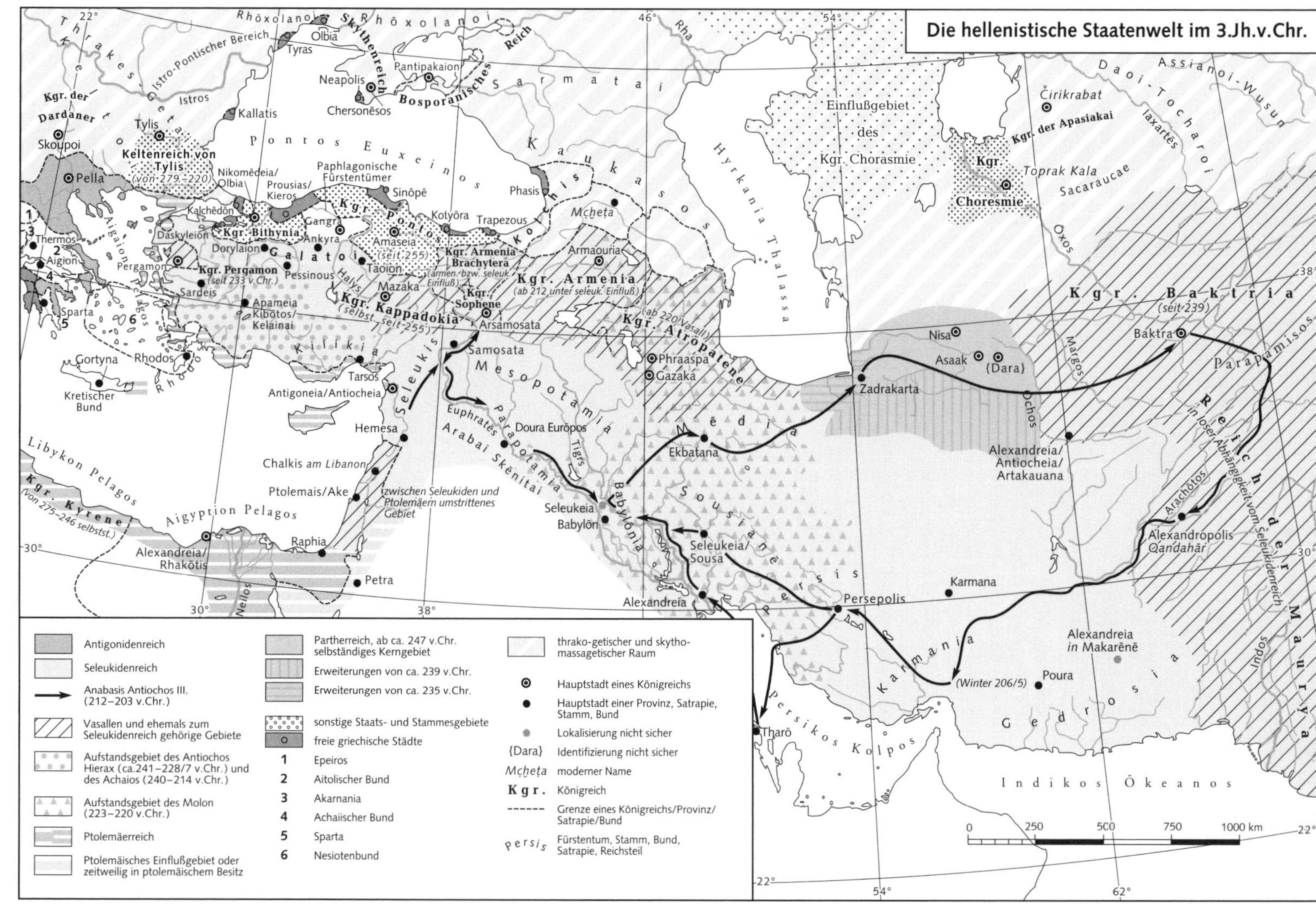
Die hellenistische Staatenwelt im 3.Jh.v.Chr.
Antigonidenreich
Seleukidenreich
Anabasis Antiochos III. (212–203 v.Chr.)
Vasallen und ehemals zum Seleukidenreich gehörige Gebiete
Aufstandsgebiet des Antiochos Hierax (ca.241–228/7 v.Chr.) und des Achaios (240–214 v.Chr.)
Aufstandsgebiet des Molon (223–220 v.Chr.)
Ptolemäerreich
Ptolemäisches Einflußgebiet oder zeitweilig in ptolemäischem Besitz
Partherreich, ab ca. 247 v.Chr. selbständiges Kerngebiet
Erweiterungen von ca. 239 v.Chr.
Erweiterungen von ca. 235 v.Chr.
sonstige Staats- und Stammesgebiete
freie griechische Städte
1 Epeiros
2 Aitolischer Bund
3 Akarnania
4 Achaiischer Bund
5 Sparta
6 Nesiotenbund
thrako-getischer und skytho-massagetischer Raum
Hauptstadt eines Königreichs
Hauptstadt einer Provinz, Satrapie, Stamm, Bund
Lokalisierung nicht sicher
{Dara} Identifizierung nicht sicher
Mc̣heṭa moderner Name
Kgr. Königreich
Grenze eines Königreichs/Provinz/Satrapie/Bund
persis Fürstentum, Stamm, Bund, Satrapie, Reichsteil
0 250 500 750 1000 km
Pontos Euxeinos
Hyrkania Thalassa
Persikos Kolpos
Indikos Ōkeanos
Aigyption Pelagos
Libykon Pelagos
Kgr. der Dardaner
Keltenreich von Tylis (von 279–220)
Skythenreich
Bosporanisches Reich
Kgr. Bithynia
Kgr. Pergamon (seit 233 v.Chr.)
Kgr. Pontos (seit 255)
Kgr. Kappadokia (selbst. seit 255)
Kgr. Armenia (ab 212 unter seleuk. Einfluß)
Kgr. Armenia Brachytera
Kgr. Sophene
Kgr. Atropatene (ab 220 Vasall)
Kgr. Baktria (seit 239)
Kgr. Kyrene (von 275–246 selbstst.)
Kgr. der Apasiakai
Kgr. Choresmie
Einflußgebiet des Kgr. Chorasmie
Reich der Maurya (in loser Abhängigkeit vom Seleukidenreich)
Galatoi
Mesopotamia
Parapotamia
Babylonia
Mēdia
Sousianē
Persis
Karmania
Gedrosia
Seleukis
Kilikia
Sarmatai
Kaukasos
Thrakes
Arabai Skēnitai
zwischen Seleukiden und Ptolemäern umstrittenes Gebiet
Paphlagonische Fürstentümer
Kretischer Bund
Pella
Alexandreia/Rhakōtis
Antigoneia/Antiocheia
Seleukeia
Babylōn
Ekbatana
Persepolis
Zadrakarta
Baktra
Alexandropolis Qandahār
Alexandreia/Antiocheia/Artakauana
Alexandreia in Makarēnē
(Winter 206/5)

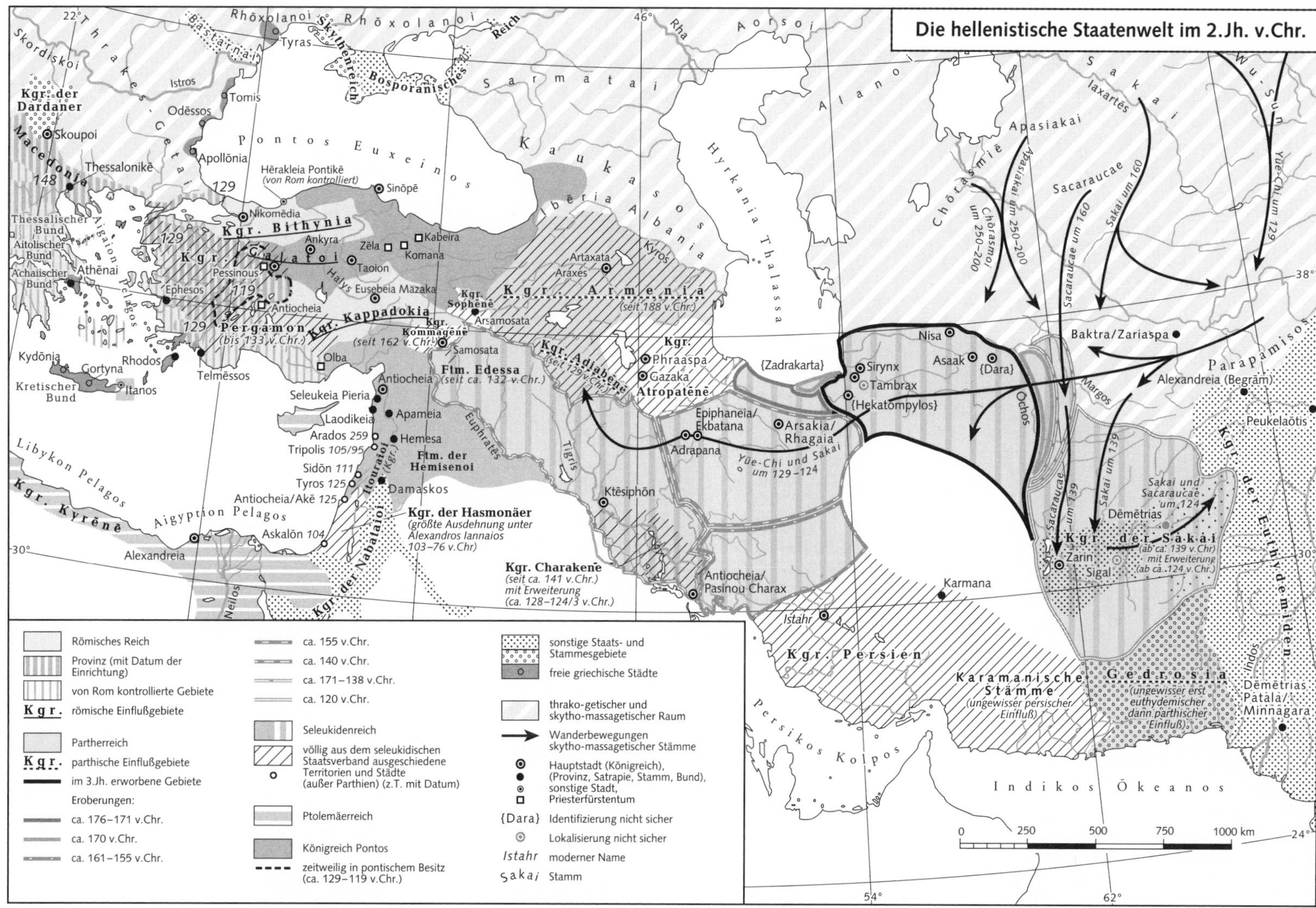
Die hellenistische Staatenwelt im 2.Jh. v.Chr.
Römisches Reich
Provinz (mit Datum der Einrichtung)
von Rom kontrollierte Gebiete
Kgr. römische Einflußgebiete
Partherreich
Kgr. parthische Einflußgebiete
im 3.Jh. erworbene Gebiete
Eroberungen:
ca. 176–171 v.Chr.
ca. 170 v.Chr.
ca. 161–155 v.Chr.
ca. 155 v.Chr.
ca. 140 v.Chr.
ca. 171–138 v.Chr.
ca. 120 v.Chr.
Seleukidenreich
völlig aus dem seleukidischen Staatsverband ausgeschiedene Territorien und Städte (außer Parthien) (z.T. mit Datum)
Ptolemäerreich
Königreich Pontos
zeitweilig in pontischem Besitz (ca. 129–119 v.Chr.)
sonstige Staats- und Stammesgebiete
freie griechische Städte
thrako-getischer und skytho-massagetischer Raum
Wanderbewegungen skytho-massagetischer Stämme
Hauptstadt (Königreich), (Provinz, Satrapie, Stamm, Bund), sonstige Stadt, Priesterfürstentum
{Dara} Identifizierung nicht sicher
Lokalisierung nicht sicher
Istahr moderner Name
Sakai Stamm

Bundes ihr Reich zu halten, bis nach drei Makedonischen Kriegen das Königtum von den Römern 168 v. Chr. aufgelöst (→ Perseus) und das Territorium 148 zur röm. Provinz Macedonia wurde.

d) Neben diesen drei großen Monarchien entstanden noch im 3. Jh., hauptsächlich auf Kosten der Seleukiden, zahlreiche z. T. kurzlebige personale Herrschaften (Antiochos Hierax und Achaios [5] in Kleinasien; Molon im Iran), aber auch dauerhafte Dynastien wie in Bithynien (Zipoites, seit 297), dem Pontos (Mithradates, seit 297/281) oder Kappadokien (Ariarathes, seit ca. 255). Die bedeutendste dieser Dynastien wurde die der Attaliden von Pergamon, nachdem → Attalos [4] I. im Bruderkrieg zwischen Seleukos II. und Antiochos Hierax nach einem Sieg über die mit Hierax verbündeten Galater ca. 241 den Königstitel annahm und sein Gebiet bis zum Taurus ausdehnte. Die guten Beziehungen zu Rom machten nach territorialen Rückschlägen das Attalidenreich seit 188 v. Chr. (Friede von Apameia) zur größten Macht in Kleinasien, bis Attalos III. es 133 v. Chr. testamentarisch den Römern vermachte.

B. Zwischenstaatliche Beziehungen

Die Beziehungen zw. den großen hell. Staaten wurden durch die von Alexander geprägte spezifische Legitimation der hell. Monarchie bestimmt (→ Basileus E.), die sich auf persönl. (mil. und organisatorische) Leistung gründete und deshalb den ständigen Nachweis des Erfolgs benötigte. Trotz dynastischer Ehen zwischen den Königshäusern, einzelner Verträge und territorialer Abkommen entstand kein Staaten-»System« mit staatsrechtl. Beziehungen. Der einzelne Monarch war vielmehr gezwungen, ständig zu expandieren, letztlich mit dem Ziel der Universalmonarchie. Der Anschein der Stabilität der h. S. im 3. Jh. ergab sich lediglich aus der Unfähigkeit des einzelnen Herrschers, sich gegen die übrigen durchzusetzen. Dieser Expansionsdrang steht bereits hinter dem Versuch des Lysimachos, nach Makedonien auszugreifen, und den gegen die Ptolemaier gerichteten Bündnissen des Seleukiden Antiochos [2] I. mit Antigonos Gonatas und Magas von Kyrene. Auch die weit über Syrien hinausgreifenden »Syrischen Kriege« (280–253) des Ptolemaios II. gegen die Seleukiden und seine »Befreiungs«-Politik in Griechenland, die gegen Antigonos zielte (→ Chremonideischer Krieg), tragen ähnliche hegemoniale Züge wie der Asienfeldzug des Ptolemaios III. (246/45) während des »Laodike-Krieges« (3. Syr. Krieg) und v. a. die »Anabasis« des Antiochos [5] III. in den östl. Iran, seine Arrondierungsversuche in Koilesyrien, Kleinasien und Thrakien und sein Eingreifen in Griechenland. Letzteres hatte das massive Eingreifen Roms in die h. S. und damit das faktische Ende einer selbständigen Politik der hell. Monarchien zur Folge.

C. Innerstaatliche Organisation

Da die polit. und ethnische Vielfalt des Alexanderreiches in der h. S. fortlebte, ergaben sich sehr unterschiedliche Verwaltungs- und Herrschaftsaufgaben. Im Reich der Antigoniden mit seiner recht homogenen Bevölkerung hatte der König rudimentäre traditionelle Gewohnheitsrechte des Volkes bzw. des Heeres und des Adels bei der Führung des Staates zu respektieren und erreichte deshalb niemals denselben Grad an Macht wie die Ptolemaier, Seleukiden und Attaliden, deren Wort Gesetz war. In deren Fall verkörperte der König den Staat, der als seine »Sache« (*ta prágmata*) galt. Da mit dem Tod Alexanders auch die Idee erlosch, einheimische Kräfte an der Staatsführung zu beteiligen, bildete sich in Asien und Äg. eine dünne Oberschicht von Makedonen und Griechen, die das Vertrauen des Königs genossen (→ Hof; Hoftitel; Hellenisierung). Diese funktionale Elite wurde – schon aus Gründen der sprachl. Verständigung mit den Indigenen – dem bestehenden Verwaltungssystem auf der unteren Ebene aufgepropft (bes. gut sichtbar in Äg., aber auch bei Seleukiden und Attaliden bezeugt), so daß gerade die mit der Eintreibung von neuen Steuern und traditionellen Abgaben verbundenen Aufgaben von Einheimischen erledigt wurden.

Obwohl die hell. Könige das Land als ihren Privatbesitz betrachteten und es (in der Regel) an die ältesten Söhne weitergaben, griffen sie wenig in bestehende Sozial- und Besitzstrukturen ein und betrieben keine zielgerichtete Politik der → Hellenisierung. Sie nutzten bei der Vergabe von Ländereien an hohe Funktionäre, bei der Ansiedlung von Kleruchenbauern (in Ägypten) oder der Neugründung von Städten (bei den Seleukiden) altes Domanialland oder neu erschlossene Gebiete und respektierten auch die Rechte der Tempel und Tempelstaaten. Erst als im 2. Jh. v. Chr. finanzielle Erfordernisse zum Zugriff auf Tempelschätze führten, kam es zu erheblichen Spannungen, die zur Minderung der königl. Autorität und damit zur inneren Schwächung der Monarchien beitrugen. Bes. Beziehungen bestanden zu den griech. Städten auf dem eigenen Territorium und außerhalb, da sie das Reservoir für die oberste Verwaltungsebene und die Rekrutierungsbasis für die in allen hell. Monarchien verwendeten Söldnerheere bildeten.

Als intakte Selbstverwaltungskörper erfüllten die Poleis subsidiäre Verwaltungsaufgaben, v. a. im Seleukidenreich, das seine Politik der Neugründung von Städten mit griech. Siedlern nicht nur aus mil. Motiven betrieb. Die Könige achteten die Autonomie der Städte, wirkten als Wohltäter (→ Euergetes) und wurden dafür in den kultischen Rang einer von mächtigen Göttern bes. geschützten Person erhoben. Die tatsächl. Machtverhältnisse zeigten sich nur im Konfliktfall. Gefördert wurde dieser »Ausgleich« zwischen Monarchie und Polis durch eine zunehmende »Plutokratisierung« der Poleis, deren reichste Bürger die höchsten städt. Ämter übernahmen und häufig als Vertraute der Könige Privilegien für »ihre« Stadt erreichen konnten. Mit einem gewissen Recht kann man von einer zweiten Blüte der Polis sprechen; sie überlebte den Niedergang der h. S. und spielte bis in die Spätant. eine bed. Rolle in Politik, Wirtschaft und Kultur.

→ Diadochen; Hellenisierung; Hellenismus

Lit.: → Hellenismus; Hellenisierung I. W. ED.

KARTEN-LIT.: H. WALDMANN, Die hell. Staatenwelt im 3. Jh. v. Chr., TAVO B V 3, 1983 • Ders., Die hell. Staatenwelt im 2. Jh. v. Chr., TAVO B V 4, 1985.

Hellenotamiai (ἑλληνοταμίαι). Den Titel H. (»Schatzmeister der Griechen«) tragen die Schatzmeister des → Attisch-Delischen Seebunds. Die von ihnen verwaltete Kasse befand sich ursprünglich in Delos, wurde aber wahrscheinlich im J. 454/3 v. Chr. nach Athen verlegt (Thuk. 1,96,2; Plut. Aristeides 25,3; Perikles 12,1; vgl. IG I³ 259 = ATL Liste 1); denn seit 454/3 zählten sich die jährlich gewählten Kollegien in fortlaufender Reihe. Die H. waren jedoch von Anfang an Athener, wurden von Athen bestellt (Thuk. ebd., vgl. [1. 44 f., 235–237]) und bildeten ein Zehner-Gremium, jeweils ein Mitglied aus je einer Phyle. Sie erhielten die Beiträge von den Bündnern und zahlten seit 453 1/60 des Beitrags jedes Staates als *aparchḗ* (»Erstling«) in den Schatz der Athena ein. Auf Weisung der Volksversammlung führten sie Zahlungen aus, hauptsächlich an die Generale für die Kriegsführung, zuweilen auch für andere Zwecke, etwa die Bauten auf der Akropolis (Parthenon: IG I³ 439; Propyläen: IG I³ 465 = ML 60). 411 v. Chr. oder kurz davor erhielt ein erweitertes Gremium von 20 H. die Verantwortung sowohl für die Kasse des Sebundes als auch für die der Polis Athen (»zukünftige« Verfassung bei Ps.-Aristot. Ath. pol. 30,2; IG I³ 375 = ML 84; vgl. [3. 391–393]).

1 R. MEIGGS, The Athenian Empire, 1972 2 ATL; jüngste Edition der Listen: IG I³ 259–290 3 RHODES 4 A. G. WOODHEAD, The Institution of the Hellenotamiae, in: JHS 79, 1959, 149–152. P. J. R.

Hellespontos (Ἑλλήσποντος, h. Çanakkale Boğazı, dt. Dardanellen). Die im Diluvium aus einem Flußtal entstandene Meeresstraße zw. Propontis im Norden und → Aigaion Pelagos (Ägäis) im Süden, der thrak. Chersonnesos [1] im Westen (Europa) und der Troas im Osten (Asien; vgl. Plin. nat. 4,49), ca. 65 km lang, zw. 1,2 (in der Höhe von Sestos und Abydos [1]) und 7,5 km breit, zw. 57 und 103 m tief. Wie im → Bosporos [1] fließt eine starke (maximal 5 Seemeilen/h; vgl. Hom. Il. 2,845; 12,30; Hesych. s. v. Ἑ.; Aristot. meteor. 2,8; Avien. 3,466), kühle (Theophr. Perí ichthýōn 5; Athen. 7,317 f.) Oberflächenströmung aus der Propontis südwestwärts und eine wärmere salzhaltigere Bodenströmung nordostwärts. In den Windungen und Buchten des H. bilden sich verschiedentlich Oberflächengegenströmungen, die das Segeln und Rudern nordostwärts erleichterten [1. 69 f.]. Der Hellespontias, ein im Sommer oft wochenlang wehender kalter Wind aus ONO (vgl. Hdt. 7,188; Aristot. meteor. 2,6,364b 19; Plin. nat. 2,121), bereitete der Seefahrt zusätzlich zu den strömungsbedingten Schwierigkeiten (vgl. Pol. 16,29,9) viele Probleme. H. bezeichnete urspr. nicht ausschließlich die Meerenge wie bei späteren Autoren (wie Pol. 16,29; Strab. 1,2,39; Plin. nat. 2,202; 205; 4,75), sondern auch angrenzende Teile der Propontis und der Ägäis (vgl. Hdt. 6,33; Thuk. 2,9; Xen. hell. 6,8,31 [2. 324]). Zum Fischreichtum des H. vgl. Hom. Il. 9,360; Athen. 1,9d; 3,105a; d; 4,157b; Avien. 3,34; 717. Menekrates von Elaia, ein Schüler des Xenokrates, hat um 300 v. Chr. dem H. eine Monographie gewidmet (*Períodos Hellespontiakḗ*, vgl. Strab. 12,3,22; FHG 2,342).

Die mythische Etym. führte den Namen H. auf Helle, die Tochter des Athamas, zurück, die im H. den Tod gefunden haben soll (vgl. die Sage vom goldenen Vlies: Pind. fr. 51; 189; Aisch. Pers. 68; Eur. Med. 1284). Hier wurde auch der Mythos von Hero und Leandros lokalisiert (Ov. epist. 17 f.).

Der H. stellte einen bed. Verkehrsknotenpunkt dar, der sowohl trennend als auch verbindend wirkte – die Schiffahrtsroute zw. Schwarzem Meer und Ägäis war etwa für die Versorgung der Athener mit Getreide von der Krim lebenswichtig; sie ließ sich jedoch leicht sperren (vgl. Pol. 4,50,6; 27,7,5). Wer den H. in westöstl. bzw. ostwestl. Richtung passieren wollte, mußte sich mit der Tiefe und den Strömungen des Gewässers, aber möglicherweise auch mit Gegnern auseinandersetzen, die auf dem gegenüberliegenden Ufer den Übergang zu verhindern suchten. Den H. überschritt beispielsweise → Dareios [1] I. im Zusammenhang mit seinem Skythenfeldzug 513/2 v. Chr. (Hdt. 4,85; 87), desgleichen → Xerxes 480 v. Chr. (Hdt. 7,33–36; 54–57), → Alexandros [4] d. Gr. im Frühjahr 334 v. Chr. von Elaion nach Ilion (Arr. an. 1,11,6) und die beiden Scipiones 190 v. Chr. (Liv. 37,33,4). Zur Sicherung dieser Seefahrtsroute legten im 8./7. Jh. v. Chr. Äoler/→ Aioleis (Sestos, Assos) und → Ioner (Kyzikos, Lampsakos, Abydos, Elaius [1]) an beiden Ufern Kolonien an.

1 W.-D. HÜTTEROTH, Türkei, 1982 2 W. SIEGLIN, Die Ausdehnung des Hellespontes bei den ant. Geographen, in: FS H. Kiepert, 1898, 323–331.

G. JACHMANN, H. als geogr. Terminus, in: Athenaeum 33, 1955, 93–111 • G. STRASBURGER, s. v. H., Lex. zur frühgriech. Gesch., 1984, 169 f. E. O.

Hellopia (Ἑλλοπία) hießen in früharch. Zeit das Gebiet um → Dodona und das h. Ioannina (Hes. cat. 240), später ein Landstrich in Nord-Euboia (Hdt. 8,23,2; Strab. 10,1,3 f.), eine Stadt der → Dolopes und eine Flur bei Thespiai in → Boiotia (Steph. Byz. s. v. Ἑ.); die aitol. Stadt Hellopion (Pol. 11,7,4) ist vielleicht mit H. der Dolopes gleichzusetzen. Diese Namen zeugen von den Wohnsitzen und Wanderungen der Hellopes, eines verschollenen, nur noch von Plin. nat. 4,2 wohl aufgrund gelehrter Rekonstruktion unter den Völkern von → Epeiros gen. Stammes. F. GSCH.

Hellotis (Ἑλλωτίς). Epiklese der → Athena in Marathon und Korinth, sowie Name einer mit → Europe [2] identifizierten Göttin in Kreta. In Marathon sind Heiligtum (Athen. 15,22,678b; schol. Pind. O. 13,56ad) und Opfer (LSCG 20) belegt; der Beiname wird von einem lokalen Sumpf (griech. *hélos*) abgeleitet. In Korinth wird für Athena H. das Fest der Hellotia mit einem Agon gefeiert (Pind. O. 13,40, nach dem schol. ad loc. ein Fackellauf der jungen Männer); das Aition leitet den Kult entweder davon ab, daß Athena hier den Pegasos einfängt (griech. *heleín*) und aufzäumt – geläufiger als Aition für den korinthischen Kult der Athena Chalinitis (von griech. *chálinos*, »Zaum«) – oder daß das Mädchen H. mit ihrer Schwester (Chryse oder Eurytione) im Tempel der Athena im Feuer umkommt, entweder weil beide Selbstmord begehen oder weil der Tempel von den Herakliden (→ Herakleidai) bei der Eroberung der Peloponnes in Brand gesteckt wird; in beiden Fällen wird das Fest als Sühneritual gestiftet (schol. Pind. O. 13,56).

Auf Kreta – namentlich genannt ist Gortyn, das urspr. H. hieß (Steph. Byz. s.v. Gortys) – ist H. auch Name eines großen Kranzes aus Myrtenzweigen, der in der Prozession der Hellotia mitgeführt wird und in dem sich angeblich die Gebeine der Europe befanden (Seleukos bei Athen. 15,678ab); wohl deswegen gilt H. als alter Name der Europe (Etym. m. s.v. H.). Auch hier sind (wie in Korinth) Fest und Gottheit mit dem Tod einer jungen Frau verbunden; die Verbindung erinnert bes. an Kult und Mythos von → Ariadne.

NILSSON, Feste, 94–96 • P. STENGEL, s.v. Hellotia, RE 8, 197 • F. WEICKER, s.v. H., RE 8, 197f. • W. BURKERT, Homo necans, 1972. F.G.

Hellusii. Bei Tac. Germ. 46,4 Name eines Fabelvolkes mit menschlichem Antlitz und tiergestaltigem Körper. Eine Etym., die auf einen Tiernamen zurückgeht, liegt somit nahe; vorgeschlagen wurde eine german. Entsprechung zu griech. ἐλλός, armen. *eln*, litau. *élnis* »Hirsch(kalb)« [1. 534–537]. Ob dieses Fabelvolk von skandinavischen Völkern oder eher von Seehunden mit ihrem menschenähnlichen Antlitz kündet, sei dahingestellt [1. 537]. Sicher nicht in Verbindung sind sie zu bringen mit den Helisii, einem Stammesteil der Lugier (Tac. Germ. 43,2).

1 R. MUCH, Die Germania des Tacitus, 3 1967. JO.S.

Helm A. ALLGEMEINES B. FRÜHE BELEGE
C. ZYPERN UND DAS HISTORISCHE GRIECHENLAND
D. ITALIEN UND ROM
E. KELTISCH-GERMANISCHER BEREICH

A. ALLGEMEINES

Helme schützen und imponieren. Ihre Gestaltung ging daher meist über eine rein waffentechnische Zweckform (→ Bewaffnung) hinaus. Individueller Schmuck diente als Rangabzeichen, Standardschmuck als Zeichen kollektiver Macht. Die Repräsentation trat in Paradeprunkhelmen als ausschließlicher Aspekt hervor, ebenfalls in als Grabbeigaben verwendeten Nachbildungen aus Ton [1]. Zeitlos war die Ledermütze (z.B. spätröm. [2. K 120, 121]); davon geben die Worte κυνέη (*kynéē*) und *galea* (beide mit der Bed. »Hundsfell«) Zeugnis. Die Schutzfunktion wurde mit aufgehefteten Plättchen verstärkt, wie z.B. bei dem homer. Eberzahnhelm. Scheibenförmige Appliken (φάλοι, *pháloi*) sind aus Homer und von Statuetten der geom. Zeit bekannt [3]. Die gängigsten anderen griech. Bezeichnungen für H. sind κράνος (*krános*), περικεφαλαία (*perikephalaía*), πήληξ (*pḗlēx*).

Die Schutzwirkung beruht auf elastischer oder plastischer Verformung, sei es der Schale, der Polsterung oder der tragenden Verspannung. Einige ital. H. zeigen, daß das Futter an der Kalotte anliegend befestigt war [4. Abb. 3 und 4]; auf der Sosiasschale (Berlin, SM) hat der verwundete Patroklos dagegen seinen H. abgesetzt, aber noch eine Lederkappe auf. Bei anliegenden Rüstungen konnte das Futter Schläge dämpfen (Beinschienenfutter aus Schwamm: Aristot. hist. an. 548b 1); besseren Schutz gaben eingespannte Futter mit einem Abstand von der Helmschale, so daß Schläge nur indirekt einwirken konnten. Ein zweischalig gefertigter H. läßt die Umsetzung dieses Prinzips in Metall erkennen [4. 240, Abb. 18]. Auch verengte Helmränder zeigen, daß die Schale einen schützenden Abstand vom Kopf hielt. Entscheidend waren auch die Eigenschaften der Helmschale; durch Treiben versprödetes, nicht nachgeglühtes Blech leistet geringeren Bruchwiderstand als weichgeglühtes, das mit seiner Zähigkeit größere Energie absorbieren kann, bevor es birst [5]. An einigen H. und Panzern des 5. und 4. Jh. v. Chr. aus It. konnte die Formung der Werkstücke durch Guß, nicht durch Treibarbeit nachgewiesen werden [6].

B. FRÜHE BELEGE

Die ältesten H. im Orient sind nur aus bildlichen Darstellungen bekannt [7]. In Griechenland lassen die meist ebenfalls aus bildlichen Darstellungen bekannten H. der minoischen und myk. Epoche oriental. Einflüsse erkennen. Es handelt sich um die sog. Pickel- und Spitzhelme und die charakteristischen kamm- und raupenförmigen Büsche [2. 11 ff.; 8]. Zahlreiche neuassyr. und urartäische H. sind durch Königsinschr. datiert; sie bestehen meist aus Br., gelegentlich auch aus Eisen [9]. Ihr Schmuck wurde in Griechenland bewundert [10]. In Ägypten erscheinen H. erst seit der Amarna-Zeit als Ausrüstung von fremden Söldnern [11].

C. ZYPERN UND DAS HISTORISCHE GRIECHENLAND

Die Formen zyprischer H. nehmen eine Mittelstellung ein; oriental. Einfluß zeigen die spitzen, von Knäufen bekrönten Kalotten, ostgriech. dagegen die Wangenklappenformen [2. 27]. Die griech. H., die frühesten seit etwa der Mitte des 8. Jh. v. Chr., sind uns als Fundstücke und aus bildlichen Darstellungen bekannt. Verschiedenen Typen ist eine Entwicklung von stereometrischer zu organischer Gestaltung gemeinsam. Helmbuschformen und getriebene, ziselierte oder applizierte Dekore sind nicht mit bestimmten Helmtypen verbunden, sondern frei kombiniert. Von den Helmformen des 8. Jh. v. Chr. lassen sich der Kegelhelm und der illyr. H. mit runder Kalotte und rechteckigem Gesichtsausschnitt in den Zusammenhang mit oriental.

Altägäis und Alter Orient 1 Mykenischer Eberzahnhelm, 2 Orientalischer Spitzhelm, 3 Orientalischer Raupenhelm, 4 Zyprischer Helm,
Griechenland 5 Geometrischer Kegelhelm, 6 Illyrischer Helm, 7 Korinthischer Helm (um 700 v.Chr.), 8 Korinthischer Helm (um 600 v.Chr.), 9 Korinthischer Helm (um 500 v.Chr.), 10 Chalkidischer Helm, 11 Pilostyp, 12 Attischer Helm, 13 Phrygischer Helm,
Etrusker und Italiker 14 Kammhelm, 15 Krempenhelm, 16 Helm mit Stirnkehle und Ohrausschnitten,
Römisches Reich 17 Typ Hagenau, 18 Typ Weisenau, 19 Gesichtshelm, 20 Gladiatorenhelm.

Vorbildern stellen. Letzterer kam wohl in der Peloponnes auf und fand in Illyrien und Thrakien besondere Verbreitung [2. 42 ff.].

Eigenständig ist der korinth. H. (Hdt. 4,180), der den Kopf bis auf die Augenöffnungen und Schlitze zw. Nasenschutz und Wangenklappen umschließt. Die ältesten Darstellungen und Beispiele stammen aus der Zeit von etwa 730–700 v. Chr. Die sog. chalkidischen [12] und att. H. unterscheiden sich von den korinth. v. a. durch die Formen des Visiers und der Wangenklappen; vom 5. Jh. v. Chr. an gewannen andere Helmformen, z. B. in Form von phrygischen oder spitzen Mützen, an Bed.; der Nackenschutz wurde wichtiger. Nicht sicher identifiziert ist der böotische H. (κράνος βοιωτιουργές, Xen.

hipp. 12,3). Das bevorzugte Material zur Anfertigung von H. war Br., zu den wenigen erh. Beispielen aus Eisen gehört der H. aus dem Königsgrab von Vergina.

D. Italien und Rom

Die villanovazeitlichen sog. »Kammhelme« (9. Jh. v. Chr.) [2. 195 ff.] zeigen Verbindungen zur mitteleurop. Urnenfelderkultur. Für das 7. bis 5. Jh. v. Chr. sind hutförmige Helme mit Krempe charakteristisch [2. 222 ff.]. Deren bekannteste Form ist der »Negauer Typ«, gen. nach dem Fundort in Slowenien. Dort und im mittleren Alpengebiet hielten sich lokale Trad. dieser Helmform bis in das 1. Jh. v. Chr. Verwandt sind die H. des 5. und 4. Jh. v. Chr. mit Stirnkehle, Ohrenausschnitten und größerer Kehle als Nackenschutz, die stärkeren griech. Einfluß erkennen lassen.

Vom 4. bis 1. Jh. herrschten die konischen H. mit Scheitelknauf und schmalem Nackenschutz bei den Römern, Etruskern und Italikern vor. Die Ausrüstung der kaiserzeitlichen Truppen [2. 293 ff.] verwendete H. der ital. (Typ Hagenau) und der kelt. (Typ Weisenau) Trad., daneben treten auch Formen aus dem östl. Mittelmeerraum auf. Kennzeichnende Merkmale sind runde Kalotten, betonter Nackenschutz, angehängte Wangenklappen und Stirnbügel. Die Kalotten sind glatt oder tragen einen Knauf, eine Kammschiene oder Federtülle. Parade-Gesichtshelme mit reichem bildlichen Schmuck dienten für Kampfspiele [2. 327 ff.]; ihr vornehmer Charakter unterscheidet sie von den Gladiatorenhelmen, die mit bizarren Visierformen ganz auf Wirkung in der Arena berechnet sind [2. 365 ff.].

1 O.-H. Frey, Ein tönerner Kammhelm aus Populonia. Überlegungen zur Verbreitung früher H. in It., in: GS J. Driehaus, 1990, 225–235 2 A. Bottini u. a., Ant. Helme. Slg. Lipperheide und andere Bestände des Antikenmus. Berlin, 1988 (Lit.) 3 A. Lebessi, Zum Phalos des homer. H., MDAI(A) 107, 1992, 1–10 4 M. Egg, Ital. H. Stud. zu den ältereisenzeitlichen H. Italiens und der Alpen, 1986 5 P. H. Blyth, Metallurgy of Bronze Armour, in: Πρακτικὰ τοῦ XII διεθνοῦς συνεδρίου ἀρχαιολογίας, Kongr. Athen 1983, 1988, Vol. 3, 293–296 6 H. Born, Ant. Herstellungstechniken. Gegossene Brustpanzer und H. aus It., in: Acta praehistorica et archaeologica 21, 1989, 989–1013 7 P. Calmeyer, s. v. H., RLA 4, 313–316 8 J. Borchardt, Helme, in: H. G. Buchholz, J. Wiesner (Hrsg.), Kriegswesen 1, (ArchHom, E 1), 1977, 57–74 9 T. Dezsö, Assyrian Iron Helmets from Nimrud now in the Britisch Museum, in: Iraq 53, 1991, 105–126, Taf. 16–20 10 S.-G. Gröschel, Der goldene H. der Athena (Ilias 5,743/4), in: AMI 19, 1986 (1988), 43–78 11 R. Krauss, s. v. H., LÄ 2, 1114 f. 12 E. Kunze, Chalkidische H., Olympiaber. 9, 1994, 29 ff.

M. Feugere, Casques antiques. Les visage de la guerre de Mycènes à la fin de l'Empire romain, 1994. MI. MA.

E. Keltisch-germanischer Bereich

Von der späten Brz. bis ans Ende der Eisenzeit (um Christi Geburt) spielt der H. im arch. Fundgut eine bedeutsame Rolle. Meist sind es Blech-H. bzw. erhaltene Metallteile von H., die bevorzugt repräsentative Prunkobjekte sind und häufig Zusammenhänge mit mediterranen H. aufweisen.

Die Bronze-H. der späten Brz. (→ Urnenfelder-Kultur 13.–8. Jh. v. Chr.) sind unterschiedlich geformt (Kamm-H., Hörner-H., Kappen-H. usw.) und z. T. mit beweglichen Wangenklappen versehen. Sie stammen häufig als Weihungen aus Flüssen und Mooren. In der kelt. → Hallstatt-Kultur (8.–5. Jh. v. Chr.) sind die H. (Doppelkamm-H., Schüssel-H., Negauer-H. usw.) Beigaben reich ausgestatteter Kriegergräber des östl. Hallstattbereiches. H.-bewehrte Krieger sind auch auf den toreutischen Arbeiten des »Situlenkreises« (→ Situla) im ostalpinen und oberital. Raum dargestellt.

In der kelt. → Latène-Kultur (5.–1. Jh. v. Chr.) sind auch eiserne H. bekannt; diese und auch die Br.-H. sind oft reich verziert mit Aufsätzen (Vogelfigur in Ciumeşti/Rumänien) oder Vergoldungen wie an Prunk-H. in Frankreich.

In der german. Kultur der Jh. um Christi Geburt ist der H. arch. kaum belegt, und erst wieder in der Völkerwanderungszeit (5.–7. Jh. n. Chr.) tauchen mehrfach reich verzierte Prunk-H. (Spangen-H.) verstreut in Europa auf, die letztlich aus spätröm.-byz. Werkstätten stammen.

→ Germanische Archäologie; Keltische Archäologie; Toreutik

K. Böhner, Die früh-ma. Spangen-H. und die nordischen H. der Vendelzeit, in: JRGZ 41, 1994 (1996), 471–549 • H. Born, L. D. Nebelsick, Ein brn. Prunk-H. der Hallstattzeit, 1991 • A. Bottini u. a., Ant. Helme. Slg. Lipperheide und andere Bestände des Antikenmus. Berlin, 1988, 181–364 • H. Hencken, The Earliest European Helmets, 1971 • M. Rusu, Das kelt. Fürstengrab von Ciumeşti in Rumänien, in: BRGK 50, 1969 (1971), 267–300 • P. Schauer, Urnenfelderzeitl. H.-Formen und ihre Vorbilder, in: Fund-Ber. Hessen 19/20, 1979/80, 521–543. V. P.

Heloris (Ἕλωρις). Syrakusier, enger Vertrauter, vielleicht sogar Adoptivvater des älteren → Dionysios [1] (Diod. 14,8,5). Während eines Aufstandes der Syrakusier gegen den Tyrannen 404/3 v. Chr. tat er nach Diodor (a.O.) den bis in die Spätantike zitierten Ausspruch: ›Ein schönes Leichentuch ist die Tyrannis‹ (*kalón entáphión estin hē tyrannís*). Später aus unbekannten Gründen verbannt, kämpfte er 394 in Rhegion gegen Dionysios, belagerte 393 vergeblich Messana und verteidigte 392 Rhegion erfolgreich gegen den Tyrannen (Diod. 14,87,1 f.; 90,4 f.). 388 fiel er als Feldherr des Italiotenbundes im Kampf gegen Dionysios [1] I. mit der Vorhut seines Heeres am Elleporos (Diod. 14,103,5–104,3).

H. Berve, Die Tyrannis bei den Griechen, 1, 1967, 222, 226, 234. K. MEI.

Heloros (Ἕλωρος).

[1] Sohn des Flußgottes Istros und Bruder des Aktaios; als Bundesgenosse des Troers → Telephos fällt er im Kampf der Myser gegen die Achaier (Philostr. Heroicus 23,13 f.,157).

A. Bettini, s. v. Aktaios II, LIMC 1.1, 470 f. J. S.-A.

[2] Fluß im östl. Sizilien, h. Tellaro. Er entspringt bei Palazzolo und mündet 20 km nördl. der Südspitze der Insel ins *mare Ionium*. Oft erwähnt wegen der Schlacht, in der → Hippokrates [4] 493/2 v. Chr. dort Syrakusai besiegte (Hdt. 7,154), und wegen dem verhängnisvollen Rückzugsweg der Athener 413 v. Chr. (sog. Ἑλωρινὴ ὁδός, *Helōrinḗ hodós*, Thuk. 6,66,3; 6,70,4; 7,80,5). GI. F.

[3] Städtchen auf Sizilien an der Mündung des gleichnamigen Flusses (Skyl. 13; Plin. nat. 32,16), im Friedensvertrag von 263 v. Chr. von den Römern Hieron II. zugesprochen (Diod. 23,4,1), 214 von Marcellus erobert (Liv. 24,35,1), von Verres ausgeplündert (Cic. Verr. 2,3,103; 129; 4,59; 5,90f.). Der Ort war schon seit dem 8. Jh. v. Chr. besiedelt. Aus archa. bis hell. Zeit stammen: Befestigungen, Agora (?) mit Portiken, Straßen, Wohnhäuser; Koreion außerhalb der Stadt, Asklepieion (?), Demeterheiligtum, Theater (4. Jh. v. Chr.). Aus byz. Zeit: Basilica. Ca. 1 km nördl. der Stadt befindet sich eine gigantische hell. Grabanlage (»La Pizzuta«), 2,5 km südwestl. eine Peristylvilla aus der späten Kaiserzeit mit polychromen Fußbodenmosaiken.

G. Voza, M. T. Lanza, s. v. Eloro, EAA² 3, 1995, 462f. • R. J. Wilson, Sicily under the Roman Empire, 1990.

GI. F./Ü: V. S.

Helos (Ἕλος, »Sumpf, Sumpfland«).

[1] Stadt im Herrschaftsbereich → Nestors (Hom. Il. 2,594); die geogr. Lage ist bereits in der Ant. umstritten (Strab. 8,3,25).

B. Mader, s. v. H., LFE. J. S.-A.

[2] Nicht lokalisierter Ort in der östl. Mündungsebene des → Eurotas (Pol. 5,19f.), einer der reichsten Agrarregionen in Lakonia. Von H. soll sich der Name der spartan. Heloten ableiten (Strab. 8,5,4; Paus. 3,20,6), was aber phonetisch nicht möglich ist [1]. Wahrscheinlich schon in der Brz. Marinestützpunkt (Hom. Il. 2,584). Jedoch machten Flußablagerungen den Hafen unbrauchbar und schon im 2. Jh. v. Chr verfiel H. Zu Pausanias' Zeiten lag H. in Ruinen (Paus. 3,22,3). Belegstellen: Thuk. 4,54,4; Xen. hell. 6,5,32; Strab. 8,3,12; 3,24; 5,2; Paus. 3,20,6f.

1 Chantraine, s. v. H.

H. Waterhouse, R. Hope Simpson, Prehistoric Laconia, in: ABSA, 55, 1960, 87–103; 56, 1961, 173. Y. L.

Heloten I. Definition II. Die Ursprünge der Helotie III. Die Behandlung der Heloten IV. Die Rolle der Heloten in Sparta

I. Definition

Die zahlreichen lit. Quellen zur Gesch. der H. sind oft widersprüchlich und ungenau. Generell werden die H. (εἵλωτες, εἱλῶται, *heílōtes*, *heilṓtai*) mit dem üblichen griech. Begriff für unfreie Personen als δοῦλοι (*dúloi*) bezeichnet, doch besteht keine Einigkeit über die Form ihrer Abhängigkeit. Bisweilen werden die H. mit anderen ebenfalls abhängigen Bevölkerungsgruppen, etwa mit den → Penestai aus Thessalien, verglichen (Plat. leg. 776cd; Aristot. pol. 1269a 36–39). Nach Pollux (3,83) standen die H. zwischen ἐλεύθεροι (*eleútheroi*, »Freien«) und *dúloi*; Strabon (8,5,4) bezeichnete sie als ›auf bestimmte Weise öffentliche Sklaven‹ (τρόπον τινα δημόσιοι δοῦλοι), nach Pausanias (3,20,6) hingegen waren sie Sklaven des spartanischen *koinón* (»Gemeinwesen«). Auch in der mod. Forschung besteht keine Einigkeit über den Status der H.; unstrittig ist aber, daß die H. als Kollektiv öffentliche Sklaven des spartanischen Gemeinwesens waren und nicht privater Besitz einzelner Spartaner sein konnten, worauf auch der offizielle Begriff δουλεία (»Knechtschaft«; Thuk. 5,23,3) als Bezeichnung für die H. hindeutet.

II. Die Ursprünge der Helotie

Im 5. Jh. v. Chr. waren die meisten H. Messenier (Thuk. 1,101). Es ist jedoch anzunehmen, daß die Helotie in Lakonien während der »Dark Ages« entstanden ist und im 8./7. Jh. v. Chr. als Folge der spartanischen Eroberung auf → Messenien übertragen wurde. Bei den H. handelte es sich nach ant. Überzeugung um die urspr. Bevölkerung Lakoniens, die im Krieg besiegt und versklavt worden war. Die Etym. des Wortes *heilṓtai* von ἑλ- (*hel-*, »gefangennehmen«) scheint diese Sicht zu bestätigen; allerdings gibt es noch eine weitere ant. Ableitung des Begriffs von → Helos, einem Ort im südlichen Eurotastal (Paus. 3,20,6). Die Spartaner haben die H. jedenfalls wie ein besiegtes Volk behandelt.

III. Die Behandlung der Heloten

Nach dem Urteil ant. Autoren waren die H. und insbesondere die Messenier eine unfreie Bevölkerung, deren richtige Behandlung sehr schwierig war (Plat. leg. 776c; 777bc; Aristot. pol. 1269a 36–b 12; Theopompos, FGrH 115 F 13). Bereits im 7. Jh. v. Chr. hat Tyrtaios die Lage der Messenier eindringlich beschrieben: ›Wie Esel unter großen Lasten erschöpft bringen sie ihren Herren, hartem Zwang gehorchend, die Hälfte der Frucht, die der Boden trägt‹ (fr. 6; Paus. 4,14,5). Dieser Text stammt aus der Zeit des ersten großen Aufstandes der Messenier; weitere Aufstände folgten, so wahrscheinlich 490 v. Chr., 465 v. Chr. und schließlich 370/369 v. Chr. mit Erfolg. Die H. Spartas nahmen an dem Aufstand 465 v. Chr. teil; sie waren jedoch weniger zum Widerstand bereit als die Messenier, denn einerseits konnten sie aufgrund der geogr. Situation leichter kontrolliert werden, und andererseits fehlte ihnen ein Zusammengehörigkeitsgefühl und Selbstbewußtsein, wie die Messenier es wohl besaßen.

Bald nach ihrem Amtsantritt erklärten die Ephoren (→ *éphoroi*) den H. alljährlich offiziell den Krieg (Plut. Lykurgos 28), um so Spartaner, die H. getötet hatten, von ihrer Blutschuld zu befreien. Die H. mußten Kleidung tragen, die sie symbolisch den Tieren gleichstellte (Myron, FGrH 106 F 2), und man zwang sie, sich völlig zu betrinken, und stellte sie so bei den Syssitien (→ Gastmahl) zur Schau (Plut. Lykurgos 28). Andererseits bestanden Möglichkeiten der Freilassung (Theopompos, FGrH 115 F 176; Myron, FGrH 106 F 1), die jedoch einen öffentlichen Akt der spartanischen Volksversammlung erforderte. Die wichtigste Gruppe freigelassener H. waren die νεοδαμώδεις (*neodamṓdeis*). Thukydides berichtet davon, daß die Spartaner, auf ihre eigene Sicherheit fixiert, H. die Freilassung für Verdienste im Krieg gegen Athen anboten und dann insgeheim 2000 H., die sich gemeldet hatten, umbrachten (Thuk. 4,80,3 f.; Diod. 12,67,4; Plut. Lykurgos 28). Diese Politik hatte keinen eindeutigen Erfolg, denn sie verstärkte den Haß der H., die nach Xenophon die Spartiaten ›am liebsten roh fressen‹ würden (Xen. hell. 3,3,6); nach Aristoteles warteten die H. wie Feinde nur auf das Unglück der Spartaner (Aristot. pol. 1269a 37 ff.). Dennoch bestand dieses System über 500 Jahre lang und trug dazu bei, daß Sparta eine Großmacht in Griechenland wurde.

IV. Die Rolle der Heloten in Sparta

H. und freigelassene H. (*neodamṓdeis*) wurden von den Spartanern als Hopliten (→ *hoplítai*, Leichtbewaffnete) sowie Ruderer im Krieg eingesetzt (Hdt. 6,80 f.; 9,28 f.; 9,80,1; 9,85; Thuk. 4,80; Xen. hell. 6,5,28 f.; 7,1,12 f.). In Sparta waren weibliche und männliche H. Diener in Haushalten der Spartiaten (Hdt. 6,63; Xen. hell. 5,4,28; Xen. Lak. pol. 7,5; Plut. Agesilaos 3,2), männliche H. auch Wächter (Hdt. 6,75,2), Pferdeknechte (Hdt. 6,68,2) und Diener, die bei Tisch aufwarteten (Kritias 88 B 33 DK).

Da die Spartaner selbst keine wirtschaftlich produktive Tätigkeit ausübten, waren Handel, Bergbau und Handwerk Aufgabe der → Perioiken; die Arbeit in der Landwirtschaft wurde von den H. geleistet. Die Spartaner waren auf die landwirtschaftlichen Produkte angewiesen, da sie zur Lieferung von Gerste, Wein, Olivenöl und Schweinefleisch für die Syssitien verpflichtet waren, worauf wiederum ihr Status als Bürger beruhte (Tyrtaios fr. 6; Aristot. pol. 1264a 32–36; Plut. Lykurgos 8,7; Plut. mor. 239de). Die H., die mit ihrer Familie das Land bebauten, arbeiteten jeweils nur für einen einzigen Spartaner, waren aber verpflichtet, auch anderen Spartanern Pferde, Hunde oder Wegzehrung zu stellen (Xen. Lak. pol. 6,3; Aristot. pol. 1263a 35–37).

Die mod. Forschung sah in der Helotie vielfach die Ursache für die Entstehung und Durchsetzung des eigentümlichen sozialen und polit. Systems Spartas; es war demnach die Furcht vor den H., die die Spartaner dazu bewog, ihre Stadt in ein Militärlager zu verwandeln und eine Art permanenten Krieges gegen die H. zu führen. Demgegenüber wurde aber auch die Auffassung vertreten, daß die Bedrohung durch die H. sowohl in der Ant. als auch in der mod. Forschung überschätzt wurde. Deutlich ist hingegen, daß Sparta mit dem Verlust Messeniens 369 v. Chr. auch seine Machtstellung unwiderruflich einbüßte. Strabon (8,5,4) war der Ansicht, daß die Helotie noch bis zur röm. Eroberung Griechenlands fortbestand. Wahrscheinlich hatten jedoch bereits Kleomenes III. (235–222 v. Chr.) und Nabis (207–192 v. Chr.) viele der H. befreit, um sie bei dem letzten Versuch, Spartas Unabhängigkeit zunächst gegen Makedonien, dann gegen Rom zu verteidigen, als Soldaten einzusetzen.

→ Sklaverei; Sparta

1 P. Cartledge, Agesilaos and the Crisis of Sparta, 1987 **2** Ders., Serfdom in Classical Greece, in: L. J. Archer (Hrsg.), Slavery and Other forms of Unfree Labour, 1988, 33–42 **3** Ders., Sparta and Lakonia, 1979 **4** P. Cartledge, A. Spawforth, Hellenistic and Roman Sparta, 1989 **5** J. Ducat, Les Hilotes, 1990 **6** J. Ducat, Les Pénestes de Thessalie, 1994 **7** M. I. Finley, The Servile Statuses of Ancient Greece, in: Ders., Economy, 133–149 **8** Y. Garlan, Slavery in ancient Greece, 1988 **9** S. Hodkinson, Sharecropping and Sparta's Economic Exploitation of the Helots, in: J. M. Sanders, H. W. Catling (Hrsg.), ΦΙΛΟΛΑΚΩΝ, FS H. W. Catling, 1992, 123–134 **10** H. Klees, Die Beurteilung der Helotie im hist. und polit. Denken der Griechen im 5. und 4. Jh. v. Chr., in: Laverna 2, 1991, 27–52; 3, 1992, 1–31 **11** D. Lotze, Μεταξὺ ἐλευθέρων καὶ δούλων, 1959 **12** P. Oliva, Sparta and her Social Problems, 1971 **13** A. Pardiso, Forme di dependenza nel mondo greco, 1991 **14** G. de Ste. Croix, The Class Struggle in Ancient Greece, 1981 **15** R. Talbert, The Role of the Helots in the Class Struggle at Sparta, in: Historia 38, 1989, 22–40 **16** K.-W. Welwei, Unfreie im ant. Kriegsdienst I, 1974 **17** M. Whitby, Two Shadows: Images of Spartans and Helots, in: A. Powell, S. Hodkinson (Hrsg.), The Shadow of Sparta, 1994, 87–126.

P. C./Ü: A. BE.

Helpidius

[1] 321–324 n. Chr. *vicarius urbis Romae* (Cod. Theod. 2,8,1; 16,2,5; 13,5,4; Cod. Iust. 8,10,6 nennt ihn *agens vicem praefectorum praetorio*). Noch 329 ist er Adressat von Gesetzen (Cod. Theod. 9,21,4; 13,5,4); da eine so lange Amtszeit als *vicarius* ungewöhnlich wäre, ist anzunehmen, daß er inzwischen ein höheres Amt innehatte, vielleicht *praefectus praetorio Italiae* war. PLRE 1, 413 (H. 1).

[2] Claudius H. Paphlagonier niederer Herkunft, Christ (er besuchte den Eremiten Antonios [5]), begann seine Karriere als *notarius*, war dann *praeses Mauretaniae Sitif.* (nach 337 n. Chr.), *consularis Pannoniae* (353), *praefectus praetorio Orientis* (360–361); bei den Soldaten war er unbeliebt, nur die Intervention Iulians verhinderte seine Ermordung. Nach dem Tod des Kaisers versuchte er dennoch, diesen zu verleumden. Bald darauf starb er (363). PLRE 1, 414 (H. 4).

[3] Anhänger Iulians, Schwager des Libanios, geb. vor 331 n. Chr. in Antiocheia; schon unter Constantius II. war er bei Hofe angesehen; unter dem Caesar Iulian, der ihn vom Christentum abbrachte, *comes rei privatae*, da er 358/9 nach Antiocheia geschickt wurde, wohl um für Iulian das Erbe des Gallus anzutreten. 363 Teilnahme am Perserfeldzug, 364 *proconsul Asiae*; er beteiligte sich am Aufstand des Prokopios, deswegen von Valens gefangengenommen, sein Vermögen wurde konfisziert. PLRE 1, 415 (H. 6). K. G.-A.

Helvecones. Neben den → Harii, Manimi, Halisiones und Nahanarvali mächtiger Teilstamm der Vandali-Lugii (Tac. Germ. 43,2); wahrscheinlich identisch mit den Eluaíōnes (Ἑλουαίωνες, Ptol. 2,11,9), obwohl sie nicht mit dem Zusatz *Lúg[i]oi* (Λοῦγ[ι]οι) versehen sind und zw. Rutíkleioi (Ῥουτίκλειοι) und Burgundiones (Βουργοῦντες) lokalisiert werden. In diesem Falle wären sie die nördlichsten Lugii. K.DI.

Helvetii. Kelt. Volksstamm, der in der röm. Kaiserzeit auf dem Boden der h. Schweiz siedelte. Grenzen des Siedlungsgebietes: im Norden der Rhein, nur zw. Aaremündung und Stein am Rhein (sog. Tafel-Jura zw. Basel und Brugg) befindet sich das Gebiet der Raurici; im Westen der Falten-Jura zw. Basel und Genf; im Süden der Genfer See ohne das Gebiet der *colonia Equestris* (Nyon); im Osten liegt die Grenze gegen Raetia auf einer Linie vom Ostufer des Genfer Sees bis Pfyn-Frauenfeld. Die H. waren in Gaue untergliedert (nach Caes. Gall. 1,12,4 vier *pagi*; nach Poseid. bei Strab. 4,3,3 drei *pagi*). Frühere Wohnsitze der H. in SW-Deutschland erschließt man aus Ptol. 2,11,2 (Ἑλουητίων ἔρημος). Einzelne Abteilungen beteiligten sich am Zug der Cimbri (Caes. Gall. 1,12,5); Reste von diesen haben sich in den Ostalpen niedergelassen; von ihnen stammen am Magdalensberg Devotions-Inschr. für die Augustus-Familie [1. 70–74]. Die innerkelt. Kämpfe 60/58 v.Chr., bei welchen rechtsrhein. Söldnertruppen angeworben wurden, gaben Caesar den erwünschten Vorwand zum Eingreifen in das freie Gallien. Nach dem Modell, das er erfolgreich als *propraetor* in Spanien verwendet hatte, deklarierte er eine interne Stammesbewegung zum *casus belli* [2]. Der Kriegsausbruch von 58 v.Chr. ist durch Caesars Darstellungskunst in eine Legende von völkerrechtlicher Korrektheit verpackt worden, welche trotz mannigfacher Kritik bis h. als histor. Wahrheit gilt. Der Kriegshistoriker HANS DELBRÜCK und andere haben längst die Unglaubwürdigkeit von Caesars Angaben über die helvetische Volksstatistik, den Charakter des Auszuges, das angebliche Ziel der Expedition erwiesen. Was in Wirklichkeit ein beschränkter mil. Auszug der H. zur Unterstützung der Haedui gegen Ariovistus war, deutete Caesar zum gefährlichen gall. Bürgerkrieg um, welcher die röm. Intervention rechtfertigte.

Nach der Niederlage des Expeditionscorps bei Bibracte wohnten die H. weiterhin in ihrem alten Stammesgebiet und nahmen auch am Vercingetorix-Aufstand teil. Zu Ende seines Lebens ließ Caesar die röm. Verkehrswege ins Gebiet der H. durch die Anlegung zweier *coloniae*, der *Colonia Iulia Equestris* (Nyon: Straße über den Großen St. Bernhard nach Genf) und der *Colonia Raurica* (Augst auf dem Gebiet der Raurici, Jurarand-Straße von Genf an den Oberrhein) sichern. Die röm. Besitznahme des H.-Gebietes geschah erst im Alpenkrieg des Augustus (15 v.Chr.). Das Territorium wurde peregrine *civitas* mit dem Hauptort Aventicum, ohne daß die innere Organisation genau bekannt ist. Beim Durchmarsch der Vitellius-Armee Anf. 69 n.Chr. geriet Aventicum in die Gefahr der Plünderung (Tac. hist. 1,67–70). Durch Vespasianus, dessen Vater bei den H. Bankgeschäfte betrieben hatte, erhielt die Stadt den Rang einer *colonia* (Suet. Vesp. 1,3): *Colonia Pia Flavia Constans Emerita Helvetiorum Foederata*. Aus welcher Zeit das *foedus* zw. Rom und den H. stammt, ist umstritten.

Seit der Flavierzeit erfolgte der monumentale Ausbau der Stadt (Stadtmauer mit fünf Toren und 73 Türmen, Amphitheater, szenisches Theater, Bäder, Tempel, Korporationshäuser, sog. *scholae*). Seit Domitianus gehörte das Gebiet der H. zur Prov. Germania Superior, die Neurömer wurden in der *tribus Quirina* eingeschrieben. Einzelne davon ließen sich in die röm. Legionen rekrutieren, während eine größere Zahl von peregrin Gebliebenen in die *auxilia* (*cohortes Helvetiorum*) eintrat. 259/260 n.Chr. hatten die Landgüter und die Hauptstadt unter den Alamannen-Einfällen zu leiden. Nach dem Fall des german. Limes schützte auch die neue Provinzialeinteilung des Diocletianus (Kleinprov. Maxima Sequanorum) die romanisierten H. nicht mehr. Um 400 n.Chr. zogen die röm. Truppen ab, und die langsame Einwanderung der burgundischen und alamannischen *foederati* begann. Das Bistum von Aventicum überlebte das Ende des röm. Reiches in Lausanne.

1 J. ŠAŠEL, Huldigung norischer Stämme am Magdalensberg in Kärnten, in: Historia 16, 1967, 70–74 **2** W. WIMMEL, Caesar und die Helvetier, in: RhM 123, 1980, 126–137; 125, 1982, 59–66.

H. DELBRÜCK, Gesch. der Kriegskunst I, 1900, 423–442 • W. DRACK, R. FELLMANN, Die Römer in der Schweiz, 1988 • G. FERRERO, Grandezza e decadenza di Roma, dt.: Größe und Niedergang Roms 2, ²1914, 1–30 • R. FREI-STOLBA, Die röm. Schweiz, in: ANRW II 5.1, 1976, 288–403 • E. HOWALD, E. MEYER, Die röm. Schweiz, 1940 • P. HUBER, Die Glaubwürdigkeit Caesars in seinem Ber. über den gall. Krieg, ²1931 • E. MEYER, Röm. Zeit, in: Hdb. der Schweizer Gesch. I, 1980, 55–92 • F. STAEHELIN, Die Schweiz in röm. Zeit, ³1948 • G. WALSER, Röm. Inschr. in der Schweiz I–III, 1979–1980 • Ders., Zu Caesars Tendenz in der geogr. Beschreibung Galliens, in: Klio 77, 1995, 217–223 • Ders., Bellum Helveticum. Stud. zum Beginn der caesarischen Eroberung von Gallien (Historia Einzelschrift 118), 1998. G.W.

Helvetum (Itin. Anton. 252; 350; Ἔλκηβος, Ptol. 2,9,18). Bisher oft gleichgesetzt mit → Helellum (Tab. Peut. 3,4) bzw. Alaia (Geogr. Rav. 26) und mit diesem schon im Itin. Anton. 354 verwechselt, ist aber nicht bei Ehl im Elsaß, sondern rechtsrhein. an der Route Mons Brisiacus – Argentoratus beim h. Riegel, Kreis Emmendingen, zu lokalisieren [1]. Kastelle aus claudischer und vespasianischer Zeit, die als Fortsetzung der Kastellreihe an der oberen Donau die Anbindung zum Rhein sicherten. Nach Eroberung der → *Decumates agri* Verlust der mil.-strateg. Bed. Aus den *cannabae* (Lagerdörfern) entwickelte sich ein größerer → *vicus* mit Handwerksbetrieben, Töpfereien, Ziegeleien sowie einem Kultbezirk mit Mithräum. Für röm. Kontinuität nach dem Limesdurchbruch 260 spricht nach neueren Unt. der Name Riegel (von *regula*, einer Funktionsbezeichnung für einen regionalen Rechts- und Verwaltungsbezirk, herzuleiten [1]).

1 H. Steger, **Regula*/Riegel am Kaiserstuhl – Helvetum?, in: Römer und Alamannen im Breisgau, (Archäologie und Geschichte 6), 1994, 233–361.

G. Fingerlin, Riegel, in: P. Filtzinger, u. a., Die Römer in Baden-Württemberg, [3]1986, 504–508. F.SCH.

Helvia

[1] Mutter Ciceros, von ihm selbst nirgends ewähnt, von seinem Bruder als penible Hausfrau bezeichnet (Cic. fam. 16,26,2), führte ein tadelloses Leben (Plut. Cicero 1,1).

[2] Frau Senecas d. Ä., den sie 40 n. Chr. verlor (Sen. dial. 12,2,4; 19,4). → Seneca d. J., einer ihrer drei Söhne, schrieb im Exil für sie die Trostschrift *Ad Helviam*. PIR[2] H 78.

[3] Ältere Schwester von H. [2]. Ihr Ehemann → Galerius [1] starb 31 n. Chr. auf der Rückreise von Ägypten nach Rom (Sen. dial. 12,19). PIR[2] H 79. ME.STR.

[4] H. Procula. Tochter des tiberischen Senators T. Helvius [II 2] Basila, den sie in Antium postum ehrte (CIL X 5056 = ILS 977). Wohl identisch mit der Frau des spanischen Senators C. Dillius Vocula, der im J. 70 n. Chr. in Germanien umkam (CIL VI 1402 = ILS 983). PIR[2] H 82. W.E.

Helvidius

[1] C. H. Priscus. Aus Cluviae stammend. Sein Vater war → *primus pilus* gewesen. Eintritt in den Senat vor dem J. 49 n. Chr. *Quaestor Achaiae* spätestens 49/50; sein Begleiter war P. → Celerius aus Histonium (IEph 7, 1, 3043/4 = [1. 67ff.]). Legionslegat in Syrien als Quaestorier im J. 51. In dieser Zeit Heirat mit Fannia, der Tochter des → Clodius [II 15] Thrasea Paetus. Erst 56 Volkstribun; dann kein anderes Amt mehr unter Nero, eine Folge der Verbindung mit seinem Schwiegervater und den stoisch beeinflußten Zirkeln in Rom. Als Thrasea Paetus sich im J. 66 selbst töten mußte, wurde H. verbannt. Rückkehr unter Galba, Praetor im J. 70. Im Senat griff er senatorische Kollaborateure der neronischen Zeit an, vor allem Eprius Marcellus; dabei vertrat er auch gegenüber Vespasian die Autonomie des Senats neben dem Princeps. Später deswegen verbannt, schließlich hingerichtet, gegen den Willen des Princeps. Eine Biographie des H. wurde von → Herennius [II 11] Senecio verfaßt. [2.; 3]

1 W. Eck, in: Splendidissima Civitas. Etudes ... à Fr. Jacques, 1996, 67ff. 2 Syme, RP VII, 568ff. 3 PIR[2] H 59.

[2] H. (Priscus). Sohn von H. [1] aus dessen erster Ehe; deshalb vor dem J. 51 n. Chr. geboren. Senator, der es trotz seines Vaters zu einem Suffektkonsulat brachte; das Jahr ist unbekannt; entweder spätestens 87 oder erst im J. 93 (wofür das Alter sprechen könnte). Ende 93 angeblich wegen eines Theaterstücks mit Anspielungen auf Domitian verurteilt und hingerichtet; vermutlich waren erbitterte Rivalitäten zwischen gegnerischen Gruppen im Senat die Ursache. Plinius attackierte 97 Publicius Certus als Ankläger; seine Rede *De Helvidii ultione* wurde später publiziert. Verheiratet mit → Anteia [2]; über zwei Töchter wurde der Name weitergegeben.

Syme, RP VII, 568ff. • W. Eck, in: Kölnische Jbb. 26, 1993, 449 • PIR[2] H 60. W.E.

Helvii (*Elvii, Elvi* oder *Ilvi*, Caes. civ. 1,35; Ἑλουοί, Strab. 4,2,1). Kelt. Volksstamm, dessen Gebiet (h. Dép. Ardèche) am rechten Ufer der Rhône im Norden an die Segusiavi, im Westen an die Vellavii und Gabali und im Süden an die Volcae Arecomici grenzte. Die Cevennen trennten sie von den Arverni (Caes. Gall. 7,8). 52 v. Chr. standen sie im Krieg gegen Vercingetorix auf der Seite Caesars. Bei der Neugliederung der Prov. unter Augustus wurden sie zu Aquitania geschlagen (Strab. l.c.), gehörten aber bald darauf (Plin. nat. 3,36) zur Gallia Narbonensis mit dem Hauptort Alba Augusta Helviorum. Unter Diocletianus wurde die *civitas Albensis* der *provincia Viennensis* zugeteilt. Im 6. Jh. n. Chr. war Vivarium (h. Viviers) ihr Hauptort. Y.L.

Helvius. Röm. Eigenname, möglicherweise abgeleitet vom Praenomem *Helvus*.

Schulze 82; 421 • Holder, 1, 1430f.

I. Republikanische Zeit

[I 1] H., C. 199 v. Chr. plebeischer Aedil, 198 Praetor in Gallia Cisalpina (Liv. 32,7,13), 189 Legat des Cn. → Manlius Vulso beim Feldzug gegen die kleinasiatischen Galater (Pol. 21,34,2–4; Liv. 38,14,4f. u. a.). MRR 1,327; 330; 364.

[I 2] H., M. 198 plebeischer Aedil, 197 Praetor in Hispania Citerior. Durch eine Krankheit bis 195 dort festgehalten, besiegte er auf dem Rückmarsch die Keltiberer bei Illiturgis am Baetis und erhielt eine *ovatio* (Liv. 34,10,1–5; InscrIt 13,1,79). K.-L.E.

[I 3] H. Cinna, C. Stammt wahrscheinlich aus Brixen in Gallia Transpadana (fr. 9 Courtney: *Genumana per salicta*). Die Helvii waren dort eine angesehene alteingesessene Familie [1. 46f.]; H.' Geburtsdatum ist unbekannt. Er könnte mit dem Kinna identisch sein, der den Dichter → Parthenios von Nikaia am Ende des Mithradatischen Krieges als Sklaven kaufte und ihm wegen seiner Gelehrsamkeit die Freiheit schenkte (Suda s. v. Parthenios). – H.' eigene Dichtung umfaßte Epigramme (Non. 124L), ein → Propemptikon für Asinius [I 5] Pollio (Char. 158B = 124K) und das Kleinepos *Zmyrna* (Catull. 95, fr. 6–8 Courtney). Wie Parthenios' war H.' Dichtung außerordentlich gelehrt: Komm. wurden zu seinem Propemptikon von Iulius → Hyginus [1] und zur *Zmyrna* von → Crassicius Pansa (Char. 171B = 134K, Suet. gramm. 18,2) geschrieben. Als enger Freund → Catulls (95; cf. 10,30; 113,1) war er wahrscheinlich ein führendes Mitglied der Dichter-gruppe, die Cicero 45 v. Chr. als »Sänger des Euphorion« kritisiert.

H. war ein Freund (Plut. Brutus 20; Caesar 68; Dio 44,50,4) und Verwandter (Val. Max. 9,9,1) Caesars. Offensichtlich wurde er nach der Bürgerrechtsverleihung an die Transpadaner 49 v. Chr. Senatsmitglied. Als Tribun schlug er 44 (Suet. Iul. 52,3) die Amtsenthebung seiner Amtskollegen, der Caesargegner Epidius Marullus und Caesetius Flavus, vor (Cass. Dio 44,10,3). Trotz eines unheilvollen Traumes nahm er am 20. März 44 an Caesars Begräbnis teil, wo ihn der Pöbel – aufgestachelt durch Antonius' Rede und im Glauben, er sei der Praetor L. Cornelius Cinna, der den Mord gebilligt hatte – ergriff und in Stücke riß (Plut. ebd.; Val. Max. 9,9,1; Suet. Iul. 85; App. civ. 2,147; Cass. Dio 44,50,4; Zon. 10,12). Ovids Anspielung auf seinen Tod (Ov. Ib. 539f.) bestätigt Plutarchs Identifikation des Dichters mit dem Tribunen [3].

H. wurde von den Dichtern der folgenden Generation geehrt (Verg. ecl. 9,35f.; Valgius fr. 2 COURTNEY; Ov. trist. 2,435), und seine *Zmyrna* wurde von Ovid in met. 10,298–502 [4] aufgearbeitet; gleichwohl war seine anspielungsreiche Gelehrsamkeit nicht nach jedermanns Geschmack (Mart. 10,21). Er wird von Antiquaren und Grammatikern bis → Isidor [9] zit. (orig. 6,12,2; 19,2,9; 19,4,7).

1 T. P. WISEMAN, C. the Poet, 1974 **2** COURTNEY, 1993 **3** J. D. MORGAN, The Death of C. the Poet, in: CQ 40, 1990, 558f. **4** G. BRUGNOLI, Ovidi Zmyrna, in: Rivista di cultura classica e medioevale 24, 1982, 47–52.

H. DAHLMANN, Über H. Cinna (AAWM 8), 1977 • R. O. A. M. LYNE, The Neoteric Poets, in: CQ 28, 1978, 167–187 • R. F. THOMAS, C., Calvus and the Ciris, in: CQ 31, 1981, 371–374 • L. C. WATSON, C. and Euphorion, in: SIFC 54, 1982, 93–110. T. W./Ü: U. R.

[I 4] H. Mancia. Sohn eines Freigelassenen aus Formiae, bekannt wegen seines Spottes (etwa über den Censor M. Antonius [I 7], Cic. de orat. 2,274) und selbst Opfer des Spottes durch C. Iulius [I 5] Caesar Strabo wegen seiner Häßlichkeit (vor 87 v. Chr., Cic. de orat. 2,266; Quint. inst. 6,3,8). In hohem Alter klagte er (wohl 55 v. Chr.) L. Scribonius Libo bei den Censoren an und griff dabei dessen Verteidiger Pompeius heftig an (Val. Max. 6,2,8). K.-L. E.

II. KAISERZEIT

[II 1] L. H. Agrippa. Senator aus der Baetica. 68/9 n. Chr. Proconsul von Sardinien. Vielleicht identisch mit dem Pontifex, der unter Domitian bei der Untersuchung sexueller Verfehlungen von Vestalinnen starb. PIR² H 64.

[II 2] T. H. Basila. Senator, der in Atina zumindest Grundbesitz hatte. Praetorische Laufbahn, vielleicht mit dem Proconsul von Achaia in AE 1949, 90 identisch. Statthalter von Galatia wohl ca. 37/8 n. Chr. [1]. Seine Tochter ist Helvia Procula. PIR² H 67; 82.

1 S. ŞAHIN, in: EA 25, 1995, 25ff. W. E.

[II 3] P. H. Pertinax s. Pertinax

[II 4] P. H. Pertinax. Geb. um 175 n. Chr., Sohn des Kaisers → Pertinax und der Flavia Titiana (CIL XIII 4323; III 14149,35+38; BGU 2,646; Cass. Dio 37,7). Er wurde nicht am Hof, sondern zusammen mit seiner Schwester im Haus des Großvaters Flavius Sulpicianus erzogen und führte gegen den Willen des Vaters die Titel *Caesar* und *princeps iuventutis* (Cass. Dio 73,7,3; Herodian. 2,4,9; [1]). Nach dem Tod des Vaters erhielt er das Priesteramt eines *flamen* des vergöttlichten Pertinax (*SHA* Pert. 15,3). Um 212 bekleidete er den Suffektkonsulat und ist im Amt von Caracalla getötet worden (SHA Carac. 4,8; Herodian. 4,6,3).

1 H. COHEN, Monnaies sous l'empire romain, Ndr. 1955, Bd. 3, 397.

PIR² H 74 • DEGRASSI, FCIR 59 • KIENAST², 153 • LEUNISSEN, 166f. T. F.

[II 5] H. Successus. Der Freigelassene und Textilhändler (in SHA Pert. 1 *lignariam* wohl Verschreibung) war der Vater des Kaisers H. → Pertinax (SHA Pert. 1; 3,3f.), der im ligurischen Apennin bei Albae Pompeiae auf dem Gut seiner Mutter, der Frau des Successus, geboren wurde (Cass. Dio 73,3,1). PIR² H 77. T. F.

Hemerologie s. Divination

Hemerologion (ἡμερολόγιον) ist ein nach den Tagen des Jahres geordneter Text. Das ant. Bed.-Spektrum reicht vom → Kalender (Plut. Caesar 59) bis zum Tagebuch (Kosmas Indikopleustes, Topographia christiana PG 88,276A, 6. Jh. n. Chr.) und wird noch im Fachlat. des 19. Jh. so genutzt. In der heutigen Wiss.-Sprache dient H. zur Bezeichnung zweier ganz unterschiedlicher Sachverhalte. In der Ägyptologie und Altorientalistik bezeichnet H. Listen mit divinatorischem (und – als entsprechendem Bezugsrahmen – kosmologischem) Interesse: Aufgrund der theologischen Qualifikation eines Tages (die nicht immer expliziert werden muß) ist eine bestimmte Handlung erlaubt/verboten (»Tagewählkalender«); in Einzelfällen kann das auch zu sachlich, nicht mehr kalendarisch geordneten Listen führen. In ihrem systematischen Interesse präsentieren → Parapegmen und (später) christl. Sanctilogien, die Heilige für jeden Tag zusammenstellen, einen vergleichbaren Texttyp. – Mit Bezug auf die griech.-röm. Ant. bezeichnet H. eine Gruppe von Texten, die erst in ma. Hss. belegt, aber sicher bis auf die Kaiserzeit zurückzuführen sind: Synopsen verschiedener Lokalkalender, die die Umrechnung der Monatstage eines Kalenders in andere Kalendersysteme erlauben.

R. LABAT, Hémérologies et ménologies d'Assur, 1939 • P. VERNUS, Omina calendériques et théorie médicale dans l'Egypte ancienne, in: RHR 199, 1982, 246f. • L. TROY, Have a Nice Day!, in: Boreas 20, 1989, 127–147 • C. LEITZ, Tagewählerei. Das Buch ḥ3t nḥḥ pḥ.wy ḏt und verwandte Texte, 2 Bde., 1994 • W. KUBITSCHEK, Die Kalenderbücher von Florenz, Rom und Leyden (= Denkschriften der kaiserlichen Akad. Wiss. Wien, phil.-hist. Kl. 57,3), 1915 (mit Ed.) • A. E. SAMUEL, Greek and Roman Chronology, 1972, 171–178. J.R.

Hemina (*emina*). Aus dem Griech. (ἡμίνα) übernommene lat. Bezeichnung für ein Hohlmaß für Flüssiges und Trockenes im Volumen von 1/96 → Amphora, 1/32 → Modius, ½ → Sextarius, entsprechend 2 → Quartarii, 4 → Acetabula, 6 → Cyathi. Sie entspricht 0,273 l; auf Wasser geeicht gehen 10 Unzen auf 1 H. Verbreitet als Maßangabe für Getränke – vergleichbar »ein Viertel« – in der Komödie und bei anderen Schriftstellern [1. 2602–2604] sowie als Mengenangabe in Rezepten bei Caelius Apicius [2. 99–100; 3. 143]. Als Ölmaß bezeichnet H. unter dem Namen λιτραῖον κέρας (Pfundhorn) ein aus Horn gefertigtes Gefäß zum Ölmessen mit einer Skala von 12 Maßstrichen.
→ Hohlmaße (Griechenland und Rom)

1 ThlL VI 3. 2 I. STRIEGAN-KEUNTJE, Concordantia et Index in Apicium, 1992. 3 A. URBÁN, Concordantia Apiciana, 1995.

F. HULTSCH, Griech. und röm. Metrologie, [2]1882 • O. VIEDEBANTT, s. v. H., RE 8, 248–249 • H. CHANTRAINE, s. v. Uncia, RE 9 A, 659–662 • Ders., s. v. H., KlP 2, 1020. H.-J. S.

Hemiobolion (ἡμιωβόλιον bzw. ἡμιωβέλιον). Münze im Wert eines halben → Obolos. Auf Silbermünzen der Peloponnes findet man häufig die abgekürzte Wertangabe HM, H oder E. In Korinth ist seit dem 5. Jh. v. Chr. der Pegasoskopf das Zeichen des H. [1. 400f.], in Athen im 4. Jh. v. Chr. die Eule statt der auf Obolos und ¼ Obolos üblichen Mondsichel [1. 374]. Das Gewicht des H. richtete sich nach den → Münzfüßen der Prägestätten.

Auf Bronzemünzen von Aigai/Achaia in röm. Zeit findet sich die Nominalbezeichnung ΗΜΙΟΒΕΛΙΝ [1. 413].
→ Obolos; Münzfüße

1 HN.

SCHRÖTTER, s. v. Hemiobol, 262. GE. S.

Hemiolion (ἡμιόλιον), wörtlich »das Anderthalbfache«. *H.* bezeichnet einen Aufschlag von 50 % einer Geld- oder Warenleistung (berechnet durch Multiplikation des Grundbetrags mit eineinhalb). In hell. und röm. Zeit trat das *h.* stereotyp in den Strafklauseln von privaten Verträgen als Buße für Nichterfüllung auf (häufig neben Zinsen), sowohl in den Papyri Ägyptens als auch in den wenigen anderweitig inschr. erh. Urkunden. Das *h.* war an die Stelle des *diplún* (διπλοῦν, das Doppelte) der älteren Vertragsklauseln getreten, was die inschr. erhaltenen Bauverträge (vgl. Plat. leg. 921d) gut illustrieren. Auch die öffentliche Verwaltung Ägyptens zur Prinzipatszeit bedient sich des *h.*, z. B. bei Säumnis in der Bezahlung von Steuern.

A. BERGER, Die Strafklauseln in den Papyrusurkunden, 1911 • G. THÜR, Bemerkungen zum altgriech. Werkvertrag, in: FS Biscardi 5, 1984, 510 • H.-A. RUPPRECHT, Einführung in die Papyruskunde, 1994, 114, 118. G. T.

Hemisphaerium (ἡμισφαίριον). Der Begriff bezeichnet eine »Halbkugel« a) in der Stereometrie als geometrischer Körper, b) in der astronomischen Kosmologie als halbe Himmelskugel beiderseits eines der großen Himmelskreise (→ Kykloi), meistens des Horizonts, also von der zentral gedachten Erde aus die obere, sichtbare Himmelshohlkugel und die untere, unsichtbare Hälfte des Himmels, dann auch c) die in der Ant. nur erschlossene konvexe Erdhalbkugel beiderseits des Horizonts. Ferner wurden auch menschliche Artefakte H. genannt: im großen d) ein Kuppelgewölbe – griech. auch → *thólos* – (Varro, Vitruv), oder e) die Form des griech. Amphitheaters (Cassiodor), im kleinen f) die konkave Mulde einer bestimmten Form der Sonnenuhr und dann synekdochisch diese selbst (= σκάφη; → Uhr; Vitruv. 9,8,1 unterscheidet davon *hemicyclium excavatum*), sowie g) ganz spät auch in latinisierter Form *duo semisphaeria* (= μαγάδεις) einer doppelten halbkreisförmigen Vorrichtung zum Spannen der Saite eines Monochords (Boeth. de institutione musicae 4,18 mit Abb. bei FRIEDLEIN).

H. DEGERING, s. v. H., RE 8, 253f. • H. H. GROTH, s. v. H., ThlL VI 3, 2604f. W. H.

Hemithea (Ἡμιθέα, »Halbgöttin«). Name einer Heilgöttin in Kastabos auf der karischen Chersonnes. Ihr Heiligtum, dessen arch. Spuren frühestens auf das späte 7. Jh. v. Chr. zurückgehen, wurde unter rhodischer Vorherrschaft ausgebaut und gelangte bis zu Rhodos' Niedergang nach 167 v. Chr. zu überregionalem Ruhm. Im Heiligtum erhielten die Kranken durch → Inkubation Heilträume (*klísis*, »Inkubation(sraum)« in einer Inschr. von ca. 150 v. Chr., SEG 14,690), auch half H. gebärenden Frauen (Diod. 5,63). Der Kult verbot Weingebrauch sowie das Opfern oder jeden anderen Gebrauch von Schweinen.

Das Kultaition leitet die Göttin von → Molpadia, der Tochter des Dionysossohns → Staphylos und Schwester von → Rhoio und → Parthenos ab (Diod. 5,62f.): Als Molpadia und Parthenos den neugefundenen Wein bewachen sollen, schlafen sie ein; ein Schwein zertrümmert den Weinkrug, die Schwestern fliehen, Parthenos wird von Apollon nach Bubastos versetzt, Molpadia nach Kastabos, wo sie als H. verehrt wird.

H. ist auch Schwester des → Ten(n)es und Sohn des → Kyknos im Gründungsmythos von Tenedos, der wohl auf die → *Kypria* zurückgeht. Danach wird Tenes von seiner Stiefmutter, die er abgewiesen hat, der Vergewaltigung angeklagt; Kyknos setzt beide in einer Truhe aus, die in Tenedos angeschwemmt wird. H. ist hier funktionslos; auf Tenedos wird sie von Achilleus verfolgt, der den Tenes tötet (Hauptstellen: Apollod. epit. 3,24f.; Konon FGrH 16 F 1,28; Plut. qu. Gr. 28; Paus. 10,14,2–4).

Staphylos und seine Töchter H. und Rhoio spielen auch eine Rolle in einem von Parthenios 1 (nach Nikainetos und Apollonios Rhodios) erzählten Mythos: Danach kehrt Lyrkos, zusammen mit seinem Schwiegervater Aibialos Herrscher über das karische Kaunos, nach dem Besuch des Orakels von Didyma bei Staphylos ein; Lyrkos war kinderlos geblieben, und das Orakel hatte vorausgesagt, die erste Frau, mit der Lyrkos schlafe, werde seinen Sohn gebären – also legt Staphylos ihm H. ins Bett, die mit einem Sohn schwanger wird, der der nächste Herrscher über Kaunos wird.

A. Laumonier, Les cultes indigènes en Carie, 1958, 664–667 • J.M. Cook, W.H. Plommer, The Sanctuary of H. at Kastabos, 1966 • H.A. Cahn, s.v. Ten(n)es, LIMC 7, 892. F.G.

Hemitomos s. Gefäßformen

Hemmoor (Kreis Cuxhaven). Brandgräberfelder der jüngeren Kaiserzeit (2./3. Jh. n. Chr.) mit Br.- bzw. Messinggefäßen als Urnen. Der FO ist namengebend für die typischen H.-Eimer, die z.T. reichverzierte Randborden und Attaschen haben; sie stammen aus röm. Werkstätten des Rheinlandes.
→ Germanische Archäologie; Urna

M. Erdrich, Zu den Messingeimern vom Hemmoorer Typ, in: R. Busch (Hrsg.), Rom an der Niederelbe, 1995, 71–80 • H. Willers, Die röm. Bronzeeimer von H., 1901. V.P.

Hendeka, hoi (οἱ ἕνδεκα). Die »Elf«, eine Behörde von elf Männern, waren in Athen für das Gefängnis und die Hinrichtung der zum Tode Verurteilten zuständig. Gewöhnliche Kriminelle (*kakúrgoi*) oder Verbannte, die in Athen aufgegriffen und ihnen mittels der → *apagōgḗ* zugeführt wurden, richteten sie ohne Prozeß hin, falls sie geständig waren, oder führten den Vorsitz im Verfahren, wenn sie die Schuld leugneten. Auch in Gerichtsverfahren, die mittels → *éndeixis* eingeleitet wurden, und bei Klagen zur Erzwingung der Konfiskation von Grundstücken führten sie den Vorsitz (Ps.-Aristot. Ath. pol. 52,1). Das Amt bestand anscheinend schon zur Zeit Solons (a.O. 7,3). Die Inhaber des Amtes unter der Oligarchie der Dreißig betrachtete man als so weitgehend mit dem Regime verbunden, daß man sie zu denen zählte, die sich den → *eúthynai* zu unterziehen hatten, wenn sie in der restaurierten Demokratie leben wollten (a.O. 35,1; 39,6).

1 A.R.W. Harrison, The Law of Athens, 1971, 17f.
2 J.H. Lipsius, Das attische Recht und Rechtsverfahren, Bd. 1, 1905–1915, 74–81. P.J.R.

Hendiadyoin s. Figuren I

Hengist und Horsa (»Hengst und Roß«). Die Brüder H. und H., Söhne des Jüten (Dänen) Wihtgils, sollen die Anführer angelsächsischer Krieger gewesen sein, die von dem südbritischen König Vortigern 449 n. Chr. zur Abwehr der Scoten und Picten angeworben wurden. Nach einigen Jahren kam es zum Konflikt zwischen Briten und Germanen. In der Schlacht bei Aylesford (455) soll auf german. Seite Horsa, auf britischer Vortigerns Sohn Categirn gefallen sein. Nach der angelsächsischen Chronik hat Hengist im selben Jahr das Königreich Kent gegründet. Hengist und sein Sohn Oisc (Aesc) sollen dann 457 bei Crayford, 465 bei Wippedsfleot und 473 an unbekanntem Ort gegen die Briten gekämpft haben. 488 starb Hengist und hinterließ sein Reich Oisc, nach dem sich die späteren Könige von Kent »Oiscingas« nannten. Ob Oisc ein leiblicher Nachkomme Hengists war, ist trotz der Bezeugung bei Beda (Historia ecclesiastica 2,5) unsicher. Fraglich erscheinen auch die in der angelsächsischen Chronik überlangen Jahreszahlen, die wohl aufgrund britischer (Nennius, *Historia Brittonum*) und kontinentaler Quellen um ca. 20 Jahre zu reduzieren sind.

C. Ahrens (Hrsg.), Sachsen und Angelsachsen, 1978 • J. Morris, The Age of Arthur, [2]1977 • Ders., Studies in Dark-Age History, 1995 • K. Schreiner, Die Sage von Hengist und Horsa, 1921, Ndr. 1967. M.SCH.

Henioche (Ἡνιόχη, »Zügelhalterin«).
[1] Beiname der Hera im boiot. Lebadeia, wo man vor der Befragung des Trophonios-Orakels u.a. Zeus Basileus, Demeter und H. opferte (Paus. 9,39,5); Wagenlenkerin ist Hera auch in der *Ilias* (Hom. Il. 8,392).

Schachter 1, 240f. AN.W.

[2] Nach Ps.-Hes. scut. 83 Gattin des → Kreon (Soph. Ant. 1180: Eurydike, vgl. schol.).
[3] Tochter des Kreon (Paus. 9,10,3).
[4] Tochter des → Pittheus von Troizen, Gattin des Kanethos, Mutter des → Skiron, nach anderen des → Sinis (Plut. Theseus 25,6).
[5] Tochter des Armenios, Gattin des Andropompos, Mutter des → Melanthos, (Hellanikos FGrH 323a F 23), eponyme Heroine der → Heniochoi.
[6] Val. Fl. 5,357 hat die sonst namenlose Amme der Medea, eventuell nach den Heniochi, H. benannt.

G. Weicker, s.v. H. (1–6), RE 8, 258. T.H.

Heniochoi (Ἡνίοχοι, Ps.-Skyl. 71). Im 5. Jh. v. Chr. großer Stammesverband an der kaukasischen buchtenreichen und dichtbewaldeten Pontosküste zw. Zygoi und Achaioi im Norden und Sanigai im Süden. Im Gebiet der H. wurde → Pityus/Picunda gegr.; die H. trieben Viehzucht, daneben Piraterie mit leichten Booten (Strab. 11,2,14) und wurden gegen E. des 4. Jh. v. Chr. vom bosporanischen König → Eumelos [4] unterworfen, der die Seeräuberei im Pontos bekämpfte (Diod. 20,25,2). Im 1. Jh. v. und n. Chr. kam es zu einer starken Wanderbewegung ins nordöstl. Kleinasien, wo sich die

H. von den Pontischen Alpen bis zu den Quellen des → Kyros ansiedelten (Plin. nat 6,26; 6,30) und zumindest in hadrianischer Zeit unter röm. Suzeränität standen (Arr. per. p. E. 15).

W. E. D. Allen, Ex Ponto III, in: Bedi Kartlisa 32/33, 1959, 28–35 • E. Kiessling, s. v. Ἡνίοχοι, RE 8, 259–280.

A. P.-L.

Heniochos (Ἡνίοχος). Dichter der Mittleren Komödie, aus dessen Werk die Suda noch acht Titel kennt: Τροχίλος (›Trochílos‹), Ἐπίκληρος (›Die Erbtochter‹), Γοργόνες (›Die Gorgonen‹), Πολυπράγμων (›Der Vielbeschäftigte‹), Θωρύκιον (›Thōrýkion‹), Πολύευκτος (›Polýeuktos‹), Φιλέταιρος (›Philhétairos‹), Δὶς ἐξαπατώμενος (›Der zweimal Betrogene‹) [1. test. 1]. Neben den geringen, bei Athenaios bewahrten Resten dieser Stükke (bemerkenswert immerhin die dithyrambisierende Sprache von fr. 1 [2. 262]) überliefert Stobaios ohne Titelangabe 17 Verse (wohl aus dem Prolog) einer schwer datierbaren polit. Komödie (fr. 5).

1 PCG V, 552–557 2 H. G. Nesselrath, Die att. mittlere Komödie, 1990.

T. HI.

Henna (Ἕννα, Ἔννα).

[1] Gut befestigte Stadt der Siculi (Cic. Verr. 2,4,107; Diod. 5,3,2; evtl. aber Gründung von Syrakus, Steph. Byz. s. v. H., vgl. [1. 74[24]; 2. 395]) auf steilem, fast 1000 m hohen Berg im Zentrum von Sizilien, seit dem 5. Jh. hellenisiert, 403 vorübergehend, seit 396 dauernd von Dionysios I. besetzt (Diod. 14,14,6–8; 78,7), fiel 309 von Agathokles ab (Diod. 20,31,5). H. war im 1. Pun. Krieg umkämpft (Diod. 23,9,4 f.; Pol. 1,24,12, der es zu den πολισμάτια, »kleinen Städtchen«, zählt) und wurde 214 bei dem Versuch, zu den Karthagern abzufallen, schwer bestraft (Liv. 24,37–39; Frontin. strat. 4,7,22; Polyain. 8,21; CIL I 530). Im großen Sklavenkrieg, der 136 von H. ausging, war der Ort Residenz des Eunus (zu dessen Mz.-Prägung [2. 416 ff.]), erst 132 nach langer Belagerung durch Aushungerung genommen. Laut Cicero (Verr. 2,3,100; 4,106–115) war das *mun(icipium) Hennae* (so auf Mz.) auch ein Opfer der Machenschaften des Verres.

H. wird in byz. Berichten über die Invasion der Araber erwähnt, denen die endgültige Eroberung der Stadt 859 n. Chr. gelang. Der ma. Name Castrogiovanni (aus *Castrum Hennae* über arab. *Qaṣr Ǧanna*) ist seit 1927 durch *Enna* ersetzt. Ant. Fundstücke im Museo Alessi. Inschr.: SEG 30,1123 (Dankes-Dekret von → Entella für die von H. erfahrene Hilfe). Mz.: HN 136 f. [3. 173 ff.].

1 G. Manganaro, Mondo religioso greco e mondo »indigeno« in Sicilia, in: C. Antonetti (Hrsg.), Il dinamismo della colonizzazione greca, 1997 2 Ders., Metoikismos, in: ASNP 20, 1990, 391–408 3 V. Cammarta, H., Tra storia e arte, 1990.

BTCGI 7, 1989, 189 ff.

GI. MA./Ü: V. S.

[2] Die Blüten des von Dioskurides (1,95 Wellmann = 1,124 Berendes) als κύπρος/*kýpros* (*cypros*, Plin. nat. 12,109 u. ö.) beschriebenen, bes. aus Askalon (Palästina) und Kanopos (Unterägypten) bekannten oriental. Strauches Lawsonia inermis von ligusterartigem Aussehen liefern den heute u. a. zum Färben der Nägel und Haare benutzten orange-gelben Farbstoff. Die Herstellung des u. a. gegen Nervenleiden empfohlenen H.-Salböls (κύπρινον ἔλαιον) findet sich ebenfalls bei Dioskurides 1,55 Wellmann = 1,65 Berendes.

C. HÜ.

Henoch. Die Gestalt des biblischen Urvaters H. hat in der jüd. Exilszeit (6. Jh. v. Chr.) verschiedene Überl. von babylon. Urzeitweisen oder Kulturbringern an sich gezogen. Bereits die kurze Notiz in Gn 5,21–24 macht den Hintergrund solcher Trad. wahrscheinlich, die dann in der jüd. Lit. zw. dem 3. Jh. v. Chr. und dem 1. Jh. n. Chr. entfaltet werden. Im Mittelpunkt steht der Gedanke, daß H. nicht starb, sondern bei Lebzeiten zu Gott entrückt wurde. Sein Lebensalter von 365 J. läßt zugleich einen Bezug zu astronomisch-kalendarischen Diskussionen erkennen. Die ältesten aram. Hss. (z. B. ›Buch der Wächter‹, ›Buch der Bilderreden‹, ›Astronomisches Buch‹, ›Buch der Träume‹, ›Brief H.s‹) fanden im sog. äthiop. H.-Buch (urspr. griech., 1. Jh. n. Chr.) eine redaktionelle Zusammenfügung, wobei das Interesse am Mythos von den gefallenen Engeln und an einer apokalyptischen Geschichtsdeutung dominiert. Das sog. slav. H.-Buch (urspr. griech., 1. Jh. n. Chr.) schöpft aus diesem Schriftenkreis, erzählt die Gesch. H.s jedoch neu und in straffer Abfolge von Himmelsreise, Mahnreden und Kultgründung, wobei weisheitlich-paränetische Themen in den Vordergrund rücken. Ein sog. hebr. H.-Buch (5.–6. Jh. n. Chr.), das in den Kontext der → Hekhalotliteratur der jüd. Mystik gehört, zeigt H. als obersten Engel und Führer des Adepten bei seinem Aufstieg in die Thronwelt.

H. wird in diesen drei Schriften v. a. als Offenbarer kosmologischer und eschatolischer Geheimnisse, Lehrer der Menschheit, Schreiber beim eschatologischen Gericht, Fürbitter, Prophet oder Bevollmächtigter Gottes gezeichnet und avanciert zu einem Vorbild an Weisheit und Gerechtigkeit. Anspielungen darauf finden sich in der frühjüd. Lit. zahlreich – z. B. Sir 44,16; 49,14; Jub 4,16–26 u. ö.; LibAnt 1,13–17; TestAbrB 11,3–9; PsEupol F I 1,9; ApkEsdr 5,22; TestXII. Originalität besitzt die H.-Deutung Philons – z. B. Mut 38; Abr 23–24; Praem 15–21. Im NT wird in Jud 14 auf äthHen 1,9 Bezug genommen; Hebr 11,5 betont H.s Glauben. Kirchenväter (→ Clemens [3] von Alexandreia, → Origenes, → Tertullianus u. a.) und Chronographen (→ Synkellos) verweisen auf H. und zitieren seine Schriften. Rabbinische Texte versuchen, H.s moralische Integrität zu relativieren. Eigenständige Gestaltungen des Stoffes begegnen noch einmal in einem fragmentarisch erh. christl. Apokryphon (kopt., 5. Jh. n. Chr.), das H. als Bruder der → Sibylle zeigt, sowie in einem jüd. → Midrasch (hebr., ca. 11. Jh.), in dem H. als vorbildlicher Asket und urzeitlicher Friedenskönig auftritt. Als einer der beiden Zeugen aus Apk 11 ist H. gemeinsam mit → Elias [1] in der christl. Apokalyptik bis an die Neuzeit heran zu finden.

J. T. MILIK, The Books of Enoch. Aramaic Fragments of Qumran Cave 4, 1976 • S. UHLIG, Das äthiop. H.buch (Jüd. Schriften aus hell.-röm. Zeit V/6), 1984, 459–780 • CH. BÖTTRICH, Das slav. H.buch, (Jüd. Schriften aus hell.-röm. Zeit V/7), 1996, 781–1040 • P. SCHÄFER, K. HERRMANN (Hrsg.), Übers. der Hekhalot-Lit. I [= sog. hebr. H.buch] (Texte und Studien zum ant. Judentum 46), 1995 • CH. BÖTTRICH, Beobachtungen zum Midrasch vom »Leben Henochs«, in: Mitt. und Beitr. der Forschungsstelle Judentum Leipzig, 10–11, 1996, 44–83 • K. BERGER, s. v. H., RAC 14, 473–545 • J. C. VANDERKAM, Enoch. A Man for All Generations, 1995. CHR. B.

Henotikon (Ἑνωτικόν). Anläßlich der Amtsübernahme des Patriarchen Petros Mongos an die Kirchen Ägyptens, Libyens und der Pentapolis gerichtet, versucht das 482 n. Chr. vom oström. Kaiser → Zenon unter maßgeblicher Mitwirkung des Patriarchen Akakios von Konstantinopel promulgierte H. (CPG III, 5999; urspr. Ἤδικτον Ζήνωνος, »Edikt Zenons«, seit Zacharias Rhetor, historia ecclesiastica 5,8, H. genannt; vgl. Euagrios, hist. eccl. 3,13 f.), die nach dem Konzil von Chalkedon (→ Kalchedon) im J. 451 gefährdete Glaubens- und Reichseinheit auf der Grundlage des Nicaeno-Constantinopolitanums und der kyrillischen Christologie wiederherzustellen. Die Ablehnung durch Rom (Synode 484 unter Felix III. [II.]) führt zum Akakianischen (→ Akakios [4]) Schisma (bis 519).

ED.: E. SCHWARTZ, Cod. Vaticanus gr. 1431, 1927, Nr. 75, 52–54.
LIT.: A. GRILLMEIER, Jesus der Christus im Glauben der Kirche 2/1, 1986, 279–358 (Übers.: 285–287). J. RI.

Heosphoros s. Phosphoros

Hephaistion (Ἡφαιστίων).
[1] H. aus Pella, Freund und wahrscheinlich Geliebter von → Alexandros [4]. Ihr Verhältnis wurde schon früh dem von → Patroklos und → Achilleus [1] angeglichen und entsprechend ausgeschmückt. Ob er Jugendfreund des Alexandros war (Curt. 3,12,16), ist zweifelhaft, da er von → Philippos II. 337 v. Chr. nicht verbannt wurde. Der dem Patroklos bei Troja dargebrachte Kranz und die in der Vulgata (→ Alexanderhistoriker) ausgemalte Szene der Verwechslung von H. und Alexandros durch → Sisygambis (Arr. an. 1,12,1; 2,12,6) sind als fiktiv gekennzeichnet.

Nach kleinen Aufträgen erscheint er bei → Gaugamela, wo er verwundet wurde, als ›Führer der → Somatophylakes‹ (Diod. 17,61,3); als Kommando der → Hetairoi-Leibgarde ist das kaum zu deuten (unter den Somatophylakes ist H. später bezeugt: ›Führer‹ wohl von Diodoros hinzugefügt. Arr. an. 3,15,2 gibt keinen Rang an). Beim Prozeß des → Philotas nahm er an der Verhaftung und Folterung teil. Zur Belohnung übernahm er mit → Kleitos das Kommando der Hetairoi. In → Baktria und → Sogdiana wird er kaum erwähnt, überraschenderweise überhaupt nicht bei Kleitos' Tod, und als Ankläger des → Kallisthenes nur bei Plutarch (Alexandros 55,1), aus unbestimmbarer Quelle. Erst beim indischen Feldzug, und besonders nach der Meuterei am → Hyphasis, erscheint er in führenden Rollen. Bei → Patala und im Kampf mit den → Oreitai führte er wichtige Aufträge aus und von → Karmania führte er das Gros des Heeres und den Troß nach → Susa. Bei den Hochzeiten von Susa heiratete er eine Schwester von Alexandros' königlicher Braut → Stateira. Dort wurde er wahrscheinlich zum → Chiliarchos ernannt. In → Ekbatana starb er im Winter 324/3, vor allem an unmäßigem Weingenuß. Alexandros ließ seinen Arzt hinrichten, verbrannte die Leiche H.s auf einem königlichen Scheiterhaufen, richtete ihm mit → Ammons [1] Erlaubnis einen Heroskult ein und ließ die persischen Königsfeuer auslöschen (was als Vorzeichen seines eigenen Todes gedeutet wurde). Der »Löwe von Hamadan« könnte sein Denkmal sein.

H. war als Heerführer kompetent, doch nicht so hervorragend wie andere Offiziere, und Alexandros wußte es. Als gehässiger Intrigant vertrug er sich mit vielen der Hofleute und Heerführer nicht, doch hatte Alexandros (zum Teil auch deshalb) zu ihm volles Vertrauen. Er soll gesagt haben, daß H. ohne ihn nichts wäre (Plut. Alexandros 47,11).

BERVE 2, Nr. 357 • HECKEL, 65–90. E. B.

[2] Bildhauer aus Athen, Sohn des Myron und Vater des → Eutychides (beide ebenfalls Bildhauer). Anhand von neun erh. Basis-Inschr. in Delos ist seine Schaffenszeit von 124 v. Chr. bis Anf. 1. Jh. v. Chr. einzugrenzen. Einige seiner Werke waren Porträtstatuen, zwei davon aufgrund der Standspuren aus Bronze.

V. C. GOODLETT, Rhodian sculpture workshops, in: AJA 95, 1991, 672 • LOEWY, Nr. 252–255 • J. MARCADÉ, Recueil des signatures de sculpteurs grecs, 2, 1957, 58–62 • Ders., Au musée de Délos, 1969, 59, 65–66 • OVERBECK, Nr. 2245–2247 (Quellen). R. N.

[3] Sohn des Thrasyllos; war vor 62 v. Chr. *syngenḗs kai epistratēgós* (συγγενὴς καὶ ἐπιστρατηγός) der Thebais und agierte als → *dioikētḗs*, wohl des ganzen Landes; er wurde dann in das Amt selbst befördert, war dazu *pros tō idíō lógō kai pros procheírois* (πρὸς τῷ ἰδίῳ λόγῳ καὶ πρὸς προχείροις), 60 bis 57.
→ Hoftitel

PP 1/8, 30a; 31. • L. MOOREN, Aulic Titulature in Ptolemaic Egypt, 1975, 96 Nr. 060; 138 f. Nr. 0173 • J. D. THOMAS, The Epistrategos in Ptolemaic and Roman Egypt 1, 1975, 105 Nr. X • E. VAN'T DACK, Ptolemaica Selecta, 1988, 295 f. W. A.

[4] Metriker des 2. Jh. n. Chr., aus Alexandreia stammend, vielleicht Lehrer des Kaisers Lucius Verus (vgl. SHA Verus 2,5). Das bedeutendste Werk des Verf. ›vieler

Werke‹ (nach Suda η 659) war eine Abh. zur Metrik; diese umfaßte urspr. 48 B., wurde aber von H. selbst zunächst auf elf, dann auf drei B. und schließlich auf das h. noch erh. ›Handbüchlein‹ (*Encheirídion*; 181,11–16 Consbruch) zusammengestrichen (Suda η 659): Die Zusammenfassung ist schematisch, wenn auch reich an Beispielen aus verlorenen Werken; H. wollte sich offenbar nicht, wie → Heliodoros [3], an Anfänger wenden [5. 49–50]. Am Ende des *Encheirídion* sind zwei fragmentarische Abschnitte eines Werkes ›Über die Dichtung‹ (Περὶ ποιήματος) überliefert (eine Analyse poetischer Texte nach ihren metrischen Strukturen), dessen Verfasserschaft umstritten ist, sowie eine kurze Abh. über diakritische Zeichen, die metrische Besonderheiten ausweisen (Περὶ σημείων).

H. ist ein Anhänger der Theorie der *métra prōtótypa*, der zufolge alle Verse ausgehend von einigen grundlegenden (*prōtótypa*) Metren gebildet werden. Diese Metren werden ihrerseits aus der Kombination von kurzen Elementen mit je einer Zeiteinheit (⏑) und langen von je zwei Zeiteinheiten (–) gebildet. Nach einer Einführung zur Prosodie, in der H. auch das Phänomen der *synekphṓnēsis* (Synizese) behandelt, widmet H. jeden seiner neun *métra prōtótypa* ein Kapitel: dem Iambus (⏑–), dem Trochäus (–⏑), dem Daktylus (–⏑⏑), dem Anapäst (⏑⏑–), dem Choriambus (–⏑⏑–), dem Antispast (⏑––⏑), dem Ioniker *a maiore* (––⏑⏑), dem Ioniker *a minore* (⏑⏑––), dem Päan bzw. Kretiker (–⏑–). Aus ihnen werden die »uniformen« Verse gebildet, d. h. sie haben durchgängig denselben Rhythmus (iambisch, trochäisch, usw.) und treten in vollständiger Form (akatalektisch) auf, oder ihnen fehlt die letzte Silbe bzw. die beiden letzten (katalektisch; brachykatalektisch). Die Verse können aber auch »gemischt«, d. h. aus Metren mit verschiedenen Rhythmen zusammengestellt sein, und zwar insbes.: a) aus verwandten oder »ähnlichen« (ὁμοιοειδῆ) Metren gemischt; b) »kontrastierend« gemischt (κατ᾽ ἀντιπάθειαν) wie der sapphische Hendekasyllabus; c) asynartetisch, »nicht miteinander verbunden«, d. h. ohne homogene rhythmische Struktur (vgl. [3; 5; 7]); d) polyschematisch. H. behandelt schließlich auch die »unklaren« (συγκεχυμένα) Verse (schol. Hermog. 78,1–2 C.). Die Lehre des H. stimmt mit dem metrisch-rhythmischen System des ersten Buches des → Aristeides [7] Quintilianus überein [3; 4]. In H.' frg. 2 = 77,4–17 C., wo von der »Verwandtschaft« (συγγένεια) der Metren untereinander die Rede ist, scheinen sich darüber hinaus die Kriterien der anderen grundlegenden Theorie der griech. Metrik zu finden, nach der sich alle Verse vom daktylischen Hexameter und vom iambischen Trimeter ableiten lassen [5. 380].

Das Hdb. des H. stellte die Grundlage für die Metrik in der byz. Schule dar und wurde von → Longinos und → Choiroboskos kommentiert, mit Scholien versehen und später zu einem Kompendium zusammengefaßt (Ausg. dieser Texte in [2. 79–334]). Es beeinflußte auch die ma. Überl. poetischer Texte (vgl. [1]). Iohannes → Tzetzes verfaßte eine poetische Version des *Encheirídion*. Doch die Theorie des H. hat bis in moderne Darstellungen der Metrik hinein starke Nachwirkung gehabt: Noch das Lehrbuch von P. Masqueray von 1899 hält sich daran.

→ Lautlehre; Metrik; Philoxenos

1 J. Irigoin, Les scholies métriques de Pindar, 1958, 93–106.

Ed.: 2 M. Consbruch, 1906.

Lit.: 3 B. Gentili, L'asinarteto nella teoria metrico-ritmica degli antichi, in: P. Händel, W. Meid (Hrsg.), FS Robert Muth, 1983, 135–143 4 J. M. van Ophuijsen, H. On Metre. A translation and commentary, 1987
5 B. M. Palumbo Stracca, La teoria antica degli asinarteti, 1979 (Übers. und Komm. zu 43,5–56,3 C.)
6 R. Pretagostini, Le teorie metrico-ritmiche degli antichi, in: G. Cambiano et al. (Hrsg.), Lo spazio letterario della Grecia antica, I,2, 373–379 7 L. E. Rossi, Teoria e storia degli asinarteti dagli arcaici agli alessandrini, in: Miscellanea filologica. Problemi di metrica classica, 1978, 29–48.

S. FO./Ü: T. H.

[5] H. von Theben, verfaßte um 381 n. Chr. ein astrologisches Werk in drei B.: 1. Grundbegriffe, 2. Prognosen für Neugeborene, 3. Zeitpunkte für Handlungsbeginn (*katarchaí*). H. zitiert darin ältere Lit. über weite Strecken (fast) wörtlich: → Nechepso, → Dorotheos [5] (teilweise in Prosa umgesetzt) und → Ptolemaios. Vier verschiedene Epitomai sind erhalten.

→ Astrologie

D. Pingree (Ed.), Hephaestionis Thebani apotelesmaticorum libri tres, 1973–1974 • W. und H. G. Gundel, Astrologumena, 1966, 241–244.

W. H.

Hephaistos (Ἥφαιστος).

I. Mythos II. Kult III. Ikonographie

I. Mythos

H., der Sohn der → Hera, ist der griech. Gott des Feuers, der Schmiede und der Handwerker; die Etym. des Namens ist unbekannt.

In den min.-myk. Texten ist H. nicht belegt, auch wenn vielleicht ein theophorer Name im myk. Knossos erscheint (*apaitijo*, KN L 588; [1. 34f.]). Bei Homer ist H. eng mit seinem Element, dem → Feuer, verbunden. Er ist der Besitz des Feuers, das formelhaft φλὸξ Ἡφαιστοῖο (»Flamme des H.«) heißt (Hom. Il. 9,468 usw.), und sein Name wird überhaupt metonymisch für Feuer verwendet (Hom. Il. 2,426 usw., Formel); er greift auch auf Bitte Heras mit dem Feuer in den Kampf des Achilleus gegen Skamandros ein (Hom. Il. 21,328–382). Vor allem aber ist er als Herr des Feuers der göttliche Schmied: Er stellt den neuen Schild für Achilleus her, schafft eine Reihe wundersamer Automata für sich selbst und andere, selbstfahrende Dreifüße (Hom. Il. 18,373–379), goldene Dienerinnen (ebd. 417–421), bronzene Hunde als Wächter für König Alkinoos (Hom. Od. 7,91–94, ein altoriental. Motiv [2]); bei Hes. erg. 70f. arbeitet er außerdem mit Athena zusammen bei der Schöpfung der → Pandora.

In der Gesellschaft der »leicht lebenden« homer. Götter ist er ein Außenseiter: Er arbeitet und schwitzt dabei (Hom. Il. 18,372); beim Mahl der Götter (das wie das menschliche Symposion ges. Rollen darstellt) versucht er sich in der Rolle des → Ganymedes [1] und erntet Gelächter (Hom. Il. 1,571–600); in seiner Ehe mit → Aphrodite wird er von seinem Bruder → Ares betrogen (Hom. Od. 8,267–366). Es fehlt ihm auch die körperliche Vollkommenheit der anderen Götter: er hat verkrüppelte Füße (die archa. Vasenbilder stellen sie meist rückwärts verdreht dar). Während Homer → Zeus als Vater nennt (Hom. Il. 1,578; 14,388; Hom. Od. 8,312), hat Hera ihn bei Hesiod parthenogenetisch geboren (theog. 927), wie sie das Ungeheuer Typhaon (Hom. h. Apoll. 305–355, als Reaktion auf die Geburt der Athena) oder den Außenseiter Ares gebiert (Ov. fast. 5,229–258); dabei ist diese Geburt die Folge eines Streits mit Zeus, der mit seinem Verhältnis zu → Metis und der mutterlosen Geburt der Athena aus seinem Kopf reagiert (Hes. fr. 343, vgl. theog. 886–900). Als Hera das verkrüppelte Kind sieht, wirft sie es erzürnt aus dem Olymp ins Meer, wo Eurynome und → Thetis es aufziehen (Hom. Il. 18,395–405; ähnlich Hom. h. Apoll. 316–320); oder Zeus zürnt H., weil er sich auf Heras Seite gegen ihn stellt, und wirft ihn aus dem Olymp auf die Erde, wo er auf der Insel → Lemnos landet und von den Sinties gepflegt wird (Hom. Il. 1,590–594).

Doch darf man H. nicht unterschätzen: Er schafft nicht nur wunderbare Automaten und ist insofern sozial geschickt, als er absichtlich Lachen provoziert, um die Götter aufzuheitern; er rächt sich mit Hilfe seiner raffinierten Kunst sowohl an den Ehebrechern Aphrodite und Ares, die er ihrerseits dem Lachen aussetzt (Hom. Od. 8,267–366), wie an seiner Mutter Hera (Alkaios fr. 349 L.-P.). So zeichnet das Epos die Stellung nach, welche der durch seine Kunst unentbehrliche, hoch geschätzte und gleichzeitig heimlich gefürchtete Schmied in einer frühen aristokratischen Ges. einnahm; ähnliches findet sich in anderen Ges. [3].

Abgesehen von der Entwicklung in Athen setzt die Folgezeit dieses Bild ohne grundsätzliche Änderungen fort. Seine technischen Fähigkeiten machen ihn seit dem 5. Jh. v. Chr. zum Kulturbringer, der das tiergleiche Leben der Menschen (ein sophistisches Motiv) grundlegend veränderte (Hom. h. 20). Seine im Epos nur vage lokalisierte Werkstatt wird auf oder unter aktiven Vulkanen (etwa dem Aetna: Aischyl. Prom. 365 f., oder Hiera, eine der Liparischen Inseln: Thuk. 3,88,3) angesetzt, wo er auch einen Kult hat (Ail. nat. 11,3; Strab. 6,2,10); die → Kyklopen, die für Zeus Donner und Blitz herstellen (Hes. theog. 141), werden ihm als Arbeiter beigesellt. Ebenso kann er mit anderen natürlichen Feuern verbunden werden, wie denjenigen auf dem lykischen Olymp (Sen. epist. 79,3) oder der Gegend von Pozzuoli (Agora des H., Strab. 5,4,6 – wobei eine Trennung von → Volcanus unmöglich ist).

II. Kult

Unter den Kultorten des H. ist Lemnos, wo der Mythos ihn nach dem Fall aus dem Olymp leben ließ, bes. wichtig; hier sollen Feuer und Waffenherstellung erfunden worden sein (Hellanikos, FGrH 4 F 71; Tzetz. Lykophr. 227). Eine der beiden Städte der Insel heißt Hephaistias (Steph. Byz. s. v.), nach einem Heiligtum des H., dessen Priester eponymer Jahresbeamter ist. Er ist verbunden mit den lokalen Mysterien der → Kabeiroi, deren Vater er ist (Hdt. 3,37; auf Samothrake bezogen von Strab. 10,3,20 f.) [4]. Diese Verbindung leitet sich wohl von derjenigen archa. Schmiedebünde her. Im Hintergrund steht Un- und Vorgriechisches: die Sinties gelten als vorgriech. Thraker (Steph. Byz. s. v. Lemnos) oder als Etrusker (schol. Apoll. Rhod. 1,608). Doch darf man daraus und aus der Vielzahl der Münzen und theophoren Eigennamen in Kleinasien nicht auf außergriech. Herkunft schließen (trotz der überwältigenden Mehrheit der früheren Forscher, die ihn aus Kleinasien, vielleicht Lykien ableiteten [5. 1–3]). Vielmehr geht die Verbindung mit Lemnos mit der Marginalität des H. zusammen, und die (späten) kleinasiatischen Belege weisen auf die → Interpretatio Graeca mit einer indigenen Gottheit hin.

Besser bekannt ist der Kult in Athen, wo H. eng mit → Athena als Patronin des Handwerks und Göttin der praktischen Klugheit verbunden ist; die Handwerker können verstanden werden als »H. und Athena geweiht« (Plat. leg. 11,920d, vgl. Solon, fr. 13,49 f.). In seinem städtischen Hauptheiligtum auf dem Hügel zwischen Kerameikos und Agora, dem kurz nach 450 v. Chr. gebauten sog. »Theseion«, stand die Kultbildgruppe von H. und Athena (Hephaistia: Hesych. s. v.) nebeneinander, eine Schöpfung des → Alkamenes [2] aus dem J. 421/20 v. Chr. (Cic. nat. deor. 1,83; vgl. Val. Max. 8,11 ext. 3; Paus. 1,14,6; [5. 75–90]). Gleichzeitig mit dem Tempel wurde 429/428 das Fest der Hephaistia zu Ehren der beiden Gottheiten als Penteteris (alle vier Jahr gefeiertes Fest) neu organisiert, mit Fackellauf und großen Opfern (Aristot. Ath. pol. 54,7; das Sakralgesetz LSCG 13). Dies spiegelt die Bed. der Handwerker in der athenischen Demokratie; der Fackellauf erinnert an das Thema des neuen Feuers, das auch für Lemnos wichtig ist und mit H.' Rolle als Kulturbringer zusammengeht [6; 7]. Ebenso wichtig ist das Fest der Chalkeia (»Schmiedefest«) für H. und Athena, an dem die Handwerker in einer Prozession durch die Stadt zogen (Soph. fr. 844). Am Geschlechterfest der → Apaturia schließlich sangen die Teilnehmer in ihren schönsten Kleidern, mit einer Fackel in der Hand, einen Hymnos auf H. und opferten ihm (Istros, FGrH 334 F 2). Mit diesem Ritual hängt der athenische Mythos von H.' Versuch, Athena Gewalt anzutun, zusammen: Sein Sperma fiel dabei auf die Erde und erzeugte das Kind → Erichthonios [1], den autochthonen Ahn der athenischen Geschlechter [8].

H. wurde mit dem ägypt. Ptah in Memphis (Hdt. 2,2. 99), dem etr. Sethlans und dem röm. → Volcanus gleichgesetzt – letzteres bereits im späten 6. Jh. v. Chr., nach Ausweis einer sf. Vase mit H.' Heimführung, die am Volcanal auf dem Forum Romanum gefunden wurde [9].

1 M. Gérard-Rousseau, Les mentions religieuses dans les tablettes mycéniennes, 1968 2 C. Faraone, Hephaestus the Magician and Near Eastern Parallels to Alcinous's Watchdogs, in: GRBS 28, 1987, 257–280 3 M. Eliade, Forgerons et alchimistes, 1977 4 B. Hemberg, Die Kabiren, 1950 5 F. Brommer, H. Der Schmiedegott in der ant. Kunst, 1978 6 Deubner, 212f. 7 W. Burkert, Iason, Hypsipyle and new fire on Lemnos. A study in myth and ritual, in: CQ 20, 1970, 1–16 8 N. Loraux, Les enfants d'Athéna. Idées athéniennes sur la citoyenneté et la divison des sexes, 1981 9 F. Coarelli, Il Foro Romano. Periodo Arcaico, 1983, 177.

M. Delcourt, Héphaistos ou la légende du magicien, 1957 (Ndr. 1982) • A. Burford, Craftmanship in Greek and Roman Society, 1979 • A. Hermary, A. Jacquemin, s. v. H., LIMC 4, 257–280.

F. G.

III. Ikonographie

Die frühesten bildl. Überl. des H. auf korinth. und att. Vasen seit dem 2. Viertel des 6. Jh. v. Chr. zeigen den Gott bei der Geburt der Athena, der Hochzeit des Peleus und v.a. bei seiner Rückführung in den Olymp (François-Krater, Florenz, AM, 570/560 v. Chr.). Er wird mit oder ohne Bart dargestellt, zunächst ohne Kopfbedeckung, erst ab dem frühen 5. Jh. v. Chr. mit → Pilos, gelegentlich auch mit → Petasos; die Verkrüppelung seiner Füße ist auf wenigen archa. Vasen abgebildet. Seine Attribute wechseln entsprechend seiner dargestellten Tätigkeit: Beil bzw. Doppelhammer, seit Ende des 6. Jh. v. Chr. Schmiedewerkzeuge (Hammer und – oft glühende – Zange), die ihm wie Blasebalg und Feuerbrände auch als Waffe dienen. Pausanias beschreibt 5,19,8 die Waffenübergabe des H. an Thetis auf der → Kypseloslade in Olympia (um 600 v. Chr.) und 3,18,13 H.' Verfolgung der Athena auf dem »Thron« des Apollon in Amyklai (2. H. 6. Jh. v. Chr.). H.' Gegenwart ist bei der Erschaffung der Pandora auf der Reliefbasis der Athena Parthenos zu erwarten (447/6–439/8 v. Chr.; Paus. 1,24,7; Plin. nat. 36,18.; vgl. die Pränestinische Ciste in London, BM, Original spätes 4. Jh. v. Chr.). Im Ostgiebel des → Parthenon auf der Athener Akropolis war H. bei der Geburt Athenas dargestellt (438–432 v. Chr.), der Ostfries zeigt H. inmitten der versammelten Götter (um 440 v. Chr.). Der Nordfries des Siphnierschatzhauses in Delphi (um 525 v. Chr.) überl. H. im Gigantenkampf. Als erste freiplastische Darstellung des Gottes gilt das nicht erh. Kultbild des → Alkamenes [2], das zusammen mit Athena im Hephaisteion von Athen aufgestellt war (421/20–417/6 v. Chr.).

Von → Volcanus, der röm. Entsprechung des H., sind zahlreiche Statuetten erh. (u. a. große Mamorstatuette aus den Mithras-Thermen in Ostia, 2. Jh. n. Chr., sowie überwiegend kaiserzeitl. Bronzestatuetten); er erscheint in Werkstattszenen, oft in Begleitung der ihn bei seiner Arbeit unterstützenden → Kyklopen, auf Sarkophagen des 2.–3. Jh. n. Chr., pompejan. Wandgemälden und (wenigen) Mosaiken (z. B. Tunis, Bardo-Mus., aus Dougga; vgl. Vulcanus als Monatszeichen September: sog. Monnusmosaik, Trier, Rhein. Landesmus., um 300 n. Chr.); der Schmiedegott ist überl. auf Reliefs mit Darstellungen der Zwölf-Götter (*Dōdekátheoi/Dei* → *consentes*: »Ara Borghese«, Paris, LV, frühe Kaiserzeit?), aus den Nordwest-Prov. des Röm. Reiches bes. auf Weihreliefs und → Viergöttersteinen des 1.–3. Jh. n. Chr.; relativ häufig sind Münzbilder aus Kleinasien, überwiegend 3. Jh. n. Chr.

T. H. Carpenter, Dionysian imagery in archaic Greek art, 1986 • A. Hermary, A. Jaquemin, s. v. H., LIMC 4, 627–654 (mit ält. Lit.) • A. Schöne, Der Thiasos. Eine ikonographische Unt. über das Gefolge des Dionysos in der att. Vasenmalerei des 6. und 5. Jh. v. Chr., 1987 • E. Simon, G. Bauchhenss, s. v. Vulcanus, LIMC 8, 283–298 (mit ält. Lit.).

A. L.

Hephthalitai. Nach der Einteilung R. Göbls ([1], vgl. [2]) erlebte → Iran seit dem 4. Jh. n. Chr. vier aufeinanderfolgende »Wellen« von Einbrüchen hunnischer Völker. Während die ersten drei Gruppen dieser »iranischen Hunnen« (Kidariten, Alchon, Nezak) in den lit. Quellen wenig Spuren hinterlassen haben, gehörten die H. im 5./6. Jh. n. Chr. zu den prominentesten und gefährlichsten östl. Nachbarn der Perser. Sie sind erstmals für die Zeit des Königs Peroz ausdrücklich bezeugt und werden von Prokopios (BP 1,3) anschaulich beschrieben. Nach seinem Zeugnis waren die *Ephthalitai* ein hunnisches Volk und wurden auch ›weiße Hunnen‹ genannt. Er betont jedoch, daß sie nicht mit den sonst bekannten Hunnen vermischt waren, sich von ihnen in Aussehen und Lebensweise unterschieden und getrennt von den übrigen nördlich der Perser wohnten. Die H. seien keine Nomaden, hätten einen König und ein geordnetes Staatswesen. Die H. haben z.Z. des Peroz und seines Sohnes Cavades I. starken Einfluß auf das Sāsānidenreich genommen, bis ihre Macht um 560 durch gemeinsame Aktionen der Westtürken und der Sāsāniden unter → Chosroes I. gebrochen wurde.

1 R. Göbl, Antike Numismatik, Bd. 2, 1978, 107f.
2 F. Altheim, R. Stiehl, Gesch. Mittelasiens im Altertum, 1970, 690–698.

M. Alram, Die Gesch. Ostirans ... bis zu den iranischen Hunnen, in: W. Seipel (Hrsg.), Weihrauch und Seide, 1996, 119–140 • M. Schottky, s. v. Huns, EncIr (im Druck).

M. SCH.

Heptanomia. Von Augustus vor 11/12 n. Chr. eingerichtete Verwaltungseinheit Ägyptens, die das Gebiet zwischen Delta und Thebais umfaßte. Die sieben Gaue waren der Memphites, Herakleopolites, Aphroditopolites, Oxyrhynchites, Kynopolites, Hermopolites und vielleicht Letopolites; von Anfang an wurden diesen sieben der Arsinoites und oft auch die kleine Oase zugerechnet. Unter Marcus Aurelius und Commodus ist die Erweiterung auf elf Gaue bezeugt, doch ist die Zusammensetzung z.Z. nicht sicher feststellbar. Die H. unterstand einem Epistrategen im Rang eines *procurator Augusti*.

J.D. THOMAS, The Epistrategos in Ptolemaic and Roman Egypt 2, 1982, 19ff. W.A.

Heptateuchdichter. Der Name wurde dem Autor einer Hexameterversion der ersten sieben B. der Bibel gegeben, die in einer Hs. des 9. Jh. fälschlich → Cyprianus zugeschrieben wurde. Das wahrscheinlich in Gallien im frühen 5. Jh. verf. Gedicht ist das längste der spätant. Bibelepen (über 5700 V.). Eine Ausnahme in dieser Gattung bilden die drei Abschnitte in Hendekasyllaba, die biblischen *Cantica* entsprechen. Urspr. war das Gedicht wesentlich länger als in der jetzigen Gestalt und umfaßte alle Gesch.-B. des AT (Hss.-Kat. verweisen auf andere, h. nur in Fr. erh. B.). Der H. wurde von den angelsächsischen Autoren Aldhelm und → Beda gelesen und zit., in karolingischer Zeit abgeschrieben und exzerpiert, aber danach weitgehend vergessen.
→ Bibeldichtung

R. PEIPER, CSEL 23,1–211 (ed.) · R. HERZOG, Die Bibelepik der lat. Spätant., 1975, 53–60, 99–154. M.RO./Ü: M.MO.

Hera (Ἥρα, Ἥρη, myk. *e-ra*).
I. KULT UND MYTHOS II. IKONOGRAPHIE

I. KULT UND MYTHOS

H. ist die Tochter von → Kronos und → Rhea und Gattin des → Zeus; sie ist einerseits mit der Welt der frühen Polis (insbes. der jungen kriegerischen Männer) verbunden, andererseits und vor allem Schutzgöttin der Ehen, deren Prototyp ihre Ehe mit Zeus darstellt.

Ihre kultische (und wohl auch mythische) Verbindung mit Zeus ist bereits in den Linear B-Dokumenten faßbar, wo sie in Pylos (PY Tn 316, mit Zeus und *dirimijo* = Drimios, Sohn des Zeus [1. 94–96]) und Theben (TH Of 28) belegt ist. Bei Homer und später ist sie die Ehefrau des Zeus, in einer oft gespannten Verbindung (was auch die Wahrnehmung von Ehe in der homer. Ges. reflektiert); während Zeus in der *Ilias* über den Parteien zu stehen hat, nimmt H. resolut Partei für die Griechen, bis hin zur Täuschung ihres Gatten (Hom. Il. 14, vgl. 20,30–33). Die männl. Kinder aus dieser Ehe spiegeln diese Spannungen (Katalog Hes. theog. 921–923). Während die Tochter → Hebe als Göttin der Jugendblüte die Voraussetzung, die Tochter → Eileithyia als Geburtsgöttin die natürliche Folge der Ehe ist, sind → Ares und der bei Homer (nicht bei Hesiod) als gemeinsamer Sohn bezeichnete → Hephaistos problematische Außenseiter; den Hephaistos hat H. nach Hes. theog. 927 parthenogenetisch geboren. Eine ähnliche Ambivalenz der Göttin erscheint in ihrer (allerdings letztlich beigelegten) Feindschaft gegen den Zeussohn → Herakles und darin, daß sie Mutter oder Ziehmutter von Ungeheuern (Typhon: Hom. h. Apoll. 305–355; Hydra und Löwe von Nemea: Hes. theog. 313f.; 327f.) ist. In der späteren philos. → Allegorese wird H. regelmäßig mit der Luft identifiziert; das wird aus der Metathese der Buchstaben ihres Namens (HPA → AHP) abgeleitet und aus der homer. Erzählung über ihre Bestrafung durch Zeus: er hängt sie an einer goldenen Kette am Himmel (= Aither) auf, mit zwei Ambossen (= Wasser und Erde) an den Füßen (Hom. Il. 15,18–21; Herakleitos, Allegoriae Homericae 40 [2]).

H.s Heiligtümer gehören zu den frühesten, die durch große, oft monumentale Tempelbauten ausgezeichnet sind: das gilt für Perachora, Argos, Samos ebenso wie die großen Heraia Süditaliens (Metapontum, Kroton, Paestum); diese Heiligtümer liegen gewöhnlich deutlich außerhalb der Siedlungen, was oft mit bes. Kultformen zusammengeht [3]. Die Rolle der Tempel und der Umstand, daß in Heraia sehr oft Tempelmodelle dediziert wurden, weist auf die Bed., die H. für die archa. politische Gemeinschaft hat [4].

Der Kult H.s nimmt die beiden Aspekte auf, den der Schützerin von Städten, insbes. ihrer jungen Männer, und den der Schützerin von Ehen, Ehefrauen und Kindern; die Doppelheit von politischer Gottheit und Frauengöttin spiegelt die Rolle der Bürgersfrau in der Polis und wiederholt sich bei der früh mit ihr identifizierten röm. → Iuno. Dabei treten im Lauf der Entwicklung die polit. Aspekte zusehends hinter denen der Göttin von Brautschaft, Ehe und Mutterschaft zurück.

Als Göttin, deren mythische Biographie das normale Frauenleben spiegelt, kann H. gleichzeitig »Mädchen« (*Pais*), »Eheschließerin« (*Téleia*), »Witwe« (*Chḗra*) heißen (Paus. 8,22,2), den Beinamen »Braut« (*Nympheuoménē*) tragen (Bild im Tempel der H. Teleia von Plataiai, Paus. 9,2,7) oder gar rituell ihre Jungfräulichkeit wieder erlangen (Paus. 3,28,2). Als Ehegöttin heißt sie durchgehend Téleia (*télos*, »Vollendung« bezeichnet die Ehe), seltener Zygia; als H. Teleia wird sie zusammen mit Zeus Teleios im Hochzeitsritual angerufen (Aischyl. Eum. 214f. und fr. 383; vgl. Aristoph. Thesm. 973–976). Vereinzelte Feste sind mit der mythischen Hochzeit zwischen Zeus und H. verbunden, bes. das att. Fest der Theogamia (→ Hieros Gamos) und ein unbekanntes kretisches Fest, das als »Nachahmung« dieser Hochzeit gilt (Diod. 5,72,4) [5]. Als Empfängerin eines »Wochenbett« (*lechérna*) genannten Opfers in Argos (Hesych. s.v.) ist sie direkt, als Mutter von → Eileithyia indirekt mit den Geburten verbunden, und Weihungen aus einzelnen Heraia weisen sie als → Kurotrophos aus [6; 7]; andere Riten verbinden sie mit heranwachsenden Kindern (Hera Akraia in Korinth: schol. Eur. Med. 264; [8]), inbes. Mädchen (Foce del Sele).

Die großen Kultorte spiegeln diesen Doppelaspekt in der erh. Dokumentation wenigstens zum Teil. H.s Lieblingsstädte in der *Ilias* sind Argos, Mykenai und Sparta (Hom. Il. 4,51f.); während die Kulte in Sparta [9. 46] und Mykene blaß bleiben, ist das Heraion von → Argos ihr Hauptkultort während der ganzen Ant., neben demjenigen von → Samos und den unterital. Heraia von Kroton und Paestum (Foce del Sele).

Das zentrale argiv. Fest waren die Heraia, die nach dem Hauptopfer auch Hekatombaia genannt wurden; ihr Hauptritual war die Opferprozession aus der Stadt in das weit außerhalb gelegene Heiligtum, in dem sich die Polis Argos unter H.s Schutz darstellte und symbolisch konstituierte: In ihr wurden die hundert Kühe, deren Opferfleisch an alle Bürger verteilt wurde, mitgeführt, in ihr fuhr die eponyme Priesterin auf einem Ochsenwagen mit (Hdt. 1,31), und auserlesene junge Männer trugen den hl. Schild der Göttin, den der Urkönig → Danaos geweiht und seine Nachfolger seit → Lynkeus getragen hatten [10]. Das Thema der Ehe mit Zeus ist durch den Mythos von Zeus' Verführung der H. in Gestalt eines Kuckucks angesprochen: Der Mythos ist am argiv. Kuckucksberg (mit einem Zeusheiligtum) lokalisiert, und ein Kuckuck krönt H.s Szepter am argiv. Kultbild (Paus. 2,36,1 f.; schol. Theokr. 15, 64; [9. 42–45]); die Rolle als Geburtsgöttin spiegelt sich in der argiv. → Epiklese Eileithyia (Hesych. s. v.).

Das samische Heiligtum, dem Mythos zufolge mit Argos dadurch verbunden, daß das hochaltertümliche Kultbild (*brétas*) von dort kam (Menodotos, FGrH 541 F 1; Paus. 7,4,4), ist in archa. Zeit das Zentrum der staatl. Repräsentation. Das Hauptfest der Toneia (so die bessere hsl. Überl.) spielt ein Ausnahmeritual durch, bei dem man auf Zweiglagern aus Lygos liegt (ein Lygosbaum ist Zentrum des Heiligtums) und rituell das aus dem Tempel verschwundene Kultbild sucht, findet, wäscht und neu einkleidet (Menodotos); die Einzelheiten weisen nicht, wie die frühere Forsch. (seit Varro) meinte, auf ein Hochzeitsritual, sondern auf ein Neujahrsritual, in welchem das normalerweise gefesselte Kultbild freigesetzt wurde [11; 12].

Die von den Bewohnern von Plataiai bzw. einer größeren Zahl umliegender boiotischer Orte gefeierten kleinen (alle sieben) und großen (alle 60 Jahre) Daidala spielen nach den ausführlichen ant. Beschreibungen (Plut. fr. 157; Paus. 9,3,3–8) ein Hochzeitsritual aus, in dem bräutlich geschmückte Holzpuppen in einer Prozession auf den Gipfel des → Kithairon gefahren und dort auf einem Scheiterhaufen verbrannt werden; der Mythos versteht die Herstellung und Zurschaustellung der Puppen als Erinnerung an eine List des Zeus, um sich mit der eifersüchtigen H. zu versöhnen. Wichtiger als der Hochzeitsaspekt ist derjenige der gewaltsamen Zerstörung im riesigen Feuer, zu dem zahlreiche Parallelen existieren, und die Rolle der Städte, die sich alle mit dem Opfer einer Kuh für H. und eines Stiers für Zeus beteiligen.

1 M. Gérard-Rousseau, Les mentions religieuses dans les tablettes mycéniennes, 1968 **2** P. Lévêque, Aurea catena Homeri, 1959 **3** F. Graf, Culti e credenze nella Magna Grecia, in: Megale Hellas. Nome e immagine (Atti del Convegno di Studi sulla Magna Grecia 21, 1982), 157–185 **4** F. de Polignac, La naissance de la cité grecque. Culte, espace et société, VIIIe-VIIe siècles av. J.-C., 1984 **5** J.C. Bermejo Barrera, Zeus, H. y el matrimonio sagrado, in: Quaderni di Storia 15, 1989, 133–156 **6** T.H. Price, Kourotrophos, 1978, 138–146 **7** S.I. Johnston, Corinthian Medea and the Cult of Hera Akraia, in: J. Clauss, S.I. Johnston (Hrsg.), Medea, 1997, 44–70 **8** A. Brelich, I figli di Medeia, in: Studi e materiali di storia delle religioni 30, 1959, 213–254 **9** Nilsson, Feste **10** W. Burkert, Homo necans, 1972, 163 f. **11** G. Kipp, Zum H.-Kult auf Samos, in: F. Hampl, I. Weiler (Hrsg.), Kritische und vergleichende Studien 18, 1974, 157–208 **12** Graf, 93–96 **13** M. Cremer, Hieros Gamos im Orient und in Griechenland, in: ZPE 48, 1982, 283–290.

Nilsson, 427–433 • Ph.E. Slater, The Glory of H. Greek Mythology and the Greek Family, 1968 • K. Kerényi, Zeus und H. Urbild des Vaters, des Gatten und der Frau, 1972 • W. Pötscher, H. Eine Strukturanalyse im Vergleich mit Athena, 1987 • D.Q. Adams, Hêrôs and Hêrê, in: Glotta 65, 1987, 171–178 • A. Kossatz-Deissmann, s. v. H., LIMC 4.1, 659–719 • B.M. Fridh-Haneson, H.'s Wedding on Samos. A Change of Paradigm, in: R. Hägg, N. Marinatos, G.C. Nordquist (Hrsg.), Early Greek Cult Practice, 1988, 205–213 • J.V. O'Brien, The Transformation of H. A Study in Ritual, Hero, and the Goddess in the Iliad, 1993 • R. Häussler, H. und Juno. Wandlungen und Beharrung einer Göttin, 1995. F.G.

II. Ikonographie

Einzeldarstellungen der Göttin H. sind nur in wenigen Überl. gesichert; im myth. Gruppenkontext ist sie eindeutiger zu erkennen, v.a. als Zeus-Begleiterin, im Habitus einer Braut, in → Hieros-Gamos- und Werbungsbildern oder als matronale, hieratische Gottheit. Zu ihrer charakterist. Ikonographie gehörten der → Peplos mit Himation, der meist wie ein Schleier über ihren Kopf geführt ist, → Polos oder Stephane sowie die Attribute Zepter, → Phiale, Granatapfel. Als Kultgöttin war sie insbes. im dor.-achäischen Raum bedeutend, ihre auf Münzbildern (seit 5. Jh. v. Chr.; überwiegend kaiserzeitl.) und in Schriftquellen bezeugten Kultbilder aber sind meist nicht erh.

So liefert Pausanias Beschreibungen u.a. aus Argos von der berühmten thronenden H. des → Polykleitos aus Gold-Elfenbein (spätes 5. Jh. v. Chr.; Paus. 2. 17,4; vgl. Darstellung auf argivischen Br.-Mz.) und dem älteren Xoanon (Paus. 2,17,5), von der Kultgruppe in Olympia mit thronender H. und stehendem Zeus (Paus. 5,17,1), der Kultgruppe des → Praxiteles in Mantineia mit thronender H., stehender Athena und Hebe (etwa Mitte 4. Jh. v. Chr.; Paus. 8, 9, 3). Das Kultbild des → Alkamenes [2] im H.-Tempel bei Athen (430/400 v. Chr.; Paus. 1,1,5; 10,35,2) wurde in Kopien verschiedener Peplophoren des 5. Jh. v. Chr. erkannt (versuchte Identifizierung mit der Hestia Giustiniani, Rom, VA) und scheint auf Urkundenreliefs wiedergegeben zu sein (Vertrag zw. Athen und Samos, Athen, AM, 403/2 v. Chr.). Eine Holzstatuette aus dem → Heraion auf Samos (Vathy, Mus., 3. Viertel des 7. Jh. v. Chr.) stellt wohl H. dar, wie auch die dort geborgene Mamorstatue des späten 4. Jh. v. Chr. (Berlin, SM) und das monumentale Standbild aus der Zeit um 210/160 v. Chr. (Pythagoreion, Samos), während die von Cheramyes ebenfalls in das samische Heraion geweihte H.-Statue (Paris,

LV; 570/550 v. Chr.) auch als Kore aufgefaßt werden kann. Mit H. in Verbindung gebrachte Kopien klassischer Statuen sind ebenso auf Demeter (sog. Demeter Cherchel), Aphrodite (sog. H. Borghese) u. a. zu beziehen.

Frühe Überlieferungen der Hieros-Gamos-Gruppe vermutlich auf kretischem Reliefpithos (2. Viertel des 7. Jh. v. Chr., Basel, AM), Holzrelief aus Samos (verschollen, um 620/610 v. Chr.), Terrakottagruppe aus dem Heraion von Foce del Sele bei → Paestum (archa.), dann auf den um 470 v. Chr. datierten Metopen von Tempel E in Selinunt. Zahlreiche Vasenbilder überliefern das Götterpaar in Götterversammlungen, vgl. H. und Zeus auch im Parthenon-Ostfries (um 440 v. Chr.), Schatzhaus der Siphnier in Delphi, Ostfries (um 525 v. Chr.). Verschiedene Terrakotten aus Heraia geben mit einiger Wahrscheinlichkeit die Göttin wieder (seit dem 7. und insbes. im 6. Jh. v. Chr.).

Unter den myth. Darstellungen mit H. ist das Paris-Urteil verbreitetes Thema seit früher Zeit (Kanne des → Chigi-Malers, Rom, VG, um 630 v. Chr.); die Rückführung des Hephaistos auf den Olymp zur Befreiung der H. seit der 1. H. des 6. Jh. v. Chr. Der François-Krater (Florenz, AM, 570/560 v. Chr.) zeigt möglicherweise die gefesselte H. Relativ wenige Darstellungen zeigen H. mit Herakles: Bei der Einführung des Heros in den Olymp; Herakles schützt H. vor den sie verfolgenden Satyrn (Schale des → Brygos-Malers in London, BM, 490/480 v. Chr.); bei der Hochzeit des Herakles mit Hebe erscheint H. in ihrer Funktion als Brautmutter. Als kämpferische Göttin nimmt H. am → Giganten-Kampf teil: Schatzhaus der Siphnier in Delphi, Nordfries (um 525 v. Chr.), Parthenon, Ostmetope (um 440 v. Chr.), Ostfries des Pergamonaltars (um 160 v. Chr.), Hekataion von → Lagina, Westfries (2. H. des 2. Jh. v. Chr.).

A. DELIVORRIAS, Der statuarische Typus der sog. H. Borghese, in: H. BECK, P. C. BOL (Hrsg.), Polykletforsch., 1993, 221–252 • A. KOSSATZ-DEISSMANN, s. v. H., LIMC IV, 659–719 (mit ält. Lit.) • W. PÖTSCHER, H. Eine Strukturanalyse im Vergleich mit Athena, 1987. A. L.

Heraclianus. Weström. Usurpator im Jahre 413 n. Chr. Er ermordete 408 → Stilicho in Ravenna und wurde dafür durch die Ernennung zum *comes Africae* belohnt (Zos. 5,37,6). Trotz der dort geübten Willkürherrschaft erhielt er 413 das Konsulat (Oros. 7,42,10), erhob sich jedoch gegen → Honorius [3] und landete mit einer großen Flotte bei Rom. Er wurde besiegt und am 3. August 413 zum Tode verurteilt (Cod. Theod. 15,14,13). Er floh nach Karthago, wo man ihn tötete (Oros. 7,42,14; Zos. 6,7 ff.; Chron. min. 1,467, 654; 2,18,71 MOMMSEN).

PLRE 2, 539 f. • A. DEMANDT, Die Spätantike, 1989, 148 • ST.I. OOST, The Revolt of Heraclian, in: CPh 61, 1966, 236–242. K. P. J.

Heraclitus

[1] Septimius Severus beauftragte H. 193/4 n. Chr. damit, ihm die Herrschaft über Britannien zu sichern (SHA Sept. Sev. 6,10; SHA Pescennius 5,2 wird fälschlich Bithynia genannt) und möglicherweise dem Clodius Albinus den Caesar-Titel anzubieten. (Cass. Dio 73,15,1; Herodian. 2,15,4). Vielleicht ist er identisch mit dem *legatus* der *legio VI Ferrata* H. aus dem Jahre 196 (PIR² H 89; IGR 3,1107) bzw. mit H. [2] (PIR² H 88). T. F.

[2] Bekleidete 201 n. Chr. das Amt eines *procurator publici portorii vectigalis Illyrici*, als er von Septimius Severus und Caracalla ein Reskript bzgl. der Abgabenfreiheit der Stadt Tyras am Djnstr erhielt (CIL III 781, vgl. p. 1009 f. und Nr. 1209). Er kann identisch sein mit M. Aurelius H., dem Präsidialprokurator der Dacia Malvensis zwischen 198 und 209 n. Chr. (AE 1944, 100). Danach fungierte er offenbar als *praeses* der Provinz Mauretania Caesariensis (AE 1927, 24, 25). Daß dieser wiederum mit Aurelius Septimius H., *praefectus Aegypti* im Jahre 215, identifiziert werden kann, ist eher unwahrscheinlich (BGU II 362 col. VII 8 f, 20 f.).

PIR² H 90 • FPD 1, 91, Anm. 41 • PFLAUM, 684 ff., Nr. 253. T. F.

Heraia (Ἡραία). Westarkad. Stadt am rechten Ufer des mittleren Alpheios, kurz vor der Einmündung des Ladon, mit ausgedehntem Territorium, in dem mehrere befestigte Ortschaften lagen. Strategische Bed. hatte H. wegen seiner Lage an der großen Straße, die Elis, Arkadia und Argolis verband. Nach Paus. 8,26,1 lag H. auf einer Platte, die sanft von den Ufern des Alpheios ansteigt (geringe Reste beim h. Hagios Ioannis). Ein Bündnis mit Elis ist aus dem 6. Jh. bezeugt (IvOl 9; SGDI I, 1149; Syll.³ 9). Im 6. Jh. begann die Mz.-Prägung von H. Vom 6. bis 4. Jh. stellte H. mehrere Sieger bei den Olympischen Spielen. In klass. Zeit war die Stadt mit Sparta verbündet (Thuk. 5,67,1). Nach Strab. 8,3,2 veranlaßten die Spartaner z.Z. der Schlacht von Leuktra (371 v. Chr.) in H. einen Synoikismos von neun Dörfern (Xen. hell. 6,5,11; 22). H. war Mitglied im arkadischen Bund (IG V,2,1 = Syll.³ 183), 236 v. Chr. im achaiischen Bund (Polyain. 2,36; Ain. Takt. 18,8 ff.), wurde 227 von Kleomenes III. besetzt (Plut. Kleomenes 7,3), 222/1 von Antigonos [3] Doson (Pol. 2,54,12 f.), im Winter 219/8 von Philippos V. erobert (Pol. 4,77,5 ff.), 196 dem achaiischen Bund zurückgegeben (Pol. 18,47,10; Liv. 33,34,9). Mz. bis ins 3. Jh. n. Chr. (HN 418; 447 ff.; vgl. auch Strab. 8,8,2; Paus. 5,7,1; 8,25,12; 26,1–3).

JOST, 70–77 • E. MEYER, Peloponnes. Wanderungen, 1939, 100–106 • Ders., Neue peloponnesische Wanderungen, 1957, 20 f. • M. MOGGI, I sinecismi interstatali greci, 1976, 256–262 • A. PHILADELPHEUS, Ἀνασκαφαὶ Ἡραάς, in: AD 14, 1931/2 (1935), 57–70. Y. L.

Heraion (Ἥραιον).

[1] Allg. Begriff für Heiligtümer der Göttin → Hera; bedeutendere Heraia finden sich u. a. in → Argos,

→ Olympia, → Paestum, Perachora und auf der Insel → Samos. C.HÖ.

[2] Das äußerste Kap (h. Kap Melangavir) der von den Ausläufern der Geraneia gebildeten Halbinsel gegenüber von Korinthos mit Siedlung, Kastell und Heiligtum der Hera Akraia und Limenia (reiche Funde vom 9. Jh. v. Chr. an) an einer kleinen Hafenbucht der Südseite des Kaps (Xen. hell. 4,5,5 ff.; Xen. Ag. 2,18 f.; Strab. 8,6,22; Plut. Kleomenes 20,3; Liv. 32,23,10).

H. PAYNE u. a. (Hrsg.), The Sanctuaries of Hera Akraia and Limenia, 2 Bde., 1940/1962. C.L. u. E.O.

Heraiskos (Ἡραΐσκος). Neuplatoniker aus Alexandreia (5. Jh. n. Chr.); unter dem monophysitischen Patriarchat des Petros III. Mongos (482–489 n. Chr.) wichtige Persönlichkeit der griech. Partei (Zacharias, Vita Severi 16,22 KUGENER), obwohl er ›kein starker Streiter für die Sache der Wahrheit‹ (Damaskios, Vita Isidori fr. 182 ZINTZEN), d. h. für das Heidentum, war. H. war Schüler des → Proklos in Athen (§ 107 ZINTZEN) und Lehrer des → Isidoros (§ 37, fr. 160). Er war in den rel. Riten (fr. 162,174) und den Orakeln (§ 112–114) sehr erfahren und zeichnete sich durch die Fähigkeit zum Wahrsagen aus (fr. 171,317); in der Dialektik dagegen fehlte es ihm an Übung (fr. 163). Gemäß dem orphischen Ideal (vgl. Plat. Phaid. 69c-d) wurde er durch asketisch strengen Umgang mit der titanischen Natur (dem Körper) zum »Bakchanten« (Βάκχος; fr. 172) und »gottähnlich« (θεοειδής; fr. 161). Als Mitglied des ägypt. Priesterstands erhielt er durch seinen älteren Bruder Asklepiades ein Begräbnis nach entsprechendem Ritus (fr. 173). Proklos hielt ihn für gelehrter als sich selbst (Damaskios Vita Isidori § 107), Damaskios nannte ihn einen Philosophen aufgrund seiner Lebensführung (Damaskios Vita Isidori fr. 163).

M. TARDIEU, Le »Livre de Moïse sur le Nom« et les théologes égyptiennes d'Héraïscus et d'Asclépiade, in: Annuaire de l'École Pratique des Hautes Etudes – Sciences Religieuses 97, 1988–89, 317–319 • Ders., Formes et justifications de la fusion des dieux, in: Annuaire du Collège de France 92, 1991–92, 501–506. MI. TA./Ü: S.P.

Heraklas. Vor seiner Bekehrung zum christl. Glauben besuchte H. mit seinem Bruder Plutarchos, der später den Märtyrertod starb, zunächst den Unterricht des platon. Philosophen → Ammonios [9] Sakkas (Eus. HE 6,19,13), traf dort nach fünfjährigem Unterricht auf → Origenes als Mitstudenten und besuchte dann dessen Unterricht in Alexandreia (Eus. HE 6,3,2). Zu einem bestimmten Zeitpunkt übertrug Origenes H. die Anfänger unter seinen Schülern (Eus. HE 6,15).

H. galt selbst als gefeierter Lehrer (Eus. HE 6,31,2) und gehörte offenbar zu den Presbytern, die für die Vertreibung des Origenes aus Alexandreia verantwortlich waren; vielleicht darf man ihn sogar als ›Haupt der Antiorigenisten‹ [1] ansprechen. H. übernahm daraufhin die Leitung des christl. Unterrichts; von 231 bis 247 amtierte er als Bischof in Alexandreia. Wie eine späte Quelle zeigt, reagierte H. auch noch lange nach der Übersiedlung des Origenes nach → Caesarea [2] (Palaestina) mit großer Schärfe auf einen gottesdienstlichen Auftritt des Origenes im Nildelta (Photios, Interrogationes decem 9, PG 104, 1219–1232).

1 W. A. BIENERT, Dionysius von Alexandrien, 1978, 100–104 2 P. NAUTIN, Origène. Sa vie et son œuvre, 1977 3 C. SCHOLTEN, Die alexandrinische Katechetenschule, in: JbAC 38, 1995, 16–37. C.M.

Herakleia (Ἡράκλεια).

[1] H. Trachinia (Ἡράκλεια ἡ Τραχινία). Stadt auf einem Felsen links von und über dem Ausgang der Schlucht des → Asopos [1] in die Spercheiosebene, an der Süd- und Westflanke durch tiefe Bachbetten von der Oite (→ Oitaioi, Oite) getrennt, wo die Trachinischen Felsen mit zahlreichen Grabhöhlen aufragen. Die Unterstadt ist h. restlos verschwunden. H. wurde 426 v. Chr. von den Spartanern, die von Trachis um Hilfe gegen die Oitaioi gebeten worden waren, ca. 7 km westl. von Thermopylai bei → Trachis gegr. (Thuk. 3,92). 371 eroberte Iason von Pherai die bei den Nachbarn verhaßte Kolonie (Xen. hell. 6,4,27) und überließ sie den → Malieis und Oitaioi (Diod. 15,57,2). Hieromnemones (Delegierte im Amphiktyonenrat) aus H. erschienen seither als Vertreter der Malieis in Delphoi. Ab 280 war H. im Aitol. Bund (Paus. 10,20,9) und erlebte unter Ausdehnung auf Trachis – diese Stadt war längst verfallen – als Tagungsort der Bundesversammlung (Liv. 28,5,13) die größte Blüte. 191 wurde H. von → Acilius [I 10] nach dramatischer Belagerung geplündert. H. war ab 167 Hauptort des neu gegr. autonomen Stammstaates der Oitaioi, den der nachmalige Augustus um 30 v. Chr. mit der thessal. Phthiotis vereinigte. Iustinianus ließ im 6. Jh. die Befestigungen erneuern (Prok. aed. 4,2,17–21). Wenig später wurde H. endgültig aufgegeben.

Y. BÉQUIGNON, La vallée du Spercheios, 1937, 243 ff. • G. DAUX, Sosthenis, in: BCH 58, 1934, 156 ff. • PRITCHETT 1, 81 f. • F. STÄHLIN, s. v. H. (4), RE 8, 424 ff. • Ders., Das hellen. Thessalien, 1924, 205 ff. (Quellen) • TIB 1, 1976, 172. HE.KR.

[2] H. Lynku (Ἡράκλεια Λύγκου). Bedeutendste obermaked. Stadt, h. Bitola. Evtl. Gründung Philippos' II. Blüte in röm. Zeit (*prov. Macedonia*) wegen der Lage an der *via Egnatia* und der Querstraße nach Stoboi. Treffpunkt des Pompeius mit dem Gesandten des Dakerkönigs → Burebista 48 v. Chr. (Syll.^{3} 762). Nach den röm. Bürgerkriegen stieg die Zahl der hier residierenden röm. Bürger, die am blühenden Munizipalleben der Kaiserzeit großen Anteil hatten. H. erhielt im 3. Jh. n. Chr. den Titel *Septimia Aurelia Heraclea* [1. 162] und war spätestens vor dem Konzil von Serdica (343) Bischofssitz. Im 5. Jh. von Goten unter Theodemir (Iord. Get. 285) und Theoderich (Malchos, fr. 20 BLOCKLEY) verwüstet, wurde H. zuletzt erwähnt anläßlich des Konzils von Konstantinopel 553. In byz. Zeit war der Bischof von H. auch für Pelagonia zuständig, was gelegentlich zur Verwechslung mit Pelagonia geführt hat.

1 F. Papazoglou, Septimia Aurelia Heraclea, in: BCH 85, 1961, 162–175. 2 Ders., Les villes de Macédoine, 1988, 258–268. MA. ER.

[3] Stadt in der ostmaked. Sintike am → Strymon (Strab. 7 fr. 36). Nicht lokalisiert, vielleicht bei Neo Petritsi zu suchen. Wohl Gründung Philippos' II., von den Römern 167 v. Chr. der *Macedonia I* zugeschlagen (Liv. 45,29,6; Diod. 31,8,8). H. existierte noch im 6. Jh. n. Chr. (Hierokles, Synekdemos 639,9).

F. Papazoglou, Les villes de Macédoine, 1988, 258–268. MA. ER.

[4] Insel (19 km^2) südl. von Naxos mit befestigter Siedlung und Meter-Heiligtum (Plin. nat. 4,70; → Mater Magna, → Kybele), h. zur Inselgruppe der Nisides (ehemals Erimonisia) gerechnet.

Philippson/Kirsten 4, 13 • L. Ross, Reisen auf den griech. Inseln des ägäischen Meeres 2, 1834, 34 ff. H. KAL.

[5] Stadt in Karien am Südhang des Latmos in Nachfolge der kar. Siedlung Latmos. Mit ihrer Lage am innersten Winkel des latmischen Meerbusens (h. Bafa Gölü) war sie ein bed. Umschlaghafen für den WO-Handel. Um 300 v. Chr. von Pleistarchos, dem Bruder des Kassandros, als Residenzstadt gegr. (Steph. Byz. s. v. Πλειστάρχεια), war H. in röm. Zeit unbed. (Strab. 14,2,22), seit frühchristl. Zeit Bischofsitz. Mit orthogonalem Rasterplan: um die Agora öffentliche und sakrale Gebäude sowie vorwiegend am Hang die Wohnstadt. Überdimensionierter Festungsring aus der Zeit des Pleistarchos. Außerhalb der Stadtmauern weitläufige Nekropole. Tempel der Athena Latmia (3. Jh. v. Chr.). Buleuterion, Agora, Gymnasium, Theater, Tempel des Endymion aus dem 3./2. Jh.

F. Krischen, Die Befestigungen von H. am Latmos, 1922 • L. Bürchner, s. v. H. am Latmos, RE 8, 431 ff. • K. Wulzinger, Das Rathaus von H. am Latmos, in: F. Krischen, Ant. Rathäuser, 1941, 22 ff. • P. Romanelli, s. v. Eraclea, in: EAA 3, 1960, 390–392 • M. Wörrle, Inschr. von H. am Latmos I: Antiochos III., Zeuxis und H., in: Chiron 18, 1988, 421 ff. • Ders., Inschr. von H. am Latmos II: Das Pristertum der Athena Latmia, in: Chiron 20, 1990, 19 ff. • A. Peschlow-Bindokat, Der Latmos, 1996, 29 ff. A. PE.

[6] H. Salbake (Σαλβάκη). Stadt der östl. Karia im Grenzgebiet zu Phrygia und Pisidia am Nordrand der Ebene von → Tabai auf den südöstl. Ausläufern des Salbakos (Babadağ), die Bewohner sind inschr. als Ἡρακλεῶται ἀπὸ Σαλβάκης bezeichnet (vgl. auch Ptol. 5,2,15; Steph. Byz. s. v. H.; Hierokles 688); h. Vakıf. Gründungszeit unbekannt. Anläßlich des Besuchs des Traianus 113 n. Chr., den der aus H. stammende Leibarzt des Kaisers und Historiker T. → Statilius Criton, der bedeutendste der aus H. stammenden Ärzte, veranlaßte, wurde H. Anf. 2. Jh. n. Chr. kurzzeitig mit dem Beinamen *Ulpia* bezeichnet. Inschr. belegt sind die üblichen Stadtbeamten und die Gliederung der Bevölkerung nach Altersklassen; Mz. von Augustus bis Macrinus (217/8). Herakles war als Stadteponym Hauptgott.

Reste von Stadtmauer, Stadion sowie Blöcke mit figürlichen Reliefs von einem Heiligtum (?) nördl. bzw. östl. des Dorfes sind großenteils verschleppt.

J. Benedum, s. v. Kriton, RE Suppl. 14, 216 ff. • L. Robert, J. Robert, La Carie 2, 1954, 153–230, pl. LXV (Karte) • MAMA 6, 33 ff. Nr. 87 ff. • SNG Copenhagen Nr. 391 ff. • SNG v. Aulock Nr. 2542 ff. H. KA.

[7] H. (*Heraclea Pontica*). Ca. 560 v. Chr. von Megara aus unter boiot. Beteiligung gegr., dor. geprägte (Xen. an. 6,2,1; Ephor. fr. 44a; Arr. per. p. E. 18) Stadt an der südl. Küste des Pontos Euxeinos mit hervorragendem Naturhafen und wirtschaftlich bed. Hinterland bis zu den Akçakoca Dağları, h. Ereğli. Koloniegründungen: Panelos (Lage?), Kallatis (550/525 v. Chr.), Kalpe, Kieros, Insel Thynias oder Daphne, Chersonesos auf der Krim (ca. 422/1). Die einheimischen Mariandynoi wurden teilweise unterworfen (Status ähnlich wie Heloten oder Penesten; vgl. Strab. 12,3,4). Urspr. stark agrarisch geprägte Wirtschaft, nach Mitte 5. Jh. v. Chr. steigende Bed. im Schwarzmeerhandel (430/420 Anf. der Mz.-Prägung), wirtschaftliche Blüte im 4. Jh., nach 300 Rückgang der Exportwirtschaft. Das oligarchische Regiment wurde 364/3 von dem Platonschüler Klearchos beseitigt, der eine Tyrannis errichtete. Nach seiner Ermordung 352 folgte ihm sein Bruder Satyros, diesem Klearchos' Söhne Timotheos (ca. 345–338/7) und Dionysios (338/7–305), der 306/5 den Königstitel annahm. Ihm folgte seine Witwe → Amastris [3]. Die Alleinherrschaft wurde zunehmend akzeptiert; schließlich umfaßte das Reich die Küstenlandschaft vom östl. Teil der Thynis (östl. Hypios) bis Kotyros im Osten. Amastris, die nach kurzer Ehe mit → Lysimachos in ihrer Gründung → Amastris [4] residierte, wurde wohl von ihren Söhnen ermordet. 284 beseitigte Lysimachos deren Herrschaft und besetzte die Stadt, die er dann seiner Gattin → Arsinoe [II 3] schenkte (Verlust der Autonomie); das Reich von H. wurde aufgelöst. H. war bed. Flottenbasis und Mz.-Stätte des Lysimachos. 281 entledigte sich H. des Statthalters der Arsinoe, geriet in Konflikt mit dem seleukidischen Herrschaftsanspruch und initiierte die sog. Nördl. Liga [1. 188 ff.]. Nach dem Beitritt des bithyn. Königs kehrten dessen Eroberungen Kieros und Tios unter die Hegemonie von H. zurück. Beide Städte gingen 196/190 an → Prusias I. verloren. 190 kam es zur Aufnahme diplomat. Kontakte, nach 188 zum Freundschafts- und Bündnisvertrag mit Rom. H. war als *civitas libera* E. 74 v. Chr. von der Organisation der röm. Prov. Bithynia und dem zugehörigen Zollgesetz für Asia und Bithynia betroffen, im J. 73 unterstützte der Ort → Mithradates VI. und ging gewaltsam gegen die röm. *publicani* vor, 72 wurde H. Teil des pontischen Reichs; 72/1–70 Belagerung, Eroberung und Zerstörung durch → Aurelius [11]. Seit 65/4 war H. Teil der Prov. Pontus, ab 46/5 röm. *colonia*; Antonius gab ca. 40 den griech. Teil von Stadt und Territorium dem Ga-

laterfürsten Adiatorix, der 32/31 die Italiker ermorden ließ (Strab. 12,3,6). Nach seiner Beseitigung 31/30 war H. Teil der Prov. → Bithynia et Pontus, seit 384/387 n. Chr. gehörte die Stadt zur Prov. Honorias. Als Suffraganbistum seit 431 belegt.
→ Bithynia; Bithynia et Pontus

1 K. Strobel, Die Galater I, 1996.

D. Asheri, Über die Frühgesch. von H., in: Forsch. an der Nordküste Kleinasiens I (ETAM 5), 1972, 9–34 • A. Avram, Bemerkungen zu den Mariandynern von H., in: Studii Clasici 22, 1984, 19–28 • K. Belke, Paphlagonien und Honorias, 1996, 208–216 • A. Bittner, Eine Polis zw. Tyrannis und Selbstverwaltung: Gesellschaft und Wirtschaft in H., 1998 • S. M. Burstein, Outpost of Hellenism. The Emergence of H., 1976 • P. Desideri, Cultura Eracleotica, in: Pontica 1, 1991, 7–24 • W. Hoepfner, H.-Ereğli. Eine baugesch. Unt., in: Forsch. an der Nordküste Kleinasiens (ETAM 2.1), 1966, 3–37 • Ders., Top. Forsch. (ETAM 5), 1972, 37–60 • L. Jonnes, W. Ameling, The Inscriptions of H. (IK 47), 1994 • W. Leschhorn, Ant. Ären, 1993, 195 ff. • S. J. Saprykin, Heracleia Pontica and Tauric Chersonnesus before Roman Domination IV.-I. c. B. C., 1996.
K. ST.

[8] Von Dorieus mit lakedaimon. Siedlern am Fuß des → Eryx [1] (Sizilien) um 510 v. Chr. gegr. Stadt, wenig später von Karthago und Segesta zerstört. Belege: Hdt. 5,46; Diod. 4,23,3; Paus. 3,16,4 f.

BTCGI 7, 1989, 229 f.
GI. MA.

[9] Stadt an der Südküste Siziliens 25 km westl. von Akragas, östl. der Mündung des Halykos, h. Eraclea Minoa. Gegr. von Selinus aus (also nach 628 v. Chr.) auf dem Boden einer vorgriech., auf Minos zurückgeführten Siedlung und daher Minoa (Μινῴα) benannt. Um 505 von Euryleon besetzt und in H. um- oder zubenannt (Hdt. 5,46; Diod. 4,79,1; 4,79,5; 16,9,5). Der ON H. Minoa erscheint in den Quellen nur selten, eher noch Minoa, meist aber H. An der Identität der so bezeichneten Örtlichkeiten kann aber kein Zweifel bestehen. Infolge ihrer Lage im griech.-karthag. Grenzgebiet wechselte die Stadt mehrfach den Herrscher: Im J. 357 war sie karthag. (Diod. 16,9,4; Plut. Dion 25), in der Zeit Timoleons griech., 314 karthag. (Diod. 19,71,1), danach unter der Herrschaft des → Agathokles [2] (Diod. 20,56,3), nach seinem Tode und nach einem Zwischenspiel des Pyrrhos (Diod. 22,10,2) von den Karthagern als Flottenstützpunkt ausgebaut, nach dem Fall von Akragas 262 unter röm. Herrschaft. Im Zweiten Pun. Krieg fiel H. nach dem Tode Hierons (214) von Rom ab und wurde erst nach dem erneuten Fall von Akragas (210) wieder röm., nunmehr als *civitas decumana* (Cic. Verr. 2,3,103); nach dem großen Sklavenkrieg 132 nahm H. röm. Siedler auf (Cic. Verr. 2,2,125). Von Verres ausgeplündert, beteiligt sich H. an der Klage gegen diesen.

In Eraclea Minoa Überreste aus prähistor. (spätneolithische und frühbrz. Siedlung [1]), griech. [2] (erste Siedlungsphase Mitte 4. Jh. bis zweite H. 2. Jh. v. Chr. mit eleganten Häusern, Befestigungen, Theater mit Heiligtum; zweite Siedlungsphase E. 2. Jh. bis E. 1. Jh. v. Chr. mit bescheidenen Häusern im westl. Teil der Ebene; Nekropole, die in archa. und hell. Zeit benutzt wurde [2. 17]) und frühchristl. Zeit [3] (Friedhofsbasilika mit Nekropolen, spätestens seit 4. Jh. n. Chr. in Gebrauch, Mz. von Constans [2] II.; Siedlung im 3. Jh., Mz. des Gallienus [3. 729 ff.]).

1 D. Gullì, Primi dati sull'insedamento preistorico di Eraclea Minoa, in: Quaderni dell'Instituto di Archeologia dell'Università di Messina 9, 1993 2 G. Fiorentini, Eraclea Minoa. Necropoli arcaica, in: BCA Sicilia 9–10/3, 1988/9 3 Dies., Attività di indagini archeologiche della Soprintendenza di Agrigento, in: Kokalos 1993/4, 39 f.; 717–733.

E. De Miro, Eraclea Minoa, 1958 • Ders., La fondazione di Agrigento e l'ellenizzazione del territorio fra il Salso e il Platani, in: Kokalos 8, 1962, 144.
GI. F./Ü: V. S.

[10] Im J. 433/2 v. Chr. (Diod. 12,36,4) zw. Aciris und Siris (Plin. nat. 3,97) bei Policoro gegr. → *apoikía* von Tarentum und Thurioi, der die Siedlung Siris an der Mündung des gleichnamigen Flusses ins Mittelmeer als Seehandelsplatz diente. Ihren Namen bezog H. vom tarentinischen Herakles-Kult (Strab. 6,1,14). H. war im 4. Jh. v. Chr. Zentrum des gegen die Lucani gegr. Bundes der unterital. Griechenstädte (Strab. 6,3,4). Bei H. fand 280 v. Chr. die Schlacht zw. → Pyrrhos und den Römern statt (Plut. Pyrrhos 16; Liv. 22,59,8). Damals hatte H. schon ein *prope singulare foedus* (›ein fast einzigartiges Bündnis‹) mit Rom (Cic. Arch. 50). Vom E. 4./Anf. 3. Jh. v. Chr. datiert die in H. gefundene Verpachtungsurkunde, die für unsere Kenntnis der Organisation und landwirtschaftlichen Nutzbarmachung des Territoriums von H. wichtig ist (IG XIV 645). H. war *municipium, tribus Menenia*. In der Kaiserzeit nur noch in den Itineraria erwähnt. Arch. Grabungen haben ein Heiligtum der Demeter mit vielen Votivgaben gesichert, ebenso ein Hephaistos-Heiligtum. Der Maler → Zeuxis und der orphische Dichter → Zopyros waren wohl Bürger von H.

B. Neutsch (Hrsg.), Herakleiastudien (Arch. Forsch. in Lukanien 2), 1967 • L. Quilici, Siris-Heraclea, 1967 • A. Uguzzoni, F. Ghinatti, Le tavole greche di Eraclea, 1968 • Studi su Siris-Eraclea, 1989 • G. Camassa, I culti delle poleis italiote, in: Storia del Mezzogiorno, I/1, 1991, 467–471, 493 f. • M. Osanna, Chorai coloniali da Taranto a Locri, 1992, 97–114 • B. Otto (Hrsg.), H. in Lukanien und das Quellheiligtum der Demeter, 1996 (mit ausführlicher Bibliogr.) • A. Muggia, L'area di rispetto nelle colonie magno-greche e siceliote, 1997, 105–108 und passim.
G. CA./Ü: H. D.

[11] Ort in Akarnania am Südufer des Ambrak. Golfs, genaue Lokalisierung unsicher. Belege: Plin. nat. 4,5; Steph. Byz. s. v. Ἡ.

Pritchett 8, 97–101.
D. S.

Herakleianos. Arzt und Anatom aus Alexandreia, wirkte um 152 n. Chr. Der Sohn des Anatomen und Lehrers → Numisianos stellte einen Auszug von dessen Lehre zusammen (Gal. de musculorum dissectione 18B, 926, 935 K.), in dem er ein beachtliches anatomisches Wissen unter Beweis stellte (Gal. Admin. anat. 16,1). Er unterhielt sich mit → Galen bei dessen Ankunft in Alexandreia um 151 n. Chr., seinen anatomischen Vorlesungen folgte Galen mit anfänglichem Wohlwollen (CMG V,9,1, S. 70). Als Galen später die nachgelassenen Schriften seines Vaters sehen wollte, kühlte das Verhältnis ab. H.' Weigerung, sie vorzuzeigen, brachte schließlich das Gerücht in Umlauf, er habe kurz vor seinem Tod die Schriften seines Vaters den Flammen übergeben, um anderen den Zugriff auf dessen Entdeckungen zu verwehren (Gal. Admin. anat. 16,1).

V. N./Ü: L. v. R.-B.

Herakleidai (Ἡρακλεῖδαι). Jeder Nachfahre des → Herakles kann *Herakleídēs* heißen (s.u.). Im engeren Sinne des wohl im 7. Jh. entstandenen (Tyrtaios fr. 2 West), spätestens im 5. Jh. ausgeprägt vorliegenden Mythos von der »Rückkehr der H. auf die Peloponnes« sind H. sein Sohn → Hyllos und dessen Nachkommen bis in die vierte Generation (Hauptquellen: (Ps.-)Apollod. 2,167–180, Diod. 4, 57–58; außerdem Papyrusfunde zu → Euripides *Temenos*, *Temenidai*, *Kresphontes*, *Archelaos*).

Nach Herakles' Tod auf der Flucht vor Eurystheus, werden die H. zunächst in Trachis, dann in → Athenai (Paus. 1,32,6; (Ps.-)Apollod. 2,167–168) bzw. der att. Tetrapolis (Pherekydes FGrH 3F84) aufgenommen. Nachdem Hyllos mit Hilfe der Athener Eurystheus getötet hat, rät das delph. Orakel, mit der Rückkehr bis zur dritten Frucht zu warten. Drei Jahre später marschiert Hyllos in die Peloponnes ein und fällt im Zweikampf mit → Echemos [1] von Tegea. Daraufhin verzichten die H. vereinbarungsgemäß 50 Jahre lang auf jeglichen Rückkehrversuch und ziehen sich teils in die att. Tetrapolis, teils in die Doris zu → Aigimios [1] zurück (Diod. 4,37,3–4; Ps.-Apollod. 2,154). Erst nach Auslegung des Spruchs von der dritten Frucht als der dritten Generation gelingt den H. der Einzug in die Peloponnes unter Führung des → Oxylos.

Nach Errichtung dreier Altäre für Zeus Patroos erhält → Temenos bei der Verlosung der Halbinsel Argos, die Aristodemossöhne Prokles und Eurysthenes Lakedaimon (Aition für das spart. Doppelkönigtum: Hdt. 7,204; 8,131,2; [1. 175]), → Kresphontes Messenien.

Als Reflex der → Dorischen Wanderung läßt sich der Mythos angesichts der neueren Bewertungen des arch. Befundes, wenn überhaupt, nur eingeschränkt deuten (vgl. jedoch [2; 3; 5]). Klar erkennbar ist vielmehr seine Funktion als »charter myth« für die Aufteilung der Peloponnes unter die dor. Staaten und Begründung der spart. Hegemonie. Darüber hinaus schließt die Sage die Lücke zw. mythischer und histor. Zeit (vgl. Isokr. or. 4,54, Ephoros FGrH 70 T8; anders Thuk. 1,12).

Als Gegengewicht zum peloponnesischen Mythos (vgl. Hdt. 9,26–27) wurde in Athen die Sage von der Aufnahme der H. entwickelt, bes. in Rhet. (z. B. Lys. 2,11–16) und Trag. (Eur. Heraclid., evtl. schon Aischyl. Heraclid.). Kult der H. ist in den att. Demen Erchia (SEG 21.541 = LSCG 18, B42–43; ca. 375/50 v. Chr.) und Aixone (IG II/III[2] 1199, 23–25; ca. 325–24 v. Chr.), in Porto Rafti (IG II/III[2] 4977; 4.–3. Jh. v. Chr.) und vielleicht auch in Thorikos ([9]; 1. H. 4. Jh. v. Chr.) belegt.

Meist in propagandist. Absicht, sind H. schon früh mythische Kolonisatoren (→ Tlepolemos; → Thessalos; Rhopalos gründet Phaistos: Paus. 2,6,6–7) oder bezeichnen sich Herrscherhäuser als H. (Tyloniden und Mermnaden: Hdt. 1,7; Bakchiaden und andere in Korinth: Diod. 7,9, Paus. 2,4,3, → Hippotes; das maked. Königshaus: Hdt. 8,137–139, Hyg. fab. 219, vgl. die frei erfundene Ableitung in Eur. Archelaos; die Attaliden, über → Telephos, vgl. [4]).

H. sind auch die Söhne des → Herakles und der → Megara.

1 C. Calame, Spartan Genealogies, in: J. Bremmer (Hrsg.), Interpretations of Greek Mythology, 1987, 153–186
2 R. Drews, The Coming of the Greeks, 1988, 203–225
3 J. Chadwick, I Dori e la creazione dei dialetti greci, in: D. Musti (Hrsg.), Le origini dei greci. Dori e mondo egeo, [2]1986, 3–12 **4** T. S. Scheer, Myth. Vorväter. Zur Bed. griech. Heroenmythen im Selbstverständnis kleinasiat. Städte, 1993, 71–152 **5** C. Brillante, Il ritorno degli Eraclidi, in: Ders., La leggenda eroica e la civiltà micenea, 1981, 149–182 **6** O. Carruba, L'arrivo dei Greci, le migrazioni indoeuropee e il »ritorno« degli Eraclidi, in: Athenaeum 83, 1995, 5–44 **7** F. Kiechle, Die Ausprägung der Sage von der Rückkehr der H., in: Helikon 6, 1966, 493–517 **8** M. A. Levi, Studi Spartani, 1: Dori ed Eraclidi, in: RIL 96, 1962, 479–499 **9** R. Parker, The H. at Thorikos, in: ZPE 57, 1984, 59 **10** F. Prinz, Gründungsmythen und Sagenchronologie, 1979 **11** J. S. Rusten, The Return of the H., in: ZPE 40, 1980, 39–42 **12** B. Sergent, Le partage du Péloponnèse entre les H., in: RHR 192, 1977, 121–136; 193; 1978, 3–25.

T. H.

Herakleidas. Bildhauer aus Atrax in Thessalien, tätig im 4. Jh. v. Chr. Er signierte zusammen mit Hippokrates ein Siegesvotiv der Pharsalier in Delphi, das um die Mitte des 4. Jh. v. Chr. aufgestellt wurde. Aufgrund der Abmessungen der Basis kann es sich um die von Pausanias (10,13,5) beschriebene Bronzegruppe des Achilles zu Pferd mit Patroklos gehandelt haben. Sicherheit ist nicht zu gewinnen, da die Basis eine Umwidmung an Claudius trägt, somit Pausanias das urspr. Werk evtl. nicht mehr gesehen haben kann.

G. Daux, Pausanias à Delphes, 1936, 141–143 • J. Marcadé, Recueil des signatures de sculpteurs grecs, 1, 1953, 35 • H. Pomtow, Das Anathem der Pharsalier in Delphi, in: Philologus 7, 1921, 194–199.

R. N.

Herakleides (Ἡρακλείδης).
Bekannte Persönlichkeiten: der Politiker und Schriftsteller H. [19] Lembos, der Philosoph H. [16] Pontikos d.J., der Arzt H. [27] aus Tarent.
I. Politische Persönlichkeiten
II. Literarisch tätige Persönlichkeiten
III. Ärzte IV. Künstler

I. Politische Persönlichkeiten

[1] H. aus Klazomenai (vgl. Plat. Ion 541d) stand in persischen Diensten, darum wohl *basileús* genannt. Er hat so 423 v.Chr. wertvolle Dienste am persischen Hof für Athen leisten können, wofür er bald nach seiner Übersiedlung das att. Bürgerrecht erhielt (nach 400, Syll.[3] 118). Um die Athener für eine noch stärkere Teilnahme an der Ekklesia zu bewegen, veranlaßte er, die Zahlung von einem Obolos auf zwei für jeden Teilnehmer zu erhöhen (Aristot. Ath. pol. 41,3), für Aristoteles eine (radikal) demokratische Maßnahme (Aristot. pol. 1297a 35–38).

M.H. Hansen, Die athenische Demokratie im Zeitalter des Demosthenes, 1995, 155. PE.HÖ.

[2] Syrakusier, Sohn des Lysimachos. Er wurde 415 v.Chr. zum Feldherrn im Krieg gegen die Athener gewählt (Thuk. 6,73,1; Diod. 13,4,1), aber bereits im folgenden Jahr nach Mißerfolgen abgesetzt (Thuk. 6,103,4).

[3] Syrakusier, Sohn des Aristogenes. Einer der Führer des syrakusanischen Entsatzgeschwaders zur Führung des Seekriegs an der Westküste Kleinasiens, wo er 410 v.Chr. eintraf (Xen. hell. 1,2,8). K.MEI.

[4] H. aus Ainos. Ermordete 360/359 v.Chr. zusammen mit seinem Bruder → Python den Odrysenkönig → Kotys I., auch ermutigt durch Theorien seines Lehrers Platon zum Tyrannenmord (Diog. Laert. 3,46; Plut. mor. 1126C); die Athener ehrten ihn dafür mit dem Bürgerrecht und einem goldenen Kranz (Demosth. or. 23,119; Aristot. pol. 5,10,12 1311b 21; Plut. mor. 542f, 816e).
→ Griechische Geschichte 4. Jh.

K. Trampedach, Platon, die Akademie und die zeitgenössische Politik, 1994, 90–92. J.E.

[5] Vornehmer Syrakusier, Befehlshaber der Söldner unter → Dionysios [2] II., mit → Dion [I 1] befreundet. Floh 361/360 v.Chr. nach Griechenland und betrieb zusammen mit Dion die Rückkehr nach Sizilien 357, folgte ihm aber erst ein Jahr später mit 20 Kriegsschiffen und 1500 Mann (Diod. 16,16,2). Eine angebliche Entfremdung der beiden bereits zum damaligen Zeitpunkt (so Plut. Dion 32,4) ist kaum anzunehmen, vielmehr lag dem getrennten Vorgehen eher eine strategische Konzeption zugrunde. Erst ein Seesieg des zum Nauarchen ernannten H. über Philistos, den Admiral Dionysios' II., führte zu wachsender Rivalität. Zudem erfreute sich H. beim Demos großer Beliebtheit, während Dion des Strebens nach der Tyrannis verdächtigt wurde. Deshalb wurde H. ins Strategenkollegium gewählt, während Dion sich genötigt sah, die Stadt zu verlassen. Als Dion nach einem Sieg über die Truppen des Dionysios II. die Herrschaft über Syrakus wiedergewann, verschonte er H. Da dieser jedoch auch in der Folgezeit an der Spitze des Demos mehrfach gegen Dion opponierte – u.a. trat er durch den Spartaner Pharax sogar mit Dionysios II. in Verbindung – veranlaßte Dion 354 seine Ermordung (Plut. Dion 53) – ein Umstand, der die Autorität Dions im Volk endgültig untergrub und bald seinen gewaltsamen Tod zur Folge hatte. Quellen: Platon, 7. und 8. Brief, ebenso wie die auf Timonides von Leukas (FGrH 651), dem Angehörigen der Akademie und Teilnehmer der Expedition, beruhende Dion-Vita Plutarchs (Plut. Dion, 22,4; 30,10; 35,4) äußerst freundlich gegenüber Dion (der angeblich den platonischen Idealstaat in Syrakus verwirklichen wollte), und feindlich gegenüber H. (der als hemmungsloser Demagoge geschildert wird). Wesentlich sachlicher Diodoros 16,9–20, zumeist nach Ephoros).

H. Berve, Dion, in: AAWM, 1956, Nr. 19 • M. Sordi, in: E. Gabba, G. Vallet (Hrsg.), La Sicilia antica 2.1, 1980, 237ff. • H.D. Westlake, in: CAH [2]1994, 698ff. K.MEI.

[6] Sohn des Agathokles, nahm 310 v.Chr. am Afrikafeldzug teil und verblieb bei Ophellas von Kyrene, wodurch dieser in Sicherheit gewiegt werden sollte. Er wurde sogar von Ophellas adoptiert (Iust. 22,7,6; Polyain. 5,3,4) und später, nach der heimlichen Flucht des Agathokles aus Afrika 307, von dessen Soldaten getötet (Diod. 20,69,3).

K. Meister, Agathocles, in: CAH 7,1, [2]1984, 384–411, bes. 393ff. K.MEI.

[7] Maked. Offizier aus Bottiaia, führte im Balkankrieg → Alexandros' [4] d.Gr. (335 v.Chr.) und bei → Gaugamela eine der Ilai (→ Reiterei) der → Hetairoi (Arr. an. 1,2,5; 3,11,8).

[8] Nach dem Tod des → Hephaistion [1] von → Alexandros [4] 324 v.Chr. beauftragt, in → Hyrkanien eine Flotte zu bauen und das Kaspische Meer zu umsegeln. Alexandros' Tod verhinderte wahrscheinlich die Ausführung des Auftrags.

Berve 2, Nr. 348.

[9] H. aus Kalchedon, als Gesandter zu → Dareios [3] geschickt, begleitete ihn bis zu seinem Tod (330 v.Chr.). Von → Alexandros [4] gefangengenommen, wurde er unversehrt entlassen (Arr. an. 3,24,5). E.B.

[10] Wehrte als Kommandant der Garnison des Königs → Demetrios [2] Poliorketes, die auch nach 287 v.Chr. die Munychia und den Piräus kontrollierte, 287/6 einen Angriff der Athener erfolgreich ab (Polyain. 5,17,1; Paus. 1,29,10).

Habicht, 129f. J.E.

[11] H. aus Tarent, von Polybios (13,4; vgl. Diod. 28,2) äußerst negativ porträtiert: Um 210 v.Chr. hochverräterischer Aktivitäten bei Tarentinern und Römern verdächtigt, kam H. nach Makedonien, wo er Philippos' V. Vertrauen gewann, 204 als Agent im rhodischen Schiffsarsenal einen Brand legte (Pol. 13,5; Polyain. 5,17,2) und im 2. Maked. Krieg die Flotte des Königs befehligte (Liv. 31,16,3; 46,8), bis ihn Philipp 199/8 wohl auf Wunsch des maked. Kriegsrats absetzte (Liv. 32,5,7; Diod. 28,9) [1. 108f.].

1 S. Le Bohec, Les »philoi« des rois Antigonides, in: REG 98, 1985, 93–124.

[12] H. aus Gyrton, thessalischer Funktionär (und Königsfreund?) des Philippos V. im J. 208 v.Chr. (Syll.[3] 552). Er befehligte 197 bei Kynoskephalai die thessal. Reiterei (Pol. 18,22,2). L.-M.G.

[13] H. aus Byzanz, versuchte 190 v.Chr. als Unterhändler Antiochos' [5] III. nach dessen Niederlage bei Myonnesos vergeblich, unter territorialen und finanziellen Zugeständnissen sowie privaten Angeboten seines Auftraggebers den röm. Heerführer L. Cornelius [I 72] und dessen Bruder P. Cornelius [I 71] Scipio für einen Friedensschluß zu gewinnen (Pol. 21,13 ff.; Diod. 29,7f.; Liv. 37,34ff.; App. Syr. 29; Iust. 31,7,4ff.). A.ME.

[14] *Tōn archisōmatophylákōn, epistátēs, epí tōn prosódōn* (Τῶν ἀρχισωματοφυλάκων, ἐπιστάτης, ἐπὶ τῶν προσόδων); Epistates des Gaues Perithebas 117/6 v.Chr.

L. Mooren, The Aulic Titulature of Ptolemaic Egypt, 1975, 129 Nr. 0142 • E. van't Dack, Ptolemaica Selecta, 1988, 291, 355. W.A.

II. Literarisch tätige Persönlichkeiten

[15] Zwei aus Syrakus stammende Autoren (vermutlich aus dem 4. Jh. v.Chr.) von Abhandlungen über die Kochkunst scheinen diesen Namen zu tragen (Athen. 516c); über ihr Leben ist nichts bekannt. Nur → Athenaios [3] erwähnt sie, den einen als Autor der *Opsartytiká* (Abhandlung über die Kochkunst) im Zusammenhang mit Eiern (58b), Kuchen (114a), Fischen (105c; 328d) und der Kochkunst, die für einen Sklaven nicht geeignet ist (661e). Der andere wird als Autor eines Werkes *Perí Thesmṓn* (›Über die Gebräuche‹) mit einem Sesam-Honig-Kuchen in Form der weiblichen Scham in Verbindung gebracht, der im Ritual der → *Thesmophória* in Syrakus verwendet wurde (647a). P.S.-P./Ü: A.T.

[16] H. Pontikos d.Ä.

A. Person B. Werke C. Lehre

A. Person

Geb. um 390 in Herakleia [7] am Pontos, gest. nach 322 v.Chr. Gegen 365 in die platonische Akademie (→ Akademeia) eingetreten, stand ihr H., der stets unter denen genannt wird, die Platons Vorlesungen ›Über das Gute‹ gehört haben (F 7 und 8, vgl. F 42 Wehrli), während Platons dritter sizilischer Reise (361/60) stellvertretend vor. Er bewarb sich nach dem Tod des ihm nahe stehenden Speusippos (339/8) um dessen Nachfolge im Scholarchat, unterlag jedoch knapp Xenokrates, woraufhin er sich nach Herakleia zurückzog, um dort eine eigene Schule zu gründen. Obwohl H. offiziell niemals dem → Peripatos angehörte, ordnet ihn bereits Sotion (2. Jh. v.Chr.) – und ihm folgend Diogenes [17] Laertios – dieser Schule zu. Jedenfalls teilt H. viele wiss. Interessen mit Vertretern des Peripatos (vgl. auch Plut., Adversus Colotem XIV, 1115a = F 68 W.) [dazu 1. 60f.; 2. 523, 527]. Seiner Erscheinung und seinem Auftreten verdankt er die alternative Form seines Beinamens *Pompikós* (vgl. F 3 W.).

B. Werke

Einen (unvollständigen) Katalog des umfangreichen Œuvres bietet Diog. Laert. 5,86–88 (knapper und instruktiver Überblick über die einzelnen Schriften bei [2. 524–527]). H. bevorzugt die Dialogform, seine mit Vorliebe in der Vergangenheit angesiedelten Dialoge waren im Hinblick auf Szenerie und Gesprächssituationen offenbar reich ausgestaltet. Darauf bezieht sich Cicero, wenn er von *Herakleídeia* spricht (»Dialog nach Art des H.«, F 27a-f W.; zur Deutung [3. 10–12]).

C. Lehre

Auffällig ist bei H. durchweg die eigenwillige Verknüpfung platonischer Positionen mit neuem (bes. pythagoreischem) Gedankengut. Bemerkenswert ist im Bereich der Physik die Annahme kleinster, Veränderungen noch zulassender Partikel (ἄναρμοι ὄγκοι, »nicht festgefügte Masseteile«), die nicht mit den θραύσματα (»Bruchstücken«, F 121 W.), den eigentlichen Atomen, identisch sind (zum Verhältnis und zu den Beziehungen zum platonischen ›Timaios‹ [4. 89f.] → Atomismus). An diese spezifische Atomlehre knüpft der Arzt → Asklepiades [6] von Bithynien (1. Jh. v.Chr.) mit seiner Korpuskulartheorie an. In der Psychologie weicht H. mit der Annahme einer körperhaften Struktur der Seele von Platon ab; gleichzeitig ist jedoch die Qualifizierung der Seele als lichtartig (φωτοειδής) oder als Licht unverkennbar an akademischem Gedankengut orientiert. Probleme der Seelenlehre, insbes. das Verhältnis der Seele zum Leib, sind auch das Thema des einzigen Dialogs, der in groben Zügen rekonstruierbar ist, ›Über die Scheintote‹, in dessen Mittelpunkt die Wiedererweckung einer Scheintoten durch Empedokles [1] von Agrigent und Empedokles' anschließende Entrückung standen (zu diesem Dialog ausführlich [3. 13–36]).

Aus heutiger Sicht liegt die eigentliche Bedeutung des H. in seinen Thesen zur → Astronomie und → Kosmologie, da er hier mit der Annahme einer Achsenrotation der Erde (gegenüber Ekphantos [2], dem eine ähnliche Theorie zugeschrieben wird, kommt H. wohl die Priorität zu) sowie mit der These eines Jahresumlaufs der Erde um die Weltmitte zur Erklärung scheinbarer Unregelmäßigkeiten der Jahresbahn der Sonne spätere Theorien vorweggenommen zu haben scheint. Eine positive Würdigung der wiss. Leistung des H. wird indes durch die zahlreichen phantastischen Spekulationen, denen man in seinen Frg. begegnet (schon Cicero spricht von *pueriles fabulae*/»Märchen für Kinder«: nat. deor. 1,13,34 = F 111 W.), sehr erschwert.

1 WEHRLI, Schule (H. 7: H. Pontikos; Sammlung und Komm. der Frg.) 2 F. WEHRLI, H. Pontikos, in: GGPh² 3, 523–529 3 H. P. GOTTSCHALK, H. of Pontus, 1980 4 H.J. KRÄMER, H. Pontikos, in: GGPh² 3, 1983, 88–102. K.-H.S.

In seiner Musikschrift ([1] fr. 157–163), die auch eine mythisch-histor. Genealogie von Musikern enthält (157–160), bekräftigt H. (163) die Überlegenheit der nach hellenischen Stämmen benannten und durch ihr Ethos unterschiedenen Tonarten (*harmoníai*) Dorisch, Aiolisch, Ionisch gegenüber den barbarischen der Phryger und Lyder. Daß ein vielerörtertes Zitat zur Schalltheorie (→ Akustik) (Porph. in Ptol. harm. 30f.) von diesem H. stammt, ist nicht zweifelsfrei gesichert [1. 113].

1 WEHRLI, Schule, H. 7. F.Z.

[17] Dichter der Mittleren Komödie, von dem wir aus der großen didaskalischen Inschr. [1. test. 1] wissen, daß er um die Mitte des 4. Jh. an den Dionysien oder Lenäen hinter Alexis und vor Theophilos Dritter wurde. Erh. ist ein Fragment ohne Titel, in dem Adaios, ein General Philipps II. von Makedonien, mit dem Spitznamen »Hahn« verspottet wird.

1 PCG V, 558f. B.BÄ.

[18] H. Kretikos/Kritikos. Griech. Perieget des 3. Jh. v. Chr., Autor einer Schrift *Perí tō̂n en tē̂ Helládi póleōn* (›Über die Städte in Griechenland‹), die eine Reise durch Mittel- und Nordgriechenland nach folgendem Schema schildert: Entfernung, Straße und Landschaft, Stadtbeschreibung, Produkte der Gegend, Bewohner. Erh. sind drei anon. Auszüge zu Attika, Boiotia, Euboia und Thessalia. Wertvoll sind sie wegen der Qualität der Prosa [1. 199–219] und der eingestreuten Dichterzitate, meist aus Komödien des 4./3. Jh., v.a. aber wegen ihrer wohl auf Autopsie beruhenden Anschaulichkeit. Das Werk wurde seit der Erstausgabe durch H. STEPHANUS 1589 meist → Dikaiarchos zugewiesen, doch bezeugt eine Angabe bei dem Paradoxographen Apollonios [2. 120–142 § 19] (2. Jh. v. Chr.?) Autor und Titel.

1 G. PASQUALI, Die schriftstellerische Form des Pausanias, in: Hermes 48, 1913, 161–223 2 A. GIANNINI, Paradoxographorum Graecorum Reliquiae, 1965.

FHG II 254–264 • GGM I 97–110 • F. PFISTER, Die Reisebilder des Herakleides, in: SAWW 227.2, 1951 (Ed., Übers., Komm.) • E. PERRIN, Héracleidès le Crétois à Athènes, in: REG 107, 1994, 192–202. K.BRO.

[19] H. Lembos. Hell. Staatsmann und Schriftsteller. Nach Diog. Laert. 5,94 in Kallatis (Pontos) geb., später Bürger von Alexandreia, bekam wegen seines (sonst unbekannten) *Lembeutikós lógos* den Beinamen Lembos (»kleines Boot«). Die kurze Biographie in der Suda s.v. gibt dagegen Oxyrhynchos als Geburtsort an (weniger wahrscheinlich) und erwähnt, daß er an erfolgreichen diplomatischen Verhandlungen zw. → Ptolemaios VI. Philometor (180–145 v. Chr.) und → Antiochos Epiphanes beteiligt war. Agatharchides [6] von Knidos war sein Vorleser und Sekretär (Phot. Bibl. 213).

H.' lit. Aktivität scheint hauptsächlich kompilatorisch und popularisierend gewesen zu sein. Fragmente und Testimonien sind zu folgenden Werken erhalten: (1) Die ›Geschichten‹ (*Historíai*) in wenigstens 37 B. (nur fünf Fragmente, fast alle bei Athenaios). (2) Eine Epitome der *Bíoi* des → Satyros. (3) Eine Epitome der *Diadochaí* des → Sotion. Diogenes Laërtios bezieht sich häufig auf die beiden letztgenannten Werke und deren wertvolle Informationen zur hell. Philos. (für diese Sukzessionenlit. → Doxographie). (4) Epitomai von → Hermippos' drei Werken ›Über Gesetzgeber‹, ›Über die Sieben Weisen‹, ›Über Pythagoras‹ (POxy. 1367). (5) Kurze Auszüge aus den ›Verfassungen‹ (*Politeíai*) und ›Barbarischen Sitten‹ (*Nómima barbariká*) des Aristoteles, die in hsl. Überlieferung erh. sind. H. setzt in dem alexandrinischen Umfeld des 2. Jh. v. Chr. die Themen der peripatetischen Forsch. fort.
→ Doxographie

ED.: FHG 3, 167–171 (eine neuere Slg. der Frg. fehlt. Nicht in FGrH) • M. DILTS, Heraclidis Lembi excerpta Politiarum, 1971.
LIT.: H. BLOCH, H. Lembos and his *Epitome* of Aristotle's *Politiae*, in: TAPhA 71, 1940, 27–39 (über die Exzerpte) • P. M. FRAZER, Ptolemaic Alexandria, 1972, 514f., 741ff. • J. MEJER, Diogenes Laërtius and His Hellenistic Background, 1978, 40–42, 62ff. D.T.R./Ü: T.H.

[20] H. aus Athen (TrGF I 166), 1. Jh. v. Chr.; Sieg mit einem Satyrspiel an den von Sulla eingerichteten Amphiaraia und Romaia in Oropos kurz nach 85 v. Chr. (TrGF I: DID A 6,1). B.Z.

[21] H. Pontikos der Jüngere. Grammatiker des 1. Jh. n. Chr., Schüler des → Didymos [1] Chalkenteros, lehrte unter Claudius und Nero in Rom (Suda η 463; α 2634 [1]) und verteidigte in drei B. ›Gesprächen‹ (Λέσχαι), die in sapphischen Hendekasyllaben abgefaßt waren und die ihm den Beinamen *Leschēneutḗs* (»Quasselstrippe«: Athen. 14,649c) einbrachten, seinen Lehrer gegen die Angriffe des Aristarcheers Aper [2]. Dieses gelehrte Werk war vielleicht dialogisch angelegt und wurde wegen seiner Dunkelheit, die einen Komm. erforderlich machte (Etym. Gud. 297,50), mit den Werken des Lykophron und des Parthenios verglichen (Artem. 4,63).

Der Suda zufolge schrieb H. auch ep. Gedichte und ›Waffentänze‹ (πυρρίχαι). Er ist wahrscheinlich auch Verf. einer gramm. Schrift über δεῖ und χρή (Etym. m. s.v. δοῦλος) und eines oft H. [16] zugewiesenen [4] Werkes über Etymologien, das vom Lex. des Orion benutzt wurde.

1 M. SCHMIDT, Didymi Chalcenteri Fragmenta, 1854, 5; 8–10 2 L. COHN, s.v. Aper (6), RE 1, 2697 3 H. DAEBRITZ, G. FUNAIOLI, s.v. H. (49), RE 8, 487–488 4 A.R. DYCK,

New Light on Greek Authors from Grammatical Texts, in: MH 46, 1989, 5–6 **5** E. Heitsch, Die griech. Dichterfragmente der röm. Kaiserzeit, II, 1964, 41 **6** A. Meineke, Analecta Alexandrina, 1843, 377–381 **7** H. Schrader, Heraclidea, in: Philologus 44, 1885, 238 Anm. 3.

[22] H. Milesios. Grammatiker, um 100 n. Chr. (er zitiert → Aristonikos [5] und wird seinerseits von → Apollonios [11] Dyskolos zitiert); der Beiname findet sich bei Herodian. 2,60,24 Lenz. Verf. einer Abh. ›Über die Akzentlehre‹ (Περὶ καθολικῆς προσῳδίας), wahrscheinlich der ersten umfassenden Darstellung des Stoffes vor → Herodianos, der ihn in seinem gleichnamigen Werk zwar benutzt, aber nicht immer zitiert. Seine Abh. ›Über unregelmäßige Wörter‹ (Περὶ δυσκλίτων ῥημάτων) wurde von → Eustathios, den Lexikographen (→ Lexikographie) und den byz. Werken zu diesem Thema herangezogen. Ausgabe der Fragmente in [1]; H. scheint auch ein Anhänger der → Analogie gewesen zu sein (s. auch [2]). Er stellt eine wichtige Quelle für die Gesch. der Dialekte dar.

Lit.: **1** L. Cohn, De Heraclide Milesio grammatico, in: Berliner Studien für Klass. Philol. 1.2, 1884, 609–717 **2** W. Frye, De Heraclidae Milesii studiis homericis, in: Leipziger Studien zur class. Philol. 6, 1883, 93–188.

S. FO./Ü: T. H.

[23] Sophist aus Lykien, der dort *archiereús* (Oberpriester) des Kaiserkultes wurde (Philostr. soph. 2,26). Schüler von → Hadrianos [1] und → Chrestos in Athen, wo er ca. 193 bis 209 den kaiserlichen Lehrstuhl innehatte [1], obwohl er die Steuerfreiheit (*atéleia*) verlor, nachdem er ca. 202 in einem Rednerwettbewerb mit Apollonios von Athen vor Kaiser Septimius Severus aus dem Konzept gekommen war (soph. 2,20,601; 26,614). Von den Anhängern des Apollonios von Naukratis wurde er gewaltsam vom Lehrstuhl vertrieben und lehrte danach in Smyrna, wo er die eponyme *stephanēphoría* ausübte. Er starb mit über 80 Jahren und wurde in Lykien begraben.
→ Philostratos; Zweite Sophistik

1 I. Avotins, The holders of the chairs of rhetoric at Athens, in: HSPh 79, 1975, 322–324 **2** PIR H 87. E. BO./Ü: L. S.

[24] H. aus Sinope (Σινωπεύς). Autor eines aus dem Kranz des Philippos stammenden Epigramms. Der im Meer ertrunkenene Tlesimenes bittet in einem Gebet seine Eltern, ihm ein Kenotaph zu errichten (Anth. Pal. 7,392). Die *Anthologia Palatina* schreibt H. (ohne Ethnikon) ein weiteres Epitaphion (7,281) zu, das ebenfalls von hoher Qualität ist, sich aber außerhalb der alphabetischen Reihenfolge des Kranzes befindet. Vielleicht handelt es sich um zwei verschiedene Dichter. Auf H. bezieht sich vermutlich Diog. Laert. 5,94, der unter den 14 Personen dieses Namens einen ›musikalischen Dichter von Epigrammen‹ auflistet.

GA II,1,266 f.; II,2,300 f. M. G. A./Ü: M. A. S.

III. Ärzte

[25] H. von Kos. Arzt, Vater des → Hippokrates [6] (Soranos, Vita Hippocratis Kap. 1), wirkte um 440 v. Chr. Die Behauptung, einige hielten ihn für den Verf. der ›Aphorismen‹ wie auch des ›Prognostikon‹ [1], beruht auf einem Mißverständnis des griech. Textes bei Galen (18A,678 K.), wo beide Schriften ausdrücklich Hippokrates zugeschrieben werden.

1 H. Gossen, s. v. H. (53), RE 8, 493. V. N./Ü: L. v. R.-B.

[26] H. von Erythrai. Wirkte gegen E. des 1. Jh. v. Chr. als herophileischer Arzt (Strab. 645C). Er verfaßte eine Schrift mit dem Titel ›Über die Schule des Herophilos‹ in mindestens 7 B. (Gal. 8,746 K.). Bei der Beschreibung des Pulses als Dilatation und Kontraktion von Herz und Arterien unterstrich er die besondere Bed. des Pneuma (Gal. 8,743 f. K.). Galen hielt insbesondere H.' ausführliche Komm. zu den Epidemienb. 2, 3 und 6 aus dem *Corpus Hippocraticum* für erwähnenswert (fr. 4–10 von Staden). H. scherte aus der orthodoxen herophileischen Auslegungspraxis aus, indem er den Empirikern in der Annahme beipflichtete, daß die einzelnen Fallbeschreibungen hinzugefügten akronymen Zeichen spätere Zusätze darstellten. Galen wirft ihm Fehldeutungen und Langatmigkeit vor, räumt jedoch ein, daß er normalerweise nichts Unvernünftiges geschrieben hätte (CMG V,10,2,2, S. 378).
→ Herophilos V. N./Ü: L. v. R.-B.

[27] H. von Tarent. Bedeutendster ärztlicher Vertreter der ant. → Empiriker zw. 100 und 65 v. Chr. Als Schüler des Herophileers → Mantias, vermutlich in Ägypten, näherte er sich dem Empirismus; er verfaßte eine ausführliche Darstellung dieser Schule und ihrer Lehrmeinungen (fr. 1 Deichgräber). Diogenes Laertios (9,115 = fr. 9) berichtet zwar von einem H., der Schüler des skeptischen Philosophen Ptolemaios von Kyrene und Lehrer des → Ainesidemos war, doch kann eine Identifizierung mit H. nicht überzeugen. H.' Werke sind nur frg. überl. Er verfaßte pharmakologische Schriften (fr. 208–210), mindestens eine diätetische Abh. (fr. 241–246, vgl. fr. 187) sowie ein umfangreiches Werk, das der Ärztin → Antiochis [2] (fr. 203–207) gewidmet war. Seine Bemerkungen über den Puls, der eine sichtbare Bewegung von Herz und Arterien darstelle (fr. 172), und über das Bauchfell (fr. 185) deuten auf Sektionserfahrung oder vielmehr chirurgische Praxis hin. Seine wichtigsten therapeutischen Schriften sind die jeweils vier B. über äußerliche (fr. 174–178) und innerliche Beschwerden (fr. 179–191). Darin zeigt er die Beherrschung vielfältiger Behandlungsmethoden, die allgemeinchirurgische, augenoperative und v. a. pharmakologische Therapiemaßnahmen bei körperlichen und geistigen Gesundheitsstörungen umfassen. In diesen Schriften legte H. die Theorien der empirischen Schule dar, wobei er die Erfahrung zur Grundlage der Medizin erklärte, Kausalerklärungen jedoch nicht grundsätzlich ablehnte. Seine Darlegungen verschafften ihm Galens Anerkennung, der seine Genauigkeit und Wahrheitsliebe lobend erwähnt (fr. 175).

H. spielte auch eine gewichtige Rolle in der Gesch. der Hippokratesauslegung. Er kommentierte alle hippokratischen Werke, die er für echt hielt. Als einer der ersten wandte er sich so den ›Aphorismen‹ (fr. 365) und *De officina* (fr. 319) zu; sein Komm. zum vierten Epidemienbuch in wenigstens zwei B. (fr. 348) war für seine Zeit außergewöhnlich.

H.' nur in wenigen Fr. greifbares breites Interessenspektrum und sein argumentativer Scharfsinn lassen den Verlust fast all seiner Werke bes. schmerzlich erscheinen. Er fand Anerkennung auch bei medizinischen Autoren, die seinen theoretischen Standpunkt keineswegs teilten, wie z. B. Galen, Soranos, Caelius Aurelianus und Statilius Criton, der manche Verordnungen des H. in seinen *Kosmētiká* aufgriff (fr. 234–240). H. zählt zu den Pharmakologen, die auf dem Titel der Wiener Dioskorides-Hs. aus dem 6. Jh. (Wien, med. gr. 1, Bl. 2) dargestellt sind. Ähnliche Darstellungen seiner Person wurden bis in die muslimische Welt hinein tradiert. Im lat. Westen jedoch war von H. im 6. Jh. nichts als der Name geblieben (fr. 7; Agnellus, Comm. in Gal. de sectis, S. 22 WESTERINK).

→ Empiriker

ED./FR.: DEICHGRÄBER, 172–202, 220–249 • A. GUARDASOLE, Eraclide di Taranto, Frammenti, 1997.
LIT.: H. GOSSEN, s. v. H. (54), RE 8, 493–496.

V. N./Ü: L. v. R.–B.

IV. KÜNSTLER

[28] Griech. Maler, gen. in einer inschr. erh. Lohnabrechnung am Proskenion des hell. Theaters in Delos. Danach malte er im frühen 3. Jh. v. Chr. zwei Tafeln zum Preis von 200 Drachmen. Vermutlich handelte es sich dabei um variabel einsetzbare Kulissenbilder, wie sie zu der Zeit in der → Bühnenmalerei üblich waren.

H. BULLE, Unt. an griech. Theatern (ABAW 33), 1928 • EAA 3, s. v. H (2), 1149.

N. H.

[29] Bildhauer, Sohn des Agauos aus Ephesos. Seine Signatur und die eines Harmatios finden sich an einer in traianischer Zeit gearbeiteten, bei Neapel gefundenen Statue, jetzt in Paris (Louvre) als Mars ergänzt. Sie stellte im sog. Hüftmanteltypus vermutlich ein Porträt dar. Die Lesungen sämtlicher Namen sind umstritten, verweisen aber in jedem Fall auf eine bekannte Bildhauerfamilie aus Ephesos.

T. ASHBY, Tomas Jenkins in Roma, in: PBSR 6, 1913, 500 • CLARAC, Taf. 313, Nr. 1439 • G. CRESSEDI, s. v. H. (8), EAA 3, 1960, 1150 • LOEWY, Nr. 293 • OVERBECK, Nr. 2279 (Quellen).

R. N.

[30] Griech. Maler aus Makedonien, wirkte um die Mitte des 2. Jh. v. Chr. vielleicht als Hofmaler. Die Emigration nach Athen folgte auf den Sturz des Königs Perseus nach der Schlacht von Pydna (168 v. Chr.). Begonnen hatte der als »bekannt« beschriebene H. (Plin. nat. 35,135; 146) entweder als Anstreicher von Schiffen oder als Maler illusionistischer Darstellungen derselben. Beide Karrieren sind in der griech. → Malerei nicht unüblich. Träfe letztere zu, bleibt das Aussehen der Schiffsbilder Spekulation, denn sein Werk ist unbekannt.

L. FORTI, s. v. H. (6), EAA 3, 1150 • E. PFUHL, s. v. H. (62), RE 8, 497.

N. H.

Herakleion (Ἡράκλειον).

[1] Stadt an der kret. Nordküste, h. Iraklion. In einem Rechtshilfevertrag mit Miletos (259/250 v. Chr.) erscheint H. als souveräne, mit → Knosos verbündete Stadt (StV III 482 I) [1]. H. war im 1. Jh. v. Chr., in der Nachfolge von Amnisos, Hafenort von Knosos (Strab. 10,4,7 f.) und wohl von diesem abhängig (vgl. Strab. 10,5,1). Aufgrund von Plin. nat. 4,59 hat man geschlossen, H. habe auch den Namen Mation geführt [2]. Durchgesetzt hat sich die Auffassung, daß Plinius hier seine griech. Vorlage mißverstanden habe (πολισμάτιον Ἡ., »das Städtchen H.«) [3]. Da in der Aufzählung kret. Städte bei Plinius (und wohl auch seiner Vorlage) keine weitere Klassifizierung nach großen oder kleinen Städten vorkommt, kann man jedoch die Existenz eines nahe H. gelegenen Ortes Mation nicht ausschließen (vgl. auch Plin. nat. 4,61: die *contra Matium* gelegene Insel Dia). Ant. Reste gibt es in H. so gut wie nicht, mit der Ausnahme von röm. Gräbern und Relikten einer frühen byz. Stadtmauer zw. Odos Khandakos und Odos Daidalos [4].

1 A. CHANIOTIS, Die Verträge zw. kret. Poleis in der hell. Zeit, 1996, 448 f., Nr. 78 2 C. BURSIAN, Geogr. von Griechenland 2, 1872, 560 f. 3 N. PLATON, Δύο ὀνόματα ἀνυπάρκτων Κρητικῶν πόλεων, in: Kretika Chronika 1, 1947, 14–21 4 I. F. SANDERS, Roman Crete, 1982, 152.

H. SO.

[2] Südlichste Stadt in der maked. Pieria (Ps.-Skyl. 66) beim h. Platamon. Erwähnt in athen. Tributquotenlisten von 425/4 und 422/1 (IG I³ 71; 77); Grenzstreit mit → Gonnoi im 3. Jh. v. Chr. [1]; von den Römern im 3. Maked. Krieg (171–168 v. Chr.) erobert (Liv. 44,8,8 f.). Später wohl in der röm. Kolonie Dion [II 2] aufgegangen.

1 B. HELLY, Gonnoi II, 1973, Nr. 93.

F. PAPAZOGLOU, Les villes de Macédoine, 1988, 114.

MA. ER.

[3] Griech. Siedlung auf der östl. Krim am Südufer der Maiotis (Ptol. 3,6,4), nach Strab. 11,2,6 zw. Myrmekion und Parthenion.

[4] Zwei Vorgebirge an der kaukasischen Schwarzmeerküste: an der Mündung des Nesis die *ákra* H. (Arr. per. p. E. 9v46 DILLER) und am Fluß Achaius das *akrōtḗrion* H., das z. Z. Arrians *tá Érēma* hieß (τὰ Ἔρημα, l. c. 1014,4) hieß.

I. v. B.

Herakleios (Ἡράκλειος). Zwei angesehene, aus dem → Verres-Prozeß 70 v. Chr. bekannte Sizilier:

[1] Sohn eines Hieron, reicher Bürger von Syrakus. Erbte 73 v. Chr. von einem gleichnamigen Verwandten ein prächtiges Haus samt Einrichtung sowie 3 Millionen Sesterzen (Cic. Verr. 2,14,35). Durch die Machenschaften des Verres, der das Testament anfocht, verlor H. Vermögen und Erbschaft. Die Immobilien erhielt er durch L. Caecilius [I 13] Metellus, den Nachfolger des Verres, zurück (Cic. Verr. 2,19,47–50; 25,62).

[2] H. aus Egesta, Kapitän eines zur syrakusanischen Flotte gehörenden Schiffes, das während seiner Erkrankung von Seeräubern gekapert wurde. Auf Veranlassung des Verres verurteilt und hingerichtet (Cic. Verr. 5,44,115–45,120). K. MEI.

[3] Kyniker. Gegen ihn verfaßte Kaiser → Iulianus [11] im März 362 n. Chr. eine Rede ›Gegen den Kyniker H. über die richtige Art, Kynismus zu betreiben, und über die Frage, ob es einem »Hund« ansteht, Mythen zu erfinden‹. Als Wanderphilosoph vertrat H. mit kynischem Freimut insbes. auf dem Gebiet der Rel. Lehren, die Iulianos' Programm einer Erneuerung des Hell. zuwiderliefen. Iulianos spricht H. das Recht ab, sich auf → Diogenes [14] von Sinope zu berufen (Iul. or. 223c), wirft ihm Gottlosigkeit (204c – 205a) und mangelnde Bildung (7,235a) vor und beschuldigt ihn, er habe seine eigenen Werke im Heerlager und sogar im Kaiserpalast verbreitet (224d).

→ Kynische Schule

G. Rochefort, *Discours* de Julien l'Empereur II 1, texte établi et traduit. Collection des Universités de France, 1963, 34–90 • L. Paquet, Les cyniques grecs. Fragments et témoignages, ²1988, 271–294. M. G.-C./Ü: S. P.

[4] Sonst unbekannter kaiserzeitlicher Autor eines kurzen Epigramms, das bei Theben in Ägypten gefunden wurde: Das unvergleichlichste von allen Königsgräbern (σύριγγες) ist für den Dichter dasjenige, das mit dem Namen des mythischen Memnon verbunden wird.

EpGr 1018 • Anth. Pal. app. I 195 Cougny • J. A. Letronne, Recueil des inscriptions grecques et latines de l'Égypte, 2, 1848 (Ndr. 1974), 265 f. M. G. A./Ü: M. A. S.

[5] Hofeunuch des Kaisers → Valentinianus III., 454/5 n. Chr. *primicerius sacri cubiculi*, Feind des Reichsfeldherrn → Aetius [2], dessen Ermordung 454 von ihm betrieben wurde; bald darauf zusammen mit dem Kaiser getötet (Iohannes Antiochenus fr. 201 FHG IV 614 f.; Chron. min. 1,303,483 f.; 2,86 Mommsen; Iord. Rom. 334).

PLRE 2, 541 • A. Demandt, Die Spätantike 1989, 155 f. K. P. J.

[6] H. aus Edessa, röm. Heerführer unter den Kaisern → Leon I. und → Zenon, kämpfte vor allem 468–470 erfolgreich gegen die Vandalen. Als *magister militum per Thracias* geriet er 474 in ostgotische Gefangenschaft. Von Kaiser Zenon freigekauft, fiel er auf dem Weg nach Konstantinopel einem Anschlag der Goten zum Opfer. PLRE 2, 541 f. (Heraclius 4).

[7] Oström. Kaiser, * um 575, 610–641 n. Chr., Sohn des gleichnamigen Generals und Exarchen von Karthago, stürzte 610 den Usurpator → Phokas und begründete eine bis 711 regierende Dynastie. Von seinen Vorgängern übernahm er den Krieg mit den sāsānidischen Persern und den Avaren. Viele Details über den Verlauf der Auseinandersetzungen sind wegen der verworrenen Quellenlage [vgl. 2] umstritten, u. a. der Verlauf der Belagerung Konstantinopels durch die Avaren (mit Persern und Slaven?) 626 in Abwesenheit des H., die mit einer – als Wunder gedeuteten – Niederlage der Gegner endete, sowie die Ereignisse, die 628 zum Friedensschluß mit den Persern und zur Rückgabe des 614 in Jerusalem erbeuteten heiligen Kreuzes führten. Die Vorstöße der islamischen Araber etwa ab 634 stellten die Erfolge des H. gegen die Perser bereits zu seinen Lebzeiten wieder in Frage.

Zur Straffung der Reichsverwaltung trug er erheblich bei [1], doch begründete er nicht, wie früher angenommen, die Gliederung des Reiches in sog. Themen (θέματα, Militärprovinzen), die sich erst in der Folgezeit allmählich herausbildete. 615 führte er eine 6 röm. Gramm (= 6,81 g) schwere Silbermünze (ἑξάγραμμα) ein, die praktisch an die Stelle des großen Kupfer-Follis trat. H. war der erste Kaiser, der sich in einem offiziellen Dokument als → *Basileus* bezeichnete.

Sein Versuch, die Streitfrage um ein oder zwei Energien in Christus 638 durch die sog. Ekthesis im monotheletischen (→ Monotheletismus) Sinne beizulegen, stieß bei den Anhängern des Dogmas von Kalchedon auf Ablehnung.

Nach seinem Tod im Februar 641 führte seine Verfügung, die Macht unter seinem Sohn aus erster Ehe, Constantinus [3] III., seiner zweiten Frau Martina und seinem von ihr geborenen Sohn → Heraklonas aufzuteilen, zu Auseinandersetzungen. Als Constantinus im Sept. 641 starb, sprach der Senat dessen elfjährigem Sohn Constans [2] II. die Thronfolge zu.

1 J. F. Haldon, Byzantium in the Seventh Century, 1990 **2** P. Speck, Das geteilte Dossier, 1988 **3** A. N. Stratos, Byzantium in the Seventh Century, Bd. 1: 602–634, 1968; Bd. 2: 634–641, 1972.

PLRE 3, 586 f. (Heraclius 4) • ODB 2, 916 f. • LMA 4, 2140 f. F. T.

Herakleitos (Ἡράκλειτος).

[1] H. von Ephesos, Sohn des Bloson, herausragende Persönlichkeit der ion. Philosophie.

A. Zur Person B. Sprache C. Philosophie D. Wirkungsgeschichte

A. Zur Person

H.' Hauptschaffenszeit ist um 500–503 v. Chr. anzusetzen (Diog. Laert. 9,1). Seine Familie hatte im öffentl. Leben von Ephesos eine führende Position. Die doxographische Überl. verzeichnet zahlreiche Anekdoten über H.' Arroganz und Verachtung seiner Mitbürger wie der Menschheit im allg., die meist auf den Fragmenten des H. selbst beruhen.

B. SPRACHE

In der Ant. war H. für seine Dunkelheit bekannt, so daß man ihm die Epitheta »der Dunkle« (σκοτεινός, z. B. Strab. 14,25) und »der Rätseler« (αἰνίκτης, Timon von Phleius bei Diog. Laert. 9,6) verlieh. H. setzt die kryptische Sprache für seine philos. Reflexion bewußt ein: Statt einer durchgängigen Argumentation bietet der Text eine strukturierte Reihe änigmatischer und aphoristischer Äußerungen in einem breiten Spektrum poetischer und rhet. Kunstgriffe – von Parallelismus und Chiasmus (22 B 1 DK; B 5; B 10 usw.) bis zu Wortspielen (B 48; B 114) und Rätseln (B 56, B 34). Die Bedeutung entfaltet sich also in einem zweifachen Prozeß: Durch den kunstvollen Gebrauch der Sprache erhalten die einzelnen Äußerungen verschiedene Bedeutungsebenen, während die aphoristischen Sätze durch die Wiederkehr bestimmter Formeln oder Strukturen in ein verzweigtes System von Querbeziehungen und Überlagerungen eingeordnet sind [1. 87–95; 2].

C. PHILOSOPHIE

H. nimmt unter den ion. Philosophen eine bes. Stellung ein, da die fundamentale Frage seiner Philos. sich nicht darauf bezieht, wie das physikalische Universum aufgebaut ist, sondern wie man diese Welt verstehen soll: Die Reflexionen über die Welt, über die Natur des möglichen Wissens von der Welt und über die Mittel zum Ausdruck dieses Wissens sind eng miteinander verwoben. Ein zentraler Aspekt seiner Lehre ist die Vorstellung, ein universeller, alles durchdringender Logos strukturiere und regiere den Kosmos (B 1; B 2; B 72 usw.). Die genaue Bedeutung des Begriffs → Logos (λόγος) ist dabei nur schwer zu definieren, da H. mit Absicht das gesamte Bedeutungsfeld des Wortes ausschöpft (»Sprache«, »Rechenschaft«, »Maß«, »Proportion«, »Prinzip«, »Gesetz«, »Grund« und »Vernunft«). Da der Logos das umfassendste Prinzip des Kosmos sei, solle es das Ziel menschlichen Bemühens um wirkliches Wissen sein. Obwohl der Logos allen Menschen gemein (ξυνός) sei und sich in allen Phänomenen unserer Welt manifestiere, seien sich die Menschen seiner dennoch nicht bewußt (B 2; B 72). Sie erfaßten nicht das wirkliche Wesen (φύσις, *phýsis*), die tiefere Struktur der Erfahrungswelt, so wie eine Rede für Sprachunkundige nicht mehr als bedeutungsloses Geräusch sei (B. 107; B 17; B 34; B. 56). H. sieht eine weitreichende Analogie oder gar Identität zw. dem Verständnis der Welt und dem Verständnis der Bedeutung einer Äußerung, die etwas über diese aussagt. Der Logos sei nicht unerreichbar: Er verlange eine bes. Aufmerksamkeit und eine bewußte hermeneutische Anstrengung, vergleichbar dem Verständnis der in Gestalt eines Orakels kommenden Botschaft eines Gottes (B 18; B 35; B 86; B 93; B 113; B 115; B 116). Darüberhinaus müsse jeder für sich selbst nach einem wirklichen Verständnis streben (B 50; B 101a).

H.' Lehre vom Logos hängt mit seiner Anwendung von Gegensatzpaaren zusammen: Er führt kontrastierende Paare vor, alternierende Phasen eines Prozesses bilden konträre Qualitäten (B 57; B 88; B 126 usw.), ein einziges Objekt oder Phänomen kann einander entgegengesetzte Charakteristika aufweisen (B 48; B 59; B 60 usw.), verschiedene Beobachter können demselben Gegenstand einander entgegengesetzte Qualitäten zuschreiben (B 61; B 83). H. negiert nicht die Existenz dieser Gegensätze in den Paaren, sondern er versteht sie synthetisch als Teile eines Ganzen, schließlich als *das* Ganze, als den Kosmos selbst (B 8; B 10). Wie der Bogen in zwei entgegengesetzte Richtungen gespannt werden muß, könne laut H. überhaupt irgendetwas nur auf Grund der unaufhörlichen Spannung und Auseinandersetzung zw. den Gegensätzen funktionieren, und werde die Welt nie ihre Dynamik verlieren. Darüber hinaus garantiere der Logos zu jeder Zeit, daß der Fluß der Welt harmonisch, und die Auseinandersetzung zw. den Gegensätzen produktiv bleibe.

Der physikalische Aspekt der den Kosmos organisierenden Kraft zeige sich im → Feuer. Es wird als die höchste und reinste, göttliche Form der Materie verstanden. Als Grundstoff der Welt, der durch alle Veränderungen und Transformationen hindurch seine Natur bewahre, stelle es die materielle Seite der Einheit der Welt dar. Die Regelmäßigkeit und Proportionalität der Veränderungen des Feuers garantiere, daß das Universum ein geordnetes Ganzes bleibe (B 30; B 31). Problematisch ist jedoch, daß das Feuer in einigen Fragmenten zwar zur archetypischen Form der Materie oder zum alle physikalischen Prozesse steuernden Prinzip erklärt wird, in anderen aber mit den beiden anderen Elementen (Wasser und Erde) gleichrangig zu sein scheint. H. verneint explizit die Möglichkeit eines absoluten Anfangs der Welt (B 30); ob jedoch die These einer fortwährenden kosmischen Ordnung mit der Lehre von einem periodischen Weltenbrand (wie er H. von Aristoteles und den Stoikern zugeschrieben wird), vereinbar ist, bleibt unklar.

Die wechselseitige Beziehung zwischen dem Epistemischen und dem Physikalischen zeigt sich auch in H.' Theorie der Seele. Das kosmische Feuer, das rational und lebendig sei, wird mit der Seele gleichgesetzt (Aristot. an. 405a25), die Seele ihrerseits nehme am kosmischen Prozeß als Feuer teil (B 36). Durch das Feuer könne der Mensch an kosmischer Rationalität teilhaben: Je feuriger die Seele einer Person sei, desto intelligenter sei diese (B 1 17, B 1 18) und damit umso fähiger, das göttliche Prinzip des Kosmos zu erfassen.

D. WIRKUNGSGESCHICHTE

Obwohl → Platons Kenntnisse über H. beschränkt sind, hatte die heraklitische Flußlehre einen grundlegenden Einfluß auf seine Beschreibung der physischen Welt als von etwas ständig in Veränderung Begriffenem (vgl. Plat. Tht. 152d ff.). Diese These wurde von → Aristoteles weiterentwickelt (vgl. Aristot. metaph. Γ 3; 7; 8). Viele zentrale Thesen der → Stoiker weisen

heraklitеischen Einfluß auf. Als die wichtigste kann die Annahme vom Logos als einem aktiv regierenden Prinzip des Kosmos genannt werden. Auch → Zenon und → Kleanthes folgten H. in ihrer Annahme, daß das Feuer der physische Aspekt des Logos sei. H. kommt bei dem Skeptiker → Ainesidemos wieder in den Vordergrund. Dieser vertrat die Ansicht, daß der skeptische Weg zur heraklitischen Philos. hinführe (S. Emp. P.H. 1,210ff.).
→ Herakliteer; Herakleitische Briefe; VORSOKRATIKER

1 CH.H. KAHN, The Art and Thought of Heraclitus, 1979
2 R. MONDOLFO, The evidence of Plato and Aristotle relating to the ekpyrosis in Heraclitus, in: Phronesis 3, 1958, 75–82.

FRG.: M. MARCOVICH, Heraclitus, 1967 • S. MOURAVIEV, New readings of three Heraclitean fragments (B 23, B 28, B 26), in: Hermes 101, 1073, 114–127 • R. MONDOLFO, L. TARÁN, Eraclito, testimonianze e imitazione, 1972.
LIT.: W.K.C. GUTHRIE, A History of Greek Philosophy I, 1962, 403–492 • M. MARKOVICH, s.v. H., RE Suppl 10, 246–320 • K. REINHARDT, Heraklits Lehre vom Feuer, in: Hermes 77, 1942, 1–17 • B. SNELL, Die Sprache Heraklits, in: Hermes 61, 1926, 353–381 • J. BOLLACK, H. WISMANN, Héraclite ou la séparation, 1972 • E. HUSSEY, s.v. Héraclite, in: J. BRUNSCHWIG, G.E.R. LLOYD (Hrsg.), Le savoir grec, 1996. G.BE./Ü: T.H.

[2] Athen. 12,538f erwähnt bei einem Zitat von Chares [2] von Mytilene (FGrH 125 F 4) H. von Tarent, der als Kitharode bei der Hochzeit Alexanders d.Gr. 324 in Susa auftrat. Athen. 1,20a kennt ebenfalls einen H. von Mytilene, einen Zauberkünstler an Alexanders Hof; er trat auch beim Hochzeitsfest in Susa auf (Athen. 12,538e). Diog. Laert. 9,17 stellt Homonyme des Philosophen H. zusammen, darunter einen Hofnarren, der vorher ein Kitharöde war. Möglicherweise faßte aber Diogenes, indem er zwei Schritte in der Laufbahn des Hofnarren annahm, die zwei von Athenaios genannten Personen an Alexanders Hof zu einer zusammen. E.R./Ü: L.S.

[3] H. von Halikarnassos. Epigrammdichter, identifizierbar mit dem Elegiker bei Diog. Laert. 9,17 (ἐλεγείας ποιητὴς Ἁλικαρνασσεύς) und Freund des Kallimachos, der dessen Tod in einem bemerkenswerten Gedicht beweint (Anth. Pal. 7,80). Von H. ist ein einzigartiges Grabepigramm aus dem Kranz des Meleagros überliefert (7,465), imitiert von Antipatros [8] von Sidon (7,464); sein traditionelles Thema (eine bei der Geburt gestorbene junge Frau) ist mit großer Originalität und Eleganz behandelt.

GA I,1,106.; I,2,304f. • R. HUNTER, Callimachus and Heraclitus, in: Materiali e discussioni 28, 1992, 113–123. M.G.A./Ü: M.A.S.

[4] Komödiendichter unbekannter Zeit. Erh. ist ein Titel eines Stückes Ξενίζων (›Der Gastgeber‹), in dem eine gefräßige Frau namens Helena verspottet wird (PCG V, 560). B.BÄ.

[5] Sonst unbekannter Mythograph, unter dessen Namen im Cod. Vaticanus Graecus 305 (vgl.: [1. LII-LIII]) 39 Exzerpte aus einer Sammlung von wundersamen Dingen unter dem Titel ›Widerlegung oder Heilung von Mythen mit unnatürlichen Phänomenen‹ (ἀνασκευὴ ἢ θεραπεία μύθων τῶν παρὰ φύσιν παραδεδομένων) erh. sind. Die Mythen werden (wie auch im Werk des → Palaiphatos) rationalistisch erklärt. H. ist nicht mit dem Verf. der ›Homerallegorien‹ gleichzusetzen [2; 3].

AUSG.: 1 N. FESTA (ed.), Mythographi Graeci, Vol. III, Fasc. II, 1902, 73–87.
LIT.: 2 F. BUFFIERE, Les mythes d'Homère et la pensée grecque, 1956, 232–233 3 F. BUFFIÈRE (Hrsg.), Héraclite. Allégories d' Homère, 1962, VIII-IX. S.FO./Ü: T.H.

[6] H. von Rhodiapolis (Lykien). Arzt und Schriftsteller, 1.–2. Jh. n. Chr., »Homer der medizinischen Dichtkunst«, Verf. medizin. und philos. Schriften. Wegen seiner Werke, von denen er Abschriften zur Verfügung stellte, ehrten ihn Alexandriner, Rhodier und Athener, Areopag wie epikureische Philosophen gleichermaßen. Von seiner Heimatstadt wurde er wegen seiner Spenden, insbes. einer Stiftung von Spielen zu Ehren des Asklepios, mit einer Statue und einer ausführlichen Inschr. (TAM II,2,910) geehrt, die die einzig überl. Nachricht von diesem produktiven und weitgereisten Denker darstellt. V.N./Ü: L.v.R.-B.

[7] s. Paradoxographoi

Herakleon (Ἡρακλέων).
[1] aus Beroia, Günstling Antiochos' [10] VIII., verursachte 96 v. Chr. dessen Tod in einem Komplott, um selbst König zu werden, was aber durch die Thronbesteigung Seleukos' VI. konterkariert wurde. H.s Sohn Dionysios beherrschte Teile Nordsyriens mit Bambyke, Beroia und Herakleia (Pomp. Trog. prologus 39; Strab. 16,2; 7; Ios. ant. Iud. 13,365; Athen. 4,153b). A.ME.
[2] Seeräuberführer, siegte 72 v. Chr. über die syrakusanische Flotte (→ Herakleios [2]) und drang mit vier Schiffen in den Großen Hafen von Syrakus ein (Cic. Verr. 5,90f.; 97–100). Er wurde 70 von L. Caecilius [I 13] Metellus, dem Nachfolger des Verres, vertrieben. K.MEI.
[3] aus Ephesos. Grammatiker, Verf. eines attizistischen Lex., das von → Athenaios [3] sechsmal zitiert wird (2,52b; 3,76a; 7,303b; 7,308f; 11,503a; 14,647b); vielleicht handelt es sich um dasjenige, von dem → Didymos [3] Claudius eine Epitome angefertigt hat (was ein *terminus ante quem* für die Datierung wäre: [1], dagegen [2]).
→ Lexikographie

1 A. GUDEMAN, s.v. Herakleon (5), RE 8, 513
2 M. SCHMIDT, Didymi Chalcenteri fragmenta, 1854, 3.

F. SUSEMIHL, Gesch. der griech. Litt. in der Alexandrinerzeit, II, 1892, 22 und 190.

[4] H. von Tilotis (Ägypten). Grammatiker wahrscheinlich augusteischer Zeit, lehrte in Rom (Suda η 455). Verf. eines Komm. zu Homer κατὰ ῥαψῳδίαν (»Gesang für Gesang«), also in 48 Büchern, und zu den Lyrikern; die in den schol. zu Homer und Apollonios Rhodios überlieferten Fragmente des ersten Werkes [1] zeigen, daß H. an allen Aspekten des Textes interessiert war (Gramm., Etym., Topographie) und sich dabei zuweilen gegen die Ansichten des Aristarchos [4] von Samothrake wandte; er tendierte wohl bisweilen zur allegorischen Exegese ([2]; dagegen [5]).

1 R. Berndt, Die Fragmente des Homererklärers Heracleo, 1913 **2** Diels, DG, 1929², 91–93 **3** M. Schmidt, Didymi Chalcenteri Fragmenta, 1854, 47 **4** H. Schrader, Porphyrii Quaestiones Homericae, I, 1880, 406 **5** F. Susemihl, Gesch. der griech. Litt. in der Alexandrinerzeit, II, 1892, 20–22 **6** M. van der Valk, Researches on the text and scholia of the Iliad I, 1963, 110–111; 436–437. S.FO./Ü: T.H.

Herakleopolis magna (äg. *Nn-njswt*, h. Ihnāsiyat almadīna). Stadt auf dem Westufer des Nils im Eingangsbereich des → Fajjūm; Metropole des 20. oberäg. Gaues; Kultort des mit → Herakles geglichenen Widdergottes Harsaphes und Herkunftsstadt der herakleopolitanischen 9./10. Dyn. in der 1. Zwischenzeit. Die arch. Zeugnisse am Ort, Gräberfelder und Tempel, reichen bis in die 1. Zwischenzeit bzw. das MR (1. H. 2. Jt. v. Chr.) zurück.

F. Gomaà, s. v. H.m., LÄ 2, 1124–1127 (mit Karte) · M. C. Perez-Die, P. Vernus, Excavaciones en Ehnasya el Medina, 1992. S.S.

Herakles (Ἡρακλῆς).
[1] In Mythos und Kult der prominenteste griech. Heros (→ Heroenkult). In seinen Mythen, die sich zu keinem auf ihn fokussierten überragenden Werk der Dichtung niedergeschlagen haben, ist er bes. mit Theben, Argos und der Landschaft um Trachis verbunden, im Kult wird er fast panhellenisch verehrt, ohne daß aber ein Ort ein Heroengrab vorzeigen könnte.

I. Kult und Mythos II. Ikonographie

I. Kult und Mythos
A. Name B. Mythos C. Kult
D. Identifikationen E. Tugendlehre

A. Name

Sein Name ist schon in der Ant. mit dem der → Hera verbunden worden: er fügt sich zur geläufigen Bildung griech. Anthroponyme wie Patro-kles (»der seinem Vater Ruhm bringt«) oder Dio-kles/Zeno-kles (»der Zeus Ruhm bringt«). Die Beziehung zu Hera ist allerdings problematisch: aus Zorn auf H.' Mutter, ihre Nebenbuhlerin → Alkmene, ist sie H.' erbitterte Gegnerin (seit Hom. Il. 15,25–28; 18,119); die ant. Namenserklärung (seit Pind. fr. 291), daß H. gerade durch Heras Herausforderung zu Ruhm gekommen sei, versucht dieses Paradoxon zu verstehen. Das ist umso dringender, als (seit Pind. fr. 291) die Meinung belegt ist, H. habe urspr. Alkeides (oder Alkaios, Diod. 1,24,2) geheißen und seinen zweiten Namen eben Hera wegen erhalten; dies mißversteht das Patronymikon Alkeides, das H. als Enkel des Perseussohns Alkaios, des Vaters von Amphitryon, bezeichnet (Apollod. 2,47).

Radikaler, aber sehr hypothetisch sind einige mod. Versuche, den Namen mit *hḗrōs* im Sinne von »junger Mann« zusammenzubringen [1].

B. Mythos

Die Mythen des H. liegen in nahezu unübersichtlicher Fülle vor [2]. Obschon seit archa. Zeit mehrere Dichter H.-Epen verfaßten, die seiner Gesamtbiographie (bes. → Peisandros von Rhodos und → Panyassis von Halikarnassos) oder einzelnen Episoden (Eroberung von Oichalia, → Kreophylos von Samos; H. auf Kos, → Meropis) gelten, hat keine Dichtung die Mythen geordnet und kanonisiert, und nur wenige Trag. gelten ihm (Tod: Soph. Trach.; Wahnsinn: Eur. Herc.); zusammenfassende Darstellungen sind erst bei Diodor (4,8–39) und Apollodor (2,57–166) erhalten, die auf ältere Berichte, bes. → Herodoros (FGrH 31 F 13–37) und → Pherekydes von Athen (FGrH 3, Buch 2 und 3 der Historiai) zurückgreifen.

H. ist Sohn von Zeus und → Alkmene (Hom. Il. 14,323 f.), der Frau des theban. Königs → Amphitryon (Hom. Od. 11,266–268, vgl. Il. 5,392), vom dem sie H.' Halbbruder Iphikles, den Vater von H.' Waffengefährten → Iolaos, gebiert. Eine erste Probe seiner göttlichen Herkunft gibt er, als er zwei von Hera in seine Wiege gesandte Schlangen erwürgt (Pind. N. 1,39–59).

Im Zentrum seiner Mythen stehen die zwölf Taten, die er auf Heras Befehl im Dienste des → Eurystheus von Argos vollbrachte; diesen Dienst mit seiner Vielzahl der Taten (*áthloi*), das Heraufholen des Kerberos und den Beistand der Athena setzt bereits die *Ilias* voraus (Hom. Il. 8,362–369; 15,639; 19,132 f., vgl. Od. 11,621–626), die schlußendliche Versetzung in den Himmel und die Heirat mit Zeus' Tochter → Hebe die ›Odyssee‹ (11,601–604). Diese Taten (in mod. gelehrter Diktion der »Dodekathlos«) sind in ihrem Umfang und teilweise auch in ihrer Abfolge erst am Ende der archa. Zeit kanonisiert worden (Pind. fr. 169; Metopen des Zeustempels in Olympia, [3. Nr. 1705]), während frühere Zyklen auch später nicht zugehörige Abenteuer darstellen ([3. Nr. 1698–1703], vgl. Eur. Herc. 359–435). Fest ist schon immer der Kampf mit dem nemeischen Löwen als Jugendabenteuer, bei dem sich H. das für die Ikonographie typische, unverwundbare Löwenfell als Schutz erwirbt (vgl. Stesich. fr. 52). Daran schließt die kanonische Reihenfolge die Tötung der Hydra von Lerna, des erymanthischen Ebers, der kerynthischen Hirschkuh, der stymphalischen Vögel und die Reinigung des Stalls des → Augeias an, die alle in der Peloponnes spielen. In die vier Himmelsrichtungen greifen der kretische Stier (südl. der Peloponnes), die menschenfressenden Rosse des Thrakers Diomedes (Nord), die Erbeutung des Gürtels der Amazone (Ost) und der

Rinder des → Geryoneus (West) aus; das Heraufholen des Kerberos führt in die Unterwelt, dasjenige der Äpfel der Hesperiden an den (westl.) Rand der Welt, wo Himmel und Erde sich berühren (→ Atlas [2]). Diese Abenteuer sind alle einzeln in der archa. Lit. und Kunst faßbar: Homer erwähnt den Kerberos (Hom. Il. 8,367f.; Hom. Od. 11,623–626), Hesiod den Geryoneus, die Hydra und den Löwen von Nemea (Hes. theog. 287–294; 313–318; 327–332), für das Epos *Herakleia* des → Peisandros (7. Jh.) sind der nemeische Löwe, die Hydra, die Hindin, die Vögel und Geryoneus bezeugt (fr. 2–5), → Stesichoros verfaßte eine *Geryonēís* und einen *Kérberos*.

Nicht in diesen Zwölferkatalog aufgenommen, aber schon früh erzählt sind die Auseinandersetzungen mit den → Kentauren (Peisandros, Stesichoros), mit → Antaios, dem Sohn der → Gaia (Peisandros), die Eroberung Troias unter → Laomedon, eine Generation vor dem troianischen Krieg (Hom. Il. 5,640–651) – die seit Pindar mit dem Zug gegen die Amazonen, später auch mit H.' Teilnahme an der → Argonauten-Fahrt verbunden wurde (Pind. N. 3,36f., vgl. Hellanikos FGrH 4 F 26; Diod. 4,32) – und der Kampf gegen die Meropes, die Ureinwohner von Kos, der ausführlich in einem lokalen spätarcha. Epos, der *Meropís*, erzählt war ([4], vgl. Hom. Il. 15,25–28; Pind. I.1,31).

Die überwiegende Mehrzahl dieser Erzählungen stellt H. im Kampf mit wilden, monströsen und gefährlichen Tieren (einem riesigen Eber, menschenfressenden Pferden) oder ungeheuren Menschen (dem dreileibigen Geryoneus, den mannweiblichen Amazonen, dem unverwundbaren Antaios) dar; daraus wurde schon früh der zivilisatorische Auftrag des H. gelesen, der etwa in der Erzählung von seiner Ermordung des ägypt. Königs → Busiris [3] und Beendigung von dessen Menschenopfern bereits deutlich ist (Hdt. 2,45; Isokr. or. 11,45; [5]). Hinter vielen der Erzählungen steht traditionelles und teilweise uraltes Erzählgut, das sich in die indoeurop., gar steinzeitliche Vergangenheit verfolgen läßt [6; 7; 8]; erzählerisch bestehen auch deutliche Parallelen zum Vorderen Orient und zur ägypt. Königsideologie (zusammenfassend [9. 458–472]).

Eng mit Theben verbunden ist der Sagenkomplex um H.' Kampf gegen die → Minyer von Orchomenos und ihren König → Erginos. Als Belohnung erhält H. die theban. Königstocher → Megara, mit der er mehrere Söhne zeugt. Doch von Hera mit Wahnsinn geschlagen, tötet er (die Mutter und) seine Söhne. Diese Erzählung, die in verschiedenen, untereinander stark divergierenden Versionen vorliegt, ist mit dem theban. Kult des H. verbunden (Pind. I.4,80–86); sie wurde von Eur. Heraklid. maßgeblich dargestellt (vgl. Sen. Herc. f.).

Eine weitere Ehefrau des H. ist → Deianeira, die Tochter des Königs Oineus von Kalydon und Schwester des → Meleagros; H. kämpft um sie mit dem Mitbewerber → Acheloos [2] und gewinnt sie (Archil. fr. 286; Pind. fr. 249a; Bakchyl. 5,165). Bei einer Flußüberquerung vergreift sich der Kentaur → Nessos, der Deianeira tragen sollte, an ihr; H. erschießt ihn mit einem von der Hydra vergifteten Pfeil, der sterbende Kentaur rät ihr, sein Blut als Liebeszauber aufzubewahren. Als Deianeira ihn anwendet, um die Konkurrentin Iole abzuwehren, tötet sie H. (ausführlich Soph. Trach.; zum rel. Hintergrund [10]). Sohn aus dieser Verbindung ist → Hyllos, der Eponym der dor. Hylleis.

Die Erzählung von Iole ist in einen komplexen Handlungszusammenhang eingebunden, der die Eroberung der Stadt → Oichalia in Trachis (NO-Griechenland) mit dem Dienst bei Omphale in Lydien und dem schließlichen Flammentod auf dem Oita, dem höchsten Berg bei Trachis, verbindet. → Iole ist Tochter des → Eurytos [1] und Schwester des → Iphitos von Oichalia; H. nimmt sie zur Nebenfrau, wobei er ihren Vater und Bruder tötet – in der geläufigsten Erzählung, weil er in einem Bogenwettkampf um Iole siegt, aber ohne sie weggeschickt wird; er rächt sich durch die Ermordung von Eurytos und Iphitos (anders Hom. Od. 21,13–37, wo H. den Iphitos seiner zwölf Stuten wegen tötet, obwohl er sein Gastfreund war). Wegen dieses Mords befällt ihn eine Krankheit, über die er sich in Delphi zu informieren sucht, doch die Pythia will dem Mörder nicht antworten. Darauf raubt er den Dreifuß, und Apollon wehrt sich (häufig seit der att. sf. Vasenmalerei dargestellt, [3. Nr. 2947–3071]), bis Zeus eingreift. Heilung bringt der Sklavendienst bei → Omphale in Lydien; mit ihr hat er den Sohn Acheles, Eponym des lyd. Flusses Acheles, dessen Wasser ihn heilt (Panyassis, fr. 20) – dahinter steht wohl die Identifikation des H. mit dem lydischen Heros Masnes [11]. Ein anderer Sohn ist → Tyrsenos, der Eponym der Etrusker (Dion. Hal. ant. 1,28,1; Paus. 2,21,3); die Genealogie – die mit anderen seit Hdt. 1,94 konkurriert – ist Ausdruck der lyd. Abstammung der Etrusker.

In der seit Soph. Trach. faßbaren Vulgata erobert H. nach dem Dienst bei Omphale Oichalia und bringt die junge Iole zurück; um seine Liebe zurückzugewinnen, sendet Deianeira dem H. ein mit dem Blut des Nessos bestrichenes Gewand. Es frißt sich in seinen Körper; ein Ende der Schmerzen ist nur dadurch möglich, daß H. sich auf einem Scheiterhaufen auf dem Gipfel des Oita verbrennt. Diese Selbstverbrennung wird später als Mittel der Apotheose verstanden (Cic. Tusc. 2,20), ist aber das Aition eines Feuerkultes mit Stieropfer und Agonen auf dem Gipfel des Oita, dessen Ort arch. faßbar ist [12; 13].

In zahlreichen lokalen Mythen erscheint H. außerdem als Begründer einer königl. Genealogie. Das ist ausgeprägt für das spartan. Königtum, dessen Rolle mit der Erzählung von der Rückwanderung der Herakliden begründet wird, gilt aber auch etwa für die lyd. oder maked. Könige (Hdt. 1,7,2; 8,137f.); in diesem Zusammenhang wird die ägypt. Königslegende von der Zeugung des Pharaos durch den obersten Gott übernommen und bildet den Ausgangspunkt für die (bes. von der Bühne seit der Mittleren Komödie und Plautus ausgebeutete) Erzählung von → Amphitryon.

C. KULT

H. ist in eine Vielzahl von Kulten in der ganzen griech. Welt eingebunden (selten ist er in Kreta). Die Kultformen sind ganz verschieden und unterscheiden sich kaum von denen des Götterkults; deswegen kann Pindar ihn *hḗrōs theós* (»Heros Gott«) nennen (N. 3,22). Neben dem Feuerkult auf dem Oita steht ein ähnlicher Kult in Theben, der seinen Kindern gilt (deswegen läßt eine Version des Mythos sie im Feuer umkommen, Pherekydes FGrH 3 F 14) und als Heroenopfer (*enágisma*) in das jährliche Fest des H. einbezogen wurde [14]; die Feststruktur erinnert an die Heroenopfer, die einem Götterkult vorangehen (→ Heroenkult).

Ein bedeutendes, für die gesamte Polis zentrales Heiligtum besaß H. (Thasios, LSCG 63) auf Thasos; der Kult ist verbunden mit kult. Mahlzeiten (vielleicht von Geschlechtergruppen, weswegen er Patroios heißt) und der Verleihung von Waffen an die Söhne von Kriegsgefallenen (LSCG Suppl. 64) [15]. Überhaupt ist die Verbindung mit der mil. Jungmannschaft charakteristisch für den ostgriech. Kult des H. [16], diejenige mit den Untergruppen der Polis für H. überhaupt. So ist in Attika eine Vielzahl von kleinen, an Kultverbände gebundenen Heiligtümer für ihn bezeichnend [17]; deswegen hat gerade die athen. Komödie (aber auch Eur. Alc.) ihn zum großen Esser und Trinker gemacht. Verbreitet ist auch die Verbindung mit den Epheben (→ Ephebeia) und dem → Gymnasion; in Athen erhält H. ein Trankopfer der jungen Männer, die *oinistḗria*, und vielerorts ist er zusammen mit Hermes Schützer des Gymnasions.

Weit verbreitet ist bes. seit hell. Zeit seine Rolle als Schützer in allen möglichen Gefahren; als solcher heißt er Alexikakos (»Übelabwehrer«), und Kallinikos (»der schönen Sieg bringt«); ein im ganzen griech. sprechenden Mittelmeerraum verbreitetes (und ins Christliche transformiertes) epigrammatisches Gebet an H. Kallinikos über den Haustüren soll das Haus schützen [18].

D. IDENTIFIKATIONEN

H. ist mit einer Vielzahl ungriech. Götter und Heroen identifiziert worden; als → Hercle wurde er von den Etruskern, als → Hercules von den Römern übernommen. Bedeutsam ist die Identifikation mit dem tyrischen Melqart, die schon Herodot vorliegt (zentraler Kultort Gades in SW-Spanien); daß aber einzelne Herakleia der griech. (Thasos, Erythrai) und röm. Welt (Ara Maxima) einen Kult des → Melqart fortführen, ist unwahrscheinlich [19; 20]. Lokaler sind die Gleichsetzungen mit dem lydischen Masnes und dem bes. in Tarsos verehrten kleinasiat. Gott → Sandon [21]; inwiefern seine Popularität in It. und seine Rolle als Schützer der ital. Hirten eine indigene, sonst nicht mehr faßbare Gestalt fortsetzt, ist unklar.

E. TUGENDLEHRE

Als Vorbild des Menschen, der durch seine duldende Leistung Unsterblichkeit gewinnen kann, ist H. früh in die Moralphilos. eingegangen. Ausgangspunkt ist die von Prodikos gedichtete Gesch. von H. am Scheideweg, wonach sich der jugendliche Held zwischen (den Personifikationen von) glücklichem Sinnengenuß (*Eudaimonía, Voluptas*) und Tüchtigkeit (*Aretḗ, Virtus*) zu entscheiden hat (Xen. mem. 2,1,21–34); sie wurde in der Ant. mehrfach erzählt und ist in Renaissance und Barock auch oft bildlich dargestellt worden [22; 23]. Auch sonst hat die Allegorese die Mythen des H. in diesem Sinn ausgebeutet und an die nachant. Welt weitergegeben [24]. Spezifischer ist H. seit Alexander d.Gr. Vorbild herrscherlicher Tugend; das haben etwa der röm. Kaiser → Commodus, oder noch Karl V. (in seinem Motto »Plus Ultra«, das den Anspruch erhebt, die Säulen des Herakles zu überschreiten) übernommen [25].

→ Hercules

1 W. PÖTSCHER, Heros und Hera, in: RhM 104, 1961, 302–355 **2** PRELLER/ROBERT II 2, 421–675 **3** J. BOARDMAN et al., s. v. H., LIMC 4, 728–838. 5, 1–192 **4** H. LLOYD-JONES, The Meropis (SH 903 A), in: Ders. (Hrsg.), Greek Epic, Lyric, and Tragedy. The Academic Papers of Sir Hugh Lloyd-Jones, 1990, 21–29 (1984) **5** A.-F. LAURENS, s.v. Bousiris, LIMC 3, 147–152 **6** L. RADERMACHER, Mythos und Sage bei den Griechen, 1943 **7** F. BADER, De la préhistoire à l'idéologie tripartite. Les travaux d'H., in: R. BLOCH (Hrsg.), D'H. à Poséidon. Mythologie et protohistoire, 1985, 9–124 **8** W. BURKERT, Structure and History in Greek Mythology and Ritual, 1979, 78–98 **9** M.L. WEST, The East Face of Helicon, 1997, 458–472 **10** C.A. FARAONE, Deianira's mistake and the demise of Heracles. Erotic magic in Sophocles' Trachiniae, in: Helios 21, 1994, 115–136 **11** G.M.A. HANFMANN, Lydiaka II. Tylos and Masnes, in: HSPh 63, 1958, 68–88 **12** M.P. NILSSON, Der Flammentod des H. auf dem Oite, in: ARW 21, 1922, 310–316 **13** Y. BÉQUIGNON, La vallée du Spercheios, 1937, 204–231 **14** SCHACHTER 2, 14–30 **15** B. BERGQUIST, H. on Thasos. The Archaeological, Literary and Epigraphic Evidence for his Sanctuary, Status and Cult Reconsidered, 1973 **16** GRAF, 98 f. **17** S. WOODFORD, Cults of Heracles in Attica, in: Studies G.M.A. Hanfmann, 1971, 211–225 **18** R. MERKELBACH, Weg mit dir, H., in die Feuershölle!, in: ZPE 86, 1991, 41–43 **19** D. VAN BERCHEM, Sanctuaires d'Hercule-Melqart, in: Syria 444, 1967, 73–109; 307–336 **20** C. BONNET, Melqart. Cultes et mythes de l'Héraclès tyrien en Méditerrannée, 1988 **21** H. GOLDMAN, Sandon and H., in: Hesperia Suppl. 8, 1949, 164–174 **22** M. KUNTZ, The Prodikean »Choice of H.«. A Reshaping of Myth, in: CJ 89, 1994, 163–181 **23** E. PANOFSKY, Herkules am Scheidewege und andere ant. Bildstoffe in der neueren Kunst, 1930 **24** W. SPARN, Hercules Christianus. Mythographie und Theologie in der frühen Neuzeit, in: Wolfenbütteler Forschungen 27, 1984, 73–107 **25** W. DERICHS, H. Vorbild des Herrschers, 1950. F.G.

II. IKONOGRAPHIE

Eine um 700 v. Chr. datierte böotische Bronzefibel mit H. und der Hydra zählt zu den frühesten bildl. Überl. des Heros. Zahlreich sind die Vasenbilder seit dem späten 7. Jh. v. Chr. mit allen wesentlichen H.-Szenen: H. beim Gelage (Eurytos-Krater, Paris, LV, 7./6. Jh. v. Chr.), Einführung des H. in den Olymp durch Athena (Schale des → Phrynos-Malers, London,

BM, 550/530 v. Chr.), seine Taten und Abenteuer. Während des 6. Jh. v. Chr. wird in Attika der Heros so häufig wie sonst keine andere myth. Gestalt abgebildet, insbes. zur Zeit der Peisistratiden, deren Einfluß auf die H.-Gestalt allerdings nicht mit Sicherheit nachgewiesen werden kann (vgl. aber die an den Einzug des H. in den Olymp erinnernde Prozession des → Peisistratos). In frühen Darstellungen erscheint H. meist bärtig, gegen E. des 6. Jh. v. Chr. häufiger ohne Bart. Seine Waffen sind Keule oder Bogen, manchmal ein Schwert, eine Harpune richtet er gegen die Hydra. Er ist häufig nackt dargestellt oder mit kurzem → Chiton, mit dem Löwenfell v. a. seit E. des 6. Jh. v. Chr.

Der westliche Porosgiebel des Alten Athena-Tempels auf der Athener Akropolis (1. H. des 6. Jh. v. Chr.) zeigt H. im Kampf mit dem fischleibigen Seegreis Nereus oder Triton, im Ostgiebel des Siphnier-Schatzhauses in Delphi der Kampf zwischen H. und Apollon um den delphischen Dreifuß (um 525 v. Chr.); als Bogenschütze mit Löwenkopfhelm agiert H. im Ostgiebel des Aphaia-Tempels auf → Aigina (um 490 v. Chr.). Verschiedene Metopenfolgen haben den Tatenzyklus des H. erh.: das Athener-Schatzhaus in Delphi (Nord- und Westmetopen; um 490 v. Chr.), der Zeustempel von Olympia (um 460 v. Chr.), das Hephaisteion in Athen (450/440 v. Chr.). Seine entscheidende Mitwirkung in den → Giganten-Kämpfen wird am Parthenon in Athen (Ostmetope 11, 442–432 v. Chr.) und am Pergamonaltar, Ostfries (um 160 v. Chr.) geschildert. Auf Urkundenreliefs tritt H. fast ausnahmslos mit Athena auf – als Eponymos (von Herakleia, Theben) oder als Schutzpatron der geehrten Person.

Einzeldarstellungen des H. sind etwa seit Mitte des 6. Jh. v. Chr. überl. (insbes. Bronzestatuetten). Der H. Cherchel (wohl nach Bronze-Original des 2. Viertels des 5. Jh. v. Chr.) charakterisiert den bärtigen, das Gewicht auf sein rechtes Bein verlagernden H.; vgl. H. Farnese (Neapel, NM, frühes 3. Jh. n. Chr. nach Original des 3. Viertels des 4. Jh. v. Chr., dem → Lysippos zugeschrieben); polykletisch vermutlich der jugendl. H. aus den Caracalla-Thermen in Rom, (TM, 1./2. Jh. n. Chr., Original um 430 v. Chr.); von Lysippos die nicht erh. kolossale Sitzstatue des Heros in Tarent (vgl. Haterier-Grabrelief, Rom, VM, Anfang 2. Jh. n. Chr.; byz. Elfenbeinkästchen in Xanten). Das Herakliskos-Motiv des schlangenwürgenden H.-Kindes ist seit frühklass. Zeit wiedergegeben. Eine besondere Stellung nimmt die H.-Gestalt in der Legitimation von Herrscherdynastien und Expansionsbestrebungen verschiedener Poleis ein, v. a. seit dem 4. Jh. v. Chr.

Der ital. H./Hercules, spätestens seit frührepublikan. Zeit an der Ara Maxima auf dem Forum Boarium (→ Roma) verehrt, ist auf zahlreichen Wandgemälden und Mosaiken überliefert, oft auf Gemmen. Kleinbronzen zeigen u. a. den H. bibax (Neufund aus dem Burgus von Lich, vermutlich Motiv des 4. Jh. v. Chr.). Sein Bild gehörte zur statuarischen Ausstattung der Villa dei Papiri in Herculaneum. Sarkophagreliefs des 2.–3. Jh. n. Chr. schildern fast immer seine Taten. In der röm. Staatskunst ist H. seit republikan. Zeit faßbar (Siegesdenkmal des Bocchus auf dem Kapitol, Rom, Konservatoren-Palast, 91 v. Chr.), seit Traian wieder verstärkt in Darstellungen kaiserl. Politik (Traiansbogen in Benevent, 114 n. Chr.) und bes. populär beim Heer.

L. J. Balmaseda, s. v. H./Hercules, LIMC V, 253–262 (mit ält. Lit.) • J. Boardman et al., s. v. H., LIMC IV, 728–838; LIMC V, 1–192 (mit ält. Lit.) • P. Gros, Hercule à Glanum, in: Gallia 52, 1995, 311–331 • U. Huttner, Die polit. Rolle der H.-Gestalt im griech. Herrschertum, 1997 • P. F. B. Jongste, The twelve labours of Hercules on Roman sarcophagi, 1992 • H. Kloft, H. als Vorbild. Funktion eines griech. Mythos, 1994 • S. Ritter, Hercules in der röm. Kunst – Von den Anfängen bis Augustus, 1995 • E. Tagalidou, Weihreliefs an H. aus klass. Zeit, 1993 • R. Vollkommer, H. in the Art of Classical Greece, 1988 • S. R. Wolf, H. beim Gelage, 1993. A. L.

[2] Sohn von → Alexandros [4] und seiner Geliebten → Barsine, vom Vater nie als legitim anerkannt. Geb. 327 v. Chr. (Diod. 20,20,1), wird er zu Alexandros' Lebzeiten nicht erwähnt und lebte mit der Mutter in Pergamon. Der Vorschlag seines Onkels → Nearchos, ihn nach Alexandros' Tod (323) als Nachfolger in Erwägung zu ziehen, wurde nicht ernstgenommen (Curt. 10,6,10–12). Nach der Ausschaltung von → Alexandros [5] rief → Polyperchon H. zu sich, um ihn gegen → Kassandros als Waffe zu benützen. Doch zog er es vor, sich mit Kassandros zu einigen, und ließ H. 309 töten (Diod. 20,28; Plut. mor. 530).

P. A. Brunt, Alexander, Barsine and Heracles, in: RFIC 103, 1975, 22–34. E. B.

Herakliskos-Prägung. Gemeinsame Münzprägung von sieben Städten (Rhodos, Knidos, Iasos, Ephesos, Samos, Byzantion, Kyzikos und Lampsakos) mit lokalen Ethnika und Darstellungen auf dem Rv., ΣΥΝ (für Symmachia) und dem jungen schlangenwürgenden Herakles auf dem Av. Die Mz. werden allg. als Ausdruck einer durch andere Quellen nicht belegten Symmachie gesehen, die von den meisten in die Zeit unmittelbar nach 394 v. Chr. (Niederlage der Spartaner bei Knidos) datiert wird.

H. A. Cahn, Knidos, 1970, 173 f. • G. L. Cawkwell, A Note on the Heracles Coinage Alliance of 394 B. C., in: NC 1956, 69–75 • S. Karwiese, Lysander as Herakliskos-Drakonopnignon, in: NC 1980, 1–27 • E. Schönert, Die Münzprägung von Byzantion I, 1970, 31–35. DI. K.

Heraklit s. Herakleitos

Herakliteer. Der ion. Philosoph → Herakleitos [1] wurde in der ant. Trad. den »vereinzelten« (οἱ σποράδην) Philosophen zugerechnet, d. h. als einer von denen, die sich nicht in eine der verschiedenen Sukzessionsreihen von Lehrern und Schülern einordnen ließen.

Die Überl. erwähnt keine Schüler im eigentlichen Sinne, spricht jedoch von Anhängern des Herakleitos. Ein H. konnte jeder genannt werden, der in einer wie auch immer gearteten philos. Abhängigkeit von Herakleitos stand (vgl. die → Demokriteer). Einige der »heraklitisierenden« Denker (Ἡρακλειτίζοντες), von denen → Kratylos gewöhnlich als einziger namentlich genannt wird, scheinen die Lehre des Herakleitos vom Fluß der physikalischen Welt bis zum Extrem getrieben und jede Art von Stabilität oder Identität des Selbst geleugnet zu haben. Auf dieser Grundlage sahen sie auch ein Wissen von der Welt als unmöglich an (Aristot. metaph. 5,1010a 7ff.).

Aristoteles schreibt einigen (anderen?) Anhängern des Herakleitos jedoch auch gewisse physikalische und physiologische Lehren zu. Diese Lehren scheinen Anwendungen einer möglicherweise auf Herakleitos zurückgehenden Theorie der »Ausdünstungen« auf verschiedene Phänomene zu sein (Aristot. probl. 908a 30; 934b 34).

Auch Diogenes Laertios spricht von »H.« (Ἡρακλείτειοι, 9,6), von denen er einen gewissen Antisthenes namentlich nennt (6,19), und von einem »Heraklitisten« (Ἡρακλειτιστής), einem gewissen Pausanias (9,15). Der erste Begriff bezieht sich möglicherweise auf Anhänger, der zweite auf Kommentatoren des Heraklit.

→ Herakleitos

S. MOURAVIEV, Heraclitea II. A.1 Héraclite d'Éphese – La tradition antique et médiévale I. D' Épicharme à Platon et Héraclide le Pontique, 1993. G. BE./Ü: T. H.

(Ps.-)Heraklitische Briefe. Ein Corpus von neun pseudepigraphischen Briefen aus dem 1. Jh. und der ersten Hälfte des 2. Jh. n. Chr., von denen zwei dem Perserkönig → Dareios [1] und sieben dem Philosophen → Herakleitos zugeschrieben werden. Die Themen sind polit. Natur. Die ersten beiden Briefe sind auch bei Diog. Laert. 9,13–14 überliefert. In den vier Briefen an → Hermodoros (4; 7–9) geht es um dessen Verbannung, ebenso zuvor in Brief 3, in dem Dareios den Ephesern vorwirft, den besten Mann von ganz Ionien ins Exil gesandt zu haben. So versucht Herakleitos in Brief 4 seinen in der Verbannung lebenden Freund damit zu trösten, daß er selbst in seiner eigenen Heimatstadt vor kurzem der Gottlosigkeit (*asébeia*) angeklagt worden sei. In Brief 7 teilt er ihm mit, die Epheser hätten ein gegen ihn selbst gerichtetes Gesetz erlassen, das ›jedem Mann, der nicht lacht und ein Menschenfeind ist‹, die sofortige Verbannung androhe (eine längere Fassung dieses Briefs in Pap. Genf 271). In den Briefen 5 und 6 an seinen Freund Amphidamas schreibt Herakleitos über seine Wassersucht und greift die Ärzte an. In den ps.-H.B. finden sich zahlreiche Topoi der volkstümlichen kynisch-stoischen Ethik. Nach [3] lassen die Briefe 4, 7 und 9 auf einen jüd. Autor schließen – eine in der Forsch. sehr umstrittene Auffassung.

ED.: **1** H. W. ATTRIDGE, First-Century Cynicism in the Epistles of Heraclitus (Harvard Theological Studies 29), 1976 (Einführung, griech. Text mit engl. Übers.) **2** V. MARTIN, Un recueil de diatribes cyniques. Pap. Genev. inv. 271, in: MH 16, 1959, 77–115 **3** J. BERNAYS, Die Heraklitischen Briefe. Ein Beitrag zur philos. und religionsgesch. Litt., 1869 **4** L. TARÁN, Lettere Pseudo-Eraclitee, in: R. MONDOLFO, L. TARÁN, Eraclito. Testimonianze e imitazioni. Introduzione, traduzione e commento (Biblioteca di studi superiori 59), 1972, 279–359
LIT.: **5** I. HEINEMANN, s. v. Briefe des Herakleitos (16a), RE Suppl. 5, 228–232. M. G.-C./Ü: S. P.

Heraklonas (Ἡρακλωνᾶς). Sohn des Kaisers → Herakleios [5] und seiner zweiten Gattin Martina, * ca. 626 n. Chr., sollte nach dessen Tod 641 als Minderjähriger, vertreten von seiner Mutter, zusammen mit Herakleios' ältestem Sohn Constantinus III. die Nachfolge übernehmen, wurde aber bereits Sept. 641 auf Betreiben des Senates zusammen mit seiner Mutter abgesetzt und verbannt.

PLRE 3, 587f. • ODB 2, 918. F. T.

Heras. Griech. Arzt aus Kappadokien, der in Rom praktizierte. Seine medikamentöse Therapie, eingeordnet zw. 100 v. und 40 n. Chr., legte er in einer Abh. dar, deren Abfassung [1. 242–246] zw. 20 v. und 20 n. Chr. datiert. Die durch eine Tendenz zu Zusammensetzungen gekennzeichneten Formeln sprächen für eine Spätdatierung. H.' Herkunft und der Klassizismus seines medizinischen Stoffes legen eine Verbindung mit der evtl. so zu nennenden »Schule von Tarsos« [2] nahe oder lassen ihn zumindest der von ihr repräsentierten Strömung zuordnen.

Außer einem Papyrusfrg. [3] besitzen wir 25 Zit. bei Galen, von denen 20 direkt zu sein scheinen [1. 184–185]. Es handelt sich um Formeln von Medikamenten mit ihren Indikationen. Mehrere Zit. sind aus einem Werk gezogen, das in einem Zit. als ›Buch der Medikamente‹ bezeichnet und ›Narthex‹ bzw. ›Buch der Eigenschaften‹ betitelt wird; andere stammen aus einem als *bíblos pharmakîtis* (›Pharmazeutisches Buch‹) betitelten Werk, das mit dem vorhergehenden gleichgesetzt wird. Die Formeln werden nach den betroffenen Körperteilen oder nach Typen definiert. Der medizinische Stoff, der aus Substanzen aus den drei Reichen (der Fauna, der Flora und dem Reich der Mineralien) besteht, ist durch seinen Klassizismus gekennzeichnet, ebenso wie die Formeln, unter denen jedoch der Begriff *antídotos* erscheint, der freilich auf den toxikologischen Kontext beschränkt bleibt.

→ Galenos

1 C. FABRICIUS, Galens Exzerpte aus älteren Pharmakologen, 1972 **2** V. NUTTON, J. SCARBOROUGH, The »Preface« of Dioscorides' »Materia Medica«: Introduction, Translation, and Commentary, in: Transactions and Studies of the College of Physicians of Philadelphia Series 5, vol. 4, 1982, 187–227 **3** I. ANDORLINI MARCONE, L'apporto dei papiri alla conoscenza della scienza medica antica, in: ANRW II,37,1, num. 10.

I. ANDORLINI, Ricette mediche nei papiri, in: Atti e Memorie dell'Accademia Toscana di Scienze e Lettere »La Colombaria« 46, 1981, 41–45 und n. 36f. • MARGANNE, 134f. A.TO./Ü: T.H.

Herbessos (Ἑρβησσός). Sikulerstadt, h. Montagna di Marzo nahe Piazza Armerina (Sizilien), eindeutig lokalisiert durch Br.-Mz. und silberne *litrai*. Lit. Belege: Diod. 14,7,6–8 (404 v. Chr.); 78,7 (396 v. Chr.); 20,31,5 (309 v. Chr.); 23,8,1; Pol. 1,18,9 (bezeugt im Bericht über 262 v. Chr. die geogr. Nähe von H. zu Akragas). Weitere Belege: Mz.-Schatzfunde von 214–212 v. Chr. aus M. di Marzo; Inschr. in sikulischer Sprache und Schrift; griech. Graffiti; ein neuer, onomastisch interessanter Typ tönerner *glandes*.

G. MANGANARO, Montagna di Marzo – H., in: Sikelika (im Druck) • BTCGI 7, 1989, 278–282. GI.MA./Ü: H.D.

Herbita (Ἕρβιτα, Ἑρβίτα). Sikulische Binnenstadt. Archonides I. von H. war Mitbegründer von Kale Akte (Diod. 12,8,2; 447/6 v. Chr.); Archonides II. gründete, nach Kampf und Versöhnung mit Dionysios I., 403 v. Chr. Alaisa (Diod. 14,15,1; 14,16,1–4; 14,78,7). Weitere Belege: Cic. Verr. passim; Dekret von Entella (SEG 30, 1117); Mz. vom M. Alburchia bei Gangi [1].

1 L. DUBOIS, Inscriptions grecques dialectales de Sicile, 1989, 254f., Nr. 204 2 G. SCIBONA, Epigraphica Italaesina I (Schede 1970), in: Kokalos 17, 1971, 5f. 3 C. BÖHRINGER, Herbita, in: Numismatica e antichità classiche 10, 1981, 95ff. 4 BTCGI 7, 1989, 283–289 5 G. MANGANARO, Alla ricerca di poleis mikrai della Sicilia centro-orientale, in: Orbis Terrarum 2, 1996, 130 Anm. 9. GI.MA./Ü: H.D.

Hercle. Neben der ab Beginn des 5. Jh. v. Chr. in etr. Inschr. am häufigsten belegten Form H. sind *Hercles, Heracle, Hercele, Herchle* und *Herkle* als etruskisierte Formen des griech. Namens → Herakles [1] bekannt [1. Bd. 1, 114f.]. *H. calanice* entspricht griech. *Hēraklḗs kallínikos* (»der schön Siegende«) (Archil. fr. 324 IEG). Der Kult des H. gehört bei den Etruskern – wie der des Herakles bei den Griechen – bes. dem privaten Bereich an; er ist vorwiegend auf Werken der Kleinkunst (Spiegeln und Gemmen) dargestellt, die vor allem im Grabkult Verwendung fanden.

Trotz ähnlicher Namen und Attribute (Keule und Löwenfell) unterscheiden sich H. und Herakles: H. galt, anders als der griech. Heros, eher als Gott denn als Heros [1. Bd. 2, 329 Pa 4.2,29]. Die etr. Ikonographie, die neben der griech. belegt ist, stellt ihn als bartlosen, lokkigen Jüngling dar [2. Bd. 2,131; 3. Abb. 21; 22]. Auch der Mythos von H., der die schöne Mlacuch vom Boden aufhebt [2. Bd. 4, 344; 3. Abb. 14], ist etruskisch. Ungriech. und gemeinital. ist das Motiv des H. auf einem Floß aus leeren Amphoren mit darüber gelegtem Rost und gespanntem Löwenfell als Segel [2. Bd. 4, 398]. Mit der Zeit wuchsen lokale und griech. Mythen zusammen: H. versöhnt sich mit Uni und wird von ihr mit einem ungriech. Ritus adoptiert [2. Bd. 5, 59; 60; 3. Abb. 19f.; 1. Bd. 2, 352 Vt S.2]. Echt griech. ist hingegen die gemeinsame Darstellung der beiden Freunde H. und Vile (→ Iolaos) [2. Bd. 1, 128; 3. Abb. 15]. Von den Taten des griech. Heros führt H. nur solche aus, die als Überwindung des Todes gelesen werden konnten, z. B. die Bezwingung des Kerberos, die Fahrt (mit dem Floß?) zum Garten der → Hesperiden. Aus dieser Deutung rührt auch seine Beliebtheit über Etrurien hinaus bis in die Alpenregionen [4].

H. taucht Ende des 6. Jh. v. Chr. in der Bildkunst der Etrusker auf [5; 6]. Auf diese Zeit bezieht sich auch der Hinweis von Plinius (nat. 35,157), der Künstler Vulca [7] habe einen *Hercules fictilis* (»aus Ton«) für Veii geschaffen.

1 ET 2 E. GERHARD, G. KÖRTE, Etr. Spiegel, 1884–1897 3 A.J. PFIFFIG, Herakles in der Bilderwelt der etr. Spiegel, 1980 4 E. WALDE-PSENNER, Die vorröm. und röm. Bronzestatuetten aus Südtirol, in: Arch.-histor. Forsch. in Tirol 6, 1979, Nr. 11–14 5 W. DRÄYER, M. HÜRLIMANN, Etr. Kunst, 1955, Abb. 56 6 G. COLONNA, An Etruscan Inscription from Acquarossa, in: OpRom 16.1, 1987, 7ff. 7 M. PALLOTTINO, La scuola di Vulca, 1945.

PFIFFIG • S. SCHWARZ, s. v. Herakles/H., LIMC 5.1, 196–253 • E. SIMON, Etr. Kultgottheiten, in: M. CRISTOFANI (Hrsg.), Die Etrusker, 1995, 158ff. L.A.-F.

Herculanensische Papyri A. BESTIMMUNG B. ROLLENTYPOLOGIE C. SCHRIFT

A. BESTIMMUNG

Während der bourbonischen Ausgrabungen Mitte des 18. Jh. in einer Villa bei → Herculaneum (mit Lageplan) gefundene Papyri mit lat. und griech. Texten. Diese waren Teil der dortigen Bibliothek des Dichters und Philosophen → Philodemos von Gadara, der in den 80er–70er Jahren des 1. Jh. v. Chr. aus Athen nach Italien gekommen war und dort freundschaftliche Beziehungen zu L. → Calpurnius [I 19] Piso Caesoninus, dem Eigentümer der Villa von Herculaneum, pflegte. Philodemos versammelte in dieser luxuriösen Villa eine umfassende Bibliothek der epikureischen Philosophen (→ Epikureismus), deren gegnerischer Schulen, der Abschriften seiner eigenen zahlreichen Werke, sowie auch einer lat. Abteilung (der bekannteste Text ist das anon. *Carmen de bello Actiaco*, PHerc. 817)

Die h.P. sind von unschätzbarem Wert für die Kenntnis der hell. Philos.; sie leisten zugleich einen wichtigen Beitrag zur Typologie der Prosa-Schriftrollen sowie zur griech. und lat. Paläographie. Die Papyri wurden großenteils in der Villa selbst geschrieben, die übrigen meist außerhalb Ägyptens; sie sind eine wichtige Quelle für die Debatte, ob sich die griech. Schrift im Mittelmeerraum überall einheitlich oder regional unterschiedlich entwickelt hatte.

B. ROLLENTYPOLOGIE

Die h.P. sind für formale Fragen bedeutend, da sie neben den ägypt. und anderen griech. Funden die röm.-ital. Hss.-Praxis belegen. Papyrusrolle und Buch entsprechen sich bei den h.P. durchgehend: eine Rolle umfaßt nicht mehr als ein Buch; sehr lange Werke wurden auf zwei Rollen kopiert (PHerc. 1423 und 1007/1673; PHerc. 1538). Die Standard-Rollenlänge beträgt ca. 10 m (bisweilen etwas mehr). Die Identifikation der Klebungen (*kollēseis*) in der Schrift der betreffenden Spalten (*sélides*) bestätigt, daß die h.P. dadurch hergestellt wurden, daß man die einzelnen Papyrusblätter (*kollēmata*) zusammenklebte, um einen Streifen in einer Standardlänge herzustellen, auf dem man dann den Text schrieb. Das Verhältnis von beschriebenem zu leerem Raum hält sich an den im griech.-ägypt. Bereich üblichen Rahmen. Allerdings haben zahlreiche Rollen ein abschließendes leeres Blatt (*ágraphon*; z.B. PHerc. 1675), das in den griech.-ägypt. Papyri fehlt: dieses Blatt wurde immer mit den Papyrusstreifen in vertikaler Richtung eingeklebt. Die ant. Papyrusrollen waren offensichtlich generell mit einem Initialblatt und einem abschließenden leeren Blatt versehen. Es gibt auch beidseitig beschriebene Rollen, die mit dem gleichen Werk auf beiden Seiten beschrieben waren (PHerc. 1021; 1670).

Die Stichometrie ist schwieriger zu bestimmen: Sicher ist, daß man mindestens gegen Ende des 1. Jh. v. Chr. noch das att. System der akrophonen Numerierung benutzte. Die Überschriften wurden meist am Ende der Rolle, oft in einer → Auszeichnungsschrift, geschrieben. Diakritische Zeichen sind zahlreich verwendet.

C. Schrift

Die verschiedenen Schriftarten sind in siebzehn Gruppen zu teilen, die man alphabetisch von A bis R bezeichnet und die mindestens 34 anon. Schreibern des 3. bis zum 1. Jh. v. Chr. zuweisbar sind. Philodemos' persönliche Handschrift fehlt jedoch; erkennbare Eingriffe und Verbesserungen stammen stets vom Schreiber oder dem berufsmäßigen Korrektor (*diorthōtḗs*), nicht jedoch von Philodemos selbst. Unterschiede zu vergleichbaren griech.-ägypt. → Papyri zeigen sich im zahlreicheren Gebrauch der diakritischen Zeichen und der Verwendung der → Auszeichnungsschrift für die Titel am Ende der Rollen. Dies erklärt sich vermutlich aus der unterschiedlichen Herkunft: Die griech.-ägypt. Papyri stammen aus Randbereichen, die h.P. dagegen neben anderen Regionen aus den großen Kulturzentren des Hellenismus. Die graphische Analyse der Rollen PHerc. 255, 418, 1084, 1091 und 1112 weist Ähnlichkeiten zu den Dokumenten aus dem Zenonarchiv (3. Jh. v. Chr.) auf. PHerc. 1044 und 1746 sind im typischen »Epsilon-Theta-Stil« geschrieben, der in Äg. weit verbreitet war. Die Rollen der Gruppen A und I sind die ältesten und zeigen Ähnlichkeiten mit ptolem. Schriften der Mitte des 3. Jh. v. Chr. oder späterer Zeit (2. oder 2./1. Jh. v. Chr.). Die Gruppe K ist ins 2. Jh. v. Chr. datierbar. Die Gruppen B und C (2. Jh. v. Chr., Schriften des → Demetrios Lakon) zeigen stilistische Eigenheiten des griech. oder kleinasiat. Mittelmeergebietes, wo letzterer wirkte und wo diese Rollen vielleicht auch geschrieben wurden. Die Gruppen F, G und H enthalten Werke des Philodemos und sind somit auf das 1. Jh. v. Chr. zu datieren. Auch spätere Schriften aus der Zeit zw. dem 1. Jh. v. und 1. Jh. n. Chr. sind erhalten. Interessanterweise zeigen einige Papyri der Gruppe Q Einflüsse der lat. → Kapitale (PHerc. 380; 362). Ob hier im Herculaneum des 1. Jh. v. Chr. Schreiber am Werk waren, die gleichermaßen Lat. und Griech. schreiben konnten, oder ob die lat. Kapitale griech. Schreiber beeinflußte, ist beim derzeitigen Stand der Forsch. nicht gesichert. Immerhin zeigt die Schrift einiger lat. Papyri der Philodemos-Bibliothek eindeutige Übereinstimmungen und Einflüsse griech. Schriften (PHerc. 817; 1067; 1475).

T. Dorandi, La »Villa dei Papiri« a Ercolano e la sua biblioteca, in: CPh 90, 1995, 168–182 • G. Cavallo, Libri scritture scribi a Ercolano, 1983 (auch in: Scrittura e Civiltà 8, 1984, 5–30) • K. Kleve, An approach to the Latin papyri from Herculaneum, in: Studi M. Gigante, 1994, 313–320.

T.D./Ü: J.DE.

Herculaneum. Campanische Küstenstadt zw. Neapolis und Pompeii auf einer Anhöhe zw. zwei Flüssen (Sisenna, HRR fr. 53; Strab. 5,4,8). *Municipium* der *regio I, tribus Menenia*. H. wurde 62 n. Chr. von Erdbeben und evtl. Nachbeben heimgesucht, beim Ausbruch des Vesuvius 79 n. Chr. verschüttet.

Seit 1709 Raubgrabungen durch den Fürsten E. d'Elbœuf; eine systematische Erforschung erfolgte zuerst unter R.J. de Alcubierre (1738–1756) durch Schächte und Stollen; 1927–1958 Grabungsarbeiten unter A. Maiuri. 1961–1977 Grabungen an Palaestra und Decumanus Maximus: Basilica, Curia, Augustalencollegium.

Stratigraphische Unt. revidierten die Ansichten von den Vorgängen bei der Verschüttung 79 n. Chr: H. wurde zunächst unter einem heiß-feuchten pyroklastischen Strom begraben (der eine umfangreiche Konservierung von Holzteilen bewirkt hat); später setzten sich vulkanische Lockermassen (Ablagerungen der Glutwolke) darauf ab, so daß der ant. Ort unter bis zu 20 m mächtigem Vulkanauswurf begraben wurde. Dabei verschwanden die zwei *fluviae* (Sisenna l.c.), die Küstenlinie schob sich ins Meer vor. Die zum Wasser flüchtenden Menschen suchten Zuflucht in den Lagerhäusern der Fischer. Bis h. fand man etwa 300 Skelette.

1982 wurde am Strand die Panzerstatue des M. Nonius Balbus, des *patronus* von H., gefunden, dessen Grabmal schon 1942 auf der Terrasse vor den Thermen der Vorstadt entdeckt worden war. 1988 wurden aus dem Strandabschnitt dem hl. Bezirk gegenüber drei archa. Reliefs mit Athena, Hermes und Hephaistos geborgen. Nach der genaueren Lagebestimmung der Villa dei Papiri wurde die *villa* zunächst mithilfe der Stollen aus der Zeit der Bourbonen untersucht; die anschließenden regulären Grabungen sind bis h. nicht abgeschlossen. Zahlreiche Inschr., die z.T. durch die Lavaströme weit von ihrem urspr. Standort fortgerissen waren, wurden gefunden. In letzter Zeit konzentrierte sich

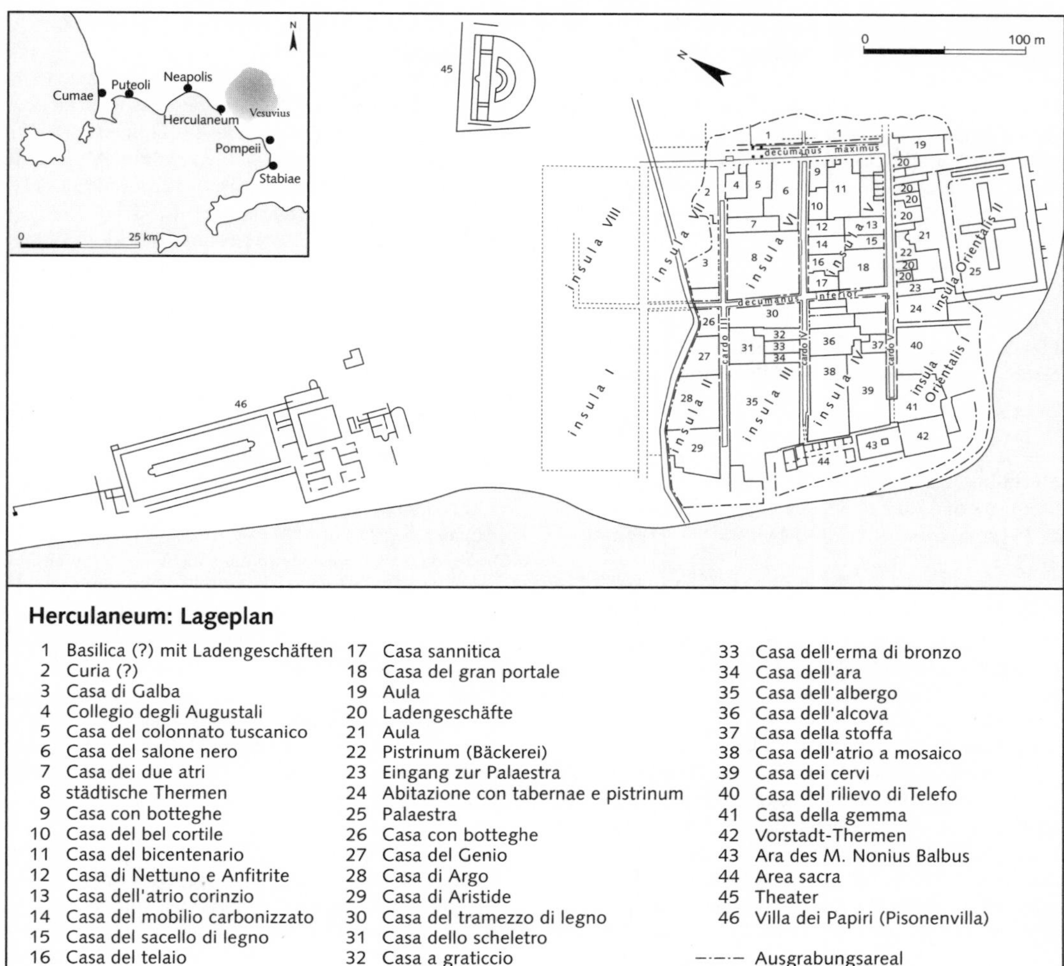

das Interesse bes. auf die Veröffentlichung der Papyri aus der Villa dei Papiri (→ Herculanensische Papyri).
→ Pompeii

L. Franchi dell'Orte (Hrsg.), Ercolano 1738–1988, 1993 · U. Pappalardo, s. v. Ercolano, EAA², Suppl. 2, 1994, 484–489 · I. C. McIlwaine, H., 1988 (mit Suppl. in: CE 20, 1990, 87–128) · E. Renna, Vesuvius Mons, 1992 · E. Lepore, Origini e strutture della Campania antica, 1989, 243–263 · G. Camodeca, La ricostruzione dell'élite municipale ercolanese negli anni 50–70, in: Cahiers G. Glotz 7, 1996, 167–178 · T. Budetta, Ercolano, in: Rivista Studi Pompeiani N. S. 3, 1989, 266 fig. 45 · H. Sigurdsson u. a., The Eruption of Vesuvius in A. D. 79, in: National Geographic Research 1, 1985, 332–387 · U. Pappalardo, L'eruzione pliniana del Vesuvio nel 79 d.C., in: Volcanologie et Arch., 1990, 198–215 · Ders., Osservazioni su un secondo grande terremoto a Pompei, in: Arch. und Seismologie, 1995, 191–194 · G. Guadagno, Documenti epigrafici ercolanesi relativi ad un terremoto, in: Arch. und Seismologie, 1995, 119–128 · S. C. Bisel, Human Bones at Herculaneum, in: Rivista Studi Pompeiani N. S. 1, 1987, 123–129 · D. Modesti, Ercolano, in: Rivista Studi Pompeiani N. S. 1, 1987, 199f. · S. Adamo Muscettola, Nuove letture borboniche, in: Prospettiva 28, 1982, 2–16 · M. Pagano, Il teatro di Ercolano, in: CE 23, 1993, 121–156 · Ders., La nuova pianta della città e alcuni edifici pubblici di Ercolano, in: CE 26, 1996, 229–248 · U. Pappalardo, Nuove testimonianze su Marco Nonio Balbo ad Ercolano, in: MDAI(R) 104, 1997, 285–297 · C. Knight, A. Jorio, L'ubicazione della Villa Ercolanese dei Papiri, in: Rendiconti Napoli 55, 1980, 51–65, Abb. 1–19 · M. Gigante (Hrsg.), La Villa dei Papiri, 1983 · A. De Simone u. a., Ercolano 1992–1997, in: CE 28, 1998, 3–55 (Vorabdruck) · M. Gigante, Catalogo dei Papiri Ercolanesi, 1979 · M. Capasso, Storia fotografica dell'Officina dei Papiri Ercolanesi, 1983 · Ders., Manuale di papirologia ercolanese, 1991.
Karten-Lit.: E. Kirsten, Süditalienkunde 1. Bd. Campanien und seine Nachbarlandschaften, 1975, 289–312, Abb. 28–30a · M. Pagano, Ercolano, 1997, bes. 8, 21 · U. Pappalardo, s. v. Ercolano, EAA Suppl. 2, 1994, 484–489, bes. 485.

U. PA./Ü: H. D.

Herculaneus rivus. Seitenarm der *aqua Marcia* in Rom hinter den *horti Pallantiani* (Frontin. aqu. 19,8) südl. der *porta Tiburtina*, die über den *Caelius mons* und die *Porta Capena* die *regiones I, XI, XII* versorgte. Wohl auf einem Irrtum beruht der Zusammenhang eines H.r. mit der *aqua Virgo* bei Plin. nat. 31,42. Ein anderer H.r. war die perennierende Quelle, die den *Anio novus* versorgte, 38 Meilen östl. von Rom an der *via Sublacensis* (Frontin. aqu. 15,4f.).

RICHARDSON, 17f. • D. CATTOLINI, s. v. H.r., LTUR 1, 1993, 69. G.U./Ü: J.W.M.

Herculem, ad. Station in Etruria an der *via Aemilia Scauri* zw. Vada Volaterrana und Pisae (Itin. Anton. 293).

M. SORDI, La via Aurelia da Vada a Pisa, in: Athenaeum 59, 1971, 302–312. G.U.

Hercules A. NAME B. VIEHZUCHT C. QUELLEN D. GRÜNDER VON STÄDTEN UND VÖLKERN E. INITIATIONSKULTE F. MANTIK G. HANDEL H. TRIUMPH

A. NAME

H. ist die röm. Form des griech. → Herakles (Ἡρακλῆς), altlat. Hercles und Hercoles, lat. Hercules, osk. Her(e)cleis/clos, etr. → Hercle.

B. VIEHZUCHT

Der Raub der Rinder des → Geryoneus, auf den sich die ältesten Zeugnisse der H.-Sage in Etrurien (ca. 600 v. Chr.) beziehen, war in It. die wichtigste Heldentat des H. Der röm. Mythos erzählt, daß H. den → Cacus, der einige seiner Rinder gestohlen hatte, tötete und zur Erinnerung daran zusammen mit → Euandros [1] und den Arkadern Opfer und rituelles Mahl an der Ara Maxima in Rom stiftete (Verg. Aen. 8,193–272; Dion. Hal. ant. 1,39f.; Liv. 1,7, vgl. Strab. 5,3,3; Ov. fast. 1,543–584; Prop. 4,9). In der euhemerist. Fassung (Dion. Hal. ant. 1,42; Solin. 1,8) wurde H. zum Feldherrn, der über Cacus siegte. Die Mythen und Kulte des H. in Rom waren auf dem Forum Boarium lokalisiert, wo ein Bronzestier an ihn erinnerte (vgl. Tac. ann. 12,24). H. war auch göttl. Geber des Salzes, das man zur Konservierung von Fleisch verwendete (Colum. 10,135; CIL IX 3961); entsprechend wohnte er bei den Salinae im Süden des Forum Boarium (Solin. 1,8).

C. QUELLEN

Dem H. waren die Quellen, bes. die warmen, heilig (Athen. 12,512f; Aristeid. 5,35; Suda s. v. Ἡράκλεια λουτρά). Bei den sabell. Völkern opferte man bei den Quellen Statuetten des H. Die Beinamen Salutaris und Salutifer (z. B. CIL VI 237) beziehen sich auf H. als Gott der heilbringenden Gewässer. Heiße Quellen des H. gab es etwa beim Orakel der → Palikoi (Diod. 4,23,5), am iapyg. Vorgebirge (Aristot. mir. 97), bei Allifae (CIL IX 2338), Caere (Liv. 22,1,10), fons Aponi (Suet. Tib. 14; Claud. carmina minora 26,23–26) und an der Mündung des Timavus [1], außerdem in Dacia bei Mehadia (CIL III 1566) und in vielen Orten Galliens, wo er häufig mit Borvo identifiziert wurde.

D. GRÜNDER VON STÄDTEN UND VÖLKERN

H.' kulturstiftende Taten verbinden ihn häufig mit lokalen Urkönigen. Oft zeugte er mit der lokalen Königstochter einen Sohn, der → Eponym einer Stadt oder Stammvater eines Volkes wurde. In Rom wurden ihm Pallas (Dion. Hal. ant. 1,43,1), Aventinus (Verg. Aen. 7,655–663, vgl. Lyd. mag. 1,34), → Latinus (Dion. Hal. ant. 1,43,1), der erste Fabius (Fest. 77; Sil. 6,633ff., vgl. Ov. fast. 2,237) und der erste Antonius (Plut. Antonius 917c) geboren.

E. INITIATIONSKULTE

Manche von H.' Kulten haben alten initiatorischen Hintergrund. H. wurde häufig von → *collegia iuvenum* verehrt (z. B. CIL IX 1681; 3578). Frauen waren von seinen Riten ausgeschlossen. Im Hochzeitsritual löste der Bräutigam den *nodus Herculaneus* am Gürtel seiner Braut als Ausdruck des Wunsches nach vielen Kindern (Fest. 55).

F. MANTIK

In der Sage von → Acca Larentia würfelte H.; im Orakel des → Geryoneus an der fons Aponi verwendete man Würfel und Lose (*sortes*) (Suet. Tib. 14); in mehreren Städten Italiens gab es H.-Orakel mit *sortes* [2] (Ostia: [3]; Tibur: Stat. silv. 1,3,79; Caere: Liv. 22,1,10; Manliana: CIL VIII 9610). Der Larentia gab H. im Traum eine Prophezeiung (Plut. qu.R. 35,273ab; Aug. civ. 6,7,2), und er wurde als *somnialis* (»H. des Traums«) verehrt (CIL XI 1449). Faunus und H. wurden als Götter der erot. Träume *incubones* genannt (Porph. Hor. comm. serm. 2,6,12; → *incubo*).

G. HANDEL

In It. war H. auch Gott des Handels, der Eide, des Rechts, der Kaufverträge und des Eigentums. Üblich war es in Rom (an der Ara Maxima) und in ganz It., nach gelungenen Geschäften und Kriegszügen dem H. den Zehnten zu weihen (*pars Herculanea*: Plaut. Bacch. 666; Fest. 237; Plut. qu. R. 18,267f; Diod. 4,21,3f.; Macr. Sat. 3,6,11). Aus diesen Einkünften gab man dem Volk – aber unter Ausschluß von Frauen (Plut. qu.R. 60,278f) oder von Sklaven und Freigelassenen (Serv. Aen. 8,179) – reichliche Festmähler (Serv. auct. Aen. 8,278; Dion. Hal. ant. 1,40). Häufig wurde ein knappes Drittel des Zehnten (Tert. apol. 14,1), das *polluctum*, auf dem Altar verbrannt; das übrige wurde unter dem Volk verteilt (*profanatum*: Varro ling. 6,54). Der Praetor vollzog das Opfer (am 12. August mit unbedecktem Haupt: *aperto capite* und *ritu Graeco*), vielleicht in Anwesenheit der → Salier (Verg. Aen. 8,285ff.) Der gesamte Kult lag anfangs bei den Potitii und Pinarii; im J. 312 v. Chr. übernahm der Staat die Leitung des H.-Kultes, und an die Stelle der Potitii wurden Staatssklaven (*servi publici*) gesetzt (Liv. 9,29,9). Die Eide in H.' Namen wurden unter freiem Himmel gesprochen (Plut. qu. R. 28,271bd); als Gott der Eide wurde H. Dius Fidius oder (Semo) Sancus (zu Sanctus verändert) genannt (Varro ling. 5,66; Prop. 4,9,73f.). Als internationaler Gott führte H. die Oberaufsicht über zwischenstaatl. Verträge. Sonst hat die Figur des H. in der Überl. viele Elemente des → Faunus übernommen.

H. Triumph

H. wurde bereits für die Tarquinii und andere etr. Adlige, bes. aber für röm. Feldherren und Kaiser (Scipio Africanus, Commodus) zum Modell des durch seine siegreichen Taten vergöttlichten Menschen. Das schlug sich im Ritual des → Triumphs nieder: Eine alte Statue des H. Triumphalis auf dem Forum Boarium wurde während den *triumphi* mit dem *habitus triumphalis* bekleidet (Plin. nat. 34,16,33), und das Mahl bei einem *triumphus* wurde *hērakleōtikós* genannt (Athen. 4,153c).

Als vergöttlichter Mensch wurde H. manchmal in den Lararia verehrt oder als Lar (→ Lares) verkleidet [5; 6]. Sein Einsatz für die leidende Menschheit und seine Vergöttlichung ermöglichten später den Vergleich mit Christus (→ Hercules Oetaeus). Zur Ikonographie vgl. → Herakles.

1 G. Cuscito, Revisione delle epigrafi di età romana rinvenute intorno al Timavo, in: Antichità altoadriatiche 10, 1976, 51 2 J. Champeaux, Sors oraculi. Les oracles en Italie sous la république et l'empire, in: MEFRA 102, 1990, 271–302 3 D. Biolchi, L'erma di Ercole del Teatro Ampiternino, in: BCAR 67, 1939, 37 ff. 4 M. Guarducci, Graffiti parietali nel santuario di Ercole Curino presso Sulmona, in: L. Gasperini (Hrsg.), Scritti in memoria di F. Grosso, 1981, 225 ff. 5 M. Floriani Squarciapino, L'ara dei Lari di Ostia, in: ArchCl 4, 1952, 204 ff. 6 O. de Cazanove, Plastique votive et imagerie Dionysiaque, in: MEFRA 98, 1986, 21 ff.

J. Bayet, Les origines de l'Hercule romain, 1926 • Ders., Hercle, 1926 • C. Jourdain-Annequin, Héraclès aux portes du soir, 1989 • Dies., Ercole in Occidente, 1993 • Dies., Héraclès, 1992 • A. Mastrocinque, Romolo, 1993 • Ders., Héraclès. Les femmes et le féminin, 1996 • M. Simon, Hercule et le Christianisme, 1955. A. MAS.

Hercules Oetaeus. Röm. Trag. eines unbekannten Verf., die im Corpus der Trag. → Senecas überl. ist. Dieses längste Drama der Ant. (1996 V.) hat höchst kontroverse Wertungen erfahren, zumeist in Abhängigkeit von der Annahme oder Ablehnung der Autorschaft Senecas (Extreme [1] und [2]; vermittelnd [3]). Das Sujet – die Ereignisse vor dem Tod des Hercules und seine Apotheose – ist trotz kunstvoller und intelligenter → Intertextualität zu Soph. Trach., Ovid (epist. 9 und met. 9) und zu Senecas *Hercules Furens* eigenständig bearbeitet. Die Stilisierung des Hercules zum Retter der Welt und zu einer fast christl. anmutenden Märtyrergestalt sowie der hochgestimmte, die Rhet. nicht verleugnende Ton passen zur Lit. des späten 1. Jh. n. Chr. Trotz der Eindrücklichkeit, mit der Hercules gezeichnet ist, ist der H. O. weder als philos. noch als rel. Lehrdrama aufzufassen: Die Intertextualität und der Wille zum Effekt rangieren vor einer weltanschaulichen Aussage.

→ Seneca, Tragödie, Hercules

1 F. Leo, Observationes Criticae, 1872, 48 ff.
2 O. Regenbogen, Schmerz und Tod in den Trag. Senecas, 1927 (Ndr. 1963) 3 C. Walde, Herculeus labor. Stud. zum Pseudosenecan. H. O., 1992. C. W.

Herculis portus. Häfen dieses Namens gibt es 1. an der ligurischen Küste (Ptol. 3,1,2 von Monaco unterschieden, vielleicht Bucht von Villafranca östl. von Nizza), 2. am Monte Argentario westl. von → Cosa (Strab. 5,2,8; Rut. Nam. 1,293; Tab. Peut. 4,4; h. Port'Ercole), 3. an der bruttischen Westküste nahe Cap Vaticano (Strab. 6,1,5; Plin. nat. 3,73) und 4. an der Südküste Sardiniens (Ptol. 3,3,3). Am bekanntesten ist 5. Herculis Monoeci portus, den schon Hekat. FGrH 1 F 57 erwähnt (Strab. 4,5,6; Plin. nat. 3,47; Verg. Aen. 6,830; Sil. 1,585 f.; Lucan. 1,405 f.; Tac. hist. 3,42; Amm. 15,10,9); die Stadt soll von Herakles bei seiner Rückkehr von → Geryoneus gegr. worden sein (h. Monaco). Y. L.

Herculius

[1] *Praefectus praetorio Illyrici* in den Jahren 408 bis 410 n. Chr. (Cod. Theod. 12,1,172; 15,1,49), dem Sophisten in Athen und Megara Statuen errichteten (IG II² 4224 f.; VII 93). → Iohannes Chrysostomos schickte ihm epist. 201. PLRE 2, 545. K. P. J.

[2] s. Maximianus

Hercynia silva I. Geographie II. Die Hercynischen Vögel

I. Geographie

Sammelbegriff für die zentraleurop. Mittelgebirge, der zuerst bei Aristot. meteor. 1,13 erscheint. In NS-Richtung neun Tagesreisen (Caes. Gall. 6,25–28; Itp. nach [1]), in WO-Richtung 60 Tagesreisen tief, erstreckte sich die an unbekannten Wildtieren reiche *H.s.* von den Grenzen der Helvetii, Nemetes und Rauraci entlang der Donau bis ins Grenzgebiet (*fines*) der Dakoi und Anartes (die übrigen Belegstellen bequem über die Indices bei [2]). Obschon die röm. Okkupation und Entdeckung des Nordens genauere Kenntnisse erbrachten (z. B. → Abnoba mons), blieben die an der Erfahrung mit den Cimbri gewonnenen, elementaren Vorstellungen von der mitteleurop. Geogr. bestimmend [3].

1 G. Götte, Die Frage der geogr. Itp. in Caesars Bellum Gallicum, Diss. Marburg 1964, 197–205, 215–222, 270–303, 337–361 2 J. Herrmann (Hrsg.), Griech. und lat. Quellen zur Frühgesch. Mitteleuropas bis zur Mitte des 1. Jt. unserer Zeit, 1988 ff. 3 D. Timpe, s. v. Entdeckungsgesch., RGA 7, 307–389, bes. 342.

F. Beckmann, Geogr. und Ethnographie in Caesars Bellum Gallicum, 1930, 86–103, 158–161, 169–171. K. DI.

II. Die Hercynischen Vögel

Die sagenhaften hercynischen Vögel mit ihren nachts leuchtenden Federn wurden seit ihrer Ersterwähnung durch Plinius (nat. 10,132) über Solin. 20,3 dem MA bekannt. Honorius Augustodunensis versetzte sie irrtümlicherweise nach Hyrkanien (Imago mundi 1,18 [1. 58]), was eine weitere Trad. begründete. Thomas von Cantimpré (5,75; [2. 213]) kennt sie unter dem urspr. Namen und (nach dem *Liber rerum*) als *lucidii aves* [3].

1 V. I. J. FLINT (Ed.), Honorius Augustodunensis Imago mundi, in: Archives d'histoire doctrinale et littéraire du moyen age 49, 1983, 7–153 2 H. BOESE (Ed.), Thomas Cantimpratensis Liber de natura rerum, 1973
3 C. HÜNEMÖRDER, Hercyniae aves, in: RhM 110, 1967, 371–384. C. HÜ.

Herd (ἐσχάρα, ἑστία, *focus, ara, lar*, vgl. auch → Altar). Bei Griechen und Römern genießen H. und H.-Feuer bes. Verehrung (→ Hestia, → Lares, → Penates, → Vesta, → Feuer), da an ihm die Hausgötter Kult und Sitz hatten. Zudem war er die zentrale Stelle im Haus, an dem die Familie sich zum Mahle treffen konnte, ferner Licht- und Wärmequelle; von daher kann H. zu einem Synonym für Haus werden. Bei der Hochzeit (→ Hochzeitsbräuche) wird die in das Haus des Bräutigams geführte Braut um den H. geleitet und mit den *katachýsmata* überschüttet, vgl. die *amphidrómia* des neugeborenen Kindes (Aristoph. Lys. 757; schol. in Plat. Tht. 160e). In Rom legte die Braut noch zusätzlich ein As auf den H. (Non. 531,8); ihre künftige Aufgabe war es u. a., den Herd sauber zu halten und abends auszufegen (Cato agr. 143,2–4). In Griechenland konnte man ferner beim H. schwören (z. B. Hom. Od. 14,159), wie auch der Schutzflehende hier Zuflucht fand (Hom. Od. 7,153.248; Thuk. 1,136,3; Plut. Themistokles 24,4–6, vgl. Plin. nat. 36,70).

Die zentrale Funktion des H. bzw. der Feuerstelle im → Haus (s. auch → Megaron) zeigen bereits die rund angelegten H. der myk. Paläste in Pylos, Mykene usw. Auch weisen bereits die Häuser des 2. Jt. v. Chr. festgemauerte H.-Stellen auf, z. T. mit Rauchabzug, ferner gab es tragbare H. und Kohlepfannen. Die Trad. des festgemauerten wie auch des tragbaren H. setzt sich in der geom., archa. und auch in der klass. Zeit fort. Daneben nutzte man die offene H.-Stelle im festgestampften Lehmboden (vgl. die Häuser in Olynth, ferner den Apollon-Tempel von Dreros). Man stellte die Töpfe auf Untersätze (Dreifüße o. ä.) oder auf eine Platte über einen Feuerungsraum.

Gemäß der Überl. stand im röm. Haus der H. urspr. im → Atrium (Ov. fast. 6,301), was später noch mindestens auf dem Land üblich war (Hor. sat. 2,6, 65–67). Allerdings haben bereits frühe röm. Häuser und erst recht die späteren großen Wohnanlagen (Haus des Faun in Pompeji; Haus auf dem Palatin; Häuser von Cosa) Kochstellen bzw. einen eigenen Küchenraum mit H. (→ Culina), so daß der Platz im Atrium frei blieb und von einem viereckigen Steintisch (*cartibulum*) eingenommen wurde. Insbes. aus den Häusern von Pompeji sind sowohl gemauerte (freistehende, an die Wand gesetzte) H. wie auch tragbare H. erhalten, die – aus Bronze oder Eisen gefertigt – unterschiedliche Formen hatten; der Rauch zog über Öffnungen in der Wand oder Schornsteine ab.

Ob man aus Prop. 4,5,26 auf die Existenz verschiedener, namentlich bezeichneter H.-Typen schließen darf, wird weiterhin diskutiert. Das Anzünden des Brennmaterials auf dem H. wird oft erwähnt, aber nie ausführlich beschrieben; auf dem H. brannte oder glimmte stets eine kleine Flamme, die man mit Blasen oder dem → Fächer (ῥιπίς, Anth. Pal. 6,306; Aristoph. Ach. 669; 888; Hesych. s. v. ῥιπίς; [1]) wieder entfachen konnte. Im Notfall konnte man zum Feuerstein (πυρίτης, Αἰθιοπικός λίθος, Plin. nat. 36,137), Feuerschwamm (ἀγαρικόν), Zunder und Holz (Plin. nat. 16,207) u. a. greifen.

Zu rel.-kult. Aspekten des H. → Altar; → Feuer.

1 V. TRAN TAM TINH, Le culte des divinités orientales à Herculaneum (EPRO 17), 1971, Taf. 27,40.

F. E. BROWN, Cosa. The making of a Roman town, 1980, 64–65 • G. BRUHNS, Küchenwesen und Mahlzeiten, ArchHom. Q, 1970, 2–6, 31 • M. CHRISTOFANI (Hrsg.), La grande Roma dei Tarquini, Ausstellungs-Kat. Rom 1990, 97–99 • G. DITMAR-TRAUTH, Das galloröm. Haus. Zu Wesen und Verbreitung des Wohnhauses der galloröm. Bevölkerung im Imperium Romanum, 1995, 83–87, 108–109 • H. DRERUP, Griech. Baukunst in geom. Zeit, ArchHom II, 1969 • R. J. FORBES, Stud. in ancient technology 6, 1958, 1–35, 57–86 • V. GASSNER, Die Kaufläden in Pompeji, 1986, 40–41 • W. HOEPFNER, E. L. SCHWANDNER, Haus und Stadt im klass. Griechenland, [2]1994, 353, s. v. H.; s. v. Hestia • J. K. PAPADOPOULOS, Lasana, tuyère and kiln firing supports, in: Hesperia 61, 1992, 203–221 • C. SCHEFFER, Cooking and cooking stands in Italy 1400–400 B. C., Acquarossa II 1, 1981. R. H.

Herdoniae (auch *Herdonia*: Strab. 6,3,7; Sil. 8,567; App. Hann. 48; Ptol. 3,1,72; *Herdonea*: Liv. 25,21,1; 27,1,6). Stadt in Apulia (*regio II*: Plin. nat. 3,105; CIL IX 689f.; 1156; Itin. Anton. 116,2), h. Ordona, an der *via Minucia* (Strab. 6,3,7; Plin. nat. 2,244), Ausgangspunkt der Straßen nach Beneventum, Aeclanum und Ausculum. Nach der Schlacht bei Cannae (216 v. Chr.) Übertritt auf die Seite Hannibals und bis 210 v. Chr. häufig in die Auseinandersetzungen des 2. Pun. Krieges involviert. Dem drohenden Abfall von H. kam Hannibal 210 v. Chr. mit der Zerstörung der Stadt und der Deportation der Bewohner zuvor (Liv. 27,1,14). Später erlebte H. als *municipium* einen bescheidenen urbanistischen Aufschwung, von dem noch einige Bauwerke zeugen. Die Einwohnerzahl wird für das 1. Jh. v. Chr. auf 7500 geschätzt [1].

1 J. MERTENS, Alba Fucens et Herdonia, in: E. OLSHAUSEN, H. SONNABEND (Hrsg.), Stuttgarter Kolloquium zur histor. Geogr. des Alt. 2/1984 und 3/1987 (Geographica Historica 5) 1991, 425.

NISSEN 2, 847 • J. MERTENS, Ordona 1978–1986, in: Ordona 8, 1988, 7–67. H. SO.

Herdonius

[1] Appius H. Ein Sabiner, besetzt 460 v. Chr. mit 2500 Exilierten und Sklaven (Liv. 3,15,5–18,11; nach Dion. Hal. ant. 10,14,1–17,1 mit 4000 Klienten und Dienern) das Capitol und kommt im Kampf gegen die Truppen des Consuls Valerius und des Dictators von Tusculum, L. Mamilius, um. Die der Verschwörung des → Catilina nachgebildete Geschichte weist vielleicht auf ethnische Spannungen im Rom der frühen Republik hin.

P. M. MARTIN, Des tentatives de tyrannies à Rome, in: EDER, Staat, 49–72, speziell 60f.

[2] Turnus H. Latiner aus Aricia, wendet sich bei einem Treffen der Latiner mit → Tarquinius Superbus gegen diesen. Von Tarquinius in den falschen Verdacht gebracht, gegen ihn und führende Latiner ein Komplott zu planen, wird H. von den Latinern getötet (Liv. 1,50,3–51,9; Dion. Hal. ant. 4,45,3–48,3). Die Episode diente wohl als röm. Ursprungslegende für eine rituelle Hinrichtung durch Ertränken.

C. AMPOLO, Un supplicio arcaico: L'uccisione di Turnus Herdonius, in: Du châtiment dans la cité (Coll. École française de Rome, 79), 1984, 91–96. W. ED.

Hereas (Ἡρέας). Aus Megara, Verf. von *Megariká*, offenbar jünger als Dieuchidas. Die Fragmente in Plutarchs *Theseus* und *Solon* stammen nach gängiger Auffassung letztlich (über Istros und Hermippos!) aus den *Megariká* oder einer anderen (antiathenischen!) Schrift des H. Wahrscheinlich ist H. mit dem in IG VII 39 (Anf. 3. Jh. v. Chr.) erwähnten Theoros identisch, schwerlich aber, wie seit [1. 8] gemeinhin angenommen wird, mit Heragoras, einem weiteren Verf. von *Megariká*.

1 U. VON WILAMOWITZ-MOELLENDORFF, Comm. gramm. 1880/1881.

FR.: FGrH 486.
LIT.: L. PICCIRILLI, Megariká, Testimonianze e Frammenti, 1975, 51ff. K. MEI.

Heredium. In der Sprache der XII Tafeln (7,3) das Bauerngut im Ausmaß von zwei *iugera* (0,5 ha; Plin. nat. 19,4,50), aus *hortus* (Bauernhof mit Garten, Paul. Fest. 91,12 L.) und *ager* (Ackerland) bestehend. Nach der Tradition hatte Romulus jedem Bürger ein unveräußerliches *h.* zugeteilt, welches jeweils dem Erben (*heres*) zufiel (Varro rust. 1,10,2); die XII Tafeln erlaubten schon die Veräußerung und Vererbung der Gesamthabe (6,1; 5,3), damit auch des *h.* Da ein *h.* zur Ernährung einer Großfamilie mit Gesinde kaum ausreichte, leuchtet MOMMSENS Annahme [1] ein, das *h.* sei nur die private Parzelle neben gemeinschaftlich genutztem Ackerland gewesen. In der späteren Sprache bezeichnet *h.* nur noch untechnisch ein sehr kleines Landgut (Paul. Fest. 89,1 L.).
→ Agrarstruktur [2]; Limitation

1 MOMMSEN, Staatsrecht, Bd. 3, 23ff. U. M.

Herennianus. Der jüngere Sohn des → Odaenathus und der → Zenobia (SHA Gall. 13,2; SHA trig. tyr. 15,2; 17,2; 24,4; 27; 28; 30). Nach dem Tod des Vaters erhielten er und sein älterer Bruder Timolaus die *ornamenta imperatoria*, während die Mutter für die unmündigen Kinder die Herrschaft führte (SHA trig. tyr. 27,1; 30,2; SHA Aurelian. 22,1; 38,1). Später übernahm aber ihr dritter Sohn → Vaballathus die Macht. H. ist wahrscheinlich von Aurelian getötet worden (SHA trig. tyr. 27,1f.).

PIR² H 95 • PLRE 1, 421 (H. 1). T. F.

Herennios Philon A. PERSON B. WERKE

A. PERSON
H. war Antiquar und Grammatiker der 2. H. des 1. Jh. n. Chr. (Hauptquelle für die Biographie: Suda s. v. Φίλων Βύβλιος, φ 447, wo der Text jedoch problematisch ist). Sein ursprünglicher Name war *Phílōn*, das Ethnikon *Býblios* (nach der Stadt Byblos/Phönizien), das Praenomen H. vielleicht von Herennius Severus Plin. epist. 4,28 übernommen [4]. Er war Lehrer des → Hermippos von Berytos.

B. WERKE
(FGrH 790): Histor.-antiquarische Werke: 1) Die ›phöniz. Gesch.‹ (Φοινικικὴ ἱστορία oder Φοινικικά), nach Eusebios in neun Büchern, in der Suda merkwürdigerweise nicht erwähnt; längere Fragmente sind von Eusebios (Pr. Ev.) überliefert. H. will die Abh. des ant. phöniz. Gelehrten → Sanchuniathon übersetzt haben, der H. zufolge um 1000 v. Chr. gelebt haben soll und unter dessen Namen 1837 sogar ein unechtes Werk veröffentlicht wurde [8]. Wenn die Fragmente auch grundlegende Bedeutung für die Kenntnis von Mythos und Rel. der Phönizier haben [17], welche nach dem Vorwurf des H. von den Griechen deformiert worden sein sollen, ist die Authentizität des Materials aus dem 2. Jt. in vollem Umfang unwahrscheinlich (wie man von 1929 an nach der Publikation von Texten aus Ugarit und Ḫattuša gedacht hatte; vgl. bes. [7] mit Lit.; zum Forschungsstand [11. 357–358]). Das Werk weist jedoch Charakteristika der hell. Geschichtsschreibung auf (Euhemerismus; Universalgesch.; nationalistische Perspektive; die Ableitung aus einer »Enthüllung«: vgl. [13]).

2) ›Über die Judäer‹ (Περὶ Ἰουδαίων) [11]. 3) ›Über die phöniz. Buchstaben‹ oder ›Über phöniz. Elemente‹ (Περὶ τῶν Φοινίκων στοιχείων) und 4) *Hypomnḗmata Ethōthiṓn* (Ὑπομνήματα Ἐθωθ(ι)ῶν), der Titel ist rätselhaft [3. 256]. 5) die ›Paradoxe Gesch.‹ (Παράδοξος ἱστορία) in 3 B., in der die »Disharmonie« (διαφωνία) der verschiedenen mythischen Überlieferungen der Griechen untersucht wurde. 6) ›Über Städte und ihre berühmten Bürger‹ (Περὶ πόλεων καὶ οὓς ἑκάστη αὐτῶν ἐνδόξους ἤνεγκε) in 30 B., von Aelius Serenus zusammengefaßt. Das wahrscheinlich buchweise alphabetisch angeordnete Werk deckte die ganze Oikumene ab; herangezogen wurde es von → Stephanos von Byzanz, → Hesychios und anderen → Lexikographen. 7) ›Über Besitz und Auswahl von Büchern‹ (Περὶ κτήσεως καὶ ἐκλογῆς βιβλίων) in 12 B., den verschiedenen Wissensgebieten entsprechend aufgebaut (→ Pinakographie). 8) ›Über Ärzte‹ (Περὶ ἰατρῶν). 9) ›Über wissenswerte Dinge‹ (Περὶ χρηστομαθείας). 10) ›Über Hadrians Herrschaft‹ (Περὶ τῆς βασιλείας Ἁδριανοῦ): dieser von der Suda überlieferte Titel trägt zur genaueren Datierung von H. bei.

Sprachwissenschaftlich-grammatisch ausgerichtete Werke: 11) ›Über nomina deverbativa‹ (Τὰ ῥηματικά). 12) ›Über den Dialekt von Rom‹ (Περὶ Ῥωμαίων διαλέκτου). 13) ein Synonymenwörterbuch (→ Lexikographie), aus dem einige byz. Exzerpte erh. sind. Das ausführlichste Werk ist jedoch das ›Synonymenlex.‹ (Περὶ ὁμοίων καὶ διαφόρων λέξεων), das → Ammonios [4] zugewiesen wird, dessen Titel auch der urspr. Titel von H.' Wörterbuch gewesen sein könnte.

Epigramme in 4 B.

1 H.W. Attridge, R.A. Oden, The Phoenician history: Introduction, crit. text, translation and notes, 1981 2 J. Barr, Philo of Byblos and his »Phoenicean History«, in: Bull. of the John Rylands Library 57, 1974, 17–68 3 A.I. Baumgarten, The Phoenician History of Philo of Byblos. A commentary, 1981 4 J. Christes, Sklaven und Freigelassene als Grammatiker und Philologen im ant. Rom, 1979, 105–106; 137–139 5 J. Ebach, Weltentstehung und Kulturentwicklung bei Philo von Byblos, 1979 6 M.J. Edwards, Philo or Sanchuniathon? A phoenicean cosmogony, in: CQ 41, 1991, 213–220 7 O. Eissfeldt, s.v. Philo Byblius, RGG³ 5, 346–347; s.v. Sanchunjaton, RGG³ 5, 1361 8 S. Faller, Der »neue« Sanchuniathon oder Die Anatomie einer Fälschung, in: T. Baier, F. Schimann (Hrsg.), Fabrica. Studien zur ant. Lit. und ihrer Rezeption, 1997, 165–178 9 A. Gudeman, s.v. H. Philon (2), RE 8, 650–661 10 E. Lipiński, The Phoenician History of Philo of Byblos, in: Bibliotheca Orientalis, 1983, 305–310 11 A. Momigliano, La storiografia greca, 1982, 357–362 12 K. Nickau, Ammonius. De adfinium vocabulorum differentia, 1966, LXVII. 13 R.A. Oden, Philo of Byblos and Hellenistic History, in: Palestine Exploration Quarterly 110, 1978, 115–126 14 V. Palmieri, »Eranius« Philo, De differentia significationis, in: Revue d'Histoire des Textes 11, 1981, 47–80 15 Ders., Herennius Philo. De diversis verborum significationibus, ²1988 16 Ders., Anonimo ›Excerptum Casanatense‹, in: Boll. dei classici III, 5, 1984, 150–168 17 S. Ribichini, Poenus advena. Gli dei fenici e l' interpretazione classica, 1985 18 Ders., Taautos et l' invention de l' écriture chez Philon de Byblos, in: Cl. Baurain, C. Bonnet, V. Krings, Phoinikeia grammata, 1991, 201–213 19 L. Troiani, L' opera storiografica di Filone da Byblos, 1974. S.FO./Ü: T.H.

Herennius. Weitverbreiteter ital. Eigenname (verbunden mit dem Praenomen *Herennus*, das mit H. oft verwechselt wird), der aber in der röm. Oberschicht erst ab dem 1. Jh. v. Chr. als Familienname bezeugt ist. Zu ihm treten häufig Beinamen als Herkunftsbezeichnungen (*Etruscus, Gallus, Picens, Siculus*). In der Kaiserzeit Name des Caesars Q.H. [II 3] Etruscus, Sohn des Kaisers → Decius [II 1], des Historikers H. → Dexippos [2], des Juristen H. → Modestinus.

Salomies 73 f. • Schulze 82; 282. K.-L.E.

I. Republikanische Zeit

[I 1] H. Centurio, der Ende 43 v. Chr. → Cicero nahe dessen Villa bei Formiae ermordete und – auf Weisung des M. Antonius [I 9] – die Leiche verstümmelte (Plut. Cicero 48,1 f.). Bei Hier. chron. Ol. 184,2 (= Suet. de oratoribus, p. 81 Reifferscheid) ist Popilius, nach Plutarch H.' übergeordneter Militärtribun, der Haupttäter. T.FR.

[I 2] H., C. Verweigerte 116 v. Chr. nach der Wahl des C. → Marius zum Praetor die Zeugenaussage in einem Prozeß wegen Amtserschleichung gegen Marius, weil er dessen Patron sei; Marius erklärte darauf, daß das Klientelverhältnis mit H. nach seiner Wahl erloschen sei (Plut. Marius 5,7 f.).

[I 3] H., C. Sonst unbekannter Verwandter und Freund des anonymen Verf. der sog. → *Rhetorica ad Herennium*, die dieser ihm um 85 v. Chr. widmete (1,1; 4,69).

[I 4] H., C. Verhinderte als Volkstribun 80 v. Chr. einen Gesetzesvorschlag Sullas über Rückkehr und Triumph des Cn. → Pompeius Magnus (Sall. hist. 2,21M; [1. 194–196]). Vielleicht ist er identisch mit dem senatorischen Geschworenen, der nach 80 wegen Bestechung verurteilt wurde (Cic. Verr. 1,39) und mit dem Legaten des Q. → Sertorius, der 76 oder 75 im Kampf gegen Pompeius in Spanien fiel (Sall. hist. 2,98,6M; Plut. Pompeius 18,3).

1 P. McGushin, Sallust: The Histories 1, 1992.

MRR 3, 101. K.-L.E.

[I 5] H., C. Volkstribun 60 v. Chr.; seine Unterstützung von P. Clodius [I 4] Pulchers Plan zum Übertritt in den Plebeierstand scheiterte an der Interzession der Amtskollegen (Cic. Att. 1,18,4; 19,5) und dem Widerstand des Consuls Q. Caecilius [I 22] Metellus (Cic. Att. 2,1,5). Unklar ist, ob auch der Antrag, das Volkstribunat generell Patriziern zugänglich zu machen (Cass. Dio 37,51,1), von H. vorgebracht wurde. T.FR.

[I 6] H., M. Obwohl nur aus unbedeutender senatorischer Familie und durchschnittlicher Redner, Praetor spätestens 96 v. Chr. und Consul 93 (Cic. Mur. 36; Brut. 166; MRR 2,14); vielleicht Münzmeister 108/7 (RRC 308). K.-L.E.

[I 7] H., M. Ratsherr (*decurio*) in Pompeii, der 63 v. Chr. von einem aus heiterem Himmel niederfahrenden Blitz erschlagen wurde (Plin. nat. 2,137). Cicero (div. 1,18) rechnet das Ereignis unter die Vorzeichen der Catilinarischen Wirren. (Der Name Vargunteius, den das Opfer bei Obseq. 61 trägt, ist in Pompeii nicht belegt).

P. Castrén, Ordo Populusque Pompeianus, 1975, 174 f., Nr. 191. T.FR.

[I 8] H. (Picens ?), M. *Cos. suff.* 34 v. Chr.; Vater von H. [II 6]. (PIR² H 118; MRR 3, 101 f.). K.-L.E.

[I 9] H. Balbus, L. 56 v. Chr. einer der Ankläger im Prozeß gegen den von Cicero verteidigten M. Caelius [I 4] Rufus (Cic. Cael. 25; 27; 49; 53; 56). Auch 52, im Prozeß gegen die Mörder des Clodius [I 4], fand sich H. in der Gegenpartei Milos und Ciceros (Ascon. 34 Clark), der H. aber gemeinhin zu seinen Freunden zählte (Cael. 25).

[I 10] H. Siculus. Wohl aus Sizilien (Katane?) stammender Opferschauer (aber Vell. 2,7,2: *haruspex Tuscus*),

Anhänger des C. → Sempronius Gracchus. 121 im Zuge der Repressalien gegen die Sympathisanten der Gracchen eingesperrt, beging H. Selbstmord, indem er seinen Schädel an einem Kerkerpfosten zerschmetterte (Val. Max. 9,12,6). Auf H.' Unbeugsamkeit und Treue zu seinen polit. Idealen spielt wohl die Münzprägung seines möglichen Nachfahren H. [I 6] an. (RRC 308).

T.FR.

II. KAISERZEIT

[II 1] C. H. Caecilianus. Aus Verona stammend, unter Hadrian in den Senat aufgenommen, 138 n. Chr. im *s. c. Beguense* erwähnt. Bei Sirmione wurde ihm auf einem Gut ein Reiterstandbild errichtet.

W. ECK, Tra epigrafia, prosopografia e archeologia, 1996, 306f. • PIR² H 102.

[II 2] C. H. Capito. Ritter aus Teate Marrucinorum, der nach einer militärischen Laufbahn Patrimonialprocurator von Livia, Tiberius und Caligula in Iamnia in Iudaea wurde (AE 1941, 105). Nach Philo verhielt er sich feindselig gegen die Juden, die er ausplünderte. Von Agrippa II. forderte er Gelder für die Patrimonialkasse ein; als dies nicht erreicht wurde, erstattete er Anzeige bei Tiberius.

PIR² H 103 • DEVIJVER, H 13. W.E.

[II 3] Q. H. Etruscus Messius Decius. Der ältere Sohn des Kaisers → Decius [II 1] und der Herennia Etruscilla, geb. zwischen 220 und 230 n. Chr. in Pannonien (Aur. Vict. Caes. 29; Ps.-Aur. Vict. epit. Caes. 29; Amm. 31,5,16; Eutr. 9,4; Oros. 7,21,3). Im Mai 250 zum Caesar und *princeps iuventutis* erhoben (CIL II 4058; XIII 6115; 9123; Cod. Iust. 5,12,9; AE 1942/3, 55), war er im Mai 251 *cos. ord.* (CIL VI 1100f.; XI 3088; Chron. min. 1, 521,39 MOMMSEN) und erhielt den Titel Augustus (CIL VI 31129 [1. 215ff., Nr. 7,16,18,19,30,37, 41]). Beim Versuch, mit seinem Vater den plündernden Goten unter Cniva den Rückweg über die Donau zu verlegen, kam es zur Schlacht bei Abrittus (Dobrudscha), in der H. noch vor seinem Vater durch einen Pfeilschuß fiel (Aur. Vict. Caes. 29,4; Iord. Get. 18; Chron. min. 1, 521,39); sein Name verfiel der *damnatio memoriae*.

1 H. COHEN, Monnaies sous l'empire romain, Ndr. 1955, Bd. 5.

PIR² H 106 • KIENAST² 206f. • M. PEACHIN, Roman Imperial Titulature and Chronology, 1990, 32f. T.F.

[II 4] M. H. Faustus Ti. Iulius Clemens Tadius Flaccus. Senator der traianisch-hadrianischen Zeit, der u. a. Legionslegat in Apulum war und, wohl im J. 121 n. Chr., *cos. suff.* wurde. Er dürfte Hadrian im J. 130 nach Ägypten begleitet haben.

PIR² H 107 • PISO, FPD 214ff.

[II 5] H. Gallus. Legat der *legio I* in Bonna im J. 69/70 n. Chr. Kämpfe gegen die aufständischen Bataver verliefen unglücklich. 70 wurde er von den eigenen Soldaten ermordet. PIR² H 108.

[II 6] M. H. Picens. *Cos. suff.* 1 n. Chr.; entweder er oder sein Vater, *cos. ord.* 34 v. Chr., war Proconsul von Asia unter Augustus (THOMASSON, Laterculi I 209). Veii hatte ihm öffentliche Gebäude zu verdanken. PIR² H 118.

[II 7] P. H. Pollio. *Cos. suff.* im J. 85 n. Chr., Vater von H. [II 8].

AE 1975, 21 • W. ECK, s. v. H. (35b), RE Suppl. 14, 197.

[II 8] M. Annius H. Pollio. Zusammen mit seinem Vater (H. [II 7]) *cos. suff.* im J. 85 (AE 1975, 21; VIDMAN, FO² 44, 79). Unter Traian klagte er den Proconsul von Pontus-Bithynien, → Iulius [II 28] Bassus, im Senat an. PIR² H 119.

[II 9] H. Rufinus. Bürger von Oea in Africa. Schwiegervater des Sicinius Pontianus, des Stiefsohnes von Apuleius. Er veranlaßte die Anklage gegen Apuleius wegen Magie. PIR² H 123.

[II 10] L. H. Saturninus. Proconsul von Achaia im J. 98 n. Chr., *cos. suff.* 100, consularer Statthalter von Moesia superior ca. 104–106 [1. 330, 340ff.]. Ihm widmete Plutarch sein Werk gegen die Epikureer. PIR² H 126.

1 W. ECK, in: Chiron 12, 1982, 281–362.

[II 11] H. Senecio. Aus der Baetica stammend; Senator, der es nur bis zur Quaestur brachte; mit Plinius zusammen klagte er wohl im J. 93 n. Chr. Baebius Massa wegen Repetunden an. Angeblich wegen seines Buches über → Helvidius [1] Priscus von Mettius Carus im Senat angeklagt und von Domitian getötet. PIR² H 128.

[II 12] P. H. Severus. Spanischer Senator, der vielleicht unter Hadrian zu einem Suffektkonsulat gelangte; möglicherweise mit dem von Plin. epist. 4,28,1 genannten *vir doctissimus* identisch. PIR² H 130.

CABALLOS, Senadores I, 156f. W.E.

Hergetion (Ἐργέτιον). Kleine Stadt im Landesinnern von Sizilien bei Grammichele, nördl. von → Hybla [1] Heraia, erwähnt in der Delph. Liste der *theōrodókoi* (col. IV 106; vgl. [1. 434f.] mit dem Vorschlag der Lokalisierung in Ferla, [2. 133ff.[32]]), in einem Orakel von Dodona [4. 85f.] und bei Steph. Byz. s. v. Segesta. Zum Ethnikon vgl. die Bronzemz. aus Syrakus [3. 203].

1 G. MANGANARO, Città di Sicilia e santuari panellenici nel III e II sec. a.C., in: Historia 13, 1964, 414–439 2 Ders., Alla ricerca di poleis mikrai della Sicilia centro-orientale, in: Orbis Terrarum 2, 1996, 129–144 3 R. CALCIATI (Hrsg.), Corpus nummorum Siculorum 3, 1987
4 J. VOKOTOPOULOU, in: A. STAZIO (Hrsg.), La Magna Grecia e i Grandi Santuari della Madrepatria. Atti XXXI Conv. Studi Magna Grecia, 1991, 62–90.

M. GIANGIULIO, s. v. Ergezio, BTCGI 7, 1989, 344ff.

GI. MA./Ü: V. S.

Herillos von Karthago (Kalchedon). Stoischer Philosoph des 3. Jh. v. Chr., Schüler des → Zenon von Kition. Wie Ariston von Chios entwickelte er einen auf Ethik konzentrierten → Stoizismus. Nachdem sich die

von Kleanthes und Chrysippos vertretene Richtung dieser Schule durchgesetzt hatte, wurde der Ansatz des H. als von Zenon abweichend betrachtet. Die Lebensbeschreibung des H. bei Diogenes Laertios enthält eine Liste von Werktiteln, die anscheinend überwiegend auf ethische Themen bezogen waren (über den Inhalt seiner Dialoge sowie der Werke ›Hermes‹ und ›Medea‹ lassen sich nur Vermutungen äußern). Die Schrift ›Über die Voraussetzungen‹ (περὶ ὑπολήψεως) behandelte vermutlich das oberste Ziel (→ *télos*), das nach H. das »Wissen« war, ›d. h. eine Lebensführung, die alles stets auf das Gebot der wiss. Einsicht ausrichtete und sich nicht durch Unwissenheit irreleiten ließ‹ (Diog. Laert. 7,165). H. wird auch die Auffassung zugeschrieben, es gebe kein bestimmtes *télos*, sondern nur ein den Umständen entsprechendes. Darin berührt er sich mit → Ariston [7] von Chios, der die Ansicht vertrat, der Weise wisse, wie man in einer bestimmten Situation richtig handle, und der bestritt, daß man allgemeingültige Handlungsrichtlinien geben könne. H. unterschied das eigentliche Endziel (*télos*), nach dem nur der Weise streben könne, von dem untergeordneten Ziel (*hypótelis*), das auch den Nicht-Weisen zugänglich sei.
→ Stoizismus

SVF 1, 91–93 • A. M. Ioppolo, Aristone di Chio e lo Stoicismo antico, 1980, 176–179. B. I./Ü: B. v. R.

Herineos. Fluß in Sicilia an der *via Elorina*, von Thukydides (7,80,6; 82,3) im Zusammenhang mit dem Rückzug der Athener 413 v. Chr. erwähnt, evtl. identisch mit dem Cavallata nördl. des Assinaros.

G. Manganaro, Alla ricerca di poleis mikrai della Sicilia centro-orientale, in: Orbis Terrarum 2, 1996, 139 mit Nr. 50 • L. Robert, Noms indigenes de l'Asie Mineure gréco-romaine, 1963, 37f. GI. MA./Ü: H. D.

Herippidas (Ἑριππίδας). Spartiat, gehörte nach 400 v. Chr. zum inneren Zirkel der spartanischen Führungsschicht [1. 154], unterdrückte 399 einen Aufstand in Herakleia Trachinia (Diod. 14,38,4–5) [2. 120f., 154], 395 einflußreichster Ratgeber des Agesilaos [2] auf dessen Kleinasienfeldzug und Kommandeur der Kyreier, die er auch 394 bei Koroneia befehligte (Xen. hell. 3,4,20; 4,1,11–14; 20–28; 4,3,15). Nach dem Tod des Nauarchen Podanemos übernahm er trotz geringer Erfahrung im Seekrieg 392/1 zeitweilig das Flottenkommando am Korinthischen Golf (Xen. hell. 4,8,11). Als einer der drei Harmostai der spartanischen Besatzung in Theben konnte er 379/8 die Befreiung Thebens durch Pelopidas nicht verhindern und wurde in Sparta zum Tode verurteilt (Plut. Pelopidas 13).

1 P. Cartledge, Agesilaos and the Crisis of Sparta, 1987
2 Ch. D. Hamilton, Sparta's Bitter Victories, 1979. K.-W. WEL.

Herkulianos (Ἑρκουλιανός). Neuplatonischer Philosoph, gest. um 408 n. Chr. Bekannt nur durch die Briefe, die ihm sein Freund → Synesios schrieb (137–146 Garyza). Mit diesem lebte er in Alexandria zusammen. Beide waren Hörer der → Hypatia, die sie bei Plotinos, Porphyrios und Iamblichos einführte.

Ch. Lacombrade, Synésios de Cyrène, Hellène et Chrétien, 1951, 50–63, 72–73. L. BR./Ü: J. DE.

Herkyna (Ἕρκυνα). Fluß in Boiotia, dessen starke, zum Teil lauwarme Quellen in → Lebadeia am Ausgang einer Felsschlucht (Höhlenheiligtum und Tempel) entspringen und eng mit dem Kult des benachbarten Orakels des → Trophonios verbunden waren. Belegstellen: Paus. 9,39,2–8; Plin. nat. 31,15; Plut. mor. 771f; Philostr. Ap. 8,19.

F. Bölte, s. v. H., RE 8, 690f. • H. G. Lolling, Reisenotizen aus Griechenland (1876 und 1877), 1989, 609–614 • N. D. Papachatzis, Παυσανίου Ἑλλάδος Περιήγησις 5, [2]1981, 244–250 • Philippson/Kirsten 1, 445–448. P. F.

Herm( ). Vielleicht Dioiket in Alexandria, jedenfalls hoher Beamter; er richtete am 5. März 112 v. Chr. einen Brief an seinen Untergebenen Asklepiades, *ho epí tōn prosódōn* (ὁ ἐπὶ τῶν προσόδων) im Fayoum, betreffs der Vorbereitungen zum Empfang des röm. Senators L. Memmius (vgl. [1], der auch die Ergänzung des Namens zu Herm(ias) ablehnt).

1 Mitteis/Wilcken I 3.

E. Olshausen, Rom und Ägypten von 116 bis 51 v. Chr., Diss. 1963, 6f. W. A.

Hermagoras (Ἑρμαγόρας).
[1] Griech. Rhetor aus Temnos (Strab. 13,3,5 = 621; Suda, s. v. H.), wohl der 2. H. des 2. Jh. v. Chr. (vor Molon, vgl. Quint. inst. 3,1,16). Welche Schriften er neben seinem Hauptwerk verfaßt hat, war bereits in der Ant. ungewiß (ebd. 3,5,14); dieses hieß wohl *Téchnai rhētorikaí* und umfaßte 6 B. (laut Suda). Sein Inhalt läßt sich teilweise rekonstruieren aus Cic. inv., Quint. inst. (bes. B. 5) und Aug. de rhetorica. H. hat die Ausbildung des rhet. Systems maßgeblich beeinflußt: Die in Ansätzen schon im 4. Jh. nachweisbare Lehre von den *stáseis* (→ Rhetorik) wurde durch ihn terminologisch fixiert; dabei habe er eine vierte *stásis* (μετάληψις, *metálēpsis*), die Zurückweisung der Zulässigkeit des Verfahrens als solchen, hinzugefügt (Cic. inv. 1,16) und der ποιότης (*poiótēs*), dem Streitstand der Handlungsqualität, auch die symbuleutische und epideiktische Redegattung untergeordnet (ebd., 1,12). Zudem habe H. nicht nur die in spezielle Gegebenheiten eingebundene Streitfrage (*hypóthesis*), sondern auch die allgemein-übergreifende Kontroverse (*thésis*) als Gegenstand der Rhet. beansprucht und damit der Philos. streitig gemacht (Quint. inst. 3,5,12–16; vgl. Cic. de orat. 3,107f.). Das Lehrsystem des H. kam den Bedürfnissen der forensischen Beredsamkeit im republikanischen Rom sehr entgegen. Deshalb und wohl auch wegen ihrer übersichtlichen Gliederung wurden die *Téchnai* zur Grundlage des rhet.

Unterrichts in Rom; daran konnte auch die Kritik an der allzu subtilen Terminologie (Quint. inst. 3,11,21 f.) und der extremen Trockenheit (Cic. Brut. 263; Tac. dial. 19,3) von H.' Lehrschrift nichts ändern.

ED.: D. MATTHES, 1962.
FORSCHUNGSBER.: Ders., H. von Temnos, in: Lustrum 3, 1958, 58–214.
LIT.: K. BARWICK, Augustins Schrift de rhetorica und H. von Temnos, in: Philologus 105, 1961, 97–110 • Ders., Zur Erklärung und Gesch. der Stasislehre des H. von Temnos, in: Philologus 108, 1964, 80–101 • Ders., Zur Rekonstruktion der Rhet. des H. von Temnos, in: Philologus 109, 1965, 186–218 • A. C. BRAET, Das Krinomenonschema und die Einseitigkeit des Begriffes στάσις von H. von Temnos, in: Mnemosyne 41, 1988, 299–317 • Ders., Variationen zur Statuslehre bei Cicero, in: Rhetorica 7, 1989, 239–259 • R. NADEAU, Classical Systems of Stases in Greek, in: GRBS 2, 1959, 51–71 • E. SCHÜTRUMPF, H. v.T. and the Classification of Aristotle's Work in the Neoplatonic Commentaries, in: Mnemosyne 44, 1991, 96–105 • W. N. THOMPSON, Stasis in Aristotle's Rhetoric, in: Quarterly Journal of Speech 58, 1972, 134–141.

[2] Griech. Rhetor des 1. Jh. v. und n. Chr., Schüler des → Theodoros von Gadara wie Kaiser Tiberius, den H. aber weit überlebt haben muß (vgl. Quint. inst. 3,1,18), später Lehrer der Rhet. in Rom. Die Suda (s. v. H.) vermischt Angaben über H. [1] aus Temnos mit solchen über den Theodoros-Schüler. Von den als Schriften des ersteren dort genannten dürften einige in Wahrheit von letzterem stammen (Περὶ πρέποντος, *Perí prépontos*: über den angemessenen Ausdruck; Περὶ σχημάτων, *Perí schēmátōn*: zur Figurenlehre; Περὶ φράσεως, *Perí phráseōs*: zur *elocutio*; Περὶ ἐξεργασίας, *Perí exergasías*: zur Ausarbeitung), da sie für H. [1] sonst nirgends bezeugt sind (so vielleicht auch eine Schrift, welche die Behandlung der *théseis* aus der Rhet. ausklammern will, vgl. Quint. inst. 3,5,12–16). Von Seneca wird H. des öfteren wegen seiner unprätentiösen, aber treffenden Sentenzen lobend erwähnt (contr. 1,1,25; 2,1,39; 2,3,22; 7, praef. 5; 7,5,14f.; 10,1,15).

ED.: D. MATTHES, 1962, 56–59.
LIT.: Ders., H. von Temnos, in: Lustrum 3, 1958, 79.

[3] Griech. Rhetor der 1. H. des 2. Jh. n. Chr., zur Unterscheidung von H. [2] als ὁ νεώτερος (»der Jüngere«) bezeichnet (Maximos Planudes bei WALZ 5,337,23). Die Datier. beruht auf Sopatros, der H. nach Lollianos und vor Minukianos und Hermogenes setzt (WALZ 5,8,20). H. verfaßte eine Monographie über die στάσις πραγματική (*stásis pragmatikḗ*), die Entscheidungsfrage, ob eine in der Zukunft mögliche Handlung stattfinden soll oder nicht (Unterabteilung der *poiótēs*, vgl. Hermog. de statibus 2,12), die noch in byz. Zeit benutzt und öfter erwähnt wird, sowie vielleicht ein Lehrbuch der Rhet. (vgl. die in den schol. Hermog. überl. Definition: WALZ 4,63,9–14; auch 2,683,25–27).

ED.: D. MATTHES, 1962, 59–65.
LIT.: Ders., H. von Temnos, in: Lustrum 3, 1958, 79–81.

M. W.

Hermai s. Hermen

Hermaios (Ἑρμαῖος).

[1] H. Soter (mittelind. *Heramaya*). Der letzte indogriech. König in Paropamisadai (h. Südosten Afghanistans) im 1. Jh. v. Chr., vielleicht Sohn des Amyntas [8]. Wie so viele indogriech. Könige ist er nur durch seine Münzen belegt, darunter eine große Menge postumer Ausgaben, geprägt von Indoskythen aus Baktrien, die ihn beseitigt hatten (nach [1] nach 30, nach [2] um 50, nach [3] um 70 v. Chr.). Seine Gemahlin war → Kalliope.

1 W. W. TARN, The Greeks in Bactria and India, 1951
2 A. K. NARAIN, The Indo-Greeks, 1958 3 BOPEARACHCHI, 112–125, 325–343.

K. K.

[2] Vielleicht 1. Jh. v. Chr. Schrieb mindestens zwei B. ›Über die Ägypter‹ und wird lediglich von Plutarch (*Isis et Osiris*) zitiert. Möglicherweise war er Vater des Grammatikers Nikanor.

FR.: FGrH 620.
LIT.: F. JACOBY, s. v. H. (4), RE 8, 712.

K. MEI.

Hermaphroditos (Ἑρμαφρόδιτος). Androgyne Gestalt, die wie Priapos (vgl. Diod. 4,6; [6. 76–79]) erst ab dem 4. Jh. v. Chr. in Erscheinung tritt. Auch wenn zweigeschlechtige Götter des Orients wie → Astarte, »dieux doubles« wie Aphrodite-Aphroditos auf Zypern, gemeinsame Kulte von Hermes und Aphrodite (s. u.), Riten des Geschlechterrollen- und Kleidertausches, Mythen von sukzessiver (→ Kaineus, → Teiresias) und simultaner (z. B. Plat. symp. 189d–192d) Bisexualität im Hintergrund stehen, bleibt die Herkunft einigermaßen unklar [6. 69].

Der Name ist nicht wie die erst ab Cicero belegte Form Hermathena usw. als Kompositum aus *hérma* (ἕρμα) und dem Gottesnamen, sondern aufgrund der Verbindung von → Hermes und → Aphrodite als seltene Zwillingsbildung analog zu *andrógynos*, *arrhenóthelys* (»mannweiblich«) zu erklären (Ov. met. 4,384).

Einzig erh. myth. Erzählung (evtl. oriental. Herkunft) ist Ov. met. 4,274–388: Als H., Sohn des Hermes und der Aphrodite (so zuerst Diod. 4,6,5), in einer Quelle badet, verschmilzt die Nymphe Salmacis mit ihm zu einem zweigeschlechtigen Körper (Aition der Androgynie des H.); daraufhin erbittet H. von seinen Eltern, daß die dort Badenden verweichlicht werden (Aition der Eigenschaft, die man der Quelle zuschrieb). Vitr. 2,8,11–12 erwähnt einen Tempel des Mercur und der Venus in der Nähe der bei Halikarnassos gelegenen Quelle, von dem sich jedoch keine Spur erhalten hat.

Als Belege für einen Kult lassen sich mit mehr oder weniger Zuversicht anführen: 1. eine Weihinschr. vom Hymettos im Demos Anagyros (385 v. Chr.); 2. evtl. Theophr. char. 16,10: Der Abergläubische bekränzt am

4. und 7. des Monats (der 4. war als Hochzeitstag Hermes und Aphrodite geweiht: Hes. erg. 800) je nach Lesart der korrupten Hs. H. bzw. Hermen; 3. ein Privataltar (Kos, 3. Jh. v. Chr.), an dem H. neben anderen Göttern inschr. benannt ist; 4. evtl. Alki. 2,35: Eine Frau bringt je nach Lesart dem H. im Demos Alopeke (Hs.) bzw. einer Person namens H. oder auch dem Steinhaufen (*hérma*) des Phaidrias eine → Eiresione dar.

Wohl nicht ganz zufällig ist die Präsenz des H. in der Ikonographie am stärksten (ab dem letzten Viertel des 4. Jh. v. Chr. [3. 283]; Überblick [3; 4. 659–661; 5; 6. 83–103]), auf die neben Ovid die Nachwirkung zurückgeht. In den H. der Alchemisten fließen die Ovid-Allegorie und weitere ant. Androgynievorbilder ein.

1 J. Kirchner, St. Dow, in: MDAI(A) 62, 1937, 7–8, Abb. 4–5 **2** R. G. Ussher, The Characters of Theophrastus, 1960, z.St. **3** A. Ajootian, s. v. H., LIMC 5.1, 268–285; 5.2, 190–198 **4** M. Delcourt, K. Hoheisel, s. v. H., RAC 14, 650–682 **5** M. Delcourt, Hermaphroditea. Recherches sur l'être double promoteur de fertilité dans le monde classique, 1966 **6** Dies., Hermaphrodite. Mythes et rites de la Bisexualité dans l'Antiquité classique, 1958 **7** J. Jessen, s. v. H., RE 7, 714–721.

T.H.

Hermarchos (Ἕρμαρχος). Geb. in Mytilene auf Lesbos, Zeitgenosse des → Epikuros. In seiner Jugend Ausbildung in Rhet.; Begegnung mit Epikur in Mytilene um 310 v. Chr. H. wandte sich der Philos. nicht sofort zu; erst nach Epikurs Schulgründung (306 v. Chr.) folgte er seinem Lehrer nach Athen. Zw. 290 und 270 v. Chr. ging er nach Lampsakos, um die dortige epikureische Schule zu besuchen. Bei seinem Tod im Jahre 270 v. Chr. übertrug Epikur H., obwohl dieser Metöke war, die Leitung der Athener Schule. H. starb im hohen Alter an Paralyse; sein Nachfolger als Leiter der Schule war Polystratos.

Diogenes Laertios (10,25 = [1. fr. 25]) überliefert folgende Werktitel: ›Abhandlungen in Briefform‹ (Ἐπιστολικά); ›Gegen Empedokles in 22 B.‹ (Πρὸς Ἐμπεδόκλεα, εἴκοσι καὶ δύο); ›Über die Wiss.‹ (Περὶ μαθημάτων); ›Gegen Platon‹ (Πρὸς Πλάτωνα); ›Gegen Aristoteles‹ (Πρὸς Ἀριστοτέλην). Hinzu kommen mindestens zwei H. zugeschriebene Sentenzen [1. fr. 23, 24], einige Briefe [1. fr. 40–42] sowie einige von Philodemos und späteren Autoren bezeugte Aussagen zu ethischen Themen [1. fr. 43–48]. Ein Werk mit dem Titel Ἐπιστολικά περὶ Ἐμπεδοκλέος (›Briefe über Empedokles‹) hat H. nie geschrieben. Es handelt sich vielmehr um zwei verschiedene Werke; deren zweites trägt den Titel Πρὸς Ἐμπεδόκλεα (›Gegen Empedokles‹) [1. 33; 3].

Seine Entstehungszeit [1. fr. 27–34] ist ungewiß. Aus Philodemos [1. fr. 29] geht hervor, daß sein letztes Buch vor dem 12. Buch von Epikurs *De natura* (vor 301 v. Chr. entstanden) geschrieben wurde. Unklar ist, ob das Werk sich gegen Empedokles' *Katharmoí* richtet. Das umfangreichste Frg. findet sich in Porphyrios' *De abstinentia* [1. fr. 34]; es geht darin um die Entstehung des Rechts in der primitiven Gesellschaft. Die übrigen Fragmente behandeln theologische Fragen [1. fr. 27 und 29–32]. Möglicherweise sind dem ›Gegen Empedokles‹ auch einige Fragmente, in denen es um die Dämonen (*daímones*) [1. fr. 50] und die Wunder (*térata*) [1. fr. 51] des Empedokles und um die Seelenwanderung [1. fr. 52] geht, zuzurechnen. Die Annahme, Epikurs Sentenzen 31–40 seien auf H.' ›Gegen Empedokles‹ zurückzuführen, ist haltlos.

Ein mit 267/6 v. Chr. genau datierter »Brief« aus den Ἐπιστολικά (›Abhandlungen in Briefform‹) an einen im übrigen unbekannten Theopheides findet sich in Philodemos' ›Rhet.‹ [1. fr. 35; 36; vgl. fr. 37–39]. Er enthält eine Polemik des H. gegen den Megariker → Alexinos von Elis, in der H. wie Epikur und Metrodoros die Auffassung vertritt, nur der sophistischen Rhet. sei der Status einer Kunst (τέχνη) zuzuerkennen. Auf das Werk ›Gegen Platon‹ (Πρὸς Πλάτωνα) bezieht sich eine Stelle bei Proklos [1. fr. 48], in der es um die Zweckmäßigkeit von Gebeten geht.

Von den übrigen Werken ist nichts erhalten. Immerhin finden sich in den ant. Quellen Zeugnisse von Aussagen H.' zu Zorn [1. fr. 43], Schmeichelei [1. fr. 44], Freundschaft [1. fr. 45] und zur Notwendigkeit eines genügsamen Lebens [1. fr. 47]. Darüber hinaus gibt es Belege für die Existenz eines Briefwechsels [1. fr. 40–42].

→ Epikuros; Epikureische Schule

1 F. Longo, Ermarco. Frammenti, 1988 **2** M. Erler, GGPh² 4.1, 227–234 **3** D. Obbink, H., Against Empedocles, in: CQ 38, 1988, 428–435.

T.D./Ü: S.P.

Hermas, Hermae Pastor. Bei dem Werk ›Der Hirt des H.‹ (griech. nur Ποιμήν/*Poimḗn*, lat. *Liber pastoris nuntii paenitentiae* bzw. *Liber Hermae prophetae*) handelt es sich um eine christl. prophetische Schrift, mit Stilmerkmalen einer → Apokalypse, ohne jedoch diesem Genre ganz zu entsprechen. Sie wird h. zu den Apostolischen Vätern (→ Apostelväter) gezählt. Der Titel ›Hirt‹ (Ποιμήν) für das Gesamtwerk erscheint bereits im *Canon Muratori*, einem westl. Kanonverzeichnis (eher Ende 2. Jh. als 4. Jh.: Z. 74); der Titel deckt allerdings nur den zweiten Teil des Werkes (visio 5 bis similitudo 10) ab, in dem ein Buß-, Schutz- und Strafengel in der Gestalt eines Hirten als Offenbarer auftritt. Der Text dürfte in Rom verfaßt worden sein. Im Angesicht neuer Verfolgungen richtet der Verf. einen Bußruf an die Leser und predigt eine (damals theologisch noch heftig umstrittene) einmalige weitere Vergebung der Sünden nach der Taufe (mandatum 4,3,1).

Das Buch ist vom Verf. selbst in fünf ὁράσεις (*visiones*), zwölf ἐντολαί (*mandata*) und zehn παραβολαί (*similitudines*) eingeteilt (vis. 5); die ersten vier *visiones* erhält der Verf. auf einem Acker an der Straße nach Cumae von einer alten Frau, die er für die Sibylle hält, die sich aber als Kirche vorstellt (vis. 2,4,1); im Rest des Buches erscheint ein Hirte. Die *mandata* enthalten ethische Weisungen, die *similitudines* Gleichnisse.

Trotz verschiedener Spannungen und lit. Brüche haben sich Theorien über verschiedene Autoren des Gesamtwerkes nicht durchsetzen können. Man nimmt gegenwärtig gern eine sukzessive Entstehung durch die Hand *eines* Autors an; nach BROX [1. 27–29] sind die älteren vis. 1–4 mit dem jüngeren ›Hirtenbuch‹ (mand. und sim. 1–8) redaktionell (vis. 5) verbunden worden.

Der Autor der Schrift nennt sich Hermas (vis. 1,1,4; 2,2,2) und will von seinem Ziehvater (θρέψας) und Besitzer nach Rom an eine gewisse Rhode verkauft worden sein (vis. 1,1,1). Zur Zeit der Abfassung lebt er dort offenbar als freigelassener Geschäftsmann und stilisiert sich als bußbedürftigen Sünder; nach dem *Canon Muratori* war er ein Bruder des Pius, der anachronistisch als ›Bischof von Rom‹ bezeichnet (Z. 73–77) und dessen Amtszeit von der späteren röm. Bischofsliste auf 140–155 n. Chr. datiert wird. Nach Origenes (comm. in epistulam ad Romanos 10,31, PG 14, 1282, kritischer ist Eus. HE 3,3,6) ist sogar der im paulinischen Röm 16,14 erwähnte H. gemeint. Alle diese Angaben können nicht unbesehen als histor. Informationen verwendet werden, weil sie lit. und theologischen Interessen dienen bzw. aus gelehrter Spekulation stammen. Sicher ist, daß der Autor eine (auch sprachlich) recht schlichte, aber deswegen umso interessantere »Laientheologie« vertritt, die vermutlich dem Denken breiter Kreise der röm. Gemeinde eher entsprach als die Theologie von gebildeten Christen wie → Iustinos Martyr.

Der Text des ›Hirten‹, der zu den populärsten Büchern der christl. Ant. gehörte und offenbar in einzelnen Gemeinden sogar im Gottesdienst gelesen wurde, ist erst seit 1855 griech. wieder weitgehend durch zwei Hss. (allerdings unvollständig) belegt [3. IX-XII], dazu durch eine größere Menge von Papyri (vgl. [4; 5]). Von Bed. für die Textkonstitution sind ferner die alten Übers. (v.a. lat.: *Versio Vulgata*, 2. Jh.; *Versio Palatina*, 4./5. Jh.; dazu eine äthiop. und Fr. kopt. Übertragungen). Eine neue Textausgabe, die alle Fr. berücksichtigt, fehlt bislang.

1 N. BROX, Der Hirt des Hermas, übersetzt und erklärt (Komm. zu den apostolischen Vätern 7), 1991 **2** A. CARLINI (Ed.), Erma: Il Pastore (Ia-IIIa visione) Papyrus Bodmer XXXVIII, 1991 **3** M. WHITTAKER (Ed.), Der Hirt des Hermas (GCS 48), [2]1956 **4** A. GIACCONE, Papyrus Bodmer XXXVIII, 1991 **5** K. ALAND†, H.-U. ROSENBAUM, Repertorium der griech. christl. Papyri (Patristische Texte und Stud. 42), 1995, 232–311: KV 29–43. C.M.

Hermathena, Hermerakles. Cicero bezeichnet als H. die ihm von Atticus 67–65 v. Chr. für sein Tusculanum besorgten → Hermen der Athena und des Herakles (Cic. Att. 1,1; 4; 8; 9; 10). Die Bronzeköpfe saßen auf Marmorschäften und galten als passendes *ornamentum* für das mit der *Academia* und einem Gymnasium verglichene Peristyl. Der Terminus ist eine Wortschöpfung Ciceros. Die Aufstellung derartiger H. in röm. Villengärten fand weite Verbreitung.

R. NEUDECKER, Die Skulpturenausstattung röm. Villen in Italien, 1988, 11–18 • H. WREDE, Die ant. Herme, 1986, 59f. R.N.

Hermeias (Ἑρμείας) s.a. Hermias.

[1] von Methymna. Wohl 4. Jh. v. Chr. Erster »ausländischer« Verf. von *Sikeliká*, die 10 oder 12 B. umfaßten und bis 376/5 reichten (Diod. 15,37,3). Da nur ein einziges Fr. erh. ist, scheint er die Überl. kaum beeinflußt zu haben.

FR.: FGrH 558.
LIT.: K. MEISTER, Die griech. Geschichtsschreibung, 1990, 69. K.MEI.

[2] aus Kurion, Iambendichter aus hell. Zeit. Von ihm überliefert Athen. 13,563d-e (= CollAlex. p. 237) fünf Choliamben, die eine harsche Kritik an den Stoikern wegen deren Lebensführung enthalten, die in deutlichem Gegensatz zu ihrer eigenen Lehre stehe. Er ist vielleicht mit dem Verf. eines aus vier Kretikern bestehenden Verses gleichzusetzen, den Heph. περὶ ποιημάτων 3,5, p. 65 CONSBRUCH (= SH 484) zitiert.

M.D.MA./Ü: T.H.

Hermen. *Hermai* (ἕρμαι, »Hermesköpfe«), auch *hermádion* (»kleiner Hermes«), *schēma tetrágōnon*, *tetráglōchis*, bezeichnet in der griech.-röm. Kunst eine Sonderform anthropoider Rundplastik. Die Herme besteht aus einem Pfeiler mit Kopf, mit zumeist hölzernen seitlichen Balkenstümpfen anstelle der Arme (*cheíres*, *cunei*) und einem vorne angebrachten männlichen Geschlechtsorgan, das bei frühen H. stets ithyphallisch ist. Doppelhermen tragen zwei voneinander abgewandte Köpfe. Auch Drei- und Vierfachhermen auf einem Pfeiler sind anzutreffen. Bei arkad. H. werden bis zu fünf Pfeiler verbunden nebeneinander gesetzt. Die menschliche Gestalt ist umfangreicher ausgeführt bei Fußhermen, Schulterhermen, Hüfthermen und bei Körperhermen, an denen der Körper meist mit dem Unterleib aus dem Schaft wächst, seltener bereits an den Oberschenkeln. Gewandhermen, die den Übergang von Pfeiler zu Körper unklar lassen, werden häufig für weibliche H. verwendet.

H. leiten sich von anikonischen Steinmalen her, die seit vorarcha. Zeit an Wegkreuzungen, Grenzen, Eingängen und Gräbern für → Hermes als Gott des Übergangs aufgestellt waren. Die kanonische Form wurde in Attika geschaffen, als Hipparchos 130 H. mit Sinnsprüchen an den Straßen aufstellen ließ (522–514 v. Chr.). Ihre rasche Verbreitung ist durch die Vasenmalerei dokumentiert. Die anfangs immer bärtigen Hermes-H. waren ab dem 5. Jh. v. Chr. in Athen an Heiligtümern anzutreffen (Hermes Propylaios des → Alkamenes [2]), dienten auf der Agora zur Aufzeichnung von Urkunden und in Gymnasien als Hermes Logios zur Vermittlung eines Erziehungsideals. Ihre rel. Bed. beweist der Hermenskandal (→ Hermokopidenfrevel) von 415 v. Chr. Ab dem 4. Jh. v. Chr. wird der

Kreis der mittels H. dargestellten Götter und myth. Wesen zunehmend ausgeweitet, doch bleibt die Fruchtbarkeitssymbolik der phallischen H. durch die Beschränkung auf den dionysisch-aphrodisischen Kreis gewahrt. Theseus und Herakles schließen sich an den Hermes Logios der Gymnasien an. Priapos-H. entstanden aus Holzpfählen und sind daher als Körperhermen mit abwärts sich verjüngendem Schaft gebildet. In hell. Landschafts- und Sakralreliefs sind H. ein immer präsentes Ortsmerkmal. Dementsprechend treten H. auch als Stützfiguren an dionysisch-aphrodisischen Statuen auf.

Die Verwendung von H. für zeitgenössische Porträts setzt in der röm. Plastik im 1. Jh. v. Chr. ein, begünstigt durch die Trad. der ital. Kopfcippen (→ *cippus*). Ob sie anfangs als Hinweis auf die Fruchtbarkeit des → Genius des Porträtierten zu deuten sind, ist umstritten. Bald werden H. zu einer kostensparenden Aufstellungspraxis, weshalb wohl Kaiserporträts vor der Spätant. nicht als H. gebildet werden. Mit histor. Porträts zumeist von Geistesheroen wird die Funktion der griech. Gymnasium-H. ab dem 1. Jh. v. Chr. in die Gartenausstattung (→ Garten) der Villen übertragen (Villa dei papiri [1]). Durch Reihung entstanden H.-Galerien, die zu Geländern verbunden werden konnten. In spätant. H.-Galerien verselbständigte sich die Form mit einer beliebigen Auswahl an Köpfen (Welschbillig [2]), so daß sie auch in christl. Ambiente aufgestellt werden konnten.

Eine funktionalistische Ausweitung der H. in röm. Zeit bringt die Verwendung in architektonischem Verband als Stützen, Geländerteile, Brunnenläufe oder im Kleinformat an Möbeln.

→ Hermathena; Holz; Kultbild

1 R. Neudecker, Die Skulpturenausstattung röm. Villen in It., 1988, 65–67, 105–114 2 H. Wrede, Die spätant. Hermengalerie von Welschbillig, 1972.

J. L. Keith, Herms of Egypt, 1975 • R. Lullies, Die Typen der griech. Herme, 1931 • P. Mingazzini, s. v. erma, EAA 3, 1960, 420–421 • A. Stähli, Ornamentum Academiae. Kopien griech. Bildnisse in Hermenform, in: Acta Hyperboraea 4, 1992, 147–172 • H. Wrede, Die ant. Herme, 1986 • Ders., Die spätant. Herme, in: JbAC 30, 1987, 118–148. R.N.

Hermenericus

[1] s. Ermanarich

[2] Jüngster Sohn des Flavius Ardabur [2] Aspar (Candidus FHG 4, 135), *cos.* 465 n. Chr. (Chron. min. 3,535 Mommsen). Bei der Ermordung des Vaters rettete er sich, vielleicht mit Hilfe Zenons, dessen Tochter H. heiratete, durch Flucht aus Konstantinopel, kehrte aber später zurück (Theophanes a. 5964). PLRE 2,549 (Herminericus). ME.STR.

Hermeneutik. Im Sinne einer alltäglichen, unreflektierten Erfahrung der Interpretation von Texten gab es H. in der Ant. nicht weniger als später; verstanden dagegen als die systematische Ausarbeitung eines Regelverfahrens, das die Interpretation kontrollieren und leiten soll, entstand sie erst in der frühen Neuzeit [5]. Das Wortfeld ἑρμηνεύειν (*hermēneúein*) bedeutet urspr. »ausdrücken, übersetzen« [17] und wird wohl erst von Platon im übertragenen Sinne von »interpretieren« gebraucht [12]. Aristoteles' Περὶ ἑρμηνείας (*Perí hermēneías, De interpretatione*) ist keine Theorie der Auslegung, sondern des Ausdrucks.

Die ant. Ansätze zu einer systemat. Auslegungslehre sind spärlich und spät; bis in die Spätant. blieb die H. mit wenigen Ausnahmen das Betätigungsfeld nicht des theorisierenden Philosophen, sondern des weniger angesehenen praktischen Grammatikers [18]. In Ermangelung der Bedingungen, die die Entstehung der modernen H. im 17. Jh. begünstigten – ein immer akuter werdendes Gesch.-Bewußtsein, die sich daraus ergebende Problematisierung der Unterschiede zw. sakralem Text und geänderten Umständen, die Ablehnung der gerade zur Behebung solcher Unterschiede entwikkelten Allegorese, die Institutionalisierung und Standardisierung einer angesehenen Exegetenkaste, das mod. Vertrauen in Regelverfahren – blieb es in der ant. H. eher bei impliziten Tendenzen als ausgearbeiteten Systemen [10].

Wichtigste Tendenz der ant. H. ist die → Allegorese, die den Zeitunterschied zw. Text und Rezipienten mittels einer vermeintlich allzeit gültigen philos. ὑπόνοια (*hypónoia*, »Unter-sinn«) bzw. ἀλληγορία (*allēgoría*, »Anderes Sagen«) aufhebt [2. 16]. Schon bei Homer in Ansätzen greifbar [14], aber als lit. Gattung erst als rettende Reaktion auf die allmähliche Verschriftlichung und dadurch erhöhte Unveränderlichkeit der homer. Epen entstanden (→ Theagenes von Rhegion), blieb die Allegorese über die Ant. hinaus ein wirksames Mittel, um das Prestige der bekannten Dichter für bezweifelbare Lehrsätze einzusetzen [13]. Im späten 5. Jh. v. Chr. betrieben → Anaxagoras und → Metrodoros von Lampsakos sowie der Autor des sog. Derveni-Papyrus [15] Homer- und Orpheusallegorese; danach verschrieben sich alle ant. Philosophenschulen (außer den Epikureern und der mittleren Akademie) der Allegorese, mit einem für ihre spätere Rezeption wichtigen Höhepunkt im Neuplatonismus [6].

Daneben waren drei weitere Tendenzen von eher sporadischer Bedeutung: (1) Biographismus. Schon Aristophanes zog aus lit. Texten zu komischen Zwecken boshafte Rückschlüsse auf die Persönlichkeit ihrer Autoren. Die seriöse Ausweitung dieses Ansatzes, bes. in der peripatetischen Literaturgesch., sowie der hell. und kaiserzeitlichen Biographie [1], führte zu mancher in den ma. Dichterviten erh. (und bis in die jüngste Zeit noch wirkenden) Absurdität [7].

(2) Historisierung. Unter den vielen Ansätzen zur Lösung der Einwände gegen Homer, die Aristoteles in der ›Poetik‹ c. 25 sammelt, findet sich auch der Hinweis auf die eigentümlichen Bedingungen der heroischen Zeit (›so dachten sie‹; 60b 10; 61a2) als Entschuldigung für einzelne fragliche Details. Diese Historisierung ist

der ant. H. ansonsten eher fremd, mit der wichtigen Ausnahme des → Aristarchos [4] von Samothrake, der das Prinzip, ›Homer durch Homer zu erklären‹ durch die Auffassung eines einheitlichen Heroenzeitalters rechtfertigte [19].

(3) Formalismus. Die mikroskopische und makroskopische Analyse der formellen Elemente der Dichtung geht auf die Sophistik zurück, wurde aber für die ant. Philos. durch Platons Einwände weitestgehend disqualifiziert und blieb daher der ant. Gramm. vorenthalten [11]. Die Aufarbeitung der spärlichen Spuren dieses Ansatzes in den ant. Scholien hat begonnen [9], die Grammatiker sind dagegen meist noch unerforscht. Erst in den kaiserzeitl. Philosophenschulen (allen voran der platonisch-aristotelischen) führten verschiedene Faktoren zur Entstehung einer rudimentären H. [3. 4]: die Kanonizität eines begrenzten Textcorpus von erheblicher interpretatorischer Schwierigkeit; die lange Sukzession von Lehrmeistern, die ihre Vorgänger verehren, aber gleichzeitig korrigieren und selbst durch Interpretation derselben Grundtexte legitimiert sind; eine Tendenz zur philos. Systematisierung und didaktischer Reglementierung. In einigen Prolegomena (z. B. Anon. Prolegomena in Plat. Phil. 3,13–10,26, S. 25–49 WESTERINK; Olympiodori Prolegomena = CAG 12.1, S. 6.6–14.11 BUSSE) und Proömien zu Einzelkomm. (Ammonii in Cat. Prooemium = CAG 4.4, S. 3.20–8.19 BUSSE; Simplicii in Cat. Prooemium = CAG 8, S. 3.18–9.31 KALBFLEISCH; Eliae in Cat. Prooemium = CAG 18.1, S. 113.17–129.3 BUSSE) werden die Themen jeglicher Interpretation philos. Schriften schulmeisterhaft aufgezählt und erläutert: für Platon Schrifttum, Dialogform, Charaktere, Zeit, Ort, Stil, Methode, Titel, Werkeinteilung, Darstellungsform, Thema, Anordnung der Dialoge, Echtheit; für Aristoteles Einteilung des Corpus, lit. Gattung, Anordnung der Werke, Zweck, Eigenart des angemessenen Studenten und Interpreten, Darstellungsform, Dunkelheit, Interpretationsziele, Echtheit [8].

1 G. ARRIGHETTI, Poeti, eruditi e biografi. Momenti della riflessione dei greci sulla letteratura, 1987 **2** F. BUFFIÈRE, Les mythes d'Homère et la pensée grecque, 1956 **3** J. COULTER, The Literary Microcosm. Theories of Interpretation of the Later Neoplatonists, 1976 **4** D. DAWSON, Allegorical Readers and Cultural Revision in Ancient Alexandria, 1992 **5** H. G. GADAMER, Wahrheit und Methode, 1960 **6** R. LAMBERTON, Homer the Theologian. Neoplatonist Allegorical Reading and the Growth of the Epic Tradition, 1986 **7** M. LEFKOWITZ, The Lives of the Greek Poets, 1981 **8** J. MANSFELD, Prolegomena. Questions to be Settled before the Study of an Author, or a Text, 1994 **9** R. MEIJERING, Literary and Rhetorical Theories in Greek Scholia, 1987 **10** G. W. MOST, Rhet. und H.: Zur Konstitution der Neuzeitlichkeit, in: A&A 30, 1984, 62–79 **11** Ders., Sophistique et hermeneutique, in: B. CASSIN (Hrsg.), Positions de la Sophistique. Colloque de Cérisy, 1986, 233–45 **12** Ders., Pindar, O. 2.83–90, in: CQ 36, 1986, 308–311 **13** Ders., Cornutus and Stoic Allegoresis: A Preliminary Report, in: ANRW II 36.3, 2014–2065 **14** Ders., Die früheste erh. griech. Dichterallegorese, in: RhM 136, 1993, 209–212 **15** Ders., The Fire Next Time. Cosmology, Allegoresis, and Salvation in the Derveni Papyrus, in: JHS 117, 1997, 117–135 **16** J. PÉPIN, Mythe et allégorie. Les origines grecques et les contestations judéochrétiennes, ²1976 **17** Ders., L'herméneutique ancienne. Les mots et les idées, in: Poétique 23, 1973, 291–300 **18** R. PFEIFFER, History of Classical Scholarship from the Beginnings to the End of the Hellenistic Age, 1968 **19** M. SCHMIDT, Die Erklärungen zum Weltbild Homers und zur Kultur der Heroenzeit in den bT-Scholien zur Ilias, 1976.

G. W. M.

Hermericus. 419–438 n. Chr. König der Suebi, kämpfte 419 erfolglos gegen die Vandalen in Spanien (Hydatius Lemiensis 71). Nach Plünderungen der Gallaecia 430 und 433 (ebd. 91; 100) schloß er Frieden, trat erkrankt 438 die Herrschaft an seinen Sohn Rechila ab und starb 441 (ebd. 114; 122). PLRE 2,546 f. ME. STR.

Hermes (Ἑρμῆς, ep. auch Ἑρμείας, Ἑρμείης, Ἑρμάων)
I. KULT UND MYTHOS II. IKONOGRAPHIE

I. KULT UND MYTHOS
A. STECKBRIEF B. GOTT DER HERME
C. GOTT DER HIRTEN
D. GOTT DER BOTEN UND HEROLDE
E. HERMES ALS MYSTERIENGOTT

A. STECKBRIEF

Der mythischen Trad. nach in Arkadien beheimateter, jedoch gemeingriech. verehrter Gott, dessen Name schon auf Linear B für die myk. Zeit bezeugt ist [1. 285 f.]. Ein unter die ethnolog. Kategorie des Tricksters subsumierbarer Kulturbringer mit bes. Beziehung zum Hirtenleben; er fungierte im Epos als Bote und Herold des Zeus und galt schließlich als ein mit universalem Wissen und umfassender kommunikativer Kompetenz ausgestatteter Gott, von dem sich Händler Schutz und Beistand, Mystagogen und Verfasser esoterischer Lit. Legitimation erhofften. Mit dem röm. → Mercurius identifiziert.

B. GOTT DER HERME

Seinem Namen nach ist H. der Gott der Herme (→ Hermen; s. auch unten II.), eines teilanthropomorphen steinernen Pfeilers, der in Griechenland Hauseingänge (Thuk. 6,27; Athen. 10,437b) sowie die Grenzen von Grundstücken (z. B. Anth. Pal. 9,314) und städtischen Territorien (Paus. 2,38,7; 3,10,6; 8,34,6) markierte [2; 1. 299–306 Nr. 58, 75, 76, 78, 79, 81, 87, 92–179], wodurch er auch Wegweiserfunktion übernahm (Suda, s. v. ἑρμαῖον). Die erwünschte – eine dauernde Vigilanz des Reviereigentümers ersetzende – Signalwirkung des Grenzsteins wurde mit virilen Imponiermerkmalen, d. h. bärtigem Gesicht und erigiertem Phallos [3], verstärkt [4]. Die Sakralisierung schützte das provokante Grenzzeichen vor Übergriffen, zu denen es in Zeiten polit. Spannungen gleichwohl kam: Vor der sizil. Expedition wurden die stadtathen. Hermen verstümmelt (Thuk. 6,27) [5] (→ Hermokopidenfrevel).

Auf dem freien Land bewarfen Wanderer die Hermen mit Steinen, die sich in Haufen um sie herum ansammelten; ein solches Mal hieß Hermaion (Cornutus 16; Eust. ad Hom. Od. 16,471 [6. 48]). Der Brauch hatte die pragmat. Funktion, die Wege von Steinen zu befreien, und erlaubte zugleich, auf das herausfordernde apotropäische Signal mit einem Akt zielgehemmter Aggression zu reagieren, was im Resultat das Grenzmal verstärkte und seine Funktion gerade nicht in Frage stellte. Dem aitiologischen Mythos zufolge entstand das Hermaion durch eine symbolische Steinigung: Die Götter wagten aus Furcht vor Zeus nicht, H. wegen der Tötung des → Argos [I 5] zu verurteilen, worauf sie ihm die Stimmsteine vor die Füße warfen (schol. Hom. Od. 16,471). Als kult. Grenzzeichen zw. Gärten und Ödland waren Hermen Rastplätze (Anth. Pal. 9,314), an denen Gartenbesitzer Obst und Hirten Milch als Opfergaben für H. deponierten (Anth. Pal. 9,316; 318). Sie standen jedem, der hier ausruhte, als Proviant zur Verfügung; daher hieß ein solcher Fund *hermaíon*, was dann zu einem Namen für unverhofften Gewinn schlechthin wurde (Suda, s. v. ἑρμαῖον). Der Nahrungstribut beugte sicherlich Plünderungen vor: Er sollte die Vorbeikommenden davon abhalten, eigenmächtig in fremden Besitz einzudringen, um sich an Obstgärten und Vieh zu vergreifen.

C. Gott der Hirten 1. Beziehung zum Hirtenleben 2. Viehraubmythos
3. Kulturentstehung und Initiationsfest
4. Saturnalienartige Hermesfeste

1. Beziehung zum Hirtenleben

Weil die Herme das von Viehherden beweidete Ödland vom Kulturland trennte, wurde H. als Gott des Grenzmals insbes. zum Patron männlicher Jugendlicher, die das Vieh zu beaufsichtigen und von den Feldern fernzuhalten hatten [6. 48]. In der Dichtung wird H. regelmäßig, in der ikonograph. Überl. seit der klass. Zeit, als Jugendlicher dargestellt. Als Hirtengott war er für den Schutz (Anth. Pal. 6,334; 16,190), das Gedeihen und die Vermehrung der Viehherden zuständig (Hom. Il. 14,490f.; Hes. theog. 444; Hom. h. 4,567–573). Hirten verehrten ihn durch Opfer, so im homer. Epos der Schweinehirt Eumaios (Hom. Od. 14,435). Verbunden war H. daher auch den Hirtenfesten und ihren ästhet. Ausdrucksformen. In einem Mythos der Insel Kos bestraft er Bauern, die sich von der Hirtenfeier fernhalten, indem er sie in Vögel verwandelt (Antoninus Liberalis 15). Der arkad. Hirtengott → Pan galt als Sohn des H. (Hom. h. 19,1), desgleichen der Hirtenjüngling → Daphnis [1], der auf Sizilien als Urheber des Hirtenlieds verehrt wurde (Stesich. fr. 102 PMG; Timaios FGrH 566 F 83; Diod. 4,84,2).

2. Viehraubmythos

Der Viehraubmythos, dessen älteste Fassung der homer. H.-Hymnos bietet (behandelt u. a. auch von Alkaios nach Paus. 7,20,4; Apollod. 3,112–115), läßt sich als Begründung der Viehzucht und einiger der Hirtenfunktion eignenden technischen Fertigkeiten lesen: In einer arkad. Höhle als Sohn des → Zeus und der → Maia geboren, steigt H. gleich nach seiner Geburt aus der Getreideschwinge (Hom. h. 4,18ff.), wandert nach Thessalien, raubt dort die bislang unsterbliche Rinderherde seines älteren Halbbruders → Apollon und treibt sie, die Spuren listig beseitigend, zur Peloponnes. Dort versteckt er die Tiere in einer Höhle, mit Ausnahme von zweien, die er schlachtet und auf einem eigens hierzu mit Reibhölzern neu entfachten Feuer brät (108ff.). Das auf Spieße gesteckte Fleisch, von dem er selbst nichts ißt, teilt er in zwölf Portionen (*moírai*, Hom. h. 4,128): ein Aition des Zwölfgötteropfers, wie es in Olympia praktiziert wurde, wo H. sich mit Apollon einen Altar teilte (Paus. 5,14,8; schol. Pind. O. 5,10; [7]). Als Apollon, dem H. auf Befehl des Zeus die gestohlenen Rinder zurückgeben muß, den überführten Räuber mit Lygos-Zweigen fesselt, beginnen diese wundersam zu wachsen, verwurzeln sich im Boden, schlingen sich umeinander und um die Kühe (Hom. h. 4,409ff.). So entsteht aus der Demonstration eines aufrechterhaltenen Besitzanspruchs der mythische Prototyp des Zauns, der fortan Weidewirtschaft und Viehzucht ermöglicht [8. 1ff.].

H. gelingt es, seinen Halbbruder dazu zu überreden, ihm die Herde zu überlassen, und zwar im Tausch gegen die siebensaitige Leier und den auf ihr begleiteten theogonischen Gesang, den H. damals erstmals anstimmt (Hom. h. 4,425ff.). Diese Leier hat er vorher aus dem Panzer einer Schildkröte konstruiert, indem er sie mit den Sehnen der Opfertiere bespannte (47ff.; hiernach stammen die Saiten von Schafen, nach anderer Version hingegen von den Rindern: Apollod. 3,113). Apollon überläßt ihm außer der Rinderherde auch die Arbeitsinstrumente des Hirten, Peitsche und Stab, sowie ein ländliches Losorakel (Hom. h. 4,496ff.). So wird der jüngere Bruder sein Nachfolger im Hirtenamt, aus dem Apollon selbst nun, an der Grenze zum Erwachsenenalter stehend, ausscheidet.

3. Kulturentstehung und Initiationsfest

Die mythische Biographie des H. präformiert auf der archetypischen Ebene des Göttermythos die frühen Phasen der Kulturentwicklung vor dem Entstehen der Landwirtschaft und der Städte (→ Kulturentstehung): Als Erfinder des Feuers und des blutigen Opfers ist der Hirte H. eine Konkurrenzfigur des Tricksters → Prometheus, als Schöpfer des Saiteninstruments und des dazu angestimmten theogonischen Gesangs erscheint er als Urheber eines ästhet. Rahmenprogramms, wie es offenbar zu Festen des sozialen Statuswechsels gehörte. Wie Apollon soll auch der »Umgänger« → Amphion [1], ebenfalls ein jugendlicher Hirte, seine Leier von H. erhalten haben, worauf er mit dem bloßen Saitenspiel die Stadtmauern des siebentorigen Theben erbaute (Paus. 9,5,7f.). Daß dies als Reflex eines die Stadtgründung inszenierenden Umgangsrituals zu verstehen ist, durch das adoleszente Hirten in die Bürgerschaft aufgenommen wurden, zeigt der analoge Kult der boiot. Stadt Tanagra. Hier wurde ein H. Kriophoros (»Widderträger«) verehrt. Am Fest des Gottes trug der Ephebe, der als der schönste der Stadt galt, ein Lamm um die Stadtmauern. Das geschah in ritueller Wiederholung eines mythischen Urereignisses: Um eine Seuche abzuwehren, hatte einst der Hirtengott selbst einen Widder um die Mauern Tanagras getragen (Paus. 9,22,1). Der die Grenzen der Stadt erneuernde Umgang reinszenierte also periodisch die Überwindung einer imaginären existenzbedrohenden Krise.

Der lebensgesch. Übergangssituation der Adoleszenz war H. hier noch in anderer Weise verbunden: Er soll einst die Epheben Tanagras in die Schlacht gegen die Eritreer geführt und selbst mit dem Schaber mitgekämpft haben. Weil er den Tanagräern dadurch zum Sieg verhalf, wurde H. hier auch unter dem Beinamen Promachos (»Vorkämpfer«) verehrt (Paus. 9,22,2). Nach einer auf die gleiche mythische Schlacht bezogenen Überlieferung hieß ein städtisches Kultbild des Gottes der »Weiße H.«. Errichtet worden war die Statue angeblich zur Erinnerung an die vom Orakel befohlene Opferung eines Jünglings und eines Mädchens (Tzetz. schol. Lykophr. 680): Reflex eines im H.-Fest verankerten symbolischen Todes, den Jugendliche beider Geschlechter stellvertretend für ihre Altersklasse erlitten. Die aitiologische Bezugnahme auf einen Krieg erweist H. als göttliches Paradigma männlicher Jugendlicher, die nach dem Ausscheiden aus dem Hirtenamt in die Wehrgemeinschaft der Erwachsenen aufgenommen werden sollten, ohne ihr schon anzugehören. Daher kämpft H. nicht mit den Waffen des → Hopliten, sondern mit dem Schabinstrument des Sportlers – ein symbol. Hinweis auf den institutionellen Kontext agonistischer Übungen, die männliche Jugendliche auf den späteren Kriegsdienst vorbereiteten. Dem Ephebenheros → Herakles stand H. als Schutzgott der Palästren und Gymnasien zur Seite [9].

4. Saturnalienartige Hermesfeste

Als jugendlicher Hirte steht H. außerhalb des mit dem Ackerbau und dem Erwachsenenleben korrelierten Normensystems. Sein mythischer Viehdiebstahl war Paradigma eines allenfalls vor der Initiation tolerierten Verhaltens, wie etwa in Sparta Jugendliche ausdrücklich die Lizenz zum Raub besaßen (Plut. Lykurgos 17,50ef; vgl. 28,56e zur Krypteia). Das erklärt auch, warum saturnalienartige Feste, welche die soziale Ordnung suspendierten oder umkehrten, bisweilen H. geweiht waren: Auf Samos gab es ein Opferfest für H. Charidotes, an dem es jedem freistand zu stehlen, und zwar in angeblicher Erinnerung an eine zehnjährige Auswanderung der Samier nach Mykale in Karien, während derer sie vom Raub lebten; im Anschluß daran hätten die Exilanten ihre Insel zurückerobert (Plut. qu.Gr. 55). Dieser Mythos versetzt die lebensgesch. Lizenzperiode der Hirtenzeit in die nationale Vorgesch., da die Initianden den Übergang in die Erwachsenenrolle anscheinend in dem Bewußtsein vollzogen, auf den Spuren ihrer Samos erobernden Ahnen zu wandeln. Unklar ist, ob die Sklaven, die bei einem H.-Fest auf Kreta von ihren Herren beim Mahl bedient wurden (Athen. 14,639b), Hirten waren; wenn ja, ist die Frage, ob sich unter ihnen Freigeborene befanden, die während ihrer Hirtenzeit nominell als Sklaven galten, und ob für diese die Teilnahme am Fest einen sozialen Statuswechsel implizierte.

D. Gott der Boten und Herolde

Von sekundären Dienstleistungsfunktionen, zu denen ortsmobile jugendliche Hirten herangezogen werden konnten, läßt sich die Botenrolle ableiten, die H. im Epos zufällt. Zeus schickt ihn zu anderen Göttern und zu Menschen, um Aufträge zu überbringen (Hom. Il. 24,333 ff.; Od. 5,29 ff.). Zw. Himmel und Erde, Ober- und Unterwelt vermittelnd, wird H. zum göttl. Urbild der Dolmetscher und Herolde (Plat. Krat. 408ab). Der autorisierende Heroldstab, den er in der Hand hält, ist der mit neuem Zeichengehalt aufgeladene Hirtenstekken. Ikonographischen Ausdruck findet die Fähigkeit zur Überwindung großer Distanzen in den geflügelten Schuhen, die H. trägt (s.u. II.). Zur Funktion des Grenzen überschreitenden Boten gesellt sich diejenige des wegekundigen Führers: Wie der Viehherde, so gewährt H. ihm anvertrauten Heroen Geleitschutz (Hom. Il. 24,336 ff.; Aischyl. Eum. 90–94), er bringt das → Dionysos-Knäblein zu Aristaios oder den Nymphen (Apollod. 3,28; [1. 365 ff.]), → Pandora zu Epimetheus (Hes. erg. 84 f.), geleitet als Psychopompos die Seelen der Verstorbenen, sie mit seinem goldenen Hirtenstab treibend, in die Unterwelt (Hom. Od. 24,1 ff.); umgekehrt führt er privilegierte Figuren wie → Herakles (Hom. Od. 11,626) oder → Kore (Hom. h. 2,335 ff.) wieder aus dem Totenreich heraus.

E. Hermes als Mysteriengott

Als Gott der Übergänge und Mittler zw. Göttern und Menschen war H. die mythische Präfiguration von Kultfunktionären, die Mysterienriten organisierten. Das Priestergeschlecht der eleusinischen Keryken (»Herolde«) leitete sich von H. und der Kekropstocher Aglauros [2] ab (Paus. 1,38,3). Auf Samothrake wurde H. mit → Kadmos-Kadmilos gleichgesetzt, dem mythischen Prototyp eines bei den Initiationsriten assistierenden Kultdieners (schol. Lykophr. 162). Zwei ithyphallische Statuen des H. (Hippolytus, Refutatio omnium haeresium 5,8,10) evozierten hier das Unsagbare der im Tempelinnern verrichteten Symbolhandlungen (Hdt. 2,51; Cic. nat. deor. 3,56). Pränuptiale sexuelle Einweihungsriten spiegeln sich in einer Vielzahl von Mythen, in denen der Gott mit Nymphen (Hom. h. 5,262 f.) oder menschlichen Mädchen (Hom. Il. 16,181 ff.) Nachkommen zeugt.

Die in Pubertätsweihen verankerte → Mystagogen-Funktion des H. prädestinierte den Gott wiederum dazu, zum Archegeten hell. und spätant. Geheimüberlieferungen zu avancieren, die unter seinem Namen verbreitet waren. Mit dem ägypt. → Thot gleichgesetzt, figuriert H. unter dem Namen H. Trismegistos als pseudonymer Autor esoterischer Lit., die man heute unter dem Begriff der Hermetik (→ Hermetische Schriften) zusammenfaßt. Hierin geht es um die Vermittlung einer totalen kosmischen Schau und eines davon abhängigen Erlösungsweges. In der ersten programmat. Schrift des → Corpus Hermeticum, dem *Poimandres*, befindet sich der spätere Initiationsmeister H., vom Nus persönlich unterwiesen, selbst noch in der urbildlichen Rolle des Initianden. Das Weltbild der Hermetik ist im wesentlichen das des platonischen *Timaios*: Der Geist des Menschen ist durch sieben planetarische Sphären von seiner jenseits der Fixsternsphäre liegenden Heimat getrennt. Schon → Eratosthenes [2] interpretierte die mit sieben Saiten bespannte H.-Leier als Symbol der Sphärenharmonie und ließ H. durch seine Musik die Distanz zw. Himmel und Erde überwinden (fr. 13 CollAlex). Wird hier ein ritueller Hintergrund der hermetischen Visionslit. sichtbar? Die gleiche ägypt.-griech. Trad. setzen die spätant. → Zauberpapyri voraus, in denen sich u.a. Ritualanweisungen für ekstatische Götterschau und Himmelsreisen finden. In den Texten wird H. als Mittler kosmischen Wissens angerufen (PGM 5,401 ff.). H. Trismegistos wird hierbei zur Konkurrenzfigur des mythischen → Zoroastres, des iran. Ahnherrn der → Magier [10].

1 G. Siebert, s.v. H., LIMC 5.1, 285–387 **2** S. Eitrem, s.v. Hermai, RE 15, 696–708 **3** D. Fehling, Ethnologische Überlegungen auf dem Gebiet der Alt.skunde, 1974, 7 ff. **4** D. Furley, Andokides and the Herms, 1996 **5** M.W. de Visser, Die nicht menschengestaltigen Götter der Griechen, 1903, 102 f. **6** A. Athanassakis, From the Phallic Cairn to Shepherd God and Divine Herald, in: Eranos 87, 1989, 33–49 **7** W. Burkert, Sacrificio-sacrilegio: il »trickster« fondatore, in: Studi Storici 25, 1984, 835–845 **8** D. Baudy, Das Keuschlamm-Wunder des H., in: Grazer Beiträge 16, 1989, 1–28 **9** Burkert, 247 **10** G. Fowden, The Egyptian H., 1986.

G. Costa, H., dio delle iniziazioni, in: Civiltà classica e christiana 3, 1982, 277–295 • J. Duchemin, La houlette et la lyre, 1960 • L. Kahn, Hermès passe ou les ambiguités de la communication, 1978 • K. Kerényi, H. der Seelenführer, 1944 • Nilsson, Feste, 392–394 • J.P. Vernant, Hestia-Hermès. Sur l'expression religieuse de l'espace et du mouvement chez les Grecs, in: Ders., Mythe et pensée chez les Grecs I, (1965) 1980, 124–170 • P. Walcot, Cattle Raiding, Heroic Tradition, and Ritual: The Greek Evidence, in: HR 18, 1979, 326–351. G.B.

II. Ikonographie

In frühen Vasenbildern erscheint H. fast ausschließlich als Götterbote und Geleiter; er trägt ein langes Gewand oder einen kurzen → Chiton und eine → Chlamys, oft mit Fellumhang, den → Petasos und häufig auch Flügelschuhe (François-Krater, Florenz, AM, 570/560 v. Chr.); er wird mit oder ohne Bart dargestellt, bis sich Mitte des 5. Jh. v. Chr. der jugendliche Typus weitgehend durchsetzt. Seine charakteristischen Attribute sind der Heroldstab (*kērýkeion/caduceus*) sowie Flügel an Hut oder Stiefeln. Die seine Darstellungen häufig begleitenden Tiere sind Hahn, Hund, Ziege und Widder: als Widderträger der H. Kriophoros (u.a. Bronzestatuette aus Sparta, Boston, MFA, 510/500 v. Chr.). Als Psychopompos führt H. die Verstorbenen in die Unterwelt (Vasenbilder, wenige Reliefs; s.a. Statue des H. Andros-Farnese, London, BM und Athen, NM, nach Original um 350 v. Chr.). H. ist Führer der Göttinnen beim Paris-Urteil (Kanne des → Chigi-Malers in Rom, VG, 640/630 v. Chr.); auf vielen Vasenbildern ist H. u.a. Begleiter der Helden Perseus, Theseus, Herakles, Triptolemos. Die Götterversammlung im Ostfries des → Parthenon (442/438 v. Chr.) zeigt ihn zusammen mit Dionysos, in dessen Kreis H. meist auf Vasen des 6.–5. Jh. v. Chr. erscheint. Als Kämpfer nimmt H. an der → Gigantomachie teil (Siphnier-Schatzhaus in Delphi, um 525 v. Chr.; Parthenon in Athen, Ostmetope 1, 447–441 v. Chr.).

Statuarische Überl. sind der H. Ludovisi (Rom, NM, 2. Jh. n. Chr., nach Original um 450/440 v. Chr., die möglicherweise älteste großplastische Darstellung des Gottes, Phidias ?), der H. mit Dionysoskind (Polyklet, um 440–430 v. Chr.), wahrscheinlich die Marmorstatue Boboli (Florenz, ehem. Giardino Boboli, 2. Jh. n. Chr., vgl. Bronzestatuette von Annecy, Paris, Petit Palais, 1. Jh. v.– 1. Jh. n. Chr.); in polykletischer Trad. der H. Richelieu (Paris, LV, antonin. Kopie, Orig. um 360 v. Chr.); der H. des → Praxiteles aus Olympia, ebenfalls mit Dionysoskind (Marmor-Original?, um 340/330 v. Chr.); der sandalenbindende H. des → Lysippos (Kopenhagen/Paris, LV, Zuschreibung an Lysipp wahrscheinlich, um 310/300 v. Chr.?), der sitzende H. des Lysipp (Bronze, Neapel, NM; nach Orig. um 330/20 v. Chr.?).

Die nach dem Gott benannten → Hermen-Pfeiler sind vom späten 6. Jh. v. Chr. bis in die röm. Kaiserzeit belegt; von → Alkamenes [2] stammt der bärtige H. Propylaios (Ende 5. Jh. v. Chr.: Kopie aus Ephesos, Izmir, Mus. Basmahane, 2. H. 2. Jh. n. Chr.; Typus Pergamon, Istanbul, AM, Kopie des 2. Jh. n. Chr.). In hell.-röm. Zeit diente die Göttergestalt mehrfach als Vorbild hell. Herrscher und röm. Würdenträger (vgl. Statue des Numidierkönigs Ptolemaios in Rabat, Mus., frühes 1. Jh. n. Chr.). Der röm. H. (→ Mercurius) wird als jugendlicher Herold und Geleiter dargestellt, als Gott des Handels und Gewerbes mit → Geldbeutel (*marsupium*); der von H. übernommene *caduceus* gilt seit republikan. Zeit als Friedenssymbol.

J. Floren, Der H. des Polyklet, in: H. Beck, P.C. Bol (Hrsg.), Polykletforsch., 1993, 57–72 • J. Înan, Der Sandalenbindende H., in: Ant. Plastik 22, 1993, 105–116 • H.P. Laubscher, Ein Ptolemäer als H., in: H. Froning u.a. (Hrsg.), Kotinos. FS für E. Simon, 1992, 317–322 • C. Maderna, Juppiter, Diomedes und Merkur als Vorbilder für röm. Bildnisstatuen, 1988 • H. Oggiano-Bitar, Typologie de Mercure en Gaule. Akt. der 10. Internationalen Tagung über ant. Bronzen, 1994, 311–318 • G. Siebert, s.v. H., LIMC 5, 285–387 (mit älterer Lit.) • E. Simon, G. Bauchhenss, s.v. Mercurius, LIMC 6, 500–554 (mit älterer Lit.). A.L.

Hermesianax (Ἑρμησιάναξ). Elegischer Dichter aus Kolophon, Freund und Schüler des → Philetas (schol. Nik. Ther. 3 = fr. 12 POWELL). Er veröffentlichte ein elegisches Gedicht in drei Büchern, das den Namen der geliebten Frau, Leontion, als Titel erhielt und in dem er, aus Mythos und Gesch. schöpfend, von den Erfahrungen berühmter Persönlichkeiten in der Liebe erzählte. Aus dem dritten Buch sind über Athen. 13,597b 98 Verse (= fr. 7 POWELL) erhalten, in denen gezeigt wird, wie die Liebe sowohl Dichter (Orpheus, Musaios, Hesiod, Homer, Mimnermos, Antimachos, Alkaios, Anakreon, Sophokles, Euripides, Philoxenos, Philitas) als auch Philosophen (Pythagoras, Sokrates, Aristippos) bezwang und dazu brachte, große Opfer zu bringen. Das Werk, das sehr wahrscheinlich die *Lýdē* des → Antimachos [3] aus Kolophon zum Vorbild hatte, reiht sich in die Reihe der Katalogdichtung nach ep.-hesiodeischem Muster ein. Zugleich geht aus der chronologisch angeordneten Reihenfolge der Beispiele und der Einteilung der Dichter nach lit. Gattungen deutlich der Einfluß der biographisch-lit. Studien peripatetischer Ausrichtung hervor. Einige der Gesch. sind völlig unwahrscheinlich, reine Erfindungen oder fiktive Verbindungen: Homer soll sich z.B. in Penelope, Hesiod in Eoia (!) verliebt, Alkaios und Anakreon beide Sappho den Hof gemacht haben. Das hat die Hypothese nahegelegt [4], daß H. auf diese Weise versuche, die Vorliebe der zeitgenössischen Biographie zu karikieren, aus den Texten unbegründete Nachrichten abzuleiten und darauf völlig willkürliche Interpretationen aufzubauen. Der Einfluß des H. auf die nachfolgende alexandrinische Katalogdichtung scheint beträchtlich gewesen zu sein.

Jüngst hat man vorgeschlagen [3], H. die Frg. einer zur Gattung der *araí* (→ Fluch) gehörenden Elegie zuzuweisen, deren Autor droht, seinem Feind Bilder schrecklicher myth. Strafen einzutätowieren (PSorb. inv. 2254 und PBrux. inv. E 8934): Darin wurde unter anderem der Mythos des Eurytion behandelt, der, wie Paus. 7,18,1 bezeugt, auch Gegenstand der Elegien des H. war (= fr. 9 POWELL).

1 O. ELLENBERGER, Quaestiones Hermesianacteae, Diss. Gießen 1907 2 J.S. HEIBGES, s.v. H (2), RE 8, 823–28
3 M. HUYS, Le poème élégiaque hellénistique P. Brux. inv. E 8934 et P. Sorb. inv. 2254, 1991 4 P. BING, The bios-tradition and poet's lives in Hellenistic poetry, in: R.M. ROSEN, J. FARRELL (Hrsg.), Nomodeiktes. Greek Studies in Honor of M. Ostwald, 1993, 619–31
5 A. HARDIE, Philitas and the Plane Tree, in: ZPE 119, 1997, 21–36.

CollAlex. p. 96–106.

M.D.MA./Ü: T.H.

Hermetik s. Hermetische Schriften

Hermetische Schriften. Als h.S. (der Terminus ist neuzeitlich) gelten graeco-ägypt. Texte, deren Autor der ägypt. Gott Thot, gräzisiert als Hermes Trismegistos, gewesen sein soll. Dessen Beiname (»der dreifach große H.«), der erst kaiserzeitlich ist, leitet sich von der dreifachen Anrufung des Hermes-Thot als »des größten« her (die bereits hell. demotisch und griech. belegt ist). Clemens [3] von Alexandreia (strom. 6,4,35) beschreibt eine Prozession, in der 42 grundlegende Schriften des Hermes zur ägypt. Rel. vorgeführt wurden, welche Hymnen, Astrologie, Kosmographie, Geographie, Medizin, Ritualvorschriften und Theologie umfassen; die ägypt. Rel. wird also in gängiger griech.-röm. Perspektive als teilweise okkulte Philos. verstanden. Erh. ist das sog. → *Corpus Hermeticum*, 17 griech. Schriften, die zur Gänze allein in zwei Hss. überliefert sind und theologisch-philos. Schriften umfassen. Ihr Hintergrund ist zumeist ein »Vulgärplatonismus«, wie er unter Gebildeten bes. der Kaiserzeit geläufig war; ganz selten ist eine ägyptozentrische, fremdenfeindliche Haltung; Astrologie, Alchemie und Magie sind nur ganz am Rand wichtig. Dasselbe gilt für den lat. *Asclepius*, der im Corpus der Schriften des Platonikers Apuleius [III] überliefert ist, für die 40 griech. Texte und Textfragmente bei → Stobaios und die drei koptischen h.S. unter den Texten aus → Nag Hammadi. Neben diesem einigermaßen geschlossenen Bereich stehen astrologische, astrologisch-medizinische und alchemistische Schriften, welche die Forsch. [6] gern einem »populären« Hermetismus zuweist; auch die Slg. der *Kyranídes*, welche die okkulten Eigenschaften von Steinen, Pflanzen und Tieren darstellt, gibt sich als Offenbarung durch Hermes Trismegistos. Schließlich wird Hermes Trismegistos in den griech. und demot. → Zauberpapyri als mächtige und zauberkundige Gottheit und Gewährsmann für magische Rezepte genannt. Ob in diesem großen Bereich die traditionelle Trennung zw. philos. und populären h.S. legitim ist, wird in der Forsch. diskutiert. Die uns überkommene Slg. des *Corpus Hermeticum* ist jedenfalls wohl eine byz., durch christl.-gelehrte Autoren redigierte Auswahl.

Augustinus lehnte die Weisheit des Hermes mit nachhaltigem Erfolg ab (civ. 8,23). Durch arab. Vermittlung und über den ps.-apuleischen *Asclepius* gelangten Gedanken der h.S. ins Hoch-MA (Schule von Chartres, Johannes von Salisbury), doch erst das platonische Interesse des Florentiner Humanismus brachte das Corpus wirklich in das europ. Bewußtsein: 1463 übersetzte FICINO eine griech. Hs. mit 14 der 17 Traktate (Pimander, gedruckt 1471); es folgten Gesamteditionen (Patrizi 1591) und Kommentare (Lefèvre d'Etaples, 1494), die zu einer regelrechten »Hermolatrie« im 16. und frühen 17. Jh. führten, bis Isaac CASAUBON die angeblich uralten Schriften als spätant. enthüllte (1614). Die mod. Forsch. setzt im frühen 20. Jh. mit Richard REITZENSTEIN [5] ein.

→ HERMETIK

ED.: 1 W. SCOTT, Hermetica, 1–4, 1924–1936 2 A.D. NOCK, A.-J. FESTUGIÈRE, Corpus Hermeticum 1–4, 1945–1954 3 B.O. COPENHAVER, Hermetica. The Greek Corpus Hermeticum and the Latin Asclepius in a New English Translation, 1992 4 J. HOLZHAUSEN, Corpus Hermeticum, 1–2, 1993.

LIT.: 5 R. REITZENSTEIN, Poimandres. Studien zur griech.-ägypt. und frühchristl. Lit., 1904 6 A.-J. FESTUGIÈRE, Hermétisme et mystique païenne, 1967 7 J. DORESSE, L'Hérmetisme égyptisant, in: H.-C. PUECH, Histoire des religions 2, 1972, 430–497 8 G. FOWDEN, The Egyptian Hermes. A Historical Approach to the Late Pagan Mind, 1986. F.G.

Hermias (Ἑρμίας).

[1] Um 350 v. Chr. Nachfolger des Eubulos als Tyrann über → Atarneus und → Assos (Diog. Laert. 5,3), vielleicht Schüler Platons (Strab. 13,1,57; Theop. FGrH 115 F 250; aber dagegen Plat. epist. 6,322e). Neben anderen Philosophen holte er Aristoteles an den Hof und verheiratete ihn mit seiner Nichte → Pythias. Nachdem die Perser 343/2 Ägypten zurückerobert hatten, hielt H. auch sein Gebiet für bedroht und nahm Kontakt mit → Philippos II. auf (Demosth. or. 10,31f. mit schol.). Dareios [3] III. ließ ihn deshalb verhaften und wohl 341 hinrichten (Diod. 16,52,1ff.). Kallisthenes und Aristoteles rühmen seine philos. Bildung und vorbildliche Haltung als Herrscher und bei der Hinrichtung (vgl. Kallisthenes FGrH 124 F 2; Aristot. fr. 674f. ROSE), während Theopompos das Leben des H. als moralisches Lehrstück in den *Philippiká* kritisierte (FGrH 115 F 291). Ein Schutz- und Trutzbündnis zwischen ›H. und seinen Gefährten (ἑταῖροι)‹ und den Erythraiern (TOD, 165 = StV 322) deutet auf das ungewöhnliche Regime einer Hetairia oder eine kollektive Tyrannis hin. Didymos und Philodemos galt H. als Exempel eines platonischen Philosophenherrschers. Bei Athenaios fehlt er unter den zu Gewaltherrschern gewordenen Platonschülern; Hermippos von Smyrna erwähnt ihn jedoch in seiner Schrift über zu Herrschern gewandelte Philosophen.

H. BERVE, Die Tyrannis bei den Griechen, 1967, Bd. 2, 688f. • K. TRAMPEDACH, Platon, die Akademie und die zeitgenössische Politik, 1994, 66–79. J.E.

[2] Ptolemaiischer Nesiarch (aus Halikarnassos?), Nachfolger des → Bakchon, gründete das Fest der Philadelpheia auf Delos, wo er seit 267 v. Chr. in den Inventaren erwähnt wird.

PP 6,15042 (= 14915?) • PH. BRUNEAU, Recherches sur les cultes de Délos, 1970, 528ff. • I. MERKER, The Ptolemaic Officials and the League of the Islanders, in: Historia 19, 1970, 141–160, bes. 153 • R. BAGNALL, The Administration of the Ptolemaic Possessions Outside Egypt, 1976, 138.

[3] Vor 125/4 v. Chr. *epistátēs* (ἐπιστάτης) des äg. Gaues Perithebas, von 125/4 bis 117/6 als *stratēgós kai nomárchēs* (στρατηγὸς καὶ νομάρχης) der Gaue Perithebas, Pathyrites, Latopolites belegt; wurde vor April 119 vom Rang eines *tōn homotímōn tois syngenési* (τῶν ὁμοτίμων τοῖς συγγενέσι) zum *syngenḗs* (συγγενής) befördert (→ Hoftitel B 2).

L. MOOREN, The Aulic Titulature in Ptolemaic Egypt, 1975, 116f., Nr. 0122.

[4] Sohn eines Offiziers namens Ptolemaios (*Perses*), der um 200 v. Chr. vor den aufständischen Thebanern nach Omboi floh und dort auch nach der Niederschlagung des Aufstandes blieb. H. ist in Omboi als Soldat und Offizier, ist *tṓn perí aulḗn diadóchōn kai hēgemṓn ep' andrṓn* (τῶν περὶ αὐλὴν διαδόχων καὶ ἡγεμὼν ἐπ' ἀνδρῶν). Ein von Ptolemaios in Theben zurückgelassenes Haus war seit 153 zum größten Teil im Besitz einer Familie thebanischer Choachyten, gegen die H. auf Herausgabe klagte (die Akten des Prozesses vor den verschiedenen Instanzen in UPZ II 160ff.). H. verlor den Prozeß, der von Mai/Juni 125 bis Dezember 117 ging, da seine Besitztitel offenbar auf der Flucht verloren wurden.

P. W. PESTMAN, Il processo di Hermias e altri Documenti dell'archivio dei Choachiti, 1992 • Ders., The Archive of the Theban Choachytes, 1993.

[5] *Epí tōn prosódōn* (ἐπὶ τῶν προσόδων) im Fajjum 113 v. Chr. PP 1,978.

[6] Als *tōn diadóchōn kai epimelētḗs* (τῶν διαδόχων καὶ ἐπιμελητής) ca. 130/120 v. Chr. im Pathyrites, als *epí tōn prosódōn* (ἐπὶ τῶν προσόδων) in den Gauen Perithebas, Pathyrites und Latopolites von 112–108.

L. MOOREN, The Aulic Titulature in Ptolemaic Egypt, 1975, 144, Nr. 0187. W.A.

[7] Unbekannter, wohl christl. Verf. einer kurzen, die Lehren der griech. Philosophen in 19 Kap. verspottenden Schrift (Διασυρμὸς τῶν ἔξω [φιλο]σόφων, CPG 1113). Der doxographischen Tradition (→ Doxographie) verpflichtet, stellt H. verschiedene Schulmeinungen humorvoll vor und lehnt als Konsequenz die Philos., deren Ursprung er im Abfall der Engel von Gott (1,4f.) sieht, als falsch ab. Die Schrift, die Verbindungen zu Texten des 2./3. Jh. aufweist (vgl. [1. 23]), wird momentan meist um 200 n. Chr. angesetzt [1. 67; 4. 811].

1 R. P. C. HANSON, D. JOUSSOT, H. (SChr 388), 1993 (mit Übersicht 85–87, 94) 2 J. LEITL, A. DI PAULI, BKV 14 (Apologeten 2), 1913, 115–122 (dt. Übers.) 3 A. DI PAULI, Die Irrisio des H., 1907 4 J. H. WASZINK, s. v. H., RAC 14, 808–815. J.RI.

Herminafrid. König der Thüringer ca. 507/511–531/2 n. Chr., heiratete um 510 → Amalaberga, die Nichte des Ostgotenkönigs → Theoderich d. Gr., und ließ sich so in dessen Bündnispolitik miteinbeziehen (Anon. Vales. 12,70; Cassiod. var. 4,1; Iord. Get. 299; Prok. BG 5,12,22). H. herrschte zunächst gemeinsam mit seinen Brüdern Baderich und Berthachar. Nach deren Ermordung Alleinherrscher, wurde er ca. 531/2 vom Frankenkönig → Theoderich gestürzt und starb kurz darauf. Sein Herrschaftsgebiet wurde Teil des Frankenreichs (Greg. Tur. Franc. 3,4–8; Prok. BG 5,13,1f.). Möglicherweise war Rodelinda, die den Langobardenkönig → Audoin heiratete, H.s Tochter (Prok. BG 8,25,11f.). PLRE 2,549f. M.MEI.

Herminius. Gentilname einer röm. Familie etr. Herkunft. Sie stellte nach Vertreibung des etr. Königs am Beginn der Republik zwei Consuln, verschwand dann aber wie die meisten etr. Familien seit der Mitte des 5. Jh. v. Chr. aus der Geschichte. Der Consul von 506 (T. H. Aquilinus) wird, z. T. mit seinem Kollegen Sp. Larcius (ebenfalls etr. Herkunft), im Kampf gegen Etrusker und Latiner erwähnt (Liv. 2,10,6 f.; 11,7–10; 20,8 f.; Dion. Hal. ant. 5,22,5; 23,2 und 4; 24,1; 6,1,3). Der Consul von 448, Lar(s) H. Coritinesanus (bei Liv. Vorname Sp.), vielleicht Sohn oder Enkel des H. Aquilinus, ist inschr. bezeugt (InscrIt 13,1,366 f.), aber nur dem Namen nach bekannt (Dion. Hal. ant. 11,51). MRR 1, 6 (T. H.) und 1, 50 (Lar H.). W. ED.

Herminones. H., → Ingaevones und → Istaevones sind german. Namen für die auf die drei Söhne des Mannus zurückgeführten german. Urstämme innerhalb der (auf indigenem Kern beruhenden) ant. myth. Ethnogonie der Germanen (Mannus-Genealogie), die wohl von Poseidonios in die ant. Lit. eingeführt und stufenweise unter dem Einfluß der röm. Entdeckung des Nordens erweitert wurde (Mela 3,32; Plin. nat. 4,99 f.; Tac. Germ. 2,2). Ethnisch, räumlich und sozial bleibt der Mythos beziehungslos, und obschon die röm. Eroberer die Stammesgruppen überall dort nicht vorfanden, wo sie eigentlich zu erwarten waren, lebte das der Realität eingepaßte Mannusschema fort: Nach Plin. l.c. siedelten die H., zu denen Suebi, → Hermunduri, → Chatti und → Cherusci gehörten, im Inneren Germaniens.

D. Timpe, Romano-Germanica, 1995, 1–60. K. DI.

Herminos (Ἑρμῖνος). Peripatetiker des 2. Jh. n. Chr., Schüler des → Aspasios [1], dessen Ansicht über die Himmelsbewegung er zitierte, und Lehrer des → Alexandros [26] von Aphrodisias. Erh. sind Frg. seiner Komm. zu Aristoteles' *Categoriae*, *Analytica Priora*, *De interpretatione* und *Topica*, und zwei Bemerkungen zu *De Caelo*. Seine Annahme, daß die Ewigkeit der Himmelsbewegung von einer Himmelsseele verursacht sei, geht wohl auf Aristoteles (cael. 2,12) zurück.
→ Aristoteles-Kommentatoren; Aristotelismus

H. Schmidt, De H. Peripatetico, 1907 • Moraux II, 361–398 • H. B. Gottschalk, Aristotelian Philosophy in the Roman World from the Time of Cicero to the End of the Second Century AD, in: ANRW II 36.2, 1158 f. H. G.

Hermion(e) (inschr. und lit. Ἑρμιών und Ἑρμιόνη, Ethnikon Ἑρμιονεῖς). Stadt an der östl. Akte der Argolis, h. Ermioni, deren Territorium den SO der Akte vom Kap Thermisi 6 km östl. von H. bis zum Kap Iri südl. des Bedeni-Bachs umfaßte. H. verdankte seine Bed. den zwei gut geschützten Häfen, getrennt durch ein schmales, längliches Vorgebirge, das Gebiet der alten Stadtanlage. In röm. Zeit verlagerte sich H. nach NW um ca. 700 m zum östl. Abhang des Berges Pron, auf dem sich die Akropolis befand (Paus. 2,34,10–11). Erh. sind Teile der Stadtmauer, Tempelfundamente, Theater, Thermen, eine große Nekropole. Eine andere Nekropole belegt die Existenz des auch bei Hom. Il. 2,560 gen. Orts schon in myk. Zeit. H. war Mitglied der alten → Amphiktyonie von Kalaureia (Strab. 8,6,14), trat in gesch. Zeit aber wenig hervor. Die urspr. Bewohner sollen Dryopes gewesen sein (Hdt. 8,43; 73,2; Diod. 4,37,2; Strab. 8,6,13). H. schickte drei Schiffe 480 v. Chr. nach Salamis (Hdt. 8,43) und 300 Männer 479 v. Chr. nach Plataiai (Hdt. 9,28,4; Paus. 5,23,2; Syll.[3] 31,15). Im Peloponnesischen Krieg war H. mit Sparta verbündet (Thuk. 1,27,2; 2,56,5; 8,3,2; Xen. hell. 4,2,16; 6,2,3; 7,2,2), 229 v. Chr. Mitglied im Achaiischen Bund (Pol. 2,44,6; Strab. 8,7,3), vorübergehend mit Kleomenes III. verbündet (Pol. 2,52,2). Wurde durch Seeräuber geplündert (Plut. Pompeius 24). Purpurfischerei ist belegt (Skyl. 51; Strab. 8,6,11–14; Paus. 2,34,4–36,3; Ptol. 3,14,33).

M. H. Jameson, Inscriptions of the Peloponnesos, in: Hesperia 22, 1953, 160–167 • M. H. McAllister, A Temple at H., in: Hesperia 38, 1969, 169–173 • D. Musti, M. Torelli, Pausania. Guida della Grecia 2, 1986, 328–334 • N. Pharaklas, Ἑρμιονίς – Ἁλιάς (Ancient Greek Cities 19), 1972. Y. L.

Hermione (Ἑρμιόνη). Tochter der → Helene und des → Menelaos (Hom. Od. 4,12 ff.), Schwester des Nikostratos (Hes. fr. 175 M-W). Nach der einen Mythenversion verspricht Menelaos sie vor den Toren Troias dem → Neoptolemos (Hom. Od. 4,3 ff.), in einer anderen Version wird sie vor dem Krieg → Orestes zugesprochen (Soph. Hermione TrGF 4, 192 f.; Eur. Andr. 966 ff.; Ov. epist. 8, leicht abweichend Eur. Or. 1653 ff.). Neoptolemos raubt sie, wird aber von Orestes getötet (Eur. Andr. 993 ff.; 1085 ff.; Hyg. fab. 122 f.). Eur. Andr. thematisiert die Konkurrenz zw. der kinderlosen H. und der Kriegsgefangenen → Andromache, die dem Neoptolemos Molossos geboren hat.

Lit.: L. Kahil, s. v. H., LIMC 5.1, 388 • W. Otto, s. v. H., RE 8, 841–844.
Abb.: L. Kahil, s. v. H., LIMC 5.2, 284. R. HA.

Hermippos (Ἕρμιππος).
[1] Dichter der att. Alten Komödie, Bruder des Komödiendichters → Myrtilos. Der Beginn seiner Schaffenszeit dürfte um 440 v. Chr. liegen: Ein Dionysiensieg ist für 435 v. Chr. bezeugt [1. test. 3], auf der inschr. Dionysien-Siegerliste steht H. hinter → Pherekrates, sowie vor → Aristophanes [1] und → Eupolis [1. test. 4], auf der Lenäensiegerliste hinter → Kratinos und Pherekrates und vor → Phrynichos, Myrtilos und Eupolis [1. test. 5]. Neben dem Dionysiensieg sind insgesamt vier Lenäensiege verzeichnet [1. test 5]; insgesamt zehn Stücktitel sind erhalten. Außer Komödien wurden H. auch Iamben [1. test. 8] und Παρῳδίαι/*Parōdíai* [1. test. 7] zugeschrieben. Unter den erh. Stücktiteln weisen fünf auf die Parodie eines Mythos (Ἀθηνᾶς γοναί/›Die Geburt der Athene‹, die älteste belegte Komödie mit

dem Motiv einer Göttergeburt [2. 12–14]; Εὐρώπη/*Európē*, Θεοί/*Theoí*: ›Die Götter‹, Κέρκωπες/*Kérkōpes*: ›Die Kerkopen‹) oder einer Tragödie (Ἀγαμέμνων/*Agamémnōn*) hin, in den übrigen erweist sich H. als typischer Dichter der Alten Komödie mit viel polit. Invektive: in den ›Moiren‹ (Μοῖραι/*Moírai*) von 430 v. Chr. gegen Perikles, der des Nichtstuns angesichts der spartanischen Einfälle in Attika bezichtigt wird (fr. 42; 47), in den bald nach 421 (vgl. Aristoph. Nub. 551–559 und [1. Ἀρτοπ. test.]) geschriebenen ›Bäckerinnen‹ (Ἀρτοπώλιδες/*Artopṓlides*) gegen Hyperbolos; ein angeblicher Angriff des H. gegen Perikles' Frau Aspasia ist wohl ebenfalls als Bühneninvektive umzudeuten [1. test. 2 Anm.]. Die ›Soldaten‹ (Στρατιῶται/*Stratiṓtai*) (oder Στρατιώτιδες, ›Die Soldatinnen‹?) und die vor 424 (vgl. fr. 63,7) geschriebenen ›Korbträger‹ (Φορμοφόροι/*Phormophóroi*), aus denen fr. 63 eine lange (mit parodistischem Musenanruf eingeleitete) und vielzitierte Hexameterpartie bietet, nehmen auf die Situation Athens im Archidamischen Krieg (431–421 v. Chr.) Bezug.

1 PCG V, 561–604 2 H.-G. Nesselrath, Myth, Parody and Comic Plots: The Birth of Gods and Middle Comedy, in: G. W. Dobrov (Hrsg.), Beyond Aristophanes: Transition and Diversity in Greek Comedy, 1995, 1–27. H.-G. NE.

[2] H. aus Smyrna (Athen. 7,327c). Griech. Grammatiker und Biograph aus dem 3. Jh. v. Chr., genannt »der Kallimacheer« (ὁ Καλλιμάχειος, Athen. 2,58f; 5,213f), auch »der Peripatetiker« (περιπατητικός) – das Epitheton bezeichnet in dieser Zeit einen Gelehrten auf dem Gebiet der Lit. und der Biographie, ohne notwendigerweise eine Verbindung zum Peripatos zu enthalten. Da H. vom Tod des → Chrysippos [2] (208/204 v. Chr.: Diog. Laert. 7,184) berichtet, muß er etwa bis zum Ende des Jh. gelebt haben. Soweit wir wissen, widmete er sich hauptsächlich der Biographie, für die er Material und Ergebnisse in der Bibliothek von Alexandria heranzog (→ Philologie). H.' umfassende Sammlung von *Bíoi* berühmter Männer lehnte sich wohl an die *Pínakes* seines Lehrers → Kallimachos an, dessen Werk er wohl fortgesetzt und vervollständigt hat. Die umfangreichen Materialien scheinen in der späteren biographischen Tradition häufig benutzt worden zu sein (von → Plutarchos, → Diogenes [17] Laertios usw.): H.' Nachwirkung läßt sich auch daran erkennen, daß → Herakleides [19] Lembos im 2. Jh. v. Chr. eine Epitome verfaßte (ein Frg. in POxy. 1367). Das Werk war in Abschnitte und einzelne Biographien gegliedert: ›Über die Gesetzgeber‹ (Περὶ νομοθετῶν) und ›Über die Sieben Weisen‹ (Περὶ τῶν ἑπτὰ σοφῶν) sind bei Athen. 14,619b, Diog. Laert. 1,42 und POxy. 1367 bezeugt. ›Über Pythagoras‹, ›Über Aristoteles‹, ›Über Gorgias‹, ›Über Hipponax‹, ›Über Isokrates‹. Die Glaubwürdigkeit dieser Schriften wird allerdings bezweifelt, da die Anekdoten eindeutig erfunden sind (vgl. H.' bes. Interesse an den Todesumständen der berühmten Männer). Diese sind jedoch als lit. Gattungsmerkmal zur Charakterisierung der jeweiligen Personen anzusehen, nicht aber als Zeichen eines unseriösen und phantasiebetonten Ansatzes. H. verfaßte schließlich auch ein (verlorenes) astrologisches Gedicht.

Ed.: FHG III, 35–54 • Wehrli, Schule, Suppl. I • SH, 245–46 (Nr. 485–90) • CPF I 1**, 249–67 (Nr. 59).
Lit.: A. H. Chroust, The Vita Aristotelis of Diogenes Laertius, in: AC 34, 1965, 97–129 • Ders., Aristotle's alleged revolt against Plato, in: JHPh 11, 1973, 91–94 • I. Düring, Ariston or Hermippus? A note on the Catalogue of Aristotle's writings, in: Classica et Mediaevalia 17, 1956, 11–21 • Ders., Aristotle in the Ancient Biographical Tradition, 1957, 464 ff. • J. Engels, Der Michigan-Pap. über Theramenes und die Ausbildung des »Theramenes-Mythos«, in: ZPE 99, 1993, 125–55 • C. Fries, Zu H. von Alexandria, Wochenschrift für klass. Philol. 21, 1904, 1043 ff. • I. Gallo, in: CPF I 1, 249–257 • J. S. Heibges, s. v. H. (6), RE 8, 845–852 • F. Leo, Die griech.-röm. Biographie, 1901, 124 ff. • A. Momigliano, The Development of Greek Biography, [2]1993 • F. Montanari, in: CPF I 1, 258–265 • P. Moraux, Les listes anciennes des ouvrages d'Aristote, 1951, 221–222 • P. von der Mühll, Ant. Historismus in Plutarchs Biographie des Solon, in: Klio 35, 1942, 89–102 • G. E. Pesely, The origin and value of the Theramenes Papyrus, Ancient History Bull. 3, 1989, 29–35 • Pfeiffer, KP I, 125, 163, 188–89, 301 • F. Susemihl, Gesch. der griech. Litt. in der Alexandrinerzeit, 1891–1892, I, 492–495.

[3] H. aus Berytos (einem Dorf im Innern Phöniziens, nicht der Stadt am Mittelmeer), griech. Grammatiker aus hadrianischer Zeit (Suda ε 3045, s. v. Ἕρμιππος; ν 375, s. v. Νικάνωρ; ι 706, s. v. Ἴστρος; α 97, s. v. Ἄβρων; Etym. m. 118,14, s. v. Ἀπάμεια). Von Sklaven abstammend und später freigelassen, war H. Schüler des → Herennios Philon aus Byblos und fand so Zugang zu dem Kreis um den röm. Politiker → Herennius [II 12] Severus. Von seinen Werken sind nur wenige Frg. erh. (in einigen Fällen ist die Frage der Zuweisung an ihn bzw. an H. [2] aus Smyrna noch offen): Wichtig und berühmt war in der Ant. sein (von seinem Lehrer beeinflußtes) biographisches Werk ›Über die unterschiedliche Erziehung von Sklaven‹ (Περὶ τῶν ἐν παιδείᾳ διαπρεψάντων δούλων).

Schmid/Stählin II, 2, 805, 868 • FHG III, 35–36, 51–52 • J. S. Heibges, s. v. H. (8), RE 8, 853–54 • S. Mazzarino, Il pensiero storico classico, II/2, 134–35, 173, 177–79 • F. Sartori, Ermippo di Berito, schiavo e storiografo, in: Index 10, 1981, 260–70 • Wehrli, Schule, Suppl. I, 106. F. M./Ü: T. H.

Hermochares (Ἑρμοχάρης). Nikandros (Heteroieumena 3 = Antoninus Liberalis 1) wendet in einer Parallelerzählung bzw. Bearbeitung (1, 2 mit [1. 71 A11]) zu Akontios und → Kydippe (Kall. Aitia fr. 65–75) das Apfelwurfmotiv auf H. aus Athen und Ktesylla, die Tochter des Alkidamas aus Iulis auf Keos, an; die beiden fliehen schließlich zusammen nach Athen. Nach Tod und Entschwinden (*aphanismós*) der Ktesylla in Gestalt einer Taube (in Karthaia: Ov. met. 7,368–370, vgl. [1. 72 A20; 2]) trägt ein Orakelspruch H. die Gründung eines Heiligtums in Iulis auf (Aition für den Kult einer Aphrodite Ktesylla bzw. Ktesylla Hekaerge: vgl. [1. 72 A22] mit Hinweis auf Parallelen in Antoninus Liberalis 23: Aspalis).

1 M. Papathomopoulos (Ed.), Antoninus Liberalis, Les Métamorphoses, 1968 2 F. Bömer, P. Ovidius Naso, Metamorphosen, Komm. zu B. VI–VII, 1976. T. H.

Hermodamas (Ἑρμοδάμας). Nachfahre des Homeriden Kreophylos von Samos (vgl. [1]), wohl 6. Jh. v. Chr.. Soll in hohem Alter Lehrer des Pythagoras gewesen sein (Neanthes FGrH 84 F 29 = Porph. vita Pythagorae 1; Antonios Diogenes p. 136 Stephens-Winkler = Porph. ebd. 15; Diog. Laert. 8,2; vgl. Apul. flor. 15; Iambl. v.P. 9 und 11; [2]).
→ Homeriden; Kreophylos; Pythagoras

1 W. Burkert, Die Leistung eines Kreophylos, in: MH 29, 1972, 77f. 2 M. Detienne, Homère, Hésiode et Pythagore, 1962, 13f. C. RI.

Hermodoros (Ἑρμόδωρος).
[1] In einem Frg. des Philosophen → Herakleitos [1] von Ephesos kritisiert dieser seine Mitbürger, weil sie H., den ›wertvollsten Mann‹ unter ihnen, mit der Begründung verbannt hätten, bei ihnen solle ›niemand der wertvollste sein‹ (Diels/Kranz 22,121 = Strab. 14,1,25; Cic. Tusc. 5,105). Nach späterer Trad. soll der nach It. ins Exil gegangene H. an der Abfassung der Zwölftafelgesetze (→ Tabulae duodecim) beteiligt gewesen sein. Für Plinius war es dieser H., dessen Standbild auf dem Comitium stand (Plin. nat. 34,21).

K.-J. Hölkeskamp, Schiedsrichter, Gesetzgeber und Gesetzgebung im archa. Griechenland, 1999, 102ff. E. S.-H.

[2] H. aus Syrakus. Schüler Platons und Verf. einer der ersten biographischen Schriften ›Über Platon‹ (Philod. Academicorum index 6,6–10, nach Timaios), auf die sich auch Diogenes Laertios beruft (2,106 und 3,6). H. bietet ferner ein von der Nachschrift des Aristoteles unabhängiges Zeugnis für den platonischen Vortrag ›Über das Gute‹ (vgl. Testimonium Platonicum 31 Gaiser). Er vertrieb die Dialoge Platons in Sizilien (Philod. ebd.; ferner Zenobios 5,6 = 1, 116 Leutsch-Schneidewin); daher der Komödienvers λόγοισιν Ἑρμόδωρος ἐμπορεύεται (›mit den Dialogen (sc. Platons) macht H. ein Geschäft‹; dazu Cic. Att. 13,21,4).

Ed.: M. Isnardi Parente, Senocrate – Ermodoro. Frammenti, 1982. K.-H. S.

[3] Syr. Epigrammatiker aus dem »Kranz« des Meleager (Anth. Pal. 4,1,43 f.). Nur ein Gedicht, welches Planudes ihm zuweist, ist erh. (ebd. 16,170; das Epigramm 9,77, das ihm von diesem alternativ zu → Ariston [6] zugeschriebene stammt nicht von ihm): zwei Distichen, in denen die knidische Aphrodite des Praxiteles zu ihren Ungunsten mit der athenischen Pallas des Pheidias verglichen wird. Schwer zu entscheiden ist, ob es sich bei dem Gedicht um Variation oder Vorlage des anon. Epigramms 16,169 handelt.

GA I 1, 107; 2, 306f. M. G. A./Ü: T. H.

[4] Griech. Architekt des 2. Jh. v. Chr.; baute laut Vitruv (3,2,6) in Rom in der Porticus Metelli den Tempel des Iuppiter Stator und damit vielleicht den ersten röm. Marmortempel überhaupt (vgl. Vell. 1,11,3 und 5).

E. Fabricius, s. v. H. (8), RE 8, 861f. (Quellen) · P. Gros, H. et Vitruve, in: MEFRA 85, 1973, 137–161 · M. B. Marzani, s. v. H., EAA 4, 1961, 11. C. HÖ.

Hermogenes (Ἑρμογένης).
[1] Athener, Sohn des Hipponikos, Bruder des Kallias, tritt in den sokratischen Schriften Platons und Xenophons mehrfach als Gefährte des → Sokrates in Erscheinung. Zusammen mit der Titelgestalt ist H. Gesprächspartner des Sokrates in Platons *Kratylos*.

1 SSR VI B 71–77 2 Davies, 269–270. K. D.

[2] H. aus Aspendos, zog im Kampf des Antiochos [2] I. (gest. 261 v. Chr.) nach der Ermordung von dessen Vater Seleukos I. zur (Rück-)Gewinnung kleinasiatischer Territorien als Unterfeldherr des Patrokles gegen nordkleinasiatische Städte und schloß mit Herakleia am Pontos einen Vertrag. Im anschließenden Feldzug gegen Bithynien geriet er in einen Hinterhalt und kam samt seinem Heer um (FGrH 434 F 1,9,1–2).
[3] Einer der Kommandanten Antiochos' III. 219 v. Chr. bei der Belagerung Seleukeias in Pieria (Pol. 5,60,4). A. ME.
[4] Nach Vitruv (3,2,6) ein hell. → Architekt aus Alabanda; eine in Priene gefundene Inschr. könnte Anlaß sein, seine Herkunft aus dieser Stadt zu vermuten [2]. Strittig sind mit seinem Wirken verbundene Datierungsfragen. Als Eckdaten stehen die Zeit nach 220 v. Chr. und 130 v. Chr. zur Diskussion [9]. Für eine Frühdatier. gibt insbes. eine 1963 gefundene Inschr. deutliche Hinweise [4]. Wichtigste Quelle zu H. ist → Vitruvius, der sich wiederholt auf H. bezieht. Hiernach entwarf H. den Artemistempel in → Magnesia am Mäander (Vitr. 3,2,6), dessen Schönheit Strabon (14,647) betont und den Tempel des Liber Pater in → Teos (Vitr. 3,3,8). Über beide Bauten verfaßte H. Schriften (Vitr. 7, praef. 12). Er soll mit dem Tempel der Artemis den → Pseudodipteros erfunden haben und am Tempel in Teos bei der als hexastyl bezeichneten Ringhalle eustyle → Proportionen verwirklicht haben. Allerdings bezeichnet Vitruv (7, praef. 12) diesen Bau als → Monopteros, dessen Typus er (4,8,1) als baldachinartigen Rundbau ohne Cella definiert, so daß die typolog. Charakterisierung des Tempels in Teos als Hexastylos schwer verständlich bleibt. Zum Tempel des Liber Pater in Teos wird zusätzlich berichtet (Vitr. 4,3,1–2), H. habe das für einen Tempel dor. Ordnung bereits vorbereitete Material wegen der Probleme des Triglyphenfrieses (→ Dorischer Eckkonflikt) nachträglich umarbeiten lassen und einen Bau in ion. Ordnung errichtet. Wahr-

scheinlich darf dieser angebliche Vorgang nicht allzu wörtlich verstanden werden [7], wenngleich die Erzählung bestens geeignet ist, H. als einen Baumeister zu charakterisieren, der die ion. Bauordnung protegierte.

Da sowohl der Tempel in Teos [11] als auch der in Magnesia [6] grundsätzlich bekannt sind, können die für H. in Anspruch genommenen Ideale mit konkreten Überl. verglichen werden. Dabei stimmt der in Teos aufgedeckte Befund, der weitgehend auf eine röm.-kaiserzeitl. Erneuerung zurückgeht, eher skeptisch. Zwar handelt es sich um einen Hexastylos ion. Ordnung, doch keineswegs um einen Bau, dessen Interkolumnien mit 2¼ Säulendurchmesser eustylen Maßverhältnissen entsprechen. Statt dessen steht der Plan dem von → Pytheos entworfenen Athenatempel in → Priene so nahe, daß – sollte der in Teos bekannt gewordene Tempel tatsächlich auf einen Entwurf des H. zurückgehen – der Bau eher die Frage aufwirft, ob H. nicht vielmehr aus der Trad. des Pytheos hervorgegangen sein könnte. Mit größerer Gewißheit ist der Artemistempel in Magnesia mit H. in Verbindung zu bringen. Seine Datier. in die Zeit des H. ist ebenso unstrittig wie sein pseudodipteraler Typus. Allerdings hätte H. bei diesem Bau auf die von ihm propagierten eustylen Säulenverhältnisse verzichtet. Statt dessen konnten solche Proportionen beim kleinen Tempel des Zeus Sosipolis auf der Agora von Magnesia festgestellt werden [3].

Die Überl., nach der H. den Pseudodipteros erfunden haben soll, hält einer kritischen Nachprüfung nicht stand, denn der Weithallentempel war bereits in archa. Zeit bekannt [5. 2f.]. Zutreffender scheint zu sein, daß – nachdem die Architektur klass. Zeit von dieser Typenvariante offensichtlich keinen Gebrauch gemacht hatte – der Weithallentempel im Hell. wieder auflebte und von H. systematisiert wurde. Anscheinend kam diese Tempelform zeitgenöss. Geschmack besonders entgegen: Effektvolle Schattenwürfe und kräftige Kontraste unterstreichen die betont zur Wirkung gebrachte Weite der Ringhallen [1]. Säulenbasen und das Gebälksystem mit Fries zeigen, daß der große Tempel in Magnesia zusätzlich mit Attizismen angereichert wurde [10]. Auch die eustylen Säulenverhältnisse müssen kein erstmals und individuell von H. hervorgebrachtes Architekturideal gewesen sein. Solche Proportionen können sich aus einer Weiterentwicklung bereits in vorangegangener Zeit entstandener Entwurfsvorstellungen ergeben haben [8]. Insofern charakterisieren H. wahrscheinlich weniger neue architektonische Lösungen, sondern eher mit sicherem Zugriff entwickelte Formulierungen, durch die vielfältige Vorbilder und Quellen entsprechend zeitgenöss. Stil aktualisiert werden konnten [5. 10–16]. In den Schriften, die H. als einen Pionier der → Architekturtheorie verstehen lassen, scheint er die Summe seines Wissens und seiner Erfahrungen gezogen zu haben, um bestimmten Architekturidealen den Weg zu ebnen.

1 H. Drerup, Zum Artemistempel in Magnesia, in: MarbWPr 1964, 13–22 **2** P. Gros, Le dossier vitruvienne d'Hermogénès, in: MEFRA 90, 1978, 697–700 **3** G. Gruben, Die Tempel der Griechen, [3]1980, 388f. **4** P. Herrmann, Antiochos der Große und Teos, in: Anatolica 9, 1965, 29–33 **5** W. Hoepfner, Bauten und Bed. des H., in: W. Hoepfner, E. L. Schwandner (Hrsg.), H. und die hochhell. Architektur, 1990, 1–34 **6** C. Humann et al., Magnesia am Mäander, 1904, 39–83 **7** H. Knell, Die H.-Anekdote und das E. des dor. Ringhallentempels, in: Vitruv-Kolloquium des Dt. Archäologenverbandes, 1984, 41–64 **8** Ders., Der jüngere Tempel des Apollon Patroos auf der Athener Agora, in: JDAI 109, 1994, 228 **9** M. Kreeb, H. Quellen- und Datierungsprobleme, in: W. Hoepfner, E. L. Schwandner (Hrsg.), H. und die hochhell. Architektur, 1990, 103–113 **10** U. Schädler, Attizismen an ion. Tempeln Kleinasiens, in: MDAI(Ist) 41, 1991, 301–312 **11** D. M. Utz, The Temple of Dionysos at Teos, in: W. Hoepfner, E. L. Schwandner (Hrsg.), H. und die hochhell. Architektur, 1990, 51–61.

G. de Bonfils, H., in: Index 9, 1980, 183–192 • E. Fabricius, s. v. H. (29), RE 8, 879–881 • W. Hoepfner, E. L. Schwandner (Hrsg.), H. und die hochhell. Architektur, 1990 • W. Müller, Architekten in der Welt der Ant., 1989, 160f. • F. W. Schlikker, Hell. Vorstellungen von der Schönheit des Bauwerks nach Vitruv, 1940, 22–26 • B. Wesenberg, Beitr. zur Rekonstruktion griech. Architektur nach lit. Quellen, 9. Beih. MDAI(A), 1983, 95–100. H. KN.

[5] Bildhauer aus Kythera. Pausanias (2,2,8) sah auf der Agora von Korinth eine Aphrodite von H., die vielleicht auf Münzbildern wiedergegeben ist und dem Typus der bewaffneten Aphrodite von Kythera entspricht.

H. Brunn, Gesch. der griech. Künstler, 1, 1857, 522 • J. Flemberg, Venus armata. Stud. zur bewaffneten Aphrodite in der griech.-röm. Kunst, 1991, 102–104 • Overbeck, Nr. 2074 (Quellen) • C. K. Williams II, Corinth and the cult of Aphrodite, in: Corinthiaca, 1986, 15–18. R. N.

[6] Maler aus Antiochia, zw. 175 und 205 n. Chr. in Karthago tätig. Nach Tertullian (Adversus Hermogenem 1) schlug sich der schlechte Lebenswandel des »Weiberhelden« H. in geschmacklosen Bildinhalten nieder. Eigentlicher Grund dieser tendenziös-negativen Kritik waren aber wohl die oppositionellen Ansichten des stoischen Häretikers, der als schlechter Christ diffamiert werden sollte.

M. Durst, s. v. H., LThK[3] 5, 12 • J. H. Waszink, Tertullian: The Treatise against H., 1956. N. H.

[7] H. von Tarsos. Griech. Rhetor, ca. 160–230 n. Chr.; zuverlässige Nachrichten über sein Leben bietet allein Philostratos (soph. 2,7 = 577f.; vgl. Syrian bei Walz 4,30, Anm. 101), alle sonstigen Angaben beruhen auf Spekulation, Erfindung und Verwechslung aus byz. Zeit (vgl. [9. 868]). Mit 15 J. hatte er bereits eine solche Meisterschaft in der Redekunst erreicht, daß er mit seinen Deklamationen und improvisierten Vorträgen die Bewunderung von Kaiser Marc Aurel erregte. Im Erwachsenenalter aber betätigte er sich aus unbekannten

Gründen nicht mehr als Redner, was ihm den Spott seiner Zeitgenossen einbrachte. Bei seinem Tod in hohem Alter genoß er weder Ruhm noch Popularität.

Unter seinem Namen sind fünf Schriften überl.: 1) Περὶ ἰδεῶν (*Perí ideō̄n*), sein bedeutendstes Werk und die differenzierteste Abhandlung aus der Ant. über die systematische Erfassung und Bewertung stilistischer Eigenart. H. ersetzt das peripatetische Konzept von den drei Stilarten (→ *genera dicendi*) durch eine Kategorisierung charakteristischer Stilausprägungen (*idéai*); durch feine Unterteilung kommt er auf insgesamt 18–20 (je nach Zählweise). Jede *idéa* wird systematisch beschrieben und durch reiches Belegmaterial, meist aus Demosthenes, dokumentiert. Stilistische Meisterschaft entstehe durch gekonnte Mischung der *idéai*, wie sie in sonst nirgends erreichter Vollkommenheit bei Demosthenes vorliege.

2) Περὶ τῶν στάσεων (*Perí tōn stáseōn*): H. variiert und verfeinert die durch → Hermagoras [1] fixierte Stasislehre: Bes. durch subtile Untergliederung der Frage nach der Beschaffenheit des Sachstandes (*poiótēs*) unterscheidet er 13 → Status, die nicht für die rednerische Praxis, sondern ausschließlich für die fiktiven Streitfragen der Rhetorenschule zugeschnitten sind. Der Grad der Abhängigkeit von früheren Theoretikern und damit das Ausmaß der Eigenleistung des H. sind hier wie bei *Perí ideō̄n* nicht sicher bestimmbar, doch wird letztere neuerdings verstärkt hervorgehoben.

3) Περὶ εὑρέσεως (*Perí heuréseōs*), eine in vier Hauptteile (über Proömium, Narratio, Beweisführung, Redefiguren) gegliederte Schrift, die in der vorliegenden Form sicher nicht auf H. zurückgeht, sondern von einem Bearbeiter wahrscheinlich in byz. Zeit gestaltet wurde. Vielleicht hat derselbe auch die drei deutlich als Einzelschriften konzipierten Werke 1)–3) unter dem in den Hss. überl. Titel *Téchnē rhētorikḗ* zusammengefaßt. 4/5) Die beiden Schriften Προγυμνάσματα (*Progymnásmata*) und Περὶ μεθόδου δεινότητος (*Perí methódu deinótētos*) hält man heute übereinstimmend für zwar nicht von H., aber doch etwa zu seiner Zeit verfaßt.

Das zunächst wenig beachtete Werk des H. (immerhin schrieb aber bereits im 3. Jh. der Rhetor → Menandros einen Komm.) entfaltete seit der Spätant. (Komm. des Syrianos, Sopatros u.a.) weitreichende Wirkung und avancierte in byz. Zeit zum verbreiteten, oft komm. (Maximos Planudes, Gregorios von Korinth u.a.) und maßgeblichen Standardwerk für die Schule. Auch in Westeuropa wurde seit dem Humanismus bes. die Stillehre des H. intensiv rezipiert.

1 E. Bürgi, Ist die dem H. zugeschriebene Schrift Περὶ μεθόδου δεινότητος echt?, in: WS 48, 1930, 187–197 und 49, 1931, 40–69 **2** D. Hagedorn, Zur Ideenlehre des H., 1964 **3** G. A. Kennedy, Greek Rhetoric under the Christian Emperors, 1983, 96 ff. **4** G. L. Kustas, Stud. in Byzantine Rhetoric, 1973, 5–62; 127–199 **5** G. Lindberg, Stud. in H. and Eustathios, 1977 **6** M. Patillon, La théorie du discours chez H. le rhéteur, 1988 **7** A. M. Patterson, H. and the Renaissance, 1970 **8** L. Pernot, Anecdota rhetorica. Un résumé d'H. et d'Aphthonios, in: Révue d'Histoire des Textes 10, 1980, 55–73 **9** L. Radermacher, s. v. H. (22), RE 8, 865–877 **10** I. Rutherford, Inverting the Canon: H. on Literature, in: HSPh 94, 1992, 355–378 **11** B. Schouler, La classification des personnes et des faits chez H. et ses commentateurs, in: Rhetorica 8, 1990, 229–254 **12** B. P. Wallach, Ps.-H. and the Characterizing Oath, in: GRBS 22, 1981, 257–267 **13** C. W. Wooten, Dionysius of Halicarnassus and H. on the Style of Demosthenes, in: AJPh 110, 1989, 576–588.

Ed.: H. Rabe, 1913 (Ndr. 1985).
Übers. und Komm.: M. Heath, H. on Issues, 1995 · M. D. Reche Martinez, Téon, H., Aftonio, Ejercicios de retórica, 1991 · C. Ruiz Montero, H., sobre las formas de estilo, 1993 · C. Wooten, H. Tarsensis – On Types of Style, 1987.
M. W.

[8] Aurelius H. Proconsul von Asia zwischen 286 und 305 n. Chr. (CIL III 7069), 30. Oktober 309 – 8. Oktober 310 Stadtpräfekt von Rom (Chron. min. 1, 67 Mommsen). B. BL.

[9] *Magister equitum* unter Constantius II. (Amm. 14,10,2; Soz. 3,7,6), wahrscheinlich aus Tyros stammend (Lib. epist. 828), Arianer. Im Winter 341/2 n. Chr. erhielt er ein Kommando in Thrakien und gleichzeitig den Auftrag, den nicaenischen Bischof von Konstantinopel, Paulos, zu verbannen. Das nicaenische Stadtvolk widersetzte sich jedoch der kaiserlichen Gewalt, stellte sich vor seinen Bischof, zündete H.' Haus an und tötete ihn (Sokr. 2,13; Soz. 3,7; Lib. or. 59,94 ff.; Hier. chron. 235 Helm; Historia acephala 1,4 Martin). H. hatte einen Sohn, Herculanus (Amm. ebd.). PLRE 1, 422 f. (H. 1).

[10] Gebürtig aus Pontos, kein Christ, begann seine Karriere möglicherweise als Page des Licinius (Himerios or. 48,18 Colonna). Nach dem Studium der Philos. wurde er kaiserlicher Berater, später wohl *quaestor sacri palatii* unter Constantinus [1] d.Gr. (Himerios or. 48,28 ff.). Wahrscheinlich nach 337 n. Chr. zum *proconsul Achaeae* ernannt. U. U. ist er auch identisch mit dem Stadtpräfekten Roms von 349/350 (Chron. min. 1,68 f. Mommsen). 358 wurde H. zum *praefectus praetorio Orientis* erhoben (Lib. or. 1,115 f.; Cod. Theod. 1,7,1). Ammianus und Libanios, mit dem er befreundet war, loben seine Milde (Amm. 19,12,6; Lib. ebd.). Im Winter 359/360 gab er das Amt auf (Lib. epist. 138) und starb 361 (Amm. 21,6,9). PLRE 1, 423 ff. (H. 3, s.a. H. 2 und H. 9). M. R.

[11] s. Kleinmeisterschalen

Hermogenianus. Jurist aus dem hell. Osten des röm. Reiches, von 293 bis 295 n. Chr. *magister libellorum* (Leiter der Bittschriften-Kanzlei) Diocletians [1; 3], veröffentlichte 295 n. Chr. den *Codex Hermogenianus*, eine halbamtliche Sammlung von Reskripten Diocletians aus den Jahren 293 und 294. Die Sammlung wurde in den → *Fragmenta Vaticana*, in der → *Collatio legum Mosaicarum et Romanarum* und in der → *Consultatio* exzerpiert und vom *Codex Iustinianus* (*Haec*, pr.; *Summa* § 1) übernommen. H. verfaßte auch die wohl späteste in den Digesten Iustinians exzerpierte Juristenschrift: das Rechtsbreviar *Iuris epitomae* (6 B.; dazu [2]).

1 PLRE I, 425 f. 2 D. LIEBS, Hermogenians Iuris epitomae. Zum Stand der röm. Jurisprudenz im Zeitalter Diocletians, 1964 3 Ders., Recht und Rechtslit., in: HLL 5, 62 ff. T. G.

Hermokles (Ἑρμοκλῆς).

[1] Aus Kyzikos. Um 300 v. Chr. Dichter von → Paianen auf → Antigonos I. und → Demetrios [2] Poliorketes [4] (verloren) sowie eines Ithyphallos auf letzteren [1; 2] (vollständig erh.). Traditionelle rel. Dichtung nicht mehr nur an Götter, sondern auch an Herrscher zu adressieren, entsprach dabei der allg. üblichen Praxis des hell. Herrscherkultes [3].

ED.: 1 CollAlex 173–175 2 D. EBENER, Griech. Lyrik, 21980, 426 (dt. Übers.).
LIT.: 3 C. HABICHT, Gottmenschentum und griech. Städte (Zetemata 14), 21970, 148, 232 f. 4 L. KÄPPEL, Paian, 1992, Test. 7. L. K.

[2] Bronzebildner aus Rhodos. Laut Lukian schuf H. für Seleukos Nikator (312–285 v. Chr.) im Hera-Heiligtum von Hierapolis eine Statue des → Kombabos, des ersten Gallos (→ Kybele, → Syria Dea), der als Frau in Männerkleidung dargestellt gewesen sei.

OVERBECK, Nr. 2044 (Quellen). R. N.

Hermokopidenfrevel. Im Sommer 415 v. Chr., kurz vor der Sizilienexpedition, wurden in Athen in einer Nacht alle → Hermen beschädigt. Die Bürgerschaft sah darin ein böses Omen für das Unternehmen. Die Aussetzung hoher Belohnungen für Informanten führte zur Aufdeckung eines weiteren rel. Frevels: die Profanierung der Eleusinischen Mysterien (→ Mysteria) in den Privathäusern einiger reicher Bürger. → Alkibiades [3], Initiator der Sizilienexpedition, wurde der Beteiligung an beiden Verbrechen beschuldigt. In der folgenden »Hexenjagd« kam es zu immer neuen Denunziationen, Verhaftungen und Exekutionen. Während der H. in der älteren Forsch. oft als »Lausbubenstreich« abgetan wurde, folgen moderne Interpreten wieder dem Urteil des Thukydides und sehen in dem Anschlag auf die allgegenwärtigen, als typisch athenisch geltenden Hermen den gezielten Angriff einer oligarchischen → Hetairia auf traditionelle Rel. und demokratische Ordnung. Quellen: Thuk. 6,27–29; 53; 60 f.; And. 1.

W. D. FURLEY, Andokides and the Herms, 1996 · G. A. LEHMANN, Überlegungen zur Krise der attischen Demokratie im Peloponnesischen Krieg, in: ZPE 69, 1987, 33–73 · R. OSBORNE, The Erection and Mutilation of the Hermai, in: PCPhS 211, 1985, 47–73. E. S.-H.

Hermokrates (Ἑρμοκράτης).

[1] Syrakusanischer Staatsmann und General. Trat erstmals auf dem Friedenskongreß von Gela 424 v. Chr. hervor und forderte die sizilischen Griechen mit der Parole ›Sizilien den Sikelioten‹ erfolgreich dazu auf, die inneren Streitigkeiten beizulegen (Thuk. 4,58–64). Im J. 415 riet er zur Bildung einer über Sizilien hinausgreifenden Koalition gegen Athen (Thuk. 6,32,3–34). Zunächst zu einem der drei bevollmächtigten Strategen gewählt, doch bald ebenso wie seine Kollegen wegen Erfolglosigkeit abgesetzt (Thuk. 6,73,1; 103,4), wurde er dann der wichtigste Helfer und Ratgeber des → Gylippos und hatte maßgeblichen Anteil am Sieg über die Athener. Gegen Diokles trat er vergeblich für eine milde Behandlung der athenischen Gefangenen ein (Diod. 13,19,4–6). 412 als Admiral nach Kleinasien entsandt, wurde er nach dem Verlust seiner Schiffe in der Seeschlacht von Kyzikos (Xen. hell. 1,1,18) in Abwesenheit von den radikalen Demokraten verbannt. 408 nach Sizilien zurückgekehrt, operierte er mit Erfolg in der karthagischen Epikratie, wurde aber des Strebens nach der Tyrannis verdächtigt und deshalb nicht nach Syrakus zurückberufen (Diod. 13,63). Bei einem gescheiterten Handstreich auf Syrakus, an dem sich auch Dionysios [1] beteiligte, fiel er 407 im Straßenkampf (Diod. 13,75). Von Thukydides (4,58–64; 7,73) und Xenophon (hell. 1,1,30 f.) als Staatsmann und Patriot gerühmt.

A. ANDREWES, The Peace of Nicias, in: CAH 5, 21992, 433–463, bes. 446 ff. · D. ASHERI, Sicily, in: CAH 5, 21992, 147–170 · B. CAVEN, Dionysius I., 1990, 21 ff. · G. MADDOLI, in: E. GABBA, G. VALLET (Hrsg.), La Sicilia antica, Bd. 2.1, 1980, 74 ff. · H. D. WESTLAKE, H. the Syracusan, in: Bull. John Rylands Library 41, 1958, 239–268 = Ders., Essays on the Greek Historians and Greek History, 1969, 174 ff. K. MEI.

[2] L. Flavius H. Sophist aus Phokaia, um 200 n. Chr., Urenkel des → Polemon. Philostratos rühmt seine Fähigkeiten (soph. 2,25,608), teils um H.' Lehrer Claudius Rufinus zu kritisieren (Rufinos IK 24,1,602), sein Aussehen und seine ποικιλία (Mannigfaltigkeit), verurteilt aber seine kostspielige Lebensführung (ebd. 610). Kaiser Septimius Severus, der seine Rede bewunderte, schenkte ihm einmal 50 Talente Weihrauch, zwang ihn aber auch zu einer nur kurz dauernden Ehe (195 oder 197–199) mit einer häßlichen Tochter des Antipatros von Hierapolis, mit dem er zw. 200 und 205 an Caracallas → *consilium* (IK 16,2026) teilnahm. Vor seinem Tod mit 25 oder 28 J. wurde er im Asklepieion von Pergamon als *archiereús* und Philosoph geehrt [1; 2].
→ Philostratos; Zweite Sophistik

1 Altertümer von Pergamon 8.3,76–79 Nr. 34 2 PIR F 285. E. BO./Ü: L. S.

[3] *Syngenḗs, stratēgós* (συγγενής, στρατηγός) und *epistratēgós* (ἐπιστρατηγός) der Thebais 116/5 v. Chr.

L. MOOREN, The Aulic Titulature of Ptolemaic Egypt, 1975, 94, Nr. 057. W. A.

[4] H. aus Milet. Sohn des Alexandros, Tragödiendichter. Laut DID A 6,1b siegte er einmal bei den Amphiaraia/Rhomaia in Oropos nach 85 v. Chr.

METTE, 56 · TrGF 167. F. P.

Hermokreon

[1] Griech. Architekt des 3. Jh. v. Chr.; errichtete nach Strab. 10,5,7 und 13,1,13 aus dem Material eines aufgelassenen Tempels nahe Parion einen 1 Stadion (→ Längenmaße) langen Prunkaltar, der vermutlich auf Mz. dargestellt (London, BM) und dem hieronischen Monumentalaltar von → Syrakusai gut vergleichbar war.

OVERBECK, 2086–2087 (Quellen) • G. A. MANSUELLI, s. v. H., EAA 4, 1961, 13 (mit Abb. 18). C. HÖ.

[2] Epigrammatiker nicht sicher erwiesener Existenz; es werden ihm zwei Gedichte zugeschrieben, die nach Stil und Inhalt in das 3. Jh. v. Chr. zu setzen sind; die Zuweisung von Anth. Pal. 9,327 (eine aus dem »Kranz« des Meleager stammende Weihung von Gaben, die ein gewisser H. den Nymphen darbringt) kann jedoch aus dem Gedicht abgeleitet sein, während 16,11 (über eine Hermesstatue) von der *Sylloge Euphemiana* Platon zugeschrieben wird.

GA I 1, 106; 2, 305 f. M. G. A./Ü: T. H.

Hermolaos (Ἑρμόλαος).

[1] Sohn des Sopolis, Page (→ Basilikoi paides) von → Alexandros [4], kam dem König bei der Erlegung eines Wildschweins zuvor und wurde von ihm demütigend bestraft (327 v. Chr.). Zur Rache zettelte er unter den Pagen eine Verschwörung an, die aber fehlschlug und an den König verraten wurde. Die Beschuldigten wurden nach Folterung mit Zustimmung des Heeres zum Tode verurteilt und gesteinigt. → Kallisthenes, als Gegner der → Proskynesis dem Alexandros verhaßt, wurde, da er Lehrer der Pagen war, der Anstiftung verdächtigt. Obwohl von keinem der Knaben beschuldigt, wurde er etwas später verhaftet (Plut. Alexandros 55).

BERVE 2, Nr. 305. E. B.

[2] Bildhauer unbekannter Schaffenszeit, dessen Werke zur Ausschmückung des Kaiserpalastes am → Mons Palatinus verwendet wurden; er arbeitete zusammen mit Polydeukes.

OVERBECK, Nr. 2300 (Quellen). R. N.

Hermolochos (Ἑρμόλοχος). Autor einiger Zeilen über die Unwägbarkeiten und Hoffnungen des Lebens. Bei Stob. 4,34,66 (auch bei Phot. Bibl. 167) wird er in zwei Mss. H., in einem Ms. Hermolaos genannt. [1. 637] schreibt dieses Fragment einem Hermodotos zu und stellt zwei Verse um; [2] behält die Zuweisung an H. bei, verändert aber leicht die Kolometrie. Die daktyloepitritischen Verse weisen bei Stobaios Spuren des Dor. auf. Moderne Herausgeber haben weitere Konjekturen auf das Dor. hin vorgenommen.

1 TH. BERGK, Poetae Lyrici Graeci III, 41882 2 PMG 846 3 SH 491–493. E. R./Ü: L. S.

Hermon

[1] Bergmassiv (maximale Höhe 2814 m) im Süden des Antilibanon; hebr. *Ḥærmôn* (von *ḥrm* »Bann, Tabu«), griech. Ἀερμών, lat. *Hermon*, modern *Ǧabal aš-Šaiḫ*, »Berg des Weißhaarigen« / *Ǧabal aṯ-Ṯalǧ*, »Schneeberg«. Dt 3,9 setzt H. mit dem phöniz. *Śiriōn* und amoritisch *Śenīr* gleich, von daher wäre H. als *Šryn* im Ugarit., *Šarijana* im Hethit. und *Saniru* im Assyr. zu finden. Der biblischen Überlieferung gilt der H. als die nördl. Grenze des von Moses und Josua eroberten Landes östl. des Jordan (Jos 11,17; Dt 3,8). Aus den biblischen Belegen wird nicht deutlich, ob H. den ganzen Antilibanon (→ Antilibanos) oder nur seine nördl. oder südl. Ausläufer bezeichnet. Iosephos (ant. Iud. 5,3,1) spricht nicht von H., sondern nur vom »Berg Libanon« (→ Libanos); Eusebios (On. 20,12) bezeichnet nur den südl. Ausläufer als H. Auf dem sw Gipfel liegen die Überreste einer ant. Tempelanlage (Qasr-ʿAntar) aus dem 1.–4. Jh. n. Chr. Eine dort gefundene griech. Inschrift richtete sich an alle, die sich durch einen Fluch nicht vom Nähertreten abhalten ließen. Insgesamt wurden über zwanzig Tempelanlagen im Bereich des H. gefunden, die typologisch den kanaanäischen Freiluftheiligtümern entsprechen. Schon in der Bibel galt der H. als Sitz des Gottes Baʿal Hærmôn (Ri 3,3; 1 Chr 5,23) (→ Baal). Im 1. Jh. n. Chr. wurden Tempel des klass. Bautyps angefügt. In der hell. Zeit gehörte der H. zum Königreich der Ituräer von Chalkis (→ Ituraea).

R. ARAV, s. v. H., The Anchor Bible Dictionary 3, 1992, 158–159 • SH. DAR, s. v. H., NEAEHL 2, 616–617. TH. PO.

[2] Athener, beteiligte sich 411 v. Chr. als Befehlshaber der Besatzung in Munichia an der Erhebung des Taxiarchen → Aristokrates [2] gegen die Herrschaft der Vierhundert (Thuk. 8,92,5). Daß er 411 den Oligarchen → Phrynichos getötet haben soll, beruht auf einem Mißverständnis des Plutarch (Alkibiades 25,14). 410/409 war er Befehlshaber in Pylos (IG I³ 375,10).

[3] aus Megara, Steuermann (κυβερνήτης) auf dem Schiff des spartanischen Flottenkommandanten → Kallikratidas in der Schlacht bei den Arginusen 406 v. Chr. (Xen. hell. 1,6,32) und auf dem des → Lysandros bei Aigospotamoi 405 v. Chr. (Demosth. or. 23,212; vgl. Xen. oik. 4,20); durch eine Statue in der Gruppe des Lysandros in Delphoi geehrt (Paus. 10,9,7 f.). W. S.

[4] von Delos. Aus hell. Zeit, zw. 319 und 167 v. Chr. [1], von Porphyrios erwähnt, scheint über Vogelzeichen (schol. bT ad Il. K 274–5 ERBSE, III, 57–58; Porph. Quaestiones Homericae 1,154,23 SCHRADER = CollAlex 251–252) und Blitzmantik (Porph. ebd. 1,39,7, wo jedoch Ἕρμων ὁ Δήλιος Korrektur von MEINECKE ist) gedichtet zu haben.

1 U. v. WILAMOWITZ-MOELLENDORFF, Euripides: Herakles, Bd. II, 1889, 135 f. S. FO./Ü: T. H.

Hermonaktos kome (Ἑρμώνακτος κώμη). Siedlung an der → Tyras-Mündung (Strab. 7,3,16) oder ca. 16,5 km von ihr entfernt (Ptol. 3,10,7). Vielleicht identisch mit den Resten einer ant. Siedlung beim h. Kosovka.

M. V. ARBUNOV, K voprosu o lokalizacii bašni Neoptolema u Germonaktovoj derevni [Zum Problem der Lokalisierung des Neoptolemos-Turmes und H.k.], in: VDI 1, 1978, 43–51. I.v.B.

Hermonassa (Ἑρμώνασσα).

[1] Griech. Hafenstadt am asiat. Ufer des Kimmerischen → Bosporos [2], an der Südküste der Bucht von Taman, als Kolonie von Iones und Aioleis vor Mitte 6. Jh. v. Chr. gegr. Importe und Mz. bezeugen lebhaften Handel. H. lag im Stammesgebiet der Sindoi (Strab. 11,2,10), deren Oberschicht auch in H. lebte (reiche Kurgane). Hauptkulte: Apollon Ietros, Delphinios, Artemis, Aphrodite (Ps.-Skymn. 886–889; Arr. per. p. E. 60 u. a.).

V. F. GAIDUKEVIČ, Das Bosporanische Reich, 1971, 221–225. I.v.B.

[2] Griech. Handelsniederlassung an der Südküste des → Pontos Euxeinos im Westen von Trapezus, möglicherweise bei Akçaabat (ehemals Polathane), ›mittelgroße Kolonie‹ (κατοικία μετρία, Strab. 12,3,17), von [1] vermutungsweise mit Liviopolis (Plin. nat. 6,4,11) identifiziert.

1 W. J. HAMILTON, Reisen in Kleinasien 1, 1843, 233.

OLSHAUSEN/BILLER/WAGNER, 135 • C. MAREK, Stadt, Ära und Territorium in Pontus-Bithynia und Nord-Galatia (IstForsch 39), 1993, 19. E.O.

Hermonax

[1] Att.-rf. Vasenmaler, dessen Signatur sich auf 10 der insgesamt ca. 200 ihm von der Forsch. zugewiesenen Vasen findet. Er war zwischen 475 und 450 v. Chr. tätig und ein Schüler des → Berliner-Malers. Unter den Gefäßformen bevorzugte er Stamnoi, Peliken, Halsamphoren, Lutrophoren und Schalen, wobei bes. letztere den Einfluß des → Makron zeigen. Eine Schale in Brauron (Archäolog. Mus. A. 39) hat eine wgr. Innenseite. H. bevorzugte Verfolgungs-, Komos- und dionysische Szenen; auf einigen Vasen finden sich auch eher seltene Themen wie etwa der Schlangenbiß des Philoktet (Paris, LV G 413). Die signierten Vasen stammen aus der ersten Hälfte seines Schaffens, spätere Arbeiten sind weniger sorgfältig und abwechslungsreich gemalt. Obwohl technisch durchaus versiert, brachte H. keine Bilder von der gestalterischen Qualität hervor, für die sein Lehrer berühmt ist. Eine Pelike aus London (BM E 410), die früher für sein hochwertigstes Werk gehalten wurde, gilt h. als das namengebende Stück seines maßgeblichen Nachfolgers, des »Malers der Athena-Geburt«.

BEAZLEY, ARV², 483–492; 1655–1656; 1706 • BEAZLEY, Paralipomena, 379f.; 512 • C. ISLER-KERÉNYI, The H. in Zürich I, II, III, in: AK 26, 1983, 127–135; AK 27, 1984, 54–57; 154–165 • F. P. JOHNSON, The Late Vases of H., in: AJA 49, 1945, 491–502 • Ders., The Career of H., in: AJA 51, 1947, 233–247 • H.E. LANGENFASS, Unt. zur Chronologie, Diss. München 1972 • N. WEILL, Un cratère d'H., in: BCH 86, 1962, 64–94. J.O./Ü: R.S.-H.

[2] von Delos. Verf. von ›Kret. Glossen‹, von Athen. 3,81 f und 6,267c herangezogen (beide Male unter dem Namen *Hérmōn* zitiert, auf den vielleicht auch ein Repertorium von Synonyma zurückgeht (vgl. Athen. 11,480f) [1].

1 E. DEGANI, Hipponax. Testimonia et fragmenta, 1983, 186
2 A. GUDEMAN, s. v. H. (3), RE 8, 899–900. S.FO./Ü: T.H.

Hermonthis. Stadt auf dem Westufer des Nils, 20 km südl. von Luxor, Hauptort des 4. oberäg. Gaues, äg. *jwnj* bzw. *jwnj šmʿj*, »Oberäg. → Heliopolis«, oder *jwnw mnṯw*, das »Heliopolis des Month«, griech. H. Hauptgott ist Month, Haus- und Königsgott der Herrscher der 11. Dyn. (20. Jh. v. Chr.); sein Tempel ist seit dieser Zeit belegt, wurde in der Perserzeit zerstört, in der 30. Dyn. erneuert. Bedeutsam ist die Verehrung des Stieres Buchis mit eigener Nekropole (Bucheum). Nach dem Niedergang zw. dem 3. und 1. Jh. v. Chr. ist H. in der röm. Kaiserzeit wieder Gauhauptstadt, in kopt. Zeit Bischofssitz.

A. EGGEBRECHT, s. v. Armant, LÄ 1, 435–441 • R. MOND, O. H. MYERS, Temples of Armant, 1937 • Dies., The Bucheum, 1934. R.GR.

Hermos (Ἑρμός).

[1] Att. Asty-Demos der Phyle Akamantis, mit zwei *buleutaí*. Lage: an der »Hl. Straße« nach Eleusis am Eingang des Passes beim h. Daphni, h. Chaidari; dort befindet sich das Grabmal der Pythionike, der Gattin des Harpalos (Plut. Phokion 22,2; Paus. 1,37,5; [1]). Bei Daphni Grabinschr. von Hermeioi: IG II² 6072.

1 N. D. PAPACHATZIS, Παυσανίου Ἑλλάδος Περιήγησις. Ἀττικά, 1974, 468 mit Anm. 6.

W. KOLBE, s. v. H., RE 8, 903 • TRAILL, Attica, 47, 69, 110 Nr. 54 Tab. 5. H.LO.

[2] Fluß in West-Kleinasien, h. Gediz nehri bzw. çayı, entspringt am Dindymos (h. Murat Dağı), bildet im Mittel- und Unterlauf mit Nebenflüssen und -armen Talauen (→ Kurupedion), fließt nördl. an → Sardeis und → Magnesia am Sipylos vorbei und mündet mit oftmals verlagerten Armen in die Bucht von Smyrna (im Alt. *Hérmeios kólpos*, »H.-Bucht«); dort vorrückendes Mündungsdelta mit Nehrungen (ehemals vorgelagerte Myrmekes-, d. h. »Ameisen«-Klippen). Belege: vgl. Hom. Il. 20,392; Hes. theog. 343; Hdt. 1,55; 80; 5,101; Skyl. 98,4; Strab. 12,3,27; Plin. nat. 5,119 [1. 237]; Arr. an. 1,17,4; 5,6,4; 7; Ptol. 5,2,5 (»H. der Aiolis«).

Wegen drohender Zuschüttung der Bucht wird der Mündungsarm h. wieder weiter nördl. nach Westen zur Außenbucht geführt (1886 bei Menemen Kanalbau zu altem Flußbett), wo im Alt. die Mündung des H. südl. von Phokaia und Larisa, einst weiter flußaufwärts bei Temnos lag (Hdt.; Plin. l.c.). Der Flußgott H. ist auf Mz. von Magnesia am Sipylos und anderen Städten am H. dargestellt.

1 G. WINKLER, R. KÖNIG, C. Plinius Secundus d. Ä., Naturkunde (lat.-dt.), Bd. 5, 1993 (Komm.).

Reisekarte Türkiye-Türkei, Türk. Verteidigungsministerium/Kartograph. Verlag Ryborsch, Obertshausen bei Frankfurt/M., 1994, Bl. 2 • W.M. RAMSAY, The Historical Geography of Asia Minor, 1890, 59f., 108 • W.-D. HÜTTEROTH, Türkei, 1982, 65f. H.KA.

Hermotimos

[1] Kriegsgefangener aus Pedasa, der nach Hdt. 8,104f. als verschnittener Eunuch zu einem der engsten Vertrauten des → Xerxes I. geworden sein und sich am Sklavenhändler Panionios gerächt haben soll (Athen. 6,266e bezeugt die Bekanntheit der Geschichte). → Eunuch

1 BRIANT, 283–288 2 P. GUYOT, Eunuchen als Sklaven und Freigelassene, 1980, Register s.v. J.W.

[2] von Kolophon, Mathematiker. Er hat (nach Eudemos) die Stud. des → Eudoxos [1] und Theaitetos fortgeführt und viele in den ›Elementen‹ enthaltene Sätze und einige τόποι (*tópoi*, geometrische Örter ?) gefunden (Prokl. in Eukl. I S.67, 20–23 FRIEDLEIN).

T.L. HEATH, History of Greek Mathematics, Bd. 1, 1921, 320f. M.F.

Hermunduri. Der wohl auf Gefolgschaft beruhende german. Kampfverband, zusammen mit Suebi und Semnones im myth. Urstamm der → Herminones (Plin. nat. 4,100), in augusteischer Zeit an der Elbe lokalisiert (Strab. 7,1,3; Vell. 2,106,2), hatte seinen polit. und organisatorischen Zusammenhang damals evtl. schon verloren. Landsuchende H. siedelte → Domitius [II 2] 6/1 v.Chr. in der ehemaligen Markomannis an (Cass. Dio 55,10a,2), evtl. als strategische Hilfe gegen die durch die röm. Okkupation gesteigerte, nach Böhmen und Süddeutschland gerichtete suebische Fluktuation (nicht auf Mainfranken fixierbar: [1]). Unter Vibilius vertrieben die nördl. H. um 19 n.Chr. → Catualda (Tac. ann. 2,62f.) und stürzten um 50 Vannius (ebd. 12,29f.); kurz danach besiegten sie die → Chatti im Kampf um das Salz eines Grenzflusses (ebd. 13,57; [2]). Die der Raetia benachbarte *Hermundurorum civitas* (vgl. CIL III 14359,4) hatte *commercium* und freien Zugang zur Prov. Raetia (Tac. Germ. 41; [3; 4. 80–82; 5]). In den Markomannenkriegen waren die H. Gegner Roms (SHA Aur. 22,1; 27,10). Die mitteldeutschen H. dürften für die Ethnogenese der Thüringer maßgebend gewesen sein [6; 7. 475], während die südl. H. wohl in den Kampfverbänden der → Iuthungi aufgingen [8. 234, 236f.].

1 D. TIMPE, Erwägungen zur histor. Einordnung des augusteischen Truppenlagers von Marktbreit, in: BRGK 72, 1991, 315f. 2 J. HERRMANN (Hrsg.), Griech. und lat. Quellen zur Frühgesch. Mitteleuropas bis zur Mitte des 1. Jt. u. Z., III, 1991, 531f. 3 G. PERL, Tacitus, Germania, 1990, 240–242 4 R. WOLTERS, Der Waren- und Dienstleistungsaustausch zw. dem Röm. Reich und dem Freien Germanien, in: Münstersche Beitr. zur ant. Handelsgesch. 10, 1991, 78–132 5 K. DIETZ, in: W. CZSYZ, K. DIETZ, T. FISCHER, H.-J. KELLNER (Hrsg.), Die Römer in Bayern, 1995, 202f. 6 K. PESCHEL, Die Thüringer der Völkerwanderungszeit zw. Arch. und Gesch., in: Wiss. Zschr. Jena (Gesellschafts- und sprachwiss. Reihe) 35, 1986, 561–574 7 B. SCHMIDT, Das Königreich der Thüringer und seine Prov., in: W. MENGHIN (Hrsg.), Germanen, Hunnen und Awaren, 1988, 471–480 8 T. STICKLER, Iuthungi sive Semnones, in: Bayer. Vorgeschichtsblätter 60, 1995, 231–249. K.DI.

Hermupolis (magna). 300 km südl. von Kairo auf dem West-Ufer des Nils, äg. *Ḫmnw*, »Stadt der Acht«, nach einer Gruppe von vier Urgötterpaaren, h. al-Ašmunein, griech. H. nach dem dort verehrten → Hermes Trismegistos, der dem Stadtgott → Thot gleichgesetzt wurde. Im hl. Bezirk finden sich Reste der Tempel des Pantheons von H. vom MR bis in die röm. Kaiserzeit. H. erlebte unter den Ptolemäern und Römern erneut eine Blütezeit. Aus kopt. Zeit sind Reste einer Siedlung und einer Basilika (5. Jh. n. Chr.) erhalten.

D. KESSLER, s.v. H., LÄ 2, 1137–1147. R.GR.

Hernac (Ἡρνᾶς, Ἡρνάχ). Jüngster Sohn Attilas (Priscus fr. 8 = FHG 4, 93), siedelte nach der Niederlage der Hunnen 455 n.Chr. mit seiner Gefolgschaft im Norden der Prov. Scythia (Iord. Get. 266). Wegen eines Friedensvertrages schickten er und → Dengizich 466/7 Gesandte zu Leon I. (Priscus fr. 36 = FHG 4, 107). PLRE 2, 400f. (Ernach). ME.STR.

Hernici. Ital. Volk in Latium am → Liris und dessen Nebenfluß Trerus oder Tolerus (h. Sacco); hier lagen Anagnia, Ferentinum und Frusino an der *via Latina*, weiter im Landesinnern Verulae, Aletrium und Capitulum Hernicum. Seit Anf. der Eisenzeit faßbar, scheinen sie das älteste ital. Volk gewesen zu sein, das nach Latium eingewandert ist, evtl. im Zusammenhang mit den Wanderungen der Sabini (Serv. Aen. 7,684) oder Marsi (Paul. Fest. 89 L.). Laevus Cispius aus Anagnia unterstützte Tullus Hostilius gegen Alba Longa und gab dem Berg Cispius seinen Namen. Vorübergehend waren die H. im Latin. Bund (Liv. 2,40). 306 von Rom unterworfen (Liv. 9,43,23). Seit Augustus in der *regio I* (Plin. nat. 3,63f.). Ihr Siedlungsgebiet war die h. Ciociaria. Eisenzeitliche Siedlung bei Colleferro, Heiligtümer unterhalb Anagnia (8.–5. Jh.) und in Osteria della Fontana bei *compitum Anagninum*, wo sich wohl der *lucus Dianae* beim *circus Maritimus* befand, das Zentrum der H. (Liv. 9,42,11; 27,4,12).

M. MAZZOLANI, Anagnia, 1969 • C. LETTA, I Marsi, 1973 • S. GATTI, A. ASCENZI (Hrsg.), Dives Anagnia, 1993. G.U./Ü: H.D.

Hero (Ἡρώ). Aphroditepriesterin in Sestos, Geliebte des Leander. Da H.s Eltern einer Ehe im Wege stehen, durchschwimmt Leander jeweils in der Nacht den Hellespont von Abydos nach Sestos, wo H. ihn in einem Turm erwartet. Als einmal die wegweisende Fackel erlischt, ertrinkt er. H. stürzt sich von ihrem Turm herab, als sie den Leichnam des Geliebten am Ufer erblickt.

Zusammenhängend ist die Erzählung erst in einem Kleinepos des → Musaios aus dem 5. Jh. n. Chr. überliefert. Eine weitere Version bieten Ov. epist. 18 und 19. Erwähnungen finden sich außerdem bei Verg. georg. 3,358 ff.; Strab. 13,1,22; Ov. ars 2,249 f.; Ov. trist. 3,10,41 f. Auf einem Papyrus sind 10 Zeilen einer Bearbeitung des Stoffes erhalten [1]. Als gemeinsame Quelle wird eine hell. Elegie vermutet. Auch in der bildenden Kunst erscheint das Motiv erst seit dem 1. Jh. v. Chr.

1 H. Lloyd-Jones, P. Parson (Hrsg.), Supplementum Hellenisticum, 1983, fr. 951.

H. Färber, H. und Leander: Musaios und die weiteren ant. Zeugnisse, 1961 • A. Kossatz-Deissmann, s. v. H. und Leander, LIMC 8.1 (Suppl.), 619–622 • G. Schott, H. und Leander bei Musaios und Ovid, Diss. Köln 1956 • E. Sittig, s. v. H., RE 8, 909–916 • K. Volk, H. und Leander in Ovids Doppelbriefen (epist. 18 und 19), in: Gymnasium 103, 1996, 95–106. K. WA.

Herodas, Herondas (urspr. wohl Ἡρώιδας, später Ἡρώδας; Ἡρώνδας nur bei Athen. 3,86b).

A. Zur Person B. Werke C. Würdigung D. Nachwirkung

A. Zur Person

Der hell. Dichter verfaßte dramatische Vers-Skizzen im choliambischen Versmaß (→ Metrik). Er lebte nach zeitgenössischen Anspielungen in seinen Gedichten in der 1. H. des 3. Jh. v. Chr. und war Zeitgenosse von → Theokritos und → Kallimachos (1,30: »Zwillingstempel« von Ptolemaios II. Philadelphos und seiner Schwester Arsinoë [II 3]; 1,31: Museion in Alexandreia; 4,23–26: die Söhne des Praxiteles; 4,76–78: Apelles; 2,16: Ake in Phönikien, vor 260 in Ptolemais umbenannt). Schaffensort dürfte nach der Kulisse der Gedichte (2 und vielleicht 4 auf Kos; 6–7 in Kleinasien) sowie dem Lob Ägyptens im 1. Mimos eine Stadt oder Insel der ion. Küste Kleinasiens oder Alexandreia selbst gewesen sein. Nur in 8,75–79 redet H. von sich selbst, wobei er verkündet, das lit. Erbe des → Hipponax (2. H. 6. Jh. v. Chr.) antreten zu wollen.

B. Werke

Das Werk des H. war seit der Ant. bis zur Veröffentlichung eines vom British Museum erworbenen Papyrus, der sieben Mimiamben fast vollständig und zwei weitere bruchstückhaft enthält (London, BM Pap. 135), verloren und vergessen. Hinzu kommt POxy. 22,2326, der 8,67–75 wiedergibt. Es sind Miniaturdramen, Szenen aus dem Alltag, die in lit. Dialekt (ion.) für eine oder mehrere »Stimmen« verfaßt sind. Der Mimiambos (= M.) als Form stellt die Verbindung einer Art Straßentheater (*mímos*) einerseits, wobei der Künstler einen oder mehrere Charaktertypen durch Stimme und Gestik – ohne Maske – auf einer kleinen Schaubühne in Prosa nach-»äffte«, mit dem Hinkiambos des Hipponax von Ephesos andererseits dar, der sich dieser Form zur scharfen Kritik an zeitgenössischen Mißständen bediente. Ähnliche Miniaturdramen in Gedichtform finden sich bei Theokr. 2 (*Pharmakeútria*) und 15 (*Adoniázusai*), Hinkiambos und mimetische Form bei → Phoinix von Kolophon, *Korōnistaí* [1]. Vor H. erreichte der Mimos lit. Niveau nur bei → Sophron von Syrakus (Ende 5. Jh. v. Chr.), dessen (verlorene) Prosawerke Platon beeindruckt haben sollen. Inhaltlich ähneln die M. den ›Charakteren‹ des → Theophrastos; sonst haben sie – abgesehen von Dialekt und Metrum – am meisten mit der att. → Komödie gemeinsam [2].

Ob die M. von mehreren Schauspielern aufgeführt, von einem Darsteller mimisch rezitiert oder nur privat gelesen wurden, bleibt umstritten. Zu berücksichtigen sind folgende Faktoren: Der Mimos war in früher Zeit ein Einzelkünstler, der mehrere Figuren nachahmte; der 8. M. des H. macht nur Sinn, wenn er vom Verf. selbst vorgetragen wird; bei den M. sind zwei Stimmen die Regel, vier das Maximum. Wahrscheinlich wurden die M. im Einzelvortrag vor wenigen Hörern (Schaubühne, Symposion) dramatisch vorgetragen, wobei der Künstler durch unterstützende Gestik und Verstellung der Stimme die einzelnen »Rollen« kenntlich machte. Gegen die These, die M. seien reine Buchpoesie gewesen [3], wendet sich entschieden Mastromarco [4]. Bei Plut. mor. 712e sind zwei Mimenformen (*Hypothéseis*, *Paígnia*) als Unterhaltung beim Symposion belegt. Daß die M. auch zum Vortrag am Königshof gedacht waren, legt das Lob der Errungenschaften der alexandrinischen Kultur im 1. M. nahe. Ob die skurrilen, ans Obszöne grenzenden Szenen mancher M. auf vornehmes Publikum eher anstößig oder anregend wirkten, mag dahingestellt sein.

1. *Prokyklís* oder *Mastropós* (›Kupplerin‹) stellt den Besuch einer Kupplerin bei einer Bürgersfrau dar, deren Ehemann schon lange abwesend ist. Die Kupplerin schlägt ein Rendezvous mit einem ansehnlichen Mann vor. 2. *Pornoboskós* (›Zuhälter‹) ist die – parodistisch gefaßte – Gerichtsrede eines Zuhälters, der einen Schiffskapitän wegen mutwilliger Zerstörung seines Eigentums und Entführung einer Prostituierten auf Schadensersatz verklagt. 3. *Didáskalos* (›Schullehrer‹) stellt die Züchtigung eines faulen Jungen, der andauernd die Schule schwänzt, durch den Lehrer dar. 4. ›Frauen, die Asklepios ein Geschenk bringen und opfern‹ enthält den Dialog zweier Frauen, die zum Asklepiosheiligtum (auf Kos?) pilgern, wo sie die dort aufgestellten Kunstwerke bewundern [5] und dem Gott anschließend opfern. Parallelen mit einem Stück des → Sophron, Θάμεναι τὰ Ἴσθμια, ›Zuschauerinnen bei den Isthmien‹, bieten sich an. 5. *Zēlótypos* (›Die Eifersüchtige‹) zeigt eine eifersüchtige Herrin, die sich über die Untreue ihres Liebhabers, eines Sklaven, empört. Das Eifersuchtsmotiv ist sowohl mit Theokr. 2 (*Pharmakeútria*) als auch mit dem anon. ›Giftmischermimos‹ ([12. 47–52] = POxy. 413, col. 1–3) vergleichbar. 6. *Philiázusai* oder *Idiázusai* (›Liebende Frauen‹ oder ›Frauen unter sich‹) enthält das private Gespräch zweier Frauen über die Vorzüge eines

baubṓn (künstlichen Phallus), den eine erworben hat. 7. *Skyteús* (›Schuster‹) schließt thematisch an 6. an: Die Frauen finden sich beim Schuhmacher ein, der die *baubṓnes* herstellt, und bewundern seine Schuhe. 8. *Enhýpnion* (›Traum‹; Text sehr lückenhaft, Deutung umstritten): H. erzählt, wie er im Traum an einer ländlichen Dionysosfeier teilgenommen habe, wobei er mit einem Alten im → *Askōliasmós*-Tanz konkurriert habe; als Traumdeutung gibt H. an, er trete das lit. Erbe des »alten« Hipponax an, indem er ›krumme Gedichte für Ionier‹ verfasse (τὰ κύλλ' ἀείδειν Ξουθίδῃς) [6]. 9. *Aponestizómenai* (›Frauen nach dem Fasten‹). Nur die ersten Zeilen sind erhalten. Die Namen zweier weiterer M. – *Molpínos* und *Synergazómenai* (›Frauen bei der Arbeit‹) – sind bei Stobaios überliefert.

C. Würdigung

Der Papyrus stellt wahrscheinlich eine Auswahl aus H.' Schaffen dar. Das niedere soziale Milieu der dargestellten Figuren entspricht aller Wahrscheinlichkeit nach nicht dem des intendierten Publikums, welches imstande sein mußte, das von H. vollbrachte lit. Kunststück der Wiederbelebung einer ausgestorbenen lit. Form zu würdigen. Deshalb wendet sich Cunningham [11] entschieden gegen die These, H. sei ein »Realist«; seine Sprache sei von der Alltagssprache sehr weit entfernt. Dargestellt werden verschiedene Szenen, wobei manche reine »Frauenmimen« (Suda s.v. Sophron teilt in Frauen- bzw. Männermimen), manche gemischtgeschlechtlich sind. Vom schlauen Schuhmacher, der für seine Ware wirbt, bis zur naiven Bewunderung der ›Zu Asklepios opfernden Frauen‹ – überall läßt H. den Leser eine bestimmte Lebenssituation durch die Augen einer zwar mit Sympathie, aber auch mit ironischer Distanz gezeichneten Figur wahrnehmen. Form, Handlung, Charaktere, Gefühle sind bei H. alle eine Verkleinerungsform der att. Komödie. Der Humor ergibt sich aus der Lächerlichkeit der behandelten Situation, den erkennbaren Charakterschwächen der handelnden Personen, aber auch aus dem ästhetischen Kontrast zw. lit. Kunstsprache und alltäglichem Inhalt. Durchaus hell. wirkt H. in seiner Vorliebe für Glossen, die eher aus Speziallexika als der Mundart der Unterschicht zu stammen scheinen. Die Obszönität mancher Stellen ist auch mit Aristophanes vergleichbar.

D. Nachwirkung

Der jüngere Plinius lobt M. des Arrius Antoninus als eines H. oder Kallimachos ebenbürtig oder sogar überlegen (Plin. epist. 4,3,3). Sonst zeugen Schol., Lex.-Einträge und ant. Komm. von Kenntnis der M. bis in byz. Zeit. Als Vorbild röm. Mimiambographie darf H. gelten, sonst ist seine Nachwirkung sehr begrenzt: zw. Byzanz und Neuzeit geriet er völlig in Vergessenheit. Der umfangreiche Komm. von Headlam-Knox [9] zeugt vom Wert der M. für den Gelehrten als Fundgrube seltener Begriffe und Sprüche: Das Urteil von Cunningham [11], H. verdiene nicht zuletzt deshalb Aufmerksamkeit, weil sonst nur wenige hell. Dichter erh. sind, wird dem Autor nicht gerecht. Daß die M. nicht den allg. Ruhm erlangten, den H. sich erhoffte (8,75–79), liegt vielleicht teils am bescheidenen Anspruch der Gedichte selbst, teils an deren lexikalischen Schwierigkeiten, sicherlich aber nicht an fehlendem Darstellungs- bzw. Einfühlungsvermögen des Verfassers.

→ Hellenistische Dichtung; Mimos

1 W.D. Furley, Apollo humbled: Phoenix' Koronisma in its Hellenistic literary setting, in: Materiali e Discussioni per l'analisi dei testi classici, 33, 1994, 9–31 2 H. Krakert, H. in mimiambis quatenus comoediam graecam respexisse videatur, Diss. Freiburg/Leipzig 1902 3 G. Pasquali, Se i mimiambi di Eroda fossero destinati alla recitazione, in: Xenia Romana, 1907, 15–27 4 G. Mastromarco, The Public of Herondas (London Studies in Classical Philology vol. 11), 1984 5 T. Gelzer, Mimus und Kunsttheorie bei Herondas, Mim. 4, in: C. Schäublin (Hrsg.), Katalepton. FS B. Wyss, 1985, 96–116 6 R.M. Rosen, Mixing of Genres and Literary Program in H. 8, in: HSPh 94, 1992, 205–216.

Ed.: 7 F.G. Kenyon, London 1891 8 O. Crusius, Leipzig 1892 (Teubner) 9 W. Headlam, A.D. Knox, Cambridge 1922 10 P. Groeneboom, Groningen 1922 (nur I–VI) 11 I.C. Cunningham, Oxford 1971 (komm. Ausgabe = 1) 12 Ders., Leipzig 1987 (Teubner, cum appendice fragmentorum mimorum papyraceorum = 2) 13 B.G. Mandilaras, Athen 1986 (mit Ablichtungen des Papyrus).
Lit.: 14 O. Crusius, Unt. zu den Mimiamben des H., 1892 15 F.-J. Simon, Τὰ Κύλλ' Ἀείδειν, Interpretationen zu den Mimiamben des H., 1991 16 R.G. Ussher, The Mimiamboi of H., in: Hermathena 129, 1980, 65–76 17 Ders., The mimic tradition of »character« in H., in: Quaderni urbinati di cultura classica 50, 1985, 45–68.

W.D.F.

Herodes (Ἡρῴδης).

[1] H. I. d.Gr. Geb. ca. 73 v.Chr., Sohn des → Antipatros [4] und der Araberin Kypros. 47 zum Strategen von Galilaea ernannt, geriet er wegen eigenmächtiger Hinrichtung von Aufständischen mit dem Jerusalemer Sanhedrin in Konflikt. Der röm. Statthalter von Syrien Sex. → Iulius [I 11] Caesar machte ihn zum Strategen von Koilesyrien und Samaria. 43 erwies er sich dem Caesarmörder C. → Cassius [I 10] bei der Ausbeutung des Landes als unentbehrlich, ebenso 41, nach der Schlacht von Philippi, dem Triumvirn M. → Antonius [I 9], der ihn und seinen Bruder Phasael zu Tetrarchen erhob. Vor den Parthern und dem von ihnen eingesetzten König und Hohenpriester → Antigonos [5] floh H. nach Rom, wo der Senat ihn Ende 40 zum Gegenkönig ernannte. Mit röm. Hilfe zurückgekehrt, heiratete er 37 die Hasmonäerin Mariamme. Antonius' Landschenkungen an → Kleopatra VII. zogen auch H.' Reich in Mitleidenschaft: Neben dem Zugang zum Meer gingen 34 auch die Balsampflanzungen von Jericho verloren. Der Übergang zu Octavian/Augustus nach der Schlacht bei Actium (→ Aktion) sicherte dem H. Königswürde und Vergrößerung seines Reiches: 30 erhielt er neben Jericho auch Gadara, Hippos, Samaria, Gaza, Anthedon, Ioppa und Stratons Turm an der Küste, 23/22 die Bezirke Trachonitis, Batanaia und Auranitis sowie 20 das

Territorium des Zenodoros nördl. und nordwestl. des Sees Genezareth bis zu den Jordanquellen. H. vereinte mit dem jüd. Kernland die Gebiete der Peripherie, in denen das Zusammenleben von Juden und Nichtjuden schwerwiegende Probleme aufwarf. Die gewalttätige Effizienz der Herrschaftsausübung empfahl H. dem röm. Oberherrn ebenso wie seine unbedingte Loyalität. So herrschte er dank kaiserlicher Gunst über ein Reich, dessen Größe dem König Davids entsprach.

H. war einer der großen Bauherren der ant. Welt. Als Städtegründer, Wohltäter (→ *euergétēs*) der hell. Welt und Förderer griech. Kultur erwies er sich wie auch in seiner Herrschaftsausübung als Fortsetzer des hell. Königtums. Von seinen Großbauten und Städtegründungen sind hervorzuheben: in Jerusalem Theater, Amphitheater, Königspalast und seit 20/19 der Neubau des Tempels, der Wiederaufbau von → Samaria als Augustusstadt = Sebaste, die Gründung der Hafenstadt Caesarea (22–10/9), die Errichtung der Festung Herodion in der Nähe von Bethlehem, der Wiederaufbau der zerstörten Hasmonäerfestungen Alexandreia und Hyrkania sowie der Ausbau von Machairus und Masada. In den nichtjüd. Teilen seines Reiches und in Syrien stiftete er Tempel für den Kaiserkult, förderte den Ausbau der von Augustus gegründeten Stadt Nikopolis/Actium und errichtete u. a. eine Stiftung zugunsten der Olympischen Spiele.

Obwohl H. im jüd. Kernland das Religionsgesetz und den Einfluß der → Pharisaioi respektierte, erregten einige seiner Neuerungen den Unwillen der Frommen, vor allem die Errichtung von Theater und Amphitheater in Jerusalem sowie die Anbringung eines Adlers am Tempeleingang. Hohepriester und Sanhedrin verloren ihre traditionelle Macht. Allen Bedrohungen seiner Herrschaft, mochten sie von der priesterlichen Aristokratie, von sozialem Protest und nationalrel. Erwartungen oder dynastischen Konflikten ausgehen, begegnete er mit brutaler Härte. Aus der ehelichen Verbindung mit Mariamme und der Rivalität zwischen Herodeern und → Hasmonäern resultierte das blutige Drama dynastischer Morde und Hinrichtungen: 35 ließ H. den Hohenpriester → Aristobulos [3], Bruder der Mariamme, ermorden, 30 den ehemaligen Hohenpriester und Ethnarchen → Hyrkanos [3] II. hinrichten, 29/28 folgten Mariamme und Alexandra, deren Mutter, 27 sein Schwager Kostabar und die von ihm versteckten letzten überlebenden Hasmonäer. Der Konflikt zwischen H. und seinen Söhnen von Mariamme, Aristobulos [4] und Alexandros, endete im J. 7 mit deren Hinrichtung, und der zum Nachfolger ausersehene Antipatros wurde, einer Verschwörung überführt, wenige Tage vor H.' Tod 4 v. Chr. ebenfalls hingerichtet. In seinem letzten Testament bestimmte er H. [3] Archelaos zum König und dessen Bruder H. [4] Antipas sowie beider Halbbruder Philippos zu Tetrarchen. Hauptquellen: Ios. bell. Iud. 1,181–673; Ios. ant. Iud. 14,121–17,199. Zu den übrigen Quellen s. Lit.

Der biblische Bericht über den Kindermord von Bethlehem (Mt 2,16) entbehrt jeglicher historischen Grundlage.
→ Judentum

Schürer, Bd. 1 • H. Otto, s. v. H. 1., RE Suppl. 2, 1–158 • A. H. M. Jones, The Herods of Judaea, ²1967, 39–152 • A. Schalit, König H., 1969 • P. Richardson, H., King of the Jews and Friend of the Romans, 1997.

[2] Geb. 22 v. Chr., mit Herodias, der Tochter seines Halbbruders → Aristobulos [4], verheiratet, bevor diese die zweite Ehe mit H. [4] Antipas einging. Zeitweilig zum Thronfolger bestimmt, wurde er in der endgültigen Thronfolgeregelung seines Vaters übergangen. Er gehörte wahrscheinlich zu den Söhnen H.', die sich bei → Pontius Pilatus und Kaiser Tiberius gegen die Anbringung goldener Weihetafeln in deren Namen am Jerusalemer Königspalast wandten (Phil. legatio ad Gaium 38,300; Ios. bell. Iud. 1,557; 573; 588; 600; ant. Iud. 17,14; 19; 78; 18,109 f.; 136).

[3] H. Archelaos. Geb. um 23 v. Chr., von seinem Vater letztwillig zum König bestimmt, reiste er 4 v. Chr. nach Niederschlagung eines Aufstandes in Jerusalem nach Rom, um von Augustus die Bestätigung dieser Verfügung gegen die Ansprüche seines Bruders H. [4] Antipas zu erreichen. Während seiner Abwesenheit brach ein neuer Aufstand aus, der durch Eingreifen des Statthalters von Syrien, P. → Quinctilius Varus, niedergeschlagen wurde. Abgesandte der Priesteraristokratie forderten vergeblich, daß keiner der Herodeer die Herrschaft erhalten, sondern die hohepriesterliche Theokratie wiederhergestellt werden solle. Augustus verfügte die Teilung des Reiches. H. erhielt mit Iudaea, Samaria und Idumaea den Kern des Reiches und den Titel eines Tetrarchen. Sein gewalttätiges Regime veranlaßte die jüd. und samaritanische Aristokratie, seine Absetzung zu fordern. Im J. 6 n. Chr. verbannte ihn Augustus in das gallische Vienna. Sein Reich wurde kaiserliche Provinz, und in Jerusalem wurde, unter röm. Aufsicht, die Theokratie wiederhergestellt (Ios. bell. Iud. 1,562–2,116; ant. Iud. 17,20; 188–355; Strab. 16,765).

[4] H. Antipas. 4 v. Chr. aufgrund der letztwilligen Verfügung seines Vaters H. [1] Tetrarch von Galilaea und Peraia, gründete H. 17 n. Chr. am See Genezareth die nach Augustus' Nachfolger benannte neue Hauptstadt Tiberias. Seine zweite Ehe mit Herodias, seiner Schwägerin und Nichte, gab Anlaß zur Kritik – so von seiten Iohannes' des Täufers (Mk 6,14–29), den H. als potentiellen Unruhestifter hinrichten ließ – und verwickelte ihn in einen Krieg mit seinem Schwiegervater aus erster Ehe, → Aretas [4] IV., dem König des Nabatäerreiches. Der von Herodias initiierte Versuch, ihm anstelle ihres Bruders H. [8] Agrippa die Königswürde zu verschaffen, scheiterte und zog 39 seine Verbannung nach Lugdunum durch Kaiser Caligula nach sich (Ios. bell. Iud. 1,646; 2,20–183; ant. Iud. 17,146; 17,224–18,256; Strab. 16,765; Cass. Dio. 55,27,6).

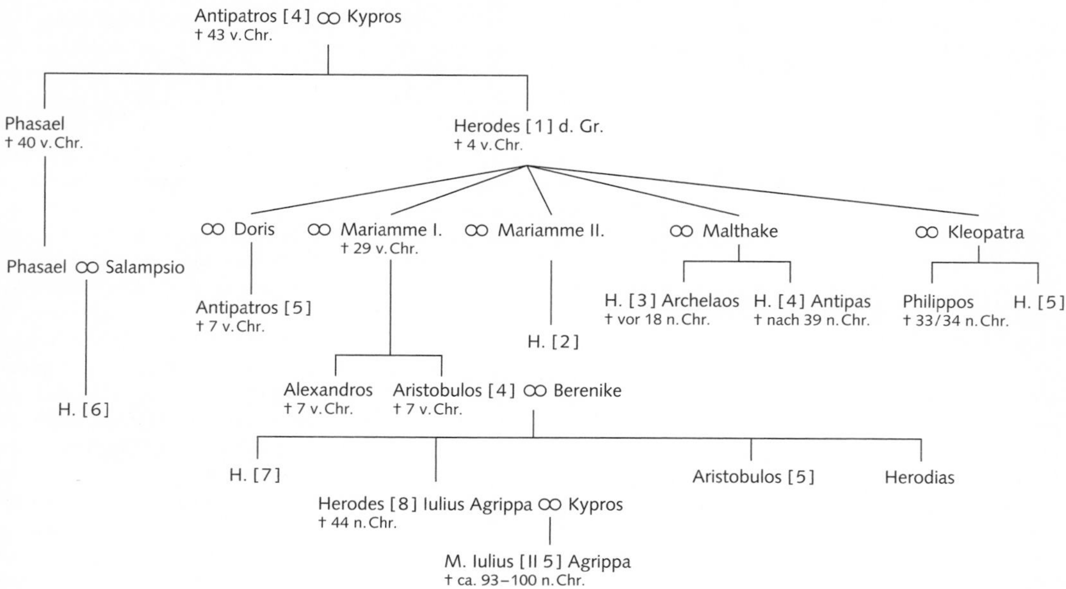

[5] Jüngerer Bruder des Tetrarchen Philippos, wurde von H. [1] d. Gr. bei der letztwilligen Verfügung über seine Nachfolger nicht berücksichtigt. Näheres ist nicht bekannt (Ios. bell. Iud. 1,562; Ios. ant. Iud. 17,21).

[6] Sohn des Phasael, des Neffen H.' [1] d. Gr., und der Salampsio, Tochter H.' d. Gr. von der Hasmonäerin Mariamme (Ios. ant. Iud. 18,130).

[7] H. (II.). Geb. zwischen 15 und 11 v. Chr., Sohn des → Aristobulos [4]. Kaiser Claudius verlieh ihm 41 n. Chr. Chalcis ad Libanum, d. h. den Rest des Ituraeerreiches, mit dem Königstitel (Ios. bell. Iud. 2,217). Als jüd. Klientelkönig und röm. Bürger mit praetorischem Rang (Cass. Dio 60,8,3) trat er für die Rechte der Juden von Alexandreia ein und erhielt 44 nach dem Tod des (H.) [8] Agrippa das Recht, die Hohenpriester einzusetzen. Nach seinem Tod wurde sein Reich 48 eingezogen und seinem Neffen → Iulius [II 5] Agrippa II. übertragen (Ios. ant. Iud. 19,279; 288; 20,15 f.; 103).

[8] (H.) Iulius Agrippa I. Geb. 10 v. Chr., Sohn des → Aristobulos [4], in Rom aufgewachsen mit engen Beziehungen zum Kaiserhaus, erhielt er nach einem wechselvollen Leben und hochverschuldet 37 n. Chr. von Kaiser Caligula die Tetrarchie des → Philippos, die Gaulanitis, Trachonitis, Batanaia und Panias mit Caesarea [2] sowie den Königstitel, 39 auch die Tetrarchie des H. [4] Antipas. Kaiser Claudius, bei dessen Kaisererhebung er eine Rolle spielte, zeichnete ihn 41 mit konsularischem Rang aus und übertrug ihm die röm. Provinz Iudaea (Cass. Dio 60,8,2), so daß er über das wiederhergestellte Reich H.' I. herrschte. Gegenüber den Juden trat er als Verehrer der jüd. Religion auf, außerhalb der Grenzen seines Reiches, aber auch in Caesarea [1] als großzügiger Förderer der nichtjüd.-hell. Kultur. Seine Versuche, seinen polit. Spielraum zu erweitern – durch Ausbau der Befestigung Jerusalems und durch Einberufung einer Konferenz östl. Klientelkönige nach Tiberias –, wurden durch Intervention des Statthalters von Syrien, C. → Vibius Marsus, zunichte gemacht. Nach seinem Tod wurde sein Reich im J. 44 eingezogen (Ios. bell. Iud. 2,178–220; Ios. ant. Iud. 18,126–366).

[9] Sohn des → Aristobulos [6] und der Salome (Ios. ant. Iud. 18,137). Näheres ist nicht überliefert.

SCHÜRER, Bd. 1 • A. H. M. JONES, The Herods of Judaea, [2]1967.

[10] H. ben Miar und **[11] H. ben Gamala.** Vornehme Bürger von Tiberias, die 66 n. Chr. bei Ausbruch des großen jüd. Aufstandes an der Loyalität zu Rom und König → Iulius [II 5] Agrippa II. festhielten (Ios. vita 33 f.).

[12] Sohn des Aumos, im Dienst von König Iulius Agrippa II., Militärbefehlshaber in der Trachonitis (OGIS 425). K.BR.

[13] *Dioikētḗs* (διοικητής) in Alexandreia, erh. sind Briefe vom Okt. 164 v. Chr. an die Untergebenen Dorion, Onias [1] und Theon zur Interpretation des königlichen *próstagma* (πρόσταγμα): SB XVI 12821, UPZ I 110.

1 V. A. TCHERIKOVER, A. FUKS (Ed.), Corpus Papyrorum Iudaicorum 1, 1957, Nr. 132 2 D. THOMPSON, Memphis under the Ptolemies, 1988, 254 f.

[14] Sohn des Demophon aus Pergamon, Bürger von Ptolemais in der Phyle Ptolemais und Deme Berenikeus. Zwischen 152 und 145 v. Chr. *tōn diadóchōn, hēgemṓn ep' andrṓn* (τῶν διαδόχων, ἡγεμὼν ἐπ' ἀνδρῶν), Phrurarch in Syene, *gerrhophýlax* (γερροφύλαξ), und Vorsteher der *ánō tópoi* (ἄνω τόποι); gleichzeitig Prophet des Chnubis und *archistolístēs* (ἀρχιστολίστης) der Tempel in Philae, Abaton und Elephantine, vor 143/2 Vorsteher des Dodekaschoinos. Auch als *epistátēs tōn metállōn* (ἐπιστάτης τῶν μετάλλων) bezeugt; wird 144/2 *archisōmatophýlax* (ἀρχισωματοφύλαξ) und Stratege der Thebais.

PP 2/8,2059 • E. VAN'T DACK, Ptolemaica Selecta, 1988, 343 ff. W.A.

[15] Aus Marathon, prominenter Athener, Vorfahr des H. [16] Atticus, Archon 60/59 v. Chr. und vierfacher Stratege, Bekannter von Cicero und T. Pomponius Atticus. 50 erwirkte er von Caesar die Stiftung von 50 Talenten für Athen (Cic. Att. 6,1,25), 45/44 verwandte sich Cicero bei ihm dafür, den Philosophen Kratippos in Athen zu halten (Plut. Cicero 24,7 f.), 44 v. Chr. war er Mentor von → Ciceros Sohn M. Tullius Cicero (Cic. Att. 14,16,3 u. a.).

HABICHT, Index s. v. H. • RAWSON, Culture, 444–449. K.-L. E.

[16] L. Vibullius Hipparchus Ti. Claudius Atticus Herodes, ca. 101/103–177 n. Chr., reichster Athener seiner Zeit, der eine röm. Karriere mit Aktivitäten als Sophist und Politiker in Athen verband. Sein Vater, Ti. → Claudius [II 10] Atticus, war der erste Grieche aus Achaia, der *cos. suff.* wurde (wahrscheinlich 108). H. wurde z. T. in Rom bei P. → Calvisius [10] Tullus Ruso ausgebildet (Fronto 1, 60 HAINES), lernte Rhet. (Philostr. soph. 2,1, 564) bei → Skopelianos (einem Hausgast zu H.' Jugendzeit, ebd. 1,21,521), → Favorinus und Secundus; → Polemon hörte er erst ca. 134 (ebd. 1,25, 537). Seine Karriere begann früh, wahrscheinlich mit einer Gesandtschaft zu Hadrian 117/118 (bei der er nervös wurde und die Nerven verlor, ebd. 2,1,565). Er wurde im folgenden »Marktaufseher« (*agoranómos*; ?124/5) und *árchōn* (126/7) seiner Heimatstadt sowie »Ausrichter der Wettspiele« (*agonothétēs*) der Panhellenia, wahrscheinlich als erster Archon des Panhellenions in den Jahren 133–137, und der → Panathenaia im Jahre 140 (ebd. 549–50); später *archiereús*. In seiner röm. Karriere war er *quaestor candidatus Caesaris* (129?), *tr. pl.*, *praetor* (?133), ca. 134 Sonderlegat zur Ordnung der Städte in der Provinz Asia, und 143 *cos. ord.*

Im Rahmen seines spektakulären Programms wohltäterischer Bauunternehmungen (vgl. Philostr. soph. 2,1,551) errichtete H. für seine Panathenaia das Stadion in Athen (ebd. 550) aus pentelischem Marmor (Paus. 1,19,6) neu. Weitere Bauten waren [1]: das Stadion zu Delphi (Paus. 10,32,1); das Nymphaion in Olympia, eingeweiht von seiner Frau Regilla (ca. 149–153 [1]); das Odeion in Athen, ihrem Gedächtnis geweiht (Paus. 7,20,6); Wiederaufbau eines Odeions in Korinth; Statuen am Isthmos und in Olympia (Paus. 2,1,7; 6,21,4); Unterstützung für Orikon in Epeiros und viele Städte in Achaia; Aquädukt für Canusium und – mit einer Spende seines Vaters von etwa 4 Millionen Drachmen – einen Aquädukt und (wahrscheinlich) Bäder für Alexandria Troas ca. 134 (Philostr. soph. 2,1,548). H.' Vermögen wurde auch sichtbar anhand seiner Besitzungen in Kephisia, Marathon (seinem *dḗmos*), Korinth, Kynuria und an der Via Appia nahe bei Rom, wo er gegen 143 der Faustina einen Tempel erbaute und Gedichte des → Markellos von Side in Inschr. festhalten ließ, die seine Frau nach ihrem Tode (späte 150er Jahre) verherrlichten.

Eine solch hohe Stellung beschwor Konflikte herauf: angeblich mit Antoninus Pius während seiner Prokonsulatszeit in Asia 134/5 (ebd. 554–555); mit dem Bruder seiner verstorbenen Frau; mit den Brüdern Quintilii, während sie Achaia (als Sonderlegaten) um 174 verwalteten (ebd. 559); mit den Freigelassenen der Familie; mit Athenern, bes. mit anderen Magnaten – (Ti. Claudius) Demostratos, Mamertinos und Praxagoras (ebd. 559) –, die zu einer Gerichtsverhandlung vor Kaiser Marcus Aurelius in Sirmium (ca. 174) und der Verbannung nach Orikon führten. Marcus' Intervention zugunsten einer Versöhnung des H. mit Athen (wie zuvor mit Fronto), dokumentiert durch eine lange Inschr. [2], bewirkte H.' Rückkehr (ca. 175), welche von Epheben mit einem überschwenglichen elegischen Hymnos (IG II² 3606) begrüßt wurde.

Von vier Kindern mit Regilla überlebte nur Regillus Atticus (*cos.* 185) H.; die anderen sowie seine Frau und seine Pflegekinder (*tróphimoi*) Polydeucio, Achilles, Memnon und Aithiops betrauerte er ostentativ.

Von → Gellius (insbes. 19,12,1) und Philostratos wird H. als herausragend auf dem Gebiet der Redekunst (vgl. Lukian. de morte Peregrini 19) gepriesen. Kaiser Antoninus Pius ernannte ihn zum Lehrer für seine Söhne Marcus Aurelius und L. Verus (Cass. Dio 72,35,1). Unter seinen Schülern waren in Rom → Aristokles und in Athen Gellius, → Chrestos, Ptolemaios von Naukratis, Onomarchos, Theodotos und evtl. Ailios → Aristeides. Ein engerer Kreis (gen. die »Wasseruhr«, *klepsýdrion*), der bes. Beachtung genoß, umfaßte → Hadrianos von Tyros, Pausanias von Caesarea und Amphikles von Chalkis. H.' rhet. Stil zeichnete sich durch reiche Einfachheit aus und erinnerte so an sein Vorbild Kritias. Philostratos (soph. 2,1,564) zählt Reden, Briefe, Tagebücher und eine Anthologie als Werke des H. auf. Erhalten sind jedoch nur noch die lat. Übers. einer Fabel, die einer Kritik des stoischen Ideals der Leidenschaftslosigkeit (*apátheia*) entstammte (Gell. 19,12), eine Rede, die Probleme im klass. Thessalien anspricht ([3], Kritias zugewiesen von [4]), sowie einige Gedichte [5].
→ Philostratos; Zweite Sophistik

1 K. W. ARAFAT, Pausanias' Greece, 1996, 37–8, 111, 195–201 **2** Hesperia, Suppl. 13, 1970 **3** U. ALBINI (Hrsg.), Περὶ Πολιτείας, 1968 **4** H. T. WADE-GERY, Kritias and H, in: CQ 39, 1945, 19 ff. **5** E. L. BOWIE, Greek sophists and Greek poetry in the second sophistic, in: ANRW II 33.1, 231–235.

P. GRAINDOR, Un milliardaire antique. Hérode Atticus et sa famille, 1930 • A. STEIN, PIR² C 802 • W. AMELING, H. Atticus, 2 Bde., 1983 • J. TOBIN, H. Attikos and the city of Athens, 1997. E. BO./Ü: C. ST.

Herodianos (Ἡρωδιανός).

[1] Ailios H. (Αἴλιος Ἡρωδιανός), aus Alexandreia, einer der bedeutendsten griech. Grammatiker, lebte im 2. Jh. n. Chr.; Sohn des → Apollonios [11] Dyskolos und dessen würdiger Schüler und Nachfolger. Eine Zeit lang hielt er sich in Rom auf und widmete Kaiser Marc Aurel (161–180) sein Hauptwerk, die Καθολικὴ προσῳδία (*Katholikḗ prosōdía*). Zu Recht sieht man in ihm zwar keinen brillanten, jedoch einen sorgfältigen und genauen Grammatiker, den großen Erben und Systematiker der alexandrinischen Tradition von Studien zur Sprache und von rationaler Analyse sprachlicher Phänomene. Das Beiwort ὁ τεχνικός (*technikós*) wird nicht nur ihm gegeben, so daß es nicht als Bezeichnung für den Grammatiker par excellence aufgefaßt werden kann: Seine Schriften waren jedoch berühmt und wurden in gelehrten Kreisen (nicht nur von Grammatikern, sondern auch in Schol., Etymologica und Lexika) oft herangezogen. Die Originalwerke sind verloren, so daß sich unsere Kenntnis seiner Lehre nur auf diese Mittelsmänner stützen kann. Grundlegend sind die Sammel- und Rekonstruktionsbemühungen von LENTZ (zu 33 Werken); diese sind trotz bekannter großer Schwächen, Irrtümer und Mängel in ihrer Gesamtheit nicht überholt und bilden den Ausgangspunkt für die Beschäftigung mit dem herodianischen Material: Papyrusfrg. und v.a. der von HUNGER veröffentlichte Text haben unser Wissen um wichtige Daten erweitert (s. DYCK 1993).

Das Hauptwerk des H. war die *Katholikḗ prosōdía* in 20 B., Frucht einer unermüdlichen Sammlung von Beispielen (über 60000 Wörter) mit einer rigorosen Formulierung der Regeln. Der größte Teil betraf die allg. Akzentlehre, doch umfaßt der Begriff *prosōdía* auch alle diakritischen Zeichen für die korrekte Lektüre von Wörtern: Akzente; Spiritūs; Zeichen für Länge oder Kürze der dichronen Vokale; Zeichen für Elision, Vereinigung oder Trennung zw. Silben. Die Bücher 1–19 behandelten die Akzentsetzung: 1–13 Substantiva; 14 Monosyllaba; 15 Numeralia und anderes; 16 Verba auf -ω und -μι; 17 Verba composita und Participia; 18–19 die übrigen Wortarten; Buch 20 beinhaltete die Quantitäten der dichronen Vokale und die Spiritūs (ein Problem besteht in seiner Beziehung zu der kleinen, separat überlieferten Abhandlung Περὶ διχρόνων, die aber wahrscheinlich aus Exzerpten aus dem größeren Werk zusammengestellt ist); schließlich scheint H. selbst eine Art Supplement über Wörter als Satzglieder hinzugefügt zu haben, von dem ein Exzerpt über die Enklitika erhalten ist.

Weitere (wahrscheinlich frühere) Arbeiten betrafen die *prosōdía* spezifischer sprachlicher Umgebungen. Nur wenig besitzen wir von der ›Att. Prosodie‹ (Ἀττικὴ προσῳδία), während von der ›Prosodie der Ilias‹ (Ἰλιακὴ προσῳδία) und (weniger) von der ›Prosodie der Odyssee‹ (Ὀδυσσειακὴ προσῳδία), die der homer. Sprache gewidmet sind, umfangreiche Frg. vorliegen: Von letzteren besitzen wir Auszüge in den Scholien zur ›Ilias‹ und zur ›Odyssee‹, da ein unbekannter spätant. Grammatiker (Sigle VMK = Viermännerkommentar) einen Homerkomm. verfaßte, indem er Schriften von Aristonikos [5], Didymos [1] aus Alexandreia, Nikanor und H. kompilierte, deren Material in byz. Schol.- und lexikographische Sammlungen einging.

H. verfaßte weiterhin eine große Zahl von Werken zu gramm. Fragen: die ›Pathologie‹ (ein Begriff, der sich auf das enorme und unzureichend definierte Gebiet der πάθη τοῦ λόγου (*páthē tu lógu*) bezieht, d.h. auf alle Phänomene phonetischer, morphologischer und dialektaler Veränderung von Wörtern, ausgehend von einer Grundform; die ›Orthographie‹ (Περὶ ὀρθογραφίας), die Nominal- und Verbalflexion, die Wortbildung, die Phonologie und weiteres mehr. Das einzige vollständig erh. Werk ist die Schrift Περὶ μονήρους λέξεως, der Wörter, die sich durch ihre Einzigartigkeit in morphologischer Hinsicht auszeichnen.

Sein Ruhm begünstigte die Zuweisung zweifelhafter oder eindeutig unechter Texte an H.: Wir kennen insgesamt etwa 20 (die nicht bei LENTZ ediert sind). Der bekannteste ist das kurze attizistische Lex. Φιλέταιρος, weitere sind Περὶ ἀκυρολογίας; Περὶ σχημάτων; Ἐπιμερισμοί.

ED.: A. LENTZ (Ed.), Herodiani Technici reliquiae, in: GG 3 · ScholiaIl. (*Iliakḗ prosōdía*) · A. LUDWICH, Herodiani Technici Reliquiarium supplementum, 1890 (Addenda zur *Odysseiakḗ prosōdía*) · K. LEHRS, Herodiani scripta tria emendatiora, 1848 · A. DAIN, Le Philetairos attribué a Hérodien, 1954 (*Philétairos*) · K. HAJDÚ, SGLG 8, 1998 (*Perí schēmátōn* (Weitere Angaben bei SCHULTZ RE (s.u.) und DYCK 1993).

LIT.: D. BLANK, Ancient Philosophy and Grammar. The Syntax of Apollonius Dyscolus, 1982, 24–25 · U. CRISCUOLO, Per la tradizione bizantina dei lessici atticisti, in: Bollettino della Badia greca di Grottaferrata, n.s. 26, 1972, 143–156 · A. R. DYCK, Herodian über die Etym. von ἴφθιμος, in: Glotta 55, 1977, 225–227 · Ders., Notes on the Epimerismoi attributed to Herodian, in: Hermes 109, 1981, 225–235 · Ders., Notes on Greek grammarians, in: RhM 124, 1981, 50–54 · Ders., Aelius Herodian: Recent Studies and Prospects for Future Research, in: ANRW II 34.1, 772–794 (sehr nützlicher Forsch.-Überblick einschl. Bibliogr.) · P. EGENOLFF, Zu Lentz' Herodian, I–III, in: Philologus 59, 1900, 238–255; 61, 1902, 77–132, 540–576; 62, 1903, 39–63 · H. ERBSE, Zu Herodian π. παθῶν, in: Philologus 97, 1948, 192 · Ders., Beiträge zur Überlieferung der Iliasscholien (Zetemata 24), 1960, 344–406 · K. HAJDÚ, SGLG 8, 1998 (s.o.) · H. HUNGER, Palimpsest-Frg. aus Herodians Καθολικὴ προσῳδία, Buch 5–7 (cod. Vindob. Hist. gr. 10), in: Jb. der österr. Byz. Ges. 16, 1967, 1–33 · D. J. JAKOB, Herakleides oder Herodian?, in: Hermes 113, 1985, 495–497 · LEHRS 1848, (s.o.) · R. REITZENSTEIN, Gesch. der griech. Etymologika, 1897, 299–312 · SCHMID/STÄHLIN II, 887–888 · M. SCHMIDT, Die Erklärungen zum Weltbild Homers und zur Kultur der Heroenzeit in den bT-Scholien zur Ilias (Zetemata 62), 1976, 32–35 · H. SCHULTZ, s.v. H. (4), RE 8, 959–973 · H. STEPHAN, De Herodiani Technici dialectologia, Diss. Straßburg 1889 · CH. THEODORIDIS, Zur Schreibernotiz im Etymologicum Genuinum (s.v. ἦχι), in: RhM 132, 1989, 409–410 · M. VAN DER VALK, Researches on the Text and

Scholia of the Iliad, 1963–64, I, 592–602 • A. Wouters, The Grammatical Papyri from Graeco-Roman Egypt, 1979, 216–224, 231–236 und passim. F.M./Ü: T.H.

[2] Geb. ca. 178/180 n. Chr., war möglicherweise ein Freigelassener oder Ritter in subalternen Positionen des kaiserlichen oder Staatsdienstes. Herkunft und Familienverhältnisse sind unsicher, er stammte vielleicht aus Alexandreia oder aus dem syrischen Antiocheia. Er verfaßte eine Gesch. Roms vom Tode des Marcus Aurelius bis zur Alleinregierung Gordians III. (180–238 n. Chr.) in acht B. (›Gesch. des Kaisertums nach Marc Aurel‹), gegliedert nach den Regierungsperioden der Kaiser (mit biographisch-historiographischem Charakter), in griech. Sprache. Das in nüchternem, leichtverständlichem und flüssigem Stil geschriebene Werk wurde nach 240 veröffentlicht.

Seine Äußerungen verraten geringe oder keine Erfahrung in Fragen der hohen Politik oder der Kriegführung. Nach seiner eigenen Aussage (1,2,5) handelt es sich um Zeitgesch., doch dürfte dieses nur für die letzten Bücher zutreffen. Nicht bekannt ist, welche Quellen H. benutzt hat; methodische Quellenkritik ist ihm fremd. Sein Werk diente der → Historia Augusta vielfach als Vorlage, hatte großen Einfluß u. a. auf Eutropius, Aurelius Victor, Ammianus Marcellinus und Iohannes Antiochenus und wurde von ant. und byz. Autoren wegen des gefälligen Stils gelobt. Während H.' Werk von der älteren Forsch. aufgrund seiner offensichtlichen historiographischen Mängel ausgesprochen ungünstig beurteilt wurde, wird es in neuerer Zeit wieder positiver bewertet und als wichtige, wenn auch nicht fehlerfreie Quelle mit unverzichtbaren Informationen zur Gesch. der 1. H. des 3. Jh. n. Chr. gesehen.

Dihle, 356f. • F.L. Müller, Herodian, 1996, 7–26. T.F.

Herodianus. *Comes*, Unterfeldherr im byz. Italienfeldzug gegen die Ostgoten, 535–540 n. Chr. unter Belisarios, seit 542 unter Maximinus. 545 lieferte er Spoleto den Goten aus. Fortan im Dienst des Gotenkönigs Totila, half er diesem 546 bei der Eroberung Roms und bewachte ab 552 dessen Schatz in Cumae (→ Kyme). Sein Schicksal nach der Eroberung Cumaes 553 durch byz. Truppen ist unbekannt. PLRE 3, 593–595. F.T.

Herodias. Tochter des → Aristobulos [4], eines Sohnes Herodes' d.Gr. In erster Ehe mit dessen Halbbruder Herodes Philippos verheiratet, verließ H. ihren Mann, um die Ehe mit → Herodes Antipas, dem Tetrarchen Galilaeas und Peraeas, einzugehen, der sich seinerseits von seiner Frau, einer Tochter des Nabatäerkönigs Aretas, scheiden ließ. Dies führte zu einem Krieg mit dem Nabatäerreich, der mit der Niederlage des Antipas 36 n. Chr. endete. Anteil dürfte H. auch an der Hinrichtung → Iohannes des Täufers gehabt haben, der ihre unrechtmäßige Ehe kritisierte. Als Antipas auf ihre Veranlassung von Caligula den Königstitel für sich erbat, wurde er 39 n. Chr. abgesetzt und nach Gallien verbannt. H. folgte ihrem Mann in das Exil.
→ Dekadenz; Fin de siècle

P. Schäfer, Geschichte der Juden in der Antike, 1983. J.P.

Herodikos

[1] *Paidotribḗs* aus Megara, der sich in Selymbria niederließ, Zeitgenosse des Protagoras. Seine Geburt wurde um 500 v. Chr. angesetzt [2. 200f.], sein im Alter eingetretener Tod um 430–420 [5. 53].

Nachdem Platon ihm die Entwicklung einer neuen Therapieform zugeschrieben hatte, sah man ihn als Verf. eines kleinen Werks an [1. 979, Z.21f.], ohne zu wissen, ob er überhaupt etwas geschrieben hatte, noch gar, ob er trotz Anon. Londiniensis IX, 20–36 eine explizite, ausgearbeitete Theorie besaß. Platon weist ihm zwei einander entgegengesetzte Behandlungsarten zu: Eine aggressive, aus Spaziergängen bestehende (Phaidr. 227d 3–4) und eine abwartende (rep. 406a-d), mit ständiger Beobachtung und Aufrechterhaltung eines Zustands, den Platon als »schwächlich« bezeichnet. Die Aufmerksamkeit, die H. der Diätetik widmet, hat dazu geführt, daß man ihn – allerdings unbegründet [3. 12–14, 16 mit Anm. 3] – als Verf. der hippokratischen Schrift ›Über Diät‹ ansah. Wenngleich der → Anonymus Londiniensis ihm eine differenzierte Lehre zuschreibt, muß man ihm doch wohl vielmehr ein großes Interesse an der Diät von Athleten zuschreiben, deren Übertragbarkeit auf den medizinischen Bereich er erkannt haben soll [5. 42–57]. In der Folge ist dann die Behauptung aufgekommen, daß er Lehrer des Hippokrates gewesen sei [4. 10] und sogar die Diätetik begründet habe [5. 42–57].
→ Diätetik; Hippokrates

1 H. Gossen, s. v. H. (2), RE 8, 978f. **2** H. Grensemann, Knidische Medizin, I, 1975 **3** R. Joly, Hippocrate, Du régime, 1967 **4** J. Rubin-Pinault, Hippocratic Lives and Legends, 1992 **5** G. Wöhrle, Stud. zur Theorie der ant. Gesundheitslehre, 1990.

[2] Arzt (?) aus Knidos; eine Datier. um 400 läßt sich nicht zwingend begründen. Das einzige explizite Zeugnis stellt der Anon. Lond. (IV,40–V,35) dar, der ihn mit → Euryphon in Verbindung bringt, ohne ihn jedoch zu seinem Schüler zu machen.

In der Aitiologie führte H. den Grund der Krankheiten wie Euryphon auf Verdauungsreste zurück; anders als dieser jedoch meinte er, daß diese *perissṓmata* sich in zwei Flüssigkeiten (sauer und bitter) auflösen, die verschiedene Krankheiten hervorrufen. Wenn die Zuweisung der Erwähnungen bei Galen und Caelius Aurelianus an diesen H. richtig ist, hat er die therapeutischen Qualitäten der Muttermilch bemerkt (Gal. 6,775; 7,701; 10,474f.), außerdem das Erbrechen als diätetische Maßnahme empfohlen, wofür er mehrere Mittel und Wege beschrieben haben soll (Caelius Aurelius, Tard. pass. 3,8,139).

Die These vom Mangel an körperlicher Betätigung hat die Verwechslung mit H. [1] von Selymbria begünstigt, ebenso der Aitiologietypus, der diesem vom Anon. Lond. zugewiesen wird. A.TO./Ü: T.H.

Herodoros (Ἡρόδωρος) aus Herakleia am Pontos. Mythograph, Vater des Megarikers → Bryson, schrieb in ion. Dialekt um 400 v.Chr., in den Hss. oft als → Herodotos zitiert. In Titeln faßbar sind Monographien zu einzelnen mythischen Gestalten (Herakles in mindestens 17 B., Pelops, Oidipus) oder Gruppen (*Argonaútai, Orphéōs kaí Musaíou historía* = ›Orpheus und Musaios‹), von denen wenige Frg. erh. sind (FGrH 31). Demnach hat H. die mythischen Traditionen insbes. von → Hellanikos und → Pherekydes von Athen übernommen. Eigenständig ist weniger die Auswahl der überkommenen Stoffe als ihre Nutzung als Rahmen für alle möglichen geogr. und naturgesch. Berichte – etwa F 2 zu Iberien, F 22 über den Geier, F 21 über die Mondwelt. Die Mythen werden rationalisiert (F 57: Der goldende Widder des Atreus ist in Wirklichkeit eine goldene Schale) und allegorisiert (F 13: Herakles lernt von Atlas Astronomie); Widersprüche in der Überl. werden durch die Ansetzung von Homonymen gelöst (F 42: zwei Orpheus, F 14: mehrere Herakles). Damit steht H. an der Schwelle zur späteren, von der Trad. stärker losgelösten Mythographie.

F. Jacoby, s.v. H. (4), RE 8, 980–987 · P. Desiderio, Cultura eracleota. Da Erodoro a Eraclide Pontico, in: R. Bernard (Hrsg.), Pontica I. Recherches sur l'histoire du Pont dans l'antiquité, 1991, 7–24. F.G.

Herodotos (Ἡρόδοτος).

[1] Der Geschichtsschreiber Herodot.

A. Leben B. Aufbau des Werkes C. Entstehung des Werkes D. Quellen und historische Methode E. Tendenz und Glaubwürdigkeit F. Weltbild und Geschichtsauffassung G. Herodot als Erzähler H. Sprache und Stil I. Nachleben

A. Leben

Quellen zum Leben von H., dem ›Vater der Gesch.‹ (Cic. leg. 1,1,5), ca. 485–424 v.Chr. (grundlegend für alles folgende: [1]) sind außer seinen eigenen Angaben vor allem die Suda s.v. H. bzw. s.v. Panyassis. H. stammte aus Halikarnassos (heute Bodrum) im Südwesten Kleinasiens. Die Namen des Vaters, Lyxes, und des Onkels, Panyassis, eines berühmten Epikers, weisen auf karische Abkunft. Wegen des mißglückten Versuchs, den Tyrannen → Lygdamis zu stürzen, flüchtete H. für einige Zeit nach Samos; nach Hause zurückgekehrt, wirkte er vor 454 am endgültigen Sturz des Lygdamis mit. Wegen Differenzen mit seinen Mitbürgern verließ er später seine Heimat für immer und wanderte in die 444 gegründete panhellenische Kolonie Thurioi aus. H. hielt nach Eusebios (Chronica Arm. 83) 445/4 in Athen öffentliche Vorlesungen aus seinem Werk und bekam dafür ein großes Honorar (vgl. Diyllos FGrH 73 F 3). In Athen fand er auch Eingang in den Kreis des → Perikles und schloß Freundschaft mit → Sophokles, der eine Ode auf H. dichtete (Anthologia Lyrica Graeca I[3] 79 Diehl) und mehrfach auf das Werk H.' Bezug nahm (vgl. bes. Soph. Ant. 903 ff. mit Hdt. 3,119; weitere Stellen: [2. 318[3]] und [3. 2 ff.]). Umgekehrt ist ein nachhaltiger Einfluß der Tragödie auf H. erkennbar, z.B. in der Geschichte des Adrastos (Hdt. 1,34 ff.) oder der Darstellung des Xerxes (B. 7 und 8). Nach Apollodoros (FGrH 244 F 7) war H. beim Ausbruch des Peloponnesischen Krieges 53 Jahre alt: Das hieraus resultierende Geburtsdatum 484 dürfte ungefähr zutreffen. H. erlebte noch die ersten Jahre des Peloponnesischen Krieges (vgl. Hdt. 6,91; 7,137; 233; 9,73). 424 lag sein Geschichtswerk vor, da einige Stellen daraus in den ›Acharnern‹ des Aristophanes parodiert werden (vgl. z.B. Aristoph. Ach. 523 ff. mit Hdt. 1,4; [4. 210[14]] verzeichnet Forscher, die für ein späteres Erscheinungsdatum plädieren). Wenig später dürfte er gestorben sein.

H. unternahm ausgedehnte Reisen, deren Chronologie unsicher ist [5. 128 ff.; 6; 7. XVff.]: 1. Ins Schwarzmeergebiet, Standquartier Olbia (Hdt. 4,17), von dort den Hypanis aufwärts ins Skythenland (4,81). Dabei lernte H. wohl auch die südl. Schwarzmeerküste, Thrakien und Makedonien kennen. 2. Nach Ägypten bis Elephantine und dem ersten Nilkatarakt. Insgesamt ca. viermonatiger Aufenthalt nach der Schlacht von Papremis 460/459 (vgl. 3,12); von Ägypten aus wohl Abstecher nach Kyrene (vgl. 2,32 f.; 181). 3. In den Vorderen Orient, nach Tyros (2,44), zum Euphrat (1,185) und nach Babylon (1,178 ff.), aber nicht ins eigentliche Persien. 4. In den gesamten griech. Siedlungsraum, u.a. ins Mutterland (Schlachtorte des Perserkrieges!), Kleinasien, die Magna Graecia und Sizilien.

B. Aufbau des Werkes

H.' Werk ist vollständig erhalten; die Einteilung in neun Bücher (vgl. Diod. 11,37,6) geht wohl auf den alexandrin. Philologen Aristarchos [4] von Samothrake zurück, der auch einen H.-Kommentar verfaßte. Das Proöm lautet: ›Dies ist die Darlegung der Erkundung (*historíēs apódexis*) des H. von Halikarnassos, auf daß das von Menschen Geschehene nicht mit der Zeit verblasse noch große Taten, aufgewiesen teils von Hellenen, teils von → Barbaren, des Ruhmes verlustig gingen, ganz besonders aber, aus welcher Schuld bzw. Ursache (*aitíē*) sie miteinander Krieg führten‹ (zum Proöm zuletzt [8. 234 ff.] mit Lit.). Die myth. Konflikte zwischen Griechen und »Barbaren« (1,1–5) schiebt H. mit einer Handbewegung beiseite und wendet sich sogleich der gesch. Zeit, d.h. der jüngeren Vergangenheit zu, und zwar dem Lyderkönig → Kroisos (ca. 560–547), ›von dem ich weiß, daß er mit den Ungerechtigkeiten gegen die Griechen begann.‹ Damit wird die Abfolge der »Barbarenkönige«, die die Griechen unterwerfen wollten, zur Leitlinie der Darstellung: Kroisos (1,6–94), Kyros (1,141–214), Kambyses (2,1–3; 70), Dareios (3,61–7,4), Xerxes (7,5–8 Ende) (zum Aufbau des Werkes vgl. bes. [1. 288 ff.] und [9; 10. 47 ff.]).

Dieser einsträngigen Haupterzählung fügt H. eine immense Fülle geogr., ethnographischen und histor. Materials in Gestalt kleinerer und größerer Exkurse (*lógoi*) ein, an deren Ende die Haupterzählung jeweils dort wieder aufgenommen wird, wo sie unterbrochen worden war. Dabei werden die einzelnen Völker (Land und Leute, Gesch. etc.) immer an der Stelle vorgestellt, an der sie erstmals mit der erobernden Macht Persien in Berührung kamen. Beispiele: 1,178–200 (Babylonier); 1,201–216 (Massageten); 2,2–182 (Ägypter); 3,20–24 (Äthiopier); 4,5–82 (Skythen); 1,142–151 (Ionier); 3,39–60; 120–149 (Samier). Die Gesch. des griech. Mutterlandes, bes. von Athen und Sparta, wird dagegen in mehreren aufeinander abgestimmten Partien dargestellt (Athen: 1,59–64; 5,55–96; 6,121 ff.; Sparta: 1,65–68; 5,39–48; 6,51–84). Im → Ionischen Aufstand (5,28 ff.) vereinigen sich Perser- und Griechenlinie: Den großen → Perserkrieg schildert H. mit einer Technik der Parallelerzählung, wonach die Vorgänge auf der einen und der anderen Seite im Wechsel bis zum Zusammenstoß der beiden Mächte dargestellt werden. Auf die Expedition des Dareios, die bei Marathon scheitert (6,102 ff.), folgt der große Feldzug des Xerxes, vom Kriegsbeschluß (7,5 ff.) über die Heeresschau (7,59 ff.), die Schlachten bei den Thermopylen (7,198–239), am Artemision (8,1–23) und bei Salamis (8,40–96) bis zu den Siegen bei Plataiai (9,19–89) und Mykale (9,90–107). Mit der Einnahme von Sestos 479, die den Übergang der Griechen von der Defensive zur Offensive markiert, endet das Werk. Ob es in der vorliegenden Form vollendet ist oder nicht, ist umstritten (vgl. den Forschungsüberblick bei [11. 152]; zum Problem zuletzt [12. 47 ff.]).

C. Entstehung des Werkes

Charakteristisch ist einerseits die außerordentlich breite Exposition mit einer großen Masse ethnographischen bzw. geogr. Materials, andererseits eine mit Fortschreiten des Werkes zunehmende Dichte der Darstellung, die in den letzten drei Büchern die Gesch. der Perserkriege im wesentlichen geschlossen erzählt. Diese Diskrepanz wird von zahlreichen Forschern biographisch gedeutet (diese sog. analytische Richtung wurde von [1. 205 ff., 467 ff.] begründet und bes. von [5. 442] weitergeführt; vgl. auch [13. 36–68]): H. sei anfänglich wie → Hekataios [3] Geograph bzw. Ethnograph gewesen und habe in dieser Eigenschaft die großen völkerkundlichen *lógoi* verfaßt, die urspr. selbständige Gebilde gewesen seien. Erst unter dem Eindruck des perikleischen Athen sei er zum Historiker geworden und habe sich entschlossen, die Perserkriege, den großen Ruhmestitel der Athener, darzustellen. Entsprechend sei ganz heterogenes Material in sein Werk eingegangen und mehr schlecht als recht zu einem Ganzen vereint worden. In Wirklichkeit spricht jedoch vieles dafür, daß H. sein Werk von vornherein in der vorliegenden Form konzipiert und verfaßt hat (Anhänger der unitarischen Richtung sind u. a. [14; 15. 360 ff.; 4. 32 ff.]).

D. Quellen und historische Methode

In den ethnographisch-geogr. Partien verwendet H. bisweilen lit. Quellen, etwa Hekataios [3], der u. a. in 2,70–73 zugrundeliegt (FGrH 324a); dagegen fehlten schriftliche Quellen für die histor. Partien fast ganz: H. benützt gelegentlich Dichtung wie die ›Perser‹ des Aischylos, er verwendet auch Inschriften (z. B. die Schlangensäule von Delphi, vgl. ML 27 mit Hdt. 8,82) und Orakelsammlungen, doch standen ihm weder nennenswerte historische Werke noch Lokalchroniken, weder Beamten- noch Siegerlisten zur Verfügung. Die altoriental. bzw. ägypt. Aufzeichnungen blieben ihm unverständlich. Seine Arbeitsweise war im wesentlichen die folgende (vgl. 2,99; dazu vor allem [16; 17; 4. 35 ff.; 13. 44 f.]): In den ethnographisch-geogr. Partien arbeitete er hauptsächlich auf der Basis von Autopsie (eigener Beobachtung) und eigenem Erleben [18], in den histor. Abschnitten auf der Grundlage von *oral tradition* (vgl. die bei [4. 211[34]] genannten Abhandlungen), die er bei ›kundigen‹ Leuten einholte, und zwar entweder bei Einzelpersonen (2,28,1; 125,6; 4,76,6; 8,65,6), Berufsgruppen (›die Priester‹) oder anonymen Bewohnern von Ländern (›die Ägypter‹, ›die Skythen‹, ›die Karthager‹) und Städten (›die Athener‹, ›die Korinther‹, ›die Kyrenaier‹ etc.) [13. 44].

Die Annahme, daß H. die geradezu unglaubliche Fülle derartiger Zitate ›ganz frei erfunden‹ habe und als bloßer ›Stubengelehrter‹ zu betrachten sei, der seine Reisen, seine Autopsie und seine Gewährsmänner nur vorgetäuscht habe, ist eine Verirrung der mod. Forsch. (diese Forsch.-Richtung wurde von [19] begründet und besitzt immer noch zahlreiche Anhänger, z. B. [20; 21; 22 sowie 23], doch vgl. zu [23] im einzelnen die von [35. 234–285] zitierten und kritisch besprochenen Aufsätze), die eigentlich keiner ernsthaften Widerlegung bedarf (mit vollem Recht wendet sich [24] gegen die in der vorangehenden Anm. genannten Forscher, die das Geschichtswerk H.' für eine große Lügenkompilation, *a compilation of lies*, halten). In Wirklichkeit liegt H.' einmalige »wiss.« Leistung gerade darin, daß er, ohne nennenswerte schriftliche Quellen zur Verfügung zu haben, aus dem Wust, der Vielfalt, der Gegensätzlichkeit mündlicher Informationen, die er von zahllosen Personen an verschiedensten Orten bezog, die Gesch. der Perserkriege als Einheit in ihrer klassisch gewordenen Form herauskristallisiert hat.

H.' methodisches Grundprinzip lautet: ›Ich bin verpflichtet, das zu berichten, was berichtet wird, alles zu glauben aber bin ich nicht verpflichtet; und dieses Wort soll für meine ganze Darstellung gelten‹ (7,152) [4. 34 ff.]. Diese Maxime führt entsprechend der Tendenz und Einstellung der jeweiligen Gewährsleute oft zur Wiedergabe divergierender, teilweise sich widersprechender Traditionen, ohne daß H. für die Richtigkeit der einen oder anderen Version eintritt. So stehen beispielsweise eine Alkmeoniden- und eine Philaiden-Trad. in Athen, eine Trad. für und gegen Demaratos in Sparta, eine spartanische, tegeatische und athenische

Überl. über die Schlacht von Plataiai gleichberechtigt nebeneinander.

E. Tendenz und Glaubwürdigkeit

Hinsichtlich des großen Rahmenthemas läßt sich feststellen, daß H. die Überlegenheit der »Barbaren«, bes. der Ägypter, gegenüber den Griechen oft anerkennt (vgl. 2,4; 32; 50; 58; 77; 82) und die Sitten und Bräuche der Nichtgriechen stets mit großer Sachlichkeit beschreibt. Ferner erweisen sich seine Berichte über fremde Völker, z.B. Ägypter, Babylonier, Skythen und Massageten, weitgehend als zuverlässig (vgl. [4. 211[36]]; zuletzt [25; 26]). Was das Hauptthema angeht, so betrachtet H. ähnlich wie Aischylos zwar die Perserkriege als Kampf zwischen Freiheit und Knechtschaft, Demokratie und Despotismus, Kargheit und Wohlleben, individueller Tüchtigkeit und anonymer Masse (vgl. bes. den Dialog Xerxes-Demaratos in 7,101–104) [27. 215ff.], aber er ist keineswegs als Panegyriker des »Nationalkrieges« zu betrachten: Die Perserkriege unter Dareios, Xerxes und Artaxerxes brachten vielmehr nach seinem Urteil größeres Unheil über Hellas als die vorangehenden 20 Generationen zusammen (6,98). Auch nennt H. die Fehler und Schwächen der Griechen beim Namen, z.B. ihre Uneinigkeit, ihren Partikularismus, ihre gegenseitigen Rivalitäten und Auseinandersetzungen, die Parteinahme zahlreicher Poleis für die Perser, die Unzulänglichkeiten der kleinasiatischen Griechen beim Ionischen Aufstand [2. 565f.]. Zwar bewundert er den *nómos* (»Recht und Sitte«) und die Tapferkeit der Spartaner sehr (vgl. 7,101–104), doch betrachtet er in dem sog. »Athenerpassus« (7,139) die Athener als eigentliche ›Retter von Griechenland‹. Freilich ist seine Bewunderung für Athen generell nicht uneingeschränkt, sein Werk darf daher keineswegs als pro-athenische Tendenzschrift gelten (nachgewiesen zuerst von [28. 474ff.]; vgl. dazu zuletzt [29]). Auch auf chronolog. Gebiet leistete H. Beachtliches (dazu [30]).

F. Weltbild und Geschichtsauffassung

Die Vergänglichkeit alles Irdischen steht als Leitmotiv über der gesamten Darstellung (1,5), der »Kreislauf der menschlichen Dinge« kommt allenthalben zum Ausdruck, besonders im Solon-Kroisos-Logos (1,207). Trotz gelegentlichem Rationalismus dominiert eine rel. Weltsicht, die sich in schicksalhafter Vorbestimmtheit der Geschehnisse, der Vorstellung von Neid und → *némesis* (»Verargen«) der Gottheit und der Bestrafung menschlicher Hybris durch »das Göttliche« manifestiert (vgl. z.B. 1,30–33: Kroisos; 3,39ff.: Polykrates von Samos; 7,35: Xerxes) (vgl. [31. 368ff.]). Das göttliche Walten kommt in Vorzeichen, Träumen, Orakeln und der Stimme des Warners zum Ausdruck, doch spielen daneben auch menschliche Motivationen und Entscheidungen eine nicht unerhebliche Rolle [32].

G. Herodot als Erzähler

Seit Cicero (leg. 1,1,5) gilt H. nicht nur als erster Geschichtsschreiber, sondern auch als erster Geschichtenerzähler des Abendlandes. Aus der Fülle von Anekdoten, Novellen und Geschichten seien hervorgehoben: Das Schelmenstück des Rhampsinitos (2,121), der Ring des Polykrates (3,40–45), der Leichtsinn des Hippokleides (6,126ff.), die Greuelmahlzeit des Harpagos (1,117ff.). Derartige Erzählungen sind kein Selbstzweck, sondern enthalten *in nuce* die Elemente der herodoteischen Weltsicht; gleiches gilt für Gespräche, Dialoge, wörtliche Reden, die mehrfach bei ihm anzutreffen sind [31; 33].

H. Sprache und Stil

Bereits die antike Stilkritik (Dion. Hal. Ad Pompeium 3,11 bzw. De Thucydide 23) hob die *poikilía* (»Buntheit«) von H.' Sprache hervor, die den großen inhaltlichen Reichtum widerspiegelt. ›Volkstümliche Erzählkunst, nüchterner Berichtsstil, die sprachlichen Mittel des Epos, der Tragödie, der Sophistik sind die Hauptmomente einer Stilsynthese, die als ganze doch ein Gepräge sui generis besitzt.‹ [34].

I. Nachleben

H. übte größten Einfluß auf die gesamte nachfolgende griech. und röm. Geschichtsschreibung aus; dazu [3; 4. 40f.]. Er regte die Entstehung histor. Spezialliteratur (z.B. Werke des Hellanikos, Antiochos) an, während → Thukydides (1,22) seine histor. Methode in Auseinandersetzung mit (dem namentlich nicht genannten) H. formulierte. Die Ausformung der rhet., dramatischen oder pragmatischen Geschichtsschreibung erfolgte zwar erst in hell. Zeit, ist aber schon im Werk H.' im Keim angelegt. Der Kommentar des Aristarchos von Samothrake (PAmherst II 12, 1901) erweist H. als anerkannten Klassiker, und auch Plutarchs Schrift ›Über die Böswilligkeit Herodots‹ bezeugt dessen hohe Autorität. Im Mittelalter existierten zwei Textrezensionen; im Humanismus und in der Renaissance wurde H. durch die lat. Übers. des Lorenzo Valla (1452–1456) bekannt, doch galt er noch bis weit ins 20. Jh. hinein als unzuverlässiger Fabulierer. Erst in der letzten Zeit beginnt H. aus dem Schatten des Thukydides herauszutreten. Dazu trugen u.a. die universalhistor. Konzeption seines Werkes, die Weite seines Geschichtsbegriffes, die eingehende Berücksichtigung der anthropologischen Dimension sowie das heuristische Prinzip ›Berichten, was berichtet wird‹ bei [4. 41].

→ Geschichtsschreibung

1 F. Jacoby, s.v. H., RE Suppl. 2, 205–520 = Griech. Historiker, 1956, 7–164 **2** Schmid/Stählin I 2 **3** K.-A. Riemann, Das herodoteische Geschichtswerk in der Antike, Diss. 1967 **4** K. Meister, Die griech. Geschichtsschreibung, 1990 **5** K. von Fritz, Die griech. Geschichtsschreibung, 1967 **6** R.P. Lisler, The Travels of Herodotus, 1980 **7** D. Asheri, Erodoto, Le storie, libro 1, 1988 **8** K. Meister, Die Interpretation histor. Quellen, Bd. 1, 1997 **9** H. Wood, The Histories of Herodotus, 1972 **10** K.H. Waters, Herodotus, the Historian, 1985 **11** H. Bengtson, Griech. Geschichte, [5]1977 **12** R. Oswald, Gedankliche und thematische Linien in Herodots Werk, in: Grazer Beiträge 21, 1995, 47–59 **13** O. Lendle, Einführung in die griech. Geschichtsschreibung, 1992 **14** J. Cobet, Herodots Exkurse und die Frage der Einheit seines Werkes, 1971 **15** Chr.

MEIER, Die Entstehung des Politischen bei den Griechen, 1980 **16** K. VERDIN, De historisch-kritische methode van Herodotus, 1971 **17** D. LATEINER, The Historical Method of Herodotus, 1984 **18** G. SCHEPENS, L' autopsie dans la méthode des historiens grecs du Ve siècle avant J.-C., 1980 **19** D. FEHLING, Die Quellenangaben bei Herodot, 1971 (engl. Übers. 1989) **20** S. WEST, Herodotus' Epigraphical Interests, in: CQ 79, 1985, 278–305 **21** F. HARTOG, The Mirror of Herodotus, 1988 **22** E. HALL, Inventing the Barbarian, 1989 **23** O. K. ARMAYOR, Herodotus' Autopsy of the Fayoum, 1985 **24** W. K. PRITCHETT, The Liar School of Herodotus, 1993 **25** Hérodote et les peuples non grecs, Entretiens 35, 1988 **26** R. ROLLINGER, Herodots babylonischer Logos (Innsbrucker Beiträge zur Kulturwissenschaft, Sonderheft 84), 1993
27 W. SCHADEWALDT, Die Anfänge der Geschichtsschreibung bei den Griechen, 1982
28 H. STRASBURGER, Herodot und das perikleische Athen, in: W. MARG (Hrsg.), Herodot, [3]1982, 574–608
29 M. OSTWALD, Herodotus and Athens, in: Illinois Classical Studies 16, 1991, 137–148 **30** H. STRASBURGER, Herodots Zeitrechnung, in: W. MARG (Hrsg.), Herodot, [3]1982, 688–736 **31** LESKY **32** L. HUBER, Rel. und polit. Beweggründe in der Geschichtsschreibung des Herodot, Diss. 1965 **33** M. LANG, Herodotean Narrative and Discourse, 1984 **34** W. SCHADEWALDT, Die Anfänge der Geschichtsschreibung bei den Griechen, in: Antike 10, 1934, 144–168, bes. 158 **35** W. K. PRITCHETT, Studies in Ancient Greek Topography, Bd. 4, 1982.

ED.: J. FEIX, 2 Bde., (Heimeran) [5]1995 · A. D. GODLEY, 4 Bde. (Loeb), 1922–1938 · K. HUDE, 2 Bde. (Oxford), 1926/7 · PH.-E. LEGRAND, 10 Bde. (Budé), 1946–1954 · H. B. ROSEN, 2 Bde. (Teubner), 1987 und 1997.
KOMM.: D. ASHEN u. a., (Mondadori) 1988 ff. (ital.), jeweils ein Buch umfassend · W. W. HOW, J. WELLS, 2 Bde., [2]1928 · H. STEIN, 5 Bde., [4–6]1893–1908 · Zu Buch 2: A. B. LLOYD, 2 Bde., 1975–1987.
LEX.: J. E. POWELL, 1938.
BIBLIOGR.: Zuletzt FR. BUBEL, Herodot-Bibliographie 1980–1988, 1991.
DEUTSCHE ÜBERS.: TH. BRAUN, H. BARTH, 2 Bde., [2]1985 · A. HORNEFFER, [4]1971 · W. MARG, 2 Bde., [3]1980 · H. STEIN, W. STAMMLER, 1984.
LIT.: T. S. BROWN, The Greek Historians, 1973, 25 ff. · A. CORCELLA, Erodoto e l'analogia, 1984 · H. DREXLER, Herodot-Studien, 1972 · H. ERBSE, Studien zum Verständnis Herodots, 1992 · Ders., Histories apodexis bei Herodot, in: Glotta 73, 1995/96, 64 ff. · J. A. EVANS, Herodotus, 1982 · Ders., Herodotus, Explorer of the Past, 1991 · K. J. GOULD, Herodotus, 1989 · Ders., Herodotus and Religion, in: S. HORNBLOWER (Hrsg.), Greek Historiography, 1994, 91–106 · F. HARTOG, Herodotus and the Invention of History, 1987 (= Arethusa, Bd. 20) · V. HUNTER, Past and Process in Herodotus and Thucydides, 1982 · H. R. IMMERWAHR, Form and Thought in Herodotus, 1966 · T. J. LUCE, The Greek Historians, 1997, 15 ff. · W. MARG (Hrsg.), Herodot, [3]1982 (WdF 26) · D. MÜLLER, Topographischer Bildkommentar zu den Historien Herodots, 1987 · B. SHIMRON, Politics and Belief in Herodotus, 1989. K. MEI.

[2] Schüler und Adressat eines Briefes des → Epikuros über die Prinzipien der Physik (erh. bei Diog. Laert. 10,29–83). Diesen Brief kann man vermutlich mit der ›Kleinen Epitome an H.‹ gleichsetzen, von der Epikur in seinem Brief an Pythokles spricht (Diog. Laert. 10,85: ἐν τῇ μικρᾷ ἐπιτομῇ πρὸς Ἡρόδοτον; vgl. auch 10,35 ohne Adressat). H. wird, zusammen mit → Timokrates, als Autor eines Buches Περὶ Ἐπικούρου ἐφηβείας (›Über die Jugend Epikurs‹) erwähnt (Diog. Laert. 10,4).

H. v. ARNIM, s. v. H. (10), RE 8, 990. T. D./Ü: J. DE.

[3] Griech. Arzt des 1./2. Jh. n. Chr., der in Rom praktizierte (Gal. 8,750–751). Er wird ohne stichhaltigen Beweis mit dem Lehrer des → Sextos Empeirikos gleichgesetzt, soll in Tarsos als Sohn eines Areios geboren sein und war Schüler des Pneumatikers → Agathinos und des Empirikers → Menodotos (Diog. Laert. 10,116). Er zeigte sich gegenüber allen medizinischen Schulen bis auf die der → Pneumatiker kritisch (Gal. 11,432).

Abgesehen von einer Äußerung, die zumindest für das Fieber einen aitiologischen Nihilismus in Betracht zieht ([Gal.] 19,343), scheint er v. a. zur Therapeutik gearbeitet zu haben, und zwar in einer Richtung, die Ähnlichkeiten mit der Schule von Tarsos aufweist; diese Verbindung ist umso eher möglich, als → Galenos ihn in einer Kritik an seiner Interpretation einer therapeutischen Tätigkeit zu → Pedanius Dioskurides in Bezug setzt (11,443).

→ Oreibasios (CMG, 4,330–331 s. v.) zit. Fr., die allesamt zur Therapeutik gehen: mechanische Heilmittel, Abführmittel und äußere Heilmittel. Obwohl man alle bekannten Zit. in diesem für ein einziges gehaltenen Werk unterbringen wollte, scheinen diejenigen bei Galen eher in eines bzw. mehrere Werke zu gehören, das bzw. die eventuell einfache und zusammengesetzte Medikamente behandelten.
→ Anonymus Parisinus A. TO./Ü: T. H.

[4] Bildhauer aus Olynth. Ihm werden von Tatian (Ad Graecos 33) die Statuen der Prostituierten Phryne und → Glykera [1] sowie der Musikerin Argeia zugeschrieben. Die grundsätzliche Unzuverlässigkeit dieser Quelle ist zwar erwiesen, doch kann aufgrund einer verlorenen Signatur an der Statue einer *hetaíra* in Rom die Existenz des H. nicht ausgeschlossen werden.

A. KALKMANN, Tatians Nachr. über Kunstwerke, in: RhM 42, 1887, 489–524 · LOEWY, Nr. 541 · OVERBECK, Nr. 1590–1591 (Quellen). R. N.

Heroenkult.
A. DIE MYTHEN
B. DER KULT C. DIE DEUTUNGEN

H. ist die kult. Verehrung einer bestimmten Gruppe übermenschlicher Wesen, welche die Griechen seit Homer als Heroen (ἥρωες, *hḗrōes*) bezeichnen; die Etym. des Wortes ist unklar, die mod. Verbindung mit → Hera problematisch [1]. Der H. benutzt sowohl die Form des gängigen olympischen Normalopfers wie spezifischere Kultformen. In der Kategorie der Heroen sind im Lauf der Entwicklung der griech. Rel. verschiedene Gruppen zusammengefaßt worden, von ursprünglichen Göttern bis zu realen Verstorbenen [2].

A. Die Mythen

Im brz. Griechenland sind Heroen vielleicht durch den Trisheros (*ti-rise-ro-e*, »Dreimalheros«, PY Tn 316) vorausgesetzt, der wie die späteren → Tritopatores als kultisch verehrter Ahn verstanden werden könnte [3]. Bei Homer erscheint *hḗrōes* durchgehend als die Bezeichnung der menschlichen Akteure des Epos, nicht Kultfiguren, doch ist dies epische Stilisierung: Die homer. Krieger sind von der Jetztzeit des Erzählers radikal getrennt, und Gräber, an die sich der Kult anschloß, sind teilweise genannt. Daß eine histor. und essentielle Distanz zum Menschen von Homers eigener Zeit impliziert ist, zeigt Hesiod, in dessen → Zeitalter-Mythos die Gruppe der *hḗrōes* die (aus dem Vorderen Orient übernommene) absteigende Reihe der Metalle von Gold zu Eisen unterbricht: Die Heroen, das vierte von fünf Geschlechtern, sind besser als das dritte, bronzene Geschlecht, sie sind Halbgötter (*hēmítheoi*), die in den epischen Kämpfen um Theben und Troia stritten und die Zeus auf die Inseln der Seligen versetzte (Hes. erg. 156–173). Damit sind sie als zwar sterblich, doch halb göttlich zw. Göttern und Menschen angesiedelt; dies bleibt die übliche griech. Auffassung, die lediglich durch die platonische Einführung der *daímones* (→ Dämonen) als niedrigere Zwischenwesen modifiziert wird. In den Genealogien der pseudo-hesiodeischen »Kataloge« (»Ehoien«, s. Hesiodos [1]) leben sämtliche Heroen zwischen der Deukalionischen Flut (→ Deukalion) und einer Generation nach dem Ende des Troianischen Kriegs; am Anfang jeder genealogischen Linie steht die Verbindung eines Gottes mit einer Heroine.

Als Verstorbenen eignet den meisten Heroen nicht nur eine Biographie, sondern auch eine Todesgeschichte und ein Grab, und sie sind weit ambivalenter als die Götter. Als ihr Wohnsitz wird die Erdtiefe gedacht, aus der sie Segen, aber auch Strafe für Missetäter senden (Aristoph. Heroes [4]) oder auch selbst auftauchen, um Hilfe zu bringen (Theseus und Marathon auf dem Schlachtbild des Polygnot, Paus. 1,15,3). Nicht erst in der Kaiserzeit, wo sie in der Magie angerufen werden, können Heroen unheimliche und gefährliche Tote sein; der Heros von Temesa in Unteritalien muß jährlich durch die Entjungferung eines Mädchens beruhigt werden (Paus. 6,6,4–11), den boiotischen Heros Aktaion muß man in seinem Bild fesseln (Paus. 9,38,5). Spätestens seit dem 5. Jh. v. Chr. können histor. Personen zu Heroen werden und einen Kult erhalten; im Lauf des Hell. breitet sich dies so weit aus, daß man in der älteren Forsch. an eine völlige Entwertung des Terminus gedacht hat. Das ist kaum zu halten, denn entscheidend bleibt immer, daß der als Heros verstandene Tote einen bemerkenswerten Tod erlitten hat (etwa, daß er jung gestorben ist) und eine Wirkung über das Grab hinaus entfaltet, die größer ist als diejenige anderer Verstorbener (so kann er besondere Schutzfunktion haben oder auch nur im Traum erscheinen) [5].

Die arch. Befunde haben immer deutlicher gezeigt, daß der H., soweit er arch. faßbar ist, erst im 8. Jh. v. Chr. einsetzt. Dabei hat sich in vielen Fällen die Verehrung epischer Heroen an wohl vorher anonyme Gräber der myk. Zeit angeschlossen, deren Inhaber längst vergessen waren. Die Renaissance des 8. Jh. gibt sich so eine Vergangenheit, die im epischen Erzählen wurzelt und Kontinuität mit der brz. Vergangenheit lediglich imaginiert [6; 7]. Dasselbe wiederholt sich in der Folgezeit immer wieder und greift auch auf Italien über; so schließt sich im 4. Jh. der Kult des Aeneas (→ Aineias [1]) in Lavinium an ein Grab des 7. Jh. an [8], auch wenn die röm. Rel. die Kategorie des Heros nicht kennt, sondern durchgehend von Göttern (*dei*) spricht und epische Heroen oft mit alten Göttern gleichsetzt (Aeneas mit den → Indiges und Romulus Quirinus). Außerdem geben sich einzelne Poleis oder ihre Unterabteilungen (bezeichnend etwa die von Kleisthenes reformierten athenischen → Phylen) mythische oder histor. Gründerheroen oder konstruieren sonst ihre Vergangenheit durch H. [9; 10; 11]; das setzt sich bis weit in die Kaiserzeit im polit. Diskurs der griech. Städte fort. Heroen stehen zudem als Tote, also ehemalige Menschen dem einzelnen mit seinen Sorgen oftmals näher als die Götter. Deswegen fassen wir zahlreiche Kulte, in denen Heroen als Segensspender, bes. als Heiler für den einzelnen tätig sind; oft sind solche Heroen kultisch nicht durch einen Eigennamen, sondern nur durch einen Funktionstitel (*hḗrōs iatrós*, »Heilheros«; *dexíōn*; *euergétēs*, »Wohltäter«) bezeichnet.

Einen Sonderfall stellt der sog. thrakische Reiterheros dar. Er ist durch zahlreiche Inschr. bezeugt, meist auf Weihreliefs mit der typischen Ikonographie eines berittenen jungen Jägers (oft mit Hund) bei einem Baum, um den sich eine Schlange ringelt. Sein Hauptverbreitungsgebiet ist der Balkanraum zwischen westl. Schwarzmeerküste und nördl. Adria, doch finden sich Reliefs auch in It. und Äg. [18]. Die griech. und lat. Dedikationen sind im Dat. *Heroi* oder (seltener) *Heroni* gehalten (wo die /*n*/-Form als Nebenform zum /*s*/-Stamm zu verstehen ist). Einen Individualnamen trägt dieser Heros nie, wohl aber gelegentlich eine lokale Epiklese, und er kann auch als *theós Hḗrō(n)/deus Hero(n)* angesprochen werden. In jedem Fall muß es sich um die (auch romanisierte) Interpretatio Graeca einer indigenen Kultfigur handeln.

B. Der Kult

Entsprechend ihrem Charakter als (imaginierte oder histor.) Tote sind die meisten H. lokal gebunden: Heroen haben Gräber, die ihre Verehrung fokussieren. Epische Heroen freilich können an mehreren Orten Grab oder Kult haben (Menelaos etwa in Therapnai und Tarent, Agamemnon in Mykenai und Tarent) und einige besondere Heroen erhalten panhellenischen Kult, werden allerdings dadurch den Göttern angenähert (→ Herakles als *hḗrōs theós*, Pind. N. 3,22; die → Dioskuroi) oder werden überhaupt zu Göttern (→ Asklepios). Die Gräber der Heroen können außerhalb der

Siedlungen liegen, sowohl myk. Tumuli (Grab des Agamemnon in Mykene, Grab der Sieben gegen Theben bei Eleusis) als auch reale Gräber. In manchen Fällen liegen sie an der Grenze der Siedlung und schützen sie so (das Grab des Iolaos in Theben an einem Stadttor, Paus. 9,23,1; Grab eines unbekannten heroisierten Adligen an einem Tor in Eretria [12]; Heroengrab an der Stadtmauer auf Naxos [13]). In zahlreichen Fällen aber befinden sie sich im Innern der Siedlung: Die Gräber von Gründerheroen liegen meist auf der Agora und sind Zentrum eines Kultes, der die Identität der Polis thematisiert.

Sehr oft sind Heroengräber mit ihren Kulten auch mit einem Heiligtum einer olympischen Gottheit verbunden: das Grab des Pelops im Zeusheiligtum von Olympia, dasjenige des Pyrrhos-Neoptolemos mit dem Apollonheiligtum in Delphi, dasjenige der Iphigeneia mit dem Artemision in Brauron. Häufig sind dabei die Kulte des Heros und des Gottes als Gegensätze konstruiert, mit nächtlichen Libationen oder Verbrennungsopfern für den Heros, ohne daß dies dem mod. Schema von »olympisch versus chthonisch« (→ Chthonische Götter) entsprechen müßte. Ebenso oft aber sind die Kulte der Heroen nicht anders als die der Götter durch Schlachtopfer mit gemeinsamen Mahlzeiten ausgestaltet, an die sich in vielen Fällen Agone anschließen; Opfergesetze können entsprechend für Götter und Heroen gemeinsame Bestimmungen erlassen (etwa das Gesetz der Salaminioi, LSCG Suppl 19) [14]. Als kult. verehrte Tote erhalten Heroen aber auch, anders als die Götter, Kultformen, die sich an Totenriten oder überhaupt an zwischenmenschlichen sozialen Riten orientieren. Weinen und Klagen sind oft belegt (was im Götterritual unmöglich wäre, wo schon geringere Abweichungen von der Norm, etwa das Fehlen der Flöte oder des Kranzes, als Hinweis auf ungewöhnliche Trauer verstanden werden), ebenso Bankette, die zusammen mit dem Heros eingenommen werden; deswegen stellt die geläufigste Ikonographie den Heros (meist zusammen mit einer Heroine und einem Mundschenk) beim Mahl liegend dar [15]. Gelegentlich ist das Bereiten eines Bades als weiteres soziomorphes Ritual bezeugt.

Blasser als Heroen sind die Heroinen: Der soziomorphen Auffassung entspricht es, wenn sehr oft einem lokalen Heros eine (oft namenlose) Heroine als Gattin beigegeben oder gar, wie bei Asklepios, eine Familie konstruiert wird. Stehen Heroinen allein, sind sie meist mit Frauenkulten verbunden (z.B. → Iphigeneia in Brauron); nur ganz selten haben sie überlokale Bed. erhalten (→ Helene) [16].

C. Die Deutungen

Gegenüber der ant. Meinung, die Heroen durchgehend als tote Ahnen verstand, hat die mod. Forsch. meist die komplexe Genese betont und verschiedene Kategorisierungen versucht; am verbreitetsten ist die pragmatisch-deskriptive von Farnell [2]. Einige Heroen können als frühere Lokalgottheiten verstanden werden (Helene), andere sind aus lokalen Ahnenkulten entstanden; zahlreiche sind aus dem Epos hervorgegangen (ohne daß in jedem Fall die Vorgesch. klar ist), wieder andere sind als eponyme Gründer frei konstruiert worden (ohne daß hier das frühere Vorurteil, das solche Kulte als weniger religiös verstand, gegenüber den Kulttatsachen Bestand hat). Die These von Nilsson, wonach die H. myk. Ahnenkult fortsetzen, hat sich in keinem Fall bestätigt, und auch die (nur in Umrissen skizzierte) Ansicht von Brelich, der H. mit initiatorischen Themen verbindet, ist zu monokausal [17].

Die mod. Terminologie versteht Heros außer im religionswiss. auch im lit. Sinn; dies geht auf die Übernahme des Wortes aus dem homer. Wortgebrauch in denjenigen des lat. Epos durch Vergil und Ovid zurück.

1 D.O. Adams, Hera and Heros. Of Men and Heroes in Greek and Indo-European, in: Glotta 65, 1987, 171–178 **2** L.R. Farnell, Greek Hero Cult and Ideas of Immortality, 1921 **3** M. Gérard-Rousseau, Les mentions religieuses dans les tablettes mycéniennes, 1968, 222–224 **4** Th. Gelzer, Zur Versreihe der »Heroes« aus der Alten Komödie (Pap. Mich. Inv. 3690), in: ZPE 4, 1969, 123–133 **5** Graf, 127–137 **6** A.M. Snodgrass, The Archaeology of the Hero, in: Annali dell'Istituto Universitario Orientale di Napoli, 10, 1988, 19–26 **7** C.M. Antonaccio, An Archaeology of Ancestors. Tomb Cult and Hero Cult in Early Greece, 1995 **8** G. Dury-Moyaers, Enée et Lavinium. A propos des découvertes archéologiques récentes, 1981 **9** S.E. Alcock, Tomb Cult and the Post-classical Polis, in: AJA 95, 1991, 447–467 **10** T.S. Scheer, Mythische Vorväter. Zur Bed. griech. Heroenmythen im Selbstverständnis kleinasiatischer Städte, 1993 **11** U. Kron, Die zehn attischen Phylenheroen. Gesch., Mythos, Kult und Darstellung, 1976 **12** C. Bérard, L'Héroon à la Porte de l'Ouest (Eretria 3), 1970 **13** V.K. Lambrinoudakis, Veneration of Ancestors in Geometric Naxos, in: R. Hägg, N. Marinatos, G.C. Nordquist (Hrsg.), Early Greek Cult Practice, 1988, 235–246 **14** A.D. Nock, The Cult of Heroes, in: A.D. Nock, Z. Stewart (Hrsg.), Essays on Rel. and the Ancient World, 1972, 575–602 (1944) **15** J.-M. Dentzer, Le motif du banquet couché dans le Proche-Orient et le monde grec du VIIe au IVe siècle avant J.-C., 1982 **16** J. Larson, Greek Heroine Cults, 1995 **17** A. Brelich, Gli Eroi Greci. Un Problema Storico-Religioso, 1958 **18** E. Will, Le relief cultuel gréco-romain, 1955.

F.G.

Heron (Ἥρων).

A. Leben B. Werke C. Nachwirkung

A. Leben

H. von Alexandreia, Mathematiker und Ingenieur. Über sein Leben sind keine Einzelheiten bekannt. Er lebte nach → Archimedes [1], den er zit., und vor → Pappos, der ihn zitiert. H. schildert in der *Dioptra*, Kap. 35, eine Methode, um den Zeitunterschied zwischen Rom und Alexandreia durch Beobachtung derselben Mondfinsternis an beiden Orten zu bestimmen. Es ist sehr wahrscheinlich, daß diese Finsternis 62 n. Chr. eintrat und daß H. sie vermutlich in Alexandreia selbst beobachtet hat [10. 21–24].

B. Werke

H. schrieb zahlreiche Werke zur Mechanik, Pneumatik, Vermessungskunde und Herstellung von Maschinen. Bei manchen Schriften ist die Autorschaft unsicher; einige dürften überarbeitete Schul-B. aus byz. Zeit sein. H. ist wenig originell. Seine Bed. liegt in der hdb.-artigen Zusammenfassung des vorhandenen Wissens.

1) H. verfaßte einen Komm. zu den ›Elementen‹ des Eukleides [3], von dem griech. Fragmente bei Proklos (In Eukl. Elem. I) und arab. im Euklid-Komm. des an-Nairīzī überl. sind. H. ging hier u.a. auf die Bed. der Axiome ein, brachte alternative Beweise und Verallgemeinerungen von Lehrsätzen [8. 310–314].

2) Als Teil einer byz. Slg. mathematischer Sätze sind die ›Definitionen‹ (Ὅροι; Ed. [1. Bd. 4, 1–169]) erh., die 133 – z.T. über Euklid hinausgehende – Erklärungen geom. Begriffe bringen. Außerdem werden Maßeinheiten umgerechnet. Der überl. Text ist vermutlich eine spätere Bearbeitung.

3) Die erst seit 1896 bekannten *Metrica* (Μετρικά, 3 B.; Ed. [1. Bd. 3, 1–185] und [3]) enthalten Anleitungen zum Vermessen von ebenen und gekrümmten Flächen (B. 1), von Körpern (B. 2) und zum Teilen von Flächen und Körpern (B. 3). Praktische Rechenregeln mit Zahlenbeispielen wechseln mit geom. strengen Beweisen ab, die stark gedrängt sind. U.a. enthält die Schrift die nach H. benannte Flächenformel für das Dreieck (1,8), die allerdings schon Archimedes bekannt war.

4) Auf den *Metrica* beruhen mehrere Slgg., die unter H.s Namen überl. werden, aber vermutlich später kompiliert wurden: Die *Geometrica* (entspricht *Metrica*, B. 1; Ed. [1. Bd. 4, 171–449]) und *Stereometrica* (entspricht *Metrica*, B. 2; Ed. [1. Bd. 5, 1–162]) enthalten praktische Beispiele, die rezeptmäßig durchgerechnet werden. *De mensuris* (Περὶ μέτρων, ›Über die Maße‹; Ed. [1. Bd. 5, 163–219]) ist eine minderwertige Kompilation geom. Rechenregeln. Die Slg. mit dem Titel *Geodaesia* (Γεωδαισία; Ed. [1. Bd. 5, LXX-XCIII]) enthält Auszüge aus den geom. Abschnitten der *Metrica*.

5) Die *Dioptra* (Περὶ διόπτρας; Ed. [1. Bd. 3, 187–315]) beschreibt sachkundig ein kompliziertes Visierinstrument, eine Art Theodolit, das für Feldmesser, Astronomen und Ingenieure vielfach verwendbar ist, z.B. bei Landvermessungen, Kanal- und Tunnelbauten und Abstandsbestimmungen am Himmel. Angehängt ist die Beschreibung eines automatischen Wegemessers.

6) Eine unter Ptolemaios' Namen überl. ›Katoptrik‹ (Ed. [1. Bd. 2, 301–365]) stammt vermutlich von H. In dieser Schrift, die nur in der lat. Übers. durch Wilhelm von Moerbeke bekannt ist, werden die Grundgesetze der Reflexion an ebenen, konvexen und konkaven Spiegeln dargestellt und auch Anordnungen von Vexierspiegeln, die an H.s »Automaten« (s. Nr. 9) erinnern.

7) Die ›Mechanik‹ (Μηχανικά) (3 B.), die (abgesehen von Fragmenten) nur aus der arab. Übers. des Qusṭā ibn Lūqā bekannt ist (Ed. bei [1. Bd. 2, 1–299]), wendet sich an Ingenieure und Baumeister. B. 1 behandelt die Konstruktion einer Winde mit Zahnradgetriebe (βαρουλκός), geom. Sätze über ähnliche Figuren, die Herstellung von Geräten zum maßstabsgerechten Wiedergeben ebener und räumlicher Figuren und elementare Sätze der Statik. B. 2 enthält die Theorie der fünf einfachen Maschinen (→ Winde, Hebel, Flaschenzug, vgl. → Hebegeräte, Keil, Schraube) und weitere Sätze der Statik. B. 3 gibt Anleitungen zu Bau, Verwendung und Bedienung von Maschinen des täglichen Gebrauchs.

8) Die ›Pneumatik‹ (Πνευματικά, 2 B.; Ed. bei [1. Bd.1, 1–333]), H.s umfangreichste Schrift, weist Beziehungen zu → Ktesibios und → Philon von Byzanz auf. Sie könnte die Vorstufe für ein Lehrbuch sein, von dem nur der Anf. in die endgültige Gestalt gebracht wurde. Hier wird die Druck- und Saugwirkung von Luft und Wasser verwendet, um Gebrauchsgegenstände anzutreiben oder Apparate für spektakuläre Vorführungen herzustellen. In der Einl. wird die Existenz des Vakuums diskutiert. H.s Auffassung von der Materie liegt zw. Aristoteles und den Atomisten.

9) In der Schrift über Automatenherstellung (Περὶ αὐτοματοποιητικῆς, 2 B.; Ed. [1. Bd. 1, 335–453]) werden zwei Arten von Automaten beschrieben: fahrende, die Prozessionswagen nachgebildet sind, und stehende in einem Schaukasten. Beide werden durch Gewichte angetrieben, die über Schnüre Wellen drehen. Nach dem Prinzip der Wasseruhren wird ein gleichmäßiger Ablauf dadurch erreicht, daß das antreibende Gewicht auf einer Sand- oder Körnerfüllung ruht, deren langsames Ausrinnen den Bewegungsablauf bestimmt (vgl. → Automaten mit Abb.).

10) Die *Belopoiika* (Βελοποιικά; Ed. [2]) behandeln die einzelnen Teile und die Herstellung von Geschützen (→ Katapulte), und zwar von bogenartigen Waffen, schweren Handwaffen sowie Pfeil- und Steinkatapulten. Die Schrift endet mit Erfahrungsformeln für das Verhältnis zw. Geschoßgewicht bzw. -länge und Kaliber.

11) Nur fr. erhaltene Schriften sind: *Barulkós* (Βαρουλκός), wahrscheinlich nur der Sondertitel eines Teils der ›Mechanik‹ (s. [1. Bd. 2, XXIII-XXV; Ed. [1. Bd. 2, 256–267]); er beschreibt eine Maschine zur Hebung schwerer Lasten. Die *Cheirobalistra* (Χειροβαλίστρας κατασκευή) geht auf die einzelnen Teile einer Wurfmaschine ein. Schriften H.s über die Wasseruhren und den Gewölbebau sind verloren.

C. Nachwirkung

Viele Regeln zur Berechnung von Flächen und Volumina, die sich bei H. finden und die in ähnlicher Weise schon den Ägyptern und Babyloniern bekannt waren, wurden auch von den röm. Agrimensoren benutzt und waren mit deren Schriften im ganzen MA im Westen verbreitet. Auch bei den Arabern waren die Werke H.s gut bekannt, v.a. die mechanischen, aber auch die *Metrica*, die u.a. von an-Nairīzī und al-Ḫwārizmī verwendet wurden. Durch die Übersetzungen aus dem

Arab. war seit dem 12. Jh. im Westen u.a. die »Heronische Dreiecksformel« wieder zugänglich [4. 635–657]. In der Renaissance waren H.s Schriften recht beliebt, v.a. die ›Pneumatik‹ und die ›Automaten‹, die als Anleitung für ähnliche Kunststücke dienten.
→ Eukleides [3]

Ed.: **1** W. Schmidt, L. Nix, H. Schöne, J. L. Heiberg, Heronis Alexandrini opera quae supersunt omnia, 5 Bde. in 6 Teilen, 1899–1914 (griech.-arab.-dt.) **2** H. Diels, E. Schramm, Herons Belopoiika (Schrift vom Geschützbau), 1918 (griech.-dt.) **3** E. M. Bruins, Codex Constantinopolitanus Palatii Veteris no. 1, 3 Bde., 1964.
Lit.: **4** M. Clagett, Archimedes in the Middle Ages, Bd. 1, 1964 **5** A. G. Drachmann, Ktesibios, Philon and Heron. A study in ancient pneumatics, 1948 **6** Ders., The mechanical technology of Greek and Roman antiquity, 1963 **7** Ders., M. S. Mahoney, Hero of Alexandria, in: Gillispie, Bd. 6, 1972, 310–315 **8** T. L. Heath, History of Greek Mathematics, Bd. 2, 1921, 298–354 **9** J. Mau, s. v. H., KlP 2, 1106–1109 **10** O. Neugebauer, Über eine Methode zur Distanzbestimmung Alexandria-Rom bei Heron, 1938/9 **11** Sezgin, Bd. 5, 151–154 **12** C. R. Tittel, s. v. H. (5), RE 8, 992–1080. M.F.

Heroninos-Archiv. Das H.-A. besteht aus über 1000 griech. Papyri, meist Briefen, Abrechnungen und Quittungen aus der Mitte des 3. Jh. n. Chr.; es handelt sich um Dokumente zur Verwaltung der großen, im *Arsinoítēs nomós* (Fajum/Äg.; → Arsinoë [III 2]) gelegenen Güter des Aurelius Appianus, der dem Rat von Alexandreia angehörte. Die zentrale Verwaltung der Güter des Appianus hatte ihren Sitz in Ptolemais Euergetis, der Hauptstadt des *nomós*, und wurde von Ratsherren aus der Region geleitet; an der Spitze der Verwaltung stand Alypios, selbst Großgrundbesitzer und kaiserlicher Procurator. Zu den Gütern des Appianus gehörten verstreut liegende Felder, Weinpflanzungen und andere Besitzungen. Der gesamte Besitz war in Verwaltungseinheiten unterteilt, die als φροντίδες (*phrontídes*) bezeichnet wurden. Jede *phrontís* wurde von einem Verwalter geführt, der gewöhnlich *phrontistḗs* genannt wurde. Das Archiv stammt aus dem Dorf Theadelphia und ist nach Heroninos benannt, der von 249–268 n. Chr. Verwalter der dortigen *phrontís* war. Das H.-A. stellt keine geordnete Sammlung von Dokumenten dar, sondern ist eher der zufällig erhaltene Überrest der Verwaltungsunterlagen des Heroninos; dennoch bietet es wichtige Informationen über die Verwaltung der Besitzungen des Appianus.

Das wichtigste Ziel der Gutsverwaltung war die Produktion von Oliven (für Öl) und Wein für den Markt, gleichzeitig wurde aber auch der eigene Bedarf gedeckt. Das Gut besaß ein zentral gelenktes Transportsystem, das Esel, Ochsen und Kamele für Arbeiten in der Landwirtschaft sowie für den Transport der Ernte und von auf den Besitzungen benötigten Gütern einsetzte. Dieses Transportsystem ermöglichte es, daß die *phrontídes* landwirtschaftliche Geräte und Instrumente gemeinsam nutzten und sich auf bestimmte Erzeugnisse spezialisieren konnten. Auf diese Weise war eine schnelle Kommunikation und zudem eine zentrale Kontrolle über den Verkauf aller Erzeugnisse gewährleistet und gleichzeitig die Voraussetzung dafür geschaffen, daß die Besitzungen des Appianus tatsächlich ein einheitlicher Wirtschaftsbetrieb wurden. Obwohl einige Felder und Einrichtungen verpachtet waren, wurden die meisten Ländereien in eigener Regie bewirtschaftet. Alle auf dem Gut eingesetzten Arbeitskräfte scheinen den Status von Freien besessen zu haben: Die *oikétai* und *metrēmatiaíoi* arbeiteten längere Zeit auf den Gütern; sie erhielten Verpflegung sowie eine monatliche Entlohnung in Bargeld, manchmal sogar Unterkunft und die Bezahlung ihrer Steuern (diese Einrichtung könnte ein Vorläufer des Colonats gewesen sein). Kurzfristig wurden auch Tagelöhner beschäftigt.

Die Wirtschaftsführung war monetär organisiert und nutzte verschiedene Formen des Kredits, Finanztransaktionen durch Banken sowie die Führung von Konten für die Arbeitskräfte mit einem Haben für die Lohnzahlungen und einem Soll für Aus- und Abgaben. Über die Anstellung von Arbeitskräften und über den Eingang sowie die Auszahlung von Geld, über Ernteerträge und den Verkauf von Erzeugnissen usw. führten die *phrontistaí* genau Buch; sie mußten diese einzelnen Rechnungsposten in einer standardisierten, in Monate unterteilten Jahresbilanz zusammenfassen und der Zentralverwaltung des Landgutes vorlegen. Diese monatlichen Abrechnungen enthielten Einträge über Verkäufe und Käufe in den Rubriken für Geld und Vorräte, womit kontinuierliche Bilanzen für Geld und Bestände vorlagen; sie ermöglichten es der zentralen Verwaltung, die wirtschaftliche Leistungsfähigkeit jeder *phrontís* zu bewerten und vielleicht sogar ihre Rentabilität einzuschätzen. Das H.-A. mit seiner hochentwickelten Rechnungsführung stellt die heute verbreitete Ansicht in Frage, daß die Gutsverwaltung der Antike einheitlich »primitiv« und »ökonomisch nicht rational« gewesen sei.
→ Colonatus; Großgrundbesitz

1 D. W. Rathbone, Economic Rationalism and Rural Society in Third-Century A. D. Egypt: The Heroninos Archive and the Appianus Estate, 1991. D.R./Ü: A.H.

Heroon s. Grabbauten; Heroenkult

Herophilos
[1] A. Leben B. Werk
C. Wissenschaftsgeschichte D. Wirkung

A. Leben
Griech. Arzt aus Kalchedon, etwa 330/320 bis 260/50 v. Chr. [5. 43–50]. Abgesehen von einer hippokratisch ausgerichteten Ausbildung bei Praxagoras verbrachte er den größten Teil seiner aktiven Laufbahn unter Ptolemaios I. und II. in Alexandreia. Er scheint jedoch nicht im → Museion gearbeitet zu haben und war auch nicht Hofarzt [5. 26 f.].

B. Werk

Von den elf Werken, die H. zugewiesen wurden, sind sechs mit großer Wahrscheinlichkeit echt: ›Anatomie‹, ›Über den Puls‹, ›Geburtshilfe‹, ›Diätetik‹, ›Therapeutik‹ und ›Gegen verbreitete Vorstellungen‹. Das siebte gehört ihm zweifellos: ›Über die Augen‹. Das achte (eine Widerlegung des dem Hippokrates zugeschriebenen *Prognōstikón*) ist ihm vielleicht zuzuweisen. Die drei letzten sind Pseudepigrapha: der ›Kommentar zu den hippokratischen Aphorismen‹, die Schrift ›Über Ernährung‹ und die ma. *Epistula ad regem Antiochum* [1].

C. Wissenschaftsgeschichte

H. hat auf dem gesamten Feld der Medizin gearbeitet, das er als Einheit auffaßte und auf neue Weise in drei epistemische Bereiche einteilte: ›Dinge in bezug auf den Zustand der Gesundheit‹ (Anatomie und Physiologie), ›in bezug auf den Zustand der Krankheit‹ und in bezug auf einen von ihm eingeführten Zustand, den ›neutralen‹ (der medikamentöse Therapeutik, Chirurgie und therapeutische Diätetik umfaßt), nach einem bald als peripatetisch [5. 100], bald als stoisch [6. 205] bezeichneten Modell. In methodologischer Hinsicht soll er in der Anatomie eine neue heuristische Methode eingeführt haben: Er soll nicht nur die Sektion an Menschen durchgeführt haben, sondern auch die Vivisektion, die er an Strafgefangenen vornahm.

Im Bereich der ›Dinge in bezug auf die Gesundheit‹ und spezifischer in der Anatomie untersuchte H. viele Organe und schuf eine beschreibende Nomenklatur, die zum Teil beibehalten wurde. Die Physiologie untersuchte H. scheinbar im Rahmen des Humoralsystems [5. 246] und identifizierte die Funktion verschiedener Organe (Nerven, Lunge, kardiovasculäres System) und körperlicher Mechanismen (Puls). Wenngleich H. auch versuchte, den Grund von Gesundheitsstörungen insbesondere durch Symptome zu erklären, bestimmte er die Krankheit einfach als ›das, was schwer aufzulösen ist, dessen Grund in den Säften zu suchen ist‹ oder als ›das, was sich mit der Zeit auflöst‹ [5. 301]; dabei kommt in bezug auf Krankheit und zweifellos auch auf Gesundheit ein zeitlicher Faktor ins Spiel.

In den ›neutralen Dingen‹ setzte er Medikamente weithin nach einem allopathischen Prinzip und auf aggressive Weise ein, als einfache oder zusammengesetzte Medikamente; sie richteten sich in ihrer Wirkung auf die »instrumentellen« Teile des Körpers und nicht auf dessen Bestandteile und wurden von H. als ›Hand der Götter‹ bezeichnet [5. 400]. Die chirurgische Praxis des H. scheint nicht von seinen anatomischen Entdeckungen profitiert zu haben und bestand wohl v.a. aus geburtshilflichen Eingriffen. Den Aderlaß soll er in großem Umfang und unter Verabreichung von Medikamenten praktiziert haben.

Zum technischen Werk des H. kommt das theoretische: die Exegese hippokratischer Texte und die medizinische Lexikographie [5. 427–442].

Man hat H., der wegen seiner anatomischen Entdeckungen geschätzt und als ›Vater der Anatomie‹ oder ›Vorläufer von A. Vesalius‹ bezeichnet wurde, als Skeptiker angesehen [3]. In der Tat bemühte er sich, hippokratisches Wissen zu vertiefen und klar darzustellen. Seine Arbeit an den Texten läßt einen von Autorität unabhängigen Pragmatismus erkennen, ohne daß es sich jedoch um Empirismus handelt [2. 48–52]. Diese Ausrichtung (insbesondere die Praxis der Sektion, die traditionell dem Kontakt mit der ägypt. Kultur und der Mumifizierung zugeschrieben wurde), hat man jüngst [5. 1–31] der Situation der alexandrinischen Welt ›an den Rändern‹ der Kulturen und Gesellschaften zugeordnet.

H.' Werk in seiner Gesamtheit ist als ›unvollendete epistemologische Revolution‹ bezeichnet worden [4. 89] und zielte wohl darauf ab, das voralexandrinische Wissen nach dem euklidischen Paradigma der Wissenschaft und seiner Beweisbezogenheit zu transformieren [4].

D. Wirkung

H.' Werk stand am Anf. einer »Schule«, zu der insbes. → Andreas [1], → Mantias und → Apollonios [17] Mys in der Pharmakologie und Bacchius in der medizinischen Lexikologie zählen. Sie wurde durch die Debatten späterer Epochen, v.a. durch die vom Herophileer → Philinos begründete empirische und durch die pneumatische »Schule«, weithin bekannt gemacht. Nach Galen blieb das Werk des H. unbekannt, bis es in der Renaissance wiederentdeckt wurde, allerdings nur, um durch die innovativen Arbeiten des A. Vésale beinahe umgehend Konkurrenz zu bekommen.

→ Anatomie; Galen; Hippokrates; Praxagoras

1 K.D. Fischer, H. von Staden, Der angebliche Brief des H. an König Antiochus, in: AGM 80, 1996, 86–98 2 M.D. Grmek, Il calderone di Medea, 1996 3 F. Kudlien, H. und der Beginn der medizinischen Skepsis, in: Gesnerus 21, 1964, 1–13 4 M. Vegetti, La scienza ellenistica, in: M.D. Grmek (Hrsg.), Storia del pensiero medico occidentale 1, 1993, 73–120 5 Staden 6 G. Wöhrle, Stud. zur Theorie der ant. Gesundheitslehre, 1990. A.TO./Ü: T.H.

[2] Kaiserzeitl. Steinschneider, Sohn des → Dioskurides [8], als der er auch signierte; erh.: blauer Glas-Kameo mit Porträt, das als Tiberius, Augustus und Drusus I. diskutiert wird.

→ Dioskurides [8], Hyllos, Eutyches [1], Steinschneidekunst

Zazoff, AG, 316 Anm. 58 (Lit.), Taf. 91,1. S.MI.

Herostratos (Ἡρόστρατος). Unbekannter Herkunft, Brandstifter bei der Zerstörung des Artemis-Tempels von → Ephesos 356 v.Chr. Auf der Folter gestand er Ruhmsucht als Motiv, weshalb die Ephesier beschlossen, daß sein Name nie wieder genannt werden dürfe. Nach Valerius Maximus (8,14 ext. 5) hielt nur Theopompos sich nicht daran (auf ihm basieren Ail. nat. 6,40; Solin. 40,2–5; Strab. 14,1,22). Tatsächlich nennen die übrigen Quellen keinen Namen (gesammelt bei [1. 262ff.]). Der Synchronismus des Brandes mit der Geburt Alexanders [4] d.Gr. ist fiktiv.

1 FiE I 2 St. Karwiese, Groß ist die Artemis von Ephesos, 1995, 57–59.
M. MEI.

Herpyllis (Ἑρπυλλίς). Lebensgefährtin (zunächst als Sklavin, dann als Freigelassene, aber wohl nicht zweite Ehefrau) des Aristoteles [6] (gest. 322 v. Chr.), in dessen Testament sie mit Geld, Dienerschaft und Wohnrecht wahlweise auf den Gütern des Philosophen in Chalkis oder Stageira bedacht wurde, da sie sich eifrig um ihn bemüht habe (ὅτι σπουδαία περὶ ἐμὲ ἐγένετο). Im Falle einer späteren Heirat sollten die Testamentsvollstrecker Sorge tragen, daß sie keinem Unwürdigen gegeben werde (Diog. Laert. 5,13). Daß H. die Mutter des Nikomachos, eines Sohnes des Aristoteles, war, ist nicht zu beweisen und möglicherweise eine Konstruktion des Timaios (FGrH 566 F 157; vgl. Athen. 13,589c).
M. MEI.

Herpyllis-Roman. Mit diesem Namen wird ein durch ein Papyrusfragment (PDubl. inv. C 3; Anf. 2. Jh. n. Chr.) bekanntes Werk bezeichnet, in dem fast [3] alle Gelehrten einen Roman erkennen. Ein Erzähler schildert, wie er selbst und eine Frau nach einer schmerzlichen Trennung an Bord zweier verschiedener Schiffe gehen. Es folgt die ausführliche, rhet. virtuose Beschreibung eines Sturmes (ein typisches Romanmotiv); mit dem Erscheinen des Elmsfeuers bricht der Text ab. Der Name der Frau wird meist als Herpyllis gelesen, andere [2. 159; 4] haben dagegen vermutet, daß er zu Derkyllis zu vervollständigen und das Fragment somit dem Roman des → Antonios [3] Diogenes zuzuweisen sei.
→ Roman

Ed.: 1 R. Kussl, Papyrusfragmente griech. Romane, 1991, 103–140 2 S. A. Stephens, J. J. Winkler (Ed.), Ancient Greek Novels. The Fragments, 1995, 158–172.
Lit.: 3 O. Crusius, Die neuesten Papyrusfunde, Beilage zur Allg. Zeitung 145 (3. Juli), 1897, 1–2 4 C. Gallavotti, Frammento di Antonio Diogene?, in: SIFC n. s. 8, 1930, 257.
M. FU. u. L. G./Ü: T. H.

Herr(in) der Tiere s. Potnia Theron

Herrschaft I. Allgemein II. Mesopotamien, Anatolien und Syrien-Palästina III. Ägypten IV. Iran V. Griechenland und Rom

I. Allgemein

H. wird hier als politische H. verstanden, d. h. als wechselseitige soziale Beziehung, die zur Herstellung und dauerhaften Bewahrung der ges. Ordnung in polit. Verbänden dient. H. ruht auf festen Regeln, die sowohl für den oder die Träger der H. als auch für die Beherrschten gelten; dabei steht der Autorität des oder der Herrscher in der Regel eine unreflektierte Zustimmung, zumindest jedoch eine tendenzielle Toleranz der Beherrschten gegenüber. Als Ordnungssystem zeigt sich H. in unterschiedlichen Formen: Im Alten Orient und Ägypten überwiegt in den Territorialreichen und in den Stadtstaaten eine monarchische Struktur (→ Herrscher); in der griech. und röm./ital. Welt entwickeln sich mit der Entstehung kleinräumiger, stadtstaatlicher Formen (→ *polis*, *urbs*) und mit zunehmender Erweiterung der an der H. Beteiligten aus urspr. monarchischen Formen zuerst aristokratisch/oligarchische, dann demokratisch/republikanische Strukturen. Diese werden seit Alexandros [4] d.Gr. bzw. Augustus erneut von monarchischen Systemen überlagert oder abgelöst (→ Hellenistische Staatenwelt; → Römisches Reich). W. ED.

II. Mesopotamien, Anatolien und Syrien-Palästina
A. Begriffe und Formen B. Begründungen
C. Beispiele für königliche Herrschaft

A. Begriffe und Formen

Die indigenen Bezeichnungen für H. werden zumeist als Abstrakta zu den Termini für → Herrscher gebildet. Im Alten Orient wird polit. H. überwiegend in Form königlicher H. realisiert. Diese ist vom ausgehenden 4. Jt. bis zum Ende der altoriental. Reiche als Organisationsform von Stadtstaaten über kleinere und größere Königtümer bis hin zu Territorialreichen belegt. Zeitweise ist sie über oligarchische bzw. aristokratische Strukturen gesetzt oder mit diesen gekoppelt. Auch die Anführer nomadisierender Stammesverbände werden in mesopot. Quellen meist als »König« angesprochen. Königliche H. wird in den ant. Quellen gewöhnl. als Administration charakterisiert. Die Qualifizierung altoriental. Königs-H. als Despotie ist ein nachaltoriental. Konstrukt.

B. Begründungen

Zentraler Bestandteil in Begründung und Darstellung von H. ist die Verknüpfung von H.-Institutionen und H.-Praxis mit rel. Deutungsmustern, insbesondere die Einbindung in die mit der Schöpfung begründete kosmische Ordnung. Die Institution an sich konnte somit nicht in Frage gestellt werden, wohingegen Kritik an individuellen Herrschern möglich war (→ Naramsin). Der H.-Auftrag besteht in der »Wahrung der Ordnung«; dieses Konzept legitimiert polit. H. nicht nur gegenüber den Göttern, sondern auch gegenüber den Beherrschten und potentiellen Gegnern. Jegliches Handeln wird in den Rahmen dieses Auftrages gestellt: die Gründung von Städten, der Bau von Tempeln und Palästen, das Vorgehen gegen polit. Gegner und die → Jagd auf wilde Tiere.

C. Beispiele für königliche Herrschaft
1. Babylonien 2. Assyrien 3. Hethiter
4. Israel

1. Babylonien

Organisation königlicher H. im 2. und 1. Jt. in Babylonien ist einerseits geprägt durch das Verhältnis zwischen Palast und Tempel, den Zentren der Wirtschaft, und andererseits durch das Verhältnis der großen, relativ autarken Städte zu einer überregional ausgerichteten H.-Form. Das Hegemoniestreben der Städte in Südmesopot. wird mit der Machtübernahme der Kassiten-Dyn. (→ Kossaioi; Anf. 16. Jh. v. Chr.) durch einen zentral verwalteten, geogr. und ethnisch relativ stabilen Territorialstaat abgelöst. Die Integration der alten Zentren und der Stammesvölker im Süden in die überregionale Form der H. bereitete dauerhaft Probleme. Die Chaldäer-Dyn. (ab 626 v. Chr.; → Nebukadnezar; → Nabonid) prägte die Überl. der klass. Antike zum altoriental. Königtum.

2. Assyrien

Die H.-Organisation des Stadtstaates Assur zu Beginn des 2. Jt. weist oligarchische Züge auf. Der Herrscher ist als aus der Versammlung der wirtschaftlich potenten Familien bestellter Vertreter *primus inter pares*. Mit der Thronübernahme durch die Amurriter-Dynastie (→ Amurru [1]; um 1800 v. Chr.) kommt es zu einer Stärkung der Machtposition des Königs. Diese Entwicklung wird durch die territoriale Expansion Assurs ab etwa 1400 v. Chr. verstärkt; eine hierarchisch organisierte, hochspezialisierte Administration bildet die logistische Grundlage eines zentral verwalteten Territorialreiches. Unterwerfung, Vasallenschaft, Klientelkönigtum und assyr. Sekundogenitur sind Mittel der Integration eigenständiger polit. Einheiten in assyr. H.

3. Hethiter

Im Verlaufe des 18. Jh. v. Chr. tritt in Zentralanatolien an die Stelle zahlreicher Kleinfürstentümer ein Territorialstaat unter einem »Groß«-König. Das Vasallitätsprinzip wird zum entscheidenden Faktor hethit. H. König und »Gemeinschaft« (hethit. *panku*-) der Großen (überwiegend Mitglieder der königlichen Familie) bilden die zentralen H.-Organe. S. auch → Ḫattusa.

4. Israel

Im 2. Jt. v. Chr. existieren in Palästina nach äg., mesopot. und indigenen Quellen Stadtstaaten, die auch während der äg. Fremd-H. ihre monarchische Struktur beibehalten. Aus der Auseinandersetzung der israelitischen Stämme (*chiefdoms*) mit den kanaanäischen Stadtstaaten geht (um 1000 v. Chr.) erneut Königs-H. hervor. Sowohl die Projektion eines israelitischen Königtums (1 Sam 8) als auch die fr. Überlieferung zu den Herrschern von → Juda und Israel im AT und in externen Quellen zeigt, daß die in Kanaan und Palästina bezeugten Formen königlicher H. auf altoriental. Traditionen gründen.

1 G. W. Ahlström, Administration of the State in Canaan and Ancient Israel, in: J. M. Sasson (Hrsg.), Civilizations of the Ancient Near East I, 1995, 587–603 2 J. B. Brinkman, Prelude to Empire, 1984 3 P. Garelli (Hrsg.), Le Palais et la Royauté, 1974 4 M. T. Larsen, The Old Assyrian City State, 1976 5 H. M. Niemann, H., Königtum und Staat, 1993 6 N. Postgate, Royal Ideology and State Administration in Sumer and Akkad, in: J. M. Sasson (Hrsg.), Civilizations of the Ancient Near East I, 1995, 395–411.

E. C.-K.

III. Ägypten

Die H.-Form im alten Äg., die auch die Kultur des Landes bestimmte, war das Königtum (→ Pharao). Ab ca. 3200 v. Chr. mit der Einheit Äg. nachweisbar, überdauerte es alle Krisen – sowohl Teilungen des Landes (während der sog. Zwischenzeiten) als auch Fremdherrschaft (→ Hyksos, Kuschiten, Assyrer, Perser, Griechen) – bis in die Zeit, als Äg. röm. Provinz wurde. Innerhalb dieser Zeitspanne war das Königtum zwar stetem Wandel unterworfen, dennoch sind in allen Epochen signifikante Grundzüge dieser H.-Form zu beobachten. Das Königtum war fest im Ordnungsprinzip des Kosmos verankert und ein nicht wegzudenkender Teil des Weltgefüges. Untrennbar vereinigte es verschiedene Aspekte polit. und rel. Macht [2]: 1. Kosmisches Königtum: Der Herrscher muß die Schöpfung bei Regierungsantritt rituell wiederholen. 2. Mythisches Königtum: Das Königtum der gesch. Zeit soll der H. von Göttern und Halbgöttern gefolgt sein; es wird als Erbe der Götter betrachtet. Der → Herrscher muß – als Sohn Gottes – die Schöpfung erhalten und bewahren. 3. Polit. und soziales Königtum: Der König gilt theoretisch als alleiniger Eigentümer des Landes in Äg.; er spricht Recht, sorgt für das Wohl des Volkes und vertritt es vor den Göttern. Die Konzeption alt-äg. H. wirkte weiter im Herrscherkult der hell. Zeit und in der H.-Idee der röm. Kaiserzeit (z. B. bei Domitian).

→ Ägypten

1 E. Blumenthal, s. v. Königsideologie, LÄ 3, 526–531 2 D. Franke, »Schöpfer, Schützer, Guter Hirte«: Zum Königsbild des MR, in: R. Gundlach, C. Raedler (Hrsg.), Selbstverständnis und Realität, 1997, 192–193 3 D. O'Connor, D. P. Silverman (Hrsg.), Ancient Egyptian Kingship, 1995.

J. KA.

IV. Iran

A. Herrschaftsform

B. Herrschaftsbegründungen

A. Herrschaftsform

War die H. der Mederkönige (→ Medai) wohl noch eher durch tribal-föderative Strukturen mit unterentwickelten bzw. verzögerten Zentralisierungstendenzen gekennzeichnet, so die der pers. Großkönige (→ Achaimenidai) unter vorderasiat. Einfluß schon früh durch ein – zumindest ideologisch und organisatorisch – »absolutes« Königtum (→ Herrscher). Der ideologisch-dichotomischen Gegenüberstellung von Herrscher und Untertanen (altpers. *bandakā*) entspricht die traditionsbedingte oder polit. opportune Vielfalt von Beziehungen zw. beiden im multikulturellen und polyethnischen Achämenidenreich allerdings nur bedingt (gestufte »Autonomie«-Regelungen, Privilegien, Sonderform der H.-Begründung etc.). Ein Verrechtlichungs- und Institutionalisierungsschub ist dabei z.Z. des → Dareios' [1] I. festzustellen (um 500 v. Chr.). In parthischer Zeit (247 v. Chr. – 227 n. Chr.) verbinden sich für die Ideologie wie die Praxis der Zentralinstanz achäm., hell.-seleukidische und »nomadische« Konzepte und bestimmen je nach Untertanengruppe (parnisch-parth. Aristokratie, Griechen, andere Untertanen) die Herrscher-Untertanen-Beziehungen in unterschiedl. Weise. Das Verhältnis von der Zentralgewalt zu den Partikulargewalten (»Vasallen-H.«) scheint dabei in bes. Weise durch ältere Vorbilder bestimmt gewesen zu sein. Für die parth. und sāsānidische Zeit (227 – 651 n. Chr.) sind die Rivalitäten zw. Herrschern und parth. (bzw. parth.-pers.) »Hochadel« kennzeichnend, wobei der Höhepunkt königlicher Machtentfaltung unter Husrav I. im 6. Jh. n. Chr. anzusetzen ist.

B. Herrschaftsbegründungen

Die Königs-H. wird Untertanen wie Nachbarn gegenüber als in bes. Weise gottgewollt, gottbegnadet und auf das Wohl der Untertanen bedacht dargestellt; königliches Handeln als Krieger/Jäger (→ Jagd), Richter/Gesetzgeber und Vermittler zw. Mensch und Göttern ist dadurch von vornherein legitimiert, Ungehorsam der Untertanen erhält den Makel der Illoyalität (altpers. *drauga*, »Lüge«) und Undankbarkeit. Die (unter hell. Einfluß konzipierte?) Idee eines Herrschers mit göttl. Abstammung und göttl. Qualitäten verstärkt später diese Vorstellung noch. Die aus langer mündlicher Überl. hervorgegangene iran.-histor. Trad. läßt die Gesch. → Irans durch die Abfolge von (z. T. mythischen) Herrscherdynastien, herausragende Herrscher- und Heldengestalten und den Grundkonflikt Irans mit dem großen Feind Turan bestimmt sein; im Verlauf ihrer Entstehung und Umformungs-Gesch. dürften in parth. Zeit durch ostiran. Königslegenden die sw-iran.-achäm. Traditionen und in spätsāsānid. Zeit durch sāsānid. Revision die parth. Bestandteile aus dieser »National-Gesch.« verdrängt worden sein. Am Ende erscheinen die → Sāsāniden als iran. Könige *par excellence*. In einem Teil der frühislamischen Universalgeschichten werden die iran. Könige – neben den biblisch-koranischen Propheten – zu Begründern wesentlicher Grundlagen der menschlichen Zivilisation.

A. Kuhrt, The Ancient Near East, 2, 1995, 647–701 • M. Springberg-Hinsen, Die Zeit vor dem Islam in arab. Universalgeschichten des 9. bis 12. Jh., 1996 • J. Wiesehöfer, Das ant. Persien, 1994 (engl. 1996) • E. Yarshater, Cambridge History of Iran, 3.1, 1993, 359–477. J. W.

V. Griechenland und Rom

A. Griechenland B. Rom

A. Griechenland

Anders als der Alte Orient und Ägypten, wo die Dominanz der monarchischen Idee eine Klassifizierung unterschiedlicher Formen von H. nicht aufkommen läßt, kennt die griech.-röm. Ant. eine Vielfalt von H.-Formen, die auch zu einer Klassifizierung und Wertung der polit. Organisationsformen führt.

In Griechenland ist die histor. Entwicklung nach der myk. Zeit geprägt von der fehlenden Bereitschaft der freien Bevölkerung, sich der H. eines einzelnen unterzuordnen, d. h. auch vom Verzicht auf einen gemeinsamen Mittelpunkt, der eine soziale Hierarchie hätte herstellen können (→ Herrscher). Die aufkeimende Aristokratie konnte ihren Status deshalb nur situativ durch Reichtum und Erfolg herstellen, tat dies jedoch in ständiger Konkurrenz, so daß sich weder ein Stand konstituieren noch eine kollektive, auf Konsens beruhende H. entwickeln konnte (→ Adel; → *aristokratía*), obgleich sich einzelne Aristokraten über ihre Standesgenossen erheben wollten und z.T. auch erhoben (→ Genealogie; → Tyrannis). Eine religiöse Legitimation von H. unterblieb. Aristokratische H. konnte nur mittelbar ausgeübt werden, und zwar über einzelne »herrschende« Mitglieder (→ *archaí*; → *árchontes*: *árchein* = »herrschen«), deren Macht zeitlich und funktional begrenzt war, und über Ratsversammlungen (→ *Áreios págos*). Diese Institutionalisierung von H., die grundsätzliche Offenheit der Aristokratie für Aufsteiger und die Existenz einer breiten Schicht nichtaristokratischer freier Gemeindemitglieder, die zu gemeinschaftlichen Aufgaben herangezogen wurden (→ *hoplítai*), aber unabhängig blieben, führten zur Erweiterung der an polit. Entscheidungen Beteiligten (*oligarchía*) und in Athen schließlich zur Entwicklung zur Demokratie seit → Solon. In der att. Demokratie lag die H., also Wahlen und Kontrolle der Funktionsträger, Gerichtsurteil und polit. Entscheidungen in Rat (→ *bulḗ*) und Versammlung (→ *ekklesía*) letztlich beim Volk (oder doch bei der überwiegenden Menge der freien Bürger, der *polítai*; → *demokratía*), obgleich die polit. Entscheidungsfindung bis weit in das 5. Jh. v. Chr. von Aristokraten bestimmt wurde (siehe z. B. → Alkibiades; → Kimon; → Perikles).

Ein Klassifikationsschema nach der Zahl der an der H. Beteiligten (Monarchie, Aristokratie bzw. Oligarchie und Demokratie) deutet sich zuerst bei Pindar (Pind. P. 2,86–88) an, verfestigt sich im ›Verfassungsdiskurs‹ bei Herodot (Hdt. 3,80–82) und erhält bei Platon (*Politeia*, *Politikos*, *Nomoi*) und Aristoteles (›Politik‹, ›Nikomachische Ethik‹) seine endgültige Form als Dreiteilung bzw. als Sechsteilung der H.-Formen, wenn den »guten« jeweils depravierte Formen gegenübergestellt werden. Die Wertung orientiert sich an der Zahl der an der H. Beteiligten, ihrem sozialen und wirtschaftl. Rang und ihren (angenommenen) ethischen Qualitäten.

B. Rom

In Rom folgt der H. von Königen (→ Herrscher; → *rex*) der Versuch einer durch Standesbewußtsein und Standesabzeichen herausgehobenen Schicht, der *patres*, H. z. T. mit religiösen Argumenten (*auspicium*) auszuüben. Dies mißlingt in den Auseinandersetzungen mit dem freien, nichtpatrizischen Teil der Bevölkerung, der → *plebs* (→ Ständekampf), doch bildet sich dabei durch die Einbeziehung der plebeiischen Oberschicht die neue Führungsschicht der Nobilität (→ *nobiles*). Ihr fehlen zwar Standesabzeichen, sie behält aber faktisch die H. durch starken polit. und sozialen Konsens (→ *amicitia*), die Beherrschung der religiösen Organisationsstruktur und feste vertikale Bindungen zu den unteren sozialen Schichten (→ *cliens*). Das Volk im Sinne des unterhalb des Rittercensus (→ *equites*) stehenden Teils der Bürgerschaft hatte trotz seiner staatsrechtlichen Qualität als Souverän (→ *populus*; → *SPQR*) kaum die Möglichkeit der Ausübung oder der Gestaltung von H. Die Versuche in der späten Republik, das Volk mehr an der H. zu beteiligen (→ *populares*; → Sempronius Gracchus) oder sogar seine Autonomie zu fördern (→ Clodius [I 4]) scheitern paradoxerweise am Zerfall des Konsens in der Nobilität, der es einzelnen Generälen (Sulla, Pompeius, Caesar) erlaubt, die H. zeitweise an sich zu ziehen, bis sie Augustus dauerhaft okkupiert. An seiner H. (und der seiner Nachfolger im Prinzipat) im Sinne einer faktischen Gestaltungsmacht der Innen- und Außenpolitik bestehen kaum Zweifel, umstritten ist die formale Einordnung als Staatsform (Republik, Monarchie, Militärmonarchie, Konstitutionelle Monokratie, Dyarchie (Zweier-H. von Senat und Princeps) oder Verfassung *sui generis*).

Zu einer eigenständigen Klassifizierung der H.-Formen kommt es in Rom nicht. Cicero orientiert sich an griech. Vorbildern (Platon), vor allem an der bereits bei Aristoteles angelegten, aber von Polybios auf die Verfassung der röm. Republik angewandten Mischverfassungslehre, die von einer gleichmäßigen Verteilung der H. auf Magistrate, Senat und Volk ausgeht. Anliegen Ciceros ist es deshalb nicht, wie Platon und Aristoteles nach der besten H.-Gestaltung zu fragen, sondern die in Rom gewachsene Form der H.-Ausübung als beste zu erweisen und damit auch Roms H. im Reich zu rechtfertigen.

Lit.: s. Herrscher IV. W. ED.

Herrscher I. Alter Orient II. Ägypten III. Iran IV. Griechenland und Rom

I. Alter Orient

A. Terminologie B. Organisation
C. Legitimation D. Herrscher-Verehrung

A. Terminologie

Als Bezeichnungen für H. finden sich 1. beschreibende Begriffe wie sumer. LUGAL (wörtlich »großer Mann«), in Vokabularen gleichgesetzt mit akkad. *šarru* (»Glänzender(?)«), *malku* (»Ratgeber«, hebr. *melek*), hethit. *ḫaššu-* (»Wohlgeborener«); des weiteren sumer. NUN und akkad. *rubā'um* (»Vornehmster«), sowie sumer. EN, akkad. *bēlu*, hethit. *išḫa-* (»Herr«); diese gelten unabhängig von Größe und Struktur des Herrschaftsbereiches. Fem.-Bildungen sind belegt. 2. kultur- und epochenspezifische Titel (darunter z. T. auch die unter 1. genannten), die auf einzelne Funktionen und Aspekte des H. Bezug nehmen: In Assyrien bezeichnet um 1900 v. Chr. *rubā'um* den H. als polit. Oberhaupt eines Herrschaftsbereiches, *waklum* (»Beauftragter«) den H. als Bevollmächtigten der Stadtversammlung der Stadt → Assur [1], *iššiakkum* (»Statthalter«) den H. als Administrator des Gottes → Assur [2]. Im internationalen Verkehr wird seit Mitte des 2. Jt. die Bezeichnung → »Großkönig« gebraucht.

B. Organisation

Organisationsgrundlage altoriental. Königsherrschaft ist die → Familie (Sippe) des H. Ab Mitte des 3. Jt. v. Chr. gewinnt die Weitergabe des H.-Amtes innerhalb der Familie (in Mesopot., Nordsyrien, Israel über die männliche, bei den Hethitern auch über die weibliche Linie) zunehmend an Bedeutung. Fehlten direkte Nachkommen, traten entferntere Angehörige des Königshauses ein; Einheirat und Adoption berechtigten ebenfalls zur Sukzession. Nachfolgeregelungen sind aus dem 2. Jt. (Hethiter) und 1. Jt. (Assyrien, Israel) erhalten. Thronfolge aufgrund von Usurpation, Eroberung und Fremdeinsetzung ist belegt. Wichtige Ämter wurden häufig von Familienmitgliedern gehalten. Trotz des in Quellen sichtbaren polit. Einflusses weiblicher Angehöriger des H. ist – anders als in Hatti (→ Ḫattusa) und bei einigen Nomadenstämmen – für Mesopot. keine Herrscherin bezeugt.

Als Staatsoberhaupt stellte der H. formal die höchste polit., mil., administrative und wirtschaftliche Autorität dar. Dies wird u. a. in → Staatsverträgen, außen- wie innenpolit. Korrespondenz, Textcorpora mit juristischer Relevanz sowie H.-Inschriften (→ Inschriften) deutlich. In der Praxis delegierte der H. die Umsetzung seines Willens an Mitglieder des Hofes. Die Interdependenz von Staat und Religion wird sichtbar: a) in der Verankerung der Position des H. im rel. Weltbild (Kosmogonien enthalten teilweise Kratogonien); b) im Status des H. als den Göttern verantwortlichen Administrators; c) in der Einbindung von H. und Hof in die Staatskulte; d) in der wirtschaftlichen Fürsorgepflicht des H. gegenüber Kulten und Tempeln. H.-Epitheta formulieren diese Verpflichtungen programmatisch: So bezieht sich z. B. »König der Könige« auf das außenpolit., »gerechter Hirte« auf das innenpolit. Wirken des H. Die »Taten« des H. bilden zentrale Themen der H.-Darstellung in Text und Bild.

Drohte dem Regenten Unheil, konnte er befristet »ersetzt« werden. Das Substitut imitierte mit Thronbesteigung, Insignien und Titulatur die physische Präsenz des Regenten und lenkte so das Unheil auf sich. Bei Eintreten oder Wegfall der Bedrohung wurde das Substitut unschädlich gemacht. »Ersatzkönige« sind histor. bezeugt in Assyrien, Babylonien und Ḫattuša (s. [4]).

C. Legitimation

In der H.-Legitimation werden bürokratisch-sakrale Konzepte und/oder dynastische Prinzipien (→ Genealogie) verbunden mit göttlicher Erwählung (überhöht als »Gottessohnschaft«). Bei seiner Einsetzung, bezeugt in Ritualen, historiographischen und administrativen Texten sowie Darstellungen, erhielt der H. u. a. »Krone«, Stab, Mantel und Thron als Insignien.

D. Herrscher-Verehrung

Die (Selbst)Bezeichnung des H. als »Sohn, Geschöpf« einer Gottheit ist gängiger Topos im Alten Orient. Eine Gleichsetzung des H. mit zentralen Gottheiten des jeweiligen Pantheons im Rahmen von Ritualen ist fallweise bezeugt. Nur für einzelne H. des späteren 3. Jt. v. Chr. belegen Texte und Bildquellen gottgleichen Status und kult. Verehrung zu Lebzeiten sowie nach ihrem Tode (z. T. bis ins 1. Jt. v. Chr.). Die gesteigerte Toten- bzw. Ahnenverehrung (→ Totenkult) verstorbener H. in Verbindung mit einem Kult an H.-Statuen impliziert nicht automatisch Vergöttlichung (anders in Ḫattuša).

→ Gottkönigtum; Herrschaft; Juda und Israel; Mesopotamien

1 R. Caplice, W. Heimpel, s. v. Investitur, RLA 5, 139–144 2 D. O. Edzard, G. Szabo, W. Nagel, s. v. H., RLA 4, 334–367 3 S. Parpola (Hrsg.), State Archives of Assyria, Bd. 1–12, 1987 ff. 4 Ders., Letters from Assyrian Scholars to the Kings Esarhaddon and Assurbanipal II, 1983, XXII-XXXII 5 J. Renger, s. v. Inthronisation, RLA 5, 129–136 6 G. Selz, Über mesopot. Herrschaftskonzepte, in: M. Dietrich, O. Loretz (Hrsg.), dubsar anta-men, FS W. H. Römer, 1998, 281–344 7 M.-J. Seux, s. v. Königtum, RLA 6, 140–173 8 TUAT I, 1–5. E. C.-K.

II. Ägypten

H. über das alte Äg. war der König (→ Pharao). Im Gegensatz zu seinem göttl. Königsamt wurde er selbst als sterblich erachtet; er spielte eine göttl. Rolle in einem immerwährenden Amt. Gottessohnschaft und die Göttlichkeit königlichen Handelns waren Grundpfeiler der H.-Idee. Der H. war stets den Göttern verpflichtet und Empfänger ihrer Gnaden (z. B. Leben, Gesundheit, Schutz, Verleihung von Amt und → Herrschaft). Er war Stellvertreter Gottes auf Erden und Stellvertreter der Irdischen im Tempel. Der H. erfuhr aber zu Lebzeiten keine den Göttern vergleichbare kultische Verehrung.

Der äg. H. führte eine fünfteilige Titulatur, die rel. bzw. polit. Verhältnisse oder Ziele umriß und deren einzelne Bestandteile sich von der 0. Dyn. (ca. 3100 v. Chr.) bis zur 4. Dyn. (ca. 2575 v. Chr.) herausgebildet hatten. Weitere häufige Bezeichnungen des H. waren »vollkommener Gott« (so wurde ausgedrückt, daß der H. in die göttl. Rolle des Königtums gereift war), »Herr der beiden Länder«, »Herr der Erscheinungen«, »Herrscher«, »Seine Person« (oftmals als »Seine Majestät« übersetzt) und »Pharao«. Die Göttlichkeit des Königsamtes machte den H. zwar nicht identisch, aber doch wesensähnlich mit den Göttern, so daß er oft auch als Sohn oder Ebenbild eines Gottes oder vergleichend »wie Gott NN« bezeichnet wurde.

Legitimation konnte der H. auf verschiedene Art erlangen: a) durch Abstammung; b) durch Designation; c) durch göttl. Erwählung mittels Mythos (dem König wurde beim Geburtsritual die Rolle des Gottessohnes zuteil), Orakel oder Traum (dem König wurde im Traum die Königswürde verheißen); d) durch Leistungsfähigkeit und damit verbunden den Besitz der tatsächlichen Regierungsgewalt (z. B. Usurpation). Dabei erforderte insbesondere die Legitimation durch Leistungsfähigkeit auch eine Legitimation durch göttl. Erwählung.

Der König war theoretisch alleiniger »Herr des Handelns«; *in praxi* delegierte er Aufgaben an Priester und Beamte, die von ihm bestimmt und eingesetzt worden waren.

Wesentliche Aufgabe des äg. H. war die Verwirklichung der → *Maat* [1], der richtigen Welt- und Lebensordnung, und der Kampf gegen das → Chaos. Dazu mußte er die Welt in Gang halten – im Innern durch die Ausübung des Kultes (zur Versöhnung der Götter und zur Gabe von Totenopfern an die Verklärten, d. h. die Verstorbenen) und durch Rechtsprechung über bzw. Fürsorge für die Menschen, nach außen durch das Niederwerfen von Feinden und die Sicherung der Grenzen. In den offiziellen → Inschriften nimmt die Schilderung der Erfüllung dieser Aufgaben durch den H. breiten Raum ein. Entsprechend dem alt-äg. Geschichtsbild wurden Ereignisse, die der *Maat* widersprachen (wie z. B. Seuchen, mil. Niederlagen, Königsmord), nicht aufgezeichnet. Nur in volkstümlichen Erzählungen wird der H. auch der *Maat* widersprechend geschildert (z. B. als homosexuell, trunksüchtig, wortbrüchig). Der Zwang zur Erfüllung seiner Aufgaben (größtenteils innerhalb des Rituals) beugte einer völligen Willkürherrschaft des Königs vor: Er war in die gesellschaftliche Ordnung fest eingebunden und trug große rel. und moralische Verantwortung.

Eine → Frau konnte Herrscherin werden, wenn sie nach dem Tod ihres königlichen Gemahls die Regentschaft für den noch unmündigen Thronfolger übernommen hatte.

→ Ägypten; Herrschaft; Kandake

1 J. Assmann, Maʾat, 1990 (dazu Rez. F. Junge, in: GGA 245, 1993, 145–160) 2 Ders., Der König als Sonnenpriester, 1970 3 J. von Beckerath, Hdb. der äg. Königsnamen, 1984 4 N.-C. Grimal, Les termes de la propagande royale égyptienne de la XIXe dynastie à la conquête d'Alexandre, 1986 5 G. Posener, De la divinité du pharaon, 1960 6 T. Schneider, Lex. der Pharaonen, 1996. J. KA.

III. Iran

A. Terminologie B. Herrschaftspraxis und -repräsentation C. Legitimation D. Herrscherverehrung

A. Terminologie

Neben 1. den einfachen Bezeichnungen für den H. wie altpers. *xšāyaθiya*, paḫlevi-mittelpers. *šāh* (»den eine Herrschaft auszeichnet«) bzw. griech. → *basileús*, βασιλεύς stehen 2. (z. T. mehrfache) Erweiterungen dieses Titels wie altpers. *x. dahyūnām* (»König der Länder/Völker«) oder Formulierungen wie *x. ahyāyā būmiyā* (*vazṛkāyā*) (*dūraiy apiy*), »König auf dieser (großen) Erde (gar fernhin)«, 3. die in Iran kennzeichnend-sten Titulaturen altpers. *x. vazṛka*, griech. μέγας βασιλεύς (*mégas basileús*; → Großkönig) und altpers. *x. xšāyaθiyānām*, pahlevi-mittelpers. *šāhān šāh*, griech. βασιλεὺς βασιλέων (»König der Könige«), in sāsānidischer Zeit z. T. noch erweitert zu *š.š. Ērān ud Anērān* (»K.d.K. von Iran und Nichtiran«) sowie 4. bes. elaborierte Formeln in spätsāsānidischer Zeit (vgl. Theophylaktos Simokat(t)es 4,8). Der einfache H.-Titel (*basileús/MLKA/šāh*) ist in parth. Zeit auch für Regional-H. (Persis, Elymais etc.) gebräuchlich.

B. Herrschaftspraxis und -repräsentation

Organisatorische und machtpolit. Stütze des H. sind die Mitglieder der eigenen Familie (Clan) unter Einschluß der (wohl realen) »Verwandten« (in achäm. Zeit συγγενεῖς, *syngeneís*) bzw. der Mitglieder des Clans ohne direkte Abkunft vom H. (sāsānidisch: *vāspuhragān*); zusammen mit Angehörigen des Hochadels werden sie bei der Vergabe von Positionen bevorzugt. Unter den Personen in der Umgebung des H. (φίλοι, συνέδριον/ *phíloi, synhédrion*, nach seleukidischem Vorbild: OGIS 430), tritt in spätsāsānidischer Zeit eine Art »Amtsadel« auf. Wird bei den Achämeniden auch die bes. Rolle der »Mutter des Königs« und zu allen Zeiten der Einfluß von Frauen des Herrscherhauses deutlich (z. B. → Atossa [1]), so sind doch erst in spätsāsānidischer Zeit Frauen auf den Thron gelangt.

Kennzeichnend für Iran sind auch der »H. auf Reisen« und mehrere H.-Residenzen. Ritualisierte Investituren sowie bestimmte Herrschaftszeichen (Tracht, Kronen, Throne, Königsfeuer u. a.m.) und Formen der Ehrbezeugung (Proskynese/Prostration) lassen die Sonderstellung des H. erkennen.

C. Legitimation

Iran. H. verbinden in ihrer Legitimation dynastisch-charismatische (medisch **farnah*, mittelpers. *xvarrah*; »Glücksglanz«, »Charisma«) und ethnisch-regionale (achäm.: *Pārsa*, sāsānidisch: *Ērānšahr*, → Iran) Konzepte mit spezifischen Konzepten der Nähe zu den Göttern (→ Herrschaft). Usurpationen sprengen dabei nie den dynastischen Rahmen.

D. Herrscherverehrung

Sind die achäm. H. allein als »H. von Gottes Gnaden« richtig charakterisiert, erscheinen die (Parther- und) Sāsānidenkönige (unter hell. Einfluß?) als H. mit göttl. Abstammung und göttl. Qualitäten (mittelpers. *bayān*), jedoch gedanklich getrennt von den eigentl. Göttern (mittelpers. *yazdān*). Opfer und Feuer ›für das Seelenheil und den Nachruhm‹ von H. und Angehörigen des H.-Hauses sind aus parth. und sāsānidischer Zeit bekannt.

→ Herrschaft

Briant • J. Wiesehöfer, Das ant. Persien, 1994 (engl. 1996) • Ders., »King of Kings« and »Philhellen«: Kingship in Arsacid Iran, in: P. Bilde et al. (Hrsg.), Aspects of Hellenistic Kingship, 1996, 55–66. J.W.

IV. Griechenland und Rom
A. Griechenland B. Rom

A. Griechenland

Das Bild vom H., der mit Zustimmung der Beherrschten über polit., richterliche und sakrale Macht verfügt, blieb bei den Griechen und Römern auf mythische und früheste histor. Phasen beschränkt und verband sich mit der Legitimation des H. als Gottessohn, Heros oder Staatsgründer (→ Herrschergeburt).

In myk. Zeit (2. Jt. v. Chr.) scheint in Anlehnung an orientalische Vorbilder eine sakrale Erhöhung des H. (→ Wanax) vorhanden gewesen zu sein. Der Wohnsitz des Königs bildete das polit., mil., wirtschaftl. und rel. Zentrum, wobei einzelne Aufgaben an hohe Funktionäre delegiert wurden (→ Basileus A.). Diese zentrale Stellung des H. verlor sich in nachmyk. Zeit (→ Dunkle Jahrhunderte) und ist in den Epen Homers und bei Hesiod (2. H. 8. Jh.) nicht mehr zu erkennen. Stellung und Machtbefugnis des bzw. der H. in den Gemeinden dieser Phase sind umstritten (→ Basileus B.) und sicher nicht gleichartig.

Mit der Ausbildung der → Polis als selbstverwalteter, von einer meist dünnen Schicht getragener polit. Einheit seit dem 8. Jh. v. Chr. (→ Bürgerrecht; → Adel) tritt in archa. Zeit in Griechenland und den von Griechen besiedelten Gebieten (→ Kolonisation) die Figur des H. zurück (→ Basileus C.), obgleich sie z. T. in der Stellung des *oikístēs* (→ *apoikía*) und zeitweise in der → Tyrannis weiterlebt. Nach der Erfahrung des Abwehrsieges gegen die Perser (490–479 v. Chr.) erscheinen H. und polit. → Freiheit der Griechen als unvereinbare Gegensätze. Die → Staatstheorie des 4. Jh. v. Chr. (Aristoteles) entwirft mehrere Typen des H., lehnt sie aber sämtlich für die griech. Polis ab, und zwar in scharfem Gegensatz zu den Barbaren, deren sklavische Natur es nötig mache, unter einem H. zu leben. H. über Griechen bleiben eine Erscheinung am Rande der griech. Welt und verschwinden selbst dort zwischen dem Tod des Hieron [1] von Syrakus (466/465 v. Chr.) und der Machtergreifung des Dionysios [1] I. im J. 405 v. Chr. vollständig (mit Ausnahme der Sonderform des Doppelkönigtums in Sparta). Das Interesse am machtvollen Einzelnen wird jedoch durch die → Sophistik (z. B. Thrasymachos) wachgehalten, dann Gegenstand der aufkeimenden Staatstheorie (Herodotos) und der Staatsphilosophie (Platon; Aristoteles; → Monarchia) und findet im 4. Jh. seinen Niederschlag in Traktaten, welche die Tugenden verstorbener oder weit entfernter H. preisen (z. B. Xenophon, ›Kyrupädie‹ und ›Agesilaos‹; Isokrates, ›Nikokles‹), mit dem Ziel, H. durch Erziehung »polisfähig« zu machen (z. B. Xenophon, ›Hieron‹; vgl. Platon, Siebter Brief) oder sie als Helfer bei der Durchsetzung polit. Ziele zu gewinnen (Isokrates, ›Philippos‹).

Alexander [4] d.Gr. verkörpert eine neue Form des H., die nach ihm im Hell. weiterlebt und in der eine neue Form der Legitimation, nämlich der mil. Erfolg, explizite Herrschaftszeichen (Diadem, Purpurgewand, Siegelring) und eine (oriental. Vorstellungen angenäherte) sakrale Überhöhung des H. zusammenfließen. Der urspr. nur dem verstorbenen hell. König zugestandene H.-Kult wird bereits in der zweiten Generation von dem lebenden H. beansprucht, auf Familienmitglieder und zum dynastischen Kult ausgedehnt. Eine staatsphilos. Reflexion des hell. H. unterbleibt, doch floriert – neben scharfer Kritik – das schon von Isokrates entwickelte Literaturgenre des → Fürstenspiegels. Die Erfahrungen der Römer mit dem hell. H.- Kult erleichtern das Aufkommen des → Kaiserkults in Rom.

B. Rom

In Rom verschwimmt das Bild der frühen Könige im myth. Dunkel (→ *rex*). Nach der Trad. folgen den vier latinischen H. (Romulus, Numa Pompilius, Tullus Hostilius, Ancus Marcius) drei etruskische H. (Tarquinius Priscus, Servius Tullius [Macstarna?], Tarquinius Superbus). Nach der Vertreibung des letzten Königs (wohl erst nach der Machtergreifung eines 4. etr. H., → Porsenna) wurde das Königtums geächtet und das Streben danach (*affectatio regni*) zum todeswürdigen Verbrechen. Erst am Ende der Republik gelang es einzelnen (→ Cornelius [I 90] Sulla; → Caesar) durch mil. Übermacht und eine Form- und Funktionsveränderung der Stellung des → *dictator*, sich faktisch zum H. zu machen.

Im → Prinzipat tritt hinter der anfangs durch Benennung (→ Princeps) und Ideologie (»Bestellung« durch den Senat; → *auctoritas*; vgl. R. Gest. div. Aug. 34) verschleierten Stellung des H. zunehmend eine Autokratisierung hervor, die durch das faktische Monopol der Verfügung über das Heer, die Zentralisierung der Verwaltung (→ Hof), Vergabe von Sondervollmachten (*lex de imperio Vespasiani*) gefördert wurde und durch die kultische Verehrung (→ Kaiserkult) auch zu Versuchen sakraler Legitimation des H. führte (bereits bei Domitianus [1], deutlicher bei Elagabalus [2], Aurelianus [3] und Diocletianus). Der Ornat des H. entwickelt sich aus der Amtstracht republikan. Magistrate, v.a. des Feldherrngewands, und wird bis zum 3. Jh. immer prunkvoller (Feldherrnmantel und Hosen in Purpur, rote Schuhe, goldbestickte Tunica). Zugleich erscheinen Zepter und Globus als H.-Insignien. Im »christlichen« H. seit Constantinus [1] I., der als erster wieder das als Königsinsignie verpönte Diadem (→ *diádēma*) trägt, und in byz. Zeit lebt im Gedanken des H. »von Gottes Gnaden« die vorchristl. Idee des H. als Schützling mächtiger Gottheiten weiter, doch verbietet das Christentum den Anspruch auf Gottessohnschaft. Die Sakralisierung der unmittelbaren Umgebung des Kaisers (z. B. *sacrum consistorium*, *sacrum cubiculum*) und die wohl am Vorbild der Sāsāniden orientierte Entwicklung des kaiserl. Ornats und des höfischen Zeremoniells (→ Proskynesis) rücken den spätant. und byz. H. jedoch weit von der irdischen Sphäre ab. Ma. H. wie Karl d.Gr. oder der Staufer Friedrich II. sehen ihr Vorbild wieder eher in Augustus oder Traianus.

→ Herrscher

Griechenland: P. Carlier, La Royauté en Grèce avant Alexandre, 1984 • P. Barceló, Basileia, Monarchia, Tyrannis, 1993 • R. Drews, The Evidence for Kingship in Geometric Greece, 1983 • H.J. Gehrke, Der siegreiche König, in: AKG 64, 1982, 247–277 • L. Mooren, The Nature of Hellenistic Monarchy, in: Studia hellenistica 27, 1983, 205–240 • K.F. Stroheker, Zu den Anfängen der monarchischen Theorie in der Sophistik, in: Historia 2, 1953/54, 381–412.

Rom: A. Alföldi, Die monarchische Repräsentation im röm. Kaiserreich, [3]1980 • J. Bleicken, Prinzipat und Dominat, 1978 • R.-J. Lilie, Byzantinische Kaiser und Reich, 1994 • B. Linke, Von der Verwandtschaft zum Staat, 1995 • P.M. Martin, L'Idée de royauté à Rome, Bd. 1, 1982; Bd. 2, 1992.

W.ED.

Herrschergeburt

I. Allgemeines II. Griechenland III. Rom IV. Byzanz V. Einzelaspekte

I. Allgemeines

Bei vielen Völkern, bes. im Vorderen Orient, aber auch bei Griechen und Römern findet sich die Vorstellung vom mythischen Urkönig, der selbst Gott oder Sohn eines Gottes bzw. einer Göttin ist. Gelegentlich wird angenommen, diese mythischen Urahnen eines Volkes oder Stammes seien Tiere gewesen oder zumindest ausgesetzt und von Tieren gesäugt worden. Sie wirkten als Kultstifter und/oder Siedlungsgründer und genossen nach ihrem Tod kult. Verehrung. Was ihnen widerfahren war – Aussetzung, Nährung durch wilde Tiere, Bewährungsproben unter Gleichaltrigen, Kämpfe gegen Ungeheuer etc. – wurde gelegentlich in Ritualen nachvollzogen; Gegenstände und Waffen, die dem Kind beigegeben waren, wurden in den Inthronisationszeremonien (oft als königl. Insignien) verwendet (z. B. → Kyros [1. 17–62]).

II. Griechenland

A. Archaische Zeit B. Klassische Zeit C. Hellenismus

A. Archaische Zeit

Könige und Herrscher wurden zwar in enge Verbindung mit Zeus gebracht; man nahm an, sie stammten von ihm ab (διογενής, *diogenḗs* / διοτρεφής, *diotrephḗs*), seien von ihm mit der Herrschaft betraut worden, er habe ihnen göttl. Charisma und damit auch die Macht verliehen. Die Vorstellung des Gottkönigs ist jedoch schon in den homer. Epen nicht mehr präsent; Göttersöhne sind trotz all ihrer Überlegenheit und Überhöhung Menschen. Auch das Konzept der Gottessohnschaft wurde in zunehmendem Maße modifiziert durch die auch aus ägypt. und jüd. Quellen bekannte Vorstellung vom Heros (→ Heroenkult). So wurden erst nur Söhne von Göttern, Wohltäter der Menschheit und gute Könige, später auch Gründer von Städten, starke Männer, die feindliche Mächte besiegt hatten, Stifter bestimmter Gebräuche, Fertigkeiten u.a. nach ihrem Tod als besondere Kraftträger und Helfer in Krisensituationen kult. verehrt. Vor allem herrschende Familien bezeichneten solche Heroen als ihre Urahnen und legitimierten damit ihre Herrschaftsansprüche.

B. Klassische Zeit

Das Muster vom ausgesetzten Urkönig (→ Aussetzungsmythen und -sagen), das bezüglich der Wohltäter der Menschheit schon lange zur Konvention geworden war, wurde auf Individuen in einer nicht so weit entfernten geschichtl. Epoche und später auch auf noch lebende Personen übertragen, bes. auf Herrscher und Stadtgründer, von denen einige nach ihrem Tod als Heroen verehrt wurden. Oft trachteten die Könige selbst danach, als von einem unbekannten Vater stammender und in den Bergen erzogener, gottähnlicher Held zu gelten. Man nahm nämlich an, Kinder, die eine Aussetzung überlebt und sich trotz schwierigster Lebensumstände bewährt hatten, seien Lieblinge der Götter, mit übernatürlichen Kräften begabt und zur Herrschaft bestimmt, zumal sie in der Regel von besonderen Eltern abstammten und ihre Geburt durch Orakel, numinose Träume und Wunder angekündigt worden war. Allmählich verbreitete sich in Griechenland die von den Ägyptern übernommene Vorstellung, daß zw. einem Gott und dem am selben Monatstag geb. Menschen ein enges Band bestehe (Hdt. 2,82), was dazu führte, daß man gleichzeitig mit dem Geburtstag (= G.) des Gottes auch denjenigen bedeutender Menschen, Herrscher, Philosophen allmonatlich öffentl. feierte [2. 15f.]. In der Regel wurde nämlich die Geburt eines Kindes nur im häuslichen Rahmen mit Opfern für den Geburtsdaimon (*daímōn genéthlios*), der den Menschen vom Augenblick seiner Geburt an begleitet und ihn beschützt, Anrufungen des guten Daimons (*daímōn agathós*), Geschenken, Festmählern, Reden und G.-Gedichten begangen, sein G. – mit denselben Bräuchen – urspr. allmonatlich, später hauptsächlich an den Jahrestagen der Geburt (→ Geburt, → Geburtstag).

C. Hellenismus

Seit → Alexandros [4] d.Gr. wurde die Idee der Gottessohnschaft der ägypt.-oriental. Vorstellung vom Gottkönigtum angenähert und damit insofern erweitert, als der Herrscher schon zu Lebzeiten als Gott, Helfer und Wohltäter der Menschen galt. Unter den → Diadochen wurde neben dem G. des Herrschers auch der Todestag des Vorgängers gefeiert, da dieser gleichzeitig als der G. eines neuen Gottes verstanden wurde (γενέσια, *genésia*). So entwickelte sich eine uniforme Art des Herrscherkults, bei dem der Herrscher oft mit mythischen Göttern gleichgesetzt, selbst als Gott verehrt und sein G. wie die G. seiner Familie (in der Regel allmonatlich) u.a. mit Opfern und Herrscheragonen (Sotereia, Ptolemaia, Demetreia) festlich begangen wurde [3. 1145]. Träger der Feste waren Städte oder Bünde.

III. Rom

In Rom wurde die Vorstellung vom Urkönig, dem Wunderkind, das nach Aussetzung und Rettung zur Herrschaft aufsteigt und zum *parens patriae* wird, bei → Romulus und Remus zusätzlich durch die Zwillingsgeburt gesteigert. Zwillinge galten als numinos, als mit übernatürl. Kräften begabte Wesen göttl. Art. Anzeichen für einen Heroenkult oder das Konzept eines Gottkönigs finden sich jedoch nicht. Der G. und seine Jahrestage waren rein private Feiern, bei denen der → *genius* von Familienmitgliedern, Freunden und Klienten mit Blumen-, Wein- und Kuchenspenden und durch das Anzünden von Lichtern verehrt wurde (urspr. wohl auch allmonatlich). Hatte sich eine Persönlichkeit um die Allgemeinheit bes. verdient gemacht, wie z.B. Marius nach seinem Sieg über die Cimbern und Teutonen, so wurden ebenfalls nicht ihr selbst als einem in göttl. Sphären emporgehobenen Individuum, sondern ihrem *genius* als dem mit ihr verbundenen und aus ihr wirkenden → *numen* Spenden dargebracht (Plut. Marius 27,9). Doch erfolgte sukzessive eine Annäherung an das Konzept des Gottkönigs: → Pompeius feierte an seinem G. einen seiner Triumphe und machte so das private Fest zu einer staatl. Feier (Plin. nat. 37,13); röm. Beamte ließen sich im Osten kult. verehren (Plut. Flaminius 16). Zudem waren die Römer in immer stärkerem Maße bereit, an die troianische Abstammung ihres Volkes zu glauben; dies bewirkte, daß einzelne Geschlechter sich auf troianische Helden und weiter auf die Gottheit zurückführten und der Gedanke der Abstammung von einem Gott über Mythos und dichterische Fiktion in Rom Einzug hielt (Aeneas, vgl. → Aineias). Caesar bediente sich der Troiasage, die gleichzeitig Familienmythos der Iulier war (Kult der → Venus Genetrix), und akzeptierte neben Auszeichnungen mit typisch röm. Charakter eine Reihe von Ehrungen, die ihn in die unmittelbare Nähe hell. Gottkönige rückten. Von Augustus wurde berichtet, er sei göttl. Abstammung (Cass. Dio 45,1; Suet. Aug. 94,4: Atia schlief im Apollotempel ein; eine Schlange glitt über sie, und sie gebar daraufhin einen Knaben, den späteren Augustus). Er lehnte zwar die offizielle Verehrung als Gott in Rom und It. ab, förderte aber die kult. Verehrung seines Adoptivvaters Caesar, wobei er der Feier von dessen G. am 12. Juli als Geste der → *pietas* besondere Aufmerksamkeit widmete, und ließ sich als *divi filius* bezeichnen. Augustus führte die Feier von Caesars G. Schritt für Schritt in den staatl. Festkanon ein, sicherte ihn gesetzlich ab und nahm ihn damit als vollgültiges Fest in den Kalender auf. Sein eigener G., der 23.9., wurde in Rom seit 8 v.Chr. (Cass. Dio 55,6) bis ins 3. Jh. gefeiert und im Osten des Reiches mehrfach als Neujahrstag gewählt. Der G. des Herrschers blieb während der Zeit des Prinzipats das wichtigste Fest im Herrscherkult; die primär rel. Zeremonie bestand aus Fürbitten, öffentl. Opfern, Gelübden zum Wohl des Herrschers, Festessen, Militärparaden und Circusspielen. Sukzessive wurden auch die G. der Mitglieder der kaiserlichen Familie in den Kult einbezogen und die Bürger des Reiches dazu verpflichtet, am Kult teilzunehmen.

IV. Byzanz

Kaiser → Constantin galt nach christl. und paganen Vorstellungen als Kaiser von Gottes Gnaden. Die christl. Legende übernahm für Constantin den alten Aussetzungs- und Reichsgründermythos, weil er das Reich zum Christentum bekehrt und für Byzanz eine neue Epoche eingeleitet habe. Obwohl er die kult. Verehrung des *genius* des Kaisers untersagte, wurde die ant.-pagane Vorstellung vom Gottkaiser (vor allem in der → Panegyrik) weitergepflegt und der Kaiser als ἥρως κτίστης (*hḗrōs ktístēs*, »göttlicher Gründer«) von Konstantinopel und *divus pater* (»göttlicher Vater«) der herrschenden Dynastie verehrt.

V. Einzelaspekte

A. Vorzeichen

Die Geburt eines Wunderkindes, das zum Herrscher ausersehen ist, wird durch Träume (vgl. u.a. → Kyros, → Agathokles, Ardašīr/Artaxerxes, → Zarathustra) und *omina* (→ Omen) angekündigt. Auch die Sterne können die Geburt eines künftigen Herrschers verkünden (Alexander d.Gr., Constantin). Während das Kind geboren wird, bebt das Weltall (vgl. Verg. ecl. 4,48–52). Die Geburt selbst ist schmerzlos, das Kind bes. schön, es lächelt sofort (→ Kypselos, Zarathustra) und wächst bes. schnell.

B. Aussetzungsmythen und -sagen

Das Grundschema (ein Gott zeugt mit einer menschl. Frau einen Sohn; das Kind wird in einem Kasten auf dem Meer ausgesetzt, der an einer Küste angetrieben wird; die Bewohner halten das Gotteskind für einen Königssohn und machen ihn zum (ersten) Herrscher oder zum Priester im Tempel des Vaters; nach seinem Tod erhält auch er göttl. Verehrung) wird insofern variiert, als die Aussetzung auch an mythischen Urzentren (Quellen, Bergen, Höhlen, Bäumen) erfolgen kann. Dort wird das Königskind in der Regel von einem Tier genährt und von Hirten gerettet, bei denen es auch aufwächst.

Das mythische Schema vom ausgesetzten Königskind ist ein typischer Zug im Königsmythos der Iraner, Inder, Griechen und Römer und wurde u.a. auf folgende histor. Herrscher übertragen: Kyros, Ardašir, Šapur, Hormizd, Ptolemaios I. Soter, Kypselos von Korinth, Hieron von Syrakus, Agathokles von Sizilien, Kaiser Constantin. Bei anderen Herrschern (Alexander, Augustus u.a.) beschränkte man sich darauf, von der wundersamen Zeugung durch einen Gott zu berichten.

1 G. Binder, Die Aussetzung des Königskindes Kyros und Romulus, 1964 2 W. Schmidt, Geburtstag im Alt., 1908
3 P. Herz, Kaiserfeste der Prinzipatszeit, in: ANRW II 16.2, 1135–1200.

L. Bieler, θεῖος ἀνήρ, 1935/36 • Chr. Habicht, Gottmenschtum und griech. Städte, 1970 • Th. Köves-Zulauf, Röm. Geburtsriten, 1990 • Ch. H. Taubert, Biographies as Instruments of Religious Propaganda in Mediterranean Antiquity, in: ANRW II 16.2, 1619–1651 • F. Taeger, Charisma, Bd. 1, 1957, Bd. 2, 1960.

R.OS.

Herrscherkult
s. Herrscher; Kaiserkult; Vergöttlichung

Herrschertod s. Kaiserkult; Tod; Vergöttlichung

Herse (Ἕρση). Tochter des → Kekrops und der → Aglauros [2] (bzw. Agraulos) (Paus. 1,2,6; Apollod. 3,14,2). Zusammen mit ihren Schwestern Aglauros (bzw. Agraulos) und → Pandrosos bildete H. in Athen die Gruppe der Kekropiden, die trotz des Verbotes der Athena den ihnen von der Göttin anvertrauten Korb mit dem neugeborenen → Erichthonios [1] öffnen, worauf sich H. und Aglauros in Wahnsinn von der Akropolis stürzen (Eur. Ion, 268–274; Paus. 1,18,2; vgl. 1,2,6; 27,2; Apollod. 3,14,6; Ov. met. 2,552–561). H. ist Geliebte des Hermes, von dem sie den Kephalos (Apollod. 3,14,3) und den Keryx zur Welt bringt (IG XIV 1389, I, 32; 54). Bei Alkman (fr. 67 PMG) erscheint eine H. als Tochter von Zeus und → Selene. H. bedeutet »Tau« (ἕρση, ep. ἐέρση).
→ Arrhephoroi

G.J. Baudy, Der Heros in der Kiste. Der Erichthonios-Mythos als Aition athen. Feste, in: A&A 38, 1992, 1–47 • D. Boedeker, Descent from Heaven: Images of Dew in Greek Poetry and Rel., 1984 • U. Kron, s.v. Aglauros, LIMC 1.1, 283–286 • E. Sittig, s.v. H., RE 8, 1146–1149.

K.WA.

Hersilia. Tochter des vornehmen Sabiners Hersilius (Dion. Hal. ant. 3,1). Beim Raub der Sabinerinnen wird sie als einzige verheiratete Frau entführt (ein Reflex hiervon ist Cass. Dio 56,5,5: H. habe die Römerinnen *tá gamiká*, »was zur Ehe gehört«, gelehrt), bleibt mit ihrer ebenfalls entführten Tochter zusammen (Dion. Hal. ant. 2,45; Macr. Sat. 1,6,16) und heiratet in Rom nach manchen Quellen einen Hostilius und wird so Großmutter des Königs Tullus → Hostilius (Dion. Hal. ant. 3,1; Plut. Romulus 18,29a); öfter findet man sie jedoch als Gattin des → Romulus (Sil. 13,812–815; Liv. 1,11,2; Serv. Aen. 8,638), was wohl auf Zenodotos von Troizen zurückgeht (FHG IV 531 = Plut. Romulus 14,26a; hier findet sich auch eine Prima als Tochter des Paares und ein Sohn Aollius, der später Avillius genannt wurde). Wie ein Ausgleich beider Versionen wirkt die Notiz, Romulus habe sie Hostilius zur Frau gegeben (Macr. Sat. 1,6,16). Bei den Friedensverhandlungen zw. Römern und Sabinern tritt sie als Sprecherin der Frauen auf (Plut. Romulus 19,29d-f; Cn. Gellius bei Gell. 13,23,13). Erst bei Ov. met. 14,829–851 wird sie nach dem Tod ihres Gatten Romulus der Hora, der Kultgenossin des Quirinus, gleichgesetzt [1. 156].

1 G. Wissowa, Rel. und Kultus der Römer, [2]1912
2 F. Bömer, P. Ovidius Naso, Metamorphosen B. XIII-XIV, 1986, 244–245.

JO.S.

Heruli. Seefahrender ostgerman. Stamm [1], der Anf. 3. Jh. n. Chr. angeblich von den Dänen aus Skandinavien vertrieben wurde und sich in Ost- und West-H.

aufspaltete. Letztere griffen 287 die Römer am Niederrhein an, wurden besiegt und überfielen von der holländisch-friesischen Küste aus mehrmals röm. Gebiet bis nach Südspanien (bes. 456/459). Von den → Franci bedroht, bemühten sie sich 476 um die Freundschaft der → Westgoten. Anf. 6. Jh. sind sie nicht mehr nachweisbar.

Die viel stärkeren Ost-H. stießen 267 als Anwohner des Asowschen Meers mit einer Flotte durch den Hellespontos verheerend über Athen [2] bis auf die Peloponnesos vor, wurden aber am Nessos von Gallienus geschlagen. Claudius II. gelang 269 ein Sieg über die »Goten« bei Naissos [3; 4]. Mitte 4. Jh. brachte sie der Ostgote → Ermanarich in seine Gewalt [5. 46]; später waren sie den Hunnen untertan. Um 454 besiegten sie diese im Verband einer antihunnischen »Koalition« am Fluß Nedao. Vermutlich im Karpatenbecken siedelnd [6. 354–356], befanden sich die H. 471 im Gefolge → Odoacers, den sie bis 491 unterstützten. Danach verbreiteten sie sich ins Wiener Becken, wo sie unter Rodulf, dem Waffensohn Theoderichs, mil. bedeutsam waren. Von den tributpflichtigen → Langobarden wurden sie um 508/9 vernichtend geschlagen [7. 28–32; 8. 211 f.]. Während das Gros der überlebenden H. von Anastasius ins östl. Reichsgebiet aufgenommen, später durch Iustinianus bei Singidunum angesiedelt und christianisiert wurde (s. aber [9]), wanderte ein kleiner Teil mit der königlichen Familie nach Skandinavien zurück [10], von wo her die Zurückgebliebenen sich einen neuen König anforderten (vgl. [11]). Negativ verzerrt charakterisiert sie Prok. BG 2,14 f., doch ist eine gewisse Roheit der unsteten und wegen ihres Muts und Kriegsgeschicks als Söldner geschätzten H. gut bezeugt.

1 P. Lakatos, Quellenbuch zur Gesch. der Heruler, 1978
2 G. E. Wilson, The Herulian Sack of Athens, A. D. 267, Diss. Univ. Washington/Seattle 1971 3 E. Kettenhofen, Die Einfälle der Heruler ins Röm. Reich im 3. Jh. n. Chr., in: Klio 74, 1992, 291–313 4 T. Kotula, Kaiser Claudius II und sein bellum Gothicum in den J. 269–270, 1994 (poln., dt. Resümee) 5 B. Tönnies, Die Amalertradition in den Quellen zur Gesch. der Ostgoten, 1989 6 J. Tejral, Probleme der Völkerwanderunsgzeit nördl. der mittleren Donau, in: W. Menghin (Hrsg.), Germanen, Hunnen und Awaren, 1988, 351–367 7 W. Menghin, Die Langobarden, 1985 8 J. Jarnut, Die langobardische Herrschaft über Rugiland, in: R. Bratož (Hrsg.), Westillyricum und Nordostit. in der spätröm. Zeit, 1996, 207–213
9 K. Düwel, s. v. Arianischen Kirchen, RGA 1, 403
10 K. Ziegler, s. v. Prokopios, RE 23, 454 f.
11 N. Wagner, Herulische Namenprobleme. Givrus, Datius und anderes, in: BN 16, 1981, 406–421.

A. Ellegård, Who were the Eruli?, in: Scandia 53, 1987, 5–34 • J. Gruber, s. v. Heruler, LMA 4, 2184 f. K. DI.

Hescanas. Etruskisches Gent. aristokratischer Familien, bes. in → Volsinii, bekannt durch die dort gelegene, figürlich ausgemalte Tomba Hescanas.
→ Etrusci, Etruria F. PR.

Hesiodos (Ἡσίοδος).
A. Person B. Werke C. Wirkungsgeschichte D. Textüberlieferung

A. Person

Der Name H., vielleicht von aiol. Ϝᾶσι (vgl. ἥδομαι), angeglichen an die ep.-ion. Form Ἡσι- und ὁδός, spielt evtl. auf die Tätigkeit des Vaters als Seekaufmann an: ›der, welcher sich über Wege (Reisen?) freut‹ [14]. Dieser hatte das aiol. Kyme wegen finanzieller Schwierigkeiten verlassen und sich im boiotischen Askra niedergelassen (Hes. erg. 635–640). Wegen der Aufteilung des väterlichen Erbes führte H. einen Prozeß gegen seinen Bruder Perses, der versuchte, die Richter zu seinen Gunsten zu bestechen (erg. 35–39). Als H. seine Herde in der Nähe des Berges → Helikon weidete, erschienen ihm die Musen und verliehen ihm dichterische Fähigkeiten: Sie trugen ihm auf, den Ursprung der Götter zu besingen (theog. 22–34). H. nahm an Agonen in Chalkis (Euboia) teil, die die Söhne des → Amphidamas zu Ehren ihres verstorbenen Vaters veranstalteten; als Siegespreis erhielt er einen Dreifuß (erg. 650–659).

Dies erlaubt eine zeitliche Einordnung: Über Amphidamas berichtet Plutarch (schol. vet. in Hesiodi opera et dies, 206, 2–3 Pertusi), daß er während des lelantinischen Krieges zw. Chalkis und Eretria (in den letzten Jahrzehnten des 8. Jh. v. Chr.) starb. Aus erg. 650–659 entstand die Tradition, daß H. und Homer am Agon für Amphidamas teilgenommen hätten und folglich Zeitgenossen gewesen seien (→ Wettkampf Homers und Hesiods). Unhaltbar ist die auch in jüngster Zeit wieder aufgegriffene These [3. 46–48], H. habe vor Homer gelebt (z. B. Ephoros, FGrH 70 F 101): 1. H. weist der Dichtung einen didaktischen Zweck zu. Dieses typische Merkmal der klass. Epoche ist bei Homer noch nicht zu finden. 2. Die Werke des H. weisen einheitlichen Charakter auf: Die ›Theogonie‹ behandelt den Ursprung der physischen Welt und der Götter, der ›Frauenkatalog‹ den der Menschen, die ›Werke und Tage‹ die Stellung und Rolle des Menschen in der Welt. Diese Themenwahl zeigt, daß H. der nachhomer. zyklischen Dichtung und der Lyrik des → Stesichoros näher steht als der homer. Dichtung. 3. Obgleich die poetische Sprache des H. im wesentlichen der ep. entspricht, fehlen ihr die mechanischen Züge und schmückende Beiworte werden weniger, Etym. von Namen und Wörter mehr gebraucht. [17. 94–100; 6].

B. Werke
1. Theogonie 2. Frauenkatalog (Ehoien)
3. Werke und Tage 4. Der Schild
5. Weitere Werke

Zwei ant. Werkverzeichnisse sind überliefert: Suda 2,592,20–22 Adler und Pausanias 9,31,5. Erhalten sind die ›Theogonie‹ (Θεογονία), die ›Werke und Tage‹ (Ἔργα καὶ ἡμέραι, *Opera et dies*) und der ›Schild‹ (Ἀσπίς, *Scutum*). Große Fragmente des ›Frauenkatalogs‹ (Γυναικῶν κατάλογος oder Ἠοῖαι, *Catalogus* oder *Ehoeae*) sind auf Papyri gefunden worden. Die Echtheit der ›Theogonie‹ und der ›Werke‹ ist gesichert; der größte Teil des ›Schildes‹ ist unecht. Die Authentizität des ›Frauenkatalogs‹ wurde zumindest in neuerer Zeit angezweifelt (vgl. [22. 125–176]); über die Echtheit der anderen dem H. zugewiesenen Werke läßt sich schwer urteilen.

1. THEOGONIE

Die ›Theogonie‹ umfaßt 1200 Verse; die V. 1021–22 bilden den Beginn des Proömiums des ›Frauenkatalogs‹. Das Proömium (V. 1–115) besteht aus der nicht mit der Tradition der homer. Dichtung konformen Erzählung von der Begegnung mit den Musen (V. 1–35), aus hymnographischen Elementen (Hymnos an die Musen, V. 36–103) und anderen traditionellen Elementen wie der Themenangabe und dem → Musenanruf (V. 104–115). Danach beginnt in V. 116 die Darstellung der verschiedenen Göttergenerationen. Am Beginn steht → Chaos, dann folgen → Gaia, → Tartaros und → Eros; zw. diesen besteht kein genealogischer Zusammenhang. Gaia ist Sitz der Unsterblichen, Tartaros wird unter der Erde angesiedelt. Eros wird als Zeugungsurkraft verstanden (V. 121–122), Chaos nicht näher bestimmt. Man hat es als den undefinierten, formlosen Zustand der Welt interpretiert [15].

Die Wesenheiten der ersten Generationen weisen im allg. eine doppelte Physiognomie auf: eine physische und eine göttliche. Die der letzten Generationen jedoch (V. 886–917) personifizieren geistige Eigenschaften oder ethische Prinzipien: → Horai (V. 901–906), → Charites (V. 907–909), → Musai (V. 915–917). Die Abfolge der Generationen strukturiert das Werk. Die Beziehung zwischen Eltern (oder Vater) und Nachkommen variiert: Bei den ersten Göttergenerationen ist sie durch Ähnlichkeit oder Gegensatz geprägt; anderswo ist sie komplizierter: vgl. die Nachkommenschaft von Nyx (V. 213–225) [7]. Diese Beziehung verflacht bis zu den letzten Generationen gänzlich, z. B. bei der Generation der Olympier, die alle von Zeus abstammen (V. 886–944). Die Episoden, die die Thronfolge der Götter beschreiben, weisen Parallelen mit den Mythen des Nahen Ostens auf [20]; sie betonen die Abfolge der Göttergenerationen: auf Uranos folgt Kronos, auf Kronos Zeus. Die Machtergreifung des Kronos wie auch des Zeus geschieht durch einen Gewaltakt (V. 154–182, 413–500).

Bei sehr wichtigen Figuren wird die Darstellung etwas ausführlicher, z.B. bei Hekate (V. 411–452), der bes. große Macht zugeschrieben wird, oder bei Prometheus (V. 521–616), der durch seinen Streit mit Zeus die Entsendung der Frau und der Übel in die Welt provoziert. Zwei Schlachten werden ausführlicher beschrieben: die der letzten Göttergeneration gegen die Titanen, die Söhne von Uranos und Gaia (V. 629–720), und jene des Zeus gegen Typhoeus, den Sohn der Gaia und des Tartaros (V. 820–868). Der letzte Abschnitt liefert eine Aufzählung der Verbindungen der Götter untereinander und der daraus entstandenen Nachkommenschaft (V. 886–962). Ein erneuter Musenanruf (V. 963–968) leitet einen weiteren Katalog von Verbindungen zw. Göttinnen und Männern ein (V. 969–1018). Schließlich folgt eine Schlußformel (V. 1019–1020) und der Anfang des ›Frauenkatalogs‹ (V. 1021–1022). ›Theogonie‹ und ›Frauenkatalog‹ wurden offensichtlich als ein Ganzes betrachtet. In der archa. Lit. hatten Werke oft keinen eindeutigen Schluß (→ Gedichttrennung) [9. 25[49]].

2. FRAUENKATALOG (EHOIEN)

Der Name *Ēhoíai* (Ἠοῖαι) leitet sich von ἢ οἵη, »oder diejenige welche«, ab; diese Formel, auf die jeweils der Name einer weiblichen Figur folgt, leitet die genealogischen Abfolgen ein. Das Werk erzählt von den Ursprüngen der verschiedenen Heroengeschlechter, die aus Verbindungen von Göttern und Frauen hervorgingen. Den Anfang bilden die Söhne des Prometheus (fr. 2–3), es folgen die Schicksale der aus diesen Verbindungen entstandenen Nachkommen bis hin zum Trojanischen Krieg. Dieser ist von Zeus ausgelöst worden, um der Vermischung von Göttern und Menschen ein Ende zu setzen (fr. 1,6–7). Das Werk sucht auch die Unterschiede zw. den Menschengeschlechtern zu begründen. Genealogien einzelner Heroen zählen schon zum Inhalt der homer. Epik; hier werden sie jedoch zum Werkzeug für die Systematisierung der gesamten myth. Tradition. Wie in der ›Theogonie‹ wird auch im ›Frauenkatalog‹ die genealogische Struktur durch die Erzählung spezieller Ereignisse unterbrochen: dies sind z. B. die Taten der Tyndareostöchter, die Rettung der Iphimede durch Artemis (fr. 23a), die Vergöttlichung des Herakles (fr. 25), der Katalog der Freier Helenas kurz vor Ausbruch des trojanischen Krieges (fr. 196–204).

3. WERKE UND TAGE

Die ›Werke und Tage‹ (828 Verse) führen in die Tradition der Heldenepik die meisten inhaltlichen und stilistischen Neuerungen ein. Das Proömium bildet ein Anruf an die Musen, → Zeus als Herrn über menschliches Glück und Mißerfolg zu preisen (V. 1–8). In V. 9–10 fordert ihn der Dichter auf, über die Gerechtigkeit der Menschen zu wachen, während er sich selbst die Aufgabe stellt, seinem Bruder Perses Wahres zu berichten. Deshalb muß H. das in theog. 225 entworfene Bild der → Eris korrigieren (V. 11–26). Sie hat zwei Formen: eine positive, die zu zuträglichem Wettbewerb anregt, und eine negative, die zu Neid und Streit verleitet und den Menschen von der Arbeit fernhält. Den Zwang zur Arbeit und die Präsenz des Bösen in der Welt erklärt H. als Folgen des Streites zw. Zeus und Prometheus (vgl. theog. 521–616). Zu den Strafen des Zeus gehört auch die Entsendung der ersten Frau (→ Pandora) und der mit ihr verknüpften Plagen (V. 80–82); diesen folgen die durch den fortschreitenden moralischen Verfall der Menschen verursachten Übel. Die Abfolge der fünf → Zeitalter (*génē*) gliedert diesen Abschnitt (V. 106–201). Weitere Übel entstehen durch den Machtmißbrauch, der den Menschen auf die Stufe von Tieren stellt, während er doch das Gesetz der → Gerechtigkeit befolgen sollte (V. 202–285).

Auf diesen ersten Teil folgen Ratschläge für das rechte Verhalten gegenüber anderen Menschen oder Göttern (V. 286–382) und Regeln für die Landarbeit; diese Tätigkeit stellt H. über alle anderen (V. 383–617). Kaum Erfahrung hat H. mit dem Seehandel (V. 618–694). Nach einer weiteren Serie von Ratschlägen (V. 695–764) belehren die ›Tage‹ (*Hēmérai*, V. 765 bis Ende) über günstige und zu vermeidende Zeitpunkte für alltägliche Tätigkeiten. Die Authentizität dieses Abschnittes, die man wegen der kleinlichen Tabus und der widersprüchlichen Zählweise der Tage in Zweifel zog [10], ist zu Recht verteidigt worden [4. 346–350], da es hier um die alltägliche Religiosität geht. Die zeitlichen Richtlinien (nicht nur für die Zählung der Tage, sondern manchmal auch für einzelne Tageszeiten) können nicht mit den sehr allg. gehaltenen Regeln eines Bauernkalenders übereinstimmen. Die Verse 826–828 kündigen den Übergang zur *Ornithomanteía* (Vogelschau) an, die Apollonios Rhodios für unecht hielt (schol. vet. in Hesiodi opera et dies, 259. 3–5 Pertusi).

4. Der Schild

Die Verse 1–56 (von insges. 480) stammen aus dem 4. Buch des ›Frauenkatalogs‹. Die darin enthaltene Ehoie von Alkmene erzählt von ihrer zweifachen Vereinigung mit Amphitryon und Zeus und der Empfängnis von Iphikles und Herakles. Der Abschnitt ab V. 57 (unecht, wie schon Aristophanes von Byzanz laut Hypothesis urteilte) geht wohl auf die ersten Jahrzehnte des 6. Jh. v. Chr. zurück [1. 34]: Er schildert das Duell des Herakles mit Kyknos, dem Sohn des Ares, der die Reisenden auf dem Wege zum delphischen Apollontempel ausraubt. Den interessantesten und bedeutendsten Teil des Werkes stellt die Beschreibung des Schildes des Herakles dar (V. 140–320), die der Schildbeschreibung in Hom. Il. 18,478–608 vergleichbar ist (→ Ekphrasis).

5. Weitere Werke

Von den Titeln, die die Suda verzeichnet, sind große Fragmente der *Melampodía* (Μελαμποδία, insges. 3 B.) erhalten, die von den berühmten Sehern Melampus, Kalchas und Mopsos (fr. 270–279) sowie den großen Ehoien (Μεγάλαι Ἠοῖαι) handelte. Über dieses Werk ist trotz der Fragmente (fr. 246–262) wenig bekannt.

C. Wirkungsgeschichte

Die beiden wichtigsten Neuerungen des H. gegenüber der lit. Tradition sind: 1. seine Berufung zum Dichter, die als feierliche Einsetzung von göttlicher Seite verstanden wird; 2. die Rolle des Dichters als Lehrer, der über privilegiertes Wissen verfügt. Dies bringt große Verantwortung, aber auch bes. Prestige mit sich. Die berühmte Erzählung von H.' Dichterweihe lieferte eine Reihe weitverbreiteter Metaphern und Symbole zur Bezeichnung des Dichters und seiner Kunst. Jeder ant. Dichter, der sich mit der eigenen Berufung und Kunst auseinandersetzte, orientierte sich an H.' Vorbild [13]. Die ›Werke und Tage‹ wurden zum Lehrgedicht schlechthin (vgl. → Vergilius, georg. 2,176). Viele weithin verbreitete Themen der ant. Lit. haben in H. ihren Ursprung: z. B. die Sehnsucht nach dem Goldenen Zeitalter, die Probleme der Theodizee oder allg. das Verhältnis der Menschen zur Gottheit. Vor allem am ›Frauenkatalog‹ orientierten sich seit → Stesichoros alle (bes. die hell. [16]) Dichter, die sich mit Mythographie befaßten. Nur wenig ist über die gelehrte Beschäftigung mit H. – angefangen mit den Peripatetikern [4. 63–71] – überliefert: Die Scholiencorpora zur ›Theogonie‹ und den ›Werken und Tagen‹ zeigen nur geringe Bearbeitungsspuren alexandrinischer Philologen. Kein einziger Papyrus enthält Fragmente von Komm. zu den Werken des H.

D. Textüberlieferung

Die Papyri bezeugen bereits für das 1. Jh. v. Chr. eine Trennung in den ›Frauenkatalog‹ einerseits und die ›Theogonie‹, die ›Werke und Tage‹ und den ›Schild‹ andererseits (vgl. PMichigan inv. 6828) [3. 51]. Der ›Frauenkatalog‹ war das in Ägypten bekannteste Werk des H.; mehr als 50 voneinander unabhängige Papyrusfragmente sind erhalten. Die ma. Überlieferung ist im allg. von schlechter Qualität. Die drei Werke des hesiodeischen Corpus sind in den Hss. ungleichmäßig vertreten: Die ›Werke und Tage‹ erscheinen häufiger. Die ältesten Codices sind der Parisinus suppl. gr. 663 (11./12. Jh.), der einen Teil der ›Theogonie‹ und des ›Schildes‹ enthält, sowie der Parisinus gr. 2771 (10. Jh.) mit den ›Werken und Tagen‹. Die übrigen bedeutenden Hss. gehen auf die Zeit zw. dem 12. und 14. Jh. zurück.

→ Aratos [4]; Lehrgedicht; Theogonie

Ed.: **1** C. F. Russo, Hesiodi Scutum, ²1965 **2** F. Solmsen, Hesiodi Theogonia, Opera et Dies, Scutum. Fragmenta selecta ediderunt R. Merkelbach et M. L. West, ³1990
3 M. L. West, Hesiod, Theogony, 1966 **4** Ders., Hesiod, Works and Days, 1978 **5** R. Merkelbach, M. L. West, Fragmenta Hesiodea, 1967.
Lit.: **6** G. Arrighetti, Poeti, eruditi e biografi, 1987, 22–36
7 Ders., Notte e i suoi figli, in: R. Pretagostini (Hrsg.), Tradizione e innovazione nella cultura greca da Omero all'età ellenistica, 1993, 101–114 **8** K. v. Fritz et al., Hésiode et son influence (Entretiens 7), 1962 **9** P. Dräger, Argo pasimelousa, 1993 **10** H. Fränkel, Wege und Formen frühgriech. Denkens, ³1968, 316–334 **11** Ders., Dichtung und Philos. des frühen Griechentums, ³1969, 104–146
12 E. Heitsch (Hrsg.), Hesiod, 1966 **13** A. Kambylis, Die Dichterweihe und ihre Symbolik, 1965
14 M. Meier-Brugger, Zu Hesiods Namen, in: Glotta 68, 1990, 62–67 **15** R. Mondi, Χάος and the Hesiodic Cosmogony, in: HSPh 92, 1989, 1–4
16 H. Reinsch-Werner, Callimachus Hesiodicus, 1976
17 I. Sellschopp, Stilistische Unt. zu Hesiod, 1934
18 F. Solmsen, The »Days« of Works and Days, in: Ders., KS I, 1968, 22–49 **19** Ders., Hesiod and Aeschylus, 1949
20 P. Walcot, Hesiod and the Near East, 1966 **21** M. L. West, The Hesiodic Catalogue of Women, 1985
22 H. Troxler, Sprache und Wortschatz Hesiods, 1964.

A. GR./Ü: M. A. S.

Hesione (Ἡσιόνη).

[1] Okeanide, Gattin des → Prometheus (Aischyl. Prom. 558).

[2] Gattin des → Nauplios, Mutter des → Palamedes (Apollod. 2,23).
[3] Gattin des → Atlas [2], Mutter der → Elektra [3], durch ihren Enkel → Dardanos [1] Stammutter des trojan. Königshauses.
[4] Tochter des trojan. Königs → Laomedon, der sie wegen eines Wortbruchs gegenüber Poseidon einem Seeungeheuer ausliefern muß (Hellanikos FGrH 26b). → Herakles befreit sie (dieses Motiv überschneidet sich mit dem → Andromeda-Mythos), ohne den versprochenen Lohn dafür zu erhalten. Er erobert deshalb Troia (Hom. Il. 5,638 ff., Pind. I,6,26 ff.), tötet Laomedon und spricht H. dem → Telamon zu, dem sie → Teukros gebiert (Apollod. 2,103 f.; 136; 3,162). Sie kann ihren Bruder → Priamos mit ihrem Schleier freikaufen (Apollod. 2,136). Die Sage war in Lit. und Kunst beliebt (Soph. Ai. 1299 ff.; Alexis fr. 88 ff. PCG II; Ov. met. 11,211 ff., Hyg. fab. 31; 89; Lykophr. 337; Eust. ad Hom. Il. 20,150 ff.).

LIT.: G. WEICKER, s. v. H., RE 8, 1240–1242 • J. H. OAKLEY, s. v. H., LIMC 8.1, 623 •
ABB.: J. H. OAKLEY, s. v. H., LIMC 8.2, 386–389. R. HA.

Hesperia (Ἑσπερία). Ant. Name von Italia, geprägt aus griech. Sicht als ›im Westen liegendes Land‹ nach der geogr. Lage der Halbinsel (Dion. Hal. ant. 1,35,3). Möglicherweise schon – nach der → *Tabula Iliaca* zu urteilen – bei Stesichoros im 6. Jh. v. Chr. verwendet, findet sich die Bezeichnung H. seither stets im poetischen Sprachgebrauch (vgl. Hor. carm. 3,6,8). Mit Zunahme der geogr. Kenntnisse bezeichnete H. aus demselben Grunde Spanien (Suda s. v. Ἱσπανία), das man manchmal zur besseren Unterscheidung als *H. ultima* kennzeichnete (vgl. Hor. carm. 36,4; Serv. Aen. 1,530).

S. EPPERLEIN, Zur Bedeutungsgesch. von Europa, H. und occidentalis, in: Philologus 115, 1971, 81–92.

G. U.

Hesperiden (Ἑσπερίδες, *Hesperides*). Nach Hesiod (theog. 215 f.; 275) hellstimmige Töchter der Nacht (→ Nyx), die jenseits des Okeanos die goldenen Äpfel hüten. Genealogie (Eltern: Nyx und Erebos, Atlas oder Hesperos; Phorkys und Keto), Anzahl (drei bis sieben) und Namen (Aigle, Erytheia, Hesperethusa: Hes. fr. 360 M.-W.; Hespere, Erytheis, Aigle: Apoll. Rhod. 4,1427 f.) variieren in den ant. Quellen. Der Garten der H., wo der vom Drachen → Ladon bewachte Baum mit den goldenen Äpfeln, das Hochzeitsgeschenk der Ge/Gaia an Hera (Pherekydes FGrH 3 F 16), stand, wurde meist auf einer mythischen Insel (Stesich. S 8 SLG) im äußersten Westen (Hes. theog. 275; Mimn. fr. 12 IEG) beim Himmelsträger → Atlas (Hes. theog. 518) lokalisiert und mit paradies. Zügen ausgestattet (Eur. Hipp. 742 ff.), aber auch in Libyen (Diod. 4,26,2), im Atlantik (Plin. nat. 6,201) oder im Land der → Hyperboreioi (Apollod. 2,113) vermutet. Als letzte seiner zwölf Taten holt → Herakles die Äpfel der H., entweder mit Atlas' Hilfe (Pherekydes FGrH 3 F 17) oder, indem er selbst den Drachen tötet (Panyassis, Herakleia EpGF F 10 = PEG I F 11; Soph. Trach. 1099 f.; Eur. Herc. 394 ff.). Bei Apollonios Rhodios (4,1396 ff.) treffen die → Argonauten auf ihrem Marsch durch die libysche Wüste am Tag nach Herakles' Tat auf die trauernden H., die sich in Staub, Bäume und zuletzt wieder in Frauen verwandeln und ihnen eine Quelle zeigen. Zu den H. in der Kunst vgl. [1; 2], zur Rezeption [3].

1 I. MCPHEE, s. v. H., LIMC 5.1, 394–406
2 G. KOKKOROU-ALEWRAS, s. v. Herakles and the Hesperides, LIMC 5.1, 100–111 3 HUNGER, Mythologie, s. v. H., 228 ff. A. A.

Hesperius. Decimius Hilarianus H., Sohn des → Ausonius; gehört zu denjenigen Familienangehörigen, die von der Nähe des Ausonius zu Kaiser → Gratianus [2] profitieren: 376/7 n. Chr. *proconsul Africae*, von 377 bis 380 als Praetorianerpraefekt im Westen mit Amtsbereichen wechselnden Zuschnitts bezeugt. Korrespondent des Symmachus (epist. 1,75–88). Epist. 19/20 MONDIN (= 16/18 PRETE) des Ausonius sind an ihn gerichtet. Wohl Christ [1]. PLRE 1,427 f.

1 V. HAEHLING, 298 f. H. L.

Hesperos s. Planeten

Hestia (Ἑστία). Griech. Göttin des → Herdes; wie → Vesta ist sie eine Personifikation, die engstens mit ihrem Gegenstand verbunden und von der rituellen Rolle des Herdes im öffentlichen und privaten Raum nicht zu trennen ist; dabei geht die kult. Verehrung des Herdes wohl bereits auf idg. Vorstellungen zurück [1].

Allgemein ist H. kultisch dadurch ausgezeichnet, daß sie in jedem Gebet zuerst angerufen und zuerst in jedem Opfer mit einer Spende bedacht wird (Pind. N. 11,5; Eur. Phaeton fr. 781,35; Plat. Krat. 401a); in Olympia erhielt sie das erste, Zeus Olympios das zweite Opfer (Paus. 5,14,5). Spezifischen Kult mit einem eigenen Tempel hat sie selten (anders als Vesta in Rom), ihre Kultorte sind die Herde im Privathaus und im öffentlichen Bereich (Prytaneia, Rathäuser); doch ist sie mit der Epiklese Temenia belegt, was auf einen eigenen Kultbezirk weist (Erythrai, [2. 363]).

Im öffentlichen Bereich besitzt jede griech. Polis ihr sakrales Zentrum im gemeinsamen Herd im → Prytaneion, wo die Göttin als H. Prytaneia verehrt wird. Für Tenedos stellt Pindar (N. 11,1, vom Schol. verallgemeinert) die zentrale Rolle der H. im Prytaneion heraus. In Athen hob Theseus beim → Synoikismos Attikas die Herde der einzelnen Demoi im einen Staatsherd im Prytaneion auf der Agora auf (Thuk. 2,15,2; Plut. Theseus 24,3). Der Kult der H. Prytaneia ist inschr. gut bezeugt und spielt auch eine Rolle in der Ephebie, indem die Epheben ihr erstes Opfer an sie richten (vgl. ihre erste Nennung im Ephebeneid von Dreros, Syll.[3] 3463,15). In Paros stand eine Statue des → Skopas, die Tiberius nach Rom brachte, am öffentlichen Herd (Cass. Dio 55,9,6; Plin. nat. 36,25; [3]). Aus dem kaiserzeitl. Ephesos stammt eine Reihe von Epigrammen, welche Kult von H., dem »Ewigen → Feuer« (*Pýr áphtharton*), Artemis, Demeter und Kore, So(si)polis (»Stadtschützer«) bezeugt [4]. Überhaupt ist wie im Vestatempel Roms auch in Griechenland an mehreren Orten ewiges Feuer belegt, so im Prytaneion von Athen (Thuk. 2,15,2) oder in Delphi (Plut. Numa 9,5; [5. 125–129]); Kolonisten nahmen vom Prytaneion Feuer für ihre neue Gründung mit [4. 114–134]; Schutzflehende suchten den dortigen Herd auf. Neben dem Prytaneion sind es die Rathäuser (*buleutḗria*), in denen ein fester Herd der H. stand, die deshalb auch die Epiklese *Bulaía* trug. Dieser Herd als Fokus der polit. Gemeinschaft steht in Zusammenhang mit dem Herd im archa. und myk. Königpalast bzw. in den kret. Männerhäusern (*andreṓnes*; Ephor. FGrH 70 F 32 = Strab. 10,4,20). Opfer wird H. dabei zu Beginn aller offiziellen Anlässe erhalten haben; mehrfach sind außerdem Opfer zu Monatsbeginn belegt, was zu ihrer rituellen Rolle bei Anfängen paßt [2. 166[31]].

Ebenso ist der → Herd mit seinem Kult der H. das Zentrum des Privathauses; nach einem für die Kaiserzeit altertüml. Hausplan lag er in der Mitte des Hauptraums (Gal. De antidotibus, Bd. 14,17 KÜHN). Er konnte Schutzflehende aufnehmen, war der Ort für den Ritus der Amphidromia [6], mit denen ein Neugeborenes dadurch in die Hausgemeinschaft aufgenommen wurde (→ Geburt), daß der Vater mit ihm den Herd umrundete, und für den Familienkult mit dem Opfer an H.; für beides war charakteristisch, daß sie sich strikt auf das Haus und seine Bewohner beschränkten (Sprichwort *Hestíai thyeín*, Paroemiographi Graeci 1,201. 242,97; 2,423,35). Nach ihrer Rolle bei den Amphidromia trug H. gelegentlich auch die Epiklese Kurotrophos (Chalkis, kaiserzeitl. [7. Nr. 88]; Etym. m. s.v.).

H.s Mythen spiegeln die kultischen Tatsachen. Entsprechend ihrer Bed. gehört H. zu den Olympischen Göttern, ist Tochter von → Kronos und → Rhea und damit Schwester von → Zeus und → Hera (Hes. theog. 454; Pind. N. 11,2; die erstgeborene, Hom. h. ad Venerem 22). Sie bleibt Jungfrau, trotz des Werbens von Poseidon und Apollon, und erhält von Zeus ihre Rolle als Hüterin und Opferempfängerin »mitten im Haus« (Hom. h. ad Venerem 22–30); ihre Jungfräulichkeit spiegelt eher die Unveränderlichkeit des Kultes als die (hypothetische und aus der Rolle der röm. Vestalinnen abgeleitete) Rolle der unverheirateten Mädchen in ihrem Kult.

1 G. NAGY, Six studies of sacral vocabulary relating to the fireplace, in: HSPh 78, 1974, 71–106 2 GRAF
3 R. MERKELBACH, Der Kult der H. im Prytaneion griech. Städte, in: ZPE 37, 1980, 77–92 4 BE 1967, Nr. 441
5 I. MALKIN, Rel. and Colonization in Ancient Greece, 1987 6 P. STENGEL, s.v. Amphidromia, RE 1, 1901 f.
7 L. VIDMAN, Sylloge Inscriptionum Religionis Isiacae et Sarapicae, 1969.

L. GERNET, Sur le symbolisme politique. Le foyer commun, in: Ders., Anthropologie de la Grèce antique, 1968 (1952) • J.-P. VERNANT, H.-Hermès. Sur l'expression religieuse de l'espace et du mouvement chez les Grecs, in: Ders., Mythe et pensée chez les Grecs 1, 1965, 124–170 (dt. 1996). F.G.

Hestiaia (Ἑστιαία). Att. Asty-Demos der Phyle Aigeis, mit einem *buleutḗs*, wegen Straßenverbindung mit Ankyle (Harpokr. s.v. τρικέφαλον) vermutlich im NO von Athen bei Cholargos.

TRAILL, Attica, 39, 70, 110 Nr. 55, Tab. 2 • Ders., Demos and Trittys, 1986, 127. H.LO.

Hestiaios (Ἑστιαῖος) aus Perinthos (4. Jh. v. Chr.), Schüler Platons (Philod. Academicorum index 6,2 nach Timaios; Diog. Laert. 3,46), der laut Simplikios neben Aristoteles und Herakleides [15] Pontikos d. Ä. Platons Vorlesungen ›Über das Gute‹ hörte und sie auch aufzeichnete. Nach dem Zeugnis Theophrasts (metaphysica 11–13 = F 2 LASSERRE = Testimonium Platonicum 30 GAISER) hat sich neben Xenokrates auch H. bis zu einem gewissen Grad um die Deduktion der Seinsbereiche aus den Prinzipien bemüht.
→ Akademeia

F. LASSERRE, De Léodamas de Thasos à Philippe d'Oponte. 1987, Nr. 9, S. 97–102, 311–316, 531–538 (Slg. und Komm. der Frg.). K.-H.S.

Hestiodoros (Ἑστιόδωρος). Sohn des Aristokleides, athenischer Stratege, belagerte seit dem J. 432/1 v. Chr. Poteidaia und nahm im Winter 430/29 die Kapitulation der Stadt entgegen (Thuk. 2,70,1). Er fiel kurz darauf in der Schlacht um Spartolos (Thuk. 2,79).

DEVELIN, 1381 • TRAILL, PAA 423910. HA.BE.

Hesychios [1]

[1] Alexandrinischer Gelehrter, Verf. eines alphabetisch angeordneten Lex., das uns zahlreiche Frg. (v.a. von Dichtung) überliefert, die Wiedergewinnung zahlreicher Textvarianten ermöglicht und eine bes. Bedeutung für das Studium der ant. Klassikerexegese sowie der Dialekte und der Gesch. der griech. Sprache einnimmt. Für die Datierung grundlegend ist die das Lex. einführende *Epistula ad Eulogium*: Manche Gelehrte setzen den Adressaten mit → Eulogios Scholastikos (5. Jh. n. Chr.) gleich, andere, darunter LATTE [3], bestreiten diese Hypothese, doch kann die Datierung nicht später als in das 6. Jh. angesetzt werden. Dieselbe *Epistula* erklärt, daß die Hauptquelle des Werks das Lex. des → Diogenianos [2] aus Herakleia oder vielleicht eine Bearbeitung davon sei (H. zitiert dieses nicht als ›Allerlei Redensarten‹/ Παντοδαπὴ λέξις, sondern unter dem merkwürdigen Titel Περιεργοπένητες/*Periergopénētes*). H. behauptet weiterhin, Glossen des → Aristarchos [4] von Samothrake, → Apion und → Heliodoros sowie Sprichwörter und orthographische Vorschriften des Herodianos hinzugefügt zu haben.

Dieses Lexikon ist durch den Cod. Marcianus Graecus 622 (15. Jh.) überliefert, der eine stark gekürzte und interpolierte Fassung enthält, in der sich bemerkenswerte Irrtümer und Unstimmigkeiten finden; die urspr. Lesarten sind darüber hinaus von den Korrekturen verdeckt, die M. MUSURUS direkt in die Hs. eintrug, als er sie für die Aldina-Edition vorbereitete. Was die Kürzungen innerhalb des Werks betrifft, das selbst schon aus der Absicht heraus entstanden war, verschiedenartige Materialien zu kondensieren, so fallen in der Fassung des Cod. Marcianus das Fehlen eines großen Teils der Zitate auf, sowie die Tendenz zu oft von Unverständnis zeugender Vereinfachung komplexer lexikographischer Strukturen (dies erklärt verschiedene anomale Glossen, in denen das Bezugsverhältnis zw. Lemma und Erklärung nicht das einer einfachen Synonymie ist; andere gehen dagegen auf spezielle Typen ant. Exegese zurück, nicht jedoch auf eine vorgebliche Irrationalität der Glossen). Unbestreitbar sind weiterhin die Interpolationen: Insbes. ist der H. des Marcianus aller Wahrscheinlichkeit nach Ergebnis einer Verschmelzung des eigentlichen Lex. des H. und desjenigen des Kyrillos. Außerdem kann man postulieren, daß die Glossen betont attizistischen Inhalts auf Interpolationen zurückgehen; dies gilt auch für solche, die mit den D-Scholien zu Homer übereinstimmen; für andere, die einem Euripides-Komm. entnommen sind, und schließlich – wie schon R. BENTLEY bemerkte – für jene biblischen Glossen, die aus einem *Onomasticum sacrum* und der Abh. des Epiphanios *De metris et mensuris ad Sacras Scripturas spectantibus* stammen. Auch die byz. Lexikographen, die H. übernahmen, kannten schon eine Fassung, die mit kyrillianischen Glossen kontaminiert war; andererseits sind einige Familien kyrillianischer Codices eben aus H. interpoliert.

ED.: 1 J. A. ALBERTI (ed.), Hesychii lexicon, I–II, Lugduni Batavorum 1746–1766 2 M. SCHMIDT (ed.), Hesychii Alexandrini lexicon, I–V, Ienae 1858–1868 3 K. LATTE (rec. et emendavit), Hesychii Alexandrini lexicon, I–II (A-O), Hauniae 1953–1966.
LIT.: 4 A. v. BLUMENTHAL, Hesych-Studien, 1930 5 F. BOSSI, R. TOSI, Strutture lessicografiche greche, in: Bollettino dell' Istituto di Filologia greca dell'Università di Padova, 5, 1979–1980, 7–20 6 E. DEGANI, Problemi di lessicografia greca, in: ebd. 4, 1977–1978, 135–146 7 K. LATTE, Neues zur klass. Lit. aus Hesych, in: Mnemosyne s. III, 10, 1942, 81–96 (= KS, 667–679) 8 B. MARZULLO, La »coppia contigua« in Esichio, in: Quaderni dell'Istituto di Filologia greca. Cagliari 3, 1968, 70–87 9 R. TOSI, Studi sulla tradizione indiretta dei classici greci, 1988.
R.T./Ü: T.H.

[2] Für das erste Drittel des 5. Jh. n. Chr. wird durch → Theophanes (p. 83,6 und 92,16 DE BOOR) und → Kyrillos von Skythopolis (p. 26,19 f. SCHWARTZ) ein Jerusalemer Presbyter H. bezeugt, der vermutlich nach 450 starb und Mönch war. Er verfaßte u. a. umfangreiche Komm. zum AT, die gegenwärtig nur teilweise befriedigend, teilweise noch gar nicht ediert sind, und Homilien, die jetzt weitgehend in einer kritischen Ausgabe vorliegen ([1] ist freilich hinsichtlich der Authentizität einzelner Zuschreibungen deutlich kritischer als CPG 3, 257–267; vgl. auch das *Menologion* des Basilios, PG 117, 373). Außerdem sind Fr. einer gegen → Nestorios gerichteten Kirchengesch. erh. (CPG 3, 6582); auch sonst ist die Theologie des H. → Kyrillos von Alexandreia verbunden, ohne jedoch dessen christologische Terminologie zu rezipieren. H. bietet in einem Teil seiner Komm. den biblischen Text nach Sinnzeilen, daneben sehr knappe, zum Teil allegorisierende Glossen (so z. B. im Obadja-Komm., CPG 3, 6558). In Jerusalem besuchte der ›Pilger von Piacenza‹ um 570 eine Hesychius-Kirche (Itin. Anton. 27).

1 G. LOESCHKE, s. v. H. (13), RE 8, 1328–1330.

ED.: CPG 3, 6550–6583 · M. AUBINEAU (Ed.), Les Homelies festales d'Hesychius de Jerusalem, 2 Bde., 1978/1980 (Subsidia Hagiographica 59) · C. RENOUX, C. MERCIER (Ed.), Hesychius de Jerusalem, Homelies sur Job: Version armenienne, 1983 (Patrologia Orientalis 42/1–2).
C.M.

[3] H. von Jerusalem. Priester (Presbyter) und Exeget, † nach 451 n. Chr. Er wirkte als ›Lehrer‹ (διδάσκαλος) und ›Theologe‹ (θεολόγος) in → Jerusalem (→ Kyrillos von Skythopolis, vita Euthymii 16,26), gewährte dem flüchtigen → Eutyches [3] Zuflucht und soll gegen die Entscheidungen der Synode zu → Kalchedon (451 n. Chr.) schriftlich Position bezogen haben. In seiner Christologie wendet er sich gegen → Nestorios (→ Nestorianismus), ohne die Terminologie → Kyrillos' von Alexandreia zu übernehmen. Seine exegetischen und homiletischen Werke sind mit reichen rhet. Stilmitteln versehen. Einige Homilien, die zeitgleich mit dem ›Armen. Lektionar von Jerusalem‹ verfaßt sind, sind bedeutsam für das ›Jerusalemer Typikon‹.

R. MENNES, H. van Jerusalem, 1971.
K.SA.

[4] H. Illustrius. Griech. paganer Geschichtsschreiber aus Milet, wohl gest. um 530 n. Chr.; daß er 582 noch lebte [1. 1322; 2. 924], ist unwahrscheinlich.

H. verfaßte eine nicht erh. Weltgesch. in sechs Büchern. Wie in der ›Bibliothek‹ des Photios (cod. 69) bezeugt, reichte B. 1 von Bel, dem mythischen Urkönig der Assyrer (zu Bel/Baal [3. 1106]), bis zum Trojanischen Krieg, B. 2 bis zur Gründung Roms, B. 3 bis zur Gründung der röm. Republik, B. 4 bis Caesar, B. 5 bis zur Gründung Konstantinopels 330 n. Chr., B. 6 bis zum Tode Anastasios' I. (518 n. Chr.).

Erh. sind nur drei Fr. aus dem 5. (FHG 4, 145 f.) und zwei aus dem 6. Buch (ebd., 154 f.). Unter dem Titel *Pátria* (›Lokalgeschichte‹) *katá Hēsýchion Illústrion* (Pseudo-H.) ist eine wohl im 10. Jh. (Alter der einzigen Hs., Palat. gr. 398) entstandene (verkürzte?) Neufassung eines Exkurses überliefert, welcher dem 6. Buch des Geschichtswerkes vorgeschaltet war. Sein Thema ist die Gesch. des alten Byzantion vor 330 n. Chr., die nach dem Vorbild der röm. Stadtsage myth. gestaltet ist. Mit Pseudo-H. beginnt eine Sammlung von Texten zur Lokalgesch. Konstantinopels, die in ihrer Gesamtheit als *Pátria Kōnstantinupóleōs* bezeichnet wird.

Ferner soll H. (nach Photios) eine Fortsetzung seines Geschichtswerkes verfaßt haben, die bis zu den ersten Jahren Iustinianus' I. (Regierungszeit ab 527) reichte.

Ein weiteres Werk des H., eine Sammlung von Kurzbiographien nichtchristlicher griech. Literaten, der *Onomatológos ē Pínax tōn en paideía onomastṓn*, lag bereits Photios (9. Jh.) nur noch in Form einer Epitome vor, deren Angaben von der Suda (um 1000) in nochmals gekürzter Form tradiert werden. Nur wenige Zitate aus dem Original sind überliefert (Angabe der Fundstellen [1. 1324]). Das in FHG 4, 155–177 edierte Werk *Perí tōn en paideía dialampsántōn sophṓn* wird dem H. fälschlich zugeschrieben.

1 H. Schultz, s. v. H. (10), RE 8, 1322–1327 **2** ODB 2, 924 **3** H. Bacht, s. v. Baal, RAC 1, 1063–1113 **4** PLRE 2, 555 (H. I. 14) **5** Hesychios, Tusculum-Lex. hrsg. von H. Buchwald, ³1982, 336f.

Zu Ps.-H.:

Ed.: **6** Th. Preger, Scriptores originum Constantinopolitanarum, 1, 1901, 1–18.

Lit.: **7** ODB 3, 1598 **8** A. Berger, Untersuchungen zu den Patria Konstantinupoleos, 1988 **9** G. Dagron, Constantinople imaginaire, 1984.

F. T.

Hetairai A. Definition
B. Geschichte des Hetairenwesens

A. Definition

Der griech. Terminus ἑταίρα (*hetaíra*) bedeutet wörtlich übersetzt »Gefährtin«. Er wird zum ersten Mal bei Herodot (2,134,1) zur Bezeichnung einer Thrakerin namens Rhodopis verwendet, die sich Männern sexuell zur Verfügung stellte und auf diese Weise zu Reichtum kam. In der Forsch. wurden H. daher häufig mit Prostituierten gleichgesetzt, wobei darauf verwiesen wurde, daß ihre Benennung als »Gefährtinnen« euphemistisch sei. Davidson [1] betont hingegen, daß der Beziehung eines Mannes zu einer *hetaíra* nach Aussage der Quellen eine Freundschaft zugrunde lag. Die *hetaíra* wird in ant. Texten von der παλλακή (*pallakḗ*, Nebenfrau) und der πόρνη (*pórnē*, Dirne) einerseits und der legitimen Ehefrau (γυνή, *gynḗ*) andererseits deutlich unterschieden (Demosth. or. 59,122; Amphis = Athen. 559a f.; Anaxilas = Athen. 572b).

B. Geschichte des Hetairenwesens

Bereits in der für das aristokratische Symposion konzipierten Lyrik der archa. Zeit (Mimnermos, → Theognis aus Megara, → Anakreon [1]) finden Frauen Erwähnung, zu denen Männer außereheliche sexuelle Beziehungen unterhalten (Mimn. fr. 1 West). In der Lyrik fehlt eine allgemeine Gruppenbezeichnung für diese teils namentlich angesprochenen (Anakr. 346 PMG fr. 1), teils mit Metaphern bezeichneten (Anakr. 417 PMG) Frauen. Auch auf korinth. und att. Vasenbildern sind seit dem 6. Jh. v. Chr. Begleiterinnen der beim Symposion abgebildeten Männer dargestellt. Erst im 5. Jh. v. Chr. wurde mit dem Begriff H. (Hdt. 2,134,1; 2,135,5) eine Gruppenbezeichnung für jene Frauen gefunden, zu denen Männer außereheliche, längerfristige erotische Freundschaften unterhielten, wobei die Benennung H. wohl in der Absicht erfolgte, auf den ideellen Wert dieser Beziehungen zu verweisen. Im übrigen finden die Prostitution in den Bordellen und auf den Straßen sowie die dort arbeitenden Frauen – im Unterschied zu den zum Teil sehr berühmten H. – in den Quellen nur selten Erwähnung (Xen. mem. 2,2,4).

Viele H. waren Sklavinnen, die von einem Kuppler bzw. einer Kupplerin (μαστροπός, *mastropós*) versorgt wurden. Sie wurden üblicherweise mittels eines Pachtvertrages für einen längeren Zeitraum vermietet (Demosth. or. 59,26). Mancher Mann kaufte dem Kuppler die begehrte Sklavin ab und ließ sie frei, damit sie im Status einer Nebenfrau in seinem Haus lebte. Bei anderen H. handelte es sich um Freie (And. 4,14; Xen. mem. 3,11) – in der Regel Fremde oder Frauen mit dem Status von → Metoiken. Die Liebhaber freier H. mußten für deren Lebensunterhalt aufkommen und versorgten sie mit Kleidern, Schmuck, Wohnungen oder Sklavinnen (Demosth. or. 59,35). Wer es sich leisten konnte, unterhielt Beziehungen zu mehreren H. gleichzeitig. Der Umgang mit H., die eine finanzielle Belastung darstellten, konnte zu Konflikten innerhalb der Familie des Mannes führen, wovon einige Prozeßreden Zeugnis ablegen (Demosth. or. 36,45; 48,53ff.; vgl. außerdem Lys. 4). Andererseits erwiesen sich kostspielige H. als geeignete Statussymbole, um den Reichtum ihrer Liebhaber zu präsentieren.

H. dienten insbesondere bei Symposien (Demosth. or. 59,33f.; → Gastmahl) und städtischen Festen (Demosth. or. 59,24) als Begleiterinnen. Als bes. Qualitäten der H. galten Schlagfertigkeit und lit. Bildung (Athen. 13,582c-d) sowie tänzerische und musikalische Talente, die in Schulen ausgebildet wurden (Isokr. or. 15,287). Zahlreiche Männer, darunter Politiker, Redner, Bildhauer und Philosophen, die Verbindungen zu H. unterhielten, sind namentlich bekannt. Über die H. hell. Herrscher kursierten bereits in der Ant. viele Anekdoten. Wichtiges Zeugnis für die rechtliche und soziale Situation der H. in Athen ist die Rede gegen → Neaira, die zusammen mit anderen Mädchen von Nikarete großgezogen worden war, um als Prostituierte für ihre Besitzerin Geld zu verdienen, die dann mehrmals verkauft wurde, zeitweise in Korinth und Megara lebte und schließlich nach Athen zurückkehrte, wo sie angeklagt wurde, weil sie sich als athenische Bürgerin ausgegeben hatte (Demosth. or. 59).

Athenaios [3] bietet zu den H. des 4. Jh. v. Chr. und des Hell. umfangreiches Material (13,566e ff.), das deutlich macht, daß das Hetairenwesen dieser Zeit ein beliebtes Thema der Komödie war. Als histor. Quellen für das griech. Hetairenwesen sind die im 2. Jh. n. Chr. verfaßten, fiktiven »Hetairengespräche« Lukians wie die »Hetairenbriefe« Alkiphrons von geringem Wert, da sie stark von den Vorstellungen der Autoren und der lit. Trad. geprägt sind.

→ Erotik; Frau; Prostitution; Sexualität

1 J. N. Davidson, Courtesans and Fishcakes, The Consuming Passions of Classical Athens, 1997 2 M. F. Kilmer, Greek Erotica, 1993 3 C. Reinsberg, Ehe, Hetärentum und Knabenliebe, 1989. E. HA.

Hetaireseos graphe (ἑταιρήσεως γραφή). In Athen bei den → Thesmotheten einzubringende Popularklage gegen Männer, die ein öffentliches Amt bekleideten oder vor dem Rat oder der Volksversammlung als Redner auftraten, obwohl sie sich gegen Geld zu homosexuellem Verkehr bereitfanden (Aristoph. Plut. 153; Demosth. or. 22,23.29; Aischin. 1,19f.; 1,29; 1,51; 1,72; 1,87). Das Gesetz (Demosth. or. 22,21) sieht Todesstrafe vor und richtet sich auch gegen einen Vater oder Vormund, der Sohn oder Mündel prostituierte. Nichtbürger fielen nicht unter diese Vorschrift.
→ Prostitution

D. Cohen, Law, sexuality, and society, 1991 (Rez.: G. Thür, in: ZRG 114, 1997, 479f.). G. T.

Hetairia (ἑταιρία, auch ἑταιρεία).
[1] In Kreta Unterabteilung der Bürgerschaft, mit Gemeinschaftsmählern (*Andreia* bzw. *Syssitia*: Aristot. pol. 1272a 12ff.; Athen. 4,143a-b = Dosiadas FGrH 458 F 2) und gemeinsamem Kult des *Zeus Hetaireíos* (Hesych. s. v. ἑταιρεῖος), aber weder ein gentilizischer Verband noch Teil einer Phyle, zu vergleichen mit der *h.* in Thera bzw. Kyrene (ML 5, Z. 16). Die Aufnahme in die *h.* erfolgte nach dem Ausscheiden der jungen Wehrfähigen aus den → *agélai* und war Voraussetzung für das Vollbürgerrecht. Die *Andreia* wurden in Lyttos z. T. aus Mitteln der Polis, z. T. aus Abgaben der landsässigen Unfreien und aus einem geringen Beitrag (1/10) der Mitglieder bestritten. Die Entstehung der *h.* ist wohl als Reaktion auf exklusive Symposien in archaischer Zeit (Hybrias bei Athen. 15,695f–696a) zu verstehen, so daß sie kaum Relikte einer vorstaatlichen Entwicklungsstufe waren, sondern eine stärkere Einbindung der Oberschicht in die sich formierende Polisgemeinschaft bewirken sollten.

H.-J. Gehrke, Gewalt und Gesetz, in: Klio 79, 1997, 23–68 • M. Lavrencic, ΑΝΔΡΕΙΟΝ, in: Tyche 3, 1988, 147–161 • St. Link, Das griech. Kreta, 1994.

[2] Seit dem 5. Jh. v. Chr. diente *h.* generell als Bezeichnung für exklusive »Clubs«. Diese bestanden nicht mehr ausschließlich aus »Aristokraten«, gehen aber letztlich zurück auf homer. *Hetairos*-Gruppen [1. 127ff.], die nicht gentilizisch organisiert waren, sondern den Kern der Gefolgschaften einflußreicherer Oikosherren bildeten [2]: Ein Funktionswandel dieser Gruppen vollzog sich im Zuge der Institutionalisierung der Polis, indem sie aktive Träger von Machtkämpfen innerhalb der Führungsschicht wurden.

In Athen waren die Handlungsräume der *h.*, die durchweg kleinere Personengruppen bildeten, seit Kleisthenes begrenzt. Exemplarisch ist der gescheiterte Versuch des Thukydides Melesiou, *h.* gegen Perikles polit. zu instrumentalisieren (Plut. Perikles 14). Durch den Hermokopidenfrevel 415 gerieten Mitglieder von *h.* generell in Verdacht, den Sturz der Demokratie zu planen [3. 7ff.]. Zu einer schweren Gefahr für die Bürgerschaft Athens wurden *h.* durch gezielten Terror im Vorfeld des oligarchischen Putsches 411 (Thuk. 8,54,4) und bei der Machtergreifung der Dreißig ([Aristot.] Ath. pol. 34,3; → Triakonta). Als Speerspitzen innerer Machtkämpfe in vielen Poleis im Peloponnesischen Krieg wertet Thukydides (3,82,4–6) die *h.*

In Theben bildeten um und nach 400 zwei *h.* größere, mit Staseis (→ *stásis*) vergleichbare Gruppierungen (Xen. hell. 5,2,25), deren Protagonisten den Boiotischen Bund zu dominieren suchten (Hell. Oxyrh. 12,2ff.) [4. 173ff.].

1 Chr. Ulf, Die homer. Ges., 1990 2 K.-W. Welwei, Polisbildung, Hetairos-Gruppen und Hetairien, in: Gymnasium 99, 1992, 481–500 3 O. Aurenche, Les groupes d'Alcibiade, de Léogoras et de Teucros, 1974 4 H.-J. Gehrke, Stasis, 1985.

G. A. Lehmann, Oligarchische Herrschaft im klass. Athen, 1997 • E. Stein-Hölkeskamp, Adelskultur und Polisges., 1989. K.-W. WEL.

[3] *H.* bezeichnet in der Kaiserzeit einen Berufsverband (lat. *collegium*) oder einen privaten Zusammenschluß, in Byzanz, belegt erst seit dem frühen 9. Jh. n. Chr., eine z. T. mit Ausländern besetzte Einheit der kaiserlichen Leibgarden, deren Funktion nicht eindeutig geklärt ist. Seit etwa 750 n. Chr. erscheint der Begriff auch, synonym mit *f(r)atría* (φ(ρ)ατρία), in der Bedeutung »Anhängerschaft, Gefolgschaft«, die man zur Erhöhung der persönlichen Macht und/oder zur Vorbereitung einer Revolte um sich scharte.

ODB 2, 925 • H.-G. Beck, Byz. Gefolgschaftswesen, SBAW, 1965, H. 5 • N. Oikonomidès, Les listes de préséance byzantines des IXe et Xe siècles, 1972. F. T.

Hetairoi. H. (ἑταῖροι, »Gefährten«) bildeten in griech. Monarchien das Gefolge des Königs, auch im Feld (z. B. Hom. Il. 1,179).

In klass. Zeit waren H. besonders in Makedonien wichtig: Vom König selbst ausgewählt, stellten sie als dessen nahe Umgebung seine engsten Berater und den Führungsnachwuchs. An ihrer Spitze zog der König in den Krieg, woraus wohl die eigentliche mil. Bedeutung des Begriffes resultierte. H. sind (oft mit dem Zusatz βασιλικοί, *basilikoí*) für die maked. Reiterei sicher erst für Alexander d.Gr. bezeugt. Ob bereits unter Alexander I. bzw. II. die → Reiterei als Ganzes oder vorerst nur ihr adliger Kern H. genannt und der Name dann auf die gesamte Truppe übertragen wurde, ist unklar. Unter Philipp II. und Alexander d.Gr. wurde die Reiterei jedenfalls erweitert (von 600 auf etwa 2000 Mann) und mehrfach reorganisiert. Spätestens unter Alexander war sie in acht Ilen mit einer Sollstärke von ca. 200 Mann, nach 328 v. Chr. (bis 324 v. Chr.?) in ebensoviel größere

Hipparchien gegliedert. 300 Mann stark war die als besonders vornehm geltende *ílē basilikḗ* (z. B. Arr. an. 3,8,1), später auch ἄγημα (*ágēma*; Arr. an. 4,24,1; 5,12,2) genannt, die der König im Kampf selbst führte. Seit dem Indienzug ergänzten bisweilen auch nichtmaked. Reiter die H. Die Diadochen behielten Organisation und Namen vorerst bei.

1 P. A. Brunt, Alexander's Macedonian cavalry, in: JHS 83, 1963, 27–46 **2** N. G. L. Hammond, The Macedonian State, 1989 **3** HM 2, 408 ff., 705 ff. **4** M. Launey, Recherches sur les armées hellénistiques, 1949, 362 f. **5** W. W. Tarn, Alexander der Große, [2]1968, 360, 383 ff.

LE. BU.

Heteroklisie s. Flexion

Hethiter s. Ḫattusa

Hethitisch

A. Überlieferung B. Geschichte, Merkmale

A. Überlieferung

Die in babylon. Keilschrift überl. Sprache der im 2. Jt. v. Chr. in Kleinasien polit. führenden Hethiter (Kerngebiet etwa der vom Halys/Kızıl İrmak umschriebene geogr. Bereich, → Ḫattusa II), von ihnen selbst *Nesumnili-* »Nesisch« gen., eine Ableitung vom ON *Nēsa-* (= altassyr. *Kaneš*, bei Kayseri; die moderne Sprachbezeichnung ist wissenschaftsgesch. bedingt); zugleich der hinsichtlich Umfang und themat. Vielfalt seines Textcorpus sowie im Hinblick auf seine philol. Auf- und Durcharbeitung (seit 1915) wichtigste Vertreter der → anatolischen Sprachen. Die ganz überwiegend aus der Hauptstadt → Ḫattusa (Boğazköy/Boğazkale; Grabungen: 1906/7, 1911/2, 1931–1939, seit 1952 andauernd, → Ḫattusa I), aber auch aus Maşat, Kuşaklı, Ortaköy, Ugarit und Emar (→ Ḫattusa II, Karte) stammende, teils in zeitgenössischen Niederschriften des 16.–13. Jh., teils in jüngeren Abschriften bes. des 13. Jh. vorliegende Textüberl. (Haupted. [1; 2]) – sie bricht mit dem Ende des hethit. Reiches um 1200 abrupt ab – umfaßt historiographische Texte polit. Themastellung, Staatsverträge, diplomatische Korrespondenz, administrative und technische Lit. (z. B. eine Verfassungsurkunde, Gesetze, Erlasse, Dienstanweisungen, Treueide, Landschenkungsurkunden, Bibliothekskataloge, Vokabulare, hippologische und medizinische Texte), Weisheitstexte, Mythen sowie eine umfangreiche rel. Lit. (Kultliturgie, Gebete, Orakel, Omina, magische Rituale, Beschwörungen) ([3], bearbeitet z. B. in den Reihen [4; 5]).

B. Geschichte, Merkmale

Sprachhistor. gliedert sich das Hethit. in die Sprachstufen Alt- (16. Jh.), Mittel- (Anf. 15.–ca. Mitte 14. Jh.) und Junghethit. (Mitte 14.–E. 13. Jh.), die im wesentlichen seit Anf. der 70er Jahre anhand einer auf keilschriftpaläographische Kriterien gestützten Textchronologie herausgearbeitet wurden (zur Keilschriftpaläographie [6; 7], zur Datierungsmethode [8]) und ungeachtet des insges. relativ kurzen Überlieferungszeitraums des Hethit. eine (gerade auch im Vergleich zu den übrigen anatol. Sprachen) sehr rasche, alle Bereiche der Gramm., insbes. aber Morphologie und Stammbildung des Nomens bzw. Verbums betreffende sprachliche Weiterentwicklung (z. B. Verkleinerung des nominalen Inhalts-/Ausdrucksparadigmas, analogische Umbildung der Nominal-/Verbalstämme) sichtbar werden lassen (z. B. [9]). Das Bestehen dieser Tendenz schon vor dem 16. Jh. zeigt der Blick auf hethit. PN und Appellativa der altassyr. Nebenüberl. Kleinasiens (18. Jh.), die noch eine Reihe im späteren Althethit. bereits obsoleter Erscheinungen bieten (z. B. Produktivität des *e*-Umlautes und verschiedener Wortbildungssuffixe, PN-Kompos.) und insofern als Repräsentanten einer »frühalthethit.« Sprachstufe in Betracht kommen [10. 24[12]], doch stehen systematische Unters. noch aus.

Gleichwohl hat das Hethit. gegenüber allen übrigen anatol. Sprachen aus der gemeinsamen uridg. bzw. uranatol. Vorstufe Altes bewahrt; z. B. noch Althethit.: Allativ auf *ă̄* (< **ō*; vgl. griech. ἄνω, κάτω), Pl. Gen. auf *-an* (< **-om*), enklit. Possessivpron.; ferner etwa: uridg. **e*, Fientiv-, Faktitiv- und Iterativ-Vb. auf *-ess-*, *-aḫḫ-* bzw. *-ske-*, differenziertere Stammbildung bei der *ḫḫi*-Konjugation. Spezifisch hethit. Neuerungen sind hingegen Assibilation **ti* > *zzi* (z. B. Verbalendung 3. Präs. Sg. *-zzi*), *i*-Prothese vor anlautendem **sC°* (z. B. *isḫiul-* »Vertrag« : *sh_2*i̯-* »binden«), Abbau bzw. Umbildung des Motionssuffixes *-i-* zur Kennzeichnung des Genus commune (z. B. *dangui-/danguu̯ai̯-* : keilschriftluw. *tanku(i)-* »dunkel« < *d^{h}*éng*$^{u̯}$*-o-*). Obwohl Mehrsprachigkeit für das hethiterzeitliche Kleinasien allg. kennzeichnend ist und speziell am Königshof in Ḫattusa der Umgang auch mit nichtanatol. Sprachen wie → Hattisch, → Hurritisch, → Akkadisch (Babylon.) ganz geläufig war, hat entgegen früherer Ansicht nur das verwandte → Luwisch in nennenswertem Umfang, und zwar vom 16.–13. Jh. ständig zunehmend, den hethit. Wortschatz (Nomen und Vb.) beeinflußt; auf luw. Vermittlung beruhen insbes. auch hurrit. Lw. und myk. EN (z. B. **Etewoklewes-* > *Tau̯aglau̯a-*) in hethit. Texten (ab 15. Jh.) [11; 12]. Während derzeit mehrere sich ergänzende lexikal. und etym. WB des Hethit. im Erscheinen begriffen sind [13; 14; 15; 16], stellt eine die hethit. Sprachstufen angemessen berücksichtigende Darstellung der Gramm. noch ein großes Desiderat dar (vgl. [17]; Orientierung über Einzelunters. s. [18; 19]).

→ Ḫattusa; Hethitologie

1 Keilschrifttexte aus Boghazköi (KBo), 1916 ff. (bisher 39 Bde.) **2** Keilschrifturkunden aus Boghazköi (KUB), 1921–1990 (60 Bde.) **3** E. Laroche, Catalogue des textes Hittites, 1971 **4** Stud. zu den Boğazköy-Texten (StBoT), 1965 ff. **5** Texte der Hethiter (THeth), 1971 ff. **6** Chr. Rüster, StBoT 20, 1972 **7** Chr. Rüster, E. Neu, StBoT 21, 1975 **8** F. Starke, StBoT 30, 1985, 21–27
9 N. Oettinger, Stammbildung des hethit. Verbums, 1979
10 F. Starke, Zur Herkunft von akkad. ta/urgumannu(m) »Dolmetscher«, in: WO 24, 1993, 20–38 **11** E. Neu, Zum

Wortschatz des Hethit. ..., in: W. MEID (Hrsg.), Stud. zum idg. Wortschatz, 1987, 167–188 **12** F. STARKE, StBoT 31, 1990 **13** J. FRIEDRICH, A. KAMMENHUBER, Hethit. WB, 1975 ff. **14** H. G. GÜTERBOCK, H. A. HOFFNER, Chicago Hittite Dictionary, 1984 ff. **15** J. PUHVEL, Hittite Etym. Dictionary, 1984 ff. **16** J. TISCHLER, Hethit. etym. Glossar, 1977 ff. **17** O. CARRUBA (Hrsg.), Per una grammatica ittita, Stud. Mediterranea 7, 1992 **18** Idg. Chronik (Abschnitt »Anatolisch«) in: Die Sprache **19** V. SOUČEK, J. SIEGELOVÁ, Systematische Bibliogr. der Hethitologie 1915–1995 (HbdOr), 3 Bde., 1996.

F. S.

Hethitische Nachfolgestaaten s. Kleinasien

Hethitisches Recht A. QUELLEN B. ZIVIL- UND STRAFRECHT C. DAS GERICHTSWESEN D. BEZIEHUNGEN ZU ANDEREN ORIENTALISCHEN RECHTEN

A. QUELLEN

1. Die sog. hethit. Gesetze 2. Der Anitta-Text 3. Die Autobiographie Ḫattušilis I. 4. Das »Polit. Testament« Ḫattušilis I. 5. Königliche Erlässe 6. Gerichtsprotokolle. 7. Königliche Briefe 8. Die Totenrituale 9. Sog. Landschenkungsurkunden 10. Die Feldertexte 11. Die Freibriefe für einzelne Vasallen 12. Die Staatsverträge.

B. ZIVIL- UND STRAFRECHT

Hierüber unterrichtet in erster Linie ein Rechtscorpus, für welches sich der Name »hethit. Gesetze« eingebürgert hat (das Wort »Gesetz« ist aber mit Vorbehalt zu verwenden, denn der Charakter des hethit. Rechtscorpus ist unklar). Es fehlt der von den mesopotam. Herrschern Urnammu, Lipit-Eštar und Ḫammurapi her bekannte Prolog, in welchem sich die Herrscher namentlich vorstellten. Der Fundort der »Gesetze« ist das Archiv der Königsburg von Ḫattusa, der Hauptstadt des Ḫattireiches; dies könnte auf eine kraft königlicher Weisung schriftlich niedergelegte Grundordnung für die Rechtsprechung des Königsgerichts als Obergericht, also auf eine Satzung hindeuten. Der Text ist in zahlreichen Varianten erhalten, die auf eine in nicht bekannten Abständen vorgenommene Überprüfung unter Anpassung an geänderte Verhältnisse hinweisen. Bedeutsam ist die dem König Telibinu (15. Jh. v. Chr.) zugeschriebene Reform, welche an der Darstellung der »früheren« und der »jetzigen« – gemilderten – Rechtslage innerhalb der einzelnen Paragraphen zu erkennen ist.

Das hethit. Rechtscorpus ist in zahlreichen mehr oder weniger vollständig erh. Tontafel-Frg. überliefert, welche schon die hethit. Schreiber als ›Tafel »Wenn ein Mann«‹ und ›Tafel »Wenn ein Weinstock«‹ bezeichneten, die jeweils rund 100 Paragraphen moderner Zählung enthalten. Ihr Aufbau folgt dem »Wenn/dann«-Schema und entspricht dem der mesopotam. Omina und gesetzlichen Regelungen.

Die Systematik der beiden Tafeln geht, abgesehen von einigen Unebenheiten, vom Prinzip des Fortschreitens vom wertvollen zum geringerwertigen Rechtsgut aus. Die beiden Tafeln enthalten Regeln für Ackerbau, Weinbau und Viehzucht, aber auch für das Handwerk. Zu Beginn der ersten Tafel stehen Vorschriften zum Schutz der Person gegen Eingriffe in ihre körperliche Integrität. Weitere Bestimmungen lassen auf eine patriarchalisch organisierte Familie schließen, zeigen aber auch, daß die hethit. Ehefrau im Verhältnis zum übrigen Alten Orient eine bedeutendere Stellung hatte. Es folgen »lehensrechtliche« Regelungen. Weitere rund 40 Paragraphen regeln den Schutz landwirtschaftlicher Güter vor Diebstahl und Sachbeschädigung. Die zweite Tafel schließt sich inhaltlich an, enthält dann aber auch Preistarife und schließlich h. dem Strafrecht zugerechnete Bestimmungen über sexuelle Vergehen (Blutschande, Vergewaltigung, Sodomie). *Leges erraticae* (Rechtssätze mit für uns nicht nachvollziehbarer Systematik) lassen erkennen, daß die Rechtssatzung nicht aus einem Guß ist. Nicht erwähnt wird der Mord, da dessen Ahndung wohl dem Sippenstrafrecht überlassen wurde. Das zeigt § 49 des Telibinu-Erlasses: Der König mischt sich nicht in Angelegenheiten des »Herrn des Blutes« (des Bluträchers). Rechtsbrüche im privatrechtlichen Bereich werden neben dem Schadensersatz im eigentlichen Sinne auch durch Geldbußen abgegolten (diese wird man in den Bereich des Privatstrafrechts stellen dürfen). Sie übersteigen den Rahmen des Schadensersatzes manchmal erheblich.

Die Todesstrafe wird nach der Rechtssatzung nur selten, nämlich in Fällen, welche einen sakralen Einschlag haben, verhängt (Auflehnung gegen ein Urteil des Königsgerichts, Diebstahl von Sakralgegenständen, Sexualdelikte). Außerhalb der o.g. Quellen zur Rechtssatzung wird die Todesstrafe bei Vergehen gegen Reinheitsvorschriften gegenüber dem König und nur gegen Personal des Palastes verhängt. An ihre Stelle treten in einzelnen Regionen des Reiches Verbannungsregeln, die der »Herr der Warte«, der Grenzkommandant, zu beachten hat.

Urkunden über Rechtsgeschäfte des Privatrechts hat man bisher nicht gefunden. Vielleicht wurden zu ihrer Aufzeichnung nicht die im Alten Orient sonst üblichen Tontafeln verwendet, sondern das vergängliche Holz (Wachstafeln?); die in einzelnen Texten überlieferte Berufsbezeichnung »Holztafelschreiber« könnte dafür sprechen.

C. DAS GERICHTSWESEN

Neben dem Königsgericht gab es eine untere Gerichtsbarkeit. Zu den vielfältigen Verwaltungsaufgaben der »inneren (inkorporierten) Länder« oblag dem Grenzkommandanten (dem »Herrn der Warte«) auch die Gerichtsbarkeit. Die »Ältesten« (wohl ein Relikt aus der Zeit des Älteren Reiches, als die Gerichtsbarkeit in den Händen lokaler Gremien gelegen hatte) standen ihm zur Seite. Ausführliche (wenn auch nach h. Vorstellungen unvollständige) Gerichtsprotokolle des 16. Jh. v. Chr. dokumentieren die Vereidigung von Zeugen und Gottesurteile in Form des Wasserordals. Gerichtsurteile sind nicht erhalten. Wer eine Entscheidung angriff, mußte mit der Todesstrafe rechnen, welche sich bei Anfechtung des Urteils des Königsgerichts auch gegen seine Familie richtete. Der König konnte Prozesse an sich ziehen und die Richter zu sich beordern: Falls sie der Vorladung nicht sofort folgten, drohte ihnen die Strafe der Blendung.

D. Beziehungen zu anderen orientalischen Rechten

Anklänge des h.R. an die übrigen zeitgenössischen Rechtsordnungen ergeben sich aus der Zugehörigkeit zum altoriental. Kulturkreis und sind nicht zu übersehen. Unterschiede zeigen sich in der verhältnismäßig milden Beurteilung von Rechtsbrüchen: So kommt die Todesstrafe ebenso selten vor wie die Verstümmelung. Die Selbsthilfe ist kaum vertreten, die Talion überhaupt nicht. Im Vordergrund stehen Schadensersatz und Bußen.

→ Ḫattusa II; Staatsverträge; Hethitologie

Rechtsgesch.: V. Korošec, Keilschriften: HdbOr, 1. Abt., Erg.bd. III), 1964, 177–219.
Hethit. Gesetze: J. Friedrich, Die hethit. Gesetze, 1959 (ed. princeps; Ndr. 1971) • R. Haase, Texte zum hethit. Recht. Eine Auswahl, 1985 • Ders., Beobachtungen zur hethit. Rechtssatzung nebst einem bibliogr. Anhang, 1995 • H. A. Hoffner, The Laws of the Hittites, 1997.
Prozess-, Staats- und Verwaltungsrecht: • G. Beckman, Hittite Diplomatic Texts, 1995 • I. Engnell, Studies in Divine Kingship in the Ancient Near East, 1967, 52ff. • H. G. Güterbock, Authority and Law in the Ancient Orient, in: Journ. of the American Oriental Society 17, 1954, 16–24 • A. Hagenbuchner, Die Korrespondenz der Hethiter, 1989 • I. Hoffmann, Der Erlaß Telibinus, 1984 • J. Klíma, La preuve dans le droit hittite, in: Recueils de la société Jean Bodin 17, 1965, 89–102 • K. K. Riemschneider, Die hethit. Landschenkungsurkunden, in: MIO 6, 1958, 321–381 • E. von Schuler, Hethit. Königserlässe als Quellen der Rechtsfindung und ihr Verhältnis zum kodifizierten Recht, in: FS J. Friedrich, 1959, 435–472 • J. Sigelová, Hethit. Verwaltungspraxis im Lichte der Wirtschafts- und Inventardokumente, 1986 • Vl. Součk, Die hethit. Feldertexte, in: Archiv orientální 27, 1959, 5–43, 371–395 • F. Starke, s. v. Labarna, RLA 6, 404–408 • R. Werner, Hethit. Gerichtsprotokolle, 1967.
Bibliogr.: R. Haase, Hethit. Recht, in: J. Gilissen, Bibliograph. Einführung in die Rechtsgesch. und Rechtsethnologie, 1967 (Kap. A/3). RI.H.

Heuneburg bei Herbertingen-Hundersingen, Kreis Sigmaringen: an der oberen Donau (Furt?) gelegene, befestigte Siedlung der späten → Hallstatt-Kultur (6./5. Jh. v. Chr.) mit offener Außensiedlung und zugehörigen, z. T. reich ausgestatteten Grabhügeln. Die H. ist eines der wichtigsten Machtzentren (→ Fürstensitz) der jüngeren Hallstattzeit in Mitteleuropa. Ausgrabungen fanden vor allem 1937/38 am Grabhügel »Hohmichele« statt, von 1950–1979 in der »Burg« und seit 1977 in der Außensiedlung (s. Karte Sp. 527f.).

Die hallstattzeitl. Befestigung besteht aus mehreren Phasen mit verschiedenartigen Holz-Stein-Erde-Mauern; eine Phase (1. H. 6. Jh. v. Chr.) wird durch eine Lehmziegelmauer mit vorgelagerten Bastionen gebildet, die auf mediterrane Bautechniken zurückgeht. Die nur z. T. freigelegte Innenfläche (ca. 300 x 150 m) war über alle Phasen dicht bebaut, mit abgegrenzten Parzellen, Handwerkerbezirken usw. nach unterschiedlichen Konzepten. Ein fürstlicher Wohnbezirk (»Akropolis«) wurde nicht gefunden.

Das reichhaltige Fundmaterial spiegelt verschiedene ortsansässige Handwerksformen (Töpferei mit der Drehscheibe, Metallhandwerk, Knochenschnitzer u. -drechsler usw.) und v. a. Beziehungen zur mediterranen Welt (att.-sf. Keramik, massaliotische Amphoren usw.). Die unbefestigte Außensiedlung war der Burg im NW und Westen großflächig vorgelagert. Sie umfaßte große Gehöfte und auch Handwerksbetriebe ähnlicher Art wie auf der Burg. In einer Spätphase der H. (E. 6. Jh. v. Chr.) wurden zumindest Teile der Außensiedlung aufgegeben und von reichen Großgrabhügeln überbaut, die z. T. auf die Gehöfte direkt Bezug nehmen. Der größte und reichste Grabhügel »Hohmichele« liegt ca. 2 km westl. der H. und enthielt mehrere z. T. beraubte, z. T. prunkvoll ausgestattete Gräber (→ Fürstengrab).

→ Befestigungswesen; Drehbank; Handwerk; Grabbauten; Ziegel

W. Kimmig u. a. (Hrsg.), H.-Studien, Bd. 1, 1962 – Bd. 10, 1996 • Ders., Die H. an der oberen Donau, [2]1983 • S. Kurz, Neue Ausgrabungen im Vorfeld der H., in: Arch. Ausgrabungen Baden-Württemberg 1995, 105–109.
Karten-Lit.: W. Kimmig, Die H. an der oberen Donau, [2]1983, Abb. 34 • S. Kurz, in: Arch. Ausgrabungen in Baden-Württemberg, 1995, 106, Abb. 58. V.P.

Heuschrecke. Das seit Hom. Il. 21,12 belegte Wort ἀκρίς/*akrís* (von κρίζειν, »schreien«) bezeichnet wie *locusta* (seit Naevius bei Varro ling. 7,39 Grundbed. »mit Gelenken versehen« bzw. »springend«) alle Arten der Saltatoria. Dies gilt auch für die Synonyme βροῦχος = *bruc(h)us*, βρύκος, μάσταξ, πάρνοψ (Aristoph. Ach. 150 und Av. 588; Ail. nat. 6,19; Paus. 1,24,8) bzw. κόρνοψ (Strab. 13,1,64 [613]) und ἀττέλαβος (Hdt. 4,172) = *attelebus* (Plin. nat. 29,92). Zur Biologie berichtet Aristot. hist. an. 5,28,555b 18–556a 7 (= Plin. nat. 11,101 f.), daß die H. nach der wie bei anderen Insekten üblichen Begattung im Herbst dicht unter den gepflügten Ackerboden ihre Eier im Paket ablegen, aus denen nach der Überwinterung unter der Erdoberfläche eiähnliche weiche Maden (μαλακὰ κυήματα) schlüpfen. Als kleine dunkle *akrídes* kommen sie dann an die Oberfläche, häuten sich und sterben nach der Eiablage am Ende des Sommers. Aristoteles erklärt ihr Hüpfen durch Strekkung der Hinterbeine (part. an. 4,6,683a 33–b 3). H. fressen Kornähren (Nik. Ther. 803) und die Blüten des Weinstocks (Aristoph. Av. 588). Sie werden ihrerseits von Eulen und Turmfalken (Aristoph. ebd.) sowie Dohlen (κολοιοί, Ail. nat. 3,12; *graculi*, Plin. nat. 11,106) verzehrt. Das durch Reiben der Hinterschenkel an den Vorderflügeln hervorgebrachte Zirpen (Aristot. hist. an. 4,9,535b 11–12; Plin. nat. 11,107) wird in Gedichten der

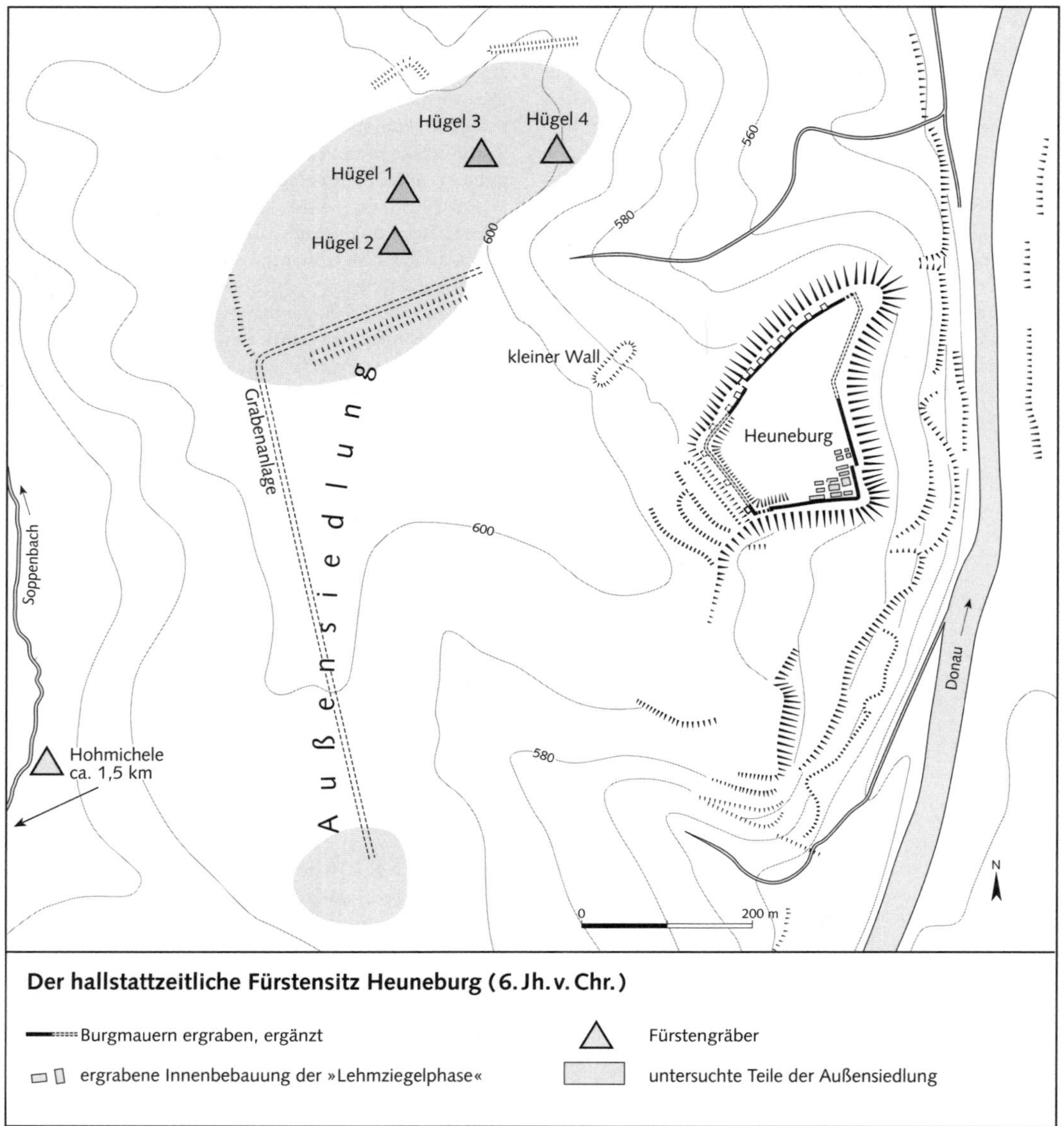

Der hallstattzeitliche Fürstensitz Heuneburg (6. Jh. v. Chr.)

Burgmauern ergraben, ergänzt

ergrabene Innenbebauung der »Lehmziegelphase«

Fürstengräber

untersuchte Teile der Außensiedlung

Anthologia Palatina mehrfach hervorgehoben (7,189; 7,192 ff.; 197 f.; 7,190: Denkmal für eine H. und eine Grille, τέττιξ; vgl. Plin. nat. 34,57).

Die It., Nordafrika, Syrien (Plin. nat. 11, 104–106), Äthiopien (Agatharchides bei Phot. bibl. c. 250) und Ägypten (Ex 10,4 ff.) heimsuchenden Schwärme (*nubes locustarum*, Pall. agric. 1,35,12) wohl von Arten der Wander-H. verdunkelten die Sonne. Einige dieser Invasionen kann man histor. datieren (125 v. Chr. in Afrika: Iulius Obsequens 30; 202 bzw. 173/72 v. Chr. in Italien: Liv. 30,2,10; 42,2,4; 42,10,7) bzw. erschließen (Athen: Paus. 1,24,8; Die Oitaier verehrten Herakles als Befreier von H.-Plagen: Strab. 13,1,64 [613]).

Als Nahrungsmittel werden H. im AT (Lv 11,22; vgl. [1. 492]) und in bezug auf Johannes den Täufer Mt 3,4 und Mk 1,6 erwähnt. Hdt. 4,172 berichtet, die Nasamonen in Lybien nähmen sie als pulverisierten Zusatz zur Milch zu sich. In Äthiopien gab es das Volk der sogen. »H.-Fresser« (ἀκριδοφάγοι, Diod. 3,29 und Strab. 16,4,12 [772]). Den Parthern (Plin. nat. 11,107) und gelegentlich den Griechen (Aristoph. Ach. 116) galten sie als Delikatesse.

1 V. Pöschl, H. Gärtner u.a., Bibliographie zur ant. Bildersprache, 1964.

H. Gossen, s. v. H., RE 8,1381 ff. • Ders., s. v. H., RE Suppl. 8,179 ff., 1956.

C. HÜ.

Hexas (ἑξᾶς). Griech. Bezeichnung für Silber- u. Aesmünzen von Sizilien und (seltener) Süditalien zu ⅙ → Litra; da das dort verwandte Münzsystem auf der Litra zu 12 Unzen basiert, auch Dionkion gen., lat. → Sextans entsprechend. Wertzeichen: 2 Punkte. Die äußerst seltenen Kleinstsilbermünzen (Durchschnittsgewicht 0,14 g) dieses Nominals sind belegt in Tarent [5. 1117–1121], Akragas [2. 122], Himera [1. 30], Leontinoi [7. 1345], Messana [7. 326], Segesta [1. 48] und Syrakus [3. 373]. – Die Aesmünzen weisen aufgrund des uneinheitlichen Standards der Bronzelitra höchst unterschiedliche Gewichte auf. Während sie im 5. und 4. Jh. v. Chr. durchschnittlich ca. 3,5 g schwer sind, kommen im 3. und 2. Jh. Gewichte zwischen 1,75 g und ca. 18 g vor. Bronzene H. werden geprägt in Brundisium [8. 68] und von den Brettii [8. 185], in Aetna [7. 1162–1165], Akragas in runder [7. 1047–1057] und konischer Form [4. 113,22–36; 9. 120], Catane [7. 1278–1284], Centuripae [7. 1322–1326], Eryx mit Wertzeichen 2 Ringe [10. 583], Gela [7. 1334], Himera [4. 139,6–7; 6. 319], Menaeum [4. 146,22; 8. 357], Messana [9. 174], Segesta [9. 199] und Selinus [4. 168,24–28], auf Lipara [6. 1087; 8. 550] sowie von den Mamertini [7. 420–422] und den Siculo-Puniern [4. 195,1–8; 6. 516].

1 BMC Sicily, 1876 2 B. V. Head, Historia Numorum, 1910 3 E. Boehringer, Die Münzen von Syrakus, 1929 4 E. Gabrici, La monetazione del bronzo nella Sicilia antica, 1927 5 O. Ravel, Descriptive catalogue of the collection of Tarentine coins formed by M. P. Vlasto, 1947 6 SNG Copenhagen, 1942 ff. 7 SNG, The Collection of the American Numismatic Society, 1969 ff. 8 H. A. Cahn, L. Mildenberg u. a., Griech. Münzen aus Grossgriechenland und Sizilien – Antikenmuseum Basel und Sammlung Ludwig, 1988 9 P. Strauss, Collection Maurice Lafaille – Monnaies grecques en bronze, 1990 10 SNG, The John Morcom Collection of Greek Bronze Coins, 1995.

K. Regling, s. v. H, RE 8, 1387. H.-J. S.

Hiarbas (Ἰάρβας).

[1] H., Iarbas. Mythischer afrikan. König über das Volk der Maxitaner (Iust. 18,6,1), Sohn Ammons und einer Nymphe (Verg. Aen. 4,198); er wirbt erfolglos um die Hand der → Dido (Verg. Aen. 4,213 ff.; Ov. fast. 3,553 f.), nach deren Tod er Karthago erobert (Ov. fast. 3,551 f.).

A. M. Guillemin, Comment Virgile construit un caractère. Iarbas, in: Humanités: revue d'enseignement secondaire et d'éducation 28, 1951, 20–22. J. S.-A.

[2] Nach Erfolgen von Marius' Anhängern wurde H. König von Ostnumidien; Vertreibung → Hiempsals [2] 87 v. Chr. Nach Durchsetzung der Anhänger → Cornelius [I 90] Sullas 83 v. Chr. wurde er wieder durch Hiempsal ersetzt; Sieg des → Pompeius, Tötung des H. [1. 63 f.] (Plut. Pompeius 12,4; Liv. per. 89).
→ Mauretania; Numidia

1 M.-R. Alföldi, Die Gesch. des numidischen Königreiches und seiner Nachfolger, in: H. G. Horn, C. B. Rüger (Hrsg.), Die Numidier, 1979, 43–74. B. M.

Hiat s. Metrik II

Hiba. Bischof von → Edessa [2] († 28.10.457 n. Chr.). Dort übertrug H., Lehrer an der »Schule der Perser« und Anhänger der antiochenischen Theologie, Schriften des → Theodoros von Mopsuestia, → Diodoros [14] von Tarsos und des Aristoteles ins Syr. Wiederholt angegriffen (u. a. mit dem Vorwurf der Häresie und Simonie), wurde er, 436 dem Ortsbischof → Rabulas (Rabbula) nachfolgend, auf der »Räubersynode« (Ephesos 449) als Anhänger des → Nestorios abgesetzt und verbannt, in Chalkedon (451) aber rehabilitiert. Bedeutsam wurde ein 433 an den Perser Mari – den späteren Archimandriten des Akoimetenklosters im Norden von Konstantinopel [3] – adressierter Brief, der auf Griech. in den Akten von Chalkedon erh. ist (CPG 6500: Acta Conciliorum Oecumenicorum II/1,3, 32–34): H. wurde im 6. Jh. (Edikt Iustinians 544, zweites Konzil von Konstantinopel 553) anon. als nestorianisch verurteilt (zweites der sog. »Drei Kapitel«: [2]). Weitere Schriften, so ein Komm. zum Buch der Spr, Homilien und Hymnen, sind verloren.

1 G. G. Blum (ed.), Rabbula von Edessa (CSCO 300), 1969, 196–205 2 A. Grillmeier, Jesus der Christus im Glauben der Kirche 2/2, 1989, 431–484 3 M. van Esbroeck, Who is Mari, the addressee of Ibas' Letter?, in: Journal of Theological Studies 38, 1987, 129–135. J. RI.

Hibernia (Irland).
A. Frühe Kenntnis B. Handel
C. Wanderungen

A. Frühe Kenntnis

Ant. Geographen berichten wenig über die NW-Küsten Europas und die küstennahen Inseln. Kenntnisse über die Insel Irland, Ierne oder H. dürften erstmals auf der Forschungsreise des Pytheas (ca. 320 v. Chr. [1; 2]) gewonnen worden sein. Pytheas hat wohl H. selbst nicht besucht, seine Berichte stammen aus zweiter Hand; seine Informationen dürften zu Strabon, Diodoros und Mela gelangt sein (Strab. 4,5,4; Diod. 5,32; Mela 3,6). Einige Elemente dieser Überl. entspringen der Phantasie (bes. die über Greueltaten, Kannibalismus und sexuelle Ausschweifungen). Geogr. Informationen, deren Quelle Pytheas war, waren spezifischer, wenn auch nicht gänzlich frei von Fehlern. Strabon und Pomponius Mela berichten, daß H. rechteckig sei und im Norden von → Britannia liege (Strab. l.c.; Mela l.c.), wovon noch Marinus und Ptolemaios überzeugt waren (Ptol. 1,6; 1,11,8). Caesar war besser über die geogr. Lage von H. zu Britannia informiert, jedoch setzte er H. zu weit südwestl. zw. Britannia und Hispania an (Caes. Gall. 5,13). Pomponius Mela berichtet über das langsame Reifen des Getreides im Klima von H.; Solinus weiß, daß es in Irland keine Schlangen gibt (Solin. 22,3). Agrippas Karte schätzt die Ausmaße H. auf 600 × 300 Meilen, eine maßlose Übertreibung. Mela verschätzt sich noch mehr, indem er die Größe von H. der von

Britannia gleichsetzt. Caesar hatte bereits eine annähernd zutreffende Schätzung geliefert: halb so groß wie Britannia.

Eine wichtige Quelle des 1. Jh. n. Chr. über H. war Philemon (zw. 20 und 50 n. Chr.), dessen Bericht von Plinius verwendet wurde und der zumindest einen Teil seines Wissens von in nordwestl. Meer tätigen Kaufleuten bezog [1. 260f.]. Als Tacitus seinen *Agricola* schrieb, war H. nur wenig besser bekannt. Ihm zufolge war H. kleiner als Britannia, aber größer als Sicilia; Boden und Klima waren ähnlich wie in Britannia (Tac. Agr. 24,2). Die polit. oder wirtschaftlichen Beziehungen zu Britannia waren nicht sehr entwickelt. 81 n. Chr. zog Agricola eine Invasion und Eroberung der Insel in Betracht, verfolgte den Gedanken aber nicht weiter (Tac. Agr. 24,3). Alle bis ca. 100 n. Chr. gesammelten Kenntnisse über H. faßte Ptolemaios in seiner *Geographia* zusammen; Hauptquellen waren Philemon und Marinus [1. 263–265]. Seine Liste der Namen von Stämmen, Flüssen und Orten ist die umfassendste, die für das ant. Irland existiert. 16 Stämme werden aufgeführt, elf *póleis*, 15 Flußmündungen und sechs Hügelketten. Es ist gewagt, seine geogr. Angaben in der h. Landschaft zu lokalisieren, in einzelnen Fällen aber zulässig: Coriondi (Coraind?); Senos (Shannon?); Limnos (Lambay?).

B. Handel

Angesichts der Tatsache, daß Irland so nahe bei Britannien liegt, kann man Handels- und andere Kontakte in gewissem Umfang erwarten. Funde röm. Ursprungs hat man in Irland gemacht, aber nicht in großer Zahl [3]. Es handelt sich dabei um Mz. und Töpferware. Für das 4./frühe 5. Jh. n. Chr. sind es hauptsächlich wertvolle Metallgegenstände; sie sind wohl als Beute zu interpretieren. So wurde z. B. der Silberschatz von Ballinrees, Coleraine, ca. 425 n. Chr. vergraben [4].

C. Wanderungen

In spätröm. Zeit wurden vielfach Raubzüge von H. nach Britannia unternommen. Der nördl. Teil von H. wurde damals von den Scotti gehalten, die die britannische Küste plünderten, bevor sie Teile Westschottlands im 5. Jh. besiedelten. In einem der ir. Raubzüge in Britannia wurde ein junger britannischer Bewohner, Patricius, gefangengenommen und nach Irland verschleppt – nachmals als St. Patrick bekannt, der in der 1. Hälfte des 5. Jh. viele der Iren zum christl. Glauben bekehrte [5; 6].

1 J. J. Tierney, The Greek geographic tradition and Ptolemy's evidence for Irish geography, in: Proceedings of the Royal Irish Academy 76, 1976, 257–266 2 R. Dion, Pytheas explorateur, in: Revue de Philologie 92, 1966, 191–216 3 J. D. Bateson, Roman Material from Ireland, in: Proceedings of the Royal Irish Academy 73, 1973, 21–97; 76, 1976, 171–180 4 J. S. Porter, Recent Discovery of Roman Coins and other Articles near Coleraine, in: Ulster Journal of Archaeology 2, 1854, 182–187 5 R. P. C. Hanson, St. Patrick, 1968 6 D. Dumville, St. Patrick, 1993.

C. Thomas (Hrsg.), The Iron Age in the Irish Sea Province, 1972.

M. TO./Ü: I. S.

Hiberus

[1] (M. Antonius?) H. Kaiserlicher Freigelassener, der ca. 26–28 n. Chr. in der Finanzadministration Ägyptens tätig war, vielleicht in einer Funktion wie der spätere → Dioiketes (POxy. 3807; er ist dort nicht als *praefectus Aegypti* erwähnt). Von Tiberius wurde er im J. 32 n. Chr. nach dem Tod des Vitrasius Pollio für einige Monate zum Praefekten von Ägypten ernannt, wo er auch kurz danach starb; sein Nachkomme soll der Consul von 133 n. Chr. M. Antonius Hiberus sein (PIR[2] H 168; wenn nicht die Inschrift AE 1975, 861 = [1] auf ihn zu beziehen ist).

1 G. Wagner, in: Bulletin de Institut Francaise d'Archeologie Orientale, 73, 1973, 183.

W. E.

[2] s. Iberus

Hiempsal

[1] Zusammen mit Bruder Adherbal [4] und Vetter → Iugurtha Erbe der Herrschaft → Micipsas; Dreiteilung des Reiches. 117 v. Chr. auf Befehl Iugurthas ermordet (Sall. Iug. 9,4; 11f.) [1. 59].

[2] Sohn Gaudas; König Ostnumidiens; 88 v. Chr. floh Marius' Sohn zu ihm. 87 von → Hiarbas verdrängt, nach dem Erfolg der Anhänger Sullas 83 erneut Herrscher. Caesar stützte 63 → Masintha gegen H., der eine Landesbeschreibung Numidiens in punischer Sprache hinterließ. [1. 63ff.] (Plut. Pompeius 12,4; Liv. per. 89).

→ Afrika; Mauretania; Numidia

1 M.-R. Alföldi, Die Geschichte des numidischen Königreiches und seiner Nachfolger, in: H. G. Horn, C. B. Rüger (Hrsg.), Die Numidier, 1979, 43–74.

B. M.

Hiera Kome, Hierokaisareia (Ἱερὰ Κώμη, Ἱεροκαισάρεια). Ort in Lydia an der ant. Straße Pergamon – Sardeis östl. des → Hyllos beim h. Sazova bzw. Beyova. H. K. entwickelte sich um ein Heiligtum der → Anaitis; der unter der Perserherrschaft eingeführte Kult war im lyd. Hermostal verbreitet und fand wegen seiner Fremdartigkeit (Feuerdienst, Magerpriester) noch im 2. Jh. n. Chr. den Zuspruch der Griechen (Paus. 5,27,5ff.; 7,6,6). 201 v. Chr. Opfer der Invasion Philippos' V. (Pol. 16,1,8), wurde der Tempel erneut 156 v. Chr. von Prusias II. geplündert (Pol. 32,27,11). Dagegen wurde seine Unverletzlichkeit (→ Asylon) von Seleukiden und Attaliden im 3./2. Jh. respektiert (Asyliegarantie Attalos' III.: [1. 68]). Seit hell. Zeit erscheint Anaitis auf Mz. (BMC, Gr, Lydia, 102,1). Dank den Verfügungen der Könige besaß das Heiligtum Territorium (Grenzstreitigkeiten mit → Thyateira, vgl. Inschr. des 2./3. Jh. n. Chr.). Spätestens im 1. Jh. v. Chr. gewann H. K. städtischen Charakter. Die Umbenennung in Hierokaisareia erfolgte aus Dankbarkeit für den nach dem Erdbeben 17 n. Chr. von Tiberius gewährten Steuernachlaß auf fünf J. (Tac. ann. 2,47,3; ILS 156). Die Bezeichnung der Bewohner als *Hierocometae* (Plin. nat. 5,126) ist im 1. Jh. n. Chr. obsolet; auf Mz. erscheint der Stadtname »H.« (unter Nero). Bei der Überprüfung sämtlicher Asylrechte 22 n. Chr. erreichte H. den Fortbestand seines Privilegs (Tac. ann. 3,62,3; Suet. Tib. 37,2).

1 WELLES.

L. BÜRCHNER, s. v. H. K., H., RE 8, 1401 f. • F. IMHOOF-BLUMER, Lyd. Stadtmz., 1897, 5 ff., 12 f. • J. KEIL, A. v. PREMERSTEIN, Denkschr. der Akad. der Wiss. Wien 53,2, 1910, Nr. 18 • MAGIE 2, 1019 f. • ROBERT, Villes, 39, 84, 266. H. KA.

Hierapolis (Ἱεράπολις).

[1] Bed. Stadt in SW-Phrygia (zu unterscheiden von der gleichnamigen Stadt in der »Pentapolis« in Zentral-Phrygia) am Rand des Lykos-Tals an der Straße im Hermos-Tal von Sardeis nach Apameia, berühmt für die warmen Quellen, deren Wasser beim Verdunsten weiße Kalksinterterassen entstehen läßt; sie haben dem Ort den h. Namen Pamukkale (»Baumwollschloß«) gegeben. Das Wasser diente zur Färbung von Wolle: Weberei und Textilhandel bildeten die Grundlage des Reichtums von H. Unter den Seleukiden gegr., erhielt H. den Namen von einer Höhle, aus der tödliche Gase entwichen (Strab. 13,4,14: *Plutṓnion*); auf ihr wurde der Tempel des Apollon Kareios errichtet, des Schutzgotts der Stadt, dessen Orakel durch Inschr. in Versform bewahrt sind und dessen Epitheton auf eine einheimische Gottheit hinweist, die von den Griechen Apollon angeglichen wurde. H. wurde oft von Erdbeben heimgesucht; das Erdbeben z.Z. Neros gab Raum für ein riesiges Bauprogramm unter Domitianus, während das Theater unter den Severern (Ende 2. / Anf. 3. Jh. n. Chr.) erneuert wurde. Eine große Nekropole mit hunderten von Sarkophagen und Grabbauten ist erh. In Steinbrüchen von Thiounta nahe H. wurde ein bekannter Marmor abgebaut. Als Ort einer großen jüd. Gemeinde wurde H. schnell christl. Zentrum; Bischofssitz, dann Metropolis in Phrygia Pacatiana. H. hatte mehrere Basiliken, ferner das Martyrion des Philippos, des Vaters von vier Prophetinnen, der sehr bald dem gleichnamigen Apostel gleichgesetzt wurde. It. Grabungen seit 1957 brachten viele Monumente, Skulpturen und Inschr. ans Tageslicht.

T. RITTI, H., Scavi e Ricerche I. Fonti letterarie ed epigrafiche, 1985 • BELKE/MERSICH, 268–272.

T. D.-B./Ü: V. S.

[2] s. Bambyke

[3] Einzig bei Plin. nat. 4,59 gen. Stadt wohl an der Südküste von Kreta, evtl. identisch mit Hierapytna oder nur als Epitheton zu Lebena gebraucht [1].

1 P. FAURE, La Crète aux cent villes, in: Kretika Chronika 13, 1959, 200. H. SO.

[4] s. Kastabala

Hierapytna (Ἱεράπυτνα). Stadt auf Kreta, h. Ierapetra, an der schmalsten Stelle der Insel, zw. Zentral- und Ostkreta (Strab. 10,4,3). In hell. Zeit bedeutender polit. Faktor, wovon zahlreiche Verträge mit anderen kret. Städten (Praisos, Itanos, Gortyn, Lyttos, Lato), vornehmlich aus der 2. H. des 3. Jh. v. Chr., zeugen [1]. Verbindungen bestanden auch mit außerkret. Mächten (Makedonien, Rhodos, Pergamon: StV III 502; 551; Syll.³ 627). Eine aggressive Territorialpolitik im O Kretas, v. a. auf Kosten von Itanos, provoziert im 2. Jh. v. Chr. das vermittelnde Eingreifen der Römer (Vertrag von 112 v. Chr. [1. Nr. 57]). 66 v. Chr. im Zuge der kret. Eroberung von Rom eingenommen (Cass. Dio 36,19,1 f.). In der Kaiserzeit beachtliche (arch. jedoch kaum erforschte) urbane Blüte mit Hafenanlagen [2], Theater, Amphitheater, Thermen, Tempeln. In byz. Zeit Bischofssitz.

1 A. CHANIOTIS, Die Verträge zw. kret. Poleis in der hell. Zeit, 1996, passim 2 K. LEHMANN-HARTLEBEN, Die ant. Hafenanlagen des Mittelmeeres, Klio Beih. 14, 1923, 201 f.

M. GUARDUCCI, Inscriptiones Creticae 3, 1942, 18 ff. • LAUFFER, Griechenland 268 f. • I. F. SANDERS, Roman Crete, 1982, 139 f. H. SO.

Hierarchie (griech. ἱεραρχία) bedeutet im eigentlichen Sinne »hl. Ordnung«. Der Begriff H., vor der Spätant. nicht belegt, wird erstmals Ende des 5. Jh. n. Chr. durch den Neuplatoniker (Ps.-)Dionysios [54] Areopagites in seinen Schriften *Perí tēs uranías hierarchías* und *Perí tēs ekklēsiastikēs hierarchías* definiert: Danach ist H. eine hl. Rangordnung, die ein Abbild der göttl. Schönheit darstellt. Alles Sein nimmt an Gott als dem Urheber der H. teil und stuft sich entsprechend der Anteilnahme an Gott ab. Der Hierarch ist der gotterfüllte Mann, in dessen Person die ganze ihm unterstellte H. gipfelt. Vorläufer dieses Denkens begegnen in der Gnosis und bei den Kirchenvätern [3].

In den paganen Priesterschaften fehlt nicht nur der Terminus H., sondern auch das Phänomen. Auch wenn in der griech. Welt in einigen Heiligtümern ein *hierárchēs* als Oberaufseher fungierte, gab es zumeist für ein Heiligtum nur einen Priester, dem allenfalls einige wenige Kultdiener unterstanden [2]. Die oberste Autorität in rel. Angelegenheiten lag bei den weltlichen Instanzen, die bes. schwierige Probleme an ein Orakel, vor allem das Delphische, verwiesen. Hier war → Apollon die Autorität, nicht einzelne Priester oder die Pythia. In Rom besaß der → *pontifex maximus* gewisse Weisungsgewalt gegenüber den Vestalinnen und einigen anderen Einzelpriestern bzw. Priesterkollegien. Ihre deutliche Verschiedenheit in Tracht, Amtsdauer und Kult resultierte statt in einer H. in einer Fragmentierung der priesterlichen Macht, wobei in der Republik die Entscheidungsgewalt beim Senat lag [1]. In der Kaiserzeit war der Herrscher *pontifex maximus* und zumeist Mitglied der vier angesehensten Priesterkollegien (*amplissima collegia*), der → *pontifices*, → *augures*, → *quindecimviri sacris faciundis* und der → *septemviri epulonum*; dadurch war das Amt des *pontifex maximus* zwar aufgewertet, doch kann von einer ausgebildeten H. nicht die Rede sein.

Eine Wende deutete sich bei den neuen Rel. der Kaiserzeit an. Im → Mithras-Kult gab es sieben verschiedene Grade der Initiation. Im → Christentum entwickelte sich bereits im 2. Jh. die Struktur → Episkopos (Bischof) – Presbyter – Diakon; Ende des 2. Jh. läßt sich erstmals der Primatsanspruch des Bischofs von Rom erkennen, der allerdings erst im 5. Jh. voll ausgebildet ist.

Zu H. im mil. Bereich s. → Heerwesen.

1 M. Beard, Priesthood in the Roman Republic, in: M. Beard, J. North (Hrsg.), Pagan Priests, 1990, 17–48
2 J. N. Bremmer, Götter, Mythen und Heiligtümer im ant. Griechenland, 1996, 31–33 3 G. O'Daly, s. v. H., RAC 15, 41–73.

H. Rausch, s. v. H., Gesch. Grundbegriffe III, 103–129.

V.RO.

Hieratisch. Kursive der äg. → Hieroglyphenschrift, neben dieser seit deren Anfängen (ca. 3000 v. Chr.) bis ins 3. Jh. n. Chr. in Gebrauch, v. a. in der Verwaltung, für rel., lit., wiss. und magische Texte sowie für Briefe. Unter Gebrauch von schwarzer Ruß- und roter Okkertinte wurde es mit einem präparierten Binsenstengel, erst in röm. Zeit auch mit der Rohrfeder, auf Papyrus, Leinen, Leder, Holz, Stein, Keramik(scherben), Kalksteinsplittern u. a. geschrieben. Es findet sich aber auch in Stein (Graffiti, Stelen) und andere harte Materialien geritzt oder geschnitten. Bei aller individuellen Variation sind Zeichenformen und Orthographie von hierat. Texten stark zeitgebunden. Sie erlauben eine Datierung nach den Epochen des AR, MR und NR, der Spätzeit und der griech.-röm. Zeit, mit mehr oder weniger großer Genauigkeit auch innerhalb davon. In der 20. Dyn. ist auch eine Unterscheidung nach ober- und unteräg. Schreibtradition möglich. Im 7. Jh. v. Chr. wird das H. durch eine neue, auch orthograph. stark abweichende Kursive, die des → Demotischen, aus dem alltägl. Gebrauch verdrängt und auf Bibliotheks- und rel. Schriften beschränkt.

→ Ägyptisch; Entzifferung

G. Möller, H. Paläographie, 4 Bd., 1936. J.OS.

Hierax (Ἱέραξ).

[1] H. aus Antiocheia, fiel von Demetrios [7] I. zu Alexandros [13] Balas ab (Diod. 33,3), von diesem 146 v. Chr. zu Ptolemaios VI., den er durch die Antiochener zum König ausrufen ließ (Diod. 32,9 c). Er hatte eine hohe Stellung am Hof und vereitelte als Stratege (?) Ptolemaios' VIII. den Aufstand des → Galestes; wurde dann vom König beseitigt (Diod. 33,22; FGrH 87 F 4). PP 1/8,264; 2, 2163; 6, 17012.

[2] 88 v. Chr. als Oberbefehlshaber Ptolemaios' IX. gegen den Aufstand der Thebais geschickt; im November war die Revolte niedergeschlagen.

Bengtson 3, 107 • E. van't Dack u. a., The Judaean-Syrian-Egyptian Conflict of 103–1 B. C., 1989, 147 ff. • U. Wilcken, Grundzüge und Chrestomathie der Papyruskunde, 1912. W.A.

[3] s. Pachom

[4] Weitgehend unbekannter Philosoph, nach [1. 617 (= 79)] ein Vertreter des → Mittelplatonismus aus dem 2. Jh. n. Chr. Verf. eines Werkes (›Über die Gerechtigkeit‹/Περὶ δικαιοσύνης?), aus dem Stobaios acht Fragmente zitiert. In diesen werden verschiedene Aspekte der Gerechtigkeit – in kritischer Auseinandersetzung mit der Stoa und dem Peripatos – untersucht.

1 K. Praechter, H. der Platoniker, in: Hermes 41, 1906, 593–618 (= KS, 1973, 55–80).

S. Lilla, Introduzione al Medio platonismo, 1992, 72 f.

M.BA. u. M.-L. L.

[5] Neuplatoniker des 5. Jh. n. Chr. Nach dem Tode des Hermias von Alexandreia kam dessen Frau, die Mutter des Syrianos, mit ihren Söhnen Ammonios und Heliodoros nach Athen, um sie dort in die Schule des Proklos zu geben (Suda s. v. Αἰδεσία, 2,161,19–163,13 Adler). Deren Freund H., Bruder des Synesios (von Kyrene?) begleitete sie (Damaskios, vita Isidori 79 und fr. 127 Zintzen) und wurde so Schüler des → Proklos (412–485 n. Chr.). L.BR./Ü: J.DE.

Hiereus s. Priester

Hieroduloi (ἱερόδουλοι, ἱεροὶ δοῦλοι). Wörtlich »Tempelsklaven«; in der ant. Realität bezeichnen sie 1. Menschen, die (nicht anders als Land) Besitz eines Tempels waren, ohne Kultpersonal zu sein, 2. Menschen, die als Sklaven (und oft als Kultpersonal) dem Tempel geschenkt wurden, 3. Sklaven, die durch Übereignung an eine Gottheit die teilweise oder völlige Freiheit erlangten (sakrale → Freilassung). In der mod. Terminologie stehen demgegenüber die sakralen Prostituierten im Vordergrund, wie sie für die Ant. etwa im Aphroditekult in Korinth (Strab. 8,6,20) oder am Eryx (Strab. 6,2,6; Diod. 4,83 – in beiden Fällen als Sache der Vergangenheit) belegt sind (→ Prostitution). In der Dokumentation zum ant. Kult sind jedoch die anderen Funktionen weit wichtiger.

Eine »große Zahl von *h.* und viel Land« ist bezeichnend für die kleinasiatischen Tempelreiche wie etwa diejenigen des Men (Strab. 12,3,31; 12,8,14), und ekstatische männliche *h.* werden für die Albanoi (Strab. 11,4,7) genannt; inschr. werden solche Menschen sowohl als *h.* wie *hieroí/hieraí* bezeichnet: sie sind einem Tempel zugeordnet, steuerfrei und unversklavbar sowie unverkäuflich. Das Phänomen geht bereits auf die Hethiter zurück.

Im griech. und röm. Ägypten sind *h.* juristisch Freie, die mit einer Gottheit verbunden sind; auch dies setzt Indigenes fort. Ähnlich besitzen bereits manche myk. Heiligtümer zahlreiche »Sklaven der Gottheit« (*teojo doero*), deren Status an denjenigen Freier erinnert; sie werden vom Palast gestiftet (ebenso handelt noch Antiochos von Kommagene im 1. Jh. v. Chr., OGIS 383,161). Bei der sakralen Freilassung wird ein Sklave aus dem Besitz eines Individuums einer Gottheit übergeben, ohne daß daraus zwingend Dienst für den Tempel folgen würde (→ *paramonē*).

P. Debord, L'esclavage sacré. Etat de question, in: Actes du colloque sur l'esclavage 1971, 1972, 135–150 · Ders., Aspects sociaux et économiques de la vie religieuse dans l'Anatolie gréco-romaine, 1982, 83–90 · W. Fauth, M.-B. v. Strutzky, s. v. Hierodulie, RAC 15, 73–82 · R. Scholl, Hierodoulos im griech.-röm. Ägypten, in: Historia 34, 1985, 466–492 · F. Bömer, Untersuchungen über die Rel. der Sklaven in Griechenland und Rom 3, 1990. F. G.

Hierogamu graphe s. Raptus

Hieroglyphen. Die Zeichen der äg. Schrift in ihrer ausführlichen, nichtkursiven Form, schon vor 3000 v. Chr. in Gebrauch und bis 394 n. Chr. nachgewiesen. Der Bestand umfaßt in älterer Zeit ca. 700 Zeichen, von denen einige aus der hierat. Kursive (→ Hieratisch) hervorgingen, in griech.-röm. Zeit durch Neubildungen und vor allem Modifikationen ca. 5000 Zeichen. Texte werden in Zeilen oder in Kolumnen und dabei links- oder rechtsläufig geschrieben. Die Schriftrichtung ist oft, v. a. bei größeren Denkmälern wie Tempeln oder Gräbern, durch die Ausrichtung auf eine Symmetrieachse oder eine dargestellte Person bestimmt.

Die Wörter werden in einer Kombination von Wort- und phonet. Zeichen geschrieben. Die Phonogramme, die selbst wieder auf Wortzeichen zurückgehen, geben allein Konsonanten wieder (im AR 24, nach lautl. Veränderungen später weniger) – in Zeichen von 1, 2, 3 oder mehr Konsonanten. Vokale sind nicht berücksichtigt, die »schwachen« Konsonanten j, w und Alef im Wortauslaut nur unregelmäßig. Zur Wiedergabe von fremden Wörtern und Namen sind schon im späten AR und dann vor allem im NR, hier auch für einige äg. Wörter und Namen, »Gruppenschreibungen« in Gebrauch, die zumindest teilweise auch Vokale zum Ausdruck bringen. Von den Wortzeichen werden viele selbständig als Ideogramme gebraucht, oft durch einen Ideogrammstrich (bei Feminina dazu mit der Endung t) markiert. Viele Wortzeichen werden zusammen mit vorausgehenden phonetischen Zeichen gebraucht und machen so als Determinative bestimmte semantische Klassen kenntlich.

Die Texte sind in *scriptio continua* verfaßt, doch dienen Determinative und Ideogrammstriche auch als Worttrenner. Nur ein geringer Teil des Wortschatzes wird allein mit phonetischen Zeichen geschrieben (vor allem Präpositionen, Präpositionaladverbien und Satzpartikeln, auch einige Substantive, Adjektive und Verben).

Die Form der Zeichen und die Orthographie der Wörter bleiben stark von der Trad. geprägt, unterliegen im Laufe der Jt. vielen zeitgebundenen Veränderungen. Die Varianz von Wortschreibungen ist teilweise sehr breit, in anderen Fällen, oft zeitgebunden, stark eingeschränkt. Lautliche Veränderungen werden allenfalls mit zeitlichem Verzug berücksichtigt. In der Spätantike ist die Kenntnis der H.-Schrift verlorengegangen (→ Horapollon).
→ Entzifferung

H. G. Fischer, s. v. H., LÄ 2, 1189–1199 · A. H. Gardiner, Egyptian Grammar, ³1957 · Unité associée au C. N. R. S. 1068 (ed.), Valeurs phonétiques des signes hiéroglyphiques d'époque gréco-romaine, 4 Bde., 1988–1996. J. OS.

Hieroglyphenschriften I. Kreta II. Kleinasien

I. Kreta

Ein früher auch »piktographisch« gen. (bisher nicht entziffertes) Schriftsystem mit oft bildhaften Zeichen (Körperteile von Mensch und Tieren, Pflanzen, Früchte, Gefäße, Waffen, Musikinstrumente usw.) ist im Rahmen der min. Hochkultur auf Kreta geschaffen und dort v. a. in der ersten Palastzeit (1900–1700 v. Chr.) benutzt worden. Doch liegen seine Anfänge früher. Anregungen mögen Ägypten oder die Levante geliefert haben, dagegen sind die »anatolischen Hieroglyphen« zeitlich später. Die Zeugnisse stammen von 34 verschiedenen Plätzen Kretas (Haupt-FO: Knosos und Mallia) sowie aus Kythera und Samothrake. Bisher sind etwa 330 Schriftträger (mit meist nur wenigen Zeichen) bekannt, darunter mehr als 130 Siegel (aus Stein oder Elfenbein); ferner aus Ton Anhänger (*médaillons*) und prismatisch geformte Klümpchen (*nodules*) mit drei oder vier Flächen (die öfters Siegelabdrücke tragen) sowie quaderförmige »Barren«; dazu kommen kurze (einwortige) Aufschriften auf Gefäßen usw., jedoch nur wenige Täfelchen. Die Inhalte sind gewiß überwiegend profan, etwa Waren-Buchungen. Die Siegel mögen PN und Titel tragen. Den Kern dieser Schrift bildet ein Fonds von fast 100 Silbenzeichen; daneben finden sich über 30 Logogramme, sowie Maß- und Zahlzeichen (Dezimalsystem). Die Zeichen sind teils sorgfältig-dekorativ (auf den Siegeln), teils flüchtig-kursiv ausgeführt. In der Epoche Mittel-Minoisch III (17. Jh.) überschneidet sich die Verwendung der kret. H. mit der von → Linear A; in Mallia und Knosos z. B. kommen beide nebeneinander vor. Zweifellos bestehen zw. beiden Systemen Beziehungen, nicht wenige ihrer Zeichen ähneln einander (und denen von → Linear B).

A. J. Evans, Scripta Minoa I, 1909 · E. Grumach, Die kret. Schriftsysteme, in: HdArch 1, 1969, 234–240 · Heubeck, 2–6 · J.-P. Olivier, L. Godart, J.-Cl. Poursat, Corpus Hieroglyphicarum Inscriptionum Cretae, Études Crétoises 31, 1996 (grundlegend, mit umfassender Bibliogr.). G. N.

II. Kleinasien
A. Luwisch B. Urartäisch

A. Luwisch

Die in Kleinasien und Nordsyrien verbreitete, vorwiegend auf Felsen, Orthostaten, Stelen und Statuen erh. luw. H. (ca. 15. Jh.-Anf. 7. Jh.), aus wissenschaftsgesch. Gründen lange Zeit zu Unrecht »hethit.« H. gen., ist eine genuine Schöpfung der Luwier und, wenngleich auch von den Hethitern im 15.–13. Jh. auf Siegeln sowie im 13. Jh. für repräsentative Inschr. (z. B. Boğazköy, Emirgazi, Yalburt/Ilgın) benutzt, speziell zur Darstellung des zu den → anatolischen Sprachen gehörigen (konventionell nach der Schrift benannten) hieroglyphenluw. Dial. (→ Luwisch) entwickelt worden, wie etwa das Fehlen eines (dem Luw. im 2. Jt. nicht eigenen) *e*-Vok. und die akrophonisch gewonnenen Silbenzeichen zeigen; z. B. setzt *u* (Zeichen: Rinderkopf, auch als Logogramm BOS dienend) ← **uu̯a-* = lyk. *uwa-* »Rind« < uranatol. **guu̯ā́-* (< uridg. Sg. Akk. *g^{u}*ṓm* < *g^{u}*óu̯-m̥*) den spezifisch luw. Schwund von **g* voraus. Das System der im 2. Jt. noch stark bildhaften, im 1. Jt. wohl in Anpassung an den Gebrauch in der Administration (vgl. die wenigen erh., auf Bleistreifen geschriebenen Briefe und Wirtschaftstexte aus Assur bzw. Kululu; 8. Jh.) zunehmend abstrakt-linearer werdenden luw. H. – Schriftrichtung links-/rechtsläufig, von Zeile zu Zeile wechselnd (Bustrophedon), Worttrenner werden nur unregelmäßig gesetzt – besteht aus einer Kombination von (h. lat. umschriebenen) Logogrammen, die auch als Determinative dienen, sowie von ca. 80, z. T. erst im 1. Jt. ausgebildeten Silbenzeichen des Typs V (*a, i, u*), CV (z. B. *ta, ti, tu*) bzw. – in geringerem Umfang – CVCV (z. B. *tara/i*), darunter auch homophone, nach ihrer Häufigkeit indizierte Zeichen (z. B. *ta, tá, tà,* ta_4, ta_5). Die graphische Differenzierung der Silbenzeichen nach *a*- bzw. *i*-Vokal ist z. T. erst Anf. des 1. Jt. (z. B. *i̯a* : *i*, *za* : *zi*), im Falle von *u̯a/i* und von (immer in Ligatur geschriebenem) *ra/i* nie erfolgt. Mehrdeutigkeit der luw. H. ergibt sich darüber hinaus durch Nichtbezeichnung einiger distinktiver Oppositionen (z. B. Tenuis/Media, *nn/n*), durch graphisch unterdrücktes antekons. *n* und durch sprachlich nicht gedeckten *a*-Vokal; im 2. Jt. kommt allg. neben verstärktem Logogrammgebrauch noch die Nichtschreibung von Nominal-/Verbalendungen hinzu, doch sind beide Erscheinungen nach Ausweis der 1996 publizierten Ankaraner Silberschale (15. Jh.; aus Karkamis stammend?, → Karkemiš) mit weitgehend syllabischer, die Endungen ausschreibender Inschr. [1] offensichtlich keine Merkmale einer noch unvollkommenen Schriftentwicklung. Eine relativ genaue, interpretierende Lesung der luw. H. ermöglicht h. die auf innerluw. Sprachvergleichung beruhende Kenntnis von Morphologie und Wortbildung; z. B. *á-za-tu [aztu]/á-ta-tu [adantu]* »er soll/sie sollen essen«, ^{ASINUS}*tara/i-ka-sa-ni-i̯a-za [tarkasnii̯anz]* »Maultiere« (Pl. Dat.), *À-sú+ra/i*^{REGIO}*-u̯a/i-na-ti*^{URBS} *[Assurau̯annadi]* »assyrisch« (Abl.), AUDIRE-*MI-ma-ti-mi-i-sa [tummantimmis]* »berühmt«. Die luw. H., die Anf. des 8. Jh. in Karkamis im Unterschied zur »assyr. (Keil-)Schrift« und zur »phöniz.« bzw. »aram. (Alphabet-)Schrift« einfach »städtische Schrift« genannt wurde [2] und die – zumindest vorübergehend und in begrenztem Umfang – auch zur Darstellung des → Urartäischen Verwendung fand [3], hat sich im 12. bis 7. Jh. als nationales Ausdrucksmittel luw. Sprachträger gegenüber Keil- und Alphabetschriften durchsetzen bzw. behaupten können; ihr Untergang ist denn wohl auch primär im Zusammenhang mit dem durch die Assyrer herbeigeführten polit. Ende der luw. Staaten Syriens und Kleinasiens zu sehen. Die Entzifferung der schon im 18. Jh. bekanntgewordenen luw. H. erfolgte im wesentlichen 1930–1950, doch vermochte erst die Anf. der 70er Jahre revidierte Lesung einer Reihe von Silbenzeichen (v. a. *i, i̯a, zi, za*; früher *a, ā, i, ī* gelesen) die bereits zuvor vermutete Zugehörigkeit der durch sie dargestellten Sprache zum Luw. schlagend aufzuzeigen. (s. auch → Kleinasien mit Karte zur Verbreitung der hieroglyph. Inschr. im 12.–8./7. Jh.).

B. Urartäisch

In Urartu ist neben der dort vornehmlich verwendeten neuassyr. Keilschrift auf Ton- bzw. Metallgefäßen aus Toprakkale (bei Van), Karmir Blur, Kayalıdere und Basṭām sowie vereinzelt auf einer Tontafel (2 ½ Zeilen) eine eigene H. bezeugt. Die sowohl einzeln wie in Gruppen erscheinenden Zeichen sind teils bildhaft, teils abstrakt. Infolge des insgesamt sehr dürftigen Materials sind bisher nur die Logogramme für die Hohlmaße *aqarqi* und *ṭerusi* (nach gleichlautenden Keilinschr. auf demselben Schriftträger) gedeutet worden.

→ Entzifferung

1 J. D. Hawkins, A Hieroglyphic Luwian Inscription on a Silver Bowl in the Museum of Anatolian Civilizations, Ankara, in: Anadolu Medeniyetleri Müzesi, 1996, 7–24 **2** F. Starke, Sprachen und Schriften in Karkamis, in: FS W. Röllig, 1997, 381–395 **3** E. Laroche, Les hieroglyphes d'Altıtepe, in: Anadolu 15, 1971, 55–61.

Luwisch: M. Marazzi, Il geroglifico anatolico, problemi di analisi e prospettive di ricerca, 1990 • A. Mopurgo Davies, J. D. Hawkins, Il sistema grafico del luvio geroglifico, in: ASNP III/VIII 3, 1978, 755–782.
Urartäisch: E. v. Schuler, s. v. Hieroglyphen, urartäisch, RLA 4, 400f. • M. Salvini, Gesch. und Kultur der Urartäer, 1995, 203–206.

F. S.

Hierokaisareia s. Hiera Kome

Hierokles (Ἱεροκλῆς).

[1] Karischer Söldnerführer des 3. Jh. v. Chr., vereitelte 287/6 mit Herakleides den Handstreich der athen. Demokraten auf den Peiraieus und die Munychia (Polyain. 5,17). Unter → Antigonos [2] Gonatas hatte H. die Position eines maked. *phrúrarchos* (»Kommandant einer fest stationierten Truppe«) im Paeiraieus inne und war mehrfach Gastgeber des Königs. Er war mit dem damaligen Leiter der Akademie, Arkesilaos [5], befreundet (Diog. Laert. 4,39f.) und mit Menedemos bekannt (Diog. Laert. 2,127).

→ Demetrios [2]

W. S. Ferguson, Hellenistic Athens, 1911 (Ndr. 1974), 150f.; 162; 234 • Habicht, 164.

J. E.

[2] Griech. Rhetor um 100 v. Chr. aus Alabanda in Karien. Zusammen mit seinem Bruder → Menekles (der aber wohl der bedeutendere war, vgl. Cic. Brut. 325) galt er als einer der Hauptvertreter des → Asianismus (Cic. orat. 231); neben Originalität der Formulierungen lobt Cicero an H. den kunstvollen Parallelismus in der Gedankenführung. Die beiden Brüder hatten zu Lebzeiten großen Erfolg; für Menekles ist bezeugt, daß er auf Rhodos so berühmte Autoren wie Apollonios [5] und → Molon zu seinen Schülern zählte (Strab. 14,2,13). H. scheint mit seinem Bruder eng zusammengewirkt zu haben (Cic. de orat. 2,95). M.W.

[3] Stoischer Philosoph (2. Jh. n. Chr.), hielt in Kleinasien und/oder Athen Vorträge und verfaßte Schriften zur Ethik. Ein Text (die ›Grundlegung der Ethik‹) ist auf Papyrus erhalten, bei Stobaios finden sich mehr als ein Dutzend Auszüge zur praktischen Ethik. Sie stammen aus Reden über Themen wie Familienbeziehungen, Ehe, bürgerliche Pflichten, Hauswirtschaft und Religion. Die ›Grundlegung der Ethik‹ behandelt die Lehren von der Selbstwahrnehmung und der → *oikeíōsis* und vertritt die Ansicht, daß die Selbstwahrnehmung die Grundlage für unsere Selbstaneignung sei. Der Text ist auch eine Quelle zu stoischen Ansichten über Wahrnehmung und Selbstbewußtsein, die Natur der Seele und das »Selbst« als einer komplexen Beziehung der Seele zum Körper. Er wirft Licht auf das Problem der Versöhnung der auf das eigene Selbst bezogenen Neigungen des Menschen (Selbstliebe, das natürliche Verlangen nach der rechten Entwicklung der eigenen Tugend) mit seinen sozialen Neigungen, die die Grundlage der auf den Anderen bezogenen Tugenden sind.

H. v. Arnim, W. Schubart, H.: Ethische Elementarlehre, 1906 • G. Bastianini, A. A. Long (Hrsg.), H., in: Corpus dei papiri filosofici Greci e Latini I.1, 1992, 268–451 • B. Inwood, Hierocles: Theory and argument in the second century AD, in: Oxford Studies in Ancient Philosophy 2, 1984, 151–183 • A. A. Long, Hierocles on *oikeiōsis* and self-perception, in: Ders., Stoic Studies, 1996 • Ders., Notes on Hierocles apud Stobaeum, in: M. Serena Funghi (Hrsg.), Ὁδοὶ διζήσιος. Le vie della ricerca. Studi in onore di F. Adorno, 1996, 299–309 • K. Praechter, H. der Stoiker, 1901. B.I./Ü: T.H.

[4] Galt als schamloser Sklave karischer Herkunft und Günstling des Kaisers → Elagabalus [2]. Er verfügte bei Hofe über großen Einfluß, konnte seiner Mutter, einer Sklavin, die Ehrenstellung einer konsularischen Frau verschaffen und sollte sogar zum Caesar ernannt werden; er wurde aber mit dem Kaiser im März 222 n. Chr. getötet (Cass. Dio 79(80),15,1; 21,1; SHA Elagabalus 6,5). PIR² H 172. T.F.

[5] Sossianus H., hoher Amtsträger in der Zivilverwaltung der tetrarchischen Epoche (Statthalter von Phoenice, Vikar, Statthalter von Bithynien und Praefekt Ägyptens); durch seine publizistische Tätigkeit und durch persönlichen Einfluß war er maßgeblicher Inspirator der Christenverfolgung von 303 n. Chr. (Lact. mort. pers. 16,4). Sein *Philalḗthēs*, eine neuplatonische Streitschrift gegen die Christen, ist nur noch aus der Widerlegung durch Eusebios' Traktat ›Gegen Hierokles‹ bekannt.

T. D. Barnes, Sossianus Hierocles and the Antecedents of the Great Persecution, in: HSPh 80, 1976, 239–259 • M. Forrat, Eusèbe de Césarée. Contre Hiéroclès, 1986 (SChr 333). B.BL.

[6] Gebildeter Jurist, Verf. einer Abh. ›Über die Pferdeheilkunde‹, zu Unrecht als Kompilator der *Hippiatriká* angesehen. Seine Lebenszeit ist unbekannt, doch liegt sie nach → Apsyrtos [2], den H. bearbeitete, und wurde aus stilistischen Gründen vor 500 n. Chr. angesetzt, genauer in die Mitte des 4. Jh. n. Chr.

Das Werk ist einem nicht näher bezeichneten Cassius gewidmet, der (zu Unrecht mit Cassianus Bassus gleichgesetzt) H. um die Redaktion gebeten haben soll. Es ist in zwei B. eingeteilt und stellt eine Neufassung des Werks des Apsyrtos in einem besseren Stil dar. Es erscheint frg. in den sog. *Hippiatrica Berolinensia* und in einer (anscheinend im Ausgang vom letztgenannten Werk) rekonstruierten Fassung in den illustrierten Hss. Leid. Voss. Q 50 und Paris. BN gr. 2244.

Die zweite Fassung ist vor dem 14. Jh. (unter verschiedenen Verformungen des Namens H.) ins Lat., It. (illustrierter Text, unter den Namen Hippokrates und Damascenus) und in die sizilischen Dial. übers. worden.

→ Hippiatrika; Veterinärmedizin A.TO./Ü: T.H.

[7] H. von Alexandreia (5. Jh. n. Chr.). Neuplatonischer griech. Philosoph, Schüler des → Plutarchos von Athen. Er unterrichtete in Alexandreia und vielleicht vorübergehend in Konstantinopel, wo er wegen seines Heidentums verfolgt und zum Exil verurteilt wurde. Wir besitzen von ihm einen Komm. zum anon. ›Goldenen Gedicht der Pythagoreer‹ und kurze, uns durch die ›Bibliothek‹ des Photios (cod. 214; 251) vermittelte Fragmente seiner sieben Bücher umfassenden Abhandlung ›Über die Vorsehung‹. Im Gegensatz zu einer im Gefolge K. Praechters [1] lange vertretenen Auffassung [2; 4] weicht das philos. System des H. nicht von den philos. Strömungen seiner Zeit ab. H. hat weder auf die Thesen der Mittelplatoniker, insbes. die des Heiden → Origenes, zurückgegriffen, noch hat er Gedanken des Christentums aufgenommen. Neuere Forsch. [3; 5; 6] sind im Gegenteil zu dem Ergebnis gekommen, daß H. über seinen Lehrer Plutarchos stark von dem Neuplatoniker Iamblichos beeinflußt wurde, und daß seine Philos. eine Mittelstelle zw. → Iamblichos und → Proklos einnimmt. Der Inhalt des 4. und 5. Buches seiner Abhandlung ›Über die Vorsehung‹, in denen er die Übereinstimmung der ›Chaldäischen Orakel‹, der Theurgie und der *Orphica* mit den platonischen Lehren nachzuweisen sucht (Phot. Bibl. cod. 214,173a), setzt ebenfalls einen Grad der Entwicklung der neuplatonischen Philos. voraus, der erst mit Iamblichos erreicht wurde.

1 K. Praechter, s. v. H. (18), RE 8, 1479–1487 2 Th. Kobusch, Studien zur Philos. des H. von Alexandrien, 1976
3 I. Hadot, Le problème du néoplatonisme alexandrin: Hiéroclès et Simplicius, 1978 4 N. Aujoulat, Le néoplatonisme alexandrin: Hiéroclès d' Alexandrie, 1986
5 I. Hadot, Le démiurge comme principe dérivé dans le

système ontologique d' Hièroclès..., in: REG 103, 1990, 241–262 6 Dies., À propos de la place ontologique du démiurge dans le système philosophique d' Hiéroclès le néoplatonicien. Dernière réponse à M. Aujoulat, in: REG 106, 1993, 430–459. I. H.

[8] Sonst unbekannter Verf. eines *Synékdēmos* (συνέκδημος, »Reisebegleiter«) gen. Verzeichnisses der 64 Prov. (ἐπαρχίαι) und 923 (nicht 935, wie der Titel angibt) Städte (πόλεις) des oström. Reichs im 6. Jh. n. Chr. Grundlage war vielleicht (so [1]) ein geogr.-beschreibendes Werk aus der Zeit Theodosios' II., das von H. zu Anf. der Herrschaft Iustinians I. (527–565 n. Chr.) unsystematisch fortgeschrieben und zur polit. Statistik umgeformt wurde. Diese lag ihrerseits → Constantinus [9] VII. Porphyrogennetos für sein Frühwerk *Perí tṓn themátōn* (*De thematibus*) vor.

1 JONES, Cities, 514–521.

PG 113, 141–156 • KRUMBACHER I, 417 • E. HONIGMANN, Le Synekdémos d'Hiéroklès, 1939 (Ed., Komm.) • HUNGER, Literatur I, 531; II, 399. K. BRO.

Hieromnemones (ἱερομνήμονες, Sg. Hieromnemon, ἱερομνήμων). Sakralbeamte mit weit gestreuter Funktion. Aristot. pol. 6,5, 1321b 35 rechnet sie, zusammen mit *mnḗmones*, *epistátai* u. a. zu den Archivbeamten; Plut. symp. 8,8,4 bezeugt den Titel für die Priester des → Poseidon Phytalmios in Leptis; das ist isoliert. Die sehr zahlreichen inschr. Belege zeigen, daß die *h.* an einigen Orten tatsächlich Archivare waren, häufiger Feste organisierten, die Tempelfinanzen führten oder den Tempelbesitz beaufsichtigten; prominent sind die *h.* der delphischen Amphiktyonie, welche die einzelnen Mitgliederstaaten vertraten (die Aufgaben in IG II^2 1126). An einigen Orten, etwa in Byzantion oder Perinthos, war der *h.* eponymer Jahresbeamter; andernorts blieben *h.* mehrere Jahre im Amt. Gewöhnlich waren sie in Kollegien organisiert; dies und die sakrale Bindung werden der Grund sein, daß *h.* gelegentlich als Übers. von lat. *pontifices* erscheint (etwa Strab. 5,3,2 oder Dion. Hal. ant. 8,55,3). Selten kommen *h.* auch als Funktionäre in privaten Kultvereinen vor.

H. HEPDING, s. v. H., RE 8, 1490–1496. F. G.

Hieron (Ἱέρων).

[1] H. I. aus Gela, → Deinomenide, Bruder Gelons [1], geb. ca. 540/530 v. Chr. Heiratete zuerst eine Tochter des Nikokles von Syrakus (vor 485), danach des Anaxilaos von Rhegion (ca. 480), schließlich des Xenokrates, eines Bruders des Theron von Akragas (ca. 475). Er siegte mehrere Male beim Pferde- und Wagenrennen in Delphi (482, 478, 470) und Olympia (476, 472, 468) [1. 208 ff.]. 485 von Gelon mit der Herrschaft über Gela betraut, folgte er diesem 478 als Tyrann von Syrakus nach. H. betrieb eine expansionistische Außenpolitik: 477/6 schützte er die Lokrer gegen Anaxilaos [1] von Rhegion (schol. Pind. P. 2,36), ca. 476 half er Sybaris im Kampf gegen Kroton (Diod. 11,48,4), 474 besiegte er die Etrusker in der Seeschlacht von Kyme entscheidend (Pind. P. 1,71–75; Diod. 11,51). In Sizilien gründete er 475 die Söldnerkolonie Aitna (Diod. 11,49,1 f.), auf Ischia 474 die Stadt Pithekussai. 472 besiegte er Therons Sohn und Nachfolger Thrasydaios von Akragas, der ihm die Hegemonie über Sizilien streitig machte (Diod. 11,53,1–5). H. trat als großzügiger Förderer von Kunst und Kultur auf, an seinem Hof weilten u. a. Simonides, Pindar, Bakchylides, Aischylos und Epicharmos (dazu [2]). H. starb 466/5 in Aitna und erhielt dort heroische Ehren (Diod. 11,66,4). Im Unterschied zum volkstümlichen Gelon galt er als despotischer und repressiver Herrscher (Diod. 11,67,2–4). Hauptquelle: Diod. 11,38,7–67,4 (vorwiegend aus Timaios, vgl. [3. 44 ff.]).

1 A. SCHENK GRAF VON STAUFFENBERG, Trinakria, 1963 2 D. A. SVARLIEN, Hieron and the Poets, Diss. Univ. of Texas at Austin, 1991 (microfilm, Zusammenfassung in Dissertation Abstracts 52, 1991/92, 2541 A) 3 K. MEISTER, Die sizilische Gesch. bei Diodor, Diss. 1967.

D. ASHERI, Sicily, in: CAH 5, ^{2}1992, 147–170 • H. BERVE, Die Tyrannis bei den Griechen 1, 1967, 148 ff.; 2, 603 ff. • G. MADDOLI, in: E. GABBA, G. VALLET (Hrsg.), La Sicilia antica, Bd. 2.1, 1980, 49 ff. K. MEI.

[2] H. II. von Syrakus, Sohn des Hierokles (Syll.^{3} 427), geb. 306 v. Chr., trat erstmals in den Karthagerkriegen des → Pyrrhos auf Sizilien ca. 278–76 durch Tapferkeit hervor. Angesichts der karthag. Bedrohung seiner Heimatstadt errichtete er 275/74 mit Hilfe von Söldnern und Teilen der Bürgerschaft eine Militärmonarchie in Syrakus und wurde zum bevollmächtigten Strategen gewählt (Pol. 1,8,1 ff.; Paus. 6,12,2). Durch die Heirat mit Philistis, der Tochter eines einflußreichen Aristokraten, stärkte er seine Position erheblich (Pol., ebd.). Nach Beilegung des Karthagerkrieges kämpfte er 271 zunächst erfolglos gegen die Mamertiner, besiegte sie dann 269 am Longanos und nahm den Königstitel an: *Basileús Hiérōn* (Syll.^{3} 427 f.). 264 erneut im Krieg gegen die Mamertiner vor Messana befindlich, verbündete er sich zunächst mit den Karthagern (Pol. 1,11,7; Diod. 23,4,1), schloß aber bald, durch die Intervention der Römer in Messana zum Rückzug gezwungen und in Syrakus belagert, mit diesen ein Bündnis, das ihm die Herrschaft über Syrakus und Teile seines ostsizilischen Einflußgebiets garantierte (Quellen bei StV III 479). H. hielt sowohl im ersten als auch im zweiten Punischen Krieg unbeirrt an seinem proröm. Kurs fest und unterstützte die Römer mehrfach mit Geld, Truppen und Getreidelieferungen. Ca. 240 erhob er seinen Sohn Gelon [2] zum Mitregenten und verlieh ihm den Königstitel. Gelon starb bereits 216/215, H. selbst im folgenden Jahr. Während seiner langjährigen Regierung, die in Titulatur, dynastischer Ordnung, Hofhaltung und sonstiger Repräsentation alle Wesenszüge einer hell. Monarchie aufweist, erlebte Syrakus eine letzte polit., wirtschaftliche und kulturelle Blüte (Bautätigkeit H.s: vgl. Cic. Verr. 2,4,118 f.; Diod. 16,83,2. Wirken des → Theokritos und → Archimedes [1] in Syrakus).

H. unterhielt enge Beziehungen zu den Ptolemaiern und bemühte sich um gutes Einvernehmen mit den Griechen des Mutterlandes. Die auf ihn zurückgehende *Lex Hieronica* regelte die Erhebung des Zehnten auf Sizilien und das Verhältnis zwischen Steuerpächtern und Grundbesitzern. Sie wurde von den Römern bei der Einrichtung der Provinz Sizilien 227 v. Chr. weitgehend übernommen.

H. BERVE, König Hieron II., in: ABAW 47, 1959 • Ders., Die Tyrannis bei den Griechen, 1, 1967, 462ff.; 2, 733ff. • J. BRISCOE, in: CAH 8, ²1989, 44ff. • E. RAWSON, in: CAH 8, ²1989, 422ff. • A. SCHENK GRAF VON STAUFFENBERG, Hieron II. von Syrakus, 1933 • H. H. SCULLARD, in: CAH 7,2, ²1989, 539ff. • G. DE SENSI SESTITO, Gerone II, 1977 • Dies., in:E. GABBA, G. VALLET (Hrsg.), La Sicilia antica II 1, 1980, 343ff. K. MEI.

[3] H. von Soloi, Steuermann (wohl unter → Nearchos) in der Flotte → Alexandros' [4] d. Gr., wurde 324/3 v. Chr. in Verbindung mit dem Plan zu einem Angriff auf Arabien zur Umschiffung der arabischen Küste ausgesandt, gelangte aber nur bis zur Straße von Hormuz (Arr. an. 7,20,7–10).

P. HÖGEMANN, Alexander der Große und Arabien, 1985, 91–93. E. B.

[4] Sohn des Simos aus Kos, wo er als ἐπίτροπος (*epítropos*) der Kinder Ptolemaios' VIII. und Kleopatras III. fungierte; zwischen 124 und 116 v. Chr. wurde er als τῶν πρώτων φίλων (*tōn prṓtōn phílōn*; → Hoftitel) für seine Verdienste von Ptolemaios VIII., Kleopatra II. und III. geehrt.

L. MOOREN, The Aulic Titulature in Ptolemaic Egypt, 1975, 207, Nr. 0383. W. A.

Hieron oros (Ἱερὸν ὄρος).
[1] Heiliger Berg, Name eines Gebirges an der → Propontis, h. Tegirdağ. Rel. Zentrum der → Thrakes (Strab. 7, fr. 55). Dort lag die gleichnamige Festung der Odrysai (Xen. an. 7,1,14). Kotys I. verschanzte sich dort 362 v. Chr. z.Z. des Aufstandes des Miltokythes (Demosth. or. 23,104). Philippos II. eroberte H. 346 (Demosth. or. 9,15; Aischin. leg. 2,82f.; 3,73f.).

C. DANOV, Altthrakien, 1976, 122f. I. v. B.

[2] Vorgebirge an der Südküste des → Pontos Euxeinos westl. von → Trapezus (Arr. per. p. E. 24), h. Fener Burnu (ehemals Yeros Burnu), wo sich nach Anon. per. p. E. 36 eine gleichnamige Stadt mit Anlegestelle befand.

OLSHAUSEN/BILLER/WAGNER, 135. E. O.

Hieron Stoma (Ἱερὸν Στόμα). Der südlichste der Donaumündungsarme (Strab. 7,5,1; 8,6,1; Ptol. 3,10,2), auch unter dem Namen → PeuKe bekannt (Lucan. 3,202; Plin. nat. 4,79; Ptol. l.c.; Mart. 7,7,1; Amm. 22,8,46; Geogr. Rav. 4,5,13), in Scythia Minor, h. Kreis Tulcea/Rumänien. Unter den sieben Mündungsarmen im Donaudelta führte das H. S. die größte Wassermenge ins Meer. Von den Christen wurde das H. S. dem hl. Georg geweiht und unter dessen Schutz gestellt; der Name des Hl. überlebte in der Bezeichnung dieses Donauarmes über das MA bis in die moderne Zeit: Sfintu Gheorghe. Peuce wurde im Alt. auch eine Insel im Donaudelta, wahrscheinlich nördl. vom H. S., bezeichnet. → Istros [2]

TIR L 35 Bucarest, 1969, 45, 57f. (mit Quellen und Lit.). J. BU.

Hieronymos (Ἱερώνυμος).
[1] Athener, einer der Stellvertreter → Konons in dessen Kommando über die persische Flotte 395 v. Chr. (Diod. 14,81,4), setzte sich in Athen für eine expansivere Politik ein (Aristoph. Eccl. 201; Ephor. FGrH 70 F 73).

TRAILL, PAA 533930.

[2] Oikist aus dem arkadischen Mainalos bei der Gründung von Megalopolis (→ Megale Polis) 370 v. Chr. (Paus. 8,27,2), gehörte zu den leitenden Staatsmännern in Megalopolis und vertrat nach 351 die Politik Philipps II. (Demosth. or. 18,295; 19,11). W. S.

[3] H. von Syrakus, geb. ca. 230 v. Chr., Sohn Gelons II. und Enkel → Hierons [2] II. Folgte diesem 215 im Alter von 15 Jahren, anfänglich 15 Vormündern unterstellt (Liv. 24,4), als König nach. Nach Aufdeckung einer Verschwörung und Hinrichtung des proröm. gesinnten Thrason gewannen die Karthagerfreunde unter seinen Beratern zusehends an Einfluß. Im Gegensatz zu seinem stets romtreuen Vorgänger wechselte er daher bald auf die Seite der Karthager über und verbündete sich mit ihnen zum Kampf gegen Rom (vgl. StV III 529). Nach Livius (24,26,1) plante er sogar ein gemeinsames Vorgehen von Syrakus, Karthago und Ägypten gegen die Römer. Bereits im Sommer 214 fiel er jedoch einer Verschwörung zum Opfer. Taten und Schicksale des H. wurden nach Polybios (7,7) in der Geschichtsschreibung nicht selten übertrieben dargestellt und sensationell aufgebauscht.

H. BERVE, Die Tyrannis bei den Griechen, 1967, 1, 471ff.; 2, 735f. • G. DE SENSI SESTITO, in: E. GABBA, G. VALLET (Hrsg.), La Sicilia antica II 1, 1980, 343ff. K. MEI.

[4] *Archisōmatophýlax* (→ Hoftitel), eponymer Offizier, *stratēgós* der Thebais (169/163 v. Chr.); sein Sohn Lysanias (PP 9,5189) war zw. 157 und 152 eponymer Priester des Königskultes in Ptolemais (zu Priesterämtern der Tochter s. PP 9,5208.). PP 1/8,192.

E. VAN'T DACK, Ptolemaica Selecta, 1988, 254, 269, 342. W. A.

[5] Tragiker und Dithyrambendichter des 5. Jh. v. Chr.; von Aristophanes (Ach. 388) wegen seiner üppigen Haarpracht verspottet. Laut Scholien (R Ald; vgl. Suda α 676 und POxy. 6,856,27) habe er in seinen inkonsequent und unklar aufgebauten Tragödien allzu pathetische Handlungsabläufe und schreckenerregende Masken verwendet, wobei ihm aber auch Publikumserfolg attestiert wird; von den Scholien (R; vgl. Suda κ 1768) zu Aristoph. Nub. 348–350 wird er als Sohn des Xenophantos identifiziert, der dort wegen seiner langen und dichten (Körper-)Behaarung und allzu wollüstigen Päderastie verhöhnt wird. Diese Gleichsetzung wird evtl. durch IG II[2] 1642, v. 16 (Mitte 4. Jh. v. Chr.) gestützt, wo ein H. als Sohn des Xenophantos erwähnt wird und es wahrscheinlich um dieselbe Familie geht (vgl. PA 7556).

TrGF 31. F. P.

[6] H. von Kardia. Griech. Geschichtsschreiber, geb. ca. 360 v. Chr. Als enger Vertrauter seines Landsmannes → Eumenes [1] (Diod. 18,50,4 = FGrH 154 T 3) leitete er 320 v. Chr. eine Gesandtschaft an Antipatros [1] (Diod. a.a.O.) und weilte nach Eumenes' Tod 316 als hoher Beamter im Hauptquartier des Antigonos [1] Monophthalmos (Diod. 19,44,3 = T 5). Nach dessen Tod 301 trat er in den Dienst des Demetrios [2] Poliorketes, der ihn 291 zum »Aufseher und Ordner« der boiotischen Städte ernannte (Plut. Demetrios 39,4 = T 8). Schließlich stand er auch bei Antigonos [2] Gonatas in Rang und Würde (Paus. 1,9,8 = T 11). Er starb bei voller geistiger und körperlicher Gesundheit im Alter von 104 Jahren (Agatharchidas von Knidos FGrH 86 F 4).

Der Titel des Geschichtswerkes ist unterschiedlich überliefert: ›Die Ereignisse nach Alexandros‹ (Suda s. v. H.), ›Geschichte der Diadochen‹ (T 3), ›Historien‹ (T 4–6). Es begann mit Alexandros' Tod 323 v. Chr. (F 2) und führte mind. bis zum Ende des Pyrrhos 272 v. Chr. (F 15). Die Schilderung von Pyrrhos' Kriegen im Westen eröffnete H. mit einer *archaiología* Roms, nach Dionysios von Halikarnassos (ant. 1,6,1) der ersten in der griech. Lit.

Vom Werk des H. sind nur 18 Fragmente erhalten, doch beeinflußte es die spätere Überlieferung nachhaltig, bes. Diodor, B. 18–20 (Vorbehalte neuerdings bei [1. 194 ff.], Arrian, Diadochengeschichte (FGrH 156) sowie Plutarch, Viten des Eumenes, Demetrios, Pyrrhos. Die neuere Forsch., bes. [2] und [3], suchte deshalb das Geschichtswerk des H. aus Diodor zu rekonstruieren und zu charakterisieren (vgl. die ausgezeichnete Gesamtwürdigung bei [2. 1557 f.]). Die Ansicht des Pausanias (1,9,8), H. beurteile die Diadochenkönige mit Ausnahme des Antigonos Gonatas tendenziell und feindlich, ist demnach zu relativieren; er erweist sich vielmehr durchweg als ›a very reliable historian‹ (so [3]). H. hatte als Mann der polit. Praxis für die Übertreibungen der rhetor. Geschichtsschreiber ebenso wenig Verständnis wie für die sensationsbetonten Berichte der »mimetischen« Historiographie und schrieb in einem schmucklosen und unpretentiösen Stil. FGrH 154.

1 F. LANDUCCI GATTINONI, Duride di Samo, 1997
2 F. JACOBY, s. v. H. (10), RE 8, 1540–1560 = Griech. Historiker, 1956, 245–256 3 J. HORNBLOWER, Hieronymus of Cardia, 1981.

T. S. BROWN, Hieronymus of Cardia, in: American Historical Review, 52, 1946, 684–696 • R. ENGEL, Zum Geschichtsbild des Hieronymos von Kardia, in: Athenaeum 50, 1972, 120–125 • F. LANDUCCI GATTINONI, Ieronimo e la storia dei diadochi, in: Invigilata Lucernis 3/4, 1981/82, 13–26 • O. LENDLE, Einführung in die griech. Geschichtsschreibung, 1992, 190 ff. • K. MEISTER, Die griech. Geschichtsschreibung, 1990, 124 ff. • I. L. MERKER, Diodorus Siculus and Hieronymus of Cardia, in: Ancient History Bulletin 2, 1988, 90–93 • K.-H. RICHTER, Untersuchungen zur hell. Historiographie, 1987, 33 ff. • K. ROSEN, Political Documents in Hieronymus of Cardia (323–302 B. C.), in: Acta Classica 10, 1967, 41–94. K. MEI.

[7] H. aus Rhodos. Peripatetiker, lebte etwa 290–230 v. Chr. Die Mehrzahl seiner Frg. stammt aus Schriften zur Ethik oder Lit.- und Kulturgesch., letztere meistens anekdotenhaft. Mit seiner Definition des Telos als ›Schmerzlosigkeit‹ (*doloris vacuitas*, fr. 8–10) und einer Schrift Περὶ ἐποχῆς (›Über die Urteilsenthaltung‹, fr. 24) schloß er sich bewußt der hell. Themenstellung an, und wir erfahren auch, daß er eine quasi-atomistische Erklärung des Sehens vertrat oder wenigstens diskutierte (fr. 53). Trotzdem scheint er im Ganzen der peripatetischen Trad. treu geblieben zu sein.
→ Aristotelismus

FRG: WEHRLI, Schule 10, 9–44 • POxy. 3656.
LIT.: F. WEHRLI, in: GGPh[2], Bd. 3, 575 ff • G. ARRIGHETTI, Jeronimo di Rodi, Studi classici ed orientali 2, 1955, 111–128. H. G.

Hieronymus A. ÜBERSICHT B. LEBEN C. WERK D. REZEPTION

A. ÜBERSICHT

Das Geburtsjahr des Eusebius H., wie er sich in chron. praef. nennt, ist umstritten und wird im Zeitraum zwischen 331 und 348 n. Chr. vermutet (Befürworter der Frühdatier. folgen der Angabe Prospers von Aquitanien, epitoma chronicon MGH AA 9,451; 469; für die Spätdatier. plädiert [1]). Ebenso ist sein Geburtsort Stridon, den H. selbst als an der Grenze zwischen Dalmatien und Panonnien liegend angibt (vir. ill. 135), nicht lokalisiert. H. starb am 30.9.419/420 in Bethlehem.

H. dokumentiert in bes. Maße die Grenzprobleme eines dem traditionellen Bildungskontext des Westens entstammenden Christen. Herausragend ist sein meist polemisches, an → Tertullian orientiertes Engagement in innerkirchlichen Auseinandersetzungen. Bes. hat er sich unter östl. Einfluß für eine asketische Ausrichtung des christl. Lebens eingesetzt [2]. H. kann unter den vier lat. → Kirchenvätern zwar nicht als der bedeutendste Theologe, jedoch als eine Persönlichkeit immenser kultureller Potenz gelten. Seine enorme schriftstellerische Produktivität über das ganze Leben hinweg ist ohne Vergleich und dient zugleich als Hauptquelle für sein Leben [3]. Er fungiert durch seine Übersetzer- sowie Kommentatorentätigkeit als Vermittler zwischen griech. und lat. Christentum [4]. Während seines Aufenthalts in Syrien lernte H. in Palästina Griech. und Hebräisch (epist. 125,12), was ihn vor den meisten christl. Autoren des Westens auszeichnet. Ebenso formte er den späteren christl. Umgang mit der traditionellen lat. lit. Kultur der Ant. zu, die er in ihrer spätant. Ausprägung völlig beherrscht [5]. Er folgt darin dem Vorbild des → Origenes, der dies für die griech. Lit. geleistet hat. So hat man H. als christl. Humanisten und Wegbereiter späterer westeurop. Rückwendungen zur Ant. bezeichnet. Freilich problematisierte er den Umgang mit dem trad. lit. Erbe durch den berühmten Ber. eines Traumes, in dem er sich vor Gottes Thron als *Ciceronianus ... non Christianus* beschuldigt und bestraft sieht (epist. 22,30).

B. Leben

H. entstammte einer christl. und offenbar begüterten Familie, denn er genoß nach Besuch der Schule in Stridon eine traditionelle lit. Ausbildung in Rom, vermutlich bei dem Grammatiker Aelius → Donatus [3], den er als *praeceptor meus* (»mein Lehrer«) bezeichnet (chron. zum Jahr 354). In Rom wurde er auch getauft. Sein Aufenthalt am Kaiserhof in Trier blieb Episode. H. scheint schnell von einer Karriere innerhalb der Verwaltung Abstand genommen zu haben. Der Entschluß zum asketischen Leben führte ihn ca. 373 zunächst nach Aquileia und anschließend auf eine Pilgerfahrt nach Jerusalem. Drei Jahre lebte er anschließend als Einsiedler in der Wüste von Chalkis in Syrien (ca. 375–377). 379 folgte die Weihung zum Priester durch Paulinus von Antiochia, den er 381 zum Konzil von Konstantinopel begleitete. Ab 382 hielt er sich wieder in Rom als Sekretär des Papstes → Damasus auf und wurde dort zur führenden Persönlichkeit eines Kreises asketisch orientierter aristokratischer Christinnen und Christen. Nach dem Tod des Damasus (384) mußte H. Rom verlassen (385) und praktizierte mit Unterstützung der über ein großes Vermögen verfügenden Paula, der Witwe eines röm. Aristokraten, und deren Tochter Eustochium seit 386 in Palästina seine asketischen Ideale. Er gründete in Bethlehem drei Frauenklöster sowie ein Männerkloster und verbrachte dort, ganz auf schriftstellerische Tätigkeit ausgerichtet, die zweite Lebenshälfte, die die Phase seiner höchsten Produktivität darstellt.

C. Werk

Zu den frühesten lit. Leistungen des H. gehört die wohl vor 381 entstandene Vita des Paulus von Theben. Sie war von großer lit. Qualität und entfaltete im Westen wie die Übers. des → Euagrios [2] der Antoniusvita eine enorme Wirkung (→ Biographie). Später (wohl noch vor 392) folgten die Lebensbeschreibung des Malchus und des Hilarion [6]. In die Zeit seines Romaufenthalts fällt die in asketischem Sinne programmatische Schrift *Adversus Helvidium de Mariae virginitate perpetua*. Die wichtigste lit. Leistung des H. besteht in der durch Papst Damasus veranlaßten Überarbeitung älterer lat. Übers. des NT anhand von griech. Vorlagen. 391–405 folgte die selbständige Übers. des AT aus dem jeweiligen hebräischen und aramäischen (Tobias, Judith) Urtext sowie aus dem Griech. (Daniel, Esther). Diese Zusammenstellung sollte ab dem 13. Jh. bis zur Mitte des 20. Jh. unter dem Namen *Vulgata* kanonisch werden. Zu den Psalmen existieren mehrere Fassungen: die Überarbeitung des *Psalterium Romanum* und die schließlich in die *Vulgata* übernommene Psalmenversion, die H. nach der *Hexapla* des Origenes anfertigte. Letztere Bearbeitung wurde wegen der Verbreitung in Gallien *psalterium Gallicanum* genannt. Es existiert auch ein wie das AT aus dem Hebräischen übers., jedoch wenig rezipiertes *psalterium iuxta Hebraeos*. Die Vollendung dieses in Rom begonnenen Übers.-Vorhabens war erst seit seinem dauerhaften Aufenthalt in Bethlehem möglich. In diese Phase fallen auch zahlreiche exegetische Schriften, die Komm. zu at. Propheten (z. B. vor 392 zu den kleinen Propheten Micha, Nahum, Habakuk, Zephania, Haggai), Briefe und 85 Predigten, auch die Streitschriften, die H. in der seit 393 tobenden Auseinandersetzung um die dogmatische Rechtmäßigkeit bestimmter Lehren des → Origenes verfaßte.

H. war stark von Origenes beeinflußt und hatte von ihm verfaßte Predigten wie die Homilien über das Hohelied übersetzt. Jetzt sprach H. sich – u. a. gegen seinen Jugendfreund → Rufinus Tyrannius – für die Verketzerung des Origenes aus. Den Bruch mit Rufinus belegt bes. die Schrift *Apologia contra Rufinum* in 3 B. (402/3). Auch sind Traktate gegen häretische Bewegungen (z. B. *Contra Pelagianos*) oder – oft unangemessen – gegen die Kritiker der asketischen Lebensform gerichtet. So griff H. 393 in der Schrift *Contra Iovinianum* eine moderate Position hinsichtlich der Ehe an. 392/3 wurde nach dem Vorbild des Sueton die christl. Lit.-Gesch. *De viris illustribus* verfaßt.

Von großer Wirkung war die Übers. der uns sonst nur noch in einer armen. Fassung überl. ›Chronik‹ des → Eusebios [7], die H. für ein westl. Publikum durch zusätzliche kulturgesch. Informationen ergänzte und bis 378 fortsetzte. Sie dürfte kurz nach diesem Datum entstanden sein und entwickelte sich zu einem unentbehrlichen Instrument christl. Chronologie. Eine einzigartige kulturhistor. und theologische Quelle sind die 154 Briefe, von denen 26 an H. gerichtet sind. Sie umspannen auch als biographisches Zeugnis – allerdings mit Lücken – das gesamte Leben des H. Von besonderer Bed. sind z. B. der an der entsprechenden Schrift Ciceros orientierte und die Bibelübers. theoretisch begleitende Brief *De optimo genere interpretandi* (epist. 57; [7]) oder der 384 an Eustochium gerichtete und als Traktat zur Jungfräulichkeit zu verstehende Brief (epist. 22). In das letzte Lebensjahrzehnt fallen die Vollendung des Jesaiakomm. (411), des Danielkomm. (407) und die großen Komm. zu Ezechiel und Jeremia.

D. Rezeption

H.' Werke wurden unterschiedlich rezipiert. Die Mönchsbiographien wurden u. a. wichtig als Vorbild für die Trad. der Heiligenvita des MA (vgl. die Praef. der ca. 641 von Jonas von Bobbio verfaßten *Vita Columbani*).

Die Schrift *De viris illustribus* erhielt zahlreiche Fortsetzungen. Grundlegend für die christl. → Geschichtsschreibung ist die Chronik des H. Umfangreich wurden die verschiedenen Komm. des H. herangezogen und verarbeitet. Auch die zahlreichen ps.-Hieronymianischen Schriften unterstreichen die Prominenz des H. Dominant ist in der H.-Rezeption die Interpretation als Typus des Asketen und Gelehrten, auch in den bildlichen Darstellungen [8] (z.B. als »Hieronymus im Gehäus« [9]). Bereits zu Lebzeiten vielbeachtet, gehört H. seit einer Unterbrechung im 6./7. Jh. im MA zu den am meisten abgeschriebenen Autoren. Auch im Zeitalter der Renaissance und des Humanismus kam H. größte Bed. zu. So gehörte er zu den von Erasmus bevorzugten Autoren. Der von diesem betreuten, bei Froben in Basel 1515 erschienenen Gesamtausgabe der *Opera Hieronymi* war eine von Erasmus selbst verfaßte Vita des H. vorangestellt worden. Sie gilt als eine erste Form histor.-kritischer Auseinandersetzung mit dem Kirchenvater [10]. Von besonderer Bed. ist auch die Rezeption des Traumes, der z.B. bei → Caesarius [4] von Arles, Odo von Cluny, Othloh von Sankt Emeram in seinem *Liber visionum* oder Hermannus Contractus als Vorbild für ähnliche Visionen gewirkt hat und bei → Gregorius [4] von Tours im ersten Buch der *Libri miraculorum* oder Peter Abaelard direkt rezipiert wird.

1 D. Booth, The Chronology of Jerome's First Years, in: Phoenix 25, 1981, 237–259 **2** P. Brown, Die Keuschheit der Engel, 1991, 372–394 **3** Ch. Favez, Saint Jérôme peint par lui-même (Collection Latomus 33), 1958 **4** W.C. McDermott, Saint Jerome and Pagan Greek Literature, in: Vigiliae Christianae 36, 1982, 372–383 **5** H. Hagendahl, Latin Fathers and the Classics, 1958, 89–328
6 M. Fuhrmann, Die Mönchsgeschichten des H., in: Entretiens 23, 1977, 41–89 **7** G.J.M. Bartelink, Liber de optimo genere interpretandi (epist. 57), 1980
8 R. Jungblut, H.: Darstellung und Verehrung eines Kirchenvaters, Diss. Tübingen 1967 **9** O. Pächt, Zur Entstehung des »H. im Gehäus«, in: Pantheon 21, 1963, 131–142 **10** J.B. Maguire, Erasmus' Biographical Masterpiece: Hieronymi Stridonensis Vita, in: RQ 26, 1973, 265–273.

Ed.: PL 22–30, Suppl. 2. • CCL 72–80 (noch nicht vollst.) • Hilberg, CSEL 54–56, 1910–1918 (epist.) • J. Labourt, 8 Bde., 1949–1963 (lat.-frz.) • CSEL 88, 1981 (neuentdeckte Briefe an Augustinus) • E. Richardson, De viris illustribus, 1896 • H. Quentin u.a., Biblia Sacra iuxta Latinam vulgatam versionem, 1926ff. (Vulgata; noch nicht beendet) • J. Wordsworth, H.J. White, F.D. Sparks, 1889–1949 • R. Helm, GCS 47, [2]1986 (Chronik) • Übersicht: H.J. Frede, Kirchenschriftsteller-Verzeichnis und Sigel, 1954, 510–532.
Übers.: BKV 15f. 18 (Auswahl).
Lit.: G. Grützmacher, H. (Stud. zur Gesch. der Theologie und der Kirche 6/10), 3 Bde., 1901–1908 • P. Jay, L'exégèse de s. Jérôme d'après son Commentaire sur Isaie, 1985 • J.N.D. Kelly, Jerome, 1975 • E.F. Rice jr., Saint Jerome in the Renaissance, 1985 • K. Sugano, Das Rombild des H., 1983. U.E.

Hierophantes s. Mysteria

Hieropoioi s. Opfer

Hieros Gamos (ἱερὸς γάμος, Heilige Hochzeit).
I. Begriff II. Alter Orient III. Griechenland

I. Begriff

Ein Terminus, der zur Bezeichnung einer rituellen sexuellen Vereinigung in der neuzeitlichen Forsch. seit dem Aufkommen des Fruchtbarkeitsparadigmas im 19. Jh. (Mannhardt, Frazer) eine große Bed. erlangt hat. Ausgehend von dem im homer. Epos erzählten Geschlechtsverkehr zwischen → Demeter und ihrem sterblichen Liebhaber → Iasion ›auf einem dreimal gepflügten Feld‹ (Hom. Od. 5, 125–128; Hes. theog. 969–971), der in Analogie mit nordeurop. Bräuchen als Reflex eines sexuellen Rituals zur Förderung der agrarischen und menschlichen Fruchtbarkeit verstanden wurde [1], wurden sowohl in Griechenland wie im Alten Orient analoge Riten gesucht. Während im Alten Orient im Kult der Inanna-Ištar-Astarte solche Riten als erwiesen angesehen wurden und dadurch das Fruchtbarkeitsparadigma bis in die jüngere Gegenwart bewahrt blieb [2], sind in der Forsch. zur griech. Rel. nach der Ablehnung dieses Paradigmas wenige und diffuse Phänomene zurückgeblieben.

1 J.W.E. Mannhardt, Der Baumcultus der Germanen und ihrer Nachbarstämme, 1875, 480–488 **2** S.N. Kramer, The Sacred Marriage Rite, 1969. F.G.

II. Alter Orient

Zunächst mit dem kult. vollzogenen *h.g.* der Inanna (→ Ištar), der Stadtgöttin von → Uruk, mit dem sagenhaften Herrscher der Stadt, Dumuzi (→ Tammuz) in Verbindung gebracht, ist der *h.g.* Thema zahlreicher Kultlieder, die sich auf die Zeit vom 21. bis 20. Jh. v. Chr. beschränken. Im Gegensatz zu der im Gefolge von Frazer fälschl. vertretenen Ansicht [2. 251f.], es handle sich dabei um einen Fruchtbarkeitsritus, stellt die Vereinigung von Göttin und Herrscher einen alten, von den Herrschern der 3. Dyn. von Ur (→ Mesopotamien) neu belebten, in Uruk beheimateten Legitimationsritus zu Beginn der Regierungszeit eines Herrschers dar [3]. Davon zu trennen sind die in Mythen und Mythologemen geschilderten Theogamien, mit z.T. kosmogonischer Relevanz.

1 E. Matsushima, Texte accadienne du rituel du marriage divin, 1985 **2** J. Renger, s.v. h.g., RLA 4, 251–259 **3** Ders., s.v. Inthronisation, RLA 5, 128–136 **4** W.H. Ph. Römer, Einige Überlegungen zur »Heiligen Hochzeit« nach altoriental. Texten (AOAT 211), 1982 **5** P. Steinkeller, On Rulers, Priests and Sacred Marriage, in: K. Watanabe, D. Yoshida (Hrsg.), Priests and Officials in the Ancient Near East, 1998 (im Druck; mit Lit.). J.RE.

III. Griechenland

Einige lokale Mythen erzählen die Hochzeit bzw. den ersten Geschlechtsverkehr der Götter → Zeus und → Hera; die homer. Erzählung von Heras Verführung des Zeus (*Diós apátē*, Hom. Il. 14,159ff.) folgt nach allg. Ansicht entsprechenden Mythen [1]. Eine Verbindung dieser Mythen mit sexuellen Riten ist jedoch sehr problematisch. Für das athenische Fest der Theogamia (»Götterhochzeit«, schol. Hes. erg. 780), das wohl identisch ist mit dem athenischen, als »heilige Hochzeit von Zeus und Hera« bezeichneten Fest [2], sind ein Ferkelopfer für Zeus Heraios (LSCG, Suppl. 1 A 20) und Festmahle bezeugt; der nur in diesem Kontext griech. belegte Terminus *h.g.* muß nicht mehr bedeuten als »für das Ritual relevante Hochzeit« in dem Sinne, daß ein ausgelassenes und üppiges Fest mit dem entsprechenden Mythos begründet wurde. Das Fest fiel in den Monat Gamelion; es mag daher Anreiz zu vermehrten Eheschließungen gewesen sein. Die boiotischen Daidala, in denen eine hochzeitliche Prozession mit Puppen stattfand, endeten mit deren Verbrennung und einem Opferfest der Nachbarstädte, haben mithin eine deutlich polit. Funktion (Paus. 9,3,8), die zum Doppelcharakter von → Hera als Polis- und als Ehegöttin paßt. Die samischen Toneia, die Varro (bei Lact. inst. 1,17,8) als Hochzeit bezeichnet, sind ein Fest der Auflösung (mit Lösung des sonst gefesselten hochaltertümlichen Kultbilds), das in der Typologie zu Neujahrsfesten gehört und wiederum allein im Mythos mit der Hochzeit der Göttin verbunden wird [3].

Entsprechende Riten hat man zum einen für Kreta, zum anderen im athenischen Dionysoskult vermutet. Auf Kreta wurde die Hochzeit von Zeus und Hera »nachgeahmt« (Diod. 5,72,4); der Ausdruck muß aber auf nichts mehr als auf ein den athenischen Theogamia entsprechendes üppiges Fest weisen. In Athen wurde am Fest der → Anthesteria die Hochzeit der Basilinna (der Ehefrau des obersten Sakralbeamten, des Archon Basileus) mit → Dionysos im Bukolion an der Agora vollzogen; die ant. Zeugnisse verwenden technisches Vokabular (»als Frau weggeben«: Demosth. or. 59,63; *symmeíxis*, »Geschlechtsakt«: Aristot. Ath. pol. 3,5), und Vasenbilder stellen dar, wie die Basilinna von einem → Satyr als Brautführer zur Hochzeit geführt wird [4]. Zur genauen Form des Rituals aber fehlen Nachrichten ebenso wie zur Funktion; die rituell vorgegebene Auflösung der Ehe des Archon Basileus mag zum Einbruch der dionysischen Ausnahmezeit und ihrer ungeregelten Sexualität gehören.

1 J. C. Bermejo Barrera, Zeus, Hera y el matrimonio sagrado, in: Quaderni di Storia 15, 1989, 133–156
2 Deubner, 177 Anm. 11 3 Graf, 93–96
4 A. Lezzi-Hafter, Anthesterien und H. G. Ein Choenbild des Methyse-Malers, in: Proc. of the 3d Symposion on Ancient and Related Pottery, 1989, 325–334.

A. Klinz, H. G., 1933 · Nilsson, GGR 1, 120–122 · Burkert, 176–178 · M. Cremer, H. G. im Orient und in Griechenland, in: ZPE 48, 1982, 283–290 · A. Avagianou, Sacred Marriage in the Rituals of Greek Rel., 1991. F. G.

Hierosolyma s. Jerusalem

Hierosylia (ἱεροσυλία). In vielen griech. Poleis »Tempelraub«, Entwendung gottgeweihter Gegenstände aus einem Heiligtum, was sehr weit ausgelegt wurde (z. B. auch Unterschlagung von Silber bei staatlicher Münzprägung, Syll.[3] 530, Dyme in Achaia, bald nach 190 v. Chr. [2]). In Athen wurde H. im 5. Jh. vermutlich mit → *eisangelía* verfolgt, später mit einer in die Zuständigkeit der → Thesmotheten fallenden ἱεροσυλίας γραφή (*hierosylías graphé*), in welcher Todesstrafe mit Verweigerung der Bestattung in Attika und Vermögensverfall drohten.

1 D. Cohen, Theft in Athenian Law, 1983, 93 ff.
2 G. Thür, G. Stumpf, Sechs Todesurteile und zwei plattierte Hemidrachmen aus Dyme, in: Tyche 4, 1989, 171–183. G. T.

Hikesie (ἱκεσία, *hikesía*; ἱκετεία, *hiketeía*). Mit dem Ritual der H. dokumentiert ein Schutzsuchender (ἱκέτης, *hikétēs*) seinen Status und bittet um Hilfe, oft um Aufnahme in eine neue Gemeinschaft. *Hiketeía* und *hikétēs* sind abgeleitet von ἵκω, ἱκνέομαι, »ankommen« (vgl. Hesych. s. v. ἱκέσθαι, ἱκετεῦσαι), und so ist der *hikétēs* zunächst derjenige, der »ankommt«. Als Institution des griech. Sakralrechts, vergleichbar mit dem Gastrecht des Fremden (Hom. Od. 8,546f.; Hes. erg. 327f.; → Gastfreundschaft, → Fremdenrecht) und eng verbunden mit der – seit hell. Zeit auch staatsrechtlichen – Einrichtung der → Asylia [7; 8], stellt die H. ein wichtiges Regulativ im ges. und zwischenstaatlichen Machtgefüge dar. Die H. ist für die gesamte griech. Ant. belegt; über die Einzelheiten des rituellen Ablaufs geben vor allem die Quellen der archa. und klass. Zeit (bes. Epos und Drama) Auskunft.

Die sitzende Haltung des Schutzflehenden an einem Herd (Hom. Od. 7,153; Thuk. 1,136,3), Altar (Hom. Od. 22,334f.; Aischyl. Suppl. 189f.; Thuk. 1,126,11) oder Götterbild (Aischyl. Eum. 259) signalisiert sein Anliegen; zudem weist er sich durch einen mit Wolle umwundenen und meist am Altar niedergelegten Ölzweig, die *hiketēría*, als *hikétēs* aus (Aischyl. Eum. 43–45; Soph. Oid. T. 3; Plut. Theseus 18,1; [1]; zum H.-Zweig vor der Volksversammlung: Aristot. Ath. pol. 43,6; vor der *boulé*: Demosth. or. 18,107). Wendet sich der Schutzflehende unmittelbar an eine Person, dann unterstreicht er seine Bitte durch rituell konnotierte → Gebärden: Neben dem Berühren von Kinn und Händen des Adressaten ist dabei das Umfassen der Knie von bes. Bed. (Hom. Il. 1,498ff.; zum Knie als Sitz der *vitalitas* bzw. als Altar vgl. Plin. nat. 11,103; [4. 21f.; 5]). Die für die H. zentrale Funktion des Kontakts zum göttlichen Bereich belegt Plutarch (Plut. Solon 12): Schutzflehende befestigen ein Seil an der Statue der Athena (vgl. Hdt. 1,26). Die Verbindlichkeit der H. beruht auf der Unverletzlichkeit aller Personen oder Gegenstände, die sich auf heiligem Grund befinden (*asylía*). *Hikétai* galten selbst als »heilig« und »rein« (*hieroí* und *hagnoí*:

Paus. 7,25,1). Ihr Schutzpatron war Zeus Hikesios. Zwar konnte die H. prinzipiell in jedem Heiligtum vollzogen werden, doch wurden bestimmte Tempel aufgrund ihrer Ausstattung und Lage zu bevorzugten Zufluchtsstätten, in denen der *hikétēs* sich bisweilen längere Zeit aufhielt [9. 95–97]. Auf die an das Heiligtum gebundene H. folgte im Idealfall die Eingliederung in die Gemeinschaft in Form der »persönlichen«, vom Staat verliehenen Asylie oder auch Metoikie (→ *métoikoi*; vgl. Aischyl. Suppl. 609 ff.; [8. 44–47]). Der Sakralschutz der H. stand nicht nur unschuldig Verfolgten, sondern auch Straftätern, ja sogar Blutschuldigen zu (vgl. Hom. Il. 16,573 f.; Hom. Od. 15,271 ff.; kritisch: Eur. Ion 1314 ff.; Tac. ann. 3,60,1; H. verbunden mit Reinigung: Orestes in Aischyl. Eum.; Iason und Medea in Apoll. Rhod. 4,692 ff.). Gewalt gegen *hikétai* galt als Sakrileg (Plat. leg. 730a; [6. 181–186]), vgl. etwa die Vergewaltigung der → Kassandra am Bild der Athena durch Aias (Alk. fr. 262,16–19 SLG) oder den → Alkmaionidenfrevel (Thuk. 1,126 f.). Das bisweilen unter Drohungen (z. B. von Selbstmord im Heiligtum) vorgetragene H.-Gesuch konnte zu einem polit. Konflikt (Krieg) führen (Aischyl. Suppl.; Eur. Heraclid.).

Aufschlußreich für eine zu erwägende Analogie von H. und → Initiation [3. 101] mag die auf Goldplättchen belegte Bezeichnung des Mysten als *hikétēs* in der Unterwelt sein [10. 303 f.: A2,6; vgl. A3,6]. Auch in lit. Texten wird der ungewisse Status des *hikétēs* häufig als ein rituell konnotierter Übergang zw. Leben und Tod veranschaulicht.

→ Gebärden; Supplicatio

1 M. Blech, Stud. zum Kranz bei den Griechen, 1982, 288–292 **2** W. Burkert, Die orientalisierende Epoche in der griech. Rel. und Lit., 1984, 68–72 **3** J. Gould, Hiketeia, in: JHS 93, 1973, 74–103 **4** J. Kopperschmidt, Die H. als dramat. Form, 1967 **5** R. B. Onians, The Origins of European Thought, 1951 (Ndr. 1988), 174–186 **6** R. Parker, Miasma, 1983 **7** K. J. Rigsby, Asylia, 1996 **8** E. Schlesinger, Die griech. Asylie, 1933 **9** U. Sinn, Greek Sanctuaries as Places of Refuge, in: N. Marinatos, R. Hägg (Hrsg.), Greek Sanctuaries, 1993, 88–109 **10** G. Zuntz, Persephone, 1971. S. G.

Hikesios. Griech. Arzt, Oberhaupt einer erasistrateischen Schule in Smyrna, frühes 1. Jh. v. Chr. (Strab. 12,8,20); schrieb über → Diätetik (Plin. nat. 14,130; 20,35; 27,31), Embryologie (Tert. de anima 25) und Zahnschmerz (Plin. 12,40). Erfinder eines berühmten schwarzen Pflasters, das »bei jeder Wundart helfe« (Galen 13,787). Galen, der vier verschiedene Rezepturen für dieses Mittel anführt (13,780; 787; 810; 812) und dabei auf vier Autoren (→ Andromachos [5] d. J., → Heras, → Herakleides [27] und Statilius Criton) zurückgreift, zerbricht sich über die Abweichungen den Kopf, die in der Tat so gravierend sind, daß sich nicht einmal zwei Rezepturen auf eine gemeinsame Quelle zurückführen lassen. V. N./Ü: L. v. R.-B.

Hiketas (Ἱκέτας).

[1] Syrakusischer Adeliger, Freund des → Dion [I 1]. In den Wirren nach dessen Tod 353 v. Chr. gewann er die Tyrannis über Leontinoi. Er unterstützte zunächst die Syrakusier im Kampf gegen → Dionysios [2] II. Bei seinem Zug gegen Syrakus 346 verständigte er sich jedoch wegen der anrückenden Karthager mit Dionysios und unterstützte dessen Hilferuf an die Korinther. Die Übermacht der Karthager bewog ihn dann zu einem neuen Frontwechsel, indem er den Kampf gegen Dionysios aufnahm und den Korinthern von der sizil. Expedition abriet. Im Kampf gegen Dionysios II. eroberte er sogar Syrakus (mit Ausnahme von Ortygia) und behielt es bis zu dessen endgültigen Vertreibung durch → Timoleon 343/342. Nach der Landung der Korinther bekämpfte er Timoleon an der Seite der Karthager, verständigte sich aber nach deren Rückzug aus Sizilien ca. 344 mit ihm. Nach dem Ausbruch neuer Kämpfe zwischen Timoleon und den Karthagern trat er erneut zu diesen über, wurde aber nach deren Niederlage am Krimissos ca. 340 von Timoleon gefangengenommen und hingerichtet.

Der ständige Frontwechsel des H. erklärt sich aus dem Bestreben, Korinther und Karthager, die beiden auswärtigen Mächte auf Sizilien, zu schwächen bzw. gegeneinander auszuspielen und so die eigene Position zu stärken. Quellen: Diodor (16,67–82) und Plutarch (Timoleon 1–33; äußerst hiketasfeindliche Tendenz, wohl nach Timaios).

H. Berve, Die Tyrannis bei den Griechen, 1967, 1, 275 ff.; 2, 664 ff.

[2] Von ca. 289/8 bis 279 v. Chr. Herrscher von Syrakus. In den Wirren nach dem Tod des Agathokles [2] erhielt H. in Syrakus die bevollmächtigte Strategie im Kampf gegen → Menon von Segesta, der die italischen Söldner des Agathokles in Dienst nahm und mit ihnen Syrakus belagerte. Nach Anfangserfolgen wurde H. durch das Eingreifen der Karthager zu einem ungünstigen Frieden und zur Aufnahme der Söldner gezwungen (Diod. 21,16,6; 18,1 ff.). Durch Verhandlungen erreichte er schließlich deren Abzug, worauf sie in Messana den Räuberstaat der Mamertiner begründeten. Später kämpfte H. erfolgreich gegen Phintias von Akragas, wurde aber nach einer Niederlage gegen die Karthager von Thoinon und Sosistratos gestürzt, die → Pyrrhos herbeiriefen und ihm die Stadt übergaben (Diod. 22,2,1; 7,2–3).

H. Berve, Die Tyrannis bei den Griechen, 1967, 1, 458 ff.; 2, 732. K. MEI.

[3] Pythagoreer aus Syrakus. Die Überlieferung über ihn ist dürftig; er scheint die – ebenfalls für den Pythagoreer → Ekphantos [2] von Syrakus (51,1 und 5 DK = Hippolytos, refutationes 1,15 und Aetia 3,13,3) und für Herakleides Pontikos (fr. 104–110 Wehrli) bezeugte – Auffassung vertreten zu haben, daß sich die Erde um ihre Achse (bzw. die des Weltalls) drehe, während die

übrigen Himmelskörper stillstünden (Theophr. fr. 240 FHSG = Cic. ac. 2,123; vgl. Diog. Laert. 8,85); außerdem soll er zusätzlich zur Erde eine Gegenerde (ἀντίχθων) postuliert haben (Aet. 3,9,2) – eine Lehre, die sonst → Philolaos zugeschrieben wird.
→ Herakleides Pontikos; Pythagoras; Pythagoreische Schule

GUTHRIE, I, 327–329 • W. BURKERT, Lore and Science in Ancient Pythagoreanism, 1972, 341 • B. L. VAN DER WAERDEN, Die Pythagoreer, 1979, 462–464. C.RI.

Hilaeira s. Leukippides

Hilarianus, Q. Iulius s. Iulius

Hilarius
[1] H. von Poitiers.
A. BIOGRAPHIE B. WERKE C. THEOLOGIE

A. BIOGRAPHIE
Wahrscheinlich wurde H. im ersten Viertel des 4. Jh. in Poitiers geb. und als Erwachsener getauft (de synodis 91). Vor 356 wurde er Bischof von Poitiers; H. ist der erste bekannte Bischof dieses Ortes, in dem es wohl nur wenige Christen gab. 356 wurde H. auf einer Synode in Béziers auf Befehl des späteren Kaisers → Iulianus [11] in die Verbannung nach Kleinasien geschickt. Während früher ausschließlich eine längere Widerstandstätigkeit gegen den kirchenpolit. Kurs des Kaisers → Constantius [2] II. und seine gegen → Athanasios gerichteten Maßnahmen als Grund des Synodalurteils postuliert wurde, vermutet man jetzt auch polit. Verdächtigungen im Zusammenhang mit der fehlgeschlagenen Ursurpation des → Silvanus oder seiner Parteinahme für den als Hochverräter verurteilten → Lucifer von Calaris [8]; sicher ist das nicht. H. verbrachte sein Exil offenbar in Phrygien, nahm allerdings an Synoden teil und korrespondierte mit gallischen Bischöfen (de synodis 1 f.). Seit 358 wurde er zum konsequenten Vertreter einer theologischen Neuorientierung am Bekenntnis von Nicaea (325 n. Chr.) und versuchte, eine bestimmte östl. trinitätstheologische Option (die der Homoiusianer) und die westl. Gegner des subordinatianischen Reichskirchenkurses des Kaisers Constantius miteinander auszusöhnen, was auf der Reichssynode von Seleukia/Rimini endgültig scheiterte. Anfang 360 kehrte H. nach Gallien zurück, möglicherweise auch aufgrund von Nachrichten über die Usurpation Iulians. Vermutlich erst nach dem Ende seines Exils nahm H. Kontakte zu → Martinus von Tours auf (Greg. Tur. Franc. 1,36; Ven. Fort. vita Hilari 9 [33]; anders Sulp. Sev. vita Martini 5,1) und versuchte, in Gallien und Nordit. die homoiische Reichskirchentheologie zurückzudrängen. 367 oder 368 starb er in Poitiers; nur über seine letzten zehn Lebensj. sind einigermaßen zuverlässige Nachrichten erhalten.

B. WERKE
H. hat v. a. exegetische Komm. und Arbeiten zu kirchenpolit. Tagesfragen vorgelegt: Erh. ist ein vor der Exilszeit entstandener Komm. zum Matthäusevangelium; trotz einer ähnlichen exegetischen Methode liegt keine direkte lit. Abhängigkeit vom Matthäuskomm. des → Origenes vor. Ferner sind *Tractatus super Psalmos* aus den letzten Lebensj. überl. (CPL 428); hier werden die entsprechenden Arbeiten des Origenes benutzt. Einige Texte dürften auf Predigten zurückgehen. Die *Tractatus in Iob* sind bis auf Fr. verloren (CPL 429), ebenso ein nt. Werk (CPL 432). Zu den Schriften zu kirchenpolit. Tagesfragen zählt eine nur noch in Teilen erh. zweiteilige, urspr. komm. Slg. von Aktenstücken zur Gesch. des trinitätstheologischen Streites (CPL 436; ed. [3]), die vielleicht posthum zu einem *Opus historicum* vereint wurden. Mit seiner Schrift *De synodis* (CPL 434) informierte H. die gallischen Bischofskollegen über die Verhältnisse im Orient. Die Schrift *Contra Constantium* (CPL 461), erst nach dem Tode des Kaisers publiziert, enthält scharfe Polemiken (Constantius als Antichrist: § 4–7) und ist ein Reflex von H.' Enttäuschung über den fehlgeschlagenen Versuch, den Monarchen von seinem kirchenpolit. Kurs abzubringen, sicher kein Manifest der ›Trennung von Staat und Kirche‹. Das theologische Hauptwerk des H., *De trinitate* (CPL 433), wurde möglicherweise erst nachträglich auf seine jetzige Form von 12 B. erweitert. Es geht vom Taufbefehl (Mt 28,19) aus und entwickelt eine biblisch begründete Trinitätstheologie in Abgrenzung von arianischen und markellischen Entwürfen; der Entwurf steht in der Trad. lat. Trinitätstheologie (→ Tertullianus, → Novatianus), rezipiert aber auch östl. Entwürfe. Von einem *Liber hymnorum* sind Reste von drei Christushymnen erh. geblieben (CPL 463).

C. THEOLOGIE
Im Mittelpunkt des theologischen Interesses stehen Trinitätstheologie und Christologie: Vater und Sohn bilden eine Einheit (*unitas*), der Sohn existiert selbständig, aber sein ganzes Dasein wird ihm vom Vater geschenkt (de trinitate 8,20). Ihr Unterschied ist lediglich durch ihr wechselseitiges Verhältnis begründet: Der Vater zeugt, der Sohn wird geboren. H. vermittelte griech. Trinitätstheologie und Exegese in den Westen; darin übte er einen prägenden Einfluß auf folgende Generationen aus. Für die Verbreitung seines Kultes, v. a. in Gallien, spielt die Vita des → Venantius Fortunatus eine zentrale Rolle; sie entstand nach der Mitte des 6. Jh.

ED.: **1** J. DOIGNON, SChr 254/258, 1978/1979 (Comm. Mt.; CPL 430) **2** A. ZINGERLE, CSEL 22, 1891 (Tract. Ps.; CPL 428 [revisionsbedürftig]) **3** A. FEDER, CSEL 65, 1916, 43–187 (hist.; CPL 436) **4** PL 10, 479–546 (syn.; CPL 434; demnächst M. DURST, CSEL) **5** A. ROCHER, SChr 334, 1987 (contra Const.; CPL 461) **6** P. SMULDERS, CCL 62/62A, 1979/1980 (trin.; CPL 433) **7** A. FEDER, CSEL 65, 227–234 (hymn.; CPL 463).
LIT.: **8** H.CH. BRENNECKE, H.v.P. und die Bischofsopposition gegen Konstantius II. (Patristische Texte und

Studien 26), 1984 **9** P.C. Burns, The Christology of H. of P. Commentary on Matthew (Studia Ephemeridis Augustinianum 16), 1981 **10** J. Doignon, H. de P. avant l'exil, 1971 **11** Ders., in: HLL 5,§ 582 **12** Ders., s.v. H.v.P., RAC 15, 139–167 **13** M. Figura, Das Kirchenverständnis des H.v.P. (Freiburger Theologische Studien 127), 1984 **14** Hilaire et son temps, Actes du Colloque de Poitiers 29.9.–3.10.1968, 1969 **15** P. Smulders, La doctrine trinitaire de Saint H., 1944 **16** Ders., H.v.P., in: M. Greschat (Hrsg.), Gestalten der Kirchengesch., Bd. 1, 1984 (Ndr. 1993), 250–265 **17** Ders., H. of P.' Preface to his Opus historicum. Translation and Commentary (= Vigiliae Christianae Suppl. 29), 1995. C.M.

[2] Bischof von Arles (429–449). Sein Onkel Honoratus von Arles hatte um 410 auf Lerinum (Insel Lérins vor Cannes) ein Kloster gegründet, in das H. eintrat. Orientiert am ägypt. Mönchtum (Pachomios) strahlte Lerinum bald auf ganz Südfrankreich aus und stellte zahlreiche Bischöfe. Honoratus wurde 424 Metropolit von Arles, ihm folgte H., dessen Grabrede auf den Onkel erh. ist. Über das Leben des H. berichtet sein Schüler, Bischof Honoratus von Marseille († nach 492). Als H. seine Vorrangstellung in Gallien ausbauen wollte (Absetzung des Metropoliten Celidonius von Besançon wegen Verstößen gegen die Kirchendisziplin), entzog ihm Papst Leo I. 445 die Metropolitanrechte, die Arles erst 450 wiedererhielt.

Ed.: Honoratus, Vita Hilarii, PL 1219ff. • H., Vita Honorati, PL 50,1249ff. • H., epist. ad Eucherium, PL 50,1271.

Lit.: H. Jedin (Hrsg.), Hdb. der Kirchengesch. Bd II/1, 1973, 398f. • G. Langgärtner, Die Gallienpolitik der Päpste im 5. und 6. Jh. Eine Studie über den apostolischen Vikariat von Arles, 1964. RO.F.

Hildericus, Hilderich. Sohn des → Hunericus und der Eudokia [2], der Tochter Valentinians III. (Theoph. 5964; 6026), König der Vandalen 523–530 n. Chr. H. beendete die katholikenfeindliche Politik seiner Vorgänger und suchte die Annäherung an Byzanz (er prägte Münzen mit dem Bild des Iustinus I. [1. 94]), während sich das Verhältnis zu den Ostgoten erheblich verschlechterte. Die vandalische Opposition unter Führung des → Gelimer nutzte daher eine Niederlage der Truppen H.' gegen Araber in der Byzacena, um ihn abzusetzen und 533 n. Chr. hinzurichten (Prok. BV 3,9,1–26; 17,12; Iord. Get. 170), was Iustinianus [1] als Vorwand für seinen Vandalenkrieg nahm.

1 W. Hahn, Moneta Imperii Byzantini 1, 1973.

PLRE 2, 564f. • Chr. Courtois, Les vandales et l'afrique, 1955, bes. 267ff. • H.-J. Diesner, Das Vandalenreich, 1966, 94–97. M.MEI.

Hillel d. Ä., babylon. Abstammung, lebte z.Z. → Herodes' [1] d.Gr. (E. 1. Jh. v. Chr./Anf. 1. Jh. n. Chr.); Schüler der Pharisäer Schemaja und Abtalion. H. zählt zu den bedeutendsten »rabbinischen« Autoritäten aus der Zeit vor der Zerstörung des Tempels von → Jerusalem (70 n. Chr.). Die Trad. schreibt ihm die stark von der griech. Rhet. beeinflußten sieben Auslegungsregeln (*Middot*) sowie die Einführung des sog. Prosbul zu: Danach konnte ein Gläubiger seine Schuld auch nach einem Erlaßjahr (vgl. Dt 15,1–11) einfordern. H. wird in der rabbinischen Lit. klischeehaft dem strengen Rabbi Schammai gegenübergestellt, da er in halakhischen Fragen (→ Halakha) weniger rigoros entschied und v. a. die Bed. der Nächstenliebe betonte (vgl. bShab 31a). In der Darstellung seines besonnenen Handelns finden sich zahlreiche Gemeinsamkeiten mit hell. Gelehrtenbiographien.

N.N. Glatzer, Hillel. Repräsentant des klass. Judentums, 1966 • G. Stemberger, Einl. in Talmud und Midrasch, [8]1992, 72 • E. Urbach, The Sages, 1979, 579–593. B.E.

Himation s. Pallium

Himera (Ἱμέρα). Den nichtgriech. ON verstanden die Siedler als ἡμέρα (*hēméra*, »Tag«) und machten den Hahn zu ihrem Wappen (Mz.), worauf auch Pind. O. 12,13 anspielt. H. war außer → Mylai die einzige alte griech. Kolonie an der Nordküste Siziliens, weit gegen den phöniz. Bereich vorgeschoben, gegr. von Zankle aus – 240 J. vor der Zerstörung 409, also 649 v. Chr. (Diod. 13,62,4) – als ion.-dor. Siedlung (Thuk. 6,5,1). Den Wohlstand von H. im 6./5. Jh. bezeugt die reiche Mz.-Prägung (HN 143–146). Eine Votivinschr. aus Samos [1] bezeugt Kämpfe um 500 v. Chr. gegen die Sikanoi. Von dem durch → Theron von Akragas bedrohten Tyrannen → Terillos gerufen, landeten die Karthager 480 bei H., wurden aber von Theron im Bunde mit → Gelon [1] von Syrakusai vernichtend geschlagen (Hdt. 7,165–167; Diod. 11,20–22). Im Peloponnesischen Krieg stand H. treu zu Syrakusai (Thuk. 3,115,1; 6,62,2; 7,1,1; 7,1,3; 7,58,2; Diod. 13,4,2; 13,7,6; 13,8,4; 13,12,4). 409 fiel H. einer großen karthag. Offensive zum Opfer und wurde zur Rache für die Rolle, die H. in der Schlacht 480 gespielt hatte, total zerstört (Diod. 11,59–62; Strab. 6,2,6); die Überlebenden wurden in der karthag. Kolonie Thermai Himeraiai angesiedelt (Diod. 13,79,8; 13,114,1).

Die Stadt [2; 3; 4; 5] entwickelte sich sowohl auf der Anhöhe (Oberstadt) als auch nahe der Flußmündung (Unterstadt). Oberstadt: 1. Phase (E. 7. bis E. 6. Jh. v. Chr.): einzelne Häuser; 2. Phase (E. 6./Anf. 5. bis E. 5. Jh. v. Chr.): parallel angeordnete isolierte Bauten auf dem ganzen Plateau. Im NO-Bereich trapezförmiges *temenos* (2. H. 7.–E. 5. Jh. v. Chr.) mit vier sakralen Bauten. Im Westen des *temenos* eine Agora (?). An der Südseite des Hügels Mauerspuren. Unterstadt (bestimmt durch die Existenz des Flußhafens): 1. Phase (Mitte 7. bis Mitte 6. Jh.): spärliche Häuser; 2. Phase (Mitte/E. 6. bis Anf. 5. Jh.): einzelne regelmäßige Bauten. Dor. Nike-Tempel (480–470 v. Chr.). Im Osten des Flusses Viertel außerhalb der Stadt (6. Jh. v. Chr.). Drei Nekropolenbereiche im Westen, Norden und Süden der Siedlung. Das Territorium von H. erstreckte sich ungefähr zw. Chephalodion und Thermai [6; 7].

1 G. Manganaro, Una dedica di Samo rivolta non a Leukaspis, ma a Hera Thespis?, in: ZPE 101, 1994, 120–126 2 N. Bonacasa, s. v. Imara, EAA[2] 3, 1995, 89–93 3 N. Allegro, H. 1989–1993, in: Kokalos 39–40, II 2, 1993/4, 1119–1131 4 Ders., Le fasi dell'abitato di H., in: H. P. Isler u. a. (Hrsg.), Wohnbauforschung in Zentral- und Westsizilien, 1997, 65–80 5 S. Vassallo, Indagini in un quartiere della città bassa di H., in: Ebd. 6 O. Belvedere, Prospezione archeologica nel territorio imerese (1986–1995), in: Ebd. 7 S. Vassallo, Il territorio di H. in età arcaica, in: Kokalos 42, 1996, 199–223. GI. F./Ü: V. S.

Himeraios (Ἱμεραῖος). Sohn des Phanostratos aus Phaleron, athen. Rhetor des 4. Jh. v. Chr., Bruder des → Demetrios [4] von Phaleron, Priester des Poseidon (Syll.[3] 289,18); Gegner der Makedonen und Ankläger des Demosthenes im Harpalosprozeß (→ Harpalos) 323 v. Chr. (Plut. mor. 846C). H. flüchtete nach der Niederlage Athens im Lamischen Krieg 322 v. Chr. nach Aigina, wurde in Abwesenheit auf Antrag des Demades zum Tode verurteilt, ergriffen und auf Befehl des → Antipatros [1] hingerichtet (Arr. FGrH 156 F 9 (13); Lukian. Demosthenis Enkomion 31; Plut. Demosthenes 28,4).

Davies, S. 108 · Develin, Nr. 1406 · PA 7578 · Traill, PPA 535130. J. E.

Himeras. Name zweier Flüsse Siziliens, die, nicht fern voneinander am S. Salvatore (1910 m) bei Polizzi in entgegengesetzte Richtungen entspringend (h. Imera Settentrionale, Imera Meridionale), als ein einziger Fluß und als NS-Mittellinie der Insel galten, obgleich die östl. Hälfte der so geteilten Insel fast doppelt so groß ist wie die westliche. Belegstellen: Pol. 7,4,2; Liv. 24,6,7; Strab. 6,2,1; Mela 2,119; Vitr. 8,3,7; Sil. 14,233. E. O.

Himerios A. Leben B. Werk C. Charakteristik

A. Leben

Aus seinen eigenen Reden und anderen Quellen (Lib., Eun. vit. soph. 14 (494), Suda) ergibt sich: Griech. Rhetor aus Prusias/Bithynien, ca. 320 bis nach 383 n. Chr., Sohn des Rhetors Ameinias. Nach seinem bis Anf. der 340er Jahre währenden Studium in Athen war H. zunächst als Lehrer der Rhet. in Konstantinopel tätig (343–352). Von mehreren in dieser Zeit unternommenen Reisen führte ihn eine nach Nikomedeia (um 350), wo er in einem Redewettstreit gegen → Libanios unterlag (Lib. epist. 742,1F = 654W; die Rede des Lib. liegt vor, decl. 46, die des H. nicht, or. 53), eine andere zu Constantius [2] II. nach Sirmium (März 351). Etwa zwischen 356 und 361 übte H. seine Lehrtätigkeit in Athen aus, wo er offenbar Erfolg hatte und hochgestellte Personen als Schüler gewinnen konnte, z. B. → Basileios [1] von Kaisareia, → Gregorios [3] von Nazianz (Soz. 6,17,1; Sokr. 4,26,6), kurzzeitig auch den späteren Kaiser Iulian (i. J. 355: Greg. Naz. or. 5,23); auch erhielt er das athenische Bürgerrecht. Die zunehmende Popularität seines christl. Konkurrenten → Prohairesios bewog H., Athen zu verlassen. In Antiocheia schloß er sich Kaiser → Iulian [11] an und folgte ihm bis zu dessen Tod (363). Bis 369 sind seine weiteren Lebensumstände unbekannt; danach, vielleicht durch den Tod des Prohairesios veranlaßt, kehrte er nach Athen zurück, wo er sich bis zu seinem Tod aufhielt. Daß er unverhohlen Nichtchrist blieb (er war in den Mithraskult eingeweiht, or. 41,1; vgl. auch Phot. 108b 42–109a 1), scheint ihm unter Valens oder Gratianus Probleme bereitet zu haben (or. 46,1 f.). Noch vor seinem Tod starb eine Tochter sowie sein begabter Sohn (or. 7 f.).

B. Werk

Die Überl. von Reden des H. stammt aus mehreren Quellen: 32 Deklamationen, z. T. verstümmelt, bietet der Cod. Par. Suppl. 352; Photios (107b 17–27 und 108a 4–b 27) nennt 72 Titel; zusammen mit dem Material weiterer Hss. (Oxon. Barocc. 131,3; Monac. 564) sowie neueren Entdeckungen sind (je nach Zählweise) 75 bzw. 80 Titel bekannt. Eine systematische Anordnung innerhalb des (vielleicht auf eine durch H. selbst oder einen seiner Schüler besorgte Auswahl zurückgehenden) Corpus ist nicht zu erkennen; es enthält sowohl Meletai (→ *exercitatio*) über gängige Themen der klass. Zeit als auch Gelegenheitsreden zu aktuellen Anlässen wie der An- oder Abreise hoher Beamter; mehrere Reden behandeln Themen des Schulbetriebes (Begrüßung/Abschied von Schülern, Auseinandersetzung mit Rivalen); Kaiser- → Panegyrik findet sich ebenso wie Lobreden auf Städte. Insgesamt bleiben die unpolit. Reden des H. im Rahmen der für die spätant. Sophistik typischen Themen. Die Konventionalität und die Vermeidung jeder präzisen Angabe beeinträchtigen den Quellenwert der meisten Reden für Zeit und Person ihres Autors und der Adressaten erheblich (Ausnahme: or. 7 f.).

C. Charakteristik

Der affektierte und in höchstem Maße gekünstelte Stil des H. rekurriert einerseits auf das Vorbild der klass. Redner, andererseits aber auch intensiv auf Platon und Rhetoren wie Aristeides [3] und Polemon. Die häufigen Musenanrufe, Selbstbezeichnungen des Autors als Poet und Sänger sowie die sehr zahlreichen Zitate aus ion. und aiol. Poesie (Sappho, Alkaios, Anakreon, Simonides) machen deutlich, daß H.' Prosa mit der Dichtung zu konkurrieren beansprucht. Gesuchte Wortwahl, künstliche Kommatisierung und Rhythmisierung (mit Übergang zu akzentbestimmten Klauseln) und die Häufigkeit gorgianischer Figuren verstärken den Eindruck des Manierismus. H. repräsentiert eine den strikten Klassizisten (wie z. B. Libanios, nach dessen Meinung der Stil des H. nicht den attizistischen Vorschriften gerecht wird, epist. 742,1F) zuwiderlaufende Stiltendenz, die zwar vielfach Anerkennung (Eun.; Phot. 107b 27–108a 3), aber keine Nachahmer fand.

ED.: A. COLONNA, 1951 (dazu: N. TERZAGHI, in: GGA 208, 1954, 72–79).
LIT.: 1 T. D. BARNES, H. and the fourth century, in: CPh 82, 1987, 206–225 2 N. BERNARDI, Un regard sur la vie étudiante à Athènes au milieu du IVe s. après J.-C., in: REG 103, 1990, 79–94 3 E. BERTI, L'esemplare di Imerio letto da Fozio, in: Studi Classici Orientali 22, 1973, 111–114 4 G. CUFFARI, I riferimenti poetici di Imerio, Università di Palermo, Istituto di filologia greca. Quaderni 12, 1983 5 S. EITREM, L. AMUNDSEN, Fragments from the speeches of H. P. Osl.inv.no.1478, in: CeM 17, 1956, 23–30 6 H. GÄRTNER, s. v. H., RAC 15, 167–73 7 C. GALLAVOTTI, Echi di Alceo e di Menandro nei retori tardivi, in: RFIC 93, 1965, 135–146 8 A. GUIDA, Frammenti inediti, in: Prometheus 5, 1979, 193–216 9 T. HÄGG, Photios als Vermittler ant. Lit., 1975, 128f., 138f., 143–159 10 G. A. KENNEDY, Greek Rhetoric under Christian Emperors, 1983, 140–149 11 J. D. MEERWALDT, Epithalamica I: De H. Sapphus imitatore, in: Mnemosyne 4 Ser. 7, 1954, 19–38 12 NORDEN, Kunstprosa, 428–431 13 E. RICHTSTEIG, H. und Platon, Byz.-Neugriech. Jbb. 2, 1921, 1–32 14 K. WEITZMANN (Hrsg.), Age of Spirituality, 1980, 53–73.

M. W.

Himeros (Ἵμερος, »Sehnsucht«). Die Personifikation des liebenden Sehnens. Zusammen mit → Eros [1] begleitet er Aphrodite (seit Hes. theog. 201); mit den → Charites (den Göttinnen der »Anmut«), wohnt er in der Nähe der Musen (Hes. theog. 64, eine poetologische Aussage). Später ist er fest mit Aphrodite und Eros verbunden, bildlich auch mit → Dionysos und → Pothos; von Eros und Pothos ist er ikonographisch ununterscheidbar. Eine H.-Statue von → Skopas stand im Aphroditetempel von Megara (Paus. 1,43,6).

A. HERMARY, s. v. H., LIMC 5, 425f. • H. A. SHAPIRO, Personifications in Greek Art, 1993, 110–120.

F. G.

Himilkon (*[ʾ]hmlkt = »Bruder des Mlkt«, Ἰμίλκων).
[1] Karthag. Feldherr, Sohn eines Hanno, Urenkel des Magoniden → Hamilkar [1] und Verwandter des → Hannibal [1], den er 407 v. Chr. als (Flotten-?)Stratege nach Sizilien begleitete und nach dessen Tod H. den Oberbefehl übernahm (Diod. 13,80; Iust. 19,2,7). H. belagerte, eroberte und zerstörte 406/5 → Akragas, anschließend → Gela und → Kamarina, scheiterte aber noch 405 bei der Belagerung von → Syrakusai an einer Seuche in seinem Heer und schloß einen Friedensvertrag mit → Dionysios [1] I. (Diod. 13,86–88; 108–111; 114; StV 2,210) [1. 159–162; 2. 116–123; 3. 60f.; 4]. Im folgenden Krieg Karthagos gegen Syrakus um die Griechenstädte West- und Südsiziliens wurde 397 v. Chr. H. erneut als Oberfeldherr entsandt; nach dem Verlust von → Motya eroberte er mit Unterstützung des → Mago im J. 396 die karthag. Positionen von Panormos aus rasch zurück und zog via Messana und Katane gegen Syrakus, wo nach anfänglichen Erfolgen und teilweisen Zerstörungen im Stadtgebiet dem H. angesichts einer neuen Epidemie im Belagerungsheer nur der (heimliche?) Rückzug seiner Bürgertruppen bei Preisgabe der restlichen Armee blieb (Diod. 14,49; 55–57; 59f.; 62f.; 70–73; 75). In Karthago wurde H. zwar nicht wegen des Mißerfolgs verurteilt, ging aber in den Freitod (Diod. 14,76) [1. 162–165; 2. 128–135; 3. 65–67].
[2] Befehligte im J. 307 v. Chr. gemeinsam mit → Adherbal [1] ein karthag. Heer gegen die syrakusanischen Invasionstruppen unter → Archagathos' [1] Feldherrn Eumachos und versperrte bei → Tunes dem → Agathokles [2] den Vormarsch ins Binnenland (Diod. 20,59–61) [1. 166f.].
[3] Verteidigte als karthag. Kommandant von Lilybaion und Vorgänger des → Geskon [3] in den Jahren 250–241(?) v. Chr. die Stadt mit Hilfe von Hanno und → Karthalo geschickt gegen die röm. Belagerer (Pol. 1,42,7–43; 45; 48; 53,5; Diod. 24,1) [1. 167f.].
[4] Karthag. Feldherr auf Sizilien 214–212 v. Chr., Vertrauter des → Hippokrates [8], mit dem H. bei Syrakus gegen den röm. Konsul M. → Claudius [I 11] Marcellus kämpfte, nachdem er persönlich die karthag. Regierung zu einer energischeren Sizilienpolitik bewogen und dann durch die Eroberung von → Akragas die Sikuler zur erneuten Allianz gebracht hatte. H. starb bei einer Epidemie im belagerten Syrakus (Liv. 24,35,3–39; 25,26) [1. 170f.; 2. 359f., 367–369].
[5] H. Phameas (Pol. 36,8: *Hamilkar*; Liv. per. 50: *Hamilco*; Eun. fr. 82: *Milkon*) [1. 22, Anm. 1300]. Als karthag. Reiterführer im 3. Pun. Krieg brachte H. den Römern im J. 149 v. Chr. am Tunes-See durch Blitzattacken immer wieder Verluste bei, bis ihn → Gulussa aufspürte und H. mit einem starken Reiterkontingent zu den Römern überlief (App. Lib. 100,471–101,473; 107,503–109,516; Diod. 32,17). Nach Rom geschickt und dort reich belohnt, kehrte H. zur weiteren Unterstützung der Römer nach Nordafrika zurück (Pol. 36,8; App. Lib. 109,517f.) [1. 171f.].
[6] Legendärer (?) karthag. Seefahrer, wohl Zeitgenosse des → Hanno [1]; erster namentlich bekannter Entdekker der Küsten NW-Europas, von dessen vermutlichem Fahrtenbericht einige Reflexe in → Avienus' *Ora maritima* enthalten sein könnten (vgl. Avien. 414) [2. 84,1]. H. erreichte sein Ziel, die *exterae Europae* (Plin. nat. 2,169), mit den sog. Zinninseln, den Oestrumniden (Avien. 113) bzw. den Kassiteriten (vgl. Hdt. 3,115), die in den h. Scilly-Inseln vermutet werden [1. 158; 2. 85,10]. Umstritten ist, inwieweit H. im offiziellen Auftrag karthag. Behörden reiste, etwa zur Monopolisierung des Zinn- und Bleihandels [2. 85], oder ob die singuläre Pioniertat ohne derartige Zielsetzungen stattfand [5. 1152; 6. 267].

1 GEUS 2 HUSS 3 L. M. HANS, Karthago und Sizilien, 1983 4 M. ZAHRNT, Die Verträge zwischen Dionysios I. und den Karthagern, in: ZPE 71, 1988, 209–228 5 H. TEIDLER, s. v. Himilkon (6), KlP 2, 1967 6 W. AMELING, Karthago, 1993.

L.-M. G.

Himjaritisch s. Altsüdarabisch

Himmelskreise s. Kykloi

Hin. Ägypt. Hohlmaß für Flüssiges und Trockenes zu 1/10 *ḥqꜣt* (Hekat) im Alten Reich bzw. 1/40 *jpt* (Oipe) im Neuen Reich, entsprechend ca. 0,48 l [3. 1201], bei geringfügigen Abweichungen nach oben [1. 1644] und unten [2. 1152]. Aus demot. Zeit ist H. als einzige durch erh. Maßgefäße gesicherte Einheit überl. Die Relationen zu → Artabe und → Choinix sind strittig [3. 1210]. Aus dem Neuen Reich sind ebenfalls Maßgefäße auf der Basis des H. überl.: *mḥt* = 1 H., *pgꜣ* = 1/4 H., *mnḏqt* = 50 H., die jedoch ohne allg. verbindliche Eichung gewesen sein dürften [3. 1202].

1 O. Viedebantt, s. v. H., RE 8, 1644–1649
2 H. Chantraine, s. v. H., KlP 2, 1152 3 W. Helck, S. Vleming, s. v. Maße u. Gewichte, LÄ 3, 1199–1214.

H.-J. S.

Hinkiamben s. Metrik

Hiob. Zentrale Figur des gleichnamigen biblischen Buches, das im hebr. Kanon zu den *Kᵉtūbīm*, den Schriften, gehört. Die Etym. des Namens führt auf ein anscheinend edomitisches Wort *Ayyab*, das in etwa mit »Büßer, Bekehrter« übersetzt werden kann. Im hebr. *ʾĪyōḇ* klingt das Wort Feind an, so daß der Name auch »der Angefeindete« (sc. »von Gott«) bedeuten kann. Der Edomiter H., dessen Gottesfurcht auf Intervention Satans auf eine harte Probe durch Gott selbst gestellt wird, beklagt zwar sein Schicksal, bleibt Gott aber stets treu ergeben und wird für seine Leiden gegen Ende seines Lebens von Gott belohnt.

Die Idee des leidenden Gerechten fand ihren Niederschlag wiederum in der nachbiblischen Lit.; im Talmud sind Person und Lebensdaten H.s allerdings umstritten – bis hin zur Aussage, H. habe nie gelebt, er und sein Los sei lediglich als Gleichnis aufzufassen. H.s Leidensweg wird in der → Haggada anschaulich geschildert; in seiner (rel.) Bed. wird er, obschon Nichtisraelit, den Patriarchen gleichgestellt.

A. Berliner, Zur Auslegung des Buches Ijob, 1913 • R. Ecker, Die arab. Job-Übers. des Gaon Saadja ben Josef, 1962 • G. Fohrer, Das Buch H., 1963 • N. Glatzer, The dimensions of Job, 1969 • P. Huber, H., Dulder oder Rebell?, 1986 • J. Lévêque, Job et son Dieu, 1970 • A. Künzli, Gotteskrise: Fragen zu H., 1998 • N. Tur-Sinai (Torcyner), The book of Job, 1957 • P. Zerafa, The wisdom of God in the book of Job, 1978 • J. Ziegler, Beitr. zum griech. Iob, 1985. Y. D.

Hipana (Ἵπανα). Kleine Sikulerstadt (Pol. 1,24,8–13; Diod. 23,9, hsl. *Sittanan*), in Zusammenhang mit den Kämpfen des 1. Pun. Krieges 261/258 v. Chr. erwähnt. Steph. Byz. (s. v. Ἵ.) bezeichnet H. als »Stadt im Gefolge Karthagos« (πόλις περὶ Καρχηδόνα). Sie wurde von den Römern 258 v. Chr. mit Mühe erobert. Die Lokalisierung am Monte dei Cavalli bei h. Prizzi ist durch Br.-Mz. mit Stier (Rv.) und Legende ΙΠΑ (Abschnitt), die auf pun. Exemplaren neu geprägt wurden, gesichert. Weitere Funde: Silberne *lítrai* nach agrigentinischem Muster (Av.: Adler auf Kapitell, umgeben vom Stammesnamen Ἱπανατᾶν), Frg. eines Kerykeion. Plin. nat. 3,8,91 erwähnt *Hyppanenses* unter den *stipendiarii* Roms.

G. Manganaro, Un Kerykeion perduto degli Hipanatai e la ubicazione di Hipana, in: Orbis Terrarum 3, 1997, 127–130, mit Taf. 1–7. GI. MA./Ü: H. D.

Hippalektryon (Ἱππαλεκτρυών, »Roßhahn«). Fabulöses → Mischwesen, aus den Körperteilen von Hahn und Pferd zusammengesetzt. Lit. frühestes Zeugnis ist Aischyl. Myrmidones fr. 134 Radt; die Erwähnungen bei Aristophanes (Pax 1177; Av. 800; Ran. 932, wie Aischyl. mit dem Epitheton *xuthós*, »bräunlich«, »blond«) sind Tragödienparodie. Bei Hesychios und Photios s. v. und den Scholien zu den Aristophanesstellen besitzt das Wesen einen Vogelkopf; dem steht der arch. Befund (Hinterteil eines Hahnes mit zwei Hahnenbeinen, Vorderteil eines Pferdes mit zwei Pferdebeinen) diametral gegenüber. Sehr oft wird H. als Reittier dargestellt. Er läßt sich beinahe nur in Attika in der Zeit zw. 560 und 470 v. Chr. nachweisen. Kompositionell verwandt sind Mischwesen wie der »Panther-Hahn« oder der »Mädchenhahn« [1. 432–433]. Ungewiß ist die oriental. Herkunft, die bei Mischwesen jedoch generell plausibel ist.

1 D. Williams, s. v. H., LIMC 5.1, 427–433.

Abb.: Ders., s. v. H., LIMC 5.2, 301–308. JO. S.

Hippalos (Ἵππαλος).

[1] Sohn des Sosos (?); Vater des Gaustrategen Theomnestos (PP 1/8, 260; 3/9, 5147) und der Athlophore Batra (PP 3/9, 5051). 185–169 v. Chr. Priester des Königskultes in Ptolemais Hermu; 182 und 173 als eponymer Offizier belegt; vor Nov. 176 (seit 185?) ἀρχισωματοφύλαξ (*archisōmatophýlax*, »Erzleibwächter«) und erster *stratēgós* der Thebais (der Hoftitel ist abhängig von der Lesung in PLond VII 2188, 214); von Nov. 176 bis wenigstens Mai 172 τῶν πρώτων φίλων (*tōn prṓtōn phílōn*) und *epistratēgós* der ganzen *chṓra*.

J. D. Thomas, The Epistrategos in Ptolemaic and Roman Egypt 1, 1975, 87 ff., Nr. 1 • PP 1/8, 193; 2/8, 1919; 3/9, 5155. W. A.

[2] Sonst unbekannter griech. Seefahrer, der dem peripl. m. r. 57 (GGM I 298 f.; → Periplus) zufolge den durch den SW-Monsun ermöglichten direkten Seeweg von Äg. bzw. Arabia nach India entdeckte; der Wind heiße nach H. ἵππαλος. Diesen Namen gibt auch Plin. (nat. 6,100; 6,104; dagegen [1]: Verschreibung für *hyphalum*), der 6,172 nach anderen dazu noch ein Vorgebirge Afrikas so nennt; Ptol. 4,7,41 kennt dort ein H.-Meer. Da u. a. Strab. (2,5,12; 17,1,13) diesen Seeweg als neuerdings rege befahren bezeichnet, ist die Entdekkung des H. wohl in das späte 2. oder frühe 1. Jh. v. Chr. zu datieren.

1 S. Mazzarino, Sul nome del vento »hipalus« in Plinio, in: Helikon 22/27, 1982/87, vii-xiv.

A. Dihle, Ant. und Orient, 1984 • A. Tchernia, Moussons et Monnaies, in: Annales: Histoire, Sciences sociales 50, 1995, 991–1009 • J. Reade (Hrsg.), The Indian Ocean in Antiquity, 1996. K. BRO.

Hipparchia (Ἱππαρχία). Kynische Philosophin aus Maroneia in Thrakien (*floruit* 111. Ol. = 336–333 v. Chr.), aus reicher Familie, Schwester des Kynikers → Metrokles, der Schüler des → Krates von Theben war. H. wollte letzteren heiraten und drohte für den Fall der Weigerung ihrer Eltern mit Selbstmord (Diog. Laert. 6,96). Sie lebte nach Art der Kyniker und begleitete Krates ständig. Mit ihm vereinigte sie sich sexuell in aller Öffentlichkeit (als κυνογαμία/*kynogamía*, »Hundehochzeit«, bezeichnet) und übte sich dadurch in Gleichgültigkeit (ἀδιαφορία, *adiaphoría*). Sie verblüffte → Theodoros von Kyrene, als sie ihm einen Trugschluß präsentierte, auf den er nichts zu antworten wußte. Damit stellte sie ihre Fähigkeiten als eine Philosophin unter Beweis, die ihre Zeit lieber zur intellektuellen Bildung nutzte als am Webstuhl zu arbeiten (Diog. Laert. 6,98). H., die einzige bekannte kynische Philosophin, verkörpert eine Auffassung von Ehe und Sexualität, die mit der von den Kynikern gepriesenen Ablehnung der menschlichen Kultur und der Rückkehr zur Natur im Einklang steht. Diog. Laert 96–98 erwähnt keine Schriften der H., doch kennt die Suda s. v. Ἱππαρχία die ›Abhandlungen der Philosophen‹ (Φιλοσόφων ὑποθέσεις), die ›Beweisführungen‹ (Ἐπιχειρήματα) und die ›Fragestellungen‹ (Προτάσεις), die an Theodoros von Kyrene gerichtet waren.
→ Kynische Schule; Philosophinnen

SSR II, 577–579 • SSR V 1 • L. Paquet, Les cyniques grecs. Fragments et témoignages, ²1988, 113–115 • A.J. Malherbe, The Cynic epistles, 1977 (von Krates an H.: 53–89) • J. M. García González, Hiparquia, la de Maronea, filósofo cínico, in: Ders., A. Pociña Pérez (Hrsg.), Studia Graecolatina C. Sanmillán in memoriam dicata, 1988, 179–187 • T. Dorandi, Figure femminili della filosofia antica, in: F. de Martino (Hrsg.), Rose di Pieria, 1991, 263–278, bes. 268–273. M. G.-C./Ü: J. DE.

Hipparchos (Ἵππαρχος).

[1] Zweiter Sohn des → Peisistratos und einer Athenerin. Zusammen mit seinem älteren Bruder → Hippias [1] und dem jüngeren Thessalos trat H. nach dem Tod des Vaters (528/7 v. Chr.) dessen Erbe an (Thuk. 6,55; [Aristot.] Ath. pol. 18,1). Anders als Hippias zeigte H. kein polit. Profil. Er widmete sich der aristokratischen Geselligkeit und Kultur und lud u. a. → Anakreon [1] von Teos und → Simonides von Keos nach Athen ein (Plat. Hipparch. 228b-d). Nach seiner Ermordung durch → Harmodios und → Aristogeiton [1] an den Panathenäen von 514 v. Chr. (Thuk. 6,54; 56; 59; [Aristot.] Ath. pol. 18,2; → Tyrannenmord) erschien H. als Tyrann schlechthin. Die Überlieferung neigte daher früh zur Legendenbildung; so kritisch schon Thukydides (1,20).

H. Berve, Die Tyrannis bei den Griechen, 1967, 63 ff., 554 ff. • L. de Libero, Die Archaische Tyrannis, 1996, 116 ff. • K.-W. Welwei, Athen, 1992, 247 ff. B. P.

[2] Komödiendichter, den die Suda der Alten Komödie zurechnet [1. test.], den aber die vier erh. Stücktitel ›Die Geretteten‹ (Ἀνασῳζόμενοι), ›Der Maler‹ (Ζωγράφος), ›Thais‹ (Θαΐς), ›Das nächtliche Fest‹ (Παννυχίς, auch: Hetärenname) und die fünf erh. Frg. als Dichter der Neuen Komödie erweisen.

1 PCG V, 605–607. H.-G. NE.

[3] Pythagoreer, dessen Historizität unsicher ist; er wird teils mit → Hippasos (Tert. anim. 5,2; Macr. somn. 1,14,19), teils mit → Archippos verwechselt (beide 5. Jh. v. Chr.) (Olympiodoros in Plat. Phaid. 61d, S. 57,8 f. Westerink, daraus Schol. in Plat. Phaid. 61d). Aus der Iambl. v. P. 73 und 246 zugrundeliegenden Überlieferung und dem gefälschten Brief des → Lysis an H. scheint die Nachricht abgeleitet, er sei wegen Veröffentlichung der pythagoreischen Lehre aus dem Geheimbund ausgeschlossen worden (Clem. Al. strom. 5,57,2 f., bei [1] auf Hippasos bezogen). Von einer neupythagoreischen Fälschung ›Über die Euthymie‹ sind Auszüge erhalten [2].
→ Pythagoreische Schule

1 Diels/Kranz, I, 108 2 H. Thesleff, The Pythagorean Texts of the Hellenistic Period, 1965, 89–91. C. RI.

[4] H. von Stageira. Schüler und Testamentsvollstrekker (s. Diog. Laert. 5,12) des Aristoteles, Verf. einer Schrift ›Was ist das Männliche und das Weibliche bei den Göttern, und was ist Heirat‹ (Τί τὸ ἄρρεν καὶ θῆλυ παρὰ θεοῖς καὶ τίς ὁ γάμος: Suda s. v.; Zum Problem der philos. Mythendeutung vgl. Aristot. metaph. 1000a 5 ff.). Er ist wohl nicht identisch mit dem H., welcher in → Theophrastos' Testament (Diog. Laert. 5,51 ff.) als sein Geschäftsführer erwähnt wird.

H. B. Gottschalk, Notes on the Wills of the Peripatetic Scholarchs, in: Hermes 100, 1972, 318 Anm. 3, 331 f. H. G.

[5] Hell. Dichter. Athenaios (3,101a; 9,393c = SH 496–497) zitiert vier Hexameter kulinarisch-gastronomischen Inhalts aus seiner ›Ägypt. Ilias‹ (über die Erlesenheit von *vulva eiecticia*, vgl. dazu Plin. nat. 11,210), und gegen den ägypt. Brauch, Wachteln zu rupfen). Er muß daher in die Homer parodierende ep.-gastronomische Dichtung eingeordnet werden.
→ Archestratos [2]; Gastronomische Dichtung; Matron von Pitane S. FO./Ü: T. H.

[6] H. aus Nikaia in Bithynien, griech. Astronom und Geograph. Seine (von Ptolemaios zitierten) Beobachtungen von Äquinoktien liegen zw. 162 und 128 v. Chr. und scheinen vorwiegend auf Rhodos stattgefunden zu haben. Seine Werke, die er selbst gesammelt hat (Ptol. syntaxis 3,1 p. 207,18: Ἀναγραφὴ τῶν ἰδίων συνταγμάτων), basieren auf bes. genauen Beobachtungen und zeichnen sich durch eine äußerst strenge Skepsis gegenüber den Theorien seiner Vorgänger sowie eine Abneigung gegen alles Hypothetische aus.

A. Logik B. Astronomie C. Geographie

A. Logik

Nach Plutarch (symp. 732f; De Stoicorum repugnatione 1047d) kritisierte H. die Lösung einer Aufgabe der Kombinatorik durch → Chrysippos [1]. Die Zuweisung algebraischer Arbeiten in arab. Quellen beruht vermutlich auf Verwechslung.

B. Astronomie

Einzig erh. Werk ist ein an einen (Schüler?) Aischrion gerichteter kritischer Komm. (3 B.) zu der Himmelsbeschreibung, die → Aratos [4] nach → Eudoxos [1] von Knidos in seinem erfolgreichen Lehrgedicht *Phainómena* gegeben hatte (Τῶν Ἀράτου καὶ Εὐδόξου Φαινομένων ἐξηγήσεως βιβλία τρία). H. berichtigt darin die geogr. Breite Athens (37°) sowie die gleichzeitigen Auf- und Untergänge (*synanatolaí* und *synkatadýseis*) der extrazodiakalen Sternbilder unter Hinweis auf die verschiedene Ausdehnung der Sternbilder und die unterschiedliche Aufgangsdauer der Ekliptikzwölftel. Der anschließende Fixsternkatalog ist auf das Zentrum der Weltkarte des → Eratosthenes, Rhodos (36°), bezogen. Angehängt ist ein Verzeichnis von markanten Sternen, an denen man die 24 Äquatorialstunden ablesen kann [2]. Die Berechnungen setzen eine Sehnen-(Sinus-) Tabelle voraus, wie sie Ptol. syntaxis 1,10f. nach H. schuf. Nach Theons Komm. zur *Sýntaxis* (1 p. 110 Halma) hat H. eine bes. Abh. darüber verfaßt (Περὶ τῆς πραγματείας τῶν ἐν κύκλῳ εὐθειῶν βιβλία ιβ'). H. ist somit Schöpfer der sphärischen Trigonometrie. Weitere theoretische Arbeiten (Liste: [3. 15f.]): über gleichzeitige Auf- und Untergänge (ἡ τῶν συνανατολῶν πραγματεία und Περὶ τῆς τῶν ιβ' ζῳδίων ἀναφορᾶς), Positionen und Entfernung von Sonne und Mond (Adrastos bei Theon Smyrnaeus 197 H.: zwei B. Περὶ μεγεθῶν καὶ ἀποστημάτων ἡλίου καὶ σελήνης), Sonnenfinsternisse (Achilleus, Commentarius in Arati relationes [4] p. 47,14), Parallaxe (Ptol. syntaxis 5,19 p. 450,21–451,5: mindestens 2 B. Παραλλακτικά), Gravitation (Simpl. In Aristot. De cael. 1,8 p. 264,25–267,6 H.: Περὶ τῶν διὰ βαρύτητα κάτω φερομένων), Präzession der Jahrpunkte (Ptol. syntaxis 7,2 p. 12,21 Περὶ τῆς μεταπτώσεως τῶν τροπικῶν καὶ ἰσημερινῶν σημείων), Länge des Sonnenjahres (Ptol. syntaxis 3,1 p. 207,20: Περὶ τοῦ ἐνιαυσίου μεγέθους βιβλίον ἕν) und des Monats (Titel erschlossen nach Galen: Περὶ μηνιαίνου χρόνου), die Breitenbewegung des Mondes (Περὶ τῆς κατὰ πλάτος μηνιαίνας κινήσεως), kalendarische Schaltmonate und -tage (Ptol. syntaxis 3,1 p. 207,7: Περὶ ἐμβολίμων μηνῶν τε καὶ ἡμερῶν). Pappos Collectio 6,70–71 p. 554–556 Hu. bezeugt ferner eine Arbeit über Größe und Entfernungen von Sonne und Mond. Sein Parapegma wurde von → Ptolemaios in den *Pháseis* benutzt. Schließlich beobachtete H. auch das Wetter (Ail. nat. 7,8). Gelegentliche Erwähnungen bei Vettius Valens (9,12,10), bes. in der zodiakalen Geographie (App. 3,14) sind ebenso zweifelhaft wie ein *Prooímion* zu Aratos. [4. 102,2 app. crit.].

Der verschollene Sternkatalog (Ptol. syntaxis 7,1 p. 3,8 Αἱ περὶ τῶν ἀπλανῶν ἀναγραφαί, vgl. Plin. nat. 2,95) fußt auf den Angaben der eratosthenischen *Katasterismoí* und rechnet mit ekliptikalen Koordinaten. Er setzt die Benutzung von Präzisionsinstrumenten, der »hipparchischen« → Dioptra (Prokl. Hypoth. 4,73.87) oder eines Globus, voraus. Sein Umfang wird auf nicht viel mehr als 850 Sterne geschätzt (die Angabe von 1080 Sternen [4. 128[13]] ist wohl falsch). Ptolemaios hat ihn erweitert und unter Berücksichtigung der Präzession korrigiert. Diese wurde von H. zuerst bei der Beobachtung von Spica (α Vir) im Vergleich mit jenen Werten, die → Timocharis und Aristyllos 160 Jahre vor ihm gemacht hatten, im Jahr 128 erkannt (Ptol. syntaxis 3,1), seine größte wiss. Leistung. Ptolemaios verbesserte den von H. gefundenen Wert, setzte ihn aber seinerseits mit 1° in 100 Jahren zu hoch an.

H. bestimmte erstaunlich genau das Sonnenjahr (Abweichung nur 6 Minuten und 26 Sekunden) und den synodischen Monat (Abweichung unter einer Sekunde). Unter Benutzung der wohl von ihm mit der Exzenter-Theorie des → Apollonios [13] von Perge verbundenen Epizykel-Theorie berechnete er die Anomalie der Sonnenbahn (Ptol. synt. 3,4 p. 233,1) und bestimmte die Mondbahn (Ptol. synt. 4,2 p. 270,19). Er konnte so → Kallippos' Schrift über Schaltmonate und -tage verbessern. Während seine Distanzbestimmung des Mondes von der Erde ziemlich genau ist, bleibt er bei der Sonne weit unter dem wirklichen Wert. Ohne seine retardierende Skepsis gegenüber dem heliozentrischen System des → Aristarchos [3] von Samos hätte sich dieses vielleicht rund 1700 Jahre früher durchgesetzt.

C. Geographie

H. schrieb drei Bücher ›Gegen die Geographie des Eratosthenes von Kyrene‹ (Περὶ τῶν Ἐρατοσθένους γεωγραφίαν). Die meisten Fragmente sind bei → Strabon erhalten, der gern für Eratosthenes [2] gegen H. Stellung nimmt. Strabons Kritik an H. ist jedoch nur teilweise berechtigt; H. bringt mit seinen überlegenen astron. Kenntnissen wesentliche Verbesserungen [3]. Er konzentriert sich auf die genaue Positionsbestimmung geographischer Einheiten anhand der *klímata* zum Zweck der Kartographie. In B. 1 und 2 übt H. Kritik an den ›Sphragiden‹ des Eratosthenes, in B. 3 stellt er seine eigene, genauere Methode der Triangulation dagegen. Die bes. schwierige Berechnung der Längen bewerkstelligte er durch Finsternistabellen. Größere Genauigkeit wäre nur in einem internationalen Netzwerk möglich gewesen, das in der Zeit des verfallenden alexandrinischen Museums nicht mehr zu verwirklichen war. Bei der Berechnung des Erdumfangs folgt er grundsätzlich dem Prinzip des Eratosthenes, berücksichtigt aber die Längenabweichung der Linie Syene – Alexandreia – Rhodos [5]. Großen Raum nimmt die Triangulation des Vorderen Orients und die ungefähre Breitenbestim-

mung Indiens ein. H. bestreitet die Annahme des Eratosthenes eines einheitlichen Weltmeeres und die mögliche Existenz weiterer Kontinente. Bei dieser überzogenen Kritik an Eratosthenes gibt er, wenn Strabon Recht hat, sogar Homer als Quelle den Vorzug.
→ Astronomie; Eratosthenes [2]

1 K.-R. Biermann, J. Mau, Überprüfung einer frühen Anwendung der Kombinatorik in der Logik, in: Journ. of Symbolic Logic 23, 1958, 129–132 2 H.C.F.C. Schellerup, Sur le chronomètre céleste d' H., in: Copernicus 1, 1881, 25–39 3 D.R. Dicks, The Geographical Fragments of H., 1960 (Bibliogr., Übers., Komm.) 4 E. Maass, Commentariorum in Aratum reliquiae, 1898 5 O. Viedebantt, Eratosthenes, H., Poseidonios, in: Klio 14, 1915, 207–256.

Ed. des Aratos-Komm. (griech.-dt.): C. Manitius, 1894.
Sternkatalog: F. Boll, Die Sternkataloge des Hipparch und des Ptolemaios, in: Bibliotheca Mathematica, 3. F. 2, 1901, 185–195 · E. Maass (Ed.), De magnitudine et positione <in>errantium stellarum, in: [4], 13–139 · St. Weinstock, in: CCAG 9,1, 1951, 189f.
Geogr. Frg.: Dicks [3].
Lit.: A. Rehm, s.v. H., RE 8, 1666–1681 · H. Vogt, Versuch einer Wiederherstellung von Hipparchs Fixsternverzeichnis, in: Astronomische Nachr. 224, 1912, 17–32 · E. Honigmann, Die sieben Klimata und die ΠΟΛΕΙΣ ΕΠΙΣΗΜΟΙ, 1929 · O. Bekker, Das mathematische Denken in der Ant., 1957 · O. Neugebauer, The Exact Sciences in Antiquity, ²1957 · Ders., A History of Ancient Mathematical Astronomy, 1975, 274–298. W.H.

[7] H., M. Antonius. Korinther, 43 v.Chr. als Freigelassener des M. Antonius [I 9] Profiteur während der Proskriptionen (Plin. nat. 35,200). Bei Actium (31) ließ H. den Wegbereiter seines Aufstiegs eilfertig im Stich (Plut. Antonius 67,10; 73,4). Unter Augustus war H. *duumvir* in seiner Heimatstadt (RPC 1, Nr. 1134ff.). T.FR.

Hipparinos (Ἱππαρῖνος).
[1] Syrakusier, Vater → Dions [I 1], 406/5 v.Chr. zusammen mit → Dionysios [1] I. zum Feldherrn gewählt (Plut. Dion 3). Unterstützte den Staatsstreich des Dionysios und gab ihm seine Tochter Aristomache zur Frau (Aristot. pol. 5,5,6). Von Platon (epist. 8, 353b) gerühmt.

H. Berve, Die Tyrannis bei den Griechen, 1967, 1, 222f.; 2, 638f.

[2] Syrakusier, Sohn des Dionysios [1] und der Aristomache, Enkel von H. [1]. Er vertrieb 353 v.Chr. Kallippos, den Mörder Dions [I 1] (Diod. 16,36,5), und kam selbst zur Herrschaft, wurde aber schon nach zwei Jahren ermordet (Theopomp FGrH 115 F 186 mit Komm.). Platon (epist. 8, 356a) urteilt über H. nicht ungünstig.

H. Berve, Die Tyrannis bei den Griechen, 1967, 1, 273f.; 2, 662.

[3] Syrakusier, Sohn Dions [I 1], überlebte wohl seinen Vater (Plat. epist. 7, 324b; 8, 355e, 357c). Umstände und Datum seines Todes sind umstritten.

H. Berve, Dion, in: AAWM, 1956, 77, 116f. K.MEI.

Hipparis. Der nördlichere, größere von zwei bei Kamarina an der SW-Küste Siziliens mündenden Flüsse, h. Íppari (→ Oanis), von Pindar (O. 5,12) als Wohltäter von Kamarina gepriesen, auf Mz. der Stadt als gehörnter Jüngling dargestellt.

J.B. Curbera, Onomastic of River-Gods in Sicily, in: Philologus 142, 1998, 59f. GI.MA.u.E.O.

Hippasos (Ἵππασος). U.a. mehrfach in ep. Texten verwendeter Name für nicht weiter individualisierte Figuren, bes. häufig in patronym. Angaben zu weniger bedeutenden Helden. Hierbei sind bes. [1] – [4] zu erwähnen:
[1] Vater des Argonauten Aktor (Apoll. Rhod. 1,112; Hyg. fab. 14).
[2] Vater des → Charops [4] (Hom. Il. 11,426).
[3] Vater des von Deiphobos getöteten Hypsenor (Hom. Il. 13,411).
[4] Vater des von Lykomedes getöteten Paionierfürsten Apisaon (Hom. Il. 17,387), Sohn der Minyastochter Leukippe, von seiner Mutter in bakchantischem Rasen in Stücke gerissen (Antoninus Liberalis 10,3).

P. Wathelet, Dictionnaire des Troyens de l'Iliade, 1988, Nr. 165. E.V.

[5] Bedeutender Pythagoreer des (frühen?) 5. Jh. v.Chr. aus Metapont (Aristot. metaph. 984a 7; Iambl. v.P. 81; Diog. Laert. 8,84; Kroton bzw. Sybaris als Herkunftsort dagegen bei Iambl. v. P. 81 bzw. 267). H. kann als Begründer der »mathematischen« Richtung der → Pythagoreischen Schule betrachtet werden (vgl. Iambl. v. P. 88 – unzutreffend 81 – und De communi mathematica scientia 25; [1. 193–197, 206f.]). Der Vorwurf, er habe das mathematische Geheimnis des Dodekaeders verraten (Iambl. v. P. 88, vgl. ferner 247), hängt mit den schulinternen Spannungen zw. »Akusmatikern« und »Mathematikern« zusammen (vgl. → Pythagoreische Schule; gegen frühere Versuche, den Verrat als Entdekkung bzw. Bekanntmachung der mathematischen Irrationalität zu deuten, wendet sich überzeugend [1. 457–461]). Man sagte H. auch die Abfassung eines »Mystischen Logos« zur Verleumdung des Pythagoras nach (Herakleides Lembos FHG 3, S.170 = Diog. Laert. 8,7; vgl. Apollonios bei Iambl. v. P. 257 und 259; [2; 1. 207 Anm. 78]; nach Demetrios aus Magnesia bei Diog. Laert. 8,84 soll H. dagegen keine Schrift hinterlassen haben). Bei Aristoteles (metaph. 984a 7) wird H. zusammen mit Heraklit als Vertreter der Lehre vom Feuer als Urstoff der Welt genannt (ebenso Theophr. Doxographia physica fr. 225 Fortenbaugh/Huby/Sharples/Gutas = Simpl. CAG 9, p.23); es heißt ferner, er habe die Seele für »feurig« gehalten (Aet. 4,3,4; Tert. De anima 5,2). H. wird auch mit dem sog. »harmonischen

Mittel« in Verbindung gebracht (Iambl. in Nicomachi arithmetica introductio p. 100 PISTELLI; [1. 441 f.]). Aus der Zuschreibung musikalischer Experimente mit bronzenen Scheiben von variierender Dicke bzw. mit unterschiedlich gefüllten Gefäßen an H. ist zu schließen, daß er die Zahlenverhältnisse der Grundkonsonanzen gekannt hat (Aristox. fr. 90 WEHRLI = Schol. in Plat. Phaid. 108d; Theon von Smyrna p. 59f. HILLER; vgl. auch Boeth. De institutione musica 2,19; [1. 377f.; 3; 4]). Die Bezeichnung der Zahl als »Paradigma« und göttliches »Werkzeug« bei der Welterschaffung (Iambl. ebd. p. 10 PISTELLI) ist wohl apokryph [1. 248f., 275 Anm. 176].
→ Pythagoreische Schule

1 W. BURKERT, Lore and Science in Ancient Pythagoreanism, 1972 2 A. DELATTE, Études sur la littérature pythagoricienne, 1915, 10f. 3 A. IZZO, Musica e numero da Ippaso ad Archita, in: A. CAPIZZI, G. CASERTANO (Hrsg.), Forme del sapere nei Presocratici, 1987, 139–145 4 G. COMOTTI, Pitagora, Ippaso, Laso e il metodo sperimentale, in: R. W. WALLACE, B. MACLACHLAN (Hrsg.), Harmonia mundi, 1991, 20–29.

DIELS/KRANZ, Nr. 18 • M. TIMPANARO CARDINI (Hrsg.), Pitagorici I, 1958, 78–105. C.RI.

Hippe (Ἵππη).
[1] Geliebte des → Theseus (Hes. fr. 147 M-W = Athen. 13,557a). Ihre Gleichsetzung mit Hippolyte (= Antiope nach Kleidemos FGrH 323 F 18 = Plut. Theseus 27,13a) ist möglich über die Entsprechung Antiope = Hippo (Kall. h. 3,239; 266) und das Auftreten der Form Hippo für Hippe (Clem. Al. strom. 1,73,4–5 und [1. Prolog Z. 21]).
[2] Tochter des Kentauren → Chiron (Hyg. astr. 2,18) und der Chariklo (nur Ov. met. 2,636); von Aiolos Tochter der weisen Melanippe (Hyg. astr. 2,18; Eur. fr. 480–488 ²NAUCK). Ihre Verstirnung in das Sternbild Equus ereignet sich auf ihre Bitte bei der Flucht vor ihrem Vater (Hyg. astr. 2,18; (Ps.-)Eratosth. Katasterismos 18); nach Kallimachos wird sie in eine Stute verwandelt, weil sie Artemis nur ungenügend diente (Hyg. astr. 2,18 = Kall. fr. 569). Eine dritte von Hyginus gegebene Variante führt ihre Verwandlung darauf zurück, daß sie ihre Sehergabe mißbrauchte, womit sich die Darstellung bei Ov. met. 2,635–675 deckt. Dort heißt sie allerdings vor der Verwandlung Ocyrhoe; nach Hyg. astr. 2,18 war ihr früherer Name bei Euripides Thetis.

1 H. v. ARNIM, Supplementum Euripideum p. 25–28 (Μελανίππη ἡ σοφή), 1913. JO.S.

Hippegos (ἱππηγός, ἱππαγωγός, lat. *hippago*, *hippagogus*). Spezielles Pferdetransportschiff ant. Kriegsflotten (Persien: Hdt. 6,48; 6,95,1; Tyros: Arr. an. 2,19,1; Demetrios Poliorketes: Diod. 20,83,1; Pergamon: Liv. 44,28,7; Rom: Pol. 1,27,9). In Athen wurden ausgediente Trieren zu H. umgebaut (z. B. Thuk. 2,56,2; IG II² 1628,466; 471); sie faßten 30 Pferde (Thuk. 6,43,2). Zu Unrecht schreibt Plinius (nat. 7,209) die Erfindung der H. Samos oder Athen zu (vgl. Hdt. 6,48; 6,95,1).
→ Flottenwesen

O. HÖCKMANN, Antike Seefahrt, 1985, 69. LE.BU.

Hippeis. Der Begriff H. (ἱππεῖς, »Reiter«) bezeichnet zunächst die zu Pferde in den Kampf ziehenden Krieger. Angesichts der großen Bed. des Hoplitenkampfes (→ *hoplítai*) spielten H. in der archa. und klass. Zeit mil. keine wesentliche Rolle; häufig wurden → Pferde nur für den Weg zum Schlachtort genutzt. Ein Grund hierfür lag in der Tatsache, daß viele Landschaften Griechenlands der Pferdezucht in größerem Stil nur begrenzte Möglichkeiten boten (Hom. Od. 4,601 ff.; Plat. leg. 625d; vgl. auch Strab. 8,8,1). Wo die Situation günstiger war, hatte die → Reiterei bezeichnenderweise einen anderen Stellenwert, so in Boiotien (Hdt. 9,68f.; Diod. 12,70), Syrakus (Pind. P. 2,1 ff.; Diod. 13,112,3; Plut. Dion 42,1 ff.; 44,2), Euboia (Hdt. 5,77; Aristot. pol. 4,3,1289b 39; 5,6,1306a 35f.; Aristot. Ath. pol. 15,2; Plut. Perikles 23,4), in verschiedenen Poleis Kleinasiens (Xen. Ag. 1,23; Aristot. pol. 4,3,1289b 39f.; Strab. 14,1,28; Polyain. 7,2,2; Ail. var. 14,46; Athen. 14,624e; IK 5,151 f.) und vor allem in Thessalien (Hdt. 5,63; Plat. Men. 70ab; Plat. leg. 625d; Aristot. fr. 456 R.).

Bes. mit dem Aufstieg der maked. Monarchie seit Philipp II. (359–336 v. Chr.) und aufgrund der durch diesen und seinen Sohn Alexander d.Gr. praktizierten Kampfweise der »verbundenen« Waffen erhielt die Reiterei zeitweise mil. ausschlaggebende Bedeutung. Xenophon widmete der Reiterei eine eigene Schrift, in der die Wahl geeigneter Pferde, die Ausbildung der Pferde und der Reiter sowie die Taktik im Kriege ausführlich behandelt werden (Xen. hipp.; vgl. mem. 3,3).

Angesichts des hohen Aufwandes, den Aufzucht und Unterhalt von Pferden erforderten, begegnet der Begriff H. auch als soziale Kategorie. Dabei kann H. als Ehrentitel für Eliteeinheiten der Fußtruppen gelten [3. 344]. Der Zusammenhang von Reichtum, adligem Lebensstil und Pferdezucht zeigte sich nicht zuletzt in der Bevorzugung der hippischen Agone durch Aristokraten und Tyrannen (Thgn. 549 ff.; 983 ff.; Aristoph. Nub. 14 ff.; 60 ff.; Thuk. 6,12,2; 15,3; 16,2; And. 4,25 ff.; Isokr. or. 7,45; 16,25; 32 ff.; Xen. Ag. 1,23; Xen. hell. 3,4,15; [3. 210f., 344f.]). Deshalb sah die polit. Theorie eine enge Verbindung zwischen aristokratisch-oligarchischen Verfassungen und einer starken Präsenz von H. (Aristot. pol. 4,3,1289b 35 ff.; 4,13,1297b 16 ff.; 6,7,1321a 6 ff.).

Diese Zusammenhänge von mil. und sozialer bzw. polit. Organisation sind für Athen bes. deutlich: In der solonischen Ordnung (→ Solon) bilden die H. die zweite Schatzungsklasse der timokratischen Verfassung (Aristot. Ath. pol. 7,3 f.). Aus ihr rekrutierten sich die 1000 H., die gemäß den → Phylen in 10 Schwadronen unter je einem Phylarchen aufgeteilt waren und von zwei Hipparchen kommandiert wurden (Aristot. Ath. pol. 61,4 f.). Sie hatten sich einer Musterung durch den Rat zu unterziehen (Xen. hipp. 1,9; Aristot. Ath. pol. 49,2). Ohne solche Musterung in der Reiterei zu dienen, war verboten (Lys. 14,4–10).

Wie der Fries mit dem Panathenäischen Festzug am Parthenon zeigt, spielten die H. in der bildlichen Selbstdarstellung der Polis Athen eine wichtige Rolle (vgl. auch Xen. hipp. 3). Auf Grabreliefs erscheinen H. oft mit ihrem Pferd, so etwa der 394 v. Chr. gefallene Athener Dexileos (Athen, Kerameikos; [8. 315]). Obwohl die Polis einen Teil der Unterhalts- und Ausrüstungskosten übernahm (nach Xen. hipp. 1,19 im 4. Jh. v. Chr. fast 40 Talente im Jahr), waren nur Angehörige der Oberschicht zum Dienst als H. in der Lage (vgl. Xen. hipp. 1,9). Infolgedessen entwickelten diese nicht nur einen entsprechenden Korpsgeist und einen aristokratischen Lebensstil, sondern scheinen der radikalen Demokratie zunehmend distanziert gegenübergestanden zu haben, bes. nachdem sie sich bei der Verteidigung Attikas im Peloponnesischen Krieg Verdienste erworben hatten (Aristoph. Ach. 5f.; 300f. und bes. Equ. passim). So waren sie auch in die Tyrannis der »Dreißig« (404/3) teilweise stark involviert (Xen. hell. 3,1,4) und galten danach eine Zeitlang als verdächtig bzw. belastet (Lys. 16,6ff.; 26,10). Im Verlauf des 4. Jh. verloren die H. in Athen zunehmend an mil. Bedeutung.

1 J. K. Anderson, Ancient Greek Horsemanship, ²1971
2 G. R. Bugh, The Horsemen of Athens, 1988
3 Busolt/Swoboda I **4** L. A. Burckhardt, Bürger und Soldaten, 1996 **5** Hasebroek, 78–81 **6** I. G. Spence, The Cavalry of Classical Greece, 1993 **7** E. Stein-Hölkeskamp, Adelskultur und Polisgesellschaft, 1989, 110f. **8** Travlos, Athen. H.-J. G.

Hippemolgoi s. Galaktophagoi

Hippias (Ἱππίας, ion. Ἱππίης).

[1] Ältester Sohn des → Peisistratos aus dessen erster Ehe mit einer Athenerin. Gemeinsam mit den Brüdern → Hipparchos [1] und Thessalos trat er 528/7 v. Chr. das Erbe des Vaters an und führte dessen gemäßigte Politik fort (Thuk. 6,54–55; [Aristot.] Ath. pol. 18,1), z. B. als Archon im J. 526/7. Als aber Hipparchos beim Panathenäenfest von 514 ermordet wurde, entwaffnete H. das Volk, ließ foltern, morden und schickte zahlreiche Konkurrenten in die Verbannung (Hdt. 5,62; Thuk. 6,59; [Aristot.] Ath. pol. 19). Die darauffolgende Verheiratung seiner Tochter Archedike mit dem Sohn des perserfreundlichen Tyrannen → Hippoklos von Lampsakos, Aiantides, läßt eine Annäherung an Persien erkennen. Die Alkmaioniden, bzw. → Kleisthenes, leiteten von Delphi aus mit Hilfe des → Kleomenes I. von Sparta den Sturz des Tyrannen ein. 510 kapitulierte H. und ging zuerst nach Sigeion, nach verfehlter Rekonziliation mit Kleomenes nach Lampsakos und Susa (Hdt. 5,63–4; 65; 91–4; 96; Thuk. 6,59; [Aristot.] Ath. pol. 19). Von dort brach er mit dem persischen Heer nach Griechenland auf und erlebte vor → Marathon das Scheitern seiner Hoffnung, nach Athen zurückzukehren (Hdt. 6,102; 107–9; 121). Die Peisistratiden wurden darauf in ganz Griechenland geächtet (Thuk. 6,55).

H. Berve, Die Tyrannis bei den Griechen, 1967, 63ff.; 554ff. • L. de Libero, Die Archaische Tyrannis, 1996, 116ff. • Traill, PPA 537810 • K.-W. Welwei, Athen, 1992, 247ff.

[2] Aus Thessalien, Anführer der arkadischen Söldner, die der Satrap Pissuthnes der propersischen Partei in Notion als Schutz gegeben hatte. 427 v. Chr. wurde H. von Paches überrumpelt und nach der Einnahme Notions erschossen (Thuk. 3,34). B.P.

[3] Makedone aus Beroia, hoher Offizier des → Perseus im 3. Maked. Krieg (Liv. 42,51,4; 44,4,1; 7,8; vgl. Pol. 18,10,1), ergab sich 168 v. Chr. dem L. → Aemilius [I 32] Paullus. Als hochrangiger Königsfreund war H. 172 zu Q. → Marcius Philippus nach Larissa (Liv. 42,39,7f.) und im Frühjahr 171 zum Senat nach Rom geschickt worden (Pol. 27,6,1–3; vgl. Liv. 42,48,1–3; App. Mac. 11,5–9). Eine weitere Mission folgte 169/8 zu → Genthios (Pol. 28,9,3; 29,3,1–3; Liv. 44,23,2). Die Identität des maked. Offiziers H. und der gleichnamigen Person(en) als Gesandte des Perseus ist umstritten [1. 156–159; 2. 113f.].

[4] Boioter, Boiotarch 187 v. Chr. (IG VII 2407; 2408; Pol. 22,4,12) [1. 156f.], wirkte 174/3 am Bündnis mit → Perseus mit; am Vorabend des 3. Maked. Krieges (172/1) von radikalen Romfreunden verbannt und angeklagt, erhielt H. mit → Ismenias und → Neon in Chalkis röm. Schutz vor feindseligen Handgreiflichkeiten (Pol. 27,1,11; 2,2f.) [3. 153f.; 157f.].

1 E. Olshausen, Prosopographie der hell. Königsgesandten, 1974 **2** S. Le Bohec, Les *phíloi* des rois Antigonides, in: REG 98, 1985, 93–124 **3** J. Deininger, Der polit. Widerstand in Griechenland gegen Rom, 1971. L.-M. G.

[5] Sophist aus Elis, ›erheblich jünger‹ als Protagoras (Plat. Hipp. mai. 382e), noch zu Beginn des 4. Jh. v. Chr. tätig – er überlebte Sokrates (vgl. Plat. apol. 19e). Zwei platonische Dialoge, *Hippias maior* und *Hippias minor*, tragen seinen Namen, er tritt auch im *Protagoras* (vgl. 337c–338b) auf sowie in einem Gespräch bei Xenophon (mem. 4,4,5–25). Er hatte eine öffentliche Stellung als Gesandter seiner Stadt (s. Plat. Hipp. mai. 281a-c)

Die ant. Tradition schreibt ihm Fachkenntnisse auf verschiedensten Gebieten zu (Arithmetik, Astronomie, Geometrie, Musik, Prosodie, Dichtung, Philologie, Rhetorik, »Archäologie«, Mnemotechnik und handwerkliche Fähigkeiten). Von seinem Werk ist nur ein einziges Fragment (Clem. Al. strom. 6,15) sowie einige Werktitel erhalten: ›Troischer Dialog‹ (Philostr. soph. 1,11,4, vgl. Plat. Hipp. mai. 286a-b), ›Völkernamen‹ (B 2 DK) eine Liste olympischer Sieger (Plut. Numa 1) und eine ›Sammlung‹ (Athen. 13,608f) vermutlich unterschiedlicher Informationen in histor. Reihenfolge. H. ist Erfinder der »Quadratrix«, deren Anwendung Proklos (in Euclidem 272,3) weniger für die annähernde

Quadratur des Kreises erklärt, als vielmehr für die Teilung eines rechten Winkels in drei gleiche Teile. Er war vielleicht der erste Doxograph (→ Doxographie) und sah schon vor Platon und Aristoteles den Dichter Homer (Okeanos und Tethys sind der Ursprung aller Dinge) als Vorgänger des Thales (alles ist Wasser).

Im 20. Jh. hat man H. eine histor. bedeutende Rolle bei der Entstehung des polit. Denkens zugewiesen [8; 10.] und ihn als ersten Theoretiker sowohl des Naturrechtes als auch des Kosmopolitismus gesehen (vgl. Plat. Prot. 337c-d: ›von Natur aus ist das Gleiche mit dem Gleichen verwandt‹; ›Das Gesetz ist der Herrscher des Menschen‹; Xen. mem. 4,4).

→ Mathematik; Platon; Politische Philosophie; Sophistik

ED.: **1** DK⁶ 86 **2** M. UNTERSTEINER, I Sofisti, Testimonianze e frammenti III, 1954, 38–109 (Ergänzungen zu DK).

LIT.: **3** H. GOMPERZ, Sophistik und Rhet., 1912 (Ndr. 1965), 68–79 **4** A. A. BJÖRNBO, s. v. H. (13), RE 8, 1707–1711 **5** A. MOMIGLIANO, Lebensideale in der Sophistik (1930), in: C. J. CLASSEN (Hrsg.), Sophistik, 1976, 465–477 **6** W. NESTLE, Vom Mythos zum Logos, ²1942, Ndr. 1975, 360–371 **7** B. SNELL, Die Nachr. über die Lehren des Thales und die Anfänge der griech. Philos.- und Literaturgesch. (1944), in: C. J. CLASSEN (Hrsg.), Sophistik, 1976, 478–490 **8** E. DUPRÉEL, Les sophistes, 1948, 185–393 **9** C. J. CLASSEN, Bemerkungen zu zwei griech. »Philosophiehistorikern«, in: Philologus 109, 1965, 175–178 **10** M. UNTERSTEINER, I Sofisti, ²1967 (Ndr. 1996), XV **11** H. BLUM, Die ant. Mnemotechnik, 1969, 48–55 **12** GUTHRIE, I 3 (The Sophists), 1971, 280–285 **13** J. MANSFELD, Cratylus 402a-c: Plato or Hippias?, in: L. ROSSETTI (Hrsg.), Atti del Symposium Heracliteum 1981, I, 1983, 43–55 **14** J. BRUNSCHWIG, H. d'Élis, philosophe-ambassadeur, in: K. BOUDOURIS (Hrsg.), The Sophistic Movement, 1984, 269–276. MI. NA./Ü: J. DE.

Hippiatrika (Τὰ ἱππιατρικά). Griech. Texte zur Medizin der Einhufer, die – abgesehen von einigen Inedita – im *Corpus Hippiatricorum Graecorum* (CHG) [1] zusammengestellt sind.

Mindestens vier Jh. trennen die hippologischen Schriften des Simon von Athen (5./4. Jh. v. Chr.) und des Xenophon sowie die wenigen Stellen, an denen Aristoteles Fortpflanzung und Krankheiten der Einhufer behandelt (bes. hist. an. 572a–577a, 604a–605a, 611a und 631a), von den ersten auf griech. erh. Schriften zur Pferdeheilkunde. Daß es für diesen langen Zeitraum keine griech. Zeugnisse gibt, wird z. T. durch die lat. Quellen aufgewogen, insbesondere die landwirtschaftlichen Abh. des Varro (2,6–8), bei dem sich der erste lit. Beleg für den Begriff ἱππιατρός (*hippiatrós*) findet (auch schon in einer Inschr. aus Lamia von 130 v. Chr. bezeugt; IG IX,2,65,9), und des Columella (6,27–38), der wiederum eine der Quellen des Eumelos ist, des ältesten der bekannten pferdemedizinischen Autoren griech. Sprache. Die Beziehungen zwischen den griech. Werken zur Pferdemedizin (etwa 2./3. bis 5. Jh. n. Chr.) und ihren lat. Entsprechungen im 4. und 5. Jh. (die *Ars veterinaria* des Pelagonius, die → *Mulomedicina Chironis* und die *Digesta artis mulomedicinalis* des Vegetius) sind zahlreich und geben Anleihen in beiden Richtungen zu erkennen. Der Einfluß der (verlorenen) Abh. des Karthagers Magon, der in diesen Texten regelmäßig zitiert wird, ist nicht zu unterschätzen.

Kein bedeutender Autor ist aus byz. Zeit bekannt, in der die H. zusammengestellt wurden; von ihnen sind vier aufeinanderfolgende Redaktionen zu erkennen. Die ersten drei heben sich durch die Anordnung nach Gegenständen von Auszügen aus verschiedenen Autoren ab. In der (1.) Redaktion M, die der urspr. Slg. am nächsten steht (Ms. Par. Gr. 2322, 11. Jh.), handelt es sich im wesentlichen um sieben Verf., die dort in alphabetischer Reihenfolge exzerpiert sind: → Apsyrtos [2] von Klazomenai, → Anatolios [1] (bei dem es sich wohl um Vindanios (oder Vindonios) Anatolios von Berytos, 4. oder 5. Jh., handelt, einen der Kompilatoren der → *Geoponika*, deren 16. B. u. a. die Pferde behandelt), Eumelos, Theomnestos (aus Magnesia, so die arab. Übers. aus der Mitte des 9. Jh.), Hippokrates, der Tierarzt, → Hierokles (ein Jurist, der sich darauf beschränkte, zahlreiche Darstellungen des Apsyrtos in eine elegantere Sprache umzuschreiben) und → Pelagonius (dessen Abh. urspr. auf Lat. abgefaßt war). Ihre Anordnung ist in der Folge modifiziert worden, und weitere Quellen sind hinzugekommen: Texte des Tiberius und eine Slg. mit dem Titel *Prognṓseis kaí iáseis* (›Prognosen und Behandlungen‹) in der (2.) Redaktion B (vertreten durch die illuminierte Hs. *Berolinensis Gr.* 134 [*Phillippicus* 1538], 10. Jh., und etwa zehn Hss. aus dem 14.–16. Jh.), außerdem Auszüge aus Iulius Africanus mit Interpolationen aus → Ailianos [2], humanmedizinische Rezepte und pferdeheilkundliche Texte, darunter die des Simon von Athen, in der (3.) Redaktion D (Hss. *Cantab. Coll. Emmanuelis* III,3,19, 12. Jh., und *Lond. Sloan.* 745, 13. Jh.). Bei der 4. Redaktion lassen sich zwei Teile abgrenzen: der 1. umfaßt drei B., die in den beiden Hss. Par. gr. 2244 und Voss. gr. Q. 50 (14. Jh.) zu jedem Kap. eine Illustration enthalten. B. 1 und 2 bringen aus den H. entnommene und in Buchform angeordnete Hieroklesstücke (nicht das Originalwerk des Hierokles). B. 3 ist eine epit. der H., konzipiert als vollständiges Hdb. der Pferdemedizin; sie liegt in mehreren Bearbeitungen vor. Der 2. (nicht illustrierte) Teil dieser 4. Redaktion bringt Auszüge, die z. T. nach Autoren (v. a. Apsyrtos und Tiberius), z. T. nach Themen angeordnet sind. Die 3 B. des ›illuminierten Zweiges‹, wie [2. 43] ihn gen. hat, haben im westl. MA eine besondere Rolle gespielt: abgesehen von einer bebilderten Übers. ins It. wurden sie auch ins Lat. und ins Sizilianische (?) übertragen.

Die Auszüge im CHG teilen uns wenig über ihre jeweiligen Autoren mit, von denen einige nur an ein oder zwei Stellen herangezogen werden. Es ist zweifellos kein Zufall, wenn die Beiträge des Apsyrtos und des Theomnestos, die selbst Tierärzte waren, besondere Bed. haben: Sie spiegeln echte praktische Erfahrung wider und enthalten einige Überlegungen zur Krankheitsentstehung, die in diesen Fachtexten, deren Ziel es ist, eine Diagnose der Krankheiten von Einhufern und ihre Behandlung zu ermöglichen, sonst sehr selten sind. → Mulomedicina Chironis; Veterinärmedizin

1 E. Oder, K. Hoppe (Hrsg.), Corpus Hippiatricorum Graecorum, 2 Bde., 1924/1927 **2** G. Björck, Apsyrtus, Julius Africanus et l'hippiatrique grecque, 1944 **3** J. N. Adams, Pelagonius and Latin Veterinary Terminology in the Roman Empire, 1995 **4** A. M. Doyen-Higuet, The Hippiatrica and Byz. Veterinary Medicine, in: Dumbarton Oaks Papers 38, 1984, 111–120 **5** K.-D. Fischer, Ancient Veterinary Medicine. A survey of Greek and Latin sources and some recent scholarship, in: Medizinhist. Journal 23, 1988, 191–209 **6** Y. Poulle-Drieux, L'hippiatrie dans l'Occident latin du XIIIe au XVe s., in: G. Beaujouan u. a., Médecine humaine et vétérinaire à la fin du Moyen Age, 1966 **7** J. Schäffer, K.-D. Fischer, s. v. Tiermedizin, LMA 8, 774–780 **8** M. Ullmann, Die Medizin im Islam, HbdOr., I, Ergbd. VI, I, 1970, 217–222.

A.D.-H./Ü: T.H.

Hippitas (Ἱππίτας). Vertrauter des spartanischen Königs Kleomenes III., den er nach der Schlacht bei Sellasia nach Alexandreia begleitete, wo er sich 219 v. Chr. nach dessen mißglückter Erhebung gegen Ptolemaios IV. töten ließ (Pol. 5,37,8; Plut. Kleomenes 37,6–13).

K.-W. WEL.

Hippo (Ἱππώ).

[1] → Okeanide, vielleicht Göttin eines »Roßbrunnens«.

[2] → Amazone (= Hippolyte, Kall. h. 3,239 ff.; 266 f.).

[3] Tochter des → Chiron (= Hippe), Geliebte des Hellen-Sohnes → Aiolos [1].

[4] Amme des Dionysos (= Hippa, Orph. h. 48; 49; Prokl. in Plat. Tim. 124c). RE. ZI.

[5] (pun. *ʾpʾ*?). Eine phönik. oder pun. Gründung oder Neugründung nordwestl. von Utica, h. Bizerte. Belegstellen: [Skyl.] 111, GGM I 89 f. (Ἵππου ἄκρα, »Burg des Pferdes« [?]); Pol. 1,82,8; 88,2 (ἡ τῶν Ἱππακριτῶν πόλις, »Stadt der Hippakritai«); Sall. Iug. 19,1 (*Hippo*); Diod. 20,55,3 (ἡ Ἵππου καλουμένη ἄκρα, »die sog. Burg des Pferdes [?]«), vgl. 57,6 (ἡ ὀνομαζομένη ἄκρα Ἵππου, ein anderer Ort); Plin. nat. 5,23 (*Hippo Dirutus*); 6,212; 9,26 (*Hippo Diarrutus*); App. Lib. 30,128 (Ἱππών); 110,520; 111,523 (Ἱππάγρετα); Ptol. 4,3,6 (Ἱππὼν διάρρυτος); Itin. Anton. 21,4 (*Hippo Zaritus*); Sol. 27,7 (*Hippo Diarrhytos*). Unter Caesar oder Augustus wurde H. *colonia* (CIL VIII 1, 1206). Inschr.: CIL VIII 1, 1206–1210, Suppl. 1, 14333–14335, Suppl. 4, 25417–25424.

W. Huss, Die pun. Namen ..., in: Semitica 38, 1990, 171–174 · S. Lancel, E. Lipiński, s. v. Bizerte, DCPP, 74 f.

W. HU.

[6] H. Regius (pun. *ʿ[p]ʾ*?). Phönik. oder pun. Gründung oder Neugründung in der Nähe der Mündung des Flusses Seybouse, h. Hippone. 205 v. Chr. landete C. Laelius im Hafen von H. und leitete damit die röm. Invasion Afrikas ein (Liv. 29,3,7; Pol. 12,1). Nach dem E. des 2. Pun. Kriegs wurde H. eine der Residenzstädte des → Massinissa (*Hippo Regius*). Belegstellen: Sil. 3,259; vgl. Plin. nat. 5,22; 6,212; Ptol. 4,3,5; Itin. Anton. 6,1; 42,4; 42,7 f.; 44,4; Solin. 27,7. Nach dem Sieg Caesars bei Thapsos (46 v. Chr.) wurde die Stadt, in deren Hafen P. Sittius die pompeianische Flotte überwältigt hatte (Bell. Afr. 96), der neuen afrikanischen Prov. eingegliedert. Zunächst war sie *municipium* [1. 1, 109], dann wurde sie *colonia* (Itin. Anton. 20,3). Sie verfügte über einen großen Hafen und ein ausgedehntes Landgebiet. Bischöfe werden seit 259 erwähnt. → Augustinus, der bedeutendste in der Reihe der Bischöfe von H., starb hier 430 n. Chr. Im J. 431 wurde die Stadt von den Vandali erobert, 533 von den Oströmern zurückerobert und Mitte des 7. Jh. von den Arabern besetzt. Zahlreiche Monumente aus vorchristl. und christl. Zeit sind erhalten. Inschr.: [1. 1–88].

1 Inscriptions latines de l'Algérie I.

S. Dahmani, H. Regius, 1973 · H. V. M. Dennis, H. Regius, 1970 (= 1924) · W. Huss, Die pun. Namen ..., in: Semitica 38, 1990, 171–174 · E. Marec, Hippone la Royale, ²1954 · K. Vössing, Unt. zur röm. Schule – Bildung – Schulbildung im Nordafrika der Kaiserzeit, 1991, 163–183.

W. HU.

Hippobotai (ἱπποβόται). Die *h.* waren die soziale Elite in → Chalkis [1] auf Euboia; ihnen wird die Gründung chalkidischer → Apoikien im 8. Jh. v. Chr. zugeschrieben (Strab. 10,1,8). Nach Aristoteles war Chalkis eine Oligarchie der Reiter, deren Macht auf ihrer mil. Überlegenheit beruhte (Aristot. pol. 1289b 36–40); im → Lelantischen Krieg konnte Chalkis allerdings nur durch die Hilfe der Thessalier die Reiterei von Eretria besiegen (Plut. mor. 760e–f; Strab. 10,1,10; 10,1,12). Aufgrund anderer Quellen ist jedoch zu bezweifeln, daß die → Reiterei in der Zeit um 700 v. Chr. eine große mil. Bedeutung besaß. Vielleicht waren die *h.* schwerbewaffnete Fußtruppen, die auf ihren Pferden in den Kampf ritten. Als die Athener Chalkis um 507 v. Chr. besiegten, siedelten sie 4000 → *klērúchoi* auf dem Land der *h.* an (Hdt. 5,77; 6,100 f.; vgl. Ail. var. 6,1, wenn sich dies nicht auf 445 bezieht). Nach Niederschlagung der Revolte von Chalkis 445 v. Chr. vertrieb Athen die *h.* (Plut. Perikles 23,4; vgl. Thuk. 1,114).

1 P. Greenhalgh, Early Greek Warfare, 1973, 90–93.

R. O./Ü: A. BE.

Hippobotos (Ἱππόβοτος). Hell. Philosophiegeschichtsschreiber unbekannten Wirkungsortes, zitiert 15mal bei → Diogenes [17] Laertios, des weiteren bei Clemens von Alexandria, Porphyrios, Iamblichos und der Suda; auch genannt in POxy. 3656. Zwei Werktitel sind bekannt: ›Über die philos. Schulrichtungen‹ (Περὶ αἱρέσεων; Diog. Laert. 1,19; 2,88) und ›Philosophenlisten‹ (Περὶ φιλοσόφων ἀναγραφή, ebd. 1,41). Im ersteren Werk stellt H. fest, es gebe neun »philos. Schulrichtungen« (→ Hairesis). Die »Liste« läßt eine Schreibtätigkeit zu Ende des 3. Jh. v. Chr., vor → Sotion vermuten. Die meisten H.-Zitate bei Diog. Laert. enthalten biographische Einzelheiten zu einzelnen Philosophen und stammen zweifellos aus dem zweiten Werk. Dieses zählt wohl zur Sukzessionen-Lit. (→ Doxographie).

Ed.: M. Gigante, Frammenti di Ippoboto, in: Omaggio a Piero Treves, 1983, 151–193 (s. auch Erg. PdP Suppl., 1985, 69).

Lit.: H. v. Arnim, RE 8, 1722f. • J. Mejer, Diogenes Laërtius and his Hellenistic Background, 1978, 45, 69–72, 77 • J. Glucker, Antiochus and the Late Academy, 1978, 176–180 (für spätere Datierung). D. T. R./Ü: J. DE.

Hippodamas (Ἱπποδάμας).
[1] Sohn des Flußgottes → Acheloos [2] und der Perimede, Vater von Euryte, Bruder des Orestes (Apollod. 1,52). In anderer Überl. Vater der Naiade → Perimele, der Geliebten von Acheloos, die, von H. ins Meer gestoßen, von Poseidon in eine der Echinadeninseln (an der W.-Küste Akarnaniens) verwandelt wird (Ov. met. 8,573 ff.).
[2] Name von Troianern: der eine H. wird von Achilleus (Hom. Il. 20,401), der andere von Agamemnon (Hyg. fab. 113) getötet; der dritte ist Sohn des Priamos (Apollod. 3,152). RE. ZI.
[3] Verf. eines hexametrischen Distichons über Herkunft und gegensätzliches Wesen von Göttern und Menschen, das durch Iambl. v. P. 82 überliefert ist. Nach Iamblichos, der H. aus Salamis (oder von Samos: Konjektur Nauck) stammen läßt, wurde diesen Versen das Lob des Pythagoras zuteil.

Anth. Pal. appendix III 17 Cougny. M. G. A./Ü: T. H.

Hippodameia (Ἱπποδάμεια, Ἱπποδάμη, lat. Hippodamia).
[1] Tochter des Königs → Oinomaos von Pisa und der Sterope (Paus. 5,10,6). Weil ein Orakel seine Ermordung durch den zukünftigen Schwiegersohn ankündigt (Diod. 4,73,2) oder weil er selbst H. begehrt (Hyg. fab. 253), verhindert Oinomaos H.s Hochzeit, indem er die zahlreichen Freier (Hes. cat. fr. 259a; Pind. O. 1,128; Paus. 6,21,10f.; Epimenides, FGrH 457 fr. 14) zum Wagenrennen herausfordert, besiegt und tötet. → Pelops jedoch besiegt Oinomaos (Pind. O. 1,67–96). Dabei hilft ihm dessen Wagenlenker Myrsilos, indem er keine oder wächserne Nägel vor die Radachsen seines Herrn steckt (Pherekydes, FGrH 3 fr. 37a). Pelops heiratet H. und tötet den Myrsilos, weil dieser versucht, H. zu vergewaltigen (Pherekydes, FGrH 3 fr. 37b), oder weil er ihm den versprochenen Lohn vorenthalten will (Paus. 8,14,11; Hyg. fab. 84). Das Paar hat zahlreiche Kinder (Pind. O. 1,144), darunter → Atreus und → Thyestes. H. überredet diese, ihren Halbbruder → Chrysippos [1] zu töten. Als die Tat entdeckt wird, flüchtet sie oder begeht Selbstmord (schol. Hom. Il. 2,105; vgl. Plat. Krat. 395b; Paus. 6,20,7; Hyg. fab. 85). Älteste erh. lit. Quelle ist Pindar, der den Betrug des Myrsilos nicht erwähnt. Sophokles (TrGF IV fr. 471–477) und Euripides (TGF fr. 571–577) schrieben einen *Oinomaos*.

In Olympia wurde H. in einem Hippodameion genannten Heiligtum verehrt (Paus. 5,22,2; 6,20,7). Nach Paus. 5,16,4 begründete sie das alle fünf Jahre in Olympia abgehaltene Herafest, an dem sich die jungen unverheirateten Frauen in athletischen Kämpfen maßen. K. WA.
[2] Tochter des Butas (Diod. 4,70,3), des Adrastos (Hyg. fab. 33,3), oder des Atrax (Ov. epist. 17,248). Frau des → Peirithoos (Hom. Il. 2,742), Mutter des Polypoites (Hom. Il. 2,40ff.; Ov. met. 12, 210ff.; Apollod. epit. 1,21; Hyg. fab. 33). Ihretwegen kommt es zum Kampf zwischen → Kentauren und Lapithen; → Eurytion [1].
[3] Frau des → Amyntor [2], Mutter des Phoinix. Da Amyntor sich wegen Phthia (Apollod. 3,175) oder Klytia (schol. Hom. Il. 9,448) von H. abwendet, stiftet H. ihren Sohn an, dem Vater die Geliebte abspenstig zu machen, was ihm gelingt. Er wird vom erzürnten Vater verflucht und geblendet und flieht (Hom. Il. 9,448 ff.).
[4] Nach schol. Hom. Il. 1,392 Eigenname der → Briseis.
[5] Dienerin der Penelope (Hom. Od. 18,182).
[6] Gattin des Autonoos. Sie wird in eine Rohrdommel verwandelt (Antoninus Liberalis 7).

M. Pipili, s. v. H. (1), LIMC 5.1, 434–435 • H. Zwicker, s. v. H., RE 8, 1725–1730. K. WA.

Hippodamos aus Milet. Griech. Architekt, Stadtplaner und Autor staatstheoretischer Schriften; das fälschlich nach ihm benannte »hippodamische System« eines rechtwinkelig angelegten urbanistischen Rasters war in den Koloniestädten des Westens und in Ionien bereits in archa. Zeit bekannt (→ Insula; → Städtebau). Die Lebens- und Schaffenszeit des H. ist ungewiß; mit ihm wird der Neuaufbau des in den Perserkriegen zerstörten → Miletos (479 v. Chr.) ebenso verbunden wie der Bau der Stadtanlage von → Peiraieus (um 450 v. Chr.) und das urbanistische Konzept von → Thurioi (445/44 v. Chr.); die ihm von Strabon (14,654) zugeschriebene Planung der Stadt Rhodos (408) ist sehr wahrscheinlich Fiktion.

Der von Aristoteles (pol. H 11,1330b 21) als neu gerühmte *hippodámeios trópos* (»nach Art des H.«) war mehr als eine bloße rechtwinklige Anordnung von Straßenzügen. In der Anlage des Peiraieus, dem einzigen durch eine Vielzahl von Quellen wirklich gesicherten »Werk« des H., findet sich erstmals ein kohärentes Konzept der Flächennutzung für eine Stadtanlage realisiert, bei der die → Insula als Modul innerhalb eines orthogonalen Rasters die gesamte Siedlungsfläche gliederte; Hausbebauung, öffentliche Bereiche für Verwaltung und Ökonomie sowie sakrale Flächen wurden voneinander getrennt und zugleich miteinander in eine geordnete Beziehung gesetzt.

Daß die Planungen des H. ein umfassenderes, auch staatspolit. verankertes Konzept und nicht eine nur bauliche Strukturierung eines Siedlungsplatzes zum Gegenstand hatten, ergibt sich aus den nur mittelbar bekannten Schriften, die in erster Linie bei Aristoteles (Pol. 1267b

24 – 1269a 29) frg. überl. sind; dies zeigt zugleich auch das weitgespannte Tätigkeitsspektrum eines → Architekten klass. Zeit. Über die staatstheroetischen Positionen des H. ist in der mod. Forsch. spekuliert worden; einem »radikaldemokratischen« H. ist mehrfach ein antidemokratisches Konzept in der Art von Platons Staatsutopie gegenübergestellt worden. Einschätzungen müssen den kritisch-ablehnenden Tenor des Aristoteles gegenüber den Ideen des H. wie den Umstand berücksichtigen, daß H. um die Mitte des 5. Jh. v. Chr. im Auftrag Athens im Peiraieus tätig war, was beides eher für demokratische Tendenzen im hippodamischen Konzept spricht. Aufgeworfen ist durch die Debatte um die Schriften des H. zugleich aber auch die Frage des Verhältnisses zwischen urbanistischer Planung und der sie begründenden und legitimierenden Staatstheorie, ein Problembereich, der über Generationen hinweg eher einseitig auf die stadtplanerischen Aspekte fokussiert geblieben ist.

P. Benvenuti Falciai, Ippodamo di Mileto architetto e filosofo. Una ricostruzione filologica della personalità, 1982 • A. Burns, H. and the Planned City, in: Historia 25, 1976, 414–428 • F. Castagnoli, Ippodamo da Mileto e l'urbanistica a pianta ortogonale, 1956 • H.-J. Gehrke, Bemerkungen zu H. von Milet, in: Demokratie und Architektur. Der hippodamische Städtebau und die Entstehung der Demokratie, 1989, 58–63 • W. Hoepfner, E. L. Schwandner, Haus und Stadt im klass. Griechenland, [2]1994 • H. R. McCredie, Hippodamos of Miletos, in: Stud. Presented to G. M. A. Hanfmann, 1971, 95–100 • I. Haugsted, H. fra Milet. Antikke graeske byplaner fra det 5. årh. f. Kr., 1978 • Ch. Schubert, Land und Raum in der röm. Republik. Die Kunst des Teilens, 1996 • J. Szidat, H. von Milet. Seine Rolle in Theorie und Praxis der griech. Stadtplanung, in: BJ 180, 1980, 31–44 • Ch. Triebel-Schubert, U. Muss, H. von Milet. Staatstheoretiker oder Stadtplaner?, in: Hephaistos 5/6, 1983/4, 37–59 • R. E. Wycherley, H. and Rhodes, in: Historia 13, 1964, 135–139. C. HÖ.

Hippodromos

[1] In der griech. Architektur bezeichnet H. (ἱππόδρομος) die Pferderennbahn, die seit dem frühen 7. Jh. (Einführung der Wagenrennen in Olympia 680 v. Chr.) als Einrichtung in den Poleis und Heiligtümern üblich wurde. Das H. war in archa. Zeit erstrangiger Ort aristokratischer Repräsentation, wo Reichtum durch den Besitz und routinierten Gebrauch edler Rennpferde weithin sichtbar vor Publikum demonstriert werden konnte. Die U-förmigen Anlagen waren von Wällen für Zuschauer umgeben und mit einer Start- und Zielvorrichtung sowie einer Wendemarkierung ausgestattet. Die erheblichen Dimensionen (ca. 250 × 600 m) machten eine Errichtung außerhalb der Heiligtümer zur Regel: Das H. von Olympia, nur aus der Schilderung des Pausanias (6,20f.) bekannt, lag zw. Stadion und Alpheios und ist vom Schwemmsand des Flusses nahezu gänzlich verschüttet worden; das H. von Delphi fand sich weit unterhalb des Apollonheiligtums in der Ebene von Kirra. Bezeugt ist ein H. ferner für die Heiligtümer von Nemea, Isthmia und Delos sowie für die Städte Athen, Sparta, Theben und Mantineia. Ebenfalls durch die Dimensionen der Anlagen bedingt war – im Gegensatz zum kleineren → Stadion – der dauerhafte Verzicht auf eine baulich-architektonische Gestaltung. Die griech. H. blieben allesamt ephemere Erd-Architekturen; bisweilen konnten, wie in Elis, Wagen- und Pferderennen sogar auf der Agora stattfinden, die dann temporär zum H. umgerüstet wurde.

Eine aufwendige architektonische Manifestation erfuhr das H. erst in Gestalt des röm. → Circus; hiervon zu trennen ist der u. a. in den Villenbriefen des Plinius überl. *h.*, der eher als Bestandteil des Gartens einer röm. Villenanlage denn als Rennbahn aufzufassen ist.

J. Ebert, Neues zum H. und den hippischen Konkurrenzen in Olympia, in: Nikephoros 2, 1989, 89–107 • R. Förtsch, Arch. Komm. zu den Villenbriefen des jüngeren Plinius, 1993, 78–80 • M. Vickers, The H. at Thessaloniki, in: JRS 62, 1972, 25–32 • H. Wiegartz, Zur Startanlage im H. von Olympia, in: Boreas 7, 1984, 41–78. C. HÖ.

[2] M. Aurelius (?) H., Sohn des Olympiodoros. Sophist aus Larissa in Thessalien, Schüler des → Chrestos von Byzantion, zweimal *agōnothétēs* der Pythischen Spiele (einmal 193 n. Chr.), hatte 209–213 den (wahrscheinlich kaiserlichen) Lehrstuhl in Athen inne [1]. Er beriet seinen Schüler Philostratos von Lemnos 213 bei den Olympischen Spielen (und weigerte sich danach, ihn durch eine eigene Rede zu beschämen); er besuchte Smyrna, um bei Megistias zu lernen. Philostratos (soph. 2,27) kennt lyrische *nómoi* und 30 Reden, rühmt H.' Erinnerungsvermögen sowie seine Hochherzigkeit, mit der er sogar seinen Feind Proklos behandelte.
→ Philostratos; Zweite Sophistik

1 I. Avotins, The Holders of the Chairs of Rhetoric at Athens, in: HSPh 79, 1975, 323 f. E. BO./Ü: L. S.

Hippokampos (Ἱππόκαμπος, *equus marinus*). Das Seepferdchen, das Paus. 2,1,9 als ›Pferd, welches von der Brust an einem Seeungeheuer (κῆτος) gleicht‹ erklärt (vgl. Serv. georg. 4,387: im ersten Teil ein Pferd, im letzten in einen Fisch übergehend). Der H. ist nicht identisch mit dem von Plin. nat. 32,58 u.ö. als Heilmittel erwähnten gleichnamigen Mittelmeerfisch (z. B. dem gefleckten Seepferdchen, Hippocampus guttulatus [1. 138]). Lit. Erwähnungen sind selten (z. B. Strab. 8,7,2 [384]). Nach Ail. nat. 14,20 stellte ein gekochter und in Wein aufgelöster Magen von einem H. für einen Trinkenden ein gefährliches Gift dar.

In der ant. Kunst dagegen begegnet das Seepferdchen auf myken. Goldplättchen und Gemmen, in archa. Zeit sehr häufig als – oft geflügeltes – Reittier für Poseidon oder einen Meergreis (→ Halios geron). Im 5. Jh. v. Chr. erscheint es selten auf Mz. und Gemmen, reichlicher in der Plastik des 4. Jh. (Figurengruppe des → Skopas mit Achilleus, Thetis, Poseidon und auf Delphinen, Seeungeheuern oder *hippocampi* sitzenden Nereiden; vgl. Plin. nat. 36,26) und auf Mosaiken und Vasen aus Olynth (vor 346 v. Chr.) sowie aus Unteritalien. Auf dem Nordfries des hell. Pergamonaltars in Berlin wird Poseidons Wagen von H. gezogen. Die Statuen-Basis des Domitius Ahenobarbus in München (35–32 v. Chr.) ist damit geschmückt. Auch in der etr. Kunst ist der H. ein häufiges Motiv, z. B. als Reittier einer Nereide auf Vasen und Spiegeln oder auf Grabsteinen und Sarkophagen. In der röm. Kaiserzeit wurden H. u. a. auf Sarkophagen, Aschebehältern, aber auch auf Wandgemälden und Mosaiken gern abgebildet (z. B. Triumphwagen des Neptunus und der Amphitrite, gezogen von 4 H., aus Utica/Tunesien, 3. Jh. n. Chr. [1. Farbabb. 22]).

1 Leitner 2 A. Driss, Die Schätze des Nationalmuseums in Bardo, 1962.

Lamer, s. v. H., RE 8, 1748 ff. • E. Boehringer, Die Mz. von Syrakus, 1929, 84 ff. • A. Rumpf, Die ant. Sarkophagreliefs 5,1: Die Meerwesen, 1939, 115 ff. C. HÜ.

Hippokleides (Ἱπποκλείδης). Sohn des Teisandros, Athener aus dem Geschlecht der Philaiden (→ Philaidai). Er warb um das J. 575 v. Chr. um → Agariste [1], die Tochter des Tyrannen → Kleisthenes von Sikyon, unterlag dabei aber, trotz guter Aussichten, dem Alkmaioniden (→ Alkmaionidai) → Megakles aufgrund eines gesellschaftlichen Affronts (Hdt. 6,126–130; Athen. 14,628d) [1]. Unter dem Archontat des H. wurden, vermutlich im J. 566/5 [2. 57 f.], die Panathenäen eingerichtet (Pherekydes FGrH 3 F 2; Hellanikos FGrH 4 F 22).

1 E. Stein-Hölkeskamp, Adelskultur und Polisgesellschaft, 1989, 118 f. 2 P. E. Corbett, The Burgon and Blaca Tombs, in: JHS 80, 1960, 52–60, bes. 57 f.

Davies, 8429, II • Develin, Nr. 1414 • Traill, PPA 538230. HA. BE.

Hippokles (Ἱπποκλῆς). H. von Kyme auf Euboia, Oikist (»Gründer«) des ital. Kyme gemeinsam mit Megasthenes von Chalkis. Nach Strabon (5,4,4) wurde die Kolonie einvernehmlich nach der Heimat des H. benannt, sollte aber als chalkid. Gründung gelten.

J. Bérard, La colonisation grecque, 1957, 38 f. M. MEI.

Hippoklos (Ἵπποκλος). H., (vermutlich erster) Tyrann von Lampsakos, von den Persern gestützt und am Skythenfeldzug des → Dareios [1] I. ca. 513 v. Chr. beteiligt (Hdt. 4,138). → Hippias [1] von Athen schloß durch die Ehe seiner Tochter Archedike mit H.' Sohn und Nachfolger Aiantides mit ihm eine Heiratsallianz, die zugleich eine Annäherung an Persien (Thuk. 6,59) bedeutete und möglicherweise ein Grund für Spartas Eingreifen in Athen 511/510 v. Chr. war [1. 301].
→ Tyrannis

1 D. M. Lewis, in: CAH 4, ²1988.

H. Berve, Die Tyrannis bei den Griechen, 1967, 87; 570 • L. de Libero, Die archaische Tyrannis, 1996, 383. J. CO.

Hippokoon (Ἱπποκόων). Sohn des → Oibalos und der Bateia (Nikostrate: schol. Eur. Or. 457), Halbbruder bzw. Bruder des → Tyndareos, den er aus Sparta vertreibt. Weil H. und die Hippokoontiden sich weigern, Herakles zu entsühnen, oder mit → Neleus verbündet sind, vor allem aber, weil sie Oionos erschlagen haben, rächt → Herakles sich an ihnen (Aition der Athena Axiopoinos) und setzt Tyndareos wieder ein (Diod. 4,33,5 f.; Paus. 3,1,4; 15,3–6; 19,7; Ps.-Apollod. 2,143; 3,123–125; schon Alkm. fr. 3 Calame [1; 2]). Mit Söhnen des H., eines »spartan. Unterweltsgotts« [3], setzt Paus. 3,14,6–7; 15,1 eine Reihe spartan. Kultheroen gleich.

1 C. Calame, Les choeurs de jeunes filles en Grèce archaïque, 1977, Bd. 2, 52 ff.; 60 f. 2 Ders., Le récit généalogique spartiate: la représentation mythologique d'une organisation spatiale, in: Quaderni di storia 13, 1987, 43–91, bes. 63–65, engl. gekürzt in: J. Bremmer, Interpretations of Greek Mythology, 1987, 153–186, bes. 170–172 3 S. Wide, Lakon. Kulte, 1893, Ndr. 1973, 322 f., vgl. 18 f. 4 H. W. Stoll, s. v. H. (1), Roscher I 2, 2677–2678. T. H.

Hippokrates (Ἱπποκράτης).
[1] Vater des → Peisistratos. H. stammte vermutlich aus Brauron, dem späteren Demos Philaidai, und führte seine Abstammung auf Neleus zurück (Hdt. 1,59; 5,65; Plut. Solon 10; 30).

Traill, PPA 538385. B. P.

[2] Sohn des Alkmaioniden (→ Alkmaionidai) → Megakles aus Athen, geb. um 560 v. Chr. H. war der Bruder des Kleisthenes, Vater des → Megakles und der Agariste [2] und dadurch Großvater des → Perikles mütterlicherseits (Hdt. 6,131; [Aristot.] Ath. pol. 22,5).

Davies 9688, X • Traill, PPA 538485.

[3] Sohn des Ariphron aus Athen, geb. vor 450 v. Chr. H. war 426/5 (SEG 10,227, Z. 3) und 424/3 Stratege. Während des Angriffs auf → Megara 424 gelang es ihm, nach geheimer Absprache mit den dortigen ›Führern des *dḗmos*‹, den Hafen → Nisaia einzunehmen (Thuk. 4,66–67). Am Ende dieses Jahres fiel er im Kampf gegen die Boioter beim Heiligtum → Delion [1] (Thuk. 4,101).

Davies 11811, II. • Traill, PPA 538615. E. S.-H.

[4] Sohn des Pantares aus Gela. H. übernahm nach der Ermordung seines Bruders Kleandros um 498 v. Chr. die Herrschaft über die Stadt und betrieb mit Hilfe eines sikelischen Söldnerheeres und einer Reiterei, die der vornehme Geloer → Gelon [1] führte, einen Territorialstaat, der sich von S nach N durch Sizilien zog: Er brachte → Kallipolis und → Naxos, Zankle und → Leontinoi in seine Gewalt und übergab sie polit. Freunden. Mit den Samiern, die 493 auf der Flucht vor dem Tyrannen → Aiakes [2] Zankle besetzten, handelte H. aus Furcht vor einem Eingreifen des Anaxilaos von Rhegion einen Vergleich aus, nach dem die Zanklaier den Samiern preisgegeben wurden, H. aber die Hälfte des Hausrats und der Sklaven der Stadt sowie aller Landbesitz zufielen. Den wahrscheinlich von ihm in Zankle eingesetzten Skythes aus Kos ließ er als Schuldigen nach Inykos bringen (Hdt. 6,23). Um 492/1 belagerte er → Syrakusai. Auf Vermittlung von Korinth und Kerkyra kam ein Vergleich zustande, nach dem Syrakus H. Kamarina abtreten mußte (Hdt. 7,154; Thuk. 6,5; 3). H. fiel 491/490 vor der Stadt Hybla im Krieg gegen die Sikeler (Hdt. 7,155).

D. Asheri, in: CAH 4, ²1988, 757–766 • H. Berve, Die Tyrannis bei den Griechen, 1967, 137ff., 597f. • T.J. Dunbabin, The Western Greeks, 1948, 106f. B.P.

[5] H. von Chios. Mathematiker und Astronom aus der 2. H. des 5. Jh. v. Chr. Nach Eudemos verfaßte H., der nach Anaxagoras und Oinopides lebte, die ersten ›Elemente‹ (Prokl. in Eucl. 1,66,7–8 Friedlein). Iamblichos (De communi mathematica scientia 25, p.78,1 Festa) nennt ihn zusammen mit → Theodoros von Kyrene als bedeutendsten Vertreter der mathematischen Sekte der Pythagoreer und macht ihn damit zum älteren Zeitgenossen des Sokrates. H. soll als Kaufmann sein Vermögen durch Betrüger oder Seeräuber verloren haben (Aristot. eth. Eud. 1247a 17–20; Plut. Solon 2; Philoponos in Aristot. phys. S.31,3–7 Vitelli). Vermutlich erwarb H. seine mathematischen Kenntnisse schon auf Chios. Später lebte er in Athen und trug zusammen mit Oinopides dazu bei, daß Athen zum Mittelpunkt der Mathematik in Griechenland wurde.

H. befaßte sich insbes. mit den sog. »klassischen Problemen«, die damals in der Mathematik behandelt wurden (Würfelverdopplung, Winkeldreiteilung, Kreisquadratur); es sind Probleme, bei denen Gleichungen gelöst werden müssen, die über den quadratischen Bereich hinausgehen. Zur Würfelverdopplung und Kreisquadratur hat H. eigene Beitr. geliefert. Obwohl seine Schriften verloren sind, lassen sich wesentliche Teile der »Möndchenquadratur« rekonstruieren [1]. Sie gelten als die ältesten erh. zusammenhängenden griech. Texte zur Mathematik. Bei der Würfelverdopplung (»Delisches Problem«) wird die Seite eines Würfels gesucht, dessen Volumen doppelt so groß wie das eines gegebenen Würfels ist. H. führte dieses Problem auf die Aufgabe zurück, zwei mittlere Proportionalen x und y zw. zwei gegebene Strecken a und $2a$ einzuschalten (Eutokios in Archim. de sphaera et cylindro, Archim. Op. 3, S.88,17–23 Heiberg; [9. 17–24]). Dies ist korrekt, weil aus $a{:}x = x{:}y = y{:}2a$ folgt: $x^3 = 2a^3$. Es ist nicht bekannt, ob H. eine Methode fand, um die beiden mittleren Proportionalen zu bestimmen.

Im Zusammenhang mit Versuchen, den Kreis zu quadrieren (d.h., ein Quadrat zu konstruieren, das flächengleich zu einem gegebenen Kreis ist), beschäftigte sich H. mit der Aufgabe, Kreismöndchen (d.h. durch Kreisbögen eingeschlossene Flächen) in flächengleiche geradlinige Figuren zu verwandeln. Der Text des H. wird von Simplikios überl. (In Aristot. phys., S.60,22–68,32 Diels), der angibt, → Eudemos wörtlich zu zitieren (zur Rekonstruktion [1; 4; 9. 25–41]). H. zeigt zunächst, daß Kreise sich wie die Quadrate ihrer Durchmesser verhalten und daß dies auch für ähnliche Kreisteile (Sektoren und Segmente) gilt. Er betrachtet dann Sehnen, deren Quadrate sich wie kleine ganze Zahlen (2:1, 3:1, 3:2) verhalten. Wenn ähnliche Kreissegmente über diesen Sehnen errichtet und voneinander abgezogen werden, so bleiben Möndchen (μηνίσκοι, *lunulae*) als Restfläche übrig, die quadrierbar sind, weil ihre Flächen einfache Zahlenverhältnisse sind. Im einfachsten Fall (Abb. 1) werden über dem gleichschenklig-rechtwinkligen Dreieck ABC ähnliche (nämlich von Viertelkreisen abgeschnittene) Segmente gezeichnet; der Außenbogen ist also gleich dem Halbkreis. Nach dem Satz des Pythagoras ist $AB^2 = AC^2 + BC^2$, und da sich die Segmente wie die Quadrate ihrer Sehnen verhalten, ist auch Segment AB = Segment AC + Segment BC. Da das Möndchen ABC dadurch entsteht, daß vom Dreieck ABC das Segment AB abgezogen und die Segmente AC und BC hinzugefügt werden, sind Möndchen und Dreieck flächengleich.

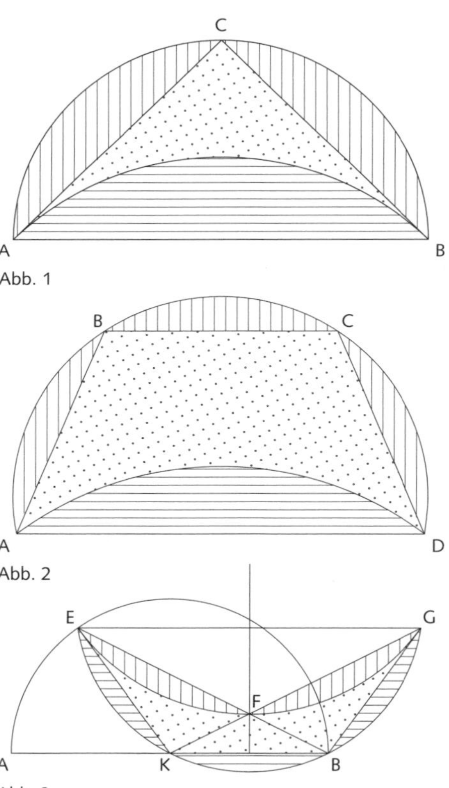

Im 2. Fall (Abb. 2) ist der Außenbogen größer als der Halbkreis, wobei gilt: AB = BC = CD und $AD^2 = 3\ AB^2$. Das Segment über AD ist also dreimal so groß wie das über AB. Wie im ersten Fall ist die Summe der kleineren Segmente gleich dem größeren Segment.

Im 3. Fall (Abb. 3) ist der äußere Bogen EKBG kleiner als ein Halbkreis. Das Möndchen wird aus zwei Kreisbögen gebildet, von denen der äußere in drei, der innere in zwei gleiche Teile geteilt ist, die die ähnlichen Segmente umschließen, wobei gilt: $EF^2 : EK^2 = 3:2$. Die von den fünf Sehnen gebildete geradlinige Figur ist flächengleich mit dem Möndchen, das demnach ebenfalls quadriert werden kann. Die Konstruktion geht von dem Halbkreis über AB aus. Die Strecke EF wird durch eine Einschiebung gefunden; dies ist das älteste bekannte Beispiel einer solchen νεῦσις-Konstruktion. – Schließlich quadriert H. noch ein Möndchen und einen Kreis zusammen. Die Anlage des Ganzen läßt vermuten, daß damit die Quadrierbarkeit jedes Möndchens bewiesen sein soll; dies trifft jedoch nicht zu, da die Beweise nicht allg. sind.

Die Möndchenquadratur des H. war im 13. und 14. Jh. im Westen in zwei Fassungen bekannt [3]. Die Frage, welche Möndchen elementar quadriert werden können, wurde seit dem 18. Jh. u. a. von D. Bernoulli und L. Euler diskutiert und im 20. Jh. endgültig gelöst (E. Landau, N. G. Tschebotarew, A. W. Dorodnow; [11]).

Die ›Elemente‹, die H. als erster verfaßt haben soll, waren vermutlich eine geordnete Zusammenstellung der im Bereich der Elementargeom. bekannten Dinge, in der alles auf gewisse Grundannahmen zurückgeführt wurde. Insofern ist H. ein Vorgänger des → Eukleides [3]. Zu den ›Elementen‹ dürften Sätze über Winkel und Kreisbögen gehört haben, die H. bei der Möndchenquadratur als bewiesene Voraussetzungen benutzt, ferner der Satz des Pythagoras und die Feststellung, daß sich Kreisflächen wie die Quadrate ihrer Durchmesser verhalten.

Als Astronom wird H. z. B. von Aristot. (meteor. 342b 36; 345b 9) gen. mit seiner Erklärung der Kometen und der Milchstraße, die der pythagoreischen ähnelt. Der Komet sei ein selten sichtbarer Planet und der Kometenschweif eine durch räumliche Bewegung hervorgerufene optische Täuschung.

→ Würfelverdopplung

Ed.: **1** F. Rudio, Der Ber. des Simplicius über die Quadraturen des Antiphon und des H., 1907 **2** M. Timpanaro Cardini, Pitagorici. Testimonianze e frammenti, fasc. 2, 1962, 28–73 **3** M. Clagett, The Quadratura circuli per lunulas, in: Ders., Archimedes in the Middle Ages, Bd. 1, 1964, 610–626.

Lit.: **4** O. Becker, Zur Textgestaltung des eudemischen Ber. über die Quadratur der Möndchen durch H. von Chios, in: O. Neugebauer u. a. (Hrsg.), Quellen und Stud. zur Gesch. der Mathematik, Astronomie und Physik, B. 3, 1936, 411–419 **5** O. Becker, Das mathematische Denken der Ant., 1957, 15; 58–60; 75 **6** A. A. Björnbo, s. v. H. (14), RE 8, 1780–1801 **7** I. Bulmer-Thomas, H. of Chios, in: Gillispie, Bd. 6, 1972, 410–418 **8** T. L. Heath, History of Greek Mathematics, 1921, Bd. 1, 183–202 **9** W. Knorr, The Ancient Trad. of Geometric Problems, 1986 **10** J. Mau, s. v. H. (7), KlP 2, 1967, 1165–1169 **11** C. J. Scriba, Welche Kreismonde sind elementar quadrierbar? Die 2400jährige Gesch. eines Problems bis zur endgültigen Lösung in den Jahren 1933/1947, in: Mitt. der Mathematischen Ges. in Hamburg 11, 1988, 517–539 **12** B. L. van der Waerden, Erwachende Wissenschaft, 1956, 216–224.

M. F.

[6] H. aus Kos, der Arzt. A. Leben B. Bildnisse C. Corpus Hippocraticum D. Wirkungsgeschichte im Altertum

A. Leben

Über die Person des H. ist außer seiner frühen Berühmtheit wenig mit Sicherheit bekannt. Aus einer Stelle bei Platon (Prot. 311b-c) ist seine Stellung als hervorragender Arzt – seine Rolle in der Medizin wird derjenigen des → Polykleitos und → Pheidias in der plastischen Kunst gleichgesetzt – gesichert; ferner ist die Kenntnis seiner Methode, die ihren Ausgang vom »Ganzen« nimmt, bei den Lesern des Phaidr. (270c-e) vorausgesetzt. H.' Geburtsort wird durch die Protagorasstelle bestätigt, die auch einen Hinweis auf seine Lebenszeit liefert: wenn sich sein Ruf zur Zeit der Dialoghandlung (ca. 433 v. Chr.) bereits etabliert hatte, ist zu schließen, daß H., selbst wenn Platon sich hier eines leichten Anachronismus schuldig macht, nicht lange nach 460 v. Chr. geboren sein kann, eher vielleicht früher. Aus Aristoteles' beiläufiger Anspielung auf den Kontrast zw. H.' körperlicher Kleinheit und seiner medizinischen Größe (pol. 1326a) erhellt, wie allg. bekannt die Figur des Arztes bis zu den zwanziger Jahren des 4. Jh. geworden war.

Alle späteren »Quellen« zum Leben des H., d. h. sowohl die Dokumentenslg. (zwei Reden, ein Erlaß und 24 Briefe), die sich direkt auf ihn beziehen will, als auch die zahlreichen Ber. – einschließlich einer biographischen Trad. – über seine Taten, Schriften und Ansichten [1], die im 3. Jh. v. Chr. anfangen und in zunehmender Fülle in der griech. und röm. Lit. der Kaiserzeit erscheinen, entbehren nennenswerter Beweiskraft. Sobald H.' zentrale Stellung in der Medizingesch. feststand und die Schriften des *Corpus Hippocraticum* in Alexandreia unter seinem Namen zusammengestellt waren, war die Voraussetzung für die Ausgestaltung eines Lebens und einer Persönlichkeit, wie sie sich für den Erfinder der Medizin ziemten, gegeben. Obwohl man dazu möglicherweise tatsächlich in koischen Archiven forschte und dabei gelegentlich Wahres zutage gefördert haben mag, läßt sich in diesen »Quellen« Echtes von Fiktivem so schwer trennen, daß ihr Wert im großen und ganzen für sehr gering zu erachten ist.

B. Bildnisse

1940 wurde in Ostia eine röm. Marmorbüste (Mus. Ostiense, Inv. Nr. 98; Helbig, Bd. 4, Nr. 3036) gefunden, die auf ein Original des 2. Jh. v. Chr. zurückgeht.

Schriften des *Corpus Hippocraticum* (Auswahl)

Abkürzung	**Lat. Titel**	**Griech. Titel**	**Deutscher Titel**
Acut.	De diaeta acutorum	*Perí diaítēs oxéōn*	Über die Diät bei akuten Krankheiten
Aër.	De aere, aquis, locis	*Perí aérōn, hydátōn, tópōn*	Über die Umwelt
Aff.	De affectionibus	*Perí pathṓn*	Über die Leiden
Alim.	De alimento	*Perí trophḗs*	Über die Nahrung
Anat.	De anatomia (De anatome)	*Perí anatomḗs*	Über die Anatomie
Aph.	Aphorismi	*Aphorismoí*	Aphorismen
Art.	De articulis	*Perí árthrōn ⟨embolḗs⟩*	Über die Einrichtung der Gelenke
Carn.	De carnibus	*Perí sarkṓn*	Über das Fleisch
Coac.	Coacae praecognitiones	*Kōakaí prognṓseis*	Koische Prognosen
Cord.	De corde	*Perí kardíēs*	Über das Herz
de Arte	De arte	*Perí téchnēs*	Über die Kunst
Decent.	De decenti ornatu	*Perí euschēmosýnēs*	Über den Anstand
Dent.	De dentitione	*Perí odontophyíēs*	Über das Zahnen
Dieb. Judic.	De diebus iudicatoriis	*Perí krisímōn ⟨hemeréōn⟩*	Über die kritischen Tage
Ep(ist).	Epistulae	*Epistolaí*	Briefe
Epid. (1–7)	De morbis popularibus (ma.: Epidemiarum 1.–7.)	*Epidēmiṓn 1.–7.*	Epidemien
Fist.	De fistulis	*Perí syríngōn*	Über die Fisteln
Flat.	De flatibus	*Perí physṓn*	Über die Winde
Foet. Exsect.	De exsectione foetus	*Perí enkatatomḗs embrýu*	Über die Zerstückelung des Kindes im Mutterleib
Fract.	De fracturis	*Perí agmṓn*	Über die Knochenbrüche
Genit.	De genitura	*Perí gonḗs*	Über den Samen
Gland.	De glandulis	*Perí adénōn*	Über die Drüsen
Haem.	De haemorrhoidibus	*Perí haimorrhoídōn*	Über die Hämorrhoiden
Hebd.	De hebdomadibus	*Perí hebdomádōn*	Über die Siebenzahl
Hum.	De humoribus	*Perí chymṓn*	Über die Säfte
Int.	De internis affectionibus	*Perí tṓn entós pathṓn*	Über die inneren Leiden
Judic.	De iudicationibus	*Perí krisíōn*	Über die Krisen
Jusj.	Iusiurandum	*Hórkos*	Eid
Liqu.	De liquidorum usu	*Perí hygrṓn chrḗsios*	Über den Gebrauch von Flüssigkeiten
Loc. Hom.	De locis in homine	*Perí tópōn tṓn katá ánthrōpon*	Über die Stellen am Menschen
Medic.	De medico	*Perí iētrú*	Über den Arzt
Morb. (1–4)	De morbis	*Perí núsōn*	Über die Krankheiten
Morb. Sacr.	De morbo sacro	*Perí hierḗs núsu*	Über die heilige Krankheit
Mul. (1–3)	De muliebribus	*Gynaikeíōn 1.–3.*	Über die Frauenkrankheiten
Nat. Hom.	De natura hominis	*Perí phýsios anthrṓpu*	Über die Natur des Menschen
Nat. Mul.	De natura muliebri	*Perí gynaikeíēs phýsios*	Über die Natur der Frau
Nat. Puer.	De natura pueri	*Perí phýsios paidíu*	Über die Natur des Kindes
Oct.	De octimestri partu	*Perí oktamḗnu*	Über das Achtmonatskind
Off.	De officina medici	*Kat' iētreíon*	Die ärztliche Werkstätte
Oss.	De ossium natura	*Perí ostéōn phýsios*	Über die Natur der Knochen
Praec.	Praeceptiones	*Parangelíai*	Vorschriften
Prog.	Praenotiones (Prognosticon)	*Prognōstikón*	Prognostikon
Prorrh. (1–2)	Praedicta (Prorrheticon)	*Prorrhētikón*	Vorhersagungen
Steril. (= Mul. 3)	De sterilibus	*Perí aphórōn ē gynaikeíōn*	Über die unfruchtbaren Frauen
Superf.	De superfetatione	*Perí epikyḗsios*	Über die Überschwängerung
Ulc.	De ulceribus	*Perí helkṓn*	Über die Geschwüre
VC	De capitis vulneribus (ma.: De vulneribus capitis)	*Perí tṓn en kephalḗ trōmátōn*	Über die Verletzungen am Kopf
Vict. (1–3)	De victu	*Perí diaítēs*	Über die Diät
Vid. Ac.	De visu	*Perí ópsios*	Vom Sehen
Virg.	De virginum morbis	*Perí partheníōn*	Über die Krankheiten der Jungfrauen
VM	De vetere medicina	*Perí archaíēs iētrikḗs*	Über die antike Medizin

Angeführt sind jeweils die (bzw. einer der) antiken lateinischen Titel; wo sich die gängige Abkürzung nach dem mittelalterlichen Titel richtet, ist dieser mit angegeben.

Sowohl der FO im Grab des Arztes Markios Demetrios als auch die auf der dazugehörenden Säule befindliche Versinschr., die als Anspielung auf den ersten hippokratischen Aphorismus zu deuten ist, unterstützen die Identifikation mit H. Drei verschiedene Bronzemünzsorten, die in der frühen Kaiserzeit auf Kos geprägt wurden, zeigen einen bärtigen Kopf bzw. eine Fig. mit der Inschr. IΠ bzw. IΠΠΟΚΡΑΤΗΣ (Bibliothèque nationale, Cabinet des médailles, Nr. 1273, 1274 = British Mus., Greek Coins, Caria, Cos, Rhodes etc., Nr. 215, 216; BN, Nr. 1246; Berlin, Staatliches Münzkabinett, Faustina II.).

C. Corpus Hippocraticum
1. Allgemein 2. Überlieferung
3. Werküberblick 4. Medizin

1. Allgemein

Das *Corpus Hippocraticum* (*CH*) entstand höchstwahrscheinlich im hell. Alexandreia als Ergebnis ptolemäischen Sammelfleißes. → Bakcheios [1] von Tanagra behandelt schon vor 200 v. Chr. in seinem hippokratischen Glossar nachweislich 21 Schriften, während → Erotianos im 1. Jh. n. Chr. eine Liste von ca. 40 Titeln bietet. Andere ant. Quellen (hauptsächlich → Galenos) nennen etwa 10 weitere Titel, so daß rund 12 Schriften der 62 im Index der ma. Hs. Vaticanus gr. 276 verzeichneten Titel ohne Erwähnung im Alt. bleiben. Wie dieses heterogene und offensichtlich von verschiedenen Verf. stammende Konglomerat, dessen Gemeinsamkeit sich auf den ion. Dial. und irgendein Verhältnis zur Medizin beschränkt, schließlich einem einzigen Autor zugewiesen wurde, bleibt unklar. Das einzige voralexandrinische Zit. eines hippokratischen Textes steht bei Aristoteles (hist. an. 512b), wo ein längerer Passus aus *Nat. Hom.* (zur Abkürzung der Titel vgl. Tabelle) dem Arzt → Polybos zugeschrieben ist.

Die hippokratische Echtheitskritik [2; 3] bedient sich sowohl äußerer wie innerer Kriterien. Als äußerer Anhaltspunkt dient erstens die o. erwähnte Äußerung zur Methode des H. im Phaidr.; jedoch ist die Stelle so unspezifisch, daß man sich bis h. nicht auf die hippokratische Schrift, die dieser Methode entsprechen soll, hat einigen können. Zweitens berichtet der 1892 bekannt gewordene → Anonymus Londinensis, ein Pap. aus dem 2. Jh. n. Chr., der teilweise auf peripatetische Schultrad. zurückgeht, in einer längeren Abh. über pathologische Lehrmeinungen (5,35–7,40) ausführlich über die Ansichten des H. Aber auch diese Quelle gibt keine mit Sicherheit auf bestimmte Werke des H. zu beziehenden Hinweise. Dritter Anhaltspunkt für die mögliche Echtheit bestimmter Schriften ist die Übereinstimmung einzelner Angaben mit Details aus H.' Leben, wie es in den biographischen Zeugen dargestellt ist; jedoch ist eher damit zu rechnen, daß die Biographie von den Schriften des *CH* inspiriert wurde, als daß ihr unabhängige histor. Bed. zukäme. Die inneren Echtheitskriterien laufen letzten Endes alle auf eine Bewertung der klinischen oder wiss. Leistung der verschiedenen Schriften hinaus: Werke, die den Vorstellungen des jeweiligen Mediziners bzw. Historikers entsprechen, gelten als koisch bzw. echt hippokratisch. Die Zeitgebundenheit dieses in der Neuzeit allzu häufig angewandten Ansatzes bedarf keiner weiteren Worte [4].

Die Einteilung der hippokratischen Schriften nach Schulrichtungen, wobei hauptsächlich eine koische und eine knidische Schule zu unterscheiden sind, geht auf Galen zurück, der die Hauptmerkmale zweier mit H. zeitgenössischer medizinischer Trad. aufstellte. Unter Heranziehung dieser und anderer Quellen versuchten in jüngster Zeit Jouanna und Grensemann scharfumrissene Bilder der konkurrierenden Schulen herauszuarbeiten, die als Zuweisungskriterien dienen könnten; doch haben diese Stud. trotz wertvoller Erkenntnisse zum Verständnis hippokratischer Medizin in diesem Punkt keine allg. Zustimmung gefunden [5; 6; 7; 8].

2. Überlieferung

Die unabhängigen Textzeugen des *CH* umfassen sechs ma. Hss., die jeweils zwischen vier und rund fünfzig der im *CH* vereinigten Schriften beinhalten: Laurentianus gr. 74,7 (9. Jh.) = B; Marcianus gr. 269 (10. Jh.) = M; Vindobonensis medicus gr. 4 (10. Jh.) = Θ; Parisinus gr. 2253 (11. Jh.) = A; Vaticanus gr. 276 (12. Jh.) = V und z. T. Parisinus gr. 2141 (13. Jh.) = I [9]. Außerdem bieten eine Anzahl von Pap. kleinere Textstücke [10].

3. Werküberblick

Da die ca. siebzig Schriften des *CH* in Form, Ziel, Wissensstand und theoretischen Anschauungen stark divergieren, läßt sich keine allg. Gliederung aufstellen, die eine sachliche oder histor. Gültigkeit beanspruchen könnte. Die folgende Einteilung ausgewählter Werke in sechs größere Kategorien nach lit. Gattung dient rein praktischen Zwecken.

(a) Handbücher (dem Umfang nach fast die Hälfte des *CH*), die sich den drei Fachgebieten der inneren Medizin, Chirurgie und der Frauenheilkunde zuordnen lassen, befassen sich jeweils mit mehr oder minder festumrissenen Krankheits- bzw. Wundengruppen. Die fünf Schriften aus dem Gebiet der inneren Medizin (*Aff.*; *Morb. 1–3* [11] und *Int.*) weisen eine gemeinsame Struktur auf, die aus einer Aneinanderreihung unabhängiger Kap. besteht, in denen jeweils ein spezifischer pathologischer Zustand abgehandelt wird, und zwar prinzipiell nach den Kategorien: Name der Krankheit bzw. Hauptmerkmal; Symptome und Verlauf; Ätiologie; Prognose; Behandlung. Die Reihenfolge der Krankheiten innerhalb einer Schrift verläuft oft *a capite ad calcem*.

In den großen chirurgischen Büchern [12] (*Fract.*; *Art.* und *VC*) werden die wichtigsten Brüche und Verrenkungen bzw. Wunden und deren Behandlung mit großer Sorgfalt und Fachkenntnis erklärt, meistens in Kapitelserien, die jeweils einer bestimmten Wundart gewidmet sind. Kleinere chirurgische Werke (*Haem.*; *Fist.*; *Liqu.*; *Vid. Ac.* und *Ulc.*) befassen sich mit verschiedenen Spezialgebieten.

Die B. *Mul.* 1–3, von denen das dritte auch den Titel *Steril.* trägt, handeln ausgiebig von Physiologie, Pathologie und Behandlung des Uterus einschließlich Hyper- und Amenorrhöe, Krebs, Gebärmuttervorfall, Unfruchtbarkeit und Schwangerschaftsleiden [13]. Ein beträchtlicher Teil dieser B. besteht aus Rezepten, die in getrennten Kap. (*Mul.* 1, 74–109; *Mul.* 2,185–212; *Steril.* 217–32) zusammengefaßt sind.

(b) Zu den Maximenslg. gehört die weitverbreiteste aller hippokratischen Schriften, *Aph.*, die aus 422 kurzen Aussagen in sieben Abteilungen besteht, welche sämtliche Aspekte der Medizin berücksichtigen. Enger gefaßt sind die zwei Werke *Coac.* und *Prorrh.* 1 [14] mit 640 bzw. 170 prognostischen, nach inhaltlich zusammengehörenden Gebieten eingeteilten Aussagen. Zwei kleinere Werke (*Dent.* und *Alim.* [15]), behandeln in 32 bzw. 55 Maximen die frühe Versorgung des Kindes und Fragen der Ernährung und des Wachstums.

(c) Ein weiteres Viertel des *CH* ist monographischen Abh. mit eindeutiger Zielsetzung gewidmet. Die Schriften *Carn.* [16] und *Genit./Nat. Puer.* [17] beschreiben die Entstehung des Menschen vom Zusammenkommen der Samen beider Eltern bis zur Formung der einzelnen Teile des Körpers samt der Ausübung ihrer Funktionen. In der Schrift *Cord.* [18], die ihrer anatomischen Kenntnisse wegen wahrscheinlich in das 3. Jh. v. Chr. zu datieren ist, gibt der Autor eine detaillierte Beschreibung des menschlichen Herzens, wobei er Herzklappen erwähnt sowie zwischen Arterien und Venen unterscheidet.

Andere Monographien befassen sich mit Fragen der Pathogenese. *Nat. Hom.* stellt ein Schema von vier Körpersäften (Blut, Schleim, gelbe Galle, schwarze Galle) auf, dem zufolge Gesundheit in der gleichmäßigen Mischung und Verteilung der Säfte, Krankheit in der Störung dieses Gleichgewichts besteht. *Morb.* 4 [17] präsentiert ein ähnliches Viererschema, allerdings mit Wasser statt schwarzer Galle als viertem Saft; *Vict.* [19] betont den zentralen Gegensatz von Feuer und Wasser im menschlichen Wesen und das im Gleichgewicht zu haltende Verhältnis von Nahrungsaufnahme und Leibesübung; *Flat.* [20] leitet alle Krankheiten von der Luft ab, die beim Atmen, Essen, Trinken oder durch Wunden in den Körper eindringt, während *Morb. sacr.* [21] die Symptome der Epilepsie als Resultat einer durch Phlegmazufluß in den Gefäßen hervorgerufenen Unterbrechung der Luftzufuhr zum Gehirn erklärt. *VM* [22] vertritt eine auf Erfahrung beruhende diätetische Medizin, wie sie die »Alten« entdeckten, gegenüber der zeitgenössischen Tendenz, sich in der Behandlung nach abstrakten Faktoren wie Hitze, Kälte, Trockenheit und Feuchtigkeit zu richten. Die Einzelheiten korrekter Diät, v.a. die Rolle der Verabreichung von Gerstenschleim, ist Thema der Schrift *Acut.*, während *Prog.* [23] die Wichtigkeit einer langen Reihe von Zeichen am Patienten sowie seiner Ausscheidungen betont, die unabhängig von der Diagnose allgemeingültige Schlüsse auf den Krankheitsausgang ermöglichen. Die Schrift *Aër.* [24] unterrichtet den Wanderarzt über die Bed. von Umweltfaktoren wie Wind, Wasser und geographischer Lage für die Gesundheit der Bevölkerung, deren Kenntnis es ihm erleichtert, in kurzer Zeit korrekte Diagnosen und Prognosen zu stellen; in einem zweiten Teil bietet die Schrift einen ausführlichen Vergleich zwischen Europäern und Asiaten, der aus den geographischen Besonderheiten der beiden Kontinente abgeleitet ist.

(d) Eine weitere Gruppe theoretischer Schriften (z. B. *Loc. hom.*, *Hum.*, *Acut.* [*Spuria*]), der es an strukturellem Zusammenhalt mangelt – Kennzeichen ist eher formale und inhaltliche Heterogenität, Verworrenheit oder sogar Widersprüchlichkeit – gibt Auskünfte über einzelne Aspekte der Heilkunde.

(e) Obwohl untereinander verschieden in Gewichtung und Ausarbeitung, teilen die B. *Epid.* 1–7 [25] den Charakter einer am Krankenbett zusammengestellten Datenslg., die hauptsächlich aus einzelnen Fallbeschreibungen und Jahresber. (*katastáseis*) über die Morbidität und Mortalität im Verhältnis zur Wetterlage in ausgewählten Gemeinden besteht. *Epid.* 1 und 3 sind gründlicher aufgearbeitet als die restlichen Epidemien-B., konzentrieren sich auf Fieberkrankheiten und unterlassen bei den Fallbeschreibungen einen ausdrücklichen Hinweis auf die Diagnose. *Epid.* 4, 5 und 7 bieten ausschließlich Krankengeschichten, die in Inhalt und Umfang stark variieren, während *Epid.* 2 und 6 [26] jeglicher inneren Ordnung entbehren.

(f) Zur letzten Gruppe gehören Dokumente (z. B. ›Eid‹ [27], Reden, Briefe [28]), deren histor. Stellenwert schwer einzuschätzen ist.

4. Medizin

Ausgangspunkt hippokratischer Physiologie und Pathologie, wie sie trotz aller Divergenzen den Schriften des *CH* zugrundeliegen, ist die implizite, aus Beobachtung und Erfahrung gewonnene Annahme [29], daß der Körper aus festen und flüssigen Bestandteilen bestehe, die in bestimmter Weise aufeinander einwirken. Anatomisch (→ Anatomie) bekannt und benannt sind die verschiedenen Körperteile, soweit sie von außen sichtbar sind oder durch Verletzungen sichtbar werden; ferner werden aus wohl zufälligen Beobachtungen an Tieren Rückschlüsse auf Form und Bau der innere Teile des menschlichen Körpers gezogen. Jedem Körperteil ist eine bestimmte Struktur eigen, die ihn – zeitgenössischen naturwissenschaftlichen Vorstellungen zufolge – mehr oder weniger befähigt, Körperflüssigkeiten anzuziehen und aufzunehmen oder abzulassen. Flüssige Körpersubstanzen sind außer den verschiedenen beobachtbaren Ausscheidungs- und Absonderungsprodukten die beiden lebenserhaltenden Stoffe Luft und Blut sowie hypothetische Körpersäfte, und zwar hauptsächlich Schleim und Galle, die sich im Krankheitszustand durch wahrnehmbare Veränderungen am Körper oder in den Ausscheidungsprodukten des Patienten bemerkbar machen [30]. Eine ausgewogene Mischung der Körpersäfte und Integrität der festen Strukturen sind

Grundlage der Gesundheit; Krankheit entsteht, wenn sich durch äußere Einflüsse Quantität oder Temperatur der Körpersäfte soweit verändert, daß deren Gleichgewicht gestört ist. In diesem Fall werden Schleim/Galle in Bewegung gesetzt, sondern sich vom Blut ab und werden von den verschiedenen Körperteilen ihrer Struktur entsprechend angezogen oder aufgesogen, bes. wenn diese erhitzt oder ausgetrocknet sind. Geraten sie in die Blutbahn, verhindern sie den regelmäßigen Fluß von Blut und Luft in den Gefäßen; setzen sie sich an einem bestimmten Körperteil fest, verletzen sie diesen und verursachen dadurch die verschiedenen Krankheitssymptome. Umgekehrt können innere oder äußere Traumata der festen Teile Krankheitsursache sein, was wiederum Auswirkungen auf die Säftebewegung hat.

Gewinnt der Körper in dem nun folgenden Kampf die Oberhand, wird der schädliche Saft, nachdem er durch einen von Fieber geförderten Kochungsprozeß »reif« geworden ist, ausgeschieden, die Verletzung heilt, und der Patient wird gesund. Die Aufgabe des Arztes ist es, diesen natürlichen Heilungsprozeß zu fördern, indem er einerseits den Körper des Patienten durch Verabreichung bzw. Entzug von Nahrung zum richtigen Zeitpunkt stärkt oder zumindest nicht schwächt, andererseits durch aktiven Eingriff, sei es diätetisch, medikamentös oder chirugisch, direkt Einfluß auf den Krankheitsvorgang nimmt mit dem Ziel, durch Entfernung oder Verdünnung des schädlichen Saftes, und/oder Wiederherstellung der natürlichen Struktur der festen Körperteile die Störung zu beheben. Das klinische Vorgehen des Arztes schreitet von der ersten Unt. des Patienten unter Berücksichtigung seiner gesamten Lebensumstände und der Ermittlung der Krankengesch. über Diagnose und Prognose zur Behandlung fort.

Über die Stellung des hippokratischen Arztes in der Ges. informieren sowohl eine Reihe deontologischer Schriften als auch beiläufige Bemerkungen in den übrigen Werken des *CH*. Die aus diesen Quellen sich ergebenden drei Hauptmerkmale des ärztlichen Selbstverständnisses sind erstens die Überzeugung von dem alleinigen Wert eines rationalen Vorgehens unter Ausschluß aller magischen bzw. rel. Erwägungen (*Morb. Sacr.*); zweitens der Glaube an die Gültigkeit theoretischen Wissens und praktischen Könnens trotz des Fehlens staatlich anerkannter Normen medizinischer Ausbildung und Qualifikation; drittens das Bewußtsein der in Ermangelung öffentlicher Bestätigung für den einzelnen Arzt bestehenden Notwendigkeit, in jedem einzelnen Fall seine Kompetenz und Vertrauenswürdigkeit unter Beweis zu stellen. Aus dieser Situation ergibt sich der besondere Wert, den der hippokratische Arzt auf seine äußere Erscheinung und sein Verhalten, auf seine Klarheit und Überzeugungskraft in Diskussionen, auf seine Kunstfertigkeit bei chirurgischen Maßnahmen aller Art und auf seine Kompetenz im Prognostizieren von Krankheitsverläufen legt. Zu diesen Bemühungen um den Nachweis eines Berufsethos gehört auch die Abfassung von Schriften wie *Praec.* und *Decent.*, die ausdrückliche Vorschriften für den praktizierenden Arzt enthalten, und vermutlich auch die Formulierung des Eides. Die medizinische Ausbildung scheint die Form des persönlichen Anschlusses an einen Meister, wie sie sowohl in Handwerker- wie Sophistenkreisen üblich war, angenommen zu haben.

D. Wirkungsgeschichte im Altertum

Schon im → Hellenismus fing eine rege Beschäftigung mit dem *CH* in Form von Komm. und Gloss. an. → Herophilos soll um 300 eine Widerlegung des *Prognostikon* geschrieben haben, und sein Schüler → Bakcheios [1] von Tanagra hat ein Spezial-WB hippokratischer Ausdrücke verfaßt. Das erste erh. Werk, das direkt auf einer Schrift des *CH* fußt, ist der mit Abb. versehene Komm. des → Apollonios [16] von Kition ›Über die Gelenke‹, in dem er H. das Epitheton »göttlichster« beimißt und ihn als den Arzt schlechthin bezeichnet. Unter den Römern erwähnt → Varro (res rusticae 1,4,5) als erster die Taten des H., während → Celsus [7] (praef. 8) und → Scribonius Largus (praef. 3; 5) im 1. Jh. n. Chr. H. als Verf. der hippokratischen Schriften einen Platz als Begründer der Medizin einräumen.

Im allg. wird der H. des *CH* und der biographischen Trad. vom 1. Jh. n. Chr. an zur Rechtfertigung eigener Lehrmeinungen von fast allen medizinischen Schriftstellern außer den → Methodikern erwähnt und zit. Der histor. bedeutendste dieser Hippokratiker ist Galen, der seiner selbsterwählten Rolle als Deuter und Verteidiger des großen Arztes aus Kos mit einer reichen Fülle histor. und interpretatorischer Komm., Propagandaschriften und einem Gloss. gerecht zu werden versucht [31]. Galens H. erreichte kanonische Gültigkeit, als → Oreibasios Galens Schriften zur bevorzugten Quelle für seine medizinischen Kompendien bestimmte, und zwar ›weil [Galen] sich an die Grundsätze und Einsichten des H. aufs genaueste anschließt‹ (Collectionum Medicarum reliquiae 1, praef.; [32]).

→ Hippokratismus; Hippokratischer Eid

1 J. Rubin, Hippocratic Lives and Legends, 1992, 1–93 **2** H. Diller, Stand und Aufgaben der Hippokratesforsch., in: Jb. 1959 der Akad. der Wissenschaften und der Lit., 271–287 **3** G. E. R. Lloyd, Methods and Problems in Greek Science, 1991, 194–223 **4** I. M. Lonie, Cos versus Cnidus and the Historians, in: History of Science 16, 1978, 42–92 **5** W. D. Smith, Galen on Coans and Cnidians, in: Bulletin of the History of Medicine 47, 1973, 569–585 **6** J. Jouanna, Hippocrate. Pour une archéologie de l'école de Cnide, 1974 **7** H. Grensemann, Knidische Medizin I–II, 1975/1987 **8** A. Thivel, Cnide et Cos?, 1981 **9** A. Rivier, Recherches sur la trad. manuscrite du traité Hippocratique »De morbo sacro«, 1962 **10** Marganne **11** R. Wittern, Die hippokratische Schrift De morbis I, 1974 **12** J. E. Petrequin, Chirurgie d'Hippocrate, 1877/8 **13** H. Fasbender, Entwickelungslehre, Geburtshülfe und Gynäkologie in den hippokratischen Schriften, 1897 **14** H. Pollack, Textkritische Unt. zu der hippokratischen Schrift Prorrhetikos I, 1976 **15** K. Deichgräber, Pseudhippokrates, Über die Nahrung, 1973 **16** Ders., Hippokrates, Über Entstehung und Aufbau des menschlichen Körpers, 1935 **17** I. M. LONIE, The Hippocratic Treatises »On Generation«, »On the Nature of the Child«, »Diseases IV«, 1981 **18** Ders., The paradoxical Text 'On the Heart', in: Medical History 17, 1973, 1–34 **19** R. JOLY Recherches sur le traité pseudo-hippocratique Du Régime, 1960 **20** A. NELSON, Die hippokratische Schrift ΠΕΡΙ ΦΥΣΕΩΝ, 1909 **21** H. GRENSEMANN, Die hippokratische Schrift »Über die heilige Krankheit«, 1968 **22** A.-J. FESTUGIÈRE, Hippocrate. L'Ancienne Médecine, 1948 **23** B. ALEXANDERSON, Die hippokratische Schrift Prognostikon, 1963 **24** H. DILLER, Wanderarzt und Aitiologe, 1934 **25** G. BAADER, R. WINAU (Hrsg.), Die hippokratischen Epidemien, 1989 **26** D. MANETTI, A. ROSELLI, Ippocrate Epidemie libro sesto, 1982 **27** G. HARIG, J. KOLLESCH, Der hippokratische Eid, in: Philologus 122, 1978, 157–176 **28** W. D. SMITH, Hippocrates. Pseudepigraphic Writings, 1990 **29** L. BOURGEY, Observation et expérience chez les médecins de la Collection Hippocratique, 1953 **30** E. SCHÖNER, Das Viererschema in der ant. Humoralpathologie, 1964, 15–58 **31** W. D. SMITH, The Hippocratic Trad., 1979, 61–176 **32** O. TEMKIN, Gesch. des Hippokratismus im ausgehenden Alt., in: Kyklos 4, 1932, 1–80.

ED.: F. Z. ERMERINS, Hippocratis ... reliquiae, 3 Bde., 1859–1864 · J. L. HEIBERG et al., CMG I, 1927ff. · R. JOLY et al., Ed. Budé, 1967ff. · W. H. S. JONES et al., Loeb Classical Library, 1923ff. · H. KUEHLEWEIN, Hippocratis Opera, nur 2 Bde. erschienen, 1894–1902 · E. LITTRÉ, Œuvres complètes d'Hippocrate, 10 Bde., 1839–1861. KONDORDANZ/INDEX: J. H. KÜHN, U. FLEISCHER, Index Hippocraticus, 1986–1989 · G. MALONEY, W. FROHN, Concordance des œuvres hippocratiques, 1984. ÜBERS. INS DT.: R. FUCHS, H. Sämtliche Werke, 3 Bde., 1895–1900 · R. KAPFERER, G. STICKER, Die Werke des H., 5 Bde., 1933–1940. BIBLIOGR.: B. BRUNI CELLI, Bibliografía Hipocrática, 1984 · S. BYL, Les dix dernières années (1983–1992) de la recherche hippocratique, in: Centre Jean-Palerne: Lettre d'informations 22, 1993, 1–39 · G. FICHTNER, Corpus Hippocraticum. Verzeichnis der hippokratischen und pseudohippokratischen Schriften, ^{2}1990 · G. MALONEY, R. SAVOIE, Cinq cents ans de bibliogr. hippocratique, 1982. GESAMTDARSTELLUNGEN: C. DAREMBERG, Œuvres choisies d'Hippocrate, ^{2}1855 · L. EDELSTEIN, s. v. H. (16), RE Suppl. 6, 1290–1345 · W. A. HEIDEL, Hippocratic medicine: its spirit and method, 1941 · J. JOUANNA, Hippocrate, 1992 (mit ausführlicher Bibliogr.) · P. LAÍN-ENTRALGO, La medicina Hipocrática, 1970 · J. A. LÓPEZ FÉREZ (Hrsg.), Tratados Hipocráticos. Actas del VIIe Colloque international hippocratique, 1992 · R. WITTERN, P. PELLEGRIN (Hrsg.), Hippokratische Medizin und ant. Philos., Verh. des VIII. Internationalen Hippokrates-Kolloquiums, 1996. P. PO. u. BE. GU.

[7] Spartiat, verteidigte 412 v. Chr. als Kommandant eines peloponnes. Geschwaders Knidos gegen die Athener (Thuk. 8,35), nahm 410 als *epistoleús* (»stellvertretender Kommandant«) des *naúarchos* (»Flottenkommandant«) Mindaros an der für Sparta äußerst verlustreichen Schlacht bei Kyzikos teil (Thuk. 8,107; Xen. hell. 1,1,23) und fiel 409 als Harmost (→ *harmostaí*) in Kalchedon bei der Verteidigung der Polis (Xen. hell. 1,3,5f.; Diod. 13,66,2). K.-W. WEL.

[8] Karthager syrakusanischer Abstammung, älterer Bruder des → Epikydes [2], mit dem gemeinsam er als Gesandter → Hannibals [4] im 2. Punischen Krieg 214 v. Chr. das syrakusanisch-karthagische Bündnis vermittelte (Pol. 7,2,3–5; Liv. 24,6,2); in den Wirren nach dem Tod des → Hieronymos [3] setzten die Brüder ihre Wahl zu Strategen durch (Liv. 24,27–32). Nachdem H. die Verhandlungen mit den Römern abgebrochen hatte und M. → Claudius [I 11] Marcellus Syrakus belagerte, übernahm er mit → Himilkon [4] die Kriegsführung (Liv. 24,33–35; Plut. Marcellus 14) und fiel schließlich der Epidemie im karthag. Heerlager zum Opfer (Liv. 25,26,4–14).

HUSS, 350–360; 369. L.-M. G.

Hippokrene (Ἱπποκρήνη, Ἵππου κρήνη, »Pferdequelle«; zu den Namen [5. 1853]). Brunnen, h. Kriopigadhi, unterhalb des Ostgipfels des → Helikon im Westen der aus ant. Spolien erbauten Kapelle Agios Elias [1. 186f.; 2. 239f.; 3. 97–99; 4. 621–624]; schon bei Hes. theog. 1 ff. als Ort der Musen und der dichterischen Inspiration bezeugt; seit hell. Zeit wird die Entstehung der Quelle auf einen Hufschlag des → Pegasos zurückgeführt [5. 1854ff.]. Belegstellen: Strab. 8,6,21; 9,2,25; Paus. 9,31,3f.; Prop. 3,3,1ff.; Ov. fast. 5,7f., met. 5,255ff.

1 V. L. ARAVANTINOS, Topographical and Archaeological Investigations on the Summit of Helicon, in: A. HURST, A. SCHACHTER (Hrsg.), La montagne des Muses, 1996, 185–192 **2** C. BURSIAN, Geogr. von Griechenland 1, 1862 **3** H. H. ULRICHS, Reisen und Forsch. in Griechenland 2, 1863 **4** H. G. LOLLING, Reisenotizen aus Griechenland (1876 und 1877), 1989 **5** E. SITTIG, F. BÖLTE, s. v. H., RE 8, 1853–1857. P. F.

Hippolochos (Ἱππόλοχος).

[1] Sohn des → Bellerophontes, Vater des Lykierfürsten → Glaukos [4] (Hom. Il. 6,206 u.ö.).

[2] Troer, fällt zusammen mit seinem Bruder → Peisandros dem Agamemnon in die Hände, der das Lösegeld-Angebot der Brüder mit einem Hinweis auf die Schuld ihres Vaters → Antimachos [1] hart zurückweist und beide tötet (Hom. Il. 11,122–148).

P. WATHELET, Dictionnaire des Troyens de l'Iliade, 1988, Nr. 173f. MA. ST.

[3] Der Thessaler H. trat im 4. Syrischen Krieg 218 v. Chr. mit 400 Reitern zu → Antiochos [5] III. über, deckte mit 5000 Infanteristen die Gegend von Samareia und befehligte 217 in der Schlacht von Rapheia etwa 5000 griech. Söldner (Pol. 5,70,11; 71,11; 79,9).

M. LAUNEY, Recherches sur les armées hellénistiques, ^{2}1987, 216. A. ME.

Hippologie s. Reiterei

Hippolyte (Ἱππολύτη).

[1] → Amazone im Herakles- und Theseusmythos, Tochter des → Ares und der Otrere. Herakles soll ihr im

Auftrag des → Eurystheus den Gürtel des Ares rauben (Apoll. Rhod. 2,778 ff.; 966 ff.; Hyg. fab. 30; Apollod. 2,98). In einigen Quellen tötet er dabei H. (Eur. Herc. 407 ff.). Im Theseusmythos konkurriert H. mit → Antiope [2] und → Glauke [3] als Gemahlin des Theseus (Isokr. or. 12,193; Plut. Theseus 27,5,13). Theseus raubt H. und zeugt mit ihr den → Hippolytos, oder er nimmt sie nach einem Friedensschluß mit den gegen Athen kämpfenden Amazonen zur Frau (Apollod. epit. 1,16). Nach Plutarch kämpft H. zusammen mit Theseus gegen die Amazonen und wird von → Molpadia getötet. Die gleichnamige Heroine von Megara (Paus. 1,41,7) steht wohl in keiner Verbindung zu den Amazonen.

Lit.: S. Eitrem, s. v. H., RE 8, 1863–1865.
Abb.: P. Devambez, A. Kauffmann-Samaras, s. v. Amazones, LIMC 1.2, 470–471, Nr. 233, 242.

[2] Tochter des → Dexamenos [1] (Diod. 4,33).
[3] Tochter des → Kretheus, Gattin des → Akastos, des Königs der Magneten, die den → Peleus vergeblich zu verführen sucht und ihn daraufhin bei ihrem Gatten verleumdet. Peleus entgeht dem Mordanschlag und tötet das Königspaar (Pind. N. 4,54 ff.; 5,26 ff.). R. HA.

Hippolytos (Ἱππόλυτος).
[1] Sohn des → Theseus und einer Amazone (→ Antiope [2] oder → Hippolyte). Sein mythisch-lit. Bild ist maßgeblich durch die H.-Dramen des Sophokles (*Phaídra*, verloren) und bes. des Euripides geprägt, den verlorenen früheren *H. Kalyptómenos* (›der verhüllte H.‹) und den erhaltenen *H. Stephanēphóros* (›der Kranzträger H.‹). Beide gehen von der Liebe der Stiefmutter → Phaidra aus, welche H. ablehnt, worauf Phaidra ihn der sexuellen Nachstellung anklagt; der erzürnte Theseus verflucht H., und Poseidon bewirkt seinen Tod, indem er ihn durch seine Pferde schleifen läßt. Die Unterschiede der beiden Stücke, von denen der *H. Kalyptómenos* durch die Echos bei Eur. Herc. 4 und Senecas *Phaedra* teilweise erkennbar ist, müssen in der Charakterzeichnung von H. und Phaidra gelegen haben – das frühere Stück muß Phaidras erotische Avancen sehr direkt dargestellt haben (aus Scham darüber hatte sich H. verhüllt, was den Titel gab), das spätere stellt H. als einseitigen Verehrer der jungfräulichen → Artemis dar (für die er einen Blumenkranz pflückt), was den Zorn der → Aphrodite provoziert; die Handlung ist letztlich durch diesen göttlichen Konflikt ausgelöst.

Nach anderen Versionen wird H. von Asklepios wieder ins Leben zurückgerufen (Apollod. 3,121, nach dem archa. Epos *Naupaktiká*), wonach er entweder nach It. auswandert und das → Diana-Heiligtum von → Aricia gründet (Paus. 2,27,3), von Artemis als Virbius in ihr Heiligtum bei Aricia gebracht (Verg. Aen. 7,761–783; Ov. fast. 6,735–762) oder als Fuhrmann (Auriga) verstirnt wird (Eratosth. Katasterismoi 6; Paus. 2,32,1).

Hinter den Mythen steht der Kult des H. in Troizen und Athen. In Athen lag sein Grab auf der Akropolis in der Nähe des Heiligtums der Aphrodite (»bei H.«, Eur. Hipp. 31–33); ein Kult, der anderswo in Attika bezeugt ist (IG I³ 255,7), ist unsicher, doch die Kombination von Grab und Tempel erinnert an die geläufige Verbindung von Heroen- und Götterkult, zumal die Göttin auch »Aphrodite im Hippolyteion« heißt (IG I³ 369,66). Weit bedeutender war der Kult in → Troizen, von dem auch der Mythos ausging: H. besaß ein prächtiges, angeblich von Diomedes [1] gestiftetes Temenos mit einem eigenen Tempel, einem Stadion und zwei weiteren Tempeln von Apollon Epibaterios und Aphrodite Kataskopia (»die Herabschauende«, weil hier Phaidra zum erstenmal H. erblickte), ferner dem Grab der Phaidra und einem Tumulus des H. (den die Troizener zu Pausanias' Zeit nicht als Grab gelten lassen wollten); H. hatte einen Priester und ein jährliches Opferfest mit Agon. Die Bräute klagten um ihn und opferten ihm ihr Haar (Eur. Hipp. 1423–1430; Paus. 2,32,1–4); er soll seinerseits den Tempel der Artemis Lykeia gestiftet haben (Paus. 1,31,4). Ein Kult in Sparta, wo er ein Heroon neben dem des Theseus hatte, ist anzunehmen (Paus. 3,12,9). Der mit ihm identifizierte → Virbius im Heiligtum der Diana von Aricia ist vor der Identifikation nicht faßbar; Pferdeopfer und Pferdeverbot im Heiligtum werden mit dem Tod des H. begründet, waren aber wohl ein Ausgangspunkt der Identifikation (Kall. fr. 190; Verg. Aen. 7,778–780; Ambr. De exhortatione virginitatis 3,5).

Durch die Wirkung der euripideischen Tragödien ist der Mythos von H. und Phaidra in der bildenden Kunst seit der frühen Kaiserzeit sehr oft dargestellt worden. Die *Phaedra* von Seneca vermittelt das Thema an die Neuzeit, wobei H. hinter dem Interesse an Phaidra zurücktritt (Racine; Gluck); eine der seltenen Ausnahmen ist J. Ph. Rameaus Oper Hippolyte et Aricie (1733).

W. Fauth, H. und Phaidra, 1958/1959 • W. Burkert, Structure and History in Greek Mythology and Ritual, 1979, 111–118 • P. Linant de Bellefonds, s. v. H. (1), LIMC 5, 445–464 • C. Montepaone, L'alsos/lucus, forma idealtipica artemidea. Il caso di Ippolito, in: O. de Cazanove, J. Scheid (Hrsg.), Les bois sacrées, 1993, 69–78.
F. G.

[2] H. von Rom. Presbyter (Oberhaupt einer christl. Gemeinde?) in Rom und griech. schreibender Kirchenschriftsteller des beginnenden 3. Jh. n. Chr.; Werkverzeichnis inschr. auf einer 1551 gefundenen Kathedra (ICUR N. S. 7, 19933) sowie bei Eus. HE 6,22 und Hier. vir. ill. 61. In der hsl. Überl. werden zahlreiche Schriften exegetischen, chronographischen, häresiologischen, apologetischen und kirchenrechtlichen Charakters mit H. verbunden, darunter:

1) Exegetische Werke zum AT, darunter Komm. zu HL und Dan (CPG 1871, 1873), die als die ältesten erh. christl. Bibel-Komm. gelten. In komplementärem Verhältnis hierzu steht:

2) *Refutatio omnium haeresium* in 10 B. (CPG 1899), von denen in unterschiedlicher Überl. B. 1 sowie die B. 4–10 erh. sind. H. sucht die ›Wiederlegung aller Häresien‹ dadurch zu erreichen, daß er sie auf nichtchristl.

Lehren zurückführt. Die häretischen Anschauungen seien somit menschlichen, nicht göttlichen Ursprungs und könnten daher nicht die Verbindlichkeit biblischer Schriften beanspruchen. Die *Refutatio* stellt h. neben den *Stromata* des → Clemens [3] von Alexandreia eine der wichtigsten frühchristl. Quellen für verlorene Schriften griech. Philosophen dar, die jedoch wegen der eigenwilligen Arbeitsweise H.' schwer auszuwerten ist [12; 15; 19. 511–524, 530].

3) Chronographische Werke, darunter eine → Chronik (CPG 1896) und die inschr. überl. Ostertafel (ICUR N.S. 7, 19934f.) für die Jahre 222–333. Die Datier. der Statue und der Buchstabenformen, der Beginn der Ostertafel und der Umstand, daß sie offenbar nur wenige Jahre in Gebrauch gewesen sein kann (vgl. [19. 508–511]), lassen den Schluß zu, daß die Inschr. (noch) in severischer Zeit auf dem Sockel der Kathedra angebracht wurde ([9. 3; 11. 536, 538, 544f.], anders [19. 542]). Sie zählt damit zu den ältesten erh. christl. Steininschr. des Westens und belegt durch ihre Monumentalität das Selbstbewußtsein der Christen Roms in der Severerzeit.

4) *Traditio apostolica* (CPG 1737): eine Kirchenordnung, deren Entstehung wohl vor dem Hintergrund innergemeindlicher Auseinandersetzungen in Rom zu sehen ist ([9. 398–457; 21. 398–402], anders [19. 525; 20]). Ausgehend von einem eigenen Verständnis des Amtes vollzieht H. erstmals in der christl. Trad. eine klare Trennung zw. Klerikern und Laien [14. 98ff.] und beschreibt die Ämter in der christl. Gemeinde (Kap. 1–14 mit einem Ritus für die Amtseinführung eines Bischofs). H. hierarchisiert den Klerus und setzt den Bischof an die Spitze, der allein über das vollständige Charisma verfügt (Kap. 8). Allein den Bekennern billigt H. eine Sonderrolle zu (Kap. 9, vgl. dagegen Kap. 10–14). Bedeutsam sind weiter Regelungen zur christl. Initiation (Kap. 15–21 mit einer Taufliturgie) sowie zum Gottesdienst und zur christl. Lebensweise (Kap. 22–42, insbes. zum Abendmahl).

Die Einheit des Werkes und H.' Stellung in der röm. Kirche sind auch in der jüngeren Forschung umstritten (neue umfassende Behandlung durch [9], vgl. auch [10; 16; 17; 18]; die Einheit des Autors vertritt SCHOLTEN gegen die Thesen von P. NAUTIN, vgl. [19. 501–504]). H., der letzte griech. schreibende Theologe des Westens, wurde im Westen wie im Osten lebhaft rezipiert, wodurch freilich auch die Überlieferungssituation komplex ist: Vielfach nachgewiesen sind Exzerpte und Zitate, weitgehende Bearbeitungen, orientalsprachliche Übers. sowie H. unterschobene Schriften. Zuerst und schwerpunktmäßig in Rom (Zeugnisse u.a. → Chronograph von 354, Epigramme von → Damasus) wurde H. auch als Märtyrer verehrt ([19. 534–549], vgl. ebd. auch Hinweise zu weiteren Märtyrern dieses Namens).

→ Häresie; Häresiologie; Kirchenordnungen

ED.: **1** CPG 1737, 1870–1925 **2** A. KELLER, Translationes Patristicae Graecae et Latinae. Bibliogr. der Übers. altchristl. Quellen 1, 1997, 448–451.
REFUTATIO: **3** P. WENDLAND, GCS 26, 1916 (griech.) **4** K. PREYSING, BKV 40, 1922 (dt.) **5** M. MARCOVICH, Patristische Texte und Studien 25, 1986 (griech.]).
TRADITIO APOSTOLICA: **6** B. BOTTE, [5]1989 (lat./griech.-frz.) **7** B. BOTTE, W. GEERLINGS, Fontes Christiani 1, 1991 (lat./griech.-dt.) **8** G. DIX, H. CHADWICK, [3]1992 (lat./griech.-engl.).
LIT.: **9** A. BRENT, Hippolytus and the Roman Church in the Third Century. Communities in tension before the emergence of a monarch-bishop (Vigiliae Christianae Suppl. 31), 1995 **10** J. FRICKEL, Das Dunkel um Hippolyt von Rom. Ein Lösungsversuch. Die Schriften Elenchos und Contra Noëtum (Grazer theol. Stud. 13), 1988
11 M. GUARDUCCI, Epigrafia greca 4, 1978, 535–545
12 J. MANSFELD, Heresiography in Context. H.' Elenchos as a Source for Greek Philosophy (Philosophia Antiqua 56), 1992 **13** M. MARCOVICH, s.v. H., TRE 15, 381–387
14 J. MARTIN, Die Genese des Amtspriestertums in der frühen Kirche, 1972 **15** I. MÜLLER, Heterodoxy and Doxography in H.' *Refutation of All Heresies*, in: ANRW II 36.6, 1992, 4309–4374 **16** Nuove Richerche su Ippolito (Studia Ephemeridis »Augustinianum« 30), 1989
17 Richerche su Ippolito (Studia Ephemeridis »Augustinianum« 13), 1977 **18** V. SAXER, s.v. H., DHGE 24, 627–635 (Lit. bis 1993) **19** C. SCHOLTEN, s.v. H., RAC 15, 492–551 (Lit. bis 1991) **20** Ders., C. SCHOLTEN, s.v. H., LThK[3] 5, 147–149 **21** E. WIRBELAUER, Die Nachfolgerbestimmung im röm. Bistum (3.–6. Jh.). Doppelwahlen und Absetzungen in ihrer herrschaftssoziologischen Bed., in: Klio 76, 1994,
388–437; 77, 1995, 555f. E.W.

Hippomanes (ἱππομανές). Von Dioskurides 2,173 WELLMANN = 2,204 BERENDES mit dem Kapernstrauch (κάππαρις) identifizierte Pflanze, deren Frucht u.a. als harntreibend galt. H. machte laut Theokr. 2,48f. und Serv. georg. 3,280 THILO in Arkadien Stuten und Fohlen toll. C.HÜ.

Hippomedon (Ἱππομέδων).

[1] Einer der → Sieben gegen Theben, Bruder oder Neffe des → Adrastos [1], aus Lerna, riesengestaltiger Held. Bei Aischylos (Sept. 486ff.) steht er gegen Hyperbios am Onkaischen, bei Euripides (Phoen. 1113ff.; 1119ff.) am Ogygischen Stadttor und an der Heeresspitze. Das Motiv seines Schildes ist → Typhon bzw. → Argos [II]. Euripides (Suppl. 881ff.) zeichnet ihn als einen auf das Physische begrenzten Krieger. Bei Statius siegt er im Diskuswettkampf (Theb. 6,646ff.), überquert als erster den Asopus (7,424ff.), verteidigt die Leiche des Tydeus, tötet Crenaeus, den Enkel des Flußgottes Ismenus, und findet, von dessen Fluten und der Thebanerübermacht bedrängt, den Tod (9,86–539). CL.K.

[2] Lakedaimonier, Sohn des Agesilaos [4], Vetter → Agis' [4] IV., der um 241 v. Chr. aus Sparta floh und in Alexandreia πάρεδρος (*párhedros*) und σύμβουλος (*sýmbulos*) Ptolemaios' III. wurde; zwischen 240 und 221 ptolem. Stratege des Bezirkes Hellespont und Thrakien.

PP 6,14605; 15048; 16115 • BENGTSON, 3, 178ff. • PH. GAUTHIER, ΕΞΑΓΩΓΗ ΣΙΤΟΥ, in: Historia 28, 1979, 76–89 • S. SAHIN, Ehrendekret für H. aus Priapos, in: EA 4, 1984, 5–8. W.A.

Hippomenes (Ἱππομένης).
[1] Boioter aus Onchestos, Sohn des → Megareus (Hyg. fab. 185) oder des Ares (schol. Theokr. 3,40) und einer Merope (Hyg. fab. 185). Vom Wettlauf des H. mit → Atalante wußte schon Hesiod (fr. 74 M.-W.). Am ausführlichsten ist die Darstellung bei Ov. met. 10,560–707 [1]: Auf seine Bitte hin überläßt ihm Venus drei Äpfel, die Atalante während des Wettlaufs jeweils aufhebt und deshalb unterliegt. H. versäumt das Dankopfer; auf Veranlassung der Venus schänden H. und Atalante den Tempel der → Kybele durch Beischlaf und werden in Löwen verwandelt (bei Hyg. fab. 185 den Tempel des Iuppiter Victor). H.' gleichnamiger Großvater ist ein Sohn Poseidons (Apollod. 3,210 WAGNER; bei Paus. 1,39,5 ist Poseidon Vater des Megareus).
[2] Kodride, der vierte der sieben Zehn-Jahres-Archonten (723/2–714/3 v. Chr. [2. 77–79]). Seine Tochter Leimone ertappte er beim Ehebruch und band sie mit einem Pferd zusammen, ohne diesem Speise zu geben, so daß sie von dem hungrigen Pferd (von *limós*/»Hunger« kommt vermutlich der Name des Mädchens) verschlungen wurde (Nikolaos von Damaskos, FGrH 90 F 49; Heraclidis Lembi epit. 1 CHAMBERS; schol. Ov. Ib. 459; ohne Namensnennung Aischin. or. 1,182).

1 F. BÖMER, P. Ovidius Naso, Metamorphosen B. X–XI, 1980, 188–190 2 P. J. RHODES, A Commentary on the Aristotelian Athenaion Politeia, 1981. JO.S.

Hippon (Ἵππων). Pythagoreischer Naturphilosoph, geb. ca. 480–470 v. Chr. Kratinos (38 A 2 DK) verspottete H. in seiner Komödie *Panóptai* (aufgeführt 435/431 v. Chr.). Laut Aristoxenos stammt H. aus Samos (38 A 1 DK), deshalb rechnen ihn viele der ion. Schule zu. Alle anderen Quellen verbinden H. mit Süditalien (38 A 1; 3; 11 DK). H. setzte die Linie der pythagoreischen Naturforsch. (Physiologie, Embryologie, Botanik) und der it. Medizin (→ Alkmaion [1], → Empedokles [4]) fort. Er schrieb mindestens zwei Werke (38 A 11 DK), von denen nur ein wörtliches Fragment erhalten ist. H.s Prinzip (eher »Feuchtigkeit«, *to hygrón*, als Wasser) ähnelt dem des → Thales nur oberflächlich: H.s Lehre war physiologisch, nicht meteorologisch orientiert. Sie scheint nicht sehr originell gewesen zu sein (vgl. Aristoteles' Geringschätzung des H., 38 A 7; 10 DK), doch war H.s Idee, daß die Gesundheit von der »Feuchtigkeit« im Organismus abhänge (38 A 11 DK), für die ant. Medizin wegweisend. Die Bezeichnung als Atheist (38 A 4; 6; 8 DK) ist spät und irreführend.

1 DIELS/KRANZ I, 385–389 (Nr. 38) 2 L. ZHMUD, Wiss., Philos. und Rel. im frühen Pythagoreismus, 1997. L.ZH.

Hipponax (Ἱππῶναξ).
A. ZUR PERSON B. METRIK
C. DIE IAMBOI D. NACHWIRKUNG

A. ZUR PERSON
H. war Iambendichter (ἰαμβοποιός) aus Ephesos (vgl. Kall. fr. 203,13). Seine Lebenszeit ist nach dem Marmor Parium 42 um ca. 541/0 v. Chr. zu datieren, Plinius (nat. 36,11) nennt Ol. 60 = 540–537 v. Chr.

B. METRIK
Anders als → Archilochos und → Semonides werden H. keine elegischen Verse zugeschrieben. In seinen *Íamboi* verwandte er hauptsächlich (1–114a, 155–155b WEST) choliambische Trimeter (x – ⏑ – x – ⏑ – x – x), durchsetzt mit gelegentlichen reinen Trimetern (z. B. 36,4; 42,4; 118a W.). Des weiteren kommen vor: trochäische Tetrameter, ebenfalls »hinkend«, d. h. auf x – x (120–127 W.) endend; ein einziger katalektischer iambischer Tetrameter (119 W.) und evtl. eine »hinkende« Version (177 W.); Epoden, die iambische Trimeter mit Hemiepes (115; 116 W.) oder mit iambischem Dimeter (117 W.) abwechseln; selten (und nur für Parodien?) Hexameter (128–129a W.).

C. DIE IAMBOI
Hauptziel der Invektiven ist ein gewisser Bupalos (vgl. Kall. fr. 191,1–4; Philippos Anth. Pal. 7,405,3). Als Ursache geben Plin. nat. 36,11 und Suda 2, 665,16 an, daß dieser zusammen mit Athenis eine obszöne Statue des H. geschaffen habe. Dies habe H. zu seinen *Íamboi* veranlaßt, die die beiden in den Selbstmord getrieben hätten. Plinius lehnt dies ab, auch lassen vergleichbare Fälle angeblicher Selbstmorde von Angriffsobjekten des Archilochos diese Überlieferung zweifelhaft erscheinen. Während Athenis nur ein einziges Mal erscheint (70,11 W.), wird Bupalos ca. zehnmal erwähnt, einmal als Bildhauer (136 W.).

Die Eröffnung des ersten *Íambos* (›Oh Klazomenier, Bupalos tötete ...‹, 1 W.) legt eine Tötung nahe, nicht eine Spottskulptur; das Gedicht scheint von einer Orgie mit Gelage, Sex und Rauferei zu erzählen, in die H. wie auch Bupalos und dessen Mätresse Arete involviert waren.

Andere *Íamboi* kritisieren heftig einen Maler Mimnes (28 W.) und einen Töpfer Aischylides (117,9 W.). Das Gedicht 115 W. verflucht heftig einen verräterischen Gefährten (*hetaíros*; das Gedicht wird jedoch auch Archilochos zugewiesen: s. [1]; für H.: [2; 3]; hell.: [4]).

Doch nimmt die Invektive nicht mehr Raum ein als die Erzählungen, die oft H.' eigenen Namen in den Vordergrund rücken (32,4; 36,2; 37; 79,9 und ?12; 117,4) und seine Person diskreditierend darstellen – als einen Armen, der Hermes um Reichtümer bittet (32–39 W.), als Opfer einer erniedrigenden Behandlung von Impotenz (92 W.), als schäbigen Protagonisten einer auf eine Rauferei folgenden Orgie (104 W). H.' Gedichte erzählen oft von bizarren Ereignissen, deren oftmals obszöne Details lebendig dargestellt und hervorgehoben werden. Die Reden der Charaktere sind mit aus dem Lydischen entlehnten Wörtern (z. B. 3 W., 92,1 W.) durchsetzt, die vermutlich in dem unter lydischem Einfluß stehenden Ephesos geläufig waren. H.' Schmähungen seiner selbst wie auch anderer sollten wohl eher sein Publikum unterhalten als »Angriffsobjekten« Unbehagen bereiten. H.' Zielgruppe ist aus den eröffnenden Vokativen (ὦ Κλαζομένιοι: 1 W.; Μιμνῆ 28 W.; Ὦθηνι

70,11 W.; ὦ Σάνν' 118,1 W.) seiner Gedichte schwer erschließbar. Dies gilt ebenso für die Frage, ob H.' Stellung in der Ges. eher aus seinem aristokratischem Namen *-anax* ableitbar ist oder aus den Adressaten aus dem Handwerkermilieu und den Erzählungen von schmutzigen Abenteuern. Plinius Bericht über die Skulpturen von Bupalos und Athenis legt nahe, daß H. eher reale Personen als typisierte Dramenfiguren auftreten läßt [5 W], doch könnte das, was H. über sich selbst äußerte, gänzlich oder größtenteils fiktiv sein (zu beachten ist die vermutete Einführung des H. von Bupalos in eine ›Odyssee‹, 74,1 W. mit 77,2 und 4 W.).

D. NACHWIRKUNG

Aristophanes erwartet vom att. Publikum, daß es die Rauferei mit Bupalos (Aristoph. Lys. 361) und H. (Aristoph. Ran. 661 wiedererkennt, und Diphilos, daß es seine Komödie genießen kann, in dem Archilochos und H. Sapphos Liebhaber sind.

H. ist derjenige archa. Iambograph, der von → Phoenix, → Kallimachos [6] und → Herodas (3. Jh. v. Chr.) am meisten nachgeahmt wurde; »Epitaphien« auf ihn verfaßten Leonidas (Anth. Pal. 7,408), Theokritos (Anth. Pal. 13,3, in Choliamben), Alkaios von Messene (Anth. Pal. 7,536) und Philippos (Anth. Pal. 7,405, in Trimetern). H.' *Íamboi* wurden in mindestens 2 B. herausgegeben; bereits im 2. Jh. n. Chr. lagen Komm. vor (POxy. 2176 = 118 W.), die von Athenaios benutzt wurden (Athen. 324a; 624b mit Hipponax 118,12 W.). Die Lexikographen (Aristophanes [4] von Byzanz?; Erotianos; Suetonius; Harpokration; Herodianos; Pollux; Phrynichos) und Athen. (15 Zitate) durchforsteten H.' Gedichte nach seltenen Wörtern und Formen. Moralisten ignorierten ihn jedoch weitgehend oder mißbilligten ihn (Clem. Alex. strom. 1,1 p. 3,11 STÄHLIN; Iul. epist. 89b BIDEZ 300c-d). Vieles jedoch konnte (vielleicht noch in einer Gesamtausg.) von Tzetzes im 12. Jh. in Byzanz gelesen werden.

1 G. M. KIRKWOOD, The authorship of the Strassburg Epodes, in: TAPhA 92, 1961, 267–282 2 G. PERROTTA, Il poeta degli epodi di Strassburgo, in: SIFC 15, 1938, 3–41 3 O. MASSON, in: REG 64, 1951, 427–442 4 C. DEL GRANDE, Note filologiche, 1942, 11–36 5 M. L. WEST, Studies in Greek elegy and iambus, 1974, 22–39, 140–149 6 A. ARDIZZONI, Callimaco »ipponatteo«, in: Ann. della Facoltà di Lettere ... Cagliari 28, 1960, 3–16.

BIBLIOGR.: D. E. GERBER, in: Lustrum 33, 1991, 108–128. ED.: E. DEGANI, Leipzig 1983 • IEG • W. DE SOUSA MEDEIROS, Humanitas 13–14, 1961–1962 (mit Komm.) • O. MASSON, 1962 • A. FARINA, 1963. LIT.: E. DEGANI, Studi su Ipponatte, 1984 • C. MIRALLES, J. PÒRTULAS, The poetry of H., 1988. E. BO./Ü: C. ST.

Hipponikos (Ἱππόνικος). Sohn des → Kallias und der → Elpinike, der (Halb)schwester → Kimons, reicher Athener (And. 1,130; Lys. 19,48) aus der Familie der Kerykes, wie sein Vater *dadúchos* in Eleusis (→ Mysteria). Als *stratēgós* 427/6 v. Chr. leitete er mit Eurymedon [4] den erfolgreichen Feldzug gegen die Tanagraier (Thuk. 3,91,4 f.; And. 1,115; Diod. 12,65,3 ff.). Er starb kurz vor 422. Seine Frau war in erster Ehe mit → Perikles verheiratet (Plut. Perikles 24,8, wo fälschlich angenommen wird, sie sei zuerst mit H. verheiratet gewesen), seine Tochter Hipparete heiratete Alkibiades [3] (Isokr. or. 16,31; Plut. Alk. 8). Reichtum und aristokratisches Auftreten des H. weckten schon zu seinen Lebzeiten Neid und Spott (Eupolis fr. 20 u. 156 PCG; Kratinos fr. 336 KOCK; And. 1,131; Athen. 5,218bc; 12,537b; Ail. var. 14,16).

PA 7658 mit Stemma 520 • DAVIES 7826, IX. • TRAILL, PPA 538910. M. MEI.

Hipponoos (Ἱππόνοος).

[1] Nach schol. Hom. Il. 6,155 DINDORF alter Name des → Bellerophontes; schol. Hom. Il. 6,155 ERBSE bietet den Namen Leophontes (Λεωφόντης).

[2] Sohn des Adrastos [1], der sich mit ihm freiwillig auf den Scheiterhaufen warf (Hyg. fab. 242). Dieses Motiv findet sich sonst in der Geschichte vom Schicksal des Kapaneus und der Euadne.

[3] Von Astynome Vater des → Kapaneus (Apollod. 3,63 WAGNER; Hyg. fab. 70) und der → Periboia (Apollod. 1,74 WAGNER). JO. S.

Hippos

[1] (Ἵππος Strab. 11,2,17; Steph. Byz. s. v. Αἶα; *Hippos* Plin. nat. 6,13; Ἵππις in Mocheresis Prok. BG 4,1,6); nördl. Zufluß des → Phasis in der → Kolchis, der h. Cʿḫeniscqali (»Pferdewasser«) in West-Georgien.

E. KIESSLING, s. v. H., RE 8, 1915–1918. A. P.-L.

[2] (ἡ Ἵππος, Eus. On. 22,21 Ἵππη; aram. *Sūsīṯā* »Stute«). Hell.-byz. Stadt(region) östl. des Sees Genezareth. Zuerst gen. bei Plinius (nat. 5,71; 74) und Iosephos (bell. Iud. 1,156); evtl. seleukidische Gründung, später zur → Dekapolis gehörig (vgl. Mz.), noch in byz. Zeit blühend (mit Bischof); h. Qalʿat al-ḥiṣn, (Mt.) Susita (Israel); Wüstung auf steiler Bergnase, reiche ant. Reste.

ABEL 2, 471 f. • M. AVI-YONAH, The Holy Land from the Persian to the Arab Conquests. A Historical Geography, 1966, 169 f. • H. BIETENHARD, Die Dekapolis von Pompeius bis Traian, in: ZPalV 79, 1963, 24–58 • SCHÜRER 2, 130–132 • G. SCHUMACHER, Der Dscholan, in: ZPalV 9, 1886, 327–334 (Plan T. VI) • P. THOMSEN, Loca sancta 1, 1907, 73. CH. BU.

Hippostratos (Ἱππόστρατος).

[1] Sohn des Amarynkeus, verführte → Periboia, Tochter des Hipponoos (Apollod. 1,74; Hes. fr. 12 M-W). J. S.-A.

[2] Neffe von → Attalos [1], Bruder von → Kleopatra, wurde nach deren Tod von → Alexandros [4] d. Gr. hingerichtet (vgl. Iust. 11,5,1). Mit anderen Männern dieses Namens nicht zu identifizieren.

BERVE 2, Nr. 390. E. B.

[3] H. Soter, einer der späteren indogriech. Könige in Ghandhara (h. Pakistan) im 1. Jh. v. Chr.; nur durch seine Münzen belegt; mittelind. Hipstrata.

BOPEARACHCHI 136f.,356–360. K.K.

[4] Wohl 3. Jh. v. Chr. Verf. eines mind. 7 B. umfassenden Werkes über sizil. Genealogien (z. B. der Emmeniden), das von den Scholien zu Pindar und Theokritos sowie den Thaumasiographen zitiert wird. Die Verwendung der Olympiadendatierung setzt wohl Timaios voraus. FGrH 568.

F. JACOBY, s. v. H. (7), RE 8, 1922. K. MEI.

Hippotai (Ἱππόται). Boiot. Siedlung (κώμη) zw. Thisbe und Koroneia, wohl mit den ant. Überresten beim h. Koukoura in einer Hochebene am Osthang des Paliaovouna gen. Südgipfels des Helikon zu identifizieren; Thebai belagerte und zerstörte H. zu unbestimmter Zeit und verteilte das Land an Thisbe und Koroneia. Nennung bei Plut. mor. 775 A-B.

A. R. BURN, Helikon in History, in: ABSA 44, 1949, 317f., 321 • FOSSEY, 339 • PRITCHETT 5, 156 • A. SCHACHTER, Reconstructing Thespiai, in: A. HURST, A. SCHACHTER (Hrsg.), La montagne des Muses, 1996, 104f. P. F.

Hippotes (Ἱππότης).
[1] Selten erwähnter Vater des → Aiolos [2]: Hom. Od. 10,2; 36; Apoll. Rhod. 4,778; 819; aufgrund einer Verwechslung von Aiolos [1] mit Aiolos [2] Sohn des Mimas (schol. Hom. Od. 10,2; Diod. 4,67,3).
[2] Sohn des → Phylas, Enkel des Antiochos, Urenkel des Herakles, Vater des → Aletes [1] ([5. 7–10]; genealog. Taf. [1; 4. 306 A 20]). In Naupaktos erschlägt H. den Seher Karnos und muß 10 Jahre in die Verbannung gehen (Ps.-Apollod. 2,174–175; Oinomaos fr. 4 H. [2]: Aition für den Kult des Apollon Karneios [3; 4. 306] bzw. zwei dazugehörige Riten [5]). Mit H. wird Korinth in die Aitiologie der Machtverteilung auf der Peloponnes (→ Herakleidai) eingebunden [4. 306].

1 C. PARADA, Genealogical Guide to Greek Mythology, 1993, Taf. Heraclides 2 J. HAMMERSTAEDT, Die Orakelkritik des Kynikers Oenomaus, 1988, z.St. 3 BURKERT, 357–358 4 F. PRINZ, Gründungsmythen und Sagenchronologie, 1979, 305–307 5 N. ROBERTSON, The Dorian Migration and Corinthian Ritual, in: CPh 75, 1980, 1–22.

[3] Sohn des → Kreon, Enkel des Lykaithos. Abweichend von der Vulgata nimmt H. Iason auf und gibt ihm seine Tochter → Medeia zur Frau (schol. Eur. Med. 19). Nach deren Flucht verlangt er von den Athenern ihre Auslieferung (Diod. 4,55,5). Nach Hyg. fab. 27 (wohl Inhalt von Pacuvius, *Medus* [1]) gibt Medus sich vor Perses als H. aus.

1 A. ARCELLASCHI, Médée dans le théâtre latin d'Ennius à Sénèque, 1990, 102–103, 127–129, 148–149. T. H.

Hippothoe (Ἱπποθόη, »die wie ein Pferd Schnelle«). Der Name weist bei [1] und [3] auf die Beziehung zu Poseidon und dem Meer.
[1] → Nereide (Hes. theog. 251; Apollod. 1,11).
[2] Eine der Töchter des → Pelias, die – durch → Medeias List getäuscht – ihren Vater zerstückelten und kochten, um ihn zu verjüngen (Apollod. 1,95; Hyg. fab. 24).
[3] Tochter des → Mestor und der → Lysidike, von Poseidon geraubt, dem sie den → Taphios (Apollod. 2,50) oder den → Pterelaos (Herodoros FGrH 31 F 15) gebar. Der Raub dient bei christl. Autoren als polemisches Exempel gegen den Anthropomorphismus der paganen Götter (Arnob. 4,26; Firm. De errore profanarum religionum 12,3). A. A.

Hippothontis (Ἱπποθοντίς). Seit der Phylenreform des Kleisthenes 8. der 10 Phylen von Attika; eponymer Heros Hippothoon. Die H. umfaßte z.Z. der 10 Phylen im 4. Jh. v. Chr. 17 (6? Asty-, 7? Paralia, 4? Mesogeia-)Demoi [1. 11f., 51f., 102] vornehmlich um Eleusis und in NW-Attika; etliche sind nicht lokalisiert [1. Karte]. 307/6 v. Chr. wechselten Koile und Oinoe (h. Myupolis) in die Demetrias, Auridai oder Korydallos in die Antigonis, 224/3 v. Chr. Oion Dekeleikon und Oinoe (aus der Demetrias) in die Ptolemaïs. Nach Auflösung der maked. Phylen 201/0 v. Chr. kehrten Koile und Auridai oder Korydallos in die H. zurück, Korydallos fiel der Attalis, Elaius 127/8 n. Chr. der Hadrianis zu [1. 11f., 27].

1 TRAILL, Attica, XVII, 11f., 21f., 24 Nr. 13, 26f., 32, 51f., 55, 57, 71, 82, 91, 102, 106, 134, Tab. 8.

P. J. BICKNELL, The City and Inland Trittyes of Phyle VIII H., in: Antichthon 7, 1973, 1–4 • J. S. TRAILL, Demos and Trittys, 1986, 1ff., 16ff., 136ff. H. LO.

Hippothoon (Ἱπποθόων).
[1] Zweiter Sohn von → Poseidon und → Alope (Hyg. fab. 187; 252). Als Säugling von seinem Großvater → Kerkyon ausgesetzt und von → Theseus aufgenommen; später König, wahrscheinlich in Eleusis (Hes. fr. 215 M-W; Hom. h. 2,153). Dafür spricht auch, daß H. dort als Kult- und Phylenheros verehrt wurde, wie das bei Eleusis am Fluß Kephisos gelegene Hippothoontion nahelegt (Paus. 1,38,4).

U. KRON, s. v. H., LIMC 5.1, 468–475. J. S.-A.

[2] H./Hippothoos (Ἱπποθόων/Ἱππόθοος). Bei Stob. (3,589,13–590,1; 3,711,15ff.; 4,496,10ff.; 4,519,5f.; 4,652,4f.; 5,1023,9f; s. auch 4,546,22–547,2) werden unter dem Lemma Ἱπποθόου, /-θόωντος, /-θόωου verschiedene sententiöse Trimeter überliefert (manche finden sich z. B. auch bei → Menandros' Monosticha), deren Zuschreibung z. T. nicht gesichert ist. So ist es überhaupt zweifelhaft, ob H. der Name eines Dichters oder der Titel eines Stückes ist (vgl. O. HENSE ad Stob. 3,589,13). F. P.

Hippothoos (Ἱππόθοος).
[1] Sohn des Priamos (Hom. Il. 24,251).
[2] Sohn des Pelasgerkönigs → Lethos Teuthamides, führt den Troianern pelasgische Hilfstruppen aus Larisa zu (Hom. Il. 2,840ff.); im Kampf um die Leiche des Patroklos vom Telamonier Aias getötet (Hom. Il. 17,288ff.).
[3] Sohn von → Aleos [1] und Neaira, vom Neffen → Telephos getötet, worauf die Mutter sich den Tod gibt (Hyg. fab. 243).
[4] Sohn von Kerkyon, Herrscher im arkad. Trapezus (Paus. 8,5,4); nimmt an der Jagd auf den kalydon. Eber teil; Darstellung von → Skopas im Giebel des Athena-Tempels von Tegea (Paus. 8,45,7).
[5] → Hippothoon [1] (Hyg. fab. 187; 252). RE.ZI.

Hippotomadai (Ἱπποτο/αμάδαι). Att. Asty?-Demos der Phyle Oineis, von 307/6 bis 201/200 v. Chr. der Demetrias, mit einem *buleutḗs*. Lage unbekannt.

E. Meyer, s. v. H., RE Suppl. 10, 325f. • Traill, Attica, 9, 19, 49, 62, 70, 110 Nr. 56, Tab. 6, 12 • Ders., Demos and Trittys, 1986, 133. H.LO.

Hippotoxotai (ἱπποτοξόται). H. waren berittene Bogenschützen. Als H. kämpften Skythen und Geten (Hdt. 4,46,3; Thuk. 2,96,1; Arr. an. 3,8,3). H. sind belegt für pers., athenische, maked. und hell. Heere (Hdt. 9,49,2; Arr. an. 4,24,1; 5,12,2; 6,6,1; Diod. 20,113,4). Während des Peloponnesischen Krieges hatte Athen eine Truppe von 200 H. (Thuk. 2,13,8); davon dienten auf Melos 20, auf Sizilien 30 (Thuk. 5,84,1; 6,94,4), wohl als Plänkler (Xen. mem. 3,3,1). H. waren Bürger und evtl. Söldner, ihr Ansehen war nach Lysias (15,6) nicht hoch.
→ Reiterei

I. G. Spence, The cavalry of classical Greece, 1993, 56f., 217. LE.BU.

Hippys (Ἵππυς) von Rhegion. Seit [1] vielbehandelter und heftig umstrittener Autor: Nach Suda s. v. = T 1 ältester westgriech. Geschichtsschreiber, der zur Zeit der Perserkriege 480/479 v. Chr. lebte und folgende Werke verfaßte: *Sikeliká* in 5 B., *Ktísis Italías* (›Gründungsgeschichte Italiens‹), *Chroniká* in 5 B., *Argoliká* in 3 B. Später habe ein gewisser Myes sein Werk epitomiert. Da die Fragmente meist rätselhaft sind (z. B. F 1–3 mit dem Komm. Jacobys), und spätere Autoren wie Dionysios von Halikarnassos, Diodor, Strabon und Pausanias H. nicht zu kennen scheinen, nahm erstmals [2] an, daß es sich um einen Schwindelautor aus hell. Zeit handle: Ihm sind zahlreiche Forscher, darunter [3], [4] und [5] gefolgt. Doch halten vor allem italienische Gelehrte wie G. de Sanctis, A. Momigliano und E. Manni (genaue Literaturnachweise bei [4. 8[23]]) nach wie vor an der Frühdatier. fest und betrachten H. nicht nur als ersten westgriech. Historiker, sondern auch als wichtige Quelle für Herodot (7,153–156), Antiochos von Syrakus (FGrH 555), Thukydides (6,2–5) und Hellanikos von Lesbos (FGrH 323a). In Wirklichkeit scheint H., selbst wenn die Frühdatierung zuträfe, die Überlieferung kaum beeinflußt zu haben. FGrH 554.

1 U. von Wilamowitz, Hippys von Rhegion, in: Hermes 19, 1884, 442–452 2 F. Jacoby, FGrH III B 3 K. von Fritz, Die griech. Geschichtsschreibung, 1967, 1, 238f.
4 L. Pearson, The Greek Historians of the West, 1987, 8–10
5 O. Lendle, Einführung in die griech. Geschichtsschreibung, 1992, 210. K.MEI.

Hipta (Ἵπτα). Eine westkleinasiatische Göttin, die sich wohl aus der altanatolischen *Ḫepat*, einer Form der Großen Göttin, entwickelt hat. Inschr. ist sie allein in Lydien genannt, wo sie als *Mḗtēr H.* und mit → Sabazios verbunden erscheint. Im orphischen Mythos taucht sie als Amme auf, welcher Zeus den neugeborenen Dionysos übergibt; sie trägt ihn in einem schlangenumwundenen Korb (*líknon*) auf dem Kopf (Orph. fr. 199). Als Amme des Dionysos – Sohn des Sabazios oder identisch mit ihm –, die auf dem Tmolos oder dem Idagebirge wohnt, rufen sie die sog. Orphischen Hymnen (→ Orphik) an (Orph. h. 48. 49), die in einer westkleinasiatischen Stadt rituell verwendet wurden.

M. L. West, The Orphic Poems, 1983, 96. F.G.

Hira (Ἱρή, Ἰρή, Εἶρα). Bergfeste in dem unzugänglichen, schluchtenreichen Gebiet im Süden der oberen Neda am Nordrand von Messenia, evtl. auf dem 864 m hohen Hagios Athanasios bei Kakaletri (Spuren ant. Befestigung). Von hier aus leitete → Aristomenes [1] 500–490/489 v. Chr. den Kampf gegen die Spartaner (sog. 3. Messen. Krieg).

Philippson/Kirsten 3,2, 357 • F. Kiechle, Messen. Studien, 1959, 86ff. C.L.u.E.O.

Hiram I. König von → Tyros (ca. 962–929 v. Chr.), der Name abgekürzt von phönik. *Aḥīram* (»mein Bruder ist erhaben«), bekannt v. a. durch die gemeinsam mit König Salomon von Jerusalem als »joint ventures« ausgesandten Handelsexpeditionen nach Ophir (Indien? Ostafrika? 1 Kg 9,26–28) und Taršiš (im Westen der Iberischen Halbinsel, → Tartessos; 1 Kg 10,22, vgl. Ez 27,12) [1. 251]. Nach glaubwürdigen, u. a. bei Iosephos (c. Ap. 1,109–121) erh. Nachrichten war er in Tyros als Städtebauer tätig und errichtete u. a. neue Tempel für → Astarte und → Melqart-Herakles, mit dessen bes. Wiederauferstehungsriten (ἔγερσις, *égersis*) er auch als Stifter verbunden ist [2. 223; 3. 326]. In den ant. Quellen ist H. bezeichnenderweise der einzige phönik. Stadtkönig, der eine auswärtige Strafexpedition unternahm, wahrscheinlich gegen die tyrische Kolonie → Kition (Ios. ant. Iud. 8,146; c. Ap. 1,119) [4. 615].
→ Salomon; Tartessos

1 H. G. Niemeyer, Expansion et colonisation, in: V. Krings (Hrsg.), La civilisation phénicienne et punique, in: HbdOr, 1. Abt., Bd. 20, 1995, 247–267 2 G. Bunnens, L'histoire événementelle *partim* Orient, in: Ebd., 222–236
3 C. Bonnet, P. Xella, La religion, in: Ebd., 316–333

4 Cl. Baurain, A. Destrooper-Georgiades, Chypre, in: Ebd., 597–631.

E. Lipinski, s. v. H., DCPP, 218. H.G.N.

Hirpini. Samnit. Stamm in Samnium vom *mons Taburnus* bis zu den Tälern des Volturnus, des Calor, des oberen Aufidus bis zum *mons Vultur*. Der Name H. leitet sich wohl von dem den H. heiligen Wolf (*hirpus*) ab, der die H. vom Norden in ihre Siedlungsgebiete geführt haben soll (Strab. 5,4,12). Die Eisenzeit ist repräsentiert von der Cairano- und der Fossakultur von Caudium. Das Gebiet der H. umfaßte Caudium, Malventum, Aec(u)lanum, Romulea, Aquilonia [2] und Compsa sowie die Abellinates Protopi und Marsi. 313 v. Chr. wurde die röm. Kolonie Saticula gegr., nach dem Sieg über Pyrrhos 268 v. Chr. auf dem Gebiet von Malventum die Kolonie Beneventum (Plin. nat. 3,105), nun Hauptzentrum der H. Im J. 180 v. Chr. wurden 47000 Liguri hierher deportiert (die sog. Baebiani und Corneliani). Große Straßen durchzogen das Gebiet: die Verlängerung der *via Appia* von Capua nach Tarentum, die *via Minucia* den Appenninus entlang, die *via Aurelia Aeclanensis*, die *via Traiana* von Beneventum nach Brundisium und die späte *via Herculia* durch Lucania. Im J. 130 wurde hier die Gracchische Ackerparzellierung durchgeführt (ILS 25). Seit der Gebietsreform unter Augustus war das Gebiet Teil der *regio II*. Von hier stammt eine *tabula alimentaria* des Traianus (ILS 6509). In der Spätant. unter der Verwaltung des *consularis Campaniae*.

B. D'Agostino, Popoli e Civiltà dell'Italia Antica 2, 1974. G.U.

Hirrius M. H. Fronto Neratius Pansa, PIR[2] N 56 → Neratius. W.E.

Hirsch. Meistens beziehen sich die Namen ἔλαφος/*élaphos* (seit Hom. Il. 11,475 u.ö.) bzw. *cervus* (= Horntier, seit Plaut. Poen. 530) und νεβρός/*nebrós* (H.-Kalb, Hom. Il. 8,248; Od. 19,228: ἐλλός/*hellós*) bzw. *inuleus* (Hor. carm. 1,23,1; Prop. 3,13,35) auf den Rot.-H. Cervus elaphus L. Der kleinere Dam-H. (oder das Reh?) Dama dama (L.) (Hom. Od. 17,295: πρόξ/*próx*), lat. *dama* (Verwechslungen mit der → Gazelle!), mit seinem Schaufeln bildenden Geweih wurde aus Asien (Indiz dafür Arr. an. 7,20,4: Herden an der Euphratmündung; Ail. nat. 5,56: syr. H. vom Libanon und Karmel schwammen nach Zypern) nach Griechenland und z. T. nach It. eingeführt.

Viele Beobachtungen zeugen von Kenntnis des H. in Griechenland (am Taygetos: Hom. Od. 6,104; in Elis: Xen. an. 5,3,10) und in It. (Verg. georg. 3,412f.) und Spanien (Mart. 1,49,26). Eine genaue Beschreibung mit vielen anatomischen Einzelheiten liefert Aristoteles (u. a. ist der H. Wiederkäuer: hist. an. 8(9),50,632b 4; hat ein großes Herz: part. an. 3,4,667a 19f.; Plin. nat. 11,183; unvollkommene Blutgerinnung: Aristot. hist. an. 3,6,515b 34–516a 4, und keine Gallenblase: 2,15,506a 22 und 31f.); beim ἀχαίνης/*achaínēs* soll diese Blase jedoch am Schwanz liegen (506a 23f.). Als Tragzeit der Kuh vor dem Wurf der 1–2 Jungen im Mai/Juni in der Nähe von Wegen (hist. an. 8(9),5,611a 15–17) gibt Aristot. etwa 8 Monate an (hist. an. 6,29, 578b 12–14). Im 2. J. wachsen dem männlichen Kalb (»Spießer«) gerade Hörner (κέρατα εὐθέα, καθάπερ παττάλους), im 3. J. (»Gabler«) gegabelte und bis zum 6. J. jeweils um eine Zacke vermehrte kompakte Geweihe. Nach dem Abwurf der alten Geweihstangen im Mai/Juni bleiben die H. im Versteck bis zum Heranwachsen des neuen Kopfschmucks, den sie an Bäumen »fegen« (hist. an. 8(9),5,611a 25–b 17). Die bekannte Langlebigkeit wurde von Plin. nat. 8,119 übertrieben (100 J.). Als charakteristische Eigenschaften des H. gelten seine Schnelligkeit, Sprungfähigkeit und Furchtsamkeit bzw. Scheu (seit Hom. Il. 1,225: κραδίην ἐλάφοιο; Aristot. hist. an. 1,1,488b 15: φρόνιμος καὶ δειλός), bes. beim Kalb (νεβρός: Hom. Il. 4,243). In ant. Vergleichen spielte der H. eine beträchtliche Rolle [1. 494].

Die Römer (wie etwa Q. Hortensius) hielten den H. in Gehegen auf ihren Landgütern (Varro rust. 3,13,3), z. T. auch als zahmes Haustier (Verg. Aen. 7,483–502, als Lieblingstier der Silvia, Tochter des Tyrrhus, Anspielung darauf bei Mart. 13,96). Ein zahmer H. diente (zusammen mit je einem Stier und Pferd) dem König Mithradates VI. von Pontos nachts als Wache. Den Tierpark des röm. Kaisers Gordianus [1] I. bevölkerten sogar je 200 Dam- und Rot-H. (SHA Gordiani tres 3,7). Das durch die Jagd mit Hunden vom Pferd aus erbeutete magere Fleisch war als angebl. Fieberprophylaktikum (Plin. nat. 8,119; 28,228) bei vornehmen Römerinnen beliebt. Galen (de facultatibus naturalibus 3,1,8 [2]) beurteilt es dagegen als hart, schwer verdaulich und schlechte Säfte erzeugend. Die Knochen des H. wurden zu Mundstükken für Musikinstrumente, das Fell zu Decken (Hom. Od. 13,436) und das Geweih als apotropäisches Mittel sowie, in verbrannter Form, zur Vertreibung der angebl. geruchsempfindlichen Schlangen (Plin. nat. 8,118 und 115) genutzt. Auch die medizinische Verwendung – z. B. das Lab eines im Mutterleib getöteten Kalbs gegen Schlangenbisse (Plin. nat. 8,118) oder die Asche des Geweihs gegen Zahnschmerzen (Plin. nat. 28,178) sowie gegen (Band-)Würmer (ebd. 28,211) – ist sehr speziell.

Im Kult der Artemis bzw. Diana ist der H. sowohl ihr Begleiter als auch ihr Reittier (Silberplatte des 4. Jh. in Berlin [3. 131 und Abb. 67]) und Jagdopfer (vgl. ihren Beinamen *elaphoktónos*, »Hirschtöterin«: Eur. Iph. T. 1113). Manchmal zogen H. auch, wie bei einer Prozession in Patras, eine auf einem Wagen sitzende Artemis-Priesterin (Paus. 7,18,12; dafür gezähmte H. erwähnen Ail. nat. 7,46 und Plin. nat. 8,117). Auch Beziehungen zu Apollon (z. B. Paus. 10,13,5 über eine Statue in Delphi), ferner zu Eros und Nemesis (Paus. 1,33,3: Statue des Pheidias in Rhamnus) liegen vor. Im Mythos des → Kyparissos trifft dieser unabsichtlich seinen Lieblings-H. (vgl. Mosaik [3. 130 und Abb. 70]). Im röm. Kult wurde vielleicht ein H. bzw. eine H.-Kuh geopfert (vgl. Fest. 57 M.: *cervaria ovis quae pro cerva immolabantur*

[4. 380]). Als Vorzeichen (*omen*) tritt die H.-Kuh bei Liv. 10,27,8 f. auf. Darstellungen von H. als Beute von Hunden, Löwen (z. B. auf ant. Münzen [5]), Panthern und vom Greif sind bekannt [6. 1948,34 ff.]; Mosaiken mit Jagdszenen aus dem 4. Jh. n. Chr. auf Sizilien [3. 131 und Farbabb. 176] sowie in England erh. [3. 131 und Abb. 72]. Auf einem Mosaik des byz. Kaiserpalastes in Istanbul kämpft ein H. mit einer Schlange [3. 132 und Abb. 71].

1 V. Pöschl, Bibliogr. zur ant. Bildersprache, 1964
2 G. Helmreich (Ed.), Galenos, de facultatibus naturalibus, 1923 (CMG 5,4,2) **3** Toynbee, Tierwelt **4** Latte
5 F. Imhoof-Blumer, O. Keller, Tier- und Pflanzenbilder auf Mz. und Gemmen des klass. Alt., 1889, Ndr. 1972
6 F. Orth, s. v. H., RE 8, 1936 ff. C. HÜ.

Hirschfeld-Maler. Att. Vasenmaler der geom. Zeit (Spätgeom. I b, nach 750 v. Chr.; → geometrische Vasenmalerei), benannt nach Gustav Hirschfeld (1847–1897), der das 1870 ausgegrabene Hauptwerk, den sog. Hirschfeldkrater (Athen, NM Inv. Nr. 990), erstmalig beschrieb [1; 2]. Der H. und seine Werkstatt standen in der Nachfolge des → Dipylon-Malers und stellten vorzugsweise monumentale Kratere her, von denen insbes. der eponyme Krater und ein weiterer in New York (MMA Inv. Nr. 14.130. 14) aufgrund der dargestellten → Prothesis- und → Ekphora-Szenen von Bed. sind. Die Anbringung von Ornamenten auf den überl. Gefäßen ist beim H. sehr reichhaltig, wobei par. Linien, Punktreihen, Swastikamotive, Mäander oder auch gefirnißte Streifen und Kreise häufig sind; im Figurenstil erscheint der Kopf als Kreis mit Punkt für das Auge, dazu treten Kinn- und Haarangabe, bei Frauen noch zusätzlich die Angabe der Brust.

1 G. Hirschfeld, Vasi arcaici Ateniesi, in: Annali del Istituto 44, 1872, 142–144, Nr. 41 **2** Monumenti inediti pubblicati dall'Instituto di Corrispondenza Archaeologica IX, 1872 Taf. 39/40.

J. N. Coldstream, Greek Geometric Pottery. A survey of ten local styles and their chronology, 1968, 41–44 • G. Ahlberg, Prothesis and Ekphora in Greek Geometric Art, 1971, 220–224 • R. Lullies, in: R. Lullies, W. Schiering (Hrsg.), Archäologen-Porträts, 1988, 88–89 • Th. Rombos, The Iconography of Attic Late Geometric II Pottery, 1988. R. H.

Hirschlanden. H.-Ditzingen, Kreis Ludwigsburg: FO einer steinernen Kriegerstatue der späten → Hallstatt-Kultur (6./5. Jh. v. Chr.). Die »Stele von H.« stellt, etwa lebensgroß (erh. H 1,50 m), vollplastisch eine nackte Männerfigur dar mit konischem Hut oder → Helm, Maske (?), Halsreif (→ Torques), → Gürtel und einem typischen Hallstattdolch. Sie lag am Rand der Umfassungsmauer eines Grabhügels der späten Hallstatt-Kultur, den sie ursprünglich bekrönte. Ihre Formgebung zeigt sowohl griech.-etr. als auch lokal-kelt. Elemente.
→ Hochdorf; Plastik; Statue

K. Bittel, S. Schieck, W. Kimmig, Die Kelten in Baden-Württemberg, 1981, bes. 87–95, 398–400 • W. Kimmig, Eisenzeitl. Grabstelen in Mitteleuropa, in: Fundber. Baden-Württemberg 12, 1987, 251–297. V. P.

Hirse s. Getreide

Hirtia. Schwester des → Hirtius, die Cicero im Jahre 46 v. Chr. nach der Scheidung von Terentia offenbar von ihrem Bruder als Ehefrau angetragen wurde. Cicero lehnte mit der Begründung, Ehe und Philosophie vertrügen sich nicht (Hieron. adv. Iovinianum 1,48), ab und heiratete die junge und reiche Publilia. Vermutlich bezieht sich auch ein Brief Ciceros (Att. 12,11) vom Nov. 46 auf H., in dem er Atticus mitteilte, er habe noch nie etwas Häßlicheres gesehen (*nihil vidi foedius*).

J. Kerschensteiner, Cicero und Hirtius, in: FS S. Lauffer, Bd. 2, 1986, 559–575. W. W.

Hirtius, Aulus. Die anfängliche Karriere des H. liegt im dunkeln. Wahrscheinlich diente er ab ca. 54 v. Chr. als Legat in Gallien (Cic. fam. 16,27,1–2). Er entwikkelte sich zu einem unbedingten Gefolgsmann Caesars, dem er schließlich auch seinen weiteren Aufstieg verdankte (Cic. Phil. 13,24). 49 begleitete er Caesar nach Spanien, 47 weilte er bei ihm in Antiocheia, ansonsten vertrat er dessen Interessen in Rom. Das Volkstribunat von 48 ist nicht gesichert, ein von ihm eingebrachtes, später aufgehobenes Gesetz (Cic. Phil. 13,32), das sich gegen die Anhänger des Pompeius richtete (*rogatio Hirtia,* CIL I² 2,604), gehört daher, gegen Cassius Dio (42,20,1), wohl ins Jahr 46, in dem H. Praetor war (MRR 2, 295). 45 avancierte er zum Statthalter (Proconsul?) der Gallia comata nebst Narbonensis (Cic. Att. 14,9,3); wohl im selben Jahr wurde er Augur, bevor er schließlich 43, noch von Caesar dazu bestimmt, das Consulat antrat (MRR 2, 334–336). In der ungewohnten Situation, nach Caesars Tod allein entscheiden zu müssen, hielt sich H. zunächst polit. zurück und widmete sich lit. Tätigkeit. Als Spannungen mit Antonius [I 9] offenbar wurden, versuchten die Caesarmörder sogar, ihn durch Vermittlung des befreundeten Cicero für sich zu gewinnen. Im Sommer erkrankte H. so schwer, daß er bei seinem Amtsantritt am 1.1.43 (zusammen mit C. → Vibius Pansa) noch nicht völlig genesen war. H. übernahm die Aufgabe, zusammen mit Pansa und Octavian (→ Augustus) den seit Dezember in Mutina belagerten D. → Iunius [I 12] Brutus zu befreien. Es gelang ihm, im März Bononia und Forum Gallorum zu besetzen und nach der Niederlage des Pansa Mitte April Antonius in einer Schlacht zu besiegen. Er fiel in einem weiteren siegreichem Treffen am 21.4. vor Mutina. ›Der schöne Soldatentod‹, schreibt von der Mühll 1913 [1. 1961], ›hat H. aus einer Stellung erlöst, deren Schwierigkeit er weder seiner Begabung noch seiner Energie nach gewachsen war‹, und faßt damit eine zumindest noch bis in die siebziger Jahre gültige Auffassung der Forschung in einem Satz zusammen.

H.' Bedeutung für die Nachwelt liegt auf lit. Gebiet. Nachdem er 45 bereits im Auftrag Caesars als Anwort auf Ciceros Laudatio eine Schmähschrift gegen Cato veröffentlicht hatte, schrieb er wohl Mitte 44 das achte Buch *De bello Gallico*, das die zeitliche Lücke (51–50) zwischen Caesars *Commentarii* über den Gallischen und den Bürgerkrieg schließt. Den in der Vorrede, einem vermutlich fiktiven Brief an Cornelius Balbus, als bereits vollendet angekündigten Plan (praef. 2), auch die Kriege bis zum Tode Caesars zu beschreiben, konnte er nicht mehr verwirklichen [2].

1 Von der Mühll, s. v. a. Hirtius, RE 8,2, 1956–1962
2 S. A. Patzer, Aulus Hirtius als Redaktor des Corpus Caesarianum, in: WJA N. F. 19, 1993, 111–130. W. W.

Hirtuleius, L. Wohl Quaestor 86 oder 85 v. Chr. (Einführung der doppelten Rechnungsführung für Schulden unter der *lex Valeria*, Cic. Font. 2), 79–75 Proquaestor des abtrünnigen Q. → Sertorius in Spanien und dessen fähigster Offizier. 79 schlug er den Statthalter M. Domitius [I 11] Calvinus am Anas, 78 den Proconsul von Gallia Transalpina, L. Manlius (MRR 2, 83; 87). 76 wurde er von Q. Caecilius [I 31] Metellus Pius bei Ilerda besiegt und fiel wenig später zusammen mit seinem Bruder bei Segontia am Duero (Liv. per. 90f.; Sall. hist. 2,31; 59M; Frontin. strat. 21,2 u.ö.; Flor. 2,10,6f.; Oros. 5,23,3–12 u. a.).

C. F. Konrad, Plutarch's Sertorius, 1994, 131f. K.-L. E.

Hispal(is, Spalis). Heute Sevilla. Zuerst gen. als Stützpunkt Caesars in seinen span. Feldzügen, sicher aber alte iber. Siedlung; phoinik. Ursprung hat man vermutet. H. gehört zu den wenigen Städten, die von der Ant. bis h. ihre Bed. bewahrt haben. Für die Ant. beweisen dies lit. Zeugnisse, Inschr. (CIL II Suppl. p. 1145f.) und Mz. [1]. Ihre Bed. beruht v. a. auf ihrer geopolit. günstigen Lage an der → Baetis-Mündung – noch h. ist H. für Seeschiffe erreichbar – und auf ihrer fruchtbaren Umgebung. Wichtigste Daten: 45 v. Chr. von Caesar zur *colonia Iulia Romula* erhoben (Isid. Etym. 15,1,71; [2. 271]). 428 n. Chr. durch die Vandali, 441 durch den Suevenkönig Rechila erobert, vorübergehend byz. [2. 411], etwa 567 vom Westgotenkönig Athanagild erobert [2. 141f.]. Eine große Rolle spielte H. als Bischofssitz; einen Höhepunkt bedeutete der Metropolit Leander (vor 579 bis etwa 600 [2. 450]); 590 fand in H. das *concilium Hispalense I*, 619 oder 620 das *concilium Hispalense II* statt [2. 217, 252]; 712–1248 stand H. unter arab. Herrschaft.

1 A. Vives, La mondeda hispánica 4, 1924 2 A. Schulten (Hrsg.), Fontes Hispaniae Antiquae 9, 1959.

Tovar 2, 140–143; 3, 411. P. B.

Hispallus. Beiname (»Spanier«) des Cn. Cornelius [I 78] Scipio H. (cos. 176); in der Form Hispanus bei seinem Sohn Cornelius [I 79]. K.-L. E.

Hispania, Iberia I. Geographie und Geschichte II. Sprachen III. Schriftsysteme IV. Religion V. Archäologie

I. Geographie und Geschichte
A. Name B. Topographie C. Wirtschaft
D. Bevölkerung E. Römische Zeit
F. Spätantike und byzantinische Zeit

A. Name

Seit dem 1. Jh. n. Chr. bezeichnet H. immer häufiger die ganze Pyrenäenhalbinsel. Der Name *Iberia* ist zwar erst z.Z. des 2. Pun. Krieges (218–201 v. Chr.) nachweisbar (Liv. 21,2; Enn. ann. 503), ist jedoch der älteste von allen, da er sich von phoinik. *í-schephanním*, »Küste der Kaninchen« (nach einer neueren Deutung »Land der Metallplatten«) ableitet. Eine weitere Bezeichnung war *Ophiussa* (»Land der Schlangen«; Avien. 148; 152; 172; 196), die wahrscheinlich die Phokaier, als sie mit einigen Regionen der Ost- bzw. Südküste in Berührung kamen, prägten (Avien. 195; 199; vgl. 156). *Ibēría* (Ἰβηρία), bedeutete urspr. nur die von Iberern besiedelten Gebiete, später das ganze Land, *Keltikḗ* (Κελτική), bezeichnete wohl immer nur das von Kelten besetzte Zentralplateau der iber. Halbinsel. *Hesperia* war ein poet. Name für It., später auch für Spanien. Näheres über diese Namensformen s. [2].

B. Topographie
1. Allgemein 2. Berge 3. Flüsse

1. Allgemein

Über die Beschaffenheit der Halbinsel hatte schon der Verf. des alten Periplus, dessen Text in der *Ora maritima* des Avienus enthalten ist, eine sehr genaue Vorstellung. Die Kenntnisse wurden für die Topo- und Ethnographie erweitert, wobei manche geogr. Irrtümer sich bis ins MA behaupteten [2. Bd. 1, 12–22]. Im folgenden werden die wichtigsten der Ant. bekannten Gebirge, Vorgebirge und Flüsse verzeichnet.

2. Berge

(*Montes*) *Pyrenaei*, *Pyrene*, Πυρηναῖα, h. Pyrenäen. Älteste Erwähnungen bei Avien. 472; 533; 555; 565. Eponym ist wohl die Stadt Pyrene. Die westl. Fortsetzung der → Pyrenaei ist das Kantabrische Gebirge, für dessen Westteil die Bez. *iuga Asturum* überl. ist (Plin. nat. 3,6). *Mons Vindius* bezeichnet das Bergland nördl. von Villafranca del Bierzo, wird aber auch umfassender gebraucht [4]. *Iuga Carpetana* (Plin. nat. 3,6) bezeichnet das Kastilische Scheidegebirge, *Idubeda* (Strab. 3,4,10; 12; Ptol. 2,6,20) das Iber. Randgebirge (h. Cordillera Ibérica). Darin liegt der *mons Caius* (h. Moncayo; Mart. 1,49,5; 4,55,2). Der *Vadavero* (Mart. 1,49,6) ist wohl die h. Sierra de Madero östl. von Numantia [3. Bd. 8, 252], *Voberca* (Mart. 1,49,14) entspricht dem h. Bubierca bei Ateca am Jalón, etwa 20 km westl. von Calatayud. Für Galicia wird der *mons Medullius* erwähnt (Flor. epit. 2,33,50; Oros. 6,21,7); seine Lage bleibt umstritten [4. 146ff.]. Die *montes Nerbasii* (Hydatius 71 = Chron.

min. 2,20) sind in der Gegend von Orense zu suchen [2. Bd. 1, 171]. Im Süden sind von Bed. die *iuga Oretana* (Plin. nat. 3,6, h. Sierra Morena), der *mons Argentarius* bei Castulo an der Quelle des → Baetis (Avien. 291; Strab. 3,2,11). *Orospéda* (Ὀροσπέδα, Strab. 3,4,12; Ὀρτόσπεδα bei Ptol. 2,6,20) bezeichnet das Gebirge von der Mitte der Ostküste bis → Cartagena (richtige Bestimmung [2. Bd. 1, 191]). Der *mons Silurus* (Avien. 433) entspricht dem *mons Solorius* (Plin. nat. 3,6), also der Sierra Nevada. *Il(l)ípula* (Ἰλ(λ)ίπουλα, Ptol. 2,4,12) ist die h. Sierra de Ronda [2. Bd. 1, 192].

Vorgebirge der Ostküste: *Prominens Pyrenae, Pyrenae(um) iugum* (Avien. 533; 472; 565; weitere Zeugnisse [2. Bd. 1, 178]). Das *promunturium Ferrarium* (Mela 2,91) ist dem *Tenébrion ákron* (Τενέβριον ἄκρον, Ptol. 2,6,16) bzw. dem h. Cabo de la Nao gleichzusetzen. Das *iugum Trete* (Avien. 452) entspricht dem *promonturium* (= *pr.*) *Saturni* (Plin. nat. 3,19) und der *Skombraría ákra* (Σκομβραρία ἄκρα, Ptol. 2,6,14), h. Cabo Palos, das *iugum Veneris* (Avien. 437) dem *Xaridḗmu akrōtḗrion* (Χαριδήμου ἀκρωτήριον, Ptol. 2,4,7), h. Cabo Gata.

Südküste: *Calpe*, h. Gibraltar (erste Erwähnung bei Avien. 344); *pr. Iunonis* (Mela 2,96; Plin. nat. 3,7), h. Cabo Trafalgar; *cautes sacra Saturni* (Avien. 215), h. Cabo Sagres; das *pr. Sacrum* (Strab. 3,1,2; Mela 3,7; Plin. nat. 2,242; 4,115) entspricht dem *iugum Cyneticum* (Avien. 201), h. Cabo San Vicente.

Westküste: Das *pr. magnum* (Mela 3,7; Plin. nat. 4,113) entspricht dem *pr. Olisiponense* (Plin. nat. l.c.) und dem *pr. Ophiussae* (Avien. 172) sowie dem *mons Sacer* (Colum. 6,27,7), h. Cabo Roca. Plinius (nat. 4,113 f.) verwechselt es mit dem *pr. Artabrum*. Das *pr. Nerium* (Strab. 3,1,3; 3,3,5) entspricht dem *pr. Celticum* (Plin. nat. 4,111; 115) und dem *pr. Artabrum* (Plin. nat. 2,242), h. Punta de Nariga westl. von La Coruña. Plinius (nat. 4,113 f.) verwechselt es mit Cabo Roca. Das *iugum Aryium* (Avien. 160) ist *Lapatía* (Λαπατία), *Kṓru ákron* (Κώρου ἄκρον) und *Tríleukon* (Τρίλευκον) (Ptol. 2,6,4), h. Cabo Ortegal, gleichzusetzen.

Nordküste: Das *iugum Veneris* (Avien. 158) entspricht *Oiassṓ ákron* (Οἰασσὼ ἄκρον, Ptol. 2,6,10), h. Cabo Higuer, dem Westteil der Pyrenaei [2. Bd. 1, 246]. Genaueres über die Küstengestaltung s. [2. Bd. 1, 207–246, 268–293].

3. Flüsse

Ostküste: *Anystus* (Avien. 547) entspricht dem *Ticis* (Mela 2,89); nicht zu verwechseln mit *Ticis*, h. Tech, bzw. *Ticer* (Plin. nat. 3,22), wahrscheinlich auch *Dilunus* (Sall. hist. 3,6; [3. Bd. 4, 232]), h. Muga; *Rubricatum* (Mela 2,90; Plin. nat. 3,21), h. Llobregat; *Subi* (Plin. nat. 3,21) entspricht wohl nicht der Gaya, sondern der h. Riera de Riudecañes oder Francoli bei Tarragona [2. Bd. 1, 306]. Der *(H)iberus* (früheste Erwähnung bei Cato; [3. Bd. 3, 186]) ist gleichzusetzen mit dem *Íbēr* (Ἴβηρ, früheste Erwähnung bei Pol. 2,13,7) und dem *flumen Oleum* (Avien. 505), h. Ebro. Linker Nebenfluß: *Sicoris* (oft gen., bes. in Caes. civ.), h. Segre, mit der *Cinga*, die h. noch Cinga heißt. Rechter Nebenfluß: *Salo*, h. Jalón. *Tyrius* (Avien. 482) entspricht der *Turia* [3. Bd. 4, 206, 213] und *Turis* (Ptol. 2,6,15), h. Guadalaviar. *Sicanus* (Avien. 469) ist der *Sucro* [3. Bd. 4, 208 f.; 5. 88], h. Júcar. *Tader* (Plin. nat. 3,19) entspricht dem *Taber* (Ptol. 2,6,14) und *Theodorus* (Avien. 456), h. Segura. Wahrscheinlich handelt es sich um den *Iber* des Hasdrubal-Vertrages (Pol. 3,21,1; 30,3; [6]).

Südküste: *Menace* (Avien. 427 vgl. 431) entspricht der *Maenuba* (Plin. nat. 3,8), h. Velez. *Chrysus* (Avien. 419) der *Barbesula* (Plin. nat. 3,8; Ptol. 2,4,7), h. Guadiaro. Der *Tartessus* (Avien. 225; 284; [3. Bd. 12, 182]) entspricht dem *Baetis*, h. Guadalquivir. Linke Nebenflüsse: *Singilis* (Plin. nat. 3,10; 12), h. Genil, und *flumen Salsum* (Bell. Hisp. 7,1; 3), h. Guadajoz. *Hiberus* (Avien. 248) entspricht *Luxia* (Plin. nat. 3,7), h. Río Tinto. *Anas* (Plin. nat. 3,6), h. Guadiana.

Westküste: *Tagus* [2. Bd. 1, 341 ff.], h. Tajo; *Tagonius* (Plut. Sertorius 17), h. Tajuña, rechter Nebenfluß des Tajo; *Munda* (Strab. 3,3,4; Plin. nat. 4,115), h. Mondego; *Durius*, h. Duero, Douro; *Urbicus* (Hydatius 173 = Chron. min. 2,28; Chronici Caesaraugustani ad a. 458 = Chron. min. 2,222; vgl. auch Isid. Historia Gothorum 31 = Chron. min. 2,279; Iord. Get. 44), rechter Nebenfluß des Astura, h. Orbigo; *Limia* (Mela 3,10; Ptol. 2,6,1; Plin. nat. 4,112), griech. Λιμαίας (*Limaías*, Strab. 3,3,4; Plin. nat. 4,115) entspricht dem *Oblivio* (Sall. hist. 3,44; Plin. nat. 4,115), dem Λήθης (*Lḗthēs*, Strab. l.c., App. Ib. 73), Βελιών (*Beliṓn*, Strab. l.c.) und dem *Aeminius* (Plin. nat. 4,115), h. Lima; *Minius* [2. Bd. 1, 354], griech. Βαῖνις (*Baínis*, Strab. l.c.) bzw. Βαίτης (*Baítēs*, App. Ib. 73), h. Miño, Minho.

Nordküste: *Navia* (Plin. nat. 4,111; Ptol. 2,6,4), h. Navia; *Melsos* (Strab. 3,4,20), h. Canero, vgl. aber [9. 590; 3. Bd. 6, 267]; *Namnasa* (Mela 3,15), h. Nansa; *Nerva* (Ptol. 2,6,7), h. Nervión bei Bilbao; *Deva* (Mela 3,15; Ptol. 2,6,8), h. Deva.

C. Wirtschaft

Top. und Vegetation der Halbinsel bestimmten ihre wirtschaftliche Bed.: Die Ost- und die Westküste waren sehr reich an Pflanzen (Strab. 3,3,4; 3,4,16). Hier herrschte der Oliven- (v.a. in der Baetica; Strab. 3,2,6), Weizen- (Strab. 3,4,16) und Weinanbau vor. Auch der Flachsanbau und die daraus resultierende Leinenproduktion waren wichtig (Plin. nat. 19,10). Vieh- und Pferdezucht ergänzten die landwirtschaftliche Produktion. An den Küsten wurde umfangreicher Fischfang betrieben; → Gades war bekannt für seinen Thunfischfang (vgl. das Wappen). Metallvorkommen konzentrierten sich im südl. und nördl. Randgebirge (Huelva, Castulo), während das Tafelland nur wenig mit Metallressourcen ausgestattet war. Im Süden bei Cartagena hat man Silber (Strab. 3,2,10) und Blei gefunden (Strab. 3,2,11), im nördl. Asturien Gold (Plin. nat. 33,78) und Silber (Strab. 3,2,10), Eisen im Ebrotal (Pol. 6,23 fr. 96) und in Kantabrien (Plin. nat. 34,149).

D. Bevölkerung

Die iber. Halbinsel war seit dem Altpaläolithikum besiedelt und hat immer wieder Einwanderungen erlebt. Deshalb bietet ihre Ethnologie zahllose Probleme. Man muß unterscheiden zw. der bodenständigen Bevölkerung und den eingewanderten Völkern, die vorübergehend als Eroberer, Kolonisten oder Händler ins Land gekommen sind, angelockt durch seine reichen Metallschätze. Einheimische: Die Iberes siedelten vornehmlich entlang der Ost- und Südküste. Sie bilden bis h. den Hauptteil der Bevölkerung ([5. 286ff.]; älteste Erwähnungen bei Avien. 250; 472; 480; 253; 613; [3. Bd. 1^2, 188f.]). Die Zugehörigkeit der Tartessier zu den Iberes wird h. nicht mehr bestritten.

→ Kelten: Sie drangen zw. 800 und 500 v. Chr. über die Pyrenaei ein und überrannten zeitweise große Teile der Halbinsel. Ob sie in einer oder – wahrscheinlicher – in mehreren Wellen kamen, ist strittig. Quellen, Funde (Hallstatt) und unzählige ON und PN bezeugen die Bed. dieser Einwanderung, die v. a. den Norden und die Mitte der Halbinsel betraf. Basken: Sie werden lit. erst im 1. Jh. v. Chr. gen., sind aber nach arch. und sprachlichen Merkmalen ein Volk rätselhafter Herkunft. Die nach den Kelten eingewanderten Völker: Viele Funde beweisen, daß schon in prähistor. Zeit Handelsimport aus den Ländern des östl. Mittelmeeres stattgefunden hat, aber ob direkt oder durch Vermittler, durch die Kreter bzw. andere Seefahrer, läßt sich nicht entscheiden. Quellenmäßig gesichert ist aber das Auftreten der Phoiniker in → Gades und an anderen Orten (vgl. Almuñecar, Sexi, Toscanos) im 8. Jh. v. Chr. Sie gründeten Faktoreien, aus denen sich mancherorts Städte entwickelten [7; 8]. Den Phoinikern folgten Griechen, bes. die Phokaier, die erst auf ihren Fahrten nach Tartessos, etwa seit 600 v. Chr. von Massalia aus einige Faktoreien und Städte, bes. an der Ost- und Südküste anlegten [5; 6. 44ff.]. Während Phoiniker und Griechen im allg. als Händler auftraten, kamen die Karthager unter → Hamilkar [3] Barkas 237 v. Chr. als Eroberer ins Land. Sie haben sich auf die alten phoinik. Niederlassungen gestützt; Neugründungen sind → Akra Leuke unter Hamilkar und → Carthago Nova unter Hasdrubal um 226 v. Chr. Ihr kultureller Einfluß wird vielfach unterschätzt [6]. Die Römer zogen 218 v. Chr. in H. ein. Bis 206 konnten sie mit Hilfe iber. Stämme die Karthager vertreiben, aber die völlige Unterwerfung der Halbinsel gelang ihnen erst unter Augustus gegen den erbitterten Widerstand der iber., keltiber. und kantabrischen Bevölkerung. H. galt frühestens um 19 v. Chr. als *provincia pacata*.

E. Römische Zeit

Das Land wurde in zwei (Ulterior, Citerior), später drei Prov. (Lusitania, Baetica, Tarraconensis) aufgeteilt. In der Folgezeit setzte die Romanisierung ein. Die alten Sprachen mit Ausnahme des → Baskischen verschwanden, so daß z.Z. Strabons (2. H. 1. Jh. v. Chr.) die Baetica als eine der am stärksten romanisierten Prov. des Imperiums galt (Strab. 3,2,15). Caesar und Augustus gründeten in H. mehr Kolonien als in anderen Gebieten – 12 in der Tarraconensis und 9 in der Baetica. Es gab 23 einheimische Städte, die röm. *municipia* wurden, und 45 latin. Gemeinden.

Die röm. Kultur wird in einer Vielzahl von Baudenkmälern wie etwa Theatern, Amphitheatern, Tempeln und Aquädukten z. B. in → Tarraco, → Augusta [2] Emerita und → Saguntum faßbar. Am Grad der Romanisierung änderten spätere Einfälle anderer Völker ab 255 n. Chr. wenig. Die Westgoten und die Sueben, die ab dem 5. Jh. eindrangen, bildeten eine nur dünne Kriegerschicht, die im Verlauf des 6. Jh. romanisiert wurde [3. Bd. 9, 195]. Die Araber, die im J. 711 ins Land kamen, wurden im Zuge der Reconquista erst 1492 aus dem Land vertrieben. Die einheimische Bevölkerung gliederte sich in Stämme, die wohl ethnologische, weniger polit. Bed. hatten und im Laufe der röm. Herrschaft allmählich verschwanden. Sie bestanden aus Clans (*gentilitas*, *gens*, *centuria*; [4. 58ff.]). Die zentrale polit. Einheit aber war die Stadt oder Burg, und aus dieser Zersplitterung erklärt sich großenteils die Gesch. des Landes. Zu den röm. Provinzen speziell s. → Hispania Baetica, → Hispania Tarraconensis, → Lusitania.

1 M. Almagro-Gorbea, Los Celtas: Hispania y Europa, 1993 2 Schulten, Landeskunde 3 A. Schulten (Hrsg.), Fontes Hispaniae Antiquae, 1925ff. 4 F.J. Lomas Salmonte, Asturias prerromana y altoimperial, 1989 5 P. Barceló, Aspekte der griech. Präsenz im westl. Mittelmeerraum, in: Tyche 3, 1988, 11ff. 6 Ders., Die Grenzen des karthagischen Machtbereichs unter Hasdrubal, in: E. Olshausen, H. Sonnabend (Hrsg.), Stuttgarter Kolloquium zur histor. Geogr. des Alt. 4. 1990 (Geographica Historica 7), 1994, 35–55 7 H. G. Niemeyer, Auf der Suche nach Mainake, in: Historia 29, 1980, 165ff. 8 Ders., Anno octogesimo post Troiam Cabotam ... Tyria classis Gadis condidit? Polemische Gedanken zum Gründungsdatum von Gades (Cadiz), in: Hamburger Beitr. zur Arch. 8, 1981, 9ff. 9 A. Schulten, s. v. Melsus, RE 15, 590.

J. Alvar, De Argantonio a los romanos, in: Historia 16, 1995 • J. Arce, El último siglo de la España romana: 284–409, 1982 • P. Barceló, Karthago und die Iber. Halbinsel vor den Barkiden, 1988 • J. M. Blázquez u. a., Historia de España Antigua, 1978 • J. L. López Castro, Hispania Poena, 1995 • A. Ruiz, M. Molinos, Los Iberos, 1995. P.B.

F. Spätantike und byzantinische Zeit

Die Eroberung der iberischen Halbinsel erfolgte zw. 711 und 712 durch vorwiegend berberische Truppenkontingente und war Ergebnis einer eher zufälligen Inkursion im Rahmen der großen islamischen Expansion nach Ägypten und Nordafrika. Nach einer kurzen, unruhigen Anfangsphase gelang es dem umayyadischen (→ Omajjaden) Prinzen ʿAbd-ar-Raḥmān das nun al-Andalus gen. islamische Spanien zu stabilisieren und dort ein von den → Abbasiden in Bagdad *de facto* unabhängiges Emirat (756–929) zu etablieren. Höhepunkt der ibero-islamischen Kultur war das umayyadische Kalifat (→ Kalif) in Córdoba (929–1030), auf dessen Auflösung eine Phase polit. Dezentralisierung (1030–1086) folgte, welche den christl. Königreichen im Norden zum ersten Mal die Gelegenheit erfolgreicher Zurück-gewinnung größerer Territorien gab. Die darauf folgenden berberischen Dyn. der Almoraviden (ab 1086) und Almohaden (ab ca. 1150) konnten sich dem christl. Expansionsdrang (»Reconquista«) nur zeitweise erfolgreich widersetzen, ab dem 13. Jh. war das islamische Spanien auf das kleine Reich der Nasriden in Granada reduziert, das 1492 schließlich in die Hände der katholischen Könige fiel.

Charakteristisch für Al-Andalus war die bes. Bevölkerungszusammensetzung und die damit zusammenhängende linguistische Situation. So bestand die einheimische Bevölkerung aus a) Christen spanisch-röm. und westgot. Herkunft, die einen roman. Dial. sprachen und Lat. als Schriftsprache pflegten – welches aber ab dem 9. Jh. zunehmend vom Arab. verdrängt wurde (= Mozaraber, d. h. »arabisierte« Christen), b) Juden, die meist sowohl die roman. wie die arab. Vulgärsprache beherrschten, als Kultursprache hingegen Hebr., bald auch Hocharab. benützten, c) eine wachsende Anzahl spanischer Neumuslime, die zumeist als gesprochenes Medium das Roman. beibehielten, aber Hocharab. schrieben. Die Herrscherschicht setzte sich a) aus arab. Stämmen zusammen, deren Schrift- und Umgangssprache das Arab. war, b) aus Berberstämmen, die als Umgangssprache lange noch Berberisch sprachen, und c) Sklaven europ. Herkunft. Diese spezifische Kommunikationssituation schuf eine der wichtigsten Rahmenbedingungen für den fruchtbaren Kulturkontakt auf der iberischen Halbinsel in islam. Zeit.

→ SPANIEN

R. ARIE, La España Musulmana, 1987 • E. ASHTOR, The Jews of Moslem Spain, 1973 • P. GUICHARD, Structures sociales »orientales« et »occidentales« dans l'Espagne musulmane, 1977 • S.KH. JAYYUSSI, The Legacy of Muslim Spain, 2 Bde., 1994 • LEVI-PROVENÇAL, Histoire de l'Espagne Musulmane, 1950–1953 • J. VERNET, Cultura hispanoárabe en Oriente y Occidente, 1987.

I. T.-N.

II. SPRACHEN

Von der einheimischen Bevölkerung der iberischen Halbinsel wurden vor der Latinisierung mind. vier verschiedene Sprachen gesprochen. Entlang der Mittelmeerküste, im Ebrogebiet, dem diesem westl. angrenzenden Binnenland und in Mittel- und Südportugal sind sie durch Inschr., vorwiegend in einer eigenen, »althispanischen« Schrift bezeugt, deren älteste ins 4. Jh. v. Chr. (in Südportugal vielleicht früher) zu datieren sind. Im Norden und NW sind Personen-, Orts- und Götternamen auf lat. Inschr. der Kaiserzeit und bei klass. Autoren die einzige Sprachquelle.

Sicher nicht-idg. ist die »iberisch« gen. Sprache, die in relativer Einheitlichkeit zw. Andalusien und Südfrankreich und im mittleren Ebrogebiet bezeugt ist. Die sehr charakteristischen PN sind normalerweise Komposita wie die phoinik. oder gall. Vollnamen. Gramm. und Lex. sind noch so gut wie völlig ungedeutet.

Durch epigraphische Denkmäler zw. oberem Ebro, Tajo und Duero ist die Sprache der keltiberischen Stämme bekannt, die zur kelt. Sprachfamilie (→ keltische Sprachen) gehört. Ihre Erschließung steckt noch in den Anfängen; dem umfangreichsten Text, vermutlich juristischen Inhalts, auf einer Bronzetafel aus Botorrita (Provinz Zaragoza), sind mehrere sicher noch nicht endgültige Übersetzungsversuche gewidmet worden. Einige Teile der Nominal- und Verbalflexion sind gut erkennbar: z. B. bei den *-o*-Stämmen Nom. Sg. *-os*, Gen. Sg. *-o*, Dat. Sg. *-ui*, Akk. Sg. *-om*, Abl. Sg. *-ud*, Gen. Pl. *-um*, Dat. Pl. *-ubos*; beim Verbum 3. Sg. Ind. *-ti*, 3. Pl. Ind. *-nti*, 3. Sg. Iptv. *-tud*.

Im mittleren Portugal zeugen drei Inschr. für eine »lusitanisch« gen. Sprache, die kelt. Merkmale, aber erh. idg. *p* vor Vokal zeigt und deswegen üblicherweise, aber vielleicht nicht zutreffend als idg. Sprache eigener Filiation angesehen wird. Die Sprache der »tartessischen« Inschr. in Südportugal, Steindenkmäler mit verhältnismäßig stereotypem Formular, deren Schrift erst spät mit einiger Sicherheit enträtselt werden konnte, ist noch nicht überzeugend identifiziert; sicher ist, daß sie nicht mit der iberischen vergleichbar ist; neuerdings versucht man – möglicherweise mit Erfolg –, sie als kelt. Sprache zu deuten. Im NW und Norden lassen die EN kelt. Züge erkennen, deren Verhältnis zur Sprache der lusitanischen und keltiberischen Denkmäler jedoch nicht klar zu bestimmen ist.

Unsicher ist der Zeugniswert einiger Namen auf lat. Inschr. aus Navarra, die zu der jenseits der Pyrenäen gut greifbaren aquitanischen Namengebung gehören, in der man eine frühe Stufe des → Baskischen zu erkennen glaubt.

ED. (INSCHR.): J. UNTERMANN (Hrsg.), Monumenta Linguarum Hispanicarum I–IV, 1975–1997.
ZU DEN SPRACHEN: J. DE HOZ, La lengua y la escritura ibéricas, y la lenguas de los íberos, in: Lengua y cultura en la Hispania prerromana. Actas del V coloquio sobre lenguas y culturas prerromanas de la Península Ibérica, 1993, 635–666 • D. E. EVANS, The identification of Continental Celtic with special reference to Hispano-Celtic, in: Ebd., 563–608 • J. UNTERMANN, Zum Stand der Deutung der »tartessischen« Inschriften, in: J. F. ESKA u. a. (Hrsg.), Hispano-Gallo-Brittonica. Essays in honour of D. Ellis Evans, 1995, 244–259 • F. VILLAR, Estudios de Celtibérico y de toponimia prerromana, 1995.

J.U.

III. SCHRIFTSYSTEME

Die vorröm. Sprachen Hispaniens werden auf den meisten ihrer epigraphischen Denkmäler durch eine eigene, »althispanische« Schrift wiedergegeben. Sie zeigt drei regionale Varianten: die südwestl. oder »tartessische« v. a. in Südportugal, die südiberische vom östl. Andalusien bis in den Süden der Provinz Valencia und, weitaus am häufigsten, die nordostiberische Schrift zw. Valencia und Béziers und im östl. Binnenland. Die letztgen. Variante wurde um 1920 von M. GÓMEZ-MORENO entziffert, und h. sind auch die beiden übrigen nahezu vollständig verständlich. Die Schrift ist gekennzeichnet durch ein System von 27 Graphemen: fünf Vokalzeichen, sieben Zeichen für Dauerlaute (je zwei Nasale,

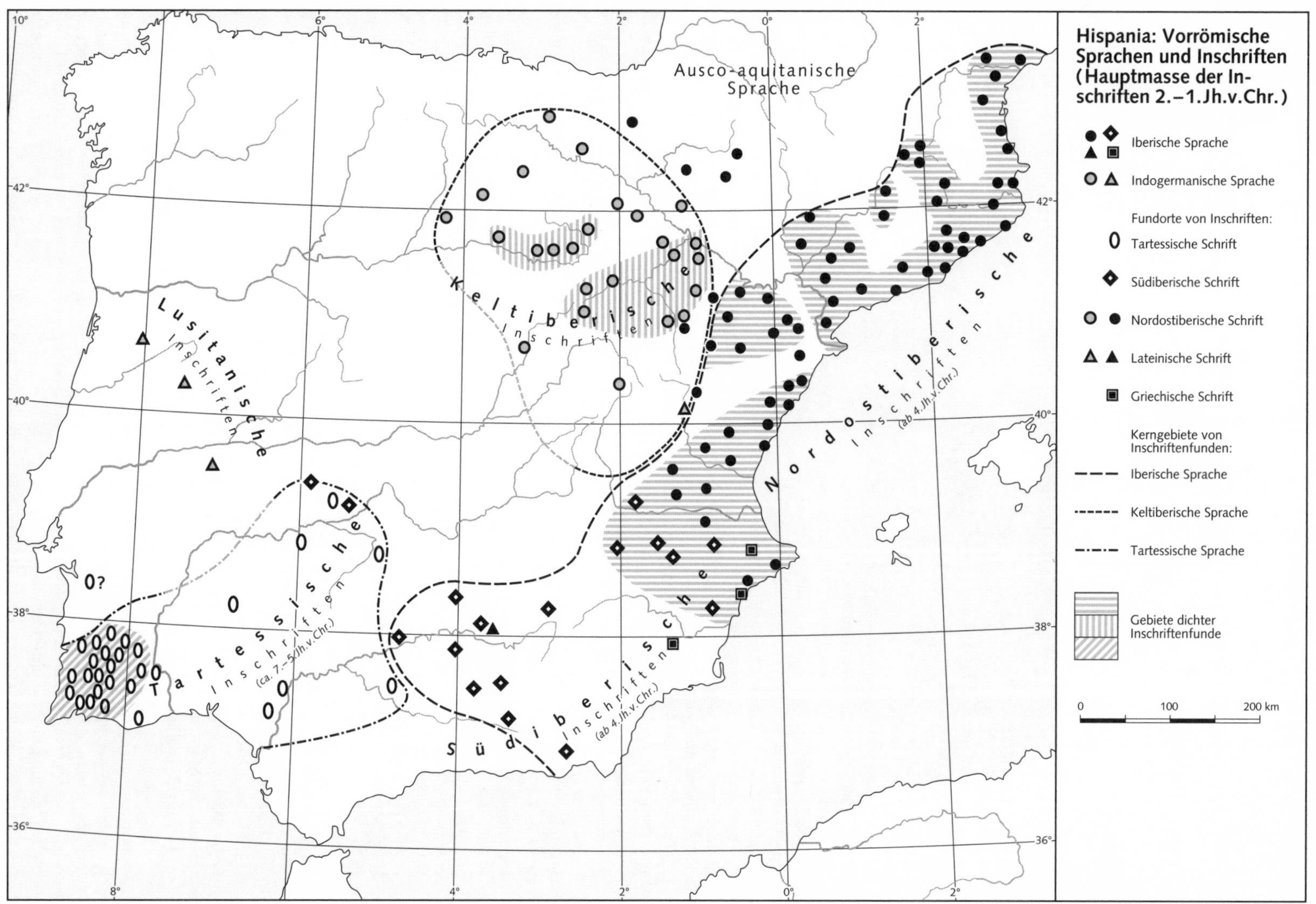
Hispania: Vorrömische Sprachen und Inschriften (Hauptmasse der Inschriften 2.–1.Jh.v.Chr.)
Iberische Sprache
Indogermanische Sprache
Fundorte von Inschriften:
Tartessische Schrift
Südiberische Schrift
Nordostiberische Schrift
Lateinische Schrift
Griechische Schrift
Kerngebiete von Inschriftenfunden:
Iberische Sprache
Keltiberische Sprache
Tartessische Sprache
Gebiete dichter Inschriftenfunde
0
100
200 km
Ausco-aquitanische Sprache
Keltiberische Inschriften
Lusitanische Inschriften
Nordostiberische Inschriften (ab 4.Jh.v.Chr.)
Tartessische Inschriften (ca. 7.–5.Jh.v.Chr.)
Südiberische Inschriften (ab 4.Jh.v.Chr.)
0?
10°
8°
6°
4°
2°
0°
42°
40°
38°
36°

Die nordostiberische Schrift (rechtsläufig)

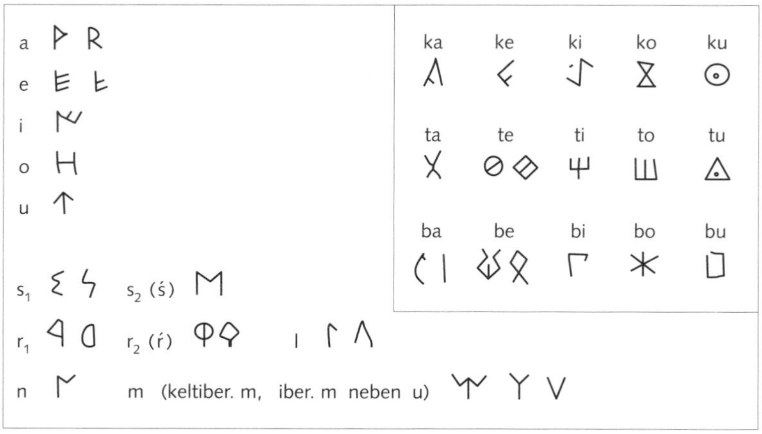

a
e
i
o
u

s_1 s_2 (ś)
r_1 r_2 (ŕ) l
n m (keltiber. m, iber. m neben u)

ka	ke	ki	ko	ku
ta	te	ti	to	tu
ba	be	bi	bo	bu

Vibranten, Sibilanten und einen Laterallaut) und 15 Silbenzeichen, mit denen drei Verschlußlautartikulationen (labial, dental, velar) jeweils kombiniert mit einem der fünf Vokale geschrieben werden; die Opposition stimmhaft/stimmlos wird nicht wiedergegeben, obwohl sie nach Ausweis anderer Quellen in den betroffenen Sprachen existierte. Entstehungszeit und -ort sind nicht sicher bekannt: wahrscheinlich übernahm ein gelehrter Erfinder im andalusischen Bereich um 500 v. Chr. das phoinik. und griech. Alphabet und gestaltete es nach Anregungen aus beiden Vorbildern unter Hinzunahme einiger frei erfundener Zeichenformen um. Eine althispanische Alphabet-Inschr. mit 27 Buchstaben, von denen die ersten 14 (von α bis υ) genau die Reihenfolge des griech. Vorbilds beibehalten, wurde in Espanca (Castro Verde, Portugal) gefunden.

J. A. Correa, El signario de Espanca (Castro Verde) y la escritura tartesia, in: Lengua y cultura en la Hispania prerromana. Actas del V coloquio sobre lenguas y culturas prerromanas de la Península Ibérica, 1993, 521–562 • J. de Hoz, El origen oriental de las antiguas escrituras hispánicas ..., in: Estudos Orientais 1, 1990, 219–246 • J. Untermann, Monumenta Linguarum Hispanicarum III, 1 1990, 132–149.

J. U.

IV. Religion

Wie in den anderen westeurop. Gebieten ist die Rel. der iberischen Halbinsel vor der Romanisierung schwer faßbar. Neben die wenigen Mitteilungen ant. Autoren (Strabon, Plinius), die fast nur das Auffallende berichten (divinatorische Menschenopfer: Strab. 3,4,6; gemeinsame Tänze von Männern und Frauen: 3,4,7; Mythos von Habis: Iust. 44,4,1), dies zudem in griech. oder röm. Interpretation, treten die naturgemäß schwer deutbaren arch., insbes. ikonographischen Befunde und die zahlreichen Inschr. röm. Zeit, die aber fast nur Götternamen enthalten; erschwerend kommt die große Vielfalt der iberischen Stämme und die unterschiedlich frühe Romanisierung dazu. Wenigstens für den Süden Spaniens ist die Lage außerdem durch die Ausstrahlung der tyrischen Kolonie → Gades mit dem zentralen Kult des → Melqart, durch die intensive punische Kolonisation und die von der griech. Kolonie Emporion (wo Strab. 3,4,8 die Artemis Ephesia belegt) ausgehende Ausstrahlung kompliziert, die bes. die Ikonographie betrifft: hinter pun. und griech. Formen und Namen können indigene Kulte stehen. Während in den punischen Städten Südspaniens insbes. der Kult des Stadtgotts Melqart, daneben wohl auch derjenige der → Tinnit (auch als Dea Caelestis inschr. faßbar) gut bezeugt ist, ergibt sich als Eigenheit der indigenen Kulte aus der Ikonographie die starke Dominanz weibl. Gottheiten (Dama de Baza, wohl auch Dama de Elche) und die Präsenz eines »Herrn der Pferde« (vgl. Strab. 3,4,15 zu den wilden Pferden).

Nach der Romanisierung bestehen die lokalen Kulte und Heiligtümer weiter (Beschreibung eines Heiligtums bei Kap Sagres in Südportugal bei Strab. 3,1,4f.); eine gewisse Bed. haben → Höhlenheiligtümer, die vorröm. Kultstätten fortsetzen. Die Inschr. belegen eine große Vielfalt lokaler Theonyme (insgesamt über 300), die sich zumeist in den → Epiklesen ausdrücken, während Grabungsbefunde die Romanisierung der Architektur und das Weiterleben der Heiligtümer bis in die Spätant. belegen. Die (zumeist nur einmal belegten) Götternamen sind oft idg. deutbar und zeigen ein Pantheon, das mit demjenigen Galliens Ähnlichkeiten aufweist (wie auch etwa der Kult von – heißen – Quellen dem kelt. Bereich von I. und Gallien gemeinsam ist); nur wenige Götternamen sind überlokal (etwa Endovellicus und Ataecina in Lusitania). Dazu tritt in den romanisierten Städten die Fülle der offiziellen röm. Kulte (kapitolinische Trias, bes. → Iuppiter Optimus Maximus; → Kaiserkult), wobei vielfach nicht nachweisbar ist, ob ein städt. Kult einen vorröm. fortsetzt. Als bes. komplex erweist sich etwa der Kult der → Diana Maxima in Saguntum, wo Indigenes mit dem griech. Kult der ephesischen Artemis verschmolzen sein kann.

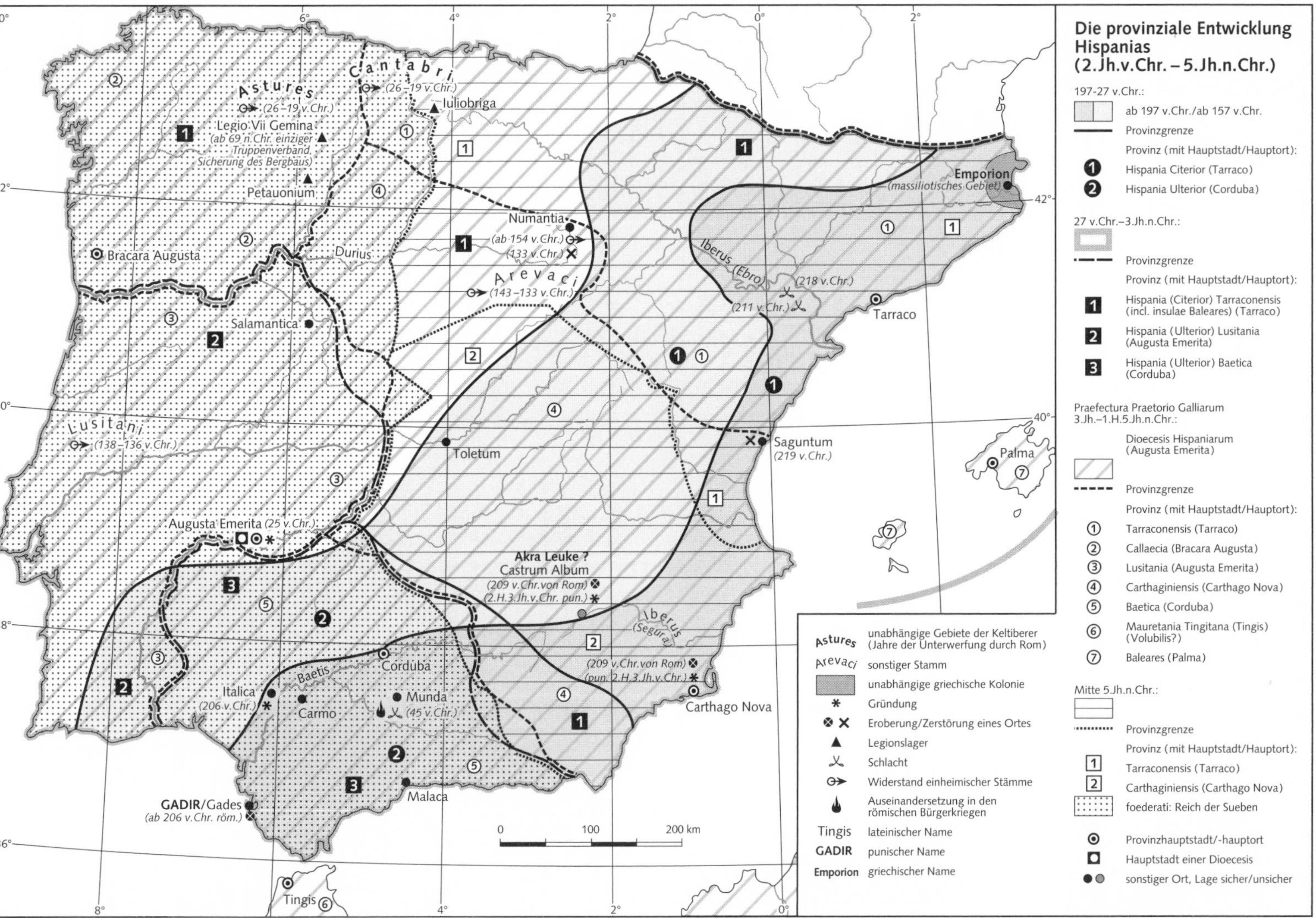
Die provinziale Entwicklung Hispanias (2.Jh.v.Chr. – 5.Jh.n.Chr.)
197-27 v.Chr.:
ab 197 v.Chr./ab 157 v.Chr.
Provinzgrenze
Provinz (mit Hauptstadt/Hauptort):
1 Hispania Citerior (Tarraco)
2 Hispania Ulterior (Corduba)
27 v.Chr.–3.Jh.n.Chr.:
Provinzgrenze
Provinz (mit Hauptstadt/Hauptort):
1 Hispania (Citerior) Tarraconensis (incl. insulae Baleares) (Tarraco)
2 Hispania (Ulterior) Lusitania (Augusta Emerita)
3 Hispania (Ulterior) Baetica (Corduba)
Praefectura Praetorio Galliarum 3.Jh.–1.H.5.Jh.n.Chr.:
Dioecesis Hispaniarum (Augusta Emerita)
Provinzgrenze
Provinz (mit Hauptstadt/Hauptort):
1 Tarraconensis (Tarraco)
2 Callaecia (Bracara Augusta)
3 Lusitania (Augusta Emerita)
4 Carthaginiensis (Carthago Nova)
5 Baetica (Corduba)
6 Mauretania Tingitana (Tingis) (Volubilis?)
7 Baleares (Palma)
Mitte 5.Jh.n.Chr.:
Provinzgrenze
Provinz (mit Hauptstadt/Hauptort):
1 Tarraconensis (Tarraco)
2 Carthaginiensis (Carthago Nova)
foederati: Reich der Sueben
Provinzhauptstadt/-hauptort
Hauptstadt einer Dioecesis
sonstiger Ort, Lage sicher/unsicher
Astures unabhängige Gebiete der Keltiberer (Jahre der Unterwerfung durch Rom)
Arevaci sonstiger Stamm
unabhängige griechische Kolonie
Gründung
Eroberung/Zerstörung eines Ortes
Legionslager
Schlacht
Widerstand einheimischer Stämme
Auseinandersetzung in den römischen Bürgerkriegen
Tingis lateinischer Name
GADIR punischer Name
Emporion griechischer Name
Astures (26–19 v.Chr.)
Cantabri (26–19 v.Chr.)
Iuliobriga
Legio VII Gemina (ab 69 n.Chr. einziger Truppenverband, Sicherung des Bergbaus)
Petauonium
Bracara Augusta
Durius
Numantia (ab 154 v.Chr.) (133 v.Chr.)
Arevaci (143–133 v.Chr.)
Salamantica
Lusitani (138–136 v.Chr.)
Toletum
Augusta Emerita (25 v.Chr.)
Akra Leuke ? Castrum Album (209 v.Chr.von Rom) (2.H.3.Jh.v.Chr. pun.)
Iberus (Segura)
(209 v.Chr.von Rom) (pun. 2.H.3.Jh.v.Chr.)
Carthago Nova
Corduba
Baetis
Italica (206 v.Chr.)
Carmo
Munda (45 v.Chr.)
Malaca
GADIR/Gades (ab 206 v.Chr. röm.)
Tingis
Emporion (massiliotisches Gebiet)
Iberus (Ebro)
(218 v.Chr.)
(211 v.Chr.)
Tarraco
Saguntum (219 v.Chr.)
Palma
0 100 200 km
10° 8° 6° 4° 2° 0° 2°
42° 40° 38° 36°

Im Lauf der Kaiserzeit dringen die oriental. Kulte ein, unter denen → Attis in der Baetica, → Mithras auf der ganzen iberischen Halbinsel gut belegt sind. Eine Sonderstellung nimmt das Heiligtum des Melqart/→ Herakles von Gades ein; gegründet von tyrischen Kolonisten, erlangt es im Lauf der hell. Zeit überlokalen Ruhm und ist in der Kaiserzeit bis zum Sieg des Christentums eines der zentralen Heiligtümer des westl. Mittelmeers. Der Kult des Melqart strahlt von hier in den ganzen tartessischen Raum aus; Hercules Gaditanus erhält Kult in ganz I. und darüber hinaus.

Quellen: J. M. Blazquez, Religiones primitivas de Hispania, I. Fuentes literarias y epigráficas, 1962 • A. M. Vázquez, La religión romana en Hispania. Fuentes epigráficas, arqueológicas y numismáticas, 1982.
Lit.: A. García y Bellído, Les religions orientales dans l'Espagne romain, 1967 • J. M. Blazquez, Diccionario de las religiones prerromanes de Hispania, 1975 • J. d'Encarnação, Divinidades indigenas sob o dominio romano em Portugal, 1975 • J. C. Bermejo Barrera (Hrsg.), Mitología y mitos de la Hispania prerromana 1–2, 1986 und 1994 • J. M. Blázquez, Einheimische Religionen Hispaniens in der röm. Kaiserzeit, in: ANRW II 18.2, 164–275 • J. Manga, Die röm. Rel. in Hispanien während der Prinzipatszeit, in: Ebd., 276–344 • M. Bendala Galán, Die oriental. Religionen Hispaniens in vorröm. und röm. Zeit, in: Ebd., 345–408. F. G.

V. Archäologie

s. Pyrenäenhalbinsel

Hispania Baetica, Hispania Ulterior. Die Anfänge der Prov. H. B. stehen im Zusammenhang mit der Neuordnung der Provinzen durch Augustus 27 v. Chr. (Cass. Dio 80,2). Das älteste Dokument, das die H. B. nennt, ist eine Inschr. vom Forum Augustum in Rom (ILS 103). Ab dem 2. Jh. n. Chr. wird die H. B. *Baetica provincia* bzw. *Hispania Baetica* gen. (ILS 269). Die Grenze der H. B. bilden im Westen der Anas (Guadiana), im Norden die Sierra Morena, im Süden Atlantik und Mittelmeer. Hauptstadt dieser senatorischen Prov. war → Corduba.
→ Lusitania

C. Castillo Garcia, Städte und Personen der Baetica, in: ANRW II 3, 1975, 601–654 • J. M. Blázquez u. a., Historia de España Antigua II, 1978 • C. Ames, Unt. zu den Rel. in der Baetica in röm. Zeit, Diss. 1998. P. B.

Hispania Tarraconensis, Hispania Citerior. Die Prov. H. T. wurde im Zuge der administrativen Neugestaltung der iber. Halbinsel durch Augustus 27 v. Chr. errichtet (Cass. Dio 80,2). Sie umfaßte zunächst die nordöstl. Hälfte von Hispania und war die größte der drei hispanischen Prov. Sie reichte im Norden bis zum Okeanos und den Pyrenaei, im Osten bildete das Mittelmeer die natürliche Grenze unter Einschluß der Baliares, im Süden wurde sie durch die Baetica begrenzt, im Westen durch die Lusitania. Mit der Vermehrung der Provinzen wurde die H. T. erheblich verkleinert; in diocletianischer Zeit umfaßte sie etwa nur die Hälfte ihrer urspr. Ausdehnung. Kerngebiete waren das Ebro-Tal und die nördl. Ostküste, Prov.-Hauptstadt war → Tarraco.

P. Bosch-Gimpera, Katalonien in der röm. Kaiserzeit, in: ANRW II 3, 1975, 572–600 • J. M. Blázquez u. a., Historia de España Antigua II, 1978. P. B.

Karten-Lit.: J. Arce u. a. (Hrsg.), Hispania Romana, Ausstellungskat. Rom, 1997 • J. M. Blázquez, Hispanien unter den Antoninen und Severern, in: ANRW II 3, 1975, 452–522 • P. Bosch-Gimpera, Katalonien in der röm. Kaiserzeit, in: ANRW II 3, 1975, 572–600 • C. Castillo Garcia, Städte und Personen der Baetica, in: ANRW II 3, 1975, 601–654 • F. Diego Santos, Die Integration Nord- und Nordwestspaniens als röm. Prov. in der Reichspolitik des Augustus, in: ANRW II 3, 1975, 523–571 • J. S. Richardson, The Romans in Spain, 1996 • A. Tovar, J. M. Blázquez Martínez, Forsch.-Ber. zur Gesch. des röm. Hispanien, in: ANRW II 3, 1975, 428–451 • W. Trillmich, Hispania Antiqua, 1993.

Hispellum. Stadt in Umbria auf einer Anhöhe des Monte Subasio, h. Spello. Seit dem 7. Jh. v. Chr. besiedelt, an die *via Flaminia* angebunden, *municipium*, *tribus Lemonia*, *colonia Iulia* (evtl. seit dem Zweiten Triumvirat). Auf dem Territorium von H. lagen die Quellen des → Clitumnus (Plin. epist. 8,8,6). Unter Constantinus war die Stadt *colonia Flavia Constans* mit einem Tempel der *gens Flavia* und dem Privileg der Feier eines umbr. Jahresfests (ILS 705 von 333/337). Arch.: Reste der Stadtmauer vom Anf. der augusteischen Zeit mit Türmen, monumentalen Toren, Amphitheater, Theater, Venusheiligtum.

P. Camerieri u. a., H., in: Atti dell' Accademia Properziana di Assisi, 1997. G. U.

Histiaia (Ἱστίαια). Stadt an der Nordküste von Euboia, noch nicht lokalisiert, wohl nahe Xirochori zu suchen, eine Gründung thessal. Hellopioi und Perrhaiboi. Das Gebiet von H. umfaßte urspr. den gesamten Norden von Euboia (Demosth. or. 23,213) und war für seinen Wein bekannt (Hom. Il. 2,537). Das Hauptheiligtum war der Tempel der Artemis Proseoa in Artemision. Nach der Seeschlacht am Kap Artemision besetzten und plünderten die Perser H. (Hdt. 8,23 f.; 66,1; Diod. 11,13,5). Dem → Attisch-Delischen Seebund trat H. 477 v. Chr. bei mit einem relativ geringen Tribut (1000 Drachmen, ATL 1,274 f.; 3,22; 197; 239; 267 f.; 288). Beim euboiischen Aufstand gegen Athen 446 v. Chr. spielte H. eine führende Rolle, wurde nach dessen Niederschlagung auch härter bestraft als z. B. Chalkis oder Eretria. Zur Vergeltung für das Kapern eines athen. Schiffes und die Ermordung der Besatzung wurden die Einwohner vertrieben. In Oreos, einem an der Küste gelegenen Demos von H. (beim h. Molos), wurden 2000 att. Kleruchen angesiedelt. Nach dem Peloponnesischen Krieg und dem Abzug der Kleruchen kehrten die vertriebenen Bewohner aus Thessalia wieder nach H. zurück. H. und Oreos schlossen sich zusammen, dokumentiert durch eine gemeinsame Mauer; als Name der Stadt bürgerte sich Oreos ein. An die Zeit der Unabhängigkeit beider Orte erinnern die Akropolen der Unter- und Oberstadt (vgl. Liv. 28,6,2; 31,46,9). Im Korinth. Krieg stand H. wie die übrigen Städte von Euboia auf seiten der Feinde der Spartaner, die H. besetzten, bis die Stadt im J. 377 von den Athenern befreit wurde (Diod. 15,30,1ff.; Xen. hell. 5,4,56f.). H. war Mitglied im 2. → Attischen Seebund, 371–357/6 unterbrochen durch das Bündnis mit Theben und 343–341 durch die Tyrannis des von Philippos II. unterstützten Philistides. In hell. Zeit war H. meist unter maked. Herrschaft. 208 v. Chr. (Liv. 28,5,18ff.) und 199 (Liv. 31,46,6ff.) wurde H. durch die Römer und → Attalos [4] I. von Pergamon erobert, nach 197 für frei erklärt (Pol. 18,47,10; Liv. 33,34,10; 34,51,1). Die weit verbreiteten Mz.-Funde und viele Proxenien weisen auf eine große handelspolit. Bed. in hell. Zeit hin. Aus röm. Zeit ist hingegen nichts mehr bekannt, Plinius (nat. 4,64) nennt H. noch, Mela und spätere Autoren erwähnen den Ort aber nicht mehr.

C. BURSIAN, Geogr. von Griechenland 2, 1872, 82ff. • KODER/HILD, 1972 • LAUFFER, Griechenland, 269f. • PHILIPPSON/KIRSTEN I, 575ff. • T. W. JACOBSEN, s. v. H., PE, 396 • A. PARADISSIS, Fortresses and castles of Greece 2, 1974, 107f. • L. ROBERT, Hellenica 11–12, 1960, 63ff.

H. KAL.

Histiaios (Ἱστιαῖος).

[1] Sohn des Lysagoras, Tyrann von Milet, Wortführer der Ionier am Istros, die Brücke für → Dareios' [1] Rückkehr vom Skythenzug ca. 513 v. Chr. zu erhalten mit dem Argument, ihrer aller → Tyrannis hänge von Dareios ab (Hdt. 4,137). Seine unverhältnismäßig ausführliche Biographie bei Herodot spiegelt zwei Tendenzen: Er ist der schlaue Held mit Ambitionen ohne Erfolg; er wird mit dem negativen Verlauf des Ionischen Aufstandes belastet [2. 486f.]. Dareios belohnte H. mit der Herrschaft von Myrkinos in Thrakien (Hdt. 5,11), berief ihn jedoch alsbald als Berater nach Susa (5,23f.); seinen Platz in Milet nahm → Aristagoras [3] ein (5,30). Angeblich durch heimliche Botschaft Anstifter des Ionischen Aufstandes (5,35), schickte ihn Dareios 496 zu dessen Beilegung (5,106f.). H. verfolgte aber nach Aristagoras' Tod eigene Pläne (6,1ff.). Vergeblich suchte er eine Basis in Chios und Milet. Mit 8 Schiffen von Lesbos setzte er sich in Byzantion fest (6,5). Nach Zerstörung Milets 494 fuhr H. gegen Chios (6,26) und Thasos, zog sich vor der persischen Flotte aber nach Lesbos zurück (6,28). Zur Nachschubbeschaffung in → Atarneus gelandet, geriet er 493 in persische Hand; der Satrap → Artaphernes [2] ließ ihn in Sardeis kreuzigen und sandte seinen Kopf zu Dareios nach Susa, der ihn ehrenvoll bestattete (6,29) [1. 102–105, 579–581; 3. 357–359, 364, 414–417].

[2] Sohn des Tymnes, Dynast von Termera in Karien, mit anderen perserfreundlichen »Tyrannen« nach der mißglückten Expedition gegen Naxos auf Veranlassung des → Aristagoras [3] von Milet zu Beginn des Ionischen Aufstandes 499 v. Chr. festgesetzt (Hdt. 5,37). Vor Salamis 480 v. Chr. zählt ihn Herodot zu den namhaftesten Anführern der persischen Flotte (7,98) [1. 121f., 590]. → Ionischer Aufstand

1 H. BERVE, Die Tyrannis bei den Griechen, 1967
2 O. MURRAY, in: CAH 4, ²1988 3 L. DE LIBERO, Die archaische Tyrannis, 1996.

J. CO.

Histonium. Küstensiedlung der samnitischen Frentani, h. Vasto. Röm. *municipium* wohl erst nach dem Bundesgenossenkrieg, *tribus Arnensis* (*quattuorviri*; irrig der Liber coloniarum 2, 260, 10f. L.: *colonia*). Kein autonomes Bistum. Im 6. und 7. Jh. byz. Stützpunkt (Kastron Reunias).

M. BUONOCORE, H., in: Supplementa Italica 2, 1983, 97–144 • A. R. STAFFA (Hrsg.), Dall'antica Histonium al Castello del Vasto, 1995 • A. R. STAFFA, Vasto (H.), in: EAA² Suppl. 5, 954f.

M. BU./Ü: J. W. M.

Historia (att. ἱστορία bzw. ion. ἱστορίη). Seit Herodot t.t., ausgehend von der Bed. »Nachforschung« (Hdt. 2,118) über »Resultat der Nachforschung« = »Kenntnis« (Hdt. 1, pr.) hin zu »schriftliche Darlegung der Nachforschung«, d.h. im Falle Herodots (7,96) »Gesch.-Werk«. Diese Bed. (Bezeichnung für Gesch.-Werke) bleibt in der griech. Lit. konstant (vgl. Pol. 1,57,5) [1; 2].

Im Lat. bedeutet *h.* (in Abgrenzung zu *fabula*) im engeren Sinne »Gesch.«/»Gesch.-Schreibung«. Daneben finden sich Zeugnisse für Versuche, *h.* in Abgrenzung von *annales* zu bestimmen: Verrius Flaccus (Gell. 5,18,1f.) postuliert als Verf. von *h.* am Geschehen Beteiligte, ähnlich Serv. Aen. 1,373 [3] (vgl. Isid. orig. 1,44,4): *H.* ist Darstellung des Zeitraums, der der Lebenszeit des Verf. entspricht, Berichte über frühere Zeiträume sind *annales*. Gellius hängt einer anderen Def. an, die *h.* als Oberbegriff, *annales* als Gesch.-Werk streng chronologischer Ordnung betrachtet (5,18,3–7), und referiert Sempronius Asellio (Fr. 1f.), der, wohl unter dem Eindruck Polybianischer Vorstellungen, zugunsten einer Präferenz von *res gestae* die *annales* verwarf, da sie keine Ursachenzusammenhänge kenntlich machen könnten.

Eine weitere terminologische Differenzierung (*h.* als histor. Monographie) läßt sich in der Ant. nicht nachweisen [4]. In der historiographischen Praxis scheint sich die anonym über Verrius/Gellius/Isidor referierte Position eingebürgert zu haben. Der Titel ›Historien‹ ist für die – ihren Lebenszeiten entsprechenden – Werke → Sallusts und → Tacitus' (Tert. apol. 16) belegt [5]; für das Werk des → Coelius [I 1] Antipater schwanken die Angaben zwischen *Annales* (Nonius) und *Historiae* [6].

1 K. KEUCK, H., Diss. 1934 2 A. SEIFERT, H. im MA, in: Archiv f. Begriffsgesch. 21, 1977, 226–284 3 D. B. DIETZ, H. in the Commentary of Servius, in: TAPhA 125, 1995, 61–97 4 G. PUCCIONI, Il problema della monografia storica latina, 1981 (dazu CR 32, 1982, 283) 5 R. P. OLIVER, The First Medicean Ms of Tacitus and the Titulature of Ancient Books, in: TAPhA 82, 1951, 232–261 6 W. HERRMANN, Die Historien des Coelius Antipater, 1979.

MA. HO.

Historia acephala. Die *H.a.*, auch *Historia Athanasii* genannt, ist eine der wichtigsten chronolog. Quellen zum Leben des alexandrinischen Bischofs → Athanasios. Erstmals 1738 von F. S. MAFFEI ediert, der ihr wegen des schlechten Überlieferungszustandes auch den Namen gab, liegt ihr nur ein einziges lat. Manuskript aus dem 8. Jh. zugrunde. Verfaßt wurde die *H.a.* wohl 386 n. Chr. zur Feier des 40. Jahrestags der Bischofsweihe des Athanasios; sie bietet eine chronograph. Geschichte des alexandrin. Bischofsstuhls seit 346. Das urspr. griech. Dokument beruht auf den bischöfl. Akten, erlebte jedoch verschiedene redaktionelle Bearbeitungen. So wurden nachträglich die Konsulardaten bis zum Tode des Athanasios eingefügt, ferner zwischen 385 und 412 Passagen über die Kirchengesch. von Konstantinopel (1,4–7; 4,5 f.) und Antiocheia (2,7) sowie ein chronolog. Anhang (5,14) eingeflochten. Zu Anfang des 5. Jh. wurde die *H.a.* in Karthago gekürzt und ins Lat. übertragen. Eine krit. Ed. mit franz. Übersetzung leistete [1], eine engl. [2]. Eine Konkordanz bietet [3. 233 f.].

1 A. MARTIN (Hrsg.), Histoire »Acéphale« et Index Syriaque des lettres festales d'Athanase d'Alexandrie, 1985 2 PH. SCHAFF, H. WACE (Hrsg.), Select Writings and Letters of Athanasius, Bishop of Alexandria, 1987 (Ndr.) 3 T. D. BARNES, Athanasius and Constantius, 1993. M. R.

Historia Apollonii regis Tyrii. Lat. → Roman eines unbekannten Verf., in dem die Wanderungen des Apollonios, des Königs von Tyros, bis zur Wiedervereinigung mit seiner totgeglaubten Frau und seiner Tochter Tarsia und zu seiner Wiedereinsetzung in sein Amt erzählt werden. In der *H.* finden sich christl. Elemente, in eine eindeutig pagane Umgebung eingebettet, ohne jedoch völlig integriert zu sein.

Die Rekonstruktion der Genese des Werks, seine Datierung und die Textkonstitution sind umstritten. Die ältesten Zeugnisse zur *H.* gehen auf das 6. Jh. n. Chr. zurück (Ven. Fort. carm. 6,8,5 f.: 566–568 n. Chr.; *De dubiis nominibus*, Ende des 6. Jh.). Die Tatsache, daß sich in der *H.* (42–43) einige Rätsel finden, die auch in der Sammlung der *Aenigmata Symphosii* (4.–5. Jh. n. Chr.) überliefert sind, stellt keine Hilfe bei der Datierung dar: Es ist denkbar, daß die Rätsel zu einer Überlieferung gehören, aus der sowohl der Verf. der *H.* als auch → Symphosios schöpfen, oder daß sie von demjenigen in die *H.* eingefügt wurden, der diese im 5.–6. Jh. umgearbeitet hat; es ist sogar die Existenz des Dichters Symphosios in Frage gestellt worden [1].

Die *H.* ist uns aus mehr als 100 Hss. bekannt, die sie jedoch in verschiedenen Redaktionen überliefern. Die ältesten dieser »Rezensionen« sind die sog. RA und RB; eine bes. Bedeutung kommt RC zu, da sie zur Konstitution des Textes von RA und RB beiträgt und weil diese Version großen Einfluß auf die spätere Lit. ausgeübt hat. RA und RB sind wahrscheinlich im 5.–6. Jh. n. Chr. abgefaßt worden; RB hängt von RA ab, schöpft aber auch direkt aus einer älteren Version. Der Redaktor von RB scheint den Text von RA, der längeren der beiden Versionen, modifiziert zu haben: RB neigt nämlich dazu, sowohl eine »klassischere« Sprache als auch eine größere narrative Kohärenz wiederherzustellen [2]. Bei der Rekonstruktion der älteren Fassung denkt KORTEKAAS [1] an einen paganen griech. Roman des 2.–3. Jh. n. Chr., von dem RA und RB zugleich eine Übers., eine Umarbeitung und eine Epitome seien; SCHMELING [2] glaubt dagegen an einen lat. Roman des 3. Jh. n. Chr., der in RA und RB christianisiert worden sei. Zwei Papyrusfragmente eines Romans (PSI 151; PMil. Vogliano 260) könnten zum griech. Original der *H.* gehören [6; 7].

In der *H.* erscheinen typische Motive des griech. Liebesromans, auch wenn das Liebespaar nicht in den Vordergrund gestellt wird. Die *H.* ist mit den *Ephesiaká* des → Xenophon von Ephesos verglichen worden, mit denen es den unprätentiösen Stil und die Trockenheit der Erzählung gemeinsam hat, die zuweilen Widersprüche und Inkohärenzen aufweist [8]. Ein Netz von Bezügen zur *Odyssee* könnte auf das eventuell griech. Original zurückgehen [9]. Ein augenfälliges Merkmal der *H.* ist die Hervorhebung von Entsprechungen zw. verschiedenen Figuren und Episoden (zuweilen zum Schaden der narrativen Kohärenz); vgl. z. B. die drei Stürme, die den Lebensweg des Apollonios markieren (11; 25; 39) [1. 125 f.]; oder die Gegenüberstellung des ruchlosen Königs Antiochos, der sich wissentlich des Inzestes mit seiner Tochter schuldig macht, und des guten Königs Apollonios, der, ohne es zu wissen, beinahe mit seiner eigenen Tochter Tarsia Inzest begeht [10].

Die *H.* hatte ein reiches Nachleben im MA, wie abgesehen von der Masse der Überlieferungsträger auch die große Zahl von Umarbeitungen und Übersetzungen zeigt. Das vielleicht berühmteste Beispiel für ihre Beliebtheit in späterer Zeit ist der Shakespeare zugeschriebene *Pericles, Prince of Tyre*.

→ Roman

ED.: 1 G. A. KORTEKAAS (Ed.), Historia Apollonii Regis Tyri, 1984 2 G. SCHMELING (Ed.), Historia Apollonii Regis Tyri, 1988.
LIT.: 3 F. MURRU, Aenigmata Symphosii ou Aenigmata Symposii?, in: Eos 68, 1980, 155–158 4 M. J. MUÑOZ JIMÉNEZ, Algunos aspectos de los »Aenigmata Symphosii«, in: Emerita 55, 1987, 307–312 5 M. JANKA, Die Fassungen »RA« und »RB« der »Historia Apollonii Regis Tyri« im Vergleich, in: RhM 140, 1997, 168–187 6 R. KUSSL, Papyrusfragmente griech. Romane, 1991, 141–159 7 A. STRAMAGLIA, Prosimetria narrativa e »romanzo perduto«, in: ZPE 92, 1992, 143–149 8 G. SCHMELING, Historia Apollonii Regis Tyri, in: Ders., The Novel in the Ancient World, 1996, 534; 541–542 9 N. Holzberg, The »Historia Apollonii regis Tyri« and the »Odyssey«, in: Groningen Colloquia on the Novel 3, 1990, 91–101 10 E. ROHDE, Der griech. Roman und seine Vorläufer, [3]1914, 447 11 E. ARCHIBALD, Fathers and Kings in »Apollonius of Tyre«, in: M. M. MACKENZIE, C. ROUECHÉ (Hrsg.), Images of Authority. Papers Presented to Joyce Reynolds on the Occasion of Her Seventieth Birthday, 1989, 33–34. M. FU. u. L. G./Ü: T. H.

Historia Augusta A. Werk B. Entstehungszeit C. Verfasserfrage D. Tendenz E. Quellen F. Überlieferung

A. Werk

H. A. ist die moderne Bezeichnung für die *Scriptores historiae Augustae* (SHA), wie Casaubonus 1603 im Anschluß an die *Vita Taciti* (10,3) die sechs sonst unbekannten Autoren Aelius Spartianus, Iulius Capitolinus, Vulcacius Gallicanus, Aelius Lampridius, Trebellius Pollio und Flavius Vopiscus aus Syrakus genannt hat. Sie erscheinen als die Verfasser einer Sammlung von → Biographien röm. Kaiser, Thronanwärter und Usurpatoren aus der Zeit von Hadrian (117–138 n. Chr.) bis Numerianus und Carinus (283–284/5). Erhalten sind 30 Lebensbeschreibungen; die der Herrscher zwischen 244 und 253 sind verloren, die der Valeriani nur bruchstückhaft, die der Gallieni nicht vollständig vorhanden. Wahrscheinlich fehlt der Anfang, da das Werk den Anschluß an die als Vorbild betrachteten Kaiserbiographien des → Suetonius gesucht haben dürfte (HA Max. Balb. 4,5; HA Prob. 2,7; quatt. tyr. 1,1–2). So ist auch der Originaltitel der Schrift nicht bekannt, vielleicht lautete er *vita principum* (HA trig. tyr. 33,8; Aurelian. 1,2; Prob. 2,7). Die Biographien bis zum Jahre 238 laufen unter den Namen der ersten 4 Autoren, die danach unter den Namen von Pollio und Vopiscus. 13 der 21 Lebensbeschreibungen der ersten Gruppe enthalten Widmungen an die Kaiser Diocletianus und Constantinus I. In den späteren Viten wird Constantius I. als lebend erwähnt (HA Claud. 1,1; 3,1; HA Aurelian. 44,5). Somit mußte man auf eine Entstehung der Sammlung in diocletianisch-constantin. Zeit zw. 293 und 330 schließen. Die moderne Forsch. nimmt ihren Ausgang von der scharfsinnigen Kritik durch H. Dessau, der 1889 die eigenen Angaben der *H. A.* verwarf und sie als das Werk eines einzigen Verf. aus dem ausgehenden 4. Jh. bezeichnete [6]. An seinem Vorschlag hat sich eine bis heute andauernde Diskussion über Entstehungszeit, Autor, Absicht, Tendenz und Quellen entzündet [10. 11–46]. Wegen der strittigen Verfasserfrage hat sich die neutrale Bezeichnung H. A. durchgesetzt.

B. Entstehungszeit

Ansatzpunkte für eine Datier. nach 330 bieten Anachronismen verschiedenster Art, Anspielungen auf Ereignisse, Gestalten und Verhältnisse späterer Zeit und vor allem Spuren nachconstantin. Schrifttums wie die vieldiskutierte Abhängigkeit der Severusvita von den 360/61 entstandenen *Caesares* des Aurelius → Victor (HA Sept. Sev. 17,5–19,3 und Aur. Vict. Caes. 20,1–30). In den letzten Jahrzehnten ist über die Benutzung von Schriften des → Hieronymus, des → Ammianus Marcellinus, → Claudianus [2] und Werken des 5. Jh. diskutiert worden. Neben dem terminus post quem 360/61 [2] bleiben Datierungsvorschläge nach 394/95 [7; 8] und nach 405 [15] von Bed. Weit verbreitet ist heute die Annahme einer Entstehungszeit der *H. A.* an der Wende vom 4. zum 5. Jh. Der äußerste terminus ante quem liegt vor 525, dem Todesjahr des Q. Aurelius Memmius → Symmachus, der das Werk benutzt hat (vgl. Iord. Get. 15,83–88). Schon 1890 hatte Th. Mommsen eine Gegenthese zu Dessaus Vorschlag entwickelt [14]. Danach handele es sich bei der *H. A.* um einen Grundstock aus diocletianisch-constantin. Zeit, der um 330 gesammelt und später überarbeitet worden sei, womit sich Anachronismen erklären ließen. In jüngster Zeit wird diese These wieder mit Nachdruck v. a. von A. Lippold vertreten [12; 13].

C. Verfasserfrage

Die Ansichten zu Verfassereinheit bzw. -vielfalt korrespondieren weithin mit denjenigen zu Spätdatier. oder Überarbeitungshypothese. Wiederum Dessau hatte zuerst auf die ungewöhnlich vielen Gemeinsamkeiten der angeblichen 6 Verf. aufmerksam gemacht. Zahlreiche Unt. zu Sprache und Stil scheinen Nachweise für einen einzigen Autor geliefert zu haben, ohne jedoch alle Zweifel ausräumen zu können. Computeranalysen erbrachten unterschiedliche Ergebnisse. Die in der Nachfolge Dessaus stehende Forschung hat den Verf. näher zu bestimmen versucht. W. Hartke sprach sich 1940 für den jüngeren Nicomachus → Flavianus [3] aus [7. 167f.], E. Demougeot 1953 für den Historiker Virius Nicomachus → Flavianus [2], vgl. [5]. J. Straub und R. Syme haben den *scriptor* als Philologen, Antiquar und Grammatiker näher charakterisiert [15; 16. 176–210]. Vieles spricht für einen im Dienst der Aristokratie schreibenden Biographen, vielleicht einen Amanuensis der Symmachi-Nicomachi [8. 412f.], mit großem Interesse an der Stadtpraefektur von Rom und deren Amtsinhabern [10. 105–147]. Der einzige der vorgeblichen Verf., der persönl. hervortritt, Vopiscus, schildert sich als den Vertrauten eines Stadtpraefekten, von dem er den Auftrag für eine Kaiservita erhält (HA Aurelian. 1,1–2).

D. Tendenz

Eine Tendenz wurde der *H. A.* erstmals 1926 von N. H. Baynes unterstellt, der sie als Propagandaschrift für → Iulianus [5] Apostata interpretierte [2]. ›Heidnische Geschichtsapologetik in der christlichen Spätantike‹, und zwar im 5. Jh., ist nach Straub das Anliegen der Biographienslg. [15]. Ein Nachweis konkreter Absichten ist jedoch bisher nicht gelungen. Generell wird die Gesch. des 2. und 3. Jh. aus dem Blickwinkel der nichtchristlichen stadtröm. Senatsaristokratie betrachtet und das Kaisertum nach dem Verhalten zu diesem Stand bewertet. Besonders idealisiert gezeichnet wird Kaiser → Severus Alexander in der längsten Vita im Kontrast zu seinem Vorgänger Elagabal.

E. Quellen

Der histor. Wert der einzelnen Biographien ist unterschiedlich. Die *H. A.* liefert gute Informationen neben offenkundigen Erfindungen und Fälschungen. Zuverlässige Nachrichten enthalten die Viten der anerkannten Herrscher von Hadrian bis Caracalla, die *vita Pii* zeigt im Aufbau die engste Anlehnung an Sueton. Bis in die Severerzeit folgt die Schrift einer verläßlichen lat.

Quelle, wahrscheinlich dem Werk des Marius Maximus, der Biographien von Traian bis Elagabal verfaßt hat und an 33 Stellen zitiert wird. Vermutet wird jedoch auch das Werk eines Anonymus als Hauptquelle [17. 30–53 mit Anm. 1]. → Herodianos' Kaisergesch. ist von allen in der *H. A.* zitierten Schriften allein erh. geblieben; sie diente als Quelle für die Biographien von Clodius Albinus bis Maximus und Balbinus. Für die Viten von Alexander bis Claudius wurde die Chronik des → Dexippos [2] benutzt. Das Werk des → Cassius [III 1] Dio wird nicht genannt, ist aber wohl herangezogen worden [11]. Für das spätere 3. Jh. standen nur noch → Eunapios und die → Enmannsche Kaisergeschichte zur Verfügung. Die Lebensbeschreibungen der Soldatenkaiserzeit und die aller Thronanwärter und Usurpatoren, die sog. Nebenviten [17. 54–77], sind unzuverlässig. Besonders hier, aber nicht nur in ihnen, häufen sich Erfindungen mit Bezügen auf die Vergangenheit (z.B. Alex. 53,5–54,3) wie auf die Gegenwart des Verfassers (z.B. Tac. 6,5). Durch eingestreute Wundergesch., Novellen und Anekdoten nähern sich Teile der *H. A.* der Romanlit. Von den ca. 130 dokumentarischen Einlagen gilt nur ein Senatsprotokoll als unverdächtig (Comm. 18f.). Trotz eines behaupteten Strebens nach Wahrhaftigkeit (trig. tyr. 11,6f.) wird einer der sog. »Dreißig Tyrannen« überhaupt erfunden (trig. tyr. 33). Die Diskrepanz zwischen histor. Wertvollem und Erfundenem ließ bereits Mommsen einen Komm. fordern, der in internationaler Gemeinschaftsarbeit [vgl. 3; 9] seit 1991 im Erscheinen ist [12; 4; 18].

F. Überlieferung

Die *H. A.* hat sich nur in einem verlorengegangenen Expl., das bereits die große Lücke aufwies, in das MA gerettet. Davon stammen die Handschriftenfamilien P und Σ ab. Cod. Palatinus Vaticanus 899 aus dem 9. Jh. ist der Archetypus für die 15 Hss. der Familie P, darunter Cod. Bambergensis des 9. Jh. Die 5 Cod. der Familie Σ entstammen dem 14. und 15. Jh. wie auch die meisten von P. Die Ed. princeps erfolgte 1475 in Mailand durch Accursius, die erste separate Werkausgabe 1603 in Paris durch I. Casaubonus.

1 T.D. Barnes, The Sources of the HA, 1978 **2** N.H. Baynes, The HA. Its date and purpose, 1926 **3** A. Alföldi, J. Straub, K. Rosen (Hrsg.), Bonner Historia-Augusta-Colloquium (BHAC), 13 Bde., 1964–1991 **4** H. Brandt, Komm. zur Vita Maximi et Balbini, 1996 **5** E. Demougeot, Flavius Vopiscus est-il Nicomaque Flavien?, in: AC 22, 1953, 361–382 **6** H. Dessau, Über Zeit und Persönlichkeit der SHA, in: Hermes 24, 1889, 337–392 **7** W. Hartke, Geschichte und Politik im spätantiken Rom, 1940 **8** Ders., Röm. Kinderkaiser, 1951 **9** G. Bonamente, N. Duval, F. Paschoud u. a., Historiae Augustae Colloquia (HAC), seit 1991 **10** K.-P. Johne, Kaiserbiographie und Senatsaristokratie, 1976 **11** F. Kolb, Lit. Beziehungen zwischen Cassius Dio, Herodian und der HA, 1972 **12** A. Lippold, Komm. zur Vita Maximini duo, 1991 **13** Ders., Die HA. Eine Sammlung röm. Kaiserbiographien aus der Zeit Konstantins, 1998 **14** Th. Mommsen, Die SHA, in: Hermes 25, 1890, 228–292 = Ges. Schriften, Bd. 7, 1909, 302–362) **15** J. Straub, Heidnische Geschichtsapologetik in der christl. Spätantike, 1963 **16** R. Syme, Ammianus and the HA, 1968 **17** Ders., Emperors and Biography, 1971 **18** S. Walentowski, Komm. zur Vita des Antoninus Pius, 1998.

Ed.: E. Hohl, Ch. Samberger, W. Seyfarth, 2 Bde., 3/51971 (maßgebend) • D. Magie, 3 Bde., 1921–1932 (Ndr. 1960/61; mit engl. Übers.) • J.-P. Callu, R. Turcan u. a., seit 1992 (mit franz. Übers.).

Übers.: E. Hohl, J. Straub u. a., 2 Bde., 1976–1985.

Lex.: C. Lessing, 1901–1906. K.P.J.

Historia Monachorum. Bericht, z. T. aus Sekundärquellen, über die Reise einiger palästinensischer Mönche zu Klosterzentren im Niltal von der Thebaïs bis zum Delta, redigiert um 395 n. Chr. von einem der Reisenden, oft zusammen mit der *Historia Lausiaca* des Palladios (um 400) überliefert (DHGE 24, 681 f.).

A.-J. Festugière, Historia Monachorum in Aegypto, 1961 (Ed.) • Lat. Übers. des Rufinus von Aquileia: PL 21, 387–462. F.T.

Historienmalerei. In der ägypt. Kunst stellen Illustrationen histor. Ereignisse eine seltene Ausnahme dar; typisierte Motive, wie z.B. das Erschlagen der Feinde durch den König, sind hier überzeitlich zu verstehen und werden über Jahrhunderte unverändert als Topoi in verschiedenen Bildmedien verwandt. Die unzureichende materielle und kunsttheoretisch-lit. Überl. zur ant. griech. H. erlaubt keine eng umrissene Definition einer ant. H. im Sinne einer Analogie zum seit der Renaissance bis ins 19. Jh. gültigen mod. Gattungsbegriff [1. 15–76]. Die neuere Forsch. hat die Frage ausführlich diskutiert, inwieweit die vielfältig-ambivalent interpretierbaren Mythenbilder v. a. att. Vasen, aber auch die von Pausanias und anderen beschriebenen monumentalen Wandgemälde z.B. in Athen (Stoa Poikile) oder Delphi (Lesche der Knidier) einen ideologischen Sinngehalt oder eine konkrete polit. Situation widerspiegeln. Dabei deutet man Darstellungen mythischer Ereignisse und heroischer Taten der Vorzeit, Bilder von Themen wie die Amazonomachie oder den Troianischen Krieg, die im kollektiven Gedächtnis der Betrachter schon Paradigmen der Gesch. geworden sind, als eine funktional und in Analogie genutzte, verklausulierte Visualisierung aktueller polit. Tendenzen.

Zu trennen ist hiervon die realistische Schilderung zeitgenössischer histor. Ereignisse in der Malerei, die, gemessen an anderen Themen, selten bleibt. Aus archa. Zeit sind nur wenige Schlachtenbilder schriftlich überliefert. Ein reflektierteres Geschichtsbewußtsein gegen E. des 6. Jh. v. Chr. als Ergebnis aus den noch aktuellen Erfahrungen der Perserkriege des 5. Jh. fördern die Entstehung der H. So hing in der Stoa Poikile, einer von der Öffentlichkeit stark frequentierten Halle in Athen, ein Bild der Marathonschlacht zusammen mit Gemälden der Amazonomachie, der Iliupersis und einer Darstellung der Schlacht bei Oinoe (Paus. 1,15,1). Die Bilder, in staatlichem Auftrag um 460/450 dorthin gekommen, zeigten den Kampf der Athener gegen äußere Feinde. Im 4. Jh. v. Chr. gaben innergriech. Auseinandersetzungen weiteren Anlaß zu Darstellungen von Kampfszenen, über deren Aussehen Schriftquellen nur lückenhaft informieren. Einziges erh. bildliches Zeugnis ant. Schlachtenmalerei ist das → Alexandermosaik aus Pompeii, eine Kopie nach frühhell. Vorbild. Weitere Sujets ant. H. waren Herrscherporträts (→ Herrscher) und genealogische Familienbilder (→ Familie), die in Heiligtümer oder für öffentliche Plätze gestiftet wurden.

Auch in röm.-republikan. Zeit gab es H. in Gräbern wie auch in Form von Tafelbildern, die bei Triumphzügen der siegreichen Feldherrn oder bei der *pompa funebris* mitgeführt wurden und Schlachten oder Personen darstellten. Die H. wurde in der röm. Kaiserzeit zunehmend durch an offiziellen Monumenten angebrachte histor. Reliefs (→ Relief) ersetzt.

1 TH. W. GAETHGENS, U. FLECKNER (Hrsg.), H. Gesch. der klass. Bildgattungen in Quellentexten und Komm., 1996.

H. BRANDT, Herakles und Peisistratos, oder: Mythos und Gesch. Anm. zur Interpretation vorklass. Vasenbilder, in: Chiron 1997, 315–334 • B. DEVELIN, The Battle of Oinoe Meets Ockham's Razor?, in: ZPE 99, 1993, 235–240 • D. CASTRIOTA, Myth, Ethos and Actuality. Official Art in 5th Century B. C. Athens, 1992 • S. GERMER, M. ZIMMERMANN, Bilder der Macht – Macht der Bilder, 1997 • A. GEYER, Gesch. als Mythos, in: JDAI 108, 1993, 443–455 • CH. HÖCKER, L. SCHNEIDER, Pericle e la costruzione dell'Acropoli, in: S. SETTIS (Hrsg.), I Greci 2/II, 1997, 1239–1274 • T. HÖLSCHER, Griech. Historienbilder des 5. u. 4. Jh. v. Chr., 1973 (dazu: B. FEHR, Gnomon 49, 1977, 179–192) • Ders., Röm. Bildsprache als semantisches System, 1987 • P. J. HOLIDAY, Narrative and Event in Ancient Art, 1993 • U. HUTTNER, Die polit. Rolle der Heraklesgestalt im griech. Herrschertum, 1997, 26–38 • R. KRUMEICH, Bildnisse griech. Herrscher und Staatsmänner im 5. Jh. v. Chr., 1997, 48f.; 83f.; 102–109; 130–134 • Ders., Namensbeischrift oder Weihinschrift?, in: AA 1996, 43–51 • R. LING, Roman Painting, 1991, 101–135 • H. MEYER, Kunst und Gesch., 1983 • K. PARLASCA, Agrippina mit der Aschenurne des Germanicus, in: E. MAI, A. REPP ECKERT, H. in Europa, 1990, 27–41 • A. ROUVERET, Les lieux de la mémoire publique, Opus VI-VIII, 1987–1989, 101–124 • I. SCHEIBLER, Griech. Malerei der Ant., 1994, 152–164 • K. STÄHLER, Griech. Geschichtsbilder klass. Zeit, 1992 • E. THOMAS, Mythos und Gesch., 1976 • L. THOMPSON, The Monumental and Literary Evidence for Programmatic Painting in Antiquity, in: Marsyas 9, 1960/61, 36–77.

N. H.

Historiographie
s. Geschichtsschreibung, s. Königsinschriften

Historiola (»Geschichtchen«). Mod. Terminus, mit dem in magische Rezepte eingebaute knappe Erzählungen bezeichnet werden, die einen mythischen Präzedenzfall für eine magisch wirksame Handlung liefern. H. sind bereits für die mesopot. und die altägypt. → Magie bezeugt. In den graeco-ägypt. → Zauberpapyri (PGM) beziehen sie sich sowohl auf die griech. (etwa PGM XX) wie die ägypt. Myth. (etwa PGM IV 1471), in christl. Riten auf christl. Legenden. Doch sind H. nicht als Verkürzungen bekannter Mythen oder als *ad hoc*-Erfindungen zu verstehen; vielmehr begreift der Erzähler sie als Verweis auf eine übergreifende Ordnung, in die er seinen Ritus einbindet.

A. A. BARB, Antaura. The mermaid and the devil's grandmother, in: Journ. of the Warburg and Courtauld Institutes 29, 1966, 1–23 • D. FRANKFURTER, Narrating power. The theory and practice of the magical h. in ritual spells, in: M. MEYER, P. MIRECKI (Hrsg.), Ancient Magic and Ritual Power, 1995, 457–476.

F. G.

Historis (Ἱστορίς). Tochter des Sehers → Teiresias (daher wohl die Ableitung von *ϝιδ-, »sehen, wissen«). Im Zusammenhang mit theban. Standbildern der Pharmakides (= Moiren) erzählt Paus. 9,11,3, daß H. sie wie → Galinthias bei Nikander überlisten konnte. Das Epitheton der Iuno Historia (CIL XI 3573) läßt sich wohl auf H. zurückführen [1].

1 M. RENARD, Iuno Historia, in: Latomus 12, 1953, 137–154.

T. H.

Historischer Roman s. Roman

Historisches Epos. Das h.E., verstanden als narrative Darstellung von Ereignissen einer nahen oder fernen Vergangenheit, kommt in der griech. Lit. meist in drei Sonderformen vor: als archaiologisch-ktistisches (→ Ktisis-Epos), histor.-mil. und histor.-enkomiastisches Epos (die letzten beiden behandeln zumeist die jüngere Gesch., das histor.-enkomiastische Epos konzentriert sich auf die Gestalt einer einzigen Person).

In archa. Zeit nahm das h.E. häufiger als den Hexameter das elegische Distichon als Versmaß an. Das beruht vielleicht darauf, daß das Distichon im symposialen Kontext als Rezitationsmetrum mehr benutzt wurde als der Hexameter; das Symposion konnte ebensosehr als Inkubator der Erinnerung an Ereignisse der öffentlichen Gesch. fungieren wie der Erinnerung an individuelle Schicksale; das gilt zumindest für Lieder von begrenztem Umfang. Bei den Vortragsgelegenheiten für längere elegische Gedichte (wie für Hexameter) wird es sich eher um rel. Feste oder öffentliche Feiern gehandelt haben.

In Hexametern waren diejenigen ältesten Werke abgefaßt, bei denen sicher ist, daß sie weiter zurückliegende »Gesch.« behandelten, in der die myth. Komponente stark oder ausschließlich war (z. B. die *Korinthiaká* des → Eumelos, die *Naupáktia* aus dem 6. Jh., die *Meropís*, über Kos, zeitgenössisch oder hell., die Genealogien der Samier des Asios; s. auch → Aristeas). In Distichen abgefaßt sind dagegen sowohl eine weitere *Archaiología* der Samier, die → Semonides von Amorgos zugeschrieben wird, als auch die ältesten epischen Gedichte, die (auch oder nur) von jüngerer Gesch. handeln: die *Politeía* (*Eunomía*) des → Tyrtaios, die vom ersten Messenischen

Krieg handelt, die *Smyrnēís* des → Mimnermos, die an die zeitgenössische Schlacht zw. den Smyrnäern und Gyges erinnert (fr. 4 G.-P.; aber vielleicht spricht das Gedicht auch von der Gründung Smyrnas), → Simonides, der die Schlacht von Plataiai und die Seeschlacht von Artemision feiert. → Xenophanes schrieb sowohl über archa. Gesch. (die Gründung von Kolophon) als auch über die zeitgenössische Gründung der Kolonie Elea (in ἔπη/*épē*: »Hexameter« oder »Distichen«), in Entsprechung zu → Panyassis, der »in Pentametern« (d.h. offenkundig »in Distichen«) sowohl von den myth. Ursprüngen der Ionier als auch ihren Kolonisationen handelte. Aus der Mitte des 5. Jh. v. Chr. stammt auch → Choirilos [1] aus Samos: er war der erste Autor, der mit Sicherheit »*épē*« von zeitgenössischem Inhalt und großem Umfang verfaßte, und einer der ersten Autoren, die histor.-enkomiastische Dichtung schrieben.

In hell. Zeit fehlen hinreichend bedeutende mil. Unternehmungen der eigenen Zeit, welche die einzelnen Städte ihrem Verdienst hätten zuschreiben und feiern lassen können. Hier besitzen wir Zeugnisse zum myth. Ktisis-Epos und zu Darstellungen der mehr oder weniger älteren Regionalgesch., die sicherlich dem zeitgenössischen Geschmack der Aitiologie entsprachen (in der Mehrzahl der Fälle läßt sich nicht ermitteln, ob es sich um Hexameter oder Pentameter handelte), z.B. über Sparta oder die Makedonen: → Phaistos; über Messenien und die messenischen Kriege: → Aischylos [2] von Alexandreia, → Rhianos; über die Argolis: → Lykeas von Argos, Telesarchos; über Elis, Achaia und Thessalien: Rhianos; über Theben: → Menelaos von Aigai; über die Troas: → Hegemon von Alexandreia (in der Troas); über Bithynien: Demosthenes von Bithynien; über Sizilien: Polykritos/ Polykleitos von Mende; über Palästina: → Theodotos; über Jerusalem: → Philon d.Ä.; über die Schlacht bei Leuktra von 371: ebenfalls → Hegemon von Alexandreia; über den marsischen Krieg: → Alexandros [22] von Ephesos; über den Kimbernkrieg des Marius und den Krieg des Lucullus gegen Mithradates: → Archias [7] von Antiocheia; über die Schlacht von Philippi: Boethos von Tarsos; s. auch → Nikandros. Die daktylische Dichtung zeitgesch. Inhalts aus hell. Zeit ist meist enkomiastisch und einzelnen Herrschern gewidmet (in vielen Fällen wahrscheinlich keine Monumentalepen, sondern Gedichte begrenzten Umfangs, vgl. [8]): z.B. über Alexander den Großen: Agis von Argos, → Anaximenes [2] von Lampsakos, → Choirilos [3] von Iasos, → Aischrion von Mytilene; über Antiochos I. Soter (oder Antiochos III. den Großen): → Simonides von Magnesia; über Eumenes II. und Attalos II.: → Musaios von Ephesos; über Kleopatra: → Theodoros; s. darüber hinaus die zahlreichen auf Papyrus überlieferten *Fragmenta adespota* in SH.

In der Kaiserzeit schwindet das regionalhistor. Epos, danach blüht praktisch nur noch die enkomiastische Form (s. [14]).

Ed.: **1** PEG **2** Gentili/Prato I²-II, **3** E. Heitsch, Die griech. Dichterfr. der röm. Kaiserzeit, I²-II, 1963–1964 **4** SH **5** CollAlex.

Lit.: **6** S. Barbantani, L'elegia encomiastica in età ellenistica, Diss. Urbino 1998 **7** E. Bowie, Early Greek Elegy, Symposium and Public Festival, in: JHS 106, 1986, 13–35 **8** A. Cameron, Callimachus and his Critics, 1995 (cap. X) **9** R. Häussler, Das h.E. der Griechen und Römer bis Vergil, 1976 **10** S. Mazzarino, Il pensiero storico classico I, 1972 (cap. I) **11** W.R. Misgeld, Rhianos von Bene und das h.E. im Hell., Diss. Köln 1968 **12** W. Rösler, *Mnemosyne* in the *Symposium*, in: O. Murray (ed.), Sympotica, 1990, 230–237 **13** T. Viljamaa, Studies in Greek Encomiastic Poetry of the Early Byzantine Period, 1968 **14** K. Ziegler, Das hell. Epos, ²1966. M.FA./Ü: T.H.

Historisches Relief s. Relief

Histria, Histri. Halbinsel (4437 km²) an der nördl. Adria zw. Tergeste und Tarsatica (Kroatien/Slowenien). H. leitet sich von den Istroi/Histri ab, die hier schon im 11. Jh. v. Chr. siedelten (erstmals von Hekataios erwähnt, FGrH 1 F 91). Ihre Siedlungen wurden auf Hügeln und an der Küste angelegt (*gradine* oder *castellieri*) und waren monumental befestigt; Brandbestattungen in Tonurnen sind nachgewiesen. Die Entwicklung der Histri zw. den Veneti im Norden, den Iapodes im NO und den Liburni im Süden und SW kann bis zur röm. Eroberung im 2. Jh. v. Chr. verfolgt werden. Im Norden (Tergeste-Region) wurde die Entfaltung ihrer Kultur durch die kelt. Carni eingeschränkt. Nachgewiesen sind importierte etr. und ital. Töpferware (im 7. Jh., teilweise aus Daunia; → Daunische Vasen), auch *situlae*, monumentale Steinskulpturen aus Nesactium unter archa. griech.-südit. Einfluß und aus dem etr. Mittel-It. Rom führte 221 v. Chr. eine erste mil. Unternehmung gegen die Histri durch, um deren Piraterie auszuschalten, dann wohl 181 v. Chr. z.Z. der Gründung von → Aquileia [1], der sich die Histri entgegenstellten. Rom eroberte das histrische Königreich 178/7 (Liv. 41,10f.); dabei wurden Mutila (evtl. Medulin), Faveria (nicht lokalisiert) und Nesactium (h. Vizače) zerstört.

Man bezeichnete die Histri in Rom als *gens inops* (›armes Volk‹, Liv. 41,11,8). Sie wurden nahe It. und den Carni bis Pola angesiedelt (Strab. 7,5,3); der Küstenstreifen, den sie besiedelten, maß 1300 Stadien. Histri ist eine Kollektivbezeichnung für mehrere verwandte Stämme wie z.B. die Menocaleni (nicht lokalisiert), Fecusses (im Hinterland von Pola), Rundictes im Norden. In der spätrepublikanischen Zeit dürften sie zur Prov. Illyricum gerechnet worden sein, zeitweise wahrscheinlich aber auch zur Gallia Cisalpina. 18/12 v. Chr. wurde die Ostgrenze It. vom Formio an die Arsia (h. Raša) verlegt (*regio X*, später *Venetia et Histria*). Konsequenz der Romanisierung war eine frühe Munizipalisierung; so wurden → Tergeste und → Pola unter Caesar *coloniae* (*Pietas Iulia Pola*; die ersten *duumviri*: C. Cassius Longinus, L. Calpurnius Piso: InscrIt X 1,81). Parentium, zuerst *municipium*, ist wohl unter dem nachmaligen Augustus *colonia Iulia* geworden, während → Nesactium schließlich in der 1. H. 1. Jh. n. Chr. *municipium* wurde. Das Hinterland war weit weniger urbanisiert; Zentrum war Piquentum (h. Buzet).

Die kommerziellen Aktivitäten wurden durch die Nachbarschaft von Aquileia, aber auch von zahlreichen Häfen, v. a. Capris (h. Koper/Capodistria), Siparis (h. Šipar), Humagum (h. Umag), Neapolis (h. Novi Grad) und Ruginium (h. Rovinj) belebt. H. war sehr fruchtbar (Olivenöl, Wein). Belegt sind viele große Landsitze von Kaisern und Senatoren, z. B. von Agrippa, Maecenas, den Statilii, Sergii, Cassii, Calpurnii, Laecanii, Calvii, Palpellii, Settidii. Während der Kriege gegen die Marcomanni wurde die *praetentura Italiae et Alpium* geschaffen, ein Verteidigungssystem, das die Regionen in Nordit., Südnoricum und NO-H. bis Tarsatica (einschließlich eines Teils von Westliburnia) umfaßte mit den Städten Albona (h. Labin), Flanona (h. Plomin) und Tarsatica. Im 4. Jh. faßte das Christentum in H. Fuß, Kirchen wurden gebaut, v. a. in Pola, Parentium (die Basilika des Euphrasius), Nesactium. In spätröm. Zeit wechselte die Herrschaft über H. häufig (Odoacer 476–493, Ostgoten 493–539, byz. Kaiser bis zur Invasion der Langobarden 568 n. Chr.). Im 7.–11. Jh. wurde das Land von Slaven kolonisiert, während sich in den Städten roman. Bevölkerung erh. hat. Inschr.: InscrIt X 1 (Pola), 2 (Parentium), 3 (Histria septentrionalis), 4 (Tergeste).

S. Gabrovec, K. Mihovilić, Jadransko-zapadnobalkanska regija. Istarska grupa [Die Adriat. West-Balkan Region. Die Istrische Kultur-Gruppe], in: Praistorija jugoslavenskih zemalja 5, 1987, 293–338 • Š. Mlakar, Istra u antici [Istria in röm. Zeit], 1962 • A. Degrassi, Scritti vari di antichità I und II, 1962; III, 1967; IV, 1971 • V. Jurkić, Priolg za sintezu povijesti Istre u rimko doba, in: Arheološka istraživanja u Istri i Hrvatskom primorju / Indagini archeologiche in Istria e nel litorale croato (Izdanja Hrvatskog arheološkog društva 11/1), 1987, 65–80 • Ders., Arheološka istraživanja u Istri [Archaeological Research in Istria] (Izdanja Hrvatskoj arheološkog društva 18), 1997 • F. Tassaux, L'implantation territoriale des grandes familles d'Istrie sous le Haut-Empire romain, in: Problemi storici e archeologici dell'Italia nordorientale e delle regioni limitrofe dalla preistoria al medioevo, 1983/4, 193–229 • R. Matijašić, Ageri antičkih kolonija Pola i Parentium, 1988.

M.Š.K./Ü: I.S.

Histrio

I. Begriff II. Entwicklung seit dem 3. Jh. v. Chr., soziale Stellung III. Anforderungen an den Histrio IV. Masken und Kostüme

I. Begriff

Bezeichnung für den röm. Schauspieler. Livius (7,2: nach Varro) berichtet, daß man nach einer Pestepidemie im J. 364 v. Chr. Tänzer (*ludiones*) mit einem Flötenspieler aus Etrurien geholt habe, um mit einer kult. Zeremonie die Stadt zu reinigen. Die einheimische Jugend habe deren Tänze nachgeahmt und mit Spottversen ausgestaltet, bis schließlich professionelle Künstler, denen man das etr. Wort *h.* beigelegt habe, ihr Stegreifspiel weiterentwickelt hätten. Dem habe → Livius Andronicus nur noch eine Fabel hinzufügen müssen, um die Tragödie zu schaffen. Diese kühne Verbindung von ital. *ludi scaenici* mit dem griech. Kunstdrama enthält einen wahren Kern, denn fortan hießen auch die Darsteller im lit. Drama *histriones*, ebenso wie in der Kaiserzeit die Tänzer des Pantomimus. In gleicher Bed. wie *h.* wird seit Cicero *scaenicus* (*s. artifex*) verwendet, selten hingegen ist *actor* (Plaut. Bacch. 213).

II. Entwicklung seit dem 3. Jh. v. Chr., soziale Stellung

Da sowohl die improvisatorischen *ludi scaenici* als auch die lit. Trag. und Komödie von außerhalb nach Rom gelangten, waren auch die Darsteller Fremde, zumeist Griechen. Als Livius Andronicus im J. 240 v. Chr. erstmals eine Trag. nach griech. Vorbild aufführte, trat er noch selbst als *h.* auf; das traf schon für Plautus nicht mehr zu. Gleichrangig hatten sich Dichter und Schauspieler mit staatlicher Genehmigung zu einem *collegium scribarum histrionumque* zusammengeschlossen, ihr Versammlungsort war der Minervatempel auf dem Aventin; doch das Gremium hatte nicht lange Bestand, vielleicht weil das Ansehen der *h.* mit dem der Dichter nicht Schritt hielt. Für einen röm. Bürger galt es als ehrlos und schändlich (Nep. praef. 5), sich auf der Bühne zu produzieren; nur Sklaven und Freigelassenen wurde das zugestanden, sie wurden dafür nicht diskriminiert. Die generelle Mißachtung der *h.* steht in bemerkenswertem Widerspruch zum Ruhm und zur gesellschaftlichen Wertschätzung einzelner »Stars«, wie Clodius → Aesopus oder Q. → Roscius, von Pantomimen der Kaiserzeit ganz zu schweigen. Daß Schauspieler auch an der polit. Meinungsbildung mitwirken konnten, zeigen die Beispiele des Mimendichters D. → Laberius und des Tragöden Diphilos (beide 1. Jh. v. Chr.); ersterer nahm im J. 46 Caesar bei einem Mimenwettstreit aufs Korn, Diphilos nutzte sein Auftreten an den → Ludi Apollinares des J. 59 zu provozierenden Versen über die Machtstellung des Cn. Pompeius (Cic. Att. 2,19,3; vgl. Val. Max. 6,2,9). Trotz einschlägiger Gesetze übte die Bühne stets eine große Faszination aus, so daß selbst Mitglieder vornehmer Familien nicht davor zurückscheuten, als Amateure zu agieren. Die Bühnenauftritte Kaiser Neros als Kitharöde und als Tragöde waren ein Skandal, den alle hinnahmen [1].

III. Anforderungen an den Histrio

Oberstes Gesetz für einen *h.* mußte es sein, dem Publikum zu gefallen. Polit. ehrgeizige Ädilen, aber auch andere Beamte in der Rolle von *ludorum curatores* investierten hohe Summen, um mit Hilfe der Aufführungen Popularität zu erlangen. Sie engagierten einen Schauspieldirektor (*actor*), der dem Autor ein Stück abkaufte, es mit seiner Truppe (*grex*) einstudierte und dabei selbst die Hauptrolle übernahm. Für Plautus tat das T. Publilius Pellio: Er spielte den Stichus (vgl. die Didaskalie, → Didaskaliai) und offenbar mehrmals den Epidicus, doch letztere Darstellung mißfiel Plautus, und er über-warf sich mit ihm (Plaut. Bacch. 214f.). Besser traf es Terenz mit L. → Ambivius Turpio, der sich unbeirrt für dessen neuartigen kultivierten Komödienstil einsetzte. Die Zahl der *h.* in einer Truppe unterlag keiner Beschränkung. Für eine Komödie benötigte man zumeist vier oder fünf Sprecher (also mehr als die obligaten drei bei den Griechen: dies beweist starke Eingriffe in die Vorlagen), dazu Statisten. Natürlich übernahmen einzelne *h.* mehrere Rollen (Plaut. Poen. 126), und alle gemeinsam sprechen bei Plautus (Plaut. Asin.; Bacch.; Capt.) einen Epilog, oder es bittet einer für die ganze hervortretende Truppe (*hunc gregem*, Plaut. Pseud. 1334) um Beifall.

Obwohl der Chor im röm. Drama kaum Fuß faßte, kam der Musik (→ *canticum*) größte Bed. zu. Alle *h.* mußten darum vortreffliche Sänger und Tänzer sein. Die Komödien des Terenz enden in unseren Ausgaben (nach Hor. ars 155 [2]) mit den Worten: *cantor: plaudite* (»ein Sänger: Klatscht Beifall«); auch mit dieser Sprecherbezeichnung dürfte ein Schauspieler gemeint sein. Der begleitende Flötenspieler (*tibicen*) war zugleich der Komponist. Im *Stichus* war es Marcipor, Sklave des Oppius (in Plaut. Stich. 755–765 wird er ins Spiel miteinbezogen), bei Terenz regelmäßig Flaccus, Sklave des Claudius.

IV. Masken und Kostüme

Der Gebrauch der → Maske ist strittig. Lediglich die improvisatorische → Atellana galt von Anfang an als Maskenspiel (*personata fabula*); darum durften junge Römer sich dieser Gattung ohne gesellschaftliche Diskriminierung widmen. Der → Mimus wiederum verzichtete ganz auf sie. Im lit. Drama scheint der *h.* zunächst nur eine Perücke (*galear*) getragen zu haben. Erst nach Terenz wird die Maske erwähnt: Für die Komödie soll sie Cincius Faliscus oder Roscius eingeführt haben [4. 155, 164]. In Plaut. Epid. 725 bekommt der Titelheld neue Kleider: Schuhe, Hemd und Mantel (*socci, tunica, pallium*), und mit der Alltagstracht ist zugleich das Bühnenkostüm umschrieben. Nach dem griech. Mantel (ἱμάτιον/*himátion*; lat. *pallium*) heißt die Komödiengattung des Plautus und Terenz *fabula palliata* (die spätere national-röm. *fabula togata* ist verloren). Das *pallium* trugen Freie, Parasiten und Sklaven ohne Unterschied; gleiches gilt für den leichten Schuh (*soccus*), der generell die Komödie bezeichnen konnte, so wie *cothurnus* (→ Kothurn) die Trag. (Hor. ars 80). Ob die Kleider je nach Rollentypus verschiedenfarbig waren (Don. De comoedia 8,6), geht aus den Texten nicht hervor. Im Auftrag der Ädilen stellte ein Kostüm- und Requisitenverleiher (*choragus*) dem Chef der Truppe das Gewünschte bereit, zumal für bes. Verkleidungen (Plaut. Curc. 4,1; Plaut. Persa 154–160; Plaut. Trin. 857f.) [3; 4].

→ Aesopus Clodius; Ambivius Turpio; Roscius, Q.

1 P.L. Schmidt, Nero und das Theater, in: J. Blänsdorf (Hrsg.), Theater und Ges. im Imperium Romanum, 1990, 149–163 2 C.O. Brink, Horace on Poetry: The »Ars Poetica« Bd. 2, 1971, 231 3 G.E. Duckworth, The Nature of Roman Comedy, 1952, 88–94 4 M. Bieber, The History of the Greek and Roman Theater, 1961, Kap. XI.

W. Beare, The Roman Stage, [3]1964 • J. Blänsdorf, Voraussetzungen und Entstehung der röm. Komödie, in: E. Lefèvre, Das röm. Drama, 1978, 92–134 • M. Ducos, La condition des acteurs à Rome. Donées juridiques et sociales, in: J. Blänsdorf (Hrsg.), Theater und Ges. im Imperium Romanum, 1990, 19–33 • Friedländer, Bd. 2, 112–147 • C. Garton, Personal Aspects of the Roman Theatre, 1972 • H. Leppin, Histrionen, 1992 • B. Zucchelli, Le denominazioni latine dell' attore, 1964.

H.-D.B.

Hochdorf. Nahe dem südwestdt. Ort Eberdingen-H. wurde 1978/9 ein verebneter Großgrabhügel ausgegraben, der sich als eines der wenigen unberaubten und modern untersuchten kelt. → Fürstengräber der späten → Hallstatt-Kultur (2. H. 6. Jh. v. Chr.) erwies. Der Hügel war von einem Steinkranz von 57 m Dm umgeben und hatte ursprünglich eine H von ca. 6 m. Im Norden fand sich ein rampenartiger Zugang, der zur 2 m eingetieften, zentralen Grabkammer führte.

Die Kammer bestand aus einem doppelwandigen Blockbau aus Eichenbalken, die mit ca. 50 Tonnen Gesteinsbrocken überdeckt war. In der quadratischen Grabkammer von 4,7 × 4,7 m war ein 40–50jähriger Mann von ungewöhnlich großer (1,87 m) und kräftiger Statur mit einer überaus reichen, fürstlichen Ausstattung beigesetzt. Er lag mit seinen persönlichen Dingen (Birkenrindenhut, Goldhalsreif-Torques, Goldarmband, Gürtel, Goldfibeln, Dolch, Köcher mit Pfeilen, Toilettenbesteck, Kleidung usw.) auf einer großen, einem Sofa ähnlichen Br.-Liege (Kline). Seine Ausstattung war z.T. speziell für die Grablege mit Gold überzogen worden (Dolch, Schuhe usw.). Die 2,75 m lange Kline, die, reich in lokaler Manier getrieben, verziert und auf anthropomorphen Füßen fahrbar war, ist bisher ein Unikat.

Die Bedeutung des Toten wird noch durch die Beigabe eines reich mit Eisen beschlagenen vierrädrigen Wagens mit zugehöriger Doppeljoch-Schirrung sowie eines reichhaltigen Trink- und Speisegeschirrs unterstrichen. Es waren neun Trinkhörner und neun Br.-Teller beigegeben, dazu drei Br.-Becken und ein großer Br.-Kessel (500 l) mit drei aufgesetzten Löwenfiguren; darin fanden sich eine Goldblechschale und Reste eines dem → Met ähnelnden Getränks. Der Kessel ist großgriech. Import, an dem aber eine Löwenfigur lokal nachgearbeitet wurde. Als zugehöriger Fürstensitz wird der ca. 10 km entfernte Hohenasperg erwogen.

→ Gold; Glauberg; Grabbauten; Heuneburg; Hirschlanden; Kline

J. Biel, Ein Fürstengrabhügel der späten Hallstattzeit bei Eberdingen-H., in: Germania 60, 1982, 61–104 • D. Planck (Red.), Der Keltenfürst von H., 1985, 31–161.

V.P.

Hochverrat s. Perduellio

Hochzeit s. Ehe

Hochzeitsbräuche und -ritual
I. Allgemeines II. Griechenland III. Rom

I. Allgemeines

Der Zweck aller ant. H. ist es, das Brautpaar kult. zu reinigen, den Bund durch Opfer zu besiegeln, die Fruchtbarkeit zu steigern und Kraft zu spenden, die Braut auf ihrem Weg zum Haus des Ehemannes vor Unheil und Schadewesen zu schützen und sie in ihren neuen Status als Ehefrau und Mutter einzuführen. Die Riten erstreckten sich über mehrere Tage, begannen im Haus der Braut, wo sie die Trennung vom elterlichen Herd signalisierten, bezogen den Weg zum Haus des Bräutigams mit ein und endeten dort damit, daß die Braut dem Schutz der neuen Hausgötter unterstellt wurde. Sie dienten nicht nur der Erleichterung, sondern auch der Akzentuierung des Übergangs und trugen somit zur Festigung der gesellschaftl. Strukturen bei [1. 75].

II. Griechenland

Nach Abschluß des Ehevertrags folgte die eigentliche Hochzeit, eine rein rel. Feier (gewöhnlich im Monat Gamelion, kurz vor Neumond). Die vorbereitenden Rituale, die προτέλεια (*protéleia*), trugen den Charakter der Entsühnung und Reinigung: Am Vorabend opferte man im Haus der Braut und betete zu den Schutzgottheiten der Ehe, insbesondere zu Zeus, Hera, Artemis, Apollon und Peitho (Plut. qu. R. 2,264b). Dabei weihte die Braut der Artemis oder – je nach Lokalbrauch – auch der Aphrodite, Nymphen oder lokalen Heroinen ihr Spielzeug, persönliche Gegenstände und Locken ihres Haares, wohl um sich so vom möglichen Zorn der jungfräulichen Artemis loszukaufen [1. 75] oder, allg. gesprochen, um nicht den von der jeweiligen Gottheit abgedeckten Lebensbereich achtlos zu übergehen. Braut und Bräutigam reinigten sich durch ein kult. Bad, das λουτρὸν νυμφικόν, *lutrón nymphikón* (→ Lutrophoros; schol. Eur. Phoen. 347). Am Hochzeitstag fand im Haus des Brautvaters ein Opfer und ein Festmahl statt. Die Braut war verschleiert und trug einen Kranz. Ein Knabe, dessen Eltern noch am Leben sein mußten (Poll. 3,43; → *amphithaleís paídes*) – sein jugendliches Alter und die Tatsache, daß er noch nicht um seine Eltern trauern mußte, gewährleisteten ungeschwächte Vitalität und Kraft – und der am Kopf einen Kranz aus stacheligen Pflanzen trug, in den Eicheln eingeflochten waren, verteilte an die Gäste Brot aus einem Korb und sprach dabei die Formel: ἔφυγον κακόν, εὗρον ἄμεινον (*éphygon kakón, héuron ámeinon*: ›Ich bin dem Übel entflohen und habe das Bessere gefunden‹). Dabei handelt es sich laut [1. 54–57] wohl um eine Reminiszenz an den Übergang von der unkultivierten Lebensweise der Jägergesellschaft zu der zivilisierteren der Ackerbaugesellschaft. Ähnlich wie bei den Initiationsriten der Mysterienkulte wurde hier der einzelne durch ein Ritual in ein neues, überindividuelles Dasein erhoben [1. 302]. Die Braut wurde im Anschluß an das Mahl entschleiert (ἀνακαλυπτήρια, *anakalyptḗria*) und erhielt vom Bräutigam Geschenke (später ebenfalls als *anakalyptḗria* bezeichnet).

Am Abend wurde die Braut zum Haus des Bräutigams geleitet. Sie nahm einen besonderen Sitz auf einem von Maultieren, später von Pferden oder Ochsen gezogenen Wagen ein, oder sie ging zu Fuß. Die Brautmutter trug eine Fackel voran, dazu wurde der Hymen (→ Hymen[aios]) gesungen. Nach Solonischem Gesetz mußte die Braut verschiedene Haushaltsgeräte mit sich führen, z. B. eine Pfanne zum Rösten von Getreide und ein Sieb; an den Türpfosten des Hauses des Bräutigams wurde eine Mörserkeule befestigt (zur Abwehr der Schadegeister). Dort hießen auch die Eltern des Bräutigams die Braut willkommen. Sie bekam einen Teil des mit Sesam und Honig gebackenen Kuchens, den der Bräutigam zerstoßen und austeilen mußte, und eine Quitte oder eine Dattel als Symbol der Fruchtbarkeit (Plut. coniugalia praecepta 1,138d). Das Zerteilen des Kuchens oder Brotes, sein Austeilen, Geben und Nehmen ist laut [1. 54–56] ein wichtiges Element des Rituals in einer Ackerbaugesellschaft und hat ähnliche Funktion wie das Schlachten vor dem Fleischgenuß, allerdings wird in der »gezähmten Lebensweise« die im Jagdritual vorhandene Aggression auf andere Objekte umgelenkt und bedient sich der Fertigkeiten und Werkzeuge der Bauern (Zerteilen, Zerschneiden, Mörserkeule).

Die Braut mußte den neuen Herd umschreiten, eine Form der magischen Umkreisung, die nach außen apotropäische und nach innen kathartische und fertilisierende Wirkung haben sollte. Auf diese Art wurde sie in die Hausgemeinschaft aufgenommen. In der Folge wurde sie mit Nüssen und getrockneten Feigen überschüttet (καταχύσματα, *katachýsmata*). Dabei, wie auch beim Bewerfen des Brautpaares mit Blumen, handelt es sich um eine Form der Kontaktmagie zur Übertragung einer unpersönlichen höheren Kraft, wobei das Bewerfen als eine bes. intensive Form der Berührung verstanden wird. Dagegen rückt z.B. das Zerschlagen von Töpfen durch Außenstehende nach dem Opfer das Brautpaar selbst ins Zentrum (gespielter) Aggression [1. 74]. Darauf begab sich das Brautpaar in den θάλαμος (*thálamos*), das Hochzeitsgemach, das während der Nacht bewacht wurde, um Schadewesen von der Braut fernzuhalten, während die Festgesellschaft derbe Scherze machte. Die Aischrologie hat sowohl lustrale und apotropäische als auch fertilisierende Wirkung (im Sinne von verbal getätigter Sexualität) [2. 239].

Am Morgen fanden von neuem Opfer und ein Festmahl statt, die ἐπαύλια (*epaúlia*); das Brautpaar empfing Geschenke von Verwandten und Freunden. Mit der Eintragung des Ehebündnisses in die → Phratrie-Liste endeten die H.

In Sparta schnitt man der Braut die Haare ab, legte ihr Männerkleidung an und ließ sie ihren Bräutigam allein und im Dunkeln auf einem Strohlager erwarten – ein

Umkehrritus, dessen Zweck es war, die Braut als einen Mann auszugeben, dem in der Hochzeitsnacht keine Gefahr durch die Defloration droht, und damit die Schadewesen zu täuschen.

III. Rom

In der Regel ging der Heirat eine Verlobungszeit voraus; der Bräutigam gab der Braut ein Handgeld (*arra*) oder einen Ring, den sie am vierten Finger der linken Hand trug. Der Tag der Hochzeit mußte sorgfältig gewählt werden, da eine Reihe von Tagen als ungünstig für die Eheschließung galt und auch Festtage nicht in Frage kamen. Am Vorabend legte die Braut ihre Kleidung ab, weihte diese samt ihren Spielsachen den Göttern und zog die *tunica recta* (*regilla*), eine lange, weiße, stolaartige *tunica* (Fest. 227; 286) an, die sie während der Nacht und auch am Hochzeitstag trug und die durch einen wollenen, mit dem *nodus Herculis* gebundenen Gürtel zusammengehalten wurde. Das Knüpfen des Gürtels war eine Aufgabe der Iuno Cinxia, der »gürtenden Iuno«, welche hier nicht als die göttl. Verkörperung der Braut, sondern als ihre Schützerin verstanden und durch die Brautmutter vertreten wurde [3. 195–206]. Das Haar der Braut wurde mit einer Lanze, durch die ein Feind getötet worden war, der *hasta caelibaris*, in sechs Strähnen geteilt und mit wollenen Bändern zusammengehalten (Plut. qu. R. 87,285c). Wolle galt wie Haare und Fell als Kraftträger, u. a. auch deshalb, weil die Haare ohne äußeres Zutun nachwachsen; die Kraft blieb auch in abgeschittenem oder zu Wolle verarbeitetem Haar erhalten (vgl. die tabuistischen Vorschriften für den *flamen Dialis* [4. 222–224]). Zum einen sollte durch die Berührung mit der »blutigen« Lanze und der Wolle die Kraft der Braut magisch gesteigert werden, zum anderen handelte es sich dabei um eine rituelle Ersatzhandlung, die das Angsterregende an der Defloration vorwegnehmend mildern sollte [1. 74]. Geschmückt wurde die Braut auch mit einem Blumenkranz und einem roten Brautschleier, dem *flammeum* (Sinnbild der Vitalität der jungen Frau).

Die eigentliche Feier, der Verwandte und Freunde beiwohnten, begann am frühen Morgen des Hochzeitstages im Hause der Braut mit Auspizien oder Eingeweideschau. Bei günstigen Vorzeichen wurde ein Opfer durchgeführt; man betete zu den Ehegöttinnen Iuno, Tellus, Ceres und vielleicht auch zu → Pilumnus und Picumnus (beide werden als *dii coniugales* bezeichnet, sie waren aber urspr. wohl eher Götter des *coniugium*, der Verbindung und des Verbundenseins in einem weiteren Sinne [3. 111–113]). Die *pronuba*, eine in erster Ehe verheiratete Frau, assistierte bei der *dextrarum iunctio* (das Ineinanderlegen der Hände) und der wechselseitigen Erklärung des *consensus* (Einigkeit). Bei der → *confarreatio* mußten die beiden Gatten auf zwei durch das Fell eines geopferten Schafes verbundenen Stühlen Platz nehmen. Das Schafsfell stellte als magisches Requisit den Kontakt zw. den beiden her und sollte als Kraftträger die Fertilität des Paares gewährleisten. Das Brautpaar teilte sich einen Speltkuchen (*farreum libum*), was Gemeinschaft

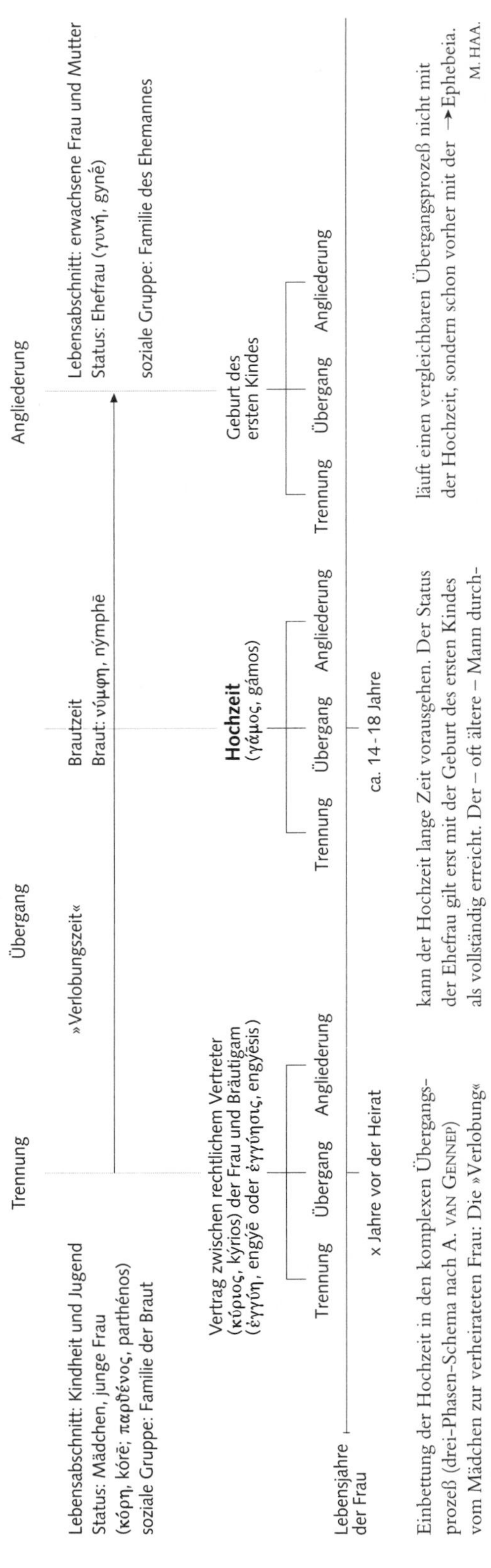

Einbettung der Hochzeit in den komplexen Übergangsprozeß (drei-Phasen-Schema nach A. van Gennep) vom Mädchen zur verheirateten Frau: Die »Verlobung« kann der Hochzeit lange Zeit vorausgehen. Der Status der Ehefrau gilt erst mit der Geburt des ersten Kindes als vollständig erreicht. Der – oft ältere – Mann durchläuft einen vergleichbaren Übergangsprozeß nicht mit der Hochzeit, sondern schon vorher mit der → Ephebeia.

M. HAA.

Metaebene: Übergangsphasen	Trennung		Übergang		Angliederung	
zeitliche Ebene	**1.Tag** Vor-Vorabend der Hochzeitsnacht	**2.Tag** Tag vor der Hochzeitsnacht (προαύλια, proaúlia)	Abend vor der Hochzeitsnacht		Hochzeits-nacht	**3.Tag** Tag nach der Hochzeitsnacht (ἐπαύλια, epaúlia)
räumliche Ebene	Haus des Brautvaters		Ortswechsel → »neutrale Zone«	Haus des Ehemanns Tür → Herd → Schlafgemach (θάλαμος, thálamos)		
beteiligte soziale Gruppen	Braut und Helferinnen unter Aufsicht der »Brautjungfer« (νυμφεύτρια, nympheútria)	Verwandte und Bekannte des Brautpaares	Polisgesellschaft		Brautpaar	- Verwandte und Bekannte des Brautpaares - Phratrie
Handlungen (in Klammern: der Akteur)	- Weihung von Gürtel, Haar, Spielzeug (Braut) (προτέλεια, protéleia) - Einholen des Badewassers (Frauen) - Brautbad (λουτρὸν νυμφικόν, lutrón nymphikón) (Braut, Bräutigam)	- Opfer und Festmahl (Familie und Gäste) - Geschenke (Ehemann an Braut) - Entschleierung (ἀνακαλυπτήρια, anakalyptéria) - Übergabe der Braut (ἔκδοσις, ékdosis) an Ehemann durch Vater	- »Heim-führung« zu Fuß oder im Wagen (Brautpaar) - Hochzeitslied (ὑμέναιος, hyménaios) (Zuschauer)	- Begrüßung (Eltern des Ehemanns) - Braut erhält Honigkuchen und Datteln - Umschreiten des Herds (Braut) - Trocken-früchte und Nüsse (καταχύσματα, katachýsmata) (Festgesell-schaft)		- Opfer und Festmahl (ἐπαύλια, epaúlia) - Geschenke an Brautpaar - Eintragung in die Phratrienliste
typische Bild-symbole in der attischen Vasen-malerei	- Wasserholen: Gefäß für Badewasser (Lutrophoros) - Schmückung der Braut		- Prozession - Fackeln - Wagenfahrt - Gestus des Ehemanns: Umfassen des Handgelenks der Braut (χεῖρ' ἐπὶ καρπῷ cheír'epì karpṓ) - Gestus der Braut: den Schleier heben (ἀνακάλυψις, anakálypsis)	- Tür - Architektur-angaben	- Brautlager (selten)	- »Hochzeitskessel« (λέβης γαμικός, lébēs gamikós) - Beschenkung

Die ideale Verlaufsstruktur läßt sich aus Texten und Bildern rekonstruieren. M. HAA.

schaffen und Übel abwehren sollte. Der *flamen Dialis* brachte dem Iuppiter ein unblutiges, aus Früchten und einem Speltbrot (*panis farreus*) bestehendes Opfer dar. Auch hier sind Gemeinsamkeiten mit den Initiationsriten in Eleusis (→ Mysterien) deutlich erkennbar, nämlich das bei Varro rust. 2,4,9 belegte einleitende Schweineopfer, das freilich nicht bei jeder Hochzeit stattgefunden haben dürfte, das Sitzen auf dem Schafsfell (Serv. Aen. 4,374) und der gemeinsame Genuß der Getreidenahrung [1. 302].

Während des Gebetes mußte das Brautpaar um den Altar schreiten (magische Umkreisung). Nachdem die Zeugen der Trauung ihre Glückwünsche ausgesprochen hatten (*feliciter*), folgte die *cena* (Festmahl). Beim Einbruch der Nacht wurde die Braut der Mutter entrissen und zum Haus des Bräutigams geleitet (*deductio*). Fakkeln aus glückverheißendem Weißdornholz (ein Mittel gegen bösen Zauber, Ov. fast. 6,129;165) wurden entzündet und nach oben gehalten, damit sie hell brannten. Die Hochzeitsgäste bemühten sich nach dem Abschluß der Überführung, die Hochzeitsfackeln zu rauben. Durch Lärm und Ausstreuen von Nüssen und die *fescennina iocatio*, derbe Scherze, denen man sowohl apotropäische als auch fertilisierende Wirkung zuschrieb, sollten die Schadewesen abgelenkt bzw. abgeschreckt werden.

Die Braut wurde von drei Knaben geleitet, deren beide Eltern noch leben mußten (*patrimi et matrimi*); ihre Vitalität sollte die Braut auf ihrem Weg beschützen und sie mit unpersönlicher höherer Kraft erfüllen. Hinter der Braut wurden Rocken und Spindel hergetragen. Dazu erklang der schon für die Römer unverständlich gewordene Ruf *talasse* oder *talassio* (Liv. 1,9; Aur. Vict. 2). Beim Haus des Bräutigams angelangt, salbte die Braut den Türpfosten und wand Wolle um ihn (Kraftsteigerung). Sie wurde über die Schwelle getragen, um unglückverheißendes Stolpern zu verhindern. Gleichzeitig sollten die Schadewesen, von denen man annahm, daß sie an der Schwelle, der Grenze zw. dem unheimlichen Draußen und der häuslichen Sphäre, lauerten, mit einem *fait accompli* konfrontiert werden. Dadurch, daß die Braut die Schwelle nicht berührte, sollte den Schadewesen vorgetäuscht werden, sie sei gar nicht im Hause anwesend. Vom Bräutigam wurde die Braut im Haus mit Wasser und Feuer empfangen, d.h. zur Teilnahme am häuslichen Kult berechtigt. Sie führte drei kleine Münzen (Asse) mit sich, von denen sie die eine dem Bräutigam gab, vielleicht um ihm als dem Repräsentanten der Vorfahren deren Eigentum symbolisch abzulösen, die zweite in den Herd, den Inbegriff der Häuslichkeit, legte und die dritte an dem nächstgelegenen *compitum* (Wegkreuzung) für die → Laren [5. 93] niederlegte (für die Fruchtbarkeit der Äcker). In der Folge wurde die Braut auf ein hölzernes *fascinum* (Phallos) gesetzt (Kontaktmagie), das personifiziert und als Mutinus Titinus (→ Mutunus Tutunus) bezeichnet wurde. Dann wurde sie zum Brautbett, dem *lectus genialis*, im Atrium geleitet. Am folgenden Tag wurde das Ehepaar von Verwandten besucht und beschenkt, ein neuerliches Opfer und ein Festmahl (*repotia*) beendeten die H.

→ Dos; Ehe; Engyesis; Frau; Gebärden; Geburt; Geschenke; Geschlecht; Geschlechterrollen; Sponsio

1 W. Burkert, Homo necans, 1972 **2** W. Pötscher, Die Lupercalia, in: Grazer Beiträge 11, 1984, 221–249 **3** Th. Köves-Zulauf, Röm. Geburtsriten, 1990 **4** W. Pötscher, Flamen Dialis, in: Mnemosyne 21, 1968, 215–239 **5** Latte.

H. Blanck, Einführung in das Privatleben der Griechen und Römer, [2]1996 • J. Bremmer, Götter, Mythen und Heiligtümer im ant. Griechenland, 1996 • J. Marquardt, Das Privatleben der Römer, 1886 (Ndr. 1990) • E. Samter, Familienfeste der Griechen und Römer, 1901 • P. Zingg, B. Woykos, Religiöser Mythos und Hochzeitsriten, 1989.

R.OS.

Abb.-Lit.: A. van Gennep, Les rites de passage, 1909, 167–207 • J.H. Oakley, R.H. Sinos, The Wedding in Ancient Athens, 1993 • C. Reinsberg, Ehe, Hetärentum und Knabenliebe im ant. Griechenland, [2]1993, 49–79 • S. Blundell, Women in Ancient Greece, 1995, 119–124 • E.D. Reeder (Hrsg.), Pandora. Frauen im klass. Griechenland, Kat. der Ausstellung Baltimore/Basel, 1996, bes. 126–128.

M.HAA.

Hodometron (ὁδόμετρον). Heron (dioptra 34) und Vitruv (10,9) beschreiben eine mechanische Vorrichtung zur Entfernungsmessung auf dem Lande, bei der eine von einem Wagenrad angetriebene Verbindung von auf verschiedenen Ebenen montierten Endlosschrauben und Zahnrädern jede Radumdrehung verlangsamend auf ein Anzeigesystem (Heron: Zeiger; Vitruv: fallende Kugeln) überträgt. Das *H.* reichte für je eine Tagesreise aus und mußte dann wieder auf die Ausgangsstellung zurückgestellt werden. Vitruv kennt eine entsprechende Vorrichtung für Seereisen, die auf einem Schaufelrad basiert.

A.G. Drachmann, The Mechanical Technology of Greek and Roman Technology, 1963, 157ff.

E.O.

Hodopoioi (ὁδοποιοί). Die *h.* (»Straßenmeister«) waren im Athen des 4. Jh. v.Chr. eine Behörde von 5 Personen (vielleicht aus paarweise gruppierten Phylen bestellt), die über öffentl. Sklaven verfügten, um die Straßen in gutem Zustand zu halten ([Aristot.] Ath. pol. 54,1). Die Behauptung des Aischines (Ctes. 25), in der Zeit des → Eubulos [1] seien die Verwalter der Theorika *hodopoioí* gewesen, könnte lediglich bedeuten, daß diese Beamten die *h.* überwachten oder ihnen die Mittel bereitstellten, nicht jedoch, daß die Behörde aufgelöst worden war [2. 237f.].

1 Busolt/Swoboda 2, 116 **2** P.J. Rhodes, The Athenian Boule, 1972.

P.J.R.

Höchstpreisedikt s. Edictum [3] Diocletiani

Höhenheiligtum. H. (= Heiligtümer auf Erhebungen oder in Bergsätteln) gab es in verschiedenen ant. Kulturen. Zu den ältesten arch. belegten Monumenten gehören die sog. Feuer-H. des → Baal im Nahen Osten [1]; es ist vermutet worden, daß von dieser Trad. möglicherweise die im 2. Jt. frequentierten H. auf Kreta beeinflußt waren [2. 60f.]. Dort hat man über 20 H. gefunden, die durch Funde von Tonfiguren und Altarspuren identifiziert werden konnten.

Eine weitere Form des H. stellen griech. Kultstätten der klass. Zeit (Festland, Inseln, Kleinasien) auf außerstädtisch gelegenen Anhöhen dar. Die Topographie stand hier in Zusammenhang mit der durch die → Epiklese ausgedrückten Eigenschaft des Gottes (z.B. Zeus Olympios) oder dem ant. Verständnis als einer Gottheit des »Draußen« vor der Stadt (z.B. Demeter) [3. 201, 368f.]. Für den röm. Bereich ist insbes. die Verehrung des Iuppiter Latiaris auf dem Mons Albanus zu nennen (Dion. Hal. ant. 4,49). In den Städten (z.B. Athen, Rom) waren Anhöhen der Ort bedeutender Kulte (in griech. Poleis die Akropolis, die Hügel in Rom). Die Höhenlage von Heiligtümern, die freilich nicht immer realisiert wurde, galt generell als die zu bevorzugende Lage (vgl. Xen. mem. 3,8,10, der als Grund den hohen Grad an Sichtbarkeit angibt).

Bei den H. der kelt. und german. Kulturen läßt sich vielfach eine Kontinuität der Kultplätze von der vorröm. bis in die christl. Zeit nachweisen, wobei die urspr. (unbebauten) H. zunächst von germano- bzw. keltoröm. Tempeln, in der Spätant. dann von frühchristl. Kirchen überbaut wurden [4; 5. 820ff.]. Von Kirchen auf Bergen entlang der Strecke des Exodus des Volkes Israel von Ägypten her gibt die → *Peregrinatio ad loca sancta* (z.B. 3,3 und 3,5 SChr 296) Zeugnis und dokumentiert die Verehrung at. Stätten in christl. Zeit.

1 R. Wenning, E. Zenger, Ein bäuerliches Baal-H. im samar. Gebirge aus der Zeit der Anfänge Israels, in: Zschr. des Dt. Palästina-Vereins 102, 1986, 75–86 2 Burkert 3 Graf 4 K.J. Gilles, Röm. Bergh. im Trierer Land. Zu den Auswirkungen der spätant. Religionspolitik, in: TZ, 1985, 195–254 5 L. Pauli, Einheim. Götter und Opferbräuche im Alpenraum, in: ANRW II 18.1, 816–871.

Th. Baumeister, s.v. Höhenkult, RAC 15, 986–1015.

C.F.u.HE.K.

Höhlenheiligtum. Ant. H. finden sich v.a. in zwei Kontexten: Einmal als »hl. Höhlen« brz. und neolithischer Kulturen sowie bes. der min. Palastzeit auf Kreta, sodann als »Initiationshöhlen« in der archa. und klass. griech. Zeit, später auch im röm. Westen.

Bes. die H. des min. Kreta sind verhältnismäßig gut erforscht. Sicher nachgewiesen sind dort 15 H. (u.a. die Höhle von Skotinó bei Knosos, Vernapheto- und Kamares-Höhle), die Existenz weiterer H. wird vermutet [1. 55ff.]. In den H. fanden sich Tongefäße, Getreidereste und Tierknochen als Weihegaben. Das bekannteste H. dürfte die sog. »Zeushöhle« am kret. Ida sein. In ihm soll nach ant. myth. Trad. Zeus von den → Kureten großgezogen worden sein (Strab. 10,4,8; Diod. 5,70,2 und 4; Paus. 5,7,6). Eine Besonderheit dieses H. ist, daß es auch in nach-min. Zeit weiter frequentiert wurde und man seit dem 8. Jh. dort »Opferfeste mit Initiationscharakter« (Mannbarkeitsriten) vollzog [1. 91].

Einem dezidiert initiatorischen Zweck dienten die H. des Mithraskultes in der röm. Kaiserzeit. Nach Porph. 6 hat → Zoroastres zu Ehren des → Mithras im pers. Bergland eine natürliche Höhle so ausgebaut, daß sie ein Abbild des Kosmos darstellte. Nach diesem Schema wurden später die röm. Mithräen gestaltet, indem man unterird. künstliche Höhlen anlegte oder die H. im Erdgeschoß von Wohnhäusern einbaute, wo die Bodenverhältnisse dazu zwangen (ausführlich [2. 133ff.]).
→ Grotte; Heiligtum

1 Burkert 2 R. Merkelbach, Mithras, 1984.

B. Rutkowski, K. Nowikki, The Psychro Cave and Other Grottoes in Crete, 1996.

C.F.

Hoenius

[1] T.H. Severus. *Cos. ord.* 141 n.Chr., möglicherweise aus Umbrien stammend (PIR[2] H 189); vielleicht verwandtschaftl. mit → Iuventius Celsus, *cos. II* 129, verbunden.

M. Gaggiotti, L. Sensi , in: EOS 2,237.

[2] T.H. Severus. Sohn von H. [1]. Patrizier, *cos. suff.* 170 n.Chr. PIR[2] H 190.

W.E.

Hörnerkrone. Während der frühdyn. Zeit (Mitte 3. Jt. v.Chr.) wird in Mesopot. die H. zur Kenntlichmachung des göttl. Charakters anthropomorpher Götterdarstellungen entwickelt. Am Anfang besteht sie aus einem Reif oder einer einfachen Kappe, an denen ein Paar Rinderhörner befestigt ist. Die in der Folgezeit entwickelte spitz zulaufende H. mit mehreren, nach innen schwingenden Hörnerpaaren übereinander wird bis weit ins 2. Jt. hinein dargestellt. Neuassyr. H. haben entweder die Form eines hohen gewölbten Helms oder sind zylindrisch mit gefiedertem Abschluß; neubabylon. Götter tragen, abgesehen von archaisierenden Darstellungen, Poloi (hohe, meist zylindrische Hüte; → Polos) ohne Hörner. Während die H. als Attribut allen Gottheiten dient, ist sie (seit dem 12. Jh. v.Chr.) isoliert Symbol nur für die Götter → Enlil, Anu und → Assur [2]. In benachbarten Kulturen werden Hörner mit eigenständigen Kronenformen kombiniert. Vgl. Abb. Sp. 659f.

R.M. Boehmer, Die Entwicklung der H. von ihren Anfängen bis zum Ende der Akkad-Zeit, in: Berliner Jb. für Vor- und Frühgesch. 7, 1967, 273–291 • Ders., s.v. H., RLA 4, 431–434 • U. Seidl, Die babylon. Kudurru-Reliefs (OBO 87), 1989, 116f., 230 • J.M. Asher-Greve, Reading the Horned Crown, in: AfO 42/43, 1995/96, 181–189.

U.SE.

Formen altorientalischer Hörnerkronen: zeitliche und räumliche Verteilung

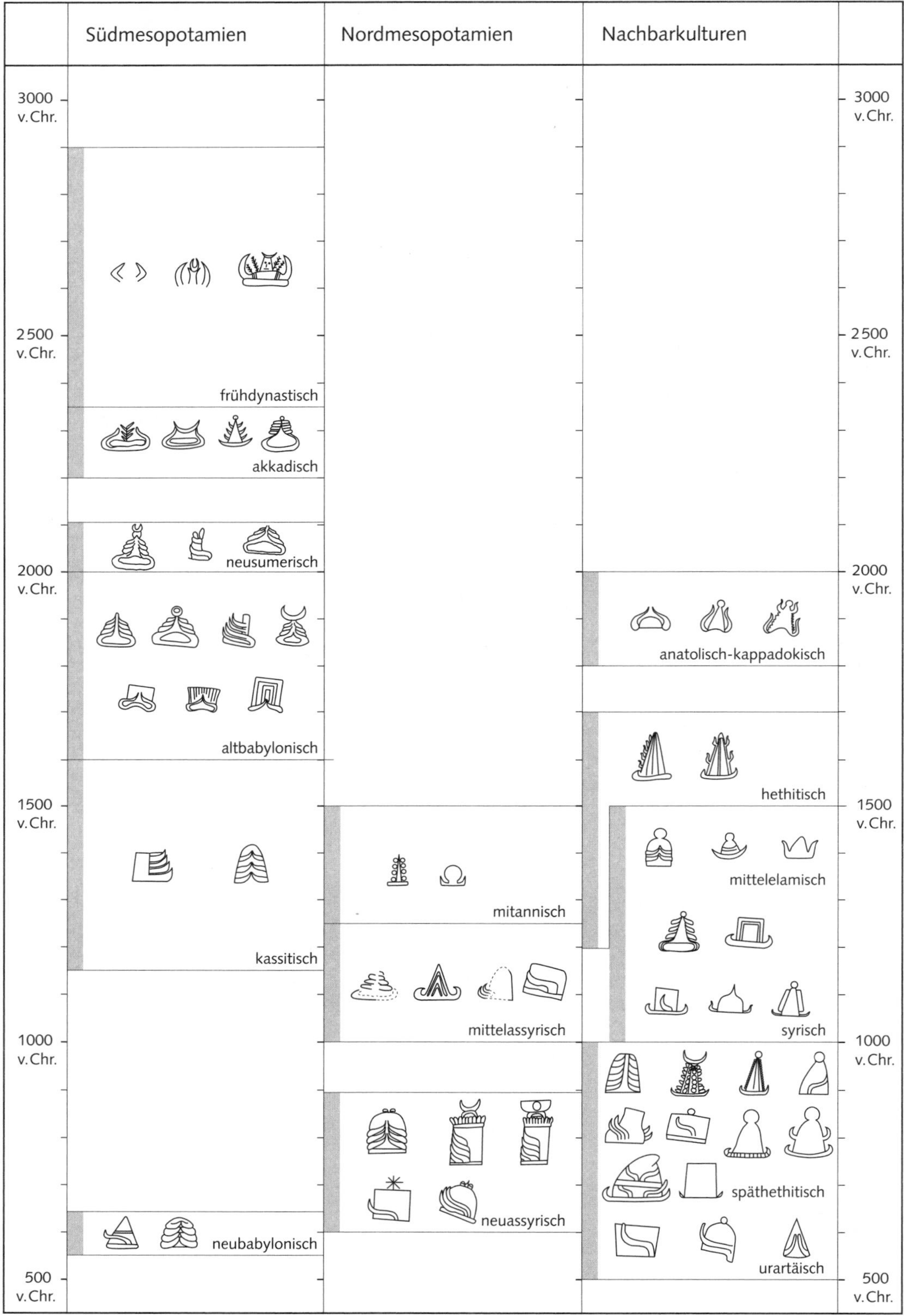

Hof (griech. αὐλή/*aulḗ*, lat. *aula, comitatus*).
A. Allgemeines B. Hellenismus C. Prinzipat D. Spätantike E. Rezeption

A. Allgemeines

Wie die territoriale → Monarchie, so ist auch der H. als »erweitertes Haus« eines Monarchen ein nachklass., erst mit dem Ende der polit. Dominanz städtischer Gemeinwesen auftretendes Phänomen der ant. Gesch. Hervorgegangen aus dem → *oíkos* eines griech., der → *domus* eines röm. Adligen, waren H. im Gegensatz zu jenen »Häusern« nicht mehr in die Stadtgemeinde eingebunden, sondern etablierten sich als eigenständige Zentren polit. Entscheidung und Herrschaft über Städte, Völkerschaften und Reiche. Die aus der persönlichen Nähe zu einem König oder Kaiser resultierenden Chancen auf Einfluß, Reichtum und Ansehen machten die Anwesenheit am H. attraktiv auch für Mitglieder der aristokratischen Oberschichten, wenngleich sie dort meist mit sozial niedriger stehenden Personengruppen zu konkurrieren hatten. Die höf. Kommunikationsbedingungen, die Bedeutung der Gunst des Herrschers, die Labilität der erlangten Stellung sowie Schmeichelei und Intrigen im Streben nach Aufstieg und Sicherung der Position wurden schon von Zeitgenossen als Spezifikum des H. beobachtet und kritisiert (vgl. Pol. 4,87,3 f.; 5,26,12 f.; Lucan. 8,493 f.; Amm. 22,4,2). Die Entfaltung höf. Pracht, die Förderung von Wiss. und Kunst dienten der Manifestation der Stellung der Monarchen; im Gegensatz zur späteren europ. Gesch. entstand in der Ant. jedoch keine eigenständige höf., die städtisch-polit. Prägungen der klass. Zeit überwindende Oberschichtkultur: Das ant. Äquivalent zu »Höflichkeit« (mhd. *höveschheit*, mlat. *curialitas*) blieb »Urbanität« (griech. ἀστειότης, *asteiótēs*; lat. *urbanitas*).

B. Hellenismus

Z. T. prachtvoll und großräumig gestaltete Palastanlagen (→ Palast-Anlagen) in meist neugegründeten Residenzstädten (Alexandreia, Seleukeia, Antiocheia, Pella, Aigai, Pergamon u. a.) bildeten den räumlichen Rahmen der Hofhaltungen. Die neben den Verwandten des Königs wichtigste Gruppe der höf. Ges. bestand aus seinen »Freunden« (φίλοι, *phíloi*), deren gemeinsames Merkmal ihre griech. (bes. bei den Antigoniden auch maked.) Herkunft war, die ansonsten in freier Auswahl nach persönl. Qualitäten aus den städt. Oberschichten, oft auch aus Künstlern, Literaten und Wissenschaftlern rekrutiert wurden. Sie bildeten die ständige Umgebung des Königs vom morgens zusammentretenden »Rat« (συνέδριον, → *synhédrion*) bis zum abendlichen Symposion. Aus ihrem Kreis wurden für Aufgaben außerhalb des H. Provinzstatthalter, mil. Führungspersonal und Gesandte ausgewählt. Weitere Personen am H. waren stärker in organisatorische Zusammenhänge eingebunden: die für den königl. Schutz zuständige Leibgarde (σωματοφύλακες, *sōmatophýlakes*), das zentrale Sekretariat (ἐπιστολογραφεῖον, *epistolographeíon*) und das umfangreiche, oft aus Sklaven und → Eunuchen bestehende Dienstpersonal. Das anfangs meist egalitäre Verhältnis zw. den Königen und ihren »Freunden«, das aus der gemeinsamen Fremdherrschaft über eine indigene Bevölkerung und aus der Konkurrenzsituation zw. den H. resultierte, wurde seit Beginn des 2. Jh. v. Chr. stärker hierarchisiert. Am ptolem. und seleukid., in Ansätzen auch am maked. H. entstand ein System von bis zu acht → Hoftiteln, die die gesamte, mit administrativen Funktionen betraute Oberschicht in eine nach formalisierter Nähe zum Monarchen gegliederte Rangordnung einbanden. Die im Gegenzug erkennbare Heranziehung von Personen niedrigen sozialen Status, z. T. von Eunuchen, in die engste Umgebung der Könige ist als Reaktion auf das zunehmende polit. Eigengewicht der H.-Ges. zu deuten, sichtbar an höf. Parteiungen, oft um einzelne »Freunde«, die zeitweise den Königen selbst zur Gefahr wurden.

C. Prinzipat

Im Unterschied zu den hell. Königshöfen entstand der röm. Kaiser-H. innerhalb einer städtischen Adelsges., deren Hierarchie auf senatorischen Rangklassen basierte. Den räumlichen Rahmen des H.s bildete ein Komplex zweier großräumiger Palastbauten, die im Laufe des 1. Jh. n. Chr. den Palatin (→ Palatinus mons), das vornehmste Wohngebiet Roms, belegten und mit dessen Namen (*palatium*) bezeichnet wurden. Charakteristisch für die soziale Zusammensetzung der H.-Ges. ist, daß die engste Umgebung des Kaisers im 1. Jh., abgesehen von Mitgliedern seiner Familie, weitgehend aus Personen niedrigerer Stellung in der aristokratischen Hierarchie, phasenweise sogar vornehmlich aus kaiserl. Sklaven und → Freigelassenen bestand. Deren auf kaiserlicher Gunst basierende Stellung war häufig mit Positionen in den neuentstandenen höf. Organisationsstrukturen verknüpft. Die ritterlichen Praefekten der Praetorianergarde (→ *praefectus praetorio*), die Leiter der zentralen Sekretariate für Finanzen (*a rationibus*), Korrespondenz (*ab epistulis*) und Bittschriften (*a libellis*), aber auch andere Personen der umfangreichen kaiserl. Palastdienerschaft, etwa Kammerdiener (*cubicularii*), konnten (ähnlich wie die Frauen des Kaiserhauses) zeitweise zu entscheidendem polit. Einfluß und großem Reichtum gelangen. Die am H. stattfindenden Kontakte des Kaisers mit der Mehrzahl der Mitglieder der senatorisch-ritterlichen Aristokratie beschränkten sich anfangs auf die traditionellen Interaktionsformen des aristokratischen Hauses: auf die Morgenbegrüßung (→ *salutatio*) und das abendliche → Gastmahl (*convivium*), die sich jeweils zu umfangreichen, häufig die gesamte Aristokratie einbeziehenden Veranstaltungen ausweiteten, sowie auf die gelegentliche Zuziehung zu einem kaiserlichen Rat (→ *consilium*). Freunde (*amici*, → *amicitia*) des Kaisers waren damit in einer unspezifischen Weise alle (am H. erscheinenden) Mitglieder der senatorisch-ritterlichen Aristokratie, in einem engeren Sinne diejenigen, die in einer näheren Beziehung zu ihm standen. Hierarchisierungen entsprechend den H.-Rangtiteln der hell. Zeit hat es im kaiserzeitlichen Rom nicht gegeben. Vielmehr ging die im Laufe des 2. Jh. feststellbare vorübergehende Integration der führenden Mitglieder der Senatsaristokratie in die tägliche Umgebung der Kaiser einher mit einer Durchsetzung der traditionellen ges. Hierarchie auch am H.

D. Spätantike

Ein entscheidendes Merkmal der spätant. Kaiserhöfe ist ihre räumliche Distanz von der Stadt Rom und die damit verbundene Emanzipation von der dortigen senatorischen Gesellschaft. Mit der Ausbildung neuer Residenzen in Konstantinopel, Mailand, Ravenna und weiteren Städten des Reiches entwickelten sich die frühkaiserzeitl. höf. Organisationsstrukturen zu umfangreichen Zentralen der zivilen und mil. Administration des Reiches, die die traditionellen röm. Magistraturen in ihrer polit. Funktion ersetzten. Ihre Leiter – der für den inneren Bereich des H.s zuständige *praepositus sacri cubiculi*, sodann der *magister officiorum*, der *quaestor sacri palatii*, der *comes sacrarum largitionum*, der *comes rerum privatarum* und die zwei *magistri militum praesentales* – bildeten neben anderen den offiziellen kaiserlichen Rat (→ *consistorium*).

Parallel dazu etablierte sich seit diocletianischer Zeit (um 300 n. Chr.) ein differenziertes H.-Zeremoniell, das z. B. bei der → *adoratio purpurae* oder bei festlichen Banketten stattfand. Es umgab die Kaiser mit einer sakralen Aura, distanzierte sie von ihrer Umgebung und manifestierte zugleich die gegebene ges. Rangordnung am H. Organisatorische Strukturen und zeremonielle Hierarchien wurden dabei konterkariert durch eine informelle, nach kaiserl. Nähe und Gunst strukturierte Hierarchie, sichtbar an der Einflußnahme rivalisierender Gruppierungen auf die kaiserl. Entscheidungen. Die soziale Rekrutierung der engsten kaiserl. Umgebung und der obersten Ämter am H. war durch das weitgehende Fehlen von Personen vornehmer Geburt gekennzeichnet. Die Kämmerer (*cubicularii*), die aufgrund ihrer Funktion die größten Chancen auf kaiserl. Nähe hatten, bestanden fast ausschließlich aus → Eunuchen, ehemaligen Sklaven ausländischer Herkunft. Im Unterschied zur Prinzipatszeit erlangten jedoch die führenden höf. Funktionsträger mit der Bekleidung ihrer Ämter die Aufnahme in die höchsten ges. Rangklassen, was die spätant. Kaiserhöfe zu Orten außergewöhnlicher sozialer Mobilität werden ließ. Der Versuch Constantins [1] d.Gr., eine durch formalisierte Nähe zum Kaiser strukturierte höf. Rangordnung nach *comites primi, secundi* und *tertii ordinis* und damit eine dem späthell. H.-Rangsystem vergleichbare Hierarchisierung der Oberschicht zu etablieren, setzte sich nicht durch. Mit den Ranggesetzen Valentinians I. (372) wurde stattdessen eine modifizierte senatorische Rangordnung nach *clarissimi, spectabiles* und *illustres* bzw. *illustrissimi* als Prinzip der Hierarchie der Oberschicht festgeschrieben (→ Hoftitel C).

E. Rezeption

Die Bedeutung der H. der Ant. für die Ausprägungen höf. Zentren im Europa des MA und der frühen Neuzeit ist noch weitgehend unerforscht. Unmittelbare Kontinuität ant. H.-Haltung läßt sich in Byzanz und bei der päpstlichen Kurie, in Ansätzen auch im Merowingerreich greifen. Versuche eines bewußten Anknüpfens an spätant. Herrschaftssymbolik, zeremonielle Regelungen und höf. Amtsbezeichnungen, wie sie für das fränkisch-dt. Kaisertum des 9. und 11. Jh. oder für it. Renaissancefürsten feststellbar sind, dienten der Herrschaftslegitimation; die adaptierten Formen gingen jedoch einher mit veränderten Inhalten und Funktionen. Kontinuierliche Plausibilität behielten die Topoi ant. H.-Kritik, die in MA und früher Neuzeit häufig zitiert wurden. Entsprechend zeigt ein typologischer Vergleich der ant. mit ma. und frühneuzeitlichen H.en strukturelle Ähnlichkeiten insbes. hinsichtlich der Verlagerung von Macht vom Herrscher auf die in seiner unmittelbaren Umgebung agierenden Personen und bezüglich der daraus resultierenden Kommunikationsstrukturen. Ein Grundproblem der H.e der Ant., die Konkurrenz zwischen Monarch und Aristokratie, läßt sich in ähnlicher Weise nur bei ma. Königshöfen feststellen, sichtbar an der Heranziehung unfreier Ministerialen. Demgegenüber zeichneten sich die europ. H.e im Zeitalter des Absolutismus durch weitgehende Integration des Adels in die Umgebung der Monarchen und damit durch die Möglichkeit der Beeinflussung polit.-sozialer Rangverhältnisse im H.-Zeremoniell aus. Dies deutet darauf hin, daß sich die epochenübergreifenden Gemeinsamkeiten v. a. aus äquivalenten Problemlösungen bei der Organisation monarchischer Großhaushalte und vormoderner Alleinherrschaft erklären lassen, die eine Annahme unmittelbarer Wirkungen nicht erfordert.

→ Adel; Comes, comites; Freundschaft; Herrschaft; Herrscher; Hoftitel; Sklaverei; Verwaltung

A. Allg.: E. Lévy (Hrsg.), Le système palatial en Orient, en Grèce et à Rome, 1987 • A. Winterling (Hrsg.), Ant. H. im Vergleich, 1997.

B. Hell.: Berve 1, 10–84 • E. Bikerman, Institutions des Séleucides, 1938, 31–50 • G. Herman, The Court Society of the Hellenistic Age, in: P. Cartledge u. a. (Hrsg.), Hellenistic Constructs, 1997, 199–224 • L. Mooren, The Aulic Titulature in Ptolemaic Egypt, 1975 • H. H. Schmitt, s. v. H., Kleines Lex. d. Hell., [2]1993, 253–259 • G. Weber, Dichtung und höf. Ges., 1993.

C. Prinzipat: A. Alföldi, Die monarchische Repräsentation im röm. Kaiserreiche, 1970 • Friedländer 1, 33–103 • Mommsen, Staatsrecht 2.2, 833–839 • Saller, 41–78 • A. Wallace-Hadrill, The Imperial Court, CAH 10, [2]1996, 283–308 • A. Winterling, Aula Caesaris, 1999.

D. Spätant.: Hopkins, Conquerors, 172–196 • H. Löhken, Ordines dignitatum, 1982 • O. Treitinger, Die oström. Kaiser- und Reichsidee nach ihrer Gestaltung im höf. Zeremoniell, 1938 • A. Winterling (Hrsg.), Comitatus, 1998.

E. Rezeption: R. A. Müller, Der Fürstenhof in der frühen Neuzeit, 1995 • W. Paravicini, Die ritterlich-höf. Kultur des MA, 1994 • P. E. Schramm, Kaiser, Rom und Renovatio, [3]1962 • P. Schreiner, Charakteristische Aspekte der byz. Hofkultur, in: R. Lauer, H. G. Majer

(Hrsg.), Höf. Kultur in Südosteuropa, 1994, 11–24 • A. WINTERLING, H., in: Ders. (Hrsg.), Antike Höfe im Vergleich, 1997, 11–25 • Ders., Vergleichende Perspektiven, in: Ebd. 151–169. A. WI.

Hofdichtung. Für H. im engeren Sinn ist die Genese an einem Königs- oder Fürstenhof inhaltlich konstitutiv. Der Autor als Teil der (je unterschiedlich konstituierten) höfischen Ges. trägt mit oder ohne expliziten Auftrag zur Herrschaftslegitimation bei, indem er Machtstrukturen lit. überformt oder durch sein bloßes Wirken um eine kulturelle Dimension erweitert. Frühestes Beispiel ist die Nennung der Aineaden in der Ilias, bes. ausgeprägt ist H. bei den griech. Chorlyrikern (→ Pindaros, → Bakchylides, → Simonides) an den Höfen in Sizilien und Griechenland und dann im Hell. (bes. Alexandreia) [1]. Dagegen läßt sich bei lat. Autoren (z.B. → Statius, → Martialis) nur bedingt von H. reden, da sich im Prinzipat republikanische Komponenten erhielten [2]. Griech. Autoren im kaiserzeitl. Rom (z.B. → Krinagoras) dagegen übertragen die Konventionen der H. von den griech. Königshöfen nach Rom.
→ Propaganda

1 G. WEBER, Dichtung und höfische Ges., 1993 (grundlegend) 2 E. FANTHAM, Lit. Leben im ant. Rom, 1998. U. SCH.

Hofrangwesen s. Hof, s. Hoftitel

Hoftitel A. VORGÄNGER IM ALTEN ORIENT B. HELLENISMUS C. RÖMISCHES REICH UND SPÄTANTIKE D. BYZANZ

A. VORGÄNGER IM ALTEN ORIENT

H. und Hofrangwesen der Ant. sind zur Bezeichnung und Herstellung persönl. Nähe von Mitgliedern der Hofgesellschaft zum → Herrscher bzw. zur hierarch. Ranggliederung der an der Verwaltung beteiligten Oberschicht eine Folge der Entstehung territorialer Monarchien seit Alexandros [4] d.Gr. und der damit verbundenen Organisation von Höfen (→ Hof) als Zentren polit. Herrschaft. Die Frage nach altoriental. Vorgängern und Vorbildern für die H. der Ant. muß anhand der beiden wesentlichsten Eigenschaften des Hofrangwesens in den unmittelbaren Nachfolgern altoriental. Reiche, d.h. in den hell. Monarchien, beantwortet werden: H. sind nicht an Ämter gebunden; Hofrang und H. einer Person enden mit dem Tod ihres Verleihers. Unter diesen Prämissen scheiden nach h. Forschungsstand die vorhell. Monarchien im mesopot.-syrischen Raum als Vorbilder aus, da hier Titel und Amt gekoppelt erscheinen und z.B. an der Tafel des Assyrerkönigs nur Amtsinhaber Platz finden. Im Perserreich der → Achaimenidai sind zahlreiche Titel üblich. Einige gleichen oder ähneln den hell. H., doch bezeichnet »Verwandte des Königs « wirkliche, nicht fiktive Verwandte [1] des Perserkönigs, und Titel sind im Sinne eines Dienstadels stets mit Ämtern und Funktionen verbunden. Achäm. Vorbilder für die Organisation von griech. Tyrannenhöfen in archa. und klass. Zeit (vgl. Plat. epist. 7,334c, wo *phíloi* (»Freunde«) und *syngeneís* (»Verwandte«) des Dion [I 1] von Syrakus erwähnt werden) sind möglich (so [2]), aber nicht zwingend, da diese Erscheinungen auch als bloße Elementarparallelen gedeutet werden können.

Hingegen wird bereits im Alten Reich des pharaonischen Ägypten eine Tendenz stark, nicht nur ein Rang- und Titelwesen zu entwickeln, das die Nähe zum Herrscher differenziert, sondern auch das Amt zugunsten des Titels zu entwerten und Funktionen und Kompetenzen an Titel statt an Ämter zu binden. Der Rückgang der erreichten feinen Differenzierung unter den Titeln bzw. Rängen ab der 12. Dynastie führt zu einer für alle Höflinge gleichen Rangtitelkette, die daher nicht zur Bezeichnung konkreter Ämter geeignet ist. Reine Rangbezeichnungen kennt noch das unter persischer Herrschaft stehende Ägypten [3]. Diese haben aber wohl nicht als Vorbilder für die ptolem. H. gedient.

1 J.-D. GAUGER, Zu einem offenen Problem des hell. Hoftitelsystems, in: FS J. Straub, 1977, 137–158
2 V. FADINGER, Griech. Tyrannis und Alter Orient, in: K. RAAFLAUB (Hrsg.), Anfänge polit. Denkens in der Antike, 1993, 263–316 3 W. HUSS, Ägyptische Kollaborateure in persischer Zeit, in: Tyche 12, 1997, 131–143.

W. HELCK, Untersuchungen zu den Beamtentiteln des ägyptischen Alten Reiches, 1954 • Ders., Zur Verwaltung des Mittleren und Neuen Reiches, 1958, 281 ff. • W. KLAUBER, Assyrisches Beamtentum nach Briefen aus der Sargonidenzeit, 1910 • LÄ 2, s.v. Hofrang, 1237; 5, s.v. Rang, 146 f.; 6, s.v. Wedelträger, 1161–63 • J. RENGER, s.v. Hofstaat, RLA 4, 435–446 • J. WIESEHÖFER, Das antike Persien, 1993. A. ME.

B. HELLENISMUS
1. ALLGEMEIN 2. PTOLEMÄISCHES ÄGYPTEN
3. SELEUKIDENREICH

1. ALLGEMEIN

Die hell. H. der Antigoniden (→ Antigonos) in Makedonien, der Attaliden (→ Attalos) von Pergamon, der Ptolemäer (→ Ptolemaios) und Seleukiden (→ Seleukos) knüpften an das Vorbild des Alexanderreiches an; Bezeichnungen wie φίλος (*phílos*, »Freund«), σωματοφύλαξ (*sōmatophýlax*, »Leibwächter«) und συγγενής (*syngenḗs*, »Verwandter«) haben daher anfangs und weit in das 3. Jh. v. Chr. hinein einen realen Hintergrund in den Nahbeziehungen zum Monarchen. Die Titel konnten widerrufen werden und waren prinzipiell nicht erblich, doch konnte persönl. Umgang *de facto* weitere Mitglieder einer Familie in die nächste Umgebung des Königs bringen. Durch Morgengruß, Tischgesellschaft und Reisebegleitung entstand polit. Einfluß und die Verwendung bei polit., mil. und diplomat. Aufgaben. Die Entwicklung in den hell. Reichen verlief nicht gleichförmig, da etwa den maked. Antigoniden die einheimische Aristokratie zur Verfügung stand, die von den anderen Herrschern nicht herangezogen wurde. Auch die an der Wende vom 3. zum 2. Jh. v. Chr. bei Ptolemäern und Seleukiden sichtbare Formalisierung der H. läßt sich bei Antigoniden und Attaliden nicht in gleicher Weise beobachten.

2. Ptolemäisches Ägypten

Im ptolem. Ägypten blieben – wie in allen Nachfolgestaaten des Alexanderreiches – die H. während des 3. Jh. prinzipiell Individualtitel, obwohl die Beibehaltung der Titel während der Abwesenheit vom Hof bereits einen ersten Schritt zur Verbindung von H. und Amt darstellte. Erst unter Ptolemaios V. wurden wohl mit einem einzigen Verwaltungsakt H. als Klassenbezeichnungen für Beamtengruppen eingeführt und die Ämter mit den H. in Beziehung gesetzt (vor 197/4 v. Chr.). Die Zugehörigkeit zu einer Gruppe rückte in den Vordergrund, ersichtlich im Gebrauch des genitivus partitivus (τῶν φίλων, *tōn phílōn*, besagt, daß der Titelträger zur »Gruppe der Freunde« gehörte). Sechs Titel sind belegt bzw. anzunehmen (Rangordnung von unten): τῶν διαδόχων (*tōn diadóchōn*), ἀρχισωματοφύλαξ (*archisōmatophýlax*), τῶν φίλων (*tōn phílōn*, τῶν πρώτων φίλων (*tōn prṓtōn phílōn*), τῶν σωματοφυλάκων (*tōn sōmatophylákōn*), συγγενής (*syngenḗs*). Dieses System von H. festigte in der schwierigen Situation unter Ptolemaios V., der als Kind auf den Thron kam, die Beziehung zu den Beamten, weil sie einerseits durch ihre Amtsführung in ein (fiktives, aber benanntes) Nahverhältnis zum König gerieten und damit enger an ihn gebunden wurden, andererseits ihr Prestige und ihre Autorität im Lande angehoben wurde. Zudem bildete das System der H. auch eine Art Schutzschild für die Vormünder des Königs.

Die Differenzierung der H. schritt weiter fort. 155 v. Chr. findet sich auch der H. »aus der Gruppe der Erzleibwächter« (*tōn archisōmatophylákōn*), vor 140 erscheint der H. »aus der Gruppe der Gleichrangigen mit den Freunden Erster Klasse« (*tōn isotímōn tois prṓtois phílois*) und um 120 der eines »aus der Gruppe der Gleichrangigen mit den Verwandten« (*tōn homotímōn tois syngenésin*). Die Rangfolge im ausgebauten System lautete wohl (von oben): »Verwandter«, »gleichrangig mit Verwandten«, »Freunde Erster Klasse«, »gleichrangig mit Freunden Erster Klasse«, »Erzleibwächter«, »Freunde«, »Diadochen«, »Leibwächter«. Zu Hofrangabzeichen gibt es keine gesicherte Überlieferung, doch ist ihr Gebrauch entsprechend den anderen Monarchien anzunehmen (siehe aber GVI 1152,25 f.; 1508,9 f. mit [1. 446 A. 2]). H. können auch mit Anreden kombiniert werden (der »Verwandte« als »Bruder«, *adelphós*).

Die veränderte Struktur der Titel weist auf ihre zunehmende Entwertung, der man zuerst mit einer weiteren Differenzierung des Systems, dann aber mit der Reduktion auf die drei höchsten Titel zu begegnen suchte; denn nicht viel später verschwinden die meisten dieser Titel wieder: Im 1. Jh. v. Chr. gab es nur noch die H. der »Verwandten«, der »Gleichrangigen mit Verwandten« und der »Freunde Erster Klasse«.

Das Streben nach Titeln führte schließlich zur Nivellierung, da immer niedrigere Beamtenstufen mit höheren Titeln bedacht wurden (die Entwicklung in Äg. scheint hier rascher und konsequenter verlaufen zu sein als in den äußeren Besitzungen der Ptolemäer). Mit dem Ansteigen der H. der unteren Chargen mußten aber auch die H. ihrer Vorgesetzten erhöht werden (157/6 und 135/4 sind wichtige Einschnitte).

Mit den H.n ging eine Differenzierung des Beamtenapparates einher. Gerade bei den Strategen (στρατηγοί) wird deutlich, daß Umfang und Bedeutung des Verwaltungsbezirkes den Grad des H.s bestimmten. Mit dem Aufgabenbereich veränderte sich auch der H., so daß sich Beförderungen an den Titeln ablesen lassen. Die höchsten Ämter (und damit H.) hatten die Epistrategen (ἐπιστρατηγοί) und der Statthalter Zyperns inne, bei denen mil. Funktionen mit der zivilen Aufsicht über mehrere Gaue verbunden waren.

1 L. Robert, Noms indigènes, 1963.

Chr. Habicht, Die herrschende Ges. in den hell. Monarchien, in: Vierteljahresschrift für Sozial- und Wirtschaftsgesch. 45, 1958, 1 ff. • L. Mooren, in: Proc. XIVth Int. Congress of Papyrologists, 1974, 233 ff. • Ders., The Aulic Titulature in Ptolemaic Egypt, 1975 • Ders., La hiérarchie de cour ptolémaique, 1977 • M. Trindl, Ehrentitel im Ptolemäerreich, Diss. 1942.

W.A.

3. Seleukidenreich

Das Titel- und Rangwesen am Seleukidenhof wurde bürokratisch verwaltet (1 Makk 10,65). In den oberen Rängen drückten die H. wie im hell. Ägypten (fiktive) Verwandtschaftsbeziehungen aus: Der »Verwandte« (*syngenḗs*) und der »Mitaufgezogene« (*sýntrophos*: MAMA 3,62) wurde vom König als »Bruder« (*adelphós*) angeredet (2 Makk 11,22). In den unteren Rängen wurden Grade der persönl. Nähe zum König benannt: »Freunde Ersten Ranges« (*prṓtoi phíloi*), »Geschätzte Freunde« (*timṓmenoi phíloi*) und »Freunde« (*phíloi*) (OGIS 255; 256; Welles 45; 1 Makk 10,20 mit 65); die dem Gesamtrang der »Freunde« Angehörenden bildeten ein Korps (Pol. 30,25 (31,3),7; vgl. 30,26 (31,4),9). Das Durchlaufen der Rangstufen vom »Freund« bis zum »Verwandten« war möglich (1 Makk 10,20; 65; 89). Die Verbindung von Titeln mit Attributen (Purpurgewand, Goldschmuck, goldenes Eß- und Trinkgeschirr) erscheint in der diesbezügl. Hauptquelle (1 Makk 10,20; 62–65; 89; 11,57 f.) nicht eindeutig. Offen muß auch bleiben, inwieweit die im Vergleich zum Ptolemäerreich eher lockere Struktur des Seleukidenreiches dessen Titel- und Rangwesen geprägt hat, und ob die (nur ein Mal belegte) Vergabe eines griech. Personennamens durch den König an einen Nichtgriechen auch dazu gehörte [1. 150, vgl. 132].

Der Verleihung eines H. konnten Gaben an den Titelgeber vorausgehen (1 Makk 11,24–27; vgl. 13,34 ff.); sie konnte kombiniert sein mit der Beschenkung bzw. Belehnung des Erhöhten oder mit dessen Einsetzung in ein Amt (1 Makk 2,18; 10, 20; 65; 89; 11,26 f.; 57). Titel, Attribute und materielle Beigaben waren nicht erblich, sie konnten vom Geber zurückgenommen werden und bedurften wie sonstige Privilegien der Bestätigung durch Nachfolger (1 Makk 10–11; 2 Makk 4,38). Obwohl ein H. nicht Voraussetzung für die Teilnahme am Hofleben war (Athen. 155b), bildeten die Titelträger doch den Kern der Hofges., warteten dem König auf, lebten mit ihm zusammen und berieten ihn in Frieden und Krieg (Pol. 5,56,10; 83,1; 8,21,1; 29,27; Diod. 34,1; 16; Ios. ant. Iud. 12,263); sie konnten aber auch fern vom Hof eine Aufgabe der Reichsverwaltung erfüllen, ein mil. Kommando gegen einen Feind erhalten oder gar eine mit dem Titelgeber locker verbundene, aber *de facto* selbständige Herrschaft ausüben (1 Makk 10–11). In Krisensituationen konnte sich das persönl. Geschick von Titelträgern mit dem Schicksal des Gebers verknüpfen (OGIS 219,15; Liv. per. 50; Ios. ant. Iud. 13,368).

1 S. Sherwin-White, A. Kuhrt, From Samarkhand to Sardis, 1993.

E. Bikerman, Institutions des Séleucides, 1938, 40–50.

A. ME.

C. Römisches Reich und Spätantike

Schon in republikan. Zeit konnte *titulus* hohe Amtsstellungen (etwa *t. consulatus*: Cic. Pis. 9,19) und generell ehrenhaften Status und erworbene Verdienste (z. B. *perpetrati belli t.*: Liv. 28,41,3) bezeichnen. Mit Beginn der Kaiserzeit entstand neben dem republikanischen → *cursus honorum* und den Statusrechten des Senatoren- oder Ritterstandes ein »höfisches« System ehrenhafter Hofdienste und Auszeichnungen. Es faßte sowohl Angehörige der kaiserlichen *familia* im privatrechtlichen Sinne als auch die den Kaiser ständig umgebenden Amtspersonen, sei es des Ritter-, sei es des Senatorenstandes, in einer im Laufe der Zeit vielfältig gegliederten Hoffunktionärs- oder Dienerschaft. Das Muster der hell. Königshöfe und ihr Zeremonienwesen wurden dabei nachgeahmt; so bei einem aus Ehrengründen gestuften Kreis der Freunde (*amici*), Berater und engen Gefolgschaftsangehörigen (*consiliarii*, später *consistoriani*, *comites*, → *comes*, entsprechend *hetaíroi*, *hepómenoi*). Anders als im Hell. war es aber im röm. Prinzipatskaisertum nötig, das System höfischer Ämter, Ehren- und Vertrauensstellungen auf ein fortbestehendes System »republikanischer« Rangklassen (*senatores*, *equites*) und Ämter (*cursus honorum*) abzustimmen. Dies geschah a) durch titulare Gleichstellung der i.e.S. kaiserl. Verwaltungsfunktionäre mit traditionell-republikanischen Beamten (der *legatus pro consule* eines kaiserlichen Provinzverwalters entsprach im Range dem *proconsul* einer Senatsprovinz), b) durch kaiserl. Erhebung höfischer Funktionäre in den Ritter- bzw. in den Senatorenstand, oft nach einem nur ehrenhalber und kurz ausgeübten entsprechenden republikan. Amt und c) – mit Beginn des → »Dominats« – durch Schaffung einer einheitlichen Ordnung der öffentl. Ämter und Würden (*ordo dignitatum*), wobei der → Hof als Zentrum aller staatlichen Tätigkeit und somit als Quelle auch aller Anerkennung polit. Leistungen oder Geltungsansprüche begriffen wurde.

Diese spätant. Ordnung fand in vielfältigen gesetzlichen Regelungen und zusammenhängend etwa im Codex Theodosianus des 4. Jh. (B. 6) sowie im → Codex Iustinianus (B. 12) auch rechtlichen Ausdruck. Seit der Regierung Constantinus' I. im 4. Jh. gab es dabei einmal eine Ordnung der *comites* des Kaisers, die zahlreiche Reichsämter erfaßte und zugleich drei Rangstufen enthielt (Eus. vita Const. 4,1); sie bestand in vielem auch später fort. Ein weiteres Element war der von Constantin zum Zweck einer außerordentlichen, höchsten Ehrung aktualisierte Titel eines *patricius* (Zos. 2,40). Zu den hauptsächlichen, im ganzen kontinuierlichen Elementen gehörten aber die drei Haupt-Rangklassen des fortbestehenden, wenn auch funktionell veränderten senatorischen Standes (*illustres*, *spectabiles*, *clari*) sowie eine Schichtung von *dignitates* (»Würden«) unter ihnen, innerhalb deren die *perfectissimi* an der Spitze stehen, gefolgt von anderen Stufen bis hin zu der eines einfachen *egregius* innerhalb eines formell fortbestehenden *ordo equester* (Cod. Iust. 12,31).

Innerhalb der *illustres* wurde seit ca. 400 folgendermaßen gestuft: An der Spitze standen die tätigen Amtsinhaber der ersten senatorischen Rangklasse (*in actu positi illustres*), gefolgt von den zum kaiserlichen Gefolge gehörenden amtlosen *illustres* (= *i.*) mit dem Zeichen eines höheren Amtes (*cingulum*), den nicht an den Hof berufenen *i.* mit *cingulum*, den am Hofe anwesenden *i.* ohne *cingulum* und den vom Hofe abwesenden *i.* ohne *cingulum*. Amtsinhaber (*administratores*) und sogar Amtlose, aber mit mil. oder zivilen Aufgaben Betraute gingen im Rang den Inhabern reiner Ehrenstellungen (*honorarii*) stets vor (Cod. Iust. 12,8,2). Die darin erkennbaren Rangkriterien »Handlungsmacht« und »Nähe zum Hof« gab es aber auch schon früher. Zur ersten senatorischen Rangklasse gehörten seit den diocletianisch-constantinischen Reichsreformen (E. des 3. bis Anf. des 4. Jh. n. Chr.) in jedem Reichsteil etwa 20 der höchsten aktiven zivilen und mil. Reichsbeamten. Zu den *spectabiles* zählten vor allem die Ratgeber des Kaisers, viele Vertreter der höchsten Reichsbeamten oder die Vorsteher der Hofkanzleien. Der dritten Rangstufe der »einfachen« Senatoren sind überwiegend die Provinzverwalter zuzurechnen. Alle nachgeordneten Amtsfunktionen eines höheren Dienstes am kaiserlichen Hof pflegten mit Angehörigen nicht-senatorischer *dignitates* besetzt zu sein. Das System der H. verband sich mit einem differenzierten Privilegienwesen (abgestufte Befreiungen von den gesetzl. → *munera*, gerichtl. Sonderbehandlung, materielle Zuwendungen und öffentl. Ehrungen verschiedener Art; vgl. im einzelnen: Cod. Iust. 1,28 ff. und 12,1 ff.).

→ Illustris vir

1 Alföldi 2 Jones, LRE, 366 ff., 411 ff., 607 ff.
3 A. Winterling (Hrsg.), Ant. Höfe im Vergleich, 1997
4 H. Löhken, Ordines Dignitatum, 1982 5 R. Scharf, Comites und comitiva primi ordinis, 1994 6 W. Heul, Der constantinische Prinzipat, 1966.

C. G.

D. Byzanz

H. sind wie in der Ant. auch im byz. Reich (4.–15. Jh. n. Chr.) im Gegensatz zum Amt als reine Ehrung zu verstehen, die an keine bestimmte Tätigkeit oder Funktion gebunden war. Doch bestand auch hier zwischen Titel und Amtsbezeichnung nicht in allen Fällen eine deutliche Grenze.

Das urspr. Cognomen *Caesar* (Καῖσαρ, *Kaísar*) wurde zunächst zu einem Bestandteil der Kaisertitulatur; im diocletianischen System der → Tetrarchie ab 293 n. Chr. bezeichnete es die beiden »Unterkaiser« in Ost und West. Nach 550 wurde es als höchster H. für kaiserl. Mitregenten bzw. designierte Thronfolger, in der Regel Kaisersöhne, verwendet [1. 363].

Von → Constantinus [1] I. wurde in Anknüpfung an den röm. Patriziat der vom Kaiser frei verleihbare hochrangige H. *patricius* (πατρίκιος) geschaffen, der bis ins 11. Jh. überdauerte [3. 1600].

In der Spätantike bezeichneten die Titel *illustris* (ἰλλούστριος), *spectabilis* (περίβλεπτος, *períbleptos*) und *clarus* bzw. *clarissimus* (λαμπρότατος, *lamprótatos*) die drei Rangklassen des Senatorenstandes. Angehörige der kaiserlichen Familie trugen seit Constantinus [1] I. häufig den Titel *nobilissimus*, der in späteren Jh. allgemein als hochrangiger H. (νωβελίσσιμος) verwendet wurde [3. 1489 f.].

An das relativ subalterne Amt der *cura palatii* (zuständig für das Palastgebäude) knüpfte der H. κουροπαλάτης (*kuropalátēs*) an, den erstmals → Iustinianus I. seinem Neffen und späteren Nachfolger Iustinus II. verlieh [2. 1157].

Erst längere Zeit nach dem Erlöschen des hohen Amtes *magister officiorum* wurde der rein byz. H. μάγιστρος (*mágistros*) geschaffen, der ab dem 9. Jh. sicher bezeugt ist [2. 1267].

Das bereits in der Kaiserzeit de facto zu einem Ehrentitel degradierte Konsulat erscheint in Byzanz als der H. → *hýpatos* (ὕπατος, mit den höheren Rängen δισύπατος, *dishypatos* und ἀνθύπατος, *anthýpatos*).

Im → *Kletorologion* des Philotheos, einem Handbuch der Hofetikette von 899 n. Chr. [3. 1661 f.], wird für die oben behandelten H. die nachstehende Rangfolge angegeben (von oben): *kaísar, nōbelíssimos, kuropalátēs, mágistros, anthýpatos, patríkios, dísypatos, hýpatos*. Hier werden auch die spezifischen Insignien (βραβεῖα, *brabeía*) beschrieben, die bei der Verleihung überreicht wurden.

1 ODB 1 **2** ODB 2 **3** ODB 3.

ODB 1, 623 • R. Guilland, Titres et fonctions de l'Empire byzantin, 1976 • W. Heil, Der konstantinische Patriziat, 1966 • N. Oikonomidès, Les listes de préséance byzantines des IXe et Xe siècles, 1972 • Stein, Spätröm. R. I–II • F. Winkelmann, Byz. Rang- und Ämterstruktur im 8. und 9. Jh., 1985.

F. T.

Hohlmaße

I. Alter Orient II. Ägypten III. Griechenland IV. Rom

I. Alter Orient

Mit H. wurden neben Flüssigkeiten v. a. Getreide und andere Schüttgüter (Datteln usw.) gemessen. Dementsprechend werden H. insbesondere in der Administration von Getreide, darunter der Ausgabe von Rationen, eingesetzt. Die üblichen Maßgefäße (besonders *Sea*) sind nach keilschriftl. Quellen aus Holz. Eigene H. für Flüssigkeiten sind nur lokal begrenzt feststellbar; ein Standard-»Gefäß« enthält dabei meist 20 oder 30 Liter. In Mesopot. darf man trotz aller zeitlichen und lokalen Unterschiede beim H.-System vielleicht von einer relativ konstanten absoluten Größe der kleinen Einheit sumer. SÌLA, akkad. *qû* »Liter« = ca. 0,8–1,0 Liter ausgehen. In Babylonien wird von den ersten Zeugnissen (um 3000 v. Chr.) an das Verhältnis zwischen den Maßeinheiten meist durch die Faktoren 5 oder 10, aber auch durch den Faktor 6 bestimmt, der eine leichte Teilbarkeit ermöglicht. Fest steht dabei die Relation 6 BAN/*sutu*, »Sea« = 1 BARIGA/*parsiktu*, »Scheffel«, das gewissermaßen das Grundmaß jedes Systems darstellt. Je nach Periode ist 1 Sea = 10 oder 6 Liter. Das große H. ist das *Kor* zu 4 (im 3. Jt., 144 oder 240 l) oder 5 »Scheffel« (300 l im späten 3. und in der 1. H. des 2. Jt., 180 l im 1. Jt.).

Ein Bezug zwischen H. und Mine (→ Gewichte) scheint (auf der Grundlage von Gerste) bestanden zu haben (TUAT Bd. 1, 19:144–6; 21. Jh. v. Chr.). In Nord-Mesopot. (der syr. Ǧazīra, Assyrien) gilt regelmäßig: 10 Sea = 1 *imēru* »Eselslast«; dabei ist 1 Sea = 10, auch 8 oder 9 Liter (ein dezimales System ist in Syrien schon im 3. Jt. belegt). Im spätbrz. NW-Syrien (→ Ugarit, Alalaḫ) und in hethit. Texten wird das *parīsu* als übliches, dem babylon. *parsiktu* entsprechendes H. verwendet. Ugarit kennt daneben in keilalphabetischen Texten ein H. *dd* (»Sack«?). Das H.-System in hethit. Texten beruht auf den Verhältniszahlen 2, 4 und 6 mit dem *parīsu* als höchstem H. [1. 522 ff.]. Für Palästina im 1. Jt. liegt nur das AT als Quelle vor, wo sich ein dezimales (»assyrisches«) (1 *Chomer* »Eselslast« = 10 *ʾepah* = 100 *ʾomer*) und ein »babylonisches« H.-System (1 *kor* = 30 *seʾah* = 180 *qab*) erkennen lassen [2. Bd. 1,320–26].

1 M. A. Powell, Th. van den Hout, s. v. Maße und Gewichte, RLA 7, 492–530 **2** R. de Vaux, Die Lebensordnungen des AT, [2]1964.

WA. SA.

II. Ägypten

Das geläufigste äg. H. basiert, wohl schon seit dem AR [2], auf der Einheit *Heqat* (ca. 4,8 l). Zehn *Heqat* bezeichnet man in der älteren Zeit als »Sack« (*Char*, ca. 48 l). Es sind Doppel- und Vierfach-*Heqat* (»großes Maß«) belegt, von denen 10 bzw. 5 einen (Doppel-) »Sack« von ca. 96 l ergeben. Im NR beinhaltet ein Sack 4 *Oipe*, d. h. 4 Vierfach-*Heqat* (ca. 76,8 l); die Relationen gründen nun auf dem Faktor 4. Gemessen werden mit diesem H. v. a. Getreide, aber auch Früchte, Mineralien und Pigmente. Ein *Heqat* besteht aus 10 → *Hin*, ein H., das auch für Flüssigkeiten verwendet wurde. Seit dem 5. Jh. v. Chr. ist die → *Artabe* (belegt in verschiedenen Größen, wohl meist ca. 32 l) ein urspr. pers. Maß, anstelle des »Sacks« das größte Trocken-H. Daneben sind zahlreiche Gefäße als H. für flüssige und trockene Substanzen belegt, deren Normgröße nicht sicher zu erschließen ist.

1 W. Helck, S. Vleeming, s. v. Maße und Gewichte, LÄ 3, 1201–1205 und 1210–1211 2 P. Posener-Kriéger, Les mesures de grain, in: C. Eyre u. a. (Hrsg.), The Unbroken Reed, GS A. F. Shore, 1994, 269–271.

HE. FE.

III. Griechenland

Bei den Griechen sind Maße für Trockenes (Getreide, Früchte – μέτρα ξηρά) und Maße für Flüssiges (Wein, Öl – μέτρα ὑγρά) zu unterscheiden. Sie besitzen durch die Ableitung von geläufigen Größen (Krug, Kanne bzw. Korb, Sack o.ä.) sowie durch Form und Material der verwendeten Gefäße unterschiedliche Bezeichnungen, die nur in den kleinsten Werten gemeinsam sind. Ihre Normierung ist im Rahmen der Solon. Reform erfolgt (um 600 v. Chr.). Je nach Landschaft, Ort und Zeit sowie in der Ableitung aus bestimmten Gewichtssystemen weisen die H. unterschiedliche Werte auf, ebenso sind die absoluten Größen z. T. strittig. An Maßen für Trockenes [1. 104–107] finden sich: → Medimnos (ca. 52,53 l) = 6 → Hekteis (ca. 8,75 l) = 48 → Choinikes (ca. 1,09 l) = 96 → Xestai (ca. 0,54 l) = 192 → Kotylai (ca. 0,27 l); an Maßen für Flüssiges [1. 101–104]: → Metretes (ca. 39,39 l) = 12 Choes (→ Chus, ca. 3,28 l) = 72 → Xestai (ca. 0,54 l) = 144 → Kotylai (ca. 0,27 l) = 576 → Oxybapha (ca. 0,07 l) = 866 → Kyathoi (ca. 0,04 l). Die angegebenen Umrechnungen entsprechen dem weiträumig verbreiteten att. Standard [1. 505, 703 Tab. X], wobei regionale Sonderformen (→ Kypros) sowie örtliche und zeitliche Abweichungen [1. 102] nicht berücksichtigt sind. Für den von Hultsch [1. 501–505] angenommenen, bis zu 40 % von der Norm abweichenden äginet. Standard konnte bislang kein arch. Belegmaterial nachgewiesen werden [4. 28 Anm. 84].

Maßgefäße sind in größerem Umfang v. a. aus Athen [2. 39–45] und Olympia [4. 28 Anm. 84] bekannt, wobei als frühestes Stück eine argivische Vase aus dem späten 8. oder frühen 7. Jh. v. Chr. angesehen wird [3. 465]. Bei den Trockenmaßen überwiegen Gefäße mit zylindrischer Form, die mit den Aufschriften μέτρον (*métron*) oder δημόσιον (*dēmósion*) versehen sind und in Athen als staatliche Garantie ein Siegel mit Athenakopf und Eule tragen [3. 467 f. und Abb. 111–112]. Bei den Maßgefäßen (→ Eichung) für Flüssiges handelt es sich in der Regel um Olpen, Oinochoen oder Amphoren, die ebenfalls mit entsprechender Inschr. und Siegel versehen sind [3. 467]. Die Funde zahlreicher Maßgefäße aus hell. Zeit im Bereich des Tholos auf der athen. Agora lassen dort einen Maßtisch mit Mustermaßen (σηκώματα/*sēkṓmata*) vermuten [3. 469]. Derartige Steintische mit unterschiedlich großen Aushöhlungen zur Aufnahme metallener Mustermaße sind aus Chios, Delos und Thasos [3. 471 und Abb. 113] bekannt. Ein aus dem 2. Jh. n. Chr. stammender Maßtisch aus Gythion in Lakonien enthält fünf Aushöhlungen für die Maßeinheiten Modios, Chus, Kotyle und Hemihekteus sowie ein weiteres, unleserliches Maß [3. 472].

IV. Rom

Die röm. Hohlmaße stehen nach den Namen, den Werten und ihrer Staffelung in engem Zusammenhang mit dem griech. System. Standardmaß für Trockenes ist der → Modius (ca. 8,75 l) = 2 Semodii (ca. 4,37 l) = 16 → Sextarii (ca. 0,54 l) = 32 → Heminae (ca. 0,27 l) = 64 → Quartarii (ca. 0,13 l) = 128 → Acetabula (ca. 0,06 l). Als Großmaß ist bei Plaut. Men. Prolog 14 das der → Amphora entsprechende Trimodium (ca. 26,26 l) erwähnt. Hauptmaß für Flüssiges ist die Amphora (ca. 26,26 l) oder das → Quadrantal = 2 → Urnae (ca. 13,13 l) = 8 → Congii (ca. 3,28 l) = 48 Sextarii (ca. 0,54 l) = 96 Heminae (ca. 0,27 l) = 192 Quartarii (ca. 0,13 l) = 384 Acetabula (ca. 0,06 l) = 576 → Kyathi (ca. 0,04 l). Kleinste Einheit ist das → Cochlear (ca. 0,011 l) = ¼ Cyathus = 1/48 Sextarius [1. 112–126, 704 Tab. XI], das auch als Medizinermaß Verwendung fand (vgl. Tab. zu → Cochlear). Als Großeinheit existiert der hauptsächlich als Maß für Weinfässer verwandte → Culleus (ca. 525,2 l) = 20 Amphorae. Die Umrechnungen auf absolute Größen weichen bei den Metrologen geringfügig nach oben bzw. unten ab. So rechnet [1] den Modius zu 8,754 l und die Amphora zu 26,26 l [1. 703 Tab. XI], [5] zu 8,733 l bzw. 26,196 l [5. 844 Tab. XII] und [6. 94 Beiblatt I] zu 8,697 bzw. 26,092 l. Die von [6] erschlossenen speziellen Maße für Öl sind strittig.

Maßgefäße ohne und mit Inschr. (ILS 8627–8628) sind wie aus dem griech. Kulturkreis bekannt, wobei vornehmlich der zylinderförmige Modius ein auf kaiserzeitlichen Münzen im Kontext der stadtröm. Getreideversorgung (→ Cura annonae) weit verbreitetes Motiv ist. Bildliche Darstellungen von Modii finden sich ferner auf Grabsteinen von Angehörigen der Berufsgruppen Bäckerei und Getreidehandel [7. 24]. Die Eichtische mit ihren Aushöhlungen zur Aufnahme metallener Mustermaße (→ Eichung, → Ponderarium) entsprechen den aus Griechenland bekannten Formen. Ein Beispiel für einen solchen Maßtisch befindet sich am Rande des Forums von Pompeji (CIL X 793). Vornehmlich in der Spätant. begegnen Sonderformen (Modius castrensis), die in ihren Standards stark umstritten sind.

→ Hohl- und Längenmasse

1 F. Hultsch, Griech. und röm. Metrologie, ²1882
2 M. Lang, M. Crosby, The Athenian Agora 10. Weights, Measures and Tokens, 1964 3 M. Guarducci, Epigrafia Greca 2, 1969 4 H. Büsing, Metrologische Beiträge, in: JDAI 97, 1982, 1–45 5 H. Nissen, Griech. und röm. Metrologie, HbdA I² 6 A. Oxé, in: BJ 147, 1942

7 G. ZIMMER, Röm. Berufsdarstellungen, 1982
8 H. CHANTRAINE s. v. H., KlP 2, 1198 f. 9 LAW, s. v. Maße und Gewichte, 3422–3426 10 D. P. S. PEACOCK, D. F. WILLIAMS, Amphorae and the Roman Economy, 1986 11 R. F. DOCTER, Amphorae Capacities and Archaic Levantine Trade, Hamburger Beitr. zur Arch. 15/17, 1988/1990, 143–188 12 N. SPICHTIG, P. KAMBER, Zur Berechnung und Interpretation von Gefäßvolumina, Jb. der Schweizerischen Ges. für Urgesch. 74, 1991, 226–228.

H.-J.S.

Holofernes. Eine der wichtigsten Figuren des wahrscheinlich in der Makkabäerzeit abgefaßten Buches → Judith, einer apokryphen jüd. Schrift, deren Inhalt histor. als nicht gesichert gilt. H., Feldherr → Nebukadnezars, beabsichtigt, während einer Strafexpedition die Juden zu vernichten. Dieser Plan wird durch Judith (hebr. »Jüdin«) vereitelt, indem sie H.' Vertrauen gewinnt, mit ihm speist und ihn anschließend enthauptet.

Dieser Haupterzählstrang des Judith-Buches wurde vielfach wieder aufgegriffen, so auch in Parallelerzählungen in der Midrasch-Lit.

S. DUBNOW, Weltgesch. des jüdischen Volkes 2, 1925, 208 f. • E. HAAG, Studien zum Buche Judith: seine theologische Bed. und lit. Eigenart, 1963 • E. ZENGER, Das Buch Judit: histor. und legendarische Erzählungen, 1981.

Y.D.

Holunder. In Europa kommen aus der Familie der Caprifoliaceae zwei Sträucher der Gattung Sambucus vor, nämlich der schwarze H. (Sambucus nigra L., *sa(m)bucus*, ἀκτῆ) und der rotfrüchtige Trauben-H. (Sambucus racemosa L.; Verg. ecl. 10,27: Pan sei rot durch die Beeren des *ebulum*, eine laut Serv. z. St. vergleichbare Pflanze). Eine dritte Art ist der krautige schwarzfrüchtige Attich (Sambucus ebulus L., *ebulus/um*, χαμαιάκτη bei Dioskurides 4,173,2 WELLMANN = 4,172 BERENDES; Plin. nat. 24,51: *chamaeactis* oder *helion acte*). Eine gute Beschreibung der Arten liefert Theophr. h. plant. 3,13,4–6.

Ihre medizinische Verwendung (Dioskurides, ebd.; Plin. nat. 24,52) war umfangreich: Die Wurzeln und die Rinde wurden als Abführ- und Brechmittel empfohlen. Die Blätter, in Wein getrunken, sollten gegen Schlangenbisse helfen und, auf entzündete Wunden gelegt, kühlend wirken. Die Beeren galten als harntreibend und dienten zum (Schwarz-)Färben des Haares. Das Mark (*medulla*) des Stengels wurde zum Verschließen von Ästen mit kostbaren Äpfeln (Plin. nat. 15,64) bzw. Granatäpfeln (Colum. 12,46,3; Pall. agric. 4,10,9,) zum Zwecke der Lagerung verwendet. Pfähle aus H.-Holz waren den Weinstöcken eine dauerhafte Stütze (Plin. nat. 17,151 und 174; Colum. 4,26,1). Der Rauch des Attichs sollte Schlangen vertreiben (Plin. nat. 25,119). Nichts mit dem H. zu tun hat die unbestimmbare *actaea* (Plin. nat. 27,43). C.HÜ.

Holz A. ALLGEMEIN B. LANDWIRTSCHAFT, HANDWERK, HAUSBAU C. HOLZ ALS MATERIAL IN DER PLASTIK D. SCHIFFBAU UND LANDTRANSPORT E. SONSTIGE VERWENDUNGEN F. HOLZ ALS BRENNSTOFF G. TRANSPORT UND VERARBEITUNG VON HOLZ H. HOLZ UND POLITIK I. DENDROCHRONOLOGIE J. BAUSTOFF K. MÖBEL

A. ALLGEMEIN

H. war in der Ant. wie allg. in vorindustriellen Gesellschaften ein universell verwendeter Werkstoff, der sogar als Ersatzstoff für Metall und für Verschleißteile eingesetzt wurde und gleichzeitig neben der tierischen und menschlichen Muskelkraft die wichtigste Energiequelle war. Zusammenfassend werden die Baumarten und ihre wirtschaftliche sowie technische Nutzung von Theophrastos (h. plant. 5), Vitruvius (2,8,20; 2,9 f.) und Plinius (nat. 16) behandelt.

B. LANDWIRTSCHAFT, HANDWERK, HAUSBAU

Landwirtschaft und Gewerbe waren in großem Umfang auf H. als Material für Werkzeuge und Geräte angewiesen. Schon bei Hesiod (erg. 420 ff.) finden sich Ratschläge, aus welchem H. die Teile des Wagens (vgl. Hom. Il. 4,485 f.) und des Pfluges jeweils hergestellt werden sollen; Wein- und Olivenpressen waren mit langen Preßbäumen aus H. ausgestattet (Cato agr. 31,2). Darüberhinaus wurde H. für eine Vielzahl anderer Werkzeuge benötigt, etwa für Hacken, Dreschflegel und Dreschschlitten; auch für die handwerkliche Produktion war der Gebrauch von Geräten und Instrumenten aus H. charakteristisch.

H. wurde beim Hausbau vielseitig für Türen, Türrahmen und -schwellen, Decken- und Dachbalken, Dielen und Treppen verwendet (Theophr. h. plant. 5,7,4); auch einfache Dachschindeln bestanden aus H. (Plin. nat. 16,36). In Rom war Hausbau ursprünglich fast reiner Holzbau; erst später wurde das Mauerwerk meist aus Steinen oder Ziegeln hergestellt; einfache Nutzbauten (Baracken, Ställe) bestanden aber weiterhin häufig aus H. Für das *diribitorium* (→ Saepta Iulia) auf dem Marsfeld in Rom wurden freitragende Deckenbalken von 100 Fuß Länge und 1,5 Fuß Dicke verwendet; es galt als das größte überdachte Gebäude der Welt (Plin. nat. 16,201; 36,102; Cass. Dio 55,8,4). Ein von Tiberius für den *pons naumachiarius* (→ Naumachie) bestimmter, aus den Alpen stammender Balken besaß eine Länge von 120 Fuß und eine Dicke von 2 Fuß (Plin. nat. 16,190; 16,200). Der Mangel an langen Deckenbalken wurde normalerweise durch Dachkonstruktionen mit Zwischenständern sowie durch Nut- und Zapfverbindungen mit H.-Dübeln ausgeglichen. In röm. Städten hat man H. überdies als Baumaterial für den Fachwerkbau (Vitr. 2,8,20; 2,9,16) sowie für hervorkragende Balkonkonstruktionen (Amm. 27,9,10) gebraucht. Großkonstruktionen, die wie das drehbare Doppeltheater des P. Scribonius Curio (*tr. pl.* 50 v. Chr.; Plin. nat. 36,116 ff.) nicht für eine längere Nutzung bestimmt waren, wurden ebenfalls aus H. errichtet. Diese Bauweise wurde selbst nach dem Einsturz des H.-Theaters von Fidenae (Tac. ann. 4,62f.; Suet. Tib. 40) beibehalten. Zahlreiche Brücken wie etwa die Moselbrücke in Trier oder die Donaubrücke des Traianus besaßen eine Trägerkonstruktion aus H. Trotz der hohen Brandgefahr blieb H. immer ein wichtiges Baumaterial; nach Brandkatastrophen wurde von Nero und später von Zenon die Verwendung von H. im Hausbau eingeschränkt (Tac. ann. 15,43,3f.; Cod. Iust. 8,10,12). Große Mengen an H. wurden im Baugewerbe auch für die Gerüste, die Verschalung (→ *opus caementicium*) und die Sicherung von Fundamenten auf feuchtem Untergrund mit Hilfe von Pfählen benötigt.

H. lieferte außerdem das Material für Stühle, Tische, Klinen, Bettgestelle, Kisten und Truhen; in der Zeit der späten Republik und des frühen Prinzipats führte der allg. Ausstattungsluxus zur Herstellung bes. wertvoller Möbel. So sollen Tische aus Zitrus-H. bis zu 1,3 Mio. Sesterzen gekostet haben (Plin. nat. 13,91–99).

→ Architektur; Bautechnik; Bauwesen P.H.

C. Holz als Material in der Plastik

H. bleibt nur unter Luftabschluß erh., weshalb die zeitliche und räumliche Verteilung der Funde nicht repräsentativ für die Gesamtheit ant. Holzskulptur ist. Viele bedeutende Funde aus H. stammen wegen günstiger Lagerungsbedingungen aus Randgebieten der griech.-röm. Welt.

Während aus der altägypt. Produktion reiche Funde vorliegen, läßt sich Holzplastik in der minoischen Kunst nur erschließen. Dagegen blieben figürliche Schnitzereien der asiatischen Steppennomaden in vereisten Gräbern konserviert (Altai, 6.–5. Jh. v. Chr). In luftdichten Feuchtlagen von Quellheiligtümern fanden sich bes. in Gallien Tausende von Votivstatuetten aus H. (Seine-Quelle, Chamalières, 1. Jh. v. Chr.), zumeist einfache Figuren der Pilger. In pun. Gräbern erhielten sich anthropoide Sarkophage (Kerkouane, 4.–3. Jh. v. Chr.; [1]). Die Grabbauten griech. Kolonisten am Schwarzen Meer bargen Sarkophage mit farbig gefaßten figürlichen Holzattachen (Krim, 4.–3. Jh. v. Chr).

Eine künstlerische Entwicklung erlebte die H.-Plastik in Griechenland ab dädalischer Zeit in Form von Kultbildern, → Xoana, die eine lange Pflege und auch Nachschöpfungen erfuhren. Die schriftliche Überl. verband sie mit den frühesten, legendären Künstlernamen wie → Daidalos und → Theodoros von Samos (Plin. nat. 7, 198) und berichtet insgesamt von ca. 50 teilweise noch in der Kaiserzeit bekannten Exemplaren. Ihre Ursprünge liegen vielleicht in früher Dendrolatrie, weshalb für Athena Olivenholz und für Dionysos der Weinstock als passend galt. Das berühmteste Bildwerk aus H., das Troianische Pferd des Epeios, existierte nur im Epos; sagenhaft waren auch die meisten Werke des → Endoios. Glaubwürdiger sind Nachr. über die samische Hera des Smilis (6. Jh. v. Chr.) und einen Apollon des → Kanachos. Der Fachterminus *aiginētiká érga* verweist auf Aigina als frühes Zentrum der Holzschnitzkunst. In delischen Tempelinventaren werden 48 Holzstatuen vermerkt. Von all diesen Werken ist keines erh. Dafür lieferte Samos Depots qualitätvoller Votivstatuetten aus dem 7. Jh. v. Chr., Einzelstücke stammen aus Pitsa bei Korinth (6. Jh.) und aus Sizilien (7.–6. Jh.).

Stil und Entwicklungsstand dieser frühen Werke werden kunstgesch. konträr beurteilt. Gegen einen ausschließlichen Ursprung griech. Rundplastik aus H. wird die geringe Größe der Votive und der Xoana angeführt sowie die bald einsetzende Entwicklung der Stein- und Bronzeplastik. Auch die hölzernen Siegerstatuen des 6. Jh. v. Chr. werden durch Bronzen abgelöst. Als spezifisch geeignet galt H. später nur für Priapos-Statuen. Als billiger Ersatz hingegen wurde H. mit Stucküberzug auch bei anderen Götterstatuen verwendet, etwa im marmorarmen Ägypten für Sarapis.

Aus Rom berichten die Quellen ebenfalls von frühen Xoana (Servius Tullius, Veiovis). In der Kaiserzeit galten Götterbilder aus H. als kunstlos (Lucan. 3,412–413). Die wenigen erh. Statuetten aus H. entstammen dem häuslichen Bereich und sind als billiger Ersatz zu werten, z. B. Holzporträts aus Herculaneum, Statuetten eines Larariums (→ Lares) aus einem Schiffsfund [2] und Puppen.

Von der kunsthandwerklichen Dekoration von Möbeln und Gebrauchsgegenständen bewahrte bes. das koptische Ägypten eine Fülle aus spätant. Zeit. Als einziges erh. Beispiel in Rom bezeugen die Holztüren von S. Sabina (1. H. 5. Jh. n. Chr.; [3]) eine hohe Qualität spätant. Reliefkunst in H.

→ Akrolithon; Bildhauertechnik; Hermen; Sarkophag

1 M. Fantar, Un sarcophage en bois à couvercle anthropoïde découvert dans la nécropole punique de Kerkouane, in: CRAI 1972, 340–354 2 M. L'Hour, Les statuettes de bois de l'épave Planier I à Marseille, in: Archaeonautica 4, 1984, 53–73 3 G. Jeremias, Die Holztür der Basilika S. Sabina in Rom, 1980.

Blümner, 238–347 • G. Bermond Montanari et al., s. v. legno, EAA 4, 1961, 530–537 • S. I. Rudenko, Frozen tombs of Sibiria, 1970 • M. Vaulina, Bois grecs et romains de l'Ermitage, 1974 • H. V. Herrmann, Zum Problem der Entstehung der griech. Großplastik, in: Wandlungen. FS Homann-Wedeking, 1975, 35–48 • H. Kyrieleis, Neue Holzfunde aus dem Heraion von Samos, in: ASAA 61, 1983, 295–302 • S. Deyts, Les bois sculptés des sources de la Seine, 1983 • A. M. Romeuf, Ex-voto en bois de Chamalières et des sources de la Seine, in: Gallia 44, 1986, 65–89 • M. H. Rutschowskaya, Musée du Louvre. Catalogue des bois de l'Egypte copte, 1986 • Fuchs/Floren, 205; 309; 369–371. R.N.

D. Schiffbau und Landtransport

Die Griechen bevorzugten beim Bau von Kriegsschiffen (→ Flottenwesen) Eiche für den Kiel, Tanne und Bergkiefer für die Beplankung, Esche, Maulbeerbaum oder Ulme für die Belastungsteile sowie Tanne oder Zeder für die Masten (Theophr. h. plant. 5,7). Die Ruder wurden aus Tannen gefertigt. Zeder und Zypresse, die vor allem von Phöniziern und Persern verwendet wurden, galten als weniger geeignet, da sie zu schwer waren. Entscheidende Kriterien für die Auswahl des H. bei Kriegsschiffen waren Belastbarkeit und Gewicht. Für den Kiel versuchte man ganze Stämme zu verwenden; der wohl längste Kiel wurde von → Demetrios [2] Poliorketes aus einer zypriotischen Zeder mit 130 Fuß Länge hergestellt (Plin. nat. 16,203). Reisewagen und die schweren Wagen für den Gütertransport zu Lande wurden ebenfalls aus H. gebaut; obgleich der Einsatz von Tragtieren (Eseln, Maultieren und im Osten Kamelen) im Lastentransport bis in die Spätant. nachweisbar ist, gewann die H.-Verarbeitung damit auch für den Güteraustausch an Bedeutung.

E. Sonstige Verwendungen

In diesem Zusammenhang sind außerdem die Waffenherstellung und der Bereich der Militärtechnik zu erwähnen: Einfache Waffen wie z. B. Stoßlanze und Wurfspeer bestanden aus H., und Schilde waren aus Brettern zusammengefügt (Pol. 6,23). Aber auch die großen Belagerungsgeräte (→ Poliorketik) der hell. Zeit, darunter die fahrbaren Türme (→ Helepolis) und die Katapulte, wurden aus H. errichtet. Wie unentbehrlich H. für alle Bereiche der ant. Zivilisation war, zeigen beispielhaft → Musikinstrumente wie Flöten, Harfen oder Lyren. H.-Täfelchen und H. waren ein wichtiger Beschreibstoff und damit von erheblicher Bedeutung für die amtliche und private Kommunikation.

F. Holz als Brennstoff

H. war neben → Holzkohle der wichtigste Brennstoff der Ant.; als Heizmaterial dienten vor allem Abfall-H. (P. Köln 52) und Reisig. Der Großverbrauch in den stadtröm. Thermenanlagen (zu Misenum vgl. CIL X 3678 = ILS 5689) führte in der Spätantike zu einem → *munus* der H.-Lieferung (Cod. Theod. 14,5,1; Symm. epist. 10,40), zum Import von Brenn-H. aus Afrika, das als Ballast in Getreidetransportern angeliefert wurde, und zu Sparmaßnahmen beim Verbrauch. So wurde für die Thermen von Catania eine Reduzierung von 32 (4960 kg) auf 18 *pensae* (2790 kg) angeordnet (IG XIV 455). Im holzarmen Äg. wurde H. weitgehend durch Schilf oder Papyrus ersetzt.

G. Transport und Verarbeitung von Holz

Entästete Stämme wurden auf kürzeren Strecken durch Ochsen- und Maultiergespanne mit Nachläufern transportiert (CIL IV 485 = ILS 6417b: *lignarii plostrari*). Daneben ist der Flußtransport von Einzelstämmen und Flößen belegt (*ratiarii* auf Rhône und Isère: CIL XII 2597; 2331). Der Transport auf dem Meer erfolgte als Decklast, aber auch als Floß. Meist kam bereits zugeschnittenes H. (Bretter, Balken) in den Handel (Edictum Diocletiani 12 ff.); mit Bau-H. handelten die *negotiatores materiarii* oder *n. lignarii*; teilweise wurde Bau-H. von hoher Qualität aus entfernten Gebieten herangeschafft, etwa für den Parthenon von der Insel Karpathos (Syll.[3] 129). Stämme aus den Alpen wurden auf dem Po nach Ravenna und dann weiter in die Städte an der Adria – bis nach Ancona – gebracht (Vitr. 2,9,16). Die Stadt Rom erhielt auf dem Tiber H. aus Etrurien und Umbrien (*porticus inter lignarios*; Liv. 35,41,10). Daneben gab es in Ostia organisierte *navicularii lignarii* (CIL XIV 4549,3), die für den H.-Import zuständig waren.

Bei den holzverarbeitenden Berufen ist eine starke Differenzierung und Spezialisierung nach den hergestellten Produkten (*carpentarius*, *cuparius*, *scandularius*), aber auch nach den bearbeiteten H.-Arten (z. B. *citrarius*, *eborarius*; insgesamt sind mehr als 50 Berufsbezeichnungen belegt) feststellbar. Einige Berufe wurden später von den *munera civilia* (öffentl. Belastungen) befreit (Cod. Theod. 13,4,2 = Cod. Iust. 10,66,1).

Der Zeitpunkt, an dem die Bäume gefällt werden sollten, sowie die Bedeutung des Standortes und des Alters der Bäume für die Qualität des H. werden von Theophrastos und Plinius thematisiert (Theophr. h. plant. 5,1 f.; Plin. nat. 16,188 ff.; 16,197 f.; vgl. Veg. mil. 4,34 ff.). Bereits in den Epen Homers wird die Tätigkeit der H.-Fäller in den Gebirgen in Vergleichen beschrieben (Hom. Il. 11,86 ff.; 13,178 ff.; 13,390 ff.; 16,482 ff.; 16,633 f.; 17,742 ff.; vgl. Hom. Od. 5,234 ff.; Verg. Aen. 2,626 ff.); Organisation und Umfang der H.-Gewinnung für den Flottenbau im Hell. veranschaulicht der Bericht über die Rüstungen des Antigonos 315 v. Chr. (Diod. 19,58).

H. Holz und Politik

Da für den Flottenbau große Mengen Schiffbau-H. benötigt wurden, war der Zugang zu Waldgebieten, die geeignete Stämme in hinreichender Zahl liefern konnten, für die Seemächte eine entscheidende machtpolit. Frage (Thuk. 6,90,3; Xen. hell. 6,1,11; Plat. leg. 705c ff.). Flottenbauprogramme waren stets mit der Aufgabe verbunden, das dafür notwendige H. zu beschaffen (Thuk. 8,1,3; Diod. 14,42,4 f.; 19,58), und es gehörte im Krieg zu den strategisch wichtigen Zielen, die Versorgung des Gegners mit Schiffbau-H. zu unterbinden oder seine H.-Vorräte zu vernichten (Thuk. 4,108,1; 7,25,2). Athen war im Peloponnesischen Krieg auf die Hilfe der maked. Könige angewiesen (IG I[2] 105; vgl. And. 2,11); so war es verständlich, daß die Römer den Makedonen im Jahre 168 v. Chr. untersagten, H. für den Schiffbau zu schlagen oder dies anderen zu erlauben (Liv. 45,29,14). Für den Bau röm. Kriegsschiffe wurden Stämme aus den Apenninen verwendet (Sidon. carm. 5,441 ff.), in der Prinzipatszeit konnten die Römer dann auf die Ressourcen des gesamten Mittelmeerraumes zurückgreifen.

Ein großer Teil der Wälder war Königsbesitz (in Makedonien, *regiae silvae* in Bithynien) bzw. → *ager publicus* wie etwa der Sila-Wald in It. (Cic. Brut. 85) oder der Libanon. Daneben existierte auch Wald im Besitz von Gemeinden oder Privatleuten. Schutzprogramme für die Wälder im Libanon-Gebirge sind für die Zeit Hadrians belegt (IGLS 5001–5187). Ebenso gab es einen gezielten Schutz und eine Förderung von Anpflanzungen im hell.-röm. Ägypten. Durch die Sekundärnutzung des Waldes als Weide wurden die H.-Ressourcen aber nachhaltig geschädigt.

I. Dendrochronologie

H.-Funde sind in der mod. Arch. ein wichtiges Hilfsmittel der Chronologie. Da in verschiedenen Jahren Baumringe entsprechend den jeweiligen Witterungsbedingungen eine unterschiedliche Stärke aufweisen, sind »charakteristische Jahrring-Abfolgen« feststellbar; auf diese Weise kann für einzelne Regionen eine relativ genaue Chronologie (Dendrochronologie) erstellt und so der Zeitpunkt, an dem H. verarbeitet wurde, bestimmt werden.

1 J.-C. Beal (Hrsg.), L'arbre et la forêt, le bois dans l'antiquité, 1995 2 Blümner, Techn. 2, 238–356 3 W. Eck, Inschriften auf Holz. Ein unterschätztes Phänomen der epigraphischen Kultur Roms, in: P. Kneissl, V. Losemann (Hrsg.), Imperium Romanum, 1998, 203–217 4 H.-C. Grassmann, Wirkungsweise und Energieverbrauch ant. röm. Thermen, in: JRGZ 41, 1994, 297–321 5 B. Kramer, Arborikultur und Holzwirtschaft im griech., röm. und byz. Ägypten, in: APF 41, 1995, 217–231 6 F. G. Maier, Neue Wege in die alte Welt – Methoden der modernen Archäologie, 1977, 305 ff. 7 R. Meiggs, Trees and Timber in the Ancient Mediterranean World, 1982 8 H. v. Petrikovits, Die Spezialisierung des röm. Handwerks, in: H. Jankuhn (Hrsg.), Das Handwerk in vor- und frühgesch. Zeit (AAWG 122), 1981, 63–132 9 J. Radkau, Technik in Deutschland, 1989, 59 ff. 10 Zimmer, Katalog-Nr. 56–74.

P. H.

J. Baustoff

s. Architektur, Bautechnik, Bauwesen

K. Möbel

s. Hausrat, s. Möbel

Holzfässer. Während im Mittelmeerraum Flüssigkeiten wie Wein und Öl in großen Tonkrügen (πίθος, *dolium*) gelagert und in Tierhäuten oder Amphoren transportiert wurden, hat man seit dem frühen Prinzipat in den westl. Prov. und in Nordit. für die Lagerung und den Transport von Wein zunehmend auch H. verwendet (Oberit.: Strab. 5,1,8; 5,1,12; Alpen: Plin. nat. 14,132).

Wie zahlreiche Reliefs und Grabskulpturen zeigen, wurden Weinfässer mit schweren, von Pferden gezogenen Wagen (Grabreliefs in Langres und Augsburg) oder auf Flüssen wie der Mosel mit Ruderschiffen oder Treidelkähnen (Grabdenkmal aus Neumagen, Trier, Rhein. Landesmuseum; Grabrelief, Avignon, Musée Calvet) befördert; dabei bestand die Fracht eines Wagens wohl häufig aus einem einzigen großen Holzfaß. Gegenüber der → Amphora [1] hatte das Holzfaß den Vorteil, daß die Relation zwischen dem Eigengewicht des Flüssigkeitsbehälters und dem Gewicht der Ladung günstiger war; außerdem mußten Fässer etwa beim Beladen eines Schiffes nicht wie Amphoren getragen werden, sondern konnten über eine Planke auf das Schiff gerollt werden (Relief, Landesmuseum Mainz).

1 H. Cüppers (Hrsg.), Die Römer in Rheinland-Pfalz, 1990, 181, Abb. 89 2 Die Römer in Schwaben, ²1985, 127, Abb. 96 3 W. Selzer, Röm. Steindenkmäler. Mainz in römischer Zeit, 1988, 35, Abb. 18 4 White, Technology, 133, Abb. 132 5 Zimmer, 149, Anm. 151, Katalog-Nr. 177 (Ancona), 196, 197 (Turin).

H. SCHN.

Holzkohle (ἄνθραξ, *carbo*) war neben dem → Holz der wichtigste in der Ant. genutzte Brennstoff; H., die bereits in Äg. und Mesopot. bekannt war, wurde durch einen kontrollierten Reduktionsprozeß (Holz: 50 % Kohlenstoff, H.: 80–90 %) aus ausgewählten Hölzern (Theophr. h. plant. 5,9,1 ff.: Eiche, Walnuß, Kiefer, Fichte) gewonnen. Dabei wurde eine erhebliche Steigerung des Heizwertes gegenüber Holz erzielt (29 000 gegenüber 16 500 kJ/kg). H. wurde in Meilern (κάμινος, *calyx*) produziert, die aus geradem und eng geschichteten Stammholz aufgebaut und dann mit Erde luftdicht abgedeckt wurden (Theophr. h. plant. 5,9,4; 9,3,1 f.; Plin. nat. 16,23), um ein Durchbrennen des Meilers zu verhindern. Technisch eng damit verbunden war auch die Teerproduktion durch das Schwelen von Fichtenstämmen (Plin. nat. 16,52 f.). Die Verkohlung führte zu einer deutlichen Gewichtsreduzierung, was den Transport der H. erleichterte. Die Ant. kannte qualitativ unterschiedliche Typen von H., je nach dem verwendeten Holz. Die beste H. stammte von Bäumen, die dichtes und festes Holz besaßen und beim Fällen noch im vollen Saft standen. Alte Bäume galten für die Gewinnung von H. als unbrauchbar. Zum Bearbeiten von → Eisen bevorzugte man H. aus Walnuß-, bei Silber H. aus Fichtenholz (Theophr. h. plant. 5,9,1 ff.).

H. war für viele technische Zwecke unentbehrlich, so etwa für die Metallgewinnung und -verarbeitung (→ Metallurgie), aber auch bei der Münzherstellung. In geringerem Umfang wurde sie auch für Heizzwecke (H.-Becken) sowie im Kultbereich verwendet: Da das Verlöschen eines Opferfeuers ominöse Bedeutung gehabt hätte, wurde H. für diesen Zweck sorgfältig ausgewählt (Plin. nat. 16,24). Für Delos sind Angaben über den Kauf von H. für die Kulthandlungen erhalten (IDélos 287; 338; 372; 442); im Jahr wurden etwa 100 Drachmen für diesen Zweck ausgegeben.

In der Spätant. war der Transport von H. eine Aufgabe von hoher Priorität, die als *munus sordidum* (niedere öffentliche Verpflichtung) Grundbesitzern auferlegt wurde (Cod. Theod. 11,16,15; 11,16,18; von 382 bzw. 390 n. Chr.). Wenn die H. für die Münzstätten oder die Waffenproduktion bestimmt war, gab es keinen Entschuldigungsgrund (*excusatio*) von dieser Aufgabe (Cod. Theod. 11,16,18: *carbonis ab eo inlatio non cogetur nisi vel monetalis cusio vel antiquo more necessaria fabricatio poscit armorum*; d. h. die Lieferung von Holzkohle sollte nicht erzwungen werden, außer wenn die Prägung von Münzen oder die notwendige Herstellung von Waffen dies erforderte). Unsicher ist, ob man diese H. als Sachsteuerleistung ablieferte oder ob sie direkt in öffentlichem Auftrag produziert wurde.

→ Brennstoffe

1 Blümner, Techn. 2, 347–356 2 Meiggs, 451 ff.

P. H.

Homarion (Ὁμάριον, Ἀμάριον). Heiligtum des Zeus bei Helike (Pol. 5,93,10 bzw. Strab. 8,7,3; 7,5; Syll.[3] 490, [1]), Zentrum des Achaiischen Bundes, nach dem Untergang von Helike (373 v. Chr.) im Besitz von Aigion. Trotz mehrerer Inschr.-Funde nordwestl. von Aigion nicht zu lokalisieren [2; 3; 4; 5. 191–193]. Nicht zu verwechseln mit Homagyrion bei Paus. 7,24,2. Vgl. aber das achaiische Heiligtum des Zeus Homarios in Unterit. (Pol. 2,39,6) [6].

1 A. Aymard, Le Zeus fédéral achaien Hamarios-Homarios, in: Mélanges Navarre, 1935, 453–470 2 P. Aström, Ἀ βουλὰ τῶν Ἀχαιῶν. Une inscription d'Aigion, in: OpAth 2, 1955 (1956), 4–9 3 J. Bingen, Inscriptions du Péloponnèse, in: BCH 77, 1953, 616–628 4 Ders., Inscriptions d'Achaie, in: BCH 78, 1954, 402–407 5 A. Stavropoulos, Ἱστορία τῆς πόλεως Αἰγίου, 1954 6 M. Osanna, Sull'ubicazione del santuario di Zeus Homarios in Magna Grecia, in: Dialoghi di archeologia 7, 1989, 55–63. Y.L.

Homeridai (Ὁμηρίδαι). Spezielle → Rhapsoden-Gruppe (für uns erstmals erwähnt bei Pind. N. 2,1, ca. 485/480 v. Chr.), die sich laut späten Nachr. (schol. z.St., Harpokration s. v., u. a.) in der ersten Generation biologisch direkt auf → Homer [1] zurückgeführt haben soll, danach als »Nachlaßpfleger« der Homerischen Epen galt. Sitz: Chios; bekanntester Vertreter: Kynaithos. Homer-Vereine dieses Namens (eher Bewunderer als Rhapsoden: Plat. Ion 530d; Plat. rep. 599e) sind bis in hell. Zeit bezeugt [1. 87[6]].

1 Schmid/Stählin I 1, 157f. 2 H. T. Wade-Gery, The Poet of the Iliad, 1952, 19–21 3 W. Burkert, Die Leistung eines Kreophylos, in: MH 29, 1972, 74–85 4 M. Haslam, in: I. Morris, B. Powell (Hrsg.), A New Companion to Homer, 1997, 81. J.L.

Homerische Becher s. Reliefkeramik

Homerische Sprache A. Altertümlichkeit B. Dialekte C. Sprache und Vers D. Uneinheitlichkeit E. Überlieferung und Nachwirkung

A. Altertümlichkeit

Infolge des hohen Alters von *Ilias* und *Odyssee* enthält die h.S. Altertümlichkeiten, die im Griech. früh zurückgegangen und in späteren Texten gewöhnlich nur aufgrund von Homernachahmung (s.u. E.) bezeugt sind: im Nomen den Instr. auf -φι (ἶφι, ναῦφι; sonst nur im Myk.), Ζῆν' Akk. »Zeus« (am Versende vor Vok.) = altind. *dyā̃m*, das Suffix von ἀνδρο-μέος; im Vb. einen zusätzlichen Bestand an Wz.-Präs. (ἔδ-μεναι, στεῦ-ται) und -Aor. (ἔ-κτα-το, ὦρ-το), das *nā*-Präs. (δάμ-νη-μι), den kurzvok. Konj. (ἐρεί-ο-μεν, δαμάσσ-ε-ται), die freiere Tmesis (ἄπο λοιγὸν ἀμῦναι, λίπω κάτα), die augmentlosen Präteritumsformen (φέρε, ἴδεν; μὴ ἔνθεο injunktivisch). Ältere Lautzustände liegen in ἀέκων, φιλέει, νόος offen zutage (att. kontrahiert ἄκων, φιλεῖ, νοῦς; φ. und ν. auch in der h.S., s.u. D.). Andere derartige Lauterscheinungen sind dagegen noch in vorhomer. Zeit erneuert worden und nur noch an Störungen des Versmaßes zu erkennen: θυγατέρα ἥν (–⏑⏑–?–) mit positionsbildendem ἥν < **su̯ām*, ἀνδροτῆτα (⏑?⏑––⏑) offenbar mit ἀνδρο- < **anr̥*-. Hierher gehören v. a. die Spuren des → »Digamma« bei Homer: κατὰ ἄστυ anstelle von älterem κατὰ ϝάστυ.

Auf Vorstufen ep., und zwar mündlicher Dichtung, weisen außerdem die zahlreichen schmückenden Beiwörter, die z. T. semantisch verblaßt sind (ἀγέρωχος, ἀμιχθαλόεις, ἀτρύγετος, μέροψ, νῶροψ), sowie die formelhaften, aber z. T. abwandelbaren Versgruppen, Verse und Versstücke; manche Fügungen lassen sich bis zur → indogermanischen Dichtersprache zurückverfolgen.

B. Dialekte

Die h.S. ist keinem festumrissenen griech. Dial.-Gebiet zuzuordnen. Sicher ist eine starke Prägung durch das → Ionische, und zwar v. a. wegen η < *ā* auch hinter *e* / *i* / *r* (νεηνίης, πρῆξις) und wegen εω < *āŏ* (Πηλείδεω, πυλέων). Andere Erscheinungen stimmen dagegen nicht zum bekannten Ion.; ihre Einordnung und Erklärung ist z. T. noch strittig. Offensichtlich enthält die h.S. Züge aus älterer aiol. Dichtung, z. B. πίσυρες mit π- < **kʷ*- (→ Gutturale), ἐρεβεννή mit -εvv- < *-*esn*-, ἤμβροτε »verfehlte« mit -ρο > *-*r̥*-, Gen. auf -οιο wie ἠελίοιο, Dat. auf -εσσι wie νήεσσι. Die vier letzten Formen zeigen allerdings zugleich ein ion. η, sind also ans Ion. angepaßte Mischformen.

Außer Ion. und Aiol. haben wohl noch weitere Dial. zur h.S. beigetragen.

C. Sprache und Vers

Bestimmte Formen, die sich dem daktylischen Hexameter kaum einfügen lassen, fehlen der h.S. nicht zufällig (κτημάτων –⏑–); andere sind für das Versmaß künstlich umgestaltet. Ein rein lautliches Mittel ist die → metrische Dehnung eines Kurzvokals, sichtbar in οὔνομα = ὄνομα, unsichtbar in ἀνέρα (*ā*-). In der Forschung nicht immer davon getrennt wird die analogische Umgestaltung zugunsten einer langen Silbe (ἠνεμόεσσα aus ἀνεμόεσσα, etwa nach ποδ-ήνεμος); fernzuhalten sind auch rein metr. Freiheiten wie die Füllung einer Arsis durch kurze Auslautsilbe (ἦλθες ––? vor Vok.). Ein weiterer Kunstgriff der h.S. ist die Einsparung einer Silbe im Wortinnern durch Synizese: βουλέων (–⏑– > βουλέων (––).

Anders bedingt sind die künstlichen Lautungen αα, οω in ὁράασθαι, ὁρόων; auch an ihnen zeigt sich, daß die h.S. Vorstufen hat. Im Vers stand zunächst normalsprachliches ὁράεσθαι (⏑⏑⏑–⏓), ὁράων (⏑⏑–). Nach der Kontraktion wurde ὁρᾶσθαι, ὁρῶν gesprochen. Durch »ep. Zerdehnung« (διέκτασις) von ᾱ ω wurde daraus die urspr., für den Vers nötige Silbenfolge wiederhergestellt. Künstlich ist u. a. wohl auch die Umwertung des vor Ζῆν' (s.o. A.) stehenden Akk. εὐρύοπα zum Indeclinabile, das dann an gleicher Versstelle auch vor Ζεῦ Vok. bzw. Ζεύς Nom. stehen konnte.

D. Uneinheitlichkeit

Die h.S. hat also eine längere Vorgesch., sie trägt Spuren verschiedener Zeiten, verschiedener Dial. und verschiedenartig prägender Dichter. Infolgedessen enthält sie Älteres neben Jüngerem, Aiolisches neben Ionischem, Künstliches und Persönliches neben Üblichem. Dadurch hatte Homer gleichbedeutende Formen mit verschiedener Lautstruktur zur Verfügung, deren verschiedene Einsatztechnik im Hexameter ihm willkommen war, z. B. für »erhob sich« älteres ὦρτο und jüngeres ὤρετο mit verschiedener Silbenzahl, für »vier« aiol. πίσυρες (⏑⏑– vor Kons.) und ion. τέσσαρες (–⏑⏑), für »sehen« künstliches ὁράασθαι (⏑⏑–⏓) und normalsprachliches ὁρᾶσθαι (⏑–⏓). Prosodisch immerhin gleichwertig sind z. B. aiol. αἰ und ion. εἰ »wenn«; ἀνέρα ist gegenüber normalsprachlichem ἄνδρα einerseits altertümlicher (-ε-), andererseits künstlich ($\bar{a}$-); auch das künstliche ὁράασθαι ist strukturell älter als ὁρᾶσθαι (s.o. C.). Angesichts dieser verwickelten Verhältnisse ist die Bestimmung manchen Wechsels in der h.S. begreiflicherweise noch strittig (ὀμόσσαι / ὀμόσαι).

Verstreut finden sich in den homer. Werken auffällige, meist junge Einzelerscheinungen: μον-ωθείς (Il. 11,470); τέμ-νειν (Od. 3,175); νοῦς (Od. 10,240); ποντοπορ-ούσ-ης (Od. 11,11); Ὀδυσεῦς (Gen.) (Od. 24,398); häufig sind dagegen: μουν-, ταμ-, νόος, -ευσ-, Ὀδυσ(σ)ῆος. Ähnlich merkwürdig und vereinzelt ist z. B. βούλεται (Konj.) (Il. 1,67).

E. Überlieferung und Nachwirkung

Die h.S. ist namentlich in der Ilias sorgfältig überliefert. Auch in kleinen, nicht durchs Versmaß geschützten sprachlichen Einzelheiten ist der Überlieferungsbefund in der Regel eindeutig; z. B. gilt Augment in δ'ἔκλυε (Il. 1,43) oder ἐπέπλεον (Il. 1,312), wo auch augmentlose Formen einsetzbar wären (*δὲ κλύε sogar mit identischen Buchstaben), umgekehrt gilt augmentloses γε φάμεν (Il. 23,440). Am Versende wechseln z. B. -εν -ιν und -ε -ι regelmäßig je nach folgendem Laut; vgl. auch das feste einmalige τέμνειν (s.o. D.). Seit wann der Text diese überl. Gestalt hat, ist freilich ungewiß. Da zu ihr auch Akzentbesonderheiten gehören, z. B. ἔνθά κεν, ist mit genauer mündlicher Weitergabe der h.S. zu rechnen. Zurückhaltung ist daher gegenüber allen früheren Versuchen geboten, die h.S. noch altertümlicher zu machen, z. B. durch die Einführung von γιγνώσκω für γῑν- oder gar von κατὰ ϝάστυ für κατὰ ἄστυ. Der Endfassung Homers sind auch verhältnismäßig junge Lautungen wie γῑνώσκω zuzutrauen (s.o. D. Ende), und das »Digamma« ϝ ist an vielen Stellen verstechnisch nicht einsetzbar, gehörte also der Endfassung wohl nicht mehr an.

Die h.S. hat das griech. Epos bis in die Spätant. beherrscht. Von Anfang an beeinflußt hat sie ferner die übrige griech. Dichtung, v. a. die hexametrische (Elegie, Epigramm), aber auch Lyrik und Tragödie, ja teilweise die Prosa: Im Herodottext stehen sogar Formen mit metrischer Dehnung wie οὔνομα. Ferner hat die h.S. seit Ennius auf das Lat. gewirkt und durch Übersetzungen auch auf neuere Sprachen: nhd. »geflügelte Worte« geht auf homer. ἔπεα πτερόεντα zurück.

→ Aiolisch (Lesbisch); Digamma; Griechische Dialekte; Griechische Literatur-Sprachen; Indogermanische Dichtersprache; Ionisch; Metrische Dehnung

P. Chantraine, Grammaire homérique Bd. 1, [3]1958, Bd. 2, 1953 • H. Ebeling, Lex. Homericum, 1880–1885 • B. Forssman, Schichten in der homer. Sprache, in: J. Latacz (Hrsg.), Zweihundert Jahre Homerforschung (CollRau 2), 1991, 259–288 (mit Lit.) • A. Gehring, Index Homericus, [2]1970 • J. P. Holoka, Homer, Oral Poetry Theory, in: J. Latacz, s.o., 456–481 (mit Lit.) • J. La Roche, Die homer. Textkritik im Alterthum, 1866 • LFE • J. R. Tebben, Concordantia Homerica, 1994ff. • J. Untermann, Einf. in die Sprache Homers, 1987. B. F.

Homeros

[1] (Ὅμηρος, lat. *Homērus*, frz. *Homère*, danach dt. *Homér*). I. Kurzdefinition II. Person, Heimat, Zeit, Herkunftsmilieu III. Werke IV. Stoff, Sprache und Vers V. Mündlichkeit und Schriftlichkeit VI. Überlieferung

I. Kurzdefinition

Homer ist der erste Dichter des europ. Kulturkreises, von dem vollständige Werke größeren Umfangs (rund 28000 hexametrische Verse in griech. Sprache) stammen, die seit ihrer Entstehung vor ca. 2700 Jahren kontinuierlich in der gesamten europ. geprägten Welt rezipiert wurden und die Kulturentwicklung bis h. offen und latent beeinflußt haben [11; 39; 17. 274].

II. Person, Heimat, Zeit, Herkunftsmilieu
A. Identität und Name des Autors B. Heimat C. Zeit D. Herkunftsmilieu

A. Identität und Name des Autors

Da das echte Œuvre (d. h. mindestens die *Ilias*, evtl. auch die *Odyssee*) in einer Zeit entstand (um 700 v. Chr.), die erst seit wenigen Jahrzehnten die Schrift kannte (→ Alphabet) und noch keine Textualität (somit auch kein Urkundenwesen usw.) entwickelt hatte [18. Kap. 1], kann mit zeitgenöss. Nachr. zur Person des Autors nicht gerechnet werden. Die durch das Œuvre Homers wohl erst in Gang gesetzte [18. 26–29] Textualität versuchte diese Informationslücke später durch Rekonstruktionen nachträglich auszufüllen; die frühesten Stufen dieser Rekonstruktionsversuche sind verloren; uns liegen lediglich Endprodukte vor, die sämtlich aus dem ausgehenden Hell. und der röm. Kaiserzeit stammen, d. h. etwa 700 Jahre vom Autor getrennt sind und daher keinerlei Authentizität beanspruchen können: sieben Lebensbeschreibungen (βίοι, *vitae*) und ein → ›Wettkampf Homers und Hesiods‹ (*Certamen Homeri et Hesiodi*). Sorgfältige sprachliche und inhaltliche Analysen dieses ganzen von Wilamowitz [1] zusammengestellten Erzählguts [38; 30; 33; 12; 34] haben wahrscheinlich gemacht, daß einzelne Kern-Informationen daraus bis ins 7. Jh. zurückreichen können (Quelle: → Homeriden und → Rhapsoden?): Der ion. Name Ὅμηρος (*Hómēros*, für uns erstmals indirekt und nicht ganz sicher belegt bei → Kallinos Test. 10 GENTILI-PRATO, um 650 v. Chr., dann sicher bei Xenophan. 21 B 10 und B 11,1 DK und Heraklit 22 B 42, 56, 105 DK, beide etwa 2. Hälfte des 6. Jh. v. Chr., sowie Sim. 564,4 PMG, um 500) ist ein gängiges (hier als PN verwendetes) Subst. (zur Etym.: [7. s. v.]), das »Bürge«, »Unterpfand« bedeutet (z. B. Hdt. 8,94,3); die äol. Form Ὅμαρος (*Hómāros*) ist als Männername auch inschr. belegt ([38. 372; 7. s. v.]; typologisch ähnliche Namen sind *Próxeinos*, *Prýtanis*, *Synhístōr* u. ä., s. [4. 513 ff.]); der Verdacht, der Name könnte eine bloße Kollektivbezeichnung für Angehörige einer Sängerzunft gewesen sein (so schon CURTIUS 1855 [8]; zuletzt WEST [36. 217[43]]), stützt sich bisher auf nichts; den traditionellen Autor-Namen Homeros gegen einen anderen (oder gar keinen) Namen auszutauschen, wäre ohne Sinn [5. 447].

B. HEIMAT

Die ion. Namensform, der Grunddial. (das Ion.), dazu die weitgehende Übereinstimmung des biographischen Erzählguts darüber, daß die Heimat des Autors Ionien gewesen sei (von den zahlreichen Städten, die Homers Geburtsort gewesen sein wollten – und später unter die Siebenzahl gestellt wurden –, sind die meisten ion.), weisen auf das kleinasiatische Ionien als Stammland des Autors hin [38. 372; 18. 33 f.]; andere vorgeschlagene Regionen – Oropos: [24]; Euboia: [25. 31] – haben wegen der dort weit geringeren Kulturdichte wenig für sich. Über die Genealogie ist nichts Brauchbares überliefert.

C. ZEIT

Großflächige Vergleiche der in *Ilias* und *Odyssee* widergespiegelten Grundschicht des Kultur- und Gesellschaftszustandes mit den Einzelphasen der von der modernen Arch., Sprach- und Geschichtswiss. rekonstruierten frühgriech. Gesch. machen als Lebens- und Schaffenszeit des Autors die 2. Hälfte des 8. Jh. v. Chr. wahrscheinlich [29; 21. bes. 693; 13; 18. 74–90; 26. bes. 625]. Mit einzelnen Werkstellen und bestimmten Objekten argumentierende Herabdatierungen, v. a. ins 7. Jh. [6; 36], haben sich bislang nicht durchgesetzt [25. 3 f.].

D. HERKUNFTSMILIEU

Der Autor steht auf einem gedanklich, sprachlich, ästhetisch, wertethisch, emotional und geschmacklich so hohen Niveau und reflektiert so dominant und zugleich affirmativ die Weltsicht einer Oberschicht, daß er innerhalb der von BOWRA [5. 444–468] aus dem Vergleich mündlicher Dichtung aller Völker und Zeiten abgeleiteten sozialen Hierarchie von Sängerdichtern auf der obersten Stufe angesiedelt werden muß: Er hat wohl – als → Aoide wie Achilleus in Il. 9,186–188 – dem Adel entweder selbst angehört oder ständig in seinem Umkreis gelebt [18. 43–47].

III. WERKE A. ZUGESCHRIEBENE WERKE B. ECHTE WERKE 1. ILIAS 2. ODYSSEE

A. ZUGESCHRIEBENE WERKE

Ilias und *Odyssee* galten die ganze Ant. hindurch als echt (zu der schon ant. Hypothese, nur die *Ilias* sei von Homer, s. → Chorizontes). Zahlreiche weitere Produkte (die z. T. auch uns noch vorliegen, im folgenden Katalog mit Sternchen versehen) liefen zwar ebenfalls unter H.s Namen, wurden ihm aber bereits von der H.-Philol. der Ant. ganz oder teilweise abgesprochen. Im spätant. Lex. → Suda werden als »zugeschrieben« aufgezählt: → *Amazónia*, → *Iliás mikrā́*, → *Nóstoi*, *Epikichlídes*, *Ethiépaktos* oder *Íamboi* (unklar, was gemeint), *Batrachomachía* (gemeint: die → **Batrachomyomachía*), *Arachnomachía*, *Geranomachía*, *Kerameís*, → *Amphiaráu exélasis*, *Paígnia* (»Spielereien, Scherzgedichte«), → *Oichalíās Hálōsis*, *Epithalámia*, *Kýklos* (gemeint: → *Epischer Zyklus), *Hýmnoi* (gemeint: die → *Homerischen Hymnen), → *Kýpria* (dazu tritt in anderen Quellen noch der → **Margítēs*). Schon ant. Lit.-Kritiker sprachen allen diesen Dichtungen aus Stil- und Qualitätsgründen die Echtheit ab (z. B. H.-Vita Nr. 5 [1. 29, 19–22]). Die neuzeitliche H.-Philol. ist zum gleichen Urteil gelangt (Forsch.-Ber.: [21. 821–831]).

B. ECHTE WERKE

1. ILIAS

a) UMFANG UND EINTEILUNG

Das Werk umfaßt (in [2]) 15 693 Hexameter, aufgeteilt in 24 »Gesänge« (ῥαψ-ῳδίαι, *rhaps-ōdíai*, zu je zw. ca. 450 und ca. 900 V.), entsprechend den 24 Buchstaben des griech. Einheitsalphabets seit → Eukleides [1]; schon die – offenbar uralte – Bezeichnung der Einheiten als »Rhapsodien«, die auf die → Rhapsoden verweist, macht wahrscheinlich, daß die Einteilung als solche nicht erst von den alexandrinischen Philologen vorgenommen wurde, sondern sich schon früh aus natürlichen »Vortragseinheiten« [21. 839,15] entwickelt hatte (vgl. das schon bei Herodot belegte Zitiersystem »H. *in der Diomedes-Aristie*«: Hdt. 2,116) und durch die institutionalisierte Werk-Rezitation am Fest der Panathenäen in Athen seit → Hipparchos [1] (um 520) befestigt wurde [37]; die Kanonisierung der Zahl 24 kann aber erst nach 403 (Buchstabenzahl-Fixierung durch → Eukleides [1]) erfolgt sein, so daß die Vita Ps.-Plutarchea 2,4 (›*Ilias* und *Odyssee* sind beide entsprechend der Zahl der Buchstaben aufgeteilt, nicht vom Dichter selbst, sondern von den Grammatikern um Aristarchos‹) im Grundsatz (autor-unabhängige Gelehrten-Erfindung) etwas Richtiges bewahrt haben könnte.

b) TITEL

Ἰλιάς (*Iliás*, für uns zum ersten Mal belegt bei Hdt. 2,116 (ἐν Ἰλιάδι), ist ein fem. Adj., das Herodot unterminologisiert auch zu anderen Subst. setzt (χώρη 5,94; γῆ 5,122: ›ilisches Land‹; vgl. Ἰλιὰς γυνή Eur. Hel. 1114: ›ilische Frau‹); zu ergänzen ist hier ποίησις (*poíēsis*: ›ilische Dichtung‹, ›Gedicht mit dem Thema Ilios‹ (analoge

Zeitliche Binnenstruktur der Ilias

Tag	Nacht	Anzahl der Verse	Partie	Inhalt
1. Tag	–	41	1, 12b – 52	Chryses-Vorspiel
2.–9. Tag	7 Nächte	1	1, 53	Pest im Achaier-Lager
10. Tag	Vorgeschichte (21 Tage)	422	1, 54 – 476	Streit. Gesandtschaft nach Chryse
11. Tag	646 Verse	16	1, 477 – 492	Rückkehr der Gesandtschaft/Groll d. Achilleus
12.–20. Tag	8 Nächte	(1)	(1, 493)	Götter bei den Aithiopen
21. Tag und	Nacht zum 22. Tag	165	1, 493 – 2, 47	Thetis-Bitte/Agamemnons Traum
22. Tag		3.653	2, 48 – 7, 380	Heeres-Test *(Peíra)*
			(fast 6 Gesänge)	Kataloge
				Vertrag: Kriegsentscheidung durch
				Zweikampf Menelaos – Paris
	Erster Kampftag			Teichoskopie (Mauerschau)
	(Einblendung)			Zweikampf Menelaos – Paris
				Vertragsbruch: Pandaros
				Diomedie / Homilie
				Zweikampf Hektor – Aias
23. Tag		52	7, 381 – 432	Waffenruhe/Bestattung
24. Tag		50	7, 433 – 482	Mauerbau der Achaier
25. Tag und	Nacht zum 26. Tag	1.857	8, 1 – 10, 579	Zurückdrängung der Achaier
	Zweiter Kampftag		(fast 3 Gesänge)	Troer lagern in Ebene
				Bittgesandtschaft zu Achilleus *(Litaí)*
				(Dolonie)
EPOS-KERN				Aristie des Agamemnon
(6 Tage)				Aristie Hektors
13.444 Verse		5.669		Verwundung der Achaier-Führer
26. Tag und	Nacht zum 27. Tag		11, 1 – 18, 617	Achilleus sendet Patroklos zu Nestor
	Dritter Kampftag		(8 Gesänge)	Kampf um die Lagermauer (Teichomachie)
				Einbruch der Troer ins Achaier-Lager
				Kampf vor den Schiffen
				Heras Verführung des Zeus *(Diós apátē)*
		2.163		Patroklie/Schildbeschreibung
27.Tag und	Nacht zum 28. Tag		19, 1 – 23, 110a	Beilegung des Streits *(Mḗnidos apórrhēsis)*
	Vierter Kampftag	147	(fast 5 Gesänge)	Neue Schlacht/Hektors Tod
28. Tag		662	23, 110b – 227a	Patroklos' Bestattung
29. Tag und	Nacht zum 30. Tag	9	23, 227b – 24, 21	Leichenspiele *(Ā́thla)*
30.– 40. Tag	10 Nächte	646	24, 22 – 30	Hektors Mißhandlung
41. Tag und	Nacht zum 42. Tag	105	24, 31 – 676	Priamos ins Achaier-Lager
42. Tag	Nachgeschichte		24, 677 – 781	Hektors Heimführung
	(24 Tage)			
	1.592 Verse	3		
43.– 50 Tag	7 Nächte	20	24, 782 – 784	Waffenruhe/Holzsammeln
51. Tag			24, 785 – 804	Hektors Bestattung

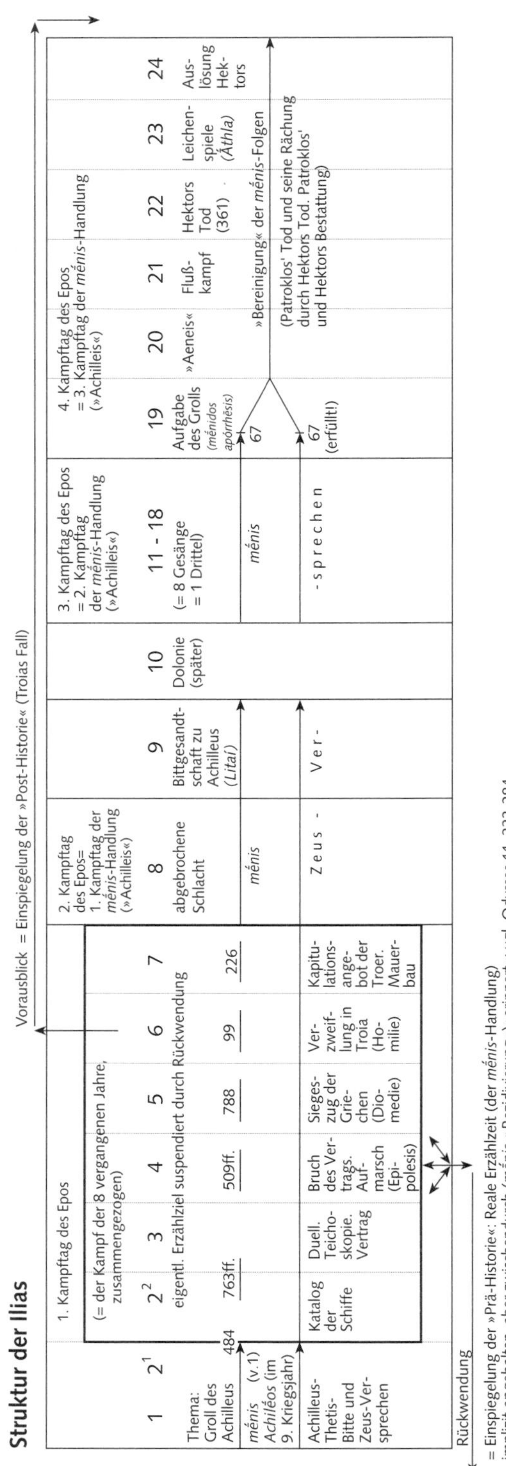

Titel: *Minyás*, *Dionysiás* usw., mit *i*-Suffix: *Thēbaís*, *Aeneis* usw.). Da Titelgebung erst mit wachsender Textualität überhaupt erforderlich wird, kann der Titel nicht vom Autor selbst stammen (ebenso [31. 24[3]]); daß dieser Titel den Kernpunkt verfehlt (Thema ist ja nicht Ilios, sondern die *mēnis Achilēos*, der Groll des Achilleus, Il. 1,1), ist evident [32. 93[5]]; treffend wäre *Meniás* oder *Achillēís*. Der Titel wird also zu einem nicht mehr bestimmbaren Zeitpunkt vor Herodot, vermutlich von Rhapsoden zu Unterscheidungszwecken, gegeben worden sein; er griff das vordergründige Faktum auf, daß die Teilhandlung ›Groll des Achilleus‹, die den Gegenstand der Dichtung bildet, in eine Rahmenhandlung eingebettet ist, die vor Ilios spielt und in der es um Ilios geht (Genaueres zur Frage: [19. 30–32]).

c) Inhalt und Komposition

Bei einer gemeinsamen Flotten-Expedition einer achaiischen mil. Allianz gegen Ilios (Troia) kommt es im 9. Jahr der Stadtbelagerung zu einem Grundsatzstreit zw. zwei achaiischen Adelsherren, dem Oberbefehlshaber Agamemnon von Argos/Mykene und dem jungen thessal. Königssohn Achilleus, der mit seinem Heeresteil, den Myrmidonen, für die Kampfkraft der Allianz entscheidend ist. Der Streit geht um die richtige Auslegung von bis dahin allgemeinverbindlichen Grundnormen der adeligen Oberschicht wie Ehre, Rang, Würde, Einsatzbereitschaft für das Ganze u.ä. Achilleus wird in seiner Ehre und in seinem Ranganspruch von Agamemnon so tief gedemütigt, daß er sich gezwungen sieht, aus der Kampfgemeinschaft auszuscheiden. Er verfällt in tiefen Groll (*mēnis Achilēos*), fährt aber nicht nach Hause, sondern hofft, die Wiederherstellung der durch seine persönliche Entehrung verletzten überpersönlichen Norm durch eine äußerste Gefährdung der Gesamtheit und die dadurch bei ihrem Führer zu erwartende Erkenntnis seines Fehlhandelns (= öffentliche Abbitte) erreichen zu können. Es gelingt ihm, seine göttl. Mutter Thetis und über sie den Göttervater Zeus für diesen radikalen Plan zu gewinnen.

Aufgrund der Unterstützung durch Zeus machen die belagerten Troianer daraufhin einen erfolgreichen Ausfall. Als sie unter ihrem Führer Hektor, dem Sohn des greisen troianischen Königs Priamos, bereits die ersten Schiffe der Achaier in Brand zu stecken versuchen, tritt der erhoffte Effekt tatsächlich ein: Agamemnon erkennt seine damalige Verblendetheit und leistet öffentlich Abbitte. Inzw. haben aber alle Beteiligten – nicht nur die beiden Kontrahenten, sondern die gesamte Allianz – so schwere äußere und innere Verluste erlitten (Achilleus selbst hat seinen geliebten Freund Patroklos verloren), daß alle Wiedergutmachungsversuche überholt sind. Achilleus greift zwar wieder in den Kampf ein, tötet Hektor und treibt die Troianer in ihre Burg zurück, so daß der alte Zustand äußerlich nicht nur wiederhergestellt, sondern mil. sogar noch verbessert ist, aber die Gemeinschaft ist durch den Streit im Innersten geschwächt, und der einst selbstverständliche Verbund ist vielfältig problematisiert und verunsichert worden.

Diese Gesch. ist keine unterhaltsame Wiedererzählung des ›Kriegs um Troia‹, sondern eine Reflexion der Oberschicht-Problematik des 8. Jh. angesichts eines rasanten wirtschaftlichen und ges. Neuaufbruchs (»Renaissance des 8. Jh.«) und des damit verbundenen allgemeinen Wertewandels: ›Wie soll die Oberschicht sich in der neuen Zeit neu orientieren?‹. Als Rahmen, in den diese Gesch. sich einbettet, ist die allbekannte Gesamtgesch. Troias (vom Paris-Urteil und dem Raub der Helena durch Paris bis zu Troias Fall) gewählt. Diese Technik wiederholt sich in der Weltlit. hundertfach (eine bekannte Großgesch. wird segmentiert, und im Segment wird ein Problem der Gegenwart entfaltet: »Mythenreprisen-Lit.«, vgl. etwa auch die Bibelnutzungslit.); zur ganzen Frage [20. 12–18].

Die Handlung der Ilias umfaßt 51 Tage. Der Handlungsablauf, die zeitl. Binnenstruktur, das Verhältnis zw. Raffung und Dehnung, zw. einlässig erzählter und nur summierter bzw. benannter Zeit usw. gehen aus der Abb. (Zeitliche Binnenstruktur der Ilias) hervor.

Die Komposition im einzelnen kann die zweite Abb. (Struktur der Ilias) verdeutlichen:

Streit der Fürsten sowie Achilleus- und Thetis-Bitte nehmen eineinhalb Gesänge ein. Ab 2,484 werden Achilleus- und Thetis-Bitte sowie das zugehörige Zeus-Versprechen für 5½ Gesänge (2^2 bis 7) suspendiert und dafür in einer Rückwendung die Hauptereignisse der vergangenen 8 J. (von der Flottensammlung in Aulis bis zum Kapitulationsangebot der Troianer *vor* Achilleus' Ausscheiden) hereingeholt (wobei die Gegenwartshandlung – der Groll des Achilleus – durch »Rezidivierungsstellen« immer wieder präsent gemacht wird). Im 8. Gesang wird die Hauptlinie (die *mē̓nis*-Handlung) wieder aufgenommen und (über den späteren Einschub des 10. Gesangs hinweg, s. [9]) nunmehr zügig bis zum Plan-Ziel des 1. Gesanges (äußerste Gefährdung der Achaier und Abbitte des Agamemnon) in 19,67 weitergeführt. Danach wird in 5½ Gesängen die Bereinigung der *mē̓nis*-Folgen bis zu Hektors Tötung durch Achilleus (22), den Leichenspielen für Patroklos (23) und dem versöhnlichen Abschluß der Herausgabe von Hektors Leichnam an Priamos durch Achilleus sowie Hektors Bestattung in Troia (24) erzählt.

In der Hauptstruktur ist die Erzählung als offensichtlich wohlgeplante Einheit – ohne wirkliche Überlappungen, Dubletten, logische Lücken und Widersprüche im Grundplan – durchkomponiert [18. 168 f.]; Längen und Ausmalungen können durchaus die sukzessive Arbeit des Original-Autors an seinem Riesenwerk widerspiegeln und müssen nicht Einschübe von fremder Hand sein [27. 209–211, 462–466, 533; 5. 483 f.; 24. 234; 18. 168 f.; 37]. Die Meinung setzt sich durch, daß die Ilias schriftlich verfaßt und das Werk *eines* großen Dichters ist [37].

2. Odyssee

a) Umfang und Einteilung

Das Werk umfaßt (in [3]) 12 109 Hexameter, eingeteilt wie die Ilias in 24 Gesänge im Umfang von je ca. 350 bis ca. 900 V. Für die Entstehung der Einteilung gilt dasselbe wie bei der Ilias (s.o.).

b) Titel

Ὀδυσσείη/*Odysseíē* (später häufiger Ὀδύσσεια/ *Odýsseia*) ist für uns zum ersten Mal belegt bei Hdt. 2,116 (ἐν Ὀδυσσείῃ). Der Titel bereitet hier keine Probleme: Benennung nach dem Hauptthelden ist von früh an üblich (*Hērakléīs* oder *Hērakleía*, *Alkmaiōnís*, *Aithiopís*: Gedicht vom Aithiopen-König Memnon, usw.) und trifft sachlich zu.

c) Inhalt und Komposition

Nach der Eroberung Troias geraten die Achaier in Streit und fahren getrennt und auf unterschiedlichen Routen in die Heimat zurück. Ihre Abenteuer auf der Heimfahrt (*nóstos*) bildeten das Thema einer Reihe von Einzel-Vorträgen der Aoiden (vgl. Od. 1,325 ff.), z.B. ›Die Heimkehr der Atriden‹, ›Die Heimkehr des Nestor‹, ›Die Heimkehr des Menelaos‹ usw.; später wurden solche Einzelvorträge auch zu einem Gesamtwerk → *Nóstoi* (›Heimkünfte‹) zusammengestellt; als Heimkunft-Erzählung allein erh. geblieben ist unsere *Odyssee*, als offenbar ebenfalls durch die Schrift ermöglichte großdimensionierte Ausarbeitung einer ›Heimkehr des Odysseus‹.

Die *Odyssee* erzählt die kritischen letzten 40 Tage der Heimkehr des Troia-Kämpfers Odysseus auf seine Heimatinsel Ithaka und ›zu seiner Frau‹ (= Penelope; 1,13) im 20. Jahr (16,206 u.ö.) nach seinem Aufbruch gen Troia (10 Jahre Troianischer Krieg und 10 Jahre Irrfahrten und Zwangsaufenthalte, zuletzt bewirkt durch den Zorn des Meeresgottes Poseidon: 1,68–75). Von den 40 Handlungstagen werden nur 16 Tage und 8 Nächte erzählt, der Rest ist benannte Zeit; die Vorgesch., d. h. die fast 20 Jahre vor dem Einsetzen der Handlung, wird – ähnlich wie in der *Ilias*, aber technisch entwickelter – in Rückblicken, v. a. in der großen Ich-Abenteuer-Erzählung des Odysseus bei den Phaiaken (Gesänge 6–12: sog. *Phaiakís*) die Abenteuer an die Handlung herangeholt:

Handlung nach Odysseus' Abfahrt mit 12 Schiffen von Troia
(6.–12. Gesang)

1. Das Land der Kikonen: Zerstörung der Stadt Ismaros. Schlacht mit den Kikonen der Umgebung. Verlust von 72 Gefährten.

   Vom Sturm bei Kap Melea (= Südspitze der Argolis auf der Peloponnes) an der Insel Kythera vorbei »neun Tage lang« abgetrieben: Ausfahrt aus der realen Welt, Einfahrt ins Land der Schiffermärchen.

2. Das Land der Lotophagen (= Lotos-Esser): Durch Genuß der Droge Lotos die Heimkehr fast vergessen.

3. Die Insel der Kyklopen (= Einäug-Riesen): der Kyklop Polyphem (Πολύφημος, *Polýphēmos*, »der Vielberüchtigte«): Mit 12 Gefährten in der Höhle des Riesen eingeschlossen. 6 Gefährten vom Kyklopen verspeist. Dem Riesen mit einem angespitzten, glühendheiß gemachten Ölbaumpfahl das einzige Auge ausgebohrt. Der »Niemand«-Trick. Unter dem Bauch je 3 zusammengebundener Schafe aus der von Polyphem bewachten Höhlenöffnung entkommen. Mutwillige Reizung des blinden Riesen vom Schiff aus. Polyphem bittet seinen Vater Poseidon um Rache.

4. Die schwimmende Insel des Herrn der Winde Aiolos: Beschenkung mit dem Windschlauch.
   In Sichtweite der Heimat öffnen die törichten Gefährten den Windschlauch: Wirbelwind trägt die Schiffe zurück zu Aiolos. Fluch des Aiolos über Odysseus.
5. Das Land der Laistrygonen (= Riesen): 11 Schiffe durch Feldsteinwürfe der Riesen vernichtet, die schwimmenden Gefährten aufgefischt und aufgefressen. Nur noch das Schiff des Odysseus ist übrig.
6. Die Insel Aia mit der Zauberin Kirke (Tochter des Sonnengottes Helios): 22 Gefährten von Kirke in Schweine verwandelt. Hermes schenkt Odysseus das Gegenkraut Moly (Μῶλυ, eine Wunderpflanze). Odysseus erliegt Kirkes Anziehung. Ein Jahr lang Wohlleben bei Kirke. Bei der Abfahrt verweist Kirke den Odysseus an den Seher Teiresias im Totenland.
7. Die Totenbeschwörung jenseits des Ringstroms Okeanos: Prophezeiung des Teiresias. Begegnung mit der Mutter, mit Agamemnon, Achilleus, Patroklos, Aias. Betrachtung des Totenrichters Minos, der Übeltäter Tityos, Tantalos, Sisyphos; des Wohltäters Herakles.
   Rückkehr zu Kirke. Kirkes Warnung vor den Sirenen, den Plankten, vor Skylla und Charybdis, den Herden des Helios.
8. Die Insel der Sirenen: Durch Verstopfen der Ohren mit Wachs und durch Festbinden des Odysseus an den Mastbaum der Verführung des absoluten Wissens entkommen.
9. Skylla und Charybdis (= Meeresstrudel): Verlust von 6 Gefährten.
10. Die Helios-Insel Thrinakia: Gefährten schlachten vor Hunger die verbotenen Rinder des Helios. Helios fordert Rache von Zeus. Zeus schlägt das Schiff mit seinem Blitz, alle Gefährten ertrinken. Odysseus kommt, auf Kiel und Mastbaum reitend, als einziger Überlebender nach Ogygia zu Kalypso.

Das Werk gliedert sich in die zwei Hälften ›Heimkehr vor Erreichen Ithakas‹ (1–12) und ›Heimkehr auf Ithaka selbst‹ (in der von Athene bewirkten Tarnung eines Bettlers, 13–24); das Hauptgewicht liegt auf der zweiten Hälfte, die in ihren 12 Gesängen lediglich 6 Tage erzählt. Der 5. Tag von Odysseus' Aufenthalt auf Ithaka – der Tag der Entscheidung mit dem Höhepunkt der Wiedererkennungsszene Odysseus-Penelope – nimmt allein 4 Gesänge (20–23) mit 1701 Versen ein: die äußere Heimkehr (mit der Abenteuer-Erzählung) wird der inneren Heimkehr (Überwindung der Entfremdung nach 20 Jahren Abwesenheit) untergeordnet.

Verfugt mit der zentripetalen Haupthandlung »Rückkehr des Vaters« ist die zentrifugale Nebenhandlung »Suche des Sohnes (Telemachos) nach dem Vater« (sog. ›Telemachie‹: Gesänge 3 und 4 plus ein Teil von 15), die den vaterlos aufgewachsenen Sohn durch die Begegnung mit dem *Bild* seines Vaters in den Erinnerungen von Odysseus' alten Troia-Kampfgenossen Nestor in Pylos (3. Gesang) und Menelaos in Sparta (4. Gesang) für die *reale* Begegnung mit seinem Vater (16. Gesang) innerlich reif macht. Die Gliederung im einzelnen zeigt folgende Übersicht:

Die Handlung besteht aus 5 großen Handlungsblöcken:

	Handlungsimpuls: Götterversammlung	Gesang
I.	Ithaka vor Odysseus Wiederkehr	1 und 2
II.	Telemachos' Reise nach Pylos und Sparta, um Gewißheit über den Verbleib seines Vaters zu erhalten (I + II, dazu noch ›Telemachs Rückkehr‹ im 15. Gesang, werden als ›Telemachie‹ bezeichnet)	3 und 4
III.	Odysseus' Floßfahrt von Ogygia bis Scheria	5
IV.	Odysseus auf Scheria bei den Phaiaken (sog. ›Phaiakis‹): Odysseus erzählt seine Abenteuer von Trojas Fall bis zur Ankunft auf Scheria	6 bis 12
V.	Odysseus auf Ithaka	13 bis 24

Deutlich ist eine grundlegende strukturelle Zweiteilung zu erkennen:

(A) 12 Gesänge Vorbereitung der Heimkehr bei allen, die beteiligt sind (Frau, Sohn, Hausgesinde, Freier, Volk von Ithaka, die Außenwelt befreundeter Adelshäuser; die Götter; Odysseus selbst),

(B) 12 Gesänge Rückkehr in der Heimat selbst: Wiedererwerb und Sicherung des einst mit Selbstverständlichkeit Besessenen.

IV. Stoff, Sprache und Vers

Den stofflichen Hintergrund der *Ilias* bildet die → Troia-Sage, den der *Odyssee* die → Odysseus-Sage; beide Sagen gehen auf myk. Zeit (→ Mykenai) zurück und wurden zw. ihr und der Entstehungszeit beider Epen, dem 8. Jh., im Medium des mündl. improvisierten hexametrischen → Aoiden-Vortrags von Generation zu Generation weitergegeben (→ Epos II).
Zur Sprache s. → Homerische Sprache.

V. Mündlichkeit und Schriftlichkeit

Troia-Sage und Odysseus-Sage waren Einzelstücke in einem gewaltigen Heldensagen-Reservoir (z. B. Argonauten-Sage, Theben-Sage, Herakles-Sage), aus dem die Aoiden ihre mündlichen Vorträge auf Anforderung stets aufs neue formten (Einspiegelung dieser Praxis in die *Odyssee* selbst z. B. 8,250–255 und 8,488–498 [18. 42]). Vor der Einführung des Alphabets (um 800) waren diese Vorträge Unikate, die mit dem letzten Wort des Sängers für immer verronnen waren (→ Mündliche Dichtung; M. Parry). Unsere *Ilias* und unsere *Odyssee* sind Jahrzehnte nach Einführung des Alphabets entstanden, höchstwahrscheinlich mit Hilfe der Schrift komponiert, jedenfalls aber mittels der Schrift fixiert (ob vom Autor diktiert oder selbst niedergeschrieben, bleibt offen; für die Diktat-These z. B. Janko [14. 37f.] nach Lord [22], für eine differenzierte Autographie-These z. B. Latacz [16. 12f.]) und tradiert worden. Die Schrift mit ihren Vorstudien- und Planungsmöglichkeiten [10] erlaubte die Schaffung logisch kohärenter, kunstvoll durchkomponierter Thematisierungen von

Einzelmotiven, die aus der Erzähltradition herausgegriffen und vielfältig ausgeweitet und vertieft wurden. Aus den urspr. wohl linear-narrativen Sagen-Erzählungen konnten so Reflexionen über Fragen der eigenen Zeit werden, die sich im traditionellen Erzählraum ansiedelten und auf diese Weise eine konzentrierte und kondensierte Qualität erreichten, die ihnen ihr Überleben sicherte [20].

VI. Überlieferung

Mit der Überführung eines Teiles der traditionellen mündlichen hexametrischen Erzähltradition in die Schriftlichkeit in Form der beiden Groß-Epen *Ilias* und *Odyssee* war die Zeit der freien Improvisation grundsätzlich beendet; folgerichtig wurden aus den bisherigen Aoiden (d.h. Improvisationskünstlern) nunmehr Rhapsoden (d.h. *Ilias*- und *Odyssee*-Rezitatoren). Da das Autograph des Autors mangels eines Urheberrechts nicht wortwörtlich wiedergegeben werden mußte, konnten die Rhapsoden je nach Rezitationsumständen und Selbstdarstellungsehrgeiz Modifikationen (Zusätze, Omissionen usw.) vornehmen. Solche Modifikationen scheinen sich jedoch – abgesehen vom 10. Ilias-Gesang, der → Dolonie – nach Ausweis der generellen Stimmigkeit beider Erzählverläufe auf nur wenige Stellen und meist auf Einzelverse oder Formelvarianten beschränkt zu haben.

Die große Popularität beider Epen bes. in Athen (Darstellungen von Epen-Szenen in der att. Vasenmalerei seit vor 600 [15]) führte zu ihrer Integration in das Festprogramm der att. Panathenäen unter Hipparchos (um 520): vollständige Rezitation durch Rezitations-Ensembles alle 4 J. Dadurch und durch die Einführung der Epen als Pflichtlektüre ins Ausbildungsprogramm der athenischen Oberschichtjugend wurde Athen für die weitere Homerüberlieferung prägend; möglicherweise wurde den Panathenäen-Rezitationen ein bestimmter Einheitstext zugrunde gelegt. Dennoch gab es – anders als im Falle der att. Tragiker – kein eigentliches H.-»Staatsexpl.«, so daß die Überlieferung (die ja nicht nur in Athen stattfand), wie H.-Zitate bei Platon, Aristoteles u.a. zeigen, grundsätzlich uneinheitlich blieb.

Die Philologen-Akademie des Museions von Alexandreia nahm sich des »National-Autors« intensiv an: die drei berühmtesten Bibliotheksvorstände der Museionsbibliothek, → Zenodotos, → Aristophanes [4] von Byzanz und → Aristarchos [4] von Samothrake, beschäftigten sich krit. mit dem H.-Text und hinterließen in den uns erh. → Scholien ihre Spuren. Seit ca. 150 v.Chr. bieten die H.-Papyri eine wesentlich einheitlichere Textgestalt als zuvor (und unsere ma. Mss. weichen davon in nur noch geringem Ausmaß ab); dies dürfte die Buchhandelsreaktion auf Aristarchos' Vereinheitlichung des H.-Textes sein. Die Text-Arbeit der drei »Großen« wurde fortgeführt von den alexandrinischen Philologen → Aristonikos [5] und → Didymos [1] (unter Augustus) und (neben anderen) von → Nikanor und → Herodianos (im 2. Jh. n. Chr.). Die Arbeit dieser vier Philologen wurde in einem Komm. zusammengefaßt (→ Viermännerkommentar), der den Scholien in unseren Hss. A und T zugrunde liegt. Trotz dieser krit. Arbeit am Text kam es nie zu einer standardisierten Einheitsausgabe H.s; das zeigen die rund 2000 H.-Papyri (3. Jh. v. – 7. Jh. n. Chr.), die in vielen (wenn auch nicht gravierenden) Einzelheiten nicht unerheblich differieren.

Die ma. Cod. setzen im 9. Jh. ein; ihre genaue Anzahl ist bis h. unbekannt (allein zur *Ilias* sind bisher über 200 Hss., zur *Odyssee* weit über 70 registriert), und eine Kollation auch nur aller bekannten liegt in weiter Ferne. Die *editio princeps* erfolgte 1488 in Florenz durch Demetrios Chalkondyles auf der Basis einer h. verschollenen Hs. Verbreitetste Lesetexte sind h. [2] und [3]; im Entstehen begriffen ist eine neue Teubner-Ausgabe der *Ilias* von M. L. West. Da die Erfassung und Kollationierung sämtlicher H.-Hss. eine Utopie bleiben muß, geht die H.-Philol. h. von einer Vulgata aus, deren mangelnde Fundiertheit ihr zwar bewußt ist, die sie aber angesichts der relativ geringen Diskrepanzen in den bisher untersuchten H.-Hss. als Arbeitsgrundlage für ausreichend erachtet.

→ Epos; Homerische Sprache; Allegorese; Epik; Homerische Frage

Ed.: **1** U. de Wilamowitz-Moellendorff, Vitae Homeri et Hesiodi in usum scholarum, 1915 u.ö. **2** D.B. Monro, T.W. Allen (ed.), Homeri Opera, Tom. I/II (Ilias), 1902 u.ö. (Oxford Classical Texts) **3** P. Von der Mühll (rec.), Homeri Odyssea, 1946 u.ö. (jetzt Bibliotheca Teubneriana).
Lit.: **4** F. Bechtel, Die histor. PN des Griech. bis zur Kaiserzeit, 1917 **5** C.M. Bowra, Heldendichtung, 1964 (Heroic Poetry, 1952) **6** W. Burkert, Das hunderttorige Theben, in: WS 89, 1976, 5–21 **7** Chantraine **8** G. Curtius, De nomine Homeri, 1855 **9** G. Danek, Studien zur Dolonie, 1988 **10** A. Dihle, Homer-Probleme, 1970 **11** G. Finsler, Homer in der Neuzeit von Dante bis Goethe, 1912 **12** K. Heldmann, Die Niederlage Homers im Dichterwettstreit mit Hesiod, 1982 **13** R. Janko, Homer, Hesiod and the Hymns, 1982 **14** Ders., The Iliad: A Commentary, Vol. IV: books 13–16, 1992 **15** R. Kannicht, Dichtung und Bildkunst. Die Rezeption der Troja-Epik in den frühgriech. Sagenbildern (1979), in: Ders., Paradeigmata, 1996, 45–67 (engl.: Poetry and Art, in: Classical Antiquity 1, 1982, 70–86) **16** J. Latacz, Hauptfunktionen des ant. Epos in Ant. und Moderne, in: AU 34(3), 1991, 8–17 **17** Ders., Hauptfunktionen ... (Langfassung, 1991), in: Ders., Erschließung der Ant., 1994, 257–279 **18** Ders., Homer. Der erste Dichter des Abendlands, 1985, ³1997 (engl.: Homer. His Art and His World, 1996; ital.: 1990; niederländ.: 1991) **19** Ders., Achilleus, (1995) ²1997 **20** Ders., Troia und Homer. Neue Erkenntnisse und neue Perspektiven, in: Grazer Morgenländische Studien 4, 1997, 1–42 **21** A. Lesky, s.v. H., RE Suppl. 11, 687–846 **22** A. Lord, Homer's Originality: Oral Dictated Texts (1953), in: Ders., Epic Singers and Oral Tradition, 1991, 38–48 **23** Ders., Der Sänger erzählt. Wie ein Epos entsteht, 1965 (The Singer of Tales, 1960) **24** M. Peters, in: Die Sprache 33, 1987, 234ff. **25** B. Powell, Homer and Writing, in: I. Morris, B. Powell (Hrsg.), A New Companion to Homer, 1997, 3–32

26 K. RAAFLAUB, Homeric Society, in: Ebd., 624–648
27 K. REINHARDT, Die Ilias und ihr Dichter, 1961
28 W. SCHADEWALDT, Iliasstudien, (1938) ³1966 u.ö.
29 Ders., Homer und sein Jh. (1942), in: Ders., Von Homers Welt und Werk, (1944) ³1959, 87–129 30 Ders., Legende von Homer dem fahrenden Sänger (1942), 1959
31 E. SCHMALZRIEDT, Περὶ φύσεως. Zur Frühgesch. der Buchtitel, 1970 32 SCHMID/STÄHLIN I 33 E. VOGT, Die Schrift vom Wettkampf Homers und Hesiods, in: RhM 102, 1959, 193–221 34 Ders., Homer – ein großer Schatten? Die Forschungen zur Person Homers, in: J. LATACZ (Hrsg.), Zweihundert Jahre Homer-Forschung, 1991, 365–377
35 S. WEST, The Transmission of the Text, in: A. HEUBECK, S. WEST, J. B. HAINSWORTH, A Commentary on Homer's Odyssey, I, 1988, 33–48 36 M. L. WEST, The Date of the Iliad, in: MH 52, 1995, 203–219 37 Ders., Die Gesch. des Textes, in: J. LATACZ und Mitarbeiter, Homer, Ilias. Ein Gesamtkomm., I 2, 1999 38 U.v. WILAMOWITZ-MOELLENDORFF, Die Ilias und H., in: Ders., Die Ilias und Homer, 1916, 356–376 39 W. WIMMEL, Die Kultur holt uns ein. Die Bedeutung der Textualität für das gesch. Werden, 1981. J.L.

[2] H. aus Byzantion. Nach Suda o 253 (vgl. Tzetz. chil. 12,399, v. 202) Sohn des Andromachos und der Dichterin Myro (Suda μ 1464), Grammatiker und Tragiker, Hauptschaffenszeit 284/1–281/0 v. Chr. H. war Mitglied der trag. Pleias (CAT A 5a,1 und b,6) und Konkurrent des Sositheos (TrGF 99; vgl. Suda σ 860), er soll 45 (Suda o 253) oder 57 (Tzetz. vita Lycophronis p. 4,30 SCH.) Tragödien und ein Epos ›Eurypyleia‹ (Tzetz. vita Hesiodi p. 49,25 WIL.) verfaßt haben; von einer Ehrenstatue in Byzantion wird berichtet (Anth. Pal. 2,407 ff.). Er trug den Beinamen *neós/neṓteros* (»der Jüngere«; vgl. Tzetz. vita Lycophronis, ebd.; vita Hesiodi, ebd.). Timon (TrGF 112) soll u. a. ihn beim Abfassen von Tragödien unterstützt haben (Diog. Laert. 9,113). Vielleicht ist er identisch mit dem in DID A 3a, 66 genannten H., der an den Dionysien siegte (TrGF 109).

METTE, 163 • TrGF 98 und 109. F.P.

Homerphilologie s. Philologie

Homicidium. Das lat. Wort *h.* (»Mord, Totschlag«, auch »unbeabsichtigte Tötung«) ist nicht vor Seneca d. Ä. (1. Jh. v. Chr.) nachweisbar (bei Cicero dreimal *homicida*) und begegnet bei den Juristen vor 250 n. Chr. noch selten, häufig dagegen in den Kaiserkonstitutionen. Bis zur spätrepublikanischen Zeit war die Bezeichnung für vorsätzliche Tötung → *parricidium*. Schon eine Norm der Priester vor den 12 Tafeln (ca. 450 v. Chr.) bestimmte, daß nur der absichtliche Täter *parricida(s)* sein solle. Er verfiel nach altröm. Recht der vom Gemeinwesen kontrollierten Privatrache. Der absichtslose Täter mußte vor versammeltem Volk den Agnaten (→ *agnatio*) des Getöteten einen Schafsbock anbieten, den diese anstelle des Täters töteten. Der privaten Verfolgung des Mordes trat seit dem Beginn des 2. Jh. v. Chr. allmählich eine Verfolgung von Amts wegen an die Seite, welche sie schließlich völlig verdrängte. Die ihr zugrunde liegenden materiellrechtlichen Normen werden nicht anders ausgesehen haben als diejenigen des Kernstücks der *lex Cornelia de sicariis et veneficis* (81 v. Chr.), das in erster Linie das Bewaffnetsein in verbrecherischer Absicht und erst an zweiter Stelle die vorsätzliche vollendete Tötung eines (auch unfreien) Menschen sowie die Giftmischerei betraf. Die *lex Cornelia* blieb mit mancherlei Veränderungen bis Iustinian (6. Jh. n. Chr.) in Kraft. Seit Hadrian (Anf. 2. Jh. n. Chr.) ist die Tendenz zur Bestrafung auch der fahrlässigen Tötung zu beobachten.
→ Mord

W. KUNKEL, Unters. zur Entwicklung des röm. Kriminalverfahrens in vorsullanischer Zeit, 1962 • Ders., s. v. quaestio, RE 24, 720–786 • A. VÖLKL, Die Verfolgung der Körperverletzung im frühen Röm. Recht, 1984, 98 f. • WIEACKER, RRG, 246. DI.S.

Homilia s. Predigt

Homo mensura-Satz s. Protagoras

Homoioi
I. HOMOIOI BEI ARISTOTELES II. SPARTA

I. HOMOIOI BEI ARISTOTELES
Mit dem Begriff *h.* (bei Homer, im Ion. und im frühen Att. ὁμοῖοι, später ὅμοιοι, »die Gleichen«) bezeichnet Aristoteles in einem Abschnitt über die Voraussetzungen politischer Stabilität (Aristot. pol. 1308a 11–13) eindeutig eine Elite, also eine rechtlich oder sozial definierte, durch Geburt oder Reichtum klar abgegrenzte herrschende Schicht. Wenn viele einer solchen Elite angehören, so stellt sie nach Aristoteles selbst eine Art Volk dar (ὥσπερ δῆμος ἤδη οἱ ὅμοιοι); es sei dann von Nutzen, durch eine Beschränkung der Amtszeit möglichst alle *h.* an der Regierung zu beteiligen (Aristot. pol. 1308a 13–17; vgl. auch 1332b 27–29).

II. SPARTA
Wie der Wortgebrauch bei Xenophon nahelegt (hell. 3,3,4 f.; Lak. pol. 10,7; 13,1; 13,7; an. 4,6,14; vgl. Aristot. pol. 1306b 30, allerdings vielleicht ein Einschub), gehörte die Bezeichnung *h.* zu den Begriffen, mit denen die spartanische Gesellschaft beschrieben wurde. Weitere Belege für die Verwendung des Wortes im übertragenen Sinn (Hdt. 7,234,2; Demosth. or. 20,107; vgl. Isokr. or. 7,61) bestätigen dies. Offensichtlich handelte es sich um ein eher inoffizielles Synonym für Σπαρτιᾶται (→ *Spartiátai*) – ein Ausdruck, der in amtlichen Dokumenten Verwendung fand (SEG XI, 1204a, ca. 600–550 v. Chr.) – und bezeichnete demnach spartanische Bürger mit allen polit. und sozialen Rechten. Der entsprechende Begriff für die Unterschichten (ὑπομείονες, *hypomeíones*) erscheint nur ein einziges Mal bei Xenophon (hell. 3,3,5).

Der Begriff *h.* kann nicht mit »Gleiche« übersetzt werden, denn die Spartaner waren nicht ἴσοι (*ísoi*) und haben sich selbst nicht als solche bezeichnet. Sie waren auch nicht ὁμοί (*homoí*, »identisch«), sondern *h.*, Gleiche zwar nicht in jeder Hinsicht, aber gleich unter einigen entscheidenden Aspekten. Dazu gehörten vor allem Herkunft, Erziehung und Lebensweise. Jeder der *h.* hatte einen spartanischen Vater und (mit der möglichen Ausnahme der μόθακες, → *móthakes*) eine spartanische Mutter. Sie alle mußten – abgesehen von den Thronfolgern aus den beiden Königsfamilien – die obligatorische Erziehung (ἀγωγή, → *agōgḗ*) durchlaufen. Sie trugen dieselbe Kleidung, aßen dieselben Speisen bei den gemeinsamen Mahlzeiten (συσκάνια, συσσίτια; *syskánia, syssítia*) und kämpften gemeinsam in einheitlicher Ausrüstung als → Hopliten in der Phalanx.

Tatsächlich aber bestanden auch für die *h.* in Sparta erhebliche Ungleichheiten in sozialer, polit. und zunehmend vor allem in wirtschaftlicher Hinsicht. Das Wort *h.* betonte demnach in einer Polis, die sowohl nach ihrer Selbstauffassung als auch im alltäglichen Leben stets auf Homogenität und Gleichheit der Bürger bedacht war, in ideologischer Weise die Gemeinsamkeiten der Spartiaten, womit wahrscheinlich die wachsenden Unterschiede verhüllt werden sollten. Es spricht viel dafür, daß der Begriff *h.* im 5. Jh. v. Chr. aufkam, in einer Zeit also, in der die Gegensätze und Ungleichheiten tatsächlich eher zunahmen. Gerade jene Faktoren, die eigentlich Gleichheit unter den Spartiaten bewirken sollten, nämlich Herkunft, Erziehung und Lebensweise, wurden zur Ursache dieser Ungleichheit. Einige Spartiaten, unter ihnen die Könige, waren Aristokraten (Thuk. 5,16,2), während die meisten dem δᾶμος (*dámos*, Volk) angehörten. Auch im Erziehungssystem kam es zu einer Differenzierung zwischen denen, die erfolgreich waren, und denen, die versagten und sogar zu den *hypomeíones* zurückgestuft wurden. Einige Spartiaten waren extrem reich und so in der Lage, sich den Pferderennen zu widmen oder auch Weizenbrot für die gemeinsamen Mahlzeiten beizusteuern (Xen. Lak. pol. 5,3), während andere zu arm waren, um den vorgeschriebenen Beitrag an Gerste zu leisten (Aristot. pol. 1270a 30ff.). Diese Disparitäten unter den *h.* trugen zuletzt dazu bei, den berühmten spartanischen κόσμος (*kósmos*) zu destabilisieren.

→ Sozialstruktur; Sparta

1 P. Cartledge, Agesilaus and the Crisis of Sparta, 1987
2 Ders., Hopliten und Helden: Spartas Beitrag zur Technik der antiken Kriegskunst, in: K. Christ (Hrsg.), Sparta, 1986, 387–425, 470 **3** K. Christ (Hrsg.), Sparta, 1986 **4** M. I. Finley, Sparta, in: K. Christ (Hrsg.), Sparta, 1986, 327–350
5 S. Hodkinson, Social order and the conflict of values in Classical Sparta, in: Chiron 1983, 239–81 **6** S. Link, Der Kosmos Sparta: Recht und Sitte in klass. Zeit, 1994
7 M. Nafissi, La nascita del Kosmos: Studi sulla storia e la società di Sparta, 1991 **8** P. Oliva, Sparta and her Social Problems, 1971 **9** L. Thommen, Lakedaimonion Politeia, 1996.

P.C./Ü: A.H.

Homoioprophoron, Homoioteleuton s. Figuren

Homole, Homolion (Ὁμόλη, Ὁμόλιον). Berg am Nordende der thessal. → Ossa. Am Ausfluß des Peneios aus dem Tempetal (→ Tempe) lag am Abhang (nicht am Meer, Strab. 9,5,22) die gleichnamige Stadt, nachgewiesen oberhalb vom h. Omolion (früher Laspochori). H. war die nördlichste Stadt der → Magnesia und damit Griechenlands. H. überwachte den Flußübergang nach Niedermakedonien (Liv. 42,38,10; Brückenreste ca. 1 km nördl. von Omolion). Funde belegen eine Besiedlung seit archa. Zeit. Als bedeutendster Ort der Magnetai außerhalb des Golfs von Pagasai entsandte H. meist einen der Hieromnemones (Delegierte im Amphiktyonenrat) des Stamms nach Delphoi. H. entging nach Ausweis von Mz. des 3. Jh. (HN 296) dem → Synoikismos von → Demetrias [1] um 290 v. Chr. Im J. 172 fanden an der Peneiosbrücke Verhandlungen zw. Q. Marcius Philippus und Perseus statt (Liv. 42,39ff.). In byz. Zeit lag oberhalb von H. eine Einsiedelei.

H. Biesantz, Die thessal. Grabreliefs, 1965, 130f. • F. Stählin, s. v. H. (1–2), RE 8, 2259ff. • Ders., Das hellen. Thessalien, 1924, 46 (Quellen) • D. Theocharis, in: AD 17, 1961/2,2, 17ff. und 20,2, 1965, 319 (Fundber.) • TIB 1, 1976, 1973.

HE.KR.

Homologia (ὁμολογία), wörtlich »Gleichsprechen«, bezeichnet in der griech. Umgangssprache die schlichte mündliche Zustimmung oder Vereinbarung. Im rechtlichen Sinn wurde H. bald auch für schriftliche Vereinbarungen gebraucht (→ *syngraphḗ*, → *synthḗkē*). Die rechtliche Bindung an die *h.* ging, wie in Athen ersichtlich, vom vorprozessualen Zugeständnis einzelner Behauptungen des Gegners aus. Im Vorverfahren (→ *anákrisis*, s. → *diaitētaí* [2]) hatten die Parteien die Pflicht, einander auf Fragen zu antworten (Demosth. or. 46,10). Die Bejahung einer solchen Frage war, von Zeugen bestätigt, als *h.* im Hauptverfahren (s. → *dikasterion*) maßgeblich (κυρία/*kyría*, Demosth. or. 42,122). Die gleiche Wirkung hatte eine vor dem Prozeß, also ohne Antwortzwang (ἑκών/*hekṓn*, freiwillig), abgegebene *h.* (Demosth. or. 56,2). Aus der *h.* als bloßer »Vereinbarung« konnte also nicht geklagt werden, allenfalls auf der Grundlage hierin als unbestreitbar zugestandener haftungsbegründender Tatsachen. In den Papyri Ägyptens lebt dieser Rechtszustand fort. Häufig ist der Text von Geschäftsurkunden (bes. die bei den → *agoranómoi* hinterlegten) und das → *cheirógraphon* mit der Klausel eingeleitet, eine oder beide Parteien »gestehen zu« oder »anerkennen«, weshalb diese Dokumente nach ihrer Formulierung *h.* bezeichnet werden. Aber auch ohne diese Einleitung bezeichnen die Geschäftspartner selbst eine Vertragsurkunde oft als *h.*

Die im röm. Formular am Schluß der Urkunde übliche Stipulationsklausel (→ *stipulatio*) wird in griech. Sprache mit ὁμολογεῖν (*homologeín*, anerkennen) wiedergegeben, im Babatha-Archiv (PYadin) vom Toten Meer bereits zu Beginn des 2. Jh. n. Chr., in Ägypten erst nach der Constitutio Antoniniana 212 n. Chr.

H. J. Wolff, Die Grundlagen des griech. Vertragsrechts, in: ZRG 74, 1957, 26–72 • G. Thür, Beweisführung vor den

Schwurgerichtshöfen Athens, 1977, 152–158 • H. A. RUPPRECHT, Einführung in die Papyruskunde, 1994, 113 f. 138 f. G.T.

Homonoia (Ὁμόνοια). Das Wort *h.* (»Einigkeit«) wird in Athens Krise von 411 v. Chr. (darauf bezogen bei Thuk. 8,75,2; 93,3) als Mahnung der Demokraten zum inneren Zusammenhalt offenbar neu geprägt (vgl. Antiphon 87 B 44–71; Thrasymachos 85 B 1; Gorgias 82 B 8a DK).

Polisinterner H. liegen von da an meist sozioökonom. Konflikte (Gegenbegriff → *stásis*: Lys. 18,17–18) zugrunde, bi- und trilateraler H. (seit hell. Zeit) neben Grenzkonflikten v. a. im kaiserzeitlichen Kleinasien Rangstreitigkeiten, aber auch Interesse an ökonom. Beziehungen. Panhellenische H. formiert sich im 4. Jh. gegen die pers., dann makedon. Bedrohung, erneut im Chremonideischen Krieg gegen Antigonos Gonatas.

Instrumente einträchtiger Regelungen sind v. a. Eide, Verträge, Beschlüsse und die Anrufung auswärtiger Schlichter, seit hell. Zeit auch auswärtiger Richter (H.dikasten), später auch röm. Instanzen. H. in all ihren Formen beschwörende Funktion hat bes. der im 4. Jh. entstandene Kult des polit. Abstraktums, darunter die Sonderkulte der »H. der Hellenen« [1; 2] und der kaiserlichen H. (*H. Sebastḗ*, → Concordia Augusta).

1 R. ETIENNE, M. PIÉRART, Un décret du Koinon des Hellènes à Platées, in: BCH 99, 1975, 51–75 **2** R. ETIENNE, Le Koinon des Hellènes à Platées, in: La Béotie antique, 1985, 259–263.

P. R. FRANKE, Zu den H.-Münzen Kleinasiens, in: Stuttgarter Kolloquium zur histor. Geogr. des Alt.s. 1, 1980, 1987, 81–102 • R. PERA, H. sulle monete da Augusto agli Antonini, 1984 • A. R. R. SHEPPARD, H. in the Greek Cities of the Roman Empire, in: Ancient Society, 1984–86, 15–17; 229–252 • G. THÉRIAULT, Le culte d'H. dans les cités grecques, 1996. T.H.

Homo novus s. Novus homo

Homosexualität

I. DEFINITION II. GRIECHENLAND III. ROM IV. CHRISTENTUM UND SPÄTANTIKE

I. DEFINITION

Der Terminus H. zur Bezeichnung der auf Partner des gleichen Geschlechts gerichteten körperlichen Liebe ist nicht antik. Er verfehlt insofern die typischen Züge ant. Geschlechtslebens, als darin ein individuelles Charakteristikum festgelegt wird. Das sexuelle Verhalten eines Menschen wurde in der Ant. aber weniger durch seine individuellen Neigungen als durch seine soziale Stellung als Freier oder Unfreier, als junger oder alter Mensch, als Mann oder Frau determiniert. Der Ant. war die Vorstellung weitgehend fremd, daß Sexualität sich auf ein einziges Geschlecht bezieht. Unter bestimmten ges. Rahmenbedingungen konnten sowohl Frauen als auch Männer ihrem erotischen Interesse an beiden Geschlechtern nachgehen.

II. GRIECHENLAND

A. WEIBLICHE HOMOSEXUALITÄT B. MÄNNLICHE HOMOSEXUALITÄT

A. WEIBLICHE HOMOSEXUALITÄT

Homoerotische Begegnungen unter Frauen werden von der Dichterin → Sappho von Lesbos (um 600 v. Chr.) beschrieben (Sappho 1 LP/D): Sie sind hier gemäß der Auffassung, Wissen könne nur durch eine affektive Beziehung zwischen Lehrenden und Lernenden vermittelt werden, Bestandteil der Erziehung junger Mädchen aus aristokratischen Familien in einem Zirkel, dem die Dichterin selbst vorstand. In der Folgezeit galt »lesbische Liebe« als Umschreibung für weibliche H. (Lukian. dialogi meretricii 5). Auch die Chorlieddichtung Alkmans spielt auf homoerotische Begegnungen unter den Frauen Spartas im pädagogischen Kontext an (Alkm. 1 D). Spätere Quellen belegen, daß dort junge Mädchen, bevor sie heirateten, ältere Frauen als Liebhaberinnen hatten, die ihre Tugenden und erotischen Erfahrungen auf die Jüngeren zu übertragen wünschten und diesen als Vorbild galten (Plut. Lykurgos 18,9; Athen. 602d-e). Aus der Perspektive männlicher Autoren werden homoerotische Ambitionen von Frauen meist als widernatürlich (παρὰ φύσιν) und als Zeichen der Ausschweifung beurteilt (Plat. leg. 636c; Anth. Pal. 5,207). Artemidoros zählt ebenfalls körperliche Liebe unter Frauen zu den sexuellen Beziehungen »wider die Natur« (Artem. 1,80).

B. MÄNNLICHE HOMOSEXUALITÄT

Mehr Quellen liegen über die erotischen Beziehungen unter Männern vor, die vor allem in Form der Knabenliebe (Paiderastie) in verschiedenen Poleis gepflegt wurden. Beide am paiderastischen Verhältnis beteiligten Männer hatten den Status von Freien, unterschieden sich aber hinsichtlich ihres Alters beträchtlich. Der Liebhaber (ἐραστής, *erastḗs*) war älter als 30 und nahm gegenüber dem 12–18jährigen Geliebten (ἐρώμενος, *erṓmenos*) die Rolle des Erziehers ein. In Sparta war die Paiderastie strukturell mit der Erziehung der Jungen verbunden (Plut. Lykurgos 17 f.; vgl. Plat. leg. 836b), auch in Theben war männliche H. bekannt (Plut. Pelopidas 19; vgl. Plat. symp. 182b). Die Werbung um einen Jungen war normalerweise mit Geschenken verbunden (Aristoph. Plut. 147 ff.). Der Stellenwert des sexuellen und des pädagogischen Aspektes der Knabenliebe wird in der Forsch. verschieden gewichtet, indem diese teils als »erotisch gefärbte Mentorschaft«, teils als pädagogisch verbrämte sexuelle Beziehung gedeutet wird. Wer Männer begehrte, die dem Alter eines *erṓmenos* bereits entwachsen waren, wurde als weibisch verspottet (Aristoph. Thesm. 49 f.; 97 f.). Platon, der im *Symposion* die Beziehung zwischen Liebhaber und Geliebtem unter dem Aspekt des Strebens nach dem Schönen gerechtfertigt (Plat. symp. 178c–179b) und die verschiedenen Formen sexuellen Begehrens noch mit Verständnis beschrieben hat (symp. 191c–193c), äußert sich in den *Nómoi* kritisch auch über die männliche H. (Plat.

leg. 636c); unter Berufung auf die Natur und besonders auf das Verhalten der Tiere tritt Platon für eine Ächtung männlicher H. in der von ihm beschriebenen Polis ein (leg. 835b–842a). Für den homosexuellen Verkehr unter Männern gab es auch Prostituierte, denen in Athen durch Gesetz untersagt war, Ämter zu bekleiden und im Rat oder in der Volksversammlung zu sprechen (Aischin. Tim. 19f.).

In der griech. sf. und rf. Vasenmalerei ist männliche H. ein zentrales Thema, wobei gerade die Darstellung des umworbenen Jungen mit den überreichten Geschenken, oft Tieren (Hahn oder Hase), weit verbreitet ist.

III. Rom
A. Weibliche Homosexualität B. Männliche Homosexualität

A. Weibliche Homosexualität

Homosexueller Verkehr unter Frauen wird in Quellen der röm. Zeit nur äußerst selten, dabei stets aus männlicher Perspektive thematisiert und durchweg negativ beurteilt (Mart. 1,90; 7,67). Weibliche H. betreffende Gesetze sind nicht überliefert.

B. Männliche Homosexualität

Die in der älteren Forsch. vertretene, bereits bei röm. Autoren (Cic. Tusc. 4,70) angedeutete Auffassung, daß das erotische Interesse der Römer an jungen Männern auf den Einfluß der griech. Kultur zurückzuführen sei, wird in neueren Untersuchungen zurückgewiesen. Die Komödien des Plautus belegen als gängige Praxis, daß röm. Herren sexuelle Beziehungen zu ihren jungen Sklaven (*pueri meriti*) unterhielten. Wie in Griechenland fanden auch in Rom die sexuellen Begegnungen zwischen Männern unterschiedlichen Alters statt; Leidenschaften gegenüber dem Jünglingsalter entwachsenen Männern (*exoleti*) waren verpönt (Sen. epist. 47,7). Im Unterschied zur griech. Paiderastie wurden in Rom homosexuelle Verhältnisse zu Freien (*ingenui*) abgelehnt; auch thematisiert der röm. Diskurs zur männlichen H. keine erzieherischen Absichten des Liebhabers. Mit der Heirat des Liebhabers sollte sein Verhältnis zu seinem Sklavenliebling beendet sein (Catull. 61,141ff.); dies scheint jedoch nicht immer der Fall gewesen zu sein. Es war durchaus möglich, daß ein Herr zu mehreren Sklaven gleichzeitig homoerotische Beziehungen unterhielt. Der sexuelle Umgang mit männlichen Prostituierten war auch in Rom verbreitet. Wie die Griechen unterschieden auch die Römer im Hinblick auf die Stellungen der Partner beim Verkehr sinngemäß zwischen aktivem und passivem Sexualverhalten. Letzteres schickte sich zwar für Frauen, bei einem Mann galt es jedoch als Indiz für Unmännlichkeit, deren negative Bewertung sich an der Charakterisierung der Männer als *mollis* (weichlich) ebenso wie an den pejorativen, dem Griech. entlehnten Bezeichnungen *cinaedus* und *pathicus* (Catull. 16) ablesen läßt.

Neuere Stud. betonen, daß die homoerotische Dichtung der späten Republik und des frühen Prinzipats durchaus Verhaltensweisen der Autoren widerspiegelt und nicht – wie früher vermutet – als reine Fiktion aufzufassen ist. Der Vorwurf der sexuellen Verfügbarkeit (*impudicitia*) erwies sich insbesondere in Verbindung mit der Behauptung, jemand habe sich seine sexuellen Dienste bezahlen lassen, als verbreiteter Topos der forensischen Rhet. Solche Vorwürfe fehlten selten in Auseinandersetzungen polit. Gegner. Caesar wurde z.B. sowohl von seinen Kontrahenten im Senat als auch von seinen Soldaten wegen einer angeblichen sexuellen Beziehung zum König Nikomedes von Bithynien verspottet (Suet. Iul. 49; Cass. Dio 43,20). Unterstellungen dieser Art sind gerade für die ges. Moralvorstellungen aufschlußreich (Sall. Catil. 13; Cic. Catil. 2,23). Offen thematisiert Petronius die H. im *Satyrikon* (Petron. 8ff.; 23; 79,9ff.; 114,7ff.). Eine wichtige Quelle zur H. in der Prinzipatszeit sind die Epigramme von Martialis (zur weiblichen H.: 1,90; 7,67; Analverkehr: 9,47; 9,57; 11,43; ein Hochzeitsritual im homosexuellen Milieu: 12,42). Die Satiren Iuvenals belegen, daß männliche H. in der Zeit um 100 n.Chr. Anlaß zum Spott bot; sie kritisieren insbesondere die Doppelmoral der ges. Elite, die ihre H. hinter einer Fassade altröm. Tugenden zu verbergen suchte (Iuv. 2; 9).

Inwieweit gesetzliche Regelungen des homosexuellen Umgangs vorlagen, ist nicht genau zu rekonstruieren. Sowohl die Datier. als auch die konkreten inhaltlichen Bestimmungen der in verschiedenen Texten (Cic. fam. 8,12,3; Suet. Dom. 8,3; Iuv. 2,44) erwähnten *lex Scantinia* sind umstritten. Dieses Gesetz war spätestens seit der Mitte des 1. Jh. v.Chr. in Kraft getreten und stellte die Unzucht (*stuprum*) mit minderjährigen Freien unter Strafe. Ein röm. Bürger konnte gegen jeden vorgehen, der sexuelle Beziehungen zu seinen Sklaven aufnahm. Suetonius berichtet von homosexuellen Aktivitäten fast aller Principes (Suet. Tib. 43f.; Cal. 24,3; 36,1; Nero 28f.; Galba 22). Auch in der *Historia Augusta* wird H. von Principes erwähnt (Hadrianus: SHA Hadr. 11,7; 14,5ff.). Kaiser Hadrian gründete dort, wo sein junger Geliebter → Antinoos starb, die Stadt Antinoupolis und richtete ihm in Mantineia einen Kult ein (Paus. 8,9,7f.; Amm. 22,16,2). Die *lex Scantinia* blieb – obgleich von den Principes nur zeitweise angewendet (Suet. Dom. 8,3) – gültig und wurde im Laufe der Zeit durch den Erlaß weiterer Vorschriften aktualisiert.

IV. Christentum und Spätantike

Bereits das AT erkennt nur in Menschen, die sich als Mann und Frau verbinden, Gottes Abbild (Gn 1,27; 2,18–24) und verurteilt es, mit einem Mann geschlechtlich zu verkehren »wie mit einer Frau« (Lv 18,22; 20,13). Auch in nt. Schriften wird H. als widernatürlich abgelehnt, ohne daß dabei auf das AT verwiesen wird. H. stellte für Paulus eine mögliche Verfehlung unter vielen dar, die dem Sündigen den Zutritt zum Reich Gottes verwehrte (Röm 1,27; 1 Kor 6,9f.). Die von christl.

Autoren wie Clemens von Alexandria (Clem. Al. strom. 2,23) vertretene Auffassung, daß Lust allein dem Zweck der Zeugung zu dienen habe, findet sich auch in der paganen Lit. (Musonius Rufus 12). Die Kirchenväter verwiesen stets auf den lasterhaften Charakter der H. (Aug. epist. 211). In mehreren Synoden des 4. Jh. wurden Kirchenstrafen gegen Homosexuelle festgelegt. Kleriker hatten beim Vorwurf der H. ihre Absetzung zu befürchten.

Unter den christl. Kaisern fand die Verurteilung der H. (insbesondere des passiven Partners) Eingang in verschiedene Gesetze: Eine Regelung im Codex Theodosianus (9,7,6, 390 n. Chr.) sah die Todesstrafe vor. Um die Anwendung und Auswirkungen dieser Regelung beurteilen zu können, mangelt es an Quellen. Im 5. Jh. beklagt Salvianus, daß Männer in Karthago sich ganz offen zu ihren homosexuellen Neigungen bekennen, ohne eine Strafe fürchten zu müssen (Salv. gub. 7,18). Als besonders unerbittlicher Verfolger der H. aus rel. Gründen gilt Kaiser Iustinianus (527–565). Seine Auslegung des AT, die in der durch die H. heraufbeschworenen Rache Gottes eine Gefahr für die ganze Menschheit erkannte, blieb bis in die Neuzeit wirksam.
→ Erotik; Geschlechterrollen; Hetaireseos graphe; Päderastie; Prostitution; Sexualität

1 G. Bleibtreu-Ehrenberg, Sexuelle Abartigkeit im Urteil der abendländischen Religions-, Geistes- und Rechtsgeschichte, 1970 2 E. Cantarella, Secondo natura, La bissessualità nel mondo antico, 1988 3 P. Cartledge, The Politics of Spartan Pederasty, in: PCPhS 207, N.S. 27, 1981, 17–36 4 K.J. Dover, Greek Homosexuality, 1978 5 D.M. Halperin, One Hundred Years of Homosexuality, 1988 6 K. Hoheisel, s.v. H., RAC 16, 289–364 7 G. Koch-Harnack, Erotische Symbole, 1989 8 Dies., Knabenliebe und Tiergeschenke, 1983 9 W. Kroll, Röm. Erotik, in: Zschr. für Sexualwissenschaft und Sexualpolitik, 17, 1930, 145–178 10 E. Meyer-Zwiffelhoffer, Im Zeichen des Phallus, 1995 11 H.P. Obermayer, Martial und der Diskurs über männliche »Homosexualität« in der Lit. der frühen Kaiserzeit (Classica Monacensia 18), 1998 12 H. Patzer, Die griech. Knabenliebe, 1982 13 C. Reinsberg, Ehe, Hetärentum und Knabenliebe, 1989 14 A. Rousselle, Porneia, 1983, dt. 1989 15 J.M. Snyder, Lesbian Desire in the Lyrics of Sappho, 1997 16 P. Veyne, Homosexualität im ant. Rom, in: P. Ariès, A. Béjin (Hrsg.), Die Masken des Begehrens und die Metamorphosen der Sinnlichkeit, 1984, 40–50 17 J.J. Winkler, The Constraints of Desire, 1992, dt. 1994.

E. HA.

Honestiores/Humiliores. Während in der frühen Prinzipatszeit das röm. → Strafrecht vor allem zw. Bürgern und Nichtbürgern unterschied und somit ein personenrechtliches Kriterium für die Festlegung des Strafmaßes entscheidend war, bestimmte seit Ende des 2. Jh. n. Chr. der soziale Rang die Behandlung des einzelnen vor Gericht. Die Differenzierung der Strafen verbindet sich in den juristischen Texten und in der mod. Forschung vor allem mit zwei Termini, den *humiliores* und *honestiores*. Zu den *honestiores* zählten die Angehörigen der privilegierten Stände (Senatoren, Equites, Decurionen, Veteranen); sie waren von der Folter, entehrenden Strafen, Zwangsarbeit, weitgehend auch von der Todesstrafe ausgenommen und wurden selbst bei Kapitalverbrechen zumeist lediglich mit der Verbannung bestraft, während die *humiliores* der ganzen Schärfe des Gesetzes unterworfen waren.

In den juristischen Texten des 2. und 3. Jh. n. Chr. dient eine Vielzahl von Termini und Umschreibungen zur Bezeichnung der *honestiores* und *humiliores*. Für den *honestior* finden sich u. a.: *honestiore loco natus, in aliquo honore positus, in aliqua dignitate positus, altior*. Der *humilior* wird u. a. als *humiliore loco positus, qui humillimo loco est, plebeius, sordidior, tenuior* bezeichnet. Als durchgängiges Konzept wird die *h./h.*-Terminologie erst in den um 300 n. Chr. entstandenen Sentenzen des Ps.-Paulus verwendet. Die röm. Juristen bieten keine exakte Definition der beiden Gruppen; es blieb in der Gerichtspraxis zumeist dem einzelnen Richter überlassen, darüber zu entscheiden, wer zu den *honestiores* bzw. *humiliores* gehörte. Wenn zu den *honestiores* auch die Veteranen zählten, die in der Regel lediglich über einen bescheidenen Besitz verfügten und damit an sich nicht zu den besitzenden Schichten gerechnet werden können, so erklärt sich ihre Privilegierung, die derjenigen der Decurionen entsprach (Marcianus, Dig. 49,18,3), aus der großen polit. Bedeutung der röm. Armee.

Ihren sichtbaren Ausdruck findet die Unterscheidung zwischen *honestiores* und *humiliores* in den unterschiedlichen Strafen. Die Angehörigen der privilegierten Bevölkerungsschichten erhielten für dieselbe Straftat eine geringere Strafe als der Rest der Bevölkerung: Verbannung und allenfalls Enthauptung anstelle der verschärften Todesstrafe (*summa supplicia* waren: Kreuzigung, Feuertod, Verurteilung *ad bestias*), Befreiung von der Verurteilung *ad metallum* (der Arbeit in Bergwerken oder Steinbrüchen) oder zur Zwangsarbeit (*opus publicum*). Die *lex Iulia de vi publica* des Augustus bekräftigte den Schutz der röm. Bürger vor Züchtigungen noch einmal (Ulpian, Dig. 48,6,7). Spätestens mit dem Ende des 2. Jh. n. Chr. hatten sich für die Angehörigen der einfachen Bevölkerungsschichten jedoch Körperstrafen durchgesetzt: Züchtigung mit *fustes* (Stöcken; Cod. Iust. 2,11(12),5 – 198 n. Chr.; Callistratus, Dig. 48,19,28,2 und 5). Die Folter, die vor Gericht ursprünglich auf Sklaven beschränkt gewesen war, drohte seit dem 2. Jh. auch den armen Freien. Bes. häufig wird von den Juristen die Befreiung der Decurionen von der Folter diskutiert; da diese in der Hierarchie der privilegierten sozialen Gruppen am weitesten unten standen, waren ihre Privilegien am ehesten gefährdet (Paulus, Dig. 50,2,14). Gegen Ende des 3. Jh. konnten Zeugen, sofern sie niedriger sozialer Herkunft waren, gefoltert werden (Arcadius Charisius, Dig. 22,5,21,2). *Humiliores* wurden eher inhaftiert als *honestiores*, die zumeist durch Bürgenstellung einer Untersuchungshaft entgingen (Ulpian, Dig. 48,3,1; 26,10,3,16). Vor Gericht, sowohl in Straf- wie in Zivilsachen, wurde den Zeugenaussagen von Angehörigen der Oberschichten ein größeres Gewicht beigemessen (Callistratus, Dig. 22,5,3,pr.). Eine Rechtsverletzung (*iniuria*) galt dann als bes. schwerwiegend, wenn der Täter ein Angehöriger der Unterschichten und das Opfer ein Senator oder ein Eques war (Ulpian, Dig. 47,10,35).

Obgleich die Angehörigen der Oberschichten vor Gericht stets sehr viel besser gestellt waren als der Rest der Bevölkerung, kam es erst im 2. Jh. n. Chr. zu der klaren Unterscheidung zwischen *honestiores* und *humiliores*. Sie ist eng verbunden mit der Durchsetzung der → *cognitio extra ordinem*: Während die Strafgesetze der späten Republik ein einheitliches Strafmaß unabhängig vom sozialen Stand des Angeklagten fixiert hatten, war der Richter in der *cognitio extra ordinem* bei der Festlegung der Strafen völlig frei und nicht an gesetzliche Vorgaben gebunden. Die Differenzierung zwischen den *honestiores* und *humiliores* hat sich zunächst in der Strafpraxis herausgebildet und ging erst dann in die Gesetzgebung der Principes ein: Hadrianus und Antoninus Pius waren die ersten, die die Unterscheidung zw. *honestiores* und *humiliores* im Strafrecht voraussetzten (Callistratus, Dig. 47,21,2; Papinian, Dig. 48,5,39(38),8).

Das Prinzip, bei der Strafbemessung nach sozialem Rang zu differenzieren, wurde in der Spätantike beibehalten: Während die Angehörigen der Oberschichten mit Geldbußen belegt wurden, wurden die Armen am Körper gestraft. Wenngleich die Strafen, die den *humiliores* drohten, denen glichen, die für Sklaven vorgesehen waren (vgl. Macer, Dig. 48,19,10,pr.), darf hieraus doch nicht gefolgert werden, daß die personenrechtlichen Unterschiede zwischen Sklaven und armen Freien sich verwischt hätten. Gerade in der spätant. Gesetzgebung ist die Tendenz zu beobachten, auch im Strafmaß wieder sehr viel stärker zwischen diesen beiden Gruppen zu differenzieren.

1 Alföldy, RG, 69–81 **2** P. Garnsey, Social Status and Legal Privilege in the Roman Empire, 1970 **3** Ders., Why Penalties Become Harsher: The Roman Case, Late Republic to Fourth Century Empire, in: Natural Law Forum 13, 1968, 141–162 **4** J.-U. Krause, Gefängnisse im Römischen Reich, 1996 **5** R. Rilinger, Humiliores – Honestiores. Zu einer sozialen Dichotomie im Strafrecht der röm. Kaiserzeit, 1988. J.K.

Honestus. Epigrammatiker aus dem »Kranz« des Philippos, unter dessen seltenem Namen Ὄνεστος (wahrscheinlich Assimilation des röm. Cognomens H.) – er wird bald als *Korínthios* (vgl. Anth. Pal. 9,216), bald als *Byzántios* (vgl. ebd. 7,274) bezeichnet – zehn größtenteils epideiktische Gedichte erh. sind, die oft in Bezug zu Böotien stehen und sich durch Antithesen und lexikalisch wie phraseologisch originelle Wortprägungen auszeichnen. Beinahe sicher ist die Identität mit dem homonymen Verf. der in Thespiai ans Licht gekommenen inschr. Epigramme, von denen neun den Musen gewidmet sind, eins der Thamyris und eins einer Σεβαστή (*Sebastē*), d. h. einer *Augusta*, sehr wahrscheinlich Livia, der dritten Gattin des Augustus.

GA II 1, 268–279; 2, 301–309. M.G.A./Ü: T.H.

Honig (μέλι, *mel*).

I. Alter Orient

Im Alten Orient und Äg. terminologisch nicht immer von Sirup-Arten (Dattel- oder Feigensirup) getrennt. Mit einem Wert von 1–2 Liter pro Sekel Silber (21. Jh. v. Chr.) gehörte H. in Mesopot. zu den wertvollsten Nahrungsmitteln und stand vor allem Göttern (Opfer) und hohen Beamten zu. Die lit. Trad. kennt H. als Kostbarkeit besonders zusammen mit dem hochgeschätzten Butteröl (»Milch und Honig«).

H. A. Hoffner, Alimenta Hethaeorum, 1974, 123 • J. Leclant, s. v. Biene, LÄ 1, 1975, 786–789 • D. T. Potts, Mesopotamian Civilization, 1997, 50. R.K.E.

II. Griechenland und Italien

Bienen-H., ein seit prähistor. Zeit überall in der ant. Welt verbreitetes Nahrungsmittel, stieg seines hohen Zuckergehalts wegen zum wichtigsten Süßmittel des Alt. auf. Als hervorragend galt Thymian-H. (Varro rust. 3,16,26), dessen beste Qualitäten aus Attika, Sizilien und von den griech. Inseln stammten und im Mittelmeerraum gehandelt wurden (Plin. nat. 11,32–33; Dioskurides 2,101). Obwohl Bienenzucht zu einem bäuerlichen Vollbetrieb dazugehörte (Cic. Cato 56) und sich der Berufszweig des Imkers herausgebildet hatte, überstieg die Nachfrage nach H. stets das Angebot. H. gehörte deshalb das ganze Alt. hindurch zu den hochwertigen Nahrungsmitteln (Hes. erg. 233 über Bienen; Aristoph. Pax 252–254; Athen. 4,36a). *Mel optimum* (»Spitzen-H.«) kostete zu Beginn des 4. Jh. n. Chr. soviel wie bestes Olivenöl (Edictum Diocletiani 3,10; vgl. 3,1a). Die wesentliche Funktion des H. in der Küche war die eines Süßmittels (Apicius, Excerpta, brevis pimentorum). Apicius gibt H. an nahezu alle Saucen, Fleisch- und Fischgerichte sowie Gemüsespeisen. Außerdem war H. substantieller Bestandteil von Gebäck, Süßspeisen, Marmeladen und bildete die Grundlage von Getränken wie → Met und *mulsum*. H. wurde auch als Konservierungsmittel für Obst und Fleisch verwendet (Colum. 12,10,5; Apicius, De re coquinaria 1,8 André).

Außerhalb der Küche erfüllte H. wichtige Funktionen in der Heilkunde (Plin. nat. 22,106): Ärzte machten sich seine entzündungshemmenden (Theophr. h. plant. 9,11,3) und stärkenden Wirkungen (Dioskurides 2,104) zu eigen. H. wurde außerdem zu kosmetischen Zwekken eingesetzt, etwa als Mittel gegen Haarausfall und Sommersprossen (nach Plin. nat. 25,18; Dioskurides 2,102). Auch im Kult war H., der als Himmelstau (Aristot. hist. an. 5,553b 27–29) und als Geschenk der Götter (Verg. georg. 4,1) angesehen wurde, von Bed., er wurde insbes. bei Übergangsriten etwa anläßlich des Todes (vgl. Hom. Il. 23,170; Hom. Od. 10,519) geopfert.

J. André, L'alimentation et la cuisine à Rome, [2]1981 • O. Böcher, A. Sallinger, s. v. H., RAC 16, 433–473 • A. Dalby, Siren Feasts. A History of Food and Gastronomy in Greece, 1996 • G. Lafaye, s. v. Mel, DS 3, 1701–1706 • M. Schuster, s. v. Mel, RE 15, 364–384. A.G.

Honorarium s. Vergütungen

Honoratus

[1] Beamter unter Constantius [2] II. *Consularis Syriae* (vor 353 n. Chr.; Lib. epist. 251), *comes Orientis* (353–354; Amm. 14,1,3; 7,2; Lib. epist. 386), *praefectus praetorio Galliarum* (355/357; Lib. epist. 386 FOERSTER). Von 359–361 war er der erste *praefectus urbis Constantinopolitanae* (Chron. min. 1,239 MOMMSEN) und richtete in diesem Amt über die Ketzerei des Aetius (Soz. 4,23,3). PLRE 1, 438f. (H. 2).

[2] Sohn des Sophisten und Beamten Quirinus (Lib. epist. 358; 359), um 355 n. Chr. Schüler des Libanios (Lib. epist. 405; 535). Von 358–361 war er im Staatsdienst, wahrscheinlich als *notarius* (Lib. epist. 358; 359 FOERSTER). Evtl. ist er identisch mit dem für 368 bezeugten *consularis Byzacii* gleichen Namens (Cod. Iust. 1,33,1). PLRE 1, 439 (H. 3 und 4). W. P.

Honoria. Iusta Grata H., weström. Kaiserin. Tochter → Constantius' [6] III. und der → Galla [3] Placidia, ältere Schwester → Valentinianus' III., 417 oder 418 n. Chr. geb. (Olympiodor fr. 34 FHG IV 65; Soz. 9,16,2), wurde wohl vor dem Jahre 437 Augusta (ILS 817f.). Sie wurde zum Gelübde ewiger Jungfrauenschaft gezwungen, 449 jedoch wegen einer Affäre mit ihrem Prokurator vom Hofe verstoßen und mit einem Senator verlobt. Daraufhin bat sie den Hunnenkönig → Attila um Hilfe und gab ihm ein Heiratsversprechen (Iord. Rom. 328; Iord. Get. 42,223f.; Iohannes Antiochenus fr. 199 FHG IV 613f.). Als Attilas Forderung nach ihrer Auslieferung und der Hälfte des Westreiches als Morgengabe verweigert wurde, fiel er 451 mit großer Heeresmacht in Gallien ein (Prisc. fr. 15f. FHG IV 98f.; Chron. min. 1, 662, 139; 2, 79, 434 MOMMSEN).

PLRE 2, 568f., 1308 • J. B. BURY, Iusta Grata Honoria, in: JRS 9, 1919, 1–13 • A. DEMANDT, Die Spätantike, 1989, 149, 154 • ST. I. OOST, Galla Placidia Augusta, 1968 • STEIN, Spätröm. R., Bd. 1, 494–498. K. P. J.

Honorius

[1] Bei [Aur. Vict.] Epit. Caes. 48,1 als Vater des Kaisers Theodosius I. bezeichnet, dürfte aber sein Großvater gewesen sein. PLRE 1,441.

[2] Älterer Bruder Theodosius' I., verh. wohl mit → Maria, Tochter war → Serena; beide wurden in den Haushalt des Kaisers aufgenommen wurden. PLRE 1,441. H. L.

[3] Flavius H., weström. Kaiser 393–423 n. Chr., wurde am 9.9.384 n. Chr. als jüngerer Sohn Kaiser → Theodosius' I. und der Aelia Flavia Flacilla in Konstantinopel geboren (Sokr. 5,12,2). Schon 386 bekleidete er als *nobilissimus puer* das erste seiner 12 Konsulate (CIL XIV 231). Im Januar 393 wurde er zum Augustus proklamiert (Sokr. 5,25,8; Chron. min. 1, 298 MOMMSEN). Kurz vor seinem Tode ließ ihn Theodosius nach Mailand kommen und übergab ihm die Herrschaft des westl. Reichsteils unter der Vormundschaft → Stilichos (Ambr. obit. Theod. 34f.; Claud. carm. 7,151ff.; Zos. 4,59,1). Die faktische Reichsteilung vom 17.1. 395 mit seinem älteren Bruder → Arcadius wurde nicht wieder rückgängig gemacht.

Anders als Theodosius und dessen Vorgänger zogen seine Söhne und deren Nachfolger nicht mehr persönl. ins Feld, sondern lebten als *principes clausi* (Sidon. carm. 5,358) nur noch im Palast. H. residierte anfangs in Mailand, ab 402 in Ravenna, das sich unter seiner Regierung zur Hauptstadt des Westreiches entwickelte. Diese Residenz verließ er fast nur zu Reisen nach Rom, z. B. 403/4 (Claud. carm. 28) und 407/8 (Cod. Theod. 16,2,38; 1,20,1). Der Kaiser stand zeitlebens unter dem Einfluß seiner Feldherren und Berater und handelte kaum selbständig. Bis 408 wurde der junge H. von dem *magister utriusque militiae* Stilicho beherrscht, der sich als *parens* des Kaisers bezeichnen ließ (ILS 795) und 398 seine ältere Tochter Maria (Claud. carm. 10), nach deren Tode seine jüngere Tochter Thermantia mit ihm verheiratete (Zos. 5,28,1–3; 35,3); beide Ehen blieben kinderlos.

Unter Stilichos Regentschaft bestanden durchweg Spannungen mit dem östl. Reichsteil. Die Angriffe des Gotenkönigs → Alaricus [2] wurden abgewehrt, 398 → Gildo in Afrika, 406 → Radagaisus in Italien besiegt. Nicht verhindert werden konnten 406 der Einfall zahlreicher Germanen über den Rhein nach Gallien (Oros. 7,38; Greg. Tur. Franc. 2,9; Chron. min. 1, 299) und 407 die faktische Aufgabe Britanniens. Nach Stilichos Ermordung 408 drangen Alaricus' Westgoten nach Italien ein und eroberten am 24.8.410 Rom (Soz. 9,9; Chron. min. 1, 300; 466). Die Plünderung der »Ewigen Stadt« rief zwischen paganen und christl. Denkern heftige Kontroversen hervor. H. blieb auch nach dem Tode seines Schwiegervaters von Ratgebern abhängig. 408/9 leitete der *magister officiorum* → Olympios die Politik, 409/10 der *praefectus praetorio* → Iovius [2], 411–21 der schließlich zum Mitregenten erhobene *patricius* → Constantius [6] III., seit 417 Gatte von H.' Schwester Galla [3] Placidia. Zwar konnten die Usurpationen von → Constantinus [3] III., → Attalos [11], → Iovinus [2] und → Heraclianus niedergeworfen werden, doch das weitere Eindringen von Germanen und anderen Barbaren ließ sich nicht mehr aufhalten. 409–11 drangen Vandalen, Alanen und Sueben in Spanien ein, Westgoten, Franken, Burgunder und Alamannen in Gallien, Hunnen in Pannonien (Soz. 9,12f.; Oros. 7,40–43; Chron. min. 2,17f.) Die Bildung von Föderatenstaaten begann, z. B. 418 bei den Westgoten in Aquitanien (Chron. min. 1, 654; 2, 19).

Der fromme H., der in jungen J. nachhaltig unter dem Einfluß des Bischofs → Ambrosius von Mailand gestanden hatte, förderte die Kirche und die Privilegien des Klerus (Cod. Theod. 16,2,29ff.). Er ließ Nichtchristen ebenso energisch bekämpfen (Cod. Theod. 16,10,15ff.) wie Häretiker, v. a. die Donatisten (Cod. Theod. 16,5,37ff.). 404 erfolgte die Abschaffung der Gladiatorenspiele (Theod. hist. eccl. 5,26), 407 wurden die Sibyllin. Bücher verbrannt (Rut. Nam. 2,52–56). 419 entschied H. ein Schisma zugunsten von Papst → Bonifatius [2] 1. Der Kaiser starb im August 423 an der Wassersucht (Sokr. 7,22,20; Olympiodor fr. 41 FHG IV 67). Zu seinen Münzen RIC 10, 1994, 123–37; 317–42; zum Münzbildnis Taf. 34–42; vgl. [1].

1 R. Delbrueck, Spätant. Kaiserportraits, 1933, 32, 96f., 206ff., 211ff.

PLRE 1, 442 (H. 3) • TH.S. BURNS, Barbarians within the Gates of Rome, 1994 • A. CAMERON, Claudianus, 1970 • A. DEMANDT, Die Spätantike, 1989, 137–150 • E. DEMOUGEOT, De l'unité à la division de l'Empire Romain, 1951 • v. HAEHLING, 593ff. • H. WOLFRAM, Die Goten, ³1990, 158–180. K.P.J.

Honos. Personifikation der Ehre. H. wird nur von Ovid (fast. 5,23 ff.) als Gatte der Reverentia und Vater der Maiestas in eine Genealogie eingebunden. Sonst spielt H. vor allem im mil. Umfeld eine Rolle, wo er für ehrenhaftes und tugendhaftes Verhalten in Kriegssituationen steht und eng mit → Virtus verbunden ist. So erstaunt es nicht, daß der Gottheit, die oft mit Lanze und Füllhorn dargestellt wird [1], von bedeutenden Feldherren Tempel geweiht wurden. Q. Fabius [30] Maximus Verrucosus errichtete H. 233 v. Chr. bei der → Porta Capena in unmittelbarer Nähe des Marstempels ein Heiligtum (Cic. nat. deor. 2,61). Dieses war der Ausgangspunkt der → *transvectio equitum* (Aur. Vict. De viris illustribus 32) und wurde 212 v. Chr. mit der Beute aus der Eroberung von Syrakus (Liv. 25,40,1 ff.) von M. Marcellus ausgeschmückt und mit einer Cella für Virtus erweitert (Liv. 27,25,7 ff.; Plut. Marcellus 28; Val. Max. 1,1,8). Der Tempel wurde noch von Vespasian renoviert (Plin. nat. 35,120). C. Marius errichtete nach den Cimbernkriegen aus der Beute einen Tempel für H. und Virtus (CIL XI 1831), dessen Proportionen von Vitruv (7 praef. 17) gelobt werden. In diesem Tempel fand die Senatssitzung statt, die Cicero erlaubte, aus dem Exil zurückzukehren (Cic. Sest. 116).

H. wurde schon in früher Zeit verehrt. Aus der Gegend der Porta Collina stammt eine altlat. Weihinschr. (CIL I² 31), die vermutlich zu einem alten H.-Heiligtum gehörte (vgl. Cic. leg. 2,58). Nach Plutarch (qu.R. 266f) opferte man H. nicht wie üblich mit verhülltem Haupt; zudem konnten der männl. Gottheit weibl. Opfertiere geopfert werden (CIL VI 2044 I 5). Dies spricht für einen Kult nach griech. Art (*Graeco ritu*).

1 C. LOCHIN, s. v. H., LIMC 5.2, 341 Nr. 6; 10; 13. B.SCH.

Hopfen (Humulus lupulus L., Familie Cannabinaceae). H. kommt in Mitteleuropa häufig in Auwäldern als Schlingpflanze wild vor. Die zapfenartige Frucht der weiblichen Pflanze wird wegen ihrer aromatischen und konservierenden Bitterstoffe dem Bier zugesetzt. Dies sollen finnisch-ugrische Stämme erfunden haben, von denen diese Würzung im 5.–7. Jh. in Westeuropa übernommen wurde. Der erste H.-Garten (*humularium*) in der Abtei St. Denis bei Paris ist für 768 nachgewiesen [1. 216]. Der einzige ant. Beleg findet sich bei Plinius, der den an Weiden rankenden *lupus salictarius* als Lekkerbissen erwähnt (nat. 21,86). Die jungen Triebe wurden wie Spargel (→ Asparagos) als Gemüse genossen.

1 J. BECKMANN: H., in: Beyträge zur Gesch. der Erfindungen, Bd. 5.2, 1803, 206–234. C.HÜ.

Hopletes s. Iones

Hoplitai. Das Wort ὁπλίτης (*hoplítēs*, Pl. *hoplítai*) ist abgeleitet von ὅπλον (*hóplon*, »Gerät, Schild«; bes. im Plur. ὅπλα, *hópla* »Waffen«) und bezeichnet schwerbewaffnete Fußsoldaten. Ihre aus Bronze gefertigte Rüstung (Panhoplie) bestand aus einem runden Schild von 0,9 m Durchmesser mit Armschiene (πόρπαξ, *pórpax*) im Zentrum und Haltegriff (ἀντιλαβή, *antilabḗ*) am Rand, einem Helm, einem Brustpanzer, Beinschienen, welche von den Knöcheln bis über die Knie reichten, einer Stoßlanze sowie einem Kurzschwert für den Kampf auf engstem Raum. Waffen dieser Art sind seit dem späten 8. Jh. v. Chr. arch. bezeugt, und die damit verbundene Kampfweise ist auf der Chigi-Kanne, einer protokorinthischen Olpe (um 650/40 v. Chr.; Rom, VG) bildlich dargestellt; man kann allerdings annehmen, daß der Dichter der Ilias diese Waffen bereits kannte.

Charakteristisch für den Kampf der *h.* war die geschlossene Schlachtreihe (→ Phalanx), in der die Krieger in breiter Linie und einer Tiefe von 8 oder mehr Mann angeordnet waren. Sie rückten gleichzeitig gehend oder laufend nach dem Rhythmus der Flötenbläser vor. Gefechtsentscheidend war das koordinierte Vorgehen bis zum Aufprall auf den Gegner sowie die Standfestigkeit im folgenden Nahkampf. Da ein Hoplit mit der linken Hälfte seines Schildes die ungeschützte Seite seines Nachbarn deckte, kam es auf höchste Verläßlichkeit an. Zugleich ergab sich daraus im Verlauf des Gefechtes ein Abdriften nach rechts, zur ungeschützten Seite hin (Thuk. 5,71,1), so daß von hier aus auch die gegnerische Flanke angegriffen werden konnte. Der rechte Flügel war daher der Platz für die Eliteeinheiten, der zugleich als ehrenvoll galt. Mit dieser Kampfweise war eine spezifische Ethik wechselseitiger Solidarität verbunden, die sich auf die → Polis bezog (Tyrtaios 6; 7; 8,11 ff; 9,13 ff. D.). Diese Kampfform war – zusammen mit dem entsprechenden Kriegerethos – zuerst in Sparta (7. Jh. v. Chr.) ausgeprägt, breitete sich dann als bes. erfolgreich aus und führte zu den wichtigen Siegen gegen die Perser (Marathon 490, Plataiai 479 v. Chr.). Die Phalanx verlor erst mit dem Siegeszug der maked. Taktik, die der → Reiterei mehr Gewicht gab (Schlacht von Chaironeia 338 v. Chr.), an Bedeutung.

Da die Krieger sich im wesentlichen selbst auszurüsten hatten, setzte der Status von *h.* eine gewisse ökonomische Leistungsfähigkeit voraus. Aufgrund der Größe der archa. Heere rekrutierten *h.* sich nicht allein aus dem Adel, sondern auch aus der Schicht begüterter Bauern, die dann die aristokratischen Vorstellungen und Normen übernahmen. Zugleich wurde die wechselseitige Solidarität und die Bindung an die Polis zunehmend positiv bewertet. Deshalb hat man die Polisentwicklung häufig mit der gleichzeitigen Entwicklung der H.-Phalanx in Verbindung gebracht. Die Urteile in der modernen Forsch. darüber sind kontrovers, doch kann insgesamt kein Zweifel daran sein, daß sich diese Kampfweise integrativ im Sinne der Stärkung auch der polit. Solidarität ausgewirkt hat.

Der Begriff *h.* hatte auch eine soziale Bedeutung: Wer als Hoplit diente, gehörte zu einer sozial herausgehobenen, mittleren Schicht zwischen den → Theten (Besitzlosen) und dem Adel, bei der es sich um wohlhabende Gespannbauern handelte; so bezeichnet wohl die dritte der solonischen Klassen (die → Zeugitai) diese Gruppe. In verschiedenen Poleis war dieser Zusammenhang formalisiert; ein bestimmter Zensus, der den H.-dienst ermöglichte bzw. dazu verpflichtete, verlieh auch bes. polit. Rechte, etwa die eines Voll- oder Aktivbürgers (Aristot. pol. 2,6,1265b 26ff.; 4,3,1291a 28ff.; 6,7,1321a 12f.); man spricht dann von einer Hoplitenpoliteia, die in der demokratiekritischen polit. Theorie (Aristoteles) eher positiv eingeschätzt wurde. Beim oligarchischen Umsturz in Athen (411 v. Chr.) war die Einrichtung einer solchen Verfassung geplant (Thuk. 8,97,1; Aristot. Ath. pol. 33,1), im Jahre 322 v. Chr. scheint eine solche Ordnung realisiert worden zu sein. Eine Alternative zur Demokratie bildete sie in Athen allerdings nicht.

1 J.K. ANDERSON, Hoplites and Heresies, in: JHS 104, 1984, 152 **2** P. CARTLEDGE, Hoplites and Heroes, in: JHS 97, 1977, 11–27 **3** P. DUCREY, Guerre et guerriers dans la Grèce antique, 1985 **4** H.-J. GEHRKE, Phokion, 1976, 90–93 **5** Ders., Stasis, 1985, 317f. **6** A.J. HOLLADAY, Hoplites and Heresies, in: JHS 102, 1982, 94–103 **7** J. LATACZ, Kampfparänese, Kampfdarstellung und Kampfwirklichkeit in der Ilias, bei Kallinos und Tyrtaios, 1977 **8** O. MURRAY, Das frühe Griechenland, 1982, 159–174 **9** J. SALMON, Political Hoplites?, in: JHS 97, 1977, 84–101 **10** A.M. SNODGRASS, The Hoplite Reform and History, in: JHS 85, 1965, 110–122 **11** P. SPAHN, Mittelschicht und Polisbildung, 1977. H.-J. G.

Hoplites (Ὁπλίτης).
[1] Ort im NO von Sparta (Pol. 16,16,2), evtl. nach der archa. Kultstatue des Apollon im nahegelegenen Thornax (»Soldat«) benannt.

F. W. WALBANK, A Historical Commentary on Polybius 2, 1967, 521. Y. L.

[2] Kleiner Fluß in Boiotia, dessen Lokalisierung bei Haliartos oder Koroneia schon in der Ant. umstritten war; mit einem Orakel über den Tod des Lysandros verbunden (Plut. Lysandros 29,3 ff.; mor. 408A-B).

F. BÖLTE, s. v. H. (2), RE 8, 2296f. • S. LAUFFER, Kopais 1, 1986, 80f. P. F.

[3] s. Hoplitai

Hor. Ägypter aus dem Gau → Sebennytos, Dorfschreiber und vielleicht auch Schreiber des Gaues, begann 173 v. Chr. eine fünfjährige Reise, die ihm durch Orakel aufgetragen war. → *Pastophóros* der Isis und ab 167/6 Priester (κάτοχος/*kátochos*?) am Ibis-Heiligtum von Saqqara/Memphis, wo er eine Stelle in der Tempelverwaltung hatte. Er gab Traumorakel, die bis an den Hof gelangten. U.a. reiste er 168 zum Sarapeion von Alexandreia, wo er ein gegen Antiochos IV. gerichtetes, die Sicherheit Alexandreias und der Dynastie betreffendes Orakel vor den Königen vortrug. 158 schrieb er ein Enkomion für den Geburtstag (und erwarteten Besuch) Ptolemaios' VI. Erhalten ist ein Archiv demotischer Orakelmitteilungen.

D. KESSLER, Die hl. Tiere und der König 1, 1989, 110ff. • J. D. RAY, The Archive of Hor, 1976 • Ders., Observations on the Archive of Hor, in: JEA 64, 1978, 113 ff. W. A.

Horai (Ὧραι). Göttl. Wesen des Zeitenwechsels, zunächst drei, wohl im Anschluß an die Unterscheidung einer vierten Jahreszeit (Alkm. fr. 12 CALAME; Hippokr. De aere aquis et locis 1. 10; Aristot. gen. an. 784a 19) später meist vier (eine Hora als Göttin der Jugendschönheit: Pind. N. 8,1; rekapitulierend die Reihen von 9 bzw. 10 Namen: Hyg. fab. 183). Appellativum und Personifikation sind zuweilen kaum zu unterscheiden (z. B. Hom. Il. 21,450; Od. 10,469).

Wie andere Göttervereine treten die H. oft in Begleitung olymp. Götter auf, bes. Demeter (Hom. h. 2,54; 192; 492), Apollon (SEG 33, 115, 13; Lykophr. 352; Anth. Pal. 9,525,25; [1]), Aphrodite und Dionysos.

Ihre verschiedenen Erscheinungsformen überlagern sich zum Teil. In der *Ilias* sind sie Wächterinnen der Tore des Olymp (5,749–751 = 8,393–395; 433–435), seit Hesiod (theog. 901–903) wahren die H. → Eunomia, → Dike und → Eirene, Töchter des → Zeus und der → Themis, wohl im Anschluß an den Gedanken eines inneren Zusammenhangs zw. Beachtung des Rechts und blühender Natur (Hom. Il. 16,384–392; Hom. Od. 19,109–114), die Einhaltung der menschlichen Rechtsordnung. Daneben sind die H. schon früh zusammen mit den → Charites schmückende Göttinnen (Aphrodite: Hes. erg. 74–75; Kypria 1, fr. 4; Hom. h. 6, 5–13; Pandora: Hes. erg. 70–76) und werden mit dem Frühling assoziiert (ebd.; Pind. fr. 75,14–15). Mit Geburt (z. B. Aphrodite, Hermes), dem Aufziehen von Kindern (z. B. Pind. P. 9,59–65: Aristaios) und Hochzeiten (z. B. Peleus und Thetis, Dionysos und Ariadne) stehen die H. wohl wegen des Zeitenwechsels, der in diesen Lebensstationen zum Ausdruck kommt, in Verbindung.

Im klass. Athen werden die H. während eines Fests, bei dem man das Fleisch nicht brät, sondern kocht, um mäßige Wärme und gedeihlichen Regen zur Förderung des Wachstums gebeten (Philochoros FGrH 328 F 173). Nach Pausanias (9,35,1–2) scheinen es jedoch nur zwei H. gewesen zu sein, → Karpo und → Thallo, während Auxo zusammen mit Hegemone eine der → Charites ist (zum Problem [2]). Die Namen weisen sie aber als Vegetationsgottheiten aus.

Kult der H. ist nicht nur in Attika (z. B. ein Heiligtum der H. mit einem Altar des Dionysos Orthos: Philochoros FGrH 328 F 5b; IG II/III²: 4877; [3; 4]), sondern, meist in Verbindung mit anderen Göttern, auch andernorts belegt (z. B. Opus, Olympia, Megalopolis, Argos, Kyrene). In hell. Zeit gingen vier H. in der großen Prozession des Ptolemaios II. Philadelphos [5].

Ikonographisch erscheinen die H., Chariten und Nymphen oft zum Verwechseln ähnlich (vgl. Artem. 2,44), v. a. auf den bekannten Mosaiken und den kaiserzeitl. Jahreszeitensarkophagen. Als H. deutet [9] die drei Figuren auf dem Relief an der Südostecke der → Ara Pacis, die Hauptfigur als Pax Augusta (= Eirene). Zur Nachwirkung sind auch H.-Feste in ma. Kalendern [8] zu zählen.

1 F. Williams, A Theophany in Theocritus, in: CQ 21, 1971, 142 **2** Chr. Habicht, Stud. zur Gesch. Athens in hell. Zeit, 1982, 87–90 **3** Farnell, Cults 5, 425 **4** Deubner, 190f., 201 **5** E. E. Rice, The Grand Procession of Ptolemy Philadelphus, 1983, 49–51; 57 **6** M. Pessoa, Villa romaine de Rabaçal, Penela (Coimbra-Portugal): réalités et perspectives, in: Conimbriga 30, 1991, 109–119 **7** J. Engemann, Ein Missorium des Anastasius, FS für K. Wessel zum 70. Geburtstag, hrsg. von M. Restle, 1988, 103–115 **8** G. Comet, Les calendriers médiévaux: une représentations du monde, in: Journal des Savants 1992, 35–98 **9** N. Th. de Grummond, Pax Augusta and the Horae on the Ara Pacis Augustae, in: AJA 94, 1990, 663–677.

V. Machaira, s. v. H., LIMC 5.1, 502–510 · L. Abad Casal, s. v. H./Horae, LIMC 5.1, 510–538 · Chr. Bauchhenss-Thüriedl, Jahreszeiten, Kotinos, FS für E. Simon, 1992, 429–432 · M. Dufková, Noch zu Jahreszeiten-Sarkophagen, in: Listy filologické 115, 1992, 161–163 · G. M. A. Hanfmann, The Season Sarcophagus in Dumbarton Oaks, 1951 · A. Jolles, s. v. H., RE 8, 2300–2313 · P. Kranz, Jahreszeiten-Sarkophage. Entwicklung und Ikonographie des Motivs der vier Jahreszeiten auf kaiserzeitlichen Sarkophagen und Sarkophagdeckeln, 1984 · M. T. Marabini Moevs, Penteteris e le tre H. nella Pompè di Tolemeo Filadelfo, in: BA 72, 1987, 1–36 · A. Rapp, s. v. H., Roscher 1.2, 2712–2731 · M. Schleiermacher, Die Jahreszeitenfresken von Nida-Heddernheim, in: Kölner Jb. für Vor- und Frühgesch. 24, 1991, 213–218. T. H.

Horapollon. Der Ägypter H., Autor der *Hieroglyphiká*, evtl. identisch mit H., dem Sohn des Asklepiades, entstammte einer Familie von Grammatikern und Philosophen aus Phenebythis im Panopolites; wirkte um 500 n. Chr. in Alexandreia. H. ist u. a. bekannt aus der Vita des Proklos-Schülers → Isidoros [4], verfaßt vom Neuplatoniker → Damaskios, und aus einer zw. 491 und 493 gemachten griech. Eingabe an einen Beamten von Phenebythis (Pap. Cairo 67295).

Der griech. Text der *Hieroglyphiká* ist durch Hss. des 14. Jh. überliefert und soll nach dem Buchtitel von Philippos aus dem Äg. übersetzt worden sein. Ein äg. (kopt.) Urtext ist aufgrund äußerer Umstände und der Sprache des griech. Textes aber nicht anzunehmen. Im ersten Buch des Werkes sind 70, im zweiten 30 → Hieroglyphen und 89 Phantasiezeichen, wohl eine Ergänzung des Philippos, beschrieben nach dem Schema: ›Wenn sie x ausdrücken wollen, malen sie y‹. Dieser Teil basiert wohl auf einem äg. Zeichenpapyrus und spiegelt das im griech.-röm. Äg. erweiterte Bedeutungsspektrum einzelner Schriftzeichen wider. Es folgt eine Begründung, die auf den neuplatonischen Hintergrund des Autors und seine Vertrautheit mit ant. Bestiarien hinweist. Diese allegorisch-symbolischen Erklärungen prägten die Vorstellung von den Hieroglyphen als zum geheimnisvollen Bild verdichteter Weisheit. Sie förderten die Entstehung der Hieroglyphik bzw. Emblematik im Kreise der Humanisten, die bis in die Neuzeit der Entzifferung der Hieroglyphen entgegenwirkte.
→ Ägyptologie; Entzifferung

1 F. Sbordone, Hori Apollinis Hieroglyphica, 1940 **2** H.-J. Thissen, Vom Bild zum Buchstaben – vom Buchstaben zum Bild. Von der Arbeit an H.s Hieroglyphika, 1998 **3** E. Winter, s. v. Hieroglyphen, RAC 15, 90–94. HE. FE.

Horatius. Name einer schon im 5. Jh. v. Chr. erloschenen patrizischen *gens*. Spätere Träger des Namens verdanken ihn der Provenienz aus der nach dieser *gens* benannten Tribus.

[1] Horatii (Königszeit). Der Sage nach (Liv. 1,24–26; Dion. Hal. ant. 3,13,4–22,10) entschied unter König Tullus → Hostilius [I 4] ein Kampf der Drillinge der Horatier gegen die Drillinge der Curiatier statt einer Schlacht den Streit zwischen Rom und → Alba Longa. Nachdem zwei Brüder gefallen waren, überwand der letzte H. seine Gegner. Bei der Rückkehr nach Rom erkannte H.' Schwester unter den mitgeführten Beutestücken ein Gewand ihres Verlobten (eines der Curiatier), beklagte diesen und wurde daraufhin vom Bruder getötet als Warnung, nicht mit einem Feind Mitleid zu empfinden. Vor Gericht als Mörder verurteilt, wurde er nach Berufung an das Volk unter der Auflage, Sühne zu leisten, freigesprochen. C. MÜ.

Das Sühneopfer wurde regelmäßig auf einem Altar unter einem beim *compitum Acilii* in Forumnähe über die Straße gespannten Balken, dem Tigillum Sororium, eingerichtet. Die Erzählung ist Aition für eine Reihe alter Tumuli in Latium und für das Ritual am Tigillum Sororium, hinter dem sich initiatorische Thematik verbirgt; die Verbindung von *sororium* mit *soror* (»Schwester«) ist eine Volksetym. Quellen: Liv. 1,24–26; Dion. Hal. ant. 3,13,4–22,10.

1 T. J. Cornell, The Beginnings of Rome, 1995

H. J. Rose, De religionibus antiquis questiunculae tres, in: Mnemosyne 53, 1925, 407–410 · G. Dumézil, Horace et les Curiaces, 1942 · F. Coarelli, Il Foro Romano. Periodo Arcaico, 1983, 111–117 · J. Poucet, Les origines de Rome, 1985, 219–221. F. G.

[2] H., P. Wohl aufgrund einer Verwechslung mit einem P. Curiatius nur von Dion. Hal. (ant. 10,53,1; 56,2) als Consul 453 v. Chr. und Decemvir 451 erwähnt. MRR 1, 43 f.; 45 f.

[3] H. Barbatus, M. Cognomen [Tu]rrin(us) ? (vgl. Fasti feriarum Latinarum, CIL I², 56). Nach Ende der Herrschaft der → *decemviri* [1] führte er als *cos.* 449 mit seinem Kollegen L. Valerius Potitus (MRR 1, 47) die Gesetzgebung der *decemviri*, als deren Gegner beide vorher aufgetreten waren, durch Hinzufügung der letzten zwei Gesetzestafeln und Aufstellung aller 12 Tafeln (→ *tabulae duodecim*) zu Ende (Diod. 12,26,1; Liv. 3,57,10). Die ihnen zugeschriebenen *leges Valeriae Horatiae* (Liv. 3,55,3–7) sind als mögliche Rückprojektionen der Ergebnisse der → Ständekämpfe in ihrer Historizität umstritten [1. 276–278; 2. 213–220]. Als Sieger über die Sabiner soll H. vom Senat ein Triumph verweigert, dann aber vom Volk gewährt worden sein (Liv. 3,57,9; 61,11–63; Dion. Hal. ant. 11,48–50,1).

1 T.J. Cornell, The Beginnings of Rome, 1995
2 D. Flach, Die Gesetze der frühen römischen Republik, 1994.

[4] H. Cocles. In der röm. lit. Trad. als Inbegriff altröm. *virtus* gesehen. Die früheste Darstellung der Sage gibt Polybios (6,54): Im Kampf gegen die vor Rom stehenden Etrusker unter → Porsenna verteidigte H. den → *pons sublicius* gegen die Angreifer, bis die Brücke hinter ihm abgerissen war, sprang danach ins Wasser und fand hierbei den Tod. Nach Livius (2,10,2–11) verteidigte H. die Brücke zunächst mit zwei Kameraden, konnte sich unversehrt retten und erhielt eine Reihe von Ehrungen. Sein Cognomen *Cocles* (»der Einäugige«) wird von den ant. Autoren meist damit erklärt, daß er in einem früheren Kampf bereits ein Auge verloren habe.

[5] H. Pulvillus, C. *Cos.* 477 und 457 (MRR 1, 26f.; 41; Liv. 3,30,1 und Diod. 11,91,1 mit dem Praenomen M. für den *cos.* 457). Aufgrund der Schwankung hinsichtlich des Praenomens ist die Identität des *cos.* 477 mit dem von 457 nicht völlig gesichert. 477 soll H., vorher im Kampf gegen die Volsker, nach der Schlacht an der Cremera durch seine Rückkehr Rom vor den Etruskern geschützt haben (Liv. 2,51,1–3). In H.' zweitem Consulat 457 erfolgte die Verdopplung der Volkstribunenzahl auf zehn; er selbst eroberte im Aequerkrieg Corbio (Liv. 3,30; Dion. Hal. ant. 10,28–30).

[6] H. Pulvillus, M. Als Stellvertreter des Königs Tarquinius vor Ardea stellte er sich nach dessen Vertreibung aus Rom gegen ihn (Dion. Hal. ant. 4,85). Polybius (3,22,1) führt H. mit L. Iunius [I 4] Brutus als erste Consuln der Republik an und setzt den ersten röm.-karthagischen Vertrag in ihr Consulat. Die übrige Überl. kennt H. als *cos. suff.* 509 mit seinem Kollegen P. Valerius Poplicola, mit dem er 507 ein zweites (bei Livius übergangenes) Consulat bekleidete (MRR 1, 3; 6). Aufgrund einer Weihinschr. wurde H. die Weihung des capitolinischen Iuppitertempels zugeschrieben. Uneins ist die Überl., ob dies in seinem ersten oder zweiten Consulat geschah bzw. ob H. hierbei als Consul oder Pontifex handelte (Cic. dom. 139; Liv. 2,8,6–8; Dion. Hal. ant. 5,35,3; Val. Max. 5,10,1; Sen. dial. 6,13,1; Tac. hist. 3,72,1 f.; Plut. Poplicola 14). C.MÜ.

[7] H. Flaccus, Q., der Dichter Horaz.
A. Leben. B. Werke C. Wirkung

A. Leben

Die ant. Informationen über H. sind vergleichsweise reich. Er selbst gibt in seinen Werken nicht wenige Darstellungen und Hinweise. Freilich muß davor gewarnt werden, diese Angaben, v.a. diejenigen der Lyrik, als gesicherte Daten anzusehen; sie sind poetische Aussagen und müssen als solche gewertet werden. Hinzu kommen Mitteilungen in den spätant. Schol. des → Porphyrio, des → Pseudo-Acro und eine indirekt überl. Vita des → Suetonius. Der volle Name Q. Horatius Flaccus ist im Zusammenhang des *Carmen saeculare* (s.u.) inschr. bezeugt; seine Elemente erscheinen auch alle in den Dichtungen (*Quintus*: sat. 2,6,37; *Horatius*: epist. 1,14,5; carm. 4,6,44; *Flaccus*: epod. 15,12; sat. 2,1,18). H. wurde am 8. Dez. 63 v.Chr. in Venosa/Venusia (an der Grenze zw. Lukanien und Apulien) als Sohn eines Freigelassenen geb.; er starb am 27. Nov. 8 v.Chr.

H. genoß dank der Fürsorge seines Vaters eine außergewöhnlich gute Erziehung, zunächst in seiner Heimat (epist. 2,1,70f.), darauf in Rom im Kreis hochgestellter Mitschüler (sat. 1,6,71–78; epist. 2,2,41 f.), schließlich als Student in Athen (epist. 2,2,43–5). Er wurde durch das Vorbild seines Vaters zu ständiger Selbstprüfung, aber auch zu intensiver Beobachtung und moralischer Bewertung der Lebenshaltung anderer angeleitet (sat. 1,4,103–143). Die Lage der Heimatstadt an der Grenze hat in H. Unsicherheit hinsichtlich seiner Stammeszugehörigkeit geweckt und ihn auch die Heftigkeit seines Charakters an diese Herkunft anknüpfen lassen (sat. 2,1,34ff.). Nach den Jahren der Ausbildung geriet er in die Wirren der Bürgerkriege (epist. 2,2,46–48): Dem Studenten in Athen übertrug Iunius [I 10] Brutus ein erstaunlich hohes mil. Kommando als *tribunus militum* (sat. 1,6,48). H. verlor nach der Niederlage bei → Philippoi das gesamte väterliche Erbe und arbeitete für seinen Lebensunterhalt bei der Staatskasse. Die Armut habe ihn, sagt er (epist. 2,2,51 f.), dazu geführt, Verse zu machen – eine eher ironische Aussage, wie der Kontext zeigt.

In der Tat sind H.' erste Dichtungen in der 1. H. der 30er Jahre v.Chr. entstanden. Sie führten ihn in einer Kette von Begegnungen aus der materiellen Not heraus. Die Dichter → Vergilius und → Varius wurden auf ihn aufmerksam; durch diese neuen Freunde wurde er an → Maecenas (M.) und durch diesen an Octavian, den späteren → Augustus, empfohlen. Eine erste Begegnung mit M. i.J. 37 (sat. 1,6,52–64) führte 9 Monate später zur Aufnahme des H. in den Freundeskreis des M.; etwa 32 schenkte dieser ihm das → Sabinum, ein (nach damaliger Auffassung bescheidenes) Landgut in den Sabiner Bergen bei Vicovaro, das von einem Verwalter geleitet, von fünf Pächterfamilien bearbeitet und von acht Sklaven bedient wurde. H. hatte damit neben einem Auskommen eine zweite Heimat, die er hochschätzte und in freundlichen Farben feierte (sat. 2,6,1–

15; 60–70; epist. 1,16,5–16; carm. 3,13). Er gab sie auch nicht auf, als er später, wie die *Vita* berichtet, ein höchst ehrenvolles Angebot auf eine einflußreiche Stellung erhielt: Augustus selbst wünschte ihn als Privatsekretär bei sich zu haben. Die Ablehnung führte nach Sueton zu keiner Verstimmung.

Der 44jährige H. schildert sich selbst als klein von Statur, wohlbeleibt und früh ergraut (epist. 1,20,24; epist. 1,7,26; epist. 1,4,15; vita). Als einen bes. Charakterzug nennt er seinen Jähzorn (epist. 1,20,25; carm. 3,9,23; sat. 2,3,323), der freilich rasch erlischt. Philos. bekannte sich H. zur Schule des → Epikuros (epist. 1,4,16); Gedankengut aus der → Stoa und der kynischen → Diatribe ist verschiedentlich eingeflossen und amalgamiert [25]. Der Tod traf den 57jährigen zwei Monate nach M. Als Erben benannte er Augustus; die Beisetzung erfolgte auf dem Esquilin.

B. Werke
1. Graeca 2. Satiren 3. Epoden
4. Oden 5. Carmen saeculare
6. Episteln und ars poetica

1. Graeca

Möglicherweise liegt in dem Epigramm Anth. Gr. 7,542 eines Dichters namens Flaccus ein Poem des jungen H. vor [18]. In jedem Falle hat H. sich selbst zu derartigen früheren Versuchen bekannt und sich später deutlich von eigenem griech. Dichten distanziert (sat. 1,10,39–43).

2. Satiren

Folgte H. in seinen etwa gleichzeitig entstehenden Epoden mit → Archilochos einem griech. Modell, so nutzte er in den → ›Satiren‹ eine röm. Form. Doch setzt er sich theoretisch und praktisch in deutlichen Abstand zu → Lucilius. Der Titel ist *sermones*, die Entstehungszeit beider B. etwa 41–35/3 bzw. 35–30 [22]. H. lobt an Lucilius den Freimut, kritisiert aber die allzu leichtfertige Schreibart und die ungefeilte Überproduktion (sat. 1,10; 1,4,8–13). Er ist jedoch gerecht genug, den Zeitfaktor zu berücksichtigen und die frühe Epoche für die Defizite mitverantwortlich zu machen, nicht den Autor allein (1,10,64–69). B. 1 enthält 10, B. 2 nur 8 Stücke; der Einzelumfang wechselt zwischen 35 (1,7) und 326 Versen (2,3). Widmungsträger ist M. (1,1,1 und 1,6,1); Octavian findet ehrenvolle Erwähnung in 2,1,11 und 2,5,62–64. Beide haben so je am Anfang und am Beginn der zweiten Buchhälfte ihren Platz [34]. – Die vielleicht früheste Satire (1,2) hat Unzucht und Ehebruch zum Hauptthema (wobei 69–71 sogar der Penis zu Wort kommt), die längste (2,3) fünf verschiedene Formen der Verrücktheit (*insanire* 81), nämlich Habsucht (82–160), Ehrgeiz (160–223), Luxus (224–246), Verliebtheit (247–280), Aberglauben (281–297). Hexentreiben wird gegeißelt (1,8); eine Unterweltsbefragung des Teiresias attackiert die Erbschleicherei (2,5). Neben der Kritik an derlei Untugenden sind aber auch freundschaftliche Szenen einbezogen, z.B. in der heiteren Beschreibung der Reise nach Brundisium (1,5). Traditionelle Satirenthemen wie *cena* (2,8) oder *iter* (1,5; vgl. Lucilius, *Iter Siculum*) erscheinen mehrfach. Eine Fabel (›Stadtmaus und Landmaus‹) beschließt beschaulich den Diskurs über Luxus und Bescheidung, über unbequem urbanes und geruhsam rustikales Leben (2,6). Ein Kabinettstück ist auch die ›Schwätzersatire‹ (1,9), in der ein lästiger Zeitgenosse H. auf der → Via Sacra aufhält und um Protektion bei M. angeht.

3. Epoden

Auch als ›Iamben‹ (→ Iambographen) bezeichnet, enthält das Buch, das ebenfalls aus den 30er Jahren stammt, 17 Dichtungen, die alle in unterschiedlicher Weise jambische Maße verwenden: Die ersten 10 benutzen jambische Disticha (Trimeter und Dimeter), am Ende (17) steht ebenfalls ein rein jambisches Gedicht (Trimeter); 11–16 dagegen verbinden verschiedene, teils jambische Zeilen mit dem Hexameter (13–16), teils mit dem sog. Elegiambus (11), teils erscheint auch (12) eine rein daktylische Versform (Hexameter und Tetrameter [5; 16]). Damit ist bereits ein erstes Gliederungsprinzip angesprochen: die metrisch begründete Anordnung, die auch in den Oden hervortreten wird. Wiederum ist hier, wie zuvor in den ›Satiren‹ und auch späterhin, M. Widmungsträger (1, 2 und 4). Der große Gönner wird noch dreimal angesprochen, jeweils dem Inhalt entsprechend in Heiterkeit (*iocose M.*, 3,20), in Siegesfreude (*beate M.*, 9,4), in vertrauter Nähe (*candide M.*, 14,5). Im übrigen kontrastieren im Eingangsgedicht die Lebensbahnen des hohen Freundes und die des gesellschaftlich geringer gestellten Schützlings; ein derartiges Konfrontationsmuster unterschiedlicher Lebenswege wird ebenfalls in späteren Werken wiederkehren. H. hat selbst rückschauend das poetische Programm seiner ›Iamben‹ theoretisch eingeordnet (epist. 1,19,19–25): Er rühmt sich, als erster (*princeps, primus*) Iamben aus Paros nach Latium gebracht zu haben und dabei dem Archilochos gefolgt zu sein – wenn nicht in den eigentlichen Themen und der namentlichen Schelte, so doch in der Versform und dem poetischen Impetus (*animus*). Damit ist eine Grundhaltung der augusteischen Kultur gekennzeichnet: Anknüpfung an griech. Muster einerseits, Humanisierung des archa. Vorbilds andererseits. Zugleich greift die Modellwahl, aus der hell. verengten Perspektive der → Neoteriker ausbrechend, mit energischem Griff in eine wesentlich frühere, frischere Vorzeit. Auch dies wird sich in den ›Oden‹ fortsetzen. Die augusteische »Klassik« (als eine Art »Renaissance«) zeichnet sich ab (→ Literatur, augusteische; → Klassizismus).

4. Oden

23 v.Chr. veröffentlichte H. 3 B. *Carmina* mit insgesamt 88 lyrischen Gedichten; ein 4. B. mit 15 Liedern wurde, angeblich auf Drängen des Augustus, um 15 oder kurz danach publ. Zuvor war im Sommer 17 als Auftragswerk das Lied zur Jahrhundertfeier (→ *saeculum*) entstanden (s.u.). Es waren ›äolische‹ Gesänge (carm. 3,30,13; 4,3,12; *Lesboum ... barbiton* 1,1,34), die

sich an poetischen Modellen wie → Alkaios [4] (carm. 2,13,27; 4,9,7) und → Sappho (carm. 2,13,25) orientierten [41] und auch deren metrische Formen aufnahmen. Neben ihren Strophen fanden v.a. die des → Asklepiades [1] Verwendung; auch → Pindaros wurde zum Vorbild oder besser Gegenbild (carm. 4,2). Die Zuwendung zur griech. Frühzeit ist bezeichnend; mit dem großen Gestus dieser Gedichte distanziert sich H. von der Zierlichkeit hell. Poesie und ihren Verkünstelungen, er wächst zum »Klassiker«. Im Umfang sind die Dichtungen unterschiedlich konzipiert: zweistrophigen Achtzeilern stehen Lieder mit über 10 vierzeiligen Strophen gegenüber; das *Carmen saeculare* umfaßt 76 V., die 4. ›Römer-Ode‹ (3,4) 80. Doch ist Kürze im allg. bevorzugt.

Wie die ›Römeroden‹ am Anfang von B. 3 als geschlossener Block mit nur einem Versmaß [52] und die Eingangsgedichte von B. 2 mit zwei Versmaßen in regelmäßigem Wechsel, so bilden am Beginn von B. 1 die ersten Oden einen Zyklus (die sog. ›Parade-Oden‹), indem sie die von H. neu erschlossenen Versformen vorführen [39; 45]. Als Themen der Lyrik definiert H. (ars 83–85): → Hymnoi und → Paiane auf Götter und Heroen, ferner → Epinikien und → Enkomien, erotische und sympotische Dichtung, schließlich auch (carm. 4,2,21–24) → Threnoi. Hinzu treten Huldigungen an den Herrscher und sein Haus; Gespräche mit Freunden verschiedener Rangstufen; Reflexionen und moralische Mahnungen; Gedanken an die Vergänglichkeit des Lebens und Aufmunterung zu seinem Genuß; Mahnungen zum Maßhalten, zur rechten »goldenen« Mitte (*aurea mediocritas*, carm. 2,10,5). Private und polit. Gedichte verbinden sich zu einem weiten Panorama poetischer Produktion (die ›Kleopatra-Ode‹ *Nunc est bibendum* 1,37; das Lied auf die → Bandusia-Quelle 3,13; die Mahnung *carpe diem*, 1,11 und die Ode *Integer vitae*, 1,22). Am gewichtigsten die sog. »Römer-Oden« (3,1–6), in denen der Dichter sich an sein Volk wendet (*Romane* 3,6,2) und die Jugend (*virginibus puerisque canto* 3,1,4) zu den traditionellen Werten des Staates aufruft, die er später als *Fides/Pax/Honos Pudorque/Virtus* (carm. saec. 57f.) zusammenfaßt.

5. Carmen Saeculare

736 a.u.c. (= 17 v. Chr.) veranstaltete Augustus unter Berufung auf einen → Sibyllenspruch nach fast 2 Jh. eine Säcularfeier (→ *saeculum*). Das Komitee zur Vorbereitung, dem er vorstand, beauftragte H. mit der Abfassung eines Kultliedes, das von je 27 (= 3×3×3) Mädchen und Knaben aus der Nobilität auf dem Palatin vorgetragen und auf dem Kapitol wiederholt wurde; es wurde vom Dichter einstudiert und möglicherweise auch von ihm selbst instrumental begleitet (carm. 4,3,29–44; vgl. epist. 2,1,132). Die Autorschaft ist inschr. belegt (CIL VI,32323 = ILS Nr. 5050), der Text der Bezeugung im Kreuzgang des Thermenmuseums in Rom einsehbar. Das dreitägige Fest begann am Abend des 31. Mai; der Dreizahl entsprechend gliedert sich H.' Festlied in 2×3×3 (sapphische) Strophen mit einer Schlußstrophe als Abgesang. In der ersten H. erscheint Apollo als Gott der Sonne am Anfang, er und Diana als Göttin des Mondes am Ende; sie umrahmen so die in der Mitte angerufenen unterirdischen Gottheiten → Eileithyia, Parzen (→ Parcae) und → Tellus. In der 2. H. wird Roms Gesch. beschworen. Den Beschluß in der letzten Strophe macht eine Spielart der → Sphragis: Der Chor spricht von seiner sicheren Hoffnung auf Erhörung des Gebets. – Gegen ältere Positionen ([14]: ›geistige Zusammenfassung‹ der Feier; [23]: ihr ›ideales Abbild‹), in denen das Lied als selbständiger Teil der Begehung erschien, betont und belegt [15] die Einheit von Ritual und Lied.

6. Episteln und Ars poetica

Buch 1: Möglicherweise mitveranlaßt durch die ungünstige Aufnahme seiner Lyrik (epist. 1,19,35–41), wandte H. sich nach 23 v. Chr. erneut hexametrischer Kleinform zu. Im J. 20 erschienen zwanzig Dichtungen (zwischen 13 und 112 V. Umfang) als 1. Epistel-B., später gefolgt von B. 2. Einleitend wird in dem wiederum dem M. gewidmeten Buch betont (1,1,10f.), ›Verse und all der übrige Tand‹ würden nun beiseite gelegt; die Aufmerksamkeit gelte nun dem, was wahr und geziemend sei. Angeredet werden Personen aller Stände: der Prinz Tiberius (9), der Gönner M. (1; 19), der Freund Lollius (2; 18), der Dichterfreund Tibull (4), andererseits der namenlos bleibende Gutsverwalter (14) und sogar das eigene Buch (20). Die Kontraste von Hoch und Niedrig, Stadt und Land werden in der Mitte erörtert (9f.), mehrfach auch die rechte Haltung dem Patron gegenüber (13; 17f.) und andererseits Maximen wie die Distanz des *nil admirari* (6,1). Eine Art Ringkomposition zeichnet sich ab: 1 und 19 sind M. gewidmet, 2 und 18 dem Lollius; der Schlußbrief (20) gibt als Sphragis Auskunft über Person und Lebensumstände des Verf. und über sein Verhältnis zum Werk. Die Ausgewogenheit seiner vielfältigen Aspekte zwischen Ernst und Heiterkeit macht das B. zum ›harmonischsten aller Bücher des H.‹ ([23. 364]; ähnlich [28; 29; 30]).

Buch 2 und *Ars poetica* [31]: In drei längeren Gedichten (270, 216 und 476 V.) erörtert H. nach zweieinhalb Jahrzehnten poetischer Produktion am Ende seines Schaffens das ihm teuerste Thema: die Poesie. Epist. 1, das erste Augustus gewidmete horazische Eingangsgedicht, enthält nach dem einleitenden Lob des Herrschers eine Auseinandersetzung mit archaisierenden Tendenzen und in der Mitte (V. 126–138) den Preis des Poeten in seiner Position als Pädagoge, Priester und Prophet der Gemeinschaft, gefolgt von Gedanken über die Entstehung des röm. Dramas im Rahmen ländlicher Feste und über seine Entwicklung unter der Einwirkung des griech. Schauspiels. Der Brief, eine Art Ber. über die poetische Lage der Nation, mündet in eine Selbstdefinition des H. in seiner → *recusatio*, Augustus nicht wie Vergil und Varius im → Epos feiern zu können. – In Epist. 2 an Florus, dem schon epist. 1,3 gewidmet war, bespricht H. seinen Bildungsweg und seinen Abschied von der Lyrik; in der Mitte wird (V. 109–125) der Blick auf die Regeln zur Schaffung guter Dichtung gelenkt, im letzten Teil auf die Philos. und ihre Warnung vor Habgier, Ehrgeiz, Zorn, Aberglauben, Todesfurcht. Im heiteren Finale (V. 213–216) spricht der Poet sich selbst zu, seine Rolle des Gealterten recht zu erfüllen. Praktische Philos. und Poesie, die beiden großen Grundgedanken im Leben des H., sind nirgends so deutlich in seiner persönlichen Prägung zu erfassen wie in den beiden Briefbüchern.

→ Quintilian hat als erster die *Ars poetica* als solche benannt (inst., praef. 2; 8,3,60); sie heißt auch nach den Widmungsträgern *Ad Pisones*, ›An die Pisonen‹. Nach Porphyrio hat H. ›nicht alle, aber die wichtigsten Regeln des → Neoptolemos von Parion in diesem B. zusammengestellt‹. Fragmente der → Herculanensischen Papyri haben Teile einer Widerlegung des Neoptolemos durch den Epikureer → Philodemos von Gadara erhalten, so daß eine indirekte Kenntnisnahme möglich ist. Freilich ist die *Ars* kein versifiziertes Hdb., sondern humanes Gespräch mit Freunden über ein gemeinsames Thema. Immerhin scheint der Gegensatz Dichtwerk-Dichter in H.' *Ars* wieder aufgenommen zu sein und die Gliederung beeinflußt zu haben; dem Gegensatz *de arte poetica* (V. 1–294) versus *de poeta* (V. 295–Ende nach NORDEN) entspricht moderner der zw. Werkästhetik und Produktions- und Wirkungsästhetik. Beide Hauptteile widmen sich einer gemeinsamen Frage: Wie ist das vollkommene Kunstwerk zu kreieren möglich? Aus der Fülle der Gedanken sind vier hervorzuheben. 1) Der zweifache Zweck der Poesie: Sie soll das Angenehme mit dem Nützlichen verbinden (V. 343f.), wie der Dichter nützen und zugleich auch erfreuen will (V. 333f.). 2) Die Bed. des Bezugs röm. Dichtung auf griech. Modelle (V. 268f.). 3) Die Betonung der Behutsamkeit des Produktionsprozesses, der konstanten Korrektur, Kritik und Selbstkritik (V. 385–390). 4) Schließlich die Gedanken über Wert und Wirksamkeit der Wörter und ihre Neuschöpfung bzw. Wiederbelebung (V. 47f.; V. 240–243).

C. WIRKUNG

Bereits in der Ant. avancierte H. zum Schulbuchautor; Quintilian zollte sowohl dem Satiriker (inst. 10,1,94) wie dem Lyriker (10,1,96) hohe Anerkennung: Er sei *verbis felicissime audax*, ›im Gebrauch der Wörter von höchst erfolgreicher Kühnheit‹. → Petronius spricht von H.' *curiosa felicitas*, der Verbindung von Mühe und glücklichem Erfolg, NIETZSCHE von seinem ›feierlichen Leichtsinn‹ (›Menschliches, Allzumenschliches‹ I,109). → Ovid nennt ihn *numerosus Horatius*, ›rhythmenreicher H.‹ (trist. 4,10,49). Das Christentum bewundert seine Form, distanziert sich von seinen Gedanken: *Quid facit cum psalterio Horatius?* ›Was hat denn H. mit dem Psalter zu schaffen?‹ (Hieron. epist. 22,29). Erst → Prudentius vermag den Zwiespalt zu lösen, indem er in den Strophen des H. christl. Lieder dichtet. Wurde noch am Anf. des 6. Jh. von → Mavortius (*cos.* 527) eine Textrevision vorgenommen, so blieb H. im beginnenden MA [43] vergessen.

Erst in der → karolingischen Renaissance begann neue Beachtung; hier setzen auch die Zeugnisse der Textüberl. ein. Das Röm. Brevier enthält vier → Hymnen in Versmaßen des H., in denen auch im 12. Jh. der Tegernseer Mönch Metellus Oden auf den Hl. Quirinus schuf. DANTE schließt H. (›Inferno‹ 4,94) in die erlauchte Gruppe der sieben größten Dichter ein mit dem Beiwort *satiro*: Der Satirendichter als *ethicus* ist dem MA präsent, nicht der Lyriker, wie Hugo VON TRIMBERG (gest. 1313) in seinem Autorenregister (2,66ff.) bestätigt. Hingegen wird H. in Renaissance und Barock neu entdeckt: PETRARCA gestaltet seine 67 *epistole* nach dem Vorbild der Briefe des H.; Humanisten wie CELTIS und MELISSUS im 16. Jh., Jesuiten wie BALDE und FABRICIUS im 17. Jh. schaffen umfangreiche Liederslgg., in Metrik, Strophenform, Wortwahl und Gedankenführung horazischem Muster folgend [46]. Der Erstausg. von 1470 folgen Übers. seit 1535. Vertonungen in der Art der sog. »Humanistenoden« (Chorsätze mit Übertragung der Silbenquantität in Notendauer) durch TRITONIUS, SENFL, HOFHAIMER setzen ein; ihnen stellen andere, wie GLAREANUS und JUDENKÜNIG, taktfreies monodisches Melos entgegen. Der weitere Weg führt durch viele musikalische Stile über ORLANDO DI LASSO zu Carl LOEWE, Peter CORNELIUS und Zoltán KODÁLY. In der bildenden Kunst ist H. ebenfalls Anreger [51; 53]: 1498 erschien in Straßburg die mit Holzschnitten geschmückte Ausg. des Jacob LOCHER, 1607 in Antwerpen 103 Emblemata des Rubensschülers Otto VAN VEEN, in London 1733 229 Kupferstiche des John PINE, in der Pariser Prachtausg. von 1799 12 Bilder von C. PERCIER/GIRARDOT.

Parodien verpflanzten H.' Gedichte z. B. ins Bayerische oder ins Berliner Milieu (MORGENSTERN), auch ins Jiddische. Das Bild des H. wandelte sich vielfältig: vom *ethicus* im MA zum lyrischen Vorbild der Humanisten, zum Anakreontiker der Romantik, zum polit.-patriotischen Poeten im 20. Jh. Bald stand der hell., bald der national-röm. Dichter im Vordergrund. Wurde der »Hofdichter« und »Epigone« hier getadelt, so dort der Philosoph anerkannt; da der Dichtungstheoretiker bewundert, dort der Ges.-Kritiker gefeiert. WIELAND, NIETZSCHE, BRECHT bewunderten H.; Primo LEVI hat ihm am 14. April 1985 einen Brief ins Jenseits geschrieben. Der 2000. Todestag 1993 gab Anlaß zu verschiedenen Veranstaltungen [27; 35; 44].

ED.: **1** S. BORZSÁK, 1984 • D. R. SHACKLETON-BAILEY, 1985 • B. KYTZLER, 1992 (mit Übers.).
SCHOLIEN: **2** A. HOLDER, O. KELLER (Hrsg.), Scholia Antiqua in Q. Horatium Flaccum, 1894 (Ndr. 1979).
GESAMTBIBLIOGR.: **3** W. KISSEL, in: ANRW II 31.3, 1981, 1403–1558.
FORSCH.-BER.: **4** E. DOBLHOFER, H. in der Forsch. seit 1957, 1992 **5** A. SETAIOLI, Gli Epodi di Orazio nella critica dal 1937 al 1972 (con un appendice fino al 1978), in: ANRW II 31.3, 1674–1788.
LEXIKON: **6** D. BO, 1965/6.
KONKORDANZ: **7** I. ECHEGOYEN, 1990.
KOMM.: **8** A. KIESSLING, R. HEINZE, [11]1964 **9** H. P.

SYNDIKUS, Die Lyrik des H., 2 Bde., 1972/3 **10** R. G. M. NISBET, M. HUBBARD, Odes I/II, 1970/78 **11** C. O. BRINK, H. on Poetry, 3 Bde., 1963–82.

LIT.: **12** R. ANCONA, Time and the Erotic in H.'s Odes, 1995 **13** D. ARMSTRONG, H., 1989 **14** C. BECKER, Das Spätwerk des H., 1963 **15** H. CANCIK, Carmen und sacrificium, in: B. SEIDENSTICKER, R. FABER (Hrsg.), Wörter – Bilder – Töne. FS B. Kytzler, 1996, 99–113 **16** R. W. CARRUBBA, The Epodes of H., 1969 **17** N. E. COLLINGE, The structure of H.'s Odes, 1961 **18** F. DELLA CORTE, Fra Statilio e Orazio, in: RFIC 101, 1973, 442–450 **19** G. DAVIS, The Rhetoric of Horatian Lyric, 1991 **20** H. DETTMER, H.: A Study in Structure, 1983 **21** J. DRAHEIM, G. WILLE, H.-Vertonungen vom MA bis zur Gegenwart, 1985 **22** K. FREUDENBURG, The Walking Muse. H. on the Theory of Satire, 1993 **23** E. FRAENKEL, H., 1963 (engl. 1957) **24** O. GALL, Die Bilder der horazischen Lyrik, 1981 **25** O. GIGON, H. und die Philos., in: Die ant. Philos. als Maßstab und Realität, 1977 **26** T. HALTER, Vergil und H., 1970 **27** S. J. HARRISON (Hrsg.), Homage to H., 1995 **28** H. J. HIRTH, H., der Dichter der Episteln, 1985 **29** W. R. JOHNSON, H. and the Dialectic of Freedom, 1993 **30** R. S. KILPATRICK, The Theory of Friendship, 1986 (epist. 1) **31** Ders., The Poetry of Criticism, 1990 (epist. 2) **32** B. KYTZLER, H., 1996 **33** E. LEFÈVRE, H. – Dichter im augusteischen Rom, 1993 **34** W. LUDWIG, Die Komposition der beiden Satirenb. des H., in: Poetica 2, 1968, 304–335 **35** W. LUDWIG (Hrsg.), H. (Entretiens 39), 1993 **36** R. LYNE, H.: Behind the Public Poetry, 1995 **37** D. MANKIN, H.'s Epodes, 1995 **38** D. MULROY, H.'s Odes and Epodes, 1994 **39** F. H. MUTSCHLER, Beobachtungen zur Gedichtanordnung in der ersten Odenslg. des H., in: RhM 117, 1974, 109–132 **40** W. OTT, Metrische Analysen zur Ars poetica, 1970 **41** G. PASQUALI, Orazio Lirico, 1920 (Ndr. 1964) **42** V. PÖSCHL, Horazische Lyrik, 1991 **43** M.-B. QUINT, Unt. zur ma. H.-Rezeption, 1988 **44** N. RUDD (Hrsg.), H. 2000, 1993 **45** M. S. SANTIROCCO, Unity and Design in H.'s Odes, 1986 **46** E. SCHÄFER, Deutscher H., 1976 **47** E. SIMON, H. und die Bildkunst seiner Zeit – ein Stilvergleich, in: Quaderni ticinesi di numismatica e antichità classiche 23, 1994, 211–221 **48** E. STEMPLINGER, Das Fortleben der horazischen Lyrik seit der Renaissance, 1906 **49** Ders., H. im Urteil der Jahrhunderte, 1921 **50** R. STORRS, C. TENNYSON, Ad Pyrrham, 1959 (154 Übers. in 25 Sprachen von carm. 1,5) **51** O. VAN VEEN, Quinti Horati Flacci Emblemata, 1607 (Ndr. 1972) **52** C. WITKE, H.'s Roman Odes, 1983 **53** P. VON ZEESEN, Moralia Horatiana, 1656 (Ndr. 1963). B. KY.

Horaz s. Q. → Horatius [7] Flaccus

Hordeonius

[1] M. H. Offensichtlich Patrimonialprokurator der Narbonensis unter Tiberius (CIL VI 92 = 30690). Wohl Vater von H. [2]; aus Puteoli stammend.

G. CAMODECA, in: EOS 2, 128 f.

[2] M. H. Flaccus. Sohn von H. [1]. *Cos. suff.* im J. 47 n. Chr. (AE 1988, 325; 1991, 474; [1]). Im Sommer 68 löste er, bereits *senex*, Verginius Rufus als Legat des obergerman. Heeres ab. Als die Truppen am 1. Jan. 69 in Moguntiacum den Eid auf Galba [2] verweigerten, unternahm er nichts; möglicherweise war er bereits in die Planungen des → Vitellius eingeweiht, dem er sich Anf. Januar offen anschloß. Von Vitellius als Legat des gesamten Rheinheeres zurückgelassen, wurde er mit der Proklamation Vespasians und dem Aufstand der Bataver unter Civilis konfrontiert. In Tacitus' Bericht in den *Historien* erscheint H. als unsicher, schwach und in seiner Treue schwankend. Doch ist sein Bild vielleicht im Nachhinein von Civilis und mehr noch von den Flaviern aus Eigeninteresse verfälscht worden. Er vereidigte die Truppen am Rhein nach der Niederlage des Vitellius bei Cremona auf Vespasian. Als er ein Donativ, das noch Vitellius gesandt hatte, im Namen Vespasians an die Truppen auszahlte, wurde er von den betrunkenen Soldaten während der Nacht erschlagen. Tac. hist. 1–4 passim.

1 G. CAMODECA, in: L. FRANCI DELL'ORTO (ed.), Ercolano 1738–1788, 1993, 525.

PIR² H 202 · O. SCHMITT, in: BJ 193, 1993, 155 ff. W. E.

Horeia, Horia s. Binnenschiffahrt

Hormisdas (neupers. *Hormizd*, arab. *Hurmuz*; Sasaniden).

[1] H. I., lat. *Odomastes* (HA trig. tyr. 2,2). Sohn → Sapors I., in dessen Auftrag er einen Einfall nach Armenien unternahm. Er amtierte dort seit ca. 252 n. Chr. unter dem Titel eines »Großkönigs« als pers. Statthalter und folgte seinem Vater nach dessen Tod (Herbst 272) für ca. ein Jahr auf den pers. Thron.

[2] H. II., Neffe von [1], Perserkönig 302–309 n. Chr. (Agathias 4,25,1).

[3] Sohn von H. [2] II. Als sein älterer Bruder Adanarses nach sehr kurzer Herrschaft noch 309 gestürzt wurde, wurde auch H. eingekerkert. Er konnte jedoch durch eine List seiner Gattin entkommen und floh kurz vor 324 zu Constantinus [1] d.Gr. (Zos. 2,27). Von Constantius [2] II. zum Anführer einer Reiterabteilung ernannt, diente er diesem im Kampf gegen Persien und begleitete den Kaiser 357 nach Rom (Amm. 16,10,16). 363 war er bei Kaiser → Iulianus [5] in Antiocheia (Lib. or. 18,258), der erwogen haben soll, H. anstelle von dessen Bruder Sapor II. zum Perserkönig zu machen (Lib. epist. 1402 FOERSTER). H. nahm dann an Iulianus' Perserkrieg teil und leistete ihm vielfältige Dienste.

[4] Sohn von H. [3], von dem Usurpator Prokopios 365 zum *proconsul Asiae* ernannt. Er kämpfte tapfer gegen Valens (Amm. 26,8,12; Zos. 4,8,1). Um 380 ist er als Feldherr des Kaisers Theodosius I. belegt (Zos. 4,30,5).

[5] H. III., (ältester?) Sohn Yazdgirds II. und Statthalter von Sistan, wurde 457 nach dem Tod des Vaters Großkönig. Gegen ihn erhob sich sein jüngerer Bruder Peroz, dem es mit Hilfe der → Hephthalitai 459 gelang, H. zu entthronen.

[6] H. IV., Sohn und seit 579 Nachfolger Chosroes' [5] I. Die Quellen zeigen ihn als sozial eingestellten Herrscher, der die Armen förderte, aber zarathustrische Priesterschaft (→ Zoroastres) und Adel bekämpfte. Der vom Vater ererbte Krieg gegen Byzanz ging zunächst ohne greifbare Ergebnisse weiter, ein Einfall der Türken, die 588 bis Balch und Herat vorgedrungen waren, konnte durch den Feldherrn → Wahram Tschobin abgewehrt werden. Als Wahram bald darauf eine unbedeutende Niederlage in Kaukasien gegen Byzanz erlitt, wurde er von H. abgesetzt. Der hochadelige General unternahm daraufhin den Versuch, in Verbindung mit Militär, Adel und Priesterschaft selbst die Macht zu ergreifen, und marschierte nach Ktesiphon. H. wurde im Frühjahr 590 durch eine Palastrevolution gestürzt und wohl mit stillschweigender Billigung seines Sohnes Chosroes [6] II. getötet.

[7] H. V., Urenkel von H. [6] und Enkel Chosroes [6] II., wurde von den pers. Truppen in Nisibis zum König ausgerufen und hielt sich, ohne allg. anerkannt zu werden, von 631–632.

M. H. Dodgeon, S. N. C. Lieu, The Roman Eastern Frontier and the Persian Wars AD 226–363, 1991 • W. Felix, Antike lit. Quellen zur Außenpolitik des Sāsānidenstaates, Bd. 1, 1985 • O. Klíma, Ruhm und Untergang des alten Iran, 1988 • Th. Nöldeke, Geschichte der Perser und Araber zur Zeit der Sasaniden, Ndr. 1973 • K. Schippmann, Grundzüge der Gesch. des sasanid. Reiches, 1990 • M. Schottky, Dunkle Punkte in der armen. Königsliste, in: AMI 27, 1994, 223–235, bes. 232.

M. SCH.

[8] Röm. Bischof und Papst (514–523 n. Chr.) z.Z. der Herrschaft des → Theoderich. Als Nachfolger des → Symmachus gelang es H. innerhalb weniger Jahre, sowohl innerhalb der röm. Gemeinde (→ Symmachianische Fälschungen) wie im Verhältnis zu Byzanz (Beendigung des sog. Akakianischen Schismas durch den *Libellus fidei*, CPL 1684) Frieden zu stiften. Seine Amtszeit gehört dank der in der → Collectio Avellana erh. Korrespondenz zu den bestdokumentierten Phasen im spätant. röm. Episkopat. H. verstand es zudem, sich der Mitarbeit des fähigsten Kirchenrechtlers seiner Zeit, → Dionysios [55] Exiguus, zu versichern, und förderte die Verbreitung von → Collectiones canonum, v. a. in Italien, Gallien und Spanien. Insgesamt gesehen trug H. wesentlich zur Umsetzung der leonisch-gelasianischen Vorstellungen vom Papsttum als universaler Herrschaft bei. Sein Sohn Silverius wird 536/7 einer seiner Nachfolger.

→ Akakios [4]; Leo (Papst)

Regesten/Überblicke: Jaffé, [Kaltenbrunner], 101–109 mit Nr. 770–871 • CPL 1683 f. • H. J. Frede, Kirchenschriftsteller. Verzeichnis und Sigel, [4]1995, 550–554 • A. Keller, Translationes Patristicae Graecae et Latinae. Bibliogr. der Übers. altchristl. Quellen 1, 1997, 452 f.

Brief-Ed.: A. Thiel, Epistolae Romanorum pontificum 1, 1867, 741–990 (größtenteils überholt) • O. Günther, CSEL 35, 1895–1898, Nr. 105–243.

Lit.: G. Prinzing, s. v. H., LThK[3] 5, 279 f. (mit Hinweisen auf die vor 1996 erschienene Lit.) • E. Wirbelauer, Zwei Päpste in Rom. Der Konflikt zw. Laurentius und Symmachus (498–514). Stud. und Texte (Quellen und Forsch. zur Ant. Welt 16), 1993.

E. W.

Hormus. (Flavius) H. Freigelassener Vespasians, der die flavischen Truppen bei ihrem Vorrücken in Italien begleitete und neben → Antonius [II 13] Primus großen Einfluß hatte (Tac. hist. 3,12,3; 28,1). Vom Senat wurde er am 1. Jan. 70 n. Chr. mit dem Ritterrang belohnt. Tac. hist. 4,39,1; PIR[2] H 204.

W. E.

Horoi (ὅροι). Grenzsteine, die im gesamten griech. Bereich die Grenzen (ebenfalls *h.* genannt) des Staatsgebietes, von Tempelbezirken und -grundstücken, öffentlichen Plätzen und privatem Grund, markierten. Sie tragen oft nur die Aufschrift *hóros*, manchmal mit näheren Zusätzen, und standen unter dem Schutz des Zeus Horios. Nach zw.-staatlichen Schiedssprüchen in Grenzstreitigkeiten [4] und Revision von verpachtetem Tempelland [8] traten häufig Kommissionen von *horistaí* auf, die *h.* im Gelände setzten.

Da die griech. Poleis kein → Grundbuch kannten, erfüllten *h.* auch als »Warnsteine« die Funktion, Belastungen von Grundstücken und Häusern publik zu machen. Es waren gewöhnlich unbearbeitete Kalksteinplatten, die Inschr. von ungeübter Hand trugen. Zur Kreditsicherung dienten »Hypothekensteine« (→ *hypothékē*, → *prâsis epí lýsei*); vermerkt wurde auch, wenn ein Vormund für das empfangene Mündelvermögen oder ein Ehegatte für den Wert der Mitgift (→ *proíx*) durch Schätzung (*apotímēma*) Sicherheit leisteten [6; 7]. Auch zur Kennzeichnung eines als Mitgift oder zur Pacht [1. 52 f.] empfangenen Grundstückes wurden *h.* aufgestellt. Entehrenden Zweck verfolgte die Aufstellung von *h.* auf den Grundstücken von verurteilten Hochverrätern (Plut. vita X oratorum 834a; Antiphon).

1 D. Behrend, Att. Pachturkunden, 1970 **2** M. I. Finley, Studies in Land and Credit in Ancient Athens, o.J. (1951, [2]1985) **3** A. R. W. Harrison, The Law of Athens I, 1989, 257–279 **4** K. Harter-Uibopuu, Das zwischenstaatliche Schiedsverfahren im Achäischen Koinon, 1998
5 F. Pringsheim, Gesammelte Abh. II, 1961, 339–368
6 H. J. Wolff, Verpachtung von Mündelvermögen in Attika, in: FS H. Lewald, 1953, 201–208 **7** Ders., Das att. Apotimema, in: FS. E. Rabel II, 1954, 293–333
8 A. Uguzzoni, F. Ghinatti, Le tavole greche di Eraclea, 1968.

G. T.

Horologium s. Uhr

Horologium (Solare) Augusti. Die von Plinius (nat. 36,72 f.) beschriebene, in der Regentschaft des Augustus auf dem Marsfeld in Rom (→ Roma) entstandene, im 1. und 2. Jh. n. Chr. mehrfach erneuerte Sonnenuhr mit Kalenderfunktionen; der Gnomon (→ Uhr) bestand aus einem Obelisk, der seinen Schatten auf eine gepflasterte Fläche mit einem Liniennetz warf, das mittels Bronzeeinlagen markiert war. Die im Anschluß an verschiedene Ausgrabungen und Interpretationen der ant. und neuzeitlichen Textüberl. vorgestellte Rekonstruktion von [1], der hier ein komplexes dynastisches Monument annahm (welches auch die → Ara Pacis Augustae mit einschloß) ist von [3] unter Hinweis auf verschiedene

Fehler in der mathematischen und physikalischen Berechnung in Zweifel gezogen worden.

1 E. Buchner, Die Sonnenuhr des Augustus, 1982
2 Richardson, 190f. 3 M. Schütz, Zur Sonnenuhr des Augustus auf dem Marsfeld. Eine Auseinandersetzung mit E. Buchners Rekonstruktion ..., in: Gymnasium 97, 1990, 432–457. C.HÖ.

Horoskop I. Alter Orient II. Griechisch-römisch

I. Alter Orient

Derzeit sind 32 H. aus Babylonien aus der Zeit von 410 bis 69 v. Chr. bekannt. Sie beginnen meist mit dem Datum, an dem ein Kind geboren wurde. Es folgt die Position von Mond, Sonne und den Planeten in der Reihenfolge Jupiter, Venus, Merkur, Saturn, Mars. Die Position wird nach Tierkreiszeichen, manchmal auch nach Grad innerhalb eines Zeichens gegeben. Mitunter folgen weitere astronomische Phänomene aus dem Monat oder dem Jahr der Geburt. Die Positionen sind berechnet und könnten aus den sog. Almanachen stammen. Nur wenige H. enthalten Vorhersagen für das Leben des Kindes. Es gibt aber Omina, die aus den (auch astronomischen) Umständen bei der Geburt Vorhersagen ableiten. Daher kann man die H. als Sammlungen von Zeichen auffassen, zu denen die Vorhersagen auf anderen Tafeln zu finden waren.

→ Astrologie; Astronomie; Divination

F. Rochberg-Halton, Babylonian Horoscopes, in: Orientalia 58, 1989, 102–123. H.HU.

II. Griechisch-römisch

Die ca. neun ägypt. (zw. 38 v. Chr. und 93 n. Chr.) und 180 griech. H. sind auf Stein, Papyrus, als Ostrakon oder Graffito, ferner im Lehrgedicht (bei → Manethon als Sphragis in B. 6) oder in Texten der Fachlit. überliefert (→ Vettius Valens, → Rhetorios, »Palchos« = Abū Ma'šar). Sie betreffen die Geburt einzelner Menschen, die Krönung von Herrschern, die Gründung oder Einweihung von Städten oder ganzen Ländern bis hin zum *thema mundi* (Firm. mathesis 3,1 nach Nechepso-Petosiris) und beginnen 62 v. Chr. (Krönungshoroskop des Antiochos von Kommagene). Wir kennen z. B. die H. von → Manethon, → Hadrianos [1] von Tyros und → Proklos. Das Standardwerk von [2] reicht bis zum Jahr 621, für das → Stephanos philosophos ca. 150 Jahre später die Herrschaft des Islam voraussagt. Das erste arab. H. datiert vom 18.8.531. Zahlreiche H. sind auch aus byz. Zeit bekannt. Firm., mathesis 2,29,10–20, überliefert das einzige erh. lat. H. für Ceionius [7] Rufius Albinus (*13.3.303) und bietet mathesis 6,30,1–26 auch eine Reihe fiktiver Ideal-H.

→ Astrologie; Firmicus Maternus; Horoskope

1 A. Bouché-Leclercq, L'astrologie grecque, 1899
2 O. Neugebauer, H. B. van Hoesen, Greek Horoscopes, 1959 3 O. Neugebauer, The Horoscope of Ceionius Rufius Albinus, in: AJPh 74, 1953, 418–420 4 T. D. Barnes, Two Senators under Constantine, in: JRS 55, 1975, 40–49. W.H.

Horrea

[1] s. Speicheranlagen

[2] H. Agrippina s. Speicheranlagen, s. Roma

Horsa s. Hengist und Horsa

Horsabad s. Dur Scharrukin

Horsiesi. Generalabt des von → Pachomios in Oberäg. gegr. koinobitischen Klosterverbandes († nach 386 n. Chr.). Zunächst Vorsteher des Klosters in Šenesēt (Chenoboskion); dann wurde H. durch Abt Petronios zum Nachfolger bestimmt. Nach Konflikten im sog. Armutsstreit übernahm Theodoros die »stellvertretende Leitung« [3. 527] für H. Später führte dieser erneut die *koinōnía* (»Gemeinschaft«), zunächst gemeinsam mit Theodoros, nach dessen Tod allein. Als geistliches Testament verfaßte er den *Liber Orsiesii* (lat. Übers. durch → Hieronymus, im J. 404; Text und dt. Übers. [2. 58–189]). Daneben sind in kopt. Sprache Briefe, Katechesen-Fr. sowie Instruktionen für Mönche (Text und frz. Übers. [1. 63–99]) erh. 1972 wurden zwei weitere Briefe entdeckt (frz. Übers. [4. 9–16]).

Ed.: 1 L. Th. Lefort, Œuvres de S. Pachôme et de ses Disciples, 1956 (CSCO 159f.).
Lit.: 2 H. Bacht, Das Vermächtnis des Ursprungs. I, 1972 3 Ch. Joest, Pachom und Theodoros, in: Theologie und Philos. 68, 1993, 516–529 4 A. de Vogüé, Les nouvelles lettres d'Horsièse et de Théodore, in: Studia monastica 28, 1986, 7–50. J.RI.

Horta (*Hortanum*, Plin. nat. 3,52). Etr. Stadt auf einem Vulkanberg rechts des Tiberis, h. Orte; handelspolit. wichtiger Kreuzungspunkt mehrerer Straßen. Besiedelt seit dem 6. Jh. v. Chr. (Nekropole von Le Piane), *municipium* nach dem → Bundesgenossenkrieg [3], *tribus Stellatina* [1. 85]. Über eine Brücke mit dem *vicus* des Flußhafens am linken Flußufer verbunden, als *Castellum Amerinum* auf der Tab. Peut. verzeichnet. Reste von Kais, Magazinen, Thermen.

1 W. Kubitschek, Imperium Romanum tributim discriptum, 1889.

G. Nardi, Le antichità di Orte 1–2, 1980 · Ders., Orte, in: EAA² 4, 1996, 132f. G.U./Ü: J.W.M.

Hortarius. König der Alamannen, der zusammen mit anderen alamann. Königen 357 n. Chr. dem Heer Iulians bei Straßburg unterlag (Amm. 16,12,1). Er unterwarf sich 358 (Amm. 17,10,5–9) und erstrebte sowohl mit den Römern wie mit den ihm benachbarten Germanenstämmen ein friedliches Übereinkommen (Amm. 18,2,2; 13f.). PLRE 1, 444 (H.1). W.P.

Hortensia. Tochter des bekannten Redners Q. Hortensius [7] Hortalus. Man rühmte sie, die Fähigkeiten des Vaters ererbt zu haben (Val. Max. 8,3,3; Quint. inst. 1,1,6): 42 v. Chr. trat H. auf dem Forum erfolgreich als Wortführerin gegen eine von den Triumvirn verhängte außergewöhnliche Kriegssteuer für wohlhabende Römerinnen auf (App. civ. 4,135–146).

M. H. Dettenhofer, Frauen in polit. Krisen, in: Dies. (Hrsg.), Reine Männersache?, 1994, 140f. T. FR.

Hortensius. Name einer röm. plebeischen Familie, wohl nicht abgeleitet von *hortus*, sondern von Ortsnamen *Hortense, Hortenses* [1. 660; 2. 175; 177; 534]. Der erste sicher bezeugte Namensträger ist H. [4], prominentester Angehöriger der Redner H. [7]. Stammbaum: [3. 75].

1 Walde/Hofmann 1 2 Schulze 3 Drumann/Groebe, Bd. 3.

[1] H., L. Führte 170 v. Chr. als Praetor das Kommando über die Flotte im 3. Maked. Krieg (Ehrungen in Athen: IG II^2 907, und Delos: IDélos III 461 Aa 83). Er eroberte Abdera, verkaufte dessen Bevölkerung in die Sklaverei und drangsalierte Chalkis, mußte aber auf Weisung des Senats seine Anordnungen zurücknehmen (Liv. 43,4,8–13; 7,5–8,7). Im J. 155 Mitglied einer Dreiergesandtschaft an Attalos II. und Prusias (Pol. 33,1,2).
[2] H., L. Kämpfte 86 v. Chr. als Legat Sullas erfolgreich in der Schlacht von Chaironeia (MRR 2,56).
[3] H., L. oder Q. Wohl spätestens 111 v. Chr. Praetor (gute Verwaltung Siziliens, Cic. Verr. 2,3,42), vielleicht identisch mit dem Consul H., der 108 vor Amtsantritt verurteilt wurde (MRR 1,541, Anm. 2).
[4] H., Q. Wurde anläßlich des letzten Auszuges der Plebs auf das Ianiculum 287 v. Chr. Dictator und brachte ein Gesetz durch, das die Beschlüsse der Plebs (*plebiscita*) für das röm. Gesamtvolk verbindlich erklärte (Liv. per. 11; Laelius Felix bei Gell. 15,27,4; Plin. nat. 16,37; Gai. inst. 1,3 u. a.). Die *lex Hortensia* erleichterte die Gesetzgebung durch die plebeische Volksversammlung unter Leitung der Volkstribunen. Sie gilt damit gewöhnlich als Zeichen der Integration des Tribunats in die staatliche Ordnung und so als Abschluß des → Ständekampfes, kann aber auch im Eigeninteresse des niederen Volkes gegen die patrizisch-plebeische Elite gelegen haben [so 1]. H. wird auch ein Gesetz zugeschrieben, das an Markttagen Gerichtsverhandlungen erlaubte (Granius Licinianus bei Macr. Sat. 1,16,30). Er starb im Amt.

1 K.-J. Hölkeskamp, Die Entstehung der Nobilität und der Funktionswandel des Volkstribunats: Die histor. Bed. der *lex Hortensia de plebiscitis*, in: AKG 70, 1988, 271–312. K.-L. E.

[5] H. (Hortalus), Q. (Zum Cognomen: Catull. 65,2). Sohn des Q. H. [7] Hortalus. Während der fünfziger Jahre aufwendiger Lebenswandel inmitten von Roms *jeunesse dorée*; 51/50 v. Chr. (als Quaestor? MRR 3,103) in Asia (Cic. Att. 6,3,9). Im Bürgerkrieg Parteigänger Caesars; erstürmte Ariminum (Plut. Caesar 32,1; vgl. Caes. civ. 1,8,1). 49 wurde er von Caesar mit dem Flottenkommando im Tyrrhenischen Meer betraut (App. civ. 2,166), scheiterte aber in der Adria beim Entsatz des auf Curicta/Krk zernierten C. Antonius [I 3] (Oros. 6,15,8). Praetor 45 (oder früher? MRR 3,103), danach als Proconsul in Macedonia. Nach Caesars Tod Wechsel der polit. Orientierung: H. übergab die Provinz nicht an M. Antonius' Bruder C. Antonius, sondern an M. Iunius [I 10] Brutus, unter dessen Oberbefehl er in Macedonia bis 42 sein proconsularisches Imperium ausübte (Cic. Phil. 10 passim; Plut. Brutus 25,2; Cass. Dio 47,21,4; delisches Ehrenmal: ILS 9460). Den in Gefangenschaft geratenen C. Antonius ließ er exekutieren. Nach Philippi ergriffen (Herbst 42), wurde H. auf Weisung des M. Antonius am Grab von dessen Bruder getötet (Plut. Antonius 22,3; Brutus 28,1; vgl. Liv. per. 124; Vell. 2,71,2).

M. H. Dettenhofer, Perdita Iuventus, 1992, 18.

[6] (H.) Hortalus, M. Sohn von H. [5]. Im Zuge von Augustus' Förderung des Weiterbestands altehrwürdiger *gentes* wurde H. großzügig mit Geldmitteln versehen, die ihm eine Familiengründung erlaubten. 16 n. Chr. erneut in prekären Finanzverhältnissen, zeigte sich Tiberius seinem Ersuchen um weitere Subventionen allerdings wenig zugänglich (Suet. Tib. 47; Tac. ann. 2,37f.). T. FR.
[7] H. L. f. Hortalus, Q. (114–50 v. Chr.). Der berühmteste Redner Roms vor Cicero. Seine rednerische Tätigkeit begann i. J. 95 mit der Verteidigung einiger Afrikaner vor den Consuln (Cic. de orat. 3,229). 86 verteidigte er Cn. Pompeius, der ihn gegen die Sullanischen Proskriptionen schützte. Als Sohn eines Consuls optierte er polit. für die aristokratische Linie [9. 764]; er heiratete eine Schwester des Sullaners Q. Lutatius Catulus (seine zweite Frau wurde Marcia, die vormalige Gattin des M. Cato). 81 klagte er P. Quinctius an – seine erste Konfrontation mit Cicero, dem Verteidiger. Im J. 80 war er Quaestor, 75 Aedil (glänzende Spiele; Getreideversorgung: Cic. Verr. 2,3,215), 72 Praetor und 69 Consul. Im Wahljahr 70 hatte H. die Verteidigung seines Freundes C. → Verres übernommen; er unterbrach Ciceros Anklage in der *actio prima*, bevor die Zeugen aufgerufen werden konnten (ebd., 2,1,71), Verres ging ins Exil. Wie schon in den Vorjahren blieb H. in Rom, statt in eine Prov. zu gehen; hier widersetzte er sich den Ermächtigungen für Pompeius [6. 50–52]. Ciceros Konsulat (63) brachte eine Annäherung zwischen H. und Cicero, die nun auch zusammen vor Gericht agierten (Verteidigung des C. Rabirius, 63, L. Licinius Murena und P. Sulla, 62). Dank Atticus' Bemühen [2. 91f.] überstand die Beziehung auch die Belastungen von Ciceros Exil. 53 setzte sich der Augur Hortensius erfolgreich für die Kooptation Ciceros (als Nachfolger des gefallenen P. Crassus) ein (Cic. Brut. 1; Cic. Phil. 2,4; [2. 95]). Im Konflikt zwischen Milo, der den Tribun Clodius [I 4] getötet hatte, und Pompeius trat H. auf Milos Seite; die Verteidigung Mi-

los übernahm Cicero. In seinen letzten Lebensjahren verteidigte H. in Bestechungsprozessen (*de ambitu*) M. Valerius Messalla (51) und Ap. Claudius (50). H. starb zwischen E. April und Anf. Juni 50 (zum Tod s. Cic. Att. 6,6,2).

H. war 44 Jahre als Redner tätig (Cic. Brut. 229). Bis zu seinem Konsulatsjahr an der Spitze der röm. Redner, trat er dann allmählich hinter Cicero zurück (ebd., 320). Cicero begründete das mit dem → Asianismus des H., die besser zu jungen als zu alten Rednern passe (ebd., 325); dazu [5. 97–100]. Bekannt sind 25 Reden [1], dazu verfaßte er ein B. zu Fragen der Rhet. (*Quaestiones generaliter tracta<tae>*, Quint. inst. 2,1,11; vgl. [9. 764–766]) und Gedichte (Plin. epist. 5,3,5; Varro ling. 8,14; 10,78). – H., von Hause aus reich, wurde im Alter zunehmend wegen seines Luxus angegriffen, wovon einige Anekdoten zeugen; er liebte Fische und soll seine Platanen mit Wein »gewässert« haben (Macr. Sat. 3,13,3). Seine Kleidung war immer so sorgfältig geordnet, daß ihn L. Torquatus mit dem Namen einer Tänzerin, Dionysia, verspottete (Gell. 1,5,3; [2. 98–102]). Dieser Episode verdanken wir das einzige direkte Zitat des H.

Fr.: **1** ORF⁴, 310–330.
Lit.: **2** Drumann/Groebe, 3,6, 78–102 **3** A.E. Douglas, M. Tulli Ciceronis Brutus, 1966 **4** E.S. Gruen, The Dolabellae and Sulla, in: AJPh 87, 1966, 385–399 **5** G. Kennedy, The Art of Rhetoric in the Roman World 300 BC-AD 300, 1972 **6** E.S. Gruen, The Last Generation of the Roman Republic, 1974 **7** I. Shatzman, Senatorial Wealth and Roman Politics, 1975, 355 f. **8** C.J. Classen, Recht – Rhet. – Politik, 1985 **9** J.-M. David, Le patronat judicaire au dernier siècle de la république romaine, 1992, 763–766.
G.C.

Hortfunde

I. Keltisch-germanischer Bereich II. Italien

I. Keltisch-germanischer Bereich

In Mitteleuropa bilden von der Brz. an H. (Depot-, Schatz-, Verwahr-, Massen-, Versteckfunde usw.) v.a. von Metallobjekten (Kupfer, Br., Eisen, Edelmetalle) eine wichtige arch. Fundgruppe. Die Vielzahl der Bezeichnungen spiegelt die Breite der Diskussion um die Bed. der H. Als Indizien für die Funktion gelten sowohl die verschiedenartigen Fundplatzsituationen, wie z.B. fester Boden, Moore, Flüsse, besondere Plätze (Felsen, Spalten, Höhlen, Verkehrswege usw.), als v.a. auch die Zusammensetzung der Objekte (→ Schmuck, Waffen, Geräte, Gußreste, → Barren, Bruchmaterial, neue oder beschädigte Stücke), anhand derer versucht wird, die Gründe für die Niederlegung der H. zu ermitteln. Zwei Bereiche stehen im Mittelpunkt der Diskussion; einmal »profane« H., die man wieder bergen wollte (Wertanhäufungen, Hausschätze, Händler- oder Handwerkerbesitz, Rohmaterial usw.) und »rituelle« H., deren Wiederaufnahme nicht vorgesehen war (Weihungen, → Opfer, Kult- oder Totenschätze usw.).

Das Vorkommen der H. ist auf bestimmte Zeiten konzentriert und verschiedenartig. In der frühen Brz. (1. H. 2. Jt. v. Chr.) sind es im südl. Mitteleuropa v.a. H. mit typischen Barrenformen aus Kupfer bzw. Br. (Ring- und Spangenbarren), im Norden kommen mehr Geräte und Schmuck in den H. vor. In der späten Brz. (12.–8. Jh. v. Chr.) sind zunächst Brucherz-H. bes. häufig und dann Waffen (Panzer, → Helme usw.) und andere Prestigeobjekte aus Flüssen und Mooren und, bes. im nördl. Mitteleuropa, Br.- und Goldgefäße (Eberswalde). In der jüngeren kelt. Eisenzeit (3.–1. Jh. v. Chr.) dominieren Eisen-H. (Waffen und Gerät sowie verschiedene Barrenformen) und Goldfunde mit Münzen und Halsreifen (→ Torques). In der Kaiserzeit (1.–4. Jh. n. Chr.) gibt es in Germanien zahlreiche Münz-H. (Wertanhäufung), dazu prunkvolle röm. Silbergefäß-H. (z.B. → Hildesheimer Silberfund) und v.a. H. aus Brunnen und Mooren (→ Thorsberger Moor), in denen Waffen, Gerät usw. überwiegen. Für das MA sind die wichtigsten H. die Hacksilberfunde im östl. und nördl. Europa, die mehr eine geldähnliche Funktion haben.

→ Germanische Archäologie; Gold; Handwerk; Keltische Archäologie; Kult; Münzen

H. Geislinger s. v. Depotfund, H., RGA 5, 320–338 • A. und B. Hänsel (Hrsg.), Gaben an die Götter – Schätze der Brz. Europas, 1997 • S. Hansen, Stud. zu den Metalldeponierungen während der älteren Urnenfelderzeit zwischen Rhône und Karpatenbecken, 1994 • G. Kurz, Kelt. H.- und Gewässerfunde in Mitteleuropa, 1995 • F. Stein, Brz. H. in Süddeutschland, 1976 • Dies., Kat. der vorgesch. H. in Süddeutschland, 1979.
V.P.

II. Italien

In Italien sind H. seit der Brz. belegt (z.B. auf Lipari). Die wenigsten von ihnen sind als Niederlegungen in Notsituationen, wie bei feindlichen Angriffen, oder in kultischem Kontext zu verstehen. Vielmehr scheinen H. in Zusammenhang mit den Handelswegen des Kupfer- und später des Eisenerzes zu stehen. Anschaulich wird dies mit der sog. »Straße der H.« (*via dei ripostigli*) umschrieben, die während der Brz. mit Slgg. von Äxten und »Br.-Kuchen« die reichen Erzlagerstätten in den Colline Metallifere in der Toskana mit der Küste bei Vulci (→ Volcae) verband. In der Folgezeit weitete sich diese Verbindung zu den Erzvorkommen in den → Tolfabergen im heutigen Latium und v.a. nach Elba (→ Ilva) aus (Protovillanova-Kultur mit qualitätvollen Metallgefäßen). Diese H. befinden sich meistens in der Nähe der Altstraßen außerhalb der Siedlungen und deuten in ihrer Zusammensetzung eher auf die zeitweise vorgenommene Deponierung der Waren von Händlern oder Handwerkern entlang ihrer Handelswege hin (wichtige FO: Ardea, Coste del Marano, Goluzzo, Piano di Tallone, Santa Marinella). Der chronolog. Rahmen umfaßt die E.-Brz. und den Beginn der Eisenzeit (11.–8. Jh. v. Chr.) im Raum der → Villanova-Kultur. Eine Sonderstellung nimmt der H. von San Francesco in Bologna ein. Er umfaßt ca. 14800 Br., die gemeinsam in einem → Pithos gelagert wurden, darunter zerschnittene Bruchstücke, Halbfabrikate, fertige Waffen, Geräte und Trachtgegenstände, die auch aufgrund ihrer unterschiedlichen Zeitstellung (11.– 7. Jh. v. Chr.) als Vorratslager einer Br.-Werkstatt innerhalb einer Siedlung anzusehen sind.

→ Etrusci, Etruria (mit Karten)

M. A. Fugazzola Delpino, Ripostigli »protovillanoviani« dell'Italia peninsulare, in: A. Radmilli (Hrsg.), Popoli e civiltà dell'Italia antica 4, 1975, 43–49, 57–60 · M. Cristofani, Economia e società, in: G. Pugliese Carratelli (Hrsg.), Rasenna, 1986, 79–156, bes. 80–88 · G. Bartoloni, La cultura villanoviana, 1989. C.KO.

Horti Agrippinae, Horti Caesaris s. Gartenanlagen; Ianiculum; Roma

Hortikultur I. Alter Orient und Ägypten II. Klassische Antike

I. Alter Orient und Ägypten

In den Nutzgärten im vorderen Orient und Äg. wurden im sog. Stockwerksbau unter dem schattenspendenden Dach der Dattelpalmen Obstbäume (v. a. Apfel, Feige, Granatapfel; dazu in Äg. Johannisbrotbaum, Jujube; → Obstbau) und darunter → Gemüse (v. a. Zwiebel- und Gurkengewächse, Hülsenfrüchte, Blattgemüse wie Kresse, sowie Gewürzkräuter, z. B. Koriander, Thymian, Kümmel, Minze) angebaut. Die Dattelpalme lieferte nicht nur Datteln als wichtigstes Süßmittel, sondern auch Bast, Palmblätter, Blattrispen und Stämme zum Herstellen von Matten, Körben, Seilen und Abdeckmaterial für Dächer. Nicht mit einem Wohnhaus verbundene Dattelgärten wurden in Mesopot. oft verpachtet. Verträge regelten den Pachtzins, der in Naturalien zu leisten war. Zusätzlich waren Nebenprodukte wie Palmblätter, Bast usw. abzuliefern. Weingärten (→ Weinbau) existierten in den bergigen Regionen Assyriens und Syrien-Palästinas, dort gab es auch Olivenpflanzungen.

→ Landwirtschaft

1 F. Daumas, s. v. Früchte, Gemüse, LÄ 2, 344–348, 522–524
2 I. Gamer-Wallert, s. v. Palme, LÄ 4, 658–659
3 W. Helck, s. v. G., LÄ 2, 378–380 4 H. A. Hoffner, Alimenta hethaeorum, 1974, 95–112 5 N. Postgate (Hrsg.), Bull. on Sumerian Agriculture 2, 1985; 3, 1987. J.RE.

II. Klassische Antike

A. Allgemein B. Hortikultur und Ernährung
C. Anbaumethoden und Bewässerung
D. Naturbeherrschung und Innovation
E. Hortikultur als Fach

A. Allgemein

Der Gartenbau war in der Ant. ein wichtiger Zweig der Landwirtschaft; der Garten (κῆπος, *hortus*) leistete einen wesentlichen Beitrag zur menschlichen Ernährung, indem er zusätzlich zu den Grundnahrungsmitteln → Getreide, → Wein und Öl weitere pflanzliche Produkte lieferte, wobei zu beachten ist, daß in der Ant. Hülsenfrüchte nicht dem Gartenbau, sondern dem Feldbau zugerechnet wurden (vgl. bereits Hom. Il. 13,588 ff.). Zwischen dem Feldbau, insbesondere dem Getreideanbau, und der H. bestanden in den Methoden der Düngung und des Anbaus sowie hinsichtlich der Bewässerung grundlegende Unterschiede.

B. Hortikultur und Ernährung

Die H. bot normalerweise die Ergänzung zur Hauptnahrung (vgl. Cic. Cato 56: der eigene Garten als eine *succidia*, als »zweite Speckseite«), aber bei sinkendem sozialen Status mußte die H. die Hauptnahrung ersetzen: Die Auffassung des Plinius, der Garten sei der Acker des Armen (*ager pauperis*) und → *macellum* der Plebs (Plin. nat. 19,52), verdeutlicht die Not, die den *hortus* zur zentralen Nahrungsquelle werden ließ. Die Unterschicht mußte immer mehr auf Gartenprodukte ausweichen (Colum. 10, praef. 2) und konnte so Brot sparen (Plin. nat. 19,58; vgl. auch Apul. met. 9,32 ff.). Größte Bed. hatte die → Feige, sie war Brot und Beilage in einem; Cato kürzte seinen Sklaven die Brotration, sobald die Feigen reif wurden (Cato agr. 56). Roh eßbares → Gemüse wie Salate, Zwiebeln, Kresse, Lauch, Gurken, Karotten und Rettich faßte Plinius als *acetaria* zusammen, deren Vorteil darin bestand, daß man zu ihrer Zubereitung kein Brennholz benötigte (Plin. nat. 19,58). Auch garantierte die H. die Ernährung im Winter: So werden eingelegtes Gemüse (Kohlsprossen, Selleriestengel, Möhren, Spargel, Lattich- und Endiviensalat, Zwiebeln) sowie getrocknetes oder eingemachtes → Obst bei → Columella erwähnt (Colum. 12,6 f.; 9 f.). Einlagern konnte man Weißkohl, Kohl, Rüben und Zwiebeln. Wie für einen Bauern, der nur *pauca iugera* besaß, war auch für den Wohlhabenden das ungekaufte Essen aus dem eigenen Garten etwas Erstrebenswertes und entsprach dem weitverbreiteten Autarkiebedürfnis (Verg. georg. 4,125–133; Hor. epod. 2,47 ff.; Colum. 11,3,1). Bei den Griechen galt Rohkost als Philosophenkost (Diog. Laert. 6,58: Diogenes; 7,26: Zenon; 8,13: Pythagoras).

C. Anbaumethoden und Bewässerung

Als → Düngemittel wurden bevorzugt Mist von Esel und Taube sowie Holzasche verwendet, die wie auch Taubenmist zugleich als Mittel gegen Schädlinge galt; außerdem wurde auch mit Kompost gedüngt. Damit wurde der Zwang zur Brache aufgehoben, durch die im Ackerbau mindestens jedes zweites Jahr etwa die Hälfte der Felder unbebaut blieb, wobei der Boden aber weiter bearbeitet werden mußte (Brachpflügen). Auf diese Weise sollte die im Feldbau nicht mögliche regelmäßige Düngung ersetzt werden. Im Garten wurde wohl auf den einzelnen Beeten auf Fruchtwechsel innerhalb des Jahres geachtet. Dies legt die Landwirtschaft Campaniens nahe, die mit saisonalen Fruchtfolgen der H. nahekam (Plin. nat. 18,191). Außer Kraft gesetzt war im Gartenbau vor allem die Abhängigkeit des Feldbaus vom Herbst- und Winterregen, weswegen normalerweise im Herbst ausgesät wurde.

Durch die Wahl des Ortes sollte die erste Grundbedingung der H., die Möglichkeit zur → Bewässerung, erfüllt werden, am besten durch einen Wasserlauf, sonst durch das Graben eines Brunnens, im ungünstigsten Fall durch Zisternen (Colum. 11,3,8 ff.; vgl. allgemein 1,5,1 ff. und außerdem Theophr. c. plant. 3,8,3 f.; Plin. nat. 19,60). Seit augusteischer Zeit wirkte sich die bessere Wasserversorgung auch auf die H. positiv aus. Das hohe Alter der wichtigsten Gartentechnik, der Bewässerung, zeigt sich in den alten Verben ἄρδειν bzw. *rigare* (vgl. Hom. Il. 21,257 ff.). Somit gab es in der H. nicht nur die alljährliche Bestellung, sondern auch das wichtige Ziel, den Anbau auf das ganze Jahr auszudehnen. So erreichte man bei Blumen ganzjähriges Blühen (Theophr. h. plant. 6,8,2; c. plant. 1,13,12), frühes oder spätes Blühen durch spezielles Gießen, durch verschieden tiefes Eingraben oder durch mehrmaliges Setzen einer Blumenart in Monatsabständen. Bei → Obst gab es frühe und späte Sorten, beim Gemüse ging man zu Zweitsaaten neben der Aussaat an den üblichen Hauptterminen über (Theophr. h. plant. 7,1,2 f.). Aristophanes hatte diese Verfügbarkeit vieler Produkte gegen die natürliche Ordnung des Jahres (›mitten im Winter‹) in den *Horai* kritisiert, weil dies zu Begehrlichkeit und luxuriösem Aufwand verleite; Athen sei nun zu Ägypten verwandelt (fr. 581,1–11 PCG = Athen. 372bff.; vgl. 653 f.). In einem Gemüsekalender (Geop. 12,1) wird von Januar bis Dezember in jedem Monat gesät, sogar im August (Endivie, Mangold, Weißkohl). Manche Gemüse baute man also das ganze Jahr über an, z. B. Lattich, Karotten, Rettich, weiße Rüben, Rauke (verwendet für eine Art Spinat). War Bewässerung unmöglich, so empfahl man Speicherung der Feuchtigkeit durch besonders tiefes Umgraben oder durch Beete mit nach unten abschließender Ziegelschicht. Abgesenkte Gärten, die bis zu einem Stockwerk tiefer als die Erdoberfläche lagen, waren wohl selten.

Trotz der Möglichkeit, Gartenland zu bewässern und zu düngen, sollte der Boden schon von sich aus fruchtbar und leicht zu bearbeiten sein (Colum. 11,3,8; Plin. nat. 17,36 f.). Als ideal galt die Lage in einer Ebene am Fuße eines Berges, was die Anlage von Bewässerungssystemen erleichterte. Die Erde sollte umgegraben werden (Colum. 10,45 f.); der Spaten war also für die H. charakteristisch. Vom intensiven Durcharbeiten des Bodens hing die Qualität des Gartenlandes ab. Für den Gemüsegarten waren Beete typisch (πρασιά; *area, porca, pulvinus*), die aber wegen Jätens von Hand nicht allzu breit sein sollten. Als Regel galt es, κατὰ γένος (jede Art für sich) zu pflanzen, nicht ἀτάκτως (durcheinander). Doch gab es zur Schädlingsbekämpfung die Methode des ἐπισπείρειν/*una serere, intermiscere*: Rettiche und Rüben sollten durch Erven geschützt werden, Kohl durch Kichererbsen oder durch Minze, Zwiebeln durch Saturei, *brassica* durch Mohn, Lattich durch Rauke (Theophr. h. plant. 7,5,4; Plin. nat. 19,107; 19,168; 19,179). Das Umsetzen von Jungpflanzen (μεταφυτεύειν/*transferre*) gehörte bei Kohl, Rüben, Salat und anderen Gemüsepflanzen zu den üblichen Methoden, um den Ertrag zu steigern und eine Degenerierung zu verhindern; bei der Samenzucht wurde sie stets angewandt (Theophr. h. plant. 7,5,3).

Blumen waren offenbar zunächst dem Baumgarten zugeordnet, wo sie in Nachahmung heiliger Haine und Wiesen in natürlichen Blumenpolstern Schatten und Feuchtigkeit fanden; in den Gärten der Villen sowie in kommerziellen Gärten wurden Beete angelegt. Bis in die byz. Zeit wurden, auch wegen ihrer wirtschaftlichen Bed., etwa dieselben Blumen bevorzugt (Rosen, Lilien, Veilchen, Krokus, etc.; Theophr. h. plant. 6,6–8); in Form von Kränzen und Girlanden, auch gestreut (nicht als Sträuße) brauchte man sie für Kult, Fest und Beerdigung. Schon bei Cato lieferten die suburbanen *villae coronamenta* (Blumen aller Art für Kränze) und anderen Bedarf der Stadt (Cato agr. 8,2; vgl. Varro rust. 1,16,3: *violaria ac rosaria*). Blumengärten dienten auch als Bienenweide, zu der auch Thymian zählte.

Eine Umzäunung war gartentypisch (vgl. die Etymologien von ὄρχατος und *hortus*), sie bestand oft aus Dornenhecken, wie bei Columella empfohlen (Colum. 11,3,3 ff.). Bei Selbstversorgern dürfte eine Fläche von etwa 400 qm den Jahresbedarf einer Familie (ca. 8–10 Personen) gedeckt haben.

D. Naturbeherrschung und Innovation

Während im Ackerbau die Grundregel galt, sich klug den natürlichen Bedingungen von Boden und Klima anzupassen, gab es in der H. schon früh Versuche, die Beschränkungen der Natur durch Anstrengung und Ideen zu überwinden, ja Unmögliches zu versuchen. Selbst der einfache Gärtner aus Corycus bei Vergil lehnt sich gegen die Natur auf, wenn er im Stolz auf seine frühe Ernte die naturgegebenen Erntezeiten als zu spät verhöhnt (Verg. georg. 4,127–138). Dabei konnte die H. in Kritik geraten, wenn sie sich vor allem an dem Bedarf an teuren Speisen für die luxuriösen Gastmähler der Reichen orientierte (Colum. 10, praef. 2; Plin. nat. 19,52–56) oder die Ordnung der Natur nicht achtete.

Im Garten ergaben sich durch neue Methoden, durch Einführung neuer Arten (Plin. nat. 15,35 ff.) und durch neue Sorten aufgrund von Veredelung viele Fortschrittsmöglichkeiten. Zum frühen Bestand an Obst (Apfel, Birne, Feige, Traube) kamen Edelkirsche, Pfirsich, Citrus, Aprikose, Quitte, Pistazie und viele andere hinzu. Die Lust am Experiment war besonders beim Pfropfen groß (Pfropfen und Okulieren: Colum. 5,11; Plin. nat. 17,99–122; 17,135–138). Höchstens der → Weinbau läßt sich mit dieser Entwicklung vergleichen, während sich der Ackerbau mit seinen Haupterzeugnissen → Getreide und Hülsenfrüchten durch die ganze Ant. wenig veränderte. In der H. herrschte dagegen eine positive Einstellung zu Innovationen (Plin. nat. 15,35; 15,49); soziale Bedenken gab es zwar, da die Verfeinerung der Produkte sie für die Armen teurer machte (Plin. nat. 17,8; 19,53 f.), aber die Neuerungen fanden gesellschaftliche Akzeptanz: Neue Sorten wurden nach ihrem Urheber benannt, ›als ob dieser in seinem Leben etwas Bedeutendes vollbracht hätte‹ (*tamquam ob egregium aliquod in vita factum*, Plin. 15,49). So gab es nun etwa *Appiana* (Quitten; Plin. nat. 15,49), *Corelliana* (Kastanien; Plin. nat. 17,122) und *Caeciliana* (Lattich; Colum. 11,3,26). Erreichte man einmal keinen Fortschritt, so wurde dies als Ausnahme betrachtet (*minimum in hac arbore ingenia profecerunt*, Plin. nat. 15,97).

E. Hortikultur als Fach

Kluge alte Gärtner kannte schon Homer, so etwa Penelopes Diener Dolios oder Laertes (Hom. Od. 4,735–741; 24,219–247; 24,336–344). Doch erscheint die Berufsbezeichnung κηπουρός (*kēpurós*) zuerst im 5./4. Jh. v. Chr., allerdings noch selten. Gartenbücher werden erst nach Platon erwähnt (Ps.-Plat. Min. 316e). Offenbar wurden sie immer wieder in landwirtschaftliche Werke eingearbeitet. So sind die von Plinius als Quellenschriftsteller für Buch 19 der *Naturalis Historia* erwähnten Autoren von *Cepurica* kaum noch faßbar (vgl. Plin. nat. 19,177: Sabinus Tiro). Die ausführlichsten Partien zur H. finden sich in der Agrarliteratur: bei Columella in B. 10 und 11,3 (zum Vorrat aus dem Garten B. 12; zum Obstgarten 5,10–11), bei Plinius (Plin. nat. 14–15; 17 und 19), bei Palladius in den Rubriken *de hortis* und *de pomeris*, in Geop. 9–12 (Ölbaum, Obst, Zierbäume und Blumen, Gemüse); hinzu kommen die Schriften des → Theophrastos über die Pflanzen. Die Gartenlit. muß auch die Konservierung der Produkte behandelt haben (vgl. Colum. 12,4–10; 12,14–15; 12,44–50; 12,56). Dies war für die private Versorgung wichtig, aber auch ökonomisch interessant, um nach der Erntezeit gute Preise zu erzielen.

→ Agrarschriftsteller; Garten, Gartenanlagen; Gemüsebau; Landwirtschaft

1 J. André, Les noms de plantes dans la Rome antique, 1985 2 B. Andreae, »Am Birnbaum«. Gärten und Parks im ant. Rom, in den Vesuvstädten und in Ostia, 1996
3 M. Carroll-Spillecke (Hrsg.), Der Garten von der Ant. bis zum MA, 1992 4 Dies., ΚΗΠΟΣ, Der ant. griech. Garten, 1989 5 L. Farrar, Gardens of Italy and the Western Provinces of the Roman Empire, 1996 (British Archaeological Reports International Ser. 650) 6 V. Hehn, Kulturpflanzen und Haustiere in ihrem Übergang aus Asien nach Griechenland und Italien, 1911 7 W. F. Jashemski, The Gardens of Pompei, Herculaneum and the Villas Destroyed by Vesuvius, 2 Bände, 1979/1993 8 J. Koder, Gemüse in Byzanz, 1993 9 R. Osborne, Classical Greek Gardens: Between Farm and Paradise, in: Garden History, 1992, 373–391 10 W. Richter, Die Landwirtschaft im homerischen Zeitalter, in: ArchHom 2 H, 1968, 123–127; 140–146 11 A. Sarpaki, The Palaeobotanical Approach. The Mediterranean Triad or is it a Quartet?, in: B. Wells (Hrsg.), Agriculture in Ancient Greece, 1992, 61–76
12 M. C. Shaw, The Aegean Garden, in: AJA 97, 1993, 661–685 13 White, Farming. E. C.

Hortona. Frentanische Küstenstadt (*regio IV Samnium*, Plin. nat. 3,106), h. Ortona. Erwähnt im Zusammenhang des byz.-got. Kriegs (535–540 n. Chr.) während der Eroberung des Küstenstreifens durch die Byzantiner (Marcellinus Comes zum J. 538); gegen E. 6. Jh. Bistum.

M. Buonocore, G. Firpo, Fonti latine e greche per la storia dell'Abruzzo antico 1, 1991, 528–537 • A. R. Staffa, Ortona, in: EAA² Suppl. 4, 1996, 133. M. BU./Ü: J. W. M.

Horus. Bedeutendster äg. Falkengott, dessen Name (äg. *Ḥrw*, »der Ferne«) und Gestalt auf seine Funktion als Himmelsgott hinweisen. Die Spur seiner Herkunft verliert sich im Dunkel der Vorgesch. Der bekannteste H.-Gott histor. Zeit ist H. Behedeti (*Bḥdtj*) aus dem oberäg. → Edfu, doch sprechen Indizien für einen unteräg. Ursprung. Früh erfolgte die Vereinnahmung anderer Falkengötter durch H. sowie seine enge Verbindung mit dem Sonnengott. H. gilt auch als morgendliche Sonne; sein Name ist Appellativ im Sinne von »Herrscher/Höchster/Erhabener« (z. B. in Harachte, »Horizontischer Horus«). Später wird der H.-Falke mit dem Himmelsgewölbe gleichgesetzt; seine Augen werden als Sonne und Mond gedeutet. Schon die Pyramidentexte kennen eine H.-Form als Morgenstern.

Als Königsgott steht H. seit der Frühzeit neben → Seth für das Gottkönigtum der beiden Landeshälften. H. vertritt im Sinnbild der Vereinigung der beiden Länder Unteräg., Seth, als Gott von Ombos, Oberäg. Andere Quellen weisen H. die Herrschaft über Äg., Seth die über die Fremdländer zu. Der Königsthron gilt als Thron des H. und der regierende König ist die Verkörperung des H. auf Erden. Dies zeigt u. a. der älteste der fünf Königsnamen, der sog. H.-Name. H. und Seth, als typisches Götterpaar der äg. Myth., stehen für zahlreiche Oppositionen (Inland/Ausland; Himmel/Erde; Herrschaft/Macht aufgrund von Körperkraft; Ordnung/Unordnung). Zu ihren Auseinandersetzungen, in denen u. a. das Auge des H. verletzt bzw. geraubt wird, geben die Pyramidentexte erste bruchstückhafte Hinweise. Das H.-Auge – die Opfergabe schlechthin – wird wieder geheilt bzw. zurückgegeben und damit die Sicherung des Lebens (durch Kontinuität des Königtums, Versorgung der Götter und Toten, Regeneration des Sonnengottes) verbürgt. In den mythischen Fragmenten um H. und Seth überlagern sich unterschiedl. Traditionsstränge. Ein großer oder älterer H. (Haroeris) und ein »H.-Sohn-der-Isis« (Harsiese) existieren nebeneinander. Nach der einen Trad. gehören H. und Seth einer Generation an, nach der anderen ist Seth als Bruder des → Osiris und der → Isis der »Onkel« des H., dem er das Anrecht auf das Erbe, die Königsherrschaft, streitig macht. Kämpferische Aspekte verbinden beide H.-Formen.

Seit dem späten NR ist der Kindgott »H.-das-Kind« (Harpokrates) belegt, der sich besonders im Volksglauben großer Beliebtheit erfreut. Er ist Sohn von Isis und Osiris, Ideal des Sprosses einer Götterfamilie, auch jugendlicher Sonnengott und zuständig für Fruchtbarkeit und Nahrung.

Genealogische und funktionale Differenzierungen und neue Götterverbindungen führen zur Ausbildung vieler selbständiger H.-Formen. Die durch lokale Kulte belegten H.-Götter unterscheiden sich z. T. durch die

Betonung bestimmter Wesensmerkmale (z. B. H. von Letopolis als vorübergehend blinder Gott und nächtlicher Sonnengott). H. wird als Falke, als Mensch mit Falkenkopf oder anthropomorph dargestellt; als Krieger kann er auch die Gestalt eines Löwen, z. T. mit Menschenkopf annehmen. Er wurde u. a. mit → Apollon, → Herakles und → Eros [1] identifiziert. Er ist bis in christl. Zeit in PN belegt.
→ Herrschaft; Herrscher; Mandulis

1 W. Brashear, s. v. H., RAC 16, 574–597 2 J. G. Griffiths, The Conflict of H. and Seth from Egyptian and Classical Sources, 1960 3 D. Kurth, Treffpunkt der Götter. Inschr. aus dem Tempel des H. von Edfu, ²1998 4 W. Schenkel, s. v. H., LÄ 3, 14–25. HE. FE.

Hosidius
[1] C. H. Geta. Münzmeister vielleicht im J. 54 v. Chr. (MRR 2, 441); von den Triumvirn 43 geächtet, aber von seinem Sohn gerettet; später von der Proskriptionsliste gestrichen (App. civ. 4,171).
[2] [H.] Geta. Senator, dessen fragmentar. *cursus* wegen des Amtes eines *quaesitor* wohl in die augusteisch-tiberische Zeit gehört. CIL IX 2844; PIR² H 215.
[3] C. H. Geta. Legionslegat während Claudius' Britannienfeldzug im J. 43 n. Chr., nach dem er, obwohl noch Prätorier, *ornamenta triumphalia* erhielt. ILS 971 dürfte sich auf ihn beziehen; dann wurde er von Claudius unter die Patrizier aufgenommen; später leitete er einen Feldzug gegen die Hiberer. Birley, 222 ff.; PIR² H 217.
[4] Cn. H. Geta. Legat des Claudius in Mauretanien; nach seinen Erfolgen wurde das Land in zwei Provinzen organisiert. Wenn AE 1997, 76 sich auf ihn bezieht, auch Teilnahme am Britannienfeldzug des Claudius. *Cos. suff.* von Juli-Dez. 47–n. Chr.

PIR² H 216 · Birley, 365 · G. Camodeca, in: Epigraphia. Actes...A. Degrassi, 1991, 70.

[5] M. Vitorius H. Geta s. Vitorius
[6] Cn. H. Mauricus. Vielleicht Sohn von H. [4]. *Cos. suff.* in einem unbekannten J., vielleicht in flavischer Zeit. PIR² H 220.
[7] C. H. Severus. Sohn eines Gnaeus, *tribus Claudia*. Ritter aus Sala in Mauretania Tingitana. Nach vier ritterlichen *militiae* wurde er *procurator ad census* in Britannia. Vermutlich ins 2. Jh. zu datieren. Das Bürgerrecht der Familie geht auf H. [4] zurück. AE 1991, 1749; 1750. W. E.

Hospes. Cognomen in den kaiserzeitlichen Fasten in den Familien der Iulii und Vettii (→ Iulius; Vettius).

Degrassi, FCIR 255. K.-L. E.

Hospitalitas. Ursprüngliche Bed. »Gastlichkeit«. Mil. bedeutet *h.* »Einquartierung«. Soldat und Wirt wurden als *hospes* bezeichnet, letzterer auch als *dominus* oder *possessor*. Der Wirt hatte ⅓, bei *illustres* ½ seines Hauses dem *hospes* als Obdach zu überlassen. Nicht jedes Haus durfte von den *mensores* (*mediatores*) als Quartier herangezogen werden. Privilegiert waren Senatoren, hohe Amtsträger, kaiserliche und öffentliche Beamten, teils auch Gewerbetreibende (Cod. Theod. 7,8,1 f.; Cod. Iust. 12,41 f. [3. 40–55]).

H. begegnet auch als Terminus bei der Ansiedlung von *foederati* (i.e. Barbaren) nach 418 n Chr. in den Quellen. u. a. [5], jüngst [4] deuteten *h.* als eine Neuverteilung des Grundeigentums nach den genannten Prinzipien. [3] und [1] bezweifelten, daß der Literalsinn der Quellen die Form der Barbarenansiedlung erkläre. U. a. Cassiodor (var. 2,16), Ennodius (epist. 9,23), Prokop (BG I [V], 1,4 ff.; 28; Cod. Euricianus 276; 277; Lex Romana Burgundionum 54 f.) ließen die Aufteilung als Steuerreform verstehen, die den Barbaren statt Eigentum Steueranteile (*sortes*) zuwies und keine größeren Enteignungen vorsah [1; 2; 3 passim].

1 J. Durliat, Le salaire de la paix sociale dans les royaumes barbares, in: H. Wolfram, A. Schwarcz (Hrsg.), Anerkennung und Integration, 1988, 21–73 2 Ders., Cité, impôt et intégration des barbares, in: W. Pohl (Hrsg.), Kingdoms of the Empire, 1997, 153–179 3 W. Goffart, Barbarians and Romans. A. D. 418–584, 1980
4 W. Liebeschütz, Cities, Taxes and the Accomodation of the Barbarians, in: W. Pohl (Hrsg.), Kingdoms of the Empire, 1997, 135–141 5 F. Lot, Du régime de l'hospitalité, in: Revue belge de philologie et d'histoire 7, 1928, 975–1011. U. HE.

Hospitium s. Gastfreundschaft

Hostia s. Immolatio, s. Opfer

Hostilia. *Vicus* in SO-Venetia am Padus auf dem Territorium von Verona (Tac. hist. 3,9), Flußhafen auf der Strecke Ticinum – Ravenna (*ab H. per Padum*, Tab. Peut. 4,5), h. Ostiglia. Beginn des südl. Zweigs der *via Claudia Augusta* (ILS 208, *Padana*). Erwähnt im Zusammenhang der Kämpfe von 69 n. Chr. (Tac. hist. 2,100). Eine bes. Technik der Honiggewinnung wurde hier betrieben (Plin. nat. 21,73).

G. Paviani Buganza, Storia e topografia di Ostiglia, in: Atti e Memorie dell'Accademia Virgiliana di Mantova 39, 1971, 7–41 · R. De Marinis, Villaggi e necropoli dell'età del Bronzo, 1987 · Quaderni del Gruppo Archeologico Ostigliense, 1991 ff. G. U.

Hostilia, Quarta. In zweiter Ehe Gattin des C. Calpurnius [I 9] Piso (Consul 180 v. Chr.); vergiftete angeblich ihren Mann im Amt, um ihrem Sohn aus erster Ehe, Q. Fulvius [I 11] Flaccus, zum Konsulat zu verhelfen, und wurde deshalb verurteilt (Liv. 40,37,5–7). K.-L. E.

Hostilianus. C. Valens H. Messius Quintus war der jüngere Sohn des Kaisers → Decius [II 1] und der Herennia Etruscilla. Im Sept. 250 n. Chr. wurde er zum Caesar und *princeps iuventutis* ernannt (AE 1942/43, 55; ILS 518) und nach dem Tod seines Vaters im Juni 251 von → Trebonianus Gallus adoptiert und zum Augustus erhoben (Zos. 1,25,1; RIC 4,3, 143 ff.), wohl um von der Mitschuld des Trebonianus am Tode seines Vaters und Bruders abzulenken. Er starb kurz darauf in Rom an der Pest (Aur. Vict. Caes. 30,1; [Aur. Vict.] epit. Caes. 30; Eutr. 9,5) oder eher auf Betreiben des Trebonianus (Zos. 1,25,1).

PIR V 8 • KIENAST, 207 • M. PEACHIN, Roman Imperial Titulature and Chronology, 1990, 33 f. • R. ZIEGLER, Aigeai, der Asklepioskult, das Kaiserhaus der Decier und das Christentum, in: Tyche 9, 1994, 187–212, bes. 188 ff. T.F.

Hostilius. Alter lat. Familienname, dessen Herkunft ungeklärt ist, inschr. auch *Hostillius* und *Hostilus* [1. 30; 175]. Das hohe Alter des Namens bezeugen der dritte röm. König Tullus H. [4] und Bezeichnungen wie *Curia Hostilia*, *Lares Hostilii* und die Göttin *Hostilina*. In histor. Zeit ist die Familie plebeisch und seit dem 2. Jh. v. Chr. besonders in den Zweigen der Tubuli und Mancini polit. aktiv; am Ende des 1. Jh. v. Chr. erloschen.

1 SCHULZE

[1] H. Praetor oder Volkstribun im 2. Jh. v. Chr. (?), brachte eine *lex Hostilia* durch, die die Vertretung des Klägers vor Gericht in Diebstahlprozessen erlaubte.

KASER/HACKEL, RZ, ²1996, 63.

[2] H. (Tubulus?), C. Mitglied der Dreiergesandtschaft unter Führung von C. Popillius Laenas im J. 168 v. Chr. nach Alexandreia, die dort den sofortigen Abzug des Antiochos [6] IV. Epiphanes aus Ägypten erwirkte. MRR 1, 430. P.N.

[3] H., Hostus (oder Hostius). Legendärer Großvater des Königs Tullus H. [4], angeblich aus der albanischen Kolonie Medullia stammend, treuer Anhänger des → Romulus, fiel auf dem Forum als röm. Führer im Abwehrkampf gegen die wegen des Frauenraubes angreifenden Sabiner und wurde dort begraben. Seine Frau war Hersilia (Liv. 1,12,3 f.; Dion. Hal. ant. 3,1,1–3). Er ist wohl zur Gänze Erfindung der älteren Annalistik. K.-L.E.

[4] Tullus H. ist der dritte König Roms, nach → Romulus und → Numa; nach der Überl. regierte er 672–641 v. Chr. Sein Großvater, Hostus H., ein Kampfgenosse des Romulus, soll auf dem Forum beim Lapis Niger begraben sein. Der Ableitung seines Namens von *hostis* (»Feind«) verdankt er seinen kriegerischen Ruf, der ihn ›wilder als Romulus‹ sein ließ (Liv. 1,22,2). Von Numa wird er dadurch abgesetzt, daß er das kriegerische Ritual, insbes. die Riten der → *fetiales*, eingerichtet haben soll. Er kämpfte gegen Fidenae, Veii und die Sabiner, vor allem aber eroberte und zerstörte er Roms Mutterstadt → Alba Longa (Endpunkt des Kriegs war der Zweikampf der Horatii und Curiatii, → Horatius [1]) und siedelte die Albaner auf dem von ihm zum Stadtgebiet geschlagenen → Mons Caelius an: das legitimiert Roms Herrschaft über ganz Latium, die Existenz von albanischen Familien in Rom und die Aufsicht über albanische Kulte einschließlich desjenigen des → Iuppiter Latiaris auf dem Albanerberg. Als sein Wohnsitz gelten die Velia oder der Caelius. An städtischen Bauten werden ihm das erste Senatsgebäude (*curia Hostilia*), das *comitium* und eine beides umfassende Einzäunung (*saepta*) zugeschrieben, was zeitlich ungefähr zum arch. Befund (erste Pflasterung des *comitium* noch im 7. Jh.?) paßt, ohne daß daraus ein Argument für die Historizität des H. gewonnen werden könnte. Den Tod fand er, indem er zusammen mit Frau und Kindern in seinem Haus verbrannte, entweder durch einen Anschlag seines Nachfolgers Ancus → Marcius oder weil das Haus wegen eines Religionsfrevels (der unterschiedlich erzählt wird) durch einen Blitz getroffen wurde. Quellen: Enn. ann. 120–126; Cic. rep. 2,31 f.; Liv. 1,22–31; Dion. Hal. ant. 3,1–35.

R. M. OGILVIE, A Commentary on Livy I–V, 1965, 105–125 • F. COARELLI, Il Foro Romano. Periodo Arcaico, 1983, 121 f. • J. POUCET, Les origines de Rome, 1985. F.G.

[5] H., Tullus. Volkstribun 42 v. Chr. (MRR 2,359; 3,103). Vor Mutina im Stab des M. Antonius [I 9]; Cicero (Phil. 13,26) bezichtigt H. des versuchten Verrats an seinem früheren Heerführer (D. Iunius [I 12] Brutus?). T.FR.

[6] H. Cato, A. Bekleidete die Ämter zusammen mit seinem Bruder L.; 207 v. Chr. Praetor (Sardinia), 201 Decemvir zur Aufteilung eingezogenen Landes in Apulien und Samnium, 190 Legat unter L. Cornelius [I 72] Scipio im Krieg gegen Antiochos [5] III. 187 wurden die Brüder im Zusammenhang mit den Prozessen gegen die Scipionen wegen Unterschlagung angeklagt, A. freigesprochen, L. verurteilt (Liv. 38,55,4–6; 58,1 nach Valerius Antias). K.-L.E.

[7] H. Mancinus, A. Praetor 180 v. Chr. Als Consul 170 wurde ihm der Krieg gegen → Perseus von Makedonien übertragen (MRR 1, 419 f.), in dem er zunächst einem Hinterhalt in Epeiros entging. Er beschränkte sich im wesentlichen auf Verteidigungmaßnahmen sowie auf die Festigung des röm. Einflusses in Griechenland und führte deswegen keine mil. Entscheidung herbei, stellte aber die Heeresdisziplin wieder her und sicherte die Zusammenarbeit mit den Bundesgenossen (Liv. 44,1,5–8). Q. Marcius Philippus löste ihn im folgenden J. ab.

[8] H. Mancinus, C. Sohn von [7], Praetor um 148 v. Chr. Bekam als Consul 137 Hispania Citerior zugelost und nahm den Krieg gegen die Numantiner (→ Numantia) wieder auf, nachdem ein von Q. Pompeius ausgehandelter Friedensvertrag im Senat gescheitert war (MRR 1, 482). H. wurde wiederholt geschlagen, zog seine Truppen schließlich ab und wurde trotz numerischer Überlegenheit von den Feinden eingeschlossen (Liv. per. 56; App. Ib. 80; Vir. ill. 59,1–3). Seine Kapitulation gegen freien Abzug (*foedus Mancinum*), die sein Quaestor Ti. → Sempronius Gracchus maßgeblich ausgehandelt hatte, rettete unzähligen Römern das Leben, wurde aber in Rom als Schmach empfunden und vom

Senat verworfen (Cic. har. resp. 43; Vell. 2,2,1; Plut. Ti. Gracchus 5–7). Ein Volksbeschluß 136 ordnete seine Auslieferung an die Numantiner an, die diese jedoch ablehnten (Cic. Caecin. 98; Liv. per. 56). Nach seiner Rückkehr wurde er aus dem Senat verwiesen (Cic. de orat. 1,181), in den er später durch erneute Wahl zum Praetor zurückkehrte (Vir. ill. 59,4). Vorher war ihm vom Volk sein Bürgerrecht bestätigt worden (Dig. 50,7,18).

[9] H. Mancinus, L. Erhielt 148 v. Chr. als Legat (MRR 1, 462 Anm. 3) den Oberbefehl über die Flotte im 3. Pun. Krieg, blieb aber erfolglos. Beim gescheiterten Versuch, Karthago von See her einzunehmen, konnte er nur durch das Eingreifen Scipios gerettet werden (App. Lib. 113–14; Plin. nat. 35,23; Zon. 9,29). Consul 145.

[10] H. Tubulus, C. *Praetor urbanus* 209 v. Chr. Sein *imperium* wurde bis 204 jedes Jahr erneuert. Im J. 208 besetzte er auf Verdacht hin → Arretium und ließ sich Geiseln stellen (Liv. 27, 24,1–8). 207 wurde er nach Tarent und später nach Capua versetzt, wo er bis 204 blieb.

[11] H. Tubulus, L. Wohl Enkel von H. [10]. 142 v. Chr. *praetor de sicariis* und somit einer der ersten Vorsitzenden des ständigen Gerichtshofes für Mordprozesse (MRR 1, 475); bis weit ins 1. Jh. v. Chr. berüchtigt wegen seiner Bestechlichkeit. Im J. 141 wurde gegen ihn eine außerordentliche Untersuchung angestrengt [1]. Einer Verurteilung versuchte er durch freiwilliges Exil zu entgehen, wurde jedoch zurückgeholt und nahm sich daraufhin mit Gift das Leben (Ascon. 23 C).

1 ALEXANDER, 5. P.N.

Hostis. H. bezeichnete urspr. den Ausländer (*peregrinus*), also den Feind (*perduellis*) ebenso wie den Gast (*hospes*), wie Cicero (off. 1,37) richtig aus den Bestimmungen der XII Tafeln (→ *tabulae duodecim*) schließt (*aut status dies cum hoste*: 2,2; *adversus hostem aeterna auctoritas*: 6,4). Sie zeigen zugleich, daß auch ein Fremder ohne → *commercium* vor dem röm. Magistrat prozessieren konnte. Ebenso ist für den zwischenstaatlichen Bereich die ältere Auffassung, daß ein »dauernder Kriegszustand« (MOMMSEN) oder eine »natürliche Feindschaft« (TÄUBLER) erst durch einen förmlichen Freundschaftsvertrag aufgehoben wurde, durch den Nachweis von HEUSS widerlegt, daß das Verhältnis der → *amicitia* ›durch jede Art friedlichen zwischenstaatlichen Verkehrs gegeben‹ war. Die Frage der Möglichkeit eines reinen Freundschaftsvertrages bleibt nach ZIEGLER freilich umstritten. Ein Feind im Rechtssinne – *iustus et legitimus hostis* (Cic. off. 3,107) – konnte nur ein staatlich organisiertes Gemeinwesen sein, dem gegenüber Verpflichtungen der → *fides* (NÖRR) und das *ius fetiale* (→ *fetiales*) galten und mit dem ein »gerechter Krieg« (*bellum iustum*) zu führen war, ansonsten handelte es sich um Piraten oder Räuber (Dig. 49,15,24).

In der Krise der späten Röm. Republik kam es zu einer Übertragung des Begriffs *h.* auf röm. Bürger, obgleich es innerhalb des röm. Gemeinwesens doch allenfalls einen persönlichen Feind (*inimicus*) geben sollte. Bereits das gewaltsame Vorgehen des → Scipio Nasica gegen Tiberius Gracchus und seine Anhänger im J. 133 v. Chr. und die Erklärung des Notstands durch das *senatusconsultum ultimum* im J. 121 v. Chr. gegen Gaius → Sempronius Gracchus implizierten eine solche Übertragung auf die inneren Konflikte. Seit dem J. 88 v. Chr. ergingen beim Zustand drohender Gefahr wiederholt förmliche *h.*-Erklärungen durch Senatsbeschluß gegen Gegner außerhalb des Stadtbereichs. Cicero ging im Fall der inhaftierten und damit bereits unschädlich gemachten Catilinarier im J. 63 v. Chr. noch weiter, indem er den gesetzlichen Schutz des röm. Bürgers vor magistratischer → *coercitio* (*lex Sempronia de capite civis*) durch die These vom automatischen Verlust des Bürgerrechtes bei feindlichem Handeln gegen das Gemeinwesen zu beseitigen suchte. Die extreme Form, Bürger in *h.* umzuwandeln, wurde in den Proskriptionslisten Sullas und der Triumvirn Antonius, Caesar (C. Octavius) und Lepidus erreicht (vgl. auch Flor. epit. 2,16 zu L. Antonius 41 v. Chr.).

1 S. ALBERT, Bellum iustum, 1980 2 J. BLEICKEN, Lex Publica, 1975, 473 ff. 3 W. DAHLHEIM, Struktur und Entwicklung des röm. Völkerrechts im dritten und zweiten Jahrhundert v. Chr., 1968, 136f. 4 A. DRUMMOND, Law, Politics and Power. Sallust and the Execution of the Catilinarian Conspirators, 1995 5 C. HABICHT, Cicero der Politiker, 1990, 51 (zum Begriff *hostis domesticus*)
6 J. HELLEGOUARC'H, Le vocabulaire latin des relations et des partis politiques sous la république, 1972 7 A. HEUSS, Die völkerrechtlichen Grundlagen der röm. Außenpolitik in republikanischer Zeit, 1933, 46 8 M. KASER, Ius gentium, 1993 9 Ders., K. HACKL, Das röm. Zivilprozeßrecht (HdbA 10.3.4), ²1996, 62, Anm. 15 10 W. KUNKEL, R. WITTMANN, Staatsordnung und Staatspraxis der röm. Republik, 2. Die Magistratur (HdbA 10.3.2.2), 1995, 238f.
11 M. MANTOVANI, Bellum iustum. Die Idee des gerechten Krieges in der röm. Kaiserzeit, 1990 12 MOMMSEN, Staatsrecht, Bd. 3, 590ff. 13 D. NÖRR, Aspekte des röm. Völkerrechts. Die Bronzetafel von Alcántara (ABAW N. F. 101), 1989, bes. 102 14 E. TÄUBLER, Imperium Romanum 1, 1913 15 J. v. UNGERN-STERNBERG, Das Verfahren gegen die Catilinarier oder: Der vermiedene Prozeß, in: U. MANTHE, J. v. UNGERN-STERNBERG (Hrsg.), Polit. Prozesse in Rom, 1997, 85–99, bes. 93 ff. 16 Ders., Untersuchungen zum spätrepublikanischen Notstandsrecht. *Senatusconsultum ultimum* und *hostis*-Erklärung, 1970, 18 ff.; 63 ff. (mit einer Liste der *hostis*-Erklärungen: 116, Anm. 153) 17 F. VITTINGHOFF, Der Staatsfeind in der röm. Kaiserzeit, Untersuchungen zur »damnatio memoriae«, 1936 18 WIEACKER, RRG, 266, Anm. 139 19 K.-H. ZIEGLER, Das Völkerrecht der röm. Republik, in: ANRW I 2, 68–114, bes. 87f. J.v.U.-S.

Hostius

[1] Schrieb ein → Epos mit dem Titel *Bellum Histricum* in mindestens 2 B., von denen 7 Fr. erh. sind. Es handelte verm. von dem Krieg, der 129 v. Chr. von C. Sempronius Tuditanus geführt worden war. H. stand wahrscheinlich in Beziehung zu ihm wie → Ennius [1] zu Fulvius [15] Nobilior und → Furius [I 7] Antias zu Lutatius Catulus; das Epos war wohl panegyrischen Typs, wie es in der hell. Dichtung üblich war. Prop. 3,20,8 erwähnt den *doctus avus* eines Mädchens, mit dem er eine Beziehung hat, und aufgrund der zweifelhaften Annahme, daß das Mädchen Cynthia sei, deren wirklicher Name Hostia war, ist oft behauptet worden, der Dichter sei ihr Vorfahr gewesen. Das ist jedoch unwahrscheinlich.

M. A. VINCHESI, Il Bellum Histricum di Ostio, in: V. TANDOI (Hrsg.), Disiecti Membra Poetae Bd. 1, 1984, 35–59 · COURTNEY, 52. ED.C./Ü: M.MO.

[2] H. Capito, Q. s. Capito [1]

Hostus. Seltenes lat. Praenomen unbekannter Herkunft (in den Quellen häufig mit Hostius verwechselt), → Hostilius [3] und H. Lucretius Tricipitinus (Consul 429 v. Chr.)

SALOMIES, 30f. K.-L.E.

Hülsenfrüchte s. Ernährung; Erve

Hufeisen s. Landtransport

Huhn (Hahn). Das urspr. in Südasien aus mehreren Wildhühnern, v. a. dem Bankiva-H. der Sunda-Inseln und Indiens, gezüchtete Haus-H. wurde um 1400 v. Chr. nach China und noch vor 1200 nach Baktrien und Iran (daher die Bezeichnung »persischer Vogel« von Kratinos bei Athen. 9,374d und Aristoph. Av. 485; 707; sowie »medischer Vogel« Aristoph. Av. 276) und von dort nach Mesopot. und Kleinasien eingeführt. Dort lernten es die Griechen kennen und brachten es im 6. Jh. in ihr Mutterland sowie nach Sizilien und Unteritalien. Die Vielzahl der Namen spiegelt die Verbreitung: ἀλέκτωρ, »der schlaflos Machende« (Batr. 192; Pind. O. 12,14; Aischyl. Ag. 1671 und Eum. 861, stets nur poetisch), ἀλεκτρυών (seit Theognis 864; seit Aristoph. Nub. 662 auch fem.), ἡ ἀλεκτορίς (Hippokr. Int. 27 und Nat. Puer. 29; Epicharmos 152,172; Hekat. 58); als gewöhnliches Federvieh seit den Tragikern: ὁ ἐνοίκιος ὄρνις (Aischyl. Eum. 866; Soph. El. 18) und ἡ ὄρνις (θήλεια) (Soph.). Die Einbürgerungszeit wird auch durch Hahn-Abb. auf Mz. (Himera [1. Taf. 5,40–42], Anf. 5. Jh.; Phaistos und Dardanos [1. Taf. 5,38 und 43], Mitte 5. Jh.) bestätigt. Prächtige Hähne zieren Mosaiken aus der Spätant. [8. 250f. und Taf. 131].

Kampf-Hähne, auf deren Sieg auf öffentlichen Plätzen man wettete, wurden an verschiedenen Orten, z. B. auf Rhodos und in Tanagra (Plin. nat. 10,48) gezüchtet. Angeblich soll Themistokles – vielleicht nach kleinasiatischem Vorbild (Ail. var. 2,28, vgl. Plin. nat. 10,50) – die als Volksbelustigung (vgl. Aristoph. Av. 759; Lucil. 300f. M.) beliebten H.-Kämpfe eingeführt haben, welche Platon (leg. 7,880) und u. a. Aischines (Tim. 53) kritisierten. Ein Silberstater von Leukas [1. Taf. 5,46] zeigt einen Hahn in Kampfstellung, Gemmen bieten auch echte Kampfszenen (z. B. [1. Taf. 21,33 und 35]; vgl. [2]). Seinen oft gerühmten Kampfesmut (Pind. O. 12,14; Aischyl. Eum. 813; Plin. nat. 10,47; Ail. nat. 4,29) unterstützte man durch entsprechende Fütterung mit Knoblauch (σκόροδον) und Zwiebeln (κρόμμυον; Xen. symp. 4,9; Schol. Aristoph. Equ. 494). Man schenkte sich unter Freunden auch gerne einen Hahn (mit erotischer Nebenbedeutung; vgl. die Darstellungen von H. und Eros auf Gemmen [1. Taf. 16,31; 21,47–50; 21,54], seine stete Paarungsbereitschaft: Aristot. hist. an. 1,1,488b 4, ebenso beim Stein-H.: hist. an. 8(9),8,613b 25f.).

Als Vogel der Lichtgottheit, da sein Krähen ja den kommenden Morgen verkündet (Theognis 863f.; Plin. nat. 10,46), war der Hahn nach persischer Sitte Attribut von Hermes, Helios-Apollon, Eos und Mithras und sollte Dämonen wie den Basilisken fernhalten (Ail. nat. 3,31). In dieser apotropäischen Eigenschaft ziert er oft Grabsteine, Urnen, Waffen usw. Die Furcht des Löwen vor ihm (Aisop. 84 und 292 HAUSRATH; Ail. nat. 3,31 und 5,50; Plin. nat. 8,52 und 10,47; Lucr. 4,710–17) bzw. seinem Krähen ist vielleicht auch rel. Ursprungs. Dem Asklepios wurden ebenso wie Herakles Hähne geopfert (Plat. Phaid. 118; Ail. nat. 17,46; Artem. 255,24; Plut. symp. 4,10,1). Als Lichtvogel war er auch bei den Christen ein Attribut Christi (Prud. liber cathemerinon 1).

Als Lieferant von Eiern und Fleisch spielte das H. in Griechenland eine geringere Rolle als in Rom seit dem 1. Jh. v. Chr., auf Delos soll die H.-Zucht und Mästung aber bedeutsam gewesen sein (Varro rust. 3,9,2; Colum. 8,2,4; Plin. nat. 10,139). Das H.-Fleisch galt Galen (de bonis malisque sucis 3,1; de alim. fac. 3,18,3) als leicht verdaulich und nahrhaft. Nach 3,21,1 waren die frischen und nur wenig gekochten Eier ebenfalls empfehlenswert. In It. entstand aus Kreuzungen die h. noch »Italiener« gen. bräunliche Rasse mit hoher Legeleistung. In Germanien, Gallien und Britannien gab es, vermutlich seit der späten Hallstatt- und frühen Latène-Zeit, ebenfalls schon Haus-H. (Caes. Gall. 5,12; vgl. [3. 69ff.; 4. 6ff.]). Erst seit dem 1. Jh. n. Chr. sind die größeren Rassen der Römer dort durch Funde belegt. Aristoteles hat die Fortpflanzung der H. ebenso wie die Entwicklung des Kükens im Ei sehr genau biologisch untersucht (Hauptstellen: hist. an. 5,13,544a 31–33 und 6,1,558b 10–22 über Fortpflanzung und Eibildung; hist. an. 6,3,561a 6–562a 20 über die Kükenentwicklung; hist. an. 4,9,536a 30–32 über das Verhalten des H. nach seinem Sieg über Nebenbuhler; 8(9),49,631b 8–18 über sexuelle Verhaltensstörungen beider Geschlechter usw.). Die kristallinen Magensteine *alectoriae* sollen den Athleten Milon von Kroton unbesiegbar gemacht haben (Plin. nat. 37,144). Einzelheiten der Zucht finden sich bei Colum. 8,2,2–15 bis 7,5 und Pallad. 1,27.

Plinius (nat. 10,48ff.) beleuchtet die Rolle der heiligen H. (*pulli*), das sog. *auspicium ex tripudiis*, d. h. die Erforschung des Götterwillens durch das Freßverhalten der Tiere im röm. Kult vor staatlichen Unternehmungen (→ Divination). Dies ist zuerst für 325 v. Chr. nach-

weisbar (Liv. 8,30). Cicero (div. 1,28; 2,72; nat. deor. 2,7) läßt durch seinen ironischen Ber. erkennen, daß man dieses Verfahren [5. 1,82ff.; 6. 532; 7] oft manipulierte und auch nicht mehr ernst nahm.
→ Hahnenkampf

1 F. Imhoof-Blumer, O. Keller, Tier- und Pflanzenbilder, 1889, Ndr. 1972 2 K. Schneider, s. v. Hahnenkämpfe, RE 7, 2210 3 O. F. Gandert, Zur Abstammungs- und Kulturgesch. des Hausgeflügels, insbes. des Haushuhns, in: Beitr. zur Frühgesch. der Landwirtschaft 1, 1953 4 W. Schweizer, Zur Frühgesch. des Haushuhns in Mitteleuropa, Diss. München 1961 5 Mommsen, Staatsrecht 6 G. Wissowa, Religion und Kultus der Römer, [2]1912 7 Marbach, s. v. Tripudium, RE 7 A, 230ff. 8 Toynbee, Tierwelt.

B. Lorentz, Kulturgesch. Beitr. zur Tierkunde des Alt. Die Hühnervögel, 1904, III-XIV (Jb. Kgl. Gymn. Wurzen).

C.HÜ.

Hulchnie. Etruskisches Gent. aristokratischer Familien, bes. in → Volsinii und → Tarquinii (Tomba dell' Orco), evtl. syn. mit den lat. Fulginii. F.PR.

Humanistische Schrift. In der griech. Schrift der Humanistenzeit des 15. und 16. Jh. läßt sich oft die Fortsetzung älterer Tendenzen und Stilrichtungen verfolgen. Abgesehen von der otrantinischen Schrift (→ Süditalienische Schrift), die in der Renaissancezeit noch überlebt, aber kaum eine Rolle spielt, dauern auch andere traditionelle Schriftarten immer noch an. Zur archaisierenden Schrift gehört der sog. Hodegonstil (14. Jh), der nicht nur in den östl. Klöstern bes. bei liturgischen Hss., sondern auch im Westen von führenden Kopisten der Renaissance, wie z. B. Ioannes Rhosos, bis in die 1. H. des 17. Jh. benutzt wurde. Daneben entwickelt sich seit der Palaiologenzeit eine klassizistische Stilrichtung, die durch allg. Ausgewogenheit, leichte Rechtsneigung, sorgfältige Wort- und Buchstabentrennung, stark reduzierte Ober- und Unterlängen, sowie kleinen Mittelbau der Buchstaben gekennzeichnet ist. Dieser Schriftstil wurde in den Westen durch die ersten Hss. klass. Autoren, welche die it. Humanisten aus Konstantinopel mitbrachten, und durch die byz. Kopisten, die nach Italien flüchteten, übertragen und lebte bei vielen Gelehrten und Berufskopisten des 15. und 16. Jh., wenn auch mit unterschiedlichen Ergebnissen, weiter (z. B. Manuel Chrysoloras, Michael und Aristobulos Apostoles).

Mit diesem Schriftstil verwandt, aber mit einigen Elementen der → Fettaugenmode, ist die Schrift mancher griech. und it. Schreiber (wie z. B. Stephanos von Medeia, Demetrios Sguropulos), dabei aber gezierter und flüssiger. Ähnlich, aber mit ausgeprägten Ober- und Unterlängen, sehen insbes. die Schriften des Andronikos Kallistos, Demetrios Chalkondyles, Demetrios Moschos und Zacharias Kallierges aus. Diese kursivere Schreibrichtung läßt sich auch bei vielen produktiven Kopisten des 16. Jh. beobachten (z. B. Camillo Zanetti). Bei einigen hauptsächlich in Paris wirkenden Schreibern (den sog. »grecs du roi«) entwickelt sich eine ausladende, ligaturenreiche Schriftvariante, die durch größere Verschnörkelung und kräftige Oberlängen bestimmt wird (z. B. bei Ange Vergèce). In diesem Zusammenhang sind auch die Vertreter der sog. Barockschrift zu nennen: Gegensatz von Groß- und Kümmerbuchstaben, Schnörkel und Einrollungen, ausgeprägte Ober- und Unterlängen kennzeichnen die meistens gedrängt aussehende Schrift vieler Berufskopisten des 16. Jh. (bes. in Venedig).

It. Humanisten versuchen oft, das Schriftmuster ihrer griech. Lehrer nachzuahmen, ihre Schrift verrät aber lat. Schreibgewohnheiten. Das Ergebnis ist gewöhnlich eine kleinformatige, viereckige Schrift mit regelmäßigem Duktus, reduzierten Ober- und Unterlängen, deutlicher Wort- und Buchstabentrennung sowie wenigen Kürzungen (z. B. Giovanni Aurispa, Lorenzo Valla, Poggio Bracciolini). Ausnahmefälle sind die individuellen Züge einiger Gelehrten, wie Ciriaco von Ancona und Angelo Poliziano.
Zur lat. humanistischen Schrift → Schriftstile.

D. Harlfinger, Zu griech. Kopisten und Schriftstilen des 15. und 16. Jh., in: La paléographie grecque et byzantine 1977, 327–341 • P. Eleuteri, P. Canart, Scrittura greca nell'Umanesimo italiano, 1991. P.E.

Humanitas
A. Definition B. Bedeutungsebenen
C. Komplementärer Charakter

A. Definition
In *h.* als »Menschlichkeit« treten folgende Merkmale hervor: 1. philanthropische Rücksicht, speziell Barmherzigkeit (*misericordia*), 2. geistreiche und taktvolle Umgänglichkeit (*urbanitas*), 3. Gefühl für natürliche menschliche Verbundenheit (*sensus humanitatis*), 4. gebildetes Menschsein (*eruditio, doctrina*), 5. Zivilisation (*cultus*). Schon in Ciceros Rede *Pro Sex. Roscio* (84 v. Chr.) finden sich fast alle Schattierungen.

B. Bedeutungsebenen
1. *H.* als Zuwendung zum Bedürftigen (griech. *philanthropía*) fächerte sich als »Rücksichtnahme auf Unterlegene«, die auch in altröm. Tradition (v. a. der *clementia*) verwurzelt war, unter griech. Einfluß in eine Fülle verwandter Tugenden auf: Barmherzigkeit, Sanftmut und Versöhnlichkeit, Nachgiebigkeit, Wohlwollen, Freigebigkeit usw. Es gehört zur *h.*, für die Bedürfnisse und Nöte seiner Mitmenschen empfindsam zu sein und sich entsprechend zu verhalten (Plin. epist. 8,16,3). Als Voraussetzung dafür galt allg. das Bewußtsein einer allen Menschen gemeinsamen Unvollkommenheit, worauf die Wechselfälle des Lebens, die Wiederkehr von Auswegslosigkeit und Zufall (Liv. 45,8,5 f.) ebenso verweisen wie Irrtümer und Verfehlungen (Plin. epist. 9,12,1; 8,22,1 ff.), Schwäche und Sterblichkeit (*condicio humana*). Der *h.* lag das Adjektiv *humanus* im zunächst vorherrschenden Sinn von »zerbrechlich, hinfällig«

(Cic. Lael. 102) zugrunde. Entsprechend ist *h.* als Appell an die Richter, für den Angeklagten angesichts des Glückswechsels mildernde Umstände durch Barmherzigkeit walten zu lassen, schon beim Auctor ad Herennium (ca. 84 v. Chr.) fester Topos der Gerichtsrede. In einer anderen Trad. (der hell. Königstugenden) wird philanthropische *h.* als Sorge für die Wohlfahrt der Beherrschten von Cicero wiederholt an staatlichen Verantwortungsträgern (Feldherrn, Magistraten) hervorgehoben. Hartherzigkeit, Hochmut und Grausamkeit sind der *h.* entgegengesetzt.

2. *H.* als Urbanität kennzeichnete eine feine, lockere, zuvorkommende Lebensart, wie sie beim Stadtrömer allg., bes. aber bei seinen Eliten in der von Berufs- und Amtspflichten entlasteten Geselligkeit der Freizeit (*otium*) in Erscheinung treten konnte (→ Muße). Zu ihr gehörten Heiterkeit (*hilaritas*), Freundlichkeit (*comitas*) Umgänglichkeit (*facilitas, dexteritas*), Liebenswürdigkeit (*venustas, lepos, iucunditas*), feiner Witz (*facetiae*), Eleganz (*elegantia*), Scherz (*iocus*) und dergleichen. Die Verbindung mit lit. Bildung, wie sie Cicero im sog. → Scipionenkreis maßgeblich vorgeprägt sah (vgl. Cic. Mur. 66; de orat. 2,22; 154; rep. 1,14 ff.). *Urbanitas* gab ihr ein bes. Profil und ergab sich prägnant aus der Verbindung von philanthropischer und gebildeter *h.* (z. B. in Cic. fam. 11,27,6).

3. *H.* als (Sinn für) Gemeinschaftlichkeit aller Menschen (*communis h.*) wurde v. a. von Cicero im Anschluß an stoische Theorie von der natürlichen, gleichsam organischen Gemeinschaft des menschlichen Geschlechts (*societas humani generis*), der sich der einzelne rücksichtsvoll einzufügen habe, in seinen philos. Schriften erläutert (Cic. fin. 3,62–65; off. 1,50–56; s. → *oikeíōsis*). Der Schutz von ›Vereinigung und Gemeinschaftlichkeit ist sogar dem Erkenntnisstreben überlegen‹ (off. 1,157). Es zeugt von einer ›alle Menschlichkeit zurückweisenden Ungeheuerlichkeit‹ (off. 1,62; 3,32), den eigenen Vorteil dem Gemeinnutz vorzuziehen, wie es umgekehrt zur *h.* gehört, über alle sozialen, polit. und nationalen Grenzen hinweg die Lebensinteressen aller Menschen zu schützen, die der persönlichen Gegner (Quinct. 51) ebenso wie die der unterworfenen Völker (ad Q. fr. 1,1,27). Die Erfahrungen der Bürgerkriege des 1. Jh. v. Chr. ließen solche *h.* schmerzlich vermissen (vgl. Cic. S.Rosc. 154). Seneca hat sowohl im konkreten (epist. 95,51; vgl. Cic. off. 1,51 f.) als auch im allg. Ciceros Ansichten zur *h.* wiederholt (epist. 5,4; 95,52).

4. *H.* als vervollkommnete Menschlichkeit wurde, wieder zuerst von Cicero, in Aufnahme aristotelisch-stoischer Tradition, die dem Menschen in der Vernunft seine ausgezeichnete Eigentümlichkeit (*proprietas, praestantia*) zuspricht, seit 63 v. Chr. mit Bildung (*doctrina*) in Zusammenhang gebracht. Die ihr eigenen »Künste« und »Studien« (*studia humanitatis*) bilden die menschliche Vernunftnatur zur vollkommenen Gestalt (Cic. Arch. 4,15; Cic. de orat. 3,58) bzw. führen durch ihren »Schliff« (Cic. rep. 1,28) zum eigentlichen Menschsein. Im Zusammenhang mit *virtus* qualifiziert sie die Eliten.

Bes. relevant wurde die durch lit. Bildung ausgeprägte *h.* für Ciceros Ideal eines vollkommenen Redners (*in omni genere sermonis et humanitatis perfectum*; de orat. 1,35; 1,71). Angefangen von der Muße, wo es für *h.* als menschliche Kultur ›nichts Bezeichnenderes geben kann als eine elegante, nirgends rohe Unterhaltung‹ (de orat. 1,32) bis hin zu ordnendem Einfluß in öffentlichen Angelegenheiten erweist sich vernünftige Rede (*ratio et oratio*, off. 1,50) als humanisierende Kraft sozialer Kommunikation, weil sie Sachkenntnis, Gedankenreichtum und Wertorientierung einschließt. Seneca sprach den *studia liberalia* eine bes. Bedeutung für philanthropische *h.* ab, bevorzugte im übrigen im Moralischen eher altröm. Tugendbegriffe wie *simplicitas, modestia, clementia* (epist. 88,30). Plinius d. J. konnte in der *h.* wieder philos. Lehre und Menschenfreundlichkeit zusammensehen (epist. 1,10,2). Wie Cicero sah auch er wahre Menschlichkeit und v. a. lit. Kultur in Griechenland beheimatet (epist. 8,24,2; ähnlich Cic. ad Q. fr. 1,1,27). Irrtümlich setzte Gellius (13,17) den Sinn von »Ausbildung und Unterweisung in den guten Künsten« gegenüber dem »vulgären« philanthropischen Sinn als ursprünglich an.

5. *H.* als zivilisatorische Verfeinerung des menschlichen Lebens wurde mit kunstvoll gestalteten Gefäßen (Varro, ling. 8,31), Handelsgütern des höheren Lebensstandards (Caes. BG 1,1,3), Säulenhallen, Bäderanlagen und geschmackvollen Gastmälern (Tac. Agr. 21) verbunden (in den beiden letzten Fällen auch mit der Folge der Lähmung der Widerstandskraft von Unterworfenen).

C. Komplementärer Charakter

H. war zwar immer ein wichtiger, nie aber ein beherrschender Wertbegriff. Um sie im sozialen Kontext vom Verdacht einer leichtfertigen Offenheit zu schützen, wurde sie gern mit »Tugend« (*virtus*) und ihr traditionell zugehörigen altröm. Wertbegriffen wie Unbestechlichkeit, Standfestigkeit, Rechtschaffenheit u. ä. verknüpft, so wie sie umgekehrt dazu diente, diese Werte vor starrer Anwendung zu bewahren und ihren Druck komplementär zu erleichtern (bes. eindrücklich in Cic. Mur. 65 dokumentiert). Als Ideal galt – bes. bei Cicero (Mur. 66; fam. 12,27 und Plinius d.J. (epist. 4,3,2; 8,21,1; 9,9,2) – das Gleichgewicht bzw. die Mischung von »Ernst«, *gravitas* (oder »Strenge«, *severitas*) und *h.* im Sinne von Freundlichkeit und Umgänglichkeit).

→ Scipionenkreis; Humanismus

1 H. Haffter, Die röm. H., in: H. Oppermann (Hrsg.), Röm. Wertbegriffe, 1967, 468–482 2 F. Klingner, Humanität und h., in: Ders., Röm. Geisteswelt, [5]1965, 704–746 3 W. Schadewaldt, H. Romana, in: ANRW I 4, 1973, 43–62.

H.ST.

Humbaba s. Gilgamesch, Gilgamesch-Epos

Humiliores s. Honestiores

Hummer. Diese edle Krebsart (Homarus vulgaris) gehörte nach Aristoteles (hist. an. 1,6,490b 12) unter dem Namen ἀστακός/*astakós* (nach FRISK »mit Knochen versehen«) zu den Weichschalern (μαλακόστρακα), nach Ailianos (nat. 9,6) aber zu den Schaltieren (ὀστρακόδερμα). Seine präzise Beschreibung (schwarze Sprenkelung auf weißem Grunde, acht Füße, große Scheren mit Zähnen darauf, aus verschiedenen Teilen zusammengesetzter Schwanz) bei Aristot. hist. an. 4,2,526a 11–b 18 ermöglicht die Bestimmung. Man findet den H. im seichten Meerwasser im Hellespont, bei Thasos und Alexandreia (Athen. 1,7b) und den Liparischen Inseln (549b 14). Diokles von Karystos (bei Athen. 3,105b = fr. 134 WELLMANN) lobt seinen Wohlgeschmack. Weitere Erwähnungen bietet Athen. 3,104f–105d. Die Römer schätzten sein Fleisch weniger bis auf Heliogabal, der eine Mayonnaise davon erfand (SHA Heliog. 19,6), und Apicius 2,37, der eine Art Haché kennt. Varro (rust. 3,11,3) nennt den *cammarus* (nach κάμμαρος) nur als Entenfutter. Bei Mart. 2,43,11f. und Iuv. 5,84f. ist er Armenspeise.

KELLER 2,490f. C.HÜ.

Hund

[1] (κύων, κυνίδιον, κυνίσκος, σκύλαξ, σκυλάκιον, *canis, canicula, catellus*).

A. RASSEN B. LITERATUR, RELIGION, MEDIZIN

A. RASSEN

Eines der ältesten, wahrscheinlich schon im Mesolithikum, an verschiedenen Stellen der Erde aus h. ausgestorbenen Wildhund-Arten gezüchtetes Haustier. Die Ableitung vom Goldschakal (Canis aureus) [2] ist heute wieder aufgegeben. Aus Knochenresten und Abbildungen können mehrere Frührassen, von denen die heutigen Rassen abzuleiten sind, erschlossen werden: 1. *Canis familiaris Putjatini Studer*, dingo-ähnlich, breit und robust, Typus der »Eberjagd« von Tiryns (14. Jh. v. Chr.) 2. *Canis familiaris matris optimae Jeitteles*, der »Bronze-H.«, nach HAUCK Stammvater der Pariah- und Wind-H. 3. Die *Bracken* (*bracci*), schwere Hetz-H. mit Hängeohren, entstanden durch Kreuzung mit einem weiteren Wild-H. 4. Der große *Hirten-H.*, aus einer Kreuzung mit dem *Canis inostranzewi Anutschin* hervorgegangen, Stammart für die Bullenbeißer und Doggen. 5. *Canis familiaris palustris Rütimeyer*, der Torf-H. oder Pfahlbautenspitz, der Stammvater der Spitze und ähnlicher Rassen.

Um 3000 v. Chr. lassen sich einige dieser Rassen im Alten Orient auf Abbildungen wiedererkennen, nämlich Doggen in Mesopot. und Äg. sowie Wind-H. und terrierartige Formen in Äg. (3. Jt. v. Chr.). PLACHT [1] unterscheidet nach dem griech. Bildmaterial unter Zuhilfenahme ant. Beschreibungen vier Gruppen, nämlich Melitäer (Zwergspitze), Lakonier (d. h. καστόριαι und ἀλωπεκίδες), Kreter (Wind-H.) und Molosser (Doggen und Schäfer-H.). HAUCK spricht dagegen von sechs Typen (Pariah- und Schäfer-H.-, Wind-H.-, Bracken-, Doggen-, Spitz- und Hirten-H.-Typus) und warnt davor, die Abbildungen als zu realistisch einzustufen. Homer (etwa 90 Stellen) und andere ant. Autoren klassifizieren die H. nur nach ihren Aufgaben, etwa der Jagd (Hom. Il. 8,338–340; 10,360–362; 11,292f.; Hom. Od. 19,428ff. u.ö.), der Bewachung und Verteidigung der Herde (Il. 5,476; 10,183f. u.ö.) oder eines Anwesens (Od. 14,29–36; 20,13–15 u.ö.). Erst seit dem 5. Jh. werden Rassen unterschieden, nämlich Lakonier (Pind. fr. 106 B. = 121 TU.; Soph. Ai. 8), Inder (Hdt. 1,192), Molosser (Aristoph. Thesm. 416). Aus der zoologischen und Jagd-Literatur ergeben sich folgende Charakteristika für bekannten Rassen:

1. Molosser (Epiroten): die größte, schärfste und stärkste Rasse mit der Verwendung als Hirten- und Hof-H., aber auch zur Jagd auf Großwild. Sie gehören eindeutig zum Doggen-Typus, doch muß man an Kreuzungen mit Lakoniern denken. Der Hof-H. des Eumaios (Hom. Od. 14,29–36) gehörte sicherlich dazu, ebenso die »indischen« H. (Aristot. gen. an. 2,7,746a 34f.; Xen. kyn. 10,1).

2. Lakonier (spartanischer H.): wohl eine Kreuzung von Doggen mit anderen Arten. Sie waren stark wie Bullenbeißer, aber kleiner und schneller und dienten der Jagd. Infolge ihrer sorgfältigen Zucht (vgl. Xen. kyn. 4) waren sie sehr kostbar. Xenophon (kyn. 3) unterscheidet zw. der Hauptform, der kastorischen (nach ihrem angeblichen Erstzüchter Kastor), und der (nach ihrem – auf vielen klass. Vasenbildern abgebildeten – fuchsähnlichen Kopf) Alopekiden genannten.

3. Kretische und sizilianische H. waren Wind-H. Bes. die kretischen wurden oft mit Lakoniern gekreuzt und eigneten sich vorzüglich als Begleit-H. berittener Jäger. Mz. aus Panormos, Segesta und Eryx zeigen als Hinweis auf die dort florierende Zucht den sizilianischen Typ.

4. Melitäer H., benannt nach Malta als ihrem ersten Zuchtort, stellten kleine, schwache, langhaarige Spitze mit kurzen Beinen dar, die als Wach-H., hauptsächlich aber als Schoß-H. (Strab. 6,277; Ail. nat. 7,40) dienten.

5. Der Hirten-H. aus Kreuzungen war ein billiges Nutztier und wird in der landwirtschaftlichen Fachlit. (Varro rust. 2,9; Colum. 7,12; vgl. Verg. georg. 3,404f.; Colum. 7,12,3) behandelt.

In Griechenland züchtete man seit alters H. für die Jagd, im Gegensatz zum Orient aber nicht für den Kampf im Krieg bis auf seltene Ausnahmen (Hdt. 5,1; Plin. nat. 8,143; Plut. De sollertia animalium 13 = mor. 969; Ail. nat. 7,38: Schlacht bei Marathon). Nur die Britannier besaßen Kampf-H. (Claud. De Consulatu Stilichonis 3,301). Die Kelten hatten außer dem gewöhnlichen und häßlichen »segusischen« H. (Arr. cyn. 3,4) den schnellen und edlen Wind-H. *vertragus* (Arr. cyn. 3,6f.; Opp. kyn. 1,373; Plin. nat. 8,148; Grattius 156; Mart. 3,47). Hinweise auf verwilderte, umherstreunende, von Aas und Abfall lebende H. gibt es aus dem Orient (Ps 59,7 und 15; Jer 15,3; Ex 22,31; 1 Kg 21,19ff.), Griechenland (Hom. Il. 8,379f.; 17,241;

18,271 f.; 22,66; Hom. Od. 3,259; 14,133 f.) und It. (Liv. 41,21,7; Hor. epod. 5,23). In archa. Zeit ließ man H. nicht nur die Leichen der Feinde, sondern auch deren ausgerissene Genitalien fressen (Od. 18,86 und 22,476; vgl. Il. 22,75).

B. Literatur, Religion, Medizin

Der zahme H. galt als Inbild der Treue (Hom. Od. 17,291 ff.; Plin. nat. 8,143 f.; Ail. nat. 6,25; 7,40 u.ö.) und der Klugheit (z.B. Xen. oik. 13,8; Aristot. hist. an. 8(9),1,608a 27; Theokr. 21,15; Plin. nat. 8,147; Plut. soll. an. 19 = mor. 973e-f; Ail. nat. 7,13). Sein Herr verwöhnte ihn (Od. 10,216 f.; Arr. kyn. 9,1; 18,1) und gab ihm einen Eigennamen (Xen. kyn. 7 [3]; Plin. nat. 8,143 f.). Treue und wachsame Menschen konnte man positiv als H. bezeichnen (Aischyl. Ag. 607; 896; Aristoph. Equ. 1023), aber auch Tiere wie den Adler als H. des Zeus (Aischyl. Prom. 1021 f.; Soph. fr. 884) oder den Greif (Aischyl. Prom. 803). Negativ steht der H. für das dreiste, gemeine und »hündische« Wesen (bei Frauen: Hom. Il. 6,344; 356; 8,423; 21,481; Hom. Od. 18,338; Aristoph. Vesp. 1402; bei Männern: Hom. Il. 8,299; 13,623; Od. 17,248). Auch Angriffslust wird durch den Vergleich mit H. charakterisiert (Aischyl. Suppl. 758: κυνοθρασεῖς; Soph. fr. 885; Eur. fr. 555; Theokr. 15,53: κυνοθαρσής; mit Bezug auf die Furien: Soph. El. 1388; Eur. fr. 383). Daß *kýōn* als Beiname des → Antisthenes [1], → Diogenes [14] und der kynischen Philosophen negativ anzusehen ist (Aristot. rhet. 3,10,1411a 24; Anth. Pal. 7,65; 413; Plut. mor. 717c), liegt auf der Hand.

Als beliebtes Haustier des Menschen (vgl. Hom. Od. 17,309; Prop. 4,3,55; Phaedr. 3,7,22; Mart. 1,109) regte der H. zu vielen Sprichwörtern an [4] und begegnet in Tierfabeln (Aisop. 41; 52; 64; 93; 94; 129; 134–139; 283 Hausrath; Phaedr. 1,4,17–19; 22; 3,7; Babr. 42; 48; 74; 79; 85; 87; 99; 104; 110). In histor. Zeit wurde er (im Gegensatz zu Ostasien) nirgendwo mehr gegessen (vgl. die Fehlinterpretation im röm. Kult [5. 68[1]]). Die Aufforderung des Dareios I. an die Karthager, auf Menschenopfer und den Genuß des H.-Fleisches zu verzichten, erklärt sich aus dem rel. Schutz des H. im Iran als Wächter gegen böse Geister (Iust. 19,1,10). Als Opfertier wurde er wohl nur bei Reinigungsriten verwendet (Klearchos bei Ail. nat. 12,34; Athen. 3,99e; Plut. qu. R. 52,277b; Plin. nat. 29,58 [6. 27 f.; 40 ff.].

In der Kunst charakterisierte er – als deren Begleiter – den Jäger sowie Götter des Waldes und der Jagd (Apollon, Pan, Priapos, Silvanus und Diana) und natürlich auch den Iuppiter Custos auf dem röm. Kapitol. Auch mit → Hekate war der H. verbunden. Der H. des Hades war → Kerberos. Im röm. Aberglauben wurden bes. dem heulenden, schwarzen und trächtigen Hund wichtige Funktionen beigelegt [7. 32 ff.]. Die reichliche magisch-organotherapeutische Verwendung einzelner Körperteile und von Blut, Fett, Milch, Urin u.a.m. bei Plin. nat. 29,99–101 u.ö. sprechen wie beim → Geier für die dem H. zugeschriebenen geheimen Kräfte.

Die zoologischen Kenntnisse über den H. waren dagegen eher dürftig. Aristot. hist. an. 3,7,516a 16f. behauptet sogar, sein Schädel bestehe nur aus einem Knochen. Den Zahnwechsel erörtern Aristoteles (hist. an. 2,2,501b 5–14) und Plinius (nat. 11,160; vgl. Cic. nat. deor. 2,134). Das Unterschlagen des Schwanzes unter den Körper versteht Plin. nat. 11,265 nicht als allg. Demutsgeste und schreibt es nur minderwertigen H. zu. Die auch auf Menschen übertragbare Tollwut (rabies canum) wurde genau beobachtet (Aristot. hist. an. 7(8),22,604a 4–8; Plin. nat. 2,207; 7,64; 8,152 f. u.ö.) und – erfolglos – mit vielen Heilmitteln bekämpft (z.B. Plin. nat. 24,95; 28,156; 29,99–101 u.ö.). Über die Aufzucht und Abrichtung der H. informiert die ant. Lit. recht gut (z.B. Varro rust. 2,9; Opp. kyn. 1,376–538; Plin. nat. 8,151; Colum. 7,12,11–14; Sen. clem. 1,16). Den H.-Krankheiten widmet Columella ein kurzes eigenes Kap. (7,13).

1 W. Placht, Die Darstellung des H. auf griech. Bildwerken, Diss. Wien 1933 (Masch.) **2** K. Lorenz, So kam der Mensch auf den H., 1950, [28]1966 **3** E. Baecker, H.-Namen des Alt., Diss. Königsberg 1884 **4** Otto, Sprichwörter **5** Latte **6** H. Scholz, Der H. in der griech.-röm. Magie, Diss. Berlin 1937 **7** E.E. Burriss, The Place of the Dog in Superstition, in: CPh 30, 1935, 32 ff.

Keller 1, 91–151 • O. Antonius, Grundzüge einer Stammesgesch. der Haustiere, 1922, 89–138 • F.E. Zeuner, Gesch. der Haustiere, 1967, 69–98 • Toynbee, Tierwelt, 94–109.

C.HÜ.

[2] s. Sternbilder

Hunericus, Hunerich. Ältester Sohn des → Geisericus, als dessen Nachfolger 477–484 n.Chr. König der Vandalen (*rex Vandalorum et Alanorum*; Victor Vitensis 2,1). H. war zunächst mit einer Tochter des Westgotenkönigs Theoderich I. vermählt (Iord. Get. 184), seit 456 mit Eudokia [2], der Tochter Valentinians III. (Prok. BV 3,5,6), eine Ehe, die wohl beschlossen wurde, als H. als Geisel bei diesem weilte, um die Einhaltung des Vertrags von 442 zwischen Römern und Vandalen zu sichern (Prok. BV 3,4,13). H. suchte nur zu Beginn seiner Regierung den Ausgleich mit Ostrom (Malchus fr. 13 FHG 4,120 f.), seit 482 verfolgte er blutig die Katholiken (Victor Vitensis 2 f.). Die Loslösung maurischer Stämme vom Vandalenreich konnte er nicht verhindern (Prok. BV 3,8), auch seine auf Stärkung des Königtums zielende Politik scheiterte trotz scharfen Vorgehens gegen oppositionelle Adlige: Auf den Thron folgte ihm nicht sein Sohn → Hildericus, sondern → Gunthamundus (Iord. Get. 170).

PLRE 2,572 f. • Chr. Courtois, Les vandales et l'Afrique, 1955, bes. 262 ff. • H.-J. Diesner, Das Vandalenreich, 1966, 75 ff.

M.MEI.

Hunger s. Mangelernährung

Hunimundus

[1] *Dux*, später *rex* der Donausueben, ca. 465 n.Chr. nach einem Raubzug in Dalmatien vom Gotenkönig Thiudimer besiegt und »adoptiert«. Bot eine mehrstämmige, auch von Ostrom unterstützte Kriegskoalition gegen die Goten auf, unterlag ihnen aber ca. 469 (Iord. Get. 273–279). Wohl mit dem gleichnamigen Plünderer von Batavis (Eugippius, vita Severini 22,4) identisch. PLRE 2, 574 (H. 2).

H. Wolfram, Die Goten, [3]1990, 264ff. P.KE.

[2] H. d.J., König der Ostgoten, Sohn des → Ermanarich, Vater des Thorismud (Iord. Get. 250; [1. 255f.]), aus der jüngeren Amalerlinie, Nachfolger des Vinitharius. H. ist wohl nicht identisch mit H., dem Vater des → Gesimund (so [2. 574]; anders [3. 27f.]).

1 H. Wolfram, Die Goten, [3]1990 2 PLRE 2,573, H. 1 3 P. Heather, Goths and Romans 332–489, 1991, 27, 57, 240 4 B. Tönnies, Die Amalertrad. in den Quellen zur Gesch. der Ostgoten, 1989, 43. ME.STR.

Hunni (Οὖννοι, Χοῦννοι), die Hunnen.
A. Geschichte B. Kultur

A. Geschichte

Nomadenvolk, Ursprung umstritten. Höchstwahrscheinlich kamen sie kurz nach der Zeitwende aus Zentralasien. Als Χοῦννοι (*Chúnnoi*) zuerst bei Ptol. 3,5,25 zw. → Bastarnae und Roxolani gen. (weitere spätere Lokalisierungen bei Amm. 2,1; Iord. Get. 36f.). Einige der hunn. Stämme zogen ins Kaukasosgebiet; aus dem osthunn. Zweig gingen mehrere Staaten hervor (Hephthalitai, Avaren, Chazaren und Protobulgaren). Um 376 n.Chr. überquerten hunn. Stämme die Wolga, besiegten die Alani und das Ostgotenreich des → Ermanarich und vernichteten das westgot. Heer des → Athanarich (Amm. 31,2,13). Sie errichteten ein Reich in dem unterworfenen Gebiet, von dem aus sie ab 395 n.Chr. Einfälle in den Kaukasos und die unteren Donaugebiete unternahmen. Von dort aus stießen sie um 400 nach Westen vor. Das von Khan Uldin angeführte Heer unterstützte Rom in der Valachei gegen Gainas (400) und → Stilicho gegen → Radagaisus (405); 408 fiel es in Thrakia ein (Oros. 7,37; Zos. 5,22; Soz. 9,5). Zw. 402 und 404 vertrieben sie die Burgundiones und die Vandali von der Weichsel und Oder und lösten damit eine Kettenreaktion von Stammeswanderungen aus. Nach dem Tod des Arcadius wandten sie sich ab 408 gegen die Oströmer, nahmen Festungen ein und besetzten Castra Martis südl. der Donau. Erst 412 wurde ein Friedensvertrag zw. Khan Karaton und Byzanz geschlossen. 422 drangen die H. erneut in Thrakia ein. 424 verlegte der Khan Rua seine Residenz in die Ebene östl. der Theiß. Der ihm folgende Khan Bleda und Attila schlossen mit Ostrom 435 bei Margos (Moesia) einen Vertrag, der den H. viele polit. und wirtschaftliche Privilegien sicherte. 440/1 eroberte Bleda Moesia Prima und Pannonia Secunda. Sein Bruder Attila half ihm an der östl. Flanke und nahm im Jahr darauf Ratiaria ein. Zusammen besiegten sie das oström. Heer Aspars (→ Ardabur [2]). Der »Erste Frieden des Anatolios« im J. 443 brachte dem hunn. Staat sehr großen Reichtum. Das hunn. Reich, nach Stämmen organisiert und zentralistisch beherrscht, umfaßte die Gebiete von der h. Ukraine bis zur Donau und reichte im Westen bis zum Rhein. Ein System von Vasallenkönigen hielt das Reich zusammen. Seit Rua wurde versucht, die vielen Stämme der H. bis zur nördl. Waldzone zu vereinen. Höhepunkt der hunn. Macht war die Regierungszeit des → Attila (434–453). 447 drang er mit german. Bundesgenossen auf die Balkanhalbinsel vor und besetzte Moesia Prima und Dacia Ripensis. Nach dem »Zweiten Frieden des Anatolios« im J. 450, in dem er auf seine Eroberungen südl. der Donau verzichtete, zog er mit german. Bundesgenossen gegen Gallien und Norditalien. Im Sommer 451 wurde er von den vereinigten Streitkräften des Aetius auf den Katalaunischen Feldern (→ Campi Catalauni) geschlagen und mußte sich auf die rechte Rheinseite zurückziehen (Iord. Get. 194–218). Damit begann der Verfall des hunn. Reiches. 452 gelang es noch, → Aquileia [1] einzunehmen und bis Mailand vorzudringen, doch der Angriff des Kaisers Marcianus auf sein Kernland an der Donau ließen ihn umkehren. Nach seinem Tod begannen Thronkämpfe, die die von den H. unterworfenen Gepidae, Rugi, Suebi und Sarmatae ausnutzten. Unter Attilas Söhnen Ellak und Dengitzik, die beide 454 in der Schlacht am Nedao in Pannonia gegen german. Stämme starben, zerfiel das hunn. Reich in Europa. Viele der H. wurden Söldner im oström., später auch im german. Heer, andere wurden in Dacia Ripensis angesiedelt. Beiderseits des Dnjepr siedelten noch H., deren Herrscher nach 494 wahrscheinlich Attilas jüngster Sohn Hernac war (Iord. Get. 259ff.). Von dort ging der letzte nachgewiesene Einfall der H. unter Zenon aus (Euagrios, historia ecclesiae 3,2).

B. Kultur

Ihre histor. Bed. erlangten die H. durch die Auslösung der »Großen Völkerwanderung«. Durch ihre schnellen berittenen Bogenschützen besaßen sie bei ihren Eroberungszügen eine sehr große Stoßkraft. Exemplare der mit Goldblech beschlagenen »goldenen Bogen« sind als Machtsymbole aus hunn. Fürstengräbern bekannt. Ihre Sprache, auf die man nur aufgrund von Namen schließen kann, war Altaltaisch und eng mit dem Alttürk. verwandt. In der ant. Lit. als ›barbarisches und wüstes‹ Volk allg. negativ dargestellt (Iord. Get. 123) und arch. nur stellenweise faßbar, ist nur wenig über die H. und ihre Kultur bekannt. Elemente des Nomaden- und Kriegerlebens waren offensichtlich vorherrschend, ihr Leben war durch Jagd und Viehhaltung geprägt. Sāsānid. Einflüsse sind gegen E. des 4. Jh. nachzuweisen. Wichtigste Quellen: Priscus aus Panion; Konstantinos Porphyrogennetos, Excerpta de legationibus; Iord. Get.; Amm. 31,2; Zos. 4,20.

F. ALTHEIM, Gesch. der Hunnen 1–5, 1959–1962 · O.J. MAENCHEN-HELFEN, Die Welt der Hunnen, 1978 · A. ALFÖLDY, Funde aus der Hunnenzeit und ihre ethnische Sonderung, 1932 · E.A. THOMPSON, A History of Attila and the Huns, 1948 · J. WERNER, Beitr. zur Arch. des Attilareiches, 1956. I.V.B.

Hunsrück-Eifel-Kultur. Sondergruppe der kelt. Eisenzeit im westl. Mittelgebirgsraum zw. Luxemburg, dem Rhein, der Hocheifel und dem Nahetal. Die H. ist sowohl Teil der späten → Hallstatt-Kultur als auch der frühen → Latène-Kultur (6. bis Mitte 3. Jh. v. Chr.). Sie wird v. a. durch kontinuierlich belegte Grabhügelfelder mit Körperbestattungen charakterisiert. Weitere Eigenständigkeiten sind bes. Keramikformen sowie eigene Grabausstattungen (viel Ringschmuck, wenige Fibeln, häufige Lanzenbeigabe usw.). Im Verlauf der H., bes. im 5./4. Jh. v. Chr., bildet sich eine Gruppe von → Fürstengräbern in der H. heraus, die durch reichen Goldschmuck, griech.-etr. Importe, Schwert- und Wagenbeigabe (v. a. zweirädrige Streitwagen) ausgezeichnet sind (z. B. Schwarzenbach, → Waldalgesheim).

Siedlungen sind für die H. nur vereinzelt als befestigte Höhenburgen bekannt, von denen bisher keine als → Fürstensitz einzuordnen ist. Die Gründe für die Herausbildung dieser Gruppe werden oft in lokalen Eisenvorkommen gesehen. Der H. kommt offensichtlich eine wichtige Rolle bei der Herausbildung der Latènekultur zu.

→ Eisen; Keltische Archäologie; Wagen

A. HAFFNER, Die westl. H., 1976 · Ders., A. MIRON (Hrsg.), Studien zur Eisenzeit im Hunsrück-Nahe-Raum, 1991 · H.-E. Joachim, Die H. am Mittelrhein, 1968. V.P.

Hurriter. Altorientalische Sprachgemeinschaft, die seit der Akkad-Zeit (um 2200 v. Chr.) nachweisbar ist. Die Vorfahren der H. lebten wohl schon im frühen 3. Jt. v. Chr. in Ostanatolien. Durch die Expansion der mesopot. Großreiche kamen die H. in den Gesichtskreis der altorientalischen Hochkulturen (Kriegsgefangene, Tributsendungen; hurrit. Beschwörungen um 1750 v. Chr.). Besonders im Zuge des Zusammenbruchs der mesopot. Großreiche strömten H. in die nördl. Teile des »Fruchtbaren Halbmonds«. Seit der späten Akkad-Zeit sind Stadtstaaten unter hurrit. Herrschern in Obermesopot. und Assyrien (Urkeš) bezeugt. Anfang des 2. Jt. breiteten sich die H. nach Westen aus. In Nordsyrien entstand noch vor der Mitte des 2. Jt. eine hurrit. Schriftkultur, die althurrit. Traditionen mit bodenständig-syrischen verband und seit etwa 1400 v. Chr. die Kultur der Hethiter (→ Ḫattuša) stark beeinflußte. Im 16. Jh. v. Chr. entstand in Obermesopotamien ein H.-Reich (→ Mittani), das um 1400 vom Mittelmeer bis zum Zagros reichte. Seine Geschichte ist im 16. Jh. von der Auseinandersetzung mit dem althethit. Reich geprägt, im 15. Jh. vom Konflikt mit Äg. und im 14. Jh. von der Abwehr hethit. und assyr. Expansionsbestrebungen, die wohl den Anlaß zu friedlicher Übereinkunft mit Äg. (→ Amarna-Briefe) gaben. Um 1335 wurde Mittani von Hethitern und Assyrern erobert und bestand danach nur als rasch an Bedeutung verlierender Reststaat (Hanigalbat) fort. Die hurrit. Sprache verschwand weitgehend, hielt sich aber in Teilen Ostanatoliens wohl noch bis mindestens ins 7. Jh. v. Chr.

→ Hurritisch

G. WILHELM, The Hurrians, 1989. GE.W.

Hurritisch. Altoriental. Sprache, verschriftet in babylon. und ugarit. Keilschrift, mit großer Verbreitung in Ostanatolien, Obermesopotamien und Nordsyrien während des späten 3. und v. a. des 2. Jt. v. Chr. Zu den bisher bekannten hurrit. Texten gehören Briefe, Mythen, Beschwörungen, Gebete, Rituale, Omina, Weisheitstexte und lexikalische Listen. Eng verwandt ist das → Urartäische, das in assyr. Keilschrift geschrieben und von ca. 820 bis 600 v. Chr. v. a. für Königsinschr. in Ostanatolien und NW-Iran verwendet wurde. Das H. ist eine agglutinierende und ergativische Sprache, die ausschließlich Suffixe in einer strikten Sequenzordnung verwendet. Die Nomina unterscheiden zwei Numeri (Sg., Pl.), aber kein grammat. Geschlecht. Bisher sind mindestens 11 Kasus beobachtet worden. Das Verb des Dialekts von → Mittani unterscheidet drei Tempora, der Dialekt der Tafeln aus → Ḫattuša und andere ältere Texte anscheinend Aspekte und Aktionsarten. Dazu tritt ein komplexes System nicht-indikativ. Formen.

F. W. BUSH, A Grammar of the Hurrian Language, 1964 · I. M. DIAKONOFF, Hurrisch und Urartäisch, 1971. GE.W.

Hussain (Ḥusain). Enkel des Propheten → Mohammed (Muḥammad), Sohn von dessen Tochter → Fatima (Fāṭima) und Vetters → Ali (ʿAlī). Dritter → Imām der → Schiiten. Nach dem Tod des → Kalifen → Muʿāwiya von den Parteigängern seines Vaters zur Machtübernahme gegen die → Omajjaden (Umayyaden) gedrängt, wurde H. von deren Truppen 680 in Kerbela (ʿIrāq) getötet. Seines Märtyrertodes gedenken die Schiiten jährlich in Passionsspielen, die unterlassene Hilfeleistung der Parteigänger wird in Geißlerprozessionen gesühnt.

H. HALM, Der schiitische Islam, 1994 · Ders., Shiism, 1991 · L. VECCIA VAGLIERI, Ḥusayn b. ʿAlī b. Abī Ṭālib, EI 3, 607a–615b. H.SCHÖ.

Hut s. Kleidung

Huwawa s. Gilgamesch, Gilgamesch-Epos

Hyaden (Ὑάδες, erst seit Statius *Hyas*, sonst *Suculae*, nach Plin. nat. 18,247 volkstümlich *sidus Parilicium*). Sternbild im Kopf des Stieres, welcher sich, weil der Stier umgekehrt aufgeht, am Ende des Zeichens befindet, in der Nachbarschaft des Orion und der → Pleiaden (neben diesen werden die H. schon bei Hom. Il. 18,486 auf dem Schild des Achilleus erwähnt). Ihr Name wird abgeleitet von ὗς (*hys*; »Schwein«; »Ferkelchen«) oder von ὕειν (*hýein*; »regnen«; »Regenzeichen«) oder von der Form des Buchstabens Y als Abbild des Stierschädels. Die Zahl der H. schwankt zw. zwei und sieben. Der hellste Stern erster Größe (α Tau, h. Aldebaran) hieß ὁ λαμπρός τῶν Ὑάδων sim., nach Ptol. apotelesmata 1,9,3 Λαμπαύρας/*Lampaúras* (Λαμπαδίας varia lectio). Er ist einer der sechs rötlichen (ὑπόκιρροι) und liegt nach Ptol. syntaxis 7,5 dem ebenfalls rötlichen Antares (α Sco) gradgenau gegenüber. Daher gehören diese beiden Sterne zu den vier »königlichen Sternen« (*stellae regales*, Firm. mathesis 6,2). Der rötlichen Farbe verdankt das Sternbild auch seine Zuordnung zum Planeten Mars (Ptol. apotelesmata 1,9,3), wozu Rhetorios später Venus hinzufügt (vgl. schon Manil. 4,151). Der Frühuntergang der H. Mitte November kündigte den Beginn des Pflügens an (Hes. erg. 614–617), die H. galten ferner als Sturm- und Regenzeichen. Nach Teukros (Anon. De stellis fixis 1,2,2) verheißen die H. βροχάς ὑδραγωγούς, περιχύτας, nach Manil. (5,118, danach Firm. mathesis 8,6,6) aufrührerische Menschen und Schweinehirten.

Hesiod (frg. 291 MERKELBACH/WEST bei schol. Arat. 172 p. 166,7 MARTIN) nennt als Namen der einzelnen H.: Phaisyle, Koronis, Kle(e)ia, Phaio, Eudore, anders Pherekydes bei Hyg. astr. 2,21 l.824 VIRÉ: Ambrosia, Eudora, Pedile, Coronis, Polyxo, Phyto, Thyone (mit einigen anderen Lesarten; weitere Varianten bei [2. 2620]). Eratosthenes (katasterismoi 14) und Dichter kennen sie als Töchter des → Atlas und Schwestern der → Pleiaden und des → Hyas (Musaios) oder als Töchter des Hyas (Alexandros), des Erechtheus (Euripides) des Kadmos (Myrtilos), des Lamos (Nonnos) oder des Okeanos (schol. Germ.). Sie gelten als Nymphen und Ammen des kleinen Dionysos, der auf Naxos und in Dodona als Ὕης (*Hýēs*) verehrt wurde. Als Begleiterinnen des reiferen Gottes wurden sie gezwungen, sich ins Meer zu stürzen. Philochoros (frg. 31) berichtet, daß den H. in Athen zusammen mit Dionysos geopfert wurde.

→ Pleiaden

1 F. BOLL, Ant. Beobachtungen farbiger Sterne, 1916
2 W. GUNDEL, s. v. H., RE 8, 2615–2624 3 A. LE BOEUFFLE, Les noms latins d'astres et de constellations, 1977, 155–159, 207f. 4 W. HÜBNER, Grade und Gradbezirke der Tierkreiszeichen, 1995.

W.H.

Hyäne (ὕαινα, von ὗς/*hys*, »Schwein«). Ersterwähnung Hdt. 4,192; γλάνος (Aristot. hist. an. 7(8),594a 31); κ(ο)ροκόττας, zuerst bei Ktesias frg. 87 M. und Agatharchides, Periplus maris rubri 39. Lat. *hyaena* und *c(o)rocotta(s)* bei Plin. nat. 8,72 und 107; nachklass. *belua (belva)* (SHA Gord. 33,1). Bekannt war wohl nicht nur die häufigere Streifen-H. (Hyaena striata in Vorderasien und Afrika), sondern nach Opp. kyn. 3,288 (Περὶ στικτῇσιν ὑαίναις) auch die Tüpfel-H. (Hyaena crocuta in Afrika). Sie galt irrtümlich als Kreuzungsprodukt von Wolf und Hündin bzw. Hund und Wölfin (Plin. ebd.; Ktesias ebd.; Diod. 3,35,10). Das Aussehen der H. beschreiben Aristoteles, der sie wohl selber gesehen hat (hist. an. 6,32,579b 15–29; 7(8),5,594a 31–b 5), und Plinius (nat. 8,105f.): Sie besitzt die Färbung und Größe eines Wolfes, eine pferdeartige, aber dichtere, härtere und über das ganze Rückgrat – das durch seine Starre (Plin. nat. 8,105) ein Verdrehen des Halses verhindere – verlaufende Mähne sowie (Plin. ebd.) Augen von unterschiedlicher Art und offenbar wechselndem Ausdruck.

Die ant. Lit. erwähnt zahlreiche absonderliche Vorstellungen. Dem verbreiteten Aberglauben, die H. sei zwittrig und wechsle jedes Jahr das Geschlecht (noch bei Ov. met. 15,409f.; Ail. nat. 1,25; Physiologos 24) treten schon Aristoteles (hist. an. 6,32,579b 16–29; gen. an. 3,6,757a 2–13) und Diodoros (32,12,2) mit dem Argument einer anatomischen Besonderheit entgegen; weibliche Tiere könnten zudem selten erbeutet und genauer untersucht werden. Als einziges Tier grabe die H. sogar Leichen aus. Ihre Zähne zerbrächen jeden Knochen (Diod. 3,35,10). Weitere Absonderlichkeiten: Sie imitiere das Erbrechen eines Menschen (zur Anlockung von Hunden) sowie seine Rufnamen (Diod. 3,35 mit Zweifel daran; Plin. nat. 8,105; Ail. nat. 7,22) und banne durch Berührung mit einer Tatze bzw. durch ihren Schatten andere Tiere an ihren Platz (Plin. nat. 8,106; Ail. nat. 6,14; Geop. 15,1,12; Variante: ebd. 15,1,10) oder lasse die sie verfolgenden Hunde verstummen. Alle diese Motive sind dem MA v.a. durch Plinius und Solinus 27,23–26 übermittelt worden (vgl. Thomas von Cantimpré 4,53 [1. 138f.]).

Die Körperteile der H. wurden vielfach zu magischen und organotherapeutischen Zwecken (Plin. nat. 28,92–106) verwendet, etwa die Haut gegen Kopfschmerz oder die Zähne gegen Zahnschmerzen. Eine Umkleidung des Aussaatgefäßes mit einem H.-Fell sollte ein Aufgehen des Korns bewirken (Colum. 2,9,9 = Pall. agric. 10,3,1) und, um das Land herumgetragen, Hagelschaden verhindern (ebd. 1,35,14). Ihr oberster Halswirbel (»Atlas«) führte angeblich zur Versöhnung Streitender (Lucan. 6,672; Plin. nat. 28,99). Der Edelstein *hyaenia* aus ihren Augen sollte, unter die Zunge eines Menschen gelegt, die Zukunft vorhersagen lassen (Plin. nat. 37,168; Isid. orig. 16,15,25). Als Traumbild bedeutete die H. die Ankündigung von sexuell abnormen Wesen.

Den Römern tatsächlich vorgeführt wurden H. erst unter den röm. Kaisern Antoninus Pius (SHA Antoninus Pius 3,10,9), Alexander Severus (Cass. Dio 77,1,3) und Philippus (SHA Gord. 33,1), hier mit 10 Exemplaren aus der Menagerie des Gordianus III. Auf Mosaiken ist die H. selten abgebildet, z.B. auf einem aus Praeneste [2] und die Streifen-H. auf der sogenannten Worcester-Jagd aus Antiochia am Orontes [3. 364, Abb. 151 nach 4. 382].

1 H. BOESE (ed.), Thomas Cantimpratensis, Liber de natura rerum, 1973 2 H. BESIG, s. v. H., RE Suppl. 8, 1248f.
3 D. LEVI, Antioch Mosaic Pavements I, 1947 4 TOYNBEE.

C.HÜ.

Hyagnis. Myth. Musiker aus Kelainai in Phrygien, »Erfinder« des Aulos, soll als erster die phryg. Tonart (*harmonía*) sowie *nómoi* der Kybele und des Pan einge-

führt haben (Aristox. fr. 78; Marmor Parium 10); zusammen mit → Marsyas und → Olympos gen. (Pseudo-Plut. mus. 1132f; Anon. Bellermanni 28).
→ Musikinstrumente II (Aulos) F.Z.

Hyakinthia s. Hyakinthos

Hyakinthides (Ὑακινθίδες). Name einer Gruppe athenischer Göttinnen, denen zu Ehren ein jährliches Opferfest mit Mädchentänzen stattfand sowie vor dem Auszug in eine Schlacht weinlose Spenden dargebracht wurden. Der Mythos begründet diese Riten damit, daß die H. zur Abwehr eines kriegerischen Einfalls von → Erechtheus geopfert worden seien. Ihre Zahl und ihre Namen schwanken; aus einigen Namen ist eine Beziehung auf Artemis (die in Sparta Opfer vor der Schlacht erhält) lesbar. Sie können auch einfach Parthenoi, »Mädchen«, oder Erechtheides heißen und gelten gewöhnlich als Töchter des Erechtheus, die ihren Namen von ihrer Opferung auf einem Hyakinthos genannten Hügel haben. In wohl späterer, aus der Homonymie mit → Hyakinthos [1] von Amyklai entwikkelten Auffassung gelten sie als seine Töchter (mit dem doppelten Problem, daß Spartanerinnen Athen retten und Hyakinthos gewöhnlich als Ephebe stirbt). Der Mythos folgt einem geläufigen Schema [2].

Quellen: die Erechtheustradition (Euripides, Erechtheus fr. 65,65–98 [1]; Phanodemos, FGrH 325 F 4; Philochoros, FGrH 328 F 12; Demosth. or. 60,27); die Hyakinthos-Tradition (Apollod. 3,212; Hyg. fab. 128).

1 C. Austin, Nova Fragmenta Euripidea, 1968
2 W. Burkert, Homo necans, 1972, 76–80. F.G.

Hyakinthos (Ὑάκινθος).
[1] Heros, dessen Grab und Kult in → Amyklai [1] bei Sparta beheimatet, dessen Fest, die Hyakinthia, und der damit zusammenhängende Monatsname (*hyakínthios*, kret. *bakínthios/wakínthios* [1]) aber in vielen dor. Orten bekannt sind; diese Verbreitung weist auf eine alte, überlokale Bed. des Heros. Nach Ausweis des Suffixes *-nth-* ist der Name vorgriech.; das amykläische Heiligtum aber ist zwar vordorisch, doch erst seit spätmyk. Zeit faßbar [1].

Im Mythos ist H. entweder Sohn des Lokalheroen Amyklas und der Lapithin Diomede (Hes. fr. 171; Apollod. 3,116) oder der Muse Klio (→ Kleio), die Aphrodite im Zorn mit → Pieros, dem Sohn des Magnes, verbindet (Apollod. 1,16); als Geschwister sind die Brüder Argalos und Kynortes (Paus. 3,1,3; Apollod. 3,116f.) und die jung verstorbene Schwester Polyboia genannt (Paus. 3,19,4). Dominant ist H.' Rolle als homoerotischer Geliebter entweder des Sängers → Thamyris, der damit diese Praxis erfand (Apollod. 1,16), oder, in der verbreiteten Version, des → Apollon, der ihn versehentlich mit einem Diskuswurf tötet (Ov. met. 10,162–219); gelegentlich heißt es, → Zephyros, der erfolglose Rivale des Apollon bei H., habe den Diskos auf H. gelenkt (Paus. 3,19,5). Zur Erinnerung an den Geliebten setzt Apollon den amykläischen Kult mit seinem Jahresfest der Hyakinthia ein (Eur. Hel. 1469–1474) und läßt aus seinem Blut die Hyazinthe (s.u. H. [2]) wachsen, in deren Blütenblätter er das klagende *AIAI* einschreibt. Dieser Tod des jungen H. macht den att. Mythos, nach dem er Vater der → Hyakinthides ist, unmöglich; deswegen steht daneben auch eine von H. losgelöste Überlieferung.

Das amykläische Fest der Hyakinthia verbindet H. und den Hauptinhaber des Heiligtums, Apollon, unter dessen altarartigem »Thron« mit einem archa. Bild des gerüsteten und mit Lanze und Bogen bewaffneten Gottes H. begraben war (Paus. 3,19,1–5), im oft belegten Nebeneinander von Gott und Heros. Es ist das spartanische Hauptfest in dem nach der Fülle der Opfer benannten Monat Hekatombaion, während dessen Sparta keine Kriege führte (Beschreibung: Polykrates, FGrH 588 F 1 [2]). Das Fest dauerte drei Tage. Der erste galt bes. H.; einige der von griech. Norm abweichenden Festgebräuche wurden mit der Trauer um H. erklärt, und vor dem Hauptopfer an Apollon erhielt H. auf seinem Altar im »Thron« ein Totenopfer (Paus. 3,19,3). Der Haupttag war der mittlere, mit einer Prozession von Sparta nach Amyklai (*pompa*, Ov. met. 10,219), mit musischen und agonistischen Vorführungen der Knaben und jungen Männer sowie einem Bankett mit Bewirtung der Sklaven und Fremden [3]. Die jungen Frauen (*parthénoi*) fuhren auf Wagen in der Prozession mit, die Frauen brachten Apollon ein neues Gewand dar (Paus. 3,16,2), und nächtliche Tänze der Frauen und Mädchen sind ebenfalls bezeugt (Eur. Hel. 1468). Irgendwann wurde auch der Panzer des Timomachos, der Amyklai für Sparta eroberte, vorgeführt (Aristot. fr. 532). Insgesamt spielt das Fest dieselbe Rolle staatlicher Selbstrepräsentation für Sparta wie die Panathenaia für Athen [4].

An anderen dor. Orten ist außer dem Monatsnamen wenig faßbar. Die spartanische Kolonie Thera feierte die Hyakinthia; in der spartanischen Kolonie Tarent wurde ein Grab des H. oder gar des Apollon H. gezeigt, das östlich der Stadt lag (Pol. 8,28); man wird dieselbe Kultkonstellation wie in Amyklai vermuten. In Knidos hieß Artemis inschr. *Hyakinthotróphos* und hatte ein Fest der Hyakinthotrophia, was auf einen Mythos weist, in dem sie H. aufzieht (SGDI 3501; 3502; 3512).

Ikonographisch wird H. immer als junger Mann dargestellt, mit Ausnahme der Darstellung auf dem amykläischen Thron (Paus. 3,19,4; s. → Amyklai).

1 W. Burkert, Resep-Figuren, Apollon und Amyklai und die »Erfindung« des Opfers auf Cypern: Zur Religionsgesch. der »Dunklen Jh.«, in: Grazer Beiträge 4, 1975, 51–79
2 Samuel, Index s.v. 3 Nilsson, Feste, 129–140
4 L. Bruit, The Meal at the Hyakinthia. Ritual Consumption and Offering, in: O. Murray (Hrsg.), Sympotica, 1990, 162–174 5 P. Brulé, Fêtes grecques. Périodicité et initiation. Hyakinthies et Panathénées, in: A. Moreau (Hrsg.), L'initiation. Actes du colloque international, 1992, 19–38.

M.J. MELLINK, H., 1943 • B.C. DIETRICH, The Dorian Hyacinthia, in: Kadmos, 14, 1975, 133–142 • L. VILLARD, F. VILLARD, s.v. H., LIMC 5, 546–550 • M. PETTERSSON, Cults of Apollo at Sparta. The Hyakinthia, the Gymnopaidia and the Karneia, 1992. F.G.

[2] Der Pflanzenname H., der sich durch sein Suffix als vorgriech. erweist [1. 510], bezeichnet verschiedene Blumen mit »purpurnen« (blauen, dann auch roten), traubig angeordneten Blüten. Die archa. griech. Lit. erlaubt wegen ihres Naturrealismus eindeutige Identifikationen: Der in den Bergen wildwachsende H. von Homer (Il. 14,348) und Sappho (105b VOIGT) ist die Sternhyazinthe Scilla bifolia L., ein bis 20 cm hohes, blaublühendes, duftloses Liliengewächs, das im Frühling – meist zusammen mit anderen Geophyten wie Krokussen – auf manchen Gebirgen Südeuropas und Kleinasiens farbenprächtige Massenbestände bildet. In der ›Odyssee‹ hingegen ist der von Dioskurides (4,62 WELLMANN = 4,63 BERENDES) beschriebene, ebenfalls blaublühende Hyacinthus orientalis L. gemeint, also unsere – urspr. nur in Kilikien und Syrien wild wachsende – Gartenhyazinthe, die schon früh nach Griechenland importiert und dort kultiviert worden sein muß. Hom. Od. 6,231 und 23,158 werden die Haarlocken des Odysseus trefflich mit den rückwärts gebogenen Perigonzipfeln der traubig gehäuften Blüten verglichen. Ihr Wohlgeruch wird zuerst in den Kyprien erwähnt (4,3 DAVIES); Theognis 537 stellt sie als edle Kulturpflanze mit der Rose auf eine Stufe; der att. Komödie war sie wohlvertraut. Auch Theophrast (h. plant. 6,8,1 f.) unterscheidet die auf Bergen wildwachsende und die künstlich durch Brutzwiebeln vermehrte Art. Die letztere findet sich dann immer wieder in der späteren griech. und röm. Lit. als Gartenpflanze, deren Besitz Wohlstand verrät (z.B. Catull. 61,91–93; Longos 4,2,6).

Am E. des 4. Jh. v. Chr. taucht bei Palaiphatos 46 (MythGr III 2, S. 68) zum ersten Mal die Verbindung der Blume mit dem von Apollon geliebten und versehentlich getöteten Heros H. [1] auf: Den Anfangsbuchstaben seines Namens glaubte man in den Spalten der zurückgebogenen Perigonzipfel wiederzufinden. Seit Euphorion (40 POWELL) heißt dann auch die aus dem Blut des Aias entstandene Blume H.: Auf den Blüten waren die beiden ersten Buchstaben seines Namens lesbar, die zugleich einen Klagelaut (*AIAI*) darstellen.

Unter H. verstand man in der Ant. sowohl rosablühende Siegwurzarten wie Gladiolus italicus Mill. (*Iridaceae*) als auch den blaublühenden Acker-Rittersporn Consolida orientalis (Gay) Schröd. (syn. Delphinium ajacis L., *Ranunculaceae*) und verwandte Arten, auf deren Blüten die Buchstaben durch dunkle Adern tatsächlich deutlich gezeichnet sind. Bei allmählichem Überhandnehmen der symbolischen und mythischen Bed. des H. in der späteren Ant. schwand das Bewußtsein der realen Identität und es entstand als botanisches Monstrum eine dichterische Phantasiepflanze, welche die Trauer über den tragischen Tod der beiden Heroen verkörperte (Ov. met. 10,164–166; 206–216; vgl. Plin. nat. 21,66).

1 SCHWYZER, Gramm.

S. AMIGUES, H. – Fleur mythique et plantes réelles, in: REG 105, 1992, 19–36. B.HE.

Hyampolis (Ὑάμπολις). Stadt der östl. → Phokis, h. Bogdanou auf der Hochebene von Kalapodi; in der Ant. Hauptzugang von Nordgriechenland in das Kephisos-Tal (Hdt. 8,28; Paus. 10,1,11) über Thermopylai und die Ebene von Opus. Die Akropolis von H. liegt auf einer Anhöhe an der Vereinigung des zur Ebene von Exarchos hinabführenden (→ Abai, Entfernung ca. 2,5 km) Durchgangs mit dem Tal, das von der Straße nach Orchomenos durchquert wird. Etym. von *Hyántōn pólis* abgeleitet (Paus. 10,35,5; Strab. 9,2,3; 9,3,15). Im Schiffskat. (Hom. Il. 2,519–523) erwähnt. Wegen der Lage am Ausgang eines Grenzpasses war H. (wie Abai) für die Kontrolle der Phokis und des Übergangs nach Süd- und Mittelgriechenland von strategischer Bed. Die thessal. Herrschaft über Phokis fand mit dem phok. Sieg bei Kleonai ihr Ende. 480 v. Chr. von den Persern gebrandschatzt (Hdt. 8,33–35), 395 von den Boiotern, 371 von Iason von Pherai, im 3. Hl. Krieg geplündert (Hell. Oxyrh. 18(13),5; Xen. Hell. 6,4,27; Diod. 16,56), 346 von Philippos II. zerstört (Paus. 10,3,1–2), 196 von Flamininus erstürmt (Liv. 32,18,6).

Stadtmauerreste stammen aus dem 4. Jh. v. Chr. Die Überreste eines klass. Tempels (46 × 19 m) auf einer Höhe am Rande der Ebene von Kalapodi, 5 km nördl. von H., gehören zum Heiligtum der Artemis Elaphebolos, der Hauptgottheit von H. (Paus. 10,35,7; Plin. nat. 4,27), zu deren Ehren die Elaphebolia gefeiert wurden (IG IX, I, 90; vgl. Plut. De mulierum virtutibus 24b, symp. 4,1,1 660d). Anhand von Weihegaben und Inschr. läßt sich die Gesch. des Heiligtums bis in die geom. Zeit mit verschiedenen Bauphasen vom 9. Jh. bis in klass. Zeit verfolgen [1]: Ausbauphase 575/550 v. Chr.; Errichtung des klass. Tempels, der durch Erdbeben 426 v. Chr. beschädigt, gegen E. des Jh. restauriert wurde. Noch in der Kaiserzeit war H. besiedelt und wurde der Tempel aufgesucht; in der Nähe des Tempels liegen byz. Gräber [2].

1 R.C.S. FELSCH, H.J. KIENAST, H. SCHULER, Apollon und Artemis oder Artemis und Apollon?, in: AA 1980, 30–123
2 R.C.S. FELSCH, Kalapodi, in: AA 1987, 1–99.

P. ELLINGER, La légende nationale phocidienne, 1993 • J.M. FOSSEY, The ancient topography of Eastern Phokis, 1986, 72–76 • P. SIEWERT, Inschr. aus dem Heiligtum von H. bei Kalapodi, in: AA 1987, 681–687. G.D.R./Ü: J.W.M.

Hyantes (Ὕαντες). Alter nicht-griech. Volksstamm in Boiotien, von den Phöniziern unter Kadmos vertrieben, gründete Hyas bzw. → Hyampolis in der östl. Phokis (schol. Pind. O. 6,148; schol. Apoll. Rhod. 3,1242; Strab. 7,7,1; 9,2,3; Paus. 10,35,5).

G. HUXLEY, Aetolian H. in Phrynichus, in: GRBS 27, 1986, 235 ff. HE.KA.

Hyas (Ὕας). Sohn des → Atlas [2] und der → Aithra, kam in Libyen auf der Jagd um. Mehrere seiner Schwestern starben aus Trauer und wurden darauf von Zeus als Sternbild (→ Hyaden) an den Himmel versetzt (Timaios FGrH 566 F 91; Hyg. astr. 2,21; fab. 192; Ov. fast. 5,170–182).

E. SIEBERT, s. v. H., LIMC 5.1, 550f. HE. KA.

Hybadai (Ὑβάδαι). Att. Mesogeia(?)-Demos der Phyle Leontis, mit zwei (einem) → *buleutaí*. Lage unbekannt.

E. MEYER, s. v. H., RE Suppl. 10, 327 • TRAILL, Attica, 6, 18, 46, 62, 69, 110 Nr. 57, Tab. 4 • Ders., Demos and Trittys, 1986, 131. H. LO.

Hybla (Ὕβλα).

[1] H. Megale/Heraia (Ὕ. Μεγάλη, Ἡραία). Die Existenz von H. ist unbestreitbar (anders [6]), die Lokalisierung des Ortes bei Ragusa (auf Sizilien) aber nicht gesichert. Hippokrates, der Herrscher von H., starb während der Belagerung durch die Sikuler 491 v. Chr. (Hdt. 7,155,1). H. hat drei Br.-Münzemissionen mit der Legende Ὕβλας Μεγάλας herausgegeben, deren Umlauf auf einen kleinen Bereich (um Ragusa, Modica, Vizzini) beschränkt war. Entscheidend ist die Liste der Theorodokoi von Delphoi, in der Υβλας nach Kamarina und vor Hergetion geführt wird. Nicht eindeutig ist Nonn. Dion. 13,311–313. Vgl. Itin. Anton. 89; Paus. 5,23 (»größer«).

1 G. MANGANARO, Alla ricerca di poleis mikrai della Sicilia centro-orientale, in: Orbis Terrarum 2, 1996, 130 mit Nr. 12 **2** Ders., Un Kerykeion perduto degli Hipanatai e la ubicazione di Hipana, in: Orbis Terrarum 3, 1997, 128 mit Nr. 11. **3** BTCGI 14, 1996, 538ff. **4** BTCGI 8, 1990, 220f. **5** R. J. A. WILSON, Sicily under the Roman Empire, 1990 **6** E. MANNI, Geografia fisica et politica della Sicilia ant. (Testimonia Siciliae antiqua 1,1), Kokalos Suppl. 4, 1981, 184–186 **7** S. NICITA, Dossier Ibla, Prov. Reg. Ragusa, 1997.

[2] H. Geleatis/Gereatis (Ὕ. Γελεᾶτις, Thuk. 6,62,5; Γερεᾶτις, Paus. 5,23,6: »Siedlung der Katanaioi«). Stadt auf Sizilien nahe釘Posternò bei Inessa-Aitna (h. Civita). Die Athener verwüsteten 414 v. Chr. H. und H. [1] (Thuk. 6,94,3; 63,2). Nach Paus. 5,23 gab es in H. ein Heiligtum der Göttin Hyblaia mit Priestern als Traumdeutern (vgl. FGrH 556 F 57). H. soll in archa. Zeit Olympia eine Zeusstatue mit Zepter geweiht haben. Hyblaia war eine Aphrodite (wohl die mit einem Vogel auf der ausgestreckten Hand dargestellte Figur auf dem Rv. von katanischen Br.-Mz. des 2. Jh. v. Chr.), in einer Weihinschr. als *Venus Victrix Hyblensis* bezeichnet (CIL X 2,7013) und im → *Pervigilium Veneris* verehrt.

R. J. A. WILSON, Sicily under the Roman Empire, 1990, 410 Nr. 79 • BTCGI 13, 1994, 383ff. • BTCGI 8, 1990, 226f.

[3] Eine dritte Stadt dieses Namens hat es nie gegeben. Ihre Existenz wurde irrig aus Steph. Byz. s. v. Ὕ. gefolgert, der verschiedene geogr. und historiographische Trad. kontaminiert, wenn er, um Megara im Norden von Syrakusai von der gleichnamigen Mutterstadt in Griechenland zu unterscheiden, den Beinamen οἱ Μεγαρεῖς Ὑβλαῖοι κληθέντες (»die sog. megarischen Hyblaier«) nach dem Namen des Sikulerkönigs Hyblon (Ὕβλων, Thuk. 6,4,1) hinzufügt. GI. MA./Ü: H. D.

Hybreas (Ὑβρέας). Griech. Redner und Politiker des 1. Jh. v. Chr. aus Mylasa in Karien. Er kam aus einfachsten Verhältnissen (Strab. 14,2,24 = 659), genoß aber in Antiocheia Unterricht bei dem Rhetor Diotrephes. In seine Heimatstadt zurückgekehrt, kam er zu Einfluß und Vermögen und wurde nach dem Tod seines Rivalen Euthydemos zum mächtigsten Mann in Mylasa; er hatte u. a. das Amt des → Agoranomos inne (ebd.). In den Auseinandersetzungen nach Caesars Ermordung stand H. auf seiten der Triumvirn, wies aber im Jahre 41 als Wortführer kleinasiatischer Städte Tributforderungen des M. Antonius [I 9] zurück (Plut. Antonius 24,7f.). Ein Jahr später mußte er vor Labienus nach Rhodos fliehen, kehrte nach dessen Ende aber wieder nach Mylasa zurück und baute die Stadt wieder auf (Strab. 14,2,24 = 660). H. genoß zu seinen Lebzeiten außerordentlichen rhetor. Ruhm (Strab. 13,4,5 = 630; Hier. chron. z.J. 32 v. Chr.), der einige auf ihn bezogene Anekdoten erklären kann (vgl. Strab. 14,2,24 = 659f.; Val. Max. 9,14). Die wenigen, bei Seneca (z. B. contr. 1,2,23; 2,5,20; 9,1,12; 9,6,16) überl. Proben sind Musterbeispiele des asianischen Stiles (→ Asianismus). Sen. suas. 7,14 kennt auch H.' gleichnamigen Sohn als Rhetor und Anwalt in der Prov. Asia. M. W.

Hybrias (Ὑβρίας). Am Ende einer Scholiensammlung fügt Athen. 695f ein Gedicht von H. von Kreta hinzu, das ›manche für ein Scholion halten‹ [1]. H. brüstet sich darin, Herr über die öffentlichen Sklaven (δεσπότας μνοΐας) zu sein und vom Soldatenberuf zu leben. Das Gedicht wurde früher als das Kriegerlied eines dor. Adligen, jetzt gemeinhin als Prahlerei eines Mannes angesehen, der aus der Schicht stammt, die er nun beherrscht [2]. Ein Bezug auf den pers. Großkönig legt die Mitte des 6. Jh. als *terminus post quem* nahe. Die zwei Strophen bestehen hauptsächlich aus Trochäen, Choriamben und Glykoneen; der Dialekt weist Spuren des Dor. auf.
→ Arbeitslieder

1 PMG 909 **2** D. L. PAGE, The Song of H. the Cretan, in: PCPhS 191, 1965, 62–65. E. R./Ü: L. S.

Hybride Münzen, auch als »Zwittermünzen« bezeichnet. Es handelt sich um Mz., bei denen Av. und Rv. nicht zusammen gehören. Teils entstanden h.M. durch ein Versehen des Personals einer Prägestätte, indem Prägestempel gleichzeitiger Emissionen miteinander gekoppelt wurden (Quinar, Rom, 261 n. Chr., Av. Gallienus, Rv. Salonina, s. [1]), teils wurden Stempel eines früheren Herrschers unter seinem Nachfolger weiter verwendet (Rv. des Aemilianus unter Gallienus, [2]). Letztere kann man als offizielle h.M. bezeichnen. In

Inflationszeiten mit hohem Münzausstoß begegnen h.M. häufig, wie die Antoniniane des → Gallienus zeigen, die während seiner Alleinherrschaft (261–268 n. Chr.) geprägt wurden. Hier war die mangelnde oder gar fehlende Kontrolle der Münzprägung ursächlich.

Ein nicht unbeträchtlicher Teil der h.M. sind bewußte → Münzfälschungen, die mit Kopien von Originalstempeln oder gestohlenen Stempeln hergestellt wurden.

1 Göbl II, 141 Nr. 304 2 C. Brenot, M. Christol, Un antoninianus de Gallien au revers d'Émilien, Bulletin de la Société Française de Numismatique, 1976, 84f.

Göbl I,55,222 • Schrötter, s. v. Zwittermünzen, 761 f. GE.S.

Hybris (ὕβρις). Ethischer Begriff zur Bezeichnung absichtlich entehrenden Verhaltens einschließlich erniedrigender körperlicher Übergriffe wie z.B. Vergewaltigung (maßgebliche Definition: Aristoteles rhet. 1378 b; lat. *superbia*). Etym. ist *h.* wohl von hethit. *huwap-*: »mißhandeln« mit Subst. **huwappar* > **huppar* abzuleiten [1]. Positive Gegenbegriffe: → *aidṓs*, → *díkē*, → *eunomía*, → *sōphrosýnē*.

I. Allgemein II. Juristisch

I. Allgemein

In der frühgriech. Lit. erscheint *h.* in der vielfach variierten Begriffskette *ólbos – kóros – hýbris – átē* (»Reichtum« – »Sattheit« – »Übermut« – »Verderben«; z.B. Aischyl. Ag. 750–771). Als eindeutige Personifikation läßt sich appellativer Gebrauch in metaphor. Kontext dort (z.B. Hes. erg. 213–218; Sol. fr. 6,3–4 IEG; Aischyl. Pers. 821; Pind. O. 13,10; Hdt. 8,77) jedoch nicht bestimmen (ikonograph. erst im 3. Jh. n. Chr., in der Nähe frühchristl. Kunst [4]). Ein Kult ist auch durch die z.B. schon von Cicero (leg. 2,11,28) mißverstandenen *líthoi hýbreōs kai anaideías* (»die Steine der H. und der Schamlosigkeit« als Standort von Angeklagten bzw. dem Ankläger auf dem Areopag) nicht zu belegen.

1 O. Szemerenyi, The Origins of the Greek Lexicon: ex oriente lux, in: JHS 94, 1974, 154 2 D. L. Cairns, Aidôs. The Psychology and Ethics of Honour and Shame in Ancient Greek Literature, 1993 3 M. L. West (ed.), Hesiod, Works & Days, 1978, zu V. 213 4 H. A. Shapiro, Personifications in Greek Art. The Representation of Abstract Concepts 600–400 B.C., 1993, 41 mit Anm. 29.

N. R. E. Fisher, H. A Study in the Values of Honour and Shame in Ancient Greece, 1992 (ausführliche Bibliogr.) • E. H. Loeb, s. v. H. (1), LIMC 5.1, 551–553 • J. Procopé, s. v. Hochmut, RAC 15, 795–858. T.H.

II. Juristisch

In Demosth. or. 21,47 ist ein Gesetz überliefert, das den weiten Tatbestand der *h.* als mit Schriftklage (→ *graphḗ*) zu verfolgendes Verbrechen gegen die staatliche Ordnung umschreibt: ›Wer ein Kind, eine Frau oder einen Mann, seien sie Freie oder Sklaven, tätlich beleidigt oder gegen sie etwas Gesetzeswidriges unternimmt . . .‹. Wie bei der → *asébeia* handelte es sich um eine Vorschrift, die dem Geschworenengericht (→ *dikastḗrion*) einen weiten Beurteilungsspielraum ließ. Der Täter mußte die körperliche Integrität des Opfers in herabwürdigender, sich selbst überhebender Gesinnung verletzt haben; auch sexuelle Angriffe fielen darunter. Bloße empfangene Schläge konnten nur vom Opfer selbst mit der privaten → *aikeías díkē* verfolgt werden. Daß für ein Opfer von *h.* jeder Bürger mit Popularklage eintreten konnte, machte die γραφὴ ὕβρεως (*graphḗ hýbreōs*) zu einem wirksamen Instrument, die Egalität in der athenischen Gesellschaft zu kontrollieren. Die Klage war bei den → Thesmotheten einzubringen, die schätzbare (→ *timētós agṓn*) Geldbuße fiel an den Staat. Der Kläger hatte also materiell nichts zu gewinnen, jedoch 1000 Drachmen zu zahlen, wenn er die Klage fallen ließ oder nicht ein Fünftel der Richterstimmen erhielt.

A. R. W. Harrison, The Law of Athens II, 1997 • D. Cohen, Law, Violence and Community in Classical Athens, 1995. G.T.

Hydarnes (altpers. *Vidṛna*, elam. *Miturna*, *Mitarna*). Häufiger pers. Name mehrerer Personen unterschiedlicher sozialer Stellung in den Persepolis-Täfelchen. Ktesias erwähnt passim Heiraten zwischen Hydarniden und der königlichen Familie. Wichtigste Namensträger sind:

[1] H., Sohn des Bagabigna, Helfer des Dareios [1] [2. DB 4.84] gegen (Pseudo)-Bardiya [2](→ Gaumāta), der 522 v. Chr. die rebellierenden Meder besiegte [2. DB 2.19, 21]; nach Hdt. 3,70 handelt es sich bei ihm um einen von Aspathines in das Komplott einbezogenen Mitverschwörer gegen (Pseudo-) → Smerdis. Ktesias' Idernes ist wohl der einzig korrekte Name in dessen Liste der sieben Verbündeten des Dareios (FGrH 680 F 13.16). H. war während der Regierung des Dareios [1] in Medien tätig, wahrscheinlich als Satrap [3. PF 1483; 4. 84]. Das schließt sein gleichzeitiges Agieren in Thrakien und die Identifizierung mit dem von Hdt. 6,133 erwähnten H. [2] aus [3. PF 1363, 2055].

[2] Perser, der nach Hdt. 6,133 in Thrakien aktiv war; nicht, wie zu Unrecht [4. 84] in der Lit. behauptet wird, identisch mit H. [1], der zu dieser Zeit wahrscheinlich als Satrap in Medien tätig war [3. PF 1363,2055].

[3] Sohn des H. [1], empfing als *stratēgós* in Sardis Sperthias und Bulis; kommandierte 480 v. Chr. das Elitekorps der 10000 »Unsterblichen« und führte diese bei den → Thermopylen entlang dem von Ephialtes gewiesenen Weg (Hdt. 7,215).

[4] Vater des Tissaphernes.

[5] Kommandant z. Z. Dareios' III.

1 Briant, 607 2 R. Kent, Old Persian, 1953, 208 (zu Familien-Beziehungen der Hydarniden) 3 R. T. Hallock, Persepolis Fortification Tablets, 1969 4 D. Lewis, Sparta and Persia 1977. A.KU.u.H.S.-W.

Hydaspes (Ὑδάσπης; Βιδάσπης bei Ptol.), wahrscheinl. aus altind. *Vitastā* (wohl durch iran. Vermittlung); einer der Hauptflüsse des Pandschab, h. Jhelum in Pakistan, entspringt im West-Himalaya und mündet in den → Akesines [2]. An einer nicht mehr sicher identifizierbaren Stelle an dessen linkem Ufer kämpfte Alexander gegen → Poros, nachdem er den Fluß bei heftigem Monsunregen überschritten hatte. Nach der Schlacht wurden die Zwillingsstädte → Nikaia und → Bukephala gegründet (Arr. an. 5,9–19; 29; Diod. 17,87–89; 95; Curt. 8,13f.; 9,3). Nach Alexanders Rückkehr vom → Hyphasis wurde hier die Stromflotte gebaut; der Feldzug ging dann weiter flußabwärts zum Akesines und → Indos. Aus der Alexandergesch. war der H. so allgemein bekannt, daß man den Namen in der röm. Lit. als Synonym für ganz Indien gebrauchen konnte (z. B. Hor. carm. 1,22,8).

K. KARTTUNEN, India and the Hellenistic World, 1997, Index s. v. H. K. K.

Hydatius

[1] (Ydacius). Bischof von Emerita (Merida/Spanien), † vor 392. Vehementer Gegner des → Priscillianus, gegen den er 380 die Synode von Saragossa einberief. H. erreichte dessen Verurteilung und später (385) Hinrichtung durch den Imperator Maximus. Seine Härte gegen die Priscillianer, genährt von persönl. Abneigungen, wurde von etlichen Bischöfen (→ Martinus von Tours, → Ambrosius, → Siricius) verurteilt und führte zu seiner Absetzung 388.

Sulpicius Severus, Chronica II, 46–51, CSEL 1,99–105 • Priscillianus, Liber ad Damasum, CSEL 18,34–43 • A. FRANZEN, s. v. Priscillianismus, LThK[2] 8, 769–771 • J. MARTIN, s. v. Priscillian, LThK[2] 8, 768–769 • O. SEECK, s. v. H. (1), RE 9, 39f.

[2] Chronist, * um 394 in Limia (Xinzo de Limia/Nordwestspanien), 427 Bischof von (vermutlich) Aquae Sextiae (Aix-en-Provence), † nach 468. Als Jugendlicher lernte er auf einer Palästinareise → Hieronymus kennen. Die *Chronica*, die H. später abfaßte, schließen an die Chronik des Hieronymus (abgebrochen 378) an und reichen bis 468. Sie sind für die Gesch. Spaniens im 5. Jh. die wichtigste Quelle. Die *Fasti* bieten ab Ende 3. Jh. bis 468 ein Konsularverzeichnis von Konstantinopel, kompiliert aus mehreren Quellen.

Chronica: PL 74,701–750 • Fasti: MGH AA IX, 197–247 • O. SEECK, s. v. H. (2), RE 9, 40–43. RO. F.

Hydra

[1] (Ὕδρα, »Wasserschlange«). Ungeheuer, das von den Ungetümen → Typhon und → Echidna (»Schlange«) geboren und von → Hera aus Groll über Zeus aufgezogen wird. Sie haust an der Quelle der → Amymone in den Sümpfen von Lerna, raubt Vieh und Menschen und wird schließlich von → Herakles getötet (Hes. theog. 313–318; Diod. 4,11,5f.; Apollod. 2,77–80; Hyg. fab. 30), trotz der Hilfe einer von Hera gesandten Krabbe; in der kanonischen Reihenfolge ist dies Herakles' zweite Tat. Das Gift der H., gegen das sich Herakles mit seinem Löwenfell schützt, benutzt er, um seine Pfeile tödlich zu machen; ein von Herakles getroffener Kentaur flieht zum eleischen Fluß Anigros, dessen übler Geruch von diesem Gift stammt (Paus. 5,5,9). Seit dem frühesten Bild (boiot. Fibel um 700 v. Chr. [1]) ist die H. vielköpfig; in die Lit. ist dies zuerst von → Peisandros von Rhodos, einem Epiker des mittleren 7. Jh., übernommen worden (Paus. 2,37,4). Die Zahl der Köpfe schwankt (meist sind es neun, doch auch fünfzig, Verg. Aen. 6,576, oder hundert, Eur. Herc. 1190), und sie wachsen nach; doch → Iolaos sengt sie ab, nur der neunte Kopf ist unsterblich und wird von ihm unter einem Felsblock vergraben (sichtbar an der Straße von Lerna nach Elaious, Apollod. 2,80). In den Sternsagen werden sowohl die H. (als Sternbild der H.) wie die Krabbe (als Krebs) verstirnt (Eratosth. Katasterismoi 11.13.16; Hyg. astr. 2,23).

Der Kampf des Herakles gegen die H. ist seit der orientalisierenden Kunst oft bildlich dargestellt worden. Er nimmt sowohl in der Erzählung vom Kampf des Heroen gegen ein Schlangenungeheuer wie in der spezifischen Ikonographie vorderasiatische Motive auf, etwa vom Kampf → Ninurtas gegen eine siebenköpfige Schlange, → Baals Kampf gegen ein Meerwesen (Tiamat, Leviathan) oder die hethit. Erzählung vom Kampf gegen die Schlange Iluyankas [2; 3]. In der allegorischen Deutung ist die Gesch. meist auf die Trockenlegung des lernäischen Sumpfes durch den Kulturbringer Herakles bezogen worden (Serv. Aen. 6,287), was sich bis in die mod. Forsch. gehalten hat.

1 K. SCHEFOLD, Frühgriech. Sagenbilder, 1964, Abb. 6a
2 J. FONTENROSE, Python. A Study of Delphic Mythology, 1959 3 M. L. WEST, The East Face of Helicon. West Asiatic Elements in Greek Poetry and Myth, 1997, 461.

G. KOKKOROU-ALEWAS, s. v. Herakles IVC, LIMC 5.1, 34–43. F. G.

[2] See im Westen der Aitolia, auch → Konope und (wie h.) → Lysimacheia gen. (Strab. 10,2,22; Ov. met. 7,371–373; Antonius Liberalis 12).

C. ANTONETTI, Les Étoliens, 1990 • F. BÖLTE, s. v. H., RE 9, 50–52. D. S.

Hydraletes s. Mühlen

Hydraotes (Ὑδραώτης bei Arr., Ὑάρωτις/*Hyárōtis* bei Strab., *Hiarotis* bei Curt. beruht auf einer mittelind. Form für altind. *Airāvatī*/Irāwatī, wohl durch iran. Vermittlung und in Anlehnung an griech. ὕδωρ); einer der Hauptflüsse des Pandschab, h. Rāvī in Pakistan; entspringt im West-Himalaya, mündet in den → Akesines [2] (Chenāb) und wurde den Griechen durch den Alexanderzug bekannt.

E. KIESSLING, s. v. Hyarotis, RE 9, 23f. K. K.

Hydrargyrum s. Quecksilber

Hydraulis s. Musikinstrumente

Hydrea (Ὑδρέα). Insel vor der Ostküste der argolischen Akte, felsig, wenig fruchtbar, schon in myk. Zeit besiedelt, h. Hydra; gehörte zunächst zu → Hermione, dann zu Troizen. Belegstellen: Hdt. 3,59; Paus. 2,34,9; Steph. Byz. s. v. H.; Inschr.: SEG 1, 79f.; 17, 172–177.

N. PHARAKLAS, Ἑρμιονίς, 1972. Y. L.

Hydria (ἡ ὑδρία). Dreihenkliger Wasserkrug mit enger Mündung, wie er inschr. in der Troilos-Szene des Klitias-Kraters (Florenz, AM) als H. bezeichnet ist. Die Form kommt schon in der FH-Keramik und auf myk. Tontafeln von → Pylos vor (dort mit der Bezeichnung *ka-ti*). Die ältere Kugelform wurde im 6. Jh. v. Chr., nun auch in Bronze und Silber, durch die gestreckte Schulter-H. und etwas später die »Kalpis« mit durchlaufendem Profil abgelöst (→ Gefäße Abb. B 11–12). Sehr schlanke H. gab es noch im 4. Jh. v. Chr. bis in den Hell.; in der röm. Kaiserzeit waren H. dagegen nicht mehr gebräuchlich. Verwendet wurde die H. primär an Quelle und Brunnenhaus (→ Brunnen), nicht aber am Schöpfbrunnen. Den Gebrauch illustrieren Bilder, insbes. auf att. H. selbst. Das horizontale Henkelpaar diente zum Anheben der gefüllten H., der Vertikalhenkel zum Tragen des leeren Gefäßes und zum Kippen. Frauen trugen sie mit Polster, der τύλη (*týlē*), auf dem Kopf, Männer in der Regel auf der Schulter. Zum tägl. Wasserholen benutzte man grobkeramische und bronzene H., nicht die bemalter Feinkeramik. Gemäß der Bed. des Wassers als lebenerhaltendes und reinigendes Element sowie als Mischwasser für Wein übernahm die H. zahlreiche kult. Funktionen, zu denen auch feierliche Hydrophorien gehörten. H. sind außerdem als Siegespreise, Weihgaben, Grabbeigaben, Brautgeschenke und als Behälter von Totenasche bezeugt.

E. DIEHL, Die H. Formgesch. und Verwendung im Kult des Alt., 1964 • E. MANAKIDOU, Athenerinnen in sf. Brunnenhausszenen, in: Hephaistos 11/12, 1992/93, 51–91 • C. ROLLEY, Hydries de Bronze dans Péloponnèse du Nord, in: BCH 87, 1963, 459–484. I. S.

Hydromanteia s. Divination

Hydruntum I. BRONZE- BIS KAISERZEIT II. BYZANTINISCHE ZEIT

I. BRONZE- BIS KAISERZEIT

Hafenstadt an der iapygischen Küste (angeblich von Kretern gegr., Steph. Byz. s. v. Βίεννος), ca. 70 km südl. von → Brundisium im Bereich zw. adriat. und ion. Meer (Liv. 36,21,5; Plin. nat. 3,100; CIL X 1795; Ps.-Skyl. 14; 27; Strab. 6,3,4), wo die Überfahrt nach Griechenland am kürzesten ist (Plin. nat. 3,100f.; vgl. Cic. Att. 15,21,3; aber Lucan. 5,375: *avius Hydrus* [1]), h. Otranto. H. spielte in der Br.- (myk. Funde) [2; 3] und Eisenzeit (Siedlungsreste des 9./8. Jh. v. Chr., älteste euböische, korinth., aber auch alban. Keramik-Importe in It.) [2; 4; 5], in archa. [5; 6], bes. aber in spätant. und byz. Zeit eine wichtige Rolle (Cassiod. var. 1,2; Prok. BV 1,1; Prok. BG 1,15) [2; 8]. Im 4./3. Jh. befestigt [7]. Das *municipium* war in der Kaiserzeit eine wichtige See- und Landstation der *via Appia Traiana* (Itin. Anton. 119; 323; 329; Itin. Marit. 489; 497; 521; Itin. Burd. 609; Tab. Peut. 6f.) [1; 2; 8].

1 F. D'ANDRIA, D. MORESCHINI, s. v. Otranto, BTCGI 13, 1994, 127–142 (mit ant. Quellenbelegen und Bibliogr. bis 1993) 2 F. D'ANDRIA, s. v. Otranto, EAA² Suppl. 2, 148–150 3 M. A. ORLANDO, L'età del Bronzo recente e finale a Otranto, in: Studi di Antichità 4, 1983, 67–118
4 F. D'ANDRIA, Salento arcaico, 1979, 18–24 5 Ders. (Hrsg.), Archeologia dei Messapi, 1990, 21–48
6 G. SEMERARO, Otranto dal 6. secolo a.C. all'età ellenistica, in: Studi di Antichità 4, 1983, 125–212 7 F. D'ANDRIA, Otranto, in: Studi di Antichità 8,2, 1996, 189–206
8 D. MICHAELIDES u. a. (Hrsg.), Excavations at Otranto, I–II, 1992. M. L.

II. BYZANTINISCHE ZEIT

Der Hafen von H. gewann seit dem 6. Jh. für die Byzantiner als Anlaufstelle für mil. Unternehmungen nach Italien zu Lasten von → Brundisium überragende Bed. Vom 9.–11. Jh. führten alle bekannten byz. Expeditionen über diesen Brückenkopf, bis H. im J. 1068 endgültig von den Normannen erobert und nun umgekehrt zum Ausgangspunkt für Fahrten nach Osten (auch bei Kreuzzügen) gemacht wurde. Die mil. Bed. wird auch durch die Anwesenheit eines *tribunus* (im J. 599, Greg. epist. 9,201; 206 NORBERG) und die Einrichtung eines Dukats im 8. und 9. Jh. bezeugt, doch wurde nach 876 Bari der Hauptort des → Themas Langobardia. Das Bistum H. ist erst seit 595 nachgewiesen (Greg. M. epist. 6,21; 9,170; 201; 11,57 NORBERG); es wurde im 9. Jh. (bald nach 876?) zum autokephalen Erzbistum, 968 zur Metropolis einer eigenen Kirchenprovinz erhoben. Auch nach dem Abzug der Byzantiner blieb H. eines der Zentren griech. Kultur in Süditalien, wovon bed. Kirchenbauten und eine vielfältige Wissens- und Buchkultur zeugen.

T. S. BROWN, D. KINNEY, s. v. Otranto, ODB 3, 1541 • G. CAVALLO, Libri greci e resistenza etnica in Terra d'Otranto, in: G. CAVALLO (Hrsg.), Libri e lettori nel mondo bizantino. Guida storica e critica, 1982, 155–178, 223–227 • N. KAMP, s. v. Otranto, LMA 6, 1592 (Lit. vor 1993) • S. PALESE, s. v. Otranto, LThK³ 7, 1217 • J. WEISS, s. v. H., RE 9, 87. E. W.

Hydrussa (Ὑδροῦσσα; auch Ὑδρόεσσα, Ὑδροῦσα, Ὕδρουσα, *Hydróessa*, *Hydrúsa*, *Hýdrusa*; »die Wasserreiche«). Name mehrerer Inseln, in Attika nach Strab. 9,1,21 → Aixone vorgelagert. Die Bezeichnung paßt indes auf keines dieser Felseilande vor der Westküste von Attika.

L. BÜRCHNER, s. v. H., RE 9, 79 • W. KOLBE, s. v. H., RE 9, 87. H. LO.

Hyettos (Ὑηττός). Stadt in Boiotia nördl. der Kopais, nordöstl. von Orchomenos, östl. vom h. Loutsi; Lokalisierung durch Inschr. für Septimius Severus und Caracalla gesichert (IG VII 2833 f.). Mindestens von archa. bis in byz. Zeit besiedelt, im 5. und 6. Jh. n. Chr. Bischofssitz. Zahlreiche Überreste, reiches Inschr.-Material (IG VII und [1]). Mitglied des Boiot. Bundes, stellte im 5/4. Jh. v. Chr. gemeinsam mit Orchomenos zwei Boiotarchen (Hell. Oxyrh. 19,3,390: Ὑσιαῖοι). Herakleshеiligtum mit Heilkult (Paus. 9,24,3; 36,6 f.; [2. 2 f.]). Spuren von Erzbergbau.

1 R. Etienne, D. Knoepfler, Hyettos de Béotie et la chronologie des archontes fédéraux entre 250 et 171 avant J.-C., 1976 2 Schachter 2.

O. Davies, Roman Mines in Europe, 1935, 246 • Fossey, 257–261 • Lauffer, Griechenland, s. v. H. • N. D. Papachatzis, Παυσανίου Ἑλλάδος περιήγησις 5, ²1981, 163–166. M. FE.

Hygiaion (Ὑγιαίων). Herrscher des Bosporan. Reiches (→ Regnum Bosporanum), ca 220–200 v. Chr. Nachfolger des → Leukon II., jedoch nicht als König, sondern als *árchōn*, auch ohne Königsdiadem dargestellt. Vielleicht kein Spartokide. Auf Ziegelstempeln und Münzen ἄρχοντος Ὑγιαίοντος.

V. F. Gaidukevič, Das Bosporan. Reich, 1971, 93, 95. I. v. B.

Hygieia (Ὑγίεια). Personifikation der Gesundheit und neben → Akeso, Iaso und Panakeia eine der Töchter von → Asklepios und → Epione; eine eigene Myth. besitzt sie nicht. Während ihre Schwestern verschiedene Formen des Heilens (griech. *iáomai, akéomai*) in ihrem Namen tragen, ist H. die »Gesundheit« schlechthin und verdrängt als solche seit dem späten 5. Jh. den Rest der Familie mindestens in ihrer kult. Bed. (Aristeid. 38,22). Im Kult wird gewöhnlich nur sie zusammen mit Asklepios angerufen, H. erhält aber auch allein Dedikationen für Heilungen. Auf den Weihreliefs ist sie als seine alleinige weibliche Gefährtin dargestellt; die späte Überl. macht sie gar zu seiner Frau (Orph. h. 67). Die älteste Darstellung ist eine von Mikythos von Rhegion geweihte Gruppe von H. und Asklepios in Olympia (vor 450 v. Chr., Paus. 5,26,2). Auffallenden Kult hat sie in Titane, wo sie in einem von → Machaons Sohn Alexanor gegr. Asklepieion mit Haaropfern verehrt wurde, die ihr Bild völlig verdeckten; das Alter des Kultes ist unklar, wenigstens Asklepios' Statue ist hochaltertümlich (Paus. 2,11,6). Auf der athenischen Akropolis stand ihr Bild neben demjenigen der Athena H., deren Kult seit dem späten 6. Jh. v. Chr. inschr. belegt und damit deutlich älter ist als derjenige von Asklepios (und damit H.), der 421/20 v. Chr. eingeführt wurde; spätere Autoren verbinden die Statue der Athena H., nicht aber die Einführung des Kults, mit → Perikles (Plut. Perikles 13). Athenas Epiklese H. ist neben der Personifikation eine andere, ältere Form, eine Gottheit mit dem Schutz der Gesundheit zu betrauen.

H. Sobel, H. Die Göttin der Gesundheit, 1990 • F. Croissant, s. v. H., LIMC 5, 554–572 • H. A. Shapiro, Personifications in Greek Art, 1993, 125–131. F. G.

Hygiene s. Körperpflege

Hyginus, C. Iulius I. Leben und Werk II. Hyginus als Agrarschriftsteller

I. Leben und Werk

a) Philologe und Polyhistor der augusteischen Zeit aus Spanien oder Alexandreia, Freigelassener des Augustus, nach 28 v. Chr. Präfekt der palatinischen Bibl. bei gleichzeitiger ausgedehnter Lehrtätigkeit (zur Biogr. vgl. Suet. gramm. 20). Dennoch mußte er zeitlebens von Clodius [II 6] Licinus unterstützt werden und starb arm; Ov. trist. 3,14 ist an ihn gerichtet. Sein umfangreiches Œuvre umfaßte philol. (Komm. zum *Propempticon Pollionis* des → Helvius [I 3] Cinna; Besprechung ausgewählter Stellen aus → Vergil, vgl. [5. 51–67]), histor.-antiquarische (Exempla, vgl. [9. 63 ff.]; *De familiis Troianis*, vgl. [6]; über ital. Städte; *De proprietatibus deorum; De dis penatibus*) und landwirtschaftliche Werke (*De agricultura; De apibus*); zahlreiche Fr. sind erh. Von seiner polit. Biographienslg. *De viris illustribus*, die 9 B. zu je 21 Viten enthielt, ist das anon. überl., h. überwiegend Cornelius → Nepos zugeschriebene B. *De excellentibus ducibus exterarum gentium* bewahrt (vgl. [7. 1645 ff.]). Zum Weiterwirken (Elogien des Augustus-Forums; → Valerius Maximus; → Ampelius, HLL § 530; die spätant. *Viri illustres*, HLL § 532.3) dieser wichtigen frühaugusteischen, von → Livius weitgehend verdrängten Gesch.-Quelle vgl. [7. 1636 ff., 1647 ff. und Stemma 1654; 8. 1,52 ff.; 2,9 ff.]; zu den Exempla bei Valerius Maximus sowie bei Frontinus s. [9].

b) Wohl vom gleichen Verf. [10. xxxi ff.] stammt ein astronom.-myth. Hdb. in 4 B. (B. 1 und 4: astronom. Erklärungen; B. 2 und 3: Sternsagen und -kataloge). Als Quelle diente eine → Arat-Einführung des → Eratosthenes [2]. Zahlreiche, auch bebilderte Hss. vom 9. Jh. an zeugen für die Beliebtheit des Textes im MA.

c) Damit (vgl. Hyg. astr. 2,12: *De quo in primo libro Genealogiarum scripsimus*) hat auch ein myth. Hdb. seinen Autor und seinen urspr. Titel *Genealogiae* (*Fabulae* in der Überl.) gefunden: Es umfaßt a) Stammbäume von Göttern und Heroen und b) 277 kurze Erzählungen und Listen myth. Inhalts, die ab Nr. 221 dominieren. Bei der Umarbeitung der griech. mythographischen Quelle kam nur wenig Röm. hinzu. Allerdings ist infolge zahlreicher Veränderungen und Interpolationen die urspr. Form des überl. lat. Textes nicht immer feststellbar; so mag von der griech. Fassung der *Hygini Genealogia* in CGL 3,56–69 [18. 172 ff.] einiges auf den Text der dem Erstdruck [17] zugrundeliegenden Hs. (um 900) zurückführen, von der nur Frgg. wiederentdeckt worden sind.

Zu a)
Frgg.: 1 GRF 525–537 2 HRR 2, p. 72–77

3 R. Reitzenstein, De scriptoribus rei rusticae librorum deperditis, 1884, 18 ff.; 53 f.
Lit.: 4 P.v.d. Woestijne, Hyginiana, 1930
5 S. Timpanaro, Per la storia della filologia virgiliana antica, 1986, 51–67 6 P. Toohey, Varro, H. and Horace, in: Arethusa 17, 1984, 5–28 7 P. L. Schmidt, s. v. H., RE Suppl. 15, 1978, 1644–1659 8 J. Fugmann, Königszeit und Frühe Rep. in der Schrift De viris illustribus, 2 Bde., 1990/1997
9 A. Klotz, Stud. zu Valerius Maximus, 1942.
Zu b)
Ed.: 10 A. Boeuffle, 1983 (mit frz. Übers.) 11 G. Viré, 1992.
Lit.: 12 M. Chiabò, L. Roberti, Index verborum, 1990
13 W. Hübner, Nachlese zu H., in: Hermes 113, 1985, 208–224 14 G. Viré, La transmission du De astronomia, in: Revue de l'histoire du texte 11, 1981, 159–276 15 Dies., Informatique et classement des manuscrits. Essai méthodologique sur le De astronomia d'H., 1986 16 Dies., Le texte du De astronomia, in: Latomus 51, 1992, 843–856.
Zu c)
Ed.: 17 J. Micyllus, 1535 18 H. I. Rose, [2]1963 19 P. K. Marshall, 1993 (mit Bibliogr.) 20 J.-Y. Boríaud, H. Mythographus, 1997.
Lit.: 21 H. Matakiewicz, De Hygino mythographo, in: Eos 34, 1932/33, 93–110 22 J. Schwartz, Ps.-Hesiodeia, 1960, 297–314 23 C. Desmedt, Fabulae Hygini, in: RBPh 48, 1970, 26–35 und Bollettino di Studi Latini 3, 1973, 26–34
24 A. B. Breen, The »Fabulae Hygini« reappraised, 1991.
P. L. S.

II. Hyginus als Agrarschriftsteller

H. wurde als → Agrarschriftsteller hochgeschätzt, wie aus seiner Erwähnung in der Liste der älteren Agronomen bei → Columella hervorgeht (Colum. 1,1,13). Bei Plinius wird er als Quellenautor zu den Büchern 10–21 der *Naturalis Historia* aufgeführt. Columella, der H. oft namentlich nennt, bezeichnet ihn als *paedagogus* der Landwirtschaft und rühmt ihn als Autor zusammen mit Vergil und → Celsus [7] (Colum. 9,2,1). Wie die Erwähnungen bei Columella und Plinius zeigen, hat H. wohl alle Zweige der Landwirtschaft behandelt (Colum. 3,11,8: Bodenqualität im Weinbau; Colum. 11,2,83: Ochsenhaltung; Colum. 11,3,62: Rübenanbau; Plin. nat. 13,134: Schneckenklee; Plin. nat. 16,230: Werkzeug aus Holz; Plin. nat. 18,232: Wein). Besonders berühmt war das Buch über die → Bienenzucht (*Liber de apibus*, Colum. 9,13,8), dem Columella in seiner eigenen Darstellung an vielen Stellen gefolgt ist. H., der die Schriften anderer Autoren umfassend ausgewertet hat (Colum. 9,2,1; 9,13,8 zu Aristomachus), widmete dem mythischen Ursprung der Bienenzucht längere Ausführungen, was Columella deswegen kritisiert, weil derartige Schilderungen für den Landwirt wenig nützlich seien (Colum. 9,2,2–5). Ein Charakteristikum seiner Darstellung der Bienenpflege scheint die Genauigkeit der Vorschriften gewesen zu sein (Colum. 9,14,1; 9,14,18).

1 W. Richter (Hrsg.), L. Iunius Columella, Zwölf Bücher über Landwirtschaft, Bd. 3, 1983, 586; 619. H. SCHN.

Hyksos (Ägypt. *Ḥq3.w-ḫ3s.wt* »Herrscher fremder Länder«; griech. Ὑκσώς) werden seit dem späten AR sporadisch Herrscher fremder Völker genannt: Der Turiner Königspap. bezeichnet so eine Dyn. fremdstämmiger Herrscher von sechs Königen (15. Dyn., ca. 1650–1540 v. Chr.) der 2. Zwischenzeit, deren erste Vertreter diesen Titel vor der späteren vollständigen Übernahme der äg. Königstitulatur selbst führten. Iosephos (c. Ap. 1,14,82 ff.), auf → Manetho fußend, bezieht den Terminus inkorrekt und mit ungenauer Etym. auf das Volk, dem diese Könige entstammten. Vor dem Hintergrund einer (arch. nachweisbaren) ausgedehnten kanaanäischen Infiltration im Ostdelta seit der 13. Dyn. gelang es (nach Manetho und durchaus plausibel) in einer Periode dynastischer Schwäche nach dem MR einer Linie asiatischer Invasoren, gewaltsam die Macht in Äg. zu übernehmen. Ausgehend von ihrer Hauptstadt Auaris (Tall aḍ-Ḍabʿa) im Ost-Delta gelang es ihnen, ein bedeutendes Reich aufzubauen, das im Norden wohl Süd-Kanaan erfaßte und im Süden zumindest zeitweise auch das südl. Ober-Äg. bis al-Ǧabalain einschloß. Der ethnische Hintergrund der H. wird anhaltend kontrovers diskutiert; gegenüber Helcks [1. 95] These eines → hurritischen Ursprungs wird heute überwiegend westsemit. Herkunft angenommen. Arch. sind die Träger der H.-Herrschaft der syro-palästin. Mittel-Br.-II-Kultur zuzuordnen; die fortschreitende Anpassung an äg. kulturelle Muster ist deutlich, die Usurpation älterer Denkmäler durch die H. verbreitet. Unter dem vorletzten H.-König Apophis nahm die einheim. 17. Dyn., die sich im südl. Ober-Äg. hatte halten können, den Kampf gegen die Fremdherrschaft auf, der mit dem Sieg des Ahmose und der Gründung des NR (um 1540 v. Chr.) endete. Die Periode der H.-Herrschaft hat z. B. mit der Einführung von Pferd, Streitwagen und Sichelschwert im kulturellen Inventar, v. a. aber im polit. Bewußtsein Ägyptens, wie es sich in polit.-ideologischen Texten ausspricht, tiefe Spuren hinterlassen.
→ Ägypten

1 M. Bietak, s. v. H., LÄ 3, 93–103 2 Ders., Avaris, The Capital of the H., 1996 3 K. S. B. Ryholt, The Political Situation in Egypt During the Second Intermediate Period, 1997, 118–150. S. S.

Hylaia (Ὑλαία). Bewaldetes Gebiet östl. des Borysthenes (Hdt. 4,17; 19; Ps.-Skymn. 844 f.) zw. der Kinburn-Halbinsel und Skadovska in den Steppen des unteren Dnjestrs, zu → Olbia gehörig. Es war in archa. und klass. Zeit für → Skythai und griech. Kolonisten bedeutsam. Der skyth. Name für H. war Abika (Steph. Byz. s. v. Ὑ.). Große Rolle spielte H. in der skyth. Myth. (vgl. Hdt. 4,9; 76). Es wurde ein großes Pruduktions- und Handelszentrum mit Hafenanlagen wohl aus dem 6./5. Jh. v. Chr. entdeckt (Jagorlyckoe poselenie).

J. G. Vinogradov, Olbia, 1981, 14–18. I. v. B.

Hylaios (Ὑλαῖος, »Waldmann«). → Kentaur, dargestellt im Kampf gegen die Lapithen (Verg. georg. 2,457) auf der Françoisvase (6. Jh. v. Chr.); getötet von Theseus (Serv. Aen. 8,294), Herakles (Hor. carm. 2,12,6) oder von → Atalante (Apollod. 3,106; Kall. h. 3,221), der er mit Rhoikos nachstellte. RE. ZI.

Hylas (Ὕλας). Sohn des → Theiodamas (Apollod. 1,117; Apoll. Rhod. 1,1212 f.) und der Menodike (Hyg. fab. 14,11); Lokalheros von → Kios. → Herakles erschlägt wegen Hunger (des Sohns: Kall. fr. 24) Theiodamas im Streit (Apollod. 2,153; Apoll. Rhod. 1,1212–1219, wo Herakles einen Vorwand zum Krieg gegen die Dryoper sucht).

Das weitere nach Apollod. 1,117; Apoll. Rhod. 1,1153–1283: Herakles nimmt H. als Geliebten mit auf die → Argonauten-Fahrt. In Mysien wird H. beim Wasserholen von Nymphen geraubt (in ein Echo verwandelt, Nikandros fr. 48; Antoninus Liberalis 26); während der Suche durch Herakles und → Polyphemos, der H.' Schrei gehört hat, fahren die Argonauten am selben Abend ab, ohne den Verlust zu bemerken. Herakles verpflichtet die Myser durch Geiseln zur Suche nach H.

Von Apollodoros und Apollonios Rhodios hängen ab (unter Weglassung des Polyphemos): Theokr. 13 [1. 177 f.], Prop. 1,20 (wo → Kalais und Zetes H. mit Küssen verfolgen) sowie Val. Fl. 3,481 ff. (3,182 ff. Aristie des H.), wo Iuno einen Anschlag gegen H. durchführt, die Argonauten erst nach sechs Tagen Beratung abfahren und H. dem Herakles auf Iuppiters Veranlassung im Traum erscheint [2. 47 ff.]. Rationalistische Deutung läßt H. vom Schiff oder in die Quelle fallen und ertrinken [3. 112].

Der H.-Mythos bildet das Aition eines lokalen Kultbrauchs, verwandt mit dem des mariandynischen Vegetationsdämons → Bormos [3. 113 f.; 4. 429 f.; 5. 35 f.; 6. 58 f., 218]: Die Einheimischen opfern dem H. an der Quelle und streifen in Wäldern umher, wobei der Priester dreimal H. ruft und das Echo antwortet (Strab. 12,4,3). Daher ist Ὕλαν κραυγάζειν (*Hýlan kraugázein*) sprichwörtlich für vergebliches Suchen [3. 113]. H. in der Kunst: [3. 113; 7].

1 U. v. Wilamowitz-Moellendorff, Die Textgesch. der griech. Bukoliker, 1905 2 J. Adamietz, Zur Komposition der Argonautica des Valerius Flaccus, 1976 3 E. Sittig, s. v. H. (1), RE 9, 110–115 4 Nilsson, Feste 5 P. Kretschmer, Mythische Namen, in: Glotta 14, 1925, 33–36
6 M. Alexiou, The Ritual Element in Greek Tradition, 1974 7 J. Oakley, s. v. H., LIMC 5.1, 574–579. P. D.

Hyle (Ὕλη).

[1] Ort in Boiotia (Hom. Il. 2,500; vgl. Strab. 9,2,26; Steph. Byz. s. v. H., nach Hom. Il. 5,707 ff. (mit Paus. 9,38,7; Strab. 9,2,27) an der Kopais, nach Strab. 9,2,20 an der → Hylike (s. auch Stat. Theb. 7,267 f.); Identifizierungsversuche bei Wallace und Knauss [3. 82 f.; 2. 243–278] mit einem der prähistor. Siedlungsplätze zw. der ehemaligen Kopais und der h. Hylike setzten H. mit den prähistor. Siedlungsresten im Stadtareal von Akraiphia gleich, während Fossey [1. 225–229, 235–243] H. zw. den h. Seen Paralimni und Hylike bei Oungra (mit einer Nachfolgesiedlung weiter südl. bei Klimatariai) sucht.

1 Fossey 2 J. Knauss, Die Melioration des Kopaisbeckens durch die Minyer im 2. Jt. v. Chr., 1987 3 P. W. Wallace, Strabo's Description of Boiotia, 1979. P. F.

[2] Begriff der Naturphilosophie s. Materie

Hylike (Ὑλικὴ λίμνη). Boiot. See westl. der Kopais, nördl. von Thebai (Strab. 9,2,20); wohl der ehemals Likeri und h. wieder H. gen. See [2. 494 f.; 3. 81 f.]; Fossey [1. 225–229] identifiziert unter Verweis auf Nikandros (Theriaka 887 ff.) H. mit dem nördlicher gelegenen, meist mit der ant. Trephia gleichgesetzten h. Paralimni-See.

1 Fossey 2 Philippson/Kirsten 1,2 3 P. W. Wallace, Strabo's Description of Boiotia, 1979. P. F.

Hylloi (Ὕλλοι). Illyr. Stamm, erstmals im 4. Jh. v. Chr. unter den *bárbaroi* erwähnt (Skyl. 22); andere Schreibweisen *Hylleís* (Steph. Byz. s. v. Ὑλλεῖς) und *Hyllaíoi* (Ὑλλαῖοι, Ptol. 2,16,5). Ihr Siedlungsgebiet wird ungefähr zw. den Flüssen Titius (h. Krka) und Nestus (h. Cetina) lokalisiert. Wie andere kleinere illyr. Stämme wurden die H. nach dem 4. Jh. v. Chr. von den → Dalmatae absorbiert, so daß in röm. Zeit nur noch die Bezeichnung der Küste südl. von Šibenik als Halbinsel *Hyllica/Hyllis* (Plin. nat. 3,141; Skymn. 405) an die H. erinnerte. Eine Verbindung zw. den illyr. H. und der dor. Phyle Hylleis ist nicht nachweisbar [1].

1 G. Neumann, s. v. H., KlP 2, 1266.

M. Fluss, s. v. H., RE Suppl. 6, 115–117 • J. Wilkes, The Illyrians, 1992. D. S.

Hyllos (Ὕλλος).

[1] Sohn des → Herakles und der → Deianeira, Bruder der Makaria. Als seine Brüder werden Ktesippos, Glenos und Oneites (Hes. fr. 25,19 M-W; Apollod. 2,165 Wagner) oder Gleneus und Odites (Diod. 4,37,1) genannt, als seine Tochter Euaichme (Hes. fr. 251b M-W). Von Herakles gebeten, ihn auf einem Scheiterhaufen auf dem Oita zu verbrennen und Iole zur Frau zu nehmen (Soph. Trach. 1179–1258; (Ps.-)Sen. Hercules Oetaeus 1481–1491), flieht er nach dessen Tod mit den anderen Herakliden vor → Eurystheus erst zu Keyx, dem König von Trachis (Apollod. 2,167 Wagner), und von dort unter Führung des Iolaos und unter Begleitung der greisen Alkmene (Eur. Heraclid. 1–47) nach Athen. Dort werden sie von Theseus (Paus. 1,32,6; Diod. 4,57,6) oder dessen Sohn Demophon (Eur. Heraclid. 115–122; Antoninus Liberalis 33 = Pherekydes FGrH 3 F 84) aufgenommen. Die Athener verteidigen die Herakliden im Kampf gegen Eurystheus, der dabei am Skironischen Fels getötet wird (von H.' eigener Hand: Apollod. 2,168 WAGNER; von Iolaos: Paus. 1,44,10; von letzterem gefangen und später auf Befehl Alkmenes hingerichtet: Eur. Heraclid. 859–863 und 928–1052); für den erfolgreichen Ausgang des Kampfes war der freiwillige Opfertod der Makaria notwendig (Eur. Heraclid. 408–601; Paus. 1,32,6). Die Herakliden erobern die Peloponnes, ziehen sich aber alsbald zurück (Apollod. 2,169–170 WAGNER).

Ein Orakel verheißt H. Wiedereroberung »nach der dritten Frucht« (τὸν τρίτον καρπόν), was dieser als »drei Jahre« interpretiert. Am Isthmos wird von den beiden Heeren der Sieg durch einen Zweikampf zw. H. und dem Tegeaten Echemos entschieden (Hdt. 9,26; Diod. 4,58,1–5), bei dem H. stirbt. Den dadurch auf 50 bzw. 100 J. in Kraft getretenen Waffenstillstand brechen die Herakliden, doch hat erst die dritte Generation unter Aristodemos, dem Urenkel des H., Erfolg (Hdt. 6,52), denn »nach der dritten Frucht« bedeutete eben dies (Apollod. 2,172 WAGNER).

H. ist Eponym der spartan. Hylleer; auf dieses Konstrukt weist seine bei Strab. 9,4,10 erwähnte Adoption durch den spartan. König Aigimios. H.' Grab wurde in Megara gezeigt, ein Heroon befand sich in Athen in der Nähe des Olympieions (Paus. 1,41,2).
→ Herakleidai

M. SCHMIDT, s. v. H., LIMC 5.1, 579–582.

[2] Sohn des → Herakles und der kerkyräischen Naiade Melite, Eponym der illyrischen Hylleer. Nach Apoll. Rhod. 4,522–551 verläßt er das von Nausithoos beherrschte Kerkyra und siedelt mit seinen Begleitern an der NO-Küste der Adria, wo sein Tod durch die Mentores, ein Volk zwischen Liburnern und Hylleern, erfolgt.
JO.S.

[3] Röm.-kaiserzeitl. Steinschneider, Sohn des → Dioskurides [8] mit entsprechender Signatur auf Karneol-Intaglii mit Barbaren-Kopf (Florenz, AM), klassizistischem Apollo-Kopf (St. Petersburg, ER), frontaler, komischer Maske (Frg., Paris, CM), Triton und Nereide (Boston, MFA), schreitendem Löwen (Nikosia, Arch. Mus.) sowie auf Chalcedonen mit statuarischem Bild des Theseus (verschollen) und geschmücktem Opferstier (Paris, CM). Der von ihm signierte Sardonyx-Kameo mit Satyr (Berlin, SM) belegt zudem, daß sich H. auch in dieser Technik versuchte; zugeschrieben wird ihm weiterhin der Kölner Divus-Augustus-Kameo [1. 31 ff. Anm. 221 Taf. 10, 58–61].
→ Steinschneidekunst

1 E. ZWIERLEIN-DIEHL, Der Divus-Augustus-Kameo in Köln, in: Kölner Jb. für Vor- und Frühgesch. 17, 1980, 12–53.

O. NEVEROV, Master H. and the Sculptures on the Apollo Temple on the Palatine, in: Soobščenija Gosudarstvennogo ordena Lenina Ermituža 36, 1973, 43–47 • ZAZOFF, AG, 317f. Anm. 71 ff., Taf. 92,4–93,2.
S.MI.

[4] Nördl. Nebenfluß des → Hermos in Lydia, h. Kum Çayı (Sandfluß); sein Mündungsgebiet befindet sich nordöstl. von → Magnesia am Sipylos. Der Fluß war im Alt. fischreich. Er hieß später *Phrygios* (Strab. 13,4,5; *Phryx*, bei Plin. nat. 5,119); so wird er zusammen mit dem Hermos als Aufmarschgebiet der Römer vor der Schlacht bei Magnesia 190 v. Chr. gen. (Liv. 37,37,9f.; App. Syr. 30). Ein anderer, wie dieser vom Temnos (h. Simav Dağları) herabziehender H. (h. Demirci Çayı) mündet nordöstl. von Sardeis in den Hermos; in der wasserreichen Ebene dort (Hdt. 1,80) wurde 547 v. Chr. Kroisos von Kyros geschlagen und nach Sardeis zurückgetrieben. Die Landschaft nordöstl. von Salihli ist h. durch die Talsperre Demirköprü wesentlich verändert.

K. BURESCH, Aus Lydien, 1898, Karte • W. M. CALDER, G. E. BEAN, A Classical map of Asia Minor, 1958 • MAGIE 2, 783 f.
H. KA.

Hymenaios (ὑμέναιος). Hochzeitsgott oder Hochzeitslied (Sappho: ὑμήναος, Kallimachos: ὑμήναιος).

[1] Griech. Gott der Hochzeit, dessen Name vom griech. Wort für Hochzeitslied, *hyménaios*, stammt. Die Etym. ist unklar. H. ist eine relativ späte Schöpfung: Erstmals taucht er als eine Personifikation des Hochzeitsliedes bei Pindar (fr. 128c) und Euripides (Tro. 310; 314) auf. In der innovativen Chorlyrik des 4. Jh. v. Chr. scheint er ein Lieblingsthema gewesen zu sein [1. 56], dennoch wird er vor Catull (61) und Seneca (Med. 67) nicht als Gott der legitimen Hochzeit angerufen. In Analogie zu den Musen, Satyrn u. ä. Gruppierungen nennt ein Graffito in Dura-Europos sogar Hymenaioi im Plural (SEG 17,772).

Der Hintergrund des Hochzeitslieds zeigt sich in den verschiedenen Genealogien: Üblicherweise wird H. als Sohn einer Muse dargestellt, kann aber auch Sohn der Musiker Apollon oder → Magnes sein [1. 55; 2. 583]. Interessanterweise wird er auch zum Sohn des → Dionysos (Sen. Med. 110; Serv. Aen. 4,127), des Gottes, der auch in der *Anthologia Palatina* (9,524,21) das Epitheton *hymenḗios* erhält: Tatsächlich wird H. in späteren Repräsentationen mit dionysischen Zügen dargestellt [3]. Der Ursprung dieser Genealogie ist offensichtlich auf die heitere Sphäre der dionysischen Welt zurückzuführen. Ein Kult für H. ist nicht bekannt und seine Myth. beschränkt sich auf wenige Details.

Serv. Aen. 4,99 erwähnt, daß eines Tages ein Athener H. und eine Gruppe Mädchen, die nach Eleusis unterwegs sind, von Piraten gefangengenommen werden. H., der seiner Schönheit wegen kaum von einem Mädchen zu unterscheiden ist, tötet die Piraten und heiratet das Mädchen, in das er sich verliebt hat. Von diesem Abenteuer an hätten die Athener den H. während ihrer Hochzeitszeremonien mit Namen angerufen. Die Motive des Sieges über die Piraten und des mädchenhaften Aussehens des H. lassen einen starken Einfluß des homer. Dionysos-Hymnos vermuten (ein weiteres Zeugnis für die Verbindung von H. und Dionysos in der späteren Ant.). Im 1. Jh. n. Chr. berichtet Cornelius

Balbus (bei Serv. Aen. 4,127), daß H. während der Hochzeit von Dionysos und Althaea, auf der er sang, gestorben sei: Der Gott der Hochzeit sollte wohl selbst nicht älter als das Brautpaar sein. Der Mythos um den Tod des Gottes geht mindestens auf die Zeit des Hell. zurück: Apollodoros (FGrH 244 F 139) erwähnt, in den orphischen Quellen (fr. 40 KERN) werde H. von Asklepios auferweckt. Der Name H. war unter röm. Sklaven und Freigelassenen weitverbreitet [4. Bd. 1, 522f.; Bd. 3, 1369].

1 A. HENRICHS, Ein neues Likymniosfragment bei Philodem, in: ZPE 57, 1984, 53–57 **2** P. LINANT DE BELLEFONDS, s.v. H., LIMC 4.1, 583–585 **3** Ders., Hyménaios: une iconographie contestée, in: MEFRA 103, 1991, 197–212 **4** H. SOLIN, Die griech. Personennamen in Rom, Bd. 1–3, 1982.

J.B./Ü: B.S.

[2] Hochzeitslied I. GRIECHISCH II. LATEINISCH

I. GRIECHISCH
A. ETYMOLOGIE B. HYMENAIOS UND EPITHALAMION C. FORMEL

A. ETYMOLOGIE

Die Bedeutung von *h.* hat auch ὑμήν, wie man es gewöhnlich in dem Ausruf Ὑμὴν ὦ Ὑμέναιε findet [1. Bd. 2,361]. Der Ursprung des Wortes ὑμήν ist umstritten: Die einen behaupten, es sei vorgriech. und nicht idg. Ursprungs [2], die anderen, es sei griech. und gleichbedeutend mit *hymḗn* = Membran (und somit der Jungfernhaut), auch wenn diese Bedeutung erst bei späten Autoren auftaucht [3. 964–965]. DIEHL, der eine Verbindung mit dem lat. *suo* annimmt, sieht einen weiteren Zusammenhang mit ὕμνος (*hýmnos*), das ebenfalls von »nähen, weben« abgeleitet ist [4. 90]. Pindar und Sophokles gehen von einer Verbindung zw. Ὑμέναιος und ὕμνος aus (Pind. fr. 128c; Soph. Ant. 813–816).

B. HYMENAIOS UND EPITHALAMION

Der *h.* als Lied ist zuerst bei Hom. Il. 18,491–496 erwähnt, wo er Bestandteil einer Prozession zum Geleit der Braut ist. Er konnte auch bei der Ankündigung der Hochzeit gesungen werden (Eur. Hel. 1433–1435) oder sonst von den Gästen bei dem Hochzeitsmahl, das gewöhnlich im Hause der Braut stattfand (Hom. Od. 4,17).

Der Gesang vor der Tür des Brautgemachs in der Nacht des Vollzugs der Ehe wird häufig *epithalámios/-ion* genannt, doch dieser Wortgebrauch ist alexandrinisch. Der Begriff *h.* bürgerte sich als Bezeichnung für alle Arten von Hochzeitsliedern ein, und die Zuweisung der *epithalámia* der → Sappho zu bes. Zeitpunkten der Hochzeitszeremonie ist schwierig [5. 116–126]. Das längste erh. Fragment Sapphos (44 VOIGT [6]) beschreibt, wie Hektor Andromache nach Troia geleitet; im allg. hält man das Gedicht für ein Hochzeitslied, obwohl es keinen Hinweis auf einen Anlaß gibt [7. 102–109]. *Epithalámios* ist als Titel für Theokr. 18 überliefert, einen von Jungfrauen vor der Tür des Brautgemachs des Menelaos und der Helena gesungenen H. Das Hochzeitslied war häufig eine scherzhaft-zweideutige Angelegenheit: Theokr. 18 enthält ebenso harmlosen Spott wie Sapphos *epithalámia* (110 (a) V.). Obszönes hat man in Sappho 111 V. entdecken wollen [8].

C. FORMEL

Das Hochzeitslied soll angeblich mit den Worten ἐκκόρει κόρει κορώνας oder ἐκκορὶ κορὶ κορώνη (881 PMG) angestimmt worden sein, was man unterschiedlich als obszöne oder als Fruchtbarkeit und Treue heraufbeschwörende Worte aufgefaßt hat, doch vermutlich handelt es sich nur um sinnlos aneinandergefügte Silben [9. 92–96]. Ein für den Morgen nach der Hochzeitsnacht bestimmtes Lied ist mit Sappho 30 V. fragmentarisch überliefert. Aus Aischyl. TrGF III 43 ist ersichtlich, daß das Morgenlied die Formel σὺν κόροις τε καὶ κόραις enthielt, was viele mit ἐκκορὶ κορὶ κορώνη in Verbindung gebracht haben, aber es ist sehr viel wahrscheinlicher, daß diese Worte auf die Zusammensetzung des Chors von Jünglingen und Mädchen hinweisen, die das Lied sangen, Freunde der Braut und des Bräutigams.

1 A. S. F. GOW, Theocritus, 1965 **2** R. MUTH, »H.« und »Epithalamion«, in: WS 67, 1954, 5–45 **3** FRISK II **4** E. DIEHL, »... fuerunt ante Homerum poetae«, in: RhM 89, 1940, 81–114 **5** D. L. PAGE, Sappho and Alcaeus, 1955 **6** E.-M. VOIGT, Sappho et Alcaeus, 1971 **7** E. CONTIADES-TSITSONI, H. und Epithalamion, 1990 **8** G. S. KIRK, A fragment of Sappho reinterpreted, in: CQ n.s. 13, 1963, 51 f. **9** G. LAMBIN, La chanson grecque dans l'antiquité, 1992.

E.R./Ü: A.WI.

II. LATEINISCH

Der H. (bzw. Hochzeitshymnos) war kein Bestandteil des röm. Hochzeitsrituals, und das lit. *epithalamium* hat nur eine geringe Beziehung dazu. Wo sich Hochzeitsprozessionen mit glykoneischen Refrains finden, in denen der Gott H. [1] angerufen wird, liegt offensichtlich eine Nachahmung griech. Originale vor (vgl. Plaut. Cas. 798–854 mit Aristoph. Av. 1720–1765; Pax 1316–1357). Wir besitzen Zitate glykoneischer Epithalamien von → Licinius Calvus (FPL [3]1995, 211f.) und Ticidas (FPL 226), sowie von → Catullus (61); dieses für Manlius Torquatus und Iunia Aurunculeia verfaßte Gedicht führt unter Fackelschein vom Haus der Braut zu dem des Bräutigams. Während dieser *deductio* werden → fescenninische Verse gesungen, was den starken it. Einfluß dokumentiert. Das normale Metrum für die lat. Hochzeitsdichtung ist jedoch der Hexameter: Calvus verwendet ihn; Catull. 62, ist zudem nicht an eine spezielle Hochzeit und einen bestimmten Ort gebunden: der Großteil des Gedichtes besteht aus einem *carmen amoebaeum* zw. zwei Chören, einem Jungen- und einem Mädchenchor. Catull. 64, ein → Epyllion über die Hochzeit von Peleus und Thetis, enthält ein Epithalamium, das von den Parzen bei dieser Hochzeit gesungen wurde (323–381). Stat. silv. 1,2 ist ein Hochzeitslied in Hexametern. Einige Verse sind aus dem Epithalamium des Kaisers Gallienus erh. (FPL 378f.). Der → Cento nuptialis (lib. 18 PRETE = lib. 17 LOEB) des Ausonius reiht

Vergilverse zu einer Erzählung einer Hochzeit zusammen. → Claudianus [2] schrieb sowohl daktylische Epithalamien für die Hochzeiten von Honorius und Maria, sowie Palladius und Celerina, dazu fescenninische Verse für die Erstgenannten.

Christl. Schriftsteller wie Dracontius, Ennodius, Sidonius Apollinaris und Venantius Fortunatus verwenden in ihren Epithalamien die Bildersprache und Myth. der früheren Dichter.

FPL ³1995 · A. D'Errico, L'epitalamio nella letteratura latina, dal fescennino nuziale al c. 62 di Catullo, in: Annali della Facoltà di Lettere e Filosofia dell' università di Napoli 5, 1955, 73–93 · R. Muth, H. und Epithalamion, in: WS 67, 1954, 5–45. E.R./Ü: J.S.

Hymettos (Ὑμηττός, Name vorgriech. [17]). Gebirge in Attika, h. Imittos, früher Trelovuni, türk. Deli Dağ (H 1027 m). Der h. weitgehend entwaldete H. besteht aus Triaskalken, Glimmerschiefer, Marmor und anderen Metamorphiten [19]. Er riegelt das Pedion von Athen im SO von der att. Mesogaia ab. Vom Defilée zw. Pentelikon und H. bei Stavro im Norden erstreckt er sich über 22 km bis an den Saron. Golf bei Kap Zoster im Süden [14]. Der Pirnaripaß trennt den nördl. »großen H.« (μέγας Ὑ.) vom südl. »wasserlosen H.« (ἄνυδρος Ὑ.; Theophr. De signis tempestatum 1,20). Mehrere ant. Wege führten über den H. [8. 135]. Am NW-Hang des H. enspringt der → Ilis(s)os. Der (obere) blaugraue hymettische Marmor (μάρμαρος ... Ὑμεττίας, Strab. 9,1,23) wird in der Plastik seit früharcha. Zeit verwendet, in der Architektur (Asklepieion, Dionysos-Theater, Attalos-Stoa) seit dem 4. Jh. v. Chr. bevorzugt [21]. Die ant. Steinbrüche liegen im Westen des H. [11; 15. 25ff.; 21. 191].

Um den H., der nie systematisch erforscht wurde (das bis 1971 Bekannte bei [18]), lagen zahlreiche Demoi (→ Demos [2]) in → Attika, von einigen sind Horos-Inschr. erh. [4; 10; 20]. Luftbilder zeigen im südl. H. bei Aixone (h. Glyphada) ausgedehnte ant. Terrassenkulturen [1]. Entwaldung bezeugt schon in klass. Zeit Platon (Kritias 111c), → Bienenzucht noch in der Kaiserzeit Pausanias (1,32,1). Der → Honig war berühmt (Hor. carm. 2,6,15; Plin. nat. 11,32; Strab. 9,1,23) [5].

Der Kult des Zeus Hymettios (Paus. 1,32,2), offenbar identisch mit dem des Epakrios (Etym. m. s.v. ἐπάκριος Ζεύς) [8. 138; 3. 610, 624 (E 60)], ist auf dem Gipfel zu lokalisieren, der des Zeus Ombrios (Paus. 1,32,2) bei der Kapelle des Prophitis Elias oberhalb Koropi ([8. 139; 12; 15. 32], anders [9; 21. 191 Abb. 246–248]). Der »H.-Tower« [12; 16] ist kein Signalturm, sondern evtl. der Kultplatz des Apollon Proopsios (Paus. 1,32,2; zu weiteren Kultstätten des Apollon [8. 139]). Die Stelle eines Aphroditeheiligtums mit Fruchtbarkeit bewirkender Quelle nimmt das Kloster Kaisariani ein [8. 139f.; 19. 807; 21. 192]. Im SO-Hang des H. in Anagyrus liegt die Nymphengrotte von Vari (Synes. epist. 136; [21. 447 Abb. 581–586; 23. 90ff.]), an der NO-Spitze eine Panhöhle [23. 175ff.], nach Vanderpool [22] identisch mit der bei Men. Dysk. 407ff. in Paiania (h. Liopesi) erwähnten Höhle. Rätsel geben ein »Drachenhaus« auf dem Westhang [2. 189ff.; 21. 191] und eine Wehranlage [13] auf dem Grat des »großen H.« auf. In byz. Zeit entstanden am H. zahlreiche Kirchen und Klöster [6; 21. 192].

1 J. Bradford, Fieldwork on Aerial Discoveries in Attica and Rhodes, in: Antiquaries Journal 36, 1956, 172–180
2 J. Carpenter, D. Boyd, Dragon Houses: Euboia, Attika, Ikaria, in: AJA 81, 1977, 179–215 3 G. Daux, La grande démarchie, in: BCH 87, 1963, 603–634 4 H.R. Goette, Neue att. Felsinschr., in: Klio 76, 1994, 120–134 5 J.E. Jones, Hives and Honey of H., in: Archaeology 29, 1976, 80–91 6 Kirsten/Kraiker, 203ff. 7 U. Knigge, Eine prähistor. Siedlung am H., in: AA 1977, 137–141
8 W. Kolbe, s.v. H., RE 9, 135–140 9 M.K. Langdon, A Sanctuary of Zeus on Mount H., in: Hesperia Suppl. 16, 1976 10 Ders., Hymettiana I, in: Hesperia 54, 1985, 257–270
11 Ders., Hymettiana II. An ancient quarry on Mount H., in: AJA 92, 1988, 75–83 12 H. Lohmann, Atene, 1993, 234
13 J.R. McCredie, Fortified Military Camps in Attica, in: Hesperia Suppl. 11, 1966, 48ff. 14 E. Meyer, s.v. Zoster (1), RE 10A, 848–853 15 A. Milchhöfer, Karten von Attika. Text II, 1883 16 M.H. Munn, The Defense of Attica, 1993, Index s.v. H. tower 17 G. Neumann, s.v. Vorgriech. Sprachen, KlP 5, 1336 18 M. Petropolakou, E. Pentazos, Ἀττική (Ancient Greek Cities 21), 1973, 101–111, 142–152 (Planquadrate X7–Y3 und X7–Y4) 19 Philippson/Kirsten 1, 802–814 20 J.S. Traill, Demos and Trittys, 1986
21 Travlos, Attika 22 E. Vanderpool, Pan in Paiania, in: AJA 71, 1967, 309–311 23 J.M. Wickens, The Archaeology and History of Cave Use in Attica 2, 1986. H.LO.

Hymnos, Hymnus I. Der griechische Hymnos
II. Der lateinische Hymnus
III. Der christliche Hymnus
IV. Der byzantinische Hymnus

I. Der griechische Hymnos
A. Kulthymnen B. Literarische Hymnen
C. Isis-Aretalogien

A. Kulthymnen

Obgleich griech. *hýmnos* (ὕμνος) im frühen Stadium allg. »Gesang« bedeutet, wobei ein ep. Lied oder pindarisches → Epinikion gleichermaßen als »H.« bezeichnet werden kann, zeichnet sich spätestens im 5./4. Jh. v. Chr. die für uns relevante Begriffsspezifizierung als »Gesang für einen Gott« ab (Plat. rep. 10,607a: ὕμνους θεοῖς καὶ ἐγκώμια τοῖς ἀγαθοῖς: ›Hymnen für Götter und Lobpreisungen für hervorragende Menschen‹; Plat. leg. 700b 1–2: εὐχαὶ πρὸς θεούς, ὄνομα δὲ ὕμνοι ἐπεκαλοῦντο) [1]. H. wird zum Oberbegriff für »rel. Lied«, dem einzelnen Kulten zugeordnete Gesangsformen, z.B. der → Paian oder der → Dithyrambos, angehören (vgl. Didymos [1] von Alexandria bei Orion 155–6 Sturz; Proklos bei Phot. Bibl. 320 a9–17 Henry). H. bezeichnet sowohl das Gesungene – also die Worte und die Melodie – als auch den Vortrag des Liedes selbst: Im Kultus singt eine Kultgemeinde zu Aulos- oder Kitharabegleitung um den – oder auf dem Weg zum – Altar eine an eine oder mehrere Gottheiten gerichtete Dichtung, die zusammen mit anderen Kulthandlungen (wie z.B. Opfer, Weinspende, Gebet) als Bestandteil des Gottesdienstes anzusehen ist. Die angesprochene Gottheit soll durch den Gesang auf die Verehrung seitens der Menschen aufmerksam gemacht und gnädig gestimmt werden. Als diesem Zweck dienlich hat sich seit unseren frühesten Quellen eine typische Form durchgesetzt, die mit unterschiedlicher Gewichtung in fast allen Kulten und lit. Gattungen erkennbar ist:

(1) zunächst spricht der H. die Gottheit(en) an, indem er Namen, Beinamen, Genealogie und beliebte Aufenthaltsorte des Gottes angibt (*invocatio*); da der H. eine Kommunikationsform ist, können wir diese Eröffnung als mündliche »Adresse« für die folgende Botschaft verstehen, die den Angesprochenen möglichst genau bestimmt. (2) Als nächstes werden verschiedene Gründe vom Bittsteller angeführt, weshalb gerade diese Gottheit imstande sei, seine Wünsche zu erfüllen; es wird die von E. Norden analysierte Prädikation göttlicher Eigenschaften vorgenommen: Partizipien, Relativsätze, ganze Erzählungen werden entweder im »Du-« oder »Er-Stil« aneinander gereiht, um die göttliche Potenz zu beschreiben und zu preisen (*pars epica, aretalogia, sanctio* [2]). (3) Nach dieser Vorbereitung wird die Bitte gestellt (*precatio*) – sei diese sehr allg. (›Herr, schenke deinen Verehrern Wohlsein‹) oder spezifisch (›Herr, erlöse uns von dieser Plage‹).

Bereits die Ilias kennt verschiedene Arten von Götterhymnen: Paiane an Apollon, um die Pest zu bannen (Hom. Il. 1,472–4); den Linos – ein Erntedank-Lied (ebd. 18,570); Mädchenchöre für Artemis (ebd. 16,183). Lyriker wie → Pindaros, → Bakchylides, → Simonides komponierten eine Vielzahl von verschiedenen Kultliedern, die von ihren alexandrinischen Hrsg. getrennt gesammelt wurden, die aber mit Ausnahme einiger Papyrusfunde (Paiane und Dithyramben von Pindar und Bakchylides), verloren sind: → Paian, → Prosodion, → Nomos, → Dithyrambos, Adonidion, Iobakchos und Hyporchema gehören nach der ant. Klassifizierung des Proklos zu den Hymnen, die ausschließlich Götter preisen; → Partheneion, → Daphnephorikon, Tripodephorikon, Oschophorikon und Euktikon zu denen, die sowohl Götter als auch Menschen lobpreisen (Prokl. Chrestomathie, Zusammenfassung bei Photios, Bibliothek).

Diese Kultlieder waren mit jeweils charakteristischem Inhalt, mit Melodie-, Tanz- und Tonart größtenteils spezifischen Göttern bzw. Festen zugeordnet; dabei spielten der Dithyrambos zu Ehren von Dionysos mit seiner eher turbulenten Vortragsweise und der Paian, der Apollon (v.a.) in eher gediegenem Stil rühmte, eine besondere Rolle, die durch die erh. Überreste teilweise rekonstruierbar ist [3; 4]. Aus spätklass./hell. Zeit häufen sich die Funde inschr. überlieferter echter Kulthymnen (Paiane, Prosodia, Hymnen); von Delphi besitzen wir die Hymnen des Korinthers Aristonoos (→ Aristonus [4]) auf Apollon und Hestia; die zwei berühmten Paiane (im kretisch-paionischen Versmaß: -˘-) und Prosodia auf Apollon mit musikalischer bzw. melodischer Partitur von → Athenaios [7] und → Limenios. Aus Epidauros sind namenlose Hymnen auf die Mutter der Götter, Pan, Alle Götter, ein Paian auf Asklepios im ion. Maß (˘˘--) von → Isyllos, sowie → Ariphrons Paian auf Hygieia erhalten. Der bei Palaikastro in Ostkreta gefundene H. der Kureten auf »den größten Kuros« (= den jugendlichen Zeus) erregte am Anfang des 20. Jh. u.a. bei J.E. Harrison zu Recht großes Aufsehen [5].

B. Literarische Hymnen

Außer den (meist verlorenen) Kulthymnen sind eine Anzahl lit. H. überliefert, deren formale Merkmale der jeweiligen lit. Gattung angepaßt sind, der sie angehören [6]. Die hexametrischen »Homerischen« Hymnen, darunter die vier »großen« auf Demeter, Apollon, Hermes und Aphrodite, stammen zwar sicherlich nicht von Homer, stehen aber fest in der Tradition ep. Rezitationskunst des 7. und 6. Jh. (→ Epos). Sie stellen ein Eröffnungslied (*prooímion*) des → Rhapsoden dar, mit dem er das Wohlwollen mithörender Götter vor seinem eigenen Beitrag zum Homerwettbewerb sichern wollte [7]. Aus den Federn von → Alkaios [4], → Sappho, → Anakreon [1] und → Ibykos stammen verschiedene hymnische Gedichte und Fragmente, die analog zu den Homer. H. wahrscheinlich als Eröffnungsstücke ihres kitharodischen Vortrags (beim Fest oder Symposion) anzusehen sind [8]. Dazu gehören die zwei berühmten Aphrodite-Lieder der Sappho (fr. 1 und 2). Aus hell. Zeit stammen mehrere ausgesprochen lit. Dichtungen, die von den Autoren in archaisierender Absicht der Gattung Götter-H. zugeordnet sind: die H. des → Kallimachos knüpfen an die narrative Tradition des Homer. H. bzw. des kitharodischen Prooimion, um gelehrte Einzelheiten aus dem Leben und Kultus von Zeus, Artemis, Leto (Delos-H.), Apollon, Athena (in elegischen Distichen) und Demeter zu berichten, wobei 2, 5 und 6 sich einer mimetischen Erzähltechnik bedienen, die den Anschein erweckt, als finde die beschriebene Kulthandlung im Augenblick des Erzählens statt [9]. Zwei »Adonis-Klagen« – eine am Ende von Theokrits 15. Gedicht, die andere von → Bion [2] aus Smyrna (Hauptschaffenszeit ca. 100 v. Chr.; Ed.: [10]) – zeugen von der bewußten Förderung oriental. Kulte durch das ptolemäische Herrscherhaus in Alexandria (vgl. Theokr. 15,106–111).

Im 4. Jh. v. Chr. setzt mit des → Aristoteles [6] H. auf die Arete (Tugend), den er zu Ehren seines verstorbenen Freundes Hermeias im daktylo-epitritischen Maß schrieb, und Ariphrons Paian auf Hygieia (Gesundheit), eine Reihe von hymnischen Dichtungen auf abstrakte oder personifizierte Begriffe ein, die in den folgenden Jh. an Bedeutung gewinnt. Es finden sich H. auf Tyche (Glück), die Moiren (Schicksal), Mnemosyne (Erinnerung), später auch ein H. auf Rom von → Melinno (SH 541). Die traditionelle Gestalt des Zeus wird im Zeus-H. des Stoikers → Kleanthes (331–232 v. Chr.) zu der dem Kosmos innewohnenden *archḗ* (Prinzip) radikal umgestaltet. In diesem Zusammenhang sind auch die naturphilos. Dichtungen des → Mesomedes (hadrianische Zeit) zu nennen, z. B. auf Physis (Natur), die Adria oder die Sonne, sowie die Dichtungen des Neuplatonikers → Proklos (5. Jh. n. Chr.). Diesen Werken gemeinsam ist das Bestreben, moral- bzw. naturphilos. Begriffe in die Würde althergebrachter hieratischer Anredeformen zu kleiden.

C. Isis-Aretalogien

Sublit., aber dennoch von großem Interesse sind eine Anzahl mag. H., die in den aus Ägypten stammenden → Zauberpapyri des Späthell. (30. v. Chr. – 600 n. Chr.) gefunden wurden [11]. Es sind hauptsächlich hexametrische Dichtungen, die Götter (Apollon, Hermes, Selene, Hekate) durch wiederholtes Herbeirufen beschwören, damit diese den Zauberpraktiker unterstützen. Der Synkretismus dieser Texte verbindet Ägyptisches, Syrisches, teilweise auch Christliches mit den Namen des griech. Pantheons. Die sog. Isis-Aretalogien – mit Ausnahme des Textes aus Andros in Prosa verfaßt (vgl. [12]) – belegen den Einzug dieser ägypt. Göttin aus Memphis in den offiziellen griech. Kultus, wobei → Isis mit verschiedenen griech. Göttinnen – vorzugsweise Artemis, aber auch Aphrodite oder Demeter – in ähnlich synkretistischem Geist assimiliert wird. Die »orphischen Hymnen« (→ Orphik) gehören nach gelehrter Meinung zum Gottesdienst einer Gemeinde praktizierender »Orphiker« in Kleinasien im 3. Jh. n. Chr. [13; 14].

1 K. Thraede, s. v. H. (1), RAC 16, 916f.; 922–924.
2 E. Norden, Agnostos Theos, 1913, 143–176 3 L. Käppel, Paian, Studien zur Gesch. einer Gattung, 1992
4 B. Zimmermann, Dithyrambos, Gesch. einer Gattung (Hypomnemata Bd. 98), 1992 5 J. E. Harrison, Themis, A study of the social origins of Greek religion, 1911
6 W. D. Furley, Types of Greek Hymns, in: Eos 81, 1993, 21–41 7 R. Böhme, Das Prooimion. Eine Form sakraler Dichtung der Griechen, Diss. Heidelberg 1937
8 J. Danielewicz, De elementis hymnicis in Sapphus Alcaei Anacreontisque carminibus obviis quaestiones selectae, in: Eos 62, 1974, 23–33 9 W. Albert, Das mimetische Gedicht in der Antike. Gesch. und Typologie von den Anfängen bis in die augusteische Zeit (Beiträge zur Klass. Philol. 190), 1988 10 M. Fantuzzi, Bionis Smyrnaei ›Adonidis epitaphium‹, 1985 11 PGM 2, 237ff. 12 W. Peek, Der Isis-Hymnus von Andros und verwandte Texte, 1930
13 W. Quandt, Orphei Hymni, 1962 14 A. N. Athanassakis, The Orphic Hymns, 1988.

J. M. Bremer, Greek Hymns, in: H. S. Versnel, E. T. van Straten (Hrsg.), Faith, Hope and Worship, 1981, 193–215 • W. Furley, Praise and persuasion in Greek hymns, in: JHS 115, 1995, 29–46 • W. Burkert, Griech. Hymnoi in: W. Burkert, F. Stolz (Hrsg.), Hymnen der Alten Welt im Kulturvergleich (Orbis Biblicus et Orientalis 131), 1994, 9–17 • A. C. Cassio, G. Cerri, L'inno tra rituale e letteratura nel mondo antico, in: Atti di un colloquio Napoli 21–24 ottobre 1991, 1991 • CID III • M. Lattke, Hymnus. Materialien zu einer Gesch. der ant. Hymnologie (NT et Orbis antiquus 19), 1991 • P. Maas, Epidaurische Hymnen, 1933.

W. D. F.

II. Der lateinische Hymnus

A. Begriffsbestimmung B. Der Hymnus in der paganen römischen Literatur

A. Begriffsbestimmung

Im Lat. stammen die ältesten sicheren Belege für den Begriff *hymnus* aus dem 2. Jh. n. Chr. (Apul.; Sen. fr. 88 ist unsicher); noch im 7. Jh. kann er als griech. Fremdwort gelten (Isid. orig. 1,39,17: *hymni autem ex graeco in latinum »laudes« interpretantur*). Als lit. Gattung – in Dichtung (in verschiedenen Versmaßen) und Prosa – war der H. jedoch schon früh bekannt und wurde sowohl benutzt (Catull. 34) als auch beschrieben (Hor. carm. 4,2,13: ›Götter oder Könige besingen‹; Hor. ars 83), doch stehen wohl meist griech. Vorbilder im Hintergrund. Die begriffliche Unterscheidung des H. als Götterlob von den *laudes* für Menschen ist spät (Porph. Hor. epist. 2,1,134 zählt den H. zu den *carmina quibus dii placantur*, ›Lieder, mit denen Götter gnädig gestimmt werden‹), wird aber faktisch (zumal in den lit. H.) zu keiner Zeit gewahrt. Auf den griech. H. gehen auch formale und inhaltliche Charakteristika zurück [3]: Anrede, Prädikation, meist im anaphorischen Du-Stil und oft als Polyptoton (*tu/ad te/a te/per te/nec sine te*; auch im Er- oder Ich-Stil), Polyonymie (z. B. Catull. 34,21 f.: *sis quocumque tibi placet sancta nomine*), Relativstil, Allmachtsformeln (z. B. Lucr. 1,31: *tu sola potes*), Aretalogie mit Nennung der Kultstätten, Genealogie und Aufzählung der Machtbereiche, Epiphanieschilderungen (z. B. Tiberianus, carm. 4,5 f.: *quem maxima tellus intremit*; Apul. met. 11,25: *tuam maiestatem tremescunt aves*), Gebet, evtl. mit dem Verweis auf frühere Hilfeleistung (Hypomnese; vgl. Catull. 34,23: *antique ut solita es, bona sospites ope gentem*). Diese H.-Topoi finden sich einzeln oder in Kombination auch in anderen lit. Gattungen (s. u. B.) sowie in → Parodien von H. Hymnische Elemente enthalten auch einfache → Gebete, Kultlieder, → Flüche, Lobreden an verschiedenste Adressaten usw. Oft sind die Grenzen zwischen H. und anderen lit. Genera fließend, und eine eindeutige Zuordnung zur Gattung H. ist schwierig. Im Zweifelsfall wird man sich auf die Diagnose der hymnischen Formeln und Motive beschränken müssen [5. 922–924].

B. Der Hymnus in der paganen römischen Literatur

Eine röm. H.-Trad. ist in den Kultliedern (→ Carmen Arvale; → Carmen Saliare) faßbar. Die lit. H. sind dagegen auch bei röm. Einkleidung von Kult und Szenerie griech. inspiriert, so auch das »Salierlied« Verg. Aen. 8,293–302. Fast modellhaft gebaut ist Catulls H. an Diana in glykoneischen Strophen (carm. 34), der einem Chor von Mädchen und Knaben in den Mund gelegt wird: Er weist fast alle der o.g. hymnischen Elemente auf und evoziert die Vorstellung einer chorlyrischen Darbietung in kultischem Rahmen. Trotz abschließender Bitte um Wohlergehen für die *Romuli gens* handelt es sich mit größter Wahrscheinlichkeit (gegen [3. 166]) um lit. Fiktion und Stilisierung nach griech. Vorlagen. So sind auch die als H. gestalteten lyr. Gedichte des → Horatius – mit Ausnahme des *Carmen saeculare* – nicht für einen kult. Anlaß bestimmt, wodurch die H.-Form flexibler und freier verwendbar wird: Neben den Götter-H. im konventionellen Stil (carm. 1,10 an Merkur; 1,12 an ein Götter-Kollektiv; 1,21 an Diana und Apollo; 1,30 an Venus; 1,35 an Fortuna; 2,19 und 3,25 an Bacchus; 3,18 an Faunus) finden sich auch H. an die Leier (1,32), an die Bandusia-Quelle (3,13) oder an den Weinkrug (3,21); auf den Formenschatz des H. greifen auch 3,4 (an die Musen mit Darstellung der Gigantomachie) und 3,22 (Weihung einer Pinie an Diana) zurück. Die Loslösung von der kult. Funktion erlaubt auch stärker die Einbeziehung urspr. gattungsfremder Motive, z.B. aktueller polit. Ereignisse (so in Hor. carm. 1,21; 1,35; 3,4), oder die Umfunktionierung der H.-Form (3,21 ist ein Geburtstagsgedicht für Messalla). So benutzt auch Propertius einen H. an Bacchus, um die Qualen des *servitium amoris* zum Ausdruck zu bringen (3,17). Ovid gestaltet zwei Einträge in die *Fasti* als H. an Merkur (5,663–692) und an Augustus (2,119–144).

Öfter sind H. in den Text einer anderen lit. Gattung eingebettet: Als Proömium dienen H. an Venus in Lucr. 1,1–43 und an Bacchus in Verg. georg. 2,1–8; ein H. an Apollo findet sich in Stat. Theb. 1,696–720. In eine Prosa-Erzählung eingebaut sind H. an Priapus in Petron. 133 (in Hexametern), an Hymenaeus in Mart. Cap. 1,1 (eleg. Distichen), zwei Prosa-H. an Isis in Apul. met. 11,2 und 25 (vgl. die Isis-Aretalogie im Ich-Stil ebd. 5). Aus der Kaiserzeit stammen zwei lyrische Gebete in H.-Form: Caesius Bassus, FPL 2 (an Bacchus, ithyphallisch) und Septimius Serenus, FPL 23 (an Ianus, choriambisch). Die hymnischen Stilmerkmale werden nun z.T. bis zum Exzeß verwendet (z.B. Anth. Lat. 385,38–60 mit 23fachem anaphorischem Anruf an Sol). Für die Spätant. repräsentativ sind neben der christl. Hymnik (s.u.III.) philos. (neuplatonische) H. (Tiberianus carm. 4, mit einer Ethopoiie Platons, und Boeth. cons. 3 carm. 9 an den Lenker des Weltalls; s.u. III.).

Häufig ist die Verwendung von einzelnen Elementen des H. in einem gattungsfremden Kontext wie z.B. im Musenanruf in Enn. ann. 1,1, im Epithalamium Catull. 61,46–75 (an Hymenaeus), in einer Invektive Catull. 36,11–17 (an Venus), in der Personifikation der *Patria* in Cic. Catil. 1,18 [4], im Proömium Tusc. 5,5 (an die Philos.), in Festschilderungen Tib. 1,7 und 2,1 (an Osiris bzw. Bacchus). Den Formenschatz des H. beutet Ovid zumal in den met. aus [1]: In 4,11–17 mit einer Liste von Bacchus-Epiklesen (Topos der Polyonymie), in 5,341–345 mit einer Ceres-Aretalogie; öfter verwendet Ovid die hymnische Selbstaretalogie (Ich- und Relativstil) in Prahlreden eines Gottes vor einer Sterblichen (1,515–524: Apollo zu Daphne; 1,589–597: Iuppiter zu Io; 4,226–228: Sol zu Leucothoe; usw.). Plin. nat. 2,154–159 beschreibt die physikalischen Qualitäten der Erde in Anlehung an den H. Hymnisch stilisiert ist auch das → *Pervigilium Veneris*. Nach griech. Vorbild gibt Seneca gewissen Passagen der Trag.-Chorlieder H.-Form [6. 178]. Hymnische Elemente finden sich auch in Enkomien für Menschen (vgl. z.B. Lucr. 3,1–30: an Epikur; Verg. georg. 1,24–42; 3,26–36; Aen. 6,791–807: an Augustus).

Immer wieder wird der H. als Gattung oder der H.-Stil auch parodiert [1; 2], wie z.B. Hor. carm. 3,21 (an den Weinkrug); Anth. Lat. 682 (an Pan); Mart. 5,24 (an den Gladiator Hermes mit Parodie der H. an Hermes Trismegistus) [6]; Maximianus elegiae 5,87–104 (an den Penis, *mentula*); CE 1504 (an Priapus); Priap. 85 (Ich-Aretalogie des Priapus).

→ Gebet; Lied

1 T. Fuhrer, Der Götterh. als Prahlrede, in: Hermes 126, 1998, 1–12 **2** H. Kleinknecht, Die Gebetsparodie in der Ant., 1937 **3** E. Norden, Agnostos Theos, 1913 **4** C. Ratkowitsch, Ein 'H.' in Ciceros erster Catilinaria, in: WS 15, 1981, 157–167 **5** K. Thraede, s.v. H. I, RAC 16, 915–946 **6** R. Wünsch, s.v. H., RE 9, 140–183. T.FU.

III. Der christliche Hymnus
A. Begriffsbestimmung B. Griechisch C. Lateinisch D. Mittelalter und frühe Neuzeit

A. Begriffsbestimmung
In der LXX, z.T. im NT und in der frühchristl. Lit. werden die Begriffe ὕμνος (*hýmnos*), ψαλμός (*psalmós*) und ᾠδή (*ōdḗ*) bzw. lat. *psalmus, hymnus, canticum/carmen* meist unterschiedslos für alle möglichen Arten der Danksagung und des Lobgesangs in (rhythmisierter) Prosa oder Dichtung verwendet. So ›mißlingt heute auch hier die wiss. Definition einer »Gattung«‹, und für die Spätant. muß man mit einer ›allg. Mischung der Gattungen‹ rechnen [9. 918 bzw. 940]. Den als H. bezeichneten Texten gemeinsam sind Merkmale inhaltlicher Art (Lobpreis, Danksagung, evtl. Bitte) sowie formale Merkmale wie Gottesanruf (Akklamation), Prädikations- und Partizipialstil, Doxologie (entsprechend der Aretalogie im paganen H.). Seit dem 3.Jh. weisen griech. wie lat. H. öfter alphabetische Akrosticha auf, weshalb man von → Abecedarien spricht. Hymnische Elemente können auch als Teile eines → Gebetes oder anderer Textsorten erscheinen. Im Prinzip ist zu unterscheiden zwischen liturgischem (→ Lied) und lit. H. Eine klare Trennung ist jedoch keineswegs immer möglich.

B. Griechisch
Wie einige at. Psalmen als H. bezeichnet werden können [1. 97–121], läßt sich der Begriff auch auf eine Reihe von nt. Texten anwenden: die (z.T. vorpaulinischen) Christus-H. in Prosa in den Paulus-Briefen (v.a. Phil 2,6–11; Hebr 1,3; Kol 1,15–20) und die hymnischen Gesänge bei Lukas (1,46–55: Magnificat; 1,68–79: Benedictus; 2,29–32: Nunc dimittis) u.a. [2]. Von hymnischen Gesängen bithynischer Christen berichtet Plin. epist. 10,96,7; 1 Clem. 59,3–61,3 zit. ein solches lobpreisendes Gebet. → Ignatios [1] von Antiocheia (Anf. 2.Jh.) fügt in seinem Epheserbrief 19,1–3 seinen

›Stern-H.‹ ein. Als H. können die 24 Oden Salomons gelten (frühes 2. Jh.?). H. und Psalmen spielen auch in der christl. → Gnosis eine wichtige Rolle [1. 254–260]. Die griech. (vorwiegend mündl.) H.-Produktion der ersten Jh. ist jedoch zum größten Teil verloren oder nur frg. in späteren Zit. oder auf Pap. (z. T. mit Notenschrift) erh. [1. 261 f.; 275]. Zu erwähnen ist auch die syr. H.-Trad. (→ Bardesanes, → Aphrahat u. a.) [1].

Seit dem E. des 2. Jh. entstanden neben der liturgischen H.-Trad. auch (rein lit.?) H. in klass. lyrischen Metren: Clemens [3] von Alexandreia schließt den *Paidagōgós* (um 190 n. Chr.) mit einem Christus-H. ab (3,12,101,3 in lyr. Anapästen; platonisierende Epitheta in der Prädikation). Pagane Formen weist auch der ›Abend-H.‹ φῶς ἱλαρόν (*Phṓs Hilarón*) auf (2. od. 3. Jh.), der bis h. in der byz. Liturgie seinen Platz hat. Einen Christus-H. (Abecedarius in iamb. Strophen mit Refrain) stellt auch Methodios (3./4. Jh.) an den Schluß des *Symposions*; hier tritt die seit dem 3. Jh. vordringende akzentuierende neben die quantitierende Aussprache. Unter den Gedichten des → Gregorios [3] von Nazianz (4. Jh.) finden sich H. in versch. Metren (u. a. Anakreonteen); berühmt ist der philos. H. ὦ πάντων ἐπέκεινα (*ō pántōn epékeina*, carm. 1,1,29). Gregor rekurriert stark auf den Formenschatz der paganen H. → Synesios von Kyrene (4./5. Jh.) schrieb neun (neuplaton.-christl.) H. in dor. Dialekt und in versch., z. T. entlegenen lyrischen Metren [4].

C. Lateinisch

Auch im lat. Westen steht am Anf. einer Formengesch. des H. die liturgische Praxis (das *Gloria in excelsis* gilt als ältester bekannter H. in lat. Sprache). Seit dem 4. Jh. wurde auch für die H.-Dichtung das Prinzip der χρῆσις (*chrḗsis*) paganer Formen wirksam. Der erste uns als Persönlichkeit faßbare Dichter von lat. H. ist → Hilarius [1] von Poitiers, aus dessen *Liber hymnorum* (entstanden um 360) Frg. von 3 H. in klass. Metren überl. sind. Der theologische (anti-arianische) Inhalt, die Länge und die Kunstsprache machten diese H. für den Kirchengesang ungeeignet. Von → Marius Victorinus sind 3 H. *De trinitate* in psalmodischer Prosa erhalten; → Nicetas von Remesiana wird das *Te Deum* zugeschrieben. Doch erst → Ambrosius gilt als »Vater der lat. H.-Dichtung« [3]. Neu ist, daß er H. speziell für den Gemeindegesang verfaßte, in einer einheitlichen und eingängigen Form (8 vierzeilige Strophen in zweifüßigen Jamben) und mit anti-arianischer Tendenz (→ Arianismus). Anlaß für diese kirchenpolit. Funktion der ambrosianischen H. waren wohl die Pressionen gegen die Mailänder Kirche, die von der arianischen Kaiserin → Iustina ausgingen. Explizite »Kampf-H.« sind jedoch erst der anti-donatistische Abecedarius des → Augustinus (*psalmus contra partem Donati*) in 16silbigen V. und der anti-arianische *Psalmus abecedarius* des → Fulgentius [2] von Ruspe (5. Jh.). Der Erfolg der »ambrosianischen« Strophe (vgl. Aug. conf. 9,7,15) führte bereits damals zu zahlreichen Nachahmungen (von ca. 40 ambrosianischen H. gelten 14 als echt), und v. a. im MA wurde sie zur beherrschenden Form der H.-Dichtung.

Die (z. T. überlangen) H. des → Prudentius sind sicher nicht allein auf die Liturgie ausgerichtet, vielleicht sogar reine Lesedichtung (gegen [10]). Die Slg. *Cathemerinon* stellt H. für die Stunden des Tages bzw. für bestimmte Tage des liturg. Jahres zusammen; der Zyklus *Peristephanon* enthält H. auf Märtyrer. Beide Gedichtbücher sind nach einem sorgfältig durchdachten Plan aufgebaut. Indem Prudentius teilweise komplizierte lyrische (horazische) Strophen und auch eine kunstvolle Sprache verwendet, macht er seine H. zur hohen Poesie. Vergleichbar ist Paulinus von Nolas carm. 6, ein H. an Johannes den Täufer.

Ins 4. Jh. gehören noch die formal der paganen H.-Trad. verpflichteten, aber inhaltlich klar christl. H. des → Ausonius (ephem. 3) und des → Claudianus [2] (carmina minora 32). Ab dem 5. Jh. sind viele H. wieder anonym bzw. ohne gesicherte Autorschaft. Zu erwähnen sind die zwei H. des → Sedulius (5. Jh.), die 12 H. des → Ennodius (5./6. Jh., vorwiegend in ambros. Trad.), 2 H. des Flavius (6. Jh.). → Venantius Fortunatus (6. Jh.) knüpft in seinen H. wieder an die röm. Lyrik an; von seinen beiden Kreuz-H. steht das berühmte *Pange lingua gloriosi* in der Nachfolge von Prud. cathemerinon 9.

D. Mittelalter und frühe Neuzeit

Die H.-Form entwickelte sich außer- oder innerhalb der Liturgie (im Stundengebet) in den verschiedenen Regionen des lat. Westens z. T. eigenständig weiter [7; 8]: v. a. in Frankreich (Chilperich [2]; Theodulf von Orléans; Fulbert von Chartres; Marbod von Rennes; Balderich von Bourgeuil; Marien-H. des Bernard von Cluny), Italien (Schule von Monte Cassino; Petrus Damiani), Spanien (unter dem Einfluß des Prudentius; H. der mozarabischen Liturgie), Irland (St. Patrick-H.; Antiphonar von Bangor), England (Aethelwald; Beda; Alkuin; Stephen Langtons *Veni Sancte Spiritus*) und Deutschland (Hrabanus Maurus; Walahfrid Strabo; Lupus von Ferrières; Gottschalk der Sachse). Als H. (auch »Hymne«) können verschiedene Formen metrischer oder rhythmischer (seit dem frühen MA auch mehrstimmiger) Lieder gelten, aber auch Lobgesänge in rhythmischer Prosa. Die beliebte Form des Abecedarius hielt sich bis ins dt. Kirchenlied des 17. Jh. Immer wieder wurde auf die klass. Metren zurückgegriffen: Hildebert von Lavardin dichtete einen nicht-liturgischen H. in 200 Strophen. Abaelard schrieb eine H.-Slg. für das Kloster Heloïses mit 20 verschiedenen Strophenformen. Als H. wurden neben anderen liturgischen Formen auch die Tropen (Glossen auf liturgischen Liedern) und Sequenzen (Texte zur Melodie, die urspr. auf dem Schluß-a des Alleluja gesungen wurde) bezeichnet (Notker Balbulus; Reim-Sequenzen der Schulen von St. Victor und Notre-Dame; Hildegard von Bingen). Einen Höhepunkt erreichte die lat. H.-Dichtung im Zuge der Gründungen neuer Orden im 13. Jh. durch Thomas von Aquin, Thomas von Celano, der als Verf. des *Dies Irae* gilt, und Jacopone da Todi, dem das *Stabat Mater* zugeschrieben wird.

Die frühchristl. H. wurden seit dem frühen MA und v. a. im Humanismus immer wieder mit verschiedenen Melodien versehen [10]. Der H.-Gesang behielt seine Bed. auch im protestantischen Gottesdienst (dt. Umdichtungen, v. a. durch Martin LUTHER). Im Humanismus benutzten verschiedene Dichter die H.-Form für ihre eigene (nicht-liturgische) lat. Dichtung (Mathias FUNCK, Sebastian BRANT, Jakob WIMPFELING, Rudolf AGRICOLA, u. a.).
→ Gebet; Lied; Liturgie; HYMNOS, HYMNUS

1 M. LATTKE, H., 1991 2 R. DEICHGRÄBER, Gottesh. und Christush. in der frühen Christenheit, 1967 3 J. FONTAINE, Ambroise de Milan. Hymnes, 1992 4 J. GRUBER, H. STROHM, Synesios von Kyrene. Hymnen, 1991 5 M. KILEY, Prayer from Alexander to Constantine, 1997 6 E. NORDEN, Agnostos Theos 7 J. SZÖVÉRFFY, Die Annalen der lat. H.-Dichtung, 2 Bde., 1964/5 8 Ders., Latin Hymns, 1989 9 K. THRAEDE, s. v. H. I, RAC 16, 1994, 915–946 10 G. WILLE, Musica Romana, 1967. T. FU.

IV. DER BYZANTINISCHE HYMNUS

Als H. werden in byz. Zeit zunächst alle liturgischen Gesänge, später nur solche mit nichtbiblischen Texten bezeichnet. Die Verwendung der ant. quantitierenden Versmaße endet mit Synesios und Gregorios [2] von Nyssa. Seit dem 5. Jh. entsteht unter dem Einfluß der gesprochenen Sprache und nach syr. Vorbildern das Kontakion, formal eine versifizierte Predigt, bestehend aus einem Prooimion (Einleitung) und zahlreichen rhythmisch parallel aufgebauten Strophen, die durch einen Refrain und zumeist eine Akrostichis zusammengehalten werden. Bedeutendster Vertreter der Gattung ist im 6. Jh. Romanos Melodos. Aus der Praxis, bei der Matutin neben den Psalmen auch die neun biblischen Oden zu singen, entwickelt sich seit dem Ende des 7. Jh. der Kanon, von dem das Kontakion allmählich verdrängt wird. Der Kanon besteht aus neun, später meist nur acht kurzen Kontakia mit wenigen Strophen, die die biblischen Oden paraphrasieren oder auf das Fest des Tages Bezug nehmen. Bed. Dichter von Kanones sind im 8. Jh. Andreas [2] von Kreta und Iohannes [33] von Damaskos, im 9. Jh. Iosephos [9] von Thessalonike und die Hymnographen Ioseph und Kosmas. Neben den Kanones wurden auch kleinere Formen wie das Sticheron (→ Syntomon) und Troparion weitergepflegt. Die Dichtung von H. für die Liturgie endet mit wenigen Ausnahmen im 11. Jh.
→ Andreas [2] von Kreta; Gregorios [2] von Nyssa; Iohannes [33] von Damaskos; Kanon; Kontakion; Romanos Melodos; Synesios; Troparion

W. CHRIST, M. PARANIKAS, Anthologia graeca carminum christianorum, 1871 • E. FOLLIERI, Initia hymnorum ecclesiae graecae, 1960–1966 • E. WELLESZ, A History of Byzantine Music and Hymnography, 1961 • K. MITSAKIS, Βυζαντινή ὑμνογραφία, 1971. AL. B.

Hyoskyamos s. Bilsenkraut

Hypallage s. Figuren

Hypallagma (ὑπάλλαγμα). Wörtlich »Austausch«, ein im röm. Äg. durch Vertragsklauseln bestimmtes Sicherungsrecht des Gläubigers. Anders als die → *hypothḗkē* gewährte das *h.* dem Gläubiger kein eigentumsähnliches Beherrschungsrecht über das im Besitz des Schuldners verbleibende Sicherungsobjekt, in der Regel ein Grundstück, sondern verpflichtete den Schuldner lediglich, bestimmte Gegenstände für die Befriedigung des Gläubigers im Wege der Zwangsvollstreckung bereitzuhalten. Die Verträge enthalten keine Verfallsklausel, jedoch unterliegt der Schuldner wie bei der *hypothḗkē* gewissen Verfügungsbeschränkungen über die ebenfalls in seinem Besitz verbleibenden Gegenstände.
→ Schulden, Verschuldung

A. B. SCHWARZ, Hypothek und H., 1911 • H.-A. RUPPRECHT, Einführung in die Papyruskunde, 1994, 134 • Ders., Die dinglichen Sicherungsrechte nach der Praxis der Papyri, in: FS H. Ankum II, 1995, 425–436, bes. 428 f. G. T.

Hypanis (Ὕπανις).

[1] Fluß in der Ukraine (h. Bug). Nach Hdt. 4,47,52 von Westen nach Osten fließend, neben → Istros (Donau) und → Tyras (Dnjestr) dritter der dem Pontos zufließenden skythischen Ströme. Weitere Quellen: Hdt. 4,17,18; Skymni periegesis V. 804 (= GGM 1,229); Strab. 2,107; 7, 298; 306; Ptol. 3,5,2; Anonymi periplus Ponti Euxini 60 (= GGM 1,417); Steph. Byz. s. v. → Borysthenes; Mela 2,6; Plin. nat. 4,83 f.

[2] Der im nördl. Kaukasus entspringende h. Kuban, der beim alten Phanagoreia (h. Gebiet von Sennaja) ins Schwarze Meer mündet.

[3] s. → Hyphasis

E. KIESSLING, s. v. H., RE 9, 210 ff. B. B. u. H. T.

Hyparchia (ὑπαρχία). Hell. Begriff für »Unterbezirk« einer Satrapie, vornehmlich im → Seleukidenreich. In der durch OGIS 1, 238 bezeugten *h.* Eriza (Kleinasien) war der »Gouverneur« (*hýparchos*, ὕπαρχος) direkt dem Satrapen von Karien unterstellt (OGIS 1,224), so daß es hier keine Zwischeninstanz zwischen beiden Funktionsträgern gab [1. 176]. Der Beleg kann allerdings auch aus der Attalidenzeit stammen, doch wären in diesem Fall Rückschlüsse auf die seleukid. Verwaltung möglich, in der ein *hýparchos* (OGIS 1,225) als Verwalter einer von der → *eparchía* zu differenzierenden *h.* wohl auch mil. Aufgaben hatte [2. 93].

Die *h.* ist in der 1. H. des 3. Jh. v. Chr. zudem in dem damals ptolem. beherrschten »Syrien und Phoinikien« (SB V 8008) und in parth. Zeit in Media Atropatene und Mesopotamien [3. 28, 30; 4. 4] belegt. Aus Arrian (Ind. 12,7) ist eine Übertragung des Begriffs *h.* auf indische Verhältnisse zu erschließen.

1 K. BRODERSEN, Appians Abriß der Seleukidengesch., 1989 2 B. BAR-KOCHVA, The Seleucid Army, 1976 3 E. H. MINNS, Parchments of the Parthian Period, in: JHS 35, 1915, 22–65 4 M. ROSTOVTZEFF, C. B. WELLS, A Parchment

Contract of Loan from Dura-Europos on the Euphrates, in: YClS 2, 1931, 1–78.

BENGTSON, 2, 22ff. • D. MUSTI, in: CAH 7,1,²1984, 184ff.

K.-W. WEL.

Hypata (Ὑπάτα). Erst im 5. oder Anf. 4. Jh. v. Chr. nachweisbarer Hauptort der Ainianes (HN 296) auf einer durch Schluchten abgetrennten Terrasse über dem Spercheiostal am Nordhang der Oite (→ Oitaioi, Oite), h. Hypate. Die Geschicke von Stadt und Stamm fallen weitgehend zusammen (Belege [1; 2; 3]). Um 344 begann die maked. Herrschaft, nach dem Intermezzo des Lamischen Krieges seit ca. 273 von der des Aitol. Bundes abgelöst. Im J. 191 verwüstete → Acilius [I 10] das Territorium von H. (Liv. 36,14,15; 16,5). 189 kam es dort zu röm.-aitol. Verhandlungen (Pol. 20,9f.; 21,4f.). Nach dem Friedensschluß war H. der einzige aitol. Posten nördl. der Oite. Mit der Neugründung des Ainianischen Bundes 168 durch Rom begann der Aufschwung von H. Der nachmalige Augustus vereinte den Stamm um 30 v. Chr. mit Thessalia. Bereits im 1. Jh. n. Chr. besaß wenigstens eine Familie in H. das röm. Bürgerrecht, im 2. Jh. scheint H. die bedeutendste thessal. Stadt gewesen zu sein. Unter Hadrian legte der Statthalter von Macedonia die Grenze zw. H. und Lamia fest (ILS 5947a, dazu [4. 199]). Seit dem 3. Jh. gab es in H. einen Bischof. Iustinian ließ die Befestigungen erneuern (Prok. aed. 4,2,16). Im 10. Jh war H. als »Neai Patrai« Metropolis, evtl. seit Neubesiedlung nach zeitweiliger Wüstlage z.Z. der Slaveneinwanderung.

1 E. MEYER, s. v. H, KlP 2, 1271f. 2 F. STÄHLIN, s. v. H., RE 9, 236ff. 3 Ders., Das hellen. Thessalien, 1924, 220ff. 4 W. ECK, Jahres- und Provinzialfasten der senatorischen Statthalter von 69/70 bis 138/9, in: Chiron 13, 1983, 143ff.

J. A. O. LARSEN, A Thessalian Family under the Principate, in: CPh 48, 1953, 86ff. • P. LAZARIDIS, in: AD 16,2, 1960, 166 und 27,2; 1972, 390; 28,2, 1973, 321 (Fundber.) • P. PANTOS, in: G. D. DELOPOULOU (Hrsg.), 1. Συνέδριο Φθιωτικών Ερευνών (1. Synédrio Phthiōtikōn Erevnōn), 1990, 74ff. (Lageber. zur hell.-röm. Stadt) • P. PANTOS, in: BCH 119, 1990, 772 (Fundber.) • TIB 1, 1976, 223ff.

HE. KR.

Hypatia. Neuplatonische Philosophin in Alexandria [2] (gest. 415 v. Chr.), Tochter des vor allem als Mathematiker bekannten Philosophen → Theon von Alexandria. Die Ausgabe des *Almagest*, die dem Komm. des Theon vorangestellt war, besorgte sie ab Buch III [1]. Sie verfaßte (heute verlorene) Komm. zu → Diophantos [4], zu den ›Kegelschnitten‹ des → Apollonios [13] von Perge und den ›Handlichen Tafeln‹ des Ptolemaios (Suda I.4,664–646 ADLER). Großen Erfolg hatte ihr philos. Unterricht (darin auch die mathematischen Wiss.), den sie höchstwahrscheinlich privat erteilte. Dieser bestand zwar in der üblichen Kommentierung der Werke des Platon, des Aristoteles oder anderer Philosophen, erregte jedoch dadurch Aufsehen, daß sich eine Frau in dieser Weise hervortat. Ihre moralische Strenge wurde ebenfalls bewundert. Einen kynischen Zug von Schamlosigkeit hat man darin sehen wollen, daß sie einem in sie verliebten Schüler ihre von Menstruationsblut befleckte Wäsche gezeigt habe, doch kann man darin ebenso gut plotinischen Einfluß sehen (Suda I.4,664–646 ADLER) [3]. Sie dürfte sich in ihrem neuplatonischen Denken, wie auch ihr Schüler → Synesios, eher an Plotin und Porphyrios als an Iamblichos angeschlossen haben. Wir besitzen sieben Briefe (10; 15; 16; 46; 81; 124; 154 GARYZA) des Synesios an H., in denen er sie als seine Mutter, Schwester, Lehrerin und Wohltäterin bezeichnet. H. wurde durch den christl. Pöbel von Alexandria gelyncht. Die Hetze des Bischofs der Stadt, Kyrillos I., gegen den Stadtpräfekten Orestes, der als Freund der H. bekannt war (Sokrates hist. eccl. 7,13–15), ist zumindest als mittelbare Ursache dafür anzusehen.

Durch die dramatischen Lebensumstände der H. in der Konfrontation von Heidentum und Christentum war die Nachwirkung schon in der Spätant. groß, bes. aber dann im religionskritischen Kontext der Aufklärung [4]. Der Roman ›H.‹ (London 1853) von Chr. Kingsley (1819–1876) machte H. auch breiten Kreisen bekannt. Heute ist eine 1986 gegr. Zschr. der feministischen Philos. nach ihr benannt.

→ Philosophinnen

1 A. CAMERON, Isidore of Miletus and H.: On the Editing of Mathematical Texts, in: GRBS 31, 1990, 103–127 2 M. DZIELSKA, H. of Alexandria, 1995 3 D. SHANZER, Merely a Cynic Gesture?, in: RFIC 113, 1985, 61–66 4 CH. LACOMBRADE, s. v. H., RAC 16, 965.

P. HA.

Hypatios

[1] Schüler des → Libanios, von dem er Briefe empfing (Lib. epist. 137; 157; 158). 360/361 n. Chr. war er *consularis Palaestinae primae* (Lib. epist. 156; 159). PLRE 1, 447 (H.us 1). W. P.

[2] Flavius H. Bruder der Kaiserin → Eusebia. Zusammen mit seinem Bruder Fl. Eusebius war er 359 n. Chr. Consul (Amm. 18,1,1). 363 war er evtl. *vicarius urbis Romae* (Cod. Theod. 3,5,8). Er wurde zusammen mit seinem Bruder 371 in einem Hochverratsprozeß verurteilt, aber bald wieder amnestiert (Amm. 29,2,9–16). Im Jahr 379 war er *praefectus urbis Romae* (Cod. Theod. 11,36,26), 382/383 *praefectus praetorio Italiae et Illyrici* (Cod. Theod. 11,16,15; 6,26,3 u.a.). Ammian lobt seinen edlen Charakter (29,2,16). Libanios hat ihm eine Lobrede gewidmet (vgl. Lib. or. 1,179–181). PLRE 1, 448 (H.us 2 und 4). W. P.

[3] *Praefectus Augustalis* 383 n. Chr., vielleicht nochmals 392 (Cod. Theod. 12,6,17; 11,36,31). Der gleichzeitig in diesem Amt belegte Potamius scheint ihm kurzzeitig sein Amt übergeben zu haben [1. 166–168]. PLRE 1, 448 (H.us 3).

1 C. VANDERSLEYEN, Chronologie des préfets d'Egypte de 284 à 395, 1962.

K. G.-A.

[4] Sohn des Secundinus und der Caesaria, einer Schwester des Kaisers → Anastasios [1] I., gest. 532 n. Chr., oström. General und Usurpator. Nachdem er 500 das Konsulat bekleidet hatte, kämpfte er 503 glücklos als *magister militum praesentalis* gegen die Perser und in Thrakien. 513 von Kaiser Anastasios mit einer Armee gegen den Usurpator Vitalianus gesandt, wurde er dessen Gefangener, aber 514 vom Kaiser losgekauft. Seit ca. 516 *magister militum per Orientem*, erhielt er spätestens 526 den → Hoftitel πατρίκιος (*patríkios*). Nach erfolglosen Verhandlungen und Kämpfen mit den Persern wurde er 529 durch → Belisarios abgelöst. Während des Nika-Aufstandes (Januar 532) wurde er von einer Gruppe von Senatoren unter Beteiligung des Volkes von Konstantinopel am 17.1. gegen → Iustinianus [1] I. zum Kaiser erhoben, aber nach dem Scheitern der Revolte am 19.1. hingerichtet. ODB 2, 962f.; PLRE 2, 577–581 (H.us 6). F.T.

Hypatodoros (Ὑπατόδωρος). Bronzebildner aus Theben, tätig im mittleren 5. Jh. v. Chr. In Delphi schuf H. zusammen mit Aristogeiton die ›Sieben gegen Theben‹, die als Siegesvotiv der Argiver nach der Schlacht von Oinoe (um 460 v. Chr.) aufgestellt wurden (Paus. 10,10,3–4), und deren Basis am Beginn der Hl. Straße identifiziert wurde, sowie laut einer erh. Signatur das Votiv für einen Boioter. Berühmt für ihre Größe und Schönheit war H.' Bronzestatue der Athena in Aliphera in Arkadien (Paus. 8,26,7), deren Basis aufgefunden wurde. Polybios (4,78,3–5), der den Künstler allerdings Hekatodoros nennt, gibt als Mitarbeiter einen Sostratos an. Ein von Plinius (nat. 34,50) 372–369 v. Chr. datierter H. ist entweder ein späterer gleichnamiger Künstler oder beruht auf Irrtum.

H. Brunn, Gesch. der griech. Künstler, 1, 1857, 293–295 • G. Daux, Pausanias à Delphes, 1936, 89–90 • Loewy, Nr. 101 • J. Marcadé, Recueil des signatures de sculpteurs grecs, 1, 1953, 8; 38 • H. Pomtow, Stud. zu den Weihgeschenken und der Topographie von Delphi 3, in: Klio 8, 1908, 187–205 • A. K. Orlandos, Η αρκαδική Αλίφειρα και τα μνημεία της, 1967–68, 125–132 • Overbeck, Nr. 1569; 1570–73 (Quellen) • C. Vatin, Monuments votifs de Delphes, 1991, 139–148. R.N.

Hypatos (Ὕπατος).

[1] Das republikanische Amt des Consul (griech. ὕπατος, *hýpatos*) bestand unter Augustus und seinen Nachfolgern scheinbar weiter, aber *de facto*, bis 541 n. Chr., nur noch als Ehrentitel, der nach 541 ausschließlich dem regierenden (oström.) Kaiser (bis zum 7. Jh) vorbehalten blieb. Bereits ab dem 7. Jh. ist auf byz. Siegeln H. als → Hoftitel belegt, der mit dem alten Konsulat nichts mehr gemein hat. Er ist gemäß den Ranglisten des 9. und 10. Jh. relativ niedrig und den Titeln ἀνθύπατος (*anthýpatos*, Proconsul) und δισύπατος (*dishýpatos*, Doppelconsul) untergeordnet. Ab dem 11. Jh. erhalten angesehene Gelehrte und Lehrer gelegentlich den Titel ὕπατος τῶν φιλοσόφων (*h. tōn philosóphōn*).

ODB 2, 963f. • N. Oikonomidès, Les listes de préséance byzantines des IXe et Xe siècles, 1972. F.T.

[2] Oberhalb von Glisas gelegener, h. Sagmatas gen. südl. Ausläufer des Messapion in Boiotia, auf dem sich wohl an der Stelle des h. Klosters (mit vielen ant. Spolien) ein Heiligtum des Zeus H. befand (Paus. 9,19,3).

Fossey, 223–225 • H. G. Lolling, Reisenotizen aus Griechenland (1876 und 1877), 1989, 506f. • N. D. Papachatzis, Παυσανίου Ἑλλάδος Περιήγησις 5, ²1981, 122–125. P.F.

Hyperbolos (Ὑπέρβολος). Athenischer Staatsmann (411 v. Chr.) aus dem Demos Perithoidai. Entgegen den gegen ihn vorgebrachten Anschuldigungen war er gebürtiger Athener. Er scheint sein Vermögen mit Herstellung oder Verkauf von Lampen erworben zu haben (vgl. Aristoph. Equ. 1315). Sowohl Aristophanes (etwa Equ. 1304) als auch Thukydides (8,73,3) beschreiben ihn als gemein (*mochthērós*). Als → Demagoge nach Art des Kleon erstrebte er nach dessen Tod 422 v. Chr. eine führende Position und war 421/420 Mitglied des Rates (Platon comicus 166f. CAF = 182 PCG; vgl. IG I³ 82). Nach Plutarch beantragte er in der Hoffnung, Alkibiades oder Nikias beseitigen zu können, einen → Ostrakismos, wurde aber selbst ostrakisiert, als sich die beiden zusammentaten (Plut. Alkibiades 13; Nikias 11; vgl. Plut. Aristeides 7,3–4). H. war das letzte Opfer eines Ostrakismos. Der Zeitpunkt ist umstritten, doch muß er im J. 415 oder ein bis zwei J. früher liegen. 411 wurde H. auf Samos von den athen. Oligarchen ermordet (Thuk. 8,73,3).

PA 13910 • Davies 517 • LGPN 2, s. v. H. (5) • W. R. Connor, The New Politicians of Fifth-Century Athens, 1971 • P. J. Rhodes, The Ostracism of Hyperbolus, in: R. Osborne (Hrsg.), Ritual, Finance, Politics. FS D. Lewis, 1994, 85–98 • E. Vanderpool, in: Semple Lectures 2, 1966–1970, 215–270, 242f. mit Abb. 32, 64f. P.J.R.

Hyperboreioi (Ὑπερβόρε(ι)οι). Die Hyperboreer, ein mythisches Volk, das man sich am Rand der Welt (Pind. I. 6,23) »jenseits des Nordwinds (Boreas)« wohnend dachte (so die ant. Etym., die h. als unsicher gilt [1]). Mit den übrigen Randvölkern (wie den Aithiopen, ihrem südlichen Gegenstück) teilen die H. Züge der Idealvorstellung von einer paradiesischen, götternahen Existenz in einem klimatisch begünstigten Land [2; 3; 4]. Durch ihre Beziehung zu → Apollon sind die H. eng mit dessen beiden wichtigsten Kultzentren Delphi und Delos verbunden.

Neben ihrer frühesten Bezeugung bei Hes. cat. fr. 150,21 M-W lassen sich die H. in einem Paian des Alkaios (fr. 307c V.) fassen, der den Aufenthalt Apollons bei den H. und seine Rückkehr nach Delphi auf einem Schwanenwagen besingt – die → Epiphanie des Gottes wird nach bekanntem Schema als Ankunft aus der Fremde repräsentiert [5. 230]. Die Idee, daß das Land der H. ›weder zu Schiff noch zu Fuß‹ (Pind. P. 10,29) zu erreichen, sondern nur Göttern oder Heroen zugänglich sei (vgl. die Legende vom Flug des Hyperboreers → Abaris), begegnet sowohl bei Pindar, wo Perseus die von Musik begleiteten Opferfeste der von Krankheit und Alter freien H. für Apollon besucht (Pind. P. 10,29ff.; zu den Eselsopfern vgl. Kall. fr. 186,10; 492) und Herakles den Ölbaum von den H. nach Olympia holt (Pind. O. 3), als auch bei Bakchyl. 3,58–62, wo Apollon den frommen → Kroisos vom Scheiterhaufen zu den H. entrückt. Hier nähert sich das wohl von orphisch-pythagoreischen Lehren beeinflußte Bild der »H.-Glückseligkeit« (Aischyl. Choeph. 373) den eschatolog. Vorstellungen von den Inseln der Seligen (→ Makaron nesoi) und vom → Elysion an [6].

Den ausführlichsten, von vorsichtiger Skepsis geprägten Bericht über die H. liefert Hdt. 4,32–36, der sich auf delische Trad. beruft (vgl. IG II 813): Die H. senden alljährlich in Stroh gebundene Opfergaben, die von Volk zu Volk weitergereicht werden, nach → Delos; urspr. sei der Tribut an → Eileithyia von zwei H.-Mädchen, Hyperoche und Laodike, deren Grab (*sḗma*) beim Heiligtum der Artemis seither Haaropfer von del. Mädchen und Knaben empfängt, zusammen mit fünf Begleitern (*perpherées*) persönlich überbracht worden; noch früher seien Arge (→ Hekaerge) und → Opis gekommen, die in einem anderen Grab, der sog. *thḗkē*, begraben worden seien und in einem Hymnos des → Olen angerufen würden [5. 92f., 311; 7]. An die Prozessionsroute, die in ähnlicher Form auch bei Kall. h. 4,278ff. (vgl. fr. 186) und Paus. 1,31,2 erscheint, knüpfen sich ant. und mod. Spekulationen über die Identität der H., die schon bei → Aristeas [1] von Prokonnesos als nördl. Nachbarn der → Arimaspoi, Issedonen und Skythen galten (Hdt. 4,13). Im Hell. dienten die H. als utopisches Modell (→ Hekataios von Abdera), später verblaßten sie zum Symbol des Hohen Nordens.

1 Frisk, s.v. H., Bd. 2, 967 2 B. Gatz, Weltalter, goldene Zeit und sinnverwandte Vorstellungen, 1967, 189–200
3 J. Ferguson, Utopias of the Classical World, 1975, 16–22
4 J.S. Romm, The Edges of the Earth in Ancient Thought, 1992, 60–67 5 Burkert 6 E. Krummen, Pyrsos Hymnon: festliche Gegenwart und mythisch-rituelle Trad. als Voraussetzung einer Pindarinterpretation, 1990, 255–263
7 W. Sale, The Hyperborean Maidens on Delos, in: Harvard Theological Review 54, 1961, 75–89.

O. Crusius, s.v. H., Roscher 1.2, 2805–2835 • H. Daebritz, s.v. H., RE 9, 258–279 • H.M. Werhahn, s.v. H., RAC 16, 967–986 • Ph. Zaphiropoulou, s.v. H., LIMC 8.1, 641–643. A.A.

Hyperechios. Steinschneider der röm. Kaiserzeit (antoninisch/1. Jh.). Signierte roten Jaspis mit Sokrates-Büste (Berlin, SM) und gelben Jaspis (eine für die spätere Kaiserzeit typische Steinvarietät) mit Löwe (Boston, MFA).

→ Steinschneidekunst

Zazoff, AG, 322, Anm. 106, Taf. 96,4;5. S.MI.

Hypereides (Ὑπερείδης). Att. Redner, Sohn des Glaukippos, aus dem Demos Kollytos, geb. 390/89 (da 330/29 Diaitet und damit 60jährig, IG II 941), gest. 322 v.Chr.

A. Leben B. Werk
C. Charakteristik und antikes Urteil

A. Leben

Von der reichen biographischen Tradition der Ant. (Hermippos, Dionysios von Halikarnassos, Kaikilios) sind nur die *vita* bei Ps.-Plutarch (mor. 848d–850b) sowie kurze Notizen bei Athenaios, Photios (495b–496a) und in der Suda erhalten; dazu kommen biographisch verwertbare Angaben in den erh. Reden und inschr. Zeugnisse.

H. entstammte einer begüterten Familie (Häuser in Athen und im Piräus; Besitzungen in Eleusis; Grabstätte vor dem »Ritter-Tor«) und leistete in den Jahren 340 und 339 gleich drei aufwendige → Leiturgien (Trierarchien, Choregie; weitere sind allerdings nicht bezeugt). Ohne materiell darauf angewiesen zu sein, betätigte er sich sein ganzes Leben lang auch als → Logograph in Privatprozessen. Die Quellen bezeichnen ihn als Schüler sowohl des → Isokrates als auch des Platon, aber nur der Einfluß des ersteren ist in Gedankenwelt und Stil des H. deutlich zu spüren. Ansonsten notiert man Anekdotisches und Pikantes aus seinem Privatleben (Vorliebe für kulinarische Genüsse, Affären mit Phryne und anderen Hetären).

Nach erstem polit. Hervortreten auf Seiten der Gruppe um → Timotheos (Prozesse gegen Aristophon 362 und Autokles ca. 360) scheint sich H. in den folgenden 17 Jahren ganz auf die Logographie konzentriert zu haben, wo er zum Spezialisten für kleinere Privatprozesse und bes. Synegorien (Unterstützung einer Prozeßpartei durch einen Außenstehenden) wurde. Ganz auf der Linie des → Demosthenes [2] und gegen → Eubulos [1] agierte H. in den Jahren vor der Schlacht von Chaironeia (→ *eisangelía* gegen Philokrates 343, Vertretung athenischer Interessen vor der delphischen Amphiktyonie 343/2 sowie auf Chios und Rhodos 341; Bündnis mit Theben im Herbst 339). An der Schlacht von Chaironeia nahm H. nicht teil, da er Buleut war, organisierte aber nach der Niederlage den Widerstand bis zum äußersten (u.a. Befreiung von Sklaven), was sich angesichts der Zurückhaltung Philipps nach seinem Sieg als überflüssig erwies, H. aber eine → Paranomie-Klage wegen der Sklavenbefreiung durch Aristogeiton und wegen der Einbürgerung von Metöken (vgl. Ps.-Plut. mor. 849a 1–4) einbrachte, von der er freigesprochen wurde. Auch nach Philipps Tod (336) und während des Alexanderzuges blieb H. entschieden antimakedonisch. Die wohl mit der Kontroverse um Chares und die Söldner am Tainaron (kurz vor 324) beginnende Entfremdung zw. ihm und Demosthenes führte über Meinungsverschiedenheiten bezüglich Alexanders Dekrete zur Vergöttlichung seiner Person und der Rückführung aller Expatriierten zum offenen Bruch im Zusammenhang mit der Harpalos-Affäre: H. erreichte als einer der Ankläger die Verurteilung des Demosthenes zu einer hohen Geldstrafe, der dieser sich durch Flucht entzog (Jan. 323). In der auf Alexanders Tod (Juni 323) folgenden Rebellion gegen die Makedonenherrschaft war H. der Wortführer (Grabrede auf die Gefallenen, 323/2) Nach dem Sieg der Makedonen bei Krannon (Sept. 322) entzog sich H. wie Demosthenes durch Flucht der geforderten Auslieferung, wurde aber noch im Oktober desselben Jahres von Häschern des Antipatros [1] wohl auf Aigina ergriffen und grausam getötet.

B. Werk

Nach Ps.-Plutarch kannte die Ant. 77 Reden des H., davon galten 52 als echt. Wir haben 71 Titel (z. T. mit einigen Fragmenten), unter denen nur eine der epideiktischen (→ Epideixis), 15 der symbuleutischen, alle übrigen der gerichtlichen Gattung zuzuordnen sind. Noch im 16. Jh. soll nach Aussage des Humanisten Brassicanus eine H.-Hs. in der Bibliothek des ungarischen Königs vorhanden gewesen sein, was heute aber bezweifelt wird. Erst durch Papyrusfunde, die in fünf Etappen zwischen 1848 und 1892 publiziert wurden, kamen große Reste von vier Rollen zutage. Sie enthalten den Schluß der Rede gegen Pheidippides (wohl kurz vor Philipps Tod 336; Paranomieklage), den Schluß der Rede für Lykophron (333; Erbschaftsstreit), die vollständige Rede für Euxenippos (330; Eisangelie), mit geringen Lücken die Rede gegen Athenogenes (nach 330; Streit um Kaufvertrag), umfangreiche Abschnitte der Rede gegen Demosthenes (323) und den größeren Teil des *Epitáphios* (323/2). Alles Erhaltene entstammt also den letzten 14 Lebensjahren des H.

C. Charakteristik und antikes Urteil

Soweit ein Urteil auf dieser immer noch schmalen Basis möglich ist, zeichnet sich H. durch eine dem → Lysias ebenbürtige Kunst der Ethopoiie und der anschaulichen Schilderung (→ Ekphrasis) aus. Er meidet auffälligen rhet. Schmuck und vermittelt den Eindruck ungekünstelter Einfachheit. Die Argumentation ist geschickt, die Gliederung klar und an der Sache orientiert. In seine Sprache läßt H. Wörter des Alltags und Anleihen aus der Komödie einfließen, gelegentlich auch Neologismen oder in neuer Bedeutung gebrauchte Wörter. Fast allgegenwärtig ist sein Humor, der zw. feiner Ironie und bissigem Sarkasmus oszilliert. Polemische »Tiefschläge« nach Art des Demosthenes oder Aischines findet man dagegen nicht (was aber auch Folge des Überlieferungszustandes sein kann). Der *Epitáphios* mit seinem gesteigerten Pathos und seiner isokrateisch-gorgianisch gefärbten Diktion fällt gattungsbedingt aus diesem Rahmen.

Die ant. Lit.-Kritik gibt H. meist den zweiten Platz in der Beredsamkeit nach Demosthenes, in mancher Hinsicht wird er sogar über diesen gestellt (in der Heuresis, Dion. Hal. De imitatione 5,6; in der Menge und Vielseitigkeit seiner Vorzüge, Ps.-Longinos, Περὶ ὕψους 34) und als Muster zur Nachahmung empfohlen (Dion Chrys. 18,11). Das weniger positive Urteil des Hermogenes (ebd. 2,382) bleibt demgegenüber ebenso eine Randerscheinung wie die polit.-moralische Verurteilung des H. wegen seiner Attacken gegen Demosthenes (Lukian. Demosthenis Encomium 31).

Ed.: C. Jensen, 1917 (Ndr. 1963) • G. Colin, 1946 • J. O. Burtt, 1954 • M. Marzi, P. Leone, E. Malcovati, 1977. Komm.: V. de Falco, 1947 (*Euxenippos* und *Athenogenes*) • A. N. Oikonomides, 1958 (*Euxenippos*) • G. Schiassi, 1959 (*Epitáphios*).
Forsch.ber.: G. Bartolini, Iperide. Rassegna di problemi e di studi (1912–1970) (Proagones studi 13), 1977.
Lit.: J. Engels, Studien zur polit. Biographie des H., 1989.
Zu einzelnen Reden: G. Bartolini, I papiri e le edizioni dell' orazione di Iperide Contro Demostene, in: A&R 17, 1972, 103–113 • L. Braccesi, L'epitafio di Iperide come fonte storica, in: Athenaeum 48, 1970, 276–301 • S. Salomone, Originalità dell' epitafio Iperideo, in: A&R 22, 1977, 15–25 • Ders., Osservazioni sull' orazione Iperidea »Per Licofrone«, in: Maia n. s. 25, 1973, 55–63.

M. W.

Hyperion (Ὑπερίων; zur Etym. [1]). In der Trad. Hesiods einer der → Titanen, der mit seiner Schwester Theia die Lichtgötter Helios (→ Sol), → Selene und → Eos zeugt (Hes. theog. 134; 371–374; Apollod. 1,2,8). Die Überl. ist hinsichtlich seiner Teilnahme an der → Titanomachie gespalten (schol. Hom. Il. 14,274 Dindorf contra Serv. Aen. 6,580). Bei Homer hingegen ist H. sowohl Beiwort (Hom. Od. 1,8) als auch selbständige Bezeichnung des Helios (Hom. Il. 19,398, bes. aber in der röm. Dichtung: z. B. Ov. met. 8,565; Stat. Theb. 3,35). H. ist der Titel eines Briefromans von J.Ch. Hölderlin (1797–1799), in dem H. der im Sinn der Lichtmetaphorik bedeutungsvolle Name eines Kämpfers im griech. Befreiungskrieg ist.

1 O. Jessen, s. v. H., RE 9, 287 2 A. Kossatz-Deissmann, s. v. H., LIMC 5.1, 587–588.

C. W.

Hypermestra (auch Hypermnestra; Ὑπερμήστρα, Ὑπερμνήστρα).

[1] Tochter des → Danaos, Ehefrau des → Lynkeus (oder Lyrkeus). Einzige der Töchter des Danaos, die in der Hochzeitsnacht ihren Ehemann gegen den Befehl des Vaters nicht tötet (Pind. N. 10,6; Aischyl. Prom. 866; Apollod. 2,1,5). Sie verschont ihn, weil sie ihn liebt (Aischyl. Prom. 865–868; schol. Pind. P. 9,195b; vgl. Hor. carm. 3,11,33–52) oder weil er sie unberührt läßt (Apollod. 2,1,5; vgl. Ov. epist. 14,64). H. wird von Danaos vor Gericht gestellt, durch die Hilfe der Aphrodite jedoch freigesprochen (Paus. 2,20,7), was vermutlich in den ›Danaiden‹ des Aischylos dargestellt war (TrGF III fr. 43–46). H. weiht deshalb im Tempel des Apollon eine Statue der Aphrodite Nikephoros (Paus. 2,19,6) und stiftet der Artemis-Peitho ein Heiligtum (Paus. 2,21,1). Nach einer anderen Version tötet Lynkeus den Danaos und seine übrigen Töchter, wird König von Argos und zeugt mit H. den → Abas [1] (schol. Eur. Hec. 886; Paus. 2,16,1 f.). Das Paar wird so zu den Stammeltern argiv. Helden (vgl. Paus. 10,10,5).

[2] Heroine, deren Grabmal in Argos neben demjenigen von H. [1] gezeigt wurde, Tochter des → Thestios, Ehefrau des → Oikles, Mutter des → Amphiaraos (Paus. 2,21,2; Diod. 4,68,5; Apollod. 1,7,7; Hyg. fab. 73).
[3] Tochter des → Erysichthon bei Antoninus Liberalis 17, sonst Mestra genannt.

G. Berger-Doer, s. v. H., LIMC 5.1, 588–590 • O. Jessen, s. v. H., RE 9, 289–292 • Ch. Rohweder, Macht und Gedeihen: Eine polit. Interpretation der Hiketiden des Aischylos, 1998. K. WA.

Hyperocha. Wörtlich »Überschuß« (τὰ ὑπέροχα, *tá hypérocha*, oder ἡ ὑπεροχή, *hē hyperochḗ*), bezeichnet technisch den Mehrwert, um den der Wert der Pfandsache den Betrag der gesicherten Forderung übersteigt, lat. *superfluum*. Da das griech. Pfand dogmatisch als Verfallspfand aufzufassen ist (vgl. → *hypothḗkē*), bedurfte es bes. vertraglicher oder gesetzlicher Regelungen, wenn der Mehrwert einem weiteren Gläubiger als Sicherung dienen oder nach Pfandverkauf an den Pfandschuldner fallen sollte. Mehrfache Verpfändung ist bereits im 4. Jh. v. Chr. aus Athen belegt (vgl. → *hypothḗkē*), ohne daß dort allerdings der Ausdruck *h.* gebraucht würde. *H.* tritt erstmals im sog. Getreidegesetz aus Samos auf (Syll.[3] 976, Z. 66; um 260 v. Chr.), wo Pfandverkauf vorgeschrieben ist [3. 87; 5]. Konsequenterweise haftet der Schuldner dort auch für den durch das Pfand nicht gedeckten Fehlbetrag persönlich. Zu *h.* und Fehlbetrag (ἐλλεῖπον, *elleípon*) in den Papyri s. [2. 134]; vgl. auch SB 18,13167, Z. 25f. (Alexandreia?, Mitte 2. Jh. n. Chr.), wo dem Fehlbetrag statt *h.* ein Mehrerlös (πλεόνασμα, *pleónasma*) gegenübergestellt wird [4. 243]. Zu Überschuß im röm. Recht → *pignus*.

1 A. Manigk, s. v. H., RE 9, 292–321, bes. 306ff. 2 H.-A. Rupprecht, Einführung in die Papyruskunde, 1994
3 G. Thür, H. Koch, Prozeßrechtlicher Komm. zum »Getreidegesetz« aus Samos, Anzeiger der Oesterr. Akad. der Wiss. 118, 1981, 61–88 4 G. Thür, Hypotheken-Urkunden eines Seedarlehens, in: Tyche 2, 1987, 229–245
5 St. Tracy, The Date of the Grain Decree from Samos, in: Chiron 20, 1990, 97–100. G. T.

Hyperochos (Ὑπέροχος) aus dem unterital. Kyme, Zeit unbekannt (nach Jacoby, Komm. zu H., FGrH 576) frühestens 3. Jh. v. Chr., spätestens 2. Jh. n. Chr.). Verfasser einer Lokalgeschichte von Kyme (*Kymaiká*), von der nur 3 Fr. erh. sind. K. MEI.

Hypeuthynos (ὑπεύθυνος) wird in Strafbestimmungen griech. Dekrete für »haftbar, schuldig« gebraucht (gemeint: zur Zahlung von Geldstrafen, z. B. IPArk 11,37), speziell in Athen für »rechenschaftspflichtig«. Jeder Athener, der ein Amt innehatte, mußte sich nach Ablauf der Amtszeit einem Rechenschaftsverfahren (εὔθυναι, → *eúthynai*) unterziehen, bis zu dessen Abschluß er nicht ins Ausland reisen und über sein Vermögen keine Verfügungen treffen durfte. In den Papyri Ägyptens bedeutet *h.* einfach »leistungs- oder zahlungspflichtig«.

A. R. W. Harrison, The Law of Athens 2, 1971, 208–211 • IPArk. G. T.

Hyphärese s. Sandhi

Hyphasis (H. bei Arr., → Hypanis bei Strab., Diod. und Dion. Per., Hypasis bei Curt. und Plin. nat., Bipasis bei Ptol.; alle wohl durch iran. Vermittlung aus altind. *Vipāśā-*); einer der fünf Hauptflüsse des Pandschab, h. Satlağ/Beas. Am Oberlauf (h. Beas) lag der Punkt, von dem Alexander zum → Hydaspes zurückkehrte. Daher blieb der noch weiter östl. gelegene Satlağ (→ Zaradros des Ptol.) den Alexanderhistorikern unbekannt und auch der gemeinsame Unterlauf bis zum → Akesines [2] galt als H. Im 2. Jh. n. Chr. sah Ptol. mit etwas weiter reichenden geogr. Kenntnissen richtig im Bipasis einen Nebenfluss des Zaradros.

E. Kiessling, s. v. H., RE 9, 230–236. K. K.

Hyphen s. Lesezeichen

Hypios (Ὕπιος).
[1] (*Hyp(p)ius*). Fluß, h. Melen Çayı, der den See Daphnusis (h. Efteni Gölü) zum Schwarzen Meer entwässert; der Oberlauf des H. ist mit dem Küçük Melen Çayı gleichzusetzen (anders [1]).
[2] (*Hypius mons*). Gebirge nördl. von → Prusias am H. (Plin. nat. 5,148; anders [1]).

1 L. Robert, A travers l'Asie Mineure, 1980, 11–106.

K. Belke, Paphlagonien und Honorias, 1996, 217f. • W. Ruge, s. v. H., RE 9, 322f. K. ST.

Hypnos s. Somnus

Hypoboles graphe (ὑποβολῆς γραφή). Popularklage gegen eine Person, die einem Bürger als dessen eigenes Kind unterschoben worden war. Untergeschobene Kinder, meist gekaufte Sklaven, werden in den att. Gerichtsreden und → Komödien häufig erwähnt: Kinderlose Ehefrauen suchten so ihre Stellung im Hause zu festigen, doch ist die *h.g.* nur in den *Lexica Segueriana* V [2] überliefert. Die Sanktion gegen den Untergeschobenen war der Verkauf als Sklave.

1 I. Bekker (ed.), Anecdota Graeca I, 1814/1865, 311
2 Lipsius, 417. G. T.

Hypocaustum s. Heizung

Hypogäum. Sammelbezeichnung für unterirdisch angelegte Architekturen. Das H. bildet im mod. Verständnis überwiegend einen Teilbereich der → Grabbauten, wobei mit H. eine unter das Erdniveau gesetzte Architektur gemeint ist und nicht eine mit Erdreich überschüttete, zunächst oberirdisch erbaute im Sinne des Tumulus mit einer Grabkammer darin; ferner können (mit einem Grab wesensmäßig eng verwandte) Heroa (z. B. dasjenige von → Kalydon) sowie Baulichkeiten

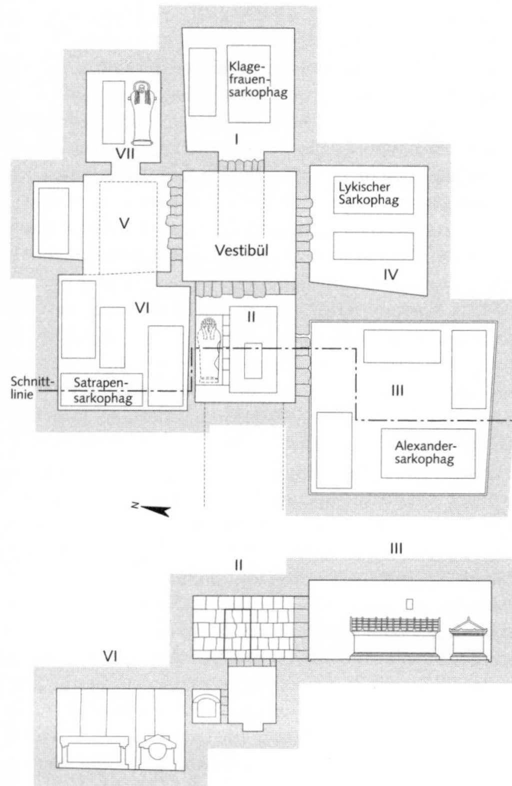

Königsnekropole von Sidon, Hypogäum A, Ende 6. Jh. – Ende 4. Jh. v. Chr. (Grundriß und Schnitt). (Die röm. Ziffern bezeichnen die einzelnen Kammern.)

für besondere Kultanlagen (z.B. das Nekromanteion von → Ephyra [3] oder, aus röm. Zeit, das Mithräum von → Capua/S. Maria Capua Vetere) als H. in Erscheinung treten.

Das H. tritt seit der 2. H. des 4. Jh. v. Chr. im griech. Kulturraum wie in den Nachbarkulturen der Thraker oder der indigenen Kulturen Süditaliens (Apulien; H. von Paestum, → Poseidonia) immer häufiger auf; eine Herleitung der zahlreichen alexandrinischen H. aus älteren ägypt.-byz. Vorbildern (Königsmetropole von Sidon, vgl. Abb.) wird diskutiert, wäre aber kaum eine Erklärung des Phänomens insgesamt. In der frühchristl. Architektur spielt das bisweilen zur → Katakombe erweiterte H. eine bedeutende Rolle als Begräbnis- und Kultplatz und fixiert damit den Ort des Entstehens erster Coemeterial-Kirchen.

H. Alon el-Atta, The Relations between the Egyptian Tombs and the Alexandrine H., in: Études et travaux 16, 1992, 11–19 • A. Barbet u. a., L'hypogée paléochrétien des Orants à Constanta, in: MEFRA 108, 1996, 105–158 • W. A. Daszewski, The Origins of the Hellenistic H. in Alexandria, in: FS für E. Winter, 1994, 51–68 • U. Kron, Zum H. von Paestum, in: JDAI 86, 1971, 117–148 • J. L. Lamboley, Les hypogeés indigènes apuliens, in: MEFRA 94, 1982, 91–194 • L. Reekmans, Spätröm. H., in: O. Feld (Hrsg.), FS für F. W. Deichmann, 1986, 11–37.

C. HÖ.

Hypokrites (ὑποκριτής).

I. Begriff II. Entwicklung in Athen III. Aufgaben (einschliesslich Statisten) IV. Entwicklung ausserhalb Athens seit dem 4. Jh. v. Chr. V. Masken und Kostüme

I. Begriff

Das zugrundeliegende Verbum ὑποκρίνομαι (*hypokrínomai*) bedeutet bei Homer »auf Anfrage eine Entscheidung treffen«, »deuten« (von Vorzeichen: Hom. Il. 12,228 oder Träumen: Hom. Od. 19,535; 555) bzw. »antworten« (Hom. Od. 2,111). Als Grundbed. für das erst im 5. Jh. v. Chr. bezeugte Nomen *h.* wurde darum bald »Antworter« (auf Fragen des Chorführers), bald »Deuter« (des Mythos, den der Chor vortrug) postuliert. Es bezeichnet den Sprecher, der den Sängern des Tragödien- oder Komödienchors entgegentrat und einen Dialog ermöglichte, d. h. den Schauspieler in allen dramatischen Gattungen.

II. Entwicklung in Athen

Die ersten *hypokritaí* waren die Tragiker selbst: von → Thespis (TrGF 1,49: DID D1) bis zu → Aischylos war der Dichter zugleich Komponist, Regisseur und Darsteller. Aischylos führte neben sich einen zweiten Sprecher ein, die Namen Kleandros und Mynniskos nennt die Vita Aeschyli 15 (TrGF III, Testimonia A 1). → Sophokles verzichtete darauf, selbst die Hauptrolle zu übernehmen; er erhöhte die Sprecherzahl auf drei, setzte also auf Professionalität der Darstellung und begründete so den Berufsstand des *h.*, der gleiches Ansehen genoß wie die Dichter. Bei der Dreizahl von *h.* ist es geblieben, sie garantierte Chancengleichheit im dramatischen Agon. Dem ersten *h.* (→ Protagonistes) fiel die Hauptrolle zu, die beiden anderen (→ Deuteragonistes, → Tritagonistes) mußten eine Fülle von Personen – Männer wie Frauen – darstellen. Die Aufteilung einer Rolle auf verschiedene Sprecher wurde zunächst vermieden (vgl. aber Theseus in Soph. Oid. K. 551–667, 887–1043), bei Menander ist sie geläufige Praxis. Die länger am Improvisatorischen festhaltende Komödie hat sich erst nachträglich der Beschränkung auf drei *h.* unterworfen – schwerlich schon durch → Kratinos (PCG IV Cratinus, Testimonia 19).

III. Aufgaben (einschliesslich Statisten)

Im Lauf der Entwicklung des Dramas nehmen Dialogpartien auf Kosten des Chors ständig zu. Vom *h.* wurde darum vor allem perfekte Stimmbeherrschung verlangt. Er mußte in einer tragischen Tetralogie hintereinander ganz unterschiedliche Personen verkörpern: bald argumentierend, bald zur Aulos-Begleitung deklamierend, seit Sophokles auch singend. Die von der Bühne her vorgetragenen (τὰ ἀπὸ τῆς σκηνῆς, *tá apó tḗs skēnḗs*, Aristot. poet. 12,1452b 18) Arien oder Monodien waren zunächst strophisch gegliedert, im Spätwerk des Euripides effektvoll durchkomponiert (Eur. Or. 1369–1502: Phryger-Arie) [1]. Lebhaftes Agieren und Gebärdenspiel, Gesangskunst und sprachliche Virtuosität erforderte vor allem die Alte Komödie. Allmählich galt das Publikumsinteresse dem Darsteller ebenso wie seiner Rolle. Um 449 v. Chr. richtete man darum an den Dionysien einen Agon der tragischen Protagonisten ein, wenig später an den Lenäen einen für die der Komödie. Der Starkult war geboren. Nunmehr wurde den konkurrierenden Dichtern ihr Protagonist zugelost (Hesych. N 286), die beiden anderen *h.* wählten sie in ihrer Eigenschaft als Regisseure selbst aus [2. 93–95]. Die Besoldung übernahm der Staat, nur die Statisten (κωφὰ πρόσωπα, *kōphá prósōpa*) bezahlte der → Choregos als Extraleistung (παραχορήγημα, *parachorḗgēma*). Zwei Gruppen von Statisten sind zu unterscheiden: Darsteller von Personen der Handlung, die zeitweise oder dauernd stumm bleiben, da keiner der drei *h.* zur Verfügung steht (z. B. Ismene in Soph. Oid. K. 1096–1689; Pylades durchweg in Aischyl. Choeph.; Soph. El.; Eur. El.), und Statisten im engeren Sinne (Leibgarde, Dienerschaft, Kinder) [3]. Ob die stummen Frauenrollen bei Aristophanes, wie Opora und Theoria im ›Frieden‹, von Männern gespielt wurden oder nicht (schol. Aristoph. Pax 849 nennt Prostituierte), bleibt umstritten.

IV. Entwicklung ausserhalb Athens seit dem 4. Jh. v. Chr.

Aufführungen in Theatern att. Gemeinden (Peiraieus, Thorikos, Ikarion) und seit 386 v. Chr. Reprisen auch an den Städtischen → Dionysien begünstigten die Bildung von Repertoires. Als im gesamten griech. Sprachraum neue Theater entstanden, erwarben sich durch den lebhaften Tourneebetrieb einige *h.* Ruhm und Reichtum: Kallippides, Neoptolemos, Polos und Theodoros in der Trag., Lykon und Satyros in der Komödie. Als Protagonisten schufen sie sich eigene Ensembles und spielten Stücke, in denen sie glänzten [4]. Während die Stars im Brennpunkt öffentlichen Interesses standen, wie es Ehrendekrete und viele Anekdoten bezeugen, war das Leben der übrigen *h.* (wenn wir glauben dürfen, was Demosthenes über → Aischines [2] berichtet, vgl. [5]) mühsam und glanzlos. Das schloß nicht aus, daß Aischines später als Politiker und Redner zu hohem Ruhm gelangen konnte. Im Hell. war aus dem att. Berufsstand des *h.* ein panhellenischer geworden; damals schlossen sich alle in Athen, am Isthmos und in Nemea, in Ionien und am Hellespont tätigen dionysischen Künstler (→ Technitai) zu Gilden zusammen. Diese garantierten den Wandertruppen Rechtsschutz und Privilegien und wahrten das künstlerische Niveau der Aufführungen, solange noch vollständige Dramen und nicht bravouröse musikalische und tänzerische Solodarbietungen vorgeführt wurden.

V. Masken und Kostüme

Die mit dem Kult des → Dionysos [I. C. 7.] eng verbundene → Maske ließ den *h.* hinter der von ihm verkörperten Gestalt zurücktreten. Masken erleichterten ihm die Übernahme auch von Frauenrollen und den schnellen Rollenwechsel. Die für Trag. und Satyrspiel identischen Masken waren in klass. Zeit verhalten im Ausdruck, seit Ende des 4. Jh. von immer stärkerem Pathos geprägt; umgekehrt büßten die Komödienmasken ihre urspr. grotesken und dämonischen Züge allmählich ein und wurden natürlicher.

Das Kostüm des tragischen *h.* scheint nach Ausweis der spärlichen Bildquellen [2. 177–231; 6] zunächst von der Alltagstracht (→ Kleidung, → Chiton, → Peplos) wenig abgewichen zu sein; im ausgehenden 5. Jh. aber ist ein prunkvolles Trag.-Kostüm bezeugt: ein knöchellanges, reich dekoriertes, oriental. anmutendes Ärmelgewand vielleicht dionysischer Herkunft; ein solches trug auch der Aulosspieler. Dazu kam als Bühnenschuh (→ Kothurn) ein weicher schmiegsamer Schnürstiefel, zum Schreiten und Tanzen bestens geeignet; erst im späten Hell. wurde daraus der hohe Stelzschuh. – Der *h.* der Alten Komödie trat in drastischer Sinnlichkeit in Erscheinung: Bauch und Hinterteil waren grotesk gepolstert, und über einem enganliegenden Trikot trug er einen lächerlich kurzen Chiton, unter dem ein Phallos hervorbaumelte. Das typische Frauengewand war ein langer safrangelber Chiton. Im Lauf des 4. Jh. wurde analog zur Maske auch das Kostüm des komischen *h.* dezent. Ein Kleiderverzeichnis und einen Maskenkatalog für die Neue Komödie überliefert Poll. 4,118–120; 133–154 [7].

→ Lykon; Neoptolemos; Polos; Theodoros

1 W. Barner, Die Monodie, in: W. Jens (Hrsg.), Die Bauformen der griech. Trag., 1971, 277–320 **2** A. Pickard-Cambridge, The Dramatic Festivals of Athens, ²1968, 126–176 **3** D. P. Stanley-Porter, Mute Actors in the Tragedies of Euripides, in: BICS 20, 1973, 68–93 **4** P. E. Easterling, From repertoire to canon, in: Dies. (Hrsg.), The Cambridge Companion to Greek Tragedy, 1997, 211–227 **5** H. Wankel, Demosthenes. Rede für Ktesiphon über den Kranz, 1976, zu §180 und §262 **6** B. A. Trendall, T. B. L. Webster, Illustrations of Greek Drama, 1971 **7** T. B. L. Webster, J. R. Green, A. Seeberg, Monuments Illustrating New Comedy Bd. 1, ³1995, 1–51.

M. Bieber, The History of Greek and Roman Theater, ²1961 • H.-D. Blume, Einführung in das ant. Theaterwesen, ³1991, 77–106 • P. Ghiron-Bistagne, Recherches sur les acteurs dans la Grèce antique, 1976 • A. Lesky, Hypokrites (1955), in: W. Kraus (Hrsg.), Gesammelte Schriften, 1966, 239–246 • J. B. O'Connor, Chapters in the History of Actors and Acting in Ancient Greece, 1908 (Suppl.: I. Parenti, in: Dioniso 35, 1961, 5–29) • F. Poland, s. v. Technitai, RE 5, 2473–2558 • K. Schneider, s. v. H., RE Suppl. 8, 187–232 • B. Zucchelli, Ὑποκριτής. Origine e storia del termine (Pubblicazioni dell' Istituto di Filologia Classica dell' università di Genova 15), 1962.

H.-D. B.

Hypomnema (ὑπόμνημα, seltener ὑπομνηματισμός; lat. *commentarius* oder seltener *commentarium*). Das Wort h. (von der Wurzel von μιμνῄσκω, »sich erinnern«) hat die abstrakte Grundbedeutung »Erinnerung«, Anwesenheit im Gedächtnis oder Aufruf/Stütze für das Gedächtnis (in diesem Sinne schon bei Thuk. 2,44,2 sowie Isokrates, Demosthenes, Xenophon usw.), nimmt jedoch im Laufe der Zeit eine große Zahl verschiedener Konnotationen und Nuancen an, bes. die verbreitete (konkrete) Bedeutung »Erwähnung, Hinweis«, auch in verbalem Sinn (z. B. Thuk. 4,126,1), »Notiz, Gedächtnisstütze, Aufzeichnung« zur Bezeichnung eines schriftlichen *memorandum* privater oder öffentlicher Natur: ökonomische Verzeichnisse, Konten, Listen von Personen oder Sachen, gesetzliche Aufzeichnungen, auch formale Dokumente, z. B. Gesuche oder Protokolle [3; 16]. Beispiele für diese Verwendung finden sich vor allem in den Papyrusurkunden. Zumindest von alexandrinischer Zeit an bezeichnet das Wort auch die offiziellen Register, d. h. die Archive von Höfen und öffentlichen Behörden (wofür auch der Begriff *ephemerídes* gebraucht wird). Das lat. Äquivalent *commentarius* deckt alle Bed. des griech. Wortes ab – einschließlich der Bezeichnung offizieller Archive (von Priesterkollegien, z. B. die → *commentarii pontificum*, oder von Magistraten oder Staatsorganen, z. B. die *commentarii senatus*; die *commentarii principis* waren die Archive des Kaisers); für diese kam in der Kaiserzeit auch der Begriff *acta* in Gebrauch.

Die Bedeutung »Notiz, Aufzeichnung zur Unterstützung des Gedächtnisses« kann *h.* mit Bezug auf verschiedene Gelegenheiten und Situationen privater Natur annehmen, wie z. B. Stichwortzettel für eine Rede, Lektürenotizen oder Aufzeichnungen von neuerworbenem Wissen, Unterrichtsmaterialien usw., z. B. wird »Aufzeichnungen schreiben« (ὑπομνήματα γράφειν) in Plat. polit. 295c von einem Arzt oder einem Gymnastiklehrer gesagt, die schriftliche Aufzeichnungen für die Kranken bzw. die Schüler hinterlassen; in Plat. Phaidr. 276d sind *hypomnémata* schriftliche Notizen zur Unterstützung des eigenen Gedächtnisses gegen das Vergessen, das mit dem Alter einhergeht, also eine Art persönliches Tagebuch. Die Konnotation »Notiz privater Natur« rechtfertigt den Gebrauch des Worts *h.* im Sinne einer nicht für die Verbreitung in der Öffentlichkeit bestimmten Schrift, im Gegensatz zu einem veröffentlichten Werk. Auf dieser Grundlage beruht auch der Gebrauch des Begriffs i.S. von »Entwurf, Skizze« zur Vorbereitung eines noch auszuarbeitenden Werks im Bereich der Historiographie und Philos. Für die Historiographie ist er gut dokumentiert; einer Theorie zufolge hatte der Historiker zunächst ein grobes Schema der Fakten, ein *h.*, vorzubereiten, das dann rhet. auszuarbeiten war.

Die Konnotation »erinnernswerte Dinge« führt leicht zur Bedeutung »Erörterung, Darstellung, Abh.« verschiedener Art (außer Rede und Dialog), nunmehr als tatsächlich abgeschlossenes und veröffentlichtes Buch. Wir besitzen Beispiele mit Bezug auf Werke histor. (z. B. Pol. 1,1,1), geogr. (z. B. Ptol. Geographica 1,6,2), medizinischen (z. B. oft bei → Galenos), philos. (Diog. Laert. 4,4 definiert einen Teil der Werke des Speusippos als *h.* im Unterschied zu dessen Dialogen) und rhet. (Ps.-Longinos De Sublimitate 44,12) Inhalts oder mit Bezug auf Werke vermischten Inhalts, wie die *Sýmmikta hypomnémata* des → Aristoxenos oder die *Hypomnémata* des → Kallimachos. Die Definition *h.* wird im speziellen Sinne auch für autobiographische Schriften und Erinnerungen großer Männer gebraucht: Pol. 2,40,4 erwähnt die *hypomnēmatismoí* des Staatsmanns Aratos von Sikyon (weitere Fälle in FGrH 227–238). Schwer zu sagen ist jedoch, ob und wann der Begriff auf den Autor zurückging und wirklich der Titel des Werks war oder eine sekundäre Gattungsbezeichnung ist, die auf die → indirekte Überlieferung zurückgeht.

Von hell. Zeit an wird der Begriff *h.* zur Bezeichnung des fortlaufenden exegetischen Komm. zu lit. Texten gebraucht, der auf eine vom kommentierten Text getrennte Rolle von meist beträchtlichem Umfang geschrieben wurde: Dies ist eines der charakteristischsten Produkte der gelehrten philol. Arbeit der alexandrinischen Grammatiker (zusammen mit der Textausgabe, *ékdosis*), das sich mit → Aristarchos [4] von Samothrake (ca. 215 – 144? v. Chr.) definitiv durchsetzte. Hier steht das *h.* dem *sýngramma* gegenüber, das eine monographische Abh. bezeichnet (s. z. B. Galen, Komm. zu Hippokrates, De acutorum morborum victu 15,515 K.; Scholia Il. 2,111). Die Originale dieser Schriften sind verloren; die vielfältige Masse ihres gelehrten Materials ist durch die scholiographischen und gelehrten Slgg. der Byzantiner überliefert worden. Nur durch Papyrusfunde kennen wir bedeutende Reste von *hypomnémata*. Sie sind normalerweise nach dem Aufbaumuster Lemma – Exegese gegliedert, das dem komm. Text folgt, und sie weisen verschiedene Interessen und Inhalte auf, von der einfachen glossographischen Erklärung einzelner Wörter bis zur Erörterung philol., exegetischer, antiquarischer, mythographischer Probleme; von Sprach- und Wortgebrauch, rhet. Figuren, stilistischen Beobachtungen, Sprichwörtern, Anekdoten und biographischen Fragen bis hin zu ästhetischen und moralischen Urteilen über das Werk und auch zur → Allegorese. Oft setzt sich die gelehrt-doxographische Anhäufung durch, nicht selten in gekürzter und brachylogischer Redaktion. Erh. Beispiele ausführlicher Komm. aus der Kaiserzeit sind die medizinisch ausgerichteten des → Galenos (seine Komm. zu philos. Themen sind verloren) und die des → Alexandros [26] von Aphrodisias zu Aristoteles; erh. sind auch zahlreiche spätant. Aristoteles- und Platonkommentare.

→ Commentarii

G. Arrighetti, Poeti, eruditi e biografi. Momenti della riflessione dei Greci sulla letteratura, 1987, 161–231 • G. Avenarius, Lukians Schrift zur Geschichtsschreibung, 1956, 85–104 • E. Bickermann, Beiträge zur ant. Urkundengesch., in: APF 9, 1930, 164 ff. • F. Bömer, Der Commentarius, in: Hermes 81, 1953, 215–250 • M. Del

FABBRO, Il commentario nella tradizione papiracea, in: Studia Papyrologica 18, 1979, 69–132 • ENTRETIENS XL, 1994, • FGrH 227–238 • K. MCNAMEE, Sigla and Select Marginalia in Greek Literary Papyri, 1992 • G. MISCH, Gesch. der Autobiographie, I 1, [3]1949, 209 ff. • F. MONTANARI, Filologia omerica antica nei papiri, Proc. of the XVIII Congress of Papyrology at Athens, Athenai, Greek Papyrological Soc., 1988, 337–344 • Ders., Zenodotus, Aristarchus and the Ekdosis of Homer, in: G. W. MOST, Editing Texts – Texte edieren (Aporemata 2), 1998, 1–21 • PFEIFFER, KP I • J. RÜPKE, Wer las Caesars bella als commentarii?, in: Gymnasium 99, 1992, 201–226 • E. G. TURNER, Greek Papyri. An Introduction, [2]1980, 63–126 • E. ZIEBARTH, s. v. H., RE Suppl. 7, 281–82. F.M./Ü: T.H.

Hypomosia (ὑπωμοσία). In Athen zwei Arten von eidlichen Erklärungen: 1. Im Prozeß konnte eine Partei selbst oder durch einen Vertreter den Antrag auf Vertagung stellen (Demosth. or. 48,25 f.; schol. Demosth. or. 21,84), wenn wichtige Gründe vorlagen, wie Reise oder Begräbnispflichten. Der Gegner konnte dies durch ἀντωμοσία (*antōmosía*, Gegeneid) bestreiten.

2. Wurde im Rat (→ *bulḗ*) oder in der Volksversammlung (→ *ekklēsía*) über einen Antrag verhandelt, konnte jeder Bürger bis zum Schluß der Verhandlung durch *h.* erklären, er werde gegen den Antragsteller eine Klage wegen Gesetzwidrigkeit des Beschlusses (→ *paranómōn graphḗ*) oder wegen Unzweckmäßigkeit des Gesetzes einbringen. Dadurch wurde entweder die Abstimmung oder, wenn diese bereits erfolgt war, die Wirksamkeit des Beschlusses ausgesetzt, bis das Geschworenengericht entschieden hatte.

A. R. W. HARRISON, The Law of Athens 2, 1971, 155 • H. J. WOLFF, »Normenkontrolle« und Gesetzesbegriff in der att. Demokratie, 1970. G.T.

Hyporchema (ὑπόρχημα). Altgriech. Chorlyrik, die urspr. mit dem Waffentanz in Verbindung gebracht wurde. Das Wort *h.* ist zuerst bei Plat. Ion 534c belegt, wo es zusammen mit Dichtungsformen genannt wird. → Thaletas von Gortyn (7. Jh. v. Chr.) verfaßte als erster *hyporchḗmata* zur Begleitung von Waffentänzen der → Kureten (schol. Pind. P. 2,127). Da Kriegertänze kunstvoller und mimetischer als andere Chortänze waren, sang vermutlich ein Solist (Athen. 1,15d-e). Thaletas brachte wohl das *h.* nach Sparta, wo er mit Xenodamos von Kythera verantwortlich für die zweite Organisation der Musik für den Staat war: Beide verfaßten auch → Paiane (Plut. De musica 1134b-c). Das längste erh. Fragment eines *h.* stammt von → Pratinas von Phleius (Athen. 14,617c-f), vermutlich aus einem Satyrspiel: Es betont die Verbindung mit Dionysos und ordnet die Musik dem Gesang unter. *H.* haben somit vielleicht eine Rolle im Drama gespielt: Einige wollen in Abschnitten wie Soph. Ai. 693 ff. und Trachin. 205 ff. *h.* sehen [1. 342]. Die Zitate bei Plut. mor. 747a–748d wurden → Simonides [2. 399–401] und Pindar [3. 100–102] zugewiesen. Das Wesen des → Kastoreion bei Pind. P. 2,69 ist bes. problematisch: Das Scholion nennt es ein *h.* und zitiert die Eingangsverse mit der Feststellung, daß die Dioskuren mit Kriegertänzen assoziiert wurden. Nach anderen ist dieses Kastoreion das Epinikion selbst [4. 96–101]. Die Zuweisungen an Bakchylides beruhen manchmal darauf, daß überwiegend das kretische Versmaß verwendet wird, das angeblich für das *h.* charakteristisch ist [5. 90–91] und ein Zeichen für dessen kret. Ursprung.

1 E. DIEHL, s. v. H., RE 9, 338–343 2 TH. BERGK, Poetae lyrici Graeci III, [4]1882 3 H. MAEHLER, Pindari Carmina II, 1989 4 G. W. MOST, The Measures of Praise, 1985
5 B. SNELL, H. MAEHLER, Bacchylidis Carmina cum Fragmentis, [10]1970. E.R./Ü: L.S.

Hyporon. Stadt in Bruttium (Bronze-Mz. um 300 v. Chr.: HN 105), wohl identisch mit Hipporum im Itin. Anton. 115.

NISSEN 2, 949. E.O.

Hyposkenion s. Theater

Hypostase

[1] s. Wortbildung

[2] (ὑπόστασις/*hypóstasis*; *substantia, subsistentia*). In der Spätant. – durch den Neuplatonismus und in den Auseinandersetzungen des 4. Jh. n. Chr. um das Wesen der Trinität – wurde H. von einem mehrdeutigen, von keiner Schule genau definierten (vgl. Sokr. 3,7) zu einem der wichtigsten Begriffe des philos. und theologischen Denkens (Trinitätslehre, Christologie).

Der Begriff H. erscheint zuerst in medizinisch-naturwiss. Texten (→ Hippokrates, → Aristoteles [6]) und bezeichnet das Sich-Absetzen fester Stoffe aus Flüssigkeit (z. B. im Urin), aber auch den in Erscheinung tretenden Stoff selbst (»Sediment«, »Niederschlag«) [1. 24–26]. Hieran knüpft die erstmals im 2. Jh. v. Chr. bei → Okellos und → Demetrios [21] Lakon faßbare philos. Bedeutung (»dauerhafter Bestand«, »Wirklichkeit«, »Existenz«) an. Trotz Versuchen, die Einführung von H. als philos. Begriff der Alten Stoa zuzuschreiben, scheint er dort – wie auch in der späteren Stoa – keine Rolle gespielt zu haben [2]. Die hell. Philosophen gebrauchen H. als nachdrücklichere Bezeichnung für »Existenz«. Gelegentlich scheint H. sogar mit οὐσία (*usía*) austauschbar. Als lat. Übers. kommt im 1. Jh. n. Chr. *substantia* auf, das aber bald auch *usía* wiedergibt. Daher wird von Marius Victorinus im 4. Jh. n. Chr. zur Unterscheidung *subsistentia* geprägt, das sich aber nicht allg. durchsetzt.

Obgleich auf Plotin die neuplaton. H.-Lehre zurückgeht, nach der aus dem Einen durch → Emanation der Geist und aus diesem die Seele hervorgehen, wendet er den Begriff H. darauf noch nicht an. Erst → Porphyrios bezeichnet im Titel von Plot. Enneades 5,1 (Περὶ τῶν τριῶν ἀρχικῶν ὑποστάσεων) das Eine, den Geist und die Seele als H., Plotin dagegen spricht von *phýseis*.

In der christl. trinitarischen Diskussion bezeichnet als erster → Origenes Gottvater, Sohn und Hl. Geist als H.; für ihn ist jedoch H. noch mit *usía* austauschbar, er versteht also darunter noch nicht »individuelle Existenz« im Sinne von »Person« [3]. Der arianische Streit (→ Arianismus) löste Kontroversen aus, wie in Gott Einheit und Trinität zu denken seien. Dabei bediente man sich des H.-Begriffs, um das innertrinitarische Verhältnis zu beschreiben (μία οὐσία, τρεῖς ὑποστάσεις, ›eine Substanz, drei *h.*‹). Abweichend von neuplaton. Vorstellungen aber sind die H. in der Trinität gleichrangig, der Gedanke an eine Stufung ist aufgegeben.

In der Christologie unterschied man anfangs nicht zw. H. und Natur (*phýsis*), bis schließlich das Konzil von Chalkedon (451) definierte, daß beide Naturen (des Gott- und des Menschseins) in einer Person und H. zusammenkommen.

1 H. Dörrie, Ὑπόστασις. Wort- und Bedeutungsgesch., 1955 (auch in: Ders., Platonica minora, 1976, 12–69) **2** J. Hammerstaedt, Das Aufkommen der philos. H.bedeutung, in: JbAC 35, 1992, 7–11 **3** Ders., Der trinitarische Gebrauch des H.begriffs bei Origenes, in: JbAC 34, 1991, 12–20 **4** Ders., RAC 16, 986–1035 **5** F. Romano, D. P. Taormina (Hrsg.), Hyparxis e hypostasis nel neoplatonismo, 1994 **6** R. Witt, Ὑπόστασις, in: Amicitiae corolla ... J. R. Harris, 1933, 319–343.

S.M.-S.

Hypostigme, Hypoteleia s. Lesezeichen

Hypotheke (ὑποθήκη).
[1] Juristisch
A. Griechisches Recht B. Graeco-Ägyptisches Recht C. Römisches Recht

A. Griechisches Recht

Die *h.* (wörtlich »Unterlage«) begegnet im att. Recht als eine Belastung von Liegenschaften, Häusern, Unternehmen zur Sicherung von Darlehensforderungen. H.-Steine (→ *hóroi*) zeigten die hypothekarische Belastung an. Die *h.* war ein gemeingriech. Institut, die Kennzeichnung des belasteten Anwesens durch *hóroi* wurde jedoch außerhalb von Attika nur auf einigen wenigen Inseln der Ägäis befolgt. Die *h.* war Verfallsrecht. Dies erweisen den Verfall an den Gläubiger aussprechende Zusätze auf manchen *hóroi*, z.B. [1. Nr. 1]. Die *h.* war weiter Ersatzrecht; der Schuldner übernahm bes. die Haftung auf den »Fehlbetrag« (ἐλλεῖπον, *elleípon*). Das Belastungsobjekt (die *h.*) blieb im Besitz des Schuldners, im Gegensatz zur Sicherheit (ἐνέχυρον/*enéchyron*), die in den Besitz des Gläubigers gelangte. Mit der *h.* verband sich teilweise ein gesetzliches Veräußerungs- und Nachverpfändungsverbot; z.B. in → Gortyn (Große Gesetzesinschr. 10,25). In Athen beispielsweise konnte ein Pfandnehmer gegen Weiterverfügungen Einspruch erheben (κωλύειν συμβάλλειν; Reminiszenz in Cod. Iust. 8,44,24 aus dem J. 294 n. Chr.). Beim → Seedarlehen war es üblich, die Nachverpfändung (ἐπιδανείζειν, *epidaneízein*) zu verbieten (Demosth. or. 35,11).

B. Graeco-Ägyptisches Recht

Auch die graeco-ägypt. *h.* war Verfallsrecht. Der Gläubiger erhielt bei Nichtbezahlung das Recht zur Ergreifung von Besitz und Eigentum (κρατεῖν καὶ κυριεύειν o. ä.). Gelegentlich begnügte man sich mit einer Verweisung auf die allg. Regeln des H.-Rechts, verbunden mit der Eröffnung persönlicher Haftung des Schuldners auf den Fehlbetrag (FIRA III Nr. 119 aus den J. 143/4 n. Chr.). Das ansonsten verbreitete Veräußerungsverbot an den Schuldner fehlt in den von Römern in Ägypten errichteten Urkunden. Seine Zulässigkeit war unter den röm. Juristen strittig: Marcianus ließ es zu (Dig. 20,5,7,2), ebenso Justinian und die byz. Jurisprudenz. Hypothezierungen aus röm. Zeit nehmen das spätere sog. »Gordianische Pfand« (→ *pignus Gordianum*) vorweg. Der *h.* steht die → *ōnḗ en pístei* (ὠνὴ ἐν πίστει, Sicherungsübereignung) nahe, die der altgriech. → *prā́sis epí lýsei* (πρᾶσις ἐπὶ λύσει, Verkauf auf Ablösung) entspricht. Von der *h.* zu unterscheiden ist das → *hypállagma* (wörtlich: Austausch).

C. Römisches Recht

Erstmals bei Cicero begegnet *h.* als Lehnwort (fam. 13,56,2) für eine griech. Verfalls-*h.* Anfragen aus den östl. Provinzen an die röm. Juristen verwenden die Ausdrücke *hypothḗkē* und *hypotíthesthai* (Scaevola Dig. 20,1,34,1; 17,1,60,4) und fördern den Eingang des Wortes *h.* in die jurist. Fachsprache der Römer. Erstmals in einem jurist. Text nachweisbar ist das Wort im 2. Jh. n. Chr. bei Julian (Dig. 41,3,33,4). Danach wird es oft von Gaius und Marcianus, seltener bei anderen Juristen verwendet.

Mit *h.* bezeichnen die Römer das röm. → Pfandrecht, das aber kein Verfallsrecht ist. Dabei soll *»hypotheca« proprie* das besitzlose Pfandrecht bezeichnen (Ulp. Dig. 13,7,9,1); das Wort wird jedoch vielfach in einer das Besitzpfandrecht einschließenden Bedeutung verwendet (z.B. im Titel der Monographien von Gaius und Marcianus), wie umgekehrt das Wort → *pignus* auch für das besitzlose Pfandrecht gebraucht wird, da zw. diesem und dem Besitzpfandrecht kein wesentlicher Unterschied besteht (Marcianus Dig. 20,1,5,1; Inst. Iust. 4,6,7); in beiden Fällen ist der Gläubiger durch die dingliche Pfandklage (*actio Serviana*) geschützt, und in beiden Fällen steht ihm bei Pfandreife, wenn die Sicherheit zur Verwertung fällig wird, das Verkaufsrecht zu (*ius distrahendi*).

1 M. Finley, Studies in Land and Credit in Ancient Athens 500–200 B.C. The Horos-Inscriptions, o.J. (1951), [2]1985.

A. Biscardi, Appunti sulle garanzie reali in diritto romano, 1976, 150–156, 218–254 • Honsell/Mayer-Maly/Selb, 196 mit Anm. 10, 203–206 • Kaser, RPR I, 459 mit Anm. 8, 463–473; II, 312–321 • H.-A. Rupprecht, Einführung in die Papyruskunde, 1944, 134f. • Ders., Die dinglichen Sicherungsrechte nach der Praxis der Papyri, in: FS H. Ankum II, 1995, 425–436 • Taubenschlag, 271–291.

D.SCH.

[2] Rhetorisch, s. Gnome [2]

Hypothesis (ὑπόθεσις). Einleitung, Inhaltsangabe.
A. Literaturhistorisch B. Rhetorisch

A. Literaturhistorisch

Für die Trag. kann man drei Typen unterscheiden: 1. die in peripatetischer Tradition (→ Dikaiarchos fr. 78 Wehrli) stehenden *hypothéseis* des → Aristophanes [4] von Byzanz; sie enthalten eine knappe Inhaltsangabe, verweisen auf die Behandlung desselben Stoffes bei einem anderen Tragiker, benennen den Schauplatz, die Identität des Chors und den Prologsprecher und geben weitere Informationen zur Aufführung (Datierung, Titel der anderen gleichzeitig aufgeführten Stücke des Autors, Konkurrenten und Plazierung im Agon, → Choregos). Teilweise folgt eine kritisch-ästhetische Würdigung. Quellen dürften die *Pínakes* des → Kallimachos und die → *Didaskalíai* des Aristoteles sein. Eine vollständige H. dieses Typs ist nicht erhalten. 2. Die vor allem mit Euripides verbundenen, alphabetisch angeordneten und teilweise in Versform abgefaßten *h.* Sie benennen den ersten Vers des Stücks und enthalten eine im Praeteritum abgefaßte Inhaltsangabe; namenlose *dramatis personae* werden identifiziert. Sie sind – wohl als myth. Kompendium – als Ersatz für die Dramentexte und nicht als einführende Information gedacht. Sie dürften aus dem 1. Jh. v. Chr. stammen. 3. Auf der Basis des zweiten Typs entstanden in byz. Zeit (13./14. Jh.: Demetrios Triklinios, Manuel Moschopoulos) für den Schulunterricht bestimmte *h.*

Die den Komödien vorangestellten *h.* entsprechen dem Schema der tragischen. Die *h.* vom Typ 1 scheinen auf Aristophanes [4] von Byzanz zurückzugehen. Sie wurden von → Symmachos umgearbeitet und enthalten mehr didaskalische Informationen als die entprechenden trag. H. Daneben gibt es umfangreichere Inhaltsangaben (Typ 2, vgl. POxy. 663 zu → Kratinos' *Dionysaléxandros*, PCG IV, p. 140), zu → Menandros wohl auch in alphabetischer Ordnung (POxy. 1235 zu *Hiéraia* und *Ímbrioi*), und (Typ 3) in moralisierend, didaktischer Absicht verfaßte byz. *h.* (z.B. *h.* II zu Aristophanes' *Aves*). Häufiger als bei der Tragödie erscheinen in gerader (10 oder 12) Verszahl geschriebene *h.*, deren Zuweisung an Aristophanes von Byzanz – vielleicht mit Ausnahme von Aristophanes' ›Thesmophoriazusen‹ – zweifelhaft ist.

Zu nicht-dramatischen Texten sind *h.* erhalten zu Pindar (wohl von → Didymos [1]), Ps.-Hesiods *Aspís*, Theokrit (von → Artemidoros [4] aus Tyana und dessen Sohn → Theon), Apollonios [2] Rhodios, Lykophron und zu den Rednern Isokrates, Isaios, Antiphon, Andokides, Lykurgos. Zu den Reden des Demosthenes gibt es *h.* des → Libanios, die in byz. Zeit als Einleitungen zu den Ausgaben verwendet wurden.

B. Rhetorisch

In der → Rhetorik versteht man unter H. einen Spezialfall (*quaestio specialis*) im Gegensatz zu einer allg. Frage (*thésis*). Systematisch wird die H. von → Hermagoras von Temnos behandelt.

→ Argumentum

N. Dunbar (ed., comm.), Aristophanes, Birds, 1995, 31–37 • Pfeiffer, KP I, 238–242 • E. Pöhlmann, Einführung in die Überlieferungsgesch. und in die Textkritik der ant. Lit. I, 1994, 33 f. • L. Radermacher (Ed.), Aristophanes' Frösche, 1967, 74–85 • G. Zuntz, The political plays of Euripides, 1954, 129 ff. B.Z.

Hypsaeus. Cognomen (inschr. auch *Ypsaeus*) wohl griech. Herkunft in republikanischer Zeit in der Familie der → Plautii. K.-L.E.

Hypseus (Ὑψεύς). König der thessal. → Lapithen (Pind. P. 9,13–31; gemäß schol. ad loc. nach einer *Ehoie* des Hes. fr. 215 M-W), geboren im thessal. Pindos-Gebirge als Sohn des Flußgottes → Peneios und der Naiade → Kreusa (einer Tochter des Okeanos und der Gaia), oder Tochter der Philyra (schol. Pind. P. 9,27); Vater von → Kyrene und Alkaia (schol. Pind. P. 9,31), die er mit Chlidanope zeugt; auch Vater der Themisto (Apollod. 1,84; Hyg. fab. 1). J.S.-A.

Hypsikles (Ὑψικλῆς). Hell. Mathematiker und Astronom. Aus der Einl. zu dem von ihm stammenden B. 14 von Euklids ›Elementen‹ folgt, daß H. um 175 v. Chr. in Alexandreia lebte.

Durch Hss. wird bezeugt, daß er die Schrift verfaßt hat, die später als B. 14 den ›Elementen‹ des → Eukleides [3] zugefügt wurde (Ed. [1]). Sie behandelt wie B. 13 das Einbeschreiben regulärer Körper in eine Kugel und war als Erklärung zu einem verlorenen Werk des → Apollonios [13] über Dodekaeder und Ikosaeder gedacht. H. zeigt, daß die Flächen, die einen derselben Kugel einbeschriebenen Ikosaeder und Dodekaeder bilden, von demselben Kreis umbeschrieben werden. Ferner weist er nach, daß sich Oberflächen und Volumina von Dodekaeder und Ikosaeder zueinander verhalten wie die Kante des in dieselbe Kugel einbeschriebenen Würfels zur Ikosaederkante. Die auf arab. Überl. fußende Vermutung, daß H. auch an dem sog. B. 15 der ›Elemente‹ beteiligt war, ist unwahrscheinlich.

Erh. ist auch eine kurze und vermutlich unvollständige Schrift über die Aufgangszeiten der Gestirne (*Anaphorikós*, Ἀναφορικός; Ed. [2; 3]). Es ist das früheste bekannte griech. Werk, bei der die → Ekliptik (wohl nach babylon. Vorbild) in 360 Grad geteilt wird. H. gibt ein Verfahren an, um die Zeiten zu berechnen, welche die verschiedenen Zeichen und Grade der Ekliptik zu ihrem Auf- und Untergang brauchen. Seine Methode beruht nicht auf exakter Rechnung, sondern auf einer groben Annäherung. Er geht davon aus, daß die Dauer des längsten Tages für Alexandreia 210 Zeitgrade beträgt, und nimmt (unzutreffend) an, daß die Aufgangszeiten der Zeichen von Widder bis Jungfrau eine aufsteigende und von Waage bis Fische eine absteigende arithmetische Reihe bilden. Zur Berechnung benutzt er Hilfssätze über arithmetische Folgen. Trotz der falschen Annahme, daß die Tageslängen monoton zu- und abnehmen, kommt er zu Ergebnissen, die für praktische Anwendungen (z.B. in der Astrologie) ausreichen. Die

Schrift ist im Stil des Euklid mathematisch korrekt gearbeitet und stellt astronomisch ein interessantes Zwischenglied zwischen der babylon. und hell. Wissenschaft dar: Da H. die trigonometrischen Hilfsmittel des Ptolemaios noch nicht zur Verfügung standen, um die Auf- und Untergangszeiten genau zu berechnen, benutzte er Annäherungen durch arithmetische Folgen, d. h. lineare Zackenfunktionen, mit deren Hilfe die Babylonier ihre Ephemeriden berechneten. – Der *Anaphorikós* wurde als eines der »mittleren Bücher«, die man nach dem Studium des Euklid zur Vorbereitung von → Ptolemaios' ›Almagest‹ lesen sollte, im 9. Jh. ins Arab. (Ed. [3]) und von dort im 12. Jh. durch Gerhard von Cremona ins Lat. übers. (*Liber Esculei de ascensionibus*; Ed. [2]).

Die Vertrautheit des H. mit arithmetischen Folgen und Reihen bezeugt auch → Diophantos [4], der erwähnt, daß H. den Wert einer beliebigen Polygonalzahl (→ Gnomon [3]) bestimmt hat (De polygonis numeris, S. 470,27 TANNERY).

ED.: 1 J. L. HEIBERG, Hypsiclis liber, sive Elementorum liber XIV qui fertur, 1888 (= Euclidis opera omnia, Bd. 5; griech.-lat.) 2 K. MANITIUS, Des H. Schrift Anaphorikos nach Überl. und Inhalt kritisch behandelt, Programm Gymnasium Dresden, 1888 (griech. Text und lat. Übers. von Gerhard von Cremona) 3 V. DE FALCO, M. KRAUSE (Hrsg.), H.: Die Aufgangszeiten der Gestirne, in: AAWG, 3. Folge, Nr. 62, 1966 (griech.-dt. mit Schol., arab. Übers. und Komm.).

LIT.: 4 A. A. BJÖRNBO, s. v. H. (2), RE 9, 427–433 5 I. BULMER-THOMAS, H. of Alexandria, in: GILLISPIE, Bd. 6, 1972, 616 f. 6 T. L. HEATH, History of Greek Mathematics, 1921, Bd. 1, 84; 419 f.; Bd. 2, 192; 213–218; 515 7 J. MAU, s. v. H., KlP 2, 1967, 1289 f. 8 SEZGIN, Bd. 5, 143–145; Bd. 6, 80 9 B. L. VAN DER WAERDEN, Erwachende Wissenschaft, 1956, 445–448. M. F.

Hypsikrates (Ὑψικράτης) von Amisos. Historiker und Grammatiker, der 92 J. alt wurde ([Lukian.] makrob. 22). Die wenigen Fragmente seines Geschichtswerkes weisen auf die Zeit des Caesar bzw. Augustus (E. 1. Jh. v. Chr.). Er schrieb auch über Homer, den er als Zeitgenossen Hesiods betrachtete, und gab Etymologien griech. und lat. Worte, die Varro ablehnte. Dabei leitete er den lat. Sprachschatz aus dem griech. her. FGrH 190.

R. GIOMINI, Ipsicrate, in: Maia 8, 1956, 49–55. K. MEI.

Hypsipyle s. Iason; Lemnische Frauen; Thoas

Hypsistos (ὕψιστος, »der Höchste«) kann als Adjektiv jedem Gott beigelegt werden, ist aber vor allem inschr. seit dem späteren Hell. belegte Epiklese des → Zeus als Berggott oder Hochgott und Name eines Gottes (*theós h.*), der identisch mit Zeus H. sein, aber auch den jüd. oder christl. Gott bezeichnen kann; im einzelnen ist eine Abgrenzung oft schwierig. Eine Gesamtstudie des seit den ersten Analysen gewaltig angewachsenen Materials, die L. ROBERT mehrfach angekündigt hat, steht noch aus [1].

Zeus wird durchgehend als höchster Gott bezeichnet; seit der *Ilias* ist das Adjektiv *hýpatos*, seit Pindar (Pind. N. 1,60; 11,2) *h.* bezeugt, und zwar sowohl für Zeus als höchsten Gott überhaupt wie auch spezifisch als Berggott (Soph. Trach. 1091: Kult auf dem Oita); kult. trägt der Berggott Zeus häufiger die Epiklese *Hýpatos* [2. 875 f.] als H. Die inschr. Belege für H. (Zeus und *theós*) verteilen sich auf verschiedene Bereiche:

1. Seit dem mittleren Hell. ist Zeus als Gott des maked. Königtums mit der Epiklese H. bezeugt; die Inschr. stammen aus den Königsstädten Edessa und Aigai wie aus anderen Städten Makedoniens. Solche Dedikationen wiederholen sich in einigen Orten des griech. Mutterlands, wobei die Beziehung zu Makedonien nicht sicher erweisbar ist. In Theben stand ein Tempel in der Nähe eines danach benannten Stadttors (Paus. 9,8,15), in Korinth befanden sich die Altäre von Zeus Chthonios, des Gottes der Erdtiefe, und seines Gegenstücks Zeus H., des Gottes des obersten Himmels, nebeneinander, in Olympia mehrere Altäre von Zeus H. (Paus. 2,2,8; 5,15,5).

2. Seit der frühen Kaiserzeit finden sich in Kleinasien zahlreiche Inschr., die zumeist einem *theós h.* gelten, insbes. im Pontosgebiet, in Lykien und Phrygien. Wenigstens ein Teil dieser Inschr. kann einen der lokalen Hochgötter umschreiben (analog erscheint die lokale Muttergöttin auch als *hypsístē*). Gelegentlich wird die Epiklese → Helios als oberstem sichtbaren Gott beigelegt. Andere Texte, bes. aus dem phrygisch-lydischen Grenzgebiet, sind Ergebnis spezieller rel. Entwicklungen in einem Gebiet Anatoliens, das sich in der Kaiserzeit auch sonst durch rel. Innovation auszeichnet. Das gilt vor allem dort, wo einem *theos h.* als dem höchsten Gott eine Mittlergestalt (*theós ángelos, tó theíon angelikón, tó theíon epiphanés*) [3] beigesellt wird, ohne daß dies als jüd. oder christl. erkennbar ist; es reflektiert vielmehr die auch in der philos.-theologischen Spekulation der Kaiserzeit faßbare Tendenz, den obersten Gott aus der direkten menschlichen Reichweite wegzubewegen.

3. Im Vorderen Orient werden zahlreiche lokale Baalim (→ Baal), insbes. wenn sie Höhengötter sind, in einer → Interpretatio Graeca als Zeus H. angesprochen [2. 886–888]; so ist eine große Zahl solcher Dedikationen etwa aus → Palmyra erhalten. Das strahlt in die Ägäis aus, etwa wenn auf Delos Zeus auf dem Kynthos H. heißt oder wenn auf Kalymnos Zeus H., Hera Urania (Tanit) und Poseidon Asphaleios für Rettung aus einem Erdbeben gedankt wird ([4], unter Antoninus Pius).

4. In der Septuaginta, der jüd. hell. Lit. und (seltener) dem NT, aber auch den graeco-ägypt. → Zauberpapyri wird der jüd. Gott als *theós h.* angesprochen; außerhalb der LXX erweist sich die Form oft als Beschreibung durch Nichtjuden [5]. Theos H. findet sich auch in jüd. und christl. Inschr. der Kaiserzeit, bes. in Kleinasien, wo seit der Diadochenzeit große jüd., dann auch christl. Diasporagemeinden existierten; jüd. sind etwa die beiden Inschr. von Rheneia, welche Theos H., »den Herrn

der Winde und jeden Fleisches«, als Rächer in einem Mordfall anrufen (Syll.³ 1181).

Diese verschiedenen Gruppen lassen sich in der kult. Realität nicht sauber voneinander abgrenzen: Angesichts der Evidenz des Konzepts ist mit der Interaktion verschiedener, spontan entstandener Gruppen zu rechnen. In der Forsch. hat die Herleitung aus dem jüd. (und danach christl.) Wortgebrauch dominiert. Das ist insofern wohl überzeichnet, als jüd. und christl. Nennungen nur dann sicher identifizierbar sind, wenn der Kontext die Zuordnung ermöglicht; eine Differenzierung zw. Zeus H. und Theos H. ist ebenfalls nicht überall nachweisbar, zumal an verschiedenen Orten tendenziell offizielle Inschr. Zeus H., private Dedikationen Theos H. anreden, Theos H. also die private Version des Zeus H. sein kann. Religionsgesch. ebenso wichtig wie die saubere Scheidung der Gruppen ist aber gerade der Umstand, daß in der Kaiserzeit und bes. in Kleinasien die verschiedenen rel. Gruppen den Namen oder die Epiklese H. zum Ausdruck eines heno- oder monotheistischen rel. Ideals benutzten, in dem pagane, jüd. und christl. Traditionen konvergieren konnten und sich so von der offiziellen Polisreligion distanzierten. Bezeichnend ist, daß die Kulte des (Zeus oder Theos) H. sehr oft als private Kultvereine mit gemeinsamen Banketten konstituiert waren, in denen der einzelne soziale und rel. Identität finden konnte (etwa Ägypten PLond. 2710 [6]; Thessaloniki IG X 2 Nr. 68–71, spätes 1. Jh. n. Chr.; Milet OGIS 755 f. [7]), daß Zeus oder Theos H. als → Soter und Nothelfer angeredet (Thessaloniki IG X 2 Nr. 67, Rettung aus Seenot durch einen Traum) und mit Heilkulten verbunden war, in denen sich private rel. Anliegen bes. deutlich niederschlugen: so in Athen auf der Pnyx [8], in Kos (zusammen mit → Asklepios und → Hygieia [9]) oder im syro-phöniz. Raum (Ešmun [6. 62 f.]). So überrascht auch nicht, daß sich umgekehrt das kleinasiatische Christentum von Splittergruppen wie den kappadokischen Hypsistarioi oder Hypsistianoi polemisch abgrenzt (Greg. Naz. or. 18,5; vgl. Greg. Nyss. Contra Eunomium 38 [10]).

1 C. Colpe, A. Löw, s. v. H. (Theos), RAC 16, 1036–1056 **2** A. B. Cook, Zeus. A Study in Ancient Rel. 2: Zeus God of the Dark Sky, 1925 **3** L. Robert, Reliefs votifs et cultes d'Anatolie, in: Anatolia 3, 1958, 112–120 (Opera Minora Selecta 1, 411–419) **4** M. Segre, Tituli Calymnii, in: ASAA 6/7, 1944/45, 31 Nr. XXXIII **5** M. Simon, Theos H., in: Ex orbe religionum. Studia Geo Widengren, 1972, 1, 372–385 **6** C. Roberts, Th. C. Skeat, A. D. Nock, The Gild of Zeus H., in: Harvard Theological Revue 29, 1936, 39–88 **7** L. Robert, in: CRAI 1968, 594 f. (Opera Minora Selecta 5, 610 f.) **8** B. Forsén, The Sanctuary of Zeus H. and the Assembly Place of the Pnyx, in: Hesperia 62, 1993, 507–521 **9** M. Segre, Iscrizioni di Cos, 1994, EV 127 **10** M. Simon, s. v. Gottesfürchtiger, RAC 11, 1068–1070. F. G.

Hypso (Ὑψώ). Nach Val. Flacc. 1,365 ff. Mutter der Argonauten-Zwillinge → Deukalion und → Amphion aus Pella; abweichend davon die Version bei Apoll. Rhod. 1,176, der Asterion (anstelle von Deukalion) und Amphion aus Pellene Söhne des Hyperasios nennt. J. S.-A.

Hyria (Ὑρία). Im homer. Schiffskatalog erwähnte boiot. Stadt am → Euripos nahe Aulis und Chalia. Heimat des Lykos, Nykteus, Orion, Euphemos und der Antiope. In klass. Zeit von Thebai, seit hell. Zeit von Tanagra abhängig; die Lokalisierung nördl. des h. Paralia Avlidas (früher Dhramesi) oder auf einem Tseloneri (auch Glypha) gen. Hügel an der Westseite der Chalkis gegenüberliegenden Euriposbucht bleibt unsicher. Belegstellen: Hom. Il. 2,496; Hes. fr. 181; 253 West; Strab. 8,6,17; 9,2,12; 9,2,21; Plin. nat. 4,26; Apollod. 3,5,5; Nonn. Dion. 13,96 ff.; Steph. Byz. s. v. Ὑ., s. v. Χαλία).

S. C. Bakhuizen, Salganeus and the Fortification on its Mountains, 1970, 16 f., 145–147 · Fossey, 75 f. · Lauffer, Griechenland, 234 f., 509. · P. W. Wallace, Strabo's Description of Boiotia, 1979, 52 f. P. F.

Hyrie (Ὑρίη). Aitol. Nymphe. Nach dem Sprung ihres Sohnes Kyknos vom Felsen zerfließt sie vor Trauer in Tränen und wird zum See, der nach ihr benannt wird (Ov. met. 7,371 ff.). Bei Antoninus Liberalis 12 heißt sie (nach Nikandros und Areus von Lakonien) Thyria; als Kyknos, ihr und Apollons Sohn, sich in den See Kanope stürzt, folgt sie ihm; Apollon verwandelt beide in Schwäne.

F. Bömer, P. Ovidius Naso, Metamorphosen, B. VI–VII, 1976, 292. RE. ZI.

Hyrieus (Ὑριεύς). Sohn von → Poseidon und → Alkyone [1], Gründer der boiot. Stadt → Hyria(i). → Trophonios und Agamedes erbauen ihm ein Schatzhaus, doch so, daß sie heimlich daraus stehlen können; daran schließt sich eine Gesch. an, welche die Erzählung vom Meisterdieb (Hdt. 2,121) variiert (Paus. 9,27,5–7). Oft erzählt ist, wie H. zu seinem Sohn Orion kommt: Den kinderlosen Witwer besuchen Zeus und Apollon, und zum Dank für seine Gastfreundschaft (er schlachtet ihnen sein einziges Rind) urinieren sie in die Rindshaut; daraus entsteht das Kind Orion (Wortspiel mit *ourein*, »urinieren«; ausführlich Ov. fast. 5,495–536; zuerst belegt Pind. fr. 73, Sonderrolle des Hermes: Hyg. fab. 195). F. G.

Hyrkania (Ὑρκανία < altpers. *varkāna-*, »Wolfland«; mittelpers. *gurgān*). Historisch-geogr. wichtige Region Irans (Bewohner: Ὑρκάνιοι, Ὑρκανοί, *Hyrcani*) am SO-Winkel des Kaspischen Meeres (Hekataios FGrH 1 F 291: Ὑρκανίη θάλασσα), wird im Süden und SO durch den östl. Elburzflügel abgeschirmt und öffnet sich nach NO hin zur aralokaspischen Steppe. Sie war klimatisch wie naturräumlich begünstigt durch die auf der Nord-Seite des Elburz abregnenden Niederschläge (Plin. nat. 31,43), zahlreiche kleinere Gewässer und die größeren Flüsse Sarnios (h. Atrak) und Maxeras (h. Rōd-i Gurgān), die beide ins Kaspische Meer münden. Apollodor von Artemita (Strab. 11,7,1 ff.) und Ptolemaios (6,9) kennzeichnen H. als fruchtbar, tierreich (vgl. auch Ail. nat. 7,38; 16,10 zu den für Krieg und Jagd abgerichteten Hunden und Curt. 3,2,6 zur hyrkanischen Reiterei) und dichtbesiedelt. Unter den Städten ragten die achäm. satrapale Residenzstadt Zadrakarta, später Syrinx und Tambrax heraus (bis h. nicht exakt lokalisiert). Laut Arrianos (an. 3,23,1) führte die wichtigste Überlandstraße von Ekbatana nach Baktra nicht durch H., vielmehr zweigte in Parthien eine für Wagen und Troß geeignete Königsstraße nach Zadrakarta hin ab, die über das Elburzgebirge führte.

Wohl unter Kyros d.Gr. dem Achämenidenreich einverleibt, rebellierte H. (zusammen mit Parthien) 521 v. Chr. vergeblich gegen Dareios I. [4. DB 2,92 ff.]. 480 v. Chr. kämpften die Hyrkanier im Heere des Xerxes in pers. Ausrüstung (Hdt. 7,62). Unter Dareios III. fungierte → Phrataphernes als Satrap von Parthien und H. (Arr. an. 3,23,4) und befehligte als solcher 331 v. Chr. die Parther, Hyrkanier und Tapurer in der Schlacht bei Gaugamela (Arr. an. 3,8,4). Zusammen mit seinen Söhnen ging er nach dem Tode des Dareios vor Zadrakarta zu Alexander über, von dem er kurz darauf die Satrapie zurückerhielt.

Eine bemerkenswerte Nachricht bei Polybios (10,28,3) bezeugt nicht nur achäm. Bewässerungsanlagen in H., sondern auch königl. Privilegien für die sie unterhaltenden Dorfgemeinschaften. Unter Seleukos I. wurde H. seleukidische Satrapie (App. Syr. 57; zw. 311 und 304 v. Chr.), griech. Verwaltung ist inschriftl. (SEG 20,325), griech. Besiedlung lit. bezeugt (etwa in → Syrinx: Pol. 10,31,5, wo sich auch ein »Palast«, βασίλειον befand). Einige Zeit vor dem Ostfeldzug Antiochos III. fiel H. vorübergehend an die Parther (Iust. 41,4,8), endgültig aber wohl erst zu Beginn des 2. Jh. v. Chr.

In parth. Zeit (ab dem 2. Jh. v. Chr.) erscheint H. als Sommeraufenthalt der Könige (Strab. 16,1,16) und als Exilort des Seleukidenherrschers Demetrios II. (Iust. 36,1,6; 38,9,3–9). Isidor von Charax gibt in seinem Itinerar (*Mansiones Persica* 14) die Ausdehnung H.s mit 60 Schoinen an und erwähnt dort elf Siedlungen mit Halteplätzen; bei Ptol. 6,9,2–8 werden 13 hyrkan. Städte namentlich erwähnt, von denen allerdings bis jetzt keine zuverlässig lokalisiert werden konnte. War der Partherkönig Artabanos II. entgegen landläufiger Meinung wohl nicht hyrkanischer Herkunft [7. 63–78], so doch dessen Nachfolger und Ziehsohn Gotarzes II. [8. 445], der dort seine Machtbasis besaß (Tac. ann. 11,8–10). Ein Aufstand in H. – unter dem Sohn Vardanes I.? [so 7. 118 f., anders 3. 77] – hinderte in den 50er-Jahren des 1. Jh. n. Chr. den Partherkönig → Vologaises I. an einer erfolgreichen Kriegführung gegen die Römer in Armenien (Tac. ann. 13,37,5; 14,25,1 f.; 15,1,1; 15,2,4); im Verlauf dieser Erhebung schickten die Hyrkanier auch Gesandte nach Rom, die um ein vertraglich vereinbartes Bündnis (*societas*) nachsuchten (Tac. ann. 14,25,2). Verm. kam es Anfang der 60er-Jahre zu einem Kompromiß zw. Hyrkaniern und Parthern, nach dem erstere wieder unter die Botmäßigkeit des Arsakidenkönigs zurückkehrten; für ein hyrkan., mit Rom verbündetes Sonderreich [9. 18–20] spricht nichts [3. 88].

Schon seit achäm. Zeit stellte sich für die iran. Könige das Problem, H. gegen Angriffe und Beutezüge aus der Steppe zu verteidigen [6]. Dies war auch der Zweck des imposanten »Alexander-Walls« nördl. des Gurgān-Flusses mit über 180 km Länge und rund 40 Kastellen. Verm. in (spät?-)parth. Zeit erbaut [6. 240 f.], wurde er wohl in sāsānidischer Zeit gründlich restauriert. Arsakidenzeitliche Siedlungsreste sind in H. gleichfalls nachweisbar [5], allerdings in der Regel weder genauer datierbar, noch mit Städten der schriftl. Parallelüberlieferung identifizierbar. Die Bedrohung aus dem NO blieb auch in sāsānidischer Zeit bestehen, in der H. (Gurgān) eine Provinz (*šahr*) bildete, deren Funktionäre z. T. durch ihre Siegel bezeugt sind [2. 50,84]. Seit Yazdgird II. (438–457) hören wir wiederholt von mil. Unternehmungen der Könige zur Abwehr nomadisierender Gruppen und Völkerschaften. Gurgān zählte zu den Regionen, in denen christl. Deportierte angesiedelt wurden, sprechen christl. Zeugnisse doch von einem Bistum »Gefangenschaft/Deportation von Gurgān« zu Beginn des 5. Jh. [1. Bd.4. 382–384]; aus der Mitte des 7. Jh. ist uns in Gurgān sogar eine jakobitische Diözese bezeugt [1. Bd.5. 332–334].

→ Parther; Sāsāniden

1 J. M. Fiey, Communautés syriaques en Iran et Irak, 1979 **2** R. Gyselen, La géographie administrative de l'Empire sassanide, 1989 **3** M. Heil, Die oriental. Außenpolitik des Kaisers Nero, 1997 **4** R. G. Kent, Old Persian, 1953 **5** M. Y. Kiani, Parthian Sites in H., 1982 **6** M. J. Olbrycht, Parthia et ulteriores gentes, 1998 **7** M. Schottky, Parther, Meder und Hyrkanier, in: AMI N. F. 24, 1991, 61–134 **8** Ders., Quellen zur Gesch. von Media Atropatene und H. in parth. Zeit, in: J. Wiesehöfer (Hrsg.), Das Partherreich, 1998, 435–472 **9** W. Schur, Die Orientpolitik des Kaisers Nero, 1923.

J. W.

Hyrkanos. Beiname von Juden, nach → Hyrkania am Kaspischen Meer, eingebürgert durch Rückwanderer aus der dortigen Diaspora.

[1] Sohn des ptolem. Generalsteuerpächters von Koilesyrien und Phoinikien Iosephos aus der jüd. Magnatenfamilie der Tobiaden. Er zog sich nach der Eroberung des ptolem. Syriens durch → Antiochos [5] III. im J. 200 v. Chr. in das Transjordanland zurück, wo der Großvater Tobias als Kommandeur jüd. Militärsiedler die Machtstellung der Familie begründet hatte. H. bewahrte vermutlich eine proptolem. Haltung und konnte sich in weitgehend unabhängiger Stellung behaupten, bis → Antiochos [6] IV. seiner Herrschaft ein Ende bereitete und er sich das Leben nahm (ca. 170 v. Chr.). Der Palast in → ʿIrāq al-Amīr war wahrscheinlich seine Residenz im Transjordanland. H. und sein Vater sind die Hauptpersonen des von Flavios Iosephos (ant. Iud. 12,154–236) ausgeschriebenen sog. »Tobiadenromans«, einer Erzählung nach Art der hell. Biographie.

E. Bikerman, The Jews in the Greek Age, 1988, 231–234 • M. Hengel, Judentum und Hell., [2]1973, 486–503.

[2] Iohannes H. Jüd. Hohepriester aus dem Hause der → Hasmonäer 135–104 v. Chr., wurde von → Antiochos [9] VII. Sidetes nach mehrjährigem Krieg gezwungen, die seleukid. Oberhoheit zu akzeptieren (131/30 v. Chr.). Wohl auf Grund röm. diplomat. Intervention (die Datier. der betreffenden Dokumente bei Iosephos, ant. Iud. 13, 260–265 und 14, 247–255, ist jedoch strittig) behielt H. gegen Zahlung von Tributen Ioppe und andere Orte außerhalb Judaeas. H. mußte 130/29 Antiochos VII. bei dessen Partherfeldzug Heeresfolge leisten. Nach dessen Niederlage und Tod zog H. Gewinn aus dem Niedergang des Seleukidenreiches, eroberte Gebiete im Ostjordanland, → Samaria, wo er die Stadt und den schismatischen Tempel der Samaritaner zerstörte, ohne daß → Antiochos [11] IX. dies verhindern konnte, und gewann Skythopolis und Idumaia, wo er die Bevölkerung judaisierte. Im Inneren geriet er in Konflikt mit den → Pharisaioi (Quellen: Ios. bell. Iud. 1,54–69; ant. Iud. 13,230–300).

Schürer 1, 200–215.

[3] Iohannes H. II. folgte seinem Vater → Alexandros [16] Iannaios 76 v. Chr. in der Hohepriesterwürde, nach dem Tod seiner Mutter → Alexandra Salome 67 v. Chr. in der Königswürde. Im Streit mit seinem Bruder → Aristobulos [2] II. gewann er durch Vermittlung des Idumäers → Antipatros [4] die Hilfe → Aretas' [3] III. und erhielt durch Pompeius' Entscheidung 63 v. Chr. das Hohepriesteramt und die Herrschaft über das erheblich verkleinerte Hasmonäerreich. 57 v. Chr. wurde ihm die weltliche Herrschaft entzogen, doch erhielt er sie durch Caesar, dem Antipatros in Alexandrien mil. Hilfe geleistet hatte, in territorial vergrößertem Rahmen mit dem Titel eines »Ethnarchen und röm. Bundesgenossen« zurück. Beim Parthereinfall im J. 40 wurde H. durch Abschneiden der Ohren für das Amt des Hohenpriesters untauglich gemacht. Von König → Herodes [1] aus der Gefangenschaft zurückgeholt, wurde er 31/30 v. Chr. auf dessen Befehl hingerichtet (Quellen: Ios. bell. Iud. 1,199–273; ant. Iud. 14,80–369).

Schürer 1, 267–280.

[4] Sohn des → Herodes v. Chalkis und der Berenike, geb. vor 48 n. Chr. H. ist auf Grund der Bevorzugung seines Halbbruders → Aristobulos [6] polit. nicht hervorgetreten (Ios. bell. Iud. 2,221; ant. Iud. 20,104). K.BR.

Hyrnetho (Ὑρνηθώ). Eponymos der argiv. Phyle Hyrnathioi; Heiligtümer in Argos und Epidauros. Tochter des → Temenos und Gattin des Herakliden → Deïphontes. Von den Brüdern wurde H. getötet, weil sie im Familienstreit zu ihrem Mann hielt (Paus. 2,28,3–7). RE.ZI.

Hyrtakos (Ὕρτακος). Im Verbündetenkatalog der *Ilias* als Vater des Asios genannt, des Herrschers über das am Hellespont gelegene Arisbe (Hom. Il. 2,835–839). H. selbst taucht nur in patronym. Angaben zu Asios auf; sein Name ist möglicherweise mit einer kret. Stadt namens Hyrtakina in Verbindung zu bringen. Ein Held gleichen Namens tritt in der *Aeneis* Vergils als Vater des Nisus auf (Verg. Aen. 9,176f.).

Kamptz, 313f. • P. Wathelet, Dictionnaire des Troyens de l'Iliade, 1988, Nr. 325. E.V.

Hysiai (Ὑσίαι). Boiot. Stadt am Nordhang des → Kithairon östl. von Plataiai, westl. von Erythrai (Eur. Bacch. 751; Thuk. 3,24,2; Paus. 9,1,6), ca. 2 km östl. vom h. Erythres (früher Kriekouki) bei der Kirche Pantanassa. Vor der Schlacht bei Plataiai 479 v. Chr. erstreckte sich das pers. Feldlager am Asopos von Erythrai über H. bis Plataiai, während das griech. Heer zunächst bei Erythrai Stellung bezog, dann über H. zum dortigen Demeter-Heiligtum zog (Hdt. 9,15,3; 25,3; Plut. Aristeides 11,6). H. galt als von Nykteus gegr. *apoikía* von Hyria (Strab. 9,2,12; Steph. Byz. s. v. Ὑ., s. v. Ὑρία); seit 519 v. Chr. mit Plataiai zu Athen gehörig (Hdt. 5,74,2; 6,108,6 mit Thuk. 3,68,5), kam H. mit den übrigen Orten südl. des Asopos spätestens 447 zu Thebai (Hell. Oxyrh. 19,3,391 verwechselt H. mit → Hyettos); in röm. Zeit lag H. mit seinem Apollon-Heiligtum und Quell-Orakel in Trümmern (Paus. 9,2,1).

Fossey, 112–115 • Lauffer, Griechenland, 274f. • Müller, 499 • N. D. Papachatzis, Παυσανίου Ἑλλάδος Περιήγησις 5, ²1981, 24–30 • Pritchett 1, 104–106; 3, 74–77; 5, 101–103 • Schachter 1, 49, 152–154 • P. W. Wallace, Strabo's Description of Boiotia, 1979, 54f. P.F.

Hyspaosines (griech. Ὑσπαοσίνης, Σπασίνης, Πασίνης; lat. *Spaosines*; keilschriftl. *Aspasine*; Name iran. Herkunft). Sohn des Sagdo(do)nacus; Begründer einer Dyn. selbständiger lokaler Herrscher in der → Charakene; nach Plinius (nat. 6,139) König (*rex*) der Araber, die zwar in den Keilschrifttexten seiner Zeit wiederholt erwähnt werden, aber nicht in Verbindung mit ihm. Ca. 165 v. Chr. von Antiochos IV. als Verwalter der Eparchie am Roten Meer eingesetzt, gelang es ihm, im Zusammenhang mit dem Übergang Südmesopot. von den Seleukiden an die Arsakiden (141 v. Chr.) weitgehende Unabhängigkeit (Königstitel) zu erlangen. Seine Münzprägung beginnt um diese Zeit; ab 138/7 [1. 168–171 u.ö.] wird er auch in Keilschrifttexten erwähnt. Babylon stand kurzzeitig unter seiner Herrschaft (Frühjahr 127, er wurde aber wohl noch im gleichen Jahr zurückgedrängt [1. 254f.]). Neben den Auseinandersetzungen mit den Arsakiden gab es kriegerische Konflikte auch mit der → Elymais. Nach kurzer Krankheit starb er – nach der Überlieferung – in hohem Alter (vielleicht in Gefangenschaft? [1. 274f.]) am 11. Juni 124, Nachfolger wurde ein unmündiger Sohn [1. 282f.]. Die Münzprägung endet erst 121/20 [2. 91].

1 A. J. Sachs, H. Hunger, Astronomical Diaries 3, 1996
2 S. A. Nodelman, A Preliminary History of Charakene, in: Berytus 13, 1959/60, 85–91. J.OE.

Hystaspes (Ὑστάσπης, altpers./avest. *Vī/īštāspa-*, »mit (zum Rennen) losgebundenen Rossen«). Name verschiedener iran. Persönlichkeiten.

[1] Als *kauui-* (Kavi, Prinz) der entscheidende Förderer Zarathustras (→ Zoroastres [4. 13,100]); Sohn des *Auruuat̰.aspa-*, Gatte der Hutaosā. Unter seinem Namen liefen in der griech.-röm. Welt auch vielbenutzte und vielzitierte »Orakel« um, die sich mit den letzten Dingen befaßten, vgl. zuletzt [1. 376–381].

[2] Sohn des Arsames (altpers. *Aršāma-*), Enkel des Ariaramnes (*Ariyāramna-*), Vater des → Dareios I., schlug 521 v. Chr. nach der Thronbesteigung seines Sohnes in zwei Schlachten in Parthien einen parthisch-hyrkanischen Aufstand nieder (TUAT 1, 436 §§ 35 f.).

[3] Sohn des Dareios [1] I. und der Atossa, Statthalter von Baktrien und Sogdien (Hdt. 7,64).

[4] Sohn des → Xerxes I. (und der Amastris?), der sich z.Z. der Ermordung seines Vaters (465 v. Chr.) in seiner Satrapie Baktrien aufgehalten (Diod. 11,69,2) und später vergeblich gegen seinen Bruder und neuen Großkönig → Artaxerxes [1] I. aufgelehnt haben soll (Ktes. FGrH 688 F 14: dort wird allerdings von einem »anderen Artabanos« gesprochen [2. 581–588]).

[5] Verwandter (*propinquus*) Dareios' III. und mit der Tochter des Bisthanes, einer Enkelin des Artaxerxes Ochos, vermählt; von Dareios mit einem hohen mil. Kommando versehen (Curt. 6,2,7), wurde H. im Jahre 324 von Alexander mit der Führung des orientalischen Teiles des Agema der Hetairenreiterei betraut (Arr. an. 7,6,5).

[6] Nach Xen. Kyr. 2,2,2–5 u.ö. Freund und Feldherr Kyros' d.Gr., u.a. in Kleinasien (Hystaspas).

1 M. Boyce, F. Grenet, A Hist. of Zoroastrianism, vol. 3, 1991 2 Briant, Index s.v. H. 3 R. G. Kent, Old Persian, 1953 4 W. W. Malandra, The Fravaši Yašt, 1971. J.W.

Hysterie. Das Substantiv »Hysterie« kommt in klass. Zeit nicht vor. Allerdings hielt man die Gebärmutter (ὑστέρα, *hystéra*) für die körperliche Ursache einer Reihe von körperlichen und geistigen Gesundheitsbeeinträchtigungen, die vom Kopfschmerz über Zähneknirschen, Stimmverlust und Atemnot bis zum ausgeprägten Anfall reichten. Das Ausbleiben der Monatsblutung, Übermüdung, unzureichende Ernährung, sexuelle Enthaltsamkeit und eine abnorme Leichtigkeit bzw. Trokkenheit der Gebärmutter ließen dieses Organ, wie man glaubte, auf Wanderschaft durch den Körper gehen (vgl. z.B. Hippokr. Mul. 1,7 = 8,32 L.). Nach Lehrmeinung der hippokratischen → Gynäkologie waren ältere Frauen gefährdeter, da ihre Gebärmutter angeblich leichter war (Mul. 1,7 = 8,32 L.); Aretaios dagegen meinte, jüngere Frauen seien eher betroffen, da deren Lebenswandel und Weltverständnis »umherirrend« (ῥεμβώδης, De causis et symptomatibus morborum 2,11 = CMG 2,34,5) seien. Die hippokratischen Autoren unterschieden eine ganze Reihe von Gesundheitsstörungen je nach dem Körperteil, an dem der umherwandernde Uterus seine Reise unterbrach (Mul. 2,123–131 = 8,266–278 L.): Wenn die Gebärmutter sich in Richtung Leber auf die Suche nach Feuchtigkeit mache, könne sie den Atemfluß im Körper unterbrechen; wandere sie zu den Rippen, komme es zu Hustenanfällen, Seitenstechen und einem Gefühl, als liege eine Kugel in der Seite. Platon (Tim. 91a-d) beschreibt die Gebärmutter als ein Lebewesen, das, wenn es unbefruchtet bleibe, durch den Körper wandern, Passagen blockieren und so Krankheiten verursachen könne. In hell. Zeit kannte die Medizin eine Krankheit namens ὑστερικὴ πνίξ, »Erstickung der bzw. durch die Gebärmutter«.

Die Entdeckung der den Uterus in der Bauchhöhle fixierenden Haltebänder durch Herophilos (fr. 114 von Staden) führte keineswegs zur Aufgabe dieser Krankheitsentität. Stattdessen bemühte man allerlei Erklärungen, wie der Uterus andere Körperorgane affizieren könne, ohne diese Organe tatsächlich als Wanderuterus zu erreichen. → Aretaios sprach von einer »Sympathie« zw. der Gebärmutter und den kranial gelegenen Organen und behauptete, die Haltebänder seien besonders elastisch, so daß der Uterus dennoch frei beweglich sei (De causis et symptomatibus morborum 4,11 = CMG 2,81,31). Galen (De loc. aff. 6,5 = 8,420–424; 432 Kühn) unterschied zw. einem durch weibliche Samenverhaltung und einem durch Ausbleiben der Monatsblutung verursachten Erstickungsanfall, wobei ersterer als der gefährlichere galt, da seine Auswirkungen auf den Körper einer Vergiftung gleichkamen. Die Behandlung eines angeblich durch die Gebärmutter verursachten Anfalls bestand in Maßnahmen, die geeignet schienen, die scheinbar tote Patientin wieder zum Leben zu erwecken; dazu gehörten insbesondere Mittel, mit deren Hilfe man die Patientin zum Niesen bringen konnte (z.B. Hippokr. Aph. 5,35 = 4,544 Littré), wozu auch Senf zählte (Plin. nat. 20,87,238). In bes. schweren Fällen wurde vor Beginn der Therapie erst einmal geprüft, ob die Patientin überhaupt noch am Leben war; zu diesem Zwecke hielt man ihr Federn oder Wollfetzen unter die Nase oder stellte eine Wasserschüssel auf ihren Brustkorb. Die Anwendung übel riechender Substanzen an der Nase sollte das Hinunterdrängen der Gebärmutter unterstützen: Knoblauch, Dürrkraut und Bibergeil fanden breite Verwendung. Der Behandelnde wikkelte Bandagen um den Körper der Patientin (Mul. 2,127 = 8,272 L.) oder gebrauchte seine Hände (Diokles von Karystos, in: Soranos, Gynaikeia 3.4.29 = CMG 4,112,18–23), um die Gebärmutter an ihren angestammten Platz zurückzudrängen. Im Kontext galenischer Medizin hielt man Aderlässe am Knöchel für heilsam. Als beste Vorbeugung gegen die krankhafte Wanderschaft der Gebärmutter galten jedoch in weiten Kreisen Heirat und Schwangerschaft.

→ Frau; Gynäkologie; Hippokrates (mit Schriften-/Abkürzungstabelle)

H. King, Once Upon a Text: Hysteria from Hippocrates, in: S. Gilman et al., Hysteria Beyond Freud, 1993, 3–90.

H.K./Ü: L.v.R.-B.

Hysteron proteron s. Figuren

I

I (sprachwissenschaftlich)
A. Lautwerte B. Herkunft der i-Laute; Weiterentwicklung

A. Lautwerte

Der zehnte Buchstabe des griech. → Alphabets hatte folgende Lautwerte: 1. son. (silb.) *ĭ* in δίκη, τίς; 2. son. *ī* in ἶς »Kraft«; 3. kons. (unsilb.) *i̯*; letzteres gilt in Kurzdiphthongen (*ai̯*; frühklass. *ei̯*; *oi̯*), Langdiphthongen (*āi̯*; *ę̄i̯*; *ǭi̯*) sowie hinter son. *i* (nichtphonematisch): αἴθω, δείκνυμι, οἰνή, τοῖο; χώρᾱι Dat., τιμῆι, ἀγρῶι, ἠῶιος; pamphyl. διια [5. 312].

Ähnliche Geltung hatte *I* im Lat.: 1. *ĭ* in *dictus*, *quis*; 2. *ī* in *uīs* »Kraft«, *fīo*; 3. *i̯* in altlat. *aide* Akk. »Tempel«, *ex-deicendum*, *oino* Akk. »einen«; wie διια lat. inschr. *Fabiius*; dazu 4. anlautendes *i̯*- in *iecur*, *iocus* (zweisilbige Formen); 5. -*i̯i̯*- in Formen wie *ai(i)o*, *ei(i)us* (zweisilbig, mit positionslanger erster Silbe); *aiio* ist eine auch von Cicero verwendete Schreibweise [2. 127; 6. 124].

Nicht als eigener Buchstabe anerkannt, aber inschr. gut bezeugt ist die Variante *I longa* [1; 2. 13 f.], namentlich für *ī* (FELICI), *i̯* (IVSSV, EIIVS), *i̯i̯* (EIVS), *ii̯* (PIETAS).

B. Herkunft der i-Laute; Weiterentwicklung

i̯ und *ĭ* waren im Uridg. Allophone, z. B. in der Wz. **dei̯ḱ* / *diḱ* »zeigen« (→ Ablaut); der Wechsel ist in δείκνυμι /δίκ-η sowie in altlat. -*deic-endum* / *dic-tus* erhalten.

Anlautendes *i̯*- ist in lat. *iecur* ererbt (vgl. altind. *yákr̥t* »Leber«), auch im älteren Myk. war es noch vorhanden: *jo-qi* Relativpron. (vgl. altind. *yát* »welches«), hieraus homer. ὅτ-τι. Dagegen war *ī* im Uridg. wohl marginal; häufiger ist *ī* < *ii̯ə* (→ Laryngal), so wohl auch im Wz.-Nomen **u̯ī–s* »Kraft« < **u̯ii̯ə-s*; etwas anders *fīo* < **bhūi-i̯ō* < **bhu̯ə-i̯ō* [4. 108]; kontrahiert ist πόλῑ Dat. < *-*ii*. Nicht ursprünglich ist antesonantischer i-Diphthong: τοῖο < **tosi̯o*; *aiio* < **agi̯ō*, *eiius* < **esi̯o-s*, *maiior* < **magi̯ōs*. Langdiphthonge wie in ἀγρῶι sind durch (z. T. vorurgriech.) Kontraktion (-ῶι < *-*o-ei̯*, mit Dat.-Endung) entstanden. Lat. *ĭ* hat außer *ĭ* (*dictus*, *quis*) und *ī* (gekürzt z. B. in *fierem*) noch weitere Ursprünge: In unbetonter Stellung kann es aus anderem Kurzvok. entstanden sein (*ce-cid-ī*, *col-lig-o*, *per-fring-o*; *ag-it*), in betonter durch Assim. (*ni-sī*); in *medius* (dreisilbig) geht es auf *i̯* zurück (altind. *mádhya*-); in *fac-i-lis* ist es eingeschoben (»Anaptyxe«).

Son. *ĭ* und *ī* blieb im ant. Griech. und Lat. weitgehend fest. Dagegen werden *ai̯ ei̯ oi̯* in beiden Sprachen nach und nach zu Monophthongen; z. B. altlat. *oi̯no*- > klass.-lat. *ūno*-; *dei̯k*- > griech. lat. *dẹ̄k*- > *dīk*- (klass.-lat. *dīc-ere*). Dadurch kann <EI> Zeichen für /ī/ werden (τειμη, *feilia*). Die nur griech. Langdiphthonge *āi̯ ę̄i̯ ǭi̯* verlieren im Hell. hingegen das *i̯*: ἀγρῶι > ἀγρω, hierfür im MA wieder ἀγρῷ mit stummem »Iota subscriptum« [3. 814].

Im zunächst durchaus vok. klingenden *i̯* von *iocus*, *mai(i)or* entwickelt sich in der Spätant. ein Reibegeräusch (it. *gioco*, *maggiore*).

→ Aussprache; E (sprachwissenschaftlich); Itazismus; J (sprachwissenschaftlich)

1 P. Flobert, Le témoignage épigraphique des apices et des I longae, in: G. Calboli (Hrsg.), Latin vulgaire – latin tardif II, 1990, 101–110 2 Leumann 3 LSJ 4 H. Rix, Südpiken. *kduíú*, in: HS-ZVS 107, 1994, 105–122 5 Schwyzer, Gramm. 6 Sommer/Pfister.

ThlL VII 1,1–4. B. F.

J (sprachwissenschaftlich). Schon in der Ant. gab es Ansätze, die verschiedenen Lautwerte des lat. Buchstabens *I* auch in der Schrift verschieden auszudrücken. Im allg. galt jedoch dasselbe Zeichen für son. Laute (*i*, *ī*) wie für kons. (*i̯*, *i̯i̯*), eine Schwierigkeit, die den ant. Grammatikern bewußt war [2. 2, 12–44]. Einen neuen Anlauf machten Grammatiker der frühen Neuzeit, bes. P. Ramus (P. La Ramée), indem sie die zunächst rein graph. Variante *J* dem kons. Laut zuordneten [1. 12]. Dadurch konnten *jam*, *jocus*, *jubeo*, *Julius*, *cujus* von *etiam*, *iaspis*, *io*, *Iulus*, *Latoius* äußerlich unterschieden werden. Die Scheidung hat jedoch, anders als die entsprechende von *V* und *U*, keine weite Verbreitung gefunden.

→ I (sprachwissenschaftlich); U (sprachwissenschaftlich); V (sprachwissenschaftlich)

1 M. Niedermann, Histor. Lautlehre des Lat., 1953
2 ThlL VII 1. B. F.

Iabadiu (Ἰαβαδίου; altindisch *Yavadvīpa*, h. Java oder Sumatra); große Insel in SO-Asien (Ptol. 7,2,29). Während die Identifizierung immer noch strittig ist, wußte Ptol., daß der Name »Gersteninsel« (altind. *yava*, Gerste) bedeutet; sie sei reich an Gold; ihre Hauptstadt heiße Argyre.

A. Herrmann, s. v. I. nesos, RE 9, 1175–77. K. K.

Jabne (Ἰάμνια). Stadt, südl. des h. Tel Aviv gelegen, bildete nach der Zerstörung des Jerusalemer Tempels im J. 70 n. Chr. das neue Zentrum, in dem sich das Judentum zunächst unter Rabbi Jochanan ben Zakkai sowie später unter Gamaliel [2] II. als rabbinisches Judentum neu konstitutierte. Eine erste Formulierung des Materials, das später in die Mišna eingehen sollte, wurde hier vorgenommen, wobei der Aspekt einer Ordnung des rel. Lebens ohne Tempelkult und Priester sowie der Aufbau einer jüd. Selbstverwaltung eine bes. Rolle spielte. Nach dem gescheiterten Bar-Kochba-Aufstand (132–135 n. Chr.; → Bar Kochba) verlagerte sich das Zentrum des Judentums nach Galilaea.

Die These einer »Synode von Javne«, bei der man formell die zum Kanon der hebr. → Bibel gehörigen Bücher zur Abgrenzung vom Christentum festgelegt habe, wird in der neueren Forschung nicht mehr akzeptiert.

S. SAFRAI, Das Zeitalter der Mischna und des Talmuds (70–640), in: H. HILLEL BEN-SASSON (Hrsg.), Gesch. des jüd. Volkes, 1978 (Ndr. 1992), 377–469, bes. 391–405 • P. SCHÄFER, Gesch. der Juden in der Antike, 1983, 151–155.

B.E.

Iactus. Der t.t. des röm. Rechts für den »Seewurf«, das Abwerfen von Ladung aus einem in Seenot geratenen Schiff. Die sog. *lex Rhodia de iactu* sah in diesen Fällen eine Gefahrengemeinschaft zw. allen Beteiligten vor: dem Geschädigten, dem Schiffer (*nauta*) und den Eigentümern der geretteten Ladung. Diese *lex* war in Wahrheit Gewohnheitsrecht, das im ganzen hell. Gebiet verbreitet war. Im einzelnen konnte der Geschädigte vom Schiffer anteiligen Ersatz mit der Werkvertragsklage (*actio locati*) verlangen, der Schiffer dafür von den anderen Wareneigentümern einen Ausgleich mit der *actio conducti*. Als »Große Havarei« ist die röm.-hell. Regelung des *i.* Bestandteil des europ. Seerechts seit dem MA, zunächst im Mittelmeer, dann auch in Atlantik, Nord- und Ostsee geworden.

G. WESENER, Von der Lex Rhodia de iactu zum § 1043 ABGB, in: J. BÄRMANN, H. LUTTER (Hrsg.), Recht und Wirtschaft in Gesch. und Gegenwart: FS J. Bärmann, 1975, 31–51.

G.S.

Iader (τὰ Διάδωρα, *tá Diádōra*). Liburnische Gründung der Eisenzeit, später die bedeutendste Stadt von Liburnia, Prov. Dalmatia, h. Zadar (it. Zara) in Kroatien (Mela 2,57; Plin. nat. 3,140 *colonia Iader*, vgl. 141; 152; Itin. Anton. 272,1 f.; vgl. 496,7; 497,2; CIL III 2925). Die Einwohner (*Iadertini*) kämpften auf seiten Caesars gegen Pompeius (Bell. Alex. 42).

I. wurde wohl unter Caesar röm. *colonia* (*colonia Iulia*; schon zuvor ist ein *conventus civium Romanorum* nachgewiesen). Spuren der Zenturiation auf dem Territorium der *colonia* (einschließlich der Insel Ugljan). Augustus (als *parens coloniae*) stiftete Stadtmauer und Türme (CIL III 13264; 2907). Dokumentiert sind Karrieren von Stadtmagistraten wie C. Vetidius Maximus (*eques, pontifex, duumvir, duumvir quinquennalis*, Stadtpatron: CIL III 2932; *ordo Iadestinus* CIL III 2919). Kaiserkult ist belegt (Cossutia, *flaminica divae Faustinae* [1]). Reiche Architektur: Forum (vgl. CIL III 2922) mit *capitolium, nymphaeum, basilicae* (augusteisch, severisch) und anderen Gebäuden (zahlreiche Spolien in der Kirche St. Donatus verbaut), Bäder, Bögen, reiche Nekropolen, *villae rusticae* in der Umgebung. I. war frühchristl. Zentrum (St.-Thomas-Kirche, 5. Jh., St.-Petrus-Kirche, später St. Anastasia): Bezeugt sind die Bischöfe Felix (E. 4. Jh.) und Andreas (1. H. 6. Jh.).

1 Inscriptiones Latinae Iugoslaviae 210.

M. SUIĆ, Zadar u starom vijeku [Zadar in der Ant.], 1981.

M.Š.K./Ü: I.S.

Jaffa s. Ioppe

Jagd I. ALTER ORIENT II. KLASSISCHE ANTIKE

I. ALTER ORIENT

Arch. Funde belegen Treib-J. mit Fallen in Vorderasien seit dem 7. Jt. v. Chr. Andererseits finden sich nur wenige keilschriftl. Hinweise auf den Beruf des Jägers, wie z.B. im → Gilgamesch-Epos (TUAT 3. 676, I iii 9 ff.). Gejagt wurden Wildrinder, Wildziegen, Wildesel, Gazellen, Löwen, → Elefanten u.v.m. Als J.-Waffen verwendete man neben Fallen, Netzen und Schlingen auch Pfeil und Bogen, Wurfhölzer, Lanzen, Schwerter und Dolche, als J.-Hunde Doggen und Windhunde. Bildliche Darstellungen von J. finden sich seit Beginn des 3. Jt. v. Chr. vor allem auf mesopot. → Rollsiegeln.

Schon im 3. Jt. galt die J. als königlicher Sport. Assyr. Texte berichten – im Umfeld der Feldzüge – ab Tiglatpilesar I. (1114–1076 v. Chr.) über königl. J. zu Fuß oder vom Wagen aus. Bevorzugte J.-Gebiete waren das Euphrattal und die angrenzende Steppe. Seit Assurnasirpal II. (883–859 v. Chr.) finden sich Darstellungen dieser J. und der anschließenden J.-Opfer auch auf den → Reliefs assyr. Paläste. Die Kunst von → Urartu übernahm das Motiv der königl. J. Unter → Sargon II. (722–705 v. Chr.) wurde die J. erstmals in höfischer Umgebung dargestellt. Sie bezeugte wie der kriegerische Kampf die Macht des Herrschers; die Tiere erlitten das gleiche Schicksal wie die Feinde: Tod oder Gefangenschaft. Parallel dazu forderte auch das ägypt. Königsdogma die Löwenjagd als rituelle Überhöhung des Herrschers. → Assurbanipals (668–627 v. Chr.) Löwenjagden – zu Fuß, zu Pferd, vom Wagen oder vom Schiff aus – fanden in eigenen J.-Parks mit herbeigebrachten Tieren statt. Die Löwen scheinen als Symbol der Bedrohung Assyriens betrachtet worden zu sein. Der Zusammenhang der königl. J. mit dem rituellen Schutz des Kulturlandes und der Herden wird auch in den Inschr. und Reliefs der assyr. Könige deutlich. → Achaimeniden und → Sāsāniden (Taq-i Bustan) übernahmen die Tradition der umzäunten oder ummauerten J.-Gehege (→ Paradeisos).

H. ALTENMUELLER, s. v. J., LÄ 3, 221–233, spez. 221 • J. K. ANDERSON, Hunting in the Ancient World, 1985 • H. D. GALTER, Paradies und Palmentod, in: W. SCHOLZ (Hrsg.), Der oriental. Mensch und seine Beziehungen zur Umwelt, 1989, 237–253 • W. HEIMPEL, L. TRÜMPELMANN, s. v. J., RLA 5, 234–238 • S. W. HELMS, A. PETTS, The Desert »Kites« of Badiyat esh-Sham and North Arabia, in: Paléorient 13, 1987, 41–67 • U. MAGEN, Assyr. Königsdarstellungen, 1986, 29–36.

HA.G.

II. KLASSISCHE ANTIKE

In der frühen griech. Lit. und im Mythos wurde die J. zunächst als Abwehr von Tieren, die den Menschen Schaden zufügen, gesehen; das heroische Geschehen der Tötung des gefährlichen Tieres wurde oft bildlich, auf Vasen und Reliefs, dargestellt und steht im Zentrum der lit. Zeugnisse. So tötet → Herakles den Nemeischen Löwen und fängt den Erymanthischen Eber (Apollod.

2,5,1; 2,5,4). Berühmt war auch die J. des → Meleagros auf einen Eber, der, von → Artemis geschickt, die Felder um Kalydon verwüstete (Hom. Il. 9,533–549; vgl. Apollod. 1,8,3; Ov. met. 8,273–424; bildl. Darstellung: François Vase, Florenz AM, BEAZLEY, ABV 76,1; BEAZLEY, Paralipomena 29). Noch bei Platon ist diese Sicht erkennbar: In seiner Fassung des Prometheusmythos drohen die wilden Tiere die schwächeren Menschen auszurotten; prononciert wird hier vom »Krieg gegen die Tiere« gesprochen (τὸν τῶν θηρίων πόλεμον; Plat. Prot. 322b; vgl. noch Anth. Gr. 6,168). Ohne Zweifel diente die J. auch der Ernährung (Hom. Od. 9,152–162: Ziegen; 10,156–184: Hirsch; vgl. Verg. Aen. 1,180–213). Als Waffen des Jägers werden Pfeil und Bogen sowie der Speer erwähnt. Das J.-Geschehen selbst wird im Epos dramatisch dargestellt (Hom. Od. 19,428–458). Die att. Vasenmalerei zeigt in der archa. Epoche eine Vielzahl von J.-Szenen, darunter Gruppen von Reitern, die Hirsche und Wildschweine jagen (etwa sf. Hydria, London BM, BEAZLEY, ABV 266,4). Die J. gehörte in Athen in den Kontext aristokratischen Lebensstils (Aristoph. Vesp. 1194–1204) und zur Lebensweise der Spartaner (Xen. Lak. pol. 4,7).

Umfassende Informationen über die J. im 4. Jh. v. Chr., die Ausrüstung der Jäger, die Hunde und das Wild bietet eine Schrift von Xenophon (Κυνηγετικός, *Kynēgetikós*). Bei der J. wurden Netze, in die das Wild hineingetrieben wurde (Xen. kyn. 2,3–9; 6,5–10; 10,19), und auch Fußangeln (9,11–19) verwendet; ausführlich wird die Wahl und Zucht geeigneter J.-Hunde behandelt (3 f.; 7). Im Zentrum steht die J. auf Hasen (5 f.), Hirsche und Wildschweine (9 f.), während die J. auf Löwen, Leoparden oder Bären nur kurz erwähnt wird (11). Den Wert der J. sieht Xenophon darin, daß sie für einen gesunden Körper, gute Augen und Gehör sorgt und so den Jäger körperlich für alle Aufgaben des Kriegsdienstes vorbereitet; aus Jägern, resümiert Xenophon, werden στρατιῶταί τε ἀγαθοὶ καὶ στρατηγοί, gute Soldaten und Feldherren (Xen. kyn. 12,1–9; vgl. Xen. Lak. pol. 4,7). Ähnliche Überlegungen zur J. finden sich auch in der *Kyrupaideía* (Xen. Kyr. 1,2,10; 1,6,28; 6,2,5; 8,1,34); die J. dient hier explizit als Vorbild für das Vorgehen im Krieg (Xen. Kyr. 2,4,25). Platon, der eine Systematik der verschiedenen Arten der J. – darunter auch die J. auf Menschen – aufstellt, lehnt Fischen (→ Fischerei) und Vogelfang ab, da sie weder Anstrengung noch Tapferkeit erforderten, und hält nur die J. mit Pferden und Hunden auf Landtiere für ehrenvoll (Plat. leg. 823a–824a).

Eine neue Epoche in der Geschichte der J. begann mit Alexander d.Gr. und den hell. Königen; für Alexander, der sowohl auf maked. als auch pers. Traditionen zurückgriff, war die J. zu Pferde und insbesondere die Löwen-J. eine königliche Betätigung mit herrschaftslegitimierender Funktion (Plut. Alexander 40; Arr. an. 4,13,2). Wie der → Alexandersarkophag aus Sidon (Istanbul, AM) mit seinen Schlacht- und J.-Szenen zeigt, gehörte seit dem späten 4. Jh. v. Chr. die Darstellung der Überwindung des wilden Tieres zur bildlichen Repräsentation hell. Herrscher.

In der röm. Oberschicht scheint das Interesse für die J. erst durch die Begegnung mit der hell. Kultur geweckt worden zu sein; so war P. Scipio Aemilianus nach 169 v. Chr. in Makedonien ein begeisterter Jäger geworden und widmete sich nach seiner Rückkehr nach Italien – zusammen mit Polybios – intensiv der J. (Pol. 31,29). Im bäuerlichen Milieu wurde der Winter zur J. genutzt (Verg. georg. 1,307–310; vgl. auch die idyllisierende Schilderung des Jägerlebens bei Dion Chrys. 7,10–80). Die J. stieß zwar auch auf Ablehnung (Sall. Catil. 4,1), aber es war für Senatoren der frühen Prinzipatszeit wohl nicht unüblich, während der Aufenthalte auf dem Land zu jagen (Plin. epist. 1,6); dafür spricht auch der Hinweis des Plinius auf den Wildbestand seiner Ländereien in Etrurien (*frequens ibi et varia venatio*: Plin. epist. 5,6,7).

Von erheblicher Bedeutung für den Principat war die Tatsache, daß die Principes selbst sich zunehmend der J. widmeten. Dies gilt zunächst für Traianus, der von Plinius gerühmt wurde, weil er nicht gefangene Tiere tötete, sondern das Wild in den Wäldern selbst aufstöberte (Plin. paneg. 81). Hadrianus soll mehrere Löwen mit eigener Hand getötet haben, erlitt bei der J. aber auch Verletzungen (SHA Hadr. 26,3; vgl. Cass. Dio 69,10,2). Auf den großen Relieftondi, die später am Konstantinsbogen angebracht wurden, ist der Princeps bei der J. auf einen Bären, einen Eber und einen Löwen dargestellt, wobei die Opferszenen den Bezug zum Mythos und zur Religion herstellen. Es entsprach dieser Neigung der Principes, daß seit dem 2. Jh. mehrere Werke zur J. geschrieben wurden, so von Arrianos (*Kynēgetikós*) und von Oppianos (frühes 3. Jh.), dessen in Hexametern geschriebene *Kynēgetiká* im Gegensatz zu Xenophons Schrift nun auch dem J.-Pferd und der J. auf Löwen größere Aufmerksamkeit schenken (Opp. kyn. 1,158–367; 4,77–211). Fragmentarisch überliefert sind die lat. *Cynegetica* des Nemesianus (spätes 3. Jh.). Die Löwenjagdsarkophage des 3. Jh. sind ein Beleg dafür, daß J.-Szenen auch in der spätant. Kunst ein bevorzugtes Bildthema waren.

1 J. K. ANDERSON, Hunting in the Ancient Greek World, 1985 2 A. DEMANDT, Das Privatleben der röm. Kaiser, 1996, 146 ff. 3 J.-L. DURAND, A. SCHNAPP, Schlachtopfer und rituelle Jagd, in: C. BÉRARD u. a. (Hrsg.), Die Bilderwelt der Griechen, 1985, 73–99 4 R. L. FOX, Ancient Hunting: From Homer to Polybios, in: G. SHIPLEY, J. SALMON (Hrsg.), Human Landscapes in Classical Antiquity, 1996, 119–153.

H.SCHN.

Jagd-Maler. Hauptmeister der → lakon. Vasenmalerei, tätig um 560–540 v. Chr., der v.a. Schalen, aber auch → Hydrien bemalte; typisch sind seine Schaleninnenbilder mit einem tondoförmigen Bildausschnitt. Nach Bildern einer (mythischen?) Eberjagd benannt (Schale Paris, LV, E 670 und Frg. Leipzig T 302/Florenz 85118), bevorzugt der J.-M. ansonsten Kampf-, Tanz- und Gelagebilder, aus dem Mythos Heraklestaten. Häufiges Füll- und Nebenmotiv bilden Vögel und Fische. Die sorgfältige und dekorative Malweise des J.-M. hat die Vasenmalerei in Sparta nachhaltig beeinflußt. Die etwa 80 ihm zugewiesenen Werke stammen v.a. aus Samos, Sparta und Italien.

P. Settimi, Il pittore della caccia, in: Studi sulla ceramica laconica: atti del seminario; Perugia, 23–24 febr. 1981, 1986, 33–44 • E. Simon, Die griech. Vasen, [2]1981, Taf. 36 • C.M. Stibbe, Lakon. Vasenmaler des 6. Jh. v.Chr., 1972, 121–150, 280–285 • Ders., Das andere Sparta, 1996, 175–178. M.ST.

Jahr s. Kalender; Zeitrechnung

Jahresnamen s. Zeitrechnung

Jahreszeiten (ὧραι, *hṓrai*; *tempora anni*).
I. Vorderasien/Ägypten
II. Griechenland und Italien

I. Vorderasien/Ägypten

Die J. und die Zeiteinheit Jahr richteten sich v.a. nach den regelmäßig wiederkehrenden Naturerscheinungen, wie z.B. dem Hochwasser von Tigris und Euphrat in Mesopot. (einer kurzen Vegetationsperiode und der sommerlichen Dürre, Thema des sumer. Streitgedichtes von Sommer und Winter, s. Kindler 19, 604) und des Nils in Äg. (Nilüberschwemmung, Vegetationsperiode, Sommerhitze von je vier Monaten). Von den vorherrschenden Niederschlagsperioden hingen in Iran, Anatolien (vier J. [2. 13]), Assyrien und Syrien/Palästina (AT: Winter und Sommer, [4. 1, 305]) Feldbestellung und Ernte ab (→ Bewässerung). Auch die oft jährlich unternommenen Feldzüge beschränkten sich meist auf die günstigen J. Der Wechsel der J. spiegelte sich in der Myth. und in den kult. Festkalendern wider, bes. in Vorstellungen vom Verschwinden und von der Wiederkehr von Fruchtbarkeits- und Vegetationsgöttern, wie Dumuzi (→ Tammuz) in Mesopot., Telipinu in Ḫattuša und → Baal in Ugarit.
→ Kalender; Zeitrechnung

1 W. Helck, s.v. J., LÄ 3, 240f. 2 H.A. Hoffner, Alimenta Hethaeorum, 1974 3 H. Hunger, s.v. Kalender, RLA 5, 297–303 4 R. de Vaux, Die Lebensordnungen des AT, [2]1964. H.FR.

II. Griechenland und Italien
A. Astronomisch und kalendarisch
B. Kulturgeschichtlich und literarisch

A. Astronomisch und kalendarisch

Die Einteilung des Sonnenjahres war wichtig für Landarbeit, Schiffahrt und Kriegsführung und geschah astronomisch, meteorologisch oder kalendarisch. Die J. bestimmten die rel. Feste. Ausgehend von einer Zweiteilung in Sommer und Winter mit ihrer höchsten Entfaltung bei den Solstitien und den Grenzen in den Äquinoktien wurden die vier Jahrpunkte selbst zu den Grenzen der J., wobei die vier Abschnitte infolge der Anomalie der scheinbaren Sonnenbewegung ungleich groß sind, nach Hipparch (bei Geminus Astronomicus 1,9–41 und Ptol. Syntaxis Mathematica 3,4–6) Frühling 94 1/2, Sommer 92 1/2, Herbst 88 1/8, Winter 90 1/8 Tage (andere Werte [3. 281–285; 7. 55–61, 595, 929, 953, 963]).

Obgleich die vier Jahrpunkte die Mitte der J. markieren sollten, bilden sie in der astronomischen Einteilung den Anf.: Frühling ab Frühlingsgleiche, Sommer ab Sommerwende, Herbst ab Herbstgleiche, Winter ab Winterwende. Vereinzelt begegnet auch die um 90° verschobene Einteilung (Mart. Cap. 8,874): Frühling ab Winterwende bis zur Frühlingsgleiche usw. Die kalendarische Zeitrechnung war bei Griechen [3. 308–315] und Römern [3. 182–191] örtlich verschieden und zudem überall so unzuverlässig, daß man andere Orientierungsmittel suchte: das Erscheinen von Vögeln (Schwalbe oder Nachtigall) am Frühlingsanf., die erste oder letzte Sichtbarkeit bestimmter Sternbilder nach Sonnenuntergang (akronychisch) oder vor Sonnenaufgang (heliakisch: → Paranatellonta). So begann etwa nach Hes. erg. 383 die Saatzeit des Bauern mit dem <Früh>Aufgang der → Pleiaden, nach Hes. erg. 565f. der Frühling mit dem Spätaufgang des Arktur, nach Theophrast (De signis tempestatum 6) der Winter mit dem Frühuntergang der Pleiaden und der Sommer mit dem Frühaufgang der Pleiaden. Varro (bei Plin. nat. 18,271 u.ö.) ließ den Herbst mit dem <Früh>Untergang der Leier beginnen. In seiner von Sosigenes erarbeiteten Kalenderreform setzte Caesar (bei Plin. nat. 18,211; 246; 256; 311) den Beginn der J. jeweils *a.d. VIII Kal.* fest, was im einzelnen die Daten 24.12 – 25.3. – 24.6. – 24.9. ergibt, doch finden sich auch andere Daten [3. 281]. Nach der Inschr. auf der Sonnenuhr des Augustus (→ Horologium Augusti) fällt der Sommeranfang (ΘΕΡΟΥΣ ΑΡΧΗ) etwa auf den 7. Mai [1. 79]. Schalttage rangierten im allgemeinen außerhalb der J.

In der Astrologie spielen die J. eine geringere Rolle als das alternierende System mit den »stabilen« Tierkreiszeichen in der Mitte der J., die jeweils von den »tropischen« vorbereitet und von den »doppelten« Übergangszeichen abgelöst werden [6. 74–87]. Das analogisierende Denken parallelisierte die J. mit den Himmelsrichtungen, den Lebensaltern und den Elementen, bes. aber mit den Farben der Zirkus-Parteien: Frühling grün, Sommer rot, Herbst blau, Winter weiß [2. 336–338; 10].
→ Kalender

1 E. Buchner, Die Sonnenuhr des Augustus, 1982
2 A. Cameron, Circus Factions. Blues and Greens at Rome and Byzantium, 1976 3 F.K. Ginzel, Hdb. der Chronologie II, 1911 4 J. Gunning, s.v. J., RE Suppl. 3, 1164–1175 5 W. Hübner, Die Eigenschaften der Tierkreiszeichen in der Ant., 1982 6 A. Le Bœuffle, Le ciel des Romains, 1989 7 O. Neugebauer, A History of Ancient mathematical Astronomy, 1975 8 A. Rehm, Parapegmastudien, 1941 9 B.L. van der Waerden, Erwachende Wiss., [2]1966 10 P. Wuilleumier, Cirque et Astrologie, in: MEFRA 44, 1927, 184–209. W.H.

B. Kulturgeschichtlich und literarisch
1. Allgemeines 2. Jahreszeiten in der Literatur 3. Bildliche Darstellungen

1. Allgemeines

Die Gliederung des Jahres in J. diente urspr. dazu, Zeit im Hinblick auf bestimmte Tätigkeiten zu strukturieren. Zunächst erhielt nur der für Landwirtschaft, Schiffahrt und Kriegführung klimatisch ungünstige Abschnitt des Jahres eine eigene Bezeichnung (χειμών/*cheimṓn*), dann auch die zunächst nur als ὥρα/*hṓra* bezeichnete restliche Zeit (θέρος/*théros*) [7. 1165 f.]. Diese Zweiteilung des Jahres in Sommer und Winter blieb im mil. Kontext trotz fortschreitender Differenzierung der J. erhalten (Thuk. 2,1 κατὰ θέρος καὶ χειμῶνα). In den homer. Epen ist mit dem Frühling (ἔαρ/*éar*) eine Dreiteilung des Jahres faßbar [7. 1168 f.]. Die ebenfalls früh belegte (Alkm. fr. 20) Einteilung in vier J. setzt sich unter dem Einfluß wiss. Erkenntnisse der ion. Naturphilos. über den Rhythmus des Sonnenjahres durch und war im 4. Jh. v. Chr. etabliert; der Herbst heißt μετόπωρον/*metópōron* oder φθινόπωρον/*phthinópōron* nach der alten Bezeichnung des Hoch-/Spätsommers, ὀπώρα/*opṓra* [7. 1169 f.]. Vier J. erscheinen auch bei den röm. Autoren, wobei bisweilen eine ältere Gliederung in Sommer- und Winterhalbjahr erkennbar ist [8].

2. Jahreszeiten in der Literatur

Sowohl der J.-Zyklus als auch einzelne J. werden in der Lit. thematisiert und funktionalisiert. Der Wechsel der J. ist bes. in der Dichtung Bild für Vergänglichkeit (Hom. Il. 6,146–149; Hor. ars 60–62) oder für die Kürze der Jugend (Mimn. fr. 2 Allen); ein beliebtes Motiv ist auch die zyklische Erneuerung der Natur im Lauf der J. im Kontrast zur Endgültigkeit des Todes (Ps.-Mosch. Epitaphios Bionos 99–104; Hor. carm. 4,7) [6]. Die Parallelisierung verschiedener Lebensaltersstufen mit den J. (Ov. met. 15,199–213; Diog. Laert. 8,10) ist möglicherweise pythagoreisches Gedankengut. In der ant. Philos. von den Vorsokratikern bis zum Neuplatonismus gilt der Kreislauf der J. als Beweis für die Existenz einer kosmischen Ordnung [10. Bd. 1, 91–93, 107–109, 152 f.]; Seneca (epist. 36,11) dient er zur Illustration der stoischen Lehre von der → Palingenesie. Entsprechend betrachten christl. Autoren den konstanten Zyklus der J. als Beweis für die teleologische Ordnung der Welt durch den Schöpfer [10. Bd. 1, 198–205] oder verwenden ihn zur Veranschaulichung des Auferstehungsgedankens (Tert. apol. 48,7 f.; Min. Fel. 34,10–12) [1; 3]; hinzu tritt vom 3. Jh. n. Chr. an eine genuin christl. Funktionalisierung der J. durch allegorische Schriftauslegung (greifbar etwa bei Hrabanus Maurus, De universo 10,11) [10. Bd. 1, 205 f.]. Die ant. Medizin stellt Beziehungen zw. den J. und dem Auftreten bestimmter Krankheiten, dem Lebensalter des Menschen sowie den geogr. Klimazonen her [10. Bd. 1, 89 f., 122]. Vielleicht im Rückgriff auf eine verlorene Schrift Suetons erwähnt Tertullian (De spectaculis 9) eine Deutung des Wagenrennens im Circus als kosmische Allegorie, die den vier *factiones* (→ Factiones [II]) jeweils eine der J. zuordnet [10. Bd. 1, 159–163].

Unter den einzelnen J. entfaltet bes. der Frühling breite Wirkung als lit. Motiv. Er ist Gegenstand zahlreicher poetischer Schilderungen (z. B. Pind. fr. 75,14–19; Catull. 46; Hor. carm. 4,7,1–4; Ov. trist. 3,12,1–30; Stat. silv. 4,5,5–12; Anth. Pal. 9,363; 10,5) und erscheint in doppeltem Sinne als Zeit des Anfangs: Zum einen markiert er das Wiedererwachen der Natur (als Wirken der Venus interpretiert z. B. von Lucr. 1,1–20 [15. 147 f.]), zum andern gilt er als die J., die am Anfang der Welt herrschte (Lucr. 5,801 f.; 818–820; Verg. georg. 2,336–342; Pervigilium Veneris 2). Der Frühling gilt als die angenehmste der J. (Hippokr. De aere aquis locis 12,3–9; Bion fr. 2,15–18); das Motiv des langen/ewigen Frühlings oder eines frühlingshaften Idealklimas (als »Mischung der J.«, κρᾶσις τῶν ὡρῶν /*krā̂sis tōn hōrō̂n* in Verbindung mit Elementen des Herbstes) ist häufig in Schilderungen entlegener, mythischer oder idealisierter Landschaften (Hom. Od. 7,117–128; Verg. georg. 2,149; Hor. carm. 2,6,17 f.; Ov. met. 5,390 f.), der Inseln der Seligen und des → Elysions (Hom. Od. 4,566–568; Hor. epod. 16,53–56; 61 f.), des Goldenen → Zeitalters (Ov. met. 1,107 f.), schließlich in christl. Texten als Merkmal des → Paradieses [9; 14].

In Schilderungen des Herbstes (als Personifikation bes. bei lat. Dichtern [2]) begegnen zwei Aspekte: Der Herbst gilt einerseits als schön, farbenfroh, fruchtbringend und als Zeit der Reife [13. 272–275] (die er auch in erotischem Sinn symbolisieren kann: Sappho fr. 105a; Philod. Anth. Pal. 5,124; Hor. carm. 2,5). Negativ vermerkt werden Regenwetter (Hes. erg. 414–416) und die Gefahr von Krankheiten (Bion fr. 2,13); ähnlich wie der Wechsel der J. symbolisiert der herbstliche Laubfall Vergänglichkeit (Aischyl. Ag. 79–82; Aristoph. Av. 685–687) sowie schwindende Vitalität (Ov. trist. 3,8,27–31) und Attraktivität (Hor. carm. 1,25,17–20) [13. 276–278].

Ebenso wie der oft als quälend heiß gezeichnete Sommer (wo *théros*/*aestas* nicht lediglich den schönen Teil des Jahres bezeichnet) erscheint auch der Winter als unangenehme J. Er wird als abstoßend und feindlich erlebt (Hes. erg. 504–563; Schnee-Gleichnisse für Kampfhandlungen Hom. Il. 12,156–161; 278–289). Das Motiv des langen/ewigen Winters dient zur negativen Charakterisierung von Landschaften (Verg. georg. 3,349–370; Ov. trist. 3,10); Merkmale des Winters kommen auch in Beschreibungen der Unterwelt vor [13. 281 f.]. Unter den zahlreichen Behandlungen des Themas durch röm. Autoren findet sich keine durchweg positive Darstellung [5].

3. Bildliche Darstellungen

Die J. werden (anders als die in Mythos und Kult beheimateten, mit den J. erst sekundär verknüpften → Horai) nicht vor Ende der klass. Zeit dargestellt. Im Festzug zur Feier der Ptolemaia 271/70 v. Chr. treten als J. kostümierte Personen auf (Athen. 198b); für diese Zeit läßt sich vielleicht auch eine bildliche Darstellung der in Frauengestalt personifizierten J. (männliche Personifikationen der J. finden erst ab dem 2. Jh. n. Chr. Verbreitung) mit entsprechenden Attributen (Frühling: Blumen; Sommer: Ähren; Herbst: Trauben; Winter: warme Kleidung) rekonstruieren [10. Bd. 1, 112–114; anders 11. 355]. Von der Mitte des 2. Jh. v. Chr. an nehmen solche Darstellungen bes. auf ital. Boden, später auch in den Provinzen erheblich zu, im 1. Jh. n. Chr. unter Erweiterung des ikonographischen Repertoires [10. Bd. 1, 127–141]; sie finden sich auf Reliefs, Wandgemälden, Mosaiken und vom 2. Jh. n. Chr. an auch auf Sarkophagen [10; 12]. Im Dienst der kaiserlichen Propaganda erscheinen die J. auf Bauwerken und Münzen u. a. als Symbol der *felicitas temporum* [10. Bd. 1, 163–184] und werden auch in andere Bildmotive integriert [4].

1 E. Ahlborn, Naturvorgänge als Auferstehungsgleichnis bei Seneca, Tertullian und Minucius Felix, in: WS 103, 1990, 123–137 **2** E. Aust, s. v. Autumnus, RE 2, 2613 f. **3** C. P. Bammel, Der Tod, die Gestirne und die J. in ant. und christl. Dichtung, in: JbAC 39, 1996, 5–12 **4** C. Clay, Nilus and the Four Seasons on a New As of Septimius Severus, in: NC 130, 1970, 71–87 **5** P.-J. Dehon, Hiems Latina, 1993 **6** M. Fantuzzi, Caducità dell'uomo ed eternità della natura, in: Quaderni Urbinati di cultura classica 26,2, 1987, 101–110 **7** J. Gunning, s. v. J., RE Suppl. 3, 1164–1175 **8** R. Gustin, Le nombre des saisons chez les poètes latins, in: Les Études Classiques 15, 1947, 114–119 **9** R. Gustin, Le printemps chez les poètes latins, in: Les Études Classiques 15, 1947, 323–330 **10** M. A. Hanfmann, The Season Sarcophagus in Dumbarton Oaks, 1951 **11** R. Horn, Rezension von [10], in: Gnomon 27, 1955, 351–359 **12** P. Kranz, J.-Sarkophage, 1984 **13** K. Preston, Aspects of Autumn in Roman Poetry, in: CPh 13, 1918, 272–282 **14** H. Reynen, Ewiger Frühling und goldene Zeit, in: Gymnasium 72, 1965, 415–433 **15** R. Thurow, Frühlingsbilder, in: A&A 33, 1987, 140–162.

H. H.

Jahrhunderte, Dunkle (500–800 n. Chr.)
s. Textgeschichte

Jahwe. Eigenname des Gottes der Israeliten und Judäer und nach dem Untergang dieser Staaten (722/720 bzw. 586/582 v. Chr.) des Gottes der Hebr. Bibel (AT).
A. Name B. Herkunft, Ursprünge
C. Verhältnis zu anderen Gottheiten

A. Name

Das AT gibt nur die Konsonanten des Gottesnamens (*Yhwh*; epigraphisch seit dem 9. Jh. v. Chr. bezeugt), die Aussprache ist im rabbinischen Judentum tabuisiert. Gelesen wird *Yhwh* gewöhnlich als »Herr« (*ʾadōnāy*, daher das Κύριος (*kýrios*) der LXX und das »HErr« der Lutherbibel sowie das irrige »Jehova«: Die Konsonanten der »Schreibung« *Yhwh* werden mit den Vokalen der »Lesung« *ʾadōnāy* versehen. Die Lesung **Yahwē* stützt sich auf die morphologische Analyse des Konsonantengerüstes als Lang-Impft. einer Wurzel *HWY* sowie auf griech. Transkription bei den Kirchenvätern (Ἰαουέ, Clem. Al. strom. 5,6,34; Ἰαβέ, Ἰαβαί, Theodoretos in Exodum 15; → Theodoretos von Kyrrhos). Neben der Langform stehen Kurzformen in PN (judä. -**yahū*, keilschriftl. *Ia-u* wie in *ḫa-za-qi-ia(-a)-ú/u* = *Ḥizqīyāhū* (Hiskia) von Juda, israelitisch -*Yau/Yō*-, keilschriftl. *Ia-* wie in *Ia-ʾa-su* = Joas von Israel) wie selbständig (**Yahō* bei den Juden von → Elephantine im 5. Jh. v. Chr., in den graeco-äg. Zauberpap. Ἰάω; *Ya[h]* im biblischen Hebr.). Die Kurzformen sind aus der Langform hervorgegangen. Als Impft.-Einwortname macht der Name eine Aussage über den Bezeichneten. Diese archa. Namensbildung hat sich in Arabien bis in unmittelbar vorislamische Zeit gehalten. Da der Gott J. aus NW-Arabien stammt und in den ältesten Belegen als Wettergott agiert (Ri 5,4 f; 1 Kg 8,12 f.), hat von den vielen Vorschlägen die Deutung J. Wellhausens die meiste Wahrscheinlichkeit für sich: »Er weht, stürmt«, nach arab. *HWY* »wehen«. Daß diese Wurzel im Hebr. fehlt, spricht angesichts der Herkunft des Gottes eher für diesen Vorschlag. In Ex 3,14 wird mit ›Ich bin, der ich bin‹ der Name nicht etwa durch hebr. *HYY* »sein« erklärt, sondern die Frage des → Moses nach Name und Bedeutung abgewehrt – ein früher Beleg für die Tabuisierung des Gottesnamens.

B. Herkunft, Ursprünge

Der Gott ist älter als das Volk Israel. In ON-Listen des → Amenophis [3] III. (14. Jh. v. Chr.) erscheint ein »Schasu-Land Yhwȝ« (»Land der Yhw-Nomaden«?; ȝ steht hier für beliebigen langen Vokal) im Kontext des »Schasu-Landes Seïr«. In Seïr/Edom vermutet einer der ältesten Texte des AT, Ri 5,4 (10. Jh. v. Chr.), die Heimat J.s, im südl. anschließenden Midian die jüngeren Texte Hab 3,7; Ex 3; 18. Durch ihre Bergbauinteressen in Wadi l-ʿAraba kamen die Ägypter im 13. und 12. Jh. v. Chr. mit den Bauern und Viehzüchtern Edoms und Midians in Kontakt, zugleich kontrollierten sie die Provinz Kanaan und unterwarfen 1208 den zentralpalästin. Stamm Israel. Äg. als Ort der Begegnung des nw-arab. Gottes J. mit Israeliten ist histor. plausibel (vgl. Hos 11,1; Ez 20,5). Seit der Ankunft der »Exodusgruppe« in Kanaan (nach 1185 v. Chr.?) war J. der Gott Israels, Israel das Volk J.s.

C. Verhältnis zu anderen Gottheiten

Die offizielle Theologie Jerusalems von David oder Salomo bis zum 7. Jh. v. Chr. reflektiert Dt 32,8 f. (LXX), wonach der Höchste Gott (*El Elyon*) bei der Schöpfung die Völker als Lehen an seine Söhne verteilt hat, so daß J. Israel erhielt (und damit implizit zu einem Bruder anderer Nationalgötter wurde). In der Volksreligion Judas war J.s Gemahlin Aschera (Verschmelzung von J. und → El; Inschr. von Kuntillat ʿAǧrūd und Ḫirbat al-Qōm). Im Nordreich Israel übernahm J. → ʿAnat, die Schwester und Geliebte → Baals (unter der Voraussetzung, daß die Rel. der Militärkolonie von Elephantine im 5. Jh. v. Chr. die Trad. von Bethel fortführt) als Gemahlin. Bei J. und Baal handelt es sich urspr. um zwei Erscheinungen des Wettergottes → Hadad. Sie trafen in Gegnerschaft aufeinander, als seit dem 9. Jh.

v. Chr. in Israel, seit dem 8. Jh. in Juda konservativ-sippenbäuerliche Kreise im Namen J.s den unter Zufluß phöniz. Kapitals um sich greifenden Staats- und Rentenkapitalismus kritisierten, dessen Träger sie als Verehrer Baals identifizierten. Neben der Ausdifferenzierung von J. und Baal steht eine Aufspaltung J.s in lokale Manifestitationen, in Kuntillat ʿAğrūd J. von Samaria neben J. von Teman (= »Süden« = Juda?).

Der Staatsgott Israels wie Judas war weder einziger Gott noch bildlos. Der Durchbruch zum biblischen Monotheismus erfolgte frühestens nach dem Untergang des Staates Israel (722/720 v. Chr.) und spätestens nach dem Untergang des Staates Juda (586/582 v. Chr.). Wie die Münzemissionen der persischen Provinz Yehud zeigen, hat sich dort seit dem 2. Viertel des 4. Jh. neben der Einzigkeit J.s auch seine Bildlosigkeit durchgesetzt (anders als im gleichzeitigen Samaria), womit die von der Bibel in seine Anfänge zurückprojizierten Wesensmerkmale J.s nunmehr historische Realität geworden waren.

→ Juda und Israel; Judentum

W. DIETRICH, M. A. KLOPFENSTEIN (Hrsg.), Ein Gott allein? JHWH-Verehrung und biblischer Monotheismus, 1994 • O. KEEL, CH. UEHLINGER, Göttinnen, Götter und Gottessymbole, ³1995 • E. A. KNAUF, Midian, 1988, 43–63; 97–141 • H. NIEHR, Der höchste Gott, 1990 • K. VAN DER TOORN, s. v. J., Dictionary of Deities and Demons, 1995, 1711–1730 • CH. UEHLINGER, Anthropomorphic Cult Statuary in Iron Age Palestine and the Search for Yahweh's Cult Image, in: K. VAN DER TOORN (Hrsg.), The Image and the Book 1997, 97–155 • M. WEIPPERT, J. und die anderen Götter, 1997. E. A. K.

Iakchos (Ἴακχος). Eine der Gottheiten der Mysterien von → Eleusis [1]. I. ist die Personifikation des ekstatischen Kultrufs (*íakchos*, onomatopoetisch) der Mysten während ihrer Prozession von Athen zum eleusinischen Heiligtum, um dort die Mysterienweihe zu begehen (Hdt. 8,65; Aristoph. Ran. 316–353). Sein Bild, das in einem Tempel von Demeter, Kore und I. beim Pompeion am Heiligen Tor aufbewahrt war (Paus. 1,2,4, wohl identisch mit dem Iakcheion Plut. Aristeides 27,4), wurde dieser Prozession vom *iakchagōgós* (»Führer des I.«) vorangetragen: Daher wird sie mit »I. herausführen« umschrieben (etwa Plut. Themistokles 15,1; Alkibiades 34,4), und att. Inschr. bezeichnen das Geleit, das die Epheben der Prozession geben, auch als »Geleit für I.« (etwa IG II 2 1028,10). Sein Attribut ist die Fackel, in deren Licht die Mysten in Eleusis ankamen (Aristoph. Ran. 340–353, vgl. Paus. 1,2,4); charakteristisch für ihn ist der ekstatische Tanz (Aristoph. Ran. 316–353; Strab. 10,3,10). Dies spiegelt die ekstatischen Erlebnisse der Mysten auf ihrem langen Marsch (24 km), den sie am letzten von drei Fasttagen vollzogen. Deswegen wird I. in der Lit. seit Soph. Ant. 1152 und Eur. Ion 1074–1077 mit → Dionysos gleichgesetzt (vgl. Strab. 10,3,10); erst spät bezeugt ist die Identifikation in einem Kultruf des eleusinischen *dadúchos* (schol. Aristoph. Ran. 479).

Die Ikonographie des I. ist umstritten, da kein Vasenbild mit Beischrift erhalten ist. Die eleusinischen Bilder stellen zwei junge Männer in Ependytes, thrak. Stiefeln und (oft) mit Fackeln dar, von denen einer meist als I. verstanden wurde, doch kann auch der mehrfach in eleusinischem Kontext abgebildete Dionysos I. sein.

→ Mysterien

F. GRAF, Eleusis und die orphische Dichtung Athens, 1974, 40–59 • E. KEARNS, The Heroes of Attica, 1989, 170f. • E. SIMON, s. v. I., LIMC 5, 612–614 • K. CLINTON, Myth and Cult. The Iconography of the Eleusinian Mysteries, 1992, Kap. 2f. F. G.

Jakob

[1] Nach Gn 25,26 einer, »der die Ferse (Esaus) hält«; ansonsten ist die Etym. des Wortes ungeklärt. Der Sohn Isaaks und Rebekkas, dritter und herausragendster Patriarch neben → Abraham [1] und → Isaak sowie Vater der zwölf Stämme Israels, wird nach seinem Kampf mit dem Engel *Israel* (»der mit Gott ringt«) genannt. Seit der Königszeit ist auch J. auch Metapher für das Volk Israel.

J., der – nach traditioneller Auffassung – einerseits Tugendhaftigkeit, Wahrheit und Gottesfurcht verkörpert, andererseits aber auch als egoistisch, ja hinterlistig gesehen wird, gilt in seinem Lebenswandel als Vorbild für die künftige Gesch. des jüd. Volkes sowie als Personifikation des Volkes Israel. Eine der wenigen moralischen Schwächen J.s wird in der Bevorzugung seines Sohnes → Josef gesehen. In einigen haggadischen Quellen (→ Haggada) wird die starke Bindung J.s an Gott bereits in die Zeit vor seiner Geburt verlegt: Wenn Rebekka während ihrer Schwangerschaft an einem Lehrhaus vorbeigegangen sei, habe sich J. bewegt; sei sie an einem Götzentempel vorübergegangen, habe sich sein Zwillingsbruder Esau geregt. Während die biblische J.-Gesch. eine eigenständige Erzählung darstellt, ist in der islam. Trad. das Geschehen um J. ganz in die Josefsgesch. eingebettet. J. – im → Koran nur zweimal *Israil* gen. – wird dort als ein von Gott erwählter Prophet gesehen.

H. GAUBERT, Isaac et Jacob, les élus de Dieu, 1964 • L. GINZBERG, The legend of the Jews 1, 1968 • D. GOLDSTEIN, Jewish folklore and legend, 1980 • A. PURY, Promesse divine et légende culturelle dans le cycle de Jacob, 1975. Y. D.

[2] J. Baradaeus (*Burdʿānā*). Syr.-orthodoxer Bischof von Edessa, geb. in Tella, aufgewachsen im Kloster von Phesilta (nahe Nisibis; ca. 500–578 n. Chr.). Er lebte 15 Jahre als Protegé der Kaiserin → Theodora in Konstantinopel. Im J. 542 n. Chr., als der ġassānidische König einen Bischof verlangte, wurde er heimlich geweiht. Da sich durch seine heimlich vollzogenen Priesterordinationen eine gegen Chalkedon gerichtete Hierarchie bildete, wurden die Angehörigen der syr.-orthodoxen Kirche von den Anhängern des Konzils von Chalkedon »Jakobiten« genannt. Sein Leben beschreibt → Iohannes [26] von Ephesos in seiner Biographiensammlung

›Gesch. der oriental. Heiligen‹ (Kap. 49f.). Erh. sind einige Briefe und ein Glaubensbekenntnis.
→ Monophysitismus

Patrologia Orientalis 18–19 (Biographie) • H.G. Kleyn, J.B. de stichter der syrische Monophysitische Kerk, 1882 • A. Baumstark, Gesch. der syr. Lit., 1922, 174f. • E. Honigmann, Évêques et évêchés monophysites du VIe siècle (CSCO Subs. 227), 1951, 157–177 • D. Bundy, J.B. The state of research, in: Le Muséon 91, 1978, 45–86.

[3] J. von Sarug (Sᵉrūḡ). Syr. Dichter, gest. 521 n. Chr. Ausgebildet in der »Pers. Schule« in Edessa, wurde er syr.-orthodoxer Chorbischof (Chorepiskopos) im Gebiet von Sarug und 519 Bischof von Baṭnān-da-Sarug. Er verfaßte mehrere hundert vorzügliche Vershomilien (*memrē*) meist über biblische Themen (ca. 225 sind publiziert); außerdem sechs Festhomilien in Prosa (*turgāmē*), 43 Briefe und zwei Biographien lokaler Heiliger (unveröffentlicht). Darüber hinaus werden ihm drei *Anaphorai* und der maronitische Taufritus zugeschrieben.

Ed.:
Memre: P. Bedjan, I–V, 1905–1910 (nur Text) • C. Moss, in: Le Muséon 48, 1935, 87–112 (›Über das Theater‹, Fr.) • M. Albert, Patrologia Orientalis 38, 1976 (›Gegen die Juden‹) • W. Strothmann, Göttinger Orientforschungen 12, 1976 (›Über den Apostel Thomas‹) • K. Alwan, CSCO Scr. Syri 214f., 1989 (›Über die Schöpfung‹) • J. Amar, Patrologia Orientalis 47, 1995 (›Über Ephraem‹).
Turgame: F. Rilliet, Patrologia Orientalis 43, 1986.
Briefe: J. Olinder, CSCO Scr. Syri 57, 1937 (nur Text).
Lit.: A. Vööbus, Hsl. Überl. der Memre-Dichtung des J.v.S. I–IV CSCO Subs. 39f. und 60f., 1973 bzw. 1980 • W. Cramer, Irrtum und Lüge. Zum Urteil des J.v.S., über Reste paganer Rel. und Kultur, in: JAC 23, 1980, 96–107 • T. Bou Mansour, La Théologie de J. de S. I, 1993 • T. Kollamparampil, J. of S.: Select Festal Homilies, 1997.
Bibl.: K. Alwan, in: Parole de l'Orient 13, 1986, 313–383 • Dictionnaire de spiritualité 8, 1974, 56–60 • TRE 16, 1987, 470–474.

[4] J. von Edessa (ca. 640–708 n. Chr.). Syr. Schriftsteller und Gelehrter, geb. bei Antiocheia. Nach seinem Studium im Kloster von Qennešrē (am Euphrat) und in Alexandreia wurde er um 684 syr.-orthodoxer Bischof von Edessa, gab aber wegen der nachlässigen Haltung der Priesterschaft gegenüber den Ordensregeln das Amt bald wieder auf. Zunächst zog er sich in ein Kloster bei Kaisūm (nahe Samosata) zurück, anschließend nach Tel ʿAda. Aus der Vielzahl seiner erh. Werke sind von bes. Interesse: seine Kommentierung des *Hexaemeron*, Scholien zum AT, eine Vielzahl von Briefen über verschiedenste Themen, ein philos. Encheiridion sowie zahlreiche kanonistische Bücher (meist im Frage-Antwort-Stil). Nur fragmentarisch erh. sind seine Chronik und Grammatik. Darüber hinaus revidierte er ältere Übers. aus dem Griechischen, darunter solche der Homilien und Hymnen des Severus, einiger Bücher des AT, verschiedener liturgischer Texte und vielleicht auch der ›Kategorien‹ des Aristoteles. Seine eigenen Übers. aus dem Griech. enthalten das *Testamentum Domini*.

Ed.: J.B. Chabot, A. Vaschalde, CSCO Scr. Syri 44 und 48, 1928 bzw. 1932 (Komm. zum Hexaemeron) • A. Merx, Historia artis grammaticae apud Syros, 1889, 48–62, 73*–84* (Grammatik) • E.W. Brooks, CSCO Scr. Syri 5f., 1905 bzw. 1907 (Chronik) • G. Furlani, in: Rendiconti della R. Accademia Nazionale dei Lincei (Cl. Sc. mor. 6:4), 1928, 222–249 (Encheiridion) • K. Georr, 1948 (Übers. der ›Kategorien‹ des Aristot.) • C. Kayser, 1886 (dt. Übers. der *Kanones*).
Lit.: E.J. Revell, The Grammar of Jacob of E. …, in: Parole de l'Orient 3, 1972, 365–374 • Dictionnaire de spiritualité 8, 1974, 33–35 • TRE 16, 1987, 468–470.
S.BR./Ü: S.Z.

Iakobos Psychrestos. Arzt, Sohn des Hesychios von Damaskos, wechselte im frühen 6. Jh. n. Chr. den Wohnsitz, um in die Arztpraxis seines Vaters in Konstantinopel einsteigen zu können. Er behandelte Kaiser Leo und wurde → *comes* und → *archiatros* (Chr. pasch. 8254a; Malalas, Chronographia 370 Dindorf; Photios, Bibliotheca 344A). Als paganer Philosoph, der in Athen und Konstantinopel mit Statuen geehrt wurde, befahl er den Reichen, den Armen zu helfen, die er im übrigen ohne Honorar behandelte. Sein Spitzname leitet sich ab von einer neuen Radikalkur mit kalten Bädern, die körperliche Spannungen und seelische Sorgen, v.a. Geldsorgen, abbauen sollte. V.N./Ü: L.v.R.-B.

Ialemos (Ἰάλεμος). Sohn des → Apollon und der Muse → Kalliope, somit Bruder mehrerer mythischer Sänger: des → Hymenaios, → Linos, → Orpheus (schol. Eur. Rhes. 985). Wie Hymenaios Personifikation des Hochzeitslieds und Linos der Totenklage ist, so ist auch I. Personifikation der Totenklagen, die dichterisch *iálemoi* heißen. Der Mythos drückt die Beziehung entweder dadurch aus, daß I. früh stirbt und damit zur Totenklage Anlaß gibt (wie Linos) (Pind. fr. 139,8) oder daß I. das Klagelied erfindet. Gelegentlich wird er überhaupt mit Linos gleichgesetzt (schol. Eur. Or. 1390). F.G.

Iallius. M. I. M. f. Volt(inia tribu) Bassus Fabius Valerianus. Senator, der aus Alba Helviorum in der Narbonensis stammt. 156–159 n. Chr. leitete er als prätorischer Statthalter Pannonia inferior (AE 1976, 542; RMD II 102; 103). *Cos. suff.* kurz danach; *curator operum publicorum* 161; konsularer Statthalter von Moesia inferior; anschließend *comes Augustorum* während des Partherkrieges. Am Ende der Laufbahn konsularer Statthalter von Pannonia superior, wo er mit eingedrungenen Germanenstämmen Frieden schloß (Cass. Dio 71,3,1; PIR[2] J 4).

Kolb, Bauverwaltung, 1993, 213f. • J. Fitz, Die Verwaltung Pannoniens…, II, 1993, 488ff. W.E.

Ialmenos (Ἰάλμενος). Sohn des → Ares und der → Astyoche, zusammen mit seinem Zwillingsbruder → Askalaphos [2] Anführer des minyischen Kontingents vor Troia (Hom. Il. 2, 511), dementsprechend auch als Freier der → Helene aufgeführt (Apollod. 3,130). Läßt sich nach der Einnahme Troias mit minyischen Siedlern im Gebiet der Krim nieder (Pherekydes, FGrH 3 F 143; Strab. 9,2,42). Wie sein Bruder ist I. vermutlich schon eine Figur des voriliad. Mythos.

W. KULLMANN, Die Quellen der Ilias, 1960, 70f. • KAMPTZ, 252. E.V.

Ialysos (Ἰάλυσος). Stadt an der Nordküste der Insel Rhodos, gehört mit → Lindos und → Kamiros zu den drei alten Städten von Rhodos. Lage ca. 15 km südwestl. der Stadt Rhodos, auf dem Westabhang des 267 m hohen, als Akropolis von I. fungierenden Berges Filerimos (ant. Name *Achaía*, Diod. 5,57,6; Athen. 8,360e). Siedlung und Nekropole aus myk. Zeit beim h. Dorf Trianda. Als legendärer Stadtgründer wird der Heraklide → Tlepolemos gen. (Hom. Il. 2,653–656; Pind. O. 7). Zusammen mit Lindos, Kamiros, Kos, Knidos und Halikarnassos war I. Mitglied der dor. Hexapolis (Hdt. 1,144). Für 591 v. Chr. ist ein Söldner aus I. im ägypt. Abu Simbel bezeugt [1]. Aus I. stammte der zu Beginn des 5. Jh. v. Chr. wegen Medismos (hochverräterische Zusammenarbeit mit den Persern) verbannte Lyriker Timokreon. In dieser Zeit verfügte I. über ein ausgedehntes Territorium: bezeugt sind 11 Demen, dazu die Insel Syme (Athen. 7,296c) und Teile der festländischen Peraia [2].

Im 5. Jh. v. Chr. war I. Miglied des → Attisch-Delischen Seebundes mit Tributzahlungen zw. 5 und 10 Talenten (ATL 1,290f.; 3,185, 191 A.26, 213, 242, 349). 412/1 v. Chr. überredeten die Spartaner I. zusammen mit Lindos und Kamiros zum Abfall von Athen (Thuk. 8,44,2). 408 v. Chr. initiierte → Dorieus [2] aus I., der Sohn des Olympioniken Diagoras, einen → Synoikismos mit Lindos und Kamiros, aus dem die neue Polis Rhodos hervorging. I. existierte danach weiter als Siedlung mit dörflichem Charakter (Strab. 14,2,12). Außer (bis in die klass. Zeit belegten) Nekropolen findet sich an arch. Überresten auf der Akropolis ein Tempel der Athena Ialysia (mit Vorgängerbau aus dem 6. Jh. v. Chr., seinerseits ersetzt durch eine christl. Basilika) sowie ein dor. Brunnenhaus aus dem 4. Jh. v. Chr.

1 A. BERNAND, O. MASSON, Les inscriptions grecques d'Abou Simbel, in: REG 70, 1957, 1–46 2 P. M. FRASER, G. E. BEAN, The Rhodian Peraea and Islands, 1954, 80f.

FR. HILLER VON GÄRTRINGEN, Die Demen der rhodischen Städte III: Jalysos, in: MDAI(A) 42, 1917, 179ff. • LAUFFER, Griechenland, 275f. H.SO.

Iambe (Ἰάμβη). Magd im Haus des → Keleos, wo die um ihre entführte Tochter Persephone trauernde → Demeter nur den von I. angebotenen einfachen Stuhl akzeptiert (Hom. h. 2,192–197; Umkehr-Ritual mit Bezug zur *thrónōsis*, »Setzen« des Initianden auf einen Schemel [1]). Mit ihren frechen Späßen und provozierenden Beschimpfungen bringt I. Demeter zum Lachen und stimmt sie wieder gnädig (Hom. h. 2,202–204, vgl. SH 680,51ff.). Darin spiegelt sich die kultische Praxis der Aischrologia (rituelle Beschimpfung). Daß ein Zusammenhang zwischen der mythischen Figur I. und der lit. Gattung des Iambos (→ Iambographen) bestehen muß, ist evident, auch wenn die Richtung der Abhängigkeit ebensowenig geklärt ist wie die Etymologie.

1 W. BURKERT, Homo necans, 1972, 294–297.

N. RICHARDSON, The Homeric Hymn to Demeter, 1974, 213–223 • CH.G. BROWN, Iambos, in: D. E. GERBER (Hrsg.), A Companion to the Greek Lyric Poets, 1997, 16–25 (mit Lit.). RE.N.

Iamben s. Metrik, s. Iambographen

Iambenkürzung s. Lautlehre

Iambia (Ἰαμβία κώμη). Hafenstadt an der Westküste der arab. Halbinsel, nach Ptolemaios zum Gebiet der Arsai (Ἄρσαι, Ptol. 6,7,3) gehörig. Ebenso dürfte I. mit der nach Plin. nat. 6,168 vor Berenike gelegenen und sonst unbekannten Insel Iambe gemeint sein. Während die Gesch. von I. in hell. und röm.-byz. Zeit weitgehend unbekannt ist, erlangte der Ort unter dem arab. Namen Yanbuʿ al-baḥr als Hafen für Medina (Ἰάθριππα/Yaṯrib) v. a. für den Pilgerverkehr einige Bed.
→ Berenike [9]; Erythra thalatta; Yaṯrīb

J. TKAČ, s. v. I., RE 9, 636–639 • S. E. SIDEBOTHAM, Roman Economic Policy in the Erythra Thalassa, 1986. J.P.

Iamblichos (Ἰάμβλιχος). Personenname (zur Form vgl. [1]).
[1] I., syr.-arab. Dynast, wohl identisch mit dem vor Cicero (fam. 15,1; 2) gen. Phylarchos I. von Arethusa und Emesa, wurde 31 v. Chr. im Heer des Antonius vor Actium hingerichtet. Sein gleichnamiger Sohn erhielt von Augustus im J. 20 Emesa zurück (Cass. Dio 50,13,7; 51,2,2; vgl. Strab. 16,753).

1 SCHÜRER 1, 234f., 25. H.G.G.

[2] Neuplatoniker des 3./4. Jh. n. Chr.
A. PERSON B. WERKE C. PHILOSOPHIE
D. WIRKUNGSGESCHICHTE

A. PERSON
I. lebte wahrscheinlich zw. 240 und 325 n. Chr. und erreichte ein Alter von 85 Jahren. Geb. in Chalkis in der Provinz Syria Coele (wahrscheinlich Chalcis ad Belum, heute Qinnasrīn). Sein Name ist eine Transkription von syr. oder aram. *ya-mliku*, »er ist König« oder »er sei König«. Über die Herkunft seiner Eltern ist so gut wie nichts bekannt. Seine Lehrer waren zunächst Anatolios, dann → Porphyrios (Eun. vit. soph. 5,1,2). Er soll in Syrien eine Schule gegründet haben, und zwar in Apa-

meia (Ps.-Iul. epist. 40 HERTLEIN = 184 BIDEZ-CUMONT; Lib. epist. 1389 FÖRSTER; or. 52,21 FÖRSTER) oder, weniger wahrscheinlich, in Daphne, einer Vorstadt Antiocheias (Malalas, Chronographia 12,312,11–12). Sein bekanntester Schüler war Sopatros. Weil dieser auf Befehl Kaiser Konstantins hingerichtet wurde, trat zuerst → Aidesios [1], der sich später in Pergamon niederließ, dann → Eustathios [2] die Nachfolge des I. an (Eun. vit. soph. 6,4,5–7). Weitere Schüler waren → Theodoros von Asine und → Dexippos [4].

B. WERKE

Die zeitliche Reihenfolge der Werke läßt sich nicht sicher bestimmen. Das wichtigste Werk scheint eine aus zehn Büchern bestehende Schrift über den Pythagoreismus gewesen zu sein. Von den vier erh. Büchern ist das erste, das wohl als Einleitung diente, ein ›Leben des Pythagoras‹ (Περὶ τοῦ Πυθαγορικοῦ βίου). Es folgen ein ›Aufruf zur Philos.‹ (Λόγος προτρεπτικὸς ἐπὶ φιλοσοφίαν), eine Schrift ›Über die allg. mathematische Wiss.‹ (Περὶ τῆς κοινῆς μαθηματικῆς ἐπιστήμης) und ein Komm. ›Über die Einführung in die Arithmetik des Nikomachos‹ (Περὶ τῆς Νικομάχου ἀριθμητικῆς εἰσαγωγῆς). Die verlorengegangenen Bücher handelten über Physik, Ethik, Theologie, Geometrie, Musik und Astronomie. Bei Psellos finden sich Auszüge aus dem 5.–7. Buch (vgl. D. O'MEARAS Ausgabe der beiden Fragmente ›Über die Zahl in der Natur‹/Περὶ τοῦ φυσικοῦ ἀριθμοῦ, B. 5 und ›Über die ethische und theologische Arithmetik‹/Περὶ τῆς ἠθικῆς ἀριθμητικῆς καὶ τῆς θεολογικῆς, B. 6 und 7]). ›Die Theologie der Arithmetik‹ (Τὰ θεολογούμενα τῆς ἀριθμητικῆς) ist eine Zusammenstellung von Auszügen aus dem gleichnamigen Werk des Nikomachos von Gerasa sowie aus einem Werk des Anatolios (wahrscheinlich des Lehrers des I.) ›Über die Dekade und die darin enthaltenen Zahlen‹ (Περὶ δεκάδος καὶ τῶν ἐντὸς αὐτῆς ἀριθμῶν).

I.' originellstes Werk ist seine Antwort auf → Porphyrios' ›Brief an Anebon‹, die in den Hss. den Titel ›Antwort des Lehrers Abammons auf den Brief des Porphyrios an Anebon und Lösung der darin enthaltenen Schwierigkeiten‹ (Ἀβάμμωνος διδασκάλου πρὸς τὴν Πορφυρίου πρὸς Ἀνεβὼ ἐπιστολὴν ἀπόκρισις καὶ τῶν ἐν αὐτῇ ἀπορημάτων λύσεις) trägt. Die zehn Bücher umfassende Schrift tritt unter Berufung auf die chaldäische und ägypt. Weisheit für die »wahre« → Theurgie ein.

Bei Stobaios finden sich umfangreiche Fragmente eines Traktats ›Über die Seele‹ (Περὶ ψυχῆς), über Wesen, Kräfte und Wanderungen der Seele in einem Körper oder unabhängig davon, in dem I. auf die Positionen einiger zeitgenössischer und älterer Philosophen eingeht. Erh. sind ferner Fragmente eines 28 B. umfassenden Traktats ›Über die chaldäischen Orakel‹ (Περὶ τῆς τελειοτάτης Χαλδαϊκῆς θεολογίας) sowie eines Traktats ›Über die Götter‹ (Περὶ θεῶν), auf den zwei Reden (or. 4 und 5) Kaiser Julians und Synesios' ›Über die Götter und das Universum‹ zurückgehen.

Bei Stobaios finden sich außerdem Fragmente von neunzehn Briefen des I. an elf verschiedene Empfänger, darunter seinen Lehrer Anatolios und seine Schüler Sopatros, Dexippos und Eustathios. Der Brief an Makedonios über das Schicksal ist von großem philos. Interesse.

I. scheint in der Kommentartechnik die Lehre entwickelt zu haben, daß jeder Dialog genau ein Thema behandle (Elias, In Aristot. cat. 131,10–15 BUSSE), welches das für alles übrige maßgebliche Ziel (σκοπός, *skopós*) darstelle (Anon. prolegomena § 26,13–44 WESTERINK). Auf I. geht die Anordnung der platonischen Dialoge zurück, die er wohl auch in seinem eigenen Unterricht anwandte, und die für alle späteren Neuplatoniker maßgebend war: Der Schüler gelangt über die traditionellen drei Bereiche der Philos. – Ethik (*Alkibiades 1*, *Gorgias*, *Phaidon*), Logik (*Kratylos*, *Theaitetos*) und Physik (*Sophistes*, *Politikos*) – zur höchsten philos. Disziplin, der Theologie (*Phaidros*, *Symposion*), und zum höchsten Gut der Theologie, dem Guten (*Philebos*). Den Abschluß bilden der *Timaios* und der *Parmenides* mit einer Zusammenfassung der gesamten platonischen Lehre in den Bereichen Physik und Theologie.

Erh. sind eine beträchtliche Zahl von Frg. eines *Timaios*-Komm. sowie mehrere Frg. eines *Parmenides*- und eines *Phaidros*-Kommentars. Hinzu kommen einige Bemerkungen zu exegetischen Detailfragen in Abschnitten von *Alkibiades 1*, *Phaidon* und *Philebos*, und in einem Scholion zum *Sophistes* findet sich eine Anspielung auf das Ziel (*skopós*), das I. diesem Dialog zuschrieb. I.' Interpretation der Hypothesen des *Parmenides*, wo es nach der Auffassung der → Neuplatoniker um die Organisation der ersten Prinzipien geht, ist sehr eigenständig. Um den Trägern der Theurgie (Erzengeln, Engeln, Dämonen und Heroen), die er »höhere Wesen« nennt, in der Hierarchie der Götter einen sehr hohen Rang zuzuweisen, erhöht er die gesamte Götterhierarchie um eine Stufe. Da er gezwungen ist, außerhalb der Hypothesen des *Parmenides* einen unaussprechlichen Gott anzunehmen, verläßt er sogar den Rahmen dieses Dialoges. Dieses wichtige interpretatorische Problem wurde später von → Damaskios aufgegriffen.

Wahrscheinlich hat I. einen Komm. zu Aristoteles' *Categoriae* sowie den *Analytica priora* geschrieben. Für *De interpretatione* und *De caelo* ist dies weniger klar, auch wenn Stephanos von Alexandreia in seinem Komm. zu *De interpretatione* Bemerkungen I.' zu interpretatorischen Detailfragen und Simplikios in seinem Komm. zu *De caelo* seine Auffassung des *skopós* der Schrift zitiert.

C. PHILOSOPHIE

I.' philos. System ist im wesentlichen eine Verfeinerung des Systems des Plotin, die auf einer eigenständigen, stark vom Neupythagoreismus und von den Chaldäischen Orakeln (→ *Oracula Chaldaïca*) beeinflußten Interpretation beruht. I. nimmt vor dem Einen (Damaskios, De principiis § 43, Bd. II, 1. 1–9 WESTERINK-COMBÈS) ein ›vollkommen unaussprechliches‹ (πάντῃ ἄρρητος) Prinzip an. Zw. dem Einen und dem Intelligiblen stehen für ihn die beiden Prinzipien des Begrenzten (πέρας, *péras*) und des Unbegrenzten (ἄπειρον, *ápeiron*). So ist das ›eine Sein‹ (ἕν ὄν), das an der Spitze der intelligiblen Triade steht, eine Verschmelzung (μικτόν, *miktón*) dieser beiden Prinzipien (Damaskios De principiis § 50f.). Mit dieser Sichtweise könnte I. die Henadenlehre, die im späteren Neuplatonismus eine wichtige Rolle spielte, vorbereitet haben.

Auf den Bereich des Einen folgt der des Seins, d.h. der des Intelligiblen und des Intellektuellen. Nach Prokl. in Plat. Tim. I 308.17f. nimmt I. hier sieben Triaden an: drei Triaden intelligibler Götter, deren erste die des einen Seins (ἕν ὄν, *hén ón*) ist, drei Triaden intelligibler und intellektueller Götter sowie eine Triade intellektueller Götter. Letztere umfasse Kronos, Rhea und Zeus, den die Neuplatoniker als den Demiurgen ansähen. Ob diese Darstellung zutrifft, ist fraglich, denn Proklos (in Plat. Tim. I 307.14–308.17) führt sie an, um zu zeigen, daß I. sich zu ungenau ausdrückt, wenn er in seiner Auseinandersetzung mit Porphyrios die gesamte intelligible Welt als Demiurgen bezeichnet.

Es folgt der Bereich der Seele, der Seele als Hypostase ebenso wie der anderen Arten von Seelen. Hinsichtlich der Einzelseelen weicht I. in einem wesentlichen Punkt von Plotin und Porphyrios ab: Er widerlegt die These, ein höherer Teil der Seele verbleibe auf der Stufe der intelligiblen Welt; für ihn vereinigt sich die Seele vollständig mit dem Körper. Diese Auffassung, die der aristotelischen entspricht, hat zur Folge, daß das Seelenheil notwendigerweise anderswoher kommen muß. Der Konflikt zw. Porphyrios und I. hinsichtlich dieses Problems verschärfte sich. Während Porphyrios dem plotinischen Rationalismus treu blieb, gab I. gegenüber der Philos. der Theurgie den Vorrang; diese verstand er als geistige Bewegung, mit deren Hilfe man sich mittels genau festgelegter Riten direkt an die Götter wendet, um die Vereinigung der Seele mit den Göttern zu erlangen. Deshalb maß er den ›Chaldäischen Orakeln‹ eine so große Bedeutung zu.

Was die Natur betrifft, so ist I. hinsichtlich der Fähigkeiten des Intellekts weniger optimistisch als Plotin. Dennoch ist er der Auffassung, daß das Schicksal nur über die niedere (nichtrationale) Seele Macht hat und die höhere Seele sich mit Hilfe der Praxis der Theurgie von seinem Einfluß befreien kann.

Die Materie schließlich, die bis auf die Dyade im Bereich des Einen zurückgehen könnte (Prokl. in Plat. Tim. I 77.24–78.12), ist als das anzusehen, was den *lógoi* Andersheit verleiht (Prokl. in Plat. Tim. I 87.6–15); diese sind die Manifestationen der Formen in der Seele und im Sinnlichen.

D. Wirkungsgeschichte

I. übte einen bestimmenden Einfluß auf die Philosophen der neuplatonischen Schule von Athen, insbes. auf → Proklos und → Damaskios aus.

Edd.: L. Deubner, Iamblichi De vita Pythagorica liber, 1937 (korr. Ausg. von U. Klein, 1975) • É. des Places, Protreptikos, texte et traduction, 1989 • N. Festa, De communi Mathematica Scientia, 1891 (korr. Ausg. von U. Klein, 1975) • H. Pistelli, In Nicomachi *Arithmeticam Introductionem* liber, 1894 (korr. Ausg. von U. Klein 1975) • D. O'Meara, Pythagoras revived, 1989, App. I: The excerpts from Iamblichus' *On Pythagoreanism* V–VII in Psellus: text, translation and notes • V. de Falco, Theologoumena Arithmeticae, 1922 (korr. Ausg. von U. Klein, 1975) • B.D. Larsen, Jamblique de Chalcis, Exégète philosophe, Diss. Aarhus, mit App.: Testimonia et fragmenta exegetica • J.M. Dillon, Iamblichi Chalcidensis In Platonis Dialogos commentariorum fragmenta, ed. with translation and commentary (Philosophia Antiqua 23), 1973 • De anima, trad. A.J. Festugière, in: La révélation d'Hermès Trismégiste III, 1953, App. I.

Lit.: J.M. Dillon, Iamblichus of Chalcis (c. 240–325 A.D.), in: ANRW II 36.2, 862–909 • H. Blumenthal, E.G. Clark (Hrsg.), The Divine Iamblichus. Philosopher and Man of Gods, 1993.

L.BR./Ü: S.P.

[3] Verf. der ›Babylonischen Geschichten‹ (Βαβυλωνιακά, *Babylōniaká*). Nach schol. Phot. cod. 94 ein Syrer, der von einem Erzieher Sprache, Kultur und Erzählungen Babyloniens gelernt habe; erst als Schreiber des Königs habe er Griech. und Rhet. gelernt. Hierbei scheint es sich jedoch um eine Biographie zu handeln, die darauf ausgerichtet ist, dem an phantastischer Erfindung bes. reichen Roman histor. Authentizität zu verleihen. Wenig zuverlässig erscheinen auch die von I. selbst in sein Werk eingefügten autobiographischen Daten; er gibt sich dort als babylon. Magier mit griech. Bildung aus, der den Ausgang des Krieges des Lucius Verus gegen den Partherkönig → Vologaeses III. (166 n. Chr.: *terminus post quem*) vorausgesagt hatte, d.h. als Romanfigur.

Von den ›Babylonischen Gesch.‹ sind nur die Zusammenfassung des Photios, einige Zitate in der Suda und drei umfangreiche Fragmente erhalten. Der nach Photios in 16, nach der Suda in 35 oder 39 Bücher eingeteilte Roman handelt von dem Brautpaar Rhodanes und Sinonis, die von Garmos, dem babylon. König, verfolgt werden, und von ihren parallelen Erlebnissen, die immer stark übertrieben sind (Kreuzigungen, Folter, Kannibalismus, Hinrichtungen: Der Ton erinnert an die *Phoinikiká* des → Lollianos). Viele der Mißverständnisse, die der Handlung zugrundeliegen, leiten sich aus der physischen Ähnlichkeit des Rhodanes mit den beiden Zwillingen Tigris und Euphrates, sowie der Sinonis mit ihrer Rivalin Kore her: I. benutzt das das Doppelgänger-Motiv in derselben verwirrenden Funktion der dominierenden Logik, die es später auch in der erzählenden Lit. des Barock und in der romantischen Phantastik hat. Zudem scheint der Roman dem Erwartungshorizont der Leser bisweilen nicht entsprechen zu wollen: Die Heldin, die es fertigbringt, einen anderen nur aus Eifersucht zu heiraten (und nicht aus Notwendigkeit, wie die Protagonistin des → Chariton), wird als ungewöhnlich grausam und barbarisch dargestellt, während ihre Doppelgängerin einen positiveren Eindruck erweckt. Die Grenze zw. Illusion und Wirklichkeit wird durch einen fast paroxystischen Gebrauch von Topoi (z.B. Verwechslung von Personen, Scheintod, Verkleidung und unerwarteter Rollentausch) ständig offengehalten. MERKELBACHS [1] These, daß sich hinter dieser Handlung ein Roman der → Mithras-Mysterien verberge, scheint nicht überzeugend, weil diese Rel. u. a. sieben Initiationsstufen vorsah, während es im Roman keine Spur einer aufsteigenden Hierarchie gibt.

Die Photios-Ausgabe des Jahres 1601 und die lat. Übers. des Andreas SCHOTT von 1606 führten zu einem gewissen Nachleben des Romans in der Barocklit., bes. im Gesang XIV der ›Adone‹ des Gianbattista MARINO (1623) und in der ›Histoire africaine de Cléomède et Sophonisbe‹ des François GERZAN (1627–28).

→ Roman

1 R. MERKELBACH, Roman und Mysterium in der Ant., 1962 **2** U. SCHNEIDER-MENZEL, Jamblichos' »Babylonische Gesch.«, in: F. ALTHEIM, Lit. und Ges. im ausgehenden Alt. I, 1948 **3** E. HABRICH (ed.), I. Babyloniaka, 1960 **4** R. BECK, Soteriology, the mysteries, and the ancient novel, in: U. BIANCHI, M. J. VERMASEREN, La soteriologia dei culti orientali nell'impero romano, 1982 **5** S. STEPHENS, Fragments of Lost Novels, in: G. SCHMELING, The Novel in the Ancient World, 1996 **6** G. SANDY, The Heritage of the Ancient Novel in France and Great Britain, in: ebd.

M. FU. u. L. G./Ü: T. H.

Iambographen A. PERSONENKREIS B. BEGRIFF UND METRIK DES IAMBOS C. THEMENBEREICHE D. REZITATIONSBEDINGUNGEN UND ZIELGRUPPE E. NACHKLASSISCHER IAMBOS

A. PERSONENKREIS

Unter den archa. griech. Dichtern wurden vornehmlich → Archilochos, → Semonides und → Hipponax, aber auch → Ananios und später im 5. Jh. v. Chr. → Hermippos als Verfasser von Iamben (*íamboi*) bezeichnet. Der Begriff *iambopoioí* ist mit Sicherheit nicht vor die byz. Lexika zu datieren.

B. BEGRIFF UND METRIK DES IAMBOS

Der Begriff »Iambos« (ἴαμβος) scheint anfänglich einen Gedichttypus zu identifizieren, der eher durch seinen Inhalt (vgl. Plat. leg. 935e) als durch das Metrum definiert werden kann (bei Hdt. 1,12 ἐν ἰάμβῳ τριμέτρῳ spezifiziert wahrscheinlich nur τριμέτρῳ das Metrum). Die erste Verwendung (Archil. 215 W.) ist diesbezüglich allerdings nicht eindeutig.

Diejenigen Dichter, die man später *iambográphoi* (»I.«) nannte, benutzten meistens (iambische) Trimeter und (trochäische) Tetrameter, so z. B. Ananios und Hermippos; eine anapästische Zeile weist Epicharmos (fr. 88 KAIBEL) den *Íamboi* des Aristoxenos von Selinos zu; ein Trimeter und Hemiepes werden vom Etym. m. und Etym. gen. einem *Íambos* des Anakreon (5. Iambos W.) zugeschrieben. Die alexandrinischen Philologen schlossen in die *Íamboi* von Archilochos und Hipponax auch Epoden (davon einige asynartetische), Trimeter und Tetrameter mit ein. Nur der Trimeter wird in den iambischen Frg. des dritten der kanonischen I., Semonides, verwendet und herrscht (in seiner choliambischen Form) bei Hipponax vor.

C. THEMENBEREICHE

Diese Prädominanz war wahrscheinlich Grundlage der metrischen Bezeichnung *iambeíon*, die bereits vor Kritias 4,4 W. geprägt (?ca. 420 v. Chr.; danach bei Aristoph. Ran. 1204) und von Aristoteles (polit. 1448b 33) erklärt wurde: ›da sie in diesem Metrum einander verspotteten‹ (ἰάμβιζον). Dies zeigt auch, daß Aristoteles den Spott als ein Merkmal der *Íamboi* ansah (vgl. ὡς Ἀρχίλοχος ψέγει rhet. 1418b 27): Eine Definition von *íambos* als »Spottgedicht, das beabsichtigt, ein Publikum zu unterhalten und/oder ein Opfer zu beschämen«, paßt sowohl auf den Namen → Iambe, einer alten Frau im Homer. Hymnos an Demeter, deren scherzender Spott (χλεύῃς ... παρασκώπτουσ' 202–3) Demeter zum Lachen bringt, als auch auf viele der auf uns gekommenen Frg. In diesen ist Obszönität (*aischrología*) ebenfalls geläufig, aber weder die rituelle Assoziation mit Dionysos und Demeter noch der Name Iambe belegen die rituelle Herkunft, die von vielen stets für den Iambos beansprucht wird und von WEST noch immer für den Kontext von Archilochos' *Íamboi* gehalten wird ([6], vgl. [7], dagegen [8]). Thema der Frg. sind vorgeblich autobiographische Erzählungen, einige mil. (Archil. 88–113 W. in Tetrametern), andere sexueller Art, gelegentlich frei von Spott (Hipponax 92 W.) oder Obszönität (Archil. 196A W.), manche anscheinend frei von beidem (Archil. 23–24 W., 48 W.). Sie enthalten allg. (Semonides 7 W., Susarion 1 W., gegen Frauen) oder entlegeneren Spott (→ Hermippos 4 W. zu Herakleion). Reflexionen, die denen der Elegie ähneln (Semonides 1 W.), betreffen das Essen (id. 22–23 W.; Ananios 5 W.; Hermippos 2 W.) oder sympotische Spiele (Hermippos 7 W.). Hieraus folgt, daß die Iamben – von Anfang an oder erst von einzelnen Dichtern entwickelt – entweder mehr als nur Spott enthielten, oder daß die alexandrinischen I.-Editionen auch solche Gedichte enthielten, die von ihren Verf. nicht als *íamboi* gedacht waren.

Trimeter und Tetrameter werden jedoch auch von Dichtern verwendet, die später nicht als I. klassifiziert worden sind: vielleicht von Mimnermos (vgl. 11a W.) und sicher von → Solon (für spezifischer als in seinen Elegien formulierte polit. Selbstverteidigung) wie auch im Drama, im lit. und inschr. Epigramm, und im → Margites.

D. REZITATIONSBEDINGUNGEN UND ZIELGRUPPE

Häufige Anreden an genannte Personen (z. B. Archil. 48; 88; 96; 105; 124; 131; 168; 172; ?175 W., wahrscheinlich 124 und 196 W.; Hipponax 28; 70,11 W.), bisweilen in einem sympotischen Zusammenhang (Archil. 124 W.; Semonides 22 W.), sprechen gegen WESTS Ansicht, daß diese Gattung dramatisch ist, und weisen auf das Symposion als einen primären Vortragskontext (vgl. das σκώπτειν, »spötteln«, in Adespota elegiaca 27,6 W., jedoch nicht notwendigerweise iambisch), wenn auch einige Gedichte an eine ungenannte Person gerichtet sind (Semonides 1 W. ὦ παῖ), oder an eine wahrscheinlich nicht anwesende, ob nun genannt (Archil.

172 W.: Lykambes) oder nicht (ebd. 188 W.), oder an eine größere Gruppe (Archil. 109 W.: ὦ... πολῖται; Hipponax 1 W. ὦ Κλαζομένιοι; Susarion 1 W. ἀκούετε λεῴι) adressiert sind. Von einer Aufführung in öffentlichem Rahmen wird zum ersten Mal gesichert im 4. Jh. v. Chr. berichtet: Aristot. polit. 1336b 20–2 »Zuschauer«; Lysanias »in den Aufführungen«; vielleicht Klearchos bei Athen. 620c über Archilochos' Gedichte (nicht notwendigerweise *íamboi*), die »in den Theatern« aufgeführt wurden, bei einem Festival nur in der Archilochos-Biographie des Mnesiepes aus dem 3. Jh. v. Chr. (251 W.). Rezitative Aufführung, vom *aulós* begleitet, wird für Tetrameter durch Xen. symp. 6,3 bestätigt; Theokr. epigr. 14 könnte implizieren, daß Archilochos' *Íamboi* gesungen wurden; Ps.-Plut. de musica 1141a berichtet von einer »Überlieferung« (φασί), nach der Archilochos sowohl das Singen iambischer Metren als auch ihre Rezitation mit begleitender Streichmusik eingeführt habe; und Phillis bei Athen. 636b behauptet, Iambyke und Klepsiambos hätten die jeweiligen Aufführungsarten begleitet. Vielleicht wurden charakteristischerweise Tetrameter und Epoden gesungen, Trimeter rezitiert [9], aber Sicherheit gibt es darüber nicht [10].

E. Nachklassischer Iambos

Einige spätere Iamben enthalten noch Züge der archa. *íamboi*. Ca. 200 v. Chr. schrieb → Alkaios von Messene *íamboi*, um die Plagiate des Ephoros zu kritisieren (Porphyrios ap. Euseb. Pr. Ev. 10,3,23 [11. 8]), und Hermeias von Kurion verwendete Choliamben, um die Stoiker anzugreifen (Athen. 563d = CollAlex S. 237).

Die typischen Iamben-Merkmale – Kritik, Fabeln und konkrete Adressaten – werden im frühen 3. Jh. v. Chr. in den moralisierenden choliambischen *Íamboi* des → Phoinix (CollAlex S. 231–236) und des Parmenon (ebd. S. 237f.) beibehalten. Entwickelt wurde die Gattung von → Kallimachos in seinem Buch der 13 *Íamboi*; im Eingangsgedicht spricht der vom Tode zurückgekehrte Hipponax, dessen ion. Dialekt (und bisweilen Diktion) mit archilocheischen Metren und Themen gekreuzt ist, die nach und nach weniger iambisch werden. Ungefähr zur selben Zeit verwendete → Herodas Choliamben und manchmal auch »niedere« iambische Themen (Prostitution in 1 und 2, Dildos in 6) in seinen dramatischen Mimiamben (imitiert von Arrius Antoninus ca. 100 n. Chr.: Plinius, epist. 4,3). → Machon behielt den Humor und die Skurrilität der *íamboi* in seinem Trimeter *Chreíai* (›Anekdoten‹) bei. Im späten 3. Jh. könnten Invektiven der Inhalt der Choliamben des → Kerkidas gewesen sein (nur eine einzige Zeile ist erh.: CollAlex fr. 14 p. 213). Einiges mehr ist von seinen Meliamben erh. geblieben, die kritische Reflexionen (wie diejenigen der Iamben) in lyrischem Metrum wiedergaben. Choliamben wurden im 1. Jh. n. Chr. von → Babrios, der den Gebrauch der *Mythíamboi* einführte, in zwei Büchern dieses Titels mit äsopischen Fabeln, und dann im 4. Jh. n. Chr. von → Gregorios von Nazianz für paränetische Spottgedichte und Selbstverteidigung eingesetzt.

Die Gedichte vieler Autoren sind jedoch allein bezüglich ihres Metrums iambisch. Choliamben verwendete bereits im späten 4. Jh. → Aischrion in einem Epigramm [11. 3–4] und in einer mythischen Erzählung (SH fr. 5), ebenso im 3. Jh. → Asklepiades (SH fr. 216f.) und → Apollonios [2] Rhodios (in seinem *Kanobos*, evtl. einer Gründungserzählung); später finden sie sich im Alexander-Roman und sogar in Epitaphien (GVI 722, ca. 117 n. Chr.). Trimeter wurden in Epigrammform über alle Epochen hinweg eingesetzt, im 4. und 3. Jh. v. Chr. dann von Philosophen und Moralisten: → Chares [3]; → Krantor; → Krates; → Zenon; → Kleanthes; vgl. die *Gnṓmai* des → Menandros und → Epicharmos. Im 2. Jh. v. Chr. führte → Apollodoros' *Chroniká* die Tradition didaktischer Dichtung in Trimetern ein, gefolgt von (Ps.-)→ Skymnos,→ Damokrates, → Dionysios [26] und anderen. In der späten Kaiserzeit wurden sie für Hymnen, Enkomien, narrative Dichtung und für Prologe hexametrischer Gedichte verwandt.

Im 2. Jh. v. Chr. schrieb Eratosthenes' Lehrer → Lysanias von Kyrene ›Über die Iambendichter‹ (Περὶ ἰαμβοποιῶν) mehr als ein Buch (Athen. 620c), und die frühen I. wurden von Metrikern und von Lexikographen (auf seltene Worte oder Formen) genau untersucht.
→ Invektive

Bibliogr.: **1** D. E. Gerber, in: Lustrum 33, 1991, 9–18 (für 1921–1989)
Ed.: **2** IEG I² und 2² **3** CollAlex **4** SH **5** A. D. Knox, Herodes, Cercidas and the Greek Choliambic poets, 1929.
Lit.: **6** M. L. West, Studies in Greek Elegy and Iambus, 1974, 22–39 **7** G. Nagy, The Best of the Achaeans, 1979, 243–252 **8** C. Carey, Archilochus and Lycambes, in: CQ n. s. 36, 1986, 63–65 **9** A. M. Dale, Stichos and stanza, in: CQ n. s. 13, 1963, 46–50 **10** K. Bartol, Greek Elegy and Iambus, 1993, 61–65 **11** GA I.2.
E. BO./Ü: C. ST.

Iambulos (Ἰαμβοῦλος). In seiner Bibliothek der Weltgesch. (2,55–60) erwähnt → Diodoros [18] Siculus einen Händler I., der auf einer Reise in Arabien von Äthiopiern, die damit einen schon mehr als 20 Generationen alten Reinigungsritus vollzogen, auf eine glückselige Insel verschleppt wurde. Die Beschreibung der Insel (hinter der sich vielleicht Ceylon verbirgt) enthält alle Charakteristika der ant. Utopie: ideales Klima, außergewöhnliche Fruchtbarkeit und eine kommunistische Gesellschaftsstruktur. Paradoxe Elemente fehlen nicht: Die Einwohner haben eine (im wörtl. Sinne) gespaltene Zunge, mit der sie gleichzeitig zwei verschiedene Gespräche führen können. Nach sieben Jahren auf der Insel wird I. wegen eines nicht näher bezeichneten Vergehens von ihr verbannt und kehrt über Indien und Persien nach Griechenland zurück.

Der Roman, der Diodoros vorlag, dürfte eine sorgfältig ausgearbeitete Gestalt besessen haben, die ihm selbst in Lukians satirischem Pastiche der ›Wahren Gesch.‹ (1,3) zuerkannt wird. Rohde hatte das Werk (wie die *Hierá anagraphḗ* des → Euhemeros) als utopischen Roman etikettiert, doch ist dies heute nicht mehr unumstritten, da nur schwer bestimmbar ist, wie weit Diodoros die urspr. Struktur verändert hat, um der polit. Beschreibung größeren Raum zu geben, und in welchem Verhältnis der narrative Teil (einschließlich der Rückreise) zum theoretischen stand.

→ Roman; Utopie

E. ROHDE, Der griech. Roman und seine Vorläufer, [2]1914 • W. W. EHLERS, »Mit dem Südwestmonsun nach Ceylon«: Eine Interpretation der Iambul-Exzerpte Diodors, in: WJA 11, 1985, 73–84 • B. KYTZLER, Zum utopischen Roman der klass. Ant., in: Groningen Colloquia on the Novel 1, 1988, 7–16 • N. HOLZBERG, Novel-like Works of Extended Prose Fiction II, in: G. SCHMELING (Hrsg.), The Novel in the Ancient World, 1996. M. FU./Ü: T. H.

Iamos (Ἴαμος). Ahnherr des eleischen Sehergeschlechts der Iamidai, das in Olympia zusammen mit den → Klytiadai (Hdt. 9,33) bis zum Untergang des Heiligtums aktiv war. Diese prophezeiten gewöhnlich aus der Flamme des Opferfeuers (vgl. Pind. O. 8,2f.), doch erfand Thrasybulos die Divination aus den Eingeweiden eines Hundes (Paus. 6,2,4); ihre Prophezeiungen schlugen sich auch in ausführlichen Orakeln (*lógia*) nieder (Paus. 3,11,6). Sie sind eng mit Sparta verbunden (dort das Grab der Iamidai, Paus. 3,12,8), aber auch im Dienst Messenes (Paus. 4,16,1) und Mantineias (Paus. 10,5,8) faßbar.

I. ist Sohn → Apollons und der → Euadne, der Tochter Poseidons und der spartanischen Lokalheroine Pitane. Die Mutter bringt das Kind beim Wasserholen zur Welt und setzt es in Veilchen (*ía*, daher der Name) aus, und Schlangen nähren es mit Honig; auf Geheiß Apollons zieht → Aipytos [1] das Kind groß; erwachsen, fleht er Poseidon und Apollon um ein Amt an, und Apollon schenkt ihm die Sehergabe (Pind. O. 6,28–72).

H. HEPDING, s. v. I., RE 9, 685–689 • H. W. PARKE, The Oracles of Zeus, 1967, 174–178 • E. SIMON, s. v. I., LIMC 5, 614f. F. G.

Ianeira (Ἰάνειρα, »Mannskraft«). → Nereide (Hom. Il. 18,47; Apollod. 1,12) oder → Okeanide (Hes. theog. 356), die auch zu den Gespielinnen der Persephone gehörte (Hom. h. 2,421). RE. ZI.

Ianiculum. Einer der sieben Hügel Roms (→ Roma); am rechten Tiberufer gelegen und bereits in republikanischer Zeit durch vier Brücken mit dem → Campus Martius verbunden. Wegen seiner mil. Bed. wurde der I. bereits früh in den *ager Romanus* mit einbezogen (Cass. Dio 37,27,3 – 37,28,1). Der Name I. geht vermutlich auf eine Kultstelle für Ianus zurück; seit der späten Republik war der von der Via Aurelia überquerte Hügel Ort verschiedener großer → Gartenanlagen (*horti Agrippinae; horti Caesaris*).

P. LIVERANI, s. v. I., LTUR 3, 1996, 89f. (Quellen) • RICHARDSON, 205f. C. HÖ.

Ianitor s. Hochzeitsbräuche

Jannes und Jambres (Jamnes und Mambres). Das Pseudepigraph von J.u.J. fußt auf Ex 7,8ff. und wurde breit rezipiert: Die in *Exodus* nicht namentlich gen. beiden ägypt. Zauberer, Gegner des → Moses und des Aaron, figurieren als J.u.J. (die Schreibweise variiert je nach griech., lat. oder hebr. Vorlage) in jüd., griech. und röm. Schriften sowie im NT und anderen christl. Dokumenten. Auch in der rabbin. und targumischen (Targum Ps.-Jonathan) Lit. wurde der J.u.J.-Stoff verarbeitet.

A. PIETERSMA (ed.), The Apocryphon of Jannes and Jambres, the magicians, 1994 • SCHÜRER 3, 781–783. Y. D.

Ianthe (Ἰάνθη, »Veilchenblüte«). Tochter von → Okeanos und → Tethys (Hes. theog. 349; Hyg. fab. praef. 6; Paus. 4,30,4); Spielgefährtin der → Persephone (Hom. h. 2,418). J. S.-A.

Ianuarius Nepotianus. Bearbeiter der Exempla-Slg. des → Valerius Maximus für den Rhetorik-Unterricht, wohl aus dem 4. Jh. n. Chr. (so mit sprachlichen Argumenten [1]). Bei Bewahrung der Anordnung wurde die Vorlage stilistisch bearbeitet und – z. T. aus Cicero – ergänzt (vgl. 7,3; 9,24 etc.). Der Auszug, im *Codex unicus* (*Vaticanus Latinus* 1321, s. XIV) nur bis Val. Max. 3,2,7 erhalten, ist von Landolfus Sagax (um 1000) noch in einem vollständigeren Expl. benutzt worden.

1 F. BUECHELER, Kleine Schriften 3, 1930, 331–335 ([1]1906) **2** D. M. SCHULLIAN, I. Nepotianus, in: F. E. CRANZ, P. O. KRISTELLER (Hrsg.), Catalogus translationum et commentariorum 5, 1984, 251f. **3** M. IHM, Zu Valerius Maximus und I. Nepotianus, in: RhM 49, 1894, 254.

ED.: C. KEMPF, Valerius Maximus, 1888, XVIIf., 592–624 • H. DROYSEN, Nachträge, in: Hermes 13, 1878, 122–132. P. L. S.

Ianus A. KULTORTE B. MYTHOS C. KULT D. DARSTELLUNGEN

Röm. Gott des Durchgangs im top., zeitlichen und übertragenen Sinn. Sein Name wird von *ianua* (»Durchgang, Tor«) hergeleitet und mit dem → Ianiculum verbunden; der Name wird sowohl für den Gott wie für die mit ihm verbundenen kult. relevanten Tordurchgänge verwendet. Die seit republikanischer Zeit belegte Ikonographie stellt I. regelmäßig mit zwei, gelegentlich mit vier Gesichtern dar (*bifrons, quadrifrons*).

A. KULTORTE

Sein Kult ist praktisch ausschließlich öffentlich-politisch; allein zwei private Dedikationen an ihn sind erhalten. Zwei alte Altäre des I. in Rom sind lit. bezeugt: einer auf dem Ianiculum, dem Ort seines Königspalasts (Varro bei Aug. civ. 7,4; Ov. fast. 1,245f.), ein zweiter beim sog. Tigillum Sororium auf dem Mons Oppius, einem die Straße überspannenden Holzbalken, der an den Mythos von den Horatii und Curiatii (→ Horatius) erinnert, zusammen mit einem Altar der → Iuno Sororia. I. trug hier die Epiklese Curiatius (Liv. 1,26,13; Dion. Hal. ant. 3,22,7f.) und erhielt am 1. Oktober ein Opfer; der Kult hängt mit Durchgangsriten der Pubertät zusammen, welchen urspr. die jungen → *nobiles* unterworfen waren; → Cornelius [II 19] Labeo versteht den Beinamen Curiatius, der mit der urspr. männerbundartigen *curia* < **co-viria* zusammenhängt, als »Schützer der Adligen« (Lyd. mens. 4,1) [1].

Der wichtigste Kultbau war der I. Geminus am Forum Romanum (dessen genaue Lage noch immer unklar ist [2]), ein vermutlich urspr. hölzerner, bronzebeschlagener Doppeltorbau, der in augusteischer Zeit ganz aus Bronze erneuert und zu einer Art Schrein für die archa., über 2 Meter hohe Bronzestatue des I. gemacht wurde (Beschreibung: Prok. BG 5 (1) 25,20f.; Münzbilder [3]); er hatte im Osten und im Westen je ein Flügeltor, in deren Richtung die beiden bärtigen Gesichter der Statue schauten. Die Statue selbst, eine der ältesten Roms (Plin. nat. 34,33; bezeugt im 2. Jh. v. Chr. durch den Annalisten L. → Calpurnius [III 1] Piso (fr. 9 HRR)), trug als Attribute Schlüssel und Stab (Ov. fast. 1,99). Unter Augustus (dann wieder unter Nero und noch öfter in der Kaiserzeit) wurden die Flügeltore geschlossen, wenn im ganzen Reich Friede herrschte – ein Ritus, der von Numa hergeleitet wurde (Piso, fr. 9 HRR; Liv. 1,19,2), zum erstenmal für das J. 235 v. Chr. belegt ist (Varro ling. 5,165) und von Augustus zu einem wichtigen rituellen Ausdruck seiner Friedenspolitik gemacht wurde (vgl. Verg. Aen. 1,293–297). Seit der augusteischen Erneuerung trug I. hier die (sprachlich ebenso mit *curia* verwandte) Epiklese Quirinus (R. Gest. div. Aug. 2,42; Suet. Aug. 22; [4. 421–424]), die von den ant. Interpreten auf seine kriegerische (bzw. Frieden bringende) Funktion zurückgeführt (Macr. Sat. 1,9,16) und entsprechend mit dem Namen des griech. Kriegsgottes → Enyalios übersetzt wurde (Plut. qu. R. 25, vgl. Lyd. mens. 4,1: *prómachos*). Die im Gebet des *flamen Cerialis* verwendeten Epiklesen Patulcius (»Öffner«) und Clusivius (»Schließer«) beziehen sich ebenfalls auf diesen Ritus (Ov. fast. 1,129f., Macr. Sat. 1,9,16; [4. 416–420]). Domitian verlegte den Kult in ein neues Heiligtum auf dem → Forum Transitorium.

Einen eigentlichen Tempel hatte I. auf dem Forum Holitorium beim Marcellustheater in Rom. Dieser war in der Seeschlacht von Mylae (260 v. Chr.) von M. Duilius gelobt worden; Augustus restaurierte ihn, Tiberius weihte ihn neu und verlegte den Stiftungstag vom 17. August auf den 18. Oktober. Es war wohl dieser Tempel, der zwölf Altäre enthielt, welche M. Terentius Varro (Macr. Sat. 1,9,16) und Fonteius [I 9] (Lyd. mens. 2,2) auf die zwölf Monate bezogen.

B. Mythos

Der Mythos macht I. zum Urkönig von Latium, der über die → Aborigenes herrscht und in seinem Palast auf dem Ianiculum den nach Westen geflohenen → Saturnus aufnimmt, der den Ackerbau und damit die Zivilisation nach Latium bringt (Macr. Sat. 1,7,19–22): Damit wird das Thema der Durchgänge auf den absoluten Anfang von Roms Gesch. projiziert, I. auch als urröm. Gottheit ausgezeichnet, der jede griech. Entsprechung fehlt. Ein nur von Ov. fast. 6,101–168 erzählter Mythos macht I. zum Liebhaber der Carna, der Göttin der Türangel. Die spielerische, wenn auch naheliegende Beziehung (wohl eine ovidianische Erfindung) ist Aition für den röm. Brauch, durch Aufhängen einer Weißdornrute an der Tür die kinderraubenden Striges vom Haus fernzuhalten [5].

C. Kult

Im röm. Kult spielt I. eine regelmäßige Rolle bei rituellen Anfängen. Er erhält bei jedem Opfer jeweils das Voropfer von Wein oder Weihrauch (Cic. nat. deor. 2,67; Ov. fast. 1, 171f.; Beispiele etwa Cato agr. 134. 141; Liv. 8,9,6; [6]), und er wird zu Beginn jedes Opfers angerufen, Vesta am Schluß [7]; deswegen versteht ihn der Antiquar Gavius [I 2] Bassus als Gott der Luft, der die Gebete von den Menschen zu den Göttern befördert (Lyd. mens. 2,2). Das hohe Alter und die umfassende Bed. seines Kultes wird durch die Anrufung im Lied der Salii (→ Carmen Saliare) nahegelegt (Varro ling. 7,27: *divom deus*, »Gott der Götter«; vgl. Macr. Sat. 1,9,14). Der erste Jahresmonat ist nach übereinstimmender ant. Meinung dem I. geweiht (Bedenken: [8]), auch wenn das Hauptopfer des 1. Januar dem Iuppiter Optimus Maximus auf dem Kapitol gilt (Ov. fast. 1,79f.) und von I. in der Feier der Kalendae Ianuariae keine Spur zu finden ist [9]. *Ludi* werden ihm dann allerdings am 7. Januar gefeiert, und er erhält das erste *agonium* des Jahres am 9. Januar (Ov. fast. 1,317f.). Erst spät ist belegt, daß er an jedem Monatsersten ein Opfer erhielt und dabei den Beinamen Iunonius trug, weil die Kalenden → Iuno geweiht sind (Macr. Sat. 1,9,16, allegorisiert bei Lyd. mens. 4,1).

D. Darstellungen

I. wird seit jeher doppelköpfig dargestellt, sowohl bei der archa. Bronzestatue im I. Geminus wie auf der Vorderseite des alten → As (mittlere und späte Republik), dessen Rückseite eine Schiffsprora schmückte [10]. Ov. fast. 1,229–254 deutet dies aus dem Mythos von I. und Saturnus; die mod. Forsch. versteht die Doppelköpfigkeit teilweise als heraldische Übernahme aus griech. Münzprägung. Selbst wenn dies zutreffen sollte, ist aber mit dem Bild mehr ausgedrückt, nämlich die grundlegende Funktion des Gottes der Anfänge und Durchgänge, aus der man dann sogar seine Begleiterinnen Antevorta und Postvorta konstruierte (Macr. Sat. 1,7,20). Zudem besteht wohl ein Zusammenhang zum etr., ebenfalls doppelköpfigen Gott Culsan [11; 12]. Das Attribut des Stabs zeichnet I. als Autoritätsfigur (*I. pater* im Gebet bei Cato agr. 134), dasjenige des Schlüssels als Gott der Eingänge; wenn seine Finger die Zahl der Tage des Jahres, 365, ausdrücken sollten, ist dies eine erst nach der caesarianischen Kalenderreform denkbare Allegorie, welche aus dem Gott des ersten Monats den Jahresgott überhaupt macht (Plin. nat. 34,44; Macr. Sat. 1,9,10). Noch weiter geht Ov. fast. 1,101–114, der I. zum kosmologisch ersten Gott (Chaos) macht und in der Doppelgesichtigkeit einen Hinweis auf dessen Formlosigkeit sieht.

1 H.J. Rose, De religionibus antiquis quaestiunculae tres, in: Mnemosyne 53, 1925, 407–410 2 E. Tortoria, s.v. I. Geminus, LTUR 4, 92f. 3 RRC I 487 Nr. 478f.; II 739 4 G. Capdeville, Les épithètes cultuels de Janus, in: MEFRA 85, 1973, 395–436 5 C.M. McDonough, Carna, Proca and the Strix on the Kalends of June, in: TAPhA 127, 1997, 315–344 6 J. Cels-Saint-Hilaire, Auguste, Diane et Hercule. A propos d'une inscription de Tibur, in: M.-M. Mactoux, E. Geny (Hrsg.): Mélanges P. Lévêcque 6, 1992, 45–71 7 Latte, 134 8 RRC II 718 9 Latte, 134f. 10 F. Graf, Kalendae Ianuariae, in: Ders. (Hrsg.), Ansichten griech. Rituale. Geburtstagssymposium für W. Burkert, 1998, 199–216 11 E. Simon, Culsu, Culsans und Ianus, in: Dies., Schriften zur etr. und ital. Kunst und Rel., 1996, 41–53 (1989) 12 I. Krauskopf, Culsan und Culsá, in: R. Altheim-Stiehl, M. Rosenbach (Hrsg.), Beiträge zur altital. Geistesgesch. FS Gerhard Radke, 1986, 156–163.

G. Wissowa, Rel. und Kultus der Römer, ²1912, 103–113 • L.A. Holland, Janus and the Bridge, 1961 • M. Guarducci, I. Geminus, in: Dies., Scritti scelti sulla religione greca e romana e sul cristianesimo, 1983, 165–179 (1966) • R. Schilling, Janus. Le dieu introducteur, le dieu des passages, in: Ders., Rites, cultes, dieux de Rome, 1979, 220–262 (1960) • R. Turcan, Janus à l'époque impériale, in: ANRW II 17.1, 374–402 • E. Simon, s.v. I., LIMC 5, 618–623. F.G.

Iao s. Jahwe

Iapetos (Ἰαπετός). Die Etym. ist unsicher; vielleicht »der Herabgeschleuderte« (zu ἰάπτειν, »schleudern« [1]); die häufig postulierte Beziehung zum at. Japheth, dem dritten Sohn Noahs (Gn 5,32 u.ö.), läßt sich nicht beweisen [2; 3]. Titan, der zusammen mit → Kronos von Zeus in den Tartaros geschleudert wurde (Hom. Il. 8,479). Sohn der → Gaia und des → Uranos (Hes. theog. 134); mit der Okeanide Klymene hat er die Söhne → Atlas [2], → Menoitios, → Prometheus und Epimetheus (Hes. theog. 507–511). Als seine Gattin werden u.a. auch Asia (Apollod. 1,8; Lykophr. 1283) und Themis (Aischyl. Prom. 18) genannt. Er spielt für die Myth. nur im Zusammenhang mit seinen Söhnen, den Iapetiden, eine Rolle (vgl. Ov. met. 1,82). Kultisch verehrt wurde er nur vereinzelt (auf Imbros: IG XII 8,74). In der Bildkunst ist I. vielleicht am Südfries des Pergamonaltars (1. Hälfte 2. Jh. v. Chr.) dargestellt [4].

1 Frisk 1, 705 2 M.L. West, Hesiod. Theogony (Komm.), 1966, 202–203 3 W. Burkert, The Orientalizing Revolution, 1992, 177 4 E. Simon, s.v. I., LIMC 5.1, 623–624, Nr. 1.

Graf, 81–82. R.B.

Iapis. Sohn des → Iasos und Liebling Apollons. Der Gott will ihm die Gabe der Weissagekunst, des Leierspiels und des treffsicheren Pfeilschießens verleihen. I. aber bittet um Heilkunst, um dem Vater das Leben zu retten. Mit Hilfe der Venus heilt er Aeneas von seinen Wunden (Verg. Aen. 12,391 ff.; Serv. Aen. 12,391 (Iapyx); Macr. Sat. 5,15,12). RE.ZI.

Iapodes. Indoeur. Volk, seit dem 9./8. Jh. v. Chr. nachgewiesen, oft irrig den Illyrern zugeordnet, in Lika, den Karstebenen von Gacko, Ličko, Krbavsko (Westkroatien), am Una nahe Bihać (Westbosnien) und Notranjska (Innerkrain/Slowenien) ansässig. Verwaltungstechnisch zählten sie zum *conventus Scardonitanus* der Prov. → Illyricum, später Dalmatia. Die Zrmanja und die Velebit-Berge trennten sie von den → Liburni im Süden. Mit diesen setzten sie sich im 3. Jh. v. Chr. mit nur vorübergehendem Erfolg auseinander, um in der Bucht von Kvarner einen Zugang zum Meer zu gewinnen. Im Norden grenzten sie an die Colapiani entlang der Colapis (= Kolpa/Kupa), nach Westen reichten sie bis zum Ocra-Paß unterhalb des Nanos im Hinterland von Tergeste, das sie öfters plündernd durchzogen (vgl. Caes. Gall. 8,24,3; App. Ill. 18; 52 v. Chr.). Der Einfluß der Latène-Kultur hinterließ bei ihnen nur geringe Spuren (gegen Strab. 7,5,2, der behauptet, sie seien keltisiert worden). Den Römern grundsätzlich feindlich, scheinen die I. vor 171 v. Chr. eine Art Übereinkunft mit Rom gehabt zu haben, als sie von C. Cassius Longinus angegriffen wurden; denn sie beklagten sich beim Senat über diese Ungerechtigkeit. C. Sempronius Tuditanus zog 129 v. Chr. gegen sie in den Kampf. Sie wurden 35/4 v. Chr. durch den nachmaligen Augustus endgültig unterworfen (App. Ill. 18–21; Cass. Dio 49,35), der ihre Festungen Monetium (= Brinje), Avendo (= Crkvina bei Brlog), Arupium (= Prozor) und Terponus (= Gornji Modruš) eroberte und ihren Zentralort Metulum (= oberhalb Viničica nahe Ogulin gelegen) zerstörte. Diese Zentren der I. existierten in röm. Zeit als städtische Gemeinden fort; Metulum erlangte sogar den Status eines *municipium* (vgl. CIL III 10060).

R. Drechsler-Bižić, Japodska grupa [Die Iapodische Kultur-Gruppe], in: Praistorija jugoslavenskih zemalja 5, 1987, 391–441 • S. Grabovec, Notranjska grupa [Die Innerkrainische Kultur-Gruppe], in: Ebd., 151–177 • M. Šašel Kos, A Historical Outline of the Region between Aquileia, the Adriatic, and Sirmium in Cassius Dio and Herodian, 1986, 128–145. M.Š.K./Ü: I.S.

Iapyges, Iapygia. Volk und Landschaft im äußersten SO von It. (h. Puglia). Erstmals von Hekataios (FGrH 1 F 86f.) mit den nicht lokalisierbaren Gemeinden *Eleútioi* (Ἐλεύτιοι), *Peukaíoi* (Πευκαῖοι, entspricht evtl. Πευκέτιοι) und *pólis Chandánē* (πόλις Χανδάνη) erwähnt; evtl. meint Hekataios (l.c.) I. auch mit ›Stadt in Italia‹ (πόλις ἐν τῆι Ἰταλίαι). Nach Hdt. 4,99 ist ein Akroterion von I. die Halbinsel südl. des Isthmus zw. Tarentum und Brundisium [7. 170–172]. Antiochos (FGrH 555 F 12) setzt die Grenze zw. It. und I. bei Metapontum an (vgl. F 3b; Aristot. pol. 7,9,2) und rechnet Tarentum zum Land der I. (F 3a), während Skyl. 14 in I. (von Lucania bis zum Garganus) auch Herakleia und Metapontum miteinschließt. Nach Strabon (6,3,1; 5) ist I., auch Messapia gen., nur die Halbinsel südl. des Isthmus zw. Tarentum und Brundisium [8. 47f.]. I. ist meist, und vielleicht urspr. [4], mit Kap Leuca (Ἄκρα Ἰαπυγίας) verbunden (vgl. Thuk. 6,30,1; Skyl. 27; Aristot. mir. 97; Diod. 13,3,3; Strab. 2,5,20; Plin. nat. 3,100). In griech. Quellen bezeichnet I. meist die ganze Bevölkerung in SO-It. (Hdt. 4,99; Skymn. 363) mit den Messapii, Peucetii und Dauni (Pol. 3,88; Strab. 6,3,2), aber v.a. die südl. Messapii, gegen die die griech. Ansiedler von Tarentum kämpften (Gründungsorakel bei Antiochos, FGrH 555 F 13; Diod. 8,21, vgl. Hdt. 7,170) [8; 10]. Zw. I. und Messapii unterscheidet nur Pol. 2,24,10.

Meist schreibt die Überl. den I. kret. Ursprung und Herkunft aus minoischer Zeit zu [4; 8; 11]. Hdt. 7,170 weiß von einer Landung von Kretern in I. (Gründung von Hyrie – Uria oder wahrscheinlicher Veretum, vgl. Strab. 6,3,2 – u.a. *poleis*) sowie deren Umbenennung zu *Iḗpyges Messápioi* (Ἰήπυγες Μεσσάπιοι, vgl. auch Konon, FGrH 26 F 1,25; Athen. 12,522f.). Nach Strab. 6,3,2 (vgl. 6,3,6) und Sol. 2,7 stammen die I. von Iapyx (→ Iapis), einem Sohn des Daidalos, ab. Nikandros (bei Antoninus Liberalis, metamorphoses 31) schreibt den I. einen arkad. und illyr. Ursprung und die Abstammung von Iapyx, dem Sohn des Lykaon, zu. Nach Hellanikos von Lesbos (FGrH 4 F 79) vertrieben die I. die Ausonii aus It., was vielleicht mit der Bezeugung von *Iapýgōn ákrai* im Raum von Kroton durch Ephoros (Ἰαπύγων ἄκραι, FGrH 70 F 140) übereinstimmt.

Gut überliefert sind die Kämpfe von Tarentum gegen die I. in spätarcha. Zeit: die Eroberung der Stadt Karbina (Klearchos bei Athen. 12,522 e-f) und anderer *poleis* (Hdt. 7,170); die Siege über die Messapii, die Peucetii und Opis, den König der I. (Paus. 10,10,6; 13,10); die blutige Niederlage, die Tarentum um 470 hinnehmen mußte (Hdt. 7,170; Aristot. pol. 5,2,8; Diod. 11,52). 413 v.Chr. stellte der iapyg.-messap. Fürst Artas den Athenern Hilfstruppen im Kampf um Syrakusai (Thuk. 7,33,4; 57,11). Gegen E. 4. Jh. wurde auch I. in die Kämpfe zw. Rom und Samnites hineingezogen (Diod. 20,35; 80). Zu Anf. des 3. Jh. verbündete sich Agathokles [2] mit den I. und Peucetii (Diod. 21, fr. 4).

Herakles-Sagen in I. bezeugt Aristot. mir. 97; einheimische Mythen finden sich bei Antoninus Liberalis (metamorphoses 31,3; vgl. Ov. met. 14,514–526). Die Annahme illyr. Herkunft der I. [2; 4; 6; 7. 75–84] und ihrer Sprache, wahrscheinlich die der sog. messap. Inschr., läßt sich nicht beweisen [7. 107–110; 8; 11]. Die arch. Quellen belegen vom 8. Jh. an wichtige kulturelle Entwicklungen in I. mit einer fortschreitenden Differenzierung zw. den Messapii im Süden, den Dauni im Norden und den Peucetii in der Mitte sowie ihre Beziehungen zu den Griechen [5; 6; 7; 8; 9].

1 NISSEN 1, 539–542 **2** G. SUSINI, Fonti per la storia greca e romana del Salento, 1962 **3** G. NENCI, Il βάρβαρος πόλεμος tra Taranto e gli Iapigi, in: ASNP III, 6, 1976, 719–738
4 Ders., Per una definizione della Ἰαπυγία, in: ASNP III, 8, 1978, 43–58 **5** F. D'ANDRIA, Greci e indigeni in Iapigia, in: Forme di contatto ... Atti Convegno Cortona, 1983, 287–305 **6** E. DE JULIIS, Gli Iapigi, 1988 **7** M. CONGEDO (Hrsg.), Salento Porta d'Italia. Atti del convegno di Lecce 1986, 1989 **8** M. LOMBARDO, I Messapi, in: A. STAZIO (Hrsg.), Atti XXX Convegno sulla Magna Grecia, 1991, 35–109 **9** D. YNTEMA, The Matt-Painted Pottery of Southern Italy, 1990 **10** M. LOMBARDO, I Messapi e la Messapia nelle fonti letterarie greche e latine, 1992
11 Ders., La Puglia prima dei Greci, in: P. BRONI (Hrsg.), La Puglia prima della colonizzazione, 1997, 15–37. M.L.

Jargon s. Fachsprache

Jariri. Prinzregent aus Karkamis, Anf. 8 Jh. v. Chr., Erzieher des Kamani, des Sohnes des Astiruwa. Bildliche Darstellung J.s mit Kamani: KARKAMIS B 7. In seiner hieroglyphenluwischen Inschrift (KARKAMIS A 6,2–3) (→ Hieroglyphenschriften (Kleinasien)) rühmt er sich, im Ausland wohl bekannt zu sein: in Äg., Urartu, bei Lydern, Phrygern und Phoinikern, deren Länder J. auch wohl bereist hat. Denn in seiner zweiten Inschrift (KARKAMIS A 15b, 4), in der er von sich behauptet, vier Schriften (*SCRIBA-lalija*): hieroglyphenluwisch, phoinikisch, assyrisch und aramäisch schreiben und 12 Sprachen (*lalati-*) sprechen zu können, ist von »(diplomatischen) Reisen« (*ḫarwatāḫid-*) die Rede.
→ Karkemiš

J. D. HAWKINS, Rulers of Karkamis 1986, 259–271 •
F. STARKE, Sprachen und Schriften in Karkamis, in: FS W. Röllig, 1997, 381–395. PE.HÖ.

Iasdius

[1] L. I. Aemilianus Honoratianus Postumus. Sohn von I. [2]. *Frater Arvalis* 240–241 n. Chr. CIL VI 41225.

SCHEID, Collège 464ff.

[2] L.? I. Domitianus. Kam als *homo novus* in den Senat. Nach der Prätur kommandierte er zwei Legionen, wurde *curator viae Aemiliae* und gleichzeitig *praefectus alimentorum*. Prätorische Statthalterschaft und Suffektkonsulat fallen zwischen ca. 215 u. 225 n. Chr. Anschließend konsularer Legat von Germania inferior oder Pannonia inferior, anschließend Legat der Tres Daciae (vor 235), CIL VI 1428 = 31651 + 31805 = 41225; PISO, FPD I 192ff. W.E.

Iasion (Ἰασίων, auch Ἰάσιος und Ἴασος). Ein adoleszenter Heros aus dem Bereich der Ackerbau-Mysterien. Nach einer auf Kreta lokalisierten Überl. zeugt I. mit → Demeter auf dreimal gepflügtem Brachland den → Plutos (Personifikation des Getreidereichtums); Zeus erschlägt ihn deswegen mit dem Blitz (Hom. Od. 5,125–128; Hes. theog. 969–974; vgl. schol. Theokr. 3,49–51d; Ov. am. 3,10,25ff.). Der Mythos begründete die Entstehung des Ackerbaus nach der Sintflut (schol. Hom. Od. 5,125). Die ältere Forsch. hat dahinter Bräuche vermutet, die durch sympathetische Agrarmagie die Feldfruchtbarkeit erneuern sollten [1; 2]. Adäquater deutet man den Mythos als Reflex pränuptialer bäuerlicher

Initiationsriten, die den Übergang ins Erwachsenenleben mit dem Neubeginn des agrarischen Jahres synchronisierten. Der Blitztod des I. dürfte myth. Aition einer Mysterienweihe gewesen sein, welche die doppelte Legitimation zu Ackerbau und Kinderzeugung vermittelte.

Aus diesem Grund ließ I. sich mit dem samothrak. Eetion (Ἠετίων), dem Bruder des → Dardanos und der → Harmonia, gleichsetzen, einem Mysterienheros, welchen Zeus nach der Sintflut mit dem Blitz erschlägt, weil er in sexueller Begierde ein Kultbild (Hellanikos von Lesbos, FGrH 4 F 23; Strab. 7,49 [50]; Apollod. 3,138) oder ein »Phantom« (Konon, FGrH 26 F 1, 21) der Demeter umarmt hat. Nach einer alternativen Version führt I. auf → Samothrake die ihm von Zeus gezeigte Mysterienweihe ein (Diod. 5,48,4) – einen Initiationsritus, der durch das Geschenk von Saatgut (ebd. 5,49,1 und 4) einerseits ins bäuerliche Leben einwies (zu Unrecht geleugnet von [3]) und andererseits die symbolische Lizenz zur Kinderzeugung erteilte.

Eine weitere Erzählung, derzufolge Dardanos seinen Bruder I. ermordet und dann Samothrake verläßt, um in Kleinasien am Fuß des Ida eine Stadt zu gründen (Serv. Aen. 3,167; Mythographici Vaticani 1,135), evoziert den Mythos der Korybantes und → Kabeiroi (vgl. Clem. Al. strom. 19,1–4) [4]. Wie dieser läßt er sich als Aition eines den Adonisgärten analogen Brauchtums deuten, nämlich einer in interregional verbreiteten Pubertätsriten benutzten *cista mystica* (→ Adonis).

Mit dem eleusinischen Ackerbauheros → Triptolemos parallelisiert, wurde I. neben diesem im Zodiakalzeichen der Zwillinge wiedererkannt (Hyg. astr. 2,22). Anschluß an entferntere Kulttraditionen erlangte die Figur des I. durch Wandermythen, die ihn zusammen mit Dardanos aus Arkadien (Dion. Hal. ant. 1,61) oder Etrurien (Verg. Aen. 3,167–171 mit Serv. ad loc.) nach Samothrake gelangen ließen.

1 W. Mannhardt, Myth. Forsch., 1884, 238ff. **2** Nilsson, GGR, 121, 462 **3** A. Avagianou, Sacred Marriage in the Rituals of Greek Religion, 1991, 165ff. **4** Burkert, 177, 424f.

W. Gundel, s. v. I., RE 9, 752–758 · B. Hemberg, Die Kabiren, 1950, 89ff. · E. Simon, s. v. I., LIMC 5.1, 627–628.

G.B.

Iaso s. Iatros

Iason (Ἰάσων).

[1] Thessal. Heros aus → Iolkos, Führer der → Argonauten, Teilnehmer an der Kalydonischen Jagd (Apollod. 1,68), Sohn des → Aison [1] und der Polymela (Hes. cat. 38–40; Apollod. 1,107) bzw. → Alkimede (Pherekydes 3 F 104 FGrH; Apoll. Rhod. 1,47); Bruder des → Promachos (Apollod. 1,143); von → Hypsipyle Vater des → Euneos (Hom. Il. 7,468) und Nebrophonos (Apollod. 1,115), von → Medeia Vater des Medeios (Hes. theog. 1001), des → Mermeros und Pheres (Apollod. 1,146).

I. wird bei → Chiron erzogen (Hes. cat. 40) und lebt mit Aison ohne Thronrechte in Iolkos (Hes. theog. 997; Apollod. 1,107). Dort regiert rechtmäßig Pelias als ältester Sohn der → Tyro und des Poseidon, der beim Tod des → Kretheus wegen seiner Feindschaft zu Hera (Apollod. 1,92) durch das Orakel vor einem Einschuhigen [1. 112ff.; 2. 132ff.] gewarnt worden war. Als sich I. nach dem Durchwaten des Anauros als dieser entpuppt, beauftragt Pelias auf Grund einer I. von Hera eingegebenen Selbstverpflichtung diesen, das Goldene Vlies aus → Aia herbeizuholen. Mit Heras Hilfe (Hom. Od. 12,72) unternimmt I. den Argonautenzug, der Medeia als Heras Rächerin an Pelias nach Iolkos bringt (Pherekydes 3 F 105 FGrH; Apollod. 1,107–109 [1. 12ff.]). Nur bei Pindar (Pind. P. 4,106–108) hat I. Thronansprüche, da Pelias Aison als den ältesten legitimen Sohn des Kretheus vom Thron gedrängt hat. Neben dem delph. Einschuhigen-Orakel, das I. mit seiner Rückkehr vom 20jährigen Exil bei Chiron erfüllt (ebd. 71–120), hatte Pelias eine Traumerscheinung des Phrixos; auf Grund dieser Erscheinung und auf Delphis Weisung beauftragt er I. gegen das Versprechen der Rückgabe der Herrschaft, den gegen die Aioliden gerichteten Zorn der Unterirdischen durch Heimholung der ins Goldene Vlies übergegangenen Seele des Phrixos zu beschwichtigen (ebd. 158–167 [1. 150ff.; 3]). Bei Apollonios Rhodios, wo erst die pindarische Traumerscheinung des Phrixos zum delph. Orakel führt (Apoll. Rhod. 1,5–17), muß der Hera-Freund I. (3,60–75) im Auftrag des rechtmäßigen Herrschers, aber Hera-Verächters Pelias (1,14) nach Kolchis reisen, um den durch die skythische Baumbestattung (3,200–209) des Phrixos erregten Zorn des Zeus zu sühnen (2,1192–1195; 3,336–339 [1. 93ff.]). Der ruhmsüchtige I. stellt eine Gefahr für den rechtmäßigen Herrscher Pelias dar (Diod. 4,40; Val. Fl. 1,22–62), so daß er diesen ohne Orakel beauftragt [1. 328ff.]. Nach dem Bau der → Argo startet der Zug der Argonauten unter Leitung I.s, der zuvor das Orakel von Dodona (Apollod. 1,110; Val. Fl. 1,544; 3,299) bzw. Delphi (Apoll. Rhod. 1,412–414; Val. Fl. 3,299; 617f.; vgl. Hdt. 4,179 [1. 336ff.]) befragt hat.

Auf den Abenteuern der Hinfahrt (→ Argonautai) tritt I. auf Lemnos als Geliebter der Hypsipyle (Apollod. 1,114f.; Apoll. Rhod. 1,774–908ff.; Val. Fl. 2,72ff.; → Lemnische Frauen), bei den → Dolionen als Kampfgegner des → Kyzikos (Apoll. Rhod. 1,1030–1034; Val. Fl. 3,239ff.), sowie bei der von Apollonios Rhodios (2,1093ff. [1. 326f.]) erfundenen Begegnung mit den Phrixos-Söhnen auf der Ares-Insel bes. in Erscheinung. In Aia/Kolchis stellt → Aietes als Bedingung für die Herausgabe des Vlieses das Jochen der Stiere, Pflügen, Säen der Zähne des → Kadmos-Drachens (Pherekydes 3 F 22 FGrH) und den Kampf gegen die → Gegeneis ([2. 137; 4. 450ff.]; bei Pindar (Pind. P. 4,232–237) nur Jochen und Pflügen [1. 182ff., 191[140]]; bei Valerius Flaccus (5,541ff.) zusätzlich Beistand im Bruderkrieg gegen Perses). I. erfüllt dies mit Hilfe (Salbe/Kräuter) bzw. Ratschlägen (Steinwurf unter Gegeneis) Medeias, die sich durch Aphrodites Eingreifen in I. verliebt und der I. die Ehe versprochen hatte. Durch die Weigerung des Aietes, das Vlies herauszugeben, erhält I. das Recht, es mit Hilfe Medeias zu rauben und sich der Verfolger (auch durch Tötung des Apsyrtos) zu erwehren (Apollod. 1,127–133; Pind. P. 4,211 ff.; Apoll. Rhod. 3,482–502; 4,410ff.; Val. Fl. 7,58ff.). Die Heirat I.s und Medeias ([5. 197ff.] auf der → Kypseloslade, Paus. 5,18,3) findet in Iolkos (Hes. theog. 997–999) oder schon in Kolchis (Antimachos fr. 75), Byzantion (Dionysios Skytobrachion fr. 31 RUSTEN), auf Kerkyra/Drepane (Timaios 566 F 87 FGrH; Apollod. 1,138; Apoll. Rhod. 4,1128ff.) oder Peuke (Val. Fl. 8,217ff.) statt.

Nach Übergabe des Vlieses und Weihung der Argo am Isthmos (Apollod. 1,143 f.; Diod. 4,53,2) rächt I. mit Hilfe Medeias den Selbstmord seiner Eltern und die Tötung seines Bruders durch Pelias (Apollod. 1,143f.; Diod. 4,50; Val. Fl. 1,700ff.). I. wird (nach Drachenkampf: Lykophr. 1315 [5. 160]) von Medeia verjüngt (Sim. fr. 548 PMG; Pherekydes 3 F 113 FGrH [2. 137]).

Nach Teilnahme an den Leichenspielen für Pelias (Ringkampf mit → Peleus auf der Kypseloslade, Paus. 5,17,10) geht I. mit Medeia, von Akastos aus Iolkos vertrieben, nach Korinth (Apollod. 1,144f.); nach Diod. 4,53 von sich aus, nachdem er Akastos als Herrscher eingesetzt hat; nach Eumelos (fr. 5 PEG) regiert I. dort dank Medeia, die die Korinther als Tochter des Korinthers Aietes aus Iolkos herbeigeholt und mit der Herrschaft betraut hatten; doch kehrt I. nach der Entfremdung von Medeia nach Iolkos zurück. Nach Naupaktos (fr. 9 PEG) siedelt I. nach Pelias' Tod von Iolkos nach Korkyra über; nach Apollod. (244 F 180a FGrH) mit Medeia ins thesprotische → Ephyra; nach Iustinus (42,2,12f.) kehrt I. mit Medeia und deren Sohn Medos nach Kolchis zurück, setzt Aietes wieder ein und vergrößert dessen Reich durch Kriegszüge. Als I. nach 10 Jahren in Korinth → Glauke heiraten will, tötet Medeia diese und deren Vater sowie ihre und I.s Kinder Mermeros und Pheres (Apollod. 1,145; Diod. 4,54f.). Mit Peleus und den → Dioskuren zerstört I. Iolkos unter Akastos (Pherekydes 3 F 62 FGrH; Apollod. 3,173). Tod von I.: nicht in Kolchis durch Drachen [3]; sondern er wird durch einen Balken der Argo erschlagen (Eur. Med. 1386f. mit schol.); Selbstmord (Diod. 4,55,1) durch Erhängen (Neophron fr. 3 TGF) bzw. Trinken von Stierblut (Apollonius Sophista 156,18); Verbrennen mit Braut (Hyg. fab. 25,3).

Einziges Telos der Existenz I.s bildet der Argonautenzug, den I. urspr. als Vertreter des binnenthessal. Hera-Kultes gegenüber der neu aufkommenden Poseidon-Verehrung der durch Pelias repräsentierten Küstenbewohner unternimmt [1. 136ff.]. Am Ende steht I. als Führer eines Gemeinschaftsunternehmens, der nach Aeneas geformt ist [6. 237ff.], der seinerseits Züge I.s aus Euripides' ›Medeia‹ ([7. 13ff.] vgl. Sen. Med. [8. 371ff.]) sowie des alexandrinischen »passiven«, realistischen »Anti-Heros« des Apoll. Rhod. [4. 215; 9; 10. 210f.] widerspiegelt (vgl. Goethe, Faust II, 7373f.).

Die ant. (schol. Pind. P. 4,211a) und neuzeitliche Ableitung des Namens von ἰάομαι (*iáomai*/»heilen«; I. als Heilgott [11. 759; 12]) ist weder gesichert noch berechtigt [5. 244], ungriech. Herkunft nicht ausgeschlossen [13. 156, 373]. I. in der Kunst: [14; 16. 39ff.].

1 P. DRÄGER, Argo pasimelousa, I, 1993 2 A. MOREAU, Le Mythe de Jason et Médée, 1994 3 P. DRÄGER, »Abbruchsformel« und Jona-Motiv in Pind. 4. Pyth. Ode, in: WJA 21, 1996/97, 1–7 4 R. HUNTER, Short on Heroics, in: CQ 38, 1988, 436–453 5 U. v. WILAMOWITZ-MOELLENDORFF, Hell. Dichtung, II, 21962 6 E. BURCK, Die ›Argonautica‹ des Valerius Flaccus, in: Ders. (Hrsg.), Das röm. Epos, 1979, 208–253 7 A. BURNETT, Medea and the Tragedy of Revenge, in: CPh 68, 1973, 1–24 8 K. v. FRITZ, Die Entwicklung der I.-Medea-Sage und die Medea des Euripides, in: Ant. und mod. Trag., 1962, 322–429 9 G. LAWALL, Apollonius' Argonautica, in: YClS 19, 1966, 121–169 10 J.J. CLAUSS, The Best of the Argonauts, 1993 11 O. JESSEN, s. v. I. (1), RE 9, 759–771 12 LFE s. v. I. 13 KAMPTZ 14 J. NEILS, s. v. I., LIMC 5.1, 629–738 15 M. VOJATZI, Frühe Argonautenbilder, 1982.

P.D.

[2] Tyrann von → Pherai in Thessalien, Anf. 4. Jh. v. Chr.; Prototyp der jüngeren → Tyrannis im Mutterland, der sich nicht mit Stadtherrschaft begnügte, in vielem Dionysios [1] I. von Syrakus vergleichbar. Er müsse hungern, wäre er nicht Tyrann (Aristot. pol. 1277a 24). Die Überlieferung stattete ihn mit sophistischer Gedankenschärfe und thukydideischem Machtkalkül aus und zeichnete ihn als fähigen Feldherrn, der Charisma und Rationalität zu verbinden wußte (Xen. hell. 6,1; 4). Wer im Großen gerecht handeln wolle, müsse im Kleinen Unrecht tun, wird als seine sprichwörtliche Maxime überliefert (Plut. mor. 817f; Aristot. rhet. 1373a 26). Anders als Dionysios konnte er mit seiner Politik auf die Trad. des thessalischen Bundes zurückgreifen.

Der Anschluß des I. an → Lykophron, den Begründer der Tyrannis in Pherai, als Sohn oder Schwiegersohn nach dessen Tod 390 v. Chr. ist unklar. Die Überlieferung setzt groß ein mit dem vergeblichen Hilfegesuch des Polydamas von Pharsalos gegen ihn in Sparta 375 (Xen. hell. 6,1). Mit dessen Einlenken gewann I. ganz → Thessalien; er wurde zum → *tagós* (ταγός), dem obersten Heerführer des Bundes, gewählt. Seine Machtgrundlage, 6000 auf ihn eingeschworene Söldner, erweiterte er um das durch ihn neu festgelegte Aufgebot des thessalischen Bundes: 20000 Hopliten, zahllose Peltasten und 8000 Reiter; hinzu kamen Tribute der Perioiken. Verbündet mit Makedonien, Theben und wohl auch Athen, vermittelte er doch nach der Schlacht bei Leuktra 371 in wohlverstandenem Eigeninteresse den freien Abzug des geschlagenen spartan. Aufgebots (Xen. hell. 6,4,20–26). Im Begriff, bei den Pythien in Delphi 370 Macht und Pracht zu demonstrieren, wurde er, weil er eine Bedrohung Thebens darstellte, ermordet; die Verschwörer wurden vielerorts als Tyrannenmörder (→ Tyrannenmord) gefeiert (vgl. Xen. hell. 6,4,31f.; Diod. 15,60,5). Die Überlieferung schrieb I. größere Pläne zu: Flottenbau, die Hegemonie über

Griechenland, einen panhellen. Zug gegen die Perser (Xen. hell. 6,1,8–12; Isokr. or. 5,119f.; Diod. 15,60,1; Val. Max. 9,10, ext. 2).

H. Berve, Die Tyrannis bei den Griechen, 1967, 285–290, 668–670 • B. Helly, L'état thessalien, 1995, 240–256, 334f., 345–353 • J. Mandel, Jason, the Tyrant of Pherae, tagus of Thessaly, in: Rivista storica dell' Antichità 10, 1980, 47–77 • C. Tuplin, The Failings of Empire, 1993, 117–121, 180f., 207–213. J. CO.

[3] I. von Kyrene. Jüd. hell. Historiker, dessen einziges bekanntes Werk – eine Gesch. des Makkabäeraufstandes (175–161 v. Chr.; → Iudas [2] Makkabaios) in fünf B. – nicht erh. ist. Es bildete die Grundlage für das zweite Makkabäerbuch (2 Makk 2,23; [1.1 71f.; 4]). I. greift wohl auf Augenzeugenberichte zurück und dürfte demnach in der Mitte des 2. Jh. v. Chr. gelebt haben. Zu der Abhängigkeit zw. 1 Makk und 2 Makk sowie I.s Werk, ihren Quellen und den verwendeten Urkunden vgl. [1. 177; 5. 531f.].

1 Ch. Habicht, Das zweite Makkabäerbuch (JSHRZ I,3), 1976 **2** M. Hengel, Judentum und Hellenismus, 1969, 176–183 **3** B. Niese, Kritik der beiden Makkabäerbücher, 1900 **4** R. Pfeiffer, History of New Testament Times, 1949, 506–518 **5** Schürer 1, 19; 3/1, 531–537 **6** M. E. Stone (Hrsg.), Jewish Writings of the Second Temple Period, Apocrypha, Pseudepigrapha, Qumran Sectarian Writings, Philo, Josephus, 1984, 176–183. I. WA.

[4] I. von Argos. Nach der Suda s. v. I. jünger als Plutarch und deshalb vermutlich ins 2. Jh. n. Chr. zu datieren. Verf. einer Schrift ›Über Griechenland‹ in 4 B. Dabei handelt es sich kaum um den *Bíos tēs Helládos*, dessen Autor eher Iason von Nysa war, sondern um einen Abriß, der bis zur Einnahme Athens durch Antipatros 322 v. Chr. reichte und im letzten Teil sehr ausführlich war. FGrH 94. K. MEI.

[5] Bildhauer aus Athen im 2. Jh. n. Chr. Er signierte eine Personifikation der ›Odyssee‹ in weiblicher Gestalt mit einem Panzer, der Odyssee-Szenen trägt. Zusammen mit ›Ilias‹ bildete sie eine Gruppe, die vermutlich in der Pantainos-Bibliothek in Athen aufgestellt war.

Loewy, Nr. 329 • K. Stemmer, Unt. zur Typologie, Chronologie und Ikonographie der Panzerstatuen, 1978, 115–116 • H. A. Thompson, The Athenian Agora, Bd. 14: The Agora of Athens, 1972, 115. R. N.

Iasos (Ἴασος/Ἰάσιος).

[1] Könige von Argos: a) Sohn von Argos und Euadne, Vater Agenors (Apollod. 2,3); b) Sohn von Argos und Ismene, Vater der → Io (ebd. 2,5); c) Sohn von Triopas, Bruder Agenors, Vater der Io (Paus. 2,16,1).

[2] Arkader, Sohn von Lykurgos und Kleophile, Bruder von Ankaios, Epochos und Amphidamas, Gemahl der Minyas-Tochter Klymene, Vater der → Atalante (Hes. theog. 1288; Kall. h. 3,216; Apollod. 3,105; 109).

[3] Führer der Athener vor Troia, von Aineias getötet (Hom. Il. 15,332, 337.). Das Patronym Iasides haben die Könige Amphion von Orchomenos (Hom. Od. 11,283) und Dmetor von Kypris (17,443), Iapyx (Verg. Aen. 5,843), Palinurus (12,391). *Iason Argos* (Hom. Od. 18,246) ist eine Landschaft, deren Bestimmung unsicher ist [1]; nach [2] ist damit das »Jonierland« gemeint.

[4] Einer der → Daktyloi Idaioi (»Däumling«: Schmiedekobold der großen Göttin Kybele) neben Herakles, Paionaios, Epimedes, Idas, denen der 1. Wettlauf in Olympia zugeschrieben wird (Paus. 5,7,6).

1 B. Mader, s. v. Iason, LFE, 2, 1109 **2** Ed. Meyer, Forsch. zur Alten Gesch. I, 1892. RE. ZI.

[5] (Ἰασός). Kar. Hafenstadt im Nordwinkel des Golfs von I. (h. Güllük körfezi) auf kleiner, felsiger Insel (seit röm. Kaiserzeit Halbinsel), h. Asın Kalesi gegenüber Kuren. Die sagenhafte Gründung von Argos her (Pol. 16,12,1f.) weist auf spätmyk. Zeit, seine griech. Siedler setzten sich erst mithilfe von Miletos gegen die einheimischen Karer durch. Ion. Charakters (Sprache der Inschr.), teilte I. weitgehend die Gesch. von Karia: Anfangs unter lyd., ab 546 v. Chr. unter pers. Herrschaft; Mitte 5. Jh. v. Chr. Mitglied im → Attisch-Delischen Seebund, 412 als »altbegütert« (Thuk. 8,28) von der spartanischen Flotte geplündert und Tissaphernes übergeben; 405 von Lysandros zerstört, die Männer getötet, Frauen und Kinder versklavt (Diod. 13,104,7); nach 387/6 gehörte I. zur Satrapie des → Hekatomnos, verhängte 367/6 über flüchtige Verschwörer gegen → Maussollos lebenslange Verbannung mit Güterkonfiskation (Syll.[3] 169). 334 von → Alexandros [4] d.Gr. eingenommen; die Brüder Gorgos und Minnion, Bürger von I., erwirkten 333/323 von Alexandros die Rückgabe des »kleinen Meeres« (Fischbucht bei I.) und machten sich um die in I. aufgenommenen Vertriebenen aus Samos und deren Repatriierung 322/1 verdient [1. Bd. 1, 30; 1. Bd. 2, T 50]. E. 4. Jh. von → Antigonos [1] I. beansprucht (Diod. 19,75), ab 309/306 mit Ptolemaios I. verbündet [1. Bd. 1, 2f.]; wahrscheinlich seit 227/220 unter maked. Herrschaft [2. 16, 20]; nach Abzug der Besatzung Philippos' V. 197/6 (Pol. 18,2,3; 8,9; 44,4; Liv. 32,33,7) und der nachgerückten Garnison Antiochos' [5] III. (Liv. 37,17,3–7) war I. 189/8 frei. 190 hatten Flüchtlinge aus I. Rom zum Verzicht auf die Erstürmung ihrer Heimat bewogen (Liv. 37,17,5–8). 129 v. Chr. wurde die Stadt der röm. Prov. Asia eingegliedert, im J. 85 mit Duldung Sullas von Seeräubern geplündert (App. Mithr. 63).

Die Bewohner lebten von Handel und Fischfang (Strab. 14,2,21). Aus I. stammte der Hofpoet Alexandros' d.Gr. → Choirilos [3] und der Philosoph und Dialektiker → Diodoros [4]. I. hatte eine kleine jüd. Gemeinde und war im 4. Jh. Bischofssitz (Not. episc. 1,340; 3,295; 8,392; 9,302; 10,409; 13,259).

Einen gewissen Wohlstand in hell. und Kaiserzeit lassen it. Grabungen (seit 1960) erkennen. Arch. Reste: unter der Agora über brz. Mauerwerk Gräber submyk. und geom. Zeit; Stadtmauer mit Türmen und Toren (4. Jh. v. Chr. und hell.); hell.-röm. Theater am terrassierten Osthang des Stadtbergs. Wohnquartiere, am Südhang *villae*, teils mit Wanddekoration und Bodenmosaik (1.–2. Jh.); ein Propylaion und Demeter-Kore-Heiligtum. An der hell.-röm. Agora ein Buleuterion (128 und 138 n. Chr.), daneben ein Heiligtum für die Hauptgöttin Artemis Astias, nahe dem Osttor zum äußeren Hafen ein Zeus-Megistos-Tempel. Im Nord- und Ostteil von I. vier frühbyz. Basiliken (6. Jh. und später), eine inmitten der Agora, deren Vorgängerbau ein Martyrium (5. Jh.), deren Nachfolgerin eine verkleinerte Kirche (11. Jh.); eine weitere Basilika auf dem Festland. Im 10./11. Jh. war I. noch stark befestigt: byz. Sperrfort am Isthmos, Festung auf der Akropolis-Höhe, Molen zum Schutz des inneren Hafens, auf deren östl. die Ruine eines byz. Hafenturms.

Landseitig vom Isthmos befinden sich ein monumentales röm. Heroon (2. Jh. n. Chr.) und ein Teil eines Aquädukts (Balık Pazarı, »Fischmarkt«), im NW von Kuren eine ausgedehnte Wehranlage mit hell. 2,5 km langer Landmauer; südl. jenseits der westl. Hafenbucht hell.-röm. Gräber. Die Gebäude von I., bes. Stadtmauer und Theater, unterlagen im 19. Jh. planmäßigem Steinraub.

1 W. Blümel, Die Inschr. von I. 1–2 (IK 28), 1985
2 H. Bengtson, Die Inschr. von Labranda und die Politik des Antigonos Doson, in: SBAW 1971, 3.

G. E. Bean, M. Cook, The Carian Coast III, in: ABSA 52, 1957, 100 ff. • G. E. Bean, Kleinasien 3, 1974, 71–84 • F. Berti, V. Graziano, I. [Führer], 1994 • L. Bürchner, s. v. I. (15), RE 9, 786–790 • C. Crowther, I. in the (early) second century B. C., I–II, in: BICS 36, 1989, 136 ff.; 37, 1990, 143 ff. • G. Jost, I. in Karien, Diss. Hamburg, 1935 • D. Levi, G. Pugliese Caratelli, Le due prime campagne di scavo a I. (1960–61). Nuove iscrizione di I., in: ASAA 39/40, 1961/2, 505–571; 573–632 (und fortlaufend, Grabungsber.) • Ders. u. a., I. Studi su I. di Caria, in: BA Suppl. 31/2, 1986 (mit Lit. XI-XIII) • W. Koenigs, Westtürkei, 1991, 230 ff. • Magie 2, 906 f. • W. Radt, Siedlungen und Bauten auf der Halbinsel von Halikarnassos, unter bes. Berücksichtigung der archa. Epoche, in: MDAI(Ist) Beih. 3, 1970, 208 ff. • H. H. Schmitt, Antiochos d.Gr., 1964, 243, 247. H. KA.

Jastorf-Kultur. Bezeichnung für Kulturgruppen der vorröm. Eisenzeit in Norddeutschland (→ Germanische Archäologie, mit Karte) nach dem Urnengräberfeld von Jastorf, Kreis Ülzen (Niedersachsen). Die Grabanlagen und -ausstattungen mit Schmuck, Tongefäßen und vereinzelt auch Waffen und Geräten sind typisch für die german. J. Sie ist die erste eisenverarbeitende Kultur im nordischen Raum.
→ Eisen; Jevenstedt

H-J. Hässler (Hrsg.), Ur-und Frühgesch. in Niedersachsen, 1991, 380 • G. Schwantes, Die Urnenfriedhöfe in Niedersachsen I 2, 1911, 95–139. V. P.

Iathrippa s. Yaṯrīb

Iatraleiptes. Masseur, ein Beruf, der im 1. Jh. n. Chr. in Mode gekommen zu sein scheint (z. B. CIL 6,9476); doch reicht die Verknüpfung von Medizin und Gymnastik bis Herodikos [1] von Selymbria (5. Jh. v. Chr.) zurück. Trimalchio wurde von drei *aliptae* behandelt (Petron. 28), Plinius betrachtete diesen ganzen Zweig der Medizin als Quacksalberei (nat. 29,4–5). Vespasian hingegen garantierte allen, die diese Kunst ausübten, diverse Privilegien (FIRA 1,77), und Plinius d. J. gelang es, Traian zu veranlassen, seinem ägypt. *i.* Harpocrates, dem er die Heilung von einer ernsten Erkrankung zu verdanken meinte, das röm. (und alexandrinische) Bürgerrecht zu verleihen (Epistulae 10,5–7,10).

V. N./Ü: L. v. R.–B.

Iatrokles (Ἰατροκλῆς).

[1] Athener, floh 411 v. Chr. nach der demokrat. Erhebung auf der athen. Flotte vor Samos mit dem Trierarchen → Eratosthenes [1] u. a. von der im Hellespont operierenden Flotte nach Athen, wo er sich für die Oligarchie einsetzte (Lys. 12,42).

Traill, PAA 531050. W. S.

[2] Sohn des Pasiphon, 348 v. Chr. von → Philippos II. bei der Eroberung von → Olynthos gefangengenommen, aber danach freigelassen (Aischin. leg. 15–16); 347/46 zweimal einer der athen. Gesandten zur Aushandlung des Philokratesfriedens (→ Philokrates) von 346 (Aischin. leg. 20 und 126; Demosth. or. 19,197 f.).

Develin Nr. 1443 • PA 7442. J. E.

[3] Bei → Athenaios [3] (2./3. Jh.) mehrfach als Verf. eines Brot- und/bzw. Kuchenbackbuches (Ἀρτοποιικόν, *Artopoiikón*, nur 326e; Περὶ πλακούντων, *Perí plakúntōn*) genannt; seine Lebenszeit ist nicht bestimmbar. Die Erwähnungen Athen. 646a und 647b enthalten den Titel des Kuchenbackbuches, zwei dazwischen liegende Notizen ohne Titelangabe sind demnach wohl demselben Werk entnommen. Die Informationen beziehen sich auf Namen von Backwerk: »Kalmar« (Tintenfisch) 326e; κριμνίτης πλακοῦς (*krimnítēs plakús*), ein Gerstenschrotkuchen 646a; παῖσον (*paíson*), ein Kleingebäck von der Insel Kos 646 f. Unter dem Stichwort »Muscheln« bzw. »Schnecken« ist 647b ein aus Weizen und Honig hergestelltes Gebäck (vgl. 114a) genannt, das als »Siegespreis« erhielt, wer ein Gelage am besten durchwacht hatte (*pyramís, pyramús*: vgl. Aristoph. Equ. 277; Thesm. 94). Die Zutaten 646b lassen auf eine Art Käsekuchen mit Weizenteigboden und einem Belag aus Wasser, Honig, Sesam und Quark schließen. G. BI.

Iatromaia (»Geburtshelferin«, »Hebamme«). Geburtshilfe wurde gewöhnlich von Frauen geleistet, lag jedoch nicht ausschließlich in ihren Händen. So berichtet eine parische Inschr. von zwei männlichen Geburtshelfern (IG 12,5,199), außerdem richten sich die erh. geburtshilflichen Schriften an ein männliches Publikum. *I.* als Berufsbezeichnung taucht auf zwei röm. Inschr. aus dem 3. bzw. 4. Jh. n. Chr. auf (CIL 6,9477 f.); in ersterer wird Valeria Verecunda die ›erste *i.* in ihrer Gegend‹ gen., ein Epitheton, das eher auf die Qualität ihrer Arbeit als auf einen Posten im Rahmen eines *collegium* hinweist.

→ Hebamme V. N./Ü: L. v. R.-B.

Iatromathematik A. Definition B. Quellen C. Wissenschaftsgeschichte D. Wirkung

A. Definition

Iatromathēmatiká (Herm. Trism. 1,387,1 Ideler) oder *nosúntōn perignostiká ek tēs mathēmatikēs epistēmēs* (ebd. 1,430,2–3) u. ä. bezeichnen die medizinischen Implikationen der Astrologie: Erkennung der nosologischen Prädisposition von Patienten oder Prognostik aktueller Erkrankungen, je nach Fall in Verbindung mit Prävention oder Therapeutik.

B. Quellen

Die der I. zugrundeliegenden B. sind die vorgeblichen Enthüllungen des → Hermes, dem evtl. Asklepios beistand; die Enthüllungen sind in zwei *corpora* aufgezeichnet: demjenigen, das unter dem Namen des Hermes läuft und in zwei Fassungen existiert (Herm. Trism. 1,387–396, 430–440 I.), und demjenigen des Königs → Nechepso, der vom Priester → Petosiris unterstützt wurde [9; 1]. Diese Texte scheinen in der Tat im griech. Umfeld Ägyptens entstanden zu sein (Ptol. Apotelesmatika 1,3,12), vielleicht vom 2. Jh. v. Chr. an, und entwickelten sich bis zum 2. Jh. n. Chr. durch Anreicherung, während zur gleichen Zeit eine anonyme Produktion florierte.

Informationen über die I. besitzen wir darüber hinaus in den Überblicken über die Astrologie, die nur wenig später als diese *corpora* entstanden und mehr oder weniger detailliert sind; dies sind v. a. (in der wahrscheinlichen chronologischen Abfolge): → Manilius 2,453–465, 4,701–710; → Dorotheos [5] von Sidon 5,37–41 Pingree; → Ptolemaios, Tetrabiblos 3.12; → Sextos Empeirikos, Adversus mathematicos 5,21 f.; Vettius Valens, Anthologiae 2,37 (=2,36 Pingree); → Firmicus Maternus 2,24; 4,22,1–2; [Galenos], Prognostica de decubitu (19,529–573) [2]; und der ps.-ptolemäische *Karpós* (8; 19–21).

C. Wissenschaftsgeschichte

Im Rahmen der Theorie von der Entsprechung von Mikro- und Makrokosmos (menschlichem Körper und Universum) und – genauer – im Rahmen der astrologischen Theorie von der Entsprechung von Körperteilen sowie inneren Organen mit den Tierkreiszeichen oder Planeten, mit den Zwölfgöttern und den Ländern der Oikumene, sowie im Zusammenhang mit dem Aufblühen der Magie scheinen sich diese Techniken, deren Entstehung seit der Ant. den Ägyptern zugeschrieben wurde (Ptol. Tetrabiblos 1,3 = 30,20–32,22 Robb.), im griech. Ägypten von hell. Zeit an entwickelt zu haben.

Die Erkennung der nosologischen Prädispositionen gründete sich auf das Prinzip der Melothesie, d. h. der Entsprechung vom Typ Mikro-/Makrokosmos zwischen den Körperteilen oder inneren Organen und den Tierkreiszeichen [7; 8], die ihrerseits der griech. Astrologie zufolge mehr oder weniger passend zu den Planeten (zodiako-planetarische Melothesie) oder der ägypt. Astrologie zufolge zu den Dekanen (zodiakodekanische Melothesie) in Beziehung gesetzt wurden (die Entsprechungen waren dabei variabel; ein Beispiel bei [4. 27]). Ausgehend von dem Geburtshoroskop des Patienten (Genethliologie) mußten die Einflüsse auf die Zeichen und über sie auf die entsprechenden Körperteile oder Organe erkannt werden, um zu einer Frühdiagnose nach Art der prädiktiven Medizin zu gelangen.

Die Prognose aktueller Erkrankungen war dadurch bestimmt, daß die der Krankheit zugeschriebenen Phasen zu verschiedenen astronomischen Phasen in Beziehung gesetzt wurden: den Phasen des Mondes, seinen planetarischen Konjunktionen und den astralen Einflüssen, denen er seinen Phasen entsprechend ausgesetzt ist; bestimmte Stunden, Tage, Monate und Jahre wurden als gefährlich und sogar tödlich (*klimaktēres*) angesehen und zunächst auf einfache mathematische Weise, dann elaborierter durch den Einfluß der Planeten und Fixsterne im Geburtshoroskop ermittelt.

Auf diese diagnostische Phase folgte eine weitere, interventionistische und präventivtherapeutische, in mehreren Formen: Die Melothesie führte zu Ratschlägen für die Prävention; sie konnte auch, wie die Prognostik der Krankheiten, zu Interventionen in therapeutischer Absicht Anlaß geben, die auf dem Prinzip der kosmischen Sympathie beruhten und aus der Verabreichung von Medikamenten bestanden; dabei ging man nach zwei einander entgegengesetzten Strategien vor: Auffüllung der Einflußkarenzen des Zeichens, das für den kranken Körperteil oder das kranke Organ verantwortlich ist (Homöopathie; *corpus* des Herm. Trism.), bzw. antagonistische Zufuhr, die darauf abzielt, eine Reaktion auf die negativen Einflüsse auszulösen (Allopathie; *corpus* des Nechepso und Petosiris).

Das Prinzip der *klimaktēres* wurde auch umgekehrt und dazu benutzt, die für therapeutisch-chirurgische Interventionen günstigen Zeitpunkte nach dem allgemeineren astrologischen System der *katarchaí* zu ermitteln.

Das Prinzip der kosmischen Sympathie brachte Rezepte mit sich, die in der Therapie unbedingt zu befolgen waren und bis zur Magie im strengen Sinne reichten; das umso mehr, als eine andere Form der Therapie darin bestand, zu versuchen, einen direkten Einfluß auf die hinter den Erkrankungen stehenden Planeten, Sterne und anderen Phänomene auszuüben.

D. Wirkung

Die Disziplin wurde aus dem griech. Milieu Ägyptens in den gesamten Mittelmeerraum hinein verbreitet, in Rom kultiviert und in Byzanz wie im Westen fortgeführt, wo die Traktate des Hermes Trismegistos zu einem ungewissen Zeitpunkt, jedoch nicht vor dem 6. Jh., ins Lat. übersetzt wurden (Ausg.: [5]). Von Byzanz aus wurde die I. in die arab. Welt vermittelt und dort übersetzt, woraufhin sie dort eine außerordentliche Entwicklung nahm [6]. Das läßt sich auch vom MA im Westen, und zwar umso mehr, als die Disziplin wie die gesamte Astrologie christianisiert wurde, und von der Renaissance sagen, die sie in besonderem Maß reaktivierte [10].

1 F. Boll, Excerpta ex Nechepsone et Petosiride de Solis et Lunae defectionibus, in: CCAG 7, 1908, 129–151 **2** F. Cumont, Les »Prognostica de decubitu« attribués à Galien, in: BIBR 15, 1935, 119–131 **3** A. Delatte, Herbarius, [3]1961 **4** H. G. Gundel, Zodiakos, 1992 **5** W. Gundel, Neue astrologische Texte des Hermes Trismegistos, 1936 **6** F. Klein-Franke, Iatromathematics in Islam, 1984 **7** O. Neugebauer, Melothesia and Dodecatemoria, in: Studia biblica et orientalia 3, Oriens antiquus, Analecta Biblica 12, 1959, 270–275 **8** A. Olivieri, Melotesia planetaria greca, in: Memorie e Rendiconti dell' Accademia di Architettura, Lettere e Arti di Napoli 5, 1936, 21–580 **9** E. Riess, Nechepsonis et Petosiridis fragmenta magica, in: Phil. Suppl. 6, 1891–1893, 325–394 **10** L. Welker, Das iatromathematische Corpus, 1988.

CCAG, 11 Bde., 1898–1934 • S. Fazzo, Un'arte inconfutabile: la difesa dell'astrologia nella Tetrabiblos di Tolomeo, in: Rivista critica di storia della filosofia 46, 1991, 213–244 • W. Hübner, Eine unbeachtete zodiakale Melothesie bei Vettius Valens, in: RhM N. F. 120, 1977, 247–254 (mit Bibliogr.) • Ders., Manilius als Astrologe und Dichter, in: ANRW II 32,1, 1984, 126–320 • A. J. Festugière, La révélation d'Hermès Trismégiste, [2]1950, 1 • H. G. Gundel, Weltbild und Astrologie in den griech. Zauberpap., 1968 • W. Gundel, H. G. Gundel, Astrologumena, 1966.

A. TO./Ü: T. H.

Iatros (griech. ἰατρός, »Arzt«).

[1] Arzt, → Medizin.

[2] Epiklese des → Apollon als Heilgott. Sie ist bes. im ion. Osten und in den griech. Kolonien entlang der Westküste des Schwarzen Meeres verbreitet; in Olbia verdrängt Apollon I. seit hell. Zeit den milesischen Apollon Delphinios. Diese Form Apollons wurde im frührepublikanischen Rom als Apollo Medicus übernommen.

[3] Funktionsbezeichnung und Titel von vier att. Heilheroen. Die (wenigen und späten) Texte geben ihnen auch Eigennamen: Amphilochos (Athen, in der Nähe der Agora), Aristomachos (Marathon), Oresinios (Eleusis), Aristomachos (Rhamnus; auch identifiziert mit → Amphiaraos). Die Inschr. benutzen fast immer den Funktionstitel: Für die jeweiligen Verehrer zählte allein die Heilkraft, eine allfällige Myth. war sekundär.

E. Kearns, The Heroes of Attica, 1989, 171 f.

F. G.

Iatrosophistes. Urspr. Bezeichnung eines Lehrers der Medizin (v. a. in Alexandreia), konnte sich *i.* in späterer Zeit auf jeden erfahrenen Praktiker beziehen (*medicus sapientissimus*, Corpus Glossatorum Latinorum 3,600,32 Goetz), sei es in der Schulmedizin (z. B. → Agnellus, In Galeni De sectis commentarium 33) oder in der magischen Heilkunst (Ps.-Kallisthenes, Vita Alexandri 1,3) [1]. Entgegen der Emendierung durch v. Arnim in Dion Chrys. 33,6 dürfte der Begriff nicht vor dem späten 4. Jh. n. Chr. geprägt worden sein (Epiphanios, Adversus haereses 56,10; Cassius Felix, De medicina 182; Fulg. Mythologiae 3,7). Er wird von christl. Autoren häufig sarkastisch verwendet (z. B. *Vita Archelai*, PG 10,12) und gegen den medizinischen Gegner gerichtet, z. B. gegen → Gesios (Suda, s. v. Gesios). Als erstem Lehrer wurde der Titel *i.* dem um 360 n. Chr. wirkenden → Magnus von Nisibis beigegeben (Palladas, Anth. Pal. 11,281, jedoch nur in einem Lemma). Dieser war bekannt für seine Rednergaben und sein Lehrtalent: In galenischer Trad. legte man großen Wert auf die Doppelrolle des Arztes als Philosoph und Praktiker. Mit Beginn des 6. Jh. wurden zumindest in Alexandreia die *iatrosophistaí* als die führenden Ärzte angesehen [2].

1 A. Grilli, I., in: RIL 122, 1988, 125–128 **2** J. M. Duffy, Byzantine medicine in the sixth and seventh centuries, in: Dumbarton Oaks Papers 38, 1984, 22–25.

V. N./Ü: L. v. R.-B.

Iavolenus

[1] C. I. Calvinus Geminius Kapito Cornelius Pollio Squilla Q. Vulkacius Scuppidius Verus. Senator, der unter Hadrian und Antoninus Pius eine längere prätorische Laufbahn absolvierte, die mit der Statthalterschaft in Lusitanien, dem Prokonsulat in der Baetica und einem Suffektkonsulat abschloß. ILS 1060; PIR[2] J 13.

W. E.

[2] C. Octavius Tidius Tossianus L. I. Priscus. Jurist, Nachfolger des Caelius Sabinus (→ Arulenus [1]) und Vorgänger des → Fulvius [II 2] Aburnius Valens als Schulhaupt der Sabinianer (Dig. 1,2,2,53, → Rechtsschulen), war Konsiliar Traians und wohl noch Hadrians, bekleidete städtische Magistraturen (*cos. suff.* 86 n. Chr.) und Statthalterschaften in Obergermanien, Syrien und Afrika [1]. Damit verkörperte I. den seit Vespasian häufigen Juristentypus des Mitglieds der kaiserlichen Justizbürokratie [5. 165 ff.]. Er schrieb eine Responsen- und Quästionensammlung *Epistulae* (14 B.; dazu [2]) und kritische Komm. zu den Juristenschriften: *Ex Cassio* zum *Ius civile* des → Cassius [II 14] Longinus (15 B.; dazu [3]), *Ex Plautio* zur Quästionensammlung des → Plautius (5 B.) und zu den *Posteriora* des → Antistius [II 3] Labeo (10 B.; dazu [4]). Sowohl seiner kasuistischen Veranlagung als auch der sabinianischen Schultradition (Dig. 50,17,1) folgend hielt I. »Definitionen« (im Sinne aller abstrakten Juristensätze) für »gefährlich« (Dig. 50,17,202) und falsifizierte in seinen Komm. viele derartige »Festlegungen« der früheren Jurisprudenz. I. war Lehrer des Salvius → Iulianus [5] (Dig. 40,2,5).

1 PIR IV, 1952–1956, 108 f. **2** B. Eckardt, Iavoleni epistulae, 1978 **3** U. Manthe, Die libri ex Cassio des I. Priscus, 1982 **4** D. Mantovani, Sull'origine dei libri posteriores di Labeone, in: Labeo 34, 1988, 271–322 **5** R. A. Bauman, Lawyers and Politics in the Early Roman Empire, 1989.

T. G.

Iaxartes. Fluß im westl. Zentralasien, h. Syr-darja, 2860 km lang; entspringt am Taidyk-Paß im östl. Altaigebirge, nimmt nach kurzem nördl. Lauf von Osten den unweit des Sees Issyk-Kul entspringenden Naryn auf, betritt sw von Taschkent (wo er schiffbar wird) die Ebenen von Kasachstan und mündet in den → Aralsee (Amm. 23,6,59). Die einheimischen Skythen nannten den I. Silis bzw. Orxantes, Alexander d.Gr. Tanais (Plin. nat. 6,49; Arr. an. 3,30–7–8 u.ö., aber auch I. Arr. an. 7,16,3 u.a.), im Hinblick auf den europ. Tanais (h. Don), an dem auch Skythen wohnten; pers. Yaḫšart. Nach Ptolemaios (6,12,1) fiel der I. in das Gebiet der Sogdiana, berührt aber tatsächl. nur den Norden des Landes.

A. Herrmann, s. v. I., RE 9, 1181–1189. B.B.u.H.T.

Iazyges, Iazuges (Ἰάζυγες). Iran.-sarmatischer Volksstamm, lit. erstmals um die Zeitenwende belegt. Vermutlich siedelten sie frühestens seit dem 3. Jh. v. Chr. an der → Maiotis östl. des Tanais in der Nachbarschaft der Roxolani (Ptol. 3,7; Amm. 22,8,31). Wohl im 1. Jh. v. Chr. wandte sich ein Zweig der I. nach SW, überquerte die Karpaten und ließ sich in der Ebene zw. der unteren Donau und dem Tibiscus (spätere Prov. Pannonia) nieder (vgl. Ov. Pont. 4,7,9; trist. 2,191; Ἰάζυγες μετανάσται mit Liste der iazyg. Städte, Ptol. 7,1 f.; Strab. 7,2,4; Plin. nat. 4,12,80). Tacitus erwähnt *principes* und *eques* (ann. 12,29; hist. 3,5). Seit Domitianus sind die I. als ständige Feinde Roms bekannt: Von 166–180 n. Chr. fielen sie wiederholt zusammen mit Langobardi, Marcomanni und Sarmatae über die Donau ins röm. Reich ein; 292 kämpfte Diocletianus, 294 Galerius gegen I. und Sarmatae (Eutr. 9,25; Aur. Vict. 39,43), desgleichen Maximinus Thrax, Gordianus III., Gallienus, Aurelianus, Probus und Carus.

J. Harmatta, Studies on the History of the Sarmatians, 1950, 3 ff. • A. Mócsy, Pannonia and Upper Moesia, 1974 • M. Rostovtzeff, Iranians and Greeks in South Russia, 1922, 113 ff., passim • Ders., The Sarmatae and Parthians, in: CAH 11, 1936, 91 ff. I.v.B.

Ibas s. Hiba

Iberer (Ἴβηροι, Ἴβηρες). I. sowie *Iberia* (Ἰβηρία) als Bezeichnungen der Bewohner und des Landes Ostgeorgiens kommen nur in griech.-röm. und byz. Quellen vor; etym. möglicherweise mit *virk*ᶜ (armen.) bzw. *Sáspeires* (Σάσπειρες, Hdt. 4,37; 40) verwandt [1. 146]. Iberia grenzte im Norden an → Sarmatia, im Westen an → Kolchis, im Süden an Groß-Armenien (→ Armenia) und im Osten an → Albania [1] (Ptol. 5,10,1 f.).
→ Armenien; Georgien, Georgier; Georgisch

1 O. Lordkipanidse, Arch. in Georgien (Quellen und Forsch. zur prähistor. provinzialröm. Arch. 5), 1991.

K.SA.

Iberia

[1] (Ἰβηρία Strab. 11,3,1–6; Ptol. 5,10,1–2; georg. *K*ᶜ*art*ᶜ*li*, parth. *Virčan*, armen. *Virk*ᶜ). Land im Zentrum Süd-Kaukasiens, begrenzt durch den Großen → Kaukasos im Norden, die nord-südl. vom Gr. zum Kleinen Kaukasos verlaufende Lichikette im Westen, das Kyrosbecken im Osten und den Kleinen Kaukasos im Süden, wobei v. a. Süd- und West-Grenze fließend waren; etwa das h. Ost-Georgien. Hauptstadt war bis E. 5. Jh. n. Chr. → Mestleta mit → Harmozike am Zusammenfluß von → Kyros und → Aragos, seither das Kyros-abwärts gelegene Tbilisi (»warme Quellen«). In achäm. Zeit im Strahlungsbereich persischer Kultur, aber polit. unabhängig (Plut. Alexander 34,7), in hell. Zeit teilweise in Abhängigkeit von den Seleukiden, später den Parthern.

Nach der im 9./10. Jh. n. Chr. kompilierten georg. Überl. gründete → Pharnabazos ca. 290/80 v. Chr. das Königreich I. [6. 70 ff.]. Nach einer Blüte im 3. Jh. hatte dieses im 2./1. Jh. v. Chr. Gebietsverluste, v. a. an die → Armenia maior → Tigranes' d.Gr., hinzunehmen. Bei Strabon 11,3 ist I. ein volkreiches Land mit schönen Städten, entwickeltem Handwerk und Landwirtschaft. Mit dem Orientfeldzug des Pompeius (66/65 v. Chr.) kam I. in den Interessenkreis Roms (App. Mithr. 101 ff.; Plut. Pompeius 34); es lavierte seither geschickt zwischen Parthern und Römern, die beide das Land als Vasallen betrachteten. Seit der Neuordnung der Provinzen unter den Flaviern war I. stärker in röm. Sphäre; inschr. überliefert ist die Befestigung der Mauern von Mcᶜḫeta 75 n. Chr. durch Vespasian [1. 214] im Zusammenhang mit der Sicherung der Kaukasuspässe gegen die nördl. Steppenvölker. Als Höhepunkt der Kontakte gilt der Rombesuch König → Pharasmanes' von I. z. Z. des Antoninus Pius (Fasti Ost. [6]; Cass. Dio 70,2,1). Mit dem sāsānidischen Machtantritt verstärkte sich der Druck aus dem Osten erneut; in der Felsinschrift von → Paikuli (vor 298) gehört I. zu den dem Perserkönig tributpflichtigen Ländern [5. H15,03]. 298 gelangte es wieder unter röm. Oberhoheit; 370 kam es zur röm.-persischen Teilung (Amm. 27,12,16–18). Bei Prokopios sind die Iberer seit alters persische Untertanen (BP 1,12,3); um 455–510/18 herrschte König Vaxtang Gorgasal (»Wolfshaupt«; → Gurgenes). Im Lazischen Krieg war I. persisches Aufmarschgebiet; 579/80 beseitigten die Perser mit Zustimmung des iber. Adels die Monarchie; Verwaltung der *de facto* persischen Provinz geschah durch Vertreter des iber. Adels.

Belegt ist die Verehrung von Astralgottheiten, daneben → Mazdaismus (frühhell. Feuertempel von Cixiagora) und → Mithras-Verehrung; zur offiziellen Einführung des Christentums kam es bereits 337 oder 356. Ausgrabungen belegen eine entwickelte Stadtkultur in hell. und v.a. röm. Zeit; in letzterer ist eine deutliche Romanisierung der bislang iran. geprägten Oberschicht festzustellen.

1 A. I. Boltunova, Quelques notes sur l'inscription de Vespasian trouvée à Mtskhetha, in: Klio 53, 1971, 213–222
2 D. Braund, Georgia in Antiquity, 1995

3 O. Lordkipanidse, Archäologie in Georgien, 1991, 146–176 4 Ders., H. Brakman, s. v. I., RAC 17, 12–106 5 E. Humbach, P. O. Skjaervo, The Sassanian Inscription of Paikuli, 1983 6 H. Nesselhauf, Ein neues Fr. der Fasten von Ostia, in: Athenaeum 36,1958, 219–28 7 G. Pätsch, Das Leben Kartlis, 1985. A.P.-L.

[2] s. Hispania

Iberisch s. Hispania

Iberische Archäologie s. Pyrenäenhalbinsel

Iberoi s. Georgier

Iberus (Hiberus). Name zweier span. Flüsse, von dem gleichlautenden Völkernamen abgeleitet, nicht – wie ant. Gelehrte (Plin. nat. 3,21; Iust. 44,1,2) glaubten – umgekehrt [1. 307–315].

[1] Heute Ebro. Alle Quellen stimmen darin überein, daß der ant. I. mit seinen Nebenflüssen fast völlig dem h. Ebro entspricht. Der einzige Unterschied: Der ant. Fluß war bis Vareia (h. Varea östl. von Logroño) schiffbar (Plin. nat. 3,21), h. nur bis Tortosa (andere neuere Auffassungen widersprechen dieser Identifizierung, u. a. [2]). Ein rätselhafter alter Name des I. war Oleum (Avien. 505; Erklärungsversuch bei [1. 307–315]).

[2] Heute Rio Tinto (Avien. 248). Dazu [1. 336]. Späterer Name: Luxia (Plin. nat. 3,7).

1 Schulten, Landeskunde 1, ²1974 2 P. Barceló, Die Grenzen des karthagischen Machtbereichs unter Hasdrubal, in: E. Olshausen, H. Sonnabend (Hrsg.), Stuttgarter Kolloquium zur histor. Geogr. des Alt. 4 (1990, Geographica Historica 7), 1994, 35–55. P.B.

Ibis (ägypt. *hbj* > griech. ἶβις).
I. Ägypten II. Griechenland und Rom

I. Ägypten

Der I. galt in Ägypten als hl. Vogel (Hdt. 2, 65; 67; 75 und andere ant. Schriftsteller), wo er in drei Arten vorkam. v. a. der »weiße I.« (Threskiornis aethiopicus) wird als das hl. Tier des Schreiber- und Mondgottes → Thot verehrt und oft dargestellt. I.-bestattungen sind seit dem NR bekannt; in der Spätzeit gab es überall in Ägypten Brutkolonien und Tierfriedhöfe mit mumifizierten I., bes. reichhaltig an den Hauptkultstellen des Thot.

D. Kessler, Die heiligen Tiere und der König, 1989 • A.-P. Zivie, s. v. I., LÄ 3, 115–121. K.J.-W.

II. Griechenland und Rom

Die Römer kannten den I. nur aus Ägypten (Plin. nat. 8,97), und zwar den dunklen (d. h. den Braunen Sichler, Plegadis falcinellus Kaup) nur von Pelusium, den weißen von überall (Plin. nat. 10,87, nach Aristot. hist. an. 8(9),27,617b 27–31) als Schlangenfresser (Plin. nat. 10,75). Durch Isid. orig. 12,7,33 wurde seine angebliche Selbstpurgierung mit dem gebogenen Schnabel an das MA weitergegeben. Der früher in den Alpen brütende Schopf-I. oder Waldrapp (Gerontius eremita L.) wird erstmals von Plin. nat. 10,134 erwähnt.
→ Storch

J.-C. Savigny, Histoire naturelle et mythologique de l'Ibis, 1805. C.HÜ.

Ibykos (Ἴβυκος), geb. in Rhegion, 6. Jh. v. Chr., der zweite wichtige Dichter Großgriechenlands nächst → Stesichoros. Er kam in der 54. Ol. (564–561 v. Chr.) nach Samos (Suda: ›als Polykrates, der Vater des Tyrannen, dort herrschte‹, ist wahrscheinlich in Πολυκράτους zu verbessern, was geläufigeres Griechisch ergibt und, in Übereinstimmung mit Hdt. 3,39, der den Namen des Vaters mit Aiakes angibt, heißen würde: ›als der Vater des Tyrannen Polykrates dort herrschte‹). Eusebios' davon abweichende Datierung, I. sei in den Jahren der 61. Ol. (536–533 v. Chr.) berühmt gewesen [1. 206–220], wird man kaum zustimmen können.

Das fr. 1 PMGF [2], dessen 48 auf einem Pap. erh. Zeilen im allg. dem I. zugeschrieben werden, sind an Polykrates gerichtet. Man wird sie am ehesten für ein Preislied auf die Schönheit des Jünglings und künftigen Tyrannen halten, verfaßt bei der Ankunft des Dichters an jenem Hofe, an dem später → Anakreon [1] mit seiner erotischen Dichtung zu Ruhm gelangte. Das Gedicht ist in Form von Triaden abgefaßt, und man hat es daher für Chorlyrik gehalten, was jedoch unwahrscheinlich ist [3]. Nach einer kunstvollen *praeteritio* zu trojanischen Themen führt I. die Personen des Kyanippos und Zeuxippos ein, die in dem homer. Bericht vom trojanischen Krieg keine Rolle spielen, und stützt sich demnach auf eine andere als die übliche ep. Überlieferung [4]. Der Ruhm des Adressaten sei, so wird gesagt, abhängig von dem Ruf des höfischen Dichters. Mit dieser Selbstdarstellung und dem Gebrauch myth. Beispiele zu Zwecken der Lobpreisung ist I. ein wichtiger Vorläufer der späteren Gelegenheitsdichtung und bes. des → Epinikions. Angeblich hat I. die Gesch. des Raubs des Ganymedes und des Tithonos in einem Gedicht erzählt, das einem gewissen Gorgias gewidmet ist (289a PMGF).

Die Alexandriner ordneten die Gedichte des I. in sieben Büchern an und nahmen ihn in den Kanon der neun lyrischen Dichter auf. Die erh. dürftigen Fragmente zeigen übereinstimmend einen kunstvollen Stil mit einer großen Zahl von Epitheta. Die Sprache weist ep., dor. und aiol. Elemente auf, das Versmaß ist häufig daktylisch.

Die Gedichte 286 und 287 PMGF (evtl. vollständig erhalten) gehören zu den schönsten überlieferten Beispielen griech. Lyrik. Es handelt sich um sorgfältig und einander ähnlich gestaltete Stücke erotischer Dichtung [5. 323–326]. In der Suda wird I. wohl deshalb als ἐρωτομανέστατος περὶ μειράκια, »rasend verliebt in Knaben« bezeichnet (TB1 PMGF; vgl. Cic. Tusc. 4,71 = TB2 PMGF). Wie bei Stesichoros empfand man seine Myth. als äußerst eigenwillig, bes. in seinen erotischen Erzählungen: Bei I. ist Idomeneus der Liebhaber Helenas (297 PMGF), Achilleus heiratet Medea in den Elysischen Gefilden (291 PMGF), Menelaos, von der Schönheit Helenas überwältigt, läßt sein Schwert fallen (296 PMGF). Man geht im allg. davon aus, daß I. (ganz wie Stesichoros) erzählende Dichtung schrieb, daher ist die Zuweisung einzelner Gedichte wie z.B. der Ἆθλα ἐπὶ Πελίᾳ (Stesichoros, 179(i) PMGF) unsicher. Er behandelte Themen wie Herakles, Meleagros und die Argonauten; doch läßt sich aus den wenigen Zeugnissen weder bestimmen, wie er mit diesen Gegenständen umging, noch läßt sich die gängige Einteilung seines Werkes in eine frühe it. Periode erzählender Dichtung im Stile des Stesichoros sowie eine samische Periode erotischer Verse rechtfertigen.

Einer Legende nach wurde I. von Räubern getötet, deren Verbrechen durch Kraniche ans Licht kam (TA5–11 PMGF); die Gesch. findet sich in bekannt einprägsamer Weise in Schillers Ballade ›Die Kraniche des Ibykus‹.

1 L. Woodbury, Ibycus and Polycrates, in: Phoenix 39, 1985, 193–220 **2** PMGF, p. 235–305 **3** M. Davies, Monody, choral lyric, and the tyranny of the hand-book, in: CQ, n.s. 38, 1988, 55 **4** E. Cingano, Tra epos e storia, in: ZPE 79, 1989, 27–38 **5** H. Fränkel, Dichtung und Philos. des frühen Griechentums, [2]1962. E.R./Ü: A.WI.

Icauna. Linker Nebenfluß der Seine, h. Yonne, auch Name der Flußgöttin (CIL XIII 2921: *dea Icauna*, Weihinschr. aus Autessiodurum; Vita S. Germani 12, E. 5. Jh. n. Chr.: *flumen Ycaunense*). Y.L.

Iccius. Fürst der seit 57 v. Chr. mit Rom verbündeten → Remi (*primus civitatis*), hielt im selben J. als Kommandant von Bibrax die Stadt bis zum Eintreffen röm. Hilfe gegen einen Angriff der Belger (Caes. Gall. 2,3,1; 6,4; 7,1).
→ Caesar W.W.

Icelus. Mit vollem Namen (Ser. Sulpicius) I. Marcianus. Freigelassener → Galbas [2], der während dessen Statthalterschaft in der Tarraconensis in Rom zurückgeblieben war. Von Nero nach der Akklamation Galbas ins Gefängnis geworfen; nach Neros Tod befreit, eilte er in sieben Tagen nach Spanien, um Galba die Nachricht zu überbringen. Von Galba erhielt er den Goldring der Ritter und wohl die *restitutio natalium*. Er übte größten Einfluß auf Galba aus, angeblich konnte er ihn beherrschen – ein Urteil, das eher ein Reflex sozialer Voreingenommenheit der Überlieferung ist. Tacitus spricht von seiner Grausamkeit und Habgier (hist. 1,37,5; 2,95,3). Nach Galbas Tod wurde I. von Otho hingerichtet.

PIR[2] I 16 • Demougin, Prosopographie, 546f. W.E.

Iceni. Kelt. Stamm im Gebiet von Norfolk und Suffolk (SO-England). Erstmals erwähnt unter dem Namen Cenimagni als einer der Stämme, die sich Caesar 54 v. Chr. unterwarfen (Caes. Gall. 5,21,1). Zur Zeit der claudischen Eroberung (43 n. Chr.) waren sie bereit, die Allianz mit Rom zu akzeptieren. 47 n. Chr. rebellierten sie und wurden unterworfen, blieben aber im Status eines verbündeten Königreiches (Tac. ann. 12,31). Nach dem Tod ihres Königs Prasutagus ca. 59 n. Chr. wurde ihr Gebiet in die röm. Administration einbezogen, nicht nur die Hälfte, die Prasutagus Nero überlassen hatte. → Boudicca, seine Witwe, und ihre Töchter veranlaßten die I. dazu, sich der Revolte der Trinovantes gegen Rom 60–61 n. Chr. anzuschließen (Tac. ann. 14,31–38; [1. 70–74]). Unter der Führung Boudiccas zerstörten die I. und ihre Verbündeten die *colonia* in → Camulodunum und die beiden Städte → Verulamium und → Londinium. Die Revolte wurde durch Suetonius Paullinus niedergeschlagen. Die I. wurden in einer *civitas* mit Zentrum *Venta Icenorum* (h. Caister-by-Norwich) organisiert.

1 S.S. Frere, Britannia, [3]1987.

G. Webster, Boudicca, 1978. M.TO./Ü: I.S.

Ichana (Ἴχανα). Ortschaft auf Sizilien, geriet unter die Herrschaft von Syrakusai (Steph. Byz. s.v. I.). Belege: Griff eines br. Kerykeion mit der Aufschrift Ιχανινοδαμοσιον; silbernes *hēmílitron* (Av. gehörnter Kopf, Personifikation eines Flusses, zu dessen Rechten auf einigen Prägungen ΣΙΧΑ, auf dem Rv. ein Schiffsbug mit der Legende ΝΙΚΑ, datierbar E. 5. Jh. v. Chr., I. feierte also einen Seesieg); in einer sikulischen Inschr. aus Herbessos steht ΘΙΚΑΝΑ.

G. Manganaro, in: JNG 33, 1984, 31–33 • Ders., Alla ricerca di poleis mikrai della Sicilia centro-orientale, in: Orbis Terrarum 2, 1996, 140–141 • Ders., Modi dell'alfabetizzazione in Sicilia, in: Medit. Ant. I, 1998, 22f. GI.MA./Ü: J.W.M.

Ichara (Ἰχάρα, h. Failaka). Insel im Persischen Golf an der Ostküste Arabiens. Das bei Ptolemaios (6,7,47 N) genannte I. wird heute allg. als Variante zu → Ikaros aufgefaßt. Während die Identifikation lange zwischen Failaka, Kharg und Qaru schwankte, ist die Gleichung von Ikaros (und damit Ichara?) mit Failaka inzwischen inschr. bestätigt. Nach Arrianos (an. 7,20,2–3) erhielt die Insel ihren Namen von Alexander nach einer Insel in der Ägäis. Vermutlich geht der Name jedoch auf ein Heiligtum É-KARA zurück, das in assyr. und aram. Quellen bezeugt ist.

D. T. Potts, The Arabian Gulf in Antiquity I, 1990, 349; II, 1990, 179–196 • J. Tkač, s.v. I., RE 9, 821–829. H.J.N.

Ichnai (Ἴχναι). Befestigte Siedlung am Balissos (Balīḫ), nach → Isidoros von Charax zwischen Alagma und → Nikephorion gelegen (Isidoros von Charax 1 Schoff; Plut. Crassus 25,17; Cass. Dio 40,12,2). Angeblich maked. Gründung; trotz Anlehnung an griech. Ortsnamen ist der Name vielleicht identisch mit altbabylon. Aḫūnā [1. 6]. Bei I. gewann → Licinius Crassus 54 v. Chr. ein Gefecht gegen den parth. Satrapen Silakes. Publius, dem Sohn des Crassus, wurde geraten, in das römerfreundliche I. zu fliehen. Die alte Gleichsetzung [2] mit dem modernen Toponym Ḥnez ist zweifelhaft.

1 B. Groneberg, Répertoire Géographique des Textes Cunéiformes, 3, 1980 2 F. H. Weissbach, s. v. I., RE 9, 830.

K. KE.

Ichneumon. Pharaonsratte oder Mungo (Herpestes ichneumon, unter dem Namen ἰχνεύμων zuerst von Aristot. hist. an. 6,35,580a 25, sonst auch ἰχνευτής/-ήρ erwähnt), sich wie ein Hund ernährende Schleichkatze in Äg. und nach Vitr. 8,2,7 auch in Marokko. Der I. hält sich meistens im Schilf auf und räubert gerne in Geflügelzuchten. In Äg. war er als grimmiger Feind des Krokodils bekannt, in dessen offenen Rachen er hineinschlüpfe und dieses durch Verzehr seiner Innereien töte (Strab. 17,812; Diod. 1,87; Opp. kyn. 3,407–432; Ail. nat. 8,25; 10,47; Plin. nat. 8,90; Plut. De sollertia animalium 10 = mor. 966d). Als *enhydros* ging er durch Isid. orig. 12,2,36 in die lat. Lit. des MA ein (u. a. als *ydros* bei Thomas von Cantimpré 8,21 [1. 283 f.]). Ferner kämpfte der I. in Äg., geschützt durch eine Schlammschicht, gegen die Viper ἀσπίς (Theophr. bei Aristot. 8(9),6, 612a 15–20; Nik. Ther. 190 ff.; Strab. ebd.; Plin. nat. 8,88; Ail. nat. 3,22; vgl. Mosaik aus Pompeji [2. 81 und Abb. 33]). Der I. war der → Leto und der → Eileithyia hl. und wurde bes. in Herakleopolis verehrt und sogar in Ehren beigesetzt (Hdt. 2,67; Strab. 17,812; Ail. nat. 10,47; Cic. nat. deor. 1,101). Als magisches Mittel zweifelhaften Wertes gegen Schlangen erwähnt Plinius (nat. 29,68) sein Fett. In hadrianischer Zeit schmückte der I. als Symbol Äg.s eine Bronzemünze aus Panopolis [3. Taf. 1,25] und mehrere ant. Siegelsteine [3. Taf. 16,5 und 6 u.ö.].

1 H. Boese (Ed.), Thomas Cantimpratensis, Liber de natura rerum, 1973 2 Toynbee, Tierwelt 3 F. Imhoof-Blumer, O. Keller, Tier- und Pflanzenbilder, 1889, Ndr. 1972.

H. Gossen, s. v. I., RE Suppl. 8,233.

C. HÜ.

Ichor (ἰχώρ). Das Wort ist zur aram. bzw. hebr. Wurzel mit der Bed. »Würde«, »Glanz« in Bezug gestellt worden, mit möglichen etym. Überlagerungen von der sumer. Wurzel mit der Bed. »Blut« und der akkad. Wurzel mit der Bed. »gießen« her.

Bei Homer (Il. 5,340; vgl. 416) bezeichnet das Wort den Lebenssaft der Götter und nicht das Blut, dessen Produktion an ebendieser Stelle an das Essen von Brot und das Trinken von Wein gebunden ist. Der *i.* erscheint auch bei Aischylos (Ag. 1479 f., 458 v. Chr.), wo das Wort eine Flüssigkeit bezeichnet, die aus einer sich nicht schließenden Wunde austritt. Im 4. Jh. wird es häufiger und bezeichnet pathogene Flüssigkeiten und das dünne Blut, d. h. vielleicht den serösen Teil des Bluts; in dieser Bed. wird es auf andere Flüssigkeiten von der Galle bis zur Milch angewandt. Spätestens von 395 v. Chr. an bezeichnete es jedwede physiologische Flüssigkeit ohne diagnostische Bewertung und hielt sich danach in dieser Bed., mußte aber zur genauen Angabe seiner Natur näher bestimmt werden und konnte daher jede pathologische Sekretion bezeichnen, die durch einen beliebigen pathogenen Mechanismus bedingt war.

A. TO./Ü: T. H.

Ichthyas (Ἰχθύας). Schüler des Eukleides [2] aus Megara, 4. Jh. v. Chr., → Megariker; Titelfigur eines Dialoges des → Diogenes [14] aus Sinope. I. wird üblicherweise mit dem in den Hss. als Icthydias oder Ychtyas bezeichneten Mann identifiziert, der bei einer Revolte gegen seine Vaterstadt (Megara?) ums Leben kam (Tert. apol. 46,16).

1 K. Döring, Die Megariker, 1972, 15, 91–94, 100–101
2 SSR II H.

K. D.

Ichthyes (Fische) s. Sternbilder

Ichthyokentauros s. Triton

Ichthyophagoi (Ἰχθυοφάγοι, »Fischesser«). Ethnographischer Sammelname für Küstenvölker, die sich vorwiegend von Fischen ernähren. Als utopisches Volk mit Wohnsitz an den Enden der im Alt. bekannten Welt werden die I. einerseits als vorbildlich gerecht, andererseits mitunter als tierähnlich und auf einer sehr niedrigen Kulturstufe stehend beschrieben (Agatharchides von Knidos, De Mari Erythro, fr. 31–49 = GGM 1, 129–141). Am häufigsten genannt sind die aithiop. I. am Roten Meer, von denen Herodot berichtet, sie seien von → Kambyses (vergebens) als Spione zu den – ebenfalls in utopischen Bildern beschriebenen – Aithiopen gesandt worden (Hdt. 3,19–25).
→ Utopie

O. Longo, I mangiatori di pesci, in: Materiali e discussioni per l'analisi dei testi classici 18, 1987, 9–55 • J. S. Romm, The Edges of the Earth in Ancient Thought, 1992, 38–40.

R. B.

Ichthys

[1] Der Fisch (griech. ἰχθῦς, lat. *piscis*) war in Griechenland und Rom ein Volksnahrungsmittel, bestimmte Fische in Rom auch ausgesprochene Luxusnahrung. Das erklärt das griech. Interesse an Nachbarkulturen wie der ägypt. oder syrischen, wo auffallende Speiseverbote festgestellt und oft verallgemeinert wurden (Priester in Ägypten: Hdt. 2,37; Plut. Is. 7, 353b; Plut. symp. 8,8,2; Syrien: Ov. fast. 2,473 f.; Porph. De abstinentia 2,61 usw.) und wo oft die Fischverehrung damit zusammenging (Ägypten: Strab. 17,1,40, vgl. PSI 8 Nr. 901; Syrien seit Xen. an. 1,4,9, extrem Clem. Al. Protreptikos 2,39,9). Insbes. gilt dies für die syrische Göttin Atargatis sowohl an ihrem Hauptkultort Hierapolis (Lukian. De Dea Syria 14) wie anderswo in Syrien und der Mittelmeerwelt (Smyrna LSAM 17; Delos LSCG Suppl. 54).

In Griechenland wie in Rom selbst werden Fische sehr selten geopfert (verallgemeinert Plut. symp. 8,8,3).

Der Genuß bestimmter Fische ist in einigen Kulten oder für bestimmte Priester verboten, etwa die Seebarbe (*triglē*) für die Mysten in Eleusis (Plut. mor. 983f; Ail. nat. 9,51) oder für die Herapriesterin in Argos (Ail. nat. 9,51), alle Fische für den Priester des Poseidon in Leptis (Plut. symp. 8,8,4); ebenso befolgen die Pythagoreer das Eßverbot bestimmter oder aller Fische (Plut. symp. 8,8,1–3). Die Seltenheit von Fischopfern erklärt sich mit der Seltenheit von Opfern nichtdomestizierter Tiere; bezeichnend ist, daß Fische entweder dem Meergott Poseidon oder aber marginalen Gottheiten wie Pan oder Priapos geopfert werden; das Fischtabu ist umgekehrt auf dem Hintergrund des verbreiteten Fischgenusses als rituelle Auszeichnung bestimmter Personen zu verstehen.

Bereits in der altchristl. Ikonographie ist der Fisch sehr häufig, sowohl eingebunden in umfassendere Szenen als auch allein; letztere Darstellung findet sich einerseits an den Wänden von Katakomben (als Ausdruck der Zugehörigkeit zum Christentum), andererseits als apotropäisches Zeichen über Haustüren, auf Grabsteinen, Amuletten und Ringen. Durch den Fischzug Petri (Mt 4,19) ist die Symbolisierung des einzelnen Gläubigen durch einen Fisch schon im NT angelegt und bald lit. belegt (etwa in der Bilderliste bei Clem. Al. Paidagogos 3,101,3). Bereits Tertullian (De baptismo 1) verbindet diese Bildlichkeit – die Christen sind *pisciculi* (»Fischlein«) – mit dem griech. Wort *i.* Dieses ist als Akronym, gebildet aus den Anfangsbuchstaben von *Iēsús Christós Theú Hyiós Sōtḗr* (»Jesus Christus, Gottes Sohn, Retter«) etwa gleichzeitig mit Tertullian inschr. und in den *Oracula Sibyllina* (8,217–250) faßbar, geht also auf das 2. Jh. zurück; es findet sich noch öfter in der ant. christl. Lit. und erfährt verschiedene allegorische Auslegungen, etwa daß Christus als Fisch im Meer menschl. Sterblichkeit leben konnte (Aug. civ. 18,23). Angesichts der komplexen Lage der Zeugnisse muß offen bleiben, ob das Akronym oder die Auslegung des NT den Ausgangspunkt für die christl. Fischsymbolik bildeten; sie haben sich jedenfalls schon früh gegenseitig gestützt.

F.J. Dölger, I., 5 Bde., 1910–1943 • J. Engemann, s.v. Fisch, RAC 7, 959–1097. F.G.

[2] Kap an der elischen Westküste der Peloponnesos, h. Katakolo (Thuk. 2,25,4; Xen. hell. 6,2,31).

Philippson/Kirsten 3, 345. C.L.u.E.O.

Icilius. Name eines wohl schon im 4. Jh. v. Chr. erloschenen, nach der Tradition für seine patrizierfeindliche Haltung bekannten (Liv. 4,54,4) plebeischen Geschlechts.

[1] I., L. Volkstribun 456, 455, 449 v. Chr. (MRR 1,42; 48). I. soll 456 die *lex de Aventino publicando*, die den Aventin der *plebs* zur Nutzung zuwies, durchgesetzt haben (Liv. 3,31,1; 32,7; Dion. Hal. ant. 10,31,2–32,5), als Verlobter der → Verginia mutig gegen die Willkür des Decemvirn Appius Claudius [I 5] aufgetreten (Liv. 3,44,3; 45,4–46,8; 48,7–49,3; Dion. Hal. ant. 11,28,2; 31,3–5; 38,2) und danach Wortführer der *plebs* bei der 2. → Secessio (449) gewesen sein (Liv. 3,51,7–10; 53,2f.). Auch sollen 449 auf sein Betreiben die Konsuln Valerius und Horatius durch Volksbeschluß einen Triumph erhalten haben (Liv. 3,63,8–11).

[2] I., L. Beantragte als Volkstribun 412 v. Chr. ein Akkergesetz (Liv. 4,52,1–3). 409 gehörte er wahrscheinlich zu den drei I. unter den Volkstribunen, welche die Besetzung von drei der vier Quaestorenstellen mit Plebeiern und für 408 die Wahl von Konsulartribunen durchsetzten (Liv. 4,54–56,3). Letzteres war insofern bedeutsam, als bis zu den Licinisch-Sextischen Gesetzen 367 mit Ausnahme der Jahre 393 und 392 an Stelle von Konsuln Konsulartribune gewählt wurden.

[3] I., Sp. Nach Dion. Hal. (ant. 6,88,4, hier wie auch sonst bei Dion. durch Verwechslung bzw. Textverderbnis wohl fälschlich als Sicinius oder Sicilius bezeichnet) war er einer der Gesandten der Plebeier nach dem Auszug auf den Mons Sacer. Als Volkstribun 492 v. Chr. soll I. ein Gesetz eingebracht haben, das die Störung plebeischer Versammlungen unter Strafe stellte (Dion. Hal. ant. 7,17,4f.; 10,31,1); möglicherweise ist dieses Gesetz aber eher in das Jahr 470 zu datieren, für das die ersten vollständigen Volkstribunenlisten (Calpurnius Piso fr. 23 HRR [= Liv. 2,58,1f.]; Diod. 11,68,8) vorliegen, welche ebenfalls I. aufführen. MRR 1,31. C.MÜ.

Icorigium. Röm. Straßenstation (Itin. Anton. 373,1: *Egorigio*; Tab. Peut. 3,1) am Kyllübergang der Straße Trier – Köln, h. Jünkerath. Seit dem 1. Jh. n. Chr. wurden Streifenhäuser beiderseits dicht aneinander mit der Schmalseite zur Straße hin erbaut. Während der Germaneneinfälle im 3. Jh. zerstört, in spätkonstantinischer Zeit durch eine kreisförmige Befestigung (135 m Dm) mit 13 Rundtürmen und zwei Torbauten geschützt. Die Wehranlage ähnelt denen in → Beda und → Noviomagus. Gegen E. des 4. Jh. wurde I. aufgegeben. Als Spolien verbaute Grabreliefs zeigen für das Moselland typische Szenen aus dem Alltagsleben der Bewohner.

H. Koethe, Straßendorf und Kastell bei Jünkerath, in: Trierer Zschr. Beih. 11, 1936, 50–106 • W. Binsfeld, Jünkerath, in: Führer vor- und frühgesch. Denkmäler 33, 1977, 300–304 • H. Cüppers, Jünkerath, in: Ders. (Hrsg.), Die Römer in Rheinland-Pfalz, 1990, 403–405. RA.WI.

Icosium (Ἰκόσιον, pun. *ʾj ksm*, »Insel der Eulen«?). Phönik. oder pun. Gründung in der späteren Mauretania Caesariensis, h. Algier. Belegstellen: Mela 1,31; Plin. nat. 5,20; Ptol. 4,2,6; Itin. Anton. 15,5; Sol. 25,17 (mit verkehrter Etym.); Amm. 29,5,16 (mit Anspielung auf diese Etym.); Geogr. Rav. 40,44; 88,12. Während der Regierungszeit → Iubas II. wurde eine röm. Veteranen-Kolonie nach I. deduziert (Plin. nat. 3,19; 5,20). Unter Vespasianus wurde die Stadt *colonia Latina* (CIL VIII Suppl. 3, 20853). In ihrem Gebiet wurde ein Münzhort von 158 Mz. aus der Zeit ca. 150–50 v. Chr. gefunden [1]. Inschr.: CIL VIII 2, 9256–9268; Suppl. 3, 20852f.

1 M. Thompson, O. Mørkholm, C. M. Cray, (Hrsg.), An Inventary of Greek Coin Hoards, 1973, 2303.

S. Lancel, E. Lipiński, s. v. I., DCPP, 226. W. HU.

Icovellauna. Durch Namen und Fundort mit Wasser verbundene kelt. Lokalgöttin. Inner- (CIL XIII, 1.2, 4296–4298) und außerhalb (CIL XIII, 1.2, 4294f.) eines oktogonalen Brunnengebäudes in Sablon bei Metz-Divodurum kamen vier kleine Br.- bzw. Marmortäfelchen sowie Reste eines Altares mit Weihungen an Dea I. zutage. Das einzelne Marmortäfelchen für Dea I. aus Trier, Altbachtal (CIL XIII, 1.2, 3644) spricht nicht gegen die lediglich lokale Bed. der Göttin im Gebiet der → Mediomatrici.

W. Binsfeld et al., Kat. der röm. Steindenkmäler des Rhein. Landesmus. Trier, 1988, 55ff. • J. DeVries, Kelt. Rel., 1961, 115 • J.B. Keune, s. v. I., RE 12, 856f. • Ders., Sablon in röm. Zeit, in: Jb. der Ges. für lothring. Gesch. und Altertumskunde, 1903, 365ff. • F. Moeller, Ein Nymphaeum in Sablon bei Metz, in: Westdt. Zschr. 2, 1883, 249ff. M. E.

Ictis. Bei Ebbe mit dem Festland verbundene brit. Insel, auf der nach Diod. 5,22,2 die Bewohner von Belerion (Land's End in SW-Britannien) → Zinn aus eigenen Minen vertrieben – dies waren die Anfänge des Zinnhandels zw. Britannia und dem Mittelmeerraum. Die Lokalisierung von I. wird immer noch diskutiert. Zur Wahl stehen St. Michael's Mount in der Mounts Bay/ Cornwall [1. 176], bei Ebbe mit dem Festland verbunden, und Mount Batten im Plymouth Sound/Devon, wo Handelsbeziehungen mit dem Kontinent in der späten Eisenzeit gesichert sind [2]; denkbar sind weiterhin Portland Bill und Hengistbury Head/Dorset. I. ist jedenfalls in der Nähe der Zinnvorkommen von Devon und Cornwall zu vermuten.

1 H. O'N. Hencken, The Archaeology of Cornwall and Scilly, 1932 2 B. Cunliffe, Mount Batten/Plymouth, 1988. M. TO./Ü: I. S.

Ida (Ἴδη, Ἰδαῖον ὄρος).

[1] Höchster Gebirgszug Kretas, h. Psiloritis, mit dem Gipfel Timios Stavros (2456 m). In der Ant. noch stark bewaldet (vgl. den Namen I. = »Waldgebirge«), bes. durch Zypressen (Eur. Hipp. 1253; Theophr. h. plant. 3,2,6; 4,1,3; Plin. nat. 16,142). Schon früh Abbau von Metallen (FGrH 239,11; Diod. 5,64,5) und landwirtschaftliche Nutzung (Theophr. de ventis, fr. 5,13 Wimmer; [1]). Bes. Verehrung genoß die als Geburtsstätte des Zeus angesehene Höhle an der Ostflanke des I.-Massivs, am Rande der Nida-Hochebene (Diod. 5,70,2; 4; Strab. 10,4,8; Mela 2,113; Paus. 5,7,6; Arat. 31ff.; Pind. O. 5,42; Diog. Laert. 8,13; Porph. vita Pythagorae 17). Hier fanden sich zahlreiche Votivgaben v. a. aus archa. Zeit, u. a. die sog. »kretischen Bronzen« aus dem 8./7. Jh. v. Chr.

1 A. Chaniotis, Die kret. Berge als Wirtschaftsraum, in: E. Olshausen, H. Sonnabend (Hrsg.), Stuttgarter Kolloquium zur Histor. Geogr. des Alt. 5 (1993), 1996, 255–266.

P. Faure, Noms de montagnes crétoises, (L'Association G. Budé, Lettres d'Humanistes 24), 1965, 426–446 • Lauffer, Griechenland, 277 • R. F. Willetts, Cretan Cults and Festivals, 1962, 143f., 239ff. H. SO.

[2] Gebirgszug in der südl. Troas (h. Kazdağları), durch Homer (Il. 2,824; 4,103; 8,170; 8,410; 12,19ff.; 14,283ff.) lokalisiert (vgl. Strab. 13,1,5). Westl. Ausläufer ist das Kap Lekton, der nordöstl. reicht bis Zeleia, im Süden reicht er bis ans Meer bei Antandros und Gargara. Die I. ist »quellenreich« (Hom. Il. 8,47; 14,157; 283ff.); hier entspringen u. a. Aisepos, Granikos, Simoeis und Skamandros (Hom. Il. 12,19ff.). Der Waldreichtum der I. war für den Schiffbau von großer Bed. (Thuk. 4,52; Strab. 13,1,51) und daher für Pergamon wichtig, obwohl sie, im Winter unpassierbar, den Landweg an die Westküste der Troas erschwerte. Auf den höchsten Gipfel der I. wurden → Kybele und → Zeus verehrt (Hom. Il. 8,48). Idaia hieß eine Nymphe, die Gattin des Flußgottes Skamandros, Mutter des Teukros, des ersten Königs von Troia (Apollod. 3,139; Diod. 4,75), Idaios der Sohn des Dardanos und der Chryse, der den Kult der Kybele auf der I. eingeführt haben soll (Dion. Hal. ant. 1,61; 1,68; Paus. 8,44,5).
→ Aisepos; Granikos; Idaia; Idaios; Simoeis; Skamandros; Teukros

L. Bürchner, s. v. I., RE 17, 862–864 • J. M. Cook, The Troad, 1973, 443 • W. Leaf, Strabo on the Troad, 1973, 352 • A. Philippson, Petermanns geogr. Mitt., Ergh. 167 1910, 104 • J. Stauber, Die Bucht von Adramytteion 1 (IK 50), 1996, 362. E. SCH.

Idaia (Ἰδαία).

[1] Einer der vielen Beinamen der Göttermutter (→ Kybele), nach ihrem Kult auf dem phryg. → Ida [2] (z. B. Eur. Or. 1453; Strab. 10,469). C. W.

[2] Nymphe der Ida [2] in zu Phrygien, Gattin des Flußgottes Skamandros, Mutter von → Teukros, dem ersten König in der Troas, nach dem das Volk der Teukrer benannt ist (Apollod. 3,139; Diod. 4,75).

[3] Tochter des Dardanos, Urenkelin von [2], zweite Gattin des → Phineus; sie schwärzt ihre Stiefkinder Plexippos und Pandion bei ihrem Gatten an; dieser blendet seine Söhne, wofür er von den Argonauten bestraft wird (Soph. Ant. 966ff.; Apollod. 3,200; Diod. 4,43f.).

[4] Nymphe, die dem Hirten Theodoros die → Sibylle Herophile in einer Grotte bei Erythrai zur Welt bringt (Paus. 10,12,3f.). RE. ZI.

Idaioi Daktyloi s. Daktyloi

Idaios (Ἰδαῖος).

[1] Beiname des → Zeus vom Ida auf Kreta (Eur. fr. 472 TGF; Inscr. Creticae 1,12,1) oder bei Troia (Hom. Il. 24,291; Verg. Aen. 7,139; in Kelainai: Plut. mor. 306e f.) und von → Herakles als Daktylos I. und Gründer der

Olymp. Spiele (Paus. 5,7,6ff.; 8,31,3; auch in Elis und Erythrai: Paus. 6,23,3; 9,27,8). AN.W.

[2] Sohn der Chryse und des → Dardanos [1], mit dem er aus Arkadien über Samothrake ins → Ida-Gebirge [2] auswandert, das nach I. benannt sein soll. Dort richtet I. den Kult der Göttermutter ein (Dion. Hal. ant. 1,61).

[3] Name von zwei Troianern in der *Ilias*: a) Herold: holt → Priamos mit Opfertieren zum Zweikampf von Paris und Menelaos (3,245ff.); unterbreitet den Griechen Paris' Kompromißvorschlag (7,372ff.); begleitet Priamos bei der Herausgabe von Hektors Leiche ins griech. Heer (B. 24). b) Sohn des → Dares [1], eines Priesters des Hephaistos, der I. im Kampf gegen → Diomedes rettet (5,9–24).

P. WATHELET, Dictionnaire des Troyens de l'Iliade 1, 1988, 598–601. RE.N.

[4] I. von Rhodos. Epiker, der Homers Dichtung »verdoppelte«, indem er zu jedem Vers einen weiteren hinzufügte (Suda II, 608,12–14 = SH 502); auch Verf. von *Rhodiaká* in 3000 Versen.

FGrH 533 F 10. S.FO./Ü: T.H.

Idalion (Ἰδάλιον). In assyr. Inschr. 672 v.Chr. gen. griech.-phoinik. Stadt im Innern von Kypros, der ant. Lit. als ein Hauptsitz des Aphrodite-Kults bekannt (Theokr. 15,100; Verg. Aen. 1,681; 692). Besiedelt seit der späten Brz. Ruinen beim h. Dali zw. Larnaka und Nikosia mit zwei Akropolen, Stadtmauer, Häuserresten und Nekropolen [1]. In den Heiligtümern von Anat-Athena, Rešef-Apollon und Aphrodite wurden griech., phoinik. und kypro-syllabische Inschr. sowie zahlr. Skulpturen gefunden (CIS I 88–94; [2; 3; 4]). Mz.-Prägung [5]. Seit E. 5. Jh. v.Chr. Teil des Königreichs von → Kition. In ptolemaiischer Zeit Einrichtung des Herrscherkultes, Nymphenheiligtum in der nördl. gelegenen Höhle von Kafizin [6]; z.Z. des Plinius (nat. 5,130) offenbar verlassen.

1 V. KARAGEORGHIS, R.P. CHARLES, P. DUCOS, Excavations in the Necropolis of I., 1963, in: RDAC 1964, 28–113 **2** MASSON, 233–257 **3** O. MASSON, Kypriaka, Le sanctuaire d'Apollon a Idalion, in: BCH 92, 1968, 386–402 **4** R. SENFF, Das Apollonheiligtum von I. (Studies in Mediterranean Archaeology 94), 1993 **5** G. HILL, BMC, Gr Cyprus XLVIII-LIII, 24–28 **6** T.B. MITFORD, The Nymphaeum of Kafizin (Kadmos Suppl. 2), 1980.

E. OBERHUMMER, s.v. I., RE 9, 867–872 • M. OHNEFALSCH-RICHTER, Kypros, die Bibel und Homer, 1893, passim • L.E. STAGER, A.M. WALKER u.a., American expedition to I.: Cyprus. First Preliminary Report. Seasons of 1971 and 1972, 1974 • Dies. u.a., American expedition to I., Cyprus 1973–1980, 1989. R.SE.

Idas (Ἴδας). Sohn des → Aphareus [1], des Königs von Messene, und Bruder des → Lynkeus. Das messenische Brüderpaar wird als Apharetidai dem spartanischen Brüderpaar der → Dioskuroi gegenübergestellt, was die Rivalitäten und Auseinandersetzungen Spartas und Messenes spiegelt. I. wird durchweg als nahezu übermenschlich stark (seit Hom. Il. 9, 556) und streitsüchtig charakterisiert, er gilt auch als Sohn Poseidons (Apollod. 3,117). Als er mit Apollon um → Marpessa, die Tochter des Flußgottes Euenos, freit, bedroht I. den Gott mit seinem Bogen (Hom. Il. 9,556–560). Marpessa wird entweder von Apollon entführt (Paus. 5,18,2, auf der Kypseloslade), oder von I. mit Hilfe eines Flügelwagens, den er von Poseidon erhält (Apollod. 1,60); von Zeus vor die Wahl zwischen Gott und Heros gestellt, wählt sie den Heros, um nicht im Alter vom ewig jungen Gott verlassen zu werden (Apollod. 1,60f.).

Beide Brüder nehmen an den Unternehmungen der kalydonischen Jagd (Meleagros ist I.' Schwiegersohn, Hom. Il. 9,556f.) und der Fahrt der → Argonauten teil (Apoll. Rhod. 1,151). Beide sterben im Kampf mit den Dioskuren, der verschieden erzählt wird. Nach Theokr. 22,137–213 entführen die Dioskuren die Töchter des → Leukippos, welche den Apharetidai versprochen waren; im Zweikampf zwischen Kastor und Lynkeus am Grab des Aphareus fällt letzterer, doch als I. regelwidrig eingreifen will, erschlägt ihn Zeus mit einem Blitz. Sonst ist Rinderdiebstahl der Anlaß: Nach Pind. N. 10,60–72 streitet I. mit Kastor um eine Herde, und im darauffolgenden Kampf am Grab des Aphareus fallen I., Lynkeus und Kastor; wieder wird I. von Zeus getötet. Apollod. 3,134–137 gibt als Grund des tödlichen Streites an, daß alle vier gemeinsam eine Rinderherde rauben, doch I. die Dioskuren bei der Verteilung betrügt. Daß die so verschiedenen Erzählungen alle den Kampf an Aphareus' Grab ansiedeln und I. vom Blitz erschlagen lassen, weist auf die Existenz dreier Gräber, von denen eines als Blitzmal verstanden wurde.

C. SCHWANZAR, s.v. Apharetidai, LIMC 1, 877f. F.G.

Ide (Ἴδη, Ida).

[1] Eponyme Nymphe des → Ida-Gebirges [2] in der Troas (Ps.-Plut. 13,3 = GGM 2,652), bei Vergil (Aen. 9,177) Mutter des → Nisos und Jägerin; Bildnis mit Beischrift auf Münzen von Skamandria und Skepsis [1].

[2] Eponyme Nymphe des kret. → Ida [1], Tochter des Melisseus/Melissos oder des Korybas, Mutter der → Daktyloi Idaioi von Daktylos (schol. Apoll. Rhod. 1,1129) oder Zeus (Stesimbrotos FGrH 107 F 12); nach anderen Quellen Frau des Lykastos und Mutter des Minos, Rhadamanthys und Sarpedon (Sokrates von Argos FGrH 310 F 1; vgl. Diod. 4,60,2f.); zusammen mit ihrer Schwester → Adrasteia Amme des Zeus (Orph. fr. 105; Apollod. 1,5; Plut. symp. 3,8,657e; Paus. 8,47,3: Bild am Altar der Athena Alea in Tegea [2]).

1 CH. PAPAGEORGIADOU, s.v. I. (2), LIMC 5.1, 643 **2** Dies., s.v. I. (1), ebd., 642f. A.A.

Ideenlehre. Die moderne (19. Jh.) Bezeichnung für einen Teilbereich der Ontologie → Platons. Zu den jeweils vielen wahrnehmbaren Dingen gleicher Art gibt es je ein nicht wahrnehmbares, allein im Denken erfaßbares »Vorbild«, das die Beschaffenheit der »Abbilder«

erklärt und ihr Sein begründet. Dieses Vorbild nennt Platon »Idee« (ἰδέα/*idéa*, gleichbedeutend εἶδος/*eídos*). Die Idee ist ungeworden und unvergänglich, unveränderlich, eingestaltig und unteilbar, außerhalb von Raum und Zeit; sie ist, was sie ist, ohne Einschränkung und Zweideutigkeit (Plat. symp. 211a; Plat. Phaidr. 247c u.ö.). Sie ist zugleich das voll Erkennbare und das eigentlich Reale, das Allg. und zugleich das ideale Paradigma der Einzeldinge, schließlich auch deren »Ursache« (αἰτία/*aitía*). Die Beziehung zwischen Ding und Idee wird durch Begriffe wie »Teilhabe«, »Gegenwart« und »Gemeinschaft« umschrieben (μέθεξις, παρουσία, κοινωνία Plat. Phaid. 100c–d; aporetisch diskutiert Plat. Parm. 130b ff.). Über die Notwendigkeit der I.: Plat. Phaid. 96a–102a; rep. 474b–480a.

Zw. den Erkenntnisweisen und den ontologisch getrennten Objektklassen besteht strikte Entsprechung (von Wahrnehmbarem ist nur »Meinung«, *dóxa*, von den Ideen nur »Wissen«, *epistḗmē*, möglich: Plat. rep. 477b ff.; 511e; 534a; Plat. Tim. 51d–e), was der modernen Kritik als die eigentliche Achillesferse der I. gilt. Die Ideenerkenntnis ist die Voraussetzung und Grundlage aller richtigen Entscheidungen in Ethik, Politik, in den Wiss. und der Technik. Die »göttliche« Ideenwelt enthält »Teile« ungleichen Ranges (rep. 485b), ist ein wohlgeordnetes (ebd. 500c) organisches Ganzes, dem Leben (soph. 248e) und Vernunft zukommt: Sie ist als das »vollkommene Lebewesen« (παντελὲς ζῷον, Tim. 30c–31b) das allumfassende Modell des Kosmos, dessen Vollkommenheit und Glückseligkeit (ebd. 34b) die entsprechenden Züge seines Vorbildes widerspiegeln. Die obersten dialektischen Begriffe (*mégista génē*), darunter Sein, Bewegung, Ruhe, Selbigkeit und Verschiedenheit (Plat. soph. 254c–d), erlauben eine Annäherung an die Spitze der Ideenwelt, die alles Erkennen und Sein ermöglichende Idee des Guten, die selbst ›jenseits des Seins‹ steht (ἐπέκεινα τῆς οὐσίας, rep. 509b 9). Die Ideenerkenntnis wird als »Schau« (θέα, θεᾶσθαι) verstanden, die am Ende eines »Aufstiegs« »plötzlich« eintritt (rep. 518d; symp. 210e–212a; Phaidr. 247a ff.).

Nach Aristoteles (metaph. A 6; MN) war die I. Teil einer umfassenderen Theorie, in der alle Dinge aus zwei Prinzipien hergeleitet werden, dem Einen (identisch mit dem Guten: ebd. 1091b 14) und der Unbestimmten Zweiheit (→ Dyas). Die (Ideen-)Zahlen sind das erste Produkt der Begrenzung der Dyas durch das Eine, es folgen die übrigen Ideen, dann die Gegenstände der Mathematik als eigener Seinsbereich, dann die wahrnehmbare Welt. Aristoteles kritisiert die I. der Dialoge (ebd. A 9) ebenso scharf wie die Ideenzahlenlehre der mündlichen Philos. (ebd. MN). In seiner eigenen Konzeption bleibt das *eídos* das voll Erkennbare und wahrhaft Reale, jedoch nicht als transzendente Idee (εἶδος χωριστόν), sondern als immanente Form des Einzeldings.

Im Hell. traf die I. auf Unverständnis und Spott. Im Mittelplatonismus verstand man die Ideen überwiegend als Gedanken Gottes; zugleich versuchte man, die aristotelische Position mit der platonischen zu verbinden: Das immanente *eídos* erkläre das Sinnending, die transzendente Idee das wahrhafte Sein. Der stark vom Mittelplatonismus beeinflußte Philon von Alexandreia faßte den Ideenkosmos als den vor Erschaffung der Welt entworfenen Bauplan des Schöpfers (Phil. de opificio mundi 16; 19). → Plotinos bemühte sich u.a. um das Problem der Herleitung der Ideenwelt aus dem Einen, wobei er die aristotelischen Nachrichten mit den Kernsätzen der Dialoge verband (u.a. Plot. Enneades 6,7 Πῶς τὸ πλῆθος τῶν ἰδεῶν ὑπέστη; 6,6 Περὶ ἀριθμῶν). Christl. Autoren lehnten die I. anfangs ab (Iust. Mart. dial. 2,6; Tert. De anima 18; 23,5f.; 24), akzeptierten sie aber zunehmend ab dem 3. Jh. [6. 238ff.]: Die Ideen sind, wie bei Philon, von Gott vor der Welt erschaffen (Clem. Al. strom. 5,93,5; Mar. Victorin. Adversus Arium 4,5), oder waren von jeher im Geist Gottes vorhanden (Aug. diversae quaestiones 46,2).

→ Platonismus

1 L. Robin, La théorie platonicienne des idées et des nombres d'après Aristote, 1908 2 P. Natorp, Platos I., [2]1922 3 D. Ross, Plato's Theory of Ideas, 1951
4 A. Graeser, Platons I., 1975 5 H.J. Krämer, Dialettica e definizione del Bene in Platone, 1989 6 M. Baltes, s.v. Idee (Ideenlehre), RAC 17, 213–246. T.A.S.

Idicra. Ort in Numidia südl. der Linie Milev – Cuicul, h. Azziz-ben-Tellis (Itin. Anton. 28,4). Zwei Inschr. informieren über einen Opfertarif für den Kult afrikan. Götter (CIL VIII 1, 8246f.); weitere Inschr.: CIL VIII 1, 8243–8266. Im 4. und 5. Jh. war I. Bischofssitz (Optatus 2,18, p. 53,4; 19, p. 54,14; Notitia episcopatuum Numidiae 16[a]).

AAAlg, Bl. 17, Nr. 214. W.HU.

Idios Logos (Ἴδιος λόγος). Der I.L. wurde unter → Ptolemaios VI. als »Sonderkonto« eingerichtet (zuerst belegt am 5.1.162 v.Chr., [1]). Eingezahlt wurden nahezu alle Einnahmen aus dem Verkauf von Staatseigentum, v.a. verlassener oder eingezogener Ländereien (ἀδέσποτα, γῆ ἐν ὑπολόγῳ / *adéspota, gē en hypológōi*); spätestens im 1. Jh. v.Chr. gab es ein Amt πρὸς τῷ ἰδίῳ λόγῳ (*pros tōi idíōi lógōi*), das für die Verwaltung des zu Gunsten des I.L. konfiszierten Landes und dessen Weiterverkauf zuständig war (Kontoführung wie Verwaltung gehörten früher zum βασιλικόν (*basilikón*, »Sache der Könige«); der I.L. wurde vielleicht eingerichtet, um buchhalterisch die steigenden irregulären von den regulären Einkünften zu trennen).

Verwaltung und Verkauf von *adéspota* und anderem Regierungsbesitz sowie Untersuchung der damit zusammenhängenden Fragen und die entsprechende Jurisdiktion waren auch in augusteischer Zeit die wichtigste Funktion der Amtsstelle des I.L. (ein Konto des I.L. gab es nicht mehr, die Einkünfte wurden unter dem δημόσιον, *dēmósion*, »Sache des Volkes«) gebucht). Von hier aus entwickelte sich die im 2. Jh. n.Chr. belegte Zuständigkeit des I.L. für alle Erbschaftsangelegenheiten, schließlich auch für Fragen des zivilrechtlichen Status. War der I. L. anfangs für die *bona caduca* (→ *caducum*) zuständig, so kam später auch die Konfiszierung der *bona damnatorum* in seine Zuständigkeit. Land wurde von ihm nicht mehr nur verkauft, sondern auch verpachtet. In röm. Zeit wurden auch Priestertümer vom I. L. verkauft und damit zusammenhängende Gebühren und Strafsummen eingezogen; der I. L. hatte daher auch die Jurisdiktion in solchen Fällen. Erhalten ist ein auf Augustus zurückgehendes Regelbuch, das Zusätze bis 161 n. Chr. enthält, der sog. ›Gnomon des I. L.‹ (BGU V 1, 1210; POxy. 3014). In röm. Zeit unterstand der I. L. einem ritterlichen *procurator* (*ducenarius*); die letzten Amtsinhaber sind unter den Severern (Anf. 3. Jh. n. Chr.) belegt.

1 L. Mitteis, U. Wilcken, Grundzüge und Chrestomathie der Papyruskunde, Bd. 1, 1912 (Ndr. 1962), 162 **2** W. Uxkull-Gyllenband, Der Gnomon des I. L.; Komm. (BGU 5,2), 1934 **3** S. Riccobono, Il Gnomon dell'Idios Logos, 1950 **4** P. R. Swarney, The Ptolemaic and Roman Idios Logos, 1970 **5** O. Montevecchi, L'amministrazione dell' Egitto sotto i Giulio-Claudi, in: ANRW II 10, 1, 413–471, bes. 432 ff. W. A.

Idiotes (ἰδιώτης). Als *i.* wurde ein Privatmann bezeichnet, der kein Amt ausübte und nicht am polit. Leben teilnahm; im mil. Bereich war *i.* bei den Historikern ein gebräuchlicher Begriff für den einfachen Soldaten im Gegensatz zu den Inhabern der Befehlsgewalt (Xen. an. 1,3,11; 3,2,32; Pol. 5,60,3; Diod. 19,4,3). In Mannschaftslisten der Armee des ptolem. Äg. wird der einfache Soldat als *i.* bezeichnet (z. B. Pap. Hib. 1,30,21). LE. BU.

Idistaviso. Ort einer Schlacht zw. Germanen unter → Arminius und Römern unter → Germanicus. Dieser hatte im Sommer 16 n. Chr. die Truppen über See zur Ems und weiter zu Land über die Weser geführt. In der I. gen. Ebene (*campus*) zw. Weser und hügeligem Gelände (Tac. ann. 2,16,1) siegten die Römer. I. läßt sich nicht lokalisieren, wird jedoch allg. im Umfeld der Porta Westfalica angenommen.

B. Rappaport, s. v. I., RE 9, 903–905 · E. Koestermann, Die Feldzüge des Germanicus, in: Historia 6, 1957, 429–479, bes. 425–455. RA. WI.

Idmon (Ἴδμων).

[1] Sohn der → Asteria [2] (Tochter des thessal. → Lapithen Koronos) und des Apollon (Val. Fl. 1,228 ff.), Vater des → Thestor, Großvater des → Kalchas (Pherekydes, FGrH 3 F 108.); als menschl. Putativvater gilt der Argiver → Abas [1] (Apoll. Rhod. 1,139 ff.; Orph. Arg. 187 ff.; Hyg. fab. 14,11). Als Seher mit sprechendem Namen (»Der Wissende«: Wilamowitz) nimmt er in der wohl urspr. Version des → Argonauten-Mythos trotz des Wissens um seinen bevorstehenden Tod an der Fahrt teil und stirbt an einem Eberbiß bei den Mariandynern (Apollod. 1,126; Apoll. Rhod. 2,815 ff.; bei Sen. Med. 652 f. ist sein Tod durch Schlangenbiß in Libyen mit → Mopsos verwechselt) bzw. an einer Krankheit (Val. Fl. 5,1 ff.); an seinem Grab gründen Megarer und Boioter die Stadt Herakleia (Herodoros von Herakleia, FGrH 31 F 51; nach F 53 könnte er erst auf der Rückfahrt dort gestorben sein). Das (spätere) Epos läßt ihn nach Kolchis gelangen und dort eine wichtige Rolle bei der Flucht der Argonauten spielen (Naupaktika F 5–7 PEG I, vielleicht Eumelos F 19 PEG I).

[2] Purpurfärber aus Kolophon, Vater der → Arachne, Ov. met. 6,8.

U. von Wilamowitz, Hell. Dichtung II, [2]1962, 237 f. Anm. 4 · P. Dräger, Argo pasimelousa, I, 1993, 348 Anm. 38. P. D.

Idomenai (Ἰδομεναί, *Idomene*, *Eidomene*). Stadt in der maked. Amphaxitis an der Straße von Thessalonike zur Donau (Strab. 8,8,5; Tab. Peut. 8,1), vielleicht beim h. Marvinci. I. ist schon im 5. Jh. v. Chr. bezeugt (Thuk. 2,100,3), wurde im 3. Jh. v. Chr. von delph. *theōroí* (»Opfergesandten«) besucht [1] und war noch im 6. Jh. n. Chr. bekannt (Hierokles, Synekdemos 639,5).

1 BCH 45, 1921, 17 Z. 68.

F. Papazoglou, Les villes de Macédoine, 1988, 177. MA. ER.

Idomeneus (Ἰδομενεύς).

[1] Sohn des → Deukalion, Enkel des → Minos; der Name ist indirekt bereits in Linear B bezeugt [1]. I. gehört zu den Freiern der → Helene (Hes. fr. 204,56 ff. M-W) und ist ein Gastfreund des Menelaos (Hom. Il. 3,230–233). Er befehligt das mit 80 Schiffen relativ große kretische Kontingent auf dem Troiafeldzug, unterstützt von seinem treuen Gefolgsmann → Meriones (Hom. Il. 2,645–652); nach Nestor ist er der älteste Grieche vor Troia, aber immer noch kampftüchtig (Aristie in Il. 13); I. gehört zum engeren Kreis der griech. Heerführer, hat aber keine »sprechende Rolle« in ihren Debatten. Daß I. einen Lyder namens Phaistos (= kret. Städtename) tötet (Hom. Il. 5,43–47), dürfte eher freie Namensassoziation [2] als der Bezug auf einen in der Lokalsage verankerten Städtekrieg sein [3].

Nach Hom. Od. 3,191 f. kehrt I. sicher nach Hause zurück; nach anderer Version (Serv. Aen. 3,121) gelobt er Poseidon im Sturm, im Fall einer glücklichen Heimkehr das erste ihm begegnende Lebewesen zu opfern – wie sich herausstellen wird, seinen Sohn (ein gängiges Märchenmotiv [4]). I. wird daraufhin vom Thron verjagt und flieht nach Süditalien (Serv. Aen. 3,400 f.; 11,264).

In der ›Odyssee‹ ist I. regelmäßig Gegenstand von Odysseus' Trugreden: Als »Kreter« will dieser I.' Sohn Orsilochos getötet haben (13,256–270) und gemeinsam mit I. als gleichberechtigter Heerführer nach Troia gezogen sein (14,229–238); gegenüber Penelope gibt er sich als I.' jüngeren Bruder aus (19,181–202).

Spätere Quellen erweitern das I.-Bild zusätzlich: Dictys Cretensis will in Anlehnung an Odysseus'

Trugreden I.' Gefährte gewesen sein und von diesem den Auftrag zur Aufzeichnung eines Kriegstagebuchs erhalten haben (p. 2,9–11 EISENHUT). Quintus von Smyrna ergänzt u. a., daß I. bei den Leichenspielen für Achilleus kampflos dessen Gespann gewinnt (4,284 ff.) und Insasse des hölzernen Pferdes ist (12,320). In einer dem → Paris-Urteil nachempfundenen Szene (Ps.-Athenodoros bei Phot. 150a-b) bestraft die unterlegene Medea das Geschlecht des I. – d. h. die (sprichwörtlich lügnerischen) Kreter – damit, fortan immer zu lügen.

1 DMic, s. v. i-do-me-ne-ja 1,272 2 G. S. KIRK, The Iliad 2, 1990, 58 3 W. KULLMANN, Die Quellen der Ilias, 1960, 104 4 M. L. WEST, The East Face of Helicon, 1997, 441–442. RE. N.

[2] Epikureer, geb. in Lampsakos um 325 v. Chr. Begegnung mit → Epikuros während dessen Aufenthalt in Lampsakos 310/09 v. Chr. Nach dessen Rückkehr nach Athen leitete I. die → epikureische Schule in Lampsakos; er blieb seinem Lehrer durch einen lebhaften Briefwechsel verbunden und nahm an dessen Auseinandersetzungen mit den konkurrierenden Philosophenschulen teil. Von seinen Schriften sind vier Auszüge von Briefen sowie Teile eines Buchs ›Über die Sokratiker‹ erhalten. Die Identität mit I. [3] ist umstritten.

A. ANGELI, I frammenti di Idomeneo di Lampsaco, in: CE 11, 1981, 41–101 • Dies., L'opera ›Sui demagoghi in Atene‹ di Idomeneo, in: Vichiana 10, 1981, 5–16. T. D./Ü: S. P.

[3] I. von Lampsakos. Ca. 350–270 v. Chr., vielleicht Peripatetiker, in seiner Heimat als Politiker tätig. Verf. dreier biographischer Werke: 1. ›Über die Sokratiker‹, daraus bei Diogenes Laertios (2,20) ein Frg. über den Sokratiker Aischines. 2. ›Über Volksführer‹ (*Perí demagōgōn* in mind. 2 B., von Plutarch und Athenaios benützt. 3. ›Geschichte von Samothrake‹; sie enthielt nach Art der peripatetischen Biographie eine Sammlung von Anekdoten und Skandalgeschichten, letztere wohl zur Diffamierung der polit. Gegner. Vielleicht identisch mit I. [2].

FRG.: H. USENER, Epicurea 128–38 • FGrH 338 F 1–18.
ED.: A. ANGELI, Bolletino del Centro internazionale per lo studio dei Papiri Ercolanesi (Cronache Ercolanesi), 1981, 41–101 (mit vita). K. MEI.

Idrias (Ἰδριάς). Kar. Gebirgslandschaft mit dem Marsyas-Tal östl. von Mylasa (Hdt. 5,118; Strab. 14,5,23) mit gleichnamiger kar. Stadt. Deren angeblich älterer Name Chrysaoris (Steph. Byz. s. v. I.; s. v. Chrysaoris) wird auch der Stadt Stratonikeia und deren Landschaft zugeschrieben (Paus. 5,21,10), wohl in dem Sinne, daß I. in einem Gebiet lag, dessen Dörfer sich um das Heiligtum des Zeus Chrysaoreus zum kar. Bund der Chrysaoreis zusammengeschlossen hatten; die in der 1. H. 3. Jh. v. Chr. gegr. Stadt Stratonikeia lag nahe dem Bundesheiligtum (Strab. 14,2,25) und I., in der Landschaft Chrysaoris.

L. BÜRCHNER, s. v. I., RE 9, 912 • MAGIE 2, 1031 f. • H. OPPERMANN, Zeus Panamaros (RGVV 19,3), 1924, 9 ff. • L. ROBERT, Ét. Anatoliennes, 1937, 571 Anm. 2. H. KA.

Idrieus (Hidrieus; Ἱδριεύς); Sohn des → Hekatomnos und jüngerer Bruder des → Maussolos, zusammen mit seiner Schwester und Gemahlin Ada Satrap von Karien zw. 351 und 344. I. half Artaxerxes III. in den 340er Jahren, die zyprische Erhebung gegen Persien niederzuschlagen, und stellte zu diesem Zweck Euagoras II. und Phokion von Athen Schiffe und Truppen zur Verfügung (Diod. 16,42,6 f.). Als *euergetes* (»Wohltäter«) und *proxenos* (»Staatsgastfreund«) geehrt im ionischen Erythrai (SEG 31,969); Weihinschr. des I. in → Labraunda (Labraunda 16) und Amyzon (OGIS 235). Auch in Sinuri sind I. und Ada bezeugt. 344/3 starb I. eines natürl. Todes (Diod. 16,69,1; Strab. 14,2,17).

S. HORNBLOWER, Mausolus, 1982, Index s. v. • F. G. MAIER, Cyprus and Phoenicia, in: CAH² 6, 1994, 329 f. • L. ROBERT, Le sanctuaire de Sinuri, 1, 1945, 94 ff. • Ders., Fouilles d'Amyzon, 1983, 93 ff. • S. RUZICKA, Politics of a Persian Dyn., 1992, Index s. v. J. W.

Idumaea s. Edom

Idus s. Kalender, s. Monat (röm.)

Idyia (Ἰδυῖα, auch Εἰδυῖα, »die Wissende«). → Okeanide (Hes. theog. 352), Gattin des → Aietes, Mutter der → Medeia (Hes. theog. 960; Soph. fr. 546 TrGF; Apoll. Rhod. 3,243; Lykophr. 1024; Cic. nat. deor. 3,48; Ov. epist. 17,232; Apollod. 1,129; Hyg. fab. 25) und der → Chalkiope [2], nur bei Tzetz. Lykophr. 798, 1024 auch des → Apsyrtos [1]. A. A.

Idylle s. Bukolik, s. Eidyllion

Idyma (Ἴδυμα). Alte kar. Siedlung (Ptol. 5,2,15; Steph. Byz. s. v. I.) am östl. Ende des Golfs von Keramos nahe Gökova, 4 km landeinwärts bei İskele, in der Nähe das Flüßchen Idymos. Erh. sind Mz. (ab 6. Jh. v. Chr.) mit Panskopf, aus hell. Zeit mit rhod. Apollon und Feigenblatt. Mitte 5. Jh. v. Chr. gehörte I. zum → Attisch-Delischen Seebund, damals von Paktyes beherrscht. Im 3.–2. Jh. zur rhod. Peraia gehörig, wurde I. nach Inbesitznahme durch Philippos V. 201 vermutlich um 197 durch den Rhodier Nikagoras zurückgewonnen und gehörte auch nach 167 v. Chr. zu Rhodos. I. bildete mit Nachbarorten einen Gemeindeverbund (→ *Koinón*). Arch.: Auf der hochgelegenen Akropolis Gebäudereste und Teile des Mauerrings, in einer Nekropole Felsgräber, z. T. mit ion. Tempelfassade (4. Jh. v. Chr.).

G. E. BEAN, J. M. COOK, The Carian Coast 3, in: ABSA 52, 1957, 68 ff. • P. M. FRASER, G. E. BEAN, The Rhodian Peraea and Islands, 1954, 71 f. • F. IMHOOF-BLUMER, Kleinasiat. Mz., 1901/2, 137 • MAGIE 2, 879; 1030 • E. MEYER, s. v. Peraia, RE 19, 566 ff. • L. ROBERT, Études Anatoliennes, 1937, 472 ff. H. KA.

Idyros s. Pamphylia

Jehuda ha-Nasi. Meist einfach »Rabbi« oder »unser heiliger Rabbi« gen., ca. 175–217 n. Chr.; Sohn und Nachfolger von Simeon ben Gamaliel [2] II., der bedeutendste der jüd. Patriarchen, unter dessen Herrschaft das Amt seine größte Macht erfuhr. Er war offiziell von den Römern als Repräsentant des Judentums anerkannt und fungierte außerdem als Vorsitzender des Sanhedrin (*Bēt Dīn*; → Synhedrion) und höchste Autorität in Lehrfragen (*Ḥakham*). J. verfügte über eine solide wirtschaftliche Grundlage, pflegte ausgedehnte Handelsbeziehungen und Kontakte mit der → Diaspora, der gegenüber er seine Macht v.a. durch die Festsetzung des Kalenders demonstrierte. Der Verweis auf die Abstammung J.s aus dem Hause → Davids diente ebenfalls der Sicherung und Legitimierung seiner Herrschaft. J. verlegte den Sitz des Patriachats von Uša (Untergalilaea, in der Nähe des h. Haifa) zunächst nach → Beth Shearim (ab ca. 175) und schließlich – ca. um 200 – in das bedeutendere → Sepphoris, das stark von griech.-röm. Lebensstil und Kultur geprägt war. Die → Haggada erzählt von guten Beziehungen zw. J. und dem severischen Kaiserhaus. Unsicher ist, ob und in welcher Form J. Steuern erhob. Rabbi J. gilt traditionell als Redaktor der Mischna (→ Rabbinische Literatur).

M. JACOBS, Die Institution des jüd. Patriarchen. Eine quellen-und traditionskritische Studie zur Gesch. des Judentums in der Spätant. (Texte und Stud. zum Antiken Judentum 52), 1995, 115 ff., 124 ff. • L. I. LEVINE, The Rabbinic Class of Roman Palestine in Late Antiquity, 1989, 33–37 • S. SAFRAI, Das Zeitalter der Mischna und des Talmuds (70–640), in: H. H. BEN-SASSON (Hrsg.), Gesch. des Jüd. Volkes, 1978 (Ndr. 1992), 377–469, hier: 415–417 • P. SCHÄFER, Gesch. der Juden in der Ant. Die Juden Palästinas von Alexander dem Großen bis zur arab. Eroberung, 1983, 182–184. B.E.

Jenseitsvorstellungen. Ansichten darüber, was den Menschen nach seinem Tod erwartet, sind in den meisten Kulturen vorhanden. In der griech.-röm. Welt fanden sie in Lit. und Bildender Kunst, in philos. Reflexion, theologischer Propaganda und nicht zuletzt in den Grabinschr. Ausdruck; dabei sind die lit. und philos. Meinungen in sich kohärenter als die alltäglichen Vorstellungen, die sich in den Grabinschr. niederschlugen. Festzuhalten ist auch, daß ein fester Konnex zwischen J. und Grabriten in dem Sinne, daß Veränderungen des Grabrituals (etwa Erdbestattung statt Kremation) mit Veränderungen der J. verbunden sind, kaum auszumachen ist.

Zentrale lit. Form zum Ausdruck solcher Vorstellungen ist seit der altoriental. Lit. (Jenseitsgang der Inanna, → Gilgamesch-Epos) die Erzählung von einer Jenseitsreise des Helden, wie sie maßgeblich in der *Nekyia* der homer. ›Odyssee‹ (B. 11) vorliegt, die vom Unterweltsgang des Odysseus erzählt; Vergil schließt sich im 6. Buch der *Aeneis* ebenso an diese Erzählform an wie Platon (rep. B. 10, sog. → Er-Mythos) oder Plutarch, und noch Dante in der *Divina Commedia* folgt ihr, obwohl seit der Kaiserzeit und bes. in der jüd.-christl. Lit. in immer stärkerem Maß das Medium der Vision zum Ausdruck solcher Vorstellungen wurde (christl. faßbar seit der Passion der → Perpetua, dominant seit den *Dialogoi* von → Gregorios [3] d.Gr.).

Die homer. Unterwelt ist ein dunkler Raum am Rande der Welt, bevölkert von kraftlosen Schatten, deren Los ohne Rücksicht auf ihr Vorleben identisch ist, mit Ausnahme von positiv oder negativ ausgezeichneten Toten wie → Minos, der weiterhin als König im Amt ist (Hom. Od. 11,568–571), und → Teiresias, der als Seher Erinnerung und Bewußtsein behält, andererseits die großen Frevler → Tityos, → Tantalos, → Sisyphos (und später → Ixion). Diese Vorstellung, die im Vorderen Orient im Bild der düsteren und staubigschmutzigen Unterwelt ihre Entsprechungen hat, ist bis an das Ende der paganen Welt präsent. Bereits bei Homer steht daneben ein Paradies (→ Elysion), in das auserlesene Menschen entrückt werden können (→ Menelaos, Hom. Od. 4,561–569). Der homer. Demeterhymnos kennt die Jenseitsstrafe für Vergehen, deren jeder Mensch schuldig werden kann und über die → Persephone urteilt (Hom. h. ad Cerem 366–369), verspricht vor allem dem in die → Mysterien Eingeweihten ein bes. Los (480–483). In der Folgezeit werden diese Jenseitsversprechen stärker artikuliert, indem das Elysion zum paradiesischen Ort für alle Eingeweihten wird; in den bakchischen Mysterien (→ Dionysos) schlägt sich dies bes. in den als eigentliche Jenseitsführer ausgestalteten Texten der sog. orphischen Goldblättchen (→ Lamellae Orphicae) nieder. Moralistische Reflexion ihrerseits übernimmt das Elysion als Ort, an dem gute Menschen belohnt werden. Das führt seit Platon, der in seinen Bildern die seit dem Pythagoreismus faßbare Seelenwanderungslehre (→ Pythagoras, → Empedokles [1]) übernimmt, zu einem Neben- und Ineinander moralischer und religiöser Kriterien, wobei der (wohl ägypt.) Vorstellung eines Totengerichts eine Schlüsselrolle zukommt. In der Folgezeit stehen diese Vorstellungen in den ant. Kulturen nebeneinander, ergänzt bes. durch → Epikurs materialist. Lehre, wonach der Tod ein absolutes Ende sei (was Lucr. 3,978–1094 zur Allegorese der J. zwingt).

Die etr. Kultur kannte urspr. eine weit grausamere Unterwelt, wie aus den Bildern auch der gräzisierten Unterweltsgötter (Aita = → Hades mit Wolfskappe, Charun als Dämon, → Vanth) hervorgeht, und auch die röm. Totengöttin → Libitina weist auf alte Besonderheiten; im Lauf der Hellenisierung Italiens wurden sie aber zurückgedrängt; die in den Grabepigrammen sichtbaren J. tragen keine Spuren mehr davon. Dagegen tritt in der Kaiserzeit die → Vergöttlichung, bes. die Verstirnung ausgewählter Toter stärker auf; sie betrifft vor allem junge Verstorbene, die tendenziell schon immer ein bes. Los hatten und als frustrierte Totenseelen (*áhoroi, biaiothánatoi*) auch Instrumente der → Magie wurden.

Während das AT sich im allg. das Jenseits (*šeʾôl*) dunkel und einförmig vorstellt, nicht anders als die umgebenden vorderoriental. Kulturen, finden sich ansatzweise Verweise auf eine bes. Belohnung des Frommen (Ps 16,8–10), vor allem auch auf eine Differenzierung am Ende der Zeiten zwischen den einen, deren Leben ewig, und den anderen, die in »Schmach und Abscheu«

sein werden (Dan 12,1–3). Einzelne jüd. Sekten sind hier weit expliziter, insbes. die → Essener, denen Flavios Iosephos die Unterscheidung zwischen einem den griech. Inseln der Seligen nachgebildeten Paradies und einem dunklen Erdloch als Strafort für die moralisch Schlechten zuschreibt (Ios. bell. Iud. 2,154–165). Ausführlicher sind dann die Visionen in Schriften wie dem apokryphen Henochbuch und im *Sefer ha-Razîm*, in denen ausführliche und detaillierte Jenseitsbilder erscheinen.

Das NT schließt in seinen ältesten Bildern der Endzeit an jüd. Vorstellungen an: Die Trennung der Guten und Schlechten am Ende der Zeit in Mt 25,31 erinnert an Dan 12,1–3. Die Visionen der Märtyrer seit Perpetua verbinden jüd.-nt. mit paganen Vorstellungen, konzentrieren sich indessen fast ausschließlich auf das selige Los der Verfolgten im Paradies, während nur gelegentlich die Unterwelt als Strafort der Ungetauften, bald auch der abgefallenen Christen (*lapsi*) in Erinnerung gerät. Mit dem Durchbruch des Christentums verändert sich auch der Charakter der Jenseitsbilder: Es geht nun um das Los der Seele direkt nach dem Tod und immer stärker auch um eine Moralisierung der Christen selbst; die Jenseitsbilder werden zu Mitteln der moralischen Erziehung, wobei immer mehr die Jenseitsstrafen als Mittel der Abschreckung in den Vordergrund treten. Seit Gregor d.Gr. geht die Entwicklung geradlinig in Richtung auf eine Dreiteilung von Himmel, Hölle und Fegefeuer mit Einzelheiten, die bereits auf Dante vorausweisen.
→ Bestattung; Eschatologie; Hades; Inferi; Katabasis; Makaron Nesoi; Paradies; Tod; Totenkult; Unterwelt

M. Herfort-Koch, Tod, Totenfürsorge und J. in der griech. Ant. Eine Bibliogr., 1992 • J.M. Bremer, Th.P.J. van den Hout, R. Peters (Hrsg.), Hidden Futures. Death and Immortality in Ancient Egypt, Anatolia, the Classical, Biblical and Arabic-Islamic World, 1994 • E. Rohde, Psyche. Seelencult und Unsterblichkeitsglaube der Griechen, ²1898 (1890–1894) • D. Kurtz, J. Boardman, Greek Burial Customs, 1971 • J.M.C. Toynbee, Burial in the Roman World, 1971 • G. Binder (Hrsg.), Tod und Jenseits im Altertum, 1991 • A. Bottini, Archeologia della Salvezza. L'escatologia greca nelle testimonianze archeologiche, 1992 • C. Sourvinou-Inwood, »Reading« Greek Death. To the End of the Classical Period, 1995 • Pfiffig, 162–208 • M. Himmelfarb, Ascent to Heaven in Jewish and Christian Apocalypses, 1993 • Dies., Tours of Hell. An Apocalyptic Form in Jewish and Christian Literature, 1985 • M.P. Ciccarese, Visioni dell'aldilà in Occidente, 1987 • A.E. Bernstein, The Formation of Hell. Death and Retribution in the Ancient and Early Christian Worlds, 1993 • J. Le Goff, La naissance du purgatoire, 1981 • C. Colpe, E. Dassmann, J. Engemann, P. Habermehl, K. Hoheisel, s. v. Jenseits, RAC 17, 246–408. F.G.

Ientaculum s. Mahlzeiten

Jeremia (hebr. *Jirm*ᵓ*jāhū*). PN und Titel des vom gleichnamigen Autor verfaßten biblischen Buches. In einigen haggadischen Quellen (→ Haggada) wird der Name des herausragenden zweiten der »großen Propheten« mit der Vernichtung → Jerusalems, die zu seinen Lebzeiten stattfand, in Verbindung gebracht. Nicht gesichert ist die mögliche Bed. »Gott möge erhöhen«. J.s Geburt wird um 650 v. Chr., in die Regierungszeit König Jošijas, angesetzt. J. führte in seiner Eigenschaft als Weissager ein bewegtes Leben zw. höchster Anerkennung und heftiger Ablehnung bis hin zur mehrfachen Todesdrohung. Seine Prophetie weist im wesentlichen zwei Grundtendenzen auf: Charakteristisch ist 1) die Überzeugung, nur ein Unglücksprophet sei ein wahrer Prophet, 2) unterscheidet ihn seine Individualprophetie markant von anderen Propheten: Der einzelne steht in seiner Beziehung zu Gott im Vordergrund; die innere Umkehr jedes einzelnen führt letztlich zur Rettung des gesamten Volkes. Mit seinem Wirken wurde J. für weite Teile der haggadischen Lit. prägend.

J. Breuer, Das Buch Jirmejah, übers. und erläutert von J. Breuer, 1914 • G. Brunet, Les lamentations contre Jérémie, 1968 • J. Carlebach, Die drei großen Propheten Jesajas, Jirmija und Jecheskel, 1932 (Ndr. 1994) • S. Herrmann, J., 1986 • B. Huwyler, J. und die Völker: Unt. zu den Völkersprüchen in Jeremia 46–49, 1997 • N. Ittmann, Die Konfessionen J.s, 1981 • J. Kastein, Jeremias: der Bericht vom Schicksal einer Idee, 1938 • C. Kuhl, Israels Propheten, 1956 • H. Lamparter, Prophet wider Willen, 1964 • A. Néher, Jérémie, 1960 • T. Odashima, Heilsworte im J.-Buch, 1984 • L. Prjis, Die J.-Homilie Pesikta Rabbati Kap. 26, 1966 • S. Soderlund, The Greek text of Jeremiah, 1985 • C. Wolff, J. im Frühjudentum und Urchristentum, 1976. Y.D.

Jericho (hebr. *Y*ᵊ*riḥō*; griech. Ἱεριχώ, Ἱερικοῦς, Ἱεριχοῦς; arab. *ar-Rīḥā*; von westsem. *yrḥ*, »Mond«?). Palmenreiche, für Datteln und Balsam berühmte (Strab. 16,2,41; Pomp. Trog. 3,2–3; Plin. nat. 13,44; Ios. bell. Iud. 1,138; 4,452–475; Ios. ant. Iud. 14,54; 15,96) Oase 8 km westl. des Jordan, 10 km nördl. des Toten Meeres, 250 m unter dem Meeresspiegel, bewässert durch die Quelle ʿAin as-Sulṭān am nw Rand der Oase. J. ist besiedelt seit dem Natufium (9100–8500 v. Chr.), im präkeramischen Neolithikum (8500–6300) wurde der Ort mit einer Schutzmauer umgeben; zur Neubesiedlung kam es im keramischen Neolithikum (6300–4500), im späten Chalkolithikum (ab 3500) und in der Früh-Brz. II-III (3100–2250; massive Lehmziegelstadtmauer). Während des Übergangs von der Früh- zur Mittelbrz. (2250–2000) ist nur lockere Bebauung nachgewiesen; in der Mittel-Brz. II (1800–1570) war J. eine bed. Stadt (von 11 m hohem Wall umgeben). Um 1570 wurde sie zerstört, zu einer kurzen Nachbesiedlung kam es in der Spät-Brz. II (1400–1350/25); eine Wiederbesiedlung erfolgte erst zw. 1200–1000.

Da die biblisch erzählte Zerstörung der Stadt (Jos 2–6) nach innerbiblischer Chronologie während der spätbrz. Siedlungsunterbrechung stattgefunden haben müßte, wurde sie zunächst als Ätiologie oder als Historisierung eines jährlichen Pesach-Massot-Festes (→ Pesah) interpretiert, doch deuten neuere Untersuchungen auf rein lit. Erzählbildungen frühestens des späten 8. Jh. v. Chr., als der Jordan Grenzfluß und J. Grenzstadt geworden war und in einer fiktionalen Landnahmeerzählung nicht ohne Erwähnung einer Zerstörung passiert werden konnte.

Für die achäm. Zeit (5./4. Jh.) wurde am nördl. Abhang des Tells eine unbefestigte Siedlung nachgewiesen (Esr 2,34; Neh 3,2; 7,36). Nach Beteiligung am Aufstand gegen → Artaxerxes [3] III. (344–343) wurden Teile der Bevölkerung deportiert (Kaspisches Meer, Babylonien). Bereits in hasmonäischer Zeit war sw der Oase (*Tulūl Abī l-ʿAlāʾiq*) ein von → Herodes d.Gr. erweiterter (Ios. bell. Iud. 1,407), von → Archelaos [10] erneuerter (ant. Iud. 17,340) und teilweise freigelegter Winterpalast mit Garten- und Badeanlagen (ant. Iud. 15,54), in dem Herodes starb (bell. Iud. 1,665), sowie ein Hippodrom (*Tall as-Samarat*; bell. Iud. 1,659; 2,3) und ein Amphitheater (unlok.; bell. Iud. 1,666; ant. Iud. 17,161; 194) entstanden. Für die seit hell. Zeit anzunehmende Zivilsiedlung im Bereich der Oase und ihre spätant. Umfassungsmauer liegen außer drei Kirchen und einer Synagoge kaum arch. Befunde vor. Unter Hišām Ibn ʿAbd al-Malik wurde ab 742 n. Chr. nördl. der Oase der Bau eines Winterpalastes (*Ḫirbat al-Mafǧir*) begonnen, nach dem Erdbeben von 746 und Ende der umayyadischen Dyn. 750 aber nicht mehr vollendet.

K. M. KENYON u. a., s. v. J., NEAEHL II, 674–697 • K. BIEBERSTEIN, Josua – Jordan – J., 1995. K.B.

Jerusalem I. NAME II. LAGE UND GESCHICHTE III. STÄTTEN IN DER UMGEBUNG

I. NAME

Hebr. *Yᵉrūšālēm*, vermutl. »Gründung des (Gottes) Šalēm«, masoretisch (→ Masora) stets als Dualform *Yᵉrūšālayim* vokalisiert; griech. Ἱερουσαλήμ, Ἱεροσόλυμα; lat. *Ierusalem*, *[H]ierosolyma*), archaisierend *Šālēm* (Gn 14,18; Ps 76,3) oder *Yᵉbōs* (Ri 19,10–11; 1 Chr 11,4–5), unter Hadrian als *Colonia Aelia Capitolina*, unter Commodus als *Colonia Aelia Commodiana* neu benannt, schon in frühislam. Zeit zumeist als *al-Quds*, »die Heilige«, bezeichnet.

II. LAGE UND GESCHICHTE
A. VOREXILISCHE ZEIT B. NACHEXILISCHE ZEIT

A. VOREXILISCHE ZEIT

J. liegt wenig östl. der Wasserscheide des westjordanischen Berglandes, im Osten vom Ölberg überragt, und wenig südl. eines über → Jericho in das ostjordanische Hochland führenden Handelsweges an der Grenze zw. den Gebieten der Stämme Benjamin und Juda (Jos 15,8; 18,16). Bereits Ende d. 4. Jt. entstand auf dem schmalen Bergsporn westl. oberhalb des Gihon (ʿAin al-Sitt Maryam), der einzigen perennierenden Quelle im Stadtgebiet, eine offene Siedlung, die aber schon nach wenigen Jahrzehnten wieder aufgegeben wurde. Eine Neugründung um 1800 v. Chr. wurde bald durch einen Mauerring befestigt und vielleicht schon in äg. → Ächtungstexten der 12. Dyn. (19. Jh. v. Chr.) als *ȝwšȝmm* [3. 53 Nr. e27 und e28, 58 Nr. f18], sicher aber im frühen 14. Jh. in den Briefen ihres Stadtfürsten Abdi-Ḫepa an → Amenophis [4] IV. als *ú-ru-sa-lim* [2. Nr. 285–290] erwähnt. Nachdem J. um 1000 v. Chr. von David eingenommen und zur Hauptstadt von Israel und Juda erhoben (2 Sam 5,6–9) worden war (so die späteren, retrospektiven Darstellungen), errichtete → Salomo an einem auf der Bergkuppe nördl. der Davidsstadt gelegenen Kultort den → Jahwe-Tempel sowie zw. diesem und der Davidsstadt seinen Palast und umgab beide mit einem erweiterten Mauerring (1 Kg 6–8). Die frühesten arch. Befunde aus dem fraglichen Gelände stammen jedoch erst aus dem 9. oder 8. Jh. v. Chr. Ein neuer, teils als Tunnel, teils als offene Rinne geführter Kanal leitete das Wasser des Gihon am Fuß der Davidsstadt nach Süden, bewässerte die im Kidrontal gelegenen königlichen Gärten und ergoß sich am südl. Ende der Stadt in ein Rückhaltebecken (*al-Birkat aš-Šamra*); vermutl. bezog sich Jesaja mit seinem Wort von den ruhig dahinfließenden Wassern von Šiloaḥ (Jes 8,6) auf dieses Rinnsal.

Von einem Doppelkammergrab am Ölberg (16.–14. Jh. v. Chr.) abgesehen, lag die früheste bekannte Nekropole mit Schachtgrabkammern nach phöniz. Vorbild (10.–9. Jh. v. Chr.) unmittelbar westl. der salomonischen Oberstadt, westl. des Tyropoiontales. Nur die Gräber des Königshauses (zumindest bis Ahas (734/3–715/4 v. Chr.), abweichende Grabnotizen in 2 Chr sind tendenziös konstruiert) waren im SO der Davidsstadt situiert, doch ist die Gleichsetzung mit dort ergrabenen Felskammern umstritten. Zwar entstand im späten 8. Jh. vis à vis der Davidsstadt östl. des Kidrontales ein neues Gräberfeld mit Grabkammern nach phryg. und urartäischen Parallelen, doch wurde in neueren Grabungen im Oberlauf des Hinnomtales westl. der Stadt ein neues Gräberfeld entdeckt, das im 8. Jh. einsetzt und sich bis in hell. Zeit langsam das Tal hinunter bis zu dessen Mündung ins Kidrontal verschob. Dieses ist insofern von religionsgesch. Bedeutung, als in seinem Bereich auch der Molechkult (→ Moloch) stattfand, der wohl weniger in Analogie zu pun. *mlk*-Opfern, sondern eher als Verehrung des aus → Ebla, → Mari und → Ugarit bekannten Gottes Mālik zu interpretieren ist und dem Hinnomtal seine chthonische Konnotierung verlieh (Jer 7,26–35).

Mit dem Untergang des Aramäerreiches von → Damaskos im Jahre 733 und des Nord-Reiches Israel 722 v. Chr. geriet Juda unter unmittelbaren assyr. Druck: Wohl auch um die Flüchtlinge des ehemaligen Nord-Reiches aufzunehmen, erweiterte Hiskija (725–697 v. Chr.) den Stadtmauerring nach Westen und schuf in der »Neustadt« (Zeph 1,10; 2 Kg 22,14) und im »Mörser« (Zeph 1,11) eine neue Oberstadt, die vom »Oberen Teich« (Betesdateich oder *Birkat Šammām al-Baṭraq*?) ihr Wasser erhielt (Jes 7,3; 36,2; 2 Kg 18,17). Auch leitete er das Wasser des Gihon durch einen 533 m

Karte A: **Jerusalem: Mittlere Bronzezeit bis zur Zerstörung durch Nebukadnezar II. (1800 v.Chr.–587 v.Chr.)**
Karte B: **Jerusalem: Neuerrichtung in achämenidischer Zeit bis zur Zerstörung durch Titus (520 v.Chr.–70 n.Chr.)**

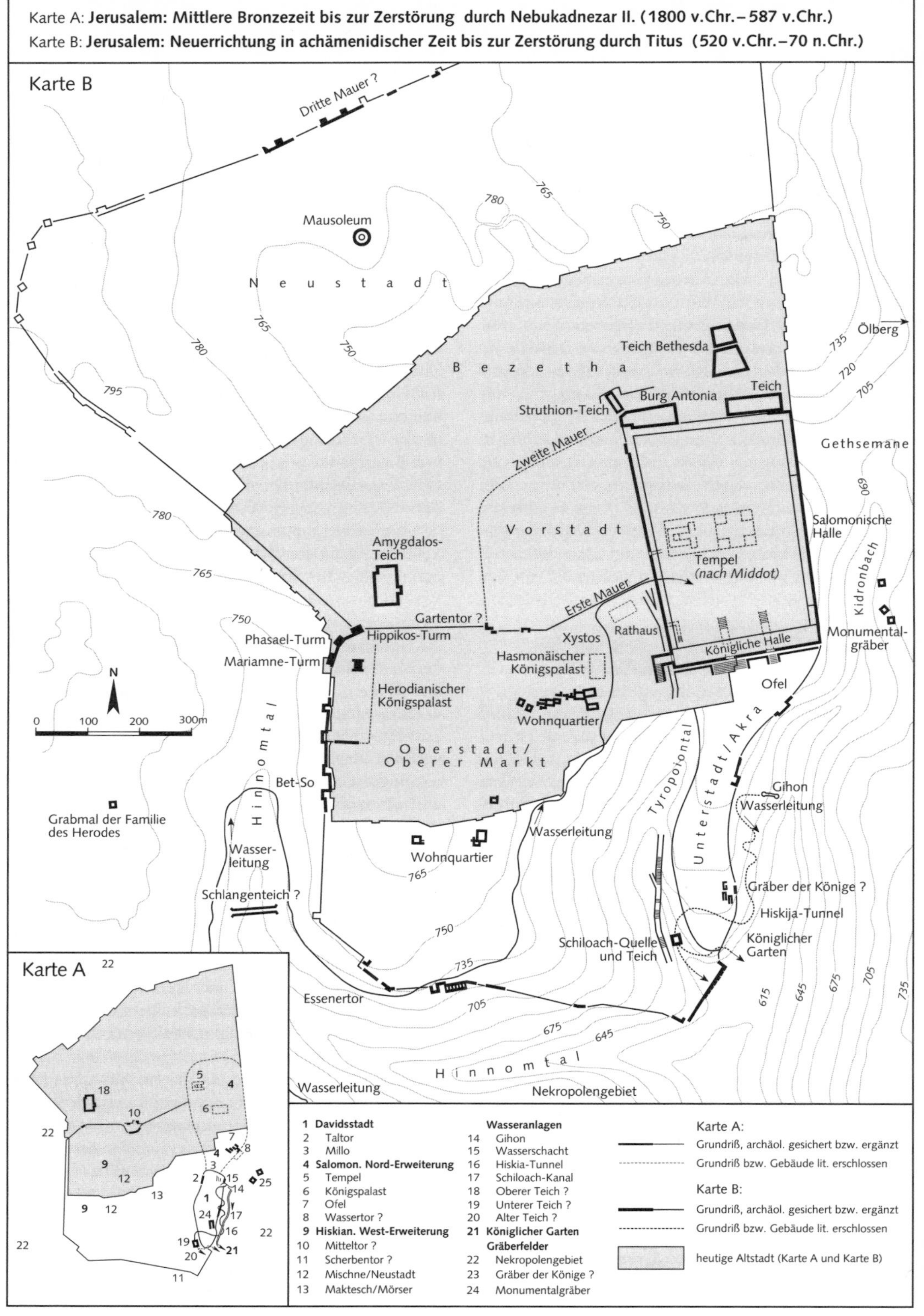

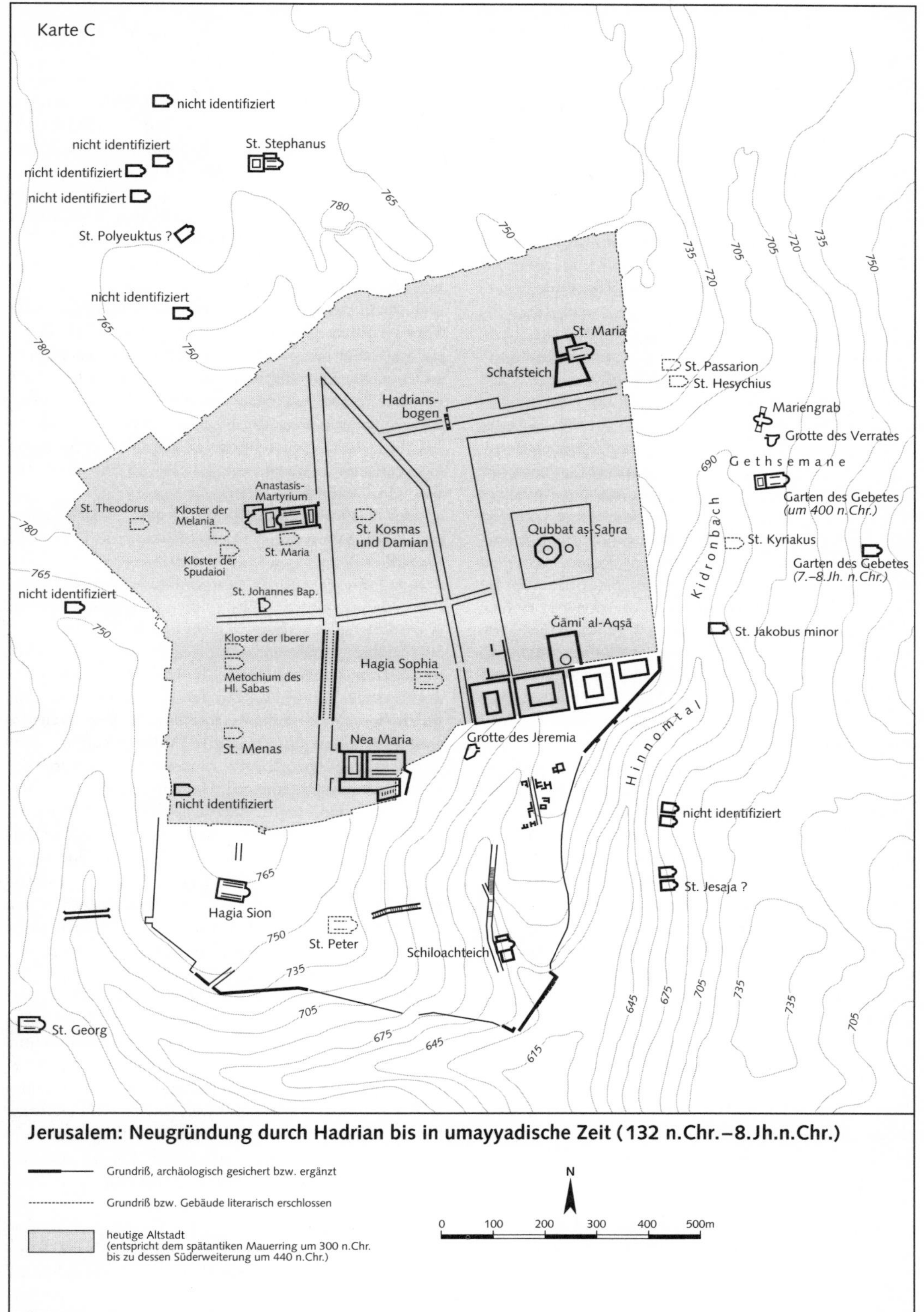

Jerusalem: Neugründung durch Hadrian bis in umayyadische Zeit (132 n.Chr.–8.Jh.n.Chr.)

Grundriß, archäologisch gesichert bzw. ergänzt

Grundriß bzw. Gebäude literarisch erschlossen

heutige Altstadt (entspricht dem spätantiken Mauerring um 300 n.Chr. bis zu dessen Süderweiterung um 440 n.Chr.)

langen Tunnel in die Stadt (KAI 189), verschloß die außerhalb der Stadt gelegene Quelle (2 Kg 20,20; 2 Chr 32,3–4.30; Sir 48,47) und sicherte die Stadt so gegen einen Angriff. Allerdings verzichtete → Sanherib 701 v.Chr. nach Tributzahlungen auf eine Stürmung der Stadt. Unter dem babylon. Herrscher → Nebukadnezar II. wurde König Jojachin mit einem Teil der judäischen Oberschicht nach Babylon deportiert (597 v.Chr.) und die Stadt nach erneuten Autonomiebestrebungen im Jahre 587 vom babylon. Heer eingenommen und nach weiteren Deportationen zerstört (2 Kg 24–25).

→ Jahwe; Juda und Israel; Judentum; Palaestina

1 K. Bieberstein, H. Bloedhorn, Jerusalem I–III, 1994 2 W.M. Moran, The Amarna Letters, 1992 3 K. Sethe, Die Ächtung feindlicher Fürsten, Völker und Dinge auf altäg. Tonscherben des MR, 1926. K.B.

B. Nachexilische Zeit

Im J. 538 v.Chr. kehrten die ersten Deportierten unter Führung von Šešbazzar zurück, 520–515 wurde z.Z. Serubabels und des Priesters Jošua unter der Ägide der Propheten Haggai und Sacharja sowie unter kritischer Opposition tritojesajanischer Kreise der Tempel wiederaufgebaut (Esr 1–6). 445 wurde → Juda zur pers. Prov. erhoben; Nehemia stellte die Stadtmauer J.s im Umfang der vorhiskijanischen Stadt wieder her (Neh 2–6; 12,27–43). 175 erwirkten führende Kreise von → Antiochos [6] IV. Epiphanes die Erlaubnis, ein Gymnasion einzurichten, was die Gründung einer Polis vorbereitete (1 Makk 1,33). Im J. 168 errichtete die seleukidische Besatzung am Aufgang zum Tempelgelände als Zwingburg die Akra (1 Makk 1,29–37), und 167 folgte die Widmung des Jahwe-Tempels an Zeus Olympios (1 Makk 1,54–61). Nach 3½-jährigem Kampf der orthodoxen Opposition eroberte → Iudas Makkabaios 164 v.Chr. die Stadt und stellte den orthodoxen Jahwe-Kult wieder her (1 Makk 4,36–61), 141 konnte Simon Makkabaios die Akra bezwingen und die volle Souveränität erringen (1 Makk 13,49–51). Unter Iohannes → Hyrkanos [2] I. (135–104) wurde die Akra abgetragen und nordwestl. des Tempelgeländes die Festung Baris errichtet (Ios. ant. Iud. 18,91 f.), die noch → Aristobulos [2] II. (67–63 v.Chr.) als Palast diente (Ios. bell. Iud. 1,120–122). Vermutlich erst unter seiner Herrschaft wurde die Stadt nach Westen erweitert (»Erste Mauer«, Ios. bell. Iud. 5,142–145), womit sie wieder den Umfang der spätvorexilischen Zeit erreichte, sowie in der neuen Vorstadt ein neuer, arch. noch nicht gesicherter Palast errichtet (Ios. bell. Iud. 1,142–144; 2,344; ant. Iud. 14,58–63; 20,189–198); kurz darauf wurde die Stadt nochmals nach Norden erweitert (»Zweite Mauer«, Ios. bell. Iud. 5,146; 158).

→ Herodes [1] d.Gr. (37–4 v.Chr.) sicherte zu Beginn seiner Herrschaft die nördl. Flanke des Tempelgeländes durch den Ausbau der Baris zur Burg Antonia (Ios. bell. Iud. 1,401; 5,238–245); außerdem baute er sich in seinem 13. Jahr am NW-Eck der Stadt einen neuen Palast (Ios. bell. Iud. 1,402; 5,161–183; ant. Iud. 15,318), der auch den röm. Statthaltern als Residenz diente (Sabinus: Ios. bell. Iud. 2,46; Ios. ant. Iud. 17,257; Pontius Pilatus: Phil. legatio ad Gaium 299–306; Gessius Florus: Ios. bell. Iud. 2,301), und ersetzte seit seinem 15. (Ios. bell. Iud. 1,401) oder 18. (ant. Iud. 15,380) Jahr den Jahwe-Tempel durch einen Neubau, wobei er dessen Temenos zu seiner noch h. erh. Größe erweiterte (Ios. bell. Iud. 5,184–237; ant. Iud. 380–402). Im Tyropoiontal zw. dem ehemaligen hasmonäischen Königspalast und dem Tempelgelände lagen der Xystos (Ios. bell. Iud. 2,344; 4,581; 5,144; 6,191; 325; 377; ant. Iud. 20,189) und das Rathaus (Ios. bell. Iud. 5,144; 6,354), beide arch. nicht nachgewiesen. Nach einem abgebrochenen Versuch unter → Herodes [8] Agrippa I. (41–44 n.Chr.), die Stadt abermals großzügig nach Norden zu erweitern (»Dritte Mauer«, Ios. bell. Iud. 2,218 f.; 5,146–160), wurden Tempel und Stadt infolge des Jüd. Aufstandes nach mehrmonatiger Belagerung durch Titus im J. 70 n.Chr. zerstört, bis auf einen Teil der westl. Befestigung geschleift und in deren Schutz die *legio X Fretensis* stationiert (Ios. bell. Iud. 5,67–7,5).

Der 2. Jüd. Aufstand unter Šimon → Bar Kochba (132–135) wurde durch Hadrians Beschluß, J. als *Colonia Aelia Capitolina* und Hauptstadt der Prov. Palaestina neu zu gründen und am Ort des Jahwe-Tempels einen Tempel für Iuppiter Capitolinus zu errichten, ausgelöst (Cass. Dio 69,12,1–3), griff aber nicht auf die Stadt über. Nach seiner Niederschlagung wurde der Baubeschluß modifiziert und der Iuppiter-Tempel (Hier. epist. 58,3) neben einem Aphrodite-Tempel (Eus. vita Const. 3,26) westl. des → *cardo* gebaut. Trotz eines angeblichen gegenläufigen, aber nur von christl. Autoren kolportierten Verbotes (Eus. HE 4,6,3 u.ö.) scheint es seit severischer Zeit wieder eine kleine jüd. Gemeinde gegeben zu haben. Dagegen dürfte die judenchristl. Gemeinde nur bis zum Bar Kochba-Aufstand bestanden haben (Eus. HE 4,5,1–4; 4,6,4; 5,12). Die von Eusebios überl. durchgängige, zunächst judenchristl. (Eus. HE 4,5,3) und anschließend heidenchristl. (HE 5,12) Bischofsliste ist nur eine unter Bischof Narcissus oder seinem Nachfolger Alexander erstellte Konstruktion zur Sicherung der apostolischen Autorität im Osterfeststreit (HE 5,22–25).

Nach Verlegung der *legio X Fretensis* nach Aila (Eus. On. 6,17–20) unter Diocletian wieder mit einem Stadtmauerring versehen, wurde die Stadt unter Constantin zu einem christl. Mnemotop: Im Anschluß an das Konzil von Nikaia (325) wurden in Bethlehem eine Basilika zum Gedenken der Menschwerdung, im Bereich der Tempelanlagen westl. des *cardo* eine Kirchenanlage zum Gedenken der Auferstehung und am Ölberg eine Basilika zum Gedenken der Himmelfahrt Christi errichtet (Eus. vita Const. 3,33–43) und von einer Stifterin namens Poimenia noch vor 374 n.Chr. durch eine Rotunde ergänzt; im Anschluß an das Konzil von Konstantinopel (381) wurde zum Gedenken der Herabkunft des Hl. Geistes die Hagia Sion und noch vor 391 am Fuß des Ölberges die Gethsemane-Kirche gebaut. Trotz Erhebung der Stadt zum Patriarchat auf dem Konzil von Chalkedon (451) schlug sich die monastische Bewegung zunächst zur antichalkedonensischen Opposition; aus dem Kontext der anschließenden Wirren stammt die erstmalige Erwähnung des Mariengrabes; etwa zur selben Zeit wurden das Haus des Kaiphas (St. Petrus) und das Praetorium des Pilatus (Hagia Sophia) mit Kirchen markiert und der Stadtmauerring durch Kaiserin → Eudokia [1] nach Süden erweitert. Nicht zuletzt zur Versorgung der Pilgerströme wurde unter Iustinian (543) im Süden der Stadt die Nea Maria als größte Kirche der Stadt mit Hospizanlagen fertiggestellt (Prok. aed. 5,6). Die Verwüstungen des Sāsānideneinfalles (614) wurden in kurzer Zeit mit sāsānidischer Hilfe beseitigt. Zwar kehrte die Stadt 630 oder 631 nochmals in byz. Hände zurück, mußte dem islamischen Heer unter Führung von Ḫālid ibn Ṯābit al-Fahmī zw. 635 und 638 aber seine Tore öffnen. Die Kirchen blieben dabei unangetastet. Am ehemaligen Tempelplatz (al-Ḥaram al-Ašraf) entstand unter Anknüpfung an jüd. Tempeltrad. eine Moschee (Ǧamiʿ al-Aqṣā), die unter Abd al-Malik durch einen Steinbau ersetzt und mit dem im J. 692 vollendeten Felsendom (Qubbat aṣ-Ṣaḫra) ausgestattet wurde.

→ Jerusalem

K. Bieberstein, H. Bloedhorn, J. I–III, 1994 · Ders., J. Baugesch., TAVO B IV 7, 1992 · K.M. Kenyon, Digging Up J., 1974 · E. Otto, J., 1980 · Y. Shiloh, A. de Groot, D.T. Ariel, Excavations at the City of David I–IV, 1980–1996 · J.J. Simons, J. in the Old Testament, 1952 · H. Vincent, Jérusalem I, 1912 · H. Vincent, F.-M. Abel, Jérusalem II, 1914–1926 · L.-H. Vincent, A.-M. Steve, Jérusalem de l'Ancien Testament I–III, 1954–1956. K.B.

III. Stätten in der Umgebung
A. Gethsemane B. Golgotha

A. Gethsemane

Gethsemane (griech. Γεθσημανεί, von hebr. גתשמנים, »Ölpresse«) ist der Name eines am Fuße des Ölberges östl. von J. gelegenen Ölgartens, der nur im NT Erwähnung findet. Laut Mk 14, 26–53 (und Parallelüberl.) ist es der Ort des Gebetes → Jesu und seiner Jünger sowie der Ort, wo Jesus, durch → Judas [1] Iškariot verraten, gefangen wurde. Seit E. des 4. Jh. ist ein Kirchenbau an dieser Stelle beschrieben (u.a. durch die → *Peregrinatio ad loca sancta* der Egeria und durch → Hieronymus) [1. 183–217; 2. 338–346; 3. 387–399].

B. Golgotha

Golgotha (griech. Γολγοθᾶ; entweder von aram. גולגעתא, »Steinkreis«, oder גולגולתא, »Schädel«) ist die im NW von J. (außerhalb der Stadttore) gelegene Hinrichtungsstätte, an der → Jesus gekreuzigt wurde (Mk 15,22 und Parallelüberl.); seit → Herodes [1] Agrippa (41–44 n. Chr.) aufgrund der Ausdehnung des Stadtgebietes eingemeindet. Unter → Constantinus [1] d.Gr. wurde der seit der Stadtumgestaltung durch Hadrianus verschüttete Ort (136 n. Chr.) wieder ausgegraben und als christl. Wallfahrtsort verehrt (ab 326 n. Chr.). 336 wurde die Grabeskirche, in deren sog. innerem Atrium der G.-Felsen lag, geweiht. Erst seit dem Neubau der Grabeskirche unter den Kreuzfahrern (1140–1149) aber befanden sich Hinrichtungsstätte und Grab unter demselben Dach. Eine Beschreibung des Ortes sowie der Jerusalemer Liturgie, in der Golgotha einen wichtigen Platz einnimmt, bietet der Reisebericht der Egeria (→ *Peregrinatio ad loca sancta*, um 400 n. Chr.); die erste bildliche Darstellung findet sich auf dem Stadtplan J.s im Madaba-Mosaik (6. Jh. n. Chr.) [1. 183–217; 2. 183–217; 3. 422–444].

1 K. Bieberstein, J. 2, 1994 2 G. Dalman, Orte und Wege Jesu, [4]1924 3 C. Kopp, Die hl. Stätten der Evangelien, 1959. I. WA.

Jesaja (hebr. Jəšāʿāhū, etwa »Gott hat errettet«). Hebr. PN, auch Titel des gleichnamigen biblischen Buches, das zum einen J. selbst zum Verfasser hat, zum anderen einen unbekannten Propheten, der als Deutero-J. in die Forsch. eingegangen ist. Daneben gibt es weitere Teile, die weder von J. noch von Deutero-J. stammen und mit Trito-J. bezeichnet werden; das Buch wirkt als ganzes sehr heterogen. Der erste der »großen Propheten«, Sohn des Amoz und Nachfahre von Juda und Tamar, wirkte im 8. Jh. v. Chr. Nach rabbinischer Legende geht sein Ursprung auf einen königlichen Stamm zurück. J.s universalistische Prophetie (Gott als alleiniger Lenker der Weltgesch.) zeichnet sich durch ausgeprägtes soziales Denken aus. Politisch plädierte er für Neutralität gegenüber den Großmächten. In der rabbinischen Überl. (z.B. Deut. rabba 2,3) gilt J. uneingeschränkt – neben Moses – als der größte Prophet.

→ Rabbinische Literatur

H. Barth, Die J.-Worte in der Josiazeit, 1977 · J. Becker, Isaias, der Prophet und sein Buch, 1968 · J. Begrich, Studien zu Deuterojesaja, 1963 · J. Carlebach, Die drei großen Propheten Jesajas, Jirmija und Jecheskel, 1932 (Ndr. 1994) · R. Clements, Isaiah and the deliverance of Jerusalem, 1980 · C. Evans, To see and not perceive: Isaiah 6.9–10 in early Jewish and Christian interpretation, 1989 · H. Haag, Der Gottesknecht bei Deuterojesaja, 1985 · J. Hirsch, Das Buch J., 1911 · F. Huber, Jahwe, Juda und die anderen Völker beim Propheten J., 1976 · C. Kuhl, Israels Propheten, 1956 · D. Millar, Isaiah 24–27 and the origin of Apocalyptic, 1976 · E. Vincent, Studien zur lit. Eigenart und zur geistigen Heimat von J., Kap. 40–55, 1977 · H. Wildberger, Königsherrschaft Gottes, J. 1–39, 1983. Y.D.

Jesus A. Die Quellen und ihre Beurteilung B. Jesus von Nazareth: Historische Rekonstruktion C. Jesus Christus: Älteste Christologie

Im Zuge der historistischen Aufklärung wurde die urchristl. Überl. über J. einer eingehenden Quellenkritik unterzogen. Der dogmatischen Einheit der göttl. und menschl. Natur J. Christi trat eine »historische Jesusfrage« zur Seite, in der nach der authentischen geschichtl. Gestalt J. im Kontext des zeitgenössischen Judentums gesucht wird. Zugleich zeigt die Gesch. der Leben-Jesu-Forschung jedoch, daß die Rekonstruktion eines »historischen J.« nicht nur abhängig von Entscheidungen in der Quellenkritik ist, sondern hermeneutischen Vorgaben unterliegt, die epochal bedingten Vorverständnissen folgen [3; 19]. Innerhalb der Theologie ist zudem strittig, welche Bed. den relativen und relativierenden histor. Aussagen über J. für die christl.-theologische Wertung seiner Person zukommt. Dies gilt um so mehr, als die histor. Untersuchungen die Gestalt J. zunehmend in den Gruppenpluralismus des zeitgenössischen Judentums einzeichnen, nicht zuletzt vermittelt auch durch die Ergebnisse jüd. Forscher [10; 11; 25].

Insgesamt sind nach den Anfängen im 18. Jh. mindestens drei intensive Phasen der Jesusforschung zu unterscheiden [23. 21 ff.]: Die erste ist geprägt durch die liberale Leben-Jesu-Theologie des 19. Jh. und die Ausarbeitung einer quellenkritischen Grundlage. Die zweite antwortet in den fünfziger und sechziger Jahren auf die in der Dialektischen Theologie und insbes. von Rudolf Bultmann erklärte theologische Irrelevanz der histor. Jesusfrage, was seinerseits eine Konsequenz aus dem Scheitern des histor. Optimismus der Leben-Jesu-Theologie hinsichtlich der Rekonstruktion einer Biographie J. war. Diese »neue Frage« ist gekennzeichnet durch den Versuch, mit Differenzkriterien J. histor. sowohl im Kontrast zum Judentum wie zum Urchristentum einzuordnen. Die dritte Phase hat vor etwas mehr als zehn Jahren im englischsprachigen Raum (»third quest«) begonnen [26]. Sie ist gekennzeichnet durch erneute quellenkritische Diskussionen, insbes. durch die Einbeziehung nicht-kanonischer urchristl. Lit., die selbstverständliche Einordnung J. in den religiösen, sozialen und kulturellen Kontext des zeitgenössischen Judentums und die damit verbundene Einbeziehung sozialgesch. und kulturanthropologischer Methoden. Dementsprechend zeichnet sich gegenwärtig ein Methodenpluralismus ab, der durch eine Kombination litergesch. mit religions-, sozial-, wirtschaftsgesch. und kulturanthropologischen (inklusive »Gender-Studies«) Fragestellungen geprägt ist.

A. Die Quellen und ihre Beurteilung

J. selbst hat nichts Schriftliches hinterlassen. Nichtchristl. ant. Zeugnisse über ihn sind spärlich, so daß sich die histor. Rekonstruktion vor allem auf nt. und außerkanonische altchristl. Texte [1; 2; 23. 35 ff] stützen muß. Sie wiederum sind literarhistor. kritisch zu sichten und im Kontext der Quellen über das Judentum im Land Israel und des frühen Christentums auszuwerten.

1. Nichtchristliche Zeugnisse

a) Der jüd. Historiker Flavius → Iosephos erwähnt um 93 n. Chr. in seinen ›Jüdischen Altertümern‹ im Zusammenhang des Berichtes über die Hinrichtung des Jakobus (62 n. Chr.), dieser sei ›der Bruder J., der Christus genannt wird‹ (Ios. ant. Iud. 20,200). Der Beiname *Christus* verdeutlicht den häufig vorkommenden Namen *Jesus* (wie Kol 4,11: ›J., der Iustus genannt wird‹), ist also kaum als Anerkennung einer messianischen Bed. J. durch Iosephos gemeint.

Umstritten ist die Authentizität des *Testimonium Flavianum* im selben Werk (Ios. ant. Iud. 18,63 f.). Anläßlich der Behandlung der Amtszeit des Präfekten von Iudaea, → Pontius Pilatus, referiert es in Kurzfassung eine im wesentlichen christl. Version des Lebens J. Die Orientierung am christl. Bekenntnis hat zur Auffassung geführt, daß die Stelle – zumal sie auch einen kompositionellen Zusammenhang unterbricht – sekundäre christl. Interpolation sei. In jüngster Zeit mehren sich jedoch Stimmen, die sie als in irgendeiner Form redigierte Fassung eines urspr. von Iosephos selbst stammenden Textes ansehen. Doch bleibt äußerst hypothetisch und umstritten, was denn der von Iosephos stammende Grundbestand sein soll. Sicher unecht sind Texte in der altruss. Version des ›Jüdischen Krieges‹, die in der griech. nicht enthalten sind und auf J. Bezug nehmen.

b) Der röm. Senator und Epistolograph C. → Plinius Caecilius Secundus (Plinius d. J.) erwähnt in seiner amtlichen Korrespondenz mit dem Kaiser Traian als Legat mit außerordentlichen Vollmachten in der Provinz → Bithynia et Pontus (um 111/113 n. Chr.) Prozesse gegen Christen. Diese gaben nach Plinius an, sich vor Sonnenaufgang an einem bestimmten Tag zu versammeln, um auf ›Christus als ihrem Gott ein Lied wechselweise anzustimmen‹ (*carmenque Christo quasi deo dicere secum invicem*, Plin. epist. 10,96,7). Da Plinius im Zuge der fortgeschrittenen röm. Kriminalisierung der Christen [22. 272 ff.] Christsein selbst (*nomen ipsum*) als Kapitalverbrechen beurteilte und bei Weigerung des Abschwörens mit der Todesstrafe ahndete, ist diese Angabe als Versuch der Verteidigung von Christen zu verstehen, die ihre Harmlosigkeit unter Beweis stellen wollten.

c) Der röm. Historiker Cornelius → Tacitus erwähnt in seinen ›Annalen‹ (ca. 115/117 n. Chr.) im Zusammenhang mit der Schilderung des Brands Roms (64 n. Chr.) und Neros Beschuldigung der Christen, daß dieser ›Name von Christus stammt, der unter Tiberius vom Procurator Pontius Pilatus hingerichtet worden war‹ (*auctor nominis eius Christus Tiberio imperitante per procuratorem Pontium Pilatum supplicio adfectus erat*, Tac. ann. 15,44,3). Sein Hauptinteresse gilt der Kennzeichnung der Christen als Menschen, ›die wegen ihrer Untaten (*flagitia*) verhaßt‹ waren und des Christentums als eines ›verhängnisvollen Aberglaubens‹ (*exitiabilis superstitio*), was dadurch unterstrichen wird, daß der Namensurheber als Verbrecher durch den röm. Statthalter von Iudaea hingerichtet wurde. Woher Tacitus seine Angaben über *Christus* hat, ist unsicher.

d) Der röm. Schriftsteller C. → Suetonius Tranquillus erwähnt in seinen Kaiserbiographien (um 120 n. Chr.), daß Claudius ›die Juden aus Rom vertrieb, weil sie, von Chrestus aufgehetzt, fortwährend Unruhe stifteten‹ (*Iudaeos impulsore Chresto assidue tumultuantes Roma expulit*, Suet. Claud. 25,4). Bemerkenswert ist hier zweierlei: 1. Die *i/e*-Verschiebung (→ »Itazismus«), die zwar nicht ungewöhnlich ist, aber, da *Chrestus* ein beliebter Sklavenname war, gewisse Assoziationen freisetzt. 2. Sueton scheint anzunehmen, daß *Chrestus* selbst hinter den Unruhen in Rom steckt. Vermutlich bezieht sich die Stelle auf eine auch in der Apostelgeschichte (18,2) erwähnte administrative Maßnahme des Kaisers Claudius (»Claudius-Edikt«), bei der jüd. Christusgläubige (wie das in Apg 18,2 genannte Ehepaar → Aquila [4] und Priscilla) aus Rom ausgewiesen wurden, weil sie wegen ihrer missionarischen Aktivität unter Juden Roms Unruhen hervorriefen. Wahrscheinlichstes Datum dafür ist das J. 49 n. Chr.

e) Der Chronograph → Iulius Africanus (um 170–240) erwähnt (vgl. FGrH II B 1157) mit Bezug auf ›das dritte Buch der Historien‹ eines Thallos (der um 52 n. Chr. eine dreibändige Weltgesch. verfaßt hat) dessen Deutung der Finsternis, die während der Kreuzigung J. weltweit hereingebrochen sein soll, als natürliche »Sonnenfinsternis«. Iulius Africanus bezeichnet dies als »unlogisch« und beharrt auf dem Mirakulösen, weil J. zur Zeit des Pessachfestes, mithin des Frühlingsvollmondes gekreuzigt wurde, was eine natürliche Sonnenfinsternis ausschließt. Ist die Quellenangabe authentisch, dann zeigt sie, daß christl. Deutungen der Passionsgeschichte J. schon früh auf Widerspruch stießen.

f) Eine syrische Hs. im Britischen Museum (Text bei [1. 2ff.]), die auf das 7. Jh. n. Chr. datiert wird, enthält den Text eines Briefes, den ein sich als stoischer Philosoph gebender Mara bar Sarapion an seinen Sohn aus einer röm. Gefangenschaft schreibt. Er parallelisiert die Hinrichtungen des Sokrates, eines Bildhauers (!) Pythagoras und J., der freilich immer nur der »weise König« der Juden genannt wird. Alle drei Tötungen hätten Unglück für ihre Landsleute zur Folge gehabt und die Hingerichteten lebten gleichwohl in ihrer Lehre oder ihrem Werk fort. Die Formulierung, die sich auf J. bezieht, deutet in Aufnahme christl. Geschichtstheologie die jüd. Niederlage im ersten großen Aufstand gegen Rom (66–70 n. Chr.), die Tötungen der Juden und deren Vertreibung in die »Zerstreuung« (→ Diaspora), als Strafe für die Hinrichtung J. Auch der Königstitel nimmt christl. Deutung auf, die etwa schon im Johannesevangelium mit weisheitlicher Trad. verbunden wird. Sein Fortleben wird zwar nicht in der Auferstehung, aber in ›den neuen Gesetzen, die er (sc. der weise König der Juden) gegeben hat‹, gesehen. Auch hier reflektiert sich weisheitliche Trad., wie der Brief zuvor deutlich macht: ›Das Leben der Menschen, mein Sohn, geht aus der Welt, ihr Lob und ihre Gaben bleiben in Ewigkeit‹. Da der Brief den Anschein erweckt, kurz nach 73 n. Chr. verfaßt worden zu sein, halten ihn manche Forscher für das älteste nichtchristl. Zeugnis (zuletzt [23. 84ff.]), andere datieren ihn auf das zweite oder dritte Jh. Letzteres erscheint am plausibelsten, zumal die Parallelisierung mit → Sokrates (und anderen Philosophen) ein Motiv aufgreift, das erst in der christl. Apologetik nachweisbar ist. Deshalb muß auch die Frage gestellt werden, ob nicht der Brief insgesamt christl. Herkunft ist.

g) Bezugnahmen auf J. in rabbinischen Quellen (→ Talmudim, → Midraschim) sind selten und hinsichtlich ihres Alters sehr umstritten. Die umfassenden Untersuchungen von Johann MAIER kommen zu dem Ergebnis, daß es keine J.-Stellen in Texten aus tannaitischer Zeit, also vor 220 n. Chr., gibt und daß auch die amoräischen eher auf spätere Interpolationen zurückzuführen sind [13. 268ff.]. Dabei wäre der Name *Jeschu* oder *Jeschu-han-nozri* später eingefügt, und es wären bestimmte rabbinische Polemiken gegen Zauberei und Verführung zum Götzendienst nachträglich auf J. umgedeutet worden. Dies gilt nach MAIER auch etwa für die Ben-Stada/Ben-Pandera-Figur. In jedem Fall dürfte die umfassende Polemik, die das in zahlreichen Versionen und Variationen verbreitete Volksbuch → *Toledot Jeschu* enthält, insgesamt erst ma. sein. Als tannaitisch gilt jedoch einigen Forschern etwa eine Baraita zum Talmudtraktat *Sanhedrin* (bSanh 43a), nach der J. am Vorabend des Pessachfestes wegen Zauberei und Verführung (zum Abfall) vor dem Sanhedrin angeklagt, gesteinigt und anschließend aufgehängt wurde (etwa [11]); freilich dürfte hier antichristl. Polemik vorliegen und kein histor. plausibles Zeugnis.

2. CHRISTLICHE ZEUGNISSE

a) Die ältesten kanonischen Zeugnisse über J. finden sich in Briefen (ca. 50–60 n. Chr.) des Paulus, einige mit dem Anspruch, vom »Herrn« selbst zu stammen, was möglicherweise heißt, daß sie ihm als durch »Offenbarung« vermittelt gelten (vgl. 1 Thess 4,15–17; 1 Kor 7,10; 9,14; 11,23–25).

b) Die umfangreichste kanonische Überl. bewahren die eine eigene christl. Literaturgattung bildenden → Evangelien (ca. 70–100 n. Chr.). Die im Zuge der ersten Phase der Leben-Jesu-Forschung ausgearbeitete Quellenkritik hat grundsätzlich eine Präferenz für die histor. Rekonstruktion den Synoptischen Evangelien (Mt, Mk, Lk) gegenüber dem Johannesevangelium zuerkannt, wobei jene zugleich nach einer »Zwei-Quellen-Theorie« (d. h. zwei Quellen für den histor. J.) literargesch. differenziert wurden. Diese Theorie besagt, daß Mk das älteste und von Mt und Lk benutzte Evangelium ist und darüber hinaus eine zweite, meist deutlich vor 70 n. Chr. datierte Quelle (manchmal auch nur als mündliche Überlieferungsschicht angesehen) Mt und Lk zugrundeliegt, die wegen der vorherrschenden Textsorte von Aussprüchen und Reden J. »Reden-« oder »Logienquelle« (»Q«) genannt wurde. Grundsätzlich wird ihr die wichtigste Rolle für die Rekonstruktion der Lehre J. zugemessen. Daneben wird aber auch zum Teil dem »Sondergut« bei Lk und Mt Gewicht für die histor. Rekonstruktion gegeben. Während zunächst Mk für den chronologisch-geographischen Aufriß der Vita Jesu histor. Vertrauen geschenkt wurde, hat sich durch literar-, form- und redaktionsgesch. Analyse gezeigt, daß dieser Rahmen sekundär ist. Hinter diesen ältesten lit. Quellen wurden aufgrund der Unterscheidung von redaktionellen Rahmungen und älteren Trad. Überl.-Komplexe oder Slgg. mit unterschiedlichen redaktionellen oder kompositorischen Stadien erschlossen. Die diachrone literar- und formkritische Analyse hat zudem den Überl.-Stoff der Synoptischen Evangelien insgesamt in einzelne kleine Einheiten von Worten (Logien, Gleichnisse) und Geschichten zerlegt, die charakteristische Formelemente aufweisen und literatursoziologisch den Bedürfnissen des Urchristentums entstammen. Diese Überl.-Lage bedeutet, daß der histor. Rückschluß auf J. selbst besonderer Kriterien bedarf, da die diachrone Analyse allenfalls zu Überl. der ältesten Gemeinden führt.

c) Nicht-kanonische altchristl. Zeugnisse wurden in den ersten beiden Phasen der histor. Jesusfrage zwar auch beachtet und unter dem Begriff der → *Agrapha* gesammelt. Doch erst durch einige Vertreter des »third quest« in Amerika werden sie erstmals als gleichberechtigt berücksichtigt, zum Teil aufgrund von umstrittenen Frühdatierungen [12]. Bes. Bed. kommt folgenden Texten zu:

Papyrus Egerton 2: Hier handelt es sich um Fragmente aus einem unbekannten Codex mit einem Streitgespräch und Wundergeschichten J., die freilich deutliche Beeinflussung durch die kanonischen Evangelien aufweisen und kaum vor 150 n. Chr. entstanden sein dürften. POxy. 840: Ein 1905 in Äg. gefundenes Pergament(!)-Blatt, das aus einem nach 400 geschriebenen Codex stammt und Variationen synoptischen Stoffes (Mk 7; Mt 23) enthält. Die Datier. in das 1. Jh. ist unsicher.

Thomasevangelium: Eine der synoptischen »Logienquelle« verwandte Sammlung von 114 Logien, 1945 in → Nag Hammadi gefunden und Teil der dortigen Bibliothek koptischer Schriften (NHCod II/2). Griech. Fragmente waren schon aus den Oxyrhynchos-Papyri (POxy. 1; 654; 655) bekannt, weswegen das Thomasevangelium nicht nach etwa 140 n. Chr. entstanden sein dürfte. Umstritten ist angesichts der Konvergenz von etwa 50 % der Logien mit dem Stoff der kanonischen Evangelien, ob das Thomasevangelium als unabhängiges Zeugnis gelten kann – so vor allem Vertreter des »third quest« in Amerika – oder nur eine gnostisch überarbeitete und erweiterte Version insbes. der synoptischen Trad. darstellt.

Petrusevangelium: Griech. Fragmente vor allem der Passionsgeschichte eines Evangeliums, dessen Erzähler vorgibt, Petrus zu sein, wurden 1886 in Oberägypten gefunden. Die Hs. wird auf das 8./9. Jh. datiert. Die Entstehungszeit dürfte vor 200 n. Chr. (wegen paralleler Fragmente in POxy. 2949 und 4009), frühestens jedoch um 150 n. Chr. liegen. Ob im Petrusevangelium ein sehr altes »Kreuzevangelium« überliefert wird (so [7. 506 ff.]), ist sehr fraglich. Plausibler ist, daß es die vier kanonischen Evangelien voraussetzt.

Geheimes Markusevangelium: Ein im Kloster Mar Saba bei Jerusalem 1958 von Morton SMITH entdeckter und später edierter Brief des → Clemens [3] von Alexandreia enthält ein Zitat aus einem »geheimen Markusevangelium«, in dem die Auferweckung eines Jünglings in → Bethania [1] (im Anschluß an Mk 10,34) erzählt wird [21]. Die Hs. ist seit ihrer Entdeckung nicht mehr einsehbar gewesen. Selbst wenn der Brief echt sein sollte, dürfte das Zitat keiner Vorstufe des Mk-Evangeliums entstammen, sondern einer (gnostischen) Überarbeitung desselben (in Variation von Jo 11) aus dem 2. Jh.

3. BEURTEILUNG

Die nichtchristl. Zeugnisse sind allesamt Reaktionen zum Teil sehr polemischer Art auf das entstehende Christentum bzw. dessen »Stifter« Christus und reflektieren selbst schon christl. Deutungen. Am meisten Gewicht ist für die histor. Rekonstruktion der Tacitus-Stelle zu geben, da sie u. a. für die Historizität J. und dafür spricht, daß er in einem röm. Prozeß vom Procurator von Iudaea verurteilt und als Verbrecher hingerichtet wurde. Bei den christl. Zeugnissen dürfte trotz mancher gegenteiliger Tendenz in der gegenwärtigen Forsch. weiterhin historisch am ergiebigsten und verläßlichsten die kanonische, insbes. die synoptische Überl. sein, wobei in Einzelfällen nicht ausgeschlossen werden soll, daß nicht-kanonische Überl. miteinbezogen werden kann. Die diachrone Analyse der kanonischen Überl. läßt trotz mancher gegenteiliger Annahmen [15] einen direkten Rückschluß auf den histor. J. nicht zu. Vielmehr bedarf es dafür eines differenzierten methodischen Vorgehens, so daß Rekonstruktionen immer hypothetisch bleiben. Gleichwohl ist extreme Skepsis, die jeglicher Rekonstruktion widerrät, nicht angezeigt. Die literarhistor. zusammen mit rel.- und sozialgesch. Methoden können Kriterien entwickeln, die J. und seine erste Anhängerschaft (»Jesusbewegung«) sowohl im Kontext des zeitgenössischen Judentums im Land Israel als auch in dem seiner Wirkung im frühen Christentum verorten lassen [24]. Histor. Plausibilität ist dabei jedoch neben den quellenkritischen Entscheidungen immer davon bestimmt, wie man die Korrespondenz mit diesen Kontexten und die Differenz zu ihnen beurteilt.

B. JESUS VON NAZARETH: HISTORISCHE REKONSTRUKTION

1. HERKUNFT UND PRÄGUNG

J. stammt aus einer jüdischen, als davidisch geltenden Familie (Vater Joseph, Mutter Maria bzw. Mirjam; neben Schwestern werden vier Brüder Mk 6,3 namentlich genannt, unter ihnen der später für die Jerusalemer Gemeinde wichtige Jakobus). Der griech. Name Ἰησοῦς (*Iēsús*) ist in der LXX Wiedergabe von hebräisch *Yᵉhōšuaʿ* (»JHWH hilft«) sowie der späteren Form *Yēšuaʿ* und war bis zum 2. Jh. n. Chr. im Judentum verbreitet. Geboren vielleicht noch vor 4 v. Chr. (weil noch zu Lebzeiten Herodes' [1] d.Gr., wenn Mt 2/Lk 1,5 historisch; doch steht dagegen der Lk 2,1 erwähnte Census unter Quirinius in der Provinz Iudaea, der nicht vor 6 n. Chr., eher später stattfand), wuchs J. auf in → Galilaea, und zwar in oder bei → Nazareth (Mk 6,1 »seine Heimatstadt«; deshalb zur Unterscheidung von anderen

Namensträgern Ἰ. ὁ Ναζαρηνός/*Nazarēnós* oder Ναζωραῖος/*Nazōraíos* u.ä. in den Evangelien; auch »J. von Nazareth«). → Aramäisch war die Umgangssprache in Galilaea zur Zeit J.; → Hebräisch war die heilige Sprache bzw. die Sprache der rel. Lehre, weswegen Hebräischkenntnisse bei J. vorausgesetzt werden können. Nicht gleich wahrscheinlich sind Griechischkenntnisse. Unterricht im Hebräischen und Kenntnisse der Bibel und der rel. Traditionen wurden J. wohl wie vielen Kindern durch den Vater (vielleicht auch in einer Schule) vermittelt; auszuschließen ist eine höhere Gelehrsamkeit, wie sie z.B. der aus der Priesteraristokratie stammende → Iosephos besaß. Nach Mk 6,3 war J. wie der Vater (Mt 13,55) *téktōn*, d.h. ein Bauhandwerker, was ihn sozialstratigraphisch der Unterschicht und ökonomisch den relativ Armen (*pénētes*), aber nicht den Bettelarmen (*ptōchoí*) zuordnet.

Der Charakter des → Judentums im Land Israel war zur Zeit J. einerseits geprägt durch gemeinsame Institutionen (Tempel, → Synagoge, Haus), Überzeugungen (→ Monotheismus, Erwählung, Tora) und Praktiken (Tempelkult, Beschneidung, → Sabbat-Heiligung, Torastudium, Speise- und Reinheitsvorschriften), andererseits durch einen Pluralismus von Gruppen (Pharisäer/→ *Pharisaíoi*, → Sadduzäer, → Qumran-Essener, prophetisch-charismatische Gruppen usw.), in denen diese gemeinsamen Identitätsmerkmale unterschiedlich und kontrovers interpretiert wurden, abhängig auch von der sozioökonomischen Position. J. galiläischer Kontext war Teil dieses »common Judaism« [16] und seines Pluralismus. Er war kaum hell.-urban, sondern eher konservativ jüdisch und ländlich; die hellenistischer geprägten Städte Sepphoris und Tiberias z.B. sind keine Stätten der Wirksamkeit J. Unplausibel ist darum ebenso J. Charakterisierung als eines »jüdischen Kynikers«, der Weisheit und Magie verbunden hat [7. 119ff.; 553f.], wie seine Kennzeichnung als »marginaler Jude« [14]. Die mit seinem öffentl. Auftreten (nach Lk 3,23 im 30. Lebensjahr) verbundene Wandertätigkeit hat mit dem religionssoziologisch als Charismatismus [22. 171ff.; 23. 175ff.] zu kennzeichnenden Charakter seiner Bewegung zu tun, der typisch für sozioökonomische und damit verbundene Traditionskrisen ist. Rel. entscheidend geprägt wurde J. durch den Priester Iohannes den Täufer, der in Anknüpfung an biblische Mose-Elia-Typologie eine messianisch-prophetische Bußbewegung ins Leben gerufen hatte. Seine Erwartung eines radikalen Endgerichtes, aus dem nur die durch die Taufe im Jordan symbolisch Entsühnten gerettet würden (Mt 3,7ff./Lk 3,7ff.), nimmt frühjüdische-apokalyptische Vorstellungen auf; seine asketische Lebensweise weist zusammen mit der Sammlung einer engeren Anhängerschaft, zu der J. gehörte (nach Jo 3,22ff. hätte J. dem Täufer sogar »assistiert«), der Mobilisierung von Massen und herrschaftskritischen Aspekten (Mk 6,17f.: Kritik der verbotenen Verwandtenehe des Herodes Antipas) charismatische Züge auf. Andere Einflüsse auf J., vor allem pharisäische in der Tora-Auslegung, dürften durch die Breitenwirkung dieser Gruppen vermittelt sein, die bei den Pharisäern am intensivsten war.

2. Grundzüge des Wirkens und der Lehre

J. öffentliches Auftreten – wahrscheinlich unmittelbar nach dem Martyrium des Täufers (Mk 1,14) – ist verbunden mit der Manifestation charismatischer Heilungskräfte (*dynámeis*: Mk 6,2. 5. 14 u.ö.), insbes. Exorzismen (Mk 1,21ff. u.ö.), die als Ausweis seiner göttlich legitimierten Sendung und Vollmacht (*exusía*: Mk 1,22 u.ö.) gelten. Insofern wurde in jüngster Zeit mit Recht die Nähe J. zu thaumaturgischen Heilern gegen die vor allem in der protestantischen Forsch. vorherrschende Stilisierung J. als eschatologischer »Prediger« betont (so zuletzt aber wieder [17]). Entscheidend ist aber, daß er diese außeralltäglichen Kräfte im Kontext einer wandercharismatischen, wirtschafts- und familienfremden (wohl auch sexualasketischen) Bewegung einer engeren Jünger- und weiteren Anhängerschaft entfaltet und prophetisch als partielle und punktuelle Gegenwart des endzeitlichen Gottesreiches apokalyptisch deutet.

Die Evangelien verbinden Jesu Auftreten von Beginn an mit der Berufung von Jüngern als Nachfolgern (Mk 1,16ff.), wobei deren Kern möglicherweise aus dem Jüngerkreis des Täufers kam (Jo 1,35ff.). Nicht wenige waren Fischer vom Nordufer des Genezareth, also auch aus der Unterschicht. Sie bildeten mit J. eine Lebens- und Schicksalsgemeinschaft und nahmen an seinem charismatischen Heilen teil (Mk 6,7ff.). Dies impliziert das Verlassen der Familien – auch zeitweise der Ehefrauen – und eine »vagabundierende« Lebensweise in Armut entsprechend der religionssoziologisch beschriebenen »Selbststigmatisierung« charismatischer Bewegungen. Hat J. selbst einen Zwölferkreis geschaffen, so dürfte er das eschatologisch restaurierte Zwölfstämmevolk Israel repräsentieren. Eine weitere Anhängerschaft, die zum größten Teil ortsstabil blieb, aber auch die »Nachfolge« antrat, unterstützte diese engere Jüngerschaft mäzenatisch; zu ihnen gehörten auch Frauen (Mk 15,40f.; Lk 8,2f.). Manchmal wird eine frauenfreundliche, emanzipatorische Tendenz in der Jesusbewegung vermutet [18]. Egalitäre Züge verdanken sich jedoch hauptsächlich dem Charismatismus.

Mit dem Stichwort »Gottesreich« oder »Königsherrschaft Gottes« (*basileía tu theú*) akzentuiert J. in seiner Verkündigung und insbes. in Gleichnissen die neue Situation im eschatologischen Drama gegenüber Iohannes. Dieser apokalyptische Horizont der Botschaft J. wird zwar neuerdings wieder bestritten, zumal durch Vertreter des »third quest« und nicht zuletzt aufgrund der Präferenz für das (gnostische) Thomasevangelium [4; 7], aber schwerlich mit Recht. Denn die Einbettung der Gottesreichverkündigung J. in apokalyptische Zusammenhänge, insbes. ihre Verbindung mit der Gerichtspredigt, kann kaum als nur nachträgliche christl. Interpretation gelten. Seine charismatischen Heilungen kommentiert J. als partielle und punktuelle Gegenwart des endzeitlichen Gottesreiches (Mt 12,28/Lk 11,20), das nahegekommen, aber insgesamt noch zukünftig ist

(Mt 6,11; Lk 11,2f. u.ö.). Das Stichwort ist biblisch vorbereitet, kommt ansonsten nur gelegentlich im nachbiblisch-jüdischen Schrifttum vor und stellt offenbar ein in Krisensituationen aktualisierbares Symbol für eine göttl. (ideale) Herrschaft dar, in der die bösen Kräfte besiegt und Not und Mangel jeglicher Art aufgehoben sind. Die Bettelarmen und Notleidenden sowie die (Waisen-)Kinder, denen das Gottesreich bedingungslos zugesprochen wird (Lk 6,20f.; Mk 9,33ff.; 10,14f.), gelten als Kern der eschatologischen Sammlung des Gottesvolkes. Hier zeigt sich der Anspruch J., Mandatar und Vollstrecker einer die jüd. Gesellschaft von Armut, ökonomischer und religiöser Not heilenden Herrschaft Gottes zu sein. Dem entspricht eine sozialintegrative Verhaltensweise, wie seine Mahlgemeinschaften mit »Sündern und Zöllnern« (Mk 2,13ff.) zeigen. Er verteidigt dies gegen Kritik in Gleichnissen (Lk 15,1ff.; Mt 20,1ff.). Hier finden sich zwar für die spätere Ausbreitung des Christusglaubens unter Nichtjuden in den mediterranen Zentren Anknüpfungspunkte, doch kommen die Völker im apokalyptischen Konzept Jesu allenfalls marginal vor, nicht programmatisch.

Die Institutionen und Grundüberzeugungen sowie die gemeinsamen Praktiken des Judentums werden von J. nicht grundsätzlich in Frage gestellt. Freilich findet sich Kritik, etwa an Vorgängen im Tempelbezirk, verbunden möglicherweise mit unheilsprophetischer Ansage einer göttl. Strafaktion (Mk 11,1ff.; 14,58), und eine teilweise abweichende Auslegung der Tora, insbes. der Sabbat → *halakha* (der pharisäische Grundsatz, daß Lebensgefahr den Sabbat verdrängt, wird auch auf die Notsituation des Hungers ausgedehnt: Mk 2,23ff. u.ö.), des Scheidungsrechtes (Scheidung ist, ähnlich wie in der pharisäischen Schule Schammais, nur im Fall des Ehebruchs erlaubt: Mt 5,32 u.ö.) und der Speise- und Reinheitsvorschriften (ethische »Herzensreinheit« wird über rituelle Reinheit gestellt: Mk 7,1ff.). Radikalisiert werden entsprechend dem sozialintegrativen Zug der Lehre Jesu auch die traditionellen Solidaritätsgebote des Judentums (»Nächstenliebe« auch gegenüber dem Feind, Gewaltverzicht, Pflicht zur Versöhnung, Schulderlaß: Lk 6,20–49/Mt 5–7). Eine Auseinandersetzung mit den machtpolitischen und sozioökonomischen Problemen fehlt ebenso wie weithin auch eine Kritik der jüd. Elite. Kritisiert werden pauschal Reiche. Konflikte mit Pharisäern, Sadduzäern und Schriftgelehrten sind, wo nicht überhaupt Retrojektionen aus späteren christlich-jüdischen Konflikten, motiviert durch unterschiedliche Auffassungen über Grundüberzeugungen und Praktiken des Judentums.

3. Das Schicksal Jesu

Das Ende J. in Jerusalem steht im Zusammenhang einer traditionellen Frömmigkeitsübung, nämlich der Wallfahrt zum Pessachfest. Die Darstellungen der Passionsgeschichte in den Evangelien sind zum Teil widersprüchlich, die Annahmen über ältere Überlieferungskomplexe hinter ihnen höchst hypothetisch. Sehr wahrscheinlich gestalten tendenziöse Retrojektionen aus Konflikterfahrungen späterer Zeit die Darstellungen, wobei apologetische Interessen der Abwehr römischer Kriminalisierung von Christen eine Rolle spielen. Als gesichert kann nur gelten, daß J. in einem röm. Prozeß (→ *coercitio*) von dem wegen des Wallfahrtsfestes in Jerusalem weilenden Procurator Pontius Pilatus als Aufständischer (»Räuber«) bzw. sozialbanditischer Gegenkönig (Kreuztitulus: »König der Juden«) verurteilt und durch die für Provinziale übliche Kreuzigung hingerichtet wurde. Ein vorgängiger jüd. Prozeß (vor dem → Synhedrion) ist ausgeschlossen, eine auch nur »offiziöse« jüd. Beteiligung unwahrscheinlich [6; 8]. In der Datierung des Todestages stimmen die Evangelien insofern überein, als sie denselben Wochentag (Freitag) nennen. Strittig ist, ob dies der Vorabend des Pessachfestes (14. Nisan, so Jo 18,28; 19,31) oder der erste Tag des Pessachfestes (15. Nisan, so die synopt. Evangelien) war. Dementsprechend variiert die Datierung des Todesjahres. Es muß ein Amtsjahr des Procurators Pontius Pilatus sein (27–34 n.Chr.). Die johanneische Chronologie legt das Jahr 30 (was heute weithin als Todesjahr angenommen wird) oder 33 näher, die synoptische 27 oder 34 n.Chr. [23. 152ff.].

C. Jesus Christus: Älteste Christologie

Als apokalyptisch-charismatische Bewegung erhebt J. Auftreten von Beginn an einen Sendungsanspruch: Er ist der gesandte und autorisierte Vollstrecker der endzeitlichen Herrschaft Gottes. Das Stichwort »Glaube« haftet dementsprechend in der synoptischen Überl. an der Wundertradition: Glauben heißt, J. die charismatischen Heilungskräfte zuzutrauen, die er als Ausweis des Gekommenseins des endzeitlichen Reiches hat. Möglicherweise hat J. sich selbst auch als Prophet gesehen. Auch hat er angesichts des Schicksals seines Lehrers vermutlich mit dem eigenen Martyrium gerechnet, freilich – wenn die Einsetzung des »Herrenmahls« authentisch ist – verbunden mit der Erwartung, daß sein Tod eine heilsgesch. Rolle zur Aufrichtung des Gottesreiches unter seiner Anhängerschaft spielt (vgl. 1 Kor 11,23ff.; Mk 14,22ff.; Mt 26,26ff.). Wenig wahrscheinlich, aber umstritten ist, ob er sich als → Messias/Gesalbter im Sinne der Erwartung eines idealen Herrschers in davidischer Linie verstand. Vieles spricht dafür, daß diese Deutung erst nach seiner Hinrichtung als »König der Juden« und nur verbunden mit einer Reihe anderer messianischer Erwartungen (insbes. der des »Menschensohns«) auf ihn angewandt wurde.

Fraglos historisch ist, daß bald nach der Hinrichtung J. unter seiner Jünger- und Anhängerschaft zahlreiche visionäre Erfahrungen einsetzten (1 Kor 15,3ff.), die, weil sie als Erscheinungen vom Himmel her galten, so gedeutet wurden, daß der tote J. auferweckt und in den Himmel versetzt wurde. Diese Interpretation orientiert sich an jüd. Märtyrertheologie. Doch zugleich entfaltet sie das apokalyptische Selbstverständnis weiter, insofern als sie mit der Entrückung in den Himmel die Einsetzung in eine himmlische Herrschaftsstellung als »Sohn

Gottes« und → Kyrios (Röm 1,3 ff.) verbindet. Nach der ältesten synoptischen Trad. wird J. auch die Rolle des »Menschensohnes« zugeschrieben, einer himmlischen Gestalt, die nach jüd. Apokalyptik (äthiop. Hen 37–71; 4 Esra 13 in Aufnahme der eher metaphorischen Menschensohn-Trad. in Dan 7) Vermittler des endzeitlichen Gerichts und der Rettung vom Himmel her und Anführer des himmlischen Heeres ist (äthiop. Hen 48,10; 52,4 identifiziert ihn auch mit dem »Messias«). Strittig ist, ob. J. selbst schon auf eine solche Gestalt hingewiesen und sich in Beziehung zu ihr gesetzt hat [23. 447 ff.]. Jedenfalls stehen alle auf J. angewandten »Titel« im Kontext einer messianisch-apokalyptischen Deutung, nach der sein irdisches Auftreten und Schicksal Teil einer endzeitlichen Heilsinitiative Gottes ist, die mit der baldigen Parusie des Auferstandenen als Herrscher ihr Ende findet. Dementsprechend wird J. schon früh (Phil 2,6 ff.) in ein umfassendes Konzept eingeordnet, wonach er als präexistenter Gottessohn zur Rettung auf die Erde gesandt, nach seinem (sühnenden) Tod in den Himmel zurückgekehrt ist und dort als der eschatologische Richter, Retter und Herrscher zur Vollendung bereit steht. Diese christologische Entwicklung ist religionssoziologisch verbunden mit der »Entpersonalisierung« des Charismas in der Jesusbewegung und enthält zugleich Elemente der Universalisierung, die ihre Ausbreitung in die urbanen Zentren des Mittelmeeraums begünstigte.

→ Bibel; Christentum; Evangelium; Jerusalem; Judentum

1 J. B. Aufhauser, Ant. J.-Zeugnisse (Kleine Texte 126), ^{3}1925 **2** F. F. Bruce, Außerbiblische Zeugnisse über J. und das frühe Christentum, ^{3}1993 **3** M. J. Borg, J. in Contemporary Scholarship, 1994 **4** Ders., J. Der neue Mensch, 1993 **5** C. Burchard, J. von Nazareth, in: J. Becker (Hrsg.), Die Anfänge des Christentums, 1987, 12–58 **6** C. Cohn, Der Prozeß und Tod J. aus jüdischer Sicht, 1997 **7** J. D. Crossan, Der histor. J., 1994 **8** Ders., Who Killed J.?, Exposing the Roots of Anti-Semitism in the Gospel Story of the Death of J., 1995 **9** C. A. Evans, Life of J. Research. An Annotated Bibliography (New Testament Tools and Studies 13), 1989 **10** D. Flusser, J. in Selbstzeugnissen und Bilddokumenten, 1968 **11** J. Klausner, J. von Nazareth, ^{23}1952 **12** H. Koester, Ancient Christian Gospels. Their History and Development, 1990 **13** J. Maier, J. von Nazareth in der talmudischen Überl., 1978 **14** J. P. Meier, A Marginal Jew. Rethinking the Historical J., Vol. 1, 1991; Vol. 2, 1994 **15** R. Riesner, J. als Lehrer. Eine Unt. zum Ursprung der Evangelien-Überl. (WUNT 2. Reihe 7), ^{4}1993 **16** E. P. Sanders, Judaism. Practice and Belief 63 BCE – 66CE, 1992 **17** Ders., Sohn Gottes. Eine histor. Biographie J., 1996 **18** E. Schüssler-Fiorenza, Zu ihrem Gedächtnis ... Eine feministische Rekonstruktion der christl. Ursprünge, 1988 **19** A. Schweitzer, Gesch. der Leben-Jesu-Forschung, ^{9}1984 **20** E. Schweizer, J., das Gleichnis Gottes. Was wissen wir wirklich vom Leben J.?, 1995 **21** M. Smith, Auf der Suche nach dem histor. J, 1974 **22** E. Stegemann, W. Stegemann, Urchristl. Sozialgesch. Die Anfänge im Judentum und die Christusgemeinden in der mediterranen Welt, ^{2}1997 **23** G. Theissen, A. Merz, Der histor. J. Ein Lehrbuch, ^{2}1997 **24** G. Theissen, D. Winter, Die Kriterienfrage in der Jesusforsch. (Novum testamentum et orbis antiquus 34), 1997 **25** G. Vermes, J. der Jude, 1993 **26** B. Witherington III, The J. Quest. The Third Search for the Jew of Nazareth, 1995. E. STE.

Ietragoras (Ἰητραγόρας/Ἰητραγόρης) aus Milet, wurde 499 v. Chr. von den aufständischen Ioniern beauftragt, die aus Naxos heimkehrende persische Flotte abzufangen und die perserfreundlichen Tyrannen auf den Schiffen gefangenzunehmen (Hdt. 5,36 f.).

U. Walter, Herodot und die Ursachen des Ionischen Aufstandes, in: Historia 42, 1993, 257–278. E. S.-H.

Jeu s. Nag Hammadi

Jevenstedt im Kreis Rendsburg (Schleswig-Holstein). Gräberfeld der german. vorröm. Eisenzeit (6.–4. Jh. v. Chr.) mit Beigaben von bemalten Tongefäßen und Eisenschlacken in den Gräbern, was eine Sonderstellung innerhalb der → Jastorf-Kultur bedeutet und als Hinweis auf frühe Eisenverarbeitung durch Kontakte zur → Hallstatt-Kultur verstanden wird. Raseneisenerzlager und Schlackenanhäufungen in der Nachbarschaft sind bekannt, aber nicht sicher zuweisbar.

→ Eisen; Germanische Archäologie

H. Hingst, Jevenstedt, 1974. V. P.

Iezdegerd s. Yazdgird

Jezira, Sefer ha- (hebr. »Buch der Schöpfung«). Versuch einer systematischen Beschreibung der fundamentalen Prinzipien der Weltordnung. Das nur wenige Seiten umfassende hebr.-sprachige Werk, das in drei verschiedenen Rezensionen vorliegt, entstand wohl zw. dem 3. und 6. Jh. und gehört damit zu den ältesten Texten der jüd. Esoterik. Als Elemente der Schöpfung werden im ersten Teil die zehn Urzahlen sowie im zweiten Teil die zweiundzwanzig Buchstaben des hebr. Alphabets vorgestellt, durch deren Kombination Gott ›auf geheimen Wegen der Weisheit‹ die Welt schuf. Bes. bei den Ausführungen über die Kombination der Buchstaben, die mit geheimen Kräften ausgestattet seien, spielen Mikrokosmos-Makrokosmos-Spekulationen, die Verbindungen zw. dem menschlichen Körper, der Welt der Gestirne sowie der Ordnung der Zeit herstellen, eine bed. Rolle. Neben frühjüd. Schöpfungsvorstellungen finden sich in diesem Werk auch Gedanken späthell. und spätneuplatonischer → Zahlenmystik. Das Werk, das in seiner Ausdrucksweise oft sehr opak und dunkel wirkt, bildete ab dem frühen MA die Grundlage zahlreicher Komm.

J. Dan, The Ancient Jewish Mysticism, 1993, 198–211 • L. Goldschmidt, Sepher Jezirah. Das Buch der Schöpfung, 1894 (Ndr. 1969) • I. Gruenwald, Some Critical Notes on the First Part of the Sēfer Yezīrā, in: Rev. des Études Juives 132, 1973, 475–528 • J. Maier, Die Kabbalah. Einf. – Klass. Texte – Erläuterungen, 1995, 38–43 • Ph. Merlan, Zur

Zahlenlehre im Platonismus und im Sefer Yezira, in: Journ. of the History of Philosophy 3, 1965, 167–181 • G. SCHOLEM, Die jüd. Mystik in ihren Hauptströmungen, 1967, 81–84. B.E.

Ifriqiya s. Afrika

Igel (ἐχῖνος χερσαῖος, *ericius*, *ire-* oder *erinaceus*, selten *echinus*), Erinaceus europaeus L., ein Säugetier aus der Ordnung der Insektenfresser. Seine typischen Eigenschaften werden von Aristoteles u. a. Autoren beschrieben: die Stacheln (Aristot. hist. an. 1,6,490b 29 und 3,11,517b 24, vgl. Emp. fr. 83 DIELS/KRANZ; Aristoph. Pax 1086), die Lage der Hoden im Körperinneren (Aristot. hist. an. 3,1,509b 9) und seine Begattung in aufrechter Haltung, Bauch gegen Bauch (ebd. 5,2,540a 3 f.; Plin. nat. 10,174). Sein Stachelfell wurde zum Kämmen von Tuchen benutzt (Plin. nat. 8,135), deshalb wurde er gejagt (Nemes. cynegetica 48). Er zerstöre sein Fell mit seinem angeblich giftigen Urin, sobald er zum Jagdziel werde; daher erhängte man ihn (Plin. nat. 8,134 und 30,65; Anth. Pal. 6,45 und 169). Daß er Obst und Trauben sammle (Plin. nat. 8,133; Plut. de sollertia animalium 16 = mor. 971e-f), ist natürlich ein oft wiederholtes Märchen. Das Fleisch des I. wurde gegessen (Plin. nat. 30,65), doch verordnete man es in erster Linie medizinisch: u.a. bei Wassersucht (Plin. nat. 30,105) und Harnverhalten (Plin. nat. 30,65) sowie Spasmen (Plin. nat. 30,110), Geschwüren und Narben. Die Asche des I. benutzte man gegen Haarausfall (Plin. nat. 29,107). Als Schlangenvertilger hielt man den I. schon in früher Zeit als Haustier (vgl. Aristot. hist. an. 8(9),612b 6) und bewunderte sein kluges Verhalten als Vorratssammler (Plin. nat. 8,133; Plut. l.c. 16 = mor. 971 e-f), als Wetterprophet (Aristot. hist. an. 8(9),6,612b 4–10) sowie bei der Selbstverteidigung durch »Einigeln« (Archilochos 118 BURCK = 103 DIEHL; Lykophr. 1093; Plin. nat. 8,133; Ail. nat. 6,54). Eine altkorinth. Vase [1. 1,19; Abb. 2,279] bildet ihn mit anderen Tieren als Unglückspropheten bei der Ausfahrt des → Amphiaraos ab. Der I. wurde im Analogiezauber gegen Wahnsinn verwendet (Plin. nat. 30,95). In christl. Zeit hat man oft den Lv 11,5 und Dt 14,7 erwähnten unreinen Klippschliefer (*choerogryllus*) teils als → Hase, teils als I. gedeutet.

1 KELLER. C.HÜ.

Igeler Säule s. Säulenmonumente

Igilgili (pun. *ʾj glgl[t]*?, »Insel des Schädels«?). Phönik. oder pun. Gründung, in der späteren → Mauretania Sitifensis – westl. von der Mündung des Ampsaga – gelegen, h. Djidjelli. Belegstellen: Plin. nat. 5,20; Ptol. 4,2,11; Itin. Anton. 39,7; 40,5; Tab. Peut. 3,1; Amm. 29,5,5; Notitia episcopatuum Mauretaniae Sitifensis 4[a]; Anon. Geographia 40 (GGM II 505); Geogr. Rav. 40,22; 88,20; Guido p. 132,29. Augustus (?) erhob I. zur *colonia*. Inschr.: CIL VIII 2, 8367–8373, 10330–10333; Suppl. 3, 20211–20213.

S. LANCEL, s. v. I., DCPP, 228 • P. SALAMA, s. v. Djidjelli, EB, 2469–2476 • L. TEUTSCH, Das Städtewesen in Nordafrika, 1962, 194. W.HU.

Igilium. Insel im *mare Tyrrhenum*, dem *promonturium Argentarium* vorgelagert, h. Giglio. Besiedelt seit dem Neolithikum. I. gehörte zum Gebiet der *colonia* → Cosa und war 49 v. Chr. im Besitz der Domitii, die dort eine Flotte gegen Massilia ausrüsteten (Caes. civ. 1,34,3). Zum Schiffsverkehr vgl. das *corpus codicariorum* (CIL XI 2643). Abgelegen und dicht bewaldet, diente I. den Römern z.Z. Alaricus' [2] (Rut. Nam. 1,325) als Zufluchtsort. Arch.: eine prächtige *villa* am Hafen, eine weitere bei Campese; etr. und röm. Überreste in den umliegenden Gewässern.

R. BRONSON, G. UGGERI, Isola del Giglio, in: SE 38, 1970, 201–214 • L. CORSI, s. v. Giglio, BTCGI 7, 123–132. G.U./Ü: J.W.M.

Ignatios (Ἰγνάτιος).

[1] Bischof von Antiocheia, Märtyrer, wird zu den Apostolischen Vätern (→ Apostelväter) gezählt.

A. BIOGRAPHIE B. BRIEFE C. THEOLOGIE

A. BIOGRAPHIE

Person und Werk können bei I. nicht voneinander getrennt werden, da sich gesicherte biographische Informationen einzig in Verbindung mit dem ihm zugeschriebenen Briefcorpus gewinnen lassen. So bestimmt der Standpunkt in der sog. »ignatianischen Frage«, d. h. in der Diskussion um Einheit und Echtheit der unter seinem Namen überl. Briefe (s. [4], mit Antwort [5; 6]), auch das jeweilige Bild des histor. I., seines Werkes und seiner Theologie. Andere Hinweise haben untergeordnete Bed.: So berichtet → Eusebios [7] von Kaisareia, I. sei nach Evodios der zweite Bischof von Antiocheia gewesen (Eus. HE 3,22,1) und habe, gefangen nach Rom gebracht, unter Kaiser Traian (98–117 n. Chr.) das Martyrium erlitten (Eus. HE 3,36,3). Bereits früh wurde der lit. Nachlaß des I. gesammelt (vgl. Polyk. 13,2). Eusebios kennt z. B. sieben Briefe, die I. auf seiner Reise nach Rom verfaßte; dabei entstanden vier in Smyrna und drei in der Troas (Eus. HE 3,36,5–15).

B. BRIEFE

Das Briefcorpus liegt in drei Rezensionen vor. Neben einer in Syr. erh. Kurzfassung dreier Briefe ist eine *recensio longior* überliefert, die neben den sieben bei Eusebios erwähnten Briefen sechs weitere enthält. Diese geht zurück auf eine mittlere Rezension, deren Inhalt mit Eusebios übereinstimmt. Seit dem späten 19. Jh. werden die sieben Briefe der mittleren Rezension als authentische Schriften des I. dem frühen 2. Jh. zugeordnet [3. 65]. Innere und äußere Gründe (Textüberl., Stilistik u. a.) haben immer wieder zu Zweifeln an der Echtheit der Ignatianen geführt (vgl. [9. 285–292]), jüngst durch R. M. HÜBNER [4].

C. THEOLOGIE

Bestimmend für das Gemeindeverständnis des I. ist die auf verschiedenen Ebenen sich manifestierende Einheit (ἕνωσις/ἑνότης, Ign. epist. ad Magnesios 1,2; 13,2 u.ö.; καθολικὴ ἐκκλησία, Ign. epist. ad Smyrnaeos 8,2). Vergegenwärtigt wird sie in der von ihm angemahnten Ämtertrias (Bischof/Presbyter/Diakon) mit dem monarchisch beschriebenen Bischofsamt an der Spitze. Die Zusage des Heils durch Christus geschieht für die Gemeinde in der Eucharistiefeier (φάρμακον ἀθανασίας, Ign. epist. ad Ephesios 20,2). Die Eschatologie des I. ist von seiner starken Sehnsucht nach dem Martyrium geprägt. Ed.: zu *Epistulae VII genuinae* (CPG 1025) s. z.B. [1. 109–225], zu *Epistulae interpolatae et epistulae suppositiciae* (CPG 1026) s. [2. 83–269].

ED.: 1 J.A. FISCHER, Die Apostolischen Väter, [9]1986 2 F.X. FUNK, F. DIEKAMP, Patres Apostolici II, 1913.
LIT: 3 M. GÜNTHER, Einl. in die Apostolischen Väter, 1997, 64–75, 122f. 4 R.M. HÜBNER, Thesen zur Echtheit und Datier. der sieben Briefe des I., in: Zschr. für ant. Christentum 1, 1997, 44–72 5 A. LINDEMANN, Antwort auf die »Thesen zur Echtheit und Datier. der sieben Briefe des I. von Antiochien«, in: Ebd., 185–194 6 G. SCHÖLLGEN, Die Ignatianen als pseudepigraph. Briefcorpus, in: Zschr. für ant. Christentum 2, 1998, 16–25 7 CH. MUNIER, Où en est la question d'I.?, in: ANRW II 27.1, 359–484 (Bibliogr. 360–376) 8 H. PAULSEN, s. v. I., RAC 17, 933–953 9 W.R. SCHOEDEL, Polycarp of Smyrna and I., in: ANRW II 27.1, 272–358. J.RI.

[2] I. Magister. Diakon und Skeuophylax in Konstantinopel (784–815), dann Metropolit von Nikaia (gest. nach 845). Die unter seinem Namen erh. Werke werfen auf Grund konkurrierender Homonyme häufig Zuweisungsprobleme auf (vgl. [1]). Zu den verlorenen Werken gehören die Iamben gegen Thomas den Aufständischen (vgl. Suda ι 84 ADLER). I. verfaßte Viten der Patriarchen Tarasios [2] und Nikephoros [3], ein Anakreontion auf den vorzeitigen Tod seines Schülers Paulos [4], einen iambischen Dialog über die Erbsünde [5], iambisch-tetrastichische Kurzfassungen äsopischer Fabeln [6], iambische Sentenzen rel. Inhalts in alphabetischer Anordnung [7] und ein Gedicht über den reichen Mann und den armen Lazaros [8]. Er schrieb auch einige weitere Grabepigramme (Anth. Pal. 15,29–31), die in Stil und Wortwahl klassizistisch, wenn auch nicht frei von metrischen Mängeln sind (vermutlich war es I., der dem elegischen Distichon nach zwei Jh. der Vernachlässigung zu erneutem Ansehen verhalf). Vielleicht stammen auch die beiden Hexameter mit dem anschließenden Pentameter (Anth. Pal. 15,39) von ihm, in denen er Ruhm dafür beansprucht, ›die Gramm., die in einem Meer des Vergessens verborgen war‹, wieder ans Licht gebracht zu haben.

1 W. WOLSKA-CONUS, De quibusdam Ignatiis, in: Travaux et mémoirs. Byz. 4, 1970, 329–360 2 I.A. HEIKEL, in: Acta Societatis Scientiae Fennicae 17, 1889, 395–423 3 PG 100, 41–160 4 Matranga II 664–667 5 J. BOISSONADE, Anecdota Graeca 1, 1962, 436–444 6 C.F. MÜLLER, O. CRUSIUS, Babrii fabulae Aesopeae, 1897, 264–285 7 C.F. MÜLLER, in: RhM 46, 1891, 320–322 8 L. STERNBACH, in: Eos 4, 1897, 151–154 • A. CAMERON, The Greek Anthology from Meleager to Planudes, 1993, 308, 331–333.

[3] Kanzleivorsteher in Konstantinopel, Verf. eines aus zwei iambischen Trimetern bestehenden Epigramms (Anth. Pal. 1,109). Dieses feiert die Restaurierung der berühmten, schon von Iustinian erbauten Kirche der hochheiligen Gottesmutter an der Quelle (am Selymbria-Tor in Konstantinopel) unter der gemeinsamen Herrschaft, wie aus Vers 2 hervorzugehen scheint, des → Basileios [5] I. und seiner beiden Söhne Konstantinos und Leon (und stammt somit aus dem Zeitraum von ca. 870–879).

A. CAMERON, The Greek Anthology from Meleager to Planudes, 1993, 151. M.G.A./Ü: T.H.

Ignorantia. Von der *i.*, auch *ignoratio* (Unkenntnis), handelt eine alte röm. Rechtsregel. Nach Paulus (3. Jh. n. Chr., Dig. 22,6,9 pr.) lautet sie: *iuris i. nocet, facti vero i. non nocet* (›Rechtsunkenntnis schadet, Tatsachenunkenntnis aber nicht‹). Seit dem MA spricht man eher von Irrtum (*error*). Bei den Römern hat man *error* und *i.* vermutlich gleich bewertet: Der Rechtsirrtum hindert weder die Verantwortlichkeit für eigenes (»straf«- wie zivilrechtliches) Verhalten, noch die Wirksamkeit des → *consensus* bei Rechtsgeschäften unter Lebenden oder bei der rechtsgeschäftlichen Erklärung für Regelungen nach dem Tode. Die *i. facti* hingegen führt wie der Tatsachenirrtum meist zur Entschuldbarkeit des Verhaltens und zur Unwirksamkeit der rechtsgeschäftlichen Erklärung. Bei Testamenten wurde freilich vielfach mit wohlwollender → *interpretatio* geholfen. Generell unbeachtlich sollte der bloße Benennungsirrtum (*error in nomine*) sein (Ulp. Dig. 18,1,9,1). Daraus hat sich im MA die Regel *falsa demonstratio non nocet* (›Falschbezeichnung schadet nicht‹) entwickelt.

HONSELL/MAYER-MALY/SELB, 122–126 • J.G. WOLF, Error im röm. Vertragsrecht, 1961 • L. WINKEL, Error iuris nocet, dt. 1985 (Orig. Diss. Amsterdam 1983). G.S.

Iguvinische Tafeln s. Tabulae Iguvinae

Iguvium. Stadt der Umbri auf einer Anhöhe im oberen Tal des Tibers, kontrollierte einen wichtigen Verkehrsweg, der das tyrrhenische mit dem adriat. Ufer über den Paß von Scheggia (63 m) verband, h. Gubbio. Prägte eigene Mz. (*IKVVINI, IKVVINS* [1. 140–152]). Nach 268 v. Chr. *civitas foederata* (Cic. Balb. 47). 167 v. Chr. wurde hier der Illyrerkönig Genthios interniert (Liv. 45,43,9). Nach dem Bundesgenossenkrieg *municipium, tribus Clustumina*. Stützpunkt des Pompeius im Bürgerkrieg; von Caesar besetzt (Caes. civ. 1,12,1). Unter Augustus wurde I. in die Ebene am Fuß des Monte Ingino verpflanzt und urbanistisch reorganisiert. Daß die *via Flaminia* I. nicht tangierte, verursachte deren Niedergang. Überreste: Ein Theater im SW von I. (1. Jh.

n. Chr.), Hausanlagen, Nekropolen, Brennöfen. Großer Tempel am Rand des Territoriums von I. (in Monteleto).

1444 wurden die berühmten → *Tabulae Iguvinae* in der Nähe des Theaters gefunden, sieben unterschiedlich große, teilweise beidseitig in umbr. Sprache beschriftete Br.-Tafeln, die teils linksläufig in umbr. Alphabet (240/150 v. Chr.), teils rechtsläufig in lat. Alphabet (150/89 v. Chr.) abgefaßt sind. Sie enthalten Anweisungen für rel. Zeremonien des Priestercollegiums der *fratres Atiedii*, mit reichen Informationen über Institutionen, Zeremonien, Kulte (Iuppiter, Pomonus, Vesuna), über die *gens Petronia*, über die Top. und über die Sprache.

1 F. Catalli, Monetazione preromana in Umbria, in: Antichità Umbre, catalogo di Perugia, 1989.

J. W. Poultney, The Br. Tables of I. (TAPhA 18), 1959 • G. Devoto, Tabulae Iguvinae, ³1962 • A. Pfiffig, Religio Iguvina, 1964 • A. L. Prosdocimi, Le Tavole Iguvine, 1984 • M. Cipollone, Gubbio, in: NSA 38 f., 1984 f., 95–167 • C. Malone, S. Stoddart, Territory, Time and State, 1994 • P. Micalizzi, Storia dell'architettura e dell'urbanistica di Gubbio, 1988 • D. Manconi, Gubbio, EAA, Suppl. 2,2, 895–897 • A. Ancillotti, R. Cervi, Le tavole di Gubbio e la civiltà degli Umbri, 1996. G. U.

Ikarion (Ἰκάριον; Ἰκαρία nur Steph. Byz. s. v. Ἰ.).
[1] Att. Mesogeia-Demos der Phyle Aigeis, 307/6 bis 201 der Antigonis, ab 200 v. Chr. der Attalis am NO-Hang des → Pentelikon (h. Dioniso). Nur ein Demos namens I. ist bezeugt [7. 115 Nr. 16]. Mit fünf (sechs) *buleutaí* mittelgroß, aber (durch Kultbetrieb?) wohlhabend [9. 160 Anm. 77, 163]. 1888/9 wurde das Dionysos-Heiligtum [9. 221] mit einem der ältesten Theater von Attika [2; 3; 8] und archa. Kultbild des Dionysos (IG I³ 254, IG II² 2851 [5; 9. 215]) freigelegt [1; 8]. Der Tragödiendichter → Thespis stammte aus I. Dramatische Agone bezeugt IG I³ 254 (2. H. 5. Jh. v. Chr.). Zum Kult des eponymen Heros Ikarios s. [3; 6], zu dem des Apollon Pythios s. [4]. Inschr.: IG I³ 253 f.; IG II² 1178 f., 2851, 3094 f., 3098 f., 4976; SEG 22, 44 Nr. 17.

1 W. R. Biers, T. D. Boyd, I. in Attica, 1888–1981, in: Hesperia 52, 1982, 1–18 2 H. R. Goette, Griech. Theaterbau der Klassik, in: E. Pöhlmann (Hrsg.), Stud. zur Bühnendichtung und zum Theaterbau der Ant., 1995, 10 f., Abb. 1a bzw. 1b 3 F. Kolb, Agora und Theater, 1981, 70 ff. 4 E. Meyer, s. v. Pythion (5), RE 24, 561 f. 5 I. B. Romano, The Archaic Statue of Dionysos from I., in: Hesperia 51, 1982, 398–409 6 A. Shapiro, Art and Cult under the Tyrants in Athens, 1989, 95 f. 7 Traill, Attica, 7, 15, 33, 41, 59, 67, 83, 110 Nr. 58, 115 Nr. 16, Tab. 2, 11, 14 8 Travlos, Attika, 85 ff. Abb. 96–100 9 Whitehead, Index s. v. I. H. LO.

[2] s. Ikarios

Ikarios (Ἰκάριος).
[1] Att. Heros, dessen Kult (wohl im Demos Ikaria) bereits im 5. Jh. belegt ist (IG I³ 253, 6.9); Opfer an ihn, seine Tochter → Erigone [1] und ihren Hund erwähnt Ail. nat. 7,28. Sein Mythos ist seit der nur frg. erh. ›Erigone‹ des Eratosthenes in verschiedenen Brechungen bekannt (Hyg. astr. 2,4; Apollod. 3,192 f. usw.). Der Gott → Dionysos kehrt bei I. ein, wird von ihm bewirtet und gibt ihm zum Dank den ersten Wein. Als I. diesen ungemischt seinen Nachbarn kredenzt, werden sie betrunken; wieder nüchtern, erschlagen sie ihn als Giftmischer. Sein Hund Maira führt die Tochter → Erigone zur Leiche; Erigone bestattet ihn und erhängt sich aus Kummer. Dionysos kommt zurück und lehrt das Mischen des Weins mit Wasser; Zeus versetzt I. als Bootes, Erigone als Virgo und Maira als Sirius (Hundsstern, Prokyon) an den Himmel.

Der Kult des I. ist älter als Eratosthenes. Seine Erzählung benutzt geläufige Motive (Einkehr des göttlichen Gasts, Erhängen des Mädchens) für eine Reihe von Aitien: neben der Sternsage steht die Einführung des Weins und des Mischens mit Wasser, die kult. Verehrung des I., der Brauch des → Askoliasmos, des Springens auf einem eingefetteten Weinschlauch (Hyg. astr. 2,4), und das Ritual der → Aiora am dritten Tag der Anthesteria, für die das Erhängen der Erigone Aition ist.
[2] Vater der → Penelope. Die ›Odyssee‹ gibt ihm kaum Gestalt. Später wird er mit wechselnder Genealogie in Sparta lokalisiert, und man erzählte, daß er seine Tochter nur ungern mit Odysseus gehen ließ (Paus. 3,10,10 f.).

D. Flückiger-Guggenheim, Göttliche Gäste. Die Einkehr von Göttern und Heroen in der griech. Myth., 1984, bes. 108–116 • E. Kearns, The Heroes of Attica, 1989, 172 • D. Gondicas, s. v. I., LIMC 5, 645–647 • A. Rosokoki, Die Erigone des Eratosthenes. Eine komm. Ausgabe der Frg., 1995. F. G.

Ikarisches Meer (Ἰκάριος πόντος). Südöstl. Teil des Ägäischen Meeres von Samos bis Mykonos (Plin. nat. 4,51) bzw. von Ikaros mit Korassiai (Korseai, h. Fourni) und Samos über Patmos, Leros und Kalymnos bis Kos (Strab. 10,5,13). Belegstellen: Hom. Il. 2,145 (Ἰκάριος πόντος); Sen. Hercules Oetaeus 694; Auson. epist. 23 (*Icarius pontus*); Ov. fast. 4,283; 566; Plin. nat. 4,68; 6,215 (*Icarium*); Hdt. 6,96; Strab. 2,5,21; Ptol. 5,2,1–6; 17,2; Diod. 4,77,6 (Ἰκάριον πέλαγος); Claud. in Eutropium 2,265 (*Icarium pelagus*).

Das I. M. bespült die Küsten der westkleinasiat. Landschaften Ionia, Karia, Doris; daran liegen im Norden Teos, Lebedos, Kolophon (Hafen Notion), die Kaystros-Mündung, Ephesos, Kap Trogilion an der Mykale, die Maiandros-Mündung (Ptol. l.c.). Unterabteilungen des I. M. sind der Latmische Golf (im MA großenteils verlandet, h. Bafa-See als verbliebener Rest) mit den Städten Miletos, Myus und Herakleia am Latmos, südl. anschließend die Buchten von Iasos und Bargylia und der Keramische Golf mit Halikarnassos, Keramos, Idyma, Kedreai. Von der Schiffahrt gefürchtet waren die zahlreichen Felsklippen (Hor. carm. 3,7,21; Theaitetos, Anth. Pal. 7,499) und die stürmischen Etesien (*Icarii fluctus*, Hor. carm. 1,1,15); der Name ist von der Insel Ikaros (Ikaria) abgeleitet (Strab. 10,5,13; Plin. nat. 4,68).

L. Bürchner, s. v. I. M., RE 9, 972 f. • C. Bursian, Geogr. von Griechenland 2, 1872, 351 Anm. 2. H. KA.

Ikaros (Ἴκαρος).

[1] Sohn des → Daidalos [1]. Von → Minos auf Kreta festgehalten, baut Daidalos für sich und I. je ein Flügelpaar, mit dem sie Minos entkommen. Doch I. kommt trotz der Mahnungen seines Vaters der Sonne zu nahe; dadurch schmilzt das Wachs der Flügel, er stürzt in der Nähe der Insel → Ikaros/Ikaria [2] ab und ertrinkt. Daidalos (oder Herakles, Apollod. 2,132) bestattet ihn; die Insel und das sie umgebende Meer sind nach I. benannt.

Diese Erzählung ist für uns durch Ov. met. 8,183–235 gültig formuliert worden (vgl. Apollod. Epitome 1,12 f.); etwa gleichzeitig ist ein pompejanisches Wandbild. Wie frühere Erzählungen aussahen, ist schwierig auszumachen: Zuerst, aber nur in Umrissen erkennbar ist der Mythos in der att. Tragödie (seit Aischyl. Pers. 890; wichtig waren die verlorenen ›Kreter‹ des Euripides), und ob die seit dem 4. Jh. belegte Version, daß das Ikarische Meer den Namen davon habe, daß I. aus dem Schiff seines Vaters gefallen und ertrunken sei (Menekrates von Xanthos, FGrH 769 F 1) der Flugerzählung vorangeht oder sie eher rationalisiert (vgl. Diod. 4,77,6; Paus. 9,11,2), ist unklar; die älteste bildliche Darstellung (ein att. sf. Skyphos um 600) bildet nur Daidalos ab. Trotz der eindeutig auf die Insel Ikaros/Ikaria und die Ikarische See bezogenen Aitiologie gehört I. wohl erst in das att. Ikaria (→ Ikarios), dem der Demos Daidalidai benachbart war; Daidalos selbst ist Athener, Sohn des Metion (Pherekydes FGrH 3 F 146).

In der nachant. Moralisierung ist I. Bild jugendlicher Selbstüberschätzung (Natalis Comes), seit der Renaissance und insbes. dem 19. Jh. Bild für die Gefahren der sich selbst überschätzenden Technik, oft auch in optimistischer Wendung zum Bild des technischen Höhenflugs geworden.

F. Bömer, P. Ovidius Naso, Metamorphosen, Buch VIII-IX, 1977, 66–70 • J. E. Nyenhuis, s. v. Daidalos et I., LIMC 2, 313–321, bes. 316–319. F. G.

[2] I., Ikaria (Ἴκαρος, Ἰκαρία). 257 km² große, von Ost nach West 40 km verlaufende felsige, bis 1041 m aufragende Insel vor der kleinasiat. Küste mit drei größeren milesischen Kolonien, nämlich dem Hauptort Oine (beim h. Kampos) an der Nordküste, Thermai (h. Therma) an der SO-Küste und Drakanon am gleichnamigen Ostkap. Ant. und byz. Reste findet man v. a. bei Kampos, aber auch bei Therma (Reste der alten Badeanlagen; der Hügel Kastro bildete die Akropolis). An der Westküste wurden die Fundamente eines Tempels freigelegt, der zum Heiligtum der Artemis Tauropolos gehörte [1]. Der Sage nach ist I. nach dem hier bestatteten Ikaros benannt, dessen Grab noch in röm. Zeit gezeigt wurde. Oine und Thermai waren Mitglieder im → Attisch-Delischen Seebund mit 4000–8000 bzw. 3000 Drachmen Tribut (ATL 1,282 f.; 360 f.; 490; 528; 2,86; 3,190; 204). Wohl seit dem 2. Jh. v. Chr. gehörte I. zu Samos; Thermai scheint damals den Namen Asklepieis geführt zu haben (Strab. 10,5,13; 14,1,6; 14,1,19; HN 602). Oberhalb von Oine lag die ma. Siedlung mit der teilweise erh. Kirche Hagia Irini aus dem 11. Jh. Die Insel, die im MA Nikaria hieß, war Verbannungsort, seit 1204 fränk. Baronie, dann genuesischer Besitz und von Chios abhängig. 1481 fiel I. an die Johanniter von Rhodos und schließlich 1523 an die Türken. An die jahrhundertelange Seeräuberplage erinnern die fast bis zum Dach in den Boden eingesenkten Piratenschutzhäuser.

1 U. Jantzen, Arch. Funde vom Sommer 1937 bis Sommer 1938. Griechenland, in: AA 53, 1938, 581–583 (L. Politis).

K. Hopf, Veneto-byz. Analekten, in: SAWW 32, 1859, 144 ff. • Lauffer, Griechenland, 277 f. • I. Lehmann, Ägäische Wanderungen, 1985 • J. Melas, Istoria tis nisu I., 2 Bd., 1955–1958 • G. B. Montanari, s. v. I., PE 406 • Philippson/Kirsten 4, 269 ff. • H. W. Pleket, The hot springs at Icaria, in: Mnemosyne 13, 1960, 240 f. • L. Ross, Reisen auf den Inseln des ägäischen Meeres 2, 1843, 156 ff. H. KAL.

Ikelos s. Morpheus

Ikkos s. Olympionikai

Ikonion (Ἰκόνιον, h. Konya). Aus einem vor- und frühgesch. Tall (Alāettintepe) mit phryg. Besiedlung (8. Jh. v. Chr.) entwickelte sich die bedeutendste Stadt in Lykaonia, nur bei Xen. an. 1,2,19 als östlichste Stadt von Phrygia gen., am Schnittpunkt wichtiger Handels- und Militärstraßen. I. kam 25 v. Chr. mit den übrigen Besitzungen des Königs → Amyntas [9] zur neuen Prov. Galatia. Schon unter Augustus wurde das Stadtgebiet zw. der griech. *pólis* und der von ihm gegr. Kolonie geteilt; Neugründung der Kolonie unter Hadrianus [1. 51–59; 75–90]. Nach Missionierung durch den Apostel Paulus (Apg 14,1–5,28; 16,1–5) kam es zu einem raschen Anwachsen der christl. Gemeinde [2. 773 f.]; Bischöfe sind seit Anf. 3. Jh. bekannt (Eus. HE 6,19,17 f.). I. wurde 260 von den Sāsāniden erobert. Unter Diocletianus wurde I. der neuen Prov. Pisidia zugeschlagen, um 370–372 war I. polit. und kirchliche Metropole der neuen Prov. Lykaonia. Im späten 7. Jh. Stadt des Thema Anatolikon; 723 erstmalig von den Arabern eingenommen [3. 176–178].

1 H. v. Aulock, Mz. und Städte Lykaoniens, 1976 2 A. v. Harnack, Die Mission und Ausbreitung des Christentums in den ersten drei Jh., [4]1924 3 Belke 4 F. Prayon, A. M. Wittke, Kleinasien vom 12. bis 6. Jh. v. Chr., TAVO B 82, 1994. K. BE.

Ikonoklasmus s. Constantinus [7] V.; Leon III; Syrische Dynastie

Ikos (Ἰκός). 62 km² große Insel der nördl. Sporaden, h. Halonnesos (auch Chelidromia oder Chilidromia); Mitglied im 1. Att. Seebund (→ Attisch-Delischer Seebund) mit einem Tribut von 1500 Drachmen, desgleichen im 2. → Attischen Seebund. Seit dem Friedensschluß der Athener mit Philippos II. 338 befand sich die Insel unter maked. Oberhoheit, seit 42 v. Chr. bis in die späte röm. Kaiserzeit in athenischem Besitz. Nach dem Fall von Konstantinopel stand I. unter venezianischem, seit 1537 unter türk. Einfluß. Nach schweren Verwüstungen im Unabhängigkeitskrieg wurde I. 1830 dem Königreich Griechenland eingegliedert. Überreste der ant. Stadt haben sich an der SO-Seite bei Kokkinokastro erh. (Mauerreste des 4. Jh. v. Chr.). Bei der nördl. von I. gelegenen Insel Pelagos wurde 1970 ein Schiffswrack (Mitte 12. Jh. n. Chr.) mit vollständiger Ladung entdeckt und geborgen.

C. Bursian, Geogr. von Griechenland 2, 1868–1872, 389 • Philippson/Kirsten 4, 47 ff. • Koder/Hild, 147 • Lauffer, Griechenland, 256. H. KAL.

Ikrion s. Schiffbau, s. Theater

Iktinos (Ἰκτῖνος). Architekt klass. Zeit. Als Hauptwerk gilt der 447–438 v. Chr. errichtete Athener → Parthenon (Strab. 9,395–396; Paus. 8,41,9), den er anscheinend gemeinsam mit → Kallikrates, dessen Anteil neuerdings stärker betont wurde [1], entworfen hat (Plut. Perikles 13,7). Mit einem sonst unbekannten Karpon soll er über den Parthenon eine Schrift verfaßt haben (Vitr. 7 praef. 12). Wiederholt ist I. als Architekt des um 440 v. Chr. entworfenen Telesterion in → Eleusis überl. (Strab. 9,395; Vitr. 7 praef. 16), für dessen Bau allerdings auch andere Verantwortliche genannt werden (Plut. Perikles 13). Außerdem entwarf er den nach 429 v. Chr. begonnenen Apollontempel bei Phigalia (Paus. 8,41,8–9), dessen Schönheit ausdrücklich gerühmt wird. Aus allgemeineren Gründen wurde ihm das Odeion des Perikles in Athen zugeschrieben [2]. Eine späte, wahrscheinlich auf Varro zurückgehende Quelle (Auson. Mos. 309) zählt ihn zu den bedeutendsten Architekten, eine Auszeichnung, die durch mit seinem Namen in Verbindung gebrachte Bauwerke bestätigt wird.

V. a. der Parthenon charakterisiert I. als einen Architekten, der über herausragende technische Kompetenz und besondere gestalterische Kreativität verfügte. Dies zeigt sich sowohl im Umgang mit durch den Vorparthenon erzwungenen Vorgaben als auch im konsequent durchproportionierten Parthenonentwurf und nicht zuletzt in einem neu thematisierten Verständnis von Innenräumen [3]. Dies kennzeichnet nicht weniger den unvollendet gebliebenen Entwurf für den Saalbau des Telesterion in Eleusis [4; 5] und den erst nachträglich fertiggestellten Apollontempel bei Phigalia. Dessen neuartige Cella erweist sich als ein prunkvoll ausgestatteter Festsaal [6; 7; 8], für dessen aufwendige Rauminszenierung anscheinend das korinth. Kapitell kreiert worden ist. Bauten und Entwürfe des I. vermittelten ant. Architektur einen Entwicklungsschub, dessen Wirkung die folgende Zeit nachhaltig beeinflussen sollte.

1 B. Wesenberg, Wer erbaute den Parthenon?, in: MDAI(A) 97, 1982, 99–125 2 A. L. Robbin, The Odeion of Pericles: Some Observations on its History, Form and Function, 1979 3 G. Gruben, Die Tempel der Griechen, ³1980, 163–178 4 A. Corso, Gli architetti di telesterion di Eleusi nell' età di Pericle, in: Atti. Istituto veneto di scienze, lettere ed arti 140, 1981/82, 199–215 5 Travlos, Attika, 94–95 6 A. Mallwitz, Cella und Adyton des Apollontempels in Bassae, in: MDAI(A) 77, 1962, 140–177 7 G. Roux, L'architecture de l'Argolide aux IVe et IIIe siècle avant J.-C., 1961, 21–56 8 Ch. Hoffkes-Brukker, A. Mallwitz, Der Bassaefries, 1975, 24–37.

E. Fabricius, s. v. I., RE 19,995 f. • H. Knell, I.: Baumeister des Parthenon und des Apollontempels von Phigalia-Bassae?, in: JDAI 63, 1968, 100–117 • R. Martin, L'atelier Ictinos-Callicratès au temple de Bassae, in: BCH 100, 1976, 427–442 • W. Müller, Architekten in der Welt der Ant., 1989, 165–170 • H. Svenson-Evers, Die griech. Architekten archa. und klass. Zeit, 1996, 157–211 • C. Weickert, s. v. I., in: U. Thieme, U. Becker, Allg. Lex. der bildenden Künstler 18, 560–566 • F. E. Winter, Trad. and Innovation in Doric Design 3. The Work of I., in: AJA 84, 1980, 399–416. H. KN.

Ilai s. Reiterei

Ilerda. Alte Ibererstadt am Sicoris (h. Segre), h. Lérida (Abstoßung der iber. Vorsilbe *I*). Überreste finden sich hauptsächlich oberhalb der neuen Stadt. Inschr.: CIL II Suppl. p. 1146. Evtl. schon bei Avien. 475 angesprochen. I. spielte in der röm. Kriegsgesch. mehrfach eine Rolle, bes. in den Kämpfen Caesars mit den Legaten des Pompeius. Von Augustus wurde I. zum *municipium* erhoben (Mz., Plin. nat. 3,24). Noch Ausonius erwähnt I. öfters (z. B. commemoratio professorum Burdigalensium 23,10; epist. 29,59 Peiper), und in den Konzilsakten erscheint sie regelmäßig als westgot. Bistum [2]. Schulten [1] vermutet eine zweite, noch ältere Stadt I.

1 Schulten, Landeskunde 1, 309 2 J. D. Mansi (Hrsg.), Sacrorum conciliorum collectio IX-XII.

A. Schulten (Hrsg.), Fontes Hispaniae Antiquae 1, 1925, 3–9 (Indices) • R. P. Merce, Datos arqueológicos ilerd., in: Ilerda 2, 1952, 99–110; 12, 1954, 201–218 • J. B. Keune, s. v. I., RE Suppl. 3, 1207–1210 • Tovar 3, 212, 420 f. • A. Vives, La moneda hispánica 2, 1924, 52 ff.; 4, 1924, 43 f. P. B.

Ilergetes. Iber. Stamm um → Ilerda in der h. Prov. Huesca. Die I. werden oft im Zusammenhang mit dem 2. Pun. Krieg gen., standen zunächst auf seiten der Karthager, wurden 205 v. Chr. von den Römern besiegt (Liv. 29,3) und waren später *socii* (Liv. 34,11). Erwähnt bei Strab. 3,4,10 und Plin. nat. 3,21, später nicht mehr.

A. Schulten (Hrsg.), Fontes Hispaniae Antiquae 3, 1935, 232 • Tovar 3, 1989, 46 f. • Schulten, Landeskunde 1, ²1974, 309 • A. Vives, La moneda hispánica 2, 1924, 52. P. B.

Ilex s. Eiche

Ilia s. Rea Silvia

Ilias s. Homeros [1]

Ilias Latina. Der Name wurde von BAEHRENS einem lat. Gedicht gegeben, das Homers ›Ilias‹ auf 1070 Hexameter verkürzt. Es wird von → Lactantius Placidus zu Stat. Theb. 6,114 (121) unter dem Namen Homerus zit., der auch in den Titeln der meisten früh-ma. Hss. auftaucht. Die späteren schreiben es aus unbekannten Gründen Pindar zu. Die einzige weitere Spur der *I. L.* aus der Ant. ist die Imitation durch → Dracontius. Der Prolog (= Il. 1,1–7) bietet das Akrostichon ITALICPS, der (unhomer.) Epilog SCQIPSIT. Letzteres kann leicht in SCRIPSIT emendiert werden, ersteres steht vielleicht absichtlich fehlerhaft für ITALICUS [1]. Unterschiede in Stil und Metrum schließen eine Identifizierung mit → Silius Italicus aus. Der Rubrikator (jetzt als J. Cuspinianus identifiziert [2. 31]) einer späten und wertlosen Hs. betitelt das Werk *Bebii Italici poetae clarissimi Epithome* ... [2. tav. vi]. Die Gleichheit des Namens mit dem aus dem Akrostichon entnommenen (nicht vor dem 19. Jh. entdeckt) hat nahegelegt, daß Cuspinianus ihn aus einer unbekannten, von der hsl. Trad. unabhängigen Quelle gewonnen haben könnte. Im 20. Jh. ist ein → Baebius [II 7] Italicus, dessen h. bekannte Laufbahn unter Vespasian begann, als *cos.* des J. 90 n. Chr. aufgetaucht (PIR[2] B 17). Die Identifizierung muß jedoch unsicher bleiben.

Stil und Metrum liefern keine feste Basis für eine Datier. Die Kürzung von *-o* wird vermieden, ist aber wahrscheinlich auf eine künstliche Theorie, nicht auf Gewohnheit zurückzuführen [3]. V. 899–902 spielen wahrscheinlich (auch wenn das angezweifelt wurde) auf die Vergöttlichung des Augustus an, können aber jederzeit geschrieben worden sein [2. 52, Anm. 103]. Deutliche Anklänge an Senecas Trag. schließen eine vorneronische Datier. aus. Eine zu späte Datier. wird durch die Klassizität von Stil und Metrik verwehrt. Ein Argument für eine neronische Datier. ist die Möglichkeit, daß V. 261 f. zu der homer. Erzählung als Anspielung auf Neros *Troica* hinzugefügt wurden.

Große Uneinheitlichkeit besteht in der Länge der Bearbeitung. Die ersten acht B. der ›Ilias‹ verbrauchen ⅔ der *I. L.*, die B. 13 und 17 bekommen je nur 5 und 3 Zeilen. Diese Ungleichheit zeigt, daß der Autor sich nicht als Epitomator betrachtete, doch diente sein Werk im MA zu diesem Zweck, als → Epitomai gewöhnliche scholastische Texte waren. Im Epilog beansprucht der Verf. eigenes Dichtertum, was mit einigen Abweichungen von der homer. Erzählung übereinstimmt [2. 81 ff.; 4. 60 ff.]. Es gibt z. B. neun Gleichnisse, von denen nur vier Gegenstücke in Homer haben [2. 117]. Die Schildbeschreibung (862 ff.) hat ausgeprägt unhomer. Merkmale. Vergil und Ovid haben die Ausdrucksweise der *I. L.* stark beeinflußt; das Werk ist der ›Ilias‹-Übers. des → Matius (vgl. [5]) einigermaßen verpflichtet.

1 E. COURTNEY, Greek and Latin Acrostichs, in: Philologus 134, 1990, 12 f. 2 G. BROCCIA, Prolegomeni all'»Omero Latino«, 1992 3 D. ARMSTRONG, Stylistics and the date of Calpurnius Siculus, in: Philologus 130, 1986, 130–35 4 M. SCAFFAI, Baebii Italici I. L., 1982 5 COURTNEY, 100 f.

ED. C./Ü: M. MO.

Ilias mikra (Ἰλιὰς μικρά, Kleine Ilias). Verlorenes Teil-Epos des → Epischen Zyklus; außer Kurz-Inhaltsangaben in der ›Chrestomathie‹ des → Proklos und der Epitome des → Apollodoros [7] sowie einigen Testimonien stehen nur sieben direkte Zitate mit insgesamt 26 Hexametern [1; 2; 3. 95] für Rekonstruktion und Datierung zur Verfügung. Umfang nach Proklos 4 B., Einsatzpunkt offenbar (darin Proklos einig mit Aristot. poet. 1459a 37–b 7 [4. 2411]) die *Hóplōn krísis* (Entscheidung, wem Achilleus' Rüstung gebührt). Demnach muß das Opus unmittelbar an die → *Aithiopís* angeschlossen haben (die mit Achilleus' Tod und Bestattung endete). Erzählverlauf laut Proklos (gekürzt): Statt des → Aias erhält Odysseus Achilleus' Rüstung: Aias verliert den Verstand, schlachtet (im Glauben, sich an den Atriden zu rächen) das Beutevieh der Achaier und bringt sich – wieder klar geworden – vor Scham und Schande selber um. Odysseus fängt → Helenos, der verrät, Troia könne nur durch → Philoktetes eingenommen werden: Diomedes holt Philoktetes von Lemnos, → Machaon heilt ihn, und Philoktetes tötet Paris. Helena fällt an → Deïphobos. Odysseus holt Achilleus' Sohn → Neoptolemos von Skyros, der Troias neuen Helfer → Eurypylos tötet. Es folgt die Gesch. vom Hölzernen Pferd bis zu dessen Einholung nach Troia und dem Freudenmahl der Troer. Nach Aristot. poet. 1459a 37 ging das Werk weiter bis zur Abfahrt der Achaier nach der Eroberung der Stadt (s. → Iliupersis). Als Verf. wurden Homer, → Kinaithon und u. a. (spät) ein → Lesches von Lesbos genannt (s. dazu → Epischer Zyklus). Der Stoff ist alt, das Werk aber frühestens im 6. Jh. v. Chr. entstanden [3. 100].
→ Epischer Zyklus (mit weiterer Lit.).

ED.: 1 PEG 2 EpGr.
LIT.: 3 M. DAVIES, The Date of the Epic Cycle, in: Glotta 67, 1989, 89–100 4 A. RZACH, s. v. Kyklos, RE 11, 2410–2422 5 E. BETHE, Homer. Dichtung und Sage II 2.4 (»Der Troische Epenkreis«), 1929, 245–261.

J. L.

Iliberis

[1] I., Iliberri. Ibererstadt, wahrscheinlich nahe Granada in der Sierra de Elvira. Erwähnt bei Plin. nat. 3,10 und Ptol. 2,4,9. In christl. Zeit Bistum, Tagungsort des *concilium Eliberitanum* (306 n. Chr.?) [1]. Oft gen. auf Mz. und Inschr., hier mehrfach als *municipium Florentinum* (z. B. CIL II 1572; 2070). Nach der arab. Invasion scheint die Stadt allmählich verfallen und die Bevölkerung nach Garnatha, h. Granada, übergesiedelt zu sein. Inschr.: CIL II p. 285 ff., Suppl. p. 1146.

1 A. SCHULTEN u.a. (Hrsg.), Fontes Hispaniae Antiquae 8/9, 1959/1947.

J. B. KEUNE, s. v. I., RE Suppl. 3, 1210–1215 · TOVAR 1, 137f. · A. VIVES, La moneda hispánica 2, 1924, 162. P. B.

[2] Ibererstadt nördl. der → Pyrenaei nahe am Mittelmeer, h. Elne am gleichnamigen Fluß, h. Tech. I. wird erstmals 218 v. Chr. als Station Hannibals auf seinem Marsch nach It. gen. (Liv. 21,24,1; 3; 5); z.Z. des Plinius (nat. 3,32) verfallen, wurde die Stadt zweifellos von Constantinus I. wiederaufgebaut und nach dessen Mutter Helena (davon Elne) benannt. Kaiser Constans fand in I. 350 den Tod (Zos. 2,42,5; Oros. 7,29,7). Seit dem 7. Jh. Bistum [1; 2].

1 A. SCHULTEN (Hrsg.), Fontes Hispaniae Antiquae 8, 69; 9, 319 2 J. B. KEUNE, s. v. I. (2), RE Suppl. 3, 1215. P. B.

Ilici. Alte Ibererstadt, in der Spätant. Elece, h. Elche. Man nimmt an, daß hier Hamilkar [3] Barkas 228 v. Chr. den Tod fand, doch ist dies zugunsten von Helike (Elche de la Sierra) zu korrigieren [2. 11 f.]. In röm. Zeit war I. *colonia immunis* (Plin. nat. 3,19). In ihrem Hafen wurde 460 n. Chr. die Flotte des Maiorianus von Vandali vernichtet [3. 81 f.]. In westgot. Zeit wird I. oft als Bistum gen. [3. 449]. Der ant. Ort lag etwas näher am Meer auf dem Hügel La Alcudia. Die Ausgrabungen zeugen von seiner Bed. Berühmt wurde Elche v. a. durch einen Fund, die Marmorskulptur »la dama de Elche« [1]. Inschr.: CIL II p. 479; Suppl. p. 1146f.
→ Pyrenäenhalbinsel: Archäologie

1 A. GARCÍA Y BELLIDO, La dama de Elche, 1943
2 A. SCHULTEN (Hrsg.), Fontes Hispaniae Antiquae 3, 1935
3 Ders. (Hrsg.), Fontes Hispaniae Antiquae 9, 1947.

J. B. KEUNE, s. v. I., RE Suppl. 3, 1217–1221 · TOVAR 3, [2]1974, 198ff. · A. VIVES, La moneda hispánica 4, 1924, 39ff. P. B.

Ilienses. Alter (Mela 2,123), neben den Corsi der einzige nicht von Rom unterworfene sardin. Stamm (Paus. 10,17,8f.). Plinius (nat. 3,85) nennt unter der Rubrik *provinciae* drei nicht urbanisierte Völker, darunter die I. Livius erinnert an die siegreichen Feldzüge von 181 v. Chr. (Liv. 40,34,12ff.) und 178–176 (Liv. 41,6,5ff.; 12,4ff.). Zweifelhaft ist die Lage ihrer Siedlungen – evtl. vom Marghine im Norden (vgl. die Inschr. auf dem Nuragen von Aidu Entos *Ili(ensium) iur(a)*) bis zur Ogliastra im Süden (Flor. epit. 1,22,35, Nennung der I. im Zusammenhang mit den zw. Dorgali und Baunei gelegenen *montes Insani*).

P. MELONI, Sardegna romana, 1990, 75ff., 229ff. · L. GASPERINI, La scritta latina del nuraghe Aidu Entos, in: M. BONELLO LAI (Hrsg.), Sardinia Antiqua. Studi in onore di P. Meloni, 1992, 303ff. P. M./Ü: R. P. L.

Ilion, Ilios s. Troia

Ilione (Ἰλιόνη). Älteste Tochter des → Priamos und der → Hekabe, Ehefrau des Thrakers Polymestor (Verg. Aen. 1,653f. erwähnt ihr Zepter, das Aeneas von Ilion mitbringt; vgl. Hyg. fab. 90). Ihr jüngster Bruder → Polydoros wächst bei I. auf, zusammen mit ihrem und Polymestors Sohn → Deïpylos. Nach Ende des troian. Krieges veranlaßt Agamemnon den Polymestor, Polydoros zu töten. Dieser ermordet den eigenen Sohn, da I. den Deïpylos für ihren Bruder ausgegeben hatte. Der echte Polydoros stiftet I. dazu an, ihren Ehemann zu töten. I. begeht nach dieser Tat Selbstmord (Hyg. fab. 109; vgl. 240; 243, 254; Serv. Aen. 1,653). Pacuvius schrieb eine Tragödie *Iliona* [1] (vgl. Hor. sat. 2,3,60).

1 I. D'ANNA, M. Pacuvii Fragmenta, 1967, 109–115, fr. 221–250.

S. EITREM, s. v. I., RE 11, 1066. K. WA.

Ilioneus (Ἰλιονεύς). Troian. Krieger, Sohn eines durch enge Verbindung mit → Hermes besonders reichen Bauern namens Phorbas, der in der Schlacht vom Minyerfürsten → Peneleos getötet wird (Hom. Il. 14,487–507). Vergil verwendet diesen Namen für den ältesten Anführer der troian. Flüchtlinge (Aen. 1,521 u.ö.).

P. WATHELET, Dictionnaire des Troyens de l'Iliade, 1988, Nr. 161. E. V.

Ilipa. Heute Alcalá del Río (arab. Umbenennung »Festung des Flusses«) am rechten Ufer des → Baetis. Name und die Stadt sind iber. [1. 1221]. I. war wichtig für die Schiffahrt (Strab. 3,2,3; CIL II 1085), ferner bed. aufgrund nahe gelegener Silbergruben (Strab. l.c.), Landwirtschaft und Fischfang (Mz.) und führte daher den Beinamen *Magna* (Ptol. 2,4,10; Plin. nat. 3,11?). Bei I. siegte P. Cornelius Scipio 206 v. Chr. über die Karthager. In westgot. Zeit wird I. als Bistum erwähnt [2. 216].

1 J. B. KEUNE, s. v. I. (1), RE Suppl. 3, 1221–1225
2 A. SCHULTEN (Hrsg.), Fontes Hispaniae Antiquae 9, 1947.

A. SCHULTEN (Hrsg.), Fontes Hispaniae Antiquae, 1925ff., bes. Bd. 2, 5–9 · Ders., Forsch. in Spanien I/2, 1940, 113ff. · SCHULTEN, Landeskunde 1, 489 · TOVAR 2, 162f. · A. VIVES, La moneda hispánica 3, 1924, 87ff. P. B.

Ilipula. Es gab in der Prov. → Hispania Baetica mehrere Ortschaften dieses Namens [3. 1225]. Oft sind sie schwer zu unterscheiden von *Ilipa, Ilipla, Elepla, Elipla* [1]. Hier werden nur die wichtigsten kurz angeführt.
[1] I. Magna (Ptol. 2,4,9) oder I. Laus (*Iulia*?, Plin. nat. 3,10). Lage unbekannt.
[2] I. Minor (Plin. nat. 3,12; CIL II 1469f.), h. Repla, südl. von Osuna.
[3] I., Ilipla ([2]; Ptol. 2,410). Zw. → Baetis und Anas, h. Niebla. Die Ruinen der alten Stadt stammen hauptsächlich aus arab. Zeit, doch gehen Funde bis ins 7. Jh. v. Chr. zurück.
[4] Gebirge südl. des → Baetis (Ptol. 2,4,12), h. wohl Sierra de Ronda.

1 A. SCHULTEN (Hrsg.), Fontes Hispaniae Antiquae 9, 1947, 12, 446 2 A. VIVES, La moneda hispánica 3, 1924, 81 3 J. B. KEUNE, s. v. I. (2–5), RE Suppl. 3, 1225f.

J. P. DROOP, Excavations at Niebla, in: AAA 12, 1925, 175–206 • SCHULTEN, Landeskunde 1, 192 • TOVAR 1, 129, 139. P.B.

Ilis(s)os (Ἰλισός, Ἰλισσός). Neben dem Kephisos Hauptfluß der Ebene von Athen (Strab. 9,1,24), der am NW-Hang des → Hymettos entspringt und am S-Rand von Athen nach SW zieht (h. vollständig überbaut und wie im Alt. nicht perennierend). Strittig ist, ob der I. bei Phaleron ins Meer oder nördl. des Peiraieus in den Kephisos mündete [2. 164 Abb. 213]. Nebenfluß des I. war der Eridanos (Paus. 1,19,5). Am I. lagen das Stadion von Athen und mehrere Tempel [2. 112, 278, 289ff. Abb. 379]. Brücken über den I.: [2. 498 Abb. 155, 630, 634]. Auf einer Insel im I. unterhalb des Olympieion entsprang die Kallirhoe [2. 114, 204 Abb. 154, 268]. Den Gerbern am I. verbot ein Dekret (IG I³ 1257), den I. zu verschmutzen [1. 257f.; 2. 340f. Abb. 442]. Kult des I.: IG I³ 369e Z. 89, 383 Z. 206.
→ Athenai (mit Plan)

1 H. LIND, Neues aus Kydathen, in: MH 42, 1985, 249–261
2 TRAVLOS, Athen, Index s. v. I.

W. JUDEICH, Top. von Athen, ²1931, 48 • W. KOLBE, s. v. I., RE 9, 1067f. • PHILIPPSON/KIRSTEN 1, 877, 889, 899ff., 922, 1001. H.LO.

Iliupersis (Ἰλίου πέρσις, Die Zerstörung von Ilios [= Troia]). Verlorenes Teil-Epos des → Epischen Zyklus; außer Kurz-Inhaltsangaben in der ›Chrestomathie‹ des → Proklos und der Epitome des → Apollodoros [7] von Athen sowie einigen Testimonien steht nur ein wörtliches Zitat mit acht Hexametern [1; 2; 3. 96] für Rekonstruktion und Datierung zur Verfügung. Umfang nach Proklos: 2 B., Einsatzpunkt nach Proklos: die Beratung der das Hölzerne Pferd in Troia umstehenden Troianer (vgl. Verg. Aen. 2,31–249). Die *I.* schloß damit unmittelbar an die → Ilias mikra an [5. 214]. Weiterer Erzählverlauf nach Proklos (gekürzt und z. T. ergänzt oder modifiziert aus Apollodoros): Beschluß, das Pferd der Athene zu opfern, Freudenfest, → Laokoon-Episode, Auswanderung des Aineias, Sinon-Episode (Sinons Feuerzeichen), Rückkehr der Flotte von Tenedos, Straßenkampf in Troia, die Achaier stecken Troia in Brand und opfern Polyxena am Grab des Achilleus, Neoptolemos tötet Astyanax, Beuteverteilung, Abfahrt der Griechen (Athene sendet einen Seesturm, Dezimierung und Zerstreuung der griech. Flotte: wohl spätere Zusatznotiz [5. 214³]). Aristot. poet. 1459a 37–b 7 kennt ›Iliupersis, Abfahrt, Sinon und Troerinnen‹ (d. h. die Beuteverteilung) als Teile der *Iliás mikrá*. *Iliupérsis* war also wohl nur Sondertitel des letzten Teils der *Iliás mikrá*; Differenzen in Einzelheiten zw. den Inhaltsreferaten zur *Iliás mikrá* und die *I.* gehen zu Lasten der ant. Referenten ([5. 218–225]; andere Hypothese: → Aithiopis). Als Verf. wird meist → Arktinos angegeben, Aristot. ebd. sagt nur ›der Dichter der Kleinen Ilias‹. Zur Datierung s. → Ilias mikra.
→ Epischer Zyklus (mit weiterer Lit.).

ED.: 1 PEG 2 EpGr.
LIT.: 3 M. DAVIES, The Date of the Epic Cycle, in: Glotta 67, 1989, 89–100 4 A. RZACH, s. v. Kyklos, RE 11, 2405–2410 5 E. BETHE, Homer. Dichtung und Sage II 2.4 (»Der Troische Epenkreis«), ²1929. J.L.

Iliupersismaler. Apul. Vasenmaler des 2. Viertels des 4. Jh. v. Chr., benannt nach einem Volutenkrater in London (BM Inv. F 160 [1. 193 Nr. 8]) mit Darstellung der → Iliupersis. Der I. gehört zu den innovativ tätigen Vasenmalern mit bahnbrechenden Neuerungen für die Entwicklung der späteren → apulischen Vasenmalerei; hierunter fallen u. a. die Einführung von Grabszenen (→ Naiskosvasen), ferner die Riefelung von Gefäßen in ihrem unteren Teil und die Verzierung der Henkel an Volutenkrateren mit runden Medaillons, die er mit bemalten oder reliefierten Kopfappliken bzw. figürlich verziert, und schließlich der aus dem Blütenkelch aufsteigende Frauenkopf zw. Ranken. Der I. stellte mythische wie dionysische Szenen dar, dazu Genreszenen mit Eroten, Männern und Frauen. Durch ihn wird der Volutenkrater zu einem der wichtigsten Bildträger der apul. Vasenmalerei.
→ Dareios-Maler, Baltimore-Maler

1 TRENDALL/CAMBITOGLOU.

K. SCHAUENBURG, Zu Werken des I. und seines Umkreises in einer Privatsammlung, in: N. BASGELEN, M. LUGAL (Hrsg.), FS J. Inan, 1989, 511–515 • Ders., Diesseits und Jenseits in der ital. Grabkunst, in: JÖAI 64, 1995, Beiblatt, 57 • TRENDALL/CAMBITOGLOU, Suppl. I, 1983, 25–26 • Dies., Suppl. II, 1991, 43–48. R.H.

Illos (Ἴλλος oder Ἰλλοῦς). Isaurier, hoher Beamter und General im oström. Reich. Er unterstützte im Februar 474 n. Chr. zusammen mit → Verina, der Witwe → Leons I., die Erhebung seines Landsmannes → Zenon zum Kaiser, schloß sich aber bereits 475 zusammen mit ihr dem Usurpator → Basiliskos an. Nach dessen Scheitern 476 alsbald wieder auf seiten Zenons, wurde I. 477 *magister officiorum* und *patricius*. Auf seine Veranlassung wurde Verina, die 478 zusammen mit Epinikos [2] versucht hatte, ihn zu beseitigen, nach Isaurien verbannt. Als er 480/81 einem weiteren Anschlag entgangen war, ernannte ihn Zenon 481 zum *magister utriusque militiae per Orientem*, geriet aber wegen seines Bruders Longinus, den I. inhaftiert hatte und nicht freilassen wollte, mit ihm in Streit und setzte ihn 483 wieder ab. Obwohl er sich zum chalkedonischen Christentum bekannte, war I. dem nichtchristl. Dichter und Magier → Pamprepios von Panopolis ergeben, der 484 seinem erneuten Versuch, Zenon zu stürzen, gute Chancen prophezeite. Daraufhin erhob I. zusammen mit Verina, die er inzwischen freigelassen hatte, am 19. Juli zu Tarsos den General Leontios zum Gegenkaiser, der aber zusammen mit I. noch im gleichen Jahr von Zenons General Iohannes besiegt und in der isaurischen Festung Papyrios eingeschlossen wurde. Leontios und I. verhängten dort über Pamprepios wegen seiner unzutreffenden Prognose die Todesstrafe, wurden aber nach der Einnahme des Kastells 488 auf Geheiß Zenons ihrerseits hingerichtet.

ODB 2, 986 • PLRE 2, 586–590 • STEIN, Spätröm. R. 1, 535–539; Histoire du Bas-Empire 2, 8–31. F.T.

Il(l)urco. Ibererstadt in der Prov. → Hispania Baetica, h. Pinos Puente bei Illora la Vieja westl. von Granada (Plin. nat. 3,10). Ihre Lage ist inschr. gesichert (CIL II p. 284; Suppl. p. 1147). Mz. [1. 107f.; 2. 1234].

1 A. VIVES, La moneda hispánica 3, 1924 **2** J.B. KEUNE, s. v. I., RE Suppl. 3, 1233–1235.

TOVAR 1, 136; 3, 163 ff. P.B.

Illustration s. Buchmalerei

Illustris vir. Schon in röm.-republikanischer Zeit kann das Wort *illustris* – wie die Worte *clarus*, *spectabilis* oder *egregius* – einen hohen ges. Rang bezeichnen. Im spätant. *ordo dignitatum* bezeichnet *illustris, illustrissimus* aber speziell die allerhöchste Rangstufe für die Amts- und Würdenträger (Not. dign. or. 2–15 und occ. 2–13; Cod. Theod. 6,7; 9,1; 14,1; Cod. Iust. 12,8,2; griech. adapt. Wort: *illústrios* Nov. Iust. 13,3; 15,1). Pflegen bis zur Mitte des 4. Jh. n. Chr. gleichermaßen alle Angehörigen des senatorischen Standes als *clari* oder *clarissimi* tituliert zu werden, so vollzieht sich danach allmählich eine Differenzierung nach senatorischen Inhabern hoher und höchster Hof- und Reichsämter, senatorischer Provinzialverwaltern und Senatoren ohne Karriere im Reichsdienst (Cod. Theod. 6,4,12). Am Ende dieser Entwicklung wird von Valentinian I. eine später in den Cod. Iust. (12,8,1, *lex* d.J. 440/1) übernommene Ordnung der höfischen Ränge eingeführt, in der die schon seit Mitte des 4. Jh. – wenn auch nicht exklusiv – verwendeten Rangbezeichnungen *spectabiles* und *illustres* (Cod. Theod. 11,30,31; 7,6,1) nunmehr strikt von denen für einfache Angehörige des senatorischen Standes abgegrenzt werden.

Nach dieser Ordnung werden in der *illustres*-Klasse ferner unterschieden: *illustres* kraft ihres Amtes (*in actu*), ferner die *vacantes* und die *honorarii* (Cod. Iust. 12,8,2). Zu den *i. in actu* gehören nach dieser Ordnung, teilweise aber auch schon früher, u.a. die Consuln (in der spätantiken Amtsform), der *praefectus urbi*, die *praefecti praetorio*, die *magistri militum*, der *praepositus sacri cubiculi*, der *quaestor palatii*, der *magister officiorum*, der *comes sacrarum largitionum*, der *comes sacri patrimonii* und die *comites domesticorum*.

Bis zum 6. Jh. wird die Stimmberechtigung im Senat auf die amtsinhabenden und die mittlerweile zahlreich gewordenen honorarischen *illustres viri* begrenzt (*qui a patriciis et consulibus usque ad omnes illustres viros descendunt, ... soli in senatu sententiam dicere possunt* – Dig. 1,9,12,1, ein auf die Redaktionszeit zu beziehendes Ulpian-Zitat). Honorarisch einbezogen in die *illustres* schon der Zeit Theodosius' I. (gest. 395 n. Chr.) ist u.a. der jüd. Patriarch (Cod. Theod. 16,8,8 d.J. 392); auch christl. Bischöfe können diesen Rang erhalten.

Mit dem Titel sind die Befreiung von *munera sordida* (→ *munera*) und anderen Lasten (z.B. Cod. Theod. 7,8,16; 11,16,23), ferner Privilegien im Zivil- und Kriminalprozeß und eine Anzahl weiterer Ehrungen verbunden (Cod. Iust. 12,1,16f.). Diese Privilegien gehen prinzipiell auch auf die Frauen über (Cod. Theod. 2,1,7; Cod. Iust. 12,1,13).
→ Comes; Hoftitel

A. CHASTAGNOL, Le sénat romain à l'époque impériale, 1992, 293–324 • JONES, LRE 528–536 • H. LÖHKEN, Ordo Dignitatum, 1982, 112–147. C.G.

Illyricum (auch *Hilluricum*, *Hillyricum*, *Illuricum*). Die erste röm. Prov. an der O-Küste der Adria, 167 v. Chr. als röm. Herrschaftsgebiet organisiert, ehemals Teil des illyr. Königreichs.

A. FORSCHUNGSLAGE B. VORRÖMISCHE GESCHICHTE C. RÖMISCHE PROVINZ D. NACHPROVINZIALE ZEIT E. KULTUR

A. FORSCHUNGSLAGE

Der Begriff I. wird unterschiedlich verstanden. Die Diskussion über die »illyr. Frage« erreichte ihren Höhepunkt mit dem Panillyrismus, der in den Illyrern Träger der Urnenfeld-Kultur sah (vgl. die Publikationen von H. KRAHE, dessen Schlußfolgerungen seither aber gründlich revidiert wurden). In der Zeit von den Anfängen bis zum Zusammenbruch des illyr. Königreichs zeigen sich die Illyrer in variierenden Allianzen mit Stämmen gemeinsamer oder ähnlicher Herkunft und Sprache. Nur PN und geogr. Namen blieben von ihnen übrig; es ist nicht sicher, ob die illyr. Sprachen zu der Kentum- oder der Satem-Gruppe (→ Kentumsprache, → Satemsprache) gehörten; auch der Begriff »Illyrisch« ist nicht mehr gesichert, man spricht vielmehr höchstens von »illyrisch«, vorkeltisch oder einheimisch. Wichtig sind die onomastischen Studien von KATIČIĆ, in denen der Versuch unternommen wird, verschiedene onomastische Regionen gegeneinander abzugrenzen, darunter auch die illyr. Namen, die für die südöstl. Regionen der Adriaküste mit Hinterland bezeugt sind – nur diese lassen sich mit Recht als illyr. bezeichnen. Ein zentrales Forschungsproblem ist die Frage nach einem illyr. Urstamm (vgl. *Illyrii proprie dicti*, Plin. nat. 3,144; Mela 2,56; vgl. auch die Sage von → Kadmos und Harmonia); denn von Anf. an wird das Wort »Illyrer« bei den ant. Autoren in der Bed. eines Stammesverbands gebraucht. Sie werden nach Plin. l.c. im *conventus* von Narona zw. Epidauros und Lissos lokalisiert, wo die ersten Kontakte zw. griech. Kaufleuten und/oder Forschungsreisenden einerseits und Einwohnern der Region, die nachmals als Illyris/Illyria bekannt war, andererseits geknüpft wurden. Jedoch waren die Illyrer in der griech. Welt kaum bekannt, weil die griech. Kolonisation an der ostadriatischen Küste nur sehr begrenzt (Epidamnos/Dyrrhachion, Apollonia) oder spät (z.B. Issa, Pharos) eingesetzt hat.

B. Vorrömische Geschichte

Die frühesten Erwähnungen der Illyrer finden sich bei Hekat. (FGrH 1 F 98–101, vgl. 93–97) und Hdt. (1,196; 4,49); die meisten Angaben über illyr. Stämme enthält der Periplus des Ps.-Skyl. (ca. 330 v. Chr., GGM 1,26 ff.) und Ps-Skymn. (2. Jh. v. Chr., GGM 1,211 ff.). Ihr Territorium soll sich nach Ps.-Skyl. von der Enchelei bis zu den → Chaones (Nord-Epeiros) erstreckt haben. Von den im Landesinnern lebenden Völkern werden nur die → Autariatae als illyr. bezeichnet. Im Bereich dieser illyr. Stämme konstituierte sich ein illyr. Königreich in Süd-I. (5. Jh. v. Chr.), dessen bekannteste Vertreter sich in der letzten, der ardiaeischen Dynastie des Agron (Sohn des Pleuratos) und der Teuta finden. Ihr Name wurde eponym für viele benachbarte Stämme, die nur lose mit ihnen in Verbindung standen. Die früheren Dynastien (mit Bardylis, Grabos, Kleitos, Glaukias) sind hauptsächlich durch ihre Auseinandersetzungen mit den Makedonen bekannt, und zwar seitdem sie ca. 393 v. Chr. in Makedonien eingedrungen waren; ihre frühen Kontakte sind nicht dokumentiert, später aber waren sie im allg. Feinde der Makedonen.

Das Protektorat, das die Römer nach dem Fall des Genthios 167 v. Chr. über einen Teil des illyr. Gebiets errichteten (Teile des Gebiets der Parthini und → Atintanes südl. von Lissos im Hinterland von Dyrrhachion, vgl. Liv. 45,26,15), wurde griech. *Illyrís*, lat. *Illyria* genannt. Nach der Niederlage des Perseus 168 wurde es der *prov. Macedonia* als *4. merís* einverleibt. Dieses Protektorat ist wohl der Ursprung der röm. Vorstellung von I. gewesen. Alle folgenden röm. Eroberungen, zuerst des Restes des illyr. Königreiches, dann der nördl. Küstenregionen und des dalmat. Hinterlandes, wurden Illyris/Illyria allmählich hinzugefügt. Verwaltungstechnisch wurden zahlreiche Stämme und Völker, die zu den Illyrern keine ethnischen Verbindungen hatten (→ Liburni, → Histria), I. zugerechnet und illyr. gen., weil sie in I. lebten. Griech. und lat. Autoren der Zeit nach der Gründung des Protektorats von I. im 2. Jh. v. Chr. (aus dem die Prov. I. im 1. Jh. v. Chr. entstand), die Illyris/Illyria und/oder I. und Illyrer erwähnten, taten dies nur in bezug auf die Verwaltungsorganisation des Balkans oder in geogr. Sinn, denn der NW der Halbinsel gehörte größtenteils zu I. *Illyrís* war nach Strabon ein Land, das sich von den oberen Gebieten des Adriaraums bis hinunter zum Rhyzonischen Golf und dem Land der Ardiaei erstreckte, zw. dem Meer und den pannon. Völkern (7,5,3; vgl. App. Ill. 1; Cass. Dio 12; Zon. 8,19,8). Ihre Feldzüge führten die Römer hauptsächlich von ihren Stützpunkten an der ital. Küste der Adria aus. Die röm. Armee operierte auch von → Gallia Cisalpina aus; diese Angriffe richteten sich gegen verschiedene Stämme und Völker, die später in die Prov. I. eingingen, v. a. die Histri, die schon 177 v. Chr. unterworfen wurden. Im allg. war das gesamte Territorium südl. des Formio als I. bekannt; unter Augustus, wahrscheinlich 18/12 v. Chr., wurde Histria It. zugeschlagen und zusammen mit Venetia der 10. Region eingegliedert.

C. Römische Provinz

Es ist nicht möglich, ein exaktes Datum der Schaffung der Prov. I. anzugeben: nach Th. Mommsen dürfte die Prov. von Sulla (CIL III p. 279) eingerichtet worden sein. Caesar war wohl der erste, der I. einem ausschließlich diese Prov. verwaltenden Unterstatthalter übertrug (Vatinius 45–43), denn er selbst leitete seit 58 v. Chr. beide Prov. Gallien und I. Die Senatsprov. I. umfaßte große Teile der späteren Prov. Dalmatia und Teile von Pannonia. Nach dem pannon.-dalmat. Aufstand 9 n. Chr. dürfte I. in *I. superius* und *I. inferius* geteilt worden sein (vgl. ILS 938). Als unter Vespasianus die Prov. Dalmatia und Pannonia aus I. gebildet wurden, behielt keine der neugebildeten Prov. den alten Namen bei. Schon unter Augustus hatte der Name I. nichts mehr mit dem urspr. illyr. Territorium im Süden von Dalmatia zu tun; er bezeichnete vielmehr den ganzen Nord- und Zentralbalkan (vgl. Suet. Tib. 16,4). I. umfaßte ein größeres Territorium als Pannonia und Dalmatia zusammen, wohl auch die Gebiete, die durch die Proconsuln von Macedonia im 2./1. Jh. erobert worden waren, und deckte sich mehr oder weniger mit der künftigen Prov. Moesia. Der Name I. wurde jetzt für andere administrative Einheiten verwendet, so z. B. für die Zollgebiete (*publicum portorii Illyrici*), die den größten Teil von Raetia bis zum Pontos Euxeinos umfaßten (App. Ill. 6).

D. Nachprovinziale Zeit

Der Begriff I. war wohl der einzig verfügbare mit dem notwendigen Bedeutungsbereich, um auch nur annähernd die in Betracht kommenden Gebiete abzudecken; es ist sicher, daß diese Bezeichnung den Weg für den spätant. Wortgebrauch freigab, als »illyrisch« unter Septimius Severus die auf dem Balkan stationierte Armee und später mehrere Kaiser, die vom Balkan stammten, bezeichnete. Seit Diocletianus deckte sich I. mehr oder weniger mit den Regionen des *publicum portorii Illyrici*; denn in der pannon. Balkanregion wurden drei Diözesen der neuen territorial-verwaltungstechnischen Gliederung des Reiches geschaffen (Pannonia, Moesia, Thracia): sie rechneten zum I., einer der vier von Constantinus geschaffenen Präfekturen. In der *Notitia dignitatum* (ca. 395 n. Chr.) umfaßt die Präfektur I. (*Illyricum orientale*) aber die Diözesen Macedonia (mit Griechenland) und Dacia, während die Diözese I. (*Illyricum occidentale*) zur Präfektur Italia rechnet, mit den zwei Prov. von Noricum, den vier Prov. von Pannonia sowie Dalmatia, aber ohne Praevalitana (→ Diocletianus, Karte).

E. Kultur

Fast nichts ist über die illyr. Sprache bekannt (→ Balkanhalbinsel, Sprachen, mit Karte); bei Hesychios wird nur ein Wort als illyr. definiert, während über 100 als maked. bezeichnet werden. Es gibt große onomastische und kulturelle Unterschiede der einzelnen Völker in I. Einige erreichten einen höheren Entwicklungsgrad; das Zivilisationsgefälle war bes. groß zw. den Küstenvölkern und den Stämmen im Landesinneren. Der verbindende Faktor war hauptsächlich die lokal unterschiedlich starke Romanisierung.

G. ZIPPEL, Die röm. Herrschaft in Illyrien bis auf Augustus, 1877 • H. KRAHE, Lexikon altillyr. PN, 1929 • Ders., Die Sprache der Illyrier 1: Die Quellen, 1955 • M. SUIĆ, Istočna Jadranska obala u Pseudo Skilakovu Periplu [Eastern Adriatic Coast in Pseudo-Scylax's Periplus], in: Rad Jugoslavenske akademije znanosti i umjetnosti 306, 1955, 121–186 • A. MAYER, Die Sprache der alten Illyrier 1, 1957; 2, 1959 • F. PAPAZOGLOU, Les origines et la destinée de l'état illyrien, in: Historia 14, 1965, 143–179 • R. KATIČIĆ, Ancient Languages of the Balkans 1, 1976 • H. PARZINGER, Arch. zur Frage der Illyrier, in: Ber. der Röm.-german. Kommission 72, 1991, 205–246 • J. WILKES, The Illyrians, 1992 • M. ŠAŠEL KOS, Cadmus and Harmonia in Illyria, in: Arheološki vestnik 44, 1993, 113–136. M.Š.K./Ü: I.S.

Illyrisch s. Balkanhalbinsel, Sprachen

Illyrische Kaiser. Als I. K. wird eine Gruppe von röm. Herrschern bezeichnet, deren gemeinsames Merkmal ihre Herkunft aus dem illyrischen Raum, im weiteren Sinne das Gebiet zwischen der Adria und der unteren Donau, ist. Die Reihe beginnt bereits mit → Decius [II 1] (249–251 n. Chr.), umfaßt aber im wesentlichen die Kaiser → Claudius [III 2] Gothicus, → Aurelianus [2], → Probus, → Diocletianus, → Maximianus und → Constantinus [1] I. Diesen Herrschern schrieb man bereits in der Ant. wenig Bildung, andererseits aber Vertrautheit mit dem Kriegsdienst und beste Eignung zur Staatsverwaltung zu (Aur. Vict. Caes. 39,26). Sie verdankten ihren Aufstieg in der Regel ihrer mil. Tüchtigkeit und trugen durch innere Reformen und außenpolit. Erfolge stark zur Behebung der Krise des 3. Jh. bei. Ihre Herkunft aus längst romanisierten, aber schwach christianisierten Provinzen erklärt auch, warum einige (Decius, Diocletianus, Maximianus) die Verfolgung der Christen systematisch und reichsweit betrieben. T.F.

Ilorci. Ibererstadt in der Gegend des oberen → Baetis mit dem Grabmahl eines der beiden 211 v. Chr. gefallenen Scipiones, wahrscheinlich des Cn. Scipio (Plin. nat. 3,25). Die Gleichsetzung von I. mit h. Lorca (Prov. Murcia) ist nicht unumstritten. CIL II p. 476.

A. SCHULTEN (Hrsg.), Fontes Hispaniae Antiquae 3, 1935, 91 • J. B. KEUNE, s. v. I., RE Suppl. 3, 1229 • G. ALFÖLDY, Röm. Städtewesen auf der neukastilischen Hochebene, 1981, 38. P.B.

Ilos (Ἶλος).

[1] Heros Eponymos und Gründer von Ilios/Ilion (→ Troia); Sohn des → Tros, Vater des → Laomedon (Hom. Il. 20,231 ff.; → Dardanidai). Sein Grab ist in der *Ilias* (11,166 u.ö.) als topograph. Fixpunkt in der Ebene vor Troia genannt. Die ausführlichste Version der Gründungslegende bietet Apollod. 3,140 ff.; eine Münze Kaiser Caracallas aus Ilion zeigt I. opfernd vor dem → Palladion, das er laut Apollodor bei der Gründung der Stadt von Zeus erhielt.

[2] Nach Verg. Aen. 1,267 f. urspr. Name des Aineias-Sohnes → Iulus/Askanios, über den sich die *gens Iulia* auf das troische Herrschergeschlecht und Aphrodite zurückführte [1. 317 ff.].

1 G. BINDER, Der brauchbare Held: Aeneas, in: H.-J. HORN, H. WALTER (Hrsg.), Die Allegorese des ant. Mythos, 1997, 311–330.

R. VOLLKOMMER, s. v. I., LIMC 5.1, 650 • P. WATHELET, Dictionnaire des Troyens de l'Iliade, 1988, Nr. 162. MA.ST.

Iltis. Ob mit γαλῆ/*galḗ* bzw. ἰκτίς/*iktís*, lat. *mustela* bzw. *viverra* das Große Wiesel (Mustela erminea L.) oder der Iltis (M. putorius L.) gemeint ist, bleibt unklar. Der I. kommt aber h. in Griechenland nicht vor [1. Bd. 1, 163]. Fest steht, daß dieses Tier bei den Römern als gefürchteter Räuber unter dem Federvieh bekannt war und deshalb schon bei Varro (rust. 3,12,3) als *faelis* (bei Colum. 8,14,9 sind es *viverra, faelesve ... mustela*) von deren Gehegen ferngehalten werden mußte. Aristoteles kennt die *galḗ* jedenfalls recht gut (knochige Rute: hist. an. 2,1,500b 24 = Plin. nat. 11,261; guter Mäusejäger: Aristot. hist. an. 6,37,580b 26; Kampf mit Schlangen, gegen deren Gift er sich mit einer Pflanze schützen soll: 8(9),6,612a 30 = Plin. nat. 8,98 und 20,132; beißt Vögeln den Hals durch: Aristot. hist. an. 8(9),6,612b 1). Plinius empfiehlt seine Körperteile vielfach in der Medizin [2. 2,64].
→ Frettchen

1 KELLER 2 O. SCHNEIDER, In C. Plini Secundi naturalis historiae libros indices, 1857 (Ndr. 1967). C.HÜ.

Iluraton (Ἰλούρατον). Griech.-skyth. Siedlung nördl. des Curubas-Sees im Inneren von h. Kerč, ca. 17 km von Pantikapaion entfernt. Siedlungsspuren seit dem Neolithikum; gegr. Mitte des 1. Jh. n. Chr. Die Befunde der Ausgrabungen sind repräsentativ für andere Binnensiedlungen im Bosporanischen Reich zur röm. Zeit: I. war natürlich und künstlich stark befestigt. Die Einwohner waren Wehrbauern, die Ackerbau und Viehzucht betrieben, hellenisierte Nachkommen der Skythen: Lebensart, rel. Vorstellungen und Kulte waren vorwiegend skyth., die Muttersprache griech. 266–268 n. Chr. von den Goten zerstört.

V. F. GAIDUKEVIČ, Ilurat, in: Materialy instituta arheologii 85, 1958, 9–148 • Ders., Das Bosporan. Reich, 1971, 409 f. I. v. B.

Ilurcavones (Ilercavones). Ein Ibererstamm um Dertosa am unteren Ebro. 218 v. Chr. unterwarfen sie sich den Römern (Liv. 21,60,3; für spätere Zeiten vgl. auch Liv. 22,21,6; Caes. civ. 1,60,2; Ptol. 2,6,16; Plin. nat. 3,21).

A. SCHULTEN (Hrsg.), Fontes Hispaniae Antiquae 4–8, 1925 ff. (Index) • TOVAR 3, 34 f. P.B.

Ilva. Insel im *mare Tyrrhenum* vor Populonia (Αἰθάλη, Αἰθαλία: Hekat. FGrH 1 F 59; Ps.-Skyl. 6), h. Elba. Der *limēn Argōos* (λιμὴν Ἀργῷος) soll von den → Argonautai gegr. worden sein (Strab. 5,2,6; andere führen den Namen auf die weiße Farbe des Strandes zurück). Besiedelt seit dem Neolithikum. I. war berühmt für die seit etr. Zeit ausgebeuteten Eisenerzminen (Verhüttungsschlakken auf Pithekussai und in Populonia). 453 v. Chr. wurde I. kurzfristig von Syrakusai besetzt (Diod. 11,88,4f.). Befestigungen liegen bei Monte Castello und Castiglione San Martino, ein Heiligtum bei Monte Serra, in Grotte di Portoferraio und Cavo di Rio Marina prachtvolle röm. *villae*; in den Gewässern um die Insel zahlreiche Schiffswracks.

V. MELLINI, Memorie storiche dell'isola d'Elba, 1965 • M. ZECCHINI, Gli Etruschi all'isola d'Elba, 1978 • Ders., L'isola d'Elba, 1982 • L. CORSI, s. v. Elba, BTCGI 7, 127–146. G.U./Ü: H.D.

Ilvates. Ligur. Stamm zw. Appenninus, Placentia und Regium. 200 v. Chr. Aufstand gegen Rom unter pun. Führung (Liv. 31,10,2), 197 v. Chr. unterworfen (Liv. 32,29,7; 31,4). Evtl. identisch mit den Eleiates der *Fasti Triumphales*.

Fontes Ligurum et Liguriae antiquae, 1976, s. v. I. L.S.A./Ü: J.W.M.

Imachara (Ἰμάχαρα). Kleine Stadt auf Sizilien (Cic. Verr. 2,3,47; Plin. nat. 3,91; Ptol. 3,4,12,3; erh. sind Kerykeion, IG XIV 589, Litrai in zwei Versionen). Die Identifikation mit der Grabungsstätte bei Nissoria ist denkbar. Im Gebiet von I. befand sich ein Fluß (Rv. der Litra).

E. MANNI, Geografia fisica e politica della Sicilia antica (Testimonia Siciliae antiqua 1,1), Kokalos Suppl. 4, 1981, 190 • R. J. A. WILSON, Sicily under the Roman Empire, 145, 378 Nr. 14 • S. CATALDI, s. v. I., BTCGI 8, 238–247 • G. MANGANARO, Alla ricerca di poleis mikrai della Sicilia centro-orientale, in: Orbis Terrarum 2, 1996, 144 Nr. 74. GI.MA./Ü: H.D.

Imaginarius (wörtlich: »bildlich«) war im röm. Recht die Bezeichnung für ein Rechtsgeschäft, das etwas anderes ausdrückte als von den Parteien eigentlich gewünscht war. Das plastischste Beispiel ist die → *mancipatio nummo uno*, eine Übereignung gegen und durch Zahlung mit einer bloß symbolischen Kupfermünze (*aes*). In ihrem äußeren Bild war sie ein Barkauf; in der realen Wirkung konnte sie Übereignung zu beliebigen Zwecken, also »abstrakt« sein – dann lag eine *imaginaria venditio* (Gai. inst. 1,113) vor. Haftung bedeutete im frühen röm. Recht Unterworfenheit unter die Zugriffsgewalt des Gläubigers. Die Lösung von ihr (*solutio*) bedurfte ebenfalls eines formalen Geschäftes. Wurde die Schuld einfach bezahlt, gelang die Lösung von der Haftung nur durch eine *imaginaria solutio*, bei der wiederum symbolisch mit einer Münze an eine Waage geschlagen wurde (→ *libripens*). Später war die *imaginaria solutio* die Form des Erlasses einer bestehenden Schuld. Neben dieser sehr alten legitimen Verwendung rechtlicher Formen zu neuen Zwecken bezeichnet z. B. *imaginaria venditio* seit dem 2. oder 3. Jh. n. Chr. auch ein mißbilligtes Geschäft, das bloß zum Schein vorgenommen wird, um damit eine verbotene Gestaltung (z. B. Schenkung unter Ehegatten) zu verbergen (z. B. Paul. Dig. 18,1,55).

HONSELL/MAYER-MALY/SELB, 100f. • A. BERGER, s. v. I., RE 9, 1094–1097. G.S.

Imagines maiorum A. BEGRIFF B. FUNKTION C. WIRKUNG AUF ANDERE DARSTELLUNGSFORMEN

A. BEGRIFF

Obwohl *imago* grundsätzlich jedes Abbild, häufig auch Porträtbüsten aus verschiedenem Material bezeichnet, versteht man unter *i.m.* (oft einfach *imagines*) vornehmlich die Wachsbilder (daher auch *cerae*: Ov. am. 1,8,65; Iuv. 8,19) der → Ahnen, die im → Atrium vornehmer röm. Häuser aufbewahrt wurden. Ob aus Cicero (Verr. 2,5,36 *ius imaginis ad memoriam posteritatemque prodendae*) mit MOMMSEN [7. 442–4] gefolgert werden darf, daß solche Bilder nur von kurulischen Magistraten existierten, ist nicht gesichert (kritisch [3. 108; 9. 32f.]). Der Brauch galt als alt, bestand mindestens seit dem 3. Jh. v. Chr. und wird von Polybios (6,53,4–10) ausführlich beschrieben. Da arch. Funde fehlen, bleibt unklar, ob es sich um Gesichts- oder (wahrscheinlicher) Ganzmasken handelte, ob sie zu Lebzeiten (so zuletzt [5. 2[38]]) oder als Totenmasken abgeformt oder vielmehr ohne Gipsform frei modelliert wurden.

B. FUNKTION

Die Bilder, die von *fictores* (Serv. Aen. 8,654) hergestellt wurden und die Verstorbenen lebensecht repräsentierten, wurden einzeln in Schränken aufbewahrt (Pol. 6,53,4; Plin. nat. 35,6), die an Festtagen geöffnet (Pol. 6,53,6; *imagines aperire* ist t.t. von Cic. Sull. 88 bis SHA Tac. 19,6) und aus bes. Anlaß mit Lorbeer bekränzt wurden (Cic. Mur. 88). Für eine kult. Verehrung der *i.m.* gibt es jedoch nicht den geringsten Anhaltspunkt [1. 115–7]. Den Bildern waren *tituli* beigegeben (Hor. sat. 1,6,17; Val. Max. 5,8,3), die Namen und Ämter, manchmal auch Taten der Dargestellten erwähnten (bes. Liv. 10,7,11; zur vermutlichen Entwicklung der *tituli* [5. 180–84]) und manchmal auch Übertreibungen oder Erfindungen enthielten (Liv. 8,40,4–5). Die *i.m.* hielten den nachwachsenden Generationen Leistung und Ruhm der Familie eindrucksvoll gegenwärtig und spornten sie zu entsprechenden Leistungen an (Sall. Iug. 4,5f.; weiteres bei [6]).

Wichtigste Funktion der *i.m.* war nach Plinius (nat. 35,6) die Verwendung bei der → Bestattung (D. 2) der Nachkommen. Die magistratischen Vorfahren des (oder der) Verstorbenen, repräsentiert durch Personen, die Masken mit den Zügen der Ahnen und die diesen zustehende Amtstracht trugen, begleiteten den Leichenzug (auf Wagen: Pol. 6,53,8; später wohl auf Bahren getragen) zum Forum und nahmen vor den *rostra* (→ Rednerbühne) auf ihren → *sellae curules* Platz, um der Leichenrede (→ *laudatio funebris*) zuzuhören, an deren Ende auch ihre Taten lobend aufgezählt wurden. Das war nicht nur ein nachdrücklicher Ansporn für die jüngeren Zuhörer (Pol. 6,54,3), sondern auch eine machtvolle Demonstration gentilizischen Ruhmes vor der ganzen Bürgerschaft (weitergehende Deutungen z.B. in [4; 5]).

Die Teilnahme der *i.m.* am Leichenzug blieb auch in der Kaiserzeit üblich. Bei den Begräbnissen prominenter *privati* wurden öfter die Bilder verwandter Familien mitgeführt (z.B. Tac. ann. 3,76,2), bei Kaiserbegräbnissen sogar solche von beliebigen Größen der röm. Geschichte (z.B. Cass. Dio 56,34,2). Unberücksichtigt blieben die vergöttlichten Mitglieder des Kaiserhauses, da sie nicht als Verstorbene galten. Die Teilnahme der *i.m.* bestimmter verurteilter Straftäter (Caesar-Mörder: Tac. ann. 3,76,2; M. → Scribonius Libo Drusus: Tac. ann. 2,32,1; Cn. → Calpurnius [II 16] Piso: *SC de Cn. Pisone patre* 76–82) an Leichenzügen war ausdrücklich verboten. Für die Spätant. ist die Teilnahme der Ahnen am Leichenzug nicht mehr bezeugt, doch gab es weiter *i.m.* in den vornehmen Häusern [5. 264–269].

C. Wirkung auf andere Darstellungsformen

Da keine *i.m.* erhalten sind, lassen sich Auswirkungen auf Porträtdarstellungen in anderen Medien schwer nachweisen. Auf röm. Mz. finden sich seit etwa 60 v.Chr. realistische Bilder von Vorfahren der Münzmeister, denen *i.m.* als Vorlage gedient haben können (RRC 437,1–4; 439,1; 450,3; 455,1; 494,26–31: dazu [10]). Ganz umstritten ist die Beziehung der republikanischen Porträt-Plastik (→ Porträt) zu den *i.m.*; auch wenn die früher oft vertretene Herleitung des realistischen Porträts von der Totenmaske heute meist abgelehnt wird ([2]; gegen die abweichende Position von [3] z.B. [8. 30f.]), ist ein Zusammenhang mit (frei modellierten) *i.m.* nicht auszuschließen.

1 F. Bömer, Ahnenbild und Ahnenglaube im alten Rom, 1943, 104–123 **2** F. Brommer, Zu den röm. Ahnenbildern, in: MDAI(R) 60/61, 1953/54, 163–171 (= Röm. Porträts, 1974, 336–348) **3** H. Drerup, Totenmaske und Ahnenbild bei den Römern, in: MDAI(R) 87, 1980, 81–129 **4** E. Flaig, Die Pompa Funebris, in: O. G. Oexle (Hrsg.), Memoria als Kultur, 1995, 115–148 **5** H. I. Flower, Ancestor Masks and Aristocratic Power in Roman Culture, 1996 (umfassende Bibliogr.) **6** G. Lahusen, Zur Funktion und Rezeption des röm. Ahnenbildes, in: MDAI(R) 92, 1985, 261–289 **7** Mommsen, Staatsrecht 1, 442–447 **8** R. R. R. Smith, Greeks, Foreigners and Roman Republican Portraits, in: JRS 71, 1981, 24–38 **9** A. N. Zadoks-Josephus Jitta, Ancestral Portraiture in Rome and the Art of the Last Century of the Republic, 1932 **10** H. Zehnacker, Moneta, 1973, 994–1007.

W.K.

Imaginiferi, Imaginifarii. Der *imaginifer* war ein Soldat, der zumindest bei Festen ein Bildnis (*imago*) des Princeps trug (Veg. mil. 2,6; 2,7; Ios. ant. Iud. 18,55); sicherlich besaßen die *i.* keine direkt mil. Aufgaben. In jeder Legion gab es einen *imaginifer*, der jedoch nicht unbedingt der ersten Kohorte (→ *cohors*) angehörte (CIL III 2553: 3. Kohorte). Nach Vegetius (mil. 2,7) waren *i.* auch in anderen Einheiten vertreten. Inschriftlich sind *i.* für die *cohortes urbanae* und die → *vigiles* in Rom sowie für die Legionen und die Einheiten der → *auxilia* (*alae*, *cohortes* und *numeri*), nicht aber für die Praetorianer nachgewiesen. Die bildliche Darstellung eines *imaginifer* findet sich auf dem Grabrelief des Genialis, der die an einer langen Stange befestigte *imago* in der rechten Hand hält (Landesmuseum Mainz Inv.Nr. S.509; ILS 9167). Die *imagines* sind wohl nicht identisch mit den Bildern auf den *signa* (→ Feldzeichen). Unklar ist, ob das Heer auf diese Weise nur den regierenden Princeps oder auch einige seiner Vorgänger ehrte. Nach Constantinus I. hat es im röm. Heer wahrscheinlich keine *i.* mehr gegeben.

1 Domaszewski, 69 **2** Domaszewski/Dobson, 43 **3** M. Durry, Cohortes prétoriennes, [2]1968, 206 **4** R. O. Fink, Roman Military Records on Papyrus, 1971 **5** G. Walser, Röm. Inschrift-Kunst, 1988, 228f.

Y.L.B./Ü: C.P.

Imam (arab. *imām*, allg. »Leiter, Anführer«). 1. Leiter des Gebets, d.h. Vorbeter in der Moschee; 2. Leiter der Gemeinde aller Muslime in der Nachfolge des Propheten → Mohammed (Muḥammad), d.h. rel. und polit. Oberhaupt. Unterschiedliche Auffassungen der Rechtsschulen und Glaubensrichtungen bezüglich Qualifikationen, Investitur und Funktionen/Pflichten des I. lassen sich erkennen. Bei den → Sunniten: Bewahrer von Glaube, (rel.) Recht und Gerechtigkeit. Die auf die vier rechtgeleiteten → Kalifen folgenden I. waren zunehmend weltliche Herrscher. Bei den Zwölfer- und anderen → Schiiten: Die Qualitäten des unfehlbaren I. sind – abgesehen von der Offenbarungsvermittlung – prophetische. Der seit E. 9. Jh. »verborgene« zwölfte I. wird als Mahdī (eine Art → Messias) zurückerwartet.

W. Madelung, s.v. Imāma, EI 3, 1163b–1169b. H.SCHÖ.

Imaon. Griech. Name des Himalaja, altind. Himavān, → Emodos. K.K.

Imbrasos (Ἴμβρασος). Fluß auf Samos (Plin. nat. 5,135), ant. auch als Parthenios (Strab. 10,2,17) bezeichnet, in der Nähe des Hera-Tempels, h. Imvrasos. Unter dem Lygosbaum (Keuschlammbaum) am Ufer des I. soll gemäß ant. Trad. Hera geboren worden sein (Paus. 7,4,4; Apoll. Rhod. 1,187), was Anlaß zu periodisch wiederkehrenden kult. Handlungen im Wasser des I. gab.

E. Buschor, I., in: MDAI(A) 68, 1953 (1956), 1–10 • H.J. Kienast, Zum heiligen Baum der Hera auf Samos, in: MDAI(A) 106, 1991, 71–80 • G. Shipley, A History of Samos 800–188 B.C., 1987, 280. H.SO.

Imbrios (Ἴμβριος). Sohn des Mentor aus Pedaion, der die Priamos-Tochter Medesikaste zur Frau hat und seit Beginn des troian. Krieges bei seinem Schwiegervater wohnt. Er wird beim Kampf um die Schiffe von → Teukros getötet (Hom. Il. 13,170ff.; Paus. 10,25,9).

C. W.

Imbros (Ἴμβρος, h. türk. *Imroz adası*). Insel der nördl. Sporaden am Südausgang des Hellespontos, 30 km lang, 13 km breit, 225 km² groß, Hügelland bis 597 m ansteigend. Die Stadt I., h. Kastro, lag im Osten der Nordküste; Reste der Stadtmauer. Als urspr. Bewohner werden Pelasgoi oder Tyrrhenoi gen. Wohl durch Miltiades wurde I. um 500 v. Chr. athenisch und blieb es bis in die Kaiserzeit (Hdt. 6,41; 104; Thuk. 7,57,2; Xen. hell. 5,1,31). Im → Attisch-Delischen Seebund erscheint I. mit Tributsummen zw. 3300 Drachmen und 1 Talent (ATL 1, 292f.; 3, 289f.). Belege: Hom. Il. 13,33; 14,281; Skyl. 67; IG XII 8 Nr. 46–149, S. 2ff. Suppl. S. 148; HN 261f.

K. Fredrich, s. v. I., RE 9, 1105–1107 • Ders., I., in: MDAI(A) 33, 1908, 81ff. • E. Oberhummer, I., in: Beitr. zur alten Gesch. FS für H. Kiepert, 1898, 81ff.

H. KAL.

Imitatio s. Intertextualität, s. Mimesis

Immarados (Ἰμμάραδος/Ἴσμαρος). Eleusinier, Sohn des → Eumolpos. I. führt allein oder mit dem Vater ein thrak. Heer gegen die Athener und wird in diesem »Eleusinischen Krieg« von → Erechtheus getötet (Apollod. 3,202). Der Zweikampf war in einer Bronzegruppe des → Myron auf der Akropolis von Athen dargestellt (Paus. 1,5,2).

RE. ZI.

Immiscere, se (*alicui rei*, »sich in etwas einlassen«). Ein *suus heres* (Hauserbe, → Erbrecht III A) konnte eine gesetzliche oder testamentarische Erbschaft nicht wirksam nach → *ius civile* ausschlagen (*semel heres semper heres*), wurde aber, wenn er vor dem Prätor die Ausschlagung erklärte, von diesem so behandelt, als sei er nicht Erbe geworden (→ *abstentio*). Hatte er sich aber einmal äußerlich wie ein Erbe verhalten (*i.*), so verlor er das → *beneficium abstinendi*. Ferner bezeichnet *i.* den Beginn der Wahrnehmung sonstiger Geschäfte. Erst seit dem 4. Jh. n. Chr. bedeutet *i.* soviel wie »sich unbefugt einmischen« oder »strafbare Handlungen begehen« (anders [1]).

1 A. Berger, s. v. I. se, RE 9, 1107–1112 2 Kaser, RPR I, 715.

U. M.

Immolatio ist die lat. Bezeichnung für den Vorgang des Opferns, die Opferhandlung, im Gegensatz zu der Opfergabe (Früchte, Brot, Wein) oder dem Opfertier (*hostia*). Das Opfer war eines der einfachsten Arten, sich im röm. Privat- wie Staatskult gegenüber einer Gottheit zu äußern. Der lat. Ausdruck *i.* umschreibt diesen Vorgang; urspr. Bed.: das Bestreuen des Opfertieres mit gesalzenem Spelt, dem Opferdinkel (*immolare* = mit Opfermehl, *mola salsa*, bestreuen; vgl. Fest. 124 L.; Fest. 97 L. s. v. *immolare*; Serv. Aen. 10,541). *I.* bezeichnet somit den Akt der Reinigung vor der eigentlichen Tötung. Der Begriff zeigt, daß die Römer das Wesentliche am Opfer nicht in der Schlachtung, sondern in der Darbringung, der Weihung der Opfertiere, sahen; seine Ausweitung auf die Tötung des Tieres erfolgte erst später.

Die *i.* diente unterschiedlichen Zielen: Mehrung der Kraft der Götter durch die Opfergabe (*mactare*), Bitte (Cato agr. 139; 141), Dank, Versöhnung eines zürnenden Gottes, Sühne für ein falsches Verhalten gegenüber einer Gottheit. Vor jedem wichtigen Akt von staatlich-polit. Interesse wurde eine Opferung durchgeführt: bei Amtsantritt der Beamten (Consuln, Censoren), vor Kriegshandlungen (Auszug in den Krieg, → *Lustratio*, → *Suovetaurilia*), seit Augustus vor Senatssitzungen (Rauchopfer; Suet. Aug. 35; Cass. Dio 54,30,1), sowie z. B. bei Götterfesten, Tempelgeburtstagen oder Einlösung von Gelübden. Zu unterscheiden ist zwischen unblutigen und blutigen Opfern. Erstere fanden hauptsächlich im Hauskult statt; da die urspr. Rel. bzw. die Götter zum großen Teil dem alten Bauernkalender entlehnt waren, wurden hierbei in erster Linie landwirtschaftliche Güter (Feldfrüchte, Herdentiere) geopfert. Im bes. Maße zählten hierzu die Erstlingsopfer (*primitiae*) zum Dank für eine gute Ernte. Wegen ihres engen Bezugs zum häuslichen Umfeld bestanden die Gaben häufig aus Anteilen vom Eßtisch, d. h. den Mahlzeiten, die den Hausgöttern (→ *lares*, → *penates*) dargebracht wurden. Hierzu gehörten ebenso Rauchopfer, bei denen den Göttern der Wohlgeruch bestimmter Pflanzen (Weihrauch, Gewürze) gespendet oder Früchte und andere feste Gaben (Brot, Kuchen) auf dem Altar verbrannt wurden. Trankopfer (Wein, Most, Milch) konnten allein oder als Voropfer vor jedem anderen Opfer vollzogen werden. Voraussetzung war in jedem Fall die Eignung der Gaben zum Opfer, bes. Makellosigkeit.

Blutige Opfer, d. h. Tieropfer, herrschten im Staatskult vor. Geopfert wurden vor allem Schweine, Rinder und Schafe. Die Tiere mußten neben ihrer Makellosigkeit bestimmte Kriterien (Alter, Geschlecht, Farbe; Plin. nat. 8,183) erfüllen. Die *i.* wurde nach einem festgelegten Ritus vollzogen. Zu einem Tieropfer gehörten viele verschiedene Handlungen, die sowohl durch die ant. Schriftquellen wie auch durch die arch. Quellen gut dokumentiert sind: a) Beginn des Opfervorgangs: *probatio hostiae* oder *victimae* (vgl. Plin. nat. 8,138; Cic. leg. agr. 2,93), die Prüfung des Tiers auf seine Eignung zum Opfer (dargestellt in einer Statuettengruppe im Vatikan, wo ein *pontifex minor* einen Stier auf seine Zeugungskraft prüft [1]). b) Schmückung des Tiers/der Tiere mit Binden (→ *infulae*) oder Girlanden aus Blumen. Rindern wurden die Hörner umwunden oder vergoldete Gestelle (*frontale*) zwischen sie gesetzt. Rindern und Schweinen wurde eine reichverzierte Schmuckborte (*dorsualis*) über den Rücken gelegt (vgl. Rückseitenreliefs der sog. Anaglypha Traiani [2; 3]). c) Feierliche Prozession zum Opferplatz.

Nach einleitenden Aufforderungen zur Ruhe durch einen Herold (Don. ad Ter. Andr. 24) und Gebeten des Opferherrn begann die eigentliche Opferhandlung: d) Reinigung der am Opfer beteiligten Personen durch Handwaschung mit Wasser aus einem fließenden Gewässer. e) Weihung des Opfertiers (die eigentl. *immolatio*) als zentrale Handlung, indem man ihm *mola salsa* (und später auch Wein) über den Kopf goß. Ebenso wurden die Opfermesser (*culter*; vgl. Serv. Aen. 12,173; Iuv. 12,84) und andere Opfergaben (z.B. Kuchen; Varro bei Non. 114,17) mit dem gesalzenen Spelt bestreut. Nach Entfernung des Schmucks zog der Opferherr mit dem Messer von der Stirn zum Schwanz des Tieres einen imaginären Strich, die symbolische Opferung (Diskussion der Bed.: [4]). f) Schlachtung: Betäubung des Tieres mittels eines Schlags mit dem Opferhammer (*malleus*) durch den Opferschlächter (*popa, victimarius*), Durchtrennen der Halsschlagader mit einem Messer; damit war die eigentliche Opferung abgeschlossen. g) Eingeweideschau (*extispicium*), bei der anhand der Eingeweide (*exta*) der Götterwille erkundet wurde. h) Kochen der Eingeweide und Verbrennen auf dem Altar als Anteil für die Gottheit (Mahlzeit, Götterspeisung = *epulum*), Zubereitung und Verzehr des genießbaren Fleisches durch die Opferteilnehmer.

Plätze für das Opfer waren speziell dafür geweihte Orte, die entweder dauerhaft (→ Heiligtum), nur zeitweilig (Marsfeld bei Lustration) oder einmalig (im Felde während Kriegshandlungen) genutzt wurden; → Altar. Jeder freie Bürger, der kultisch rein war, durfte ein Opfer darbringen: Private oder familiäre Opferungen wurden vom *pater familias* vollzogen, bei staatlichen vollzog der Opferherr (Magistrat, Priester) lediglich die symbolische Opferung (vgl. e), Opferschlächter erledigten die tatsächliche Schlachtung.
→ Opfer

1 H.R. Goette, Kuh und Stier als Opfertier. Zur probatio victimae, in: Bullettino della Commissione archeologica comunale di Roma 91, 1986, 61–68 **2** U. Rüdiger, in: AntPl 12, 1973, 161 ff. **3** G.M. Koeppel, Die histor. Reliefs der röm. Kaiserzeit. II: Stadtröm. Denkmäler unbekannter Zugehörigkeit aus flavischer Zeit, in: BJ 186, 1986, 20; 23 f. Abb. 3. **4** Latte, 388 Anm. 1.

Latte, 45 f., 375–393 • H. Petersmann, Zu einem altröm. Opferritual (Cato de agricultura c. 141), in: RhM 116, 1973, 238–255, hier 243–246 • A.V. Siebert, Instrumenta sacra, 1998 • F. Fless, Opferdiener und Kultmusiker auf stadtröm. histor. Reliefs, 1995. A.V.S.

Immunitas. Die Freistellung von öffentlichen Dienst-, Leistungs- und Duldungspflichten einzelner Rechtspersonen, lat. *i.* (*... vacationem militiae munerisque ... immunitatem appellari*: Dig. 50,16,18; griech. *atéleia, aneisphoría, aleiturgeisía*: Dig. 27,1,6,2), kann auf gesetzlich allg. formulierter Nichteinbeziehung eines Kreises, dem sie zugehören, oder auf einem zeitweiligen oder dauerndem persönlichen Dispens beruhen (Dig. 50,6: *de iure immunitatis*; 50,5: *de vacatione et excusatione munerum*). Je nach den gemeinten Pflichten befreit *i. personae* von Lasten, die den einzelnen körperlich oder geistig beanspruchen, *i. patrimonii* von Pflichten, die einem Vermögen und damit dessen jeweiligem Inhaber auferlegt sind. Ungeachtet dieser Ordnungsgbegriffe sind die Freistellungsregeln im einzelnen aber sehr differenziert. Zu den gesetzlichen Freistellungsgründen können Alter, Geschlecht, Standeszugehörigkeit (z.B. Senatoren, Ritter; in christl. Zeit auch Priester und Mönche), Zugehörigkeit zu versorgungswichtigen Korporationen (z.B. den *navicularii*), zu den Dispensgründen körperliche Schwäche, Armut, anderweitige öffentliche oder allgemeinnützliche berufliche Inanspruchnahme (z.B. bei Professoren, Rhetoren, Ärzten) oder auch bes. Verleihung ehrenhalber (z.B. verdiente hohe Beamte, Veteranen) oder sonst belohnungshalber (z.B. bei Athleten, Schauspielern) gehören.

Neben der *i.* der Einzelpersonen gibt es – bes. zur Zeit der röm. Republik häufig und vom Senat gewährt – die zumeist auf einem röm.-ant. Staatsvertragsrecht basierende Freistellung einer ganzen Stadtgemeinde. So haben eine *i. ipso iure* etwa in Italien die röm. → *coloniae*, desgleichen – wegen ihrer Autonomie – ital. Städte mit dem Status einer *civitas foederata et libera*. Röm. *coloniae* und andere – auch autonome – Städte in den Provinzen haben *i.* dagegen nur bei bes. vertraglicher Einräumung oder hoheitlicher Verleihung (Tac. ann. 2,47; Liv. 45,26,13 f.). In der Kaiserzeit erfolgt diese Art Freistellung durch kaiserliches Edikt oder Epistula (Dig. 27,1,17,1; ILS 423).
→ Leiturgia; Munera

F.F. Abbott, A.C. Johnson, Municipal Administration in the Roman Empire, 1926, 504 (Ndr. 1968) • Jones, LRE 535 f., 734–737 • Mommsen, Staatsrecht 3, 224–244. C.G.

Impasto. Mod. t.t. für eine Keramikgattung der Villanova-, der etr. und lazialen Kultur (→ Etrusci II. Archäologie), der Gefäße aus schlecht gebranntem, ungereinigtem Ton bezeichnet. I. ist überwiegend mit der Hand, nicht mit der → Drehscheibe geformt. Typische Gefäße der Villanova-Zeit sind bikonische Aschenurnen, Amphoren und Schalen. In der orientalisierenden Periode erscheinen in Etrurien neue Formen, die dem griech. und phöniz. Repertoire entliehen sind und oft mit dem Weinkonsum zusammenhängen. Sie verbinden sich mit dem Aufkommen des adligen Symposion. Gleichzeitig erscheinen Varianten des I., bes. der »Impasto rosso«. Der dünnwandige »buccheroide« I. markiert den Übergang zum → Bucchero. Trotz ihrer im allg. eng auf die nördl. und mittlere Apennin-Halbinsel begrenzten Verbreitung begegnet die I.-Keramik gelegentlich sogar an weit entfernten Fundorten wie etwa Karthago [1].

1 H.G. Niemeyer, R.F. Docter, Die Grabung unter dem Decumanus Maximus von Karthago. Vorber. über die Kampagnen 1986–1991, in: MDAI(R) 100, 1993, 227–229, Abb. 11,e, Taf. 58,3.

A. RATHJE, A Banquet Service from the Latin City of Ficana, in: Analecta Romana Instituti Danici 12, 1983, 7–29 • R. D. DE PUMA, Etruscan Tomb-Groups, 1986, 8–10.

R.D.

Impedimenta s. Marschgepäck

Imperator. Altlat. *induperator*; griech. στρατηγός (*stratēgós*), seit Sulla jedoch αὐτοκράτωρ (*autokrátōr*); auch transkribiert ἰμπεράτωρ. Allg. Bezeichnung des mil. Oberbefehlshabers röm. oder peregriner Herkunft.

A. REPUBLIK B. PRINZIPAT C. KAISERZEIT AB DEM 3. JH.

A. REPUBLIK

I. ist kein Amtstitel. Imperiumsträger verwenden diesen Ausdruck allerdings seit dem 2. Jh. v. Chr. in Dekreten und Dedikationen vor allem außerhalb Roms und Italiens anstelle der nur für Rom relevanten regulären Amts- bzw. Funktionsbezeichnung wie (Pro-)Consul oder (Pro-)Praetor (CIL I^2 614: *L. Aimilius L.f. inpeirator decreivit*, 189 v. Chr.; I^2 2951a: *iudicium addeixit C. Valerius C.f. Flaccus imperator*, ›Tabula Contrebiensis‹, 87 v. Chr.). Dieser untechnische Gebrauch findet in spätrepublikan. Zeit auch Eingang in offizielle Verlautbarungen (CIL I^2 593, *lex Iulia municipalis*). Die röm. Soldaten dürften ihren Feldherrn mit *i.* angeredet haben.

Von diesem allg. Funktionsbegriff äußerlich nicht geschieden ist die Verwendung von *i.* als Ehrentitel. Die Ausrufung zum *i.* durch die eigenen Soldaten nach erfolgreicher Schlacht erlaubt es dem Imperiumsträger, diese Anrede als Titel seinem Namen nachzustellen. Lit. bezeugt ist der Brauch der imperatorischen Akklamation zuerst für das Jahr 209 v. Chr. (Pol. 10,40,2–5; Liv. 27,19,3–6; in ihrer Historizität umstritten). Sichere epigraphische und numismatische Nachweise liegen für das 1. Jh. v. Chr. vor, als es seit Sulla üblich wird, die I.-Akklamationen zu zählen. Der Ursprung der soldatischen Ausrufung (hell. oder genuin röm.) und ihre Bedeutung (Anerkennung, Bestätigung der feldherrlichen Qualitäten) sind nicht sicher. Die Begrüßung als *i.* durch die Soldaten begründet keine rechtlichen Ansprüche.

Der Senat kann einer solchen Akklamation zustimmen und einen Triumph für den siegreichen Feldherrn bewilligen. Es steht ihm jedoch auch frei, diese Anerkennung zu verweigern. Seit den 60er Jahren des 1. Jh. v. Chr. beschließt der Senat unabhängig von der soldatischen Akklamation auch selbst den I.-Titel für erfolgreiche Heerführer (Cic. Pis. 44). Der I.-Titel wird für die Dauer des → *imperium* als sichtbares Zeichen der *virtus* getragen. Mit Überschreiten des → Pomeriums wird mit dem Verlust des *imperium* auch der I.-Titel abgelegt. Der Triumphator darf sich jedoch für einen Tag in Rom *i.* nennen (so etwa CIL I^2 626). Seit Sulla wird es üblich, die Iteration der imperatorischen Akklamationen im Titel zu dokumentieren (z. B. RRC 359: *L. Sulla imper. iterum*; CIL XI 2104: *Cn. Pompeio Cn. f. Magno imper. iter.*).

Seit den 70er Jahren des 1. Jh. v. Chr. wird neben dem I.-Titel immer häufiger die Amtsbezeichnung geführt, wobei auch gewesene Ämter in der Titulatur verzeichnet werden. Das erste bekannte Zeugnis liegt in einer Inschr. aus Oropos für den Consul des J. 79 v. Chr. P. Servilius Vatia Isauricus vor: ὕπατον, αὐτοκράτορα (*hýpaton, autokrátora*, IG VII 244, um 75 v. Chr.). Die Position des I. variiert in den einzelnen Titulaturen (z. B. CIL VI 1316: *cos. imp. iter.*; CIL IX 5837: *imp. cos. ter*). Caesar führt schließlich nach 49 v. Chr. den absoluten Gebrauch ein. *I.* steht nicht mehr nur für einen einmaligen Sieg, sondern für die mil. Autorität seines Trägers. Die Zählung fällt daher weg, der Titel wird nun auch in Rom geführt. *I.* wird aber wohl noch nicht zu einem Namensbestandteil Caesars (so jedoch Suet. Iul. 76; Cass. Dio 43,44,2), auch wenn es äußerlich die Stelle des Cognomens einnehmen kann (CIL I^2 788: *C. Caesare imp.*; so aber eben auch AE 1991, 168: *Q. Scipio imp.*; allg. [5]).

In der Triumviratszeit zeichnet sich die Titulatur der drei Machthaber Roms bis etwa 39 v. Chr. durch eine strikte Ebenbürtigkeit aus. Mit spätestens 38 v. Chr. wird jedoch der I.-Titel im Machtkampf der einzelnen Potentaten auf neuem Wege instrumentalisiert. C. Iulius Caesar (Octavianus) setzt nun *i.* an die Stelle des ererbten Praenomens und fügt als neues Gentilicium das Cognomen *Caesar* hinzu. Die positiven Assoziationen, die diese beiden Namen hervorrufen, sollen allein mit seiner Person verbunden werden. Charakteristisch für die Titulatur Octavians wird das Nebeneinander von I.-Namen und I.-Titel (z. B. CIL V 526: *Imp. Caesari divi f. imp. V*). 29 v. Chr. sanktioniert der Senat offiziell das *praenomen imperatoris* des nunmehrigen Alleinherrschers und beschließt 27 v. Chr. den Ehrennamen »Augustus«, so daß sich Octavian gleich der republikanischen *tria nomina* »Imperator Caesar Augustus« nennen kann [9]. Die rein mil. Gewalt, auf die sich der Princeps stützt, kommt nur in seinem Namen und in der gezählten Imperatur zum Ausdruck.

B. PRINZIPAT

Während in der Triumviratszeit eine gewisse Inflation des I.-Titels anzutreffen ist [10], setzt im frühen Prinzipat allmählich eine gewollte Beschränkung auch des *titulum imperii* (Ov. fast. 4,675 f.) auf den Herrscher und seine männlichen Familienangehörigen ein. Q. Iunius Blaesus ist 22 n. Chr. der letzte Feldherr, der – ohne der Kaiserfamilie anzugehören – die imperatorische Akklamation seiner Soldaten annehmen darf (Tac. ann. 3,74). In Rom selbst übt Augustus nach 27 v. Chr. Zurückhaltung in der Verwendung des I.-Namens. Seine Nachfolger Tiberius, Gaius und Claudius verzichten sogar mit Blick auf die propagierte *res publica restituta* gänzlich auf das *praenomen imperatoris*. Nero führt es dagegen wieder, wenn auch nur zeitweilig. Erst mit Vespasian wird *i.* endgültig fester Namensbestandteil. Wie einst Augustus stellt dieser Princeps wieder das Cognomen *Caesar* dem *praenomen imperatoris* nach. Diese Kombination setzt sich bei seinen Nachfolgern rasch durch [8].

Im 2. Jh. n. Chr. entwickelt sich *i.* in dieser Wortverbindung unter Marc Aurel und L. Verus zu einem Titel. *I.* wird nun zusammen mit *Caesar* vor den eigentlichen Namen des Kaisers gesetzt (z. B. AE 1992, 1184: *Imperator Caesar M. Aurelius Antoninus Augustus*; griech. AE 1993, 1554). Die Kaisertitulatur setzt sich jetzt zusammen aus dem Wortpaar *i.* und *Caesar*, dem Namen des Herrschers, Ehren- sowie Amtstiteln. Bis zum Ende des Prinzipats im 3. Jh. n. Chr. wird diese Form beibehalten, die durch zusätzliche Beinamen, Triumphal- und Amtstitel im Laufe der Zeit mit überladender Ausführlichkeit ergänzt wird. In der lit. Überlieferung wird *i.* als nichttitulare Bezeichnung für »Kaiser« schlechthin vom 2. Jh. n. Chr. an immer gebräuchlicher.

C. Kaiserzeit ab dem 3. Jh.

Gegen Ende des 3. Jh. wird die imperatorische Akklamation schließlich einem Bedeutungswandel unterzogen. Nicht auf einen konkreten Sieg hin, sondern unabhängig hiervon erfolgt jetzt jedes Jahr die *salutatio* des Heeres. Diese alljährliche Ausrufung des Kaisers zum *i.* dient äußerlich nur noch der Zählung der Regierungsjahre. Ebenfalls im 3. Jh. tritt an die Stelle der traditionellen Herrschaftsübertragung durch den Senat, der in dieser Zeit an Einfluß einbüßt, die Kaisererhebung durch das Heer. Legitime Herrschaft wird nun allein durch die soldatische Akklamation begründet. *I.* stellt jetzt die korrekte Bezeichnung für den Kaiser dar [6]. Auch wenn sich seit dem Dominat *dominus noster* (*d.n.*) als Titel allmählich durchsetzt [8], bleibt *i.* bis zum Ende der Ant. als Appellativ im Gebrauch.

1 R. Combès, Imperator, 1966 **2** J. Deininger, Von der Republik zur Monarchie, in: ANRW 1,1, 982–997 **3** Chr. Gizewski, Zur Normativität und Struktur der Verfassungsverhältnisse in der späteren röm. Kaiserzeit, 1988 **4** D. Kienast, Imperator, in: ZRG 78, 1961, 403–421 **5** J. Linderski, Q. Scipio Imperator, in: Imperium sine fine, 1996, 145–185 **6** F. De Martino, Storia della costituzione romana, 4.1, ²1974, 212 ff.; 5, ²1975, 241 f. **7** D. McFayden, The History of the Title Imperator under the Roman Empire, Diss. 1922 **8** D. A. Musca, Le deno minazioni del principe nei documenti epigrafici romani, 1979 **9** Syme, RP 1, 361–377 **10** L. Schumacher, Die imperatorischen Akklamationen der Triumvirn und die auspicia des Augustus, in: Historia 34, 1985, 191–222. L. d. L.

Imperios(s)us. Röm. Cognomen, übermäßige persönliche Härte bezeichnend, in republikanischer Zeit in der Familie der Manlier (→ Manlius) im 4. Jh. v. Chr.

Kajanto, Cognomina, 266. K.-L. E.

Imperium. Im weiteren Sinne die allg. mil. Kommandogewalt eines beliebigen (auch nichtröm.) Befehlshabers; i.e.S. die mil. Befehlsgewalt der höchsten Beamten Roms (Consul, Praetor, Dictator, Magister equitum).

In der frühen Republik ist *i.* ein Teilaspekt der röm. Amtsgewalt (*auspicium*). Spätestens seit dem Ende des 4. Jh. v. Chr. führen außenpolit. Konflikte mit den Nachbarn zur Betonung und Hervorhebung der mil. Kompetenz der Oberbeamten (*auspicium imperiumque*: Plaut. Amph. 192; 196). In der späten Republik bezeichnet *i.* schließlich die gesamte Amtsgewalt, d. h. es steht nun für die Einheit von mil. und ziviler magistratischer Gewalt [1]. Dieses sog. »totale *i.*« gehört also – anders als es die ältere Forsch. noch sah [2] – in eine spätere Phase der röm. Verfassungsentwicklung, und nicht in die Königszeit oder frühe Republik [3]. Die zivilen, v. a. die jurisdiktionellen Befugnisse der höheren Beamten leiten sich daher nicht aus dem *i.* ab [4]. Die I.-Träger werden in der urspr. Heeresversammlung (→ *comitia centuriata*) vom röm. Volk gewählt. Sie erhalten mit dieser Wahl auch das Recht der Götterbefragung (Auspizien). Ihre mil. Kompetenz (*auspicia militaria*) müssen sie jedoch nach Amtsantritt durch ein Gesetz in der Kurienversammlung (*comitia curiata*) bestätigen lassen (sog. *lex curiata de imperio*). Dieses Gesetz ist ein Relikt älterer Zeit, als die Wahlen der höchsten Beamten noch in dieser Volksversammlung vorgenommen wurden [1].

Die äußeren Zeichen der Amtsgewalt röm. Magistrate *cum imperio* sind die ihnen vorangehenden Lictoren mit den Rutenbündeln (*fasces*), in die außerhalb Roms auch das Beil als Hoheitssymbol hineingenommen wird. Die Zahl der *fasces* richtet sich nach dem Rang der Beamten (Dictator: 24, Consul: 12, Praetor: 6) [5]. Die Lictoren setzen die Polizeigewalt (→ *coercitio*) der I.-Träger um. Diese *coercitio* ist durch die Provokationsgesetzgebung zum Schutz des röm. Bürgers vor magistratischer Willkür seit 300 v. Chr. eingeschränkt worden [6]. Wie alle Beamten unterliegen auch die I.-Träger verschiedenen Kontrollmechanismen, die sich in Rechtsprinzipien ausdrücken: Prinzip der Annuität und Kollegialität, Verbot der Kontinuation und Iteration des Amtes sowie der Kumulation von Ämtern [7]. Gegenüber niederen Beamten besitzen die ranghöheren das Verbietungsrecht (*ius intercessionis*, → *intercessio*). Ihre Amtsgewalt wird daher im Rahmen dieses Bezugssystems als *potestas* (*maior* gegenüber *minor*) charakterisiert [1].

In der Republik ist eine wesentliche Aufgabe der Magistrate *cum imperio* die vorwiegend mil., aber auch immer mehr administrative Tätigkeit im außerstädtischen Bereich (*militiae*). Da durch die zunehmende Entfernung der Amtsbereiche die Aufgaben von den amtierenden I.-Trägern kaum noch bewältigt werden können, werden von der Mitte des 3. Jh. v. Chr. an neue Beamtenstellen geschaffen (*praetor peregrinus*, Praetoren für die neu eingerichteten Provinzen Sicilia, Sardinia et Corsica, Hispania citerior und Hispania ulterior) [1]. Bevorzugt wird jedoch die seit 327/26 praktizierte Verlängerung der Amtsgewalt über das reguläre Amtsjahr hinaus (*prorogatio imperii*), die in der Regel von Senat und Volk beschlossen wird. Die gewesenen Magistrate sind nun, »anstelle eines Consuls« (*pro consule*) oder »anstelle eines Praetors« (*pro praetore*) → Promagistrate, die im außerstädtischen Bereich weiterhin zumeist als mil. Befehlshaber tätig sind. Sie sind den ordentlichen Oberbeamten gleichen Ranges nachgeordnet. Ihre Tätigkeit ist entsprechend ihres Auftrags von unterschiedlicher Dauer. Unabhängig hiervon erlischt ihr proconsularisches oder propraetorisches *i.* mit dem Überschreiten der röm. Stadtgrenze (*pomerium*). Promagistrate, denen ein Triumph in Rom zuerkannt wird, erhalten daher für einen Tag durch besonderen Volksbeschluß das *i.* im Bereich *domi* ([4. 15–21]; grundlegend [8]).

Seit Cornelius [I 90] Sulla erfolgt eine geogr. Trennung der magistratischen Aufgabenbereiche. Ihr reguläres Amtsjahr haben jetzt die I.-Träger in Rom selbst (*domi*) abzuleisten. Anschließend folgt ein weiteres Jahr als Promagistrat im außerstädtischen Bereich (*militiae*), d.h. als Statthalter in den röm. Provinzen [9]. Durch diese Trennung verlieren die Oberbeamten jedoch nicht ihr *i. militiae*. Die mil. Kommandogewalt kommt in den Jahren zw. 80 und 49 v.Chr. weiterhin zum Tragen [9; 10]. Durch ein *senatus consultum* d.J. 53 und eine *lex Pompeia* d.J. 52 werden Magistratur und Promagistratur durch ein 5jähriges Intervall voneinander getrennt. Die Promagistratur verliert nun den Charakter einer verlängerten Amtsgewalt, das proconsularische und propraetorische *i.* werden damit faktisch vom regulären Oberamt losgelöst.

Diese Entwicklung findet mit Augustus ihren Abschluß. Die Oberbeamten führen im Prinzipat de facto das mil. Kommando nicht mehr [9]. Dieser Verlust an Substanz führt daher die röm. Juristen im 3. Jh. n. Chr. zu der Konstruktion eines *i. merum* und eines *i. mixtum*. Diese Begriffe nehmen inhaltlich Bezug auf die magistratische Rechtsprechung, die als wesentliches Element der auf das Zivile beschränkten Amtsgewalt der höheren Magistrate gesehen wird (Dig. 2,1,3 f.; Dig. 1,21,5,1; 50,1,26) [4. 27 f.].

Das proconsularische *i.* der Triumvirn und des Princeps geht zurück auf die außerordentlichen Kommandos der späten Republik. Die unbewältigten Probleme eines großen Herrschaftsgebietes, aber auch der polit. Ehrgeiz führender Aristokraten Roms erzwingt die Übertragung von solchen *imperia extraordinaria* oder *infinita* an einzelne Persönlichkeiten, die zumeist als Promagistrate oder *privati* proconsularischen Ranges über eine provinzübergreifende Militärgewalt verfügen (Cn. Pompeius, C. Iulius Caesar). Diese außerordentliche Gewalt im Bereich *militiae* konkurriert mit dem *i.* der einzelnen Provinzstatthalter, sie ist kein *i. maius*. Vorstöße zur Verleihung eines solchen übergeordneten Kommandos (57 und 43 v.Chr.; Cic. Att. 4,1,7; Cic. Phil. 11,30) sind nicht erfolgreich [9]. Erst in der Prinzipatszeit findet sich das *i. maius* im Sinne einer *potestas maior* gegenüber den Proconsuln [11]. In den Bürgerkriegen verbindet dann das Triumvirat (43–33 v.Chr.) aufgrund der *lex Titia* als Sondergewalt neben dem Consulat die proconsularische Befehlsgewalt, die über mehrere Provinzen gebietet, mit magistratischen Befugnissen innerhalb des *pomerium*. Die sullanische Trennung der Amtsbereiche, *domi* und *militiae*, wird mit dieser Regelung beseitigt [12].

Das *i. consulare* bzw. *proconsulare* (so zuerst bei Val. Max. 6,9,7; 8,1, amb. 2) ist neben der *tribunicia potestas* das rechtliche Fundament des Prinzipats. Es steht für die absolute Befehlsgewalt des Herrschers über die Legionen und seine alleinige Verfügung über die wichtigsten Provinzen. Ein Privileg verleiht diesem *i.* seit 23 v. Chr. Gültigkeit auch innerhalb der Stadt Rom (Cass. Dio 53,32,5). Dem neuen Herrscher wird diese Gewalt vom Senat übertragen. Der Tag der Verleihung bzw. später auch der Tag der Erhebung durch das Heer wird als Tag des Regierungsantritts (*dies imperii*) angesehen. Das *i. proconsulare* wird in der Kaisertitulatur nicht aufgeführt. Der Princeps nennt sich bis zur Regierungszeit Neros bzw. Traians nicht »Proconsul«. Erkennbar wird die mil. Macht nur in der Führung des *praenomen imperatoris* und der Aufzählung der imperatorischen Akklamationen. Die einzelnen Teilgewalten, Rechte und Privilegien des Princeps verschmelzen früh zu einer Einheit monarchischer Gewalt (*imperatoria potestas*). Diese Entwicklung wird bereits in dem sog. Bestallungsgesetz Vespasians, der *lex de imperio Vespasiani*, aus dem Jahr 69 n. Chr. deutlich ([13]; vgl. CIL VI 930). Im 3. Jh. n. Chr. verliert mit der Entmachtung des Senats die Übertragung des *i.*, d.h. der kaiserlichen Gewalt und damit ihre Legitimierung durch dieses Gremium an Bedeutung. An ihre Stelle tritt die Akklamation zum → *imperator* durch das Heer [14].

Neben seinem mil. und staatsrechtlichen Gehalt findet sich für *i.* schon in der Republik eine Verwendung im räumlichen Sinne, *i. Romanum*.

→ IMPERATOR

1 J. BLEICKEN, Zum Begriff der röm. Amtsgewalt, 1981 **2** MOMMSEN, Staatsrecht 1, 22 ff., 116 ff. **3** A. HEUSS, Gedanken und Vermutungen zur frühen röm. Regierungsgewalt, 1982 (= Gesammelte Schriften 2, 1995, 908–985) **4** W. KUNKEL, Die Magistratur, 1995 **5** TH. SCHÄFER, Imperii insignia, 1989 **6** J. MARTIN, Die Provokation in der klass. und späten Republik, in: Hermes 98, 1970, 72–96 **7** J. BLEICKEN, Die Verfassung der röm. Republik, [7]1995 **8** W. F. JASHEMSKI, The Origins and History of the Proconsular and Propraetorian Imperium to 27 B.C., 1950 **9** J. BLEICKEN, Imperium consulare/proconsulare, in: FS A. Heuß 1993, 117–133 **10** A. GIOVANNINI, Consulare imperium, 1983, 83 ff. **11** W. ECK, A. CABALLOS, F. FERNANDEZ, Das senatus consultum de Cn. Pisone patre, 1996 **12** J. BLEICKEN, Zw. Republik und Principat, 1990 **13** P. A. BRUNT, Lex de imperio Vespasiani, in: JRS 67, 1977, 95–116 **14** F. DE MARTINO, Storia della costituzione romana, 4.1, [2]1974, 460 ff.; 5, [2]1975, 228 ff.

L.d.L.

Imperium Romanum s. Römisches Reich

Impluvium. Das Wasserbecken im → Atrium des röm. Hauses, in dem sich das vom → Compluvium, der Lichtöffnung des Atriums, zusammengeführte Regenwasser sammelte und das oft Teil einer → Zisterne war.

E. M. EVANS, The Atrium Complex in the Houses of Pompeii, 1980 • R. FÖRTSCH, Arch. Komm. zu den Villenbriefen des jüngeren Plinius, 1993, 30 f.

C.HÖ.

Import – Export. Im Kern der von M.I. FINLEY [1] ausgelösten Debatte über die ant. Wirtschaft geht es um die quantitative und qualitative Einordnung von Gewerbe und → Handel im gesamten ant. Wirtschaftsgeschehen. Folgerichtig gilt das Interesse der neueren wirtschaftshistor. Forschung vorrangig den Städten und ihrer Stellung in der ant. Wirtschaft. Von den »Primitivisten« und »Neoprimitivisten« wurden die Städte in Anlehnung an MAX WEBER als Konsumenten- oder Verbraucherstädte bezeichnet. Diese Sicht konnte vor allem mit den umfangreichen Getreideimporten nach Athen und Rom begründet werden.

Demgegenüber zeigen viele Texte, daß ant. Städte Güter sowohl importierten als auch exportierten. In der polit. Theorie werden I. und E. nebeneinander erwähnt; dies gilt sogar für die ideale Polis bei Platon (Plat. rep. 370e–371b; vgl. Plat. leg. 847b-d; Aristot. pol. 1257a 31–34; 1327a 25–27). Große Bedeutung für den I., aber auch für die exportorientierte städtische Produktion und den E. hatten der Zugang zum Meer und ein günstig gelegener Hafen (→ Hafenanlagen).

Korinth exportierte schon im 8. und 7. Jh. v. Chr. Keramik bis nach It. und zu den Schwarzmeerküsten; die günstige Lage von Korinth förderte ebenso den Zwischenhandel und den I. Auch Athen hatte sich bis zum 5. und 4. Jh. v. Chr. nicht nur zum wichtigsten Handelszentrum im östlichen Mittelmeerraum, sondern ebenso zu einem Produktionszentrum entwickelt. Seit spätarcha. Zeit exportierte Athen in bedeutendem Umfang Keramik in Gebiete außerhalb Griechenlands. Die in Megara hergestellten Mäntel (Xen. mem. 2,7,6) waren sicherlich ebenfalls für den E. bestimmt. Gleichzeitig mit den wachsenden Exportchancen kam es zu einer starken Differenzierung und Spezialisierung im → Handwerk (Xen. Kyr. 8,2,5). Unter den Städten, die Handwerkserzeugnisse exportierten, nahm Alexandreia eine Sonderstellung ein; Strabon, der diese Stadt als ›größten Handelsplatz der Welt‹ (μέγιστον ἐμπόριον τῆς οἰκουμένης) bezeichnet, stellt ausdrücklich fest, daß der E. einen größeren Umfang besaß als der I. (Strab. 17,1,7; 17,1,13; vgl. Cic. Rab. Post. 40). Daneben produzierten auch kleinere Städte in Äg. für den Verkauf auf fremden Märkten; dies gilt etwa für die Textilproduktion in → Oxyrhynchos, dessen Handels- und Kommunikationskontakte über Äg. hinaus reichten.

Selbst Rom in der Prinzipatszeit kann nicht als ausschließliche I.- oder Konsumentenstadt bezeichnet werden; allein die Grabinschriften (vgl. bes. CIL VI) dokumentieren mehr als 200 Gewerbe und Berufe. Erzeugnisse der Bronzeverarbeitung in Rom erreichten Britannien, reliefverzierte Tonlampen aus stadtröm. Produktion wurden im 1. Jh. n. Chr. im ganzen Mittelmeerraum gehandelt, und importierte Rohstoffe – etwa Papyrus in der *officina* des Fannius (Plin. nat. 13,75) – wurden in Rom aufbereitet und zumindest teilweise exportiert. Viele Städte im Imperium Romanum sind als Produktionsstätten von Waren, die weite Verbreitung gefunden haben, bekannt, so etwa → Capua mit den Bronzegefäßen des L. Ansius Epaphroditus und des P. Cipius Polybius. Dabei ist zuzugestehen, daß es aufgrund der Quellenlage nicht möglich ist, eine auch nur annähernd genaue Handelsbilanz ant. Städte zu erstellen.

→ Wirtschaft

1 FINLEY, Ancient Economy **2** P.M. FRASER, Ptolemaic Alexandria, 1972 **3** F. KOLB, Rom. Die Geschichte der Stadt in der Ant., 1995, 464–507 **4** J. KUNOW, Die capuanischen Bronzegefäßhersteller L. Ansius Epaphroditus und P. Cipius Polybius, in: BJ 185, 1985, 215–242 **5** P. v. MINNEN, The Volume of Oxyrhynchos Textile Trade, in: MBAH 5,2, 1986, 88–95 **6** L. NEESEN, Demiurgoi und Artifices, 1989 **7** H. PARKINS, C. SMITH, Trade, Traders and the Ancient City, 1998 **8** ROSTOVTZEFF, Roman Empire **9** I. SCHEIBLER, Griechische Töpferkunst, 1983, 150–186.

H.-J.D.

Imuthes

[1] s. Petobastis IV.

[2] (Imhotep; äg. *Jj-m-Ḥtp*; griech. Ἰμούθης). In zeitgenössischen Inschriften und Papyri am Anfang der 3. Dyn. (um 2650 v. Chr.) unter → Djoser und Sechemchet als höchstrangiger Beamter, Oberdomänenverwalter und Hoherpriester von → Heliopolis, vielleicht auch in der (kult.?) Rolle als Oberbildhauer und Bauleiter belegt. Im Licht der späteren Trad. wird ihm eine maßgebliche Rolle beim Bau des Pyramidenbezirks des Djoser, des ersten großen Steinbauwerks, zugeschrieben; sein Grab wird in Nord-Saqqara vermutet. Schon im NR gilt I. als großer Weiser und Patron der Schreiber; seit der Saïtenzeit (7.–6. Jh. v. Chr.) genießt er als Sohn des Gottes Ptah zunächst in Memphis göttl. Verehrung. Der mit diesem Kult assoziierte Bildtypus zeigt ihn als auf einem Blocksitz thronenden Schreiber, der eine Papyrusrolle auf seinem Schoß entrollt. In ptolem. Zeit breitet sich sein Kult (mit → Asklepios gleichgesetzt) auch in den anderen Kultorten des Landes aus.

D. WILDUNG, s. v. I., LÄ 2, 145–148 • Ders., Imhotep und Amenhotep, 1977.

S.S.

In Genesin ad Leonem papam (204 Hexameter), in den Hss. fälschlich → Hilarius von Poitiers zugeschrieben, ist Papst Leo I. (440–461) gewidmet. Nach einer hymnischen Einl. erzählt der größte Teil des Gedichts die Schöpfungsgesch.; ein kurzer Schluß berichtet Sündenfall, Sintflut und die Aussicht auf Erlösung. Die Naturdarstellung zeigt den Einfluß von → Lukrez, → Vergil (bes. *Georgica*) und der Kosmogonie in Ov. met. 1.

→ Bibeldichtung

ED.: R. PEIPER, CSEL 23, 231–239.

M.RO./Ü: C.P.

In iure cessio. Die *i.i.c.* des röm. Rechts ist ein Akt der Rechtsübertragung in der Form eines Scheinprozesses, der → *legis actio sacramento in rem*. Sie ist – wie die → *mancipatio* – nicht abhängig vom Bestehen eines Rechtsgrundes (*causa*), z.B. eines Kaufvertrages, vielmehr »abstrakt«. Die *i.i.c.* betrifft Gegenstände, an welchen quiritisches Eigentum möglich ist (z.B. nicht Provinzialgrundstücke), und ist nur röm. Bürgern zugänglich (Gai. inst. 2,65). Manche Gegenstände, wie der → *ususfructus*, können nur durch *i.i.c.* übertragen werden (Gai. inst. 2,30). Vor einem röm. Magistrat (→ Praetor) ergreift der Erwerber die Sache und spricht z. B. die Worte *Hunc ego hominem ex iure Quiritium meum esse aio* (›Ich behaupte, daß dieser Sklave der meine ist nach dem Recht der röm. Bürger‹). Der Veräußerer wehrt sich nicht, woraufhin der Praetor oder auch der Provinzstatthalter (Gai. inst. 2,24) die Sache dem Erwerber zuspricht. Schon zur Zeit des Gaius im 2. Jh. n. Chr. (Gai. inst. 2,25) wird die *i.i.c.* als zu umständlich gemieden. Das justinianische Recht kennt sie nicht mehr.

Honsell/Mayer-Maly/Selb, 104–106 · Kaser, RPR I 40, 48f., 134, 415; II 50, 274f. · M. Kaser, K. Hackl, Das röm. Zivilprozeßrecht, ²1997, 42, 72 Anm. 18, 94 Anm. 34, 187. D.SCH.

Inachos (Ἴναχος; Etym. ungeklärt).

[1] Sohn des → Okeanos und der → Tethys, welcher dem Hauptfluß von → Argos [II] und der → Argolis den Namen gab (schol. Eur. Or. 932). Erster König von Argos (Akusilaos, FGrH 2 F 23c) und Stammvater der argiv. Könige und Helden (»Inachiden«: Eur. Iph. A. 1088). Im Streit zwischen Poseidon und Hera um Argos entscheidet I. zugunsten der Göttin und führt deren Kult ein, weshalb Poseidon den Fluß trockenlegt (Paus. 2,15,4–5). I.' Frau ist entweder seine Schwester Argeia (Hyg. fab. 143; 145) oder die Okeanide Melie (Apollod. 2,1). Als Vater der → Io (Aischyl. Prom. 589–590; 705; Hdt. 1,1; Kall. h. 3,254; Apollod. 2,5) ist I. in deren Ikonographie aber kaum nachweisbar [1]. Als weitere Kinder werden genannt: Phoroneus, Aigialeus (Apollod. 2,1), Pelasgos (schol. Apoll. Rhod. 1,580), Argos (Asklepiades von Tragilos, FGrH 12 F 16), Phegeus (schol. Eur. Or. 932), Mykene (Paus. 2,16,3). Sophokles benannte ein Satyrspiel nach I. (TrGF IV F 269a–295a).

1 St.E. Katakis, s. v. I., LIMC 5.1, 653–654. R.B.

[2] Hauptfluß der Ebene von Argos, entspringt im Lyrkeion nördl. von Artemision (Malevo), fließt östl. von Argos vorbei in den Golf von Nauplia bei Nea Kios. Er führte schon im Alt. oft kein Wasser. Die griech. Myth. erhob den Fluß zum Stammvater der argiv. Könige (Steph. Byz. s. v. Λάκμων; Strab. 6,2,4; 7,5,8; 7,8; 8,6,7f.; Hekat. FGrH 1 F 102; Paus. 2,15,4f.; 18,3; 25,3; 8,6,6).

R. Baladié, Le Péloponnèse de Strabon, 1980, 69–72 · D. Musti, M. Torelli, Pausania. Guida della Grecia. II. La Corinzia e l'Argolide, 1986, 263f. Y.L.

Inanna s. Ištar

Inaros (Ἰνάρως). Libyscher König, Sohn des → Psammetichos, veranlaßte 460 v. Chr. die Ägypter zum Aufstand gegen die Perser. Die von I. zu Hilfe gerufenen Athener beteiligten sich an dem zunächst erfolgreichen Unternehmen und schlossen → Memphis ein. Diese Belagerung zog sich über Jahre hin. Erst 456 sandten die Perser ein Heer nach Memphis, das die Athener auf der Insel → Prosopis einschloß. Doch erst mit der Trockenlegung eines Nilarmes zwangen sie diese schließlich, ihre Schiffe zu verbrennen und sich geschlagen zu geben. I. geriet durch Verrat in Gefangenschaft und wurde später gekreuzigt (Thuk. 1,104; 109f.; Hdt. 3,12; 7,7).

P.J. Rhodes, in: CAH V², 1992, 54ff. E.S.-H.

Inauguratio. Im eigentlichen Sinne »der Anfang«, vgl. auch *inaugurare*: »Augurien anstellen«, »Weissagevögel befragen«; »einweihen«.

Im röm. Sakralrecht ist *i.* die priesterliche Amtseinführung, die seit histor. faßbarer Zeit nur bei den → *flamines maiores* (*Dialis*: Gai. inst. 1,130; 3,114; Liv. 27,8,4; 41,28,7; *Martialis*: Liv. 29,38,6; 45,15,10; Macr. Sat. 3,13,11), dem → *rex sacrorum* (Labeo bei Gell. 15,27,1; Liv. 40,42,8) und den → *augures* (Liv. 27,36,5; 30,26,10; 33,44,3; Cic. Brut. 1; Suet. Cal. 12,1), nicht aber bei den anderen Priesterschaften (*pontifices*, *Vestales*) angewandt wurde. In einer bes. Zeremonie vor den *comitia curiata/centuriata* wurde um die Zustimmung Iuppiters für die Amtseinführung des neuen Priesters gebeten. Der urspr. Gedanke war die Übertragung der dem weihenden Auguren innewohnenden Macht auf das Amt des neu antretenden Priesters; dies hat aber in histor. Zeit keine Relevanz mehr. Die dabei gesprochene Formel war geheim und wurde immer an den nachfolgenden Auguren weitergegeben (Fest. 14 L.); für die bei Liv. 1,18,9 wiedergegebene Formel für die *i.* des Numa Pompilius stellt sich die Frage, ob es sich überhaupt um einen authentischen Wortlaut handelt. Während des Akts, der von den *pontifices* vollzogen wurde, stand der inaugurierende Priester zur Linken des neuen Priesters und berührte sein Haupt mit der rechten Hand.

F. Richter, s. v. I., RE 9, 1220ff. · Latte, 141; 403ff. · B. Gladigow, Condicio und I.: Ein Beitrag zur röm. Sakralverfassung, in: Hermes 98, 1970, 369–379. A.V.S.

Inaures s. Ohrschmuck

Incantatio s. Magie

Incendium. Lat. »Brand«, auch »Brandstiftung«. Als Notsituation mehrfach von Bed.: entlastend für den Schuldner bei Untergang der Leistungsgegenstände (neben Zerstörung/*ruina*, und Schiffbruch/*naufragium*, ein typ. Beispiel für Höhere Gewalt/→ *vis maior*; Dig. 2,13,6,9), haftungsverschärfend (Verwahrung/*depositum*, Dig. 16,3,1,1, Raub/*rapina*, Dig. 47,9) und u.U. rechtfertigend für eine Beschädigung (Ulp. Dig. 9,2,49,1).

Für vorsätzliche Brandstiftung sahen schon die Zwölftafelgesetze (8,10) die Todesstrafe vor. Später fiel die Tat unter die *lex Cornelia de sicariis et veneficis* (Marcianus Dig. 48,8,1 pr.), auch unter die *lex Iulia de vi privata* (Marcianus Dig. 48,6,5 pr.). Ob die von Gaius (Dig. 47,9,9) erwähnte bes. Behandlung bei Fahrlässigkeit schon den Zwölftafeln angehört, ist strittig, die → *lex Aquilia* ist jedenfalls anwendbar. Die Strafen werden später nach Ort, Gegenständen und Personen abgestuft, zuständig sind die *praefecti urbi* und *praefecti vigilum* (Ulp. Dig. 1,15,5).

VIR III, 675–678, s. v. i., incendiarius • U. BRASIELLO, La repressione penale nel diritto romano, 1937, 205 ff. • MOMMSEN, Strafrecht, 840 f. C.E.

Incensus (»nicht geschätzt«) ist derjenige, der in Rom seine Vermögensschätzung durch den Censor versäumt (→ *census*: Dig. 1,2,2,17) und deshalb wegen Nichtfeststellung seiner Wählerklassenzugehörigkeit und seiner Kriegsdienstverpflichtung evtl. nicht zu seinen wesentlichen Bürgerpflichten herangezogen werden kann. Der *i.* wird nach einem legendären Gesetz des Servius Tullius (Liv. 1,44,1) mit dem Tode bestraft. In republikanischer Zeit kann die Konsequenz einer unterlassenen Steuererklärung Vermögenseinzug und Verkauf in die Sklaverei sein (Cic. Caecin. 99; Val. Max. 6,3; 4; Suet. Aug. 24.; Gai. inst. 1,160). Doch hängt dies von den Umständen des Einzelfalles, bes. vom Vorliegen eines Betruges gegenüber der Allgemeinheit oder einer Fälschung ab. Die normale Folge dürfte die von Amts wegen vorgenommene Schätzung eines namentlich bekannten Bürgers gewesen sein, die, wie heute, zu seinen Lasten zu gehen pflegte, und deswegen als Sanktion ausreichte.

→ Census

MOMMSEN, Staatsrecht 2 (3), 367, 434; 3 (3), 548. C.G.

Incestus (auch *incestum*, »unrein«; aus *in* und *castus*). *I.* stammt aus dem Bereich des rel. Verbotenen (*nefas*, s. → *fas*); insbes. ist *i.* die Verletzung des Keuschheitsgebots durch eine Vestalin, die vom Pontifikalcollegium geahndet wurde. Sie selbst wurde lebend begraben, der Komplize vom *pontifex maximus* zu Tode gepeitscht (Liv. 22,57,3; Plin. epist. 4,11).

Außerhalb des *fas* ist *i.* die geschlechtliche Verbindung zw. Verwandten und Verschwägerten und eng mit dem betreffenden Eheverbot verbunden, das auf die *veteres mores* (»Sitten der Alten«) zurückgeführt wird (Paul. Dig. 23,2,39,1); die Herkunft aus dem *fas* ist in der Wendung *incestae et nefariae nuptiae* (›inzestuöse und rel. verbotene Ehe‹, Gai. inst. 1,59,64) wie auch im direkten Verweis auf das *fas* (Marcianus Dig. 48,18,5) spürbar. Erfaßt ist urspr. die gerade Linie, Geschwister und Halbgeschwister, insges. bis zum sechsten Grad. Nach Ulp. (reg. 5,6) reicht das Verbot im 3. Jh. n. Chr. bis zum vierten Grad, abgesehen von der durch ein SC von Claudius in eigener Sache erwirkten Ausnahme für die Ehe zw. Onkel und Tochter des Bruders (Tac. ann. 12,5–6; Gai. inst. 1,62). Jedenfalls im 2. Jh. n. Chr. waren auch Verschwägerte betroffen (Gai. inst. 1,63). Seit E. des 3. Jh. n. Chr. häufen sich gesetzgeberische Maßnahmen zur Verschärfung: Diocletian (coll. 6,4; Cod. Iust. 5,4,17), Constantius II. (Cod. Theod. 3,12,1.2 – mit Nachdruck hinsichtlich der Ehe mit der Schwägerin), Theodosius I. (Cod. Iust. 5,5,5), Arcadius (Cod. Theod. 3,12,3), Theodosius II. (Cod. Theod. 3,12,4), Zenon (Cod. Iust. 5,5,9). Zweck war die Abwehr der oft üblichen Verwandtenehen, womit auch die Kategorien des *i. iure gentium* und *i. iure civili* (Paul. Dig. 23,2,68; → *ius*) zusammenhängen könnten. Die verbotswidrige Ehe war nichtig, die Kinder illegitim ohne Erbrecht, die Testier- und Erbfähigkeit der Partner beschränkt. Begünstigungen für die Kinder (Nov. 12,3 aus 535) wurden 539 (Nov. 89,15) abgeschafft.

Die Verfolgung lag (trotz genereller Formulierung bei Cic. leg. 2,22) wohl nur für die Vestalin beim Pontifikalcollegium, gerichtliche Maßnahmen waren die Ausnahme, Strafen wurden im allg. vom Hausgericht verhängt [2. 31]. Geahndet wurde *i.* mit der Todesstrafe (Felssturz: Tac. ann. 6,19; Quint. inst. 7,8,3), später regelmäßig ersetzt durch Deportation, endlich Vermögensstrafen (Cod. Theod. 3,12,3). Nov. 12 regelt die Strafen neu. Entgegen älterer Meinung scheint die → *lex Iulia de adulteriis* den *i.* nicht nur bei Konkurrenz mit Ehebruch (→ *adulterium*) erfaßt zu haben [2]. Sonderregeln betreffen die teilweise geringere Bestrafung der Frau, die Berücksichtigung von Rechtsunkenntnis und das Sklavenverhör.

1 A. GUARINO, Studi sull' »incestum«, in: ZRG 63, 1943, 175–267 2 L. SCHUMACHER, Servus Index, 1982, 13 ff., 175 ff. 3 Y. THOMAS, Mariages endogamiques à Rome. Patrimoine, pouvoir et parenté depuis l'époque archaique, in: Révue historique de droit français et étranger 58, 1980, 345–382.

P. BONTE (Hrsg.), Épouser au plus proche, Inceste, prohibitions et stratégies matrimoniales autour de la Méditerranée, 1994. C.E.

Incitaria. Schiffsanlegestelle (Itin. Maritimum 499) auf dem *promonturium Argentarium* in Etruria, h. Porto Santo Stefano. Der ON ist zu deuten als »*in cetaria*« und bezeichnet also eine Thunfischfangstation.

R. BRONSON, G. UGGERI, Isola del Giglio, in: SE 38, 1970, 208 f. G.U./Ü: J.W.M.

Incubatio s. Inkubation

Incubus oder **Incubo** (abgeleitet aus lat. *incubare*, »auf etwas liegen«) bezeichnet im Spätlat. sowohl den Sender der Alpträume, der dem griech. Ephialtes (→ Aloaden) entspricht, als auch den von ihm verursachten Alptraum. Als Kobold und Bringer obszöner Träume wird *I.* u.a mit → Faunus bzw. mit dem sog. *Faunus ficarius* (»Faunus der Feigenbäume«; Isid. orig. 8,11,103–104) [1], mit → Inuus und mit → Silvanus gleichgesetzt (Serv. Aen. 6,775). Christl. Autoren haben bes. die Gier der *Incubi* nach Geschlechtsverkehr mit Frauen hervorgehoben (Aug. civ. 15,23,108). Man glaubte, daß Pflanzen oder andere Heilmitteln (Plin. nat. 25,4,29; 30,10,84) vor ihrem Einfluß schützten. Petron. 38 deutet auf eine Funktion des *I.* als Schatzhüter. *I.* sowie *Succubus* (von lat. *succumbere*, »unter etwas liegen«) haben ein Nachleben in der ma. Dämonologie [2].

1 W. Otto, s. v. Faunus, RE 6, 2060 2 D. Müller, s. v. I. und Succubus, Enzyklopädie des Märchens 7, 113–117.

FR. P.

Index

[1] Von lat. *dicere, in-dicere* »anzeigen«; Anzeiger, Angeber, Verräter (Cic. Cluent. 21; Cic. Verr. 2,5,161; Cic. Mur. 49), Register, kurze Inhaltsangabe (Cic. de orat. 2,61: Paul. Dig. 22,4,2; Quint. inst. 10,1,57); Zeigefinger (*digitus i.*, Cic. Att. 13,46,1).

Personen, die Anzeigen erstatteten, stammten aus unteren sozialen Schichten, die meist nicht das Recht oder die Mittel hatten, eine Klage selbst zu führen. Denunzierende Ritter wurden durch die Bezeichnung *i.* abqualifiziert (Cic. Att. 2,24,2); häufig findet sich die Verbindung von *testis* (Zeuge) und *i.* (Iuv. 10,69 f.); als *potestas indicandi* (»Möglichkeit, anzuzeigen«) wird eine belastende Aussage eines Unfreien bezeichnet (Cic. Cluent. 187). Der Anzeige durch einen *servus i.* bediente man sich trotz des Verbotes in der *l. Cornelia de falsis* später auch gegen den Eigentümer (*contra dominum*) zum Zweck des Verrates, des Zwanges, der Diffamierung (etwa im Prozeß der Octavia, Gemahlin des Nero, nach der *l. Iulia de adulteriis*), oder bei Fiskaldelikten (vor allem unter Caligula, durch dessen sog. *l. de servis indicibus* (Rotondi, 467) im Ergebnis in den Schutz des Privateigentums eingegriffen wurde). War der *i.* selbst an der Missetat beteiligt (vgl. Ulp. Dig. 48,18,1,26), so wurde ihm in späterer Zeit bei einzelnen Delikten unter bestimmten Voraussetzungen Straffreiheit gewährt (vgl. Liv. 8,18; 39,19; Cod. Iust. 9,8,5,7). Bisweilen erhielt der *i.* auch eine Belohnung (vgl. etwa Ulp. Dig. 47,10,5,1; 29,5,3,13–15; Modestinus Dig. 37,14,9,1).

Bei Amm. 29,1,41 sind juristische Werke in Buchform überliefert, die als *indices iuris* bezeichnet wurden. Als Lit.-Gattung begegnet *i.* vor allem in byz. Zeit. Iustinian (Const. Deo auctore § 12) gestattete Bearbeitungen seiner *Digesta* nur in Form von wortgetreuen griech. Übers. (κατὰ πόδα), von Sammlungen von Parallelstellen (παράτιτλα) und von Zusammenfassungen, die streng dem Wortlaut der einzelnen Fragmente angepaßt sein mußten (*indices*). Verf. solcher *indices* zu den *Digesta* waren Theophilos, Dorotheos, Stephanos und Kyrillos. Der heute nach seinem Fundort, der florentinischen Digesten-Hs., sog. *i. Florentinus* geht auf die Const. Tanta/Δέδωκεν § 20 zurück, wo Iustinian die Anfertigung eines Registers aller in die *Digesta* aufgenommenen Autoren und Schriften anordnet.

ThlL VII 1, 1140–1156, s. v. i., indicium, indicare • A. Berger, Studies in the Basilica, in: Bull. dell' ist. di diritto Romano 55/56, 1952, 65–184 • M. Kaser, s. v. testimonium, RE 5A, 1047 ff. • Mommsen, Strafrecht 195, 504 f. • Schulz, 404 • L. Schumacher, Servus I., 1982 • Wenger, 578 f., 681 f. • F. Wieacker, Textstufen klass. Juristen, 1960, 106.

FR. R.

[2] s. Rolle

India I. Name II. Frühe Beziehungen III. Alexanderzug und Hellenismus IV. Römische Kaiserzeit V. Spätantike

I. Name

Altindisch *Sindhu* als Name des Indus-Flusses ist (mit iran. *h*) als *Hindu* in den altpers. Inschriften belegt, daraus entstand griech. Ἰνδός (mit ion. Verlust des *h*) für den Fluß und dann Ἰνδική für das Land. Die lat. Bezeichnungen sind Indus bzw. India.

II. Frühe Beziehungen

Während Beziehungen zwischen NW-I. und Mesopot. bis ins 3. Jt. v. Chr. zurückreichen, wurde I. in Griechenland erst im späten 6. Jh. durch Skylax (FGrH 709) bekannt, der NW-I. im Dienst des Dareios [1] I. selbst besuchte. Die späteren Autoren Hekataios, Herodotos und Ktesias benutzten Informationen aus Persien ohne eigene Anschauung. Hinter den sagenhaften und übertriebenen Berichten bei Hdt. und besonders Ktesias lassen sich oft ind. Sagen als Vorbilder nachweisen [2. 157 ff.]. Trotz seiner gelegentlich scharfen Kritik war noch Aristoteles in seinen wenigen Angaben weitgehend von Ktesias abhängig. In dieser Zeit war I. ein Teil der Sagenethnographie, ein Land am Weltrand mit gänzlich anderen Verhältnissen als Griechenland und andere bekannte Länder. Auch die geogr. Lage war unklar, wobei I. oft als Nachbarland Äthiopiens galt. Die wahre Herkunft der wenigen ind. Tiere (wie Huhn und Pfau) und Produkte (Zimt und Pfeffer), die schon damals Griechenland erreicht hatten, blieb meist unerkannt.

III. Alexanderzug und Hellenismus

Durch den Alexanderzug wurde I. den Griechen erstmals genauer bekannt. Das bereits früher einmal zum Achäm.-Reich gehörige Industal wurde von → Alexandros [4] erneut erobert. Nach der Unterwerfung des oberen Industals drangen die Makedonen durch den Pañjab bis zum → Hyphasis (h. Sutlej) vor, fuhren den → Hydaspes (h. Jilam) und den Indus hinab und eroberten das untere Industal bis ans Meer. Als fernste und merkwürdigste von Alexanders Eroberungen wurde I. ausführlich in vielen Alexander-Erzählungen behandelt. Die immer wieder für I. zitierten Autoren waren in der Ant. Aristobulos, Onesikritos, Nearchos und Kleitarchos mit wichtigen Angaben über Zeitgeschichte, Ethnographie und Naturkunde. Der Schwerpunkt lag auf dem von Alexander in erster Linie eroberten NW (h. Pakistan); vom Gebiet jenseits des Hyphasis konnte man sehr wenig berichten. Die verlorenen Werke dieser frühen → Alexanderhistoriker sind meist nur durch Arrianos (an. und Ind.), Diodorus, Curtius Rufus und Strabon bekannt.

Die ind. Satrapien Alexanders wurden schon kurz nach seinem Tod ein Zentrum des Aufruhrs des Candragupta Maurya (→ Sandrakottos), der bald große Teile Nord-I.s in sein neues Maurya-Reich eingliederte. Ein gescheiterter Versuch des → Seleukos, die ind. Satrapien wiederzugewinnen, endete mit einem Abkommen zwischen ihm und Candragupta, das letzterem nicht nur die eigentlichen ind. Satrapien, sondern auch Gedrosien, Arachosien und Paropamisadai zuschlug. Seleukos erhielt 500 Kriegselefanten, die in den folgenden Diadochenkriegen zu einer wichtigen Waffe wurden. Rege diplomatische Beziehungen zwischen den beiden Reichen dauerten mindestens bis zur Zeit des → Aśoka, des Enkels Candraguptas. → Megasthenes, Gesandter des Seleukos I. Nikator am Maurya-Hof in → Palimbothra, schrieb eine ausführliche und viel zitierte Monographie (FGrH 715) über das Land mit einer Beschreibung des Maurya-Reiches und des Gangestals. (Von den *Indiká* des Daimachos wissen wir leider sehr wenig.) Im NW des Maurya-Reiches erhielt sich eine griech. Bevölkerung (wohl in Siedlungen Alexanders) und Aśoka ließ dort seine königlichen Edikte auch auf Griech. (und Aram.) eingravieren.

Die Entstehung eigener Reiche in Parthien und Baktrien (→ Graeco-Baktrien) um die Mitte des 3. Jh. trennte die Seleukiden von I., obwohl Antiochos III. noch einmal die ind. Grenzregionen erreichte. Zu Beginn des 2. Jh. v. Chr. eroberten die baktrischen Griechen unter Demetrios [10] und Menandros NW-I. Die → Indogriechen bildeten bald mehrere Teilstaaten, und als sie zuletzt von den Parthern, Sakas und Indoskythen abgelöst wurden, interessierte das niemanden im Westen: Große Teile ihrer Geschichte müssen fast ausschließlich aufgrund von Münzfunden rekonstruiert werden. Als nachhaltigste Auswirkung kann die spätere hell.-buddhistische Kunst (sog. Gandhāra-Kunst) gelten.

IV. Römische Kaiserzeit

Die wichtigste Verbindung zwischen I. und dem Westen war jetzt der rege Seehandel zwischen I. und Äg. (z. T. auch Mesopot.), der sowohl aus dem Westen (ind. Elfenbeinstatuette in Pompeii, Brāhmī-Inschr. in Äg.) als auch aus dem Osten (hell.-röm. Keramik, Lampen und Glaswaren, große Mengen von röm. Münzen bes. in Süd-I.) bekannt ist. Berühmt sind neben weiteren Fundstätten bes. die Funde von → Arikamedu. In der Lit. sind Strabon, Plinius, Ptolemaios und bes. der *Periplus maris rubri* die wichtigsten Quellen. Der Beginn dieses Handels ist schon im 2. Jh. v. Chr. anzusetzen, als das Monopol der südarab. Zwischenhändler durch direkten Handel zwischen I. und dem ptolem. Äg. gebrochen wurde; bis zur Zeit des Augustus war der Umsatz allerdings bescheiden. Die wichtigsten Häfen in I. waren Barabara an der Indus-Mündung, → Barygaza und → Kalliena, und im Süden → Muziris und → Nelkynda; von Muziris an der Kerala-Küste wurden die Waren zu Lande nach Tamilnadu transportiert.

Der Landweg durch Parthien nach NW-I. spielte eine geringere Rolle. Aus I. wurden meist Luxuswaren wie Parfüme, Heilmittel und Gewürze, Perlen, Elfenbein und Edelsteine eingeführt und gegen Textilwaren, Wein, Glas und Korallen, häufig auch Silber- und Goldmz. getauscht. Die Verteilung und Zusammensetzung der Münzfunde gibt wichtige Hinweise auf die Geschichte des Handels [3]. Griech. Papyri aus Äg. und die klass. Tamil-Dichtung, aber auch das arch. Material [4] zeugen von griech. Händlern, die sich in Süd-I. aufhielten. Im 1. Jh. n. Chr. besuchten griech. Schiffe meist nur die Westküste, später wurden bisweilen auch die Ostküste und → Taprobane (Sri Lanka), seltener sogar SO-Asien erreicht. Auch ind. Schiffe beteiligten sich an diesem Fernhandel. Ind. Waren waren in den Häfen Südarabiens und Ostafrikas erhältlich. In der Lit. werden mehrere ind. und eine taprobanische Gesandtschaft erwähnt, die Augustus, Claudius und spätere Kaiser besuchten.

Das lit. Bild I.s im Westen blieb so gut wie unverändert und die frühen Alexanderhistoriker mit Megasthenes waren weiter die Hauptquellen [1. 32–36]. So ist z. B. Strabons I.-Abschnitt (15,1), eine der wichtigsten ant. Schilderungen I.s, ganz von diesen abhängig, was auch für Arrianos gilt, der seine *Indiká* als Anhang seiner Alexandergesch. schrieb. Nur im Bereich der Geogr. wurden neue Erkenntnisse berücksichtigt: Plinius (Buch 6), der Verfasser des *Periplus maris rubri* und Ptolemaios (Buch 7) benutzten neue Seefahrerinformationen. Besonders im *Periplus maris rubri* stammen die genauen Angaben von Häfen und Handel der ind. West-Küste deutlich aus erster Hand. Erst mit Ptolemaios, der (dem verlorenen Werk des Marinos folgend) einen Teil seiner Informationen von einem gewissen Alexandros erhielt, bekam man genauere Kenntnis von der Ost-Küste und von SO-Asien.

Für den gebildeten Leser blieb I. dennoch immer ein Land in äußerster Ferne, das man zudem nicht immer von Äthiopien trennen konnte; ein Land der vielen Naturwunder (darunter wertvolle Handelsgüter), der nackten Asketen und immer noch auch der goldgrabenden Ameisen des Herodot. Die ind. nackten Asketen oder → Gymnosophisten, die Alexander in Taxila getroffen hatte, und darunter besonders Kalanos, der Alexander folgte und sich dann selbst verbrannte, wurden immer wieder staunend in der Lit. erwähnt. Philostratos widmete dem Besuch des Apollonios bei den ind. Brahmanen zwei Bücher (Philostr. Ap. 3 und 4). Ein beliebtes Thema, urspr. Teil der Alexandergeschichte, waren auch die angeblichen I.-Feldzüge des Herakles und besonders des → Dionysos. Dieser wurde gern mit ind. Tieren wie Tigern und Leoparden abgebildet, und ep. Dichter wie → Dionysios [27] und → Nonnos beschrieben seinen I.-Zug. Daß die ind. Natur, von der die Alexanderhistoriker so ausführlich berichtet hatten, immer noch die Leser reizte, erkennt man an den Tierbüchern des Plinius und Ailianos.

V. Spätantike

Die christl. Mission in I. begann vielleicht mit Bartholomaeus im 2. Jh. n. Chr. [1. 37–39]; erst seit dem 5. Jh. wurde dem Thomas, ursprünglich Apostel von Edessa und Parthien, auch die ind. Mission anvertraut. Während der Handel nach und nach in die Hände der Axumiten (→ Axum) und anderer Zwischenhändler fiel, gab es doch auch direkten Kontakt zwischen der

Mittelmeerwelt und I. Der Reisebericht des Scholastikos von Theben ist bei Ps.-Palladius erhalten und christl. Schriftsteller wie Clemens Alexandrinus konnten oft Neues über I. berichten. Der Syrer → Bardesanes schrieb angeblich *Indiká* (FGrH 719). Auch die alten Traditionen der Gymnosophisten blieben beliebt bei Schriftstellern, die sich für die Askese interessierten. Einiges wurde wohl auch durch die Manichäer (→ Mani) vermittelt. Im 6. Jh. gab → Kosmas Indikopleustes in seiner ›Christl. Kosmographie‹ die letzten Primärnachrichten von I. und Sri Lanka.

Während einige Verfasser noch echte (und sogar neue) Kenntnisse aus I. vermittelten, wurde I. in der Lit. immer öfter mit Äthiopien verwechselt, ein Irrtum, der seine Wurzeln bereits in den frühesten griech. und altoriental. Quellen hat. Ganz sagenhaft war I. in den verschiedenen Rezensionen des → Alexanderromans und in dem fiktiven Brief Alexanders an Aristoteles. In der christl. Lit. wurde I. mit Paradiesvorstellungen vermischt und der → Ganges (oder Indus) mit dem Paradiesfluß Phison identifiziert. Nach Kosmas war das I.-Wissen in Byzanz meist, und im lat. Westen ausschließlich von ant. Quellen abhängig [5; 6].
→ Indienhandel (mit Karte); INDIEN

1 A. DIHLE, s. v. I., RAC 18, 1–56 **2** K. KARTTUNEN, I. in Early Greek Lit., 1989 **3** P. J. TURNER, Roman Coins from I., 1989 **4** V. BEGLEY, R. D. DE PUMA (Hrsg.), Rome and I. The Ancient Sea Trade, 1991 **5** N. V. PIGULEWSKAJA, Byzanz auf den Wegen nach I. Aus der Geschichte des byz. Handels mit dem Orient vom 4. bis 6. Jh., 1969
6 H. GREGOR, Das Indienbild des Abendlandes (bis zum Ende des 13. Jh.), 1964.

J. ANDRÉ, J. FILLIOZAT, L'Indie vue de Rome. Textes latins de l'Antiquité relatifs à l'Indie, 1986 • B. BRELOER, F. BÖMER, Fontes historiae religionum Indicarum, 1939 • R. M. CIMINO (Hrsg.), Ancient Rome and I. Commercial and Cultural Contacts between the Roman World and I., 1994 • P. DAFFINÀ, Le relazioni tra Roma e l'I. alla luce delle più recenti indagini. Conferenze Istituto Italiano per il Medio ed Estremo Oriente, 1995 • A. DIHLE, Ant. und Orient. Gesammelte Aufsätze (Supplemente zu den SHAW 2), 1984 • Ders., I. und die hell.-röm. Welt (Literaturbericht), in: Geographia antiqua 1, 1992, 151–159 • K. KARTTUNEN, Graeco-Indica. A survey of Recent Work, in: Arctos 20, 1986, 73–86 • Ders., Graeco-Indica 2, in: Topoi 3, 1993, 391–400 • Ders., I. and the Hellenistic World, 1997 • F. F. SCHWARZ, Neue Perspektiven in den griech.-ind. Beziehungen, in: OLZ 67, 1972, 5–26 • J. SEDLAR, I. and the Greek World, 1980.

K. K.

Indibilis (Ἀνδοβάλης). Stammesfürst der → Ilergetes; er und sein Bruder → Mandonius waren *omnis Hispaniae principes* (Liv. 27,17,3); I. geriet als Verbündeter der Karthager im 2. Punischen Krieg 218 v. Chr. in röm. Gefangenschaft (Pol. 3,76,6 f.), war 211 am Sieg von → Hasdrubal [3] und → Mago über P. → Cornelius [I 68] Scipio beteiligt (Liv. 25,34,6–9) [1. 319], fiel dann aber nach Repressalien seitens → Hasdrubals [5] und umworben von P. → Cornelius [I 71] Scipio zu den Römern ab (Pol. 9,11; 10,18; 35,6–8; 40,1–6; Liv. 26,49; 27,17; 19,1–7). Nachdem I. sich im J. 206 wieder gegen die Römer gewandt hatte, aus einer mil. Niederlage aber hatte entfliehen können (Pol. 11,29–33; Liv. 28,24–34,11; App. Ib. 37,147 f.), wiegelte er nach dem Abzug Scipios und seiner Truppen [1. 409[49]] die Ausetaner und Sedetaner gegen die Römer auf und fiel im J. 205 im Kampf gegen L. → Cornelius [I 36] Lentulus und L. → Manlius Acidinus, denen sein Bruder Mandonius dann zur Hinrichtung ausgeliefert wurde (Liv. 29,1,19–3,5; Diod. 26,22; App. Ib. 38,156 f.).

1 J. SEIBERT, Hannibal, 1993. L.-M. G.

Indictio. Eigentlich »Auflage, Steuer« (Dig. 19,1,13,6; Cod. Iust. 1,51,11 und 12,52,3), seit dem 4. Jh. n. Chr. auch, seit dem 6. Jh. nur noch ein Begriff der Zeitrechnung.

Indictiones temporariae waren in der Kaiserzeit außerordentliche Getreidesteuern. Kaiser → Diocletianus führte 287 einen alljährlichen, auf jeweils fünf Jahre festgesetzten Steuercensus ein, der zunächst ἐπιγραφή (*epigraphḗ*), nach 297 auch *i.* (ἰνδικτίων, *indiktíōn*) genannt wurde. Ein 15jähriger Steuerzyklus wurde 314 mit rückwirkend auf Sept. 312 festgelegtem Beginn eingeführt, nicht, wie meist angenommen, durch → Constantinus I., sondern (gemäß [5]) durch → Licinius in Nikomedeia, der als ersten Tag des I.-Jahres den 23. Sept. (Geburtstag des Kaisers Augustus, in Kleinasien verbreiteter Jahresbeginn) festsetzte. Erst im 5. Jh. (zw. 452 und 459), als die urspr. Bed. dieses Termins vergessen war, wurde der Beginn des I.-Jahres auf den rechnerisch bequemeren 1. Sept. verlegt [5. 193–202].

Bereits im 4. Jh. (erstmals in einem Gesetz von 356, Cod. Theod. 12,12,2) wurde das Indiktionssystem für Datier. verwendet, indem man das Jahr des Datums durch seine Ziffer im betreffenden 15-Jahres-Zyklus bezeichnete. So gilt z. B. das Jahr von Sept. 312 bis Sept. 313 als »erste I.«, das folgende Jahr als »zweite« usw.; im Sept. 327 beginnt die Zählung von neuem usw. Die Angabe »in der xten I.« gibt also nur das xte Jahr in einem beliebigen 15-Jahres-Zyklus ab 312 an, nicht aber, um welchen Zyklus es sich handelt. Darin besteht für den Historiker der Nachteil dieses Datierungssystems.

Die I. (griech. auch ἐπινέμησις/*epinémēsis*) wurde durch → Iustinianus [1] I. im J. 537 (Nov. 47) verbindlich für die Datierung aller öffentlichen Urkunden eingeführt. Bis in die Spätzeit des oström. Reiches wurden Dokumente mit der Angabe der I. datiert. Im Abendland verwendete man, nach Gebieten und Zeiten verschieden, teils diese sog. *i. Graeca*, teils andere I.-Systeme.

1 P.-J. SCHALLER, s. v. Indiktion, LMA 5, 405 f. **2** ODB 2, 993 **3** O. SEECK, s. v. I., RE 9, 1327–1332 **4** R. S. BAGNALL, K. A. WARP, The Chronological Systems of Byzantine Egypt, 1978 **5** V. GRUMEL, La chronologie, 1958, 192–206. F. T.

Indienhandel. Bereits Herodot hat die Informationen über Indien (→ India) zusammengefaßt und ein farbiges Bild von den Sitten und Ernährungsgewohnheiten der Inder sowie der Art ihrer Goldgewinnung entworfen (Hdt. 3,97–106), aber erst durch den Alexanderzug wurde das Interesse der Griechen an Indien nachhaltig geweckt (Arr. Ind.; Diod. 2,35–42; Strab. 15,1; Plin. nat. 6,56–106). Ein umfangreicher und regelmäßiger Handel im frühen Hell. hat kaum existiert, wenngleich Handelskontakte über den griech.-baktrischen Raum möglich sind. Mit der Erschließung der Monsunrouten gegen Ende des 2. Jh. v. Chr. vom Roten Meer zum Mündungsgebiet des → Indos [1] und an die Malabarküste setzte ein regelmäßiger maritimer Handelsverkehr zwischen dem ptolem. Äg. und Indien ein (Strab. 2,3,4; peripl. m. r. 57; → Periplus). → Palmyra begann in dieser Zeit bei der Organisation des → Karawanenhandels zwischen Indien und dem Mittelmeerraum eine zunehmend wichtige Rolle zu spielen. In dieser Zeit wurden vor allem Luxusgüter aus Indien importiert, während etwa vielfältige Keramikprodukte aus dem Mittelmeerraum sogar in das Landesinnere Indiens gelangten.

Ohne Zweifel existierten in der Zeit des frühen Prinzipats (1./2. Jh. n. Chr.) intensive Handelsbeziehungen zwischen der griech.-röm. und der indischen Welt. Sri Lanka und der hinterindische Raum waren bereits in diesen Handel einbezogen. Schon in augusteischer Zeit sollen nach Strabon jährlich 120 Schiffe von Myos Hormos am Roten Meer nach Indien gefahren sein (Strab. 2,5,12; vgl. 17,1,13; 17,1,45). Nach Plinius gab es drei Schiffahrtswege: von Syagron, einem Vorgebirge an der Südküste Arabiens (h. Ras Fartak), nach Patale an der Indosmündung, dann von Syagron nach Zigeros (Melizeigara, südlich von Bombay) und schließlich von Okelis (am Bab el-Mandeb) nach Muziris (an der Küste von Malabar, h. Cranganore; Plin. nat. 6,100; 6,101; 6,104; vgl. peripl. m. r. 57). Von Myos Hormos wurden die Waren mit Kamelen nach Koptos am Nil und dann weiter nach Alexandreia transportiert (Strab. 17,1,45; Plin. nat. 6,102 f.). Der Karawanenhandel über Palmyra wurde nun umfassend organisiert und gewann an Bedeutung; die palmyrenischen Kaufleute unterhielten Handelsstationen in Seleukeia, Babylon, Vologesias und Spasinu Charax.

Seit Beginn des Prinzipats waren die Handelsbeziehungen zum südindischen Raum intensiver als zu den zentral- und nordindischen Gebieten, wie sowohl die imposanten Funde röm. Mz. seit augusteischer Zeit als auch der *Periplus maris Erythraei* bezeugen. Auch in Sri Lanka wurden zahlreiche Mz. gefunden. Der Geld- bzw. Edelmetallexport wurde von Plinius den Luxusbedürfnissen der Frauen angelastet und wegen seiner wirtschaftlichen Folgen kritisiert: Nach Plinius wurden im Jahr 100 Mio Sesterzen für Waren aus Indien, China und Arabien aufgewendet (Plin. nat. 12,84; vgl. 6,101; 21,11); Aristeides hingegen rühmte den Import aus Indien als Beispiel dafür, daß Waren aus aller Welt nach Rom gebracht wurden (Aristeid. 26,12). In der Tat kamen vornehmlich Luxusprodukte (→ Gewürze, → Seide, → Elfenbein) aus dem fernen Osten in das Röm. Reich; im Gegenzug wurden landwirtschaftliche Produkte (Öl, Oliven, Getreide, Wein) und Textilien ausgeführt. Außerdem ist durch arch. Funde in Indien ein nicht unerheblicher Import röm. Keramik-, Metall- und Glasprodukte nachgewiesen. Der Papyrus Vindob. G 40822 aus dem 2. Jh. n. Chr., ein in Muziris und Alexandreia aufgesetzter Kaufvertrag, ist ein Zeugnis für diese Handelsbeziehungen. Da nur ein kleiner Käuferkreis die durch lange Transportwege sowie fiskalische Zugriffe bedingten hohen Preise bezahlen konnte, sollte das Volumen des I. nicht überschätzt werden; die Handelsbilanz war keineswegs ausgeglichen. Der Zoll für das *mare rubrum* (→ *Erythrá thálatta*) wurde vom *fiscus* verpachtet (Plin. nat. 6,84).

Von der Krise des 3. Jh. n. Chr. ist der I. stark beeinträchtigt worden. Die palmyrenischen Handelsstationen am Persischen Golf fielen seit 224 n. Chr. in den sāsānidischen Herrschaftsbereich, Palmyra – kurzlebiges Zentrum eines Nebenreiches – wurde 272 n. Chr. von den Römern zerstört; in Äg. kam es bis zum Ende des 3. Jh. zu Unruhen und mil. Auseinandersetzungen. Mit der Konsolidierung des Imperium Romanum unter Diocletianus und Constantinus I. (E. 2. bis Anf. 3. Jh. n. Chr.) wurden die Handelsbeziehungen mit Südindien und Sri Lanka, allerdings in geringerem Umfang, wiederhergestellt (Amm. 14,3,3). Wahrscheinlich hat ein Edikt von 356 oder 352 n. Chr. (Cod. Theod. 9,23,1), das die Ausfuhr von Geld gänzlich untersagte, den I. beeinträchtigt.

→ Handel

1 V. Begley, Ceramic Evidence for Pre-Periplus Trade on the Indian Coasts, in: V. Begley, R. D. De Puma (Hrsg.), Rome and India. The Ancient Sea Trade, 1991, 157–196
2 L. Casson, The Periplus Maris Erythraei, 1989
3 A. Dihle, Antike und Orient, 1984 **4** Ders., Die entdeckungsgeschichtlichen Voraussetzungen des I. der röm. Kaiserzeit, in: ANRW II 9.2, 546–580 (= Ders., Antike und Orient, 1984, 118–152) **5** R. Drexhage, Untersuchungen zum röm. Osthandel, 1988 **6** A. H. M. Jones, Asian Trade in Antiquity, in: Ders., Economy, 140–150 **7** K. Karttunen, Early Roman Trade with South India, in: Arctos 29, 1995, 81–91 **8** J. I. Miller, The Spice Trade of the Roman Empire, 1969 **9** Rostovtzeff, Roman Empire, 94–97 **10** P. J. Turner, Roman Coins from India, 1989 **11** R. Walburg, Ant. Münzen aus Sri Lanka (Ceylon). Die Bedeutung röm. Münzen und ihrer Nachahmungen für den Geldumlauf auf Ceylon, in: Studien zu Fundmünzen der Antike 3, 1985, 27–260.
H.-J. D.

Karten-Lit.: L. Casson, The Periplus Maris Erythraei, 1989 • P. Högemann u. a., Nordostafrika und Arabische Halbinsel. Staaten und Kulturen (4.–1. Jh. v. Chr.), TAVO B V 22, 1987 • I. Pill-Rademacher u. a., Vorderer Orient. Römer und Parther (14–138 n. Chr.), TAVO B V 8, 1988 • H. Waldmann, Die hell. Staatenwelt im 3. Jh. v. Chr., TAVO B V 3, 1983.

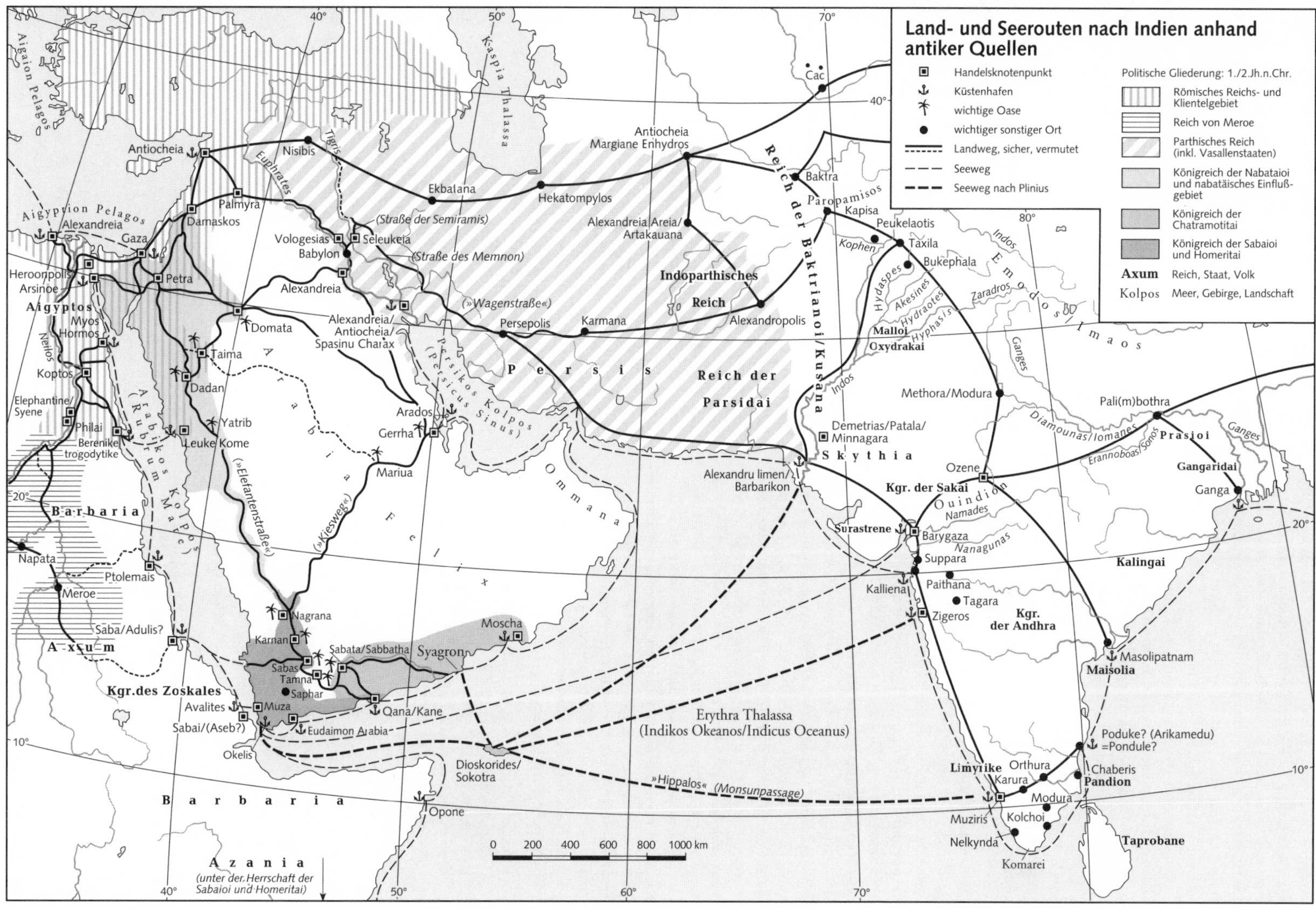
Land- und Seerouten nach Indien anhand antiker Quellen
Handelsknotenpunkt
Küstenhafen
wichtige Oase
wichtiger sonstiger Ort
Landweg, sicher, vermutet
Seeweg
Seeweg nach Plinius
Politische Gliederung: 1./2.Jh.n.Chr.
Römisches Reichs- und Klientelgebiet
Reich von Meroe
Parthisches Reich (inkl. Vasallenstaaten)
Königreich der Nabataioi und nabatäisches Einflußgebiet
Königreich der Chatramotitai
Königreich der Sabaioi und Homeritai
Axum Reich, Staat, Volk
Kolpos Meer, Gebirge, Landschaft
Aigaion Pelagos
Aigyption Pelagos
Kaspia Thalassa
Persikos Kolpos (Persicus Sinus)
Arabikos Kolpos (Rubrum Mare)
Erythra Thalassa (Indikos Okeanos/Indicus Oceanus)
»Hippalos« (Monsunpassage)
Reich der Baktrianoi/Kusana
Indoparthisches Reich
Reich der Parsidai
Persis
Skythia
Arabia Felix
Ommana
Barbaria
Azania (unter der Herrschaft der Sabaioi und Homeritai)
Kgr. des Zoskales
Axum
Aigyptos
Kgr. der Sakai
Kgr. der Andhra
Kalingai
Prasioi
Gangaridai
Taprobane
Limyrike
Pandion
Maisolia
Malloi
Oxydrakai
Surastrene
Antiocheia
Alexandreia
Gaza
Petra
Heroonpolis
Arsinoe
Myos Hormos
Koptos
Elephantine/Syene
Philai
Berenike trogodytike
Damaskos
Palmyra
Nisibis
Tigris
Euphrates
Vologesias
Babylon
Seleukeia
(Straße der Semiramis)
(Straße des Memnon)
(»Wagenstraße«)
Ekbatana
Hekatompylos
Antiocheia Margiane Enhydros
Alexandreia Areia/Artakauana
Alexandropolis
Persepolis
Karmana
Alexandreia/Antiocheia/Spasinu Charax
Domata
Taima
Dadan
Yatrib
Leuke Kome
(»Elefantenstraße«)
(»Kiesweg«)
Arados
Gerrha
Mariua
Nagrana
Karnan
Sabata/Sabbatha
Syagron
Moscha
Sabas
Tamna
Saphar
Muza
Qana/Kane
Eudaimon Arabia
Avalites
Sabai/(Aseb?)
Okelis
Dioskorides/Sokotra
Opone
Napata
Meroe
Ptolemais
Saba/Adulis?
Neilos
Cac
Baktra
Paropamisos
Kapisa
Kophen
Peukelaotis
Taxila
Bukephala
Hydaspes
Akesines
Hydraotes
Hyphasis
Zaradros
Indos
Emodos
Imaos
Ganges
Demetrias/Patala/Minnagara
Alexandru limen/Barbarikon
Methora/Modura
Pali(m)bothra
Diamounas/Iomanes
Erannoboas/Sonos
Ozene
Ouindion
Namades
Nanagunas
Barygaza
Suppara
Kalliena
Paithana
Tagara
Zigeros
Ganga
Masolipatnam
Poduke? (Arikamedu) =Pondule?
Chaberis
Orthura
Karura
Modura
Muziris
Kolchoi
Nelkynda
Komarei
0 200 400 600 800 1000 km

Indiges und sein Plural **Indigetes** bezeichnen eine Gottheit oder eine Gruppe von Gottheiten, deren Identität schon in der Ant. unterschiedlich gedeutet wurde (Serv. Aen. 12,794). Umstritten ist auch die Etym.: Die heute am meisten vertretene Hypothese ist diejenige, nach der I. wie auch → Indigitamenta von *indigitare* < **end-ag-itare* [1] (»rufen«; Fest. 101 L.: *indigitanto imprecanto*) abzuleiten sind, wobei I. mit passivischer Bed. als »gerufen« (**indag-et-*) zu verstehen ist [2. 59].

Bei Lavinium am Fluß Numicus ist ein dem Iuppiter I. (Liv. 1,2,6) oder dem Sol I. (Plin. nat. 3,56) [3] gewidmeter Kult belegt. Er wird später mit dem des Aeneas I. gleichgesetzt [2. 67f.], wobei Aeneas als Pater I. verehrt (Dion. Hal. ant. 1,64,5: πατὴρ θεὸς χθόνιος) oder mit Iuppiter I. identifiziert wird (Serv. Aen. 1,259). Der Beiname I. wird Aeneas nach seiner Vergöttlichung zugeschrieben (Verg. Aen. 12,794; Gell. 2,16,8–9). Auf dem Quirinal gab es einen Tempel des → Sol I., dessen Geburtstag am 9. August [4] gefeiert wurde. Der I., dem zu Ehren am 11. Dezember die Agonalien begangen wurden [5], kann auf der Basis von Lyd. mens. 4,155, demzufolge mit diesem Fest Helios geehrt wird, mit Sol I. identifiziert werden. Außer für Lavinium und Rom sind die *dii I.* auch für Arpinum (CIL X 1, 5779) und nach Serv. Aen. 7,678 für Praeneste belegt. Mehrmals werden die *dii I.* neben anderen Göttern erwähnt (von Verg. georg. 1,498; Ov. met. 15,861; Claud. De bello Gildonico 15,131). In dem vom Consul Decius Mus vor dem Selbstopfer (*devotio*) ausgesprochenen Gebet (Liv. 8,9,6) werden die *dii I.* nach den *novensides* angerufen. Darauf beruft sich [6], um die I. als einheimische (*indigenae*) Götter von diesen anderen – neuangesiedelten – zu unterscheiden. Diese Interpretation wie auch die von [7. 78ff.], nach der I. »Stammvater« bedeutete, hat sich jedoch nicht durchgesetzt.

1 Ernout/Meillet, s.v. aio 2 R. Schilling, Le culte de l'indiges à Lavinium, in: REL 57, 1979, 49–68 3 Enea nel Lazio. Archeologia e mito (Ausstellungs-Kat.), 1981, 167ff. 4 InscrIt. 13,2,493 5 Ebd., 13,2,535–537 6 G. Wissowa, Gesammelte Abh. zur röm. Rel.- und Stadtgesch., 1904, 175–191 7 C. Koch, Gestirnverehrung im alten Italien, 1933.

S. Borzsák, Zur Indigetes-Frage, in: Hermes 78, 1943, 245–257 · Latte, 43ff. · B. Liou-Gille, Cultes »héroïques« romains, 1980, 99ff. · Radke, 149ff. · S. Weinstock, s.v. Novensides di, RE 17, 1185–1189.

R. SCH.

Indigitamenta. Zur Etym. s. → Indiges. Nach Wissowa bezeichnet das Wort I. Sammlungen von Anrufungsformeln, mit denen sich röm. Priester bei verschiedenen Anlässen an Gottheiten wenden und die wegen ihrer zwingenden Gewalt vom Staat geheimgehalten werden [1; 2]. Unter Berufung auf Varro (Antiquitates 14, fr. 87 Cardauns) werden aber in den I. häufig Verzeichnisse von Gottheiten gesehen, die zu Pontificalbüchern gehören. Viele von diesen Göttern, sog. »Sonder- oder Augenblicksgötter«, haben eine beschränkte Funktion, welche meist durch ihren Namen ausgedrückt wird: z.B. die nach der Furcht der Kinder benannte Paventia (Aug. civ. 4,11,161), oder Iterduca und Domiduca, die dafür zuständig sind, auf den Weg und nach Hause zu führen (Aug. civ. 7,3,276). Der prädeistischen Theorie, nach der I. die erste Stufe in der Personifikation der Götter darstellen [3; 4], ist zu widersprechen; vielmehr sind sie als untergeordnete Gottheiten zu begreifen, die im Dienst höherer agieren, als ob sie ihrer *familia* angehörten [5]. Sie haben weder eigene Priester noch Kulte. Selten werden sie in Gebeten an andere Götter erwähnt, wie die von Fabius Pictor und Varro (durch Serv. georg. 1,21; Aug. civ. 4,8) überlieferten zwölf Götter, die während des Opfers für → Ceres (*sacrum Cereale*) angerufen werden [6], und diejenigen, die von den → Arvales fratres während des Sühneopfers für das Entfernen eines Baumes aus dem *lucus* (Hain) der → Dea Dia genannt werden (CIL VI 2099: Adolenda, Conmolenda, Deferunda; 2107a: Adolenda, Coinquenda) [7].

Die Werke, die direkte Informationen über die I. enthielten, wie z.B. Varros *Antiquitates rerum divinarum*, deren primäre Quelle, die *Libri iuris pontificii* des → Fabius [I 34] Pictor, und auch das Caesar gewidmete Buch *De indigitamentis* von → Granius [I 3] Flaccus (Cens. de die natali 3,2), sind nicht überliefert. Einige Fragmente davon wurden jedoch von christl. Autoren, vor allem von Augustinus (civ. bes. B. 4; 6; 7), tradiert, denen diese Werke als Grundlage ihrer Kritik am Polytheismus der heidnischen Religion dienten.

1 G. Wissowa, Rel. und Kultus der Römer, [2]1912, 37; 397; 513 2 Ders., Gesammelte Abh. zur röm. Rel.- und Stadtgesch. 1904, 304ff. 3 L. Deubner, Altröm. Rel., in: Die Ant. 2, 1926, 61–78 4 H. Usener, Götternamen (1896), 1948, 301ff. 5 Dumézil, 50ff. 6 J. Bayet, Croyances et rites dans la Rome antique, 1977, 181ff. 7 Latte, 54.

C. Koch, Gestirnverehrung im alten Italien, 1933, 78ff.

R. SCH.

Indiktion s. Zeitrechnung

Indirekte Überlieferung. Die Edition ant. Texte stützt sich gewöhnlich auf → Handschriften, die aus der Ant. (→ Papyrus) oder dem MA stammen. Häufig ist man jedoch auf die indirekte oder Nebentradition angewiesen.

A. Übersetzungen B. Textzitate
C. Literarische Zitate

A. Übersetzungen

In der Spätant. oder dem frühen MA wurden zahlreiche griech. Texte, vor allem philos. oder wiss. Inhalts, ins Lat. (bzw. eine oder mehrere oriental. Sprachen) übersetzt. Die Vorlagen für den Übersetzer waren nicht unbedingt älter als die frühesten heute greifbaren Texte der direkten Hss.-Tradition, und es waren auch nicht alle Übersetzer ihrer Aufgabe gewachsen. Doch mißt man den Übersetzungen h. einigen Wert bei. Übersetzungen aus dem Lat. ins Griech. dagegen fertigte man selten an. Planudes übersetzte beispielsweise einige Werke des Ovid (so die *Metamorphoseis*, ed. [1]; *Heroides*, gedruckt in der postumen Ed. von [2] mit einer neuen Ed. durch [3]; die Liebesdichtungen, ed. von [4] als *Ovidiana Graeca*). Die Herausgeber sahen diese seinerzeit als wertvoll an, doch werden heute deren Vorlagen als minderwertiger eingeschätzt (vgl. [5; 6]).

Bereits aus der klassischen Antike stammen Catulls Übertragungen von Sappho (fr. 31 LOBEL-PAGE/VOIGT = Catull. 51) und Kallimachos (*Coma Berenices*, fr. 10 = Catull. 66); Cicero übersetzte zahlreiche Abschnitte aus griech. Tragödien.

B. TEXTZITATE

Meist anon. Zitate finden sich – außer auf Papyrus und Pergament – nur in sehr geringer Zahl und hauptsächlich als Graffiti aus Pompeii. Ein schönes Beispiel ist die Wandinschrift CIL 4,1950 mit der besten Lesart von Prop. 3,16,13–14 (dazu jetzt [7]). Schreiber dieser Art fühlten sich natürlich nicht an den Originalwortlaut gebunden und kombinierten Textstücke aus unterschiedlichen Werken, wie etwa das pompeianische Graffito CIL 4,1520 zeigt. Hier gab man Prop. 1,1,5 wieder als *candida* (*donec* Prop.) *me docuit nigras* (*castas* Prop.) *odisse puellas*, und fügte noch eine korrupte Version eines weiteren Hexameters aus Ov. am. 3,11,35 hinzu (HEINSIUS tilgte diese Verse): *odero, si potero; sed* (*si* Ov.) *non invitus amabo*. Ein seltener Fall ist der einer Sokrates-Statue, die ein Platonzitat Krit. 46b 4–6 trägt, das die Editoren sogar in die Platonausgaben übernehmen.

C. LITERARISCHE ZITATE

Diese häufigste und wichtigste Quelle der i.Ü. liegt zeitlich oft noch vor den ältesten Textzeugen der direkten Überlieferung, und man übernimmt im Zweifelsfall gerne, und oft zu Recht, die ältere Variante. Diese ist sorgfältig zu prüfen, da die ant. und ma. Schriftsteller die Korrektheit ihres Zitats kaum nachprüften und ihrem umfangreichen, aber unzuverlässigen Gedächtnisschatz vertrauten, zumal sich das Volumenformat der Codices für eine schnelle Belegprüfung nicht eignete und die genaue Stellenangabe nach Kapitel und Zeile unbekannt war. Wenn jedoch die i.Ü. dort eine Variante bietet, wo das Zitat eine spezifische Eigenheit belegen soll, ist ein Fehler weniger wahrscheinlich. Doch ist auch hier Vorsicht geboten, wie das bekannte Beispiel des Zitats von Verg. ecl. 4,62–3 bei Quint. inst. 9,3,8 zeigt: die Quintilian-Hss. lesen mit Vergil alle *cui non risere parentes, / nec deus hunc mensa, dea nec dignata cubili est*. Doch der Zusammenhang (Numeruswechsel) und die eingeflochtene Bemerkung (*ex illis enim »qui non risere« hic quem non dignata*) zeigen, daß Quintilian selbst *qui* las. Nun paßt aber *ridere* mit dem Akk. in der Bedeutung »jemanden auslachen« (und nicht »jemandem zulächeln«) nicht zu *parentes* (Versuch dennoch bei [8; 9]). Die meisten Editoren übernehmen daher SCHRADERS Lesung *parenti* und vermuten, daß die Quintilian-Hss. durch diejenigen des Vergil doppelt verderbt wurden. Doch möglicherweise ist Quintilians Lesart eher in einer eigenen Fehlinterpretation als einem unverderbten Text begründet, wenn die Argumente von [10] gegen das heute übliche *qui ... parenti* richtig sind.

Die Bandbreite von Gründen für ein Zitat reicht von den Lemmata von Scholien über technische Zitate bei Grammatikern und Metrikern und den Bezug auf die Autorität eines älteren Schriftstellers bis hin zur freien Umgestaltung der Vorlage.

1. SCHOLIEN

Da Schol. am Rand der zu kommentierenden Texte notiert sind, sind sie nicht in wünschenswertem Maße unabhängig, doch können sie nützlich sein, um Entscheidungen über den Wert von Textabweichungen bereits in der Ant. zu treffen (auch wenn moderne Editoren sie nur selten als verbindlich betrachten), und um von der Haupttradition nicht überliefertes Material zu bieten (vgl. [11] für Verg. Aen., zur i.Ü. des Vergil allgemeiner [12; 13]). Diskussion der ant. Varianten vgl. schol. Aristoph. Thesm. 162.

2. GRAMMATIKER UND METRIKER

Grammatiker und Metriker nutzen unabhängigere Überlieferungen und interessieren sich für eine spezifische Besonderheit, die sie durch ihr Zitat bestätigen, und geben so dem Herausgeber wenig Anlaß zu Zweifel. Charisius z.B. (1,107,27–8 KEIL) bestätigt das Femininum *demissae ... sertae* der ältesten Hs. zu Prop. 2,33,37 gegen das Neutrum in allen übrigen Hss., und die Diskussion um die Konjugation von *necto* bei Diomedes (1,369,21 KEIL) und Priskian (2,536,7–15 KEIL) zeigt, daß bei Prop. 3,8,37 die Lesart *nexisti retia lecto* zu übernehmen ist, nicht aber die überlieferte (aber gramm. regelwidrige) Vereinfachung *tendisti*. Solche Autoren bemühen sich um eine sorgfältige Quellenangabe, doch kommen gelegentlich Fehler vor, wie etwa Diomedes' falsche Zuweisung des o.g. Textes an »Maecenas«. Ursache für diese Irrtümer ist, daß man Quellenzitate in Tabellen auflistete. In manchen Fällen reicht die Zahl der Zitate eines sonst über die direkte Überlieferung nicht greifbaren Werkes für eine Edition seiner Fragmente aus. Ein herausragendes Beispiel ist die *Hekálē* des Kallimachos: A. HECKER [14] wies scharfsinnig nach, daß nicht nur die zugewiesenen, sondern auch die nicht zuweisbaren Zitate in der → Suda (sofern nicht anderweitig bekannt) alle aus diesem verlorenen Gedicht stammten (vgl. auch [15]). Die grundsätzliche Richtigkeit dieser Erkenntnis wurde später durch Papyrusfunde des Originaltextes bestätigt.

Metriker zitieren gewöhnlich die ersten Zeilen eines Gedichtes oder Buches (wie auch alle Gelehrten dazu neigen, bei Referenzen sich auf den Beginn einer Buch- oder Gedichtserie zu beziehen), so daß die Form des Zitates Aussagen über die Buch- und → Gedichttrennung erlaubt [16]. Die Rezeption von Catull 1 ist ein gutes Beispiel: Verse seines 10-Zeilen-Gedichtes werden (wiederholt) wegen ihrer Metrik zitiert, des weiteren in einer Abhandlung über ant. Buchproduktion (Isid. 6,12,3) und schließlich, um das Vorwort von Ausonius (1,4,1) und des älteren Plinius einzuleiten (nat.

praef. 1; mit einer expliziten Änderung der catullischen Wortreihenfolge, die ihrerseits wiederum in der Plinius-Überlieferung korrumpiert wurde, um für Vers 4 einen eher spondeischen als iambischen Beginn herzustellen).

3. UMARBEITUNG DER VORLAGE

Eine durchdachte Form der kreativen Umgestaltung ist der → Cento. Hier schafft man durch die Neukomposition unterschiedlicher Einzelteile älterer Gedichte ein neues. Diese Zitate entsprechen meist dem korrekten Wortlaut, nutzen den Editoren jedoch kaum, da gerade die Texte von Homer und Vergil, die häufigste Grundlage für den Cento, bereits in der ant. Überlieferung erhalten sind. So ist Ausonius' *Cento nuptialis* (ed. [17]) mit seinen 131 Zeilen nur als zusätzlicher Beleg für eine bestimmte Schreibvariante aus verschiedenen Gruppen von Vergil-Hss. brauchbar. Umgekehrt kann man die Vergiltradition als indirekte Zeugen zu dem Ausoniustext nutzen. Bedeutender ist der Beitrag des ma. Spiels *Christus patiens*, dessen Text insbes. die große Lücke in Euripides' *Bakchai* nach Vers 1329 schließen hilft.

Der Cento gibt den Wortlaut der Vorlage exakt wieder; die Parodie kommt dem Original ebenfalls recht nahe: vgl. Eur. Hel. 570 in Aristoph. Thesm. 910 und andere paratragische Passagen in dieser Komödie; vgl. Catull. 4 bei [Verg.] catal. 10. Auch unpräzisere Wiedergaben können zur i.Ü. beitragen, wie z.B. der überlieferte Text von Verg. georg. 1,513 zeigt: Die meisten Hss. des 9. Jh. geben *addunt in spatia* – trotz syntaktischer Schwierigkeiten und obwohl die beiden erh. ant. Hss. R und M das *in* auslassen, und M mit einigen späteren Hss. *spatio* bietet. Die Quintilian-Hss. zu inst. 8,3,78 belegen hierbei durch ihre eigenen beiden Textvarianten (*in spatio* und *in spatia*) eine Beeinflussung durch die direkte Vergilüberlieferung. Damit kann PULBROOKS kühne Konjektur *invadunt spatia* [18] eine gewisse Plausibilität nicht abgesprochen werden, doch müßte dann die Korruptel bereits entstanden sein, bevor Silius Italicus 16,373 *in spatia* (oder *-o*) *addebant* schrieb.

Auch wenn man der Ansicht von WEST [19] folgt und annimmt, daß Soph. Oid. T. 1278–1279 interpoliert sei (→ Interpolation), muß man die Ergänzung bereits für ant. halten, da diese Verse bei Sen. Oedipus 978–979 paraphrasiert werden. Gelegentlich verwendet man die Zitatvorlage zur Textkonstitution des Zitates. So liest im Falle von Ov. am. 1,15,25 der Herausgeber J.C. MCKEOWN [20] gemäß der Aldina-Ausgabe von 1502 *Tityrus et* segetes *Aeneiaque arma legentur* statt des überlieferten *fruges*, um hier eine Anspielung auf Verg. georg. 1,1 herzustellen (*Quid faciat laetas segetes*) und um es dem Reflex von ecl. 1,1 und Aen. 1,1 anzupassen. Andererseits ist gerade die Ersetzung durch ein Synonym eine gelungene Variation, und selbst Vergil spielt am Ende eines Werkes auf das nächste an, wie ecl. 10,76 zeigt (*nocent et frugibus umbrae*). Diese Beispiele zeigen, wie schwierig es ist, die Grenzen der i.Ü. abzustecken.

→ Autorenvarianten; TEXTÜBERLIEFERUNG

1 J. BOISSONADE (ed.), Paris 1822 (Metamorphosen) **2** A. PALMER (ed.), 1898, 161–274 (postume Ed. der Heroides) **3** M. PAPATHOMOPOULOS (ed.), Ioannina 1976 (Heroides) **4** P.E. EASTERLING, E.J. KENNEY, Ovidiana Graeca (PCPhS suppl. 1), 1965 (Liebesdichtung) **5** R.J. TARRANT, Text and Transmission 281, n. 20 **6** E.J. KENNEY, in: Hermes 91, 1963, 214–216 **7** J.L. BUTRICA, in: CQ 47, 1997, 181–182 **8** TH. BIRT, in: Berliner Philologische Wochenschrift 1918, 186–192 **9** R.G.M. NISBET, Collected Papers, 1995, 73, Anm. 135 **10** G.P. GOOLD, A skullcracker in Virgil, in: Classica et Mediaevalia: Studies in honor of Joseph Szövérffy, 1986, 67–76 **11** R.A.B. MYNORS (ed.), P. Vergili Maronis Opera, 1969, p. XII **12** S. TIMPANARO, Per la storia della filologia virgiliana antica, 1986 **13** M.L. DELRIGO, Testo virgiliano e tradizione indiretta. Le varianti probiane, 1987 **14** A. HECKER, Commentationum Callimachearum capita duo, 1842, 79–148 **15** A.S. HOLLIS (ed.), Callimachus, Hecale, 1990, 41–44 **16** J.L. BUTRICA, in: Illinois Classical Studies 21, 1996, 94–96 **17** R.P.H. GREEN, The Works of Ausonius, 1991, 518–526 **18** M. PULBROOK, in: Hermathena 120, 1976, 39–40 **19** M.L. WEST, in: BICS 25, 1978, 121 **20** J.C. MCKEOWN, Commentary on Ovid, Amores, 1989, z. St.

S. TIMPANARO, Alcuni casi controversi di tradizione indiretta, in: Maia 22, 1990, 351–359 • L.D. REYNOLDS, N.G. WILSON, Scribes and Scholars, ³1991, 219–221.

S.H. u. N.W./Ü: J.DE.

Indischer Ozean. Der h. I.O. war den Griechen meist als → *Erythrá thálatta* [1] bekannt, was eigentlich nur dessen westl. Teil bezeichnete. Mit der Erweiterung des geogr. Wissens wurde *Erythrá thálatta* auch für den ganzen Ozean gebraucht (z.B. peripl. m. r.), der aber sonst Indische See (Ἰνδικὸν πέλαγος, Ptol. 7,1,1; 7,2,1) oder I.O. (Ἰνδικὸς ὠκεανός, Agathemeros 2,4; *Oceanus Indicus*, Mela 1,9, Sen. nat. 4,2,4) genannt wurde. Mit den großen Meerbusen (Sinus Gangeticus, Sabaracus und Perimulicus) formte er für die ant. Autoren die Südgrenze Indiens. Im Osten reichte der → Magnus Sinus bis zur Küste der Sinai (China). Nach Marinos (bei Ptol. 7,3,6 u.a.) war dieser Ozean ein geschlossenes Meer mit einer Landverbindung zwischen Ostasien und Afrika – eine Vorstellung, die auch für den Alten Orient zu gelten scheint, wo der Name Meluḫḫa, im 3. Jt. v. Chr. für die → Indus-Kulturen gebraucht, im 1. Jt. auf Äthiopien übertragen wurde.

→ Hippalos; Sachalites; Indienhandel (mit Karte)

J. READE, The Indian Ocean in Antiquity, 1996. K.K.

Indoarische Sprachen. Die i.S. umfassen die Mehrzahl derjenigen → indogermanischen Sprachen, die auf dem ind. Subkontinent seit der Einwanderung aus NW im 2. Jt. v. Chr. gesprochen werden. Sie bilden zusammen mit den → iranischen Sprachen den indoiran. Zweig dieser Sprachfamilie. Das Altindoarische (weniger genau: Altind.) beginnt gegen 1200 v. Chr. mit dem Vedischen und setzt sich im Sanskrit fort [1. 16–48]. Als altertümliche und frühbezeugte idg. Sprache hat es viele nicht nur formale Übereinstimmungen mit dem Lat. und v.a. auch mit dem Griech.; daher kommt ihm auch bei der Rekonstruktion der idg. Grundsprache große Bed. zu: vgl. die nominalen (bzw. pronominalen) Ausgänge im Sg. der *-o*-Stämme

	uridg.	altindoar.	homer.	altlat.
Nom.	*-*os*	-*as*	-ος	-*os*
Akk.	*-*om*	-*am*	-ον	-*om*
Gen.	*-*osi̯o*	-*asya*	-οιο	-*osio*

Im Hinblick auf das Griech. sind folgende Merkmale des älteren Vedischen bes. hervorhebenswert: freier musikalischer Wortakzent (→ Akzent) sowie formale und funktionale Opposition zw. augmentierten und nicht augmentierten Präteritalformen (Ind. als Modus des Berichts : Injunktiv als Modus der Erwähnung) [2], vgl. beim Präs.-Stamm

	uridg.	indoar.	homer.
Sg. 1.	**bʰér-o-m*	*bhár-a-m*	φέρ-ο-ν
	**é-bʰer-o-m*	*á-bhar-a-m*	ἔ-φερ-ο-ν
2.	**bʰér-e-s*	*bhár-a-s*	φέρ-ε-ς
	**é-bʰer-e-s*	*á-bhar-a-s*	ἔ-φερ-ε-ς
3.	**bʰér-e-t*	*bhár-a-t*	φέρ-ε
	**é-bʰer-e-t*	*á-bhar-a-t*	ἔ-φερ-ε

Ferner bestehen in der Zeit des Mittelindoarischen geringe wechselseitige Lehnbeziehungen zw. den i.S. und v.a. dem Griech., u.a. bei EN (z.B. *Milinda-* aus griech. Μένανδρος oder Σανδρόκοττος aus indoar. *Candragupta-*) oder bei Fachtermini: vgl. *khalīna-* »Trense« aus griech. χαλῑνός oder σάκχαρ(-ι, -ον) »Zucker« (entlehnt ins Lat. als *saccharum*) aus Pāli *sakkharā-* »Sandzucker« < altindoar. *śárkarā-* »Kies, Geröll, Grieß« [3. 155f.].

→ Griechisch; Latein

1 H. Bechert, G. von Simson (Hrsg.), Einführung in die Indologie, ²1993 2 K. Hoffmann, Der Injunktiv im Veda, 1967 3 Schwyzer, Gramm. R.P.

Indogermanen. A. Definition, Allgemeines, Methoden B. Urheimat und Ausbreitung C. Materielle und geistige Kultur

A. Definition, Allgemeines, Methoden

Mit I. meint man sowohl die Träger einzelner → indogermanischer Sprachen als auch die des rekonstruierten Uridg. (uridg. Grundsprache) oder etwa des Urgriech. Der zu Beginn des 19. Jh. erbrachte Nachweis der sprachlichen Verwandtschaft hat die Frage nach den Sprechern der Grundsprache aufkommen lassen. In die Vorgesch. wurde mit diesem neuen Begriff das Postulat eingeführt, daß ein Volk mit einer charakteristischen Kultur zu suchen sei. Doch hängt die Definition eines Ethnos nicht ausschließlich vom Faktor Sprache ab. Aussagen über rassische Zusammensetzung des Urvolks sind unzulässig. Die unabdingbare interdisziplinäre Forsch. wird durch verschiedene Methoden in den (vor)histor. Fächern erschwert. Die Sprachwiss. bestimmt die Prämissen [1], indem sie Elemente des uridg. Wortschatzes rekonstruiert, sie gegebenenfalls etym. deutet, zu Sinnbezirken ordnet oder durch wechselseitigen semantischen Bezug zu präzisieren versucht. Das Verfahren, Schlüsse vom grundsprachlichen Wortschatz auf Lebensbedingungen und Umwelt der Sprecher zu ziehen, nennt man »linguistische Paläontologie«. Nicht scharf davon zu trennen ist die idg. Altertumskunde, die gemeinsame kulturelle Trad. auf urzeitliche Quellen zurückführt: Texte transportieren überkommene Inhalte. Kritiker wenden prinzipiell ein, daß immer auch die Möglichkeit von Polygenese bzw. sekundärer Ausbreitung von kulturellen Errungenschaften und ihren Benennungen bestehe. So ist die Diskussion noch zu keiner exakten Festlegung von Raum und Zeit gelangt. Alte Lw. im Uridg., die vorhistor. Kontakte aufdecken könnten, sind nicht zu sichern.

B. Urheimat und Ausbreitung

Neben der linguistischen Paläontologie gestattet die histor. Verteilung Schlüsse über die vorhistor. Sitze. Das zu Beginn des 2. Jt. nachweisbare Auftreten von I. in Kleinasien (→ anatolische Sprachen), das selbst nicht Urheimat (falsch [2]) war, richtet die Suche auf benachbarte Regionen. Vertretbar erscheint eine weiträumige Lokalisierung in südruss. und ukrain. Gegenden, ohne daß es genug Anhaltspunkte für Abgrenzungen gegenüber benachbarten Räumen gibt. Die genannten Areale gestatten es, die Ausbreitung nachzuvollziehen. Abwechselnd haben allmähliche, Dialektkontinua erzeugende, oder weit ausholende Wanderungen bei abreißender Kommunikation (Modelle: »Wellentheorie« versus »Stammbaumtheorie«) stattgefunden. Da Griech. und ihm nahestehende Sprachen, wie das → Makedonische, bei der sprachwiss. Klassifikation [3. 244f.] an die Seite von → Phrygisch und → Armenisch zu stellen sind, bietet sich als Urheimat dieser Gruppe der Raum zw. Balkan und Kleinasien an. Sehr wahrscheinlich lag das Verbreitungsgebiet der vorhistor. »Gräkoarmenier« nördl. des Schwarzen Meeres, nicht fern vom Ausgangspunkt der Ur-I. Eine andere Abspaltung durch NW-Wanderung bildete im 2. Jt. v.Chr. ein Epizentrum in Mittel- und Osteuropa, das einem modifizierten Konzept des → Alteuropäischen entspricht. Von da aus erfolgte die Besiedlung europ. Randgebiete, d.h. des Westens durch die Kelten und Italiens durch die Italiker, nach deren Lösung aus dem Verband mit den Kelten. Die Triebkräfte bei der vorhistor. Ausbreitung sind schwer bestimmbar. Vermutlich bestanden die Ur-I. in einer verhältnismäßig starken Population, wahrscheinlich unter günstigen natürlichen Bedingungen gewachsen, dabei vielfache Errungenschaften ausnützend. Auf der Suche nach anderen Plätzen haben sie fremde Stämme verdrängt oder unterjocht, bis sie die aus histor. Zeit bekannte Verbreitung einnahmen.

C. Materielle und geistige Kultur

Die Kriterien für die zeitliche Einordnung der Ur-I. (ausgehendes Neolithikum, ca. 3. Jt.) ergeben sich aus Fragen nach technischen Errungenschaften. Neben der noch ohne Töpferscheibe produzierten Keramik kannten sie an Metallen **(h₂)ái̯es-* »Bronze, Kupfer« (altind. *áyas-*, lat. *aes*) und **h₂arĝn̥tóm* »Silber« (altind. *rajatám*, lat. *argentum*), doch fehlen aussagekräftige Wörter im Umfeld der Herstellung oder Verarbeitung der Metalle. Hinsichtlich der materiellen Grundlagen bieten sich Termini der Ernährung an, um etwas über die Lebenswelt der I. auszusagen. Neben Ackerbau und Viehzucht haben Jagd und Fischfang den Speisezettel bereichert. Zu den Haustieren zählten Hund, Pferd, Rind, Schaf, Schwein und Ziege. Wörter für »Milch«, »melken«, »Wolle«, »spinnen«, »weben« legen nahe, daß es sich um domestizierte Arten der genannten Tiere handelt. Rekonstruierbare Vokabeln für Pflug und Wagen (Rad, Deichsel usw.) deuten auf Nutzung von Pferd und/oder Rind als Zugtiere. Zur Fauna gehörten u.a. noch: Adler, Bär, Biber, Biene, Fuchs, Hase, Kranich, Wolf. Blaß bleibt die Rekonstruktion rechtlicher, gesellschaftlicher oder polit. Begriffe bzw. der diesen zugeordneten Zustände. Als verfehlt gelten die Ansichten Dumézils (dagegen ausführlich [4]), daß die idg. Ges. und ihre Widerspiegelung im Mythos von einer funktionalen Dreiteilung geprägt war. Es lassen sich Spuren vergleichbarer ritueller Praktiken und rel. Vorstellungen sichern. Man vermutet ein Pantheon von Natur- und Gestirngottheiten (griech. → *Eos*, lat. *Aurora*). Die Epiklese »Vater« des höchsten Gottes »Tag(-Himmel)« (lat. *Diespiter*/→ *Iuppiter*, griech. → *Zeus*) weist mit der Erschließung eines Systems von Verwandtschaftsbezeichnungen auf eine patriarchalisch organisierte Familie. Trotz Unsicherheiten in bezug auf die Methodik bleiben die materielle und geistige Kultur der Ur-I. bzw. der sich bereits in vorgesch. Zeit herauskristallisierenden Ethnien legitime Forsch.-Objekte. Es ist durchaus relevant zu wissen, inwieweit Institutionen, Traditionen und Bräuche aus der Urzeit ererbt, organisch entwickelt oder von anderswoher übernommen sind. Da Griech. und Lat. innerhalb der idg. Sprachfamilie nicht enger verwandt sind, müssen Übereinstimmungen im Wortschatz entweder auf die Urzeit zurückgehen oder auf Entlehnung in histor. Zeit beruhen.

→ Indogermanische Dichtersprache; Indogermanische Sprachen; Sprachverwandtschaft; Indogermanistik

1 W. Dressler, Methodische Vorfragen bei der Bestimmung der »Urheimat«, in: Sprache 11, 1965, 25–60
2 C. Renfrew, Archaeology and Language, 1987
3 G. Klingenschmitt, Die Verwandtschaftsverhältnisse der idg. Sprachen, in: J. E. Rasmussen (Hrsg.), In honorem H. Pedersen, 1994, 235–251 4 B. Schlerath, Georges Dumézil und die Rekonstruktion der idg. Kultur, in: Kratylos 40, 1995, 1–48; 41, 1996, 1–67.

E. Benveniste, Indeur. Institutionen, 1993 (frz. 1969) • T.V. Gamkrelidze, V.V. Ivanov, Indo-European and the Indo-Europeans, 1995 • B. Hänsel, S. Zimmer (Hrsg.), Die I. und das Pferd, 1994 • W. Meid, Arch. und Sprachwiss., 1989 • A. Scherer (Hrsg.), Die Urheimat der I., 1968 • S. Zimmer, Ursprache, Urvolk und Indogermanisierung, 1990.
Zschr.: The Journal of Indo-European Studies. D.ST.

Indogermanische Dichtersprache. Unter i.D. versteht man etym. meist übereinstimmende Formeln, die sich in den ältesten Dichtungen verschiedener idg. Sprachen, insbes. des Griech. und Indoiran., finden. Ein Beispiel ist griech. κλέος ἄφθιτον (*kléos áphthiton*) bei Homer und altind. *ákṣitaṃ śrávas*, beides »unsterblicher Ruhm«. Für das hohe Alter der Formel spricht, daß *ákṣitam* im Altind. nur noch in dieser Verbindung vorkommt. So kann man für die i.D. ein **kléu̯os n̥g*^{wh}*δ*^{h}*itom* rekonstruieren. Weitere Formeln aus dem gleichen inhaltlichen Bereich, beispielsweise griech. κλέα ἀνδρῶν (*kléa andrṓn*) bei Homer und altind. *śrávo...nr̥ṇā́m*, was beides wörtlich »Ruhm der Männer«, in Wahrheit aber »berühmte Taten von Heroen« bedeutet, sichern die Hypothese. Auch die Existenz der Dichtung selbst wird durch Formeln indirekt bestätigt, denn im Griech. können Dichter als ἐπέων τέκτονες (*epéōn téktones*) »Zimmerleute der Worte« bezeichnet werden, und im Altind. heißt es *vácāṁsi...takṣam* »Worte will ich zimmern«. Weitere Formeln stammen offensichtlich aus Hymnen bzw. Gebeten, andere, nicht im engeren Sinne dichtersprachliche, aus metr. oder prosaischer Spruchweisheit, Mythenüberl. und dgl.

Meillet hat gezeigt, daß der elfsilbige Vers der äolisch-griech. Dichterin Sappho mit dem altind. Triṣṭubh-Vers gleicher Silbenzahl zusätzlich auch in der Verteilung der langen und kurzen Silben innerhalb der zweiten Advershälfte übereinstimmt. Auch wenn die letztere Eigenschaft von der altiran. Dichtung nicht geteilt wird, so findet sich doch auch hier der elfsilbige Vers, so daß das silbenzählende Metrum bereits der i.D. zugeschrieben werden kann.

→ Homerische Sprache; Indogermanen; Indogermanische Sprachen; Metrik

R. Schmitt, Dichtung und Dichtersprache in idg. Zeit, 1967 • Ders., (Hrsg.), I.D., 1968 • C. Watkins, How to Kill a Dragon. Aspects of Indo-European Poetics, 1995. N.O.

Indogermanische Sprachen

A. Allgemeines, Definition B. Vertreter
C. Laut- und Formenbestand
D. Gemeinsame Grundsprache

A. Allgemeines, Definition

Seit Beginn des 19. Jh. v.a. im dt. Sprachraum (vgl. engl. *Indo-European languages* bzw. frz. *langues indo-européennes*) übliche Bezeichnung für eine Gruppe genetisch verwandter Sprachen, die sich in Ant. und MA auf einer gedachten, von SO nach NW verlaufenden Linie von Indien bis nach Nordeuropa (Germanen) erstreckte. Dieses Verbreitungsgebiet lieferte den Namen für diese Sprachfamilie, die alt- und spätbezeugte sowie im Lauf der Zeit ausgestorbene und noch lebende Fortsetzer umfaßt. Die i.S. umfassen demnach nicht nur einen weiten geogr. Raum, sondern besitzen auch eine große zeitliche Erstreckung.

B. Vertreter

Die i.S. gliedern sich im wesentlichen in zehn Sprachzweige (jeweils mit Angabe über Bezeugungsdauer der spracheigenen Quellen): (1) *Indoiranisch*, bestehend aus den → indoarischen Sprachen (Altindoar. seit ca. 1200 v. Chr., beginnend mit dem Vedischen, im Sanskrit fortgesetzt) und den → iranischen Sprachen (Altiran. mit dem Altpers. ab dem 6. Jh. v. Chr. und dem Avestischen seit der 1. H. des 1. Jt. v. Chr.); (2) → *Anatolische Sprachen* (→ Kleinasien, Sprachen) mit den ältesten Zeugnissen einer idg. Sprache, darunter das → Hethitische (ab dem 18. Jh. v. Chr.); (3) → *Griechisch*, beginnend mit dem → Mykenischen (etwa 1400–1200 v. Chr.), kontinuierliche Überl. seit der 2. H. des 8. Jh. v. Chr. mit alphabetischen Zeugnissen; (4) *Italisch* (→ Italien, Sprachen) von ca. 500 v. Chr. an, zerfallend in die osk.-umbr. und latino-falisk. Gruppe (→ Oskisch-Umbrisch, → Latein); (5) → *Germanische Sprachen*, zerfallend in das Ostgerman. mit dem → Gotischen (E. 4. Jh. n. Chr.), das Nordgerman. mit den skandinavischen Sprachen (seit dem 3. Jh. n. Chr.) und das Westgerman., darunter das Ahd., ab 700 n. Chr.; (6) → *Keltische Sprachen* mit zwei Ausprägungen: Insel-Kelt. (Irland, Britannien) seit 400 n. Chr. und Festland-Kelt. (Gallien, Spanien, Norditalien) ab dem 2. Jh. v. Chr.; (7) *Balto-Slavisch*, bestehend aus den → slavischen Sprachen (seit dem 9. Jh. n. Chr. mit drei Gruppierungen: Ost-Slav. z. B. mit Russ.; Süd-Slav. u. a. mit Bulgar. und Serbokroat.; Westslav.) und den → baltischen Sprachen (Litau., Lett., Altpreuß., seit dem 14. Jh. n. Chr.); (8) → *Armenisch* vom 5. Jh. n. Chr. an; (9) → *Tocharisch* (in West-China, Tarim-Becken: 6.–8. Jh. n. Chr.) mit zwei Dial.: A oder Ost-Tochar. und B oder West-Tochar.; (10) → *Albanisch* seit dem 15. Jh. n. Chr. Dazu kommen (11) noch einige Sprachen des ant. Mittelmeerraumes, die nur aus wenigen, z. T. nicht sicher gedeuteten Zeugnissen (Inschr., EN, Glossen, Lw.) bekannt oder erschlossen sind und deren Verhältnis zu (1)–(10) sich nicht exakt bestimmen läßt: z. B. → Makedonisch, → Messapisch, → Phrygisch.

C. Laut- und Formenbestand

Die Zusammengehörigkeit der i.S. zeigt sich in deren Rückführbarkeit auf eine gemeinsame, nicht überlieferte Grundsprache: das Uridg. Aus dem Zusammenspiel der einzelnen Tochtersprachen kann man infolge des Umstandes, daß sich das Lautsystem im allg. lautges. und damit regelmäßig verändert, für das Uridg. folgendes Phoneminventar gewinnen:

I. Sonanten			
1. kurz:	*e*	*a*	*o*
2. lang:	*ē*	*ā*	*ō*
II. Resonanten			
1. Halbvokale			
a) sonantisch:	*i*	*u*	
(selten lang:	*ī*	*ū*)	
b) konsonantisch:	*i̯*	*u̯*	
2. Liquiden			
a) sonantisch:	*l̥*	*r̥*	
b) konsonantisch:	*l*	*r*	
3. Nasale			
a) sonantisch:	*m̥*	*n̥*	
b) konsonantisch:	*m*	*n*	
III. Laryngale	h_1	h_2	h_3
IV. Konsonanten			
1. Labiale	*p*	*b*	b^h
2. Dentale	*t*	*d*	d^h
3. Velare	*k*	*g*	g^h
4. Palatale	*ḱ*	*ǵ*	$ǵ^h$
5. Labiovelare	k^w	g^w	g^{wh}
V. Sibilanten	*s*	*z*	

Als Eigentümlichkeiten des idg. Lautsystems sind festzuhalten: quantitativer und qualitativer → Ablaut bei den Sonanten; sonant. bzw. kons. Realisierung der Resonanten; Bildung von Kurz- oder Langdiphthongen durch Kombination von Sonanten und Halbvokalen; Trias von → Laryngalen; Aufgliederung der Kons.-Reihen nach Artikulationsart in stimmlose (Tenues), stimmhafte (Mediae) und stimmhaft-aspirierte (Mediae aspiratae) Laute. In allen i.S. wird bei den → Gutturalen die erschlossene grundsprachliche Dreiheit (Velar, Palatal, Labiovelar) durch den Zusammenfall von Palatal bzw. Labiovelar mit dem Velar zu einer Zweiheit reduziert. Nach dem lat. bzw. avest. Wort für »100« unterscheidet man → Kentum- (d. h. Labiovelar-)Sprachen und → Satem- (d. h. Palatal-)Sprachen:

Kentumsprachen		Satemsprachen	
lat.	*centum*	avest.	*satəm*
griech.	ἑ-κατόν	altind.	*śatám*
altir.	*cét*	aksl.	*sŭto*
got.	*hund*	litau.	*šim̃tas*
tochar. A	*känt*	lett.	*sìmts*

Dieses Merkmal gestattet eine Einteilung in östl. und westl. i.S., ohne daß diese Klassifizierung allzu viel besagt. Keineswegs aussagekräftiger ist das Kriterium der übereinstimmenden Gewässernamen in Europa, in denen man die Basis der alteuropäischen Sprachen (→ Alteuropäisch) sehen wollte.

Aus dem Lautsystem und den einzelsprachlichen Zeugnissen kann der Formenbestand der i.S. oft bis in Details festgelegt werden. So ermöglichen die einzelsprachlichen Kontinuanten

altind.	*ásti*	:	*sánti*
jungavest.	*asti*	:	*hə̨nti*
altpers.	*astiy*	:	ha_ntiy
hethit.	*ešzi*	:	*ašanzi*
griech.	ἐστί	:	*/ehensi/* (myk.)
osk.-umbr.	*est*	:	*sent*

zusammen mit noch weiteren einzelsprachlichen Vertretern die uridg. Ansätze *h_1*és-ti* »er, sie, es ist« und *h_1*s-énti* »sie sind«. Durch den Sprachvergleich kann zudem eine bestimmte Klasse der Präs.-Stammbildung (athemat. Wz.-Präs.) mit einem bestimmten flexivischen Kennzeichen (→ Ablaut in der Wz.-Silbe) und eine bestimmte Endungsreihe (Primärendungen *-*ti* in der 3. Sg., *-*énti* in der 3. Pl.) ermittelt werden.

D. Gemeinsame Grundsprache

Infolge der von den idg. Tochtersprachen gelieferten breiten Materialbasis kann die erschlossene gemeinsame Grundsprache Uridg. lexikalisch (und damit phonetisch und morphologisch) sowie syntaktisch erschlossen wer-

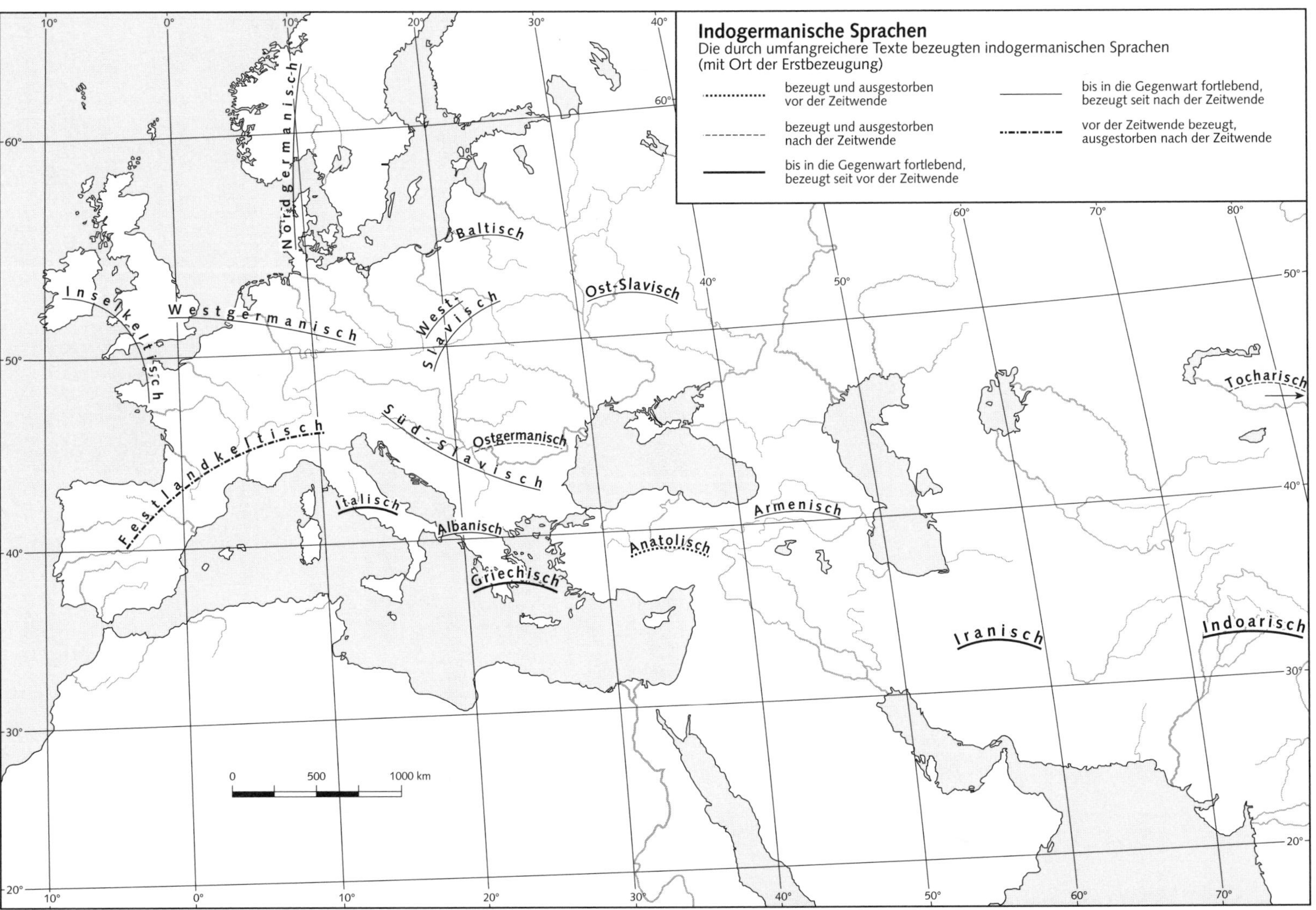

Indogermanische Sprachen
Die durch umfangreichere Texte bezeugten indogermanischen Sprachen (mit Ort der Erstbezeugung)
bezeugt und ausgestorben vor der Zeitwende
bezeugt und ausgestorben nach der Zeitwende
bis in die Gegenwart fortlebend, bezeugt seit vor der Zeitwende
bis in die Gegenwart fortlebend, bezeugt seit nach der Zeitwende
vor der Zeitwende bezeugt, ausgestorben nach der Zeitwende
Nordgermanisch
Baltisch
Ost-Slavisch
Inselkeltisch
Westgermanisch
West-Slavisch
Tocharisch
Süd-Slavisch
Ostgermanisch
Festlandkeltisch
Italisch
Albanisch
Armenisch
Anatolisch
Griechisch
Iranisch
Indoarisch
0 500 1000 km

den. Ferner berechtigen Stilmerkmale (u.a. bei bestimmten Wortverbindungen) zum Ansetzen einer → indogermanischen Dichtersprache. Das Ermitteln grundsprachlicher Fakten und die damit zusammenhängenden sprachhistor. Fragen stellen eine der Aufgaben der Indogermanistik dar. Dank ihrer Forschungen kann man aus dem für die Grundsprache angenommenen Wortschatz Rückschlüsse auf reale Gegebenheiten bei den Sprechern des Uridg. ziehen, so etwa auf Lebensweise und Sozialstruktur (→ Indogermanen).
→ INDOGERMANISTIK

R.S.P. BEEKES, Comparative Indo-European Linguistics, 1995 • BRUGMANN/DELBRÜCK • W. COWGILL, Idg. Gramm. I,1: Einl., 1986 • POKORNY • O. SZEMERÉNYI, Einführung in die Vergleichende Sprachwiss., [4]1990. R.P.

Indogriechen. Die Griechen der hell. Baktria (→ Graeco-Baktrien), die im 2. Jh. v. Chr. SO-Afghanistan (Paropamisadai und Arachosien) und NW-Indien (h. Pakistan) eroberten. Nach den ersten und wichtigsten Königen (→ Demetrios [10] und Menandros) zerfiel das Reich in mehrere Teile, deren zahlreiche Herrscher (fast 40) meist nur durch Mz. belegt sind. Die I. hielten sich bis zum 1. Jh. v. Chr. oder gar 1. Jh. n. Chr.; ihre Territorien wurden dann von den → Parthern und den zentralasiatischen Sakas und Indoskythen erobert. Ihre Wirkung auf Indien und Zentralasien blieb gering, doch stammt die hell. Formsprache der späteren buddhistischen Gandhāra-Kunst letztlich von ihnen.

BOPEARACHCHI • K. NARAIN, The Indo-Greeks, 1957. K.K.

Indos (Ἰνδός).
[1] Der Indus. Wohl aus altind. *Sindhu* (zur Etymologie vgl. → India); der ind. Name ist besser als *Sindus* bei Plin. nat. 6,71, als Σίνθος bei peripl. m. r. 38; 40 und als Σίνδων/Σίνθων bei Ptol. 7,1,2 (hier ein Delta-Arm) belegt. Nach allgemeiner griech. Meinung (mit Ausnahme von → Megasthenes) ist der I. der größte Fluß Indiens, den Griechen seit Ende des 6. Jh. v. Chr. (Skylax bei Hdt. 4,44) bekannt. Der Unterlauf etwa vom Zusammenfluß mit dem Kabul-Fluß abwärts und das Delta wurden von → Skylax und danach von Alexander d.Gr. erforscht. Die wirklichen Quellen in West-Tibet blieben unbekannt; man glaubte, daß der Strom erst kurz vor seinem Durchbruch zur Ebene entspringe. Die große Bedeutung des I. für Natur und Wirtschaft der Stromebene wurde von Alexanderhistorikern und Naturwissenschaftlern richtig erkannt, der Strom mit dem Nil verglichen. Wie dieser war der I. auch wichtig als Verkehrs- und Handelsweg; → Patala und → Barabara im Delta waren wichtige Handelshäfen.

1 K. KARTTUNEN, The Name of India, in: Cracow Indological Stud. 1, 1995, 151–163 **2** O. WECKER, s.v. I. (1), RE 9, 1369–73. K.K.

[2] Lyk. Fluß im Grenzbereich zu Karia, h. Dalaman Çayı, im Oberlauf Koca Çayı bzw. Morzon Çayı. Er entspringt auf den Bergen im Norden der Kibyratis (am Eşler Dağı, 2254 m), von Plin. nat. 5,103 als ausnehmend wasserreich geschildert, da er 60 perennierende Nebenflüsse und über 100 Wildbäche auf seinem Lauf aufnimmt. Am I. lag das Kastell Thabusion (Liv. 38,14,2).

G. WINKLER, R. KÖNIG (Hrsg.), C. Plinius Secundus. Naturalis Historiae Libri XXXVII, Bd. 5, 1993, 220 (Komm.). E.O.

Indoskythen (in chin. Quellen *Yuezhi*); urspr. ein zentralasiatisches Volk, im 2. Jh. v. Chr. nach Westen gewandert. Die I. eroberten → Graeco-Baktrien und zogen später nach Indien, wo sie die mächtige Kuschanen-Dynastie (→ Kuschan) gründeten (→ Kanischka). Ihr indisches Reich wird als Indoskythia bei Ptolemaios u.a. genannt.
→ Skythes

J.E. VAN LOHUIZEN-DE LEEUW, The Scythian Period, 1949. K.K.

Indulgentia. Seit Anfang des 3. Jh. n. Chr. der t.t. für die strafrechtliche Begnadigung durch den röm. Kaiser (z.B. Cod. Iust. 9,23,5 aus dem J. 225). Begnadigungen hat es jedoch schon lange vorher in Rom gegeben. Sie konnten wohl während eines laufenden Strafverfahrens (z.B. Mod. Dig. 48,16,17) ebenso wie nach dessen Beendigung zur Aufhebung der verhängten Sanktion und sogar noch vor Eröffnung jeglicher Verfolgungsmaßnahmen erfolgen. So veranlaßte Iulius Caesar M. Antonius, als Volkstribun ein Plebiszit herbeizuführen, durch das die nach dem Gesetz des Pompeius wegen Wahlfälschung (→ *ambitus*) Verurteilten begnadigt wurden (Caes. civ. 3,1,4; Cic. Phil. 2,98). An dieser Form der Begnadigung, die für die Zeit seit Sulla mehrfach überliefert ist, wird deren Zusammenhang mit der gesetzgebenden Gewalt deutlich. So erscheint die einem einzelnen durch den Kaiser gewährte *i.* noch in den Inst. Iust. (1,2,6) bei dessen gesetzgeberischen Befugnissen. Darin unterscheidet sich die *i.* von der bloßen Einstellung des Verfahrens (vgl. → *abolitio*), die auch vom Richter verfügt werden konnte, trifft sich aber mit der gesetzmäßig bestimmten griech. → *amnēstía*. Vor dem 3. Jh. n. Chr. bezeichnete man die *i.* wohl nach ihrer Rechtsfolge, der → *restitutio*. Sie bedeutet im allg., daß der Begnadigte in vollem Umfang in seine frühere Rechtsstellung eingesetzt wurde, nicht jedoch in sein eingezogenes Vermögen (vgl. Cod. Iust. 9,51,2: Erstattung nur durch bes. → *beneficium*). Bei Massenbegnadigung (*i. communis* oder *generalis*) blieb demgegenüber die Nebenfolge des Ehrverlustes (→ *infamia*) bestehen. Außerhalb streng juristischer Bed. bezeichnet *i.* die generell dem Kaiser zugeschriebene Eigenschaft der Gnade als Inhalt beliebiger begünstigender Maßnahmen.

W. WALDSTEIN, Unt. zum röm. Begnadigungsrecht, 1964 • J. GAUDEMET, I. principis, 1962. G.S.

Indus-Kultur. Vorgesch. Hochkultur im 3. Jt. im NW Südasiens, vom Pandschab bis Baluchistan und Gujarat, mit Harappa und Mohenjo-daro als den wohl wichtigsten Zentren. Reger Überseehandel (ein Hafen wurde bei Lothal in Gujarat ausgegraben) bestand mit Makan (h. Oman), → Dilmun (h. Baḥrain), der Insel Failaka (h. zu Kuwait) und Mesopotamien [1. 107ff.]. Die berühmte Indus-Schrift ist nur in Form sehr kurzer Siegellegenden belegt; die zugrundeliegende Sprache wahrscheinlich – wenn auch ungesichert – eine Form des Proto-Dravidischen [2].

1 J. Reade (Hrsg.), The Indian Ocean in Antiquity, 1996
2 A. Parpola, Deciphering the Indus Script, 1994. K.K.

Industria. *Oppidum* (*regio IX*, Plin. nat. 3,49; ab 124/3 v. Chr.?) nahe dem ligurischen Bodincomagus gelegen (Plin. nat. 3,122), *municipium* (*tribus Pollia*), h. Monteu da Po. Isis- und Serapis-Heiligtum (hadrianische Zeit), Straße, *insula*. CIL V 7468; 7469; Suppl. Italica, XII 1994, 41–61.

Fontes Ligurum et Liguriae antiquae, 1976, s. v. Bodincomagus, Industria • E. Zanda u. a., Studi su Industria, in: Quaderni Soprintendenza Archeologica Piemonte 11, 1993, 29–97 • E. Zanda, Il santuario isiaco di Industria, in: E. A. Arslan (Hrsg.), Iside, 1997, 352–357. L.S.A./Ü: J.W.M.

Indutiae. Im Unterschied zur bloßen Kampfpause (*quies a proeliis*) meint *i.* im Kriegs- und Völkerrecht den vereinbarten Waffenstillstand (*cessatio pugnae pacticia*: Gell. 1,25,8) bzw. das diesem zugrundeliegende Abkommen (*pactio indutiarum*). Die Historizität von über das Amtsjahr des Feldherrn hinaus gültigen *i.*, die gemäß annalistischer Tradition wie Friedensverträge den Krieg für 2 bis 100 Jahre beendeten, ist umstritten [2. 43 f.]. Das entwickelte röm. Völkerrecht kennt nur die »vertraglich vereinbarte, befristete Unterbrechung der Kampfhandlungen« [2. 45] bei fortdauerndem Krieg (Gell. 1,25,4; vgl. Dig. 49,15,19,1). Die Befristung von einem Tag bis zu mehreren Monaten war funktional, um z. B. Gefallene zu bestatten, Verhandlungen und Kapitulationen einzuleiten oder nach Abschluß eines Präliminarfriedens ein *foedus* zu ratifizieren. In der Spätant. dienen *i.* u. a. als kurzfristige Kriegsbeendigungsverträge [3. 73 f.].

1 Martino, SCR 2,63 ff. 2 K.-H. Ziegler, Kriegsverträge im ant. röm. Recht, in: ZRG 102, 1985, 40–90 3 Ders., Völkerrechtsgesch., 1994. P.KE.

Indutiomarus

[1] Kelt. Namenskompositum aus *-marus*, »groß« [1. 96–98]. Führer einer Gesandtschaft der → Allobroges, die M. → Fonteius [I 2] 69 v. Chr. in einem Repetundenverfahren (→ *repetundarum crimen*) anklagte. Cicero verteidigte diesen offenbar erfolgreich (*pro M. Fonteio*) [2. 83–104].

1 Evans 2 B. Kremer, Das Bild der Kelten bis in augusteische Zeit, 1994.

[2] Fürst der → Treveri, Schwiegervater und Gegner des → Cingetorix [1]. 54 v. Chr. war er am Aufstand unter → Ambiorix beteiligt, mußte aber nach einem Vorstoß Caesars die Belagerung des → Labienus im Trevərergebiet zunächst abbrechen. I. fiel 53 bei einem erneuten Angriff, doch behielten seine Anhänger die Kontrolle im Stamm und konnten auch german. Unterstützung anwerben (Caes. Gall 5,53; 55–58; 6,2; Flor. 1,45; Cass. Dio 40,11; Oros. 6,10,10).

H. Heinen, Trier und das Trevererland in röm. Zeit, 1985, 23–25. W.SP.

Inessa (Ἴνησσα). Stadt der Siculi am Südhang des Ätna (→ Aitne [1]) zw. Katane und Kentoripa; nach dem Tode Hierons I. 461 v. Chr. von den aus Katane vertriebenen Siedlern besetzt, in Aitne [2] umbenannt, mit Konsekrierung Hierons als »Gründer« (οἰκιστής, Diod. 11,76,3; Strab. 6,2,3; Steph. Byz. s. v. I.; vgl. Thuk. 3,103,1; 6,94,3). Eher mit Cività bei S. Maria di Licodia als mit Poira zu identifizieren.

G. Manganaro, La caduta dei Diomenidi e il Politikon nomisma in Sicilia nella prima metà del V sec.a.C., in: Annali dell'Istituto Italiano di Numismatica 21/2, 1974/5, 35 Nr. 89 • Ders., Metoikismos, in: ASNP 20, 1990, 394 Nr. 18 • R. J. A. Wilson, Sicily under the Roman Empire, 1990, 410 Nr. 79 • M. Massa, BTCGI 8, 286–293. GI.MA./Ü: H.D.

Infamia (von *infamis*, *in* und *fama*), Ehrlosigkeit; i.e.S. eine Minderung der Rechtsstellung durch Ehrverlust. Ältere Quellen bevorzugen *ignominia*, insbes. für die Folgen der Rüge des → Censor (*nota censoria*, Cic. rep. 4,6,6). *I.* ist direkte Folge mancher Verhaltensweisen und Tätigkeiten (z. B. als Schauspieler, Schuldner im Konkurs, unehrenhaft entlassener Soldaten), von einigen Verurteilungen im öffentlichen Strafverfahren (*iudicium publicum*), im Privatrechtsprozeß von solchen aus sog. *actiones famosae* (→ *actio*), u. a. aus vorsätzlicher Schädigung (*dolus*), treuhänderischer Übertragung (*fiducia*). *I.* bedeutet den Ausschluß von Ämtern, der Geschworenen- und Anklägerfunktion und beschränkt die Befugnis zur Antragstellung und Vertretung im Zivilprozeß. *I.* entwickelt sich seit Constantin d.Gr. zu einer bes. Ehrenstrafe.

M. Kaser, K. Hackl, Die röm. Zivilprozeßordnung, [2]1997, 207 f. • M. Kaser, I. und ignominia in den röm. Rechtsquellen, in: ZRG 73, 1956, 220–278. C.E.

Inferi. Etymologisch mit *infra* (»unten«) verbunden, ist I. ein Sammelbegriff für alle Götter der Unterwelt (→ *manes*); es entspricht den griech. Bezeichnungen *katachthónioi* und *hypochthónioi*. Die *dii i.* werden den oberirdischen Göttern (*dii superi*: CIL IX 5813) oder den Göttern des Himmels (*dii caelestes*) und der Erde (*terrestres*) (z. B. bei der Kriegserklärung durch die → *fetiales*: Liv. 1,32,9) gegenübergestellt. Beim Kult wird ihr unterirdischer Charakter durch die Art und Weise gekennzeichnet, wie ihnen die Opfergabe dargebracht wird: sie

wird auf den Boden (Fest. 27 L.; 440 L.) geworfen (Serv. Aen. 6,244) [1]. Der Kontaktpunkt zwischen Ober- und Unterwelt ist der → *mundus*, eine Grube, die als Altar der *dii i.* (Serv. Aen. 3,134) oder als Tür der Unterwelt (Cato bei Macr. Sat. 1,16,18) verstanden wird. Metonymisch bezeichnen I. auch die Unterwelt, deren ausführlichste Beschreibung in der lat. Lit. das 6. Buch der *Aeneis* Vergils darstellt [2; 3]. Ausgehend von den zwei nt. Stellen 1 Petr 3,19f.; 4,6 entwickelt das frühe Christentum die Anschauung vom Abstieg Christi nach seiner Auferstehung in die Unterwelt als ein Stück der christlichen Glaubensüberzeugung, die auch in Bekenntnissen wie dem Apostolicum (*descendit ad inferos/inferna*) Eingang gefunden hat. Der Abstieg Christi und seine Predigt vor den Verstorbenen werden als Vollendung seiner Erlösungstat verstanden und eröffnen allen Menschen das Heil [4. 182–189].
→ Jenseitsvorstellungen; Unterwelt

1 J. Scheid, Romulus et ses frères, 1990, 587ff.
2 E. Norden, P. Vergilius Maro. Aeneis B. 6, ²1916
3 J. Amat, Songes et visions. L'au-delà d'après la littérature latine tardive, 1985 4 N. Brox, Der erste Petrusbrief, 1979.

G. Binder (Hrsg.), Tod und Jenseits im Alt., 1991 · H.-J. Drexhage, J. Sünskes Thompson (Hrsg.), Bestattung und Jenseits in der griech.-röm. Ant., 1994 · H. Vorgrimler, Gesch. der Hölle, 1994. R. SCH.

Infibulation (κρίκωσις, κρικοῦσθαι, *infibulare*). Anlegen eines Rings (κρίκος) oder einer *fibula*, leichte chirurgische Intervention am männlichen Glied, die von Celsus (7,25,2) und von Oreibasios (50,11) beschrieben wurde. Der Eingriff bestand im Durchstechen der Vorhaut, durch deren Perforationen man bis zum Abschluß der Vernarbung einen Faden hin- und herzog, damit diese weiter wurden und sich nicht mehr wieder schlossen; dann brachte man einen Ring (oder eine *fibula*) an, der (bzw. die) die Entblößung der Eichel verhindern sollte; zumindest in manchen Fällen konnte diese Vorrichtung wieder entfernt werden.

Celsus hält den Eingriff für ›weit häufiger unnütz als notwendig‹ und sieht dahinter gesundheitliche Motive und ein Bemühen um die Erhaltung der Stimme bei präadoleszenten Jungen. Plinius macht aus der Vorrichtung einen Keuschheitsgürtel (vgl. Mart. 11,75), dessen Gebrauch ziemlich weit verbreitet war, da er sich bis zu Tertullian (De corona 24) wiederfindet.

J. Jüthner, s. v. I., RE 9, 2543–2548. A. TO./Ü: T. H.

Infrastruktur I. Allgemeines II. Technik III. Verwaltung IV. Bewertung V. Bronzezeit VI. Griechenland und Hellenismus VII. Rom

I. Allgemeines

Mit dem mod. Begriff I. bezeichnet man Anlagen und Einrichtungen, die flächendeckend die materiellen Voraussetzungen für die gesellschaftlichen Produktions- und Austauschprozesse schaffen. Diese Definition, unter der sich für die Ant. die Anlagen der Verkehrs-I. (Straßen, Brücken, Häfen) subsumieren lassen, betont die ökonomische Funktion von I. Selbstverständlich diente I. immer auch mil. Zwecken. Es ist sinnvoll, daneben auch Anlagen für die Trinkwasserversorgung, die der Verbesserung der Lebensqualität (*utilitas, salubritas, securitas, voluptas*; »Nützlichkeit«, »Hygiene«, »Sicherheit«, »Schönheit«) dienten und bei denen ökonomische Rationalität eine untergeordnete Rolle spielte, zur I. zu zählen. Dem mod. Begriff I. entspricht in der röm. Lit. ziemlich genau die Auffassung, bestimmte Bauten dienten dem öffentlichen Nutzen (*ad usum rei publicae pertinent*, Cic. off. 2,60; vgl. Frontin. aqu. 1: *salubritas* und *securitas*). In der Architekturtheorie des Vitruvius werden die öffentlichen Bauten in drei Gruppen eingeteilt: in Bauten für die Verteidigung (*defensio*), für die Gottesverehrung (*religio*) und für den allgemeinen Nutzen (*opportunitas*; Vitr. 1,3,1; vgl. 5,12,7); dem Bau von Häfen und von Wasserleitungen sind dementsprechend eigene Kapitel gewidmet (Vitr. 5,12; 8,5f.).

Der Bau von I.-Anlagen hing eng mit dem Prozeß der Urbanisierung zusammen, wobei in spätarcha. Zeit mehrfach Tyrannen die Initiative ergriffen. Bei der Gründung von Städten nutzten die hell. Könige die Möglichkeit, dadurch als Wohltäter (→ Euergetes; Euergetismus) aufzutreten. In Rom gehörte der vielleicht nach etr. Vorbild angelegte Entwässerungskanal (*cloaca maxima*) in die Frühzeit der Stadtwerdung. In der röm. Republik waren I.-Bauten Gegenstand aristokratischer Konkurrenz (Frontin. aqu. 5; 7), später Teil der öffentlichen Selbstdarstellung des Princeps (R. Gest. div. Aug. 20; vgl. ferner zahlreiche Meilensteine, Bauinschr. und Mz.) und ein zentrales Feld des Prestigewettbewerbs zwischen den Städten. Die Tatsache, daß trotz wachsenden Bedarfs nach 126 v. Chr. (*aqua Tepula*) zunächst keine neue Wasserleitung mehr nach Rom geführt wurde, und die Sorglosigkeit, mit der die bestehenden Wasserleitungen behandelt wurden, obwohl ihr Nutzen für das Gemeinwesen unbestritten war (Frontin. aqu. 9; 76), spiegelten auch die Handlungsunfähigkeit und das Versagen der polit. Elite in der späten Republik. Umgekehrt galten die Initiativen und Maßnahmen des M. Vipsanius → Agrippa [1] vor allem dem Neubau von Straßen, Häfen und Wasserleitungen. Das Imperium Romanum als ein Reich von Städten war auf eine vernetzende Verkehrs-I. und → Wasserleitungen zur Versorgung der Bevölkerungszentren aus weit entfernten Quellgebieten angewiesen. Wegen der hohen Kosten (vereinzelte Angaben aus der Prinzipatszeit sprechen von 340000 HS/km für eine Straße und von 2 Mill. HS/km für eine Wasserleitung) konnten I.-Bauten schon in der Ant. nur von Gemeinwesen oder Herrschern finanziert werden, oft mit großzügigen privaten Spenden für einzelne Bau- oder Reparaturmaßnahmen (Philostr. soph. 548). Zum Bau und zur Erhaltung von Straßen zog man die Anrainer heran, vor allem in den röm. Provinzen. Nicht unterschätzt werden darf für diese Epoche die ästhetische und repräsentative Dimension von I.; diese war auch Ausdruck von Zivilisation und Naturbeherrschung (Aristeid. 26,182 f.).

II. Technik

Planung und Bau von I.-Anlagen setzten eine hohe technische Kompetenz der Architekten voraus. So wurden Berge von beiden Seiten durchstochen, was beim → Eupalinos-Tunnel auf Samos (6. Jh. v. Chr.; Hdt. 3,60) auf Anhieb glückte, nicht aber im Fall von Saldae (Mauretania Caesariensis) um 150 n. Chr., als der Princeps erst einen im Heer dienenden → *mensor* schicken mußte, um einen Tunnelbau mit *patientia, virtus* und *spes* (»Geduld«, »Tatkraft«, »Hoffnung«) zum Abschluß zu bringen (ILS 5795). Noch heute beeindruckt die Nivellierung röm. Wasserleitungen mit ihrem extrem niedrigen Gefälle (Kaikos-Leitung in Pergamon: 31 cm/km; Nîmes: 34 cm/km) sowie die Planung und Konstruktion solcher Aquaedukte wie des Pont du Gard, doch gab es auch kostspielige Fehlplanungen, die zu Bauruinen bzw. stark erhöhtem Investitionsbedarf führten (Plin. epist. 10,37 f.). Zu den technisch bedeutenden Leistungen gehört auch der Bau von Straßenbrücken, die teilweise in Höhen von über 25 m (Narni: 30 m; Alcántara: 48 m) bei Spannweiten der Bögen von über 20 m (Narni: 32,1 m; Alcántara: 28,5 m) über einen Fluß geführt wurden. Auch die → Hafenanlagen von Puteoli oder Ostia sind mit großem technischen Aufwand errichtet worden.

Bedeutsam war die in der Kaiserzeit bei der Wasserversorgung Roms erreichte systemische Vernetzung und Hierarchisierung der insges. ca. 500 km langen Wasserleitungen (*aquae*), so daß bei Teilausfällen die flächendeckende Versorgung gewährleistet blieb (Frontin. aqu. 87; 92); dem Ausgleich von Dargebot und Nachfrage dienten Reservoire.

III. Verwaltung

I.-Bauten erforderten nicht nur einen hohen Einsatz von technischem und organisatorischem Können sowie erhebliche Ressourcen an Material und Arbeitskraft bei ihrer Errichtung, sondern auch eine leistungsfähige Verwaltung und ständige Aufsicht für ihren dauerhaften Betrieb; dies galt vor allem für Bauten der Wasserversorgung. Seit dem 4. Jh. v. Chr. überwachten daher vielerorts die städt. Aufsichtsbeamten (Agoranomen, Astynomen) die entsprechenden Anlagen, oder es gab spezielle Beauftragte wie den ἐπιμελητὴς τῶν κρηνῶν (»Aufseher der Brunnen«; Aristot. Ath. pol. 43,1) in Athen. Sie hatten im Rom der Prinzipatszeit ihre Entsprechung in den hochrangigen *curatores* (*c. viarum, c. aquarum*; → *cura* [2]). Bereits M. Agrippa sorgte für eine geordnete und überdurchschnittlich professionalisierte Administration im Bereich der stadtröm. Wasserversorgung (Frontin. aqu. 98), für die nach seinem Tod durch mehrere Senatsbeschlüsse eine rechtliche Grundlage geschaffen wurde (Frontin. aqu. 99 ff.; 104; 106; 108). Die damit einsetzende Tendenz zur Zentralisierung und Verrechtlichung wurde durch punktuelle Eingriffe in die lokale Selbstverwaltung zur Korrektur von Fehlplanungen noch verstärkt. Die hohe Priorität von I.-Bauten zeigt sich darin, daß ein Besitzer, der Schwierigkeiten machte (*difficilior possessor*), zum Verkauf seines benötigten Grundstückes gezwungen werden konnte (Frontin. aqu. 128,1). Im Laufe des 2. Jh. n. Chr. wurden größere I.-Projekte aus öffentlichen Mitteln generell genehmigungspflichtig; in der Spätantike ordneten Statthalter Neubauten oder Reparaturen von sich aus an.

IV. Bewertung

Nutzbauten wurden in der ant. Lit. vielfach außerordentlich positiv bewertet (Strab. 5,3,8; Dion. Hal. ant. 3,67,5; Anth. Gr. 7,379; 9,708; Plin. nat. 36,104 ff.; Frontin. aqu. 1; 16; Cassiod. var. 7,6). Die Architekten rühmten sich ihrer Leistungen für die I., so etwa Mandrokles aus Samos (Hdt. 4,88), Lacer, der die Brücke von Alcántara errichtet hatte (ILS 287b) oder Nonius Datus, der den Tunnel für die Wasserleitung für Saldae vermessen hatte (ILS 5795).

V. Bronzezeit

Den engen Zusammenhang zw. I. und der Zentralisierung von Herrschaft zeigen bereits die brz. I.-Bauten, z. B. das Straßennetz auf Kreta oder die befestigten, mit Brücken und seitlichen Einfassungsmauern versehenen Straßen, die z. T. in zwei parallelen Trassen von Mykene ausgingen und wahrscheinlich für Streitwagen gebaut waren. Ein Straßennetz ist bisher für Messenien, Phokis und Boiotien nachgewiesen. In Knossos gab es Wasserleitungen aus Tonrohren. Bedeutsame myk. Wasserbauten waren eine in den Felsen gehauene Wasserleitung nach Theben, ein Hochwasserdamm bei Tiryns und das komplexe Wasserregulierungs- und Drainagesystem am Kopais-See in Boiotien.

VI. Griechenland und Hellenismus

Die überwiegend kleinen Poleis verfügten nicht über die Ressourcen zur Errichtung größerer Systeme von Verkehrs-I.; ein Netz befestigter Wege mit einfachen Brücken ist aber für einige Landschaften in klass. Zeit nachweisbar. Für die Bürgergemeinschaft wichtige Strecken wurden aufwendiger ausgeführt, so die »Heilige Straße« zwischen Athen und Eleusis. Auf dem Isthmos von Korinth diente der spätarcha. Diolkos, eine gepflasterte Straße, dem Transport von Schiffsladungen zwischen der Ägäis und dem Korinth. Golf. Die Städtegründungen Alexanders d.Gr. und der hell. Könige knüpften das Straßennetz aus persischer Zeit enger, v. a. im Seleukidenreich. Vornehmlich dem Handel und der Versorgung der Bevölkerung dienten Hafenanlagen; wo die natürlichen Gegebenheiten nicht ausreichten, schuf man bereits in spätarcha. Zeit durch ins Meer hinausgebaute Molen künstliche Hafenbuchten (Samos, Eretria). In Alexandreia wurden zwei Hafenbecken künstlich ausgehoben (Strab. 17,1,6–10).

In spätarcha. Zeit wurde in einigen größeren Poleis (Samos, Athen, Megara) die bestehende Wasserversorgung mit Quellen, Brunnen, Zisternen oder Sickergalerien durch unterirdische Leitungen ergänzt; aus klass. Zeit sind diese für Aigina, Korinth, Akragas und Syrakus bekannt. Die zeitgenössische Wahrnehmung der wohl unter Hippias (vor 510 v. Chr.) begonnenen, bis zum Verteiler knapp 8 km langen Leitung nach Athen spiegelt sich in zahlreichen Darstellungen von Brunnenhäusern auf att. Vasenbildern. Die meisten Städte erhielten jedoch erst in der Prinzipatszeit eine Versorgung mit Fließwasser, die dann zum Standardinventar einer Polis gehörte (Paus. 10,4,1); daß auch auf die Funktionstüchtigkeit der privaten Speichereinrichtungen geachtet wurde, zeigt die Astynomeninschrift aus Pergamon (OGIS 483).

VII. ROM

Die ersten stadtüberschreitenden I.-Bauten Roms sind in der Tradition mit Ap. → Claudius [I 2] Caecus verbunden (*Aqua Appia, Via Appia*). Die öffentlichen Fernstraßen (*viae publicae*) dienten zunächst primär der mil.-polit. Durchdringung eroberter Gebiete, doch in der Prinzipatszeit überwogen zumind. in Italien die zivilen Bedürfnisse (Handel, Reisen). Der Gütertransport zwischen den Zentralorten und ihrem Umland wurde durch die regionalen Netze der *viae vicinales* erleichtert. Die Principes verbesserten die in der späten Republik vernachlässigte Verkehrs-I. durch Neubauten, Reparaturen und die Verstetigung der Administration wesentlich. Bei Großvorhaben wie dem Ausbau des Hafens von → Ostia unter Claudius verbanden sich technische Neuerungen (Gußmörtel), enorme finanzielle Ressourcen und polit. Wille (Cass. Dio 60,11,1–5). Unter Traianus dominierten Projekte mit dem Akzent auf Nutzen und Funktionalität das imperiale Bauprogramm. Die röm. I.-Bauten waren tatsächlich *magnitudinis imperii Romani praecipuum indicium* (›hervorragendes Kennzeichen für die Größe des Imperium Romanum‹, Frontin. aqu. 119). Da I.-Anlagen durch einschneidende polit. oder kulturelle Umbrüche kaum überflüssig wurden, bedeutete ihr Verfall in der Spätant. einen einschneidenden Verlust an Wohlfahrtseffekten und war gleichzeitig ein Indiz für den Niedergang der Verwaltung. Dies galt besonders für die Wasserversorgung, während die Fernstraßen und die Brücken das Ende des Imperium Romanum im Westen teilweise lange überdauerten (vgl. aber Rut. Nam. 37ff.). Immerhin übten die Ruinen ant. I.-Anlagen noch bis in die Neuzeit eine große Faszination aus, die etwa in den Radierungen von G. PIRANESI sowie in den Gemälden von H. ROBERT und in einer Vielzahl von Texten wie der Beschreibung des Pont du Gard bei ROUSSEAU zum Ausdruck kommt.

→ Straßen- und Brückenbau; Verkehrswesen; INFRASTRUKTUR

1 R. CHEVALLIER, Roman Roads, 1976 **2** D. P. CROUCH, Water Management in Ancient Greek Cities, 1993 **3** W. ECK, Die staatliche Organisation Italiens in der hohen Kaiserzeit, 1979, 25–87 **4** Ders., Die Wasserversorgung im röm. Reich, in: Ders., Die Verwaltung des röm. Reiches in der hohen Kaiserzeit 1, 1995, 179–252 **5** FRONTINUS-GESELLSCHAFT (Hrsg.), Die Wasserversorgung ant. Städte, 1987 **6** Dies. (Hrsg.), Die Wasserversorgung ant. Städte, 1988 **7** Dies. (Hrsg.), Wasserversorgung im ant. Rom, 1982 **8** A. NÜNNERICH-ASMUS, Straßen, Brücken und Bögen als Zeichen röm. Herrschaftsanspruchs, in: W. TRILLMICH (Hrsg.), Hispania Antiqua. Denkmäler der Römerzeit, 1993, 121–157 **9** H. SCHNEIDER, Die Gaben des Prometheus, in: W. KÖNIG (Hrsg.), Propyläen Technikgeschichte 1, 1991, 267–297 **10** Ders., I. und polit. Legitimation im frühen Prinzipat, in: Opus 5, 1986, 23–51 **11** Ders., Einführung in die ant. Technikgeschichte, 1992, 171–193 **12** H. CHR. SCHNEIDER, Altstraßenforschung, 1982 **13** R. TÖLLE-KASTENBEIN, Ant. Wasserkultur, 1990 **14** Dies., Das archa. Wasserleitungsnetz für Athen, 1994 **15** Y. TSEDAKIS u. a., Les routes minoennes, in: BCH 113, 1989, 43–75; 114, 1990, 43–65.

U. WAL.

Infula. (Woll-)Binde mit vielseitiger Verwendung. Neben Girlanden ist die *i.* das am häufigsten verwendete Schmuckutensil im röm. sakralen Bereich: an Opfertieren, sakralen Gebäuden, teilweise auch Altären (Fest. 100 L.); sie ist auch Schmuck des Hochzeitshauses (Lucan. 2,355; Plin. nat. 29,30; Serv. Aen. 4,458). Als Bestandteil der Priestertracht (Kopfbinde [1]) ist die *i.* eine diademartige Binde, von der beiderseits der Enden Quasten (*vittae*) herabhängen, teilweise zweifarbig aus roten und weißen Fäden gedreht, teilweise in einzelne Segmente (sog. Astragalbinde) untergegliedert (Isid. orig. 19,31,6). Vestalinnen tragen sie als ständige Kopfbedeckung (vgl. Vestalinnenbüste, Florenz, UF [2]; sog. Cancelleria-Relief B, Rom, VM [3]). Häufig wird (in erster Linie in der Dichtersprache) für *i.* der Begriff *vitta* synonym verwendet. Der Unterschied zwischen *i.* und *vitta* ist aber differenziert: *i.* ist das Band, *vitta* die Quaste an den Enden.

1 H. FREIER, Caput velare, 1965, 71–75 **2** H. JUCKER, Bildnisbüste einer Vestalin, in: RhM 68, 1961, 93–113 Taf. 28–29 **3** G. M. KOEPPEL, Die histor. Reliefs der röm. Kaiserzeit. II: Stadtröm. Denkmäler unbekannter Zugehörigkeit aus flavischer Zeit, in: BJ 184, 1984, 31 Nr. 8.

H. DRAGENDORFF, Die Amtstracht der Vestalinnen, in: RhM 51, 1896, 281–302 • H. FREIER, Caput velare, 1965 • B. I. SCHOLZ, Untersuchungen zur Tracht der röm. matrona, 1992, 123f. mit Anm. 233 • A. V. SIEBERT, Quellenanalytische Bemerkungen zu Haartracht und Kopfschmuck röm. Priesterinnen, in: Boreas 18, 1995, 77–92.

A. V. S.

Ingaevones. Wohl schon bei Pytheas von Massilia bezeugte (Plin. nat. 37,35 DETLEFSEN mit Konjektur) myth. Stammesgruppe der Germani (Plin. nat. 4,96; 99; Tac. Germ. 2,2; → Herminones), die – obwohl die realste der drei Mannusgruppen – nur noch als fiktiver Oberbegriff für Cimbri, Teutones und Chauci fungierte.

D. TIMPE, Romano-Germanica, 1995, bes. 20–24.

K. DI.

Ingenuus

[1] Statthalter von Pannonien und Moesien, wurde 260 n. Chr. von den moesischen Legionen gegen → Gallienus zum Kaiser ausgerufen, nachdem → Valerianus in persische Gefangenschaft geraten war und die Sarmaten mit einem Einfall drohten (SHA trig. tyr. 9,1; Aur. Vict. Caes. 33,2; Zon. 12,24, p. 143 D). Der Reiterführer des Gallienus, → Aureolus, besiegte ihn bei Mursa in der Nähe von Sirmium; auf der Flucht verlor I. sein Leben (Zon. a.O.; Aur. Vict. Caes. 32,2; Eutr. 9,8,1; Oros. 7,22,10; Chron. min. 1, 521,45 MOMMSEN).

PIR^{2} I 23 • PLRE 1, 457 (I. 1) • B. BLECKMANN, Die Reichskrise des 3. Jh., 1991, 226ff. • J. FITZ, I. et Régalien, 1966 • KIENAST^{2}, 223. T.F.

[2] Urspr. wurden die → *patricii ingenui* genannt (Cincius bei Fest. p. 277), doch spätestens in der Kaiserzeit galt der Grundsatz, daß Freigeborene als *ingenui* bezeichnet wurden: *ingenui sunt qui liberi nati sunt* (Gai. inst. 1,11), wobei im Zweifelsfall die Geburt von einer freien Mutter den Ausschlag gab. Noch im 2. Jh. v. Chr. waren anscheinend Ehen von *i.* und → Freigelassenen (*liberti*) verboten, doch spätestens ab der augusteischen *lex Papia Poppaea* sind sie, außer für Senatoren, erlaubt (so [1. 429ff.], der sich auf den Fall der Fecennia Hispala im Bacchanalienskandal stützt, Liv. 39,19,3–5; anders ein Großteil der mod. Forsch., z.B. [2. 82ff.] unter Berufung auf Dig. 23,2,23). Die privatrechtliche Lit. macht keine weitere Unterscheidung innerhalb der *i.*, denen die *libertini* gegenübergestellt werden (*libertinus* ist ursprünglich der Sohn eines Freigelassenen; als diese später als *ingenui* angesehen wurden, wurden *libertus* und *libertinus* synonym). Im Staatsrecht werden von den »normalen« *i.* jedoch diejenigen abgehoben, die einen freigeborenen Vater und einen freien Großvater besaßen (Suet. Claud. 24,1f.; Plin. nat. 33,32). Freie Geburt war Voraussetzung für die Bekleidung munizipaler Ämter und Priesterschaften. Die »gesteigerte Ingenuität« (MOMMSEN) war jedoch bei der Aufnahme in den Ritterstand und dementsprechend auch in den Senat nachzuweisen. Ausnahmsweise kam es immer wieder zur Aufnahme von Freigelassenensöhnen, denen der Kaiser die Ingenuität verliehen hatte, in den Senat.

1 MOMMSEN, Staatsrecht 3.1 **2** S. TREGGIARI, Roman Freedmen during the Republic, 1969 **3** B. KÜBLER, s.v. I., RE 9, 1544–1552 **4** KASER, RPR 1, 118, 296 **5** G. VITUCCI, s.v. libertus, RUGGIERO 4, 1957, 925f., H.GA.

Inguiomerus. Angesehener, anfangs romfreundlicher cheruskischer Stammesadliger, Bruder des → Segimerus, der später mit seinem Neffen → Arminius den Kampf gegen → Germanicus [2] anführt (Tac. ann. 1,60,1). Schwer verwundet bei dem vergeblichen Versuch, gegen den Rat des Arminius das Lager des Aulus → Caecina [II 8] Severus zu stürmen (Tac. ann. 1,68), flieht I. aus der Schlacht bei → Idistaviso (Tac. ann. 2,17,5) und bleibt erfolglos am Angrivarierwall (Tac. ann. 2,21,2). Da er seinem Neffen Arminius nicht weiter gehorchen will, wechselt er 17 n. Chr. »mit einer Schar von Gefolgsleuten« (*cum manu clientium*) zu dessen Gegner, dem Markomannenkönig → Maroboduus, wodurch nach dem Abfall der Semnonen und Langobarden von Maroboduus das Kräfteverhältnis zwischen den Rivalen zunächst wieder ausgeglichen wird (Tac. ann. 2,45).

A. BECKER, Rom und die Chatten, 1992 • D. TIMPE, Der Triumph des Germanicus, 1968. V.L.

Ingwer. Durch Plin. nat. 12,28 wissen wir, daß die Römer den Wurzelstock des *zingiber* oder *zimpiber* (Zingiber officinalis L.) nicht wie heute aus Asien, sondern aus Arabien und Troglodytien (dem südl. Ägypten) als bitter schmeckendes Gewürz importierten. Palladius würzte damit eingekochte Quitten (agric. 11,20,2). Dioskurides schreibt dem *zingíberi* eine erwärmende und magenfreundliche Wirkung zu (2,160 WELLMANN = 2,189 BERENDES). Es helfe bei grauem Star und in Gegengiften.

R. STADLER, s.v. I., RE 9, 1554. C.HÜ.

Ininthimaios (Ἰνινθίμαιος). Bosporanischer König, ca. 234–239 n. Chr. aus der Dynastie der Tiberii Iulii. Wie sein Wappen ist auch sein Name sarmatisch. Bezeugt auf Mz. und Inschr. (IOSPE 2, 334, 433 u.a.).

V. F. GAIDUKEVIČ, Das Bosporanische Reich, 1971, 458 • A. N. ZOGRAPH, Ancient Coinage, 1977, II, 333. I.v.B.

Initiale (von *initium*, »Anfang, Beginn, Eingang«). Der hervorgehobene Anfangsbuchstabe einer Textsequenz. Die Gesch. der abendländischen I. beginnt in der Spätantike. Der Cod. *Virgilius Augusteus* (5. Jh. n. Chr.; Rom, Bibliotheca Vaticana, Vat. lat. 3256) ist die älteste Hs., die schon ausgebildete I. besitzt [2. 51–56]: von der Schrift gesondert, mit Zirkel und Lineal umrissen und mit geometrischen Ornamenten ausgefüllt (»Füllornamente« [1. 135, 153–161]).

In der 1. H. des 6. Jh. entwickelt sich dann im ravennatischen Umfeld die zoomorphe I.: Schäfte und Bögen des Buchstabens werden durch zoomorphe Motive ersetzt (»Ersatzornamente« [1. 135, 161–180]). Die zoomorphe I. verbreitet sich zunächst auf den britischen Inseln und weiter in merowingischen und westgotischen Skriptorien (7. und 8. Jh.). Das ornamentale Repertoire umfaßt anfangs nur stilisierte Fische und Vögel (»Fisch- und Vogelbuchstaben« [2. 60–63]); später wird die Darstellung der Tiere lebendiger.

Das anthropomorphe Ersatzornament findet sich ab dem späten 8. Jh. Die Figuren-I., bei denen der Buchstabenkörper durch das Zusammenspiel von Tier- oder Menschenfiguren, Pflanzen und anderen Objekten gebildet wird, stellen ganze Szenen narrativen Inhalts dar, die auch in Beziehung zum Text stehen können. Die Lebewesen können sich im fließenden Übergang ineinander verwandeln (nach dem Prinzip der »kaleidoskopischen Metamorphose«) [3. 53]. Figuren- und kaleidoskopische I. entwickeln sich in karolingischer und ottonischer Zeit wegen des programmatischen Rückgriffs auf die klass. Ant. nicht weiter, ihre Gesch. setzt sich erst ab Anfang des 12. Jh. fort. Der Polymorphismus gefährdet die Lesbarkeit des Buchstabens (die Vermischung von Schrift, Schmuck und Bild ist der klass. Norm fremd). Die karolingische und ottonische Buchmalerei hält die Sphären von Ornament und Schrift streng getrennt; die geometrische Form der I. ist klar erkennbar. Flächig dargestellte phytomorphe Füll- und Besatzornamente (unter denen das klass. Akanthusornament vorherrscht) setzen sich als Verzierung durch.

In der Romanik entwickeln sich zwei I.-Typen: 1. Die »bewohnte I.«, die auf den brit. Inseln ausgebildet wird (10.–11. Jh.): Der Körper und der Binnenraum des Buchstabens werden von plastisch gestalteten Ranken gefüllt, in denen figürliche Darstellungen abgebildet sind. Diese I. verbreitet sich im kontinentalen Europa und blüht bes. im Nordwestfrankreich des 11. Jh., vor allem in den zahlreichen normannischen Zentren. 2. Die »historisierte I.«: Der Buchstabenkörper dient als Rahmen für das in der Regel mit dem Text verbundene Bild; die klare Form des Buchstabens wird nicht von Ornamenten beeinträchtigt. Vorstufen dieser I. sind schon im 8. Jh. in einigen figurgefüllten I. der insularen Buchmalerei zu finden, die eigentliche Blüte erlebt sie vom 12. bis 15. Jh.

Die I. ist Teil des komplexen dekorativen Systems differenzierter Ornamenttypologien, das der hierarchischen Unterteilung des Textes entspricht. Dazu gehören auch eher standardisierte I., wie z. B. die Filigran-I. (zuerst im Frankreich des 13. Jh.) und einfache flächige Farben-I. Kennzeichen humanistischer Initialornamentik (15. Jh.) sind die Facetten-I., Buchstaben, deren Körper dreidimensional gestaltet ist, und die I. mit weißen Weinlaubranken auf farbigem Grund.

→ Buchmalerei

1 C. Nordenfalk, Die spätant. Zierbuchstaben, 1970
2 Ders., Studies in the History of Book Illumination, 1992
3 O. Pächt, Buchmalerei des MA, 1984, 45–95.

J. J. G. Alexander, The Decorated Letter, 1978 • S. Maddalo, s. v. Iniziale, Enciclopedia dell'arte medievale 7, 375–386.

G. d. F.

Initiation A. Allgemeines B. Riten für Heranwachsende C. Forschungslage

A. Allgemeines

I. bezeichnet a) in einer auf die griech. und röm. Religion beschränkten Perspektive die rituelle Einweihung in einen Mysterienkult, b) in weiterer, ethnolog. und sozial-anthropolog. Terminologie den Komplex von Riten, mit denen in archa. Ges. Heranwachsende beiden Geschlechts in die Ges. der Erwachsenen aufgenommen werden (dt. früher auch Pubertätsweihe). Für die erste Funktion existiert eine entsprechende ant. Terminologie (griech. μύησις/*mýēsis*, seltener τελετή/*teletḗ*, lat. *initia* N.Pl.), für die zweite nicht. Das schließt nicht aus, daß entsprechende Riten existierten, entsprechend der Annahme der Sozialanthropologie, daß diese fast allen Ges. gemeinsam sind; doch weist der lexikographische Befund darauf, daß die ant. Ges. die ethnolog. I. nur in Transformationen und Adaptationen an die eigenen Sozialstrukturen kannten. Dabei sind diese Riten eine Untergruppe der sehr weiten Kategorie der »Passageriten« (rites de passage) [1]. Zu den Transformationen zählen u. a. die I.-Riten der → Mysterien-Kulte, welche die bes. Existenz der Mysten begründen [2]. In keinem Fall sind sie auf Heranwachsende beschränkt (doch hält sich in Eleusis wohl ein Rest in der Einweihung des sog. παῖς ἀφ' ἑστίας/*paîs aph' hestías*, eines auf Kosten des athen. Staates eingeweihten Knaben).

B. Riten für Heranwachsende

Im Bereich der Riten und Mythen, welche die Heranwachsenden betreffen, ist zwischen den beiden Geschlechtern zu trennen. Für die jungen Männer sind bes. die Kulte → Apollons (des ewig jungen Gottes), daneben des → Hermes und des → Herakles relevant. Als erwiesen kann gelten, daß die Institutionen der archa. kretischen Städte im Bereich der Jungkrieger und der Männerhäuser (*andreō̆nes*) formal und funktionell eng mit den I. zusammengehen (locus classicus: Ephoros FGrH 70 F 149); die dienende Rolle der Knaben in den *andreō̆nes*, insbes. aber die Einführung eines adligen jungen Mannes in die Welt erwachsener Krieger durch eine Periode im Draußen, die durch homoerotisches Zusammenleben mit einem erwachsenen Mann und gemeinsame Jagd gekennzeichnet ist, hat deutliche ethnographische Parallelen. Ähnliches gilt für die spartan. → Agoge, die allerdings im Interesse der Militarisierung des spartan. Staatswesen stark transformiert wurde. Ebenso lassen sich in den Institutionen um die athenische → Ephebeia Formen finden, die phänomenolog. mit der I. zusammenhängen, wobei sich hier das kaum lösbare Problem stellt, wie diese vor der Reform der Ephebie im 4. Jh. ausgesehen haben könnten [3]; jedenfalls spiegelt der aitiologische Mythos der → Apaturia, eines Festes, das durch die gemeinsame attisch-ionische Bezeugung auf die Zeit vor der ionischen Wanderung zurückgeht (Hdt. 1,47), initiatorische Themen [4], [5]. Ein ähnliches Problem stellt die Mythologie des → Theseus dar, der in mancher Hinsicht myth. Vorbild des att. Epheben ist, dessen Mythen jedoch in spätarcha. Zeit stark umgeformt wurden [6].

Im Bereich der Mädcheninitiation wurden die zahlreichen Mythen und Kulte, in denen Tänze der Mädchen in Heiligtümern (bes. von → Artemis und → Hera) außerhalb der Städte eine Rolle spielten, mit den I. verbunden [7]; bes. gut erforscht sind dabei die athenischen Verhältnisse, wo einerseits der Kult der Artemis von Brauron, andererseits die Riten der → Arrhephoren im Kult der Athena Polias auf diesem Hintergrund zu verstehen sind [8]. – Generell kann gelten, daß in den meisten griech. Stadtstaaten die I.-Riten ihre allg. Gültigkeit eingebüßt hatten und auf die adlige Oberschicht in ihrer Allgemeinheit (Kreta) oder in einzelnen Vertretern (Knaben- und Mädchenpriester, Arrhephoren) beschränkt wurden; damit wurden sie zu einem Instrument adliger Repräsentation, was sich auch in der att. Ephebie seit dem Hell. als Einführung der Angehörigen der Oberschicht in die Traditionen der Stadt ausdrückt.

Im Rückgriff auf die Arbeiten zur griech. Religion sind analoge Riten auch in Rom aufgewiesen worden (etwa bei den → Salii oder den Riten am *tigillum sororium*, Liv. 1,26,13). Angesichts der relativ späten Bezeugung (arch. seit der mittleren, lit. seit der späten Republik und der frühen Kaiserzeit) sind diese Riten weit stärker transformiert [9].

Im christl. Ritual leben I. funktionell und formal weiter, wobei in der älteren Forsch. die Verbindung mit den Mysterienriten diskutiert war [10]. Die → Taufe kann durchaus als I.-Ritual verstanden werden, das den einzelnen (im ant. Christentum als Erwachsenen) in eine neue Gemeinschaft aufnimmt und seinen Status im Hier und im Jenseits verändert. Weit stärker ausgeformt wurden dann die I. in den Mönchsorden, in denen etwa auch Vorstellungen von Tod und Wiedergeburt rituell ausgespielt wurden [11]. Noch wenig beachtet ist schließlich, daß auch manche Heiligenleben (z. B. Athanasius, Vita Antonii Eremitae) sich in ihrer narrativen Struktur wie I.-Erzählungen geben.

C. Forschungslage

Die Forsch. zu I.-Riten der Ant. ging aus der »myth and ritual«-Forsch. der sog. Cambridge School hervor; die entscheidenden Anstöße verdankte sie Jane Ellen Harrison, die in ihren ›Prolegomena to the Study of Greek Religion‹ (1903) die Verbindung des Kuretenhymnos von Palaikastro und der in ihm gespiegelten Riten mit Hilfe ethnologischer Befunde herausarbeitete. In ›Couroi et Courètes‹ (1939) weitete der Durkheim-Schüler Henri Jeanmaire dies zu einer Studie der entsprechenden Mythen und Riten in den dorischen Ges. Kretas und Spartas wie auch in anderen griech. Orten (Aitolien, Athen) aus; er verstand die griech. Phänomene als histor. Fortsetzung ethnolog. Riten (und suchte sie in Rückgriff auf die Kulturkreislehre von Leo Frobenius zu begründen). Schließlich vertiefte Angelo Brelich in der (nie vollendeten) Synthese ›Paides e Parthenoi‹ (1968) den Ansatz. Während diese Arbeiten die These einer Transformation der ethnolog. I. in griech.-röm. Riten und Mythen im ganzen schlüssig aufgewiesen haben, leidet eine große Zahl von neueren Arbeiten daran, daß I.-Riten mit den Passageriten (mit denen sie die dreiphasige Grundstruktur teilen) praktisch gleichgesetzt werden; im einzelnen ist es insbes. bei den Mythen allerdings schwer, über die Feststellung dieser Grundstruktur hinauszukommen.

→ Initiation

1 A. van Gennep, Les rites de passage, 1909 **2** W. Burkert, Ant. Mysterien. Funktion und Gehalt, 1990 **3** C. Pélékides, Histoire de l'éphébie attique, 1962 **4** P. Vidal-Naquet, Le chasseur noir et l'origine de l'éphébie athénienne, in: Annales. Economies, Sociétés, Civilisations 23, 1968, 947–964 **5** Ders., Retour au chasseur noir, in: J.-P. Vernant, P. Vidal-Naquet, La Grèce ancienne. Bd. 3: Rites de passage et transgressions, 1992, 215–251 (1989) **6** C. Calame, Thésée et l'imaginaire athénien. Légende et culte en Grèce antique, 1990 **7** Ders., Les choeurs de jeunes filles en Grèce archaïque. 1: Morphologie, fonction religieuse et sociale, 1977 **8** P. Brulé, La fille d'Athènes. La religion des filles à Athènes à l'époque classique, 1987 **9** M. Torelli, Lavinio e Roma. Riti Iniziatici e Matrimonio tra Archeologia e Storia, 1984 **10** D. H. Wiens, Mystery concepts in primitive Christianity and its environment, in: ANRW II 23.2, 1248–1284 **11** V. Saxer, Les rites de l'i. chrétienne du IIe au VIe siècle. Esquisse historique et signification d'après leurs principaux témoins, 1988.

B. Lincoln, Emerging From the Chrysalis. Studies in Rituals of Women's I., 1981 • C. Sourvinou-Inwood, Studies in Girls' Transitions. Aspects of the Arkteia and Age Representation in Attic Iconography, 1988 • K. Dowden, Death and the Maiden. Girl's I. Rites in Greek Mythology, 1989 • A. Moreau (Hrsg.), L'i. Actes du colloque international de Montpellier 11–14 avril 1991, 1992 • F. Graf, Initiationsriten in der ant. Mittelmeerwelt, in: AU 36,2, 1993, 29–40 • J. N. Bremmer, Greek Religion, 1994, 44–48 • S. I. Johnston, Restless Dead, 1999, Kap. 6.

F. G.

Iniuria. Einerseits ein Sammelbegriff für widerrechtliches Verhalten im allg. und für Rechtswidrigkeit und Verschulden bei der → *lex Aquilia*, andererseits die Bezeichnung für ein Delikt, unter das vorsätzliche Körperverletzungen und Ehrenbeleidigungen fielen. Die Zwölftafeln sahen für schwere Fälle der *i.* die reale Vergeltung vor (→ *talio*; Talionsprinzip); diese entfiel bei Einigung über eine Buße (→ *pactum*). In leichteren Fällen gab es nur Geldbußen, die schließlich die *talio* generell ablösten. Die Höhe der Buße variierte mit der Schwere der Tat und dem sozialen Status des Opfers (Gai. inst. 3,225). Manche Formen der *i.* wurden in der Kaiserzeit auch strafrechtlich verfolgt.

→ Culpa; Delictum; Dolus

M. Balzarini, De iniuria extra ordinem statui, 1983 • Mommsen, Strafrecht, 784 – 808 • F. Raber, Grundlagen klass. Injurienansprüche, 1969 • A. Völkl, Die Verfolgung der Körperverletzung im frühen Röm. Recht, 1984 • R. Zimmermann, The Law of Obligations, 1990, 1050–1062.

R. GA.

Inklination. Mod. t.t. der arch. Bauforsch.; bezeichnet wird hiermit die bei einigen dor. Ringhallentempeln der klass. Zeit (z. B. → Parthenon) zu beobachtende geringfügige Einwärtsneigung der → Säule im äußeren Säulenkranz; zusammen mit der → Entasis, der Verstärkung des Durchmessers der Ecksäulen und der → Kurvatur ein Element der → Optical Refinements im griech. Säulenbau.

D. Mertens, Der Tempel von Segesta und die dor. Tempelbaukunst des griech. Westens in klass. Zeit, 1984, 255 s. v. Säulenneigung • W. Müller-Wiener, Griech. Bauwesen der Ant., 1986, 136f. • E. Rankin, Geometry enlivened. Interpreting the Refinements of the Greek Doric Temple, in: Acta classica 29, 1986, 29–41.

C. HÖ.

Inkrustation. Bei Vitruv (7,5) mißverständlich als Stuckverblendung im Sinne des 1. pompejanischen Stils (→ Stuck; → Wandmalerei) beschriebene Wanddekoration mit architekturimitierendem Aufbau; als arch. t.t. bezeichnet I. (von lat. → *crustae* sc. *marmoreae*, griech. πλάκωσις) hingegen ausschließlich die Innenverkleidung von Wänden minderen Materials mit flachgeschnittenen Marmorplatten (wobei das Verhältnis dieser »echten« I. zum 1. pompejanischen Stil, der I. imitiert und deshalb häufig auch I.-Stil gen. wird, weiterhin unklar ist). Die bei Plin. (nat. 36,48) überl. Nachricht, ein gewisser Mamurra habe erstmalig um 60 v. Chr. Wände mit *crustae* verkleidet, ist legendär: Die Technik läßt sich im griech. Kulturraum verschiedentlich seit der Archaik (Delos) nachweisen, wird wohl im 4. Jh. v. Chr. zunehmend häufig (Palast des Maussollos in Halikarnassos, Plin. nat. 36,47; Vitr. 2,8,10) und spätestens im hell. Alexandreia Gemeingut; sie war hier jedoch zunächst ein Surrogat, das Marmormangel kaschierte oder durch hohe Baugeschwindigkeit begründet war [3. 229].

I. sind aus ihrer Frühzeit selten erh.; sie bestanden nicht nur aus flachen Marmorplatten, sondern konnten auch Gesimse, Pilaster und Architrave umfassen und auf diese Weise zu ganzen Scheinarchitekturen zusammengefügt werden. Die einzelnen Elemente wurden mit Mörtel, meist zusätzlich auch mit Haken und Dübeln an der Wand fixiert [1. 286]. In republikanischer Zeit werden I. als ideale Verkleidungselemente der neuentwickelten Zement- und Ziegelbauweise (→ Bautechnik) zu einem wesentlichen Bestandteil der röm. Architektur und dann schnell zu einem Repräsentationsmittel. Sie konnten mit prachtvoll ornamentierten → Intarsien und figürlichen Einlegearbeiten aus buntfarbenem Stein versehen sein und sind dem spätrepublikanischen Phänomen des Marmorluxus zuzuordnen [2. 13 f.; 34]; der o. zit. Mamurra könnte hier insofern Pionier gewesen sein, als er möglicherweise der erste war, der diese Art des Bauluxus in einem Privathaus ausführen ließ.

I. finden sich seit der Zeitenwende an allen repräsentativen öffentlichen Architekturen des Imperium Romanum, etwa an Basiliken, Thermen und Theatern, darüber hinaus zahlreich an Privathäusern der Reichen und an kaiserlichen Palästen. In der spätant. Architektur bilden I. ein ebenso durchgängiges Element (u.a. die Palast-Villa von Stobi) wie im frühchristl. Kirchenbau (Rom: Santa Sabina, 5. Jh. n. Chr.; Ravenna: San Vitale, 6. Jh.; Konstantinopel: → Hagia Sophia, 6. Jh.).

Ein nachant. Wiederaufleben der I.-Technik erfolgte unter den Cosmaten in Rom (12.–14. Jh.) und an verschiedenen Bauten der Proto-Renaissance Norditaliens [4]. Zur ant. I. außerhalb des Genres der Architektur → *crustae*; → Intarsien.

1 O. Deubner, s. v. I., RE Suppl. 7, 285–293 **2** H. Drerup, Zum Ausstattungsluxus in der röm. Architektur, [2]1981 **3** W. Hoepfner, E. L. Schwandner, Haus und Stadt im klass. Griechenland, [2]1994 **4** E. Huston, The Cosmati, 1951.

A. Andreou, Griech. Wanddekorationen, 1988 • W. Drack, Zum Farbenspiel röm. Marmor- und I.-Imitationen, in: Von Farbe und Farben, FS A. Knoepfli, 1980, 31–36 • A. Kleinert, Die I. der Hagia Sophia, 1979 • B. Wesenberg, Certae rationes picturarum, in: MarbWPr 1975/6, 23–43.

C.HÖ.

Inkubation (von lat. *incubare*, griech. ἐγκοιμᾶσθαι, »in einem Tempel schlafen«). Die Bezeichnung für eine in vielen Rel. geübte Methode, um Offenbarungen zu erhalten: der Schlaf an einem hl. Ort, während dem der übermenschliche Inhaber des Ortes im Traum erscheint, Information und Rat gibt (selbst in der komischen Brechung bei Aristoph. Plut. 698–747 tritt Asklepios selber auf). In der griech.-röm. Ant. ebenso wie im byz. Christentum wurde die I. bes. in den → Heilkulten gepflegt, vor allem im Kult des → Asklepios und der → Isis, aber auch etwa des → Amphiaraos in Oropos, der → Hemithea von Kastabos, im daunischen Kult des → Kalchas am Monte Gargano (Strab. 6,3,9) oder des Podaleirios (Lykophr. Alexandra 1050); in byz. Kirchen setzt sich dies bis in die Neuzeit fort [1; 2]. Da der Zugang zu göttl. Wissen in vielen Lebenssituationen erwünscht ist, ist selbst die I. bei Asklepios – wenigstens nach Ausweis der Wunderberichte von → Epidauros – nicht auf Krankenheilung beschränkt [3]. Hingegen ist die I. ein ritueller Weg, durch den jedes Individuum in direkten und nicht durch Priester vermittelten Kontakt mit der Gottheit treten kann (Philostr. Ap. 1,7); deswegen stehen die persönlichen und oft intimen Probleme, insbes. Krankheiten, im Vordergrund. Während die I. durch den Ort (Heiligtum) und die vorbereitenden Riten meist in einen institutionellen Rahmen eingebettet sind, führen die griech.-ägypt. → Zauberpapyri mit den Riten der außerhalb eines institutionellen Zusammenhangs im privaten Schlafraum stattfindenden Traumsendung die Individualisierung noch einen entscheidenden Schritt weiter.

Das Ritual der I. ist komplex; für die meisten Kulte fehlen Einzelheiten, am aufschlußreichsten ist ein Sakralgesetz aus dem Asklepieion von Pergamon (LSAM 14, vgl. [4]); eine burleske Beschreibung der I. im Asklepieion im Peiraieus gibt Aristoph. Plut. 653–747. Der I.-Raum selbst (*enkoimētérion* oder *ádyton*) ist ein besonderer Raum im Heiligtum, der oft nach Geschlechtern getrennt (Amphiaraion, Asklepieia) und zumindest so weit ummauert ist, daß man nicht hineinsehen kann. Hier schläft man auf Zweigbetten (*stibádes*) oder auf dem Fell eines Opfertiers (Amphiaraion, Paus. 1,34,5), nicht auf einem Bett, mit einem Kranz und in einem bes. Gewand ohne Gürtel oder Ringe. Zugang erhält man nach Reinigungsriten (im Peiraieus nach einem Bad im Meer: Aristoph. Plut. 656–658; Voropfer an eine große Zahl von Göttern im Amphiaraion: Paus. 1,34,5), spezifischen Opfern unmittelbar vor dem Betreten des Raums (Kuchen an Asklepios und seinen Kreis in Pergamon, einen Widder an Amphiaraos, Kalchas, Podaleirios), aber auch nach einem Opfer an → Mnemosyne, um das Gedächtnis an den Traum zu bewahren (Pergamon). Das unterstreicht das Außerordentliche der Erfahrung: Einen Kranz trägt man bei Opfer und Symposium, *stibádes* werden in den Riten des Dionysos und der Demeter verwendet. Nach der Nacht bezahlte man die fällige Gebühr an den Tempel (in Oropos warf man Geld in die hl. Quelle, Paus. 1,34,4) und besprach den Traum mit den Priestern des Heiligtums (Aristeid. Hieroi Logoi).

1 F. R. TROMBLEY, Hellenic Rel. and Christianization c. 370–529, 1993, Bd. 1, 165–168; Bd. 2, 5–15 **2** P. MARAVAL, Lieux saints et pèlerinages d'Orient, 1985, 224–229 **3** L. R. LIDONNICI, The Epidaurian Miracle Inscriptions. Text, Translation and Commentary, 1995 **4** C. VELIGIANNI, Lex sacra aus Amphipolis, in: ZPE 100, 1994, 391–405.

L. DEUBNER, De incubatione capita quattuor, 1900 · E. ROOS, De incubatione ritu per ludibrium apud Aristophanem detorto, OpAth 3, 1960, 55–93 · M. F. G. PARMENTIER, Incubatie in de antieke hagiografie, in: A. HILHORST (Hrsg.), De heiligenverering in de eerste eeuwen van het christendom, 1988, 27–40 · F. GRAF, Heiligtum und Ritual. Das Beispiel der griech.-röm. Asklepieia, in: O. REVERDIN, B. GRANGE (Hrsg.), Le sanctuaire grec (Entretiens sur l'antiquité grecque 37), 1992, 159–199 · P. ATHANASSIADI, Dreams, Theurgy and Freelance Divination. The Testimony of Iamblichus, in: JRS 83, 1993, 115–130. F.G.

Inkuse Münzen. Ca. 550–440 v. Chr. in Unteritalien (Sybaris, Kroton, Kaulonia, Metapont, Tarent, Laus, Siris-Pyxos, Poseidonia, Velia, Rhegion, u. a.) geprägte Münzen, bei denen auf dem Rv. das Bild des Av. vertieft erscheint. Es handelt sich dabei um eine bewußte Rückansicht, keine einfache Verdoppelung. Die Bed. ist umstritten. Es werden zum einen rein technische Gründe vermutet; mit den i.M. habe man eine saubere, genau zentrierte Mz. schlagen wollen. Andere nehmen einen weltanschaulichen Zusammenhang zumeist mit der Lehre des Pythagoras an, nach der die ganze Welt in Antithesen aufgebaut ist. Pythagoras kommt als Erfinder der i.M. aber nicht in Frage. Die Schrötlinge der i.M. sind bedingt durch die Prägetechnik groß und dünn. In der Spätphase erscheint inkus ein zweites Münzbild, in den 430er Jahren wird die inkuse Prägung aufgegeben.

L. BREGLIA, La coniazione i., Annali dell' Istituto Italiano di Numismatica 1956, 23–37 · G. GORINI, La monetazione i., 1975 · A. JOHNSTON, in: S. P. NOE, The Coinage of Metapontum, 1984, 36–46 · N. F. PARISE, Struttura e funzione delle monetazioni arcaiche de Magna Grecia, in: Atti del XII. convegno di studi sulla Magna Grecia, 1975, 87–124 · W. SCHWABACHER, Zur Prägetechnik und Deutung der I. M., Actes Congrès International de Numismatique, Rom 1961, 1965, 107–116. DI.K.

Innocentius I. Papst 402–417, geb. in Alba bei Rom, Sohn des Anastasius (Papst 399–402). Wie schon Siricius (384–399) versuchte er, die Bischöfe des Westens an den Apostolischen Stuhl zu binden: der Bischof von Rom sei *caput et apex episcopatus* (epist. 37,1), ihm verdankten alle Bischöfe Italiens, Galliens und Spaniens ihre Einsetzung (epist. 25,2), ihm seien alle wichtigeren Fälle zur Entscheidung vorzulegen (epist. 2,3). Seine Dekretalen wollten in der westl. Reichshälfte eine einheitliche Kirchendisziplin durchsetzen. Bemühungen, Leitungsansprüche auch in Konstantinopel zur Geltung zu bringen (Eintreten für den verbannten Iohannes Chrysostomos), scheiterten. Unterstützt von Augustinus, bezog I. Stellung gegen Donatisten und Pelagianer.

Innocentius, Briefe und Dekrete: PL 20,463–612; 84,639–674 · M.-R. GREEN, Pope Innocent I., 1973 · H. JEDIN (Hrsg.), Hdb. der Kirchengesch. Bd. II/1, 1973, 265–268. RO.F.

Ino s. Leukothea

Inquilinus. Der – nicht notwendigerweise sozial schlecht gestellte – Mieter (*conductor*) einer Wohnung. Im röm. Recht ist der *i.* mit dem Vermieter (*locator*) durch einen Konsensualvertrag (→ *locatio conductio*) verbunden. Auf dessen Grundlage ist er berechtigt, die Wohnung zu gebrauchen. Als t.t. verwenden die röm. Juristen *i.*, um innerhalb des weit umfassenderen Vertragstyps *locatio conductio* (modern-rechtlich auch Pacht, Dienst- und Werkvertrag) eine trennscharfe Bezeichnung gerade für den Wohnungsmieter zu haben.

Der *i.* wird von den röm. Juristen vom *colonus* (→ *colonatus*), dem Pächter eines Landguts, unterschieden, der auch zur Fruchtziehung berechtigt ist. Dem *i.* steht hingegen ein → *interdictum de migrando* gegen die Beschlagnahme von Einrichtungsgegenständen durch den Vermieter zu.

B. FRIER, Landlords and Tenants in Imperial Rome, 1980 · T. MAYER-MALY, Locatio Conductio. Eine Unt. zum klass. röm. Recht, 1956 · W. SCHEIDEL, Grundpacht und Lohnarbeit in der Landwirtschaft des röm. Italien, 1994 · P. PANITSCHEK, Der spätant. Kolonat: Ein Substitut für die »Halbfreiheit« peregriner Rechtssetzungen?, in: ZRG 107, 1990, 137–154. N.F.

Inschriften I. ALTER ORIENT II. GRIECHISCH III. LATEINISCH

I. ALTER ORIENT
A. ALLGEMEIN B. MESOPOTAMIEN, KLEINASIEN, SYRIEN/PALÄSTINA C. ÄGYPTEN

A. ALLGEMEIN
I. im engeren Sinne sind aufgrund ihrer Funktion für die Dauer bestimmte Texte meist monumentalen Charakters, bzw. Texte, die auf einem anderen als den üblichen Schriftträgern – Tontafel, → Papyrus, → Ostrakon usw. – geschrieben sind. Gemeinsamkeiten in Schrift, Form und Inhalt verbinden I. eng mit anderen Texten. Deshalb hat sich trotz spezifischer Forschungsansätze altorientalische Epigraphik – mit Ausnahme der hebr.-aram. Überlieferung aus dem 1. Jt., wo I., Ostraka usw. neben dem AT stehen – nicht als eigenständige Teildisziplin herausgebildet.

B. Mesopotamien, Kleinasien, Syrien/Palästina

I. stammen vor allem aus dem keilschriftlichen Bereich, in geringerem Umfang auch aus den alphabetischen Schriftkulturen. I. werden vom Herrscher, selten von Beamten für ihren Amtsbereich oder von Privatpersonen (z.B. Siegel-, Weih-, Grab-I.) in Auftrag gegeben.

I.-Träger bestehen aus gebranntem Ton, Stein, Metall (meist Bronze) oder Bein; selten sind I. in Malerei oder Ziegelglasur; Holz ist nicht erhalten. Seit dem frühesten 3. Jt. v. Chr. sind I. in Mesopot. häufig mit bildlichen Darstellungen verbunden (Statuen oder Reliefs). I. finden sich auf Weihgaben oder Objekten des täglichen Lebens wie Gewichten, Siegeln, Gefäßen und Waffen. Mesopot. Bau-I. sind oft in gleichlautenden Exemplaren auf identischen oder auch verschiedenen I.-Trägern (Ziegeln, Tonnägeln, Zylindern, Stein- oder Metallplatten, Figurinen) überliefert. Ziegelstempel erlaubten zudem eine Vervielfältigung von I. Bau-I. wurden oft in Depots im Fundament niedergelegt oder zwischen den Ziegeln vermauert. Außer auf Bauteilen aus Stein (Türangelsteinen, Schwellen, Wandorthostaten) sind I. an sichtbaren Bauteilen in der Lehmarchitektur nur ausnahmsweise bekannt.

In I. wird die → Keilschrift in repäsentativen, normierten, auch archaisierenden Zeichen geschrieben und immer in die Oberfläche eingegraben. Oft bei luw. Hieroglyphen (→ Luwisch; → Hieroglyphenschriften, Kleinasien), seltener bei Alphabetschriften (phöniz., aram., altsüdarab.; → Alphabet) sind die Zeichen in Stein erhaben herausgearbeitet. Die → altpersische Keilschrift wird ausschließl. in achäm. I. gebraucht. I. sind üblicherweise in der/den Landessprache(n) (→ Bilinguen, Trilinguen) oder Sprachen mit hohem kulturellen Prestige gehalten.

Eine Gliederung von I. läßt sich aufgrund der Textfunktion erreichen. Dabei sind die einfacheren Formen (1., 2.) auch jeweils in den folgenden impliziert: 1. Identifizierende I.: Der Text nennt den Auftraggeber (Name, Titulatur des Herrschers), Besitzer und/oder den Gegenstand bzw. das auf den Reliefs Dargestellte. 2. Berichtende I.: Genannt werden Taten des Herrschers (Bauten, Kriegsberichte – wichtig v.a. in neuassyr. und achäm., auch in phöniz., hebr. und aram. I.). 3. Weih-I. betreffen Gegenstände oder Bauwerke – in Babylonien die häufigste Form der I. 4. Deklarative I. etablieren rechtliche Verhältnisse; im einzelnen handelt es sich dabei um Stelen mit Rechtsnormen (spätes 3. bis frühes 2. Jt.; → Hammurapi, → Keilschriftrechte), Urkundensteine betr. Land-Transaktionen oder Vergünstigungen (3. Jt., 2. H. 2. Jt. bis 7. Jh.) und → Staatsverträge. 5. Appellative I.: Hier spricht der Auftraggeber im Text selbst zu einem Adressaten, d.h. im Rahmen von anderen I.-Formen zur Gottheit (→ Gebet) oder zum Nachfahren (Segens- und Fluchformeln; → Fluch); Amulette und magische Figurinen richten sich an Dämonen. Bau- und Weih-I. erfüllen den intendierten Zweck, ohne daß sie (vor)gelesen oder gesehen werden müßten; sichtbare Monumental-I. sind nicht unbedingt auch lesbar (→ Bisutun).

→ Entzifferung; Geschichtsschreibung

R. Borger, Hdb. der Keilschriftlit., 1967–1975 · CIS · Corpus Inscriptionum Iranicarum, 1985 ff. · J. Naveh, Early History of the Alphabet, 1982 · Royal Inscriptions of Mesopotamia, 1987 ff. · TUAT. WA. SA.

C. Ägypten

Äg. I. wurden in Schriftträger eingeschnitten, aus ihnen herausgearbeitet, mit Tinte oder Farbe aufgeschrieben oder aus anderen Materialien eingelegt. Belegt sind v.a. Stein, Holz, Metall, Ton, Stuck, Kartonage, Stoff und Fayence. Beschriftet wurden Architekturteile, Ausstattungselemente von Sakral-, Profan- und Grabbauten, Grabbeigaben, Weihgeschenke und Objekte des täglichen Lebens (Tongefäße, Siegel, Amulette).

Typisch sind I. in → Hieroglyphen (seit der Frühzeit), seltener in → Hieratisch (Aufschriften, Graffiti) und seit der 2. H. 1. Jt. v. Chr. in → Demotisch. Hieroglyphen-I. sind vom NR an meist in archaisierender Sprache abgefaßt. I. des 1. Jt. v. Chr. vereinen z. T. verschiedene Sprach(form)en und Schriften [5]. Der Aspekt der Veröffentlichung ist bei äg. I. von geringer Bed., angestrebt wird ewige magische Aktualität der Textinhalte [2]. Hieroglyphen-I. entfalten teilweise die Wirkmacht von Darstellungen. Einzelheiten ihrer Anbringung (Ort, Ausrichtung) sind durch Regeln bestimmt, die sich im Laufe der Zeit ändern [4].

Eine inhaltliche Aufteilung des umfangreichen in I. belegten Schrifttums ist problematisch. Drei nicht klar voneinander zu scheidende Gruppen können bestimmt werden: 1. Beischriften, Aufschriften und Listen (identifizierende und erklärende Angaben zu Darstellungen, Eigentümer-, Herkunfts- und Inhaltsangaben, Opferlisten, Festkalender); 2. histor.-biographische Texte (→ Autobiographien von Privatleuten, königliche Tatenberichte und Erlasse); 3. rel. Texte (Weihformeln, Hymnen, Gebete, Ritualtexte, Totentexte usw.). Durch Herkunft aus Grab- bzw. Tempelkontext und Anspruch auf ewige Dauer sind die meisten I. rel. konnotiert.

→ Bilingue; Entzifferung; Geschichtsschreibung; Trilingue

1 Annual Egyptological Bibliography, 1948 ff.
2 J. Assmann, Sprachbezug und Weltbezug der Hieroglyphenschrift, in: Ders., Stein und Zeit, ^{2}1995, 76–92 (bes. 86–88) 3 A. Farid, Fünf demot. Stelen, 1995
4 H. G. Fischer, L'écriture et l'art de l'Égypte ancienne, 1986 5 J. Horn, s. v. Bilingue, Trilingue, LÄ 7, 1–8
6 J. Kahl et al., Die I. der 3. Dyn., 1995 7 B. Porter, R. L. B. Moss, Topographical Bibliography, ^{2}1960 ff.
8 Textes et langages de l'Égypte pharaonique, Bd. 2 und 3, 1972. HE. FE.

II. GRIECHISCH
A. ALLGEMEIN B. BEDEUTUNG C. TECHNIK
D. SCHRIFT E. INHALT F. DATIERUNG
G. GESCHICHTE DER GRIECH. EPIGRAPHIK

A. ALLGEMEIN

Mit griech. Buchstaben geschriebene I. sind Gegenstand der griech. → EPIGRAPHIK (ἐπιγραφή, *epigraphḗ*: »Aufschrift«); Sondergebiete sind griech. Texte in nichtgriech. → Schrift (→ Linear B, → kyprische Silbenschrift [26]). Ihre räumliche Verbreitung entspricht der der griech. Sprache; Schwerpunkte sind griech. Mutterland und östl. Mittelmeergebiet, die größte Anzahl liefert Athen (ca. 18000). Die ältesten I. stammen aus dem 8. Jh. v. Chr. (Nestorbecher), die untere Zeitgrenze ist unscharf, in den Corpora meist auf die Zeit des Iustinianus (6. Jh. n. Chr.) festgelegt. Spätere I. gehören der byz. Epigraphik. Schriftträger sind vor allem Stein und Metall, selten Holz. Für I. auf Keramik (Vasenbeischriften, → Ostraka) gibt es spezielle Sammlungen. Mit I. auf Mz. beschäftigt sich die → NUMISMATIK, auf Papyri die → PAPYROLOGIE.

B. BEDEUTUNG

I. sind Primärquellen; sie ergänzen, illustrieren, korrigieren die erh. Schriften ant. Autoren. Jede I. ist ein Original. Meist verstümmelt gefunden, sind sie in hohem Maße der Ergänzung und Interpretation bedürftig. Hierzu nötig ist neben Kenntnis der epigraph. Parallelen v. a. Autopsie (persönl. Ansicht) der I. oder des → Abklatsches. Der Zustrom an neuen griech. I. hält unvermindert an: jährlich werden ca. 1000 neu publiziert. Erschöpft dagegen ist der Bestand der bei den ant. Autoren zitierten I. [35; 36].

C. TECHNIK

I. sind in der Regel auf Metall eingeritzt oder punziert, in Stein eingemeißelt und mit Farbe (rot, blau) ausgelegt. Qualität und Menge der I. ist abhängig von den zur Verfügung stehenden Gesteinen (in Attika pentelischer und eleusinischer Marmor). Metallplatten (teils mit Nagellöchern) sind bes. auf der Peloponnes verbreitet. Bleiplättchen werden – zusammengerollt – für Verwünschungen bevorzugt. Silber und Gold sind äußerst selten (in röm. Zeit gibt es vergoldete Bronzebuchstaben, *litterae auratae*).

Die ältesten I. [27] laufen von rechts nach links (linksläufig), längere Texte abwechselnd links- und rechtsläufig in »Schlangen-Schrift« (βουστροφεδόν, *bustrophedón*; → Schriftrichtung); in Attika werden die Buchstaben vertikal und horizontal genau untereinandergesetzt (στοιχεδόν, *stoichedón*, 5.–3. Jh. v. Chr. [28]). Es gibt keinen Zwischenraum zwischen den Worten (*scriptio continua*); Interpunktionen finden sich in frühester Zeit willkürlich, in der Kaiserzeit nach röm. Vorbild gelegentlich; dann auch Abkürzungen.

D. SCHRIFT

Die griech. → Schrift wurde im 10. Jh. v. Chr. (?) aus der phoinikischen entwickelt. Die archa. → Alphabete sind regional verschieden ausgeprägt [28], ihre Chronologie umstritten; ihre Verbreitung entspricht nicht der der Dialekte [8]. Seit dem 4. Jh. v. Chr. sind bei offiziellen I. Berufsschreiber an ihren Eigenheiten erkennbar [29]. Weitere Vereinheitlichung der Schrift parallel zur Bildung der → *Koiné*, Auszierung (verdickte und gespaltene Hasten, sog. *apices*), Vergröberung; in der Kaiserzeit dringen kursive und unziale, später eckige Formen und → Ligaturen ein.

E. INHALT

Inhalt und Zweck der I. sind äußerst mannigfach. Grab-I. (am häufigsten) mit dem Namen der Toten und einem Gruß auf Grabstelen (mit Relief), -säulen und -altären. Eine bes. Form bilden Grabgedichte (Grabepigramm) [14; 15]; Weih-I. an Götter, oft auf dem geweihten Gegenstand und häufig nach einem Sieg bei einem sportl. oder musischen Agon (→ Wettkampf) gestiftet [16]; Ehren-I., vor allem als Unterschriften von Statuen, treten erst seit dem 4. Jh. v. Chr. häufiger, in röm. Zeit massenhaft auf; Bildhauer-I., in denen sich der Künstler selbst nennt [17; 18]; Dekrete (mit unterschiedl. Formularen in den einzelnen Poleis) mit den Beschlüssen der Gesamtgemeinde oder ihrer Abteilungen und Vereine [31]. Dabei überwiegen Ehrendekrete für Bürger anderer Poleis, Könige, röm. Magistrate, denen das Ehrenbürgerrecht (→ *proxenía*) verliehen wird; Freilassungsurkunden von Sklaven (→ Freilassung), oft als (fiktiver) Verkauf an eine Gottheit vollzogen und in deren Tempel dokumentiert (bes. in Delphi und Nordgriechenland); Grenz- und Hypothekensteine (→ *hóroi* [32]); Gesetze und Regelungen betreffend privatrechtl., öffentl. [19] und sakrale Angelegenheiten [20] bis hin zur Kodifizierung geltenden Rechts [33]; rel. Texte, Hymnen (mit Noten) [34]; Briefe von Königen [22] und röm. Kaisern [23]; Bau-I., Abrechnungs-Urkunden, Inventarlisten von sakralem Gerät; Listen und Kataloge von Gegenständen (z. B. auf den Schiffen der athen. Flotte) und Personen (z. B. von eponymen Beamten, Priestern); zwischenstaatliche Urkunden (Asylieurkunden [24], Staatsverträge [25], Akten der Rechtssprechung).

F. DATIERUNG

Meist ist man allein auf die Buchstabenformen angewiesen. Sie erlauben die Datierung auf etwa ein Jh. genau; gegenüber engeren Zeitstellungen ist Skepsis angebracht. Innere Indizien sind ferner Inhalt, Sprache, Formeln, prosopographische Relationen. Nicht selten ist Datierung nach eponymen Beamten möglich (→ eponyme Datierung). Listen der von Polis zu Polis unterschiedl. Eponyme sind bruchstückhaft erhalten oder rekonstruierbar: für die athen. Archonten (480–301 bei Diodoros Siculus genannt, danach durch I., aber im Detail umstritten [37]), für die Archonten von Delos (326–168) und von Delphi [38] sowie die Stephanephoren in Milet (525–259 [39]). Daneben wird seit der Zeit der → Diadochen nach Regierungsjahren der Könige, später nach → Ären [40] datiert: der seleukidischen (ab 312), maked. (ab 148), sullanischen (ab 85), aktischen oder Kaiser-Ära (ab 32 v. Chr.).

G. Geschichte der griechischen Epigraphik

Ant. I.-sammlungen gab es (→ Philochoros, → Krateros, → Polemon von Ilion), sie sind aber nicht erhalten. Griech. I. wurden zuerst wieder von Cyriacus von Ancona (1391–nach 1455) gesammelt. Die Corpora des 16.–18. Jh. waren Kompilationen verstreuter Abschriften von Griechenland- und Orientreisenden; hinzu kamen wenige Stücke in Museen. 1815 gründete A. Böckh (1785–1867) das ›Corpus Inscriptionum Graecarum‹ (CIG) an der Preuß. Akademie der Wissenschaften. In vier Bd. wurden 1828–1859 alle Inschr. geogr. geordnet gesammelt und kommentiert. Mit der Unabhängigkeit Griechenlands (1832) und dem Beginn systemat. Ausgrabungen wuchs das Material drastisch. U. v. Wilamowitz-Moellendorff vereinte 1902 das Prinzip der Autopsie mit dem der Vollständigkeit, beschränkte zugleich die ›Inscriptiones Graecae‹ (IG) auf Griechenland, Italien und die Inseln der Ägäis [1]. Daneben entstand eine Vielzahl von Corpora unterschiedlichster Qualität. Die daraus entstehende Unübersichtlichkeit nimmt weiter zu und setzt sich fort in den epigraph. Datenbanken, die zudem nur bereits publizierte Inschr. zu erfassen suchen (am vollständigsten 1998 die CD ROM #7 des Packard Humanities Institute). Für die Forsch. umso wichtiger wird daher die Behandlung der jährlichen Neupublikationen im ›Bulletin épigraphique‹ (BE) der REG (referierend) und im ›Supplementum epigraphicum Graecum‹ (SEG, seit 1923 lückenhaft, seit 1976 vollständig, mit Texten und Indices). Ohnehin kann der technische Fortschritt die zwar aufwendige, aber notwendige Autopsie nicht ersetzen; dabei wird die museale Sicherung der ständig wachsenden Bestände an I. zum Problem. Umfangreiche Sammlungen befinden sich in Athen (Epigraphisches Museum, EM), London, Paris und Berlin; über das größte epigraphische Archiv verfügen die ›Inscriptiones Graecae‹ an der Akademie in Berlin.

→ Epigraphik; Inschriften

Corpora: **1** IG, 15 Bde. (bisher 45 Faszikel, teils in 2. und 3. Aufl.) **2** TAM, 6 Bde. **3** IK, 52 Bde.
Auswahlsammlungen: **4** Syll.^{3}, 4 Bde, 1915–24 **5** OGIS, 2 Bde. 1903–05 **6** Tod, 2 Bde., 1933–48 **7** ML, 1969. **8** SGDI, 4 Bde., 1884–1915.
Übers.: **9** Histor. griech. I. in Übers. (HGIÜ), 2 Bde., 1995–97.
Lit.: **10** Guide de l'épigraphiste, 1986 (mit Suppl. 1993)
Hdb.: **11** W. Larfeld, Hdb. der griech. Epigraphik, 3 Bde., 1902–07 **12** M. Guarducci, Epigrafia greca, 4 Bde., 1967–78 **13** G. Klaffenbach, Griech. Epigraphik, ^{2}1966.
Sachcorpora: **14** CEG, 2 Bde., 1983–89 **15** GVI, 1955 **16** L. Moretti, Iscrizioni agonistiche greche, 1953 **17** E. Loewy, I. griech. Bildhauer, 1885 **18** J. Marcadé, Recueil des signatures des sculpteurs grecs, 1953–57 **19** R. Koerner, Inschr. Gesetzestexte der frühen griech. Polis, 1993 **20** LSCG, 1969 **21** LSAM, 1955 **22** Welles, 1934 **23** Oliver, 1989 **24** K. Rigsby, Asylia. Territorial Inviolability in the Hellenistic World, 1996 **25** StV, Bd. 2–3, 1962–69 **26** Masson, 1961 **27** LSAG, ^{2}1990 **28** R. P. Austin, The Stoichedon Style in Greek Inscriptions, 1938 **29** St.V. Tracy, Attic Letter-Cutters of 229 to 86 BC, 1990 **30** A. Kirchhoff, Studien zur Gesch. des griech. Alphabets, ^{4}1887 **31** P.J. Rhodes, The Decrees of the Greek States, 1997 **32** M. I. Finley, Studies in Land and Credit in Ancient Athens 500–200 BC, 1951 **33** R. F. Willetts, The Law Code of Gortyn, 1967 **34** M. L. West, Ancient Greek Music, 1992 **35** C. Meyer, Die Urkunden im Geschichtswerk des Thukydides, 1955 **36** Ch. Habicht, Pausanias und seine ›Beschreibung Griechenlands‹, 1985 **37** B. D. Meritt, The Athenian Year, 1961 **38** G. Daux, Chronologie delphique, 1943 **39** IMilet I 3, Nr. 122–123 **40** W. Leschhorn, Antike Ären, 1993. K.H.

III. Lateinisch
A. Allgemein B. Geschichte
C. Überlieferung D. Herstellung
E. Entwicklung der lateinischen Epigraphik

A. Allgemein

Unter I. (lat. *titulus*, selten *inscriptio*) im engeren Sinn versteht man in Stein oder Metall eingetragene, für Dauer bestimmte Mitteilungen. Nicht auf Dauer angelegt waren auf Holz oder auf Wänden aufgemalte Wahlaufrufe oder Bekanntmachungen (z. B. in Pompeii). Im weiteren Sinn gehören zu dieser Quellengattung die häufig als Klein-I. oder *instrumentum domesticum* bezeichneten Produzentenvermerke auf Keramik und Ziegeln (»Stempel«), Glas und Metallgegenständen, ebenso Namensgraffiti auf Keramik, die zusammen mindestens ebenso zahlreich sein dürften wie die Stein-I. [1; 2]. Obige I. sind meist in Großbuchstaben (*Capitalis*, → Kapitale) geschrieben [3]. Bei Petronius (58,7) sagt Hermeros von sich: *lapidarias litteras scio*. Wir kennen auch eine in monumentaler *Capitalis* geschriebene I.-Vorlage auf Papyrus [4. 13]. Die mit dem Pinsel aufgemalten Abfertigungsvermerke auf Amphoren sowie Mitteilungen auf Keramikscherben (Bou N'Djem) und auch die auf Holztäfelchen mit Tinte geschriebenen Dokumente (wie z. B. aus Vindolanda) sind in Kleinbuchstaben (→ Minuskeln) geschrieben.

Im Gegensatz zu den – quellensystematisch nahe verwandten – Papyri sind I. aus dem ganzen röm. Reich erhalten, wobei im Osten die wenigen lat. I. durch gleichzeitige griech. ergänzt werden.

Die I. erweitern unser Quellenmaterial für Gebiete, die in der lit. Überlieferung nur spärlich behandelt werden: Sozial- und Wirtschaftsgesch., Religionen sowie die Organisation des Reiches außerhalb der Hauptstadt. Gelegentlich bieten sie auch parallel zu den Berichten der Historiker die Primärquellen: das → *Senatus consultum de Bacchanalibus*, das → *Monumentum Ancyranum*, das → *Senatus consultum de Pisone patre* und die Tafel von Lyon (*Tabula Lugudunensis*), das Höchstpreisedikt Diocletians (→ *Edictum* [3] *Diocletiani*).

B. Geschichte

Am Ende des 8. Jh. v. Chr. übernahmen die Etrusker von den Griechen in Cumae mit leichten Veränderungen deren Schrift. Von dort drang sie ab der Mitte des 7. Jh. in weitere Gebiete Italiens vor, zu den Venetern um Este, den Umbrern und an die mittlere Adria (die I. des Kriegers von Capestrano aus dem 7. Jh.). Im 6. Jh. übernahmen auch die Römer die Schrift, allerdings mit Rückanleihen bei den Griechen (B, D und X sind im etr. Alphabet nicht vorhanden). Z wurde 312 von Ap. Claudius [I 2] getilgt; an dessen Stelle im Alphabet trat Mitte des 3. Jh. die Media G (C mit Strich). Y und Z wurden im 1. Jh. zur Schreibung griech. Namen (wieder) eingeführt. Der Versuch des Kaisers Claudius, drei neue Buchstaben einzuführen, blieb erfolglos, wenn auch nach Ansicht z. B. des Quintilian der röm. Buchstabenvorrat der Aussprache seiner Zeit nicht mehr angepaßt war, und so ist das Alphabet der Zeit Ciceros auch das unsrige geblieben (Prisc. 2,15 GL).

Die ältesten erhaltenen lat. I. finden sich auf der in ihrer Echtheit umstrittenen (Zweifel bei [5]; anders [6]) *fibula Praenestina* (CIL I²,3 = ILLRP 1) aus dem 7. Jh. v. Chr. und dem → *lapis niger* vom Forum Romanum, einer Kultsatzung vom Ende des 6. Jh. v. Chr. Auf Bronzeplatten waren der erste Karthagervertrag (507?) und das Zwölftafelgesetz (451/50, → *tabulae duodecim*), auf einer Bronzesäule das → *foedus Cassianum* von 486 veröffentlicht. Erst um die Mitte des 4. Jh. nimmt langsam die Zahl der → Weihinschriften, noch später die der → Grabinschriften zu. Aus fünf Jh. der Republik stammen etwa 3000 I., aus der Kaiserzeit 300 000. Ab der Mitte des 3. Jh. n. Chr. folgt ein rapider Rückgang mit nur geringer Belebung im 4. Jh.

C. Überlieferung

Erhalten sind von den ehemals vielen Millionen auf dauernden Bestand angelegten I. hauptsächlich solche auf Stein, am wenigsten die auf bes. wertvollem Material (Gold, Silber). Von den über 300 000 bislang bekannten röm. Stein-I. (mit einem jährlichen Zuwachs von ca. 1000) stellen die Grab-I. die weitaus größte Gruppe dar. Vom Rest dürften die Weihungen an Götter und an die Kaiser den Hauptanteil stellen, dann Bau-, Stifter-I. usw. Die trad. Ordnung der I., wie sie vom CIL über die ILS bis in viele moderne Corpora übernommen wurde, beginnt mit den republikanischen I., führt dann über Götterweihungen, Kaiser-I., solche, die Senatoren, Ritter und das Militär betreffen, *tituli municipales* und Grab-I. schließlich zu den überall reichlich vertretenen Fragmenten. I. ephemerer Bedeutung wie die meist auf geweißten Holztafeln (den *tabulae dealbatae*) publizierten Sitzungsprotokolle, Mitgliederlisten usw. fehlen fast völlig, ebenso – außerhalb Pompeiis – die Wahlaufrufe [7]. Die lokale Verbreitung ist sehr unterschiedlich: Rom selbst lieferte bislang ein knappes Drittel der bekannten lat. I., das lat. Nordafrika etwa 50 000, der gallisch-german. Raum um 25 000. Von Einzelstädten dürfte Pompeii mit rund 10 000 I. (davon nur 800 auf Stein) am besten bekannt sein; für mittlere Städte wie Köln oder Italica (bei Sevilla) sind 500 bis 1000 Stein-I. schon eine gute Quellenbasis. Die Zahl der überlieferten I., ob sie erhalten blieben, verbaut, verkauft oder zu Kalk gebrannt wurden, hängt entscheidend von der späteren Gesch. der Stadt ab und ist deshalb kaum generalisierbar.

D. Herstellung

Über die Arbeit der Werkstätten (*officinae lapidariae*) ist wenig bekannt. Sie erhielten die Vorlagen wohl meist in Kursive geschrieben, was eine Quelle für Übertragungsfehler sein konnte. Manche Steinmetze (*lapicidae*) konnten selbst nicht lesen, andere dürften für des Schreibens unkundige Auftraggeber deren Texte (nach Musterbüchern?) verfaßt haben. Die Anordnung der I. auf dem Stein (*ordinatio*) umfaßte die Einteilung des Schriftfelds, die Ausmessung und Vorzeichnung von Zeilen und Buchstaben und die Planung der Abkürzungen, die Kosten sparten und sprachliche Unsicherheiten verbergen konnten (Gell. 10,1). Als Schrift wählte man meist die *Capitalis* (*quadrata* oder *rustica*, daneben die schlankere *actuaria*); nur gelegentlich, bei Klein-I. oder Graffiti, wird auch die → Kursive verwandt. Die Buchstaben wurden mit Mennigerot bei Stein-I. oder mit Bleiweiß bei solchen aus Brz. gefüllt, um sie besser sichtbar zu machen; bei sehr aufwendigen I., z. B. der Dedikation des Colosseums, fanden sich auch versenkte oder aufgesetzte, häufig vergoldete Bronzebuchstaben (*inscriptiones caelatae*) [8].

Auch die Christen setzten I., doch – aus begreiflichen Gründen – zunächst nur Grab-I., die sich – außer in Symbolen und manchen Formeln – wenig von den paganen unterscheiden. Ab Constantinus I. begegnen auch Bau-I. für Basiliken, als erste 324 eine für eine Kirche in Castellum Tingitanum [9] und *elogia* (→ *elogium* [1]) für Päpste und Märtyrer, bes. qualitätvoll von Papst Damasus (→ Epigrammata Damasiana) verfaßt und von → Filocalus verfertigt (ILCV 963 und [10]).

Die Datierung der I. ist nur in wenigen Fällen durch Eponymenangabe, d. h. Nennung von Consuln, einer *tribunicia potestas* des Kaisers o.ä. direkt möglich. Indirekte Kriterien sind, in absteigender Reihenfolge der Präzision, Nennung von histor. bekannten Geschehnissen oder Sachverhalten (Kriege, Kaiser, Einzelheiten von der Gesch. von Personen oder Truppeneinheiten), Stil und Formular (z. B. die Superlative späterer Zeit), Buchstabenformen, Steinart sowie Verzierung und Abbildungen auf dem Träger der I. Nicht zuletzt aus diesem Grund sollte die Publikation der I. nie, wie früher weitgehend üblich, ohne eine genaue Beschreibung des gesamten Monuments erfolgen.

E. Entwicklung der lateinischen Epigraphik

Erste Sammlungen lat. I. (vor allem aus Rom) scheint es in der Spätant. gegeben zu haben, aus denen die sog. ›Einsiedler-Sylloge‹ aus der Zeit um 800 n. Chr. einen Teil ihres Materials bezog. Nach Jh., in denen die röm. Monumentalschrift nicht einmal mehr gelesen werden konnte, folgen ab dem ausgehenden 14. Jh. immer umfangreichere und präzisere Slgg., unter denen die des Cyriacus von Ancona, später die des Ligorius, des Alciatus und des Pighius weitreichende Wirkung hatten. Die wiss. → Epigraphik setzte nach Vorläufern im 18. Jh. wie Scipione Maffei und Bartolomeo Borghesi ab 1845 mit dem ›Corpus Inscriptionum Latinarum‹

(CIL) der Preuß. Akademie der Wiss. ein, in dem Theodor MOMMSEN mit einer Reihe von Mitarbeitern nach den Prinzipien von Vollständigkeit und Autopsie (persönl. Sichtung) nahezu alle damals bekannten lat. I. publizierte. Die Publikation erfolgte in Latein und umging so das schon damals virulente Problem der »Nationalcorpora in nationaler Sprache«, die dann in der zweiten Hälfte des 20. Jh. das Feld für sich zu beanspruchen schienen und zu wachsender Unübersichtlichkeit führten. Die jetzt in Arbeit befindliche Neuauflage des CIL kehrte deshalb wieder zu Latein als Publikationssprache zurück.

Andererseits entstehen im Moment, kaum koordiniert und nur beschränkt kompatibel, vielerorts epigraph. Datenbanken; es ist eine der wichtigsten forschungspolit. Aufgaben der Zukunft, diese Bemühungen zu koordinieren und in ein auf allseitigem Geben und Nehmen beruhendes I.-Corpus im Internet einmünden zu lassen. Dessen Sprache wird dann wahrscheinlich nicht mehr das Lateinische sein.
→ EPIGRAPHIK; INSCHRIFTEN

1 M. ORMOS (Hrsg.), Instrumenta Latina Inscripta, Specimina Nova VII.1, 1992 **2** W.V. HARRIS (Hrsg.), The Inscribed Economy, Journal of Roman Archeology, Suppl. 6, 1993 **3** G. SUSINI, The Roman Stonecutter, 1973 **4** L. KEPPIE, Understanding Roman inscriptions, 1991 **5** M. GUARDUCCI, La cosidetta Fibula Praenestina: elementi nuovi, in: Memorie della Classe di Scienze morali e storiche dell' Accademia dei Lincei, VIII 28, 1984, 127ff. **6** A. E. GORDON, The Inscribed Fibula Praenestina: Problems of Authenticity, 1975 **7** W. ECK, I. auf Holz, in: Imperium Romanum (FS K. Christ), 1998, 203–217 **8** G. ALFÖLDY, Eine Bauinschrift aus dem Kolosseum, in: ZPE 109, 1995, 195–226 **9** L. LESCHI, Atti del IV Congr. Internazionale di Archeologia Cristiana I, 149ff. **10** C. M. KAUFMANN, Hdb. der altchristl. Epigraphik, 1917, 327f.

CORPORA UND AUSWAHLSAMMLUNGEN: Corpus Inscriptionum Latinarum (CIL; in inzw. über 60 Foliobänden, teilweise in 2. Aufl.; zum Aufbau E. MEYER (s.u.), 131ff.) • H. DESSAU (ed.), Inscriptiones Latinae Selectae (ILS; nach Sachgruppen zusammengestellte Auswahl) • L'Année Épigraphique (AE; jährliche Neupublikationen).
BIBLIOGR.: J. BÉRARD u.a., Guide de l'épigraphiste. Bibliographie choisie des épigraphies antiques et médiévales, ²1989.
HANDBÜCHER UND LIT.: R. CAGNAT, Cours d'épigraphie latine, ⁴1910 • I. CALABI LIMENTANI, Epigrafia latina, ⁴1991 • A. E. GORDON, Illustrated Introduction to Latin Epigraphy, 1983 • E. MEYER, Einführung in die lat. Epigraphik, ³1991.
H.GA.

Inschriften-Maler. Hauptmeister der frühen → chalkid. Vasenmalerei, um 560–540 v. Chr. tätig, der v.a. Amphoren, Hydrien und Kratere bemalte. Der I.-M. ist nach den Namensbeischriften auf seinen Mythenbildern benannt. Bevorzugt werden die Sagen um Troia [1. 118–140], hinzu kommen Bellerophon [1. 114–117], Perseus [1. 113] oder der Kampf des Zeus gegen Typhon [1. 84–85]; zweimal findet sich der Kampf des Herakles gegen Geryoneus [1. 90–96]. Außer Mythen (etwa die Hälfte aller chalkid. Mythenbilder stammt von der Hand des I.-M.), Satyrn und Mänaden begegnen häufig Reiter- und Tierfriese, oft heraldisch um ein pflanzl. Ornament geordnet. Der Stil des I.-M. ist von kraftvoller Geschmeidigkeit, seine Bilder sind großflächig angelegt. Hauptfundorte der etwa 50 dem I.-M. zugewiesenen Vasen sind Vulci und Reggio di Calabria.

1 J. KECK, Studien zur Rezeption fremder Einflüsse in der chalkid. Keramik, 1988.

M. IOZZO, La ceramica »calcidese«, 1994, 15–31 • E. SIMON, Die griech. Vasen, ²1981, Taf. 18f., 39f.
M.ST.

Inschriftenstil. Als I. wird die Schriftart der ältesten griech. lit. → Papyri und Papyrus-Dokumente bezeichnet (ca. 4.–3. Jh. v. Chr.), eine → Majuskel, die den Stil der zeitgenössischen Inschr. nachahmt. Zeugnisse sind der Papyrus der *Perser* des → Timotheos aus Milet [3], der Papyrus von Derveni [1], die sog. Klage der Artemisia [4] und einige wenige andere Papyri von Sakkara und Hibeh [2]. Der Inschr.-Charakter zeigt sich im bilinearen, starren, einförmigen und schweren Schriftzug: in den Formen des E (in vier Strichen), des Z (zwei horizontale Striche verbunden durch einen vertikalen), des Θ (ein Kreis mit einem Punkt in der Mitte), des M (in vier getrennten Linien), des eckigen Σ, des Ξ (in drei parallelen Strichen) und des Ω, in der für die Inschr. typischen archa. Form. Im Laufe des 3. Jh. v. Chr. entwickelt sich das Inschriftenmodell infolge der größeren Verbreitung der Schrift zu weicheren Formen, und eine schnellere → Kursive beginnt sich von der Buchschrift zu unterscheiden.

1 S. G. KAPSOMENOS, Ὁ ὀρφικὸς πάπυρος τῆς Θεσσαλονίκης, in: AD 19, 1964, 17–25. **2** E. G. TURNER, Ptolemaic Bookhands and Lille Stesichorus, in: Scrittura e Civiltà 4, 1980, 26–27. **3** U. VON WILAMOWITZ-MOELLENDORFF (Hrsg.), Timotheos, die Perser, aus einem Papyrus von Abusir, 1903 (Faksimile: Der Timotheos-Papyrus gefunden bei Abusir am 1. Februar 1902, 1903) **4** U. WILCKEN, Urkunden der Ptolemäerzeit, I, 1927, 97–104.

E. CRISCI, Scrivere greco fuori d'Egitto (Papyrologica Florentina XXVII), 1996, 9–15. • E.G TURNER, Ptolemaic Bookhands and Lille Stesichorus, in: Scrittura e Civiltà 4, 1980, 19–40.
G.M./Ü: P.P.

Inscriptio. Der t. t. für die Quellenangaben am Anf. der Frg. der Digesten (→ *Digesta*) und der Konstitutionen des *Cod. Iustinianus* (→ Codex II C). Bei den *Digesta* wird der Autor aus klass. Zeit (z. B. Ulpian), sein Werk (z. B. *ad edictum* = Ediktskomm.) und das »Buch« daraus (z. B. *libro quinto* für 5. B.) angegeben, beim Cod. Iustinianus – wie schon im Cod. Theodosianus – der Kaiser, der die Konstitution erlassen hat, und der Adressat. Die *i.* der *Digesta* waren die wichtigste Hilfe zur Rekonstruktion der klass. Juristenschriften aus dem 1. Jh.

v. Chr. bis zur Mitte des 3. Jh. n. Chr. (bis heute mustergültig [1]).
→ Constitutiones

1 O. Lenel, Palingenesia iuris civilis, 1889, Ndr. 1960.

G.S.

Insekten. Diese Tierklasse wurde von Aristoteles (hist. an. 1,1,487a 32–34; 4,1,523b 13–15) erstmals nach ihren Kerben (ἐντομαί/*entomaí*) auf der Bauch- oder Bauch- und Rückenseite ἔντομα/*éntoma* (sc. ζῷα) gen., woher die mod. Bezeichnungen »Entomologie« und »Kerbtiere« abgeleitet sind. Die wichtigsten von Aristoteles zusätzlich angeführten Merkmale sind: I. atmen keine Luft ein (hist. an. 1,1,487a 30–32; 4,9,535b 5; das von den höheren Tieren abweichende Atemsystem mit Tracheen war ihm offensichtlich unbekannt), sind blutlos (ἄναιμα, hist. an. 1,6,490b 14) und oft vielfüßig (πολύποδες, ebd. 490b 15). Die h. als systematisch wichtig angesehenen drei Beinpaare (daher der mod. Name Hexapoda für diese Klasse) erwähnt Aristot. lediglich part. an. 4,6,683b 2f. für die Spring-I. (→ Heuschrecken und → Flöhe). Varro (rust. 3,16,5) vermutet jedoch eine Beziehung zwischen den sechseckigen Waben im Bienenstock und ihren sechs Beinen. Die Flügel (vgl. Aristot. hist. an. 4,7,532a 19–26) können dauernd vorhanden sein (z. B. → Biene, μέλιττα; [Mist?]→ käfer, μηλολόνθη; → Wespe, σφήξ) oder nur zeitweilig (bei → Ameisen, μύρμηκες, und Leuchtkäfern [= → Glühwürmchen?], πυγολαμπίδες, ebd. 4,1,523b 20f.). Ihr Körper, der nach heutiger Kenntnis von einer aus Chitin bestehenden festen Haut umhüllt ist, besitzt keine Knochen, sondern stützt sich selbst (ebd. 523b 15–17; 4,7, 532b 1–3). Irrtümer, wie z. B. die Zuordnung des stets ungeflügelten Tausendfüßers (σκολόπενδρα, ebd. 523b 18) zu den I. (statt zu der eigenen Klasse der Myriopoda), sind angesichts der systematischen Schwierigkeiten verständlich. Die teils sexuelle, teils parthenogenetische Fortpflanzung mit mehreren Entwicklungsstadien läßt Aristot. bei den Bienen und Wespen sowie den → Fliegen oder → Bremsen mit der Made (σκώληξ, hist. an. 5,1,539b 11; 5,19,552a 21 = *vermiculus* bei Plin. nat. 10,190), bei anderen mit der Raupe (κάμπη) beginnen (Hauptstelle: Aristot. gen. an. 3,9,758a 29– b 759a 7, die sich nach dem unbeweglichen Puppenstadium (χρυσαλλίς) zum fertigen I. (ζῷον ἐπιτελεσθέν, z. B. gen. an. 3,9,758b 26f.) umgestaltet (Metamorphose).

Den »Hochzeitsflug« der Bienenkönigin (bei Aristot. βασιλεύς, »König«; er hält das Tier also für mask.) mit den (danach absterbenden) Drohnen (κηφῆναι) hat Aristoteles nie beobachtet, weshalb er nach längerer zweifelnder Überlegung (ἀπορία, gen. an. 3,10,759a 8–b 31) die Drohnen von den mit männlichen (Stachel!) und weiblichen Eigenschaften ausgestatteten Arbeitsbienen parthenogenetisch erzeugen läßt. Auch sonst vermutete er vielfach ungeschlechtliche Entstehung aus anderer Materie, z. B. hist. an. 5,19,552a 15 aus der Quecke (ἀγρώστις) bei den »Schafläusen« (κρότωνες).

Plinius (nat. 11,1 ff.) übernimmt von Aristoteles (hist. an. 4,1, s.o.) nicht nur die Bezeichnung *insecta*, sondern auch viele Einzelheiten. Dem angeblichen Nichtatmen und Fehlen einer Stimme widerspricht er hingegen ausdrücklich (nat. 11,5–7). Vieles verstand jedoch auch Plinius nicht. Wenn etwa Vergil (georg. 4,284f.) Bienen aus verdorbenem Rinderblut entstehen läßt, so bezieht sich Plinius (nat. 11,70) darauf und erweitert diese auf ungenügender Beobachtung beruhende sonderbare Entstehung auf die Wespen (*vespae*) aus dem Fleisch von Pferden (Servius georg. 4,286: von Eseln) sowie auf die Hornissen (*crabrones*) und Drohnen aus dem von Maultieren (*muli*; vgl. auch Nik. Ther. 740f.; Archelaos bei Varro rust. 3,16,4; vgl. ebd. 2,5,5; Ov. fast. 1,377f.; met. 15,364–366; Ail. nat. 1,28 und 2,57) sowie z. T. aus dem Fleisch anderer Tiere (Isid. orig. 11,4,3 und 12,8,2). Die ungeschlechtliche Herkunft galt im MA als wesensbestimmend für die in *vermes* (»Würmer«; spätestens seit Isid. orig. 12,5,1–19) umbenannten und meistens als lästige Parasiten bekämpften I.
→ Grille; Laus; Mücke; Schabe; Schmetterling; Wanze; Zikade

1 Keller 2,395–460.

C.HÜ.

Insel der Seligen s. Makaron Nesoi

Insteius. Name einer röm. *gens*, häufiger bezeugt erst seit der späten Republik, gleichwohl in der Frühzeit Roms verwurzelt, worauf die Bezeichnung eines Straßenzugs deutet: *vicus Instei(an)us* auf der Südkuppe des Quirinal, dem *collis Latiaris* (Varro ling. 5,52; Liv. 24,10,8).

I. Republik

[I 1] I., L. Diente 89 v. Chr. im → Bundesgenossenkrieg [3] unter Cn. Pompeius Strabo vor Asculum (ILLRP 515); wohl identisch mit dem Legaten, der 76 auf → Sertorius' Seite in Spanien kämpfte (Liv. 91, fr. 22: hier auch ein C. I. als *praefectus equitum*, Bruder des L. I.?). MRR 3,104.

[I 2] I., M. Volkstribun 42 v. Chr. (MRR 2,359). Während des → Mutinensischen Kriegs (43) im Lager des M. Antonius [I 9], von Cicero (Phil. 13,26) verhöhnt. Bei Actium (31) operierte I. im Zentrum von Antonius' Flotte (Plut. Antonius 65,1; MRR 3,104: als *praefectus classis*?).

[I 3] I. Cato. Ein Führer der Italiker im → Bundesgenossenkrieg [3] (ab 90 v. Chr.); nur bei Velleius (2,16,1) bezeugt und wohl irrtümlich für P. → Vettius Scato überliefert (vgl. App. civ. 1,181).

T.FR.

II. Kaiserzeit

[II 1] M. I. Bithynicus. Senator aus Volcei in Unteritalien [1]; *cos. suff.* 162 n. Chr. Mit ihm könnte der *frater Arvalis* im J. 186–187 identisch sein [2].

1 G. Camodeca, in: EOS 2, 154f. 2 Scheid, Collège, 102 3 PIR² I 30.

[II 2] I. Capito. Centurio im syrischen Heer, der von Ummidius Quadratus mit der Übernahme parthischer Geiseln beauftragt wurde; unter → Domitius [II 11] Corbulo *praefectus castrorum*. PIR² I 31.

[II 3] Q. I. Celer. *Cos. suff.* in hadrianischer Zeit, vielleicht im J. 128 n. Chr. (AE 1973, 36). Auf ihn wohl CIL XIV 2924 und Dig. 26,5,12,1 zu beziehen: dann war er konsularer Provinzstatthalter; wenn er auch in RMD II 90 genannt ist, ist er Legat von Germania superior im J. 130 n. Chr. gewesen.

Eck, Statthalter, 54. W.E.

Institor. Als *i.* wird der vom Geschäftsherrn eingesetzte Leiter eines auf fortdauernde Geschäftstätigkeit gerichteten Handels- oder Gewerbebetriebes (vergleichbar einem leitenden Angestellten bzw. einem Geschäftsführer) bezeichnet (vgl. Ulp. Dig. 14,3,3). Es können sowohl Gewaltunterworfene (Sklaven und Freie) als auch gewaltfreie Personen beiderlei Geschlechts als *institores* eingesetzt werden (vgl. Dig. 14,3,7). Für die Erfüllung der im Rahmen des Geschäftsbetriebes durch den *i.* gegenüber Dritten eingegangenen Verpflichtungen haftet auch der Geschäftsherr (»Unternehmer«), und zwar infolge der adjektizischen (»angelehnten«) *actio institoria*, welche der Vertragspartner des *i.* gegen den Geschäftsherrn anstellen kann (vgl. Dig. 14,3; Cod. Iust. 4,25; Gai. Inst. 4,71). Auf Papinianus (Dig. 14,3,19 pr.) geht eine *actio ad exemplum institoriae actionis* zur Erweiterung der institorischen Haftung auch auf zuvor nicht den *i.*-Tätigkeiten zugerechnete Geschäfte des → *procurator* zurück; eine generelle direkte Stellvertretung durch Freie bleibt dem röm. Recht jedoch unbekannt.
→ Actio (*adiecticiae qualitatis*)

J. Aubert, Business Managers in Ancient Rome. A Social and Economic Study of Institores, 200 BC–AD 250, 1994 • N. Benke, Zu Papinians actio ad exemplum institoriae actionis, in: ZRG 105, 1988, 592–633 • Honsell/Mayer-Maly/Selb, 380f. • Kaser, RPR I, 606 ff; Bd. 2, ²1975, 103 ff. • A. Wacke, Die adjektizischen Klagen im Überblick, in: ZRG 111, 1994, 280–362. V.T.H.

Institutiones. Aus dem Begriff *institutio* (Unterricht) haben wohl als erste die röm. Juristen *I.* im 2. Jh. als Werktitel für einführende Lehrbücher abgeleitet. Die Bed. dieser röm. Lit.-Gattung für die europ. Rechtsgesch. geht weit über diejenige hinaus, die man im allg. von ant. didaktischen Einführungswerken erwarten kann: Als die Arbeiten zur Kodifikation des röm. Juristenrechts in der Gestalt der → *Digesta* so weit fortgeschritten waren, daß deren Gelingen sicher erscheinen mochte, beauftragte Kaiser Iustinian im J. 533 n. Chr. seinen Gesetzgebungsminister → Tribonianus, gemeinsam mit den byz. Rechtslehrern → Theophilos und → Dorotheos [10] für den Rechtsunterricht zur Einführung in das Recht der *Digesta* ein Lehrbuch mit Gesetzeskraft herzustellen. Hierdurch haben die *I.* eine einzigartige Autorität erhalten, die sie auch im Rechtsunterricht an den westeurop. Universitäten seit dem 12. Jh. bewahrt haben. *Institutio* wurde so aus einem Begriff für eine lit.-gesetzgeberische Form zum Synonym für die grundlegenden Einrichtungen des (röm.) Rechts selbst.

Iustinian teilt ausdrücklich mit (Const. *Imperatoriam* § 6), daß diese *I.* in wesentlichen Teilen auf dem gleichnamigen Werk des → Gaius [2] aus der Mitte des 2. Jh. n. Chr. beruhen. Während aber die Juristenschriften, die als Vorlagen für die *Digesta* dienten, fast ganz verschollen sind, sind die *I.* des Gaius als einzige klass. Juristenschrift nahezu vollständig überliefert. Die *I.* des Gaius sind seit ihrer Wiederentdeckung 1816 in der Dombibliothek von Verona für die Rekonstruktion des klass. röm. Rechts und dessen Entwicklung im Rahmen des republikan. Prozesses fast so wichtig geworden wie die *I.* Iustinians für den akadem. Rechtsunterricht und das »System« des gemeinen Rechts seit dem Hoch-MA.

Das System der *I.* von Gaius und dadurch auch von Iustinian ist noch die Grundlage der modernen Privatrechtssysteme. Unterschieden werden *personae* (Personen- und Familienrecht), *res* (Sachen- und Erbrecht, teilweise auch das Schuldrecht) und *actiones* (Prozeßrecht und wiederum Teile des Schuldrechts). Die Systematisierung wird aber auch weiter in Einzelheiten hinein betrieben. Ein Beispiel ist die Unterteilung in Konsensual-, Real-, Formal- sowie Litteralverträge (→ *contractus*). Mit dieser »flächendeckenden« systematischen Haltung stehen die überlieferten *I.* der Rechtslit. wie wohl auch ihre weitgehend verschollenen Parallelen von anderen Autoren (z. B. → Florentinus [3], → Pomponius, → Ulpianus) in der Trad. der hell. Lehrbücher (→ Isagoge).

O. Behrend, R. Knütel, B. Kupisch, H. H. Seiler, Corpus Iuris Civilis, Text und Übersetzung I: Institutionen, ²1997 (mit Erläuterungen 273–298). G.S.

Instrumentum. Der Begriff *i.* (»Errichtetes«, »Eingerichtetes«) hat in der röm. Rechtssprache sehr unterschiedliche Bed.: 1. In der Kaiserzeit, vor allem in der Spätant., ist das *i.* die von einem Urkundenschreiber (→ *tabellio*) über ein privates Rechtsgeschäft oder (als *i. publicum*) von einer Behörde über private oder öffentliche Angelegenheiten aufgenommene Urkunde. Das *i. publicum* und das von drei Zeugen schriftlich bestätigte und vom *tabellio* gleichfalls schriftlich als echt bezeugte *i.* des Urkundenschreibers hatten im spätant. Prozeß bis zum Beweis einer Fälschung vollen Beweiswert. Ein bes. wichtiger Anwendungsfall privater *instrumenta* ist das Versprechen einer Mitgift (→ *dos*). An die Stelle der früher üblichen → *dictio dotis* und deren abstrakt-verbindlicher Erklärung in der Form der → *stipulatio* trat in der Spätant. das *i. dotalium*. Dessen Errichtung war zugleich ein wichtiges Indiz für das Ehebewußtsein (*affectio maritalis*; → Ehe III.).

2. Meist in der Verbindung *i. fundi* bezeichnet der Begriff das Zubehör, vor allem bei einem landwirtschaftlichen Grundstück. Dort umfaßt es jedenfalls alle landwirtschaftlichen Geräte und Aufbewahrungsvor-

richtungen (Cato agr. 1,5; Colum. 1,8; 15,3). Die meisten Juristen verstehen *i.* weiter, u.a. einschließlich der zum Betrieb gehörenden Arbeitssklaven (→ Hausrat). Praktische Bed. hatte der Begriff bei der Auslegung von Rechtsgeschäften, durch die mit Zubehör (*cum instrumento*) veräußert, vermacht oder pachtweise überlassen werden sollte. Aus Anlaß von Vermächtnissen als offenbar wichtigstem Anwendungsgebiet ist dieser Frage ein ganzer Digesten-Titel (Dig. 33,7) gewidmet. Ulpian berichtet noch Anf. des 3. Jh. n. Chr. von einem Entscheidungsvorschlag des Q. → Mucius Scaevola von Anf. des 1. Jh. v. Chr., bei dem danach unterschieden wurde, ob ein Sklave zeitweilig an ein Landgut versetzt (dann kein *i.*) oder dauerhaft speziell für das Gut gehalten war (dann *i.*; Dig. 28,5,35,3). Aber auch ganz ohne Erwähnung des *i.* konnte die Auslegung ergeben, daß Zubehör beim Rechtsgeschäft nach dessen typischem Zweck mitgemeint sein sollte. In diesem Sinn entschied man z. B. bei Pacht, anders hingegen bei Vermächtnissen.

KASER, RPR II, 677ff. • A. STEINWENTER, Fundus cum instrumento, 1942. G.S.

Insubres. Großes kelt. Volk (Pol. 2,17,4; Strab. 5,1,6; nach Liv. 5,34,9 Gau der Haedui) einfacher Lebensart (Pol. l.c.) in Oberit., östl. der Salassi (Ptol. 3,1,34) und Libici (Ptol. 3,1,36), westl. der → Cenomanni [3] (Ptol. 3,1,33; Pol. 2,17,4; Strab. 5,1,9) und des Flusses Klusios (Κλούσιος, Pol. 2,32,4) mit dem Hauptort Mediolan(i)um (Liv. 5,34,9; Plin. nat. 3,124; Strab. 5,1,6). Weitere Städte der I. (Ptol. 3,1,33): Comum, Ticinum (Cic. fam. 15,16,1), Novaria, Acerae (Pol. 2,24,4 f.), Victumulae (Liv. 21,45,3). Die I. kämpften 225 v. Chr. gegen Rom (Pol. 2,22–35; bei Telamon), desgleichen 223 (Pol. 2,32 f.) und 222 (Pol. 2,34; bei → Clastidium). Sie schlossen sich Hannibal an (Liv. 21,39,1) und blieben den Karthagern bis 203 treu (Liv. 30,18,1). Auch in den folgenden Jahren bildeten sie den Kern des kelt. Widerstandes gegen Rom und wurden 197 (Liv. 33,23,4), 196 (33,37,10), und 194 (34,46,1; Cic. Balb. 32) geschlagen (Triumphe: CIL I^2, p. 47 f.). Der Jurist T. Catius (Cic. fam. 15,16,1) und der Komödiendichter Statius Caecilius (Hier. chron. 1838) waren I.; nach Tac. ann. 11,23,3 stellten die I. auch Senatoren.
→ Gallia Cisalpina

C. PEYRE, La Cisalpine gauloise du IIIe au Ier siècle av. J.-C., 1979. Y.L.u.G.RA.

Insula. Von lat. *insula* (»Insel«, »Wohnhaus«) abgeleiteter mod. t.t. der Urbanistik, der beim → Städtebau die allseits von Straßen umgebene und durch diese Struktur markierte Fläche für die Bebauung bezeichnet. Insulae sind nicht ausschließlich ein Produkt städtebaulicher Gesamtplanungen. Sie sind innerhalb eines orthogonalen Straßennetzes zwar in der Regel von rechteckiger oder trapezoider, seltener quadratischer Form, zugleich heißt aber auch der Terrain-Ausschnitt des unregelmäßigen Straßensystems einer »gewachsenen« Stadt I. (wie z. B. in Delos oder in Teilen Pompeiis).

Im griech. Städtebau findet sich die I. als Resultat orthogonaler oder pseudo-orthogonaler Einteilung des Siedlungsgebietes in Streifen erstmals im Kontext früher Koloniestädte des Westens. Die Stadtanlage von Megara Hyblaea auf Sizilien gilt als frühester Beleg; bereits im späten 8. Jh. v. Chr. durchzog hier ein Raster teils par., teils sich kreuzender Straßen weite Teile des Gebiets innerhalb der ummauerten Stadt. Vermutlich diente dies Verfahren der gleichmäßigen Landverteilung an die Kolonisten und korrespondierte mit einer ähnlichen, h. nur noch selten rekonstruierbaren Rasterung der Chora außerhalb der Stadt (vgl. bes. → Metapont).

Im Zusammenhang mit ersten städtebaulichen Gesamtkonzeptionen der griech. Stadt, meist verbunden mit der durch → Hippodamos von Milet erbauten Stadtanlage im → Peiraieus bei Athen, wird die I. zum Nukleus eines Konzepts der Flächennutzung und bildet, wie etwa in Priene noch gut nachvollziehbar, innerhalb eines übergeordneten Planungsrasters ein Modul, das mittels Addition oder in Bruchteilen das gesamte Stadtgebiet mit proportional aufeinander abgestimmten Flächen überzieht und auch den öffentlichen und rel. Raum der Stadt definiert. War in den griech. Koloniestädten der archa. und frühklass. Zeit die gerechte Teilung von Land unter den Kolonisten Ursache für das Entstehen der I., so sind die Überlegungen von [5] zur Normgröße der I. in den urbanistischen Gesamtplanungen des 5. und 4. Jh., zum darauf erbauten uniformen Typen-Haus und zur damit verknüpften Idee einer Gleichsetzung von Demokratie, Isonomia und Besitzgleichheit von arch. und histor. Seite nicht unwidersprochen geblieben. Wahrscheinlich ist indessen, daß das System der von mehreren Häusern bestandenen I. ursächlich zur Ausrichtung des Wohnhauses auf einen inneren Lichthof wie Pastas, Peristyl oder Atrium führte (→ Haus).

Die I. der röm. Stadt fügt sich ein in das zunächst sakral, später eher als pragmatischer Herrschaftsakt gehandhabte Konzept der Landnahme und Landvermessung (*centuriatio*; → Limitation); die in I. gegliederte Stadtstruktur nimmt ihren Ausgang am Kreuzungspunkt von → *cardo* und → *decumanus* im Zentrum der Stadt und entspricht als ein übergeordnetes Flächennutzungskonzept einerseits dem traditionellen röm. Militärlager, andererseits zumindest in Grundzügen der griech. Urbanistik des späten 5. und 4. Jh. v. Chr. Teile des Konzeptes sind dabei dem etr. Ritus der Städtegründung und Siedlungsstrukturierung entlehnt; bereits in Etrurien finden sich als Produkte eines rituellen Aktes der Städtegründung orthogonale, an Decumanus und Cardo ausgerichtete Bebauungen mit I. (z. B. in Marzabotto, 6. Jh. v. Chr.). Die I. waren dicht bebaut, in Ballungszentren wie Rom oder Ostia z. T. mit mehrgeschossigen Mietshäusern, in Landstädten wie Pompeii mit maximal zweigeschossigen, z. T. großflächigen Stadthäusern, die zur Straße hin Läden aufwiesen, ansonsten aber durch hohe, fensterlose Mauern von der Außenwelt abgetrennt waren.

In zahlreichen lat. Schriftquellen bezeichnet I. darüber hinaus auch ein Einzelmietshaus und steht im Gegensatz zur *domus*, dem Herrensitz; diese Häuser wurden an die ärmere Bevölkerung (*insularii*) vermietet und meist von einem Sklaven (*servus insularius*) verwaltet.

1 D. Asheri, Distribuzioni di terre nell'antica Greca, 1966 2 T. Boyd, M. Jameson, Urban and Rural Land Division in Ancient Greece, in: Hesperia 50, 1981, 327–342 3 K.-V. v. Eickstedt, Beitr. zur Top. des ant. Piräus, 1991 4 B. Fehr, Kosmos und Chreia. Der Sieg der reinen über die praktische Vernunft in der griech. Stadtarchitektur des 4. Jh. v. Chr., in: Hephaistos 2, 1980, 155–185 5 W. Hoepfner, E. L. Schwandner, Haus und Stadt im klass. Griechenland, [2]1994 6 F. Lang, Archa. Siedlungen in Griechenland, 1996, 58–63 7 Th. Lorenz, Röm. Städte, 1987 8 D. Mertens, E. Greco, Urban Planning in Magna Grecia, in: G. Pugliese Caratelli (Hrsg.), The Western Greeks, 1996, 243–262 9 F. Prayon, Die Etrusker, 1996, 85–89 10 Ch. Schubert, Land und Raum in der röm. Republik. Die Kunst des Teilens, 1996. C. HÖ.

Insula Columbaria. Insel im *mare Tyrrhenum* bei Ilva (Plin. nat. 3,81). G. U.

Insulae Aegates. Inselgruppe zw. Lilybaion und Karthago (h. Favignana und Levanza). Hier ging 250 v. Chr., von Lilybaion zu Hilfe gerufen, die karthag. Flotte vor Anker (Pol. 1,44,2). In Sichtweite von Favignana fand 241 v. Chr. die den 1. Pun. Krieg entscheidende Seeschlacht zw. C. Lutatius Catulus und Hanno statt (Pol. 1,60,4 ff.) [1. 248 f.].

1 Huss.

R. J. A. Wilson, Sicily under the Roman Empire, 1990, 228, 393 Nr. 179 • G. Purpura, in: SicA 15/48, 1982, 56 f.; 18/57–58, 1985, 59–86 • A. M. Fallico, Sicilia: XII. Favignana e Marettimo (Isole Egadi), in: NSA 23, 1969, 321. GI. MA./Ü: H. D.

Insulae fortunatae s. Makaron Nesoi

Insulae Gorgades. Nicht lokalisierte Inselgruppe, erwähnt von Plinius (nat. 6,200; Mela 3,99: *Dorcades*), der sich auf → Xenophon von Lampsakos (Lage der Inseln zwei Tagesfahrten vor der afrikan. Westküste; Rückführung des Namens der I. G. auf die dort einst lebenden Gorgonen) und → Hanno [1] (Charakterisierung der Bewohner als Wilde, ihre Frauen hätten behaarte Haut) beruft. In Hannos Bericht, der uns in vielfach veränderter Form vorliegt (peripl. 18, GGM 1,1–14), werden die Frauen auf den I. G. als *Gorillai* (Γορίλλαι, möglicherweise Verschreibung der griech. Übers. für *Gorgades*) bezeichnet.

S. Gsell, Histoire ancienne de l'Afrique du Nord 1, [3]1921, 499 ff. • K. Bayer, in: G. Winkler, R. König (Hrsg.), C. Plinius Secundus, Naturalis historiae libri XXXVII, Bd. 5, 1993, 360–363 (Lit.). E. O.

Intaglio s. Steinschneidekunst

Intaphernes (altpers. *Vindafarna*, elam. *Mindaparna*). Helfer des Dareios I. im Komplott gegen (Pseudo-) Bardiya [2] (→ Gaumata) [1. DB 3.84] im J. 522 v. Chr., zerschlug die zweite babylon. Rebellion [1. DB 83–91]. Herodot (3,118–119) erzählt von einer angeblichen Empörung des I., weshalb die ganze Familie ausgerottet wurde; nur der Bruder seiner Frau wurde auf ihre Bitte hin gerettet (Parallele zu Sophokles' Antigone).

1 R. G. Kent, Old Persian, 1953 2 M. Mayrhofer, Onomastica Persepolitana, 1973, 8.1078
3 H. Sancisi-Weerdenburg, »Exit Atossa«, in: A. Cameron, A. Kuhrt, Images of Women in Antiquity, 1983, 32 ff. A. KU. u. H. S.-W.

Intarabus (Entarabus). Kelt. Gott, nur inschr. bezeugt (CIL VIII, 3632, 4128), im Gebiet der Treverer (Trier) verehrt. Die Inschr. bezeugen dem I. geweihte Bauwerke (*porticus, aedes, fanum, simulacrum*), woraus die Beliebtheit des Gottes geschlossen wird. In CIL VIII, 3653 erhält I. den Beinamen Mars. RE. ZI.

Intarsien I. Alter Orient
II. Klassische Archäologie

I. Alter Orient

Als I. bezeichnet man in der Vorderasiatischen Arch. die Auf- oder Einlage von dekorativen Elementen aus unterschiedlichen Materialien auf bzw. in einem Trägermaterial. Um bes. Farbkonstraste zu erzielen, wurden Kombinationen unterschiedlicher Stoffe, insbes. farbige Steine, Weichtiergehäuse, Knochen, Elfenbein, Metalle, Keramik, Glas und Kieselkeramik genutzt; die häufigsten Trägermaterialien waren Stein, Metall, Holz und Ton/Keramik. Als Bindemittel diente zumeist Bitumen. Älteste Beispiele für I. sind aus dem präkeramischen Neolithikum Palästinas (ca. 8000 v. Chr.) bekannt (z. B. aus Jericho gipsüberzogene Menschenschädel mit Augeneinlagen aus Muscheln). I. finden sich seit dem ausgehenden 4. Jt. v. Chr. häufig bei Steingefäßen, in der Kleinkunst (u. a. Siegel), bei Skulpturen, als Wanddekoration, bei Luxusgütern (sog. Standarte und Spielbrett von Ur), bei äg. Mumienmasken. Eine Sonderform baugebundener I. stellen die Wanddekorationen in Form von Stiftmosaiken (z. B. Uruk, Ende 4. Jt.) dar. R. W.

II. Klassische Archäologie

Als I. bezeichnet die klass. Arch. Einlegearbeiten nicht nur aus Holz, sondern aus unterschiedlichsten Materialien wie Glasfluß, Alabaster, Bernstein, Elfenbein, Schildpatt, Blattgold und Buntmarmor auf Holz, Metall oder Steinplatten als den Trägern; I. finden sich in den verschiedensten Kunst- und Kunstgewerbegattungen. Am häufigsten finden sich I. im Bereich der → Möbel (hier v. a. bei → Klinen); auch Brettspiele, Musikinstrumente und verschiedene weitere Gerätschaften konnten Träger von I. sein. Nur weniges ist hiervon erh. geblieben, vieles aber lit. beschrieben oder in der Vasenmalerei abgebildet. Die Einlagen wurden gesägt, geschnitten oder gegossen und dann auf dem Träger mit einem Binder (Bitumen, Pech, verschiedene Harze) fixiert; das Ganze wurde schließlich homogen verschliffen bzw. poliert. I. konnten ornamentales Dekor (→ Ornament), aber auch figürliche Szenen, ja ganze Bildsequenzen darstellen.

I. sind spätestens im 3. Jt. v. Chr. im Vorderen Orient entstanden, finden sich, wenn auch selten, in der minoischen Kultur Kretas und waren im nachmyk. Griechenland bis in die Klassik hinein Bestandteil der »östl.«, importierten Luxus-Kunst mit ihrem ambivalent beurteilten farbenprächtig-ornamentalen Bildreichtum. Erst ab dem 4. Jh. v. Chr. häufen sich I. auch aus griech. Werkstätten; sie werden im Hell. wie auch im Imperium Romanum in den verschiedensten Formen zum Gemeingut einer vermögenden Oberschicht. Insbes. in der frühchristl. Kleinkunst, bei Devotionalien und liturgischem Gerät fanden Einlegearbeiten in unterschiedlichsten Formen und Techniken Verwendung.

Ein grundsätzlich den I. zuzuordnendes Phänomen ist darüber hinaus das → Mosaik in seinen verschiedenen technischen Ausführungen, bes. in der *opus sectile*-Technik (vgl. auch → Pavimentum). Zu I. in architektonischen Kontexten (Wandverkleidungen) → Inkrustation.

H. S. Baker, Furniture in the Ancient World, 1966 • E. Bielefeld, Eine Patene aus dem frz. Krönungsschatz. Ein Versuch zur Kleinkunst des 4. Jh. n. Chr., in: Gymnasium 79, 1972, 395–445 • F. Guidobaldi, L'intarsio marmoreo nella decorazione pavietale e pavimentale di età romana, in: E. Dolci, Il marmo nella civiltà romana, 1990, 55–67 • H. Kyrieleis, Throne und Klinen (24. Ergh. JDAI), 1969 • H. Mielsch, Buntmarmore aus Rom im Antikenmus. Berlin, 1985 • H. W. Müller, Koptische Glas-I. mit figürlichen Darstellungen aus Antinoe, Mittelägypt., in: Pantheon 20, 1962, 13–18 • G. M. A. Richter, The Furniture of the Greeks, Etruscans and Romans, 1966, 122–126 • R. L. Scranton, Glass Pictures from the Sea, in: Archaeology 20, 1967, 163–173. C. HÖ.

Intellekt. Der I., bei Homer verkörpert in Athene auf göttl. und Odysseus auf menschl. Ebene – diese Doppelung bleibt auch später bewahrt im Begriff des *nus* (νοῦς: I., Geist, Vernunft) als (a) göttl. Substanz und (b) menschl. Erkenntnisvermögen –, wird in der Vorsokratik zur weltlenkenden Macht bei → Xenophanes (21 B 23–25 DK) und vor allem bei → Anaxagoras, für den der göttl. *nus* alles erkennt, ordnet und beherrscht (59 B 12 DK). Zugleich betont Anaxagoras die Sonderstellung des Menschen, der das Leben des I. lebt (59 A 29–30 DK). Platon nimmt die *nus*-Spekulation auf: aus dem Ungenügen an ihrer anaxagoreischen Form läßt er die → Ideenlehre erwachsen (Plat. Phaid. 97b ff.). Die Ideenwelt selbst hat I.-Natur, verfügt sie doch über *nus* (Plat. soph. 248e f.). Der die sichtbare Welt gestaltende → Demiurgos wird häufig als ein göttlicher I. verstanden [3]. Er konstruiert die Welt als ein mit I. begabtes Lebewesen (ζῷον ἔννουν, Plat. Tim. 30b). Die Göttlichkeit der innerkosmischen Götter beruht auf ihrer Seinsweise als I. (Plat. Phaidr. 249c). Des *nus* teilhaftig sind die Götter und jener seltene Menschentyp (Plat. Tim. 51e), der dank seiner Ausrichtung auf die Ideenwelt »gottgeliebt« (θεοφιλής) ist (Plat. symp. 212a), d. h. der Philosoph, der zur Ideenerkenntnis fähig ist. Die Idee des Guten steht noch über dem I. (ebd. 508e 3–509a 7, wo *epistḗmē* (»Wiss.«) dasselbe meint wie *nus* 508c 1; 511d 4). Daß Gott ›entweder I. oder etwas jenseits des I. ist‹ (ἢ νοῦς ἐστὶν ἢ ἐπέκεινά τι τοῦ νοῦ), erwog Aristoteles in ›Über das Gebet‹ fr. 1 Rose. Im übrigen bestimmt Aristoteles als das höchste Prinzip, von dem die Welt abhängt, den sich selbst denkenden göttl. I. (metaph. 12,7,1072a 19–19,1075a 10). Zugleich ist der *nus* das (von außen eintretende: Aristot. gen. an. 736b 28) Göttliche im Menschen, das ihm die beglückende theoretische Lebensform und die Unsterblichkeit (ἀθανατίζειν) ermöglicht (eth. Nic. 10,1177b 26–1178a 2).

Die Stoa fordert, daß der Mensch vollständig vom I. bestimmt sei; auch hier ist die Übereinstimmung zw. menschl. Vernunftgebrauch und göttl. Vernünftigkeit der Welt die leitende Vorstellung. Die Vernunft im Menschen ist »göttl.« (SVF I 40,5; II 307,24), die (feurige) Vernunft des Kosmos ist Gott (ebd. I 42,7); ›eines ist Gott und *nus* und *heimarménē*‹ (I 28,22). Der Aristotelismus wirkte, vor allem durch die Auslegung des *nus politikós* (vgl. Aristot. an. 3,5,430a 10–25) durch Alexandros von Aphrodisias (an. 81,24 ff.; 888,22 ff.; 106,19 ff.), nachhaltig auf alle spätere, bes. auch die ma. Diskussion. Der Mittel- und Neuplatonismus betont im Anschluß an den platonischen ›Timaios‹ die Funktion des I. als Ursache der Welt und nimmt die von Platon (Charm. 166a ff.) und Aristoteles (metaph. 12,9) begonnenen Überlegungen zur Reflexivität des *nus* auf (zu Numenios s. [5]). Plotinos erörtert den *nus* als zweite → *hypóstasis* seines Systems immer wieder vor allem hinsichtlich seiner Herkunft vom Ursprung (»Überfließen« des Einen und »Rückwendung«) und seiner Struktur (Dualität von Denkendem und Gedachtem und ihre Einheit im Denkvollzug, »alles zusammen« (ὁμοῦ πάντα), als durchgehende wechselseitige Durchdringung und Verbundenheit aller Inhalte mit allen, Plot. Enneades 5 und 6 passim). → Proklos' Philos. des I. versucht die triadische Struktur des *nus* (Verharren – Hervorgang – Rückwendung: μονή – πρόοδος – ἐπιστροφή) als umfassendes Strukturprinzip der intelligiblen (und mittelbar der sensiblen) Welt zu erweisen. Unter den lat. christl. Autoren verstand Marius Victorinus in neuplatonischer Weise Gott als den I. übersteigend (Adversus Arium 3,7,15–17), während Augustinus in *De trinitate* (B. 10, 14,15) den Nachweis zu führen versuchte, daß der menschliche I. (die *mens humana*) als Abbild des göttlichen über eine »trinitarische« Struktur verfüge.

1 W. Jaeger, Die Theologie der frühen griech. Denker, 1953 **2** H. J. Krämer, Der Ursprung der Geistmetaphysik, [2]1967 **3** G. Reale, Zu einer neuen Interpretation Platons, 1993 **4** K. Oehler, Subjektivität und Selbstbewußtsein in der Ant., 1997 **5** J. Halfwassen, Geist und Selbstbewußtsein. Studien zu Plotin und Numenios (AAWM), 1994 **6** TH.A. SZLEZÁK, Platon und Aristoteles in der Nuslehre Plotins, 1979 **7** W. BEIERWALTES, Proklos. Grundzüge seiner Metaphysik, ²1979 **8** P. MORAUX, Alexandre d'Aphrodise, exégète de la noétique d'Aristote, 1942. T.A.S.

Intentio, das Klagebegehren, legt innerhalb der den röm. Formularprozeß kennzeichnenden Prozeßformel (→ *formula*) den (ggf. zu beweisenden) Streitgegenstand fest (Gai. inst. 4,41). Im Falle einer Feststellungsklage beschränkt sich diese Formel auf die *i.* (Gai. inst. 4,44), während bei Leistungsklagen danach zu unterscheiden ist, ob sie auf ein *certum* (d.h. eine bestimmte Summe, Sache oder Warenmenge) oder ein *incertum* (d.h. ein *quidquid dare facere oportet*, ›alles, was er zu leisten verpflichtet ist‹), gerichtet ist. Letzterenfalls wird die *i.* zur Präzisierung des Begehrens durch einen vorangestellten Hinweis auf den Sachverhalt (→ *demonstratio*) ergänzt. Diese Unterscheidung ist überdies auch für die »Rechtsfolge« der Formel, die → *condemnatio* (Verurteilung), von Bedeutung: Während es bei den auf ein *incertum* gerichteten Klagen dem Richter übertragen ist, den durch die *bona* → *fides* gebotenen Leistungsumfang festzusetzen, obliegt diese Aufgabe bei den auf ein *certum* gerichteten Klagen dem Kläger. Eine mangelhafte Präzision seines in der *i.* umschriebenen Begehrens wird mittels der → *pluspetitio* (Prozeßverlust bei Zuvielforderung) sanktioniert (Gai. inst. 4,54), wobei allerdings zu beachten ist, daß die *i.* ausgelegt werden kann – und zwar grundsätzlich (zumindest nach Ansicht von Iulianus bzw. Paulus) zu Gunsten eines Prozeßfortgangs (Dig. 34,5,12; 50,17,172,1). Den beiden Varianten der Leistungsklage ist jedoch gemeinsam, daß das in der *i.* ausgedrückte klägerische Begehren mit der in der *condemnatio* ausgesprochenen Leistungspflicht korrespondiert, sofern der Kläger tatsächlich obsiegt – er ist also in diesem Fall der Gläubiger dieser Pflicht. Hiervon gibt es einige wenige Ausnahmen, die auf eine ant. Form der Prozeßstandschaft hinauslaufen: So ist bei der *actio Rutiliana* der *bonorum emptor* (Vermögenserwerber) nicht in der *i.* genannt, wohl aber als der Begünstigte der *condemnatio* (Gai. inst. 4,35).

M. KASER, K. HACKL, Das röm. Zivilprozeßrecht, ²1997, 311–314 • W. SELB, Formeln mit unbestimmter I. Iuris, Bd. I, 1974. C.PA.

Interamna

[1] (*I. Nahars*, CIL XI 4213; ethnische Bezeichnung *Interamnates Nartes*, CIL VI 140). Stadt in Umbria, h. Terni. Der ON ist auf die Lage am Zusammenfluß von Nera (umbr. *Nahar* [1], lat. *Nar*) und Serra zurückzuführen (in der Ant. mit anderem Flußverlauf). In Pentima und in San Pietro in Campo sind Siedlungsphasen aus dem 10.–7. Jh. nachgewiesen. Eine im Stadtteil Clai entdeckte Siedlung aus dem 7. Jh. scheint die Überl. zu bestätigen, nach der I. 672 v. Chr. gegr. wurde (vgl. CIL XI 4170: 704 J. seit der Gründung = 32 n. Chr.). *Municipium, tribus Clustumina*. Streitigkeiten mit → Reate sind bekannt, das 54 v. Chr. (Cic. Att. 4,15,5) und 15 n. Chr. (Tac. ann. 1,79) durch den über die Ufer getretenen Nar in Mitleidenschaft gezogen worden war. Arch.: Reste röm. Mauern unter dem öffentlichen Park; Reste des *cardo*, des *decumanus maximus* und des Theaters; in der Nähe der Mauern im SW Amphitheater aus der Zeit des Tiberius; *villa* unter der Kirche San Salvatore; Heiligtum aus dem 6. Jh. v. Chr. bei Monte Torre Maggiore. Inschr.: CIL XI 4170–4344.

1 G. DEVOTO, Il nome Naharko, in: SE 33, 1965, 369–377.

E. ROSSI-PASSAVANTI, I. Nahars, 1932 • P. RINALDI, Materiali per il museo archeologico di Terni, 1985 • L. BONOMI PONZI, Terni, in: EAA² 5, 1997, 674–677.

[2] I. Lirenas, I. Sucasina. Seit dem 7. Jh. v. Chr. von Aurunci, Volsci und Samnites bewohnte Stadt bei Casinum auf einer kleinen Anhöhe am linken Ufer des Liris beim h. Termini bei Pignataro I. Seit 312 v. Chr. latin. Kolonie (Liv. 9,28,8; Diod. 19,105,5; Vell. 1,14,4), erhielt den Beinamen *Lirenas* (CIL X 4960) bzw. *Sucasina* (Plin. nat. 3,64), *regio I.* Weigerte sich, gegen Hannibal Hilfe zu leisten, wurde deshalb von Rom bestraft (Liv. 27,9,8). Seit 90 *municipium, tribus Teretina* (Cic. Phil. 2,105; CIL X 4860). Inschr.: CIL X 5331–5365.

M. CAGIANO DE AZEVEDO, I. Lirenas vel Sucasina, 1947 • G. LENA, I. L., in: Quaderni del Museo Civico di Pontecorvo 2, 1982, 57–75 • E. M. BERANGER, I. L., in: EAA² 3, 1995, 115 f. G.U./Ü: H.D.

[3] I. Praetuttiorum. Stadt der Praetuttii (Ptol. 5,1,58) am Zusammenfluß von Tordino und Vezzola, h. Teramo (unzutreffend die Bezeichnung *Interamnia*). Das *conciliabulum civium Romanorum* wurde nach 268 v. Chr. gegr., als den Praetutii die *civitas optimo iure* verliehen wurde (*VIII viri*, ILS 5666 aus frühaugusteischer Zeit), die *Interamnates* oder *Interamnites Praetuttiani* waren in der *tribus Velina* eingeschrieben. Nach dem Bundesgenossenkrieg wurde I. *municipium*, dann eine sullanische *colonia* mit *praetores* und *II viri*; das Nebeneinander von *municipes* und *coloni* ist inschr. bis ins 2. Jh. n. Chr. bezeugt.

A. MIGLIORATI, Municipes et coloni, in: Archeologia classica 28, 1976, 242–246 • J. B. DE SMET, Interamnia Praetuttiorum (Teramo) et le problème des communautés à statut juridique double, in: Acta archaeologica Lovaniensia 38/9, 1989/1990, 63–74 • P. SOMMELLA, Teramo, in: EAA² Suppl. 5, 1997, 665 f. • M. BUONOCORE, Un' inedita testimonianza di munificentia femminile a Teramo, in: Athenaeum 86, 1998 (im Erscheinen). M.BU./Ü: J.W.M.

Interamnium. Straßenstation im Tal des Sybaris in Lucania (Tab. Peut. 7,1; Geogr. Rav. 4,34).

NISSEN 2, 918. E.O.

Interaspiration s. Lesezeichen

Intercessio I. Staatsrechtlich II. Privatrechtlich

I. Staatsrechtlich

Im röm.-republikanischen Staatsrecht bedeutet *i.* (von *intercedere* = dazwischentreten) das Veto gegen magistratische Dekrete (→ *decretum*), gegen Senatskonsulte (→ *senatus consultum*) und gegen → Rogationen aller Art an die verschiedenen Volksversammlungsarten. Dekrete werden dadurch unwirksam, soweit nicht gesetzlich eine *i.* ausgeschlossen ist, wie z. B. gegen magistratische Gerichtsdekrete während eines laufenden Gerichtsverfahrens. Senatsbeschlüsse werden zur reinen Empfehlung (→ *auctoritas*) und Rogationen gegenstandslos, soweit das Volk über sie noch nicht beschlossen hat. Dieses Verbotsrecht hat a) jeder Amtsträger im Verhältnis zu seinen gleichrangigen Kollegen, b) jeder Amtsträger im Verhältnis zu niederrangigen Amtsträgern, c) jeder Amtsträger gegenüber Beschlüssen des Senats, soweit sie nicht von höherrangigen Senatsmitgliedern mitgefaßt wurden, d) jeder Volkstribun im Verhältnis zu jedem Amtsträger mit Ausnahme der Dictatoren, ferner gegenüber allen Senatsbeschlüssen und gegenüber allen Rogationen an die Volksversammlung. Die *i.* ist seit dem Ende der Königszeit als Folge des Prinzips kollegialer Gewaltenteilung anzunehmen, wird aber seit den Ständekämpfen des 5. Jh. v. Chr. auch zur wichtigen Handhabe der Volkstribunen zum Schutze der *plebs* gegen Übergriffe der Magistrate. Allg. ist sie ein Mittel der Regierungs- und Verwaltungskontrolle im Interesse der dadurch Verletzten, denn auf deren Antrag kann sie von allen Magistraten so eingesetzt werden; in den latinischen Munizipien gibt es ebenfalls eine *i.*, obwohl sie keine Tribunen haben.

Mommsen, Staatsrecht, 266–292. C. G.

II. Privatrechtlich

Im Privatrecht versteht man unter *i.* das »Dazwischentreten« durch Übernahme einer Schuld im fremden Interesse, z. B. durch Bürgschaft, Schuldbeitritt, Übernahme einer fremden Schuld durch → *novatio*, Aufnahme eines Kredits für einen anderen, sowie Bestellung eines Pfandes (→ *pignus*) für eine fremde Schuld.

Unter Augustus sowie durch Edikte des Claudius soll Frauen die *i.* für ihre Ehemänner verboten gewesen sein (Ulp. Dig. 16,1,2 pr.). Durch das (zw. 41 und 65 n. Chr. erlassene) *SC Velleianum* wurde Frauen die *i.* generell verboten (Paul. Dig. 16,1,1; Ulp. Dig. 16,1,2,1). Die aus einer *i.* beklagte Frau konnte eine Einrede (→ *exceptio, SC Velleiani*) erheben. Zur Reichweite des Verbotes der *i.* existiert eine reiche Kasuistik (vgl. Dig. 16,1; Cod. Iust. 4,29).

→ Bürgschaft

Honsell/Mayer-Maly/Selb, 292–294 • D. Medicus, Zur Gesch. des Senatus consultum Velleianum, 1957 • J. Beaucamp, Le statut de la femme à Byzance I, 1990, 54–78 • R. Zimmermann, The Law of Obligations, 1990, 145–152. F. ME.

Intercisa

[1] Mil. Lager, Zollstation und Zivilsiedlung am Limes der Pannonia Inferior an der Straße Aquincum – Altinum – Mursa (Itin. Anton. 245,3; Not. dign. occ. 33,25 f.; 38), h. Dunaújváros, Kreis Fejér in Ungarn. Das urspr. Holz-Erde-Kastell wurde wohl in der ausgehenden flavischen Zeit von der *ala I Augusta Ituraeorum sagittariorum* errichtet. Stützpunkt der *ala I Flavia Augusta Britannica* (105–106 n. Chr.), der *ala I Tungrorum Frontoniana* (bis 118/9) und der *ala I Thracum veteranorum sagittariorum*. Im späteren Steinlager (176 × 205 m) war nach den Markomannenkriegen die *cohors milliaria Hemesenorum* stationiert. Damals erfolgte ein reger Ausbau inner- und außerhalb des Lagers. Seit E. 3. Jh. sind hier *cuneus equitum Dalmatarum, cuneus equitum Constantianorum* und *equites sagittarii* bezeugt. Im Lager und in der Umgebung der Siedlung wurden Gebäudereste, Wachttürme, *villae*, Meilensteine, Gräber, zahlreiche Inschr. und zwei Münzschatzfunde nachgewiesen. Noch im 5. Jh. n. Chr. war I. bewohnt.

L. Barkóczi (Hrsg.), Intercisa, 2 Bde., 1954/1957 • TIR L 34 Budapest, 1968, 66 ff. (mit Quellen und Lit.) • J. Fitz (Hrsg.), Der röm. Limes in Ungarn, 1976, 101 ff. J. BU.

[2] Straßenstation der *via Flaminia* zw. Forum Sempronii und Pitinum Mergens bei Gola del Furlo, benannt nach dem 37 m langen Tunnel, den Vespasianus 77 n. Chr. bauen ließ (CIL XI 6106; Claud. carm. 281; 502; daher auch die ON Petra Pertusa bzw. Pertunsa petra, Aur. Vict. Caes. 9,10, und Furlo). Im Gotenkrieg byz. Stützpunkt (zum J. 538 vgl. Prok. BG 2,11,2; 10–13; zum J. 552 vgl. 4,28,13).

Nissen 2, 383 • T. Ashby, R. A. L. Fell, The via Flaminia, in: JRS 11, 1921, 125–190. G. U./Ü: J. W. M.

Intercisi dies s. Fasti

Interdictum. Anordnung des → Praetors oder Provinzstatthalters aufgrund seines → *imperium* (z. B. Iulianus, Dig. 43,8,7) zur raschen Beendigung von Streitigkeiten, v. a. über → *possessio* (Besitz) oder *quasi possessio* (Gai. inst. 4,139); dabei sind immer auch öffentliche Interessen berührt. Erste Spuren von *interdicta* finden sich bei Plautus (Stich. 696; 748–750; Asin. 504–509), Terenz (Eun. 319 f.) und in der *lex Agraria* von 111 v. Chr. (Z. 18); eine Anspielung enthält Cic. de orat. 1,10,41.

I. sind teils Gebote: *exhibeas* (auf Vorweisung) oder *restituas* (auf Rückgewähr), daher *i. exhibitoria, restitutoria* (auch *decreta*), teils Verbote (*i. prohibitoria*, auch einfach *i.*), z. B. *vim fieri veto* (Verbote von Gewalt). Gewalt darf nicht gegen den »fehlerfreien«, durchaus aber gegen den »fehlerhaften« Besitzer geübt werden (*i. uti possidetis* für Grundstücke, *i. utrubi* für bewegliche Sachen, jeweils mit der Möglichkeit zur Einrede fehlerhaften Besitzes). Weitere Beispiele: Verbot an den Wohnungsvermieter, den auszugsbereiten Mieter an der Mitnahme pfand-freier Sachen zu hindern (*i. de migrando*); Verbot *ne quid in loco sacro fiat* (Störung eines geweihten Ortes, zu all dem Gai. inst. 4,139f.).

I. zielen auf (erstmalige) Erlangung, Erhalt oder Wiedererlangung des Besitzes (*i. adipiscendae, retinendae, reciperandae possessionis causa conparata*; Gai. inst. 4,143). Der Besitzerlangung dient etwa das *i. quorum bonorum* des *bonorum possessor* (»praetorischen Besitzers«, Gai. inst. 4,144), ferner das *i. Salvianum* des Landverpächters für ihm vom Pächter wegen des Pachtzinses verpfändete Sachen (Gai. inst. 4,147). Dem Besitzerhalt dienen die *i. uti possidetis* und *utrubi*; sie bereiten auch den Eigentumsstreit durch Verteilung der Parteirollen vor (Gai. inst. 4,148–153). Der Wiedererlangung des Besitzes dienen das *i. unde vi* (»auf Grund von Gewalt«; mit seinen schon von den »Vorvätern«, *maiores*, anerkannten *duo genera causarum*, zwei Arten von Gründen, Cic. pro Caec. 30,86) und das *i. de vi armata* (über Waffengewalt), jenes mit, dieses ohne Einrede des fehlerhaften Besitzes. *I.* richten sich entweder nur an eine der Parteien oder an beide (*i. simplicia, duplicia*): nur an eine die *i. exhibitoria* und *restitutoria*; teils an eine, teils an beide dagegen die *i. prohibitoria*, nur an eine etwa das *i. de migrando*, ferner das *i. ne quid in loco sacro fiat*, an beide Parteien *i. uti possidetis* und *i. utrubi* (Gai. inst. 4,157–160).

Der Wortlaut der *i.* enthält ihre Voraussetzungen, die der Magistrat nur summarisch geprüft hat. Ob sie tatsächlich vorliegen und dem *i.* zuwidergehandelt worden ist oder wird, ist daher zu diesem Zeitpunkt noch offen. Ggf. wird das Verfahren auf der Grundlage von Formeln des Praetors vor dem Richter (→ *iudex*, → *recuperatores*) fortgesetzt; es kann für den Zuwiderhandelnden mit einer Strafe (*poena*) enden (so immer im Verfahren mit Strafstipulationen, *per sponsionem*, nach *i. prohibitoria*, Gai. inst. 4,141) oder mit Freispruch oder Verurteilung (so im Verfahren mit Klagformel auf Naturalleistung, *formula arbitraria*, nach *i. exhibitoria* und *restitutoria*, Gai. inst. 4,162–164). Das Verfahren *per sponsionem* ergänzen Klagen auf Wiedergutmachung: das *iudicium Cascellianum sive secutorium* und das *iudicium de re restituenda vel exhibenda* (Gai. inst. 4,165,166a,169). Gegen eine Verweigerung der Mitwirkung an der Durchführung dieses Verfahrens hilft das *i. secundarium* (Gai. inst. 4,170).

Gegen E. der Republik wird der Schutz gegen gewaltsame Eingriffe in den Besitz verschärft. Schon das *i. de vi armata* schützt auch den fehlerhaften Besitzer (s.o.). 76 v. Chr. führt der Praetor M. Lucullus für Fälle der Schädigung durch bewaffnete oder zusammengerottete Leute eine Strafklage ein (Cic. Tull. 3,7–5,11; 13,31). Eine *lex Iulia de vi armata* des Augustus bedroht die außergerichtliche Selbsthilfe mit Kriminalstrafe (Mod. Dig. 48,7,8; Inst. Iust. 4,15,6); ein Dekret des Marc Aurel ordnet darüber hinaus den Verlust etwa bestehender Ansprüche des Täters an (Callimachus Dig. 4,2,13 = 48,7,7).

Seit der nachklass. Zeit (ab Mitte 3. Jh.) gehen die *i.* in den *actiones* (→ *actio*) auf. Das wichtigste *i. unde vi* wird in einem Zivilprozeß erlangt und als »vorläufige Klage« (*actio momentaria*) o.ä. bezeichnet. Constantin schafft 319 die Einrede des fehlerhaften Besitzes ab (Cod. Theod. 9,10,3). Unter Constantin schreitet auch die Kriminalisierung von Gewaltakten fort (Cod. Theod. 9,10,1 = Cod. Iust. 9,12,6; Cod. Theod. 9,10,2); so verliert der Selbsthilfe verübende Eigentümer sein Eigentum an den *fiscus* (Cod. Theod. 9,10,3). Iustinian behält die nachklass. Neuerungen bei und verknüpft die kriminelle Verfolgung mit dem Interdiktenverfahren (Cod. Iust. 9,12,7; Inst. Iust. 4,15,6). Das Verfahren ist jetzt die *actio* des allg. Zivilprozesses (Inst. Iust. 4,15 pr.; 8).

A. BERGER, s. v. I., RE 9, 1609–1707 • HONSELL/MAYER-MALY/SELB, 551–553 • KASER, RPR I 396–400, 472, 740; II 256–261 • M. KASER, K. HACKL, Das röm. Zivilprozeßrecht, [2]1997, 408–421, 637f. • O. LENEL, Das Edictum perpetuum, 1927 (Ndr. 1974), 446–500 (Tit. XLIII De interdictis) • WIEACKER, RRG, 249–251.

D.SCH.

Interesse. Das *i.*, der Schadenersatz, wurde bei Vertragsverletzungen im röm. Recht häufig nach dem Interesse des Klägers an der ordnungsgemäßen Erfüllung (*quod eius interest*) bemessen. Zur Berechnung griffen die röm. Juristen weder auf starre Richtlinien noch auf einen schematischen Vermögensvergleich (sog. Differenzmethode) zurück, sondern ermittelten das *i.* nach den konkreten Umständen des Falles. Einbezogen wurden dabei z. B. der Wert der nicht geleisteten Sache, der Minderwert einer mangelhaften Sache, die durch den Verzug verursachten Nachteile, die Kosten eines Dekkungsgeschäftes, ein entgangener Gewinn oder mittelbare Schäden. Auch die Schadensberechnung nach dem 3. Kap. der → *lex Aquilia* stellte auf das *i.* ab.
→ Damnum

HONSELL/MAYER-MALY/SELB, 224–228 • R. ZIMMERMANN, The Law of Obligations, 1990, 824–833, 961f.

R.GA.

Interkalation s. Kalender

Interkolumnium s. Joch, s. Säule

Interpolation. Mit I. wird üblicherweise jede Einwirkung auf den Text bezeichnet, die nicht rein mechanische Ursachen hat, sondern die durch Schreiber oder Leser bewußt (oder weniger bewußt) vorgenommen wurde, bes. die Hinzufügung fremden Textes, doch auch die Änderung einzelner Wörter (vgl. aber [5]). Eine weitere Möglichkeit des Eingriffs ist das Auslassen oder Löschen von Textteilen durch die Schreiber.

I. ist eine häufige Erscheinung in der Textwiss. Man kann mit TARRANT drei Kategorien der I. im Sinne der Einfügung bezeichnen: Kollaboration (oder »Imitation«), Emendation (d. h. Ersatz eines verderbten Textes) und Anmerkung (unterteilt in »Glosse«, »Komm.« und »Zitat«) [13]. Leser verschönerten den Text, Theaterschauspieler brachten an einem etablierten

Werk Verbesserungen an. Leser bemerkten Fehler (oder was sie als solche ansahen) in Metrik, Grammatik, Stil oder Gedankengang und versuchten sie zu verbessern. Mißfallende Textpassagen wurden zensiert (gerade hierdurch entstanden Auslassungen). Wurden Textteile wiederholt, erweiterte man den Umfang der Wiederholung (»Konkordanz-I.«). Komm., Glossen oder Parallelstellen wurden in einer späteren Phase in den Lesetext selbst hineingeschrieben. Insbesondere Fachliteratur wurde als lebendiger Text angesehen; jede Generation paßte somit den Inhalt an ihre Bedürfnisse an oder erweiterte ihn (z. B. → Eukleides' ›Elementenlehre‹; vgl. → Auflage, zweite).

Bereits die Erwähnung Athens im homer. Schiffskatalog (Hom. Il. 2,546 ff.) war ein Problem für die ant. Gelehrten, und die Bürger von Megara beschuldigten die Athener, den Text der Zeilen 557–558 verändert zu haben. Allg. bieten die exzentrischen (»wilden«) homer. Papyri aus ptolemäischer Zeit eine große Zahl zusätzlicher Verse, die in der späteren Tradition nicht mehr erscheinen ([15]; allg. [1]).

Schauspieler und Produzenten bearbeiteten seit dem 4. Jh. v. Chr. tragische Texte (etwa die vieldiskutierte Stelle Soph. Ai. 1028–1039; zu Sophokles generell [6], zu Euripides [9]). Auch schrieb man sehr oft erklärende Glossen in den trag. Text hinein (in Aischyl. Ag. 549 z. B. hat die Hs. *F* τυράννων, eine Glosse zu dem von Triklinios wiederhergestellten κοιράνων). Die sog. »Binnen-I.« (die darin besteht, daß vermutlich eingefügte Textteile inmitten eines Verses beginnen und enden) liegt erstaunlich häufig vor: bei Soph. Oid. K. 1321 f. ist dies nachweisbar, weil die zweifelhaften Wörter in einem wichtigen Überlieferungszweig fehlen. In den Komödientexten dagegen wurde wohl weniger interpoliert: vgl. jedoch die Unordnung am Ende von Aristophanes' ›Fröschen‹, wo die nicht zusammen passenden Varianten eine Einfügung des Autors selbst vermuten lassen (→ Autorenvariante). Eine weitreichende I. des überlieferten Plautus-Textes hat O. Zwierlein nachzuweisen versucht ([19] und spätere Publikationen).

In Prosatexten dagegen sind Zusätze und Veränderungen gewöhnlich schwerer auszumachen, insbes. bei Autoren mit langatmigem Stil (informative Diskussion eines bes. komplizierten Textes bei [10]; s. auch für lat. Texte die Petronius-Edd. von [11] und die Bemerkungen von [12]).

In Prosa und Dichtung gleichermaßen muß man mit ant. oder ma. Lesern rechnen, die eine Alternative oder Verbesserung zur überlieferten Lesart beisteuern – eine Folge u. a. der rhet. orientierten Ausbildung [6; 17]. Dies gilt auch für die lat. Dichtung, wie Tarrant feststellt: Die für Erweiterungen bes. »anfälligen« Texte sind »rhet.« Natur – Ovid, Senecas Tragödien und Iuvenal ([14] mit kurzem einleitenden Abriß der »Jagd« nach I.). Insbes. für Iuvenal steht nach langer Diskussion [3; 7; 8; 12] eine weitreichende I. fest [16]. Hexameter unterlagen der I. mehr als Lyrik, doch wagten sich offenbar vereinzelte Leser auch an schwierigere Metren (vgl. Hor. carm. 3,11,17–20 und 4,8; Catull. 61,92–96, entfernt durch [4]).

Die Bekanntheit der vergilischen Dichtung führte zu häufiger Konkordanz-I. (z. B. Verg. Aen. 3,230: die Wiederholung von 1,311 wurde dadurch angeregt, daß die letzten Wörter von 1,310 *sed rupe cavata* auch in 3,229 erscheinen). Gerade die Halbverse der *Aeneis* wurden oft vervollständigt: die Worte *de collo fistula pendet* (Verg. Aen. 3,661) wären eine schöne Ergänzung zur Darstellung des Polyphemos als eine Figur der theokriteischen Pastorale, wenn sie nicht in den Majuskel-Hss. fehlten. Doch erhalten andererseits Herausgeber den Text Verg. Aen. 11,309 in vollem Umfang, trotz des anomalen Rhythmus von *ponite* vor *spes* (Burgess und Porson tilgten die letzten acht Wörter).

Christl. Glaube und Wissen der Leser führten etwa zur kaum überraschenden Wandlung des Flusses Iardanos (Hom. Il. 7,135) in den Jordan im A-Schol. z. Stelle. Auch Fälle von Zensur entsprangen – allerdings eher selten – dieser Geisteshaltung [18]. So bieten die Properz-Hss. eine Reihe kleinerer, aber bezeichnender Fälle von Textverderbnis, die wahrscheinlich der Prüderie eines Schreibers oder Lesers zuzuschreiben sind: In Prop. 2,31,3, fehlt das Epitheton *Poenis* (in ma. Hss. meistens *penis* geschrieben) in den von Petrarcas verlorener Abschrift abhängigen Hss. *F* und *L*; in Prop. 4,4,47 ist Palmers *potabitur* der beste Ersatz für das im Kontext sinnlose *pugnabitur*.

1 M. J. Apthorp, The Manuscript Evidence for I. in Homer, 1980 **2** W. V. Clausen (ed.), A. Persi Flacci et D. Iuni Iuvenalis Saturae, 1959 **3** E. Courtney, The interpolations in Iuvenal, in: BICS 22, 1975, 147–162 **4** B. Georg, Catullus 61.90–6, in: CQ 46, 1996, 302–304 **5** H. C. Günther, Quaestiones Propertianae, 1997, 96 **6** Ders., Exercitationes Sophocleae, 1997 **7** G. Jachmann, Studien zu Juvenal (Nachr. der Akad. der Wiss. in Göttingen, philol.-histor. Kl.), 1943, 187–266 **8** U. Knoche (Ed.), D. Iunius Iuvenalis, Satirae, 1950 **9** D. J. Mastronarde (Ed.), Euripides, Phoenissae, 1994, 39–49 **10** K. Maurer, I. in Thucydides, 1995 **11** K. Müller (Ed.), Petronius, 1983 **12** R. G. M. Nisbet, in: JRS 52, 1962, 227–238 (Rez. und Diskussion von [2] und [11]; = Ders., Collected Papers, 1995, 16–28, vgl. dort auch 283–284 **13** R. J. Tarrant, Towards a typology of i. in Latin poetry, in: TAPhA 117, 1987, 281–298 **14** Ders., The reader as author: collaborative i. in Latin poetry, in: J. N. Grant (Hrsg.), Editing Greek and Latin Texts, 1989, 121–162, hier: 158–162 **15** S. R. West, The Ptolemaic papyri of Homer, 1969, 12–13 **16** J. Willis (ed.), D. Iuni Iuvenalis Saturae selectae, 1997 **17** N. G. Wilson, Variant readings with poor support in the manuscript tradition, in: Révue d'histoire des textes 17, 1987, 1–13 (bes. 8 ff.) **18** Ders., Scholars of Byzantium, [2]1996, 12–18, 276 **19** O. Zwierlein, Zur Kritik und Exegese des Plautus I (AAWM 4), 1990.

N. W. u. S. H./Ü: J. DE.

Interpolationenkritik. Mit I. bezeichnet man in der röm. Rechtsgesch. v. a. die Unt. der Texte des *Corpus Iuris* in der überlieferten Fassung auf Verfälschungen gegenüber dem Original. In bes. Maße betrifft dies die Frg. aus den Schriften klass. Juristen (1. Jh. v. Chr. – 3. Jh. n. Chr.) in den → *Digesta*, aber auch die → *Institutiones* im Vergleich zu ihren Vorlagen und sogar die älteren Kaisergesetze, die im → *Codex Iustinianus* zusammengestellt worden sind. Hinsichtlich der Digesten gab Kaiser Iustinian selbst schon in seinem Auftrag an die Gesetzgebungskommission aus dem J. 530 (Const. Deo auctore §§ 4/10) ausdrücklich die Anweisung, die Texte zu »bereinigen«, nämlich veraltete Rechtsinstitutionen wegzulassen oder durch modernere Entsprechungen zu ersetzen, eigene Gesetzgebungsentscheidungen Iustinians einzuarbeiten, Fälle und Regeln zu verknappen oder in verallgemeinernde Sätze zu bringen und Streit unter den Juristen zu tilgen, so daß aus einem größeren Diskussionszusammenhang jeweils nur eine einzige Auffassung übrig blieb. Die Aufgabe der I. besteht zunächst darin, diese Veränderungen gegenüber den Vorlagen in den Digestentexten aufzuspüren. Darüber hinaus ist die I. erforderlich, um Veränderungen der Texte herauszuarbeiten, wie sie sich geradezu selbstverständlich aus der Länge der Überlieferungszeit zwischen dem Entstehen der Originalwerke, vor allem im 2. und beginnenden 3. Jh. n. Chr., und deren Verwendung im *Corpus Iuris* ergeben haben. Diese Art der Textverderbnis ist gelegentlich auch an den wenigen außerhalb des *Corpus Iuris* auf uns gekommenen Sammlungen und Einzelwerken, insbes. den → *Institutiones* des → Gaius [2], zu beobachten.

Die I. seit dem → HUMANISMUS, vor allem aber in der → RECHTSGESCHICHTE (ROMANISTIK) seit dem ausgehenden 19. Jh. ist selbst ein wesentlicher Teil der Wirkungs- und Wissenschaftsgesch. des röm. Rechts. Für eine Reihe von Sammlungen und Werken lassen sich heute aufgrund genauer, teilweise computergestützter Analysen »Lebensgesch.« des Textes rekonstruieren (sog. Textstufenforschung); mit ihnen ist die I. wesentlich verfeinert worden. Der 1929–1935 erschienene Interpolationsindex ([1], vgl. [2]) repräsentiert demgegenüber aus heutiger Sicht eher eine Fülle scharfsinniger Sachkritik am Inhalt der Texte als methodisch gesicherte I. Teilweise betrachtet man die vorhandene Überlieferung inzw. wieder sehr konservativ (repräsentativ [3]). Mit äußerst differenziertem histor.-philol. Methodenbewußtsein (vgl. insbes. [4]) wird man aber die I. stets bei der Quellenarbeit am röm. Recht berücksichtigen müssen.

→ INTERPOLATIONENFORSCHUNG

1 E. LEVY (Hrsg.), Index interpolationum quae in Iustiniani Digestis inesse dicuntur I, 1929, II, 1931, III 1935, Suppl. I, 1929 2 G. BRUGGINI (Hrsg.), Index Interpolationum quae in Iustiniani Codice inesse dicuntur, 1969 3 M. KASER, Zur Methodik der röm. Rechtsquellenforsch., 1974
4 WIEACKER, RRG, 154–182. G.S.

Interpretatio I. RECHT II. RELIGION

I. RECHT
A. BEGRIFF B. INTERPRETATIO UND GESETZ
C. INTERPRETATIO ALS RECHTSQUELLE
D. METHODEN E. INTERPRETATIO VON RECHTSGESCHÄFTEN
F. DAS INTERPRETATIONSVERBOT DER SPÄTANTIKE

A. BEGRIFF

I. ist die Auslegung von Texten, aber auch von mündlichen Erklärungen und von sonstigen rechtserheblichen Fakten. Der Topos einfacher Wahrheit, die keines Vermittlers bedarf (Petron. 107,15), gilt nicht für das Spezialwissen von Astrologen (vgl. → Divination), Philologen (zu beiden: Cic. div. 1,34; 2,92) und Juristen (Cic. leg. 2,59). Am Ende der Republik verdichten sich die Worte *interpres* (»Ausleger«) und *interpretari* (»Auslegen«) zum Abstraktum *i.* [3. 80ff., 91ff.], so für die Rechtsdeutung bereits der Könige (Cic. rep. 5,3) und der Priester (Dig. 1,2,2,6), dann der Säkularjurisprudenz (Cic. de orat. 1,199), des Richters (Cic. Cluent. 146), schließlich des Praetors (Dig. 46,5,9). Im ersten röm. jur. Komm.-Werk, den *Tripertita* des Sex. → Aelius [I 11] Petus Catus (um 200 v. Chr.), folgt dem Text des Zwölftafelgesetzes dessen *i.* Man kennt außer der *i. iuris* auch die *i. legum, edicti* oder *senatus consulti*. Laut Pomponius (Dig. 1,2,2,12) ist aber die *i. prudentium* mit dem *sine scripto* (ungeschrieben) geschaffenen (Dig. 1,2,2,5) *ius civile* »im eigentlichen Sinne« identisch.

B. INTERPRETATIO UND GESETZ

Die neuzeitlichen Konzepte der wiss. Auslegung haben die rechtspolit. Rolle der röm. *i.* als Gesetzgebungsersatz verdunkelt. Schon in Rom umfaßte die »Gesetzeskenntnis« über den Wortlaut hinaus »Sinn und Zweck der Gesetze« (*legum vis ac potestas*, Dig. 1,3,17). Der Satz *clara non sunt interpretanda* (»Klares bedarf keiner *i.*«) war noch unbekannt: Da selbst die »evidenten« Edikte (Dig. 25,4,1,11) der *i.* bedurften, wurde die *verborum i.* (Wort-*i.*) zum Kern des Ediktkomm. (Dig. 12,1,1 pr.).

Angesichts der geringen Rolle der Legislation vollzog sich die Rechtsänderung im Prinzipat hauptsächlich durch den Interpretationswechsel, der auf die jurist. Logik mit ihrem Anknüpfungsdenken angewiesen war. Zw. Rechtssicherheit und Billigkeit war nur eine graduelle Rechtsfortbildung durch Interpretation der Interpretation, unter Voraussetzung der Fortgeltung alten Rechts, möglich: *minime sunt mutanda, quae interpretationem certam semper habuerunt* (›auf keinen Fall darf geändert werden, was immer eine feste Auslegung gehabt hat‹, Dig. 1,3,23). Auch das gesetzte Recht paßte man nur in kleinen Schritten an: *optima legum interpres consuetudo* (›die beste *i.* der Gesetze ist die Gewohnheit‹, Dig. 1,3,37). Freilich stellte man in versteckter Rechtskritik den histor. Gesetzgeber zugunsten des »rationalen« zurück. Man bediente sich dazu nicht nur der Auslegung »nach dem Sinn« (*ex sententia*), sondern auch der Textumdeutung durch die sog. identifizierende Interpretation, die mit Hilfe von *intellegitur, videtur* (»man versteht darunter«) oder *continetur* (»enthalten ist darin«) in alte Begriffe einen neuen Inhalt hineinverlegte [2. 42 ff.]: Diese mit dem Text zusammenwachsende *i.* [7. 287] verschmolz Buchstabe und Geist zu einer Einheit.

C. Interpretatio als Rechtsquelle

Die jurist. *i.*, die dem Volk sein Recht typischerweise in Form von → *responsa* (Gutachten) vermittelt (Cic. leg. 1,14: *interpretari et responsitare*; vgl. Dig. 34,1,20,1), beruht auf ihrer formalisierten Kompetenz und auf spezifischen Methoden. Die Interpretationskompetenz der → *pontifices* ergab sich aus ihrer Priesterweihe, die der spätrepublikanischen Jurisprudenz aus ihrer Honoratiorenstellung (→ *iuris prudentia*) und die der Prinzipatsjurisprudenz aus der → *auctoritas principis*. Volle Geltung erlangte die *i.* aber erst mit dem Konsens der Interpretengemeinschaft [8. 81 ff.], ausgedrückt mit *a plerisque respondetur* (›von den meisten wird begutachtet‹) oder *placet/placuit* (›ist anerkannt‹). Auf dieses Kollektiv beziehen sich in den röm. Katalogen von Rechtsquellen Pomponius' *i.*, Gaius' (inst. 1,2) *responsa* und Papinians (Dig. 1,1,7 pr.) *auctoritas prudentium*.

D. Methoden

Die jurist. *i.* richtete sich, anders als von der Rhet. nahegelegt [2. 22 ff.; 6. 669 ff.], nicht auf den histor. Gesetzgeber, sondern auf den »rationalen« Gesetzeswillen (Dig. 1,3,18). Deshalb folgte sie methodisch, gelegentlich von der *cognitio* (Erkenntnis) abgesetzt (Cic. off. 2,65), dem eigenständigen Regelkanon der juristischen Logik, die das Recht durch Analogie-, Größen-, Umkehr- und Absurditätsschlüsse fallgemäß zu »verbessern« vermochte. Als Ziel geben die Prinzipatsjuristen die Präzisierung des gesetzten Rechts an (Dig. 1,3,11 *certius statuere*, »genauer bestimmen«) sowie weitergehend dessen Unterstützung (Dig. 35,1,64,1 *adiuvari*), Ergänzung (Dig. 1,3,13 *suppleri*), Ausdehnung »auf Ähnliches« (*ad similia*, Dig. 1,3,12) und Vervollkommnung (Dig. 23,5,4 *plenius* oder Dig. 1,4,3 *plenissime interpretari*). Die *i.* umfaßt sowohl die Restriktion (Dig. 50,16,120 *interpretatione coangustatum*) als auch die Analogie (Gai. inst. 1,165).

Von der Auslegungsfreiheit zeugt die Formel *aliter interpretantibus* (Dig. 18,1,77; 18,1,80 pr.; 34,2,39 pr.), mit der man eine alternative *i.* wegen ihrer unannehmbaren Folgen verwirft. Mit vielen wertbezogenen Adjektiven (wie *durior, severa* für Härte, *benignior, humanior* für Milde) orientiert man sich am Ergebnis. Die *i.* dient dem Nachteilsausgleich (Dig. 13,5,17 *aequum est succurri reo ... iusta i.*, ›es ist gerecht, dem Beklagten mit rechter *i.* zu helfen‹); Strafgesetze deutet man *benignius* (»wohlwollender«) zugunsten des Angeklagten (vgl. Dig. 50,17,155,2), Freilassungen zugunsten der Freiheit (z.B. Dig. 40,5,24,10: *favor libertatis suadet, ut interpretemur*, ›der Vorrang der Freiheit rät uns zur *i.*‹). Die Auslegung zugunsten des Mündels heißt *propter utilitatem benignior* (Gai. inst. 3,109) oder *pro favore pupillorum latior i. facta* (Dig. 22,1,1,3).

Die bereits der altröm. Wortauslegung eigentümliche Kreativität bezeugen die sog. nachgeformten Rechtsgeschäfte der Priesterjurisprudenz [6. 330 ff., 581 ff.]. Vor diesem Hintergrund tadelt Q. → Mucius Pontifex die »Perversion« von *scripta simplicium* (›Geschriebenem der einfach Denkenden‹) durch eine *i. disertorum* (*i.* der Wortgewandten, Cic. Brut. 196), Cicero die spitzfindige *i. malitiosa*, die das *summum ius* (»das höchste Recht«) zur *summa iniuria* (»zum höchsten Unrecht«) werden läßt (off. 1,33).

E. Interpretatio von Rechtsgeschäften

Die Rechtsgeschäfte handhabte man grundsätzlich ebenso wie das gesetzte Recht [6. 330, 580], nämlich – vom sog. konkludenten Verhalten (Dig. 23,3,30; 28,4,2; dazu [4. 260, 269 f.] abgesehen – als einen Normtext im Spannungsfeld zw. Gesagtem und Gewolltem. Zwar war hier der Rückgriff auf die *voluntas* (»Willen«) über die vom *communis usus* (»allg. Gebrauch«) abweichende *opinio singulorum* (»Einzelmeinung«, Dig. 33,10,7,1 f.) eher möglich (dazu [4. 253, 256; 6. 653 f., 672 f.]), der sog. interpretative Formalismus wurde aber auch hier bis zum Ende des Prinzipats nicht völlig überwunden [1. 34 ff., 92 ff., 155 ff.; 6. 581]. Selbst bei Testamenten hatte der eindeutige Wortlaut (Dig. 32,29 pr. *verborum i.*) Vorrang. Erst recht bürdete die dem Vertrauensschutz verpflichtete Auslegung der Geschäfte unter Lebenden (Dig. 50,16,125 *ad id quod actum est interpretationem redigendam*: ›die *i.* zu dem hinzuführen, was verhandelt worden ist‹) dem Erklärenden die Selbstverantwortung auf [4. 264]: Ein unklares *pactum* deutete man *contra venditorem* (»gegen den Verkäufer«, Dig. 50,17,172 pr.), die Stipulation *contra stipulatorem* (»gegen den Versprechensempfänger«, Dig. 45,1,38,18) oder *secundum promissorem* (»zugunsten des Versprechenden«, Dig. 45,1,99 pr.).

F. Das Interpretationsverbot der Spätantike

Wegen der großen Bedeutung der *i.* bezeichnet man das Recht der Prinzipatszeit als Juristenrecht [6. 495 ff.]. In dessen Umwelt war auch der Princeps nur ein Rechtsinterpret [5. 379 ff.], der dem Mehrheitsvotum der Interpretengemeinschaft folgte [7. 149 ff.] und in das Privatrecht nur punktuell eingriff [7. 168 f.]. In der Spätant. gipfelt aber der kaiserliche Patronat über die *i.* in einem Interpretationsmonopol: Seit Diocletianus (ab 284 n. Chr.) wurde die interpretative Rechtsfindung durch die obrigkeitliche Rechtsfixierung verdrängt [1. 362 f.]. Der spätant. Beamte pflegte die Kaisergesetze eher »anzubeten« (*venerari*) als zu interpretieren (Symm. rel. 30,4; dazu [5. 389, 403]). Die *Interpretationes* zum → *Codex Theodosianus* und zu den *Pauli Sententiae* (→ Iulius [IV 16] Paulus) sind westgot. Ursprungs (→ *Lex Romana Visigothorum*). Constantin d. Gr. verbot die zw. Recht und Billigkeit »vermittelnde« *i.* (*interposita i.*, Cod. Theod. 1,2,3; dazu [5. 392 f., 404]); Marcianus verläßt sich nur auf die *imperatoria i.* (Nov. Marciana 4 pr.; dazu [8. 163 f.]); Iustinian nennt die Interpreten eine Streitquelle und untersagt die *legum interpretationes*

(Const. Tanta § 21) als *perversiones* [3. 98; 5. 405f.]: Zulässig war nur die sog. authentische Interpretation durch den Kaiser selbst als den alleinigen »Schöpfer wie Interpret der Gesetze« (*tam conditor quam interpres legum*, Cod. Iust. 1,14,12,5).

1 Schulz **2** U. Wesel, Rhet. Statuslehre und die Gesetzesauslegung der röm. Juristen, 1967 **3** M. Fuhrmann, I., in: Sympotica F. Wieacker, 1970, 80–110 **4** P. Voci, Interpretazione del negozio giuridico, Enciclopedia del Diritto 22, 1972, 252–277 **5** J. Gaudemet, Études de droit romain I, 1979, 375–409 **6** Wieacker, RRG **7** M. Bretone, Gesch. des röm. Rechts, 1992 **8** F. Gallo, Interpretazione e formazione consuetudinaria del diritto, ²1993.

T.G.

II. Religion

Interpretatio Graeca (I.G.)/Interpretatio Romana (I.R.) ist die bei Griechen und Römern verbreitete Identifikation einer fremden Gottheit mit einem Mitglied des eigenen Pantheons. Ant. belegt ist der Terminus I.R. in Zusammenhang mit germanischen Göttern in Tacitus' *Germania* (Kap. 43). Analog hierzu verwendet die heutige Wissenschaft für das griech. Phänomen den Ausdruck I.G. Die (wenig erforschte) Erscheinung ist urspr. Zeichen für den selbstverständlichen Umgang polytheistischer Systeme miteinander; sie wird sekundär zur Feststellung des Ursprungs der Götter und zum Ausdruck henotheistischer Tendenzen benutzt.

In ihrer eigentlichen Form behandelt die I.G./I.R. Theonyme wie Appellativa, übersetzt also einen Götternamen aus der fremden in die eigene Sprache; analog können in bilinguen Texten Anthroponyme aus der einen in die andere Sprache übersetzt werden (lyd. Bakivalis = griech. *Dionysiklēs*). Das ist bereits durch altoriental. sumerisch-akkadische Götterlisten gesichert, welche sich in die lexikographische Trad. der altorientalischen Schreiberkulturen einordnen. Im Griech. ist dies durch die Übernahme vorderoriental. Mythen(motive) in die Göttermythologie von Anfang an vorauszusetzen; der hesiodeische Sukzessionsmythos etwa legt die Gleichsetzung von → Uranos mit Anu, → Kronos mit Enki (oder dem hethit. Kumarbi), → Zeus mit → Marduk (oder dem hethit. Wettergott) nahe. Explizit ist die I.G. dann bei Herodot, der regelmäßig auch für nichtgriech. Götter griech. Götternamen verwendet [1], in seltenen Fällen den fremden Namen als → Epiklese gebraucht (Zeus Belos in Babylon, Hdt. 1,181,2). Ausnahmen sind nicht nur möglich, wenn eine Gottheit keine Entsprechung findet (etwa Ianus im Griech., der pers. Mithras im griech.-röm. Westen), sondern auch, wenn die betreffende Gottheit in ihrem indigenen Namen überlokal bekannt ist, sei es dank ihrer Bed., sei es, daß der Kult in fremder Umgebung durch seine urspr. Verehrer weitergeführt wird oder daß die Verehrung unter dem indigenen Namen eine zusätzliche Bed. erhält. So verwendet Herodot die Namen von Isis und Osiris, obwohl er die Übersetzung als Demeter und Dionysos anerkennt (Hdt. 2,59,2, vgl. 2,42,2); in Athen behält die von den Thrakern verehrte → Bendis trotz ihrer I.G. als Artemis gewöhnlich ihren indigenen Namen, und die seit hell. Zeit verbreiteten Mysterien der → Isis bauen, wie die späteren des → Mithras, auf der exotischen Färbung auf, die durch Beibehaltung des Namens erreicht wird.

Bei der Hellenisierung bzw. Romanisierung der ant. Mittelmeerwelt erfährt die I.G./I.R. die Ausweitung, daß lokale indigene Gottheiten auch im Kult mit ihrer griech. bzw. lat. Entsprechung benannt werden, und zwar auch von den lokalen Verehrern, wie Bilinguen aus Lydien oder Lykien zeigen. Die lokalen Besonderheiten werden in der Differenzierung durch Epiklesen aufgefangen; das gilt für das hellenisierte Anatolien nicht anders als für das romanisierte Gallien [2]. Umgekehrt ist auch die I.G./I.R. einer Gottheit der politisch dominanten Macht in den Termini der Eroberten belegt, so im Fall eines griech. verfaßten Sakralgesetzes für pers. Kult aus der Zeit der pers. Besetzung von Sardis, in dem durchweg von Zeus die Rede ist [3].

Die Gründe, die zu einer bestimmten I. führen, sind keineswegs einheitlich und nicht immer leicht feststellbar, wie der Vergleich der herodoteischen Identifikationen mit den entsprechenden Gottheiten zeigt; in jedem Fall werden einzelne Züge des Rituals, gelegentlich auch des Mythos herausgegriffen. Unter dem Druck einer dominanten rel. Kultur können lokale Besonderheiten, die nicht in die I. aufgenommen wurden, im Laufe der Zeit zurücktreten oder gar verschwinden, wie dies mit den meisten röm. und wohl auch mit zahlreichen kelt. Göttern geschehen ist. – Gewöhnung an die I. führt auch dazu, daß in den griech. oder lat. Texten die Verwendung des indigenen Namens so speziell ist, daß sie den Interpreten regelmäßig große Probleme aufgibt; das zeigt sich bes. schön an der Vielfalt der Scholien zum Katalog der kelt. Götter mit Menschenopfern bei Lucan. 1,445 [4].

Herodot bezeugt auch die erste Weiterführung der I.G. zu einer Diffusionshypothese von Riten und Götternamen: demnach kamen fast alle Namen der griech. Götter ebenso wie ihre Riten von den Ägyptern zu den → Pelasgern und von diesen zu den Griechen (Hdt. 2,50–52). Eine solche Herleitung hält sich in Teilbereichen bis in die Spätant., wenn etwa Iamblichos die »wahren« Götternamen, die im magischen und theurgischen Ritual verwendet werden, aus dem Ägypt. und Assyr. als den Sprachen, die den Göttern am nächsten seien, herleitet (Iambl. de myst. 7,4).

Die Zuspitzung einer solchen Diffusionshypothese führt, in einer wichtigen theologischen Entwicklung, zu henotheistischen Ansätzen [5]. Wenn die Namen übersetzbar sind, muß hinter den verschiedenen Namen eine einzige göttl. Essenz stehen. Dies ist bes. für den Kult der → Isis ausgearbeitet worden; sie wuchs im Lauf ihrer hell. und kaiserzeitl. Expansion zu einer umfassenden Göttin heran, der in Kult und Theologie die Epiklese Polyonymos (»vielnamig«) oder Myrionymus (»zehntausendnamig«) gegeben wurde; in einer langen Liste setzt Apul. met. 11,4 sie mit zahlreichen anderen Göttinnen gleich (vgl. auch Simpl. In Aristotelis Physica, CAG 9, 641,33).

I.G./I.R. ist mithin ein Phänomen im sprachlich-konzeptuellen Bereich. Sie kann Folgen für die Ikonographie haben: Die Ikonographie der fremden Gottheit kann die eigene verdrängen oder sie überhaupt erst schaffen – so übernehmen die etr. und röm. Gottheiten praktisch ausschließlich die Ikonographie ihrer griech. Entsprechungen. Umgekehrt kann trotz der Übernahme Wert darauf gelegt werden, indigene Attribute beizubehalten; dies trifft bes. auf den gallischen Raum zu.

1 W. Burkert, Herodot über die Namen der Götter: Polytheismus als histor. Problem, in: MH 42, 1985, 121–132 **2** G. Wissowa, Interpretatio Romana, in: ARW 19, 1918, 1–49 **3** L. Robert, Une nouvelle inscription grecque de Sardes. Règlement de l'autorité perse relatif au culte de Zeus, in: CRAI 1975, 306–330 **4** F. Graf, Menschenopfer in der Burgerbibliothek. Anmerkungen zum Götterkatalog der »Commenta Bernensia« zu Lucan 1,445, in: Arch. der Schweiz 14, 1991, 136–143 **5** H. S. Versnel, Inconsistencies in Greek and Roman Rel., Bd. 1: Ter Unus. Isis, Dionysos, Hermes. Three Studies in Henotheism, 1990. F. G.

Interpunktion s. Lesezeichen

Interregnum s. Interrex

Interrex (wörtl. »Zwischenkönig«). Der röm. Beamte, der bei Ausfall eines höchsten Amtsträgers die Wahl eines *suffectus* vorzunehmen hat. Das Wort und der nicht kollegiale Amtscharakter weisen auf eine Herkunft aus der Königszeit hin (Liv. 1,17,12; Cic. rep. 2,12,23; Plut. Numa 2). In der Republik tritt der *i.* ein, wenn durch den Tod beider Consuln das Oberamt vakant wird (*interregnum*) und Ersatzwahlen stattfinden müssen, die im Normalfall für Consuln ein noch amtierender Consul abhält. Dies beruht vor allem auf der Annahme, daß nur Consuln die Auspikation, bei der die Götter ihre Zustimmung zu dem Wahlakt geben, vornehmen können. Gibt es keinen Consul mehr, so erhält sich aber doch die Qualifikation zur Auspikation bei denjenigen, die jedenfalls zur Übernahme des Konsulats qualifiziert sind. Dies sind in der Frühzeit die patrizischen Senatoren des Senats. Auch später, als Plebejer das Konsulat bekleiden können, verbleibt die Qualifikation, die Auspizien der Consuln wieder aufleben zu lassen, bei den patrizischen Senatoren. So kehren bei Vakanz die Auspizien gleichsam zum Senat zurück (*auspicia ad patres redierant*, Liv. 1,32,1; Cic. leg. 3,4,9), dessen Aufgabe es nun ist, aus seinem Kreis eine Exekutive zu erzeugen, die ›nach Durchführung der Auspizien‹ (*auspicato*) die Wahlleitung für die Suffect-Wahl der Consuln übernehmen kann. Das geschieht in der Weise, daß die patrizischen Senatoren einen der ihren zum *i.* bestimmen, der nach fünftägiger Regierung einen anderen ernennt, der ebenfalls wiederum fünf Tage regiert und so fort, bis die Consulwahlen erledigt sind. Diese Wahlen werden unter Wegräumung aller verfassungsmäßigen Hindernisse schnellstens abgehalten, jedoch darf sie nicht der erste *i.* abhalten, wohl weil er als einziger in der Kette der *interreges* ohne Auspikation gewählt ist. Die Auffassung, daß der (patrizische) Senat die urspr. Quelle der höchsten Beamtengewalt ist, zu der bei Erledigung der höchsten Magistratur die Initiative zur Beamtenernennung zurückkehrt, ist wohl als der Reflex einer starken Abhängigkeit der Exekutive vom Senat aufzufassen. Der letzte *i.* fungiert im J. 52 v. Chr.; jedoch hat man noch 43 v. Chr. an die Möglichkeit eines Interregnums gedacht.

I. gibt es in Analogie zu Rom auch in den Munizipien bei Vakanz des höchsten Munizipalamtes; sie werden von Augustus durch Praefekten ersetzt.

→ Magistratus

A. Heuss, in: ZRG 64, 1944, 79 ff. • Mommsen, Staatsrecht 1 (3), 647–661 • P. Willems, Le Sénat de la république romaine, 1885 (2), 2, 10 ff. (Verzeichnis der *i.*). C. G.

Interrogatio meint allg. die Befragung vor Gericht und hat im röm. Strafprozeß des → *iudicium publicum* als *i. legibus* und im Zivilprozeß als *i. in iure* eine engere technische Bedeutung. Erstere bezeichnet die Frage an den Angeklagten, ob er sich schuldig bekenne; sie wird in den Quellen der späten röm. Republik mitunter geradezu als Bezeichnung für die Anklage der → *quaestio* verwendet. Mit der letzteren, der Befragung des Beklagten vor dem Gerichtsmagistrat, will der Kläger Klarheit über die Passivlegitimation schaffen, also darüber, ob er wirklich den richtigen Beklagten vor sich hat. Bes. Bedeutung hat diese *i. in iure*, der ein eigener Digestentitel (Dig. 11,1) gewidmet ist, im Fall der Klage gegen den Erben und im Fall der Noxalklage. Bei dieser muß sichergestellt werden, daß der Beklagte den Täter in seiner rechtlichen und tatsächlichen Gewalt hat, bei jener dagegen, ob und zu welchem Teil er sich als Erbe bekennt. Hat der Beklagte falsch geantwortet, so ist zu unterscheiden: Ist dadurch der Eindruck einer Haftung entstanden, die in Wirklichkeit gar nicht oder nicht so umfangreich besteht, wird er durch eigene *actiones interrogatoriae*, die die Richtigkeit der falschen Antwort fingieren, an ihr festgehalten. Hat er dagegen seine in Wahrheit bestehende Haftung ganz oder zum Teil geleugnet und kann dies der Kläger beweisen, treffen ihn Nachteile, die im allg. in einer Steigerung der Haftung bestehen.

M. Kaser, K. Hackl, Das röm. Zivilprozeßrecht, [2]1997, 251 ff. • M. Lemosse, Actiones interrogatoriae, in: Labeo 34, 1988, 7–17. A. VÖ.

Intertextualität A. Begriff
B. Intertextualität und klassische Philologie C. Produktions- und rezeptionsästhetisches Potential

A. Begriff

In den 1960er Jahren fand die Kritik an der werkimmanenten Interpretation lit. Texte als abgeschlossener Systeme ihren Ausdruck in der Rezeptionsästhetik von H. R. JAUSS und der von der Semiotikerin Julia KRISTEVA geprägten I. Beeinflußt wurde KRISTEVA von Michail BACHTINS Konzeption des lit. Textes als eines offenen Systems: Kein Text entsteht in einem soziohistor. Vakuum; er repräsentiert schon im Augenblick seiner Entstehung eine dialogische Auseinandersetzung mit anderen lit. wie nichtlit. Texten und stellt zugleich die (gebrochene) Verarbeitung gesellschaftlicher Realität dar. KRISTEVA radikalisierte diese Position; die traditionelle Interpretation des Textes als eines geschlossenen Systems mit einer einzigen festen Bed. ersetzte sie durch die Vorstellung des Textes als Intertext: Jeder Text sei bereits im Augenblick seiner Produktion ein Mosaik aus verschiedenen vorliegenden Texten und Zit. Er repräsentiere daher keine statische Entität, sondern sei ein Prozeß kontinuierlicher Produktivität, in dessen Verlauf andere (Prae-)Texte absorbiert und transformiert werden, sich überkreuzen und durchdringen. Die Beeinflussung des Textes durch vorliegende Praetexte resultiere in seiner Arbeit an sich selbst – und damit letzten Endes in einem permanenten Bed.-Wandel [9]. In Weiterführung von BACHTINS Position entgrenzte KRISTEVA nicht nur den immanenten Textbegriff – jedes kulturelle System, jede außerlit. Struktur und schließlich die Ges. als ganze wurde als »Text« definiert, der den Intertext durchdringt –, sondern sie ersetzte auch den in der traditionellen Textanalyse allmächtigen Autor durch die subjektlose Produktivität der Texte (der Einfluß des Strukturbegriffs der marxistisch orientierten Ges.-Theorie ist hier unverkennbar): Das Zeichen im Text, losgelöst von seinem referentiellen Signifikat, kommuniziert mit anderen Zeichen in einem potentiell unendlichen Prozeß der intertextuellen Kommunikation ohne Rückbindung an die Intentionalität des Subjekts/Autors.

B. INTERTEXTUALITÄT UND KLASSISCHE PHILOLOGIE

KRISTEVAS Programm des universalen Intertextes fand seine Fortführung im Dekonstruktionismus. Gleichzeitig wurde in kritischer Auseinandersetzung mit diesem universalistischen Ansatz die an den Bedürfnissen der Philologien orientierte textanalytische Methode einer spezifischen I. formuliert, welche die bewußten, intendierten und markierten Bezüge zwischen einem Text und vorliegenden lit. Praetexten beschreibt. Dieser deskriptive I.-Begriff macht nicht nur die Entgrenzung des Textbegriffes rückgängig, sondern behält gleichzeitig den Begriff der auktorialen Intentionalität bei. Wichtig ist, daß unter Unterscheidung einer produktionsästhetischen und einer rezeptionsästhetischen I. zwar an der relativen Offenheit der Sinnproduktion des lit. Textes festgehalten wird: Nicht alle vom Autor intendierten intertextuellen Bezüge müssen zum unmittelbaren Verständis des Textes vom Rezipienten erfaßt werden, ebenso wie der Rezipient aufgrund vorheriger Texterfahrungen intertextuelle Bezüge herstellt, die von der Produktionsseite nicht vorgegeben oder intendiert sind. In der Praxis versprach die I. damit zwar eine verfeinerte Methodik zur Beschreibung der Bezüge zwischen lit. Texten bereitzustellen [3; 7; 14], das Instrumentarium der Textanalyse war allerdings aus der traditionellen philol. Arbeit hinlänglich bekannt (Adaption, Allusion/Anspielung, Imitation, Parodie, Travestie, Übers., Zitat) – häufig zumal unter Aufgabe der für KRISTEVA zentralen Perspektive der textlichen Auseinandersetzung mit außerlit. Systemen [6; 12].

Die Intention des Autors sowie die Einheit des überl. Textes haben ihre Anziehungskraft auf die Klass. Philol. nicht eingebüßt. I. findet hier zumeist in ihrer eingeschränkten textanalytischen Form Anwendung bei der Analyse der Verarbeitung griech. Vorgänger und Modelle in der lat. Literatur. Mit dem I.-Begriff läßt sich aber auch die explizite oder implizite Bezugnahme lat. Autoren auf ihre röm. Vorgänger als Gattungsgesch. darstellen: etwa die Sukzessionsreihe Ennius – Lukrez – Vergil – Ovid – Lukan – Statius (→ Epos). Die Kompatibilität des Begriffes I. mit dem Vokabular der traditionellen philol. Arbeit (Allusion, Einfluß, *imitatio*, Nachleben, Quellenkritik) läßt manche Kritiker allerdings den Neuigkeitswert einer auf die ant. Texte applizierten I. bezweifeln.

C. PRODUKTIONS- UND REZEPTIONSÄSTHETISCHES POTENTIAL

Dieser schleichenden Nivellierung des I.-Begriffs sollte durch die Rückbesinnung auf sein produktions- wie rezeptionsästhetisches Potential begegnet werden. Unter Berufung auf das Konzept der μίμησις (→ *mímēsis*)/*imitatio* in Ant. und Renaissance untersucht eine traditionelle Philol. Anspielungen und Parallelen unter dem Gesichtspunkt der Imitation kanonischer Vorbilder. Wie die Gesch. der ant. Lit. gezeigt hat, führt diese klassizistische Lit.-Vorstellung häufig zur impliziten oder offenen Entwertung der Nachahmer als Epigonen. Im Gegensatz hierzu vermag I. die Textproduktion als eine – entweder affirmative oder subversiv negierende – Adaption und als Neubewertung vorliegender lit. Traditionen in einem gewandelten sozio-polit. Rahmen zu untersuchen: etwa die Uminterpretation des homer. Helden und der ep. Trad. durch Vergil vor dem Hintergrund der augusteischen Ges. [1; 10]; oder die intertextuelle Collage verschiedenster Textsorten in Senecas *Apocolocyntosis* [2]; oder die Adaption der vergilischen Trad. durch Ovid und die Autoren der sog. »Silbernen Latinität« nicht zum Zweck der *imitatio* eines lit. Kanons, sondern als kritische Infragestellung eben dieser Trad. [8].

Gleichzeitig problematisiert I. auch die Rezeptionsseite. In der klass. Trad. der Werk- und Autororientierung wird dem Text eine ästhetische Autonomie zuerkannt. Interpretationsziel ist die Rekonstruktion seiner Intention. Komplementär dazu läßt sich die Attraktivität der Rezeptionsästhetik von JAUSS mit deren Versuch erklären, einen histor. konkreten Horizont der Lesererwartung zu rekonstruieren. Aber wie für den Leser die Autorintention nicht unmittelbar zugänglich ist, so bleibt auch die Vorstellung eines homogenen Erwartungshorizonts einer histor. faßbaren Leserschaft heuristisch uneinlösbar [11; 13]. Zentrale Analysekategorie bleibt damit der Text als Intertext, als die Akkumulation und Aufbereitung früherer Texterfahrungen und -erwartungen, die weder vom Autor noch vom Leser vollständig gesteuert wird. Zwar hat sich die Maximalforderung des universalen und subjektlosen Intertextes für die Praxis nicht fruchtbar machen lassen. Trotzdem hat der I.-Begriff mit seinem Bild vom Text als Produktivität das Potential, die statischen Vorstellungen der traditionellen Lit.-Wiss. durch eine dynamische Produktions- und Rezeptionsästhetik, die auch die Ergebnisse der Produktions- und Lesepsychologie berücksichtigt, zu ersetzen.

1 A. BARCHIESI, La traccia del modello, 1984 **2** J. BLÄNSDORF, Senecas *Apocolocyntosis* und die I.-Theorie, in: Poetica 18, 1986, 1–26 **3** U. BROICH, M. PFISTER, I., 1985, 1–58 **4** G. B. CONTE, Memoria dei poeti e sistema letterario, ²1985 **5** Ders., A. BARCHIESI, Imitazione e arte allusiva, in: Dies. (Hrsg.), Lo spazio letterario di Roma antica, 1989, 1, 81–114 **6** O. ETTE, I., in: Romanist. Zeitschr. f. Lit.-Gesch. 9, 1985, 497–522 **7** J. HELBIG, I. und Markierung, 1996 **8** S. HINDS, Allusion and intertext. Dynamics of appropriation in Roman poetry, 1998 **9** J. KRISTEVA, Sémeiotiké, 1969 **10** R. O. A.M. LYNE, Further voices in Vergil's Aeneid, 1987 **11** Ders., Vergil's Aeneid: subversion by intertextuality, in: G&R 41, 1994, 187–204 **12** H.-P. MAI, Bypassing intertextuality, in: H. F. PLETT (Hrsg.), Intertextuality, 1991, 30–59 **13** R. R. NAUTA, Historicizing reading: the aesthetics of reception and Horace's 'Soracte Ode', in: I. DE JONG, J. P. SULLIVAN (Hrsg.), Modern critical theory and Classical literature, 1994, 207–230 **14** H. F. PLETT, Intertextualities, in: Ders. (Hrsg.), Intertextuality, 1991, 3–29. A.BEN.

Intestabilis. Im röm. Recht: rechtlich unfähig, Zeuge (*testis*) zu sein. In den Inst. Iust. (2,10,6) werden als *intestabiles* aufgezählt: Frauen, Unmündige, Sklaven, Stumme, Taube, Geisteskranke, entmündigte Verschwender und die von einem bes. Gesetz für *improbus* (unehrlich) und *i.* Erklärten. Solche gesetzlichen Anordnungen ergeben sich z. B. (nach Ulp. Dig. 47,10,5,9) aus der *l. Cornelia de iniuriis* gegen Verf. oder Verbreiter von Schriften mit beleidigendem Inhalt oder (nach Cassius Dig. 1,9,2) aus der *l. Iulia de repetundis* gegen die wegen Sittenlosigkeit aus dem Senat Entfernten. Schon die Zwölftafelgesetze (ca. 450 v. Chr.) verbanden *i.* mit der Unfähigkeit, ein → *testamentum* zu errichten (Gell. 15,13,11). G.S.

Intestatus. Ohne die Hinterlassung eines wirksamen Testaments Verstorbener. Der Nachlaß eines *i.* fiel nach röm. *ius civile* zuerst den → *sui heredes* an, sonst den gradnächsten agnatischen Verwandten (*agnati proximi*). *Sui* wurden nach den XII Tafeln (5. Jh. v. Chr.) mit dem Erbfall *heredes*, *agnati* erwarben nur das Vermögen (*familia*, XII 5.4) und wurden durch → *usucapio* Erben; im klass. Recht (1.–3. Jh. n. Chr.) wurden Agnaten durch → *aditio hereditatis* Erben. Agnatinnen ab dem 3. Grade hatten ab dem 2. Jh. v. Chr. kein Erbrecht (→ *lex Voconia*). Wenn alle *agnati proximi* ausschlugen, wurden nicht die gradferneren berufen; vielmehr fiel die Erbschaft den Gens-Angehörigen an. Das Erbrecht der Gentilen war noch im 1. Jh. v. Chr. lebendig (Suet. Caes. 1,1; Cic. de orat. 1,39,176), starb aber dann ab (Gai. inst. 3,17). Die Intestaterbschaft eines Freigelassenen fiel an seine *sui*, sonst an den *patronus* und seine agnatischen Abkömmlinge. → Latini Iuniani wurden nicht beerbt, da sie mit ihrem Tode wieder wie Sklaven angesehen wurden (Gai. inst. 3,56).

Seit der späten Republik schuf der Praetor eine neue Erbfolgeordnung, die teilweise das Zivilrecht verdrängte (→ *bonorum possessio*). Er berief (1) die *sui heredes* und zugleich die emanzipierten Kinder, welche durch Emanzipation aus dem Agnatenverband ausgetreten waren (*liberi*), (2) die zivilen Intestaterben (*legitimi*: *sui* und *agnati*), (3) die Blutsverwandten bis zum 6. Grade sowie die Kinder von *sobrini* (von denselben Urgroßeltern abstammende Urenkel, → *cognati*), (4) den *patronus* und die Patronsabkömmlinge (*familia patroni*) sowie (5) den *patronus* eines selbst freigelassenen *patronus* und seine Kinder und Eltern (*patronus patroni*), (6) den Ehegatten (*vir et uxor*), (7) die Kognaten des *patronus* (*cognati manumissoris*). Für jede Klasse galten Antragsfristen; wer den Antrag in einer Klasse versäumt hatte, konnte ihn in einer weiteren, zu der er berufen war, stellen (*sui* z. B. in den Klassen der *liberi, legitimi* und *cognati*).

Die *lex Papia* (9 n. Chr.) gab einem Patron eines wohlhabenden Freigelassenen sowie einer Patronin und Patronstochter mit *ius liberorum* (Kinderprivileg) ziviles Erbrecht neben den *sui* eines Freigelassenen (Gai. inst. 3,42; 46; 50). Das *SC Tertullianum* (unter Hadrian) gab einer Mutter (die, wenn sie → *manus*-frei war, kein ziviles Erbrecht hatte) mit *ius liberorum* ziviles Erbrecht nach ihren Kindern; das *SC Orfitianum* (178 n. Chr.) gab den Kindern ziviles Erbrecht nach ihrer Mutter. Das Kadukarrecht (→ *caducum*) beeinträchtigte nicht die Intestaterbfolge. Ein Intestaterbe konnte nur mit Fideikommissen beschwert werden

Das klass. Intestaterbrecht wurde durch Nov. 118 und 127 (543, 548 n. Chr.) zugunsten einer Kognatenerbfolge aufgehoben, welche noch im Gemeinen Recht (bis 1889) galt.

→ Agnatio; Cognatio; Consanguinei; Erbrecht III. C.

1 HONSELL/MAYER-MALY/SELB, 442 ff. **2** KASER, RPR I, 95 ff.; 695 ff.; II, 497 ff. **3** H. L. W. NELSON, U. MANTHE, Gai Institutiones III 1–87, 1992, 51 ff., 214 ff. **4** P. VOCI, Diritto ereditario romano II, ²1963, 3 ff. **5** A. WATSON, The Law of Succession in the Later Roman Republic, 1971, 175 ff. U.M.

Intrige (τὸ μηχάνημα, τὸ τέχνημα, *mēchánēma, téchnēma*). Bereits Hom. Od., B. 19–24 weist die enge Verbindung von Wiedererkennungsszenen (→ Anagnorisis) und I. auf, wie sie für die att. Trag. charakteristisch ist. *Locus classicus* ist Aischyl. Choeph. Bei Euripides fehlt

in fast keinem Stück die I., so daß ihn Aristoph. Thesm. 94 zu Recht »Meister des Intrigenspiels« nennen kann. Vor allem im Spätwerk konzipiert Euripides Anagnorisis-I.-Dramen: Nach der Wiedererkennung wird die Rettung durch eine I. bewerkstelligt (z.B. Eur. Iph. T. 1017ff.; Eur. Hel. 1034ff.). Im *Ion* findet sich eine spielerische Umkehrung: Die erste (falsche) Anagnorisis setzt eine I. nicht zur Rettung, sondern Ermordung des Protagonisten in Bewegung. Aristophanes parodiert in den ›Thesmophoriazusen‹ in Form und Inhalt diesen Tragödientyp. Beeinflußt von Euripides entwickeln die Autoren der Neuen Komödie (→ Menandros, → Plautus, → Terentius) die I. zu einem handlungsbestimmenden Element (vgl. den stereotypen *servus fallax*, den intriganten Sklaven), das von der Komödie seinen Weg auch in den Roman findet.
→ Roman

TH. PAULSEN, Inszenierung des Schicksals, 1992, 172–192 • F. SOLMSEN, Zur Gestaltung des Intriguenmotivs in den Tragödien des Sophokles und Euripides, in: E. R. SCHWINGE (Hrsg.), Euripides, 1968, 326–344. B.Z.

Inula s. Helenion

Inuus. Neben → Pales röm. Schutzgott der Viehherden (Arnob. 3,23); nach dem rutulischen Kultort *Castrum Inui* (Verg. Aen. 6,775 und Serv. ad loc.) wohl altlatin. Herkunft. Der Name leitet sich nach Servius von *inire* (= »bespringen«) her (Serv. l.c.). I. wurde vielfach identifiziert mit → Pan oder → Faunus (Liv. 1,5,2; Serv. l.c.; Prob. in Verg. georg. 1,10,16; Macr. Sat. 1,22,2). Nach Livius galten ihm die → Lupercalia (Liv. l.c.). J.S.-A.

Invektive. Die I., als Begriff (*invectiva oratio*) seit dem 4. Jh. n. Chr. belegt, ist nicht scharf definiert. Sie sucht am Maßstab eines allg.-gültigen Wertekanons vor einer breiten oder begrenzten Öffentlichkeit einen (u.U. nur indirekt bezeichneten) Gegner ernsthaft zu diskriminieren (welcher Mittel auch immer sie sich dabei bedient, s. → Satire) bzw. zu vernichten. In einer auf Platon zurückgehenden Trad. bildet ψόγος (*psógos*, Tadel) den Kontrast zu ἔπαινος (*épainos*, Lob), Enkomion und Hymnos; doch verbietet es sich nach Plat. leg. 934d–936b in dem unter dem Aspekt der Belehrung stehenden Konzept, einen anderen ernstlich schlecht und lächerlich zu machen: Lob und Tadel affirmieren den Wertekodex und haben pädagogische Funktion (leg. 829c–e). Als festes Gegensatzpaar sind Lob und Tadel in der Rhet. ausgebildet und dem *genos epideiktikon* (*genus demonstrativum/laudativum*) zugeordnet (Aristot. rhet. 1358b 12f.), wobei die Bestimmung des *psógos* (der *vituperatio*) sich durch Kontrastbildung aus der des *épainos* (der *laus*) ergibt (ebd. 1368a 33–37). Beide Elemente bleiben in der rhet. Theorie erh., wenn auch zumal im Rahmen der Progymnasmata der Tadel eine eigene Ausarbeitung erfährt. Im Hinblick auf eine Definition der I. ist dabei bes. unbefriedigend, daß weder die konkrete Intentionalität der I. erfaßt wird, noch die spezielle Form der Identifikation Berücksichtigung findet, welche für das Publikum angestrebt wird. Im Fall der I. übernimmt der Hörer/Leser zugleich die Funktion des Richters. Ein festes Inventar der Beschimpfungstopik ist nachweisbar [4. 358ff.; 13. 245ff.; 10. 81].

Im lat. Bereich (für den griech. ist auf die → Iambographen, → Spottgedichte, aber auch die alte → Komödie und die att. Redner zu verweisen) ist die poetische wie prosaische I. stark ausgebildet (*in tam maledica civitate*, Cic. Cael. 38), mit einem polit. bedingten Höhepunkt im 1. Jh. v. Chr. I.-Elemente finden sich von früher Zeit an nicht nur bei den Rednern (Cato Censorinus 213, Scipio Aemilianus 17, C. Gracchus 43; 58, jeweils [4]ORF), sondern in allen lit. Gattungen mit öffentlicher Wirkung (Bühnenstücke, Epigramme, Satiren). Eine Sonderstellung nimmt in diesem Zusammenhang → Lucilius ein. C. Licinius Calvus und → Catull (c. 29; 57 u.a., wobei die ges. und pol. Implikationen immer klarer erkannt werden [12; 14]) richten direkt oder indirekt Schmähgedichte gegen Caesar und Pompeius (Suet. Iul. 73; vgl. auch 49 und COURTNEY 210), M. → Furius [I 9] Bibaculus gegen Augustus (Tac. ann. 4,34,4). Catull, Bibaculus und Horaz werden von Quint. inst. 10,1,96 in einem Atemzug gen., gemeinsam mit Archilochos, Hipponax und Lucilius von Diomedes [4] (ars gramm. 1,485). Zu ihrem Gipfel gelangt die I. in Ciceros Reden (s.a. M. Caelius Rufus 17 [4]ORF gegen C. Antonius), in denen die rhet. Theorie von der abschätzigen Darstellung eines ganzen Lebenslaufs [4. 14ff.] Berücksichtigung findet. Quint. inst. 3,7 hebt die nicht erh. Reden gegen die Mitbewerber um das Konsulat, C. Antonius und Catilina, und *In Clodium et Curionem* sowie die *Pisoniana* eigens hervor. Seit den Grammatikern des 4. Jh. n. Chr. und in den Hss. werden die catilinarischen Reden als *invectiones/invectivae* bezeichnet. Die *Pisoniana* (zu den konventionellen antiepikureischen Elementen [1]) und die (ps.-?)sallustianische Cicero-I. sind zum prägenden Muster geworden.

Die I.-Produktion fand in der Kaiserzeit ihre Fortsetzung und führte nicht selten zu Tod und Verbannung (Tac. ann. 6,39; 14,48ff.; Suet. Dom. 8,3). Eine Wiederbelebung der durch die Machtkämpfe bedingten I. nach dem Muster Octavian – Antonius ist unter Iulian (vgl. aber auch die rel. bedingten »Reden« Greg. Naz. or. 4f. gegen Iulian [5. 18ff.]) festzustellen (Amm. 21,10,7f.; vgl. 22,14,2f.). Signifikant ist die Integration der I. in das »sekundäre« → Epos mit affektiver Profilierung des Erzählers: Claudians *In Eutropium* und *In Rufinum* sind die bedeutsamsten Beispiele. Auch die christl. polemische Lit. ist bei Verknüpfung von ideologisch-gruppenspezifischer und persönlicher Schmähung der I. verpflichtet (z.B. → *Carmen ad quendam senatorem*, → *Carmen contra paganos*), ebenso Hieronymus, der selbst die Glaubensgenossen nicht schont (s.a. Sidon. epist. 2,1; vgl. 1,11). Schmähende und diffamierende Dichtung war nicht nur im MA – bis hin zu den Anthologien – außerordentlich verbreitet; Schmähschriften lassen sich zu allen Zeiten nachweisen (der Fall Tho-

mas BERNHARD zeigt es [16]), bes. aber im 16. Jh. (Pamphlet, Pasquill).
→ SATIRE

1 PH. DELACY, Cicero's invective against Piso, in: TAPhA 72, 1941, 49–58 2 S. GOZZOLI, La In Pisonem di Cicerone, in: Athenaeum 78, 1990, 451–463 3 J. A. HOLLAR, The traditions of satire and invective in Catullus, Diss. Washington Univ. 1972 4 S. KOSTER, Die I. in der griech. und röm. Lit., 1980 5 A. KURMANN, Gregor v. Nazianz, Oratio 4 gegen Julian, 1988 6 H. L. LEVY, Claudian's In Rufinum and the rhetorical ψόγος, in: TAPhA 77, 1946, 57–65 7 J. F. LONG, Claudian's In Eutropium, 1996 8 N. W. MERRILL, Cicero and early Roman invective, Diss. Cincinnati, 1975 9 R. G. M. NISBET, M. Tulli Ciceronis in L. Calpurnium Pisonem oratio, 1961, bes. 192ff. 10 U. SCHINDEL, Die I. gegen Cicero und die Theorie der Tadelrede, in: Nachrichten der Akademie der Wiss. in Göttingen, Phil.-Histor. Klasse, 1980, 77–92 11 K. SCOTT, The political propaganda of 40–33 B. C., in: Memories of the American Academy in Rome 11, 1933, 7–49 12 M. B. SKINNER, Parasites and strange bedfellows. A study in Catullus' political imagery, in: Ramus 8, 1979, 137–152 13 W. SÜSS, Ethos, 1910 14 W. J. TATUM, Catullus 79, in: Papers of the Leeds International Latin Seminar 7, 1993, 31–45 15 G. BEBERMEYER, s. v. Schmähschrift (Streitschrift), Reallexikon der dt. Lit.-Gesch. 3, [2]1977, 665–678 16 F. VAN INGEN, Thomas Bernhards *Holzfällen* oder die Kunst der I., in: Amsterdamer Beitr. zur neueren Germanistik 36, 1993, 257–282. W.-L. L.

Inventio (εὕρεσις, *heúresis*: Erfindung, Findung sc. der Gedanken). Mit *i.* wird im rhet. System das erste von fünf Produktionsstadien beim Verfassen einer Rede bezeichnet (→ *partes orationis*; neben *i.* → *dispositio*, → *elocutio*, → *memoria*, → *pronuntiatio*). In der die gesamte ant. Rhet. durchlaufenden Trennung von sprachlicher Ausführung (*verba*) und Gedanken (*res*), die diese Fünfteilung unterläuft, ist die *i.* gemeinsam mit der nicht von ihr zu trennenden *dispositio* den *res* zuzuordnen, denen ein eigentümlich konkreter Status zugestanden wird. Die *i.* dient dem Auffinden der zum Stoff passenden (*aptum*) Gedanken, wobei auch ein Mißverhältnis zwischen unbedeutender *materia* und Argumentationsaufwand bestehen kann. Die Nutzung von Argumenten ist nicht auf einen bestimmten Personenkreis beschränkt, doch sollten sie an der Wahrscheinlichkeit und Glaubwürdigkeit orientiert sein und im Idealfall vom Ethos des Redners kontrolliert werden. Die *i.* wird in der Ant. nicht als autonomer kreativer Akt gesehen, wie in den Dichtungstheorien der Neuzeit, wo *i.* in einer Bed.-Änderung die Imaginationskraft schlechthin bezeichnet. Vielmehr wird *i.* als Finden durch Erinnerung (analog der platonischen Auffassung vom Wissen) aufgefaßt. Danach sind die für eine Rede geeigneten Gedanken in der Seele als Fundus von Meinungswissen und kulturell determinierten Denk- und Wahrnehmungsmustern (*copia rerum*) schon vorhanden. Ein guter Redner muß sich dieses Wissen durch gründliches Studium (wieder) aneignen und durch permanente Wiederholung wachhalten und aktivieren, wozu er sich einer Erinnerungstechnik bedient (Cic. inv. 1,69). Das Gedächtnis wird als Raum imaginiert, in dessen Teilen (lat. *loci*, griech. *tópoi*) die einzelnen Gedanken verteilt sind.

Die *i.* ist die vollständige gedankliche Durchdringung des Redegegenstandes, der als Konstrukt aus typischen Möglichkeiten gesehen wird. Deren spezifische Zusammensetzung erschließt sich nicht auf den ersten Blick, sondern muß gefunden werden. Die *i.* orientiert sich neben der Person, der Sache, der Zeit etc. (z. B. Quint. inst. 5,8,4) auch an Fragen nach Begriffsverwandtschaft (Cic. inv. 1,41 ff. *adiunctum*: nach dem Vergleich, dem Gegensatz, der Deduktion und der Induktion). Aus der Fülle der Ereignisse und Situationen (*materia*) wird die den Einzelfall konturierende Hypothese gewonnen. Daraus ergibt sich die Frage nach dem → Status des behandelten Falles. Quintilianus (inst. 5,10,20 f.) vergleicht die *i.* mit der Jagd, bei der ein guter Jäger immer schon wisse, wo er das Wild findet. Durch geeignete Suchkategorien (→ Topik) werden die in den *loci* verborgenen Gedanken in Erinnerung gerufen. Die röm. Rhet. vereinfacht im Dienste einer praktischen Anwendung die dialektischen und sehr diffizilen Suchkategorien der in dieser Hinsicht einschlägigen Topik des Aristoteles und unterteilt nach sach- und personenbezogenen Argumentationsmustern: Während Cicero (inv. passim) die Menge der Fundstätten für begrenzt hält, weil sich jeder spezielle Fall auf einen allg. zurückführen lasse, postuliert Quintilian, daß das Eigentümliche am Fall selbst gelernt werden müsse und daß es Beweisgründe gebe, die durch Suchformen vage oder gar nicht abgedeckt seien. Zuweilen müsse man eher der Natur denn der Kunst folgen (Quint. inst. 5,10,103). Die Vorgegebenheit der Gedanken schließt Originalität (*ingenium*) des einzelnen Redners keineswegs aus.

Die *i.* dient dem »Auffinden« und groben Vorsortieren der Gedanken, die schon hier auf ihre Überzeugungskraft und Tauglichkeit überprüft werden. Gleichzeitig orientiert sich die *i.* bereits an den Teilen der Rede (→ *partes orationis*: → *exordium*, *narratio*, → *argumentatio*, *peroratio*), denen eine bestimmte Funktion in der Argumentation zugewiesen wird und auf die die gefundenen Argumente verteilt werden. Die Feinarbeit des Gedankenaufbaus bleibt der *dispositio* vorbehalten. Mag auch die *i.* im Rahmen der Rhet. eine eher künstliche Position haben, so handelt es sich bei näherer Betrachtung um grundsätzliche Modi der geistigen Produktivität und Problemlösung.

1 K.-H. GÖTTERT, Einführung in die Rhet., [2]1991, 26 f. 2 M. HEATH, I., in: S. E. PORTER (Hrsg.), Handbook of Classical Rhet. in the Hell. Period 330 B.C– A. D. 400, 1997, 89–119 3 J. MARTIN, Ant. Rhet., 1972, 13–51 4 G. UEDING, Klass. Rhet., 1995, 55–65. C. W.

Invocatio s. Musenanruf

Inykon (Ἴνυκον). Ort auf Sizilien (Hesych. s. v. Ἰνυκῖνος οἶνος; Steph. Byz. s. v. I.), dessen Wein berühmt war. → Charax identifiziert I. mit Kamikos, der

Residenz des Kokalos (FGrH 103 F 58). → Hippokrates [4] von Gela hielt Skythes von Kos und Pythogenes in I. gefangen, bevor diesen die Flucht nach Himera gelang (Hdt. 6,23 f.). Der Sophist Hippias soll bei dem ›kleinen Dorf I.‹ mehr als 20 Minen besessen haben (Plat. Hipp. mai. 282e). Zw. Selinus und Akragas, möglicherweise in der Nähe von Kamikos (h. S. Angelo Muxaro) zu lokalisieren.

M. Massa, BTCGI 8, 1990, 303–308 • E. Manni, Geografia fisica et politica della Sicilia antica (Testimonia Siciliae antiqua 1,1), Kokalos Suppl. 4, 1981, 192. GI.MA./Ü: H.D.

Inzest s. incestus

Io (Ἰώ). Tochter des → Inachos, des Königs von Argos (Aischyl. Prom. 589f.; Bakchyl. 19,18 u.a.), oder des → Peiren (bzw. Peras oder Peirasos), des Königs von Tyrins (Hes. cat. fr. 124), und der Melia (Johannes Antiochenus FHG IV 544 fr. 14). Zeus verliebt sich in sie und verführt sie, dabei nimmt er die Gestalt eines Stieres an; Hera verwandelt I. aus Eifersucht in eine Kuh (Aischyl. Suppl. 299); nach Hes. cat. fr. 124 wird I. erst nach dem Liebesabenteuer von Zeus selbst verwandelt, um Hera zu täuschen (so auch Apollod. 2,1,3). Nach Aischyl. Prom. 645–686 wird I. von ihrem Vater aufgrund von Orakelsprüchen aus dem Haus gejagt und bereits vor ihrer Begegnung mit Zeus verwandelt. Zeus schwört Hera den Meineid, nicht mit I. geschlafen zu haben, und macht ihr die weiße Kuh zum Geschenk, in die er I. verwandelt hat (Hes. cat. 124; vgl. Aischyl. Prom. 589–592). Hera schließt diese in einem Hain ein und läßt sie vom Riesen → Argos [I 5] bewachen (Soph. El. 4f.; Akusilaos FGrH 2 F 26f.; Apollod.). Doch Hermes tötet Argos im Auftrag von Zeus und befreit I. (Aischyl. Suppl. 305; Bakchyl. 19,25–33; Apollod. 2,1,3). Hera schickt nun eine Bremse, welche die wahnsinnige I. verfolgt (Aischyl. Prom. 589). Nach Aischyl. Prom. 567–573 handelt es sich dabei um den Schatten des toten Argos (vgl. Ov. met. 1,725–727). I. durchwandert Nordgriechenland, das ion. Meer, das nach ihr benannt sein soll (Aischyl. Prom. 839–841), ebenso wie den Bosporos (Aischyl. Prom. 733). Über Skythien und Asien gelangt I. weiter nach Ägypten (Aischyl. Suppl. 540–573; Prom. 707–735; 790–815; 829–847). Dort wird sie von Zeus durch Berührung mit der Hand oder durch Anhauchen wieder in menschliche Gestalt verwandelt und gebiert den Epaphos, von dem u.a. Libye (oder Libya) und → Danaos, der Vater der Danaiden, abstammen (Aischyl. Suppl. 313ff.; Prom. 848–858; Bakchyl. 19,39–43 u.a.).

Älteste Quelle für den Mythos von I. sind Epen des 7. Jh.: *Aigimios* (Hes. fr. 294; 296), *Danais* (EpGF p. 141) und *Phoronis* (EpGF p. 153–155). Darauf basieren die Berichte der Historiker (Akusilaos FGrH 2 fr. 26f.; Pherekydes FGrH 3 fr. 67; Hdt. 1,1; 2,41; 3,27) ebenso wie die Behandlung des Stoffes bei Lyrikern und Dramatikern (Pind. N. 4,35; Bakchyl. 19; Aischyl. Suppl. 291–315; Prom. 561–900; Soph. Inachos TrGF IV fr. 269a; Eur. Phoen. 247f.; 676–681; 828; Iph. T. 394). Der Titel *Io* ist für zwei Komödien überliefert (Sannyrion, CAF I 795 fr. 10–11; Platonius, De Differentia comoediarum, CAF I 615 fr. 55). Aufgrund der geogr. Dimension des Mythos und weil bereits Herodot I. mit Isis gleichsetzt, wurde nahöstlicher und ägypt. Einfluß vermutet. Für den rituellen Hintergrund ist die Situierung in Argos, die Verbindung zum Herakult und die Parallele zum Mythos der → Proitides von Bed. [1].

1 W. Burkert, Homo Necans, 1972, 181–189.

M. v. Albrecht, Die Erzählung von I. bei Ovid und Valerius Flaccus, in: WJA, N.S. 3, 1977, 139–148 • K. Dowden, Death and the Maiden, 1989, 117–145 • S. Eitrem, s.v. I., RE 9, 1732–1743 • N. Icard-Giarolia, s.v. I. (1), LIMC 5.1, 661–665 (mit Bibliogr.) • F. Wehrli, I., Dichtung und Kultlegende, in: H. Hommel (Hrsg.), Wege zu Aischylos, Bd. 2, 1974, 136–148. K.WA.

Iobakchoi s. Mysterien

Iobaritai (Ἰωβαρῖται, Ἰοβαρῖται). Ethn. Gruppe im südl. Arabien; nur bei Ptol. 6,7,24 als Nachbarn der Sachalitai (→ Sachalites) erwähnt.

J. Tkač, s.v. I., RE 9, 1832–1837. J.RE.

Iobates (Ἰοβάτης, »der kraftvoll einherschreitet«). Namenloser König von Lydien (Hom. Il. 6,155–197), zu dem Proitos den → Bellerophontes mit dem Uriasbrief sendet (Apollod. 2,30ff.; Hyg. fab. 57; vgl. Plut. mor. 248a-d). Vater von → Stheneboia und Philonoe. Eine gleichnamige Trag. von Sophokles ist fragmentarisch überliefert (TrGF IV 297–299), von Euripides eine *Stheneboia* (TGF p.567).

T.R. Bryce, The Lycians in Literary and Epigraphic Sources I, 1986, 16–20; 209. RE.ZI.

Joch. Mod. t.t. in der arch. Bauforsch., der im ant. Säulenbau den Achsabstand zweier Säulen bezeichnet (im Gegensatz zum lichten Raum dazwischen, dem auch in der ant. Architekturterminologie als Begriff bezeugten Interkolumnium; vgl. [1]); in der angelsächs. Fachlit. wird das J. meist als »interaxial space« bezeichnet. Das J. war, bes. im Konzept des griech. Peripteraltempels klass. Zeit (→ Tempel), als eine notwendigerweise klar definierte Teilmenge der Achsweiten (d.h. der Distanzen zwischen den Mittelpunkten der vier Ecksäulen) eine der zentralen Planungsgrößen im Bauentwurf (→ Bauwesen); der planerische Nukleus archa. Tempel des 6. Jh. v. Chr. war demgegenüber meist der langrechteckige → Stylobat. Das J. findet sich häufig als → Aufschnürung (Markierung der Säulenmittelpunkte, z.B. am Zeustempel in Olympia) auf dem Stylobat. Es präjudizierte im systematisierten Maßverbund des Säulenbaus dor. Ordnung das Maß- und Proportionsgefüge der Metopen und Triglyphen im → Fries, wo ein J. regelhaft aus der Maßsumme zweier Triglyphen und zweier Metopen bestand (wobei sich die arithmetische Beziehung zwischen J. auf der einen und Metope bzw. Triglyphe auf der anderen Seite meist in einem einfachen, kleinsten gemeinsamen Nenner spiegeln, der wiederum als »Grundmaß« oft geeignet ist, das gesamte Maßgefüge der Architektur transparent zu machen). Eine zentrale Rolle spielt das J. als planerisch relevante Distanz darüber hinaus auch im → dorischen Eckkonflikt. Trotz dieser aus Befunden und der Systematik des griech. Gliederbaus erschlossenen eminenten Bed. für Bauplanung und Baurealisation hat sich aus der schriftl. Überl. zur ant. Architektur bis h. kein zeitgenöss. Begriff für das J. gefunden; selbst bei Vitruv (z.B. 3,3,1 ff. und öfter) dominieren umständliche Umschreibungen mithilfe des Interkolumniums und des unteren Säulendurchmessers.

Die Tendenz zu Systematisierung, zu maßlicher und proportionaler Verkettung der einzelnen Bauelemente und Strecken im griech. Ringhallentempel wird an der sich zwischen dem 6. und späten 4. Jh. v. Chr. erheblich wandelnden Auffassung des J. besonders offensichtlich. Bis ins späte 6. Jh. v. Chr. bleiben unterschiedliche J.-Weiten an Fronten und Flanken der Ringhalle in der Folge additiver, noch wenig systematisierter Baukonzeptionen üblich; in der Regel wird dabei die Tempelfront durch weitere Abstände der Säulenachsen gegenüber den dichter gefaßten Langseiten betont. Im Athenatempel von Paestum (um 510 v. Chr.) findet sich an einem wegweisenden Pionierbau des Westens als Innovation erstmals das ringsum identische Normal-J., das mit dem älteren Poseidontempel von Kap Sunion (um 490 v. Chr.) im griech. Mutterland erstmalig auftritt und hier fortan zum Regelfall wird; die daraus resultierende Kommensurabilität von J.-Weiten mit den Teil-Maßen im Fries und der proportionalen Verkettung mit Säulen- und Gebälkhöhe findet im Zeustempel von Olympia, dem → Parthenon in Athen und dem großen Tempel von Segesta ihre Höhepunkte in der 2. Hälfte des 5. Jh. v. Chr. Der reißbrettkonzipierte, nunmehr meist in ion., später auch in korinth. Ordnung ausgeführte Rasterbau, der seit dem mittleren 4. Jh. v. Chr. den dor. Gliederbau ablöst, ordnet das J. in ein den gesamten Plan durchziehendes Gitternetz ein und macht das J. als zentrale Planungsgröße zunehmend obsolet.

1 K. Nohl, Index Vitruvianus 1876, s. v. *intercolumnium*.

H. Büsing, Eckkontraktion und Ensembleplanung, in: MarbWPr 1987, 14–46 • J. J. Coulton, Towards Understanding Doric Design: The Stylobate and Intercolumniations, in: ABSA 69, 1974, 61–86 • Ch. Höcker, Planung und Konzeption der klass. Ringhallentempel von Agrigent, 1993, 72–74; 119–141 • H. Knell, Vitruvs Architekturtheorie, 1985, 63–114 • D. Mertens, Der Tempel von Segesta und die dor. Tempelbaukunst des griech. Westens in klass. Zeit, 1984, 252 s. v. J. • W. Müller-Wiener, Griech. Bauwesen in der Ant., 1986, 29–31 • H. Riemann, Zum griech. Peripteraltempel, 1935 passim • Ders., Hauptphasen in der Plangestaltung des dor. Peripteraltempels, in: G. E. Mylons (Hrsg.), Stud. presented to D. M. Robinson, Bd. 1, 1951, 295–308 • B. Wesenberg, Beitr. zur Rekonstruktion griech. Architektur nach lit. Quellen, 9. Beih., MDAI(A), 1983.

C. HÖ.

Iocheaira s. Artemis

Iodama (Ἰοδάμα). Lokalgottheit von Koroneia (Boiotien), von Athene verdrängt. Im Mythos Tochter des → Itonos, Enkelin des → Amphiktyon [2], Priesterin der Athena Itonia; von dieser mit dem Gorgoneion versteint (Paus. 9,34,2); in anderer Überl. Mutter der Thebe von Zeus, Schwester der Athene, von ihr aus Eifersucht getötet (Simonides, FGrH 8 F 1). RE. ZI.

Iohannes (Ἰωάννης). Bekannte Personen u. a.: I. [1] der Evangelist, I. [4] Chrysostomos, der Bischof von Konstantinopel und Homilet, I. [18] Malalas, der Verf. der Weltchronik, I. [25] von Gaza, der Rhetor und Dichter, I. [33] von Damaskos, der Theologe.

[1] I. der Evangelist A. Tradition und Kritik B. Das Selbstzeugnis des Evangeliums C. Rekonstruktion D. Wirkung

A. Tradition und Kritik

Der Verf. eines → Evangeliums (Jo), dreier Briefe und der Apokalypse im NT heißt nach den Inschr. I. (= J.; der Name steht im Text nur Apk 1,1; 1,4; 1,9; 22,8). Seit Ende des 2. Jh. (Iren. adversus haereses 3,1,1; Polykrates von Ephesos nach Eus. HE 3,31,3; Clem. Al. nach Eus. HE 6,14,7; Canon Muratori 9 Lietzmann) sieht man in ihm weithin den ›Jünger des Herrn‹, den Sohn des Zebedaios und Bruder des Iakobos, der im Jüngerkreis und der Urgemeinde den zweiten Rang nach Petrus innehatte (Mk 1,19; 9,22; Apg 3–4; Gal 2,9). Unter Domitian sei er nach Patmos verbannt worden (Tert. De praescriptione haereticorum 36,3; Eus. HE 3,18,1; vgl. Apk 1,9), habe dann bis in die Zeit Traians in Ephesos gelebt und dort sein Evangelium geschrieben (Iren. adversus haereses 2,22,5; Eus. HE 3,23,3 f.). Einer anderen Trad. zufolge wurde J. (wie sein Bruder: Apg 12,2) von Juden getötet (Papias, fr. 10 und 17 [13]). Diese Nachricht wurde durch die einflußreiche Verf.-Trad. zurückgedrängt und verdient daher histor. eher Vertrauen [11. 88–91]. Auch viele inhaltliche Gründe (v. a. die Differenzen zu den Synoptikern in Stoffauswahl und Diktion) stehen der Abfassung des Jo durch den Zebedaiden entgegen.

B. Das Selbstzeugnis des Evangeliums

Das Vf.-Problem des Jo ist eng mit der Zuschreibung der drei Briefe (1–3 Jo) und der Frage der lit. Einheitlichkeit des Jo verknüpft. Gegenüber den Schichtenanalysen der älteren Forsch. [6; 2; dazu 11; 10] wird neuerdings die Einheit des Jo wieder stärker gesehen [11; 20; 22], strittig ist jedoch, ob die in Jo 21,24 erkennbaren Hrsg. nur Kap. 21 (so [11; 19]) oder auch weitere kleinere (Jo 5,28 f.; 6,51c–58 etc.) und größere (Kap.

15–17) Zusätze einfügten [2; 18]. Die außergewöhnliche sprachlich-stilistische Einheitlichkeit und Eigenständigkeit des Jo [17; 11; 10. 429–445] macht umfangreichere Nachträge (außer Kap. 21) unwahrscheinlich und legt die Annahme eines sprachlich und theologisch gestaltenden Autors nahe. Dieser wird meist »Evangelist« genannt (anders [22]: der Hrsg. als der eigentliche »Evangelist«). In 21,24 identifizieren die Hrsg. den Autor mit dem ›Jünger, den Jesus liebte‹, der ab dem letzten Mahl (13,23–25; 19,26f.; 20,2–10; 21,7.20–23) auftritt (1,40 und 18,15 sind unklar) und sich vor Petrus durch seine größere Nähe zu Jesus auszeichnet. Als idealer Jünger und Zeuge verkörpert er den Anspruch des Jo, die älteren Evangelien zu überbieten. Er ist aber kaum eine bloße lit. Fiktion (gegen [14; 22]), sondern ein den Hrsg. wie den Adressaten noch bekannter christl. Lehrer, der als Trad.-Träger der ersten Zeit galt, aber z.Z. der Herausgabe des Jo wohl schon verstorben war (Jo 21,22f.). Er hat sein Werk unvollendet hinterlassen, so daß es von Schülern behutsam ergänzt, mit einer Beglaubigung versehen (21,24f.) und verbreitet wurde [11].

C. Rekonstruktion

Die meisten Versuche, den ›Jünger, den Jesus liebte‹, mit textlichen Figuren (z.B. Lazaros, Thomas) oder anderen bekannten Personen (z.B. Johannes Markos: Apg 12,12) zu identifizieren [8. 72–85; 7. 127–224], sind reine Spekulation. Der am ehesten verwertbare Hinweis findet sich bei Papias (fr. 5 [13]: Eus. HE 3,39,4), der außer dem Apostel noch einen anderen J., den »Presbyter« (Πρεσβύτερος) J., erwähnt, den er noch gehört hat und dessen Überlieferungen er in seinem weithin verlorenen Werk mitgeteilt haben soll (Eus. HE 3,39,7). Dieser »Presbyter J.« läßt sich histor. mit den Verf.-Angaben 2 Jo 1,1 und 3 Jo 1,1 verbinden. Dann wäre jener kleinasiatische »Presbyter« J. der Autor der beiden kleinen Briefe [19; 21] oder eher aller drei Briefe [11], der als Schulhaupt autoritativ in den Konflikt in dem ihm verbundenen Gemeindekreis eingreift. Strittig ist, ob die Briefe mit der Redaktion des Jo zu verbinden [5; 12; 18] oder in seine Vorgesch. einzuordnen sind [11; 19; 21], d.h., wie sich Briefautor und Evangelist zueinander verhalten. Wenn man die 1 Jo sachlich nahe stehenden Kapitel Jo 15–17 nicht als sekundäre Zusätze aus dem Jo herauslösen kann, wird auch die Nachordnung der Briefe fraglich, zumal der in 1 Jo 2,18ff. thematisierte Konflikt auch in Jo 6,60ff. u.ö. reflektiert sein dürfte [19]. Dann liegt es näher, im Autor der Briefe zugleich jenes Schulhaupt zu sehen, das die mit ihm verbundenen Gemeinden prägte und aus dessen Wirken das Jo hervorging, den Evangelisten [11].

Die Apk stammt aus sprachlichen und theologischen Gründen sicher von einem anderen Verf., der entweder ein sonst unbekannter Prophet J. ist oder, vielleicht noch von der Schule des »Presbyters« beeinflußt, sein Werk dem in Kleinasien bekannten J. nach dessen Tod zuschrieb [9].

Der Name J., die Sprache und die rezipierten Orts- und Auslegungstraditionen legen nahe, daß J. palästinischer Jude (am ehesten aus Jerusalem) war. Seine Verbindung zu Jesus und zur Urgemeinde bleibt jedoch unklar. Er mag im Zuge des jüd. Krieges nach Ephesos gekommen sein und dort von ca. 70 bis ca. 100 n. Chr. als Verkündiger und Lehrer gewirkt haben. Sein Werk dürfte dort über einen längeren Zeitraum hinweg entstanden und dann wohl in der Zeit Traians um oder kurz nach 100 herausgegeben worden sein [19]. Es erweist seinen Autor als theologischen Denker von Rang und führt die nt. Christologie zu ihrem Höhepunkt.

D. Wirkung

Die kunstvoll gewahrte Anonymität des Autors im Jo hat der Zuschreibung an den Apostel J. den Weg bereitet. Diese liegt nicht erst bei Irenaeus (→ Eirenaios [2]), sondern schon bei dem Valentinianer Ptolemaios (epist. ad Floram: Epiphanius, Panarion 33,3,6 Holl) um 150 vor [11. 38]. Für die kleinasiatische Kirche hatte J. und die mit ihm verbundene Trad. grundlegende Bed. (Polykrates von Ephesos nach Eus. HE 5,24,7). Seit Origenes (in Ioannem, fr. 1) trägt J. den Beinamen »der Theologe« (ὁ θεόλογος). Die spätere Legende malt sein Bild mit vielfältigen Zügen aus [1; 8].

1 W. Bauer, in: E. Hennecke, W. Schneemelcher (Hrsg.), Neutestamentliche Apokryphen II, ⁴1971, 24–27 **2** J. Becker, Das Evangelium nach J. I–II, ³1991 **3** J. Beutler, s.v. J.-Evangelium, RAC 18, 646–670 **4** F.-M. Braun, Jean le théologien I, 1959 **5** R.E. Brown, The Epistles of John, 1982 **6** R. Bultmann, s.v. Johannesevangelium, RGG³ III, 840–850 **7** J.H. Charlesworth, The Beloved Disciple, 1995 **8** R.A. Culpepper, John, the Son of Zebedee, 1994 **9** J. Frey, Erwägungen zum Verhältnis der Johannesapokalypse zu den übrigen Schriften im Corpus Johanneum, in: [11], 326–429 **10** Ders., Die johanneische Eschatologie I, 1997 **11** M. Hengel, Die johanneische Frage, 1993 **12** H.-J. Klauck, Die Johannesbriefe, 1991 **13** U.H.J. Körtner, Papiasfragmente, in: Ders., M. Leutzsch, Schriften des Urchristentums III, 1998, 3–103 **14** J. Kügler, Der Jünger, den Jesus liebte, 1988 **15** R. Kysar, The Fourth Gospel. A Report on Recent Research, in: ANRW II 25.3, 2389–2480 **16** K.H. Rengstorf (Hrsg.), J. und sein Evangelium, 1973 **17** E. Ruckstuhl, P. Dschulnigg, Stilkritik und Verfasserfrage im Johannesevangelium, 1991 **18** R. Schnackenburg, Das Johannesevangelium I–IV, 1965–1984 **19** U. Schnelle, Einleitung in das NT, 1994 **20** Ders., Das Evangelium nach J., 1998 **21** G. Strecker, Die Johannesbriefe, 1989 **22** H. Thyen, Noch einmal: Johannes 21 und »der Jünger, den Jesus liebte«, FS Lars Hartman, 1995, 147–190.

J.FR.

[2] I. von Gischala (hebr. *Giš/Guš Ḥālāḇ*). Gischala gilt als die Hochburg des Zelotentums in Galiläa z.Z. des jüd. Krieges, in dem I. eine nicht unumstrittene Rolle als Wortführer der jüd. Aufständischen gegen Rom spielte. Werden einerseits seine Tatkraft, sein Mut und seine Intelligenz (so z.B. [1]) herausgestrichen, so sieht ihn Iosephos [2] Flavios, dessen Widersacher I. war, als Ränkeschmied und Heuchler. I.' Leistung bestand bes.

im Wiederaufbau der Stadt Gischala, die vor dem Ausbruch des jüd. Krieges von Nichtjuden zerstört worden war. Quelle: Ios. bell. Iud.

→ Bar Kochba; Iosephos [2] Flavios; Zeloten

1 H. GRAETZ, Gesch. der Juden 3/2, 1906 2 SCHÜRER 1, 490f., 496–498, 501–509. Y.D.

[3] I. von Lykopolis. Einsiedler im Gebiet von Lykos in der Thebais am Ende des 4. Jh. n. Chr. In kirchenhistor. und monastischer Lit. wird sehr oft berichtet, daß er, als ihn Kaiser Theodosius I. über die Zukunft befragen ließ, diesem die Siege über Maxentius im J. 388 und Eugenius im J. 394 weissagte (Rufin. Historia ecclesiastica 11,19 und 32; Soz. 6,28,1; 7,22,7–8; 7,29,1; Aug. civ. 5,26; Aug. De cura pro mortuis gerenda 17,21; Historia monachorum 1,1; Pall. Laus. 35 p. 101,1–15 BUTLER; Theod. hist. eccl. 5,24,1 f.; Iohannes Cassianus, Collationes 24,26; Chron. min. 1, 463,607 MOMMSEN; Claud. in Eutr. 1,312–316 und 2, praef. 37–40). Die → *Historia monachorum* (1,1–65) berichtet weitere Szenen aus I.' Leben und teilt Apophthegmata des Mönches mit. Ihm zeitweilig zugerechnete Texte werden jetzt dem Einsiedler Iohannes von Apamea (2. H. 5. Jh.) zugeschrieben.

A.-J. FESTUGIÈRE (ed.), Historia Monachorum in Aegypto (Subsidia Hagiographica 34), 1961. C.M.

[4] I. Chrysostomos. Bischof von Konstantinopel (397–404); seit dem 6. Jh. als *Chrysóstomos* (»Goldmund«) bezeichnet; bedeutendster Homilet der griech. Kirche.

A. LEBEN B. WERKE (AUSWAHL) C. THEOLOGIE

A. LEBEN

Geb. in Antiocheia (wohl 349), fand I. durch den Unterricht im Asketerion des → Diodoros [14] aus Tarsos Zugang zur antiochenischen Exegese. Seit 372 Mönch, verließ I. im J. 378 – gesundheitlich angeschlagen – die klösterliche Gemeinschaft wieder, wurde 381 Diakon und im Februar 386 Priester. Die Predigt war nun seine Hauptaufgabe. 397 wurde er Nachfolger des Nektarios als Bischof von Konstantinopel. Hier galt sein bes. Augenmerk pastoralen und sozialen Problemfeldern (u. a. Gründung mehrerer Hospize). Unzufriedenheit im Klerus, das Eintreten für die sog. »Langen Brüder« (des Origenismus verdächtigte ägypt. Mönche, → Origenes) sowie der Konflikt mit der Kaiserin → Eudoxia [2] führten im Herbst 403 zu seiner Absetzung durch die sog. »Eichensynode« [8. 211–227]. Nach Aufhebung einer ersten Verbannung erfolgte am 8. Juni 404 die endgültige Exilierung. I. starb am 14. September 407 im pontischen Komana.

B. WERKE (AUSWAHL)

An Zahl nur denen des Augustinus vergleichbar, unterteilen sich die Werke des I. in drei Gruppen: Abhandlungen, Predigten und Briefe. Bereits als Diakon verfaßte er erste Traktate, so die Mahnschrift *Ad Theodorum lapsum* (CPG 4305). An → Gregorios [3] von Nazianz ausgerichtet, veröffentlichte er die Reformschrift *De sacerdotio* (CPG Suppl. 4316; Datier. unsicher, 385–391 n. Chr.), in der er ein Idealbild des Priesteramtes zeichnet. Mehr als 700 Predigten gelten als authentisch. Als eigenes Genos gelten die zu bes. Anlässen (Heiligenfeste u. a.) gehaltenen Reden, z. B. die ›Säulenhomilien‹ (CPG Suppl. 4330), die Taufkatechesen (CPG Suppl. 4460–4472) sowie die gegen judaisierende Christen gerichteten ›Acht Reden gegen die Juden‹ (CPG 4327). Unter dem Namen des I. befinden sich 242 Briefe, darunter 17 Trostbriefe an die Diakonisse Olympias. Als Ps.-Chrysostomica sind mehr als 1000 Schriften bekannt.

C. THEOLOGIE

Exegetisch der → antiochenischen Schule und ihrer ethischen Ausrichtung verpflichtet, beschreibt I. das Heilswerk Gottes, in dessen Zentrum das Kreuz steht, als συγκατάβασις/*synkatábasis* [7. 467 f.]. Vornehmlich praktisch orientiert, betont der in Belangen der Lehre eher Zurückhaltende die soziale Dimension des Evangeliums. Dabei kommt der Urgemeinde und dem mönchischen Leben Modellcharakter zu. Ziel ist eine neu formierte, auf christl. Solidarität aufgebaute Gesellschaft.

ED.: 1 CPG 4305–5197 bzw. CPG Suppl. ebd. 2 H. SAVILE, Eton 1610–1612 (Gesamtausg.) 3 MONTFAUCON PG 47–64 4 R. BRÄNDLE, V. JEGHER-BUCHER, J., Acht Reden gegen die Juden, 1995, 274–301 (Übersicht der Ausg./Übers., nach CPG).

LIT.: 5 J. A. DE ALDAMA, Repertorium pseudochrysostomicum, 1965 6 CH. BAUR, Der hl. Johannes Chrysostomus und seine Zeit, 2 Bde., 1929/1930 7 R. BRÄNDLE, V. JEGHER-BUCHER, s. v. Johannes Chrysostomus I., RAC 18, 426–503 (Lit. 495–503) 8 J. N. D. KELLY, Golden mouth, 1995 9 R. A. KRUPP, Shepherding the flock of God, 1991 10 J. H. LIEBESCHUETZ, Barbarians and bishops, 1990 11 K.-H. UTHEMANN, s. v. Johannes, Biographisch-Bibliogr. Kirchenlex. 3, 1992, 305–326 12 S. J. VOICU, s. v. Johannes Chrysostomos II. (Ps.-Chrysostomica), RAC 18, 503–515. J.RI.

[5] *Tribunus et notarius*, ging 394 n. Chr. als Gesandter des Theodosius nach Mailand (Paulinus von Mailand, Vita S. Ambrosii 31). I. war 408 *primicerius notariorum* und führte eine Gesandtschaft an Alarich (Zos. 5,40,2). 409 *magister officiorum* des Usurpators Attalos [11] (Soz. 9,8,3), aber 412–413 *praefectus praetorio Italiae* des Honorius (Cod. Theod. 13,11,13; 7,8,10). Evtl. 422 ein zweites Mal *praef. praet. Italiae* (Cod. Theod. 2,13,1). PLRE 1, 459 (I. 2).

[6] *Comes*, Berater des → Arcadius, angebl. Liebhaber der Kaiserin → Aelia [4] Eudoxia und Vater Theodosius' II. (Zos. 5,18,8). Während des Gotenaufstands 400 n. Chr. suchte I. kirchl. Asyl, wurde aber von Iohannes [4] Chrysostomos an Gainas ausgeliefert. 404 *comes sacrarum largitionum* (Palladius Monachus, Dialogus de vita Ioannis Chrysostomi 3).

PLRE 2, 593 f. (I. 1) • AL. CAMERON, A Misidentified Homily of Chrysostom, in: Nottingham Mediaeval Studies,

32, 1988, 34–48 • J. LIEBESCHUETZ, Friends and Enemies of John Chrysostom, in: A. MOFFAT (Hrsg.), Maistor, 1984, 85–111.

[7] I. Primicerius. Weström. Kaiser 423–425 n. Chr. Nachdem Honorius [3] am 15. Aug. 423 gestorben war und Theodosius II. zunächst keinen Westkaiser ernannt hatte, wurde I., der bisher *primicerius notariorum* gewesen war, am 20. Nov. 423 in Rom zum Augustus ausgerufen (Sokr. 7,23,3; Ann. Rav. sub anno 423; Olympiodor FHG fr. 41; Chron. min. 1,470; 523; 658 MOMMSEN). Wahrscheinlich wurde die Akklamation auf Senatsbeschluß vorgenommen. Auch die in Italien stationierten Truppen unter dem *magister utriusque militiae* Castinus folgten I. (Chron. min. a.O.). Theodosius dagegen verweigerte die Anerkennung und ließ die Gesandten des I. verhaften und in die Verbannung schicken (Philostorgius 12,13; Sokr. 7,23,4). Der *comes Africae* Bonifatius stellte daraufhin die Getreidelieferungen nach Rom ein, so daß I. ein Expeditionskorps gegen ihn rüstete, das aber scheiterte (Chron. min. 1,470). Das Konsulat des I. 425 wurde im Osten nicht anerkannt. Wohl im Mai 425 gelang Aspar (Ardabur [2]) die Eroberung Ravennas, I. wurde gefangengenommen und hingerichtet (Prok. BV 1,3,7f.; Chron. min. 1,470). Nach Nikephoros Kallistos 14,7 war er Gote, möglicherweise Arianer (Cod. Theod. 16,2,47). PLRE 2, 594f. (I. 6).

[8] *Comes rei privatae* ca. 426–429 n. Chr. (Cod. Theod. 5,16,35), 429–431 *comes sacrarum largitionum.* Auf dem Konzil von Ephesos (431 n. Chr.) als kaiserl. Schlichter tätig und dort in das *magisterium officiorum* erhoben (Acta conciliorum oecumenicorum 1,1,7, S. 74), in dem er bis 433 nachweisbar ist (Cod. Theod. 7,8,15). Vor 450 gestorben (Nestorius, Liber Heracl. 306 NAU). PLRE 2, 596 (I. 12). M.R.

[9] I. Stobaios s. Stobaios

[10] I. von Skythopolis. Zeitgenosse des → Iohannes [15] von Kaisareia; er schrieb wie dieser eine Apologie des Konzils von Chalkedon 451 n. Chr. (CPG 3, 6851) auf der Basis neuchalkedonensischer Theologie. Seine Scholien zu den Traktaten des → Ps.-Dionysios [54] Areopagites (CPG 3, 6852; kritische Ed. durch B. R. SUCHLA in Vorbereitung) sind seit dem frühen 6. Jh. n. Chr. in den entsprechenden Hss. überliefert und haben die Rezeption des Corpus des Dionysios bis in die Gegenwart tief geprägt.

J. LEBON (Ed.), Contra impium grammaticum, 1952, 202–204 (CSCO 94) • L. PERRONE, La Chiesa di Palestina e le controversie cristologiche, 1980, 239–250 • B. R. SUCHLA, Verteidigung eines platonischen Denkmodells einer christl. Welt (Nachr. der Akad. der Wiss. in Göttingen, Phil.-histor. Klasse 1), 1995. C.M.

[11] I. I. Mandakuni. Als Erzbischof in → Armenia (478–490 n. Chr.) verlegte er 484 seine Residenz nach Dvin/Zentralarmenien. I. gilt als Reformer der armen. Kirchenordnung und Liturgie und wird in der armen. Kirche als Hl. verehrt. Seine Schriften verfaßte er in der klass.-armen. Schriftsprache (→ Armenisch). Viele ihm zugeschriebene Homilien, Hymnen und Kanones stammen u. a. aber von Ioannes von Mayragom und Iohannes von Odzun.

K. SARKISSIAN, The Council of Chalcedon and the Armenian Church, ²1975, 186–195 • R. W. THOMSON, A Bibliography of Classical Armenian Literature to 1500 A. D. (CCG 0,1), 1995, 224f. (Lit.). K.SA.

[12] I. II., Bischof von Jerusalem († 10.1.417 n. Chr.). Als junger Mönch 387 zum Bischof geweiht, wurde I. seit 394 durch → Epiphanios [1] von Salamis und → Hieronymus wegen seines vorgeblichen Origenismus angegriffen (sog. ›Apologie des I.‹ als Verteidigung, s. CPG 3620). Nach Ankunft des Pelagios in Jerusalem und der Feststellung seiner Rechtgläubigkeit auf der von I. geleiteten Synode von Diospolis (415) kam es zum wohlwollenden Briefwechsel mit Augustinus. Unter dem Namen des I. sind mehrere Symbola und z. T. in ihrer Zuweisung umstrittene Homilien ([2. 411]; CPG Suppl. 3624–3626) überliefert. I. gilt als Verf. der seinem Vorgänger Kyrillos zugeschriebenen sog. mystagogischen Katechesen (CPG 3622). Lit. s. [1; 2].

[13] Bischof von Antiocheia (429–441/2 n. Chr.). Mit → Theodoros von Mopsuestia und → Nestorios erzogen, unterstützte I. letzteren in seinem theologischen Anliegen. Verspätet zum Konzil in Ephesos (431) eingetroffen, verurteilte I. → Kyrillos von Alexandreia und den Ortsbischof Memnon auf einer Gegensynode. Nach kaiserlicher Intervention akzeptierte er 432 die Verurteilung des Nestorios und bemühte sich um Verständigung mit den früheren Gegnern (Union von 433). Über die nestorianische Kontroverse liegt ein umfangreicher Briefwechsel vor (CPG 6301–6360). Lit. s. [3].

[14] I. Diakrinomenos (»Separatist«), monophysitischer Kirchenhistoriker (6. Jh. n. Chr.). Nach Photios (Phot. Bibl. 41) verfaßte I. eine ansprechend gestaltete Kirchengesch. in 10 Bd. Deren erste fünf B. reichten, beginnend mit dem Konflikt um Nestorios (Konzil von Ephesos 431), bis in die Regierungszeit Kaiser Zenos (474–491). Geschrieben nach 526 ([6. 69], bislang meist: 512–518) haben sich Fr. bei byz. Historikern erh.; Fr. s. [4], Lit. s. [5; 6].

1 E. A. CLARK, The Origenist Controversy, 1992, 132–137 2 K.-H. Uthemann, s. v. Johannes, Biographisch-Bibliogr. Kirchenlex. 3, 1992, 402–413 3 L. I. SCIPIONI, Nestorio e il concilio di Efeso, 1974, 195–299 4 G. C. HANSEN, Theodoros Anagnostes Kirchengeschichte, 1995 152–157 (GCS N. F. 3) 5 A. JÜLICHER, s. v. Johannes (46), RE 9, 1806 6 W. T. TREADGOLD, The Nature of the Bibliotheca of Photius, 1980, 69f. J.RI.

[15] I. von Kaisareia. Der Grammatiker I., Presbyter aus Kaisareia in Kappadokien (so [2]), verfaßte zw. 514 und 518 n. Chr. eine Apologie der Synode von Chalkedon, von der in der Schrift *Contra impium grammaticum* des Severos von Antiocheia 44 Zitate erh. sind. Außerdem sind einige weitere kleine Schriften überl. (CPG 3, 6855–6862). I. ist ein früher Vertreter der sog. »neuchalkedonensischen Christologie«, die zw. → Kyrillos von Alexandreia und der von seinen Anhängern als »nestorianisch« (→ Nestorianismus) empfundenen Christologie vermitteln wollte. Er prägte die Formel von den zwei ›enhypostatisch geeinten Naturen Christi‹ [2. 53 Z. 118–120].

1 J. Lebon (Ed.), Severi Antiocheni Liber contra impium grammaticum, 1952 (CSCO 111, 93, 101) 2 M. Richard (Ed.), Iohannis Caesariensis Presbyteri et Grammatici Opera quae supersunt, 1977 (CCG 1) 3 A. Grillmeier, Jesus der Christus im Glauben der Kirche 2/2, 1989, 54. C. M.

[16] Flavius I., »der Kappadokier«, seit 531 n. Chr. *praefectus praetorio per Orientem* unter Kaiser → Iustinianus [1]. I. betrieb, v. a. zur Finanzierung der kaiserl. Kriegsunternehmen, eine sparsame und auf hohes Steueraufkommen gerichtete Finanzpolitik, die ihn dem Kaiser unentbehrlich, beim Volk aber unbeliebt machte. So verlor er im → Nika-Aufstand (Jan. 532) vorübergehend sein Amt, in dem er aber seit Okt. 532 wieder bezeugt ist. Auch die zeitgenössischen Geschichtsschreiber beurteilen ihn negativ und werfen ihm u. a. Habsucht und persönl. Bereicherung vor. Intrigen der Kaiserin → Theodora führten im Mai 541 zu seiner Absetzung und Verbannung. Nach deren Tod 548 zurückgerufen, starb er einige Zeit später in Konstantinopel.

PLRE 3, 627–635 (I. 11) • E. Stein, Histoire du Bas-Empire 2, 879, Index, s. v. Jean de Cappadoce. F. T.

[17] Neffe des Usurpators → Vitalianus, 537–549 n. Chr. *magister militum vacans* im Krieg des Kaisers → Iustinianus [1] I. gegen die Ostgoten unter → Belisarios in Italien; heiratete 545 in Konstantinopel Iustina, eine Tochter des → Germanus [1] (Vetter des Iustinianus). Als *mag. mil. per Illyricum* hielt er sich von Herbst 550 bis 552 in Salona (Spalatum) auf, von wo aus er im Sommer 551 zusammen mit dem *mag. mil.* Valerianus an der Küste Italiens bei Sena Gallia einen Seesieg über die Goten errang. Seit 552 kämpfte er unter Narses in Italien, wo er 553 zuletzt erwähnt ist. PLRE 3, 652–661 (I. 46). F. T.

[18] I. Malalas. Verf. der ältesten erh. byz. Weltchronik. Geb. in Antiocheia um 490/500 n. Chr., syr. Herkunft (der Name *Malalas* < syr. *mallāl* bedeutet »Rhetor«), wahrscheinlich dort als Verwaltungsbeamter tätig, gest. nach 570. Seine Chronik behandelt in 18 B. die Gesch. von der Erschaffung der Welt bis zum J. 563. Sie ist nur in einer einzigen Hs. aus dem 11. Jh. erh., aber, wie ein Vergleich mit der etwa gleichzeitigen, vollständigeren aksl. Übers. zeigt, in leicht gekürzter Form. Urspr. endete der Text im Jahr 565, vielleicht auch erst 574. Die Gesch. der Mittelmeervölker im Alt. ist nach zumeist namentlich gen., überwiegend wohl aus zweiter Hand benutzten Quellen zusammengestellt. Griech. Mythen werden als histor. Ereignisse dargestellt, häufig in rationalisierter Form. Antiocheia wird in der Darstellung bevorzugt und nach lokalen Quellen behandelt. Die Sympathien des Autors für den → Monophysitismus sind deutlich erkennbar. Das letzte B. über die Regierungszeit → Iustinianus' [1] I. (527–565) zeigt eine abweichende Tendenz: Es stellt Konstantinopel stärker in den Mittelpunkt, als Quellen dienen zeitgenössische Berichte und vielleicht eigenes Erleben des Autors; in der Darstellung der Ereignisse folgt es der offiziellen staatlichen Propaganda, und die monophysitischen Neigungen treten nicht mehr so klar zutage.

Diese Unterschiede sind dadurch erklärt worden, daß I. seit etwa 530/540 in Konstantinopel gelebt und seine polit. Anschauungen entsprechend revidiert habe oder daß dieser Teil von einem anderen Verf. stamme. Die ältere Vermutung, dies könnte der aus Antiocheia stammende Patriarch → Iohannes [28] III. Scholastikos (565–577) von Konstantinopel gewesen sein, wird h. nicht mehr vertreten. Die Chronik nimmt durch häufiges Erzählen von Anekdoten und Wundergesch. auf den Geschmack eines breiteren Publikums Rücksicht; sie verzichtet weitgehend auf lit. Anspruch und ist durch die Verwendung der zeitgenössischen Umgangssprache von großer sprachhistor. Bed. Sie übte starken Einfluß auf die Entwicklung des Genres auch im Westen aus. Späteren byz. Werken wie dem → *Chronicon Paschale* und → Theophanes diente sie als Quelle. Außer ins Slavische wurde sie auch ins Georgische übersetzt.

L. Dindorf (ed.), Ioannis Malalae Chronographiae, 1831 • A. Schenk von Stauffenberg, Die röm. Kaisergesch. bei Malalas, 1930 • E. Hörling, Mythos und Pistis: Zur Deutung heidnischer Mythen in der christl. Weltchronik des Johannes Malalas, 1980 • E. Jeffreys, B. Croke, R. Scott (ed.), Studies in John Malalas, 1990. AL. B.

[19] Philoponos s. Philoponos

[20] I. Abbas Biclarensis, * um 540, † um 621. Der nach Isid. De viris illustribus 31 aus Scallabis stammende Gote I. studierte in Konstantinopel und wurde nach seiner Rückkehr um 576 wegen seines katholischen Glaubens (Anhänger des Chalkedonense) mit dem arianischen König Leovigild in → Barcino interniert. Unter König Reccared gründete er 586/7 das Kloster im spanischen Biclaro, für das er eine nicht mehr erh. Regel verfaßte. Spätestens 592 wird I. Bischof von Gerunda. Um 590/1 schrieb er als Fortsetzer des → Victor Tonnunensis eine Chronik für die J. 567–589. Sie ist in ihrem bündigen Stil (so Isidor) eine wichtige Quelle für Byzanz und das Westgotenreich im 6. Jh.
→ Chronik

Ed.: J. Campos, Juan de Biclaro, 1960 (Einl., Komm.) • Th. Mommsen, MGH AA XI, 1894, 207–220 • K. B. Wolf, Conquerors and Chroniclers of Early Medieval Spain, 1990, 1–11, 61–80 (engl. Übers.) • (Neued. von C. Hartmann geplant).
Lit.: A. Kollautz, Orient und Okzident am Ausgang des 6. Jh., in: Byzantina 12, 1983, 464–506 • S. Teillet, Dès Goths à la nation gothique, 1984, 421–455. JÖ. RI.

[21] I. von Antiocheia. Verfassername, der mit zahlreichen Fr. in byz. Geschichtswerken verbunden wird. Die Texte lassen sich mind. zwei Autoren zuweisen, von denen der erste um 520/530 n. Chr. schrieb, der zweite im 9./10. Jh. Der ältere I., über dessen Leben keine Nachrichten vorliegen, ist sicher nicht identisch mit → Iohannes [18] Malalas, aber auch nicht, wie früher zuweilen angenommen wurde, mit dem jakobitischen Patriarchen von Antiocheia Iohannes I. (631–649). Sein Werk enthält einige sonst nicht überl. Nachrichten über die spätröm.-frühbyz. Zeit und diente als Quelle u. a. für die Exzerptensammlung des → Konstantinos VII. Porphyrogennetos und die Chronik des Iohannes → Zonaras (12. Jh.).

FHG 4, 535–622 • Suppl. FHG 5, 27–38 • P. Sotiroudis, Unt. zum Geschichtswerk des Johannes von Antiocheia, 1989 • ODB 2, 1062. AL. B.

[22] Verf. einer liturgiegeschichtlich wichtigen *Epistula ad Senarium*, vielleicht identisch mit Papst I. I. (523–526). Text [1. 170–179].

[23] Verf. eines Katenenkommentars *Expositum in Heptateuchum* mit teils nur hier überlieferten Textfragmenten; setzt Victor von Capua (541–554) voraus, vielleicht identisch mit Papst I. III. (561–574). Auszüge [2. 278–302] und [3. 165–176].

1 A. Wilmart, Analecta Reginensia, Studi e testi 59, 1933 2 J. B. Pitra, Spicilegium Solesmense I, 1852 3 Ders., Analecta sacra et classica I, 1888 4 CPL, Nr. 950–952 und Register (Lit.). M. HE.

[24] I. Alexandrinus. → Iatrosophist und Schriftsteller in Alexandreia, wirkte zwischen 530 und 650 n. Chr. Obwohl er sich verschiedentlich auf seinen Lehrer bezieht (CMG 11,1,4, p. 12), bleibt → Gesios doch nur eine Mutmaßung. Sein überl. Werk besteht aus einem Komm. zu Galens *De sectis* (seine lat. Fassung [1] weist große Ähnlichkeit mit der des → Agnellus auf und wird auch dem Gesios zugeschrieben) und einem ebenfalls ins Lat. übers. Komm. [2] zum 6. Epidemien-B. des Hippokrates, wovon Fr. in griech. Sprache überl. sind [3]. Weitere griech. Fr. eines Komm. zu *De natura pueri* von Hippokrates wurden erstmalig von [4] publiziert. Ein umfangreiches medizinisches Kompendium, das in einer Hs. der Bibliothèque Nationale (Fond. gr. 2316) I. dem Iatrosophisten und in anderen Hss. dem I. Archiatros zugeschrieben wird, dürfte jedoch kaum von dem hier gemeinten I. stammen, der in arab. medizin. Texten ebenfalls mit Iohannes → Philoponos und dem sogar noch schwerer faßbaren I. Grammaticus verwechselt wurde [1]. Seine Komm. stellen typische Beispiele spätalexandrinischer Gelehrsamkeit dar: Während er sich streng an die galenischen Deutungsangebote des Hippokrates hält, ist I. doch unabhängiger Gedanken fähig, die auf Vorkommnissen in seiner eigenen Praxis gründen. Trotz seines christl. Namens hält er in den Komm. Anspielungen auf den rel. Bereich mit Bedacht neutral.

1 C. D. Pritchet (ed.), Iohannis Alexandrini commentaria in librum De Sectis Galeni, 1982 2 Ders. (ed.), Iohannis Alexandrini commentaria in sextum librum Hippocratis Epidemiarum, 1975 3 J. M. Duffy (Hrsg.), CMG 11,1,4,25–107 4 Ders., CMG 11,1,4,127–175.

O. Temkin, Gesch. des Hippokratismus im ausgehenden Alt., in: Kyklos 4, 1932, 66–71. V. N./Ü: L. v. R.-B.

[25] I. von Gaza. Griech. Rhetor und Dichter des 6. Jh. n. Chr., Verf. von anakreontischen Gelegenheitsgedichten [1; 3] und einer zwischen B. 14 und 15 der Anth. Pal. überl. poetischen → Ekphrasis [2] eines Kuppelgemäldes im Winterbad zu Antiocheia (vor 526: [4]), das den Kosmos in allegorischen Figuren darstellte [5]. Das Gedicht, 2 B. in Hexametern mit je einer iambischen Einl., lehnt sich in Stil und Metrik an → Nonnos an [6].

Ed.: 1 T. Bergk, Poetae Lyrici Graeci 3, [4]1882, 342–348 2 P. Friedländer, 1912.
Lit.: 3 R. Gentile Messina, Note alle Anacreontee di Giovanni di Gaza, in: Studi di filologia bizantina 4, 1988, 33–39 4 A. Cameron, On the date of J. of G., in: CQ 43, 1993, 348–351 5 C. Cupane, Il κοσμικὸς πίναξ di Giovanni di Gaza, in: Jb. der österreich. Byzantinistik 28, 1979, 195–207 6 C. Caiazzo, L'esametro di Giovanni di Gaza, in: Ταλαρίσκος. FS A. Garzya, 1987, 243–252. P. L. S.

[26] I. von Ephesos (ca. 507–ca. 588 n. Chr.). Syr. Autor, geb. bei Amida, wurde schon in jungen Jahren Mönch. Er unternahm weite Reisen, hielt sich mehrmals in Konstantinopel auf (u. a. Gefängnishaft unter Iustinus [4] II.). Trotz seiner Zugehörigkeit zur syr.-orthodoxen Kirche wurde er von Iustinianus [1] (ca. 542 n. Chr.) damit beauftragt, die pagane Bevölkerung in der Gegend um Ephesos zu bekehren.

I. verfaßte zwei wichtige Werke: 1) ›Leben der oriental. Heiligen‹: 58 Kurzbiographien syrisch-orthodoxer Heiliger (Männer und Frauen), zumeist aus dem Gebiet von Amida. 2) Eine Kirchengesch. in drei Teilen: der erste Teil, von Iulius Caesar bis zum J. 449, ist verloren; der zweite, von 449 bis 571, teilweise erh. – interessanterweise als Einfügung in die Chronik von Zuqnīn aus dem 8. Jh. (→ [Ps.-]Dionysios [23] von Tell-Maḥrē, → Iošua Stylites) –; der dritte (bis 588) ist erhalten.
→ Monophysitismus

Ed.: ›Leben der oriental. Hl.‹: E. W. Brooks, Patrologia Orientalis 17–19, 1923 f. • Kirchengesch.: J. B. Chabot, E. W. Brooks R. Hespel, CSCO Scr. Syri 53 und 213, 1933 bzw. 1989 (Teil 2) • W. Witakowski, 1996 (engl. Übers.) • E. W. Brooks, CSCO Scr. Syri 54 f., 1935 f. (Teil 3).
Lit.: A. D'yakonov, Ioann Yefesskiy, 1908 • S. A. Harvey, Asceticism and society in Crisis: John of Ephesus and the Lives of the Eastern Saints, 1990 • L. M. Whitby, John of Ephesus and the pagans, in: M. Salomon (ed.), Paganism in the Later Roman Empire and in Byzantium, 1991, 111–131 • J. J. van Ginkel, John of Ephesus. A Monophysite Historian in Sixth-Century Byzantium, Diss. Groningen 1995. S. BR./Ü: S. Z.

[27] I. IV. Nesteutes. Patriarch von Konstantinopel (582–595). Bereits zu Lebzeiten aufgrund seiner asketischen Lebensführung – daher Beiname »der Faster« (νηστευτής, *ieiunator*) – im Ruf der Heiligkeit stehend, wurde der Mönch und Kleriker der → Hagia Sophia 582 Nachfolger des Eutychios. Gegen den von ihm ab 587 offiziell verwendeten Titel οἰκουμενικὸς πατριάρχης (»ökumenischer Patriarch«) protestierten die Päpste Pelagius II. und Gregorius [3] I., d.Gr. Mit I.' Namen verbindet die byz. Tradition diverse pseudepigraphische Schriften (vgl. [2. 423 f.]; CPG 7555–7560), bes. zur Bußdisziplin, u. a. das sog. *Protokanonarion* (Bußbuch, wohl 9./10. Jh.; Text: [1. 23–129]).

1 M. Arranz, I penitenziali bizantini, 1993 2 H.-G. Beck, Kirche und theologische Lit. im byz. Reich, [2]1977, 423–425 3 D. Stiernon, s. v. Jean (129) le Jeuneur, in: Dictionnaire de Spiritualité 8, 1974, 586–589. J. RI.

[28] I. Scholastikos. Als Sohn eines Geistlichen bei Antiocheia geb., war I. zuerst als *scholastikós* (Rechtsgelehrter) tätig, wurde dann (um 550 n. Chr.) Presbyter in Antiocheia und nach einer Tätigkeit als *apokrisiarios* (kirchlicher Botschafter) des antiochenischen Patriarchen in Konstantinopel dort als Iohannes III. im J. 565 Patriarch. 577 starb er. I. schrieb sowohl juristische wie theologische Texte (κατηχητικὸς λόγος, bezeugt bei Photios, bibl. cod. 75); erh. geblieben sind freilich nur zwei kirchenjuristische Werke (CPG 3, 7550/51): die älteste erh. Slg. der → *Kanones* der kirchlichen Konzilien und Provinzialsynoden (samt den *Canones Apostolorum*) ist seine *Synagōgḗ kanónōn* (Συναγωγὴ κανόνων), die freilich ihrerseits auf einer verlorenen Slg. beruhte; dazu erstellte I. eine Sammlung kirchlich relevanter Texte aus den Novellen des Kaisers → Iustinianus [1].

V. N. Beneševič (Ed.), Sinagogá v 50 Titulov i drugie juridičeskie sborniki Joanna Scholastika, 1914 (Ndr. 1972) • E. Schwartz, Die Kanonessammlungen der alten Reichskirche, in: Ders., Gesammelte Schriften 4, 1960, 159–176 • Ders., Die Kanonessammlung des Johannes Scholastikos, SB der bayerischen Akad. der Wiss. (Phil.-histor. Klasse 6), 1933. C. M.

[29] I. Moschos, besser I. Eukrates. Sohn des Moschos, wurde bald nach 550 n. Chr. (vielleicht in Damaskos) geb. und war Mönch im Kloster des Theodosios zw. Jerusalem und Bethlehem. Er ging später in die neue Laura (Mönchssiedlung) des Sabas, verließ Palaestina nach der pers. Eroberung im J. 614 endgültig und starb nach einer regen Reisetätigkeit im Frühjahr 619 (oder 634) in Rom. Sein einziges Werk ist die ›Geistliche Wiese‹ (*Leimṓn, Leimōnárion* bzw. *Néos parádeisos, Pratum spiritale*, PG 87/3, 2852–3112; CPG 3, 7376); sie wurde von seinem Schüler und Reisebegleiter, dem späteren Jerusalemer Patriarchen → Sophronios († 638) herausgegeben und enthält nach dem Vorbild anderer Mönchsgeschichten (wie der → *Historia monachorum*) Lebensbeschreibungen, Erzählungen und Worte bed. zeitgenössischer Mönche. I. verteidigte das Konzil von Chalkedon inmitten von eher chalkedonkritischem Mönchtum; sowohl für die entsprechenden Auseinandersetzungen wie für die Krisenzeit vor der pers. Invasion ist die ›Wiese‹ eine einzigartige Quelle. Sie wurde eines der meistgelesenen Bücher des byz. MA.

H. Chadwick, John Moschus and his Friend Sophronius the Sophist, in: Journal of Theological Studies 25, 1974, 41–74 • H. Usener, Der hl. Tychon, 1907, 83–107. C. M.

[30] I. Klimakos, auch Scholastikos oder Sinaïtes gen. (Κλῖμαξ, ὁ τῆς κλίμακος bzw. σχολαστικός oder σιναΐτης).

A. Leben B. Werk und Theologie

A. Leben

I. wurde um 579 n. Chr. geb. und starb nach 654. Seinen Beinamen erhielt er nach seinem Hauptwerk ›Himmelsleiter‹. Er wurde mit 16 J. koinobitischer Mönch des Katharinenklosters auf dem Sinai u. a. unter Anastasios [5] von Antiocheia und lebte nach dessen Tod 40 J. dort als Eremit; gegen Ende seines Lebens wurde er Abt des Sinai-Klosters.

B. Werk und Theologie

Sein Hauptwerk ›Himmelsleiter‹ (Κλῖμαξ τοῦ παραδείσου, *Klímax tú paradeísu*), das er auf Anregung seines Freundes Iohannes von Raithu verfaßte, erlangte normativen Wert für die Theorie der mystagogischen Lebensführung. Das Werk beschreibt in Anlehnung an die »Jakobsleiter« des AT (Gn 28) das Leben des Mystikers als einen Aufstieg zu Gott über 30 Stufen (entsprechend der 30 J. des verborgenen Lebens Christi). In Abhängigkeit v. a. von → Euagrios [1] Pontikos und unter Einbringung eigener mystischer Erfahrung gibt I. den Mönchen eine Anleitung zur »Seelenruhe« (ἀπάθεια, *apátheia*), zur Heiligung ihres Lebens, das aus dem inneren Kampf mit den eigenen Affekten (πάθη, *páthē*) hervorgehen muß; dieses Motiv beeinflußte die Ikonographie, die die *páthē* als personifizierte Dämonen darstellt, wie sie den Mystiker von der Leiter, an deren Ende Christus die Aufsteigenden erwartet, reißen. Eine Fortsetzung dieser Schrift ist das sog. ›Handbuch für den Abt‹ (λόγος πρὸς τῶν ποιμένα), das sich auf eine Anfrage des I. von Raithu bezieht.

Ed.: PG 88, 631–1210.
Lit.: W. Völker, Scala Paradisi, 1968 • H. G. Beck, Kirche und theologische Lit., [3]1989, 451 f. K. SA.

[31] I. von Thessalonike. Im Titel der Erzählung über die Wunder des hl. Demetrios von Thessalonike *Miracula S. Demetrii* als Verf. gen. hl. Erzbischof. Er ist wohl identisch mit dem im zweiten B. der Schrift erwähnten, bereits verstorbenen, wunderwirkenden Abt I., dem Erretter von Thessalonike bei einer Belagerung durch die Slaven im frühen 7. Jh. n. Chr. Erst von einem späteren Redaktor wurde er zum Autor des Textes gemacht und mit dem histor., um 680 bezeugten Erzbischof I. von → Thessalonike identifiziert. Der Kult des hl. Demetrios war urspr. in → Sirmium beheimatet und wurde beim endgültigen Verlust der Stadt 582 n. Chr. nach der Stadt Thessalonike übertragen, zu deren Schutzheiligen Demetrios im Lauf des 7. Jh. wurde. Die Wundererzählung spiegelt diese Entwicklung wider, indem sie eine Reihe von urspr. anderen Personen zugehörigen Wundern auf Demetrios überträgt; in der h. vorliegenden Form wurde sie im 9. Jh. aus älterem Material zusammengestellt und muß deshalb als Quelle vorsichtig interpretiert werden.

P. Lemerle, Les plus anciens recueils des miracles de Saint Démétrius, 2 Bde., 1979–1981 • P. Speck, De miraculis Sancti Demetrii, qui Thessalonicam profugus venit, in: Varia IV, Poikila Byzantina 12, 1993, 255–532. AL.B.

[32] I. Eleemon, der Barmherzige. Geboren in Amathus auf Zypern, orthodoxer Patriarch von Alexandreia seit 610 n. Chr., floh 619 bei der Eroberung Ägyptens durch die Perser in seine Heimat, wo er bald danach starb. I. erhielt den Beinamen Ἐλεήμων (der Barmherzige) aufgrund seiner karitativen Tätigkeit in Alexandreia, wo er u. a. mehrere Hospitäler stiftete und Flüchtlinge betreute. I. wird von der orthodoxen Kirche als Hl. verehrt. Seine von Leontios von Neapolis verfaßte Vita ist erh., zwei weitere Viten von → Iohannes [29] Moschos und → Sophronios sind dagegen nur in Auszügen überliefert.
→ Leontios von Neapolis

A.-J. Festugière, L. Rydén (ed.), Léontios de Néapolis, Vie de Syméon le Fou et Vie de Jean de Chypre, 1974, 257–637 • ODB 2, 1058f. AL.B.

[33] I. von Damaskos. A. Leben B. Werk

A. Leben

I. wurde um 650 n. Chr. als Sohn der wohlhabenden Familie Manṣūr in → Damaskos geboren. Er genoß zusammen mit seinem Adoptivbruder → Kosmas von Maiuma eine Allgemeinbildung im Sinne des hell. Fächerkanons. Sein Vertrauensamt am Hof des Kalifen Yazīd (680–683) legte er nach Verschlechterung der Lage der Christen unter ʿUmar II. (717–720) nieder und zog sich mit Kosmas nach Mar Saba zurück. Dort widmete er sich dem kontemplativen Leben und verfaßte Werke zur Darstellung und Verteidigung der Orthodoxie. Als Berater in kirchenpolit. Fragen wurde er sehr geschätzt. Von Iohannes V. von Jerusalem wurde er auf den Titel der Anastasis-Kirche in der hl. Stadt geweiht. Während des Bilderstreites (→ Leo III., → Syrische Dynastie) entwickelte er eine dezidierte Theologie des Bildes, die maßgeblich für die Ikonentheologie wurde. Ebenso setzte er Maßstäbe in der kirchlichen Hymnendichtung (Blüte des → Kanon). Sein Todesjahr ist nicht bekannt; er wurde in Mar Saba beigesetzt. Die Siebte Ökumenenische Synode von → Nikaia (787) hob das dreifache Anathema, das die Ikonoklastensynode in Hiera (754) über ihn verhängt hatte, auf.

B. Werk

Die kompilatorische Hauptschrift *Pēgḗ gnṓseōs* (Πηγὴ γνώσεως), die er seinem Bruder Kosmas widmete, behandelt die griech.-röm. Philos. und bietet eine genaue Auslegung des rechten Glaubens in Abgrenzung zu den Häresien. In den ›Drei Reden an die Schmäher der hl. Ikonen‹ (CPG 8045) wird die Ikonentheologie entwikkelt: Dem dialektischen Verhältnis von Prototyp und Antityp entspricht die Unterscheidung von Verehrung des Bildes (προσκύνησις, *proskýnēsis*) und Anbetung der Gottheit (λατρεία, *latreía*). Im Roman von → ›Barlaam und Ioasaph‹ werden Buddha-Legende und ind. Fabeln christl. gedeutet. Die meisten Hss. und die älteste Vita (arab.) sprechen sich für I. als Autor dieses Werkes aus.

Ed.: B. Kotter (ed.), Die Schriften des J. von Damaskos I–V (Patristische Texte und Stud. 7, 12, 17, 22, 29), 1969–1986.
Lit.: R. Volk, Urtext und Modifikationen des griech. Barlaam-Romans, in: ByzZ 86/7, 1993/4, 442–461 • F. R. Gahbauer, Die Anthropologie des Johannes von Damaskos, in: Theologie und Philos. 69, 1994, 1–21. K.SA.

[34] I. von Nikiu († kurz nach 700 n. Chr.). In der Zeit der arab. Eroberung Ägyptens (639–642) geb., wirkte I. als Bischof der auf einer Insel im westl. Hauptarm des Nils gelegenen unterägypt. Stadt Nikiu. 696 zum Generalaufseher der Klöster bestellt, wurde er wenig später wegen Amtsmißbrauchs abgesetzt. Der Monophysit (→ Monophysitismus) ist Verf. einer urspr. wohl kopt. [4. 1367] abgefaßten Weltchronik, die in einer verstümmelten äthiop. Übers. (Anf. 17. Jh.) – basierend auf einer arab. Übertragung – erh. ist. Von verschiedenen Quellen (→ Iohannes [18] Malalas u. a.) abhängig, ist I. trotz Lücken ein Hauptzeuge für die polit. und kirchlichen Vorgänge in Äg. zw. 580 n. Chr. und der arab. Eroberung.

Ed.: **1** H. Zotenberg, Chronique de Jéan, évêque de Nikiou. Texte éthiopien publiés et traduit, 1883 **2** R. H. Charles, The chronicle of John, Bishop of Nikiu, 1916 (engl. Übers.; Ndr. 1980).
Lit: **3** A. Carile, Giovanni di Nikiu, cronista bizantino-copto del VII secolo, in: N. A. Stratos (Hrsg.), Byzantion: aphieroma ston Andrea N. Stratos 2, 1986, 353–398 **4** P. M. Fraser, s. v. John of Nikiu, The Coptic Encyclopedia 5, 1991, 1366f. J.RI.

[35] I. I. Tzimiskes. Byz. Kaiser 969–976; geb. um 925 n. Chr.; Armenier; General unter seinem Onkel und Vorgänger → Nikephoros II., den er im Dez. 969 ermordete. I. siegte 971 über Fürst Svjatoslav von Kiev und kämpfte 972 und 974–975 erfolgreich in Syrien gegen die äg. Fatimiden. ODB 2, 1045. F.T.

[36] I. Philoponos s. Philoponos

[37] I. Skylitzes s. Skylitzes

[38] I. Mauropus s. Mauropus

Iokaste (Ἰοκάστη, in älteren Quellen auch Epikaste/ Ἐπικάστη). Tochter des → Menoikeus, Schwester des → Kreon, Gemahlin des → Laios, Mutter und später Gattin des → Oidipus. Trotz des negativen Orakelspruchs des Apollon in Delphi zeugt Laios mit I. Oidipus, der nach der Geburt ausgesetzt wird, später den Vater tötet und, nachdem er das Rätsel der → Sphinx gelöst hat, die Mutter heiratet. In den älteren Quellen offenbaren die Götter den Inzest (Hom. Od. 11,271–280), worauf sich I. tötet. I. hat hier meist zwei Söhne (Phrastor, Laonytos), die im Krieg mit den Minyern umkommen. Seine Kinder (→ Eteokles [1], → Polyneikes, → Antigone [3], → Ismene [1]) zeugt Oidipus mit seiner zweiten Gattin → Euryganeia, der Schwester der I. (Pherekydes, FGrH 3 F 95; Peisandros, FGrH 16 F 10; Epimenides, FGrH 457 F 13; Paus. 9,5,10f.). Erst die Tragiker machen I. zur Mutter der Kinder des Oidipus (Aischyl. Sept. 926ff.; Soph. Oid. T.); bei Sophokles erhängt sie sich nach der Aufdeckung des Inzests (Oid. T. 1235ff.), während spätere Quellen sie als Vermittlerin im Krieg zw. Eteokles und Polyneikes zeigen, wo ihr Scheitern sie in den Selbstmord treibt (Eur. Phoen.; Hyg. fab. 243; Stat. Theb. 7,470ff.; 11,315ff.; 642ff.).

LIT.: E. BETHE, s.v I., RE 8, 1841–1842 • J.M. BREMER, A.M. VAN TAALMAN KIP, S.R. SLINGS, Some Recently Found Greek Poems, 1987, 164–172 • I. KRAUSKOPF, s.v. I., LIMC 5.1, 682–683.
ABB.: I. KRAUSKOPF, s.v. I., LIMC 5.2, 458. R.HA.

Iolaos (Ἰόλαος).
[1] Neffe des → Herakles, Sohn von dessen Halbbruder → Iphikles und der (schattenhaften) Automedusa. Er begleitet Herakles auf praktisch allen seinen Abenteuern (v.a. als Wagenlenker), wird der erste Olympionike (Bild in Olympia, Paus. 5,17,11), erhält von Herakles → Megara zur Frau und tötet schließlich → Eurystheus in Attika (Paus. 1,44,10, Grab), wozu er eigens für einen Tag verjüngt wurde (Eur. Heraclid. 843–863, vielleicht nach Aischyl. fr. 361); er starb in Theben (Pind. O. 9,80) oder Sardis (Paus. 9,23,1). Entsprechend hat I. wenig eigene mythische Statur; immerhin soll er nach Herakles' Tod Kolonisten aus Athen und Thespiai nach Sardinien geführt und die Nuraghen gebaut haben (Diod. 4,29. 5,15; Paus. 7,2,2; Aristot. mir. 100).

Auch im Kult ist I. meist mit Herakles verbunden (Plut. mor. 492c); wo Einzelheiten faßbar sind, erscheint er spezifisch als ein Heros der jungen Männer. In Theben hat er ein → *témenos*, das mit einem Gymnasion und einem Stadion verbunden ist (Arr. an. 1,7,7; Paus. 9,23,1; Pferderennen: Pind. N. 5,32; Kult: Pind. P. 9,79) und sein Grab enthält, das auch dasjenige seines Großvaters → Amphitryon ist (Pind. O. 9,81); hier besiegeln Erastes und Eromenos ihren Liebesbund (Aristot. fr. 97; Plut. mor. 761de). Er ist in das große Fest der Herakleia so einbezogen, daß diese auch Iolaeia heißen (schol. Pind. O. 7,53). Die Forsch. nimmt gewöhnlich an, daß I. der Vorgänger des Herakles im theban. Kult ist; wichtiger ist, daß das Miteinander der beiden Heroen die Riten der thebanischen jungen Männer spiegelt. Selbständiger ist sein Kult in Agyrion auf Sizilien mit einem von Herakles eingerichteten Heiligtum an einem See vor der Stadt, wo jedes Jahr ein bedeutendes Opferfest stattfand und wo die Epheben ihre Haare opferten. Zwar paßt auch hier die Betonung der Riten der jungen Männer zum theban. Befund, doch ist vielleicht ein älterer Lokalkult auf I. übertragen worden (Diod. 4,24,4).

NILSSON, Feste 449f. • SCHACHTER 2, 17f.; 64f. • M. PIPILI, s.v. I., LIMC 5, 686–696. F.G.

[2] Von → Perdikkas 432 v.Chr. mit 200 Mann als Oberbefehlshaber der Kavallerie bei → Poteidaia abgesandt, nahm aber an der Schlacht gegen die Athener dann nicht teil. Wahrscheinlich Vater von → Antipatros [1] (Thuk. 1,62f.; oft mißverstanden).

S. HORNBLOWER, Commentary on Thucydides 1, 1991, 165 • J. SUNDWALL, s.v. Iolaos (4), RE 9, 1847. E.B.

[3] Sohn des → Antipatros [1], Enkel von I. [2], Mundschenk des → Alexandros [4] d.Gr. in dessen letztem Lebensjahr; wurde später vom Kreis der → Olympias beschuldigt, ihn vergiftet zu haben (verworfen von Arr. an. 7,27,1f.; akzeptiert z.B. von Diod. 17,118,1 und im → Alexanderroman ausgesponnen). 322 v.Chr. führte er seine Schwester → Nikaia dem → Perdikkas als Braut zu (Arr. an. 21; Diod. 18,23,3). 317 wurde sein Grab von Olympias demonstrativ geschändet (Diod. 19,11,8). E.B.

[4] Nur inschr. bezeugter [1. test.] Komödiendichter, der 177 v.Chr. an den Dionysien den zweiten Preis erhielt.

PCG V, 608. H.-G.NE.

Iolaos-Roman. Als I.-R. wird ein Werk bezeichnet, das uns nur aus einem einzigen Papyrusfragment (POxy. 3010, Anf. 2. Jh. n.Chr.) bekannt ist. Darin begibt sich jemand zu einem gewissen Iolaos und hält ihm einen Vortrag in sotadeischen Versen: er sei ein Gallus geworden, d.h. ein entmannter Anhänger der Kybele [1. 57] und wisse alles. Der Papyrus bricht mit einem Euripideszitat (Eur. Or. 1155–7) über den Wert der Freundschaft ab. Die Bedeutung des Fragments liegt in der Verwendung des → Prosimetrums (der Unterschied zw. Prosa und Versen ist auch graphisch gekennzeichnet) in einer komischen Erzählung: Man hat deswegen eine Verbindung zum *Satyricon* des → Petronius vermutet; jedenfalls ist damit die Existenz eines realistisch-komischen Romans bei den Griechen belegt (wie auch die *Phoinikiká* des → Lollianos).
→ Roman

1 P. PARSONS, A Greek Satyricon?, in: BICS 18, 1971, 53–68
2 Ancient Greek Novels. The Fragments, ed. S.A. STEPHENS, J.J. WINKLER, 1995, 358–374.
M.FU. u. L.G./Ü: T.H.

Joldelund im Kreis Nordfriesland. Ein mod. untersuchtes german. Eisenproduktionszentrum der späten Kaiser- und frühen Völkerwanderungszeit (ca. 350–450 n. Chr.). Im Bereich einer dörflichen Siedlung mit mehreren bäuerlichen Gehöften erfolgte eine spezialisierte Verhüttung lokal vorkommender Raseneisenerze in mehreren hundert Rennfeueröfen, die auf ca. 8 ha verteilt gefunden wurden. Das gewonnene Roheisen wurde auf mehreren Schmiedeplätzen am Ort weiter aufbereitet. Die erforderliche Holzkohle wurde in J. auf mindestens einem nachgewiesenen Meilerplatz erzeugt. → Eisen; Germanische Archäologie

S. Backer u. a., Frühgesch. Eisengewinnung und -verarbeitung am Kammberg bei J., in: M. Müller-Wille, D. Hoffmann, Der Vergangenheit auf der Spur, 1992, 83–110 • H. Jöns, Frühe Eisengewinnung in J., Kr. Nordfriesland, 1997. V. P.

Iole (Ἰόλη). Tochter des → Eurytos [1], des Königs von Oichalia, und der Antioche (Hes. cat. fr. 26,31a), Schwester des von Herakles ermordeten → Iphitos (vgl. Hom. Od. 21,11–41). Obwohl Herakles I. in dem von Eurytos veranstalteten Bogenkampf gewinnt, verweigert ihm dieser seine Tochter (Pherekydes FGrH 3 F 82a; Apollod. 2,6,1–3; Diod. 4,31,37). Aus Rache für den ihm zur Sühne des Mordes an Iphitos auferlegten Sklavendienst bei → Omphale zerstört Herakles Oichalia und entführt I. als seine Geliebte (Soph. Trach. 68–75; 254–260; 856–862; Bakchyl. 16). Seine Gattin → Deianeira tötet darauf Herakles durch ein vergiftetes Gewand, das sie von → Nessos erhält und mit dessen Hilfe sie seine Liebe zurückgewinnen will (Soph. Trach.). Der sterbende Herakles gibt I. seinem Sohn → Hyllos [1] zur Frau (Soph. Trach. 1219–1228). Herakles' Werbung um I. und die Zerstörung von Oichalia waren sehr wahrscheinlich Inhalt des verlorenen, dem Kreophylos von Samos zugeschriebenen Epos *Oichalías hálōsis* (»Die Einnahme von Oichalia«, EpGF, p. 149–153). Ein korinth. Krater (600–590 v. Chr.) zeigt Herakles, Eurytos, seine Söhne und I., vgl. [1]. Bei Sophokles und Bakchylides steht Deianeiras Reaktion auf die Ankunft der I. im Mittelpunkt. Vielleicht erzählte auch Panyassis von Halikarnassos in seinen *Herakleia* den Mythos.

1 R. Olmos, s. v. I. (1), LIMC 5.1, 700.

A. Beck, Der Empfang I.s, in: Hermes 81, 1953, 10–21 • L. Bergson, Herakles, Deianeira und I., in: RhM 136, 1993, 102–115. • S. Eitrem, s. v. I., RE 9, 1847–1848. K. WA.

Iolkos (Ἰωλκός). Schon in ältesten Sagen (Aison, Alkestis, Argonautai, Iason, Neleus, Peleus, Pelias) gen. Residenzstadt am Nordausgang des Golfs von → Pagasai am Anauros (h. Xerias). Ein großer Siedlungshügel in der Altstadt von Volos (Kastro Volo) bezeugt Siedlungskontinuität spätestens seit der frühen Brz. – zahlreiche myk. Gräber, zwei Palastanlagen, ein dor. Tempel (Artemis Iolkia). Große myk. Anlagen bei Dimini lassen den myth. Ort I. auch dort vermuten. Pevkakia Magula (→ Neleia) an der Küste bei → Demetrias [1] kommt aufgrund von Funden evtl. als Hafen zumindest des myk. I. in Betracht, so daß I. möglicherweise ein Name mehrerer zusammengehörender Siedlungskerne ist.

Gräber in und um Kastro Volo zeigen eine Blüte des Orts in myk. und der Kaiserzeit. Der Rückgang Anf. der histor. Zeit erklärt sich evtl. aus der Verlandung des Hafens und der Gründung von Pagasai als Hafen der Thessaloi (vgl. Peleussage). Diese boten Anf. 5. Jh. I. dem Hippias an (Hdt. 5,94,1). Um 290 v. Chr. wurde I. Demetrias [1] eingemeindet (Strab. 9,5,15). 169 v. Chr. landete die röm. Flotte bei I., um von dort aus Demetrias anzugreifen (Liv. 44,12,8; 13,4). In byz. Zeit befestigter Bischofssitz. Im 14. Jh. hieß die Stadt Golos (später Volos).

B. G. Intzesiloglou, Ιστορική τοπογραφία της περιοχής του κόλπου του Βόλου [Istoriki topographia tis periochis tou kolpou tou Volou], in: La Thessalie, Quinze années de recherches archéologiques 1975–1990, 1994, 31 ff. • K. Liapis, Το κάστρο του Βόλου μέσα στους αιώνες [To kástro tou Volou mesa stous aiones], 1991, 14 ff. • Philippson/Kirsten 1, 154 f. • F. Stählin, s. v. I., RE 9, 1850 ff. (dort Quellen) • Ders., Das hellen. Thessalien, 1924, 62 ff., 75 f. • D. Theocharis, I., whence sailed the Argonauts, in: Archaeology 11, 1958, 13 ff. • TIB 1, 1976, 165 f. HE. KR.

Iomedes (Ἰομήδης). Sonst unbekannter Verf. einer im syr. Nemra (Namarae Batanaeorum) gefundenen Grabinschr. aus dem 2. oder 3. Jh. n. Chr. (fünf teilweise beschädigte Distichen). Der Dichter, der sich selbst als ›Herr (*prýtanis*) der ausonischen Muse‹ (V. 10) bezeichnet, feiert dort die eigenen Vorväter, die einst am selben Ort ein Denkmal der Tyche geweiht hatten. Am Ende (V. 9) zeichnet er mit seinem Namen (τήνδ' Ἰομήδης), hinter dem man – angesichts seiner absoluten Singularität – eine beabsichtigte und geistreiche Änderung von »Diomedes« vermutet hat [1].

1 EpGr 440 2 Anth. Pal. appendix II 665 Cougny.

M. G. A./Ü: T. H.

Ion (Ἴων).

[1] Eponymer Heros der Ionier (→ Iones). Über seine Abstammung gibt es verschiedene Traditionen, die den polit. Primat Athens in den Vordergrund stellen. In den frühen und prägendsten Versionen erscheint I. als Sohn des → Xuthos und der Kreusa und damit als Enkel des → Hellen, des Stammvaters der Hellenen, und des athen. Königs → Erechtheus (Strab. 8,383; Paus. 7,1,2). I.s Bruder ist Achaios [1], der Stammvater der Achaier, seine Onkel von Vaterseite sind → Aiolos [1] und → Doros. Mit seiner Gattin → Helike, der Tochter des peloponnes. Königs Selinos, zeugt I. die Söhne Geleon, Hoples, Argades und Aigikores, nach denen die vier att.-ionischen Urphylen benannt sind (Arist. Ath. pol. 41,2). Paus. 7,1,5 berichtet, daß I. den Athenern von der Peloponnes her gegen die Eleusinier zur Hilfe gekommen und dabei gefallen sei. Durch ihre Abstammung vom gemeinsamen Vater Xuthos wird den Achaiern und Ioniern innerhalb des griech. Stämmegefüges eine engere Zusammengehörigkeit zugesprochen. Indes werden die Insel- und kleinasiat. Ionier erst ganz spät als Nachkommen des I. bezeichnet (Vell. 1,4; Vitr. 6,1).

In der anderen Version der Genealogie, wie sie in der Trag. *I.* des Euripides und bei Platon (Euthyd. 302c) zutage tritt, wird der Führungsanspruch Athens über das griech. Mutterland sogar noch klarer formuliert, indem jegliche nicht-athen. Abstammung eliminiert ist (inwiefern eine gleichnamige Trag. des Sophokles denselben Stoff behandelte, ist ungeklärt): Im Unterschied zu seinen Brüdern Aiolos und Doros wird I. zum Sohn des Gottes → Apollon gemacht. Kreusa hatte den von Apollon empfangenen und heimlich geborenen Sohn unmittelbar nach der Geburt in einer Höhle ausgesetzt. Hermes übergibt I. aber zur Aufzucht dem Apollon-Tempel in Delphi, wo er Tempelwächter wird. Kreusa heiratet später den König Xuthos; ihre Ehe bleibt aber vorerst kinderlos. Ein Besuch beim Apollon-Orakel in Delphi soll Aufschluß bringen. Nach einigen Verwicklungen kommt es schließlich zur Anagnorisis von Mutter und Sohn: Xuthos erkennt I., der nach Gebot des Apollon der → Eponym der kleinasiat. Ionier werden soll (Eur. Ion 74; 1581–1588), an Sohnes Statt an.

Für I. und seine Söhne ist ein Kult aus Samos bezeugt; im ostatt. Potamoi zeigte man zudem das Grab des I. (Paus. 1,31,3), was ebenfalls auf einen Heroenkult deutet. Auch steht I. in direkter Verbindung mit dem Kult des → Apollon als Patroos, wie er in Athen, auf Delos und in Kleinasien verehrt wurde und der mit dem Apollon Pythios und Hypoakraios identisch ist, der am Nordwesthang der Akropolis einen Höhlenkult besaß. Dort soll Kreusa ihren Sohn I. ausgesetzt haben.

1 W. A. OLDFATHER, s. v. I. (3), RE 9, 1857–1860
2 R. PARKER, Myths of Early Athens, in: J. BREMMER (Hrsg.), Interpretations of Greek Mythology, 1987, 206–207
3 E. PRINZ, Gründungsmythen und Sagenchronologie, 1979, 356–370; 446–450 4 E. SIMON, s. v. I., LIMC 5.1, 702–704. C. W.

[2] I. aus Chios, ca. 480–423/2 v. Chr. Bereits als junger Mann kam er nach Athen (zw. 465–462, TrGF 19 T 4a). Er ist eine Ausnahmeerscheinung unter den Literaten des 5. Jh., da er sich in verschiedenen Gattungen – sowohl in Prosa wie in der Poesie – betätigte. Kallimachos würdigt in den Iamben ausdrücklich die Vielfalt von I.s Werk (fr. 203,43 ff. PFEIFFER). I. hat vermutlich zehn trag. Tetralogien verfaßt; in Alexandreia waren wohl nur noch zwölf Stücke bekannt. Sein Debut als Tragiker erfolgte zw. 451 und 448, an den Dionysien 428 unterlag er → Euripides und → Iophon [2] (T 5), ein nicht datierbarer Sieg im Tragödien- und Dithyrambenagon im selben Jahr ist bezeugt (T 3). Erhalten sind 68 Fragmente, darunter auch aus lyrischen Partien (F 10; F 14); bekannt sind 11 Titel, darunter das Satyrspiel *Omphálē* und der singuläre Titel *Méga Dráma* (›Das große Drama‹). Ps.-Longinos (33,5) betont, daß I. untadelige und elegante Trag. verfaßt habe, der poetische Schwung und die Inspiration eines Sophokles hätten ihm jedoch gefehlt. Die Scholien-Notiz, I. habe auch Komödien gedichtet, bezieht sich wohl auf seine Satyrspiele (PCG V, p. 608).

Als lyr. Dichter hat I. Dithyramben, Hymnen und Enkomien verfaßt (PMG 740–746). Aristoph. Pax 828 ff. bringt I. in Zusammenhang mit den durch die Neue Musik des ausgehenden 5. Jh. v. Chr. beeinflußten Dithyrambikern (vgl. auch → Kinesias in Aristoph. Av. 1372 ff). Bezeugt ist ein Hymnos auf den günstigen Augenblick (*Kairós*) und ein Enkomion auf einen sonst unbekannten Skythiades. Die Elegien (IEG II 26–32) scheinen sympotischen Anlässen zuzuordnen zu sein. Fr. 27 wurde vermutlich für ein von König → Archidamos [1] II. von Sparta veranstaltetes Symposion verfaßt. Ob die Gründungsgesch. von Chios (*Chíu ktísis*) ebenfalls eine Elegie oder ein Prosawerk gewesen ist, läßt sich nicht entscheiden (FGrH 392).

Sichere Prosawerke sind der *Triagmós* und die *Epidēmíai*: Im *Triagmós* gibt I. eine der pythagoreischen Lehre verpflichtete Welterklärung, der er die Dreizahl zugrunde legt (36 B 1 DK). Wie der Titel genau zu verstehen ist (Dreikampf, Dreiheit, Dreiteilung), ist unklar. Die *Epidēmíai* (›Reisebilder bzw. -erinnerungen‹) sind das erste Memoirenwerk der Lit.-Gesch. In ihnen berichtet I. über Begegnungen mit Größen seiner Zeit. Sie sind teils wichtige Quelle für die Biographie von I.s Zeitgenossen (fr. 5a BLUMENTHAL zu Aischylos' Teilnahme an der Schlacht von Salamis), teils geben sie Details zu deren Gewohnheiten und Aussehen (zu Kimon fr. 2 f. BLUMENTHAL, fr. 6 zu Perikles, fr. 11 zu Sokrates), teils weisen sie anekdotische Züge auf (fr. 8 B. zu Sophokles auf Chios).
→ Dithyrambos; Geschichtsschreibung; Tragödie; Satyrspiel; Pythagoreismus

A. v. BLUMENTHAL, Ion von Chios, 1939 · B. GAULY u. a. (Hrsg.), Musa tragica, 1991, 64–81, 274 f. · O. LENDLE, Einführung in die griech. Geschichtsschreibung, 1992, 28–32 · A. LEURINI, Ionis Chii testimonia et fragmenta, 1992 · M. L. WEST, Ion of Chios, in: BICS 32, 1985, 71–78. B. Z.

[3] I. aus Thessalonike, im 3. Maked. Krieg hoher Offizier des → Perseus (Liv. 42,58,10), dessen Kinder er 168 v. Chr. auf Samothrake den Römern auslieferte (Liv. 45,6,9; Plut. Aemilius Paulus 26,6). L.-M. G.
[4] Oberhalb von → Aiginion in den → Peneios mündender (Strab. 7,7,9) linker Nebenfluß im Chassiagebirge, h. Mourgani; an seinem Oberlauf die Stadt Oxyneia.

L. DARMEZIN, Sites archéologiques et territoires du massiv des Chassia, in: Topographie antique et géographie historique en pays grec, 1992, 139–155 · F. STÄHLIN, Das hellen. Thessalien, 1924, 114. HE. KR.

Jonathan (von hebr. *Yeho natan*, »Gott gab«). Name mehrerer biblischer Figuren sowie nachbiblischer Personen insbes. von Rabbinern aus dem 2. und 3. Jh.

n. Chr. Die wichtigsten biblischen Figuren dieses Namens sind 1) J., der Sohn des Gerschom, nach Ri 18,30 Priester des Stammes Dan, und 2) J., der Sohn Sauls, des ersten Königs von Israel (1 Sam 13 und 14). Der Sohn Sauls gilt als eine der edelsten Gestalten der Bibel. Seine aufrichtige und innige, von Saul jedoch nicht geschätzte Freundschaft zu → David [1] ist Gegenstand haggadischer Erzählungen (→ Haggada), die deren selbstlosen und wertfreien Aspekt gegenüber materialistisch-utilitaristisch geprägten Freundschaften betonen.

K. BUDDE, Das Buch der Richter, 1897 · Ders., Die Bücher Samuel, 1902 · W. DIETRICH, Die Samuelbücher, 1995 · L. GINZBERG, The Legends of the Jews, 1968 (Index). Y. D.

Iones (Ἴωνες, Ionier). Name eines griech. Stammes (ältere Form *Iāwones*), erstmals belegt in einem Knosos-Text (B 164, Z. 4) wohl als Bezeichnung einer fremdstämmigen Kriegerschar. Homer (Il. 13,685) bezieht den Namen auf die Athener, im del. Apollonhymnus (Hom. h. 5,147–155) ist die del. Festversammlung der I. gemeint, in der Amphiktyonie ist I. der Name des Stammes, den Athen und die euboi. Städte vertreten. In den weiteren Quellen der archa. und klass. Zeit heißen I. im engeren Sinn die Griechen Kleinasiens von Phokaia und Smyrna (beide auf vorher aiol. Gebiet) bis Milet mit den vorgelagerten Inseln Chios und Samos, im weiteren Sinn die Bewohner aller Gebiete, in denen seit alters Dial. der ion.-att. Gruppe (→ Attisch, → Ionisch) gesprochen wurden. Das waren neben Ionia in Kleinasien die Kyklades ohne Kythnos und den dor. Inselbogen von Melos bis Astypalaia, Euboia ohne die Dryoperstädte Styra und Karystos, Oropos und schließlich Athen mit seinem großen Gebiet.

Die kleinasiat. I. haben als loser Staatenbund institutionelle Relikte eines frühgesch. Stammverbandes bis in röm. Zeit bewahrt; daß aber nicht nur sie, sondern mit ihnen alle anderen I. einst eine polit. Einheit bildeten, beweisen einerseits ihre nahe verwandten Kalender (deren Vergleichung einen ur-ion. Fest- und Monatskalender erschließen läßt), andererseits die Tatsache, daß in vielen ion. Städten gleiche Phylennamen belegt sind. So kehren die Namen der vier vorkleisthenischen Phylen Athens, Aigikoreis, Argadeis, Geleontes und Hoplētes, in vielen ion. Städten wieder; die kleinasiat. Städte, jedenfalls Miletos, Ephesos und Samos, hatten dazu noch zwei weitere Phylen, Bōreis und Oinōpes. Demnach spricht viel dafür, daß die I. einst ein Stamm im östl. Mittelgriechenland waren, der sich im Verlauf der nachmyk. Wanderungen hier nur in Attika und Euboia behauptete, in seiner Masse aber über die Kykladen nach Kleinasien auswich und dort eine gewisse polit. Einheit noch längere Zeit bewahrte (woraus sich der engere Gebrauch des Namens erklärt). Seit dem frühen 1. Jt. war der Name der I. (in einer älteren Form *Jāwan*; früheste Erwähnung in keilschriftlichen Quellen E. 8. Jh. v. Chr., s. [1]) weithin in Vorderasien als der Name aller Griechen in Gebrauch; das geht wohl darauf zurück, daß es v. a. I. (aus Kleinasien und Euboia) waren, die den griech. Orienthandel trugen.

1 RLA 5, 150.

F. CASSOLA, La Ionia nel mondo miceneo, 1957 · M. B. SAKELLARIOU, La migration grecque en Ionie, 1958 · C. TRÜMPY, Unt. zu den altgriech. Monatsnamen und -folgen, 1997, 10–119. F. GSCH.

Jongleure s. Unterhaltungskünstler

Ionia (Ἰωνία, Ἰωνίη). Westanatol. Landschaft zw. Aiolis im Norden, Lydia im Osten, der Ägäis im Westen und Karia im Süden; sie umfaßt das kleinasiat. Siedlungsgebiet der im Zusammenhang der nachmyk. Wanderung dort eingezogenen und etwa seit 700 v. Chr. in der panion. Amphiktyonie zusammengeschlossen → Iones (vgl. die Beschreibungen von I. bei Strab. 14,1; Plin. nat. 5,112–120) mit den küstennahen Städten (vgl. Hdt. 1,142–148; Aischyl. Pers. 771) Miletos, Myus, Priene, Ephesos, Kolophon, Lebedos, Teos, Erythrai, Klazomenai, Symrna und Phokaia (die beiden zuletzt gen. urspr. aiol.) sowie den Inseln Samos und Chios (also unter Ausschluß der ion. Griechen auf den Kyklades, Euboia, in Oropos und Attika). I. war nie ein verwaltungstechnischer Terminus.

J. M. COOK, The Greeks in Ionia and the East, 1962. E. O.

Ioniapolis (Ἰωνιάπολις). Miles. Hafenstadt am Südufer des ehemaligen Latmischen Golfes, h. Bafa Gölü. Über diesen Hafen wurde das aus den nahegelegenen Marmorbrüchen stammende Baumaterial für den Apollon-Tempel von → Didyma verschifft. Am Seeufer und im Wasser bei Pınarcık Yayla (ehemals Mersinet İskelesi) sind zahlreiche didymäische Säulentrommeln innerhalb einer spätant. Siedlung erh. Der ant. Hafen ist wegen des gestiegenen Wasserspiegels weiter seewärts anzunehmen. Der Name ist in zwei hell. Inschr. aus Milet [1] und einer Bannurkunde aus Didyma überliefert.

1 IMilet I 3, 1914, Nr. 149 Z. 45, Nr. 150 Z. 103 f.
2 IDidyma II, 1958, Nr. 40 Z. 16.

A. PESCHLOW-BINDOKAT, I., in: Istanbuler Mitt. 27/8, 1977/8, 131–136 · Dies., in: JDAI 96, 1981, 186 f. · Dies., Der Latmos, 1996, 55–57, 59 f. A. PE.

Ionicus von Sardes. Lehrer und Arzt, wirkte um 390 n. Chr. Als Sohn eines Arztes und Schüler von Zenon von Zypern stand er in hohem Ansehen, v. a. wegen seiner Verdienste in der praktischen Therapie, Drogenkunde, Bandagierungskunst und Chirurgie. Er war auch Philosoph mit besonderen Fähigkeiten sowohl in medizinischer Prognostik als auch in Wahrsagerei (Eunapius, Vitae philosophorum 499). Zudem soll er als bekannter Redner und Dichter hervorgetreten sein, auch wenn keines seiner Werke überl. ist. V. N./Ü: L. v. R.-B.

Ionidai (Ἰωνίδαι). Att. Mesogeia-Demos der Phyle Aigeis, stellte zwei (einen) *buleutaí*. MEYER [1] lokalisiert I. bei Charvati, SIEWERT [2] bei Lutró, TRAILL [3; 4] bei Draphi (?) und VANDERPOOL [5. 24 ff.] bei Vurva. Genealogische Beziehungen seines eponymen Heros Ion zu Gargettos (Paus. 6,22,7) könnten I. allg. in die Gegend von Charvati südl. von Pallene verweisen.

1 E. MEYER, s. v. I., RE Suppl. 10, 329 **2** P. SIEWERT, Die Trittyen Attikas und die Heeresreform des Kleisthenes, 1982, 87 Anm. 2, 172 ff. **3** TRAILL, Attica, 5, 15 f., 41, 69, 110 Nr. 59, Tab. 2 **4** Ders., Demos and Trittys, 1986, 127 **5** E. VANDERPOOL, The location of the Attic deme Erchia, in: BCH 89, 1965, 21–26. H. LO.

Ionios Kolpos (Ἰόνιος κόλπος), Adria (ὁ Ἀδρίας, *mare Adriaticum* oder *supernum*), Ionisches Meer. Der I. K. wird anders als h. schon von Hekat. (FGrH 1 F 91 f.) bei Istria, von Hellanikos (FGrH 4 F 4) bei der Mündung des Spines angesetzt; im Süden wird der Name des I. K. bisweilen auf das sikilische Meer (Mela 2,37; 48; 110) übertragen. *Adria* (= A.) bezeichnete urspr. nur den innersten Winkel des adriatischen Meeres vor der Po-Mündung und dem Siedlungsgebiet der Veneti, von deren Stadt → Atria sich die Bezeichnung A. ableiten soll (Strab. 5,1,8). Im 4. Jh. v. Chr. werden A. und I. K. synonym gen. (Skyl. 14; 27), später auch die Gewässer über die Straße von Otranto hinaus als A. bezeichnet (Ptol. 3,1,1; Paus. 5,25,3). Wegen unzureichender N-S-Verbindungen auf der Balkan-Halbinsel diente der I. K. schon in der Brz. als Handelsweg zw. Mitteleuropa und Griechenland. Seit dem 8. Jh. erschlossen griech. Seefahrer und Kolonisten den I. K., der wichtiger Verkehrsweg zw. It. und Hellas wurde. In der Spätant. ist das I. K. Grenze zw. west- und oström. Reich.

J. PARTSCH, s. v. Adria, RE 1, 417–419 · W. M. MURRAY, s. v. Adriatic Sea, [3]OCD, 14. D. S.

Ionisch I. VON DER VORKLASSISCHEN ZEIT BIS ZUR KOINE II. NEUIONISCH-PONTISCH

I. VON DER VORKLASSISCHEN ZEIT BIS ZUR KOINE

Das I. ist seit vorklass. Zeit in drei Hauptgebieten belegt, von denen aus es sich im Laufe der Zweiten → Kolonisation bis ans Ende des Pontos und bis nach Hispania ausgebreitet hat: (1) West-I.: Euboia (und Oropos) mit Kolonien in der Chalkidike (Olynthos), Unteritalien (Kyme, Pithekussa) und Sizilien; (2) Insel-I. (ion. Kykladen): u. a. Keos, Delos, Paros (mit Thasos), Naxos (mit Amorgos); (3) Ost-I. (Ionien mit vorgelagerten Inseln Chios und Samos): u. a. Phokaia (mit Massalia und dessen Siedlungen Emporiae im NO Spaniens und Pech Maho im Süden Frankreichs), Smyrna, Klazomenai, Erythrai, Teos, Ephesos, Priene, Milet, Halikarnassos. Lehrreich für das I. sind v. a. die archa. Inschr.; denn das I. wird schon seit der 2. H. des 5. Jh. durch das als Grundlage der *Koinḗ* geltende → Attisch stark beeinflußt bzw. ersetzt, so daß es oft schwierig ist, in nicht-archa. Inschr. das Echt-I. aufzuspüren. Das lit. I., das die ep. Sprache und daher alle Gattungen der Dichtersprache und der Kunstprosa prägt (→ Griech. Literatursprachen), ist eher künstlich, läßt aber echt-ion. Wortschatz erkennen (z. B. bei Hipponax).

Das I. zeigt neben (a) einer ostgriech. Komponente und (b) einer Reihe von Übereinstimmungen mit dem Att., die eindeutig auf eine urspr. Einheit (das »Ion.-Att.«) etwa um die Wende zum 1. Jt. v. Chr. zurückgehen, (c) eine Reihe spezifischer Merkmale, die es vom Att. unterscheiden.

Zu (a): **-ti(-)* > *-si(-)*; *$t^{(h)}$*i̯* (Typ τόσος), **ts* > *s*; Nom. Pl. οἱ, αἱ; 1. Pl. auf -μεν; athemat. Inf. auf -ναι (aber westion. z. T. auch -ν); ὅτε; ἄν; **g*^{u}*ol-* »wollen«; πρῶτος; ἱερός (aber ostion. auch ἶρος); εἴκοσι »20«.

Zu (b): **ā* > *ǟ*; Metathese **āo* > *eō* (mit sog. »att.« Dekl. λεώς) bzw. **ēa* > *eā*; früher Schwund von **u̯*; Ny ephelkystikon; ἡμεῖς, ὑμεῖς; 3. Sg. ἦν »er war«; 3. Pl. -σαν (ἔθε-σαν); πρός; einige weitere hierher gehörende Erscheinungen hat das I. mit dem Dor. (**r̥* > *ra* im Kontext *Cr̥C*; Verba vocalia auf -άω, -έω; ἀπό; *ἐν-ς mit Akk., woraus ion. ἐς), bes. mit dem »milden« Dor. (*ē̩/ō̩* aus Ersatzdehnung und Kontraktionen, Typ βουλή, τοῦ), gemeinsam.

Zu (c): *ǟ* > *ę̄* auch hinter *e*, *i*, *r* (z. B. νέη, οἰκίη, χώρη); Erhaltung von *ea*, *eo*, *eō* (aber *eo* > *o* durch Hyphärese seit dem 5. Jh., *eu̯* seit dem 4. Jh., z. B. Θοκλος, θευπροπος = Θέοκλος, θεοπρόπος); Gen. Sg. Mask. vom Typ πολίτεω, -ω (ostion. auch -ευ); Gen. Sg. der *-i*-Stämme auf –ιος (aber auch auf -εως, -εος); nur *-*i̯on*- im Komparativ (μέζονα); themat. Flexion im reduplizierten athemat. Präs. (Typ διδοῖ); Aor. ἤνεικα; Konj. auf **-s-o/e-*; Ptz. ἐών »seiend«; ἤν (= ἐάν); τέσσε/αρες »vier«; ἱστίη (= ἑστία).

Die Dialektgeogr. des I. wird dadurch erschwert, daß der Belegstand der verschiedenen Städte (Milet als maßgebende Norm im Ost-I.!) bzw. Inseln in vielen Punkten lückenhaft ist und daß oft att. statt echt-ion. Formen vorkommen. Weder die vierfache Gruppierung bei Herodot (1,142,3) noch die herkömmliche, rein geogr. Aufteilung in (1) West-, (2) Insel- und (3) Ost.-I. entspricht der dialektalen Situation, die aus den Inschr. hervorgeht. Eher bilden in mancher Hinsicht (2) und (3) eine (allerdings unvollständige) Einheit gegenüber (1), das näher am Att. (*-rs-* > *-rr-*; ἐκεῖνος; χῑ́λιοι »1000«), z. T. auch am Boiot. (*$t^{(h)}$*-i̯*, *$k^{(h)}$*i̯* [Präs. auf -ττω], **tu̯* > *tt*; ξένος; Dat. Pl. -αις, -οις) steht, vgl. demgegenüber insel- bzw. ostion.: *-rs-*; κεῖνος; χείλιοι; *ss* (-σσω); ξεῖνος; -η(ι)σι(ν), -οισι(ν). Typisch westion.: *u*, nicht *ü* (ϙύϙνυς = Κύκνος); Kürzung von *-ēi̯*, *-ōi̯* zu *-ei̯* (wie im Att.), *-oi̯*; τουτα, τουτει, εντουθα (= ταῦτα, ταύτῃ, ἐνταῦθα); Inf. τιθεῖν, διδοῦν, εἶν (= τιθέναι, διδόναι, εἶναι); βόλομαι. Spezifisch für Eretria: *-s(-)* > *-r(-)*. Typisch ost- und inselion.: <αο>, <εο> für *au̯*, *eu̯* (αοτος, ταοτα, εο°, βασιλεος = αὐτός, ταῦτα, εὐ°, βασιλεύς), was auf eine Aussprache *ü* von **u* weist; γῑ́νομαι. Nur ostion. ist die → Psilose (daher rührt der Gebrauch von <H> für *ę̄* aus *ǟ* < **ā* im milesischen Alphabet, das sich später ausgebreitet hat); ὀκο- aus **i̯o-k*^{u}*o-* (z. B. οκοια für ὁποῖα); Flexion vom Typ ἱέρεως, Gen. -εω; ἑωυτο-, aber auch ἑαυ/οτο-; ἶρός, aber auch ἱερός (auch in ein- und derselben Inschr.). Vorwiegend im Norden Ioniens (Phokaia und Kolonien, Chios, Smyrna, Erythrai), das urspr.

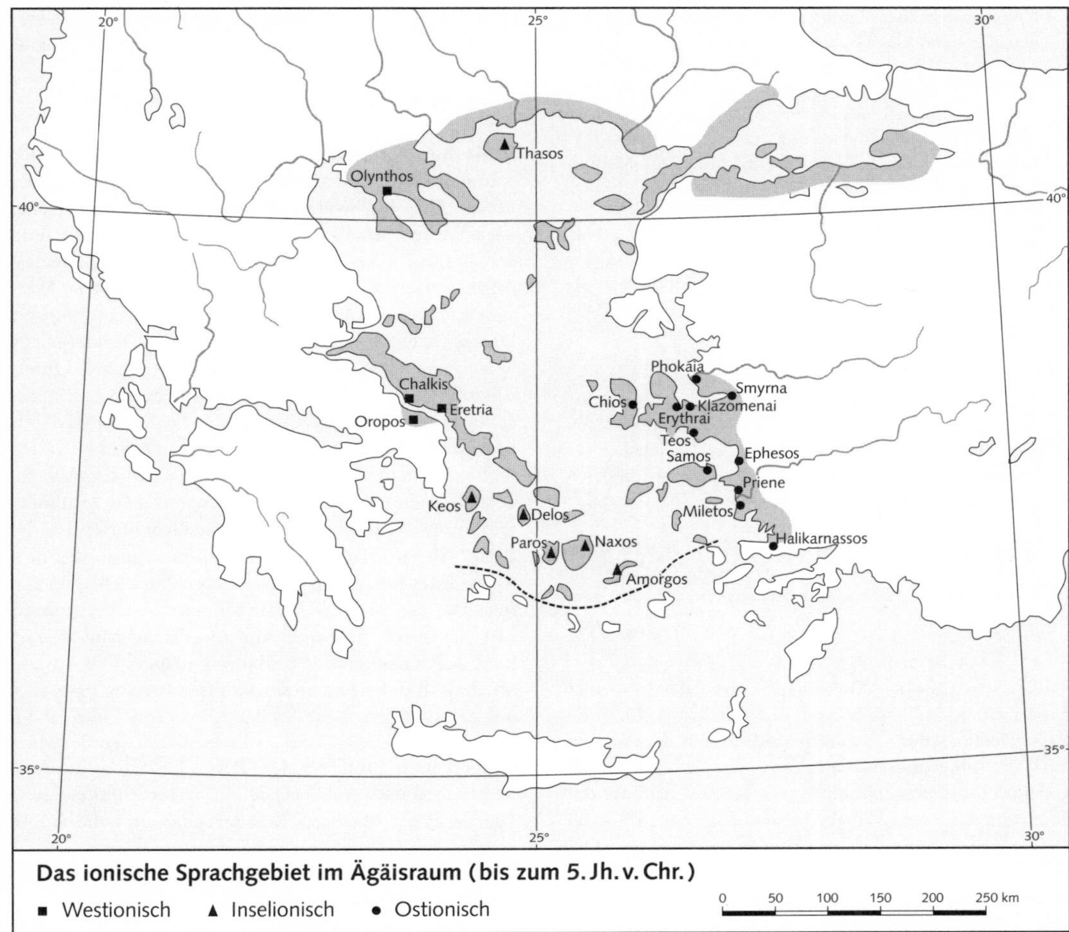

Das ionische Sprachgebiet im Ägäisraum (bis zum 5. Jh. v. Chr.)

■ Westionisch ▲ Inselionisch ● Ostionisch

von aiol. Stämmen bewohnt war (Hdt. 1,149–150), kommen sporadisch Übereinstimmungen mit dem Lesb. vor, die auf Substrat oder Adstrat beruhen dürften: *-ons-* > *-oi̯s-* (3. Pl. -οισι, -ωισι aus *-*onti*, *-*ōnti*); flektierte Numeralia (z. B. τεσσ[ερ]ακοντων); Dat. Pl. -αισιν; athemat. Flexion im Ptz. der Verba vocalia (διψαντ[ι in Emporiae); vielleicht Ζιονυ[σιος] (Phokaia), ἀί und αἰί »immer«.

Proben:

West-I.: Kyme (7. Jh.) Ταταιε̄ς ε̄μι λε̄ϙυθος · Hος δ' αν με κλεφσει θυφλος εσται. – Eretria (411) εδοξεν τει βο̄ληι · … και σιτηριν ειναι και αυτωι και παιριν, οταν ε[π]ιδημεωριν και ατελεην και προεδριην ες το̄ς αγωνας. (Um 340) οπωρ αν τα Αρτεμιρια … αγωμεν και θυωριν οι πλειστοι εδοξεν τει βουλει και τοι δημοι · τιθειν την πολιν αγωνα μουσικης …

Insel-I.: Naxos (7.–6. Jh.: hexametrisch) Νικανδρη μ' ανεθε̄κεν Hηκηβολοι ιοχεαιρηι / ϙορη Δεινιδικηο του ΝαHσιο εHσοχος αληον / Δεινομενεος δε κασιγνε̄τη ΦHραHσο δ' αλοχος ν[υν] (<η> = <H>!). Entsprechend Νικάνδρη μ' ἀνέθηκεν ἑκηβόλῳ ἰοχεαίρῃ / κούρη Δεινοδικε̣ω τοῦ Ναξίου ἔξοχος ἀλλέ̣ων / Δεινομένε̣ος δὲ κασιγνήτη Φράξου δ' ἄλοχος νῦν.

Ost-I.: Milet (6. Jh.) Εοθρασ[ης] … Λεωδαμας Οναξο̄ πρυτ[α]νευοντες ανεθεσαν τἠκατηι. (Um 450) ην δε η πολι[ς ε]γκρατης γενηται, κατακτε̄ναι [αυτ]ο̄ς το̄ς επιμηνιο̄ς επ' ων αν λαφθεωσιν. (Um 344) ειναι δε … τωι βουλομενωι εισαφιξιν ες Σαρδις … κατα τα αοτα. – Chios (5. Jh.) [οι πε]ντεκα[ιδεκ]α ες βο̄λη[ν εν]ειкαντων [εν] πεντ' ημερη[ι]σιν · το̄ς δε κηρυκας διαπεμψαντες ες τας χωρας κη[ρ]υσσοντων και … αποδεκνυντες την ημερην ην αν λαβωισιν και το πρηχμα προσκηρυσσοντων ο τι αν μελλη πρηξεσθαι. – Didyma (6. Jh.) —κα]θαιρε̄ν και : το̄ : ιρεως : γι[νεσθαι — απο ιερηιο̄ : κ[α]ι νεφρ[ον. – Pech Maho (2. H. 5. Jh.) και κειν' ελαβεν εν τωι ποταμωι · τον αρραβων' ανεδωκα οκο̄ τἀκατια ορμιζεται.

→ Aiolisch (Lesbisch); Attisch; Griechische Dialekte; Griechische Literatursprachen; Homerische Sprache; Psilose

Quellen (Auswahl): IG XI, 2–4; XII, 5; XII, 7; XII, 9; XII, Suppl. • IK 1–2; 11/1; 12; 15; 17/1; 17/3; 24/1 •
L. Dubois, Inscriptions grecques dialectales de la Sicile, 1989 (1–20 euböische Kolonien) • Ders., Inscriptions grecques dialectales de Grande Grèce I. Colonies eubéennes.

Colonies ioniennes. Emporia, 1995 • Ders., Inscriptions grecques dialectales d' Olbia du Pont, 1996 • J. Pouilloux, M. Lejeune, Une transaction commerciale ionienne au Ve siècle à Pech-Maho, in: CRAI 1988, 526–535 • R. A. Santiago, Epigrafía dialectal emporitana, in: E. Crespo u. a. (Hrsg.), Dialectologica Graeca Miraflores, 1993, 281–295.
Lit.: M. del Barrio, El dialecto de Eubea, Diss. Madrid UCM 1987 • Bechtel, Dial.² 3 • Cl. Brixhe u. a., Bulletin de dialectologie grecque, in: REG 98, 1985, 274–279 (Forsch.-Ber.) • K. A. Garbrah, A Grammar of the Ionic Inscriptions from Erythrae, 1978 • P. Hualde, Eolismos en Jonia: revisión de un problema de geografía intradialectal, in: Emerita 65, 1997, 221–256 (als Belegslg. nützlich) • E. Knitl, Die Sprache der ion. Kykladen nach den inschr. Quellen, Diss. München 1938 • M. Lejeune, La dédicace de Νικάνδρη et l'écriture archaïque de Naxos, in: RPh 97, 1971, 209–215 • A. López Eire, Géographie intradialectale de l'ionien-attique, in: Verbum 10, 1987, 154–178 • A. Scherer, Zur Laut- und Formenlehre der milesischen Inschr., Diss. München 1934 • K. Stüber, Zur dialektalen Einheit des Ostion., 1996 • Thumb/Scherer, 194–284, bes. 245–284.
Karten-Lit.: M. del Barrio, El dialecto de Eubea, Diss. Madrid UCM 1987 • K. Stüber, Zur dialektalen Einheit des Ostion., 1996 • Thumb/Scherer, 194–284, bes. 245–284.

J. G.-R.

II. Neuionisch-Pontisch

Wie im Falle des Tsakonischen und des h. Griech. Unteritaliens stellt sich auch für den pont. Dial. des Neugriech. an der Schwarzmeerküste (seit dem griech.-türk. Bevölkerungstausch in den 20er Jahren dieses Jh. gefährdet) die Frage, inwieweit er Reste erhält, die zeitlich hinter die *Koinḗ* zurückgehen, oder gar als Fortsetzer des ant. I. bezeichnet werden kann; für diesen Dial. ist diese Frage bes. kompliziert zu klären, da schon das Großatt., erst recht die *Koinḗ* stark unter ion. Einfluß standen, so daß Koineisierung und Bewahrung alten Dialektgutes im Ergebnis oft identisch sein mußten. Insgesamt präsentiert sich das Pont. als bes. altertümlicher Dial.: Geminatenerhalt wie in den übrigen Randzonen des neugriech. Dialektgebiets; Erhalt des urspr. Akzentsitzes in παιδία für Standardneugriechisch (= SNgr.) παιδιά, Erhalt von <η> als /e/ wie in νύφη zu altgriech. νύμφη; Erhalt von /o/ z. B. in lat. LW wie καρβώνιν, σαπώνιν gegen SNgr. καρβούνι, σαπούνι; Erhalt alter Bedeutungen etwa in παιδεύω als »erziehen« gegen SNgr. »quälen«; aber auch einige Chrakteristika des alten I. sind erh. geblieben wie etwa die Verneinung κιτ < ion. οὐκί (att. wäre οὐχι; das SNgr. hat δέν < οὐδέν), auslautendes -η etwa in αἴγειρη »Schwarzpappel«, die Hauchversetzung etwa in ἀχαντώνα für ἀκανθών wie in ion. βάθρακος gegen att. βάτραχος oder Ersatzdehnung der Gruppe *ολϝ in οὖλον statt SNgr. όλος wie in ion. οὖλος gegen att. ὅλος.

N. Andriotis, Lex. der Archaismen in den neugriech. Dial., 1974 • N. Kontosopoulos, Διάλεκτοι και ιδιώματα της νέας ελληνικής, 1981 • J. Niehoff-Panagiotidis, Koine und Diglossie, 1995 • D. E. Oikonomidis, Γραμματική της ελληνικής διαλέκτου του Πόντου, 1958 • A. Papadopoulos, Ιστορική γραμματική της ποντικής διαλέκτου, 1955 • A. Semenov, Der nordpont. Dial. des Neugriech., in: Glotta 23, 1935, 91–107.

V. BL.

Ionische Wanderung s. Kolonisation

Ionischer Aufstand. Die griech. Städte in → Ionia waren seit 546/5 v. Chr. willfährige Untertanen der Perser. Erst die weitere Expansion des Perserreiches nach Westen, daraus resultierende Einschränkungen ihres Handels, steigende Steuern und Zwang zur Heeresfolge führten dazu, daß viele Städte sich 499 → Aristagoras [2], dem Initiator der Revolte, anschlossen. Dieser hatte in → Miletos die Tyrannis niedergelegt, → *isonomía* proklamiert und dem Aufstand mil. Unterstützung aus Athen und Eretria gesichert. 498 griffen die Milesier und ihre Verbündeten → Sardeis an und zerstörten es. Weitere Städte am Hellespont und in Karien schlossen sich ihnen daraufhin an. Gleichzeitig revoltierten die griech. Städte auf Zypern. Mit der Rückeroberung der Insel begann 497 die Gegenoffensive der Perser. Ihren Erfolgen am Hellespont und in der Propontis folgte allerdings ein schwerer Rückschlag in Karien, der die persischen Aktivitäten zunächst stoppte. Erst 494 waren die Perser zum Angriff auf Milet bereit. Ineffektive Kommandostrukturen, mangelnder Zusammenhalt und die Flucht der von den Persern bestochenen Samier führten zur Niederlage der ion. Flotte in der Seeschlacht bei der Insel → Lade. Dann wurde Milet belagert und vernichtet. Die Perser bestraften die Aufständischen mit großer Härte und richteten ihre eigene Vorherrschaft über die Küstenregion und die Inseln wieder auf.

Der Bericht des Herodot (5,28–6,32), die einzige ant. Quelle zum I., beruht auf lokaler mündlicher Überlieferung. Herodot spielt die Leistungen der Ionier herunter, betont ihren Mangel an Kooperationsfähigkeit und spricht dem Unternehmen von vornherein jede Erfolgschance ab. Die Existenz des *koinón*, einer zentralen Institution zur Koordinierung der Revolte, und die beachtlichen Anfangserfolge der Ionier zeigen jedoch die Einseitigkeit seines Urteils.

O. Murray, in: CAH 4, ²1988, 461–490 • P. Tozzi, La rivolta ionica, 1978.

E. S.-H.

Iophon (Ἰοφῶν)

[1] Sohn des → Peisistratos aus zweiter Ehe mit der Argiverin Timonassa, Tochter des Gorgilos und Witwe des → Kypseliden Archinos von Ambrakia. Von I. ist im Gegensatz zu seinem Bruder → Hegesistratos [1] nur der Name überliefert ([Aristot.] Ath. pol. 17,3; Plut. Cato maior 24,8; Hdt. 5,94 f.).

L. de Libero, Die Archaische Tyrannis, 1996, 88 • Traill, PAA 537360.

B. P.

[2] Tragiker aus Athen (TrGF I 22), Sohn des → Sophokles; verfaßte 50 Stücke (TrGF I T 1). Als Titel sind bezeugt: *Achilleús*, *Tḗlephos*, *Aktaíōn*, *Iliu Pérsis*, *Dexamenós*, *Bákchai*, *Pentheús* (möglich Doppeltitel ›Bakchen oder Pentheus‹), Satyrspiel ›Die Satyrn als Sänger zum Aulos‹; eventuell kommen die wohl fälschlich → Kleophon (TrGF *77 T 1) zugeschriebenen Titel *Amphiáraos, Ērigónē, Thyéstēs, Leúkippos* dazu. Erhalten sind insgesamt nur fünf Verse. I. siegte an den Dionysien 435 v. Chr. und wurde 428 Zweiter hinter → Euripides und vor → Ion. In der Komödie wird häufig gespottet, daß er nicht die Qualität seines Vaters besitze oder gar dessen Stücke als seine eigenen aufgeführt habe (T 5a). Die in der Sophokles-Vita des → Satyros überlieferte Gesch., I. habe seinen Vater wegen Altersschwachsinn entmündigen lassen wollen und Sophokles habe dies durch Rezitation aus seinem ›Oidipus auf Kolonos‹ entkräftet, geht wohl auch auf Komödienspott zurück.

K.J. Dover (ed., comm.), Aristophanes, Frogs, 1993, 199 • B. Gauly u.a. (Hrsg.), Musa tragica, 1991, 88–93, 280f.

B.Z.

Iophossa (Ἰοφῶσσα). Nach Hesiod und Akusilaos ein anderer Name der → Chalkiope [2]. Tochter des Aietes von Kolchis und der Idyia. Schwester Medeias, Gattin des Phrixos, mit dem sie vier Söhne hat (schol. Apoll. Rhod. 2,1122; 2,1149; Apollod. 1,83). RE.ZI.

Ioppe (äg. *ypw*, assyr. *yāpu, yappû*, hebr. *yāpô* »schön sein«), griech. bzw. lat. Bezeichnung des h. Jaffa südl. von Tel Aviv. Vom 2. Jt. v. Chr. bis zur hell.-röm. Zeit besiedelt, ist I. der einzige Schauplatz eines griech. Mythos in → Palaestina. In ihm wird die einem Meeresungeheuer ausgelieferte → Andromeda von Perseus gerettet (Ov. met. 4,772 ff.). Eine vergleichbare Konstellation in der Jonageschichte.

O. Keel, Orte und Landschaften der Bibel, 2, 1982, 12–28 • J. Kaplan, H.R. Ritter-Kaplan, s.v. Jaffa, NEAEHL 2, 655–659.

R.L.

Iordanes

[1] Schriftsteller justinianischer Zeit (6. Jh. n. Chr.). German., wohl got. Herkunft, Enkel des Paria (des Sekretärs des Alanenherzogs Candac), Sohn des Alanoviamuth. Geb. wohl im späteren 5. Jh. n. Chr., war I. selbst Sekretär von Cantacs Neffen Gunthigis (Iord. Get. 265). Nach seiner *conversio* (vom Arianismus zur Orthodoxie? Vom weltlichen in einen geistlichen Stand?) wird er 551 (Iord. Rom. 4. 363; vgl. Iord. Get. 104) in Konstantinopel von einem Freund Vigilius (kaum dem gleichnamigen zeitgenöss. Papst) um eine Leidensgesch. der Welt (Rom. 2) und während dieser Arbeit (Get. 1) von einem gemeinsamen Freund Castalius um eine Kurzfassung der Gotengeschichte → Cassiodorus' gebeten, die er mit *De summa temporum vel origine actibusque gentis Romanorum* (Rom. 4) zusammenarbeitet und etwa 552 Vigilius widmet.

Das Buch *De summa temporum vel origine actibusque gentis Romanorum* (= Rom.) kombiniert Auszüge aus dem AT (8–61), der Chronik des Hieronymus (12–85; 256–314), aus Florus und Festus (87–254), Eutropius (vgl. [5]) und Orosius (255–318) sowie Marcellinus Comes (315–384; auch in Get. benutzt). Gescheitert ist der Versuch von [4], dieses »Quellenmosaik« auf die *Historia Romana* des Memmius Symmachus zurückzuführen (vgl. [6]). Der Tenor der Schrift ist – entsprechend dem Wunsch des Adressaten und auf dessen *conversio* abzielend (Rom. 4) – im Sinne der augustinischen Geschichtstheologie (→ Augustinus) auf die *clades* und *casus* (»Unglücks-« und »Wechselfälle«) der Weltgeschichte (als im Resultat römischer Gesch.) bis zum byz.-gotischen Krieg (535–553 n. Chr., Rom. 368 ff.) gestimmt.

Das parallel entstandene und die Weltgesch. mikrokosmisch ergänzende Buch *De origine actibusque Getarum* (= Get.) behandelt die Gotengesch. im Blick auf die Amaler-Dynastie (→ Amali) bis zu deren Katastrophe im J. 540. Basis ist die Gotengeschichte des Cassiodorus, die I. allerdings nur drei Tage eingesehen und insofern nicht wörtlich übernommen und auch durch andere Quellen ergänzt hat (Get. 2f., vgl. [3. 234f.]). Wie [4] dort hat hier [7] eine Eigentätigkeit des I. geleugnet (vgl. aber [8]; [9. 25ff.]; [11]; [17. 38ff.]; dagegen noch [16. 14ff.]). Eine progotische [7] bzw. durchgehend proiustinianische [9], ja überhaupt ausgeprägt polit. Tendenz ist wie in *De summa temporum* nicht auszumachen.

Dieses »Diptychon« hat als handliche Zusammenfassung der röm. Gesch., kombiniert mit einer Heroisierung eines quasi-mythischen Volkes (»Gotizismus«, vgl. [14]), schon im MA einigen Erfolg gehabt. Die *Getica* gelten auch der h. Forsch. (vgl. [15]–[17], aber [10. 19ff.]) als Hauptquelle für die Gotengesch.

Mommsen basierte seinen Text auf die am wenigsten »klassische« »Klasse 1«, zumal auf Heidelberg, Pal. 921 (s. VIII/IX; 1880 bei Mommsen verbrannt); die sprachlich normgerechtere »Klasse 3« ist indes jetzt durch den älteren Bobiensis Palermo, Archivio dello Stato, Cod. Basile (s. VIII², Codices Latini Antiquiores Suppl. 1741) vertreten. Erst die geplante Ausgabe von Bradley (vgl. [13]) verspricht einen stemmatisch ausgewogenen Text, der die Untersuchung von Sprache und Stil auf eine neue Grundlage stellen sollte.

1 N. Wagner, Getica, 1967 **2** W. Suerbaum, Vom ant. zum frühma. Staatsbegriff, ³1977, 268–278, 380ff.
3 J.J. O'Donnell, The Aims of Jordanes, in: Historia 31, 1982, 223–240 **4** W. Ensslin, Des Symmachus Historia Romana als Quelle für Jordanes, 1949 **5** S. Ratti, Les Romana de Jordanès et le Bréviaire d'Eutrope, in: AC 65, 1996, 175–187 **6** L. Várady, Jordanes-Studien, in: Chiron 6, 1976, 441–487 **7** Momigliano 2, 207ff. **8** B. Croke, Cassiodorus and the Getica of Jordanes, in: CPh 82, 1987, 117–134 **9** W. Goffart, The Narrators of Barbarian History, 1988, 20–111 **10** Ders., Two Notes on Germanic Antiquity Today, in: Traditio 50, 1995, 9–30
11 G. Zecchini, Ricerche di storiographia Latina tardoantica, 1993, 193–209 **12** D.R. Bradley, The Getica of Jordanes, in: Hermes 121, 1993, 211–236 **13** Ders., Manuscript Evidence for the Text of the »Getica« of Jordanes, in: Hermes 123, 1995, 346–362, 490–503
14 J. Svennung, Zur Gesch. des Goticismus, 1967
15 S. Teillet, Des Goths à la nation gothique, 1984, 305–334

16 B. Tönnies, Die Amalertradition, 1989, 8–20 17 P.J. Heather, Goths and Romans, 1991, 1–67.

Ed.: Th. Mommsen, 1882 • F. Giunta, A. Grillone, 1991 (nur Get.; Bibliogr. XLI-XLVII). P.L.S.

[2] Der Fluß Jordan, hebr. *hay-Yardēn*; griech. ὁ Ἰορδάνης; arab. *al-Urdunn* oder *aš-Šarīʿat al-Kabīra*, »die große Tränke«. Die Etym. ist umstritten; möglicherweise von aram. *RDY* oder hebr. *YRD* (»fließen«). Perennierendes Gewässer im syr.-afrikan. Grabenbruch mit mehreren Quellflüssen. Der I. führt durch den h. trokkengelegten Semechonitis-See (Buḥair al-Ḥūla, +70 m) und den See Gennesaret (–208 m), nimmt von Osten Jarmuk und Jabbok auf und mündet ins Tote Meer (–395 m; → Asphaltitis limne). Das Tal zwischen See Gennesaret und Totem Meer hat subtropisches Klima, südl. des Jabbok, von Oasen abgesehen, ist es weitgehend wüstenhaft. Bewässerungsfeldbau ist wegen der tiefen Lage des Bettes nur aus seitlichen Zuflüssen möglich. Das Tal diente aus klimatischen Gründen nie als Verkehrsachse; der I. war nie schiffbar. Selbst im Ost-West-Verkehr bildete er allenfalls während der Frühjahrshochwasser ein Hindernis; eher verband er die östl. und westl. Regionen zu einer ökonomischen Einheit. Die geläufige Vorstellung vom I. als Ost-Grenze des dem Volk Israel verheißenen Landes und seiner Überschreitung als Auftakt der Landnahme setzt die Einrichtung der assyr. Provinz Galʾad (um 733 v. Chr.) voraus und wurde erst in exilisch-nachexilischen Grenzbeschreibungen (Nm 34,12; Ez 47,18) festgeschrieben.
→ Juda und Israel

K. Bieberstein, Josua – Jericho – Jordan, 1995. K.B.

Ios (Ἴος). Wenig fruchtbare Insel der südl. Kykladen zw. Naxos und Thera, 103 km² groß, 735 m hoch (Pirgos). Die Stadt I. lag an der Ostseite beim h. Hauptort. Wenige Reste, Haupttheiligtum des Apollon Pythios [2. 308 f.; 311 f.] sind erh., ferner prähistor. Funde [1. 24] und die Ruine eines ant. Wachturmes (Psaropyrgos). I. beanspruchte, die Heimat des → Homeros zu sein, und zeigte sein Grab unweit der Nordspitze der Insel in der h. Flur Plakato (Paus. 10,24,2). Im 5. Jh. v. Chr. war I. Mitglied im → Attisch-Delischen Seebund mit einem Tribut von zunächst einem, dann einem halben Talent (ATL 1, 288; 3, 33; 48; 198). Weitere Belege: IG XII 5 Nr. 14 und 217 (Kopie des großen Isishymnos); Skyl. 58; Strab. 10,5,1; Stadiasmus maris magni 273; 284 (GGM I 497; 500); Ps.-Plut. Vita Homeri 3 f. (= Aristot. fr. 76 R.); Steph. Byz. s. v. Ἴ.; Ptol. 3,14,23; IG XII 5 Nr. 1–23, Suppl. Nr. 167–176. I. prägte Mz. mit dem Kopf Homers (HN 486).

1 D. Fimmen, Kret.-myk. Kultur, ²1924 2 P. Graindor, in: BCH 28, 1904.

L. Bürchner, s. v. I., RE 9, 1930 ff. • Lauffer, Griechenland, 279 • Philippson/Kirsten 4, 141 ff. H.KAL.

Josef (hebr. PN, vom hebr. Verbalstamm *jasaf*, »hinzufügen«). Die biblische Überl. der J.-Geschichte (Gn 30 ff.), einer novellenhaften Lehrerzählung, zeigt in ihrer Kernaussage, wie hinter dem Schicksal eines einzelnen das verborgene Walten Gottes steht: J., Lieblingssohn → Jakobs und Rachels, Vater Ephraims und Manasses; wird von seinen Brüdern in die Sklaverei nach Äg. verkauft, wo er als Bediensteter des Pharao wirkt, nachdem er vom Vorwurf der Vergewaltigung der Frau des Potiphar entlastet weden konnte.

Der Stoff der J.-Geschichte, die u. a. auf ägypt. Vorbilder zurückgeht, wurde auf vielfache Weise in der jüd., islam. sowie christl. Trad. bis ins 20. Jh. hinein verarbeitet (z. B. von Th. Mann). In der jüd.-hell. Lit. wird J. als einer der Urheber der ägypt. Zivilisation dargestellt; Philon schildert ihn vornehmlich als Staatsmann und Politiker. In den Midrašim (→ Rabbinische Literatur) und der → Haggada wird eher seine Frömmigkeit und Gerechtigkeit akzentuiert. Die Ursache für die Leiden J.s wird in seiner Bevorzugung durch seinen Vater Jakob gesehen. Bes. der Verkauf J.s durch die neidischen Brüder und seine Verschleppung nach Äg. sind Gegenstand phantasievoller und bildreicher Ausschmückungen im Midraš. Im Koran (12. Sure) wird die J.-Erzählung, die in der muslimischen Trad. einen zentralen Stellenwert besitzt, mit Einzelheiten ausgestaltet, die nicht in der biblischen Vorlage zu finden sind; eine andere Gewichtung erfährt beispielsweise die Verführungsszene, in der J. zwar heftiges Verlangen nach Potiphars Frau verspürt, diesem aber – als Gottesfürchtiger – um Allahs willen widersteht.

M.J. Bin-Gorion, Die Sagen der Juden, 1935 u.ö. • H. Donner, Die lit. Gestalt der at. Josephsgesch., 1976 • L. Ginzberg, The Legends of the Jews 2, ⁹1969; 5, ⁸1968 • D. Goldstein, Jewish Folklore and Legend, 1980 • J. Horovitz, Die Josefserzählung, 1921 • L. Ruppert, Die Josephserzählung der Genesis, 1965 • I. Schapiro, Die haggadischen Elemente im erzählenden Teil des Korans, 1907. Y.D.

Iosephos (Ἰώσηπ(π)ος, Ἰώσηφ(ος)). Von hebräisch *josep josipjah*, »Gott möge (weitere Kinder) hinzufügen«; in Erinnerung an den bibl. Patriarchen J. (Gn 35; 37–50) verbreiteter jüd. Name, u. a. in der herodian. Familie.
[1] Onkel und Schwager → Herodes' [1] d.Gr. (Ios. ant. Iud. 15,65; 81), fungierte 34 v. Chr. während dessen Reise zu M. → Antonius [I 9] als sein Stellvertreter, geriet in die Intrigen um die Königin → Mariamme und wurde auf Anzeige seiner Frau Salome wegen Ehebruchs mit Mariamme hingerichtet (Ios. bell. Iud. 1,443; Ios. ant. Iud. 15,87).
[2] Jüngerer Bruder Herodes' [1] d.Gr., vertrat Herodes, als dieser sich nach dem Parthereinfall 40 v. Chr. nach Italien begeben hatte, und fiel 38 im Kampf gegen den von den Parthern eingesetzten König und Hohenpriester → Antigonos [5] (Ios. bell. Iud. 1,266–323; Ios. ant. Iud. 14,413–450 passim).

[3] Sohn von I. [2], Gemahl der Herodestochter Olympias (Ios. bell. Iud. 1,562; Ios. ant. Iud. 17,20), stand während der Unruhen nach Herodes' [1] Tod 4 v. Chr. auf röm. Seite (Ios. bell. Iud. 2,74; Ios. ant. Iud. 17,294). Seine Tochter Mariamme war mit dem Tetrarchen → Herodes [7] von Chalkis verheiratet (Ios. bell. Iud. 2,221; Ios. ant. Iud. 18,134). K.BR.

[4] I. Flavios. A. Leben B. Werke

A. Leben

Jüd. hell. Historiker, der 37/8 n. Chr. in Jerusalem geb. wurde (gest. vermutlich 100 n. Chr. in Rom) und dessen Familie zur Priesteraristokratie gehörte; seine von ihm behauptete Verwandtschaft mit dem hasmonäischen Königshaus wird angezweifelt (vita 2). Obwohl als Priester eher der Religionspartei der → Sadduzäer nahestehend, schloß I. sich den Pharisäern an (→ Pharisaioi, vita 12; [22]). Seine Muttersprache war Aram.; seine Griechischkenntnisse muß er bereits in früher Jugend erworben haben. Lateinkenntnisse eignete er sich vermutlich erst während seiner diplomatischen Mission in Rom an (64–66 n. Chr.), die die Freilassung jüd. Priester erreichte. Im J. 66 n. Chr. trat er auf die Seite der sich gegen den röm. Procurator → Gessius Florus und den syr. Statthalter Cestius Gallus erhebenden Aufständischen und erhielt im ausbrechenden Krieg gegen Rom eine führende Position als General der galiläischen Festung → Iotapata (Ios. bell. Iud. 2,568, vita 29). I.' polit. und mil. Rolle sowie seine Loyalität zu → Iohannes [2] von Gischala und der Zelotenpartei aber sind umstritten [12. 181–231; 23. 144–173; 28. 231 f.]; Widersprüche treten auch in seiner Selbstdarstellung hervor (vita 28, bell. Iud. 2,562–571). Nach der Einnahme von Iotapata durch Vespasian im Frühjahr 67 wurde I. gefangengenommen (bell. Iud. 3,340–391). Während seiner Gefangenschaft weissagte er Vespasian das Kaiseramt, wurde daher 69 n. Chr. nach der Ausrufung Vespasians zum Kaiser freigelassen und nahm an der Eroberung Jerusalems 70 n. Chr. durch Titus auf röm. Seite teil (bell. Iud. 5). Ab 71 n. Chr. in Rom lebend, erhielt er das röm. Bürgerrecht, eine Jahrespension und Landgüter.

B. Werke

Die Werke des I. sind vollständig erh. Sie sind in Griech. verfaßt; lediglich für das *Bellum Iudaicum* ist eine nicht erh. aram. Erstfassung (ca. 75 n. Chr.) anzunehmen. Keine seiner Schriften ist im Judentum in nennenswerter Weise rezipiert worden. Die einzige Ausnahme stellt das ma. hebr. *Sefer* → *Josippon* dar.

Bellum Iudaicum: Die griechische Fassung des *Bellum* (Περὶ τοῦ Ἰουδαϊκοῦ πολέμου) erschien zw. 79 und 81 n. Chr. und richtete sich an die hellenisierte gebildete Oberschicht des röm. Reiches. Sie behandelt die Vorgesch. und Gesch. des jüd.-röm. Krieges bis zum Fall der Bergfestung Massada. Unverkennbar ist die apologetische Grundhaltung ([17. 198 ff.], anders z. B. [23. 132 ff.]), deren Ziel es ist, jüd. Splitterparteien für die Erhebung gegen Rom verantwortlich zu machen und dadurch sowohl das jüd. Volk und die Aristokratie zu entlasten als auch die Flavierkaiser zu verherrlichen. I.' Quellen sind seine eigenen Aufzeichnungen des Kriegsgeschehens, die Kriegsdarstellung von Vespasian und Titus sowie die Darstellung der Weltgesch. des → Nikolaos von Damaskos [6. 392–419].

Antiquitates Iudaicae: ›Die Jüd. Altertümer‹ (Ἰουδαϊκὴ ἀρχαιολογία), 93/4 wahrscheinlich gemeinsam mit der *Vita* erschienen, schildern in 20 B. die jüd. Gesch. (B. 1–10: von der Weltschöpfung bis zur Perserherrschaft; B. 11–20: von Alexander d. Gr. bis zum jüd.-röm. Krieg), wobei in der ersten Hälfte bes. die hebr. → Bibel [14. 50–58] (hebr. und aram. Fassung sowie vorrangig die Septuaginta [14. 97–115] und eine unbekannte griech. Übers. [25. 773]) als Vorlage und in der zweiten Hälfte u. a. Nikolaos von Damaskos [14. 147–172], Polybios, Strabon, 1 Makk [14. 116–131] und der → Aristeasbrief [14. 97–115] sowie auch jüd. Dokumente [24. 367–400] als Quellen nachweisbar sind [11. 80 ff.; 27. 256–283]. Die von I. verwendeten Urkunden und Dokumente werden als weitgehend authentisch eingeschätzt [11. 100]. Als Zielpublikum der *Antiquitates* sind sowohl gebildete Römer und Griechen, denen das → Judentum nahegebracht werden sollte, als auch hellenisierte jüd. Kreise anzunehmen.

Vita Josephi: Die Autobiographie des I. (Ἰωσήπου βίος) ist als Anhang zu den *Antiquitates* 93/4 zum ersten Mal erschienen und stellt das älteste Beispiel ihrer Gattung dar. Zielrichtung I.' ist es, sein Verhalten im jüd.-röm. Krieg zu rechtfertigen sowie seine Befähigung als Autor herauszustellen.

Contra Apionem: Im Zentrum der zw. 93/4 und 96 erschienenen Schrift ›Gegen Apion‹ (Πρὸς Ἀπίωνα) – unter diesem Titel seit Hieronymus (epist. 70,3) bekannt – steht in noch deutlicherer Weise als in den *Antiquitates* die Apologie des Judentums. Das hohe Alter der jüd. Rel. und die Tatsache, daß sie philos. Grundsätzen entspreche, werden herausgestellt (c. Ap. 1,165; 2,145–286; [10. 220–232]).

Ed.: **1** B. Niese, Flavii Josephi Opera, 7 Bde., 1885–1895 **2** S. A. Naber, Flavii Josephi Opera Omnia, 6 Bde., 1888–1896.
Übers.: **3** H.St.J. Thackeray, R. Marcus, L. H. Feldman, Josephus, 9 Bde., 1926–1965 **4** O. Michel, O. Bauernfeind, Flavius Josephus: De Bello Judaico. Der jüd. Krieg, 3 Bde., 1963–1982.
Konkordanz: **5** K. H. Rengstorff (Hrsg.), A complete concordance to Flavius Josephus, 4 Bde., 1973–1983.
Bibliogr.: **6** L. H. Feldman, Josephus and Modern Scholarship (1957–1980), 1984 **7** L. H. Feldman, Josephus. A Supplementary Bibliography, 1989
8 H. Schreckenberg, Bibliogr. zu Flavius Josephus, 1968
9 Ders., Bibliogr. zu Flavius Josephus. Suppl. mit Gesamtregister, 1979.
Lit.: **10** O. Betz, K. Haacker, M. Hengel (Hrsg.), Josephus-Studien: Unters. zu Josephus, dem ant. Judentum und dem NT, 1974 **11** P. Bilde, Flavius Josephus between Jerusalem and Rome. His life, works and their importance, 1988 **12** S. J. D. Cohen, Josephus in Galilee and Rome. His

vita and development as a historian, 1979 **13** L.H. Feldman, G. Hata (Hrsg.), Josephus, Judaism, and Christianity, 1987 **14** Dies. (Hrsg.), Josephus, the bible, and history, 1989 **15** F.J. Foakes Jackson, Josephus and the Jews: The Religion and History of the Jews as Explained by Flavius Josephus, 1930 (Ndr. 1977) **16** C. Gerber, Die Heiligen Schriften des Judentums nach Flavius Josephus, in: M. Hengel, H. Löhr (Hrsg.), Schriftauslegung im ant. Judentum und im Urchristentum, 1994, 91–113 **17** M. Goodman, The Ruling Class of Judaea, 1987 **18** M. Hadas-Lebel, Flavius Josephus, le juif de Rome, 1989 **19** G. Hölscher, Die Quellen des Josephus für die Zeit vom Exil bis zum jüd. Kriege, 1904 **20** K.-S. Krieger, Geschichtsschreibung als Apologetik bei Flavius Josephus, 1994 **21** R. Laquer, Der jüd. Historiker Flavius Josephus, 1920 (Ndr. 1970) **22** S. Mason, Flavius Josephus on the Pharisees: A Composition-Critical Study, 1991 **23** T. Rajak, Josephus: the Historian and his Society, 1983 **24** A. Schalit (Hrsg.), Zur Josephus-Forschung, 1973 **25** H. Schreckenberg, s.v. Josephus (Flavius Josephus), RAC 18, 762–802 **26** B. Schröder, Die »väterlichen Gesetze«. Flavius Josephus als Vermittler von Halachah an Griechen und Römer, 1996 **27** Schürer 1, 43–63, 428–441, 485–496; 3/1, 186, 545f. **28** G.E. Sterling, Historiography and Self-Definition. Josephos, Luke-Acts and Apologetic Historiography, 1992 **29** H.St.J. Thackeray, Josephus. The Man and the Historian, 1929 (Ndr. mit Einl. von S. Sandmel, 1967). I.WA.

[5] I. von Thessalonike. Jüngerer Bruder des Theodoros Studites, geb. 762 n. Chr., seit etwa 780 Mönch, seit 798 im Studioskloster in Konstantinopel, 807–809 Erzbischof von Thessalonike, wurde dann gestürzt und mehrfach verbannt, gest. 832. Nach dem Ende des Bilderstreits 844 (Ikonoklasmus, → Syrische Dynastie) wurden seine Gebeine ins Studioskloster nach Konstantinopel überführt. Schriftsteller und bed. Hymnendichter der orthodoxen Kirche; die unter dem Namen Iosephos überl. Dichtungen lassen sich teils ihm, teils dem jüngeren Iosephos, dem Hymnographen (ca. 810 in Sizilien – 886 Konstantinopel) zuweisen.

→ Hymnos; Theodoros Studites

H.-G. Beck, Kirche und theolog. Lit. im byz. Reich, 1959, 50f. AL.B.

[6] I. Genesios. Konventioneller Name eines anon. byz. Geschichtswerks über die J. 813–886 n. Chr., das wohl in der Mitte des 10. Jh. entstanden ist. Ein *Genesios* wird nur von einem Zusatz einer erheblich jüngeren Hand in der aus dem 11. Jh. stammenden Hs. als Autor bezeichnet. Eine Identifizierung mit dem von Iohannes Skylitzes als Vorgänger erwähnten I. Genesios ist möglich, aber nicht beweisbar. Der Name Genesios ist armen. Herkunft. Das Werk verwendet als Quelle Georgios Monachos, einige andere erh. Texte und eine verlorene Chronik, die auch von der Fortsetzung des Theophanes benützt wurde.

→ Georgios [5] Monachos; Skylitzes; Theophanes Continuatus

Ed.: A. Lesmueller-Werner, I. Thurn (ed.), Iosephi Genesii regum libri quattuor, 1978.
Übers.: A. Lesmüller-Werner, Byzanz am Vorabend neuer Größe ... Die vier Bücher der Kaisergesch. des Ioseph Genesios, 1989. AL.B.

Jossipon. Diese in Hebr. vermutlich im 10. Jh. in Südit. verfaßte geschichtliche Darstellung des Weltgeschehens (von Adam bis zur Zerstörung des jüd. Tempels in Jerusalem durch Titus 70 n. Chr.) basiert auf den Werken des → Iosephos [4] Flavios (*Antiquitates Iudaicae, Bellum Judaicum, Contra Apionem*). Als hauptsächliche Vorlage sind neben der lat. Fassung des *Bellum* (sog. lat. Hegesippus, 4. Jh. n. Chr.) diverse ma. Chroniken auszumachen. Im Zentrum stehen die Auseinandersetzungen zw. Rom und Israel. Ma. Übers. ins Arab., Äthiop. und Lat. liegen vor; editio princeps: Mantua vor 1480 (kurze hebr. Fassung); Konstantinopel 1510 (lange hebr. Fassung).

Ed.: • J.F. Breithaupt, Josephus Gorionides, sive Josephus Hebraicus, Latine Versus, 1707 • H. Hominer, Shearith Yisrael complete, the second volume of Josiphon, 1967, (Einl. von A.J. Wertheimer).
Lit.: S. Bowman, »Yosippon« and Jewish Nationalism, in: Proceedings of the American Academy for Jewish Research 61, 1995, 23–51 • D. Flusser, Der lat. Josephus und der hebr. J., in: O. Betz u.a. (Hrsg.), Josephus-Studien, 1974, 122–132 • H. Schreckenberg, Rezeptionsgeschichtliche und textkritische Unters. zu Flavius Josephus, 1977, 48–53 • Schürer 1, 117f. • S. Shulamit, From Joseph son of Mathias to Joseph son of Gorion, in: Tarbiz 64, 1994/5, 51–63 • S. Zeitlin, J., in: Jewish Quarterly Review 53, 1953, 273–297. I.WA.

Iošua Stylites (»der Säulenheilige«). Eine syr. Chronik, die ausführlich Auskunft über die Lokalgesch. Edessas für die Jahre 495–507 enthält (z.B. über die Belagerung von Amida), ist eingebettet in die Chronik von Zuqnīn, auch bekannt als ›Chronik des → [Ps.-]Dionysios [23] von Tell-Maḥrē‹. Sie wird häufig I. Stylites zugeschrieben. Er wird wohl zu Recht auch für den Verf. der gesamten Chronik gehalten.

Ed.: J.B. Chabot, CSCO Scr. Syri 43 und 66, 1927 und 1949 • W. Wright, 1882 (mit engl. Übers.) • J. Watt (im Erscheinen).
Lit.: W. Witakowski, The Syriac Chronicle of Ps.-Dionysius of Tel-Mahre, 1987. S.BR./Ü: S.Z.

Iota subscriptum s. Lesezeichen

Iotapata (Ἰωτάπατα, Ἰωταπάτη, hebr. *Yodp̄at, Yotpat*), Ort in Untergalilaea 10 km nördl. von → Sepphoris, h. Ḥirbat šifāt. Laut arch. Befund bereits in der späteren Brz. besiedelt [4], nach rabbinischer Überl. (Mišna ʿArakin 9,6) schon z.Z. Josuas befestigte Stadt; evtl. identisch mit *Yotbah* 2 Kg 21,19 [5]. Im jüd. Krieg unter Führung des → Josephos [4] ein Zentrum des antiröm. Widerstandes (Ios. bell. Iud. 3,141–288), 67 n. Chr. nach 47tägiger Belagerung durch Vespasianus eingenommen und weitgehend zerstört (ebd. 3,316–338). Als Ort mit jüd. Bevölkerung (u. a. Sitz einer der 24 Priesterklassen [2]) auch später noch bis ins 3. Jh. erwähnt (vgl. babylon. Talmud Zebahim 110b; Me^cila 13 b).

1 SCHÜRER 1, 477, 490, 493 2 S. KLEIN, Beitr. zur Gesch. und Geogr. Galiläas, 1909, 50 3 G. DALMAN, Palästina-Jb. 8, 1912, 40–43 4 A. SAARISOLO, Journ. Palest. Orient Soc. 9, 1929, 37, 39 5 ABEL 2, 336 6 D. R. EDWARDS, M. AVIAM, D. ADAN BAYEWITZ, Yodefat 1992, in: Israel Exploration Journal 45, 1995, 191–197. BE.SCH.

Iotape (Ἰοτάπη).

[1] Tochter des Antiochos [18] IV. von Kommagene; wurde Gattin des Alexandros, der Sohn des Herodes-Nachfahren und kurzzeitigen armen. Königs Tigranes war, durch den röm. Kaiser Vespasian (= 79 n. Chr.) König einer kleinen Herrschaft in Kilikien wurde und Münzen mit seinem und seiner Frau Abbild prägen ließ (Ios. ant. Iud. 18, 139–141).

R. D. SULLIVAN, The Dynasty of Commagene, in: ANRW II 8, 1977, 794 f. A.ME.

[2] Küstenstadt in Kilikia Tracheia, h. Aydap İskelesi, 8 km nordwestl. von Selinus. Ptol. 5,7,2; Plin. nat. 5,92; Hierokles 709,7.

1 HILD s. v. I. 2 E. ROSENBAUM, G. HUBER, S. ONURKAN, A Survey of Coastal Cities in Western Cilicia. Preliminary Report, 1967, 35 ff. (mit Planskizze). K.T.

Iotapianus. I., der sich der Abstammung von (Severus?) Alexander gerühmt haben soll (Aur. Vict. Caes. 29,2), ist 248/49 n. Chr. in Kappadokien oder Syrien (Chron. min. 1, 521,38 MOMMSEN; Zos. 1,20,2; Aur. Vict. Caes. 29,2) zum Gegenkaiser des → Philippus Arabs erhoben und im Sept./Okt. 249 von den Soldaten getötet worden (Zos. 1,21,2; RIC 4,3, 105).

PIR[2] I 49 • KIENAST[2], 202 • X. LORIOT, Les premières années de la grande crise du IIIe siècle, in: ANRW II 2, 1975, 657–797, bes. 794. T.F.

Iovianus. Flavius I., röm. Kaiser 363–364 n. Chr., geb. 331 in Singidunum, Sohn des *comes domesticorum* Varronianus. Sein Schwiegervater war der Heermeister Lucillianus, seine Frau hieß evtl. Charito (vgl. Zon. 13,14). Unter Constantius [2] II. war er *protector domesticus* (Amm. 21,16,20), unter Iulianus [11] *primicerius domesticorum* (Amm. 25,5,4). Einen Tag nach Iulianus' Tod im Kampf gegen die Perser wurde I. am 27.6.363 noch auf pers. Gebiet vom Heer zum Kaiser erhoben. Er beendete den Perserkrieg und ging auf die von Sapor II. angebotenen Bedingungen für einen 30jährigen Friedensvertrag ein, bei dem die Römer auf alle Gebiete jenseits des Tigris sowie auf die Städte Nisibis und Singara verzichteten (Amm. 25,7,9–11; Zos. 3,30 f.). Den Zeitgenossen galt der Vertragsschluß als Schmachfrieden (Amm. 25,7,10; 13; Eutr. 10,17; Lib. or. 18,278 ff.). I., selbst Christ, ließ die von Iulianus getroffenen antichristl. Maßnahmen aufheben und die verbannten Kleriker zurückkehren (Theod. hist. eccl. 4,2; Philostorgios 8,5; Soz. 6,3). Anfänglich ergriffene Maßnahmen gegen die Altgläubigen (Schließung der Tempel: Sokr. 3,24,5) nahm I. später zurück, nur Zauberei und Magie blieben verboten (Them. or. 5,70b). Von Edessa zog I. über Antiocheia nach Ankyra, wo er zusammen mit seinem Sohn Varronianus das Konsulat für 364 antrat. Themistios hielt dabei die noch erh. Festrede (or. 5). Schon am 17.2. 364 starb I. auf dem Weg nach Konstantinopel in Dadastana (Sokr. 3,26,5).

PLRE 1, 461 (I. 3) • G. WIRTH, Jovian – Kaiser und Karikatur, in: Vivarium, FS Th. Klauser, 1984, 353–384. W.P.

Iovinus

[1] Flavius I., 361 n. Chr. *magister equitum* des → Iulianus [11] (Amm. 21,8,3; 22,3,1), 363 *mag. mil. per Gallias* (Amm. 25,8,11; 10,6–17; 26,5,1–3); I. behauptete seine Ämter auch unter Valentinianus und Valens; 366 Sieg über die Alamannen an der oberen Mosel (Amm. 27,2); 367 Consul; noch bis 369 war er in Gallien und Britannien tätig. Er war Christ und erbaute in Reims die Kirche des hl. Agricola (CIL XIII 3256). PLRE 1, 462 f. (F. I. 6). K.G.-A.

[2] Gallischer Usurpator der J. 411–413 n. Chr., entstammte der provinzialen Aristokratie (Oros. 7,42,6) und wurde unter Mitwirkung des Burgunderkönigs Guntiarius und des Alanen Goar zum Gegenkaiser des → Honorius [3] erhoben (Olympiodor fr. 17 FHG IV 61). Mit einem Heer aus Alanen, Burgundern, Alamannen und Franken eroberte er Arelate (Greg. Tur. Franc. 2,9). Weite Teile Galliens fielen ihm zu; in Trier, Arelate und Lugdunum wurden seine Münzen geprägt. Er suchte Kontakt zu dem Gotenkönig → Ataulfus, geriet aber 412 mit ihm in Konflikt und mußte sich 413 unterwerfen; an den gall. Praefekten des Honorius [3] ausgeliefert, wurde er in Narbo getötet (Olympiodor fr. 19 FHG IV 61; Soz. 9,15,3; Iord. Get. 32,165; Chron. min. 1, 523, 654; 2, 18, 71 MOMMSEN). Zu seinen Münzen RIC, 10, 1994, 152–54; 352–54, zum Münzbildnis ebd., Taf. 46.

PLRE 2, 621 f. (I. 2) • A. DEMANDT, Die Spätantike, 1989, 148 • S. ELBERN, Usurpationen im spätröm. Reich, 1984 • H. WOLFRAM, Die Goten, [3]1990, 168 f. K.P.J.

Iovis epulum. Festmahl zu Ehren → Iuppiters (beteiligt waren auch Iuno und Minerva: Val. Max. 2,1,2) an den Iden des November während der → Ludi plebeii; wie diese von den plebejischen Aedilen veranstaltet (s. bes. Liv. 30,39,8). Die kaiserzeitlichen Kalender [1] belegen ein *I. e.* auch für die → Ludi Romani an den Iden des September.

Bei diesem Fest konstituierten sich die Senatoren auf dem Capitol als Mahlgemeinschaft. Der bandstiftende Ritus (Gell. 12,8,2) war im Falle eines extremen Konflikts nicht mehr durchführbar (Cass. Dio 39,30,4). Vergleichbar ist die im häuslichen Rahmen vor der Hirse-,

Knoblauch- und Linsensaat veranstaltete *daps* für Iuppiter (Cato agr. 132).
→ Epulo; lectisternium.

1 InscrIt 13,2,509; 530.

W. K. Quinn-Schofield, Observations upon the Ludi Plebeii, in: Latomus 26, 1967, 677–685. D. B.

Iovius
[1] Beiname des Diocletianus, → Tetrarchie. B. BL.

[2] Praetorianerpraefekt des Kaisers → Honorius [3]. Von Stilicho 407 n. Chr. zum *praefectus praetorio Illyrici* ernannt, um diese Praefektur dem Ostreich zu entreißen, blieb dort aber vom Gotenkönig → Alaricus [2] abhängig (Soz. 8,25,3; 9,4,3; Zos. 5,48,2). Im Jahre 409 wurde er *praef. praet. Italiae* und *patricius* (Cod. Theod. 2,8,25; 16,5,47; Zos. 5,47,1). Als einflußreichster Berater des Kaisers führte er ergebnislose Friedensverhandlungen mit Alaricus (Zos. 5,47–49; 51; Soz. 9,7). 410 lief er zu dem Usurpator → Attalos [11] über, wurde in seinen Ämtern bestätigt, bewegte dann aber den Gotenkönig zu dessen Absetzung (Olympiodor fr. 13 FHG IV 59 f.; Zos. 6,8 f.). Er ist evtl. identisch mit dem *comes*, der 399 in Africa pagane Tempel zerstörte (Aug. civ. 18,54) und von → Symmachus die Briefe 8,30; 50; 9,59 erhielt.

PLRE 2, 622–24 (I. 2 u. 3) • v. Haehling, 314 f., 471 f. • Stein, Spätröm. R. 1, 391–94. K. P. J.

Iphianassa (Ἰφιάνασσα).
[1] Tochter des → Proitos und der → Stheneboia (Hes. fr. 129,16–24 M-W), wird mit ihren Schwestern Lysippe und Iphinoe wegen Mißachtung des Kults des Dionysos (Hes. fr. 131 M-W) oder Beleidigung der Hera (Bakchyl. 11,40 ff.) mit Wahnsinn geschlagen. Schließlich bringt Proitos Artemis mit einem Opfer dazu, Hera umzustimmen. Nach einer anderen Version (Pherekydes, FGrH 3 F 114; Hdt. 9,34) heilt der Seher → Melampus die Töchter, nachdem er länger um die Belohnung gefeilscht hat. Gemäß Diodor (4,68) erhält er auf diesem Weg I. zur Frau (zu den verschiedenen Versionen [1. 196–202]).
[2] Tochter des → Agamemnon und der → Klytaimestra (Hom. Il. 9,145); I. vertritt oder ersetzt die bei Homer nicht erwähnte → Iphigeneia (vgl. [2]). Den *Kypria* (fr. 24 Bernabé) zufolge ist sie ihre Schwester.

1 H. Maehler, Die Lieder des Bakchylides 1.2, 1982
2 A. Heubeck, Zur neueren Homerforsch. (V), in: Gymnasium 71, 1964, 63. RE. N.

Iphianeira (Ἰφιάνειρα). Name verschiedener griech. Heroinen: Zum einen der Tochter des argiv. Königs Megapenthes, von der dasselbe erzählt wird wie von → Iphianassa [1] (Diod. 4,68,4), zum anderen heißt I. die Schwester des → Amphiaraos (Diod. 4,68,5). C. W.

Iphidamas (Ἰφιδάμας). Gestalt aus dem troischen Sagenzyklus, Sohn des → Antenor [1] und der Theano. Bei Kisses, dem Vater seiner Mutter, im thrak. Perkote aufgewachsen, verläßt er seine Heimat gegen den Willen seiner Frau, um den Troern beizustehen. Der in Hom. Il. 11,218–263 beschriebene Schlachtentod des I. und seines Bruders → Koon durch → Agamemnon war auch auf der → Kypselos-Lade dargestellt (Paus. 5,19,4).

I. Espermann, Theano, Antenor und Antenoriden, 1980, 71–80 • P. Wathelet, Dictionnaire des Troyens de l'Iliade, 1988, Nr. 180. E. V.

Iphigeneia (Ἰφιγένεια).
A. Mythos B. Kult C. Nachleben

A. Mythos

Tochter von → Agamemnon und → Klytaimestra (Prokl. Cypriorum enarratio, 55–62 EpGF S. 32; Aischyl. Ag.; vgl. aber Stesich. fr. 191 PMGF und Nikandros fr. 58 = Antoninus Liberalis 27, wo Theseus und Helena ihre Eltern sind und I. lediglich von Klytaimestra adoptiert wird), Schwester von → Orestes, → Chrysothemis [2] und → Elektra [4]. Obwohl sie dem Achilleus [1] zur Ehe versprochen ist, wird sie von Agamemnon auf Rat des Kalchas der Artemis geopfert, um die durch eine unnatürliche Windstille verzögerte Abfahrt der Griechen nach Troia zu ermöglichen.

Als Ort der Opferung wird zumeist Aulis genannt (Prokl. loc. cit. 55; Eur. Iph.A.; Lucr. 1,84; Phanodemus fr. 10; 11 FHG, etc.), doch Brauron (Euphorion fr. 91 CollAlex), Megara (wo sie ein Grab hatte: Paus. 1,43,1) und vielleicht auch Aigira und Hermione (wo I. verehrt wurde: Paus. 7,26,5; 2,35,1 f.) erhoben darauf ebenfalls Anspruch. Dies legt nahe, daß I. nur ein Name des archetyp. sterbenden Mädchens ist, das deshalb bekannter als die anderen wurde, weil sie früh ihren Eingang in den panhellenischen Mythos fand [1. Kap. 2]. Andere Namen: → Iphianassa (Lucr. 1,85; schol. Eur. Or. 22), Iphigone (Eur. El. 1023), Iphimede (Hes. cat. fr. 23a, 17–26; vgl. Iphimedeia, für die auf einer Linear B-Tafel aus Pylos ein Opfer belegt ist: PY 172 = Tn 316; vgl. auch die Gesch. über Mädchen aus Brauron und Munichos (Suda s. v. Ἔμβαρός εἰμι und Ἄρκτος ἢ Βραυρωνίοις, [1. 20–22]).

Was das Opfer angeht, ist I. anderen Mädchen, die vor einer Schlacht geopfert werden, z. B. Makaria, zur Seite zu stellen [4. 57–63]. In einigen Versionen rettet Artemis I. im letzten Moment dadurch, daß sie sie durch ein Hirschkalb, einen Bär, Stier oder ein Eidolon (»Trugbild«) ersetzt (Proc. l.c. 62; Eur. Iph.T. 28 und Iph.A. 1587; Phanodemus 325 F 14 FGrH; Nikandros loc. cit; Hes. cat. fr. 23a). Entweder wird die entrückte I. zur Göttin, die Orsilocheia, Artemis Einodia oder → Hekate genannt wird (Nikandros l.c.; Stesich. fr. 215 PMGF; Hes. cat. fr. 23a, 17–26; vgl. 23b = Paus. 1,43,1); oder sie wird zur Priesterin der Artemis im Taurerlande (Prokl. l. c. 61), zu deren Pflichten auch die Opferung aller dorthin gelangenden Griechen gehört (Eur. Iph.T. 72 ff.; vgl. Hdt. 4,103).

I.s Gesch. kulminiert in der Ankunft ihres Bruders Orestes und seines Begleiters Pylades im Taurerlande. Gerade als I. diese für das Opfer vorbereiten will, kommt es zur Wiedererkennung. Die drei fliehen nach Griechenland und führen auf Geheiß der Athena die Statue der Artemis mit sich (Eur. Iph.T.; [5]). Der Mythos ist Aition für eine Reihe von Artemiskulten, in denen ein kleines hochaltertümliches Bild verwendet wurde (Artemis Orthia und Sparta, Phalekitis in Tyndaris und Diana Nemorensis in Aricia; [5]). Bis zu ihrem Lebensende bleibt I. Priesterin der Artemis in Brauron (Eur. Iph.T. 1462–1467; vgl. Euphorion l.c.); nach anderer Quelle wird sie nach ihrem Tod dem Achilleus anvermählt und verbringt mit ihm die Ewigkeit auf → Leuke, der paradies. »weißen Insel« (Nikandros l.c.). Eine Verbindung zu Achilleus wird auch in der Trad. sichtbar, in der I. durch die Vortäuschung ihrer bevorstehenden Heirat mit Achilleus zum Platz ihrer Opferung gelockt wird (Prokl. l.c. 59–60; Eur. Iph.A. 98–105).

B. Kult

Von allen Kulten im Zusammenhang mit I. ist der von → Brauron am besten bezeugt. Nach Euripides (Iph.T. 1462–1467) sollten der I. nach ihrem Tod als ihr *ágalma* die Webarbeiten von Frauen dargebracht werden, die im Wochenbett starben; dies vielleicht im Kontrast zu Artemis, die die Kleider der überlebenden Frauen empfing (schol. Kall. h. 1,77). Tempelaufzeichnungen aus Brauron sind noch nicht veröffentlicht, doch wird diese Sitte möglicherweise widergespiegelt durch den Brauch, nicht fertiggestellte Kleider am Brauronion in Athen zu weihen [6. 17–19]. Dies, aber auch der Name Orsilocheia (»Erregerin der Geburtsschmerzen«) und vielleicht sogar der Name I., der von den Griechen der histor. Zeit als »stark in Geburt« (vgl. aber [1. 46]) verstanden wurde, legen eine Funktion als Geburtsgöttin nahe [2. Kap. 6; 4. 27–28]. In dieselbe Richtung deutet ihre Verbindung mit der Geburtsgöttin und *kurotróphos* → Hekate [2. Kap. 6]. Wahrscheinlich dient I. in Brauron auch als mythischer Archetyp für die Mädchen, die sich dort Initiationsriten an der Schwelle zur Heiratsfähigkeit unterzogen.

C. Nachleben

In Nachfolge der beiden Trag. des Euripides, die I. in verschiedenen Phasen ihres Lebens (Opferung: Iph.A., Taurerland: Iph.T.) vorführten, ist das Schicksal der I., die zum Paradigma der »Fremden« schlechthin avancierte, bis in die Neuzeit immer wieder Stoff von Dramen und Opern gewesen. Unter diesen ist sicher Goethes ›Iphigenie auf Tauris‹ (1779), in der die Sehnsucht der Heldin nach Griechenland programmatisch für die zeitgenössische Idealisierung und Verklärung der griech. Ant. steht, die prägendste gewesen.

1 K. Dowden, Death and the Maiden. Girls' Initiation Rites in Greek Mythology, 1989 **2** S. I. Johnston, Restless Dead, 1999 **3** S. G. Cole, The Social Function of Rituals of Maturation: The Koureion and the Arkteia, in: ZPE 55, 1984, 233–244 **4** E. Kearns, The Heroes of Attica, in: BICS Suppl. 57, 1989 **5** F. Graf, Das Götterbild aus dem Taurerland, in: Ant. Welt 4, 1979, 33–41 **6** T. Linders, Studies in the Treasure Records of Artemis Brauronia found in Athens, 1972 **7** W. Sale, The Temple legends of the Arkteia, in: RhM N. S. 118, 1975, 265–284.

A. Athanasios, Symbole sten historia tou hierou tes Brauronias Artemidos, 1990 (Quellensammlung) · L. Kahil et al., s. v. I., LIMC 5.1, 706–734 · J. Larson, Greek Heroine Cults, 1995.

S.I.J.

Iphikles (Ἰφικλῆς, auch Ἴφικλος). Sohn → Alkmenes von → Amphitryon, der Zwillings(halb)bruder des → Herakles, für dessen Gottmenschentum er als Folie dient. Er flieht vor den Schlangen in ihrem Kinderbett, die Herakles erwürgt (Pherekydes FGrH 3 F 69). I. ist Teilnehmer an der kalydon. Jagd und am Troiazug des Herakles (Diod. 4,49,3). Von Automedusa, der Tochter des Alkathoos, ist er Vater des → Iolaos; nach dem Kampf gegen Erginos bekommt Herakles die ältere Tochter Kreons, Megara, I. die jüngere zur Frau. Im Wahnsinn wirft Herakles auch zwei Kinder des I. ins Feuer (Apollod. 2,61 ff.). I. fällt im Kampf gegen die Söhne des Hippokoon (Apollod. 2,145) oder stirbt in Pheneos, wohin er nach einer Verwundung im Kampf gegen die Molionen gebracht wird und wo er ein Heroon erhält (Paus. 8,14,9 f.).

S. Woodford, s. v. I., LIMC 5.1., 734–737.

C.W.

Iphikrates (Ἰφικράτης). Sohn des Timotheos, Athener aus Rhamnous, bedeutender General in der 1. H. des 4. Jh. v. Chr. I. zeichnete sich im Korinth. Krieg durch die Schaffung eines schlagkräftigen Korps von Peltasten aus, mit dem er zwischen 393 und 390 in der Peloponnes operierte und eine spartan. → *móra* bei Korinth vernichtete (Xen. hell. 4,5,11–18; Diod. 14,91,2; 15,44; Nep. Iphikrates 1). 389 kämpfte er als Stratege siegreich am Hellespont gegen → Anaxibios (Xen. hell. 4,8,34–39). Nach dem Königsfrieden (387/386 v. Chr.; → Antalkidas) trat I. in den Dienst des Thrakerkönigs → Kotys, heiratete dessen Schwester und erhielt die Städte Drys und Antissa (Demosth. or. 23,132). 374/3 diente er (wieder im Auftrag Athens) als Söldnerführer unter dem Satrapen → Pharnabazos gegen die Ägypter (Diod. 15,41,1 f.; 42,4 f.; 43,1–6), kehrte aber bald aufgrund persönl. Differenzen mit Pharnabazos nach Athen zurück und erhielt mehrere wichtige Kommanden: 372 ins Ion. Meer, 370/69 gegen → Epameinondas in die Peloponnes und seit 369 gegen Amphipolis. 365 durch seinen innenpolit. Kontrahenten → Timotheos ersetzt, zog sich I. wieder nach Thrakien zurück. Im → Bundesgenossenkrieg (→ Bundesgenossenkriege [1]) wurde er erneut Stratege (vgl. IG II[2] 124), söhnte sich mit Timotheos aus und wurde gemeinsam mit diesem nach der Schlacht von Embata 356–355 des Hochverrates angeklagt, aber freigesprochen (Diod. 16,21,1–4; Nep. Iphikrates 3; vgl. Lys. fr. 45–9). Er starb kurz nach dem Prozeß.

→ Antalkidas; Konon

DAVIES, 7737 • DEVELIN, 1449 • J. HESKEL, The North Aegean Wars, 1997 • L. KALLET, Iphikrates, Timotheos, and Athens, in: GRBS 24, 1983, 239–52 • TRAILL, PAA 542925.
HA. BE.

Iphimedeia (Ἰφιμέδεια).
[1] Tochter des Triops, Gattin des Aloeus, Geliebte Poseidons, dem sie die → Aloaden, Otos und Ephialtes, gebiert (Hom. Od. 11,304; Pind. P. 4,89; Apollod. 1,53; Hyg. fab. 28). I. und ihre Tochter Pankratis (Pankrato) spielen in der Vorgesch. von Naxos eine Rolle (Diod. 5,50f.; Parthenios 19): Die Aloaden verfolgen die Thraker, die ihre Mutter und Schwester nach Naxos entführt haben, und befreien I., während Pankratis umkommt. Pausanias bezeugt I.s Grab in Anthedon, einen Kult im karischen Mylasa und ein Bild von Polygnotos in Delphi (Paus. 9,22,5; 10,28,8).
[2] → Iphigeneia. C.W.

Iphinoe (Ἰφινόη). Name verschiedener Heroinen in Mythos und Kult: zum einen eine Tochter des megarischen Königs → Alkathoos [1], an dessen Grab Mädchen vor ihrer Hochzeit Trankopfer und Haarlocken opferten (Paus. 1,43,3f.); zum anderen die Tochter des Königs → Proitos (Apollod. 2,29), die bei einem Versuch des Melampus, sie und ihre Schwestern vom Wahnsinn zu heilen, stirbt. Vielleicht wurde sie mit Riten während der argiv. Agrigonia geehrt (Hesych. s. v. Agrania).

W. BURKERT, Homo Necans, 1972, 189–200 • K. DOWDEN, Death and the Maiden. Girls' Initiation Rites in Greek Mythology, 1989. S.I.J.

Iphion. Griech. Maler aus Korinth, durch zwei rühmende Epigramme aus Anth. Pal. 9,757 und 13,17 namentlich überliefert. Seine Schaffenszeit, nur aus der Quellenkritik zu rekonstruieren, ist umstritten, lag jedoch vermutlich in der 1. H. des 5. Jh. v. Chr. Über sein Werk wissen wir nichts, doch genoß die korinth. Malerschule dieser Zeit, der er entstammte, hohes Ansehen.

L. GUERRINI, s. v. I., EAA 4, 178 • G. LIPPOLD, s. v. I., RE 9, 2023. N.H.

Iphis (Ἶφις). Name einer Reihe von kleinen Heroen (Gen. Ἴφιος) und Heroinen (Gen. Ἴφιδος). Auf der Ambivalenz des Genus basiert die Erzählung von Ov. met. 9,666–797 über die Geschlechtsverwandlung der Tochter des Lygdus und der Telethusa in Phaistos, die eine dichterische Transformation des von Antoninus Liberalis 17 nach → Nikandros erzählten Aitions für das Ritual der Ekdysia im Kult der Leto von Phaistos ist; dort heißt die Heroin Leukippe [1].

Daneben tragen mehrere argivische Heroen, ein Argonaut, ein Mitkämpfer der Sieben vor Theben und eine Sklavin des Patroklos diesen Namen. Aus Antoninus Liberalis 39 (dort sind die Hauptgestalten nach → Hermesianax von Kolophon Arkeophron und Arsinoe) stammt die Erzählung bei Ov. met. 14,698–761: Der nichtadlige I. wird von der adligen Anaxarete (»Herrschertugend«, ein sprechender Name) abgewiesen und erhängt sich vor ihrer Tür; als Anaxarete von ihrem Fenster aus dem Grabzug zusehen will, wird sie zu Stein – Aition einer Statue der Venus Prospiciens, also der Aphrodite Parakyptusa [2].

1 D. LEITAO, The perils of Leucippus. Initiatory transvestism and male gender ideology in the Ekdysia at Phaistos, in: Classical Antiquity 14, 1995, 130–163 2 W. FAUTH, Aphrodite Parakyptusa. Untersuchungen zum Erscheinungsbild der vorderasiatischen Dea Prospiciens, Abh. Mainz 1966. F.G.

Iphistiadai (Ἰφιστιάδαι). Att. Asty-Demos der Phyle Akamantis, stellte einen Buleuten. Ein Grundstück Platons grenzte im Süden an das Herakleion von I. (Diog. Laert. 3,41), das aufgrund einer Horosinschr. (IG II² 2611) 4 km südwestl. Kephisia am SW-Rand vom h. Iraklion (ehem. Arakli) anzusetzen ist und den ant. Namen bewahrte [1; 2; 3. 47]. Einen eponymen Heros Iphistios bezeugt Hesychios s. v. Ἰ. [4. 210].

1 G. KLAFFENBACH, Zwei neue Horossteine aus Attika, in: MDAI(A) 51, 1926, 21–25 2 P. SIEWERT, Die Trittyen Attikas und die Heeresreform des Kleisthenes, 1982, 96 3 TRAILL, Attica, 47, 69, 110 Nr. 60, Tab. 5 4 WHITEHEAD, 75 Anm. 37, 84, 207 Anm. 183, 210. H.LO.

Iphitos (Ἴφιτος). Sohn des → Eurytos [1] von Oichalia und der Antiope (oder Antioche), der von Herakles getötet wird, weil der Vater und die Brüder (I. ausgenommen: Apollod. 1,128) diesem nicht wie versprochen als Preis für einen Sieg im Bogenschießen → Iole zur Frau geben. Die Sage erzählen Hom. Od. 21,14ff. (danach ist der Bogen des Odysseus ein Gastgeschenk I.'), das verlorene Epos *Oichalías hálōsis*, ferner Soph. Trach. 225ff., Diod. 4,31,2ff. und Apollod. 2,127ff. Nach einer anderen Version kommt I. auf der Suche nach seinen Stuten zur Burg Tiryns, wo Herakles ihn auf den Mauern herumführt und dann von einem Turm herabstürzt. I. als Argonaut: Apoll. Rhod. 1,86.

R. OLMOS, s. v. I. (1), LIMC 5.1, 738–741. C.W.

Iphthime (Ἰφθίμη). Tochter des → Ikarios (Hom. Od. 4,797) und möglicherweise der Asterodia; Schwester der → Penelope (schol. Hom. Od. 4,797); ihr Abbild sendet Athene als Traumbild, um Penelope zu trösten (Hom. Od. 4,799ff.). J.S.-A.

Ipsos (Ἴψος). Stadt beim türk. Dorf Çayırbağı (früher Sipsin unter Bewahrung des ant. Namens) nahe Afyon in Zentral-Phrygia. Berühmt als Ort der Schlacht, in der → Lysimachos und → Seleukos 301 v. Chr. dem Vorhaben des → Antigonos [1] und seines Sohnes Demetrios, den durch Alexander d.Gr. geschaffenen Staat zu erhalten, ein Ende setzten (Plut. Demetrios 29f.). I., lokalisiert auf einem Hügel mit phryg. Spuren und byz. Mauern in der Ebene des Kaystros, war in hell. Zeit eine Stadt, doch nicht als solche in der röm. Kaiserzeit bestätigt, da I. Teil der großen kaiserlichen Domäne, *regio*

Ipsina et Moeteana, war, der einen Teil von Zentral-Phrygia mit den Marmorsteinbrüchen von Dokimeion und Soa umfaßte. I. ist in byz. Zeit als Stadt gut nachweisbar, Suffraganbistum von Synnada in Phrygia Salutaris, von der Synode von Chalkedon 451 an bis ins 12. Jh.

Belke/Mersich, 282. T.D.-B./Ü: I.S.

Iran (mittelpers. *ērān*, Gen. Pl. von *ēr*, in *Ērān-šahr*, »Land der → Arier/Iranier« < mittelpers. *ēr*, sāsānidische Inschr. und Paḫlavī-Lit. des 9. Jh. n. Chr. < alt-iran. **arya-*, altpers. *ariya-*, avest. *airya-*).
I. Begriffsgeschichte II. Geographie
III. Geschichte IV. Kulturelle und religiöse Traditionen

I. Begriffsgeschichte

Obgleich bereits *ariya-* ethnischen Wert besitzt (Selbstbezeichnung der Achaimeniden als *ariya-* bzw. *ariyaciça-*, »arisch« bzw. »von arischer Abstammung«), ist I. (bzw. *Ērān-šahr*) als zugleich ethnischer, rel. und polit. Begriff eine frühsāsānidische Schöpfung. Schon unter Sapor I. (240–272 n. Chr.) tritt zu *Ērān* das Gegenstück *Anērān*, etwa im Titel *Šāhān šāh Ērān ud Anērān* (»König der Könige von Ērān und Nicht-Ērān«). *Ērān* wird aber auch zum Bestandteil von Funktionärstitulaturen oder ON; dabei dokumentiert z. B. das Toponym *Ērān-xwarrah-Šābuhr* (»Glorie der Arier des Sapor«) das Bemühen der Sāsāniden, die neue Idee des Königtums mit einer rel. Tradition zu verbinden, die zugleich zarathustrisch, kayanidisch und arisch ist (*Ērān xwarrah* < avest. *airyanąm x*ᵛ*arənō*). Nach dem Untergang des Sāsānidenreiches verschwindet auch der polit. Begriff I. Die islamischen Geographen und Historiographen, aber auch der pers. Epiker Firdausī benutzen ihn allein als historisierende Bez. für das Sāsānidenreich. Als polit. Konzept taucht er erst wieder im Reich der Īl-Khāne (1265–1335) auf; in der Herrschaftsideologie der Paḫlavī-Dyn. begründet liegt die von Rezā Šāh 1934 angeordnete Ersetzung des frz. Namens *Perse* durch I. in offiziellen Zusammenhängen.

II. Geographie

Unter I. verstanden die dort lebenden Menschen der Antike nicht nur die Regionen des h. Nationalstaates I., sondern auch von Iraniern bewohnte Landschaften des h. Afghanistan, Pakistan, Turkmenistan, Usbekistan, Tadschikistan und Kirgistan.

III. Geschichte

Unter den iran. Dyn., die in vorislamischer Zeit alle oder große Teile I.s beherrschten, ragen fünf heraus: a) die der Meder (→ Medai; Anfang 7. bis Mitte 6. Jh. v. Chr.) mit einem Reichsgebiet wohl von Ost-Iran bis zum Halys in Anatolien und dem/einem Zentrum in → Ekbatana; b) die der → Achaimeniden (559–330 v. Chr.) mit einem Territorium vom → Iaxartes bis Süd-Ägypten/Nubien und von Thrakien bis zum Indus sowie Residenzen/Königszentren in → Persepolis, Pasargadai, Ekbatana, Susa, Baktra (Baktrien), Sardis und Babylon; c) die der Arsakiden (239/8 v. Chr. – 224 n. Chr.; → Arsakes), deren Reich sich vom Euphrat bis nach Ost-Iran und von den Grenzen Parthiens und der Margiane bis zum Persischen Golf (mit Zentren v. a. in → Nisā (Turkmenistan) und → Ktesiphon) erstreckte; schließl. d) die der Sāsāniden (224–651 n. Chr.), die ein Territorium von Ost-Iran bis ins Zweistromland und von → Chorezmien bis zum Persischen Golf kontrollierten; Hauptorte waren → Istachr (Fars), → Merv (Turkmenistan) und Ktesiphon/al-Madāʾin. Vom Ende des 3. Jh. bis ca. 140 v. Chr. befanden sich Teile I.s (vor allem West-I.) unter der Herrschaft der Seleukiden, von ca. 240 bis ca. 130 v. Chr. Teile Ost-I.s (Baktrien) unter derjenigen der Graeco-Baktrer, denen dort die Sākā, die → Kušānas und Indo-Parther folgten.

Da die Reiche der Achaimeniden, → Parther und Sāsāniden immer auch Gebiete umschlossen, in denen nicht-iran. Bevölkerungsgruppen zu Hause waren, war das Problem des Umgangs mit fremden Sprachen, Trad. und Glaubensvorstellungen, aber auch mit den polit. Hoffnungen und Bestrebungen ehemals unabhängiger Völker für alle iran. Dyn. von Anfang an gegeben. Die lange Dauer ihrer Herrschaft über »I. (und Nicht-I.)« spricht, aufs ganze gesehen, für eine eher behutsame und weitsichtige sowie insgesamt erfolgreiche Politik der Könige gegenüber kulturellen, rel. oder polit. Minoritäten. Ihre Rel.-Politik ist ein Indiz unter vielen für diese These: Kult. Einheitsgebote waren danach nie Mittel der Herrschaftssicherung, Leitgedanke war vielmehr zu allen Zeiten die Förderung zuverlässiger und die Bestrafung illoyaler Gruppen und Gemeinschaften. Der vorislamische I. ist auch dadurch charakterisiert, daß er nicht nur eigene Trad. und Überl. pflegte (etwa die zoroastrische Sicht kosmischen und weltlichen Geschehens, die Ideale alt-iran. Königtums oder das Interesse an unterhaltsamer und zugleich belehrender Darstellung iran. Geschichte), sondern auch bereitwillig solche anderer Kulturen aufnahm, mischte, umgestaltete oder weitergab.

Reichs- und Herrschaftskrisen waren nur z. T. eine Folge äußeren Drucks durch Griechen, Makedonen und Römer im Westen, Steppenvölker im Norden und Osten (vgl. den in der Trad. maßgeblichen Gegensatz zw. I. und Tūrān) und zuletzt durch die Araber im Süden; mindestens ebenso wichtig waren Probleme und Konflikte im Inneren des Reiches: die Spannungen zw. Königshaus und grundbesitzender Aristokratie, die polit. Ambitionen von Mitgliedern des Königshauses und des Hochadels sowie von unzuverlässigen oder der Illoyalität verdächtigen Teilen der Bevölkerung, zuweilen auch Seuchen, Hungerkrisen und soziale Konflikte. Dabei konnten sich äußere und innere Faktoren dieser Art zu bestimmten Zeiten miteinander verbinden, wie etwa während der großen Krise des Sāsānidenreiches im 5. Jh. n. Chr. Während die Herrschaft der Achaimeniden mit den Siegen Alexanders (334–331 v. Chr.) eher überraschend zu Ende ging – nicht etwa als Folge unlösbarer Probleme im Inneren des Reiches – und die

Ursache für die Ablösung der Parther durch die Sāsāniden mehr im polit. und mil. Geschick Ardašīrs I. als in der Schwäche arsakidischer Herrschaft lag, waren im 7. Jh. äußere und innere Faktoren gemeinsam für das Ende der Sāsānidenherrschaft in I. verantwortlich: Partikulare Interessen von Angehörigen des Hochadels, Konflikte innerhalb des Herrscherhauses, die Überbeanspruchung der Kräfte durch Husrav II. im Kampf gegen Byzanz und schließl. die Auflösung des laḫmidischen Pufferstaates (→ Lachmiden) begünstigten die Vorstöße der schlagkräftigen Heere des Propheten gegen Mesopot. und I.

IV. Kulturelle und religiöse Traditionen

Achaimeniden, Arsakiden und Sāsāniden haben die kulturellen Traditionen I.s in höchst unterschiedlichem Maße bestimmt: Während letztere in der von ihnen zusammengestellten »Nationalgeschichte« als iran. Könige *par excellence* weiterlebten, wurden die Parther in ihr zu »Teilkönigen« abgewertet; → Kyros und seine Nachfolger mußten gar erst in unserer Zeit wiederentdeckt werden und als fragwürdige »Vorfahren« legitimationsbedürftiger Herrscher dienen.

Der Zoroastrismus (→ Zoroastres) wurde in I. selbst schon früh zur Minderheiten-Rel. und erlangte nie die Bedeutung von Christentum, Judentum und Islam, obwohl die Botschaft Zarathustras zu allen Zeiten Bewunderer und Anhänger gefunden hat.

In Europa haben (früh-)neuzeitliche Reisende, Schriftenentzifferer und Archäologen die Zeugnisse des alten I. in die Erinnerung zurückgerufen, von Iranisten und Historikern wurden die Charakteristika der iran. Kulturen neu bestimmt und bewertet.

→ Familie; Frau; Geschichtsschreibung; Graeco-Baktrien; Hyrkanien

B. G. Fragner, Histor. Wurzeln neuzeitlicher iran. Identität, in: M. Macuch u. a. (Hrsg.), Studia Semitica nec non Iranica Rudolpho Macuch dedicata, 1989, 79–100 • Dies., Der polit. Begriff »Iran« in der Neuzeit, in: G. Gnoli, A. Panaino (Hrsg.), First European Conference of Iranian Studies, 2, 1990, 365–376 • G. Gnoli, The Idea of I., 1989 • Ders., I. als rel. Begriff im Mazdaismus, 1993 • J. Wiesehöfer, Das ant. Persien, 1994.

J. W.

Iranische Sprachen. Das Iran. bildet zusammen mit dem Indoarischen den indoiran. Zweig der idg. Sprachfamilie. Er gehört zu den Satemsprachen. Das Iran. hat sich in zahlreiche Einzelsprachen aufgespalten, die sich im Alt. über ein noch wesentlich weiteres Gebiet als h. erstreckten, und zwar von Ungarn und der Ukraine im Westen über Kasachstan und Chinesisch-Turkestan im Osten bis Balutschistan im Süden. Zwei altiran. Sprachen sind relativ gut bekannt, nämlich das Avestische der hl. Schriften der Anhänger Zarathustras (→ Zoroastres) und – in geringerem Umfang – das Altpers. des Achämenidenreiches (→ Achaimenidai, mit Karte). Das Avest. besteht aus dem Altavest., auch Gathisch genannt, und dem Jungavestischen. Ersteres enthält 17 Hymnen (Gāthās) und den Liturgietext Yasna Haptaŋhāiti, die dem Propheten Zarathustra selbst zugeschrieben werden und spätestens um das Jahr 800 v. Chr. abgefaßt sein dürften. Auf jungavestisch sind ebenfalls v. a. Hymnen und andere Gebete sowie das kirchliche Gesetzbuch, der Videvdad, überliefert. Diese Texte sind um mindestens zwei Jh. jünger. Das Avest. wurde wahrscheinlich in Ariana (→ Areia [1], h. Westafghanistan) gesprochen und ist schon früh ausgestorben. Die ältesten Avesta-Mss. stammen erst aus dem 13. Jh. n. Chr. und sind zudem sehr fehlerhaft, so daß der Textkritik große Bed. zukommt. Der Archetypus der Mss. ist von Hoffmann in das 4. Jh. n. Chr., also in die sāsānidische Zeit, datiert worden. Die Avestaschrift besitzt im Gegensatz zu ihrem Vorbild, der Pahlavischrift, Vokalzeichen.

Anders als das Avesta können die altpers. Inschr. genau datiert und lokalisiert werden. Sie sind in einer speziell für die Abfassung repräsentativer Königsinschr. in altpers. Sprache geschaffenen Keilschrift aufgezeichnet, deren Erfindung um 520 v. Chr. im Auftrag des Großkönigs → Dareios [1] erfolgt sein dürfte. Von ihm und seinem Nachfolger → Xerxes I. (486–465) stammen die meisten Inschr., deren Fundorte v. a. die Hauptstädte → Persepolis (in der Persis) und → Susa sowie → Bīsutūn westl. von Hamadān sind. In ihnen schildern die Herrscher ihre Taten, wobei der Bericht des Dareios teilweise mit Angaben von Herodot übereinstimmt. Altpers. ist eine sw-iran. Sprache und Vorläufer des Mpers. und h. Pers. In NW-Iran wurde das Medische gesprochen, das uns nur durch einige ins Altpers. entlehnte Formeln sowie durch im Altpers., Griech. und anderen Sprachen überl. Namen bekannt ist.

In den klass. Sprachen sind altiran. EN – wie z. B. griech. Δαρεῖος (*Dareios*), lat. *Darius* < altpers. *Dārayavau-š*, wörtlich »Bewahre (*dāraya*) das Gute (*vau*)!« – auf uns gekommen. Aus dem Medischen (vgl. avest. *pairidaēza-*, »Umwallung«) ist griech. παράδεισος (*parádeisos*), »ummauerter Tierpark, Park«, später »Paradies«, entlehnt. Griech. εὔξεινος πόντος (*eúxeinos póntos*, eigentlich »gastfreundliches Meer«) als Bezeichnung des Schwarzen Meeres ist → Euphemismus für πόντος ἄξεινος (*póntos áxeinos*, eigentlich »ungastliches Meer«), das volksetym. aus einem iran. Namen, der »dunkelfarbiges Meer« bedeutete, entlehnt und umgedeutet worden sein dürfte: Man vergleiche avest. *axšaēna-*, »dunkelfarbig«. Durch Vermittlung der in der Ukraine ansässigen Skythen lernten die Griechen das Wort κάνναβις (*kánnabis*), »Hanf«, kennen.

→ Altpersische Keilschrift; Avestaschrift; Indogermanische Sprachen; Indoarische Sprachen; Satemsprache

K. Hoffmann, Altiran., in: HbdOr, 1,4,1, 1958, 1–19 (= Ders., Aufsätze zur Indoiranistik I, 1975, 58–76) • K. Hoffmann, B. Forssman, Avest. Laut- und Flexionslehre, 1996, 31–38 • W. Brandenstein, M. Mayrhofer, Hdb. des Altpers., 1964 • R. G. Kent, Old Persian, 1953 • R. Schmitt (Hrsg.), Compendium linguarum Iranicarum, 1989.

N. O.

ʿIrāq al-Amīr (Arak al-Amir). Die Ruinen I. und Qaṣr al-ʿAbd befinden sich im Wādī as-Sīr westl. vom h. Amman. Seit achäm. Zeit befand sich dort eine Domäne der → Tobiaden (Neh 2,10; 2,19; 3,33; 3,35). I. besteht aus zwei ca. 300 m langen künstlichen Höhlengalerien. Die oberhalb auf einem Plateau liegende Palast- oder Grabmalsstruktur mit Tierreliefs (Qaṣr al-ʿAbd) gehörte zu der 181 v. Chr. gegründeten Befestigung (βάρις) Tyros des Tobiaden → Hyrkanos [1] (Ios. ant. Iud. 12, 229–234).

E. Will, F. Larché u. a., I.: Le château du Tobiade Hyrcan, 1991. T. L.

Irenaeus s. Eirenaios

Irenaios Referendarios. Epigrammdichter des 6. Jh. n. Chr., Verf. von drei erotischen Epigrammen, die aus dem »Kyklos« des Agathias stammen: Anth. Pal. 5,249 (die Liebe mit der hochmütigen Rhodope wird als eine Verschmelzung von Seele und Körper dargestellt); 5,251 (über eine Namenlose, deren Stolz nicht einmal durch ihre schwindende Schönheit gebrochen wird) und 253 (Aufforderung an die schamhafte Chrysilla, sich den Wünschen der Kypris zu unterwerfen); dieses letzte Gedicht wurde von Niketas Eugenianos imitiert.

Al. und Av. Cameron, The ›Cycle‹ of Agathias, in: JHS 86, 1966, 8. M. G. A./Ü: T. H.

Irene (Εἰρήνη). Byz. Kaiserin (797–802 n. Chr.; geb. in Athen ca. 752, gest. auf Lesbos 803), seit 768 Gattin → Leons IV.; nach dessen Tod 780 Regentin für ihren minderjährigen Sohn → Constantinus [8] VI. Das auf ihr Betreiben einberufene und von Tarasios, dem Patriarchen ihrer Wahl, geleitete Konzil von Nicaea 787 gelangte zu einer gemäßigten Beilegung des byz. Bilderstreites (→ Syrische Dynastie) zugunsten des Bilderkultes. 790 erzwang ihr Sohn die Übergabe der Macht, wurde aber von ihr 797 abgesetzt und geblendet. Die Annahme, sie könnte Karl d.Gr. die Kaiserkrone des Westens angeboten haben, wird zuletzt von [1. 206 f.] befürwortet. 802 wurde sie von dem Usurpator → Nikephoros I. abgesetzt.

1 R.-J. Lilie, Byzanz unter Eirene und Konstantin VI., 1996
2 P. Speck, Kaiser Konstantin VI., 1978. F. T.

Iria. Ligurisches *oppidum* und Fluß (nicht der Taurini, Ptol. 3,1,35 irrig), *regio IX* (Plin. nat. 3,49), ca. 25 km vor → Dertona (Itin. Anton. 288), h. Voghera. Forum wohl seit Augustus; unsicher, seit wann *colonia Forum Iulium Iriensium* (CIL V 785; 7375). Vorröm. Reste, Brücke der *via Postumia* über den I.

Fontes Ligurum et Liguriae antiquae, 1976, s. v. Forum Iulii Iriensium • P. Tozzi, Per la topografia di Forum Iuli Iriensium, in: Rendiconti Istituto Lombardo 109, 1975, 342–346. L. S. A./Ü: J. W. M.

Iris (Ἶρις, »Regenbogen«)

[1] Der vergöttlichte Regenbogen. In Hesiods Genealogie (Hes. theog. 266) ist sie Tochter des → Thaumas (vgl. θαῦμα/*thaúma*, »Wunder«) und der → Elektra [1] (vgl. das glänzende Metall Elektron) und Schwester der windschnellen → Harpyien. Ihre Genealogie kennzeichnet sie: sie selbst gilt als schnell, und in der griech. Physik kann der Regenbogen Winde erzeugen. In den myth. Erzählungen ist sie von ihrem Element weitestgehend gelöst und hat die Funktion einer Götterbotin (Hom. Il. 2,786 usw.), die sie sich nachhomer. mit → Hermes so teilt, daß sie bes. Hera zugeordnet ist. Erst die röm. Dichtung ruft spielerisch gelegentlich das Natursubstrat in Erinnerung (Ov. met. 11,589).

A. Kossatz-Deissmann, s. v. I, LIMC 5, 741–760. F. G.

[2] Die aromatische Wurzel zahlreicher Sorten der in den Regenbogenfarben blühenden Schwertlilien (z. B. I. florentina und germanica L.) stammen meist vom Balkan, aus Libyen und Kleinasien. Man zerkleinerte sie (Plin. nat. 21,40–42; Dioskurides 1,1,1–3 Wellmann = 1,1 Berendes) oder verwendete sie in Form von Öl (*oleum irinum*: Plin. nat. 15,30; Dioskurides 1,56 Wellmann = 1,66 Berendes) v. a. für die Herstellung von Salben (*unguenta*, Plin. nat. 13,5). Äußerlich soll die I. (Plin. nat. 21,140–144) u. a. Geschwüre am Kopf sowie Hundebisse heilen, innerlich (mit Honig eingenommen) bei Husten und Verdauungsbeschwerden helfen. Gekaut beseitige sie Mundgeruch und Rausch. Zahnenden und hustenden Kindern solle man sie umbinden. Dem Pech für die Fässer zum Aufbewahren des Weines konnte man I.-Wurzel und -Öl zusetzen (Plin. nat. 14,128). Theophrast (h. plant. 9,9,2, vgl. De odoribus 24) kennt ein aus dem Samen oder Rhizom gewonnenes I.-Parfüm (ἴρινον μύρον). C. HÜ.

[3] (Ἶρις). Fluß in Pontos, h. Yeşil Irmak (»Grüner Fluß«). Er entspringt am Westhang des Köse Dağları und nimmt 12 km südl. von → Amaseia den Skylax (h. Çekerek Irmağı) und ca. 70 km nordöstl. von Amaseia den Lykos (h. Kelkit Çayı) auf, bevor er nach dem Durchbruch durch das Nordanatol. Randgebirge mit einem ca. 60 km breiten Delta ins Schwarze Meer mündet. Mit diesen beiden Nebenflüssen prägt der I. die pont. Landschaft, Kernzelle des Mithradatiden-Reiches. E. O.

Irland s. Hibernia

Ironie (griech. εἰρωνεία, *eirōneía*, urspr. »Kleintuerei«, lat. *simulatio, dissimulatio, illusio*).
I. Rhetorik II. Philosophie

I. Rhetorik

Die I. wird im rhet. System wie z. B. die Metapher (→ Vergleich) zu den Tropen (→ Tropus) gerechnet (Rhet. Her. 4,46 ordnet sie der Allegorie zu). Während die Metapher durch Ähnlichkeit von Gesagtem und Gemeintem operiert, ist I. durch das Verhältnis des Ge-

gensatzes (*contrarium*) gekennzeichnet (Anaximen. Ars rhetorica = [Arist.] rhet. Alex. 21,1,1434a, 17f.; Quint. inst. 8,6,54–56; Aquila rhetor 7 p. 24,21 f. H). I. ist kontextabhängig und muß zur Vermeidung von Mißverständnissen (*obscuritas*) durch Signale des Vortrags (*pronuntiatio*) verstärkt werden. Wort-I. ist die ironische Verwendung einzelner Wörter aus dem Vokabular der Gegenpartei; I. als Gedankentropus tritt in zwei Formen auf: Die *simulatio* macht sich entweder in provozierender oder betont harmlos gebender Weise die Meinung des Gegners zueigen, der im besten Fall mit seinen eigenen Worten *ad absurdum* geführt wird; die *dissimulatio* verheimlicht die eigene Meinung durch Vortäuschung von Unwissenheit (bes. durch Fragen im Sinne der sokrat. Fragekunst, → Maieutik), durch eine ostentative Mehrdeutigkeit oder durch Herunterspielen der eigenen Fähigkeiten und Anliegen (*detractio*). Ziel beider Formen kann es sein, daß der Rezipient entweder die I. als gegensätzlichen Sinn verstehen soll oder daß in einer handlungstaktischen I. der Zustand des Mißverständnisses bewußt aufrechterhalten wird, weil der Sprecher seine Meinung nicht oder noch nicht preisgeben will (Cic. Brut. 292f. 298f). Die Ethik verwirft handlungstaktische I., auch ihre habitualisierten Formen wie Höflichkeitsfloskeln. Das Gegenteil von *simulatio/dissimulatio* ist die redetaktische Offenheit (*sinceritas*), deren gedankliches und sprachliches Ausdrucksmittel die *perspicuitas* ist. C.W.

II. Philosophie

Ausdruck einer Sache durch ihr Gegenteil. *Eirōneía* [1. 381 ff.] wurde urspr. negativ gewertet (Aristoph. Vesp. 174; Plat. rep. 337a) als mit Täuschungsabsicht verbundenes Verstellen zum Geringeren [2. 341 ff.] (vgl. Theophr. char. 1 ad fin.). Aristoteles sieht die Verstellung durch Untertreibung etwas weniger negativ als die durch Übertreibung (eth. Nic. 1127a 20–32). Bisweilen – wohl mit Blick auf die Sokratesgestalt [3. 29] – wird I. auch positiv gewertet (Aspasios CAG 19, 54). Bei Platon findet sich I. als Darstellungsmittel in vielfältiger Form: zur Bestimmung der Handlung, Charakterisierung von Personen, Relativierung von Meinungen, als Selbstironie [4. 129ff.]. Diese I. ist nicht zu verwechseln mit der I. der Romantik als Ausdruck eines grundlegenden, alles relativierenden Bewußtseinsgehaltes. Bei Platon finden sich keine I.-Signale, wenn es um Ideen geht. Er verwendet die I. als Darstellungsmittel, das als Hinweis für die Leser dienen, nicht aber eine Lösung der angesprochenen Probleme ermöglichen kann (Aporie) [5. 1 ff., 280ff.]. Adressat ist, wie bei tragischer I., der Rezipient, für den Bemerkungen oder das Gesprächsverhalten dank überlegter Informiertheit an Zusatzbedeutung gewinnen [6. 87–90]. In den Rhetoriken findet sich die I. seit → Anaximenes [2] von Lampsakos. Tryphon von Alexandreia unterscheidet zw. Fremd- und Selbst-I. (De Tropis III 205,12 Spengel). Spätere Rhetoriken trennen zw. I. als Gedanken- und als Wortfigur [7. § 582–585, 902–904]. Cicero sieht in I. ein Mittel forensischer Auseinandersetzung und beansprucht sie als Lebensform für sich (Brut. 292f.; 298f.). In der Neuzeit ist I. wichtig in der Erzähllit.: Der Romantik dient die I. zum Ausdruck der Spannung endlichen Bewußtseins und unendlicher Wahrheit (Schlegel) [8. 23–36] und hat als »Neuformulierung« [9. 123] der sokratischen I. die Sokrates- und Platoninterpretationen (Kierkegaard, Friedländer) beeinflußt.

→ Ironie

1 O. Ribbeck, Über den Begriff des Εἴρων, in: RhM 31, 1876, 381–400 **2** W. Büchner, Über den Begriff der Eironeia, in: Hermes 76, 1941, 339–358 **3** G. Vlastos, Socrates. Ironist and Moral Philosopher, 1991, 21–44 **4** Th.A. Szlezák, Platon lesen, 1993 **5** M. Erler, Der Sinn der Aporien in den Dialogen Platons, 1987 **6** M. Pfister, Das Drama, [5]1988 **7** Lausberg **8** W. Boder, Die sokratische I. in den platonischen Frühdialogen, 1973 **9** E. Behler, Klass. I., Romantische I., Trag. I., 1972.

B. Allemann, s. v. I., Fischer Lex. Bd. 35/1 Lit. II/1, 1965, 305 • S. Kierkegaard, Über den Begriff der I. mit ständiger Rücksicht auf Sokrates, 1841 • J. Martin, Ant. Rhet. (HdbA 2.3), 1974, 262–264 • H. Weinrich, s. v. I., HWdPh 4, 578–582. M.ER.

Iros (Ἶρος).

[1] Sohn des Aktor aus Opus, Vater des Argonauten Eurytion, den → Peleus auf der Jagd versehentlich tötet (Pind. fr. 48). Das aus Schafen und Rindern bestehende Sühneangebot lehnt I. ab (Antoninus Liberalis 38).

[2] Spottname (sekundäres Maskulinum zum Namen der Götterbotin → Iris: »Herr Iris«) für den Bettler Arnaios, weil er für jedermann Botendienste verrichtet (Hom. Od. 18,6f.). Verfressen, anmaßend, aber gleichzeitig feige, versucht I., dem »Bettler« → Odysseus den Platz streitig zu machen, unterliegt aber in einem von den Freiern provozierten Boxkampf kläglich (18,1–116). RE.N.

Iroschottische Mönche. Irische Mönche, die seit dem 7. Jh. n. Chr. an die Westküste des heutigen Schottland, nach Nordhumbrien und auf den Kontinent gingen, um in der → *peregrinatio* ein gottgefälliges Leben zu führen. Im Gegensatz zu den abendländ. Mönchen auf dem Kontinent lebten sie nicht nach der Regel des → Benedictus, sondern nach der Regel, die Columban d. Ä. um 600 in Form eines Bußbuchs zusammengestellt hatte. Außerdem hatten sie eine andere Osterrechnung, eine andere Tonsur (Jakobstonsur) und betonten Buße und Askese, die sie nicht nur durch Fasten und Abhärtung, sondern auch durch die *peregrinatio* verwirklichten. Diese *peregrinatio* hatte eine große Bedeutung für das Abendland, denn durch die damit verbundene Predigt verbreiteten und stärkten die Mönche den christl. Glauben. Sie gingen zuerst an die Westküste Schottlands (Columban d. Ä. Anf. 7. Jh. nach Iona), dann nach Nordhumbrien (Aidan von Iona aus), Gallien (Columban d. J. von Bangor aus), Italien (622 Bobbio) und in die Schweiz (St. Gallen); sie predigten bei den Franken, Alamannen, Bayern und in Böhmen. Die *peregrinatio* führte sie meistens in die Einsamkeit, so ging Aidan nicht in die nordhumbr. Königsstadt, sondern nach Lindisfarne, wo er ein Kloster gründete. Die i. M. entfalteten eine große Kulturtätigkeit in Buchmalerei und Schrift, die die insulare Schriftentwicklung stark beeinflußte, auch auf dem Kontinent noch lange nachwirkte und die insularen Merkmale beibehielt (z. B. in St. Gallen, St. Emeram, Bobbio, Mainz, Fulda). Irisch-nordhumbrische Mönche wirkten am Hofe Karls d. Gr. (z. B. Alkuin, Dicuil, Dungal, Sedulius Scottus). Im 12. und 13. Jh. kamen noch einmal i. M. auf den Kontinent, wo sie die »Schottenklöster« gründeten (z. B. Würzburg, Regensburg, Wien).

L. Bieler, Irland, Wegbereiter des Mittelalters, 1961 • J. Blair, R. Sharpe, Pastoral Care before the Parish, 1992 • H. Löwe (Hrsg.), Die Iren und Europa im früheren MA, 2 Bde., 1982. G. SP.

Isaak (von hebr. *Yiṣḥāq*, »er wird lachen«).

[1] Sohn → Abrahams [1] und Saras, Halbbruder → Ismaels (Gn 17ff.), Vater Esaus und → Jakobs und der zweite der Patriarchen Israels. Hauptereignis in I.s Leben ist der an seinen Vater ergangene Befehl Gottes, ihn zu opfern. Diese Opferbindung (hebr. *Akeda*), mit der Gott Abrahams Treue auf die Probe stellt, wurde in den Talmūdīm und Midrašīm ausführlich verarbeitet: Anders als in der biblischen Darstellung wird in manchen haggadischen Erzählungen (→ Haggada) die Probe nicht durch Gott, sondern durch Satan veranlaßt. Hier ist es I., der seinen Vater auffordert, ihn Gott zu opfern. Auch soll I. Abraham gebeten haben, ihn festzubinden, damit er nicht beim Anblick eines Opfermessers erschrecke, fliehe und dadurch die Opferung vereitle. Ein anderer Midraš berichtet, wie I. dem hochmütigen Ismael, der sich im Alter von 13 J. freiwillig habe beschneiden lassen und auf I. herabsehe, weil dieser im Beschneidungsalter von acht Tagen keinen freien Willen habe ausdrücken können, verkündet, er werde sich Gott zum Opfer bringen. Im biblischen Bericht erblindet I. im Greisenalter; die rabbinische Lit. bringt den Verlust des Augenlichtes mit der Opferbindung in Zusammenhang: Die Tränen der bei dieser Bindung anwesenden Engel seien auf I.s Augen gefallen, die daraufhin erblindeten. In der muslimischen Trad. herrscht die Auffassung, daß nicht I., sondern Ismael geopfert wurde.

→ Circumcisio; Rabbinische Literatur

A. Agus, The binding of Isaac and Messiah: law, martyrdom and deliverance in early rabbinic religiosity, 1988 • H. Gaubert, Isaac et Jacob, les élus de Dieu, 1964 • G. Vermes, Scripture and tradition in Judaism: Haggadic studies, 1983 • W. Zuidema, Isaak wird wieder geopfert, 1987. Y. D.

[2] I. von Antiocheia. Unter dem Namen I.s sind fast 200 syr. Homilien (*memrē*, → Predigt) erhalten. Bereits im 7. Jh. unterschied man drei verschiedene Autoren namens I.: I. von Amid (frühes 5. Jh.), wohl Verf. einer → *Memrā* auf Konstantinopel; I. »der Große« von Edessa, allerdings in Antiocheia tätig (spätes 5. Jh.), Verf. einer *Memrā* auf einen Papagei, der das »Trishagion« sang, sowie einer weiteren I. von Edessa aus dem frühen 6. Jh.

Ed.: P. Bedjan, 1903 (67 Memrē; nur Text) • G. Bickell, I–II, 1872/1877 (37 Texte mit lat. Übers) • C. Moss, in: Zschr. für Semitistik 7, 1929, 298–306 (Homilie auf Konstantinopel) • S. Kazan, in: Oriens Christianus 45, 1961, 298–306 (Homilie gegen die Juden).
Lit.: A. Baumstark, Gesch. der syr. Lit., 1922, 63–66 • A. Klugkist, Pagane Bräuche in den Homilien des I. von Antiochia, in: Journ. of Semitic Studies 32, 1987, 279–313 • M. van Esbroeck, The Memra on the Parrot by Isaac of Antioch, in: Journ. of Theological Studies N. S. 47, 1996, 464–476.

[3] I. von Niniveh (I. Syrus). Ostsyr. Autor und Mönch des späten 7. Jh., geb. in Qaṭar. Nach kurzer Zeit als Bischof von Niniveh (Mosul) zog er sich als Einsiedler zurück. Er verfaßte umfassende Schriften über das spirituelle Leben, erh. in zwei ›Teilen‹. Eine im Kloster Mar Saba (Palaestina) angefertigte griech. Übers. eines Großteils des aus 82 Kap. bestehenden ›Ersten Teils‹ erwies sich als äußerst einflußreich sowohl im Griech. wie auch in Übers. aus dem Griech. (25 Kap. wurden ins Lat. übersetzt). Der ›Zweite Teil‹ umfaßt 42 Kap., darunter vier Versionen der *Kephalaia Gnostica*. Das ebenfalls I. zugeschriebene ›Buch der Gnade‹ stammt möglicherweise von seinem Zeitgenossen Šemʿōn dᵉ-Taibūṯeh.

Ed.:
Erster Teil: P. Bedjan, 1909 • A. J. Wensinck, Mystic Treatises by Isaac of Niniveh, 1923 (Ndr. 1969; engl. Übers. aus dem Syr.) • N. Theotokes (ed.), 1770 (griech.; Ndr. I. Spetsieris, 1895 und 1977) • [D. Miller], The Ascetical Homilies of St. Isaac, 1984 (engl. Übers. aus dem Griech.) • J. Touraille, 1981 (frz. Übers. aus dem Griech.) • PG 86.1, 811–886 (lat.).
Zweiter Teil: P. Bettiolo, Isacco di Ninive, Discorsi Spirituali, ²1990 (it. Übers. der *Kephalaia Gnostica*) • S. Brock, (CSCO Scr. Syri 224f.), 1995 (Kap. 4–42, mit engl. Übers.).
Lit.: K. Treu, Remnants of a majuscule codex of I. Syrus from Damascus, in: TU 129, 1985, 114–120 • Y. de Andia, Hesychia et contemplation chez Isaac le Syre, in: Collectanea Cisterciana 93, 1991, 20–48 • S. P. Brock, Theoria in the writings of Isaac of Niniveh, in: Parole de l'Orient 20, 1995, 407–419 • Dictionnaire de Spiritualité 7, 1971, 2041–2054. S. BR./Ü: S. Z.

Isadas (Ἰσάδας). Spartiat, Sohn des Phoibidas, bewährte sich 362 v. Chr. bei der Verteidigung Spartas im Kampf gegen die Streitkräfte des → Epameinondas (Plut. Agesilaos 34; Ail. var. 6,3); bei Polyainos (2,9), der die theban. Einfälle von 370/69 und 362 offenbar verwechselt, fälschlich als Isidas bezeichnet. K.-W. WEL.

Isagoge A. Definition B. Funktionen C. Formelemente D. Fächer E. Christentum

A. Definition

Der Begriff εἰσαγωγή (*eisagōgḗ*, »Einführung«) ist in Buchtiteln zuerst bei den Stoikern belegt (Chrysippos, Περὶ τῆς εἰς τὰς ἀμφιβολίας εἰσαγωγῆς/›Über die Einführung in die Mehrdeutigkeiten‹ u.a. logische Themen, SVF II S. 6, 28; 30; S. 7, 15; 16; 28; 34; 35; Περὶ ἀγαθῶν καὶ κακῶν εἰσαγωγή SVF III S. 196, 34; Apollodoros [11] von Seleukeia Εἰς τὰ δόγματα εἰσαγωγαί SVF III S. 259, 8–9; Poseidonios Εἰσαγωγὴ περὶ λέξεως F 44 Edelstein-Kidd). Kaiserzeitliche Belege zeigen, daß sich damit eine feste Gattungsvorstellung verbindet: Die I. gehört zur Lehrbuch-Lit. und stellt die Grundlagen eines Faches für Anfänger dar. Hiervon unterscheiden sich die eigentlichen Lehrbücher durch Vollständigkeit und professionelle Darstellungsweise. Im Lat. findet sich der Begriff als Fremdwort (erster Beleg: Gell. 14,7,2: Varros *commentarius* εἰσαγωγικός (›Einführungs-Notizen‹: s.u. B.3 u. D.8), latinisiert *isagoga*, später in der Übers. *introductio*. Dagegen kann *institutio* sowohl ein umfassendes Unterrichtswerk (Quintilian) als auch eine Einführungsschrift (s.u. D.8) bezeichnen. Das Aufkommen der I. scheint mit der Entstehung eines gestuften Unterrichtssystems zusammenzuhängen [10. 5]. Damit gliederte sie sich von dem älteren Begriff des Lehrbuchs ab. Eine isagogische Lehrschrift konnte auch einem nicht-professionellen Bildungsinteresse dienen, bei dem eine Fortgeschrittenen-Stufe gar nicht angestrebt wurde [4. 1454].

B. Funktionen

Die Abgrenzung der I. von anderen Lehrbuch-Formen ist schwierig. Die ant. Terminologie ist nicht fest; Wörter wie στοιχείωσις (*stoicheíōsis*, »Elementarbuch«), ἐγχειρίδιον (*encheirídion*, »Handbüchlein«) u.a. (s. auch D.7) kommen synonym vor; umgekehrt werden mit I. auch andersartige Schriften bezeichnet. Auch formale Elemente sind uneinheitlich. Es empfiehlt sich daher, die Funktion zum Kriterium zu machen (so [4] und [1]). 1. Als primären Zweck kann man die Begleitung des mündlichen Anfangsunterrichts ansehen. So lassen sich Schriften mit abstrakt formulierten Begriffsschemata erklären, die für sich allein kaum verständlich sind, aber als schriftliche Orientierungshilfe und Gedächtnisstütze beim Unterricht nützlich sein können [1. 324f.] (Beispiel: Kleoneides, s.u. D.3). 2. Andere I. sind leicht lesbar, anschaulich formuliert im Stil eines mündlichen Vortrags (Beispiel: Kleomedes, s.u. D.4). Sie können dem Nachvollzug eines Einführungskurses dienen, ihn aber auch ersetzen [1. 320f.]. Hier grenzen die Gattungen der enzyklopädischen Lit. (→ Artes liberales, → Enzyklopädie) und der Kompendien an. 3. In einen anderen pragmatischen Kontext gehören praktische Anweisungen für bestimmte Aufgaben, insbes. für die Amtsführung; Interessenten sind Personen, die eine fachliche (etwa juristische) Ausbildung nicht haben und nicht anstreben. Typisch ist Varros I. (s.o.) über das Verfahren der Senatsberatung, welche Pompeius bei Antritt seines Konsulats erbeten hatte (→ Fachliteratur).

C. Formelemente

Allg. wird Kürze und Beschränkung auf das Wesentliche angestrebt. Die Darstellungsweise ist entweder anschaulich, lebendig, eindringlich (s.o. B.2) oder trokken, schematisch, an Einteilungen (Dihäresen) und abstrakten Definitionen orientiert (s.o. B.1). Reine Definitionssammlungen: Ps.-Plat. Ὅροι; Ps.-Galen (s.u. D.7). 3. Am Anfang steht manchmal eine Anrede: der Belehrende wendet sich an den Schüler oder Widmungsempfänger. 4. Es kommen Dialog-Formen vor, schematisiert zur Katechismus-Form. 5. Die I. ist manchmal direkt mit einem größeren Lehrwerk verbunden, etwa das 1. Buch des Almagest von → Ptolemaios oder die Prolegomena zu Aristoteleskomm. (s.u. D.1).

D. Fächer

Hier sei ein gedrängter Überblick über das Material gegeben (mehr Einzelheiten bei [10] und [11]).

1. Philosophie. Hier ist der Titel I. zuerst belegt (s.o. A., ferner → Galenos, Εἰσαγωγὴ λογική, ›Einf. in die Logik‹?). Einführungen ins Platon- und Aristoteles-Studium [7]: Zu Platon seit → Alkinoos [2] (oder Albinos?) Εἰσαγωγὴ εἰς τοὺς Πλάτωνος διαλόγους (›Einf. in die Dialoge Platons‹) [12. VII f.]; zu einzelnen Dialogen seit → Calcidius [10. 27–30]. Eine Einführung in die aristotelische Logik verfaßte → Porphyrios (Εἰσαγωγὴ εἰς τὰς Ἀριστοτέλους κατηγορίας, hierzu auch eine Schrift in Katechismus-Form Εἰς τὰς Ἀριστοτέλους κατηγορίας κατὰ πεῦσιν καὶ ἀπόκρισιν, ›Zu den Kategorien des Aristoteles in Frage und Antwort‹); diese wurde ihrerseits mit Komm. und Einleitungen versehen, welche sich zu allg. Einführungen in die Philos. ausweiteten [10. 59–68]. Prolegomena zu Aristoteles: [2. 444–476; 10. 9–20; 12. 341–348].

2. Mathematik. Wieweit die Gattung der Στοιχεῖα (*Stoicheía*, *Elementa*) hierher gehört, ist unklar. Das Werk des → Eukleides [3] geht jedenfalls über die Funktionen einer I. hinaus. → Nikomachos von Gerasa, Ἀριθμητικὴ εἰσαγωγή; → Heron von Alexandreia, Εἰσαγωγαὶ τῶν στερεομετρουμένων (›Einleitungen zu den Themen der Stereometrie‹); Ὅροι τῶν γεωμετρίας ὀνομάτων (›Definitionen der geometrischen Fachwörter‹); → Theon von Smyrna, Τὰ κατὰ τὸ μαθηματικὸν χρήσιμα εἰς τὴν Πλάτωνος ἀνάγνωσιν (›Nützliches für die Platonlektüre aus der Mathematik‹). Auch Neuplatoniker verfaßten für die Propädeutik ihrer Studenten mathematische Einführungen.

3. Musik. → Kleoneides, Εἰσαγωγὴ ἁρμονική; → Nikomachos von Gerasa, Ἁρμονικὸν ἐγχειρίδιον; → Bakcheios, Εἰσαγωγὴ τέχνης μουσικῆς (in Katechismus-Form); → Alypios [3], Εἰσαγωγὴ μουσική.

4. Astronomie. → Geminos, Εἰσαγωγὴ εἰς τὰ φαινόμενα; → Kleomedes, Κυκλικὴ θεωρία μετεώρων (oder Μετέωρα?) (›Kreistheorie der Himmelserscheinungen‹); → Porphyrios, Εἰσαγωγὴ εἰς τὴν ἀποτελεσματικὴν τοῦ Πτολεμαίου (Astrologie).

5. Grammatik. → Dionysios [17] Thrax, Τέχνη γραμματική (wahrscheinlich als I. zu betrachten, weil sie als abstraktes Begriffsgerippe zur Begleitung eines Anfangsunterrichts geeignet ist). Sie blieb das elementare Schulbuch; im 12. Jh. kam die Katechismus-Form der *Erōtḗmata* auf (Moschopulos), die bis zu den Humanisten vorherrschend blieb (weiteres: [10. 30–46]). Einführungen zu einzelnen Dichtern wurden wahrscheinlich in der Kaiserzeit als *Prolegomena* den Ausgaben vorangestellt [10. 20–26; 7.43–57]. (Daß es eine isagogische Lit. zur Poetik gab, wie E. NORDEN [9] sie als Quelle von Horazens *Ars poetica* vermutete, wird heute nicht mehr angenommen).

6. In der Rhet. sind → Ciceros *Partitiones oratoriae* (in Katechismus-Form) zu nennen, später die *Prolegomena* zu → Hermogenes.

7. Medizin. → Galenos hat den Anfängern mehrere Unterrichtswerke gewidmet (Aufzählung: De librorum ordine 19,54 KÜHN), dergleichen Einführungsschriften. Sie liefen unter Titeln wie ὑποτύπωσις, εἰσαγωγή, σύνοψις, ὑφήγησις (›Skizze, Einführung, Überblick, Hinführung‹) um; er selbst zog es vor, dem Sachtitel jeweils hinzuzufügen τοῖς εἰσαγομένοις (»für die Einzuführenden«, De libris propriis 19,11 KÜHN). Ps.-Galen, Ὅροι ἰατρικοί (›Medizinische Definitionen‹) läßt vielleicht auf ältere medizinische Einführungen schließen [3. 179f.; 5]. Ps.-Galen, Εἰσαγωγὴ ἢ ἰατρός, auch in lat. Bearbeitung (in Katechismus-Form) als Ps.-Soranus, *Quaestiones medicinales*.

8. Jurisprudenz. Die Lit. der → *Institutiones* gehört hierher, weil sie für die untere Stufe des Rechtsunterrichts bestimmt ist [6]. Schriften mit Anweisungen für Amtsinhaber (*De officio proconsulis* usw., z. B. von → Ulpianus) zählen zu dem unter B.3 besprochenen Typus. Erste Beispiele: Varro (s.o. A.), Q. Cicero, *Commentariolum petitionis* (›Kleiner Aufsatz über die Amtsbewerbung‹; mehr bei [11. 876f.]).

E. CHRISTENTUM

1. Isagogische Züge haben kurzgefaßte Texte, die beim Taufunterricht verwendet wurden (z. B. Glaubensbekenntnisse).

2. Die Vorstellung von Stufen eines Unterrichts findet sich bei → Clemens von Alexandria, der seinen Παιδαγωγός (*Paidagōgós*) an Neubekehrte (»Kinder«) richtet; die höhere Stufe der »Lehre« (Διδάσκαλος, »Lehrer«) sollte folgen. Noch deutlicher sind die Verhältnisse bei → Origenes, der einen zweistufigen Unterricht organisierte, wobei er die Einführung (εἰσαγωγή) Anfänger dem Helfer Heraklas anvertraute (Eus. HE 6,15). Eine entsprechende Schrift verfaßte → Eusebios [7] von Kaisareia (Καθόλου στοιχειώδης εἰσαγωγή, ›Allg. elementare Einführung‹). Zweistufig ist dessen Werk *Praeparatio evangelica/Demonstratio evangelica*. Die Einordnung der *Divinae institutiones* des → Lactantius ist nicht ganz klar. Dieser schließt sich an juristische Institutionen an (1,1,12), verbindet dies aber mit Zügen des Protreptikós (→ Protreptik); an eine höhere Stufe der wiss. Theologie (wie Origenes) scheint er nicht zu denken.

3. Schriften zur Vorbereitung auf das Bibelstudium (vgl. D.5: Einführungen in die Dichterlektüre): Hieronymus Epist. 53; → Tyconius, *Liber regularum*; → Augustinus, *De doctrina Christiana*, B. 1; → Hadrianos [2], Εἰσαγωγὴ εἰς τὰς θείας γραφάς (›Einleitung in die hl. Schriften‹); → Eucherius [3], *Instructiones*; Iunilius, *Instituta regularia divinae legis*; → Cassiodorus, *Institutiones*, B. 1: *De institutione divinarum litterarum* (mit Rückblick auf diese Gattung 1,10). In der neuzeitlichen Theologie hat sich hieraus das Fach der »Einleitungswiss.« (engl. »isagogics«) entwickelt (TRE 9, 460f.). d) Praktische Anweisungen für die Führung kirchlicher Ämter lassen sich mit den röm. Schriften *De officio* (s.o. B.3) vergleichen (Einzelheiten [11. 888–897]).

1 M. ASPER, Zur Struktur und Funktion eisagogischer Texte, in: W. KULLMANN u. a. (Hrsg.), Gattungen wiss. Lit. in der Ant., 1998, 309–340 **2** I. DÜRING, Aristotle in the ancient biographical tradition, 1957 **3** M. FUHRMANN, Das systematische Lehrbuch, 1960 **4** Ders., s. v. Isagogische Lit., KlP 2, 1453–1456 **5** J. KOLLESCH, Zur Gesch. des medizinischen Lehrbuchs in der Ant., in: R. BLASER, H. BUESS (Hrsg.), Aktuelle Probleme aus der Gesch. der Medizin, 1966, 203–208 **6** D. LIEBS, Rechtsschulen und Rechtsunterricht im Prinzipat, in: ANRW II 15, 1976, 197–286, hier: Das Aufkommen juristischer Elementarlit., 229–236 **7** J. MANSFELD, Prolegomena: Questions to be Settled before the Study of an Author, or a Text, 1994 **8** L. MERCKLIN, Die isagogischen Schriften der Römer, in: Philologus 4, 1849, 413–429 **9** E. NORDEN, Die Composition und Literaturgattung der horazischen Epistula ad Pisones, in: Hermes 40, 1905, 481–528 **10** M. PLEZIA, De commentariis isagogicis (Archiwum filologiczne 23), 1949 **11** K. TH. SCHÄFER, s. v. Eisagoge, RAC 4, 862–904 **12** L. G. WESTERINK, The Alexandrian commentators and the introductions to their commentaries, in: R. SORABJI (Hrsg.), Aristotle transformed, 1990, 325–348 **13** L. G. WESTERINK, J. TROUILLARD (Hrsg.), Prolégomènes à la philos. de Platon, 1990.

H. GÖ.

Isagoras (Ἰσαγόρας).

[1] Sohn des Teisandros, konkurrierte nach dem Sturz der Tyrannis mit → Kleisthenes um die Vormacht in Athen. Der Konflikt wurde zunächst zwischen ihren Hetairien (→ Hetairia) ausgetragen. Erst als I. für 508/7 v. Chr. zum Archon gewählt wurde, bemühte sich Kleisthenes erfolgreich um die Unterstützung des *dḗmos*. Auch I. mußte nun weitere Machtressourcen mobilisieren und veranlaßte nach traditionell aristokratischer Manier seinen Gastfreund → Kleomenes I. von Sparta zur Intervention in Attika und zur Exilierung des Kleisthenes und weiterer 700 Familien. I.' Plan, die *bulḗ* aufzulösen und ein konsequent oligarch. Regime einzurichten, scheiterte am Widerstand des Rates. Es kam zu einer spontanen Volkserhebung; I. und das spartan. Heer wurden zum Abzug gezwungen, seine übrigen Anhänger getötet. Ein späterer Versuch des Kleomenes, I. mit mil. Gewalt als Tyrannen einzusetzen, blieb erfolglos, und I. wurde danach in Abwesenheit zum Tode verurteilt (Hdt. 5,66; 70; 72–74; [Aristot.] Ath. pol. 20; schol. Aristoph. Lys. 274–281).

Develin, 51 • Rhodes, 242 ff. • E. Stein-Hölkeskamp, Adelskultur und Polisges., 1989, 154–167 • Traill, PAA 539700. E.S.-H.

[2] Nach Philostr. soph. 2,11 (p. 94f) Kayser war I. Tragödiendichter und Schüler des Redners → Chrestos aus Byzantion; seine Lebenszeit wird ungefähr um das Ende des 2. Jh. n. Chr. angesetzt [1. 135,24].

1 F. Solmsen, s. v. Philostratos (9), RE 20, 135 2 TrGF 195. F.P.

Isaios (Ἰσαῖος).

[1] Att. Logograph etwa der 1. H. des 4. Jh. v. Chr., Sohn des Diagoras. Spärliche Informationen über sein Leben bieten Viten in den Hss., bei Ps.-Plutarch (mor. 839e–f), Harpokration, Suda und Photios (490a), die aber allesamt von Dion. Hal. De Isaeo und Kaikilios abhängen. Die genauen Lebensdaten sind unbekannt, unter den datierbaren der erhaltenen Reden kann die früheste auf etwa 389, die späteste vielleicht auf 344/3 gesetzt werden. Als Geburtsort werden Athen und Chalkis auf Euböa genannt; die Tatsache, daß I. sein ganzes Leben hindurch sich in keiner Weise polit. engagiert hat, spricht aber dafür, daß er (wie → Lysias) als Metöke in Athen gelebt hat. I. soll Schüler des Lysias und Lehrer des → Demosthenes gewesen sein, was sich weder beweisen noch widerlegen, immerhin als eine chronologisch naheliegende (und damit auch leicht zu erfindende) Konstruktion bezeichnen läßt.

Die Ant. kannte von I. 64 Reden, von denen 50 als echt galten; wir haben 56 Titel, vollständig erh. sind zehn Reden, dazu eine weitere unvollständig, sowie Fragmente, darunter ein sehr umfangreiches, das durch Dion. Hal. überliefert ist (or. 12 in modernen Ausgaben). Alle erh. Reden sind für Prozesse geschrieben, in denen Erbschaftsstreitigkeiten verhandelt wurden. So geht es immer um dieselben Kernfragen, nämlich Gültigkeit und Stellenwert von Testamenten sowie Erbanspruch auf Grund von Blutsverwandtschaft gegenüber Erbfolge gemäß Adoption. Dazu werden – je nach Interessenlage des von I. bedienten Klienten – konträre Standpunkte in subtiler, von profunder juristischer Sachkenntnis getragener Argumentation vertreten. Eine Bemerkung bei Dion. Hal. De Isaeo 4,16, wonach sich bei I. unter der zur Schau gestellten treuherzigen Wohlanständigkeit eine bes. ausgekochte Verschlagenheit verberge, hat sich auf seine Beurteilung bis in unser Jh. ausgewirkt; erst in neueren Arbeiten wird die Möglichkeit erwogen, daß I. auch einmal für eine tatsächlich berechtigte Position eine Rede geschrieben haben könnte. Seine Plädoyers zeichnen sich durch klare, logisch sauber nachvollziehbare Gliederung aus, der im ganzen schlichte Stil wird durch Meidung des → Hiatus, den Einsatz von Sinnfiguren und die Verwendung polit.-jurist. Fachtermini über das Niveau der Alltagssprache erhoben. Von wie auch immer gearteter Nachwirkung des I. ist nichts bekannt, was wohl an der sehr speziellen, für die Nachwelt wenig anziehenden Thematik eines Großteils seiner Reden lag; daß er überhaupt zur Kenntnis genommen und sein Werk tradiert wurde, dürfte dem Umstand zu verdanken sein, daß man ihn für den Lehrer des größten aller Redner hielt.

Ed.: Th. Thalheim, 1903 (Ndr. 1963) • P. Roussel, 1922 • E. S. Forster, 1927 (Ndr. 1957).
Komm.: W. Wyse, 1904.
Indices: W. A. Goligher, W. S. Maguiness, 1964 • J. M. Denommé, 1968.
Lit.: S. Avramović, Plaidoyer for Isaeus, or. IX, in: G. Nenci, G. Thür (Hrsg.), Symposion 1988, 1990, 41–55 • J. M. Denommé, Le choix des mots dans les discours d'I., in: Les études classiques 42, 1974, 127–148 • J. M. Lawless, Law, argument and equity in the speeches of I., Diss. Brown Univ., 1991 • R. F. Wevers, I. Chronology, prosopography and social history, 1969.
Zu einzelnen Reden: L. Huchthausen, Betrachtungen zur II. Rede des I., in: Klio 46, 1965, 241–262 • N. Lewis, Pro Isaeo XI,50, in: AJPh 80, 1959, 162–168 • W. E. Thompson, De Hagniae hereditate (Mnemosyne Suppl. 44), 1976 • D. Welsh, Isaeus 9 and Astyphilus' last expedition, in: GRBS 32, 1991, 133–150. M.W.

[2] Griech. Rhetor des 1. und frühen 2. Jh. n. Chr., der wohl aus dem äußersten Osten des Imperiums stammte (Beiname »der Assyrer«). Was wir über ihn wissen, fließt aus zwei Quellen: Philostr. (soph. 1,20 = 512–514) bietet außer Anekdotischem (wie der vollkommenen Wandlung des I. von einem allen Genüssen ergebenen Jugendlichen zu einem asketisch-ernsthaften Mann) die wichtige Nachricht, daß I. seinen Schüler → Dionysios [40] von Milet getadelt habe, weil er seine Deklamationen ›in einem Singsang‹ (ξὺν ᾠδῇ) vortrug; I. selbst erstrebte und erreichte äußerste Kürze und Präzision des Ausdruckes. Dazu paßt, daß Plinius, der den schon 60jährigen I. selbst hörte (epist. 2,3; vgl. auch Iuv. 3,74), seine Sprache als *Graecus immo Atticus* bezeichnet. I. dürfte also ein früher Vertreter des aufblühenden Attizismus gewesen sein. Die beiden Hauptquellen widersprechen sich aber insofern, als Philostr. behauptet, I. habe niemals improvisiert, während er nach Plin. *semper ex tempore* sprach. Durch Inschr. (IG 2/3² 3632 und 3709) wissen wir, daß I. einen gleichnamigen Sohn hatte, dessen Tochter Isidote z.Zt. des Marc Aurel in Eleusis Hierophantin war und daß der spätere Kaiser Hadrian zu den Hörern des I. gehörte.

P. Grimal, Deux figures de la correspondance de Pline, in: Latomus 14, 1955, 370–383. M.W.

Isar(a)

[1] Linker Nebenfluß des Rhodanus, h. Isère, entspringt in den → Alpes Graiae als Bergstrom (*torrens*: Plin. nat. 3,33; *maximum flumen*: Cic. fam. 10,15,3) und durchfließt das Gebiet der Allobroges. Hannibal zog 218 v. Chr. von der Mündung der I. in den Rhodanus flußaufwärts (Pol. 3,49; Liv. 21,31), hier schlug Q. Fabius Maximus 121 v. Chr. die Arverni (Flor. epit. 1,37,4). Weitere Belege: Strab. 4,1,11; 2,3; 6,6; Ptol. 2,10,4; Cass. Dio 37,47.

P. Guichonnet (Hrsg.), Histoire de la Savoie, 1973. Y.L.

[2] Heute Oise, Nebenfluß der Seine, auf einem Meilenstein aus Tongeren (CIL XIII 9158) erwähnt, im Itin. Anton. 384 Straßenstation *Briva Isarae*, h. Pont-Oise.

M. ROBLIN, Le terroir de l'Oise aux époques gallo-romaine et franque, 1978. F.SCH.

[3] Nebenfluß der Donau in Raetia, h. Isar (Strab. 4,6,9). Entgegen der Meinung Strabons entspringt er aus demselben See wie der in die Adria mündende Ἀτησῖνος (h. Etsch). Der Name I. kann mit den raet. → Isarci bzw. dem Isarcus in Zusammenhang gebracht werden; vgl. auch den röm. ON *Iovisura* (Itin. Anton. 259,5), dessen Lage nur annähernd ausgemacht ist.

F. HAUG, s. v. Isar (3), RE 9, 2053 • Ders., s. v. Isarci, RE 9, 2053 f. • U. PHILIPP, s. v. Isarcus, RE 9, 2054 • TIR M 33, 1986, 46. J.BU.

Isarci. Raet. Stamm im Eisacktal/Südtirol; von Augustus im Alpenkrieg (25–14 v. Chr.) unterworfen. Der Name steht auf der Inschr. des *Tropaeum Alpium* von La Turbie.

E. MEYER, Die röm. Schweiz, 1940, 70f., 80f., Taf. I • Ders., Tropaeum Alpium, RE Suppl. 11, 1269. G.W.

Isauria, Isauroi (Ἰσαυρία, Ἴσαυροι). Landschaft im südl. Kleinasien zw. Pisidia, Lykaonia und Kilikia Tracheia, zunächst auf das Bergland im Tauros um die beiden Vororte *Ísaura palaiá* (Ἴσαυρα παλαιά, h. Zengibar Kalesi) und *Ísaura néa* (Ἴσαυρα νέα, h. Aydoğmuş, vormals Dorla) beschränkt [1. 109ff.]. Erste Erwähnung bei Diodoros (18,22): *Ísaura* (unklar, welches) sei 322 v. Chr. von Perdikkas eingenommen worden. Beim ersten röm. Vorstoß nach I. eroberte P. Servilius Vatia 75 v. Chr. *Ísaura néa* [2. 287ff., 1167ff.]. Nach der Schlacht von Aktion fiel I. dem Galaterkönig Amyntas zu, der *Ísaura palaiá* zur Residenz ausbauen ließ (Strab. 12,6,3); nach dessen Tod 25 v. Chr. kam es zur neu eingerichteten Prov. Galatia [2. 453ff., 1303ff.]. Cass. Dio 55,28,3 erwähnt für 6 n. Chr. den Anf. von Aufständen der Isauroi. Seit 138 n. Chr. bildete I. einen Teil der gemeinsam verwalteten *eparcheíai Kilikía, I.* und *Lykaonía* (OGIS 576). Unter Probus (276–282) begannen die spätant. Isaurierkriege mit dem Aufstand des Lydius (Zos. 1,69f.; nach SHA Prob. 16,4 unter Palfuerius). Anf. des 4. Jh. wurde eine Prov. I. geschaffen, die auch die südl. Lykaonia und die Kilikia Tracheia umfaßte [3. 34f.]. Zunächst unter einem *praeses*, wurde I. etwa Mitte des 4. Jh. einem *comes rei militaris per Isauriam et praeses* (Not. dign. or. 29) unterstellt und erhielt eine Besatzung von zuerst drei, später zwei Legionen [3. 35; 4. 29ff.]. Die Isauroi unternahmen regelmäßig Raubzüge (Amm. 14,2; 19,13,1f.; 27,9,6f. zu den J. 354, 359 und 368 sowie Zos. 4,20,1f.; 5,25 zu den J. 377 und 404). Um 370 wurde die Prov. I. verkleinert und der Norden mit dem isaurischen Kerngebiet der neuen Prov. Lycaonia zugeschlagen [3. 37]. Seit Theodosios II. wurden Isauroi zum Heeresdienst herangezogen, 474 gelangte der Isauros Tarasikodissas unter dem Namen Zenon auf den Kaiserthron, den er in langen Kämpfen gegen den ebenfalls aus I. stammenden General Illos behaupten konnte [3. 40f.; 1. 116f.]. Nach Zenons Tod 491 wurden die Isauroi aus dem Heer entfernt, in schweren Kämpfen bis 498 endgültig unterworfen und in großer Zahl nach Thrakien umgesiedelt [3. 41f.].

1 W. D. BURGESS, Isaurian names and the ethnic identity of the Isaurians, AncSoc 21, 1990, 109–121 2 MAGIE 3 HILD/HELLENKEMPER 4 W. D. BURGESS, The Isaurians in the fifth century AD, Diss. 1985 5 G. E. BEAN, T. B. MITFORD, Journeys in Rough Cilicia 1964–1968, 1970. K.T.

Isauricus. Siegerbeiname (»Isauriersieger«) des P. → Servilius Vatia (Consul 79 v. Chr.), auf seinen Sohn P. Servilius I. (Consul 41) vererbt. K.-L.E.

Isaurische Kaiser. Byz. Dynastie von 717 bis 802 n. Chr. (Leon III., Constantinus [7] V., Leon IV., Irene und Constantinus [8] VI.). Ihr Begründer Leon III. stammte gemäß einer unzuverlässigen Quellennotiz aus Isaurien, in Wirklichkeit aber, wie seit langem bekannt, aus dem syrischen Germanikeia. Dennoch ist der Dynastie bedauerlicherweise – denn es gab ja in der Person von Kaiser Zenon (474–91) einen wirklichen Isaurier auf dem Kaiserthron – ihr traditioneller Name verblieben. Die beiden ersten Vertreter der Dynastie gelten als Gegner der Bilderverehrung (sog. Ikonoklasten); doch plädiert [5] mit guten Gründen dafür, überhaupt erst Constantinus [7] V. habe mit einiger Konsequenz Kultbilder aus Kirchen entfernen oder übertünchen lassen. Aus der Sicht der neueren Forsch. waren die »Isaurier« nicht die bedeutenden Reformer, welche eine von der Aufklärung beeinflußte Historiographie in ihnen vermutete. Doch erwarben sich Leon III. und Constantinus [7] V. Verdienste als Verteidiger des Reiches gegen die Araber und die Bulgaren, aber auch als Gesetzgeber; unter beider Namen wurde 741 (nach neuerer Datier.) die *Ecloga*/→ *Eklogḗ* (Ἐκλογή) als ein Gesetzbuch vorgelegt, das aus der iustinian. Rechtsüberlieferung in origineller Weise die für den Rechtsalltag des 8. Jh. relevanten Normen auswählt und neu formuliert.

1 ODB 2, 1014f.; zur Ecloga: 1, 672f. 2 L. BURGMANN, Ecloga, 1983 3 R.-J. LILIE, Byzanz unter Eirene und Konstantin VI., 1996 4 I. ROCHOW, Kaiser Konstantin V., 1994 5 P. SPECK, Ich bin's nicht, Kaiser Konstantin ist es gewesen, 1990. F.T.

Isca Silurum. Ca. 74 n. Chr. angelegtes röm. Legionslager in Britannia, h. Caerleon (Süd-Wales). Hier war die *legio II Augusta* stationiert [1; 2]. Um 100 n. Chr. wurden die Verteidigungsanlagen in Stein erneuert, dann die Innenbauten. Außerhalb der Lagermauern wurde ein Amphitheater ausgegraben, desgleichen Kaianlagen am Ufer des Usk [3; 4]. Seit 300 wurde die Besatzung reduziert und im 4. Jh. ganz abgezogen. Seit dem 2. Jh. entwickelte sich ein ausgedehnter *vicus*.

1 G. C. BOON, I., [3]1972 2 M. G. JARRETT, Legio II Augusta in Britain, in: Archaeologia Cambrensis 113, 1964, 47–63

3 R. E. M. Wheeler, T. V. Wheeler, The Roman Amphitheatre at Caerleon, in: Archaeologia 78, 1928, 111–218 4 J. D. Zienkiewicz, The Legionary Fortress Baths at Caerleon, 1986.

R. J. Brewer, Caerleon-I.: The Roman Legionary Museum, 1987. M. TO./Ü: I. S.

Ischagoras (Ἰσχαγόρας). Spartiat, konnte 423 v. Chr. seinen Auftrag, → Brasidas in Thrakien Verstärkungen zuzuführen, infolge der Gegenaktionen des Perdikkas von Makedonien nicht ausführen, erreichte aber mit wenigen Begleitern das dortige Kriegsgebiet und ließ durch Brasidas in einigen Poleis Spartiaten als Kommandanten einsetzen (Thuk. 4,132). Nachdem er 421 den Nikiasfrieden mitunterzeichnet und die Ausführung der Bestimmungen in Thrakien überwacht hatte, beschwor er im selben J. das auf 50 Jahre geschlossene athenisch-spartan. Bündnis (Thuk. 5,19,2; 21; 24,1). K.-W. WEL.

Ischolaos (Ἰσχόλαος). Spartiat, kämpfte im Korinthischen Krieg gegen Chabrias in Thrakien (Polyain. 2,22), fiel im Winter 370/69 v. Chr. in der Skiritis im Kampf gegen Arkader (Xen. hell. 6,5,24–26; Diod. 15,64,3 f.). K.-W. WEL.

Ischys (Ἰσχύς). Ehemann (Hes. fr. 30) oder Geliebter von Apollons Geliebter → Koronis. Apollon, der von der Beziehung durch einen Raben erfährt, versteht es als Ehebruch (*adulterium*, Ov. met. 2,545) und tötet die mit → Asklepios schwangere Koronis, rettet aber das Ungeborene vom Scheiterhaufen (Pind. P. 3,31–46; Apollod. 3,118). F. G.

Isidoros (Ἰσίδωρος).

[1] Piratenkapitän, organisierte die kilikischen Seeräuber im Raum um Kreta, wurde 78 v. Chr. von P. Servilius Isauricus besiegt (Flor. 1,41,3), trat später in den Dienst des Mithradates und wurde 72 in der Seeschlacht von Tenedos (am Eingang der Dardanellen) von Lucullus geschlagen (App. Mithr. 77, Memnon 42,2 = FHG 3,548) und getötet (Plut. Lucullus 12.2). ME. STR.

[2] I. aus Charax. Geograph, wohl der augusteischen Zeit (Ende 1. Jh. v. Chr.). Über seine Person ist nichts Näheres bekannt. Überliefert werden unter seinem Namen: 1. Frg. einer Vermessung der *oikuménē* (Teile bei Plin. nat.); 2. eine kleine Schrift ›Parthische Stationen‹ (*Stathmoí Parthikoí*) – Beschreibung und Vermessung der im Partherreich von Zeugma am Euphrat bis nach Alexandreia in Arachosien führenden Straße; 3. Frg. über die Perlenfischerei im Pers. Golf (bei Athen. 3,93d =GGM 1,254); 4. Angaben über angebliche langlebige oriental. Könige (Ps.-Lukian. macrob. 15,15 = GGM 1, 256).

I. gibt ein Resümee der Entdeckungen des späten Hell., wobei er das Ergebnis der Erdvermessung des Eratosthenes [2] zugrundelegt, worauf Plinius dann zurückgreift. Die beiden letztgenannten Werke enthalten Material bis in die Zeit um 100 n. Chr. Teilweise wird versucht, die dadurch entstehenden Datierungsschwierigkeiten durch Annahme von zwei Autoren gleichen Namens zu lösen.

→ Charakene; Charax Spasinu

F. H. Weissbach, s. v. I. (20), RE 9, 2064–2068 • Übers.: W. H. Schoff, Parthian Stations by I. of Charax, 1914. J. OE.

[3] Alexandrinischer Grieche. Gymnasiarch, d. h. er gehörte zu einer führenden Familie der Stadt. In den Auseinandersetzungen mit dem jüd. Bevölkerungsteil im J. 38 n. Chr. benutzte er zunächst den *praefectus Aegypti* Avillius Flaccus für seine Zwecke; später hetzte er die Bevölkerung gegen den Praefekten auf, den er schließlich auch vor Caligula in Rom anklagte. Als er spät in der Regierungszeit des Claudius König → Iulius [II 5] Agrippa II. anzuklagen suchte, wurde er selbst verurteilt und hingerichtet, PIR² J 53. W. E.

[4] Frühchristl. Gnostiker (2. H. des 2. Jh.). In Alexandreia beheimatet, führt I. die Lehrtätigkeit seines Vaters → Basileides [2] in dessen Sinne fort. Wie dieser rezipiert er selektiv philos. Lehrgut, vor allem platonischer und stoischer Provenienz, und setzt es – unter dem Blickwinkel seelsorgerlichen Ertrages – in Beziehung zur jüd.-christl. Tradition. Verschiedene, einander z. T. überlappende Traditionsstränge machen eine sinnvolle Differenzierung zwischen Anschauungen des Basileides sowie des übrigen Schülerkreises um I. weitgehend unmöglich (Zuordnung der Fragmente: [2. 326[5]]; nach Löhr stammen sämtliche Schülerzitate von I.). I. veröffentlicht – nicht vor 160 [1. 291] – mehrere eigenständige, für uns nur in wenigen Fragmenten greifbare Monographien. In seiner Schrift *Perí prosphyoús psychḗs* spricht er, auf platonisierender Grundlage, von zwei Seelenteilen. Dabei versuchen die dem niederen Seelenteil als Anhängsel beigegebenen Leidenschaften den Menschen zum Bösen hin zu beeinflussen. Mit den *Ethiká* verfaßt I. wohl erstmals im 2. Jh. einen ›Traktat über Fragen der praktischen, christl. Moral‹ [2. 107[26]] und optiert gegen einen verkrampften Enkratismus mit 1 Kor 7,9 für die Ehe als *remedium concupiscentiae*. In seiner Schrift *Toú prophḗtou Parchṓr exēgētiká* interpretiert er Aussprüche eines ansonsten unbekannten Propheten Parchor, wobei er die Philos. als Vermittlerin dieser vorzeitlichen Weisheit ansieht. Viele der bei Basileides und I. angesprochenen Themen finden sich später bei → Clemens [3] von Alexandreia und → Origenes wieder.

1 A. Harnack, Gesch. der altchristl. Lit. bis Eusebius, ²1958, Bd. I/1, 157–161; Bd. II/1, 290f. 2 W. A. Löhr, Basilides und seine Schule, 1996 (Sammlung und Übers. sämtlicher Testimonien und Fragmente) 3 W. Völker, Quellen zur Gesch. der christl. Gnosis, 1932, 38–44. J. RI.

[5] Flavius Anthemius Isidorus aus Alexandreia, war *proconsul Asiae* zw. 405 und 410 n. Chr., *praefectus urbis Constantinopolitanae* 410 bis 412 (Cod. Theod. 8,17,2;

15,1,50), *praefectus praetorio Illyrici* 424 (Cod. Theod. 15,5,4), *praef. praet. Orientis* 435–36 (Cod. Theod. 6,28,8; 12,1,192) und 436 *consul* (Acta conciliorum oecumenicorum 1,1,3 p. 67, 69). Er starb vor dem Jahre 447 (Theod. epist. 42; 47).

PLRE 2, 631–33 (Isidorus 9) • v. HAEHLING, 86f. K.P.J.

[6] I. aus Pelusion. Offenbar kein Vorsteher eines Klosters (so die Einl. in den → *Apophthegmata patrum*), sondern Presbyter in Pelusion/Äg. (so jedenfalls Severos von Antiocheia (Contra impium grammaticum 3,39 [1; 2]). Er lebte wohl zw. 360 und 435 n. Chr., hat wahrscheinlich in Alexandreia studiert und wohl als Mönch in Pelusion gelebt. I. hinterließ ein umfangreiches Briefcorpus von 2016 Schreiben guten Stils (CPG 3, 5557) sowie Apophthegmata (CPG 3, 5558), anderes ist verloren. Die Briefe verwenden u.a. Fr. der ›Hypotyposen‹ des → Clemens [3] von Alexandreia; außerdem kennt und zitiert I. → Basileios [1] von Kaisareia und → Gregorios [3] von Nazianz. Direkter Schüler des → Iohannes [4] Chrysostomos war er aber wohl nicht (anders Nikephoros Kallistos, historia ecclesiastica 14,30,53). Er folgte theologisch der alexandrinischen Trad. (epist. 4,99), aber wendete auch die hermeneutischen Regeln der antiochenischen Exegese an (epist. 4,117).

1 E.W. BROOKS (Ed.), The Sixth Book of the Select Letters of Severus 2/2, 1904, 251 2 I. LEBON (Ed.), Severi Antiocheni liber Contra impium grammaticum (CSCO 102), 1933, 183.

P. ÉVIEUX (Ed.), Lettres 1: 1214–1413 (SChr 422), 1997 • Ders., Isidore de Péluse (Théologie Historique 99), 1995 • A.M. RITTER, s.v. Isidore de Péluse, Dictionnaire de Spiritualite 7, 1971, 2097–2103 • L. BAYER, Isidors von Pelusium klass. Bildung (Forsch. zur christl. Lit.- und Dogmengesch. 13/2), 1915. C.M.

[7] Neuplatoniker aus Alexandreia (5. Jh. n. Chr.); Sohn des Theodotes, deren Bruder Aigyptos mit → Hermeias von Alexandreia befreundet war (Damaskios Vita Isidori fr. 119 ZINTZEN). Schüler des → Heraiskos und des → Asklepiades (ebd. fr. 160 ZINTZEN), später in Athen des → Proklos (ebd. fr. 129–137 Z.) und des → Marinos [1] (ebd. fr. 90 Z.). Nach Proklos' Tod (485) kehrte I. nach Alexandreia zurück. In den ersten Monaten des monophysitischen Patriarchats Athanasios' II. Keletes (489) verließ er die Stadt und ließ sich nach einer achtmonatigen Reise mit → Damaskios durch Syrien und Kleinasien erneut in Athen nieder (§§ 195–219 Z.). Nach dem Tod des Marinos wurde er zum Diadochen der Akademie gewählt (ebd. § 226 Z.). Aus seiner Ehe mit Domna ging ein Sohn, Proklos, hervor (fr. 339 Z.). I. verfaßte Hymnen (fr. 113 Z.) sowie einen Brief an Marinos über dessen Auslegung der Hypothesen des *Parmenides* (fr. 245 Z.). Seine Schüler waren Theodora (der Damaskios' *Vita Isidori* gewidmet ist) und ihre Schwestern aus der Familie des → Iamblichos, des Doros von Arabien und des Damaskios, den er zur Philos. bekehrte und der sein Biograph wurde. I. war ein erklärter Gegner des Christentums (§ 38 Z.; Zacharias Vita Severi 16,22 KUGENER). Seine Bewunderung galt vor allem den Philosophen, die den Aufstieg zum Göttlichen vollzogen hatten: Platon, Iamblichos, Syrianos (fr. 77 Z.) und Heraiskos, ›seinem einzigen Lehrer‹ (§ 37 Z.). Für Zacharias ist H. ›offenkundig ein Zauberer und Unruhestifter‹ (Vita Severi 22), für Damaskios dagegen ein ›wahrer Philosoph‹ (Vita Isidori §§ 160; 164 Z.).

ED.: M.-A. KUGENER (ed.), Zacharie Rhéteur (ou: le Scholastique), Vita Severi, texte syriaque et traduction française (Patrologia Orientalis t. II/6, 1903 • C. ZINTZEN (ed.), Damascius, Vita Isidori, 1967 • R. ASMUS, Das Leben des Philosophen I., 1991 (dt. Übers.) • Ders., in: ByzZ 18, 1909, 424–480 und 19, 1910, 264–284.
LIT.: P. CHUVIN, Chronique des derniers païens, 1990, [2]1991 • M. TARDIEU, Les Paysages reliques. Routes et haltes syriennes d'Isidore à Simplicius, 1990 • R. DONCEEL, M. SARTRE, Théandrios, dieu de Canatha, in: Electrum 1, 1997, 21–34. MI.TA./Ü: S.P.

[8] Bei Stobaios (3,590,11f.; 5,731,2ff.; vgl. Men. 343 JAEKEL) werden unter dem Lemma Ἰσιδώρου (vgl. O. HENSE zu Stob. 5,731,2) fünf sententiöse Trimeter überliefert.

TrGF 211. F.P.

[9] Isidorus, Bischof von Hispalis (Sevilla).
A. THEOLOGISCHE UND ENZYKLOPÄDISCHE SCHRIFTEN B. MUSIKTHEORIE

A. THEOLOGISCHE UND ENZYKLOPÄDISCHE SCHRIFTEN

Theologe und Sachschriftsteller der ausgehenden Spätant., * um 560, † 636. Seine Familie gehörte zur hispano-röm., konfessionell orthodoxen Führungsschicht; auch seine älteren Brüder Leander und Fulgentius waren Bischöfe. Die Familie wurde nach 550 aus Cartagena vertrieben und lebte in Sevilla, wo I. seinem Bruder Leander als Bischof 599/600 nachfolgte. Das Verhältnis der kath. Elite zu den Westgoten hatte sich nach dem Übertritt des Königs Reccared zur Großkirche 589 normalisiert, und I. hat zwei westgotischen Königen, Sisebut und Suinthila, Werke gewidmet.

Die beiden Schwerpunkte von I.' lit. Aktivität [1] werden mit »Gestalt der Kirchengesch.« [2] bzw. »Enzyklopädist« [3] gekennzeichnet. Dem ersten Bereich sind eine Reihe von exegetischen, dogmatischen und praktisch-seelsorgerlichen Schriften zuzurechnen (hervorzuheben die Synonyma *De lamentatione animae peccatricis* und *De origine officiorum*); dem zweiten, von der säkularen Bildung herkommenden Bereich grammatikalische (*Differentiae*), histor. (*Chronica, De origine Gothorum, De viris illustribus*) und naturwiss. Werke (*De natura rerum*). Hierzu zählt auch die umfassende, die Vorarbeiten z.T. einschließende Behandlung von Bildung, Gott, Mensch und Welt in den *Etymologiae* (vulgo *Origines*), die – von I. unfertig hinterlassen – von seinem

Freund Braulio in 20 B. zur Publikation bearbeitet wurden [4]. In dieser Ausgabe behandeln B. 1–4 der Enzyklopädie die → *Artes liberales* (einschließlich der Medizin), B. 5–6 die Institutionen des polit.-ges. und kulturellen Lebens (Recht und Gesetz, Zeit, Bücher und Bibliotheken, Festkalender und Gottesdienst), B. 7–8 Gott und die Kirche, B. 9 die ges. Differenzierungen, B. 11–12 die Biologie (Mensch und Tier), B. 13–14 Geographie, B. 15–20 Stadt und Land, Krieg und Spiele samt Werkstoffen, Gerätschaften, Kleidung und Nahrungsmitteln. Eine textkritisch befriedigende Ausgabe steht noch immer aus (vgl. [5]; zur Ordnung der Hss. [6]). Dieses am nachhaltigsten wirkende und die ma. Bildung fundierende Werk I.' muß in seinem systematischen Anspruch, aber auch von seinen Quellen her (etwa → Cassiodorus, → Servius, → Solinus, ältere Autoren überwiegend indirekt, Kirchenväter häufiger namentlich zit.) bzw. als christl. Antwort auf Plinius' *Naturalis historia* und Suetons *Pratum* [7] sowie dessen Horizont → Varro gewürdigt werden; auch in der Quellenfrage ist über FONTAINE (1983) hinauszukommen [8]. ›Jedenfalls erscheint I. überall als der Mann, der das Überkommene kritisch sichtete und praktisch zusammenfaßte und so dem MA behutsam und zielsicher den Weg ebnete‹ [9. 3].
→ Enzyklopädie

1 C.H. LYNCH, P. GALINDO, San Braulio, 1950, 356ff. (Werkliste Braulios) 2 M. REYDELLET, I., in: M. GRESCHAT (Hrsg.), Gestalten der Kirchengesch. 3, 1983, 47–57
3 C. CODOÑER, L'encyclopédisme, 1991, 19–35
4 W. PORZIG, Die Rezensionen der Etymologiae, in: Hermes 72, 1937, 129–170 5 U. SCHINDEL, Zur frühen Überl.-Gesch. der Etymologiae I.' von Sevilla, in: StM 3,29, 1988, 587–605 6 M. REYDELLET, La diffusion des Origines d'I. de Séville au haut moyen âge, in: MEFRA 78, 1966, 383–437, Stemma 437 7 P.L. SCHMIDT, in: HLL 4, 1997, 19ff. 8 U. SCHINDEL, Die Quelle von I.' »rhet.« Figurenlehre, in: RhM 137, 1994, 374–382, hier 375 Anm. 4 9 A. BORST, Das Bild der Gesch. in der Enzyklopädie I.', in: Deutsches Archiv für Erforschung des MA 22, 1966, 1–62.

ED.: CPL 1186–1212 • W.M. LINDSAY, 2 Bde., 1911 (Etym.) • P.K. MARSHALL, 1983 (B. 2) • M. REYDELLET, 1984 (B. 9) • J. ANDRÉ, 1986 (B. 12; 17) • M. RODRÍGUEZ-PANTOJA, 1995 (B. 19) • C. CODOÑER, 1992 (Diff. 1) • J. FONTAINE, 1960 (Nat. rer.) • C. RODRÍGUEZ ALONSO, 1975 (Orig. Goth. Vand. Sueb.) • T. MOMMSEN, MGH AA 11, 424–488 (Chronica) • C. CODOÑER, 1964 (Vir. ill.).
BIBLIOGR.: J.N. HILLGARTH, in: StM 24, 1983, 817–905 (1936–1975) • A. FERREIRO, The Visigoths, 1988, 325–413.
LIT.: Miscellanea Isidoriana, 1936 • M.C. DIAZ Y DIAZ (Hrsg.), Isidoriana, 1961 • Los Visigodos (Antiguedad y cristianismo 3), 1986, 303–413 • L. HOLTZ (Hrsg.), De Tertullien aux Mozarabes 2, 1992, 9–98 • J. FONTAINE (Hrsg.), L'Europe héritière de l'Espagne wisigothique, 1992, 195–283 • J. MADOZ, San I. de S. Semblanza de su personalidad literaria, 1960 • H.-J. DIESNER, I. von S. und seine Z., 1973 • Ders., I. von S. und das westgot. Spanien, 1978 • J. FONTAINE, I. de S. et la culture classique dans l'Espagne Wisigothique 1–3, [2]1983 • Ders., Tradition et actualité chez I., 1988 • P. CAZIER, I. de S. et la naissance de l'Espagne catholique, 1994. P.L.S.

B. MUSIKTHEORIE

De musica (orig. 3, 15–23), im MA viel gelesen, unterrichtet über das Elementarwissen: die *musica*, ihre Erfinder, ihre Macht, ihre Teile *harmonica*, *rhythmica*, *metrica* (18), ihre Einteilung in *harmonica* (20), *organica* (21), *rhythmica* (22) und ihre Zahlen (23). I. stützt sich hier bes. auf → Cassiodorus und ältere Quellen. Im Kapitel *De officiis* (orig. 6,19) werden liturgisch-musikalische Begriffe erklärt.
→ Musik III (Rom)

LIT.: 1 M. BERNHARD, Überl. und Fortleben der ant. lat. Musiktheorie im MA, in: GMth 3, 1990, 33–35
2 W. GURLITT, Zur Bed.-Gesch. von »musicus« und »cantor« bei I. von Sevilla, 1950 3 M. HUGLO, Les diagrammes d'harmonique interpolés dans les manuscrits hispaniques de la Musica Isidori, Scriptorium 48, 1994, 171–186 4 H. HÜSCHEN, Der Einfluß I. von Sevilla auf die Musikanschauung des MA, in: Miscellanea H. ANGLÉS, 1958–1961, B. 1, 397–406 5 O. STRUNK, Source Readings in Music History, 1950, 93–100 (engl. Übers. von orig. 3, 15–23) 6 G. WILLE, Musica Romana, 1967, 709–715. F.Z.

[10] I. Scholastikos von Bolbythia (Bolbitine in Ägypten?). Ins 6. Jh. n. Chr. zu setzender Verf. eines Epigramms aus dem »Kyklos« des Agathias: fiktive Weihung des nunmehr nutzlosen Betts samt Decke an die geliebte Mondgöttin Mēnē durch den völlig ergrauten Endymion (Anth. Pal. 6,58). Die Zuweisung von Anth. Pal. 9,11 ist abzulehnen; vgl. I. [11] von Aigeiai.

AL. und AV. CAMERON, The ›Cycle‹ of Agathias, in: JHS 86, 1966, 8. M.G.A./Ü: T.H.

[11] I. von Aigeiai. Verf. von fünf eleganten Epigrammen (vier sepulchralen und einem epideiktischen), die thematische Bezüge zum »Kranz« des Philippos aufweisen: zu Anth. Pal. 7, 280 (in iambischen Trimetern, wie auch das Gedicht 7,293, bei dem es sich vielleicht um eine wirkliche Inschr. handelt) vgl. Antiphilos, ebd. 7,175f. und Herakleides, ebd. 7,281; zu Anth. Pal. 9,94 (ein Fischer bekommt als Beute einen vom Polypen gefaßten Hasen) vgl. Antiphilos, ebd. 9,14 und Bianor, ebd. 9,227. Zweifelhaft ist die Zuweisung eines sechsten Epigramms (9,11: über das alte Motiv des Blinden und des Lahmen), das im Lemma einem I. (ohne Ethnikon), alternativ dazu Philippos von Thessalonike zugewiesen wird.

GA II 1, 432–435; II 2, 459–461. M.G.A./Ü: T.H.

[12] – [13] Die zwei bei Prokop (aed. 1,1,24; 50; 70; 2,3,7 und 2,8,16–18) überlieferten, miteinander verwandten und aus Milet stammenden, aufeinander folgenden Architekten der → Hagia Sophia in Konstantinopel (6. Jh. n. Chr.).

H. KÄHLER, Die Hagia Sophia, 1967, 15–19. C.HÖ.

Isigonos s. Paradoxographoi

Isinda (Ἴσινδα).
[1] Zentrallyk. Ort beim h. Belenli, lyk. Name *isñt*. Durch Steph. Byz. (s. v. Σινδία) identifizierte Polis, die zusammen mit Simena und Apollonia Bestandteil einer Sympolitie um Aperlai war. In archa.-klass. Zeit Dynastensitz mit ummauerter Akropolis. Drei Pfeilergräber, eines mit Reliefplatten (Jagd-, Kampf-, Musik- und Ringerszenen) aus der 2. H. des 6. Jh. v. Chr., zwei Felsgräber mit lyk. Inschr. und Sarkophage, z. T. mit Inschr.

C. Deltour-Levie, Les Piliers funéraires de Lycie, 1982, 171 ff. • M. Zimmermann, Unt. zur histor. Landeskunde Zentrallykiens, 1992, 24 f., 30 ff. KA.GE.

[2] Pisidische Stadt westl. von Termessos, h. Kışlar bei Korkuteli. Erstmals gen. im Zusammenhang des Feldzugs unter Cn. Manlius Vulso 189 v. Chr. (Pol. 21,35; Liv. 38,15,4), später zeitweise wohl im galat. Reich des → Amyntas [9], dann in der Prov. Lycia-Pamphylia(-Pisidia). Relativ reiche späthell. und kaiserzeitliche Mz.-Prägung ist erh. [1] mit nicht sicher deutbaren Ära-Angaben im späten 1. Jh. v. Chr. [2], im 3. Jh. n. Chr. mit einem zeittypischen, auch auf Inschr. erscheinenden Abstammungsanspruch (»Iones«). Spätant. Suffraganbistum von Perge.

1 Aulock 1, 29–32, 76–101 2 W. Leschhorn, Ant. Ären, 1993, 395–397.

W. Ruge, s. v. I. (3), RE 9, 2083. P.W.

Isindos (Ἴσινδος, Ἴσινδα). ON, nur bei Steph. Byz. s. v. I. mit diesen beiden Namensformen als Stadt in → Ionia bezeugt. E.O.

Isis I. Ägypten
II. Griechenland und Rom

I. Ägypten
Herkunft, Deutung des Namens und urspr. Funktion der ägypt. Göttin I. sind nicht eindeutig geklärt. Vieles spricht für ihre Heimat im 12. unteräg. Gau mit seiner Hauptstadt Per-Hebit (*pr-ḥbjt*), lat. Iseum, h. *Bahbīt al-Ḥiǧāra*. Der mit dem Bild eines Thrones geschriebene Name hat lange die Annahme bestimmt, I. personifiziere den königlichen Thron. Doch die sehr wahrscheinliche Grundform des Namens (*ȝst*) charakterisiert I. als »die, die herrschaftliche Macht hat«. Bedeutsam ist die Einbindung in den Osiris-Mythos, in dem mehrere durch Zusammenwirken und Spannung charakterisierte Götterpaare (I.-Osiris, I.-Horus, Horus-Seth, Osiris-Horus, Osiris-Seth) ein komplexes, teilweise widersprüchliches Ganzes ergeben. Danach sucht und findet I. den toten Gatten → Osiris, empfängt von ihm den Sohn → Horus, bestattet Osiris und betrauert ihn zusammen mit ihrer Schwester → Nephthys, zieht den Sohn im Verborgenen auf und tritt vor den Göttern für dessen Rechte ein. Als Gattin des Osiris und Mutter des Horus wird sie zu einer Mutter- und Schutzgöttin. Im 1. Jt. v. Chr. ist die Darstellung der I. als stillende Gottesmutter mit dem Horusknaben sehr beliebt. Auch in ihrer Bindung an → Min (Horus) von Achmim erscheint sie früh als Gottesmutter; zusammen mit Nephthys, → Neith und → Selkis als Schutzgöttin des Sarges. Bedeutsam ist ihre Rolle als Mutter und Amme, die Geburt und Wiedergeburt bewirkt. Die Gleichsetzung mit → Sothis macht sie zur Bringerin der Nilüberschwemmung und des neuen Jahres.

Mythische Erzählungen schildern ihre Weisheit und List. In der äg. Zauberlit. führt sie häufig den Beinamen »die Zauberreiche«. I. erscheint anthropomorph, stehend oder sitzend, und theriomorph als Falkenweibchen, Schlange, Skorpion oder weibliches Nilpferd. Zahlreiche ägypt. Kultstätten und Feste zeigen ihre herausragende Rolle.

→ Heilgötter; Mandulis; Philai; Seth

J. Bergman, s. v. I., LÄ 3, 186–204 • M. Münster, Unt. zur Göttin I., 1968 • R. E. Witt, I. in the Ancient World, 1997. R.GR.

II. Griechenland und Rom
A. Griechenland B. Italien und Rom
C. Reaktionen gegen den Isiskult
D. Isis und die domus Augusta
E. Feste und Priesterschaft

A. Griechenland
Die Griechen hatten schon vor den Ptolemäern ägypt. Götter kennengelernt und Gemeinsamkeiten zw. den bekannten griech. und unbekannten ägypt. Göttern festgestellt (Hdt. 2.42 ff.). I. wurde z. B. der → Demeter gleichgesetzt. Ein piräisches Dekret (333 v. Chr., SIRIS 1) zeigt, daß die ersten Kultanhänger der I. in Attika Ägypter waren, die wirtschaftl. Verbindungen mit Attika hatten. Ende des 3. Jh. v. Chr. und Generationen nach Ptolemaios I. Soters Wahl des → Sarapis als Beschützer der maked. Pharaonen war der Kult in Athen etabliert und die Priester selbst athen. Bürger; ähnliches gilt für Delos. Am Anfang des 3. Jh. waren Ägypter Priester des Kultes, ihnen folgten Delier und Athener. Die ägypt. Götter hatten während des 3. und 2. Jh. nicht nur Anhänger auf den verschiedenen Inseln oder in Hafenstädten, sondern auch im Innern Griechenlands und in Kleinasien. Die Peloponnes weist den geringsten Einfluß auf [1]. Delos ist für die ägypt. Götter außerhalb Äg. am aufschlußreichsten. Kaufleute, die zu diesem kommerziellen Zentrum der Ägäis kamen, brachten zum Teil auch den I.-Kult mit sich. Der wichtigste Impuls in seiner Verbreitung war die Einnahme von Delos durch Archelaos [4], einen General Mithradates' VI. von Pontos, im Jahre 88 v. Chr. [2]. So kamen ägypt. Götter mit zurückkehrenden ital. Kaufleuten nach Italien.

B. Italien und Rom
Wie für den östl. Mittelmeerbereich gilt für Sizilien, Sardinien und Italien, daß mit der hell. Zeit eine intensivere Periode der Rezeption des I.-Kultes beginnt.

Epitheta der Isis

Apuleius, Metamorphosen 11,2

Apuleius, Metamorphosen 11,2		Isis-Aretalogie	Ägypt. Epitheta
regina caeli	Himmelskönigin		nbt pt (MR, NR) Herrin des Himmels
Ceres alma *frugum parens originalis*	nährende Ceres Urmutter der Feldfrüchte	Ἐγώ εἰμι ἡ καρπὸν ἀνθρώποις εὑροῦσα. Ich bin es, die die Feldfrucht für die Menschen gefunden hat.	
caelestis Venus *quae... sexuum diversitatem generato Amore sociasti*	himmlische Venus die Du mit Hilfe des von Dir geborenen Amor die verschiedenen Geschlechter vereint hast	Ἐγὼ γυναῖκα καὶ ἄνδρα συνήγαγον. Ich habe Frau und Mann zusammengeführt. Ἐγὼ στέργεσθαι γυναῖκας ὑπὸ ἀνδρῶν ἠνάγκασα. Ich habe erzwungen, daß die Frauen von den Männern geliebt werden.	ḥnwt ḥmwt Herrin der Frauen (3.Jh.v.Chr., Philae)
Phoebi soror... *partu fetarum medelis lenientibus recreato*	des Phoebus Schwester [= Diana] mit lindernden Mitteln die Niederkunft der Schwangeren erleichternd	Ἐγὼ γυναικὶ δεκαμηνιαῖον βρέφος εἰς φῶς ἐξενεγκεῖν ἔταξα. Ich habe den Frauen auferlegt, ein zehnmonatiges Kind zu gebären.	
Proserpina	[Gattin des Hades]	Ἐγώ εἰμι γυνὴ καὶ ἀδελφὴ Ὀσείριδος βασιλέως. Ich bin Frau und Schwester des Königs Osiris.	snt nt Wsr Schwester des Osiris
solis ambagibus dispensans incerta lumina	nach dem Umlauf der Sonne Dein wechselndes Licht richtend [Mond]	Ἐγὼ ἡλίου καὶ σελήνης πορείαν συνεταξάμην. Ich habe die Bahn der Sonne und des Mondes geregelt.	
tu fortunam conlapsam adfirma *tu saevis exanclatis casibus pausam pacemque tribue*	laß Du mein zusammengebrochenes Glück wieder erstarken nach Erduldung der grimmigen Schicksalsschläge gib Du mir nun Rast und Ruhe	Ἐγὼ τὸ εἱμαρμένον νικῶ. Ich besiege das Schicksal. Ἐμοῦ τὸ εἱμαρμένον ἀκούει. Auf mich hört das Schicksal.	

Apuleius, Metamorphosen 11,5

Apuleius, Metamorphosen 11,5		Isis-Aretalogie	Ägypt. Epitheta
rerum naturae parens	Mutter der Schöpfung		
elementorum omnium domina	Herrin aller Elemente	Ἐγὼ ποταμῶν καὶ ἀνέμων καὶ θαλάσσης εἰμὶ κυρία. Ich bin die Herrin der Flüsse und der Winde und des Meeres. Ἐγὼ κεραυνοῦ κυρία εἰμί. Ich bin die Herrin des Donners. Ἐγὼ ὄμβρων εἰμὶ κυρία. Ich bin die Herrin der Regenfälle.	
saeculorum progenies initialis	Ursproß der Jahrhunderte		wrt š;ʿt ḫpr die Älteste, die das Entstehen begann
summa numinum	Höchste der Gottheiten		ḥnwt nṯrw nbw Herrin aller Götter
regina manium	Königin der Geister		ḥnwt jmntt; ḥnwt ḏsr Herrin des Westens; Herrin der Nekropole
prima caelitum	Erste der Himmlischen		
deorum dearumque facies uniformis	Erscheinung der Götter und Göttinnen in einer Gestalt		
		Εἶσις ἐγώ εἰμι ἡ τύραννος πάσης χώρας. Isis bin ich, die Herrscherin jedes Landes.	ḥnwt t;w nbw Herrin aller Länder
		καὶ γράμματα εὗρον μετὰ Ἑρμοῦ τά τε ἱερὰ καὶ τὰ δημόσια. ...und ich erfand die Schrift mit Hermes, sowohl die hieratische als auch die demotische.	ḥnwt mdwt nṯrw Herrin der Gottesworte [=Hieroglyphen]
		Ἐγώ εἰμι Κρόνου θυγάτηρ πρεσβυτάτη. Ich bin des Kronos älteste Tochter.	s;t Itm Tochter des Atum
		Ἐγώ εἰμι μήτηρ Ὥρου βασιλέως. Ich bin die Mutter des Königs Horus.	mwt Ḥrw (MR; NR) Mutter des Horus
		Ἐγὼ παρεδρεύω τῆι τοῦ ἡλίου πορείαι. Ich bin bei der Fahrt der Sonne dabei.	m ḥ;t wj; n Rʿ vorn in der Barke des Re

Ausgangspunkt des Vergleichs ist Apuleius (2.Jh.n.Chr.; [1; 5]). Die Isis-Aretalogie [2; 3] ist am vollständigsten in der Inschrift von Kyme/Kleinasien (1.–2. Jh.n.Chr.) überliefert; der Text geht wohl auf das 2. Jh.v.Chr. zurück ([3.1f.]). Sofern nicht anders angegeben, sind die ägypt. Epitheta ([4]) im Neuen Reich (ca. 1550–1070 v.Chr.) nachgewiesen. Nebeneinandergestellt sind nicht nur wörtliche Entsprechungen, sondern auch vergleichbare Inhalte.

M. HAA.

Romanisierung ist für alle anderen Gebiete ausschlaggebend. In Hafenstädten (Puteoli, Pompeji und Ostia) ist I. schon vor 88 v. Chr. gut etabliert [3; 4; 5; 6]. Das Iseum von Pompeji wurde gegen Ende des 2. Jh. v. Chr. erbaut, der Tempel für die alexandrin. Götter in Puteoli ist auf 105 v. Chr. zu datieren. Mit der erzwungenen Rückkehr der ital. Kaufleute war es somit nur noch eine Frage der Zeit, bis der I.-Kult sich in Rom etablierte. Apuleius' Lucius berichtet, daß das erste *collegium pastophorum* in Rom zur Zeit des Sulla gegründet wurde (Apul. met. 11,30). Eine nun leider verlorene Inschr. (SIRIS 377) erlaubt eine Verbindung zw. Delos und Rom: sie wurde überzeugend in die Zeitspanne 90–60 v. Chr. datiert [7]. Sullas Zeit mag für den ägypt. Kult günstig gewesen sein [8], doch waren es kaum die entfesselten Leidenschaften des einfachen Volkes, die diese Akzeptanz herbeiführten. Ägypt. Szenen und Darstellungen wie die Kopfbedeckung der I., Sistra, Uraei, Obeliske und Lotusblumen waren Bestandteile des artistischen Repertoires. Kontrollmarkierungen auf Münzen sind nicht Ausdruck einer Sozialrevolution, sondern artistische Verwirklichung einer (spätrepublikanischen) kulturellen Realität [9].

C. Reaktionen gegen den Isiskult

Die Reaktionen in Rom gegen den I.-Kult in den J. 58, 53 und 48 v. Chr. (Tert. nat. 1,10; Cass. Dio 40,47; 42,26) waren polit. Natur: Der Senat sah sich zunehmend seiner polit. Macht beraubt. Einer seiner Privilegien war die Zustimmung und darausfolgende Einführung eines fremden Kultes in das röm. Religionssystem. Selbstbestätigung und Sicherstellung der urspr. Autorität diktierte in diesem Fall die Vertreibung der I. auf Staatsebene. Daß I. nicht einfach verschwand, zeigt die Befürwortung eines I.-Tempels durch das 2. Triumvirat im J. 43 v. Chr. (Cass. Dio 47,15,4) [10]. Die zwei späteren Regelungen (28 und 21 v. Chr.: Cass. Dio 53,2,4; 54,6,6), den Kult innerhalb Roms nicht zuzulassen, sind als augusteische Maßnahme der Sicherstellung des *mos maiorum* und der einheim. Götter gesehen worden. Diese Stipulationen sollten aber eher als sozialpolit. Kontrollmechanismen verstanden werden, vor allem angesichts Augustus' noch recht unsicherer polit. Position.

Tiberius Anordnung, Juden und Verehrer der I. aus Rom zu vertreiben (Tac. Ann. 2,85,5; Ios. ant. Iud. 18,72; Suet. Tib. 36,1), mag als weiterer Versuch der Aufrechterhaltung röm. Moral gelten, hatte aber wohl mehr mit Geschehnissen in Äg. zu tun: Alexandreia hatte die größte Anzahl jüd. Einwohner im röm. Reich, und I. war die mächtigste ihrer Stadtgötter. Germanicus hatte die Kornspeicher öffnen lassen und so eine Hungersnot in Rom ausgelöst (Tac. Ann. 2,67). Der auserkorene Nachfolger des Augustus hatte ohne Erlaubnis Memphis besucht. Die memphit. Priester, die Hüter des lebenden und der toten Apisstiere, konnten Pharaonen küren sowie entmachten. Die Entfernung von I.-Anhängern und Juden aus Rom demonstrierte öffentlich die polit. Macht des *princeps* und symbolisierte die Wiederherstellung von Ordnung.

Die Möglichkeit, den I.-Kult als → *superstitio* zu erklären, verschwand mit der Konsolidation des augusteischen Staatsmodells und der Vorstellung von Äg. als integralen Bestandteil des Imperium Romanum. Am Ende der Regierung des Gaius Caligula oder am Anfang der Regierungszeit des Claudius wurde der I.-Kult zu einem *sacrum publicum*, einem öffentlichen Kult [11].

D. Isis und die domus Augusta

Die Verbindung der I. mit der *domus Augusta* vollzog sich während der Regierungszeit des → Vespasian. Dieser wurde in Alexandreia zum Kaiser ausgerufen. Er verbrachte die Nacht vor dem *triumphus* mit Titus in Rom im Iseum Campense (Ios. bell. Iud. 7,123 f.). Als eine Variation dieser Pietätsbekundung den alexandrinischen Göttern gegenüber kann auch Domitians Renovation verschiedener I.-Heiligtümer gesehen werden. → Hadrians Interesse an Äg. kann mit dem Tod des → Antinoos [2] in Zusammenhang gebracht werden; außerdem war Hadrian Philhellene (Alexandreia besaß die außerordentlichsten Bibliotheken der ant. Welt und konnte als Hüter der griech. Kultur betrachtet werden). Die hadrian. Zeit brachte wie die domitian. ein zunehmendes Interesse an ägypt. und ägyptisierenden Gegenständen mit sich [12; 13]. Inschr. zum Wohle der *domus Augusta* im Namen vor allem des Sarapis tauchen in den danubischen Provinzen nach dem Sieg des Marcus Aurelius über die Quadi auf. Dedikanten waren seine Generäle [14]. Der Grund scheint das vom *hierogrammateús* Arnouphis im Kampf gegen die Quadi herbeigeführte Regenwunder gewesen zu sein (Cass. Dio 71,8). Die unabsichtliche und unbewußte Verwirklichung der pharaon.-ptolem. Ideologie fand z.Z. der Severer ihren Abschluß.

E. Feste und Priesterschaft

Zwei große mit I. verbundene Feste sind bekannt: das öffentl. *navigium Isidis*, »Schiff der I.« (→ *ploiaphésia*, »I.' Seefahrt«) am 5. März (Apul. met. 11,8–17) und die *inventio* (*heúresis*) Osiridis (»das Finden des Osiris«) vom 28. Okt.–3. Nov. Beide sind eng mit dem Mythos von I. und → Osiris verbunden: Das Frühlingsfest, das zugleich mit der Eröffnung der Seefahrt zusammenfällt und von dessen Prozession Apuleius ein farbiges Bild zeichnet (Apul. met. 8,17), erinnert an I.' Seefahrt nach Byblos, um Osiris zu suchen, das zweite in seinem Verlauf von Trauer zu Freude an das Ende dieser Suche, als I. den zerstückelten Leichnam des Osiris findet, ihn zusammensetzt und zum Leben erweckt. Demgegenüber sind die Mysterienriten naturgemäß nur schwer faßbar. Apuleius (met. 11) zeichnet ein ausführliches Bild der vorbereitenden (Traumbefehl zur Einweihung, kultisches Bad, Fasten, Einkleidung in ein Leinengewand) und abschließenden Riten (Einkleidung mit zwölf – kosmischen? – Roben, Präsentation vor der Gemeinde), während er das entscheidende nächtliche Ritual als Jenseitsreise und Begegnung mit dem Tod und den Göttern lediglich umschreibt; es fügt sich jedenfalls in gängige Mysterienriten.

Eine Kultverbindung hatte wahrscheinlich fünf *antistites*, Priester oder *pastophori* (*hierophóroi*), die in der Hierarchie unter dem *sacerdos* standen. Diese trugen unterschiedliche Insignien in Prozessionen (Apul. met. 11,10). Ein *sacerdos* (Mann oder Frau) hatte diese Stellung meistens für ein Jahr, manchmal aber auch auf Lebenszeit inne. Die unteren Priesterschaften und Amtsstellungen waren eher auf Lebenszeit. In Inschr. kommen Tempelwächter, *neōkóroi* oder *zákoroi*, die vielleicht auch bei Opfern halfen, vor. Die im Westen und aus der Kaiserzeit bezeugten *pastophori* (Statuenträger) wurden mit *hierophóroi* bzw. *hagiophóroi* gleichgesetzt. Griechen in Äg. übersetzten den Titel des höchsten Priesters als *prophḗtēs*. Dafür gibt es außerhalb Äg. sehr wenig Belege, und es scheint, daß ein *prophḗtēs* einem *pastophorus* gleichzusetzen ist. Nach dem Propheten hatte der *stolistḗs* (»Bekleider«) unter den ägypt. I.-Priestern den zweithöchsten Rang; Stolisten kommen nur in Athen in der Kaiserzeit des 2. und 3. Jh. vor. Eine *ornatrix fani* (»Schmückerin des Heiligtums«) ist im Westen nur einmal bezeugt (SIRIS 731). Der *scriba* (*grammateús, hierogrammateús*, »Schreiber«; Apul. met. 11,17) folgt dem Stolisten in der ägypt. Priesterhierarchie, er ist aber wie Astrologen (*hōroskópoi, hōrológoi*) und Sänger (*hymnōdoí*) außerhalb Äg. inschr. nicht belegt. *therapeutaí* (*cultores*) waren Kultanhänger ohne Rang und Funktion. Der *naúarchos* (*triḗrarchos, hieronaútēs, naubátēs*), der nur aus Inschr. der Kaiserzeit bekannt ist [15], war kein Priester, sondern Kultvereinsmitglied und Offiziant der Ploiaphesien. Im allgemeinen ist festzuhalten, daß Priester und Funktionäre der Kultvereine (Laien) die gleichen Bezeichnungen tragen konnten. Auch ist nicht jeder Widmende oder Adressat einer Inschr. ein Kulteingeweihter. Die meisten persönl. Inschr. sind *ex voto* und die meisten offiziellen (z. B. *pro salute imperatoris*) polit. Natur.

I.-Tempel (Isea) findet man in röm. Zeit meistens außerhalb der *pomeria* (»Stadtgrenzen«) und in einem wasserhaltigen Gebiet (Marsch, Hafen, nahe eines Flusses oder einer wichtigen Wasserquelle) [16]. Isea waren nicht wie griech.-röm. Tempel auf Straßen und öffentl. Plätze hin orientiert. Auch öffnete sich die *cella* (*naós*) eines Iseums nur nach innen. Der Tempel war Ort der Einweihung. Die Tempeltüren wurden mit einer Morgen- und Nachmittagszeremonie geöffnet und geschlossen. Während dieser Zeremonien wurden Opfer dargebracht. Ob der Kult dem Initianden wirklich drei Initiationsrituale abverlangte (Apul. met. 21 ff.), muß offen bleiben. Wie in anderen → Mysterien beinhalteten die Vorbereitungen Reinigung und Abstinenz. Der *mýstēs* erlebte danach den rituellen Tod und fand so neues Leben. Im Unterschied zu den öffentl. Kulten gab es in der I.-Religion keinen Standesunterschied. Die verschiedenen I.-Aretalogien unterstreichen die Schöpfungskräfte der henotheistischen Göttin »mit tausend Namen« (*myriónyma*), die in kosm. Verbindung mit Sothis (Sirius) stand [17].

Dominant sind in Kult, Mythos und Erscheinungsbild der I. bei allen Überlagerungen die ägypt. Elemente; in der Erotik muß ein Teil der Anziehungskraft gelegen haben. Sie wirkte über die Ant. hinaus: die Ikonographie der Maria mit ihrem Kind ist ohne diejenige der I. mit dem Horusknaben undenkbar. In der frühen Neuzeit nahm insbes. Athanasius KIRCHNER die mysteriosophen Ansätze der I.-Mysterien wieder auf; in der künstlerischen Umformung von MOZARTS ›Zauberflöte‹ sind sie Gemeingut geworden.

1 F. DUNAND, Le culte d'I. dans le bassin oriental de la Méditerranée, 1973 **2** M. MALAISE, La diffusion des cultes Égyptiens dans les provinces européennes de l'empire romain, in: ANRW II 17.3, 1615–1691 **3** L. ROSS TAYLOR, The Cults of Ostia, Bd. 2, 1985 **4** M. FLORIANI SQUARCIAPINO, I culti orientali ad Ostia, 1962 **5** V. TRAN TAM TINH, Essai sur le culte d'I. in Pompei, 1964 **6** Ders., Le culte de divinités orientales en Campanie, 1972 **7** F. COARELLI, Iside Capitolina, Clodio e i mercanti di schiavi, in: Studi e materiali dell'Instituto di Archelogia Università di Palermo 6, 1984, 461–475 **8** L. VIDMAN, I. und Sarapis bei den Griechen und Römern, 1970 **9** S. TAKACS, I. and Sarapis in the Roman World, 1995 **10** K. LEMBKE, Das Iseum Campense in Rom, 1994 **11** A. BARRETT, Caligula, 1989, 220–221 **12** R. TURCAN, Les cultes orientaux, 1989, 77–127 **13** A. ROULLET, The Egyptian and Egyptianizing Monuments of Imperial Rome, 1972 **14** I. TÓTH, Marcus Aurelius' Miracle of the Rain and the Egyptian Cults in the Danube Region, in: Studia Aegyptiaca 2, 1976, 101–113 **15** C. MAYSTRE, Les grands prêtres de Ptah Memphis, 1992 **16** R. WILD, Water in the Cultic Worship of I. and Sarapis, 1981 **17** M. TOTTI, Ausgewählte Texte der I.- und Sarapis-Rel., 1985 **18** L. Vidman (Hrsg.), Sylloge inscriptionum religionis Isiacae et Sarapiacae (SIRIS), 1969.

J. GWYN GRIFFITHS, Apuleius of Madauros, The I.-Book, 1975.

S. TA.

ABB.-LIT.: **1** J. GWYN GRIFFITHS, Apuleius of Madauros, The Isis-Book (Metamorphoses, Book XI), EPRO 39, 1975 **2** J. BERGMAN, Ich bin Isis. Stud. zum memphitischen Hintergrund der griech. Isis-Aretalogien, 1968 **3** D. MÜLLER, Ägypten und die griech. Isis-Aretalogien, 1961 **4** M. MÜNSTER, Unt. zur Göttin Isis. Vom AR bis zum Ende des NR, 1968 **5** R. HELM, Apuleius, Metamorphosen (lat. und dt.), 51961.

M. HAA.

Islam (*islām*).

I. DEFINITION II. GESCHICHTE III. WESTLICHES ISLAMBILD UND ISLAMWISSENSCHAFT

I. DEFINITION

I., »vollkommene, vorbehaltlose Unterwerfung, Hingabe an Gott«, als *nomen agentis*: *muslim*; beide Termini sind koranisch. Die jüngste der drei monotheistischen Weltreligionen, h. über eine Milliarde Anhänger.

II. Geschichte
A. Entstehung B. Verbreitung C. Religion und Recht
D. Orthodoxie und Glaubensrichtungen

A. Entstehung
In der überwiegend nomadischen Ges. Arabiens vor dem 7. Jh. n. Chr. wurde eine Anzahl von Göttern und Göttinnen verehrt, meist Stammes- oder Lokalgottheiten. Zu Lebzeiten des Propheten → Mohammed (Muḥammad, um 570–632) zeichnete sich aber in einer Übergangsphase zu seßhafter Lebensform unter dem Einfluß der auf der Arab. Halbinsel schon seit Jahrzehnten verbreiteten christl. Konfessionen (nördl. Randgebiete) sowie durch das Judentum eine Tendenz zum → Monotheismus (Allāh = »*der* Gott«) ab. Die vorislamische Zeit wird rückblickend als *ǧāhiliyya* bezeichnet, was soviel wie »Unwissenheit« (nämlich bezüglich der »wahren« Rel.) bedeutet. Mohammed verstand sich als Empfänger und Vermittler göttl. Offenbarungen, nämlich des → Koran, der nach seinem Tode schriftlich fixiert und redigiert wurde (→ Othman).

B. Verbreitung
Offenbarungen eschatologischen Inhalts und eine Ausrichtung auf das jenseitige Leben motivierten die ersten Anhänger des Propheten (v. a. nach der → Hedschra) sowie die gläubige Gemeinde nach seinem Tod. Durch Eroberungszüge (zuerst der vier »rechtgeleiteten«, dann der umayyadischen → Kalifen) fanden eine rapide territoriale Ausbreitung des I. statt: Eroberungen seit Mitte des 7. Jh.: Arab. Halbinsel, Syrien-Palästina, Ägypten, ʿIrāq; Iran; Anf. 8. Jh.: Nordafrika, Spanien (bis 1492, Fall von Granada); Transoxanien, Vorderindien; 11. Jh.: Kleinasien; 14. Jh.: Vordringen bis SO-Europa. Die anfänglich positiv-tolerante Einstellung zu Juden und Christen als Anhänger der beiden anderen großen Offenbarungsrel. auf der Basis einer gemeinsamen »Heiligen Urschrift« verhinderte eine Zwangsbekehrung dieser Minderheiten, denen gegen Zahlung einer Kopfsteuer Schutz garantiert wurde. Die Verbreitung des I. beschränkt sich auch h. vornehmlich auf Afrika und Asien. Durch Arbeitsmigration in der 2. H. des 20. Jh. bildeten sich daneben zahlenstarke muslimische Gemeinden in Europa und Amerika.

C. Religion und Recht
Im I., der sich als letzte Offenbarungsrel. nach denen der anderen »Schriftbesitzer« versteht, sind alle Bereiche des menschlichen Lebens, ob des Individuums oder der (rel. und polit.) Gemeinschaft der Gläubigen (*umma*), reglementiert. Der I. umfaßt Glaube und Hingabe an den einen Schöpfergott sowie Gehorsam gegenüber dem rel. Gesetz. Die islam. Gesetzeswiss. regelt die Pflichten des Muslims in jeder Beziehung. Gesetzesgrundlage sind an erster Stelle die rel. Schriften: Koran und »Tradition« (*ḥadīṯ*, d. h. die Überlieferungen der Worte und Taten des Propheten und seiner engsten Gefährten als Verhaltensmaßgabe). Die rel. Pflichten des Muslims sind in den fünf »Säulen« des I. formuliert: 1. Das Glaubensbekenntnis – ›Ich bezeuge, daß es keinen Gott außer Allah (= dem einen Gott) gibt und daß Muḥammad der Gesandte Gottes ist‹ – betont den monotheistischen Charakter (allmächtiger Schöpfergott). 2. Das rituelle Gebet ist fünfmal am Tag nach Verrichtung der rituellen Waschung in Richtung Mekka (anfangs kurzzeitig → Jerusalem; → Kaaba) zu sprechen. Freitags findet das Mittagsgebet in der Moschee statt. 3. Die gesetzliche Almosensteuer wird an Bedürftige weitergeleitet. 4. Fasten im Monat Ramaḍān von Sonnenaufgang bis -untergang, d. h. Sich-Enthalten von Speisen, Getränken, Rauchen, Geschlechtsverkehr. 5. Die Wallfahrt nach Mekka sollte jeder Muslim nach seinem Vermögen mindestens einmal im Leben durchführen.

Erst die Absichtserklärung macht jedoch die folgende Tat im religionsgesetzlichen Sinn gültig. Eine (koranisch belegte) rel. Pflicht ist auch der »Heilige Krieg« (*ǧihād*, wörtl. »Mühe«, »Anstrengung auf dem Weg Gottes«) zur Verteidigung und Ausbreitung des I., der dem Kämpfer Verdienst im Jenseits verspricht und den Gefallenen zum Märtyrer macht.

D. Orthodoxie und Glaubensrichtungen
Unter der Herrschaft der → ʿAbbāsiden gedieh eine arab.-iran.-islam. Kultur, die ihre Blüte im 10. Jh. erreichte. Eine seit dem 8. Jh. verstärkte Übersetzertätigkeit förderte entscheidend die Rezeption des ant. Erbes und die Auseinandersetzung mit hell. Gedankengut – v. a. in den Bereichen Medizin, Naturwiss. und Philos. (z. B. Aristoteles-Rezeption, → Textgeschichte) – welches dann Einfluß nahm auf die Diskussion theologischer Fragen (→ Kalām) sowie auf die Ausbildung und Ausprägung der islam. Mystik (→ Sufismus). Schon früh entstanden rel.-polit. Bewegungen, die sich in Opposition zur herrschenden Orthodoxie befanden. Dies führte zur Herausbildung der Haupt-Glaubensrichtungen der → Sunniten (mehr als vier Fünftel aller Muslime) und → Schiiten. Im 8./9. Jh. entstanden vier sunnitische Rechtsschulen: Ḥanafiten, Mālikiten, Šāfiʿiten, Hanbaliten, die jeweils leicht modifizierte Auslegungen des Rechts vornahmen.

III. Westliches Islambild und Islamwissenschaft
Nach einer langen Phase der Unkenntnis und Ignoranz setzte erst z. Z. der Kreuzzüge eine offensivere Auseinandersetzung mit dem I. ein. Sie fand ihren schriftlichen Niederschlag in ersten lat. Übers. arab. naturwiss.-medizinischer und philos. Texte, aber auch des → Koran. Trotzdem überwogen noch Polemik, Mißverständnisse und wenig Sachkenntnis, verstärkt im 15. Jh. durch Orientierung des Westens auf das griech. und röm. Erbe und damit Überhöhung der eigenen Tradition. Gemeinsamkeiten des ant. Erbes und etwaige Wechselbeziehung wurden erst in neuerer Zeit hinterfragt. Eine objektiv-kritische I.-Wiss. bildete sich erst seit der Aufklärung aus. Ende des 19. Jh. lieferten Texteditionen, Quellenanalysen und -kritik, deren Grundstein der Begründer der arab. Philol., Johann Jakob

Reiske (1716–1774), gelegt hatte, Informationen für zahlreiche Propheten-Biographien und später Koranstudien. Heute hat sich die I.-Wiss., die seit über einem Jh. auch an den Universitäten etabliert ist, über den rein religionswiss. Kontext hinaus zu einer multidisziplinären Forschung entwickelt.

→ Judentum; Textgeschichte; Arabisch-Islamische Kulturregion (Al-Andalus)

C. Cahen, Der I. i (Fischer Weltgesch. 14), 1995 • W. Ende, U. Steinbach (Hrsg.), Der I. in der Gegenwart, 1996 • G. Endress, Der I. Eine Einführung in seine Gesch., [2]1991 • G. E. von Grunebaum, Studien zum Kulturbild und Selbstverständnis des I., 1969 • B. Lewis (ed.), The World of I. Faith, People, Culture, 1976 • E. W. Said, Orientalism, 1979 • A. Schimmel u. a., Der Islam III, 1990 • D. Waines, An Introduction to I., 1995 • W. M. Watt, A. T. Welch, Der Islam I, 1980 • Ders., M. Marmura, Der Islam II, 1985.

H. SCHÖ.

Ismael, Ismaeliten (PN, von hebr. *Yišmaᶜel*, »Gott hört«). Sohn → Abrahams [1] und Hagars (Gn 16,11). Nach Gn 17,20 und Gn 25,15 ff. zeugte der Stammvater der Ismaeliten zwölf Stämme. Trotz der Blutsverwandtschaft mit den Israeliten erachteten diese die als freiheitsliebend und kriegslustig geltenden Abkömmlinge I.s als nicht gleichberechtigt, da I. von einer ägypt. Magd geboren und mit ihr von Abraham vertrieben wurde. Gerade diese Vertreibung I.s wird in der → Haggada facettenreich verarbeitet; bes. Augenmerk wird auf den Charakter I.s gerichtet: I. erscheint als Götzendiener und Bruderhasser, der durch den bösen Blick Saras krank wird. Eine Wende tritt ein, als I. bereut und seinen Bruder → Isaak zu verehren beginnt (Midraš ha-gadol 381). Im → Islam erscheint I. mit dem Namen Ismail als Prophet. Als Erstgeborener Abrahams ist er Verkünder einer neuen, abrahamitisch gen. Religion. Nach der Überl. soll Abraham gemeinsam mit I. in → Mekka die → Kaaba errichtet haben.

L. Ginzberg, The legends of the Jews, Bd. 1, Bd. 5, 1968 • J. Longton, Fils d'Abraham: panorama des communautés juives, chrétiennes et musulmanes, 1987 • F. Peters, Children of Abraham: Judaism, Christianity, Islam, 1982 • S. Stern, Studies in early Ismailism, 1983.

Y. D.

Ismaris (Ἰσμαρίς). See an der Küste der Ägäis zw. Maroneia und dem Strymon (Hdt. 7,109) mit Heiligtum des Maron (Strab. 7, fr. 44), wahrscheinlich nahe dem h. Paguria.

I. v. B.

Ismaros (Ἴσμαρος). Im thrak. Kikonien (SO-Thrakien) gelegene Stadt, bei Maroneia (Strab. 7 fr. 44) oder identisch mit dieser (schol. Hom. Od. 9,39 f.); I. wird als Verbündete Troias (Hom. Il. 2,846; schol. Hom. Od. 9,40) von Odysseus zerstört (Hom. Od. 9,40). Nach Archilochos eine offenbar bekannte Weingegend (Archil. fr. 2 W.). Später erwähnt u. a. bei Verg. Aen. 10,381 und Prop. 3,12,25.

J. Wiesner, Die Thraker, 1963, 16 f., 44.

J. S.-A.

Ismene (Ἰσμήνη).

[1] Theban. Heroine, die sich wegen ihrer Liebesbeziehung zu → Periklymenos den Zorn der Athene zuzieht und von → Tydeus getötet wird (Mimn. fr. 21 IEG; Pherekydes FGrH 3 F 95). Im 5. Jh. v. Chr. wurde sie v. a. durch die Tragiker in den Oidipusmythos integriert: Als Tochter des → Oidipus und der → Iokaste oder → Euryganeia, als Schwester der → Antigone [3], des → Eteokles [1] und → Polyneikes überlebt sie mit Antigone den Angriff der Sieben gegen Theben (Aischyl. Sept. 861 ff.; Soph. Ant.; Oid. K.). Sophokles stellt sie als sehr an die soziale Norm angepaßte Gegenfigur zu Antigone dar. Nach Ion von Chios (fr. 740 PMG) wird sie zusammen mit Antigone von → Laodamas verbrannt.

[2] Quellnymphe in Theben, Tochter des Flußgottes Asopos, Gemahlin des → Argos [I 5], Großmutter der → Io (Hes. fr. 294 M-W; Apollod. 2,6); sie wurde wohl erst sekundär in die argiv. Genealogie eingefügt und ist wahrscheinlich mit der Heroine I. [1] zu verbinden.

Lit.: G. Berger-Doer, s. v. I. (2), LIMC 5.1, 799 • E. Bethe, s. v. I., RE 8, 2135–2136 • I. Krauskopf, s. v. I. (1), LIMC 5.1, 796–797.
Abb.: I. Krauskopf, s. v. I. (1), LIMC 5.2, 527.

R. HA.

Ismenias (Ἰσμηνίας oder Ἰσμηνίας).

[1] Prominenter theban. Politiker, für seinen Reichtum berühmt (Plat. Men. 90a). Nach dem E. des Peloponnes. Krieges (431–404 v. Chr.) trat I. mit → Androkleidas als Führer einer Hetairie hervor, die gegen die prospartan. Politik des → Leontiades opponierte. Ziel waren die Zurückdrängung der Leontiades-Faktion und die außenpolit. Neuorientierung an Athen (Hell. Oxyrh. 12,1 f.; 13,1; Xen. hell. 3,5,1–6) [1]. Unter seiner Regie schloß Theben 395 v. Chr. ein Bündnis mit Athen und wurde (mit persischen Geldern ausgestattet) zu einem der Hauptprotagonisten der antispartan. Allianz im → Korinthischen Krieg (StV 2,223–5) [2]. Als im J. 382 I. und Leontiades beide als theban. Polemarchen fungierten und I. in der Olynth-Krise erneut für einen antispartan. Kurs eintrat, führte Leontiades mit Hilfe des Spartaners → Phoibidas einen Staatsstreich durch (Xen. hell. 5,2,27–31; Plut. Pelopidas 5; u. a.). I. wurde verhaftet, durch ein Sondergericht des Peloponnes. Bundes in einem Schauprozeß wegen persischer Gesinnung (im Korinth. Krieg) zum Tode verurteilt und hingerichtet (Xen. hell. 5,2,35 f.) [3].

1 H. Beck, Polis und Koinon, 1997, 231 2 P. Funke, Homonoia und Arche, 1980, 67–73 3 H.-J. Gehrke, Stasis, 1985, 175–7.

M. Cook, Ancient Political Factions, in: TAPhA 118, 1988, 57–85 • R. J. Buck, Boiotia and the Boiotian League, 1994, 27 ff.

HA. BE.

[2] Thebaner, Sohn des I. [1]. Mit → Pelopidas im J. 368 v. Chr. nach Thessalien entsandt, um mit dem Tyrannen → Alexandros [15] von Pherai über die Unabhängigkeit der thessal. Städte zu verhandeln. Dabei wurden beide von Alexandros festgesetzt und erst im J. 367 durch die mil. Intervention des → Epameinondas wieder freigegeben (Diod. 15,71,2–7; Plut. Pelopidas 27–29). Noch im selben Jahr wurde I. (erneut mit Pelopidas) eine Gesandtschaft zum Großkönig nach Susa übertragen (Plut. Artaxerxes 22,8; vgl. Xen. hell. 7,1,33–7; Plut. Pelopidas 30–1). 340/39 fungierte er als boiotischer *hieromnémōn* im *synhédrion* der delphischen → *amphiktyonía* (Syll.[3] 243 D14) und bekleidete kurz darauf das eponyme Archontat des Boiotischen Bundes (SEG 3,333). Sein Sohn erhielt (offenbar aus Verehrung für Pelopidas) den Namen Thettaliskos (Aristot. rhet. 1398b 5–8).

J.Buckler, The Theban Hegemony, 1980, 120–8, 135.

HA.BE.

[3] I. aus Theben. Ihm als »princeps der anderen Partei« unterstellten seine innenpolit. Gegner 172 v. Chr. gegen den Willen der Römer das Bündnis zwischen dem Koinon der Boioter und → Perseus zu betreiben (Liv. 42,38,5; 43,9f.; zw. 174 und 172). I. war Verfechter der Erhaltung des Boiotischen Bundes (→ Boiotia) und stand der promaked. Gruppierung um Neon, Hippias und Diketas nahe ([1. 372; 377]: »alter Demokrat«). Als Archon des Bundes 173–172 (Liv. 42,43,9) schlug er einen geschlossenen Übertritt zu den Römern bei der Konferenz in Chalkis vor (Pol. 27,1f.; Liv. 42,44,1f.), obgleich die röm. Gesandten Einzelverhandlungen mit den Städten forderten. Vor einem Attentat mußte er zu den Römern fliehen. Auch das von ihm und seinen Anhängern Neon, Hippias und Diketas in Theben mühsam errungene und aufrecht erhaltene Übergewicht war nicht zu halten; Theben sowie alle anderen boiotischen Städte außer Haliartos, Thisbe und Koroneia verhandelten einzeln mit den röm. Gesandten und dem Senat: der Bund war aufgelöst. Soweit sich die Promakedonen nach Chalkis begaben, wurden sie angeklagt und gefangengesetzt; mit anderen zusammen nahm sich I. in Gefangenschaft das Leben (Pol. 27,2,9).

1 P. Roesch, Études Béotiennes, 1982, 372–77
2 J. Deininger, Der polit. Widerstand gegen Rom, 1971, 153–59 3 F. Walbank, A Historical Commentary on Polybius, Bd. 3., 1979, ad loc.

BO.D.

[4] Thebanischer Aulosspieler und -lehrer des 4. Jh. v. Chr. (Plut. Demetrios 1, 889b; Diog. Laert. 7,125), auch Gemmensammler (Plin. nat. 37,6). I. soll als Kriegsgefangener dem skythischen König → Ateas vorgespielt, dieser aber gesagt haben, das Wiehern von Pferden höre er lieber (Plut. mor. 174f, 334b, 632c, 1095f).

→ Musik II F.Z.

[5] Griech. Maler aus Chalkis, tätig im letzten Viertel des 4. Jh. v. Chr. Nach Plutarchos (mor. 843e-f) stammte von seiner Hand ein monumentales Tafelbild im Erechtheion zu Athen, das Ahnen und Familienmitglieder des → Lykurgos zeigte. Ob das genealogische Thema die Verdienste der Dynastie der Eteobuteaden in Form eines Stammbaums repräsentierte, wie teilweise von der Forsch. angenommen wurde, muß Spekulation bleiben.

G. Lippold, s. v. I., RE 9, 2141 • R. Pincelli, s. v. I., EAA 4, 242 • I. Scheibler, Griech. Malerei der Ant., 1994, 160 • K. Stähler, Griech. Geschichtsbilder der klass. Zeit, 1992, 112.

N.H.

Ismenos (auch *Hismenos*; Ἰσμηνός, Ἱσμηνός). Boiot. Fluß mit Quelle in → Thebai [1] nahe der Kadmeia. Außerhalb der Stadt vereinigte er sich mit der → Dirke und mündete in die → Hylike. In der Dichtung wird der I. häufig erwähnt. Im Ismenion südöstl. der Kadmeia oberhalb des I. wurde der Apollon Ismenios verehrt. Der Flußgott I. ging allmählich im Orakelkult des Apollon auf. Ein geom. Tempel im Ismenion wurde ca. 700 v. Chr. durch Brand zerstört, ein zweiter Tempel im 6. Jh. errichtet. Im 4. Jh. blieb ein Peripteros unvollendet. Belegstellen: Pind. P. 11,7; Hdt. 1,52; 1,92; 5,59–61; Paus. 9,10,2–6; Strab. 9,2,24.

1 S. Symeonoglou, The Topography of Thebes, 1985, 302.

Schachter 1, 77ff. (mit weiteren Quellen).

K.F.

Isodaites s. Pluton

Isoglosse s. Dialekt; Sprachverwandtschaft

Isokrates. Logograph, Rhetoriklehrer und Publizist aus Athen, Demos Erchia, Sohn des Theodoros und der Hedyto, 436–338 v. Chr.

A. Biographisches B. Werk C. Wirkung und Bewertung

A. Biographisches

Die auf Hermippos zurückgehende biographische Tradition über I. ist im wesentlichen dokumentiert durch: Dion. Hal. De Isocrate 1, Ps.-Plut. mor. 836e–839d, eine anon. Vita in einigen Hss., Phot. 486b–488a und einen Suda-Artikel s. v. I.; dazu kommen biographisch verwertbare Angaben im Werk des I. selbst, bes. in or. 15. Als Sohn eines begüterten Flötenfabrikanten erhielt I. eine standesgemäße Ausbildung, → Prodikos, → Teisias und → Theramenes werden als seine Lehrer genannt; am stärksten wurde er aber durch → Gorgias geprägt, bei dem er wohl mehrere Studienjahre in Thessalien verbrachte. Näherer Kontakt mit Sokrates ist unwahrscheinlich. Infolge des Dekeleischen Krieges finanziell ruiniert, war I. gezwungen, seine erworbenen Kenntnisse gewinnbringend einzusetzen. So betätigte er sich zw. ca. 403 und dem Ende der 90er Jahre des 4. Jh. als Logograph. Als um 390 die Grundlage für wirtschaftliche Unabhängigkeit von neuem geschaffen war, wandte sich I. von der Logographie ab und eröffnete in Athen eine Schule der Redekunst. Die folgenden 50 Jahre konnte er sich einerseits auf seine Lehrtätigkeit konzentrieren (berühmte Schüler waren → Timotheos, → Lykurgos, → Theopompos, → Ephoros, → Isaios und → Theodektes), andererseits auf das Verfassen von Reden über die großen polit. Themen der Zeit sowie über seine Bildungskonzeption. Diese Reden trug er nie selbst vor, da er sich konstitutionell den Anforderungen an einen Redner (Stimmkraft, Sicherheit des Auftretens) nicht gewachsen fühlte; sie wurden stattdessen vor größerem oder kleinem Publikum vorgelesen und waren auch als Muster für den Unterricht sowie für die private Lektüre bestimmt. I. heiratete erst in vorgerücktem Alter und adoptierte einen der Söhne seiner Frau namens Aphareus. Dem Politikgetriebe seiner Heimatstadt hielt sich I. fern, erfüllte aber die ihm aufgrund seines Reichtums zuwachsenden Pflichten durch Übernahme kostspieliger Leiturgien. I. soll nicht lange nach der Schlacht von Chaironeia (August 338) gestorben sein; ob er seinen Tod wirklich mit Absicht durch Verzicht auf Nahrung herbeigeführt hat, ist ungewiß.

B. Werk

1. Logographie 2. Philosophie
3. Politik 4. Stil

Im 1. Jh. v. Chr. lagen unter dem Namen des I. 60 Reden vor, von denen man 25 (Dion. Hal.) bzw. 28 (Kaikilios) für echt hielt. Bereits während der Kaiserzeit scheint sich das Corpus auf seinen heutigen Umfang reduziert zu haben, nämlich 21 Reden und 9 Briefe, darunter wohl einiges Unechte (or. 1; epist. 6 und 10).

1. Logographie

Sechs Reden aus I.' Logographenzeit sind erhalten: or. 21 (403/2), or. 18 (402/1), or. 20 (zw. 400 und 396), or. 16 (wohl 395/4), or. 17 (zw. 393 und 391) und or. 19 (391/0). Ihr Reichtum an allg. Sentenzen empfiehlt sie als Werbungs- und Unterrichtsmaterial für die Schule. Wahrscheinlich hat I. selbst diese (und vielleicht weitere seiner) Gerichtsreden veröffentlicht (Dion. Hal. De Isocrate 18).

2. Philosophie

Von den nach der Schulgründung entstandenen Reden befassen sich einige vornehmlich oder ausschließlich mit I.' eigenständigem Entwurf eines Bildungsprogrammes und dessen Abgrenzung gegen Konkurrenten der sophistischen (→ Alkidamas) bzw. der sokratischen Richtung (→ Antisthenes, → Platon), nämlich: or. 13 (ca. 390), or. 10 (zw. 390 und 380); or. 11 (zw. 380 und 375), or. 3, 2 und 9 (zw. 371 und 367) sowie or 15 (353). Grundlage von I.' Bildungskonzept ist ein auf → Protagoras und → Gorgias zurückgehender erkenntnistheoretischer Pessimismus, demzufolge sicheres Wissen nicht erreichbar sei, man also sein Handeln von wohlbegründeten Meinungen und dem Wahrscheinlichen leiten lassen müsse. Im Mittelpunkt der Bildung steht die rhet. Schulung, weil nach Überzeugung des I. »gut reden« und »gut denken« einander bedingen. Für einen Erfolg sind Begabung, Unterweisung und Übung gleichermaßen notwendig. Ziel ist sowohl die Fähigkeit, vernünftige Gedanken zu wichtigen Themen in angemessener Form und zum Nutzen der Adressaten formulieren zu können, als auch die Kompetenz zu davon ausgehendem Handeln, geleitet von einem gesunden Streben nach Ruhm, das sich ethischen Anforderungen verpflichtet weiß. Mit diesem, von ihm selbst als *philosophía* bezeichneten Konzept setzt sich I. deutlich ab einerseits vom sokratisch-platonischen Optimismus bezüglich des Tugendwissens, andererseits von einem auf das Formale beschränkten Rhet.-Unterricht. Konflikte mit den Vertretern beider Richtungen, bes. mit Platon (dessen Meinung über I. aber noch immer umstritten ist) waren die Folge.

3. Politik

In den übrigen Reden tritt die Stellungnahme zu polit. Themen stärker in den Vordergrund: In or. 4 ›Panegyrikos‹ (380 nach 10jähriger Arbeit fertiggestellt) entwickelt I. erstmals sein Konzept eines panhellenischen Kriegszuges gegen das Perserreich. Die kurzlebige Vorherrschaft Thebens verfolgt I. mit Ablehnung (or. 14 ›Plataikos‹ von 373, or. 6 ›Archidamos‹ von 366). Die beiden in kurzem Abstand aufeinander folgenden or. 8 ›Über den Frieden‹ (355) und or. 7 ›Areopagitikos‹ (355/4 oder 358/7) formulieren das Konzept einer außen- und innenpolit. Neuorientierung Athens (Verzicht auf hegemoniale Ambitionen, Rückkehr zur *pátrios politeía*). Auf den Aufstieg Makedoniens reagiert I. in or. 5 ›Philippos‹ (346) und epist. 2 ›An Philippos‹ (344). Die letzte Rede des I. (or. 12 ›Panathenaikos‹, 339) entzieht sich durch ihre Themenvielfalt und (teilweise noch nicht befriedigend geklärte) gedankliche Komplexität einer knappen Zusammenfassung. Die polit. bedeutsamen unter den Briefen entstammen dem Zeitraum zw. Anfang 367 und Herbst 338 (falls epist. 3 echt ist) und haben als Adressaten neben Philipp den syrakusanischen Herrscher Dionysios (epist. 1; 367), die Söhne des Iason von Pherai (epist. 6; ca. 358) und den spartanischen König Archidamos (epist. 9; 356); die Echtheit der meisten wird mit mehr oder weniger Grund bezweifelt. Das polit. Denken des I. ist von einem mehr kulturell als ethnisch begründeten Panhellenismus geprägt, der auf die Eintracht der Poleis unter Wahrung ihrer Autonomie bedacht ist und als gemeinsames Ziel den Kriegszug nach Osten proklamiert; als eine von dessen positiven Folgen erwartet I. die Beseitigung der sozialen Spannung in Hellas, die er vom Standpunkt der Besitzenden aus mit Sorge beobachtet. Die für den Krieg notwendige einheitliche Führung möchte er zunächst von den traditionellen Vormächten Athen und Sparta wahrgenommen wissen, zieht aber seit den 60er Jahren – wohl unter dem Eindruck der Machtentfaltung Thebens – mehr und mehr die Hegemonie eines Alleinherrschers in Betracht, zuletzt die des Philippos. Dennoch wird I. nicht zum Monarchisten, sondern bleibt verfassungspolit. Anhänger einer eingeschränkten Demokratie in der »konservativen« att. Tradition eines Theramenes, Nikias oder Kimon; die Form der Verfassung gilt ihm allerdings als sekundär im Vergleich zur ethischen Beschaffenheit derjenigen, die die Politik bestimmen. Wie stark I. die reale Politik beeinflußt hat, ist umstritten; für eine eher geringe Wirkung seiner Konzepte auf die polit. Praxis scheint mehr zu sprechen als für das Gegenteil.

4. Stil

Zu seinen sprachlich-stilistischen Prinzipien äußert sich I. selbst an mehreren Stellen: In der Wortwahl erstrebt er Reinheit und Genauigkeit, im Satzbau Harmonie und Ausgewogenheit (Antithesen, Parallelismen usw.). Die gorgianischen Figuren werden geschätzt, aber sparsam eingesetzt. I. will durch seine Kunstprosa mit der Poesie konkurrieren, worauf auch die Tendenz zur Rhythmisierung und die zunehmend strikte Hiatmeidung deuten. Die Entwicklung dieses unverwechselbaren Stiles läßt sich bereits in den Gerichtsreden beobachten; seine volle Entfaltung ist im ›Panegyrikos‹ erreicht.

C. Wirkung und Bewertung

I. wurde in den Kanon der att. Redner aufgenommen, obwohl er nach ant. Maßstäben nur die ersten drei der fünf Aufgaben des Redners (*officia oratoris*) erfüllt hat. Sein Einfluß auf das Bildungswesen der Ant. sowie deren normative Ansprüche an die Kunstprosa ist kaum zu überschätzen. Seine Schule prägt z.B. weithin die hell. Historiographie, erlebt in der → Zweiten Sophistik eine neue Blüte und wirkt von hier aus auf die Spätantike und Byzanz. Gelegentlich geäußerte Kritik an der Monotonie des isokrateischen Periodenstils (Dion. Hal. De Isocrate 13 f.; 20) hat daran nichts geändert. Auch in Rom gelangte spätestens seit und durch → Cicero der Rhet.- und Bildungsentwurf des I. zu bestimmender Geltung, die ihm bis in die frühe Neuzeit (Erasmus von Rotterdam) erhalten blieb. Seit der Renaissance wurde I. als Sprachmeister und moralische Autorität (bes. aufgrund der wohl unechten or. 1 ›An Demonikos‹) geschätzt. Erst im 19. Jh., im Zusammenhang mit dem wachsenden Interesse an Platon, mehren sich die Stimmen, die das »philos.« Denken des I. für banal und oberflächlich, seine polit. Konzepte für illusionär erklären. Andere glaubten im Kontext der dt. Bemühungen um nationale Einigung im Hellas des 4. Jh. eine historische Analogie zu erkennen und glorifizierten entsprechend I. als deren Vorkämpfer. In jüngerer Zeit wurde dergleichen richtiggestellt; zugleich regt sich neues Interesse an einem genaueren Verständnis des isokrateischen »Philos.«-Entwurfes und seiner Position im geistigen Leben des 4. Jh. sowie an der rezeptionsästhetischen Sonderstellung seiner zum Vorlesen und Lesen, nicht aber für den rednerischen Vortrag geschriebenen »Reden«.

Gesamtausg.: G.B. Norlin, L. van Hook, 1928–45, 3 Bde. (mit engl. Übers.) • G. Mathieu, E. Brémond, 1928–62, 4 Bde. (mit frz. Übers.) • J. Castellanos Vila, 1971–91, bisher 3 Bde. (orr. 1–8, mit katalan. Übers.).
Einzelne Reden: or. 1: A. Morpurgo, 1960 • or. 2: F. Seck, 1965 • orr. 2, 3: S. Usher, 1990 • or. 7: V. Costa, 1983 • or. 10, 11, 13, 16, 18: R. Flacelière, 1961 • or. 13: S. Cecchi, 1959 • or. 15: K.Th. Arapopoulos, 1958 • or. 18: E. Carlotti, in: Annali del Liceo classico G. Garibaldi di Palermo 3/4, 1966/67, 346–79 • or. 19: F. Brindensi, 1963.
Übers: M. Marzi, 1991, 2 Bde. (ital.) • Chr. Ley-Hutton, K. Brodersen, 1993–1997, bisher 2 Bde. (dt.).
Index: S. Preuss, 1904 (Ndr. 1963).
Schol.: W. Dindorf, 1852.
Lit.: E. Alexiou, Ruhm und Ehre, 1995 • K. Barwick, Das Problem der isokrateischen Techne, in: Philologus 107, 1963, 43–60 (auch in: F. Seck (Hrsg.), Isokrates (WdF 351), 1976, 275–95) • Blass 2,1 ff. • K. Bringmann, Studien zu den polit. Ideen des I., 1965 • P. Cloché, I. et son temps, 1963 • N.D. Dimitriadis, Ἀνατομία τῆς ῥητορικῆς. Ἡ διαφωνία Πλάτωνος καὶ Ἰσοκράτους, 1983 • W. Eder, Monarchie und Demokratie im 4. Jh. v. Chr. Die Rolle des Fürstenspiegels in der athenischen Demokratie, in: Eder, Demokratie, 153–173 • H. Erbse, Platons Urteil über I., in: Hermes 99, 1971, 183–97 (auch in: F. Seck (Hrsg.), Isokrates (WdF 351), 1976, 329–52) • Ch. Eucken, I. und seine Positionen in der Auseinandersetzung mit den zeitgenössischen Philosophen, 1983 • P. Frolov, Das Problem der Monarchie und der Tyrannis in der polit. Publizistik des 4. Jh. v. Chr., in: E.Ch. Welskopf (Hrsg.), Hellenische Poleis, Bd. 1, 1974, 401–434 • A. Fuks, Isocrates and the social-economic situation in Greece, in: Ancient Society 3, 1972, 17–44 • G. Heilbrunn, I. on rhetoric and power, in: Hermes 103, 1975, 154–78 • H. Kehl, Die Monarchie im polit. Denken des I., 1962 • M.A. Levi, Isocrate, 1959 • J. Lombard, Isocrate. Rhétorique et éducation, 1990 • A. Masaracchia, Isocrate. Retorica e politica, 1995 • G. Mathieu, Les idées politiques d'Isocrate, 1925 (Ndr. 1966) • E. Mikkola, I., 1954 • Norden, Kunstprosa 113 ff. • S. Perlman, Panhellenism, the Polis, and Imperialism, in: Historia 15, 1976, 1–130 • F. Pointner, Die Verfassungstheorie des I., Diss. 1969 • W. Steidle, Redekunst und Bildung bei I., in: Hermes 80, 1952, 257–96 • Yun Lee Too, The rhetoric of identity in I., 1995 • M. Tulli, Sul rapporto di Platone con I., in: Athenäum 68, 1990, 403–22 • S. Usener, I., Platon und ihr Publikum, 1994 • S. Usher, The style of I., in: BICS 20, 1973, 39–67 • H. Wilms, Techne und Paideia bei Xenophon und I., 1995.
Zu einzelnen Reden: or. 1: B. Rosenkranz, Die Struktur der Ps.Isokrateischen Demonicea, in: Emerita 34, 1966, 95–129 • or. 4: E. Buchner, Der Panegyrikos des I., 1958 • D. Gillis, I.' Panegyricus, in: WS 5, 1971, 52–73 • C.W. Müller, Platon und der Panegyrikos des I., in: Philologus 135, 1991, 140–56 • F. Seck, Die Komposition des ›Panegyrikos‹, in: Ders., I. (WdF 351), 1976, 353–70 • or. 5: G. Dobesch, Der panhellenische Gedanke im 4. Jh. v. Chr. und der Philippos des I., 1968 • D. Gillis, Isocrates, the Philippos, and the evening of democracy, in: Centro ricerche documentazione sull' antichità classica 8, 1976/7, 123–33 • M.M. Markle, Support of Athenian intellectuals for Philipp, in: JHS 96, 1976, 80–99 • or. 7: M. Silvestrini, Terminologia politica isocratea II, in: Quaderni di storia 4, 1978, 169–83 • or. 8: J. Davidson, Isocrates against imperialism, in: Historia 39,1990,20–36 • D. Gillis, The structure of arguments in Isocrates De pace, in: Philologus 114, 1970, 195–210 • or. 9: D.K. Mason, Studies in the Evagoras of Isocrates, Diss. 1975 • W.H. Race, Pindaric encomium and I.' Evagoras, in: TAPhA 117, 1987, 131–55 • or. 10: L. Braun, Die schöne Helena, wie Gorgias und I. sie sehen, in: Hermes 110, 1982, 158–74 • G. Heilbrunn, The composition of Isocrates' Helen, in: TAPhA 107, 1977, 147–59 • F. Parodi Scotti, Auctoritas del mito, in: Studi E. Corsini, 1994,79–90 • or. 11: S. Usener, I.' Busiris, in: W. Kullmann, J. Althoff, Vermittlung und Tradierung von Wissen in der griech Kultur, 1993, 247–62 • or. 12: M. Erler, Hilfe und Hintersinn, in: II. Symposium

Platonicum, ed. L. Rosetti, 1992, 122–37 • V. Gray, Images of Sparta, in: A. Powell, S. Hodkinson, The shadow of Sparta, 1994, 223–71 • H.-O. Kroener, Dialog und Rede, in: A&A 15, 1969, 102–121 (auch in: F. Seck, I. (WdF 351), 1976, 296–328) • C. Schäublin, Selbstinterpretation im Panathenaikos des I., in: MH 39, 1982, 165–78 • or. 13: M. Dixsaut, I. contre des sophistes sans sophistique, in: L. Brisson (Hrsg.), Le plaisir de parler, 1986, 63–85 • or. 17: G. Thür, Komplexe Prozessführung dargestellt am Beispiel des Trapezitikos (I. 17), in: Symposion 1971, 1975, 157–88 • or. 18: J. H. Kuehn, Die Amnestie von 403 v. Chr. im Reflex der 18. I.-Rede, in: WS 80, 1967, 31–73.

Briefe: R. N. Gaines, Isocrates, Ep. 6. 8, in: Hermes 118, 1990, 165–70 • M. Marzi, Isocrate e Filippo II di Macedonia, in: A&R 39, 1994, 1–10. M. W.

Isonomia (ἰσονομία). Der Begriff *i.* (»Gleichheit vor dem Gesetz«) scheint neben anderen mit *iso-* (»gleich«) gebildeten Komposita im späten 6. und frühen 5. Jh. v. Chr. eine bedeutende Rolle im polit. Diskurs in Griechenland gespielt zu haben. Herodot benutzt *i.* in der Verfassungsdebatte am Perserhof, um auf die Demokratie zu verweisen (Hdt. 3,80,6; 83,1), und bezieht an anderen Stellen (3,142,3; 5,37,2) I. auf eine verfassungsmäßige Regierung im Gegensatz zur → Tyrannis; im letzteren Sinn nutzt er auch *isēgoría* (»Gleichheit der Rede«) und *isokratía* (»Gleichheit der Macht«) (5,78; 92a,1). Für Thukydides ist *i.* ein Begriff, der sich auf eine solide Oligarchie auf breiter Grundlage ebenso anwenden läßt wie auf eine Demokratie. Die → *skólia* (Trinklieder) auf Harmodios und → Aristogeiton preisen diese, weil sie sowohl den Tyrannen getötet als auch den Athenern die *i.* gebracht haben (PMG 893–896): Wahrscheinlich nutzte man das Wort I. anfangs, um den Gegensatz zwischen polit. Freiheit im Innern und der Abhängigkeit von einem Tyrannen darzustellen, doch könnte es von → Kleisthenes als Schlagwort für seine Reformen übernommen worden sein.

1 V. Ehrenberg, Origins of Democracy, in: Historia 1, 1950, 515–548 2 C. Meier, Die Entstehung des Polit. bei den Griechen, 1980, 281–284 3 M. Ostwald, Nomos and the Beginnings of the Athenian Democracy, 1969, bes. 96–136 4 K. A. Raaflaub, Einleitung und Bilanz, in: K. H. Kinzl (Hrsg.), Demokratia, 1995, 49–51. P. J. R.

Isopoliteia (ἰσοπολιτεία). Der Begriff *i.* (»gleiches Bürgerrecht«), wird seit dem 3. Jh. v. Chr. verwendet, um (anstelle von → *politeía*) die Vergabe des Bürgerrechts durch einen griech. Staat an Einzelpersonen (z. B. IG V 2,11 = Syll.[3] 501) oder aber hauptsächlich an ganze Gemeinden (z. B. IG V 2, 419 = Syll.[3] 472) zu bezeichnen. Die moderne Forsch. unterscheidet zw. der *i.*, dem Austausch von Rechten zwischen Staaten, die ihre Unabhängigkeit bewahrten, und der → *sympoliteía*, dem Zusammenschluß von zwei oder mehreren Staaten zu einem einzigen. Der ant. Sprachgebrauch ist jedoch vielfältiger. Der Aitolische Bund gebrauchte das Mittel der *i.*, um weit entfernte Staaten anzugliedern, wobei die *i.* entweder mit dem gesamten Bund oder einer einzelnen aitolischen Stadt vereinbart wurde.

1 Busolt/Swoboda 225 f., 1245, 1510–9 2 V. Ehrenberg, Der Staat der Griechen, [2]1965, 319 f. 3 J. A. O. Larsen, Greek Federal States, 1968, 202 ff. P. J. R.

Isos (Ἶσος). Nicht sicher lokalisiert, z.Z. Strabons bereits wüster Ort (ἴχνη πόλεως, Strab. 9,2,14) nahe Anthedon in Boiotia. Überreste am NO-Ende des Paralimni-Sees sind wohl mit I. zu identifizieren ([1. 457 f.; 2. 257–261], anders [3. 62 f.]).

1 F. Noack, Arne, in: MDAI(A) 19, 1894, 405–485 2 Fossey 3 P. W. Wallace, Strabo's Description of Boiotia 1979. M. FE.

Isoteleia (ἰσοτέλεια, »Gleichheit der Pflichten«, d. h. der Bürgerpflichten) war ein Privileg, das ein griech. Staat an Nicht-Bürger vergeben konnte, wenn er sie zwar über den normalen Status von Metoiken (→ *métoikoi*) heben, aber doch nicht mit vollem Bürgerrecht ausstatten wollte. Da die *i.* üblicherweise von Steuern und anderen Belastungen befreite, denen Nicht-Bürger unterlagen, konnte der gleiche Status entweder als *i.* oder als → *atéleia* (»Freiheit von Pflichten«) bezeichnet werden (etwa in Athen: IG II[2] 53: *atéleia*, 287: *isotéleia*). In Athen konnte *isotelḗs* als statusspezifische Bezeichnung dem Namen eines Mannes angefügt werden (z. B. [Demosth.] or. 34, 18; 44; IG II[2] 791,51 an der Stelle der Demos-Angabe in einer Liste von Spendern). Die *i.* wurde auch von vielen anderen griech. Staaten vergeben (z. B. Boiotien: Syll.[3] 644, 30–31), manchmal zusammen mit dem Bürgerrecht, um die volle Gleichstellung des Empfängers mit den Bürgern zu betonen (etwa in Kalchedon: Syll.[3] 645, 71–72). In Ephesos finden sich im Jahr 86 v. Chr. die *isoteleís* unter den Einwohnern, denen das Bürgerrecht angeboten wurde, falls sie sich zum Kampf gegen Mithradates VI. von Pontos verpflichteten (Syll.[3] 742, 44–48). P. J. R.

Išōʿyahḇ III. Syr. Autor und Patriarch der Ostkirche (649–659 n. Chr.), Sohn von Landeigentümern. Er wurde Mönch am Kloster Beṯ ʿAbē, in der Folgezeit 627 Bischof von Niniveh (Mosul), 639 Metropolit von → Arbela [1]; im J. 649 wurde er schließlich zum Patriarchen gewählt. Eine umfangreiche Sammlung von 106 Briefen liefert zahlreiche Informationen über die Ostkirche in der Übergangszeit von sāsānidischer zu arab. Herrschaft. I. führte weitreichende liturgische Reformen durch, ferner verfaßte er ein Werk über das Leben des Märtyrers Išōʿsabrān.

Ed.: R. Duval, CSCO Scr. Syri 11 f., 1904 f. (Briefe) • J. B. Chabot, in: Nouvelle archives des missions scientifiques et littéraires 7, 1897, 485–584 (Leben Ishoʿsabrans).

Lit.: A. Baumstark, Gesch. der syr. Lit., 1922, 197–200 • J.-M. Fiey, Ishoʿyaw le Grand, in: Orientalia Christiana Periodica 35, 1969, 305–333; 36, 1970, 5–46 • DHGE 150, 1995, 179–181. S. BR./Ü: S. Z.

Israel s. Juda und Israel; Judentum

Issa (Ἴσσα). Insel und Stadt vor der dalmatischen Küste, h. Vis, Kroatien. Die im späten 4. Jh. v. Chr. aus Syrakus nach I. kommenden Siedler (Skymn. 413f; Diod. 15,14,2) [3; 4] legten ihrerseits Kolonien an: Tragurion, Epetion und eine Siedlung auf Korkyra Melaina (SEG 43, 348) [3]. 230/229 v. Chr. von Rom zur *civitas libera et foederata* [1. 100] erhoben, wurde I. 167 v. Chr. für steuerfrei erklärt. 56 v. Chr. ging eine Gesandtschaft aus I. zu Caesar (SEG 43, 350). Seit dem 1. Jh. v. Chr. zum Verwaltungsgebiet von → Salona gehörend [1. 106f.], wird I. in die Prov. → Illyricum eingegliedert. Mz.: [2. 58–68; 4]. Inschr.: SEG 31, 593–604; 35, 681–693; 40, 510–515; 42, 549; CEG 2, 662 [2; 3].
→ Epetion; Korkyra Melaina; Tragurion

1 G. Alföldy, Bevölkerung und Ges. der röm. Prov. Dalmatien, 1965 2 J. Brunšmid, Die Inschr. und Mz. der griech. Städte Dalmatiens, 1898 3 P. M. Fraser, The Colonial Inscription of I., in: P. Cabanes (Hrsg.), L' Illyrie méridionale et l'Épire, 1993, 167–174 4 P. Visonà, Colonization and Money Supply at I., in: Chiron 25, 1995, 55–59.

J. Wilkes, The Illyrians, 1992. D. S.

Issedones (Ἰσσηδόνες, Ἰσσηδοί, Ἐσσηδόνες). Skythisches Volk asiatischer Herkunft. Nach Hdt. (1,201; 4,13–26) südöstl. des Aralsees zu lokalisieren; der Schwerpunkt ihrer Wohngebiete lag aber in Mittelasien. Ptolemaios (6,16,5; 16,7; 8,24,3; 24,5 N) rechnet ihnen die im chinesischen Ost-Turkestan (Tarimbecken) an der Seidenstraße gelegenen Städte Ἰσσηδὼν Σκυθική (h. Kutscha) u. Ἰσσηδὼν Σηρική (h. Tscharchlik) südwestlich des Lobnor zu.
→ Skythai J. RE. u. H. T.

Issorion (Ἰσσώριον). Hügel an der nördl. Stadtgrenze von Sparta mit Heiligtum der Artemis Issoria (Plut. Agesilaos 32,3; Polyain. 2,1,14; Nep. Agesilaus 6,2), evtl. die h. Klaraki gen. Anhöhe.

F. Bölte, s. v. Sparta, RE 3A, 1350ff. C. L. u. E. O.

Issos. Stadt östl. der Kilikia Pedias zw. Amanides (Amanikai) und Kilikiai Pylai, h. der Siedlungshügel Yeşil Hüyük (früher Kinet Hüyük), 2 km nnw. der Mündung des → Pinaros, wo → Alexandros [4] d.Gr. 333 v. Chr. → Dareios [3] III. besiegte; danach später auch Nikopolis gen. 194 n. Chr. siegte hier Septimius Severus über Pescennius Niger und ließ zur Erinnerung einen *Kodrigai* (nach *Quadriga*) gen. Triumphbogen in den Kilikiai Pylai errichten. Nikopolis, 260 n. Chr. von den Sāsāniden erobert (Res Gestae divi Saporis 30), erlebte im 9./10. Jh. eine Blüte als Ḥiṣn at-Tīnāt, von wo man Holz aus dem → Amanos nach Syria und Äg. ausführte.

F. Hild/H. Hellenkemper, 277f. F. H.

Istachr (*Iṣṭaxr*, h. *Taxt-i Ṭā'ūs*). Ruinenstätte in der Persis (Fārs) an der Straße von Iṣfahān nach Šīrāz, bei → Naqš-e Rostam; seit prähistor. Zeit besiedelt, hat sich laut arab. Überl. in spätparth. Zeit dort ein Feuerheiligtum der → Anāhitā befunden (arch. nicht nachzuweisen), als dessen Vorsteher der Eponym der → Sāsānidendynastie, Sāsān, gewirkt haben soll. Inschr., Münzfunde, Siegellegenden und lit. Überl. erweisen I. als einen polit.-administrativ, rel.-kultischen sowie »ideologisch« wichtigen Platz, der von den Muslimen erst nach schweren Kämpfen eingenommen wurde. I. war Sitz eines nestorianischen Bischofs.

M.-L. Chaumont, Le culte d'Anāhitā à Staxr, in: RHR 153, 1958, 154–175 • J. M. Fiey, Communautés syriaques en Iran et Irak, 1979, Index s. v. • R. Gyselen, La géographie administrative de l'empire sassanide, 1989 • J. Wiesehöfer, Die »dunklen Jahrhunderte« der Persis, 1994, Index s. v. J. W.

Istaevones. Myth. Urstamm der Germani (Plin. nat. 4,100; Tac. Germ. 2,2), ohne histor. faßbaren Realitätsbezug. Nach Plin. l.c. hätten sie *proximi Rheno* (nahe des Rheins) gewohnt.
→ Herminones K. DI.

Ištar. Die semit. Göttin I. ist etym. mit → Astarte (*Aṯtarat*) zu verbinden; gramm. ist der Name mask. (zu vergleichen mit west-semit. *Aṯtar*). Im südl. Mesopot. wurde sie mit der sumer. Stadtgöttin von → Uruk, Inanna, gleichgesetzt, ihre Verehrung dort ist bis in achäm. Zeit bezeugt. Im nördl. Babylonien und Assyrien wurden I.-Gestalten in zahlreichen Städten verehrt (I. der Stadt NN; u. a. der Städte → Akkad, → Arbela [1], → Niniveh) und z. T. mit anderen Göttinen gleichgesetzt. Daraus ist zu erklären, daß der Name als *Ištar(t)u* in Mesopot. als genereller Terminus für Göttin gebraucht wird. I. (und Inanna) – im Pantheon keinem Gott ehelich verbunden, eine jugendhafte Gestalt – gilt als Göttin der Liebe, verkörpert aber auch kriegerische Züge und wird in ihrer astralen Erscheinung als Venusstern verehrt. Die Verbindung der Ištar-Inanna mit dem Ritual des → Hieros Gamos wird in der akkad. geprägten Überlieferung kritisch gesehen.

F. Bruschweiler, Inanna, 1987 • C. Wilcke, U. Seidl, s. v. Inanna, RLA 5, 74–88. J. RE.

Ištar-Tor. Nördl. Haupttor von → Babylon; gewaltige, turmbewehrte Doppeltoranlage mit rechtwinklig zueinander liegenden Torräumen und tunnelartigem Durchgang von ca. 46 m Länge. Das gesamte Torgebäude war mit farbig glasierten Ziegeln verkleidet. Auf der dunkelblauen Grundfarbe hoben sich geom. Ornamente, Rosetten und Tierdarstellungen (Stiere, Schlangendrachen) in Hoch- und Flachrelief verschiedenfarbig ab. Aufgrund beschrifteter Ziegelstempel kann das I. in die zweite Regierungshälfte → Nebukadnezars II. (604–562 v. Chr.) datiert werden; ebenfalls inschr. belegt ist der Name des Tores nach der Göttin → Ištar. Das I. stellte zusammen mit der Prozessionsstraße einen architektonischen Gesamtkomplex dar, der den baulichen Höhepunkt des babylon. Neujahrsfestzuges (→ Neujahrsfest) bildete. Dieser zeremoniellen

Funktion verdankte das Tor seine Größe und prachtvolle Ausstattung. Eine Rekonstruktion befindet sich im Vorderasiatischen Museum, Berlin.

R. KOLDEWEY, Das I. in Babylon, 1918 • Ders., Das wiedererstehende Babylon, [5]1990, 43 ff. • J. MARZAHN, Das I. von Babylon, 1994. J.BÄ.

Isthmia. Die im Heiligtum des → Poseidon am Isthmos von Korinth seit 582 v. Chr. ausgetragenen I. gehören der → Periodos (περίοδος, »Umlauf«) der panhellenischen Agone an. Der Mythos bringt die Gründung der Isthmischen Spiele mit Leichenspielen für den ertrunkenen Melikertes (Paus. 2,1,3) oder mit Theseus (Plut. Theseus 11e) in Verbindung [1]. Arch. Befunde für sportliche Wettkämpfe gehen nicht vor das 6. Jh. v. Chr. zurück [2. (Sprunggewicht); 1. 76 (Wagen)]. Bereits 229 v. Chr. wurde den Römern aus Dankbarkeit für die Vernichtung der Seeräuber Teilnahmerecht an den I. gewährt (Pol. 2,12,8). Nach der Zerstörung Korinths 146 v. Chr. fanden die I. eine Zeitlang unter dem Vorsitz von Sikyon statt.

Das Programm bestand aus gymnischen, hippischen und musischen Disziplinen, gelegentlich auch aus Vorträgen und Wettbewerben in der Malerei. Ein (sonst selten bezeugter) Lauf »Hippios« über vier Stadien wurde hier (vielleicht zu Ehren des Poseidon als Patron der Pferde) ausgetragen [3]. Eine Episode bei Thukydides (8,9) berührt den Festfrieden der I. Den Siegern wurden Kränze verliehen, anfangs aus Pinienzweigen, später aus Sellerie [4]. Die Wettkampfsieger (Isthmioniken) aus Athen erhielten 100 Drachmen (Plut. Solon 91b; Diog. Laert. 1,55) von ihrer Heimatstadt, gegenüber 500 Drachmen, die man dort für einen Olympiasieg auszahlte. In jüngerer Zeit kamen mit den Namen von Athleten beschriftete Bleiplättchen ans Tageslicht, mit denen Kampfrichter ihr Urteil in der Frage der Einteilung in Altersklassen abgaben [5; 6]. Von großer Bed. ist die noch *in situ* befindliche Startanlage (Hysplex) des archa. Stadions in Form eines gleichschenkligen Dreiecks, die eine kontrollierte Startfreigabe für 16 Läufer ermöglichte. Sie wurde von einem zentral postierten Starter ausgelöst, der durch Ösen geführte Seilzüge bewegen konnte und den gleichzeitigen Fall von hölzernen Startschranken bewirkte [7]. In hell. Zeit wurde ein neues Stadion errichtet [7. 32 f.]. Der Hippodrom wird ca. 2 km westlich vom Heiligtum vermutet [8].

Unter den berühmten Athleten, die bei den I. an den Start gingen, verdienen Milon [9. Nr. 122] und Theogenes [9. Nr. 201; 2. Nr. 37] mit je 10 Siegen bes. Erwähnung, aber auch Kleitomachos [9. Nr. 584] erregte mit drei Erfolgen in den Kampfsportarten an einem Tage Aufsehen. Vor Ort haben sich agonistische Inschr. [10; 11], jedoch keine Siegerstatuen erhalten.

1 E. R. GEBHARD, The Early Stadium at Isthmia and the Founding of the Isthmian Games, in: W. COULSON, H. KYRIELEIS (Hrsg.), Proc. of an International Symposium on the Olympic Games, 5–9 September 1988, 1992, 73–79 **2** J. EBERT, Epigramme auf Sieger an gymnischen und hippischen Agonen, 1972, Nr. 1 **3** I. WEILER, Der Sport bei den Völkern der alten Welt, [2]1988, 131 **4** O. BRONEER, The Isthmian Victory Crown, in: AJA 66, 1962, 259–263 **5** D. R. JORDAN, A. J. S. SPAWFORTH, A New Document from the Isthmian Games, in: Hesperia 51, 1982, 65–68 **6** D. R. JORDAN, Inscribed Lead Tablets from the Games in the Sanctuary of Poseidon, in: Hesperia 63, 1994, 111–126 **7** D. G. ROMANO, Athletics and Mathematics in Archaic Corinth: The Origins of the Greek Stadion, 1993, 24–33 **8** E. R. GEBHARD, The Sanctuary of Poseidon on the Isthmus of Corinth and the Isthmian Games, in: O. TZACHOU-ALEXANDRI (Hrsg.), Mind and Body, 1979, 82–88; bes. 87 **9** L. MORETTI, Olympionikai, 1957 **10** B. D. MERITT, Greek Inscriptions 1896–1927 (Corinth VIII, I) 1931, Nr. 14–18 **11** J. H. KENT, The Inscriptions 1926–1950 (Corinth VIII, III) 1966, 28–31.

W. DECKER, Sport in der griech. Ant., 1995, 52–55 • J. H. KRAUSE, Die Pythien, Nemeen und Isthmien, 1841, Ndr. 1975 • K. SCHNEIDER, s. v. I., RE 9, 2248–2255.

W.D.

Isthmos (Ἰσθμός, ὁ oder ἡ) meint zunächst grundsätzlich jedes Verbindungsglied zw. zwei Dingen (so z. B. den Hals, Plat. Tim. 69e); im engeren Sinne jeden Landstreifen zw. zwei Meeren, so z. B. die thrak. Chersonesos [1] (Hdt. 6,36), bes. aber den I. von Korinthos (z. B. Hdt. 8,40; Thuk. 1,13,5; 108,2; 2,9,2; 10,3).

Dieser I. entspricht der grundsätzlichen Definition in doppelter Hinsicht – er verbindet einerseits den Korinth. Golf mit dem Saron. Golf, andererseits Mittelgriechenland mit der Peloponnesos. Der I. von Korinthos besteht aus stark verworfenen Schichten neogener Mergel und Sanden mit alluvialen Anlandungen, ist quellen- und bachlos und an seiner schmalsten Stelle etwa 6 km breit, bis zu 80 m hoch und Durchgangsgebiet wichtiger Verkehrswege (h. Auto- und Eisenbahn). Schon in der Ant. ist der Versuch, den I. mit einem Kanal zu durchstechen, mehrfach vergeblich unternommen worden, so von Periandros (Diog. Laert. 1,7,99), Demetrios [2] Poliorketes (Strab. 1,3,11), Caesar (Plut. Caesar 58,4), Caligula (Suet. Cal. 21), Nero (Suet. Nero 19; einziger bis zum Baubeginn gediehener Plan, dessen zahlreiche Spuren aber durch den modernen Kanalbau 1881–1893 verdeckt worden sind) und Herodes Atticus (Philostr. soph. 2,6). Stattdessen diente zur Überleitung von Schiffen vom westl. in den östl. Golf der Anf. 6. Jh. v. Chr. angelegte Diolkos, eine Rillenschleifbahn, auf der man kleinere Schiffe über den I. zog (Thuk. 3,15,1; 8,7; 8,8,3; Aristoph. Thesm. 647 f.; Pol. 4,19,7 ff.; 5,101,4; Strab. 8,2,1; Plin. nat. 4,10; Cass. Dio 51,5,2); er war bis 883 n. Chr. in Benutzung. Längere Strecken dieses Diolkos sind an seinem Westende freigelegt [1. 2259 f.; 2; 3; 4].

Schon in spätmyk. Zeit wurde der I. durch eine Mauer gegen den Durchzug von Norden nach Süden gesperrt (vgl. Hdt. 9,26 f.). Am bekanntesten ist die Befestigung von 480 v. Chr. zur Abwehr der Perser (Hdt. 8,40,2; 71; 9,7; Diod. 11,16,3), die bis in die Neuzeit mehrfach erneuert wurde. Was davon h. noch zu sehen ist, stammt aus iustinianischer Zeit (Prok. aed. 4,2,27 f.;

IG IV 204f.). Südl. vom Ostende des h. Kanals hat man Reste des Heiligtums des Isthmischen Poseidon (7./5. Jh. und spätere Bauten) und des Palaimon, Theater, Stadion, Thermen und weitere Bauten ausgegraben (IG IV 203). 390 v. Chr. besetzte → Agesilaos [2] das Heiligtum; bei dieser Gelegenheit ging der Tempel in Flammen auf (Xen. hell. 4,5,1 ff.). Im Stadion wurde 196 v. Chr. bei den Isthmischen Spielen (→ Isthmia) die »Freiheit der Griechenstädte« durch T. Quinctius Flamininus verkündet (Pol. 18,46,4ff.; Liv. 33,32; Plut. Titus Quinctius Flamininus 10,3 ff.; App. Mac. 9,4). Intensive Bautätigkeit in der röm. Kaiserzeit ist belegt (Strab. 8,6,4; 6,22; Paus. 2,1,5–2,2; Plin. nat. 4,9f.).

1 D. Fimmen, s. v. I. (2), RE 9, 2256–2265 2 E. Meyer, s. v. Diolkos (2), RE Suppl. 11, 534 3 N. M. Verdelis, Der Diolkos am I. von Korinth, in: MDAI(A) 71, 1956, 51 ff.; 1958, 140ff. 4 G. Raepsaet, M. Tolley, Le diolkos de l'Isthme à Corinthe, in: BCH 117/1, 1993, 233–261.

O. Broneer, s. v. Isthmia, PE, 417f. • Ders., s. v. Isthmus of Corinth, PE, 418f. • B. v. Freyberg, Geologie des I. von Korinth, 1973 • A. Philippson, Der I. von Korinth, in: Zschr. der Ges. für Erdkunde 25, 1890, 1 ff. • Philippson/Kirsten 3, 71 ff.

C. L. u. E. O.

Istros

[1] (Ἴστρος). Bei Steph. Byz. s. v. I. bezeugte Insel mit gleichnamiger Stadt vor dem Vorgebirge Triopion (Deveboynu Burnu bzw. Kıriyo Burnu) bei Knidos. E. O.

[2] (ὁ Ἴστρος, *Hister*, *Danuvius*, *Danubius*, Δάνυβις, h. Donau). Nach Apoll. Rhod. 4 sollen die → Argonautai (mit Karte zur Argonautenfahrt) vom Schwarzen Meer über den I. und seine Nebenflüsse zurückgekehrt sein, um zum *mare Adriaticum* zu gelangen. Hdt. 4,33 beschreibt wohl denselben Weg, den die → Hyperboreioi von Skythia aus nach Dodona zurücklegten. Lange Zeit kannten die Griechen vornehmlich den Unterlauf des I. Hdt. 4,48f. beschreibt den I. als den bedeutendsten der ihm bekannten Flüsse und lokalisiert seine Quelle im Land der Kelten. Er nennt viele seiner Nebenflüsse, v. a. die südlichen Save-abwärts (Hdt. 2,33). Dem Feldzug des → Dareios [2] gegen die Skythen von 512 v. Chr. war es zu verdanken, daß der Unterlauf des I. besser bekannt wurde: Die Ioner errichteten oberhalb des Deltas eine Ponton-Brücke über den I. (Hdt. 4,89). Die griech. Kolonien am Schwarzen Meer (besonders Histria-Istros, Tomis, Kallatis) profitierten vom Handel, der im unteren Flußtal betrieben wurde. Die maked. Könige Philippos II. und sein Sohn Alexandros d.Gr. unternahmen Feldzüge durch Thrakia bis zum rechten I.-Ufer, ohne daß es ihnen gelang, die thrak. Bevölkerung dauerhaft zu unterwerfen. Pol. 4,41 f. erwähnt den I. nur im Zusammenhang mit Schwemmlandbildungen im Deltabereich.

Tiberius entdeckte 15 v. Chr. die Quellen des I., nach Strab. 7,1,5 einen Tagesmarsch nördl. des Bodensees. Strab. l.c. unterscheidet zw. dem Abschnitt des I. von der Quelle bis zum »Eisernen Tor« und dem Unterlauf des I. 45 n. Chr. annektierte Claudius Thrakia und weitete die Prov. Moesia bis zur Flußmündung aus, was Rom in die Lage versetzte, den Lauf des I. mit Hilfe der Prov. Noricum, Pannonia und Moesia von der Quelle bis zur Mündung zu kontrollieren. Der I. war jedoch schon bald eine durchlässige Grenze: Strab. 7,3,10 berichtet von der Ansiedlung von 50000 Getae von jenseits des I. durch Aelius [II 7] in Thrakia z.Z. des Augustus. Unter Nero ließ der Legat von Moesia, Plautius Silvanus, 100000 Männer und Frauen (Roxolani, Bastarnae) die Donau passieren; andere Überquerungen waren bedrohlicher, z. B. die der Sarmatae 67–69 n. Chr. Unter Vespasianus wurde eine Reihe von Lagern entlang des I. errichtet, aus denen später der Limes entstand. Die *classis Moesica*, in → Noviodunum am Westende des Deltas stationiert, und die *classis Pannonica* in Taurunum nahe dem Zusammenfluß von I. und Save sicherten die Flußgrenze. Dacia unter → Decebalus stellte eine ständige Gefahr für das Reich dar: 101 begann Traianus seinen Feldzug gegen ihn, und sein Königreich nördl. des I. wurde 106 röm. Prov.

E. 2. Jh. überschritten Quadi und Marcomanni den I.; sie durchzogen 167 Noricum und Pannonia; 174 kämpfte Marcus Aurelius gegen die Sarmate, wodurch der I. seine Funktion als Grenze wiedergewann. Seit Mitte 3. Jh. erfolgte eine Goteninvasion in Griechenland und Kleinasien, der erst Constantinus 332 erfolgreich entgegentreten konnte. Seit 375 konnte die I.-Grenze den Westgoten nicht mehr standhalten; Valens wurde in der Schlacht von Adrianopolis 378 besiegt und getötet.

J. Wilkes, Les provinces danubiennes, in: Rome et l'intégration de l'Empire, 44 av. J.-C.–260 ap. J.-C. 2, in: Nouvelle Clio, 1998, LIII-LVII und 231–297.

PI. CA./Ü: S. F.

[3] (Ἴστρος, Ἰστρίη, Ἰστρόπολις, *Histria*, *Histropolis*). Griech. Kolonie an der westl. Schwarzmeerküste südl. der Donaumündung, h. Caranasuf (Caranasif), Kreis Constanţa/Rumänien. I. wurde von Milesiern im letzten Drittel des 7. Jh. v. Chr. gegr. Im Laufe des 6. Jh. entwickelte sich I. zu einer bed. Hafenstadt, die in regen Handelsbeziehungen mit Miletos, Rhodos, Samos, Korinthos und bes. Athen stand. Um 512 unterlag I. Dareios I. auf seinem Skythenfeldzug. Der Verlauf der Perserkriege hatte eine Stärkung des athen. Einflusses auf die westpontischen Städte zur Folge. Im 5. Jh. wurde die Stadt in großem Stil ausgebaut. Zu E. des 5. Jh. wurden hier Silbermz. geprägt. Damals verstärkte sich in der Umgebung der Stadt die Macht der thrak. Odrysai, die sich bemühten, ihren Einfluß auch über I. auszuweiten. Seit Anf. 4. Jh. gewannen in Scythia Minor die Skythai an Macht; sie waren aber bald einem steigendem Druck der Makedones ausgesetzt. Philippos II. besiegte zwar die Skythai, mußte jedoch darauf verzichten, sich die westpontischen Städte zu unterwerfen. Die Makedones setzten sich hier erst unter Alexandros durch und festigten sich unter Lysimachos (Diod. 29,73). Nach dem Tode des Lysimachos gewannen die westpontischen

Städte ihre Selbständigkeit zurück. Im J. 260 unterstützte I. die damals mächtigste westpontische Stadt Kallatis in ihrem Kampf gegen Byzantion. In der Folge war I. einem immer stärkeren Druck der benachbarten einheimischen Stämme ausgesetzt, die sich auch innerhalb der Stadt ansiedelten. Im 2. Jh. wurde I. von den → Bastarnae angegriffen. Nach der Niederlage Mithradates' VI., der seinen Einfluss bis I. ausgedehnt hatte, machte sich seit 72 v. Chr. die röm. Macht auch an der westpontischen Küste geltend. Um 50 v. Chr. hatte die Stadt unter den Angriffen des Dakers → Burebista schwer zu leiden, der sich für kurze Zeit I. bemächtigte. Über die Gesch. der Stadt unter röm. Herrschaft ist wenig bekannt. I. gehörte zum westpontischen Städtebund (κοινόν) und scheint Anf. 3. Jh. noch eine Blütezeit erlebt zu haben. Autonome Münzprägung ist noch unter → Gordianus [3] III. bezeugt. Mitte 3. Jh. n. Chr. wurde die Stadt von den Goti gebrandschatzt, im ausgehenden 6. Jh. von avaro-slavischen Stämmen zerstört. Anf. des 7. Jh. wurde die Siedlung verlassen.

Im rel. Leben des ant. I. spielte der Kult von Apollon, Zeus, Helios, Dionysios, Demeter, Dioskuren, Kabeiroi und Hermes eine Rolle. Gebäudereste (Thermen, Basilika), Stadtbefestigungen, Straßen und Nekropolen sind erh., ferner zahlreiche Inschr. und Münzfunde.

C. Danoff, s. v. Pontos Euxeinos, RE Suppl. 9, 1082 ff. • T. W. Blawatskaja, Westpontische Städte im 7.–1. Jh. v. Chr., 1952 (russisch) • D. M. Pippidi, Epigraph. Beitr. zur Gesch. Histrias in hell. und röm. Zeit, 1961 • TIR L 35 Bucarest, 1969, 45 f. (Quellen und Lit.). J. BU.

[4] Schüler des → Kallimachos (»Der Kallimacheer«) unbestimmter Herkunft, verfaßte ca. Mitte des 3. Jh. v. Chr. in Alexandreia mit Hilfe der dortigen Bibliothek zahlreiche Schriften vorwiegend histor.-antiquar. Inhalts. Sie sind nur fragmentarisch erh. und werden vornehmlich von Plutarch, Pausanias und den Lexikographen zitiert. Sein Hauptwerk, eine ›Zusammenstellung der Atthiden‹ in mind. 14 B., beruhte größtenteils nicht auf eigener krit. Forschung, sondern enthielt eine vergleichende Zusammenstellung der Überlieferungen zur Gesch. Athens und Attikas. Ähnlich hat man sich die *Argoliká* und die *Eliaká* in mind. 5 B. vorzustellen. Weitere Schriften galten dem alten Ägypten (z. B. ›Äg. Kolonien‹), religionsgesch. Fragen (›Erscheinungen Apollons‹, ›Erscheinungen des Herakles‹, ›Zusammenstellung der kretischen Opfer‹) und biograph. Themen (›Über lyrische Dichter‹); wieder andere betrafen gramm. bzw. lexikograph. Probleme (›Attische Wörter‹, ›Vermischtes‹, ›Ungeordnetes‹). In den ›Entgegnungen auf Timaios‹ warf er diesem Historiker zahlreiche Irrtümer vor und bezeichnete ihn wegen seiner maßlosen Polemiken geistreich als *Epitímaios* (»Ehrabschneider«). FGrH 334 (mit Komm.).

F. Jacoby, s. v. I., RE 9, 2270–2282 = Ders., Griech. Historiker, 1956, 305–311 • K. Meister, Die griech. Geschichtsschreibung, 1990, 130. K. MEI.

Isuwa (Išuwa). Name einer anatolischen Landschaft in hethit. und assyr. Quellen des 15.–9. Jh. v. Chr. I. lag zwischen Euphrat und Tigris im Bereich des Murat su, Zentrum war die Ebene von Elazığ (Arsanias, h. Keban-See).

I. wird zuerst in Texten des hethit. Königs Tudḫaliya I./II. (spätes 15. Jh.) erwähnt, war aber schon früher zw. dem hethit. Reich und dem obermesopot. → Mittani-Reich umstritten. Texte dieser Zeit nennen »Älteste von I.« und berichten über die Flucht ganzer Dorfgemeinschaften aus I. Tudḫaliya I./II. eroberte I., Tudḫaliya III. verlor es; sein Sohn Šuppiluliuma nahm es Mitte des 14. Jh. wieder ein. Unter der hethit. Herrschaft wurde I. spätestens um 1250 ein Königreich, dessen Herrscher (Ari-šarruma, Eḫli-šarruma) wohl der hethit. Königsfamilie entstammten. Nach dem Ende des Hethiterreichs (um 1190) eroberte der assyr. König Tiglatpilesar I. (1114–1077) »Enzata im Lande I.«. Die letzte Erwähnung findet sich in einer Inschr. Salmanassars III. (858–824 v. Chr.).

H. Klengel, s. v. I., RLA 4, 214–216. GE. W.

Isyllos (Ἴσυλλος) aus Epidauros, Sohn des Sokrates. Um 300 v. Chr. Dichter einer fortlaufenden Folge von inschr. erh. Gedichten (in trochäischen Tetrametern, daktylischen Hexametern, Ionikern, elegischen Distichen) für den → Asklepios-Kult von → Epidauros (IG IV 1^2 128 = [1. 380–383]). In ihnen schafft I. einerseits eine spezifisch epidaurische Asklepiosmyth., die die Wurzeln des Gottes an den Ort des seit dem 5. Jh. v. Chr. aufstrebenden Heilheiligtums verlegt: Während der traditionelle Mythos in Thessalien spielt (Koronis, die Tochter des Königs Phlegyas von Trikka in Thessalien, wird von Apollon schwanger, betrügt den Gott und wird von ihm getötet. Das Kind wird vom göttlichen Vater gerettet und vom Kentauren Cheiron zum Arzt erzogen: so Hom. h. 16; Pind. P. 3 etc.), gibt bei I. Zeus die Muse Erato dem Malos zur Frau; deren Tochter Kleophema heiratet Phlegyas, der in Epidauros wohnt; deren Tochter Aigle, genannt Koronis, wird von Apollon verführt und gebiert den Asklepios im Heiligtum von Epidauros. Damit ist der Asklepios-Kult eng an Epidauros und den dortigen Kult des Apollon Maleatas geknüpft [2]. Andererseits stellt I. eine enge polit. Bindung zu Sparta her: Apollon Maleatas habe Sparta vor Philipp von Makedonien gerettet. I.' Hauptwerk, der → Paian an Asklepios, weist strukturelle Ähnlichkeiten mit dem → Erythräischen Paian sowie dem Paian des → Makedonios auf [1. 200–206; 382].

1 L. Käppel, Paian, 1992 2 R. A. Tomlinson, Epidauros, 1983, 13–15.

U. v. Wilamowitz-Moellendorff, I. von Epidauros (Philol. Unt. 9), 1886 • E. J. und L. Edelstein, Asclepius, 2 Bde., 1945. L. K.

Itala s. Bibelübersetzungen

Italia

I. Geographie und Geschichte II. Religion

I. Geographie und Geschichte

A. Der Name und seine Entwicklung
B. Geographie C. Naturprodukte
D. Vorrömische Völker E. Romanisierung
F. Italia seit Augustus G. Spätantike und byzantinische Zeit

A. Der Name und seine Entwicklung

In augusteischer Zeit erlangte der Name I. seine h. Bed., während er urspr. das auf die bruttische Halbinsel von Sila bis Skylletion beschränkte Reich des oenotrischen Fürsten Italos bezeichnete (Antiochos FGrH 555 F 5; nach Hekat. FGrH 1 F 41,51–53 liegen Medma, Locris, Caulonia und Krotalla in I.). Hellanikos bringt I. mit dem Wort *vitulus* (»Kalb«) und der Sage vom dem Herakles entflohenen Kalb des → Geryoneus in Zusammenhang (Dion. Hal. ant. 1,35), Timaios mit dem Reichtum an Rindern in dieser Gegend (Gell. 11,1; vgl. Fest. 94 s. v. I.); daher prägten die Italiker im → Bundesgenossenkrieg [3] (90–88 v. Chr.) Mz. mit dem Bild eines Kalbs und der Legende *Viteliu*. Die Verbreitung des Namens I. hängt mit der griech. Kolonisation und der pythagoreischen Schule zusammen, die von → Kroton nach → Metapontum wechselte. In der 2. H. 5. Jh. bezeichnete I. die Halbinsel im Westen bis zum Fluß → Laus im Gebiet der Opici und im Osten bis zum Bradanus im Gebiet der → Iapyges (Thuk. 7,33,4; Antiochos FGrH 555 F 3) [1; 2; 3]. Im 4. Jh. umschloß er mit dem Italiotischen Bund Tarentum und Poseidonia (Dion. Hal. ant. 1,73,4). 306 garantierte der Vertrag mit Karthago Rom den herrschenden Einfluß in I.; im 3. Jh. herrschte bei den Griechen inzwischen eine einheitliche geogr. Vorstellung von I., das bis zu den Alpen reichte (Pol. 1,6,2; Strab. 5,3,5; [4; 5]); I. war aber immer noch ein Gemisch aus verschiedenen Völkern und Sprachen, welches Rom ebenso wie die Institutionen zw. dem 3. und 1. Jh. zu vereinheitlichen suchte. Für Cato sind die Alpen die Mauer von I. (fr. 85); in seinen *Origines* behandelt er alle Völker von den Alpen bis nach Sizilien. Polit. allerdings umfaßte I. nur die Halbinsel (bis zum → Aesis), deren Bewohner im J. 89 v. Chr. das Bürgerrecht erhielten; 81 verlegte Sulla die Grenze nach Norden an den Arnus und den Rubico. Das Bürgerrecht wurde 49 auf die Transpadani ausgeweitet (Cass. Dio 41,36), jedoch bestand die Prov. *Gallia Cisalpina* bis 43 weiter (Cic. Phil. 3,4,5). Seit 42 reichte I. vom Varus bis zum Formio und in spätaugusteischer Zeit bis zum Arsia. Somit war die polit. Einheit des ›schönen Landes, vom Appennin geteilt, vom Meer und den Alpen umschlossen‹ (Petrarca), vollendet. Die ethnischen Einheiten sind die *Itali* im Gegensatz zu den *Italiotai* gen. griech. Kolonisten und *Italici* im Gegensatz zu den Römern. In der Dichtung finden sich archaisierende Bezeichnungen für I.: *Hesperia*, *Ausonia*, *Opicia*, *Oinotria* (Hekataios, Antiochos) [6]; *Saturnia tellus* ist anfangs auf Latium beschränkt.

B. Geographie

I. ist eine im wesentlichen gebirgige Landschaft mit kleinen Ebenen, abgesehen von der Poebene.

1) Vulkanische Erscheinungen

Colli Albani, Pithecusa (Ausbruch nach der Kolonisation, Timaios FGrH 566 F 58), Vesuvius (Ausbruch von 79 n. Chr.), Aitne, Stromboli; Nutzbarmachung von Thermalquellen. Häufige Erdbeben, Bradyseismos, hydrographische Veränderungen und Änderungen im Küstenverlauf.

2) Gebirge

Die Alpes, von Westen nach Osten: Maritimae (mit *tropaea Augusti* bei Monaco und dem *mons Caenia*), Cottiae (*mons Vaesulus*; Paß des *mons Matrona*), Graiae (Paß des Kleinen St. Bernhard), Poeninae (Paß des Großen St. Bernhard, Poeninus), Carnicae, Iuliae (*mons Ocra*). Appenninus, von Norden nach Süden: *mons Auginus*; Tetrica, Fiscellus, Ceraunii und Tifernus in Samnium; Taburnus, Voltur, Alburnus, Sila bis zum *promonturium* von Leukopetra.

3) Meere, Küsten und Inseln

Mare Adriaticum bzw. *Superum* mit dem *mons Garganus*; *mare Ionium* mit dem *promonturium Iapygium*, dem *sinus Cocynthum*, dem *promonturium Zephyrium* und dem *fretum Siculum*; Sizilien und die umliegenden Inseln (Aeoliae oder Liparaeae; Aegusae oder Aegates: Cossura, Melita und Gaulos); *mare Tyrrhenum*, *Tuscum* oder *Inferum* mit dem *sinus Terinaeus*, *sinus Laus*, *sinus Paestanus*, dem *promonturium Minervae* und der Insel Capreae, dem *sinus Puteolanus* und der Insel Aenaria; *sinus Formianus*, *sinus Amyclanus*, *promonturium Circei* und Insel Pontia, *mons Argentarius* und den Inseln Igilium und Dianium, das *promonturium* von Populonia, die Inseln Elba, Corsica und Sardinia, *mare Ligusticum* mit *portus Lunae*.

4) Zuflüsse zum mare Adriaticum

Der von Turin bis zum Meer schiffbare Padus, der am *mons Vesulus* entspringt, aufgefüllt durch seine in den Alpes entspringenden linken Nebenflüsse: Duria minor, Stura, Orgus, Duria maior, Sesites, Ticinus, Lambrus, Addua, Sarius, Ollius (mit Mella und Clesis), Mincius, Tartarus; seine im Appenninus entspringenden rechten Nebenflüsse: Tanarus (mit Stura), Trebia, Nure, Tarus, Parma, Incia, Secia, Scultenna, Rhenus, Idex, Silarus, Vatrenus. Venetische Flüsse alpinen Ursprungs im Norden des Padus: Athesis (schiffbar), Meduacus, Plavis, Liquentia, Tiliaventus, Natiso, Isontius (mit dem Frigidus), Formio, Ningus, Arsia. Im Süden des Padus die kleinen Flüsse appenninischen Ursprungs Rubico, Ariminus, Pisaurus, Metaurus, Aesis, Flusor, Cluentus, Tinna, Truentus, Vomanus, Aternus, Sagrus, Trinius, Tifernus, Frento, Aquilo, Cerbalus, Aufidus.

5) Zuflüsse zum *mare Ionium*

Galesus, Bradanus, Casuentus, Acalandrus, Aciris, Siris, Sybaris, Crathis, Trais, Naethus, Sagras.

6) Zuflüsse zum mare Tyrrhenum

Sabatus, Laus, Silarus (mit Calor und Tanager), Sarnus, Volturnus (mit Calor und Tamarus), Savo, Liris (mit Trerus und Melpis), Amasenus, Astura, Numicius,

Tiberis (mind. bis Castellum Amerinum schiffbar; mit seinen Zuflüssen Anio, Cremera, Fabaris, Nar, Pallia, Clanis, Tinia), Minio, Marta, Arminia, Albinia, Umbro, Caecina, Arnus (schiffbar), Auser, Macra; in Liguria die kleinen Flüsse Entella, Tavia, Rutuba und Varus.

7) Seen (lacus)

In den Alpen: Verbanus, Ceresius, Larius, Sebinus, Benacus. In Etruria: Trasimenus, Volsiniensis, Ciminius, Sabatinus. In Latium: die kleinen Seen Regillus, Albanus, Nemorensis. Im Gebiet der Marsi: Fucinus. Größere Lagunen sind die *VII maria* in Venetia. Die Malaria muß ein der Urbarmachung und der Besiedlung entgegenstehendes endemisches Phänomen gewesen sein, vgl. die Interpretation von Graviscae, den Pomptinischen Sümpfen (*paludes Pomptinae*) oder der Maremma (Plin. epist. 5,6) [7].

C. Naturprodukte

Einige bekannte Naturprodukte (Marmor aus den ligur. Alpen im Gebiet der Apuani, Pozzolanerde, Alaun, Salz) und landwirtschaftliche Erzeugnisse, vermehrt durch Urbarmachung, Centuriationen und intensive Bebauung (Übergang von Getreide zum Oliven- und Weinanbau); Viehzucht, auch Transhumanz, zur Versorgung von Märkten und Messen. Das Land wurde in den lit. Quellen als bes. fruchtbar gepriesen (bei Varro rust. 1,2,6; Verg. georg. 2,136–176; Dion. Hal. ant. 1,36f.; Strab. 6,4,1; Plin. nat. 3,39–42; 60; 37,13; 77) [8; 9].

D. Vorrömische Völker

(Ohne Berücksichtigung der prähistor. Kulturen [10; 11; 12]). Ungeachtet der großen, an das → *ver sacrum* gebundenen Mobilität sind zu unterscheiden: die weitläufig über die westl. Alpes, den nördl. Appenninus und die Gallia Narbonensis verteilten Ligures; Euganei und Veneti nördl. des Padus (Zentren Ateste und Patavium mit der Atestina-Kultur und venet. Inschr.); → Etrusci, die sich zw. Tiberis und Arnus niedergelassen hatten und dann nach Campania und in die Cisalpina vordrangen (mit bildender Kunst eigener Prägung und reichem inschr. Material); Umbri, früher weiter zw. Padus und Tiberis (von ihrer Sprache zeugen die → *Tabulae Iguvinae*), Picentes im Picenum (Stele von Novilara), Falisci (→ Faliskisch) um den Soracte; Latini um den *mons Albanus*, deren Sprache (→ Latein) sich im Zuge der röm. Eroberungen durchsetzte; Samnites (Sabini), Vestini, Paeligni, Marrucini, Aequi und Aequiculi, Marsi, Hernici, Carricini, Pentri, Hirpini im bergigen Innern, Ausones (Aurunci), Oinotres, Opici, ferner die Osci in Campania (→ Oskisch-Umbrisch); Lucani und Bruttii im äußersten Süden; Iapyges (Hekataios), Daunii, Peucetii und Messapii illyr. Ursprungs (messap. Inschr., → Messapisch) in Apulia. Bezeichnungen wie *Megálē Hellás* (Μεγάλη Ἑλλάς) oder → *Magna Graecia* spiegeln die im 8. Jh. einsetzende Kolonisation wieder, die Begriffe selbst scheinen aber nur polit. Tendenzen des 4. Jh. zu entsprechen [13; 14]. Die → Gallia Cisalpina bildete sich während der Kelteninvasion im 5.–4. Jh. v. Chr. heraus, der Begriff aber setzte sich erst mit der Einrichtung der röm. Prov. durch; in den Tälern der Alpes repräsentieren die Raeti den Rest der etrusk. Okkupation.

E. Romanisierung

I. ist das Ergebnis eines Romanisierungsprozesses verschiedener Völker durch Bündnis oder Eroberung (vgl. Begriffe wie *socii, civitates sine suffragio* oder auch *ager publicus populi Romani* und *coloniae maritimae* [15] und *Latinae*). Die Römer bewirkten die Errichtung eines leistungsfähigen Straßensystems, die Massendeportation (→ Verschleppung) von Völkerschaften, die Umsiedlung von Bergbewohnern in die Täler und von auf Anhöhen gelegenen Ortschaften in die Ebene, das Phänomen der Verstädterung in großem Ausmaß und die städtebauliche Neuordnung im 2. und 1. Jh., die Gewährung des Bürgerrechts an die *municipia Italicorum*, die Ausdehnung des Bürgerrechts auf die Gallia Cisalpina und Transalpina.

F. Italia seit Augustus

Augustus verdanken wir die *discriptio totius Italiae* in 11 *regiones*, gestützt auf die vorröm. Völker, aufgezeichnet in einer Karte, von Süden nach Norden voranschreitend (Süden oben), versehen mit laufenden Nummern (die Namen der Regionen setzten sich erst später durch). Für jede Region unterschied man *coloniae* und *municipia*, in alphabetischer Reihenfolge, möglicherweise aus praktischen Anforderungen zur Archivierung von Censusdaten, ohne direkten Nutzen für die Administration (Plin. nat. 3,46). Für die Rechtsverwaltung führte Hadrianus vier *consulares* ein; dagegen verfügte man von Marcus Aurelius bis zu Aurelianus über Gerichtsbezirke mit Richtern [16; 17; 18]; es gab einen einzigen *corrector* in I. Im J. 297 n. Chr. leitete Diocletianus die Provinzialisierung von I. ein; Rom war nicht mehr Hauptstadt, I. eine der 12 *dioeceses* des Reiches, aufgeteilt in zwei *partes* (*annonaria* im Norden, *suburbicaria* im Süden) und 12 Provinzen: Venetia et Histria, Aemilia et Liguria, Alpes Cottiae, Flaminia et Picenum, Tuscia et Umbria, Campania et Samnium, Apulia et Calabria, Lucania et Bruttii, Corsica, Sardinia, Sicilia, Raetia. Im 4. Jh. wurden daraus 17: Venetia et Histria, Aemilia, Liguria, Flaminia et Picenum annonarium, Alpes Cottiae, Raetia I, Raetia II, Tuscia et Umbria, Campania, Samnium, Apulia et Calabria, Lucania et Bruttii, Picenum suburbicarium, Valeria, Sardinia, Corsica, Sicilia.

Beschreibung von I. nach den Regionen des Augustus:

Regio I: Latium et Campania vom Tiberis zum Silarus; man unterscheidet *Latium vetus* bis zum *promonturium Circei* und *Latium adiectum* bis zum *mons Massicus*; Haupthafen Puteoli, später Militärhafen Misenum und Handelshafen Ostia; Rom drängte nach und nach die anderen Zentren in den Hintergrund, viele verschwanden; in Campania Cumae und das gegenüberliegende Pithecusa, die Metropole Capua im Zentrum eines unermeßlich reichen Landes, das eine an astronomischen Gegebenheiten orientierte Centuriation besaß; Nola, die Häfen von Neapolis und Salernum.

Regio II: Apulia, Calabria, Sallentini, Hirpini: Es handelte sich dabei ungefähr um das h. Apulien vom Tifernus bis zum Bradanus mit der Halbinsel Sallentina und dem *mons Garganus*; in Daunia die Kolonie Luceria; in Hirpinum die Kolonie Beneventum; in Peucetia die Häfen Barium und Egnathia, im Landesinnern Canusium und Venusia; in Calabria die Metropole Taras-Tarentum und die Kolonie Brundisium, Endpunkt der *via Appia* und der *via Traiana* sowie Hafen für den Orient.

Regio III: Lucani et Bruttii; h. Basilicata und Calabria vom Silarus bis zum Bradanus; griechische Kolonien am *mare Tyrrhenum* waren Poseidonia-Paestum, Elea-Velia, Pyxus-Buxentum, Laos, Terina, Hipponion-Vibo Valentia, Medma; am *fretum Siculum* Rhegium; am *mare Ionium* Locri, Caulonia, Croton, Crimisa, Sybaris-Thurii-Copia, Siris-Heraclea, Metapontum. In röm. Zeit Niedergang, außer Rhegium und Croton und im Landesinnern Potentia, Grumentum, Consentia.

Regio IV: Samnites, Sabini, Marsi, Vestini, Paeligni, Marrucini, Frentani; im Apenninus vom Tiberis zum Volturnus, am *mare Adriaticum* vom Salinus zum Tifernus; als Häfen dienten Ostia Aterni, Hortona, Histonium; Städte der Sabini waren Reate und Nursia, der Marrucini Teate, der Paeligni Corfinium, der Pentri Bovianum; bei den Aequiculi die Kolonie Alba Fucens am *lacus Fucinus*.

Regio V: Piceni et Praetuttii, entlang dem *mare Adriaticum* vom Aesis zum Salinus und im Landesinnern bis zum Appenninus (Tetrica, Fiscellus); Haupthafen Ancona, im Landesinnern Auximum, Firmum, Asculum und Interamna. Endpunkt der *via Salaria* und der *via Caecilia*.

Regio VI: Umbria et ager Gallicus; von Pisaurum zum Aesis am *mare Adriaticum* und im Appenninus vom Arnus bis zum Tiberis und Nar; Städte: Interamnia Nahars, Carsulae, Ameria, Spoletium, Camerinum, Sassina und an der See Pisaurum, Fanum Fortunae, Sena Gallica.

Regio VII: Etruria; vom Macra zum Tiberis und bis zum Appenninus; die Städte Caere, Veii, Tarquinii, Volci, Volsinii, Rusellae, Vetulonia, Volaterrae, Clusium, Perusia, Cortona, Faesulae waren zum Teil verfallen. Röm. Kolonien bei den Häfen Cosa und Luna; Pisae, Florentia und Arretium am Arnus und Kolonie latinischen Rechts Luca am Auser. Durchquert von den *viae Cassia, Clodia* und *Aurelia*.

Regio VIII: Gallia Cispadana, deren Name Aemilia von der gleichnamigen Straße stammt, die sie auf ganzer Länge von Ariminum bis Placentia durchquerte, flankiert durch reiche, centurierte Territorien; vom Appenninus bis zum Padus. Etrusk. Zeit: Felsina, Spina, Marzabotto. Röm. Kolonien waren Ariminum, Placentia und Bononia. Ravenna war Stützpunkt der *classis praetoria* seit Augustus und Verwaltungszentrum seit 403.

Regio IX: Liguria; vom Varus zum Macra, vom Appenninus bis zum Padus; Genua war Haupthafen; im Landesinnern Dertona, Verkehrsknotenpunkt der *via Postumia* und der *via Iulia Augusta*.

Regio X: Venetia, Carni et Histri; vom Padus bis zu den Alpes, vom Ollius bis zum Arsia; bed. Häfen in chronologischer Folge waren Adria, Altinum und Aquileia; Verona und Tridentum am Athesis; Kolonie Cremona und Hostilia am Padus, Brixia am Mella, Mantua am Mincius, Patavium am Meduacus. Ausgedehnte centurierte Territorien; Straßen über die Alpes (*via Iulia, via Claudia Augusta*), *fossae* in den *VII maria*.

Regio XI: Gallia Transpadana; vom Padus bis zu den Alpes Graiae et Poeninae und dem Ollius; Hauptzentren: Ticinum, Augusta Taurinorum und Augusta Praetoria, an den Straßen nach Gallien Comum, Mediolanum, letzteres Verwaltungszentrum von 286 bis 402 n. Chr.

Inschr. Belege zu I.: CIL I; IV; IX–XI; XIV; XV.

1 L. Matteini, L' I. nel Περὶ Ἰταλίας di Antioco, in: Helikon 18/9, 1978/9, 293–300 **2** F. Prontera, Antioco di Siracusa, in: Geographia Antiqua 1, 1992, 109–136 **3** C. Cuscunà, Quale I. per Antioco?, in: Kokalos 41, 1995, 63–78 **4** G. De Sanctis, Storia dei Romani 1, 1956, 111 **5** E. Lepore, L' I. nella formazione della comunità romano-italica, in: Klearchos 5, 1963, 89 **6** M. Ameruoso, La visualizzazione geografica di I., in: Miscellanea greca e romana 17, 1992, 65–131 **7** P. Fraccaro, La malaria e la storia dell' I. antica, in: SE 2, 1929, 197ff. **8** Toynbee, Hannibal 2, 373f. **9** Ph. Desy, Grec et Latin en 1991 et 1992, 1994
10 G. Giacomelli, Gli etnici dell' I. antica, 1960
11 M. Cristofani, Etruschi e altre genti nell' I. preromana, 1996 **12** R. Pittioni, Italien. Urgeschichtliche Kulturen, RE Suppl. 9, 105–372 **13** G. Pugliese Carratelli (Hrsg.), Magna Grecia, 1985 **14** D. Musti, Strabone e la Magna Grecia, 1988 **15** E. T. Salmon, The coloniae maritimae, in: Athenaeum 41, 1968, 3–38 **16** R. Thomsen, The Italic Regions, 1947 **17** M. Corbier, Les circonscriptions judiciaires de l' I., in: MEFRA 85, 1973, 2 **18** W. Eck, Die regionale Organisation ital. Iuridikate, in: ZPE 18, 1975, 155–166.

B. Flavio, I. illustrata, 1453 (Romae 1471) (Beginn der topogr. Rekonstruktion des ant. Italien) • L. Alberti, Descrittione di tutta I., 1550 • Ph. Cluverii, I. antiqua, 1624 • L. Holstenii, Adnotationes ad Cluverium, 1666 • H. Kiepert, A Manual of anc. Geography, 1881, 209–256 • K. J. Beloch, Der ital. Bund, 1880 • Nissen • Ruggiero • G. De Sanctis, Storia dei Romani, 1907–1923; 1956–1964 • E. Pais, Storia della colonizzazione di Roma antica, 1923 • Ders., Storia dell' I. antica, 1925 • Carta archeologica d'I., 1927ff. (= Forma Italiae ser. 2) • Forma Italiae, 1928ff. • G. Devoto, Gli antichi Italici, 1929 • ESAR • J. Whatmough, The Prae-Italic Dialects of I., 1933 • Ders., The Foundations of Roman I., 1937 • B. Pace, Arte e civiltà della Sicilia antica, 1935–1949 • E. Wikén, Die Kunde der Hellenen, 1937 • Syme, RR • J. Bérard, La Colonisation grecque, 1941 • T. J. Dunbabin, The Western Greeks, 1948 • E. Sereni, Comunità rurali nell' I. antica, 1955 • P. Fraccaro, Opuscula, 1957 • F. Castagnoli, Le ricerche sui resti della centuriazione, 1958 • EAA[1] • EAA[2] • U. Kahrstedt, Die wirtschaftliche Lage Großgriechenlands in der Kaiserzeit, 1960 • L. R. Taylor, The Voting Districts of the Roman Republic, 1960 • A. Degrassi, Scritti vari di antichità, 1962–1971 • G. Schmiedt, Atlante aerofotografico delle sedi umane in I.,

1964ff. • A.H. TOYNBEE, Hannibal • E.T. SALMON, Roman Colonization under the Republic, 1969 • G.A. MANSUELLI, Popoli e Civiltà dell' I. Antica, 1971ff. • P.A. BRUNT, Italian Manpower, 1971 • W.V. HARRIS, Rome in Etruria and Umbria, 1971 • ANRW II 11.2 • H. GALSTERER, Herrschaft und Verwaltung im republikanischen I., 1976 • C. NICOLET, Les structures de l' I. romaine, 1977 • BTCGI • G. TIBILETTI, Storie locali dell' I. romana, 1978 • W. ECK, Die staatliche Organisation Italiens, 1979 • A. GIARDINA, A. SCHIAVONE, L' I., insediamenti e forme economiche, 1981 • E.T. SALMON, The Making of Roman I., 1982 • R. CHEVALLIER, La Romanisation de la Celtique du Pô, 1983 • L. KEPPIE, Colonisation and Veteran Settlement in I., 1983 • A. KEAVENEY, Rome, 1987 • P. SOMMELLA, I. antica, l'urbanistica romana, 1988 • F.M. AUSBÜTTEL, Die Verwaltung der Städte und Prov. im spätant. I., 1988 • M. AMERUSO, Megale Hellas, 1996.

G.U./Ü: H.D.

G. Spätantike und byzantinische Zeit

Nach ihrem Einfall in I. (488 n. Chr.) eroberten die Ostgoten → Ravenna, wodurch I. unter → Theoderich nur noch unter formeller Oberherrschaft des röm. Kaisers blieb. Im Rahmen seiner Politik der *restauratio* mußte es daher → Iustinianus' erklärtes Ziel sein, I. und die Prestigestadt Rom wieder unter die Botmäßigkeit Ostroms zu bringen. Die langen und verlustreichen Kriege (bis 555), geführt von → Belisarios und → Narses und beschrieben von → Prokopios, waren jedoch nur ein vorübergehender, wenn auch in seinen Konsequenzen weitreichender [1. 20ff., 54ff.] Erfolg: 568 erfolgte der Langobardeneinfall, am Ende desselben Jh. begann die Niederlassung der → Slaven in Istrien (→ Histria). Byzanz behielt nur Venedig und Ravenna mit ihren Territorien, die Küste Istriens und den Süden (Kampanien, Apulien, Kalabrien, Lukanien und Sizilien); das Papsttum erkannte die byz. Oberherrschaft an. Bis gegen die Mitte des 8. Jh. [2] blieb diese Situation stabil: Erst 751 ging Ravenna, Sitz des Exarchen (→ Exarchat), verloren. Byzanz übertrug die kirchliche Jurisdiktion des Südens dem Patriarchen von Konstantinopel, was u.a. dazu führte, daß sich der Papst nunmehr der neuen Macht im Norden näherte, dem Frankenreich. Die Schwäche der langobardischen Herzogtümer im Süden trug dazu bei, daß Byzanz seine Präsenz dort verstärkte und das Themensystem (→ Thema) einführte. Damit war gegen 800 die geogr. Zweiteilung I.s perfekt: Im Norden herrschte der fränkische König bzw. deutsche Kaiser, im Süden Byzanz; dazwischen der selbständige Kirchenstaat. Lediglich Venedig blieb nominell bei Byzanz, was im Frieden von Aachen (812), der B. den Verlust Istriens brachte, bestätigt wurde. Mit dem Beginn der Eroberung Siziliens [3] (abgeschlossen 902: Fall Taorminas) kam ein weiterer Faktor ins Spiel: Im äußersten Süden herrschte nun eine griech.-lat.-arab. Mischkultur. Das restliche Süd-I. blieb byz. (vor 969 → Katepanat), trotz der Versuche der Ottonen, das *regnum Italiae* [4] ganz zu kontrollieren. Das fragile Gleichgewicht in I. wurde erst durch die Eroberungen und anschließend durch die Rebellion des G. Maniakes (1038–1042) unterbrochen, wodurch die Normannen, die die byz. und arab. Besitzungen vereinen sollten, ihre Eroberungen sichern konnten.

Kulturell-sprachlich blieb der Süden somit integraler Bestandteil der griech. Welt, auch über das 11. Jh. hinaus; während der Zeit des Ikonoklasmus (→ Syrische Dynastie) flohen zahlreiche verfolgte Bilderverehrer nach I. Eine bes. Erscheinung blieb die südit. Klosterkultur (Neilos von Rossano † 1004). Der Einfluß von Byzanz auf die südit. Kultur wurde erst in den letzten Jahrzehnten positiv gewürdigt [5; 6]: Neben der Kunst (wobei die meisten Denkmäler stauferzeitlich sind) und der Buchkultur [7] ist hier auch die Anwesenheit von Griechen bis in unsere Tage zu erwähnen [8]. Entscheidend ist die byz. Kultur jedoch für das Stauferreich geworden. Ebenbürtig ist der byz. Einfluß in Venedig: Auch hier überdauerte der kulturelle Einfluß die polit. Herrschaft bei weitem (Markusdom; venez. *gondola* < κοντοῦρα). Am dauerhaftesten war freilich die Tatsache, daß I. durch den byz.-fränkischen Gegensatz jahrhundertelang zwei, später drei Kulturräumen angehörte – die Folgen davon dauern bis h. an.

→ Italien

1 R. HODGES, D. WHITEHOUSE, Mohammed, Charlemagne and the Origins of Europe. Archaeology and the Pirenne Thesis, 1983 2 P. CLASSEN, Karl der Große, das Papsttum und Byzanz, 1985 3 V. v. FALKENHAUSEN, La dominazione bizantina nell'Italia meridionale dal IX all XI secolo, 1967/1978 4 R. HIESTAND, Byzanz und das regnum italicum im 10. Jh., 1964 5 G. CAVALLO (Ed.), Bizantini in Italia, 1982 6 W. BERSCHIN, Griech.-Lat. MA, 1980 7 G. CAVALLO, Libri e lettori nel mondo bizantino, 1982 8 G. ROHLFS, Grammatica storica dei dialetti italogreci (Calabria-Salerno), 1977.

J.N.

II. Religion

Die ital. Religionen aus der Bronze- und frühen Eisenzeit sind nahezu unbekannt: Teilweise belegt sind der Totenkult, andere Kulte in Höhlen, Weihgaben in Form von bronzenen Waffen in Flüssen (Norditalien) und von Pferden und Ochsen aus Ton innerhalb von Siedlungen. Die Priesterämter reichen in die Epoche der indoeurop. Einheit zurück (vgl. lat. *flamen* = altind. *brahman*). Der *rex* führte priesterliche Aufgaben aus, doch die Priesterämter wurden im Laufe der Zeit differenzierter und zahlreicher. In Etrurien und Latium belegt die arch. und epigraph. Dokumentation zunehmende rel. Aktivität ab dem 7. und 6. Jh. v. Chr., bei den Sabelli, Umbri und Veneti erst ab dem 5. Jh. v. Chr. Ab dem 7. Jh. zeigen die ital. Kulte eine fortlaufende Hellenisierung: Zunächst wurden griech. Mythen – bes. die von → Odysseus und → Herakles – hauptsächlich von der Oberschicht aufgenommen; darauf folgte die Gleichsetzung einheimischer Gottheiten mit griech. (z.B. des Iuppiter mit Zeus, der Minerva mit Athena, der Venus mit Aphrodite); es wurden aber auch Götter aus dem griech. Pantheon neu eingeführt (z.B. Herakles, Dioskuren, Hermes). Es ist nicht immer einfach, alte latin. und etr. Züge der Gottheiten aufzuzeigen, die griech. Ikonographie und Mythologie übernommen haben (wie z.B. Ceres und die etr. Turan vor der Gleichsetzung mit Demeter bzw. Aphrodite). Auch bei neu eingeführten Gottheiten wurden die urspr. Züge griech. Götter in Hinblick auf rel. und sozio-ökonomischen Bedürfnisse uminterpretiert. Castor wurde z.B. der Gott der jungen röm. Ritter, auch Herakles wurde in Bezug zu lokalen Gottheiten gesetzt. Zu den wichtigsten einheimischen Gottheiten zählen Herren/Herrinnen der Tiere, die auch Unterwelt- und Fruchtbarkeitsnumina waren, etwa Faunus und Diana in Latium, Suri in Etrurien, eine mit Artemis Aitolike gleichgesetzte Göttin bei den Veneti. Ferner verehrte man Gottheiten, deren Namen Personifikationen sind, wie z.B. Ceres (Göttin des Wachstums), Liber (Gott-Sohn), Venus (Göttin der Liebesverzauberung), Salus, Spes, Victoria etc.

Im 6. Jh. v. Chr. entstanden in Etrurien und Latium die ersten monumentalen Tempel, in anderen Regionen erst später. Die heiligen Haine, in denen Asylrecht für Mensch und Tier galt, bestanden weiterhin. Die Städte organisierten ihr Pantheon um Stadtgottheiten, die die höchsten Bürgerwerte verkörperten: z.B. Iuppiter in Rom, Iuno Regina in Veii, Fortuna in Praeneste. Ähnlich gruppierten sich Völkerbünde um föderale Kulte, z.B. die etr. Städte um den Voltumnakult, die Latiner um Iuppiter Latiaris und Diana. Andere Götter spielten eine ges. wichtige Rolle bei Initiations- und Hochzeitsriten, hier vor allem Minerva und Venus in antithetischer und komplementärer Funktion, aber auch Mars, Hercules, Liber. Vom 5. bis zum 1. Jh. v. Chr. war der Brauch verbreitet, Statuetten, die Götter, Menschen oder Körperglieder darstellten und die Suche nach *sanatio* (Heilung) dokumentierten, als Votivgabe darzubringen. *Sanatio* wurde nicht nur bei → Heilgottheiten im engeren Sinne, wie Aesculap oder Apollo, sondern bei allen Göttern gesucht. Auf der gesamten ital. Halbinsel wurde die Praxis der *auspicia* im öffentlichen Bereich geübt, die Mantik der *sortes* bei privaten Konsultationen. Für die Interpretation der Prodigien und der Leber von Opfertieren waren in Etrurien und in Rom etr. → *haruspices* zuständig, die dafür eine komplexe Lehre entwickelt hatten.

Radke · Italia omnium terrarum alumna, Antica madre 11, 1988 · Italia omnium terrarum parens, Antica madre 12, 1989.
A. MAS./Ü: F. P.

Italica. Stadt in der Nähe von Santiponce bei Sevilla. 206 v. Chr. von P. Cornelius Scipio gegr. und mit Veteranen besiedelt (App. Ib. 38) als *vicus civium Romanorum* (CIL II 1119). Seit Caesar erscheint I. als *municipium* (Bell. Alex. 52,4; Mz.), seit Hadrianus (117–138 n. Chr.) als *colonia* (Gell. 16,13,4; CIL II 1135; XI 2699; XII 1856). I. war die Heimat der Kaiser Traianus und Hadrianus, aber schwerlich auch des Dichters Silius. In I. waren die *legio VII* (CIL II 1125 f.) und die *cohors III Gallica* (CIL II 1127) stationiert. Nach den arch. Überresten, bes. dem großen Amphitheater, zu urteilen, war I. bed., z.B. aufgrund von Ölexport (CIL XV 2631) und seiner Steinbrüche (CIL II 1131). In westgot. Zeit spielte I. 584 als Festung und als Bischofssitz eine Rolle [1. 449]. Nach 711 n. Chr. verfiel die Stadt [2. 49 ff.].

1 A. Schulten (Hrsg.), Fontes Hispaniae Antiquae 9, 1947
2 A. García y Bellido, Colonia Aelia Augusta Italica, 1960.

A. Parladé, Excavaciones en el anfiteatro de Itálica, in: Memorias de la Junta Superior de Excavaciones y Antigüedades, 1920/1, Nr. 2, 1–7; 1921/2, Nr. 7, 1–6; 1923/4, Nr. 10; 1924/5, Nr. 11, 1–6 · A. Schulten, Forsch. in Spanien, in: AA 1940, I/2, 112 f. · Tovar 1, 1974, 163 ff. · F. Chaves Tristán, Las monedas de Italica, 1973.
P. B.

Italicus. Weitverbreitetes röm. Cognomen. Am bekanntesten der Dichter → Silius I.

Kajanto, Cognomina, 180.
K.-L. E.

[1] Sohn des Cheruskers → Flavus (dem Bruder des → Arminius) und einer Tochter des Chattenprinceps Actumerus, in Rom geboren und aufgewachsen. Da I. vom zerstrittenen Adel als König der → Cherusci verlangt wird, setzt Kaiser → Claudius [III 1] den letzten Sproß der *stirps regia* 47 n. Chr. als König ein (Tac. ann. 11,16); das zeigt die neue Entwicklung der röm.-german. Beziehungen seit der Varusschlacht. Nach Parteikämpfen vertrieben, von den → Langobardi wieder eingesetzt, kann I. seine Herrschaft behaupten (ann. 11,17).

R. Wolters, Röm. Eroberung und Herrschaftsorganisation, 1990.
V. L.

[2] *Rex Sueborum*, wohl Sohn und Nachfolger von → Vangio; im J. 69 n. Chr. zusammen mit → Sido zum Anschluß an die Bürgerkriegspartei des → Vespasianus gebracht, kämpfte er für diese bei → Betriacum (Tac. hist. 3,5,1; 21,2).
→ Suebi P. KE.

Italien, Alphabetschriften A. Einführung B. Etrusker C. Latiner D. Falisker E. Veneter (Lepontier, Räter) F. Umbrer G. Osker H. Diverse

A. Einführung

Das Alphabet (A.) wurde durch euboiische Griechen nach It. eingeführt und unreduziert (→ Alphabet, II. B.) von den Etruskern übernommen. Das Alphabetar von Marsiliana d'Albegna (ca. 700–650 v. Chr.; s. Tab.) entspricht dem ital. Prototyp. Aus den Alphabetaren (*I.1 ff. in [1], so auch im folgenden zit.) läßt sich die ital. Schriftgesch. am besten ablesen. Neben den vom etr. A. abhängigen Schriften finden sich v.a. griech. in Süditalien (auch in weiter nördl. Handelssiedlungen und auf Importwaren) – darunter die angeblich früheste griech. Inschr., ευλιν (vollständig), 770 v. Chr. [2] –, ferner semit. z.B. auf Sardinien (→ Alphabet, p. 541 o.), auf Ischia [3] und in Pyrgi [4].

B. Etrusker

Die Etrusker [5. 234 f.] lernten bis nach 600 v. Chr. das A. in unreduzierter Form (s. auch *I.4, *I.6 mit Silbenübung *ci ca cu ce vi va vu ve* usw., *I.3), gebrauchten aber mehrere Zeichen (praktisch) gar nie (in der Tab. Zeichen Nr. 2, 4, 15, 16; s. die Übung!) oder (in Südetrurien) als Varianten (Nr. 24) bzw. in einer orthographischen Distribution (Nr. 3, 11, 19 [6. 15 ff.]). Dann erfolgten Reduktionsreformen: Nord- und Südetrurien gaben die Zeichen Nr. 2, 4, 15, 16, 24 auf, der Norden (= N) zudem Nr. 3 und 19 (s. *II.5, *III.21; *III.2, *III.19). Die Bemühungen um die Schrift spiegeln sich auch in der didaktischen Maßnahme der sog. Silbenpunktierung wider [7]. Einige Jahrzehnte nach der Reduktionsreform (im Süden *II.5, s. Tab., im N *II.7, *II.12, s. Tab.; s.u. E.) wurde – bald nach Mitte 6. Jh. – für /f/, das vorher HF bzw. FH geschrieben worden war, im Süden (= S) und N ein Zeichen 8 angehängt (im S *III.2, im N *III.1, s. Tab.). Wohl noch im 5. Jh. wurden im S schließlich Nr. 11 und 19 eliminiert (*III.19., s. Tab., kurz vor, *III.20 wohl bald nach der Reform). Damit hatten die A. ihre endgültige Gestalt (im N z. B. *III.8b; im S z. B. *IV.1, s. Tab., und *IV.6).

Im N und S waren seit alters Nr. 18 und 21 funktionell vertauscht [4. I 38 f.]. Im S wurden die *u*-Diphthonge ab ca. 500 v. Chr. mit F notiert (z. B. im S *avle*, im N *aule*). Ab ca. 400 wurde auch im N statt K immer mehr C verwendet; da dieses aber den Platz von K (Nr. 11) einnahm (*IV.4, ca. 200 v. Chr., s. Tab.; [8. 54[73]]), handelt es sich nicht um eine Schriftreform, sondern nur um einen Spezialfall einer Buchstabenformänderung.

C. Latiner

Das lat. A. wurde von einem unreduzierten etr. A. (also noch im 7. Jh.) abgeleitet, wobei ein griech. A. für die Lautwerte von B, D, O, X (aber nicht für C, dessen Hauptlautwert /k/ die Abhängigkeit vom etr. A. beweist) Pate gestanden haben muß [6. 20 ff.]. Wir wissen nicht genau, wann in der Folge die Umstellung von FH/HF zu F für /f/ (und gleichzeitig von F zu V für /w/) sowie die Elimination von Nr. 9, 15, 18, 25, 26 vorgenommen wurden [6. 23 ff., 32 f.]. Erst gegen Mitte 3. Jh. wurde für Zeta (Nr. 7, »tot«; s. Tab.) ein Zeichen G für /g/ substituiert (durch den Lehrer Sp. → Carvilius [2], einen Freigelassenen wohl griech. Herkunft [6. 324–333]). Für griech. Lw. und Namen wurden im späteren 1. Jh. v. Chr. Y und Z angefügt. Die von Kaiser → Claudius [III 1] konzipierten Zusatzbuchstaben [9. 12 § 10] hatten dagegen keinen Erfolg. Die lat. Schrift hat als einzige der von der etr. abgeleiteten Schriften den Schritt zur Rechtsläufigkeit vollzogen (wohl bald nach 500 nach griech. »Mode«).

D. Falisker

Das falisk. A. [6. bes. 37 ff.] ist wegen der Verwendung von Nr. 3 für /k/ ebenfalls vom etr. A. abgeleitet, am ehesten (früh) über das lat., mit dem es bes. die Verwendung von V für /w/ teilt (daneben die südetr.-lat.-falisk. archa. orthograph. Distribution von Nr. 3, 11, 19 und später die Generalisierung von Nr. 3 für /k/, im Falisk. auch in /k^w/, z. B. *cuicto* »Quintus«). Ein Alphabetar fehlt bislang, deshalb wissen wir nicht, ob die »toten« Buchstaben (Nr. 2, 6, 15, 18, 25, 26) je eliminiert worden sind (die seltene Verwendung von Nr. 9 spricht eher dagegen) und ob der spezielle Buchstabe ↑ (*f*) (Nr. 27) am Ende angehängt oder z. B. auf Platz Nr. 6 substituiert war (immerhin beweist er eine Reform); s. Tab.

E. Veneter (Lepontier, Räter)

Die Veneter übernahmen ein reduziertes, aber – angesichts der Schreibung FH für /f/ – noch nicht um Nr. 8 (*f*) erweitertes nordetr. A. (also in der 1. H. 6. Jh.) und fügten O (*o*) an. /b/ schrieben sie mit Nr. 25, /g/ mit Nr. 26 und /d/ mit Nr. 7 oder 22. Die kleinen lokalen Besonderheiten sind sekundär entstanden. Das Heiligtum »Fondo Baratela« in Este hat zahlreiche Votivinschr. mit Alphabetaren (s. Tab., Es 23 [10. 28, 195 Nr. 4a; 11. 97 ff., 95–142]) und Silbenlisten geliefert [10. 187–202; 11 *passim*]. Die sekundär aus Südetr. eingeführte Silbenpunktierung ist im Venet. zum orthographischen Standard erhoben.

Ebenfalls von nordetr. Alphabeten stammen die lepontischen [12] und rätischen A. [13; 14], von denen aber bislang keine Alphabetare gefunden worden sind.

F. Umbrer

Ein umbr. Alphabetar steht ebenfalls noch aus. Das Fehlen von Nr. 16 (*o*), eines Zeichens, das für die umbr. Sprache nützlich wäre, legt die Annahme nahe, daß die Reduktionsreform des etr. A. bei der Schaffung des umbr. schon vollzogen war. Der (seltene) Gebrauch von Nr. 9 und 18 als graphische Varianten für /t/ und /s/ weist darauf hin, daß keine weitere Reduktion mehr stattgefunden hat (also wurden wohl – mind. – auch Nr. 25 und 26 als »tote« Buchstaben noch gelernt). Wo in der Reihe das in südumbr. Inschr. verwendete C, die beiden Zusatzbuchstaben (von denen der erste sehr alt sein muß) und das (wohl als letztes aufgenommene) B standen, ist unsicher; s. Tab.

→ Iguvinum; Tabulae Iguvinae

G. Osker

In Kampanien wurde die osk. Sprache zunächst etr. geschrieben (z. T. mit Silbenpunktierung). Vermutlich wurde dann (gegen 400) von den Samniten das geeignetere »osk.« A. mitgebracht (wegen der Buchstabenformen von Nr. 4 und 20 war es wohl urspr. mit dem umbr. A. identisch) und reformiert (»Restitution« von Nr. 2, 3, 4 zweifellos nach griech. Vorbild; evtl. gleichzeitig Elimination von Nr. 18). Eine deutlich spätere [15] Reform brachte noch die zwei Zusatzbuchstaben (um 300 v. Chr.). Es sind mehrere (unvollständige) Alphabetare gefunden worden [16]; s. Tab. mit einer Synthese.

H. Diverse

Nicht einzugliedernde ital. A. (und weitgehend unverständliche Sprachen) zeigen ferner die Stele von → Novilara (bei Pisaurum) [17], der Helm von Negau [18], das → Messapische [19] und das → Sikulische [20]; zum Ital. gehört ferner auch das Südpikenische (→ Oskisch-Umbrisch).

Italien: Alphabetschriften

	← Westgriechisch = archaisch etruskisch (*I.1 Marsiliana, c. 675–50)	→ Lateinisch (Monteroni di Palo, Ende 4. Jh.)	← Faliskisch (kein Alphabetar; ca. 4. Jh.)	← Südetruskisch reduziert (*II.5 Gravisca, 1. H. 6. Jh.; mit 8 *III.19 Nola, 1. H. 5. Jh.)	← Nordetruskisch reduziert (*II.12 Perugia, 2. H. 6. Jh.)	← Venetisch (P = Padua, V = Vincenza, E = Este; Es 23, Anf. 3. Jh.)	← Südetruskisch definitiv (mit 8; ohne K Q) (*IV.1 Bomarzo, 3. Jh.)	← Nordetruskisch definitiv (mit 8; später z. T. mit C statt K) (*III.1 Magliano, 2. H. 6. Jh.; *IV.4 Vetulonia, c. 200)	← Umbrisch (kein Alphabetar; Tab. Iguv.)	← Oskisch (mit í ú) (Pompeji, 1. Jh.)
1	𐌀	𐌀	𐌀	𐌀 𐌀	𐌀	𐌀	𐌀	𐌀 𐌀	𐌀	𐌀
2	𐌁 †	B		– –	–	–	–	– –		𐌁 /b/
3	/g/ 𐌂 /k/	C /k/	𐌂	[c] 𐌂	–	–	𐌂	– –		𐌂 /g/
4	𐌃 †	D	𐌃	– –	–	–	–	– –		𐌃 /d/
5	𐌄	E	𐌄	[e] 𐌄	𐌄	𐌄	𐌄	𐌄 𐌄	𐌄	𐌄
6	𐌅 /w/	F /f/		[v] 𐌅	𐌅	𐌅	𐌅	𐌅 𐌅	𐌅	𐌅
7	𐌆	𐌆 †	𐌆	[z] 𐌆	𐌆	𐌆 PV † E /d/	𐌆	𐌆 𐌆	𐌆 /ts/	𐌆 /ts/
8	𐌇	H	𐌇	ḥ 𐌇	𐌇	𐌇 𐌇	𐌇	𐌇 𐌇 ⊘	⊘	𐌇
9	⊗	–	⊙	○ ⊗	⊙	P ⊙ E V X /t/	○	⊙ ○	⊙ /t/ (†)	⊙
10	I	I	I	I I	I	I	I	I I	I	I
11	𐌊	K	𐌊	𐌊 𐌂	𐌊	𐌊	–	𐌊 𐌂	𐌊 𐌂	𐌊
12	𐌋	L	𐌋	𐌋 𐌋	𐌋	𐌋	𐌋	𐌋 𐌋	𐌋	𐌋
13	𐌌	M	𐌌	𐌌 𐌌	𐌌	𐌌	𐌌	𐌌 𐌌 Λ	𐌌 Λ	𐌌
14	𐌍	N	𐌍	ṇ 𐌍	𐌍	𐌍	𐌍	𐌍 H	𐌍	H
15	† ⊞ †	–		– –	–	–	–	– –		–
16	O †	O	O	– –	–	–	–	– –		–
17	𐌐	P	𐌐	[p] 𐌐	𐌐	𐌐	𐌐	𐌐 𐌐	𐌐	Π
18	† M /σ/	–		[σ] 𐌑	M /ś/	M	M /σ/	M M /ś/	M /s/ (†)	–
19	𐌒	Q	𐌒	[q] 𐌒	–	–	–	– –		–
20	𐌓	R	𐌓	[r] 𐌓	𐌓	𐌓	𐌓	𐌓 𐌓	𐌓	𐌓
21	𐌔 /s/	S	𐌔	[s] 𐌔	𐌔 /ś/	𐌔	𐌔 /s/	𐌔 𐌔 /ś/	𐌔 /s/	𐌔
22	𐌕	T	𐌕	𐌕 𐌕	𐌕	𐌕 PV /d/ E †	𐌕	𐌕 𐌕	𐌕 𐌕 /t/	T
23	𐌖	V	V /u w/	V V	V	Λ	V	V V	V	V
24	/ks/ X /s/(†)	+ /ks/	X	– –	–	–	–	– –		–
25	𐌘	–		𐌘 𐌘	𐌘	𐌘 /b/	𐌘	𐌘 𐌘	? †	–
26	𐌙	–		𐌙 𐌙	𐌙	𐌙 /g/	𐌙	𐌙 [χ]	? †	–
27			↑ /f/	8 /f/		◇ /o/	8 /f/	8 [f]	8 /f/	8 /f/
28+									𐌛 /ř/	𐌝 /í/
									𐌜 /ç/	𐌞 /ú/
									𐌁 /b/	

1 M. PANDOLFINI, A. L. PROSDOCIMI, Alfabetari e insegnamento della scrittura in Etruria e nell'Italia antica, 1990, bes. 3–94 2 A. M. BIETTI SESTIERI, The Iron Age community of Osteria dell' Osa, 1992, 184 f., 259 (Bibliogr.) 3 G. BUCHNER, D. RIDGWAY, Pithekoussai I, 3 Bde., 1993 4 ET, Nr. Cr 4.4 5 H. RIX, La scrittura e la lingua, in: M. CRISTOFANI (Hrsg.), Gli Etruschi: una nuova immagine, 1993, 199–227 6 WACHTER 7 R. WACHTER, Die etr. und venet. Silbenpunktierung, in: MH 43, 1986, 111–126 8 Ders., Zur Vorgesch. des griech. Alphabets, in: Kadmos 28, 1989, 19–78 9 LEUMANN 10 M. LEJEUNE, Manuel de la langue vénète, 1974 11 A. MARINETTI, Le tavolette alfabetiche di Este, in: [1], 95–142 12 PROSDOCIMI (bes. M. G. TIBILETTI BRUNO, Ligure, Leponzio e Gallo, 129–208) 13 M. G. TIBILETTI BRUNO, Camuno e dialetti retico e pararetico, in: [12], 209–255 14 E. RISCH, Die Räter als sprachliches Problem, in: Das Räterproblem in geschichtlicher, sprachlicher und arch. Sicht, 1984, 22–36 15 VETTER Nr. 117, 120, 128, 131 16 R. ANTONINI, Gli alfabetari oschi, in: [1], 143–153 17 M. DURANTE, Nord Piceno: La lingua delle iscrizioni di Novilara, in: [12], 393–400 18 A. L. PROSDOCIMI, L'iscrizione »germanica« sull'elmo B di Negau, in: [12], 381–392 19 O. PARLANGELI, C. SANTORO, Il Messapico, in: [12], 913–947 20 A. ZAMBONI, Il Siculo, in: [12], 949–1012.

M. PANDOLFINI, A. L. PROSDOCIMI (oben [1]) • M. CRISTOFANI, L'alfabeto etrusco, in: [12], 401–428. R. WA.

Italien, Sprachen

A. ALLGEMEINES B. GEOGRAPHISCHE VERTEILUNG C. OBERITALIEN UND ETRURIEN D. DER ITALISCHE SPRACHZWEIG E. UNTERITALIEN UND SIZILIEN F. AUSKLANG

A. ALLGEMEINES

Das vorröm. It. weist eine erstaunliche Sprachenvielfalt auf, an der wenigstens vier idg. Sprachzweige teilhaben, der ital. (→ Latein, → Faliskisch, → Oskisch-Umbrisch, → Venetisch), kelt. (→ keltische Sprachen: → Lepontisch, Gallisch), messapische (Illyr.?) und der griechische (s. Stemma Sp. 1173 f.). Idg. Sprachen (noch) unbekannter Zuordnung sind die indigenen Idiome Siziliens (s.u. E.) sowie (verm.) das noch unentschlüsselte → Nordpikenische [1]. An nichtidg. Gruppen sind die tyrsen. durch das → Rätische und das → Etruskische, die semit. durch das Punische (ca. 170 Inschr. aus archa. Handelskolonien Siziliens, Sardiniens und Pyrgi/Cerveteri [2]) bezeugt. Unklar ist die Zugehörigkeit des »Camunischen« (ca. 70 Inschr.; 5.–1. Jh. v. Chr.) der Valcamonica [3]. Insgesamt sind uns dank der frühen Alphabetisierung – vor 700 in Südetrurien (Tarquinii, Caere/Cerveteri) einsetzend, erfaßt sie im 7. Jh. den gesamten etr. Sprachraum einschließlich Poebene und Kampanien, spätestens im 6. Jh. ganz Italien (→ Italien: Alphabetschriften) – ca. anderthalb Dutzend Sprachen (und weitere zugehörige Dial.) unmittelbar in inschr. Zeugnissen überliefert. Von einigen anderen, etwa dem Daunischen (→ Daunia) oder → Ligurischen kennen wir wenig mehr als den Namen. Glossen und onomastisches Material [4; 5], die für solche, aber auch für direkt überl. Sprachen als Sekundärquellen in Betracht kommen, haben meist geringen Informationsgehalt und sind in ihrer sprachlichen Zugehörigkeit vielfach problematisch.

B. GEOGRAPHISCHE VERTEILUNG

Die buntscheckige Sprachenkarte des ant. Italien (s. Sp. 1171 f.) ist durch viele einander teilweise überlagernde Migrationsbewegungen entstanden. Diese sind nur gelegentlich in histor. Quellen faßbar, so im 6.–4. Jh. der Einbruch der Gallier in die Poebene (Liv. 5,34) oder die Südexpansion der Samniten (Strab. 5,242). Wohl ins 2. Jt. fällt die Einwanderung der »Italiker« (s.u. D.), möglicherweise in zwei Wellen, deren eine die Latiner, die andere die Sabeller (Osko-Umbrer) ins Land brachte, doch sind für diesen Zeitraum Migrationsbewegungen arch. (noch) nicht nachweisbar [6. 75 f.]: Das Eindringen der Brandbestattung (von den Etruskern und Latinern bevorzugt, während die Sabeller an der Körperbestattung festhielten) um die Mitte des 2. Jt. von Norden her weist nicht notwendig auf eine entsprechende Bevölkerungsverschiebung hin. Wohl vor der latinisch-sabellischen Trennung hat sich das Venetische abgespalten (s.u. D.). Die Etrusker sind ausweislich der epigraphischen Überl. und der Onomastik von der tyrrhen. Küste ins vorher von Umbrosabinern bzw. im Süden von Latinern besiedelte Binnenland vorgedrungen (was u. a. die Abwanderung der Volsker nach Süden auslöste, vgl. [7. 14, 48 f.]); dieser Prozeß war im 7. Jh. weitgehend abgeschlossen. Ihr Übergreifen auf die Poebene sowie Kampanien schon im 9. Jh. bezeugen dort vereinzelte Siedlungen der → Villanova-Kultur [6. 138, 149]. Für die Herkunftsfrage des Etr. – autochthon oder (aus dem Osten) eingeführt – bleibt das geogr. Verhältnis zum nächstverwandten Rätischen ein Problem.

C. OBERITALIEN UND ETRURIEN

Im Umkreis von 50 km um Lugano ist das kelt. Lepontische in ca. 100 Inschr. (6.–1. Jh.) bezeugt [8; 9; 10], vgl. *uvamokozis*: *plialeθu*: *uvltiauiopos*: *ariuonepos*: *sitesˇ*: *tetu* ›Uvamogostis Bl. setzte diese »Sitze« für die Uvlt. Ar. (Dat. Pl.)‹ (Prestino, ca. 500 v. Chr.). Seit der Eroberung durch die Gallier im 4. Jh. ist die Poebene gall. Sprachgebiet, die wenigen Inschr. (3./2. Jh.) entstammen bis auf die Bilingue von Todi dem an das Lepont. angrenzenden Raum links des Po [11; 12].

Das Rätische, südl. und nördl. des Brenner bezeugt, ist ausweislich morphologischer und lexikalischer Übereinstimmungen dem Etr. eng verwandt, jedoch kein etr. Dialekt [13; 14; 15]. Das Etr. ist in Oberit. (Felsina/Bologna, Adria, Spina, Mantua) und Kampanien seit dem 7. Jh., in seinem Kernland im westl. Mittelit. schon früher durch insgesamt knapp 9000 Inschr. dokumentiert.

D. DER ITALISCHE SPRACHZWEIG

Die Einheit des ital. Zweiges mit den beiden Untergruppen »latin.« und »osk.-umbr.« wird durch Gemeinsamkeiten wie das strukturell und materiell weitgehend gleiche Flexionssystem (mit spezif. Neuerungen wie Konj. Impft.), typische Lautentwicklungen wie die

Vertretung der uridg. Mediae Aspiratae $d^h\, b^h\, g^{wh}\, g^h$ (zunächst als Spiranten, Zusammenfall von $d^h\, b^h\, g^{wh}$ im Anlaut zu *f* usw.), v. a. aber durch viele Wortbildungsgleichungen erwiesen. Ein wichtiger Unterschied ist etwa die Entwicklung der Labiovelare $k^w\, g^w$ (> latin. *qu u̯*, sabell. *p b*, vgl. lat. *quis*, osk. *pis*).

Das östl. Mittelitalien ist die Zone der umbrosabin. Dialekte (→ Oskisch-Umbrisch), denen neben dem Umbrischen (»Paläoumbr.« seit dem 7. Jh.) Südpikenisch (6.–4. Jh.), »Sabinisch« (v. a. Glossen), Äquisch (der Äquikuler), Marsisch (seit 4. Jh.), weiter im Süden Volskisch (Velitrae) und »Präsamnitisch« (der vorosk. Italiker Kampaniens; 6./5. Jh.) angehören. Östl. bzw. südl. liegt das Kernland der osk. sprechenden Samniten, deren Idiom sich im 5. Jh. über fast ganz Südit. ausbreitet (s.o. B.) und dabei neben dem »Präsamnit.« noch weitere ital. Dial. überlagert (greifbar etwa in [16], vgl. [17]), sowie die eng verwandten Dial. des Pälignischen, Vestinischen und Marrukinischen. Die latin. Gruppe ist v. a. durch das stadtröm. Latein und das Faliskische vertreten; die spärlich bezeugten Dial. der latin. Gemeinden unterscheiden sich in Einzelzügen vom Lat.

Zum ital. Zweig gehört aufgrund lautlicher Übereinstimmungen etwa in der Entwicklung der uridg. Mediae Aspiratae auch das Venetische (ca. 300 Inschr. des 6.–1. Jh. v. Chr.) in Venetien (Hauptorte Este, Padova). Die flexivischen Divergenzen (z. B. Verbalendungen *do-to*, *dona-s-an*: »gab«, »schenkten«) deuten jedoch auf eine frühe Abspaltung [18; 19].

E. Unteritalien und Sizilien

Durch ca. 300 Inschr. ist in Apulien die Sprache der aus Illyrien eingewanderten → Messapii bezeugt (6.–1. Jh.) [20].

Die ant. Einteilung der indigenen Bevölkerung Siziliens in → Elymoi (NW), Sikanoi (W) und Sikuli (O) wird durch den sprachlich-epigraphischen Befund (im allg. 7.–5. Jh. v. Chr.) nur bedingt gestützt. Auf idg. Charakter des Elymischen führen die Ausgänge Dat. Sg. *-ai* < *-āi̯*, *ōi̯* (?), Pl. *-ib* (< uridg. Instr. Pl. *-i-bʰi*) sowie *emi* »ich bin«, vgl. [21] *]xsilai emi* »ich gehöre *-ksila*.« Hier wie bei den übrigen, wohl ebenfalls idg. Idiomen, für die → Sikulisch als Sammelbegriff gelten mag, sind engere Beziehungen zum »Italischen« nicht erkennbar. Eine Ausnahme bildet in dieser Hinsicht der Dial. der Bauinschr. von Mendolito [22], vgl. *iam* »eam«, *teuto* ~ osk. *touto*, *verega* ~ osk. *vereiia*, *verehasio*, Perf.-Endung in *geped* ~ osk. *-ed*. Sizilische Glossen und toponymisches Material bietet z. B. Zamboni ([23]; vgl. noch [21. Anm. 13; 24; 25; 26]).

F. Ausklang

Im Gefolge des → Bundesgenossenkrieges 90/89 v. Chr. wurde allen Italikern das Bürgerrecht verliehen, was den Gebrauch des Lat. einschloß. Spätestens im Laufe des 1. Jh. v. Chr. ist daher allenthalben die Aufgabe der einheimischen Idiome zugunsten des Lat. zu beobachten; um die Zeitenwende hat sich dieses in fast ganz It. durchgesetzt [27]. Neben ihm konnte sich auf Dauer lediglich das Griech. Süditaliens und Siziliens behaupten.

→ Daunia; Elymisch; Etruskisch; Faliskisch; Griechisch; Italien: Alphabetschriften; Keltische Sprachen; Latein; Lepontisch; Ligurisch; Messapisch; Oskisch-Umbrisch; Rätisch; Sikulisch; Venetisch

1 M. Durante, Nordpiceno, in: Prosdocimi, 393–400 **2** S. Moscati, Le iscrizioni fenicio-puniche, in: Le Iscrizioni prelatine, 1979, 45–55 **3** A. Mancini, Le iscrizioni della Valcamonica, in: Studi Urbinati di storia, filosofia e letteratura, Supplemento linguistico 2, 1980, 75–167 **4** J. Untermann, Namenlandschaften im alten Oberit., in: BN 10, 1959, 74–108, 121–159; 11, 1960, 273–318; 12, 1961, 1–30 **5** J. B. Pellegrini, Toponymi ed etnici ..., in: Prosdocimi, 79–127 **6** M. Pallottino, Etruscologia, 71985 **7** I Volsci. Quaderni di Arch. Etrusco-Italica 20, 1992 **8** M. Lejeune, Lepontica, 1971 **9** F. Motta, Vues présentes sur le celtique cisalpin, in: Études Celtiques 29, 1992, 311–317 **10** V. Daniele (Hrsg.), Celti ed Etruschi nell'Italia centro-settentrionale dal V. secolo alla romanizzazione, 1987 **11** P.-Y. Lambert, La langue Gauloise, 31997 **12** M. Lejeune, Recueil des Inscriptions Gauloises. 2,1: Textes Gallo-étrusques ..., 1988 **13** S. Schumacher, Die rät. Inschr. ..., 1992 **14** Ders., Sprachliche Gemeinsamkeiten zw. Rät. und Etr., in: Der Schlern 72, 1998, 90–114 **15** H. Rix, Rät. und Etr., 1998 **16** Vetter, Nr. 186f. **17** P. Poccetti, Per un' identità culturale dei Brettii, 1988, 89–124 **18** M. Lejeune, Manuel de la langue vénète, 1974 **19** G. Fogolari, A. L. Prosdocimi, I Veneti antichi, 1988 **20** C. Santoro, Nuovi Studi Messapici, 3 Bde., 1982–1984 **21** L. Agostiniani, Le iscrizioni anelleniche di Sicilia, 1977, Nr. 312 **22** M. Durante, Il Siculo e la sua documentazione, in: Kokalos 10/1, 1964/5, 440ff. **23** A. Zamboni, Il Siculo, in: Prosdocimi, 971ff. **24** L. Agostiniani, Epigrafia e linguistica anelleniche di Sicilia ..., in: Kokalos 26/7, 1980/1, 503ff. **25** R. van Compernolle, L'apporto dell'epigrafia e della linguistica anelleniche ..., in: Kokalos 39/40, 1993/4, 143ff. **26** U. Schmoll, Die vorgriech. Sprachen Siziliens, 1958 **27** P. Bruun et al., Studies in the romanisation of Etruria, 1975.

Prosdocimi, passim • Le Iscrizioni prelatine. Atti dei Convegni Lincei 39, 1979 • A. Morandi, Epigrafia Italica, 1982 • M. Pallotino, Storia della prima Italia 1981 [dt.: Italien vor der Römerzeit, 1987]. GE.ME.

Italisch s. Oskisch-Umbrisch

Italischer Bund s. Bundesgenossensystem

Italus (Ἴταλος). Bedeutende Gestalt der mythisch-histor. Siedlungsgesch. und Eponym Italiens (Dion. Hal. ant. 1,35,1; Verg. Aen. 1,533; Steph. Byz. s. v. Ἰταλία). Dem König und Gesetzgeber der Oinotrer, der späteren Italer, (Antiochos, FGrH 555 F 5f.) schreibt Aristoteles die Stiftung von Syssitien und des Ackerbaus zu (Aristot. pol. 1329b 8–20; [1]). I. (Thuk. 6,2,4), bzw. sein Sohn Sikelos (Philistos, FGrH 556 F 46), gilt auch als König der aus Italien vertriebenen Sikeler. Als König Siziliens soll er zudem nach Latium gekommen sein; weitere Identifizierungen bei Servius (Aen. 1,533).

1 G. Huxley, Antiochos on Italos, in: Φιλίας χάριν, FS Eugenio Manni, Bd. 4, 1197–1204. C.R.

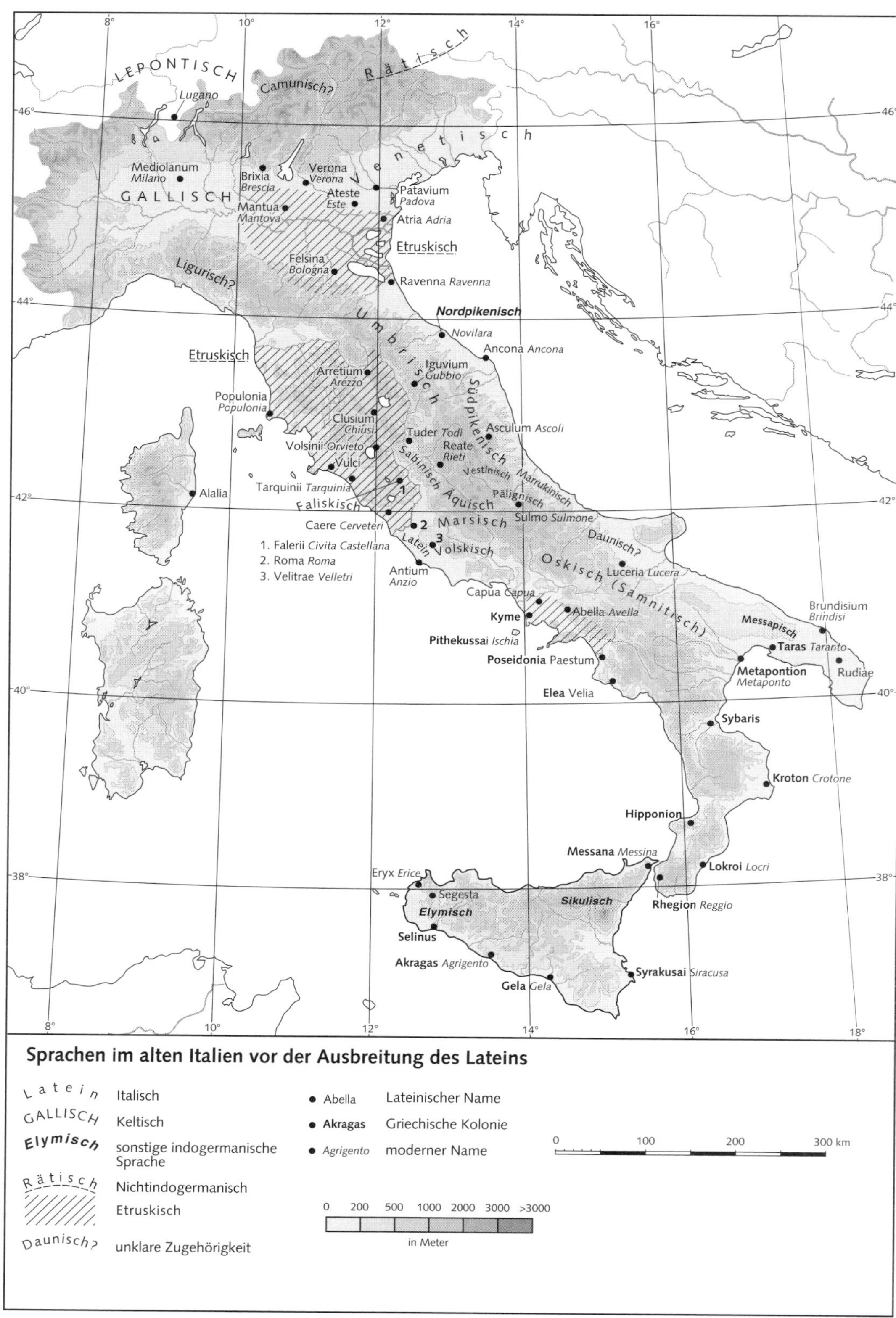
Sprachen im alten Italien vor der Ausbreitung des Lateins
Latein Italisch
GALLISCH Keltisch
Elymisch sonstige indogermanische Sprache
Rätisch Nichtindogermanisch
Etruskisch
Daunisch? unklare Zugehörigkeit
Abella Lateinischer Name
Akragas Griechische Kolonie
Agrigento moderner Name
0 100 200 300 km
0 200 500 1000 2000 3000 >3000
in Meter
LEPONTISCH
Rätisch
Camunisch?
Lugano
Venetisch
Mediolanum Milano
GALLISCH
Brixia Brescia
Verona Verona
Ateste Este
Patavium Padova
Mantua Mantova
Atria Adria
Etruskisch
Felsina Bologna
Ligurisch?
Ravenna Ravenna
Nordpikenisch
Novilara
Ancona Ancona
Umbrisch
Etruskisch
Arretium Arezzo
Iguvium Gubbio
Südpikenisch
Populonia Populonia
Clusium Chiusi
Tuder Todi
Asculum Ascoli
Volsinii Orvieto
Reate Rieti
Vulci
Vestinisch
Marrukinisch
Sabinisch
Alalia
Tarquinii Tarquinia
Äquisch
Pälignisch
Faliskisch
Sulmo Sulmone
Caere Cerveteri
Marsisch
Daunisch?
1. Falerii Civita Castellana
2. Roma Roma
3. Velitrae Velletri
Latein
Volskisch
Oskisch (Samnitisch)
Luceria Lucera
Antium Anzio
Capua Capua
Brundisium Brindisi
Kyme
Abella Avella
Messapisch
Pithekussai Ischia
Taras Taranto
Poseidonia Paestum
Metapontion Metaponto
Rudiae
Elea Velia
Sybaris
Kroton Crotone
Hipponion
Messana Messina
Lokroi Locri
Eryx Erice
Segesta
Sikulisch
Elymisch
Rhegion Reggio
Selinus
Akragas Agrigento
Syrakusai Siracusa
Gela Gela
8° 10° 12° 14° 16° 18°
46° 44° 42° 40° 38°

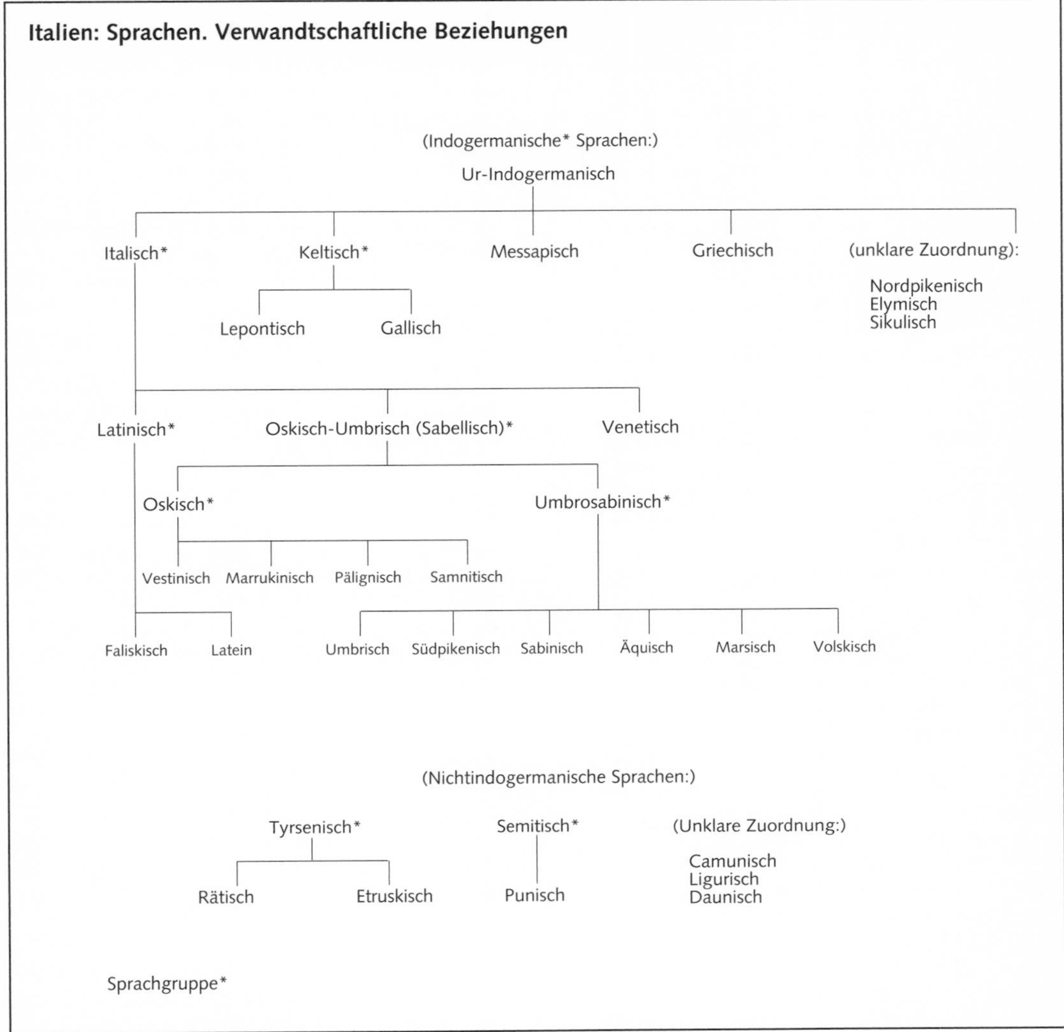

Itanos (Ἴτανος). Hafenstadt im äußersten NO von Kreta, zw. zwei Akropoleis gelegen, h. Erimupolis. Siedlungsspuren bereits aus min. Zeit. Im 7. Jh. v. Chr. soll der Purpurfischer Korobios aus I. Kolonisten aus → Thera nach → Kyrene geführt haben (Hdt. 4,151). In hell. Zeit ägäischer Stützpunkt der Ptolemäer [1]. 112 v. Chr. werden Rivalitäten mit → Hierapytna auf röm. Initiative hin geschlichtet [2. Nr. 57]. Wenige Reste, u. a. eine byz. Basilika.

1 S. Spyridakis, Ptolemaic I. and Hellenistic Crete, 1970
2 A. Chaniotis, Die Verträge zw. kret. Poleis in der hell. Zeit, 1996.

Lauffer, Griechenland, 281 f. • I. F. Sanders, Roman Crete, 1982, 138. H. SO.

Itazismus. I. (geprägt nach ἰωτακισμός, zu ἰωτακίζω < *ἰωτατίζω, »wie ἰῶτα, *iōta*, aussprechen«) bedeutet zunächst die »Aussprache des Buchstabennamens ἦτα, *ēta*, als ['ita]« und somit des Buchstabens η als [i]. Man versteht darunter 1) in engerem Sinne die unterschiedslose Aussprache der Buchstaben bzw. Buchstabenkombinationen ει, η, ηι (ῃ), ι, οι, υ als [i], wie sie im Griech. gegen E. des 10. Jh. erreicht ist; 2) im weiteren Sinne die Aussprache aller Buchstaben bzw. bestimmter Buchstabenkombinationen (außer den erwähnten z. B. αι, αυ, ευ; γκ, μπ, ντ), wie sie zu der genannten Zeit im Griech. feststellbar ist und – von dialektalen Besonderheiten abgesehen – im wesentlichen unverändert bis auf die Gegenwart fortgilt: die byz.-ngr. Aussprache.

Das dieser Aussprache zugrundeliegende Phonemsystem ist das Ergebnis der zeitlich, räumlich und schichtenspezifisch unterschiedlich erfolgten Veränderungen, die das Phonemsystem des Att. seit dem Ausgang der klass. Zeit erfahren hat und die zugleich vom Verlust der vok. Quantitätsoppositionen und vom Ersatz der Intonationsoppositionen durch einen Druckakz. begleitet waren.

Die itazistische Aussprache, die byz. Gelehrte im 15. Jh. nach Westeuropa brachten, wurde von den meisten Humanisten, so JOHANNES REUCHLIN (1455–1522) übernommen (daher reuchlinische Aussprache), bes. aber von PHILIPP MELANCHTHON (1497–1560) gefördert und in katholischen wie protestantischen Kreisen verwendet. Ihr entgegen traten schon E. des 15. Jh. u.a. ALDUS MANUTIUS D.Ä. (1448–1515), v.a. jedoch 1528 ERASMUS VON ROTTERDAM (1469?–1536). Dieser forderte die Einführung der für das klass. Griech. näherungsweise erschließbaren Aussprache (Etazismus, da ἦτα als [ˈɛ:ta] bzw. η als [ɛ:] auszusprechen sei; erasmische Aussprache). Sie fand durch den Calvinismus Verbreitung, konnte sich gegen den I. aber erst seit Beginn des 19. Jh. dank der Bemühungen der Neuhumanisten im gelehrten Sprachgebrauch und im Unterricht in Deutschland (mit den Ausgangspunkten Leipzig und Berlin) und weitgehend international durchsetzen.

E. DRERUP, Die Schulaussprache des Griech. von der Renaissance bis zur Gegenwart, 2 Bde., 1930/1932 • SCHWYZER, Gramm., bes. 174ff., 392ff. • E.H. STURTEVANT, The Pronunciation of Greek and Latin, 1940 • A. MIRAMBEL, La langue grecque moderne, Description et analyse, 1959.

C.H.

Ithake (Ἰθάκη, *Ithaca*).
A. GEOGRAPHIE B. GESCHICHTE
C. DIE ITHAKA-FRAGE D. QUELLEN

A. GEOGRAPHIE

Eine der mittleren Ion. Inseln im Westen Griechenlands, h. auch Thiaki gen., 23 km lang und etwa 6 km breit, ca. 94 km² groß, östl. der Insel → Kephallenia und von dieser durch einen 2–5 km breiten Sund getrennt. I. teilt sich in eine größere Nordhälfte mit dem Berg Neriton (808 m) und eine Südhälfte mit dem Merovigli (671 m); die Verbindung stellt der nur 600 m breite Isthmos mit dem Berg Aetos (380 m) her. Die steil nach Westen abfallende Seite ist wenig gegliedert (Buchten beim Aetos und der Polis-Ebene), während im Osten gute Häfen vorhanden sind, so beim h. Frikes, Kioni und in der von NO eindringenden Bucht von Molo, von der nach SO die Bucht von Skinos und der vorzügliche Hafen Vathy ausgehen. Die felsige und wenig fruchtbare Insel ist h. fast waldlos und von dürrer Phrygana- und Macchienvegetation bewachsen.

B. GESCHICHTE

Frühe Siedlungsreste aus der Zeit um 2200 v.Chr. finden sich auf dem Hügel von Pelikata; hier wie auch im nahegelegenen Tris Langadas (SH III A-Haus, Grabungsber. in [4]) und am Aetos (Grabungsber. in [5]) wurden myk. Funde gemacht, ein Palast trotz intensiver Suche aber nicht entdeckt [17. 302]. Da sich der Stil der lokal gefertigten protogeom. Keramik aus dem der submyk. entwickelt hatte, ist Besiedlungskontinuität nicht ausgeschlossen. Der wichtigste Ort im 10.–8. Jh. v.Chr. war die Siedlung auf dem Isthmos am Aetos (späterer Name → Alalkomenai [2]), in der mind. zwei Heiligtümer des 10./9. Jh. nachgewiesen sind [5]. Die Funde von Keramik, Br., Elfenbein, Bernstein, Fiebeln, Nadeln etc. des 9.–7. Jh. v.Chr. weisen auf Seefahrer aus dem gesamten ägäischen und adriatischen Raum [1]; vermutlich waren die Häfen am Aetos eine wichtige Station auf dem Weg von Griechenland nach It. [9]. Im Norden läßt der Name der Polis-Bucht auf die Hauptsiedlung von I. schließen, doch fehlen bisher markante Funde [4; 17]. Wichtigster FO ist hier die Grotte am Nordufer der Polis-Bucht, in der ca. 14 Dreifüße aus dem 9.–8. Jh. v.Chr. ausgegraben wurden (Grabungsber. in [6; 2]). Eine hier gefundene späthell. Weihung an Odysseus führte zur Vermutung, daß in der Grotte seit (spät-)myk. Zeit ein → Heroenkult ausgeübt wurde. Erste nachweislich kult. verehrte Götter sind aber Athena und Hera ([7] um 550 v.Chr.), im Hell. die Nymphen und Artemis. Der Bezug auf → Odysseus ist v.a. ein hell.-röm. Phänomen, als auf I. allenthalben ep. Reminiszenzen gepflegt wurden: Es gab Odysseia-Spiele [10] und einen Odysseus-Kult (Heliodoros 5,16,22; vgl. die Mz.); die Verfassung von I. nimmt bewußt Bezug auf die Verhältnisse der hom. Epen [3]. In späterer Zeit tritt I. nicht hervor, scheint aber das Schicksal der Nachbarinsel Kephallenia geteilt zu haben: 226 v.Chr. Mitglied im Aitolischen Bund (→ Aitoloi, Aitolia, mit Karte), 189 Erklärung zur *civitas libera*, in der frühen Kaiserzeit Zuordnung zur Prov. → Achaia, später zur Prov. Epirus (Ptol. 3,13,9; Tab. Peut. 7,4; Hierokles, synekdoche 652,7) [12].

C. DIE ITHAKA-FRAGE

Seit der Ant. wird versucht, das histor. I. als Vorbild des ep. I. der Odyssee (→ Homeros) zu erweisen (Strab. 10,2,10–16). Einige Angaben der Odyssee sind tatsächlich – wenn auch nicht detailgenau – auf dem h. I. wiederzufinden [15]: z.B. der Hafen des Phorkys in der Bucht von Vathy, die Schweineställe des Eumaios und der Korax-Felsen auf der Marathia-Hochebene. Andere Beschreibungen verdanken sich dichterischer Phantasie (z.B. der Palast des Odysseus) oder der Übertragung bekannter geogr. Besonderheiten der Ion. Inseln auf I. (der Berg Ainos auf Kephallenia ähnelt dem → Neriton der Od.; die Nymphenhöhle hat Vorbilder auf I. und Kephallenia). Versuche, das I. der Odyssee auf Kephallenia, → Leukas oder → Korkyra zu suchen, führen daher in die Irre. Wenn überhaupt eine Ion. Insel Anspruch auf die Identität mit dem homer. I. erheben kann, dann ist dies nach Meinung des Verf. das h. Thiaki [11; 16]. Ob es in histor. Zeit einen Herrscher Odysseus auf I. (oder Kephallenia) und sein bei Homer (Od. 9,21–26; Il. 631–637) beschriebenes Reich [14] gegeben hat, kann beim h. Forsch.-Stand nicht entschieden werden.

D. Quellen

Skyl. 34; Plut. de sera 12 (557C); Skymn. 466; Dion. Kalliphontis 51 f.; Dion. Per. 495 f.; Cic. de orat. 1,196; Plin. nat. 4,55; Mela 2,110; Porph. de antro Nymph.; Steph. Byz. s. v. Κροκύλειον. Mz.: BMC, Gr (Peloponnes), 105–106; Inschr.: SEG 38, 432; 43, 228 [8; 10; 13].

1 J. N. Coldstream, Geometric Greece, 1977
2 W. Coulson, The »Protogeometric« from Polis reconsidered, in: ABSA 86, 1991, 42–64 3 O. Gigon, Aristotelis Opera 3, 1987, 645 f. Nr. 68 fr. 509–514 4 ABSA 35, 1934–35, 1–44 (Pelikata); 47, 1952, 227–242 (Stavros); 68, 1973, 1–24 (Tris Langadas) 5 ABSA 33, 1932–33, 22–65; 40, 1939–40, 1–13; 43, 1948, 1–124; 48, 1953, 255–361; Praktika 1990, 271–278; 1992, 200–210; Ergon 1995, 63–67 6 ABSA 35, 1934–35, 45–73; 39, 1938–39, 1–51 7 LSAG 231, 234 Nr. 3 8 E. Meyer, s. v. I., KlP 2, 1487 9 C. Morgan, Corinth, the Corinthian Gulf and Western Greece during the Eighth Century B. C., in: ABSA 83, 1988, 313–338
10 K. J. Rigsby, Asylia, 1996, Nr. 86 11 W. Sieberer, Zur Lokalisation des homer. I., in: Tyche 5, 1990, 149–164
12 Soustal, Nikopolis, 168 f. 13 D. Strauch, Aus der Arbeit am Inschr.-Corpus der Ion. Inseln: IG IX 1², 4, in: Chiron 27, 1997, 217–226 14 E. Visser, Homer. Kat. der Schiffe, 1997, 574–598 15 A. J. B. Wace, F. H. Stubbings (Hrsg.), A Companion to Homer, 1962, 398–421
16 H. Warneke, Die histor.-geogr. Lösung des I.-Problems, in: Orbis Terrarum 3, 1997, 77–99 17 H. Waterhouse, From Ithaca to the Odyssey, in: ABSA 91, 1996, 301–317.

H. Beister, s. v. I., in: Lauffer, Griechenland, 282 f. • J. Partsch, Kephallenia und I., Petermanns Mitt. Ergh. 98, 1890 • Philippson/Kirsten 2, 491–502. D. S.

Ithobalos (Ἰθόβαλος, Εἰθώβαλος u. ä., phöniz. *ʾittōbaʿal*, »mit ihm ist Baʿal«). Name verschiedener phöniz. Fürsten.

[1] König von Byblos um 1000 v. Chr., bekannt aus seiner Inschr. auf dem Sarkophag seines Vaters Aḥīrām (KAI Nr. 1).

[2] I. I. von Tyros (und Sidon). Astartepriester und – durch Revolte – sechster Nachfolger Hirams I. (Ios. c. Ap. 1,123). Jedenfalls identisch mit Ethbaal, Vater der Izebel (1 Kg 16,31) und Zeitgenosse Ahabs von Israel im 9. Jh. v. Chr. Nach Menander von Ephesos (Ios. ant. Iud. 8,324) soll er → Botrys in Phönizien und Auza in Libyen gegründet haben.

[3] I. II. von Tyros (*ˡTu-ba-ìl*) erscheint ca. 737 v. Chr. unter den Tributären → Tiglatpilesars III.

[4] I. von Sidon (und Tyros?). 701 v. Chr. von → Sanherib eingesetzt (*ˡTu-ba-ʾa-lu* [1]).

1 D. Luckenbill, The Annals of Sennacherib, 1924, 30, 47.

[5] I. III. von Tyros. Wurde angeblich 13 Jahre lang (von 587–574 v. Chr.) von → Nebukadnezar II. belagert (Ios. ant. Iud. 10,228; c. Ap. 1,156).

H. J. Katzenstein, The History of Tyre, 1973 • M. Weippert, Menahem von Israel und seine Zeitgenossen in einer Steleninschr. des assyr. Königs Tiglathpileser III. aus dem Iran, in: ZPalV 79, 1973, 46 ff. • M. Cogan, Tyre and Tiglath-Pileser III, in: JCS 25, 1973, 97 f. W. R.

Ithome (Ἰθώμη).

[1] Der 802 m hohe Kalkberg (h. Vurkano), der die messenische Ebene beherrscht, mit Eua, seinem südl. Nebengipfel (h. Hagios Vassilios), bildet die natürl. Akropolis der gesamten Landschaft Messenia und ist in Sage und Gesch. deren Mittelpunkt. Die langdauernde Belagerung des Berges I. ist das Hauptthema im Prosaroman des Myron von Priene über den sog. 1. Messen. Krieg (Paus. 4,9–13). Beim großen Helotenaufstand von 464 v. Chr. konnten sich die Messenier hier zehn Jahre lang behaupten (Hdt. 9,35,2; Thuk. 1,101–103; Diod. 11,64,4; 15,66,4; Plut. Kimon 17,2), und nach der Befreiung von Messenia wurde der Hauptort Messene als eine der stärksten Festungen Griechenlands am Fuß des Berges I. angelegt: Paus. 4,26,6–27,8; 29,5; 31,4; 33,1 f.; Diod. 15,66; Plut. Pelopidas 24,5; Arat. 50,2 ff.; Pol. 7,12,3; Strab. 8,4,1; 4,8; IG V 1, 1399. Auf dem Gipfel befand sich ein Heiligtum des Zeus Ithomatas mit einem Kultbild des Ageladas (Paus. 4,33,1 f.). Ein Fest, die *Ithōmaía*, ist inschr. belegt: SEG 23,208,22 f.; [1. 96, 9 f.].

1 P. Themelis, Ausgrabungen in Messenia, in: Praktika 146, 1991 (1994).

E. Meyer, s. v. Messene, RE Suppl. 15, 149 f. • W. K. Pritchett, Thucydides' Pentekontaetia and other Essays, 1995, 268–279. Y. L.

[2] (Ἰθώμη, Θώμη, Θαμαι, Θούμαιον). Stadt in der thessal. Hestiaiotis beim h. Phanarion. E. 5. Jh. v. Chr. mit Onthyrion und anderen Orten in den → Synoikismos von Metropolis einbezogen. Arch.: Ant. Quadermauerreste, ma. Kastell. Belegstellen: Hom. Il. 2,129; Strab. 9,5,17; Steph. Byz. s. v. I.

Philippson/Kirsten 1, 52 ff., 291 ff. • F. Stähelin, Das hell. Thessalien, 1924, 129 • Koder/Hild, 237 s. v. Phanarion. E. O.

Ithoria (Ἰθωρία). Befestigter Ort in Aitolia, zerstört 219 v. Chr. von Philippos V. (Pol. 4,64,9 f.). Innerhalb des hell. Mauerzugs am linken Ufer des → Acheloos [1] auf dem Berg oberhalb des h. Dorfes Hagios Ilias Funde von myk. bis frühröm. Zeit.

S. Bommeljé (Hrsg.), Aetolia and the Aetolians, 1987, 74 • Pritchett 7, 15 f. • R. Scheer, s. v. I., in: Lauffer, Griechenland, 284. D. S.

Itinerare

I. Alter Orient II. Imperium Romanum

I. Alter Orient

Einige mesopot. Texte kommen späteren Reisebeschreibungen sehr nahe. Ein altbabylon. Text beschreibt detailliert eine 38tägige Reise vom babylon. Dūr-Apil-Sîn bis zum nordsyr. Emar [1], zwei altbabylon. Tafeln eine Reise von über 6 Monaten Dauer vom babylon. Larsa nach Nordsyrien und zurück [2]. Im neuassyr. »Zamua-I.« [5] wird eine 4tägige Wegstrecke durch das → Zagros-Gebirge mit exakten Distanzangaben beschrieben.

Besonders neuassyr. Feldzugsberichte des 9./8 Jh. v. Chr. enthalten oft längere Passagen mit Nennung von Tagesetappen. In Verwaltungstexten und Abrechnungen seit dem Ende des 3. Jt. v. Chr., aber auch etwa in neuassyr. Briefen, finden sich häufiger kurze Notierungen über Reisestrecken. So lassen sich Teile der Wegstrecke zwischen Assur und den altassyr. Handelskolonien in Anatolien (→ Kaneš) durch die Spesenabrechnungen der Transporteure rekonstruieren.

Hethit. Texte zeigen nur indirekt Elemente von I. in Orakelanfragen, die Feldzüge oder kultische Rundreisen des Königs und Kultpersonals betreffen. Echte I. sind auch aus Äg. nicht erhalten, doch ist ihre Existenz durch Angaben im Pap. Anastasi I (XVIII 7ff.; [4]) zu erschließen. Die äg. ON-Listen und die Toponymenlisten, welche auf Feldzügen basieren, zeigen oft deutlich die Abhängigkeit von I.

1 D. O. Edzard, G. Frantz-Szabó, s. v. I., RLA 5, 216–220 2 A. Goetze, An Old Babylonian Itinerary, in: JCS 7, 1953, 51–72 3 W. W. Hallo, The Road to Emar, in: JCS 18, 1963, 67–88 4 W. Helck, s. v. I., LÄ 3, 206 5 L. Levine, K 4675+. The Zamua-Itinerary, in: State Archives of Assyria Bulletin 3, 1989, 75–92. K. KE.

II. Imperium Romanum

A. Allgemeines B. Römische Itineraria
C. Christliche Itineraria D. Itineraria picta

A. Allgemeines

Itineraria (*I.*), Reisekarten bzw. »Reiseführer« für das röm. Imperium, deren Angaben zivilen wie auch mil. Zwecken dienen konnten, Handbücher, in denen die Richtungen der wichtigsten Straßen mit ihren Abzweigungen und daran liegenden Orten (Raststätten) verzeichnet waren. Wichtig waren Angaben der Entfernungen zw. einzelnen Ortschaften, über nahegelegene Flüsse, über das Wesen der betreffenden Landschaft. In der zivilen Sphäre waren diese Auskünfte bes. für Kaufleute und in der christl. Spätant. für Pilger von Bed. Die Funktion der *I.*, in mil. Sinn »Marschkarten«, veranschaulicht Vegetius (mil. 3,6,1; 4): ›Diejenigen, die sich mit dem Kriegswesen intensiver befaßt haben, versichern, daß auf den Wegstrecken gewöhnlich mehr Gefahren lauern als in der Schlacht selbst ... Zuallererst muß (ein Feldherr) von all den Gegenden, in denen Krieg geführt wird, so vollständige Wegeverzeichnisse haben, daß er sich mit den Entfernungen zw. den Orten nicht nur nach der Zahl der Meilen, sondern auch nach der Wegebeschaffenheit vertraut machen kann und sich von den Abkürzungen, Umgehungsmöglichkeiten, Bergen und Flüssen anhand einer zuverlässigen Beschreibung soweit ein Urteil bilden kann; (die Bed. der Ortskenntnis ist so wichtig,) daß geschicktere Feldherrn bestätigten, Wegebeschreibungen von den Prov., in denen Aufgaben zu erledigen waren, nicht nur in schriftlicher, sondern auch in bildlicher Form zur Hand gehabt zu haben, so daß man nicht nur mit Hilfe des Verstandes, sondern auch aufgrund des Augenscheins den Weg auswählen konnte, den man zu gehen beabsichtigte.‹

Die Kenntnis der geogr. Bedingungen war bes. dort unentbehrlich, wo sich ein Heer feindnah bewegte. Vegetius unterscheidet zw. *I. adnotata* (verbal beschriebene Situation oder ziemlich generelle Skizzen) und *I. picta* (bildhafte Zeichnungen), die er deutlich bevorzugt. Aus Veg. l.c. ergibt sich, daß bei der Anwendung des Begriffes I. bestimmte sachliche Kriterien erfüllt sein müssen. Von diesem Standpunkt aus können die Angaben auf Meilensteinen oder Wegweisern nicht als *I.* bezeichnet werden. Ebenfalls können die überwiegend lit. orientierten Reisebeschreibungen oder -erinnerungen nicht zu den *I.* im eigentlichen Sinn gezählt werden. Dies ist der Fall beim sog. → *Itinerarium Alexandri*, dessen Autor (um 340 n. Chr.) durch die Beschreibung der Ostfeldzüge Alexanders d.Gr. und Traians seinem Kaiser Constantius II. beim Antritt des Perserfeldzuges die Erfahrungen dieser Herrscher vor Augen stellen wollte.

B. Römische Itineraria

Den Kern aller *I.*, gleich ob es sich um *I. adnotata* oder *I. picta* handelte, bildete das Straßennetz mit seinen Stationen, deren Entfernungen in *milia passuum* (»Meilen«) angegeben wurden. Die Auskunft erfolgte in runden Zahlen und war mehr oder weniger approximativ. Ein Sonderfall der *I.* sind die vier silbernen Becher, die in Vicarello in der Nähe des *lacus Sabatinus* entdeckt wurden. Auf den Bechern ist auf die für die *I.* charakteristische Art die Verbindung zw. Gades und Rom notiert (CIL XI 3281; 3283 f.; 32828). Hier wird auch der Begriff *itinerarium* (3281) bzw. *intinerare* (3282, 3283) ausdrücklich gen. Bei aller grundsätzlichen Übereinstimmung der Darstellung auf den Bechern lassen sich doch im Detail auch Unterschiede feststellen. Die erstgen. drei Becher (CIL XI 3281–3283) weisen einen inneren Zusammenhang auf. Der vierte, in dessen Text weder *itinerarium* noch *itinerare* vorkommt, ist offensichtlich älter (vor 333–337 n. Chr. entstanden) und weicht in seiner äußeren Form und Darstellung von den anderen ab. Die Frage nach dem Vorbild dieser *I.* ist bisher nicht überzeugend geklärt. Ein weiteres inschr. überl. *I.* ist die Inschr. aus Autun, ein *I.* der Strecke Rom – Augustodunum aus dem 3. Jh. n. Chr. (CIL XIII 2681).

Unter den hsl. überl. *I.* repräsentiert das sog. *I. provinciarum Antonini Augusti* eine wichtige Quelle für unsere Kenntnis der Top. des röm. Reiches, obwohl im einzelnen Ungenauigkeiten, Verwechslungen und andere Fehler darin vorkommen. Diese sind jedoch nicht nur auf den Verf. selbst, sondern auch auf den Stand der ihm zur Verfügung stehenden Vorlagen und auf die zeitgenössischen und späteren Entstellungen der Überl. zurückzuführen. Die Darstellung folgt einem territorialen Prinzip, ohne jedoch eine einheitliche, systematische Gliederung des Materials zu beachten. Das Werk unterscheidet 17 Hauptstrecken, wobei sein Horizont durch die Grenzen des Imperiums beschränkt wird. Es ist wenig wahrscheinlich, daß das *I. provinciarum* als ein offizielles Handbuch dienen sollte. In seiner h. Form ist das Werk zu Anf. der diocletianischen Zeit entstanden und geht offensichtlich auf eine Vorlage aus der Regierungszeit Caracallas zurück. Zusammen damit ist in den Hss. auch das *I. maritimum Antonini Augusti* überliefert. Es handelt sich um eine kleinere Schrift, in der v.a. Raumdistanzen, nicht Fahrtdauer zw. den Hafenstädten und Inseln des Mittelmeerraums, wiedergegeben werden. Abschließend werden die Inseln, von den Orkaden im NW und weiter in östl. Richtung aufgezählt und summarisch charakterisiert.

C. Christliche Itineraria

Die christl. Pilgerkultur hat zahlreiche *I.* entstehen lassen, von denen uns noch einige erh. sind. Eine Vorstufe solcher *I.* dürfte das geogr. Handbuch sein, das → Eusebios [7] von Kaisareia vor 331 verfaßt hat (GCS 11,1,1904; von Hier. lat. bearbeitet, PL 23,903–976). Im J. 333 ist das *I. Hierosolymitanum sive Burdigalense* entstanden, in dem ein christl. Pilger seine Reise von Burdigala nach Jerusalem und zurück über Rom nach Mediolanum beschreibt. Es enthält nicht nur die für die *I.* charakteristischen Angaben über die an der Strecke liegenden Stationen und die Entfernungen zw. ihnen, sondern macht auch auf Sehenswürdigkeiten, bes. auf hl. Orte aufmerksam (PL 8,783–795). Hieronymus hat in das Trostschreiben an Eustochium, die Tochter der verstorbenen Paula, ein *I.* eingefügt: Paulas Reise von Rom nach Jerusalem (PL 22,881–883). Reich an Detailangaben ist das *I. Egeriae* (auch *Peregrinatio Aetheriae*, 395–398 oder 415–418 entstanden, CSEL 89,37–101, → *Peregrinatio ad loca sancta*). Andere Palästinapilger waren der Archidiakon Theodosius (*I. De situ Terrae Sanctae*, um 525, CSEL 39,135–150), der Anonymus, der ein *I. Ad loca sancta* verfaßt hat (irrtümlich mit dem Märtyrer Antonius von Piacenza identifiziert, zw. 560 und 570, CSEL 39,157–218). Der Bischof Arculf ist Autor eines *I. De locis sanctis* (von Adamnanus von Iona/Hy aufgezeichnet, aus dem J. 674 oder 685, PL 88,779–814).

D. Itineraria picta

Eine ungefähre Vorstellung von der Darstellungsweise der *I. picta* bietet die *Tabula Peutingeriana*. Es handelt sich dabei um die Kopie einer röm. Straßenkarte, deren Ursprung etwa im 2./3. Jh. n. Chr. zu suchen ist und deren Original später (im 4. Jh.?) überarbeitet wurde. Eine Hs. dieser Karte aus dem 12./13. Jh. hat Konrad Celtis entdeckt, der sie im J. 1508 dem Augsburger Ratsherrn Konrad Peutinger übergab. 1737 wurde sie von der Wiener Hof- bzw. Nationalbibl. erworben, wo sie bis h. aufbewahrt wird. Die Karte bestand urspr. aus 12 Segmenten, deren erstes (Marokko, Spanien, ein großer Teil von Britannien und Irland) verlorengegangen ist. Die erh. 11 Segmente erfassen die ant. Welt bis nach Indien. In ihrer h. Form ist die Peutingersche Tafel ein 6,82 m langer und 34 cm breiter Streifen [1]. Auf eine ähnliche Karte geht offensichtlich auch die *Cosmographia* des *Anonymus (Geographus, Cosmographus) Ravennas* aus dem 7./8. Jh. zurück [2; 3].

→ Katalog

1 E. Weber, Tabula Peutingeriana. Codex Vindobonensis 324, 1976 2 J. Schnetz, Ravennatis Anonymi Cosmographia et Guidonis Geographia, Itineraria Romana 2, 1940 3 Ders., Ravennas Anonymus, Nomina Germanica 10, 1951 (Übers.).

K. Brodersen, Terra Cognita, 1993 • O. Cuntz, I. Romana, 1, 1929 • J. Schnetz, I. Romana 2, 1940 • B. Kötting, Peregrinatio religiosa, 1950 • W. Kubitschek, s. v. Itinerarien, RE 9, 2308–2363 • K. Miller, I. Romana, 1916 • Schanz/Hosius 4,1, 112–115.

J. BU.

Itinerarium Alexandri. Im Anschluß an den → Alexanderroman des → Iulius [IV 23] Valerius überl. der Ambrosianus P 49 Sup. unter dem Titel *I. A.* eine anon. Kurzfassung (*breviarium*, § 3) der Alexandergesch., basierend auf → Arrianos' [2] *Anabasis*, aber auch Iulius Valerius' Übers. des (Ps.)→ Kallisthenes u.a. Die → Constantius II. gewidmete Schrift datiert sich auf 340 (im April stirbt der Kaiser) und verspricht als Ermutigung zum geplanten Partherkrieg auch den Ber. des Partherfeldzugs Traians; indes bricht der Text mit Alexanders Fahrt zu den Säulen des Hercules ab. Der Stil erinnert an → Dictys und → Dares: einfach, parataktisch, meist im histor. Präsens, ohne die senile Betulichkeit des Iulius Valerius, gleichwohl prätentiös und in der Praefatio rhet. überzogen.

Ed.: A. Mai, 1817 • K. Müller, 1846 (in F. Dübner, Arrianus 2, 155–167) • D. Volkmann, 1871 (mit dem neuen Wolfenbüttler Frg.) • H.J. Hausmann, I. A., Diss. 1970.

Lit.: R. Tabacco, Per una nuova ed. critica dell' I. A., in: Pubbl. Ist. Filol. Ling. Trad. class. di Torino, 1992, 1–23 • R. Merkelbach, Die Quellen d. Alexanderromans, 1954, 179 ff. • H. Tonnet, Le résumé et l'adoption de l'Anabase d'Arrien dans l' I. A., in: Revue d'Histoire des Textes 9, 1979, 243–254.

KL. SA.

Itium, Itius portus. Vorgebirge und Hafen der Morini in Gallia → Belgica, Ausgangsbasis für Caesars Flotte für die britannischen Expeditionen (Caes. Gall. 4,21–23; 5,2). Caesar erwähnt I. nur anläßlich der zweiten Expedition 54 v. Chr., τὸ Ἴτιον bei Strab. 4,5,2 ist auf das Unternehmen vom Vorjahr zu beziehen. Das Vorgebirge (Ἴτιον ἄκρον, Ptol. 2,9,1) ist eher bei Cap Gris-Nez als bei Cap d'Albrech zu lokalisieren. Von vielen Theorien zur Lage des Hafens (etwa in Flandern und der Calaisis) sind nur zwei ernsthafter in Betracht zu ziehen: die breite Lianebucht von Boulogne [1], wo sich später der röm. Übersetzhafen befand, oder – neuerdings favorisiert – 20 km nördl. davon die Lände von Wissant-Sangatte [2; 3].

→ Gesoriacum

1 R. Delmaire, Civitas Morinorum, in: Latomus 33, 1974, 269–275 2 R. Dion, Les campagnes de César en l'année 55, in: REL 41, 1963, 186–209 3 A. Grisart, Portus Itius, 1986.

F. SCH.

Iton (ὁ/ἡ Ἴτων, Ἴτωνος). Eine der ältesten griech. Städte, im thessal. Kerngebiet der Tetras Thessaliotis (Strab. 9,5,14) im Tal des Kuralios/Kuarios, eines rechten Nebenflusses des → Peneios. Zu ihrem Gebiet gehörte das thessal. Stammesheiligtum der Athena Itonia (Strab. 9,5,17). Die Stadt und ihr Heiligtum wurden lange wegen einer irrigen Entfernungsangabe Strabons (9,5,8) bei → Halos (Achaia Phthiotis) vermutet [1; 2; 3], sind jedoch inzwischen durch Grabungen beim h. Philia, ca. 16 km südöstlich von Karditsa ca. 10 km flußaufwärts von → Kierion nachgewiesen. Grabungen erbrachten Scherben, Weihegaben, Baureste von der frühmyk. bis in die röm. Kaiserzeit. Reste einer frühchristl. Basilika weisen auf eine Fortsetzung der Kulttradition hin.

I. wird schon im Schiffskatalog der Ilias Homers gen. (Il. 2,696). Das Heiligtum genoß überregionales Ansehen. Dort wurden Weihegaben und Beute niedergelegt, u.a. von Pyrrhos 274 v.Chr. nach seinem Sieg über → Antigonos [2] Gonatas (Paus. 1,13,2; Plut. Pyrrhos 26,5), oder Verlautbarungen aufgestellt (z.B. die Amnestie des Perseus von 179: Pol. 25,3). Es gab Kultspiele und Festversammlungen. »Athena Itonia« war der thessal. Schlachtruf, ein thessal. Monat hieß Itonios. Das Bild der Göttin erscheint ab 196 auf Mz. des erneuerten Thessal. Bundes (Quellen: [1; 2; 3]). Die von den Thessaloi aus dem Kuariostal nach Süden abgedrängten Boiotoi (→ Arne [2]) nahmen den Kult der Athena Itonia in ihre histor. Sitze mit. Er ist auch sonst in Griechenland bezeugt [1].

1 E. Meyer, s. v. I., KlP, 1492 **2** F. Stählin, s. v. I., RE 9, 2371 ff. **3** Ders., Das hellen. Thessalien, 1924, 175 f.

H. W. Catling, Archaeology in Greece, in: Archaeological Reports for 1982/3, 35 und 1983/4, 36 • J.-C. Decourt, La vallée de l'Enipeus en Thessalie, 1990, 154 f. • C. Habicht, Ambrakia und der thessal. Bund z.Z. des Perseuskrieges, in: V. Milojčić, D. Theocharis, Demetrias 1, 1976, 175 ff. • B. G. Intzesiloglou, (Fundber.), in: AD 40,2, 1985, 197 (= Ders., in: Programme, rapports et communications du Colloque international sur la Thessalie, 1990, 99 f.) • D. Theocharis, (Grabungsber.), in: AD 22,2, 1967, 296 (= Ders., in: AAA 1, 1968, 240). HE. KR.

Itonos (Ἴτωνος). Vater des → Boiotos (nur bei Diod. 4,67,7 dessen Sohn); Eponym des nahe dem boiot. Koroneia gelegenen Ortes → Iton mit dem bedeutenden Heiligtum der Athena Itonia [1]. Die Homonymie mit einem Ort und einem Heiligtum gleichen Namens in Thessalien (zwischen Larisa und Pherai gelegen) ist ein wesentliches Indiz für die angeblich 60 Jahre nach dem Fall Troias beginnende Landnahme Boiotiens von Norden her (Thuk. 1,12,3). Als eponymer Heros wird I. allerdings nur im Zusammenhang mit der boiot. Siedlung erwähnt.

1 Schachter, 1, 117–127.

E. Visser, Homers Katalog der Schiffe, 1997, 272; 665. E. V.

Ituraea (Ἰτουραία). Landschaft, benannt nach einem arab. Stamm, dessen Eponym Jeṭūr (hebr. *Yᵉṭūr*) als Sohn → Ismaels galt (Gn 25,15; 1 Chr 1,31). In frühhell. Zeit noch östl. des Jordan belegt (1 Chr 5,19; Eupolemos bei Eus. Pr. Ev. 9,30), wurde er im Bereich des Antilibanon, der Ebene Massyas (h. Biqaʿ) und des Libanon seßhaft und unternahm, als räuberisch berüchtigt (Cic. Phil. 2,112), aus befestigten Stützpunkten auf dem Libanon Raubüberfälle auf → Byblos und Beirut (→ Berytos; Strab. 16,2,18) und aus der Trachonitis gegen → Damaskos (Ios. bell. Iud. 1,398 f; ant. Iud. 15,344).

Ptolemaios, Sohne des Mennaios (ca. 85–40 v.Chr.), begründete in Chalkis (h. Anǧar?) eine Herrschaft, die im Osten auch die Abilene und im Süden Paneas und Ulatha umfaßte (Strab. 16,2,10; Ios. ant. Iud. 14,126). Bereits von Pompeius 63 v.Chr. zu Tribut gezwungen (Ios. ant. Iud. 14,39 f), ließ Antonius 36 oder 34 v.Chr. Ptolemaios' Sohn und Thronfolger Lysanias hinrichten und beschenkte Kleopatra mit seinem Gebiet (Cass. Dio 49,32,5; Ios. bell. Iud. 1,440; ant. Iud. 15,92 f.). Zur weiteren Stabilisierung der Region wurde in der Biqaʿ die Kolonie von Heliopolis (→ Baalbek) gegründet und das übrige Gebiet bis zur Eingliederung in das röm. Provinzialsystem ergebenen lokalen Dynasten vergeben: Das ehemalige Gebiet des Lysanias um Paneas und Ulatha wurde an Zenodoros verpachtet. Augustus übertrug zunächst die Trachonitis und nach dem Tod des Zenodoros um 20 v.Chr. das gesamte Gebiet bis Galiläa an → Herodes d.Gr. (Ios. bell. Iud. 1,398–400; ant. Iud. 15,344; 359 f.), nach dessen Tod es an seinen Sohn Philippus kam (Lk 3,1; Ios. ant. Iud. 17,319). Die Abilene oblag unter Tiberius einem Lysanias (Lk 3,1), später gemeinsam mit der Tetrachie des Philippus den Herodianern Agrippa I. und II. (Ios. ant. Iud. 18,237; 19,275; 20,138). Das ›Gebiet der ituraeischen Araber‹ – wohl nördl. von Heliopolis bis nach Laodikeia – wurde von Caligula im J. 38 n.Chr. einem gewissen Soaimos verliehen (Cass. Dio 59,12,2). Es wurde nach dem Tod dieses Sohaemus (Tac. ann. 12,23) 49 n.Chr. in die Prov. Syria eingegliedert. Das Kerngebiet um Chalkis unterstand 41–48 n.Chr. Herodes von Chalkis (Ios. ant. Iud. 19,277) und wurde vermutlich um 92 n.Chr. als letztes der Prov. Syria eingegliedert.

G. Schmitt, Zum Königreich Chalkis, in: ZPalV 98, 1982, 110–124 • W. Schottroff, Die Ituräer, ebd., 125–152. K. B.

Iturius. *Cliens* der Iunia Silana, der im J. 55 n.Chr. nach Agrippinas [3] erstem Machtverlust Anklage gegen sie erhob. Auf Forderung Agrippinas wurde er von Nero verbannt; nach ihrem Tod 59 wurde ihm die Rückkehr gestattet, Tac. ann. 13,19; 21 f.; 14,12,4; PIR² J 62. W. E.

Itylos (Ἴτυλος). Sohn des → Zethos und der → Aëdon (Hom. Od. 19,518; Pherekydes FHG 1,95); auch als Sohn der → Prokne überliefert, der sonst Itys genannt wird (Cat. 65,14). RE. ZI.

Itys (Ἴτυς). Sohn von → Tereus und → Prokne (anders Antoninus Liberalis 11); I. (bzw. Itylos: schol. Thuk. 2,29,3) wird von der Mutter getötet und dem Vater als Essen vorgesetzt (Apollod. 3,193 ff.; Ov. met. 6,424 ff.);

er wird zum Fasan verwandelt (Serv. ecl. 6,78). I. ist der Klageruf der Nachtigall (Aischyl. Ag. 1144; schol. Aristoph. Av. 212). AN.W.

Iuba (Ἰόβας, Ἰούβας, Ἰόβα).

[1] Geb. ca. 85 v. Chr., gest. 46 v. Chr., König von Numidien, Sohn und Nachfolger von Hiempsal. 63 vertrat I. in Rom numidische Interessen (Cic. leg. agr. 2,59). 62 wurde er zum Feind Caesars, welcher → Masintha schützte und I. am Bart zog (Suet. Iul. 71; zu seinem Aussehen [1; 2]). 50 war I. schon König, aber von Rom noch nicht anerkannt [3. 126–128]. C. → Scribonius Curio forderte Numidiens Annexion; der Senat verwarf dies, ließ I.s Status aber offen. Im Bürgerkrieg stand der König zu Pompeius. Sein Feind Curio landete am 19.6.49 bei Utica; I. und sein General → Saburra lockten ihn in eine Falle und töteten Curio mit dem Großteil seines Heeres (Caes. civ. 2,23–44). Der Rest ergab sich den Pompeianern, doch I. ließ die meisten hinrichten. Pompeius erkannte ihn nun als *rex* an, während Caesar ihn zum Staatsfeind und I.s Feinde Bocchus [2] und Bogudes [2] von Mauretanien zu Königen erklären ließ. Nach der Schlacht von Pharsalos sammelten die Pompeianer sich unter Q. → Caecilius [I 32] Metellus Scipio in Africa; die Quellen reden von Führungsansprüchen I.s, welche erst das Eintreffen des jüngeren Cato beendet habe (Plut. Cato minor 57f.; Cass. Dio 42,57,1–4). Der König stand bei Caesars Landung Ende 47 in Africa mit starken Truppen bereit, zog aber mit dem Gros seiner Armee ab, als Bocchus und P. Sittius in Numidien einfielen (Bell. Afr. 25,2–5). Nur Scipios Versprechen, er werde ganz Africa erhalten (Cass. Dio 43,4,6), soll ihn zur Rückkehr bewogen haben. Nach Caesars Sieg bei Thapsos floh I. ohne Heer in sein Reich, wo die Stadt Zama ihm jedoch angesichts seiner völligen Niederlage die Tore verschloß. Verzweifelt suchte er nahe Zama den Tod im Zweikampf mit dem Pompeianer M. Petreius (vgl. [4]). Caesar zog Numidien als Provinz Africa Nova ein (→ Afrika 3) und triumphierte noch 46 in Rom über I.

1 Richter, Portraits III, 280 2 J. Mazard, Corpus nummorum Numidiae Mauretaniaeque, 1955, 49–52 3 H. W. Ritter, Rom und Numidien, 1987 4 W. C. McDermott, M. Petreius and Juba, in: Latomus 28, 1969, 858–862.

H. G. Horn, C. B. Rüger (Hrsg.), Die Numider (Kat. Bonn, RLM), 1979. JÖ.F.

[2] Geb. ca. 50 v. Chr., gest. wohl 23 n. Chr. Sohn von I. [1], König von Mauretanien und Schriftsteller. I. wurde in → Caesars Triumphzug 46 v. Chr. gezeigt. Er wurde in Octavianus' (→ Augustus) Umgebung hell.-röm. erzogen, erhielt durch ihn das Bürgerrecht (vgl. PIR² I 65) und zog 32 mit ihm in den Krieg (Avien., De ora maritima, 279; Cass. Dio 51,15,6). 25 setzte Augustus I. als Klientelkönig Mauretaniens ein und wies ihm Teile Gaetuliens zu ([1]; früher schloß man aus Cass. Dio 53,26,2 irrig, er habe zuvor Numidien regiert [2]). 20 v. Chr. heiratete I. → Kleopatra Selene, deren königl. Herkunft sich auch im Namen ihres gemeinsamen Sohnes und Erben → Ptolemaios spiegelt. Die Existenz einer Tochter Drusilla ist unsicher.

I. schloß sich in der Münzprägung [3] Augustus' Vorbild an. Residenz und kulturelles Zentrum im hell. Stil wurde Iol, nun → Caesarea [1] genannt; der Status von → Volubilis als Zweitsitz ist umstritten [4]. Die Romanisierung Mauretaniens (→ Mauretania) schritt unter I. zügig voran; er erschloß als Einnahmequelle die Purpurgewinnung (Plin. nat. 6,201; [5]). Nach offenbar ruhigen Jahren mußte Cossus → Cornelius [II 26] Lentulus 3–6 n. Chr. eine Erhebung der Gaetuler gegen den König bekämpfen; seit 17 n. Chr. folgte der Aufstand unter → Tacfarinas, der zu I.s Lebzeiten [6. 2386f.] nicht mehr beendet wurde. Kleopatra starb spät, und I. heiratete für kurze Zeit → Glaphyra [2], Tochter des → Archelaos [7] von Kappadokien.

I.s lit. Werk [6. 2388–2395] konzentriert sich auf die Ethnographie: Bekannt sind Bücher über Assyrien, Arabien (Augustus' Enkel C. Caesar gewidmet), Afrika (anders als die übrigen Werke aus eigener Anschauung geschöpft). Hinzu kommen ein Kurzabriß der röm. Gesch., eine vergleichende Sittengesch. und Naturkundliches (→ Elefant), große Kompendien über Theater, Musik und Malerei. I.s Quellen sind Berosos, Onesikritos, punische Autoren, vielleicht auch Varro und Verrius Flaccus. Fragmente von I.s Werk bietet vor allem Plinius d. Ä., daneben Plutarch, Athenaios und andere.

1 R. Desanges, Les territoires gétules de Juba II, in: REA 66, 1964, 33–47 2 H. W. Ritter, Rom und Numidien, 1987, 137–142 3 J. Mazard, Corpus nummorum Numidiae Mauretaniaeque, 1955, 71–121 4 H. Ghazi-Ben Maissa, Volubilis et le problème de regia Jubae, in: L' Africa Romana 10, 1992, 243–261 5 J. Gattefossé, La pourpre gétule, invention du roi Juba de Maurétanie, in: Hespéris 44, 1957, 329–334 6 F. Jacoby, s. v. Iuba 2, RE 9,2, 2384–2395.

Ed.: FGrH 275 • PIR² I 65.

Lit.: H. G. Horn, C. B. Rüger (Hrsg.), Die Numider (Kat. Bonn, RLM), 1979. JÖ.F.

[3] Verf. eines metriktheoretischen Werkes in mindestens vier, wahrscheinlich acht oder mehr B. (Rufin. gramm. 6,561,11 K; Prisc. gramm. 3,420,24 K). Die einzige Aussage über I. bietet → Marius Victorinus (→ Asmonius) gramm. 6,94,6: ›Unser Iuba, der, den Vorgaben Heliodors folgend, unter den Metrikern aufgrund seiner Gelehrsamkeit eine führende Autorität ist‹. I. folgte also dem von Heliodoros und Hephaistion vertretenen System der *métra prōtótypa* (→ Metrik), was die erh. Fr. bestätigen. Der Titel des Werkes war vielleicht *ars metrica* (*I. artigraphus* bei Serv. Aen. 5,522); die Abfassungszeit liegt zwischen → Heliodoros [6] und → Plotius Claudius Sacerdos (Ende 3. Jh.), der ihn zit.; daß I. den Dichter → Septimius Serenus (Beginn 3. Jh.) zit., ist unsicher [4. 63 f]. Das Werk des I. war von erheblichem Einfluß; nach → Terentianus Maurus ist er der von den späteren lat. Grammatikern am häufigsten zit. lat. Metriktheoretiker. Einen Eindruck von seiner Darstellung, die auch ausführlich griech. Beispiele einbezog, vermitteln die wörtlichen Exzerpte bei Rufin. gramm. 6,561 ff.

Ed.: **1** O. Hense, De I. artigrapho (= Acta Soc. Lipsiensis 4), 1875 **2** Siehe GL 7,602.
Lit.: **3** P. L. Schmidt, in: HLL, § 442.2 **4** J.-W. Beck, Annianus, Septimius Serenus und ein vergessenes Fr., 1994.
Teilindex: **5** P. R. Díaz y Díaz, Varro, Bassus, I., ceteri antiquiores (= Scriptores Latini de re metrica. Concordantiae, Bd. 7), 1990. J. LE.

Jubiläenbuch s. Liber Iubilaerorum, s. Liber antiquitatum biblicarum

Iucundus
[1] Nach Ios. bell. Iud. 1,527 einer der Reiterkommandeure, nach Ios. ant. Iud. 16,314 einer der Leibwächter → Herodes' [1] d.Gr. I. wurde der Verschwörung mit Herodes' Sohn Alexandros gegen den König verdächtigt, gefoltert und nach einem erpreßten Geständnis hingerichtet (9 n. Chr.).
[2] Offizier der röm. Besatzung in → Caesarea [2], versuchte 66 n. Chr. dort vergeblich, die Kämpfe zwischen Griechen und Juden zu beenden (Ios. bell. Iud. 2,291); möglicherweise identisch mit dem bei Iosephos (bell. Iud. 2,544) genannten *praefectus alae* Aemilius I., der 66 bei dem Rückzug aus Jerusalem fiel. K. BR.
[3] s. Terra Sigillata

Iudaea s. Palaestina

Juda und Israel I. Alter Orient
II. Hellenistische und spätantike Zeit

I. Alter Orient
A. Definition B. Vormonarchische Zeit
C. Monarchische Zeit
D. Postmonarchische Zeit

A. Definition

Juda (= J.) und Israel (= I.) sind Bezeichnungen, die im gesch. Wandel geogr., politische, ethnische und theologische Komponenten aufweisen. J. war zunächst im südl. → Palaestina ein Landschaftsname, der später den fiktiven Ahnherren eines Stammes bezeichnete und damit zum Namen des Stammes selbst wurde. Ein polit. Gebilde wurde J. mit Davids Königtum (10. Jh. v. Chr.). Der Name J. (im AT *yhwdh*, in althebr. Texten außerhalb des AT *yhd/yhwd*, assyr. *ia-u/ʾu-da-a-a*, babylon. *ia-a-ḫu-du*) hat möglicherweise die Bedeutung »→ Jahwe ist siegreich/möge siegreich sein« (vgl. Gn 49,9; Dt 33,7) und wäre damit semantisch mit dem Namen I. (»Gott herrscht/möge herrschen«; vgl. Gn 32,29; Hos 12,4) verwandt.

Zum ersten Mal für eine Menschengruppe im mittelpalästin. Raum ist der Name I. (*jsʾr/jsirʾr*) am Ende des 13. Jh. v. Chr. auf der »Israel-Stele« des Pharao Merneptah bezeugt (4,552). In assyr. Inschr. des 1. Jt. v. Chr. steht neben *Ḫumri* bzw. *Bīt Ḫumri* (Omri bzw. Haus Omri) und *Samerina* (Samaria) einmal *Sirʾilajja*. Die mit I. bezeichnete Größe ist im biblischen Sprachgebrauch mehrdeutig: Als PN erscheint der Name nur bei der nachträglichen Umbenennung des Stämme-Ahnherrn Jakob in I. (Gn 32,29). Dabei ist schon ein einheitliches Volk I. im Blick, das die Bücher Ex bis Ri, die die vormonarchische Zeit repräsentieren sollen, als rel. Gemeinschaft in die Frühzeit projizieren. Erst in der Königszeit (1. H. 1. Jt. v. Chr.) wird I. ein selbständiger Staat neben J. (1 Sam 17,52; 18,16), nach David und → Salomon besteht das Nordreich I. neben dem Südreich J. (1 Kg 12 – 2 Kg 17). Auch in jener Zeit kann I. über die territorialen Grenzen hinaus durch Ethos (2 Sam 13,12) und Religion (Jes 5,19; 5,24) bestimmt werden, bes. bei den Propheten (Hos 9,1 u.ö.). Nach dem Untergang von Nord- und Süd-Reich (722 bzw. 587/86 v. Chr) wird I. Bezeichnung für das von Jahwe erwählte Volk (Jes 41,8 u.ö.), während als polit. Terminus nur noch der Name J. dient (Neh 2,7 u.ö.), der in der aram. Form *Jehud* als pers. Prov.-Bezeichnung und in der Form *Iudaia* unter den Ptolemäern und → Seleukiden in der hell. Zeit weiterlebt.

B. Vormonarchische Zeit

Das biblische Geschichtsbild für die Zeit nach der »Urgeschichte« (Gn 1–11) ist ein Produkt, das seine endgültige Gestalt erst nach dem Zusammenbruch von I. u. J. und dem Verlust des Landes für einen Teil des Volkes gewann. Die neuere Forschung äußert Zweifel an der Darstellung des AT [6. 68–73]: Die Erzählungen über die »Väter« Abraham, Isaak und Jakob enthalten keine histor. verwertbaren Hinweise; sie spiegeln soziale und kulturelle Gegebenheiten verschiedener Epochen und Regionen des alten Orients wider, ihr Bild vom »Gott der Väter« (»der Gott des NN«/»der Gott meines Vaters« u. a.) ist nicht Indiz für eine Religionsepoche, sondern zeitunabhängiger Ausdruck familiärer Frömmigkeit [2. 146–148]. In den Erzählungen werden v. a. Erfahrungen und Hoffnungen des exilischen »Israel« (2. H. 1. Jt. v. Chr.) auf Individuen einer fernen Vergangenheit projiziert. Trotz des at. Grundbekenntnisses zur Befreiung des versklavten Volkes (Ex 1,11) aus Äg. (Hos 11,1; 13,4 u. a.) bestreiten extreme Meinungen die Historizität des Exodus oder transformieren die Befreiung in eine Vertreibung [6. 52–68]. Bei gemäßigterem Urteil wird mit einer kleinen Exodusgruppe (vgl. dagegen Ex 12,37 f.) gerechnet, die unter → Moses aus Äg. floh und nach der Theophanie ihres Befreiergottes Jahwe und nach Wüstenwanderungen in das verheißene Land (Ex 3,8 u. a.) einzog [1. 68–104].

Histor. gesehen war die Entstehung »Israels« ein komplexer Vorgang. Als um 1200 v. Chr. das System von Stadtstaaten in Syrien-Palaestina im Zusammenhang der → Seevölkerwanderung weitgehend kollabierte, bildeten sich im Übergang von der Brz. zur Eisenzeit in den Gebirgsregionen Palaestinas die Stämme I. Sie rekrutierten sich nach Maßgabe der materiellen

Kultur, die Kontinuität (Gebrauchsgegenstände) und Diskontinuität (Hausbau, Anlage der Ortschaften) zwischen vorisraelitisch-kanaanäischer und israelitisch bestimmter Kultur aufweist, aus der Bevölkerung kanaanäischer Städte und sozial desintegrierter Gruppen in der Umgebung von Städten (*Ḫapiru*) sowie aus Nomaden, die am Rande des Kulturlandes in Symbiose mit der Stadtbevölkerung lebten [2.104–121]. Falsifiziert sind inzwischen Modelle einer friedlichen Infiltrierung bzw. kriegerischen Invasion von Nomaden aus der Wüste oder einer Revolution von *Ḫapiru* sowie die Theorie einer anschließenden, das ganze Land erfassenden → Amphiktyonie in Analogie zu altgriech. und altital. Beispielen [2. 121–128]. Das frühe »Israel« war eine fiktional aus Verwandtschaftsgruppen bestehende, segmentäre, d.h. aus einzelnen Teilen bestehende, akephale Gesellschaft von Ackerbau und Viehzucht treibenden Bauern, die sich infolge sippenübergreifender polit. Allianzen zu einer geschichteten Stammesgesellschaft, schließlich zum Häuptlingstum und zum Staat entwickelte.

C. MONARCHISCHE ZEIT

Politische (→ Philister), wirtschaftliche (Zusammenbruch des internationalen Handels, Überbevölkerung) und gesellschaftliche (soziale Komplexität) Faktoren begünstigten zu Beginn der Eisenzeit individuelle Herrschaftsformen; zunächst Häuptlingstümer (Gideon: Ri 6–8, Abimelech: Ri 9), zu denen auch die Herrschaft Sauls (1 Sam 8–31) gehörte, strenggenommen sogar diejenige Davids in → Hebron (2 Sam 2,1–11) [5. 111]. Während Sauls Herrschaft auf das Territorium des späteren Nord-Reiches beschränkt war (2 Sam 2,9), regierte David (2 Sam 1–24) zunächst in Hebron über J. (2 Sam 2,1–4), dann auch über I. (2 Sam 5,1–5), mit → Jerusalem als Regierungssitz (2 Sam 5,6–12). Die 40jährige Regierungszeit (1 Kg 2,11) → Davids [1] (um 1000 v. Chr.) könnte ebenso eine Idealisierung sein wie seine außenpolit. Erfolge (2 Sam 8; 10,1–11,1; 12,26–31). Er hielt sich über den Heerbann der Bauern hinaus ein Söldnerheer (Krethi und Plethi: 2 Sam 8,18 u.a.) und einen Beamtenstab (2 Sam 8,15–18; 20,23–26). Nachfolger Davids wurde durch Hofintrigen sein Sohn Salomon (1 Kg 1). Das dynastische Prinzip wurde (später) hoftheologisch sanktioniert (2 Sam 7). Salomon (1 Kg 1–11), der ebenfalls 40 Jahre regiert haben soll (1 Kg 11,42), wird der Bau von Tempel und Palast zugeschrieben (1 Kg 6–7); eine rege Bautätigkeit (1 Kg 9,15–19) konnte aber arch. für seine Zeit nicht nachgewiesen werden.

Der schon unter David im Aufstand seines Sohnes Absalom aufbrechende Gegensatz zwischen I. u. J. (2 Sam 15–19, vgl. 2 Sam 20) wurde unter Salomos Sohn Rehabeam (926–910 v. Chr.) durch eskalierende Fronmaßnahmen akut (1 Kg 12). Das Ergebnis war eine Spaltung zwischen I. u. J. Rehabeam wurde in Jerusalem König über J., Jerobeam I. (927–907 v. Chr.) in Sichem über I. Anders als im Süd-Reich, wo das dynastische Prinzip während der gesamten Königszeit Bestand hatte, schuf im Nord-Reich die Grundlagen für eine dauerhaftere Dynastiebildung erst Omri (882–871 v. Chr.), der → Samaria zur Hauptstadt des Nord-Reichs machte, dessen polit. Leistung (vgl. 1 Kg 16,21–28) aber zusammen mit der seines Sohnes → Ahab (871–852 v. Chr.) durch die Darstellung prophet. Opposition (Jahwe contra → Baal, 1 Kg 17–19; 21; 2 Kg 1; 2) verdeckt wird. Im 9. Jh. wurde Assyrien zur permanenten Bedrohung für I. 853 v. Chr. beteiligte sich Ahab an einer gegen Salmanassar III. (858–824 v. Chr.) gerichteten Opposition [4. 361], 842 entrichtete Jehu, der eine weitere Dyn. begründete (2 Kg 10,29–36), an Salmanassar Tribut [4. 363], 738 Menahem (2 Kg 15,17–22) an Tiglatpilesar III. (745–727 v. Chr.) [4. 371], unter dem I. Gilead, Dor und Galiläa verlor. Bald darauf wurde der verbliebene Rumpfstaat Efraim assyr. Provinz; als der letzte israelitische König Hosea (732–722 v. Chr.) Tributzahlungen verweigerte, eroberte Salmanassar V. (727–722 v. Chr.) Samaria (2 Kg 17, vgl. [4. 382 f.]) und bewirkte damit das polit. Ende des Nord-Reichs.

Entgegen der Darstellung in den Königsbüchern war J., das in der Zeit der Nachfolger Rehabeams mit I. um die Grenze der Territorien rang (z. B. 1 Kg 15,21 f.), dem Nord-Reich I. polit. und wirtschaftlich unterlegen. Es erlebte im Städtebau und bei den Kulturgütern erst ein Jh. später als Israel einen vergleichbaren Standard [9. 518–30]. 701 eroberte der Assyrer → Sanherib (705–681 v. Chr.) J., aber nicht Jerusalem [4. 390], dessen Herrscher Hiskia (725–697 v. Chr.) bes. gewürdigt wird (2 Kg 18–20), wie später auch Josia (639–609 v. Chr.; 2 Kg 22–23), als die assyr. Macht im Niedergang begriffen war. Die Nachfolge der Assyrer traten die Babylonier an, die J. mit seiner Hauptstadt Jerusalem 587/6 eroberten und zur Prov. machten. Beide Teilreiche, I. mit 19 Königen in einer 200jährigen Gesch. und J. mit 19 Königen und 1 Königin in einer 350jährigen Gesch., hatten damit ihre polit. Existenz verloren.

D. POSTMONARCHISCHE ZEIT

Während des babylon. Exils gehörte Juda zur Prov. Samaria; in pers. Zeit unter → Nehemia wurde es selbständige Prov. mit Jerusalem als Hauptstadt, in der der Tempel neu erbaut und das lit.-rel. Erbe von I. u. J. auf der Grundlage der Tora (Gn-Dt) gesammelt und kodifiziert wurde. Die untergegangenen Staaten wurden in den Texten nicht wiederbelebt; allenfalls in vielfältigen messianischen Erwartungen fand die Restauration der Herrschaft Davids Gestalt. ›Dieses Israel hat im Versuch, sich zu definieren und einzugrenzen, der mit der Perserzeit begann und mit dem Abschluß des Kanons endete, ... das »biblische Israel« entworfen: eine Utopie, die seitdem zwei Religionen mit jeweils mehreren Konfessionen als für sich verbindlich ansehen. Es ist ein Aspekt der Wirkungs- und Rezeptionsgesch. des biblischen I., daß es seit 1948 wieder einen Staat – und jetzt auch eine Nation – Israel gibt‹ [5. 189].

→ Bethlehem

1 R. ALBERTZ, Religionsgesch. Israels in at. Zeit, 1992
2 V. FRITZ, Die Entstehung I. im 12. und 11. Jh. v. Chr.,

1996 3 S. HERRMANN, Gesch. Israels in at. Zeit, [2]1980 4 TUAT 5 E. A. KNAUF, Die Umwelt des AT, 1994 6 N. P. LEMCHE, Die Vorgesch. Israels, 1996 7 H. M. NIEMANN, Herrschaft, Königtum und Staat, 1993 8 TH.L. THOMPSON, Early History of the Israelite People, 1992 9 H. WEIPPERT, Palästina in vorhell. Zeit, 1988. R.L.

II. HELLENISTISCHE UND SPÄTANTIKE ZEIT

Ab 332 v. Chr. unter der Herrschaft Alexanders d.Gr., fiel I. nach dessen Tod zunächst an die Ptolemäer, ging aber Anfang des 2. Jh. v. Chr. zusammen mit ganz → Palaestina in seleukidischen Besitz über. In I., dem Kernland jüd. Siedlung, brach als Reaktion auf die Maßnahmen zur Zwangshellenisierung und die Entweihung des Jerusalemer Tempels 167 v. Chr. durch → Antiochos [6] IV. Epiphanes (175–164 v. Chr.) der makkabäische Aufstand aus (→ Iudas Makkabaios). In der Folge gelang es den → Hasmonäern (mit Stemma), eine zunächst auf I. beschränkte Herrschaft zu errichten. Ab Simon (142–135/4) begann sich das hasmonäische Einflußgebiet über I. hinaus auszudehnen. Der auf griech. *Iudaía chṓra* (Ἰουδαία χώρα) zurückgehende Begriff *Iudaea* bezeichnete dabei sowohl die Landschaft im engeren Sinn als auch das hasmonäische Reich.

63 v. Chr. besetzte Pompeius → Jerusalem. Nach der Auflösung des Reichs der Hasmonäer bildete I. zusammen mit Idumaea und Teilen von → Galilaea einen röm. Vasallenstaat. Als Verbündeter Roms dehnte → Herodes [1] nach Abwehr der parthischen Invasion 37 v. Chr. seine Herrschaft über ganz Palaestina aus. Infolge der Reichsteilung auf der Grundlage des Testaments des Herodes fiel I. zusammen mit Idumaea und → Samaria 4 n. Chr. dessen Sohn → Archelaos [10] zu, der jedoch 6 n. Chr. von Kaiser Augustus verbannt wurde. I. kam unter direkte röm. Verwaltung und wurde Teil der prokuratorischen Prov. Iudaea unter der Oberaufsicht der Prov. Syria. Der 1. Jüd. Krieg (66–70/74 n. Chr.) führte schließlich zur Umwandlung Iudaeas in eine selbständige prätorische Prov. und zu der Stationierung der *legio X Fretensis* bei Jerusalem. Zahlreiche Siedlungen I.s wurden im Verlauf des Krieges verwüstet. Nach der Niederschlagung der Revolte fiel der Grundbesitz zum großen Teil an den Kaiser, der röm. Veteranen bei Emmaus [3] ansiedelte. Die Zerstörung des Tempels (70 n. Chr.) bedingte die Neugründung des Judentums als rabbinisches Judentum. Noch weitreichender waren die Folgen des Bar Kochba-Aufstandes (132–135, → Bar Kochba). Jerusalem wurde zur röm. *colonia Aelia Capitolina*, Juden war das Betreten der Stadt und ihres Umlandes verboten, so daß sich das Zentrum des Judentums nach Galilaea verlagerte. Die je nach Gegebenheiten auf Wein- bzw. Getreideanbau und Schafzucht spezialisierte Wirtschaftsstruktur I.s wurde weitgehend zerstört. Unter Constantinus [1] d.Gr., der zahlreiche Kirchenbauten an den christl. hl. Stätten errichtete, begann die Christianisierung I.s. Um 400 n. Chr. gehörte I. zur neu eingerichteten Prov. Palaestina prima.

→ Jerusalem; Judentum

H.-P. KUHNEN, Palästina in griech.-röm. Zeit, 1990 • F. MILLAR, The Roman Near East, 1993 • J. A. SOGGIN, Einf. in die Gesch. Israels und Judas, 1991 • G. STEMBERGER, Juden und Christen im Heiligen Land, 1987. J.P.

Judas

[1] J. Makkabaios (Der Beiname wohl von hebr. *maqqaebaet*, »der Hammer« wegen mil. Erfolge). Dritter Sohn des Priesters Mattathias (→ Hasmonäer), übernahm 167/166 v. Chr. die Führung der jüd. Aufständischen, die sich gegen die Schändung des Jerusalemer Tempels, das Verbot der jüd. Religion und den Steuerdruck unter → Antiochos IV. [6] erhoben. I. erwies sich als Meister der Guerillataktik und der Politik sowie als charismatischer Führer. Seine mil. Erfolge bewogen Antiochos IV., eine Amnestie und die Wiederherstellung der alten rel. Lebensordnung unter der Bedingung in Aussicht zu stellen, daß die Aufständischen die Waffen niederlegten. J. konterkarierte die diesbezüglichen Verhandlungen durch die Rückeroberung Jerusalems, wo der jüd. Kultus im Dezember 165 wiederaufgenommen wurde (an den Tag der Wiedereinweihung des Tempels, den 25. Kislew, knüpft das Chanukkafest an), und durch Ausweitung des Krieges zur Rettung und Umsiedlung jüd. Minderheiten. Dies veranlaßte → Lysias, den »Kanzler« → Antiochos' [7] V., mit großem Heeresaufgebot den Frieden zu erzwingen: J. wurde im Sommer 163 bei Beth-Sacharja geschlagen, die jüd. Festung Beth-Zur eingenommen und in Jerusalem mit Zustimmung der Ḥasidim, die sich von dem Bündnis mit J. lösten, ein Hoherpriester namens Alkimos [4] eingesetzt. J. ging mit seinen Anhängern in den Untergrund. Der Aufstand gewann unter dem neuen seleukid. Oberherrn → Demetrios [7] I. wieder an Boden. Im März 161 schlug J. ein seleukid. Heer unter → Nikanor bei Adasa (am 13. Adar, der als Nikanortag in den jüd. Festkalender einging) und erwirkte durch eine Gesandtschaft ein Bündnis mit Rom. Demetrios [7] I. kam jedoch einer röm. Intervention zuvor. Im April 160 wurde J. von dem seleukid. Strategen → Bakchides vernichtend geschlagen und fiel in der Schlacht. Quellen: 1 und 2 Makk.

→ Jerusalem; Judentum

1 SCHÜRER 1, 158–179 2 K. BRINGMANN, Hell. Reform und Religionsverfolgung in Judäa, 1983 3 B. BAR-KOCHVA, Judas Maccabaeus, 1989. K.BR.

[2] J. Iškariot. Wahrscheinlich hebr. *Iš kariot* bzw. *keriot*, ein Mann »aus Kariot« (im Gebiet des Stammes Juda), einer der zwölf Jünger → Jesu. In der Lit. zum Leben Jesu ist die Figur des J. umstritten: er soll Jesus an die Behörden ausgeliefert und danach Selbstmord begangen haben. Doch trotz mancher nt. Belegstellen können weder die Figur des J. noch die Tat selbst als histor. gesichert gelten. Durch die große (theologische) Bed., die J. im Christentum erhalten hat, wurde der Name J. gleichbedeutend mit »Verräter«; in neueren

Forsch. (z.B. [2]) wird ausgeführt, der Jude J. habe aufgrund der Weigerung Jesu, gegen die Römer einen Aufstand zu organisieren, aus Enttäuschung den Verrat begangen. Eine andere, eher christl. Sichtweise versteht J. als jemanden, der im Glauben, der Tod Jesu bringe die ersehnte Erlösung, ihn verriet. In der nachbiblischen Lit. erlangte J. nicht zuletzt gerade wegen der Ungeheuerlichkeit der vermeintlichen Tat große Popularität.

1 C. Cohn, Der Prozeß und Tod Jesu aus jüd. Sicht, 1997
2 D. Flusser, Die letzten Tage Jesu in Jerusalem, 1982
3 W. Fricke, Standrechtlich gekreuzigt, 1986 4 W. Jens, Der Fall J., 1975 5 Schürer 6 S. Zeitlin, Who Crucified Jesus?, 1964. Y.D.

Judentum A. Allgemeines, Begriff
B. Grundpfeiler des Judentums
C. Das Judentum von Alexander d.Gr. bis 800 n.Chr.

A. Allgemeines, Begriff

Der Begriff J. leitet sich vom hebr. *Yehuda* (vgl. die Stammesbezeichung Juda, → Juda und Israel) ab, dessen Etym. nicht vollständig gesichert ist. Er bezeichnet nicht nur die jüd. Rel., sondern auch – und dies ganz bes. – die aus heutiger Sicht als nicht unproblematisch zu bewertende ethnische Zugehörigkeit zum jüd. Volk sowie dessen gesamtes kulturelles, polit. und philos. Umfeld sowohl im Alten Israel als auch in der → Diaspora. Eine allg. anerkannte, griffige Definition von J. fehlt bis heute, da nicht zuletzt auch innerhalb des J.s selbst aufgrund der verschiedenen Strömungen – von der Ultraorthodoxie bis zum Reform-J. – kein einheitliches Verständnis des J.s existiert. Am ehesten läßt sich der Begriff wohl über die → Halakha, das jüd. Religionsgesetz, fassen. Hier wird stets das rel. Moment mit der Idee einer jüd. Volkszugehörigkeit, (die letztlich in der Gründung des Staates Israel ihren Höhepunkt erreicht zu haben scheint), verquickt. Problematisch ist der Begriff des J.s bes. auch mit Blick auf die verschiedenen Gruppierungen innerhalb des J.s (Aschkenazim, Sepharadim, Jemeniten), die keine einheitliche Vorstellung *eines* jüd. Volkes zulassen.

B. Grundpfeiler des Judentums

Voraussetzung für ein *rel.* Verständnis des J.s ist eine streng monotheistische Gottesauffassung, die eine Vermittlungsinstanz zw. Gott und Mensch im Sinne eines → Jesus oder → Mohammed nicht kennt. Die von Gott dem Volk Israel gegebene Tora (→ Pentateuch) bestimmt durch ihre Ge- und Verbote sowie ihre sittlichen Pflichten, deren oberste die *Zedaḳa*, die Gerechtigkeit, ist, das gesamte Leben des jüd. Menschen. Zwar kennt das J. keine dogmatischen Lehren, wohl aber Vorschriften, die bereits in der Tora angelegt sind und später in der Halakha ausgeführt, kommentiert und – ganz im Sinne der Tora – ergänzt wurden (→ Talmud): Da Gott als Schöpfer Mittelpunkt der Welt ist, gilt es, ihm in Dankbarkeit und Demut zu huldigen; so ist das gesamte jüd. Jahr mit seinen Festen auf die Heiligung und Verehrung des Ewigen ausgerichtet. Der höchste jüd. Feiertag, der *Yom Kippur*, verlangt von jedem einzelnen, in reumütiger Umkehr Buße zu tun. Denn der Mensch mit seinem Hang zum Bösen (*jeṣær hā-rāʿ*), von Gott ausgestattet mit dem freien Willen, Gutes, aber auch Schlechtes zu tun, sündigt stets, und nur durch Umkehr (*tᵉšuḇāh*) kann er sich vor dem Bösen retten.

Neben der Ausstattung des einzelnen mit dem freien Willen ist eine weitere Grundlage des J.s die (oft als überhebliche Erhöhung über die anderen Völker mißverstandene) Erwählung des gesamten Volkes Israel. Diese Erwählung hat ihren Sinn darin, daß die dem J. Zugehörigen zu absolut strikter Einhaltung der Gesetze verpflichtet sind – bes. auch im Hinblick auf den Bund (*bᵉrīṯ*), den Gott mit Israel geschlossen hat und der durch die Beschneidung eines jeden neugeborenen Jungen im Alter von acht Tagen besiegelt wird. Auch die in der Bibel geschilderten Leiden des jüd. Volkes sind nur vor dem Hintergrund dieser Auserwähltheit (zum Leiden) angemessen zu verstehen.

Eine systematische Theologie, wie sie im Christentum definiert wird, kennt das J. nicht; wohl aber gab (und gibt) es Versuche, rel. Inhalte zu systematisieren (so bei → Philon von Alexandreia).

F. Bautz (Hrsg.), Gesch. der Juden von der biblischen Zeit bis zur Gegenwart, 1983 • G. Fohrer, Gesch. Israels, 1982 • J. Maier, Gesch. des J.s im Alt., 1989 • N. De Lange, Judaism, 1986 • T. Schweer, Stichwort J., 1994 • G. Stemberger, Die jüd. Rel., 1995. Y.D.

C. Das Judentum von Alexander d.Gr. bis 800 n.Chr.
1. Problemstellung, Forschungsgeschichte
2. Äussere Geschichte
3. Kommunikationssituation
4. Geistesgeschichte

1. Problemstellung, Forschungsgeschichte

Jüd. Gesch. und Kultur zw. → Alexandros [4] d.Gr. und dem MA wurde lange Zeit als »Zwischentestamentszeit« oder »Spätjudentum« diskreditiert, Etikette, die eher die eigene theologische oder histor. Position reflektierten als daß sie dem Gegenstand gerecht wurden [16]. Die Klass. Philol. hingegen tat und tut sich mit der jüd.-hell. Lit. (→ Literatur) schwer; der ihr in den Literaturgesch. eingeräumte Raum ist im Verhältnis zu ihrer Wirkung in der Regel minimal. Dagegen ist die Theologie traditionell geneigt, die jüd.-hell. Kultur *in toto* als *praeparatio evangelica* [12; 13; 14] zu usurpieren; die Judaistik ihrerseits ist eine akademisch junge Disziplin, der klass. Bildung nicht mehr ohne weiteres zur Verfügung steht. So ist erst in den letzten Jahren ein wirklicher Wandel eingetreten [38]: Judaistik und Theologie, Klass. Philol. und Alte Gesch. [6] beginnen die jüd.-hell. Kultur als eine Erscheinung *sui generis* zu begreifen, auf der das → Christentum zwar aufbaut, welche aber gleichwohl ihren spezifisch jüd. Charakter nicht verleugnen kann. Die Stellung der Juden in der ant. Welt und zu ihrer Kultur sollte das Verhältnis von Juden, »Heiden«, Christen und Muslimen zueinander bis h. prägen (→ Antisemitismus).

2. Äussere Geschichte

Nach der Eroberung Palaestinas durch Alexander (332 v. Chr.), die strategischen Erwägungen folgte, gehörte Palaestina zuerst (312–198 v. Chr.) zum Ptolemäer-, dann zum Seleukidenreich (ab 198 v. Chr.). Bis zum Verlust Babyloniens an die Parther (160 v. Chr.; → Partherkriege) beherrschten diese somit die beiden Hauptzentren des J.s. Polit.-rel. Parteiungen, die sich auch an der zunehmenden → Hellenisierung entzündeten, gruppierten sich um die gegensätzlichen Priesterfamilien der Oniaden (von denen einer, → Onias III., in → Leontopolis/Äg. mit Erlaubnis Ptolemaios' VI. einen Tempel baute) und → Tobiaden. Der Versuch von Seleukos IV. und v. a. Antiochos [6] IV. (175–164), den Tempel zu hellenisieren, führte zum Widerstand trad. Gruppen und nach dessen Unterdrükkung zum Volksaufstand, an dessen Spitze bald → Judas [1] Mackabaios trat. Dessen Dyn., die → Hasmonäer, befand sich in demselben Dilemma wie ihre Nachfolger, die Dyn. des → Herodes [1]: Polit. Überleben in einer hell. geprägten Umwelt setzte Anpassung an diese voraus; dies rief jedoch den Widerstand eben jener trad. Kreise hervor, die dieser Dyn. zur Macht verholfen hatten und auf deren Unterstützung sie angewiesen war. So erfolgreich in gewissem Sinne die Außenpolitik der Hasmonäer auch war (Eroberung und Zwangsbekehrung der Edomiter zum J.), nach innen entlud sich die Opposition im Bürgerkrieg der → Pharisaioi gegen → Alexandros [16] Iannaios. Die röm. Herrschaft, deutlich durch Pompeius' Orientfeldzug (63) demonstriert, änderte die Grundkonstellation nicht: Die Rom gegenüber loyale Dyn. des Herodes sah sich einer stillen, jedoch wachsenden Opposition gegenüber, die sich nach der direkten Übernahme Palaestinas durch die Römer im Aufstand der → Zeloten (66 n. Chr.) entlud. Nicht der jüd. Krieg an sich, sondern dessen Konsequenzen (Zerstörung des zweiten Tempels und Erlöschen des Tempeldienstes; Zahlung der Tempelsteuer an den röm. Fiskus (→ *fiscus Iudaicus*); Verschwinden des Hohenpriesteramtes und Übergang der rel. Führung an die Rabbinen) prägen bis h. das J. (Synagogen lösten den Tempeldienst ab). Die Reaktionen des J. auf die weitere röm. Herrschaft waren uneinheitlich: Sie reichten von Zusammenarbeit (Patriarch Juda I.) bis zu weiteren, mil. erfolglosen Aufständen (115–117 n. Chr. unter Traianus; 132–135 unter Hadrianus, → Bar Kochba). Antoninus Pius hob die Strafmaßnahmen des Hadrianus zum guten Teil wieder auf; der Leiter des palaestinischen J.s, der Patriarch, residierte zunächst in Jamnia, dann (seit 3. Jh.) in → Tiberias und stand an der Spitze der jüd. Selbstverwaltung, die auch die Gerichtsbarkeit umfaßte. Wohlgesonnen war der jüd. Gemeinde die Dyn. der Severer (→ Severus).

Die Verwandlung Roms in einen christl. Staat brachte den J. unter → Constantinus [1] d.Gr. zunächst Erleichterungen (partielle Aufhebung des Verbots, sich in → Jerusalem niederzulassen), aber schon unter → Constantius [2] II. begann (mit Ausnahme von → Iulianus [11], der sogar befahl, den Tempel wiederaufzubauen) die unrühmliche Reihe gesetzlicher Einschränkungen gegenüber den Juden: Sie zieht sich, duch die antisemit. Polemik der Kirche vorbereitet, über Theodosius I., den Codex Theodosianus bis zu → Iustinianus hin, dessen Gesetze für die Politik und Legislation der folgenden Jh. gegenüber dem J. maßgeblich bleiben sollte.

Völlig anders war die Situation der zunächst unter parthischer, dann sāsānidischer Herrschaft lebende babylon. Gemeinde. Unter einem der pers. Regierung zur Loyalität verpflichteten → Exilarchen blühten dort die theologischen Schulen, so etwa Sura und Pumbeditha, in einem Ausmaß, daß sogar Palaestina in den Schatten gestellt wurde: So ist es der babylon., nicht etwa der Jerusalemer → Talmud, der sich (bis h.) durchgesetzt hat. Daß es außer der sich herausbildenden rabbinischen Orthodoxie auch synkretistische Religionsformen im alten Mesopot. gab, zeigen die jüd., in aram. Sprache verfaßten Zauberschalen, die man dort in großer Zahl gefunden hat. Die grundsätzlich tolerantere Einstellung der Perser führte schließlich dazu, daß die Unterstützung der Juden für die sāsānidische Politik zu einem Machtfaktor wurde, so bei der Eroberung Jerusalems (614 n. Chr.) und bei den Auseinandersetzung im Jemen (Ḏū Nuwās).

Blieb die byz. Einstellung gegenüber den Juden von der iustinian. Gesetzgebung geprägt, so übernahmen die arab. → Kalifen die Einstellung → Mohammeds: Christentum und Judentum sind legale Rel. der Schriftbesitzer (*ahl al-kitāb*), Proselytismus ist verboten, beide Gemeinschaften müssen eine Sondersteuer bezahlen und sind in ihren Oberhäuptern dem islamischen Herrscher zur Loyalität verpflichtet. Diese gegenüber der byz. Einstellung erheblich liberalere Einstellung und die starke Affinität zw. J. und → Islam, die v. a. in der rel. Gesetzgebung und der prinzipiell horizontalen statt zentralistisch-vertikalen Struktur der rel. Elite begründet ist, führten zu einem Aufleben des jüd. Geisteslebens unter islam. Herrschaft, v. a. in Spanien, so daß seit der Tora-Übers. des Saadja Gaon (aus dem Fajjum, *882, gest. 942 in Sura/Babylonien) nunmehr auch in der arab. Sprache ein adäquates Ausdrucksmittel zur Verfügung stand.

Im Vergleich zum Islam führten die Juden unter byz. Herrschaft ein marginales Dasein, obwohl ihre Situation dort gegenüber der im ma. Westeuropa noch als besser bezeichnet werden muß. Versuche byz. Kaiser wie → Herakleios [5] oder Basileios I., die Juden zu zwangskonvertieren, blieben Episode. Hebr. Werke wie die ›Vision Daniels‹ (*ḥᵃzōn D.*) aus dem 10. Jh. reflektieren die Verfolgungen bis zu → Konstantinos Porphyrogennetos. Trotz der Immigration aus islamischen Ländern (darunter auch Karäer aus Babylon) und der Verbindung zu den → Chazaren bildete sich in byz. Zeit ein eigenes jüd.-byz. Selbstverständnis heraus: Diese »Romanioten« (von Ῥωμανία, Byzanz) gen. Gemeinden setzen sich bis h. von den span., arab. und aškenazischen Gemeinden ab und sind in kultureller und sprachlicher Hinsicht die einzigen direkten Nachfolger des hell. J.s. Ihre nicht-hebr. synagogale Lit. ist in Neugriech. verfaßt, ihr Zentrum ist die nw-griech. Stadt Jannina (neben Chalkis). Obwohl also die Traditionslinie von hell. Zeit bis h. verläuft, hat sich die Forschung um diese Gemeinden fast nicht gekümmert.

3. Kommunikationssituation

Analog zur Expansion der jüd. Gemeinden über das gesamte Mittelmeer änderte sich die sprachliche Situation des J. seit Alexander grundlegend: Herrschten seit der nachexilischen Zeit in Palaestina nur die beiden nächstverwandten Idiome Hebr. und Aram. (letzteres als Verwaltungssprache des Nahen Ostens in immer größerer Verbreitung), so machte die Anwesenheit von Juden in den hell. Städten (v.a. Alexandreia) und dann auch im Westen (Rom) die Kenntnis dieser Sprachen rasch zu einer Sache der Gebildeten. Die Übernahme des Griech. als mündliches Kommunikationsmittel und z.T. auch als Schrift schuf nicht nur die Voraussetzung für die Entstehung der hell.-jüd. Lit. (→ Literatur), sondern war dadurch, daß die Tora durch interpretierende Übers. ins Griech. oder Aram. neu aktualisiert werden mußte, eine wesentliche Voraussetzung jüd. Auseinandersetzung mit der schriftl. Trad.: Mündliches Übersetzen durch den *meturgeman* wurde schriftlich fixiert; diese Übers. sind aber nicht unbedingt wörtlich, sondern reichen von sklavischer Nachahmung des hebr. Originals bis zu freier Nacherzählung (so etwa der *Targum šenī* zu Esther [8]). In diesem Rahmen ist auch die später christl. angeeignete Septuaginta lediglich ein griech. Targum der Tora. Trotz des zunehmenden Erlöschens des Hebr. als gesprochener Spr. in röm. Zeit pflegten die Rabbinen in Palaestina und Babylon außer dem Aram. (so im babylon. Talmud) weiter das Hebr. in seiner späteren Form; beide Idiome sind in dieser Zeit stark mit griech. und lat. Lw. angereichert (vgl. [18]). Dagegen bediente sich das Diaspora-J. überwiegend des Griech.: → Philon beherrschte das Hebr. nur wenig, die Muttersprache des Paulus war sicher das Griech. Man kann also davon ausgehen, daß durch die Verhältnisse der hell. Zeit schon die Grundkonstellation, die das J. in späterer Zeit zum Vermittler zw. Sprach- und Kulturräumen werden ließ, vorgegeben waren: Gebildete Juden waren in der Regel zweisprachig. Bes. deutlich zeigt sich dies in den mehrsprachigen Grabinschr. der Hauptstadt Rom [26]. Die Prädominanz des Griech. als zweite Sprache neben dem repräsentativen Hebr. änderte sich auch durch die Existenz von jüd. Gemeinden in der Westhälfte des Reiches nicht: die jüd. Katakomben Roms zeigen ein deutliches Übergewicht des Griech. Trotzdem ist die Existenz einer jüd.-lat. Lit. sehr wahrscheinlich (so etwa die → *Collatio legum Mosaicarum et Romanarum*). Umstritten ist hierbei die Frage, ob die Juden und später die Christen durch ihre Distanz zum röm. Staat eine bes. Art des Griech. oder Lat. sprachen; dies ist deswegen von bes. Wichtigkeit, weil die griech. und lat. Terminologie für den jüd. Monotheismus und seine Organisation nachweislich die christl. geprägt hat. Die beste Lösung scheint zu sein, daß in der gesprochenen Sprache die Unterschiede, wenn überhaupt, nur sehr gering waren: Die Vulgarismen der Katakombeninschr. in Rom sind nicht speziell »jüdisch«. Anders sieht es in der Schriftkultur aus: Gerade in einer Übersetzungslit. oder solchen nachempfundenen Originaltexten ist der Einfluß des hebr. Originals wahrscheinlich. Jedenfalls haben die lat. Targume der griech.-jüd. → Bibel, die hinter der *Vetus Latina* vermutet werden, und ihr Stil die europ. Lit. entscheidend geprägt. Durch die Bevorzugung des Hebr.-Aram. seitens der rabbinischen Orthodoxie geriet die griech.-jüd. Lit. in der Spätant. zunehmend an den Rand; auch das Aufkommen der jüd.-aram. Lit. (das Aram. wurde zu Recht als dem Hebr. ähnlich erkannt) im islam. Herrschaftsbereich brachte weitere Einbußen. Somit gewönne die griech. Lit. der Romanioten in Jannina und Chalkis als ein lebendiger Fortsetzer der hell. Trad. erhöhtes Gewicht, wenn sich die Forschung, sofern von der protestantischen Theologie getragen, nicht hauptsächlich auf die jüd.-hell. Lit. bis zum Ende des 1. Jh. n. Chr. beschränkte.

4. Geistesgeschichte

Grundproblem jüd. Kultur in hell. und röm. Zeit war die Auseinandersetzung mit der herrschenden nicht-jüd. Kultur ihrer Umwelt – insofern ist zunächst kein Unterschied zu anderen Kulturen des östl. Mittelmeers festzustellen, die, jede auf ihre Weise, die Dominanz des Hellenismus als Herausforderung annahmen oder von der Assimilierung bedroht waren (→ Hellenisierung). Wesentliches Unterscheidungsmoment war freilich der Monotheismus des J.: eine einfache → *interpretatio Graeca* wie im Falle der ägypt. oder babylon. Götter war hier, wenn man von den Bestrebungen hell. Kreise um den Hohepriester Iason unter → Antiochos [6] IV. absieht, nicht möglich. So ist die gesamte hell.-jüd. Kulturentwicklung von diesem Dilemma gekennzeichnet, das, auf anderer Ebene, auch Herrscher wie → Herodes [1] erlebten: Überleben und Expansion (Proselytismus) setzte Anpassung voraus; diese konnte aber den Kern jüd. Identität gefährden.

Wichtigstes Denkmal dieser Anpassung ist die erh. hell.-jüd. Lit.: ob ihre Verf. versuchen, jüd. Gesch. nach den Kategorien hell. Historiographie zu erzählen (→ Iosephos [4] Flavios) oder die jüd. Heilsgesch. philos. mit dem Begriffsinventar von Stoa oder Platonismus zu formulieren (→ Philon von Alexandreia) oder gar die Exodus-Episode als Trag. hell. Gattungsmustern anzugleichen (→ Ezechiel), immer steht im Hintergrund das Bestreben, die eigene Trad. und damit Identität durch partielle Übernahme zu bewahren. Dadurch macht es auch keinen Sinn, etwa die Nacherzählung der Tora durch Iosephos oder Philon von parallelen Texten der rabbinischen Trad. zu trennen: In jedem Fall liegt die speziell jüd. Trad. der »rewritten bible« vor, entstanden aus dem sprachlichen und histor. Bedürfnis, Trad. umzuformulieren, um sie zu erhalten. In Wirklichkeit ergänzen sich beide Textcorpora, die rabbinische, zumeist in Hebr.-Aram., und die »hellenisierende«, in Griech. abgefaßte. Wie schmal der Grat hierbei zw. Übers., Uminterpretation und Neuformulierung ist, zeigt etwa die Gesch. des griech. → Targums, den die Kirche als »Septuaginta« (LXX) bezeichnet: die zahlreichen, nur auf Griech. verfaßten oder erh. Teile der griech. Tora leben bis h. als kanonisch nunmehr in den griech. und oriental. Kirchen weiter.

Möglich wurde diese »Mehrzüngigkeit« des J. durch dessen fehlende hierarchisch-dogmatische Struktur, die der Islam erben sollte. Die Ereignisse um den jüd. Krieg und den Bar-Kochba-Aufstand sollten somit die jüd.-hell. Trad. zwar schwächen, aber nicht auslöschen: Zwar wird die LXX aus der jüd. Trad. ausgeschieden, aber es werden noch in der Ant. weitere griech. Targume angefertigt (→ Symmachus; → Aquila [3]). So ist es zwar richtig, daß die → rabbinische Lit. zahlreiche Anspielungen [21; 22] auf die klass. Sprachen und Lw. aus ihnen aufweist, aber in ihrer Struktur mündliche Diskussionen, wie an den rabbinischen Akademien üblich, wiedergibt [11], doch lebte das hell. J. in Form des romaniotischen J. bis h. weiter; erst kürzlich hat man den (polemischen) Gebrauch der LXX bis in die Osmanenzeit nachweisen können [19]. Auf derselben Linie liegt es, wenn zwar in der Spätant. die jüd. Lit. als Hebr.-Aram. eine neue Blüte erlebt (*Piyyūṭīm*) und die anderen Sprachen, wie Griech. und Lat., zurückgedrängt werden, doch ersteht im Jüd.-Arab. seit Saadja eine neue Literatursprache; die griech. Synagogenlieder und Targumim der heutigen Romanioten, deren älteste aus dem 12. Jh. stammen, setzen eine ältere Trad. voraus.

Somit bleibt die entscheidende Frage der Forschung die nach dem Verhältnis der Juden zu ihrer nichtjüd. Umwelt; einen Versuch, dieser Frage, lokal auf Rom begrenzt, aber aus arch., histor., lit.-wiss. und linguistischer Perspektive nachzugehen, lieferte exemplarisch [26]. Die erh. Denkmäler Roms zeigen aber bereits die Komplexität des Problems; unzweifelhaft ist eine in der Spätant. um sich greifende Rückbesinnung und Tendenz zur Abgrenzung und Rehebräisierung, die auch Gruppen wie die Judenchristen an den Rand drängte. Ebenso unbezweifelbar ist freilich auch der große Einfluß, den isolierte jüd. Gruppen wie diejenigen der arab. Halbinsel auf den entstehenden Islam ausgeübt hatten [15]. In gewissem Sinne kann auch diese Rel. als Erbin der spätant. Kulturgemeinschaft betrachtet werden, die dem J. Entscheidendes verdankt.

→ Jerusalem; Juda und Israel; Literatur (jüdische); JUDAISTIK; JUDENTUM

1 Z. ANKORI, Karaites in the Byzantine Empire: The Formative Years 970–1100, 1959 **2** M. AVI-YONAH, The Jews under Roman and Byzantine Rule, 1984 **3** D. R. G. BEATTIE, M. MCNAMARA (Ed.), The Aramaic Bible. Targums in their Historical Context, 1994 **4** J. L. BERQUIST, Judaism in Persia's Shadow. A Social and Historical approach, 1995 **5** E. J. BICKERMAN, The Jews in the Greek Age, 1988 **6** H. BOTERMANN, Das Judenedikt des Kaisers Claudius, 1996 **7** A. DIEZ MACHO, El Targum. Introducción a las traducciones aramaicas de la Biblia, 1979 **8** B. EGO, Targum Scheni zu Ester (TSAJ 54), 1996 **9** L. H. FELDMAN, Jew and Gentile in the Ancient World. Attitudes and Interactions from Alexander to Justinian, 1993
10 R. FELDMEIER, U. HECKEL (Ed.), Die Heiden, Christen und das Problem des Fremden, 1994 **11** A. GOLDBERG, Der verschriftete Sprechakt als rabbinische Lit., in: A. und A. ASSMANN, CHR. HARDMEIER (Ed.), Schrift und Gedächtnis, 1983, 123–140 **12** M. HENGEL, Die Zeloten, ²1976 **13** Ders., J. und Hellenismus, ⁴1988 **14** Ders., Paulus zw. Damaskus und Antiochien, 1998 **15** J. W. HIRSCHBERG, Jüd. und christl. Lehren im vor- und frühchristl. Arabien. Ein Beitrag zur Entstehungsgesch. des Islams, 1939
16 C. HOFFMANN, Juden und J. im Werk dt. Althistoriker des 19. und 20. Jh., 1988 **17** Italia Judaica. Atti del I. convegno internazionale, Bari 18.–22.5.1981, 1983 **18** S. KRAUSS, Griech. und lat. Lehnwörter in Talmud, Midrasch und Targum, 2 Bde., 1898/9 **19** D. J. LASKER, S. STROUMSA, The Polemic of Nestor the Priest. With an Appendix by J. NIEHOFF-PANAGIOTIDIS, 2 Bde., 1996 **20** L. I. LEVINE, The Rabbinic Class of Roman Palestine in Late Antiquity, 1989
21 S. LIEBERMANN, Greek in Jewish Palestine, 1942
22 Ders., Hellenism in Jewish Palestine, 1950 **23** J. LIEU et al. (Ed.), The Jews Among Pagans and Christians in the Roman Empire, 1992 **24** A. LINDER, The Jews in Roman Imperial Legislation, 1987 **25** M. J. MULDER (Ed.), Mikra. Text, Translation, Reading and Interpretation of the Hebrew Bible in Ancient Judaism and Early Christianity, 1988
26 L. V. RUTGERS, The Jews in Late Ancient Rome. Evidence of Cultural Interaction in the Roman Diaspora, 1995 **27** P. SCHÄFER (Ed.), Stud. zur Gesch. und Theologie des rabbinischen J.s, 1978 **28** H. SCHRECKENBERG, Die christl. Adversos Judaeos Texte und ihr lit. und histor. Umfeld (1.–11. Jh.), 1982 **29** SCHÜRER **30** S. SHAKED (Ed.), Irano-Judaica: Studies relating to Jewish contacts with Persian culture throughout the ages, o.J. **31** J. STARR, The Jews in the Byzantine Empire. 641–1204, 1939
32 M. STERN, Greek and Latin Authors on Jews and Judaism, 3 Bde., 1974–1984 **33** G. STEMBERGER, Das klass. J. Kultur und Gesch. der rabbinischen Zeit, 1979 **34** Ders., Einl. in Talmud und Midrasch, ⁸1992 **35** H. L. STRACK, P. BILLERBECK, Komm. zum NT aus Talmud und Midrasch, 4 Bde. und 2 Registerbde., 1926–1961
36 V. TSCHERIKOVER, Hellenistic Civilisation and the Jews, 1961 **37** Ders., A. FUKS, Corpus Papyrorum Judaicarum, 3 Bde., 1957–1964 **38** G. VELTRI, Eine Tora für den König Talmai. Unters. zum Übersetzungsverhältnis in der jüd.-hell. und rabbinischen Lit., 1994 **39** Ders., Magie und Halakha: Ansätze zu einem empirischen Wissenschaftsbegriff im spätant. und frühma. J., 1997
40 P. WEXLER, Three Heirs to a Judeo-Latin Legacy: Judaeo-Ibero-Romance, Yiddish and Rotwelsch, 1988
41 TH. WILLI, Juda-Jehud-Israel. Stud. zum Selbstverständnis des J. in pers. Zeit, 1995. J.N.

Iudex. Wörtlich »Rechtsprecher«, d.h. also »Richter«. Üblicherweise ist damit im röm. Recht der Einzelrichter (*i. privatus; i. unus*) gemeint, der in einem eigenen, den Rechtsstreit schließlich beendenden Verfahrensabschnitt (*apud iudicem*) die Beweisaufnahme vornimmt und das ihm vom → Praetor im ersten Verfahrensabschnitt (*in iure*, → *ius*) pauschal vorgegebene Urteil fällt. Während der Begriff des *i.* bereits zur Zeit des Zwölftafelrechts (5. Jh. v. Chr.) mit dem des → *arbiter* austauschbar ist, stellen die → *recuperatores* bzw. → *centumviri* eigene Kategorien von Richtern dar, die im Rahmen von Kollegialgerichten über Fälle von größerer, öffentlicher Bedeutung zu entscheiden hatten.

Die Bestellung des Richters erfolgt durch den Praetor (→ *addicere* bzw. *dare*), der dabei der regelmäßig einvernehmlichen Wahl der Parteien folgt, sonst einem zweistufigen Abschichtungsverfahren: wohl urspr. beschränkt auf die in die Richterliste (*album iudicum selectorum*) Aufgenommenen; im Formularprozeß dagegen mit der Möglichkeit einer Wahl listenfremder Richter. In diese Liste konnten zunächst nur Senatoren aufgenommen werden, in der Folge des von den Gracchen zum Politicum erhobenen Streitpunktes dann auch Ritter (spätestens durch eine *l. Aurelia* von 70 v. Chr.). Voraussetzung war infolgedessen nicht nur das röm. Bürgerrecht sowie ein Mindestalter (30, ab Augustus 25 J.), sondern auch ein entsprechendes Mindestvermögen. Darüber hinaus mußte der *i.* männlichen Geschlechts (Dig. 50,17,2), sowie frei von bestimmten Gebrechen (Dig. 5,1,12,2) sein, und er durfte keine Magistratur bekleiden; er sprach Recht in seiner Privatbehausung (Vitr. 6,5,2), handelte also als Privatperson. Gleichwohl war die Übernahme der Richtertätigkeit eine öffentlichrechtliche Pflicht mit eng begrenzten Befreiungsmöglichkeiten (Dig. 50,5,13 pr.).

Sofern der *i.* nicht rechtskundig war (das ist der typische Fall), wird er – zumindest in schwierigeren Fällen – ein *consilium* von jurist. Ratgebern zur Verhandlung hinzugezogen haben. Das lag schon wegen einer *culpa* (Verschuldens-)Haftung gegenüber der geschädigten Partei nahe (*lis sua facta*, ein Rechtsstreit, den der Richter zu seinem eigenen gemacht hat, Dig. 5,1,15,1). Im übrigen werden die Verfahren mit mehr oder minder großem rhet. Pomp vonstatten gegangen sein, da die eigentliche jurist. Problematik mit der Festlegung des Prozeßprogramms (→ *editio*) abgeschlossen war, so daß vor dem *i.* im wesentlichen nur noch um die angebotenen und erbrachten Beweise gestritten zu werden brauchte.

Mit der allmählichen Einführung des Kognitionsprozesses (→ *cognitio*) während des Principats wurde nicht nur das in verschiedene Zuständigkeiten fallende Verfahren (streitvorbereitende Gespräche der Parteien, *in iure, apud iudicem*) vereinheitlicht, sondern auch der private *i.* durch einen beamteten Richter ersetzt (*i. datus* bzw. *i. pedaneus*).

J. Kelly, Studies in the Civil Judicature of the Roman Republic, 1976, 112 • M. Kaser, K. Hackl, Das röm. Zivilprozeßrecht, [2]1997, 52, 192 • F. Lamberti, Riflessioni in tema di »litem suam facere«, in: Labeo 36, 1990, 218–266 • W. Simshäuser, Iuridici und Municipalgerichtsbarkeit in Italien, 1973.

C. PA.

Iudicatum. Zum einen der in einem Zivilurteil ausgesprochene Leistungsbefehl (Dig. 2,12,6: *i. facere vel solvere*), zum anderen das Urteil insgesamt; letzteres vornehmlich in der Wendung *res iudicata*; etwa Dig. 42,1,1: *res iudicata dicitur, quae finem controversiarum pronuntiatione iudicis accipit: quod vel condemnatione vel absolutione contingit* (›*res iudicata* heißt das durch Richterspruch erreichte Ende des streitigen Verfahrens, was als Verurteilung oder Freispruch vorkommt‹). In der maskulinen Form bezeichnet *iudicatus* einen Verurteilten, z.B. Dig. 42,2,1: *Confessus pro iudicato est* (›Wer anerkennt, gilt als Verurteilter‹).

Aus dem zusprechenden *i.* entsteht eine eigene Iudikatsobligation (Gai. inst. 3,180), die der Beklagte wohl bis in die justinianische Zeit (6. Jh. n. Chr.) binnen einer Frist von 30 Tagen zu erfüllen hat (lex XII tab. 3,1; derartige, im 19. Jh. 'Paritionsfristen' genannte Aufschübe begegnen auch in modernen Vollstreckungsrechten). Der Kläger muß eine *actio iudicati* (»Vollstreckungsklage«) anstrengen, sofern der Beklagte nicht leistet. Dieser wird entweder sofort seine Leistungspflicht anerkennen und damit den Weg zum Vollstreckungsverfahren ebnen, oder aber – unter Gefahr einer Litiskreszenz (Verdoppelung des Streitgegenstandes; Gai. inst. 4,9) – bestreiten (Dig. 5,1,75; 42,1,7).

Von formeller Rechtskraft läßt sich sinnvollerweise erst ab Einführung eines Instanzenzuges, d. h. einer → *appellatio* an den Princeps (zur zwei- bzw. dreitägigen Frist: Dig. 49,4,1,5), reden. Dagegen ist die Verbindlichkeit des Urteilsinhalts *inter partes* (materielle Rechtskraft) schon seit je insofern gewährleistet, als eine Klagenkonsumption bzw. die *exceptio rei iudicatae vel in iudicium deductae* (Einrede der abgeurteilten oder gerichtshängigen Sache) eine erneute Geltendmachung des klägerischen Begehrens verhindert.

H. Ankum, Pap. D. 20.1.3. pr.: »res iudicata« and full and bonitary ownership, in: Estudios en homenaje de Iglesias, 1988, 1121–1149 • M. Kaser, K. Hackl, Das röm. Zivilprozeßrecht, [2]1997, 375, 384 • D. Medicus, Zur Urteilsberichtigung in der actio iudicati des Formularprozesses, in: ZRG 81, 1964, 233–292.

C. PA.

Iudicium. Ein Zentralbegriff des röm. → Prozeßrechts, der allerdings in mehreren Bedeutungsvarianten vorkommt: im weiteren Sinne für den Rechtsstreit insgesamt, im engeren Sinne (inbes. im Kontext des Legisaktionen- und Formularverfahrens mit der Aufteilung in verschiedene Verfahrensabschnitte) für den letzten, vor dem Richter (→ *iudex*) stattfindenden Abschnitt. Mit dem Übergang zum Kognitionsverfahren (→ *cognitio*) und der damit verbundenen Beseitigung der Verfahrensabschnitte bezeichnet *i.* nur noch den Rechtsstreit insgesamt, wofür seit dem MA das Wort *processus* geläufig wurde. Weitere Bedeutungen von *i.* sind etwa die geistige Urteilskraft (Dig. 5,1,12,2; 40,2,25), ein (kirchliches) Dogma (Cod. Iust. 1,5,2,1) oder Testament im Sinne des »letzten Willens« (Dig. 10,2,20,3, *supremum i.*).

Das *i.* im engeren Sinne begegnet insbes. in Iurisdiktionsedikten und Gesetzen in Gestalt des *i. dabo.* Damit ist zum Ausdruck gebracht, daß der Rechtsprechungsmagistrat für jeden ihm vorgetragenen Einzelfall ein je individuelles Gericht einsetzen und zur Entscheidung nach Maßgabe des von ihm festgelegten Streitprogramms beauftragen wird, sofern die formalen Voraussetzungen erfüllt sind. Da beim Formularverfahren die → *formula* den von den Parteien ermittelten Richtervorschlag (s. → *iudex*) sowie das Streitprogramm enthält, können *i.* und *formula* dasselbe bedeuten. Ein *dare i.* besagt dabei also, daß der Magistrat die von den Parteien untereinander ausgehandelte oder mit seiner Hilfe zustandegekommene Formel akzeptiert. Dieser (vom Magistrat ausgesprochene) Abschluß des Verfahrensabschnitts *in iure* ist ein hoheitlicher Akt. Die Annahme der Gerichtseinsetzung durch die Parteien führt zw. ihnen zur → *litis contestatio* (Streitbefestigung). Eine derartige Formelerteilung heißt nach Maßgabe einer *l. Iulia* des Augustus aus dem Jahr 17 v. Chr. *i. legitimum* (im Gegensatz zum *i. imperio continens*, an die Amtsdauer gebundenes *i.*), wenn (1) ein Einzelrichter (*iudex*) in Rom selbst oder innerhalb des ersten Meilensteins eingesetzt ist, und wenn (2) sowohl der Richter als auch die beiden Parteien röm. Bürger sind (Gai. inst. 4,104).

I. hat noch folgende speziellere Bedeutungen: *i. calumniae*: Dieser Rechtsbehelf stellt eine dem Beklagten alternativ zur Zuschiebung eines Kalumnieneides (*non calumniae causa agere*, »nicht aus Schikane zu klagen«) an die Hand gegebene Möglichkeit dar, sich gegen eine mißbräuchliche, d.h. wider besseren Wissens (Dig. 5,1,10) erfolgte Klageerhebung zur Wehr zu setzen (Gai. inst. 4,174–179). Sofern der Beklagte damit durchdringt, muß der Kläger eine Prozeßstrafe in Höhe von (mindestens) einem Zehntel der Klagesumme entrichten.

I. contrarium: Damit kann zweierlei gemeint sein: (1) eine nur bei bestimmten Klagen zulässige, spezielle Variante des vorerwähnten *i. calumniae* (Gai. inst. 4,177). Während sie sich wegen ihres notwendigen Zusammenhangs mit dem klageweisen Vorgehen der anderen Partei als eine Widerklage im modernen Sinne erweist, stellt (2) die andere Bedeutung allein (zumindest in klass. Zeit, Dig. 13,6,17,1) auf einen materiell-rechtlichen Umstand ab – nämlich das Vorliegen eines unvollkommen zweiseitigen Rechtsgeschäfts (→ Leihe, → *depositum*, → *fiducia*, → *mandatum*, → *negotiorum gestio*, → *pignus*, → *tutela*). Dessen Besonderheit besteht darin, daß sie nur einer der beiden Parteien eine Pflicht auferlegt, während die andere lediglich berechtigt ist. Allerdings können der verpflichteten Partei aus der von ihr übernommenen Tätigkeit im Einzelfall auch einmal Ansprüche auf Aufwendungs- oder Schadensersatz entstehen, die dann mit Hilfe eines *i. contrarium* bzw. einer *actio contraria* einzuklagen sind.

I. de moribus: eine durch Justinian im Jahre 533 abgeschaffte (Cod. Iust. 5,17,11,2 b) Klage des Ehemannes gegen seine frühere Ehefrau auf Vermögensausgleich aus der bereits zurückgegebenen Mitgift (→ *dos*), sofern die Ehefrau die Scheidung wegen sittlicher Verfehlungen verschuldet hat.

I. domesticum: Damit wird das Hausgericht bezeichnet, das der → *pater familias* kraft seiner → *patria potestas* über die Gewaltunterworfenen sowohl hinsichtlich privatrechtlicher Streitigkeiten als auch wegen strafrechtlicher Vergehen abhalten konnte.

I. privatum: Damit ist im Gegensatz zum *i. publicum* das Gerichtsverfahren für Privatsachen gemeint (vgl. → *ius*). Das zivilprozessuale Verfahren hat im Verlauf der röm. Rechtsgeschichte drei Phasen durchlaufen, die nicht trennscharf voneinander abgelöst, sondern überlappend nebeneinander existiert haben. Kennzeichnend für die erste (Legisaktionen-, Spruchformelverfahren) und die zweite Phase (Formular-, Schriftformelverfahren) ist die Aufteilung in mehrere Abschnitte: Die Gewährung eines Gerichtsverfahrens durch den Magistraten (Praetor, Aedil etc.) – *in iure* – sowie die sich daran anschließende Beweisaufnahme und Urteilsfällung durch einen privaten Richter (→ *iudex*, → *recuperatores*) – *apud iudicem*. Zumindest im Formularverfahren ist freilich noch ein weiterer, dem Verfahren *in iure* vorgelagerter Abschnitt festzuhalten, nämlich die Verständigung der Parteien untereinander über den avisierten Prozeß (→ *editio*). Das Verfahren der → *legis actiones* zeichnet sich dadurch aus, daß die Parteien kontradiktorische Rechtsbehauptungen in vorformulierten und somit fixierten Spruchformeln fehlerfrei aufzusagen haben. Eine *l. Aebutia* des 2. Jh. v. Chr. schränkte den Anwendungsbereich dieses Verfahrenstyps ein, und die *l. Iulia* beseitigte ihn fast vollständig. Das stattdessen vordringende Formularverfahren zeichnet sich durch eine größere Flexibilität aus: Die Schriftformeln konnten sich nach Maßgabe der ediktalen Verheißungen den Besonderheiten des jeweiligen Einzelfalls wesentlich präziser anpassen, was insbes. bei den *bonae fidei iudicia* (→ *fides*), aber auch bei der Gewährung etwa von → *exceptiones* zum deutlichen Ausdruck kommt. Das bereits unter den ersten Principes einsetzende und seinen Vorgänger im Jahre 342 n. Chr. endgültig ablösende Kognitionsverfahren überträgt die gesamte Entscheidung über den Fall einem Richter, der in einem einheitlichen Verfahren sowohl die Sach- wie auch die Rechtsfragen zu klären hat.

I. publicum: Damit wird das klass. röm. Kriminalverfahren bezeichnet, das durch die augusteische *l. Iulia iudiciorum publicorum* neu geordnet wurde. Eingeleitet wird es durch die »Anklage« eines Bürgers, → *delatio nominis* (Dig. 37,14,10), die sodann eine Verhandlung vor einem Schwurgericht unter magistratischer Leitung nach sich zieht. Nicht alle Straftaten werden durch *i. publicum* abgeurteilt, sondern laut Dig. 48,1,1 nur diejenigen, die aus den folgenden Gesetzen abgeleitet sind: *Iulia maiestatis, Iulia de adulteriis, Cornelia de sicariis et veneficis, Pompeia parricidii, Iulia peculatus, Cornelia de testamentis, Iulia de vi privata, Iulia de vi publica, Iulia ambitus, Iulia repetundarum* und *Iulia de annona* (zum Verfahren vgl. → *quaestio*).

I. rescissorium: vom Praetor oder Provinzstatthalter gewährte Klage, um im Rahmen einer Wiedereinsetzung in den vorigen Stand (→ *restitutio in integrum*) mißbilligte Rechtslagen rückgängig machen zu können.

M. KASER, K. HACKL, Das röm. Zivilprozeßrecht, [2]1997, 288 • W. KUNKEL, Unt. zur Entwicklung des römischen Kriminalverfahrens in vorsullanischer Zeit, 1962 • M. LEMOSSE, Les deux régimes de l'instance »in iure«, in: Labeo 37, 1991, 297–304 • C. G. PAULUS, Die Beweisvereitelung in der Struktur des dt. Zivilprozesses, in: Archiv für die civilistische Praxis 197, 1997, 136–160, 151ff. • Y. THOMAS, Remarques sur la jurisdiction domestique à Rome, in: J. ANDREAU, H. BRUNS (Hrsg.), Parenté et stratégies familiale dans l'antiquité romain, 1990, 449–474.

G.T.

Judith (Ιουδιθ, *Iudith, Iudit*). Das Buch J., das uns h. nur in griech. und (davon abhängig) in lat. Sprache erh. ist und zu den Apokryphen (→ Apokryphe Literatur) zählt, geht auf ein hebr. Original zurück. In der polit. und mil. schwierigen Lage, in der die Bewohner der Gebirgsstadt Betylia von → Holofernes, dem Feldherrn Nebukadnezars belagert werden und daher unter Wassermangel leiden, erscheint J., die Heldin der Erzählung, eine junge, reiche und gottesfürchtige Witwe. Nach der Ermahnung des Volkes, Gott zu vertrauen, und einem Gebet begibt sie sich in das Lager des Feindes, wo sie vorgibt, ihr Volk verlassen zu haben und Holofernes bei der Einnahme der Stadt unterstützen zu wollen. Nach einem mehrtägigen Aufenthalt im feindlichen Lager, bei dem sie weiterhin gesetzestreu lebt, gelingt es ihr, Holofernes, der nach einem Gelage betrunken daliegt, das Haupt abschlagen, worauf die Israeliten die geschwächten Assyrer besiegen können. Ein Hymnus führt diesen Triumph auf Gottes Eingreifen zurück. Trotz der zahlreichen detaillierten Angaben zu Ort und Personen der Handlung ist der unhistor. Charakter der Erzählung unschwer zu übersehen. Nebukadnezar wird als König der Assyrer vorgestellt, der in → Niniveh residiert; Holofernes war in Wirklichkeit der Feldherr des Perserkönigs Artaxerxes [3] III. Damit handelt es sich bei dieser Erzählung um eine Art histor. Novelle, die an die Estererzählung der Septuaginta (→ Esther) erinnert: Gott erscheint als Herr der Gesch., der sein Volk prüft, aber alle mil. Gewalt demaskiert und seinem Volk Rettung widerfahren läßt, wenn es sich im Gebet an ihn wendet. Das Buch J. ist nicht vor 150 v. Chr. wohl in Jerusalem entstanden. Gerade die Schilderung J.s beim Festmahl mit Holofernes zeigt Einflüsse des hell. → Romans.

M. HELLMANN, Judit – eine Frau im Spannungsfeld von Autonomie und göttlicher Führung, 1992 • E. ZENGER, Das Buch Judit (Jüd. Schriften aus hell.-röm. Zeit: Histor. und legendarische Erzählungen I/6), 1981 • Ders., s. v. J./Judithbuch, TRE 17, 404–408 (mit weiterführender Lit.).

B.E.

Jüdisch-hellenistische Literatur s. Literatur

Jüdisches Recht A. BIBLISCHES RECHT: DIE TORA
B. DIE ENTWICKLUNG DES TALMUD
C. WEITERE QUELLEN DES JÜDISCHEN RECHTS

A. BIBLISCHES RECHT: DIE TORA

Über die histor. Anfänge des seit etwa 3000 Jahren bestehenden und in manchen Teilen der Welt noch heute befolgten j.R. läßt sich wenig feststellen. Manche seiner Regeln (z. B. bezüglich Tötung oder Diebstahl) sind in allen Kulturen vorhanden, ohne daß ihr histor. Ursprung belegt werden kann. So weist das in der Bibel enthaltene Recht Gemeinsamkeiten mit Rechtsstoff auf, der von anderen Kulturen des Nahen Ostens in der Ant. bekannt ist. Die Frage der Überschneidungen ist sehr umstritten, und überzeugende Verbindungen sind bisher nicht aufgetaucht. Der Cod. Hammurapi z. B., der bis weit in das 1. Jt. v. Chr. hinein galt, war eine akademische Rechtssammlung. Er und die biblischen Rechtsschöpfer könnten auf Grund derselben intellektuellen Haltung für Themen ihres bes. Interesses (z. B. Erlaß von Schulden alle sieben Jahre, Rückgabe von Land an seine urspr. Inhaber alle 49 Jahre) theoretische Konstruktionen geschaffen haben.

Die bibl. Rechtsregeln (das Buch des Bundes in Ex 21,2–23,19, die Gesetze in Dt 12–26, und die vielen Regeln in den Büchern Numeri und Leviticus) werden → Moses zugeschrieben; nur ausnahmsweise teilt Gott selbst Regeln mit (so gegenüber Noah und seinen Söhnen, Gn 9, Dekalog Ex 19 und Dt 5). In seinen Rechtsregeln greift »Moses« Probleme seiner eigenen Zeit (die Unterdrückung seines Volkes in Ägypten), der Zeit seiner Vorfahren (Abrahams Heirat mit seiner Halbschwester), aber auch solche viel späterer Zeiten auf (die Ernennung eines Königs in Israel). Die Bearbeiter dieses Rechtsstoffs begründen ihre eigene Rechtstradition; daher ist deren Frühgesch. sehr schwer herauszuarbeiten.

Bemerkenswert am bibl. Recht ist, daß verschiedene Rechtsquellen an unterschiedlichen Stellen in eine erzählte Gesch. eingefügt worden sind, die sich bis zu dem Zeitpunkt erstreckt, an dem Moses seinen Tod erwartet und das Volk Israel kurz vor dem Einzug in das Land Kanaan steht. Die unbekannten Autoren, die für diese Verschmelzung von Rechtsregeln und Erzählung verantwortlich sind, machen aus Moses eine legendäre Gestalt, die über vergangene Ereignisse in der Geschichte ihres Volkes urteilt (Genesis bis Deuteronomium) und zukünftige Entwicklungen voraussieht (Josua bis 2. Könige). Die lit. Überlieferung in diesen Büchern der Bibel enthält daher dieselben Themen, die in den Rechtsregeln behandelt werden. Arbeitet man die Verbindungen zw. den Rechtsregeln und einzelnen Erzählungen heraus, lassen sich der Inhalt der Rechtsregeln, ihre Sprache und ihre oftmals verwirrende Anordnung erklären: So wird etwa im Dekalog das Tötungsverbot deshalb im Anschluß an das Gebot der Ehrerbietung gegenüber den Eltern mit der Verheißung eines langen Lebens auf Erden (hebr. »dem Boden«) genannt, weil hier die Ermordung Abels durch Kain im Blickpunkt steht, mit der Folge, daß Kain den Boden nicht länger bebauen durfte.

Unter der Führung Ezras und Nehemias erreichten die Israeliten im 5. Jh. v. Chr. ihre Rückkehr aus der babylonischen Gefangenschaft. Die Tora (die ersten fünf B. Mose) wurde zur sakralen Verfassung des heimgekehrten Volkes; dies brachte strenge Reformen mit sich. Obwohl die Tora urspr. keinen Gesetzesrang hatte, werden ihre Regeln in späteren Büchern der Bibel dennoch so behandelt. Damit gelangte die Entwicklung des ant. jüd. (bibl.) Rechts zu einem Abschluß.

B. Die Entwicklung des Talmud

Das nächste große Rechtscorpus ist der Talmud. Dieser zeigt eine fortgeschrittene Stufe rechtlicher Entwicklung und beweist, daß das j. R. ein dynamisches System war, das zw. 100 v. Chr. und 500 n. Chr. gewichtige Änderungen erfuhr (Erweiterung der vertraglichen Haftung über Unehrlichkeit hinaus auf Fahrlässigkeit, schriftgemäße Vorschriften statt bloßer Beispiele als exegetischer Rechtsautorität). Der Talmud enthält Stoff vom 1. Jh. v. Chr. an, aber der Großteil seiner Rechtsregeln stammt aus der Zeit ab dem 2. Jh. n. Chr. Es gibt zwei Versionen des Talmud, den jerusalemischen oder palästinischen (um 425 n. Chr.) und den babylonischen (um 475 n. Chr.).

Beide Versionen des Talmud bestehen aus einem Komm., der Gemara, zu Mischna und Tosefta. Die Mischna ist eine Kodifikation des j.R. in hebr. Sprache, die E. des 2. Jh. n. Chr. von Rabbi → Jehuda niedergeschrieben wurde. Die Tosefta enthält Ergänzungen zur Mischna von Rabbi Jehudas Schüler, Hiyya bar Abba. Für die Mischna ist der Schwerpunkt auf den juristischen Konstruktionen der → Tannaiten (Rabbiner, die zw. 50 v. Chr. und 200 n. Chr. lebten) charakteristisch. Die Gemara gibt die Ansichten der → Amoräer (Rabbiner, die zw. 200 und 500 n. Chr. lebten) wieder. Der größtenteils in aram. Dialekt geschriebene und alle Lebensbereiche umfassende Talmud besteht aus vielfach ungelösten rechtlichen und außerrechtlichen Streitfragen. Seine diskursive und erzieherische Absicht ist unverkennbar.

Der Talmud zeigt, daß sich große Teile des j.R. unabhängig vom Inhalt der bibl. Quellen entwickelten. Ab dem 2. Jh. v. Chr. hatten die Pharisäer (→ Pharisaioi; eine gebildete Klasse, die sich vor allem dem Studium von Recht und Religion widmete) bes. Einfluß auf diese Entwicklung; ihre Traditionen werden durch den Talmud bewahrt. Die → Sadduzäer, eine einflußreiche Klasse alter, grundbesitzender Familien, widersetzten sich den Ansichten der Pharisäer. Ihre Kritik, daß die Pharisäer Vorschriften der Heiligen Schrift mißachteten, veranlaßte → Hillel (1. Jh. v. Chr.) zur umfassenden Anwendung hell. Auslegungsregeln, um zu »beweisen«, daß sich die Handhabung des Rechts durch die Pharisäer eben doch aus bibl. Rechtsregeln ableiten lasse. Rabbi Ismail (2. Jh. n. Chr.) benutzte 13 hermeneutische Regeln (hebr. *middoth*, aram. *mekilātā*, griech. *kanónes*), um Rechtssätze aus bibl. Geboten zu entwickeln. Rabbi Eliezer ben Gelili stellte später 32 Regeln zur Interpretation aller bibl. Texte auf. Diesem komplexen Prozeß der Interpretation ist die oft empfundene Schwierigkeit anzulasten, die Logik der talmudischen Argumentationsweise nachzuvollziehen. Glaubenssätze und Rechtsinstitute entgegengesetzt zu oder neu gegenüber dem, was die Hl. Schrift enthält, werden nichtsdestoweniger auf diese zurückgeführt (Glaube an die Auferstehung, Bekehrungstaufe, Arten der Todesstrafe, Schadensersatz durch Geld statt Talion).

C. Weitere Quellen des Jüdischen Rechts

Die Apokryphen, die Übers. der Bibel ins Griech. (die → Septuaginta) und Aram. (die → Targume), die Urkunden aus einer jüd. Militärsiedlung unter den Persern in Ägypten (das Recht der Papyri von Elephantine, 5. Jh. v. Chr.), aus → Qumran (die Schriftrollen vom Toten Meer) und aus judenchristl. Kreisen (NT) tragen alle zum h. Verständnis des ant. jüd. Rechts zw. der bibl. Zeit und der des Talmud bei. Die Komm. zur Hl. Schrift von → Philon von Alexandreia (20 v. Chr. bis 40 n. Chr.) und zum rechtlichen (u. a.) Inhalt des Buches Exodus von Rabbinern des 2. Jh. n. Chr. (die Mekhilta) gewähren bedeutende Einblicke. Die Apokryphen, für das j.R. als Ganzes wenig aussagekräftig, mögen regionalen Gebrauch widerspiegeln. Die Papyri aus Elephantine zeigen eine Tendenz, Facetten fremden Rechts einzubeziehen. Die Sprache der Septuaginta läßt eine größere Kenntnis rechtlicher Begriffe als bisher erkennen. Philons Allegorisierung bibl. Rechts verbindet verfeinerte rechtliche Analyse mit weitgefaßten intellektuellen Zielen. Die Schriftrollen vom Toten Meer überliefern die engen, aber sehr lebendigen Interessen sektiererischer Gruppen. Der Judaismus des NT ist unverzichtbar, um die Gesch. der im Talmud auftauchenden Begriffe und Konventionen nachzuvollziehen. Bemerkenswert in allen diesen Quellen ist die beständige Modernisierung des ant. Rechts. Bisher eng ausgelegte Regeln werden verallgemeinert. Veraltete Einrichtungen werden angepaßt: Hillels Prosbul neutralisiert die Regel zur Schuldbefreiung alle sieben Jahre (Dt 15,1–11), indem es ermöglicht, daß die Darlehensrückzahlung auch noch nach dem siebten Jahr erzwungen wird.
→ Rabbinische Literatur

C. M. Carmichael, The Spirit of Biblical Law, 1996 • D. Daube, Collected Works: Talmudic Law, ed. C. M. Carmichael, 1992 • W. Selb, Ant. Rechte im Mittelmeerraum, 1993, 157 ff., 202 ff. C. M. C./Ü: R. SCH.

Iuenna. Röm. Siedlung in Noricum, 23 Meilen von → Virunum in Richtung Celeia (Tab. Peut. 4,2), h. Globasnitz im Jauntal (Kärnten). Heiligtum des kelt. Gottes Iovenat am Hemmaberg, seit dem 5. Jh. zu einem christl. Wallfahrtsort ausgestaltet.

F. Glaser, Die röm. Siedlung I. und die frühchristl. Kirchen am Hemmaberg, 1982. H. GR.

Iugatio s. Capitatio-iugatio

Jugend I. Fragestellung und Methodik
II. Jugend und Lebensalter in der Antike
III. Jugend und Generationenfolge
IV. Jugend und Öffentlichkeit V. Mädchen

I. Fragestellung und Methodik

Die Gesch. der J. in der Ant. ist – abgesehen von einzelnen Problemen wie dem der J.-Terminologie, der J.-Erziehung oder der J.-Organisationen – ein bislang wenig erforschter Themenkomplex. Vor allem bedarf es zusätzlicher geschlechts- und schichtenspezifisch sowie zeitlich und räumlich differenzierender Einzelstudien. Im Mittelpunkt bisheriger neuerer Unt. stand das Problem, ob Adoleszenz überhaupt als ein von Kindheit und Erwachsensein geschiedener Lebensabschnitt wahrgenommen wurde, sowie ferner die Frage nach dem Verhältnis von ant. Lebensaltervorstellungen und Ausbildungsstadien einerseits und der physischen und sozialen Realität andererseits. Außerdem wurden Lebenszyklus- bzw. Übergangsriten thematisiert. Histor.- und anthropologisch-komparatistische Unt. haben gezeigt, daß die Adoleszenz als deutlich zu scheidendes, durch kritische Anpassungsprozesse an die Welt der Erwachsenen geprägtes, von ca. 12 bis 20 Jahren reichendes Stadium zwischen Kindheit und Erwachsensein ein modernes Konzept ist.

II. Jugend und Lebensalter in der Antike

J. in der Ant. ist als begrifflich wie zeitlich unbestimmter Lebensabschnitt aufzufassen, der an den Werten der Erwachsenenwelt orientiert und durch die frühe Übernahme von deren Aufgaben und Rollen geprägt war. In Griechenland wie in Rom finden sich unterschiedliche Lebensaltereinteilungen; die einzelnen Begriffe wurden dabei exakt, aber auch vage benutzt und können je nach Autor und Verwendungszusammenhang eine unterschiedliche Bedeutung besitzen. Während etwa die ἐφηβεία (→ *ephēbeía*) im Athen des 4. Jh. v. Chr. jahrgangsmäßig noch genau bestimmt war, galt dies nicht mehr in hell. Zeit; die obere Altersgrenze bei den νέοι (*néoi*) erscheint gleichfalls vage. In Rom konnte ein Kind ebenso wie ein über Dreißig- oder gar Vierzigjähriger als *adulescens* (Plin. epist. 1,14,10) angesprochen werden, ein Sechzehn- (CIL V 3189) wie ein Fünfzigjähriger (CIL VIII 9158; vgl. Gell. 10,28) als *iuvenis*. Bemerkenswert ist auch, daß im Unterrichtswesen und bei den Agonen nicht das Alter, sondern die Befähigung bzw. körperliche Entwicklung die Zusammensetzung von Gruppen bestimmt hat; für eine Ausrichtung des Unterrichts an kind- oder jugendgerechten Erziehungsinhalten oder -methoden spricht nur wenig. Die Orientierung kindlichen und jugendlichen Verhaltens am Erwachsenenleben und seinen Werten sowie das erwünschte Überspringen von frühen Lebensphasen wird auch an den in lit. (Quintilianus) und epigraphischen Zeugnissen erwähnten Wunderkindern deutlich, die Konzepte wie das des *puer-senex* bzw. παῖς τέλειος entstehen ließen.

III. Jugend und Generationenfolge

Obgleich physische Veränderungen bei Heranwachsenden wahrgenommen wurden (vor allem der Eintritt der Geschlechtsreife: ἥβη, *pubertas*), gibt es bei ant. Autoren keine Konzeption eines spezifischen Lebensstadiums Jugendlicher. Jugendliche (im heutigen Sinne) wurden in ant. Gesellschaften vor allem an Erwachsenenmaßstäben gemessen und oft genug als defizitäre Erwachsene bewertet. Wir kennen wohlwollende Charakterisierungen dieser Lebensphase (z. B. Aristot. rhet. 1389a-b) und Nachsichtigkeit gegenüber der J. (Cic. Cael. 42). Derartige Urteile bzw. Erwartungen, die oft genug von den Heranwachsenden übernommen wurden, verhinderten nicht pubertäres und rebellisches Verhalten der Jugendlichen; es fehlte aber eine ausgesprochene jugendliche »Subkultur«. Generationenkonflikte waren in der Ant. aufgrund von demographischen (geringe Lebenserwartung), sozialen (Wohnsitzwechsel), rechtlichen (Emanzipation) und kulturellen (frühe Übernahme traditioneller Werte) Faktoren bzw. Familienstrategien eher selten. Kinder der ärmeren Bevölkerungsgruppen haben wohl den Integrationsprozeß in die Erwachsenenwelt noch früher vollzogen, weil ihre Arbeitskraft von der Familie gebraucht wurde.

IV. Jugend und Öffentlichkeit

Trotz der in der Ant. gedanklich vorherrschenden Dichotomie von → Kindheit und Erwachsenenalter ist zu beobachten, daß die Lebensphase, die dem Erwachsensein und damit dem Zeitpunkt der vollständigen Integration des Heranwachsenden in die polit. Ordnung vorangeht, in den ant. Gemeinwesen nicht nur begrifflich (etwa durch νεώτατος/ἔφηβος, *neṓtatos/éphēbos*) oder *adulescens/iuvenis*) gefaßt, sondern auch polit. organisiert wurde: Bestimmte Einrichtungen zielten darauf ab, den jungen Männern eine sehr spezifische Vorstellung von ihrer zukünftigen Rolle als Bürger der *pólis* oder der *res publica* zu geben. Im archa. und klass. Griechenland spielten in dieser Phase der Sozialisation Leibesübungen, → Jagd und mil. Ausbildung (zuweilen auch die → Päderastie) eine entscheidende Rolle, im republikanischen Rom die mil. Ausbildung und für Jugendliche aus dem *ordo senatorius* oder dem *ordo equester* die rhetorische und polit. Unterweisung auf dem Forum. Bestimmungen über das Mindestalter für die Bekleidung von Ämtern und Funktionen verweisen ebenfalls auf die ant. Vorstellung vom noch defizitären J.-Alter.

Die frühe Betätigung von Jugendlichen in Berufen, die frühe Übernahme von Ämtern und Funktionen ohne Altersgrenzen sowie die frühe Präsentation von Kindern und Heranwachsenden in der Öffentlichkeit – zumindest im Milieu der polit. und intellektuellen Eliten – sind zugleich ein Beweis dafür, daß Rollen und Wertvorstellungen der Eltern von den Jugendlichen früh übernommen wurden. Die Ausdehnung der ἥβη (*hḗbē*), *adulescentia* bzw. *iuventus* weit über das physiologisch beobachtbare J.-Alter hinaus ist dabei mit der in Griechenland nur in Stufen eintretenden polit. und rechtlichen Vollmündigkeit bzw. der in Rom lange fortwirkenden Abhängigkeit der Söhne von den Vätern zu erklären.

Die Aufnahme des Heranwachsenden in die Gemeinschaft der vollwertigen Mitglieder des Gemeinwesens bzw. in den Kreis der Erwachsenen und Heiratsfähigen war in der Ant. mit bestimmten Riten bzw. Zeremonien verbunden, so etwa mit dem *kúreion*-Opfer an den Apaturien in Athen (vgl. IG II² 1237) oder mit dem Anlegen der *toga virilis* in Rom (Ov. fast. 3,771 ff.).

V. MÄDCHEN

Über das Leben der weiblichen Jugendlichen sind wir nur unzureichend informiert, nicht zuletzt deswegen, weil der Übergang der Mädchen in ein neues Lebensstadium nicht mit einer Aufnahme in das polit.-staatsbürgerliche Leben verbunden war. In Athen übernahmen sie etwa Aufgaben als *árktoi* (ἄρκτοι, → Brauron, → Artemis), → *kanēphóroi* (κανηφόροι) oder → *arrhēphóroi* (ἀρρηφόροι, vgl. Aristoph. Lys. 638–647) im Dienste an den Gottheiten der Stadt (→ Initiation).

Die Rituale der Heirat waren für Mann und Frau mehr als persönliche *rites de passage*, da die Ehe in der griech. *pólis* einen Grundpfeiler des Reproduktionssystems der Bürgerschaft darstellte. Griech. Erziehung (παιδεία) umfaßte auch – allerdings zumeist rollenspezifische – Erziehungsinhalte und -formen für junge Mädchen bzw. Frauen. Röm. Mädchen (*puellae, virgines*) waren nach allgemeiner Vorstellung dazu ausersehen, nach Eintritt der Pubertät Ehefrauen (*uxores*) und Mütter (*matronae*) zu werden; die Hochzeitsriten waren dabei Ausdruck der gesellschaftlichen Reproduktionsfunktion von Frauen.

→ Agoge; Heiratsalter; Homosexualität; Initiation; Iuvenes; Lebensalter; Lebenserwartung; Tirocinium fori; Trophima

1 E. EYBEN, Geschlechtsreife und Ehe im griech.-röm. Altertum und im frühen Christentum, in: E.W. MÜLLER (Hrsg.), Geschlechtsreife und Legitimation zur Zeugung, 1985, 403–478 2 Ders., Restless Youth in Ancient Rome, 1993 3 A. FRASCHETTI, Die Welt der jungen Römer, in: V.G. LEVI, J.-C. SCHMITT, Gesch. der Jugend von der Ant. bis zum Absolutismus, 1996, 70–112 4 M. KLEIJWEGT, Ancient Youth, 1991 5 A. SCHNAPP, Das Bild der Jugend in der griech. Polis, in: V.G. LEVI, J.-C. SCHMITT, Gesch. der Jugend von der Ant. bis zum Absolutismus, 1996, 21–69 6 B.S. STRAUSS, Fathers and Sons in Athens, 1993 7 R. ZOEPFFEL, Geschlechtsreife und Legitimation zur Zeugung im alten Griechenland, in: E.W. MÜLLER (Hrsg.), Geschlechtsreife und Legitimation zur Zeugung, 1985, 319–401.

J.W.

Iugerum. Lat. Bezeichnung für ein Flächenmaß, das ein aus zwei Quadraten (→ Actus [2]) entstandenes Rechteck von 120 × 240 Fuß = 35,52 × 71,04 m = 2523 m² = ¼ ha umfaßte [1. 84f.; 3. 9f.], nach Plin. nat. 18,3,9 die Fläche, die mit einem Ochsengespann an einem Tag gepflügt werden konnte, im übertragenen Sinne »Tagewerk«. Teilung nach dem Duodezimalsystem in 2 Actus, 12 Unciae, 288 → Scripula, wobei 1 Scripulum 100 Fuß im Quadrat entsprach. Eine vollständige Ausrechnung der Teileinheiten gibt Colum. 5,1,4–5,2,10 [2. 627]. Als Mehrfache des I. erwähnt Varro rust. 1,10,2 → Heredium (2 I.), Centuria (200 I.) und → Saltus (800 I.). Modifikationen der Norm finden sich im ägypt. Provinzialsystem, wo ein I. 2450 m² entsprach [1. 610]. In der röm. Kaiserzeit auch als Längenmaß zur Angabe von Feldlängen verwandt [2. 629]. Die Flächen der an der Peripherie der Colonia Claudia Ara Agrippinensium gelegenen Gutshöfe betragen im Durchschnitt zwischen 3 und 10 I. [4. 405–408].

→ Flächenmaße

1 F. HULTSCH, Griech. und röm. Metrologie, ²1882 2 ThlL VII 3 D. FLACH, Röm. Agrargesch. (HdbA III 9), 1990 4 W. GAITZSCH, Grundformen röm. Landsiedlungen im Westen der CCAA, in: BJ 186, 1986, 397–427 5 H. CHANTRAINE, s.v. I., KlP 2, 1512 6 F.T. HINRICHS, Die Gesch. der gromatischen Institutionen – Unt. zu Landverteilung, Landvermessung, Bodenverwaltung und Bodenrecht im röm. Reich, 1974 7 U. HEIMBERG, Röm. Landvermessung, 1977.

H.-J.S.

Iuglans oder *iugulans*. Etym. nach Varro ling. 5,102: *a Iove et glande appellata* (›nach Iuppiter und der Eichel benannt‹; vgl. Isid. orig. 17,7,21 nach Serv. ecl. 8,29f. und Plin. nat. 15,91, übersetzt aus Διὸς βάλανος, das sonst die Eßkastanie bezeichnet), die aus Persien am Schwarzen Meer über Griechenland nach It. (nach Pall. agric. 2,15,14–19 Aussaat von Ende Januar an, nach Colum. 5,10,14 im März) eingeführte Walnuß (Iuglans regia L.). Sie ist schon Theophrast bekannt. Dieser erwähnt für die καρύα ἡ Περσική (»persische Nuß«) das Austreiben aus den Seitenzweigen (h. plant. 3,6,2). Varro (rust. 1,67) empfiehlt frühzeitige Ernte der *Nux iuglans*: Viele große Bäume würden den Boden eines Landgutes steril machen (ebd. 1,16,6). Isidorus bezeichnet ihren Schatten und das Tropfwasser von den Blättern als schädlich für die nächstwachsenden Bäume (orig. 17,7,21); Plin. nat. 17,89 führt Kopfschmerzen beim Menschen auf die I. zurück (vgl. 15,87: wegen ihres starken Geruches). Nach Isidor ebd. soll die Walnuß, unter verdächtige Kräuter oder Pilze gemischt, deren Gift beseitigen. Nach Servius ebd. wurden die dem Iuppiter geweihten Walnüsse bei der Hochzeit als Omen ausgestreut. Cicero überliefert (Tusc. 5,58), der Tyrann Dionysios von Syrakus habe sich aus Furcht vor dem Schermesser Haupthaar und Bart von seinen Töchtern mit glühenden Walnüssen absengen lassen. C.HÜ.

Iugum

[1] I. (»Joch«) hieß nach Varro rust. 1,10,1 in Hispania ulterior ein Feldmaß im Betrage des → Iugerum. Seit Diocletian bildete das I. eine Steuerhufe von je nach Bodengüte wechselnder Größe. So gingen in Syrien auf ein I. 5 Iugera Weinberg, 20, 40, 60 Iugera Ackerland sinkender Bonität oder 220 bzw. 450 Perticae (zu 100 Quadratfuß?) Ölpflanzungen (FIRA 2,795f.). Andere Maße und Klassen begegnen in Palästina, Arabien und

der Inselwelt, während die entsprechenden fiskalischen Einheiten in Ägypten auf der → Arura, in Africa auf der Centuria (zu 200 Iugera), in It. auf der Millena basierten.
→ Capitatio-iugatio

J. Marquardt, Röm. Staatsverwaltung, Bd. 2, 1876 (Hdb. der röm. Alterthümer 5), 225 ff. • A. H. M. Jones, The Later Roman Empire, 1964, 62 ff.; 453 ff.; 820. HE.C.

[2] s. Landtransport

Iugum Cremonis. Heute Mont Cramont an der Route des Kleinen St. Bernhard, auf der laut Coelius Antipater (HRR fr. 14 = Liv. 21,38,7) Hannibal die Alpen überschritt. H.GR.

Iugurtha. 160–104 v. Chr.; Enkel → Massinissas, Sohn → Mastanabals, der mit → Micipsa und → Gulussa Samtherrscher in Numidien war. Von Micipsa kriegerisch erzogen, wurde er 134 v. Chr. als Kommandeur numidischer Schützen, Schleuderer und Elefanten nach → Numantia entsandt. Aufgrund seiner mil. Leistungen genoß er hohe Popularität und hatte persönl. Beziehungen zur röm. Führungsschicht, bes. zu → Cornelius [I 70] Scipio Africanus; er erlernte die lat. Sprache (Sall. Iug. 5,4–9,1; 101,6; App. Ib. 387). Nach persönl. Empfehlung durch Scipio wurde er von Micipsa adoptiert; 118 v. Chr., nach dem Tod Micipsas, kam es zur Samtherrschaft mit den jüngeren (leiblichen) Söhnen Micipsas, → Adherbal [4] und → Hiempsal [1]. Bei Auseinandersetzungen über die Besitzteilung besiegte I. Hiempsal und ließ ihn töten. Adherbal, den I. aus dem Reich vertrieb, wandte sich an den röm. Senat (Sall. Iug. 8,2–11,9; Liv. per. 62) [2. 59]. Bei der Teilung des Reiches fiel der fruchtbare Westen an I., der Osten an Adherbal (Sall. Iug. 12–16) [2. 60]. 112 v. Chr. erfolgte ein neuer Angriff I.s auf Adherbal, der in → Cirta zusammen mit ital. Geschäftsleuten getötet wurde (Sall. Iug. 20–27; Diod. 34/35,31; Liv. per. 64) [3. 165 ff.]; röm. Kriegserklärung trotz Gesandtschaft I.s (Sall. Iug. 27,1–28,2).

Die Kriegsführung des L. Calpurnius [I 1] Bestia führte im J. 111 wegen I.s Einflußnahme zum Frieden gegen geringe Zahlungen und ohne Selbstauslieferung I.s (Sall. Iug. 28,4–29,7) [1. 97 ff.]. Der Volkstribun C. Memmius erzwang I.s Einbestellung nach Rom, wo I. den Prätendenten → Massiva, Sohn Gulussas, durch → Bomilkar [4] töten ließ; I. und Bomilkar mußten Rom verlassen (Sall. Iug. 30; 32–35; Diod. 34/35,35a; App. Num. 1) [1. 99 ff.]. Sp. und Aulus Postumus Albinus führten gegen I. erneut Krieg (110 v. Chr.); I. siegte bei Suthul und erzwang den Abzug der Römer (Sall. Iug. 36–38) [1. 102 ff]. Das von I. diktierte *foedus* erkannte der Senat. nicht an [1. 103]. Die weitere Kriegsführung leitete Q. → Caecilius [I 30] Metellus (*cos.* 109), der Rüstung und Truppentraining intensivierte (Sall. Iug. 39 f.; 43–45; Cic. Brut. 127 f.), Vaga einnahm und am Muthul über I. siegte, aber I. und sein Land nicht kontrollierte (Sall. Iug. 46–69; Plut. Marius 8; App. Num. 3) [1. 103–109].

Nach ergebnislosen Verhandlungen über die Kapitulation I.s kam es zu einem Mordanschlag gegen I. durch Bomilkar; Ostnumidien wurde durch Q. Caecilius Metellus besetzt. I., der gegen die röm. Kriegsführung den Stamm der Gaetuler mobilisierte, verbündete sich mit Bocchus von Mauretanien; Metellus suchte durch Verhandlungen das gegnerische Bündnis zu schwächen (Sall. Iug. 62; 70–84). Kritik des Legaten → Marius an Metellus' Kriegführung; das Konsulat 107 und den Oberbefehl gegen I. erhielt Marius (Sall. Iug. 67,3; 69,4; 73,2; 84; 86; Plut. Mar. 7–9; Cic. off. 3,79). Marius eroberte → Capsa und konnte Angriffe bei Cirta und am → Mulucha abwehren, kontrollierte jedoch nicht die Umgebung (Sall. Iug. 87–101). Er verhandelte daher mit Bocchus über die Auslieferung I.s., die L. → Cornelius [I 90] Sulla 105 als Quaestor erwirkte (Plut. Marius 10,3–6; Sall. Iug. 103–109; 111–113; Liv. per. 66; App. Num. 4 f.; Diod. 34/35,39) [1. 113 ff.]. 104 v. Chr. wurde I. in Marius' Triumphzug mitgeführt und getötet (Liv. per. 67; Plut. Marius 12,3–6; Sall. Iug. 114,3). Bocchus überhöhte seinen Verrat propagandistisch durch figürliche Darstellung der Übergabe I.s an Sulla auf dem Kapitol (vgl. Plut. Sulla 6,1), Sulla und seine Familie durch Darstellung auf Siegelring und Münzen [1. 115 f.].
→ Numidia

1 H. W. Ritter, Rom und Numidien, 1987 **2** M.-R. Alföldi, Die Gesch. des numid. Königreiches und seiner Nachfolger, in: H. G. Horn, C. B. Rüger (Hrsg.), Die Numidier, 1979, 43–74 **3** C. Saumagne, La Numidie et Rome, 1966. B.M.